Y0-BTV-112

ENCYCLOPÆDIA
Britannica

2004
BOOK OF THE YEAR®

Encyclopædia Britannica, Inc.
Chicago · London · New Delhi · Paris · Seoul · Sydney · Taipei · Tokyo

ENCYCLOPÆDIA

Britannica

BOOK OF THE YEAR® 2004

Library of Congress Catalog Card Number: 38-12082
International Standard Book Number: 1-59339-100-5
International Standard Serial Number: 0068-1156

Britannica.com may be accessed on the Internet at http://www.britannica.com.

(Trademark Reg. U.S. Pat. Off.) Printed in U.S.A.

Foreword

Preoccupying most of the world during 2003 were the actions leading up to the U.S.-led invasion of Iraq and the worldwide repercussions emanating from the conflict. The U.S. tussle within the UN Security Council over the legitimacy of the U.S. and allied preemptive strike in Iraq loomed large in the political arena. U.S. Pres. George W. Bush's rationale for the war was also widely debated. AIDS again killed millions, while a new scourge, SARS (severe acute respiratory syndrome), led to hundreds of deaths and disrupted travel as well as the staging of sporting, theatrical, and various other events. The war in Iraq saw the inclusion of "embedded" journalists, who traveled with the troops and brought a new dimension to war-zone reporting. The year 2003 was deemed the International Year of Freshwater, and special attention was focused on finding possible solutions to ease the scarcity of this most precious commodity. To feature the major topics of the year, then, the editors selected all of these subjects for treatment in Special Reports.

In addition, former president Jimmy Carter, the recipient of the Nobel Prize for Peace in 2002, gave Britannica editors an exclusive interview in which he shares his insights on the war, world health, the activities of the Carter Center, and the state of the world in the 21st century.

Picking up the war theme again, we decided to include a Sidebar defining weapons of mass destruction, which Iraqi leader Saddam Hussein was thought to have been hiding. The history of the Indian Ocean island of Diego Garcia, a strategic base for military operations, is also highlighted (with a locator map). Technological wizardry is explored in Sidebars on virtual actors, such as the *Lord of the Rings* film character Gollum, and the ease of conducting genealogical research on the Internet. Technological failure as well as human error led to tragedy for the space shuttle *Columbia* astronauts. Social issues, such as the momentum gained by charter schools and the booming prescription-drug business from Canada to the U.S. are the focus of two other Sidebars. For sports fans the cricket World Cup comes to life again. It was also a year of rebuilding, and Daniel Libeskind's award-winning design for the World Trade Center in New York City is detailed and shown in a breathtaking image in the Sidebar that accompanies "Architecture."

Our People section contains profiles on Saddam, Libeskind, Oscar winners Catherine Zeta-Jones and Michael Moore, and Paul Martin, the new Canadian prime minister, among dozens of others. Remember with us that the entertainment industry lost some of its most luminous lights, including Katharine Hepburn, Gregory Peck, Bob Hope, Dame Wendy Hiller, Johnny Cash, and Slim Dusty.

In addition, enjoy browsing the daily Calendar, exploring the events that defined the year around the globe. Turn to your favourite article, whether it be "Theatre," "Football," "Art," or "Space Exploration," and discover what made 2003 such an amazing year.

Karen Sparks, Editor

Contents

2004

Global Challenges to the United States in a New Millennium

An Interview with Jimmy Carter

Few people in the United States have a better overview of the state of the world than Jimmy Carter. He has been a submarine officer in the U.S. Navy, a successful peanut farmer, governor of Georgia (1971–75), the 39th president of the U.S. (1977–81), and, with his wife, Rosalynn, founder of The Carter Center (1982), an organization dedicated to the well-being of the world's people. In addition to his many other honours, Carter received the 2002 Nobel Prize for Peace. Now 79 years old, Carter is still very active in The Carter Center's projects, which include monitoring national elections, promoting peace through personal diplomacy, and eradicating or preventing tropical diseases such as river blindness, Guinea worm disease, and trachoma. Since leaving the White House he has written 18 books, including political memoirs, personal reminiscences, inspirational works, poetry, and, most recently, a novel. This written interview is excerpted from a conversation with Encyclopædia Britannica (EB) Director of Yearbooks Charles Trumbull at The Carter Center in Atlanta, Ga., on June 26, 2003.

Encyclopædia Britannica: How would you characterize the state of the world in 2003?

President Carter: I think the world is deeply concerned and uncertain about the future. The number of conflicts on Earth now is close to the highest in history. There is rapidly increasing wealth in the industrialized countries and a growing gap, or chasm, between the quality of life of those nations and the nations of the developing world. The status of the international community has changed dramatically in the last year. For the first time in human history, there is one undisputed superpower that is asserting its military strength.

The strength of the United Nations has been dramatically challenged and potentially weakened. There is a lack of understanding or cooperation between Europe and the United States that is unprecedented in recent history. The effects of so-called globalization have not attenuated the disparities between the rich and poor countries but maybe have accelerated them. The ability of people now in the poorer nations to understand through mass media the degree of their economic plight has made them increasingly resentful as they can compare themselves with families in other nations and not just families in the next village. Yet the quality of life for people like me and most readers of Encyclopædia Britannica is improved every year by scientific and medical developments that hold promise for the future.

The decrease in colonial or central authority in Russia, the former Yugoslavia, and throughout Africa has unleashed ethnic strife and tribal differences that were subdued under colonial influence in Africa and under the powerful central governments of the Soviet Union and Marshal Tito. But I believe most of our individual fears of terrorism in industrialized countries are unjustified. Statistically speaking, it is highly unlikely that any of us or our friends will be directly affected by terrorism, although the aftermath of the Sept. 11, 2001, attacks has made us all extraordinarily fearful.

EB: Do you see terrorism or state terrorism as a new phenomenon?

Carter: No, I think there has been an incipient element of terrorism for a long time. When I was president, we dealt with terrorism in the form of explosions, aircraft hijackings, and things of that kind, but there was not a worldwide awareness of it. Leaders were concerned, however, and we acted to try to control it.

EB: Would you agree that the history of the 20th century was a history of the clash between various ideologies—capitalism, communism, fascism, and so on—and, if so, what do you think the arena for the 21st century is going to be? Will ideologies again be the issue, or will it be our cultural, ethnic, and social differences?

Carter: In the first few months of 2001, I gave several speeches addressing the question of the greatest challenge the world faces in the new millennium. My answer was the "growing gap between rich and poor people." This is the preeminent potential element of conflict and dispute we face in the coming years. It is exacerbated by the growing sense of a religious difference, that you have Muslims on one side and Christians on the other who have been identified, at least in the public consciousness, as adversaries. Since the 9/11 terrorist attacks, this potential difference between Islam and the Christian world has become a very important concern, almost an obsession for some people. I do not see it as justified, but it exists.

EB: Has it become an obsession on both sides, or only in the United States?

Carter: I think it is an obsession on both sides. For instance, recently I saw the results of a poll by the Pew Global Attitudes Project. The number of Jordanians who look with favour on the United States is 1%. In the past I looked upon Jordan, with Egypt, as perhaps our best friend in the Arab world. A favourable attitude overseas toward the United States is at an abysmally low level. A lot of that is a feeling not only that the United States dominates economically, militarily, and politically but also that we are trying to dominate others from a religious point of view. Within the Christian community in the U.S. certainly, and perhaps in some countries of Europe, there is a sense that Islam harbours and encourages acts of terrorism or violence to accomplish its goals.

EB: You suggested in your Nobel Prize lecture that in the new era nations will be called upon to cede some of their sovereignty to international organizations, yet in many ways the U.S. seems to be backing away from initiatives that would limit its ability to act independently—for example, in the United Nations recently over Iraq, in the World Trade Organization whenever it rules against the U.S., in regard to the International Criminal Court, and so on.

Carter: Some of my Nobel address was targeted toward the United States and its recent policies, which concern me very deeply: the inclination to bypass the United Nations or to derogate its work; an attempt to deal unilaterally with the problems of the world; trying to impose our will on others with military action as a very great and early possibility, not a last resort; a strong inclination, proven by actions, to abandon all the important international agreements that had been approved by presidents of the past and to prevent the implementation of agreements in the embryonic stage, including the International Criminal Court; and the abandonment of the agreement at Kyoto concerning global warming. The Kyoto Agreement represented consensus reached after a decade or more of analysis of scientific facts, laborious negotiation, and trying to reach a common purpose. The U.S. now has separated itself publicly from most commitments it made and is also embarking on a new effort to develop new atomic weaponry, as shown in the recent vote in Congress in support of deep-penetrating nuclear bombs, and the antiballistic-missile placements that have recently been approved in Alaska and are now facing China and North Korea. Many of these are departures from past policies and, I think, contravene the general premises espoused by the rest of the world and previous leaders of this country, regardless of our partisan commitments.

Jimmy Carter receives the 2002 Nobel Prize for Peace from Norwegian Nobel Committee Chairman Gunnar Berge.

EB: Why did this happen? Did this arrogance of power occur because the United States is the only superpower now? Is it because the Republicans are in office? Is it just a stage of history?

Carter: Well, it is not only because the United States is the only superpower. We have been the only superpower since Mikhail Gorbachev was in power in the Soviet Union and Russia. We now spend about as much on our military as the rest of the world combined. Every time we spent three dollars on our military, the Iraqis spent one cent. It is hard for me to speak in a completely objective way, but I think there have been long-standing philosophical and political commitments of some of the key players in the Bush administration whose ideas and goals are now being effectuated by national policy. Their ability to put these ideas into practice was greatly enhanced because of the 9/11 attack, which caused Americans to consider themselves to be at war against terrorism. Anytime our country is at war, we try to give the commander in chief—who is normally a civilian administrator—extraordinary public support and latitude in dealing with the threat to the country. The terrorism threat has been publicized repeatedly, such that the U.S. has never been able to get over its quite legitimate concerns after 9/11.

The U.S. is the superpower in almost every aspect of life now—not just militarily, politically, and economically—but culturally too. American music and entertainment permeate the world. Our country is in a mode of deciding how its single superpower status should be exerted.

EB: You have spoken frequently about the important role that nongovernmental organizations and private initiatives have in alleviating some of the world's problems.

Carter: A typical NGO is an organization designed for humanitarian or altruistic purposes—for example, to alleviate suffering, provide improved environmental quality, promote freedom and democracy, or guarantee human rights. Second, although some NGOs may be bound by the purposes expressed by the founder, or their heirs, many are adequately flexible and can deal without the restraints of complicated government structures, economies, and so forth and can make decisions rapidly. Third, NGO representatives quite often work in areas of the world and among people of the world who are most in need. If an NGO like The Carter Center devotes itself, say, to dealing with tropical diseases, we are on the ground in the villages, in the homes of people who suffer from these diseases.

Another aspect of NGOs is that they have no special authority and could not have it even if they wanted it. The Carter Center has now observed 45 elections in the world. We go into those countries by invitation, and the first thing I always announce when I arrive is that we have no authority. All authority rests in the local government or its national election commission.

EB: I am interested in your humble use of the word *authority*. You claim that you have no authority, yet you have enormous authority when you go into a country. The personal dimension of your involvement with The Carter Center gives you an enormous amount of sway, does it not?

Carter: Well, there is certainly moral authority and the influence of my voice, on behalf of The Carter Center. Quite often we monitor an election side by side with representatives of the United Nations. On election day, if I see something going wrong, I have no reluctance to take it up directly with the head of the ruling party, the president, or the prime minister. If that is unsuccessful, I am not shy about calling an international press conference and saying, "This is wrong, and the ruling party should take action to change it." When the election is over, I have no reticence about saying, "This election was faulty, and I do not believe the will of the people was represented."

EB: How do you view some of the other grand-scale personal efforts to alleviate suffering? I am thinking particularly of rock musician Bob Geldof, who earlier this year called for a "Marshall Plan" for Africa. Geldof said that during the Marshall Plan for Europe, 1% of the gross national product of the United States went to rebuilding Europe and that the same thing could be done in Africa with 0.16% of GNP.

Carter: I think we could do it if we invested 0.1% of the U.S. GNP for humanitarian aid. By the way, the humanitarian aid figure from the U.S. government is the lowest percentage of any industrialized country in the world. European countries give about 4 times as much; Norway gives about 17 times as much per capita.

The Carter Center

Jimmy Carter speaks with a Ghanaian mother and child in 1989 about prevention of Guinea worm disease.

EB: You set up The Carter Center 21 years ago. What was your vision then, and what is your vision now, say, looking 20 years out?

Carter: They were quite different. When we conceived of The Carter Center, Rosalynn and I had the very limited vision of creating here a Camp David in miniature. I thought I would deal exclusively with conflicts or potential conflicts in the world, analyze their causes and the principles of the parties involved, and offer my services as a mediator, as I had mediated between Israel and Egypt in the Camp David Accords in 1978 that led to the peace treaty between those countries—by the way, not a word of which has ever been violated.

We still do that. But The Carter Center has evolved, because I realized that my earlier commitments to human rights and to peace were primarily predicated on my limited viewpoint as a president and governor. I did not understand that intense personal hunger and suffering from preventable diseases was such a terrible problem. I did not know about all the poor countries I know well today. Now over half our total effort is devoted to health programs. The most remarkable progress is against Guinea worm disease. Incidences have been reduced from 3.5 million, when the eradication campaign began, to less than 50,000 today, and almost three-fourths of those are in southern Sudan, where we cannot reach some of the villages because of the civil war.

The Carter Center has extended its vision to encompass a much broader range of human rights, not only civil and political rights, such as freedom of speech, freedom of mistreatment by authorities, and the right to self-governance, but social and economic rights, including environmental concerns, alleviation of suffering, and the right to health care.

EB: Is there a connection between lack of democracy and social problems such as poor housing or unavailability of medical care?

Carter: Yes, with some caveats. The right of a people to elect their own leaders does not automatically result in a fair distribution of a nation's wealth and an alleviation of abject poverty, but it certainly gives a better opportunity for alleviation that is achieved to be more rapid and effective. If leaders of a country know they will be subject to their people's approval or disapproval in four, five, or six years, they are much more inclined to pay attention to their problems. In new democracies there is often the reverse problem too. People espousing democracy for the first time quite often are misled into extremely high expectations and believe that after they elect their own leaders, they are going to have better housing, more to eat, or better education for their children. Then they are disillusioned when change comes slowly. It is also a natural human inclination among political leaders to ally themselves with their peer group or with special interests who can provide them with funding for a reelection effort, and this can lead to favoritism or corruption. So there are some caveats about democracy, but in general it is clear that democracy is a better avenue for the solution of social problems.

EB: You have mentioned the 9/11 attacks several times today. How have those events changed your thinking or the policies of The Carter Center?

Carter: It really has not changed our policies. I was pleasantly surprised after 9/11 that the worldwide support for The Carter Center went up noticeably. Many people saw The Carter Center as an element of international stability, that we operated across ethnic and religious lines, in mundane commitments, like growing more rice on a farm or treating children for river blindness, and realized that we dealt with all kinds of governments and leaders equitably. So, as far as The Carter Center was concerned, 9/11 was a terrible atrocity but not an adverse factor on our own projects.

EB: A key aspect of The Carter Center and yourself personally, it seems, has been your dedication always to nonpartisanship. Sometimes this must have been an incredible balancing act. Often you seem to have been at cross-purposes with the White House, the State Department, and even the Democratic Party on occasion.

Carter: That is true. As president, generally I had a better relationship with the Republicans in Congress than with the Democrats, but not always. Comparatively speaking, however, there was very little partisan animosity. There was great flexibility in the House and Senate in dealing with controversial issues on their merit and how they affected people back home in their individual districts. Seldom did congressmen vote a party line. Now the Congress members go into caucus and they decide on the party's policy, and then they vote as a bloc. This is amazing to me; I never experienced that when I was in the White House.

I have always been a Democrat, and my choice is a natural one; I do not have any compunction about my choice, nor have I ever felt bound by it. My main challenge when I was president was from the liberal wing of the Democratic Party, and my strongest support was from the moderate elements in the Democratic Party.

EB: Let me ask for your quick responses to situations in a couple of hot spots around the world. Brazil—There are very interesting developments with the election of Pres. Luiz Inácio Lula da Silva.

Carter: Yes. I have very good hopes about Brazil. I understand that President Lula has chosen excellent advisers, is making good decisions, and is putting Brazil on the right track.

EB: One of Lula's first acts as president was to declare that nobody in Brazil should be without housing. As if to underline his determination, Lula canceled a very large order of military equipment.

Carter: That is a very good move. We have tried to encourage that all over Latin America. The leader in this regard is Costa Rica, a country that devotes all its resources to nonmilitary purposes.

EB: Zimbabwe—You were present at the creation, were you not?

Carter: I think I spent more time working on the issues in Zimbabwe than I did on the Middle East peace process!

EB: It seems to be a country that is on the brink.

Carter: It is because of malfeasance and maladministration of Pres. Robert Mugabe.

EB: What is the way out?

Carter: To find some means to terminate his leadership. I do not see any way out as long as he is the leader.

EB: Iraq—Do you think the Iraqis had weapons of mass destruction in the spring of 2003?

Carter: Well, I know they had weapons of mass destruction in the era of the Iran-Iraq War. They used them, I think with the knowledge of the United States. Maybe by the time this interview is published, my opinion will not amount to anything, but I am increasingly doubtful that they did have substantial weapons of mass destruction at the time of the U.S. invasion.

EB: Thank you very much, Mr. President.

Carter: I have enjoyed talking with you.

Dates of 2003

Intensive U.S. air strikes against Baghdad, Iraq, begin in March.

January

So long as there is a single Brazilian brother or sister going hungry, we have ample reason to be ashamed of ourselves.

Lula, in his inaugural address as president of Brazil, January 1

1 The Socialist Lula (Luiz Inácio Lula da Silva) takes office as president of Brazil.

•

The American Academy of Arts and Letters awards Strauss Livings to writers Gish Jen and Claire Messud; the prizes, for $250,000, are given out every five years.

2 *Nature* magazine publishes two studies showing that global warming is causing many different species of plants and animals to change their ranges or alter their reproductive habits; the scientists are alarmed at the extent of the change, given the small amount of warming that has taken place and the greater amount that is predicted.

•

Officials of Los Alamos (N.M.) National Laboratory announce the resignation of John C. Browne as director; the nuclear weapons laboratory has been under investigation because of apparent corruption and missing equipment.

3 In Caracas, Venez., a peaceful protest against the administration of Pres. Hugo Chávez Frías is intercepted by progovernment demonstrators, and a great street fight ensues, leaving at least two people dead; an antigovernment strike had begun 33 days earlier.

•

Brazil suspends the planned purchase of 12 new fighter jets, intending to devote the money to alleviating hunger instead.

•

Peru's Supreme Court issues a ruling invalidating some of the antiterrorism laws passed under former president Alberto K. Fujimori; there are expected to be a large number of retrials as a result.

•

In the annual postseason Fiesta Bowl, Ohio State University defeats the University of Miami, Fla., 31–24 in double overtime to win the national college football Division I-A championship.

4 India announces that it has created a nuclear command authority, headed by the prime minister; Pakistan already had such an entity, and the countries spent much of 2002 at loggerheads.

•

The National Society of Film Critics chooses *The Pianist* as the best film of 2002.

5 A man steals a small private airplane and threatens to crash it into the European Central Bank building in Frankfurt am Main, Ger.; much of downtown is evacuated, and the city is paralyzed for several hours until the man is talked down, saying he wished to commemorate the American astronaut Judith Resnick, who died in the *Challenger* explosion in 1986.

•

Two suicide bombers set off their bombs in downtown Tel Aviv, Israel, killing 23 people in addition to themselves and injuring scores.

•

In the runoff presidential election in Lithuania, the right-wing candidate Rolandas Paksas unexpectedly defeats incumbent Valdas Adamkus, who held the lead in the first round of voting.

6 The International Atomic Energy Agency passes a resolution demanding that North Korea readmit IAEA inspectors lest the agency be required to refer the matter to the UN Security Council.

•

Kenyan Pres. Mwai Kibaki's new cabinet is sworn in; it is the first non-KANU cabinet in 39 years.

•

The city of Louisville, Ky., merges with surrounding Jefferson county, putting it for the first time among the top 20 U.S. cities in population; other cities are considering similar changes because the metropolitan areas are finding that city and suburbs increasingly have common interests.

•

Uttar Pradesh, the most populous state in India, bans the slaughter of cows, which are held to be sacred by Hindus.

•

A large statue of the Hindu deity Krishna, under construction for the past six years and nearly complete, collapses and kills three workers outside New Delhi.

7 Great Britain mobilizes 1,500 reservists in support of a possible war against Iraq.

•

For the first time, under a presidential decree, Christmas (today on the Coptic Christian calendar) is celebrated as a national holiday in Egypt, an almost entirely Muslim country.

•

Shlomo Koves becomes the first Orthodox Jewish rabbi inaugurated in Hungary since before the Holocaust.

AP/Wide World Photos

•

The Danish Committees on Scientific Dishonesty rebukes Bjørn Lomborg for his book *The Skeptical Environmentalist,* finding that it is "clearly contrary to the standards of good scientific practice."

•

Catcher Gary Carter and switch-hitter Eddie Murray are elected to the National Baseball Hall of Fame.

8 A U.S. court of appeals rules that the government during wartime may detain indefinitely a U.S. citizen captured as an enemy combatant and deny him access to a lawyer.

•

The United States Sentencing Commission approves a plan to lengthen prison sentences for people convicted of corporate crimes, such as securities fraud.

•

The U.S. opens talks intended to lead to a free-trade agreement with Nicaragua, El Salvador, Costa Rica, Guatemala, and Honduras.

9 Chief UN weapons inspector Hans Blix and International Atomic Energy Agency head Mohamed El Baradei report to the UN Security Council that Iraq's disclosure of weapons programs was insufficiently informative but that inspectors have found no evidence of weapons or programs.

•

Astronomers announce that they have found 26 galaxies and 3 quasars approximately 13 billion light-years away, which means they date from early in the period that light first appeared in the universe.

10 North Korea announces that it is withdrawing from the Nuclear Non-proliferation Treaty; the following day one million people rally in Pyongyang in support of the decision.

•

Mexico's foreign minister, Jorge G. Castañeda, resigns, apparently as a result of his failure to achieve goals regarding relations with the U.S.; Luis Ernesto Derbéz is named as his replacement.

•

Russian Pres. Vladimir Putin and Japanese Prime Minister Junichiro Koizumi sign an agreement to improve trade relations and seek a resolution to their long-standing dispute over ownership of the Kuril Islands.

•

The Sony Corp. of America names Andrew Lack head of Sony Music Entertainment, replacing Thomas Mottola, who is a top power in the music industry.

11 In the last two days of his term of office, Illinois Gov. George Ryan commutes the death sentences of all 167 people on Death Row in Illinois, saying that the system is flawed.

12 Stephen M. Case resigns as chairman of the media conglomerate AOL Time Warner; on January 16 Richard D. Parsons, the CEO of the company, is named to succeed him. (*See* January 29.)

•

The ceremonial groundbreaking for Hong Kong Disneyland, a new theme park to be located on Lantau Island, takes place, led by Michael Eisner, chairman and chief executive officer of Walt Disney. (Photo above.)

13 The Harvard-Smithsonian Center for Astrophysics reports that astronomers at the Cerro Tololo Inter-American Observatory in Chile and in Hawaii have detected three new moons orbiting Neptune; this brings the total number of the planet's known satellites to 11.

•

FAO Inc., which owns the high-end toy-store chains F.A.O. Schwarz, Zany Brainy, and Right Start, files for bankruptcy protection.

•

The Voter News Service, owned by NBC, ABC, CBS, CNN, Fox News Channel, and the Associated Press, goes out of business; the networks plan to have a new system in place in time for the U.S. presidential election in 2004.

14 Representatives of a newly created Islamic council in France are officially welcomed to a New Year's reception by Pres. Jacques Chirac; the new council will help put Muslims in France on a more equal footing with members of other religions, which have long had their own councils.

•

The U.S. Food and Drug Administration suspends 27 gene therapy trials after a second child in a gene therapy trial in France has developed a leukemia-like disease.

•

General Electric employees nationwide begin a 48-hour strike to protest a company decision to raise employee health care costs; it is the first nationwide strike at the company since 1969.

15 In Paris, French Foreign Minister Dominique de Villepin opens peace talks between the various factions in the civil war in Côte d'Ivoire.

•

A UN investigative team says that rebel groups in the Ituri region of the Democratic Republic of the Congo last year carried out systematic atrocities, including torture, rape, and cannibalism.

•

In a televised address, U.S. Pres. George W. Bush denounces the use of racial preferences in university admission and describes plans to file a brief with the Supreme Court asking that the admissions policies at the University of Michigan, in which race is one of a number of factors considered, be found unconstitutional.

16 The space shuttle *Columbia* lifts off for a 16-day mission that is the first in three years not connected to the International Space Station or the Hubble Space Telescope; among its crew members is Ilan Ramon, the first Israeli astronaut in space. (*See* February 1.)

•

At a storage bunker in Iraq UN weapons inspectors discover 11 empty chemical warheads and a 12th that requires further testing.

17 The IMF agrees to allow Argentina to postpone a $1 billion debt payment until August in return for which Argentina agrees to a program of fiscal policies supplied by the IMF.

•

The American financier Boris Jordan is fired as CEO of Gazprom Media in Russia and as director general of the television station NTV.

18 Tens of thousands of people in cities across the U.S. demonstrate against the U.S. government's threat of war on the Iraqi regime; the biggest demonstration takes place in Washington, D.C.

•

Wildfires burning outside the city of Canberra, Australia, spread into town and destroy 402 homes; firefighters are unable to make headway against the fires.

•

In an exceptionally mistake-filled U.S. figure-skating championship competition, Michelle Kwan wins for the sixth consecutive time in the women's competition, and Michael Weiss wins the men's competition.

•

With their 55th consecutive win, the University of Connecticut Huskies set a new record for women's college basketball.

•

Emperor Akihito of Japan undergoes prostate surgery; the open reporting on the subject is a first for the Imperial Household Agency.

19 The Yuzhengong Palace in Hubei province in China burns to the ground; designated a UNESCO World Heritage Site in 1994, it exemplified a millennium of artistic and architectural achievement during the Yuan, Ming, and Qing dynasties.

•

At the Golden Globe Awards in Beverly Hills, Calif., best picture honours go to *The Hours* and *Chicago;* best director goes to Martin Scorsese for *Gangs of New York;* and the screenplay award goes to Alexander Payne and Jim Taylor for *About Schmidt.*

20 Iraq makes 10 specific commitments to the UN inspectors in response to their demands; key among them is the promise to press scientists to agree to private interviews with inspectors.

•

France announces that it will not support a UN resolution permitting military action against the Iraqi regime, should one be proposed.

•

In Geneva at a meeting of the UN Commission on Human Rights, the U.S. insists on a vote for the chairmanship for the first time in the committee's history, and, contrary to the desires of the U.S., Libya is elected.

21 The U.S. Census Bureau announces that the Hispanic population of the U.S. has grown to surpass that of the black population as a percentage of the total; at close to 13%, Hispanics are now the largest minority in the U.S.

•

Pres. Ismail Omar Guelleh of Djibouti visits U.S. Pres. George W. Bush in Washington, D.C., and is greeted with red-carpet treatment; Djibouti has become a staging area for U.S. troops in the Middle East.

•

North Korean representatives arrive in Seoul in order to resume high-level talks with their South Korean counterparts.

22 In elections in The Netherlands, the conservative Christian Democratic Party of Prime Minister Jan Peter Balkenende comes in with the most votes, followed by the Labour Party, with the Pim Fortuyn List a distant third.

•

The U.S. deploys a system called Bio-Watch that also uses Environmental Protection Agency air-quality monitoring systems to check for the presence of germs related to biological warfare.

•

Researchers in China announce the discovery of a fossilized small feathered dinosaur with four wings and a plumed tail; about 76 cm (30 in) long, the dragon-like animal has been named *Microraptor gui.*

23 Australian forces begin heading for the Persian Gulf in support of a possible U.S.-led war against Iraq.

•

McDonald's Corp., the biggest restaurant chain in the world, reports that in the last quarter of 2002 it posted a loss for the first time in its history.

•

It is reported that some 40 librettos of operas by Joseph Haydn dating from his lifetime have been serendipitously discovered in a secondhand bookstore in Budapest; these librettos were believed to have been destroyed in bombings during World War II.

24 Representatives of a number of Palestinian groups meet in Cairo under the guidance of Omar Suleiman, the head of Egyptian intelligence, to discuss a possible Palestinian cease-fire.

•

The U.S. plan to inoculate 500,000 health care workers against smallpox gets under way with the vaccination of four doctors in Connecticut.

•

A chartered plane carrying members of Kenya's new government crashes on takeoff from the airport at Busia, killing the minister of labour and two others.

25 West African leaders meet in Paris to discuss the peace agreed to by the parties in Côte d'Ivoire, and Ivorian Pres. Laurent Gbagbo accepts the appointment of Seydou Diarra as prime minister to lead the reconciliation government. (*See* February 10.)

•

Serena Williams defeats her sister Venus to win the Australian Open tennis tournament in her fourth straight victory in a major tournament; the following day Andre Agassi defeats Rainer Schüttler to win the men's title.

26 ***In San Diego, Calif., the Tampa Bay Buccaneers convincingly defeat the Oakland Raiders 48–21 to win Super Bowl XXXVII. (Photo below.)***

•

Winning films at the Sundance Film Festival awards ceremony in Park City, Utah, include *Capturing the Friedmans, American Splendor, My Flesh and Blood,* and *The Station Agent.*

27 Hans Blix, the head of the UN weapons inspectors in Iraq, reports to the UN Security Council that the Iraqi regime has been insufficiently cooperative and does not appear to accept the need to disarm.

•

Kazakhstan reaches an agreement with a consortium led by ChevronTexaco that allows the consortium to run an expansion of the Tengiz oil field.

•

A retailing group consisting of Best Buy, Tower Records, Virgin Entertainment Group, Wherehouse Entertainment, Hastings Entertainment, and Trans World Entertainment announces plans to sell music to be downloaded from the Internet.

•

In horse racing's 2002 Eclipse Awards, the filly Azeri, trained by Laura De Seroux, is named Horse of the Year.

28 In elections in Israel, there is no significant opposition to Ariel Sharon, and he retains his post as prime minister with a strong showing by Likud, his party.

•

U.S. Pres. George W. Bush delivers his second state of the union address; he stresses plans to revive the economy and his intentions to address what he portrays as the intolerable threat represented by Pres. Saddam Hussein of Iraq, and he pledges $15 billion to combat AIDS in Africa and the Caribbean.

•

A South Korean epidemiologist and expert on diseases associated with poverty, Jong Wook Lee, is named director general of the World Health Organization.

•

Claire Tomalin wins the 2002 Whitbread Book of the Year Award—given for books published in the U.K.—for her biography *Samuel Pepys: The Unequalled Self;* one of the other books in contention for the prize was the novel *Spies,* by Tomalin's husband, Michael Frayn.

•

Norio Ohga, a longtime driving force behind the company, announces that he is retiring as chairman of Sony Corp.; simultaneously, the company says that it will adopt American-style auditing arrangements.

29 AOL Time Warner announces that CNN founder Ted Turner has resigned as vice-chairman and that for the first time the number of people subscribing to AOL's services has declined. (*See* January 12.)

•

Ukrainian Pres. Leonid Kuchma is elected chairman of the Commonwealth of Independent States; it is the first time since the alliance was created in 1991 that someone other than a Russian has held the post.

•

A French court of appeals overturns the conviction for corruption of former foreign minister Roland Dumas; he was convicted as part of the enormous Elf Aquitaine scandal.

•

The government of Nepal and Maoist rebels unexpectedly agree to a cease-fire.

30 The World Food Programme says that the food crisis in sub-Saharan Africa has eased everywhere except Zimbabwe, where conditions continue to deteriorate.

•

In Boston, Richard Reid, who pleaded guilty in a trial for having attempted to blow up an airplane with a bomb concealed in his shoe, is sentenced to life in prison.

•

Irish Minister of Health Michael Martin announces that, beginning next year, smoking will be banned in all places of employment, including restaurants and pubs.

31 A mob of 5,000 people throwing stones invades the airport at Port-Bouët in Côte d'Ivoire, terrorizing hundreds of French residents trying to flee the war-torn country.

•

The American Red Cross quarantines almost all of its blood supply for the state of Georgia and some of South Carolina because of unidentified white particles that have been found in some bags of donated blood.

AP/Wide World Photos

February

The crew of the shuttle Columbia *did not return safely to Earth. Yet we can pray that all are safely home.*

U.S. Pres. George W. Bush, announcing the loss of the space shuttle *Columbia,* February 1

1 In New York City's Chinatown, the first day of the Year of the Goat, 4701, is celebrated; it is the first time in seven years that the city has allowed the traditional use of firecrackers in the New Year's festival.

•

The space shuttle* Columbia *burns up on its reentry into the Earth's atmosphere, spreading debris across Texas and Louisiana and killing all seven astronauts aboard. (Photo right.)* (See *January 16.)

2 After 13 years as president of Czechoslovakia and then of the Czech Republic, Vaclav Havel gives his farewell address.

3 Shops and factories in Venezuela begin reopening after opponents of Pres. Hugo Chávez decide to largely end the national strike that began on Dec. 2, 2002; oil workers continue to strike.

•

The trial for treason of opposition leader Morgan Tsvangirai begins in Zimbabwe; many believe that Pres. Robert Mugabe stole the 2002 presidential election from Tsvangirai.

•

Legendary rock-and-roll producer Phil Spector is arrested for the murder of a woman found dead in his home in Alhambra, Calif.

4 The legislature votes Yugoslavia out of existence as the country officially becomes Serbia and Montenegro.

•

The new African Union concludes its first meeting, in Addis Ababa, Eth., with plans to create a new peace and security council and plans to send peacekeeping troops to Burundi.

•

Marty Mankamyer, the president of the U.S. Olympic Committee, resigns; the committee has been split by bitter infighting since an inquiry early in the year into conflict-of-interest charges against the CEO of the committee.

5 U.S. Secretary of State Colin Powell appears before the UN Security Council to present photographs, recordings, and other material as evidence that Iraq possesses forbidden chemical and biological weapons as well as weapons of mass destruction and that the country therefore poses an imminent danger.

•

The rebel group Liberians United for Reconciliation and Democracy advances to within 24 km (15 mi) of Monrovia, Liberia's capital; Pres. Charles Taylor proposes peace talks and suggests that the rebels lay down their arms and run in the presidential election scheduled for October.

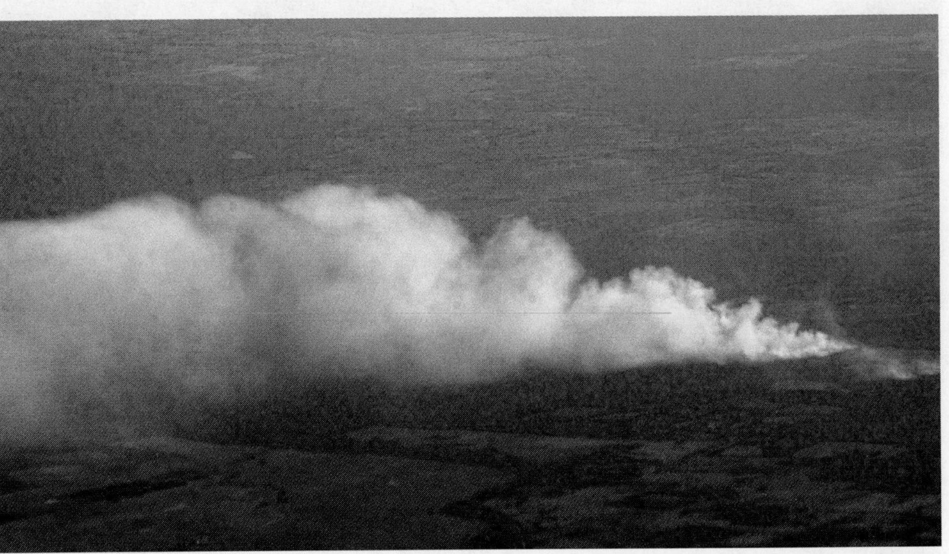

Pres. Pervez Musharraf of Pakistan meets with Pres. Vladimir Putin of Russia in Moscow; it is the first time in 33 years that the leaders of Pakistan and Russia have met.

•

Activists, including the first ladies of several African countries, gather in Addis Ababa, Eth., for a conference seeking the end of female genital mutilation, practiced in some 28 countries.

6 Brazil's flagship airline, Varig, announces plans to merge with its main competitor, TAM Linhas Aéreas, to form the biggest airline in Latin America.

•

A small private airplane carrying the Colombian minister of social welfare, Juan Luís Londoño, crashes in the Andes Mountains, killing him.

•

The Freedom Forum announces that Myanmar (Burmese) activist Aung San Suu Kyi is the winner of its annual Al Neuharth Free Spirit of the Year Award.

7 China and France indicate that they would not support a new security resolution authorizing the use of force against Iraq; both governments say they believe UN weapons inspectors should be given more time.

•

The U.S. government raises the official terror-alert level from yellow (elevated) to orange (high).

•

NASA makes a final—and futile—attempt to contact Pioneer 10, last heard from on January 22; Pioneer 10 was launched in 1972 and left the solar system in 1983.

•

In New York City, Russian chess grandmaster Garry Kasparov and the IBM computer Deep Junior agree to a draw in the final game of their six-game series, closing out the competition at a tie (one win each and four draws).

8 Members of the Islamist group Ansar al-Islam assassinate a Kurdish government minister and two other government officials as well as three civilians in Qamesh Tapa in northern Iraq.

•

The biggest Winter Asian Games to date come to a close in Aomori, Japan; athletes from 29 countries competed for eight days, with Japan, South Korea, and China winning the most gold medals.

9 Recently reelected Israeli Prime Minister Ariel Sharon officially accepts the task of forming a new government.

•

India begins the biggest mass-immunization campaign in its history in an effort to put an end to a polio epidemic in Uttar Pradesh state.

10 France, Germany, and Belgium block efforts led by the U.S. for NATO to begin planning the defense of Turkey in the event that a U.S.-led war against Iraq makes such a defense necessary.

•

Seydou Diarra is installed as prime minister of Côte d'Ivoire, as specified in the peace agreement that had been signed the previous month in Paris. (*See* January 25.)

•

Israel completely closes its borders with the West Bank and the Gaza Strip, stopping Palestinian travel during the Eid al-Adha holiday.

•

Scientists announce the discovery of the first asteroid with a solar orbit between the Earth and the Sun.

11 Philippine Pres. Gloria Macapagal Arroyo announces a suspension in the government offensive against Muslim separatists in deference to the Eid al-Adha holiday; the following day fighting erupts again.

•

The giant oil company BP agrees to a deal with the Russian oil company Sidanco and others to form a new Russian oil company in which BP will have a 50% stake.

•

A U.S. bombing raid is called in by forces under rebel ambush in the mountains of southern Afghanistan; 17 Afghani civilians are killed.

•

The English cricket team announces that it will not participate in its first World Cup game, scheduled to take place in Harare, Zimb.; it is the first time ever that a team has boycotted a venue in World Cup cricket.

•

The Kerry Blue Terrier Torums Scarf Michael, which had been favoured to win in the previous two years, is finally named Best in Show at the Westminster Kennel Club Dog Show.

12 India successfully test fires a short-range cruise missile from a naval destroyer, raising the already-high tension with Pakistan.

•

Protests against a government plan to introduce a graduated income tax explode into riots in La Paz, Bol.; by the following day 27 people have been killed.

•

The album *Get Rich or Die Trying* by the gangsta rapper 50 Cent sells 872,000 copies in its first four days; it is believed to be the fastest-selling first album on a major label ever.

•

Scientists studying the monarch butterfly announce that they have found, to their surprise, that the population of that butterfly appears to have nearly fully recovered from the enormous die-off that occurred in winter 2002.

•

Adrienne Rich is named the winner of the biennial Bollingen Prize in American Poetry.

13 The board charged with investigating the *Columbia* disaster releases preliminary findings that a breach in the skin of the space shuttle allowed superheated gases to enter the left wing, causing the breakup; the cause of the breach has not been determined.

•

A U.S. government plane carrying four Americans and a Colombian crashes in an area controlled by the Revolutionary Armed Forces of Colombia (FARC); three Americans are kidnapped and the other two passengers shot to death.

•

American microbiologist Carl R. Woese is named winner of the Crafoord Prize, for having demonstrated that the single-celled organisms now called archaea qualify as a separate major domain of life in addition to bacteria and eukaryotes.

•

The City Council of New York City approves a ban on the use of mobile telephones in such public places as theatres and museums.

14 Palestinian leader Yasir Arafat announces that he will appoint a prime minister.

AP/Wide World Photos

•

As UN weapons inspectors Hans Blix and Mohamed El Baradei report increasing cooperation from Iraq, several members of the Security Council agree with France's proposal to allow the inspectors more time.

•

Dolly the sheep, the first cloned mammal, is euthanized by veterinarians after being found to be suffering from progressive lung disease.

•

In London, Sam Mendes wins three Laurence Olivier Awards: best director, for *Twelfth Night,* best revival, for *Uncle Vanya,* and special achievement, for his leadership of the Donmar Warehouse Theatre.

15 Millions of people in more than 350 cities throughout the world rally and march against the threatened U.S. invasion of Iraq.

•

The Vatican opens archives relating to the activities of Pope Pius XII in the Vatican Secretariat of State in the years 1922–39, before his papacy, in hopes of showing that he did not shirk responsibilities to protect Jews and Roman Catholics during the rise of Nazism in Germany.

•

At the Berlin International Film Festival, the Golden Bear goes to the British film **In This World** ***directed by Michael Winterbottom (photo above), and the Silver Bear is won by the American movie*** **Adaptation.**

•

It is reported that the Internet search engine Google has bought Pyra Labs, which deals in software for creating Web logs, or blogs; it is believed that this will vastly increase the audience for blogs.

16 Greek Cypriot opposition leader Tassos Papadopoulos handily and unexpectedly defeats the incumbent president, Glafcos Clerides.

•

On a rainy day in Daytona Beach, Fla., the shortest Daytona 500 NASCAR race in history (109 of 200 laps), called because of rain, is won by Michael Waltrip.

17 Twenty-one people die in a stampede during a fire at a Chicago nightclub. (*See* February 20.)

•

Uri Lupolianski, a member of Israel's most Orthodox Jewish community, becomes acting mayor of Jerusalem.

•

Beginning this day, anyone driving a private vehicle into a demarcated area of central London between the hours of 7:00 AM and 6:30 PM on weekdays must pay a £5 (about $7.85) fee for the privilege.

•

Workers in the diamond district in Antwerp, Belg., discover that the largest safe-deposit-box robbery, as well as the largest jewel theft in Belgian history—$100 million worth of gems—has taken place over the previous two days.

18 On a rush-hour subway train in Taegu, S.Kor., a man attempts suicide by fire, igniting the train and killing at least 198 people.

•

In North Korea the Korean People's Army releases a statement saying that should the U.S. impose penalties against North Korea for its suspected illegal nuclear arms program, the North Korean military would no longer feel bound by the 1953 armistice agreement ending hostilities in the Korean War.

•

The U.S. National Academy of Engineering awards its Draper Prize to Bradford Parkinson and Ivan Getting for their work in developing the Global Positioning System satellites and its Russ Prize to Willem Kolff for his invention of the artificial kidney-dialysis machine.

19 A Russian-made Ilyushin airliner, flying from Zahedan to Kerman in Iran and carrying 302 people, mostly members of the Revolutionary Guards, crashes near Shahdad, killing all aboard; it is the worst air disaster in Iran's history.

•

In a trial in Hamburg, Ger., the first person is convicted in relation to the terrorist attacks of Sept. 11, 2001; Mounir al-Motassadeq is found guilty of 3,066 counts of accessory to murder and is sentenced to 15 years in prison.

•

It is announced at a NASA briefing that erosional gullies on the Martian surface, revealed in photographs from the Mars Odyssey spacecraft, may be the result of snowmelt running underneath a thick snow covering; a week earlier it had been reported that both polar icecaps on Mars could contain much more water than previously thought.

•

It is reported that the human remains in the Lake Mungo region of Australia, previously dated as 62,000 years old, are in fact only 42,000 years old and thus in line with theories that the great human migration out of Africa began 50,000 years ago.

20 More than 100 people die in a stampede during a nightclub fire in West Warwick, R.I. (*See* February 17.)

•

In the midst of a period of violence between Israelis and Palestinians, Israel divides the Gaza Strip into three separate security zones, which leads to fears among Palestinians of a complete takeover.

•

A new pan-Arab television news channel, al-Arabiyah, owned by the satellite television station MBC, goes on the air in the United Arab Emirates.

•

U.S. officials announce plans to send some 1,700 troops to the southern Philippines to combat the Muslim terrorist group Abu Sayyaf.

•

The U.S. government brings charges against eight people, including Sami al-Arian, a professor at the University of South Florida, accusing them of sending financial and logistic support to Palestinian terrorists in the West Bank and the Gaza Strip.

21 U.S. Secretary of State Colin Powell begins a five-day trip to Asia to persuade the leaders of South Korea, China, and Japan to go along with the U.S. approach to North Korea; he also plans to attend the inauguration of Roh Moo Hyun as president of South Korea on February 25.

•

UN weapons inspector Hans Blix orders Iraq to dismantle its al-Samoud 2 missiles, which have a range that exceeds UN-imposed limits, by the end of the month; on February 27 Iraq agrees to do so.

•

The World Health Organization suggests an increase in preparedness in response to reports that two family members in Hong Kong have contracted avian flu and one has died, though human-to-human transmission of the flu is believed to be rare and difficult.

22 The main Protestant paramilitary group in Northern Ireland, the Ulster Defense Association, declares a 12-month cease-fire and agrees to cooperate with an organization charged with monitoring disarmament of paramilitary groups.

•

In Karachi, Pak., gunmen open fire inside a Shi'ite mosque, killing nine people, in the first major sectarian attack since June 2002.

•

Sporting a new tattoo covering the left side of his face, Mike Tyson knocks out Clifford Etienne 49 seconds into the heavyweight fight in Memphis, Tenn.

23 Results of the first large-scale trial of an AIDS vaccine indicate that the vaccine is largely ineffective, though it appears to have some small efficacy among African Americans and Asians.

•

At the Grammy Awards, which are held in New York City for the first time since 1998, the top winner is Norah Jones, who wins five Grammys, including Record of the Year ("Don't Know Why"), Album of the Year (*Come Away with Me*), and best new artist; the Song of the Year goes to her recording of "Don't Know Why," written by Jesse Harris.

24 The U.S., Great Britain, and Spain request that the UN Security Council declare that Iraq has failed to disarm as required, while France, Germany, and Russia ask the Council to give inspectors greater powers and more time.

•

In Washington, D.C., the National Governors Association, which pleads that the states are facing their worst financial crisis since World War II, is told by Pres. George W. Bush that the federal government will be unable to provide fiscal assistance to them.

•

Frederick Chiluba, who was president of Zambia in 1991–2002, is arrested and accused of stealing from the state treasury.

•

The Serbian nationalist paramilitary leader Vojislav Seselj voluntarily surrenders to the UN war crimes tribunal in The Hague.

25 Roh Moo Hyun is inaugurated as president of South Korea.

•

Two months after deliveries of food aid to North Korea were halted, the U.S. announces that it will resume the shipments but at a reduced level.

•

A U.S. Army Black Hawk helicopter crashes in a sandstorm in Kuwait, killing all four crew members; the vehicle and crew were part of a troop buildup in Kuwait in anticipation of a war against Iraq.

•

The Conference Board, a private business association, reports that consumer confidence in the U.S. fell 15 points in February to its lowest level since 1993.

•

The Credit Suisse Group reports a loss of $2.4 billion in 2002, the largest one-year deficit in the bank's history.

26 In a nationally televised address, U.S. Pres. George W. Bush asserts that removing Saddam Hussein as president of Iraq would increase stability in the Middle East and could lead to the creation of a Palestinian state living in peace with Israel; he also suggests that a failure to confront Iraq on the part of the UN Security Council would weaken the authority of the United Nations.

•

U.S. intelligence officials say that North Korea has restarted a reactor at its main nuclear complex.

•

It is reported that the personal art collection of Pierre Matisse, a son of the artist Henri Matisse, has been donated to New York City's Metropolitan Museum of Art; the collection contains more than 100 pieces by the most prominent artists of the 20th century.

•

Israeli Prime Minister Ariel Sharon surprises analysts by replacing Benjamin Netanyahu as foreign minister with economist Silvan Shalom.

27 The U.S. government lowers the terror-alert level to yellow (elevated).

•

Archbishop Rowan Williams is enthroned as archbishop of Canterbury, the head of the Anglican Communion.

•

Biljana Plavsic, who served two years as president of the self-proclaimed Republika Srpska in Bosnia and Herzegovina, is sentenced to 11 years in prison by the International Criminal Tribunal for the Former Yugoslavia for crimes against humanity.

•

Officials in New York City announce that the design submitted by Studio Daniel Libeskind has been chosen for rebuilding on the site of the World Trade Center, destroyed on Sept. 11, 2001.

28 Vaclav Klaus, a former prime minister, is elected president of the Czech Republic.

•

The Ninth Circuit Court of Appeals refuses a request from the U.S. government that it reconsider its ruling that requiring children in public schools to recite the Pledge of Allegiance is unconstitutional because the pledge contains the words "under God."

March

Intelligence gathered by this and other governments leaves no doubt that the Iraqi regime continues to possess and conceal some of the most lethal weapons ever devised.

U.S. Pres. George W. Bush, in a nationally televised address on the imminence of war against Iraq, March 17

1 Authorities in Pakistan arrest Khalid Shaikh Mohammed, who is believed to be one of the top members of al-Qaeda and who is thought to have planned the terrorist attacks of Sept. 11, 2001.

•

Iraqi workers begin destroying the illegal al-Samoud 2 missiles under the supervision of UN weapons inspectors.

•

Turkey's Grand National Assembly rejects the agreement made by government officials to allow the U.S. to base troops in Turkey in order to wage war in northern Iraq.

•

The World Health Organization adopts the final text for the Framework Convention on Tobacco Control, aimed at curtailing the use of tobacco products.

2 Tens of thousands of people, mostly militant Muslims, in Islamabad, Pak., demonstrate their opposition to a U.S. war against Iraq and the possibility of Pres. Pervez Musharraf's cooperating with such an action.

AP/Wide World Photos

•

French Pres. Jacques Chirac arrives in Algiers in the first state visit by the leader of France to Algeria since the former French colony became independent in 1962.

•

The Swiss team Alinghi, led by Russell Coutts, defeats Team New Zealand to win the America's Cup, the world's most prestigious yacht race; it is Coutts's third consecutive victory (his first two wins were as the skipper for New Zealand). (Photo above.)

3 The legislative body of the new country of Serbia and Montenegro holds its first session, in Belgrade, the capital; the body consists of 91 deputies from Serbia and 35 deputies from Montenegro.

•

A radio announcer in North Korea reads a statement from leader Kim Jong Il to the effect that an attack on North Korea by the U.S. would lead to nuclear war.

•

On about 900 stages of all sizes and sorts in many countries, a reading of Aristophanes' play *Lysistrata* takes place as an organized worldwide antiwar protest.

•

A design by Julie Beckman and Keith Kaseman, featuring 184 benches with trees and reflecting pools, is chosen to memorialize the Sept. 11, 2001, terrorist attack on the Pentagon in Washington, D.C.

4 A bomb explodes at the international airport in Davao City, Phil., killing at least 21 people and wounding 170 more.

5 The foreign ministers of France, Russia, and Germany issue a statement that they would not permit passage of a UN Security Council resolution to authorize the use of force in Iraq, adding that France and Russia, permanent members of the Council, would veto such a resolution.

•

An emergency meeting of the Organization of the Islamic Conference in Doha, Qatar, which was called to try to find a way to avert a U.S. war against the Iraqi regime, breaks up in acrimony and insults.

•

A bomb destroys a city bus in Haifa, Israel, killing at least 15 passengers in the first deadly suicide attack in Israel in two months; the following day Israeli forces attack a refugee camp in the Gaza Strip, leaving 11 dead.

•

The U.S. Supreme Court upholds the constitutionality of California's "three strikes" law, which mandates lengthy prison terms for anyone who is convicted of the same type of crime three times, regardless of the severity of the crime.

•

The Supreme Court of Argentina declares unconstitutional a presidential decree converting all dollars deposited in banks into pesos; the decree had been promulgated a year earlier in an effort to bring stability to the Argentine economy.

6 In his first formal White House news conference in almost 18 months, U.S. Pres. George W. Bush says that Iraqi Pres. Saddam Hussein poses a direct threat to the U.S. and that UN opposition will not deter Washington from attacking Iraq.

•

U.S. Pres. George W. Bush and first lady Laura Bush award the 2002 National Medal of Arts to designer and architect Florence Knoll Bassett, dancer and choreographer Trisha Brown, museum director Philippe de Montebello, actress and educator Uta Hagen, architect and environmental planner Lawrence Halprin, cartoonist Al Hirschfeld (recently deceased), country singer and songwriter George Jones, painter and stage designer Ming Cho Lee, and singer-songwriter Smokey Robinson.

7 U.S. Pres. George W. Bush announces economic sanctions against the leaders of Zimbabwe's government, forbidding Americans to do business with them; the European Union had previously imposed similar measures.

•

The legislature of Serbia and Montenegro elects Svetozar Marovic president of the country; Marovic, who also holds the position of prime minister, had been an official in Montenegro's government.

•

Almost all of Broadway goes dark as stage musicians in New York City go on strike and actors and stagehands honour the strike, causing nearly all musicals to cancel performances; at issue is the minimum number of musicians a production must employ.

8 Meeting in Accra, Ghana, representatives of the warring parties in Côte d'Ivoire agree to the composition of a national reconciliation government, but fighting breaks out anew in the western region of the country.

•

Citizens of Malta approve membership in the European Union; the national referendum is the first among the proposed new members of the EU, so the vote is watched with considerable interest.

•

A judge in Argentina issues arrest warrants for four officials of the Iranian government, charging them with responsibility for the bombing of a Jewish community centre in Buenos Aires on July 18, 1994, that killed 85 people.

9 Israeli forces kill Ibrahim al-Makadmah, a leader of the Palestinian separatist group Hamas.

•

In the biggest demonstrations since 1991, tens of thousands of protesters march in the Ukrainian capital, Kiev, to demand the resignation of Pres. Leonid Kuchma.

10 Deutsche Telekom, the German telecommunications company, announces losses in 2002 of about $27.1 billion, the biggest shortfall in European corporate history.

•

The Rock and Roll Hall of Fame in Cleveland, Ohio, inducts AC/DC, the Clash, Elvis Costello and the Attractions, the Police, and the Righteous Brothers.

11 The new International Criminal Court holds its inaugural session in The Hague, attended by UN Secretary-General Kofi Annan and hundreds of other high-ranking officials.

•

Turkish Pres. Ahmet Necdet Sezer asks Recep Tayyip Erdogan, the head of the ruling Justice and Development Party, to form a government after Prime Minister Abdullah Gul resigns.

•

In a small ribbon-cutting ceremony, the European Union opens its first diplomatic office in Cuba, in Havana; the EU is Cuba's biggest trading partner.

•

The head of the U.S. House Administration Committee orders that henceforth the cafeteria in the House of Representatives will serve "freedom fries" and "freedom toast" rather than French fries and French toast; the move is intended to showcase political frustration with the French position against a U.S.-led war in Iraq.

•

In National Collegiate Athletic Association women's basketball, the Villanova University Wildcats defeat the University of Connecticut Huskies in the Big East division championship, snapping the Huskies' record winning streak of 70 games.

12 Serbian Prime Minister Zoran Djindjic is assassinated by snipers in downtown Belgrade; officials believe the killing is a response to Djindjic's crackdown on organized crime.

•

Elizabeth Smart, who was kidnapped from her home in Salt Lake City, Utah, in June 2002, is found with her kidnappers alive but apparently having been sexually abused.

13 A bomb explodes on a rush-hour train at a station in Mulund, India, a suburb of Mumbai (Bombay), killing 10 people and injuring 75.

•

Robert Sorlie of Norway wins the Iditarod Trail Sled Dog Race; unusual weather had forced the organizers to include a detour that added some 110 km (70 mi) to the race and to cut the final 80 km (50 mi) to the final line in Nome, Alaska.

14 U.S. Pres. George W. Bush says that he will adopt a peace plan, referred to as a "road map," for Israel and Palestine and will work for its acceptance as soon as Palestine has a new prime minister; he had previously said that he would not address that issue until the situation in Iraq had been resolved to his satisfaction.

•

Admitting for the first time that the weakness of Germany's economy is partially due to structural flaws, Chancellor Gerhard Schröder introduces a major reform program.

Stancliffe's Hotel, a novella written by Charlotte Brontë in 1838, appears in print for the first time, published in its entirety in *The Times* of London.

© Reuters NewMedia Inc./Corbis

15 The World Health Organization issues its first worldwide health alert in a decade, regarding a mysterious respiratory illness, SARS (severe acute respiratory syndrome), that has struck hundreds of people in China, Hong Kong, and Vietnam and has been reported in Canada.

Hu Jintao is ceremonially named China's new president, replacing Jiang Zemin, who remains head of the People's Liberation Army; the following day Wen Jiabao is named prime minister, replacing Zhu Rongji.

Opponents of war in Iraq lead large protests in several major American cities.

16 Legislative elections in Finland result in a victory for the conservative Centre Party, led by Anneli Jäätteenmäki, over Prime Minister Paavo Lipponen's Social Democratic Party. (*See* June 18.)

A referendum in Liechtenstein increases the already unusually great powers of Prince Hans Adam II, who had said he would leave the country and move to Vienna if the referendum did not pass.

Zoran Zivkovic is nominated to replace the assassinated Zoran Djindjic as prime minister of Serbia; Zivkovic was a key ally of Djindjic's.

17 In a nationally televised address, U.S. Pres. George W. Bush declares that Saddam Hussein and his sons must abandon Iraq within 48 hours or suffer a military attack; the U.S. government raises the terror-alert level from yellow (elevated) to orange (high).

After a weekend coup in the Central African Republic, rebel leader François Bozize declares himself president; French citizens flee the country.

Spain's Supreme Court bans the militant Basque political party Batasuna; it is the first time since the death of dictator Francisco Franco in 1975 that a political party has been outlawed in Spain.

18 The aluminum-producing company Alcoa reaches an agreement with Iceland to build an aluminum smelter in Reydarfjorður; the smelter is to be the sole customer for an enormous and controversial hydroelectric project in the wilderness area being undertaken by Landsvirkjun, Iceland's national power company.

An Egyptian court dismisses all charges against democracy advocate Saad Eddin Ibrahim, whose conviction and imprisonment on the same charges in 2002 evoked international protests.

19 ***The U.S. begins air strikes against Baghdad, the capital of Iraq; the first target is a complex in which Saddam Hussein was believed to be holding a meeting (photo above);*** even months later, however, Hussein's fate is unknown.

Palestinian leader Yasir Arafat names Mahmoud Abbas to the new position of prime minister.

Holmes Rolston III, a Presbyterian minister and professor of philosophy known as a founder of environmental ethics, is named the winner of the Templeton Prize for Progress Toward Research or Discoveries About Spiritual Realities.

20 U.S. and British forces push into Iraq from Kuwait, and cruise missiles are directed into Baghdad; the first coalition casualties are reported as the result of a helicopter crash in Kuwait.

Hundreds of thousands of people in cities throughout the world demonstrate against the U.S.-led invasion of Iraq; the biggest protests take place outside the U.S.

21 Avianca, Colombia's flagship carrier and the oldest airline in Latin America, files for bankruptcy protection in a U.S. court; the company plans to continue operating, however.

South Africa's Truth and Reconciliation Commission concludes its work, and commission head Bishop Desmond Tutu delivers its multivolume report to Pres. Thabo Mbeki.

22 The French petroleum company TotalFinaElf announces that it is shutting its oil facilities in western Nigeria and evacuating its employees because of increasing ethnic violence; workers at a ChevronTexaco terminal have been stranded by the violence, and ChevronTexaco and Shell have already shut down operations in the area.

23 A U.S. soldier with the 101st Airborne Division in Kuwait attacks command tents with small-arms fire and a grenade, killing one person and wounding 15.

•

The Academy Awards ceremony is only slightly overshadowed by the war in Iraq; the gala is hosted by Steve Martin, and Oscars are won by, among others, *Chicago,* director Roman Polanski, and actors Adrien Brody, Nicole Kidman, Chris Cooper, and Catherine Zeta-Jones.

•

In two referenda in Slovenia, citizens vote strongly in favour of their country's joining both NATO and the European Union.

•

A Russian-sponsored referendum on a new constitution is held in Chechnya; reported results are 96% in favour of the proposal, which envisions an elected government and a continuation of the republic's status as part of Russia.

•

Australia defeats India by 125 runs to win a record third Cricket World Cup; Australia's score of 359 for 2 is that country's highest-ever one-day total.

•

At the close of the Third World Water Forum in Japan, UNESCO announces the creation of the Water Cooperation Facility in partnership with the World Water Council; the new organization will promote mechanisms for sustainable water development and will mediate disputes over international access to fresh water.

24 U.S. forces enter and fight for control of the strategic Iraqi city of Al-Nasiriyah.

•

The Qatar-based television network al-Jazeera launches an English-language Web site, starting with coverage of the war in Iraq; the site is almost immediately hijacked by hackers.

•

In India, gunmen enter the Kashmiri village of Nadi Marg, spraying gunfire; 24 Hindu civilians are killed.

25 Officials of the World Health Organization say that China has not allowed its team of investigators to enter Guangdong province, where the SARS (severe acute respiratory syndrome) epidemic is believed to have begun; China says the outbreak in that province has already died out.

•

Boris Berezovsky, once one of the most influential people in Russia and now an expatriate billionaire in Great Britain, is arrested by British authorities for possible extradition to Russia on fraud charges.

•

The U.S. Air Force confirms that the top four commanders of the U.S. Air Force Academy in Colorado Springs, Colo., will be replaced; the action comes after months of complaints by female cadets who reported being sexually harassed or abused and claimed they themselves, rather than their attackers, were investigated.

•

A group of figure-skating professionals, including coaches, judges, and skaters, announce the formation of the World Skating Federation; the new organization hopes to replace the International Skating Union as the governing body of the sport, believing the older organization to be hopelessly corrupt.

26 U.S. forces fighting in Iraq open a northern front with 1,000 paratroopers.

•

Health officials in China double their estimate of the number of cases and deaths from SARS (severe acute respiratory syndrome) in Guangdong province as of the end of February; there are widespread complaints about the cooperation of Chinese officials in sharing information about the disease, about which almost nothing is known.

•

The World Trade Organization rules that the steel tariffs imposed by the U.S. in early 2002 are illegal under the agreements made by the organization's members.

27 Amnesty International reports escalating violence on the part of the government of Zimbabwe against opposition figures; hundreds have been arrested, and there is evidence of torture.

28 Japan launches a rocket to place into orbit two spy satellites; the move evokes strenuous objections from North Korea, whose recent bellicose policies were likely one factor behind the launching.

•

The UN Security Council places UN Secretary-General Kofi Annan in charge of Iraq's oil-for-food program for the time being; some 60% of Iraq depends on this program.

•

Argentina's government announces that it will lift the freeze on savings accounts in banks over the next three months and that depositors will get back some 80% of their assets; the freeze has been in place since 2001.

29 In Washington, D.C., Michelle Kwan wins her fifth world figure-skating championship.

•

Moon Ballad, owned by Sheikh Muhammad al-Maktoum and ridden by Frankie Dettori, wins the Dubai World Cup, the richest horse race in the world.

30 A law banning cigarette smoking in all places of employment, including restaurants and bars, goes into effect in New York City.

•

Tens of thousands of people attend opening ceremonies for the Sri Guru Singh Sabha Gurdwara in London; it is the largest Sikh temple outside India, with a capacity of 3,000 people.

•

Susan Gibson, a chemist at King's College, London, is named the first recipient of the Rosalind Franklin Award, established by the British government to honour exemplary women in science.

31 The parliament of the Czech Republic approves the treaty permitting the country to become a member of the European Union.

•

Some 100,000 city workers in Jerusalem go on strike, joining national government employees who are staging a work slowdown to protest layoffs and salary cuts promulgated by Finance Minister Benjamin Netanyahu.

•

Chicagoans are stunned to find that during the night city crews have dug up the runways of the city's Meigs Airport, stranding a few planes parked there; Mayor Richard M. Daley says the move was necessary to prevent small planes from flying over downtown in a time when the threat of terrorism is omnipresent.

April

I now inform you that you are too far from reality.

Iraqi Information Minister Muhammad Said al-Sahhaf,
after weeks of steadfastly insisting that Iraq was routing the invaders,
just before the fall of Baghdad, April 9

1 American forces advance to within 80 km (50 mi) of Baghdad, Iraq.

•

Prime Minister Recep Tayyip Erdogan of Turkey announces a new initiative to reunite Cyprus, which is seen as necessary not only to all of Cyprus joining the European Union but also to Turkey's ability to join the union.

•

Air Canada files for bankruptcy protection, though it continues to operate.

2 A peace accord is signed by the government of the Democratic Republic of the Congo and Congolese rebel groups in Sun City, S.Af.

•

China acknowledges that it has almost 400 more suspected cases of and 12 more deaths from SARS (severe acute respiratory syndrome) than it had said; for the first time, Beijing allows World Health Organization workers into Guangdong province, the epicentre of the disease.

•

In Davao City, Phil., a bomb explodes in a waiting area near a ferry terminal, killing at least 16 people and wounding dozens more; the following day, bombs go off at three of the city's mosques.

•

U.S. forces take custody of Jessica Lynch, a 19-year-old army private, who had been captured on March 23 with 14 others after the vehicle in which they were traveling made a wrong turn.

3 The bodies of 26 villagers who had been kidnapped and executed are found in Assam state in northeastern India; the killings are believed to be part of an ongoing struggle for power in the area between the Dimasa and Hmar peoples.

4 The Ituri Pacification Commission, bringing together representatives of all the groups that have tried to gain control over the northeastern district of the Democratic Republic of the Congo, is ceremonially inaugurated; three days later Pres. Joseph Kabila assumes power as interim head of state under the peace accord signed in Sun City, S.Af.

•

As violence subsides in the western Niger delta, two of the three oil companies that had shut down operations in the previous months announce plans to return gradually to their previous levels of production.

•

Authorities in Serbia and Montenegro announce that an arrest warrant for Mirjana Markovic, wife of former Yugoslav president Slobodan Milosevic, will be issued as part of the crackdown on organized crime that has been part of the response to the assassination of Serbian Prime Minister Zoran Djindjic.

•

Macedonia becomes the 146th member of the World Trade Organization.

5 U.S. ground forces reach Baghdad, Iraq, 16 days after they invaded the country.

•

A fistfight between rival gang members in a prison in Honduras soon escalates into riots that leave 86 inmates dead.

6 UN officials say that attacks in the Ituri province of the Democratic Republic of the Congo during the previous week left some 966 people dead.

•

In the worst "friendly fire" incident of the war in Iraq so far, U.S. forces mistakenly bomb a convoy of American and Kurdish soldiers and journalists, killing 18 Kurds.

•

David Hempleman-Adams becomes the first person to walk alone and unaided to the geomagnetic North Pole.

7 In Iraq, U.S. forces bomb a compound in Baghdad where they believe Pres. Saddam Hussein may be meeting with his advisers; British forces report that they have taken control of the city of Basra.

•

In New York City the winners of the 2003 Pulitzer Prizes are announced: journalistic awards go to, among others, the *Washington Post* and the *Los Angeles Times,* and winners in arts and letters include Robert Caro in biography and John Adams in music.

•

Danish architect Jørn Utzon, famed for his design of the Sydney (Australia) Opera House, is named the winner of the 2003 Pritzker Architecture Prize.

•

The National Collegiate Athletic Association (NCAA)

championship in men's basketball is won by Syracuse (N.Y.) University, which defeats the University of Kansas 81–78; in the women's final on the following day, the University of Connecticut defeats the University of Tennessee 73–68 for its second consecutive title.

8 *The Caprices,* a collection of stories by Sabina Murray, wins the 2003 PEN/Faulkner Award for fiction.

•

It is reported that studies of mitochondrial DNA show that springtails (class Collembola) are not the ancestors of insects but rather arose as a separate group before the crustaceans and insects diverged.

9 U.S.-led forces in Iraq effectively take control of Baghdad.

•

Negotiators for the U.S. and South Korea agree that the headquarters of the U.S. Army in South Korea should be moved out of Seoul as soon as it is feasible.

•

The News Corp., owned by Rupert Murdoch, agrees to buy the satellite-television distributor DirecTV from General Motors; the News Corp. owns the Fox Network and the Fox News Channel.

•

It is reported that in India Satyabhama Mahapatra, age 65, has given birth to a son, which makes her the oldest woman in the world to give birth; the previous record holder was 62 years old. (Photo right.)

10 Kurdish militiamen take over the city of Kirkuk in northern Iraq.

•

British Airways and Air France announce that they will both retire their fleets of Concorde supersonic jets this year; the Concorde first flew in commercial service in January 1976.

•

Haiti officially recognizes voodoo as a religion; henceforth the state will accept as legal voodoo baptisms, marriages, and other sacraments.

11 The World Health Organization issues a statement saying that the SARS (severe acute respiratory syndrome) outbreak appears to be under control, though it cautions that not enough is known about its spread in China; the causative agent has not been determined but is believed to be a coronavirus.

•

Ten men being held on suspicion of belonging to al-Qaeda, including two of those believed responsible for the 2000 bombing of the USS *Cole,* escape from the facility where they were imprisoned in Aden, Yemen.

12 As a three-day looting spree in Baghdad abates, it appears that the National Museum of Iraq has been thoroughly and catastrophically plundered; by the end of the month, however, it is clear that the damage is far less extensive than originally feared.

•

China allows a team of World Health Organization investigators to visit hospitals in Beijing for the first time; on April 16 the investigators announce that the prevalence of SARS (severe acute respiratory syndrome) in Beijing has been significantly underreported.

•

In legislative elections in Malta, the governing party, led by Prime Minister Eddie Fenech Adami, is reelected.

•

In Brussels, Prince Laurent of Belgium marries Claire Coombs, a British-born surveyor.

13 Rebel spokesmen say that five of the nine ministers who have been approved for Côte d'Ivoire's new coalition government have gone to the capital, Abidjan, to take up their posts; violence in the West African country continues, however.

•

As U.S. marines approach the Iraqi city of Tikrit, Iraqi soldiers abandoned by their commanding officers lead Americans to seven American prisoners of war; no other Americans are believed to have been captured.

•

The left-handed Canadian golfer Mike Weir comes from behind to win the Masters golf tournament in Augusta, Ga.

•

British runner Paula Radcliffe smashes her own world record as she finishes first among the women at the London Marathon with a time of 2 hr 15 min 25 sec; the fastest man there is Ethiopian champion Gezahegne Abera, with a time of 2 hr 7 min 56 sec.

•

Cypress Gardens, a theme park in Florida that first opened in 1936 and was best known for its water-skiing shows, closes for the last time.

14 After U.S. forces take control of Tikrit, Iraq, the Pentagon declares that major combat operations in the country have been concluded; at the same time, U.S. government officials accuse Syria of harbouring terrorists and biological and chemical weapons.

•

The Association of Computing Machinery announces that the winners of the A.M. Turing Award are Ronald L. Rivest, Adi Shamir, and Leonard M. Adleman, for their work in public-key cryptography.

•

In San Francisco the Goldman Environmental Prize is presented to Nigerian forest activist Odigha Odigha, Filipino air-pollution activist Von Hernández, Peruvian community activist María Elena Foronda Farro, Spanish physicist and economist Pedro Arrojo-Agudo, Australian Aboriginal elders Eileen Kampakuta Brown and Eileen Wani Wingfield, and American environmental activist Julia Bonds.

•

The German radio and television manufacturer Grundig files for bankruptcy protection.

•

Scientists from laboratories in China, France, Germany, Great Britain, Japan, and the U.S. announce that they have now fully sequenced the human genome to an accuracy of 99.999% and that the work of the Human Genome Project has been completed.

15 U.S. Pres. George W. Bush declares that the government of Saddam Hussein in Iraq has fallen; the following day he calls on the UN to lift sanctions against Iraq that have been in place since 1991.

•

U.S. forces in Baghdad capture Abu Abbas, the leader of the faction of the Palestine Liberation Front that attacked the Italian cruise ship *Achille Lauro* in 1985.

•

The Walt Disney Co. agrees to sell its Major League Baseball championship team, the Anaheim Angels, to Arturo Moreno, a businessman from Arizona.

16 The World Health Organization confirms that the causative agent of SARS (severe acute respiratory syndrome) is a new coronavirus first detected in Hong Kong on March 21; the agent is to be called the SARS virus, and already the genome of the virus has been mapped.

•

The U.S. government lowers the terror-alert level from orange (high) to yellow (elevated).

•

At the European Union summit meeting in Athens, the leaders of the 10 member states slated to join the EU in 2004 ceremonially sign accession treaties.

•

Partisan Review, a respected and influential political and literary journal that was first published in 1934, announces that it is ceasing publication.

•

At the age of 40, Michael Jordan, widely regarded as the best player in the history of basketball, plays his last game with the Washington Wizards and retires for the third time in his career. (*See* May 7.)

•

The Bayer pharmaceutical company pleads guilty to having engaged in a plot to overcharge Medicaid for the antibiotic Cipro and agrees to pay $257 million, a record Medicaid fraud settlement.

17 The first major contract for the postwar rebuilding of Iraq is granted to the Bechtel Group by the U.S. government.

•

U.S. forces in Baghdad, Iraq, capture Barzan Ibrahim al-Tikriti, a half brother of Saddam Hussein.

•

Anneli Jäätteenmäki is sworn in as prime minister of Finland, leading a centre-left coalition government; Finland becomes the second country, after New Zealand, to have women heads of both state and government.

•

Carnival Corp. takes over P&O Princess Cruises; P&O Princess had spent years fending off advances from Carnival.

•

The personal art collection of Surrealist André Breton is sold at auction in Paris, many pieces for record-breaking prices; the French government, which had declined to procure the collection outright, purchased pieces for 33 museums.

18 Poland signs a deal to buy Lockheed Martin F-16s to upgrade its forces to a standard acceptable to NATO, which Poland joined in 1999.

•

The world premiere of Pulitzer Prize-winning playwright August Wilson's *Gem of the Ocean* takes place at the Goodman Theatre in Chicago.

19 In presidential elections in Nigeria, Pres. Olusegun Obasanjo is reelected, defeating some 19 opposition candidates.

•

Some 3.5 million Belarusians participate in a day of voluntary unpaid work mandated by the government in order to raise money to build a new wing for the National Library of Belarus.

20 The government of China admits that the incidence of SARS (severe acute respiratory syndrome) in the country is much greater than had been reported and dismisses the health minister and the mayor of Beijing.

21 Jay Garner, who has been appointed U.S. administrator of Iraq, arrives in Baghdad.

•

Hundreds of thousands of Shi'ite Muslims make pilgrimage to Karbala, Iraq, to observe an important religious holiday on the Shi'ite calendar; it is the first time in a quarter century that they have been allowed to make this pilgrimage. (Photo below.)

•

Azerbaijani Pres. Heydar Aliyev collapses twice while giving a televised speech; he comes back each time and finishes the speech, however, and returns to work the following day.

•

The 107th Boston Marathon is won by Robert Kipkoech Cheruiyot of Kenya, with a time of 2 hr 10 min 11 sec; the winning woman is Svetlana Zakharova of Russia, with a time of 2 hr 25 min 20 sec.

•

The 46th annual *Dance Magazine* Awards are presented

to the choreographer William Forsythe, the dancers Susan Jaffe and Jock Soto, and the festival directors Charles and Stephanie Reinhart.

22 France's ambassador to the UN proposes that UN sanctions against Iraq be dropped.

•

The Yukos Oil Co., the biggest oil producer in Russia, announces that it will purchase the fifth largest company, Sibneft; YukosSibneft will be the fifth largest publicly traded oil company in the world.

•

A subtropical storm in the open waters of the Atlantic Ocean develops into a tropical storm; dubbed Ana, this is the first tropical storm to occur in April since record keeping began.

23 On the authorization of Turkish Cypriot leader Rauf Denktash, checkpoints in the divided city of Nicosia, capital of Cyprus, open for the first time since 1974; thousands of people immediately line up at both sides of the border, and the flow of visitors continues for days.

•

Alan Greenspan accepts a fifth term as chairman of the U.S. Federal Reserve Board; he has served in that position for nearly 16 years.

•

The World Health Organization adds Beijing and Toronto to its list of places that travelers should avoid because of the SARS (severe acute respiratory syndrome) outbreak.

•

A three-day general strike is called for by labour unions in Zimbabwe, and most major stores and factories close.

24 China imposes quarantines on thousands of people in the Beijing area in order to combat the spread of SARS (severe acute respiratory syndrome), sealing a hospital complex with 2,000 workers and patients inside; the following day it broadens the quarantine dramatically.

•

North Korean officials tell U.S. diplomats that the country has nuclear weapons and is making bomb-grade plutonium.

•

Iraqi Deputy Prime Minister Tariq Aziz surrenders to U.S. forces in Baghdad.

•

Japanese researchers announce that the substance pyrroloquinoline quinone (PQQ), discovered in 1979, plays a role in fertility in mice and is probably a B vitamin; it is the first new vitamin to be identified in more than 50 years.

25 Representatives of 11 Iraqi opposition groups meet in Madrid to discuss how to create a new government for Iraq.

•

The John Bates Clark Medal of the American Economic Association, given out every two years to the leading U.S. economist under the age of 40, is awarded to University of Chicago professor Steven D. Levitt.

26 At a cache of munitions collected and guarded by U.S. soldiers on the outskirts of Baghdad, Iraq, an explosion evidently set off by a flare fired into the dump kills at least six Iraqi civilians and wounds dozens more.

•

Rome inaugurates a water-taxi service on the Tiber River, which had not been navigated in nearly a century.

27 Nicanor Duarte Frutos, of the ruling Colorado Party, is elected president of Paraguay; he will take office on August 15.

•

Presidential elections in Argentina result in a near tie between Néstor Kirchner and Carlos Menem, leading a field of 18 candidates; a runoff is scheduled for May.

•

U.S. forces in Iraq arrest Muhammad Mohsen Zobeidi, who had placed himself in charge of Baghdad, in order to make clear that challenges to U.S. authority will not be tolerated.

•

U.S. military officials announce that the headquarters of U.S. air operations in the Middle East will be moved from Riyadh, Saudi Arabia, to an air base in Qatar.

•

A week after they were originally scheduled, talks open between the government of Nepal and the leaders of a Maoist insurgency.

•

In Washington, D.C., trombonist Andre Hayward wins the annual Thelonious Monk International Jazz Competition; the competition focuses on a different instrument each year.

28 Some 15 people are killed by U.S. forces during an anti-American rally in Falluja, Iraq; the occasion is the birthday of Saddam Hussein, which had traditionally been celebrated as a holiday in Iraq.

•

Armenia, Belarus, Kazakhstan, Kyrgyzstan, Russia, and Tajikistan hold a summit meeting in Dushanbe, Tajikistan, to create the Collective Security Treaty Organization, which is intended to help address terrorism and narcotics issues affecting all the states.

•

It is reported that, for the first time since magazines began being published on the World Wide Web, a Web-based magazine, *Slate*, made more money than it spent.

29 In Qatar a new constitution that provides for an elected legislature is overwhelmingly approved in a referendum.

•

The United States announces that it will withdraw all its combat forces from Saudi Arabia over the summer; the forces had been stationed there since the Persian Gulf War in 1991 in order to contain Iraq.

•

Police in Serbia and Montenegro charge 45 people with conspiracy in the assassination of Serbian Prime Minister Zoran Djindjic.

30 The U.S., Russia, the UN, and the European Union present to leaders of Israel and Palestine the "road map" for peace, a document that contains detailed steps to be taken by each entity.

•

An open-ended general strike begins in Israel; the action was prompted by austerity measures taken by Finance Minister Benjamin Netanyahu.

•

The presidency of Burundi is transferred from the Tutsi Pierre Buyoya to the Hutu Domitien Ndayizeye, as called for by the Arusha accords signed in 2000.

•

The government of Libya formally accepts responsibility for having caused the 1988 bombing of Pan Am Flight 103 over Lockerbie, Scot.; this is a step toward the ending of UN sanctions against Libya.

May

If those murderers believe that their bloody crimes will shake even one hair on the body of this nation and its unity, they are deceiving themselves.

Saudi Arabian Crown Prince Abdullah, addressing the nation on May 13, a day after the terrorist bombings in Riyadh

1 Trade unionists, communists, anarchists, and various protesters march in cities throughout Europe to mark May Day, the international labour day; this is usually the biggest holiday of the year in Beijing, but fear of SARS (severe acute respiratory syndrome), in addition to quarantines already in effect, keeps the streets and subways almost empty.

•

U.S. Pres. George W. Bush announces that the military phase of the Iraq war has ended, referring to it as "one victory in a war on terror" (photo right); on the same day, U.S. Secretary of Defense Donald Rumsfeld and Afghani Pres. Hamid Karzai announce that major combat operations in Afghanistan are over.

•

Côte d'Ivoire signs a comprehensive cease-fire agreement with rebels and representatives of Liberia, including an agreement for a joint Ivorian-Liberian patrol along the border between the two countries.

•

After questions have been raised about the integrity of his writing, Jayson Blair, a *New York Times* reporter whose work has been featured prominently in the newspaper, resigns. (*See* May 28.)

2 Indian Prime Minister Atal Bihari Vajpayee announces that India will restore diplomatic relations with Pakistan, broken off in December 2001 after an attack on Parliament; within hours Pakistani officials say that Pakistan will also restore normal diplomatic relations with India.

•

Nigerian oil workers on strike release the first of the 250 foreign oil workers they have held hostage on oil rigs since April 19; they agree to release all hostages.

3 It is agreed by the leadership of the World Health Organization, of which mainland China is a member, that WHO inspectors will be permitted to visit Taiwan to fight the outbreak of SARS (severe acute respiratory syndrome) there.

•

FIFA, the association football (soccer) governing authority, withdraws the Women's World Cup tournament from China, where it was to have been played in the fall, because of the SARS epidemic. (*See* May 26.)

•

Pope John Paul II, in a visit to Spain, makes a moving plea for peace to the half million people gathered to hear him speak; the following day at an open-air mass in Madrid, he names five new saints.

•

In the 129th running of the Kentucky Derby, the gelding Funny Cide, a long shot, outruns favourite Empire Maker by 1¾ lengths to win.

•

It is found that the Old Man of the Mountain, a famous natural granite formation on Cannon Mountain in New Hampshire, has fallen; the formation resembled a face and had been an icon of the state.

4 The astronauts who had been stranded in the International Space Station by the

grounding of the U.S. space shuttle fleet return to Earth in a Russian *Soyuz* capsule, landing in Kazakhstan.

5 When Colombian troops try to rescue hostages held by Revolutionary Armed Forces of Colombia (FARC) guerrillas, the guerrillas execute 10 of the hostages, including a provincial governor and a former cabinet member.

•

Italian Prime Minister Silvio Berlusconi testifies in his own defense in a courtroom where he is being tried on charges of bribery; it is the first time that a sitting Italian prime minister has ever testified as a criminal defendant.

•

U.S. and Iraqi officials say that just before the U.S. invasion of Iraq, one of Iraqi Pres. Saddam Hussein's sons and an adviser removed some $1 billion in cash from the central bank.

6 U.S. Pres. George W. Bush makes L. Paul Bremer III the chief U.S. administrator of Iraq, supplanting Jay Garner.

•

The discount retail chain Kmart Corp. (now Kmart Holding Corp.) emerges from bankruptcy, minus 600 stores and with a new management team.

•

A spokesman for Liberian Pres. Charles Taylor says that Liberian forces have killed Sam Bockarie, one of West Africa's most notorious warlords.

•

A new passenger terminal combining traditional Khmer and modern styles opens at Pochentong international airport near Phnom Penh, Cambodia.

•

Avery Fisher career grants are awarded to violinists Colin Jacobsen and Giora Schmidt, violinist and violist Scott St. John, flutist Demarre McGill, and pianist Natalie Zhu.

7 U.S. officials say that the government is asking members of the International Atomic Energy Agency to declare Iran to be in violation of the Nuclear Non-proliferation Treaty.

•

Michael Jordan, who had planned to return to his former job as president of basketball operations for the National Basketball Association team the Washington Wizards after retiring as a player, is fired by team owner Abe Pollin. (*See* April 16.)

•

At the National Magazine Awards ceremony, the surprise big winner is *Parenting;* other awards for general excellence go to *ESPN the Magazine, The Atlantic Monthly, Texas Monthly, Architectural Record,* and *Foreign Policy.*

8 In Morocco, Princess Salma Bennani, wife of King Muhammad VI, gives birth to a son, Hassan, who will be the chief heir to the throne.

•

Georgia's new state flag, featuring the Star and Bars of the Confederacy, which is viewed as less inflammatory than the Confederate battle flag featured on the previous two flags, flies over the capitol building for the first time.

•

In an extremely rare double birth, a woman in Cariacica, Braz., who has two wombs produces a boy and a girl, one from each womb.

9 William W. Parsons is appointed to take over management of the space shuttle program for NASA and to get the three remaining shuttles back in service; he replaces Ron D. Dittemore, who announced his resignation in April.

•

Officials in Saudi Arabia announce publicly that after a shootout during a raid on a building in Riyadh that contained a very large cache of arms, they are seeking 19 militants who are believed to be connected to al-Qaeda and to have been planning a major attack.

10 The Russian play *Nord-Ost,* which was playing to packed houses in Moscow before Chechen terrorists took over the theatre in October 2002, closes after having reopened in February; audiences were staying away from the theatre.

11 In the third round of voting, after the abolishment of the 50% threshold that invalidated two earlier elections, Filip Vojanovic is elected president of Montenegro.

•

The incomparable *Saliera,* a sculptured golden saltcellar by Benvenuto Cellini, is stolen from the Kunsthistorisches Museum in Vienna.

•

In Racine, Wis., the new Racine Art Museum, housing an internationally recognized collection of contemporary crafts, opens with an installation of baskets by glass artist Dale Chihuly.

12 A truck bomb blows up a residential complex in the town of Znamenskoye in the Russian republic of Chechnya, killing at least 59 people.

•

Suicide bombers strike three residential compounds in Riyadh, Saudi Arabia, killing 35 people from a variety of countries and injuring more than 200.

•

Clare Short, secretary for international development, becomes the second member of the British cabinet to resign because of Prime Minister Tony Blair's unstinting support of U.S. policy toward Iraq.

13 An interview with Israeli Prime Minister Ariel Sharon is published in which he says the dismantling of Israeli settlements in Palestinian territory is not being contemplated; dismantling settlements built after March 2001 is one step on the road map for peace.

•

France is paralyzed as more than one million people walk off their jobs and march in the streets to demonstrate their disagreement with proposed reforms to the state pension system.

•

The U.S. declares 14 Cuban diplomats personae non gratae; it is one of the largest diplomatic expulsions ever ordered by the U.S.

•

The U.S. Treasury Department unveils a new design for the $20 bill, featuring colours other than green in the background.

14 A suicide bomber detonates her weapon at a religious festival in Iliskhan-Yurt in the Russian republic of Chechnya in an apparent attempt to assassinate the pro-Russian regional administrator, Akhmad Kadyrov; at least 15 people are killed.

•

Taiwan's top hospital, the National Taiwan University Hospital, utterly overwhelmed by an outbreak of SARS (severe acute respiratory syndrome), shuts down as thousands are quarantined; three weeks after the last reported case of SARS in Toronto, the World Health Organization removes that city from its travel advisory list.

•

Three top executives of Banco Intercontinental, the Dominican Republic's second biggest commercial bank, are arrested after the discovery of a scheme that resulted in the embezzlement of $2.2 billion.

•

Italian Prime Minister Silvio Berlusconi officially lays the first foundation stone for the massive Venice dike project, scheduled to be completed by 2011 in order to save the low-lying city from flooding.

15 As part of an effort to make it clear that China is serious about stopping the spread of SARS (severe acute respiratory syndrome), the country temporarily suspends almost all foreign adoptions; China is a major provider of adopted babies to Westerners.

•

British forces in Iraq formally turn over control of the port city of Umm Qasr to a council made up of Iraqi volunteers.

•

France lodges a formal complaint with the U.S. government against what it sees as a formal campaign of false and hurtful information against the French being published in U.S. news sources and frequently attributed to anonymous administration sources.

16 Japan's House of Representatives passes three bills intended to strengthen the military; though Japan renounced the right to wage war in 1947, the perceived threat from North Korea has impelled lawmakers to improve Japan's defensive capabilities.

•

Suicide bombings occur at five different places nearly simultaneously in Casablanca, Mor., killing at least 41 people, including many foreigners.

17 The Vatican acknowledges for the first time that Pope John Paul II has Parkinson disease.

•

The referendum on joining the European Union passes comfortably in Slovakia.

•

Funny Cide, the Kentucky Derby winner, wins the Preakness Stakes by 9¾ lengths.

18 Four attacks by Palestinians kill nine Israelis; Israeli Prime Minister Ariel Sharon cancels a trip to the U.S. and indicates that the simultaneous concessions by each side called for by the road map for peace will be impossible.

•

Indonesian Pres. Megawati Sukarnoputri puts Aceh province under martial law; the following day the national government begins a major military offensive in the area.

•

The curtain falls for the final time after the 6,680th performance of *Les Misérables* on Broadway; the show, which opened in March 1987, was Broadway's second longest-running show, after *Cats.*

19 Thousands of Shi'ites march in downtown Baghdad in opposition to the U.S. occupation of Iraq; a number of other groups feel that change is coming too slowly.

•

MCI, as WorldCom has now been renamed, agrees to a settlement of fraud charges brought by the U.S. Securities and Exchange Commission; the telecommunications company will pay $500 million.

•

The Annual International IMPAC Dublin Literary Award goes to *My Name Is Red*; the prize will be split between the Turkish author, Orhan Pamuk, and his translator, Erdag Goknar.

•

Ari Fleischer, U.S. Pres. George W. Bush's press secretary, announces that he is stepping down.

20 Mad cow disease is diagnosed in a cow in Canada; a ban on all beef imports from Canada is immediately imposed in the U.S.

•

The U.S. government raises the terror-alert level from yellow (elevated) to orange (high).

21 The Framework Convention on Tobacco Control is unanimously adopted by the World Health Organization, committing all 192 member countries to strict limits on the advertising and sale of tobacco products; the convention will come into force once it is ratified by 40 of those countries.

•

The European Commission fines Deutsche Telekom €12.6 million (about $14 million) for having charged competitors higher prices for access to its telecommunications lines than it charged customers; though the German phone industry was deregulated five years ago, Deutsche Telekom still holds 95% of the market.

•

Jong-Wook Lee, an epidemiologist and expert on vaccines, is elected director general of the World Health Organization, replacing Gro Harlem Brundtland; he will take office on July 21.

22 The UN Security Council passes a resolution granting to the U.S.-led coalition the military occupation and administration of Iraq and abolishing economic sanctions against Iraq; an interim administration is to be set up by the Iraqi people.

•

The results of two studies published in *The New England Journal of Medicine* show that people on the low-carbohydrate Atkins diet for several months lower their triglycerides, blood fats that tend to clog arteries, and raise their HDL, or good cholesterol; researchers are surprised by these findings.

•

Annika Sörenstam becomes the first woman to play in a PGA Tour event since Babe Didrikson Zaharias in 1945 when she starts at the Colonial golf tournament; she fails to make the cut for the final two rounds, however.

23 Negotiators for the government and the opposition in Venezuela reach an agreement to hold a referendum on the presidency of Hugo Chávez after August 19 in an attempt to curtail the conflict that has been going on since last year.

•

Researchers in Hong Kong and at the World Health Organization say they have identified a virus that is at least very similar to the SARS (severe acute respiratory syndrome) virus in palm civets, which are eaten in Asia, and in a raccoon dog and a badger; meanwhile, WHO lifts its travel advisory for Hong Kong and for Guangdong province in China, but the U.S. Centers for Disease Control and Prevention reinstates the advisory for Toronto.

•

Georgian Pres. Eduard Shevardnadze ceremonially lays the first section of the Baku-Tbilisi-Ceyhan oil pipeline.

© Antoine Gyori/Corbis

24 Tens of thousands of trade-union members march in rallies across Germany to protest government plans to cut unemployment benefits and loosen job protections.

•

At the annual Eurovision song competition, held this year in Riga, Latvia, the Turkish singer Sertab Erener wins first place with her song "Every Way That I Can."

25 Néstor Kirchner is sworn in as president of Argentina.

•

Controversial legislative elections in Armenia result in a win for Prime Minister Andranik Markaryan's Republican Party of Armenia.

•

The cabinet in Israel gives its qualified approval for Prime Minister Ariel Sharon to pursue the steps of the road map for peace, supported by the "Quartet" (the U.S., the U.K., the EU, and Russia) which calls eventually for the creation of a Palestinian state.

•

At the Cannes International Film Festival, American director Gus Van Sant's film *Elephant* wins the Palme d'Or, and the Grand Prix goes to Turkish director Nuri Bilge Ceylan for *Uzak* (*Distant*).

•

Brazilian Gil de Ferran wins the Indianapolis 500 auto race by 0.2990 sec over his teammate Helio Castroneves, who was trying to win an unprecedented third consecutive Indy.

26 FIFA, the association football (soccer) governing body, chooses the U.S. to host the 2003 Women's World Cup; officials believe it will still be possible to hold the tournament within the original time frame. (*See* May 3.)

27 Belgium, France, Great Britain, Germany, Luxembourg, Spain, and Turkey join forces to acquire 180 military transport planes from Airbus in one of Europe's biggest military projects.

•

The official celebration of the 300th anniversary of St. Petersburg begins with fireworks, a laser show, and a procession of boats bearing various flags. (Photo above.)

28 A new tax law is signed by U.S. Pres. George W. Bush in which a last-minute revision prevents low-income parents from taking the child-tax credit.

•

Health authorities in Toronto quarantine some 2,000 students and staff of a parochial school where a student attended classes for two days while she had symptoms of SARS (severe acute respiratory syndrome).

•

Pres. Alejandro Toledo declares a state of emergency in Peru as strikes and protests spread throughout the country.

•

A second reporter for the *New York Times,* Rick Bragg, resigns after a controversy arises over the extent of his reliance on a freelance journalist for his reporting of a story. (*See* May 1.)

•

AC Milan defeats Juventus Turin by a score of 3–2 in the final match in Manchester, England, to win the association football (soccer) Champions League competition.

•

Krispy Kreme Doughnuts announces that its first-quarter profit grew an astonishing 48% compared with the first quarter of the previous year.

29 Scientists announce that for the first time an equine has been cloned; the baby mule, born May 4, has been dubbed Idaho Gem.

•

A gala dinner in Kathmandu attended by Sir Edmund Hillary is only one of many celebrations taking place in Nepal and elsewhere in commemoration of the 50th anniversary of the first successful ascent of Mt. Everest, by Hillary and Tenzing Norgay.

•

In the Scripps-Howard National Spelling Bee, Sai R. Gunturi of Dallas spells *pococurante* correctly to win the prize.

30 The U.S. government lowers the terror-alert level from orange (high) to yellow (elevated).

•

The U.S. opens a new embassy in Beirut, Lebanon; there has not been a U.S. consulate there since the old U.S. embassy was blown up in 1983.

31 Eric Rudolph, sought since 1996 in connection with a bombing at the Olympic Games in Atlanta, Ga., that year, is caught in Murphy, N.C.

•

The world premiere of the opera *The Little Prince,* based on the book by Antoine de Saint-Exupéry and scored by Rachel Portman, opens at the Houston (Texas) Grand Opera.

June

> *We ask the international community, most specifically the United States, to do everything within its power to help Liberia and Liberians out of this mess.*

Liberian Pres. Charles Taylor, in a radio address to the country, June 27

1 A second attempt by British forces occupying Basra, Iraq, to install a governing council is thwarted by protesters incensed that the council was chosen by the British and by disagreements between members of the council.

•

The sluice gates of the Three Gorges Dam on the Chang Jiang (Yangtze River) in China are closed, and the water level quickly rises.

2 The European Space Agency successfully launches the Mars Express orbiter and the Beagle 2, a landing vehicle, from the Baikonur Cosmodrome in Kazakhstan; the vehicles are expected to reach Mars in December.

•

Authorities in Zimbabwe arrest Morgan Tsvangirai, the opposition leader, charging him with contempt of court for planning antigovernment demonstrations; he is taken into custody again on June 6.

•

Jonathan Ive, the designer of Apple Computers' iMac personal computer, wins the Design Museum of London's first Designer of the Year award.

3 Most of Zimbabwe is shut down by a general strike that is an attempt to force Pres. Robert Mugabe to resign, but security forces effectively prevent demonstrations from taking place.

•

A wave of strikes takes place in France, Austria, Italy, and Germany; workers object to government proposals to cut retirement benefits.

•

Sammy Sosa, the only Major League Baseball player ever to hit 60 home runs in three different seasons, is ejected from a game when his bat breaks and reveals the presence of cork inside it; cork is thought to enhance batter performance, and its use is prohibited.

4 After a meeting with U.S. Pres. George W. Bush in Aqaba, Jordan, Israeli Prime Minister Ariel Sharon agrees to dismantle some unauthorized outposts of Israeli settlements in Palestinian areas; Palestinian Prime Minister Mahmoud Abbas agrees that the armed uprising on the part of Palestinians must end.

•

A UN Special Court in Sierra Leone announces that it has indicted Liberian Pres. Charles Taylor for war crimes.

•

The European Union agrees to send a force of peacekeepers, under France's leadership, to the Democratic Republic of the Congo; it is the first time the union has marshaled a force on its own to operate outside Europe.

•

In a televised speech to the country, Argentine Pres. Néstor Kirchner calls for the impeachment of the Supreme Court.

•

Good-living advocate Martha Stewart is indicted by the U.S. federal government on charges of conspiracy, obstruction of justice, and securities fraud; she resigns as chairman and CEO of her company, Martha Stewart Living Omnimedia.

5 A suicide bomber kills at least 18 people in addition to herself on a bus carrying military and civilian workers to a Russian air base just outside the republic of Chechnya.

•

The UN Security Council lifts sanctions against the import of diamonds from Sierra Leone, in the belief that Sierra Leone has taken the steps necessary to ensure that diamonds exported from the country have not been sold to finance guerrilla military activity.

•

Pope John Paul II arrives in Croatia for a five-day visit on the 100th trip of his papacy. (*See* June 22.)

6 The U.S. and Chile sign a free-trade agreement, the first such accord ever signed between the U.S. and a country in South America.

•

Leaders of Hamas, a Palestinian militia, break off cease-fire talks with Palestinian Prime Minister Mahmoud Abbas, feeling that Abbas had become too supportive of Israel.

•

In May Wal-Mart Stores announced that it would no

longer sell the men's magazines *Maxim, Stuff,* and *FHM;* now it plans to cover the fronts of women's magazines *Redbook, Cosmopolitan, Marie Claire,* and *Glamour.*

7 A car bomb strikes a bus carrying German troops from an international security force in Kabul, Afg., killing at least 4 soldiers and injuring 29.

•

An amnesty goes into effect in Russia's separatist republic of Chechnya; rebels who turn in their weapons will be guaranteed freedom from prosecution.

•

Justine Henin-Hardenne of Belgium defeats her countrywoman Kim Clijsters to win the women's French Open tennis title; the following day Juan Carlos Ferrero of Spain defeats Martin Verkerk of The Netherlands in the finals to win the men's title.

•

Empire Maker surprises observers by winning the Belmont Stakes horse race on a wet and sloppy track; Kentucky Derby and Preakness winner Funny Cide runs third.

•

The two-day referendum on joining the European Union gets under way in Poland; the results are a resounding "yes" to membership.

8 The 57th annual Tony Awards are presented in Radio City Music Hall in New York City; winners include the plays *Take Me Out, Hairspray, Long Day's Journey into Night,* and *Nine* and the actors Brian Dennehy, Vanessa Redgrave, Harvey Fierstein, and Marissa Jaret Winokur.

•

Annika Sörenstam of Sweden wins the Ladies Professional Golf Association championship on the first play-off hole, defeating Grace Park of South Korea.

9 Mexican Pres. Vicente Fox signs a bill that outlaws discrimination based on race, sex, age, or religion in all sectors of society.

•

During an investigation into questionable accounting practices at Freddie Mac, the federal mortgage insurer that is crucial to the housing market, David Glenn, the company president, is suddenly fired, and the chairman and CEO and the chief financial officer resign.

•

French forces land in Monrovia, Liberia, to evacuate hundreds of foreigners as the rebel group Liberians United for Reconciliation and Democracy continues a battle for the northern suburbs of the capital.

•

After two days of fighting in Nouakchott that followed a crackdown on Muslim extremists, the government of Mauritanian Pres. Maaouya Ould Sidi Ahmad Taya succeeds in averting an attempted coup.

•

The U.S. Centers for Disease Control and Prevention announces that the number of cases in an outbreak of monkeypox, the first ever in the Western Hemisphere, has risen to 33, with most cases occurring in Wisconsin.

•

The New Jersey Devils defeat the Anaheim Mighty Ducks to win the Stanley Cup, the National Hockey League championship; the score of the final game is 3–0.

•

With much hoopla, *Living History,* an autobiography of U.S. Sen. Hillary Clinton, goes on sale; some 200,000 copies are sold the first day.

10 Israel fires missiles into Gaza in an attempt to kill Hamas leader Abdel Aziz Rantisi; the U.S. government views the move as undermining attempts at peace.

•

In Santiago, Chile, the members of the Organization of American States vote to deny the U.S. a representative on the Inter-American Commission on Human Rights.

•

A rocket takes off from Cape Canaveral, Florida, carrying a robotic probe called *Spirit* to Mars; the robot will be looking for evidence of water.

11 A Hamas suicide bomber blows up a rush-hour bus in Jerusalem, killing 16 people in addition to himself and wounding nearly 100; meanwhile, Israeli helicopter strikes in Gaza kill 10 Palestinians.

•

At a press conference in Ethiopia, it is revealed that three skulls found in the Afar region of the country and dated at 160,000 years old are the oldest-known fossils of *Homo sapiens.*

•

Four UN monitors arrive in Tbilisi, Georgia, following their release by their kidnappers in the Kodori Gorge area some six days after they were kidnapped for ransom.

12 British Prime Minister Tony Blair abolishes the post of lord chancellor, a position that existed for 1,400 years.

•

In the first major battle since the end of the war in Iraq was announced, U.S. forces attack a site believed to be a training ground for the Iraqi resistance in an area about 145 km (90 mi) northwest of Baghdad.

•

Several items taken from the collections of the Iraqi National Museum are returned by unidentified men; the items include the Warka Vase, a particularly important artifact dating from some 5,000 years ago that depicts scenes of everyday life in ancient Uruk.

•

Investigators say that a mass grave containing the remains of hundreds of people has been uncovered at a construction site at Ulaanbaatar, Mong., dating from the 1930s, when Stalinist purges killed some 30,000 people in Mongolia.

•

A five-day celebration of the 100th anniversary of the Ford Motor Co. gets under way in Dearborn, Mich. (Photo below.)

AP/Wide World Photos

13 In Brussels, Valéry Giscard d'Estaing, head of the Convention on the Future of Europe, announces that the convention has adopted a first draft of a constitution for the European Union.

•

Science magazine publishes a report by geologists detailing evidence for what they believe was a major meteor impact on the Earth some 380 million years ago that may have caused a mass extinction of fishes.

14 A railroad linking North and South Korea is ceremonially reopened; the connection had been severed after the Korean War.

•

Sheikh Khalid ibn Saqr al-Qassami is deposed as crown prince of Ra's al-Khaymah in the United Arab Emirates in favour of his younger brother.

•

British Queen Elizabeth II publishes the list of those appointed Officers of the Order of the British Empire; they are association football (soccer) star David Beckham, musicians Sting and David Gilmour, actors Helen Mirren and Roger Moore, and fashion designer Alexander McQueen.

•

Somewhat to the surprise of their leaders, voters in the Czech Republic firmly vote in favour of joining the European Union in a binding referendum.

15 The top investigator of the UN Special Court in Sierra Leone announces that Johnny Paul Koroma, a former ruler of Sierra Leone whom the court had indicted for war crimes, has been killed in Liberia.

•

The San Antonio Spurs defeat the New Jersey Nets 88–77 to win the National Basketball Association championship; Tim Duncan of the Spurs is named MVP of the finals.

•

At the U.S. Open golf tournament at Olympia Fields (Ill.) Country Club, Jim Furyk emerges as the winner as he ties the scoring record for the tournament.

•

At the Baden-Baden (Ger.) Pentecost music festival, violinist Anne-Sophie Mutter is awarded the first Herbert von Karajan Award for outstanding contemporary musicians.

16 The death of a black motorcyclist in a high-speed police chase touches off two days of rioting in the small, mostly African American, and desperately poor town of Benton Harbor, Mich.

•

The world's first offshore tidal-energy turbine is launched off the coast of Devon in England; the turbine works on the principle of a windmill but uses water currents to generate energy.

•

At the Paris Air Show, Emirates Airline agrees to buy 41 new airplanes, among them 21 giant A380s, from Airbus Industrie; it is among the largest civil aircraft orders ever placed.

17 The government of Liberia and representatives of a rebel group sign a cease-fire agreement in which Pres. Charles Taylor promises to yield power.

•

Britons are aghast to learn that association football (soccer) sensation David Beckham (*see* June 14) is leaving Manchester United to play for Spain's Real Madrid.

18 Military officials announce that U.S. forces in Iraq have captured Abid Hamid Mahmoud al-Tikriti, believed to be Saddam Hussein's top aide.

•

The Italian Parliament passes a law making the top five government officials immune from prosecution while they hold office; this effectively stops the corruption trial of Prime Minister Silvio Berlusconi.

•

Israel's Antiquities Authority announces that the inscription written in the ancient Middle Eastern language of Aramaic on a 2,000-year-old stone box made public in October 2002 is a modern forgery; some scholars had believed that the box might be the ossuary of James, the brother of Jesus.

19 The government of the Democratic Republic of the Congo signs a cease-fire agreement in Burundi with two rebel groups backed by the government of Rwanda.

•

McDonald's Corp. announces that it will instruct its meat suppliers throughout the world to reduce their use of antibiotics in stock raising; because the fast-food chain is one of the world's largest meat purchasers, this decision is expected to cause widespread change in farming practices.

20 Pres. Nursultan Nazarbayev of Kazakhstan signs into law a controversial reform measure that for the first time permits private ownership of land.

•

The U.S. Food and Drug Administration approves the over-the-counter sale of the top-selling prescription medicine Prilosec, used for heartburn and ulcers.

21 The long-awaited and closely guarded novel *Harry Potter and the Order of the Phoenix* goes on sale; by the end of the day, a record five million copies have been sold.

•

The World Economic Forum, which prior to 2002 held its annual conference in Davos, Switz., convenes in Suweima, Jordan.

•

After months of work to dress Paris's Eiffel Tower in 20,000 new lights, the lights are switched on in a festive ceremony; the light show will be played on the tower every night. (Photo right.)

22 At an open-air mass in Banja Luka, Bosnia and Herzegovina, Pope John Paul II apologizes for crimes committed by Roman Catholics in the lands of the former Yugoslavia and exhorts his listeners to forgiveness and reconciliation in order to bring healing to the country. (*See* June 5.)

•

Voters in Tajikistan approve a number of changes to the constitution, including one that will permit Pres. Imomali Rakhmonov to serve two more seven-year terms.

•

A law goes into effect in Turkmenistan preventing people from holding both Russian and Turkmen passports; panicky Russians have been fleeing Turkmenistan for weeks.

23 In a pair of landmark decisions, the U.S. Supreme Court rules that it is constitutional for universities to consider race in deciding admissions but that the numerical weighting of "underrepresented" races is too mechanistic and therefore not permissible. (*See* June 26.)

© Reuters NewMedia Inc./Corbis

24 Matti Vanhanen is chosen by the Finnish legislature as the new prime minister, replacing Anneli Jäätteenmäki, who resigned on June 18 after a scant two months in office.

•

During a visit of Indian Prime Minister Atal Behari Vajpayee to Beijing, it is announced that India and China have agreed to reopen a border crossing between India's Sikkim state and the Tibet Autonomous Region of China that had been closed since 1962; China does not recognize India's sovereignty over Sikkim.

25 The U.S. Federal Reserve Board lowers short-term interest rates by one-quarter of a percentage point, to 1%; rates have not been this low since 1958.

•

The U.S. Internal Revenue Service releases a report showing that the 400 wealthiest taxpayers had more than doubled their share of the nation's wealth over the past eight years, while the percentage of their income that they paid in taxes dropped significantly.

•

Battles break out in the streets of Monrovia, the capital of Liberia, as rebel troops intent on overthrowing Pres. Charles Taylor attack the city.

•

The Indian Memorial at the Little Bighorn Battlefield National Monument in Montana is dedicated in ceremonies that attract thousands of Native Americans; the memorial commemorates for the first time the Indian warriors who died in the 1876 Battle of Little Bighorn, in which Lieut. Col. George A. Custer and all his men perished.

26 In another landmark decision (*see* June 23), the U.S. Supreme Court rules that states may not forbid private homosexual conduct; this overturns the precedent in this regard set in 1986.

•

Authorities in Saudi Arabia arrest Ali Abd al-Rahman al-Faqasi al-Ghamdi, believed to be the top al-Qaeda operative in the country and also thought to be behind the bombings in Riyadh in May.

•

The government of Brazil says that satellite photographs show that the area of the Amazon rainforest was reduced by about 26,000 sq km (10,000 sq mi) in the past year; the loss is 40% larger than the previous year.

•

Bonnie Fuller resigns as editor in chief of *US Weekly* to become editorial director of American Media.

27 The day after U.S. Pres. George W. Bush called on him to step down, Liberian Pres. Charles Taylor gives a radio address in which he asks for international help and declares that he will not resign, stressing his commitment to peace and security; the following day UN Secretary-General Kofi Annan calls for a peacekeeping force to be sent to Liberia.

•

A national registry for people who wish not to receive telemarketing calls opens in the U.S.; the registry is immediately overwhelmed by the volume of requests.

•

Negotiators for Israel and Palestine reach an agreement whereby Palestinian leaders will attempt to prevent attacks and Israel will begin withdrawing its troops from the Gaza Strip.

28 At a party in a three-story apartment building in Chicago, the overcrowded back decks collapse, killing 13 people.

•

Two men enter an Indian army barracks outside the city of Jammu in the state of Jammu and Kashmir and launch an attack with assault rifles and grenades; 12 unarmed Indian soldiers are killed and 7 wounded.

29 The Palestinian organizations Hamas and Islamic Jihad declare a three-month cease-fire, and al-Fatah follows suit with a six-month moratorium; in response, Israeli troops begin pulling back from the Gaza Strip.

•

China and Hong Kong conclude an economic-partnership agreement in which China agrees to open its markets to a wide variety of goods from Hong Kong.

•

France defeats Cameroon 1–0 to win the Confederations Cup in association football (soccer) in Saint-Denis, France; the occasion is overshadowed, however, by the death the previous week of Cameroon's Marc-Vivien Foe during a semifinal game against Colombia.

30 It is reported that particle physicists in Japan researching mesons may have produced subatomic particles containing five quarks; such particles are theoretically possible but have up to now not been detected.

•

The 50th anniversary of the iconic Corvette sports car is observed.

•

Hans Blix, the chief weapons inspector for the UN, retires from public life.

July

Each life that is lost is a human tragedy. No more suffering, no more death, no more pain.

Palestinian Prime Minister Mahmoud Abbas,
before his fourth meeting with Israeli Prime Minister Ariel Sharon,
in Jerusalem, July 1

1 The rotating presidency of the European Union passes from Greece to Italy.

•

Israeli Prime Minister Ariel Sharon and Palestinian Prime Minister Mahmoud Abbas appear publicly together for the first time; they express mutual respect and hope for peace before beginning a fourth round of negotiations.

•

Hundreds of thousands of people demonstrate in Hong Kong against a planned national security law that would ban subversion and other crimes against the state.

•

Pope John Paul II appoints Bishop Sean P. O'Malley to head the archdiocese of Boston, replacing Bernard Cardinal Law.

2 The European Parliament passes a law that, once ratified by the member states of the European Union, will require that food and animal feed containing genetically altered ingredients be labeled as such to alert consumers.

•

The International Olympic Committee awards the right to host the 2010 Winter Games to Vancouver, B.C.

•

The accounting firm Ernst & Young reaches an agreement with the U.S. Internal Revenue Service to pay $15 million in penalties for having failed to register certain transactions properly.

•

Argentina's Boca Juniors association football (soccer) club defeats Brazil's Santos FC to win the Libertadores Cup; it is a record-setting fourth Libertadores title for coach Carlos Bianchi.

3 The U.S. government announces a reward of as much as $25 million for the capture or proven death of Saddam Hussein and $15 million each for his sons, Uday and Qusay. (*See* July 22.)

•

Astronomers announce the discovery of a solar system 90 light-years away in the constellation Puppis centred on the star HD70642; the solar system could include terrestrial planets and thus support life.

•

The World Heritage Committee inscribes 24 new sites on UNESCO's World Heritage List; among them are the Bamiyan valley in Afghanistan, where two Buddha statues were destroyed by the Taliban in 2001, James Island in The Gambia, an important site in the historical slave trade, and the White City of Tel Aviv in Israel.

•

The U.S. National Park Service and the Nature Conservancy buy the 46,874-ha (115,828-ac) Kahuku Ranch on the slopes of Mauna Loa volcano, increasing the size of Hawaii Volcanoes National Park some 50%.

4 A bomb and grenade attack at the main Shi'ite mosque in Quetta, Pak., kills 47 people and wounds 65; Shi'ite Muslims riot in response.

•

A taped voice claiming to be Saddam Hussein and exhorting Iraqis to continue to resist the American occupation is broadcast on the al-Jazeera television channel.

•

Los Angeles Lakers basketball star Kobe Bryant is arrested in Eagle, Colo., on charges of having sexually assaulted a woman.

•

The National Constitution Center, a museum dedicated to the U.S. Constitution, opens in Philadelphia.

•

The Eads Bridge across the Mississippi River at St. Louis, Mo., reopens on its 129th anniversary with celebrations and fireworks after having been closed for renovations since 1991.

5 The World Health Organization declares that the respiratory disease SARS (severe acute respiratory syndrome) has been contained worldwide, with the last case reported to the agency on June 15; 812 people have died of the disease since the outbreak began.

•

Two bombs explode at the entrance to an annual rock festival at the Tushino Aerodrome outside Moscow, killing at least 16 people and wounding some 60 others.

•

A bomb goes off at the graduation ceremony for the first U.S.-trained Iraqi police class, killing 7 of the new police officers and wounding 70.

•

In parliamentary elections in Kuwait, Islamic traditionalists gain seats at the expense of liberals, who had hoped that with the removal of the threat from Iraq, some modernization might be possible.

•

Serena Williams defeats her sister Venus to take the Wimbledon women's tennis championship for the second consecutive year, and the following day Roger Federer of Switzerland defeats Mark Philippoussis of Australia for the men's title; Todd Woodbridge and Jonas Bjorkman capture the men's doubles in what is Woodbridge's eighth doubles title at Wimbledon, a feat that had not been achieved since 1905.

6 After a 90-minute meeting at the airport on the outskirts of Monrovia, Liberia, Pres. Charles Taylor of Liberia and Pres. Olusegun Obasanjo of Nigeria announce that Taylor will resign as president and accept an offer of safe haven from Nigeria.

•

In a referendum, citizens of Corsica reject a restructuring plan intended to increase the island's autonomy from France.

•

Sghair Ould M'Bareck, a former slave, replaces Cheikh El Afia Ould Mohamed Khouna as prime minister of Mauritania; slavery was abolished in Mauritania in 1980.

7 After numerous delays, a rover called *Opportunity* is launched; it is the second of two NASA probes intended to explore Mars.

•

Little-known American golfer Hilary Lunke wins the U.S. Women's Open golf tournament by one stroke.

•

An Iranian government official confirms Israeli press reports that Iran has successfully completed testing on a midrange missile; Israel and U.S. troops stationed in Saudi Arabia are within range of the new missile.

8 Iranian sisters Ladan and Laleh Bijani, 29-year-old twins conjoined at the head, both die after prolonged surgery to separate them in Singapore.

•

U.S. Pres. George W. Bush begins his first visit to sub-Saharan Africa in Senegal; the five-day trip will also include stops in Botswana, Nigeria, South Africa, and Uganda.

9 Tens of thousands of people demonstrate before the legislative building in Hong Kong; they call for the resignation of chief executive Tung Chee-hwa and for the institution of democratic elections.

•

The Canadian government says that it will supply marijuana to people authorized to use the drug for medical reasons.

•

The U.S. Food and Drug Administration announces that, beginning in 2006, food nutrition labels must include the amount of trans-fatty acids in the food; trans-fatty acids have been found to increase LDL, or "bad," cholesterol in the body.

10 Astronomers report that a massive planet, more than twice as big as Jupiter, has been detected by the Hubble Space Telescope in a globular star cluster in the constellation Scorpius; the planet is believed to have formed 12.7 billion years ago, not long after the big bang.

AP/Wide World Photos

•

The Great Mosque of Granada, overlooking the Alhambra, opens in the city that was once the capital of Moorish Spain; it is the first mosque to open in Spain since the end of Muslim rule in 1492. (Photo left.)

11 Director of Central Intelligence George Tenet publicly accepts responsibility for having allowed Pres. George W. Bush in his state of the union address to assert that Iraq tried to purchase uranium from an African country, an assertion based on faulty information. (*See* July 30.)

•

The World Trade Organization issues a formal finding that the steel tariffs that the U.S. imposed in 2002 violate the rules of the organization, of which the U.S. is a member.

12 Guy Verhofstadt is sworn in for a second term as Belgium's prime minister.

•

As the second annual meeting of the African Union comes to a close in Maputo, Mozambique, the delegates urge the member states to ratify a parliament for the continent by year's end.

13 Kuwaiti Emir Sheikh Jabir al-Ahmad al-Jabir al-Sabah names his brother, Foreign Minister Sheikh Sabah al-Ahmad al-Sabah, prime minister, replacing Crown Prince Sheikh Saad al-Abdullah al-Salim al-Sabah; it is the first time the post of prime minister has not been held by the heir to the throne.

•

Iraq's new governing council takes its first action, abolishing six national holidays, including the celebration on July 17 of the rise to power of the Arab Socialist Ba'th Party, and declaring April 9, the day Saddam Hussein was ousted, a national holiday.

14 It is reported that North Korea claims that it has acquired the capability to make several nuclear bombs and that it is proceeding to do so as quickly as possible.

•

The head of Iran's Oil Development and Engineering Company says that an oil field containing an estimated 38 billion bbl of oil has been discovered near the port city of Bandar-e Bushehr.

•

After an outbreak of the West Nile virus, Mexico declares a state of emergency; the horse population has been particularly hard hit, and people are asked to have their horses vaccinated.

15 The U.S. Office of Management and Budget projects a budget deficit for fiscal year 2003 of $455 billion, much higher than previously predicted and by far the biggest in U.S. history.

•

Hurricane Claudette makes landfall north of Corpus Christi, Texas, killing two people and causing damage.

16 Rebel troops seize the government of São Tomé and Príncipe in a bloodless coup while Pres. Fradique de Menezes attends a regional conference in Nigeria. (*See* July 24.)

•

Regina Ip, secretary of security, and Antony Leung, secretary of finance, announce their resignations from the government of Hong Kong; the two, who are viewed as especially close to Beijing, were among those criticized at the huge July 1 demonstration.

•

The new Church on the Blood is consecrated on the site where Tsar Nicholas II and his family were killed in 1918 in Yekaterinburg, Russia.

17 On the newly banned Ba'thist holiday in Iraq, an audiotape of Saddam Hussein exhorting his countrymen to resist the U.S. forces and the new governing council in Iraq is broadcast on al-Arabiyah television.

•

Government ally Yerodia Ndombasi, opposition leader Arthur Z'Ahidi Ngoma, and rebel leaders Jean-Pierre Bemba and Azarias Ruberwa are sworn in as vice presidents in the Democratic Republic of the Congo's transitional power-sharing government.

•

After two days of open warfare between rival gangs in shantytowns on the outskirts of Rio de Janeiro that left at least nine people dead, several battalions of police are called out to surround the area in an effort to keep the violence from growing.

18 David Kelly, a British weapons expert, is found to have committed suicide; Kelly had been questioned by the government as to whether he was the source for a BBC story asserting that the government had made unsubstantiated claims about chemical and biological weapons in Iraq in order to gain support for the U.S.-led war.

19 A cease-fire goes into effect between forces of the Philippine government and the Moro Islamic Liberation Front in order to facilitate the resumption of peace talks, which were suspended in March.

•

Rebel forces in Liberia advance into Monrovia, the capital.

•

Gabon's Parliament adopts a constitutional amendment permitting the president to run for reelection an unlimited number of times; Pres. Omar Bongo has held the office for 36 years.

20 Ben Curtis, an American golfer appearing in his first major tournament, wins the British Open.

21 Jong Wook Lee, who has announced plans to institute a division of epidemiologists trained to deal with outbreaks of contagious diseases, takes office as director general of the World Health Organization.

•

Two bombs explode in the Indian state of Jammu and Kashmir, killing 6 and wounding 38 pilgrims on their way to a Hindu temple; the following day an Indian army base is attacked, and 8 soldiers die.

•

U.S. marines land in Monrovia, Liberia, in order to evacuate Americans and other foreigners and protect the U.S. embassy, while Liberians take the bodies of people killed in the ongoing warfare to the embassy's gates in an effort to persuade the U.S. to intervene.

22 U.S. forces kill Uday and Qusay Hussein, the sons of Saddam Hussein, who are among the most-wanted former regime officials, in a house in Mosul, Iraq. (*See* July 3.)

•

Elders of Easter Island appear before the UN to seek independence from Chile, of which Easter Island has been a dependency since 1888.

23 A spokesman for the Economic Community of West African States (ECOWAS) announces that the organization will divert 774 peacekeeping troops from Sierra Leone to Liberia and that Nigeria will send in 650 soldiers.

•

The U.S. House of Representatives overwhelmingly overturns a Federal Communications Commission measure that would have increased the number of broadcast networks a single entity may own.

24 After extensive negotiations between coup leaders and international diplomats, Pres. Fradique de Menezes returns to office in São Tomé and Príncipe, having agreed to address the concerns that prompted the coup on July 16.

•

An international peacekeeping force begins arriving in the Solomon Islands in an attempt to restore order; the force, which will eventually number 2,500 troops, is led by Australians and represents the highest deployment of Australian forces in the Pacific since World War II.

•

A joint panel of intelligence committees from both houses of the U.S. Congress releases a lengthy report detailing many opportunities that were missed by intelligence services to discover or disrupt the plot that led to the terrorist attacks of Sept. 11, 2001, and suggesting substantial changes to intelligence agencies.

France's legislature passes a controversial pension-reform law requiring workers to remain on the job longer before becoming eligible to draw a full pension.

25 Palestinian Prime Minister Mahmoud Abbas meets with U.S. Pres. George W. Bush in the White House.

Argentine Pres. Néstor Kirchner revokes the decree preventing extradition of people accused of crimes related to Argentina's "dirty war" (1976–83).

At the world swimming championships in Barcelona, Spain, American swimmer Michael Phelps, who had set two world records earlier in the meet, breaks standing records for the 100-m butterfly and the 200-m individual medley; with the U.S. win in the men's 400-m medley relay on July 27, Phelps becomes the first person to establish five world records in a single championship meet.

It is reported that scientists studying the Y chromosomes of Siberians and American Indians have concluded that the first human migration to the Americas across what is now the Bering Strait happened no later than 18,000 years ago.

26 Two earthquakes measuring magnitude 5.5 and 6.2 strike Japan's northern Miyagi district hours apart, causing a great deal of damage but no fatalities.

27 In parliamentary elections in Cambodia, Prime Minister Hun Sen's Cambodian People's Party wins a majority of the seats.

Lance Armstrong becomes only the second person ever to have won the Tour de France bicycle race five consecutive times, coming in 1 min 1 sec ahead of Jan Ullrich.

Players Gary Carter and Eddie Murray, broadcaster Bob Uecker, and sportswriter Hal McCoy are inducted into the Major League Baseball Hall of Fame in Cooperstown, N.Y.

Veteran American comedian Bob Hope dies at the age of 100.

28 The UN Security Council extends for one year and strengthens its peacekeeping mandate in the Democratic Republic of the Congo, adding troops and permitting the use of force.

Indonesia gives notice that it will not seek to renew its loan agreement with the International Monetary Fund when it expires this year, believing it has reached a state of economic good health.

The two biggest U.S. banks, J.P. Morgan Chase and Citigroup, reach a settlement with the Securities and Exchange Commission and New York City's district attorney whereby they will pay some $300 million in fines and penalties to avoid prosecution on charges of having assisted Enron Corp. in concealing its precarious financial position.

New York City officials announce that Harvey Milk High School, the first public school in the U.S. exclusively for gay students, will open in the fall.

For the first time, *Bride's* magazine runs a feature article on same-sex commitment ceremonies.

29 U.S. Pres. George W. Bush signs into law the Burmese Freedom and Democracy Act, which imposes harsh economic sanctions on the government of Myanmar in response to a campaign by the government to discredit opposition leader Aung San Suu Kyi, who has been held in prison since May 30.

Members of the American Geophysical Union announce that instruments measuring the ozone layer have detected a slowdown in the rate of deterioration of the ozone in the upper stratosphere.

For the second day in a row, a number of fires sweep through the French Riviera, leaving at least four people dead; though wildfires are common this time of year, arson is suspected as the cause of many of these fires.

30 U.S. Pres. George W. Bush takes personal responsibility for the unsupported claim in his state of the union address that Iraq had tried to buy uranium from an African country; two other members of his administration had previously accepted blame for passing on the statement. (*See* July 11.)

A group of organizations headed by the Iraqi Oil Ministry and the U.S. Army Corps of Engineers announces a plan to repair and rehabilitate the infrastructure of Iraq's oil industry in hopes of resuming significant production by the end of the year.

In response to U.S. threats to move NATO headquarters out of Belgium, that country's Chamber of Representatives votes to rescind the right of Belgians to bring war-crimes charges against anyone in any country for incidents that take place anywhere in the world.

The last original-style Volkswagen Beetle rolls off the assembly line in Puebla, Mex., with a small farewell ceremony featuring a mariachi band; it is the 21,529,464th Beetle produced. (Photo below.)

31 Following the release of three of their leaders, Maoist rebels agree to resume peace talks with the government of Nepal.

Israel passes a law that forbids Palestinians who marry Israeli citizens to reside in or become citizens of Israel; besides Palestinians, the law primarily affects Israeli Arabs.

August

> *I invite all to join in my prayers for the victims of this calamity, and I exhort all to raise to the Lord fervent entreaties so that he may grant the relief of rain to the thirsty Earth.*

Pope John Paul II, responding to the catastrophic heat wave and drought gripping Western Europe, August 10

1 A suicide truck bombing takes place at a military hospital in Mozdok, Russia, a military staging area for the campaign in Chechnya; 50 people are killed.

•

The U.S. and North Korea announce that regional talks involving South Korea, Japan, China, and Russia, concerning North Korea's nuclear-weapons program, will take place; previously North Korea had resisted regional talks, insisting on only bilateral talks.

•

The UN Security Council passes a resolution to send a multinational force to Liberia to keep peace until a new government can be formed; it is to be followed no later than October 1 by a UN peacekeeping force.

•

The upper house of Belgium's legislature passes changes to the country's war-crimes law that would require that either the victim or the perpetrator be a Belgian resident in order for a crime to be charged; the new law will become effective after it is signed by the king.

•

The opening ceremony for the Pan American Games takes place in Santo Domingo, Dom.Rep.; it is the first time the Dominican Republic has hosted the games, and Juan Marichal, the only Dominican in the Major League Baseball Hall of Fame, and Pedro Martinez of the Boston Red Sox take part in the ceremony. (Photo below.)

2 Liberian Pres. Charles Taylor announces that he will leave office on August 11 in spite of ECOWAS demands that he leave a week earlier than that and says he will leave only if his war-crimes indictment is rescinded.

•

The U.S. suspends two programs under which air travelers from other countries

could fly through the U.S. and change planes within the U.S. without a U.S. visa provided that the connecting flight was to a destination outside the U.S.; the programs were seen as a security loophole.

•

The three-year-old trotter Amigo Hall, running fourth at the top of the homestretch, comes from behind to win the Hambletonian final at the Meadowlands Racetrack in New Jersey.

3 Bolivia announces that it has seized more than 5 tons of cocaine in the largest intercept in its history; the previous record was a seizure of 1.1 tons of the drug in 1985.

•

With her victory over Pak Se Ri in the Women's British Open golf tournament, Annika Sörenstam becomes the sixth female golfer to win a career Grand Slam.

•

The Pro Football Hall of Fame in Canton, Ohio, inducts running back Marcus Allen, defensive end Elvin Bethea, offensive guard Joe DeLamielleure, wide receiver James Lofton, and coach Hank Stram.

•

With a parade and reenactments, the Japanese city of Yokosuka concludes its three-day festival to commemorate the 150th anniversary of the arrival of Commodore Matthew Perry to open Japan to the West.

4 Azerbaijan's legislature confirms the appointment of Ilham Aliyev, the son of Pres. Heydar Aliyev, as prime minister.

•

A series of wildfires threatens the region around Kamloops, B.C., while other fires burn out of control in Alberta; the fires are thought to be the worst in 50 years.

5 A car bomb explodes, destroying the lobby of the JW Marriott Hotel, a top hotel in the Jakarta, Indon., suburb of Kuningan that is popular with foreign business executives; 14 people are killed and 150 are wounded.

•

The Episcopal Church in the U.S. approves the selection of V. Gene Robinson, an openly gay clergyman, as bishop of the diocese of New Hampshire.

6 The ruling coalition government in Ecuador collapses when Pachakutik, a party comprising mostly indigenous peoples, walks out with the intention of joining a new left-of-centre bloc.

•

Brazilian Pres. Luiz Inácio Lula da Silva wins a key legislative victory when the Chamber of Deputies approves by a large majority a needed overhaul of the country's overburdened public pension system.

•

Didier Ratsiraka, the former president of Madagascar living in exile in France, is sentenced in absentia to 10 years at hard labour for embezzlement.

•

A very small contingent of U.S. marines lands in Liberia to provide assessments of the circumstances and coordinate support services for the international peacekeepers.

7 A car bomb kills 19 people and wounds at least 65 outside the Jordanian embassy in Baghdad, Iraq.

•

A raid in the southern Afghani city of Deshu kills six Afghani soldiers and a driver for an American relief agency; the raid is believed to have been carried out by members of the resurgent Taliban movement.

•

A court in Indonesia sentences to death Amrozi, a suspected member of the militant Islamist organization Jemaah Islamiyah, after convicting him of involvement in the planning of the nightclub bombing in Bali in October 2002.

8 In a dramatic change in policy, the government of South Africa announces that it will begin offering antiretroviral drugs to combat HIV/AIDS through its public health system no later than October 1.

•

Pres. Ludwig Scotty of Nauru loses a no-confidence vote; he is replaced by René Harris; this is the country's fifth change of presidents in 2003.

9 Amid a severe heat wave in Europe, the temperature in Roth, Ger., reaches 40.4 °C (104.7 °F), the highest temperature ever recorded in Germany.

•

The Coalition Provisional Authority in Iraq announces the capture of former Iraqi interior minister Mahmoud Diab al-Ahmad.

•

In Anniston, Ala., the U.S. Army begins incinerating the first of thousands of tons of chemical weapons dating from the Cold War.

10 For the first time since 1659, when records began being kept, the temperature in London exceeds 100 °F, topping out at 37.9 °C (100.2 °F).

•

During two days of riots over fuel shortages in Basra, Iraq, UN officials warn that the refinery problems that are causing the shortage of gasoline will almost certainly cause a shortfall as well in kerosene, which is used for heating homes, in the coming winter.

•

Yury I. Malenchenko, aboard the International Space Station, marries Yekaterina Dmitryeva, who is at the Johnson Space Center in Houston, Texas; the ceremony is the first wedding conducted for a person in space via video hookup.

11 Charles Taylor hands over the presidency to his vice president, Moses Blah, and departs from Liberia for exile in Nigeria.

•

Riduan Isamuddin, known as Hambali, is arrested in Ayutthya, Thai.; he is believed to have been involved in a number of bombings and has been the most-wanted fugitive in Asia since the bombing on the Indonesian Island of Bali, on Oct. 12, 2002.

•

In its first major military operation outside Europe, NATO takes command of the UN-authorized peacekeeping force in Kabul, Afg.

12 The government of Serbia and Montenegro adopts a document that calls for autonomy but not independence for the UN-administered province of Kosovo.

•

A computer worm known as Blaster, designed to take advantage of vulnerabilities in recent versions of Microsoft's Windows operating systems, infects tens of thousands of personal and business computers worldwide.

•

Two Israelis are killed in suicide bombings in a grocery store and at a bus stop after a month of relative calm while the road map to peace is being discussed.

•

The ongoing drought in Europe causes water levels

in Lake Constance to drop to the point that eight unexploded British and American bombs that had been underwater for some 50 years are exposed; German military experts remove them.

13 A bomb kills 15 people on a bus in Helmand province in southern Afghanistan, and violence in other parts of the country kills more than 40 additional people.

•

On a ballot to recall California Gov. Gray Davis, 135 people register as candidates to replace him should citizens vote him out of office.

•

Police ruthlessly suppress protests as the Commonwealth summit meeting opens in Mbabane, Swaziland.

14 The power grid covering a vast swath of eight U.S. states from Michigan to Massachusetts and part of southeastern Canada crashes, dousing lights and shutting down air conditioners and refrigerators; it is the worst infrastructure collapse that the U.S. has ever suffered.

•

Bomb blasts and shootouts in remote northeastern India on the eve of Independence Day celebrations leave 34 people dead.

•

A magnitude-6.4 earthquake takes place off the Greek island of Lefkada in the Ionian Sea, injuring some 50 people.

•

The MT *Tasman Spirit,* a Greek oil tanker that ran aground on a beach off Karachi, Pak., on July 27, breaks in two, spilling some 12,000 metric tons of oil and creating an ecological disaster.

15 Nicanor Duarte Frutos is sworn in as president of Paraguay; he pledges to fight corruption.

•

Libya formally accepts responsibility for the bombing of Pan Am Flight 103 over Lockerbie, Scot., in 1988; the UN Security Council will now likely end sanctions against the country.

•

Saboteurs in Iraq blow up part of an oil pipeline between Kirkuk and the Turkish city of Ceyhan only three days after the pipeline was reopened.

16 Idi Amin, the former dictator of Uganda, dies in exile in Saudi Arabia.

•

At the annual summit meeting of the Pacific Islands Forum in Auckland, N.Z., Australian diplomat Greg Urwin is elected the organization's secretary-general.

•

At the Locarno (Switz.) International Film Festival, the top prize, the Golden Leopard, is awarded to Pakistani director Sabiha Sumar's film *Khamosh pani* (*Silent Waters*).

17 Son Kil Seung, the chairman of scandal-ridden South Korean trading company SK Global, resigns under pressure after being convicted of fraud.

•

Shaun Micheel defeats Chad Campbell by two strokes to win the first Professional Golfers' Association of America championship game he has ever played.

•

The 44th Edward MacDowell Medal for outstanding contribution to the arts is awarded to choreographer Merce Cunningham at the MacDowell Colony in Peterborough, N.H.

18 Lucien Abenhaim, France's director general for health, resigns in the face of the huge death toll caused by the record-breaking heat wave; by mid-September some 14,000 heat-related deaths have been recorded in France.

•

In Ghana, under Nigerian mediator Abdulsalami Abubakar, a peace accord between the government of Liberia and representatives of the two main rebel groups is signed.

•

Fourteen European tourists who had been kidnapped by members of a militant organization in Algeria some six months earlier are released in Tessalit, Mali.

•

In Singapore Ma Li Hua sets a new world record for solo domino toppling after having spent 45 days setting up 303,621 dominoes and 4 minutes knocking them down.

19 A truck bomb explodes at the headquarters of the UN in Baghdad, Iraq, killing at least 22 people, among them Sergio Vieira de Mello, the secretary-general's special representative in Iraq.

•

U.S. officials announce the capture of Taha Yassin Ramadan, a former vice president of Iraq regarded as one of the most ruthless members of the deposed government.

•

A suicide bomber detonates his weapon on a crowded bus in Jerusalem, killing at least 20 people.

20 A helicopter carrying government officials of Sakhalin oblast, including Gov. Igor P. Farkhutdinov, to the Kuril Islands disappears after takeoff from the Kamchatka Peninsula; the wreckage, with no survivors, is found on August 23.

•

As U.S. Secretary of Defense Donald Rumsfeld makes an official visit to Colombia, U.S. officials announce that flights backed by the U.S. government intended to intercept the trade in illegal drugs would resume over Colombia after a two-year hiatus.

21 U.S. military officials announce the capture in Iraq of Ali Hassan al-Majid, known as "Chemical Ali" for having ordered the 1988 poison-gas attack that killed 5,000 Kurds in Halabja, which is on the border with Iran.

•

Israel fires missiles from a helicopter gunship onto a busy street in Gaza, killing Hamas leader Ismail Abu Shanab and two others and wounding 17; Hamas and Islamic Jihad declare an end to their cease-fire.

•

Negotiators in Accra, Ghana, choose Charles Gyude Bryant, a leader in the Episcopal Church and a businessman, to be chairman of the interim government planned for Liberia; he will take over from Moses Blah in October.

22 The Nigerian Red Cross says that five days of sectarian violence in the port city of Warri have caused the death of some 100 people; another 1,000 people are injured.

•

A rocket being tested by the Brazilian space agency for a planned launch the following week explodes at the Alcantara Space Centre in the northeastern state of Maranhão; at least 16 people are killed.

23 Some 30,000 people are forced to flee the city of Kelowna, B.C., to escape a relentless forest fire that began with a lightning strike on August 16; British Columbia is suffering its worst fire season in decades.

•

John J. Geoghan, a defrocked priest convicted of child molestation, is killed by a fellow prisoner at a correctional centre in Massachusetts; he was accused of having molested more than 100 children over a period of decades and was emblematic of the sex scandal that rocked the Roman Catholic Church, in particular the archdiocese of Boston, in 2002.

24 The Musashi-Fuchu Little League team from Tokyo becomes the 57th Little League world champion when it defeats the team from Boynton Beach, Fla., 10–1.

•

The Washington Freedom wins the Women's United Soccer Association championship in an exciting 2–1 overtime victory over the Atlanta Beat.

•

In Amsterdam the Dutch team defeats Australia 4–2 to win the Champions Trophy in men's field hockey for the second consecutive year.

25 Two taxis wired with bombs explode in separate crowded areas in Mumbai (Bombay), killing at least 52 people.

•

Pres. Paul Kagame of Rwanda is overwhelmingly elected to an additional seven years in office; he has served as president since 2001, when he became head of an interim government.

•

Khin Nyunt is appointed prime minister of Myanmar (Burma) by the head of state, Than Shwe, who had previously held both posts concurrently himself.

AP/Wide World Photos

26 With the death of a U.S. soldier killed by a bomb near Baghdad, the number of Americans killed in Iraq since U.S. Pres. George W. Bush declared the end of major combat on May 1 has exceeded the number killed during active combat.

•

The Columbia Accident Investigation Board releases its final report on the causes of the space shuttle *Columbia* disaster in February; it blames a culture of complacency and poor communication at NASA.

27 Mars passes within 55,758,004 km (34,646,418 mi) of the Earth, the closest the two planets have been in some 60,000 years.

•

During the Kumbh Mela festival in Nasik, India, as tens of thousands of pilgrims attempt to bathe in the waters of the Godavari River, a stampede breaks out that leaves 33 people dead.

•

Maoist rebels announce their withdrawal from peace talks with the government of Nepal and the end of the cease-fire that has been in place for seven months.

•

A painting by Leonardo da Vinci,* Madonna of the Yarnwinder, *is stolen from a private collection in Scotland during a public viewing. (Photo above.)

28 The World Council of Churches chooses Samuel Kobia, a minister in the Methodist Church in Kenya, to replace Konrad Raiser of Germany as secretary-general in January 2004.

•

Peru's Truth and Reconciliation Commission reports that between 1980 and 2000, some 69,000 people were killed, slightly over half by Sendero Luminoso (Shining Path) guerrillas and the rest by the three governments that ruled Peru during those years; the vast majority of the victims were Quechua-speaking Indians.

29 In Iraq's worst atrocity since the fall of Saddam Hussein in April, a car bomb explodes outside a major Shi'ite mosque in Najaf; at least 80 people, including Shi'ite leader Ayatollah Muhammad Bakr al-Hakim, are killed.

30 A Russian nuclear submarine that had been decommissioned in 1989 sinks in the Barents Sea while being towed to a scrap yard; nine crewmen are killed, and a sole survivor is left.

•

The World Trade Organization agrees on a plan that will allow poor countries to import lifesaving medicines at low cost; the U.S., which had blocked a similar proposal in December 2002, agreed to the plan at the 2003 meeting.

31 The centennial celebration of the motorcycle manufacturer Harley-Davidson roars to an end in Milwaukee, Wis.; the four-day gala was attended by some 250,000 bikers from all over the U.S. and beyond.

•

Kenya rescinds the ban, formally in place since 1950, on the Mau Mau movement, which fought against British colonial rule in the country.

September

Colombia weeps but does not surrender.

Colombian Pres. Álvaro Uribe,
in response to a terrorist bombing in Florencia, September 28

1 In his annual state of the union address, Mexican Pres. Vicente Fox, uncharacteristically subdued, admits that he has not succeeded in producing the sweeping changes to the political system in Mexico that he believes are necessary.

•

Djibouti's ambassador to Ethiopia announces that Djibouti plans to expel more than 100,000 illegal immigrants, which amounts to about 15% of the country's population.

•

Pharmacists in The Netherlands begin offering cannabis as a prescription drug to treat those with HIV, cancer, multiple sclerosis, and Tourette syndrome; The Netherlands is the first country in the world to allow pharmacies to dispense the drug.

2 A truck bomb explodes outside the office of the police chief of Baghdad, Iraq, killing one officer and wounding 26 others; it is the fourth car bomb to go off in a month in Iraq.

•

Belgian Prime Minister Guy Verhofstadt says that Belgium plans to build the headquarters for a proposed European Union military command in 2004.

•

The Red Cross announces that the Polisario Front in Western Sahara released 243 Moroccan prisoners, some of whom the guerrilla organization had held for 28 years; it continues to hold 914 other prisoners, however.

•

Ave Maria University, established by Domino's Pizza founder Thomas Monaghan, opens in Naples, Fla.; it is the first new Roman Catholic university to open in the U.S. in 40 years.

3 A cabinet of 25 ministers chosen by the Iraqi Governing Council is sworn in, and control of five provinces is handed to a multinational force under Polish command.

•

The Supreme People's Assembly of North Korea unanimously reelects Kim Jong Il chairman of the National Defense Commission (effectively head of state) for a five-year term; spontaneous expressions of euphoria are orchestrated in Pyongyang.

•

At the Latin Grammy Awards in Miami, Fla., Colombian rock artist Juanes wins five awards, including Song of the Year and Record of the Year, both for "Es por ti," and Album of the Year for *Un día normal.*

4 U.S. Secretary of Defense Donald Rumsfeld arrives in Iraq and outlines plans to train and deploy former officers in Iraq's army to increase security in the country.

•

The CP Open Biennale opens with great success in the National Gallery in Jakarta, Indon.; it largely features paintings and sculptures by Asian artists.

5 Hong Kong chief executive Tung Chee-hwa announces the withdrawal of proposed internal-security legislation that had been pressed on Hong Kong by the government of China and massively protested against by the populace in Hong Kong.

•

Jacques Klein, the UN special representative to Liberia, says that ousted president Charles Taylor, as he departed for exile in Nigeria, stole $3 million that had been donated for the disarming of militias; a few weeks later it is revealed that Taylor stole about $100 million during his administration, which left Liberia the poorest country in the world.

•

Two bombs explode at the main courthouse in Athens; officials believe the incident is a response to the ongoing trials of members of the terrorist group November 17.

6 Unable to gain the degree of authority he deems necessary, Mahmoud Abbas resigns as Palestinian prime minister; also, Israel drops a large bomb in an attempt to assassinate the head of the guerrilla organization Hamas.

•

Tens of thousands of people demonstrate in Taipei, Taiwan, to demand that the name of the country be changed from Republic of China to Taiwan; most demonstrators are native Taiwanese, who have long resented the 1949 takeover of their country by the Nationalist government of China.

•

Justine Henin-Hardenne of Belgium defeats her countrywoman Kim Clijsters to win the U.S. Open tennis championship (*see* June 7); the following day Andy Roddick of the U.S. defeats Juan Carlos Ferrero of Spain to win the men's tournament.

7 In a nationally televised address, U.S. Pres. George W. Bush says that he plans to ask Congress for $87 billion in emergency spending for the wars in Iraq and Afghanistan.

•

Palestinian leader Yasir Arafat nominates Ahmed Qurei, the speaker of the Palestinian legislature, to replace Mahmoud Abbas as prime minister; three days later Qurei accepts the position.

8 The Recording Industry Association of America files 261 lawsuits against individuals for copyright infringement, accusing them of unauthorized sharing of files containing copyrighted material.

•

The IUCN World Parks Congress, which meets once every 10 years, opens in Durban, S.Af.; the 10-day meeting of nearly 3,000 government officials and conservationists from 140 countries will address the challenge of preserving biodiversity through protected areas worldwide. (Photo below shows Nelson Mandela [front], Jordan's Queen Noor, and South African Pres. Thabo Mbeki.)

9 Argentina defaults on a loan from the International Monetary Fund for $2.9 billion; it is the biggest default the IMF has ever suffered.

•

Six different bombs explode in Kathmandu, the capital of Nepal; a 12-year-old boy is killed and a dozen people wounded.

•

The U.S. Army announces that the tours of duty of 20,000 Army Reserve and National Guard troops stationed in and around Iraq will be extended to as much as a year; in the meantime, Pentagon officials at a hearing before Congress say that U.S. forces in Iraq are somewhat overextended.

•

Two suicide bombers in Israel, one at a bus stop near Tel Aviv and one at a café in Jerusalem, kill 15 people.

10 The border between Côte d'Ivoire and Burkina Faso, closed in 2002 after the outbreak of civil war in Côte d'Ivoire, is reopened; nearly a third of the people in Burkina Faso had relied on cross-border trade with Côte d'Ivoire.

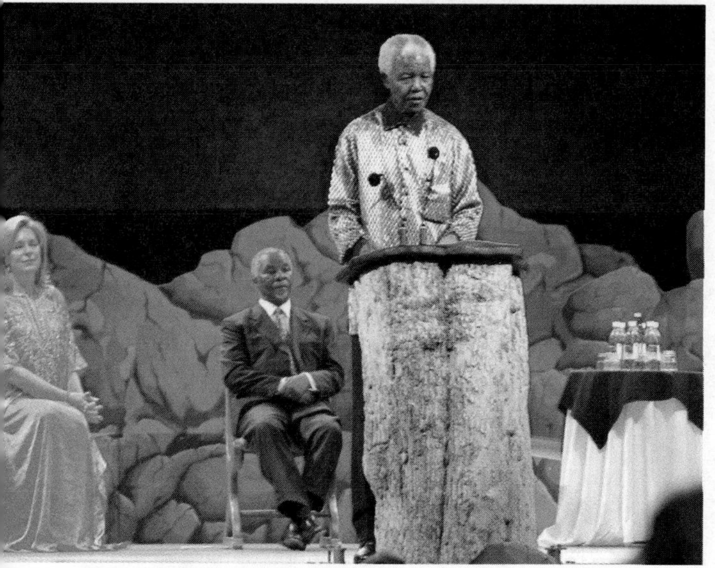

AP/Wide World Photos

•

The Prince of Asturias Award for Concord is granted to British author J.K. Rowling; the award is one of eight Prince of Asturias Awards given annually in different endeavours since 1981.

11 Popular Swedish Foreign Minister Anna Lindh dies a day after being stabbed in a department store in Stockholm, to the sorrow and horror of the Swedish public.

•

The government of Israel announces a decision in theory to remove Yasir Arafat, though no particulars are spelled out.

12 The UN Security Council votes to lift sanctions on Libya that had been imposed after the 1988 bombing of Pan Am Flight 103 over Lockerbie, Scot.; Libya has met the conditions for ending the sanctions.

•

U.S. soldiers in Iraq mistakenly kill 10 Iraqi policemen and a Jordanian security guard in a firefight in Falluja.

•

Paul Kagame is sworn in to a seven-year term as Rwanda's first elected president since 1994.

•

Police in Harare, Zimb., shut down the *Daily News*, the largest daily newspaper in the country and one of a shrinking number of independent media outlets.

13 UN Security Council negotiations on the future of Iraq reach an impasse; France will not compromise on its insistence that the UN oversee Iraq's transition to independence, and the U.S. will not compromise on its insistence that it oversee the transition.

14 A World Trade Organization meeting held in Cancún, Mex., ends without agreement after five days of negotiation, during which industrialized countries and less-developed countries were unable to compromise on a variety of issues.

•

In a referendum, Swedish voters firmly reject adoption of the euro as their currency, to the profound disappointment of Prime Minister Goran Persson and officials of the European Union.

•

The army chief of staff, Gen. Verissimo Correia Seabre, seizes power from Pres. Kumba Ialá in Guinea-Bissau the day after Ialá postponed elections for the fourth time since he dissolved the government in November 2002; a transitional government pending elections is named.

•

At the International Athletic Foundation Gala, Moroccan runner Hicham El Guerrouj and South African high jumper Hestrie Cloete are named male and female World Athlete of the Year; it is an unprecedented third consecutive win for El Guerrouj.

•

Lithuania defeats Spain 93–84 to win the European basketball championship for the first time since 1939.

•

The winners of the 2003 Albert Lasker Medical Research Awards are announced; they are Robert G. Roeder for basic medical research, for his work on gene transcription; Marc Feldmann and Ravinder N. Maini for clinical research, for discoveries leading to treatments for autoimmune disorders; and actor Christopher Reeve for public service.

15 After three seasons the Women's United Soccer

Association suspends operations; although regarded as the world's best league for association football (soccer) for women, it was unable to attract enough corporate sponsorship to keep going.

•

The first commercial flight between North and South Korea since the division of the country takes place when a North Korean Air Koryo airliner flies a South Korean tour group from Inch'on, S.Kor., to Pyongyang, N.Kor.

16 OPEC announces that representatives of the U.S.-appointed Iraqi Governing Council will take Iraq's seat at OPEC meetings, though Iraq's role may be limited, given the low production of oil as a result of constant sabotage of the infrastructure.

•

The White House reopens for tours by the general public for the first time since the terrorist attacks of Sept. 11, 2001.

•

Great Britain's Royal Botanic Gardens, Kew, inaugurates the Francis Rose Reserve, an area of sandstone outcrops that will serve as home for rare native cryptogams (spore-producing plants), including mosses, liverworts, and lichens; it is believed to be the first such botanic reserve in Europe.

•

The Bolshoi Theatre in Moscow fires celebrity ballerina Anastasiya Volochkova, maintaining that she is overweight; charges and countercharges keep the dispute on the front pages of Russian newspapers. (Photo right.)

17 Richard Grasso resigns as chairman and CEO of the New York Stock Exchange after several weeks of complaints that his remarkably high compensation package ($139.5 million) was set by some of the people whom he was responsible for regulating.

•

The scandal-plagued Dutch food retailer Royal Ahold announces the resignation of its chairman and the scaling down of its CEO's pay package in the face of widespread anger over the exceptionally high pay for the CEO coupled with deep layoffs at the company's grocery chain.

•

Spanish Prime Minister José María Aznar visits Tripoli, Libya, to meet with Libyan leader Muammar al-Qaddafi; Aznar is the first Western leader to visit Libya since international sanctions were imposed more than 10 years earlier.

18 A general strike called by Maoist rebels shuts down most of Nepal.

•

Hurricane Isabel makes landfall in North Carolina, knocking out power to millions of people in several seaboard states, cutting a wide swath of damage, and killing at least 23 people before turning north and starting to fade.

•

AOL Time Warner announces that it will change its name to Time Warner; prior to the merger with AOL in 2001, the company was also known as Time Warner.

19 In Yalta, Ukraine, the leaders of Belarus, Kazakhstan, Russia, and Ukraine sign an agreement to constitute themselves a single economic and trade zone.

AP/Wide World Photos

•

The UN Security Council approves the deployment of a peacekeeping force to Liberia, which will take over from the force from countries of the Economic Union of West African States on October 1.

•

Paleontologists report that a rodent skeleton dating to eight million years ago discovered in Venezuela has been determined to be a 680-kg (1,500-lb) ancestor of the pacarana; called *Phoberomys pattersoni,* it is by far the largest rodent ever found.

20 Japanese Prime Minister Junichiro Koizumi is resoundingly reelected leader of the Liberal Democratic Party.

•

Latvia approves membership in the European Union in a referendum; it is the last of the 10 proposed new members to hold a vote.

•

In Bosnia and Herzegovina a memorial centre is opened to commemorate the 8,000 victims of the massacre at Srebrenica in 1995 during the 1992–95 civil war in the country; former U.S. president Bill Clinton is among those on hand.

•

Akila al-Hashemi, a member of the Iraqi Governing Council, is attacked by nine gunmen and shot while on her way to work; she dies five days later.

•

Miss Florida, Ericka Dunlap, wins the title of Miss America in Atlantic City, N.J.

21 The Galileo spacecraft concludes its 14-year mission to Jupiter by diving into the planet's atmosphere and disintegrating; the destruction of the spacecraft was to avoid possible contamination of the moon

Europa, which data from Galileo suggest may have conditions for possible life.

•

The Emmy Awards are presented in Los Angeles; winners include the television shows *Everybody Loves Raymond* and *The West Wing* (its fourth win) and the actors Tony Shalhoub, James Gandolfini, Debra Messing, Edie Falco, Brad Garrett, Joe Pantoliano, Doris Roberts, and Tyne Daly.

•

Prime Minister Percival J. Patterson announces his goal of changing Jamaica to a republic with an elected head of state.

22 Dutch Foreign Minister Jaap de Hoop Scheffer is named to take over as secretary-general of NATO when Lord Robertson's term of office ends on Jan. 1, 2004.

•

A report is published in *Geophysical Research Letters* saying that the Ward Hunt Ice Shelf on the north coast of Canada's Ellesmere Island has broken up; the feature was the biggest ice shelf in the Arctic and had endured for 3,000 years.

•

Researchers at Decode Genetics in Reykjavík, Ice., say that they have discovered a gene that is linked to common forms of stroke.

23 U.S. Pres. George W. Bush addresses the UN General Assembly, defending U.S. policy on Iraq and asking for financial support to rebuild that country.

•

The worst power failure in 20 years shuts down southern Sweden and eastern Denmark for several hours.

24 Delegates from 18 religions meet in Astana, Kazakhstan, to create an organization dedicated to reducing violent confrontations between different religions.

25 UN Secretary-General Kofi Annan orders most of the non-Iraqi UN staff in Baghdad to leave the country, citing the uncertain security situation.

•

International Atomic Energy Agency inspectors in Iran report finding traces of unreported highly enriched uranium at an electrical plant outside Tehran.

•

In Naivasha, Kenya, representatives of the government of The Sudan and of the Sudan People's Liberation Army sign an accord in which the government agrees to withdraw its troops from rebel-held areas and begin the process of integrating the government's armed forces with those of the rebels.

•

Ceremonies are held in both Darwin and Sydney to mark the completion of the trans-Australia railroad, which travels between Adelaide and Darwin and is the first rail link between the north and south coasts of Australia; it has been in the works for 145 years.

•

In Nigeria an appeals court overturns Amina Lawal's conviction and sentence of death by stoning for adultery, citing irregularities in her previous trial.

26 As families sit down to celebrate the Jewish New Year, in a settlement in the West Bank a Palestinian gunman opens fire on a family, killing two people, one a baby.

•

Science magazine publishes a report that researchers in France have succeeded in cloning rats, a goal that had eluded scientists.

•

All 6,000 Segway Human Transporters are recalled because the devices have a tendency to tip forward under certain conditions when the batteries are low; the company that manufactures them intends to modify them so that they become inoperable before that point is reached.

27 In Afghanistan, Taliban guerrillas kill seven bodyguards in an apparent attempt to assassinate the governor of Helmand province, and in Nangarhar province suspected Taliban members burn down a coeducational secondary school.

•

Three missiles hit the heavily barricaded Rashid Hotel in downtown Baghdad, Iraq, which has been converted into the main compound for Americans; there are no casualties.

•

The European Space Agency launches its first vehicle to study the Moon, from Kourou, French Guiana; the probe, called Smart-1, is expected to go into orbit around the Moon in about 15 months.

•

The Brisbane Lions defeat the Collingwood Magpies 20.14 (134) to 12.12 (84) in the Australian Football League Grand Final; the victory marks an unprecedented third consecutive title for Brisbane.

•

In Sibiu, Rom., over her tearful objections, Ana-Maria Cioaba, the 12-year-old daughter of self-proclaimed Roma (Gypsy) king Florin Cioaba, is united with a 15-year-old boy in an arranged marriage that ignites outrage in Europe and North America.

28 Pope John Paul II creates 31 new cardinals, bringing the number of electors (those who may vote to choose a pope in the event of a vacancy) from 109 to 135.

•

A remote-controlled bomb kills 11 people and injures at least 40 on a crowded street in Florencia, Colom.; guerrillas in the Revolutionary Armed Forces of Colombia are blamed.

•

A power outage touched off by a tree branch in Switzerland leaves almost the entire country of Italy without electricity for several hours; in Rome the White Night festival, during which many cultural attractions are open all night, is ruined.

•

India defeats Pakistan 4–2 to win the Asia Cup in field hockey for the first time in the tournament's history.

29 The U.S. formally rejoins UNESCO, from which it had withdrawn in 1984; first lady Laura Bush represents the U.S. in a flag-raising ceremony to signal the country's return to the organization.

•

China and Hong Kong sign off on the Closer Economic Partnership Arrangement, which gives preference to Hong Kong service companies in accessing the Chinese market.

30 Paul Berenger is sworn in as prime minister of Mauritius in accordance with the provisions of a power-sharing agreement; he is the first non-Hindu to hold the position.

•

The heads of Air France and KLM Royal Dutch Airlines announce plans to merge to create Europe's biggest airline.

October

> *I will not disappoint the motherland. I will complete each movement with total concentration. And I will gain honour for the People's Liberation Army and for the Chinese nation.*

Chinese astronaut Yang Liwei, shortly before becoming the first Chinese person to orbit the Earth, October 15

1 British Energy, the biggest power company in Great Britain, reaches an agreement with its creditors that will allow the government to bail the company out in order to avoid a bankruptcy filing.

•

The U.S. Border Patrol reveals that 151 people died while attempting to cross illegally into the U.S. from Mexico at the border with Arizona during the fiscal year that just ended; this number is the most in one year and six more than in the previous fiscal year.

•

Some 900 trade-union members and activists in the Immigrant Workers Freedom Ride, demonstrating for change in U.S. immigration law and amnesty for illegal immigrants, arrive in Washington, D.C., after stops in dozens of cities throughout the country.

•

Israel approves a plan to expand the project to wall off the West Bank from Israel to include barriers built well into the West Bank that will protect several Jewish settlements.

•

Dutch cyclist Leontien Zijlaard-Van Moorsel rides 46.065 km (28.623 mi) in Mexico City to beat the world hour record set by Jeannie Longo in 2000.

2 The Nobel Prize for Literature is awarded to J.M. Coetzee of South Africa.

•

In Rwanda's first multiparty legislative elections since independence, the ruling Rwandan Patriotic Front wins the majority of seats.

•

Some 70,000 people demonstrate in Abidjan, Côte d'Ivoire, against a power-sharing agreement; the demonstrators believe that power should remain with the government and not be shared with rebels.

•

The fourth consecutive day of protests against a plan to export natural gas to the U.S. shuts down all transportation into and out of La Paz, Bol.

Zuma Press

3 The George Bush Presidential Library Foundation announces that the 2003 recipient of the George Bush Award for Excellence in Public Service will be liberal U.S. Sen. Edward Kennedy.

•

The World Health Organization reports that by using newer diagnostic tests, Taiwan has lowered the number of people who contracted SARS (severe acute respiratory syndrome) during the outbreak from 665 to 346, with only 37, rather than 180, deaths.

•

During a popular magic act featuring white tigers and lions in Las Vegas, Nev., Roy Horn of the duo Siegfried and Roy is attacked and critically injured by one of the tigers. (Photo left.)

4 A suicide bomber attacks a crowded restaurant in Haifa, Israel, killing at least 19 people and injuring 50.

•

Oman for the first time holds elections in which all citizens are eligible to vote; the elections are for the Consultative Council, which serves in an advisory capacity.

•

Iraq's central bank unveils new dinar notes, to go into circulation on October 15; the new notes, which feature Iraqi scenes rather than portraits of Saddam Hussein, are part of an attempt to stabilize Iraq's currency and reduce counterfeiting.

5 Israel conducts an air raid in Syria for the first time in 30 years, hitting a site outside Damascus that Israel asserts, and Syria denies, is a terrorist training camp.

•

Elections are held in the breakaway Russian republic of Chechnya; the handpicked incumbent and winner, Akhmad Kadyrov, faces almost no opposition and is backed by heavy-handed intimidation.

•

In the Prix de l'Arc de Triomphe, the most prestigious Thoroughbred horse race in Europe, the winner is Dalakhani; he had previously won the French Derby.

6 The Nobel Prize for Physiology or Medicine is awarded to Paul C. Lauterbur and Sir Peter Mansfield for their work that led to the development of magnetic resonance imaging (MRI).

•

Maulana Azam Tariq, a hard-line Sunnite politician and member of the National Assembly of Pakistan, is assassinated in Islamabad.

7 In Stockholm the Nobel Prize for Physics is awarded to Alexei A. Abrikosov and Vitaly L. Ginzburg for their theoretical work on the nature of superconductivity and to Anthony J. Leggett for his work on the superfluid behaviour of the isotope helium-3.

•

Voters in California choose to recall Gov. Gray Davis and install movie star Arnold Schwarzenegger as governor in his stead.

8 The Nobel Prize for Chemistry is awarded to Roderick MacKinnon, for having deduced the molecular structure of ion channels in cell membranes and to Peter C. Agre for his discovery of aquaporins, membrane channels that convey water, while the Nobel Memorial Prize in Economic Sciences goes to Robert F. Engle and Clive W.J. Granger.

•

India's National Anti-Malaria Programme reports an alarming upsurge in cases of dengue fever, with the number of infected in the vicinity of 5,000 and 78 deaths; Kerala state is bearing the brunt of the epidemic.

•

Transparency International for the third year in a row names Bangladesh the most corrupt country in the world; the least corrupt is Finland.

9 In Baghdad, Iraq, a car bomb explodes in a police compound in a Shi'ite slum, killing at least 8 people and wounding 40, and, on the other side of town, a diplomat at the Spanish embassy is assassinated at his home.

•

A British High Court judge denies a claim by islanders and their descendants for monetary compensation for having been forced by the British government to leave their homes on Diego Garcia between 1967 and 1973; Diego Garcia is now a U.S. military base.

•

The Liberty Bell is moved to its home in the newly built Liberty Bell Center in Philadelphia in time for ceremonies dedicating the building in the year of the 250th anniversary of the casting of the bell.

10 The Nobel Peace Prize is awarded to Iranian lawyer and human rights activist Shirin Ebadi; the committee cites her work on behalf of women and children.

•

The Chad-Cameroon Oil Development and Pipeline Project is officially inaugurated in a ceremony in Kome, Chad, attended by the presidents of Chad and Cameroon; the pipeline will carry oil from wells in Chad to ports in Cameroon.

•

Norwegian driver Petter Solberg wins the world rally championship when he comes in first at the Rally of Great Britain.

11 A gala celebration and opening-night concert featuring Itzhak Perlman and a world premiere by Jonathan Holland marks the opening of the new home of the Detroit Symphony Orchestra, the Max M. Fisher Music Center.

12 A car bomb explodes in Iraq outside the Baghdad Hotel, which is used by members of the Iraqi Governing Council as well as Americans; 6 Iraqi security guards die, and at least 35 people are wounded.

•

Five protesters are killed in La Paz, Bol., after Pres. Gonzalo Sánchez de Lozada calls in troops in an effort to restore order. (*See* October 17.)

•

Germany wins the Women's World Cup in association football (soccer) when it defeats Sweden 2–1 in Carson, Calif.; the tournament had been moved from its planned venue in China because of fears of SARS (severe acute respiratory syndrome).

•

The Royal Institute of British Architects announces that the Stirling Prize for 2003 goes to Jacques Herzog and Pierre de Meuron for the Laban dance centre in London.

13 Saudi Arabia announces plans to hold municipal elections; these will be the first popular elections ever held in the country.

•

Qatar's Emir Sheikh Hamad ibn Khalifah al-Thani officially opens Education City, an enormous project outside Doha that will contain branch campuses of the world's leading universities and is intended to be a hub for the entire Middle East; it is due to be completed in 2008.

14 The Man Booker Prize for Fiction, Great Britain's top literary award, goes to Australian writer DBC Pierre for his first novel, *Vernon God Little.*

•

Charles Gyude Bryant is sworn in as Liberia's new transitional leader.

15 China joins the space race more than 40 years after it got under way as it launches its first manned space flight, from a base in the Gobi Desert; the *Shenzhou 5* carries astronaut Yang Liwei into orbit around the Earth.

•

NATO formally inaugurates its new rapid-response force, which consists of 9,000 troops from all member countries and all branches of the service under a unified command; its first head is British Gen. Jack Deverell.

•

In elections in Azerbaijan, Prime Minister Ilham Aliyev is elected to succeed his father, Heydar Aliyev, as president.

•

Anglican church leaders from throughout the world gather in an emergency meeting in London called by Rowan Williams, the archbishop of Canterbury, in an effort to avoid a schism in the communion occasioned by the election of an openly gay bishop by the American province.

•

The Royal Swedish Academy announces that the winners of the Polar Music Prize, established in 1989, are B.B. King and Gyorgy Ligeti.

•

Jazz luminaries and politicians attend the opening ceremonies of the Louis Armstrong House in Queens, N.Y., where Armstrong lived from 1943 until his death in 1971; the National Historic Landmark has been renovated and serves as a museum.

16 Pope John Paul II officially celebrates 25 years on the Throne of Peter with a twilight mass in St. Peter's Square in Vatican City.

•

The UN Security Council adopts a resolution that authorizes a multinational force to go to Iraq under the command of the U.S. and requires the Iraqi Governing Council to produce a timetable for a transition to democracy by December 15.

•

Tonga's Legislative Assembly passes amendments to the country's constitution, which dates from 1875, that increase governmental control over the media and increase the monarch's power, which is already nearly absolute.

•

U.S. Secretary of the Interior Gale Norton signs an agreement that will divert water from the Colorado River away from farms in the Southwest toward large cities in southern California.

•

Patricia Ireland, a former president of the National Organization of Women, is dismissed just a few months after having been named CEO of the YWCA after her efforts to change the organization's goals prove too divisive.

17 After days of increasingly passionate demonstrations against a government plan to export natural gas, Bolivian Pres. Gonzalo Sánchez de Lozada announces his resignation; his vice president, Carlos Mesa, assumes the presidency. (*See* October 12.)

•

The German Bundestag (parliament) passes a much-needed but unpopular reform bill intended to bolster the economy and ease the country's stubborn recession.

•

In Taipei, Taiwan, a topping-out ceremony is held for the skyscraper called Taipei 101; the building, scheduled for completion in late 2004, will replace Malaysia's Petronas Towers as the tallest building in the world.

•

A fire breaks out in the 35-story Cook County Administration Building in downtown Chicago, and six people die of smoke inhalation in a stairwell, trapped by locked doors above and the fire below.

18 A Soyuz rocket takes off from Baikonur, Kazakhstan, carrying American C. Michael Foale, Russian Aleksandr Yu. Kaleri, and Spaniard Pedro Duque to the International Space Station to relieve the crew, who have been on the station for six months.

19 Tens of thousands of people gather in St. Peter's Square in Vatican City to witness Pope John Paul II's beatification of Mother Teresa of Calcutta.

•

American illusionist David Blaine, after having spent 44 days without food in a Plexiglas cube suspended near London's Tower Bridge, is lowered to the ground and released before a large crowd; the stunt attracted a great deal of attention, not all of it favourable.

20 Beset by allegations of corruption, ʿAli Abu al-Raghib abruptly resigns as prime minister of Jordan.

21 The Co-op, a British agricultural giant, declares that it will ban the production and use of genetically modified crops both for animal feed and for food sold to the public.

•

The government of Iran signs an agreement with the foreign ministers of France, the U.K., and Germany to allow increased inspection of nuclear sites and to suspend its program of uranium enrichment.

•

Louise Glück assumes her duties as U.S. poet laureate, succeeding Billy Collins.

•

France's Prix Goncourt is bestowed on Jacques-Pierre Amette for his novel *La Maîtresse de Brecht.*

22 Ukraine offers a show of force to prevent Russian workers from building a sea wall in the Kerch Strait, between the Sea of Azov and the Black Sea; the border between Ukraine and Russia in the strait has not been agreed upon.

•

After the killing of several international aid workers, the UN orders its staff in the self-declared republic of Somaliland in Somalia to remain in Hargeisa, the capital, and observe an early curfew.

•

The *Nuna II,* a solar vehicle designed by a Dutch team, wins the World Solar Challenge in Australia, covering the 3,010-km (1,870-mi) course in a record 30 hr 54 min.

23 The Walt Disney Concert Hall, designed by Frank Gehry, opens in Los Angeles; critics find it both architecturally and acoustically pleasing.

•

The first Russian military base in a foreign country since the end of the Soviet Union opens in Kyrgyzstan, only about 30 km (nearly 20 mi) from a U.S. base from which the U.S. stages operations in Afghanistan.

•

Algeria, Benin, Brazil, the Philippines, and Romania are selected as nonpermanent members of the UN Security Council.

•

U.S. government agents raid 60 Wal-Mart stores in 21 states, arresting at least 250 illegal aliens employed at the stores through outside contractors.

•

Two days after the start of the Grand Prix wildfire in southern California, hundreds of people are ordered to evacuate their homes; the fire, one of three in the area, has burned some 1,000 ha (2,500 ac) of the San Bernardino National Forest.

24 ***The final Concorde flights, for British Air, take off from Edinburgh and New York City; after their landing in London's Heathrow Airport, the supersonic era of air transport is concluded. (Photo below.)***

•

U.S. officials say they have persuaded countries and institutions to contribute a total of $13 billion for the reconstruction of Iraq's infrastructure; much of the pledged money is to be loaned, rather than donated.

25 The wild-card Florida Marlins defeat the New York Yankees in New York City 2–0 in the sixth game of the World Series to win the Major League Baseball championship; Marlins pitcher Josh Beckett is named series Most Valuable Player.

•

In response to a suit brought by a Muslim man whose sons attended an elementary school in L'Aquila, Italy, a judge rules that a crucifix should not be displayed in the classrooms of public schools, in spite of a 1923 law requiring them; public opinion is inflamed.

•

Mikhail B. Khodorkovsky, head of the Yukos oil company and reputed to be the wealthiest man in Russia, is arrested and charged with fraud and tax evasion.

•

In the Breeders' Cup Classic Thoroughbred race at Santa Anita Park in Arcadia, Calif., previously underachieving Pleasantly Perfect outruns several big-name horses to win; earlier, in the Juvenile Fillies race, Julie Krone had become the first woman jockey to win a Breeders' Cup race, riding Halfbridled to victory.

26 With the start of Ramadan, U.S. military forces lift the nightly curfew in Baghdad, Iraq, in order to accommodate observation of the Islamic fast.

•

A barrage of missiles strikes the Al-Rashid Hotel in Baghdad, Iraq, home to U.S. military officers; U.S. Deputy Secretary of Defense Paul Wolfowitz, in Iraq to highlight positive news stemming from the U.S. occupation, is a guest in the hotel.

•

The sixth annual Mark Twain Prize for American Humor is presented to Lily Tomlin in a ceremony at the John F. Kennedy Center for the Performing Arts in Washington, D.C.

27 A coordinated assault of suicide bombings in Baghdad, Iraq, targeting police stations and the Red Cross headquarters, kills at least 34 people and injures some 200.

•

Three states in Nigeria suspend a World Health Organization polio-immunization program on the grounds that there is widespread belief that the vaccine causes AIDS, cancer, and infertility.

•

Bank of America, which is under investigation for its role in the burgeoning mutual-funds mismanagement scandal, and FleetBoston Financial announce that they plan to merge to become the second largest American bank.

•

The Fukuoka Daiei Hawks defeat the Hanshin Tigers 6–2 in game seven to win the Japan Series baseball championship.

•

France's Prix Femina is awarded to Chinese-born author Dai Sijie for his novel *Le Complexe de Di.*

28 In response to a proposal from India to reestablish various links between the countries, Pakistan agrees to resume sports matches with India and to discuss air links, and it proposes to restore rail links and embassy staffs.

•

Australia announces plans to withdraw forces from the Solomon Islands, saying that its mission to restore order has been successfully accomplished.

•

After two years of searching, the New Jersey Symphony Orchestra announces that Neeme Jarvi will become principal conductor and music director.

29 One of the biggest solar storms ever recorded takes place, but in spite of widespread fears, very little disruption of electrical systems on Earth takes place.

•

Iain Duncan Smith is voted out as leader of the U.K.'s Conservative Party after two years of heading the Tories; he is replaced by Michael Howard on November 6.

•

Officials in New York City announce that they have removed 40 names from the list of victims killed in the World Trade Center in the Sept. 11, 2001, terrorist attacks, bringing the total down to 2,752.

30 Italy's highest court overturns the conviction of former prime minister Giulio Andreotti for conspiracy to murder a journalist.

•

Cooler, damper weather offers some relief in southern California, where wildfires have consumed 295,000 ha (729,000 ac) and more than 3,000 buildings, most of them houses.

31 Malaysian Prime Minister Mahathir bin Mohamad, who is in many respects the father of the country, resigns, handing the reins of government to Abdullah Ahmad Badawi.

•

In spite of a warning from Russian Pres. Vladimir Putin, Prime Minister Mikhail M. Kasyanov publicly expresses his doubts about the wisdom of the freezing of shares of the Yukos oil company.

November

Democracy needs steering. It is not good to have too much democracy.

Eduard Shevardnadze, after being forced to resign the presidency of Georgia, November 23

1 In Sri Lanka the Liberation Tigers of Tamil Eelam release a proposal for an interim governing structure for LTTE-controlled territories in the country as a step toward restarting negotiations with the government.

•

A woman with three children in her car manages to breach a security cordon and crashes into the building in which U.S. Pres. George W. Bush has just spoken in Southhaven, Miss.

2 In the deadliest single attack on U.S. forces since the start of the war in Iraq, a helicopter carrying soldiers starting furloughs is shot down outside Fallujah; 16 are killed.

•

Ignoring the threat of schism in the Anglican Communion, the Episcopal Church U.S.A. consecrates the openly gay V. Gene Robinson bishop of New Hampshire.

•

The American Academy of Arts and Letters names composer Stephen Hartke the third winner of its triennial Charles Ives Living award, intended to free recipients from having to earn a living.

3 The draft of a proposed constitution for Afghanistan is formally presented to Mohammad Zahir Shah, the country's former king; it will then be voted on in the *loya jirga.*

•

For the first time since 1969, Spain closes its border with the British enclave of Gibraltar, prompting complaints from the U.K.; the cause is the docking at Gibraltar of a cruise ship on which about a third of the passengers are ill with an intestinal virus.

•

It is reported that deCODE genetics, a company based in Iceland, has identified a gene linked to osteoporosis, with variants of the gene found to increase the odds of getting the disease threefold; a test for the gene variants is being developed.

•

James Murdoch is named CEO of the British Sky Broadcasting Group, which controls most pay-television service in Great Britain; his father, media mogul Rupert Murdoch, is chairman.

•

The French electronics company Thomson announces plans to combine its television and DVD units with those of China's TCL International Holdings to create TCL–Thomson Electronics, the biggest manufacturer of television sets in the world.

4 Sri Lankan Pres. Chandrika Kumaratunga suspends Parliament and fires several government ministers in an apparent move against Prime Minister Ranil Wickremesinghe; the following day she declares a state of emergency.

•

Alan Jackson and Johnny Cash (who died in September) each win three Country Music Association Awards, Jackson for entertainer, male vocalist, and event of the year and Cash for single, album, and video of the year; Cash also wins the Irving Waugh Award of Excellence.

•

The Giller Prize, awarded for the best novel or short-story collection published in English in Canada, is awarded to M.G. Vassanji for his novel *The In-Between World of Vikram Lall;* he also won the prize in 1994, for *The Book of Secrets*.

•

In a federal court in Birmingham, Ala., the U.S. Department of Justice indicts Richard M. Scrushy, the founder and former CEO of the hospital company HealthSouth, on 85 counts for defrauding investors.

5 Azerbaijan, Iran, Kazakhstan, Russia, and Turkmenistan sign a treaty to reduce the ecological damage to the Caspian Sea, which all the countries border.

•

U.S. Pres. George W. Bush, in a well-publicized ceremony, signs into law a measure banning a rarely used method for late-stage abortions.

•

In Seattle, Wash., Gary Ridgway pleads guilty to the murder of 48 women during the 1980s, putting an end to the mystery of the Green River killings; he is the deadliest serial killer on record.

•

The first John W. Kluge Prize for Lifetime Achievement in the Human Sciences, established by the U.S. Library of Congress to honour achievements in fields not covered by the Nobel Prizes, is awarded to Leszek Kolakowski, a Polish-born anticommunist philosopher.

6 Michael Howard is elected to lead Great Britain's Conservative Party.

•

National Public Radio announces that it is the beneficiary of the enormous bequest of at least $200 million from the estate of Joan B. Kroc, the widow of the longtime head of McDonald's Corp.

•

Bertelsmann and Sony reach an agreement to merge their music units under the name of Sony BMG and under the chairmanship of Rolf Schmidt-Holtz, with Andrew Lack as CEO.

7 Presidential elections are held in Mauritania; Pres. Maaouya Ould Sidi Ahmad Taya is declared the winner the following day.

•

A Black Hawk helicopter crashes in Tikrit, Iraq, apparently shot down, killing six U.S. soldiers; it is the third time in two weeks that an American helicopter has been brought down in Iraq.

8 A car bomb explodes at a residential compound in Riyadh, Saudi Arabia, killing at least 17 people and injuring some 120.

•

A daughter, later named Louise Alice Elizabeth Mary Mountbatten-Windsor (to be known as Lady Louise Windsor), is born to Prince Edward and his wife, Sophie, in Surrey, Eng.

9 Japanese Prime Minister Junichiro Koizumi's coalition retains power in parliamentary elections, but the size of its majority is reduced.

•

Presidential elections in Guatemala result in the need for a runoff between Oscar Berger and Álvaro Colom; former dictator Efraín Ríos Montt is out of the running.

•

France's minister of culture announces that the country is undertaking a massive 20-year renovation of the 17th-century Palace of Versailles and its gardens.

10 For the third day in a row, thousands of protesters in Tbilisi, Georgia, demand the resignation of Pres. Eduard Shevardnadze.

•

The World Trade Organization rules that the tariffs on steel imposed by the U.S. in 2002 are illegal under the rules of the organization; the European Union is thus entitled to impose sanctions on goods from the U.S.

11 The Dominican Republic is brought to a halt by a general strike, and protesters fight with police in several cities; the economic situation in the country has been deteriorating badly.

•

The Movado Watch Co. says that it is withdrawing its funding for American Ballet Theatre, transferring it to the New York City Ballet, citing financial mismanagement at ABT.

12 A car bomb destroys a compound housing an Italian police base in Nasiriyah, Iraq, killing at least 26 people, 19 of them Italian.

•

The death penalty is abolished in Turkey; the step is a prerequisite for membership in the European Union.

•

The U.S. National Medal of Arts is awarded to Ron Howard, Suzanne Farrell, Tommy Tune, Leonard Slatkin, Beverly Cleary, Buddy Guy, George Strait, Rafe Esquith, the Mormon Tabernacle Choir, and the television show *Austin City Limits*.

13 On his first official visit to Sarajevo, Bosnia and Herzegovina, Pres. Svetozar Marovic of Serbia and Montenegro apologizes to the people of Bosnia and Herzegovina for the war in 1992–95.

•

Pres. Henrique Rosa of Guinea-Bissau ceremonially opens Amilcar Cabral University, the first public university in the country; the first students will be admitted in January 2004.

•

The Hawaiian island of Kahoolawe is formally returned to the state of Hawaii by the U.S. Navy, which had used the island for weapons testing and practice from shortly before World War II until 1994, after which it began restoring the environment; the island has great meaning to indigenous Hawaiians.

14 The U.S. Central Command announces that it is enlarging its forward headquarters in Qatar, more than doubling its staff by transferring personnel from the main headquarters in Florida.

•

The Corsican National Liberation Front Combatants' Union, the main militant group seeking independence for the French enclave, announces an unconditional cease-fire.

•

The first phase of the newest contender for the title of tallest building in the world, the Taipei 101, is formally opened in Taiwan. (Photo right.)

15 Car bombs explode nearly simultaneously outside two synagogues in Istanbul during morning prayers, leaving at least 23 people dead and injuring 300.

•

Two American helicopters crash into each other over Mosul, Iraq; at least 17 U.S. soldiers are killed.

•

Grenades are thrown into two adjacent nightclubs in Bogotá, Colom., injuring dozens of people, including many tourists, but killing only one.

•

A Jewish school in the Paris suburb of Gagny is burned to the ground in the night; it is the first attack against a Jewish facility in France in close to a year.

16 Taliban gunmen in Ghazni, Afg., attack and kill a female worker for the UN

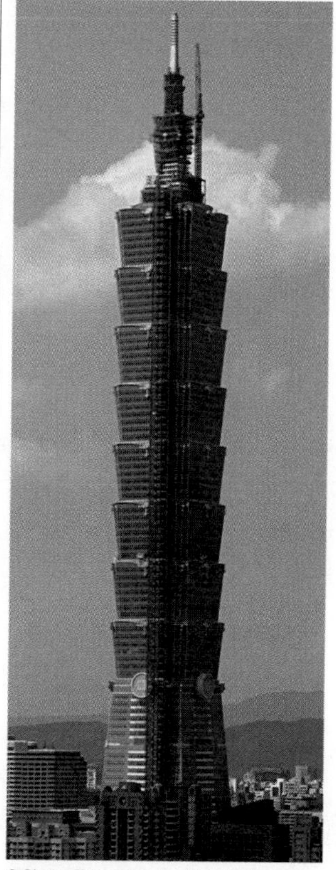

© Simon Kwong/Reuters NewMedia Inc./Corbis

High Commissioner for Refugees; the agency immediately suspends operations in the area.

•

In local elections the ruling Convergence and Union coalition and the opposition Socialist Party of Catalonia both lose seats to the small Republican Left party, which favours independence from Spain for Catalonia.

•

In Serbia's third attempt at a presidential election, the turnout is again too low for the balloting to be valid; technically the republic now has neither president nor legislature.

•

The Edmonton Eskimos defeat the Montreal Alouettes 34–22 in Regina, Sask., to capture the franchise's 12th Canadian Football League Grey Cup.

•

Donald Gordon, founder of the insurance company Liberty Life Group and the retail conglomerate Liberty International, makes the largest private gift to the arts in British history in donating some $34 million to be shared between the Royal Opera House, Covent Garden, and the under-construction Wales Millennium Centre.

17 Conrad Black, who built Hollinger International into an empire of conservative newspapers, including London's *Daily Telegraph,* the *Jerusalem Post,* and the *Chicago Sun-Times,* resigns as CEO after admitting that he and his partners were given $32 million without shareholder authorization.

•

The insurer St. Paul Companies takes control of the much larger Travelers Property Casualty Corp. to create an insurance behemoth to be known as St. Paul Travelers Companies.

•

Toys "Я" Us announces that because of declining revenues it will close all of its freestanding Kids "Я" Us clothing stores and Imaginarium educational-toy stores.

18 ***The Supreme Court of Massachusetts finds that the state constitution does not permit it to deny the benefits of civil marriage to same-sex couples. (Photo right.)***

•

It is reported that scientists at the High Energy Acceleration Research Organization in Tsukuba, Japan, have discovered a meson, a type of subatomic particle, that does not conform to any known theory of energy and matter; the new meson has been dubbed X(3872).

•

At the age of 14, Ghanaian association football (soccer) phenomenon Freddy Adu signs a contract with Major League Soccer in the U.S., becoming simultaneously the youngest and the best-paid player in the league.

•

Barry Bonds becomes the first player in Major League Baseball history to win three consecutive Most Valuable Player awards when the National League names him its 2003 season MVP.

19 The government of South Africa approves a plan to give antiretroviral medicine free of cost to people infected with HIV.

•

Law-enforcement personnel in California announce that a warrant has been issued for the arrest of pop star Michael Jackson on suspicion of child molestation.

•

The U.S. National Endowment for the Arts presents its annual Jazz Masters awards to guitarist Jim Hall, drummer Chico Hamilton, keyboardist Herbie Hancock, singer Nancy Wilson, critic Nat Hentoff, and composer Luther Henderson.

•

The National Book Awards are presented to Shirley Hazzard for her novel *The Great Fire,* Carlos Eire for his nonfiction book *Waiting for Snow in Havana: Confessions of a Cuban Boy,* C.K. Williams for his poetry collection *The Singing,* and Polly Horvath for her young-adult book *The Canning Season;* suspense novelist Stephen King is given the Medal for Distinguished Contribution to American Letters.

•

In a disagreement over Bertelsmann's agreement with Sony Music (*see* November 6), Bertelsmann's chairman, Gerd Schulte-Hillen, resigns.

20 The British consulate in Istanbul and the Istanbul headquarters of Britain's HSBC Bank are both destroyed by truck bombs; at least 27 are killed and 450 injured.

•

Tens of thousands of protesters demonstrate in London's Trafalgar Square in opposition to the policies of U.S. Pres. George W. Bush on the occasion of his state visit to the U.K.

•

Georgia's Central Election Commission reports that parties that support Pres. Eduard Shevardnadze have won the majority of seats in the parliamentary elections on November 2; opposition politicians declare the results fraudulent.

•

It is reported that researchers have succeeded in producing a draft map of protein interactions in the fruit fly; after DNA decoding, protein modeling is the next step toward understanding the processes of life.

•

Nature magazine publishes a report by Japanese scientists who, in studying whales caught during the 1970s, believe they have found a previously unnamed species of rorqual whale similar to but distinct from the Bryde's whale; they dub it *Balaenoptera omurai.*

21 Across the Middle East, Muslims observe Jerusalem Day, as they have done for many years on the last Friday of Ramadan in support of Palestinian claims to Jerusalem.

•

Brazilian Pres. Luiz Inácio Lula da Silva announces that he plans an ambitious land-redistribution project that will give parcels to 400,000 landless families.

•

A paper in *Science* magazine describes rock shards found in Antarctica that date from the Permian-Triassic boundary and that some scientists believe are fragments from a meteor as bolstering the theory that a meteorite caused the extinction of 90% of the Earth's species at the end of the Permian Period, about 245 million years ago.

22 Protesters in Tbilisi, Georgia, storm Parliament just as Pres. Eduard Shevardnadze is beginning to address the body; he is forced to flee.

•

In Sydney, Australia, England defeats Australia 20–17 to win the Rugby Union World Cup, the first team from the Northern Hemisphere ever to do so.

23 Georgian Pres. Eduard Shevardnadze peacefully relinquishes power; parliamentary speaker Nino Burdzhanadze becomes acting president, and the opposition guarantees the security of the deposed president and his family.

•

Parliamentary elections in Croatia result in a return to power of the nationalist Croatian Democratic Union led by Ivo Sanader; the party reportedly has purged itself of its more hard-line elements since it lost power in the 2000 election.

•

The San Jose Earthquakes win their second Major League Soccer title in three years with a 4–2 victory over the Chicago Fire in the MLS Cup.

•

Subway train service to the stop at the site of the former World Trade Center in New York City resumes for the first time since the station was destroyed in the terrorist attacks of Sept. 11, 2001.

•

Pakistani Prime Minister Zafarullah Khan Jamali announces that Pakistani troops patrolling the Line of Control in Kashmir will begin a cease-fire at Eid al-Fitr, the holiday that marks the end of Ramadan.

24 A jury in Virginia Beach, Va., sentences John A. Muhammad to death for having directed the sniper killings that terrorized the area around Washington, D.C., in October 2002. (*See* December 18.)

•

A group of investors led by media figure and Seagram's heir Edgar Bronfman, Jr., buys the Warner Music division of media conglomerate Time Warner.

•

A long-awaited new rule that permits mobile-phone customers to change service providers without changing their telephone numbers goes into effect in the U.S.

•

Leo F. Mullin unexpectedly announces that he will step down from his position as CEO of Delta Air Lines; he will be replaced by Gerald Grinstein.

25 A bill that will drastically revamp the Medicare system, which provides medical insurance coverage for the elderly, is approved in the U.S. Congress.

•

Israel announces that the U.S. is rescinding a small portion of its loan guarantees to Israel because of the continued building of Israeli settlements in the West Bank.

26 Legislative elections in Northern Ireland give the largest share of seats to the hard-line Protestant Democratic Unionist Party at the expense of the more moderate Ulster Unionist Party.

•

The International Atomic Energy Agency passes a resolution in which it deplores Iran's 18 years of covering up its nuclear program.

•

It is reported that four children in the U.S. state of Colorado have died of influenza in the past week, which suggests that an unusually severe flu season is in store; the worst of the flu season usually occurs in January and February.

•

A Russian court orders the Bolshoi Ballet to reinstate its star ballerina, Anastasia Volochkova, who has been appearing in concerts throughout Russia since the Bolshoi fired her. (*See* September 16.)

27 U.S. Pres. George W. Bush surprises U.S. troops—as well as the media and all but his closest advisers—by joining the soldiers in a Thanksgiving dinner at the mess hall at Baghdad International Airport in Iraq.

28 Pres. Robert Mugabe of Zimbabwe threatens to pull his country out of the Commonwealth if that organization's member states continue to shut Zimbabwe out. (*See* December 7.)

•

A study published by the U.S. Centers for Disease Control and Prevention shows that the number of new cases of HIV infection is increasing, with by far the greatest number of new cases occurring among Hispanic men.

29 Attacks in Iraq kill seven intelligence officers from Spain and two diplomats from Japan.

•

More than 40,000 people attend an all-star concert to raise money for AIDS in Cape Town, S.Af.; the highlight is a duet between Bono and Beyoncé.

30 Thousands of people in Venezuela line up at various venues to sign petitions seeking a recall of Pres. Hugo Chávez; if 20% of registered voters—about 2.4 million persons—sign the petition, a recall referendum must be initiated.

•

In the Davis Cup team tennis tournament, Mark Philippoussis of Australia defeats Juan Carlos Ferrero of Spain to give Australia its 28th Davis Cup victory; a week earlier France, led by Amelie Mauresmo, had won its second Fed Cup.

•

The Iraqi Governing Council agrees that a general election should be held in June 2004 to choose an interim government and appoints a committee to examine whether it will be possible to hold such an election.

•

Roy E. Disney, the last heir of Walt Disney, resigns from the board of the Walt Disney Co. but says he thinks CEO Michael Eisner should resign instead.

December

Ladies and gentlemen, we got him.

L. Paul Bremer III, U.S. administrator in Iraq, on December 14, announcing the capture of Saddam Hussein

1 Former Israeli minister of justice Yossi Beilin and former Palestinian minister of information Yasir Abed Rabbo unveil a far-reaching proposal for peace between Israel and Palestine.

•

The Boeing Co. announces the resignation of its CEO, Philip M. Condit; the company has been accused of ethical violations.

2 Russia signals that it will not ratify the Kyoto Protocol to limit greenhouse gases; with the cooperation of neither Russia nor the U.S., which has already announced its intention not to ratify, the treaty would not take effect.

•

A maglev train outside Tokyo on a test run reaches a speed of 581 km/hr (360 mph), breaking its own world speed record for the third time in three weeks.

3 The Canadian government approves a royal proclamation recognizing the suffering caused when some 11,000 French speakers, called Acadians, were expelled from British Canada in 1755 for refusing to swear allegiance to Great Britain.

•

After storms lashing southern France cause flooding that leaves at least 5 people dead, the area around Marseille is declared a disaster zone.

4 U.S. Pres. George W. Bush rescinds the steel tariffs that he put in place in 2002 in violation of World Trade Organization rules.

•

Interpol puts deposed Liberian president Charles Taylor on its most-wanted list by posting a so-called red notice on its Web site. (*See* September 5.)

•

South Korea's National Assembly overrules Pres. Roh Moo Hyun's veto of a measure ordering an independent investigation of corruption charges against former aides of the president; it is the first time in 49 years that a presidential veto has been overturned.

•

In Rome a synod of Chaldean Catholic bishops elects Emmanuel-Karim Delly patriarch of Babylon, head of the Chaldean Catholic Church, more than half of whose members live in Iraq; he will serve under the name Emmanuel III Delly.

•

The U.S. Presidential Medal of Freedom is awarded to Robert L. Bartley, who for some 30 years was the editorial-page editor of *The Wall Street Journal;* Bartley dies a few days later, on December 10.

5 U.S. Deputy Secretary of Defense Paul D. Wolfowitz, citing "essential security interests," issues a directive barring companies from countries that did not support the U.S.-led war in Iraq—which include France, Germany, and Russia—from bidding on contracts to rebuild Iraq's infrastructure.

•

U.S. Pres. George W. Bush names veteran statesman James A. Baker III his personal envoy to persuade creditor countries in Europe and the Middle East to restructure Iraq's foreign debt.

•

A suicide bombing takes place aboard a Russian commuter train traveling between Kislovodsk and Mineralnye Vody, near Chechnya; at least 42 people are killed, and more than 150 are injured.

•

The 22nd biennial Southeast Asian Games open in Hanoi; it is the first major international sports event to be held in Vietnam.

6 In a strike intended to kill a suspected terrorist, a U.S.-led military force in Afghanistan kills nine children but not, apparently, the intended target.

•

Saudi Arabia releases the names and photos of its most-wanted terrorists; the U.S. embassy staff in Riyadh is warned to remain in diplomatic quarters.

7 A Commonwealth summit in Nigeria declines to lift the suspension of Zimbabwe from the group, and Zimbabwean Pres. Robert Mugabe terminates Zimbabwe's membership in the Commonwealth.

•

Parliamentary elections are held in Russia, and the United Russia party, which is loyal to Pres. Vladimir Putin, wins the largest percentage of seats; observers from the Organization for Security and Co-operation in Europe say that the party's advantages in access to resources distorted the vote.

•

Arnoldo Alemán, who was president of Nicaragua in

1997–2002, is sentenced to 20 years in prison for, among other crimes, fraud and embezzlement.

•

Dutch Crown Prince Willem-Alexander and his wife, Princess Maxima, become the parents of a baby girl, who will be known as Amalia; she is second in line to the throne of The Netherlands.

•

Britain's Turner Prize is presented to the transvestite ceramics artist Grayson Perry. (Photo right.)

•

The annual Kennedy Center Honors are presented in Washington, D.C., to television star Carol Burnett, film and stage director Mike Nichols, and musicians James Brown, Loretta Lynn, and Itzhak Perlman.

8 A court in Athens finds 15 members of the militant group known as November 17 guilty of 23 killings and acquits 4 others; the group had operated virtually at liberty from 1975 to 2001.

•

In an unusually blunt statement on the subject, U.S. Pres. George W. Bush warns Taiwan against holding a referendum in support of independence from China.

•

The Right Livelihood Awards are presented in Stockholm to former New Zealand prime minister David Lange, for his work to rid the world of nuclear weapons; Walden Bello and Nicanor Perlas, Filipinos who work against corporate globalization; the Citizens' Coalition for Economic Justice, a South Korean organization that fosters inclusive economic development and promotes reconciliation with North Korea; and SEKEM, an Egyptian biodynamic farming corporation that promotes social and cultural development.

© Ian Hodgson/
Reuters NewMedia Inc./Corbis

•

U.S. Rep. Bill Janklow of South Dakota is convicted of manslaughter in a case stemming from an automobile accident in which a motorcyclist was killed; Janklow says he will resign from Congress.

9 Chinese Prime Minister Wen Jiabao is received with high honours in the White House, where he and U.S. Pres. George W. Bush discuss the crisis with North Korea and China's trade surplus with the U.S.

•

A suicide bomber detonates her weapons outside the historic National Hotel in downtown Moscow, killing at least 5 people and injuring 13, as well as destroying cars and shattering windows in the lobby of the hotel, which is located only a few hundred metres from the Kremlin.

•

The Iraqi Governing Council votes to create a national tribunal to try members of Saddam Hussein's administration on any charges stemming from that regime's crimes against humanity.

10 The U.S. Supreme Court holds that a provision of a 2002 campaign finance law that bans the unregulated donation of money to candidates for federal office or to national parties and restricts political advertising by interest groups near election time does not violate constitutional provisions protecting free speech.

•

The UN Human Rights Prize, granted every five years, is awarded to Sérgio Vieira de Mello, who was killed in Iraq; Enriqueta Estela Barnes de Carlotto of Argentina; Deng Pufang of China; Shulamith Koenig of the U.S.; the Family Protection Project Management Team of Jordan; and the Mano River Women's Peace Network of West Africa.

11 U.S. military officials reveal that an audit seems to show that Kellogg Brown & Root, a subsidiary of the Halliburton Co., overcharged the U.S. government more than $60 million for fuel delivered to Iraq.

•

Shares of the Italian food-manufacturing giant Parmalat fall nearly 50% amid a financial crisis that includes a $590 million investment loss, the resignation of the chief financial officer, a decision to sell off its American bakery assets, and a three-day suspension in stock trading. (*See* December 24.)

•

A French commission charged with making recommendations to keep state and religion separate and prevent religious turmoil turns in its report to Pres. Jacques Chirac; its most explosive recommendation is to ban the wearing of conspicuous religious symbols in schools, including skullcaps by Jewish boys, headscarves by Muslim girls, and large crosses by Christians.

•

A judge in Hamburg, Ger., orders the release of Abdelghani Mzoudi, a Moroccan on trial for having aided the planners of the terrorist attacks on Sept. 11, 2001, saying that the U.S.'s refusal to make Ramzi ibn al-Shibh, a chief witness, available for examination makes it impossible to evaluate evidence in the case.

•

Australian Foreign Minister Alexander Downer announces that the country will send nearly 300 police officers and officials to Papua New Guinea to help restore order.

12 Jean Chrétien retires as prime minister of Canada; Paul Martin assumes the office.

•

Rock singer Mick Jagger is knighted in a ceremony led by Prince Charles in London.

•

An assault takes place on the state television station in Abidjan, Côte d'Ivoire, but security forces successfully repel the attackers in a battle that leaves 18 dead; the identity of the attackers is unclear.

13 A tip leads U.S. soldiers to a farm outside Tikrit, Iraq, where they find Saddam Hussein hiding in a "spider hole" and arrest him; the capture is announced to the world the following day.

•

Meeting to vote on a proposed draft constitution for the European Union, the leaders of EU member states and those that will join the union in May 2004 adjourn without agreement; at issue is apportionment of voting power.

AP/Wide World Photos

•

The 2003 Heisman Trophy for college football is awarded to University of Oklahoma quarterback Jason White.

14 In Turkish Cypriot parliamentary elections, the vote is about evenly divided between supporters of Rauf Denktash, who rejected a UN plan to reunify Cyprus in a loose federation, and supporters of the plan.

•

Pakistani Pres. Pervez Musharraf narrowly escapes an assassination attempt when a bomb explodes on a bridge near his home in Rawalpindi just 30 seconds after his motorcade has passed that point. (*See* December 25.)

15 Bhutan begins a military campaign to remove training camps of Indian militants who conduct attacks in the Indian states of Assam and West Bengal.

•

Microsoft announces that it will no longer sell or support older products, including Windows 98, Windows NT 4, and Outlook 2000, all of which contain Java code that Microsoft agreed with Sun Microsystems to remove from its products.

•

At Washington Dulles International Airport, the Smithsonian Institution opens its Steven F. Udvar-Hazy Center, housing most of the collection of the National Air and Space Museum and more.

16 The legislature of Lithuania begins impeachment proceedings against Pres. Rolandas Paksas, who is accused of having ties with organized-crime figures.

•

CEO Harry Stonecipher announces that the Boeing Co.'s first new airplane model in more than 10 years, the 7E7 Dreamliner, will be produced in the area of Seattle, Wash.

•

In Hirtshals, Den., most of the North Sea Museum, including its most popular attraction, the Oceanarium, is destroyed by fire; the Oceanarium is Europe's biggest aquarium.

•

Afghani Pres. Hamid Karzai ceremonially cuts a ribbon to declare the reconstructed Kabul–Kandahar highway open; Taliban violence has made most of the highway too dangerous to use, however.

17 The U.S. signs the Central American Free Trade Agreement with Honduras, Guatemala, El Salvador, and Nicaragua; Costa Rica declines to join the accord.

•

The beleaguered Russian oil company Yukos and the more successful Sibneft report that they have agreed not to go forward with the merger that they had announced earlier in the year. (*See* April 22.)

•

Former Illinois governor George Ryan, known for having emptied the state's death row in January, is indicted on 18 wide-ranging counts of corruption.

•

In celebration of the centennial of the first flight, dignitaries including U.S. Pres. George W. Bush gather at Kill Devil Hills, N.C., to watch a replica of Wilbur and Orville Wright's 1903 Flyer attempt to duplicate the feat; the attempt is unsuccessful. (Photo above.)

•

In a ceremony attended by a number of celebrities, the Burbank-Glendale-Pasadena Airport in Burbank, Calif., is officially renamed the Bob Hope Airport.

•

The AirTrain, a light-rail service that will run from stations adjacent to some of New York City's mass transit stations to John F. Kennedy International Airport, opens.

•

The Lord of the Rings: The Return of the King opens simultaneously in 20 countries, breaking opening-day box-office records in a number of them.

18 A U.S. Court of Appeals in New York City declares that the government does not have the right to hold indefinitely José Padilla, a U.S. citizen who has been detained as an enemy combatant since June 2002, and must release or charge him; on the same day, a federal appeals court in San Francisco finds that holding detainees at the U.S. naval base at Guantánamo Bay, Cuba, without access to legal protections is unconstitutional.

•

NASA releases the first images from its Space Infrared Telescope Facility, launched August 25, and renames it the Spitzer Space Telescope; by operating at only about 5 °C above absolute zero, the telescope will be able to detect objects with very faint warmth.

•

Iran signs a protocol to the Nuclear Non-proliferation Treaty that will permit the International Atomic Energy Agency to make intrusive inspections to verify that Iran does not have a nuclear weapons program.

•

Teenager Lee Malvo is convicted on two counts of murder in the sniper killings in the area of Washington, D.C., in fall 2002; on December 23 he is sentenced to life in prison. (*See* November 24.)

19 Top U.S. and British government leaders announce that Libyan chief Muammar al-Qaddafi has admitted that his country has tried to create banned weapons and that he has promised to dismantle the program and permit nuclear inspections.

•

The design for Freedom Tower, intended to anchor

the replacement for the World Trade Center in New York City, is unveiled.

•

Former Argentine president Carlos Saúl Menem is charged with tax fraud.

•

Fisheries ministers of the European Union reach an agreement on long-term protection of dwindling stocks of various fishes and set catch quotas for 2004.

20 The long-awaited Hong Kong West Rail, linking the northwestern New Territories with Kowloon, opens.

•

In Boston the southbound portion of the Interstate 93 tunnel, part of the massive "Big Dig" Central Artery/Tunnel project, opens.

21 As expected, Lansana Conté wins election to a third term as president of Guinea.

•

Representatives of the government of The Sudan and of the rebel Sudan People's Liberation Army reach an agreement on the sharing of oil wealth; the question of access to natural resources has been fueling conflict in the country.

•

The U.S. government raises the country's terror alert level to orange, or high, for the first time since May.

22 A magnitude-6.5 earthquake with an epicentre near San Simeon rattles central California, collapsing a building in Paso Robles and killing two people but causing relatively little damage because of the low population in the area.

•

The Chinese government makes public a proposed amendment to the constitution stating that legally obtained private property is not to be violated; it is the first time since the beginning of communist rule that private property has had legal protection.

•

A rebel group announces that it will end its three-month boycott of the interim government in Côte d'Ivoire and again participate in the government.

23 U.S. Secretary of Agriculture Ann Veneman announces that a cow slaughtered two weeks ago near Yakima, Wash., has been found to have had bovine spongiform encephalopathy, or mad cow disease, the first case of the disease detected in the U.S.; a number of countries immediately ban the import of American beef.

•

Vivendi Universal agrees to pay $50 million to settle a suit brought by the U.S. Securities and Exchange Commission.

24 Parmalat files for bankruptcy protection under a new decree passed by the Italian government to assist the troubled food giant. (*See* December 11 and 28.)

•

Air France, in response to concerns on the part of U.S. officials, cancels six flights between Paris and Los Angeles.

•

The U.S. Department of State announces that the U.S. will give 60,000 metric tons of additional agricultural produce to North Korea through the World Food Programme.

25 Pakistani Pres. Pervez Musharraf survives a second assassination attempt in as many weeks (*see* December 14) when two suicide bombers drive into the presidential motorcade in Rawalpindi; at least 14 people, including the bombers, are killed.

•

The British-made Beagle II unmanned lander fails to signal its safe arrival on Mars as scheduled, but European scientists are pleased that the European Space Agency's *Mars Express* vehicle, which released the probe and will search for subsurface water, achieved orbit around the planet.

26 A massive earthquake measured in the U.S. at a magnitude of 6.6 nearly destroys the ancient Iranian city of Bam; estimates of the death toll reach 41,000 by the end of the year.

27 China increases health screenings of travelers in response to news that a man in Guangzhou is being treated for possible SARS (severe acute respiratory syndrome).

•

Mohamed ElBaradei, head of the International Atomic Energy Agency, arrives in Tripoli, Libya, with a team of weapons inspectors.

28 The runoff presidential election in Guatemala is won by conservative Oscar Berger.

•

In parliamentary elections in Serbia, the biggest proportion of the seats goes to the extreme nationalist Serbian Radical Party.

•

An arrest order for Calisto Tanzi, the founder and former chairman of Parmalat, is issued. (*See* December 24.)

29 The U.S. issues an emergency order requiring foreign airlines flying into, out of, or over the U.S. to put air marshals aboard the flights if so requested.

•

Japan announces that it will forgive most of Iraq's huge debt to it if other Paris Club countries will do the same.

30 The U.S. Food and Drug Administration issues a ban on the sale of the herbal supplement ephedra, which has been linked to heart attacks and sudden death.

•

U.S. Attorney General John Ashcroft recuses himself from the U.S. Department of Justice's investigation into the leak of the name of a covert CIA operative to a newspaper columnist; U.S. Attorney Patrick Fitzgerald is named as special counsel to direct the investigation.

•

Ukraine's Constitutional Court rules that Pres. Leonid Kuchma may run for a third term as president in 2004.

31 The U.S. lifts most restrictions on sending assistance to Iran for a 90-day period to allow donations in response to the December 26 earthquake.

•

In Great Britain's annual New Year Honours list, actress Joan Plowright is made a dame, while the designation of CBE goes to director Stephen Daldry, musicians Eric Clapton and Ray Davies, and wildlife activist Virginia McKenna.

•

In Baghdad, Iraq, a car bomb explodes in the Nabil Restaurant, which is filled with people celebrating New Year's Eve; five Iraqis are killed.

Disasters

Listed here are major disasters that occurred in 2003. The list includes natural and nonmilitary MECHANICAL DISASTERS that claimed ABOUT 20 OR MORE LIVES and/or resulted in SIGNIFICANT DAMAGE to property.

Aviation

January 8, Diyarbakir, Turkey. A Turkish Airlines plane crashes while attempting to land in heavy fog at the city airport; 5 people survive, but 75 are killed.

January 8, Charlotte, N.C. A commuter plane, a Beechcraft 1900 twin-engine turboprop operated by US Airways Express, crashes into a hangar on takeoff, killing 21 passengers and crew members.

January 9, Near Chachapoyas, Peru. A TANS Perú Fokker F-28 crashes in the jungle in the Andes Mountains, killing all 46 people aboard; the wreckage of the plane is not found until January 11.

February 19, Near Shahdad, Iran. An Ilyushin airliner transporting Revolutionary Guards from Zahedan to Kerman crashes, killing all 302 aboard, in the worst air disaster ever to occur in Iran.

February 20, Near Kohat, Pak. Minutes before it is due to land, a Fokker-27 aircraft carrying the head of Pakistan's air force, Mushaf Ali Mir, and 16 others crashes into the low hills outside the town; all aboard perish.

February 26, Northern Colombia. A helicopter belonging to the Colombian army crashes as it searches for guerrillas in the mountains; the 23 troops on board are killed.

March 6, Near Tamanrasset, Alg. In what is believed to be the first accident in the history of Algeria's national airline, Air Algérie Flight 6289 crashes in the Sahara shortly after takeoff, killing 102 of the 103 aboard.

May 8, Democratic Republic of the Congo. On an Ilyushin-76 cargo plane crammed with passengers flying from Kinshasa to Lubumbashi, a door opens and dozens of people fall out to their death; the death toll is later estimated to be about 160.

May 26, Macka, near Trabzon, Turkey. An airplane carrying 62 Spanish peacekeepers home from a four-month tour of duty in Afghanistan crashes into a mountain while attempting to land for refueling in bad weather; all 75 aboard are killed.

June 30, Blida, Alg. A Hercules C-130 military transport plane crashes into a row of houses shortly after takeoff; at least 17 people are killed and a further 20 injured.

July 8, Port Sudan, Sudan. A Sudan Airways Boeing 737 crashes shortly after takeoff; 116 people are killed, and one toddler survives.

August 11, Arabian Sea, near Mumbai (Bombay), India. A Russian-made helicopter ferrying employees of the Oil and Natural Gas Corp., India's biggest oil company, from an offshore rig crashes into the sea; only 2 of the 29 passengers and crew survive.

August 20, Kamchatka Peninsula, Russia. An Mi-8 helicopter carrying government officials crashes on a mountainside, and the wreckage is found three days later; the governor of Sakhalin *oblast* is among the 20 killed in the incident.

August 22, Alcântara, Braz. A VLS-3 launcher rocket that the Brazilian Space Agency is testing explodes at a military launch site just three days before its planned launch, killing 21 engineers and technicians.

August 24, Near Cap-Haïtien, Haiti. A twin-engine turboprop Tropical Airways airplane crashes into a sugarcane field, killing all 21 people aboard; reports suggest an improperly closed door may have been the cause.

November 29, Boende, Democratic Republic of the Congo. An Antonov-26 airplane crashes shortly after takeoff; all 22 passengers and the crew are killed.

December 25, Cotonou, Benin. A Boeing 727 chartered by Union des Transports Africains and carrying mostly Lebanese expatriates slides off the runway while attempting to take off, crashing into a building and ending in the sea; at least 135 people are killed in the accident, which is the worst in the histories of both Lebanon and Benin.

Fires and Explosions

January 31, Kandahar, Afg. An antitank mine blows up a minibus crossing a bridge, killing at least 16 Afghanis, including several women and children.

February 2, Lagos, Nigeria. An explosion destroys a bank and the apartment complex above it in the commercial centre, killing at least 40 people and setting off fighting and looting; authorities believe the disaster to be the result of an accident.

February 2, Harbin, China. A fire breaks out at a hotel during celebrations of the Chinese New Year, leaving 33 people dead.

February 4, Sialkot, Pak. Shipping containers packed with fireworks explode at a depot next to a school, killing at least 17 people; the containers had been labeled as holding plastic toys.

February 7, Bogotá, Colom. A bomb goes off in a fashionable nightclub; at least 32 people are killed in the blast and the ensuing fire.

February 18, Taegu, S.Kor. A man attempting to set himself on fire with paint thinner on a rush-hour subway train ignites both the train on which he is riding and a second train that pulls in next to the burning train and briefly opens its doors; most of the estimated 198 people who die are on the second train.

February 20, West Warwick, R.I. Pyrotechnics used by the hard-rock band Great White

Firefighters scamper to escape a sudden flare-up in a 40,000-ha (95,000-ac) wildfire in southern California's Simi Valley on October 29.

ignite soundproofing foam on the stage of the Station, a nightclub, and the club goes up in flames; some 100 people, including a musician in the band, perish.

April 5, Shandong province, China. A fire breaks out during the night shift at a food-processing plant; at least 21 of the 500 employees die, and the building collapses.

April 7, Sydybal, Yakutia, Russia. Fire breaks out in the cloakroom of a wooden schoolhouse, blocking the only exit; 22 children die.

April 10, Makhachkala, Dagestan, Russia. A school for deaf boys goes up in flames, killing at least 28 sleeping students and injuring more than 100; teachers had to wake the children, as they were unable to hear the alarms.

May 2, Bac Ninh, Vietnam. An explosion on a bus as it is stopping at a market to pick up passengers kills at least 19 people and seriously injures a further 19; it is believed that explosives being carried on the bus were ignited.

May 15, Mecca, Saudi Arabia. A fire breaks out in a building housing 270 pilgrims making the hajj; at least 14 people die of smoke inhalation, and 43 are injured.

May 15, Ludhiana, Punjab state, India. Fire sweeps through three cars of a train traveling from Mumbai (Bombay) to Amritsar that had pulled out of the station just minutes previously; the fire, which began in a restroom, leaves some 39 people dead and 20 injured.

June 19, Onicha Amiyi-Uhu, Nigeria. As villagers steal oil from a vandalized pipeline, a spark from a motorcycle ignites the fuel, causing an explosion; some 105 people are killed.

July 28, Wangkou, Hebei province, China. An enormous explosion destroys a fireworks factory, killing at least 29 people and injuring more than 100.

August 3, Gayal, Pak. In the area of Kashmir administered by Pakistan, a fire at a contractor's house ignites a cache of dynamite being stored there; the subsequent series of explosions destroys nearly half the village and kills at least 47 people, many of whom had rushed to the house to fight the initial fire.

August 3, Surat, Gujarat state, India. A cooking-gas cylinder explodes, causing the collapse of three buildings and killing at least 43 people.

August 26, Shadi, Fujian province, China. A cache of fireworks that had been hidden in a private home to evade safety inspections explodes; at least 20 lives are lost.

September 15, Riyadh, Saudi Arabia. A fire breaks out at a large maximum-security prison; by the time it has been extinguished three hours later, 67 inmates have died.

October 12, Randilovshchina, Belarus. A fire destroys a wing of a mental hospital, killing at least 30 patients, who were locked in the facility.

Late October, Southern California. The worst wildfire outbreak in the state's history consumes some 300,000 ha (730,000 ac) and destroys thousands of houses; at least 20 people are killed.

November 24, Moscow. A fire breaks out overnight at the Peoples' Friendship University in a five-story dormitory housing mostly Asian and African students; at least 36 people die.

Marine

January 3, Indian Ocean, off Tanzania. A boat capsizes shortly after leaving port; some 40 passengers are drowned.

January 5, Lake Victoria, Tanzania. A boat capsizes in strong winds; although 4 people are rescued, it is feared that more than 30 lives have been lost.

March 1, Niger River, Nigeria. A boat carrying about 100 people strikes a rock and sinks; some 80 people are believed to have drowned.

March 22, Lake Tanganyika, Democratic Republic of the Congo. A ferry traveling between the towns of Kalemie and Uvira sinks, drowning at least 111; 41 people are rescued.

April 3, Narmada River, Gujarat state, India. A passenger ship carrying people to a religious ceremony where the river meets the Arabian Sea capsizes in strong winds; 16 bodies are recovered.

April 4, Surma River, Bangladesh. A boat carrying seasonal quarry workers and their families collides with a cargo ship in the dark and sinks, killing more than 70 passengers, most of them women and children.

April 12, Nakchinee River, Bangladesh. A ferry is caught in a storm and sinks, killing at least 16 people, with a further 100 unaccounted for.

April 15, Cayo Arena, Dom.Rep. A boat carrying more than 150 Haitians capsizes near the northwest coast, with six passengers reported dead and dozens missing.

April 19, Off Cabo Frio, Braz. A tourist schooner returning from a day trip to Parrot Island is swamped by a large wave shortly after resuming its journey following a break for passengers to swim and snorkel; it overturns, and at least 15 passengers die.

April 21, Bangladesh. An overloaded ferry sinks in a storm in the Buriganga River, near Dhaka, killing at least 140 passengers; later another ferry, carrying a bridal party, also goes down in a storm, in the Meghna River in Kishoreganj district.

April 26, Jammu and Kashmir, India. A boat carrying children capsizes while crossing a stream; 20 children are lost.

May 2, Yellow Sea, China. China reports a "recent" submarine accident involving a diesel-powered submarine that killed all 70 aboard; the timing and nature of the accident are not disclosed.

May 25, The Philippines. Two passenger ferries collide in rough waters off the coast of Corregidor and Limbones islands, and at least 28 people drown in the accident; 203 are rescued.

June 16, Off Lampedusa, Italy. A boat loaded with illegal immigrants sinks, killing as many as 70 people.

June 20, Off the coast of Tunisia. A boat carrying illegal immigrants that is believed to have started from Libya and been bound for Italy sinks; it is feared that up to 190 people may have drowned.

July 8, Bangladesh. An overcrowded triple-deck ferry capsizes and sinks at the confluence of the Padma, Meghna, and Dakatia rivers; some 500 people are believed lost.

August 5, Lake Albert, Uganda. Two boats laden with merchandise capsize near the Ruunga landing site; 20 people, including the owner of the boats, drown.

August 11, Kishanganj, Bihar state, India. An overcrowded boat carrying 52 pilgrims to a temple in Nepal capsizes in the Kankai River, drowning at least 23 and possibly as many as 40, most of them women.

Early October, Off Lampedusa, Italy. As many as 70 Somalis attempting to immigrate to Europe perish of thirst and hunger as their boat drifts helplessly for 10 days before being spotted by an Italian fishing boat; only about 15 are rescued by the Italian coast guard.

October 7, Nagayalanka, Andhra Pradesh state, India. A boat capsizes on the Krishna River; 29 lives are lost.

October 9, Near Numan, Nigeria. A ferry strikes a pillar supporting a bridge and sinks; more than 150 passengers are missing.

October 12, China. Two cargo ships sink hours apart in heavy seas; a total of 44 crew members are missing and believed dead.

November 24, Zambia. A boat on Lake Mweru capsizes, drowning 40 people; the boat was built to carry only 32 people.

November 25, Near Inongo, Democratic Republic of the Congo. A jury-rigged and overcrowded ferry sinks in Lake Mai-Ndombe; though some 200 people survive, at least 160 are killed.

Mining and Construction

January 11, Harbin, Heilongjiang province, China. A predawn explosion in the Boaxing coal mine kills 34 miners; the previous day 8 miners had been killed in a blast in a coal mine in Baishan, Jilin province.

February 24, China. At least 49 miners die in three separate incidents: some 35 are killed in a gas explosion at the Muchonggou coal mine in Liupanshui, Guizhou province, the same mine where 162 miners died in 2001; 6 miners are killed in an explosion in a mine in Jixi, Heilongjiang province; and 14 miners are killed when a cable lowering them into a mine snaps in Shanxi province.

March 22, Xiaoyi, Shanxi province, China. A powerful gas explosion kills at least 64 of the 87 miners working in the Mengnanzhuang coal mine, 8 others are missing and likely dead.

March 30, Liaoning province, China. At least 16 coal miners are killed, with 10 others missing, after an explosion in the Mengjiagou coal mine; there were more than 40 workers in the mine at the time of the incident.

May 13, Hefei, Anhui province, China. An underground gas explosion in the Luling coal mine kills at least 81 miners, with 5 others missing.

August 11, Datong, Shanxi province, China. A gas explosion kills at least 37 workers in a coal mine; five miners are missing.

August 14, Yangquan, Shanxi province, China. A gas explosion rips through a coal mine in northern China, killing 28 workers.

August 18, Zuoquan county, Shanxi province, China. In the third accident in two weeks in Shanxi province, a gas explosion, possibly triggered by the resumption of electricity flow after an outage, kills at least 17 and perhaps as many as 27 miners in a coal mine.

November 14, Fengcheng, Jiangxi province, China. A gas explosion at the state-owned Jianxin Coal Mine kills 48 miners.

November 22, Hunan province, China. A gas explosion at the Sundian coal mine leaves 22 people dead. In all, more than 4,600 miners have died in coal mine accidents in China in 2003.

Natural

January 16, Minas Gerais state, Braz. Mud slides occasioned by heavy rains kill at least 14 people, most of them in Belo Horizonte.

January 22, Colima and Jalisco states, Mex. An earthquake of at least magnitude 7.6 strikes, collapsing scores of buildings and killing at least 29 people.

Mid-February, Northern Mozambique. Heavy flooding in Nampula province kills at least 47 people, destroys some 6,000 homes, and ruins an estimated 5,500 ha (13,600 ac) of crops.

Mid-February, Eastern seaboard of the U.S. A record-breaking snowstorm covers the area with some 60 cm (2 ft) of snow; 59 people in several states are killed.

February 17, Southern Pakistan, Kashmir, Afghanistan. In Pakistan heavy rains cause flooding and the collapse of several houses and a bridge, from which a bus is swept away; at least 16 people are killed, while in Kashmir snowstorms kill at least 8 more people; the final death toll from the storms exceeds 86 people.

February 24, Xinjiang region, China. An earthquake measured at magnitude 6.4 strikes the region, leaving 268 people dead and more than 4,000 injured in the worst earthquake in the area in 50 years; tens of thousands of buildings are destroyed as well.

March 31, Chima, Larecaja province, Bol. A gold-mining town is engulfed by a huge mud slide triggered by days of heavy rain; at least 14 people are killed, and hundreds are missing.

April 1, Flores Island, Indonesia. Flash floods and mud slides wash away 17 houses and damage hundreds of others; at least 29 people are lost.

April 20, Kurbu-Tash, Kyrgyzstan. A mud slide destroys the town in the Ozgon district, killing at least 38 residents; the site is declared a common grave, as recovery of the victims is essentially impossible.

April 22, Assam state, India. Thunderstorms leave at least 33 people dead and thousands homeless; most of the damage is concentrated in the Dhuburi district.

April 23, Chichicaste, Guat. An eroded mountain slides downhill, burying a village and killing 23 people.

Late April–early May, Kenya. Nearly two weeks of rain and torrential storms destroy water-purification systems, force thousands of people to evacuate their homes, and leave at least 30 people dead.

Early–mid-May, Horn of Africa. Days of heavy rain create havoc in several countries: in Ethiopia 117 people are killed and 100,000 left homeless; in Kenya 47 die and 60,000 are displaced, and thousands more are displaced in Somalia.

May 1, Bingol, Turkey. An earthquake of magnitude 6.4 strikes in the predawn hours, causing a boarding school to collapse and killing 167 people.

May 4–12, U.S. Midwest and South. More than 300 tornadoes and other severe storms rake through several states, destroying entire towns, damaging hundreds of homes, and killing at least 42 people.

May 4, Noabadi, Bangladesh. Tropical storms cause a landslide that destroys a village, killing at least 23 people; 31 people have been killed and more than 100 injured in the storms.

Mid-May–June 10, South Asia. A monthlong heat wave and drought across India that ends only with the unusually late arrival of the monsoon creates an acute shortage of drinking water in Karnataka state and leaves 1,522 people dead nationwide, 1,040 of them in Andhra Pradesh state; in addition, more than 60 people in Bangladesh and 40 in Pakistan have succumbed.

May 16, Wanshui, Hunan province, China. Flash floods and mud slides wash away a number of carpet factories and bury the living quarters of coal miners; at least 12 are killed, and more than 20 cannot be found.

May 17, Southern Sri Lanka. After several days of heavy rain, floods and landslides kill some 300 people, with a further 500 unaccounted for.

May 21, Thenia, Alg. A magnitude-6.8 earthquake shakes a densely populated area, killing more than 2,200 people and injuring close to 10,000; the capital, Algiers, sustains particularly heavy damage.

May 27, Luzon, Phil. Tropical Storm Linfa brings torrential rains, relieving a drought but also causing hundreds of thousands of dollars of damage and killing at least 25 people, with 12 people reported missing.

June 26, Southeastern Bangladesh. Unusually heavy monsoon rains, as much as 120 mm (4.5 in) in 24 hours, cause flash flooding and landslides, fatally sweeping away or burying at least 31 people.

July 7, Northwestern Bangladesh. The rain-swollen Jamuna River breaks through an embankment and sweeps away several villages, raising the monsoon death toll to 82.

July 11, Sichuan province, China. During the worst flooding since 1991, a mud slide leaves 51 people missing; they are among the more than 500 people the government says have been killed by rain-related disasters this year.

Mid-July–mid-August, Western Europe. A prolonged and record-breaking heat wave combined with drought is responsible for the death of some 14,800 people in France, 4,200 in Italy, 1,400 in The Netherlands, 1,300 in Portugal, 900 in the U.K., and 100 in Spain.

July 16, Himachal Pradesh state, India. A cloudburst in the mountains leads to flash flooding below, which sweeps away a camp of migrant workers employed at a hydroelectric project; more than 100 people are believed to have been killed.

July 21, Yunnan province, China. A magnitude-6 earthquake destroys tens of thousands of homes and kills at least 16 people, with a further 400 injured.

Late July, Sind province, Pak. Monsoon rains cause flooding that leaves at least 88 people dead and some 100,000 homeless.

Early August, Kassala province, Sudan. Floodwaters rise to the highest level in 70 years, leaving 20 people dead and some 250,000 homeless.

August 28, Daman, Daman and Diu union territory, India. A narrow bridge crumbles in the rain, and several vehicles, including a school van, fall into the river below; at least 23 people are killed, and several more are missing.

August 29, St. Marc, Haiti. Rains cause the St. Marc River to overflow its banks, destroying 75 houses and leaving 11 dead and 24 missing.

Late August, China. The rainy season brings floods and mud slides, killing at least 40 people in western China and perhaps as many as 70 in northern China.

Early September, Haiti. Heavy rains cause catastrophic flooding that leaves some 20 people dead and a similar number of people missing.

September 2–3, Southern China. A typhoon, after killing 2 people and causing power failures in Taiwan, sweeps onto the mainland, where it kills at least 32 more and causes destruction in the cities of Shenzhen, Guangzhou, Shantou, and Shanwei.

September 6, North-West Frontier province, Pak. During monsoon rains lightning strikes hit two villages, leaving some 27 people dead.

September 12, Southern South Korea. Typhoon Maemi slams ashore, leaving at least 124 people dead and doing tremendous economic damage to the port of Pusan; officials believe it to be the worst typhoon in 100 years.

Mid-September, Nigeria. When gates at Nigeria's biggest hydroelectric dam are opened in order to save the dam from the floodwaters of the Kaduna River, dozens of villages are inundated, and some 39 people lose their life.

September 18, Eastern U.S. Hurricane Isabel roars ashore, causing great damage, especially in North Carolina and Virginia, and leading to the death of some 40 people in seven states.

November 2, Bukit Lawang, Sumatra, Indon. Flash floods caused by days of heavy rains and exacerbated by excessive logging virtually sweep away a popular tourist village and kill some 200 people.

Mid-November, Central Vietnam. Flooding caused by several days of torrential rain leaves at least 50 people dead, 15 of them buried in a gold mine collapse.

December 16, Andhra Pradesh state, India. The first winter cyclone in 18 years leaves at least 50 people dead, while the homes and crops of some 8,000 families are destroyed.

December 19, Leyte province, Phil. After six days of rain and wind in a heavily logged mountainous area, enormous mud slides engulf towns and villages, leaving some 200 people dead.

December 23, Villa Tunari, Bol. Floodwaters cause the collapse of a bridge as four vehicles, including a passenger bus, are crossing; 29 people are confirmed dead, and a further 30 are missing.

December 26, Bam, Iran. An earthquake of magnitude 6.6 all but levels the southeastern city of 100,000 people; by year's end the death toll estimate has climbed to 41,000.

A woman laments the death of family members on December 28, two days after a massive earthquake destroyed 85% of the city of Bam, Iran.

Atta Kenare/AFP/Getty Images

Late December, Northern India. Extreme cold brings a death toll in the area of some 150 people, most of them homeless or elderly.

Railroad

February 1, Near Dete, Zimb. A passenger train traveling in the predawn hours collides with a freight train carrying flammable substances; at least 46 lives are lost.

May 8, Siofok, Hung. In one of Hungary's worst-ever accidents, an express train runs into a double-decker bus on the tracks, killing 33 elderly German tourists.

June 3, Chinchilla, Spain. On a stretch of single-track rail in Albacete province, a passenger train meets a freight train in a head-on collision; at least 19 people are killed.

June 22, Vaibhyavadi, India. A passenger train traveling from Karwar to Mumbai (Bombay) strikes a boulder left on the tracks after a landslide caused by monsoon rains; four cars derail, killing 51 passengers.

Traffic

January 18, Near Cochabamba, Bol. A bus crashes into a hill in heavy rainfall; at least 20 people are killed.

January 21, Eastern Egypt. A tourist bus traveling between resorts overturns, killing at least 20 passengers.

January 26, Ebomey, Cameroon. A bus veers into oncoming traffic and crashes into a second bus; three cars then collide with the wrecked buses; a total of more than 70 people die in the incident, which is blamed on reckless driving and excessive speed.

January 26, Near Devpur, Nepal. A bus plunges off the road, killing at least 20 people and injuring another 25.

January 28, Near Uluberia, India. A tourist bus runs head-on into a truck carrying paint; at least 40 passengers are burned to death.

February 16, Masnaa, Lebanon. The brakes fail on a Syrian military truck approaching a border crossing; the truck hits the immigration office and overturns onto several cars, catching fire; at least 17 people are killed.

March 9, Near Kaplice, Czech Rep. A bus carrying tourists home from a vacation in Austria goes off the road and falls some 7 m (23 ft), killing at least 19 passengers.

March 12, The Sudan. A bus carrying members of the al-Merreikh association football (soccer) team back from a match crashes, killing 25 people, among them the team's coach.

March 17, Yunnan province, China. A truck illegally carrying passengers goes off a mountainous road and falls into a gorge; at least 20 of the more than 40 people in the truck are killed.

March 27, Southeastern Kyrgyzstan. A double-decker bus headed for China is set upon by bandits, who kill the 21 passengers and set the bus on fire; investigators at first believed the bus had driven over a cliff.

April 13, Near Larissa, Greece. A tour bus collides with a truck carrying a load of plywood on a narrow stretch of mountainous road; 21 schoolchildren are killed.

April 15, Thailand. In three days of the Songkran festival, Thailand's biggest public holiday, more than 359 people die in traffic accidents, many of them due to drunken driving.

May 1, Near Bethlehem, S.Af. A bus carrying trade-union members to a May Day rally falls into a reservoir after the driver becomes confused and drives onto a track leading to a dam; some 80 people are believed killed.

May 9, Near Shorkot, Pak. A passenger bus and an oil tanker crash in a head-on collision after the bus driver loses control of his vehicle; at least 24 people perish.

May 17, Near Lyon, France. A bus carrying German tourists to Spain apparently skids on wet pavement and leaves the road, falling down an embankment; at least 28 passengers are killed.

June 7, Near Erzincan, Turkey. A bus crashes into a tunnel wall, killing 27 passengers and injuring 33; it is suspected that the driver fell asleep.

June 25, Madhya Pradesh state, India. A bus crossing a small bridge falls into the river below and is swept away; at least 40 people are missing.

July 9, Hong Kong. A truck collides with a double-decker bus, which then falls off a cliff; 21 passengers are killed and 20 injured, and the truck driver is arrested.

July 13, Premnagar, Jammu and Kashmir state, India. A passenger bus collides with a truck and plunges into the Chenab River; 24 passengers die, and two dozen others are reported injured.

September 7, Near Monabo, Cameroon. A truck carrying a bulldozer crashes into a bus carrying association football (soccer) players and fans returning from a tournament; 25 people are killed and some 30 injured.

September 8, Kogi state, Nigeria. Four vehicles, one of them a passenger bus, collide in a pileup that kills at least 70 people, most of whom are burned to death.

September 9, Western Venezuela. A bus crashes into a truck in an accident in which 10 people are killed and 19 injured; hours later on the same highway, another bus hits a parked truck, and 35 people die.

September 15, Nepal. A bus carrying 60 passengers goes off the road into the Bheri River; at least 36 people are missing.

September 17, Zambezi River, Zambia. At the crossing to Kazungula, Botswana, a truck overloaded with copper concentrates drives onto a pontoon, swamping it; at least 20 people are believed to have drowned.

September 22, Kyonyo, Uganda. A bus carrying Rwandan and Burundian children to school in Uganda collides at high speed with a truck carrying corn (maize) for the World Food Programme; at least 46 people, most of them schoolchildren, are killed.

October 8, East Java, Indon. A bus carrying schoolgirls on their way home from a school trip to Bali is struck head-on by a truck that lost control going downhill and is then rear-ended by a minivan; at least 54 people, most of them schoolgirls, are killed.

December 7, Near Magarkote, Jammu and Kashmir, India. An overcrowded bus loses control on a steep mountain road and falls into a gorge; at least 22 people perish.

Miscellaneous

February 17, Chicago. At a crowded nightclub on the second floor of a restaurant, the use of pepper spray in a misguided effort to stop a fight causes panic among the 1,500 patrons, who attempt to flee; the ensuing stampede leaves 21 people dead.

August 27, Nasik, Maharashtra state, India. A stampede breaks out during the Kumbh Mela festival as tens of thousands of pilgrims attempt to bathe in the Godavari River; some 40 people lose their life.

September 10, Northern Greece. The bodies of 23 would-be immigrants wash up onshore; it appears that they drowned while attempting to cross the Evros River illegally from Turkey, but the circumstances are unclear.

November 8, Port Sudan, Sudan. When a wealthy family living on a narrow street begins distributing money to the poor in observance of Ramadan, a stampede ensues in which 31 people are suffocated.

December 23–27, Gaoqiao, Chongqing province, China. A breach occurs at a gas well in a remote region, and a poisonous cloud of natural gas and hydrogen sulfide spews out and engulfs the area; some 233 people die and thousands are injured in the four days before the breach is sealed, and tens of thousands are evacuated.

People of 2003

The commander of a women's armed opposition group (in dark glasses) and her bodyguards return from a patrol in the northern area of Monrovia, Liberia, in August.

Nobel Prizes

Laureates in 2003 included an IRANIAN human rights activist, a SOUTH AFRICAN novelist, RISK analysts, pioneers of MRI technology, and scientists who made fundamental discoveries concerning the transport of WATER AND IONS in and out of cells and the behaviour of SUPERCONDUCTORS and SUPERFLUIDS.

PRIZE FOR PEACE

The 2003 Nobel Prize for Peace was awarded to Shirin Ebadi, an Iranian lawyer, writer, and teacher who had gained prominence as an advocate for democracy and human rights. She was known particularly for her efforts to establish and protect the rights of women and children in the face of a hostile Iranian government. In announcing the award, the Norwegian Nobel Committee said, "As a lawyer, judge, lecturer, writer, and activist, she has spoken out clearly and strongly in her country, Iran, and far beyond its borders. She has stood up as a sound professional, a courageous person, and has never heeded the threats to her own safety." She was the first Iranian to be awarded the Prize for Peace.

Ebadi, who was born in 1947 in Hamadān, Iran, received a degree in law in 1969 from the University of Tehran. She was one of the first women judges in Iran and from 1975 to 1979 was head of the city court of Tehran. After the 1979 revolution and the establishment of an Islamic republic, however, women were deemed unsuitable to serve as judges, and she was dismissed from the position. She then practiced law and taught at the University of Tehran, and she became known as a fearless defender of the rights of Iranian citizens. In court she defended women and dissidents, as well as a number of victims of the conservative religious regime, including the families of writers and intellectuals murdered in 1999–2000. She also distributed evidence implicating government officials in the murders of students at the University of Tehran in 1999, for which she was jailed for three weeks in 2000. Found guilty, she was given a prison term, barred from practicing law for five years, and fined, although her sentence was later suspended. Among her writings were *The Rights of the Child: A Study of Legal Aspects of Children's Rights in Iran* (1994) and *History and Documentation of Human Rights in Iran* (2000). She also was founder and head of the Association for Support of Children's Rights in Iran.

The awarding of the Nobel Prize for Peace was commonly understood to have political overtones, and this was especially evident in 2003. The choice of Ebadi was widely viewed as an attempt by the Norwegian Nobel Committee to support the reformers in Iran against that country's hard-line clerics and to promote the view that Islam was compatible with equality before the law, freedom of speech and of religion, and other democratic practices, as well as with the doctrine of human rights. The committee said, "Ebadi is a conscious Muslim. She sees no conflict between Islam and fundamental human rights. It is important to her that the dialogue between the different cultures and religions of the world should take as its point of departure their shared values." Although Muslims had earlier won the Nobel Prize for Peace—Egyptian Pres. Anwar el-Sadat shared the prize in 1978 with Israeli Prime Minister Menachem Begin, and Palestinian leader Yasir Arafat shared the prize in 1994 with Israeli Prime Minister Yitzhak Rabin and Israeli Foreign Minister Shimon Peres—Ebadi was the first Muslim woman to be given the award.

(ROBERT RAUCH)

Shirin Ebadi

PRIZE FOR ECONOMICS

The Nobel Memorial Prize in Economic Sciences was awarded in 2003 to American Robert F. Engle and Clive W.J. Granger of the U.K. for their respective contributions to the development of sophisticated techniques for the analysis of time series data. Their econometric methods enabled a chronological succession or series of values of nonstationary and volatile variables, such as household consumption, inflation, and stock prices, to be measured with greater accuracy than was possible with the standard methods previously used to find explanations of movements of variables over time. The two prizewinners spent much of their careers in the 1970s and '80s on their seminal work at the University of California, San Diego.

Engle received the Nobel for the improved mathematical techniques he developed for the evaluation and more accurate forecasting of risk, which enabled researchers to test if and how volatility in one period was related to volatility in another period. This had particular relevance in financial market analysis in which the investment returns of an asset were assessed against its risk and stock prices and returns could exhibit extreme volatility. While periods of strong turbulence caused large fluctuations in prices in stock

© Robert Pratta/Reuters/Corbis

Robert Engle

markets, these were often followed by relative calm and slight fluctuations. Inherent in Engle's autoregressive conditional heteroskedasticity (known as ARCH) model approach was the concept that while most volatility is embedded in the random error, its variance depends on previously realized random errors, with large errors being followed by large errors and small by small. This contrasted with earlier models wherein the random error was assumed to be constant over time. Engle's methods and the ARCH model had led to a proliferation of tools for analyzing stocks and had enabled economists to make more accurate forecasts.

Granger developed concepts and analytic methods to establish meaningful relationships between nonstationary variables, such as exchange rates and inflation rates. His adoption of long- and short-run perspectives increased understanding of the longer-term changes in macroeconomic indicators where, for example, a country's annual GDP might grow long term but in the short term might suffer because of a sharp rise in commodity prices or a global economic downturn. Granger demonstrated that estimated relationships between variables that changed over time could be nonsensical and misleading because the variables were wrongly perceived as having a relationship. Even where a relationship did exist, it could be a purely temporary one. Fundamental to his methods was his discovery that a specific combination of two or more nonstationary time series could be stationary, a combination for which he invented the term *cointegration.* This was in accord with the economic theory that asserts that two economic variables that share equilibrium may deviate in the short term but over the long run will adjust to equilibrium. Through his cointegration analysis, Granger showed that the dynamics in exchange rates and prices, for example, are driven by a tendency to smooth out deviations from the long-run equilibrium exchange rate and short-run fluctuations around the adjustment path.

Engle was born in November 1942 in Syracuse, N.Y., and was educated at Williams College, Williamstown, Mass. (B.S., 1964), and Cornell University, Ithaca, N.Y. (M.S., 1966; Ph.D., 1969). He was on the faculty at the Massachusetts Institute of Technology (1969–75) until he moved to the University of California, where he became a professor in 1977 and later the chair in economics. In 1999 he transferred to the Stern School of Business at New York University, and from 2000 he was the Michael Armellino Professor in the Management of Financial Services. His teaching and research interests were in financial econometrics covering equities, futures and options, interest rates, and exchange rates. Engle was a fellow of the Econometric Society, the American Academy of Arts and Sciences, and the American Statistical Association.

Clive Granger

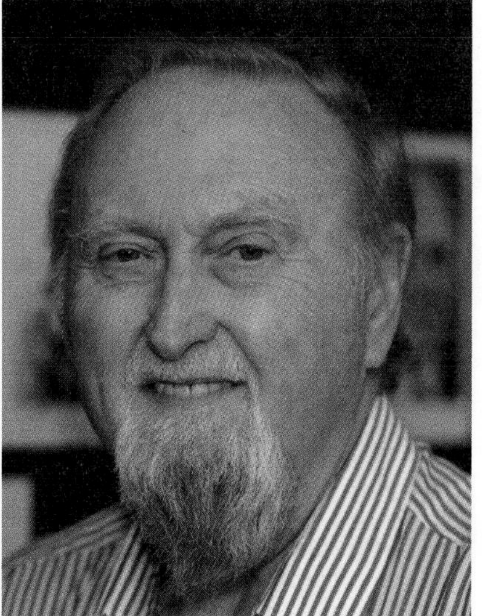

AP/Wide World Photos

He also held associate editorships on several academic journals, notably the *Journal of Applied Econometrics,* of which he was coeditor (1985–89).

Granger was born in Swansea, Wales, on Sept. 4, 1934, and was educated at the University of Nottingham, Eng. (B.A., 1955; Ph.D., 1959), where he became a lecturer in statistics in the mathematics department. In 1974 he took up a professorship at the University of California. He held fellowships at the International Institute of Forecasters, the Econometric Society, the American Academy of Arts and Sciences, and the American Economic Association, among others, and was a corresponding fellow of the British Academy. Granger's books and academic papers covered a wide range of subjects from time series analysis and forecasting to price research, statistical theory, and applied statistics. (JANET H. CLARK)

PRIZE FOR LITERATURE

The 2003 Nobel Prize for Literature was awarded to South African author J.M. Coetzee, a preeminent and uncompromising voice in the struggle for human dignity and self-preservation. An innovative and provocative novelist, essayist, and literary critic, Coetzee gained international recognition early in his career and was the first writer to receive the United Kingdom's Booker Prize (now the Man Booker Prize) twice. He belonged to the generation of South African writers—including André Brink, Breyten Breytenbach, Oswald Mbuyiseni Mtshali, and Mongane Wally Serote—that emerged during the apartheid era. Coetzee was the second South African Nobel laureate for literature and the fourth African laureate, after Wole Soyinka of Nigeria in 1986, Naguib Mahfouz of Egypt in 1988, and Coetzee's compatriot Nadine Gordimer in 1991.

Born on Feb. 9, 1940, in Cape Town, S.Af., John Maxwell Coetzee was the son of Afrikaners, but he was reared bilingual, attending English-language schools. He studied at the University of Cape Town (UCT), where he earned a B.A. in English in 1960 and another in mathematics the following year. In 1962 Coetzee left South Africa for England, where he worked as a computer programmer and completed an M.A. from UCT. He earned a Ph.D. in English in 1969 from the University of Texas at Austin. From 1968 to 1971 Coetzee taught at the State University of New York at Buffalo, and he then

© J. Bauer

J.M. Coetzee

returned to South Africa, where he became a lecturer in 1972 and, later, a professor of literature at UCT.

Highly regarded as a writer of striking originality, Coetzee experimented with diverse literary forms from historical fiction to political fable. His first published work, entitled *Dusklands* (1974), consisted of two novellas, "The Vietnam Project" and "The Narrative of Jacobus Coetzee," which examined colonialism in the 20th and 18th centuries, respectively, and incriminated the policies of both the United States and colonial South Africa. His novel *In the Heart of the Country* (U.S. title *From the Heart of the Country*) was written originally as a bilingual Afrikaans-English text but was first published in a wholly English version in 1977. The bilingual edition was issued in South Africa a year later. This work explored the emotional and psychological demise of its protagonist, whose vision of reality is distorted by the solitude and barrenness of her existence. The novel received South Africa's Central News Agency (CNA) Literary Award. The publication in 1980 of the politically inspired *Waiting for the Barbarians* established Coetzee as a major South African writer, receiving both the CNA Literary Award and Britain's James Tait Black Memorial Prize for fiction. The critically acclaimed *Life & Times of Michael K* (1983) received a third CNA Literary Award, the Prix Femina Étranger in France, and the Booker Prize.

In 1986 Coetzee published the enigmatic *Foe*, a postmodern retelling of Daniel Defoe's *Robinson Crusoe* (1719). His novel *Age of Iron* (1990) was a tour de force set in contemporary South Africa; it examined the variations and consequences of complicity with a political regime guided by racial prejudice and repression. Coetzee's allegorical narrative *The Master of Petersburg* (1994) was followed in 1999 by the Booker Prize-winning *Disgrace*, a novel of postapartheid South Africa in which a university professor charged with sexual harassment must confront the ramifications of guilt and retribution. *Elizabeth Costello* (2003), a fictional hybrid incorporating selections of Coetzee's previously published nonfiction, analyzed the relationship between the writer and society.

Coetzee published two volumes of autobiographical memoirs, *Boyhood: Scenes from Provincial Life* (1997) and its sequel, *Youth* (2002). His works of nonfiction included *White Writing: On the Culture of Letters in South Africa* (1988), *Doubling the Point: Essays and Interviews* (1992), *Giving Offense: Essays on Censorship* (1996), and *Stranger Shores: Literary Essays, 1986–1999* (2001). As a novelist Coetzee combined ambiguity with irony to produce fiction of extraordinary breadth and integrity. Cited by the Swedish Academy as a writer "who in innumerable guises portrays the surprising involvement of the outsider," Coetzee filled the void of isolation and despair with a balance of tension and empathy, as his protagonist from *In the Heart of the Country* proclaims: "We are the castaways of God as we are the castaways of history" who "wish only to be at home in the world."

(STEVEN R. SERAFIN)

PRIZE FOR CHEMISTRY

Two American scientists shared the 2003 Nobel Prize for Chemistry for discoveries about structure and operation of the many crucial porelike channels that perforate the outer surface of cells in humans and other living things. Peter Agre of Johns Hopkins University, Baltimore, Md., received half the prize for the discovery of water channels in cell membranes; and Roderick MacKinnon, of Rockefeller University, New York City, got the other half for research on ion channels.

Agre was born Jan. 30, 1949, in Northfield, Minn. He earned a medical doctorate from Johns Hopkins in 1974. In 1981, following postgraduate training and a fellowship, he returned to Hopkins, where in 1993 he advanced to professor of biological chemistry. MacKinnon, born Feb. 19, 1956, in Burlington, Mass., gained an M.D. degree from Tufts University's School of Medicine, Boston, in 1982. After practicing medicine for several years, he turned to basic research, beginning in 1986 with postdoctoral work on ion channels at Brandeis University, Waltham, Mass. In 1989 he joined Harvard University, and in 1996 he moved to Rockefeller as a professor and laboratory head. A year later he was appointed an investigator at Rockefeller's Howard Hughes Medical Institute.

Biologists realized in the mid-1800s that specialized openings must exist in cell membranes, the film of fatty material that encloses the cells of living organisms. Water, for instance, flows in and out of cells without leakage of other essential substances from inside the cell. Later in the century scientists discovered that ions also enjoy free passage in and out of cells. Ions are electrically charged atoms, such as those of sodium and potassium. Transport of ions through the membrane of motor nerve cells, for example, is needed to trigger the nerve impulses that ultimately make muscles contract or relax. Many diseases involving the kidneys, heart, and nervous system occur when ion channels do not work normally.

Peter Agre

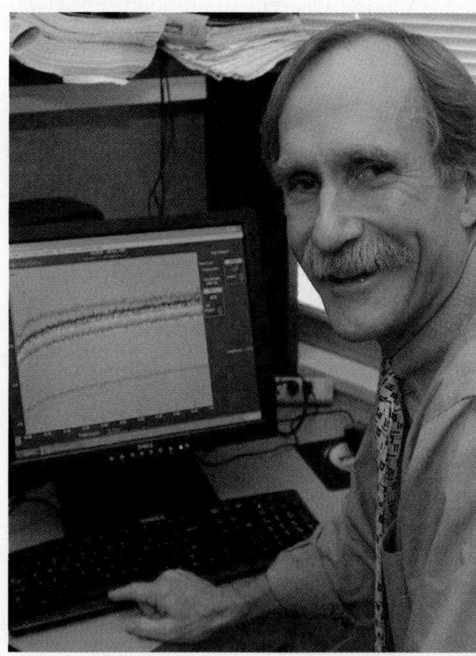

AP/Wide World Photos

AP/Wide World Photos

Roderick MacKinnon

With water and ion channels so important in health and disease, generations of scientists in the 20th century tried to find them, determine their structure, and understand how they work. Not until 1988, however, did Agre isolate a type of protein molecule in the cell membrane that he soon came to believe was the long-sought water channel. One test of his hypothesis involved comparing how cells with and without the protein in their membranes responded when placed in a water solution. Cells with the protein swelled up as water flowed in, while those lacking the protein remained the same size.

Agre named the protein aquaporin. Researchers subsequently discovered a whole family of the proteins in animals, plants, and even bacteria. Two different aquaporins were found to play a major role in the mechanism by which human kidneys concentrate dilute urine and return the extracted water to the blood.

While Agre was beginning his landmark work, MacKinnon was devoting most of his time to treating patients. He switched to research at age 30 after he had become fascinated with the studies being done on ion channels. The channels, which also proved to be proteins, not only admitted ions without allowing cell contents to seep out but also were very selective. They seemed to have "filters" that passed one type of ion—potassium, for instance—while blocking others, but no one knew how those filters worked.

MacKinnon understood that the problem could be solved by obtaining sharper images of channels with X-ray diffraction, a technique that involves passing X-rays through crystals of a material to create images of their molecular structure. He rapidly became expert in X-ray diffraction technology and within a few years astonished scientists who had spent entire careers in ion-channel research by reporting the three-dimensional molecular structure of an ion channel.

His results, obtained in 1998, allowed MacKinnon to explain how the ion filter allowed passage of potassium ions but blocked sodium ions, even through the latter are smaller. The channel, MacKinnon found, has an architecture sized in a way that easily strips potassium ions—but not sodium ions—of their associated water molecules and allows them to slip through. MacKinnon also discovered a molecular "sensor" in the end of the channel nearest the cell's interior that reacts to conditions around the cell, sending signals that open and close the channel at the appropriate times. His pioneering work allowed scientists to pursue the development of drugs for diseases—e.g., of the heart or nervous system—in which ion channels play a role.

(MICHAEL WOODS)

PRIZE FOR PHYSICS

Three scientists who explained how certain materials develop their unusual properties of superconductivity and superfluidity when chilled to very low temperatures were awarded the 2003 Nobel Prize for Physics. Their theories laid the foundation for new insights into the properties of matter and for practical applications in medicine and other areas. Sharing the prize equally were Alexei A. Abrikosov of Argonne (Ill.) National Laboratory; Vitaly L. Ginzburg of the P.N. Lebedev Physical Institute, Moscow; and Anthony J. Leggett of the University of Illinois at Urbana-Champaign.

Abrikosov was born June 25, 1928, in Moscow. He received doctorates in physics from the U.S.S.R. Academy of Sciences' Institute for Physical Problems (now the P.L. Kapitsa Institute) in 1951 and 1955. Following work spanning several decades in the former Soviet Union, he joined Argonne in 1991, becoming distinguished scientist in its materials science division. Ginzburg, born Oct. 4, 1916, in Moscow, earned a doctorate in physics at M.V. Lomonosov Moscow State University in 1938. He headed the theory group at the Lebedev Institute from 1971 to 1988. Leggett, born March 26, 1938, in London, received a Ph.D. in physics from the University of Oxford in 1964. In 1967 he joined the faculty of the University of Sussex, where he served until 1983, when he moved to the University of Illinois.

The three did their work between the 1950s and the 1970s in the field of quantum physics, which deals with effects that occur among the subatomic particles that make up matter. Usually these effects are unnoticeable in the everyday world of larger objects, but in selecting the winners for the 2003 prize, the Royal Swedish Academy of Sciences focused attention on two quantum phenomena that manifest themselves in the familiar world.

Physicists had known about superconductivity since 1911, when it was observed in the metal mercury. Superconductors are materials that lose resistance to the flow of electricity when cooled below a certain critical (and typically very low) temperature. Research on the topic had practical importance because electrical resistance accounted for costly losses in long-distance power lines. Resistance in copper and aluminum wire caused electricity to be wasted as heat en route from generating stations to consumers. Electrical resistance also was a barrier to the development of increasingly powerful electromagnets.

The 1972 Nobel physics prize went to scientists who developed the first theory explaining why certain metals, termed type I superconductors, lose electrical resistance. At temperatures near absolute zero (–273.15 °C, or –459.67 °F), the electrons in these materials form pairs (Cooper pairs) whose interaction with the material's atoms allows them to flow as electric current without resistance. The theory, however, did not explain superconductivity in another group of materials that had important potential industrial and commercial uses. Unlike type I superconductors, these materials, termed type II, remain superconducting even in the presence of very powerful magnetic fields, with superconductivity and magnetism existing within them at the same time.

Abrikosov devised a theoretical explanation for type II superconductivity. His starting point was an earlier theory about type I superconductors that Ginzburg and others had developed and refined. "Although these theories were formulated in the 1950s," stated the Swedish Academy, "they have gained renewed importance in the rapid development of materials with completely new properties. Materials can now be made superconductive at increasingly high temperatures and strong magnetic fields." Ginzberg's and Abrikosov's theoretical achievements enabled other scientists to create and test new superconducting materials and build more powerful electromagnets. Among the practical results were magnets critical for the development of magnetic resonance imaging (MRI) scanners used in medical diagnostics. (See *Prize for Physiology or Medicine,* below.) The materials used in MRI magnets are all type II superconductors.

Leggett did his prizewinning research on the related quantum phenomenon of superfluidity, in which certain extremely cold liquid substances flow without internal resistance, or viscosity. Superfluids exhibit a variety of weird behaviour, including the ability to flow up the sides and out the top of containers. Scientists had known since the 1930s that the common form of helium, the isotope helium-4, becomes a superfluid when chilled. A theoretical explanation for the phenomenon won the 1962 Nobel Prize for Physics.

In the 1970s researchers discovered that the explanation did not work for the much rarer helium isotope helium-3, which was also found to be a superfluid. Leggett filled the gap in theoretical research by showing that electrons in helium-3 form pairs in a situation similar to, but much more complicated than, the electron pairs that form in superconducting metals. His work found wide application in science ranging from cosmology to the study of subatomic particles. Research on superfluid helium-3 also "may lead to a better understanding of the ways in which turbulence arises—one of the last unsolved problems of classical physics," said the Swedish Academy.

(MICHAEL WOODS)

PRIZE FOR PHYSIOLOGY OR MEDICINE

The 2003 Nobel Prize for Physiology or Medicine was awarded to two pioneers of magnetic resonance imaging (MRI), a computerized scanning technology that produces images of internal body structures, especially those comprising soft tissues. The recipients were Paul Lauterbur of the University of Illinois at Urbana-Champaign and Sir Peter Mansfield of the University of Nottingham, Eng.

"A great advantage with MRI is that it is harmless according to all present knowledge," stated the Nobel Assembly at the Karolinska Institute in Stockholm, which awarded the prize. Unlike X-ray and computed tomography (CT) examinations, MRI avoided the use of potentially harmful ionizing radiation; rather, it produced its images with magnetic fields and radio waves. MRI scans spared patients not only many X-ray examinations but also surgical procedures and invasive tests formerly needed to diagnose diseases and follow up after treatments. More than 60 million MRI procedures were performed in 2002 alone, according to the Nobel Assembly.

Lauterbur, born May 6, 1929, in Sidney, Ohio, earned a Ph.D. in chemistry from the University of Pittsburgh, Pa., in 1962. He served as a professor at the University of New York at Stony Brook from 1969 to 1985, when he accepted the position of professor at Urbana-Champaign and director of its Biomedical Magnetic Resonance Laboratory. Mansfield was born Oct. 9, 1933, in London and received a Ph.D. in physics from the University of London in 1962. Following two years as a research associate in the U.S., he joined the faculty of the University of Nottingham, where he remained for essentially his entire career and became professor in 1979. Mansfield was knighted in 1993.

When Lauterbur and Mansfield undertook their work in the early 1970s, the technology underpinning MRI was a laboratory research tool. Called nuclear magnetic resonance (NMR) spectroscopy, it involves putting a sample to be analyzed in a strong magnetic field and then irradiating it with weak radio waves at the appropriate frequency. In the presence of the magnetic field, the nuclei of certain atoms—for example, ordinary hydrogen—absorb the radio energy; i.e., they show resonance at that particular frequency. Because the resonance frequency depends on the kind of nuclei and is influenced by the presence of nearby atoms, absorption measurements (absorption signal spectra) can provide information about the molecular structure of various solids and liquids. When the nuclei return to their previous energy levels, they emit energy, which carries additional information. NMR spectroscopy has remained a key tool in chemical analysis.

When studying molecules with NMR, chemists always had tried to maintain a steady magnetic field, because variations made the absorption signals fuzzy. Lauterbur realized that if the magnetic field was deliberately made nonuniform, information contained in the signal distortions could be used to create two-dimensional images of a sample's internal structure. While at Stony Brook, he worked evenings developing his idea, using an NMR unit borrowed from campus chemists.

MRI imaging succeeds because the human body is about two thirds water, whose molecules are made of hydrogen and oxygen atoms. There are differences in the amount of water present in different organs and tissues. In addition, the amount of water often changes when body structures become injured or diseased; those variations show up in MRI images.

When the body is exposed to MRI's magnetic field and its pulses of radio waves, the nucleus of each hydrogen atom in water absorbs energy; it then emits the energy in the form of radio waves, or resonance signals, as it returns to its previous energy level. Electronic devices detect the myriad resonance signals from all the hydrogen nuclei in the tissue being examined, and computer processing builds cross-sectional images of internal body structures, based on differences in water content and movements of water molecules. Computer processing also can stack the cross sections in sequence to create three-dimensional, solid images.

Mansfield's research helped transform Lauterbur's discoveries into a practical technology with wide uses in everyday medicine. He developed a way of using the nonuniformities, or gradients, introduced in the magnetic field to identify differences in the resonance signals more precisely. In addition, he developed new mathematical methods for quickly analyzing information in the signal and showed how technical changes in MRI could lead to extremely rapid imaging.

(Part of the 2003 Nobel Prize for Physics was awarded for advances in superconductivity with application to MRI. See *Prize for Physics,* above.)

(MICHAEL WOODS)

Biographies

The SUBJECTS of these biographies are the people who in the editors' opinions captured the IMAGINATION of the world in 2003—the most INTERESTING and/or IMPORTANT PERSONALITIES of the year.

Abbas, Mahmoud

After months of intense international pressure, Mahmoud Abbas, also known as Abu Mazen, was installed as Palestinian prime minister on April 30, 2003. As a condition for pursuing their road map to peace, the quartet (United States, European Union, Russia, and UN) had insisted on the appointment of a prime minister with wide powers in a move to circumvent Palestinian Pres. Yasir Arafat, who both Israel and the U.S. claimed was promoting terror and blocking peace negotiations.

Abbas immediately called for an end to the violent uprising against Israel but refused to disarm Islamist militants; he argued that any attempt to do so would lead to civil war. A cease-fire he negotiated with the militants in June broke down after Israel carried out a string of targeted assassinations. Undermined by Arafat and derided on the Palestinian street, Abbas's position became untenable. Blaming Israel, the U.S., and Arafat, he resigned on September 6, after slightly more than 100 days in office.

Abbas was born in 1935 in the Arab-Jewish town of Safed (now in northern Israel). During the 1948 Arab-Israeli war, his father, a prominent cheese merchant, fled with the family to Syria. Despite the family's refugee status, Abbas went on to earn a law degree at the University of Damascus.

In the late 1950s he worked in Qatar as a personnel director in the civil service before making a fortune in private business. In 1959 he was one of the founders of the al-Fatah movement, which spearheaded the Palestinian armed struggle and dominated the Palestinian Liberation Organization (PLO). In the late 1970s Abbas was instrumental in forging contacts with Israeli peace groups, a policy he fostered as head of the PLO's international department.

Abbas completed a doctorate at the Institute of Asian and African Studies of the M.V. Lomonosov Moscow State University in 1982 with a thesis titled "The Connection Between Nazism and Zionism 1933–1945." Responding in the late 1990s to accusations of Holocaust denial, he observed that "at the time we were at war with Israel. . . . Today I would not have made such remarks."

At the 1991 Madrid Peace Conference and in the Oslo peace process that followed, Abbas shaped Palestinian negotiating strategy. He gave his account of the 1993 Oslo breakthrough in *Through Secret Channels: The Road to Oslo.*

A senior member of the Palestinian delegation to the Camp David peace talks in July 2000, Abbas adamantly rejected Israel's peace offer but opposed the violent *intifadah* that erupted in its wake. In a speech in Gaza in November 2002, he had criticized the "militarization" of the *intifadah,* arguing that the violence had led to the "complete destruction of everything we built." In his inaugural address as prime minister, Abbas renounced terrorism and resolved to create a single Palestinian armed force. His failure to establish a firm hold on power, followed by his resignation, undermined the fragile peace process.

(LESLIE D. SUSSER)

Barney, Matthew

In 2003, after a year's delay, the exhibition "Matthew Barney: The Cremaster Cycle" opened at the Guggenheim Museum in New York City. Featured in its entirety for the first time in the U.S., the epic five-part film cycle—*Cremaster 4* (1994), *Cremaster 1* (1995), *Cremaster 5* (1997), *Cremaster 2* (1999), and *Cremaster 3* (2002)—was accompanied by related sculptures, photos, and drawings and required nearly seven hours of viewing time. It was a lush mélange of surreal and often perplexing imagery involving fantasy-filled reconceptions of historical events, Busby Berkeley-style dance numbers, satyrs, swarming bees, and lots of petroleum jelly. Taking its name from the muscle that raises and lowers the testicles, the *Cremaster* cycle explored sexual differentiation and the various stages of creation, central themes in much of Barney's work. Many art critics praised his inventiveness and considered him one of the most important artists of his generation. Others noted his merely workmanlike cinematic values, such as cinematography, editing, and camera placement, and considered the cycle sensational and overloaded with "potentially significant detail."

Barney was born on March 25, 1967, in San Francisco and as a child moved with his family to Boise, Idaho. He excelled at sports—which would figure prominently in his art—and attended Yale University on a football scholarship. Majoring in art, he fused performance art, film, and sculpture. For his senior thesis he submitted a two-part video in which he appeared seminude and suspended over a vat of petroleum jelly, which he applied to his various bodily orifices. He graduated in 1989 and moved to New York City. His first solo art shows, in 1991, were videotapes of various performances, notably one in which a nude Barney climbed the walls and ceiling of an art gallery. Accompanying the videos were several petroleum-jelly sculptures. Later that year at the San Francisco Museum of Modern Art, he had his first museum exhibit.

Barney's work attracted widespread attention from the outset of his career. *Drawing Restraint 7* (1993), a video that featured people in satyr costumes grappling in a limousine, was part of the 1993 Whitney Biennial at the Whitney Museum of American Art in New York City and the 45th Venice Biennale. Desiring to explore "the life cycle of an idea," Barney began work in 1994 on the *Cremaster* project. He served as writer, director, and producer and often starred in the films. The completed project first appeared at museums in Cologne, Ger., and Paris in 2002.

(AMY TIKKANEN)

Basrur, Sheela

On April 23, 2003, the World Health Organization, fearing the spread of SARS (severe acute respiratory syndrome), announced a travel advisory for Toronto. A storm of outraged protests arose from the mayor, councillors, and provincial and federal politicians. The calm eye at the centre of this turmoil was Sheela Basrur, Toronto's officer of medical health, as she stood before the City Council, refuting WHO's position step by step. With unassailable logic, she laid out her case showing that visitors to Toronto did not face a risk of acquiring SARS and asserted that the epidemic was under control. At the end of her remarks, she received a standing ovation and a bouquet of flowers. WHO lifted its advisory on April 30 and, though there was a second outbreak of SARS in May, did not reimpose it.

Basrur was no stranger to conflict. In 2000 restaurateurs objected vehemently when she

left: © AFP/Corbis; right: CP/Toronto Globe & Mail (Tibor Kolley)

introduced her colour-coded rating system for health-code infractions. She angered them again in 2001 with her support for an antismoking bylaw. In 2002 she aroused wrath in the City Council when she recommended that the city assess the public-health impact of a controversial airport expansion. In May 2003 it was the turn of gardening firms to protest when the City Council, following Basrur's observation that the "cosmetic" use of pesticides created needless public exposure to these contaminants, especially for children, passed a bylaw banning all nonessential use of pesticides.

Basrur was born in Toronto in 1956, her parents having emigrated from India the year before. Influenced by their careers (her father was a radiation oncologist, while her mother was known internationally for her work in veterinary genetics), Basrur graduated in medicine from the University of Toronto in 1982. After gaining experience as a family practitioner, she took a six-month trip to India, where her passion for preventative health care was aroused. Returning to Canada, she enrolled in a four-year residency in public health at the University of Toronto, followed by programs at the University of Western Ontario and Dalhousie University, Halifax, N.S. Basrur was East York's Medical Officer of Health for six years prior to accepting the position in Toronto in 1997.

Even though Basrur sometimes faced harsh opposition, she continued to struggle for proper public health funding and maintained her belief that it was her mission to speak for those who could not speak for themselves.

(ELIZABETH RHETT WOODS)

Bekele, Kenenisa

At the 2002 International Association of Athletics Federations (IAAF) world cross country championships in Dublin, 19-year-old Ethiopian Kenenisa Bekele, running with an apparently effortless stride, won the senior long-course (12-km [7.5-mi]) and short-course (4-km [2.5-mi]) titles—a feat never before accomplished by a male runner. Experts who wondered what such an athlete might accomplish in track races had to wait for the answer, as an Achilles tendon injury cut short Bekele's 2002 track season. In March 2003, however, he was healthy for the world cross country championships in Lausanne, Switz., where he repeated his astonishing double victory.

Bekele was born on June 13, 1982, near the town of Bekoji in the central Ethiopian province of Arsi. His parents were farmers who grew teff, wheat, sorghum, and barley and raised cattle and sheep. The young Bekele admired Ethiopian Olympic gold-medal-winning runners Haile Gebrselassie, Fatuma Roba, and Bekoji native Derartu Tulu, but his first athletic love was association football (soccer).

Bekele attended school through the ninth grade, and it was at school that he was introduced to running. He finished fourth in his first race, but in 1998 he won a provincial cross country title and placed sixth in the Ethiopian junior championships. His success led to an invitation to join the Mugher Cement Factory team, coached by Tolosa Kotu, then the Ethiopian national marathon coach.

In 1999 Bekele placed ninth in the junior race at the world cross country championships and took the silver medal in the 3,000 m at the IAAF world youth championships. Illness kept him off the Ethiopian squad for the 2000 world cross country championships, but at that year's world junior championships he won silver in the 5,000 m. At the 2001 world cross country championships, held in Ostend, Belg., he placed second in the senior short-course event and raced to a 33-sec victory margin in the junior race.

On June 1, 2003, Bekele finally showed what he could do on a track, defeating world-record-holder Gebrselassie in the 10,000-m race at the IAAF Grand Prix in Hengelo, Neth. He bested Gebrselassie again in August at the IAAF world championships in Paris, where he ran the fastest 10,000 m in championships history, timed at 26 min 49.57 sec. Bekele's time for the second half of the race, 12 min 57.24 sec, was almost a second faster than the existing world-championships record for 5,000 m. He placed third in the 5,000-m final. In September at the IAAF's World Athletics Final, held in Monaco, Bekele won the 3,000 m.

While Bekele was establishing a reputation as one of the greatest cross country runners in history, however, he faced a potential challenger in his 16-year-old brother, Tariku, who finished second in the 3,000-m final at the IAAF world youth championships in July.

(SIEG LINDSTROM)

Ethiopian champion distance runner Kenenisa Bekele sets a record in Paris.

© Paucellier-Prevosto/Photo & Co./Corbis; right: © Rune Hellestad/Corbis

Bernal, Gael García

Although he first made his name in a spate of coming-of-age films, 25-year-old Mexican actor Gael García Bernal truly arrived in 2003 with three new films—*Dot the I,* an English-language film set in London; *Diarios de motocicleta* (*The Motorcycle Diaries*), about the Cuban Revolution; and *La mala educación* (*Bad Education*), directed by Pedro Almodóvar. In his most successful film to date, *Y tu mamá también* (2001; *And Your Mother Too*), Bernal played an aimless privileged youth who sets off on a summer road trip with his best friend and a woman who is fleeing a failing marriage. The woman's forthright intimacy with the two friends sets them against each other, threatening the freewheeling fraternity they initially shared. The genuine chemistry between the two male characters was aided in part by the fact that actors Bernal and Diego Luna were longtime offscreen friends who had appeared together at age 12 in the television soap opera, *El abuelo y yo.*

Bernal's breakthrough role was in the gritty 2000 release *Amores perros.* Constructed as something of a triptych, Bernal starred in the first third of the movie as an impoverished angry teen blinded by love for his brother's pregnant wife. The following year he rose on the strength of *Y tu mamá también,* which was a runaway hit in Mexico and Guatemala and on the international festival and art-house film circuit. The movie enjoyed the highest-grossing opening in Mexico film history. In 2002 he repeated his box-office success, appearing as the title character in *El crimen del Padre Amaro* (*The Crime of Father Amaro*). The motion picture, based on the 19th-century story by Portuguese novelist José Maria Eça de Queirós of a hypocritical priest who takes up with an overly devoted parishioner, raised many eyebrows in predominantly Roman Catholic Mexico but also filled many theatre seats. Those two hits added sex appeal to Bernal's glowing marquee, and the visage of the stringy-haired youth with the soulful good looks made it onto *People en Español* magazine's list of "25 Most Beautiful People" as well as onto posters adorning the walls of his young fans.

Bernal was born on Oct. 30, 1978, in Guadalajara, Jalisco, into an acting family. As

a boy he appeared in theatrical productions with his parents, and following his preteen stint in *El abuelo y yo,* he moved to London at age 17 to study acting at the Central School of Speech and Drama. Afterward he appeared in a series of plays and short films. He portrayed Cuban revolutionary Che Guevara in the TV miniseries *Fidel* in 2002, a role he thereafter reprised in *Diarios de motocicleta.*
(TOM MICHAEL)

Blahnik, Manolo
The strappy, elegant, and sexy stiletto heels handcrafted by Spanish shoe designer Manolo Blahnik—the same signature pricey footwear featured on HBO's TV series *Sex and the City* and worn by its trendsetting star, Sarah Jessica Parker—were among the three decades of shoe designs featured at a 2003 retrospective on Blahnik at the Design Museum in London; it was Blahnik's first retrospective, and it was the first time that a shoe designer had been featured at the museum.

AP/Wide World Photos

Premier shoemaker Manolo Blahnik

Blahnik was born in 1942 in Santa Cruz de la Palma, Canary Islands. His father was Czech and his mother Spanish. He briefly studied law in Geneva but soon began concentrating on literature and architecture. In 1965 he moved to Paris and studied art. After arriving in London in 1968, he later admitted, he spent more time watching movies in Leicester Square's cavernous cinemas than working on his English, his original intention. His social life was frenetic and peopled with those at the centre of high society and fashion. His manner, however, was always rather formal—a result of his proper, disciplined upbringing.

In 1972 British dress designer Ossie Clark requested that Blahnik, then a fledgling shoe designer (who was encouraged to pursue the craft by *Vogue* editor Diana Vreeland), produce a capsule collection to accessorize dresses that would appear in his seasonal runway presentation. For Blahnik it was a watershed moment. British *Vogue* featured his work on the magazine's pages. Soon stylish young women with whom he was friendly were wearing his shoes, and in 1974 Blahnik posed with model Angelica Huston for the cover of British *Vogue,* becoming the first man to appear on the magazine's cover. He built a retail client base at a funky London boutique, Zapata, on Old Church Street. He later acquired the premises and set up his own independent shoe boutique, which he operated with his sister, Evangeline, with whom he continued to work closely. By 1979 Blahnik had opened another shoe boutique on Madison Avenue in New York City. In 1991 he added a third shop, in Hong Kong.

Blahnik taught himself to design shoes by trial and error, mastering the craft by targeting high-quality Italian shoe factories and matching their methods with his innate, artful skill. He produced the prototypes for his shoes alone, working without an apprentice, and, like a haute couturier, he sketched his collections. Those sketches were filled with bright colours and great beauty. Biannually they appeared in high-fashion magazines as his seasonal advertising campaigns. In addition to his association with Clark, Blahnik worked closely with a select group of fashion designers, including Perry Ellis and Calvin Klein in the 1980s; Isaac Mizrahi, Oscar de la Renta, and John Galliano in the '90s; and most recently young designer Zac Posen. These associations kept his designs on fashion's cutting edge. For his contribution to fashion, London's Royal College of Arts awarded Blahnik an honorary doctorate in 2001.
(BRONWYN COSGRAVE)

Brabeck-Letmathe, Peter
As head of Swiss-based Nestlé, the world's largest food company in 2003, Austrian Peter Brabeck-Letmathe likened his workday challenge to that of a world-class sprinter who measures improvements in just tenths of a second. As chief executive, his job was to keep a healthy company running even better. Despite a fall in global food prices, in the six years since he assumed the mantle in 1997, he had managed to cut manufacturing costs by $2.8 billion. Brabeck-Letmathe concentrated his efforts on fine-tuning the business rather than downsizing. During 2001–02 his appetite for acquisitions amounted to $15 billion; one of his most aggressive purchases, of the pet-food company Ralston Purina, was sealed in 2001 for $11 billion. His handiwork resulted in Nestlé's forays into bottled water and pet food but also in its abandonment of well-known brands such as Findus frozen foods and Hills Brothers coffee. Brabeck-Letmathe's latest effort was to get a handle on Nestlé's sprawling international empire by unifying practices throughout production, purchasing, and accounting. He still faced challenges, however, including mounting corporate debt and, in the view of some financial analysts, an underperforming stock.

Brabeck-Letmathe was born in Villach, Austria, on Nov. 13, 1944. He was schooled in economics at the University of World Trade in Vienna. In 1968 he joined the Austrian arm of Nestlé through the Findus division, excelling first as a salesman of ice cream and then as a new-product specialist. His adventurous spirit gave him entry into Nestlé's South American operations in the 1970s and '80s, sometimes landing him in situations that were politically unstable. He rose through the ranks, scaling to upper-management positions in Chile (1970–80), Ecuador (1981–83), and Venezuela (1983–87). One of the challenges he faced in Chile was the effort to forestall government plans to nationalize milk production, which would have undercut the company's own milk products.

Though he had returned to company headquarters several times before, in October 1987 he was drawn back to Vevey, Switz., to become vice president of the division of culinary products. On Jan. 1, 1992, he became executive vice president, with global responsibilities for marketing strategies. In this capacity, he reorganized Nestlé branding under six different headings, imposing a hierarchy that reached down to the local level. In June 1997 he was elected to the board of directors, and less than four years later he was appointed vice-chairman of the board. Brabeck-Letmathe also sat on the board of Credit Suisse Group, L'Oréal, and Roche Holding SA. An avid mountaineer, he scaled the Matterhorn in the Alps in 2002 at age 58.
(TOM MICHAEL)

Bremer, L. Paul, III
Amid criticism that the reconstruction effort in Iraq was in danger of losing the peace, L. Paul Bremer III was named the new U.S. administrator of occupied Iraq by Pres. George W. Bush on May 6, 2003, five days after the president had declared an end to major combat in the U.S.-led war there. Bremer replaced retired Lieut. Gen. Jay Garner, who had himself arrived only weeks earlier to head the Office of Humanitarian and Reconstruction Assistance in Baghdad. Before the occupation had lasted a month, it became clear that the Bush administration had not adequately planned for the reconstruction of Iraq, and Garner's team had made little headway in making the nation's capital secure. Faced with streets filled with garbage; broken electrical, water, and sewerage systems; and skyrocketing street violence that had virtually imprisoned Baghdad residents in their homes, Bremer nonetheless maintained that Iraq was "not a country in anarchy." He quickly moved to increase the number of U.S. military police in Baghdad while rebuilding the Iraqi police force, speed up fuel deliveries while repairing the country's oil infrastructure, restore basic services, deliver back pay to government workers, and remove members of the out-

lawed Ba'th Party from positions of authority. He also postponed the establishment of an Iraqi transitional government, which the Pentagon had aimed to accomplish by the end of May. Despite Bremer's decisiveness, violence continued to hamper reconstruction, and Iraqis expressed rising frustration with the occupation. In addition to increasing attacks against occupying troops, there were several confrontations in which Iraqi civilians were killed by U.S. soldiers and a number of lethal bombings, including a blast on August 19 that killed more than 20 UN workers. Fearing that the peace was once again slipping from its grasp, in early November the Bush administration summoned Bremer to the White House for talks aimed at accelerating Iraq's return to sovereignty. Bremer returned to Baghdad with a plan to transfer power to an Iraqi provisional government by the end of June 2004.

Lewis Paul Bremer III was born on Sept. 30, 1941, in Hartford, Conn. He graduated from Yale University in 1963 and received an MBA from Harvard University in 1966. He joined the Foreign Service soon after graduate school and later served as an assistant to Secretaries of State Henry Kissinger and Alexander Haig. Pres. Ronald Reagan named Bremer ambassador to The Netherlands in 1983 and ambassador-at-large for counterterrorism in 1986. From 1989 to 2000, following his retirement from the Department of State, Bremer served as managing director of Kissinger Associates, a strategic consulting firm founded by Henry Kissinger. Before his appointment to Iraq, he was chairman and CEO of Marsh Crisis Consulting. (JANET MOREDOCK)

de Villepin, Dominique

If 2003 was the year that put France back on the diplomatic map, Dominique de Villepin's was the face that placed it there. Few would forget the way that the French foreign minister, with his extravagant hand gestures and graying good looks, weighed in at the United Nations on February 5 to denounce the U.S. case for war in Iraq; he won a highly unusual round of applause in the Security Council chamber. The rebuke to the U.S. was all the more stinging because it came right after U.S. Secretary of State Colin Powell gave a full-court presentation of the evidence against the regime of Saddam Hussein.

No one could doubt after that incident that French diplomacy was back in Gaullist hands. Following the triumph of his conservatives in the June 2002 parliamentary election, neo-Gaullist Pres. Jacques Chirac chose his closest collaborator, de Villepin, who had run his Elysée office since 1995, to handle French foreign policy for him. In style and substance the two men could hardly be more similar, and it was often said that the 50-year-old de Villepin was the son that Chirac never had. One could even say, judging from de Villepin's enthusiastic literary writings on Napoleon and classic French poets, that the "son" was even more of an old-style Gaullist than the "father." One element precipitating the crisis over Iraq, therefore, was the fact that de Villepin was prone to reinforcing rather than restraining Chirac's own diplomatic impulsiveness.

De Villepin was born on Nov. 14, 1953, in Rabat, Mor., into an upper-crust family; his father represented French industry abroad before eventually securing a seat in the French Senate, and his mother fostered her son's interest in poetry. Though a late developer intellectually, de Villepin eventually passed through France's elite École Nationale d'Administration and into the Foreign Ministry in 1980. His career there led him to specialize in Africa but also to take postings in Washington, D.C., and New Delhi, India, and finally to accept appointment as top adviser to Foreign Minister Alain Juppé in 1993–95. After Chirac won the presidency in 1995, de Villepin became secretary-general of the Elysée and played a key role in many decisions, including the premature dissolution of the National Assembly in 1997. This move backfired badly when the conservatives lost rather than increased their majority, but de Villepin never admitted to any regret over his advice.

Initially, de Villepin professed confidence in his ability, based on his experience in Washington, D.C., to improve relations with the U.S. The opposite occurred, however, as the two countries went their separate ways on Iraq. De Villepin insisted that UN inspections could lead to the peaceful disarmament of Iraq, and he also argued against unilateral military action by the U.S. and the U.K. on the wider ground that such action lacked the legitimacy that only UN endorsement could confer. The war's difficult aftermath merely convinced Paris that it had been right to oppose the conflict and that it should not help rebuild Iraq without a UN mandate. De Villepin remained unrepentantly Gaullist concerning France's veto threat against Washington and London. "To go to the limit for one's principles is sometimes necessary. This is part of our rendezvous with history."

(DAVID BUCHAN)

Diouf, El Hadji

On April 1, 2003, association football (soccer) star El Hadji Ousseynou Diouf of Senegal was named African Football Confederation (CAF) Player of the Year for the second straight season. He had already established himself as either an out-and-out striker or a right-side midfield player whose strength, pace, and quick thinking often unsettled opposing defenders. Despite his reputation as a sure-shot striker, however, Diouf was occasionally something of a loose cannon off the field.

Diouf was born in Dakar, Senegal, on Jan. 15, 1981. In October 1998 he was plucked out of West Africa to play professionally for Sochaux in France. His first appearance was against Bastia on November 11. It was a difficult time for both the newcomer and the club, which found itself relegated at the end of the season. Diouf was picked up by Rennes, which enabled him to continue playing in the First Division. Despite being a teetotaler and a nonsmoker, the teenaged Diouf enjoyed partying. He acquired a criminal record after crashing a teammate's car while driving without a license; Rennes had had enough and transferred him to Lens, where he quieted down a little.

CAF Player of the Year El Hadji Diouf

Named CAF Player of the Year for 2001, Diouf became the toast of his homeland. He built a reputation as a star player with the Senegalese national team, which lost to Cameroon in the finals of the African Nations Cup in February 2002. Senegal also qualified for the 2002 World Cup finals and upset defending champion France in the first round. Although the team succumbed in overtime to Turkey in the quarterfinals, Diouf had been outstanding throughout the tournament, taking his career total for international appearances to 27 matches and 13 goals.

Liverpool, convinced Diouf was the answer to its lack of versatility in attacking positions, paid Lens £10 million (about $15.4 million) for his transfer. He was an instant success when he made his home debut for Liverpool on Aug. 24, 2002, scoring twice against Southampton. Following his initial impact, however, he lost much of his sparkle and effectiveness. During a Union des Associations Européennes de Football (UEFA) Cup quarterfinal match against Glasgow Celtic in Scotland on March 13, 2003, Diouf had the misfortune to overrun the perimeter of the pitch, and he fell into the crowd. He reacted badly to the situation and spat at a Celtic fan. Liverpool fined him heavily for his misconduct. He was charged with assault in court, pleaded guilty through an interpreter, and in September was fined £5,000 (about $8,000). The UEFA, after hearing evidence that Celtic fans had incited some of the trouble, also fined Celtic. Observers agreed that the 22-year-old Diouf could still successfully complete the transformation to English football, provided he learned to control his disturbingly wayward nature. (JACK ROLLIN)

Erdogan, Recep Tayyip

The man who formed the new Turkish government in March 2003 had to overcome a serious drawback. The parliamentary elections in November 2002 had been won by the party of Recep Tayyip Erdogan, a leader who was legally barred from standing for the parliament and therefore was not eligible to be prime minister. Erdogan had been deprived of his political rights when he was sentenced to 10 months' imprisonment in 1998 for having recited a poem that compared mosques to barracks, minarets to bayonets, and the faithful to an army. This, the court decided, made him guilty of the offense of inciting animosity between citizens on the grounds of religion. The conviction was never overturned, but a constitutional amendment in December 2002 had the effect of removing Erdogan's disqualification. In March 2003 he won a by-election in the eastern province of Siirt and a few days later was asked by the president to form a new government. "Where a brave man falls, there he rises again," Erdogan commented, for it was in Siirt that he had recited the fatal poem.

Erdogan was born in a rough neighbourhood of Istanbul on Feb. 26, 1954, the son of a captain of suburban ferries. He went to a vocational school for prayer leaders and preachers and then studied economics. In high school he became known as a fiery orator in the cause of political Islam and an accomplished association football (soccer) player. After playing with a professional soccer team, he opted for politics and became active first in the youth organization and then in the Istanbul provincial branch of parties led by the veteran Islamic politician Necmettin Erbakan. In 1994 Erdogan was elected mayor of Istanbul on the ticket of the Welfare Party. The election of the first-ever Islamist to the mayoralty shook the secularist establishment, but Erdogan proved to be a competent and canny manager. Having long ago shaved off his Islamic beard and having taken to wearing smart suits that set off his handsome appearance, Erdogan yielded to protests against the building of a mosque in the city's central square and did not enforce the ban on drinking in pavement cafés. He emerged from prison—he served only four months—as a conciliator. When Erbakan's Virtue Party was banned in 2001, Erdogan broke with him and became the leader of innovators in the Islamic camp with whom he formed the Justice and Development Party as a "democratic conservative," rather than a religion-based, political grouping. He toured the U.S. and Europe in order to prove his democratic Western credentials and advance Turkey's bid to join the European Union. He was a quick study. After a bit of fumbling in the Iraq crisis in spring 2003, which overlapped with his move to the prime minister's office, he was able to rein in his party and the parliament. In October he secured approval for the dispatch of Turkish troops to help keep the peace in Iraq. This assertion of his authority proved cost-free as Iraqi opposition prevented the deployment of Turkish peacekeepers. (ANDREW MANGO)

Recep Tayyip Erdogan, Turkey's new leader

Falconer of Thoroton, Lord

On June 12, 2003, Lord Falconer of Thoroton, a longtime friend and political ally of British Prime Minister Tony Blair, took on what was likely to be the most challenging job of his career when Blair named him lord high chancellor and keeper of the great seal. On the same day, Blair announced the abolition of this position (first created in 605), and Falconer, the 259th and last lord chancellor, was given the task of introducing the legislation that would replace the post with that of secretary of state for constitutional affairs.

Charles Leslie Falconer was born in Edinburgh on Nov. 19, 1951. He and Blair were boyhood acquaintances; at one point they even competed to date the same girl. Both men went on to study law—Blair at St. John's College, Oxford, and Falconer at Queen's College, Cambridge—and in 1976 the young barristers found themselves working in the same building. Blair moved into Falconer's apartment in south London for a time, and both became active in the same local branch of the Labour Party.

In the 1980s, after Blair had entered politics, Falconer continued to pursue a successful legal career, specializing in commercial law. The two remained close; they bought houses near each other in north London and often dined together. In 1991, at the unusually young age of 40, Falconer was appointed Queen's Counsel (the official designation of senior barristers). Ahead of the 1997 general election (with a Labour government a near certainty after 18 years in opposition), he sought to run for Parliament, but he was turned down because he sent his children to private fee-paying schools—something that active local Labour Party members overwhelmingly deplored.

Following Labour's return to power in that election, Blair arranged for a life peerage for his old friend and appointed him solicitor general. In 1998 Falconer was moved to the Cabinet Office, where he came to public attention as the minister responsible for the ill-fated Millennium Dome. He defended what many considered indefensible with good humour, a stance that evoked admiration and criticism in equal measure. After brief terms as housing minister (2001) and minister for criminal justice (2002–03), Falconer took on the post of lord chancellor and the task of reforming Britain's legal system. Within Parliament and the legal profession, there was widespread support in principle for reform. New measures would finally separate politics and the judiciary and end the ability of a government minister to appoint senior judges. Blair's appointment of his friend badly weakened the impact of a reform designed to curb patronage, but Falconer himself attracted little criticism—his skills, integrity, and easygoing style were admired across the political spectrum. In July he unveiled the first planned reforms, including the creation of a new supreme court. (PETER KELLNER)

Fierstein, Harvey

If Harvey Fierstein did not exist, the American entertainment industry would have had to invent him. The 49-year-old actor, playwright, social activist, and sometime drag queen spent 2003 eliciting bravos from Broadway audiences for his exuberant cross-dressing performance—for which he won his fourth Tony Award—in the hit stage musical version of John Waters's camp film *Hairspray,* while he simultaneously racked up accomplishments in film, television, and publishing. Having declared at one point that his drag days were over, Fierstein wisely reconsidered when offered the *Hairspray* role of teen heroine Tracy

Harvey Fierstein struts as Edna Turnblad at the Tonys.

Turnblad's plus-sized mother, Edna (played in the 1988 movie by the late Divine). Beyond Broadway, film and TV audiences heard his distinctive gravelly voice on the sound tracks of Disney's animated feature *Mulan* and Fox's *The Simpsons;* gay-rights activists welcomed his commentaries on public TV's documentary series *In the Life* and on the talk-show and lecture circuit; and children's publishing was rocked by the success of his book *The Sissy Duckling,* which was a spin-off of his Humanitas Prize-winning animated program.

Harvey Forbes Fierstein was born into a strict Jewish family on June 6, 1954, in Brooklyn, N.Y. His mother recognized his artistic potential early on, recalling, "Even as a child he was different. He was very artistic; he had hands of gold." Fierstein graduated from the Pratt Institute, Brooklyn, with a Bachelor of Fine Arts degree in 1973, but rather than becoming a teacher as his family hoped, he plunged into the world of downtown New York theatre and playwriting. Having already won a part at age 16 in Andy Warhol's play, *Pork* (1971), Fierstein went on to perform in more than 60 Off-Off-Broadway productions, inevitably appearing in drag roles. It was Ellen Stewart, doyenne of La MaMa Experimental Theatre Club, who insisted that Fierstein move beyond drag and write and act in his own work—an exhortation that led in the late 1970s to Fierstein's trilogy of plays (*The International Stud, Fugue in a Nursery,* and *Widows and Children First*), eventually performed together as *Torch Song Trilogy.* Seen all at once on Broadway (1982), in a production starring the author himself, the trilogy proved to be a powerful, profoundly moving statement that took audiences into the "exotic" world of gay families and their struggle for self-acceptance and love. With Tonys for acting and writing to his credit, Fierstein went on to appear in the 1988 screen version of *Torch Song* with Anne Bancroft and Matthew Broderick. His book for the 1986 musical *La Cage aux folles* (which won another Tony) continued to move gay issues into the mainstream. (JIM O'QUINN)

Fitz-Gerald, Sarah

In February 2003 Sarah Fitz-Gerald of Australia announced her retirement from the Women's International Squash Players Association (WISPA) world tour. The surprise announcement by the number one ranked Fitz-Gerald came one month after she was inducted into the WISPA Hall of Fame and brought to a close the most successful period in her career—in 2002 she won 12 tour events (bringing her career total to 61), her second consecutive British Open, the gold medal at the Commonwealth Games, and a record-breaking fifth World Open title. A month after her announcement, she was named Female Athlete of the Year for the second straight time by the Australia Sport Awards, which also had honoured her with the Dawn Fraser Award as sports personality of the year in 2002.

Fitz-Gerald was born on Dec. 1, 1968, and grew up in Melbourne. Her mother was a four-time Australian Open squash champion who became a coach. Fitz-Gerald's potential was apparent when she easily won the world junior championship in 1987. For a few years she languished in the lower reaches of the world top 10, but in September 1995 she broke through at the richest event of that year, the JSM Supersquash in Japan. In the five-game final, she beat her longtime Australian rival, Michelle Martin, who was then dominating the tour.

In October 1996 Fitz-Gerald, who was known for her punchy attacking style, reached the top spot in the world rankings and beat England's Cassie Jackman to win her first World Open. She retained her world crown with a victory over Martin in 1997 and again in 1998 before surgery on a troublesome knee could not be avoided. A premature return led to her losing the whole of 1999, while 2000 was marked by her gradual rehabilitation.

She returned to full strength the next season, however, and a loss to New Zealand's world number one, Leilani Joyce, in the semifinals of the Hong Kong Open in August 2001 was her last competitive defeat. From then until her "retirement" 18 months later, Fitz-Gerald was unbeaten. In October 2001 she won her fourth World Open, equaling the record of New Zealander Susan Devoy.

Fitz-Gerald was a superb ambassador for squash. In 1991, at age 23, she became president of WISPA, a position she held until she was made "patron" when she retired from the tour. Fitz-Gerald's decision to take her career in a new direction, however, had not diminished her drive to play and win. In the first half of 2003, even after she quit the world tour, she won the Welsh Open, her fourth Australian Open (matching her mother's success), and the inaugural Australian national championship. (ANDREW SHELLEY)

Franks, Gen. Tommy

After having led two successful military campaigns in as many years, U.S. Gen. Tommy Ray Franks chose to retire a national hero in May 2003. He had commanded the American forces responsible for the overthrow of the Taliban regime in Afghanistan in 2001 as well as the forces that deposed the Iraqi regime of Saddam Hussein in a blitzkrieg in March and April 2003. Franks had spent more than 36 years in uniform, his last three as commander of the Florida-based Central Command (Centcom), which was responsible for all U.S. military operations in an area comprising 25 countries, stretching from the Horn of Africa through the Middle East to Central Asia. In October he signed a book deal, reportedly worth $5 million, for his memoirs.

Franks was born on June 17, 1945, in Wynnewood, Okla. He grew up in Midland, Texas, like future president George W. Bush, and went to high school there with Bush's future wife, Laura Welch, who was one year behind him. He had a penchant for motorcycles, country music, and hunting. After studying at the University of Texas for two years, Franks dropped out and joined the army. He graduated from the Artillery Officer School in 1967 and was commissioned a second lieutenant. Shortly thereafter he was posted to Vietnam with the 9th Infantry Division. In 1969 he decided to leave the service but changed his mind following selection for the army's Bootstrap degree-completion program. He graduated with a degree in business administration in 1971. His rise through the ranks culminated in his promotion to commander of Centcom in June 2000. Franks reportedly did not get along well at first with Secretary of Defense Donald Rumsfeld, but the two developed a close working relationship after the Sept. 11, 2001, terrorist attacks in the United States. The day after the attacks, Rumsfeld ordered Franks to begin plans for retaliation, and on Oct. 7, 2001, airstrikes against Afghanistan began.

During the buildup to the invasion of Iraq, Franks was implicated in a security breach involving his wife after it was discovered that she had been present during a highly classified briefing. The Pentagon's investigation concluded that he had inadvertently allowed classified information to be discussed in front of his wife at a level for which she did not have a security clearance. Franks promised to "redouble" his efforts to protect sensitive information, and no further action was taken. Even before the investigation was finished, Rumsfeld made it clear that he would not allow the incident to interfere with Franks's war preparations.

Franks's military honours included the Defense Distinguished Service Medal; the Distinguished Service Medal (two awards); the Legion of Merit (four awards); three Bronze Star medals with "V" (for valour); three Purple Hearts; the Air Medal with "V"; and the Army Commendation medal with "V."

(PETER SARACINO)

French, Dawn

Although Dawn French had achieved her greatest renown in Great Britain for her comedic partnership with Jennifer Saunders and had also amassed a respectable list of performing credits on her own—she was sometimes referred to as the country's "first lady of television comedy"—in 2003 French took a giant step toward greater international recognition when she signed for a role—the Fat Lady, a talking painting—in the third Harry Potter movie, *Harry Potter and the Prisoner of Azkaban,* to be released in 2004. Only weeks earlier she had portrayed Potter himself in a spoof of the first two films for the BBC's Comic Relief marathon fund-raiser.

French was born on Oct. 11, 1957, in Holyhead, Wales. She and Saunders met and first teamed up in the late 1970s, when they were students at London's Central School of Speech and Drama, and they joined up again in 1980 as cast members of the Comic Strip, a London comedy club. A number of television appearances followed, especially in Comic Strip productions and the *Girls on Top* series, which French co-wrote, and in 1987 the duo began co-writing and costarring in their own series, *French and Saunders.* In 1991 French began her solo career as star of the comic drama series *Murder Most Horrid;* a second series followed in 1994. In the meantime, she had demonstrated her dramatic acting talents in 1993 in the BBC drama *Tender Loving Care.* French's most popular solo venture began in 1994 with the TV series *The Vicar of Dibley,* for which she won a British Comedy Award in 1997. From 1995 she also served as a writer for and made occasional appearances on Saunders' series *Absolutely Fabulous.* Among other TV roles were leads in the 1997 BBC drama *Sex and Chocolate* and the 2002 BBC romantic comedy *Ted and Alice.*

French had a notable stage career as well, most recently in the role of Bottom in *A Midsummer Night's Dream* in 2001 and the one-woman play *My Brilliant Divorce* in 2003. She continued to make appearances with Saunders on tour and in TV specials, and in 2002 at the Montreux (Switz.) Light Entertainment Festival, they became the first women to win an Honorary Golden Rose. She also was partner, with Helen Teague, in the French and Teague designer clothing label and in Sixteen 47, a business selling stylish clothes for large women. In 1984 French married comedian Lenny Henry—winner of the Golden Rose and the Edric Connor Inspiration Award for black achievement and founder of Comic Relief, for which he was appointed CBE in 1999.

(BARBARA WHITNEY)

Frist, Bill

On Jan. 7, 2003, Sen. Bill Frist of Tennessee formally became U.S. Senate majority leader. Two weeks earlier the surgeon turned politician had won unanimous backing from Republican Party colleagues to succeed Trent Lott as party leader and heal the fractures in Congress. Lott had resigned amid pressure stemming from his controversial statements made at Sen. Strom Thurmond's 100th birthday party, at which he praised Thurmond's 1948 presidential bid on the segregationist "Dixiecrat" ticket.

William Harrison Frist was born on Feb. 22, 1952, in Nashville, Tenn. He attended Princeton University, from which he graduated in 1974 with a specialization in health care policy from the Woodrow Wilson School of Public and International Affairs. Frist then attended Harvard Medical School, graduating with honours in 1978. He received surgical training at various hospitals and was hired in 1985 by the Vanderbilt University Medical Center, Nashville, where he founded and directed the school's renowned transplant centre. A board-certified heart surgeon, Frist performed numerous heart transplants and the first successful heart-lung transplant in the southeastern United States.

Frist was elected to the U.S. Senate on Nov. 8, 1994, defeating three-term incumbent James Sasser after mounting an aggressive campaign; he became the first physician to be elected to the Senate since 1928. In 2000 he won reelection overwhelmingly. Frist served on the health committee and specialized in health care policy, particularly ethical issues in medicine and HIV/AIDS. Opposed to cloning, Frist announced support in 2001 for strictly regulated embryonic-stem-cell research.

After the Sept. 11, 2001, terrorist attacks in the U.S. and the discovery of anthrax spores in congressional mail, Frist was increasingly consulted as a leading Senate expert on bioterrorism. He also expanded his expertise, sitting on committees dealing with such areas as foreign relations, budget, banking, commerce, finance, and education. Frist, praised for his bipartisanship and hard-working style, quickly ascended the Republican Senate hierarchy. In 2000 he was elected to head the National Republican Senatorial Committee, helping the party win majority control of the chamber in the 2002 midterm elections.

In July 1998, after a gunman opened fire in the Capitol, killing two police officers and injuring a tourist, Frist provided aid to both the victims and the gunman—even resuscitating the gunman and escorting him to the hospital. He also dispensed aid to Thurmond after the senator became ill in the Senate chamber in October 2001. Perhaps most dramatically, while vacationing in Florida just before he was to be sworn in as Senate leader in January 2003, Frist provided "invaluable" medical assistance to victims of an automobile crash.

During 2003 he was successful in shepherding much of Pres. George W. Bush's agenda through the Senate, particularly legislation on Medicare reform, but Frist drew fire from Republican colleagues for agreeing to cap Bush's proposed $726 billion tax-cut package at $350 billion. His support for a constitutional amendment prohibiting same-sex marriage (he later qualified his position) came on the heels of the U.S. Supreme Court's June ruling striking down Texas's antisodomy law. Frist's stance sparked controversy, winning praise from conservative allies and criticism from liberals.

(MICHAEL I. LEVY)

Gandolfini, James

In March 2003, when James Gandolfini—the winner of three Emmy Awards as outstanding lead actor in a dramatic series (2000, 2001, and 2003) for his portrayal of the intense, lumbering mafia boss Tony Soprano—threatened to leave *The Sopranos* over a salary dispute, production came to a halt on the most popular series in the history of cable television. Following a round of tough negotiations, however, filming resumed later that month.

Gandolfini was born on Sept. 18, 1961, in Westwood, N.J., to Italian immigrant parents. After graduating in 1983 with a degree in communications from Rutgers University, New Brunswick, N.J., he worked in New York City nightclubs as a bouncer, bartender, and manager. Persuaded by a friend to attend an acting class at the famed Actors Studio, Gandolfini was intrigued and decided to study acting, supporting himself as a deliveryman. He first gained notice on the stage in a 1992 production of *A Streetcar Named Desire* that starred Alec Baldwin and Jessica Lange. His film career began that same year with a series of small roles; he was cast in larger roles as dangerous tough guys in films that included *Terminal Velocity* (1994), *Crimson Tide* (1995), and *Get Shorty* (1995). Although respected for his work in these films and others, such as *Night Falls on Manhattan* (1997) and *A Civil Action* (1998), Gandolfini became an icon in his role-of-a-lifetime on *The Sopranos,* which debuted on HBO in 1999.

The Sopranos followed in the same tradition as Francis Ford Coppola's *Godfather* films and Martin Scorsese's *Goodfellas.* The series was as much the story of a dysfunctional family as it was of the crime syndicate as endangered species, and at the centre of both was Tony, the gangster as upper-middle-class everyman, whose sessions with his psychiatrist illuminated his deeply conflicted nature. By turns volcanic and brooding, honourable and devious, tender and cruel, a loving father and husband given to serial infidelity, Tony was one of the most complex characters in television history, and Gandolfini's performance was profoundly nuanced. How else could viewers feel such sympathy for a character capable of such tremendous violence?

Gandolfini demonstrated his range in very different roles in three films released in 2001: as a gay hitman in *The Mexican,* as the uptight military prison warden in *The Last Castle,* and as the victim of blackmail in *The Man Who Wasn't There.* All the while, the balding and hulking Gandolfini was becoming an unlikely sex symbol who changed the image of a leading man.

(JEFF WALLENFELDT)

AP/Wide World Photos

Gbagbo, Laurent

In 2003 Pres. Laurent Gbagbo of Côte d'Ivoire was, in large measure, a victim of his own success. For some 30 years he fought for the rights of workers in his native country, first as a political dissident, helping to usher in multiparty elections in 1990, and then as a political opposition leader, eventually rising to head of state in 2000. His accession was highly irregular, however, and his nationalist agenda was assailed by the leftist opposition. His regime was accused of human rights abuses, brutal political reprisals, and exploitation of differences between ethnic, religious, and immigrant groups. He clung tenaciously to power through a nine-month civil war that left his leadership on shaky ground.

Gbagbo was born to a Roman Catholic family of the Bété people on May 31, 1945, in Gagnoa in west-central Ivory Coast. In the 1960s he moved to the capital city and attended the Traditional College of Abidjan (1965) and then studied history at the University of Abidjan (B.A., 1969). He extended his studies at the Sorbonne (M.A., 1970) and returned to Abidjan to teach in the Classical College. He was arrested and imprisoned in 1971–73 for subversion, but following his release he joined the faculty at the University of Abidjan's Institute of History, Art, and African Archaeology in 1974 while simultaneously earning a doctorate (1979) from the Sorbonne. Although he was elevated to director of the institute in 1980, by 1982 his dissident activities had again raised the ire of the government. Gbagbo formed an opposition group and went into exile in France. When he returned to Côte d'Ivoire in September 1988, he was elected to lead the Ivorian Popular Front. Then, in April 1990, the country's authoritarian president, Félix Houphouët-Boigny, agreed to recognize opposition parties and, for the first time in the country's history, scheduled multiparty elections.

Houphouët-Boigny and his party dominated the elections, and Gbagbo resumed his political activism, enduring another prison sentence for having organized a public disturbance. Houphouët-Boigny died in office in 1993 and was succeeded by his finance minister, Henri Konan Bédié, who in turn was deposed in a military coup in 1999 led by Gen. Robert Gueï, who then defeated Gbagbo in an apparently fraudulent election in 2000. In the ensuing uproar Gueï fled the country, and Gbagbo took over the presidency. Almost immediately, however, rebel forces revolted, and the situation quickly deteriorated into a full-fledged civil war from September 2002. With French help, an end to the war was brokered in July 2003. In August the National Assembly voted to grant the rebels amnesty, which left Gbagbo's position secure for the moment but uncertain in the long run. (TOM MICHAEL)

Gruden, Jon

By the time the Tampa Bay Buccaneers put the finishing touches on their 48–21 rout of the Oakland Raiders in Super Bowl XXXVII, the National Football League (NFL) had discovered its latest media darling: Jon Gruden, the first-year coach of the Buccaneers. During the hype that led up to the Jan. 26, 2003, game and throughout the game itself, football fans watching TV were fed a steady diet of sideline shots of the animated coach, whom some compared to Chucky, the devilish homicidal doll featured in the *Child's Play* series of horror movies. Gruden might have frightened opponents, but he provided viewers with much more than just sideline entertainment. The fiery coach—at age 39 the league's youngest—helped to lift the Buccaneers, once the laughingstock of the NFL, to their first championship.

Gruden was born on Aug. 17, 1963, in Sandusky, Ohio. His father, Jim, coached football, including stints as an assistant at Indiana University (1973–77) and the University of Notre Dame (1978–80); from 1987 Jim was on the staff of the San Francisco 49ers. Jon attended Clay High School in South Bend, Ind., where he played baseball, basketball, and football, and then moved on to the University of Dayton, Ohio, and its football team, where he played quarterback for three years. He began his coaching career as a graduate assistant at the University of Tennessee (1986–87). He then became an offensive assistant at Southeast Missouri State University (1988) and University of the Pacific, Stockton, Calif. (1989), before he joined the 49ers (1990). In 1991 he was back at the college level at the University of Pittsburgh, Pa., but in 1992 the Green Bay Packers hired him as their wide receivers coach. In 1995 the Philadelphia Eagles made him their offensive coordinator, and in 1998 he took the Raiders' head coaching position. He guided Oakland to division titles in 2000 and 2001, compiling a record of 40–28 in his first four years as a head coach.

Though Tampa Bay had in recent years assembled some talented teams, play-off success had eluded them. The Buccaneers fired coach Tony Dungy in early 2002 and, in a move that raised more than a few eyebrows, obtained Gruden from the Raiders for $8 million and four draft picks. While Gruden was known for his offensive coaching ability, it was the fearsome Tampa Bay defense that had carried the team before he arrived, and the skilled motivator found ways to make the squad even better. The Buccaneers held opponents to fewer points (196) and fewer yards per game (252.8) than any other team in the league on the way to a 12–4 record and the National Football Conference (NFC) South division title and the Super Bowl victory. (ANTHONY G. CRAINE)

Gutiérrez, Lucio

The inauguration of former army colonel Lucio Gutiérrez as Ecuador's president on Jan. 15, 2003, marked a dramatic reversal of fortune. Just three years earlier, Gutiérrez had been imprisoned for having taken part in a failed uprising. Ecuadorans, however, hungry for fresh solutions to their country's seemingly endless difficulties, gave him a resounding mandate in the elections of 2002. He joined a growing list of political outsiders chosen to lead Latin American countries.

Lucio Edwin Gutiérrez Borbúa was born on March 23, 1957, in Quito and raised in Tena, an Amazon basin town. He was the son of a traveling salesman and attended primary and secondary school in Tena before transferring at the age of 15 to military college in Quito. Gutiérrez graduated from the Army Polytechnic School as a civil engineer after having won honours for academic and athletic prowess. He later studied in Brazil and the United States.

Gutiérrez rose steadily through the army ranks and in 1990–92 served with the United Nations observer mission to Nicaragua. As a young man he demonstrated little interest in politics, but during the 1990s he sympathized

Tampa Bay Buccaneers' head coach Jon Gruden

© AFP/Corbis

Ecuador's new top man, Lucio Gutiérrez

with fellow Ecuadorans as they became increasingly disenchanted with corruption and poverty. In 1997, as aide-de-camp to Pres. Abdalá Bucaram Ortiz, he refused an order to use force against a crowd outside the presidential palace. Bucaram fled the palace and was later removed from office by Ecuador's congress. In 1999 Gutiérrez repeatedly questioned the government's conduct and pointedly refused to shake Pres. Jamil Mahuad Witt's hand during a public ceremony in December.

On Jan. 21, 2000, after Mahuad announced the replacement of Ecuador's national currency with the U.S. dollar, Indian protesters supported by middle-ranking military officers seized the national congress building. Gutiérrez announced that he and two others had formed a "junta of national salvation." The rebellion was short-lived, however; Gutiérrez lacked the confidence of the military high command. He was replaced in the junta by Gen. Carlos Mendoza, the armed forces chief of staff, who announced that Vice Pres. Gustavo Noboa Bejarano would succeed Mahuad.

Jailed after the uprising, Gutiérrez was pardoned in June 2000 after a public campaign led by his wife, Ximena Bohórquez Romero, a physician, with whom he had two daughters. He left the army, founded the January 21 Patriotic Society movement, and plunged into civilian politics, promising an all-out war on corruption, racial inequality, and poverty. "In Ecuador, 80% of the people do not have a half-decent life," he said. Nevertheless, he dropped his early opposition to dollarization, and after his election he moved quickly to calm fears of a radical shift. In August 2003, however, he lost the congressional support of the Indian movement Pachakutik, and the future of his legislative program was thrown into doubt. (PAUL KNOX)

Hadid, Zaha

In Cincinnati, Ohio, the Lois and Richard Rosenthal Center for Contemporary Art opened in June 2003 to rave reviews—not surprisingly, in light of the fact that its architect, Iraqi-born, London-based Zaha Hadid, had been regarded as one of the stars of the design firmament long before any of her plans took concrete form.

Hadid's art centre consisted of a glassed-in ground-floor lobby topped by stacked blocks of gray concrete, black aluminum panels, and transparent glass. Monolithic chunks jutted out and cantilevered over the street corner. Inside, Hadid furnished the museum with black pedestrian ramps that angled in a zigzag manner up through a sky-lit shaft at the rear of the building. The many-angled interior spaces illustrated a core tenet of Hadid's theory that there was no reason architecture should limit itself to the 90° angle.

Hadid was born Oct. 31, 1950, in Baghdad, where her father was an industrialist and a leader of a progressive Iraqi political party. She attended a French-language Roman Catholic convent school and first attended college in Lebanon, studying mathematics at the American University in Beirut. She later moved to London, where she studied under noted Dutch architect Rem Koolhaas at the Architectural Association School of Architecture. After graduation in 1977 she worked with Koolhaas, and then in 1979 she established her own practice in London. By 2003 she was presiding over a staff of 50.

Hadid first gained acclaim for designs that were never built. Chief among them, in the early 1980s, was a mountainside sports club overlooking Hong Kong; her solution won an international competition. The design, a "horizontal skyscraper," featured two huge beams thrusting laterally from the mountain. Another, in the early 1990s, was an opera house in Cardiff, Wales, for which she also won design awards. In 1990 her design for the Monsoon Restaurant in Sapporo, Japan, was completed, and in 1993 she received international attention for the completed Vitra Fire House in Weil am Rhein, Ger. During those years she also served occasionally as a visiting lecturer and professor at several universities.

During 2003 Hadid and her staff were working on such projects as the National Center for Contemporary Art in Rome, a master plan for Singapore, and an art museum near Frank Lloyd Wright's Price Tower in Bartlesville, Okla. In addition, in May 2003 a comprehensive retrospective of her work opened at the Austrian Museum of Applied Arts in Vienna. (DAVID R. CALHOUN)

Hussein, Saddam

By early 2003 Iraqi Pres. Saddam Hussein, the Arab nationalist leader who had become infamous for atrocities against his people and who, in 24 years in power, had reduced Iraq to a state of impoverishment, devastation, and near dismemberment, had few supporters left among world leaders.

Saddam was born on April 28, 1937, in a village near Tikrit, Iraq; orphaned, he was reared by an uncle. They moved to Baghdad in the mid-1950s, and he joined the Arab Ba'th Socialist Party, an Arab ultranationalist group. By 1959 Saddam was a member of a Ba'th strike force that attempted to assassinate 'Abd

Architect Zaha Hadid and Cincinnati's Rosenthal Center for Contemporary Art

AP/Wide World Photos

al-Karim Qasim, the Iraqi prime minister and dictator. Injured in the attempt, Saddam fled to Syria and then to Egypt, where he became a political refugee. He returned to Iraq after a pro-Ba'th coup in February 1963 and again involved himself in politics. In November 1963 the Ba'th Party was ousted from power, and Saddam went underground. He spent the following years in and out of prison while remaining active in the party ranks.

In July 1968 the Ba'th Party returned to power after two successful coups. Ahmad Hasan al-Bakr became president of the Iraqi Republic, and in 1969 Saddam was elected vice-chairman of the Revolutionary Command Council, the most important political body in the country. Saddam proved to be a shrewd manipulator and survivor; between 1968 and 1979 Iraq was effectively ruled by both Bakr and Hussein. Finally, on July 16, 1979, the aging Bakr resigned, and Saddam was elected president of the republic.

Iraq was profoundly affected by the 1979 Islamic revolution in neighbouring Iran, which replaced the shah with the leadership of the Shi'ite ayatollahs. Iraqi-Iranian relations deteriorated as Baghdad feared that the new Iranian Islamic regime would encourage Iraqi Shi'ites to adopt revolutionary Islamic ideas and rise up against the Ba'th regime. After border skirmishes between the two countries, Saddam took the initiative and in September 1980 sent Iraqi troops into Iran. The ensuing war lasted almost eight years. Both sides suffered hundreds of thousands of casualties, yet the conflict ended without any noticeable gains for either side.

In August 1990 Saddam sent troops into Kuwait and annexed that country. An international coalition led by the United States evicted Iraq from Kuwait in February 1991. An uprising against Saddam's regime in the following month was harshly suppressed. The Persian Gulf War left Iraq isolated and reeling from international economic sanctions. Saddam's reaction was to clamp down further on Iraqi citizens, especially those in southern Iraq, gather more wealth and power for himself and his family, and alternately bait and submit to demands from the Western powers and international organizations, in particular a UN program to eliminate weapons of mass destruction (WMD). Despite the opposition of many members of the UN Security Council, especially France, Germany, and Russia, Iraq's failure to cooperate fully on WMD inspections as well as Saddam's obstreperousness finally resulted in the invasion of Iraq in March–April 2003. The regime collapsed, and Saddam went underground. His sons and aides, Uday and Qusay Hussein, were killed in Mosul, Iraq, on July 22, but Saddam himself eluded capture for nine months. He was finally found in a "spider hole," a covered underground bunker, just south of his hometown of Tikrit, taken without a struggle by U.S. forces, and spirited away to a secure location, where at year's end he awaited trial. (LOUAY BAHRY)

Idei, Nobuyuki

In 2003 Nobuyuki Idei, chairman and CEO of Japanese electronics giant Sony Corp., was in the midst of taking his company through a dramatic transformation. While in the past Sony had earned billions from such stand-alone electronics products as the Walkman and the Camcorder, Idei insisted that the time had come for the company to move firmly into the network age. To that end he had begun shifting Sony's emphasis to the development of an array of interconnected devices and services. A home video recorder that could be programmed from a mobile phone, a Walkman that could download music from the Internet, and a portable flat-screen gadget known as an Airboard that combined the functions of a television and a personal computer were just some of the Sony products new on the market. Idei even unveiled the prototype of a "personal entertainment robot"—the SDR-4X—that used sophisticated microelectronics and sensors to walk, sing, and interact with humans. "This is the end of the 20th-century business model," the 66-year-old CEO declared in an interview, "and the beginning of the 21st-century model."

AP/Wide World Photos

Sony's CEO, Nobuyuki Idei

Idei was born on Nov. 22, 1937, in Tokyo. He earned a B.A. degree in political science and economics from Tokyo's Waseda University in 1960. His father, an economics professor at Waseda, had intended for Idei to follow in his footsteps. Upon graduation, however, Idei instead went to work in Sony's International Division, gaining experience in several of the company's European offices. He helped establish Sony France in 1968. Four years later he was recalled to Japan to work at the company's Tokyo headquarters.

A steady succession of promotions followed. Idei was named general manager of Sony's Audio Division in 1979, senior general manager of the Home Video Group in 1988, Sony Corp. director in 1989, and managing director of the company in 1994. He was tapped as president and representative director in April 1995. He assumed CEO duties in June 1999 and a year later added chairman to his title.

Most observers had praised Idei for devoting himself to promoting the digitalization of audio and video electronics and their convergence with information technology, but he was not without his share of critics. Some wondered whether Sony would be able to sell enough of its dazzling but decidedly high-end new products to turn a profit and whether Idei was spreading the company's resources too thin. By 2003 there were some positive signs, though, as Sony's profits had begun to rebound after several down years. Idei himself remained confident that his company was on the right track, arguing that the rapid growth in Internet and mobile-phone connections would only increase the demand for Sony's new products in the future. (SHERMAN HOLLAR)

Ive, Jonathan

The man who liberated the personal computer from its gray or beige box, British designer Jonathan Ive, was named the 2003 Designer of the Year by the Design Museum. The prize, worth £25,000 (about $41,000) and awarded annually by the London museum to a designer born or based in the United Kingdom, recognized Ive's pioneering designs for the 2002 flat-panel iMac computer, Apple Computer, Inc.'s top-selling product for that year, and the 2002 iPod, the company's digital music player. In making design as integral to the appeal of a personal computer as its power and speed, Ive essentially rewrote the product standards for an industry that had, since its beginnings in the 1970s, pursued function as its grail. Ive's original 1998 iMac stunned consumers and critics alike with its translucent candy colours and a seductively rounded exterior over a functional core that was itself a product of high design. The computer's instant success—two million iMacs were sold in 1998—brought Apple its first profitable year since 1995.

Ive was born in February 1967 in Chingford, a northern London suburb. He studied art and design at Newcastle Polytechnic (now Northumbria University). After graduating in 1989, he cofounded Tangerine, a London-based design consultancy that counted Apple among its clients. In 1992 Apple offered Ive a full-time position at its headquarters in Cupertino, Calif. He accepted, but it was not until Apple cofounder Steve Jobs returned to the troubled company as CEO in 1997 that the real impact of Ive's design ethos began to be felt.

Working on the belief that the computer had become the centre of home life, Ive, since 1997 Apple's vice president of industrial design, fashioned machines that were sleek, touchable, and amenable to display. Ease and simplicity of use—his watchwords—were achieved by devoting "obsessive attention to details that are often overlooked." Ive's design for the first iMac, for example, called for reshaping the processor to fit within the machine's colourful shell and thus dramatically shrank the computer's footprint. Subsequent designs reflected his continuing effort to maximize efficiency and convenience for the user. The 2000 Power Mac G4 Cube could be easily removed from its one-piece plastic housing for internal access, and air circulated freely through its suspended core, obviating the need for noisy fans. Processor, drives, wireless technology, and even the power supply were incorporated into the 26.9-cm (10.6-in)-wide base of the 2002 flat-panel iMac. The 2003 PowerBook G4, launched as the world's lightest and slimmest laptop computer, included a 43-cm (17-in) LCD screen, a backlit keyboard, the latest wireless technology, and a bevy of other features that brought Ive's vision of the comforts of home to computing on the road.

(JANET MOREDOCK)

Jackson, Alan

By 2003 many in the music industry were touting country singer and songwriter Alan Jackson as one of country music's all-time best artists. He had responded to the tragedy of Sept. 11, 2001, by writing a song that described a range of reactions to the day's horrific events. Begun in the middle of a sleepless night, "Where Were You (When the World Stopped Turning)"—with its images of a nation shocked, grieving, and struggling to cope—went on to win the 2002 Song of the Year from the Country Music Association (CMA) and the Academy of Country Music (ACM) as well as the Grammy Award for best country song.

Jackson's first hit, "Here in the Real World," co-written by Jackson with Mark Irwin, arrived in the early months of 1990 and established the singer as a traditional artist with great talent as a composer of songs that spoke directly about the virtues of rural and small-town life, the vagaries of love, and the value of the country-music traditions inherited from predecessors such as George Jones and Hank Williams. Jackson's colleague Vince Gill described his songs as "simple truths that come from his heart."

Jackson was born on Oct. 17, 1958, in Newnan, Ga., but moved to Nashville, Tenn., in 1985 to pursue music as a career. His wife, Denise, met singer Glen Campbell in an airport, and the chance encounter eventually led to a songwriting contract for Jackson with Campbell's music-publishing company. In 1989 Jackson became the first artist signed to the country division of Arista Records, and he went on to sell more than 40 million albums and score many chart-topping hits, including "Chattahoochee." The song about summer fun in the rural South stayed at the top of *Billboard's* Hot Country Singles & Tracks chart for four weeks in 1993 and was named Song of the Year by the CMA. A traditionalist in his musical approach, Jackson became a member of the Grand Ole Opry in 1991, and he acknowledged his roots in 1999 on *Under the Influence,* an album featuring his interpretations of songs by artists such as Hank Williams Jr., Merle Haggard, Charley Pride, and Gene Watson. Jackson also recorded with George Jones, George Strait, Randy Travis, and Jimmy Buffett, among others.

Jackson's many industry awards included 13 from the CMA, which named him Entertainer of the Year in 1995 and 2002. His five victories on Nov. 6, 2002, tied a CMA record, also held by Johnny Cash and Gill, for wins in a single night. His 11th album, *Drive* (2002), included the song "Drive (for Daddy Gene)," which paid tribute to Jackson's father, a mechanic who worked in the Ford plant near the Jacksons' Georgia hometown. Jackson added 2 more ACM trophies (for a total of 14) in 2003 for album of the year and video for "Drive." In August his two-disc *Greatest Hits Volume II* entered the *Billboard* pop and country charts at number one.

(JAY ORR)

Country music superstar Alan Jackson

Jackson, Peter

During 2003 Peter Jackson joined a very exclusive group, the so-called 20/20 club. For producing, directing, and writing a remake of *King Kong,* he and his team would be paid $20 million against 20% of gross receipts—a deal usually associated only with A-list movie stars. Jackson had wanted to film his interpretation of the classic story ever since he first saw the 1933 version when he was nine years old, and his tremendous critical and financial success with *The Lord of the Rings* trilogy—which both pleased devotees of the Middle Earth saga and provided quality entertainment for those unfamiliar with J.R.R. Tolkien's epic fantasy tale and in so doing grossed billions of dollars—paved the way for him to realize this dream. *King Kong* was to be filmed in 2004 and released in 2005.

Jackson was born on Oct. 31, 1961, in Pukerua Bay, North Island, N.Z. When he was eight years old, his parents bought an 8-mm movie camera, and he began making short films, using his own inventiveness to create the special effects. At 17 he began working as a photoengraver. When he had saved enough money, he bought a used 16-mm camera and, with his friends, began work on what started out to be another short film. It kept growing, however, and, with the aid of a grant from the New Zealand Film Commission, was finally completed in 1987. *Bad Taste* won acclaim at the Cannes Film Festival and went on to become a cult horror classic. Jackson followed up with *Meet the Freebles* (1989), which featured puppets and people in animal suits engaging in the seamier aspects of human behaviour, and the zombie film *Braindead* (1992; U.S. title, *Dead Alive*), which won numerous international science-fiction awards and was said by some to be the goriest film ever made. He then turned to a real-life incident for *Heavenly Creatures* (1994), about two teenage girls who kill one girl's mother. Its screenplay garnered Academy Award nominations for Jackson and Frances Walsh, his partner and the mother of his two children. The mock documentary *Forgotten Silver* (1995) and the ghost story *The Frighteners* (1996) followed.

For *The Lord of the Rings,* Jackson took the unprecedented step of shooting all three installments simultaneously, over a 15-month period in New Zealand, the location of all his movies. The first of the three, *The Fellowship of the Ring,* was released in December 2001; the second, *The Two Towers,* followed in December 2002; and the third, *The Return of the King,* opened in December 2003.

(BARBARA WHITNEY)

Jacobs, Marc

American star designer Marc Jacobs, known for his sartorial fashion interpretations of trends in contemporary art, modeling, and the rock music scene, teamed up with Japanese artist Takashi Murakami to produce the accessories for the spring–summer 2003 collection of Louis Vuitton, the French luxury-goods house for which Jacobs had served as artistic director in Paris since 1998. Together with Murakami, Jacobs produced "eye love," a collection of handbags that merged Vuitton's traditional monogrammatic canvas—its beige and brown motif that included shapes of diamonds, stars, and flowers along with the company's initials, LV—with Murakami's modern, colourful pop-art graphics. The "eye love" handbags became instant collector's items.

Meanwhile, the advertising for Jacobs's own spring–summer 2003 collection grabbed headlines. Actress Winona Ryder, who in 2002 was discovered shoplifting several clothing items—including Jacobs's designs—at a Saks Fifth Avenue department store in Beverly Hills, Calif., was his featured model. For his autumn–winter 2003 advertising campaign for Louis Vuitton, Jacobs engaged high-profile actress and musician Jennifer Lopez as his model.

Jacobs's flair for merging fashion with the worlds of entertainment and mixed media came naturally—he was the son of two William Morris talent agents. He was born on April 9, 1963, in New York City. After graduating (1984) from the Parsons School of Design, Jacobs sold a collection of hand-knit sweaters to Charivari, the chic boutique where he worked. His 1986 debut collection received wide critical acclaim, and a year later he became the youngest recipient of the Perry Ellis Award for New Fashion Talent, bestowed by the Council of Fashion Designers of America. Predating the supermodel era, Jacobs later produced a collection inspired by the individual fashion flair of his models. Though it was a critical hit, his work was not successful on the retail front. He ceased producing clothes under his own name, and in 1989 he and Robert Duffy were appointed as a team to revive the Perry Ellis fashion label. There in 1992 Jacobs produced clothing that inspired the Seattle, Wash., grunge music scene. The collection featured prominently on the pages of *Harper's Bazaar* and American *Vogue*, and *Women's Wear Daily* dubbed Jacobs the "guru of grunge." When the designs failed to sell briskly, though, his contract was terminated by Perry Ellis. In 1994, however, Jacobs and Duffy relaunched the Marc Jacobs line, and with the help of supermodel friends Naomi Campbell and Linda Evangelista, his work again gained currency. In 1998 he signed a business deal with Bernard Arnault, the chairman of Louis Vuitton Moët Hennessy. Jacobs became artistic director of Louis Vuitton, and LVMH acquired a one-third financial stake in his eponymous line. LVMH's backing enabled the designer to thrive. By 2003 the Marc Jacobs mini fashion empire included four retail boutiques in the U.S., a complete menswear and women's wear line (which both incorporated Marc, the designer's popular diffusion label), shoes, handbags, and two fragrances.

(BRONWYN COSGRAVE)

Jansons, Mariss

In February 2003 Mariss Jansons was treated to a birthday party thrown by his cohorts at the Pittsburgh (Pa.) Symphony Orchestra to celebrate his 60th birthday. The gala included performances by such luminaries as cellist Mstislav Rostropovich, pianist Emanuel Ax, and violinist Gil Shaham. While the event celebrated a personal milestone for Jansons, it also served as a tribute to the conductor who had so greatly enhanced the orchestra's reputation since 1997, when he began his tenure as music director. It was also a farewell party of sorts; Jansons had announced in 2002 that he would be leaving his Pittsburgh post following the 2003–04 season to become principal conductor of Amsterdam's Royal Concertgebouw Orchestra. Jansons also took over as music director of the Bavarian Radio Symphony Orchestra in Munich, Ger., at the start of its season in September 2003.

Jansons was born on Jan. 14, 1943, in Riga, Latvia. The son of the respected conductor Arvid Jansons, Mariss was captivated by music as a child. He studied violin, piano, and conducting in the Soviet Union at the Leningrad (now St. Petersburg) Conservatory and graduated with honours. In 1969 he went to Austria and began studies in conducting with Hans Swarowsky at the Academy of Music and Performing Arts in Vienna and with Herbert von Karajan in Salzburg. Those efforts culminated in his winning the International Herbert von Karajan Foundation Competition in Berlin in 1971.

Two years later Jansons was invited to become associate conductor of the Leningrad (now St. Petersburg) Philharmonic; he was named its principal conductor in 1985. In 1979 Jansons began a 23-year stint as music director of the Oslo Philharmonic. As he would later do in Pittsburgh, he elevated the reputation of the Norwegian orchestra via recordings and tours in the U.S., Europe, and Japan. Over the course of his career, Jansons conducted many of the world's major orchestras, and he appeared on an annual basis at the Salzburg Festival.

Usually specializing in the Central and Eastern European repertory, Jansons made especially memorable interpretations of Dvorak, Bartok, Brahms, Stravinsky, and Shostakovich. He was a frequent visitor to the radio, television, and recording studios. His recordings with major orchestras, including those from Pittsburgh, St. Petersburg, Oslo, Philadelphia, and Berlin, were well received, and his work was honoured by receipt of the Dutch Luister Award and the French Grand Prix de Disque, among others. Perhaps the greatest honour of all came in 1995, however, when, in recognition of his work with the Oslo Philharmonic, King Harald V made Jansons Commander with Star of the Royal Norwegian Order of Merit. It was that country's highest honour for anyone not of Norwegian descent.

(HARRY SUMRALL)

Johnson, Robert

American businessman Robert L. Johnson, who had spent a quarter of a century building a national identity for Black Entertainment Television (BET), was approved in January 2003 as owner of the newest expansion team of the National Basketball Association (NBA). Johnson had bested an investment group that included basketball legend Larry Bird for ownership of the NBA franchise in Charlotte, N.C. (the city's former team, the Hornets, had just moved to New Orleans). Although he became the first African American majority owner of a major sports team, the soft-spoken hard-driving Johnson regarded it as just another rung on his ladder to increased economic prosperity.

Johnson was born on April 8, 1946, in Hickory, Miss., and grew up in Freeport, Ill. He was the 9th of 10 children and the first in his family to attend college. He graduated from the University of Illinois in 1968 and, after earning a master's degree from Princeton University, moved to Washington, D.C., where he worked for the Corporation for Public Broadcasting, the Urban League, and a local congressional delegate. He began cultivating valuable political and business connections that later helped him bankroll his vision to create a black cable television company. As a lobbyist for the nascent cable industry from 1976 to 1979, he noticed that the large African American TV audience was going unrecognized and untapped. Johnson built BET from a tiny cable outlet, airing only two hours of programming a week in 1980, to a broadcasting giant that claimed an audience of more than 70 million households.

Mariss Jansons, a conductor on the move

Top: © Mark Mainz/Getty Images; above, EFE Photos

In 1991 BET became the first black-controlled company to be listed on the New York Stock Exchange. BET thrived in the 1990s, despite lawsuits from competitors and former employees, and added more cable channels, a film division, a publisher, and a Web site. Viewership expanded along with the product line, while major media companies began to invest. Throughout the decade Johnson also attempted to purchase basketball franchises in Washington, D.C., and Charlotte. After taking BET private again in 1998, Johnson and his partners sold BET Holdings to the giant media group Viacom in 2001 for some $3 billion, though he was kept on at BET as CEO. The sale made him the first African American billionaire. Johnson then formed the umbrella group RLJ Companies, which operated widely in the media, sports, gaming, real estate, and hospitality industries.

In June 2003 the NBA franchise (which would begin competition in 2004) was given the name Bobcats, befitting its owner, who was known to his friends as Bob. Johnson's purchase, estimated at $300 million, also included the Sting, the Women's National Basketball Association team in Charlotte. The city gave Johnson a warm welcome and broke ground on the construction of a new basketball stadium, while Johnson reciprocated in May with a $1 million donation to a local YMCA community centre. (TOM MICHAEL)

Jones, Norah

In pop music the surprise of the year came at the 2003 Grammy Awards when a new star, singer-pianist Norah Jones, and her first CD, *Come Away with Me*, gathered the glory, taking eight trophies including album of the year, best new artist, and song of the year ("Don't Know Why," written by her guitarist Jesse Harris). Even before Jones's Grammy triumphs, her album had reached number one on American best-seller lists and had sold six million copies worldwide. It was an exciting ride to fame for the 23-year-old Jones, who just two years earlier had been singing for small audiences in obscure New York City clubs.

Moreover, Jones was the direct opposite of the big-voiced, flamboyant divas who usually dominated pop music. Instead of loud, lavish productions, *Come Away with Me* offered a simple, intimate music, accompanied by a small combo that included unamplified guitars. Her voice was girlish and fragile, conveying personal moods from melancholy to whimsy; critics remarked on her music's "ethereal beauty." Her style fused jazz, country, and soul in disparate Hank Williams, John D. Loudermilk, and Hoagy Carmichael songs, and most of the album was composed by Jones, Harris, and her bassist, Lee Alexander. The girlish voice and delicacy were deceptive, for Jones had the maturity to master the craft of her music. When early recording sessions proved overproduced, she threw away the results and started over with a new producer.

Perhaps good music was in Norah Jones's DNA: her mother was American concert producer Sue Jones, and her father was Indian sitar virtuoso Ravi Shankar. Jones was born on March 30, 1979, in New York City. She lived with her mother and grew up in a suburb of Dallas, Texas, where her mother's collection of jazz, blues, country, and classical albums was an early inspiration for her own eclectic musical taste. Jones was a jazz piano and vocal novice at Booker T. Washington High School for Performing and Visual Arts in Dallas when she first achieved national recognition by winning three Down Beat Student Music Awards. After two years of studying jazz at North Texas State University, Jones moved to Manhattan in 1999. There she sang and played in the underground music scene, in a funk-fusion group and with her own combos, replacing jazz standards with original songs. Bruce Lundvall, president of the Blue Note label, heard just three of her warm, soft vocals on a tape before he signed her to a recording contract.

In the midst of extensive touring and television appearances, Jones also issued a DVD, *Live in New Orleans,* in 2003. She was skeptical, however, about ever again matching her Grammy feat. (JOHN LITWEILER)

Jones, Roy, Jr.

On March 1, 2003, Roy Jones, Jr., became only the second light-heavyweight boxing champion to win a heavyweight title when he won a 12-round decision over John Ruiz in Las Vegas, Nev., to capture the World Boxing Association belt. Only Michael Spinks, who had decisioned Larry Holmes to claim the International Boxing Federation (IBF) heavyweight title on Sept. 21, 1985, preceded Jones in this distinction. Jones's historic victory over Ruiz also marked the first time since Bob Fitzsimmons knocked out James J. Corbett in March 1897 that a former middleweight champion had won a heavyweight title.

Jones was born in Pensacola, Fla., on Jan. 16, 1969. He was taught to box by his father, Roy Jones, Sr., and represented the United States at the 1988 Olympics in Seoul, S.Kor., but he was the victim of a scandalous decision in the 71-kg (156-lb) gold medal match, which the judges awarded to South Korea's Park Si Hun. The decision was so bad that the International Amateur Boxing Association levied a two-year suspension against one of the judges. Jones also received the Val Barker Award as the Games' outstanding boxer.

Heavyweight Roy Jones, Jr.

Jones made his professional debut on May 6, 1989, and was quickly recognized as a unique talent—an extremely skillful boxer with exceptionally quick reflexes and the ability to put his punches together in seamless combinations. He claimed his first major title on May 22, 1993, in Washington, D.C., when he won a 12-round decision over Bernard Hopkins for the vacant IBF middleweight belt. As his career progressed, Jones gradually added weight and won titles at super middleweight and light heavyweight.

Although Jones was widely considered one of the finest boxers of his generation, for much of his career his box office appeal was not as widespread as that of other top boxers. Owing to his vast superiority over opponents, Jones's bouts were usually one-sided. He frequently coasted after establishing his dominance in a fight and seemed content to win with a decision rather that provide fans with a knockout. Jones's focus was also questioned. He raised fighting roosters on his ranch in Pensacola and played minor league basketball for the Lakeland (Fla.) Blue Ducks and the Jacksonville (Fla.) Barracudas. He released a CD called *Round One,* the first single of which entered Billboard's Hot Rap list at number two in 2002.

The Ruiz matchup was the first of Jones's cable-TV pay-per-view fights to score a major financial success. The bout was sold to approximately 525,000 homes and generated about $26.5 million in revenue, which was more than twice as much as any previous Jones fight.

Despite the interest generated by his foray into the heavyweight division, Jones dropped back down to the light-heavyweight division to face Antonio Tarver on Nov. 8, 2003, in Las Vegas. Tarver gave Jones a surprisingly tough fight, probably the most competitive of his professional career. After being awarded a majority decision, Jones said he wanted just one more fight, against former heavyweight champion Mike Tyson, before he retired.

(NIGEL COLLINS)

Kamprad, Ingvar

While the phrase "some assembly required" might fill the average consumer with dread, in 2003 Swedish businessman Ingvar Kamprad had millions of people around the world eagerly reaching for a screwdriver. As founder of the home-furnishing company IKEA Group, he created merchandise that could be packaged flat and later put together by the customer. This innovation allowed Kamprad to lower prices significantly, which, when combined with the company's attractive contemporary designs, transformed IKEA into a global phenomenon. By the early 21st century, IKEA was the world's largest furniture retailer, with stores in some 30 countries and estimated sales of more than $15 billion. In 2003 *Forbes* magazine named Kamprad one of the richest men in the world, with a net worth of some $13 billion.

Kamprad was born in 1926 in Småland province in Sweden. He displayed entrepreneurial skills as a boy and began selling matches to neighbours. In 1943, at age 17, he founded IKEA (the name was based on his initials and the first letters of the farm [Elmtaryd] and the village [Agunnaryd] where he grew up). He initially sold such items as picture frames, jewelry, and nylon stockings over the telephone; as the business grew, he started distributing catalogs. In 1948 Kamprad began selling inexpensive furniture, and the new merchandise proved to be so popular that in 1951 IKEA began to offer only home furnishings. Two years later he opened a showroom in Almhult, Swed. IKEA's low prices, however, angered competitors, and they pressured Swedish suppliers to boycott the company. Kamprad responded by having IKEA design its own merchandise and by contracting with foreign businesses for materials.

In 1956 Kamprad introduced flat furniture to IKEA's inventory, and that proved to be the breakthrough for the company. The new items decreased shipping and labour costs dramatically and allowed customers to transport the merchandise home easily. The compact size of the packaged merchandise also meant that items could be stocked at the sales location instead of being kept in a warehouse, and in 1958 the first IKEA retail outlet opened. IKEA stores followed in Norway (1963), Germany (1974), Australia (1975), France (1981), the U.S. (1985), the U.K. (1987), China (1998), and Russia (2000). The distinctive stores—each one highlighted by a vibrant blue and yellow roof and covering on average 17,280 sq m (186,000 sq ft)—typically had more than 80,000 items in stock and were extremely customer-friendly, featuring children's play areas and Swedish restaurants. In 2000 IKEA began selling merchandise on the Internet. The company was such a phenomenon that by 2003 its catalog had the world's largest annual print run, with more than 130 million copies being produced.

To show employees his appreciation for IKEA's success, in 1999 Kamprad, who was noted for his folksy manner and work ethic, held the Big Thank You Event, in which the company's profits for one day were equally divided among them. (AMY TIKKANEN)

Kibaki, Mwai

It took him three runs for the presidency, but on Dec. 30, 2002, following general elections earlier in the month, Mwai Kibaki finally became leader of Kenya. The victory may have seemed a hollow one insofar as the sitting president, Daniel arap Moi, was prohibited by law from running for the office again. Kibaki, however, not only defeated Moi's chosen successor, Uhuru Kenyatta (a son of Jomo Kenyatta, Kenya's first president), but also routed the ruling African National Union of Kenya (KANU) party, which had dominated Kenya since the country became independent in 1963.

Ethnically a member of the Kikuyu people, Emilio Mwai Kibaki was born on Nov. 15, 1931, in the village of Gatuyaini in central Kenya. After high school he attended Makerere University in Uganda and the London School of Economics. Kibaki was active in the Kenyan struggle for independence from Great Britain, and, after that was attained, he held government positions as an MP, a minister, and a vice president. Increasingly, however, he found himself at odds with Moi. In the early 1990s, when political parties became legal, Kibaki founded the Democratic Party. He ran for president in 1992 and finished third. He ran again in 1997 and again lost to Moi, but this time he came in second. When another constitutional change made it impossible for Moi to run for the presidency yet again, Kibaki decided to participate in the election process one more time. For this race he created the National Rainbow Coalition (NARC), a party that included many experienced politicians, all united in their opposition to Moi, and this strategy of a strong, unified opposition was finally successful in unseating KANU. A few weeks before the election, however, Kibaki was involved in a car accident and suffered serious injuries. Although he was confined to a wheelchair, he continued his campaign.

As president, Kibaki pledged to focus on eliminating government corruption, although his sincerity on this issue was tested early in 2003 when legislators were permitted to vote themselves large raises. He supported constitutional reforms, including provisions that would set a maximum age for presidential candidates (Kibaki himself would be too old to run again). The president threw his support behind AIDS testing, and he even offered to take an AIDS test himself in public.

As he completed his first year as president, Kibaki still faced questions about his health, and reports were circulating about dissension within the NARC. The people of Kenya were growing tired of empty political promises, and at year's end it still remained to be seen what substance Kibaki could bring to his tenure as president. (PAMELA SMITH-IROWA)

Kirchner, Néstor

When, on May 25, 2003, Néstor Carlos Kirchner was sworn in as Argentina's sixth president in 18 months, it was an outcome that just six months earlier had seemed the least predictable of the presidential election of 2003. On April 27, in the first round of the election, Kirchner, one of three Partido Justicialista (PJ)/Peronist candidates and a little-known governor of remote Santa Cruz province in Patagonia, finished second with only 22.2% of the vote, trailing former president Carlos Menem, who won 24.4%. Shortly before the runoff scheduled for May 18, Menem withdrew his candidacy, and Kirchner became president-elect by default.

Kirchner was born on Feb. 25, 1950, in Río Gallegos, capital of Santa Cruz. In 1975 he married a fellow law student, Cristina Fernández, who went on to become his law partner and an equally powerful political actor in Santa Cruz (she was elected to the national Senate in 2001). In 1976 Kirchner graduated with a law degree from the National University of La Plata, where he was a member of the Peronist Youth organization.

Following graduation and the overthrow of the Peronist government, Kirchner and his wife returned to Santa Cruz. In 1987 Kirchner was elected mayor of Río Gallegos. In 1991 he became governor of Santa Cruz, and, after amending the provincial constitution to eliminate the article prohibiting his immediate reelection, he was reelected in 1995 and, following a second constitutional reform, in 1999.

Argentina's Néstor Kirchner (and an image of Juan Perón)

The considerable oil reserves in Santa Cruz, combined with the province's small population (197,191 as of 2001), allowed Kirchner a measure of independence from the national government, and he was frequently critical of the administration of President Menem (1989–99).

Initially, Kirchner's presidential candidacy was not taken very seriously by most observers. A skillful media campaign and the strong support provided by outgoing Pres. Eduardo Duhalde, however, helped Kirchner steadily rise in the opinion polls.

In Kirchner's first three months in office, he forced top military officials to retire, annulled legislation prohibiting the extradition of military officers accused of human rights abuses (dating to the 1976–83 military dictatorship), and engineered the resignation of the chief justice of the country's Supreme Court. These actions helped him achieve a 75% approval rating. It remained to be seen, however, if Kirchner would be able to successfully navigate between the demands of the International Monetary Fund on issues including Argentina's public-sector debt (much of which was in default) and banking system reform, and utility rate hikes and those of a citizenry still suffering from the worst economic crisis in Argentine history. (MARK P. JONES)

Kitano, Takeshi

By 2003 actor-writer-director Takeshi Kitano had established himself as one of Japan's most prominent media personalities. He appeared weekly in up to eight prime-time shows on Japanese television and was also active as a newspaper columnist and as a stand-up comedian. In addition, he had published numerous novels and collections of short stories and poetry and had even made successful forays into music and art, releasing a number of CDs and holding several exhibitions of his paintings and cartoons. It was as a film director, however, that Kitano had garnered international attention. His crime drama *Hana-bi,* winner of the Golden Lion award for best picture at the Venice Film Festival in 1997, was hailed by many critics as a masterpiece. In 2003 another Kitano film, *Zatoichi,* won the Open 2003 special award at Venice. Also released to Western audiences during the year were Kitano's *Dolls* (2002) and *Battle Royale II* (2003).

Kitano was born into a working-class family on Jan. 18, 1947, in Tokyo. He abandoned plans to become an engineer when he dropped out of college to enter show business in 1972. With friend Kyoshi Kaneko, he formed a popular comedy team called the Two Beats (later Kitano would frequently act under the name Beat Takeshi). Performing first in nightclubs, the duo soon began to appear on Japanese television and quickly attracted a national following with their irreverent, sometimes off-colour routines. In the late 1970s Kitano embarked on a solo acting career. He starred in a television series called *Super Superman* and several movies. In 1983 he appeared alongside David Bowie and Tom Conti in his first English-language film, *Merry Christmas, Mr. Lawrence.*

Kitano made his directorial debut in 1989 with *Violent Cop,* in which he also played the title role. The film, about a Tokyo detective trying to crack a *yakuza* ("gangster")-run drug ring, drew comparisons to Clint Eastwood's *Dirty Harry* and was the first in a series of Kitano-directed crime epics that included *Boiling Point* (1990) and *Sonatine* (1993). In 1994 Kitano nearly lost his life in a motorcycle accident, after which he was hospitalized for six weeks and underwent months of physical therapy. He rebounded in a big way with *Hana-bi,* another tale of policemen and *yakuza;* the film earned raves for its deft blend of comic and tragic elements and for its innovative use of flashbacks and flash forwards. Aside from winning Venice's Golden Lion, *Hana-bi* was also selected the best non-European film by the European Film Academy in 1997.

In 2000 Kitano directed *Brother,* his first film with an English-speaking cast, and *Battle Royale,* a futuristic thriller that stirred controversy in Japan with its tale of juvenile delinquents forced by authorities into deadly combat on a remote island. In *Zatoichi,* Kitano broke new ground with his first period piece, in which he played a legendary blind samurai. (SHERMAN HOLLAR)

Lagasse, Emeril

By 2003 Emeril Lagasse was perhaps the most famous chef in the United States. His name was associated with nine restaurants in five U.S. cities, seven cookbooks that had sold more than two million copies, two daily cable television shows, and his own lines of food and cooking merchandise. Lagasse's skills in the kitchen and his engaging, boisterous personality were both instrumental in his success in building a business empire. Loyal viewers of his shows became familiar with his shouts of "Bam!" and "Kick it up a notch!" as he wowed them with his latest recipes.

Chef Emeril kicks it up a notch.

Lagasse was born on Oct. 15, 1959, in Fall River, Mass., where by the age of seven he had begun to experiment in the kitchen, begging his mother to teach him how to make vegetable soup. Lagasse made several attempts before he got the soup right, and he declared that even in those first lessons, his mother taught him to cook with passion and patience. By his own admission, Lagasse was "a weird kid" because of his fascination with food. During his childhood he also excelled at music, playing percussion in a youth orchestra. When the time came to attend college, he turned down a full scholarship at the New England Conservatory of Music so that he could study cooking. He graduated from Johnson & Wales University, Providence, R.I., with a degree in culinary arts in 1978.

Following further studies in France and a series of cooking jobs in New York City, Boston, and Philadelphia, Lagasse landed in New Orleans. There he succeeded Paul Prudhomme as executive chef at Commander's Palace in 1981. Nine years later Lagasse opened his first establishment, Emeril's Restaurant, in New Orleans, and two years after that he opened a second one, Nola Restaurant, in the city's French Quarter. In 1993 he published his first cookbook, the best-selling *Emeril's New New Orleans Cooking.* In 1993 Lagasse's star really began to rise when he became a cable television personality, joining the Food Network. He hosted two programs, *Emeril Live,* which won a Cable Ace award in 1997, and *The Essence of Emeril,* which also proved to be extremely popular. In addition, he made regular appearances on ABC's *Good Morning America* and starred in a short-lived 2001 NBC sitcom, *Emeril.*

Lagasse and his restaurants received a number of awards. The James Beard Foundation named him Best Southeast Regional Chef in 1991. *Esquire* magazine and other publications heaped awards on his restaurants. He attributed his success to the fact that he made everything from scratch, including andouille, ham, and bacon from his own hogs. "This is how you do it," he told *People* magazine with characteristic forthrightness. "We're not building a rocket ship here. We're making chicken stock!" (ANTHONY G. CRAINE)

Lee Jong Wook

In January 2003, South Korean epidemiologist and public-health expert Lee Jong Wook was nominated as the next director general of the World Health Organization (WHO). Although the American-trained Lee had worked for the United Nations agency for nearly 20 years, he was not widely known in international circles, and the vote by WHO's 32-member executive board was close. Lee was chosen by a 17–15 margin over Peter Piot, the Belgian head of the UN's AIDS program, after several other prominent candidates—including Mozambican Prime Minister Pascoal Mocumbi—had been eliminated in a preliminary round of voting. After being formally approved by the WHO General Assembly in May, Lee took office and began a five-year term on July 21.

Lee was born on April 12, 1945, in Seoul. He earned an M.D. degree from Seoul National University's College of Medicine and a master's degree in epidemiology and public health from the University of Hawaii School of Public Health, where he focused on the treatment of leprosy. From 1981 to 1983 he worked as a medical officer at the LBJ Tropical Medical Center in American Samoa. Lee then joined WHO as leader of a leprosy-control team for the South Pacific. From 1987 to 1990 he served as a regional adviser for chronic disease, and in 1990 he was named director of WHO's Disease Prevention and Control office in Manila.

In 1994 Lee moved to WHO's headquarters in Geneva to direct the organization's global program for vaccines and immunizations. In this post he spearheaded the agency's efforts to combat polio and tuberculosis. In 1998 Lee became a senior policy adviser to the WHO director general. From 2000 he was the director of the agency's Stop TB program, an antituberculosis campaign that involved more than 250 international partners, including governments, academic institutions, nongovernmental organizations, and other UN agencies.

Before his election as director general, Lee had outlined his plans for WHO should he be awarded the job. He identified "poverty and AIDS, conflict and disasters, inequitable distribution of critical resources like food and safe drinking water, and environmental degradation" as the most serious current threats to public health and pledged to devote more resources to those countries in which health care systems were facing collapse. In particular, he wanted to ensure that the most basic services and drugs were available to poor communities. Organizationally, Lee called for decentralizing WHO in order to improve its effectiveness and said that by 2005 he would like to see 75% of its resources and staff based in country and regional offices rather than in Geneva. (SHERMAN HOLLAR)

Libeskind, Daniel

In February 2003 architect Daniel Libeskind triumphed over six other prominent contestants to win one of the most prestigious design competitions ever held, that for the 6.5-ha (16-ac) former site of New York City's World Trade Center. His 70-story building, topped with a 541-m (1,776-ft) spire, would become the world's tallest building. A notable feature of the Libeskind design was a sunken memorial to those who died in the Sept. 11, 2001, terrorist attacks. (*See* ARCHITECTURE: *Sidebar.*)

Libeskind was born in Lodz, Pol., on May 12, 1946, to parents who had survived the Holocaust. The family immigrated to Israel in 1957 and then to New York City in 1959. During his early teenage years, Libeskind showed his greatest interest in music, winning a scholarship to study in Israel. He soon gained recognition as a virtuoso pianist and played professionally at Carnegie Hall in New York City. At the age of 16, however, he turned his back on that career, and he later enrolled at Cooper Union for the Advancement of Science and Art in New York City, where he received an undergraduate degree in architecture in 1970. He gained an M.A. degree (1972) in the history and theory of architecture from the University of Essex, Colchester, Eng.

Libeskind began his professional career in 1971 at the Institute for Architecture and Urban Studies in New York City. In 1972 he moved to Toronto to work for Irving Grossman Associates, and from 1973 to 1975 he served as assistant professor of architecture at the University of Kentucky. He returned to Canada in 1977 as an associate professor of architecture at the University of Toronto. The next year he was appointed head of the School of Architecture and architect in residence at Cranbrook Academy of Art in Bloomfield Hills, Mich., where he remained until 1985. He then moved to Italy, where he became director of *Architecture Intermundium* in Milan and made models and drawings that he exhibited at the 1985 Venice Biennale.

AP/Wide World Photos

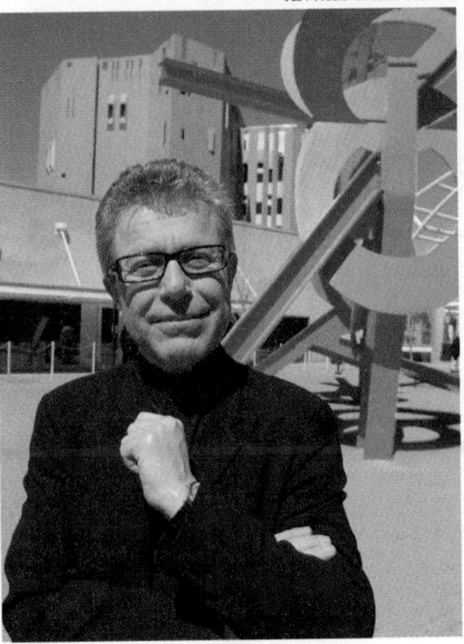

Architect Daniel Libeskind designed an expansion of the Denver Art Museum.

Libeskind achieved his first major success in 1989, when he won the competition to design Berlin's Jewish Museum. He moved to Berlin the next year and established an architectural office; by 2003 he was employing some 50 architects there. His first completed building, in 1998, was a museum in Osnabrück, Ger., dedicated to Jewish artist Felix Nussbaum, but it was the Jewish Museum, completed in 1999, that won him international renown. Libeskind followed this with the Imperial War Museum North in Manchester, Eng., completed in 2002. Constructed of steel, concrete, and asphalt, it consists of three forms derived from shattering a globe, symbolizing conflict on land, in the air, and on water.

Besides the World Trade Center project, Libeskind in 2003 was involved in designs for museums in Denver, Colo., Toronto, and London; for a large shopping centre in Switzerland; and for sets for Richard Wagner's "Ring" cycle at the Royal Opera House at Covent Garden in London. (DAVID R. CALHOUN)

Lomborg, Bjørn

A long-running environmental controversy reached fever pitch in January 2003 when the Danish Committee on Scientific Dishonesty ruled that a book challenging a number of widely held opinions was "clearly contrary to the standards of good scientific practice." The book was *The Skeptical Environmentalist* by Bjørn Lomborg, an associate professor in the department of political science at the University of Århus, Den. First published in 1998 as *Verdens sande tilstand,* the book became a best-seller in 2001 after Cambridge University Press published a revised and updated English translation.

It all began when Lomborg, a committed Greenpeace environmentalist, read a magazine interview with Julian Simon, an economist renowned for his acerbic criticisms of environmentalism. Though Lomborg and his students sought to demolish Simon's analysis, they found that much of it was accurate. A professional statistician, Lomborg then embarked on an assessment of the proposition that the world is heading for ecological catastrophe. He called the oft-recited details of this supposed deterioration "the litany" and systematically demolished them in a book of more than 500 pages with 2,930 notes and references and a 71-page bibliography. The book was subjected to the standard peer-review procedure.

Lomborg maintained that although the world faces many environmental problems, their severity is often exaggerated and the proposed remedies are inappropriate and often costly. He suggested that the money might be better invested in alleviating Third World poverty. As people became more prosperous, he wrote, they would be able to afford the technologies that would lead to environmental improvement.

The Skeptical Environmentalist received a savage review in the journal *Nature,* and in November 2001 Lomborg learned that *Scientific American* planned to publish a feature on the book in January 2002. He asked the editor of the latter to allow him a reply in the same issue, but it was to no avail. He was finally allowed a small amount of space in the May issue to rebut attacks written by four outspoken environmentalists, two of whom he had criticized in his book. His full rebuttal appeared only on his own Web site, however.

Four of his environmentalist opponents (two of the four who had contributed to the negative review in the *Scientific American*) referred the book to the Danish Committee on Scientific Dishonesty, and the committee's judgment was based primarily on the *Scientific American* articles. In April 2003 a Netherlands-based academic institution, Heidelberg Appeal the Netherlands, examined the judgment. It found that there were 27 accusations against Lomborg, of which only two minor ones might be justified. Meanwhile, Lomborg had lodged a formal complaint against the Danish Committee, and in December the Danish government overturned the committee's ruling.

Lomborg was born on Jan. 6, 1965, in Copenhagen and grew up mainly in Ålborg. The first member of his immediate family to receive a university education, he earned a Ph.D. in 1994 from the University of Copenhagen. In February 2002 he was appointed director of Denmark's Environmental Assessment Institute, which seeks to obtain the greatest environmental benefit for money spent on environmental measures. He planned to return to academic life before the end of his five-year term. (MICHAEL ALLABY)

Maher, Bill

The title of *Politically Incorrect,* the often controversial television talk show that nightly

bottom: Reprinted with the permission of Cambridge University Press

featured four outspoken guests from the world of entertainment, arts and letters, and politics, was never more appropriate than when its host, comedian Bill Maher, implied that the terrorists who had attacked the World Trade Center on Sept. 11, 2001, were braver than U.S. forces fighting in Afghanistan. Those remarks not only prompted condemnation from the White House but led ABC to cancel Maher's show, which had run on the network for more than five years after having premiered on cable television's Comedy Central. Although Maher initially tried to explain his comments, he was anything but contrite in his opposition to the war in Iraq when he returned to television with *Real Time with Bill Maher,* which first aired on Home Box Office (HBO) in February 2003. He remained steadfast in his views when he took to the Broadway stage in May with his one-man show, *Victory Begins at Home.*

Maher was born on Jan. 20, 1956, in New York City but grew up in River Vale, N.J. As a boy he idolized *The Tonight Show* host Johnny Carson but hid his aspiration to be a comedian until his junior year studying English at Cornell University, Ithaca, N.Y., when he first tried his stand-up act in a New York City comedy club. After graduating (B.A., 1978), Maher became a regular in clubs throughout the country. He also made many appearances on *The Tonight Show* and came to the attention of Steve Allen, who cast him as his sidekick on the cable series *Steve Allen's Music Room.* Beginning in 1983, Maher tried acting, appearing in several forgettable films. He also was a regular on a short-lived sitcom, *Sara,* and briefly hosted *The Midnight Hour,* a talk show on CBS. It was his cohosting of *Indecision '92,* Comedy Central's irreverent coverage of the presidential election, however, that jump-started Maher's career and led to the debut of *Politically Incorrect* in 1993.

In playing ringmaster to *PI*'s eclectic selection of notables, Maher deftly prodded his guests into heated and hilarious discussions of current events and punctuated the talks with his acerbic quips. On HBO's *Real Time,* he limited his guests to a smaller "A list," which included author Ann Coulter, journalist Christopher Hitchens, humanities professor Michael Eric Dyson, politician and author Ariana Huffington, and actor Alec Baldwin. Although less likely to satirize the left than the right, Maher was more libertarian than liberal. Above all, he was defiantly out of the mainstream. As an iconoclastic social critic he might not be the H.L. Mencken of his generation, but he might be the Mort Sahl.

(JEFF WALLENFELDT)

Mariza

In 2003 music lovers worldwide continued to awaken to the joy of melancholy through the powerful yet nuanced artistry of Portuguese fado singer Mariza. "Fado is an emotional kind of music full of passion, sorrow, jealousy, grief, and often satire," the Mozambican-born vocalist explained. Mariza appeared on the world music scene in 2002 with the international release of her critically acclaimed debut album, *Fado em mim,* which had been released in Portugal in 2001. Because of its success she was soon dubbed "the new voice of fado," and avid fans of the music even began comparing her talent to that of the legendary *fadista* Amália Rodrigues.

Mariza, a fadista *for the 21st century*

Mariza Nunes was born in Mozambique c. 1974 to parents of Portuguese, Spanish, German, African, and Indian heritage. Her family moved to Lisbon when she was three years old. There her parents ran a restaurant located in the neighbourhood where fado was said to have been born. Mariza began singing along with fado performers at the family restaurant even before she learned how to read. When she was 15, her adolescent interest in more "modern" music genres led her to explore rock, blues, jazz, and bossa nova, but by adulthood Mariza had returned to her first love. She was discovered by musician and producer Jorge Fernando when he heard her sing a fado one evening, and he persuaded her to record an entire album of fados. She appeared on Portuguese television as part of a special program in honour of Rodrigues, who died in 1999. The Portuguese public was thrilled with Mariza's performance, and in 2000 she was presented with the Voice of Fado award by Central FM (the national radio station of Portugal). Later the popular Portuguese television program *Hermansic* asked her to perform for pop star Sting in order to introduce him to fado music.

In early 2003 Mariza was the recipient of the BBC's Radio 3 world music award for best European act. Her second album, *Fado curvo,* was released in May, and she continued to tour throughout the year, appearing in major venues all over Europe and beyond.

(SHANDA SILER)

Martin, Paul

On Nov. 14, 2003, Paul Martin was chosen at the Toronto convention of the governing Liberal Party to succeed Jean Chrétien as prime minister of Canada. Martin, who headed a multinational shipping company and had also served as one of the most successful ministers of finance (1993–2002) in Canada's history, took office on December 12.

Paul Joseph Martin, Jr., was born on Aug. 28, 1938, in Windsor, Ont. His father, who had served as a minister in four Liberal governments and was a principal architect of Canada's post-World War II social policy, was an influential model for his son. Paul, Jr., attended the University of Toronto and was called to the bar in 1966. Martin did not practice law, however, and instead joined Canada Steamship Lines, a Montreal firm; he built the domestic-freight carrier into a strong multinational company and went on to purchase it.

Though he had been on the fringe of the Liberal Party, in 1988 Martin won election to the House of Commons from a Montreal riding, and two years later he made a bold bid for the leadership of the party. He lost to Chrétien. In the contest between the two men lay the roots of the tension that had bedeviled their relationship as cabinet colleagues. When the Liberals won the 1993 election, Chrétien appointed Martin minister of finance. Martin proved outstandingly successful; he wiped out a Can$42 billion (about $U.S. 32 billion) deficit, achieved five consecutive budget surpluses, and gave Canadians their largest tax cuts in history. He also won respect as an international financier, concentrating on relieving the financial crises of the Third World's emerging market economies.

Though Martin had emerged as the mainstay of the Chrétien government, he was dropped from the cabinet in 2002 when he refused to abandon leadership ambitions. He built up strong support within the party, however, and won over constituency organizations from coast to coast. As other contenders withdrew from the leadership race, the convention became more like a coronation than a contest.

Martin's goals as prime minister appeared to contradict those he had espoused as finance minister. On the one hand he spoke glowingly of the need for progressive social policies, but on the other hand he had reduced spending on health care. Though he urged that Canada play a larger role in the international community, his fiscal restraint had weakened Canada's armed forces. He also believed that Canada should act as a responsible neighbour of the United States and be prepared to cooperate in strengthening border security. What was certain was that his approach, derived from both parliamentary experience and boardroom tactics, would be prudent and pragmatic yet touched by an inherited idealism.

(DAVID M.L. FARR)

Moore, Michael

In his acceptance speech for the 2003 Academy Award for best documentary for *Bowling for Columbine* (2002), filmmaker and author Michael Moore expressed his opposition to war in Iraq and called U.S. Pres. George W. Bush "a fictitious president," prompting a mixed chorus of boos and applause. This polarized reaction to Moore, a muckraker and

© Reuters NewMedia Inc./Corbis

Media megastar Michael Moore, with Oscar

satirist, was not new. At a time when most Americans were supporting the president, Moore reached the top of the nonfiction best-seller list with *Stupid White Men* (2002), which assailed the legitimacy, methods, and motives of the Bush administration. He had similar success with *Dude, Where's My Country?* (2003), a call for "regime change" in the U.S.

Moore was born on April 23, 1954, in Flint, Mich. Following his graduation from high school, he began his populist assault on what he viewed as the injustices of American capitalism as an 18-year-old member of the Flint school board. In 1976, after having attended but not graduated from the University of Michigan at Flint, Moore started a radical weekly newspaper, the *Flint* (later *Michigan*) *Voice,* which he edited for 10 years. He also hosted a weekly radio show. In 1986 he became the editor of the San Francisco-based magazine *Mother Jones,* but he was fired after only a few months (he later accepted an out-of-court settlement for a wrongful-dismissal suit). Returning to Flint, he became newly aware of the deteriorating economic and social conditions in his hometown as a result of the closing of two General Motors (GM) factories and the company's longer-term policy of downsizing. After a quick tutorial in documentary filmmaking, Moore began chronicling the effects of unemployment on Flint, financing filming by selling his house and running a weekly bingo game. At the centre of the film were Moore's "in-your-face" efforts to gain an audience with GM's chairman, Roger Smith. Mixing humour and poignancy with indignation, *Roger & Me* (1989) was a hit with critics and at the box office and made Moore a multimillionaire.

Moving to New York City, Moore established Dog Eat Dog Films and created an organization to finance social-action groups and other filmmakers. Turning to television, Moore made three critically acclaimed but short-lived series that featured his trademark guerrilla attacks on corporate America: *TV Nation* for NBC and then Fox and *The Awful Truth* for the Bravo cable network. His lampooning of privilege and prejudice continued with another best-selling book, *Downsize This* (1996), and the documentary film *The Big One* (1997). *Bowling for Columbine* blamed gun-related violence in the United States not just on the availability of guns but on a culture of fear. Not only did the film win an Oscar and surpass *Roger & Me* as the highest-grossing documentary ever, but the International Documentary Association named it the best documentary of all time. Some of Moore's critics claimed that his research was shoddy and that he framed events to suit his political agenda, but few could dispute the fact that his work had a ring of truth for millions of readers and filmgoers.

(JEFF WALLENFELDT)

Muldoon, Paul

The U.S.-based poet from Northern Ireland Paul Muldoon—whose wit and confidence effervesced on the page, leaving readers at once amused and unsettled—won several awards and notices in 2003. His 2002 collection, *Moy Sand and Gravel,* reaped both the Pulitzer Prize for poetry and the Canadian Griffin Poetry Prize for an international writer. He was also presented with a Concert Music Award from the American Society of Composers, Authors and Publishers for the libretto of a one-act opera, *Vera of Las Vegas.* Though already at the apex of modern poetry, Muldoon displayed increasing vigour and virtuosity in his latest work. In the deft, succinct poems of *Moy Sand and Gravel,* American and Irish references cavorted, displaying pithiness with underlying seriousness. The *Irish Times* asked: "Who else can write love poems which echo [Constantine] Cavafy and Bob Dylan with equal authority?"

Muldoon was born June 20, 1951, in County Armagh, N.Ire., the son of a labourer and gardener. He began writing poems in his teenage years and went on to study at Queen's University, Belfast, where he was tutored by Nobel laureate Seamus Heaney. "Gradually I began to learn," Muldoon commented, "particularly from writers . . . who were writing about things I knew about." At the age of 19, he completed his first collection of poems, *Knowing My Place* (1971). After graduating, he worked for BBC Belfast as a radio and television producer until his immigration to the United States in 1987, following the death of his father. He and his family settled in Princeton, N.J., where he became director of Princeton University's creative-writing program; he also served as honorary professor of poetry at the University of Oxford.

Muldoon's many collections included *Meeting the British* (1987), *Madoc: A Mystery* (1990), *The Annals of Chile* (1994), for which he won the T.S. Eliot Award, *Hay* (1998), and *Poems 1968–1998* (2001). He also wrote libretti for operas and edited anthologies, and his work garnered a Guggenheim fellowship in 1990 and the Sir Geoffrey Faber Memorial Award in 1991. His oeuvre covered intensely personal and political terrain—from his wife's miscarriage to the Northern Irish conflict. He also explored elaborate imaginary encounters between historical figures, including one between Lord Byron and Thomas Jefferson, and tested himself with tight forms, such as haiku, sestinas, and sonnets. Muldoon suggested that he wrote "to sound very off-the-cuff," aiming for "clear, translucent surfaces," which, on closer inspection, held "other things happening under the surface."

(SIOBHAN DOWD)

Muralitharan, Muttiah

In May 2003 Sri Lankan spin bowler Muttiah Muralitharan became the third cricketer in history to take 450 Test wickets, placing him behind Courtney Walsh of the West Indies (with 519) and Australia's Shane Warne (with 491). His strike rate of a wicket every 60.2 balls was also a match for Warne's rate of 60.8, though his diffident, quiet, and polite manner was far removed from the flamboyance of the Australian. At the age of 31, Murali (as he was widely known) looked set to become the leading wicket taker of all time, but appreciation of his exceptional talent was tempered by concern about the legitimacy of his bowling action. To the naked eye, Murali appeared not to bowl the ball but rather to flick it with a bent arm and flexible wrist. According to the rules of cricket, if his arm was bent and then straightened at the point of delivery, the ball would be deemed a throw, but Murali's arm remained bent throughout the action. Exhaustive studies by the International Cricket Council (ICC) of both his action and the physiology of his right arm showed that the bend was natural and therefore, under Law 24, not illegal. Like his three brothers, Murali had a deformity that stopped his arm from straightening fully. "I know I am not a cheat," said the Sri Lankan, but his protest did not stop the whispers.

Murali was born on April 17, 1972, in Kandy, Sri Lanka. He attended St. Anthony's College and began bowling off-spin on the advice of his coach, Sunil Fernando. In his first school year as a spinner, he took 127 wickets. He made his Test debut against Australia at the age of 20, taking two wickets in successive balls. When England toured the following year, many players were distinctly unhappy about the way the young Sri Lankan off-spinner bowled, and batsmen found his spin difficult to read. He was also, like the more orthodox leg-spinner Warne, supremely accurate.

In 1995 Murali was finally called for "chucking" seven times in one day by Darrell Hair and again in a one-day international match by Ross Emerson and Tony McQuillan, all Australian umpires. Murali briefly thought about quitting cricket, but he fought back and, having been cleared by the ICC, resumed his career. He was not called again for throwing until Emerson was umpiring again in Australia four years later. By then, however, the peculiarities of Murali's action had been accepted within the game. At the Oval in 1998, Murali took 16 wickets against England, including 9 for 65 in the second innings. It was a virtuoso performance, matched only by his 9 for 51 against Zimbabwe on his home ground in Kandy three years later. In May 2003, in the second Test of the series against New Zealand, he took his 37th five-wicket haul, beating the record set by former New Zealand star Sir Richard Hadlee.

(ANDREW LONGMORE)

Niyazov, Saparmurad

By 2003 there were not many countries in the world that could be called the personal fiefdom of a political leader, but Turkmenistan was such a place. This Central Asian land, a former republic of the Soviet Union and an important producer of natural gas, was clenched in the grip of its president, Saparmurad Niyazov.

Niyazov was born in the village of Kipchak near Ashgabat on Feb. 19, 1940. His father, a rural schoolteacher, was killed while serving in the Red Army in World War II. His mother and two brothers died in the earthquake that devastated the Ashgabat region in October 1948, and Niyazov grew up in an orphanage. In 1967 he graduated from the Leningrad Polytechnic Institute as an engineer and returned to Turkmenistan to work at the Bezmein power plant near Ashgabat, but he soon went to work full-time for the Communist Party. In 1980 he was appointed to head the Ashgabat City Party Committee. Five years later Mikhail Gorbachev chose him to head the Turkmen republican Communist Party and carry out a cleanup campaign against corruption and mismanagement. In January 1990 Niyazov was elected chairman of the republican Supreme Soviet. When the post of executive president was created in October 1990, Niyazov received 98.3% of the vote.

In the wake of the August 1991 Moscow coup, Turkmenistan voted to go independent, with Niyazov at the helm. In 1993 he adopted the name "Turkmenbashi" ("head of the Turkmen") to stress his role as the creator of a new nation. He also launched a pervasive personality cult. In January 1994 he became the first head of state in the former Soviet republics to have his term in office extended by referendum, and in December 1999 the rubber-stamp People's Assembly gave him the right to remain in office as long as he wanted.

In the years since independence, Niyazov had gradually accumulated the power to make almost all decisions in the country; his decrees had the force of law. He was intolerant of opposition in any form; ministers who disagree with his decisions were routinely fired, and in January 2003 he decreed that anyone questioning his policies was a traitor. At the beginning of 2002, he decapitated the National Security Committee, which was the mainstay of his power, and he used an alleged coup attempt in November 2002 as justification for crushing all real or imagined domestic opposition.

Niyazov was genuinely popular with officials and many citizens, at least until he began massive reductions in the health and educational systems in 2001 and official misrepresentations about living conditions became evident. Niyazov's intention to create a national self-consciousness to unite the Turkmen tribes resulted in the establishment of a national ideology, which was expressed in his moral guide for the Turkmen people, the *Ruhnama,* which became the basis of education at all levels. (BESS BROWN)

Paksas, Rolandas

The success of Rolandas Paksas, the leader of the new populist Liberal Democratic Party, in winning the presidency of Lithuania in the second round of elections on Jan. 5, 2003, came as a surprise to many. All the major parties had backed the incumbent, the American-Lithuanian Valdas Adamkus, who symbolized the unity and the stability of the country and campaigned on his success in gaining Lithuania's integration into NATO and the European Union. Paksas, on the other hand, promised radical changes and a rise in living standards, particularly for less-fortunate people, and he appealed aggressively to younger voters, winning 54.7% of votes in a comparatively low 52.6% turnout. Still, he found himself in deep trouble at year's end.

Paksas was born on June 10, 1956, in Telsiai, northwestern Lithuania. His father was a railway clerk and later worked in the wholesale-grain trade. His mother's family was deported to Siberia but escaped Soviet concentration camps, and she worked as a nurse. Paksas graduated from Vilnius Gediminas Technical University as a civil engineer in 1979 and from the Leningrad (now St. Petersburg) Academy of Civil Aviation as an engineer-pilot in 1984. He worked as a pilot instructor and headed a flying club in Vilnius. In 1992 he founded the Restako construction company.

Paksas joined the conservative Homeland Union and won a seat in the Vilnius city council in 1997. He was elected mayor of the capital two years later and, after the resignation of Prime Minister Gediminas Vagnorius in 1999, succeeded him in office. Paksas resigned a scant five and a half months later, however, after an emotional address in which he declined to support a proposal to invite American investment in Mazeikiu Nafta, Lithuania's giant oil company. Suddenly persona non grata to the conservatives, Paksas joined a small liberal party. He worked as an adviser to President Adamkus, was reelected mayor of Vilnius, and won a seat in the Seimas (parliament). From October 2000 to June 2001 he served a second time as prime minister, but after the split of the coalition of Liberals and Social-Liberals, he resigned, remaining a member of the Parliamentary Economic Committee. Paksas founded the Liberal Democratic Party in March 2002 and under its banner became president on Feb. 26, 2003.

Paksas's short political career had been characterized by flexibility. Although he began as a communist, he became prominent in conservative circles and later emerged as a leader of the Liberals and the Liberal-Democrats. He was determined and enthusiastic on the stump, and he seemed to enjoy better relations with Russia than had his predecessors. On the other hand, his presidency was marred by allegations that he had ties with organized crime. At the end of 2003, there were calls for his impeachment after Lithuania's highest court ruled that Paksas had violated the country's constitution. (DARIUS FURMONAVIČIUS)

Papadopoulos, Tassos

On Feb. 16, 2003, with a convincing 51.5% of the vote, Tassos Papadopoulos triumphed over Glafcos Clerides, president of Cyprus for the preceding 10 years, and eight other candidates to become the island nation's fifth president. Papadopoulos had a reputation as a constitutional expert, and his skill would soon be put to the test. The elections were held at a crossroads in Cyprus history, when Greek Cyprus was looking forward to joining the European Union (EU) in May 2004 and the status of Turkish Cyprus after that date was anything but finally resolved. Papadopoulos had no honeymoon period for getting settled in the job.

Papadopoulos was born in the Cypriot capital, Lefkosia (Nicosia), on Jan. 7, 1934. He trained in law at London University's King's College and Gray's Inn and returned home to practice law. He was also drawn to politics and participated in the island's political life even before independence. A member of EOKA, the anti-British resistance group during the last years of colonial rule, Papadopoulos took part in the negotiations leading to independence in 1960. Afterward, he became minister of the interior—the youngest member of the cabinet—and he remained prominent in the island's politics for four decades. For years he was a political ally of Clerides, but he broke with him in the mid-1970s.

Papadopoulos ran for office in 2003 as leader of the moderate-right Democratic Party (DIKO). Although his EOKA credentials tended to identify him with the right, he was elected with support of the Communist and Social Democrat parties. He billed his campaign as a "ticket of change," and characterized the Clerides administration as being "in tatters." Clerides, he said, had given too much away in the UN-sponsored unification talks and had allowed domestic issues to drift while he concentrated on unifying the Greek and Turkish sectors and gaining EU membership.

As president Papadopoulos had perception problems to overcome. He was seen by some as being anti-Turkish, and allegations circulated that his law firm had assisted Serbia in circumventing the UN embargo in the 1990s. Turkish Cypriot Pres. Rauf Denktash, who had enjoyed a productive personal relationship with Clerides despite their differences, remarked that he could not do business with the new Greek Cypriot president, citing Papadopoulos's "Turk-bashing" past. Rhetoric aside, Papadopoulos established himself as a tough negotiator but rejected his anti-Turk image. He reached out to Turkish Cypriots, asking them to judge him by his actions and stressing the benefits to all Cypriots of unification and EU membership.

(GEORGE H. KELLING)

Parsons, Richard D.

In May 2003, after a year as chief executive of AOL Time Warner Inc., Dick Parsons also became the company's chairman. At the time, AOL Time Warner—formed in 2000 from the merger of the Internet service provider America Online Inc. and media conglomerate Time Warner Inc.—was not in good shape, having had to write off $54 billion in 2002. As well as being the subject of inquiries by the Securities and Exchange Commission and the U.S. Department of Justice, the company faced lawsuits filed by shareholders and had debts of $26 billion—which Parsons aimed to cut to $20 billion by the end of 2004.

Richard Dean Parsons was born on April 4, 1948, in the Bedford-Stuyvesant part of Brooklyn, N.Y. He graduated from the University of Hawaii in 1968 and studied law at Albany Law School, Union University, in Albany, N.Y., where he graduated first in his class in 1971. To help fund his tuition, Parsons worked as a part-time janitor and as an aide in the state assembly. He went on to receive top marks among 3,600 entrants to the New York state bar examination. He became a member of Gov. Nelson Rockefeller's legal team, remaining with him when Rockefeller became vice president in 1974 and becoming a senior White House aide under Pres. Gerald Ford.

In 1977 Parsons joined the New York City law firm of Patterson, Belknap, Webb & Tyler, rising to become a managing partner. One of his clients was the Dime Savings Bank of New York (later Dime Bancorp Inc.), which he joined as chief operating officer (COO) in 1988 and turned around after a period of financial difficulties. Parsons became a member of the board of Time Warner in 1991 and joined the company as president in 1995. After the merger, Parsons became co-COO of AOL Time Warner, responsible for the company's film, music, and publishing businesses. He was named CEO in May 2002.

One of the few top African American business executives, Parsons said he never considered his race as either a handicap or a focus for him. In 2001 he was appointed cochairman of the President's Commission to Strengthen Social Security. He also served as chairman of the Apollo Theater Foundation Inc. and sat on the boards of several arts, educational, and commercial organizations. Parsons, who was described as easygoing, unassuming, and generally well-liked, faced a serious challenge to pay down Time Warner's debts ("AOL" was dropped from the corporate name in September) and regain investor confidence in the struggling company, but his many supporters deemed him the right man for the job. (ALAN STEWART)

Polanski, Roman

Guy Ferrandis/H&K/CPI

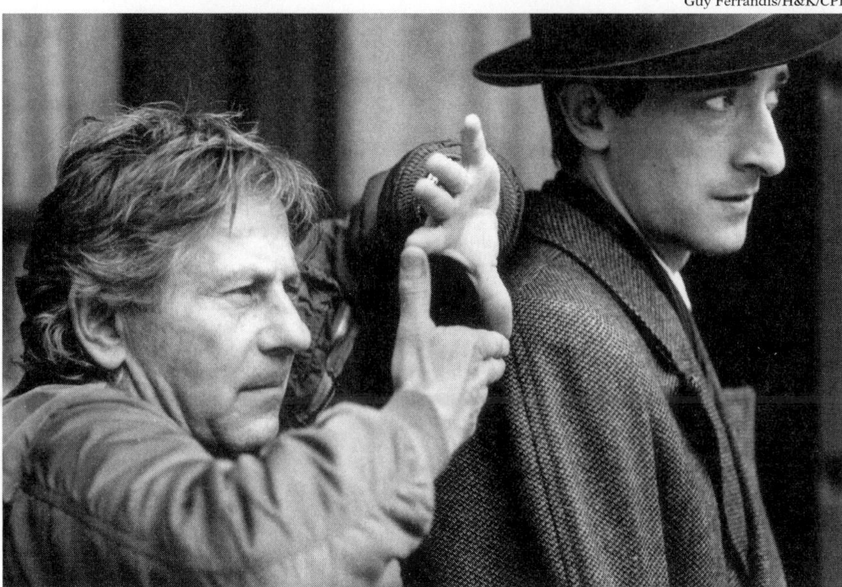

Director Roman Polanski (left) with the lead actor in The Pianist, *Adrien Brody*

Although motion picture director Roman Polanski had long been revered by critical moviegoers for his innovative, generally macabre and suspenseful films and had won numerous awards over the years, many proclaimed that with his direction of his 2002 film, *The Pianist,* he had created the film he was born to make. The tale of a Jewish pianist's struggle to stay alive during the Nazi occupation of Warsaw during World War II, it also was reflective of the horrors he himself had endured in order to survive those years. In 2003 the film won the Palme d'Or at the Cannes Film Festival and three Academy Awards, including the best director award. Polanski was unable to accept his Oscar in person, however; in 1978 he had left the U.S. to avoid sentencing for statutory rape, and he was in danger of arrest if he returned to the country.

Polanski was born Raimund Liebling on Aug. 18, 1933, in Paris and when he was three moved with his parents to Krakow, Pol. When the Nazis took over, the family was moved into the ghetto. Polanski escaped, but his parents were later imprisoned in a concentration camp, where his mother died. After living with various Roman Catholic families and sometimes on his own, he was reunited with his father after the war and began studies at a technical school. He had already done some acting, and in the 1950s he appeared on the stage and in movies and enrolled in the State School of Cinema in Lodz to study directing. One of his student films, *Dwaj ludzie z szafa* (1958; *Two Men and a Wardrobe*), won five international awards, but it was his first full-length feature, the psychological thriller *Noz w wodzie* (1962; *Knife in the Water*), winner of the Critics Prize at the Venice Film Festival, that established his reputation. The films that followed—among them *Repulsion* (1965), *Cul-de-sac* (1966), *Rosemary's Baby* (1968), and *Chinatown* (1974)—furthered his renown. Later motion pictures included *Tess* (1979), *Frantic* (1988), and *Death and the Maiden* (1995), and he also directed a number of stage plays and operas in Europe. For a change of pace, Polanski was was scheduled to begin directing a family film, a new adaptation of Charles Dickens's *Oliver Twist,* in 2004, for a 2005 release.

Polanski, whose second wife, actress Sharon Tate, was one of the murder victims of the Charles Manson gang in 1969, published an autobiography, *Roman,* in 1984.

(BARBARA WHITNEY)

Quasthoff, Thomas

In April 2003, bass-baritone Thomas Quasthoff made his opera debut singing the role of Don Fernando in a production of Beethoven's *Fidelio* with Sir Simon Rattle and the Berlin Philharmonic at the Grosses Festspielhaus in Salzburg, Austria. For any other singer, the event would have been a momentous musical watershed, but in Quasthoff's case it was also a triumph of the human spirit over immense adversity and a lifetime of struggle.

When Quasthoff was born—on Nov. 9, 1959, in Hildesheim, Ger.—he was severely disabled, the result of his mother's having taken the drug thalidomide during her pregnancy. He spent his first year in a cast to correct a right foot that faced backwards. Nothing however, could be done to fix his arms, which barely extended beyond his shoulders. For the next six years, he was confined in a residential institution for severely disabled children. Quasthoff had also been born with a voice like few others, however, a voice that would grow over the years into an instrument of singular power and emotion and one that with cultivation would make him a worldwide musical phenomenon.

Quasthoff began his vocal training in 1972 with Charlotte Lehmann in Hannover, Ger. Re-

bottom: © Wolfgang Reese

fused entry into a music conservatory because his disabilities precluded playing an instrument, he studied law for three years and spent his spare time singing with jazz bands. He became a great admirer of Frank Sinatra. Quasthoff's classical music career got its start in 1988 when he won first prize in the ARD International Music Competition in Munich, Ger. Two years later he ended his studies with Lehmann and took a day job as a radio announcer in Hannover. He began to move into the spotlight in 1996 when he won the Shostakovich Prize in Moscow and the Hamada Trust/Scotsman Festival Prize at the Edinburgh International Festival. The next year Quasthoff made his concert debut with Rattle and the Berlin Philharmonic, performing Haydn's *The Creation.* Success began to build upon success, leading to his first engagement with the New York Philharmonic, singing Gustav Mahler's *Des Knaben Wunderhorn.*

The acclaim that attended Quasthoff's performances yielded a recording contract with the Deutsche Grammophon label in 1999, and he proved to be an immediate sensation. His initial recording, of *Des Knaben Wunderhorn,* with Anne Sofie von Otter and the Berlin Philharmonic conducted by Claudio Abbado, won a Grammy Award in 2000.

Over the next three years, Quasthoff became one of the world's preeminent classical music artists, touring the U.S. and Europe, performing with major orchestras and conductors, and appearing at summer music festivals. His 2000 recording of lieder by Brahms and Liszt won a Cannes (France) Classical Award. Quasthoff was scheduled to make his Vienna State Opera debut in 2004, singing the role of Amfortas in Wagner's *Parsifal.* (HARRY SUMRALL)

Queen Latifah

During 2003 American performer Queen Latifah, already a star of the music industry as one of the first female rappers, proved that she was big-screen royalty as well. In February she received her first Academy Award nomination (best supporting actress) for her portrayal of jail warden Matron "Mama" Morton in the musical *Chicago* (2002), which later won an Oscar for best film. Soon after, the comedy *Bringing Down the House* (2003), in which she costarred with Steve Martin as a convicted bank robber seeking to prove her innocence, hit theatres. Queen Latifah, who also served as the film's executive producer, was praised for her charismatic and witty performance. The film opened atop the box office and went on to earn more than $130 million. She later signed to star in the comedy *Beauty Shop,* a spin-off of the hugely popular *Barbershop* (2002). In 2003 she was engaged in discussions about a sequel, *Barbershop 2.*

Box-office royal Queen Latifah

Born Dana Elaine Owens on March 18, 1970, in Newark, N.J., she was given the nickname Latifah (Arabic: "delicate" or "sensitive") as a child and later adopted the moniker Queen Latifah. In high school she was a member of the all-female rap group Ladies Fresh, and while studying communications at the Borough of Manhattan Community College, she recorded a demo tape that caught the attention of Tommy Boy Records, which signed the 18-year-old. In 1988 she released her first single, "Wrath of My Madness," and the following year *All Hail the Queen,* her debut album, appeared. Propelled by diverse styles—including soul, reggae, and dance—and feminist themes, it earned positive reviews and attracted a wide audience. Soon after, Queen Latifah founded her own management company. Her second album, *Nature of a Sista* (1991), however, failed to match the sales of her previous effort, and Tommy Boy did not re-sign her. After signing with Motown Records, she released *Black Reign* in 1993. The album was a critical and commercial hit, and the single "U.N.I.T.Y.," which decried sexism and violence against women, earned a Grammy Award. Queen Latifah's success launched a wave of female rappers and helped redefine the traditionally male genre.

As her achievements in the recording studio grew, Queen Latifah looked to expand her horizons. In 1991 she made her big-screen debut in *Jungle Fever,* and after several television appearances, she was signed in 1993 to costar in the series *Living Single.* After the show ended in 1998, Queen Latifah returned to the big screen, playing a jazz singer in the 1998 film *Living Out Loud.* Her commanding screen presence brought roles in more films, including *The Bone Collector* (1999) and *Brown Sugar* (2002). In 1999 she began a two-year stint of hosting her own daytime talk show, and the same year she made her debut in the publishing world, releasing the aptly titled *Ladies First: Revelations of a Strong Woman* (co-written with Karen Hunter). (AMY TIKKANEN)

Radiohead

In 2003, as it had since the late 1990s, the unofficial title of the "world's most important rock band"—bestowed by critics but confirmed by music buyers and once claimed by the Clash, U2, and then Nirvana—belonged to Radiohead, a British quintet whose experimentation with rock's sonic possibilities had begun in earnest on its masterpiece album *OK Computer* (1997). Hailed an instant classic, it fused techno electronics with guitar virtuosity and deepened the angst-ridden alienation of lyricist and operatic vocalist Thom Yorke, who reluctantly became, for some, the voice of a generation. On subsequent albums Radiohead seemed to disavow its musical past, moving away from melody and rock instrumentation to create intricately textured sound scapes, before melding this approach with its guitar-band roots on the much-anticipated album *Hail to the Thief* (2003).

Radiohead was formed in 1987 in Oxford, Eng., as On a Friday (the group's rehearsal day) by schoolmates and friends: Yorke (b. Oct. 7, 1968, Wellingborough, Northamptonshire), guitarist Jonny Greenwood (b. Nov. 5, 1971, Oxford), his brother, bassist Colin Greenwood (b. June 26, 1969, Oxford), guitarist Ed O'Brien (b. April 15, 1968, Oxford), and drummer Phil Selway (b. May 23, 1967, Hemingford Grey, Huntingdon, Cambridgeshire). Having separated when the members attended different colleges and universities, the group reconvened permanently in 1991 but received a lukewarm response from listeners and was dismissed (sometimes rudely) by the British music press. Radiohead's breakthrough came in 1993, when "Creep," a self-loathing outsider anthem, became a hit in the United States, as did the group's debut album, *Pablo Honey.* Rereleased in the U.K., "Creep" repeated its American success, and Radiohead's next album, *The Bends* (1995), was acclaimed by critics on both sides of the Atlantic.

It was *OK Computer,* however, that launched the group up the charts and garnered a Grammy Award for best alternative rock performance. In science-fiction-inflected songs such as "Subterranean Homesick Alien" and "Paranoid Android," the diminutive Yorke plaintively evoked a world whose humaneness was compromised by technology. Musically, Radiohead brought new subtlety and shading to its efforts, proving itself to be a progressive rock band in the tradition of Pink Floyd. With *Kid A* (2000), the group steadfastly refused to resort to formula. Substituting synthesized sounds and tape loops for guitars, concentrating on texture and tone, and employing increasingly reductive lyrics, Radiohead dared fans to follow it down the experimental path. Though the album was a commercial success, it met with mixed critical reaction, as would the similar *Amnesiac* (2001), produced during the same sessions as *Kid A.* Some of the Radiohead faithful wavered, but most returned to the fold with *Hail to the Thief,* which, rather than a calculated effort to return to the group's roots, was viewed by many as a logical progression in Radiohead's musical adventure.

(JEFF WALLENFELDT)

Rees, Sir Martin John

Armageddon is a favourite theme of science-fiction writers and filmmakers, but it is normally offered as escapist fantasy rather than serious prophecy. When a distinguished scientist, not known for extravagant assertions, calmly says that humankind has only a 50%

Phil Greenhalgh

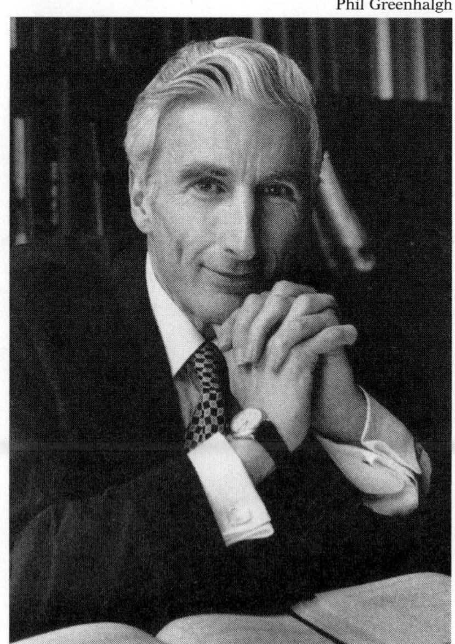

Astronomer Royal Sir Martin Rees

chance of surviving until the year 2100, his remarks are apt to make news and provoke widespread concern. That was what happened in April 2003 following the publication of *Our Final Century* (published in the U.S. as *Our Final Hour*) by Sir Martin Rees, the U.K.'s astronomer royal. Rees argued not that the human race would be wiped out by aggressive aliens but that the pace of technological change threatened to outstrip the ability of humans to control it. Specific risks included engineered airborne viruses, nuclear terrorism, new forms of "bio" and "cyber" terror, and even rogue nanomachines (or "supercomputers") that could run out of control.

Rees was born on June 23, 1942, in Shropshire, in the English Midlands. After studying mathematics at Trinity College, Cambridge (B.A., 1963), he pursued an academic career in cosmology, mainly at Cambridge but with interludes in the U.S. at Princeton and Harvard universities and at the California Institute of Technology. Rees became one of the world's leading authorities on the big-bang theory of the origins of the universe and on the related topics of black holes, quasars, pulsars, galaxy formation, and gamma-ray bursts. His early prediction that black holes would be found at the centre of the Milky Way Galaxy was borne out by subsequent observations. In 1973 he was appointed Plumian Professor of Astronomy and Experimental Philosophy at Cambridge; in 1995 he was named to the highly prestigious but essentially honorary position of astronomer royal.

Rees was never content to keep within the narrow technical bounds of cosmological theory. In his books and lectures, he explored the links between science and philosophy and humankind's place in the universe. *Our Final Century*, in some ways a logical culmination of more than 30 years' work, belonged to a long tradition in which scientists, philosophers, and mathematicians warned of the dangers of uncontrolled scientific advance. In the 1940s and '50s, Albert Einstein and Bertrand Russell feared that the newfound ability to split the atom might lead to a nuclear conflagration, and in June 1940, Prime Minister Winston Churchill spoke of "the abyss of a new Dark Age, made more sinister, and perhaps more protracted, by the lights of perverted science." In *Our Final Century* Rees warned of more varied and diffuse dangers, requiring newer and more varied responses, and argued that taken together those dangers were no less serious in 2003 than those faced by humankind 60 years earlier. (PETER KELLNER)

Rodriguez, Alex

The Most Valuable Player of Major League Baseball's American League for the 2003 season was Alex Rodriguez, the power-hitting shortstop for the Texas Rangers; the selection was a rarity in that his team finished last for the fourth consecutive year. Ten different men received at least one first-place MVP vote—but "A-Rod" prevailed because of his stellar offensive statistics. He hit 47 home runs, registered 118 runs batted in, and had a batting average of .298. At season's end, however, there was some doubt whether Rodriguez would remain with the Rangers, who had acquired him as a free agent in December 2000. His 10-year $252 million contract still made the 28-year-old star the highest-paid performer in the major leagues, but during his tenure in Texas Rodriguez had indicated on occasion that he would accept a trade to a more competitive franchise. A possible trade to the Boston Red Sox fell through in December.

Alexander Emmanuel Rodriguez was born on July 27, 1975, in New York City, where his father operated a shoe store. The family moved to his father's native Dominican Republic when Alex was four, but they later relocated to Miami, Fla. His parents separated, and Rodriguez often recounted how his mother had worked two jobs to support him and his brother and sister. He was active in the local Boys and Girls Club, where at age nine he met a counselor who helped the youngster hone his baseball skills and served as a father figure. Rodriguez became an excellent ballplayer at Westminster Christian High School in Miami, and the Seattle Mariners made him the first overall selection in the 1993 amateur draft. He began his professional career in class A at Appleton, Wis., in 1994 and then graduated in midseason to the Mariners' farm club in Jacksonville, Fla. After only 17 games there, Rodriguez was brought up from Jacksonville to play for Seattle at age 18, but he did not produce immediately and was returned to the minor leagues. In 1996, however, he became the starting shortstop for the Mariners, and his career took off. He led the major leagues with a .358 batting average and hit 36 home runs that season.

The Mariners enjoyed considerable success with Rodriguez as one of their stalwarts, but in 2000 Seattle chose not to outbid the Rangers. Texas owner Tom Hicks angered his peers with the extravagant terms of the contract that Rodriguez signed, but A-Rod hit 52 and 57 home runs, respectively, during his first two seasons in Texas (the latter a major league record for a shortstop).

Off the field Rodriguez was active in community affairs in Miami and in Dallas, Texas, where he resided with his wife. He was founder (1998) of the Alex Rodriguez Foundation and a national spokesman for the Boys & Girls Clubs of America. (ROBERT VERDI)

Rolston, Holmes

"I had to fight both theology and science to love nature," Holmes Rolston III said upon being named the recipient of the 2003 Templeton Prize for Progress Toward Research or Discoveries About Spiritual Realities. In his acceptance statement, he wrote, "We must encounter nature with grace, with an Earth ethics, because our ultimate Environment is God—in whom we live, move, and have our being." The "father of environmental ethics" had spent his life in what he called a lover's quarrel with science and religion. He had been a pastor, a philosopher, an ethicist, and a naturalist and had published articles in such varied periodicals as *Journal of Forestry* and *Theology Today*.

Rolston was born Nov. 19, 1932, in Rockbridge Baths, Va., the son and grandson of Presbyterian ministers. His boyhood home had no electricity, and water came from a cistern pump. Each summer he visited the Alabama farm where his mother had been reared; there he explored the local woods and swamps. Rolston earned a degree in physics and mathematics (1953) from Davidson College, near Charlotte, N.C., a bachelor of divinity degree (1956) from Union Theological Seminary, Richmond, Va., and a doctorate in theology and religious studies (1958) from the University of Edinburgh. He served as pastor of Walnut Grove Presbyterian Church in Bristol, Va., from 1958 until 1967. After receiving a masters degree in the philosophy of science in 1968 from the University of Pittsburgh, Pa., he joined the philosophy department of Colorado State University, where he was made a university distinguished professor in 1992.

Several journals rejected Rolston's writings on environmental ethics before "Is There an Ecological Ethic?" was published in *Ethics* in 1975. It was the first article in a major philosophical journal to challenge the idea that nature is value-free and that all values stem from a human perspective. The piece was also considered to have been seminal in launching environmental ethics as a branch of philosophical inquiry. Four years later Rolston cofounded the journal *Environmental Ethics*. In his book *Science and Religion* (1987), he wrote that "science is here to stay, and the religion that is divorced from science today will leave no offspring tomorrow." His other major works included *Environmental Ethics* (1988) and *Genes, Genesis and God* (1999), which was based on lectures he delivered at the University of Edinburgh during the 1997–98 academic year.

Rolston's field work included rafting the Grand Canyon, traversing Siberia, exploring the Amazon basin, studying tigers in Nepal, and tracking wolves through Yellowstone National Park. During his visit to Antarctica in

2000, he became the only environmental philosopher to have lectured on all seven continents. (DARRELL J. TURNER)

Romano, Ray

American actor-comedian Ray Romano, who starred as prime-time television's regular dad on the sitcom *Everybody Loves Raymond,* had reason to feel loved in 2003. CBS agreed to pay Romano nearly $50 million for the 2003–04 season and granted the show a two-year renewal, even though Romano had indicated that the upcoming season would likely be its last. *Everybody Loves Raymond,* after a quiet but critically successful debut in 1996, leapfrogged in the ratings when it was moved to Monday night in 1997, even as it competed for viewers with *Monday Night Football.* Known for its witty and insightful portrayal of the quotidian travails of family life, the show was nominated for the Emmy Award for outstanding comedy series each year from 1999 to 2003. For his role as the bumbling Ray Barone, Romano received the 2002 Emmy Award for best actor in a comedy series and the 2000 American Comedy Award for funniest male lead in a television series, as well as nominations for Golden Globe awards, Screen Actor's Guild Awards, and other honours.

Raymond Romano was born on Dec. 21, 1957, in Queens, N.Y. His upbringing in the middle-class Forest Hills section would later prove a rich mine for the wholesome, family-friendly humour that became the comedian's trademark. In the early 1980s, while studying to be an accountant and holding down a series of part-time jobs, Romano began performing stand-up comedy in New York clubs. In 1987 he decided to pursue stand-up as a career. Winning a citywide comedy contest in 1989 brought valuable exposure, and in 1990 Romano made his first national television appearance on the MTV *Half-Hour Comedy Hour.* It was an appearance on the *Late Show with David Letterman* in 1995, however, that heralded the beginning of his trajectory to superstardom. Letterman was so impressed with his guest that he had his production company, Worldwide Pants Inc., develop a situation comedy around Romano's humour. The first episode of *Everybody Loves Raymond* aired on September 13 the following year.

Having established himself at the pinnacle of American television comedy, Romano extended his humour to the big screen. In 2002 he starred as the voice of Manfred, a woolly mammoth that helps return a human baby to its father, in the animated feature *Ice Age.* In the dark comedy *Eulogy* (2003), he was cast as the maladjusted eldest son mourning the death of the family patriarch. Filming was completed in the summer of 2003 for *Welcome to Mooseport,* a comedy about a small-town political race in which Romano costarred with Gene Hackman. Romano also wrote a book, *Everything and a Kite* (1998), and released an album, *Ray Romano: Live at Carnegie Hall* (2001).

(JANET MOREDOCK)

Rove, Karl

Right-wing political operative Karl Rove, chief strategist for U.S. Pres. George W. Bush, might have gloated in 2003 over the Republican gains of the previous November. Although the party in power more often than not lost strength in midterm elections, Rove's strategy of sending Bush to campaign in key congressional races and of focusing on issues such as terrorism and tax cuts proved successful. The Republicans regained control of the Senate, if only by the narrowest of margins, and increased their majority in the House of Representatives. Rove was known for looking ahead, however, and there was no doubt that in 2003 he was concentrating on the 2004 presidential election.

Rove was born on Dec. 25, 1950, in Denver, Colo. He attended the University of Utah and other colleges but did not receive a degree. Political even as a young child, he pasted campaign stickers for Richard M. Nixon on his bicycle in 1960, and while in high school, he volunteered in a senatorial campaign. In 1971 he went to Washington, D.C., to become executive director of the College Republicans. Two years later he ran for the post of chairman in a campaign managed by strategist Lee Atwater, an early mentor. During the 1970s Rove was involved with various Republican organizations and candidates, including George H.W. Bush. Becoming involved in Texas politics, Rove worked on the failed congressional campaign of George W. Bush in 1978 and, in the same year, on the successful gubernatorial campaign of Bill Clements, the first Republican to be elected to the state's highest office since Reconstruction. Rove formed his own consulting business in 1981, with clients that included Phil Gramm, elected to the U.S. Senate in 1984, and Tom Phillips, who in 1988 became the first Republican ever elected to the Texas Supreme Court. In 1994 Rove handled Bush's successful gubernatorial campaign, and he was given much of the credit for transforming Texas from a Democratic to a Republican stronghold, with the party holding all elected state offices by 1999. Rove adroitly managed Bush's 2000 campaign for the presidency, limiting press access to the candidate and focusing on a small number of carefully chosen issues.

Rove was a master of political strategy. He exercised tight control over campaigns and brooked no dissent, even from other Republicans. Detractors cited instances of underhanded tactics that included intrigue and the spreading of disinformation, and those who had borne the brunt of his operations called him ruthless and vindictive. Rove was commonly referred to as "Bush's brain," with many people, including some Republicans, lamenting his power in the administration, in which policies and appointments appeared to be driven unduly by political considerations.

(ROBERT RAUCH)

Scardino, Marjorie

When Dame Marjorie Scardino, CEO of the British media firm Pearson PLC, accepted a bonus of £273,000 (about $452,000) in 2003, media watchers began asking if she had earned it, given that Pearson had lost £25 million (about $40 million) in 2002. After all, she had waived her bonus a year earlier following Pearson's 2001 loss of £436 million (about $633 million). Scardino's critics demanded a turnaround and pointed to declining advertising revenues at the *Financial Times* (*FT*), the firm's leading publication. Scardino spurned recommendations to sell the *FT,* insisting it would not be sold during a downturn. Her reasoned managerial approach did much to improve Pearson's standing. Her contributions to British media were recognized when she was named Dame Commander in February 2002, a month after she had adopted British citizenship.

Publisher Dame Marjorie Scardino

Scardino was born Marjorie Morris on Jan. 25, 1947, in Flagstaff, Ariz. She studied French and psychology at Baylor University, Waco, Texas (B.A., 1969), and, following a stint as an Associated Press editor, completed her legal studies at the University of San Francisco (J.D., 1975). While working as the managing partner (1976–85) of a Savannah, Ga., law firm, Scardino and her husband, Albert, launched and published a weekly newspaper, the *Georgia Gazette,* which succeeded editorially under Albert's direction. Financially, however, the paper failed. Marjorie, who served as its publisher, later said that the *Gazette*'s business losses taught her more than any success could have.

Scardino joined Pearson by way of the New York offices of the *Economist* magazine, which was half owned by Pearson. As president (1985–93) of the Economist Newspaper Group, Inc., she more than doubled the North American circulation. Upon assuming the position of CEO of the Economist Group in 1993, she moved to the magazine's London headquarters and branched into businesses such as financial research services and sector analyses.

By 1996 Pearson had become a £2.25 billion (about $3.5 billion) media firm hobbled by far-flung interests. Scardino was named CEO in 1997 and swiftly charted new directions by selling peripheral businesses such as Mindscape, a money-losing technology company; Tussaud's, famous for waxworks; and Lazard, an investment firm. Nicknamed "Marj in Charge," she made a big bet on educational publishing by purchasing Simon & Schuster's educational businesses in 1998. Despite missteps, such as overinvesting in on-line education, Scardino organized Pearson into three key divisions: consumer publishing, financial publishing, and Pearson Education—now the world's largest educational firm—comprising NCS Pearson, a testing and certification firm, and educational publishing.

When Pearson's midyear results were announced in July, Scardino predicted healthy profits by the end of 2003. New titles by key authors were scheduled for release by year-end, and payments on education contracts would be forthcoming. Luck also contributed; thanks to endorsement by Oprah Winfrey, Penguin sold 1.2 million copies of John Steinbeck's *East of Eden* in four weeks—more than had sold in 30 years, while Putnam's *Kate Remembered* by A. Scott Berg was scaling the best-seller lists. (SARAH FORBES ORWIG)

Schwarzenegger, Arnold

Austrian-born former bodybuilder Arnold Schwarzenegger, who became a Hollywood star in the film *The Terminator* (1984), saw the release of *Terminator 3* in 2003, but the debut of his latest action movie was overshadowed by his 11-week campaign to become the governor of California if the recall effort against Gov. Gray Davis was successful. Schwarzenegger triumphed over 134 other candidates and won the election with 49% of the vote. On November 17 he was sworn in as California's new governor, and he later unveiled his California Recovery Plan, which he said would address the state's staggering budget deficit of more than $15 billion.

Arnold Alois Schwarzenegger was born on July 30, 1947, in Thal bei Graz, Austria. When he began competing in bodybuilding contests, he dwarfed his competition and earned the nickname the "Styrian Oak," or "Austrian Oak." He won his first Mr. Universe (amateur) title in 1967 but moved to the U.S. the following year to compete in bigger and more lucrative events there. He captured four more Mr. Universe titles and then the professional Mr. Olympia title six years in a row (1970–75) before retiring. He returned one more time to competition to claim the 1980 Mr. Universe title.

Meanwhile, Schwarzenegger had begun to pursue his childhood dream of acting in movies. In his first film, *Hercules in New York* (1970), he played the lead, but another actor was used to dub his dialogue. Schwarzenegger's native charm and wit finally came through in the acclaimed documentary *Pumping Iron* (1977), which led to his starring role in *Conan the Barbarian* (1982). It was *The Terminator* and its sequels (1991 and 2003), however, that made him an international star. Some of his other films included *Predator* (1987), *Kindergarten Cop* (1990), *Total Recall* (1990), *True Lies* (1994), and *The 6th Day* (2000).

Schwarzenegger became a U.S. citizen in 1984 and in 1986 married TV reporter Maria Shriver, whose connection to the Democratic Kennedy political dynasty later proved helpful in his campaign. During the 1990s he became increasingly active in the Republican Party at both the state and the national level. Reports that Schwarzenegger had previously fondled and sexually harassed at least 15 women did not appreciably affect his campaign. In his first six weeks in office, the "governator" and his direct, bipartisan, tough-guy style impressed observers and confounded the Democratic-controlled legislature as he sought to overhaul California's finances. (WILLIAM L. HOSCH)

Short, Clare

In a remarkable radio interview on March 10, 2003, shortly before the U.S.-led war against Iraq began, Clare Short, the U.K. secretary of state for international development, criticized the impending war and described British Prime Minister Tony Blair's stance on Iraq as "reckless." It was widely assumed that her resignation or dismissal would follow swiftly. Instead, Blair asked her to stay on to oversee Britain's contribution to Iraq's postwar reconstruction. She agreed, on the condition that this would happen within the framework of the United Nations. On May 12, however, Short resigned. Her bitter resignation letter accused Blair of having "breached . . . the assurances you gave me about the need for a UN mandate to establish a legitimate Iraqi government. . . . This makes my position impossible." Short's resignation was the first in a series of events that provoked a continuing controversy over Blair's integrity and caused his opinion-poll ratings to plummet.

Britain's antiwar former minister Clare Short

Short was born in Birmingham, Eng., on Feb. 15, 1946. Her parents were both Irish-born Roman Catholics with strong Irish republican sympathies. After studying at the Universities of Keele and Leeds, she joined the Home Office as a career civil servant in 1970. She left five years later to enter politics. In 1983 she was elected as the Labour MP for Birmingham, Ladywood. She identified with the left wing of the Labour Party but remained an independent-minded MP, and her fiery passion helped her to stand out from the crowd. In 1985 Neil Kinnock, then leader of the Labour Party in opposition to Prime Minister Margaret Thatcher's Conservative government, appointed Short to his shadow ministerial team. Twice she resigned over Kinnock's refusal to oppose specific government policies (in 1988 over the renewal of antiterrorism legislation and in 1991 over Kinnock's support for the first Gulf War); twice she was eventually brought back into the shadow ministerial team.

Upon Labour's return to power in 1997, Blair appointed Short secretary of state for international development. Her reputation grew throughout the world as an effective minister as she secured large increases in the British government's overseas-aid budget and introduced new policies to increase the effectiveness of that aid in helping the Third World. She was especially concerned with poverty in Africa and persuaded Chancellor of the Exchequer Gordon Brown to write off the debts to Britain of Africa's poorest countries. In 1999 she gave strong support to NATO's military action in Kosovo. Given her left-wing inclinations and previous resignations, her support was vital to Blair and helped to avoid a major split in the Labour Party over Britain's involvement in the NATO action. That support ended in 2003, however, and Short quickly became one of Blair's harshest critics, denouncing the government's policies and calling for the beleaguered prime minister's resignation. (PETER KELLNER)

Skari, Bente

Norway's Bente Skari was almost untouchable during the 2002–03 World Cup cross-country skiing season. She entered 17 World Cup races and won 14, for her fourth overall crown in five years. She also went two-for-two at the 2003 Nordic world championships before dropping out because of illness. Then, on March 28, she said good-bye, retiring at age 30 after more than a decade of World Cup racing—with 42 wins (second all-time among women) and four World Cup titles, plus five world championship gold medals and five Olympic medals, including a 10-km gold at the 2002 Winter Games in Salt Lake City, Utah. "My willpower and motivation are no longer strong enough to make me want to go on," she told a farewell press conference. "I'm not the kind of athlete who does things halfheartedly."

Skari, the daughter of former Olympic ski medalist and International Ski Federation executive Odd Martinsen, was born in Oslo on Sept. 10, 1972. She skied during the 1992 season but was not an immediate hit on the World Cup circuit. She moved up during the 1994 Olympic season and won her first World Cup race in December 1997, but it was not until 1998, when she won a bronze medal at the Winter Olympic Games in Nagano, Japan, and finished the World Cup season number two in points, that she made an impact. She won the 1999 and 2000 World Cup overall titles, was second again in 2001, and won her last two years, 2002 and 2003. In mid-2000 she married Geir Skari, the 1996 National Collegiate

© Agence Zoom/Getty Images

Norway's Nordic champ, Bente Skari

Athletic Association cross-country ski champion for the University of Denver, Colo.

Early in her career, Skari was almost one-dimensional—strong in classic technique (both skis in prepared tracks) but significantly slower in skating (freestyle or free technique, where skiers kick off to the side like a speed skater). She was hard to beat, however, in skating sprints, over a 1.5-km course where four skiers duel each heat. "I don't have confidence in the longer skate races," she explained, "but when someone is right there with me, I don't want to lose and somehow I go faster, even skating."

Coincidentally, in her final season Skari emerged as an outstanding skater too. Of her 14 World Cup wins, 4 were in freestyle and 2 were in skiathlon, or double pursuit, a 10-km race that starts with 5 km of classic technique and rolls into a 5-km skate; skiers change equipment as they head into the final 5 km. She announced her retirement after winning her final race, the skiathlon at Norway's national championships. (PAUL ROBBINS)

Slim Helú, Carlos

In 2003 there was a good chance that any random consumer purchase in Mexico would eventually connect to the pocketbook of the country's leading businessman, Carlos Slim Helú. The telecommunications tycoon, through his conglomerate, Grupo Carso, SA de CV, had extensive interests in a startling number of Mexican companies, reaching deep into the fields of communications, technology, retailing, and finance. *Forbes* magazine ranked Slim the 35th richest person in the world (and the wealthiest in Latin America), estimating his net worth at $7.4 billion. This left him a few billion shy of his *Forbes* standing in 2002, which was at number 17, with $11.5 billion.

For more than a dozen years, Slim's key holding and the anchor to his success had been his ownership of the former national telephone monopoly, Teléfonos de México (Telmex), which had allowed him to broaden his portfolio into such high-technology companies as Prodigy Inc. and SBC Communications Inc. Grupo Carso had extensive interests in a long list of Mexican companies, and in the 1990s Slim also purchased shares in several American companies, including Apple Computer, OfficeMax, Circuit City, Saks, and CompUSA.

Slim was born in 1940 into a family of Lebanese Christian immigrants to Mexico, where his father made a fortune in real estate during the Mexican Revolution of 1910–20. Slim received a degree in engineering from the National Autonomous University of Mexico, and by the mid-1960s he was investing in a variety of businesses that became the foundation for Grupo Carso. He attained billionaire status on the heels of the economic crash of 1982, when the Mexican government, defaulting on foreign debts in light of a devalued peso, began nationalizing banks and scaring business investors away. Slim purchased at bargain prices controlling interests in a variety of companies, which he managed so efficiently that within the span of a decade their sum value had skyrocketed.

By the late 1980s Slim had forged close ties with then-president Carlos Salinas de Gortari and the ruling Institutional Revolutionary Party. In 1990 the Gortari administration privatized Telmex, and Slim, along with SBC and France Télécom, made the $1.76 billion purchase. He later won management control of Telmex, alienating France Télécom but keeping close relations with SBC. His tight control of Telmex upset his competitors, as well as some consumers critical of the communications giant. By 2003, however, he had turned over much of his business operations to his three sons. Slim, a noted art collector and philanthropist, was also prominent in the revitalization of the historic centre of Mexico City and supported anticrime efforts there. In late 2002 he led a group of prominent businessmen who invited former New York City mayor Rudolph Giuliani to assist in combating crime in Mexico's capital. (TOM MICHAEL)

Smith, Zadie

In 2003 *Granta* magazine named Zadie Smith one of the best young British novelists. Such praise was nothing new for the English author whose debut novel, *White Teeth* (2000), had created a sensation in the publishing world. The ambitious work teemed with eccentric characters, savvy humour, and snappy dialogue while addressing such serious issues as race, religion, and cultural identity. Set in the working-class suburb of Willesden in northwest London, *White Teeth* chronicled the lives of best friends Archie Jones, a down-on-his-luck Englishman whose failed suicide attempt opens the novel, and Samad Iqbal, a Bengali Muslim who struggles to fit into British society. Spanning some 50 years, the novel also detailed the trials and tribulations of their families. Soon after its publication, critics hailed Smith as a modern-day Charles Dickens, a comparison that seemed especially apt when the novel was adapted in 2002 (U.K.) for public television's *Masterpiece Theatre,* a long-lived program best known for its miniseries based on English literary classics.

Sadie Smith was born in London in 1975 to a Jamaican mother and an English father; at age 14 she changed the spelling of her first name to Zadie. She began writing poems and stories as a child and later studied English literature at the University of Cambridge (B.A., 1998). While there she began writing *White Teeth,* and at age 21 she submitted some 80 pages to an agent. A frenzied bidding war ensued, and the book eventually was sold to Hamish Hamilton. Smith took several more years to complete the novel, and in 2000 it was published to rave reviews. Critics applauded Smith's confident storytelling ability and her gift for creating vivid characters. *White Teeth* won numerous awards, including the Whitbread First Novel Award (2000), and was a finalist for the National Book Critics Circle Award and the Orange Prize for Fiction. Her second novel, *The Autograph Man,* was published in 2002. It centred on Alex-Li Tandem, a Chinese Jewish autograph trader who sets out to meet a reclusive 1950s starlet and in the process undertakes his own journey of self-discovery. *The Autograph Man,* which also addressed the public's obsession with celebrity and pop culture, received mostly positive reviews. In 2003 it received the *Jewish Quarterly* Wingate Literary Prize for Fiction. Soon after the novel's publication, Smith became a fellow at Harvard University's Radcliffe Institute for Advanced Study. There she began work on a collection of essays on the moral philosophy of selected 20th-century writers and on her much-anticipated third novel.

(AMY TIKKANEN)

Sukumar, Raman

After having spent more than two decades studying Asian elephants in the wild in an effort to preserve the species, Raman Sukumar, a faculty member of the Centre for Ecological Sciences at the Indian Institute of Science in Bangalore, India, was presented with the 2003 Whitley Gold Award in recognition of his commitment to conservation. Sukumar also served as honorary director of the Asian Elephant

Research and Conservation Centre, a special division of the Asian Nature Conservation Foundation, an independent organization that worked closely with many governmental and nongovernmental agencies in the region. In addition, he was chairman of the Asian Elephant Specialist Group of the World Conservation Union, and he provided technical support and advice on matters of elephant conservation to the Indian government as a member of its Project Elephant Steering Committee.

Sukumar was born on April 3, 1955, in Madras (now Chennai), India. As a young boy growing up in Madras, he was already nicknamed *vanavasi* (the Tamil word for "forest dweller") by his grandmother. It was during his secondary-school years that Sukumar first thought of working in the field of nature conservation, and he began pursuing that interest. He graduated from the University of Madras with bachelor's and master's degrees in botany. In 1979 he began studies for his doctoral thesis at the Indian Institute of Science, where he focused on the ecological conflict that occurs when elephants and humans use the same land. His thesis eventually came out as a monograph from Cambridge University Press. Sukumar believed that "if the tiger is the spirit of the jungle, the elephant is its body." He later published *Elephant Days and Nights: Ten Years with the Indian Elephant* and *The Living Elephants: Evolutionary Ecology, Behavior and Conservation* (2003); *Elephants* was scheduled for publication in 2004.

In an effort to provide a safe habitat for elephants, Sukumar carried out surveys and tried to establish protected corridors so that elephant herds could move from one area to another. He experimented with various forms of fencing around village perimeters to keep the animals away from crops and human habitation. (Annually, about 200 people lose their lives as a result of elephants on the move.) Sukumar also helped design the Nilgiri Biosphere Reserve—a first for India—where he conducted research on climate change, tropical forests, and wildlife conservation. In furthering his research, Sukumar planned to use the Whitley Award funds to help local farmers cope with elephant encroachment on their lands and to provide support for his field research team, which served as a "watchdog" in the identification of threats to the elephant population, including problems related to their health and ivory poachers.

Raman Sukumar, India's "forest dweller"

Whitley Laing Foundation

Some of Sukumar's other awards included the Presidential Award of the Chicago Zoological Society in 1989 and the Order of the Golden Ark, The Netherlands, in 1997. In 2000 he became a fellow of the Indian Academy of Sciences.
(EB-INDIA EDITORIAL)

Summers, Lawrence H.

July 1, 2003, marked the second anniversary of Lawrence H. Summers's appointment as Harvard University's 27th president, a position to which, at the young age of 46, he brought impressive credentials as an economist, academician, and public servant. He also, however, brought a reputation for viewing life from a perspective of economic efficiency and for being somewhat tactless in personal relationships. His style soon led to public controversy over the role of the modern American university.

Summers was born Nov. 30, 1954, in New Haven, Conn., the son of two economics professors. After earning a doctorate in economics at Harvard in 1982, he served on the President's Council of Economic Advisers and then returned to Harvard in 1983, at age 28 one of the youngest individuals in recent history to be awarded a tenured faculty position. In 1987 he became the first social scientist to receive the Alan T. Waterman Award of the National Science Foundation. In 1993 he received the John Bates Clark Medal, bestowed biennially on an outstanding American economist under age 40.

Summers returned to Washington in 1991 as chief economist at the World Bank, a post he held until 1993, when he was appointed undersecretary of the treasury for international affairs. He moved to the top spot in the Treasury Department in 1999 and served as the principal economic adviser to Pres. Bill Clinton.

As Harvard's newly named president, Summers scheduled interviews with prominent members of the faculty to discuss how their roles in the university might be performed most efficiently. One such interview was with Cornel West, an authority on African American studies and religion who held one of Harvard's most prestigious professorships. West was popular with students and widely acclaimed for his 1993 book *Race Matters*. During the interview Summers reportedly suggested that West missed too many classes, awarded too many A grades, failed to produce enough serious scholarship, and spent too much time in political and self-promotional activities (such as serving as chief adviser for the Rev. Al Sharpton's bid for the U.S. presidency and performing on a rap album). In response, West publicly accused Summers of racism and disrespect, identified himself as a scholar-activist, and left Harvard for a professorship at Princeton University.

By 2003 it was apparent that Summers's combination of specific aims and abrasive personal style, as seen in the West incident, would be applied as well to promoting other parts of his reform agenda. Important elements of that agenda consisted of removing key decision-making power from the university's separate schools and locating it in the president's office, tightening grading standards, pressing senior professors to teach undergraduates, focusing greater attention on societal concerns, and altering the curriculum to emphasize students' acquiring deep knowledge rather than chiefly surveying "ways of knowing" in various disciplines. Educators watched with keen interest.
(R. MURRAY THOMAS)

Sutherland, Kiefer

He might have been acting for more than 20 years, but it took only one very long day for Kiefer Sutherland to earn some of the best reviews of his career. The British-born Canadian actor starred as American counterterrorist agent Jack Bauer in *24*, the innovative television series that covered a single day in Bauer's life. Each hour-long episode aired in real time and featured nonstop action—in the series' second season, broadcast in 2002–03, Bauer saved Los Angeles from a terrorist attack, survived a nuclear blast, was tortured to death and later revived, and helped avert a war. Bordering on the outlandish at times, *24* was grounded by Sutherland's captivating performance, which combined toughness and vulnerability. Critics and audiences were riveted to their television sets, and in 2003 Sutherland earned his second consecutive Emmy nomination for his portrayal of Bauer.

Kiefer William Frederick Dempsey George Rufus Sutherland was born on Dec. 21, 1966, in London, the son of Canadian actors Donald Sutherland and Shirley Douglas. After his parents' divorce (1971), he moved with his mother and twin sister to Canada, but he left school at age 15 to pursue an acting career. He made his big-screen debut, with his father, in *Max Dugan Returns* (1983). The following year he landed a leading role in *The Bay Boy*, for which the Academy of Canadian Cinema and Television nominated him for a Genie Award as best actor. He appeared as a bully in the hit movie *Stand by Me* (1986). Sutherland's menacing performance attracted much attention, and villains became his specialty, although he typically sought out diverse roles. He starred in a series of popular films, including *The Lost Boys* (1987) and *Young Guns* (1988), and established himself as one of Hollywood's leading young actors. In 1990 he costarred with Julia Roberts in the thriller *Flatliners;* the couple's subsequent engagement and breakup became fodder for the tabloids.

Sutherland directed the TV movie *Last Light* (1993) and the feature film *Truth or Consequences, N.M.* (1997). Acting remained his primary work, however, and he made notable appearances in *A Few Good Men* (1992), *Freeway* (1996), and *A Time to Kill* (1996). He also performed with his mother onstage in *The Glass Menagerie* in 1996.

After a brief sabbatical from acting to perform in rodeos, Sutherland returned to Hollywood, and in 2001 he landed the role of Bauer on *24*. Concerns that in the wake of the attacks on Sept. 11, 2001, people would not want to see a show that dealt with terrorists proved unfounded. The series, which debuted in November 2001, was an instant hit. Many critics named it the best new show of the season, and in 2002 Sutherland won a Golden Globe Award for outstanding lead actor in a television drama. He also was praised for his role as the sinister Caller in the film *Phone Booth*, which was released in theatres in early 2003.

(AMY TIKKANEN)

Tachikawa, Keiji

After having endured months of disappointing sales, Japanese wireless provider NTT DoCoMo staged a spirited comeback in 2003 under the leadership of company president Keiji Tachikawa. NTT DoCoMo was operated by Nippon Telegraph & Telephone, Japan's main telecommunications carrier. The company had seen sales of its wireless phones plummet since 2001 as the mobile market became saturated, but Tachikawa was able to reverse NTT DoCoMo's declining fortunes in the market in part by introducing an array of innovative new products. These included the Dick Tracy-inspired Wristomo, a wristwatch that unfolded into a Web-capable cell phone. The Wristomo proved wildly popular upon its release, with the product's first two shipments of 1,000 units each taking only 10 minutes to sell out. During the year Tachikawa also presided over the completion of FOMA, a cutting-edge mobile-phone network. FOMA (Freedom Of Mobile multimedia Access) was the first network to feature high-speed "third-generation" technology capable of giving cell phones many of the same functions as a personal computer.

Tachikawa was born on May 27, 1939, in Ogaki, Gifu prefecture, Japan. After graduating from Tokyo University in 1962 with a bachelor's degree in technology, he joined Nippon Telegraph & Telephone. He later earned a master's degree in business administration (1978) from the Massachusetts Institute of Technology and a doctorate in engineering (1982) from Tokyo University. Tachikawa helped found telecommunications subsidiary NTT America, Inc., in 1987 and served as its first chief executive officer.

From 1992 to 1995 Tachikawa was a senior vice president and general manager of one of the Nippon Telegraph & Telephone's regional communications sectors. He then served as executive vice president in charge of service engineering (1995–96) and as senior executive vice president in charge of business communications (1996–97) before being tapped to run NTT DoCoMo. Initially Tachikawa was unhappy with the appointment. Up until that time, NTT DoCoMo had been a relatively obscure corporate division, but that quickly changed with Tachikawa at the helm. He soon realized that the wireless industry held tremendous potential, and he oversaw the introduction in February 1999 of i-mode, a wireless Internet service that soon had more than 15 million subscribers. By the end of 2000, NTT DoCoMo's market capitalization had far outgrown that of its parent company, and the business had emerged as one of Japan's most valuable.

NTT DoCoMo's Keiji Tachikawa

Tachikawa was named *Fortune* magazine's Asian Businessman of the Year in 2001. Despite the losses racked up by NTT DoCoMo over the next two years, he remained confident in his company's direction. In an interview in 2003, Tachikawa predicted that NTT DoCoMo would "return to the trajectory we expected when we first launched FOMA [in October 2001]." Industry analysts were equally optimistic, with some estimating that the company would triple its profits during the year.

(SHERMAN HOLLAR)

Weinstein, Harvey

In 2003 American movie executive Harvey Weinstein, the cofounder and cochairman of Miramax Films, proved that despite several missteps in the early 2000s that had led some to predict his demise, he still had the Oscar touch that he had first demonstrated years earlier. His films were nominated for an astounding 40 Academy Awards—the most nominations received by a studio in more than 60 years—and ended up winning 9 awards, including the best-picture nod for *Chicago*.

Weinstein was born March 19, 1952, in Queens, N.Y. He attended the University of Buffalo, N.Y., at which he began promoting rock concerts with his brother, Bob. Their interests soon turned to movies, and in 1979 the brothers established the Miramax Film Corp. (named after their parents, Miriam and Max) and began buying the rights to films and distributing them. Harvey proved a risk taker, purchasing films that were quirky and often controversial, and in 1989 he bought the rights to the provocative *sex, lies, and videotape,* which became Miramax's first major hit. The company's presence continued to grow in the early 1990s as the brothers began producing more films, and Harvey, who was the more flamboyant and outgoing of the two, became the public face of Miramax. In 1993 Walt Disney Inc. purchased the company for an estimated $60 million, but Harvey and his brother continued as cochairmen. A string of acclaimed films followed, including *Pulp Fiction* (1994) and *Smoke* (1995), and in 1997 Weinstein and Miramax won their first Academy Award for best picture for *The English Patient* (1996). Weinstein seemed unstoppable—releasing such hit films as *Good Will Hunting* (1997), *Shakespeare in Love* (1998; Academy Award for best picture), and *The Cider House Rules* (1999)—and by the late 1990s his movies had garnered nearly 40 Oscars. With savvy marketing and an eye for talent, he was responsible for bringing independent films into the mainstream, proving that period pieces, British accents, and character-driven dramas could wow audiences as much as car chases and explosions. Weinstein's success, however, did not come without criticism. His temper was legendary, and there were accusations that he staged overly aggressive Oscar campaigns. In addition, some filmmakers found his hands-on approach meddlesome.

As Miramax evolved from a distributor into a ministudio—with annual box-office receipts of more than $1 billion—Weinstein began to position the company as an entertainment empire. A television division was launched in 1998, and the following year *Talk* magazine, a joint venture with Hearst Publishing, hit the newsstands. In 2000 Talk Miramax Books was established. As the new ventures struggled, however, some believed that the diversion of Weinstein's attention was causing the film division to suffer, and in 2002 Miramax received only one Academy Award. That year also saw the end of *Talk*. With his success at the 2003 Oscars, however, it seemed that Weinstein was back on track.

(AMY TIKKANEN)

Wen Jiabao

At a meeting of the National People's Congress in Beijing on March 16, 2003, Wen Jiabao, a 60-year-old former geologist, was formally approved as the new premier of China, succeeding the retiring Zhu Rongji. A vice-premier under Zhu since 1998, Wen had been primarily responsible for handling agricultural, financial, and environmental matters. Viewed as a skilled and efficient administrator but one who possessed a much less forceful personal style than the often outspoken Zhu, Wen nevertheless shared Zhu's reform-minded approach to government. Restructuring China's heavily indebted banking system and continuing to reform its state-

© Reuters NewMedia Inc./Corbis

Wen Jiabao, the new Chinese premier

owned enterprises to make them more globally competitive were expected to be among his top objectives as premier.

Wen was born in September 1942 in Tianjin, China. He studied at the Beijing Institute of Geology between 1960 and 1968, eventually earning a graduate degree in structural geology. While a student at the institute, he joined the Communist Party of China (CPC), and upon graduation he went to work as a technician and political instructor at the Gansu Provincial Geological Bureau. He rose to become deputy director-general of the bureau before joining the Ministry of Geology and Mineral Resources in 1982. Wen was named deputy director of the General Office of the CPC Central Committee in 1985. The following year he was elevated to director, a post he held until 1992.

During his tenure as director of the General Office, Wen held a number of other party positions. He served as chief of staff to three general secretaries of the CPC—Hu Yaobang, Zhao Ziyang, and Jiang Zemin. In 1989, in a highly publicized incident, Wen accompanied Zhao to Beijing's Tiananmen Square while a dramatic series of pro-democracy student demonstrations were taking place. Both Wen and Zhao were photographed visiting with striking students—an act interpreted as a gesture of support for the students' cause. Although Zhao was soon placed under house arrest, and the demonstrations were forcibly repressed by the government, Wen managed to avoid being purged from the party and escaped lasting political damage from his association with Zhao. He went on to become a full member of the Secretariat of the CPC Central Committee in 1993 and a member of the Political Bureau in 1997. A year later he was appointed one of China's four vice-premiers.

As vice-premier, Wen was credited with helping launch a program aimed at lessening the tax burden on Chinese farmers. His experience in shaping agriculture policy, in particular, was believed to have helped his bid for the premiership, as one of the immediate priorities for China in 2003 was revitalizing its lagging rural economy. Upon taking office as premier, Wen cited agriculture along with banking and state-owned enterprises as areas in which he hoped to implement market-oriented reforms. According to some analysts, however, Wen's reformist agenda would likely take a backseat to national-security issues during the first years of his five-year term in office.

(SHERMAN HOLLAR)

Woese, Carl R.

For his revolutionary discovery of what the Royal Swedish Academy of Sciences termed "a third domain of life," microbiologist Carl Woese, a professor at the University of Illinois at Urbana-Champaign, was awarded the annual $500,000 Crafoord Prize in Biosciences in 2003. The award was given by the academy for accomplishments in fields other than those covered by the Nobel Prizes.

Prior to 1977 and Woese's seminal paper in *Proceedings of the National Academy of Sciences* (*PNAS*), many biologists believed that all life on Earth belongs to one of two primary lineages—the eukaryotes, which include animals, plants, fungi, and some single-cell organisms, and the prokaryotes, which include bacteria and all remaining microscopic organisms. Woese, working with microbiologist Ralph S. Wolfe, determined that prokaryotes actually comprise two distinctly different groups of organisms and should be divided into two categories: true bacteria (eubacteria) and the newly recognized archaea (archaebacteria). Archaea are aquatic or terrestrial microorganisms that differ both biochemically and genetically from true bacteria. Some thrive in—and actually require—extreme environments, including very hot or saline ones; some live in the absence of oxygen. Because such conditions resemble Earth's early environment, archaea are thought to hold important information about the evolution of cells.

In 1996 Woese and colleagues from the University of Illinois and the Institute for Genomic Research, Rockville, Md., published in the journal *Science* the first complete genome, or full genetic blueprint, of an organism in the archaea domain and concluded that archaea are more closely related "to us"—eukaryotes—than to bacteria. In two later papers that were published in *PNAS* in 1998 and 2000, Woese took his theory a giant step farther by proposing a new model to replace the standard Darwinian theory of common descent—that all life on Earth evolved from a single cell or precell. Woese proposed instead that various forms of life evolved independently from as many as several dozen ancestral precells.

Woese was born July 15, 1928, in Syracuse, N.Y. He attended Amherst (Mass.) College, from which he received a bachelor's degree in mathematics and physics in 1950; he was awarded a Ph.D. in biophysics by Yale University in 1953. After stints as a researcher at Yale (1953–60), the General Electric Research Laboratory (1960–63), and the Pasteur Institute in Paris (1962), in 1964 Woese joined the faculty at the University of Illinois, where he held the Stanley O. Ikenberry Endowed Chair. Among his many honours were a MacArthur fellowship from the John D. and Catherine T. MacArthur Foundation (1984), election to the National Academy of Sciences (1988), the Dutch Royal Academy of Science's Leeuwenhoek Medal, the highest honour in microbiology (1992), and the U.S. National Medal of Science (2000).

(ANTHONY G. CRAINE)

Yao Ming

The basketball world witnessed the emergence of an unlikely new star in 2003. In his first season in the National Basketball Association (NBA), Yao Ming, a 2.26-m (7-ft 5-in), 134-kg (296-lb) centre from Shanghai surpassed virtually everyone's expectations to become one of the league's marquee players while at the same time gaining millions of new fans worldwide for the NBA. Although the Houston Rockets selected Yao as the top overall pick in the 2002 NBA draft, many observers considered the choice to be a major gamble. With his phenomenal height, soft shooting touch, and deft passing ability, Yao undoubtedly possessed enormous potential, but prior to the draft he was largely untested against the kind of athletic big men who dominated the NBA. Any doubts about whether Yao could compete in the league were quickly erased once the season began, however. In a highly anticipated showdown against Shaquille O'Neal and the Los Angeles Lakers, Yao swatted away the first three of O'Neal's shots and scored on a dunk late in the game to help seal the Rockets' 108–104 victory.

Yao replaced O'Neal as the starting centre for the Western Conference team in the 2003 NBA All-Star game; in the fan balloting that

Houston Rockets' star Yao Ming

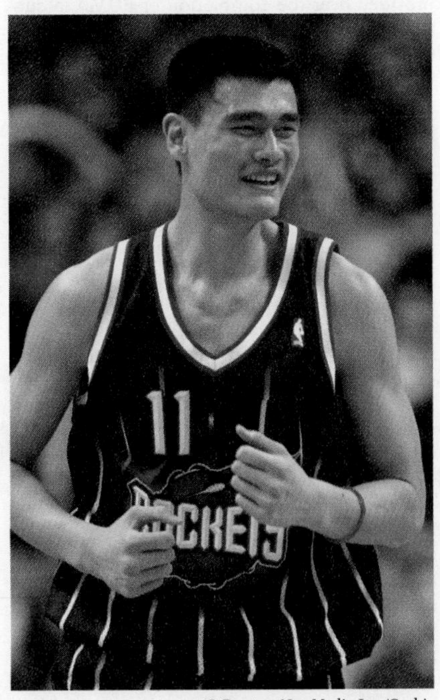

© Reuters NewMedia Inc./Corbis

determined the game's starting players, Yao bested O'Neal by nearly a quarter of a million votes. Yao was also a unanimous selection to the league's All-Rookie team. Although the Rockets narrowly missed making the NBA play-offs, Yao helped lead the team to a 43–39 record—an impressive turnaround from the Rockets' 28–54 record just one season earlier.

Yao was born in Shanghai on Sept. 12, 1980. Both of his parents stood over 1.8 m (6 ft) tall and had played basketball. From an early age Yao towered over his classmates, and by the time he was 12 years old, he was attending a local sports academy and practicing basketball several hours a day. In 1997 he joined the Shanghai Sharks of the China Basketball Association. That same year he attended Nike camps in Paris and Indianapolis, Ind., where he first attracted the notice of NBA coaches and recruiters. By the time he led the Chinese team to a respectable 10th-place finish at the 2000 Olympic Games in Sydney, Australia, Yao had become a national icon.

Soon after receiving permission from the Chinese government to join the NBA, Yao traveled to the U.S., where the media spotlight shone on him more intensely than ever. He drew large crowds wherever the Rockets played, and Houston games were broadcast to huge audiences in China and other Asian countries. He became a pitchman for Apple Computers, Visa, ESPN, and Gatorade. After the season ended, Yao made headlines again when he returned to China to host a telethon that reportedly raised more than $300,000 for SARS (severe acute respiratory syndrome) research. (SHERMAN HOLLAR)

Zeta-Jones, Catherine

For Welsh-born actress Catherine Zeta-Jones, 2003 was a year for becoming acquainted with the (desirable and not-so-desirable) wages of fame. In March she won the best supporting actress Oscar for her electrifying performance as homicidal entertainer Velma Kelly in the movie musical *Chicago* (2002). In April she and her husband, actor Michael Douglas, won their suit against a British magazine for having published unauthorized photos of the couple's wedding in November 2000.

Zeta Jones ("Zeta" is her middle name; she added the hyphen later) was born on Sept. 25, 1969, in Swansea, West Glamorgan, Wales, to Irish and Welsh parents. She performed with her church's amateur theatre group as a child and soon secured the starring role in the troupe's production of *Annie.* When she was 13 years old, she won first prize in a national tap-dancing competition. At age 15 she quit school and moved to London to pursue a career in acting. Her first major onstage role came two years later in a West End revival of the musical *42nd Street* when both the lead and the first understudy for the role were unable to perform; the producer of the musical then made her the lead for the remainder of the production run. It was not until she landed the role of Mariette Larkin in the popular British television comedy-drama series *The Darling Buds of May* during the early 1990s, however, that Zeta-Jones became well known in England. Her popularity made her a frequent target of the media; after a particularly harrowing incident in which she drove her car into a lamppost while trying to elude the paparazzi, Zeta-Jones moved to the United States.

AP/Wide World Photos

A radiant Catherine Zeta-Jones

She relocated to Los Angeles but found it initially difficult to gain a foothold in Hollywood films. She starred instead in made-for-television movies. Her performance in one such project, the miniseries *Titanic,* caught the eye of director Steven Spielberg, who thought she would be suitable for a leading role in his then-upcoming production of *The Mask of Zorro* (1998). After this breakthrough, Zeta-Jones went on to play opposite Sean Connery in the thriller *Entrapment* (1999) and to portray the wife of a drug dealer in Steven Soderbergh's Oscar-winning drama *Traffic* (2000). She received a Golden Globe nomination for her role in *Traffic,* and many felt that her performance had also merited an Oscar nomination. In a lighter vein, Zeta-Jones appeared in the romantic comedies *High Fidelity* (2000) and *America's Sweethearts* (2001).

Shortly after winning her Oscar, Zeta-Jones gave birth to her second child, Carys, in April 2003. Her next major film, *Intolerable Cruelty,* was released in October, and she was working on *Terminal* at year's end. (SHANDA SILER)

Zivkovic, Zoran

Shortly after the assassination, on March 18, 2003, of reformist premier Zoran Djindjic, the legislature of Serbia (one of the two republics that constituted Yugoslavia, which in turn was renamed Serbia and Montenegro in early 2003) elected Zoran Zivkovic prime minister. The pro-Western politician and former Yugoslav interior minister had been among Djindjic's closest allies. Prime Minister Zivkovic faced the monumental task of continuing Djindjic's reform platform, which was unpopular with many segments of the population. Zivkovic also lacked the charismatic and often controversial leadership style that had endeared Djindjic to many leaders in the international community. During his first nine months in office, however, Zivkovic governed with a high level of energy and determination, qualities that would be crucial for leading Serbia into economic recovery and civil stability.

Born in Nis, Yugos., on Dec. 22, 1960, Zivkovic completed an associates degree in economics in 1983 from the Belgrade College of Economics. In 1988 he started a company that offered supplies and maintenance for medical equipment. He began his political career in 1992 as a member of the Democratic Party and rapidly rose through its ranks, becoming party leader in his home town in 1993 and rising to party vice president in 1994. Zivkovic was elected mayor of Nis in 1996. He captured headlines in the winter of 1996–97 as an organizer of protests against Pres. Slobodan Milosevic's refusal to recognize the victory of opposition parties in local elections. In September 2000 Zivkovic was reelected mayor, but he moved to take an appointment as Yugoslav interior minister (in charge of the police) two months later. A staunch opponent of the Milosevic regime, he was a key figure in the protest campaigns that toppled the government in October 2000.

From 1993 to 1997 Zivkovic also served as a representative to the National Assembly of the Republic of Serbia, and he was a representative in the Chamber of Citizens of the Federal Assembly in 2000–03. His reputation as a politician capable of dealing with controversy and the most demanding tasks regarding party policy and state affairs earned him the ministerial appointment in 2000. During Zivkovic's tenure Yugoslavia was readmitted to Interpol. In 2002 he was elected president of the Council for Combating Terrorism and was a member of the National Council for Yugoslavia's cooperation with the UN International Criminal Tribunal for the Former Yugoslavia (ICTY) in The Hague. Together with Djindjic, he played a major role in handing indicted war criminals, such as Milosevic, over to the ICTY.

Zivkovic described the goals of his administration as a "cabinet of continuity," with a major focus on combating organized crime. He also pledged to pursue pro-market economic reforms and privatization, resolve the status of the province of Kosovo, and create institutions for the new state of Serbia and Montenegro, the loose union inaugurated in February 2003 to replace Yugoslavia. To explain the complicated situation in his country, Zivkovic made several major visits abroad, including a week conferring with U.S. and UN officials in July and a meeting with China's Wen Jiabao (*q.v.*) in November. (MILAN ANDREJEVICH)

bottom: © Reuters NewMedia Inc./Corbis

Obituaries

In 2003 the world LOST many leaders, pathfinders, NEWSMAKERS, heroes, CULTURAL ICONS, and ROGUES. The pages below RECAPTURE the lives and ACCOMPLISHMENTS of those we REMEMBER best.

Agnelli, Giovanni ("GIANNI"), Italian business tycoon (b. March 12, 1921, Turin, Italy—d. Jan. 24, 2003, Turin), as chairman (1966–96) of the Fiat SpA industrial conglomerate, was the most important Italian business leader of the 20th century and a symbol of Italy's post-

Carmaker Gianni Agnelli

World War II renaissance. Under Agnelli's leadership, diversification increased and the market for Fiat cars expanded from Italy to the rest of continental Europe. Though Agnelli had a degree in law, he embarked on a career as a jet-setting international playboy. A bad car accident in 1952 caused him to change direction, however, and in 1959 he became chairman of Istituto Finanziario Industriale, the Agnelli family's holding company. In 1963 he became managing director of Fiat. He was also well known for his stewardship of the Juventus association football (soccer) club, one of the family's holdings.

Aliyev, Heydar (GEIDAR ALI REZA OGLY ALIEV), Azerbaijani politician (b. May 10, 1923, Nakhichevan region, Transcaucasian S.F.S.R., U.S.S.R. [now an autonomous region of Azerbaijan]—d. Dec. 12, 2003, Cleveland, Ohio), was one of the most powerful men in Azerbaijan for more than 30 years, as deputy chairman (1964–67) and chairman (1967–69) of the regional KGB, as secretary (1969–87) of the Communist Party of Azerbaijan, and from 1993 as the repressive and autocratic president of independent Azerbaijan. Aliyev attained full membership in the Communist Party of the Soviet Union (CPSU) Politburo in 1982, but he opposed Soviet leader Mikhail Gorbachev's reforms, and in 1987 he was removed from office. In 1990 he denounced Soviet intervention in his homeland, and he resigned from the party the following year. When a rebellion drove Pres. Abulfaz Elchibey into internal exile in June 1993, Aliyev stepped in as acting president. He legitimized his position in a special presidential election that October and was reelected in 1998. By the time the seriously ill Aliyev stepped down in favour of his son in 2003, he had conducted protracted peace negotiations with Armenia over the status of Nagorno-Karabakh and had opened up Azerbaijan's oil industry to outside investment, but the country remained economically disadvantaged.

Allen, Ivan Earnest, Jr., American politician (b. March 15, 1911, Atlanta, Ga.—d. July 2, 2003, Atlanta), served as mayor of Atlanta from 1962 to 1970, and, having discarded his previous segregationist stance, led the city in integrating schools, businesses, and workforces at a time when other Southern cities were being troubled by racial violence. He was the only prominent Southern politician to give testimony in the Senate in support of what became the Civil Rights Act.

Amies, Sir (Edwin) Hardy, British couturier (b. July 17, 1909, London, Eng.—d. March 5, 2003, Langford, Oxfordshire, Eng.), dressed Queen Elizabeth II of England for half a century and was credited with having been a major influence on the menswear fashion revolution of the 1960s. Though his background was in business, he was hired by the design house Lachasse, known for its tailoring, in 1934, and by 1939 he was designing the entire collection. Amies founded his own design house, Hardy Amies Ltd. on Savile Row in 1945, and in 1955 he was appointed dressmaker to the queen. In 1959 he added a line of men's clothes and soon was designing for the tailoring chain Hepworth's. Amies sold his firm to the Luxury Brands Group in 2001 and retired later that year. He was knighted in 1989.

Amin, Idi (IDI AMIN DADA OUMEE), Ugandan military officer and president (b. 1924/25, near Koboko, Uganda British Protectorate—d. Aug. 16, 2003, Jiddah, Saudi Arabia), took control of Uganda in a military coup in 1971 and for eight years ruled with despotic power until he was overthrown by Ugandan nationalists supported by Tanzanian troops. Amin's often arbitrary and capricious rule of Uganda was characterized by fierce tribalism, which included the persecution of Acholi, Lango, and other peoples, and by extreme nationalism, which led him to antagonize former allies and to expel all Asians, primarily Indians, from Uganda (a move that left the already-disadvantaged country in far worse economic condition). Amin was a member of the Kakwa and had little formal education. He joined (1946) the King's African Rifles (under the British colonial army) and was made an officer after fighting for the British in Kenya during the Mau Mau revolt (1952–56). Uganda gained independence from Britain in 1962, and by 1966 Milton Obote, the new president and prime minister, had elevated Amin to major general and chief of the armed forces. Amin initially supported Obote, but in January 1971 he seized power while Obote was out of the country. Amin designated himself president in 1971, field marshal in 1975, and life president in 1976. As sole dictator, he was noted for his abrupt changes of mood, from shrewdness to buffoonery to tyranny. It was estimated that anywhere from 100,000 to as many as 500,000 Ugandans were tortured, mutilated, or murdered during his brutal regime. In April 1979, as the invading nationalist forces approached Kampala, the capital, Amin escaped to Libya; he later was given refuge in Saudi Arabia.

Aptheker, Herbert, American historian (b. July 31, 1915, Brooklyn, N.Y.—d. March 17, 2003, Mountain View, Calif.), wrote and lectured extensively on black history and on his Marxist political views. Because of Aptheker's membership in the Communist Party of the United States, which he joined in 1939, he was excluded from an academic career until 1969. He worked as an editor of various left-wing publications, and in 1964 he founded the American Institute of Marxist Studies. The best known of his many writings is *A Documentary History of the Negro People in the United States* (7 vol., 1951–94). In 1946 the sociologist and activist W.E.B. DuBois named Aptheker his literary executor; though the decision occasioned some criticism in the black intellectual community, Aptheker's editing of *The Correspondence of W.E.B. DuBois* (1973–78) was widely praised.

Armstrong, Garner Ted, American evangelist (b. Feb. 9, 1930, Portland, Ore.—d. Sept. 15, 2003, Tyler, Texas), ascended to celebrity in the 1950s as the principal evangelist on the radio and television programs of the Worldwide Church of God, which was founded by his father. The international popularity of *The World Tomorrow,* as both programs were called, helped the church achieve an estimated annual income of more than $70 million by the late 1970s. In 1978 sexual scandals and doctrinal disagreements led Armstrong's father to excommunicate him. He later formed the Church of God, International, and the Intercontinental Church of God.

Asper, Israel Harold, ("IZZY"), Canadian businessman and lawyer (b. Aug. 11, 1932, Minnedosa, Man.—d. Oct. 7, 2003, Winnipeg, Man.), transformed a bankrupt American television station (purchased in 1974 and subsequently moved to Winnipeg) into CanWest Global Communications Corp., Canada's largest media company; its holdings included more than 130 newspapers and the Global Television Network. Asper was also a noted philanthropist.

Atkins, Cholly (CHARLES SYLVAN ATKINSON), American dancer and choreographer (b. Sept. 30, 1913, Pratt City, Ala.—d. April 19, 2003, Las Vegas, Nev.), created the synchronized moves that characterized many of the Motown acts of the 1950s and '60s, including the Temptations, Gladys Knight and the Pips, the Supremes, the Shirelles, Martha and the Vandellas, and Smokey Robinson and the Miracles. He later shared a Tony Award for his work on the 1988 Broadway revue *Black and Blue.* Before Atkins turned to choreography, he had a notable career as a tap dancer, first as a member of a vaudeville act called the Rhythm Pals and later, with Charles ("Honi") Coles, in the team known as Coles and Atkins. One of the latter team's successes was a showstopping number in the Broadway production of *Gentlemen Prefer Blondes* in 1949.

Atkins, Robert Coleman, American cardiologist and nutritionist (b. Oct. 17, 1930, Columbus, Ohio—d. April 17, 2003, New York, N.Y.), wrote seven best-selling diet books—beginning in 1972 with *Dr. Atkins' Diet Revolution*—advocating that dieters adopt his controversial weight-loss plan that counseled them to consume large amounts of fats and protein and to minimize their intake of carbohydrates. Although for many years a large number of health experts deemed that diet potentially dangerous, later studies showed it to be effective and nondetrimental to health; further research was planned.

Axelrod, George, American playwright and screenwriter (b. June 9, 1922, New York, N.Y.—d. June 21, 2003, Los Angeles, Calif.), created witty, sophisticated, and sometimes satiric works for the stage and screen in the 1950s and '60s and for a time was Hollywood's highest-paid screenwriter. Among his most notable successes were the plays *The Seven Year Itch* (1952; filmed 1955) and *Will Success Spoil Rock Hunter?* (1955) and the scripts for the films *Bus Stop* (1956), *Breakfast at Tiffany's* (1961), *The Manchurian Candidate* (1962), and a black comedy that became a cult favourite, *Lord Love a Duck* (1966).

Babcock, Horace Welcome, American astronomer (b. Sept. 13, 1912, Pasadena, Calif.—d. Aug. 29, 2003, Santa Barbara, Calif.), led the effort to create, in 1969, Chile's Las Campanas Observatory, the first observatory to be built far from sources of light pollution. In the 1950s Babcock devised the system of adaptive optics that enabled telescopes to compensate for the distorting effect of Earth's atmosphere on light from distant stars and galaxies. During that time Babcock and his father, Harold Delos Babcock, invented the solar magnetograph, which measures various properties of the Sun's magnetic field.

Bachchan, Harivansh Rai, Indian poet (b. Nov. 27, 1907, Allahabad, United Provinces [now Uttar Pradesh], India—d. Jan. 18, 2003, Mumbai [Bombay], Maharashtra, India), was one of the most acclaimed Hindi-language poets of the 20th century. His long lyric poem *Madhushala* (*The House of Wine*), published in 1935, brought him legions of fans. Bachchan's public readings were attended by thousands of people, and the still-popular work was translated into English as well as many other Indian languages and was performed onstage and set to music. He continued to write poetry while teaching English at Allahabad University and working to promote the Hindi language in the government of Prime Minister Jawaharlal Nehru. In the 1970s, Bachchan published a four-part autobiography, which also created a stir in the literary world; an abridged English translation, *In the Afternoon of Time,* appeared in 1998. In his later years his fame was eclipsed by that of his son, Bollywood actor Amitabh Bachchan.

Poet Harivansh Rai Bachchan

Ballard, Hank (JOHN H. KENDRICKS), American singer and songwriter (b. Nov. 18, 1927, Detroit, Mich.—d. March 2, 2003, Los Angeles, Calif.), lit up the rhythm-and-blues (R&B) charts in the 1950s with a series of earthy blues-inspired songs and wrote the dance hit "The Twist." In 1953 Ballard was asked to step in as front man for a doo-wop band called the Royals. Ballard's first record with them, "Get It," made the top 10 on the R&B charts. The group changed its name to the Midnighters to avoid confusion with another group with a similar name. The Midnighters released the salacious "Work with Me, Annie" in 1954; it topped the R&B charts for seven weeks and made number 22 on the pop charts, though a number of radio stations refused to play it. A series of hits in a similar vein followed. In 1958 Ballard wrote and recorded "The Twist," and one year later Chubby Checker's cover of the song spawned a national dance craze. Ballard was inducted into the Rock and Roll Hall of Fame in 1990.

Banana, Canaan Sodindo, Zimbabwean Methodist minister, theologian, and statesman (b. March 5, 1936, Esiphezini, Matabeleland, Southern Rhodesia—d. Nov. 10, 2003, Harare, Zimb.), held the largely ceremonial post of president of Zimbabwe from 1980, when the country gained independence, until Prime Minister Robert Mugabe pushed through constitutional changes in 1987 that created an executive presidency for himself. In 1998, after a highly publicized and controversial trial, Banana was convicted of homosexual assault and other "unnatural acts" and was sentenced to 10 years in prison, with 9 years suspended; he eventually served eight months.

Bartley, Robert LeRoy, American journalist (b. Oct. 12, 1937, Marshall, Minn.—d. Dec. 10, 2003, New York, N.Y.), served as the editor of *The Wall Street Journal*'s editorial page for three of his nearly four decades with that paper and in that post was an avid champion of supply-side economics and increased defense spending. He won the Pulitzer Prize for editorial writing in 1980 and a few days before his death was informed that he was to be awarded the Presidential Medal of Freedom.

Bates, Sir Alan Arthur, British actor (b. Feb. 17, 1934, Allestree, Derbyshire, Eng.—d. Dec. 27, 2003, London, Eng.), was considered among the finest and most versatile performers of his generation. He was at home both in the works of such classical writers as William Shakespeare and Anton Chekhov and in those by contemporary playwrights, including Tom Stoppard, Harold Pinter, Simon Gray, and David Storey, and he excelled not only onstage but also in film and in television productions. After studying at the Royal Academy of Dramatic Arts, with an interruption for service in the Royal Air Force, Bates made his stage debut in 1955, and the following year he gained the role of a young disaffected working-class man in the play that established his reputation, *Look Back in Anger.* His edgy performance in *The Caretaker* (1960) provided further proof of the depth of his talent. Bates had his first important film role in *The Entertainer* (1960) and followed with a string of successes, among them *Zorba the Greek* (1964), *Georgy Girl* (1966), *The Fixer* (1968), *Women in Love* (1969), and *The Go-Between* (1970). Back onstage such productions as *In Celebration* (1969), *Butley* (1971), and *Otherwise Engaged* (1975) continued to showcase his versatility. Many of Bates's most acclaimed roles came late in his career, including the butler Mr. Jennings in the film *Gosford Park* (2001), the blustering Uncle Matthew in the TV miniseries *Love in a Cold Climate* (2001), and an impecunious Russian aristocrat in the Broadway production of *Fortune's Fool,* for which he won a Tony Award in 2002. Bates was made CBE in 1995 and was knighted in January 2003.

Ben Khedda, Benyoussef, Algerian independence leader (b. Feb. 23, 1920, Berrouaghia, Alg.—d. Feb. 4, 2003, Algiers, Alg.), negotiated Algeria's independence from France in 1962, but he was forced from power shortly thereafter. In 1943, after he protested against French attempts to recruit Algerians in World War II, Ben Khedda was imprisoned for eight months. After the war he became general secretary of the pro-independence organization headed by Messali Hadj, but he later broke with the party and started his own organization. After the radical National Liberation Front (FLN) launched a revolt against French rule in 1954 and France responded with mass arrests, Ben Khedda wrote in a partisan newspaper decrying the French policy. Again he was imprisoned, and on his release he joined the FLN. He joined the provisional government that the FLN set up in Tunisia, and in 1961 he replaced Ferhat Abbas as head of the provisional government. A settlement was reached whereby a referendum was held in July 1962, followed by the departure of the French and the triumphant arrival in Algiers of the provisional government. Within weeks, however, Houari Boumedienne and Ahmed Ben Bella challenged Ben Khedda for the leadership of the government, and he stepped down.

Benton, Stephen Anthony, American inventor (b. Dec. 1, 1941, San Francisco, Calif.—d. Nov. 9, 2003, Boston, Mass.), became fascinated with holograms the first time he saw one and went on to invent the rainbow hologram, the type used on credit cards, which was named the Benton hologram. He was a founding member of the Media Laboratory at the Massachusetts Institute of Technology, and his pioneering work led to uses in medical imaging and in fine arts holography.

Berio, Luciano, Italian composer (b. Oct. 24, 1925, Oneglia, Italy—d. May 27, 2003, Rome, Italy), drew on serialism, aleatoric practices, electronic sounds, musique concrète, and other sources to create a complex musical language. He received his first music lessons from his father and grandfather and beginning at age 20 studied at the Milan Conservatory. In 1952 he studied with Italian composer Luigi Dallapiccola at the Berkshire Music Center in Tanglewood, Mass. Later in the 1950s he participated in the summer sessions in Darmstadt, then in West Germany, the centre of the European avant-garde. In the mid-1950s, with Italian composer Bruno Maderna, he founded an electronic music studio in Milan, and during this time he also published the journal *Incontri Musicali.* Berio spent much of the 1960s teaching and conducting in the U.S. and from 1965 taught at the Juilliard School, New York City, where he founded the Juilliard Ensemble. Returning to Europe in 1972, he taught at the centre for experimental music established by Pierre Boulez in Paris, and in 1987 he founded an Italian counterpart, Tempo Reale, in Florence. In 2000 he became the president and artistic director of the Accademia Nazionale di Santa Cecilia in Rome. Berio wrote in many forms, from solo pieces to chamber and orchestral works to operas. Several early works for voice were written for performance by his first wife, Cathy Berberian. The *Sequenza* series (from 1958) was written for solo instruments, including the voice. His best-known work was perhaps *Sinfonia* (1968–69), which included texts taken from James Joyce and Samuel Beckett and the scherzo from Gustav Mahler's *Symphony No. 2,* among other borrowings, illustrating the range of Berio's influences and interests. Operas included *Una vera storia* (1977–81) and *Un re in ascolto* (1979–84), both collaborations with the writer Italo Calvino. Berio's completion of the final act of Giacomo Puccini's *Turandot* was debuted in 2002.

Bigelow, Julian Himely, American engineer and mathematician (b. March 19, 1913, Nutley, N.J.—d. Feb. 17, 2003, Princeton, N.J.), engineered one of the earliest computers. In 1946 John von Neumann hired Bigelow as the engineer on his project, based at the Institute for Advanced Study, Princeton, to create a stored-program computer. Bigelow was already known for being the coauthor of a paper that would become the foundation of the new field of cybernetics. He assumed overall responsibility for the design of the proposed computer, which was built in the late 1940s and came to be known as the IAS. The basic design of the IAS became the template for the modern computer.

Biswas, Anil, Indian composer and singer (b. July 7, 1914, Barisal, East Bengal, India [now in Bangladesh]—d. May 31, 2003, New Delhi, India), introduced orchestral music, often with native classical or folk elements, into popular Indian cinema. Biswas wrote music for some 100 films between 1935 and 1965, when he retired from the movie industry to take over as director of the national orchestra on All India Radio.

Blanchot, Maurice, French novelist and critic (b. Sept. 27, 1907, Quain, France—d. Feb. 20, 2003, Mesnil Saint Denis, France), was a reclu-

Composer Luciano Berio

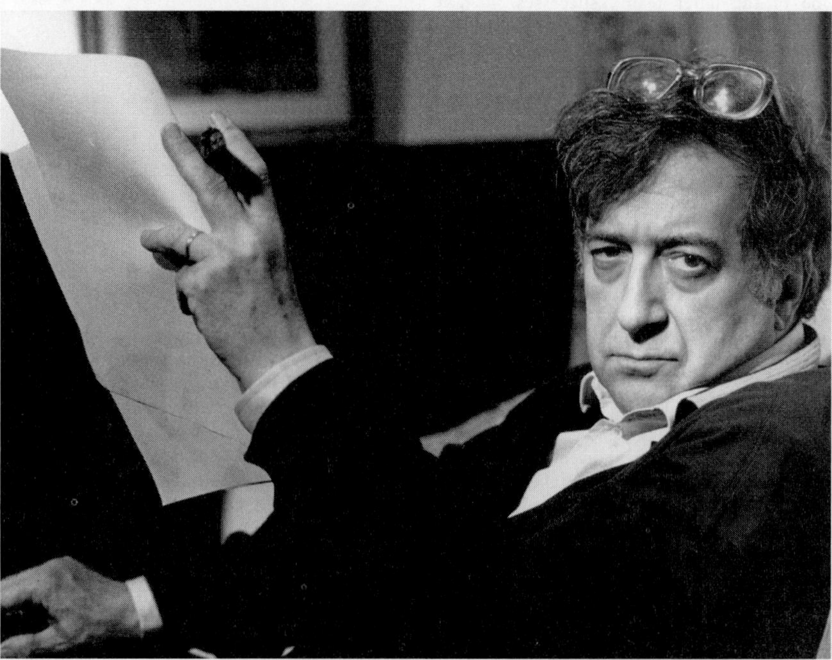

Hulton|Archive by Getty Images

sive intellectual who influenced such postmodernist thinkers as Jacques Derrida, Michel Foucault, and Roland Barthes; he also supported new writers, including Samuel Beckett and Alain Robbe-Grillet. Though Blanchot wrote for right-wing journals before World War II, after the war he opposed the French occupation of Algeria, and he joined the antigovernment demonstrations in 1968. He was associated with Jean-Paul Sartre on *Les Temps Modernes* and wrote a monthly column for *La Nouvelle Revue Française* (1953–68).

Bobetko, Janko, Croatian army chief (b. Jan. 10, 1919, Crnac, Kingdom of Serbs, Croats, and Slovenes [now in Croatia]—d. April 29, 2003, Zagreb, Croatia), was regarded as a hero of Croatia's independence, but in 2002 he was indicted for war crimes by the International Criminal Tribunal for the Former Yugoslavia (ICTY). During World War II, Bobetko rose to prominence with Josip Broz Tito's Partisan forces, which became part of Yugoslavia's army after the war. He became a general in 1954 and was made chief of staff in 1967. Bobetko was among those advocating greater autonomy for Croatia until Tito cracked down on the movement in 1972 and dismissed all of its supporters. In 1992 Bobetko assumed command of the new Croatian Defense Forces, which he led into battle in 1993 to retake Croatian territory that had been conquered by Serbian forces. In September 2002 the ICTY ordered him to stand trial in The Hague for having engaged in "ethnic cleansing" during the 1993 fighting. Bobetko refused, and in February 2003 the tribunal's medical team ruled that he was too ill to withstand a courtroom trial.

Bonds, Bobby Lee, American baseball player (b. March 15, 1946, Riverside, Calif.—d. Aug. 23, 2003, San Carlos, Calif.), was one of the first players in Major League Baseball to combine power and speed. During a 14-year career (1968–81), he was a five-time "30–30" player (he hit at least 30 home runs and stole at least 30 bases in one season), a three-time All-Star, and a three-time Gold Glove winner. His son Barry Bonds set the MLB record for most home runs in a single season (73).

Bourgault, Pierre, Canadian journalist and politician (b. Jan. 23, 1934, East Angus, Que.—d. June 16, 2003, Montreal, Que.), was a staunch supporter of Quebec's secession from Canada, writing for separatist newspapers and staging numerous protests, including a 1964 demonstration against Queen Elizabeth II that turned violent. He was president (1964–68) of the party Rassemblement pour l'Independence Nationale, but his militancy led to a falling out with the separatist leadership, and by the early 1970s Bourgault had become a marginal player in the movement.

Braidwood, Robert John, and Braidwood, Linda Schreiber, American archaeologists (respectively, b. July 29, 1907, Detroit, Mich.—d. Jan. 15, 2003, Chicago, Ill., and b. Oct. 9, 1909, Grand Rapids, Mich.—d. Jan. 15, 2003, Chicago), investigated the beginnings of settled farming communities, developed interdisciplinary methods of field research, and helped to establish Middle Eastern prehistory as a disciplined field of scholarship. While he was studying at the University of Michigan, Robert Braidwood was invited to do archaeological fieldwork near Baghdad, Iraq, in 1930. He earned an M.A. from the University of Michigan in 1933; Linda Schreiber received a B.A. from the same university in 1932. In 1933 Robert was hired by James Henry Breasted, the founder of the University of Chicago's Oriental Institute, and began work at an excavation in the Amuq Valley in northern Syria, where he established an approach that made it possible to date artifacts more precisely. In 1937 Robert and Linda Braidwood married, and henceforward they collaborated in their work. World War II brought a temporary halt to their fieldwork, and Robert directed a meteorological mapping program at the University of Chicago for the Army Air Corps. Robert received a Ph.D. from the University of Chicago in 1943, and Linda earned an M.A. from the university in 1946. In 1947 the Braidwoods established the Prehistoric Project at the Oriental Institute in order to better study the period when agriculture was first practiced and humans made the transition from hunting and gathering to agriculture and civilization. They began their fieldwork at Jarmo in northeastern Iraq with an interdisciplinary team that was an innovation in archaeological research. This led to a grant from the National Science Foundation in 1954. The work in Iraq continued until 1958. In 1963 they began work on a joint Prehistoric Project between the University of Chicago and Istanbul University at Coyonu in southern Turkey, where they discovered a farming community believed to date to about 7000 BC. Robert Braidwood was granted the Gold Medal Award for Distinguished Archaeological Achievement by the Archaeological Institute of America in 1971. The Braidwoods retired from fieldwork in 1989 but continued to work and teach at the Oriental Institute. He was a contributor to *Britannica Book of the Year* for 55 years (1943–97), a record unequaled by any other author. Robert and Linda died of pneumonia a few hours apart.

Brakhage, James Stanley ("STAN"; ROBERT SANDERS), American filmmaker (b. Jan. 14, 1933, Kansas City, Mo.—d. March 9, 2003, Victoria, B.C.), created hundreds of unique experimental films and was considered a leading figure of the American experimental cinema. Brakhage's goal in his films was to free the act of seeing from the constraints of representation and expectation. He used a variety of methods, creating films that ranged in length from a few seconds to several hours and showed visions ranging from those produced by cinematography to those made by gluing objects to the celluloid and scratching and painting the celluloid. He also taught filmmaking at the School of the Art Institute of Chicago (1969–81) and at the University of Colorado at Boulder (1981–2002). His best-known film, *Dog Star Man* (1964), is considered a key work of the American avant-garde.

Brasher, Christopher William ("CHRIS"), British athlete, journalist, and businessman (b. Aug. 21, 1928, Georgetown, British Guiana [now Guyana]—d. Feb. 28, 2003, Chaddleworth, Berkshire, Eng.), on May 6, 1954, set the pace for the first two laps of Roger Bannister's historic race breaking the four-minute mile; he later cofounded the London Marathon. Brasher discovered athletics at university and ran the steeplechase at the 1952 Olympic Games. In the 1956 Olympics, he won the gold medal in the 3,000-m steeplechase. Thereafter he worked as a sports journalist, and he was named Sportswriter of the Year in Britain in 1968 and in 1976. A successful businessman, he cofounded the British Orienteering Federation in 1966 and founded the Brasher Boot Co. in 1983. He was made CBE in 1996.

Runner Chris Brasher

Bright, William Rohl, American religious leader (b. Oct. 19, 1921, Coweta, Okla.—d. July 19, 2003, Orlando, Fla.), founded Campus Crusade for Christ in 1951 and transformed it from a college-based organization into the world's largest Christian ministry. A former self-described "happy pagan," he also wrote *The Four Spiritual Laws* (1956), a condensed version of the Christian message that became the most widely distributed religious booklet in the world. In 1996 he won the Templeton Prize for Progress in Religion.

KRT

Television newsman David Brinkley

Brinkley, David McClure, American television journalist (b. July 10, 1920, Wilmington, N.C.—d. June 11, 2003, Houston, Texas), had a dry wit, a wry, clipped delivery, and a relaxed demeanour that enhanced the effectiveness of his work and, combined with his skills as a news reporter and as a writer, made him one of the most influential news anchors and commentators in the United States. His 14-year partnership with Chet Huntley on *The Huntley-Brinkley Report* provided a format for news programs that remained the most-followed model, and their signature closing lines—"Good night, Chet," "Good night, David"—became a catchphrase, though Brinkley later admitted to having disliked the exchange. Brinkley began writing for a weekly newspaper when he was in high school, and after some university studies and a year in the army, he went to work for United Press. NBC hired him as a news writer in 1943 and in 1945 moved him to television, as moderator of a news show. He became a news commentator in 1950 and the following year was made Washington correspondent for the NBC nightly news broadcast. Brinkley was first paired with Huntley for live coverage of the political conventions in the summer of 1956, and *The Huntley-Brinkley Report* debuted in the fall. Until Huntley retired in 1970, the show was nearly always the top-ranked news program. Brinkley then served as an anchor of NBC's *Nightly News* and was host of *NBC Magazine* and *David Brinkley's Journal,* and in 1981 he moved to ABC for *This Week with David Brinkley.* He retired in 1997. Brinkley claimed that his career was summarized by the subtitle of his autobiography, *David Brinkley* (1995): *11 Presidents, 4 Wars, 22 Political Conventions, 1 Moon Landing, 3 Assassinations, 2,000 Weeks of News and Other Stuff on Television, and 18 Years of Growing Up in North Carolina.* That career, however, also included such honours as 10 Emmy Awards, 3 George Foster Peabody Awards, and the Presidential Medal of Freedom.

Brockhouse, Bertram Neville, Canadian physicist (b. July 15, 1918, Lethbridge, Alta.—d. Oct. 13, 2003, Hamilton, Ont.), won the Nobel Prize for Physics in 1994 for developing the phenomenon of inelastic neutron scattering into a technique that enabled scientists to analyze the atomic structure of matter; he shared the award with American physicist Clifford G. Shull. After serving (1939–45) in the Royal Canadian Navy during World War II, Brockhouse attended the University of British Columbia (B.A., 1947) and the University of Toronto (M.A., 1948; Ph.D., 1950). In 1950 he became a researcher at the Chalk River Nuclear Laboratory, a facility operated by Atomic Energy of Canada, and it was there that he conducted his award-winning work. In his technique a beam of neutrons all with the same energy is directed at a target material, and in the resulting collision the neutrons scatter and lose energy through inelastic collisions with atomic nuclei in the target. These energy changes are measured and analyzed to provide details about the material's atomic structure. Able to supply information not available through other analytic approaches such as X-ray crystallography, inelastic neutron scattering quickly became an important research tool and advanced the field of neutron scattering. Brockhouse utilized the technique to conduct pioneering studies on phonons (units of vibrational energy) in crystalline materials, and it was also used to study viruses and DNA. The triple-axis neutron spectrometer he created to conduct his research was later refined and became widely used. In 1962 Brockhouse joined the faculty of McMaster University in Hamilton; he became professor emeritus in 1984.

Bronson, Charles (CHARLES DENNIS BUCHINSKY), American actor (b. Nov. 3, 1921, Ehrenfeld, Pa.—d. Aug. 30, 2003, Los Angeles, Calif.), spent the early part of his movie and television career cast in small roles as quiet tough guys but later became a star, following strong supporting roles in the hit films *The Magnificent Seven* (1960), *The Great Escape* (1963), and *The Dirty Dozen* (1967), success as an action star in Europe, and the lead role in *Death Wish* (1974), which caught the American public's fancy and led to four sequels despite the controversy surrounding the films' violence and their theme of vigilante justice. His later performances were acknowledged for the humanity and tenderness apparent below the surface of his craggy-faced toughness.

Brooks, Herbert Paul ("HERB"), American ice hockey player and coach (b. Aug. 5, 1937, St. Paul, Minn.—d. Aug. 11, 2003, near Forest Lake, Minn.), guided the U.S. men's ice hockey team to one of the greatest upsets in sports as it defeated the U.S.S.R. en route to capturing the gold medal at the 1980 Winter Games in Lake Placid, N.Y.; the dramatic win became known as the "Miracle on Ice." Brooks later coached in the National Hockey League, and at the 2002 Winter Games in Salt Lake City, Utah, he steered the U.S. men's ice hockey team to a silver medal. Brooks also played (1964 and 1968) on U.S. Olympic ice hockey teams.

Brumel, Valery Nikolayevich, Soviet high jumper (b. May 14, 1942, Razvedki, Russia, U.S.S.R.—d. Jan. 26, 2003, Moscow, Russia), dominated the sport of high jumping in the early 1960s, winning two Olympic medals (silver in 1960 and gold in 1964) and setting six consecutive outdoor world records between 1961 and 1963. His final record, 2.28 m (7 ft 5¾ in), was not broken officially until 1971. Brumel, who used the traditional face-down straddle technique, also set two indoor high-jump records in 1961. He sustained multiple fractures to his right leg in a motorcycle accident in 1965. After numerous surgeries and prolonged rehabilitation, he returned to competition in 1969, and in 1970 he cleared 2.13 m (almost 7 ft). Brumel later earned a doctorate in sports psychology and wrote a semiautobiographical novel and two plays.

High jumper Valery Brumel

AP/Wide World Photos

Brunhoff, Cécile Sabouraud de, French pianist and teacher (b. Oct. 16, 1903, Paris, France—d. April 7, 2003, Paris), invented the character of Babar the Elephant and his original adventure in 1930 in a bedtime story for her two sons. The boys told the story to their father, the artist Jean de Brunhoff, the next day, and he wrote it down, with illustrations and embellishments. When a brother persuaded him to bring it out publicly, however, Cécile insisted that her name be removed from the title page, believing her contribution to have been too minor. *Histoire de Babar, le petit éléphant* (1931, *The Story of Babar, the Little Elephant,* 1933) became a worldwide children's favourite and generated many sequels, first by Jean, until his death in 1937, and then by their older son, Laurent.

Bryant, Felice (MATILDA GENEVIEVE SCADUTO), American songwriter (b. Aug. 7, 1925, Milwaukee, Wis.—d. April 22, 2003, Gatlinburg, Tenn.), with her husband, Boudleaux Bryant, formed one of the most successful and prolific songwriting teams in history. The pair met and married in 1945, and soon he began setting her poems to music. In 1950 they were persuaded to relocate to Nashville, Tenn.; they were probably the first to move there in order to make a living as songwriters. Their more than 800 songs included most of the hits of the Everly Brothers, among them "Bye Bye Love" and "Wake Up, Little Susie," as well as the bluegrass standard "Rocky Top." The Bryants were inducted into the Songwriters Hall of Fame in 1986 and into the Country Music Hall of Fame in 1991.

Buchholz, Horst, German film actor (b. Dec. 4, 1933, Berlin, Ger.—d. March 3, 2003, Berlin), enjoyed a lengthy career in several countries and was best known in the U.S. for his role in *The Magnificent Seven* (1960) and the Billy Wilder farce *One, Two, Three* (1961). The strikingly handsome Buchholz had his first screen role in *Marianne de ma jeunesse* (1954). He won a best young actor award at the Cannes Film Festival for the 1955 film *Himmel ohne Sterne* (released in the U.S. as *Sky Without Stars*). His starring role in *Bekenntnisse des Hochstaplers Felix Krull* (1957; *The Confessions of Felix Krull*) brought him international notice, and in 1959 he starred in the British movie *Tiger Bay.* In 1997 he appeared as a Nazi doctor in the Academy Award-winning film *La vita è bella* (*Life Is Beautiful*).

Bucknell, Robert Barraby ("BARRY"), British television-show host (b. Jan. 26, 1912, London, Eng.—d. Feb. 21, 2003, St. Mawes, Cornwall, Eng.), inspired do-it-yourself fans with his popular home-renovation shows in the 1950s and '60s. Bucknell was invited to appear on the BBC television program *About the Home* (1956–57), on which he gave advice about small household projects to the host, Joan Gilbert. His popularity on that show led to his own live show, *Do It Yourself,* in 1958 and to a still more popular show, *Bucknell's House,* in 1962. In the latter show Bucknell renovated a derelict Victorian house over 39 weeks. At about the same time, Bucknell designed a family sailing dinghy for the *Daily Mirror* newspaper; more than 90,000 *Mirror* dinghies were sold.

Bykau, Vasil Uladzamiravich (VASILY BYKOV), Belarusian novelist (b. June 19, 1924, Bychki, Belorussia, U.S.S.R.—d. June 22, 2003, Minsk, Belarus), eschewed the strict conventions of most Soviet-era literature in order to explore the psychology of individuals struggling with the moral dilemmas of wartime. While he ostensibly showed the heroic actions of Soviet soldiers during World War II or, after the rise of glasnost, the struggles of ordinary Belarusians living under first Nazi and then Soviet control, Bykau did not equivocate on the grim realities of war, and some of his works were banned in the Soviet Union. His translations of his own works from Belarusian into Russian served as the basis for translations from Russian into Western languages. A fierce critic of Pres. Alyaksandr Lukashenka's pro-Russian regime, Bykau lived in exile in Finland, Germany, and the Czech Republic from 1998 until shortly before his death.

Cairns, James Ford ("JIM"), Australian left-wing politician (b. Oct. 4, 1914, Melbourne, Australia—d. Oct. 12, 2003, Melbourne), was best known for his passionate antiwar activism. Cairns was first elected to Parliament in 1955 and soon became a leading light in the Labor Party. In 1970 he led a huge demonstration in Melbourne against Australian involvement in the Vietnam War. Cairns ably served in several ministerial posts in the Labor government of 1972, earning the sobriquet "minister for the castigation of wicked countries," until an ill-concealed affair with his personal secretary, Junie Morosi, coupled with financial irregularities, brought about his downfall. He retired from politics in 1977, though his commitment to left-wing causes continued unabated.

Campos, Haroldo Eurico Browne de, Brazilian poet (b. Aug. 19, 1929, São Paulo, Braz.—d. Aug. 16, 2003, São Paulo), founded a modernist literary movement known for its concrete poetry. He and his compatriots called themselves Noigandres, a word he borrowed from an Ezra Pound canto. Besides serving as the leading theorist of this group of writers, Campos was an essayist, a literary critic, and a notable translator into the Portuguese language of works in Chinese, German, Greek, Hebrew, English, Japanese, Russian, and Latin.

Carney, Arthur William Matthew ("ART"), American actor (b. Nov. 4, 1918, Mount Vernon, N.Y.—d. Nov. 9, 2003, Chester, Conn.), had a long and varied career in radio, television, theatre, and film, including an Academy Award-winning dramatic leading role in the movie *Harry and Tonto* (1974), but it was with one TV character that he would be most identified—sewer worker (or "underground sanitation expert") Ed Norton, second banana to Jackie Gleason's Ralph Kramden, in *The Honeymooners.* From 1951 to 1957—including one season (1955–56) as a half-hour sitcom—and occasionally thereafter in the 1960s and '70s, the two characters and their wives were seen in sketches on various Gleason variety shows and in a few specials. Carney began his performing career doing impressions with the Horace Heidt Orchestra and later on radio. Drafted in 1944, he was wounded on D-Day and thereafter walked with a limp. Following his military service he returned to radio performing and then expanded into TV. In addition to his *Honeymooners* appearances, Carney had roles in dozens of drama series episodes and made-for-TV movies, and he also appeared on Broadway, where his roles included the original Felix Unger in *The Odd Couple* (1965). Notable among his films were *The Late Show* (1977) and *Going in Style* (1979). Carney won seven Emmy Awards—five for his performances as Norton—and a few weeks before his death, he was inducted into the Hall of Fame of the Academy of Television Arts and Sciences.

Carter, Bennett Lester ("BENNY"), American musician and composer (b. Aug. 8, 1907, New York, N.Y.—d. July 12, 2003, Los Angeles, Calif.), was the elder statesman of jazz, one of the most original and influential swing era saxophonists, and a pioneer arranger who helped set the big band style; he was an accomplished trumpeter and also played clarinet and trombone. Most important, he was an alto saxo-

Big band pioneer Benny Carter

phonist with a pure tone and an elegant melodic style. While grace and spontaneity were his most evident qualities, a subtle yet rigorous sense of form was at the heart of his soloing; in time he adopted the fanciful rhythms of bop. He composed, arranged, and soloed with top bands before leading his own big band in 1933–34. He spent 1935–38 in Europe, with bands in England, The Netherlands, and France. Back in the U.S. during the height of the swing era, he formed more big bands and, in 1943, composed his first film score (*Stormy Weather*). For the next 29 years he composed film and television sound track music and appeared only irregularly as a soloist, He also composed for bandleader Count Basie and for many singers (including Peggy Lee and Ella Fitzgerald), and he recorded the noted album *Further Definitions* (1961). Carter was one of the first African American composers with an extensive Hollywood career. He also taught at Princeton University and was a busy jazz soloist, forming bands for festivals and worldwide tours and performing for three U.S. presidents.

Carter, Nell (NELL HARDY), American singer and actress (b. Sept. 13, 1948, Birmingham, Ala.—d. Jan. 23, 2003, Beverly Hills, Calif.), won a Tony Award in 1978 for her performance in the Broadway musical revue *Ain't Misbehavin'* and in 1982 won an Emmy Award for a TV presentation of that show. She later achieved acclaim for her role as a sassy housekeeper in the 1980s TV sitcom *Gimme a Break!*

Cash, John R. ("JOHNNY"), American singer-songwriter (b. Feb. 26, 1932, Kingsland, Ark.—d. Sept. 12, 2003, Nashville, Tenn.), was a country-and-western legend whose genre-hopping music influenced folk and rock and whose craggy baritone, simple poetics, hard-won integrity, and advocacy of the dispossessed transformed him into an American icon. Cash was the son of impoverished farmers; he grew up in Mississippi and, after high school and a stint in a Detroit factory, enlisted in the air force, where he learned to play the guitar. After his military service, he married, moved to Memphis, Tenn., and worked as an appliance salesman while pursuing a career in music. Recording for the Sun label, Cash and the Tennessee Two (Marshall Grant and Luther Perkins) scored a string of hits, including "Folsom Prison Blues" (1955) and "I Walk the Line" (1956). Moving to Columbia Records, Cash topped the country chart in 1963 with "Ring of Fire," co-written for him by June Carter (see *Cash, June Carter,* below), of the legendary musical Carter Family, who became his second wife (1968). Cash eschewed the glittery fashions typical of country performers to become the "man in black," symbolic of his intolerance of injustice. A dynamic live performer who began his shows with the simple introduction "Hello, I'm Johnny Cash," he had hits with the albums *Live at Folsom Prison* (1968) and *Johnny Cash at San Quentin* (1969). In the late 1960s and '70s he hosted a television show, collaborated with Bob Dylan, and rivaled the Beatles in record sales. Among his hits were "A Boy Named Sue" (1969) and "One Piece at a Time" (1976). Cash's popularity waned in the late '70s and '80s, but the series of critically acclaimed albums he made with producer Ric Rubin, beginning with *American Recordings* (1994), introduced a new generation to his music. The winner of 11 Grammy Awards, he was a member of both the Rock and Roll and Country Music halls of fame. Having survived earlier battles with alcohol and drugs, he died of complications from diabetes.

AP/Wide World Photos

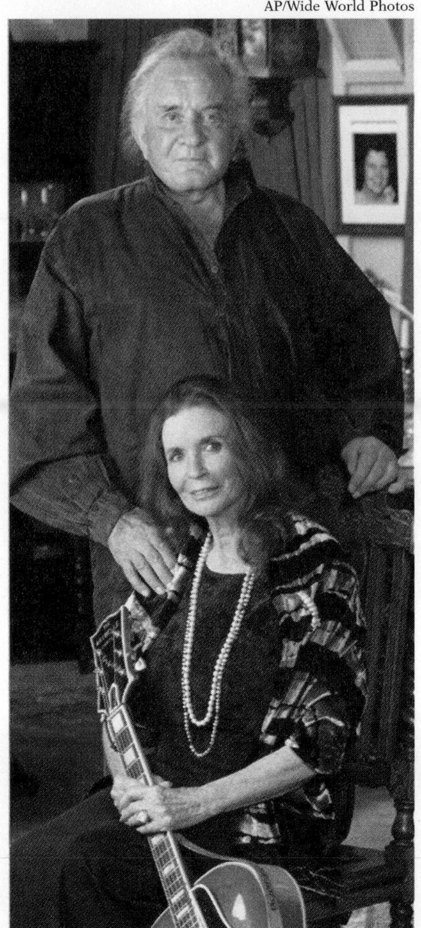

Country singers Johnny Cash and June Carter Cash

Cash, (Valerie) June Carter, American singer, songwriter, and actress (b. June 23, 1929, Maces Spring, Va.—d. May 15, 2003, Nashville, Tenn.), began her long career in country music when she was a young child, performing as a member of the legendary Carter Family, which was paramount in leading country music into the mainstream. In 1963 she co-wrote her best-known song, "Ring of Fire," to describe her feelings about singer Johnny Cash (*q.v.*), whom she married in 1968. During their more than 40-year partnership, she also acted on television and in film in addition to performing with him.

Chadwick, Lynn Russell, British sculptor (b. Nov. 24, 1914, London, Eng.—d. April 25, 2003, Stroud, Gloucestershire, Eng.), was renowned for his skeletal iron and bronze sculptures, notably animal- and humanlike forms of great emotional power. Chadwick trained as an architectural draftsman. He had his first one-man show of mobiles in 1950, and the following year he was commissioned to produce two works for the Festival of Britain and one for the Battersea Park Sculpture Exhibition. After studying welding in the early 1950s, however, he turned to stable constructions. He represented Great Britain at the 1952 Venice Biennale and was awarded the International Sculpture Prize at the 1956 Biennale, which brought him worldwide acclaim. In 1953 he was one of the 12 semifinalists for the Unknown Political Prisoner International Sculpture Competition. Chadwick was appointed CBE in 1964 and was made a Royal Academician in 2001.

Cheung, Leslie (CHEUNG KWOK-WING), Hong Kong actor and singer (b. Sept. 12, 1956, Hong Kong—d. April 1, 2003, Hong Kong), achieved enormous popularity in Hong Kong and throughout Asia, first by means of his singing and then through his performances in Chinese-language motion pictures, in which he was one of the few actors willing to portray homosexual characters. He gained worldwide fame with his performance in the 1993 film *Farewell, My Concubine,* for which he was awarded the Grand Prix at the Cannes Film Festival.

Chung Mong Hun, South Korean businessman (b. 1948, Seoul, S.Kor.—d. Aug. 4, 2003, Seoul), used his position as chairman of Hyundai Asan (part of the Hyundai conglomerate founded by his father) to push for reconciliation between North and South Korea, but he became embroiled in scandal after it was alleged that he had funneled money to the North Korean government to ensure that a 2000 summit between the two countries would take place. Indicted for falsifying his company's books to hide some $100 million in payments, he committed suicide.

Businessman Chung Mong Hun

AP/ Wide World Photos

The *Columbia* Astronauts

Anderson, Michael P., American astronaut (b. Dec. 25, 1959, Plattsburgh, N.Y.—d. Feb. 1, 2003, over Texas), was the payload commander and a mission specialist on the space shuttle *Columbia.* Anderson was educated at the University of Washington and at Creighton University, Omaha, Neb., where he earned a master's degree in physics. In 1991–95 he served in the U.S. Air Force as an instructor pilot and tactical officer, and in 1998 he flew in the space shuttle *Endeavour* on a mission to the Russian space station *Mir.*

Brown, David M., American astronaut (b. April 16, 1956, Arlington, Va.—d. Feb. 1, 2003, over Texas), was a mission specialist and flight surgeon on the space shuttle *Columbia.* Brown was educated at the College of William and Mary, Williamsburg, Va., and at Eastern Virginia Medical School, where he earned a doctorate in medicine in 1982. He was director of medical services at the Navy Branch Hospital in Adak, Alaska, and served on an aircraft carrier before beginning pilot training in 1988; he was chosen for the astronaut program in 1996.

(Clockwise from front) Astronauts Husband, Chawla, Brown, McCool, Anderson, Ramon, and Clark

Chawla, Kalpana, Indian-born American astronaut (b. July 1, 1961, Karnal, India—d. Feb. 1, 2003, over Texas), was a mission specialist on the space shuttle *Columbia.* Chawla was the first woman to study aeronautical engineering at Punjab Engineering College; she continued her education at the University of Texas at Arlington and the University of Colorado at Boulder, where she earned a doctorate in aeronautical engineering (1988). She first flew on the *Columbia* in 1997 as a mission specialist and primary robotic-arm operator.

Clark, Laurel Blair Salton, American astronaut (b. March 10, 1961, Ames, Iowa—d. Feb. 1, 2003, over Texas), was a mission specialist and flight surgeon on the space shuttle *Columbia.* Clark was educated at the University of Wisconsin at Madison, where she earned a doctorate in medicine in 1987. In the U.S. Navy she served as a diving medical officer and headed a submarine squadron medical SEAL unit before becoming a flight surgeon; she was chosen for the astronaut program in 1996.

Husband, Rick D., American astronaut (b. July 12, 1957, Amarillo, Texas—d. Feb. 1, 2003, over Texas), was commander of the space shuttle *Columbia*'s mission. Husband was educated at Texas Tech University and at California State University at Fresno, where he earned a master's degree in 1990. He joined the U.S. Air Force in 1980. In 1999 he flew on the *Discovery* on the first space shuttle mission to dock with the International Space Station.

McCool, William C., American astronaut (b. Sept. 23, 1961, San Diego, Calif.—d. Feb. 1, 2003, over Texas), was pilot of the space shuttle *Columbia.* McCool was educated at the U.S. Naval Academy; he earned a master's degree in computer science from the University of Maryland in 1985 and another in aeronautical engineering from the U.S. Naval Postgraduate School in 1992. He became a pilot for the U.S. Navy in 1986 and was chosen for the astronaut program in 1996.

Ramon, Ilan, Israeli pilot and astronaut (b. June 20, 1954, Ramat Gan, Israel—d. Feb. 1, 2003, over Texas), was Israel's first astronaut and a payload specialist on the space shuttle *Columbia.* Ramon, a graduate of the Israel Air Force Flight School, was a fighter pilot in the 1973 Yom Kippur War and in the 1982 military operations in Lebanon; he also took part in the 1981 bombing of an Iraqi nuclear reactor. He was selected for the U.S. astronaut program in 1998.

Clement, Hal (HARRY CLEMENT STUBBS), American teacher and writer (b. May 30, 1922, Somerville, Mass.—d. Oct. 29, 2003, Boston, Mass.), taught high-school science and incorporated his knowledge of science in his writing, producing "hard" science-fiction works in which situations adhered carefully and logically to the laws of science. Beginning during the Golden Age of science fiction and continuing for some 62 years, he created numerous short stories and novels, including the classic *Mission of Gravity* (1954). He also published scientific articles under his own name and created astronomical and science-fiction paintings under the name George Richard.

Codd, Edgar Frank ("TED"), British-born American computer scientist and mathematician (b. Aug. 23, 1923, Portland, Dorset, Eng.—d. April 18, 2003, Williams Island, Fla.), devised the "relational" data model, which led to the creation of the relational database, a standard method of retrieving and storing computer data. Codd interrupted his study of mathematics and chemistry at the University of Oxford to become a pilot in the Royal Air Force during World War II. Following graduation in 1948 he moved to the U.S., and he later became a U.S. citizen. Codd joined IBM Corp. in 1949 and worked as a mathematical programmer on some of the company's early computers. He invented the technique of "multiprogramming," which allows several programs to run at once. In 1967, after receiving a doctorate in computer science from the University of Michigan, Codd moved to IBM's Research Laboratory in San Jose, Calif. IBM was slow to adopt Codd's proposals, however, which allowed the Ingres and Oracle relational databases to debut before IBM's own SQL/DS was launched in 1981. The Association of Computing Machinery, the British Computer Society, the National Academy of Engineering, the American Academy of Arts and Sciences, and the Institute of Electrical and Electronics Engineers honoured Cobb for his achievements. In 1981 Codd received the A.M. Turing Award, the highest honour for computer science.

Collins, Janet, American ballet dancer and choreographer (b. March 7, 1917, New Orleans, La.—d. May 28, 2003, Fort Worth, Texas), was acclaimed for the beauty of her dancing on the Broadway stage—notably in *Out of This World*

(1950)—as well as in film and on television, but she was best known for having become (1951) the first black performer to appear on the stage of New York City's Metropolitan Opera House. As prima ballerina at the Metropolitan, she danced lead roles in such operas as *Aida* and *Carmen.*

Conable, Barber Benjamin, Jr., American politician (b. Nov. 2, 1922, Warsaw, N.Y.—d. Nov. 30, 2003, Sarasota, Fla.), served as a Republican congressman in the U.S. House of Representatives from 1965 to 1985 and in 1986 was appointed president of the International Bank for Reconstruction and Development, or World Bank. In that position, which he held until 1991, he reorganized the bank's bureaucracy, saw to the doubling of the amounts available to less-developed countries, made the environmental impact of projects a priority, and created women's economic programs.

Connor, George Leo, American football player (b. Jan. 21, 1925, Chicago, Ill.—d. March 31, 2003, Evanston, Ill.), played outstandingly at offensive and defensive tackle as well as linebacker positions, mostly with the National Football League's Chicago Bears. Already regarded as an outstanding football player in high school, Connor was an all-American for College of the Holy Cross, Worcester, Mass., for two years. After a stint in the U.S. Navy during World War II, he was an all-American (1946–47) at the University of Notre Dame; the football team was undefeated in those two years. In 1946 Connor was the first recipient of the Outland Trophy for the top interior lineman in college football. Connor briefly played professionally for the New York Giants and the Boston Yanks before embarking on a long career (1948–55) with the Chicago Bears. A two-way player throughout his career, he was an offensive and defensive tackle until 1949, when he switched to linebacker. After his retirement from football because of an injured knee, Connor worked as an assistant coach and as a broadcaster before becoming a business executive. He was elected to the Pro Football Hall of Fame in 1975.

Cooper, Art(hur), American magazine editor (b. Oct. 15, 1937, New York, N.Y.—d. June 9, 2003, New York City), as editor (1983–2003) of *Gentlemen's Quarterly* (*GQ*), created a magazine that became synonymous with suave and in the process redefined men's magazines. He filled *GQ*'s pages with a mix of fashion, sports, sex, and literary journalism, often recruiting such leading writers as David Halberstam, Gore Vidal, and Peter Mayle. In 2003 Cooper was inducted into the Hall of Fame of the American Society of Magazine Editors.

Coors, Joseph, American businessman and political patron (b. Nov. 12, 1917, Golden, Colo.—d. March 15, 2003, Rancho Mirage, Calif.), with his brother William expanded the brewery of the Adolph Coors Co. from being the producer of a local Western beer to the third largest brewer in the U.S. and was a founder in 1973 of the Heritage Foundation, a prominent conservative think tank. Coors was named to the board of the company in 1946 and served at various times as president, chief operating officer, and vice chairman. He and his brother devised and refined the company's signature cold-brewing system and played a role in the introduction of aluminum beer cans as well as in an early recycling system, begun in 1959 when the company offered a penny for each can returned. Long a financial supporter of right-wing political causes, Coors was instrumental in the rise of Ronald Reagan to the U.S. presidency in 1980.

Corelli, Franco, Italian tenor (b. April 8, 1921, Ancona, Italy—d. Oct. 29, 2003, Milan, Italy), thrilled opera audiences throughout the world with his passion, power, and charisma, particularly in heroic roles. Corelli made his opera debut in 1951 as Don José in *Carmen* at Spoleto, first sang at Milan's La Scala in 1954 with Maria Callas in Gaspare Spontini's *La vestale,* and went on to become an international star. He retired in 1976.

Coxeter, H(arold) S(cott) M(acDonald) ("DONALD"), British-born Canadian geometer (b. Feb. 9, 1907, London, Eng.—d. March 31, 2003, Toronto, Ont.), was a leading figure in the understanding of non-Euclidean geometries, reflection patterns, and polytopes (higher-dimensional analogs of three-dimensional polyhedra). His work served as an inspiration for R. Buckminster Fuller's concept of the geodesic dome and, particularly, for the intricate geometric designs of Dutch graphic artist M.C. Escher; in 1997 Coxeter published a paper in which he demonstrated that Escher's 1958 woodcut *Circle Limit III* was mathematically perfect. Coxeter studied at Trinity College, Cambridge (Ph.D., 1931). In 1936 he joined the faculty of mathematics at the University of Toronto, where he remained until he retired in 1980. Coxeter wrote some 200 papers and a dozen books, including *Non-Euclidean Geometry* (1942; 6th edition, 1998), *Introduction to Geometry* (1961), *Regular Complex Polytopes* (1974; 2nd edition, 1991), and *Kaleidoscopes* (1995). He was made a fellow of the Royal Society of Canada (1948) and of the British Royal Society (1950) and was named a Companion of the Order of Canada in 1997.

Crain, Jeanne, American actress (b. May 25, 1925, Barstow, Calif.—d. Dec. 14, 2003, Santa Barbara, Calif.), gained a best actress Academy Award nomination for her starring role as a young black woman passing for white in the controversial 1949 film *Pinky.* During her three-decade-long career, she appeared in more than 60 movies—including *State Fair* (1945), *Margie* (1946), *Apartment for Peggy* (1948), and *People Will Talk* (1951)—and in numerous television shows.

Craveirinha, José (JOSÉ G. VETRINHA), Mozambican writer (b. May 28, 1922, Lourenço Marques, Portuguese East Africa [now Maputo, Mozambique]—d. Feb. 6, 2003, South Africa), was generally considered Mozambique's greatest poet as well as one of the best contemporary poets writing in Portuguese. Craveirinha began working as a journalist, and his first poems were published in newspapers for which he wrote articles. He was chairman of the Lourenço Marques African Association in the 1950s and joined the anticolonial organization Frelimo. His first poetry collection, *Chigubo,* appeared in 1964, but Portuguese authorities jailed him for his political activities from 1966 to 1969. Craveirinha was one of the leading figures of the Negritude movement in African poetry, and his poems, most of which had a political cast, evoked an Africa ruled by Africans. He was awarded the Camões Prize for poetry in 1991, the third person to be so honoured.

Italian tenor Franco Corelli

Crenna, Richard Donald, American actor (b. Nov. 30, 1926, Los Angeles, Calif.—d. Jan. 17, 2003, Los Angeles), became known in the 1940s as such squeaky-voiced radio characters as Oogie Pringle on *Date with Judy* and Walter Denton in *Our Miss Brooks* and continued to play the latter role when that series moved to television in the 1950s. He went on to star in another TV series, *The Real McCoys,* and to acclaimed roles in such films as *The Sand Pebbles, Wait Until Dark, Body Heat,* and the Rambo movies, as well as in a number of TV series and made-for-TV movies.

Critchfield, James Hardesty, American spymaster (b. 1917, Hunter, N.D.—d. April 22, 2003, Williamsburg, Va.), employed his military, diplomatic, and intelligence skills—and readiness to make moral compromises—on many fronts in the Cold War, including Germany, Iraq, Tibet, and Cuba. Critchfield was a colonel in a U.S. Army assault battalion in World War II and joined the CIA in 1948. He was sent to Germany to act as liaison officer with the Gehlen Organization—a group of ex-Nazi officials led by Gen. Reinhardt Gehlen (formerly the Reich's anti-Soviet espionage chief)—which was forming the core of a postwar West German defense intelligence system. Gehlen's agency proved to be teeming with double agents and war criminals, but Critchfield believed that the risks posed by the Soviet Union were more dangerous and advised the Western governments to proceed anyway. The Gehlen Organization was disbanded and integrated with NATO in 1955. Critchfield was made CIA division chief for the Middle East and was among those who in the early 1960s recommended that the U.S. support the Iraqi Ba'th Party to oppose the threat of communism in that country. Critchfield retired from the CIA in 1975; the agency awarded him two medals for his services.

Cronyn, Hume Blake, Canadian-born actor (b. July 18, 1911, London, Ont.—d. June 15, 2003, Fairfield, Conn.), had a versatility that enabled him to be convincing in stage and screen character portrayals that ranged all the way from quiet and bookish to curmudgeonly to sinister. He was especially noted for his acting partnership with his wife, Jessica Tandy, during much of their almost 52-year marriage, which ended with her death in 1994. He also directed, wrote screenplays, and produced television shows. Cronyn studied at the American Academy of Dramatic Arts in New York City and in 1934 made his Broadway debut in *Hipper's Holiday.* In 1943 he went to Hollywood for his first film role, in Alfred Hitchcock's *Shadow of a Doubt.* Among the numerous films that followed were *Lifeboat* (1944), *The Postman Always Rings Twice* (1946), and *People Will Talk* (1951). During that time he also appeared with Tandy in such films as *The Seventh Cross* (1944) and *The Green Years* (1946). Cronyn and Tandy first performed together onstage in 1951 in *The Fourposter,* and they went on to star in regional theatres and on Broadway in such notable stage productions as *A Delicate Balance* (1966), *The Gin Game* (1977), *Foxfire* (1982), and *The Petition* (1986). Later films together included *Cocoon* (1985) and its sequel, *Cocoon: The Return* (1988), *Batteries Not Included* (1987), and the television feature *To Dance with the White Dog* (1994), for which Cronyn won his third Emmy Award—his first having been for *Age-Old Friends* (1989) and his second for Neil Simon's *Broadway Bound* (1992). Cronyn and Tandy were elected to the Theater Hall of Fame in 1979 and in 1986 were presented with the Kennedy Center Lifetime Achievement Medal. In addition, in 1994—many years after Cronyn had won a Tony Award for his performance in Richard Burton's 1964 production of *Hamlet*—he and Tandy were jointly honoured with the first Tony for lifetime achievement.

Cruz, Celia, Cuban-born singer (b. Oct. 21, 1924?, Havana, Cuba—d. July 16, 2003, Fort Lee, N.J.), reigned for decades as the "queen of salsa music," electrifying audiences with her wide-ranging, soulful voice and rhythmically compelling style; she shimmied as she sang, attired in flamboyant costumes, including varicoloured wigs, tight sequined dresses, and outlandishly high heels. She studied at Havana's Conservatory of Music before rising to fame as lead singer in the hit orchestra La Sonora Matancera in 1950; she appeared in five Cuban films and starred at Havana's Tropicana nightclub. After the 1959 revolution brought Fidel Castro to power, Cruz and the band moved to Mexico and then, in 1961, to the United States. Top Latin-jazz bandleader Tito Puente began featuring her in the 1960s, and her breakthrough came in the '70s with the rise of salsa, a blend of Afro-Cuban and other Caribbean musics. She recorded hits such as "Bemba Colorá" and "Quimbara" with Johnny Pacheco; was featured with Willie Colón, Ray Barretto, and other salsa stars; and was lead singer with the Fania All-Stars. She also sang with rock stars and in the Latin opera *Hommy* (a version of the Who's *Tommy*), and she included raps in her later recordings. Cruz, the subject of the 1988 BBC television documentary *My Name Is Celia Cruz,* won two Grammy Awards and three Latin Grammys and was a 1994 recipient of a National Medal of the Arts. Though her records were not allowed in Cuba and she was forbidden to return for her father's funeral, the ban on her was eased in the late 1990s. She refused to return, however, while Castro was alive.

"Queen of salsa" Celia Cruz

AP/Wide World Photos

Dacko, David, Central African Republic politician (b. March 24, 1930, Bouchia, Moyen Congo, French Equatorial Africa—d. Nov. 20, 2003, Yaoundé, Cameroon), was twice president (1960–65 and 1979–81) of the Central African Republic and twice was removed from office by a military coup. After then president Barthélemy Boganda died in a plane crash in March 1959, Dacko established himself in the top post, and from 1960 he headed an autocratic one-party state in the newly independent CAR. An ongoing economic crisis, however, led to his deposition by Col. Jean-Bédel Bokassa, who eventually declared himself emperor. In September 1979 France intervened and restored Dacko to power, but his second administration was no more successful than his first, and in 1981 Gen. André Kolingba overthrew him in a bloodless coup.

Daddah, Moktar Ould, Mauritanian politician (b. Dec. 25, 1924, Boutilimit, French West Africa—d. Oct. 15, 2003, Paris, France), as Mauritania's first postindependence president (1961–78), secured international recognition and respect for the new country while he reconciled the varied interests of Mauritania's widely dispersed, partly nomadic, and religiously diverse Arab and black African populations. Daddah trained as a lawyer in France and was elected (1957) to the territorial assembly as a member of the moderate Progressive Mauritanian Union. He became president of the Executive Council in 1958, was named prime minister in 1959, and won the first presidential election in August 1961, nine months after Mauritania gained independence. Daddah led an authoritarian one-party administration, but he was regarded as an honest and relatively enlightened leader and was reelected twice (1971, 1975). An agreement with Morocco in 1975 to divide former Spanish Sahara (Western Sahara), however, led to an expensive war in the region, and in July 1978 Daddah was overthrown in a military coup. He lived in exile in France until he was allowed to return home quietly in 2001.

right: © AFP/Getty Images

Davidson, Donald Herbert, American philosopher (b. March 6, 1917, Springfield, Mass.—d. Aug. 30, 2003, Berkeley, Calif.), applied logical and linguistic analysis to difficult problems in the philosophy of action, the philosophy of mind, and the philosophy of language. Davidson argued, against the widely held Wittgensteinian view, that reasons were the causes of actions and that, thereby, the rational and the causal domains were connected. In a related argument, he resolved Cartesian dualism (which maintains that mind and matter are completely distinct substances) with a nonreductionist physicalism in which mental events are describable in causal terms but are characterized by intentionality, which has a rational as well as a causal dimension. This position Davidson called anomalous monism. He also maintained that meaning in natural languages is understood by means of the concept of truth, for which he employed the semantic definition of Alfred Tarski. For Davidson the empirical determination of such truth requires what he called radical interpretation. Davidson earned a Ph.D. in 1949 from Harvard University. He taught at several universities, most recently the University of California, Berkeley (1986–2003). Many of his papers were collected in the volumes *Essays on Actions and Events* (1980) and *Inquiries into Truth and Interpretation* (1984).

de Weldon, Felix, Austrian-born sculptor (b. April 12, 1907, Vienna, Austria—d. June 2, 2003, Woodstock, Va.), created more than 2,000 public sculptures around the world, most notably the Marine Corps War Memorial (1954) in Arlington, Va. Based on a Pulitzer Prize-winning photograph by Joe Rosenthal, the monument depicts marines raising the U.S. flag on Iwo Jima during World War II.

DeBusschere, David Albert ("DAVE"), American basketball player (b. Oct. 16, 1940, Detroit, Mich.—d. May 14, 2003, New York, N.Y.), became the youngest coach in National Basketball Association (NBA) history when at age 24 he became player-coach for the Detroit Pistons; he later provided tenacious defense and sturdy rebounding during six seasons as a forward with the New York Knicks (1968–74). He went on to become an executive with two franchises and, in 1975, commissioner of the American Basketball Association (ABA). DeBusschere was both a basketball and baseball star in high school in Detroit and at the University of Detroit. He began as a baseball pitcher for the Chicago White Sox, winning three games and posting a 2.90 earned run average (1962–63). Uniquely, he also began a pro basketball career in 1962, with the Detroit Pistons, and two years later became the Pistons' player-coach; he led Detroit to a 79–143 record over three seasons. He was traded to the Knicks in 1968 and in 1970 sparked the Knicks to their first NBA championship; they repeated the feat in 1973. During his NBA playing career, DeBusschere averaged 16 points and 11 rebounds per game and was an eight-time all-star. After retiring in 1974, he became general manager of the New York Nets, in the ABA. As the ABA's commissioner, he was instrumental in the league's merger with the NBA in 1976. He returned to the Knicks as general manager (1982–86). DeBusschere was elected to the Basketball Hall of Fame in 1983, and in 1996 he was chosen one of the 50 greatest players in the NBA's first 50 years.

Deray, Jacques (JACQUES DESRAYAUD), French film director (b. Feb. 19, 1929, Lyon, France—d. Aug. 9, 2003, Boulogne-Billancourt, France), specialized in thrillers and film noir, making more than 30 well-constructed crime films, many starring Alain Delon. His best-known movies included the psychological thriller *La Piscine* (1969; released in the U.S. as *The Swimming Pool*) and the caper film *Borsalino* (1970).

DeTomaso, Alejandro, Argentine industrialist (b. July 10, 1928, Buenos Aires, Arg.—d. May 21, 2003, Modena, Italy), raced cars in Modena before founding (1959) DeTomaso Automobili with his wife, Isabelle Haskell, and producing a line of sports cars and a number of limited-edition cars for public roads during the 1960s, including the Vallelunga, the Mangusta, and the Pantera. The latter was distributed by the Ford Motor Co. in the U.S., but its tendency to rust and overheat coupled with stringent American emission laws soured the partnership. DeTomaso purchased a number of struggling Italian companies, including Benelli motorcycles (1971), Moto Guzzi (1972), Maserati (1975; sold to Fiat in 1990), and Innocenti (1976). A 1993 stroke sidelined him from the business, but his wife and son continued to run the company.

Dib, Mohammed, Algerian novelist and poet (b. July 21, 1920, Tlemcen, Alg.—d. May 2, 2003, La Celle-Saint-Cloud, France), was the author of some 30 books of fiction, poetry, and essays, many of which closely examined contemporary life in Algeria. Widely regarded as Algeria's foremost writer, Dib was best known for an early trilogy—*Le Grande Maison* (1952), *L'Incendie* (1954), and *Le Métier à tisser* (1957)—novels that offered a starkly realistic portrayal of Algerian peasants and workers in the years preceding World War II. Dib wrote in French—the language in which he first learned to read. He began writing poetry at the age of 15. During the war he studied literature at the University of Algeria and served as an interpreter for French and British military units. He later worked as a designer of rugs (1945–47) and as a journalist (1951) before publishing *Le Grande Maison,* his first book. Later novels included *La Danse du roi* (1968), *Qui se souvient de la mer* (1962), *Cours sur la rive sauvage* (1964), *Dieu en Barbarie* (1970), *Le Maître de chasse* (1973) and *Habel* (1977). These novels—often marked by the use of symbol, myth, and allegory—addressed subjects such as the French colonial repression of the Algerians, the war for independence and its effects, and the new Algeria after independence. Expelled from Algeria by the colonial authorities in 1959, Dib was eventually allowed to settle in southern France after fellow writers Albert Camus and André Malraux petitioned the government on his behalf. Dib's volumes of poetry included *Ombre gardienne* (1961), *Formulaires* (1970), *Omneros* (1975), and *O vive* (1987). Among his collections of essays were *Tlemcen ou les lieux d'écriture* (1994) and *L'Arbre à dires* (1998). *LA Trip,* a verse novel, appeared in 1999. Dib became the first North African writer to win the Francophone Grand Prix—the Academie Française's highest literary award—in 1994.

Algerian writer Mohammed Dib

Dillon, C(larence) Douglas, American financier, politician, and arts patron (b. Aug. 21, 1909, Geneva, Switz.—d. Jan. 10, 2003, New York, N.Y.), though a Republican, served as secretary of the treasury (1961–65) under Democratic Presidents John F. Kennedy and Lyndon Johnson; Dillon's policies were given credit for the long peacetime economic expansion of those years. Before his years of public service, he was chairman of the international banking company Dillon, Read & Co. (1946–53), and after he left the government, he served as president (1970–77) and, later, chairman (1977–83) of the Metropolitan Museum of Art, New York City, where he largely created the Chinese art collection. Dillon was awarded the Presidential Medal of Freedom in 1989.

Djindjic, Zoran, Serbian politician (b. Aug. 1, 1952, Bosanski Samac, Yugos. [now in Bosnia and Herzegovina]—d. March 12, 2003, Belgrade, Serbia and Montenegro), was a boldly pragmatic Serbian prime minister, who reformed the economy and brought former strongman Slobodan Milosevic before the UN war-crimes tribunal. As a university student in 1974, Djindjic was imprisoned for attempting to organize a noncommunist youth group. After his release he moved

to West Germany, where he earned a doctorate in 1979 from the University of Konstanz. Returning to Yugoslavia, Djindjic cofounded the Democratic Party in 1989, and in 1994 he became the party's president. When Milosevic attempted to annul the results of the 1996 legislative elections, Djindjic organized demonstrations that were sustained for 12 weeks, until Milosevic relented and recognized opposition victories. In the 2000 Yugoslav presidential election, Djindjic backed opposition leader Vojislav Kostunica, who won and named him prime minister of Serbia in January 2001. Thereafter Djindjic engaged in a power struggle with Kostunica, even while beginning to root out corruption and bringing Serbian political and social standards more in line with those of Western Europe. In the face of widespread local opposition, he allowed the extradition of Milosevic to face war-crimes charges in June 2001, which resulted in the immediate offer of millions of dollars in foreign aid. Djindjic was gunned down in downtown Belgrade.

Doby, Lawrence Eugene ("LARRY"), American baseball player (b. Dec. 13, 1923, Camden, S.C.—d. June 18, 2003, Montclair, N.J.), became the second African American player in the major leagues and the first in the American League when he joined the Cleveland Indians in 1947. The next year he starred as the Indians' centre fielder, batting .301, and his home run won a World Series game. A power hitter, he batted .326 in 1950, when he led the league in on-base percentage; twice he slugged 32 homers to lead the league; and his 126 runs batted in led the Indians to another pennant in 1954. Doby was an all-star for seven years, and he was elected to the Baseball Hall of Fame. In 1978 he became the second African American major-league manager when he took over the Chicago White Sox for half a season.

Dowiyogo, Bernard, Nauruan politician (b. Feb. 14, 1946, Nauru—d. March 9, 2003, Washington, D.C.), served six times (1976–78, 1989–95, 1996, 1998–99, 2000–01, 2003) as president of the Pacific islet nation of Nauru. Dowiyogo was twice removed from office by a no-confidence vote—once, in 1996, after only 15 days—and in January 2003 he was replaced as president for two days when the Supreme Court ruled that his election was invalid. In 1993 he reached a historic agreement with Australia over rehabilitation of Nauru's economy in the aftermath of the catastrophic damage done by phosphate mining. He later opposed French testing of nuclear weapons in the South Pacific and a proposed U.S. missile shield. In 2001 Dowiyogo faced accusations that he had allowed Nauru to become a money-laundering haven. He was returned to office in January 2003.

Dudinskaya, Natalya Mikhaylovna, Ukrainian-born Russian ballerina (b. Aug. 21, 1912, Kharkiv, Ukraine, Russian Empire—d. Jan. 29, 2003, St. Petersburg, Russia), was prima ballerina of the Kirov (now Mariinsky) Ballet. Celebrated for her virtuosity and her pure classical technique during her performing career from the 1930s to the early 1960s, she went on to renown as a cherished and highly respected teacher.

Dugan, Alan, American poet (b. Feb. 12, 1923, Brooklyn, N.Y.—d. Sept. 3, 2003, Hyannis, Mass.), wrote verse that showed his clear-eyed, irreverent, down-to-earth vision of the human predicament. His first volume, *Poems* (1961), was selected for the Yale Series of Younger Poets award and won both a National Book Award and a Pulitzer Prize, and 40 years later his collection *Poems Seven* (2001) won him a second National Book Award.

Dunne, John Gregory, American writer (b. May 25, 1932, Hartford, Conn.—d. Dec. 30, 2003, New York, N.Y.), wrote both fiction and nonfiction that showed his interest in the movie industry and his Irish-American roots. Dunne married novelist Joan Didion in 1964, and together they wrote several screenplays, including *The Panic in Needle Park* (1971), *A Star Is Born* (1976; with others), and *Up Close & Personal* (1996). He wrote *Monster: Living off the Big Screen* (1997) about his unhappy experience working on the last of these. Dunne examined Irish-American communities in a trio of gritty novels: *True Confessions* (1977; filmed 1981), *Dutch Shea, Jr.* (1982), and *The Red, White, and Blue* (1987). His other works included the autobiographical *Harp* (1988), two collections of essays, and the novel *Playland* (1994). He was a frequent contributor to *The New York Review of Books* and *The New Yorker.*

Ebsen, Buddy (CHRISTIAN RUDOLPH EBSEN, JR.), American actor, dancer, artist, and writer (b. April 2, 1908, Belleville, Ill.—d. July 6, 2003, Torrance, Calif.), began his career dancing with his younger sister, Vilma, in nightclubs, in vaudeville, on Broadway, and in a movie before going it alone in a number of musicals. Originally cast as the Scarecrow in *The Wizard of Oz,* he was reassigned the part of the Tin Man but quit because he developed a reaction to the makeup. Ebsen's greatest fame came from his television roles, however, from sidekick Georgie in Walt Disney's Davy Crockett series in 1954–55 to patriarch Jed Clampett in the hit sitcom *The Beverly Hillbillies* (1962–71) to the title character in the detective series *Barnaby Jones* (1973–80). He also appeared in numerous films and other TV series and wrote songs, plays, and books.

Ederle, Gertrude Caroline, American swimmer (b. Oct. 23, 1906, New York, N.Y.—d. Nov. 30, 2003, Wyckoff, N.J.), was the first woman to swim across the English Channel, a feat she accomplished on Aug. 6, 1926. Although blustery weather and sea conditions caused her swim from France to England to total some 56 km (35 mi)—in a straight line the distance would have been about 34 km (just over 21 mi)—her time of 14 hours 31 minutes was 1 hour 59 minutes under that of the fastest of the five men who had previously swum the Channel. Ederle's record was not broken until 1950.

AP/Wide World Photos

Channel swimmer Gertrude Ederle

Edwards, Sir George Robert, British aircraft designer (b. July 9, 1908, Chingford, Essex, Eng.—d. March 2, 2003, Guildford, Surrey, Eng.), designed a number of airplanes, notably the Viscount turboprop airliner, and in the 1970s was instrumental in persuading French and English politicians and aircraft designers to bring the supersonic Concorde project to fruition. Edwards joined the design staff of Vickers Aviation in 1935; he became chief designer in 1948 and managing director in 1953. He designed the Viking, the world's first jet-powered transport airplane; the Valetta and the Varsity, military versions of the Viking; the Viscount, in 1948, the first turboprop airliner to operate passenger services and the first British plane to have an impact on the American airline market; and the Valiant, in 1951, the first British aircraft capable of carrying a nuclear weapon and the first used in nuclear trials. When Vickers joined with other manufacturers to form the British Aircraft Corp. (1955), Edwards became managing director. He was knighted in 1957 and awarded the Order of Merit in 1971.

Elam, Jack, American character actor (b. Nov. 13, 1918, Miami, Ariz.—d. Oct. 20, 2003, Ashland, Ore.), had a sightless and wandering left eye—the result of an accident in childhood—that enhanced his maniacal portrayals as both villains and, later, comic characters in some 100 films and 200 television productions. Notable appearances were in the western movies *Rawhide* (1951), *High Noon* (1952), and *C'era una volta il West* (1968; *Once upon a Time in the West*) and in more than 20 episodes of the TV series *Gunsmoke* in the 1950s.

Faith, Adam (TERENCE NELHAMS), British pop singer, actor, and businessman (b. June 23, 1940, London, Eng.—d. March 8, 2003, Stoke-on-Trent, Staffordshire, Eng.), remained in the public eye through a succession of overlapping careers, beginning as a teen pop idol in the early 1960s. Faith landed a regular appearance on the new pop-music show *Drumbeat* in 1959. Later that year he signed with EMI's Parlophone label and released his first number one single, "What Do You Want." "Poor Me," released the following year, also made number one, and he had over a dozen more songs in the top 20 over the next five years. He also began appearing in movies, notable among them *Mix Me a Person* (1962), *Stardust* (1974), and *McVicar* (1980). He appeared onstage opposite Dame Sybil Thorndike in *Night Must Fall* (1968), starred in the 1970–72 television show *Budgie*, and briefly worked as a manager. In the 1980s he reinvented himself as a financial guru and wrote newspaper columns on investing, but this career came to an end with the '80s. In 1992–94 Faith starred in another successful TV series, *Love Hurts*, and he appeared in touring productions of *Alfie* and *A Chorus Line*.

Falkenburg, Eugenia Lincoln ("JINX"), American model and actress (b. Jan. 21, 1919, Barcelona, Spain—d. Aug. 27, 2003, Manhasset, N.Y.), had an all-American-girl quality that helped her become one of the highest-paid cover girls during World War II. She appeared in a number of movies, most notably *Cover Girl* (1944), and later—with her husband, Tex McCrary—went into radio and television broadcasting and journalism. They were pioneers of the talk-show type of program in the 1950s on both radio and TV, and they wrote a syndicated column for the *New York Herald Tribune*.

Fast, Howard Melvin, American writer (b. Nov. 11, 1914, New York, N.Y.—d. March 12, 2003, Old Greenwich, Conn.), wrote prolifically, most notably popular historical novels on themes of human rights and social justice. Fast, who was well known for his leftist political beliefs, was the author of more than 80 books in addition to poetry, screenplays, and newspaper articles. He was 19 when his first book was published, and his last work was published in 2000. He was imprisoned for three months in 1950 for refusing to cooperate with the House Un-American Activities Committee, after which he was blacklisted for some years, and in 1953 he was awarded the Stalin International Peace Prize. Fast also wrote a series of detective novels under the name E.V. Cunningham. Fast's best-known books included *Citizen Tom Paine* (1943), *Freedom Road* (1944), *Spartacus* (1951), and *The Immigrants* (1977).

Ferré, Luis Alberto, Puerto Rican politician and businessman (b. Feb, 17, 1904, Ponce, P.R.—d. Oct. 21, 2003, San Juan, P.R.), was a leading figure in the movement to gain U.S. statehood for Puerto Rico. Highly influential, he also helped to write the island's 1952 constitution, founded (1967) the New Progressive Party, served (1969–72) as governor, and was a noted patron of the arts.

Fiedler, Leslie Aaron, American literary critic (b. March 8, 1917, Newark, N.J.—d. Jan. 29, 2003, Buffalo, N.Y.), wrote the influential book *Love and Death in the American Novel* (1960), which examined underlying themes of race and sex in classic American novels and roused the ire of many commentators. After 23 years of teaching English at the University of Montana, Fiedler in 1965 moved to the State University of New York at Buffalo, where he immersed himself in the counterculture of the 1960s. Fiedler taught at several universities and published many essays on popular culture as well as collections of short stories and two novels. In 1997 the National Book Critics Circle granted him the Ivan Sandrof Award for his contributions to American arts and letters.

Freda, Vincent, American obstetrician (b. Dec. 16, 1927, New Haven, Conn.—d. May 7, 2003, New York, N.Y.), shared the 1980 Albert Lasker Award for clinical research for his pioneering work in developing a vaccine (Rhogam) that saved Rh-positive infants born to mothers with an Rh-negative blood factor from a potentially fatal condition, hemolytic disease.

Freeling, Nicolas (NICOLAS DAVIDSON), British novelist and detective-story writer (b. March 3, 1927, London, Eng.—d. July 20, 2003, Grandfontaine, France), penned 36 works of fiction and several of nonfiction. While living in Amsterdam, he developed his first and best-known protagonist, Piet Van der Valk, a Dutch policeman. A dozen books later, after Freeling had moved to France, he killed off Van der Valk and created the French sleuth Henri Castang. Freeling's awards included France's Grand Prix du Roman Policier (1964) and the Edgar Allan Poe Award from the Mystery Writers of America (1967). He also wrote two books of memoirs.

Frost, Sir Terry (TERENCE ERNEST MANITOU FROST), British abstract artist and teacher (b. Oct. 13, 1915, Leamington Spa, Warwickshire, Eng.—d. Sept. 1, 2003, Hayle, Cornwall, Eng.), created works in abstract shapes grounded in natural forms that used colour and light to produce a sense of delight in life. Frost began his career as a painter while a prisoner of war in Germany during World War II. Moving to the artist colony at St. Ives, Cornwall, he studied and later taught art. His first one-man show was at Leicester Galleries in 1952, and a major retrospective, "Terry Frost: Six Decades," was held at the Royal Academy of Arts in London in 2000. He was elected to the Royal Academy in 1992 and knighted in 1998.

Fukasaku, Kinji, Japanese filmmaker (b. July 3, 1930, Mito, Japan—d. Jan. 12, 2003, Tokyo, Japan), created a series of increasingly violent and well-received *yakuza* (gangster) movies. His first movie was *Hakuchu no buraikan* (1961; *Greed in Broad Daylight*). Standouts among the more than 60 films that he directed were *Kurotokage* (1968; *Black Lizard*), *Gunki hatameku motoni* (1972; *Under the Flag of the Rising Sun*), and *Jingi naki tatakai* (1973; *The Yakuza Papers*), the first installment in a *yakuza* series. He also made science-fiction films, including *Gamma sango uchu daisakusen* (1968; *The Green Slime*). *Batoru rowaiaru* (2000; *Battle Royale*) was shockingly violent and controversial but still well reviewed. Fukasaku was probably best known to Americans for his direction of the Japanese sequences of *Tora! Tora! Tora!* (1970).

Galtieri, Leopoldo Fortunato, Argentine military ruler (b. July 15, 1926, Caseros, Arg.—d. Jan. 12, 2003, Buenos Aires, Arg.), initiated the disastrous (for Argentina) 1982 war with Great Britain over the Falkland Islands/Islas Malvinas during his brief period as the head of the military junta that ruled Argentina in 1976–83. Argentina's ignominious defeat led to the almost immediate downfall of Galtieri and, a year later, the downfall of the junta itself and the restoration of democratic rule. Galtieri studied civil engineering at Argentina's military academy and attended the American-run School of the Americas in Panama. After a military junta seized control of the Argentine government in 1976, Gen. Jorge Videla, who had named himself presi-

dent, gave Galtieri control of the Second Army Corps in Rosario, where he vigorously suppressed any dissent from the new regime. By the end of 1979, he was commander in chief of the army. In March 1981 Videla was succeeded by Gen. Roberto Viola. By this time the initial economic gains made by the junta were fading, and public discontent with the "dirty war" against leftists and other opponents of the junta was beginning to grow. In December Galtieri forced Viola out of office and became president. Galtieri, with strong popular support, sent Argentine troops to invade the Falkland Islands; they defeated the British garrison there on April 2, 1982. Contrary to Galtieri's expectation, British Prime Minister Margaret Thatcher promptly assembled a large naval task force, and on June 14 the Argentine garrison surrendered to British forces. Nearly 1,000 people had died in the battle, about 700 of them Argentines. The junta removed Galtieri as president and commander in chief of the army on June 17, 1982. In 1986 he was sentenced to 12 years in prison for the Falkland Islands debacle, but he was pardoned in 1990. In July 2002 an Argentine judge ruled that he should face charges stemming from his role in the "dirty war" and placed him under house arrest.

García Ponce, Juan, Mexican man of letters (b. Sept. 22, 1932, Mérida, Mex.—d. Dec. 27, 2003, Mexico City, Mex.), wrote more than 40 imaginative works noted for their lush descriptions. Three of these works—*La casa en la playa* (1966; *The House on the Beach,* 1994), *Encuentros* (1972; *Encounters,* 1989 [short stories]), and *De ánima* (1984; *De Anima,* 1995)—had been translated into English at the time of his death. Although he lived with multiple sclerosis for more than 30 years, García Ponce produced art, theatre, and literary criticism, sometimes under the pen name Jorge Olmo, for such magazines as *Universidad de México* and *Revista mexicana de literatura* in addition to his works of fiction up until his death. In 2001 he won the Juan Rulfo Prize, a top award in Latin American and Caribbean literature.

Gardner, Herbert George ("HERB"), American playwright (b. Dec. 28, 1934, Brooklyn, N.Y.—d. Sept. 24, 2003, New York, N.Y.), featured eccentric characters struggling against conformity in comedies that included *A Thousand Clowns* (1962; filmed 1965), the Tony Award-winning *I'm Not Rappaport* (1985; filmed 1996), and *Conversations with My Father* (1992). Previously, in the 1950s, he had achieved renown as the creator of the syndicated comic strip *The Nebbishes,* whose creatures went on to decorate such items as greeting cards, pins, and cocktail napkins.

Gavilan, Kid (GERARDO GONZÁLEZ), Cuban-born boxer (b. Jan. 6, 1926, Camagüey, Cuba—d. Feb. 13, 2003, Miami, Fla.), was one of the most popular boxers of the 1950s and was world welterweight champion from 1951 to 1954. He began boxing at the age of 10 and fought his first professional bout in Havana in 1943. He relocated to the United States in 1947. Gavilan won the world welterweight championship in a 15-round decision against Johnny Bratton in May 1951 and successfully defended the title seven times before he lost a fight to Johnny Saxton in October 1954 in a controversial decision (almost all the boxing reporters present believed Gavilan had won the fight). Gavilan retired in 1958 with a record of 107 victories, 30 losses, and 6 draws, as well as the distinction of never having been knocked out. In 1990 he was inducted into the freshman class of the International Boxing Hall of Fame.

Hulton|Archive by Getty Images

Pugilist Kid Gavilan

Gelber, Jack, American playwright (b. April 12, 1932, Chicago, Ill.—d. May 9, 2003, New York, N.Y.), broke new theatrical ground in 1959 with his controversially raw and realistic play about drug addiction, *The Connection.* Although the plays he later wrote did not have the impact of his first effort, he had a successful career as a director and teacher.

Getting, Ivan A., American scientist (b. Jan. 18, 1912, New York, N.Y.—d. Oct. 11, 2003, Coronado, Calif.), conceived and helped develop what became the Global Positioning System while serving (1960–77) as founding president of Aerospace Corp. Using satellite transmitters and atomic clocks to pinpoint locations, the system originally was aimed at enabling the precise delivery of bombs but grew to be employed in such uses as helping pilots navigate and aiding people in finding their way to their destinations.

Getty, Sir J(ohn) Paul, Jr., American-born British philanthropist (Sept. 7, 1932, Italy—d. April 17, 2003, London, Eng.), after years of bohemian dissipation, devoted his later life to doing good works with his inherited fortune. In 1959 Getty's father, J. Paul Getty, Sr., put him in charge of the Getty Oil operations in Rome, but he soon found himself drawn into the counterculture. In 1966 he divorced his wife of 11 years and married the glamorous Talitha Pol. Their life was one of unrestrained excess, and in 1971 Getty's wife died of a drug overdose. He moved to London and became a recluse, subsisting on little more than rum and heroin. A further blow was the 1973 kidnapping of his son J. Paul Getty III; a ransom too high for Getty was demanded, and Getty's father refused to help out until after the victim's ear had been mailed to a Rome newspaper. After his father's death in 1976, Getty began gradually to pull himself together, and in the 1980s he embarked upon a career as a philanthropist. He donated millions to the National Gallery and the British Film Institute and stepped in several times to prevent art treasures from being sold to American institutions. He amassed an exceptionally fine collection of antiquarian books and built a library on his Buckinghamshire estate to house them. A serious cricket fan, he built a replica of the Oval cricket ground on the estate, contributed money to support cricket clubs, and from 1993 published the *Wisden* annual and *Wisden Cricket Monthly.* Getty was given an honorary knighthood in 1986 in recognition of his charitable contributions and, after he became a British citizen, received the full honours in 1998.

Gibb, Maurice Ernest, British singer, musician, and composer (b. Dec. 22, 1949, Douglas, Isle of Man—d. Jan. 12, 2003, Miami, Fla.), joined with his brothers to form a pop music trio and, while living in Australia, became popular as the Bee Gees (from Brothers Gibb), and they went on to be one of the most successful British groups ever. Best known for their five disco songs on the sound track of the 1977 film *Saturday Night Fever,* they sold more than 100 million albums worldwide, won seven Grammy Awards, and had number one hits in four consecutive decades. The brothers were inducted into the Rock and Roll Hall of Fame in 1997 and were made CBE in 2002.

Musician Maurice Gibb

© Lynn Goldsmith/Corbis

Gibson, Althea, American tennis player (b. Aug. 25, 1927, Silver, S.C.—d. Sept. 28, 2003, East Orange, N.J.), broke the colour barrier in tennis as the first black player to win singles ti-

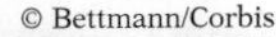

© Bettmann/Corbis

Tennis champion Althea Gibson

tles at the French Open (1956), the All-England (Wimbledon) championships (1957–58), and the U.S. national championship (later the U.S. Open; 1957–58). In 1942 Gibson, who grew up in New York City, won her first tournament, which was sponsored by the American Tennis Association (ATA), an organization for African American players. She later toured on the ATA circuit, and from 1947 to 1957 she was the ATA women's singles national champion. While attending Florida Agricultural and Mechanical University (B.S., 1953), she became the first black player to compete at the U.S. nationals (1950) and Wimbledon (1951). Tall and muscular, she possessed a powerful serve-and-volley game, and in the late 1950s Gibson came to dominate women's tennis. In addition to her landmark Grand Slam singles titles, she also won a number of doubles titles, including Wimbledon (1956–58) and the Australian Open (1957). That year Gibson became the first African American to be voted Female Athlete of the Year by the Associated Press; she also won the award the following year. In 1958 Gibson turned professional, having won 56 titles. She appeared in numerous tennis exhibitions, acted, recorded an album, and in 1962 became the first black player to compete on the Ladies Professional Golf Association tour. She was later active in sports administration for the state of New Jersey. Gibson's autobiography, *I Always Wanted to Be Somebody,* was published in 1958.

Gibson, Donald Eugene ("DON"), American singer-songwriter (b. April 3, 1928, Shelby, N.C.—d. Nov. 17, 2003, Nashville, Tenn.), was one of the creators of the "Nashville sound" and, because of his usually unhappy love songs, became known as the "sad poet." Three of his songs—"Sweet Dreams," "Oh Lonesome Me," and "I Can't Stop Loving You," the last two of which were written on the same day in 1957—came to be among country music's most popular standards, and "I Can't Stop Loving You" was recorded by more than 700 performers.

Gillman, Sid, American football coach (b. Oct. 26, 1911, Minneapolis, Minn.—d. Jan. 3, 2003, Los Angeles, Calif.), was regarded as the progenitor of the modern passing game. He became head coach at Miami University, Oxford, Ohio, in 1944 and moved to the University of Cincinnati, Ohio, in 1949, compiling a college record of 81 games won, 19 lost, and 2 ties. In 1955 Gillman started coaching professional football when he became head coach of the National Football League's Los Angeles Rams, which won a division title in his first season. He remained with the Rams until 1959 and in 1960 began coaching the new American Football League's Los Angeles Chargers. He moved with them to San Diego, Calif., in 1961, coaching them until 1969 and again in 1971, during which time they won five division titles and one league championship (1963). He coached the Houston Oilers from 1973 to 1974. Gillman was inducted into the Pro Football Hall of Fame in 1983.

Ginsberg, Harold Samuel, American microbiologist (b. May 27, 1917, Daytona Beach, Fla.—d. Feb. 2, 2003, Woods Hole, Mass.), did pioneering work in virology; his research into adenoviruses showed how viral genes function in cells and how the viruses cause disease. When Ginsberg was stationed at a U.S. Army hospital in Great Britain during World War II, he identified the hospital's plasma supply as the source of the hepatitis B infections found in a number of soldiers who had received blood transfusions. During the 1950s, at Western Reserve University (now Case Western Reserve University), Cleveland, Ohio, he discovered that several respiratory diseases were caused by adenoviruses. In 1961 Ginsberg became chairman of the microbiology department of the University of Pennsylvania, and in 1973 he moved to head the microbiology department of Columbia University, New York City. In the mid-1980s he began working at the National Institute of Allergy and Infectious Diseases of the National Institutes of Health, where he studied the simian immunodeficiency virus. Ginsberg was elected to the National Academy of Sciences in 1982.

Gironella Pous, José María, Spanish novelist (b. Dec. 31, 1917, Darníus, Spain—d. Jan. 3, 2003, Arenys de Mar, Spain), wrote the first best-selling novel published in Spain, *Los cipreses creen en Dios* (1953; *The Cypresses Believe in God,* 1955), set in the years immediately preceding the Spanish Civil War (1936–39). Gironella had fought in the war with the forces of Gen. Francisco Franco. The book, which sold three million copies and won the National Prize for Literature, attempted (and largely succeeded in) an even-handed evocation of the forces at work in Spain that led to the war. He followed it with *Un millón de muertos* (1961; *One Million Dead,* 1963), set during the war, and *Ha estallado la paz* (1966; *Peace After War,* 1969), set in the immediate postwar years; while well received, neither novel rose to the level of success of the first part of the trilogy. Gironella's output included several more novels, the last published in 2001, as well as short stories, memoirs, travel writing, and essays.

Giroud, Françoise (FRANCE GOURDJI), French journalist (b. Sept. 21, 1916, Geneva, Switz.—d. Jan. 19, 2003, Neuilly-sur-Seine, France), cofounded and edited *L'Express,* France's first weekly newsmagazine, and coined the term *nouvelle vague* to describe the French cinema of the 1950s. Giroud edited the new women's magazine *Elle* from 1946 to 1953, and in 1953, with Jean-Jacques Servan-Schreiber, she founded *L'Express,* which she edited until 1974. In the mid-1970s she briefly

© Pelletier Micheline/Corbis

Journalist Françoise Giroud

served in the government as minister of women's affairs and then as minister of culture. Giroud also wrote screenplays, some 30 books, and a column for the newsmagazine *Le Nouvel Observateur* from 1983.

Goldman-Rakic, Patricia Shoer, American neuroscientist (b. April 22, 1937, Salem, Mass.—d. July 31, 2003, New Haven, Conn.), provided the first comprehensive map of the frontal lobe of the human brain, a complex region responsible for such cognitive functions as planning, comprehension, and foresight. Her pioneering research in the 1970s led to a better understanding of working memory and offered insight into various disorders, including cerebral palsy, schizophrenia, and Alzheimer and Parkinson diseases.

Good, Robert Alan, American doctor, immunologist, and microbiologist (b. May 21, 1922, Crosby, Minn.—d. June 13, 2003, St. Petersburg, Fla.), was considered the founder of modern immunology. He performed the world's first successful bone-marrow transplant (1968) and conducted landmark research that revealed the important role tonsils and the thymus gland play in the immune system. He received the Albert Lasker Clinical Medical Research Award in 1970.

Gopal, (Bisano) Ram, Indian classical dancer (b. Nov. 20, 1917?, Bangalore, India—d. Oct. 12, 2003, Croyden, Surrey, Eng.), was for a time the toast of Europe for his beauty and grace and for the authenticity of his performances. After mastering *kathakali, bharatra natya,* and *manipuri* forms of dance, Gopal successfully toured Asia with the American dancer La Meri in the 1930s and then went to the U.S. and London, where he was also well received. In the 1940s and '50s he was feted throughout the West; a highlight of his career was a 1960 duet with ballerina Alicia Markova in which she danced Radha to his Krishna. He was appointed OBE in 1999.

Dancer Ram Gopal

Graber, Pierre, Swiss politician (b. Dec. 6, 1908, La Chaux-de-Fonds, Switz.—d. July 19, 2003, Lausanne, Switz.), as Switzerland's foreign minister (1970–78), charted a course of engaged neutrality, bringing Switzerland into the European Human Rights Convention and the Organisation for Security and Co-operation in Europe and negotiating free-trade agreements with the European Economic Community. A member of the left-leaning Social Democratic Party from 1925, Graber also pursued a policy of détente with communist countries. In 1970 Graber negotiated with Palestinian airplane hijackers and released Arab prisoners in order to secure the release of Swiss hostages.

Graham, Otto Everett, Jr., American football player (b. Dec. 6, 1921, Waukegan, Ill.—d. Dec. 17, 2003, Sarasota, Fla.), was nicknamed "Automatic Otto" for his consistently outstanding play as quarterback for the Cleveland Browns. During his 10 years as a professional player (1946–55), he never missed a game, maintained an 8.63-yd-per-passing-attempt average, and led the Browns to 10 straight championship games—four in the All-America Football Conference and six more after the Browns joined the National Football League (NFL). Graham attended Northwestern University, Evanston, Ill., on a basketball scholarship and was twice recognized (1943, 1944) as an All-American at guard. Though he had not been invited to try out for the football team, he was immediately taken onto the varsity squad after an assistant coach saw him play at an intramural game. Graham was again named an All-American, this time as a tailback. He spent his entire professional career with the Browns, with whom he collected 105 regular-season wins, with only 17 losses and 4 draws. After Graham took a late hit to the mouth during a 1953 game, trainers improvised a plastic guard for his helmet, and he thereby became the first NFL player to wear a face mask. In his final game he threw for two touchdowns and ran for two more in the Browns' 38–14 championship victory over the Los Angeles Rams. After retiring, Graham took a number of coaching positions, including stints at the U.S. Coast Guard Academy (1959–66 and 1970–84). He returned to the NFL as coach and general manager of the Washington Redskins (1966–68) but posted a lacklustre 17–22–3 record. In 1965 Graham was inducted into the Professional Football Hall of Fame, and his number (14) was retired by the Browns.

Graham, Winston Mawdsley, British novelist (b. June 30, 1910, Victoria Park, Manchester, Eng.—d. July 10, 2003, Buxted, East Sussex, Eng.), wrote a series of 12 historical novels set in Cornwall in the 18th and 19th centuries chronicling several generations of the Poldark family. These stories—when adapted for television—captured the hearts of countless viewers in more than 20 countries. Graham also wrote a number of masterful psychological thrillers, notably *Marnie* (1961), a book filmed in 1964 by director Alfred Hitchcock.

Green, Cecil Howard, British-born American seismographic engineer and philanthropist (b. Aug. 6, 1900, Manchester, Eng.—d. April 12, 2003, La Jolla, Calif.), was a cofounder of Texas Instruments Inc., the semiconductor firm that developed the first pocket-size transistor radio (1954) and the integrated circuit board (1958) that was instrumental in ushering in a wave of electrically controlled machines. After earning a masters degree (1924) in electrical engineering from the Massachusetts Institute of Technology, Green joined Geophysical Sciences Inc. in 1932. Later he and three partners bought the company, which became Texas Instruments in 1951. Green was given an honorary knighthood in 1991. He donated more than $200 million to educational and medical institutions around the globe.

Griffin, Donald Redfield, American biophysicist and animal behaviourist (b. Aug. 3, 1915, Southampton, N.Y.—d. Nov. 7, 2003, Lexington, Mass.), founded the field of cognitive ethology with his controversial claim that animals might possess the ability to think and reason. He also proved that bats navigate by using echolocation.

Griffiths, Martha Edna Wright, American politician and women's rights advocate (b. Jan. 29, 1912, Pierce City, Mo.—d. April 22, 2003, Armada, Mich.), successfully lobbied to include women on the list of those protected by the 1964 Civil Rights Act and nearly made the Equal Rights Amendment (mandating equal treatment for women) a part of the U.S. Constitution while serving (1955–75) in the U.S. House of Representatives as a Michigan Democrat. Though the measure had passed the House and the Senate, it fell three states short of the 38 needed for ratification. Beginning in 1982 Griffiths served two terms as Michigan's lieutenant governor.

Guyton, Arthur Clifton, American medical researcher and educator (b. Sept. 8, 1919, Oxford, Miss.—d. April 3, 2003, Jackson, Miss.), wrote one of the most widely used medical textbooks in the world, *Textbook of Medical Physiology* (1956), which was in its 10th edition and had been translated into 15 languages; he also contributed greatly to the understanding of hypertension. As a surgical resident at Massachusetts General Hospital in 1946, Guyton contracted polio, which resulted in permanent paralysis in his right leg, left arm, and both shoulders. While recovering from the disease, he invented a special leg brace and a motorized wheelchair, for which he received a presidential citation. He became chairman of the department of physiology and biophysics at the University of Mississippi Medical Center in 1948. In the 1950s Guyton's

Researcher Arthur Guyton

AP/Wide World Photos

right above: AP/Wide World Photos

research on hypertension yielded the insight that the amount of blood pumped by the heart is governed not by the heart itself, as had been believed, but rather by the oxygen requirements of the body's tissues. In the following decade he discovered that the kidneys are the long-term controllers of blood pressure and all other systems are subordinate to them, exerting only short-term control. His 10 children all became doctors.

Hacket, Buddy (LEONARD HACKER), American comedian and actor (b. Aug. 31, 1924, New York, N.Y. —d. June 30, 2003, Malibu, Calif.), garnered laughs for more than 50 years with a stand-up routine that utilized his physical features—pudgy physique, high-pitched voice, and rubbery face—and often featured raunchy jokes. A fixture in nightclubs and on television, he also acted in plays and movies, including *It's a Mad Mad Mad Mad World* (1963).

Columbia/The Kobal Collection

Funnyman Buddy Hacket

Hale, Sue Sally, American polo player (b. Aug. 23, 1937, Los Angeles, Calif.—d. April 29, 2003, Coachella Valley, Calif.), for nearly 20 years played in polo tournaments disguised as a man, A. Jones, because the United States Polo Association would not admit women. In 1972 the association was pressured into relenting, however, and she became the first woman to be granted membership.

Hall, Conrad L., American cinematographer (b. June 21, 1926, Papeete, Tahiti, French Polynesia—d. Jan. 4, 2003, Santa Monica, Calif.), had a half-century-long career during which he gained renown as a master of the use of light to create the desired mood of a film. Among his numerous honours were three Academy Awards—for *Butch Cassidy and the Sundance Kid* (1969), *American Beauty* (1999), and *Road to Perdition* (2002), the last awarded posthumously.

Harel, Isser (ISSER HALPERIN), Israeli spymaster (b. 1912, Vitebsk, Belorussia, Russian Empire [now in Belarus]—d. Feb. 18, 2003, Petah Tiqwa, Israel), directed the abduction from Argentina of Adolf Eichmann, the Nazi official responsible for carrying out the "final solution," the extermination of Jews in Europe. In Palestine in 1942 Harel joined the clandestine Jewish organization Haganah, and two years later he became a member of Haganah's intelligence department. When Israel became independent in 1948, Harel became the first head of Shin Bet, Israel's internal intelligence agency. In 1952 he also became head of Mossad, the foreign intelligence agency. In an operation in 1960, he found and identified Eichmann where he was living in hiding in Buenos Aires, Arg., and organized his capture and transport to Israel, where Eichmann was executed in 1962. Another campaign, against West German scientists who were helping Egypt develop weapons delivery systems at a time when the Israeli government was developing closer ties to West Germany, caused Prime Minister David Ben-Gurion to require his resignation in 1963. Harel's account of the Eichmann capture, *The House on Garibaldi Street* (1975), made him famous.

Harrison, Lou Silver, American composer (b. May 14, 1917, Portland, Ore.—d. Feb. 2, 2003, Lafayette, Ind.), was a tireless experimenter who created memorable melodies as he fused the classical Western tradition with idioms from around the world, especially music from Asia. Elements of Navajo, Korean, Indian, Indonesian, African, medieval European, and Baroque music appeared in his four symphonies and many other instrumental and vocal works. In 1946 he conducted the first complete performance of a Charles Ives symphony. He composed in many styles for unique ensembles, including all-percussion pieces, a 12-tone opera *Rapunzel* (1954), and a puppet opera *Young Caeser* (his spelling; 1971). Harrison was a proponent of the sonorous gamelan orchestra (Indonesian percussion ensemble). He composed gamelan music and, with his partner Bill Colvig, built Javanese-style gamelans out of tin cans and steel tubing.

Hatfield, Robert Lee ("BOBBY"), American singer (b. Aug. 10, 1940, Beaver Dam, Wis.—d. Nov. 5, 2003, Kalamazoo, Mich.), was one-half of the Righteous Brothers "blue-eyed soul" singing duo, whose 1964 recording "You've Lost That Lovin' Feelin'" was said to have been played on the radio in the U.S. over 10 million times, more than any other song. His tenor solo "Unchained Melody" brought them another hit in 1965 and again in 1990 after it was featured in the movie *Ghost*. The Righteous Brothers were inducted into the Rock and Roll Hall of Fame in 2003.

Hawkesworth, John Stanley, British television producer (b. Dec. 7, 1920, London, Eng.—d. Sept. 30, 2003, Leicester, Leicestershire, Eng.), was best known as the creator of the popular and acclaimed television series *Upstairs, Downstairs,* which aired in 1971–75 on London Weekend Television and in the U.S. in 1974–77 on the PBS program *Masterpiece Theatre*. Trained as a painter, Hawkesworth worked as a set designer for several movies before moving on to writing and producing; he co-wrote and produced *Tiger Bay* (1959), his final movie, and then turned his attention to television. Other TV projects for which he gained praise included *The Duchess of Duke Street* (1976–80) and *Danger UXB* (1979).

Heilbrun, Carolyn Gold, American feminist literary scholar and fiction writer (b. Jan. 13, 1926, East Orange, N.J.—d. Oct. 9, 2003, New York, N.Y.), was on the faculty of Columbia University, New York City, from 1960 to 1992 (with brief stints as visiting professor at a few other colleges during those years) and wrote a number of scholarly books and articles, including *Toward a Recognition of Androgyny* (1973) and *Writing a Woman's Life* (1988), but achieved more widespread prominence with a series of detective novels written under the name Amanda Cross, a pseudonym she adopted because she feared that mystery writing might compromise her chances for tenure. Her detective, Kate Fansler, was—like Heilbrun—a literature professor, and the mysteries not only delved into crime solving but also revealed the more unflattering aspects of academe.

Heiskell, Andrew, American publishing executive and philanthropist (b. Sept. 13, 1915, Naples, Italy—d. July 6, 2003, Darien, Conn.), had a 43-year career at Time Inc., joining the editorial department of *Life* magazine in 1937, becoming its publisher in 1946, and being named chairman of the entire company in 1960. He introduced *People* magazine and oversaw the growth of the company to also include books, newspapers, television stations, and pulp and paper mills. Following his retirement in 1980, he added to the philanthropic causes he had already begun to support, including the provision of low-income housing, and was especially noted for his efforts to improve the New York Public Library and Bryant Park.

Hemmings, David Leslie Edward, British actor, director, and producer (b. Nov. 18, 1941, Guildford, Surrey, Eng.—d. Dec. 3, 2003, Bucharest, Rom.), played the lead, a mod fashion photographer, in Michelangelo Antonioni's classic "swinging '60s" film *Blowup* (1966; U.S. title, *Blow-Up*). For many people both the actor and his character epitomized the era, and Hemmings's boyish good looks and charisma quickly made his free-wheeling lifestyle a subject for the tabloids. As a child he sang many boy soprano roles written by composer Benjamin Britten, notably that of Miles in *The Turn of the Screw*. Thereafter he attended art school and tried to make a living as a nightclub singer. He acted onstage and in several minor films before *Blowup,* which he followed with successful roles in such films as *Camelot* (1967), *The Charge of the Light Brigade* (1968), and

Barbarella (1968). Beginning in the 1970s he directed for the cinema—notably *The 14* (1973), which won a Silver Bear award at the Berlin Film Festival, and *Just a Gigolo* (1979)—and for television. By the end of the 1990s, Hemmings had grown portly, with fiendishly wild eyebrows, and he began a second career as a character actor, notably in *Gladiator* (2000), *Last Orders* (2001), *Gangs of New York* (2002), and *The League of Extraordinary Gentlemen* (2003).

Hepburn, Katharine Houghton, American actress (b. May 12, 1907, Hartford, Conn.—d. June 29, 2003, Old Saybrook, Conn.), was an extremely talented performer who exhibited a unique strength, spirit, style, and independence both in her performances and in her everyday life, attributes that gained her worldwide popularity and made her a role model for women for decades. Although Dorothy Parker was famously quoted as having claimed that a Hepburn performance "ran the gamut of emotions from A to B," Hepburn was widely considered one of the finest actresses of all time; during her more than 60-year career, she was nominated for 12 Academy Awards and won a record 4 as best actress, and many of her films came to be regarded as classics. Following her graduation (1928) from Bryn Mawr (Pa.) College, Hepburn began her performing career with small stage roles, and she played her first Broadway lead—in *The Warrior's Husband*—in 1932, the same year she made her film debut in *A Bill of Divorcement.* She won her first Oscar for her third film, *Morning Glory* (1933), but a Broadway flop and a series of unsuccessful films—including the now-classic *Stage Door* (1937) and *Bringing Up Baby* (1938)—threatened to derail her career. Undaunted, she made the film *Holiday* (1938) and returned to Broadway in a play that was written by that film's author, Philip Barry, and whose main character was modeled on Hepburn, *The Philadelphia Story.* She also starred in the film version (1940); it was a hit; and her career was back on track. In 1942 she costarred with Spencer Tracy in *Woman of the Year* and found the love of her life. Although they never married—he was already married, unhappily, but because he was a strict Roman Catholic, he would not divorce—they lived together until his death in 1967. Their onscreen relationship also endured in such films as *Adam's Rib* (1949), *Pat and Mike* (1952) and *Guess Who's Coming to Dinner* (1967), the last of which garnered Hepburn a second Oscar. Among her other outstanding performances were those in *The African Queen* (1952), *Summertime* (1955), *The Rainmaker* (1956), *Long Day's Journey into Night* (1962), *The Lion in Winter* (1968), for which she won her third Oscar, and *On Golden Pond* (1981), for which she won her fourth. Hepburn also continued her stage career—with such plays as *Coco* (1969), *A Matter of Gravity* (1976), and *The West Side Waltz* (1981) among her credits—and made several television appearances, notably in *The Glass Menagerie* (1973) and *Love Among the Ruins* (1975). She acted in motion pictures and in television films until the mid-1990s. In 1999 the American Film Institute proclaimed Hepburn the all-time number one female American screen legend.

Actress Katharine Hepburn

© Bettmann/Corbis

Hill, (John Edward) Christopher, British historian (b. Feb. 6, 1912, York, Eng.—d. Feb. 24, 2003, Oxfordshire, Eng.), changed the way generations of students understood the history of 17th-century England through his Marxist interpretations of the period of the English Civil Wars (1642–51) and their aftermath. Hill was educated at and spent almost his entire career at the University of Oxford, where he was master of Balliol College (1965–1978). He was a member of the British Communist Party from the mid-1930s until the mid-1950s and remained a convinced Marxist. Hill wrote more than 20 books upholding his belief that the mid-17th century in England saw a profound revolution that opened the way for the establishment of capitalism. Among his books were *The English Revolution 1640* (1940), *Society and Puritanism in Pre-Revolutionary England* (1964), and *The World Turned Upside Down* (1972).

Hiller, Dame Wendy (Wendy Margaret Watkin), British actress (b. Aug. 15, 1912, Bramhall, Cheshire, Eng.—d. May 14, 2003, Beaconsfield, Buckinghamshire, Eng.), was celebrated for her performances of strong, spirited women and for the slightly quavering voice in which she carefully enunciated those characters' lines. She was especially noted for being one of George Bernard Shaw's favourite leading ladies and created two of his most memorable roles, Eliza Doolittle in *Pygmalion* and the title character in *Major Barbara,* first onstage and later in the film versions. Hiller joined the Manchester Repertory Theatre when she was 18 years old, playing small roles and serving as assistant stage manager. Her first starring role, Sally Hardcastle in *Love on the Dole,* proved to be a life-altering one in many ways; she enjoyed a long, happy marriage to the coauthor of the play, Ronald Gow, and the play's production in London in 1935 brought her to the attention of Shaw, who then invited her to star in his *St. Joan* and *Pygmalion* at the Malvern Festival in 1936. Hiller never aspired to stardom and was very careful in choosing her roles. Among the most notable of her stage performances over the following few years were those in *Tess of the d'Urbervilles, The Heiress, Separate Tables,* and *A Moon for the Misbegotten.* After being persuaded to appear in the 1958 film version of *Separate Tables,* Hiller won a best supporting actress Academy Award. Other memorable film roles during her long career were in *I Know Where I'm Going!* (1945), *Sons and Lovers* (1960), *A Man for All Seasons* (1966), *Murder on the Orient Express* (1974), and *The Elephant Man* (1980). Her later roles included the imperious Lady Bracknell in *The Importance of Being Earnest,* performed onstage in 1981 and 1987 and shown on television in 1985, and the title character in *Driving Miss Daisy* on the London stage in 1988. Hiller was created OBE in 1971 and DBE in 1975.

The Kobal Collection

Dame Wendy Hiller

Hines, Gregory Oliver, American dancer and actor (b. Feb. 14, 1946, New York, N.Y.—d. Aug. 9, 2003, Los Angeles, Calif.), was widely acknowledged as the finest tap dancer of his

EPA Photos

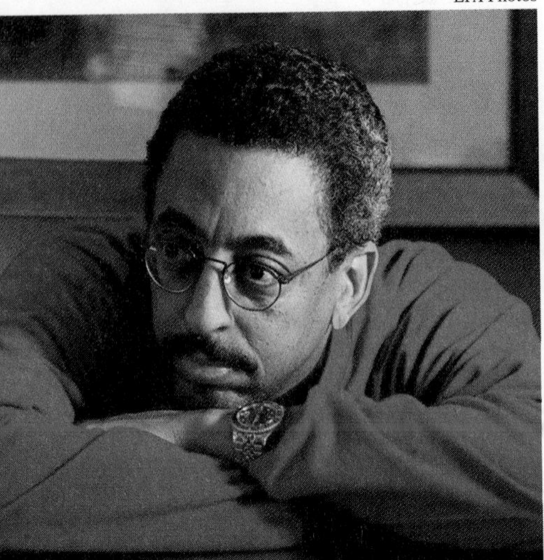

Hoofer Gregory Hines

generation, noted for his virtuosity, rhythm, and expressive style, and was credited with having modernized the form and facilitated its return to motion pictures. In addition to dancing, however, he also enjoyed a successful career as a stage, film, and television actor and a choreographer. Hines began his formal dance training when he was three years old; at age five was performing with his older brother, Maurice, as the Hines Kids; and at eight, along with his brother, made his Broadway debut in *The Girl in Pink Tights*. The boys then returned to touring, as the Hines Brothers, and in 1963 their father joined the act, playing drums. They toured and appeared on such TV showcases as *The Ed Sullivan Show* and *The Tonight Show*. In 1973 Gregory left the act, moving to California and forming a rock band, but he returned to New York in 1978 and with his brother was cast in *The Last Minstrel Show*, which closed on the road, and then in *Eubie!* Roles in *Comin' Uptown, Black Broadway*, and *Sophisticated Ladies* followed in quick succession, as did roles in such films as *The Cotton Club* (1984), *White Nights* (1985), *Running Scared* (1986), and *Tap* (1989) and television specials such as "Gregory Hines: Tap Dance in America" (1989). Hines won a Tony Award for his return to Broadway in 1992 in *Jelly's Last Jam* and was also nominated for his choreography in that show.

Hines, Jerome (Jerome Albert Link Heinz), American opera singer (b. Nov. 8, 1921, Hollywood, Calif.—d. Feb. 4, 2003, New York, N.Y), was a respected bass who sang for 41 years at the Metropolitan Opera in New York City. He made his professional debut in the role of Monterone in Verdi's *Rigoletto* at the San Francisco Opera House in 1941 and first appeared at the Metropolitan Opera in 1946 in Mussorgsky's *Boris Godunov*. In 868 appearances at the Met he portrayed 45 characters in 39 operas, and he made numerous appearances in opera houses in Europe and South America. Hines was known for his rich and flexible voice as well as his imposing stage presence. Among his best-known roles were those of Ramfis in Verdi's *Aida*, Méphistophélès in Gounod's *Faust*, and the title role in *Boris Godunov*.

Hirschfeld, Albert ("Al"), American caricaturist (b. June 21, 1903, St. Louis, Mo.—d. Jan. 20, 2003, New York, N.Y.), needed only a few strokes of his pen to capture the likenesses and the essence of the personalities of his subjects—mostly show business celebrities but also political and governmental leaders. He was internationally acclaimed for having created a visual history of the 20th-century Broadway stage. Hirschfeld's talent was recognized when he was just a young boy, and by the time he was 12 years old, his family had moved to New York City so that he could pursue his art studies. He worked in the movie industry and studied in Europe before rather offhandedly launching his career as a caricaturist; a simple sketch Hirschfeld made in 1926 during a trip to the theatre so impressed a press agent that he arranged for it to be published in the *New York Herald Tribune*. By the end of the 1920s, Hirschfeld had become a regular contributor to the *New York Times*—a status that he retained for more than 70 years, though it was only in the 1990s that he entered into a formal agreement with the paper—and he proceeded to create portraits of innumerable notables for that paper and other publications. Following the birth of his daughter, Nina, in 1945, he began hiding her name somewhere in his drawings, sometimes several times. Finding her name became a national pastime, and frustrated readers eventually persuaded Hirschfeld to indicate next to his signature just how many Ninas were to be found in a given drawing. The military even used the hidden Ninas to help sharpen the target-spotting ability of bomber pilots. Hirschfeld's work was collected in numerous books and was included in the collections of several art museums, and in 1991 his drawings graced a set of postage stamps featuring comedians. He was honoured with two Tony Awards—a special Tony in 1975 and the first Brooks Atkinson Award in 1984—and in 1996 his life and work were the subjects of a documentary film, *The Line King*. Also in 1996, Hirschfeld was declared an official New York City landmark, and at the time of his death he had just been informed that he had been elected to the American Academy of Arts and Letters and was also to be a recipient of a National Medal of Arts. On June 21, 2003, which would have been his 100th birthday, the Martin Beck Theatre in New York City was renamed the Al Hirschfeld Theatre.

Caricaturist Al Hirschfeld

© Douglas Kirkland/Corbis

Hope, Bob (Leslie Townes Hope), British-born American comic and actor (b. May 29, 1903, Eltham, near London, Eng.—d. July 27, 2003, Toluca Lake, Calif.), as one of the U.S.'s most enduring and beloved performers, delighted audiences for some seven decades with one-liners and topical monologues. A star on radio, television, stage, and screen, he was also known for the numerous tours he made (1941–90) to entertain U.S. troops, and these shows were often featured on his TV specials, which appeared regularly from 1950 to 1996. At age four Hope immigrated with his family to the U.S., settling in Cleveland, Ohio. As a teenager he began appearing in vaudeville, and he later worked as a stand-up comic. In 1927 he made his Broadway debut in *The Sidewalks of New York*, and other musicals, including *Roberta* (1933) and *Red Hot and Blue* (1936), soon followed. Hope attracted national attention in 1938 with the launch of his hugely popular radio program, *The Bob Hope Pepsodent Show*, and the release of his first feature film, *The Big Broadcast of 1938;* in that movie he sang "Thanks for the Memory," which became his trademark tune. His brash comedic style was a hit with audiences, as was his adopted persona of a cowardly braggart. In 1940 Hope costarred with Bing Crosby and Dorothy Lamour in *Road to Singapore*, a lighthearted movie that featured singing, in-jokes, and much ad-libbing. A huge success, the film catapulted Hope into superstardom and led to six more "Road" films. Later movies, including *My Favorite Blonde* (1942), *The Paleface* (1948), and *The Lemon*

The Kobal Collection

Comedy icon Bob Hope

Drop Kid (1951), helped make Hope one of the country's top box-office draws. He received numerous awards, including the Presidential Medal of Freedom (1969) and the National Medal of Arts (1995). In 1997 Hope was named an honorary veteran by the U.S. Congress, and the following year he was made an honorary CBE. Although he never won an Academy Award for his acting, he hosted the ceremony a record 18 times and received five special Oscars for his humanitarian work and contributions to film.

Hoyt, Robert Guy, American editor (b. Jan. 30, 1922, Clinton, Iowa—d. April 10, 2003, New York, N.Y.), transformed Roman Catholic journalism with the creation of the journal the *National Catholic Reporter,* the first Roman Catholic newspaper to use the standards of secular journalism. In 1967 the paper had a major scoop: the secret reports from the commission appointed by Pope Paul VI to review the church's position on birth control. Hoyt remained editor until 1971, after which he worked as executive editor and later editor in chief of *Christianity & Crisis* (1977–85) and as a senior writer at *Commonweal* (1989–2002).

Hussein, Uday, and Hussein, Qusay, Iraqi officials (respectively, b. June 18, 1964, Baghdad, Iraq—d. July 22, 2003, Mosul, Iraq, and b. May 17, 1966, Baghdad—d. July 22, 2003, Mosul), as the elder sons of Iraqi dictator Saddam Hussein, were central figures in their father's brutal 24-year rule. Despite their common goal of supporting their father's regime, the two brothers were very different. Uday was a flamboyant womanizer who financed his lavish lifestyle largely through smuggling and racketeering. His erratic and violent behaviour was widely known, and he allegedly reveled in wanton murder, rape, and particularly vicious forms of torture. Uday attended the University of Baghdad College of Engineering and the Al-Bakh Military Academy, although he showed little interest or ability in either. From the mid-1980s he controlled a radio station, a television station, and the daily newspaper *Babil* (Arabic for Babylon), as well as the Ministry of Youth. In his role as head of the Iraqi Olympic Committee in the mid-1990s, Uday reportedly jailed and tortured athletes who failed to live up to his expectations. He alienated his father in 1988 when he beat one of Saddam's personal aides to death in public. As a result, Uday was briefly imprisoned and then exiled to Switzerland. After returning to Iraq in about 1990, Uday became head of the paramilitary fedayeen. He oversaw the punishment of disloyal soldiers during and after the first Gulf War and was thought to have been responsible for the deaths of his two brothers-in-law who had defected to Jordan and then returned to Iraq. He was left partially paralyzed by an assassination attempt in 1996. Although Qusay was considered as ruthless as his older brother, he was more discreet and low-profile than Uday. Qusay studied law at the University of Baghdad and served as deputy head of Saddam's special security organization, using his power to torture and summarily execute prison inmates and political opponents. After the first Gulf War, he crushed a Shi'ite rebellion in southern Iraq and administered the destruction of the ancient marshlands in that region. After Uday was shot and crippled, Qusay took control of the fedayeen, as well as the elite Republican Guards and the National Security Council. By 2000 Uday reportedly had proved too unstable to retain his father's trust, and Qusay was generally regarded as Saddam's heir apparent. In early 2003, after the U.S.-led coalition invaded Iraq, Qusay and Uday were designated, respectively, the second and third most-wanted officials of the old regime. The brothers were in hiding in a private residence in northern Iraq when they were killed in a shootout with U.S. troops.

Imperio Argentina (MAGDALENA NILE DEL RIO), Argentine-born Spanish actress and singer (b. Dec. 26, 1906, Buenos Aires, Arg.—d. Aug. 22, 2003, Benalmádena, Spain), was one of the biggest stars of the early Spanish cinema, making the transition from silent movies to talkies and from black-and-white to colour films. She began her career on the stage but appeared in movies from 1926, starring in numerous musical comedies, notably *Melodía de arrabal* (*Suburban Melody,* 1933), in which she appeared with Argentine tango legend Carlos Gardel. She was also known as a singer of the Spanish *copla.*

Ishihara, Takashi, Japanese business executive (b. March 3, 1912, Tokyo, Japan—d. Dec. 31, 2003, Tokyo), served as president of the Nissan Motor Co. from 1977 to 1985 and helped turn the company into one of the world's largest automakers. Ishihara joined Nissan after earning a law degree from Tohoku University, Sendai, in 1937. He was named director of accounting in 1945 and director of export operations in 1957. Three years later he led the establishment of a highly successful export subsidiary in the U.S. Ishihara became a managing director of Nissan in 1963 and head of Japanese sales in 1965; in the latter position he championed the development of the Datsun Sunny, a compact one-litre-engine auto that eventually became Nissan's best-selling model. During his tenure as president, Ishihara transformed Nissan into a global power. He built the company's first plants overseas, in the U.S. and Britain—a move that was soon followed by other Japanese automakers. Besides instituting his ambitious business plans, Ishihara also helped raise the company's visibility with his forceful management style and an often brusque and outspoken manner that was in sharp contrast to most of his fellow executives in Japan. Although he stepped down as president in 1985, Ishihara continued to serve as chairman of Nissan until 1992. He also served during his career as chairman of the Japan Association of Corporate Executives and of the Japan Automobile Manufacturers Association.

Istomin, Eugene George, American classical pianist (b. Nov. 26, 1925, New York, N.Y.—d. Oct. 10, 2003, Washington, D.C.), debuted at age 17 with the Philadelphia Orchestra and the New York Philharmonic in the same week after winning awards that provided for those performances. Touring extensively, he was considered one of his generation's finest soloists, but he gained even greater renown as a member—with Isaac Stern and Leonard Rose—of a chamber trio whose recordings came to be regarded as classics.

Izetbegovic, Alija, Bosniac politician (b. Aug. 8, 1925, Bosanski Samac, Kingdom of Serbs, Croats, and Slovenes—d. Oct. 19, 2003, Sarajevo, Bosnia and Herzegovina), was a devout Muslim nationalist who was elected president of the Yugoslav republic of Bosnia and Herzegovina in December 1990; his declaration of independence in April 1992 triggered a horrifically bloody ethnic conflict between Serbs, Croats, and Muslims that lasted for more than three and a half years and left the region politically divided and economically shattered. The Dayton (Ohio) peace accords, which were signed in Paris in December 1995,

Bosnia and Herzegovinian leader Alija Izetbegovic

allocated 51% of the disputed territory to an independent Bosnia and Herzegovina. The next year Izetbegovic was elected head of the new nation's three-member collective presidency; he retired in 2000.

Jackson, Maynard Holbrook, Jr., American politician and lawyer (b. March 23, 1938, Dallas, Texas—d. June 23, 2003, Arlington, Va.), was the first African American to head a major Southern city. He was elected mayor of Atlanta in 1973, and during his three terms (1974–82, 1990–94), he oversaw Atlanta's emergence as a vital metropolis and gave voice to the city's African American majority. His notable achievements included the implementation of numerous affirmative-action policies, especially a pioneering program that reserved a portion of government contracts for minority businesses, and the expansion of Hartsfield Atlanta International Airport (one of the busiest in the U.S.). He also helped bring the 1996 Olympics to Atlanta.

Jacobsen, Josephine Winder Boylan, Canadian-born American poet, short-story writer, and critic (b. Aug. 19, 1908, Cobourg, Ont.—d. July 9, 2003, Cockeysville, Md.), from 1971 to 1973 served as consultant in poetry to the Library of Congress, a position that in 1986 became poet laureate. Over some 80 years her work, which explored universal themes of human anxieties, love, and hopes, appeared in numerous literary and college quarterlies as well as the *New York Times* and *The New Yorker.*

Jaques, Elliott, Canadian-born psychologist and social analyst (b. Jan. 18, 1917, Toronto, Ont.—d. March 8, 2003, Gloucester, Mass.), developed the concept of corporate culture and coined the term *mid-life crisis.* In 1946 Jaques became a founding member of London's Tavistock Institute of Human Relations. In 1952 he began an association with Glacier Metal, where he developed his theory of time frames and requisite organization. He believed that different individuals were capable of carrying out tasks in a variety of time frames and that organizations should be arranged hierarchically on the basis of these time-frame capabilities—that is, employees who were capable of carrying out the long-range tasks should be at the top of the hierarchy. His investigations into the lives of creative geniuses revealed that very frequently such people experienced a marked decline in activity or a major change in style at about their mid-30s; he published the paper "Death and the Mid-life Crisis" in 1965. In that same year he became head of the social sciences department of Brunel University, Uxbridge, Eng. Jaques worked with an Australian mining company, a number of government organizations, the Church of England, and the U.S. Army. He was the author of more than 20 books, among them *The General Theory of Bureaucracy* (1976) and *Requisite Organization* (1989).

Jenkins, Roy Harris (BARON JENKINS OF HILLHEAD), British politician and author (b. Nov. 11, 1920, Abersychan, Monmouthshire, Eng.—d. Jan. 5, 2003, East Hendred, Oxfordshire, Eng.), in a career that spanned half a century, was a leading figure in the Labour Party before breaking away in 1981 to help form the centrist Social Democratic Party (SDP). Jenkins was instrumental in liberalizing British society and in stabilizing the budget, promoting European monetary union, and championing British membership in the European Economic Community (EEC). Jenkins graduated from Balliol College, Oxford, in 1941. He was elected to Parliament in 1948, and in 1964 Prime Minister Harold Wilson appointed him minister of aviation. As home secretary (1965–67) Jenkins achieved the liberalization of laws banning homosexuality and abortion as well as those governing divorce and theatre censorship. In 1967, following the devaluation of the currency, he was made chancellor of the Exchequer, and, through a combination of budget cuts and tax increases, he achieved a surplus in the balance of payments by the end of 1969. In 1970 the Labour Party lost the general election, and Jenkins became deputy leader of the party. The following year Jenkins crossed party lines to vote with the Tories in favour of Britain's entering the EEC. When in 1972 the Labour Party supported a referendum calling for withdrawal from the EEC, Jenkins resigned his position. He was home secretary again when Wilson was returned to office (1974–76) and then became president of the European Commission, a position he held until 1981. That same year Jenkins joined with David Owen, Shirley Williams, and Bill Rodgers to launch the SDP. In 1982 he was elected to Parliament on the Social Democratic ticket, and thereafter he became party leader. In the 1983 elections the SDP won only six seats, and Jenkins stepped down as party leader. In the aftermath of the 1987 elections, in which he lost his seat, he was created a life peer, and in 1988 be became leader of the newly-combined Social and Liberal Democratic Party in the House of Lords, a position he held until 1997. His many well-received books included *Gladstone* (1995), which won the Whitbread award for biography, and *Churchill: A Biography* (2001). Jenkins was president of the Royal Society of Literature (1988–2003) and chancellor of the University of Oxford (1987–2003), and he was awarded the Order of Merit in 1993.

Statesman Roy Jenkins

Katz, Sir Bernard, German-born British biophysicist (b. March 26, 1911, Leipzig, Ger.—d. April 20, 2003, London, Eng.), shared (with American biochemist Julius Axelrod and Swedish physiologist Ulf von Euler) the 1970 Nobel Prize for Physiology or Medicine for discoveries concerning the chemistry of nerve transmission. Katz was singled out for his studies on the neurotransmitter acetylcholine and the mechanism by which that chemical substance transmits impulses from nerve cells to muscle fibres. Katz was born to a Russian father and Polish mother who had immigrated to Germany, but his Jewish family never held German citizenship. After graduating from the University of Leipzig (M.D., 1934), he studied under Nobel laureate A.V. Hill at University College London (UCL). Katz received a Ph.D. in 1938, briefly worked in Sydney, Australia, and served in the Australian radar corps during World War II. In 1952 he succeeded Hill as head of the UCL biophysics research unit and established the department of biophysics, where he remained until his retirement in 1978. Katz was granted British citizenship in 1941, became a fellow of the Royal Society in 1952 (winning the Copley Medal in 1967), and was knighted in 1969. His significant books included *Electric Excitation of Nerve* (1939) and *The Release of Neural Transmitter Substances* (1969).

Kazan, Elia (ELIAS KAZANTZOGLOU), American theatre and motion picture director, actor, and writer (b. Sept. 7, 1909, Constantinople, Ottoman Empire [now Istanbul, Turkey]—d. Sept. 28, 2003, New York, N.Y.), was one of the most highly acclaimed and influential directors in the history of American theatre and film—a pioneer of a naturalistic, socially conscious style. He collaborated with such playwrights as Thornton Wilder, Tennessee Williams, and Arthur Miller; was a cofounder (1947) of the Actors Studio, which provided the training ground for generations of actors; and shaped the film performances of such actors as Marlon Brando, James Dean, and Warren Beatty. For some, however, his artistic achievements were overshadowed by his naming of names when he was called before the House Un-American Activities Committee in 1952; he admitted that he had been a member of the Communist Party for two years in the 1930s and revealed the names of several fellow members. When he was four years old, Kazan moved to the U.S. with his Greek parents. He studied at the drama school at Yale University and in 1932 joined the Group Theatre in New York City, with a view toward becoming a director. In 1942 he made his breakthrough with Wilder's *The Skin of Our Teeth.* Among directorial efforts that followed were Miller's plays *All My Sons* (1947) and *Death of a Salesman* (1949)—for each of which he won a best director Tony

AP/Wide World Photos

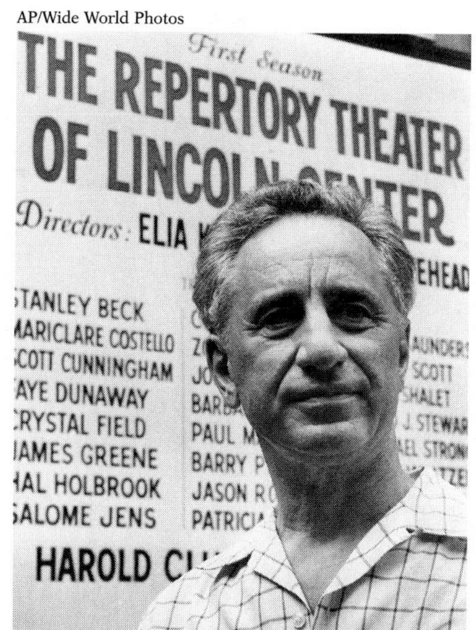

Director Elia Kazan

Award; Williams's *A Streetcar Named Desire* (1947), *Camino Real* (1953), *Cat on a Hot Tin Roof* (1955), and *Sweet Bird of Youth* (1959); William Inge's *The Dark at the Top of the Stairs* (1957); and Archibald MacLeish's *JB* (1959), for which he won another Tony. Kazan's first major film-directing credit was *A Tree Grows in Brooklyn* (1945), and he went on to guide such classics as *Gentlemen's Agreement* (1947) and *On the Waterfront* (1954)—both of which garnered him an Academy Award for best director—as well as *A Streetcar Named Desire* (1951), *East of Eden* (1955), *A Face in the Crowd* (1957), and *Splendor in the Grass* (1961). Among Kazan's awards were the Kennedy Center Honors in 1983 and a special Oscar for lifetime achievement in 1999.

Kelly, Michael, American journalist (b. March 17, 1957, Washington, D.C.—d. April 3, 2003, south of Baghdad, Iraq), was a fierce and courageous reporter, editor, and columnist. Kelly's reporting and investigative work at various publications had earned him positive notice by the time he persuaded *The New Republic* to send him as a freelance journalist to cover the Persian Gulf War in 1991. His dispatches won an Overseas Press Award and a National Magazine Award for reporting, and the book of his collected war writing, *Martyr's Day: Chronicles of a Small War* (1993), won the PEN/Martha Allbrand Award. In 1992 he became a reporter for the *New York Times,* and in 1994 he wrote from Washington for *The New Yorker* magazine. He was ferociously opposed to the administration of Pres. Bill Clinton, and his columns exuberantly expressed that opposition. He became editor of *The New Republic* in 1996, but, as he did not moderate or mute his views, he lasted less than a year at the post. Kelly then became editor of *The Atlantic* magazine, improving and broadening the publication, which won three National Magazine Awards under his tenure (1999–2002). In order to return to reporting, he became editor at large in 2002, and he returned to the Persian Gulf to report on the U.S.-led war in Iraq, this time embedded with the 3rd Infantry Division of the U.S. Army; he was the first American journalist killed in the war.

Kempson, Rachel (LADY REDGRAVE), British actress (b. May 28, 1910, Dartmouth, Eng.—d. May 24, 2003, Millbrook, N.Y.), had a distinguished stage, film, and television career in Great Britain but, especially in the U.S., became better known as the matriarch of the Redgrave acting family—the wife of Sir Michael Redgrave, the mother of Vanessa, Corin, and Lynn Redgrave, and the grandmother of Natasha Richardson.

Kenner, William Hugh, Canadian-American literary critic (b. Jan. 7, 1923, Peterborough, Ont.—d. Nov. 24, 2003, Athens, Ga.), was a leading interpreter of American poet Ezra Pound and of Modernism in general. He was probably best known for his volume *The Pound Era* (1971), though his interests and book topics ranged widely—from geodesic math to cartoonist Chuck Jones and engineer and architect R. Buckminster Fuller.

Kerimov, Kerim Aliyevich, Soviet rocket scientist (b. Nov. 14/17, 1917, Baku, Azerbaijan, Russian Empire—d. March 29, 2003, Moscow, Russia), was for many years a central figure in the Soviet space program, though his name was kept secret from the public. During and after World War II, Kerimov worked with military rockets, rising by 1959 to head the department that oversaw secret test launches. He worked under Sergey Korolyov on the space program, a position he held at the time of the launch of Sputnik, the first satellite, in 1957 and when Yury Gagarin became the first man in space in 1961. In 1966 Kerimov was put in charge of the state commission for testing of the Soyuz manned spacecraft program, intended to lead to a Moon landing. Although fatal accidents occurred in 1967 and 1971, it was not until 1974, because he continued to support the no-longer-approved lunar mission, that he was demoted. Kerimov retained his position as head of the state commission until his retirement in 1990; his name was first mentioned in public in 1987, and he wrote a history of the Soviet space program in 1995.

Kerr, Clark, American educator (b. May 17, 1911, Stony Creek, Pa.—d. Dec. 1, 2003, El Cerrito, Calif.), was chancellor of the University of California, Berkeley, from 1952 to 1958 and then served as president of the entire University of California system from 1958 to 1967. In the latter post he guided the creation of a three-tier system that guaranteed that a college education was available to all the state's high-school graduates—a plan that many other states emulated. Perceived as having been too soft on Free Speech Movement protesters, however, he was fired by then governor Ronald Reagan in 1967, whereupon he headed the Carnegie Commission on Higher Education and then chaired the Carnegie Council on Policy Studies in Higher Education.

Kerr, (Bridget) Jean Collins, American playwright and author (b. July 10, 1922, Scranton, Pa.—d. Jan. 5, 2003, White Plains, N.Y.), collaborated with her husband, drama critic Walter Kerr, on several plays but achieved her greatest success on her own. Her anecdotal book *Please Don't Eat the Daisies* (1957) was a best-seller that went on to become the basis of a 1960 movie and a mid-'60s TV sitcom, and she followed up with such successes as the book *The Snake Has All the Lines* (1960) and the plays *Mary, Mary* (1961; filmed 1963) and *Finishing Touches* (1973).

Khalkhali, Sadeq, Iranian cleric and judge (b. July 27, 1926, Givi, Azerbaijani S.S.R., U.S.S.R. [now in Azerbaijan]—d. Nov. 26, 2003, Tehran, Iran), ordered the summary execution of hundreds (perhaps thousands) of "counterrevolutionaries" in his dual role as lead prosecutor and chief justice (1979–80) of the Islamic Revolutionary Courts and as head of the Iranian antinarcotics agency (from 1982). Ayatollah Khalkhali was first elected to the Consultative Assembly in 1980, but he was ejected by the Council of Guardians in 1992 and retired. He later justified his past actions in interviews and in his autobiography, which was published in 2000.

Kindleberger, Charles Poor, II, American economist and teacher (b. Oct. 12, 1910, New York, N.Y.—d. July 7, 2003, Cambridge, Mass.), helped create the Marshall Plan, the U.S. program that provided aid to post-World War II Europe, and extensively researched historical financial events to develop economic theories. He advanced the idea that free markets are not always capable of regulating themselves, and in perhaps his best-known work, *Manias, Panics, and Crashes* (1978), he examined the role that mob psychology played in financial crises throughout history.

King, Earl (EARL SILAS JOHNSON IV), American rhythm-and-blues musician and songwriter (b. Feb. 7, 1934, New Orleans, La.—d. April 17, 2003, New Orleans), played an incandescent guitar and wrote a number of songs that became standards of the genre. His strongest influence and mentor was Guitar

R & B Legend Earl King

Zuma Press

Slim, and this influence was apparent in his early recordings, in particular the 1954 song "A Mother's Love." In 1955 King had a national hit with "Those Lonely, Lonely Nights." Among the best-known and most-covered of his subsequent songs were "Trick Bag," "Big Chief," and "Come On (Let the Good Times Roll)." His albums included *Glazed* (1988), *Sexual Telepathy* (1990), and *Hard River to Cross* (1993).

Kourouma, Ahmadou, Ivorian novelist and playwright (b. November 1927, Boundiali, French West Africa [now in Côte d'Ivoire]—d. Dec. 11, 2003, Lyon, France), wrote in a form of French that scandalized the establishment and affected French colonial policies. His first novel, *Les Soleils des indépendances* (1968; *The Suns of Independence,* 1981) was published first in Canada, having been rejected by French publishers. In it, as in the books and plays that followed, Kourouma satirized African politics and otherwise commented on postcolonial life. As a result of his writing, he spent much of his life in exile. He was probably the best-known Francophone African writer in France and was sometimes referred to as the "African Voltaire."

Kupcinet, Irving ("IRV"), American newspaper columnist (b. July 31, 1912, Chicago, Ill.—d. Nov. 10, 2003, Chicago), became a Chicago institution by way of the celebrities, politicians, and other notables he knew and reported on in "Kup's Column," his syndicated gossip column in the *Chicago Sun-Times,* which he began writing in 1943, when the paper was the *Chicago Daily Times,* and continued until a few days before his death. From 1959 to 1986 he also celebrated "the lively art of conversation" on his Peabody Award-winning syndicated television late-night talk show *At Random* (later *Kup's Show*).

Lacy, Samuel Harold ("SAM"), American sportswriter (b. Oct. 23, 1903, Mystic, Conn.—d. May 8, 2003, Washington, D.C.), was an editor and columnist for the Afro-American Newspapers in Baltimore, Md., from 1943 until shortly before his death and in that position was an influential crusader for racial integration in the major leagues. He was (1948) the first black to be accepted as a member of the Baseball Writers Association of America and, as winner of the J.G. Taylor Spink Award in 1997, became a member of the writers and broadcasters exhibit of the Baseball Hall of Fame.

French tycoon Jean-Luc Lagardère

Lagardère, Jean-Luc, French entrepreneur (b. Feb. 10, 1928, Aubiet, France—d. March 14, 2003, Paris, France), created one of France's largest industrial empires and was instrumental in the creation of the European Aeronautic Defence and Space Co. (EADS), the trans-European aerospace behemoth and manufacturer of the Airbus aircraft. Lagardère trained as an engineer and began his career in 1951, working for Avions Marcel Dassault. In 1963 he became managing director of the armaments manufacturer Matra, which he diversified into the manufacture of equipment for space exploration and automobiles, and in 1977 he became CEO. In 1980 Lagardère acquired the publishing company Hachette, which he built into one of the world's biggest magazine publishers, with such titles as *Paris Match, Elle, Woman's Day,* and *Car and Driver.* He purchased the television channel La Cinq in 1990, but it went bankrupt two years later. He salvaged the situation by merging Hachette and Matra in 1993; this became the Lagardère Group. In 1998 he merged Matra with the state-owned Aerospatiale, and he then brought it together with Germany's DaimlerChrysler and Spain's Casa to form EADS. In 2001 Lagardère handed day-to-day responsibility for the Lagardère Group to his son, but he remained chairman.

Lambert, Eleanor, American fashion publicist (b. Aug. 10, 1903, Crawfordsville, Ind.—d. Oct. 7, 2003, New York, N.Y.), helped elevate American fashion to international prominence and saw that American designers—most notably Halston, Oscar de la Renta, Anne Klein, and Bill Blass—earned the same respect as their European counterparts. A tireless promoter, she also established (1940) the International Best-Dressed List, introduced (1943) a week of New York fashion shows for the press, a precursor to the highly popular Fashion Week, and founded (1962) the Council of Fashion Designers of America.

Lange, Hope Elise Ross, American actress (b. Nov. 28, 1931/33, Redding Ridge, Conn.—d. Dec. 19, 2003, Santa Monica, Calif.), was already a veteran of stage and television when she made an impressive film debut in 1956 in *Bus Stop,* and the following year she earned an Academy Award nomination for best supporting actress for her role in *Peyton Place.* She went on to win back-to-back Emmy Awards (1969 and 1970) for her lead role in the TV series *The Ghost and Mrs. Muir* and later appeared in such films as *Blue Velvet* (1986) and *Clear and Present Danger* (1994).

Latsis, John (IOANNIS SPYRIDON LATSIS), Greek shipping and oil tycoon (b. Sept. 14, 1910, Katakolo, Greece—d. April 17, 2003, Athens, Greece), was a bold and surefooted businessman, who became one of the richest men in the world. Working his way up from deckhand to captain, Latsis used his savings to begin buying his own ships and by the 1960s he owned a fleet. In 1969 he established the Greek export-oriented refining company Petrola, and he set up an oil refinery in Saudi Arabia. By the late 1970s he was able to move into banking; he purchased the Banque des Dépots in Geneva and founded the EFG Private Bank and Trust Company in London and the Euroinvestment Bank (now Eurobank) in Athens. In his later years he used his wealth for philanthropic projects. Latsis turned over the running of his businesses to his son in 1999.

Legum, Colin, South African-born journalist (b. Jan. 3, 1919, Kestell, Orange Free State, S.Af.—d. June 8, 2003, Cape Town, S.Af.), was one of the West's most respected African affairs analysts. Legum left his homeland for England in 1949 as a protest against apartheid, and he did not return permanently until the 1990s. His work as the Commonwealth correspondent (1951–81) for the *The Observer* newspaper and as editor (from 1968) of the *African Contemporary Record,* however, led him to develop friendly personal relations with most of the top African leaders, including Julius Nyerere, Jomo Kenyatta, and Oliver Tambo. Legum's books included *Africa: A Handbook to the Continent* (1961) and *Africa Since Independence* (1999).

Liedtke, J(ohn) Hugh, American entrepreneur (b. Feb. 10, 1922, Tulsa, Okla.—d. March 28, 2003, Houston, Texas), as longtime CEO of the Pennzoil Co., became known as a takeover artist and won billions of dollars from Texaco Inc. in court. In 1953 Liedtke and his brother, William, in partnership with future U.S. president George H.W. Bush, formed the Zapata Petroleum Corp. and drilled a string of 127 successful oil wells in western Texas. The following decade the Liedtke brothers took over the South Penn Oil Co. and named the combined company Pennzoil. A series of mergers followed, the most remarkable of them being the hostile takeover of the much-larger United Gas Pipeline Co. The four-year battle for control of the Getty Oil Co. culminated in 1988 in a jury's finding that Texaco had illegally usurped a handshake deal for Pennzoil to acquire an interest in Getty; Liedtke was awarded $3 billion. He retired as CEO that same year but stayed on as chairman until 1994.

Lippert, Felice Marks, American businesswoman (b. 1929, New York, N.Y.—d. Feb. 22, 2003, Manhasset, N.Y.), with her husband and Jean Nidetch, cofounded Weight Watchers, one of the most successful weight-loss organizations in the world. In 1963 Lippert and her husband, Albert, invited Nidetch, who taught a diet program in her home, to come to the Lipperts' home and teach the program to them and some of their friends. When the Lipperts found that they successfully lost weight, they joined with Nidetch and her husband, Marty, to turn the program into a business. They began holding meetings in public places and charging membership fees; soon they trademarked the Weight Watchers name, patented the method, and began selling franchises. When the company went public in 1968, it was operating 91 franchises in 43 states. Lippert was a director and vice president of Weight Watchers International until the H.J. Heinz Co. acquired it in 1978; she continued to be chairman of the Weight Watchers Foundation.

Little Eva (Eva Narcissus Boyd), American pop singer (b. June 29, 1943, Belhaven, N.C.—d. April 10, 2003, Kinston, N.C.), achieved timeless popularity in 1962 with her recording of "The Loco-Motion." Little Eva, who was working as a babysitter for the songwriting duo Carole King and Gerry Goffin, made a demonstration recording of the dance-novelty song which they had written for another singer. The songwriters and their producers were so taken with Little Eva's version, however, that they decided to let her record it. After she demonstrated the dance steps on the television show *American Bandstand,* the song went to number one. She recorded a few other songs, but none approached the popularity of

Little Eva "Loco-Motioning"

"The Loco-Motion," which retained its popularity for decades. In the 1990s Little Eva began touring on the "oldies" circuit.

Loiseau, Bernard Daniel Jacques, French master chef (b. Jan. 13, 1951, Chamalières, France—d. Feb. 24, 2003, Saulieu, France), created a light, flavourful cuisine that was regarded as among the best in Europe; he was only the second chef ever to be admitted to the Legion of Honour (1995) and the first to put his company on the French stock exchange (1998). In 1975 Loiseau began working at La Côte d'Or in Burgundy, which had been renowned from the 1930s to the '60s. By 1991 he had earned three stars from the Michelin guide and a Gault-Millau rating of 19 (out of 20). Loiseau opened three restaurants in Paris in the late 1990s, established a line of frozen foods, and wrote a number of cookbooks. In early 2003, however, rumours circulated that Loiseau might lose his third Michelin star. In the event, he kept his star but lost two points in the *Guide Gault-Millau.* Shortly after the latest edition of the guide was published, Loiseau committed suicide; many in the culinary community blamed pressures of the rating system.

Long, Russell Billiu, American politician (b. Nov. 3, 1918, Shreveport, La.—d. May 9, 2003, Washington, D.C.), had a major influence on U.S. tax laws while serving (1948–87) as a Democratic U.S. senator from Louisiana. As the powerful chairman (1969–80) of the Senate Finance Committee, he favoured tax breaks for business and industry. He also spearheaded the creation of popular legislation that resulted in the earned income tax credit, expansion of Social Security, federal health insurance, and the massive 1986 revision and simplification of the tax laws. Besides being noted for his folksy humour and mastery of Senate rules, he was especially successful at writing laws to benefit Louisiana, particularly those involving its oil and gas industry. The last of Louisiana's historic Long political dynasty, he was the only U.S. senator whose two parents had preceded him in the Senate. Following the assassination of his father, Huey ("Kingfish") Long, his mother, Rose McConnell Long, served out her husband's term. Russell Long earned his law degree from Louisiana State University, joined the U.S. Navy during World War II, and was elected to the Senate a day before his 30th birthday. In 1956 he rewrote the Social Security Act to give benefits to disabled people, and he went on to help create Medicare. During the 1960s he opposed civil rights legislation, and while he was assistant Senate majority leader (1965–69), he favoured the Vietnam War. For a time alcoholism slowed his career, but after he stopped drinking he regained his effectiveness. Long became a successful Washington lobbyist after his retirement from the Senate.

Longden, John Eric ("Johnny"), British-born American jockey and horse trainer (b. Feb. 14, 1907, Wakefield, Yorkshire, Eng.—d. Feb. 14, 2003, Banning, Calif.), won the Triple Crown aboard Count Fleet in 1943 and was the only person to both ride and train a Kentucky Derby winner. When Longden was five years old, his family moved to Alberta. Although he had his first race—which was also his first win—in Salt Lake City, Utah, in 1927, he worked mostly in Canada until 1935, when he began to ride full time in the U.S. He rode Count Fleet to victory in 16 of 21 races, including all three of the 1943 Triple Crown races, winning the Kentucky Derby by 3 lengths, the Preakness Stakes by 8, and the Belmont Stakes by 25. In 1956 Longden broke the record, held by Sir Gordon Richards, of 4,870 career wins in Thoroughbred racing, and he was inducted into the National Thoroughbred Racing Hall of Fame in 1958. His last race was the San Juan Capistrano Handicap in March 1966, when he rode George Royal to an exciting come-from-behind victory. He retired with 6,032 wins out of 32,413 mounts, a record that stood until Bill Shoemaker broke it in 1970. After retiring as a jockey, Longden began a career as a trainer, and in 1969 one of his horses, Majestic Prince, won the Kentucky Derby and the Preakness Stakes. He retired from training in 1982, and the National Thoroughbred Racing Association honoured him with a Special Eclipse Award in 1994.

MacKenzie, Gisele (Gisele Marie Louise Marguerite LaFleche), Canadian-born singer and actress (b. Jan. 10, 1927, Winnipeg, Man.—d. Sept. 5, 2003, Burbank, Calif.), became known as Canada's first lady of song in the 1940s and appeared in the U.S. with such stars as Bob Crosby and Jack Benny before becoming one of the regulars on the weekly television show *Your Hit Parade,* on which she performed from 1953 to 1957. She then had her own show for six months, in 1963 became a regular on *The Sid Caesar Show,* and thereafter appeared as a guest on TV game shows and series.

Maddox, Lester Garfield, American businessman and politician (b. Sept. 30, 1915, Atlanta, Ga.—d. June 25, 2003, Atlanta), served as governor of Georgia (1967–71) after having garnered national attention in 1964 for refusing to serve African Americans at his Pickrick Restaurant. He later passed out pick handles as symbols of his defiance of the Civil Rights Act and eventually closed his restaurant rather than comply with the federal law. Noted for his folksy manner, he proved a surprisingly moderate governor and implemented many policies that benefited African Americans.

Mann, Herbie (HERBERT JAY SOLOMON), American musician (b. April 16, 1930, Brooklyn, N.Y.—d. July 1, 2003, Pecos, N.M.), was a full-time flutist, a rarity in jazz, and a pioneer of jazz-rock and other kinds of fusion music. Though he was a straightforward bop-oriented player in the 1950s, he had a jazz-funk hit, "Comin' Home Baby," in 1962 and began traveling widely and incorporating African and Latin American motifs into his playing; he was one of the early jazz musicians to record bossa nova. Mann's popularity spread far beyond traditional jazz boundaries, notably in a series of albums that fused jazz with soul music (in his hit album *Memphis Underground*), reggae, disco, and rock (*London Underground*). His success inspired younger flute specialists; in one of his final albums, *Eastern European Roots* (2000), he joined jazz with his own Jewish musical heritage.

Marden, Luis (ANNIBALE LUIGI PARAGALLO), American photographer, writer, and explorer (b. Jan. 25, 1913, Chelsea, Mass.—d. March 3, 2003, Arlington, Va.), discovered the wreck of the HMS *Bounty,* retraced the voyages of Christopher Columbus, and revolutionized underwater colour photography. Marden was hired as a photographer for *National Geographic* in 1934 and almost immediately introduced the use of 35-mm Kodachrome film to the magazine. He spent the 1940s on assignments in Central and South America. In the mid-1950s he worked with Jacques Cousteau aboard the *Calypso* and devised many novel photography techniques. Marden's best-known adventure was his discovery of the remains of the *Bounty* off Pitcairn Island in the South Pacific in January 1957. He also discovered a new species of orchid and a new species of sea flea, both of which were named for him. He retired in 1976, after which he and his wife, a mathematician, retraced and recalculated the first voyage of Columbus to the New World, concluding that Columbus landed at Samana Cay rather than, as had been generally accepted, at Watling Island. Marden contributed the last of his more than 60 articles to *National Geographic* in 1998.

Marinho, Roberto Pisani, Brazilian journalist and media mogul (b. Dec. 3, 1904, Rio de Janeiro, Braz.—d. Aug. 6, 2003, Rio de

Media mogul Roberto Marinho

Janeiro), transformed *O Globo* (a newspaper founded by his father in 1925) into a global media empire and in the process became one of Brazil's most influential men. The cornerstone of the company was TV Globo, Brazil's largest television network, which reached nearly every household in the country.

Marshall, Burke, American lawyer (b. Oct. 1, 1922, Plainfield, N.J.—d. June 2, 2003, Newton, Conn.), as assistant attorney general in charge of the Department of Justice's civil rights division (1961–65), played a key role in the U.S. government's attempts to desegregate the South. Practical-minded and a fine negotiator, he did much to calm racial unrest, and his notable achievements included the desegregation of interstate travel (1961) and the University of Mississippi (1962), as well as the passage of the Civil Rights Act (1964).

Mauldin, William Henry ("BILL"), American cartoonist (b. Oct. 29, 1921, Mountain Park,

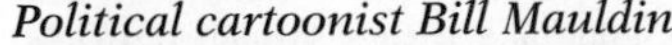

Political cartoonist Bill Mauldin

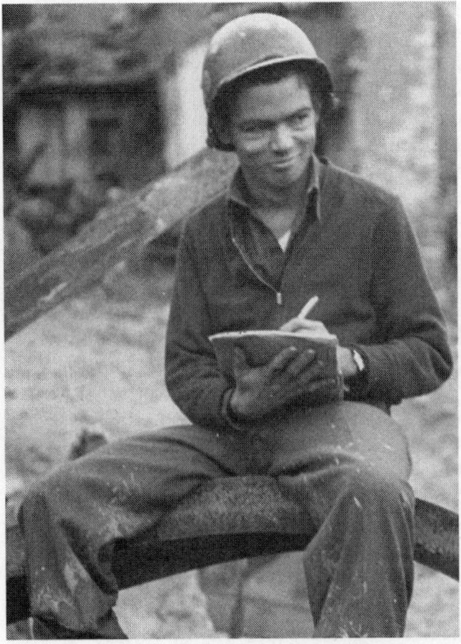

N.M.—d. Jan. 22, 2003, Newport Beach, Calif.), created Willie and Joe—two "everyman" dogfaces whose weary struggles against incompetent officers in addition to battles against the enemy made them inspiring symbols—and through them captured the reality of war and the way the infantrymen on the World War II battlefields experienced it; in 1945 these depictions won Mauldin the first of his two Pulitzer Prizes. Later, as a widely syndicated cartoonist, he turned to more general national and international political and social commentary, eloquently skewering bigotry and pomposity and expressing the emotion of historic events. Among his most memorable cartoons was one that appeared in 1963 after the assassination of Pres. John F. Kennedy; it depicted a grieving statue of Abraham Lincoln at Washington, D.C.'s Lincoln Memorial. Mauldin studied cartooning through a correspondence course and at the Chicago Academy of Fine Arts and began having some of his drawings published. The National Guard unit he had joined was federalized in 1940, and while undergoing army training he drew cartoons for military publications. Upon shipping out to Europe, he also began providing them for the army newspaper *Stars and Stripes;* in 1945 a number of those were included in his best-seller *Up Front.* After the war Mauldin concentrated on writing and on working in the motion picture business for a while, acting in the 1951 films *Red Badge of Courage* and *Teresa,* but in 1958 returned to cartooning for the *St. Louis* (Mo.) *Post-Dispatch.* The following year he won his second Pulitzer, for a cartoon depicting the U.S.S.R.'s persecution of writer Boris Pasternak. Mauldin moved to the *Chicago Sun-Times* in 1962 and remained there until his retirement in 1991.

McClendon, Sarah Newcomb, American journalist (b. July 8, 1910, Tyler, Texas—d. Jan. 8, 2003, Washington, D.C.), was a Washington institution during her more than half a century of service as White House correspondent for a group of Texas newspapers. McClendon was known for her direct, pointed questions, which she had pitched to every U.S. president since Franklin D. Roosevelt.

McCloskey, Robert, American writer and illustrator (b. Sept. 14, 1914, Hamilton, Ohio—d. June 30, 2003, Deer Isle, Maine), delighted children with a series of books noted for their detailed illustrations and universal themes. *Make Way for Ducklings* (1941), perhaps his best-known work, follows a mallard family's journey through the streets of Boston. He was the recipient of two Caldecott Medals.

McCormack, Mark Hume, American sports marketing entrepreneur (b. Nov. 6, 1930, Chicago, Ill.—d. May 16, 2003, New York,

N.Y.), began in 1960 with a handshake agreement to represent golfer Arnold Palmer as his business agent and built his enterprise into IMG (formerly International Management Group), which pioneered the idea of gaining lucrative product-endorsement deals for its clients and came to include many of the world's top sports and entertainment figures in its roster. The billion-dollar-a-year IMG also produced sports broadcasts and sponsored and promoted tournaments.

Merton, Robert King (MEYER R. SCHKOLNICK), American sociologist (b. July 4, 1910, Philadelphia, Pa.—d. Feb. 23, 2003, New York, N.Y.), made wide-ranging contributions to the field, especially the sociology of science; he coined such expressions as "self-fulfilling prophecy," "role model," "unanticipated consequences," "theories of the middle range," "opportunity structure," and "focused interview" (from whence "focus group"). Merton earned a B.A. (1931) from Temple University, Philadelphia, and a Ph.D. (1936) from Harvard University. He stayed on as an instructor at Harvard until 1939, when he moved to Tulane University, New Orleans, and then in 1941 to Columbia University, New York City, where he remained until 1985. At Columbia he collaborated with Paul F. Lazarsfeld at the university's Bureau of Applied Social Research until Lazarsfeld's death in 1976. Among Merton's publications were *Science, Technology, and Society in Seventeenth Century England* (1938), a seminal work in the sociology of science that explored the relationship between Puritanism and the rise of modern science; "Social Structure and Anomie" (1938), a widely reprinted paper that argued that some nonconformist behaviour is a result of the social structure; *Social Theory and Social Structure* (1949; rev. ed., 1968), a collection of papers that advanced a structural-functional approach to sociology; and *On the Shoulders of Giants* (1965), which traced the use of Sir Isaac Newton's statement "If I have seen farther, it is by standing on the shoulders of giants." Merton's work assisted Kenneth Brown in the preparation of the report on segregation that figured in the 1954 *Brown* v. *Board of Education* school desegregation case. Merton served as president of the American Sociological Association in 1957 and was the first sociologist to receive a National Medal of Science (1994). His son, Robert C. Merton, won the Nobel Prize for Economics in 1997.

Metcalfe, E. Bennett ("BEN"), Canadian environmentalist, journalist, and broadcaster (b. Oct. 31, 1919, Winnipeg, Man.—d. Oct. 14, 2003, Shawnigan Lake, Vancouver Island, British Columbia), was a founder of the small antinuclear Don't Make a Wave Committee. Using his broadcasting and public relations skills, he attracted international attention to the mission of the group and helped launch its growth into the three-million-member Greenpeace International.

Michaels, Leonard, American writer (b. Jan. 2, 1933, New York, N.Y.—d. May 10, 2003, Berkeley, Calif.), penned literary short stories and novels that often featured ordinary people in bizarre situations. His best-known work, *The Men's Club* (1981; filmed, 1986), centred on a group of men discussing their wives and lovers, was criticized by some as misogynistic, while others claimed it highlighted male vulnerability.

Modigliani, Franco, Italian-born American economist (b. June 18, 1918, Rome, Italy—d. Sept. 25, 2003, Cambridge, Mass.), was awarded the Nobel Prize for Economics in 1985 for his pioneering studies in the 1950s of people's saving habits. Modigliani's "life-cycle theory" holds that younger workers of all socioeconomic backgrounds—not just rich people—build up savings for their own use in retirement. Also in the '50s, Modigliani and American economist Merton H. Miller advanced the influential Modigliani-Miller theorem, which describes the effect of financial structure and dividend policy on the market value of a company's stock.

Moiseiwitsch, Tanya, British theatre designer (b. Dec. 3, 1914, London, Eng.—d. Feb. 19, 2003, London), was renowned for her visionary stage designs, including the influential thrust stage at Stratford, Ont., and for her fruitful collaboration with director Tyrone Guthrie. Moiseiwitsch's first professional design was in 1934. She designed for the Abbey Theatre in Dublin from 1935 to 1939, after which she worked for the Oxford Playhouse. In 1944 she began an association with the Old Vic Company; five years later she made her debut design for the Shakespeare Memorial Theatre at Stratford-on-Avon. In 1953 Guthrie asked her to help him design a theatre for the new Shakespeare Festival in Canada, and the result was the thrust stage in the festival tent; she designed more than 20 shows for the festival. Moiseiwitsch was appointed CBE in 1976.

Möllemann, Jürgen W., German politician (b. July 15, 1945, Augsburg, Ger.—d. June 5, 2003, Marl, Ger.), was a controversial member of the Free Democratic Party; he held several cabinet posts from 1982, but in 1993, after only a few months in office, he resigned as vice-chancellor amid accusations of corruption. During the 2002 federal election campaign, Möllemann drew sharp criticism for remarks that were perceived as anti-Semitic. He was under investigation for alleged fraud and other financial irregularities when he died in a recreational parachute jump. It was widely believed that Möllemann, an experienced and enthusiastic skydiver, had committed suicide.

Monkhouse, Robert Alan ("BOB"), British comedian and television personality (b. June 1, 1928, Beckenham, Kent, Eng.—d. Dec. 29, 2003, Eggington, Bedfordshire, Eng.), was a mainstay of British TV sitcoms and quiz shows for more than 50 years; he was admired for his comfortable on-screen affability and his seemingly endless supply of fast-talking one-liner jokes, though his critics denounced him as "smarmy." After beginning as a stand-up comic and a gag writer for other performers, Monkhouse hosted some dozen TV game shows, including *Candid Camera* (1960–67), *The Golden Shot* (1967–71, 1974–75), *Celebrity Squares* (1975–79, 1993–94), *Family Fortunes* (1979–83), and *Bob's Full House* (1984–90). He also appeared in several films and published two volumes of memoirs. Monkhouse was made OBE in 1993.

Mosley, Lady Diana (DIANA FREEMAN-MITFORD), British socialite (b. June 17, 1910, London, Eng.—d. Aug. 11, 2003, Paris, France), was the third and most beautiful of the six celebrated Mitford sisters and the wife of Sir Oswald Mosley, leader of the British Union of Fascists (1932–40) and the Union Movement (1948–80). The dazzling and witty Mitford girls, along with their brother, Tom, had a lively and eccentric childhood, which Nancy memorialized in semiautobiographical novels, notably *Love in a Cold Climate.* In 1929 Diana, despite the initial objections of her parents, married Bryan Guinness, of the wealthy and aristocratic Guinness brewing dynasty. Three years later she left him for Mosley, whom she married in 1936 at the house of Joseph

Socialite Lady Diana Mosley

Goebbels, with Adolf Hitler as an honoured guest. During World War II the Mosleys were held in Holloway Prison (1940–43) and under house arrest (1943–45); they moved to France in the early 1950s. Diana Mosley edited *The European,* a right-wing magazine, and wrote a biography of the duchess of Windsor as well as two volumes of memoirs, *A Life of Contrasts* (1977) and *Loved Ones* (1985). Even after her husband's death in 1980, she remained a committed fascist and readily acknowledged that although Hitler had done "terrible things," she was "very, very fond" of him.

Most, Mickie (MICHAEL PETER HAYES), British record producer (b. June 20, 1938, Aldershot, Hampshire, Eng.—d. May 30, 2003, London, Eng.), discovered and then molded the sound of some of the most successful young pop singers of the 1960s and '70s, including the Animals, Herman's Hermits, the Nashville Teens, Donovan, Lulu, Jeff Beck, Mud, Suzi Quatro, and Hot Chocolate. He was a member of the rock and roll group the Most Brothers in the late 1950s, but he turned to independent record producing, beginning with the Animals in 1964. In 1969 Most founded RAK Records, which released a long run of lively, optimistic hit songs. He sold RAK's back-music catalogue to EMI in 1983, but he retained control of RAK Publishing's lucrative music-copyright business. Most was also a regular judge on the 1970s television talent show *New Faces.*

Mountfort, Guy Reginald, British advertising executive, ornithologist, and conservationist (b. Dec. 4, 1905, London, Eng.—d. April 23, 2003, Bournemouth, Dorset, Eng.), co-wrote *A Field Guide to the Birds of Britain and Europe* (1954), with Roger Tory Peterson and P.A.D. Hollom; cofounded (1961) the World Wildlife Fund (WWF), with Peter Scott, Sir Julian Huxley, and Max Nicholson (*q.v.*); and spearheaded the WWF's Operation Tiger to save that species from what appeared to be imminent extinction. Mountfort served as honorary secretary (1952–62) and president (1970–75) of the British Ornithologists' Union and vice president (from 1978) of the WWF in Britain, and he wrote numerous books about his many wildlife expeditions. He also was a director at the international advertising agency Mather & Crowther (later Ogilvy & Mather) until his retirement in 1966. He was made OBE in 1970 and was awarded the WWF Gold Medal in 1978.

Moynihan, Daniel Patrick, American scholar and politician (b. March 16, 1927, Tulsa, Okla.—d. March 26, 2003, Washington, D.C.), had a long career in both academe and public service—serving in the administrations of four presidents and then being elected to four terms in the U.S. Senate—during which he was known for the depth of his intellect and for his ability to recognize and define important issues and their political ramifications ahead of other people. Among the problem areas he explored were race relations, automobile safety, and architectural preservation, and he was among the earliest to foresee the disintegration of the Soviet Union. Following navy service in World War II and education at Tufts University, Medford, Mass., and the London School of Economics, Moynihan began his political career, working on election campaigns and on the staff of New York Gov. Averell Harriman before moving (1961) to Washington, D.C., to take a post in the Department of Labor. His 1965 report titled *The Negro Family: The Case for National Action,* but more commonly known as the Moynihan Report, caused enormous controversy by focusing on single-parent families as a cause of poverty among African Americans. Moynihan joined the faculty of Harvard University in 1966, then became an adviser to Pres. Richard Nixon, and, while returning intermittently to Harvard over the following few years, also served as ambassador to India from 1973 to 1975 and ambassador to the UN in 1975–76. In 1976 he won the first of his Senate terms. Serving until 2001, Moynihan concerned himself with such issues as government secrecy, welfare reform, and the need to strengthen the Social Security system.

Mukhopadhyay, Subhas, Bengali poet (b. Feb. 12, 1919, Krishnanagar, Bengal, India—d. July 8, 2003, Kolkata [Calcutta], India), wrote poetry of social commitment. His voice, first informed by his political idealism, evolved into a personal, thoughtful, and deeply empathetic style. After the partition of India, he gave hope to a generation of Bengalis. He received two of India's highest literary awards, and his work was translated into English and Russian.

Needham, Roger Michael, British engineer and computer scientist (b. Feb. 9, 1935, Sheffield, Eng.—d. Feb. 28, 2003, Cambridge, Eng.), devised a secure way of protecting computer password files that became the basis for all systems currently used. Needham began working as a research assistant in the computer laboratory of the University of Cambridge in 1963, after having earned a Ph.D. there. In 1967, while helping to develop a time-sharing system, whereby many users can access a single computer, he developed the one-way password encryption technique—a user's access password is encrypted irreversibly during setup and stored only in that form; when someone else subsequently tries to log on, the presented password is likewise encrypted and compared against the stored version. In 1978 he and Michael Schroeder produced the Needham-Schroeder protocol for authentication of computer users through passwords. Needham succeeded Maurice Wilkes as head of Cambridge's computer laboratory in 1980 and became professor of computer systems in 1981. Upon his retirement from the computer laboratory in 1995, he set up the Microsoft Research Laboratory, the first overseas research centre established by software giant Microsoft Corp. Needham was made CBE in 2001.

Nicholson, (Edward) Max, British ornithologist, environmentalist, and civil servant (b. July 12, 1904, Kilternan, County Dublin, Ire.—d. April 26, 2003, London, Eng.), cofounded (1961), with Julian Huxley, Peter Scott, and Guy Mountfort (*q.v.*), the World Wildlife Fund (now WWF) and was instrumental in the creation of the government-sponsored Nature Conservancy (now English Nature), of which he was director general (1952–66). Nicholson studied history at Hertford College, Oxford, and was a cofounder (1932) and chairman (1947–49) of the British Trust for Ornithology. As a civil servant, he was a member of the Advisory Committee on Scientific Policy (1948–64) and chaired the organizing committee (1951) of the first Festival of Britain. He also established two think tanks, and from 1966 he served as chairman of Land Use Consultants, which sought to persuade industry to take responsibility for the environment. Nicholson was the author of several books and a contributor to the nine-volume *The Birds of the Western Palearctic* (1965–92). He was awarded the WWF Gold Medal in 1982.

Nunn May, Alan, British nuclear physicist and spy (b. May 2, 1911, Birmingham, Eng.—d. Jan. 12, 2003, Cambridge, Eng.), was one of the first Cold War spies for the Soviet Union. In 1942 Nunn May began working with the British branch of the Manhattan Project to study the feasibility of German plans to develop an atomic bomb, and the following year the members of the project were transferred to Montreal, where he was recruited by GRU, the Soviet military intelligence agency. Secrets he supplied to his handler included samples of enriched uranium and details of the bomb that was dropped on Hiroshima, Japan. In 1945, about the time Nunn May returned to Britain, a GRU agent based in Ottawa defected with documents that implicated Nunn May, and in 1946 he was arrested, convicted, and sentenced to 10 years' hard labour, of which he served 6 years.

O'Connor, Donald David Dixon Ronald, American actor and dancer (b. Aug. 28, 1925, Chicago, Ill.—d. Sept. 27, 2003, Calabasas, Calif.), was an energetic, versatile performer who spent virtually his whole life in show business. He was best known for his acrobatic song-and-dance number "Make 'Em Laugh" in *Singin' in the Rain* (1952), which showcased both his dancing skills and his loose-limbed comedic prowess and came to be considered one of the best-ever movie dance numbers. He was almost as famous for sharing the screen with a talking mule in the film *Francis* (1950) and five of its sequels.

centre: Courtesy of Microsoft; above: © Photo B.D.V./Corbis

O'Connor was carried onstage when he was only a few days old, and by the time he was three years old, he was part of his family's vaudeville act. Early film appearances included roles in *Sing You Sinners* (1938), *Beau Geste* (1939), *Mr. Big* (1943), and a series of B musicals that made him a teen idol. Among his later popular films were *I Love Melvin* (1953), in which he tap danced on roller skates, *Call Me Madam* (1953), *There's No Business like Show Business* (1954), and *Anything Goes* (1956). The 1950s also found O'Connor beginning a career on television as a host of *The Colgate Comedy Hour* (1950–55), for which he won an Emmy Award in 1953, and as the star of his own show, *The Donald O'Connor Show* (1954). Notable among his later performances were the role of Cap'n Andy in the Broadway revival of *Show Boat* (1983) and appearances in the films *Ragtime* (1981) and *Toys* (1992).

Odhiambo, Thomas Risley, Kenyan entomologist (b. Feb. 4, 1931, Alego, Nyanza province, Kenya Colony—d. May 26, 2003, Nairobi, Kenya), was one of Africa's foremost scientists; he was renowned for his research into nonchemical methods of agricultural insect control and was a pioneer in the promotion of indigenous African scientific education and research. Odhiambo studied at Makerere (Uganda) University College and Queen's College, Cambridge. He was the founding director general (1970–94) of the multidisciplinary, Nairobi-based International Centre of Insect Physiology and Ecology, the first dean (from 1990) of the University of Nairobi's department of agriculture, and founding president (1986–99) of the African Academy of Sciences. Among his numerous international awards was the African Prize for Leadership for the Sustainable End of Hunger (1987).

Olatunji, Babatunde, Nigerian-born drummer (b. April 7, 1927, Ajido, Nigeria—d. April 6, 2003, Salinas, Calif.), brought the sound of African drumming to an American audience and influenced a number of jazz and rock musicians. While studying in New York City, Olatunji formed an African drum and dance group. His seminal album, *Drums of Passion* (1959), was credited with sparking a vogue for Afro-jazz fusion music in the 1960s, and in 1964, with jazz musician-composer John Coltrane, he opened the Olatunji Center for African Culture in New York City. During the 1990s Olatunji appeared and performed on recordings with drummer Mickey Hart (of the Grateful Dead) and Hart's percussion group, Planet Drum, including an eponymous album that won a Grammy Award in 1991. In 1997 Olatunji and his troupe, Drums of Passion, released the Grammy-nominated album *Love Drum Talk*.

Drummer Babatunde Olatunji

AP/Wide World Photos

Oman, Julia Trevelyan, British stage designer (b. July 11, 1930, London, Eng.—d. Oct. 10, 2003, Much Birch, Herefordshire, Eng.), created meticulously researched and beautifully imagined sets for television, opera, theatre, and ballet and was regarded as among the best designers of the late 20th century. She began her career at the BBC in 1955. Perhaps her most admired work was for the ballet; her 1976 collaboration with Sir Frederic Ashton on *A Month in the Country* was particularly notable. She wrote several books with her historian husband, Sir Roy Strong. Oman was made CBE in 1986.

Omarr, Sydney (SIDNEY KIMMELMAN), American astrologer (b. Aug. 5, 1926, Philadelphia, Pa.—d. Jan. 2, 2003, Santa Monica, Calif.), took up his profession at the age of 15 and became probably the most widely read horoscope writer in the world. He wrote 13 books a year, one for each sign of the zodiac and one covering all 12 signs; his columns were published in more than 200 newspapers; and he served as consultant to a number of celebrities.

Onslow Ford, Gordon, British-born American painter (b. Dec. 26, 1912, Wendover, Buckinghamshire, Eng.—d. Nov. 9, 2003, Inverness, Calif.), was associated with the Paris Surrealists but came to be interested in spontaneous creation and such metaphysical concerns as psychologist Carl Jung's idea of the collective unconscious. The grandson of a sculptor, Onslow Ford served in the Royal Navy (1927–37) but, determined to pursue his interest in painting, resigned and went to Paris, where he worked briefly with André Lhote and Fernand Léger. He also met the Chilean painter Roberto Matta, who introduced him to André Breton, Yves Tanguy, Max Ernst, and other Surrealists. Onslow Ford abandoned the pictorial images of his early work and embraced techniques such as psychic automatism. In 1941 he lectured on Surrealism in New York City to an audience that included Robert Motherwell, Jackson Pollock, Mark Rothko, and other young American painters who felt his influence and went on to create some of the strongest Abstract Expressionist work of the 20th century. (Indeed, years before Pollock became famous for the technique, Onslow Ford practiced what he called *coulage,* a method of pouring paint directly onto a canvas.) Onslow Ford lived with his wife, poet Jacqueline Johnson, in Mexico (1941–47; during which time he formally broke with the Surrealists) and then in California, where Vedanta philosophy, calligraphy, and Buddhism were among the influences he absorbed. Onslow Ford also wrote about what he called a basic visual language of line, circle, and dot; his books included *Painting in the Instant* (1964) and *Creation* (1978).

Osborne, Adam, British-born American computer entrepreneur (b. March 6, 1939, Bangkok, Thai.—d. March 18, 2003, Kodiakanal, India), introduced the first portable personal computer. Osborne Computer Corp. was founded in the U.S. in 1981 with the proceeds from the sale of Osborne's previous venture in publishing computer manuals. The success of the Osborne 1 computer was short-lived, however, owing to manufacturing challenges and competition from rivals, and the company folded two years later. Osborne's next move, into low-cost software publishing, was also unsuccessful in the longer term.

Oteiza Embil, Jorge, Basque sculptor (b. Oct. 21, 1908, Orio, Spain—d. April 9, 2003, San Sebastián, Spain), examined the nature of space and emptiness in monumental minimalist sculptures that were influential in the art world of the mid-20th century. Oteiza began sculpting while studying medicine in Madrid. In 1935–48 he lived in South America, and the pre-Columbian art that he saw there informed his later work. Oteiza won the grand prize for sculpture at the 1957 São Paulo (Braz.) Bienal, but in 1959 he announced his retirement from sculpting. He continued to create small sculptures, however, in addition to publishing books on art theory and volumes of poetry. Orteiza's frieze for the Aránzazu Basilica in Spain's Guipúzcoa province, commissioned in 1950, aroused opposition but was finally completed in 1969. He was awarded the Spanish Medal of Fine Arts (1985), the Prince of Asturias Art Prize (1988), and the Gold Medal of Navarre (1992).

Pachman, Ludek, Czechoslovak chess grandmaster and political activist (b. May 11, 1924, Bela pod Bezdezem, Czech. [now in Czech Republic]—d. March 6, 2003, Passau, Ger.), had a distinguished chess career, wrote respected books on chess, and, after a conversion experience, vociferously criticized the communist government of Czechoslovakia. Pachman won the national chess championship seven times between 1946 and 1966 and three times won European Zonal tournaments in the world championship qualifying

centre: © Douglas Kirkland/Corbis

AP/Wide World Photos

Grandmaster Ludek Pachman

rounds. He earned the international master title in 1950 and advanced to grandmaster status in 1954. In addition, he played an active role in the formal organization of chess in Czechoslovakia. When Soviet tanks rolled into the country to end the Prague Spring of 1968, Pachman's political views changed; formerly a convinced communist, he became an ardent anticommunist and a Christian as well. As a result, he was imprisoned in 1969–70 and again in 1972; upon his second release he immigrated to West Germany, where he won the national chess championship in 1978.

Palmer, Robert Alan, British singer (b. Jan. 19, 1949, Batley, Yorkshire, Eng.—d. Sept. 26, 2003, Paris, France), was a respected practitioner of "blue-eyed soul," best known for his iconic 1985 song and music video "Addicted to Love." Palmer, who was known for his impeccable taste in both music and clothes, released his first solo album, *Sneakin' Sally Through the Alley,* in 1974. His hit singles included "Give Me an Inch" (1975), "Every Kinda People" (1978), "Bad Case of Loving You" (1979), and "Looking for Clues" (1980), and he won Grammy Awards in 1986 for "Addicted to Love" and 1988 for "Simply Irresistible."

Papp, Laszlo, Hungarian boxer (b. March 25, 1926, Budapest, Hung.—d. Oct. 16, 2003, Budapest), was the first three-time Olympic boxing champion; he won the middleweight (161-lb) gold medal at the 1948 Games in London and then dropped down in weight to take the gold medal in the newly created light middleweight (156-lb) division in 1952 and 1956. Papp, who was known for his devastating left hook, lost only 12 of his 300 bouts as an amateur and won the European middleweight (1949) and light middleweight (1951) amateur titles. The Hungarian government in 1957 allowed him to turn professional (the first boxer from a communist country to gain that right), and in 1962 he captured the European professional middleweight title, which he defended six times. In 1965 Papp's travel permit was revoked to prevent him from fighting American Joey Giardello for the world middleweight belt, and he retired undefeated with a professional record of 27 wins (15 knockouts) and 2 draws. Papp was inducted into the International Boxing Hall of Fame in 2001.

Parker, Suzy (CECILIA ANN RENEE PARKER), American model and actress (b. Oct. 28, 1933, Long Island City, N.Y.—d. May 3, 2003, Montecito, Calif.), had a beauty and sophistication that led to her paving the way for future supermodels by becoming the first model to make more than $100 an hour and $100,000 a year. She later had a short career as an actress in movies and on television.

Pavlov, Valentin Sergeyevich, Soviet politician (b. Sept. 26, 1937, Moscow, U.S.S.R. [now in Russia]—d. March 30, 2003, Moscow), participated in the failed coup of August 1991 against Soviet Pres. Mikhail Gorbachev. Pavlov was trained as an economist and entered the Soviet bureaucracy in 1959. In 1989 he was appointed minister of finance, and in January 1991 he became prime minister of the U.S.S.R. In this position he made the disastrous decision to withdraw 50- and 100-ruble notes from circulation. In a desperate effort to prevent the implementation of a new union treaty aimed at loosening central control, on Aug. 19, 1991, a group of eight communist hard-liners, among them Pavlov, announced that they had taken over the country and that Gorbachev was ill. Boris Yeltsin, then president of the Russian republic, rallied public support in Moscow, and the coup collapsed three days later. Pavlov was among those arrested and jailed, but the conspirators were granted an amnesty in 1994, after which Pavlov worked as an economist.

PayCheck, Johnny (DONALD EUGENE LYTLE), American country musician (b. May 31, 1938, Greenfield, Ohio—d. Feb. 18, 2003, Nashville, Tenn.), was a hard-living honky-tonk singer and songwriter who recorded more than 30 albums and had dozens of hit singles, but he was most widely recognized for his phenomenally popular 1977 rendition of David Allan Coe's workingman anthem "Take This Job and Shove It." His first top 40 song, "A-11," released in 1965, led to a series of recordings on the Little Darlin' label, which he started with producer Aubrey Mayhew, and these were regarded as his most artistically successful. He enjoyed a second period of success in the 1970s, and his last top 10 hit was "Old Violin" in 1986.

Peck, (Eldred) Gregory, American actor (b. April 5, 1916, La Jolla, Calif.—d. June 12, 2003, Los Angeles, Calif.), was most noted for portraying morally decent, dignified, and quietly strong characters. He was nominated for five Academy Awards and won one, for his performance in the role perhaps most identified with him—Atticus Finch, a small-town Southern lawyer who stands up against racism to defend a black man unjustly accused of rape in *To Kill a Mockingbird* (1962); in 2003 the American Film Institute named his Finch the all-time number one U.S. movie hero. As a student at the University of California, Berkeley, Peck had roles in several student productions. Following graduation (1939) he moved to New

Actor Gregory Peck as Atticus Finch

© Universal Studios/Courtesy of Getty Images

above right: AP/Wide World Photos

York, where he studied at the Neighborhood Playhouse, and he began to perform in stage productions. Aided by his good looks and his rich baritone voice, and also by the fact that many Hollywood actors were serving in the armed forces during World War II—a previous injury made Peck unable to join—he found himself in demand for leading roles in numerous motion pictures, among them *Days of Glory,* his debut (1944), *The Keys of the Kingdom* (1944), *Spellbound* (1945), *The Yearling* (1946), *Gentleman's Agreement* (1947), and *Twelve O'Clock High* (1949). The 1950s and early '60s saw some of his most memorable films, including *The Snows of Kilimanjaro* (1952), *Roman Holiday* (1953), *The Man in the Gray Flannel Suit* (1956), *Pork Chop Hill* (1959), *On the Beach* (1959), *The Guns of Navarone* (1961), and *Cape Fear* (1962). Later notable appearances were in *The Omen* (1976) and *The Boys from Brazil* (1978). Peck supported a number of humanitarian and political causes and film-industry activities and served them in such capacities as member of the National Council on the Arts, chairman of the American Cancer Society, cofounding chairman and board member of the American Film Institute, board member of the Motion Picture and Television Relief Fund, and governor of the Academy of Motion Picture Arts and Sciences for 15 years and president for 3 years. He was honoured with the academy's Jean Hersholt Humanitarian Award in 1968 and the Presidential Medal of Freedom in 1969, as well as several life achievement awards.

Petrassi, Goffredo, Italian composer (b. July 16, 1904, Zagarolo, Italy—d. March 2, 2003, Rome, Italy), was one of the leading creators of Italian modernist music. His progressive exploration of compositional styles was exemplified in his eight concertos for orchestra. As a child, Petrassi studied in the choir school of San Salvatore in Lauro. When he was 15, he left school to work in a music shop, though he continued to study privately. In 1928 he was admitted as a student of composition to the Conservatory of Santa Cecilia in Rome; he graduated in 1932 and began teaching there in 1934. Already his colourful *Partita* (1932) had been well received in Rome, and in 1933 it was played at the festival of the International Society for Contemporary Music in Amsterdam. His dark madrigal *Coro di morti* (1940–41) was regarded as one of his masterpieces, as was the moving cantata *Noche oscura* (1950–51), a setting of St. John of the Cross with contrapuntal textures. His *First Concerto for Orchestra* (1933–34) was similar in style to the *Partita.* During the 1950s he wrote five more concertos, ranging from pastoral delicacy to esoteric avant-garde intricacy. His later works became athematic, shaped by the timbre of the instruments. Petrassi's *Seventh Concerto for Orchestra* appeared at the beginning of the 1960s and the *Eighth* a decade later. His last major work was the large choral piece *Orationes Christi* (1974–75). Petrassi was director of La Fenice Theatre, Venice's opera house, in 1937–40. He then taught composition at the Conservatory of Santa Cecilia until 1959 and thereafter at the Academy of Santa Cecilia; he retired in 1974.

Phillips, Samuel Cornelius ("SAM"), American record producer (b. Jan. 5, 1923, Florence, Ala.—d. July 30, 2003, Memphis, Tenn.), recorded early works by blues greats Howlin' Wolf, B.B. King, and Bobby "Blue" Bland in his Memphis studio and maintained that "if I could find a white man who had the Negro sound and Negro feel, I could make a billion dollars." In 1954 he discovered Elvis Presley and issued the young singer's first records on his small, new Sun label; with the money he received from selling Presley's contract to RCA Victor, a major label, Phillips expanded Sun Records and issued the first hit singles by Jerry Lee Lewis, Johnny Cash (*q.v.*), Carl Perkins, Charlie Rich, and other rockabilly stars; he sold the Sun catalog in 1969. The day after his death, the Sun studio was designated a National Historic Landmark.

Pialat, Maurice, French film director (b. Aug. 31, 1925, Cunlhat, France—d. Jan. 11, 2003, Paris, France), created a body of work considered among the best of modern French cinema. His movies limned domestic desperation and were notable for their immediacy and difficulty. Many of the 10 feature films Pialat made were nominated for major film awards. *À nos amours* (1983) won the César Award for best film, and *Sous le soleil de Satan* (1987) won the Palme d'Or at Cannes. A television series he made in 1970–71, *La Maison des bois,* about a group of refugee children in World War I, came to be considered a masterpiece.

Plimpton, George Ames, American writer and editor (b. March 18, 1927, New York, N.Y.—d. Sept. 25/26, 2003, New York City), served as editor of the *Paris Review* from its first issue in 1953, guiding its publication of serious fiction and poetry, especially the works of new talent, and interviews with well-known writers. He was more generally renowned, however, as a participatory journalist, engaging in a host of activities—including playing baseball, boxing, circus performing, golfing, and playing percussion in an orchestra—and then writing about the experience, perhaps most notably in *Paper Lion* (1966), which recounted his stint playing football with the Detroit Lions.

Pough, Richard Hooper, American ornithologist and conservationist (b. April 19, 1904, Brooklyn, N.Y.—d. June 24, 2003, Chilmark, Mass.), served as the founding president (1954–56) of the Nature Conservatory (formerly known as the Ecologists Union), which became one of the world's leading land-conservation organizations. He also wrote best-selling bird guides for the National Audubon Society, and in 1981 he was awarded the Audubon Medal for his conservation and environmental-protection efforts.

Poujade, Pierre Marie, French political activist (b. Dec. 1, 1920, St.-Céré, France—d. Aug. 27, 2003, La Bastide-L'Evêque, France), created a short-lived movement in the 1950s the name of which, Poujadisme, remained shorthand for a kind of provincial right-wing nationalism. In 1953 Poujade, who owned a book and stationery shop, started the movement as a shopkeepers' revolt against high taxes, large commercial interests, and bureaucracy. The resulting organization, the Union for the Defense of Tradesmen and Artisans, became a national movement by the following year, and in the election of 1956, the Poujadist party won 52 seats in the National Assembly (one held by Jean-Marie Le Pen). The movement collapsed shortly thereafter, though Poujade remained politically active.

Activist Pierre Poujade

Powell, Sir (Arnold Joseph) Philip, British architect (b. March 15, 1921, Bedford, Eng.—d. May 5, 2003, London, Eng.), with his American-born longtime partner, Hidalgo Moya, designed some of post-World War II Britain's most respected structures. Their commissions included the Skylon "vertical feature" at the 1951 Festival of Britain; the award-winning Bauhaus-influenced Churchill Gardens flats in Pimlico, West London; Wolfson College, Oxford; the Chichester Festival Theatre; and the Museum of London. Powell and Moya were awarded the Gold Medal of the Royal Institute of British Architects in 1974. Powell was made OBE in 1957, knighted in 1975, and named a Companion of Honour in 1984.

Prigogine, Ilya, Russian-born Belgian physical chemist (b. Jan. 25, 1917, Moscow, Russia—d. May 28, 2003, Brussels, Belg.), was awarded the Nobel Prize for Chemistry in 1977 for contributions to the understanding of nonequilibrium thermodynamics. In particular, he helped explain how complex systems, including living organisms, could arise spontaneously from less-ordered states and maintain themselves in apparent defiance of the classical laws of physics. As a child, Prigogine moved with his family to Lithuania, Germany, and finally to

Belgium. He earned a Ph.D. in chemistry from the Free University in Brussels in 1941. He conducted research at the university and accepted a professorship there in 1947. Two years later he received Belgian citizenship. Prigogine became director of the International Solvay Institutes for Physics and Chemistry in Brussels in 1962 and, from 1967, also served as director of the Center for Statistical Mechanics and Thermodynamics at the University of Texas at Austin. The centre was later renamed the Ilya Prigogine Center for Studies in Statistical Mechanics and Complex Systems in his honour. Much of Prigogine's work dealt with the application of the second law of thermodynamics to complex systems. He theorized that the second law—which states that physical systems tend to dissolve into a state of disorder (a process known as entropy)—might be broken in certain circumstances. He argued that as long as systems receive energy from an external source—the Sun, for example—it is possible for them to evolve into more complex systems. Prigogine described how such systems, or "dissipative structures," can go through periods of instability and then suddenly evolve and become more ordered. His work was influential in a wide variety of fields, from physical chemistry to biology, and he was considered the "grandfather" of the new discipline of chaos theory. He wrote or co-wrote some 20 books and nearly 1,000 scholarly articles. King Baudouin I of Belgium made Prigogine a viscount in 1989.

Prince, F(rank) T(empleton), South African-born British poet (b. Sept. 13, 1912, Kimberley, S.Af.—d. Aug. 7, 2003, Southampton, Eng.), created a body of original poetry characterized by long lines and a quiet, though intense, voice and best exemplified by his much-anthologized war poem "Soldiers Bathing." Prince was born to British immigrants in South Africa and attended Christian Brothers College in Kimberley; the University of the Witwatersrand in Johannesburg; Balliol College, Oxford (B.Litt. with first-class honours, 1934); and Princeton University. The poets who influenced his early writing were W.B. Yeats, Ezra Pound, and T.S. Eliot, who, as an editor at Faber and Faber, brought out Prince's first volume of poetry, *Poems* (1938). Prince was a reader in English literature (1946–57) and then a professor of English (1957–74) at the University of Southampton, Eng. His famous war poem was published during World War II and again as the title poem of his second collection, which was published in 1954. After retiring from Southampton, he taught in Jamaica, the U.S., and North Yemen (now part of Yemen). In addition to his later volumes of poetry—notably *Doors of Stone* (1963) and *Collected Poems* (1993)—Prince wrote two autobiographical works, *Memoirs of Oxford* (1970) and *Walks in Rome* (1987), and an erudite critical work on John Milton, *The Italian Element in Milton's Verse* (1954).

Raine, Kathleen Jessie, British poet, critic, and scholar (b. June 14, 1908, Ilford, Essex [now part of London], Eng.—d. July 6, 2003, London), was possessed of a visionary quality that separated her from her contemporaries. Late in life (at the age of 82), she founded Temenos Academy, supported by Prince Charles, which rejected the "secular materialism" of the current age. Raine won a scholarship to Girton College, Cambridge, where she read natural sciences and psychology. Shortly after graduating she married, eloped with another man, divorced her first husband, married again, bore two children, and divorced again, not given (she later said) to domesticity. She published her first volume of poems, *Stone and Flower,* in 1943 and followed in 1945 with *Living in Time* and in 1949 with *The Pythoness.* After World War II she made a living by translating and teaching. Her passionate but platonic seven-year relationship with the gay writer Gavin Maxwell brought her both joy and great pain. While teaching she published several works of literary criticism, including many on William Blake; several more collections of poetry, notably *The Lost Country* (1972) and *Collected Poems* (2000); and four volumes of autobiography—*Farewell Happy Fields* (1973), *The Land Unknown* (1975), *The Lion's Mouth* (1977), and *India Seen Afar* (1989). She was appointed CBE in 2000.

Raphael I Bidawid, Iraqi cleric (b. April 17, 1922, Mosul, Iraq—d. July 7, 2003, Beirut, Lebanon), as patriarch of the Chaldean Catholic Church, based in Baghdad, Iraq, was known for his unstinting support of Iraqi Pres. Saddam Hussein. Raphael, who was ordained a priest in 1944, became the youngest bishop in any Catholic church in 1957 and was consecrated patriarch of Babylon of the Chaldeans in 1989. Maintaining that Hussein protected his church, Raphael supported the 1991 invasion of Kuwait and spoke out strongly against the sanctions the United Nations imposed against Iraq.

Rees, Leighton Thomas, Welsh darts player (b. Jan. 17, 1940, Ynysybwl, near Pontypridd, Wales—d. June 8, 2003, Pontypridd), was the first Embassy world professional darts champion (1978) and helped to popularize darts as a television spectator sport throughout the U.K. Rees worked in a factory before becoming a professional darts player in 1976. The following year he won the singles title at the inaugural World Darts Federation World Cup, and the Welsh team, of which he was a member, won the team championship. Rees was Welsh champion in 1970, 1974, and 1976 and represented Wales 77 times in international darts competitions.

Regan, Donald Thomas, American businessman and politician (b. Dec. 21, 1918, Cambridge, Mass.—d. June 10, 2003, Williamsburg, Va.), was the innovative chairman of Merrill Lynch & Co. (1971–80) before becoming a top aide to Pres. Ronald Reagan, serving as treasury secretary (1981–85) and chief of staff (1985–87). Regan first attracted national attention after transforming Merrill Lynch from a brokerage firm into a full-service financial company, with activities in consulting, real estate, credit cards, and checking. After joining the Reagan administration, Regan came to wield great power and in 1986 helped implement a landmark tax reform. The Iran-Contra scandal and a growing feud with first lady Nancy Reagan, however, forced Regan out of office in 1987. His autobiography, *For the Record: From Wall Street to Washington* (1988), caused a furor over its allegations that Nancy Reagan consulted an astrologer on such presidential matters as trips and personal appearances.

Reina, Carlos Roberto, Honduran politician (b. March 13, 1926, Tegucigalpa, Honduras—d. Aug. 19, 2003, Tegucigalpa), served as president of Honduras from 1994 to 1998, during which time he professionalized the armed forces and made gains in achieving a balanced budget and fighting corruption. When he was a teenager, he had been imprisoned (1944) for demonstrating against the country's dictator, and in 1963 and 1968 he also was briefly incarcerated by military governments.

Riefenstahl, Berta Helene Amalie ("LENI"), German filmmaker (b. Aug. 22, 1902, Berlin, Ger.—d. Sept. 8, 2003, Pöcking, Ger.), was the first female director to gain international renown and was acclaimed as perhaps the finest and most influential female director of the 20th century, but her association with Adolf Hitler made her almost as much reviled as admired. She employed innovative filming and editing techniques to create two documentaries—the powerful *Triumph des Willens* (1935; *Triumph of the Will*), which covered a Nazi Party rally in Nürnberg, and the two-part *Olympische Spiele* (1938; *Olympia*), which celebrated the 1936 Olympic Games in Berlin and, especially, the physical beauty of the athletes. While hailed as works of genius, these

Filmmaker Leni Riefenstahl

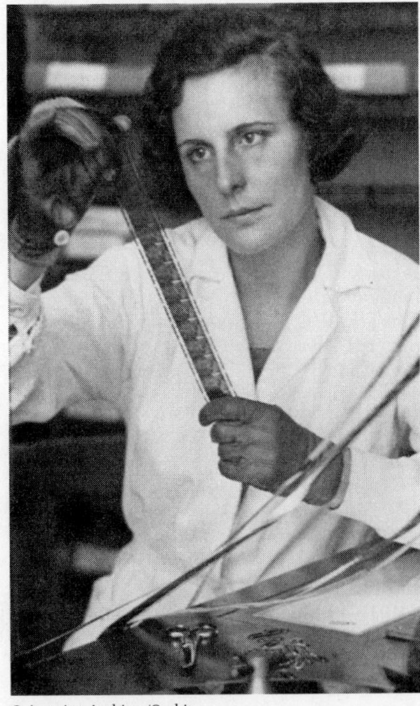

films were also reviled for their propagandistic glorification of Hitler's regime and the Nazi goal of Aryan racial purity. Riefenstahl had a brief career as a dancer in the 1920s before seeing her first motion picture. She appeared in a number of so-called mountain films while at the same time learning the technical aspects of filmmaking, and in 1931 she formed Leni Riefenstahl-Produktion. *Das blaue Licht* (1932; *The Blue Light*), which Riefenstahl wrote, produced, directed, and starred in, won a medal at the Venice Film Festival and brought her to Hitler's attention; and a short film about a 1933 Nazi rally, *Sieg des Glaubens* (1933; *Victory of the Faith*), paved the way for her two masterpieces. Following World War II she was investigated for complicity with the Nazis but, maintaining that she was unaware of the Holocaust, was finally cleared in 1952 and completed a film she had begun years earlier, *Tiefland* (1954; *Lowlands*). In 1973 Riefenstahl published *Die Nuba* (*The Last of the Nuba*), a book of photographs of the Nuba people in The Sudan that she had taken in the 1960s and '70s. She took up scuba diving and underwater photography and in 2002, at age 100, released another film, *Impressionen unter Wasser* (*Underwater Impressions*).

Ritter, Jonathon Southworth ("JOHN"), American actor and comedian (b. Sept. 17, 1948, Burbank, Calif.—d. Sept. 11, 2003, Burbank), was a master of physical comedy, a talent he put to especially good use in the best-known of his television series, *Three's Company* (1977–84), for which he won an Emmy Award in 1984. He showcased his versatility as an actor in such films as *Sling Blade* (1996) and *Manhood* (2003), in more than 25 made-for TV movies, and on Broadway in *The Dinner Party* (2000). Ritter, the son of country-and-western singer-actor Tex Ritter, collapsed on the set of his latest series, *8 Simple Rules . . . for Dating My Teenage Daughter*, and died of a previously undetected heart defect.

Robbins, Frederick Chapman, American pediatrician and virologist (b. Aug. 25, 1916, Auburn, Ala.—d. Aug. 4, 2003, Cleveland, Ohio), received the Nobel Prize for Physiology or Medicine in 1954 for successfully growing the poliovirus in tissue cultures and thereby paving the way for the development of polio vaccines; he shared the award with John Franklin Enders and Thomas H. Weller. A graduate of Harvard University Medical School (1940), Robbins interrupted his pediatric training at Children's Hospital in Boston to serve with the U.S. Army's 15th Medical General Laboratory (1942–46) during World War II. He directed studies on infectious hepatitis, typhus, and Q fever while stationed in the U.S., Italy, and North Africa and in 1945 received a Bronze Star for his work. After the war he returned to Children's Hospital, where he completed his training and in 1948 began working with Enders and Weller. At the time, viruses could not readily be grown in the laboratory, and the poliovirus could be propagated only in the nerve tissue of living monkeys. Such restrictions were inconvenient and limited the amount of virus produced for study. In 1949 the three men developed a technique for cultivating the virus in test tubes, using a mixture of human embryonic skin and muscle tissue. Their work not only helped eradicate polio in much of the world but also led to the isolation of other viruses; in 2003 scientists used the technique to identify the virus that causes SARS (severe acute respiratory syndrome). In 1952 Robbins became director of pediatrics and contagious diseases at the Cleveland Metropolitan General Hospital, a position he held until 1966. He also served as professor of pediatrics (1952–80), dean (1966–80), and professor emeritus (1985–2003) at Case Western Reserve University School of Medicine in Cleveland.

Roberts, J(ohn) M(orris), British historian (b. April 14, 1928, Bath, Somerset, Eng.—d. May 30, 2003, Roadwater, Somerset, Eng.), was a respected academician, scholar, and writer, but he captured the viewing public's fancy as the presenter of *The Triumph of the West* (1985), a 13-part television series in which he analyzed how Western civilization came to dominate the modern world. His books included *History of the World* (1976), *The French Revolution* (1978), *The Triumph of the West* (1985; an expansion of the TV series), *A History of Europe* (1996), and *The Twentieth Century* (1999). He was also editor (1967–77) of *The English Historical Review* and general editor of Purnell's *History of the 20th Century*, *The Short Oxford History of the Modern World*, and *The New Oxford History of England*. Roberts was appointed CBE in 1996.

Roc, Patricia (FELICIA MIRIAM URSULA HEROLD REISE; FELICIA REIF), British actress (b. June 7, 1915, London, Eng.—d. Dec. 30, 2003, Locarno, Switz.), was one of Britain's top box-office screen stars in the 1940s and early '50s, particularly in such dramas as *Millions Like Us* (1943), *The Wicked Lady* (1945), *Canyon Passage* (1946), her only Hollywood movie, and *When the Bough Breaks* (1947). She also made films in France until she retired in 1963.

Rocca, Roberto, Italian-born Argentine businessman (b. February 1922, Milan, Italy—d. June 10, 2003, Milan), transformed Techint, a steel corporation founded in 1945 by his father, into Argentina's largest conglomerate, with more than 100 companies worldwide operating in such fields as construction, oil and gas, engineering, telecommunications, and health care. Rocca, who was chairman of Techint from 1978 to 2003, amassed a fortune of more than $1.5 billion.

Rogers, Fred McFeely, American television host, producer, and writer (b. March 20, 1928, Latrobe, Pa.—d. Feb. 27, 2003, Pittsburgh, Pa.), was the friend of millions of children for

Neighbourly television host Fred Rogers

© Family Communications, Inc.; photo, Walt Seng

above: Zuma Press

the way he taught them how to get along with others, feel good about themselves, and cope with their fears. Singing the familiar "It's a beautiful day in the neighborhood" theme and putting on his sneakers and trademark zippered cardigan, he would open his public television program, *Mr. Rogers' Neighborhood,* and settle in with his viewers to begin the topic of the day. Besides producing, writing the scripts, and serving as host, he wrote about 200 songs for the program, some 1,000 episodes of which were broadcast between 1968 and 2001. Following graduation (1951) from Rollins College, Winter Park, Fla., with a degree in musical composition, Rogers worked first for NBC in New York City and then for the public television station WQED in Pittsburgh, where in 1954 he began what became a seven-year run of writing, producing, and serving as puppeteer for *The Children's Corner;* 30 segments of the show were broadcast on NBC in 1955–56. He earned (1962) a divinity degree from the Pittsburgh Theological Seminary and was ordained by the Presbyterian Church, which asked him to continue his TV work. Rogers made his on-camera debut in 1963 on the Canadian Broadcasting Corporation's *Misterogers* and in 1966 returned to WQED, where the show became *Misterogers' Neighborhood.* By 1968 it was being distributed nationally as *Mr. Rogers' Neighborhood.* Although the show continued to be broadcast, the last original episode was taped in December 2000 and broadcast the following August; following the Sept. 11, 2001, terrorist attacks, however, Rogers once again appeared on camera to record public-service announcements aimed at informing parents how they could help their children cope with the events. Rogers was honoured with numerous awards, including four daytime Emmys, the National Academy of Television Arts and Sciences' lifetime achievement award, and the Presidential Medal of Freedom. In addition, the Smithsonian Institution in Washington, D.C., obtained one of his red cardigans to add to its collection of Americana.

Roper, Burns Worthington ("BUD"), American pollster (b. Feb. 26, 1925, Creston, Iowa—d. Jan. 20, 2003, Bourne, Mass.), was for decades chairman (1967–93) of the polling organization founded by his father and now known as RoperASW and chairman (1970–94) of the Roper Center for Public Opinion Research at the University of Connecticut. He was instrumental in the creation of industry standards for polling methods and the wording of questions and was best known for having written the question inquiring whether one feels that "things in this country are generally going in the right direction" or that they have "seriously gotten off on the wrong track."

Rosenbluth, M(arshall) N(icholas), American physicist (b. Feb. 5, 1927, Albany, N.Y.—d. Sept. 28, 2003, San Diego, Calif.), played an important role in the development of the hydrogen bomb in the early 1950s and later attempted to find peaceful uses for nuclear fusion. A leader in the field of plasma physics, he sought to harness the process in order to generate electricity. His numerous awards included the National Medal of Science (1997).

Rosenthal, Manuel, French composer and conductor (b. June 18, 1904, Paris, France—d. June 5, 2003, Paris), championed modern composers, notably Jacques Offenbach, Igor Stravinsky, Olivier Messiaen, and Maurice Ravel, who took Rosenthal on as his third and last composition student in 1926 and who remained a close friend. Rosenthal was principal conductor of the French National Orchestra (1944–47), the Seattle Symphony (1948–51), and the Liège Symphony Orchestra (1964–67) and was professor of conducting (1962–74) at the Paris Conservatory. His best-known composition, *Gaîté Parisienne* (1938), a ballet suite based on music by Offenbach, remained a favourite with ballet companies, orchestras, and audiences around the world. Rosenthal was made a Commander of the Legion of Honour and of the Order of Merit.

Ross, Bertram, American dancer and choreographer (b. Nov. 13, 1920, Brooklyn, N.Y.—d. April 20, 2003, New York, N.Y), for 20 years (1953–73) partnered Martha Graham and was a custodian of her art before beginning a successful career as a cabaret performer. After joining Graham's company in 1949, he created dozens of roles, among them St. Michael in *Seraphic Dialogue* (1955), Agamemnon and Orestes in *Clytemnestra* (1958), and Adam in *Embattled Garden* (1958). He became a codirector of the company in 1966 and remained in that position until Graham installed a young admirer who was not a dancer, Ron Protas, as director; Ross quit the company in 1973. He had previously established his own modern dance company, and he choreographed for it and other companies and taught at many top dance schools.

Rostow, Walt Whitman, American economic historian and government official (b. Oct. 7, 1916, New York, N.Y.—d. Feb. 13, 2003, Austin, Texas), as an adviser to Presidents John F. Kennedy and Lyndon Johnson, advocated an ever-increasing American commitment to the Vietnam War (1955–75). Rostow was a Rhodes scholar who taught at several prestigious universities in the U.S. and Britain and became well known with the publication of *The Stages of Economic Growth: A Non-Communist Manifesto* (1960). Kennedy hired Rostow in 1961 as his deputy special assistant for national security affairs. Rostow chaired the State Department's policy planning council from 1961 to 1966, when he became Johnson's special assistant for national security affairs (the post later known as national security adviser). Even after most other government officials had become convinced that the Vietnam War was unwinnable, Rostow consistently pushed for its escalation, convinced that the U.S. was winning and that the war was necessary so that economic modernization could take place in Southeast Asia.

Presidential adviser Walt Rostow

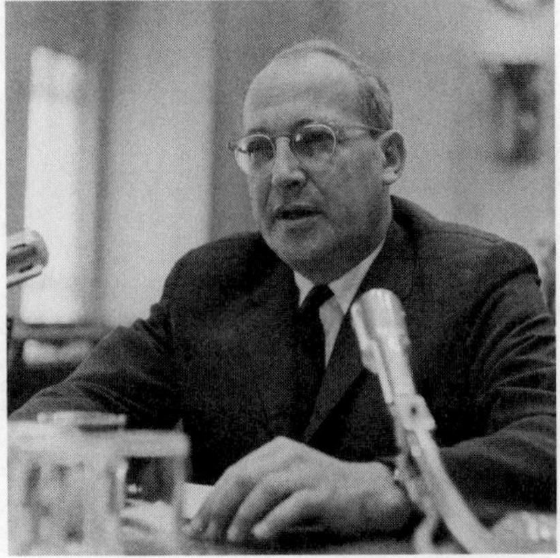

© Bettmann/Corbis

Roth, William Victor, Jr., American politician (b. July 22, 1921, Great Falls, Mont.—d. Dec. 13, 2003, Washington, D.C.), served in the U.S. Congress for 34 years—in the House of Representatives from 1967 to 1970 and the Senate from 1971 to 2001—and was best known for his attention to financial matters. He was a champion of tax cuts, revealed overspending by the Defense Department, and sponsored legislation that gave rise to a tax-sheltered retirement account that was given his name—the Roth IRA.

Sadruddin Aga Khan, Prince, UN official (b. Jan. 17, 1933, Paris, France—d. May 12, 2003, Boston, Mass.), as the longest-serving UN high commissioner for refugees (1965–77), coordinated relief and resettlement efforts throughout the world, including those in Bangladesh, Uganda, Vietnam, Angola, The Sudan, Burundi, Algeria, Chile, Cyprus, and the Middle East. He also worked with UNESCO, headed two environmental foundations, was humanitarian envoy to Afghanistan in the late 1980s, and, from 1992, served as UN chargé de mission. Prince Sadruddin was the younger son of

© Musy Gerard/Corbis Sygma

Refugee coordinator Prince Sadruddin

Sir Sultan Mohammed Shah, the Aga Khan III, imam of the Nizari Isma'ilite Shi'ite Muslim sect, and was the uncle of the Aga Khan IV.

Safar, Peter, Austrian-born anesthesiologist (b. April 12, 1924, Vienna, Austria—d. Aug. 3, 2003, Pittsburgh, Pa.), was credited with the development of such lifesaving techniques as mouth-to-mouth resuscitation and its combination with cardiac compressions, known as cardiopulmonary resuscitation, or CPR. He also pioneered means of preventing brain damage in persons suffering cardiac arrest.

Said, Edward Wadie, Palestinian American literary critic (b. Nov. 1, 1935, Jerusalem—d. Sept. 24, 2003, New York, N.Y.), reshaped scholarship in the humanities with his critique of Western studies of Oriental cultures but became more widely recognized for his staunch advocacy of Palestinian independence. In his most influential book, *Orientalism* (1978), Said argued that Western studies of the Orient, particularly the Islamic world, had been tainted by stereotypes that originated in European imperialism. The more publicly visible aspect of his defense of Islamic culture was his tireless effort to win recognition of Palestinian claims in the Middle East from Israel and the U.S. Said earned an undergraduate degree from Princeton University (1957), and, while earning his Ph.D. (1964) from Harvard University, he joined (1963) the faculty of Columbia University, New York City, where he would remain for his entire career. After the Six-Day War of 1967, much of his writing polemicized against U.S. policy in the Middle East. Elected in 1977 to the Palestine National Council (PNC), the Palestinian parliament-in-exile, Said helped to secure the PNC's adoption of the two-state solution in Algiers in 1988. This paved the way for the negotiation of the Oslo Accords by Israel and the Palestine Liberation Organization (PLO) in the 1990s. Said disapproved of the accords, however, calling them "an instrument of Palestinian surrender." Although increasingly critical of the PLO leadership, Said began to withdraw from politics—even as fighting between Israelis and Palestinians intensified—in order to concentrate on music. In 1999 he and Israeli musician Daniel Barenboim founded the West-Eastern Divan Orchestra, an organization of young Arab and Israeli performers.

Sánchez Hernández, Fidel, El Salvadoran politician and military man (b. July 7, 1917, El Divisadero, El Salvador—d. Feb. 28, 2003, San Salvador, El Salvador), as president of El Salvador (1967–72), led the country into the so-called Soccer War in 1969. After a career in the military that included stints as a military attaché in Paris and in Washington, D.C., Sánchez Hernández became minister of the interior in 1962. As the candidate of the conservative National Conciliation Party, Sánchez Hernández easily won election as president in 1967. He steered a mildly reformist course. In 1969 El Salvador and Honduras were experiencing tension over a border dispute and a plan by Honduras to forcibly repatriate hundreds of thousands of El Salvadorans. In this climate a disputed World Cup association football (soccer) qualifying match touched off rioting, and El Salvador invaded Honduras on July 14. Less than two weeks later, the Organization of American States stepped in to halt the war. Sánchez Hernández's term of office ended in 1972.

Santamaria, Ramon ("MONGO"), Cuban-born American conga drummer (b. April 7, 1922, Havana, Cuba—d. Feb. 1, 2003, Miami, Fla.), played for years with mambo stars (Perez Prado, Tito Puente, Cal Tjader) before forming his own bands and becoming a Latin jazz giant himself. He was a top percussionist in Cuba before moving to the United States in 1950. Santamaria recorded music derived from Afro-Cuban religious cults, and he composed the jazz standard "Afro Blue" in the late 1950s and recorded several hits, notably "Watermelon Man" (1963). He went on to add Latin beats to pop and soul music tunes, which led to additional hit records; his fame peaked with the 1970s popularity of salsa music, though his performances continued to be strongly influenced by jazz.

AP/Wide World Photos

Conga drummer Mongo Santamaria

Savage, John Patrick, British-born Canadian politician and physician (b. May 28, 1932, Newport, Wales—d. May 13, 2003, N.S.), ended 17 years of Progressive Conservative rule when he was elected the Liberal premier of Nova Scotia in 1993; he was the first premier of the province since confederation not to have been born in Canada. Savage's tenure was marked by turbulence; he slashed government spending and jobs and faced opposition within his own party when he refused to approve patronage jobs. When he resigned in 1997, following an opinion poll that showed that he had only a 19% approval rating among Nova Scotians, he returned to medicine and was instrumental in establishing medical centres and educational programs in Africa. He also worked extensively in Nicaragua and El Salvador. Three days before his death, he was named an Officer of the Order of Canada and was cited for his compassion and service to the less fortunate.

Schapera, Isaac, South African social anthropologist and educator (b. June 23, 1905, Garies, S.Af.—d. June 26, 2003, London, Eng.), wrote and lectured on many aspects of the culture of the Tswana people of Bechuanaland (now Botswana). His works—including *A Handbook of Tswana Law and Custom* (1938), *Married Life in an African Tribe* (1940), *Native Land Tenure in the Bechuanaland Protectorate* (1943), and *The Tswana* (1953)—earned Schapera the respect of the people he studied as well as that of his colleagues.

Schlesinger, John Richard, British director (b. Feb. 16, 1926, London, Eng.—d. July 25, 2003, Palm Springs, Calif.), won a best director Academy Award for his first American film, *Midnight Cowboy* (1969), which also was the only X-rated film to win the best picture Oscar. Considered one of the directors of British New Wave social realism, he had already made his mark with such films as *Billy Liar* (1963), *Darling* (1965), and *Far from the Madding Crowd* (1967), and following *Midnight Cowboy* he alternated between Britain and the U.S., counting *Sunday Bloody Sunday* (1971) and *Marathon Man* (1976) among his more successful later efforts. Schlesinger also directed for television and the theatre. He was made CBE in 1970.

Schonberg, Harold Charles, American music critic (b. Nov. 29, 1915, New York, N.Y.—d. July 26, 2003, New York City), considered that he wrote for himself—not for any particular audience—and led readers to think for themselves. In doing so during his half-century-long career—two decades of them (1960–80) as chief critic for the *New York Times*—he set the standard for such writing, becoming one of the most authoritative and influential music critics in the U.S. and, in 1971, the first to win a Pulitzer Prize for criticism. Schonberg also wrote about chess, reviewed mysteries and thrillers under the pseudonym Newgate Callendar, and was the author of 13 books, several of which came to be acknowledged as standard references.

Scott, Martha Ellen, American actress (b. Sept. 22, 1914, Jamesport, Mo.—d. May 28, 2003, Van Nuys, Calif.), made her Broadway debut as Emily in 1938 in the original production of Thornton Wilder's *Our Town,* made her film debut in the same role two years later, and over the

above: © Sophie Bassouls/Corbis Sygma;
right: AP/Wide World Photos

next 50 years appeared in some 20 other motion pictures, about the same number of Broadway productions, and numerous television programs, in addition to serving as producer of several plays. Her films included *The Desperate Hours* (1955) and two in which, as she delighted in pointing out, she portrayed the mother of Charlton Heston—*The Ten Commandments* (1956) and *Ben-Hur* (1959). Her last stage role was that of Goody Nurse in a 1991 production of *The Crucible.*

Scribner, Belding Hibbard, American physician (b. Jan. 18, 1921, Chicago, Ill.—d. June 19, 2003, Seattle, Wash.), revolutionized kidney dialysis by creating in 1960 the Scribner shunt, a device that allowed patients to receive long-term dialysis. Sewn into arteries and veins, the shunt eliminated the progressive damage caused by repeated insertion of tubes from the dialysis machine directly into blood vessels, the method previously used. Scribner also oversaw the creation of committees to determine which patients would receive dialysis and thereby laid the foundations for bioethics committees. In 2002 he was awarded the Albert Lasker Award for Clinical Medical Research.

Segundo, Compay (MÁXIMO FRANCISCO REPILADO MUÑOZ), Cuban musician (b. Nov. 18, 1907, Siboney, Cuba—d. July 13, 2003, Havana, Cuba), attained worldwide fame as the lusty cigar-smoking baritone who was one of the most prominent of the veteran musicians featured on the Grammy Award-winning *Buena Vista Social Club* album (1997) and in the film of the same name (1999). He was already well known throughout Cuba, where he had a thriving career as a singer and guitarist until traditional Cuban music lost favour following the Cuban Revolution, and though he had to supplement his income by working as a cigar roller for two decades, his career was revitalized when he appeared at a festival at Washington, D.C.'s Smithsonian Institution in 1989 and performed in Europe in the 1990s.

Musician Compay Segundo

Shawcross of Friston, Hartley William Shawcross, Baron, British prosecutor (b. Feb. 4, 1902, Giessen, Ger.—d. July 10, 2003, Cowbeech, Sussex, Eng.), gained renown as the chief British prosecutor on the International Military Tribunal trying Nazi war criminals in Nürnberg, Ger., in 1945–46. As Britain's attorney general (1945–51), he conducted treason trials of notorious figures, including Klaus Fuchs, Alan Nunn May, and William Joyce, known as Lord Haw-Haw. Shawcross was knighted in 1945 and served in the House of Commons from 1945 until his retirement in 1958; he was made a life peer in 1959.

Sheene, Barry, British motorcycle racer (b. Sept. 11, 1950, London, Eng.—d. March 10, 2003, Gold Coast, Queen., Australia), brought widespread popularity to motorcycle racing with his irreverent, playboy reputation and seeming indestructibility and he won two 500-cc world championships (1976 and 1977) while racing for Suzuki. Sheene entered his first motorcycle race when he was 17 years old. In 1970 he won the British 750-cc championship, and he went on to win the European championship in that category in 1973. He had already begun to attract media attention when, while being filmed for a television documentary in 1975, he suffered a horrific crash at Florida's Daytona track; his swift return to racing made him a media darling. In 1978 he was made MBE. Another accident in 1982 shattered his legs; the X-ray of his elaborately reconstructed femurs became a famous sports photo. Sheene retired from the sport in 1985, but in the '90s he began racing successfully on the veterans' circuits. In 2001 he was inducted into the Motorcycle Grand Prix Hall of Fame.

Shields, Carol Ann Warner, American-born Canadian novelist (b. June 2, 1935, Oak Park, Ill.—d. July 16, 2003, Victoria, B.C.), was celebrated for her insightful exploration of ordinary lives, attention to detail, serene humour, and impeccable style. Shields was best known for her Pulitzer Prize-winning novel, *The Stone Diaries* (1993), which attempted to capture the importance of the seemingly trivial details of living. The work also won the Governor General's Literary Award for Fiction and the National Book Critics Circle Award and was short-listed for the Booker Prize. She obtained a B.A. degree (1957) in English from Hanover (Ind.) College after having spent a year as an exchange student at the University of Exeter, Eng. There she met her future husband, Donald Hugh Shields; they married in 1957 and had five children. Shields earned an M.A. (1975) from the University of Ottawa, and she taught literature there and at the Universities of British Columbia and Manitoba. Shields's first novel, *Small Ceremonies,* received the Canadian Authors Association Award for best novel in 1977. Another novel, *Swann* (1987), won the Arthur Ellis Award for Best Novel in 1988. *Larry's Party* (1997), which explored the life of the title character in a postfeminist world, won the 1998 Orange Prize for women's fiction. Her final novel, *Unless,* exposed the unhappiness of a mother struggling with the lifestyle chosen by her daughter. It won the Ethel Wilson Fiction Prize and was short-listed for the Giller, Booker, and Orange prizes, as well as the Governor General's Literary Award. Shields was made an Officer of the Order of Canada in 1998 and a Companion of the Order of Canada in 2002.

Novelist Carol Shields

Shoemaker, William Lee ("WILLIE"; "BILL"; "THE SHOE"), American jockey (b. Aug. 19, 1931, Fabens, Texas—d. Oct. 12, 2003, San Marino, Calif.), was one of the most successful jockeys in the history of Thoroughbred horse racing. In a career that spanned 41 years, he won a record 8,833 races, including 11 Triple Crown events. Born prematurely, Shoemaker weighed less than 0.9 kg (2 lb) at birth; he eventually grew to about 1.5 m (4 ft 11 in) tall and weighed less than 45 kg (100 lb). At age 10 he moved with his father to California, which became his racing base. Noted for his self-confidence and rapport with horses, Shoemaker began racing professionally in 1949 and quickly emerged as one of the sport's leading jockeys. His notable wins included the Kentucky Derby (1955, 1959, 1965, and 1986) and the Belmont (1957, 1959, 1962, 1967, and 1975) and Preakness (1963 and 1967) stakes; with his victory at the 1986 Kentucky Derby, he became, at age 54, the oldest jockey to win that event. At the time of his retirement in 1990, he had ridden in 40,350 races and won more than $123 million. Among the horses he jockeyed were Swaps, Spectacular Bid, John Henry, and Ferdinand. In 1991 he was left a quadriplegic following an automobile accident, but he continued to train horses until

1997. Shoemaker wrote a series of mystery novels featuring a jockey-turned-sleuth protagonist, and his autobiography, *Shoemaker* (cowritten with Barney Nagler), was published in 1988. He was inducted into the National Museum of Racing's Hall of Fame in 1958.

Shukri, Muhammad (MOHAMMED CHOUKRI), Moroccan writer (b. July 15, 1935, Beni Chikar, Mor.—d. Nov. 15, 2003, Tangier, Mor.), was known for his autobiographical writings and for his friendships with other writers in Morocco. By Shukri's own account, his father sold him as a boy to a hashish addict. Shukri ran away from home and made a living by engaging in petty crime and by working at menial jobs. He did not learn to read and write until he started school at age 20. Shukri's first short story, "Al-unf ala al-shati'" ("Violence on the Beach"), was published in 1966. His major work, *Al-khubz al-hafi,* was translated by Paul Bowles as *For Bread Alone* and was published first in English in 1973. The memoir, which matter-of-factly describes his youth, was translated into many languages but was not published in Arabic until 1982 and was banned in Morocco until 2001. *Jean Genet in Tangier* (1974) and *Tennessee Williams in Tangier* (1979) record Shukri's friendships with those writers; he also wrote other autobiographical works, a play, and collections of short stories.

Simmons, Richard W., American actor (b. Aug. 19, 1913, St. Paul, Minn.—d. Jan. 11, 2003, Oceanside, Calif.), appeared in numerous movies and television series during his 40-year career, most notably the 1950s TV series *Sergeant Preston of the Yukon,* in which his crime-solving endeavours were aided by his horse, Rex, and his dog, Yukon King.

Simon, Paul Martin, American politician and educator (b. Nov. 29, 1928, Eugene, Ore.—d. Dec. 9, 2003, Springfield, Ill.), had a long career in public life that was highlighted by two terms as a U.S. senator (1985–97) and a brief run for the Democratic presidential nomination in 1988. Sporting his trademark bow tie and horn-rimmed glasses, he blended his liberal social outlook with fiscal conservatism and forged a reputation for honesty and forthright integrity. Simon entered the University of Oregon at age 16, transferred to Dana College, Blair, Neb., a year later, and at age 19 left school to buy and run a struggling weekly newspaper in Troy, Ill. Through the paper he fought against illegal gambling interests and organized crime, a crusade that attracted the attention of Democratic Party leaders interested in reform, and in 1954 he was elected to the Illinois House of Representatives. Simon was elected a state senator in 1962, and in 1968, although a Republican was elected governor, he was elected lieutenant governor—the only time in Illinois history that the two offices had been split between parties. He was defeated in the primary when he ran for governor in 1972, however, and taught college journalism for two years, but in 1974 he was elected to the U.S. House of Representatives, in which he served five terms before entering the Senate. As a senator he counted a balanced budget, job creation, reduction in violence on television, adult literacy, and federal loans for college students among his major concerns and was a firm believer in the government's power to solve social problems.

Simone, Nina (EUNICE WAYMON), American singer (b. Feb. 21, 1933, Tryon, N.C.—d. April 21, 2003, Carry-le-Rouet, France), created urgent emotional intensity by singing songs of love, protest, and black empowerment in a dramatic style, with a rough-edged voice. Originally noted as a jazz singer, she became a prominent voice of the 1960s civil rights movement with recordings such as "Mississippi Goddam" and "Old Jim Crow"; her best-known composition was "To Be Young, Gifted and Black." She also recorded songs by rock and pop songwriters. A precocious child, she played piano and organ in girlhood. She became sensitive to racism when at age 12 she gave a piano recital in a library where her parents had to stand in back because they were black. A student of classical music at the Juilliard School of Music in New York City, she began performing as a pianist. Her vocal career began in 1954 in an Atlantic City, N.J., nightclub when the club owner threatened to fire her unless she sang too. Her first album featured her distinctive versions of jazz and cabaret standards, including "I Loves You, Porgy," which became a 1959 hit. In the 1960s she added protest songs, became a friend of Martin Luther King, Jr., and Malcolm X, and performed at civil rights demonstrations. Her popularity grew as she added folk and gospel selections as well as songs by the Bee Gees, Bob Dylan, and Screaming Jay Hawkins ("I Put a Spell on You"), to her repertoire. Angered by American racism, she left the United States in 1973 and lived in Barbados, Africa, and Europe for the rest of her life. Like her private life, her career was turbulent, and she gained a reputation for throwing onstage tantrums, insulting inattentive audiences, and abruptly canceling concerts. A 1980s Chanel television commercial that included her vocal "My Baby Just Cares for Me" helped introduce her to many new, younger listeners. Despite ill health, she continued to tour and perform, and she maintained a devoted international following to the end.

Vocalist Nina Simone

Sims, Howard ("SANDMAN"), American tap dancer (b. Jan. 24, 1917, Fort Smith, Ark.—d. May 20, 2003, Bronx, N.Y.), got his nickname from dancing on sand to achieve a unique soft brushing sound. In addition to dancing, he taught footwork to such dancers as Gregory Hines (*q.v.*) and Ben Vereen as well as to boxers, including Muhammad Ali, and off and on for over three decades served Harlem's Apollo Theater in New York City as its "executioner" on amateur nights, ridding the stage of unpopular acts.

Singleton, Penny (MARIANA DOROTHY AGNES LETITIA MCNULTY), American actress (b. Sept. 15, 1908, Philadelphia, Pa.—d. Nov. 12, 2003, Sherman Oaks, Calif.), was best known for her portrayal of the comic-strip character Blondie on the radio and in 28 films between 1938 and 1950. Later, in the 1962–63 television season, she was the voice of Jane Jetson in the cartoon series *The Jetsons.*

Sisulu, Walter Max Ulyate, South African political activist (b. May 18, 1912, Engcobo, S.Af.—d. May 5, 2003, Johannesburg, S.Af.), was a political mentor of Nelson Mandela and a prominent African National Congress (ANC) member who helped lead the battle against apartheid, the South African government's policy of racial discrimination. At the age of 15, Sisulu left his Anglican mission school to work at a dairy in Johannesburg. He went on to hold a variety of other jobs before eventually opening a real-estate business. Before joining the ANC in 1940, he had been involved in trade-union activism for some years. Sisulu met Mandela in 1941 and recruited him into the ANC. Under the leadership of Sisulu, Mandela, Oliver Tambo, and Albert Luthuli, the ANC and its Youth League sponsored nonviolent demonstrations, strikes, and boycotts to protest apartheid in the 1940s and '50s. Along with Mandela and 154 others, Sisulu was arrested for treason in 1956, but he was acquitted after a four-year trial. He was arrested again with other top ANC leaders in 1963 and sentenced to life in prison the following year on charges of plotting to overthrow the government. He remained in prison until October 1989, four months before Mandela was released. Sisulu's wife, Albertina, had become a leading anti-apartheid activist herself during his imprisonment. After his release, Sisulu served as deputy president of the ANC. Although Mandela was elected president of South Africa in 1994, Sisulu declined to seek a post in the new government and formally retired from the ANC at the end of that year, though he remained one of Mandela's closest confidants.

Slim Dusty (David Gordon Kirkpatrick), Australian country music singer and songwriter (b. June 13, 1927, Kempsey, N.S.W., Australia—d. Sept. 19, 2003, Sydney, Australia), epitomized the image of a regular

© Penny Tweedie/Corbis

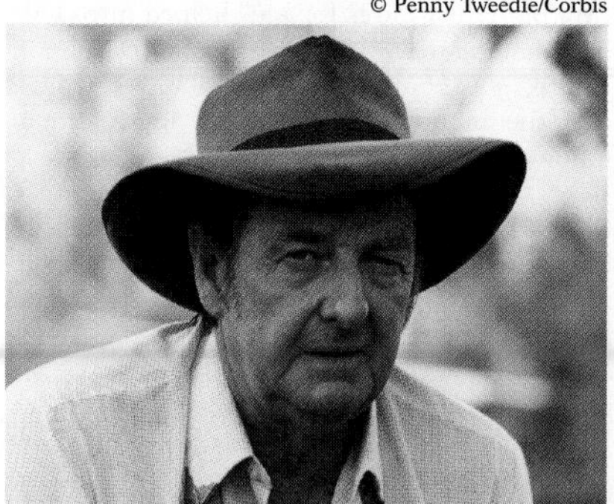

Balladeer Slim Dusty

bloke from rural Australia—a working stockman with his trademark cowboy hat, acoustic guitar, and vast repertoire of Aussie "bush ballads." He grew up on a dairy ranch, wrote his first song, "That's the Way the Cowboy Dies," at age 10, and took the stage name Slim Dusty a year later. He began singing on the radio with then partner Shorty Ranger in 1940. Slim Dusty recorded his first record, the patriotic "Song for the Aussies" (with "My Final Song" on the B-side), in 1942 and signed his first recording contract in 1946. He continued to work part-time as a ranch stockman until 1954, when he formed a full-time traveling show with his wife and other family members. Slim Dusty recorded more than 100 albums, including *Slim Dusty Sings* (1960), *Australian Bush Ballads and Other Old-Time Songs* (1965), *Beer Drinking Songs of Australia* (1986), and *G'Day, G'Day* (1989). He was the first Australian recording artist to receive a gold record (for his quintessential hit "A Pub with No Beer" in 1957), the first Australian entertainer to be granted an MBE (1970), and the first country music performer to appear at the Sydney Opera House (1978). In 2000 he sang "Waltzing Matilda" for the world at the closing ceremony of the Olympic Games in Sydney. Slim Dusty also was the founding president (1992–2001) of the Country Music Association of Australia, the author of an autobiography, *Walk a Country Mile* (1979), and the subject of a 1984 film biography. He was honoured with a formal state funeral.

Smithson, Peter Denham, British architect (b. Sept. 18, 1923, Stockton-on-Tees, Durham, Eng.—d. March 3, 2003, London, Eng.), with his wife, Alison, was among the foremost proponents of the New Brutalism style of architecture, which stressed a new respect for the functionality of materials. Smithson met fellow architecture student Alison Gill at the University of Durham; they were married in 1949. The newly created Smithson team vaulted to fame when they won a design competition for the Hunstanton Secondary Modern School in 1950; the steel-and-glass structure, built around a series of small courtyards and completely without corridors, was completed in 1954. The proposed Smithson design for rebuilding Coventry Cathedral, though never realized, was much admired. Perhaps the most successful of the Smithson team's buildings was the Economist Building Group in St. James's, Westminster, in London (completed 1964), a miniaturized high-rise complex integrated into the fabric of the surrounding neighbourhood. The Smithsons were as well known for their theories and unbuilt designs as for their relatively few realized projects. In 1956–68 they were members of the neo-avant-garde group Team X. A monograph of the Smithsons' life work, *The Charged Void,* was published in 2001.

Soong Mei-ling (Madame Chiang Kai-shek), Chinese politician (b. March 5, 1897, Shanghai, China—d. Oct. 23, 2003, New York, N.Y.), as a member of the prominent Soong family and wife (1927–75) of Nationalist leader Chiang Kai-shek, greatly influenced politics in China and later Taiwan. Educated in the U.S., she tirelessly promoted Nationalist

Copyright Robert Capa/Magnum Photos

Madame Chiang Kai-shek

China's cause in the West, and during the Sino-Japanese War (1937–45), she made highly publicized visits to the U.S., where she won much financial aid and earned the admiration of the American public. A lengthy battle with communists for control of China ended with the Nationalists' defeat in 1949. Her husband moved the Nationalist government to Taiwan, where she continued to be a formidable presence within the party and helped influence U.S. policy toward China and Taiwan for many years. After Chiang's death in 1975, however, her political power waned, and she moved to New York City, where she lived in semiseclusion.

Sordi, Alberto, Italian film actor (b. June 15, 1919, Rome, Italy—d. Feb. 24/25, 2003, Rome), depicted the vices, virtues, and foibles of post-World War II Italy in a long career of mostly comic films and was regarded as a national icon. Sordi began his career dubbing the voice of Oliver Hardy in movies in the 1930s. His breakout roles on-screen were Fernando Rivoli in Federico Fellini's *Lo sceicco bianco* (1952) and Alberto in Fellini's *I vitelloni* (1953). Among the more notable of his more than 150 films were *Un americano a Roma* (1954), *Il Conte Max* (1957), *La grande guerra* (1959), which won the Venice Film Festival's Golden Lion award, *Il diavolo* (1963), for which Sordi won a Golden Globe award for best actor in a comedy, and *Un borghese piccolo piccolo* (1977; *An Average Little Man*), for which he won a David di Donatello award for best actor. He also appeared in three English-language films. In 1995 the Venice Film Festival gave Sordi a career Golden Lion award.

Spahn, Warren Edward, American baseball player (b. April 23, 1921, Buffalo, N.Y.—d. Nov. 24, 2003, Broken Arrow, Okla.), won 363 major league games—more than any other left-handed pitcher—and baffled batters with his graceful high-kick windup and outstanding control of his fastball, curve, slider, and screwball. During his 21-year career, he led the league in victories for eight years and led in earned-run average for three years; altogether he won 20 or more games in a season 13 times, tying the major league record, and he pitched a lifetime total of 63 shutouts and 2 no-hitters. Spahn first appeared in the major leagues in 1942 with the Boston Braves. During army service in World War II, he earned a Purple Heart and a Bronze Star for heroism. Returning to the Braves in 1946, he won his first major league game, and he collected 21 victories the next season. When the Braves won the 1948 pennant, he and Johnny Sain, as the team's star pitchers, inspired the slogan "Spahn and Sain, and pray for rain." In 1957 Spahn won the Cy Young Award. He pitched winning games for Milwaukee in the 1957 World Series (the Braves beat the New York Yankees) and again in 1958, when the Braves lost the Series to the Yankees. Remarkably, he recorded 177 victories after he was 35 years old; in 1963 he won 23 games for Milwaukee, at the age of 42. After 20 years as a Brave, he pitched for the New York Mets and the San Francisco Giants in his final season. A 14-time National League All-Star, he entered the Baseball Hall of Fame in 1973; in August 2003 the Atlanta Braves dedicated a 2.7-m (9-ft)-tall bronze statue of Spahn at their ballpark.

above: © Photo File/Getty Images

Stack, Robert (Robert Langford Modini), American actor (b. Jan. 13, 1919, Los Angeles, Calif.—d. May 14, 2003, Los Angeles), had a notable six-decade-long career that saw him go from giving Deanna Durbin her first screen

Hulton|Archive by Getty Images

Actor Robert Stack

kiss in *First Love* (1939) to portraying more substantial characters in films that included *The High and the Mighty* (1954) and *Written on the Wind* (1956). The role that cemented his fame, however, was that of crime fighter Eliot Ness in the television series *The Untouchables* (1959–63), for which he won an Emmy Award in 1960. He parodied his stalwart-character type in the disaster spoof *Airplane!* (1980) but later returned to it to be the serious host and narrator of the TV series *Unsolved Mysteries* (1987–2002).

Stanfield, Robert Lorne, Canadian politician (b. April 11, 1914, Truro, N.S.—d. Dec. 16, 2003, Ottawa, Ont.), was often referred to as "the best prime minister Canada never had." As leader of the Progressive Conservative Party (PCP), Stanfield presented a dry, unassuming manner that contrasted dramatically with the charismatic Pierre Trudeau, who served as his arch political rival throughout Stanfield's 10-year career in federal politics. Stanfield, the grandson of a wealthy textile magnate, was later pegged with the unfortunate nickname "Underwear Man," a reference to the trademark long johns produced by the family business. He studied at Dalhousie University, Halifax, N.S., and graduated magna cum laude from Harvard Law School in 1939. He then worked for the Wartime Prices and Trade Board and established his own law practice. In 1946 Stanfield started moving in Conservative political circles. Within two years he was the leader of the provincial party. At the time, the PCP did not hold a single seat in the legislature. By 1956, however, Stanfield's Conservatives had won enough seats to secure the majority and start his 11-year tenure as premier of Nova Scotia. He was elected to lead the national PCP in 1967, and his first House of Commons address was a no-confidence motion against Liberal Party Prime Minister Lester Pearson. It was Pearson's successor, Trudeau, who would prove to be Stanfield's chief adversary. The 1972 federal election brought the Conservatives within two seats of a majority—the closest Stanfield would come to inhabiting the prime minister's office. He resigned as party leader in 1976 and left Parliament in 1979. For his political achievements on the provincial and federal levels, Stanfield was granted the title of Right Honourable in 1992.

Starr, Edwin (Charles Edwin Hatcher), American musician (b. Jan. 21, 1942, Nashville, Tenn.—d. April 2, 2003, Bramcote, Nottinghamshire, Eng.), achieved enduring popularity with his classic 1970 recording of the protest song "War," which topped the pop charts for 13 weeks. In 1965 Starr signed with Detroit's Ric Tic Records and released a single he had written, "Agent Double-O Soul," which made the rhythm-and-blues (R&B) top 10. The next year his "Stop Her on Sight (S.O.S.)" was also successful. Shortly thereafter Motown Records bought out Ric Tic, and Starr's 1969 single for Motown, "25 Miles," made both the R&B and pop top 10. In the 1980s Starr moved to Great Britain, where he maintained a busy touring schedule.

Steig, William, American cartoonist and writer (b. Nov. 14, 1907, Brooklyn, N.Y.—d. Oct. 3, 2003, Boston, Mass.), over a period of more than 60 years, created over 1,600 drawings and 117 covers for *The New Yorker* magazine and became known as the "king of cartoons." At the age of 60, he also branched out into writing and illustrating children's books, one of which—*Shrek!* (1990)—was made into a film (2001) that became the first winner of the Academy Award for best animated feature. In 1936 Steig began creating what he called "symbolic drawings," line drawings in which people were in some state of emotional distress. Many of these were later collected in such books as *About People* (1939), *The Lonely Ones* (1942), and *All Embarrassed* (1944) and were featured on greeting cards and party goods. Steig had also by that time begun drawing what became one of his most popular series—cartoons featuring worldly, no-nonsense children whose behaviour pointed out the idiosyncrasies of the world of their elders; they were collected in *Small Fry* (1944). Steig's first children's book, *CDB!*, was published in 1968. Among the more than two dozen that followed were *Roland, the Minstrel Pig* (1968), Caldecott Medal winner *Sylvester and the Magic Pebble* (1969), Christopher Award winner *Dominic,* his first children's novel (1972), and American Book Award winner *Doctor De Soto* (1982).

Stokes, Alexander Rawson, British mathematical physicist (b. June 27, 1919, Macclesfield, Cheshire, Eng.—d. Feb. 5, 2003, Welwyn Garden City, near London, Eng.), demonstrated mathematically that DNA has a helical molecular structure and thus provided the foundation for the 1953 discovery of DNA's double helix shape by Francis Crick and James Watson. After studying at Trinity College, Cambridge, and Cambridge's Cavendish Laboratory, Stokes in 1947 joined Maurice Wilkins (who shared the 1962 Nobel Prize with Watson and Crick) at the biophysics laboratory at King's College, London. In 1950 Stokes applied mathematical analysis to the lab's X-ray-diffraction photographs of DNA and theorized that a helical structure would create the distinctive pattern evident in the images. Stokes and Wilkins initially deferred publishing their results, but their paper (coauthored with Herbert Wilson) on experimental evidence for the double helix eventually appeared in the same issue of *Nature* as the paper by Watson and Crick describing their discovery.

Stone, Peter, American screenwriter and librettist (b. Feb. 27, 1930, Los Angeles, Calif.—d. April 26, 2003, New York, N.Y.), was the first writer to win the Emmy, Oscar, and Tony awards. He won his first award, an Emmy, for *The Defenders* in the early 1960s. His first movie script was *Charade* (1963); other notable films included *Father Goose* (1964), for which he won an Oscar for best original screenplay, *Sweet Charity* (1969), and *The Taking of Pelham One Two Three* (1974). His first Broadway success was the book for the 1969 musical *1776;* the play won that year's Tony Award for best musical. He won Tonys for his books for *Woman of the Year* in 1981 and *Titanic* in 1997. He was also well regarded as a "script doctor" and was credited with rescuing the 1983 musical *My One and Only.*

Sunderman, F(rederick) William, American scientist, physician, editor, and musician (b. Oct. 23, 1898, Juniata, Pa.—d. March 9, 2003, Philadelphia, Pa.), was honoured as the nation's oldest worker in 1999 when he reached

F. William Sunderman

AP/Wide World Photos

100. Sunderman was one of the first to treat a diabetic coma patient with insulin. He invented a widely used instrument for testing glucose levels in blood and developed quality-control methods for medical laboratories that served as the standard for 36 years. He was medical director for the Manhattan Project at Los Alamos, N.M., and later worked for the Centers for Disease Control. In addition, he taught at eight universities, served as president of the American Society for Clinical Pathology, and was a founder of the College of American Pathologists and of the Association of Clinical Scientists. Sunderman played violin in chamber music groups in Europe every summer and played in Carnegie Hall in 1998. In 1971 he founded the publication of the Association of Clinical Scientists, the *Annals of Clinical and Laboratory Science,* which he edited until early 2003.

Teller, Edward, Hungarian-born American nuclear physicist (b. Jan. 15, 1908, Budapest, Hung.—d. Sept. 9, 2003, Stanford, Calif.), spearheaded the U.S. program to develop the hydrogen bomb, the world's first thermonuclear weapon. In 1941 Teller joined Enrico Fermi and other scientists in the Manhattan Project; the goal was to create the first self-sustaining nuclear chain reaction. Teller was one of the first scientists recruited in 1943 to work on production of the atomic bomb at Los Alamos (N.M.) Scientific Laboratory. After World War II his push to develop the more powerful hydrogen bomb received little support from his colleagues, but Pres. Harry Truman authorized the effort after the Soviet Union successfully tested an atomic weapon in 1949 and British scientist Klaus Fuchs confessed that he had passed information on atomic weapons to the Soviets. On Nov. 1, 1952, a hydrogen bomb devised by Teller and physicist Stanislaw Ulam was detonated successfully at Enewetak atoll in the Pacific Ocean. Teller was among the first scientists whose research focused on the stability of the atomic nucleus. Early in his career he worked with such scientific luminaries as Niels Bohr, Werner Heisenberg, and George Gamow. Many of his colleagues turned against him, however, when his testimony before the U.S. Congress in 1954 contributed to the downfall of J. Robert Oppenheimer, the former director of the Los Alamos laboratory. Undeterred, Teller spent much of the rest of his life working to ensure U.S. superiority in the arms race. In the early 1950s he helped establish the Lawrence Radiation Laboratory (now the Lawrence Livermore National Laboratory), which became the main production facility for thermonuclear weapons in the U.S. He opposed the 1963 Nuclear Test-Ban Treaty and the Strategic Arms Limitation Talks of the 1970s. Having dealt with each U.S. president since Franklin D. Roosevelt, Teller established a strong rapport with Pres. Ronald Reagan and in the 1980s was influential in advancing the proposal for the Strategic Defense Initiative (SDI), a space-based missile defense system that was eventually abandoned because of technological difficulties. In 2003 Teller was awarded the Presidential Medal of Freedom.

Physicist Edward Teller

© Nat Farbman/Time Life Pictures/Getty Images

Thatcher, Sir Denis, British businessman and political spouse (b. May 10, 1915, London, Eng.—d. June 26, 2003, London), as the devoted husband and confidant of British Prime Minister Margaret Thatcher, was the object of public criticism and political satire, but he endured his seemingly thankless job with great style and self-deprecating good humour. Thatcher was a wealthy chemical executive when he married Margaret Roberts in 1951, and he served as a corporate director after his business was taken over by Burmah Oil in 1965. He was appointed MBE in his own right in 1944 and was made a hereditary baronet in 1991 shortly after his wife resigned from office.

Thesiger, Sir Wilfred Patrick, British explorer (b. June 3, 1910, Addis Ababa, Abyssinia [now in Ethiopia]—d. Aug. 24, 2003, Croyden, Surrey, Eng.), spent most of his life in remote regions of Africa and Asia living with the denizens of those places in the last moments before Western civilization reached and forever changed them. He twice crossed the Rubʿ al-Khali of Arabia and later spent time in Iraq, Persia (Iran), Pakistan, Afghanistan, and Kenya. Thesiger chronicled his experiences in a number of books, notably *Arabian Sands* (1959) and *The Marsh Arabs* (1964), and his photography was as well respected as his writing. He was knighted in 1995.

Thigpen, Lynne, American actress (b. Dec. 22, 1948, Joliet, Ill.—d. March 12, 2003, Los Angeles, Calif.), worked as a character actress on stage, screen, and television. Thigpen was best known for her TV roles, which included a regular part on the soap opera *All My Children* (1993–2000), the character of the Chief in the children's television programs *Where in the World Is Carmen Sandiego?* (1991) and *Where in Time Is Carmen Sandiego?* (1996), and a costarring position as Ella Farmer on the series *The District,* beginning in 2000. She won a number of awards for her stage work, among them a Tony Award for best supporting actress in 1997 for her role in *An American Daughter.*

© Gregory Pace/Corbis

Actress Lynne Thigpen

Thurmond, (James) Strom, American politician (b. Dec. 5, 1902, Edgefield, S.C.—d. June 26, 2003, Edgefield), was the longest-serving senator (1954–2003) in U.S. history and came to personify the changing political landscape of the South. After graduating from Clemson (S.C.) College (now Clemson University) in 1923, he studied law with his father and was admitted to the bar in 1930. He later served as state senator (1933–38) and circuit court judge (1938–41) before serving (1942–46) in the army; by the end of World War II, he was a highly decorated lieutenant colonel. Elected governor of South Carolina in 1946, Thurmond supported a number of progressive measures, including the improvement of African American schools and equal pay for women. In 1948 he gained national attention as the leader of a group of Southern democrats who broke with the

centre: AP/Wide World Photos; above: © Diana Walker/ Liaison

Democratic Party over civil rights. They formed the States' Rights Democratic Party—popularly known as the Dixiecrats—and adopted a segregation platform, with Thurmond as their presidential candidate. Although Thurmond lost, he captured 39 electoral votes, and the election marked the beginning decline in Southern white voters' support of the Democratic Party. After his governorship ended in 1950, Thurmond ran for the U.S. Senate but was unsuccessful. He easily won his bid in 1954, however, and became the first person elected to the Senate as a write-in candidate. He quickly aligned himself with other Southern conservatives, supporting increased military spending and denouncing civil rights legislation; in 1957 Thurmond staged a one-man filibuster, speaking on the Senate floor for more than 24 hours, to delay the passage of a civil rights bill. After Pres. Lyndon B. Johnson oversaw the enactment of the Civil Rights Act (1964), an angered Thurmond switched to the Republican Party, and in 1968 he helped Republican presidential candidate Richard Nixon win the White House. By the early 1970s, however, as integration and civil rights became inevitable, Thurmond changed his stance, hiring African Americans to serve on his staff and courting the African American vote.

Tillman, Floyd, American country singer, songwriter, and guitarist (b. Dec. 8, 1914, Ryan, Okla.—d. Aug. 22, 2003, Bacliff, Texas), was one of the pioneers of the honky-tonk sound, wrote over 1,000 songs, was one of the earliest country writers to have his songs become crossover hits, and had a style that became a major influence on generations of musicians. His best-known song was the daring-for-its-time—with its approach to adultery—"Slippin' Around" (1949). Tillman was honoured with induction into the Country Music Hall of Fame in 1984, and on his final album, *Floyd Tillman: The Influence,* which was released posthumously, he was joined in his songs by a number of fellow artists.

Tisch, Laurence Alan ("LARRY"), American entrepreneur, investor, and media executive (b. March 5, 1923, Brooklyn, N.Y.—d. Nov. 15, 2003, New York, N.Y.), bought the Loews theatre chain in partnership with his brother, Bob, and built it into Loews Corp., a multibillion-dollar conglomerate. In 1986, with CBS facing a hostile takeover, Tisch bought a controlling interest and became CEO, a move considered a rescue until his drastic restructuring, news staff and budget reductions, and sell-off of publishing and music units led to a decline in ratings and stature for the network; in 1995 CBS was sold.

Travers, Susan, British-born adventurer (b. Sept. 23, 1909, London, Eng.—d. Dec. 18, 2003, Paris, France), was the only woman to serve (1945–47) in the French Foreign Legion. From 1941 Travers was attached to the Foreign Legion as a driver during the World War II campaign in North Africa. She applied to join the Legion after the war (omitting her sex from the application) and served as a logistics officer until her resignation in 1947. Travers was awarded the Croix de Guerre, the Military Medal (1956), and the Legion of Honour (1996). She published her memoirs, *Tomorrow to Be Brave,* in 2000.

French Foreign Legionnaire Susan Travers

Trevor-Roper, Hugh Redwald (BARON DACRE OF GLANTON), British historian (b. Jan. 15, 1914, Glanton, Northumberland, Eng.—d. Jan. 26, 2003, Oxford, Eng.), was well known for his many and fruitful scholarly controversies, but he was catapulted into the public eye in an unfortunate way in 1983, when he authenticated some 60 volumes of diaries purported to be those of Adolf Hitler (and said to have been found by the German newsmagazine *Stern*) as genuine; they proved to be a forgery, and he had to issue a public apology. Trevor-Roper graduated from Christ Church College, Oxford, in 1936 and earned an M.A. from Merton College, Oxford, in 1939. During World War II he worked in intelligence. After the war the British government asked him to look into Adolf Hitler's death, and the resulting book, *The Last Days of Hitler* (1947), brought him a great deal of public notice. He began teaching history at Christ Church College in 1946, and he engaged in a long-running historical debate with R.H. Tawney and Lawrence Stone over the causes of the English Civil Wars (1642–51). In 1957 Trevor-Roper was appointed Regius Professor of Modern History at Oxford, a post he held until 1980. Considered his most remarkable collection was *Religion, the Reformation and Social Change, and Other Essays* (1967). In 1980 he became master of Peterhouse College, Cambridge, where he was at odds with the professors until his retirement in 1987. Trevor-Roper was made a life peer in 1979.

Trías Monge, José, Puerto Rican government official and judge (b. May 5, 1920, San Juan, P.R.—d. June 24, 2003, Boston, Mass.), was heavily involved with drafting the Puerto Rican constitution, which took effect in 1952. Under its terms, Puerto Rico bound itself to the U.S. and acquired approximately the same level of self-government as the 50 U.S. states. Trías Monge, who served as attorney general (1953–57) and chief justice (1974–85) of Puerto Rico, later decried the status of the island in the book *Puerto Rico: The Trials of the Oldest Colony in the World* (1997).

Trintignant, Marie, French actress (b. Jan. 21, 1962, Boulogne-Billancourt, France—d. Aug. 1, 2003, Neuilly-sur-Seine, France), specialized in portraying damaged women in a career that included more than 50 films as well as television movies and stage plays. Trintignant appeared in *Mon amour, mon amour* (1967; *My Love, My Love*) at the age of five, acting with her father, Jean-Louis Trintignant, under the direction of her mother, Nadine Trintignant. Among her more notable films were *Série noire* (1979), *L'Été prochain* (1985; *Next Summer*), and . . . *Comme elle respire* (1998; *White Lies*). She died of brain injuries, reportedly after having been beaten by her boyfriend, rock star Bertrand Cantat.

Actress Marie Trintignant

Trout, Evelyn ("BOBBI"), American aviator (b. Jan. 7, 1906, Greenup, Ill.—d. Jan. 24, 2003, La Jolla, Calif.), counted having been the first woman to fly an all-night route among her many women's flight endurance and altitude records. She was the last survivor of the pilots who in 1929 took part in the first National Women's Air Derby, which Will Rogers dubbed the "Powder Puff Derby."

Aviator Evelyn Trout

Tureck, Rosalyn, American pianist, teacher, writer, and conductor (b. Dec. 14, 1914, Chicago, Ill.—d. July 17, 2003, New York, N.Y.), sparked new interest in the composer Johann Sebastian Bach with her powerful interpretations of his music and extensive research and writings on his work. She founded (1960) the chamber orchestra Tureck Bach Players and was the first woman to conduct (1958) the New York Philharmonic.

Urbani, Carlo, Italian epidemiologist (b. Oct. 19, 1956, Castelplanio, Italy—d. March 29, 2003, Bangkok, Thai.), recognized that the SARS (severe acute respiratory syndrome) outbreak was an epidemic and raised the alarm, allowing the disease to be somewhat contained, before dying himself of SARS. Urbani began working in Africa as soon as he got his medical degree, and he became an expert in parasitic diseases. In the 1990s he undertook a number of missions in Africa for the World Health Organization (WHO) on controlling disease caused by parasitic worms. Doctors Without Borders hired him for work in Cambodia, where he made important advances in the control of parasitic worms. In 1999 he was made president of the Italian chapter of Doctors Without Borders. In 2000 WHO made him director of infectious diseases for the Western Pacific Region, based in Hanoi. In February 2003 Urbani was called to the Vietnam-France Hospital in Hanoi when an American who had arrived from Hong Kong was hospitalized with atypical pneumonia. Urbani quickly recognized the highly contagious nature of the disease, instituted strenuous anti-infection measures, and called in the health authorities. By mid-March the hospital had been quarantined. Urbani was credited with shutting down the disease in Vietnam, and his action led to WHO's worldwide alert. Urbani had just arrived in Bangkok for a conference when he realized that he had contracted SARS.

Uris, Leon Marcus, American writer (b. Aug. 3, 1924, Baltimore, Md.—d. June 21, 2003, Shelter Island, N.Y.), wrote a number of best-sellers, many of which—including *Battle Cry* (1953), *Exodus* (1958), his biggest success, *Mila 18* (1961), *Topaz* (1967), and *Trinity* (1976)—were based on events of modern history. He also wrote the screenplays for such movies as *Battle Cry* (1955) and *Gunfight at the OK Corral* (1957).

Van Steenbergen, Henrik ("RIK"), Belgian cyclist (b. Sept. 9, 1924, Arendonck, Belg.—d. May 15, 2003, Antwerp, Belg.), during a 24-year career (1943–66), won more than 900 professional races, including three world road-racing championships (1949, 1956, 1957) and eight classics—the Tour of Flanders (1944, 1946), Paris–Roubaix (1948, 1952), Flèche Wallonne (1949, 1958), Paris–Brussels (1950), and Milan–San Remo (1954). An indefatigable all-rounder, Van Steenbergen also won 25 grand-tour stages, finishing second in the 1951 Tour of Italy (Giro d'Italia), and 40 six-day track races.

Vázquez Montalbán, Manuel, Spanish author (b. July 27, 1939, Barcelona, Spain—d. Oct. 18, 2003, Bangkok, Thai.), created the complex Spanish detective Pepe Carvalho in a series of 22 novels that were translated into 24 languages. Vázquez Montalbán's astonishingly prolific output also included poetry, essays, socialistic political commentary, and plays. He received many literary awards, among them the Planeta Prize for *Los mares del sur* (1979; *Southern Seas*, 1986) and both Spain's National Literature Award and the European Literature Award for *Galíndez* (1990; Eng. trans., 1992).

Vieira de Mello, Sérgio, Brazilian diplomat (b. March 15, 1948, Rio de Janeiro, Braz.—d. Aug. 19, 2003, Baghdad, Iraq), dedicated his life to attempting to bring peace, assisting refugees, and aiding humanitarian relief in many of the most volatile trouble spots all over the world. For over 30 years he worked at resolving conflicts—guiding such notable successes as the restoration of order in Kosovo in 1999 and the transition of East Timor to independence from Indonesia in 2002—and many thought he would follow Kofi Annan as UN secretary-general. Vieira de Mello was educated at the Sorbonne, earning a degree in philosophy in 1969 and a Ph.D. in 1974. Before earning his Ph.D., however, he had already begun his UN career by taking an editorial position at the UN High Commissioner for Refugees (UNHCR) in 1969. Over the following several years, Vieira de Mello was involved in missions in such countries as East Pakistan during its transition to Bangladesh, Cyprus following the Turkish invasion in 1974, and Mozambique when its independence from Portugal in 1975 was followed by civil war, and in 1978 he went to Lima, Peru, as UNHCR regional representative for northern Latin America. From 1981 to 1983 he served as senior political adviser to the UN Interim Force in Lebanon, and he then returned to UNHCR, at its headquarters in Geneva, where he filled a number of management positions before being posted to Bosnia and Herzegovina in 1993. In 1996 Vieira de Mello was appointed UNHCR's assistant high commissioner, and two years later he became undersecretary-general for humanitarian affairs. Following his successes in Kosovo and East Timor, in 2002 he was named UN high commissioner for human rights, and in June 2003 he was sent to Baghdad as Annan's special representative in Iraq. Vieira de Mello was killed when the UN headquarters there was bombed.

Diplomat Sérgio Vieira de Mello

Vilner, Meir (MEIR VILNER-KOVNER; BER KOVNER), Lithanian-born Israeli politician (b. Oct. 23, 1918, Vilnius, Lithuania—d. June 5, 2003, Tel Aviv, Israel), was a member of the Israeli Knesset (parliament) for nearly 42 years (1949–90), secretary-general (1965–90) and chairman (1990–93) of the Communist Party of Israel, and the last surviving signatory of the Declaration of the Establishment of the State of Israel (May 14, 1948). Vilner fled to British Palestine as a refugee in 1938. He represented the Communists on the 37-member Provisional Council of State in 1948 and was, at age 29, the declaration's youngest signer.

Vladimov, Georgy (GEORGY NIKOLAYEVICH VOLOSEVICH), Russian writer, editor, and political dissident (b. Feb. 19, 1931, Kharkov, U.S.S.R. [now in Ukraine]—d. Oct. 19, 2003, Frankfurt, Ger.), was best known for his novel *Verny Ruslan* ("Faithful Ruslan"), a savage satire of the Stalinist Gulag culture from the viewpoint of a camp guard dog; it was written in the 1960s and circulated as samizdat in the U.S.S.R. until it was published in Germany in 1975 and in English in 1979. Vladimov worked as a critic for the literary journal *Novy mir* ("New World") and was elected to membership in the Soviet Writers Union in 1961, but he soon fell afoul of the authorities, both for his writings—which were not properly flattering of Soviet reality—and for his activities on behalf of and in concert with fellow dissidents Aleksandr Solzhenitsyn and Andrey Sakharov. Vladimov quit the Writers Union in 1977 and moved to Germany after his citizenship was revoked in 1983. His novel *General i yego armiya* ("The General and His Army") won the Russian Booker Prize in 1995. Vladimov's Russian citizenship was restored in 2000, and he was buried at the cemetery at Peredelkino, the writer's colony near Moscow.

Walker, Alexander, British film critic (b. March 22, 1930, Portadown, County Armagh, N.Ire.—d. July 15, 2003, London, Eng.), wrote fearlessly outspoken movie reviews for London's *Evening Standard* for more than 43 years, from 1960 until his death. He was three times named Critic of the Year by the British Press Awards. Walker was the author of more than 20 well-received books on the film industry, including histories and many biographies.

Walker, Johnny (BADRUDDIN JAMALUDDIN QAZI), Indian film comedian (b. March 23, 1924?, Indore, Madhya Pradesh, India—d. July 29, 2003, Mumbai [Bombay], India), was generally regarded as the most successful comedian of what fans called the golden age of Hindi cinema. With an unusually mobile face and a much-admired sense of timing, Walker delighted audiences with his gentle comedy in more than 300 films, beginning with *Baazi* (1951). Among his most memorable movies were *Pyaasa* (1957; *Thirst*) and *Mere Mehboob* (1963; "My Sweetheart").

Weiss, Theodore Russell, American poet and editor (b. Dec. 16, 1916, Reading, Pa.—d. April 15, 2003, Princeton, N.J.), was the founding editor in 1943 (with Warren Carrier) of the *Quarterly Review of Literature,* which published works by poets William Carlos Williams, E.E. Cummings, and Ezra Pound, as well as those of little-known poets, non-English-language writers, and especially women, including the then-unknown writers Anne Sexton, Sylvia Plath, and Joyce Carol Oates. In 1944 Weiss became sole editor, and with his wife, Renée, assisting him with editorial selections, he edited the publication until 2003. Weiss was on the faculty of Princeton University for 20 years and released more than a dozen volumes of his own poetry, mostly narrative verse.

Welch, Elisabeth Margaret, American-born British musical theatre and cabaret singer (b. Feb. 27, 1904, New York, N.Y.—d. July 15, 2003, Northolt, Middlesex, Eng.), was known for her show-stopping performances in plays by Cole Porter, Ivor Novello, and Noël Coward. Welch began her career in New York City, where she created a sensation in 1931 with her rendition of Porter's "Love for Sale." She was a cabaret singer in Paris before becoming a fixture in London's West End. From the 1930s she appeared in films and on British radio and television. Welch was particularly associated with the songs "Stormy Weather," which she introduced to English audiences in 1933, and "Solomon," written for her by Porter. Later she was a hit in the musical *Pippin* (1970), and in 1980—a half century after her last appearance in New York City—she made a triumphant return to Broadway.

West, Peter, British sports commentator (b. Aug. 12, 1920, Addiscombe, Surrey, Eng.—d. Sept. 2, 2003, Bath, Eng.), long led BBC's coverage of a number of sports, most notably cricket, and hosted *Come Dancing* (1957–72), maintaining throughout a knowledgeable and imperturbable demeanour. He began his broadcasting career on radio in 1947. For television, he covered Test cricket (1952–86), Wimbledon tennis (1955–82), Rugby Union football (1950–85), and the Olympic Games (1948, 1960, 1964, 1968, 1972, 1976).

White, Barry (BARRY EUGENE CARTER), American rhythm-and-blues singer (b. Sept. 12, 1944, Galveston, Texas—d. July 4, 2003, Los Angeles, Calif.), possessed one of the most recognizable bass-baritone voices in the musical world. Especially popular during the disco-era 1970s—an era that he helped set in motion with his Love Unlimited Orchestra's "Love's Theme" instrumental (1973)—he half sang and half spoke romantic ballads in velvety sensual tones that, in combination with lush orchestrations, created an intimate, seductive mood. Among White's numerous hit songs were two—"Can't Get Enough of Your Love, Babe" and "You're the First, the Last, My Everything"—that propelled the album they were on, *Can't Get Enough* (1974), to the top of the charts, and his album *Staying Power* (1999) won two Grammy Awards.

Williams, Sir Bernard Arthur Owen, British philosopher (b. Sept. 21, 1929, Westcliff-on-Sea, Essex, Eng.—d. June 10, 2003, Rome, Italy), sought to revitalize moral philosophy and served on public commissions investigating gambling, drug abuse, social justice, public schools, and obscenity and censorship. In opposition to the positivist and analytic approach to moral philosophy, which held that philosophers have no substantive contribution to make to ethics, Williams adopted a naturalistic position in which he attempted to embed it in history and culture. He opposed both Kantianism and utilitarianism, which both assert that there is a single valid principle of morality, arguing instead that moral life should be investigated as it is experienced rather than in terms of abstract theories. Williams was educated (1946–51) at Chigwell School and Balliol College, Oxford. He taught at the Universities of Oxford, London, and Cambridge, where he was Knightbridge Professor of Moral Philosophy (1967–79) and provost (1979–87) of King's College. After two years (1988–90) at the University of California, Berkeley, Williams returned to Oxford, where he was White's Professor of Moral Philosophy (1990–96). His principal publications included *Utilitarianism: For and Against* (edited with J.J.C. Smart, 1973), *Descartes: A Project of Pure Enquiry* (1978), *Morality* (1972), *Problems of the Self* (1973), *Moral Luck* (1981), *Shame and Necessity* (1993), and *Truth and Truthfulness* (2002). He also served (1968–86) on the board of the English National Opera, and he was elected a fellow of the British Academy in 1971 and knighted in 1999.

R&B singer Barry White

Williamson, Malcolm Benjamin Graham Christopher, Australian-born composer (b. Nov. 21, 1931, Sydney, Australia—d. March 2, 2003, Cambridge, Eng.), was an astonishingly prolific and versatile composer as well as the first non-Briton to become (1975) master of the queen's music. His body of work, which juxtaposed a deep mysticism with popular idioms and was widely, though not universally, admired, included 7 symphonies, 11 operas, 4 masses, and a large number of other choral and orchestral pieces. Williamson also composed several short operas for children as well as "cassations"—small operas for audience participation that were intended partially as teaching devices. After studying music in Sydney, Williamson moved to London in 1950, and by the early 1960s he was able to support himself by composition alone. His work during this period included the organ piece *Vision of Christ-Phoenix* (1962) and the opera *Our Man in Havana* (1963). More of his later compositions were produced for Australia, among them *The True Endeavour* (1988), for speaker, chorus, and orchestra. The song cycle *A Year of Birds* appeared in 1995. Williamson was appointed CBE in 1976 and an Officer of the Order of Australia in 1987.

Wilson, Kemmons, American businessman (b. Jan. 5, 1913, Osceola, Ark.—d. Feb. 12, 2003, Memphis, Tenn.), transformed the motel industry when in the early 1950s he founded the Holiday Inn chain, which once advertised itself as "the nation's innkeeper." In 1951 Wilson, already a millionaire from a variety of businesses, including a jukebox franchise, was appalled at the roadside accommodations he found while vacationing with his family. He determined to create a chain of clean low-priced motels that would be attractive to families. He opened the first Holiday Inn (the name came from the 1942 movie starring Bing Crosby and Fred Astaire) in Memphis, Tenn., in 1952. By 1959 there were 100 Holiday Inns nationwide, and by 1975 there were more than 1,700 operating throughout the world. Wilson retired in 1979.

Innkeeper Kemmons Wilson

The Kemmons Wilson with HOLIDAY INN® GREAT SIGN appears courtesy of InterContinental Hotels Group

Wilson, Sloan, American novelist (b. May 8, 1920, Norwalk, Conn.—d. May 25, 2003, Colonial Beach, Va.), launched a catchphrase with the title of his best-selling novel *The Man in the Gray Flannel Suit* (1955; filmed 1956), which captured the mood of the post-World War II suburban families dealing with the conformity and the sacrifice of family life seemingly necessary for the achievement of upward mobility in business and social position. Another of his successes was *A Summer Place* (1958; filmed 1959).

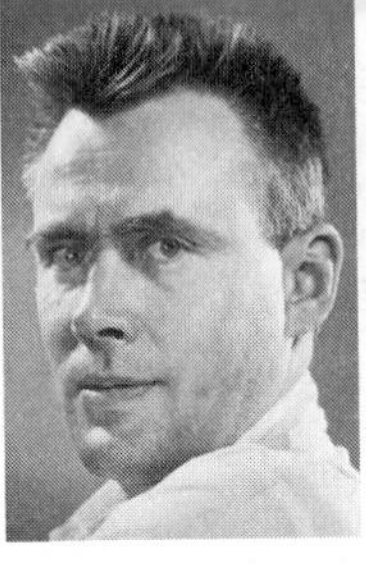

Winsor, Kathleen, American novelist (b. Oct. 16, 1919, Olivia, Minn.—d. May 26, 2003, New York, N.Y.), achieved almost instant notoriety in 1944 with *Forever Amber,* her historical saga of a sexually adventurous young woman in Restoration England, which sold 100,000 copies its first week and paved the way for the many romantic "bodice-rippers" that followed. Although it contained no explicit sex scenes, it was extremely racy for its time, and it was widely condemned.

Wittig, Monique, French avant-garde feminist writer (b. July 13, 1935, Dannemarie, France—d. Jan. 3, 2003, Tucson, Ariz.), used an experimental approach to language and subject in an attempt to break down definitions and create a language and world free of the dictates of heterosexual society. Wittig's first published work, *L'Opoponax* (1964; *The Opoponax,* 1966) won the Prix Médicis. *Les Guérillères* (1969; *The Guérillères,* 1971), a lyrical evocation of a women's society at war with men, became an iconic work of the feminist movement in France and the U.S. Her other works included *Les Corps lesbien* (1973; *The Lesbian Body,* 1975) and *Virgile, non* (1985; *Across the Acheron,* 1987), a feminist reworking of Dante's *Divine Comedy.* With her partner, Sande Zeig, she produced a dictionary, *Brouillon pour un dictionnaire des amantes* (1976; *Lesbian Peoples: Material for a Dictionary,* 1979). A collection of Wittig's essays, *The Straight Mind and Other Essays,* appeared in 1992.

Wright, G(eorg) H(enrik) von, Finnish analytic philosopher (b. June 14, 1916, Helsinki, Fin.—d. June 16, 2003, Helsinki), was the successor to Ludwig Wittgenstein's chair of philosophy (1948–51) at the University of Cambridge and one of Wittgenstein's literary executors. He was professor of philosophy (1946–61) at the University of Helsinki, research professor (1961–86) at the Academy of Finland, and professor at large (1965–77) at Cornell University, Ithaca, N.Y. Wright worked principally in inductive logic; modal logic, of which he founded a branch he called deontic logic; and the theory of action.

Young, Hugo John Smelter, British political journalist (b. Oct. 13, 1938, Sheffield, Eng.—d. Sept. 22, 2003, London, Eng.), for 30 years wrote with elegance and scholarship from a liberal perspective; his column was considered essential reading for those interested in politics. Young began working for the *Sunday Times* in 1965 and became the head writer of the paper's editorials in 1966. As the paper's political editor (1973–84), he pioneered the weekly opinion column for which he became known. He began writing a twice-weekly column for *The Guardian* in 1984. In addition, he was the author of several books, notably *One of Us* (1989; U.S. title, *The Iron Lady*), a biography of former prime minister Margaret Thatcher, and *This Blessed Plot* (1998), on Britain's relationship with continental Europe.

Zapp, Walter, Latvian-born inventor (b. Sept. 4, 1905, Riga, Latvia, Russian Empire—d. July 17, 2003, Binningen, Switz.), invented the Minox miniature camera. Zapp, essentially self-educated, invented a number of photographic improvements. In the early 1930s he conceived of the miniature camera, the first of which was produced in Latvia in 1938; a number of cameras were purchased for use by espionage agencies in several countries during World War II. Zapp relocated to Germany in 1941 and in 1945 established Minox GmbH to manufacture improved versions of the camera. After 1950 he served largely as a consultant to the firm.

Zevon, Warren, American singer-songwriter (b. Jan. 24, 1947, Chicago, Ill.—d. Sept. 7, 2003, Los Angeles, Calif.), was critically ac-

Singer Warren Zevon

claimed and much admired by a number of songwriters despite having had only one major hit, "Werewolves of London," from the album *Excitable Boy* (1978). He studied classical piano, was music director for the Everly Brothers, and wrote songs recorded by Linda Ronstadt and the Turtles before employing his rough-hewn baritone on albums such as *Warren Zevon* (1976) and *Sentimental Hygiene* (1987), featuring poetic songs that were by turns hard-boiled, humorous, tough, and tender. He survived inoperable lung cancer long enough to complete a final, touching album, *The Wind* (2003).

Zhang Aiping, Chinese general (b. 1910, Da county, Sichuan, China—d. July 5, 2003, Beijing, China), was a key player in modernizing China's armed forces. During World War II he commanded communist troops sent to rescue American aircrews after Lieut. Col. James H. Doolittle's daring raid against Tokyo. A decade later Zhang commanded an army corps that fought American forces during the Korean War (1950–53). As chairman of the National Defense Science and Technology Commission from 1975 until 1982, Zhang shepherded development of China's first nuclear-powered ballistic-missile submarine. From 1983 to 1988 he served as defense minister. Following retirement, in spring 1989 he unsuccessfully opposed the use of troops to suppress the pro-democracy protests that took place in Tiananmen Square.

Ziegler, Ronald Louis ("Ron"), American government official (b. May 12, 1939, Covington, Ky.—d. Feb. 10, 2003, Coronado, Calif.), as press secretary for Pres. Richard Nixon, characterized the infamous 1972 break-in at Democratic Party headquarters at Washington, D.C.'s Watergate Hotel as a "third-rate burglary." Ziegler worked as a press aide for Nixon when the latter was a candidate for governor of California in 1962 and again in the presidential election of 1968 before becoming the youngest-ever press secretary in 1969, at the age of 29. During this period television for the first time was playing a role in press conferences, which made Ziegler more visible than previous press secretaries. He was most remembered, however, for steadfastly holding the president's line as the Watergate scandal unraveled the administration, from the first news of the break-in until Nixon's resignation in 1974; Ziegler accompanied Nixon when he left Washington.

Press secretary Ron Ziegler

Zindel, Paul, American writer (b. May 15, 1936, Tottenville, Staten Island, N.Y.—d. March 27, 2003, New York, N.Y.), transformed incidents from his own troubled childhood and from the lives of the teenaged students whom he encountered throughout his 10 years as a high-school chemistry teacher into a Pulitzer Prize-winning play and a number of popular novels aimed at teens and addressing their issues and concerns. It was the play, *The Effect of Gamma Rays on Man-in-the-Moon Marigolds,* that first brought him to the public's attention. It was an Off-Broadway hit in 1970 before moving in 1971 to Broadway, where it ran for 819 performances and, besides the Pulitzer, won an Obie Award and the New York Drama Critics Circle Award. It was filmed in 1972. During his high-school years, Zindel wrote stories and plays, but he studied chemistry in college and became a teacher on Staten Island. He continued writing in his spare time, however, and in 1965 *The Effect of Gamma Rays on Man-in-the-Moon Marigolds* was produced in Houston, Texas. When an adaptation of it appeared on public television the following year, it attracted the attention of an editor who suggested that Zindel write a novel for teens. *The Pigman* (1968) not only was a success but was credited with having brought a heightened realism to teen fiction. Numerous novels followed, including *My Darling, My Hamburger* (1969), *Pardon Me, You're Stepping on My Eyeball* (1976), and *Confessions of a Teenage Baboon* (1977). In the meantime, Zindel was still writing plays, notably *And Miss Reardon Drinks a Little,* which opened on Broadway in 1971, and also wrote a few screenplays, including *Up the Sandbox* (1972) and *Runaway Train* (1986).

Zorina, Vera (Eva Brigitta Hartwig), German-born dancer and actress (b. Jan. 2, 1917, Berlin, Ger.—d. April 9, 2003, Santa Fe, N.M.), was a ballerina with the Ballet Russe de Monte Carlo for three years before attracting greater notice in 1936 as the star of the London production of *On Your Toes.* She went on to star in such other productions as the Hollywood film *The Goldwyn Follies* and the Broadway musical *I Married an Angel,* both in 1938, the same year she began her eight-year marriage to choreographer George Balanchine. In 1943 she originated the role of Terpsichore in Balanchine's ballet *Apollo.*

Ballerina Vera Zorina

Events of 2003

A procession of royal barges on the Chao Phraya River at Bangkok's Grand Palace welcomes delegates to the Asia-Pacific Economic Cooperation group in October.

AP/Wide World Photos

Agriculture and Food Supplies

Agricultural issues complicated international trade talks in MEXICO and common EU policies; GM FOODS were only slightly more welcome; BSE and AVIAN FLU came back; and increases in FISH FARMING offset a downturn in capture-fishery.

AGRICULTURAL PRODUCTION AND AID

Food Production. In 2003 global food production recovered from its 2002 drop but remained below 2001 levels. Severe weather conditions throughout the world hurt crops. At 883,780,000 metric tons, world coarse grain production for the 2003 crop was above the 869,910,000 metric tons of the 2002 crop but below the 892,420,000 metric tons of 2001. World rice production, at 391,300,000 metric tons (milled basis), was below the 398,600,000 metric tons of 2001 but above the 380,090,000 metric tons produced in 2002. World wheat output, at 550,510,000 metric tons, was below the 566,840,000 metric tons of 2002 and considerably below 2001's production of 581,860,000 metric tons. World oilseed production grew to 344,930,000 metric tons versus 328,960,000 metric tons in 2002 and 324,900,000 metric tons in 2001. That increase occurred despite the dry weather that reduced the U.S. soybean crop. World beef production in 2003 was 49,789,000 metric tons, slightly below the 51,033,000 metric tons of 2002 but above the 2001 level. Global pork production expanded from 86,030,000 metric tons in 2002 to 87,204,000 metric tons, while poultry meat production, at 52,833,000 metric tons, was unchanged from the previous year.

In the midst of the worst drought in more than 10 years, villagers in India's Gujarat state gather for water at a well in Natwarghad.

© Amit Dave/Reuters 2003

With global trade in crops remaining near recent levels, global ending stocks fell and prices were strong. Global wheat stocks fell from 201,110,000 metric tons at the 2001 harvest to 127,930,000 metric tons, the tightest in recent years. Global coarse grains stocks, which were 176,540,000 in crop year 2001, fell to 105,940,000 metric tons. Rice and oilseed stocks were also lower. As a result, prices strengthened, especially compared with the low prices of the late 1990s, 2000, and 2001.

Food Aid. Food assistance was again critical for some regions; southern and eastern Africa, especially, struggled with acute shortages. The 2002 crops in southern Africa were sharply reduced by inadequate precipitation, and until the 2003 crops were harvested, millions of people depended on international assistance. Drought in East Africa and political turmoil in Zimbabwe contributed to the hardships, as did the spread of HIV/AIDS in the region, which caused high death rates among the economically active population. North Korea was again unable to provide adequate food for its population. Damaged infrastructure and poor security in rural areas hindered food production and delivery in Afghanistan, and the war and its aftermath in Iraq damaged agricultural production and complicated deliveries of international food assistance.

AGRICULTURAL POLICY

International Trade Negotiations. The ongoing World Trade Organization (WTO) talks, which had been launched in Doha, Qatar, in 2001, were called the Doha Development Round because they were intended to assist less-developed countries (LDCs) in conducting trade, gaining access to markets in developed countries, and reducing trade-distorting policies of developed nations. The delegates hoped by the end of March to set a framework for a full ministerial meeting in Cancún, Mex., in September. Initial proposals by member states, however, revealed a great disparity of views on reforms. Compromise proved impossible, and the March deadline passed. A measure of agreement between the European Union and the United States reached

Greenpeace activists protest the use of genetically modified corn (maize) with a mock cornfield in front of Berlin's Reichstag.

in August revived hopes that negotiations in Cancún would succeed, but the LDCs were suspicious that the U.S. and the EU were intent on excluding them from the process.

The ministers who met in Cancún in September were unable to move forward. The Americans and the Europeans wanted a loosening of government purchasing, services, and investment as well as the establishment of rules to facilitate trade and regulate competition in exchange for liberalizing their agricultural policies. The LDCs sought specific concessions, including the elimination of export and domestic subsidies to farmers in developed countries and improved access to markets in the developed countries. The ministers adjourned without agreement but with the hope that the process might be rekindled in early 2004.

Following the collapse of the WTO negotiations, U.S. trade policy concentrated on expanding regional and bilateral trade agreements. Negotiations with several states, including Morocco and Australia, were under way, and a trade agreement with four Latin American countries was reached in mid-December. The Free Trade Area of the Americas was one regional association of interest to the U.S., but FTAA talks in November stalled partly over agricultural issues. Brazil, one of the leaders of the group that opposed the U.S. stand at Cancún, wanted agricultural issues to be prominent in the FTAA talks, while the U.S. sought to have agriculture covered in the WTO negotiations.

European Agricultural Policy. In June the EU made some changes in its Common Agricultural Policy (CAP). Beginning in 2005, farm subsidies would be partially decoupled; that is, subsidies would no longer be tied to actual farm production. The extent of decoupling would vary by commodity. Support would be cut for producers of butter and powdered milk but not for grain producers. This reform was intended to smooth the way for EU enlargement in 2004. Agricultural policy had been a stumbling block for EU expansion, because most potential entrants had large agricultural sectors.

Genetically Modified (GM) Food. The EU's moratorium on approvals of genetically modified food products continued to be an issue. In May the U.S., Argentina, Canada, and Egypt went before the WTO to challenge the legality of the moratorium. In July the EU adopted new rules on labeling and traceability of food containing GM material in July. The new rules presented an opportunity to end the moratorium, but they did not defuse the trade dispute because they expanded the scope of previous labeling requirements. Under the new rules food containing more than 0.9% GM material would have to be labeled, and processed products made from GM plants would have to be labeled. Countries that exported GM crops and food products complained of continued discrimination and pressed their case at the WTO.

Meanwhile, global production of GM crops expanded. Most of the soybeans grown in the U.S. and Argentina and a large proportion of U.S. corn (maize) were genetically modified. Farmers in Canada, China, India, Indonesia, and South Africa grew GM crops ranging from soybeans and canola to cotton. At the same time, GM research continued on vitamin-enriched rice, virus-resistant sweet potatoes, drought-resistant barley, and protein-enriched potatoes, all important crops for LDCs. Brazil, which had banned GM soybeans, seemed to be vacillating: authorities there allowed the planting and sale of GM soybeans for one year.

Livestock Disease. Animal diseases were again in the news in 2003. In February a man in Hong Kong died from avian influenza after visiting relatives in China proper. Also in February avian influenza was detected in The Netherlands, and some 20% of that nation's poultry was destroyed; production in neighbouring Belgium and Germany was also affected. In March Japan temporarily banned U.S. poultry sales following a report of an outbreak of the disease in Connecticut. Later in the year incidences of exotic Newcastle disease (END) in the western U.S. resulted in the placement of affected states under quarantine.

The beef market was disrupted with the discovery in May of a Canadian cow with bovine spongiform encephalopathy (BSE, or mad cow disease). Canadian exports of cattle and beef and other ruminant products were banned. This devastated the Canadian beef and cattle industry insofar as exports, mostly to the U.S., accounted for more than half of the industry's output. Canadian authorities traced the sick animal's history and tested other animals but found no additional cases. In August the U.S. allowed controlled imports of Canadian beef and ruminant products, although trade restrictions remained throughout 2003. In late December a cow in Washington state tested positive for BSE, the first case ever in the U.S. Beef prices and stock prices for fast-food restaurants plunged as many countries banned American beef and domestic consumers showed some nervousness. On December 30 U.S. Department of Agriculture officials sought to shore up confidence in American beef production by banning the use as food or feed additives of all animals that were too old or too sick to stand up and by inaugurating a tracking system for all American slaughter cattle.

Country of Origin Labeling. Controversy continued over country of origin labeling (COOL) mandated by the 2002 U.S. farm bill and scheduled to start in September 2004. Advocates said that COOL would certify the safety of meat products and boost demand; opponents argued that the system was too costly, violated world trade rules, and would not increase demand. Decisions on the implementation of COOL were deferred until 2004. (PHILIP L. PAARLBERG)

FISHERIES

The UN Food and Agriculture Organization (FAO) indicated that in 2001, the latest year for which figures were available, the total production for the world's capture fisheries decreased by 3.34% from the 2000 figure to a total of 92,356,034 metric tons. The marine capture fisheries recorded a fall of 2,987,823 metric tons to 83,663,276 metric tons, while the output from freshwater fisheries declined 95,963 metric tons to 8,692,758 metric tons. These results overturned the increases recorded during 2000.

Despite this decrease of nearly 2.5 million metric tons, the overall world supply of fish during 2001 remained stable at 130.2 million metric tons, with aquaculture production rising by 2.4 million metric tons to offset the capture fishery falloff. It was estimated that about 31 million metric tons, almost all from industrial marine capture fisheries, were used for reduction to fish meal and fish oil products.

The major reason for the decline in marine fishery production was the continuing fluctuation in the catch of anchoveta (Peruvian anchovy). In 2000 the anchoveta catch recorded a 29.27% increase, while the total production for 2001 declined by 4.06 million metric tons (36.03%), although it remained the top species in terms of total tonnage caught. (*See* GRAPH.) These fluctuations in the catch of anchoveta were closely related to changing natural and environmental conditions affecting the seas off the coasts of Peru and Chile, most notably El Niño. Excluding anchoveta, global capture production had remained relatively stable since 1995. Of the other top species caught, Chilean jack mackerel jumped from sixth place to third with an increase of 968,340 metric tons (62.86%) over the 2000 catch, while Atlantic herring recorded a 427,708-metric-ton (17.6%) decrease in catch and fell to fourth. Of those species outside the top five caught, blue whiting, chub mackerel, and capelin showed significant increases.

The leading fishing nation was again China, with total production of 16,529,389 metric tons, a small 2.7% decrease from the 2000 figure. There was an ongoing debate over the accuracy of the figures reported for China's output of both capture fishery and aquaculture production. Many experts believed that China's figures should be listed separately; the FAO was criticized during 2002 for reportedly overestimating significantly China's capture production in the organization's annual fishery statistics.

Peru remained the second top producing nation, despite a decline in anchoveta landings that resulted in the total catch's dropping by 2,670,000 million metric tons (25.07%) to 7,986,103 metric tons in 2001. The U.S., Indonesia, and India recorded increases in production, while Japan, Chile, and Russia declined in the total tonnage of fish landed and fell in the relative rankings. (*See* GRAPH.) Outside the top 10 producing nations, the performances of Morocco, which had a 20.8% increase in catch to 1,083,276 metric tons, and South Africa, whose fish catch rose by 17.4% to 755,345 metric tons, were worthy of note. (MARTIN J. GILL)

Production Trends for the Top 10 Catching Nations, 1992–2001
(in metric tons)

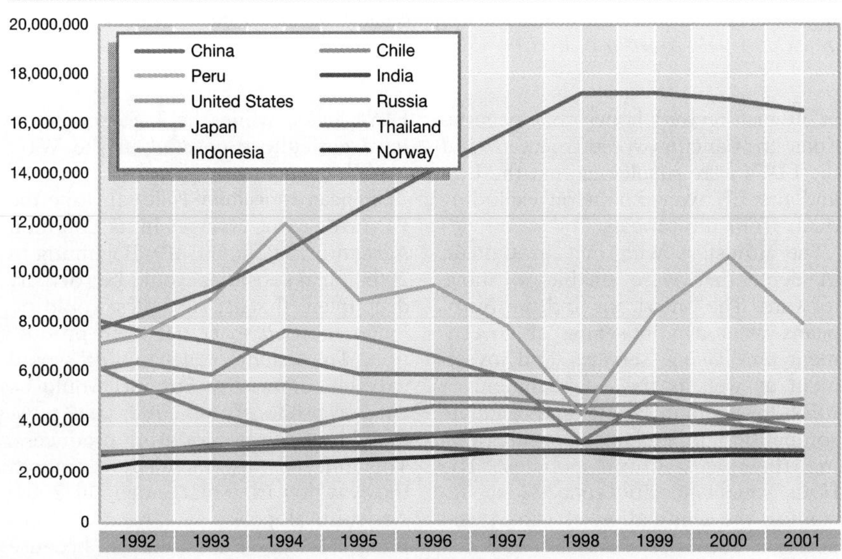

Catch Trends for the Top Five Caught Fish Species, 1992–2001
(in metric tons)

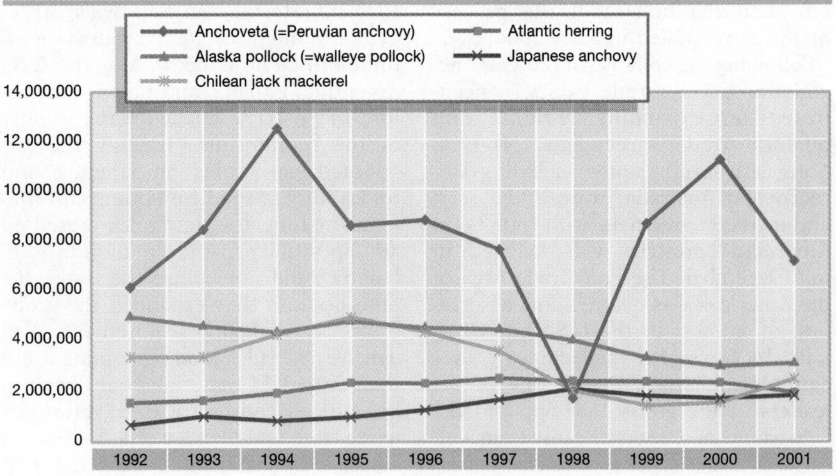

Anthropology and Archaeology

New FOSSIL FINDS strengthen the case for the OUT-OF-AFRICA model. The James ossuary—a top find in 2002—is declared a FAKE, while Iraqi historical artifacts are PLUNDERED. Discoveries in Mexico push back the date of the earliest human habitation in North America and shed more light on the OLMEC civilization.

ANTHROPOLOGY

In 2003 an international paleoanthropological research team described what were believed to be the oldest-known members of the human species. The fossilized crania of one immature and two adult individuals were recovered in 1997 along with an upper molar, an upper premolar, and a series of parietal fragments from the Herto Member of the Bouri Formation in the Middle Awash area of Ethiopia's Afar Depression. These fossils were argon-isotope dated to between 154,000 and 160,000 years ago. Associated layers of sediment contained a number of artifacts of similar age that exhibited a combination of Middle Stone Age and late Acheulean technology, as well as evidence for the butchery of large mammals. Because they were deemed to represent a population that was on the verge of anatomical modernity but were not yet fully modern, these fossils were classified as a new subspecies of *Homo sapiens, Homo sapiens idaltu*. The subspecies name (*idaltu*) means "elder" in the local Afar language. The more complete of the two adult crania had a combination of features characteristic of rugged archaic, early modern, and more recent human populations. The estimated cranial capacity was 1,450 cc (1 cc = about 0.06 cu in), at the high end of the modern human range (the second adult cranium may have been an even larger individual). The better-preserved specimen was interpreted as a male with the following features: high and especially long cranium, globular braincase, thick cranial vault, prominent browridges, large and heavily worn dentition, and a deep, tall, and broad face with moderate alveolar prognathism. All three of the Herto crania displayed extensive cultural modification consistent with mortuary practices rather than cannibalism. Overall, the Herto crania were placed somewhere between the more primitive morphology of earlier African specimens such as those from Bodo and Kabwe in Zambia and later anatomically modern specimens such as those from Klasies in South Africa and Kafzeh in Israel. The authors suggested that *H. rhodesiensis* (i.e., Bodo and Kabwe) was ultimately ancestral to *H. sapiens idaltu,* which in turn gave rise to *H. sapiens sapiens* in Africa. This would exclude Neanderthals from any significant contribution to the ancestry of modern humans and thereby strengthen the case for the out-of-Africa model rather than the multiregional model of human origins. The potential import of these Ethiopian fossils was underscored by the recently reported genetic finding that the oldest versions of human mitochondrial (mt)DNA arose some 170,000 years ago and are today found in the Sandawe people of Tanzania and !Kung San of the Kalahari, both of whom may have roots in northeastern Africa, including Ethiopia.

*This artist's rendering of a Herto man (***Homo sapiens idaltu***) shows a strikingly modern appearance, differentiated from that of modern man (***Homo sapiens sapiens***) mostly by his longer cranium and more pronounced browridges.*

Reconstruction drawing of *Homo sapiens idaltu* by Jay H. Matternes © 2003; from cover of *Nature* magazine, Vol. 423, pp. 742–747, "Pleistocene *Homo sapiens* from Middle Awash, Ethiopia," by Tim D. White et al.

Additional evidence that Neanderthals did not make a major genetic contribution to the human gene pool came from the mtDNA sequences extracted from two 23,000–25,000-year-old anatomically modern *H. sapiens sapiens* specimens that a Spanish-Italian research team recovered from the Paglicci cave in southern Italy. DNA was extracted from both a rib and a femur for the two specimens, and the results were consistent and clear-cut: the mtDNA of these individuals fell well within the range of modern human mtDNA but differed sharply from the four available sequences of the Neanderthals. (Neanderthals as a group probably died out sometime between 25,000 and 30,000 years ago.) These findings were also interpreted to support the out-of-Africa model, although some anthropological geneticists questioned whether contamination from modern mtDNA could be ruled out completely.

The Paglicci specimens brought the total sample of mtDNAs extracted from ancient anatomically modern human individuals to six, the oldest of which was reported in 2001 to be the 62,000 ±6,000-year-old Lake Mungo 3 specimen from the Willandra

Lakes region in southeastern Australia. This date proved to be erroneous (as was the 20,000–25,000-year-old date for Lake Mungo 1) according to a new analysis based on 25 dates derived from optically stimulated luminescence signals from quartz. Both Mungo burials were redated to 40,000±2,000 years ago, which would be synchronous with, or soon after, the initial human occupation of northern and western Australia some 46,000 to 50,000 years ago. Although these two Lake Mungo specimens were contemporaneous with Eurasian Neanderthals, their mtDNAs differed greatly from Neanderthal mtDNA. More perplexing, however, was the finding that three of the four Lake Mungo specimens had mtDNA closely related to the mtDNA of modern Australian Aboriginal Peoples, while the Lake Mungo 3 individual had a unique mtDNA lineage that diverged from all known fossil and contemporary human mtDNAs. Rather than supporting the multiregional model as was originally proposed, anthropological geneticists hypothesized that this was just one of many examples of an African mtDNA lineage's becoming extinct over the past 150,000–200,000 years. (STEPHEN L. ZEGURA)

ARCHAEOLOGY

Eastern Hemisphere. The year 2003 was marked not only by discovery but by scandal and wanton destruction. In early April the Iraq Museum in Baghdad was stripped of thousands of artifacts that chronicled some 6,000 years of human history. Although an estimated 3,000 of these objects were later returned, many thousands more remained unaccounted for. Hundreds surfaced in London, Paris, and New York City; others were intercepted at the Jordanian border. Still more devastating, because the uncataloged artifacts were untraceable, was the systematic looting of Iraq's archaeological sites, particularly those in the south. At the 5,000-year-old Sumerian sites of Umma, Isin, and Adab, hundreds combed the ruins for treasures to sell on the art market.

Considered by many to be "the find of the century" when it was discovered in 2002, the "James ossuary" was in 2003 declared a forgery by the Israel Antiquities Authority (IAA). The ossuary, which bore an Aramaic inscription, "James, son of Joseph, brother of Jesus," was purported to be the earliest-known artifact associated with the founder of Christianity. The IAA alleged that the ossuary was the handiwork of Oded Golan, who also was associated with the so-called Jehoash inscription, purported to be a 2,800-year-old account of repairs made to Solomon's Temple in Jerusalem following its destruction by the Babylonians. Scholars were quick to point out that the text of that inscription, written in a Hebrew-Phoenician script, was riddled with grammatical errors and, like the ossuary, was clearly a fake. The report of the IAA was generally, but not universally, accepted.

Elsewhere in Israel, excavations undertaken at Kibbutz Kfar HaHoresh near Nazareth—Jesus' boyhood home—revealed that the area was a major cult centre 9,000 years before the time of Christ. According to site investigator Nigel Goring-Morris of Hebrew University in Jerusalem, 65 enigmatic burials found in burnished lime-plaster tombs were unearthed. A headless man was interred on top of 250 aurochs (wild ox) bones, four children were buried with fox jawbones, and several other individuals were buried with flint tools. The archaeological team also found three skulls that had been defleshed shortly after death and then covered in lime plaster sculpted to resemble human facial features. Two of the plastered skulls had been painted red. Kilns used to make the lime plaster were discovered nearby.

While widening a riverbed to prevent flash floods at the ancient Macedonian site of Dion in northern Greece, contractors discovered a previously unknown sanctuary to Zeus Hypsistos, the supreme god of ancient Greece. Archaeologists subsequently excavated the site and found a 2,400-year-old headless cult statue of the god holding a thunderbolt and sceptre and bearing an inscription of his name. They also found 14 large marble column blocks decorated with eagles, a symbol of the god.

The most northerly Ice Age cave art and the first ever found in Britain—a suite of 12,000-year-old engravings of various creatures—was discovered at Creswell Crags in central England. The faint engravings were similar in style to those at Lascaux Grotto in France and Altamira in Spain. Archaeologists at the University of Innsbruck, Austria, announced the discovery of the largest-known hoard of Bronze Age weapons and jewelry to date. Dated to between 1550 and 1250 BC, the approximately 360 objects—including swords, axes, spearheads, sickles, jewelry, and part of a bronze helmet—were recovered from an offering pit at Moosbruckschrofen am Piller in Tirol. The helmet was of particular interest because only one other helmet of similar antiquity was known. The other, made of leather and boars' tusks, had been found

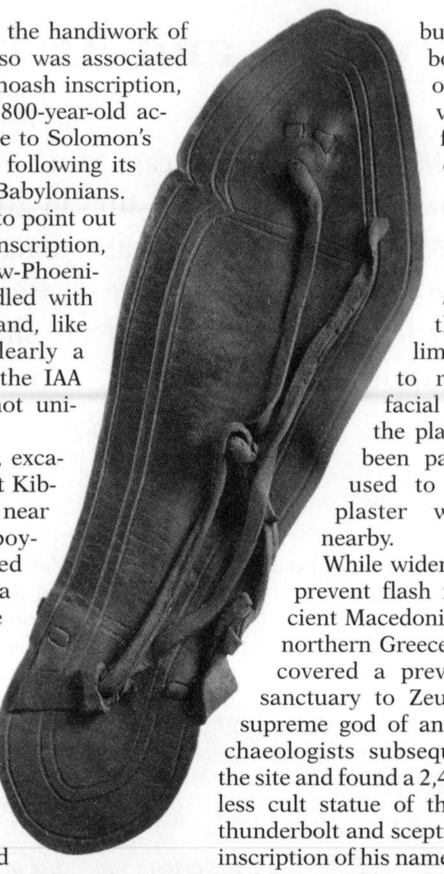

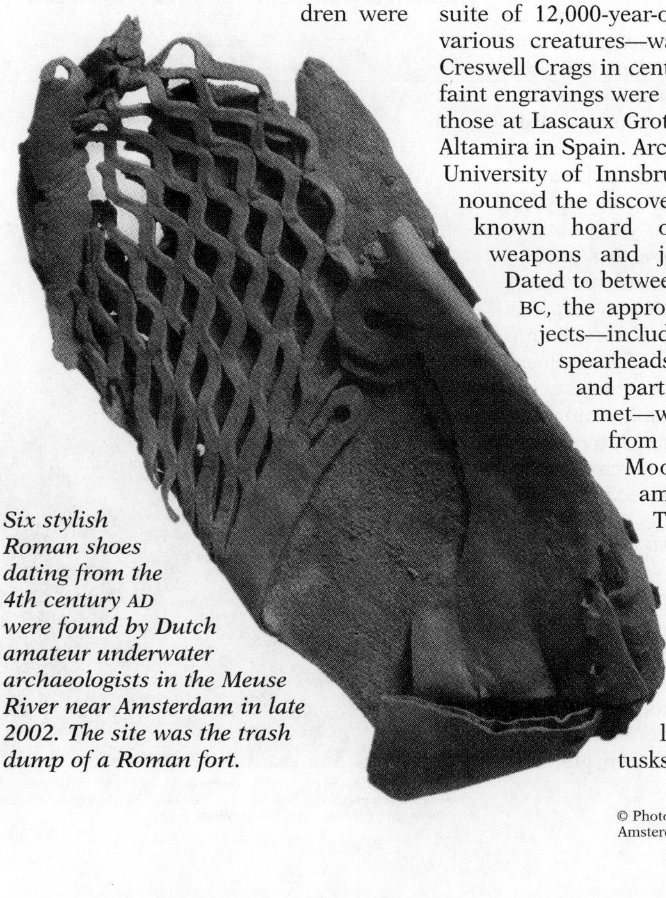

Six stylish Roman shoes dating from the 4th century AD were found by Dutch amateur underwater archaeologists in the Meuse River near Amsterdam in late 2002. The site was the trash dump of a Roman fort.

in the early 1960s at Dendra, Crete, Greece. What was believed to be the finest and largest Viking hoard ever found on the Isle of Man was brought to light in March. The cache contained 464 coins of Hiberno-Norse and Anglo-Saxon type, 25 ingots, and a large silver armlet all dating to c. AD 1020. In the Meuse River southeast of Amsterdam, a cache of 4th-century AD Roman shoes was discovered. The six complete shoes had been discarded in an ancient garbage dump near the site of a Roman fort. Archaeologists working in Hadrian's Villa at Tivoli, Italy, identified a recently excavated colonnaded building as a memorial to Antinoüs, the Roman emperor's young lover who drowned in the Nile in AD 130 and was later deified. A statue of Antinoüs dressed as the Egyptian god Osiris had been found at the site when systematic excavations began there in the 18th century.

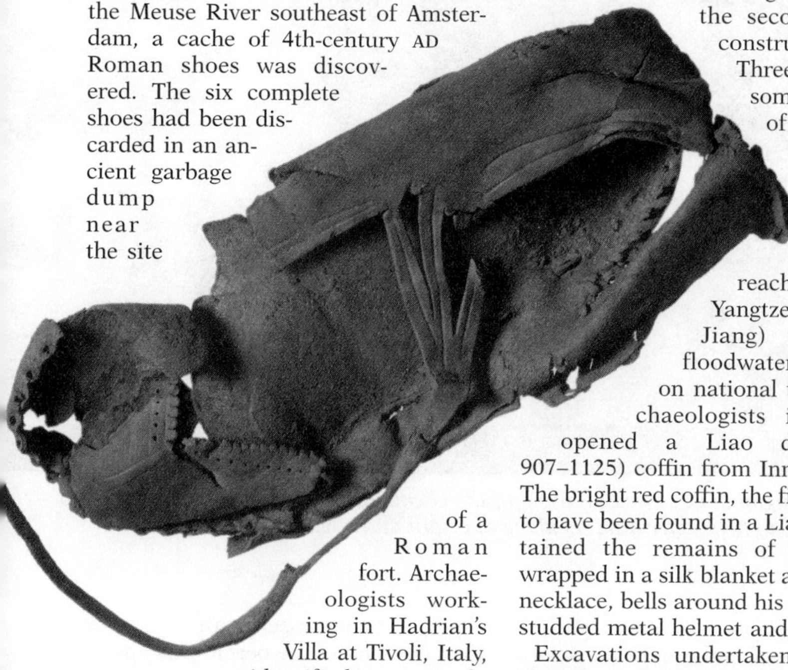

In China's Henan province archaeologists discovered a 2,500-year-old royal tomb, the largest ever found in China. The 35-m (115-ft)-long tomb, which dated to the Spring and Autumn Period (770–476 BC) of the Eastern Zhou dynasty, was composed of more than 18 pits that contained the remains of elaborate horse-drawn carriages, the bones of horses, and numerous ornate jade and metal objects. The quality of the tomb's contents, as well its location in an area thought to have been a royal cemetery, led archaeologists to posit that the burial was likely that of a king of the Zheng state. The tomb predated by some 300 years the famous tomb of China's first emperor, Shi Huangdi (c. 259–210 BC), in Xi'an. Beijing officials in the summer of 2003 enacted the first laws to protect China's Great Wall. A series of defenses built between the 7th century BC and the 16th century AD, the Great Wall, which stretched some 6,700 km (4,160 mi) across the Chinese landscape, was ravaged not only by time but by development, uncontrolled tourism, and outright vandalism. Unfortunately, the new laws protected only the famed section of the wall just outside Beijing. Following completion of the second phase of construction of the Three Gorges Dam, some 1,200 sites of historical and archaeological importance that once lined the middle reaches of China's Yangtze River (Chang Jiang) vanished as floodwaters rose. Live on national television, archaeologists in Mongolia opened a Liao dynasty (AD 907–1125) coffin from Inner Mongolia. The bright red coffin, the first of its kind to have been found in a Liao tomb, contained the remains of a nobleman wrapped in a silk blanket and wearing a necklace, bells around his ankles, and a studded metal helmet and mask.

Excavations undertaken by the Archaeological Survey of India (ASI) revealed what was purported to be evidence of a 10th-century Hindu temple at the site of the Babri Mosque in Ayodhya, Uttar Pradesh. The 16th-century mosque had been demolished in December 1992 by Hindu fundamentalists who believed that it stood atop the birthplace of Rama, one of the most revered deities of the Hindu pantheon. The ASI findings, which were called into question, only fueled what was already a highly charged political atmosphere.

(ANGELA M.H. SCHUSTER)

Western Hemisphere. A broad spectrum of archaeological discoveries absorbed the attention of archaeologists in 2003. It had long been suspected that people lived in the Americas before the well-known Clovis hunter-gatherers of 10,000 BC. A series of human skulls found in central Mexico in 1959 and stored in the National Museum of Anthropology, Mexico City, were radiocarbon dated by a team of British and Mexican researchers. The craniums date to about 13,000 years ago, to the earliest centuries of human occupation, which occurred soon after the Ice Age, perhaps as early as 15,000 years ago.

Ancient native American society was more highly developed than once suspected. For instance, it is now known that Double Ditch, a Mandan Indian site in North Dakota, was one of the largest prehistoric settlements on the Great Plains, with more than 3,000 inhabitants in the late 1300s AD. University of Arkansas archaeologist Ken Kvamme discovered hitherto-unknown earthen fortifications that once surrounded the settlement, incorporating earthen mounds and steep-sided ditches about 3 m (10 ft) deep along the defensive line. This important discovery served as eloquent testimony to the sophistication of the Mandan long before European contact.

More evidence of sophistication came from the Grossmann site in southern Illinois, a ceremonial centre of the Mississippian culture occupied in the 12th century AD. University of Illinois archaeologist Timothy Pauketat excavated a large Grossmann house with limestone flooring that contained deposits of limonite and ochre, often used as pigments for body paint. Pauketat believed this was a ceremonial structure associated with the Green Corn Ceremony, a harvest festival. Nearby lay pits containing charred seeds, cordage, and quartz crystals that may have come from Arkansas. The cordage and associated matting may have been containers for corn burned in the pit, part of the rituals and feasting that coincided with harvest.

The Olmec people of lowland Mexico contributed much to Mesoamerican civilization. It has been shown that they were pioneers of written script. The San Andrés site on the Gulf of Mexico was occupied by Olmec in about 650 BC. Archaeologist Mary Pohl of Florida State University uncovered the remains of a feast, which included some cylinder seals used to imprint objects. One of the seals depicts a bird, perhaps commemorating a royal leader. Symbols that resemble later Maya hieroglyphs emerge from the figure's mouth. One of them depicts the *ajaw* glyph, which was a name for a king and a name for a day in the Maya calendar. Pohl believed that these symbols represent words or ideas, the first stages of writing. The San Andrés symbols may be the earliest writing known from the New World.

The great city of Teotihuacán on the edge of the basin of Mexico continued to yield spectacular discoveries. Some of them testified to the city's complex relationship with Maya civilization. Three seated burials from the depths of the Pyramid of the Moon dating to the 4th century AD lay with shells, obsidian

Rollout photograph #K2784 © Justin Kerr

Archaeologists at the Smithsonian Institution in Washington, D.C., used analysis of the chemical composition of the clay in this painted vase, probably owned by a Mayan noble, to help determine its place of origin and suggest something of its provenance.

(volcanic glass), and jade ceremonial objects, including some in the Maya style. The new Moon Pyramid burials were clearly those of important people. All the previously discovered skeletons had been those of sacrificial victims. Archaeologists had long known that there were extensive contacts between the people of Teotihuacán and the cities of the Maya lowlands, documented from pottery, architectural styles, and religious imagery. The newly found burials provided confirmation from their jade beads and ear spools, as well as a jade figurine that may be of Maya origin.

High-technology archaeology and newly deciphered hieroglyphs on painted pots provided new clues about ancient Maya history. Such vessels were often formal gifts exchanged between lords. Hieroglyphic texts dedicate the vessel and list the contents—chocolate, tamales, or corn gruel, for example. The scenes on the pot contain glyphs that record the names of the individuals in the scene, their titles, and the event depicted, as well as, sometimes, its date. Using chemical fingerprinting of the clay, it is sometimes possible to trace the place of origin of the vessel. In one recent case, Smithsonian Institution scientists studied a vessel of unknown origin that depicts a red-painted building decorated with images of supernatural beings. Inside, six nobles participate in a rite of enthronement. A lord sits on a throne covered with decorated cloth and a plaited mat, his back supported by a pillow. At right, a kneeling figure, perhaps the artist, presents a tray to the lord. His signature frames his head. Chemical fingerprinting of the clay placed the vessel at the Maan site in the little-known La Florida region of Guatemala. The pot inscription suggests that the vessel may have been a formal gift from the lord of Maan to the Ikí lord Chuy-ti-Chan, an official representative of the Ik state, southwest of the city of Tikal in Guatemala's Petén.

The dry climate of Peru's desert coast continued to yield unusual discoveries. Peruvian archaeologists reconstructed a human sacrifice conducted on a beach 200 km (120 mi) north of Lima in the late 14th century AD. The skeletons of 200 men bound with ropes at the ankles and wrists lay under a thin layer of sand. The victims had knelt and then had been stabbed through the heart, toppling over forward or onto their sides into the sand. Larvae from several generations of flies infested the victims' hair, which showed that the bodies had been watched over for several days by relatives to keep away carrion-eating animals until the corpses vanished under blowing sand. A large fishing net, ropes, and clay vessels with food lay at the other end of the beach, perhaps offerings for the afterlife left by surviving family members. Textiles covering several of the victims' faces were in the Chimú style. The research team believed that the Chimú ruler Minchancaman sacrificed the fishermen in gratitude to the sea god Ni after a successful campaign of conquest in the area.

Finally, new diving technologies resulted in important underwater discoveries in the Western Hemisphere. The paddle steamer *Portland* foundered in a gale off the coast of Massachusetts in 1898 with the loss of 190 passengers and crew. Using remote diving apparatuses, National Oceanic and Atmospheric Administration (NOAA) scientists found the ship standing upright on the sea bottom. Farther south, NOAA specialists working 32 km (20 mi) off the coast of North Carolina raised the turret of the USS *Monitor,* which lay 72 m (240 ft) below the surface. Navy divers recovered the 150-ton revolving turret, the first of its kind on any ship. It rested in a tank of chilled water at the Mariners' Museum in Newport News, Va. Conservation of the turret, which contained the remains of some of the 16 seamen who perished in the wreck, was expected to take as long as 15 years.

(BRIAN FAGAN)

Architecture and Civil Engineering

Libeskind's plans for the rebuilding of the WORLD TRADE CENTER were approved, Gehry's spectacular WALT DISNEY CONCERT HALL made its debut, and Ludwig Mies van der Rohe's famous FARNSWORTH HOUSE was purchased by a preservation group.

ARCHITECTURE

The biggest architectural story of 2003 continued to be the World Trade Center (WTC) site in New York City. In February a proposal by Polish-born American architect Daniel Libeskind (*see* BIOGRAPHIES) was selected as the master plan for the rebuilding of the site, winning a design competition over proposals submitted by six other teams of prominent architects. Libeskind, best known as the architect of the Jewish Museum Berlin, proposed a semicircular group of glass towers in sharp, bold angular shapes. (*See* Sidebar.) Meanwhile, a second competition was held to choose a design for the memorial to the victims of the Sept. 11, 2001, terrorist attacks that destroyed the WTC. This was open to anyone in the world, and 5,201 designs were submitted, the most ever in a design competition. They were judged by a 14-person special jury. In November the jury announced eight designs as finalists, all of them by relatively young and little-known designers. A final winner was expected to be chosen in January 2004.

Awards. The $100,000 Pritzker Prize, regarded as the architectural equivalent of a Nobel Prize, went to 85-year-old Danish architect Jørn Utzon. He was best known for his Sydney Opera House, a dramatic building of bold curving roof forms that resemble sails on the harbour in Sydney, Australia. The Opera House took 14 years to build and cost far more than was anticipated. Utzon was fired during construction. Nonetheless, the building became a world-famous landmark, and the Pritzker Prize was seen as a vindication of the architect. Pritzker juror Frank Gehry said it "changed the image of an entire country." The American Institute of Architects awarded its annual Gold Medal for lifetime achievement to the late Samuel ("Sambo") Mockbee, who died at the age of 57 in 2001. Mockbee, a winner of the MacArthur "genius" award, was best known as the founder of the Rural Studio, where architectural students designed and built homes and other structures for low-income people in rural Alabama. "Architecture Loses Its Conscience" was the headline in one architectural magazine announcing Mockbee's death. The AIA presented its 25-Year Award, given to an American building that had proved its worth over time, to the Design Research Headquarters Building in Cambridge, Mass., a faceted glass building that functions as a transparent display case for the products inside. It was designed by the late Benjamin Thompson. The AIA also announced its annual Honor Awards for good design to 15 individual buildings. Among the more notable were the Concert Hall and Exhibition Complex in Rouen, France, by Bernard Tschumi; the American Folk Art Museum in New York City, by Tod Williams and Billie Tsien; the Diamond Ranch High School in Pomona, Calif., by Thom Mayne of Morphosis; and Simmons Hall dormitory at the Massachusetts Institute of Technology, by Stephen Holl. A new prize, the $100,000 Driehaus Prize for Classical Architecture, was awarded to Léon Krier, a prominent advocate for traditional design and an adviser to Prince Charles of the United Kingdom. The Royal Gold Medal of the Royal Institute of British Architects went to the Spanish architect José Rafael Moneo, known for such buildings as the Cathedral of Our Lady of the Angels in Los Angeles and the National Museum of Roman Art in Mérida, Spain.

Cultural and Civic Buildings. Easily the most discussed building of the year, if not the decade, was the Walt Disney Concert Hall in downtown Los Angeles, which opened in October after an agonizing 16-year period of design and construction. Designed by Gehry, the Hall won near-unanimous raves for both its architecture and its acoustics. Like Gehry's earlier Guggenheim Museum in Bilbao, Spain, the Disney's exterior featured bold curving shapes covered in shining metal and was often said to resemble a ship under full sail. The walls and ceiling of the interior concert hall were also shaped in sweeping curves. They were finished in warm-toned wood, which gave the concertgoer the sense of being inside an enormous cello. Earlier in the year, Gehry's performing arts centre at Bard

Excitement ran high in Los Angeles over the official opening on October 23 of the long-planned Walt Disney Concert Hall, distinguished by architect Frank Gehry's signature bold curving metallic shapes.

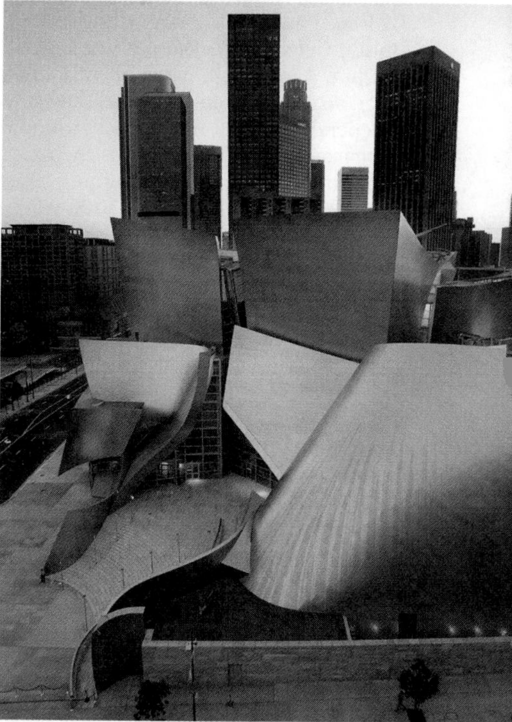

AP/Wide World Photos

College north of New York City also won plaudits for its sound. The acoustic consultant for both buildings was Yasuhisa Toyota of Japan. In Rome the Parco della Musica by Renzo Piano opened. It was a complex of three concert halls of different sizes, all in biomorphic bloblike shapes, grouped around an outdoor amphitheatre. In Fort Worth, Texas, Tadao Ando's Modern Art Museum opened; it was most memorable for its Y-shaped concrete columns that were dramatically reflected in a pool of water. Iraqi-born architect Zaha Hadid (*see* BIOGRAPHIES), who practiced out of London, won attention for her Contemporary Arts Center in Cincinnati, Ohio. It was the first major building for this architect, long known for daring designs that usually did not get built. The Arts Center was a bold composition of boxlike galleries, piled up in a seemingly precarious manner. Hadid's dramatic ski jump and aerial café in Innsbruck, Austria, opened in fall 2002, and she was in the process of completing designs for an art centre to be attached to the celebrated Price Tower by Frank Lloyd Wright in Bartlesville, Okla. In Beacon, N.Y., the Dia Art Foundation opened Dia:Beacon. This was a former printing plant converted into a museum not by an architect but by the artist Robert Irwin. Its brilliantly skylit spaces proved to be a perfect setting for the work of the minimalist artists whom the foundation sponsored. A new home for the Liberty Bell in Philadelphia was designed by Bohlin Cywinski Jackson. It was a glass pavilion, angled in such a way that when visitors looked at the bell they saw Independence Hall in the background.

Commercial Buildings. Perhaps the most remarkable commercial building was the 40-story office tower at 30 St Mary Axe in London, by Foster and Partners. Shaped like a fat cigar and covered in triangles of glass that looked like fishnet, the tower featured wedge-shaped glassed atriums that spiraled up the sides of the tower to encourage natural ventilation. In the Atacama Desert of Chile, the ESO (European Southern Observatory) hotel was a residential building for an astronomical observatory. In the moonscapelike desert, it resembled a natural rock ridge, with its surfaces of concrete coloured by iron oxide to imitate the reddish hues of the desert. In Oslo the Telenor World Headquarters was an experimental building intended as the ultimate in flexibility. Office workers did not have work stations but instead plugged in anywhere

Nigel Young

Sir Norman Foster made another eye-catching change in London's skyline with his 40-story Swiss Re tower, named 30 St Mary Axe. The spirals of glass-clad atriums not only gave the building its pineconelike appearance but also helped ventilate it.

in the building as needed, sometimes using a screensaver of family photos and notes as the equivalent of a personal tackboard. The architect was NBBJ of the United States in collaboration with Norwegian architects. In The Netherlands the architecture firm MVRDV created the Silodam housing complex, a long 10-story building on the harbour in Amsterdam. The great variety of types and sizes of apartments inside were reflected by the many colours and shapes of the facade.

Future Buildings, Competitions, and Controversies. Two young New York architects won a competition for the design of a Washington, D.C., memorial to the victims of September 11. Julie Beckman and Keith Kaseman's design provided a parklike setting with a "light bench" for each of the 184 victims of the attack on the Pentagon and the downed American Airlines Flight 77. Beneath each bench would be a pool of water, mysteriously lit from below. A competition for an Air Force Memorial was won by New York architect James Ingo Freed, designer of the United States Holocaust Memorial Museum in Washington, D.C. Freed proposed three stainless-steel spires that curved away from each other, like planes peeling off in formation. Swiss architects Herzog & de Meuron won a competition to design the Olympic stadium for the Games to be held in Beijing in 2008. One much-hyped building proposal died in New York City when it was announced that a proposed $950 million branch of the Guggenheim Museum, to be raised on piers over the East River and designed by Gehry, would not be built because of the museum's economic problems.

Preservation. The World Monuments Fund issued a list of the 100 most endangered sites. Notable entries were the Great Wall of China Cultural Landscape, all of historic Lower Manhattan, and Wright's Ennis-Brown House in Los Angeles. Meanwhile, in Buffalo, N.Y., an elaborate restoration of Wright's Darwin D. Martin House of 1904 was under way. A competition to design a visitor centre for it was won by Toshiko Mori, chairman of the architecture program at Harvard University. Also in Buffalo, it was announced that a gas station designed by Wright in 1927, but never built, would be constructed near its original site as a tourist kiosk. In Bartlesville, Okla., the landmark Price Tower was converted from offices to a boutique hotel by New York architect Wendy Evans Joseph. One of the 20th century's most famous houses, the Farnsworth House in Plano, Ill., by Ludwig Mies van der Rohe, was purchased at auction in December by a preservation group, including the National Trust for Historic Preservation, which said that the house would "be protected forever and made available to the public." Controversy surrounded a proposal by the Museum of Arts and Design in New York City to alter Two Columbus Circle as a new home for the museum. The 10-story building was designed by Edward Durell Stone and built in 1964 as the Huntington Hartford Museum. The landmark TWA terminal at John F. Kennedy International Airport, designed by Eero Saarinen and no longer in use, was the subject of talks among preservationists, JetBlue Airways, and the Port Authority in the hope of incorporating the building into a larger new terminal as a check-in hall. In Chicago a new curvy glass-and-steel football stadium was inserted into the traditional, neoclassic Soldier Field, a bizarre junction of styles that upset some and pleased others. Swedish retailer IKEA threatened to tear down a Marcel Breuer office building in New Haven, Conn. Architectural preservationists were also concerned

Rebuilding the World Trade Center

One of the most vigorously contested architectural competitions in many years ended on Feb. 26, 2003, when representatives of the Lower Manhattan Development Corp. (LMDC), the Port Authority of New York and New Jersey, and the governments of New York state and New York City chose Daniel Libeskind (*see* BIOGRAPHIES) to develop the 6.5-ha (16-ac) site of the World Trade Center, destroyed by the terrorist attacks of Sept. 11, 2001. Libeskind's design featured a park sunk 9.1 m (30 ft) below street level that would be a memorial to those killed in the attacks, and 70 stories of offices topped by a spire (Freedom Tower) that would rise to a height of 538 m (1,776 ft [The height of the structure was selected to coincide with the year that the Declaration of Independence was signed.]). Other parts of the design included visible "footprints" marking where the Twin Towers once stood, a cultural quarter with a museum at its core, a transportation hub, a performing arts centre, and four additional office towers.

UPI Photo Service

The competition for a design to rebuild "ground zero" in New York City was won by Daniel Libeskind, whose vision for a revivified World Trade Center site included a sunken park, "footprints" of the fallen Twin Towers, and a 1,776-ft-high spire.

In winning the competition, Libeskind triumphed over some of the world's most prominent architects. The six other finalists included Foster and Partners, whose design featured a single tower that appeared to be formed from two entwined buildings; Meier Eisenman Gwathmey Holl, which offered five towers, three of them connected by a walkway and two other buildings connected to each other by a walkway and erected perpendicular to the other three; the THINK Team, an international group whose design featured very tall twin towers composed of exposed steel latticework; United Architects, which submitted a plan that comprised several very high towers fused together to form a helix-shaped structure; Peterson/Littenberg, which offered tall twin towers with a promenade between them; and Skidmore, Owings, and Merrill, which presented a design featuring a cluster of 80-story buildings. Earlier, in 2002, six designs had been submitted for consideration, but all were rejected as prosaic and unimaginative.

Although Libeskind won the competition, questions remained as to who would build his design and whether it would retain all of its original elements. Though the LMDC was given the authority to oversee the restoration of the World Trade Center site, it had to share power with the Port Authority, which had built the original Trade Center and owned the land. In turn, the Port Authority had to deal with Larry Silverstein, a New York City developer who six weeks before the attacks had signed a 99-year lease on the Trade Center and held the rights to office space at the site. Silverstein was partnered with retail developer Westfield America, which was seeking maximum shopping space in any new plan and had its own well-known architect, David Childs, who envisioned some money-saving alterations to Libeskind's plan. In July, however, Libeskind and Silverstein's representatives reached an agreement whereby Childs would take the lead role in developing Freedom Tower. Later in July Spanish architect Santiago Calatrava was selected to take the lead in the construction of the train terminal. In the meantime, the federal government and the Port Authority endorsed Libeskind's plan to build the tower on the northwest corner of the site, and Mayor Michael Bloomberg agreed that the rebuilt Trade Center could expand beyond its original boundaries for a less-crowded look. In September it was announced that internationally acclaimed architects Sir Norman Foster, Jean Nouvel, and Fumihiko Maki would be designing three of the towers. Construction was scheduled to begin in the summer of 2004.

(DAVID R. CALHOUN)

---

about Beijing, where increased development for the upcoming Olympic Games of 2008 was causing older neighbourhoods of narrow twisting streets and courtyards to be demolished.

Exhibitions. A major exhibition of the work of Modernist Danish architect and furniture designer Arne Jacobsen was on view at the Louisiana Museum of Modern Art in Denmark and later in Hamburg, Ger. At the Whitney Museum of American Art in New York City, "Scanning: The Aberrant Architectures of Diller + Scofidio" presented the work of a husband-wife team whose installations explore the ironies of contemporary life. "David Adler, Architect: The Elements of Style," at the Art Institute of Chicago, displayed the work of a traditionalist American architect of the early 20th century. The National Building Museum in Washington, D.C., sponsored "Big & Green: Toward Sustainable Architecture in the 21st Century," using 50 projects from around the world to explore the impact of architecture on global climate. Architect Louis Kahn was the subject of *My Architect,* a film made by his son Nathaniel Kahn; the movie explored not only Kahn's architecture but also his complex family life.

Deaths. In March two notable figures in the field died. Sen. Daniel Patrick Moynihan was a powerful advocate of architecture and preservation, and British architect Peter Denham Smithson, together with his wife, Alison, was a leading figure in British architecture for 40 years. (*See* OBITUARIES.) Cedric Price, who designed the steel-and-mesh aviary at the London Zoo, died in August at the age of 68. Price championed a temporary, adaptable, and playful architecture that influenced later figures such as Richard Rogers and the group Archigram. Geoffrey Bawa, known for modern buildings that blended with the local culture of Sri Lanka, died in May at the age of 83.

(ROBERT CAMPBELL)

Notable Civil Engineering Projects (in work or completed, 2003)

Name	Location		Year of completion	Notes
Airports		**Terminal area (sq m)**		
Suvarnabhumi ("Golden Land")	near Bangkok, Thai.	563,000	2005	To replace Don Muang Airport—Southeast Asia's busiest airport
Pearson International (new Terminal 1)	Toronto, Ont.	340,000	2004	New horseshoe-shaped terminal at Canada's busiest airport
Baiyun ("White Cloud") Int'l (replacement)	near Guangzhou (Canton), China	305,000	2004	Main hub airport of south China (excluding Hong Kong)
Munich Int'l (new Terminal 2)	northeast of Munich, Ger.	260,000	2003	Opened June 27; Germany's busiest domestic passenger airport as of 2001
Dallas/Fort Worth Int'l (new Terminal D)	Irving, Texas	195,000	2005	New international terminal
Heathrow (new Terminal 5)	southwest of London, Eng.	70,000	2008	Biggest construction project in the U.K. from 2002
Johannesburg Int'l (new domestic terminal)	east of Johannesburg, S.Af.	70,000	2003	Opened Feb. 11; Africa's busiest passenger airport
Bridges		**Length (main span; m)**		
Hangzhou Bay	near Jiaxing, China–near Cixi, China	35,600	2008	To be world's longest transoceanic bridge/causeway; begun 2003
I-95 (Woodrow Wilson #2)	Alexandria, Va.–Md. suburbs of D.C.	1,852[1]	2005–08	2 bascule spans forming higher inverted V shape for ships; begun 2000
Nancha (1 bridge of 2-section Runyang)	Zhenjiang, China (across the Yangtze)	1,490	2005	To be world's third largest (+ China's first major) suspension bridge
Sutong	Nantong, China (100 km from Yangtze mouth)	1,088	2008	To be world's longest cable-stayed bridge
Tacoma Narrows (#3)	the Narrows of Puget Sound, Tacoma, Wash.	853	2007	Built over collapsed TN #1; longest U.S. suspension bridge since 1964
Alfred Zampa Memorial (Carquinez #3)	Crockett, Calif.–Vallejo, Calif.	728	2003	Opened Nov. 8; first major U.S. suspension bridge since 1973
Rion–Antirion	near Patrai, Greece (across Gulf of Corinth)	560	2004	To be world's longest cable-stayed bridge (incl. all spans [2,252 m])
Lupu	Shanghai, China (across the Huangpu)	550	2003	Opened June 28; world's longest steel-arch bridge
(New) Cooper River	Charleston, S.C.–Mt. Pleasant, S.C.	471	2005	To be longest cable-stayed bridge in North America
San Francisco–Oakland Bay (East Span)	Yerba Buena Is., Calif.–Oakland, Calif.	385	2007	2-km causeway + world's largest suspension bridge hung from single tower
Millau Viaduct	Tarn Gorge, west of Millau, France	342	2005	8 cable-stayed spans; world's highest (270 m) bridge
Sundøy	across the Leirfjord, Norway, at 66° N	298	2003	Opened Aug. 9; world's 2nd longest prestressed-concrete girder bridge
Buildings		**Height (m)**		
Taipei 101 (Taipei Financial Center)	Taipei, Taiwan	508	2003	If 60-m spire is included, world's tallest building, without spire, 3rd tallest; formal opening, Oct. 2004
Shanghai World Financial Center	Shanghai, China	492	2007	Begun 1997, resumed 2003; to be world's 2nd tallest building
Union Square Phase 7	Hong Kong	474	2007	Begun 2002; to be world's 3rd tallest; 16-building complex
Two International Finance Centre	Hong Kong	415	2003	Tallest building in Hong Kong and 5th in the world
Eureka Tower	Melbourne, Australia	300	2005	To be Australia's 2nd tallest building and tallest residential in world
Mok-dong Hyperion Tower A	Seoul, S.Kor.	256	2003	Opened June; tallest building in S.Kor.; #3 residential in world
Torre Mayor (Chapultepec Tower)	Mexico City, Mex.	225	2003	Opened June; tallest building in Mexico; advanced seismic engineering
Dams and Hydrologic Projects		**Crest length (m)**		
Three Gorges (end of 2 of 3 phases)	west of Yichang, China	1,983	2003	World's largest reservoir (620 km long) began filling June 1
San Roque Multipurpose	Agno River, Luzon, Phil.	1,130	2003	Opened in May; irrigation and flood control; highest embankment dam in Asia
Bakun Dam	Balui River, Sarawak, Borneo, Malaysia	740	2007	Hydroelectricity to penin. Malaysia via world's longest submarine cable
Mohale (1B; Lesotho Highlands Water Project, Leso. to S.Af. water transfer)	Senqunyane River, 100 km SE of Maseru, Lesotho	620	2003	Phase 1B transfer completed Nov. 27; phase 2 postponed
Caruachi (3rd of 5-dam Lower Caroní Development scheme)	Caroní River, northern Bolívar, Venez.	360	2003–06	Hydroelectric generation began Feb. 28
Sardar Sarovar (Narmada) Project	Narmada River, Madhya Pradesh, India	?	2007	Largest dam of controversial 30-dam project; drinking water for Gujarat
Tucuruí (upgrade)	Tocantins River, eastern Pará, Braz.	?	2005	Generating capacity to be doubled; 1st Brazilian Amazon dam (1984)
Highways		**Length (km)**		
Golden Quadrilateral superhighway	Mumbai–Chennai–Kolkata–Delhi, India	5,846	2005–07	Upgrade to 4 lanes; Mumbai–Delhi (2005), Delhi–Kolkata (2007)
Highway 1	Kabul–Kandahar–Herat, Afg.	1,000	2005?	Begun late 2002; 482-km Kabul–Kandahar section opened Dec. 16, 2003
Egnatia Motorway	Igoumenitsa–Kipi, Greece	680	2006	First Greek highway at int'l standards; 76 tunnels, 1,650 bridges
Trans Labrador Highway (Phase II of III)	Red Bay–Cartwright, Labrador, Can.	325	2000–08	Phase II opened Sept. 12–13, 2003; first all-season, gravel road
Trans Sahara (Mauritanian route)	Nouadhibou–Nouakchott, Mauritania	250	2004?	Completes road link between Tangier, Mor., and Senegal
Croatian Motorway (Section III)	Bosiljevo–Sveti Rok, Croatia	145	2004	Very difficult terrain; entire motorway (Zagreb–Split) to open 2005
Land Reclamation		**Diameter (km)**		
Palm Jumeirah + Palm Jebel Ali is.	in Persian Gulf, near Dubai, U.A.E.	5	2007	Palm-tree shaped ("17 fronds + trunk") islands; ultraexclusive
Railways (Heavy)		**Length (km)**		
Alice Springs–Darwin ("ADrail")	Northern Territory, Australia	1,420	2003	Finished Sept. 25; completes rail link (Darwin to Adelaide)
Qinghai–Tibet	China: Golmud, Qinghai–Lhasa, Tibet	1,118	2007	World's highest railway (5,072 m at summit); 86% above 4,000 m
Xi'an–Hefei	China: Xi'an, Shaanxi–Hefei, Anhui	955	2003	Completed June 18, opens 2004; for economic growth in interior
Ferronorte (extension to Cuiabá)	Alto Taquari–Cuiabá, Braz.	525	2005?	To promote agricultural exports from Mato Grosso (Braz. interior)
Bothnia Line (Botniabanan)	Nyland–Umeå, Swed.	190	2008	Along north Swedish coast; difficult terrain with 25 km of tunnels
Railways (High Speed)		**Length (km)**		
Spanish High Speed (second line)	Madrid, Spain, to France (via Barcelona)	719	2007	Opened Oct. 11, 2003; Madrid–Lleida corridor
Korea Train Express (KTX)	Seoul–Pusan, S.Kor.	412	2008	Will connect largest and second largest cities; to Taegu by 2004
Taiwan High Speed	Taipei–Kaohsiung, Taiwan	345	2005	Links Taiwan's two largest cities along west coast
Italian High Speed (second line)	Rome–Naples, Italy	205	2004	Other new lines: Milan–Bologna (2006); Florence–Bologna (2007)
Channel Tunnel Rail Link	near Folkestone–central London, Eng.	108	2007	74-km section (Folkestone–north Kent) opened Sept. 16, 2003
Shanghai maglev ("magnetic levitation")	Shanghai: city centre–int'l airport	29.9	2002	Inaug. Dec. 31, 2002; no scheduled service as of late 2003
Subways/Metros/Light Rails		**Length (km)**		
Hong Kong Railway (West Rail, phase 1)	Western New Territories to Kowloon	30.5	2003	Opened Dec. 20; 11.5 km in tunnels and 13.4 km on viaducts
Guangzhou (Canton) Metro (line 2)	Guangzhou, China (north-south line)	23.2	2003	18.3 km opened June 28; 15-line system planned
Los Angeles Metro (Gold Line)	Union Station to Pasadena, Calif.	22.0	2003	Opened July 26
Delhi Metro (Line 1)	Delhi, India	21.3	2002–04	Delhi's first subway line; 12.8 km operational by Oct. 3, 2003
Bangkok Blue Line	north-south line in central Bangkok, Thai.	20.0	2004	Thailand's first underground system
Singapore NorthEast Line	Singapore	20.0	2003	Opened June 20; world's first fully automated subway
Hiawatha Light Rail	Downtown Minneapolis–Bloomington, Minn.	19.3	2004	Difficult tunneling under M/SP airport in unstable limestone; begun 2001
Shanghai Metro (Line 1 extension)	southwest Shanghai	17.2	2003	Opened Nov. 25; "most rapidly expanding metro in world"
Bay Area Rapid Transit (extension)	Colma–San Francisco Int'l Airport, Calif.	14.0	2003	Opened June 22; first BART link to SF airport
New York Airtrain (light rail)	Kennedy Airport–subways + L.I. Railroad	13.0	2003	Opened Dec. 17; link between Kennedy terminals and Manhattan
Tunnels		**Length (m)**		
Apennine Range tunnels (9)	Bologna–Florence, Italy (high-speed railway)	73,400	2007	Begun 1996; longest tunnel, 18.6 km; tunnels to cover 93% of railway
Lötschberg #2	Frutigen–Raron, Switz.	34,577	2007	To be world's 3rd longest rail tunnel; France–Italy link
Guadarrama	50 km north-northwest of Madrid, Spain	28,377	2007	To be world's 4th longest rail tunnel; Valladolid high-speed link
Södra Länken ("Southern Link")	part of Stockholm, Swed., ring road	16,600	2004	Complex of underground interchanges
Hsüeh-shan ("Snow Mountain")	near Taipei, Taiwan	12,900	2005	To be world's 4th longest road tunnel; Taipei–Ilan expressway link
Westerscheldetunnel ("Western Schelde")	Terneuzen–Ellewoutsdijk, Neth.	6,600	2003	Opened March 14; world's longest tunnel in "bored weak soil"

1 m=3.28 ft; 1 km=0.62 mi; 1 ha=2.47 ac

[1]Length of each span.

Art and Art Exhibitions

The year in art was marked by a number of outstanding SOLO EXHIBITIONS as well as shows that JUXTAPOSED the UNEXPECTED. Several venues highlighted DOCUMENTARY and STREET PHOTOGRAPHY, and a DAGUERREOTYPE by Joseph-Philibert Girault de Prangey sold for a world RECORD PRICE for a photograph.

ART

Although dogged by persistent questions regarding everything from its relevance to the quality of art works and lack of theoretical coherence, the 2003 Venice Biennale remained the most anticipated and widely covered large-scale international exhibition. Though the early weeks of the 50th Biennale were hampered by extreme summer heat, the sprawling multicuratorial, multisite exhibition organized by Francesco Bonami and his collaborative team generally held its own. Polish-born artist Piotr Uklanski made explicit reference to this group with his red banner depicting the silhouetted figures of the 11 critics, artists, and curators who assisted Bonami. The banner, which alluded to the spread of curatorial power beyond just the Biennale, was prominently installed for maximum visibility on the facade of the offices of municipal culture facing the Grand Canal. More overt political gestures could be found elsewhere. The Mexico City-based Spanish artist Santiago Sierra commented on exclusivity and identity by turning the Spanish pavilion into an exclusive space; only individuals with Spanish passports were permitted entry. As one of two artists chosen to represent Venezuela, Javier Téllez withdrew from the Biennale in February as a gesture of protest against the government of Hugo Chávez Frías. (*See* WORLD AFFAIRS: *Venezuela*.) The other Venezuelan, Pedro Morales, whose project for the Venezuelan pavilion was censored by the government, articulated the brutal reality of political oppression; he placed a wheelbarrow full of trash on the pavilion's steps and covered the facade with "Censored" signs and Venezuelan flags; the project he would have shown could be viewed on the Internet.

Using museum display cases, a large 18th-century-style chandelier of Murano glass, and other blown-glass elements along with mannequins dressed in Renaissance-style garb, Fred Wilson's *Speak of Me as I Am* in the U.S. pavilion was a historical exploration of Venice's multicultural past and representations of Moors in Italian art. In front of the pavilion, a Senegalese man sold knockoffs of designer bags. As it turned out, the vendor was a tourist who had been hired by Wilson, and the bags had been hand made by the artist. The presence of this "vendor"—such illegal commerce was routinely shut down by the Venetian police—confused both viewers and city officials.

Not all work at the Biennale was political. Olafur Eliasson's installation for the Danish pavilion, for example, was simply dazzling. Eliasson was obsessed with the nature of perception, and his *Blind Pavilion* included numerous works intended to heighten the viewer's self-awareness and awareness of his surroundings. This the artist accomplished by requiring viewers to walk on ramps and to face devices such as camera obscuras and a multitude of mirrors, prisms, and kaleidoscopes that magnified, distorted, and sharpened spatial experience.

In New York City, Matthew Barney (*see* BIOGRAPHIES) captured the imagination of critics and the public alike. The Guggenheim Museum's exhibition featured all five films in Barney's epic Cremaster cycle as well as related sculptures, photographs, and drawings centred around Barney's elaborate narrative of procreation, sexual function, and myth. The interior of the museum's Frank Lloyd Wright-designed rotunda was itself transformed by blue Astroturf and white athletic padding—Barney's signature materials.

Two public art projects in New York City garnered significant attention in 2003. Mariko Mori's *Wave UFO* was installed in a glass atrium of 590 Madison Avenue. This translucent, tear-shaped "meditation pod" was part sci-fi fantasy and part Buddhist shrine, and it invited viewer participation. Once inside the pod, participants were attached to electrodes, and their brain activity was displayed as active light projections on the pod's ceiling. At nearby Rockefeller Center, Takashi Murakami installed *Reversed Double Helix*, composed of two 9-m (30-ft) black "eyeball" balloons, a garden of brightly coloured sculpted

Visitors to the Danish pavilion at the 50th Venice Biennale had their self-awareness and awareness of their surroundings dramatically challenged by Olafur Eliasson's sculptural installations, such as this one from the series titled **Blind Pavilion.**

Raymond Meier

An untitled installation (2003) by Tara Donovan, like her other site-specific sculptures, examines the physical properties of great quantities of common objects. Here Styrofoam cups are affixed to a skylight, creating a textured, almost underwater light effect.

flowers and mushrooms, and daisy-patterned wallpaper, all presided over by *Tongari-kun* (known in English as "Mr. Pointy"), a 9-m-tall sculpture reminiscent of a cartoon character. Like Murakami's other works, *Reversed Double Helix* combined aspects of Pop art with anime (Japanese animation) and *manga* (adult comic books), as well as more traditional art forms. Popular culture remained a crucial theme and departure point for many artists. Drawing on both his part-aboriginal Canadian ancestry and the wider commercial culture, Brian Jungen addressed questions of cultural authenticity in his sculptural works by juxtaposing the handmade and the ready-made, tribal artifacts and consumer icons. Jungen's "masks," which he called "prototypes," were fashioned from Nike athletic shoes arranged to mimic the form and appearance of tribal masks. Tom Sachs also commented on brand-name logos, as well as the commercialization of high Modernism, in his large-scale installation *Nutsy's* (2002). Basing his work on the idea that anything can be re-created in a do-it-yourself environment, Sachs fashioned a series of "stations" connected by a miniature roadway, along which one encountered a McDonald's stand where burgers and fries were prepared and consumed, a DJ booth with turntables, and a scale-model replica of Le Corbusier's housing complex in Marseille, France.

The urban context was also examined by Julie Mehretu, whose work combined aspects of cartography, architectural drawing, and painting. Her energetic works—part abstraction, part complex architectonic system—were composed of drawn lines and intersecting coloured planar shapes that together created animated topographies. Philippe Parreno's multipart installations can assume different forms depending on their context. As it was shown in 2003, Parreno's *El sueño de una cosa* (2002) consisted of a 60-second film of a Scandinavian landscape, the panels on which the film is projected, and the silence that follows. The work makes reference to Robert Rauschenberg's *White Painting* (1951) in its five white panels and to John Cage's *4′33″* (*Four Minutes and Thirty-three Seconds,* 1952) in the amount of time between showings of the film. Douglas Gordon's videos similarly explore aspects of narrative, memory, and temporality. He frequently incorporated clips from existing films (most famously, Martin Scorsese's *Taxi Driver,* 1976) but Gordon filmed the footage for *Play Dead: Real Time* himself. The installation, which alluded to Thomas Edison's shocking film (1903) of the staged electrocution of an elephant at Coney Island, consisted of two projections of a film of an elephant's death and seeming resurrection; a third projection was a small close-up of the elephant's eye.

Unlike Parreno and Gordon, Urs Fischer included readily available materials, such as wax, wood, pigment, glass, and Styrofoam as well as found objects and even organic matter, as part of his eccentric and improvisational works. In Fischer's 2003 exhibition "need no chair when walking," a life-size sculpture of three women was a clear reference to traditional themes (the female nude; the Three Graces). Fischer's figures, however, were rendered in wax and lit like giant candles at the beginning of the gallery exhibition. Gradually, hideously, the sculptures melted down to a pile of coloured wax and barely distinguishable forms. Tara Donovan also employed nontraditional art materials, such as toothpicks, pencils, Styrofoam cups, and paper plates, usually in enormous quantities. Donovan's *Haze,* which fronted a wall more than 12 m (40 ft) long, was constructed with some two million drinking straws of differing lengths sticking out horizontally from the wall. Donovan imbued mass-produced goods such as these with an organic, even atmospheric quality so that the accumulations became metaphors for growth and proliferation in the natural world.

Among the lesser-known painters who received positive critical response in 2003 were Barnaby Furnas and Dan Walsh. Furnas's watercolours were relatively small in scale, but their impact was enormous. They depicted schematic figures, sometimes solitary but also in groups, in a variety of mostly sexual or violent acts that were partially obscured by swirling clouds of bright paint spots. This abstract quality muffled their shock value only somewhat. Walsh, on the other hand, made abstract works that explored what he called "the syntax of construction." He made a notable series of handmade artist's books, a medium he considered as much a "venue" for his art as the walls of a gallery. (MEGHAN DAILEY)

ART EXHIBITIONS

It was a year of many extraordinary firsts in exhibitions in 2003. A number of shows brought together works that had never been exhibited concurrently and thereby illuminated a particular style or historical moment. One example was "Rembrandt's Journey," a show organized by the Museum of Fine Arts, Boston. Although Rembrandt is best known for his paintings, this exhibition instead highlighted his extraordinary graphic output, presenting some 150 etchings and related drawings gathered from international collections. Many of the works on view, including 20 paintings, were shown together for the first time. Another first occurred when three institutions—the Fogg Art Museum, Cambridge, Mass.; the Haggerty Museum of Art at Marquette University, Milwaukee, Wis.; and the Wallach Art Gallery at Columbia University, New York City—organized the first American retrospective of French postwar artist Jean Fautrier (1898–1964). Usually associated with Art Informel, a movement that emphasized gesture and lyrical abstraction over representation and geometric abstraction, Fautrier himself considered his work to be grounded in reality. His best-known series, *Hostages* (1944), consisting mainly of thickly impastoed paintings that suggest wounds, was a response to his deeply traumatic wartime experiences.

Several artists' works were shown at museums for the first time in years or even decades. One of the most anticipated of these "reintroductions" was a retrospective of Lee Bontecou (b. 1931), organized by the UCLA Hammer Museum, Los Angeles, and the Museum of Contemporary Art, Chicago. In the 1960s Bontecou was considered a major contemporary artist, noted for her eccentric wall-bound sculptures. Using a blowtorch and a soldering iron, she wrought metal, wire, and thick canvas into objects that were unprecedented in their originality. In the early 1970s, however, Bontecou withdrew from the art world and, though she continued to make art, exhibited rarely in the intervening decades.

A number of younger artists received their first major museum shows during the year. One of these was Laura Owens, whose works had garnered much attention, though critics often found themselves at a loss for words when attempting to describe them. The Museum of Contemporary Art, Los Angeles, showed more than 20 of her airy, freewheeling works that ranged in subject from buzzing beehives and romantic landscapes populated by bespectacled monkeys, owls, and bunnies to riffs on geometric abstraction. Japanese artist Yoshitomo Nara also was given his first major U.S. exhibition, at the Museum of Contemporary Art, Cleveland, Ohio. Nara's cartoonish renderings of children—scowling, grinning, alternately devilish and innocent—offered poignant and funny psychological portraits of a bittersweet stage of life.

Museumgoers had the opportunity to see and compare the work of some roughly contemporaneous but very different American artists. During his 50-year career, Philip Guston changed his style from representation to abstraction and back again. A major retrospective, organized by the Modern Art Museum, Fort Worth, Texas, charted Guston's early social realism of the late 1930s, his moody abstractions of the 1950s and '60s, and the stark symbolism of his disembodied heads and eyes and still-controversial hooded figures of the '70s. The show later traveled to the Metropolitan Museum of Art, New York City, and the Royal Academy of Arts, London.

Romare Bearden's Three Folk Musicians *(1967) was one of the many collages on display during the major retrospective of Bearden's work in 2003 at the National Gallery of Art, in Washington, D.C.*

By contrast, the collages of Romare Bearden (1911–88), created largely from painted paper, magazine clippings, and bits of fabric, vividly captured African American experience in the 20th century. While those works—based on his boyhood memories of life in the rural South and in New York during the Harlem Renaissance—were his signature art form, Bearden was more than an artist; he was also an art historian, teacher, composer, author, and curator, and he owned and operated an art gallery. With its presentation of its first-ever solo retrospective of a black artist and the first major retrospective of Bearden's work in more than 10 years, the National Gallery in Washington, D.C., aimed to demonstrate the full range of his contribution to American art. Another artist whose work sought to express something quintessentially American was James Rosenquist (b. 1933). Reconfiguring the iconography of advertising, Rosenquist created an extraordinary body of work that included Pop art, the movement he helped launch in the late 1950s, and his later abstractions, all painted on the grand scale that remained the former billboard painter's trademark. In addition to paintings, the exhibition offered sundry source collages (which Rosenquist made for many paintings), prints, drawings, and sculptures. The show opened in Houston, Texas, at both the Menil Collection and the Museum of Fine Arts; it then traveled to the Solomon R. Guggenheim Museum, New York City, the organizing venue.

"The Age of Watteau, Chardin, and Fragonard: Masterpieces of French Genre Painting," at the National Gallery of Canada, Ottawa, collected about 100 examples of the type of art that was most popular in 18th-century France. These were small paintings depicting scenes of everyday existence: servants going about their daily tasks, children playing games, moments of intimate conversation, and the flirtations of aristocrats. These exquisitely painted narratives remained intriguing to the modern eye.

That France in the mid-19th century had a passion for all things Spanish was evident in the more than 200 works brought together for "Manet/Velázquez: The French Taste for Spanish Painting." The show allowed viewers to see paintings by Spanish artists such as José de Ribera and El Greco side by side with those of Eugène Delacroix, Edgar Degas, and other artists working in France and to witness firsthand how one group influenced the other. Coorganized by the Réunion des Musées Nationaux and Musée d'Orsay, Paris, and the Metropolitan Museum of Art, New York City, the exhibition traveled to the Met; it was scheduled to appear at Madrid's Prado museum. In honour of the 100th anniversary of the artist's death, "Gauguin Tahiti," a major exhibition of 150

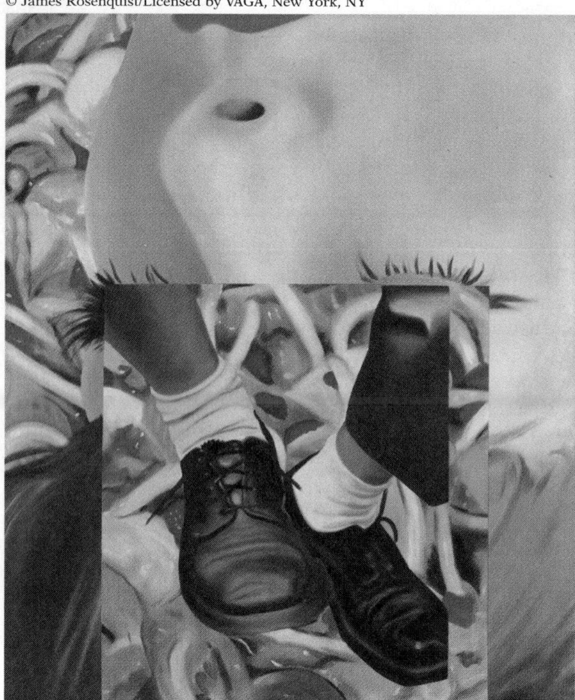

Promenade of Merce Cunningham *(1963), an oil painting by James Rosenquist, was one of the works featured in a traveling retrospective of Rosenquist's work that in 2003 opened jointly at Houston's Museum of Fine Arts and the Menil Collection.*

paintings and other items of Paul Gauguin from his last years in the Pacific, opened on October 3 at the Galeries Nationales du Grand Palais, Paris, and was slated to move to the Museum of Fine Arts, Boston, at the end of February 2004.

When Manny Farber was not writing the trenchant film criticism for which he became known, he was making abstract paintings and still lifes. He had his first solo exhibition in 1956 at Tibor de Nagy Gallery in New York City, and his career as a painter developed steadily in tandem with his work as a writer. Some 50 of his paintings, many directly inspired by the films he saw, were on view at California's Museum of Contemporary Art San Diego.

"Seventy-seven albums, twenty-seven wives, over two hundred court appearances . . . Spiritualist. Pan-Africanist. Commune king. Composer, saxophonist, keyboardist, vocalist, dancer. Would-be candidate for the Nigerian presidency. There will never be another like him." So a journalist described Fela Anikulapo-Kuti. The charismatic Fela, who died in 1997, was the subject of an engrossing show at the New Museum in New York City that explored his contributions as a musical pioneer as well as his vast influence over a generation of artists, including Sanford Biggers, Kendell Geers, Kara Walker, and Fred Wilson, all of whom contributed works inspired by Fela to the exhibition. Music was also at the heart of Christian Marclay's videos, sculptures, and installations, more than 60 of which were shown at the UCLA Hammer Museum, Los Angeles. A synthesis of visual art and sound, Marclay's work explored the contexts and significance of listening and seeing. In his *Tape Fall* (1989), for example, a reel-to-reel tape recorder placed high on a ladder plays the sound of falling water. As the "waterfall" of tape unrolls from one reel, it falls to the floor where it forms a "pool," so that the visual experience reinforces the auditory.

An encyclopaedic survey of postwar aesthetics across tendentious political and ideological lines, "Berlin-Moscow/Moscow-Berlin 1950–2000" at Martin-Gropius-Bau, Berlin, brought together nearly 500 works by 200 artists—including German artists such as Joseph Beuys and Bernd and Hilla Becher and Russian artists such as Vitaly Komar and Alex Melamid—selected by an equally diverse group of Russian and German curators. The cross-border dialogue would continue in 2004, when the exhibition was scheduled to travel to the State Tretyakov Gallery, Moscow.

German artist Dieter Roth never cared much for traditional venues—he would as readily show his work in a friend's apartment as in a gallery—or for ordinary materials—he made sculptures from materials such as sausage and chocolate—and in 1970 at a Los Angeles gallery he showed 40 suitcases filled with various types of cheese. Remarkably, hundreds of his works survived (though the rotting cheese was destroyed), and Roth's photographs, paintings, sculptures, and other works in a great variety of media were shown at Schaulager, Basel, Switz., in the first major exhibition of the artist's work since his death in 1998.

(MEGHAN DAILEY)

PHOTOGRAPHY

The year 2003 was one of resurgent interest in documentary and street photography. This trend was acknowledged in a groundbreaking exhibition at the International Center of Photography (ICP) in New York City. Entitled "Strangers: The First ICP Triennial of Photography and Video," the show—one-third of which comprised videos and two-thirds photographs—presented the works of 40 artists worldwide. It took as its theme the changed relationship of the self to others in a new technological and global environment. Many of the pieces mined the concept of the crowd, looking at the ways in which individuals respond to one another in urban public spaces. Other work, such as that of Dutch photographer Rineke Dijkstra, touched on the notion of estrangement; her portraits of adolescence struck a note of uneasy empathy.

Many of the artists in the show were contemporary photographers on the cusp of their careers. The work of Magnum photographer Luc Delahaye, whose panoramic image *Jenin Refugee Camp* (2002) featured prominently in the triennial, was exhibited in a solo show called "History" at Ricco/Maresca Gallery (New York City) in February and March. In a traveling show that had originated at the Musée d'Art Contemporain de Montréal in 2001, works by Iranian-born Shirin Neshat examined the female experience in contemporary Islamic society; her first major solo exhibition in North America included stops at the Walker Art Center, Minneapolis, Minn., in 2002 and at the Miami (Fla.) Art Museum and the Contemporary Arts Museum, Houston, Texas, in 2003. The exhibition consisted of 12 large-format photographs, six audiovisual works, and two recent films. South African portraitist Zwelethu Mthethwa showed at Jack Shainman Gallery (New York City) in February and later was featured in "Interior Portraits: Zwelethu Mthethwa Photographs" at the Cleveland (Ohio) Museum of Art.

In "Cruel and Tender: The Real in the Twentieth-Century Photograph," the Tate Modern, London, presented an exhibition exclusively composed of photography for the first time in its history. It included the work of 24 artists displayed in "sympathetic clusters" rather than chronologically. "Cruel and Tender" shared two notable artists, Philip-Lorca diCorcia and Dijkstra, with the ICP Triennial. During the summer diCorcia's pivotal exhibition, "Philip-Lorca diCorcia: A Storybook Life," opened at the Whitechapel Art Gallery in London, the first stop in a traveling show scheduled to visit Centre Nationale de la Photographie, Paris; Museum Folkwang, Essen, Ger.; and Centro de Arte de Salamanca (Spain) in 2004. The show received much popular acclaim when it was exhibited at PaceWildenstein Chelsea in New York City. The artist's book, *A Storybook Life,* contained all 76 exhibition images. Dijkstra's multiple portraits of a young female Israeli soldier and a French Foreign Legion officer were exhibited at the Marian Goodman Gallery (New York City) in the fall. The book *Rineke Dijkstra: Beach Portraits* (2002) presented the photos for which she first received recognition in the 1990s.

The influence of German photographers Bernd and Hilla Becher, the legendary instructors of Thomas Struth and Andreas Gursky, was ubiquitous throughout the exhibition "Cruel and Tender." Famous for their formalist approach, the Bechers received the Getty Images Lifetime Achievement Award, one of the highest honours presented at the 19th Annual Infinity Awards in New York City. Their work was also notably featured at DIA:Beacon (Beacon, N.Y.), a venue that opened in May 2003 to house the permanent collection of large-scale and site-specific work of the DIA Art Foundation. "Bernd and Hilla Becher: Industrial Landscapes" was on view at Sonnabend Gallery (New York City) and Fraenkel Gallery (San Francisco). The Bechers also figured in the group show "German Photography: From the Bauhaus to the Bechers" at Lawrence Miller Gallery (New York City) from January to March. The traveling show of their student Struth, organized by the Dallas (Texas) Museum of Art, visited the Metropolitan Museum of Art, New York City, and the Museum of Contemporary Art, Chicago. In 2003 *Photo District News* (*PDN*) named Struth's portrait of painter Gerhard Richter and his family, published in *The New York Times Magazine,* one of the best photos of the year.

In a technical fashion similar to that of Struth and an aesthetic in tune with the American topologists of the 1970s, the work of Edward Burtynsky was exhibited in several solo shows, including "Manufactured Landscapes: The Photographs of Edward Burtynsky," National Gallery of Canada, Ottawa; "In the Wake of Progress: Images of the Industrial Landscape," Canadian embassy, Washington, D.C.; "Oil Fields," Charles Cowles Gallery, New York City; and "Before the Flood," Robert Koch Gallery, San Francisco.

Fondation Henri Cartier-Bresson, Paris, dedicated to preserving the master photographer's legacy, was inaugurated in 2003. Its opening was accompanied by an exhibition showing 250 images by Cartier-Bresson at the Bibliothèque Nationale de France; it traveled to Caixa-Forum, Barcelona, Spain, and was scheduled to travel to Martin-Gropius-Bau, Berlin, and the Palazzo delle Esposizioni, Rome. Cartier-Bresson turned 95 in August.

In a similar documentary tradition, William Eggleston's exhibition "Los Alamos" presented his newly recovered photographs of the American South from 1965 to 1974. The exhibition traveled from Museum Ludwig, Cologne, Ger., to Museu de Arte Contemporânea de Serralves, Porto, Port.; Museet for Samtidskunst, Oslo; the Louisiana Museum of Art, Humlebæk, Den.; Albertina, Vienna; the San Francisco Museum of Modern Art; and the Dallas Museum of Modern Art. A number of images from the exhibition were published in *William Eggleston: Los Alamos,* and one was chosen by *PDN* as one of the year's best photos.

American photographer Joel Sternfeld, whose work was noted for its sense of drama and use of intense colour, had his first solo show in the U.K. at the Photographer's Gallery, London, in January. That gallery also administered the $30,000 Citibank Photography Prize, awarded in 2003 to German fashion photographer Jürgen Teller, whose exhibition "Daddy You're So Cute" was shown at Lehmann Maupin Gallery, New York City.

Portrait photographer Yousuf Karsh, who died in 2002 at age 93, was inducted into the International Photography Hall of Fame, Oklahoma City, Okla. Another noteworthy portraitist, Rosalie ("Rollie") Thorne McKenna, died on June 15, 2003, at age 84. Dylan Thomas, Truman Capote, W.H. Auden, T.S. Eliot, Sylvia Plath, and Robert Frost were among the many literary figures she captured. McKenna's work was the subject of a 2001 retrospective at the National Portrait Gallery, London. The publication of John Coplans's *Body Parts: A Self-Portrait* coincided with the artist's death.

In the auction world, Christie's of London sold *Athenes (Temple de Jupiter),* a daguerreotype by Joseph-Philibert Girault de Prangey, for $810,000, a world record for a photograph sold at auction.

(MARLA CAPLAN)

Julie Henry's **Going Down** *(1999; two video projections [left]) and Luc Delahaye's* **Jenin Refugee Camp** *(2002; chromogenic print [right]) were two of the works featured in the International Center of Photography's 2003 show "Strangers: The First ICP Triennial of Photography and Video."*

Computers and Information Systems

Consumers worldwide coped with computer **WORMS** and viruses, e-mail **SPAM**, and online **CRIME** in 2003 while savouring the advantages of **WIRELESS** Internet access, high-speed broadband, online **MUSIC** services, and high-tech **GENEALOGY** research. Meanwhile, more companies laid off workers and **OUTSOURCED** computer-technology jobs.

A flurry of legal and Internet activity swirled around the computer industry in 2003, contrasting sharply with slowed sales for computers and software. While industry sales languished and layoffs continued, consumers and businesses experienced the wrath of Internet worms and viruses. Junk e-mail, called spam, clogged e-mail inboxes everywhere, and legislators mobilized against it. The U.S. Supreme Court once again wrestled with the difficult issue of restricting Internet pornography. Music held centre stage as the battle over downloading free songs from the Internet boiled over. The Recording Industry Association of America (RIAA) filed lawsuits against 261 consumers for allegedly sharing copyrighted music.

Music and Film on the Internet. While the music industry previously had taken online file-swapping services such as Napster to court, 2003 marked the first time that the industry had sued consumers. The RIAA blamed illicit downloading—some analysts estimated that there were at least 57 million Americans sharing digital music files freely on the Internet—for a double-digit drop in sales of music compact discs (CDs) since the early 1990s. The music industry could not prove online music trading was the sole cause of the CD sales decline, however, and some research firms estimated that only a fraction of the drop was due to free downloading.

Besides struggling against free music downloading, the music industry also had to cope with what appeared to be a shift away from CDs sold in stores and toward Internet downloads. Forrester Research predicted that by 2008 about 33% of music sales would come from downloads, while CD sales would drop 30% from their peak in 1999.

The RIAA represented the five largest music companies, Universal Music Group, Sony Music Entertainment, Warner Music Group, BMG Entertainment, and EMI. As the year ended, the music industry reported that it was in the process of filing more lawsuits against consumers. It offered an amnesty program for those who had not been sued but who would admit wrongdoing and promise to delete downloaded songs.

Despite the often negative reaction to its lawsuits against consumers, the music industry complained that it had run out of legal alternatives. Napster's free online music service was stopped through court action, but new services such as Kazaa and Morpheus quickly emerged as replacements. Because they used peer-to-peer sharing between computers, they had no central Web site that could be shut down by court action. In addition, the music industry lost a case in which it tried to prove that some of the new free music services were guilty of copyright infringement. A U.S. district court ruled that those free music services were analogous to videocassette recorders that allowed consumers to make copies of TV broadcasts.

In filing the consumer lawsuits, the RIAA alleged that the potential harm caused by consumer copyright infringement was measured in the millions of dollars, but most consumers who were sued were permitted to settle the cases for a few thousand dollars. That was far less than the RIAA had demanded earlier in the year when it sued four college students for sharing music through personal Web sites; those individuals settled their suits for amounts ranging up to $17,500.

Many consumers who downloaded music seemed unmoved by the music industry's fury. The number of people using free online music services declined after the lawsuits were filed, but millions continued to use them. Informal polls indicated that many who downloaded music for free either claimed they did not understand that the action was wrong or made it clear that they did not care.

At the same time that the music industry was trying to stop free downloading, it sought to provide consumers with an alternative. Several authorized for-pay music download services debuted and claimed success. Apple Computer Corp. reported that its iTunes online service sold more than 10 million songs at 99 cents each in a five-month period. At year's end Apple

© Mannie Garcia/Reuters NewMedia Inc./Corbis

(Left to right) Mitch Bainwol of the Recording Industry Association of America, Jack Valenti of the Motion Picture Association, rapper LL Cool J, and Mike Negra of Mike's Video, Inc., are sworn in before testifying in September before the U.S. Senate Government Affairs Committee about illegal downloading of copyrighted media.

expanded its service from the niche market for Apple Macintosh computers to the broader audience who used Microsoft Corp.'s Windows operating system (OS), which accounted for well over 90% of personal computer (PC) users. Napster made a comeback as a for-pay service owned by software company Roxio. Other online sellers included consumer electronics retailer Best Buy, which resold the Rhapsody service operated by RealNetworks.

Meanwhile, the movie industry tried to avoid the illicit-downloading problem by establishing legal ways to download Hollywood films, such as the for-pay online services Movielink and CinemaNow. It was expected that movie downloads would increase after more households had high-speed broadband connections, a must for downloading large movie files. It remained unclear, however, whether the Internet movie downloads could compete with established for-pay movie sources such as cable and satellite TV, video stores, and the online rental firm NetFlix.

Security Issues. In January the Slammer worm (a worm is a malicious program that replicates without human intervention) exploited a weakness in Microsoft Web server software, spreading so quickly that it overloaded tens of thousands of business and government computer servers on the Internet. It was the largest such incident since the Code Red and Nimda worms struck the Internet in 2001.

There was worse to come in August when the Blaster worm struck hundreds of thousands of Internet-connected computers by attacking a known flaw in several versions of the Windows OS software. The worm triggered computers to shut down and restart and dramatically slowed corporate networks as it spread itself to other computers in a flood of electronic messages. Blaster and its variants collectively caused an estimated $2 billion in damage during eight days of Internet attacks that affected people ranging from employees of the Maryland motor vehicle agency to Internet users in Sweden. Experts agreed that the Blaster attack could have been prevented had corporate and home computer users downloaded and installed a Microsoft software patch for Windows. The patches often were not installed, however, typically because corporate information technology (IT) departments were too busy or consumers were unaware that the patches were available. A similar patch had been available in advance to prevent the Slammer attack on corporate servers, but it also was not widely installed. Critics asserted that these lapses revealed serious flaws in the industry's method of issuing critical software updates.

The effects of the original Blaster worm had barely begun to subside when a new variant of the worm, called Welchia, appeared. Welchia also gained entry to computers via a Windows security flaw but on an altruistic mission: it counteracted Blaster by downloading and installing the Microsoft patch that prevented future Blaster infections. Despite this, Welchia proved to be just as troublesome as Blaster because it spread itself to new computers so quickly that it clogged corporate networks.

About the same time that Welchia attacked networks, users of Internet e-mail were struck by a fast-spreading computer virus called SoBig.F. Every time a recipient opened a virus-laden e-mail attachment, SoBig.F infected the computer and e-mailed copies of itself to other computers. As a result, the virus filled e-mail in-boxes around the world and multiplied faster than had any previous computer virus.

There was wide accord on the need for more Internet security but less agreement on how to achieve it. The administration of U.S. Pres. George W. Bush favoured a cooperative partnership between government and industry to improve security rather than new government regulations. The Bush administration's plan, called the National Strategy to Secure Cyberspace, urged the creation of an emergency-response system to confront Internet attacks. The Department of Homeland Security was to be in charge of the project and later created a partnership with Carnegie Mellon University's CERT Coordination Center, which tracked Internet threats, in hopes of improving techniques for preventing, monitoring, and responding to attacks. Some data-security professionals argued that the plan's chief shortcoming was that it contained few security guidelines for industry to follow.

Despite the government's plan, private security experts worried that the Internet had entered a new era in which threats were easy to launch but had devastating impact. Some experts claimed that attacks could not be prevented until major software products had been completely redesigned to be more secure, a process that might take years. That was bad news at a time when Internet threats were increasing. According to Symantec Corp., an antivirus software firm, the number of potentially harmful software vulnerabilities discovered rose 12% in 2003 compared with the prior year. The firm also stated that about 80% of new software vulnerabilities could be exploited by someone working remotely on the Internet.

Most of the Internet attackers evaded law-enforcement officials because of the anonymous nature of the Internet. The few who were caught appeared not to be the masterminds behind the attacks but copycat attackers who adapted existing Internet worms or viruses or downloaded the building blocks for computer attacks from Internet sites devoted to hacking. Authorities arrested a 24-year-old Romanian man, an 18-year-old high-school student in Hopkins, Minn., and an unidentified juvenile for allegedly having created copycat versions of the original Blaster worm. The original authors of the Blaster or Welchia worms or the SoBig.F virus, however, had not been found by year's end.

Although not as disruptive as computer worms and viruses, the rising tide of unsolicited commercial e-mail, or spam, was a burden to e-mail users worldwide. By some estimates spam accounted for about half of the e-mail most people received daily, and pornographic spam was an increasing annoyance. As a result, there was much discussion about new laws to regulate spam or new technical solutions to limit it, such as filtering software that kept unwanted e-mail from reaching a recipient's inbox.

Some Internet service providers (ISPs) rushed to offer filters. The largest provider, America Online (AOL), claimed to have stopped more than two billion spam messages in a single day, but most software filters proved unable to block all undesirable e-mail without also deleting some "good" e-mail as well. A self-taught programmer who admitted to having sent more than 100 million pieces of spam in a 12-hour period told a U.S. Senate committee that he could easily outwit even sophisticated software filters. A survey of Internet users showed that fewer than half found spam-filtering software to be effective.

One popular legal solution discussed in Congress was a "do not spam" list similar to the Federal Trade Commission's (FTC's) "do not call" list that telemarketers were supposed to heed. Violators of the "do not spam" list would be fined or jailed. Congress passed and President Bush signed an antispam law that authorized the FTC to study the feasibility of a "do not spam" list. The law also prohibited sending bulk commercial e-mail that concealed the identity of the sender or sought to trick the recipient with a misleading subject line. In addition, the law required that commercial e-mail allow recipients to opt out of receiving future e-mail and that pornographic e-mail carry an identifying label.

Those familiar with the Internet believed that such a law would be difficult to enforce because it was too easy for senders of spam to conceal their identities. Some observers pointed out that people sending spam often made illicit use of a feature called "open relay," which was found in some computer e-mail servers around the world. Those servers would relay spam automatically to recipients and, in effect, conceal the original sources of the messages. Direct marketers opposed the creation of a "do not spam" list, arguing that it would hurt law-abiding companies and have no effect on firms that chose to ignore the list. The Direct Marketing Association, however, supported the antispam legislation, saying that a national law would result in uniform enforcement of e-mail marketing rules.

The new federal law invalidated a stricter California antispam law, which had banned sending most forms of commercial e-mail to or from the state unless the recipient had specifically requested it. The California law went farther than regulations in most other U.S. states because it attempted to regulate all e-mail advertising, not just the type that was deceptively labeled in order to encourage recipients to read it. The broad wording of the law had been expected to draw court challenges.

Spam also posed problems for e-commerce. Amazon.com filed 11 lawsuits against online marketers who allegedly forged Amazon's name to their e-mails, using a technical trick known as "spoofing." The real e-mail sender's identity was concealed, and in its place was put the name of a reputable third party—in this case Amazon—whose e-mail Internet users were more likely to open.

A new Internet business venture disturbed antispam activists and raised privacy issues, but it folded after less than a month. VeriSign, a company that assigned and administered some Web addresses, launched a for-profit service that was designed to help Internet users who typed in erroneous Web addresses. Instead of giving the users error messages, the service gave them alternative Web addresses or paid advertising links. Critics observed that the service would help defeat antispam filtering software and that it raised privacy questions by redirecting Web surfers without their permission. In the end the Internet Corporation for Assigned Names and Numbers, an Internet oversight group, pressured VeriSign to drop the service.

Corporate News. The economy made 2003 another tough year for computer technology companies. Corporate IT spending continued to be depressed, which put even more pressure on the bottom lines of companies that supplied computers and software. As the year ended, the Connecticut-based research firm Gartner Group predicted that the three-year downturn in computer-related spending was ending and that global technology spending would rise from $2.27 trillion in 2003 to $2.4 trillion in 2004.

Several corporate consolidations took place during the year. Yahoo spent $1.6 billion to buy Overture Services, Inc., which pioneered the concept of companies' paying for a favourable position on a search engine's results page. Data storage systems firm EMC Corp. bought Legato Systems, a storage software firm, for $1.3 billion and acquired Documentum, Inc., a document management software firm, for $1.43 billion. Database firm Oracle's $7.25 billion unfriendly bid to take over enterprise human resources software firm PeopleSoft was extended to February 2004, the sixth extension of the deadline. As PeopleSoft's outlook improved, its stock rose above Oracle's per-share bid price and thereby cast doubt on whether the transaction would occur. The deal also hinged on whether it was considered anticompetitive by U.S. and European Commission regulators. Oracle had launched its bid days after PeopleSoft reported that it would acquire manufacturing-integration software firm J.D. Edwards for $1.7 billion. Palm bought personal digital assistant competitor Handspring, but the value of the deal was difficult to calculate because the stock transaction excluded the value of Palm's PalmSource software operations, which were slated for a separate spinoff. Palm and Handspring were combined to form PalmOne.

Other companies reacted to the economy by trying to be more nimble. Advanced Micro Devices (AMD) sought to stay a step ahead of its larger rival, Intel Corp., by introducing its own version of the 64-bit microprocessor, the next step in boosting computer power by processing larger slices of data at one time. AMD's new 64-bit chip offered backward compatibility with 32-bit programs written for PCs and network servers, while Intel's two-year-old 64-bit chip had required new software written specifically for its architecture—a factor cited by some industry observers as the reason Intel's chip had been slow to take off.

Apple led the way as personal computer manufacturers tried to remake themselves into consumer electronics companies in order to deal with the slowed market for personal computers. Apple gained considerable publicity with its iPod MP3 music player and its iTunes authorized music-download service, especially when iTunes was adapted to the much larger Windows-based PC market late in the year; these initiatives contributed to a 36% increase in Apple's revenue over the previous year. PC companies trying to branch out into consumer electronics included Dell Inc., Gateway, Inc., and Hewlett-Packard Co. (HP). Dell, for example, introduced a music player, an online music service, a liquid crystal display television set, and a new handheld computer. While Dell made the move into consumer electronics from a position of strength in the PC business, Gateway sought to use consumer electronics devices to save its financially ailing PC business. Meanwhile, HP, fresh from its takeover of Compaq Computer Corp., released digital cameras and other digital entertainment products.

AOL's parent company, AOL Time Warner Inc., changed its name to Time Warner Inc. to shed the image of its slowing AOL Internet access business. Observers considered this an admission that the 2000 merger of AOL and Time Warner had been a failure. AOL announced plans to offer a discounted $9.95 per month dial-up Internet access service under its Netscape brand name; that represented a considerable reduction from the $23.90 a month charged for the AOL brand-name service.

Many companies reduced employment to cope with a difficult economy. Sony Corp. announced that it would eliminate 20,000 jobs, or 13% of its workforce, as part of a plan to save $3 billion over three years. EDS Corp., the second largest computer-services firm, planned to eliminate about 2% of its workforce, or some 2,700 employees. Sun Microsystems cut about 3% of its workforce to cope with more than two years of declining sales. Gateway eliminated more than 1,900 jobs and closed 80 of its retail stores. High-end computing firm Silicon Graphics laid off nearly one-fourth of its employees as it tried to cut expenses.

The number of students pursuing computer technology careers in college continued to drop, an apparent reflection of the reduction in job prospects in the field due to the economy. Colleges with big computer science and electrical engineering departments reported enrollment declines of 20–40% in those departments since 2001, which was shortly after the bursting of the Internet bubble of business activity. The lessened interest in technical fields came at the same time that the U.S. government and IT companies were defending the outsourcing of computer technology jobs to countries where wages were lower. Gartner predicted that by 2008 a quarter of all technology jobs would be located in less-developed countries with low costs.

Some technology firm executives stated that American corporations would reinvest the money saved through outsourcing and that this would lead to more American jobs in the long run. Others suggested the impending retirement of the post-World War II baby-boom generation would open up more computer technology job opportunities in the U.S., despite outsourcing. Computer executives also admitted that there was a risk that outsourcing might simply result in fewer American computer technology jobs. The U.S. government opposed any limits on the outsourcing of computer technology jobs, calling it a short-term protectionist approach, but there was some concern in Congress over the offshore outsourcing of work on government contracts.

The PC industry seemed to be on an upward trend late in the year, although there was little economic recovery in the American business market, a key segment for the PC industry's prosperity. Worldwide PC shipments grew faster than anticipated in the third quarter and were about 15% higher than in the same period a year earlier.

As the year drew to a close, IBM Corp. reported that it was beginning to see signs of economic stabilization and expected to create 10,000 new jobs in 2004. Google, the privately owned search engine company that had become nearly a household word, remained consistently profitable. Google's edge was its private computer network that periodically scoured and stored a large percentage of the Internet's Web pages and then used them to provide what were widely considered the best searches of that information. By year's end investors were expecting an initial public stock offering (IPO) from Google that some estimated could value the company at more than $15 billion.

PC industry pioneer Adam Osborne, a former technical writer who introduced the first portable personal computer in 1981, died at age 64. (*See* OBITUARIES.)

Internet Access. Wireless computer networks grew in popularity as more coffee shops, hotels, restaurants, and airports offered "hot spots" (very localized signal-coverage areas) based on a technology called Wi-Fi (for wireless fidelity). The same technology was used for home computer networks because it eliminated the need to run wires between computers. Within a radius of 9–90 m (30–300 ft) from the hot spot's antenna, computers equipped with Wi-Fi circuit cards or chips could connect to the Internet without visible communications links. Two commonly used versions of Wi-Fi, known as 802.11b and 802.11g, enabled wireless transmission speeds of 11 million bits per second (bps) or 54 million bits. Next-generation Wi-Fi standards being developed held out the promise of speeds of 200 million bps or more.

Some businesses, such as Starbucks coffee shops and McDonald's restaurants, charged customers for Wi-Fi use, while others offered the service for free in order to attract customers. Free service was practical because Wi-Fi equipment was relatively inexpensive and because many businesses already had high-speed connections to the Internet that also could handle the added Wi-Fi traffic.

Intel introduced its new Centrino microchips that provided laptops with built-in Wi-Fi capability. In addition, new Wi-Fi accessories for videogame consoles simplified playing games over the Internet by connecting game machines in the living room to a high-speed Internet connection in another part of the house.

Wi-Fi, however, was in its early days, and for-pay hot spots were expected to generate no more than $20 million–$60 million in annual revenue in the U.S. Some analysts predicted Wi-Fi revenue might reach $1 billion or more in the U.S. in only three years. Cellular telephone companies appeared poised to become significant Wi-Fi providers; T-Mobile was an early entrant that provided service in more than 2,500 bookstores and coffee shops. Conventional wired telephone companies saw Wi-Fi as an extra service they could use to keep digital subscriber line (DSL) customers from defecting to cable modems, which operated over cable TV networks. For example, Verizon Communications, the largest U.S. local telephone company, continued to add hot spots in parts of New York City. It offered free use of the hot spots to customers of its wired DSL service.

Wi-Fi also created new security problems for the unwary. People using public hot spots might have their e-mail communications intercepted by others, and home and business owners of Wi-Fi networks did not always know they should encrypt their network traffic to safeguard it from passersby with laptop computers. Sophisticated wireless snoops could sometimes steal Internet access, as well as data, user names, and passwords.

ISPs saw an increasing number of their customers switch from dial-up Internet access to high-speed broadband during the year. In the U.S., cable modems continued to outpace DSL; by

Wi-Fi *became a buzzword in 2003. Here Web surfers use the high-speed wireless Internet service in New York City's Madison Square Park, one of the 150 "hot spots" established by Verizon Communications in May.*

AP/Wide World Photos

mid-2003 cable modem connections had more than a two-to-one lead over DSL. As DSL providers such as Verizon, SBC Communications, and EarthLink began cutting prices to be more competitive, some cable systems responded by increasing the speed they offered consumers. By year's end cable companies Comcast Cable Communications and Adelphia Communications were claiming they would increase Net access speeds to 3,000,000 bps for downloads, about double the previous maximum the firms offered their consumer customers (upload speeds remained a relatively slow 256,000 bps).

South Korea, with the encouragement of its government, became a showcase for high-speed Internet access. Telecommunications companies there built what was widely considered to be the most elaborate Net access system in the world. South Koreans adapted by making online gaming and video a part of their daily lives. Experts expressed concern about the risks in broadband connections around the world because these systems were "always on" and therefore more vulnerable to hackers than traditional dial-up connections, which were connected only intermittently.

Those in the U.S. who lacked broadband connections could buy a little more speed for their existing dial-up modems. Dial-up customers, who paid about $20 a month for Internet access, had the option of paying an extra $5–$8 monthly for data-compression software that made Web pages download more than twice as fast. That was still well short of broadband speeds, but it was also cheaper, since broadband typically cost $40–$50 a month. The compression software sometimes adversely affected the quality of photographic images, a problem that could be cleared up by slowing the download speed.

Legal Decisions and Crime. The U.S. Supreme Court agreed to step into a controversial case about how to protect children from inappropriate online material. The Child Online Protection Act, passed in 1998 to punish Internet sites that failed to prevent children from seeing pornography or other inappropriate material, was overturned twice by an appeals court on the grounds that it was too restrictive of what adults had a right to see. The act, which was not in force pending the outcome of the Supreme Court case, was backed by the federal government but opposed by the American Civil Liberties Union, on the grounds that it restricted free speech. The act was the government's second effort to enact Internet protections for children. The Supreme Court had ruled in 1997 that a previous law, the Communications Decency Act (passed in 1996), was unconstitutional because it restricted free speech.

The Supreme Court upheld another controversial law restricting Internet access, the Children's Internet Protection Act, which required libraries and schools to use Internet filters to protect against inappropriate material or risk losing federal funds. Librarians lost their challenge that the law was unconstitutional.

In a closely watched legal battle that could affect the rest of the electronics industry, IBM was the subject of more than 200 lawsuits brought by employees who claimed that they were harmed by chemicals used in the firm's electronics-manufacturing processes. The case could affect other manufacturers of semiconductors and computer hard-disk drives that used similar chemicals during the 1970s and '80s. As the first of the cases went to court, IBM protested that there was no evidence that the employees became sick because they were exposed to chemicals on the job. IBM also denied plaintiff allegations that it covered up the chemicals problem.

IBM also was locked in a legal fight over OS software. The SCO Group filed a $3 billion lawsuit, charging the computer industry giant with having illegally taken pieces of SCO's Unix computer operating software code and put them into the IBM version of the Linux OS. IBM filed counterclaims alleging that SCO had violated IBM patents and engaged in unfair trade practices.

While Microsoft had settled the U.S. government's antitrust suit against it in 2001, the firm continued to have antitrust trouble in Europe. The European Commission accused Microsoft of unfairly using its dominance in media-player software and in Web and e-mail servers to improve its position in other parts of the software market. As part of a four-year antitrust case, the European Commission let it be known that it was considering a fine against Microsoft and possibly the forced disclosure of Microsoft's server software source code to other firms. Microsoft declined to comment on the likely outcome of the case but said that it would try to respond to the commission's concerns. Microsoft also described software-licensing changes that it had made in connection with its settlement of the U.S. government's antitrust lawsuit. The company asserted that the changes made it simpler and less expensive for competitors to use Microsoft source code to make sure their server software worked well with Windows OS software.

Some experts reported in 2003 that computer crime was becoming more elaborate. The head of the U.K.'s National Hi-Tech Crime Unit said organized crime had increased its presence on the Internet, where it was engaging in extortion, child pornography, and financial scams. Internet security experts affirmed that the online sale of stolen credit-card numbers, once carried out by lone hackers, had become a group activity in which large numbers of people used Internet relay chat to buy and sell the stolen card numbers as well as to check the validity of the numbers.

Adrian Lamo, a 22-year-old hacker, faced federal charges in connection with his alleged illegal accessing of the internal computer network at the *New York Times* newspaper in 2002. A 19-year-old Pennsylvania college student, Van Dinh, was accused by the Securities and Exchange Commission of having used hacking and identity theft to aid in bogus securities transactions in which he sold stock options in Cisco Systems a week before they were to expire. A 25-year-old New York City man was arrested for having stolen bank-account information from 450 customers of a photocopying shop; police said he placed software on the shop's computers that captured customers' keystrokes and thus revealed their personal information.

Sometimes security lapses made online theft easier. Microsoft acknowledged that a security flaw in its Internet Passport service, which was designed to make Internet commerce easier by identifying customers to Web merchants, had left 200 million consumer accounts vulnerable to hackers. Microsoft said that only a small number of Internet Passport users were hurt by the security lapse, but the company would not say how many.

In one of the first cases of its kind, a British man was acquitted of dealing in child pornography after convincing the court that his PC had been infected by a rogue hacker program that collected the illegal child-pornography photos and stored them on his hard drive without his knowledge. A computer security consultant who examined the man's PC found a dozen so-called "Trojan horse" programs on the hard drive that had been placed there by outsiders.

(continued on page 168)

Genealogy Takes Root on the Internet

By 2003 the number of people who had discovered the benefit of using the Internet to research their ancestry had increased dramatically. Many Web sites provide access to databases containing indexes to vital records and population censuses useful for genealogical research. For example, in September 2002 *Scotland's People,* the official Web site for the General Register Office for Scotland, became the world's first site to offer downloads of digitized copies of official birth, marriage, and death records. Scottish census records for 1891 and 1901 are also online, and baptism, marriage, and burial entries from the country's church registers were expected to become available in 2004. For a small fee, any of these images may be downloaded to a home computer and printed out. Not only is this method less expensive than ordering copies of documents for delivery by post, but it is also much more convenient than having to visit—or hiring a local researcher to visit—an archive that may be located thousands of kilometres away or in another country. In addition, a good deal of census and immigration information is available for purchase on CD-ROM, as are entries in parish and criminal registers and militia muster rolls. Many 19th- and early 20th-century trade directories and atlases had similarly been digitized and published on CD-ROM.

"Software programs also allow information to be shared with other family members by burning it on to CD-ROM or posting it to Web sites."

Specialized computer programs, including Personal Ancestral File, Family Tree Maker, and Generations, have been available to genealogists for 15 years. This software can help organize information that family historians have collected about their ancestors and facilitate the printing out of the data in family groups or various forms of family tree. Software programs also allow information to be shared with other family members by burning it on to CD-ROM or posting it to Web sites. Most programs assist in the transfer of genealogical data to and from other researchers, even when they use different software programs, through a common standard for genealogical data called GEDCOM, which was developed by the Church of Jesus Christ of Latter-day Saints (LDS). The LDS Church has long been a pioneer in genealogical research because its members believe that their deceased ancestors can be eternally reunited with their families through temple covenants, but LDS members have to identify them first.

One of the first genealogy databases to be transferred to the Internet was the International Genealogical Index (IGI), which contains birth and marriage information from around the world. The IGI was compiled by the LDS and was previously available on microfiche. Other databases on the LDS's freely accessible FamilySearch Web site include transcriptions of the 1880 federal census of the U.S. and the 1881 censuses for Canada and England and Wales.

Another major genealogy Web site, *Ancestry.com,* provides subscribers with access to a number of family history databases, including digitized images of the U.S. federal censuses from 1790 to 1930. The index to the 1930 census, which contains information about 124 million Americans, became available online in January 2003. The U.K.-oriented version of the site, *Ancestry.co.uk,* contains images from the 1891 England and Wales census. In April 2003 *Ancestry.com*'s owners, MyFamily.com, acquired the rival subscription Web site *Genealogy.com.* The site includes databases containing ships' passenger lists of immigrants to America and provides free access to the 55 million names on the U.S. Social Security Death Index 1937–1997. *RootsWeb.com,* also owned by MyFamily.com, is a free genealogy Web site providing many tools for both beginners and experienced researchers. The site also contains more than 27,000 mailing lists and 132,000 message boards through which family historians can communicate and provide help to one another.

Although full civil registration records for England and Wales are not yet accessible online, the relevant indexes have been accessible since 2003 via the *Family Research Link* Web site. The 1901 census for England and Wales has its own site, from which images may be downloaded for a fee. Searching the index is, however, free of charge. Digitized copies of wills and estate inventories for Scotland from 1500 to 1901 are downloadable from the *Scottish Documents* Web site, and all those for England and Wales from 1384 to 1858 from the *Documents Online* Web site. In both cases there is a charge for downloaded copies but not for an index search.

Other useful Web sites for genealogy researchers include that for Ellis Island, which contains a searchable database of the 22 million immigrants who arrived in the U.S. between 1892 and 1924. The Commonwealth War Graves Commission site has an index of the 1.7 million members of the armed forces of the U.K., Australia, Canada, India, New Zealand, and South Africa who died in World Wars I and II. Since 1996 American family historian Cyndi Howells has compiled a list of links to genealogical Web sites. By the end of 2003, *Cyndi's List* contained more than 200,000 links to an astonishing variety of sites throughout the world. The U.S. GenWeb Project is a network of Web sites staffed by volunteers committed to providing free genealogical information for every county in the U.S.; it is especially rich in the areas of local history, state censuses, and church and cemetery information.

In the past few years, what were referred to as "genetic genealogy" sites have appeared on the Web offering DNA testing and containing databases of previously acquired DNA samples. Mitochondrial DNA, which is principally inherited from female ancestors, may provide a link to people who lived more than 10,000 years ago. Y-chromosome DNA, which is passed down through the male line only, can be used to link families together and indicate their likely origin. All mitochondrial and Y-chromosome DNA samples obtained (so far) indicate that all humans are related, although estimates of how long ago our most recent common ancestor lived vary from 120,000 to 2 million years. Genetic genealogy is still in its infancy, but advances in the study of genetics might enable family historians a decade from now to prove scientifically their descent from historical personages and compile family trees currently beyond their wildest dreams. (ALAN STEWART)

(continued from page 166)

E-Commerce. E-commerce played a role in changing attitudes toward romance as online dating services became more socially acceptable. By midyear 45 million Americans were visiting online dating services every month, nearly a 30% increase from the end of 2002. Subscription revenues for dating Web sites were projected to total about $100 million a quarter in 2003, or 10 times more than they had been at the beginning of 2001. Genealogy software and online databases (both free and subscription) offered people new ways to investigate family history and had the potential to provide "genetic genealogy" in the search for more distant ancestry. (*See* Sidebar.)

A new approach to online book marketing rankled authors by disclosing a considerable amount of a book's content for free. An Amazon.com feature that let people search the texts of 120,000 books for specific words or phrases let users view up to 20 pages of a book at once, and sometimes much more if the user performed a series of searches. About 190 publishers took part voluntarily in the Amazon service, but some declared that they wanted to make sure the service did not hurt book sales.

Demand for online retailing led to a resurgence in IPOs. That was a welcome change for a group of companies that had not fared well with potential investors since the burst of the Internet bubble three years earlier. While the amounts raised in the IPOs were relatively modest, in the range of tens of millions of dollars, the change in investors' mood was expected to make it easier for other online sellers to raise operating capital.

Online auctions, one of the major success stories of e-commerce, were nonetheless plagued by fraud. Some law-enforcement officials reported that auctions accounted for nearly half of all Internet fraud complaints. In a crackdown on auction fraud, the FTC and 33 state and local law-enforcement agencies filed 51 criminal and civil cases for questionable auction activities. Violations ranged from sellers' failing to deliver items that had been sold to sellers' using phony third-party escrow services that purported to hold payment money from the buyer until goods had been delivered by the seller. Identity theft, in which auction accounts were set up using names and numbers from stolen credit cards, was another source of auction fraud.

E-commerce seemed likely to benefit from the U.S. government's continued philosophy of not taxing Internet access. At year's end some members of Congress were leaning in favour of extending the tax ban, but final passage of a measure was delayed until at least early 2004. The U.S. House of Representatives passed a bill that would extend and expand a five-year-old Internet tax holiday. The tax moratorium would ban state and local governments from taxing Internet access and would end legal loopholes that had allowed some states to keep their Internet taxes. Some U.S. senators were in favour of permanently banning taxes on Internet access, but the Senate bill worried state tax collectors, who feared that all telephone company voice-call charges eventually would become exempt from taxation when telephone companies converted to Internet telephony, in which calls were routed over the Internet instead of through the traditional telephone network. A complete shift to Internet telephony appeared to be years away.

Computer Games. The once-mighty Sega Corp. faced a merger with Japan's Sammy Corp., but after talks fell through, Sammy instead became the biggest shareholder in Sega. Observers alleged that Sega's sales had fallen because it tried to make too many different types of games and wound up with many that were unremarkable. The company's financial troubles also were related to its failed Dreamcast game console, which it had discontinued in 2001.

Competition also hurt Nintendo's GameCube game console, and the company temporarily stopped manufacturing it in August when GameCube sales were running behind those of Sony's PlayStation2 and Microsoft's Xbox. At year's end some analysts considered Nintendo to be in the least-favourable position of the three console makers, despite a sales spurt for GameCube following a September price drop from $150 to $99. Nintendo faced new competition in the handheld-gaming-market segment that it previously had dominated. Cellular telephone manufacturer Nokia introduced the N-Gage, a combination cell phone and game machine that competed with Nintendo's latest handheld, the GameBoy Advance SP. Sony announced plans to introduce its own portable game player, the PSP, in late 2004.

Violent videogames got an unexpected endorsement when the journal *Nature* published one of the first studies to document the benefits of playing video games. The research showed that experienced first-person shooter players were 30% better than nonplayers when it came to noticing things that happened around them by means such as peripheral vision and rapidly switching attention.

New Ideas. Hard-disk-drive manufacturer Maxtor announced that it had developed a new technique called "perpendicular recording." The technology, along with a new type of recording surface for hard disks, could more than double the amount of data on a 9-cm (3.5-in) disk to 175 billion bytes. Magink, a display technology firm, produced a sort of "electronic paper" with a surface that looked like paper but behaved like an electronic screen. The technology could produce high-resolution colour images by using electric charges to change the way surface particles reflected light.

There were some signs of technological cooperation that had long been lacking. The Reuters Group, an information services firm, announced interoperability agreements between its relatively small instant messaging (IM) service and those of IM giants Microsoft, AOL, and the Lotus division of IBM. Lack of interoperability had prevented users of one IM service from communicating with users of another.

A new wireless data service continued to blur the distinction between telephones and computers. Picture phones (cellular telephones with built-in cameras) became one of the hottest wireless products, even though the photographs they took were of low quality. The key appeared to be their immediacy; a picture-phone owner could, in a few moments, take a photo and transmit it to another wireless phone or send it over the Internet to an e-mail recipient. Other hybrid phone-data devices included phones that could send e-mail, browse the Internet, or function as palmtop computers.

The year was not without some techno-silliness. "Flash mobs"—groups of strangers who were mobilized on short notice via Web sites, online discussion groups, or e-mail distribution lists—took part in bizarre but harmless activities in public places, such as calling out the same words or eating the same food. While flash-mob antics tended to be silly, some experts conjectured that they held the promise of organizing people for more practical purposes, such as political demonstrations. (STEVE ALEXANDER)

Earth Sciences

Scientists searching for better ways to predict EARTHQUAKES began drilling a deep borehole though an INFAMOUS FAULT ZONE. The past century of GLOBAL WARMING was reported to be changing species' ranges and the timing of spring events. A LASER-BASED MAPPING technique capable of seeing the ground between trees revealed previously UNSUSPECTED GEOLOGIC FEATURES in the Puget Sound area.

GEOLOGY AND GEOCHEMISTRY

A team of earth scientists in 2003 reported the success of an experiment, begun in 1999 in western Washington state, that was revolutionizing investigations of surface-rupturing faults, landslide hazards, surface processes such as runoff and flooding, and past continental glaciation in the region. The dense forest cover in the Puget Sound area had frustrated high-resolution topographic mapping of the land surface by conventional photographic techniques. In an alternate approach, Ralph Haugerud of the U.S. Geological Survey (USGS) and five colleagues from the USGS, NASA, and the Puget Sound Regional Council synthesized topographic survey data collected from aircraft by lidar (light detection and ranging). Analogous to radar mapping with microwaves, the lidar technique measured the distance to a target by timing the round-trip travel of short laser pulses scanned across and reflected from the target area. The narrow laser beam, operating at a typical pulse rate of 30,000 per second, was able to probe between trees to reveal variations in surface height with a remarkable accuracy of 10–20 cm (4–8 in). The Puget Sound Lidar Consortium, an informal group of planners and researchers supported by the USGS, NASA, and local government, acquired the lidar topographic data for more than 10,000 sq km (3,860 sq mi) of lowlands around Puget Sound.

Ralph A. Haugerud, of the USGS, and David J. Harding, of NASA

An area of mixed forest and clearing in western Washington is shown in a digital map synthesized from lidar data. Data points representing trees were subtracted from all but the segment at left to reveal the topography of the bare earth.

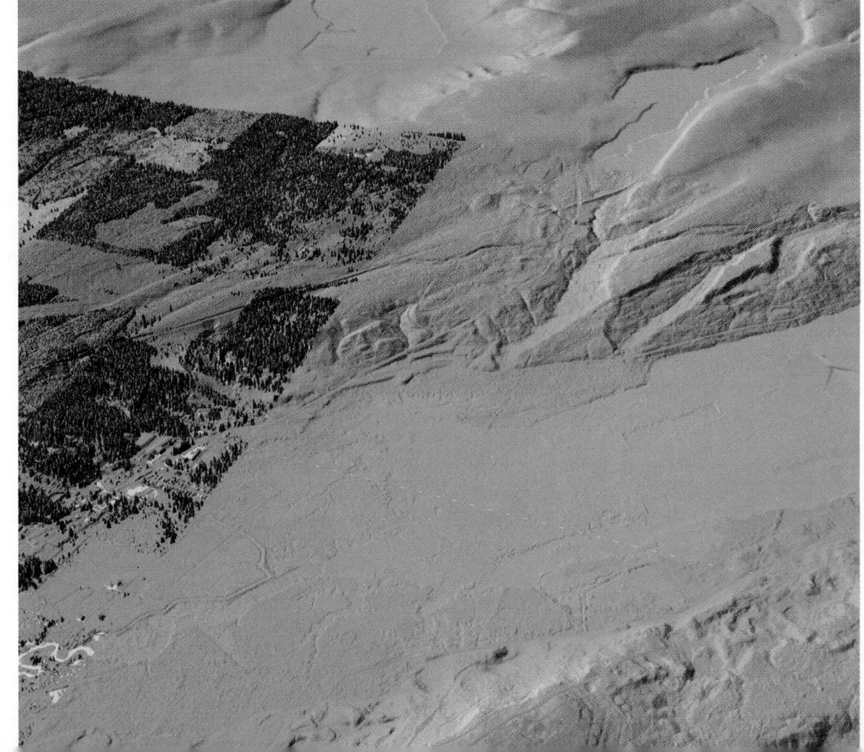

The effort resulted in the discovery of many previously unidentified geologic features, including ruptures along five known fault zones, some of which were later explored on the ground to investigate the frequency of past breaks and associated earthquakes. Among the evidence for glacial processes revealed by the lidar mapping were two intersecting sets of roughly parallel grooves spaced hundreds of metres apart in the solid land surface and having amplitudes (distances from ridge crests to valley bottoms) of metres to tens of metres. One set of older north-south grooves was overprinted by another set of younger grooves having a northeast-southwest orientation. This topography was caused by flowing ice and clearly demonstrated a significant change in the direction of ice flow.

The glaciers that spread across North America and Eurasia during the last ice age were trivial compared with the ice postulated to have covered all of Earth during so-called Snowball Earth periods about 2.4 billion years ago and again between 890 million and 580 million years ago. In 2003 John Higgins and Daniel Schrag of Harvard University used the results of a computed model of the ocean-atmosphere system to interpret the geochemistry of the global, characteristic sequence of limestone deposits—carbonate "cap rocks"—that overlie the glacial deposits of the more recent snowball period. Previous arguments had assumed that the carbon isotopes cycling between the atmosphere, the ocean, and exposed carbonate rock would be in a steady state, which did not explain the unusual changes in concentrations of carbon isotopes found in the cap rocks. The new model calculations accounted for the changes in terms of an increase in sea-surface temperature, which affected the exchange between carbon dioxide and the carbonates that form the rocks. In the early 1990s, Joseph Kirschvink of the California Institute of Technology had solved the dilemma of how Earth could have escaped its snowball condition through accumulation of carbon dioxide in the atmosphere from volcanic degassing and consequent trapping of solar radiation via the greenhouse effect. The new calculations emphasized the importance of the effect of high atmospheric carbon dioxide concentration on seawater chemistry and its relationship to the formation of the limestone cap rocks associated with the thawing of a frozen Earth.

Geochemical evidence from the deep drill cores extracted from the remaining ice sheets in Greenland and Antarctica since the 1970s have transformed investigations of Earth's climatic history. In the Vostok ice core drilled from Antarctica in the 1980s, the concentrations of hydrogen isotopes in the ice vary with increasing depth (corresponding to increasing time since the ice was deposited) in regular fluctuations that are associated with climatic cycles. Mechanisms to explain climatic cycles also involve the ocean, but scientists had found it difficult to correlate time periods that had been determined for depths within the ice core with time periods recorded in ocean sediments. During the year P. Graham Mortyn of the Scripps Institution of Oceanography, La Jolla, Calif., and four colleagues from Scripps and the University of Florida reported finding such a correlation. In so doing they clarified relationships between the Antarctic polar climate, air-sea interactions, and variability in the deep ocean and again demonstrated the important role of carbon dioxide as a greenhouse gas in past climate change. Mortyn and associates compared hydrogen isotope records from the Vostok core with their own detailed geochemical measurements of oxygen isotopes present in selected deep-sea sediment cores from the South Atlantic Ocean adjacent to Antarctica. They confirmed that the timing of the oscillations in both were synchronous over the past 60,000 years, and they extended the study of temperature oscillations through the past 400,000 years, using data from a previously drilled sediment core. The results suggested that during the last four major deglaciation events (ice-sheet retreats), changes in the temperature of polar air were synchronous with those of the nearby deep ocean and with changes in atmospheric content of carbon dioxide.

Uncertainties about Earth's internal temperature were reduced in 2003 as a result of two independent sets of experiments, by Charles Lesher of the University of California, Davis, and three colleagues and by Kyoko Matsukage of Ibaraki University, Mito, Japan, and Keiko Kubo of the Tokyo Institute of Technology. Experimental determination of the temperature at which peridotite in Earth's mantle begins to melt as a function of depth (i.e., its melting curve, or solidus) provides some calibration for thermal models of Earth's interior and for the temperatures and types of melting experienced by peridotite rising in mantle plumes. Results published between 1986 and 2000 had differed by 150 °C (270 °F) in the pressure range of 4–6 gigapascals (GPa; corresponding to depths of 120–180 km [75–110 mi]). Lesher and colleagues concluded after intricate tests that the differences had arisen from the misbehaviour of thermocouples (temperature-measuring devices) used in some of the earlier experiments. Their results indicated that the solidus temperature of mantle peridotite at the investigated pressure range was as much as 150 °C lower than usually assumed, which had significant implications for estimated temperatures in connection with mantle convection and magma generation in general.

In related experiments at lower pressures (1–2.5 GPa, corresponding to depths of 35–80 km [20–50 mi]), Matsukage and Kubo determined for the first time the systematic variation of chromium content in the mineral spinel as its parent rock, a type of dry (water-free) peridotite, was progressively melted. They compared their results with the measured chromium content in spinel from many natural peridotites and demonstrated that most of these rocks, which were known to have come from the mantle, had undergone more than one episode of partial melting. This supported the view that such rocks had experienced a complex history of successive episodes of magma generation and separation. In addition, the results of their dry experiments, compared with other experiments that included water under pressure, confirmed the generally accepted hypothesis that partial melting of peridotites originating from subduction zones (where the oceanic tectonic plates are sinking into the mantle) was accompanied by an influx of water-bearing fluid or melt. The source of the water presumably was ocean water that earlier had generated hydrated minerals in the basalt of the sinking oceanic plate.

(PETER J. WYLLIE)

GEOPHYSICS

During 2003, there were 14 major earthquakes (those of moment magnitude [M_w] 7.0 –7.9) and one great earthquake (M_w 8.0 or higher). On December 26 the deadliest earthquake of the year (M_w6.6) struck southeastern Iran, killing at least 41,000 people and injuring a comparable number. The city of Bam was hardest hit, with 85% of buildings damaged or destroyed. Another earthquake (M_w 6.8) with a high death toll rocked northern Algeria on May 21, taking more than 2,200 lives. Other earthquakes with significant fatalities occurred on January 22 (M_w 7.6) in Colima state, Mex.; February 24 (M_w 6.4) in southern Xinjiang province, China; and May 1 (M_w 6.4) in eastern Turkey. The great earthquake of the period (M_w 8.3) struck the southeastern Hokkaido region of Japan on September 25; because its epicentre was about 60 km (40 mi) offshore, injuries and damage were comparatively light.

Old observations regarding the connections between earthquakes and hydrology were discussed in new ways during the year. For instance, it had long been regarded as little more than scientific curiosities that after big earthquake tremors, nearby streams sometimes flowed more rapidly for a few days and wells located thousands of kilometres away showed permanent falls or rises in water levels. In a review of recent research on the hydrologic effects of earthquake-caused crustal deformation and ground shaking, Michael Manga of the University of California, Berkeley, and David Montgomery of the University of Washington suggested that in some instances of stream-flow surges following earthquakes, shallow seismic waves pass through groundwater-sodden soil, shaking and compacting it and squeezing the water into streams. In cases of wells drilled into solid bedrock, the researchers described how seismic waves can riddle the rock with fractures, whereupon water seeps in and well-water levels drop. In cases of wells drilled into aquifers made of unconsolidated deposits, seismic waves can compact the deposits and shrink the aquifer volume, pushing the water table upward. Manga and Montgomery concluded that the complex interactions between earthquakes and hydrologic systems offered unique opportunities for learning more about the workings of both.

An important event in seismological research was the initiation of the San Andreas Fault Observatory at Depth (SAFOD), a 3.9-km (2.4-mi)-deep instrumented borehole through California's infamous San Andreas Fault Zone, where the Pacific and North American

Juerg Alean, Eglisau, Switzerland, Stromboli online: http://www.stromboli.net

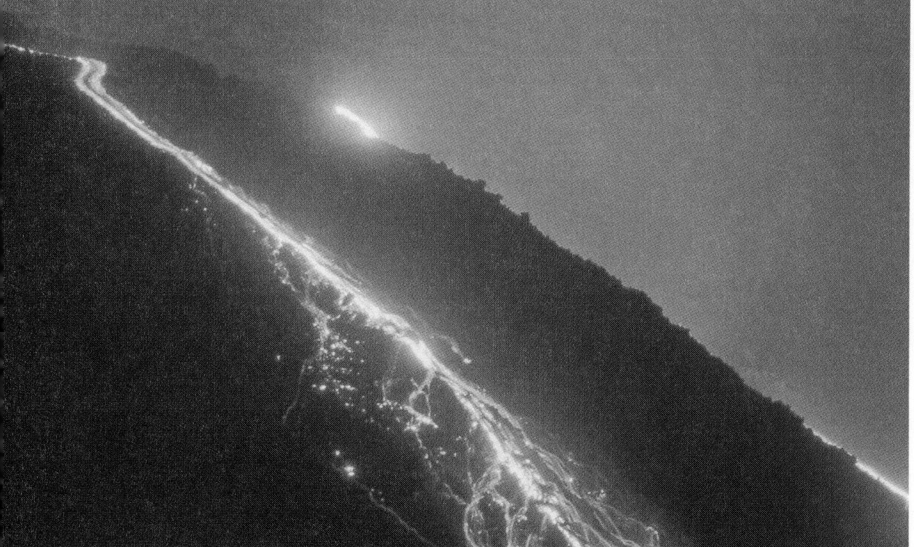

Glowing hot lava streams down a flank of the volcano on Italy's Stromboli Island on April 23. In December 2002 the volcano began a period of unusually high activity that lasted until the following July.

tectonic plates are slowly slipping past each other. Sited on private land near Parkfield, Calif., the hole would begin on the western (Pacific) side of the fault, descend vertically and then angle to the east, and eventually pierce the fault zone to end on the eastern (North American) side. It would enable scientists to install sensitive seismometers and other instruments in the fault zone to monitor seismic activity and real-time changes in rock deformation, temperature, fluid pressure, and other physical and chemical properties that occur prior to earthquakes. The findings were expected to shed new light on exactly how earthquakes work.

The year was exciting for earth scientists in Italy, considered to be the "cradle of volcanology." Stromboli Island's volcano erupted with a once-in-a-century level of intensity on April 5, showering parts of the coastline with scoria and blocks up to 2 m (about 6½ ft) in diameter but causing no human fatalities. The event was part of an unusual series of violent eruptions that had begun in December 2002. Sicily's Mt. Etna experienced major flank eruptions between October 2002 and January 2003. Lava flows destroyed ski facilities on northern and southern slopes of the volcano and near-continuous ash falls plagued two regional airports for a period of six weeks. Other significant eruptions occurred in Ecuador (Reventador), Montserrat (Soufrière Hills), Guatemala (Fuego), and the Mariana Islands (Anatahan).

A vast province lies beneath the deep ocean waters in which Earth's crust is continually renewed by volcanism and hydrothermal activities along the mid-oceanic ridge systems. Following planning meetings and workshops attended by more than 300 scientists engaged in a range of specialties in geophysics, geology, biology, chemistry, and oceanography, an integrated initiative, RIDGE 2000, was launched in late 2001 under the auspices of the U.S. National Science Foundation. The focus of the effort was "a comprehensive, integrated understanding of the relationships among the geological and geophysical processes of planetary renewal on oceanic spreading centers and the seafloor and subseafloor ecosystems that they support," and it involved far-reaching collaboration between scientists to develop whole-system models through exploration, mapping, and sampling at a limited number of representative sites.

As of 2003 three sites had been designated for the initial integrated studies: the 8°–11° N segment of the East Pacific Rise, off Central America; the Endeavor Segment of the Juan de Fuca Ridge, in the eastern Pacific Ocean off Vancouver Island, B.C.; and a segment of the East Lau Spreading Center in the Lau Basin in the western Pacific, near Fiji. Among the fundamental questions to be addressed were the relationships between mantle flow, mantle composition, and morphology and segmentation of the mid-oceanic ridges; the organization of the flow of magma in the mantle and crust underlying the seafloor; the effects of biological activity, particularly that of microorganisms, on the chemistry of hydrothermal vents and hydrothermal circulation; and the role of hydrothermal flow in influencing the physical, chemical, and biological characteristics of the biosphere from deep in the seafloor to the overlying water column.

A highlight of research related to the second question, concerning the distribution and transport of melt in the oceanic crust, was a seismic tomography study carried out by Douglas Toomey and Laura Magde of the University of Oregon and co-workers. By processing velocity data from seismic waves in a way similar to the processing of X-ray data in medical tomography, they produced vivid three-dimensional images of the magma "plumbing system" in the crust below a segment of the Mid-Atlantic Ridge.

(MURLI H. MANGHNANI)

METEOROLOGY AND CLIMATE

The drought that gripped southern Europe, southwestern Asia, and the U.S. between 1998 and 2002 appeared to be connected to temperatures in the tropical Pacific and Indian oceans, according to a study reported in 2003. Martin Hoerling and Arun Kumar of the U.S. National Oceanic and Atmospheric Administration found that during the drought years, surface waters in the eastern tropical Pacific Ocean were cooler than normal, while those in the western Pacific and Indian oceans were warmer than average. When they ran computer simulations of Earth's atmospheric circulation using the actual ocean temperature data, the jet stream in the models shifted northward, pushing wet weather north and away from midlatitude regions. Extended La Niña conditions in the east-central tropical Pacific explained the cooling observed there. In contrast, the western Pacific and Indian oceans were unprecedentedly warm, which the researchers attributed to the ocean's response to increased greenhouse gases in the atmosphere—an effect that they thought likely to continue. The results of the study reinforced the necessity for improved understanding of the links between ocean and atmosphere.

Another part of the world ocean may have been associated with drought and climate variability. Research reported during the year on the causes of multiyear "megadroughts" hinted that opposing shifts in temperatures in the tropical Pacific and North Atlantic oceans occurred while disastrous long-term droughts persisted across the North American continent. Stephen Gray of the University of Wyoming and colleagues used seven centuries of tree-ring data from the central and southern Rocky Mountains as indicators of precipitation changes having oscillations of 40–70-year periods. Their results suggested that the Great Plains, the Rockies, and the U.S. Southwest were stricken by a widespread megadrought when the tropical Pacific cooled at the same time that the North Atlantic warmed. This pattern could help explain both the long large-scale drought of the 1950s and the recent 1998–2002 drought; in each case, cool waters spread over the eastern Pacific while warmth covered portions of the North Atlantic.

The record-breaking heat wave experienced in Europe during August (*see* CALENDAR; DISASTERS), though not necessarily related to climate change, gave added impetus to scientists researching the extent and causes of the observed trends in rising global temperatures. Although much press attention was given to the possible effects of greenhouse gases, the contribution that land use makes to global climate change may have been underestimated, according to investigators from the University of Maryland. Eugenia Kalnay and Ming Cai compared two sets of 50-year temperature records for the entire U.S., one set collected from surface stations and the other from above-surface instruments (satellites and weather balloons). They concluded that not only the growth of cities but also that of agricultural activities make the world seem warmer than what could be attributed to the effects of greenhouse gases alone. The overall rise in U.S. mean surface temperatures due to such changes in land use could be as much as 0.27 °C (0.5 °F) per century—a value at least twice as high as previous estimates based on urbanization alone.

Not only do cities warm the atmosphere, but they also affect rainfall patterns. "Urban heat islands," created from solar-heat-retaining streets and buildings, were known to increase the amount and frequency of rainfall in and downwind of a number of cities. During the year a NASA-funded analysis of data from the Tropical Rainfall Measuring Mission satellite and from rain gauges on the ground corroborated this effect for the Houston, Texas, area. Average rainfall from 1998 to 2002 was 44% higher downwind of Houston than upwind and 29% higher over the city than upwind. Another study showed that the combination of increased particle pollution and higher air temperatures over large cities likely was enhancing cloud-to-ground lightning strikes in those locales. Analyzing three summer seasons (2000–2002) of lightning-flash data from three large urban areas in southeastern Brazil, Kleber Naccarato and colleagues of Brazil's National Institute for Space Research observed a 60–100% increase in flash density over the urban areas compared with surrounding regions.

Camille Parmesan

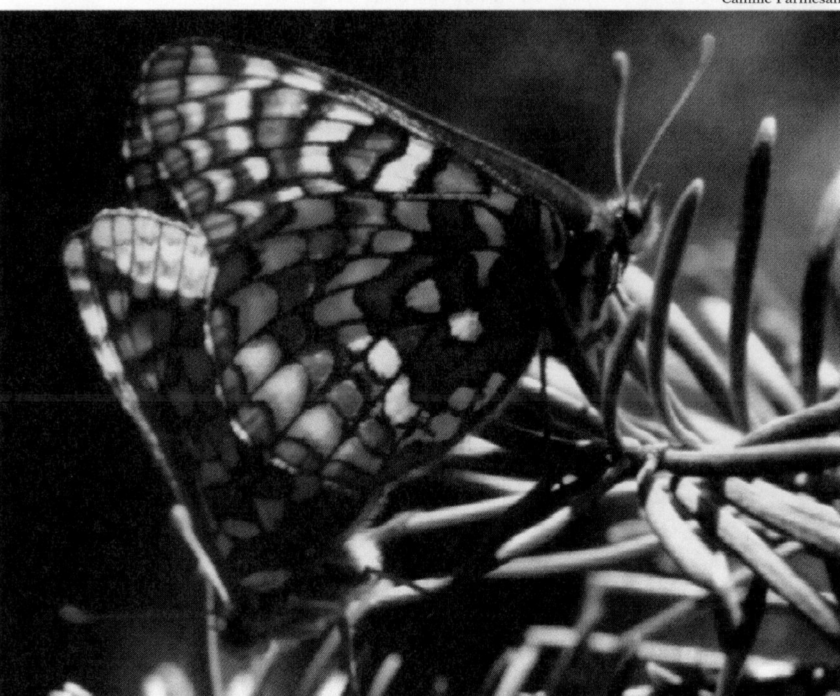

The range of Edith's checkerspot, a butterfly found in western North America, has shifted northward and to higher elevations in the past 100 years. The insect was one of 1,700 species involved in a study of the effects of climate change.

Although long-term temperature trends vary widely from region to region, evidence mounted that climate change could be affecting plants and animals across the globe. The results of one study charting the biological impact of the average rise in global temperature of 0.6 °C (1 °F) in the past 100 years suggested that the warming was moving species' ranges northward and shifting spring events earlier. After mining data from previous studies involving 1,700 species, Camille Parmesan of the University of Texas at Austin and Gary Yohe of Wesleyan University, Middletown, Conn., reported that ranges were creeping toward cooler latitudes about 6 km (3.7 mi) on average per decade. In addition, spring events such as breeding in frogs, bird nesting, bursting of tree buds, and arrival of migrating butterflies and birds were taking place about two days earlier per decade. (For discussion of a study assessing the effects of climate change on plant productivity, *see* LIFE SCIENCES: *Botany*.)

All research is based on data, and accurate global data are essential for sound climate research. In late July representatives of approximately 30 countries and 20 international organizations assembled at the Earth Observation Summit, a conference hosted by the U.S. with the goal of establishing a comprehensive and coordinated Earth observation system. The new system would focus on providing critical scientific data to help policy makers come to more-informed decisions regarding climate and the environment. Linking and expanding the many current disparate observation systems were expected to lead to better observations and models, which in turn would benefit fundamental earth science and improve its predictive power in such applications as climate change, crop production, energy and water use, disease outbreaks, and natural-hazard assessment. (DOUGLAS LE COMTE)

Economic Affairs

Despite lingering UNEMPLOYMENT and the U.S.-led war in Iraq, the world economy showed signs of RECOVERY in 2003, led by LOW interest rates and strong GROWTH in the United States. Although most stock markets rose, SCANDAL rocked the mutual fund industry, and many troubled business sectors still STRUGGLED.

In the second half of 2003, there were signs that the global economy was recovering faster than had been expected earlier in the year. In November an International Monetary Fund spokesman stated that the IMF would revise upward its 3.2% forecast for global growth in 2003. It was widely expected that the increase over 2002 would be closer to the 4% being forecast by the Organisation for Economic Co-operation and Development (OECD), which would make it the best result for the world economy since 2000. Growth in the less-developed countries (LDCs) outpaced that of the advanced countries at 5% and 1.8%, respectively.

The clearest evidence of stronger economic activity came from the U.S., which had the most expansionary policies. Annualized third-quarter growth in the U.S. was an unexpected 8.2%, the fastest pace in 20 years. This gave rise to concerns that the world was once again becoming too reliant on the U.S., where record public and current-account deficits were seen by some as unsustainable. In all regions inflation rates were falling, and in those countries where declines in consumer prices had occurred in 2002—most notably Japan—fears of deflation were receding. In the U.K. third-quarter output was running at an annual rate of 3.1%. Even in the euro zone, where several countries, including Germany, were in recession and there was limited scope for fiscal stimulus, surveys indicated that business confidence was increasing. In September the Japanese economy recorded its seventh straight quarter of expansion, growing at an annual rate of 2.2%. In Asia economic activity was returning to normal after having been disrupted by the outbreak of SARS (severe acute respiratory syndrome), which spread through some 26 countries.

Competitive pressure to attract the lacklustre flow of foreign direct investment (FDI) continued to build. This was reflected in the fact that 70 countries in 2002 made a record 236 changes in legislation as they attempted to make their economies more favourable to FDI. Several factors contributed to the slowdown in FDI. These included the continuing slow and uncertain economic growth, as well as stock market declines that discouraged cross-border mergers and acquisitions, which fell 38% in 2002 to $370 billion. There was also a decline in the number of privatizations in several countries. In 2002 global FDI inflows fell for the second straight year after a decade of rapid growth. At $651 billion, inflows were 21% less than in 2001, following a 41% decline in 2000. The developed and less-developed countries suffered similar decreases of 22% and 23%, respectively, with the U.S. accounting for nearly 90% of the FDI reduction in the LDCs. Africa suffered the sharpest drop (41%), while an 11% decline in Asia and the Pacific was due to the buoyant conditions in China, where the FDI inflow of $53 billion overtook that of the U.S. ($30 billion). In Central and Eastern Europe (CEE), the Czech Republic contributed to a modest FDI increase with its $4 billion sale of natural gas importer Transgas to Germany.

NATIONAL ECONOMIC POLICIES

The IMF projected a 1.8% rise in GDP in the advanced economies in 2003. Economic momentum in the second half of the year was building up much faster than expected, and it was likely that the rate would be exceeded.

United States. As the year drew to a close, it was clear that the rise of 2.6% projected by the IMF for the U.S. would be revised to closer to 3%. The economic recovery that began in the second quarter gathered momentum and confounded its critics. The U.S. once again became the driver of the global economy. The stimulus came from consumer spending, which was underpinned by the lowest interest rates in 45 years, reduced taxes, and an escalation in house prices. By the end of November, business confidence was reaching its highest level since the mid-1990s, and inventory stock levels were rising.

The unemployment rate rose to 6.1% (from 5.8% in 2002) as employment opportunities were slow to respond to the upturn in economic activity. The rate of nonfarm business productivity increased sharply, rising to a 20-year high in the third quarter to an annualized 9.4%. The high-tech sector continued to lose jobs but more slowly than in 2002; over a two-year period some 750,000 jobs had been lost. From the second quarter, productivity rose strongly to meet increased demand, but in September nonfarm payrolls rose by 57,000—the first increase in eight months—and first-time claims for unemployment were beginning to fall. Unemployment officially fell to 5.7% at year's end, but this was in large part because more than 300,000 people reportedly stopped looking for employment in December.

The size of the public deficit became a contentious issue. A series of tax cuts and increased defense spending—military spending rose sharply in the second quarter after the start of the U.S.-led war in Iraq, and the level was maintained in the third quarter—pushed the federal budget to an estimated $455 billion, or 4.2% of GDP. If state budgets were included, the deficit was 6% of GDP, compared with 1% in 2000.

Fears of deflation were diminishing, but the rate of inflation remained low. Consumer prices fell by 0.2% in November but rose at the same rate in December. This brought the increase over the year to 1.9%, or a core rate of 1.5% (excluding food and energy components).

United Kingdom. The U.K. economy exhibited strong resilience in 2003, as it had in 2002, with growth exceeding that of most other advanced countries. The IMF forecast a 1.7% rise in GDP, compared with 1.9% in 2002, but fourth-quarter outcomes and indications suggested that growth would at least match that in 2002. Growth in the third quarter was revised up from 1.8% year-on-year to 2%. Economic activity was being led by public and private consumption. The latter had outpaced personal disposable income since the beginning of 2002, but this was not perceived as a problem. Much of the impetus came from the services and construction industries, with the latter fueled by a booming housing sector, in which prices were rising at an annual rate of 16% in October. Despite a 25-basis-points boost in interest rates in November, the rise in house prices accelerated to 1.5% in December, bringing the increase over the year to 15.6%. Nevertheless, turnover was the lowest since 1996, largely because fewer first-time buyers entered the market.

The annual rate of inflation was falling toward year's end. It was slightly above the government's target of 2.5% but, excluding housing costs, was only 1.4%. The labour market remained tight. Unemployment was 5% in September, which was in sharp contrast to the 8.8% comparable euro-zone rate. In the year to September, the number of self-employed rose by 284,000, which accounted for most of the increase in the workforce.

A negative factor was the weakness of business investment. This was mainly because of the decline in manufacturing activity, which fell by 10% in the second quarter, the weakest performance since 1999. Subsequently, surveys suggested an improvement, but this was likely to be tempered by the need for companies to divert resources into pension funds, which had been badly depleted by earlier equity declines.

Japan. The tentative recovery in Japan strengthened and accelerated in 2003, with growth in output expected to exceed 2%. The extent of Japan's recovery surprised observers. As the year progressed, momentum increased. Even after downward revision, the second-quarter output reached 2.3% on an annual basis, with the stimulus coming from a rise in business investment and private consumption. Performance in the third quarter exceeded expectations; export demand from the U.S. and China pushed GDP by another 0.6%. This was the seventh straight quarter of recovery. Improved business confidence was reflected in rising corporate capital spending, and fixed capital expenditure jumped 14% over the 12 months to September. The stronger stock market generated capital gains, and the bankruptcy rate was falling dramatically.

Recovery was partly helped by continuing low interest rates and a ¥1.8 trillion (about $14.9 billion) tax cut, although the effects of the latter would be mitigated in 2004 by a broadening of the tax base. An upsurge in employment growth led to a drop in the unemployment rate to 5.1% by September from 5.4% a year earlier. Of continuing concern was deflation, which by some measures was in its eighth year. Prices were falling at the slowest rate in four years—down 0.2% in September, compared with 0.7% a year earlier—and in November the core consumer price index was up 0.1% from a year earlier, the first rise since 1998. Nevertheless, any strengthening of the yen could lower imported price pressures and further exacerbate deflation.

Euro Zone. In sharp contrast to the U.S., the U.K., and Japan, there were few signs of a recovery in the euro zone, and a modest rise in GDP of 0.5% was projected. The economy ground to a halt in the second quarter following a 0.1% quarter-on-quarter rise in the first. Third-quarter GDP rose by 0.4%. Industrial production in the year to September fell by 1.8%, and the unemployment rate (at 8.8%) was still rising. The rate of consumer price inflation for 2003 was revised down to 2% in October, which placed it in line with the European Central Bank's target rate of 2%.

Among the major euro-zone countries, Germany was in recession, and the economy failed to grow for the second straight year. German exports declined sharply, and domestic demand was weak. The French economy was expected to expand just 0.5%, the worst performance in a decade. Growth in France was hampered by a series of public-sector strikes in May and June when workers protested against planned pension reforms. In the third quarter, tourism, which accounted for about 7% of GDP, suffered from poor demand in Europe, with a lack of American visitors because of diplomatic tension over France's refusal to back the U.S. in the war against Iraq. Strikes in the entertainment industry, soaring temperatures, and forest fires

Table I. Real Gross Domestic Products of Selected Developed Countries
% annual change

Country	1999	2000	2001	2002	2003[1]
United States	4.1	3.8	0.3	2.4	2.6
Japan	0.2	2.8	0.4	0.2	2.0
Germany	2.0	2.9	0.8	0.2	0.0
France	3.2	4.2	2.1	1.2	0.5
Italy	1.7	3.1	1.8	0.4	0.4
United Kingdom	2.4	3.1	2.1	1.9	1.7
Canada	5.5	5.1	1.9	3.3	1.9
All developed countries	3.1	3.9	0.9	1.8	2.0
Seven major countries above	3.0	3.5	0.8	1.6	1.8
European Union	2.8	3.7	1.7	1.1	0.8

[1]Estimated.
Note: Seasonally adjusted at annual rates.
Source: OECD, *IMF World Economic Outlook*, September 2003.

Table II. Standardized Unemployment Rates in Selected Developed Countries
% of total labour force

Country	1999	2000	2001	2002	2003[1]
United States	4.2	4.0	4.8	5.8	6.1
Japan	4.7	4.7	5.0	5.4	5.3
Germany	8.0	7.3	7.4	8.1	8.9
France	10.7	9.4	8.7	9.0	9.6
Italy	11.5	10.7	9.6	9.1	8.9
United Kingdom	6.0	5.5	5.1	5.2	5.0
Canada	7.6	6.8	7.2	7.6	7.8
All developed countries	6.6	6.1	6.4	6.9	7.1
Seven major countries above	6.1	5.7	5.9	6.5	6.8
European Union	8.7	7.8	7.3	7.7	8.0

[1]Projected.
Source: OECD, *Economic Outlook*, November 2003.

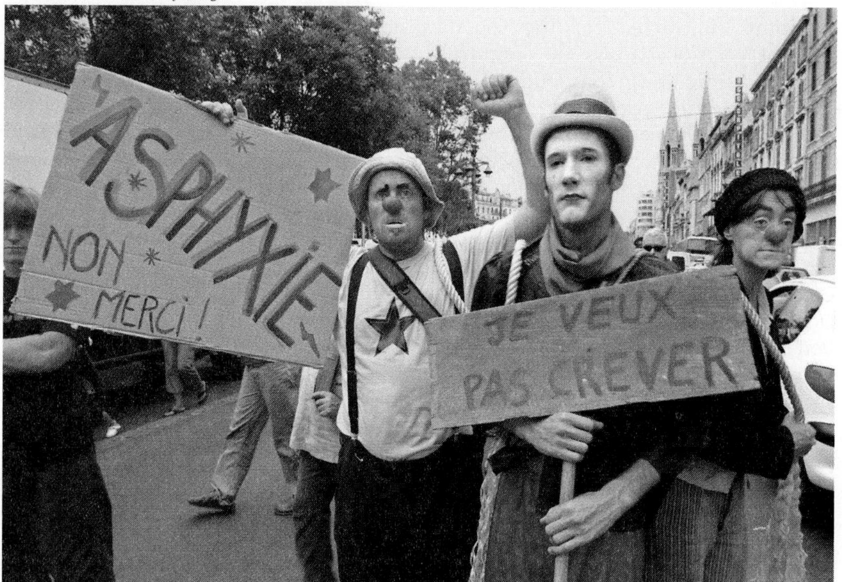

Entertainment workers in Marseille demonstrate on July 1 against a proposed change in their unemployment benefits. Strikes and protests were among the factors that threatened France's economic recovery in 2003.

also played a role. Against the general trend, Spain showed its resilience to external factors. Lifted by strong domestic demand and a buoyant construction industry, Spain's economy expanded 2.3%. The rate of employment remained high at 11.2% in September but was falling steadily (down from 11.5% in September 2002).

Throughout the year France and Germany were the joint cause of rising tension over the Stability and Growth Pact, under which budget deficits in euro-zone countries were limited to 3% of GDP. The pact had been the brainchild of Germany, but both countries breached it by a wide margin for the second consecutive year. They faced stiff penalties and sanctions for their failure to make necessary structural reforms and rein in spending. On November 26 the pact was "suspended" when European Union (EU) finance ministers succumbed to pressure from the two countries. Thereafter, tension and division between the member countries increased.

The Countries in Transition. Despite weakness in much of the global economy, growth in the countries in transition accelerated to 4.9% from 4.2% in 2002. As in earlier years, output in the Commonwealth of Independent States (CIS), at 5.8%, outpaced that in the CEE countries, which increased 3.4%. The strength of the Russian economy (up 6%) and other net energy exporters boosted the apparent robustness of the CIS economies. In the CEE much of the momentum came from strong increases in government consumption, which caused excessive fiscal deficits that were not sustainable over the longer term. Eight of the countries in transition were due to join the EU in May 2004, where they would have to exercise much more fiscal discipline.

Throughout the region inflation rates fell, with the CEE countries down to 4% (from 5.6% in 2002). The CIS rate of 13% was distorted by the high prices in Russia (14%), where the rate had steadily declined from 86% in 1999. Inflation in the group of EU accession countries was 3.2%.

Less-Developed Countries. Output in the LDCs rose by 5% (from 4.6% in 2002). Regional disparities narrowed except for Latin America, which continued to lag behind other regions following its economic contraction in 2002. Asia was the driver of growth in the LDCs. It expanded by 6.4%, although the rate was curbed by the effect of the SARS outbreak, which caused a second-quarter decline in Hong Kong, Singapore, and Taiwan, though all three recovered in the latter half of the year. China fared better, temporarily losing momentum but growing by about 9% over the year. China's industrial output surged ahead at an annual rate of close to 20%. India's output, which was expected to rise 5.6%, was supported by a recovery in agriculture and strong expansion in the service sectors, especially in information technologies. This was well below the official 8% target, however, and undermined efforts to reduce regional disparities and poverty.

In the newly industrialized countries (NICs), including Hong Kong, South Korea, Singapore, and Taiwan, output growth slowed to just 2.3% from 2002.

Table III. Changes in Output in Less-Developed Countries
% annual change in real gross domestic product

Area	1999	2000	2001	2002	2003[1]
All less-developed countries	3.9	5.7	4.1	4.6	5.0
Regional groups					
Africa	2.7	3.0	3.7	3.1	3.7
Asia	6.2	6.8	5.8	6.4	6.4
Middle East, Europe, Malta, and Turkey	0.9	6.0	2.0	4.8	5.1
Western Hemisphere	0.2	4.0	0.7	−0.1	1.1
Countries in transition	4.1	7.1	5.1	4.2	4.9

[1]Projected.
Source: International Monetary Fund, *World Economic Outlook,* September 2003.

Table IV. Changes in Consumer Prices in Less-Developed Countries
% change from preceding year

Area	1999	2000	2001	2002	2003[1]
All less-developed countries	6.5	5.8	5.8	5.3	5.9
Regional groups					
Africa	12.2	14.3	12.9	9.3	10.6
Asia	2.5	1.8	2.7	2.0	2.5
Middle East, Europe, Malta, and Turkey	23.6	19.6	17.1	15.7	13.5
Western Hemisphere	7.4	6.8	6.4	8.7	10.9

[1]Projected.
Source: International Monetary Fund, *World Economic Outlook,* September 2003.

South Korea was adversely affected by appreciation of the won against the U.S. dollar, a slowdown in the electronics industry, labour unrest, and worries over North Korea's nuclear program.

The Association of Southeast Asian Nations "group of four" (Indonesia, Malaysia, the Philippines, and Thailand) grew by 4.1%, slightly below the faster-than-expected 2002 increase of 4.3%. Thailand was likely to exceed the projected 5%, as it was helped by strong investment and export growth. In Indonesia improved income from oil helped raise output by 6.6%. It was likely that foreign investor confidence had been dented by the bombing of a Marriott Hotel in Jakarta on August 5. The rate of inflation declined in Indonesia to a more manageable 6%, while in Thailand it rose 1.4%, alleviating fears of deflation.

In the Middle East a major influence on the region was the war in Iraq, including the buildup to the war and the conflict that followed the declared end of major combat. Growth accelerated to 5.1% (from 3.9% in 2002) as oil exporters benefited from increased income. The private sector in Saudi Arabia and some Persian Gulf countries benefited from subcontracted work for the reconstruction of Iraq's infrastructure. The cost of reconstruction in Iraq up to 2007 was assessed at more than $55 billion. Tourism was another casualty of the war; arrivals in Egypt, for example, were well down in the first half of the year.

Although the African economies were resilient and expanded by 3.7% (up from 3.1% in 2002), growth was insufficient for making improvements to the inadequate social and physical infrastructure. The Maghreb countries (Algeria, Morocco, and Tunisia) grew fastest (5.7%), with those in sub-Saharan Africa (3.6%) held back by falling output in Zimbabwe (down 11%) and Côte d'Ivoire (down 3%). The best performances were in Nigeria, Tanzania, and Uganda, where outputs rose in excess of 5%. Many African countries were helped by higher commodity prices and improvements in government policies. Inflation rates were generally tame, with the notable exceptions of Zimbabwe (420%) and Angola (95.2%).

The Latin American economies made a fragile recovery from the 2002 recession and were expected to grow a modest 1.1%, helped by a real depreciation in exchange rates. High debt levels and political uncertainty continued to limit confidence in the region. Venezuela's economy contracted for the second straight year (−17%) as the country's political difficulties compounded the macroeconomic problems. Stronger copper prices helped Chile, and Mexico benefited from the U.S. upturn in the second half of the year. Many countries were in the process of making much-needed tax reforms, and inflation was gradually being brought under control. Consumer prices in Brazil (15%), the Dominican Republic (26%), and Venezuela (34%), however, rose much more sharply than in the year before.

INTERNATIONAL TRADE AND PAYMENTS

The projected 2.9% rise in the volume of world trade in 2003 was a deceleration from 2002's rate of 3.2% and was below the growth in world output for only the second time in more than two decades. For the seventh time in eight years, the export volume of the LDCs (4.3%) outpaced that of the advanced economies (1.6%). Nominal trade growth reflected the depreciation of the dollar against the major trading country currencies in Europe and Asia. In dollar terms global exports were projected to rise by 13.5% to $8,938,000,000,000 and imports by 13.7% to $7,119,000,000,000. By year's end it seemed likely that these would be revised upward. In the first half of the year, Western Europe's actual exports and imports rose by more than 20% in U.S. dollar terms. China was the major contributor to Asia's 15% increase in exports and 20% in imports. China's imports rose 45% and in value terms overtook those of Japan. The much-less-buoyant trading picture after adjustment for price and exchange-rate changes was reflected in the OECD forecast that advanced countries' exports would increase 1.5% and imports would rise 3.1%.

It was against a backdrop of sluggish real trade growth that trade ministers from 148 member countries—including new members Cambodia and Nepal—met in Cancún, Mex., for the World Trade Organization annual meeting. The agenda for talks and negotiations was wide-ranging, covering agriculture, nonfarm trade, access to patented drugs, the setting of rules for investment, and competition policy. It was hoped that the talks would pave the way for a multilateral agreement by Jan. 1, 2005. According to World Bank estimates released before the meeting, an achievable reduction of trade barriers could increase global income by $290 billion–$520 billion a year and by 2015 could take 144 million people out of poverty. The talks failed—mainly because of differences over agricultural reform.

While moves to liberalize world trade appeared to be faltering, an increasing number of regional trade agreements (RTAs) were concluded or being planned. By the beginning of 2003, there were 176 RTAs, an increase of 17 over the previous year. The internal trade of the six major regional trade groups accounted for 36.3% of world trade in 2002. The differences in degree of integration were wide, however, with nearly two-thirds of EU exports and imports and more than half of the North American Free Trade Agreement's exports being intraregional, while the other groups were trading less than a quarter of their goods internally. In November a plan to create the world's largest common market—in the Western Hemisphere—sputtered forward.

The overall current-account deficit of the balance of payments of the advanced economies rose to $245 billion. It was the fifth straight year of deficit following six years of surplus. Once again the size and increase were due to the burgeoning U.S. deficit of $553 billion, which was equivalent to more than 5% of GDP. The main counterparts to this were the current-account surpluses of Japan, China, South Korea, Taiwan, Hong Kong, and Singapore. The U.S. current-account deficit (combined with its large public deficit) was seen as unsustainable in the longer term and was a major factor in the depreciation of the U.S. dollar. In reality the U.S. was able to finance its deficit; it was uniquely placed to borrow in the world's reserve currency (the dollar) and well able to attract capital because of its large and liquid financial markets. Nevertheless, the U.S. was concerned about its expected $125 billion trade deficit with China.

The euro zone maintained a surplus ($62.4 billion) that was little changed from the year before. While most euro countries had a surplus, the deficits in Spain ($22.3 billion) and Italy ($21.4 billion) widened markedly. Germany's surplus ($62.4 billion) rose marginally, while France's ($57 billion) was up by nearly a quarter on 2002. Outside the euro zone, Japan's surplus ($121 billion) rose for the second straight year, while the U.K.'s usual deficit rose modestly to $17 billion. The surplus of the Asian NICs rose from $68 billion to

$76 billion. Overall, the countries in transition were in surplus.

The low rates of inflation in most advanced countries and actual deflation, or fears of it, in a few prompted most governments to adopt expansionary policies. In the first three quarters of the year, some central banks cut rates from what were already historically low levels. In the U.S. fears about underlying deflationary trends, mixed economic indicators following the end of major fighting in Iraq, and investor concern about the sustainability of the economic recovery led to a fall in the dollar that took it to an all-time low against the euro. At the end of May, in trade-weighted terms the dollar was 6% lower than at the end of 2002. In June the Federal Reserve (Fed) reduced interest rates to a 45-year low with a reduction of 25 basis points to 1%. Also in June, the euro-zone policy rate was cut by 50 basis points to 2%, which made real short-term rates effectively zero. In July U.K. interest rates were cut to 3.5%, the lowest level in nearly 50 years, but the move was reversed back to 3.75% in early November to curb household spending and soaring house prices.

Exchange-rate volatility persisted, however, with the euro under pressure on concerns about fiscal laxity and the fact that three of the euro-zone economies were in recession. At the end of August, the euro was at a four-year low against sterling (€1 = £0.693). In September a joint statement from the Group of Seven called for "more flexibility in exchange rates." Financial markets interpreted this as a sign of increasing concern at the growing imbalance in the global economy, especially the U.S. current-account deficit. There was also speculation that U.S. officials would try to bring the dollar down to increase output growth and would move away from the traditional strong-dollar policy.

As the year drew to a close, there was no sign of an imminent strengthening of the dollar despite increasing evidence that the U.S. economic recovery was well under way. By year's end the dollar was trading at an all-time low against the euro (€1 = $1.2579), which raised fears that euro-zone exports would be jeopardized. In Japan the authorities were containing appreciation of the yen by intervening in the markets. In September reserves of ¥4.46 trillion (about $40 billion) were sold to limit the yen's rise. The Australian dollar rose 33% over the year to a high of U.S.$0.7495 at year's end, despite two interest increases in two months. A major beneficiary of the dollar depreciation was China. It was under growing pressure from trading partners to revalue the renminbi, which was pegged to the U.S. dollar. (IEIS)

STOCK MARKETS

U.S. politics and economics weighed heavily on world stock markets in 2003. The inevitability of war with Iraq triggered a sharp rally at first, but while uncertainty had depressed major markets as the year began, in April U.S. and European stock markets fell again as investors began to calculate the cost of the war and postwar commitments to an already weak U.S. economy. Summer brought signs of a firmer market recovery, as interest rates in the U.S. and Europe hit their lowest post-World War II levels and inflation was clearly dormant. Although between the mid-March low point and mid-September the Standard & Poor's index of 500 large-company stocks (S&P 500) rose by almost 30%, some world stock markets again dipped sharply in November as a series of devastating suicide-bomb outrages in Istanbul marked another lethal twist in the war with terrorism. Despite upbeat world growth forecasts, uncertainty remained. By the end of the year, however, most markets globally had turned positive, with some

During the World Trade Organization meeting in Cancún, Mex., in September, a lampoon by individuals from Oxfam, a British-based charitable agency, criticized the trade policies of the leaders of the Group of Eight major economic powers.

making substantial gains, although still ending far off their all-time highs. (*See* TABLE V.)

Globalization posed a serious challenge to Western companies; already China and India were becoming the world's manufacturing bases. Investors worried that the long bull market had led to overcapacity, that growth in the U.S. economy was largely due to extra defense spending, and that even when companies reported profit growth, too much of this resulted from cost cutting and a weaker dollar. Many people also worried about high levels of government and consumer debt. (IEIS)

United States. Despite war with Iraq, mutual fund scandals, and economic uncertainty, 2003 saw stock prices regain much of the ground lost in the previous three years, the longest period of stock market decline since World War II. As reflected by the S&P 500 index, the broad market surged 26.38% in 2003, recovering 44% of its cumulative losses since 2000. The most widely watched index, the Dow Jones Industrial Average (DJIA) of 30 blue-chip companies' stocks, rose 25.32% for the year, while the Nasdaq (National Association of Securities Dealers automated quotations) composite index soared by 50.01%. (*See* GRAPH.) The Russell 2000, which represented small-capitalization (small-cap) stocks, did almost as well, with an increase of 45.37%. Although investors became more sanguine about the health of the U.S. economy as the year wore on, public confidence in financial markets remained tentative, with both positive and negative news (and rumours) spurring sometimes unusually volatile trading activity.

Caution dominated the market through much of the early months of the year. Ambiguous economic data did little to assuage fears of simultaneous deflation and economic stagnation, while tensions surrounding Iraq kept corporate planning in limbo and money out of the stock market. This bracing for war continued until the actual outbreak of hostilities in March allowed investors to discount the most pessimistic scenarios about Saddam Hussein's ability to fight a sustained conflict or to unleash unconventional weapons. Despite a few false starts, a surge of relief eventually became a market rally in April, sustained by government policies designed to stimulate investment. Although economic doubts lingered, tax incentives provided as part of the Jobs and Growth Tax Relief Reconciliation Act of 2003 (signed into law in May) made stocks more attractive as investments. The act lowered the rate at which capital gains and shareholder dividends were taxed and thus allowed investors to enjoy richer after-tax stock market returns.

The Fed's interest-rate-setting Federal Open Market Committee (FOMC) provided additional stimulus in June by cutting the key federal-funds rate 0.25% to a 45-year low of 1%, a move that was explicitly intended to nurture economic growth. While the already-favourable interest-rate environment meant that few if any additional cuts could be expected, FOMC officials continued to assure financial markets throughout the remainder of the year that rates would not move significantly higher in the immediate future.

Even experts found it difficult to interpret the year's economic data, which painted a widely variable and often contradictory picture of an economy that sometimes appeared more sluggish than the statistics would indicate. While business owners put expansion plans on hold before the Iraq war, leaving GDP growth—the broadest measure of all economic activity—stalled at 1.4% in the first quarter of 2003, the dam broke shortly thereafter as companies rushed both to reengage with the new business environment and to take advantage of the tax cuts, low interest rates, and other government stimuli. As a result, GDP grew at a rate of 3.3% in the second quarter and then

Table V. Selected Major World Stock Market Indexes[1]

Country and Index	2003 range[2] High	Low	Year-end close	Percent change from 12/31/2002
Argentina, Merval	1078	521	1072	104
Australia, Sydney All Ordinaries	3311	2673	3306	11
Belgium, Brussels BEL20	2244	1427	2244	11
Brazil, Bovespa	22,236	9995	22,236	97
Canada, Toronto Composite	8261	6220	8221	24
China, Shanghai Composite	1631	1317	1497	10
Denmark, KFX	263	169	244	23
Finland, HEX General	6421	4703	6032	4
France, Paris CAC 40	3558	2403	3558	16
Germany, Frankfurt Xetra DAX	3965	2203	3965	37
Hong Kong, Hang Seng	12,594	8409	12,576	35
Hungary, Bux	9914	7031	9380	20
Iceland, ICEX-MAIN	2077	1404	2075	44
India, Sensex (BSE-30)	5839	2924	5839	73
Ireland, ISEQ Overall	4921	3733	4921	23
Italy, Milan Banca Comm. Ital.	1287	959	1257	15
Japan, Nikkei Average	11,162	7608	10,677	24
Mexico, IPC	8795	5746	8795	44
Netherlands, The, CBS All Share	487	330	486	5
Pakistan, KSE-100	4604	2356	4472	66
Philippines, Manila Composite	1451	999	1442	42
Poland, Wig	22,034	13,503	20,820	45
Russia, RTS	643	336	567	58
Singapore, SES All-Singapore	490	327	476	36
South Africa, Johannesburg All Share	10,387	7361	10,387	12
South Korea, Composite Index	822	515	811	29
Spain, Madrid Stock Exchange	810	577	808	27
Switzerland, SPI General	3962	2603	3962	22
Taiwan, Weighted Price	6142	4140	5891	32
Thailand, Bangkok SET	772	351	772	117
United Kingdom, FTSE 100	4477	3287	4477	14
United States, Dow Jones Industrials	10,454	7524	10,454	25
United States, Nasdaq Composite	2010	1271	2003	50
United States, NYSE Composite[3]	6464	4487	6464	29
United States, Russell 2000	565	346	557	45
United States, S&P 500	1112	801	1112	26
World, MS Capital International	1035	705	1035	32

[1]Index numbers are rounded. [2]Based on daily closing price. [3]Index recalculated in January 2003 to a base value of 5000.
Sources: *Financial Times, The Wall Street Journal,* www.hkex.com.hk.

at the explosive pace of 8.2% in the third quarter, the most robust U.S. economic expansion reported since 1984.

The rising tide did not lift all boats, however. The unemployment rate climbed to successive nine-year highs of 6.1% in May and 6.4% in June. While labour markets historically trailed economic growth, signs of real job creation were sometimes scarce, although official unemployment slipped back to 5.7% at year's end. The pace of corporate layoffs continued, while resentment grew as it became apparent that jobs in many industries, especially manufacturing, information technology, and customer service, had been shipped overseas and would not be returning. Productivity-enhancing technology helped companies maintain and even increase their activity despite having fewer employees, but this provided little comfort for those looking for work.

Speculation that deflationary conditions in Japan could presage falling prices across the Pacific failed to materialize. U.S. inflation gauges did briefly dip into negative territory in April and again in November, which led federal bankers to note that deflation remained the primary (albeit minor) threat to the still-fragile economy.

The U.S. stock market's strength was broad based, with all 10 stock sectors tracked by Dow Jones ending the year in positive territory. Battered technology stocks enjoyed the most spectacular performance, climbing 50%, but the reduced dividend tax also drove investors into areas of the market that traditionally paid dividends. Shares in manufacturers and basic-materials producers climbed 31% and 32%, respectively. Cyclic consumer stocks also climbed 32%. After a steep three-year decline, even the telecommunications sector managed a slim 3% gain on the year, boosted by a 48% surge in wireless shares as investors (and consumers) flocked to cellular-telecoms providers. Within individual industry groups, mining companies and consumer-electronics manufacturers outperformed the rest of the market easily, soaring 156% and 148%, respectively, while the long-suffering Internet group gained 126%. Losers were limited to land-line-telecoms operators, who finished down 3% as the flight to wireless gathered momentum.

The majority of traditional blue-chip stocks performed splendidly in 2003, generally recouping their 2002 losses and in many cases recapturing levels last seen in 2001. (*See* TABLE VI.)

News that a stockbroker had allowed hedge fund Canary Capital to trade mutual fund shares after the market close (a practice considered unethical but not explicitly illegal) broke in September and gathered force throughout the remainder of 2003. The scandal quickly spread to cover a wide range of trading practices at numerous mutual fund companies. By year's end the heads of several fund companies, including Putnam Investments and Strong Financial, had resigned, and regulators were mulling both criminal charges and sweeping reforms in the previously loosely regulated fund business.

While investors were quick to shun afflicted funds, however, the news did little to dissuade investors from investing in funds managed by other companies with unblemished reputations. Despite a weak start, money flooded back into stock funds after Iraq war fears dissipated in April, creating net inflows of $138.1 billion for the year through November. Large-cap stock mutual funds gained an average of 28%, according to fund tracker Morningstar. Small-cap funds focused on capturing the investment potential of renewed economic growth and did vastly better, surging 43%. The two largest U.S. stock funds, Vanguard's 500 Index Fund and Fidelity's Magellan Fund, climbed 28.05% and 24.82%, respectively.

AP/Wide World Photos

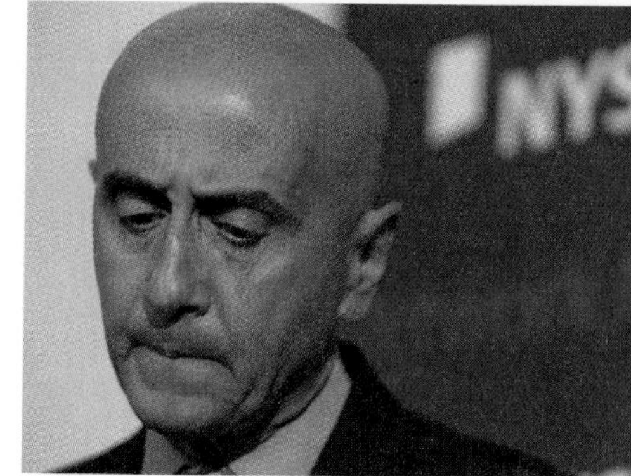

New York Stock Exchange Chairman and CEO Richard Grasso at a press conference on September 9 struggles with questions about his massive NYSE compensation package.

The New York Stock Exchange (NYSE) reported average daily trading of 1.4 billion shares in 2003, slightly less than that recorded in the previous year, for a value of $38.5 billion, down 6% from 2002. A total of 2,760 issues were listed, 24 fewer than in 2002, and there were 106 new listings, a stark decline from the previous year's figure of 152. The most actively traded issues on the exchange were Lucent Technologies, Nortel Networks, Pfizer, General Electric, and Time Warner, which officially dropped the "AOL" from its name on October 16.

The exchange was wracked by controversy after news about NYSE Chairman and CEO Richard Grasso's $187.5 million compensation package sparked public outcry and calls for fundamental

Closing Prices of Selected U.S. Stock Market Indexes, 2003

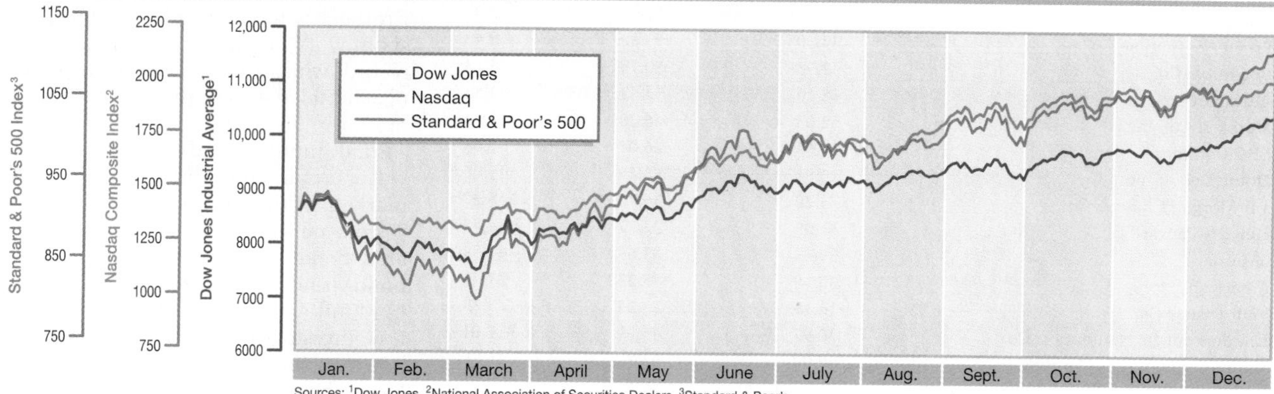

Sources: [1]Dow Jones, [2]National Association of Securities Dealers, [3]Standard & Poor's.

© Spencer Platt/Getty Images

On December 18 John Thain is introduced as the New York Stock Exchange's next CEO. Thain, who was to take command in early 2004, would earn about $4 million annually, a fraction of former CEO Richard Grasso's compensation.

reforms to the exchange's oversight and structure. Grasso resigned on September 17, and former Citigroup chairman John S. Reed was named interim CEO and chairman. Three months later Goldman Sachs president John A. Thain resigned his position and was appointed the NYSE's permanent CEO. Exchange members voted in November to create an independent supervisory board of directors in order to ensure greater operational transparency in the future.

Several NYSE seats changed hands in 2003. The last sale took place on December 18 at a price of $1.5 million, a slight improvement from a five-year low of $1.3 million set on November 5 but still nowhere near the $2.65 million such a seat fetched in the market's heyday of 1999. Short selling, wherein investors bet that a stock will decline, fluctuated through the year but ended lower—a reflection of the market's generally optimistic tone. Short interest on the exchange was 7.2 billion shares as of December 14, down 7% from the previous year. Margin borrowing rebounded in popularity after waning during the market's long retreat; in late November margin debt on the exchange stood at $172.1 billion, the highest point since debt balances began to decline in earnest in May 2001.

The Nasdaq market showed average daily trading of 1.69 billion shares through late December, a significant decline from the 1.75-billion-share pace recorded for the equivalent period of 2002. Daily dollar volume averaged $28 billion in the same period, down slightly from the previous year. Through November, 58 companies had made their Nasdaq debut, while the total number of companies listed on the exchange fell to 3,343 from 3,620, indicating the large number of companies that had been delisted for various regulatory infractions over the year. The most actively traded issues were Microsoft, Cisco, Intel, and Sirius Satellite Radio.

Table VI. Change in Share Price of Selected U.S. Blue-Chip Stocks[1] (in U.S. dollars)

Company	Starting price January 2003	Closing price year-end 2003	Percent change
General Electric Co.	23.85	30.98	29.90
Microsoft Corp.	25.62	27.37	6.83
ExxonMobil Corp.	33.98	41.00	20.66
CitiGroup, Inc.	34.29	48.54	41.56
Wal-Mart Stores, Inc.	52.85	53.05	0.38
Intel Corp.	15.51	32.05	106.64
International Business Machines Corp.	76.91	92.68	20.50
Johnson & Johnson	52.75	51.66	−2.07
Procter & Gamble Co.	84.30	99.88	18.48
Coca-Cola Co.	42.96	50.75	18.13
Altria Group	38.10	54.42	42.83
Merck & Co., Inc.	52.03	46.20	−11.21
SBC Communications, Inc.	25.64	26.07	1.68
Home Depot, Inc.	23.81	35.49	49.06
J.P. Morgan Chase & Co.	23.20	36.73	58.32
Hewlett-Packard Co.	17.08	22.97	34.48
3M Co.[2]	59.55	85.03	42.79
American Express Co.	35.10	48.23	37.41
Walt Disney Co.	16.16	23.33	44.37
E.I. du Pont De Nemours & Co.	40.97	45.89	12.01
United Technologies Corp.	60.99	94.77	55.39

[1]In order of market capitalization as of Dec. 31, 2003. [2]Price adjusted for a two-for-one stock split in 2003.

The American Stock Exchange (Amex) listed 1,121 securities at year's end, reflecting the increased popularity of various types of exchange-traded funds (ETFs), an Amex specialty. The average daily volume of equities and ETFs traded on the Amex in 2003 climbed to 67.8 million shares, compared with 60.7 million in 2002. The most actively traded issue on the exchange continued to be the Nasdaq 100 index itself. In November the National Association of Securities Dealers (NASD), owner of both the Amex exchange and the Nasdaq, announced its intention to spin off the Amex as an independent entity. A month later the company was quick to rebuff reports that it was planning to merge the Nasdaq with the NYSE.

Avenues remained bleak for companies that were seeking capital through public stock offerings. There were a total of 68 initial public offerings (IPOs) on U.S. markets, valued at a total of $15 billion, compared with 70 IPOs in 2002. By contrast, 406 IPOs had taken place in 2000.

Feelings that the securities industry had betrayed the public trust intensified in 2003, and investors filed an increased number of complaints. The number of arbitration cases that were filed with NASD, the market's regulatory organization, hit a fresh record at 8,900, a 16% increase from 2002. NASD also filed 1,352 enforcement actions and banned or suspended 830 individuals from the securities industry as a result of violations.

Once considered a refuge from weakness in the stock market and the larger economy, bonds suffered their worst reversal in a generation once stocks went back on the rise. The bond market's losses began in June and steepened through August, outstripping the bond-market crashes of 1980 and 1987 and wiping out billions of dollars in value. Bond returns, as measured by Lehman Brothers, fell 3.36% in July alone, the sixth worst monthly performance on record, while Treasury bonds in particular tumbled 4.39%, their second worst month in 30 years.

Bond mutual funds deflated as investors returned to the revitalized stock market. In the third quarter alone, investors pulled $23.8 billion out of taxable bond funds, mostly government bond funds, reversing record bond-fund inflows earlier in the year. Despite this, investors moved a total of $40 billion into taxable bond funds through November, though this was well under the previous year's inflow of $117 billion. Compared with bond funds' impressive investment returns in 2002, the rewards were meagre. According to Morningstar, long-term government bond funds returned 2.18% for the year, while short-term government bond funds returned an uninspiring 1.41%. The Lehman Aggregate bond index ended the year up 4.1%.

As demand for bonds decreased, prices fell, pushing effective yields higher in order to attract investors. Ten-year Treasuries yielded 4.26% at year's end, returning to 2002 levels and effectively erasing all progress made in the previous 12 months. The spread between the yields of investment-grade corporate bonds and similar-maturity Treasuries narrowed to under 1%, bringing the interest rates on corporate and government debt closer than they had been since 1999. The razor-thin spread reflected general optimism about the prospects of strong companies in the improved economic environment but revealed minimal room for further upside ahead in the corporate-debt market.

Canada. Canadian stock prices climbed in tandem with global equity markets in 2003, ending a two-year losing streak amid renewed investor enthusiasm worldwide. Continuing interest in mining shares combined with a rebound in technology (as embodied by market heavyweight Nortel Networks) supported the Canadian equities market, the world's seventh largest.

The broadest measure of the Canadian stock market, the S&P/TSX Composite index, climbed 24.28%. This index measured the overall performance of the Toronto Stock Exchange (TSE), Canada's largest share-trading forum. The S&P/TSX index of 60 blue-chip stocks advanced 22.93%. The Dow Jones Global index for Canada gained 25.14% in U.S. dollar terms. All sectors shared in the rebound, led by mining stocks (up 76%) and the resurgent information technology group (59%).

The TSE reported that average daily trading hit a record 220.9 million shares, a jump of 19.9% from the previous year. The dollar value of these trades, however, was only slightly better than 2002's average Can$2.5 billion (about U.S.$1.9 billion) per day, reflecting lower share prices. At the end of the year, 1,340 companies were listed on the exchange, up from 1,304 in 2002. IPOs increased to 77, compared with 75 IPOs for the same period of the previous year.

Business-information company Thomson Corp., the largest TSE stock by market capitalization, gained 28% in value to an adjusted close of Can$47.08 (about U.S.$36.38). Nortel Networks, for years the largest stock on the TSE and still the most actively traded, bounced off its 2002 lows, soaring 118% to close at Can$5.49 (about U.S.$4.24). Other heavily traded TSE stocks were Bombardier, Wheaton River Minerals, and Air Canada. The Vancouver-based TSX Venture Exchange, which focused on smaller and more speculative securities, leapt 63%, as measured by the S&P/TSX Venture Composite index. Through November, 44 companies graduated from this exchange to the larger TSE.

The soaring value of the Canadian dollar (which hit a 10-year high against the U.S. currency during the year) hampered attempts by local companies to sell their wares in foreign markets and thereby hurt the profits of exporters. The Bank of Canada raised its key overnight interest rate twice (in March and April) and lowered it twice (in July and September) in an attempt to moderate the currency's rising value, and the rate was ultimately left unchanged for the year at 2.75%.

Overall, the economy found it difficult to gain momentum in 2003 as GDP edged up 2% in the first quarter only to slip 0.7% in the second and grow 1.1% in the third. The spring outbreak of SARS (severe acute respiratory syndrome) in Toronto cost the nation an estimated Can$1.5 billion (about U.S.$1.2 billion) in lost trade and was followed by the local discovery of mad cow disease and a crippling power outage, both of which had additional negative impact on the economy.

Although Canada's securities industry remained relatively untainted by the U.S. mutual fund scandal, the general public failed to muster much enthusiasm for Canadian mutual funds until late in the year. An estimated Can$544 million (about U.S.$420 million) more was drawn out of Canadian fund accounts than was added in fresh investment. The number of such accounts shrank by 1.1 million.

(BETH KOBLINER)

Western Europe. Major European markets swayed with the vicissitudes of war, but European investors faced other worries closer to home as economic recovery in Europe lagged behind Asia and the U.S. Although stock markets generally trended upward, they remained volatile. Investors saw labour and product-market rigidities throughout the euro zone and the impact of a strong euro on exports as serious impediments to market recovery.

In January a sharp dip in the DJIA was echoed on major stock markets in London, Paris, and Frankfurt, Ger. Shares in Paris collapsed to just a third of their value at peak in 2000. Frankfurt's Xetra DAX index, which had sunk by 44% in 2002, fell further still. Analysts at the American investment bank Merrill Lynch said that the drop, which represented a 70% plunge in equity prices since March 7, 2000, made Germany's bear market worse than that of the 1930s Great Depression. Some traders blamed the declines in Europe on poor corporate news, high oil prices, and war jitters. Shares stalled again in May as investors feared a falling U.S. dollar would weaken foreign investment and dampen company earnings and that a corresponding strengthening of the euro would hit exports. Worries about deflation and coordinated terror attacks also dragged down European markets. In August the German economy dipped into recession, and in September leading stock indexes in the U.S., Japan, France, and Germany all fell in response to a call from the Group of Seven developed countries for greater flexibility in letting market forces set exchange rates. Investors feared that greater flexibility would depress the dollar further and deter foreign investment, and in response the Paris Bourse's CAC 40 index fell 2.7% and the DAX declined 3.4%.

Later in the year, levels of corporate debt in the euro zone were also seen to represent a potential brake on investment as companies used their cash to repay debt. A third successive breach by France and Germany of the European Union's Growth and Stability Pact (by which members undertake to limit government deficits to below 3% of GDP) also raised concern. Yet markets were able to regain some of the ground lost in the previous three years against a background of generally improving economic data. By year's end all major European indexes were in positive territory, and most had solid double-digit increases, with the notable exceptions of Finland (up 4.4%) and The Netherlands (5.1%). The CAC 40 and Great Britain's benchmark *Financial Times* Stock Exchange index of 100 stocks (FTSE 100) showed gains of 16.1% and 13.6%, respectively, while the DAX jumped 37.1%. (*See* TABLE V.)

Other Countries. For investors in some parts of the world, 2003 was an excellent year. In February shares on the tiny

Baghdad Stock Exchange were reported to have risen 56% since August 2002 and thus vastly outperformed the world's major stock markets. In general, emerging markets had consistently outperformed developed markets since 2001.

The pace of Asia's recovery outstripped that of the U.S. and Europe. Most Asian markets outperformed U.S. and European markets between May and August. In Japan fundamentals improved, and the benchmark Nikkei 225 index managed a 24% rise by year's end after having fallen in March to its lowest level since March 1983 on poor corporate news and war fears. Investors judged that Asian economies were in better shape than before the financial meltdown of 1997 and that Asian consumers were less burdened with debt. China, spectacularly successful in attracting foreign money, continued to fuel economic and investment activity in the region. FDI reached $33.4 billion in the year-to-end July, according to official figures, and was expected to exceed $60 billion, up from $52.7 billion in 2002. China's Shanghai Composite index gained 10% for the year.

Anxiety over terrorism and the influenza-like SARS virus took its toll on markets early in the year. In February Pakistan's stock market, having performed strongly through 2002, fell by more than 4% after a bomb attack on the head office of the Pakistan State Oil company. Indian stocks, which had undergone a rally that took prices to their highest in 29 months, crashed in August after bombs exploded in the financial centre of Mumbai (Bombay). Yet when the year ended, all the main Asian indexes had gained at least 20%—Hong Kong's Hang Seng was up almost 35%, both Pakistan and Indonesia had risen more than 60%, India had climbed nearly 73%, and Thailand had soared an astounding 117%.

Overall, the most spectacular gains were in major South American stock markets. On November 26 Brazil's Bovespa index hit its highest point since its creation in 1968, on investor confidence in a new government regime, after which it climbed even higher to finish the year up more than 97%. In October Argentina's leading Merval index surpassed its highest level since the index's launch in 1986. Argentine stocks gained more than 104% for the year, following the country's economic collapse of 2002. Debt problems and continued political instability, however, left the whole region vulnerable to reverses in investor sentiment.

Similarly, European emerging markets, particularly those countries scheduled to join the EU in May 2004, made solid gains as investors saw good value in their stock markets. Hungary, despite its budget deficit of 5% of GDP, and Poland, despite similar fiscal problems and falling bond and currency markets, recorded market gains of about 20% and 45%, respectively.

Commodities. Mined commodities traded strongly throughout 2003. Volatile stock markets, a weakening U.S. dollar, and increasing worries about the war with Iraq lifted the price of gold to a seven-year high, rising above $400 per ounce in November and ending the year at about $415. The price of gold was still far below its 1980 peak price of $850 per ounce, but some analysts believed the heavy indebtedness of Europe and the U.S. carried the potential to reignite inflation and undermine both the euro and the dollar as stores of value. China, where personal saving rates were high, was also seen as a good future customer.

Copper, nickel, and aluminum prices all rose, buoyed by demand from Asia; analysts also suspected some speculative buying by institutional investors and hedge funds. By year's end copper was trading at $2,245 a metric ton; nickel was at $16,100 a metric ton, a 14-year high. Over the year the *Economist* commodity price index for all items rose by just over 16% and for industrial metals by a little over 34%.

Crude-oil prices fell from a high of more than $37 per barrel to about $25.50 after the end of major fighting in Iraq, but they began to rise again in the autumn after OPEC unexpectedly announced a cut in output by 900,000 bbl a day beginning November 1. The oil cartel, which feared that restored Iraqi production would cause prices to fall too far, held oil prices at about $30 or higher in December. Although inventories were low—and despite the risk of oil price spikes in the event of terrorism—the price was expected to fluctuate around $25 a barrel through 2004.

Food prices generally fell, picking up with the onset of autumn as low grain stocks raised wheat prices, which were expected to fluctuate during the winter. Coffee prices rose in response to cuts in Brazil's production but later came under pressure from high stock levels and lower growth in consumption. Average overall commodity prices, which had risen by 1% in 2002, increased by about 12% in 2003, but they were predicted to fall by 5% in 2004. (IEIS)

BUSINESS OVERVIEW

Following a pair of grim years packed with all manner of economic catastrophe, 2003 was a respite for many American companies—for some it was a time of recovery, while for others it was at least a time when things did not get worse. The U.S. National Bureau of Economic Research declared during the year that the recession had ended officially in November 2001, so that the economic turmoil many companies endured in 2002 and 2003 had been actually the aftereffects of the crisis. The long-anticipated U.S.-led war in Iraq had little negative impact on the overall economy, and many battered sectors showed signs that they were stabilizing and recovering.

The U.S. GDP grew at an annual rate of 3.3% in the second quarter, but that was nothing compared with the third quarter, when GDP grew at an astonishing 8.2% annual rate, blowing away forecasts of a 4.7% increase and marking the fastest-growing quarter since 1984. A number of factors were cited for this improvement, including the impact of Pres. George W. Bush's administration's income-tax cut, the continuing mortgage-refinancing boom, and rising orders for durable goods in the manufacturing sector.

Warming economic conditions helped even sectors left shattered by the terrorist attacks of Sept. 11, 2001. One example was the airline industry, a sector that had come close to a huge multicompany collapse in 2002 and was kept alive at times only by infusions of government financing. Those harrowing days seemed to be at last over. While many airlines likely would not be profitable until 2005 at the earliest, industry analysts believed that the majority of airline companies had managed to stanch losses and had secured enough financing to get through the next few years.

There were only two major-airline bankruptcies in the U.S., both of which had taken place in 2002. U.S. Airways Group emerged from Chapter 11 bankruptcy protection on March 31, 2003, but it continued to struggle and posted a net loss of $90 million in the third quarter. U.S. Airways could point to some improvements, as its revenue per available seat mile was up 7.8% from third-quarter 2002, and its passenger load factor (the number of seats filled per plane) was up to a solid 77%. UAL, the parent company of United Airlines, was not likely to exit Chapter 11 until 2004. Throughout 2003 UAL officials implemented a major restructuring plan, which included cost-cutting measures and the implementation of such new strategies as creating a low-cost airline to compete directly with such budget carriers as Southwest Airlines and JetBlue, which remained the industry's most profitable players. Even though Southwest faced the challenge of more aggressive labour unions and an, at times, deteriorating stock price, a strong summer travel season helped the company post a 41% increase in earnings for the third quarter.

AMR, the parent company of American Airlines, came within hours of filing for bankruptcy protection in April. AMR avoided this fate only because its three main labour unions agreed to $1.8 billion in annual wage and benefit concessions. That agreement almost fell apart, however, when the unions discovered that AMR had not disclosed a controversial $41 million pension and compensation package for top executives. CEO Donald Carty resigned after the controversy. In the third quarter, AMR posted $4.61 billion in revenues and managed to squeeze out a small profit of $1 million.

Despite these slight gains, the airline industry was far from being a prosperous sector and still faced many pitfalls. In September a U.S. district court judge ruled that the families of people killed in the September 11 attacks could proceed with massive lawsuits against AMR and UAL, whose airplanes had been used in the attacks. The airlines planned to appeal the ruling, which, if it resulted in successful lawsuits, could cost them millions in settlements and legal fees.

The European airline industry also was in rocky shape, as the industry on the whole reported losses of up to $2.5 billion. The largest European airline, British Airways, reported that its annual loss in 2003 could be its worst since it became a private company in 1987. After a dismal first-quarter performance ending June 30, in which it posted a $101.5 million net loss, British Airways was hit in July by a wildcat strike that could ultimately cost the airline up to $65 million. Worse, British Airways was dethroned as the top European carrier in September when Dutch airline KLM and Air France entered a partnership that would create a massive new European air power to be named Air France–KLM. The new partnership, which would generate $22 billion in annual revenues, would run the airlines as separate companies under a single corporate umbrella. Meanwhile, Canada's largest carrier, Air Canada, filed for bankruptcy protection in April.

The airline industry's volatility had a parallel in the aircraft-production sector. Top American manufacturer Boeing faced a pair of challenges. It had to try to reclaim its formerly dominant share of commercial-aircraft production—which it had lost to its chief rival, Airbus—by pushing ahead with its new brand of aircraft, the 7E7, while also trying to boost its military-aircraft production. For the latter strategy, Boeing racked up a number of lucrative military production commissions, but the company also faced a host of controversies—politicians attacked Boeing's $20 billion contract to supply the U.S. Air Force with 100 new 767 jetliners, calling the deal overly expensive, and the Department of Justice investigated whether Boeing had won a federal rocket-launcher contract fairly. On December 1 Chairman and CEO Phil Con-

A darkened New York City skyline stands out in sharp relief against the sunrise on August 15 after a power collapse hit much of the northeastern United States and eastern Canada the previous day. Critics of the electricity industry feared that rising usage and a deteriorating power grid would lead to many more such blackouts in the future.

dit resigned in the wake of a scandal involving an air force procurement official hired by Boeing. Airbus indicated that it would make a major attempt to break into the U.S. military market.

As the woes of some industries abated, those of other sectors became a public spectacle. The power industry in 2003, for example, would be remembered for its colossal failure. On August 14 much of the Northeast and the Great Lakes region of the U.S. experienced what many called the worst blackout in U.S. history. (It also affected some areas of Canada.) The blackout, which darkened the skylines of cities such as New York, Detroit, and Cleveland, Ohio, and which endured for days in some areas, could ultimately cost $6 billion. Blame initially fell on Ohio-based First Energy Corp., the fourth largest American utility, which experienced an hour of growing failures on its Midwestern power lines before the power collapse spread outward. First Energy, which denied responsibility for the blackout, was cooperating with federal investigators into the blackout's cause. To many critics the blackout was simply a vivid indication of how decayed and overburdened the U.S. electric grid had become.

For oil producers the year was surprisingly undramatic. Most of the oil market's top players, including ExxonMobil Corp., BP Amoco PLC, and Royal Dutch/Shell Group, were in solid shape. The latter, for example, posted a 52% increase in net income for the first nine months of 2003 and in November signed a deal to explore for oil and gas in Saudi Arabia, the first such agreement between the Saudis and a Western oil company in 30 years. Just before the U.S.-led invasion of Iraq began in March, many analysts expected oil prices to skyrocket—some claimed that a price of $50 per barrel was feasible if the war went badly and Iraqi oil fields were destroyed. That never happened, and crude-oil prices remained in the $20–$28-per-barrel range for most of the year, prices that were moderate enough to cause OPEC nations to cut back production schedules. After toppling Saddam Hussein's regime, coalition forces scrambled to get Iraq back into oil production, but they had to contend with an Iraqi oil infrastructure that was blasted by war, sabotage, and decades of neglect.

Moderation and stability were not keywords for natural gas, a traditionally cheap commodity that in 2003 became quite costly. The price spiking began early in the year when, after a long, brutal winter, natural gas suppliers were left with their lowest inventory levels in 10 years. At the same time, companies consumed natural gas in ever-greater quantities, as many power plants constructed in the past decade used natural gas as their primary energy source. The result, during the summer of 2003, was that prices spiked up to $6.30 per million British thermal units (BTUs), double the typical price, and hovered at a still unnaturally high $5 per million BTU range for months. Producers benefited, notably the corporations Amerada Hess, Anadarko Petroleum, and Kerr-McGee.

Scrambling to contend with a possibly long-term period of high gas prices, companies with heavy natural gas needs, such as Dow Chemical Co., ramped up projects to import greater volumes of liquefied natural gas (LNG)—that is, natural gas that is liquefied in another country, shipped to the U.S., and then converted back to gas form at the receiving port. These receiving terminals were relatively rare in the U.S., since traditionally low natural gas prices had meant that there was no need to spend money to increase import capacity. This was no longer the case, however, as LNG imports were predicted to total about 25.5 billion cu m (900 billion cu ft) by 2005, compared with about 6.5 billion cu m (229 billion cu ft) in 2002.

In the background throughout the year was the unfolding investigation of the bankrupt Enron Corp., whose collapse in early 2002 had rattled the entire energy sector. Former Enron treasurer Ben Glisan became the first official sent to prison because of his role in the scandal, and other convictions were likely, although there were growing doubts about whether the investigation would turn up enough evidence to implicate the top Enron officials, including former CEO Kenneth Lay. A number of Enron's former rivals in energy trading either fell into bankruptcy themselves, as did Mirant Corp., or feverishly sold off many of their assets, as did Calpine Corp., Reliant Resources Inc., and former Enron merger candidate Dynegy Inc.

Steel manufacturers continued to struggle, though there were signs that growing demand could begin to push prices upward. Bankruptcies, which had become a hard fact of life for many American steel companies in the previous five years, were not as frequent in 2003, but there were still some casualties; Weirton Steel Corp., for example, filed for Chapter 11 protection in May. Worldwide steel demand increased substantially, driven mainly by China's insatiable hunger for steel products. China's steel demand was expected to be in the range of 282 million tons, up 22% from 2002. This helped American exports, as did continuing tariffs introduced by the Bush administration in 2002, which were set to remain in place until March 2005. Political pressures, however, soon put an end to the tariffs. They were watered down throughout the year until they applied to only about 25% of steel imports by the latter half of 2003, and in December the administration decided to repeal them. Steel imports to the U.S. were down substantially; there was a 22% drop in the first half of 2003 compared with the same period the previous year.

There were signs that a stronger, healthier top class of American steel producers was emerging. Most notable was International Steel Group, a two-year-old company run by mogul Wilbur Ross. ISG's business was built primarily on the ruins of two bankrupt former giants, LTV Corp. and Bethlehem Steel Corp., whose assets it had purchased. U.S. Steel Group bought the assets of bankrupt National Steel Corp. in May. U.S. Steel, formerly the largest steelmaker in the world but more recently demoted to a humble 10th place among global producers, firmed up its outlook in 2003 with a new, less-costly labour contract and boosted its prices by $20 per ton in September. Not every steel producer's health was improving—in particular, "minimills" had a mixed-to-poor year. Because these firms made steel by melting scrap, rising scrap costs drove up their expenses substantially. Top minimill Nucor Corp. posted a 59% drop in profits for third-quarter 2003.

It was an undistinguished, steady year for aluminum producers. Year to date as of August, American and Canadian aluminum shipments totaled 7 billion kg (15.5 billion lb), down 2.1% compared with the same period in 2002. Year-to-date net imports were roughly 1.9 billion kg (4.2 billion lb), up 6% from the previous year. There was a major shift among top producers as Canadian aluminum maker Alcan Inc. acquired French rival Pechiney SA for $4.7 billion. The deal would make the new combined company the world's largest aluminum company in terms of sales, dethroning Alcoa Inc., although

© Eriko Sugita/Reuters NewMedia Inc./Corbis

Nissan Motor Corp.'s president and CEO, Carlos Ghosn, presents the Nissan Fuga luxury car at the Tokyo Motor Show in October. The Japanese automaker introduced several new models in 2003 as part of its effort to increase its North American market share.

Alcoa remained the world's largest aluminum producer.

Gold had its best year since 1996 as the gold spot market broke the $400-per-ounce barrier in late 2003, and some gold producers predicted prices in the range of $450 per ounce in 2004. Analysts said price spikes were due to the plummeting value of the U.S. dollar, rising interest rates, and more consolidation among top producers, which created a more controlled supply-price environment. A projected merger would create a new industry king. AngloGold Ltd.'s $1.1 billion bid for Ghana's Ashanti Goldfields Co. in August would make it the world's largest gold-mining company, vaulting over top producer Newmont Mining Corp. South Africa's Randgold challenged the deal with its own—higher—bid, but in October Ghana approved AngloGold's final bid of $1.48 billion, despite its being lower than Randgold's offer.

The lodging industry continued to be weak, but the industry was banking on an improvement in 2004. Slow economic conditions, continuing joblessness, a vicious hurricane season, and general geopolitical fears continued to hurt travel rates, though the summer of 2003 saw an improvement in vacation activity. There were indications of a resurgence in the hotel sector. Revenue per available room (a key indicator of hotel growth) was down a mere 0.8% at the end of the third quarter, and industry players were hopeful that 2003 would ultimately be a growth year and thus end a period of contraction that had begun in 2001. Hotel occupancy rates were 65.6% in the third quarter, up from the depths of 2002, which had posted the lowest rates in more than three decades—59%. Most of the top hotel chains, however, were still on the ropes and were conservative in their outlooks. Host Marriott Corp. reported a net loss of $136 million for the first nine months of 2003. Hilton Hotels Corp., while in stronger shape, posted a 62% drop in profits for the same period.

The domestic auto industry found that a formula that had spurred sales in the past—serious price concessions, including 0% financing—could not prevent a slowdown in sales for much of 2003. Years of brutal price wars had taken their toll on the Big Three American automakers, which continued to trail their foreign competitors dramatically in terms of profitability. General Motors Corp. (GM), although it remained the most profitable of the Big Three, still earned only about $700 per vehicle, compared with the $2,000 per vehicle that Nissan Motor Corp. earned. The Big Three also continued to lose competitive ground. In the first nine months of 2003, their combined market share fell to 60.1% from 61.7% in the same period in 2002, while Japanese manufacturers' market share rose to 29% from 27.6% and that of European automakers increased to 7% from 6.8%. The Big Three did manage to close the gap in terms of productivity. By midyear 2003 GM was able to produce an average vehicle in 24.4 hours, close to Honda's rate of 22.3 hours. In addition, all of the Big Three secured favourable labour agreements with the United Auto Workers union, which agreed to some of its most serious concessions in decades in terms of layoffs and wage increases.

Ford Motor Co. officials and Ford family members who gathered in June in Dearborn, Mich., to celebrate the company's centennial could contemplate a far rosier past than future. Ford had lost two-thirds of its stock value in the past few years, and its business continued to deteriorate in 2003. In the third quarter, Ford reported a net loss of $25 million. The most battered sector of Ford's business was its European division, which lost $525 million in the second quarter alone. With such grim earnings to report, the company scrambled to reduce expenses and vowed to slash $2.5 billion in costs from its automotive division, up from an initial $500 million target. GM was in slightly stronger shape. Taking advantage of low interest rates early in the year, GM offered a colossal $13 billion debt offering to investors—the third largest corporate bond deal ever—and used the proceeds to fund its foundering pension program. GM's $901 million profit in the second quarter was due primarily to its lending unit, General Motors Acceptance Corp., and that unit's enormous mortgage-lending operation. DaimlerChrysler, the last of the Big Three, was in the most trouble; its U.S. market share had eroded each year since Daimler-Benz bought Chrysler in 1998, and such fiscal woes as a massive $1.14 billion loss in the second quarter made its stated goal to earn $2 billion in profits in 2003 a lofty one.

Japanese auto manufacturers were far healthier than their American competitors, as had been the case for many years, but the Japanese carmakers were not immune to the market's overall slowdown and the pricing wars that had become a staple of the American market. Toyota Motor Corp. reported that its North American auto sales deteriorated in the first half of 2003, but the manufacturer remained far more resilient than did its domestic rivals. Toyota's net income for the first quarter was greater than the combined income of the Big Three, and the company stated that it hoped to sell 5.85 million vehicles globally in 2003, up 60,000 from prior projections. Nissan CEO Carlos Ghosn said that his company wanted to boost its worldwide sales by 40% in the next two years and to increase its 4.7% market share in North America. To win more of the American market, Nissan still needed to find a top-tier brand of car. To that end Nissan rolled out several new models during the year.

The tobacco industry spent another year on the defensive. In March, New York City banned smoking in bars and restaurants, which essentially made it illegal to smoke anywhere but outdoors and in private residences. This type of broad prohibition, already popular in California, was emulated by other states and cities (even pub-friendly Dublin, Ire., planned to offer a similar ban in 2004). With increasing bans, growing taxation, and a huge increase in imports from areas such as Zimbabwe, it was no surprise that American tobacco production was at its lowest level since 1874. Some top producers faced a grim prognosis for future health and took radical measures. R.J. Reynolds Tobacco Holdings Inc., which had slashed its workforce by 40% and had an abysmal profit margin ($5.79 per 1,000 cigarettes, compared with Philip Morris's $21.05 per 1,000 cigarettes), reported in October that it would merge with Brown & Williamson Tobacco Corp.

If tobacco manufacturers struggled, the general mood of the textile industry was near surrender. Domestic textile companies endured another year of rising imports, bankruptcies, and layoffs. Pillowtex Corp., which filed for bankruptcy protection in July, marked its second turn in bankruptcy court in three years, and WestPoint Stevens Inc., which filed in June, had previously filed in the early 1990s. Textile industry job losses were staggering, with 26,000 jobs lost in the April-to-August period alone. While surviving textile manufacturers lobbied for new protections against competitors such as China, it seemed that the trade imbalance would likely grow more pronounced in 2004, when quotas that currently kept some low-cost imports out of the U.S. were scheduled to expire. In what could be seen as a symbolic last act for the domestic textile industry, Levi Strauss, the company that had made denim jeans one of the country's most enduring exports, announced plans to shutter all of its remaining North American plants.

AP/Wide World Photos

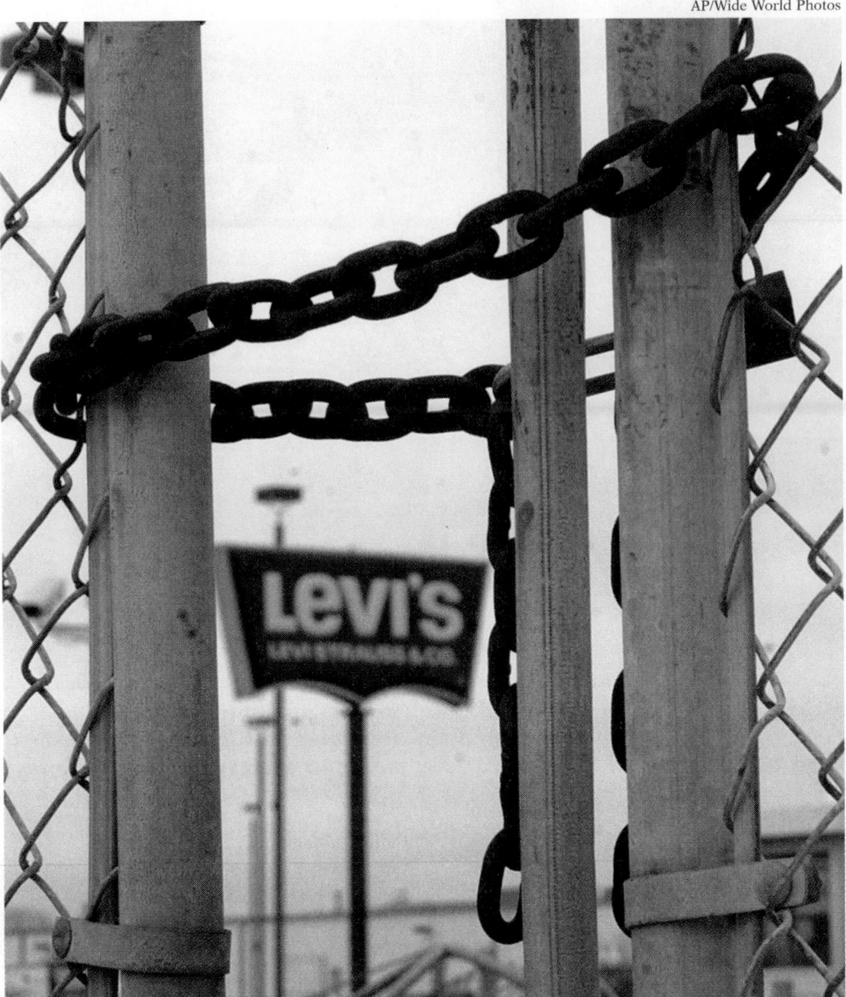

Levi Strauss & Co. the California-based company that introduced denim blue jeans to the world, in September announced plans to close its last U.S. plants. The financially ailing clothing manufacturer was one of many American companies outsourcing jobs overseas.

Even the pharmaceutical industry, which had weathered much of the economic downturn relatively unscathed, showed signs of trouble. Sales slowed for cholesterol-lowering statin drugs, which had helped drive earnings at Merck & Co. and Pfizer Inc. for a decade. After years of double-digit sales growth, analysts expected only single-digit growth in 2003. Top drugmakers such as Merck also faced a threat from generic drugs—which made up a majority of prescriptions in the U.S.—as well as from brand-name drugs from rival manufacturers, including an attempt by GlaxoSmithKline and Bayer AG to cut into Pfizer's lucrative market share for the impotence drug Viagra through a jointly developed copycat product, Levitra. Drugmakers spent much of the year lobbying against and trying to influence proposed federal legislation to add prescription-drug benefits to Medicare. What drugmakers most feared were provisions to make it easier for U.S. citizens to import prescription medicines from Canada and Europe, which could cut average drug prices significantly and upset the drug industry's elaborate pricing systems. (*See* WORLD AFFAIRS: *Canada:* Sidebar.)

In December Parmalat SpA, a global food giant based in Italy, collapsed in an Enron-like financial scandal and accepted an offer from the Italian government to file for bankruptcy protection. (CHRISTOPHER O'LEARY)

Education

The launch of a worldwide LITERACY CAMPAIGN, an increase in the use of COMPUTERS for education, funding problems, difficulties with achievement testing, DISORDER in schools, and COURT DECISIONS affecting affirmative-action policies were some of the issues that educators encountered in 2003.

PRIMARY AND SECONDARY EDUCATION

During 2003 the United Nations launched a Literacy Decade (2003–2012) campaign with the motto "Literacy for freedom" in an effort to effect a 50% reduction in numbers by 2015 of the 860 million adult illiterates and the 100 million children who had no access to schooling. Though progress during the 1990s had raised the percentage of adults (age 15 and above) who could read and write at a modest level of competence, subsequent high birthrates, economic difficulties, and traditions of not sending girls to school in sub-Saharan Africa, parts of Asia, and the Arab states caused those regions to lag behind the rest of the world in educating their populations. In the early years of the 21st century, the adult literacy rate was 60% in sub-Saharan Africa, 67% in South and West Asia, 76% in Arab states, 95% in Latin America, and more than 99% in Europe and North America.

School enrollment in the United States set a record of 73 million students in preschools, elementary and secondary schools, colleges, and universities. Ten percent of pupils aged 5 through 17 attended private schools, and 850,000 were taught at home. Nearly 20% of the country's 53 million elementary- and high-school students spoke a language other than English at home. Of three- and four-year-olds, 52% went to preschools, compared with 21% in 1970.

Worldwide the educational role of computers continued to increase. In the U.S. 98% of schools were linked to the Internet, up from 50% in 1995. Four out of five students aged 6–17 used computers at school, with four individuals sharing one school computer. Two-thirds of the students had access to a computer at home. Children from traditionally disadvantaged populations were included in the growth, with 55% of low-income households having Internet access at home, at school, or at a library. Almost all public schools in Japan were connected to the Internet, and 58% had their own Web sites. In addition, 53% of teachers there employed educational software and the Internet in class, a 5% improvement over 2002. Classroom use of computers was greater in elementary-school classes (66%) than in junior high schools (46%) and senior high schools (38%). More than 99% of England's primary and secondary schools enjoyed Internet access. The number of British students sharing a computer was reduced to 5.4 students in 2003 from 6.5 in 2002. Germany furnished one computer per 14 students, whereas Denmark provided a computer for every student.

During 2003 most U.S. school systems suffered from depressed economic conditions. States' budget deficits of $80 billion forced officials to dismiss teachers, increase class sizes, close schools, and reduce services. By midyear, plans had been laid to eliminate thousands of school personnel—notably 20,000 teachers in California, 200 in Phoenix, Ariz., 178 in Seattle, Wash., and 600 staff members in Buffalo, N.Y. Sixteen schools were slated for closure in Detroit, nine in Birmingham, Ala., and seven in Oklahoma City, Okla. Services that suffered downgrading or elimination included libraries, interscholastic sports, free bus transportation for pupils, after-school tutoring, computer purchases, musical events, and school newspapers. Some relief from the economic crisis in New York was provided by voters who, in 94% of almost 700 districts, approved proposed school budgets that often required increased taxes. In Britain more than 3,000 teachers were scheduled to lose their jobs owing to a money shortage.

A financial crisis for public schools in the Philippines was blamed partly on the inability of middle-class parents to pay the rising fees charged by the country's private schools, which resulted in

A pupil resumes her lessons when al-Amtithal Elementary School in Baghdad opens for the first formal day of instruction in May. Fear of the continued civil strife in the Iraqi capital kept many youngsters from returning to school.

an increased number of children transferring to public schools. Education officials estimated that the Philippines needed 21,000 additional classrooms and 10,000 more teachers to accommodate the new students.

The Australian government, on the other hand, increased its financial support of public schools by 8.3% above the 2002 allotment. China's Ministry of Education authorized $121 million from the sale of treasury bonds to expand 500 senior high schools, mainly in the central and western regions of the nation. Each school would accommodate another 18 classes and about 900 extra students. Owing to the lack of classrooms, about half of the 16 million junior-high-school graduates had not been able to enter senior highs in recent years. The building program would enable 450,000 additional students to enroll.

In the United States nationwide achievement testing—an important part of Pres. George W. Bush's ambitious education initiative—suffered a variety of difficulties. The most troublesome problem appeared in states that required students to pass standardized tests in reading and mathematics in order to receive high-school diplomas. Even students who had earned satisfactory marks in all of their classes could not graduate unless they also passed the exit tests. By 2003, 24 states had adopted a graduation-test plan or intended to do so. In Florida, Massachusetts, California, Nevada, New York, and North Carolina, the large numbers of students failing the exams during 2003 triggered public outcries that sent state legislators scurrying to repair their testing programs. Community activists in Florida threatened to boycott the state lottery and the tourist, citrus, and sugar industries if all 13,000 high-school seniors who had failed the Florida Comprehensive Assessment Test (FCAT) were denied diplomas. Subsequently, Florida lawmakers waived the testing requirement for students with disabilities whose individual education plans indicated that the FCAT did not accurately measure their abilities. Among the 4,178 Massachusetts high-school seniors who failed the graduation test, only 2,457 signed up for another chance to take the exam; when the retesting days arrived, just 698 showed up. The Massachusetts House of Representatives, in response to criticism, voted to allow students with "special needs" to earn diplomas even if they had not passed the exam, only to have Gov. Mitt Romney veto the measure. In New York officials cited flaws in the state's math test as the reason that thousands of seniors who had failed the exam would be granted diplomas if they had earlier passed a Math-A course. Although California lawmakers had intended to introduce a graduation-test requirement in 2004, the state board of education postponed implementing the plan until 2006 after a study suggested that at least 20% of the 2004 seniors would fail. An even higher proportion of students with disabilities or limited English skills would not graduate if the deadline went unchanged.

A variety of nations reported persistent disorder in schools, including shootings, hazing, bullying, and the disruption of classes. A study of 1,000 British children revealed that half of primary pupils and a quarter of secondary students had been bullied during the term. In a nationwide survey of police officers who were assigned to schools in the U.S., more than 70% of the respondents reported a rise over the past five years in aggressive behaviour among elementary schoolchildren.

Charter Schools Gain Momentum

By 2003 more than 684,000 U.S. students attended *charter schools*—publicly funded schools that pledged better academic results and were unencumbered by many of the regulations governing ordinary public schools. The aim of the nearly 2,700 charter schools in the U.S. was to furnish educators with the freedom to create novel ways of organizing teaching in an effort to yield better student performance and greater parent satisfaction than that typically produced by regular public schools. Operators of charter schools were granted such freedom by committing themselves—in the form of a written charter—to a variety of conditions that, they predicted, would produce superior learning outcomes. The conditions agreed with those identified in charter-school legislation passed by state or local lawmakers.

New England educator Ray Budde is often credited with having named and defined the concept of charter schools. In the early 1970s he suggested that small groups of teachers be given contracts or charters by their local school boards to explore new approaches to instruction. Budde's proposal was then publicized by Albert Shanker, president of the nation's second-largest educators' union, the American Federation of Teachers. Over the next two decades the proposal gradually attracted more enthusiasts until the first charter-school law was passed by the Minnesota legislature in 1991. By 2003, 40 states, plus the District of Columbia and Puerto Rico, had charter laws. States with the largest number of schools were Arizona (464), California (428), Florida (227), Texas (221), and Michigan (196).

The success of charter schools has been mixed. Some schools operated smoothly and reported higher student test scores than those in ordinary public schools. On the other hand, some schools provided inadequate facilities, employed poorly prepared teachers, misused funds, elicited substandard student performance, showed an unwillingness to accept students with special learning problems, and were unable to attract or retain students. In addition, controversies arose over the desirability of having for-profit education-management organizations (EMOs) operate charter schools. A study in Michigan revealed that administrative costs in EMO schools were two-to-five times higher than those in regular public schools, which resulted in lower salaries for charter-school teachers, a shortage of extra services (e.g., counseling and special learning materials), and administrators' reluctance to limit class size.

Nonetheless, charter schools were enthusiastically advocated by the federal government and endorsed by the nation's largest teachers' union, the National Education Association. In 1997 Pres. Bill Clinton called for the creation of 3,000 charter schools by the year 2002. That same year Pres. George W. Bush proposed $200 million to fund charter schools and another $100 million for a new Credit Enhancement for Charter Schools Facilities. Encouraged by such support, the charter-school movement seemed likely to continue growing.

(R. MURRAY THOMAS)

More than 41% of the officers cited a decrease in funding for safety measures in their schools, and 87% said crimes at schools were underreported to the police. The Philadelphia school system's newly imposed strict rules for reporting student misconduct resulted in a 41% increase in recorded assaults, weapons offenses, and other dangerous acts on and around school campuses. A total of 7,229 serious incidents were listed for the 2002–03 school year, including 976 weapons violations.

Authorities adopted a number of methods to stem school disorder, including expelling pupils, videotaping misconduct, teaching about the dangers of weapons, forcing bullies to pay fines, furnishing safe facilities for students, and rewarding good behaviour.

A landmark edict from the British House of Lords ruled that teachers were within their rights to refuse to teach violent pupils even if the children were legally entitled to be in school. In England over the most recent two-year period, permanent exclusions from school increased 4% from 9,135 to 9,540. Expulsions of children aged 5 to 11 increased from 1,436 to 1,450, while the figures for secondary schools rose to 7,740 from 7,305. Boys accounted for more than 80% of the expulsions.

A high-school-girls' off-campus touch-football game in Northbrook, Ill., deteriorated into a videotaped hazing melee in which members of one team kicked and punched their opponents before dousing them with paint and excrement. Many were injured; five required hospitalization. Officials responded by suspending 32 students from school.

In an effort to provide parents with visual proof of their children's misbehaviour, the Manchester, Eng., City Council authorized the installation of inconspicuous video cameras in classrooms. The Biloxi, Miss., school system became the first in the U.S. to install Internet-wired video cameras in hallways and classrooms. Less expensive than closed-circuit video cameras that record images on tape, the Biloxi equipment captured classroom scenes on a computer's hard disc. Anyone with proper Internet access could then witness the activities in any classroom.

The U.S. government allocated nearly $400 million to 97 communities to strengthen school safety and to improve mental health services for children with emotional and behavioral disorders who were at risk of becoming violent. After several Canadian youths died or committed suicide as the result of bullying by their peers, Edmonton, Ont., passed a law making bullying illegal and subjecting tormentors to a fine of at least $250. The New York City Department of Education, in an effort to relieve gay and lesbian students of ridicule by classmates, financed a special public school for homosexual, bisexual, and transgender youths; 100 students attended the new school in 2003, and enrollment was expected to grow to 170 in 2004.

Following a series of school shootings in South Africa, the organization Gun Free South Africa launched a campaign to make the nation's schools weapon-free zones. The campaign included showing the 2002 movie *Bowling for Columbine,* which director Michael Moore (*see* BIOGRAPHIES) based on a shooting incident at a high school in the United States. Ghana's nongovernmental Centre for Moral Education established a program to identify "morally upright and disciplined pupils" and reward them with the kinds of incentives typically provided for academic excellence—money, scholarships, and public recognition.

Schooling was disrupted in several nations by disasters. An outbreak of SARS (severe acute respiratory syndrome) forced schools to shut down for several weeks in Beijing, Hong Kong, Singapore, Taiwan, and Toronto. (*See* HEALTH: *Special Report.*) During the three-week closure in Hong Kong, more than 8,000 students continued their lessons from their home computers via the Internet, taking notes and speaking with their teachers and classmates by such means as Web cameras, audio-video phones, conferencing software, instant-messaging tools, and multimedia animation programs.

Successful efforts to rebuild Afghanistan's education system enabled six million children to attend school in 2003, nearly double the number of 2002. The publication of 5.8 million new textbooks helped fill the need for school supplies, as did 500,000 new desks that supplemented the 1.5 million desks purchased in 2002. There continued to be a serious shortage of qualified teachers, however, partly as the result of low pay—$35 to $45 a month. Because schooling was so badly disrupted during the 23 years of warfare prior to the defeat of the Taliban government in 2001, the number of illiterate youths and young adults in Afghanistan was believed to be in the millions. Although some 12,000 young people attended special courses in 2003, most of the unschooled were not enrolled in any program.

The Malaysian government stopped funding the nation's 206 public religious schools (Sekolah Agama Rakyat) in the belief that many of them fomented hatred and religious extremism. Prime Minister Datuk Seri Mahathir bin Mohamad stated that SAR students who transferred to national schools would receive a more-rounded education in the company of students of other races and religions. Not all of the 125,000 SAR students abandoned the religious schools after government funds were withheld, however. Some overzealous SAR teachers warned their charges that damnation awaited them if they moved to a national school.

In Europe the debate continued over the roles of the religious and the secular. French Pres. Jacques Chirac backed legislation that would prevent schoolchildren from wearing overt religious symbols, including Muslim head scarves, large crosses, or Jewish yarmulkes. In Spain, however, the administration of Prime Minister José María Aznar passed a law that required all students each year to attend a class on Roman Catholic dogma or one on world religions.

HIGHER EDUCATION

The U.S. Supreme Court justices, in a 5–4 decision, approved the affirmative-action policy that offered certain ethnic groups favoured opportunities for admission to universities. The selected groups—African Americans, Hispanics, and Native Americans—were said to need special admission provisions because they were enrolled in higher-education institutions in smaller proportions than their groups were represented in the nation's general population. Supporters of the court's ruling asserted that affirmative-action policies were necessary to provide ethnic diversity in higher-education institutions and to compensate ethnic groups that had suffered a lack of proper educational opportunities in the past. Critics of the ruling charged that the decision violated the applicants' right to be judged on their individual qualifications rather than on their membership in a particular ethnic group. The court case focused on the University of Michigan Law School's practice of taking ethnicity into account when deciding which applicants to admit. Whereas the justices endorsed the law school's affirmative-action plan, they struck

AP/Wide World Photos

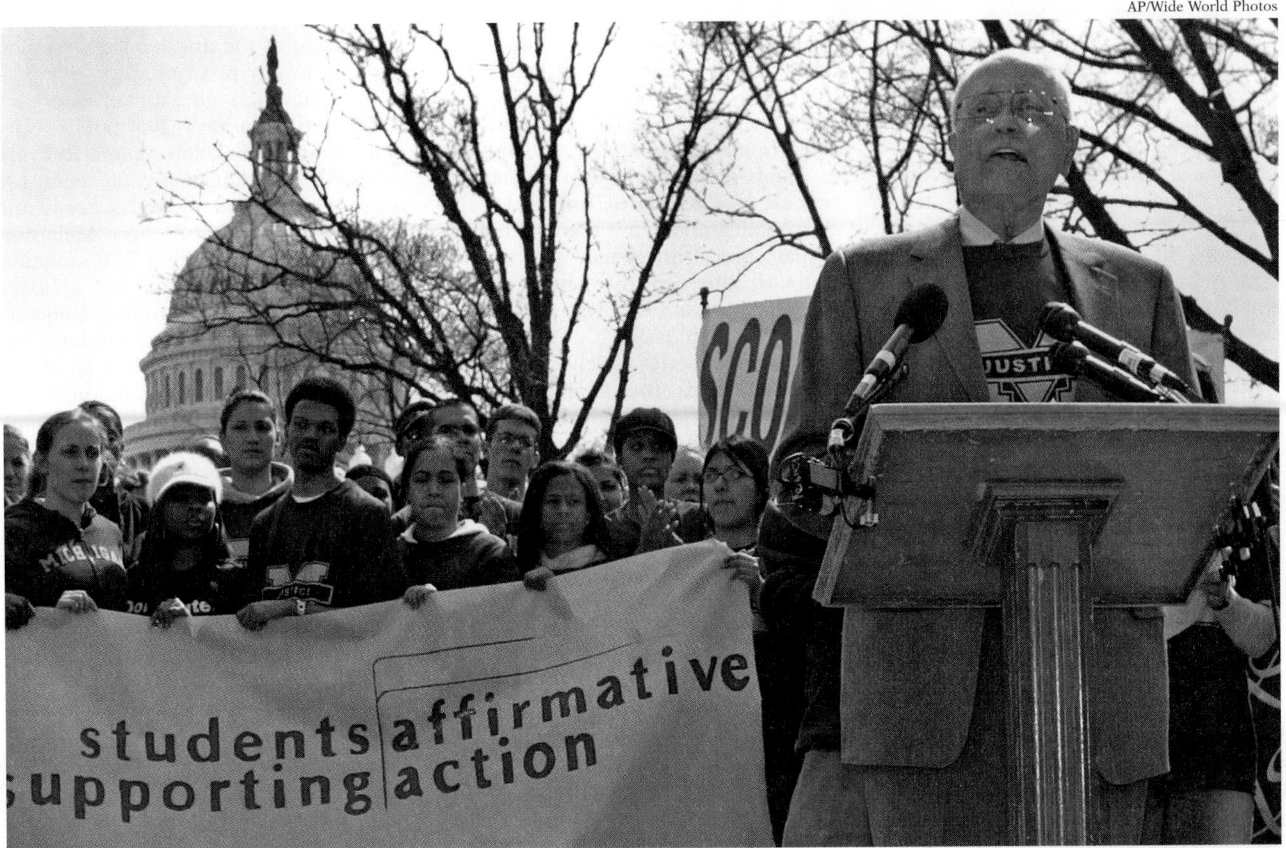

Accompanied by University of Michigan students, John Dingell, a Democratic U.S. representative from Michigan, speaks to the press in Washington, D.C., on April 1 as the Supreme Court was framing its landmark decision on whether the university may consider race as part of its admissions policy.

down the university's undergraduate-admissions policy, which awarded bonus points to applicants from underrepresented minority groups. The apparent inconsistency between these two decisions left university officials throughout the nation uninformed about precisely what criteria they would be permitted to use for granting preferential admission opportunities.

Chile's 37 private universities continued to expand their facilities, course offerings, and numbers of students. Andre Bello University added 35,000 sq m (375,000 sq ft) of new buildings for programs in medicine and biology. Diego Portales University opened new schools of medicine, nursing, and dentistry and increased the number of fields of study from 13 to 28. The University of the Americas set up its fifth campus. Over the two decades since 1981, when the Chilean government first authorized the establishment of private higher-education institutions, private universities had contributed in a major fashion to the 380% growth in the country's student population. By 2003 the private sector enrolled 53% of the country's 480,000 college students. Brazil and Colombia, which had followed Chile's lead in authorizing private universities, enrolled two-thirds of their nations' college students in such institutions by 2003.

China's Ministry of Education gave 22 universities greater freedom in student-admission decisions, permitting the institutions to include interviews and background checks rather than depending solely on applicants' entrance-exam scores. As in the past, key high schools would continue to supply recommendations about their best students as well as indicate who should be tested, interviewed, and selected for a background scrutiny. Admissions officers would then use their particular institutions' standards in choosing among the applicants. In Britain, for the first time ever, students from China outnumbered those from any other overseas country studying at universities and colleges. The 7,903 Chinese students arriving in 2003 exceeded the previous year's 5,802 by 36%.

Kenya's seven public universities gained greater autonomy when Kenyan Pres. Mwai Kibaki (*see* BIOGRAPHIES) renounced his role as chancellor of public higher-education institutions and appointed seven chancellors to replace him. Pres. Robert Mugabe's government in Zimbabwe, however, took control of Great Zimbabwe University, a private institution that had been established and operated by the Reformed Church of Zimbabwe.

In an effort to develop and preserve indigenous African languages in higher education, officials of the University of the Witwatersrand, Johannesburg, S.Af., adopted a policy that required all faculty members and students to learn a local black language. Courses would be offered in speaking, reading, and writing Sesotho, a dialect widely used in Johannesburg.

In June Myanmar (Burmese) military authorities ordered all universities and colleges closed following the detention of Nobel Peace Prize laureate Aung San Suu Kyi and 19 members of her National League for Democracy party who had clashed with pro-government protesters in northern Myanmar.

(R. MURRAY THOMAS)

The Environment

Climate change, the WORLD WATER CRISIS, and the Kyoto Protocol, which still awaited implementation, were among the unresolved environmental issues in 2003. CONSERVATION efforts to sustain APE POPULATIONS in Africa struggled against POACHING and the increased demand for bushmeat, while Iceland resumed WHALING after a 14-year suspension.

INTERNATIONAL ACTIVITIES

The governing council of the United Nations Environment Programme (UNEP) met in Nairobi, Kenya, on Feb. 3–7, 2003. The most serious of the many unresolved issues concerned legally binding action to reduce mercury pollution, an international code of conduct for sustainable production and consumption, the creation of a new intergovernmental panel on global environmental change, increased public access to information, and efforts to accelerate progress toward international chemicals management. The council learned that mercury pollution was much more widespread than had been thought and that 70% of mercury emissions were from coal-fired power stations and waste incinerators.

The third World Water Forum held a week of talks in March in three Japanese cities—Kyoto, Osaka, and Shiga. Ministers from 182 countries were among the 24,000 delegates, but the forum made little progress toward the objectives of sustainable water management agreed upon at the 2002 sustainability conference in Johannesburg, S.Af. The conference's closing declaration reaffirmed a commitment to reducing by half the number of people lacking access to basic sanitation or clean drinking water but made no reference to how this might be achieved. (*See* Special Report.)

The first of two ¥50 million (about $423,000) Blue Planet Prizes awarded in 2003 went to the 74-year-old Vietnamese ornithologist Vo Quy for his lifelong efforts to restore Vietnamese forests damaged by war. He had also helped draft Vietnam's first environmental law. A second Blue Planet Prize was shared by F. Herbert Bormann, professor emeritus at Yale University, and Gene E. Likens, director of the Institute of Ecosystem Studies in Milbrook, N.Y. They were honoured for having established the Hubbard Brook Ecosystem Study in New Hampshire. The $1 million Templeton Prize was awarded to environmental ethicist Holmes Rolston III, and the Whitley Gold Award was presented to Raman Sukumar for his conservation efforts. (*See* BIOGRAPHIES.)

NATIONAL DEVELOPMENTS

China. The sluice gates on the 190-m (630-ft)-high Three Gorges Dam began to close at midnight on June 1. The first of the dam's 26 generators was connected to the grid at 1:31 AM local time on July 10, 20 days ahead of schedule.

European Union. A European Union directive that went into effect on May 17 aimed at promoting the use of "biofuels" and other renewable fuels in transportation. Each EU member country was asked to achieve 2% biofuel use by December 2005 and 5.75% by December 2010.

The U.K. government published an Energy White Paper on February 24 setting out proposals for reducing carbon dioxide emissions to 60% of 1990 levels by 2050. This would be achieved by increasing the amount of electricity generated from renewable sources to 10% by 2010, with an "aspirational" goal of 20% by 2020. When the existing nuclear power stations reached the end of their working lives, they would not be replaced. Critics doubted that the contribution from renewable sources, especially wind power, could be achieved and considered it unwise to reduce reliance on nuclear power. Plans were also announced for the establishment of a new U.K. Energy Research Centre, with a budget of £8 million–£12 million (about $13 million–$19 million) over five years, to form the hub of a National Energy Research Network. There would also be a dedicated facility located off the coast of the Orkney Islands, costing some £5.5 million (about $8.7 million), to test ocean-wave energy. Grants to expand existing renewable technologies, such as wind power, would be increased by £60 million (about $95 million) to take government expenditure on these technologies to £348 million (about $550 million) over four years.

The Dutch government signed an agreement in March with groups representing farmers, environmentalists, and the national waterworks association; the objective was to reduce the environmental impact of chemical pesticides by 95% of 1998 levels by 2010. It was hoped that the measure would prevent the recurrence of an earlier situation wherein the criteria for pesticide use were so restrictive that farmers complained that their competitiveness was undermined and environmentalists took legal action to oppose each new pesticide introduction.

On August 21 the Danish Environment Ministry announced the appointment of Ole Christiansen to be the head of the environmental protection agency. Christiansen, deputy director of the national forest and nature agency since 1995, took over from Steen Gade, who resigned in June in protest against budget cuts.

In late August a panel of five academics published a 16-page report, commissioned by the Danish government, assessing the first eight reports from the Institute for Environmental Assessment (IMV), headed by Bjørn Lomborg (*see* BIOGRAPHIES), the controversial author of *The Skeptical Environmentalist,* which had attracted fierce criticism from environmentalists. The panel concluded that none of the reports represented scientific work or methods in the traditional sense but pointed out that the IMV had never claimed to be scientific and the IMV reports were well presented, topical, and easily accessible to the public.

Russia. On June 4 Russian Pres. Vladimir Putin told his State Council of senior advisers that 15% of Russian regions were on the brink of environmental

(continued on page 194)

World Water Crisis
Is There a Way Out?

by Peter Rogers

“Of all the social and natural crises we humans face, the water crisis is the one that lies at the heart of our survival and that of our planet Earth.”

Such was the dismal state of the world’s water supply, as presented in a press release by Koichiro Matsuura, director general of UNESCO, on March 5, 2003. Matsuura later warned, “Over the next 20 years, the average supply of water worldwide per person is expected to drop by a third.” For years there had been warnings of an ever-worsening crisis in the availability of water on planet Earth, and in making 2003 the International Year of Freshwater, the UN gave the issue global prominence. The signs are troubling. Rapid rates of population growth worldwide, rapidly growing income in many countries, and consequent rapid urbanization have led to highly stressed water systems. (*See* MAP.) It has been estimated that 2.3 billion people live in areas where there is not enough water available to meet basic needs of drinking, sanitation, hygiene, and food production—defined as 1,700 cu m (2,200 cu yd) per person per year. Some 1.7 billion people live under true water scarcity, where the supply is less than 1,000 cu m (1,300 cu yd) of water per person per year. Under conditions of scarcity, lack of water begins to hamper economic development as well as human health and well-being. All of these troubling signs are magnified by the possibility that we may be entering a period of rapid human-induced climatic change, with very uncertain implications for water-resource management in the future.

In 2000 the UN General Assembly set a goal “to halve the proportion of people without access to safe drinking water by the year 2015,” and in 2002 the UN World Summit on Sustainable Development approved a supplementary goal of halving “the proportion of people without access to basic sanitation.” The UN estimates that 1.1 billion people do not have access to safe drinking water (defined as meeting minimal standards of bacterial and chemical quality) and that 2.4 billion people do not have adequate sanitation. Cutting these numbers by 50%—while at the same time increasing food production, reducing poverty, and sustaining the ecosystem—is an ambitious goal. Hasty, ill-conceived responses may only exacerbate the problem, and so the best response at this time may be to think

FRESHWATER STRESS

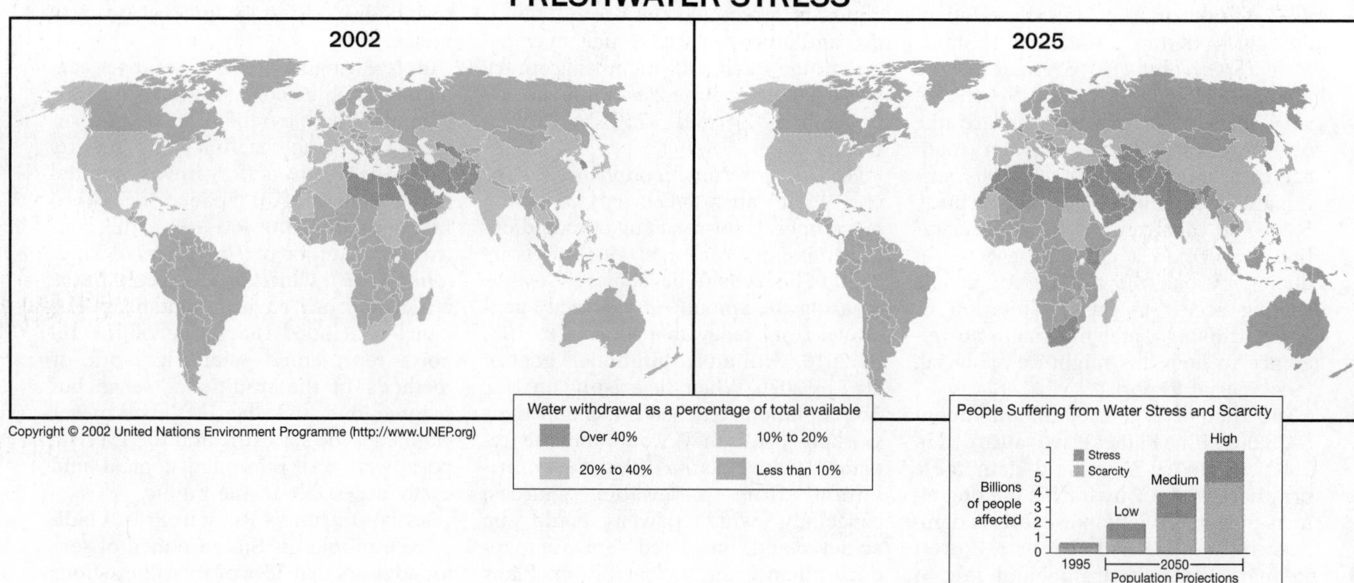

clearly about the nature of the water crisis and to evaluate possible solutions.

Do the Numbers Add Up? On the face of it, the current water crisis as presented by the UN is a classic Malthusian dilemma: a geometrically expanding population will soon meet the limits of a fixed supply of water. Yet Malthusian predictions of famine and other catastrophes have been made since the principle was first enunciated in 1798, and no such prediction has ever come true. Take the UN's claim that demand for water is growing at an unsustainable rate. This is due in part to rising population, which is due in turn to increasing life expectancy. Yet rising life expectancies are an effect of improvements in many areas, such as nutrition, hygiene, health services, and income. Could such improvements really have taken place if water supply and sanitation were deteriorating on the scale described by the UN?

Consider also the UN's drinking water and sanitation goals, described above. In order to reduce by 50% the number of people without access to safe drinking water and sanitation facilities, we need an estimate of what the current number is and what it will be over time. Unfortunately, the numbers cited above are very much in question, and even the definitions of *access, safe,* and *sanitation facilities* are open to interpretation.

Is the Water Blue, Green, or Brown? In 1995 the Swedish hydrologist Malin Falkenmark made a revolutionary contribution to hydrologic studies by distinguishing *blue* water, by which she meant all precipitation that contributes to stream runoff and groundwater and is readily withdrawn for human use, from *green* water, which is all precipitation that is transpired by vegetation or evaporated from the soil and other surfaces where it falls. Less than 40% of all rain falling each year on the land surface of the globe is blue water, and more than 60% is green water. *Brown* water, on the other hand, is all blue water that is contaminated by human use and then returned to the surface water system.

The most obvious path out of the water crisis would involve massive investments in infrastructure to store, transform, and transport blue water—in other words, more storage reservoirs, dams, desalination plants, and groundwater exploitation. Indeed, recent developments in desalination techniques—for instance, at the huge Tampa Bay (Fla.) Seawater Desalination Plant, which began operation in 2003—indicate that any urban area with access to saltwater can have a plentiful freshwater supply at reasonable cost. Another option is to expand the recycling of urban wastewater and industrial water (brown water). Yet another promising option might be to bring supplemental irrigation (blue water) to areas of rain-fed agriculture (green water). Substantial increases in food production could be achieved, and (assuming international trade was favourable) more food could be exported from rain-rich areas to rain-poor areas. This scenario leads to the concept of *virtual* water.

Consider Virtual Water. According to British hydrologist J.A. Allan, a country that imports food crops is essentially importing the water that was used to grow the crops in the exporting country. This virtual water can amount to as much as 1,000 to 5,000 tons of water per ton of crop imported. Virtual water, acquired as food and agricultural products through global food trade, can actually help to overcome disparities in water resources. Instead of spending large sums on irrigation, some countries would be better served by importing food crops from water-rich areas and saving their own dwindling water resources for human consumption.

Water Conflict. Some 40% of the global population lives within river basins that are shared by two or more countries. Often one country is water-rich and the other water-poor, or one supports heavily polluting industries while the other does not. Since there is no strong international law governing the resolution of transboundary water disputes, the potential for conflict remains high. Indeed, the *World Water Development Report* sees poor governance and lack of political will as the most important thread running through all aspects of the water crisis.

Not All Gloom and Doom. Into the gloom of the future we should project a little light by considering some successes of the past. Over the past 40 years, water resources and water quality have been greatly improved in Europe and North America. Rivers in the United States no longer spontaneously burst into flame; gross pollution of lakes and rivers has been eliminated; wetlands are protected and improved; and industrial and domestic wastes are under strict abatement levels. These achievements were not the result of immediate crash programs. Instead, they were reached step-by-step, solving the most serious problems before moving on to the next level. Such an approach might also be applicable to less-developed countries, where, unfortunately, many people expect almost instantaneous improvement. Victory in that arena would not be cheap or easy, but the benefits in health, well-being, and peaceful coexistence would be immense.

Peter Rogers is Gordon McKay Professor of Environmental Engineering and Professor of City Planning at Harvard University.

(Above) Illustration by Christine McCabe

(continued from page 191)
disaster. He urged a radical review of the country's environmental legislation.

United States. In late February a committee of the National Research Council called for substantial revisions to the draft of the Climate Change Science Program released by Pres. George W. Bush's administration. While describing the draft as a "solid foundation," the committee said it did not amount to a strategic plan, failed to present a set of clear goals, and was underfunded. The plan was issued in its final form on July 24, at twice its original length, with five goals designed to guide research and a call for 20 reports over four years to provide guidance for politicians. Critics agreed that the program was more cohesive than the earlier draft but complained that it lacked the budget and mechanisms to ensure that its results would influence policy. The program aimed to study natural climatic variability and to improve methods for measuring the climatic effect of releasing greenhouse gases and calculating the risks of global warming. Environmental groups and many climate scientists maintained that enough was already known to justify reducing greenhouse gas emissions and the program would delay necessary action.

On March 19 the Senate passed by 52–48 an amendment that removed from the 2004 budget resolution the provision that would have permitted oil drilling in Alaska's Arctic National Wildlife Refuge.

On June 23 the Environmental Protection Agency (EPA) released the *Draft Report on the Environment,* identifying indicators that could be used to track changes in environmental quality. It included some 100 indicators, such as ozone levels and levels of mercury in human blood. Owing to scientific uncertainty and political pressure, the EPA decided to omit a section of the report dealing with climate change.

Throughout the year the government continued to remove federal protections from wetlands, forests, and national parks. In December, a federal district judge voided the new rule that allowed snowmobiles in Yellowstone National Park, and other lawsuits were expected to be filed in regard to other heretofore federally protected areas.

ENVIRONMENTAL ISSUES

Climate Change. The eighth Conference of the Parties to the UN Framework Convention on Climate Change, held in New Delhi in late 2002, had been attended by representatives from about 185 countries. Some progress had been made in enabling the Clean Development Mechanism to become fully operational from the first quarter of 2003 and on harmonizing the presentation of emissions data. In 2003, however, there was no progress in the debate about how countries should respond to global warming after 2012, the target date for industrialized countries to limit greenhouse-gas emissions.

The Intergovernmental Panel on Climate Change (IPCC) Fourth Assessment Report, due to be published in 2007, was discussed at the IPCC's 20th Plenary Session, held in Paris on February 19–21. After the meeting, which was attended by some 350 government officials and climate experts, IPCC Chairman Rajendra Pachauri, of the Tata Energy Research Institute in New Delhi, said that more detailed regional models and carbon sequestration would be considered in the new assessment. A report compiled under the UN Framework Convention on Climate Change was discussed at a two-week meeting of signatories to the convention held in June in Bonn, Ger. On the basis of data supplied by governments, the report said greenhouse-gas emissions might rise by 10% between 2000 and 2010. The rising trend was attributed to economic recovery in Central and Eastern Europe and to a rapid increase in emissions in highly industrialized countries.

The approval of the Kyoto Protocol by Poland (on Dec. 13, 2002) and Canada (three days later, following an overwhelming parliamentary vote of 195–77) brought to 100 the number of countries that had ratified the protocol. This was insufficient for the protocol to come into force in 2003, however, because the ratifying countries did not account for 55% of all carbon dioxide emissions from developed countries in 1990. This goal would be reached when Russia ratified the protocol. In early December, however, Russia joined the U.S. in its opposition to the treaty.

Air Pollution. In its 2003 monitoring report, the UN Economic Commission for Europe found that the health of European forests remained little changed in 2002. Nearly 20% of trees were classified as damaged, and the proportion classified as healthy rose by 1% to 38.8% in the EU and by 1.5% to 34.1% across 30 countries.

On March 12 the Norwegian Environment Ministry announced that the volumes of sulfur transported to Norway from other countries had decreased by more than half over the previous 20 years and by 30% over the previous 5 years. Environment Minister Børge Brende said that this showed that "the international agreements on reducing atmospheric sulfur emissions in Europe are working." The statement said that acidification remained a problem, however, and further reductions in sulfur emissions would be necessary.

An EU directive limiting the amount of sulfur in road fuels to 10 parts per million by 2009 came into force in March. It called for effectively sulfur-free gasoline and diesel fuel to be available throughout the EU by 2005. In June the European Parliament voted almost unanimously to restrict the sulfur content of marine fuels further and more rapidly than had been proposed by the European Commission (EC). The EC aimed to implement a 1.5% sulfur limit (down from 2.7%) in the North and Baltic seas and the English Channel; the limit was scheduled to take effect 12 months after the directive came into force. MEPs, however, agreed that the limit should come into effect six months earlier, should be extended to all EU waters by 2010, and should be followed by a further reduction to 0.5%. This proposed lower limit also would apply to three pollution-control zones and to ferries in 2008 and throughout all EU waters from 2012. The restrictions would apply to all shipping, regardless of where a ship was registered or what its port of origin was.

Ozone Layer. It was reported on August 1 that a research team led by Michael Newchurch of the University of Alabama had found conclusive evidence that the rate of ozone depletion in the upper stratosphere had slowed markedly. Analysis of data collected over 20 years showed that ozone depletion had been occurring at 8% per decade for 20 years, but the rate had slowed to 4%. The team said it would be 50 years before the ozone concentration in the ozone layer returned to its original level.

On September 16 UNEP marked International Ozone Layer Preservation Day with a statement saying that the ozone layer was showing the first signs of recovery. The World Meteorological Organization reported that in mid-September the ozone hole over Antarctica covered about 28 million sq km (10.8 million sq mi), equal to its September 2000 area, which was the largest ever recorded, and in contrast to

NASA/Goddard Space Flight Center Scientific Visualization Studio

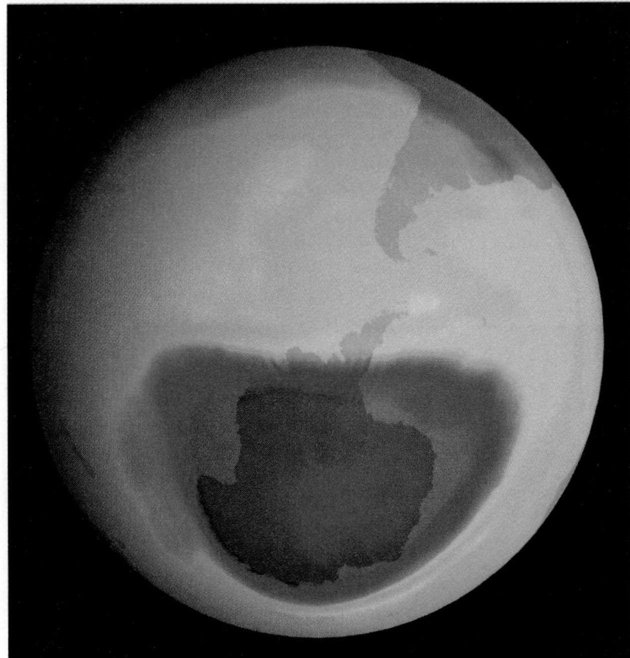

Polar scientists were mildly optimistic about the continued shrinking of the "hole" in the ozone layer of the upper stratosphere over Antarctica, which resulted for the first time in a split hole (right photo taken on Sept. 24, 2002); the ozone hole one year earlier is shown in the photo on the left.

its very small area in 2002. The increase was due to meteorological conditions in the lower stratosphere and not related to any change in the amount of ozone-depleting chemicals present.

Lead. A study of 172 young children in Rochester, N.Y., reported in April, found a significant link between intelligence and blood levels of lead even at very low concentrations. The children were given intelligence tests at ages three and five. Children with up to 10 micrograms of lead per decilitre of blood, the safe limit recommended by the World Health Organization (WHO), scored an average 7.4 points lower than children with only one microgram. The study suggested that there might be no safe level of exposure.

Marine Pollution. On Nov. 13, 2002, the single-hull tanker *Prestige,* owned by the Greek company Mare Shipping and registered in The Bahamas, was damaged in a storm off the coast of Galicia, Spain, while carrying a cargo of 77,000 metric tons of heavy fuel oil. Spanish authorities towed it out to sea, but on November 19 the ship broke in two, sinking in 3,500 m (11,500 ft) of water about 250 km (155 mi) from the Spanish coast. By mid-January 2003 an estimated 25,000 metric tons of oil had contaminated the coasts of Spain, Portugal, and France. On May 9 the International Oil Pollution Compensation Fund agreed to make €170 million (about $195 million) available to cover compensation claims. This was the maximum sum it could release, and it admitted the amount would cover only 15% of the costs of the accident, which was put at €1 billion (about $1.1 billion).

Within days after the wreck, Spanish Prime Minister José María Aznar and French Pres. Jacques Chirac had announced that authorities from both countries would inspect all vessels deemed to be dangerous. If appropriate, authorities would order them to leave the 320-km (200-mi) exclusion zone around their coasts. Portugal and Italy introduced similar measures, and within a week of the *Prestige*'s sinking, the EC had begun pressing member states for emergency action to improve maritime safety. Loyola de Palacio, the EC transport and energy commissioner, sought to impose limits on the transport of dangerous goods within 320 km of shore and a requirement, with immediate effect, that heavy fuel oil be carried in double-hulled tankers. The required measures, confirmed on December 3, included the publication of a "blacklist" of 66 substandard ships that would be banned from EU waters under safety rules proposed in 2000. Single-hull tankers carrying heavy fuel oil would no longer be permitted to enter or leave any EU port. On March 27, 2003, EU ministers reached outline agreement on the necessary legislation. Single-hulled tankers carrying fuel oil—the most polluting oil—would be banned immediately from all EU ports; the ban would apply to all single-hulled tankers by 2010. A report released in November stated that the tanker *Prestige* had spilled 64,000 metric tons of oil.

Tasman Spirit, a Greek-owned tanker chartered by Pakistan's National Shipping Corp., ran aground on July 28 close to Karachi, Pak., carrying a cargo of 67,000 metric tons of crude oil. Approximately 28,000 metric tons of oil leaked from the tanker, contaminating beaches and killing marine animals. Although 37,500 metric tons of oil were pumped from the ship in an operation lasting 15 days, a 15-km (9-mi) stretch of coast remained severely polluted. On September 1 the provincial environment minister, Faisal Malik, said that cleaning up the spill could take three years.

On February 20 the EU issued the text of a new law banning the use of organotin antifouling paints on ship hulls and oil rigs. The application of these paints was prohibited from May 9, 2003, and from Jan. 1, 2008, they had to be removed or painted over with a sealant to prevent contact with the water. The regulation did not cover warships and initially applied only to ships registered under the flags of EU member states, but from 2008 the rules would apply to all ships calling at EU ports.

In June the Swedish Commission on the Marine Environment warned that the condition of the Baltic was critical and that the sea might die unless pollution from St. Petersburg was drastically reduced. Populations of half the fish species in the sea were below the critical biological level, and pregnant Swedish women were being warned not to eat herring, a staple food, because of dioxin contamination. Some 30% of the effluent from factories and apartment blocks in St. Petersburg entered the River Neva unfiltered and drained into the sea.

Freshwater Pollution. A review released in March by UNESCO stated that if freshwater pollution increased in step with population growth, 18,000 cu km (4,300 cu mi) of water could be polluted by the year 2050, almost nine times the amount used for irrigation.

On March 29–30 at Cataguazes, in Brazil's Minas Gerais state, a chemicals reservoir burst at a wood-pulping factory. Perhaps as much as 1.5 billion litres (400 million gal) of caustic soda (although some reports said 20 million litres [5.3 million gal]), poured into the Paraiba do Sul and Pomba rivers. Much of the waste flowed over the border into Rio de Janeiro state. Animals on the riverbanks, as well as hundreds of fish, were killed, and people were warned not to drink or bathe in the water. On April 1 the company responsible was fined 50 million reals (about $15 million).

At a press conference in Göteborg, Swed., on June 27, three groups released early results from their EU-funded studies of antibiotic and other pharmaceutical contamination of European groundwater and soils. They found high concentrations of excreted antibiotics in hospital and household sewage, livestock slurry, and water used for irrigation. They also reported that antibiotics and their metabolites reached the environment directly from livestock feces and urine. EU officials said that these and other similar studies were likely to provide a basis for new management procedures for medicines, with hospitals and water companies being required to take steps to extract antibiotics from water.

It was reported in July that a team from the Shirshov Institute of Oceanology in Moscow had completed the first hydrographic survey of the Aral Sea since the early 1990s. The sea level had fallen 3.5 m (11.5 ft) more than predicted by earlier studies, to 30.5 m (100 ft) above mean sea level, and it was 2.4 times saltier than the ocean average, rather than 1.6 times saltier as expected. The sea had separated into two fragments, the North and South Aral seas.

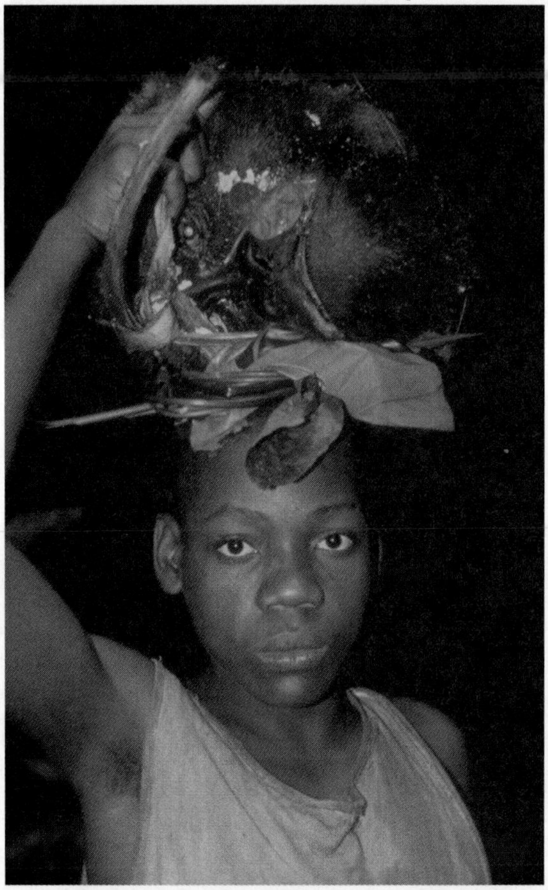

A young bushmeat hunter in equatorial Africa brings home his trophy. The hunting of endangered great apes was of particular concern to officials and environmentalists worldwide.

In August it was revealed that researchers led by Jack Ng of the University of Queensland in Australia had found that people in 17 countries were at risk of being poisoned by arsenic in the groundwater from which they were obtaining their drinking water. In Bangladesh efforts were continuing to find and replace millions of tube wells that supplied water to about 50 million people, but the government had spent less than $7 million of the $32 million provided by the World Bank in 1998 to pay for an immediate cleanup. The new evidence was from the valley of the Ganges River. In northern India, where 80% of the population relied on groundwater supplies, most of the tube wells had never been tested for arsenic. It was feared that many of the 83 million people living in Bihar state might be at risk; tests of 3,000 tube wells in Bihar had found that 40% had arsenic levels above the WHO limit and 12 wells had 20 times the limit. Parts of China, Vietnam, Argentina, and the U.S. were also at risk. (MICHAEL ALLABY)

WILDLIFE CONSERVATION

The hunting and consumption of wild animals—the bushmeat issue—was in the headlines throughout 2003, particularly with respect to Central and West Africa. Many types of wild animals were being hunted illegally. This was particularly serious for primates. Of additional concern, Ebola fever outbreaks in humans were linked during the year to the consumption of gorilla carcasses. Conservation organizations had begun to work with governments and logging companies to reduce hunting by supplying forest workers with alternative forms of protein. In April a large-scale study warned that although the forests of Gabon and the Republic of the Congo were believed to hold most of the common chimpanzees in the world and 80% of the gorillas (and that 60–80% of those forests remained intact), logging had opened up roads, which facilitated hunting. Ape populations had fared worst in the forests closest to cities, where bushmeat was sought as a delicacy. It was predicted that at current rates of decline, ape populations would fall by 80% over the next 33 years.

In January three Rwandan poachers convicted of having killed two mountain gorillas and stolen a baby gorilla from the Volcanoes National Park were sentenced to four years in prison. Six others convicted of having solicited a market for the baby gorilla abroad were sentenced to two years. The Virunga Volcanoes region, spanning Rwanda, Uganda, and the Democratic

Republic of the Congo, was home to the last 700 mountain gorillas. In 2002 the park had earned Rwanda $1.2 million from 5,895 visitors.

Also in January it was reported that climate change was affecting butterfly habitats in northern Great Britain. Some butterfly species were found to have moved as much as 41 m (135 ft) uphill in an effort to escape warmer temperatures, which were blamed on global warming. It was believed that the threatened species could experience population declines of up to 80% this century.

In February the American Association for the Advancement of Science called for the United Nations to issue a moratorium on longline and gillnet fishing, methods that were wiping out populations of fish, turtles, marine mammals, and other species in the Pacific Ocean. More than 70% of global fish populations were considered overfished, and indiscriminate commercial fishing practices harmed and killed millions of nontargeted wildlife, such as seabirds and leatherback turtles, annually.

In early August Iceland announced that it would resume whaling, and later in the month Icelandic whalers made their first kill in 14 years, slaughtering a minke whale for what were claimed to be scientific purposes. In September, 23 nations issued a démarche, one of the highest levels of diplomatic action, calling on Reykjavík to cease whaling and indicating that Iceland was acting against the will of the International Whaling Commission, of which it was a member.

In May the subantarctic Campbell Island was declared rat-free following a $2.6 million rat-eradication program. Two years earlier the New Zealand Department of Conservation had spread 120 metric tons of bait on the 11,331-ha (28,000-ac) island, which was estimated to have 200,000 Norway rats. An examination in May 2003 found no trace of rats, which had been present on the island for 200 years. It was now considered safe for the rare Campbell Island teal to be reintroduced.

In July five new natural sites were inscribed on UNESCO's World Heritage List by the UN's World Heritage Committee: Australia's Purnululu National Park, Three Parallel Rivers of Yunnan Protected Areas in China, Uvs Nuur Basin in Russia and Mongolia, Monte San Giorgio in Switzerland, and Phong Nha–Ke Bang National Park in Vietnam. Comoé National Park in Côte d'Ivoire, known for its great plant diversity, was inscribed on the List of World Heritage in Danger. The park was one of the largest protected areas in West Africa, but the unrest in Côte d'Ivoire was having an adverse effect on the site, which suffered from poaching, wildlife fires caused by poachers, overgrazing by large cattle herds, and the absence of effective management.

In August conservation and animal-welfare organizations protested about the capture of 200 bottlenose dolphins in the Solomon Islands, some of which were exported to Mexico. The trade appeared to have violated both the Convention on International Trade in Endangered Species of Wild Fauna and Flora (CITES) and Mexican law. For such export an assessment was required to ensure that the trade would not be detrimental to the species' survival. Permits issued by the Solomon Islands violated CITES regulations because so little data existed about these dolphins that the permits could not have been based on a valid nondetriment finding, while the introduction of an exotic species into a protected area violated Mexican law.

On September 26, despite earlier protests from around the world, a 5-m (16-ft) female orca, or killer whale, was captured in Avacha Gulf, off the Kamchatka Peninsula in far eastern Russia, for transport to the Utrish Dolphinarium on the Black Sea. This whale was part of a resident population that was being studied in a long-term Russian-Japanese-British initiative. Although female orcas were estimated to have an average life span of 50 years in the wild, they rarely survived beyond 6 years in captivity.

In September the fifth World Parks Congress was held in Durban, S.Af. The meeting brought together conservationists, park managers, and representatives of indigenous peoples. Recommendations covered the importance of ensuring that people who resided near protected areas had their needs considered, the recognition that protected areas also provided ecosystem services, and the need to provide tools and training to protected-area managers. The congress announced a commitment from Madagascar to bring 10% of the country under protection by 2008, plans for new national parks in South Africa, the creation of six new protected areas in Brazil, and a pledge of €5 million (about $5.85 million) for building a network of protected areas on the West African coast.

(MARTIN FISHER)

DNA sampling has shown these pygmy elephants to be a separate subspecies, different from elephants found elsewhere in Southeast Asia, that has lived in isolation in Malaysian Sabah, northern Borneo, for some 300,000 years. Dozens of new animal species and subspecies were identified every year, but this rarely occurred in mammals.

WWF-Malaysia/TH Teoh

Fashions

Trendsetting CELEBRITIES—including actors, MODELS, and sports heroes—made everything from elegant gowns to CHIPPED BLACK NAIL POLISH fashionable in 2003.

Celebrities dominated the fashion scene in 2003. Jennifer Lopez, Cate Blanchett, Liv Tyler, Christina Aguilera, Kristen Scott Thomas, and Samantha Morton promoted the work of leading fashion designers Louis Vuitton, Donna Karan, Givenchy, Donatella Versace, Giorgio Armani, and Marc Jacobs (*see* BIOGRAPHIES), respectively. Chanel appointed Oscar winner Nicole Kidman to be the face of the brand's legendary perfume, No. 5, a deal that earned the actress about $7.8 million. In July the Gap released a TV-ad campaign starring Madonna and rapper Missy Elliott, who together promoted jeans and T-shirts for the Gap's autumn-winter collection. As a part of her deal, Madonna signed a tie-in agreement that included the sale of her children's book, *The English Roses,* which was published in September. The Gap's rationale for appointing divas Madonna and Missy Elliott was shared by high-fashion designers who hired celebrity spokesmodels to attract more cash-rich female shoppers in their 30s and 40s.

Pop divas Missy Elliott and Madonna perform together in "Into the Hollywood Groove" for the Gap's fall TV campaign.

Iconic celebrity looks also proved inspirational to designers and the general public. Diana Ross's decadent 1970s early-disco style guided Tom Ford's autumn-winter 2003 collection for Yves Saint Laurent (YSL), and actress Ava Gardner's starlet glamour influenced the couture that Emanuel Ungaro presented for autumn-winter. "Hollywood, anyone!" read the program at Valentino's autumn-winter couture collection, which featured a parade of models wearing sable-trimmed dresses, embroidered-silk trouser suits, and long strapless satin evening dresses, accompanied by a retrospective video that captured movie stars Sophia Loren, Julia Roberts, and Elizabeth Taylor wearing Valentino couture at past Academy Awards ceremonies.

For sartorial inspiration, young women looked to Kelly Osbourne, the 19-year-old singer and costar of the MTV reality sitcom *The Osbournes,* whose neo-Gothic look relied on chipped black nail polish, messy hair, vintage sunglasses, and Converse running shoes, as well as the 18-year-old Canadian rock star Avril Lavigne, whose messy disheveled, layered skateboard style was composed of baggy trousers and a T-shirt over which she wore an open-neck men's-style shirt and loosely knotted tie. Dolce & Gabbana claimed David Beckham and his pop-star wife, Victoria, as muses for the menswear and women's wear collection. The English association football (soccer) star and his wife modeled clothes by the Milanese design duo's collection throughout the year and wore them when they made a high-profile joint public appearance at events such as the MTV Movie Awards in Los Angeles. In June, at the All-England (Wimbledon) Championships, tennis player Venus Williams modeled on court another fashion-celebrity tie-in—RBK by DVF, a collection of tennis wear produced by New York designer Diane Von Furstenberg together with the sportswear company Reebok.

Film proved to be a potent form of media for promoting fashion. A slew of light comedies were released during 2003 that bore similarities to the successful TV sitcom *Sex and the City,* which showcased pricey footwear, notably that of Spanish designer Manolo Blahnik. (*See* BIOGRAPHIES.) These films featured beautiful, fashionably dressed actresses and attracted audiences as much for their quirky plot lines as for the promise of viewing cutting-edge designer labels. In *Le Divorce,* Kate Hudson carried a Hermes Kelly handbag, and Reese Witherspoon wore shoes by Jimmy Choo in *Legally Blonde 2: Red White and Blonde.* Fashionable films proved to be an expanding genre; the Fox film company announced plans to make into a film the 2003 best-selling novel *The Devil Wears Prada.* The sardonic work, about an assistant who works for the irrational editor of a fashion magazine,

Britain's top pop couple, David and Victoria Beckham, attend the MTV Movie Awards show in Los Angeles on May 31, both outfitted by Dolce & Gabbana.

was written by Lauren Weisberger, a former assistant to American *Vogue* editor Anna Wintour, upon whom the central character was loosely based. Miramax acquired for £404,000 (about $670,000) the rights to *Bergdorf Blondes,* a novel written by *Vogue* writer Plum Sykes about a British fashion writer looking for love in Manhattan. New York's Killer Films announced plans to make *Simply Halston,* a biopic of the legendary American designer Roy Halston Frowick.

Red-carpet occasions, especially film premieres and awards ceremonies, greatly influenced the direction of the ready-to-wear and couture collections. Designers presented flashy clothes seemingly aimed at catching the attention of celebrity stylists, who appeared at the seasonal shows in increasing numbers. For the autumn-winter season, jewel-encrusted tops and dresses appeared in Alber Elbaz's debut collection for the House of Lanvin as well as in ensembles that were designed by Alexander McQueen. Satin clothes and accessories appeared for both day and evening wear in an array of candy colours as well as in strong shades of basic black, bright purple, electric blue, and caramel in the spring-summer and autumn-winter ready-to-wear collections of Valentino, Missoni, Prada, Gucci, Chanel, and Carolina Herrara. A standout look was Louis Vuitton's satin minidress, which, in its June issue, American *Vogue* christened "Dress of the Month," claiming it was a "luxurious upgrade of a retro diner uniform."

One of the trendsetting looks that debuted on the red carpet was the chandelier-style earrings worn by both Kidman and Julianne Moore at the 2003 Golden Globe Awards. The presence at Los Angeles Fashion Week of Hollywood stars Witherspoon, Mena Suvari, China Chow, and Anjelica Huston made the show a noteworthy occasion. In April and late October, Seventh on Sixth, the organizer of New York City fashion shows, staged its first series of centralized fashion shows in Los Angeles and attracted recognized local design-talent participants, including actress Tara Subkoff, the designer of Imitation of Christ, and designers Trina Turk, David Cardona, and Frankie B.

A wide range of global ideas pushed the boundaries of the fashion world beyond the traditional Western capitals. For Jacobs's spring-summer collection, he collaborated with Japanese artist Takashi Murakami to make "eye love," a line of handbags that merged the luxury label's iconic monogrammatic print with the artist's Pop-art graphics. During the autumn-winter ready-to-wear collections in Paris, model Alek Wek launched "1933," an accessories and handbag collection inspired by her native country, The Sudan. In May the New York City department store Lord & Taylor devoted 20 of its Fifth Avenue windows to promotion of the work of four designers from India: Tarun Tahiliani, Rina Dhaka, Vivek Narang, and Manish Arora. The *New York Times* reported that Lakme India Fashion Week in Mumbai (Bombay) attracted increasing numbers of international buyers, an advantage that helped boost the presence of native fashion talent at the annual event. Italian *Vogue*'s March 2003 issue featured a 15-page portfolio of portraits, shot by Nathaniel Goldberg, of prominent stylish Indian women dressed in traditional saris and sumptuous jewels, and a spring-summer advertising campaign produced by Valentino featured an Indian model displaying a traditional *bindhi* dot on her forehead. Yves Carcelle, head of the fashion group at LVMH Moët Hennessy Louis Vuitton, told the *New York Times* in May that "India is changing quite fast"; Louis Vuitton opened its 298th shop during the year—in New Delhi's Oberoi Hotel.

While exotic ideas and celebrity glamour helped shift high-fashion merchandise, common themes that united the year's major fashion trends were affordability and wearability. At the spring-summer collections, a safe colour palette, consisting of pretty pinks and pastel shades, dominated women's wear. Appearing on the runways at Gucci, Dolce & Gabbana, and Balenciaga were basic shapes, including combat trousers—made of parachute silk and satin—that were often accessorized with stilettos. Though some fashion critics spoke out against designers who capitalized on military-inspired styles during a time of war, cargo and combat pants proved to be an overwhelmingly popular street-fashion trend. So too were denim miniskirts, designer jeans, and basic black leggings, which first appeared as a part of Nicolas Ghesquiere's surf-inspired spring-summer collection for Balenciaga. After a slew of celebrities were spotted wearing black leggings—Chloë Sevigny at a Cannes Film Festival premiere and Stella McCartney and Kate Moss in London—British retailer Top Shop reportedly sold them by the hundreds. In summer inexpensive rubber flip flops proliferated as a unisex look on the beach and on city streets. Those made by the Brazilian company Havaianas became cult items—supermodels Naomi Campbell, Moss, and Gisele Bündchen were photographed wearing them.

For autumn-winter a greatest-hits array of safe, classic retro styles from nearly every decade of the 20th century appeared on the runways, including turn-of-the-century corsets designed by Dolce & Gabbana, Versace, and McCartney; 1940s-style fur collars and tweed separates; and 1950s-inspired pencil skirts. Evening wear inspired by one of Audrey Hepburn's most famous roles, Sabrina, appeared at Givenchy, and the 1960s mod miniskirt look proved to be a major inspiration for Jacobs.

Affordable fashion was a direct response to the continued slowdown of the global economy. A collapsing dollar and yen, the outbreak of and ongoing war in Iraq, and the epidemic of SARS (severe acute respiratory syndrome) were all factors that curbed consumer spending worldwide. (The SARS outbreak, however, started a craze in Hong Kong for the wearing of protective face masks bearing counterfeit prints of luxury fashion logos and imitation Burberry plaid.) The Hong Kong-based company Tommy Hilfiger reported losses of $513 million (in the year up to March), and the Gucci Group reportedly injected £4 million (about $6.7 million) to revive the Stella McCartney brand, which struggled to break even, reporting losses during the summer of £2.7 million (about $4.5 million) despite the high profile of the celebrity designer; her friends Gwyneth Paltrow and Hudson were known to wear her clothes. In August McCartney married Alasdhair Willis, a British entrepreneur and the former publisher of the magazine *Wallpaper.*

Not all fashion forecasts were gloomy, however. Profits soared by 52% for Hilfiger's rival Ralph Lauren. The Gucci Group announced increased profits of 75.3% for its recent acquisition, YSL, while some of its other labels, Gucci, Alexander McQueen, and Stella McCartney, each opened new boutiques in London, on New Bond Street and elsewhere. In November, however, Gucci's continued prosperity became uncertain when both Gucci creative director Tom Ford and Domenico De Sole, the company's chief executive, announced that they were leaving the company over contract disputes with Pinault-Printemps-Redoute SA, Gucci's parent company. The two, who were planning to leave in April 2004, had been credited with reviving Gucci from near bankruptcy and turning the company into the third largest seller of luxury goods in the world. In an effort to stimulate flagging sales at Jil Sander, the Prada Group—which paid €100 million (about $117 million) for the German label and then reported losses of €26.3 million (about $31 million)—hired back its original founder, Jil Sander, as a creative director and board member. In December 2000 after Prada acquired 75% of her company, Sander had departed the company swiftly, owing to what she described as the "hands-on interference of Patrizio Bertelli," Prada's chief executive.

© AFP/Corbis

Top model Naomi Campbell brings politics to the runway when she shows a peace outfit for Dolce & Gabbana's autumn-winter show in Milan in February.

In March the sportswear giant Liz Claiborne acquired for an undisclosed multimillion-dollar sum the hip Los Angeles denim and casual label Juicy Couture. Lars Nilsson, the Swedish-born designer for Bill Blass, was appointed artistic director of women's wear at the French fashion house Nina Ricci. In July, the Los Angeles designer Rick Owens debuted a new sportswear collection for Revillon, the 280-year-old French furrier; it featured experimental looks, including asymmetrically cut shrugs and stoles made from sliced sable, mink, and goat. In May, Jean-Paul Gaultier replaced Martin Margiela as creative director of the French luxury-goods house Hermes. In autumn the London-based Ghanian-born designer Ozwald Boateng became the first Savile Row tailor to open an American store on Madison Avenue in New York City. Phillips-Van Heusen acquired Calvin Klein, and in September Klein retired as design director of the company's women's wear line. He was replaced by Francisco Costa, a 34-year-old Brazilian designer who had formerly worked for Ford at Gucci. For his services to British fashion, Jimmy Choo was made an honorary OBE in June. Francesco Trussardi, the 29-year old CEO of the Italian luxury-fashion house Trussardi, was killed in a car accident in January. Eleanor Lambert, the founder of the Council of Fashion Designers of America, died in October. (*See* OBITUARIES.)

(BRONWYN COSGRAVE)

Health and Disease

The DEADLY DISEASE called SARS in 2003 vividly demonstrated the effect of a new virus on a highly mobile world society. Top-level UN health officials announced a program to deliver HIV/AIDS DRUG TREATMENT to three million people in the LESS-DEVELOPED COUNTRIES by 2005. A U.S. plan to VACCINATE health care workers and first responders against SMALLPOX got off to a fitful start.

In early 2003 a virulent new infectious disease caught the world off guard. The Chinese Ministry of Health reported to the World Health Organization (WHO) in mid-February that 305 people in Guangdong province had developed an acute pneumonia-like illness and that 5 of them had died. Laboratory tests had been negative for influenza viruses, anthrax, plague, and other infectious pathogens. By mid-March WHO realized that hundreds of people in Hong Kong, mainland China, Vietnam, and Canada had come down with the mysterious rapidly spreading disease, which was not responding to antibiotics or antiviral drugs, and for the first time in its history it issued a "global alert." Three days later WHO issued emergency guidance for travelers and airlines. By that time it was known that a doctor who had attended patients with the unusual pneumonia in Guangdong was ill with the disease when he subsequently visited Hong Kong. There he spread the illness to fellow travelers, who took it to Hanoi, Singapore, and Toronto, seeding major outbreaks in all three metropolises.

WHO called the illness severe acute respiratory syndrome (SARS). Over the next few months, SARS spread to more than two dozen countries on six continents. The last confirmed case of the outbreak occurred in Taiwan in mid-June, and by late July the SARS pandemic was considered over. The final count was 8,098 cases and 774 deaths, with health care workers accounting for 20% of cases. In fact, the first cases of SARS had occurred in Guangdong province in November 2002, but China failed to report the outbreak until three months later.

Determination of the cause—a coronavirus unlike any other known human or animal virus in its family—and sequencing of the virus's genetic makeup occurred with impressive speed. Subsequent epidemiological studies determined that Himalayan palm civets and raccoon dogs sold at food markets in Guangzhou, the provincial capital, were the likely source of SARS.

Ultimately, SARS illustrated the impact that a new disease could have in a highly mobile world. Every city with an international airport was regarded as a potential hot spot for an outbreak. Many observers noted that the public fears inspired by SARS spread faster than the virus itself. (*See* Special Report.)

Other Infectious Diseases. In May WHO extolled the Americas for having gone six months without a case of measles, the leading vaccine-preventable childhood disease. In other parts of the world, however, measles continued to take a terrible toll, affecting over 30 million children and killing some 745,000 each year, more than half of that number in Africa.

WHO and UNICEF brought together key players in the fight against measles for a summit in Cape Town in October. These leaders mapped out a strategy for reducing the number of childhood measles deaths by 2,000 a day. Shortly thereafter, all of Uganda's 12.7 million children were immunized against measles in about two weeks' time. The hugely successful campaign was carried out with support of the government, churches, kings, and tribal leaders.

The WHO-led global campaign to eradicate polio by 2005 shifted its overall strategy during the year, owing to a resurgence of the viral disease in India, Pakistan, and Nigeria. In 2001 just 329 polio cases were reported worldwide, down from an estimated 350,000 cases in 1988, the year the global campaign began. In 2002, however, the number increased nearly sixfold to 1,919 cases, with 1,556 in India. Consequently, WHO cut back immunization activity in 93 countries and concentrated it in the 13 countries where cases were still occurring and where there was a high risk of polio's return.

Although the outbreak in India was a setback, leaders of the eradication effort remained confident that their goal could be accomplished. In September WHO Director-General Lee Jong Wook (*see* BIOGRAPHIES), while attending the

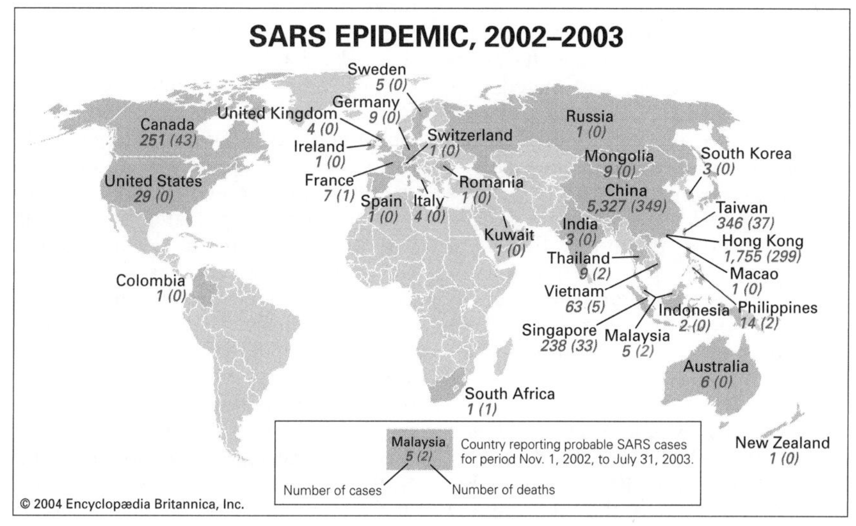

launch of a five-day immunization blitz that targeted tens of millions of Indian children, warned that even a single case of polio remaining in the world could allow the disease to spread. The scenario that Lee warned of was played out in late October when polio spread from Nigeria to neighbouring countries Benin, Burkina Faso, Ghana, Niger, and Togo. A tragedy was averted when hundreds of thousands of volunteers and health workers participated in a three-day campaign to vaccinate every child in those countries.

Between mid-May and late June, the first outbreak in the Western Hemisphere of monkeypox in humans occurred in six states in the U.S. Midwest. Of 72 cases reported, 37 were confirmed by laboratory tests. Monkeypox, so named because it was first observed in monkeys, is a relative of smallpox and occurs mainly in rainforests of central and western Africa. Those affected in the U.S. typically experienced fever, headaches, dry cough, swollen lymph nodes, chills, and sweating, followed by blisterlike skin lesions. The source of infection was traced to Gambian giant pouched rats and dormice imported from Ghana and purchased by an exotic pets dealer in Illinois, who housed them in the same facility as some 200 prairie dogs. People became infected through close contact with infected prairie dogs. The Centers for Disease Control and Prevention (CDC), Atlanta, Ga., recommended smallpox vaccines for persons who had been exposed to the virus. The CDC and the Food and Drug Administration (FDA) banned the importation of all rodents from Africa as well as the sale, transport, or release into the environment of prairie dogs.

Infection swells a child's finger at the site of a bite from a monkeypox-infected prairie dog. The child, bitten on May 13, required a week's hospitalization.

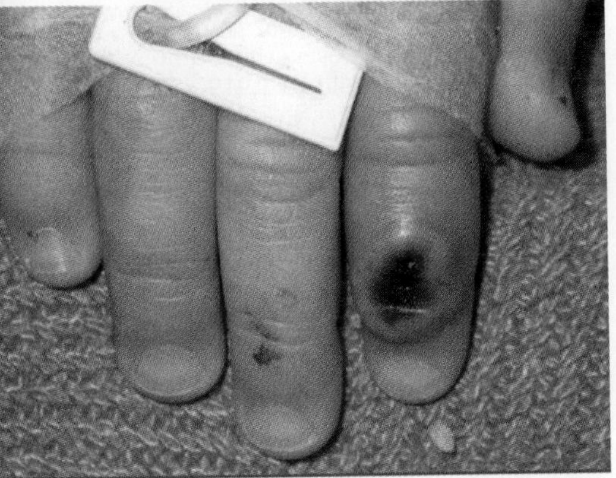

The fifth annual outbreak of West Nile virus (WNV) in the U.S. started in early July. By the end of November, 8,567 cases had been reported in 46 states, with 199 deaths; Colorado, with 2,477 cases, was hardest hit. (In 2002 there were 4,156 cases and 284 deaths in 44 states.) For the first time, rural areas were sharply affected. The mosquito that spread WNV in western states was *Culex tarsalis,* a particularly hearty species found mainly on farmland but able to travel great distances. A CDC official called the species "the most efficient vector of West Nile virus ever discovered."

During the 2002 WNV season, the virus had been found to be transmissible from person to person through blood transfusions and organ transplantation. Fortunately, by the start of the 2003 season, a new blood-screening test was available and detected WNV in more than 600 donors. Nevertheless, the screening process was not foolproof. At least two transfusion recipients developed severe West Nile illness with encephalitis (inflammation of the brain).

By mid-November Canada had experienced 1,314 probable or confirmed cases of human WNV and 10 deaths during its third annual outbreak. In 2002 the total number of laboratory-confirmed human cases had been under 100. Mexico reported having tested more than 500 people for WNV, 4 of whom were classified as WNV-positive.

HIV and AIDS. Using improved epidemiological monitoring methods, UNAIDS (Joint United Nations Programme on HIV/AIDS) and WHO revised the estimate of the number of people in the world living with HIV from 42 million to 40 million. The reduction was apparent rather than real and reflected a change in surveillance methods, not in the overall toll of the pandemic. A comprehensive report issued by the agencies in late November estimated that during the year HIV infected five million people, while AIDS killed three million—the highest numbers ever.

Although most people with HIV in developed countries were living a decade or more beyond diagnosis, thanks to life-sustaining drugs, the epidemic in those countries was far from over. In the U.S., public health officials were alarmed by a 17.7% surge in new cases among gay and bisexual men since 1999.

A mounting problem in developed countries was the appearance of strains of HIV that were resistant to available drugs. At a meeting of the International AIDS Society in Paris in July, results of the largest study ever conducted on antiretroviral drug resistance were presented. The study found that 10% of newly infected Europeans had viral strains resistant to at least one antiretroviral drug. That meant that HIV-infected people on antiretroviral therapy and carrying a virus that had developed resistance were passing on the virus by engaging in high-risk sex or needle sharing.

It had long been believed that drug-resistant strains of HIV were most likely to arise and thrive when patients took their drugs erratically. Investigators based in San Francisco found, however, that irregular drug use by individuals of low economic status, primarily the homeless, did not lead to the development of drug resistance. In fact, they found nearly twice as many drug-resistant mutations of HIV in blood samples of those who took their drugs conscientiously as in the blood of those who were noncompliant.

In March the FDA approved enfuvirtide (Fuzeon), the first in a new class of antiretroviral medications for HIV/AIDS called fusion inhibitors, which prevent HIV from entering host cells. Fuzeon had to be given by injection and was meant for those who had used other drugs but still had evidence of active disease.

While life-prolonging drugs were extending the lives of people who had access to therapy, the vast majority of those living with HIV were in sub-Saharan Africa, where only about 50,000 were receiving treatment. In September at a high-level UN meeting, representatives of WHO and UNAIDS announced their organizations' commitment to providing drug treatment to three million people in the less-developed countries by the end of 2005—a plan dubbed the "3 by 5 Initiative."

Many international public health professionals held that it would be impossible to provide AIDS drugs to people in Africa because too many were infected, the drugs were too costly, the regimens were too complicated, and there was no way to ensure compliance with therapy. Nevertheless, surveys carried out in 2002 and 2003 in Botswana, Uganda, Senegal, South Africa, and Zambia found that compliance with treatment among Africans was extremely high—higher, in fact, than among AIDS patients in developed countries. Jeffrey Stringer, working at the Center for Infectious Disease Research in Zambia, was quoted in the September 13 issue

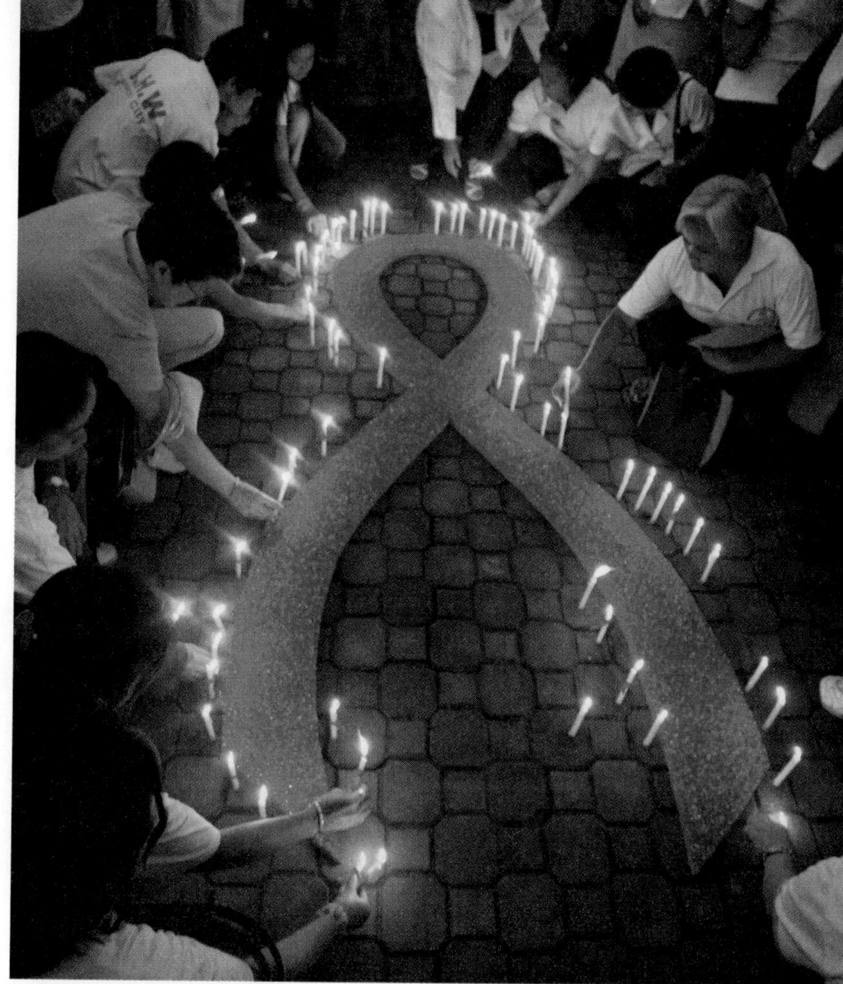

Filipinos in Manila mark World AIDS Day, December 1, with candle lightings to commemorate AIDS victims.

of *The Lancet* as saying: "High rates of antiretroviral adherence are clearly possible in African settings, and while the unique set of issues around adherence to medication in African populations should be considered carefully as we design antiretroviral treatment programs, it in no way should delay large-scale implementation."

Availability of low-cost, high-quality antiretroviral drugs would be crucial to the success of the "3 by 5" program. Thus, it was welcome news when the drug company GlaxoSmithKline said it would further cut the prices of its AIDS drugs for the world's poorest countries by as much as 47%. In addition, former U.S. president Bill Clinton announced that he had brokered a deal with four generic-drug companies to cut the cost of AIDS drugs for African and Caribbean countries by as much as one-half.

Providing medications to all who needed them was an undisputed necessity, yet most AIDS experts believed that the greatest hope for reversing the pandemic would be an effective vaccine. In 2003 more than 25 potential vaccines were being tested in some 12,000 volunteers worldwide.

In late February the California firm VaxGen Inc. announced the results of the first large-scale clinical trial of an AIDS vaccine to reach completion. The subjects were more than 5,000 North American and European volunteers; none were infected with HIV at the start of the trial, but all were at high risk for sexual exposure to the virus. Two-thirds received injections of the experimental vaccine over a period of three years, while one-third received a placebo. All participants were advised on safer sex practices.

In the study population as a whole, the vaccine did not provide protection against HIV infection. A surprising finding requiring further study, however, was that minorities other than Hispanics who received the vaccine had 67% fewer HIV infections than minorities who received the placebo. Black vaccine recipients had 78% fewer infections than black placebo recipients.

The results of a second large-scale VaxGen trial—conducted in Thailand—were released in November. Some 2,500 injection-drug users who were not infected with HIV at the start of the 36-week trial received either vaccine or placebo. This vaccine too failed to protect the recipients from becoming infected with HIV; furthermore, it did not slow the progression of AIDS in those who became infected. Although the overall results of these important trials were disappointing, vaccine proponents remained confident in the validity of an AIDS vaccine.

Bioterrorism Preparedness. In December 2002 U.S. Pres. George W. Bush announced a smallpox vaccination program to protect Americans in the event of a terrorist attack with the deadly virus. The plan called for immunizing about 500,000 health care workers first, then as many as 10 million emergency responders—police, firefighters, and paramedics. The CDC had estimated that 1.2 million immunized health care workers would be needed to vaccinate the entire U.S. population within 10 days of a smallpox attack.

The program was highly controversial because there was no imminent threat of a smallpox outbreak and because the vaccine was known to carry significant risks of life-threatening complications and death. (About 450,000 members of the U.S. military were successfully vaccinated against smallpox between December 2002 and June 2003, with very few serious adverse events.) The program to vaccinate civilian health care workers got under way in January but was riddled with problems. The federal government had estimated that each vaccination would cost $13, but state and local health officials reported the actual cost to be $75–$265. Many hospital workers initially refused the vaccine because no provisions had been made to compensate people who suffered adverse reactions. By the end of March, the CDC had reports of 72 cases of heart problems among military and civilian vaccinees—notably inflammation of the heart muscle (myocarditis)—and three fatal heart attacks. (In April Congress finally approved a bill that would ensure compensation for those who experienced short-term or permanent disability or death from the vaccine.) Although the relationship between the vaccinations and the medical problems was not clear, the CDC said that persons with heart disease or major cardiac risk factors should no

(continued on page 206)

What's Next After SARS

by Brian J. Ford

In November 2002 Huang Xingchu was working as a chef at a restaurant in Shenzhen, a thriving boomtown in China's Guangdong province, close to the Hong Kong border. Like many restaurants in southern China, Huang's establishment served up special dishes based on exotic game. One of these specialties was the civet, a catlike carnivorous animal sold openly at farmers' markets and slaughtered directly on the restaurant's premises. On December 5 Huang awoke feeling listless and uncomfortable. Soon he developed a fever of 39 °C (102 °F) and was finding it difficult to breathe. On December 15 his family took him to the People's Hospital in Heyuan City, and two days later he was transferred to the Guangzhou Military Hospital. At Guangzhou, Huang's throat was so constricted that he had to be fitted with a breathing tube. The illness eventually passed, and on Jan. 10, 2003, Huang returned home, fully recovered. Within a few months the chef from Shenzhen was to become famous as China's first reported case of SARS (severe acute respiratory syndrome), a highly contagious and often fatal illness caused by a mutant coronavirus, a type of virus usually associated with the common cold. Genetic studies now indicate that the virus probably mutated from its normal nonthreatening form after passing to humans from exotic animals such as the civet, the very creature served up as healthful fare at Huang's restaurant.

Face Masks and Quarantine. Back at Heyuan City, nine members of the People's Hospital staff had caught Huang's virus, and soon the mysterious "atypical pneumonia" appeared in five other cities in Guangdong. The authorities reacted by demolishing the restaurant where Huang had worked, by disinfecting public places and vehicles, and, in February 2003, by assuring the public that the "unidentified virus" had been contained. By then, however, it had crossed the frontier. From Guangdong the virus was taken by an infected doctor to Hong Kong, and from Hong Kong it was quickly carried throughout East Asia and to Toronto. Late in February I arrived in southern China on a lecture tour. There were face masks on many of the people, and I saw even more as I traveled across Japan. Face masks are often worn in East Asia, as protection partly against infection but mainly against traffic fumes and tree pollen. Nevertheless, many more face masks than usual were in evidence now, and the populace was avoiding many public places.

It was only a matter of time before global air travelers carried the virus to the rest of the world. On March 12, 2003, the World Health Organization (WHO) officially identified SARS as a distinct disease threat. Health authorities around the world responded by instituting strict control measures, including prohibitions on travel to and from affected countries as well as quarantines of hospitals and other places where persons were found to be infected. In Singaporean airports infrared sensors were installed to identify disembarking passengers with elevated temperatures that might indicate SARS.

The emergency measures did the job. On April 28 SARS in Vietnam was declared to have been contained (that is, no new infections had been seen in at least 20 days). On June 23 and July 2, Hong Kong and Toronto were declared safe, and on July 5, with the last remaining country, Taiwan, showing no new infections, the epidemic was officially over. By that time more than 8,000 cases—most of them in mainland China and Hong Kong—had been reported, and 774 people had died from the disease, 299 in Hong Kong alone.

Germs Without Borders. In July 2001 I spoke in Chicago to an international group of microscopists. My topic was emergent diseases in the new millennium, and the talk ended with a warning that air transportation could carry new pathogens to unsuspecting populations on opposite sides of the world. The risks seemed real. Airliners confine people in a closed environment, recirculate their expired air, and take passengers to communities unexposed to many foreign diseases. All communities harbour antibodies to infections that commonly occur there, but such resistance is usually absent from people in distant parts of the world. In an irony of modern life, Westerners are now vulnerable to exotic infections from the East, just as peoples in Asia, Africa, and the Americas were once devastated by the smallpox and

Life Cycle of the SARS Epidemic, February–July 2003*

Eating civets probably transmitted SARS from animals to humans.

February 11
WHO receives reports from the Chinese government of an outbreak of acute respiratory syndrome in Guangdong province.

February 21
A doctor from Guangzhou checks into the Metropole Hotel, Hong Kong. He will die March 4, but not before passing the SARS virus to hotel guests and hospital staff.

February 23
A Chinese Canadian woman leaves the Metropole Hotel and flies back to Toronto. She will die on March 5 and her son on March 13.

February 26
A Chinese American man who stayed at the Metropole Hotel is hospitalized in Hanoi. He will die on March 13, but not before infecting a visiting WHO official, Carlo Urbani (right).

March 11
Urbani flies from Hanoi to Bangkok. He will fall ill there and die on March 29.

March 12
WHO issues a global alert about cases of "severe atypical pneumonia." It will rename the disease SARS on March 15.

March 15
A Singaporean doctor, on a return flight from New York City, is quarantined in Frankfurt.

March 20
The first case of SARS is reported in the United States.

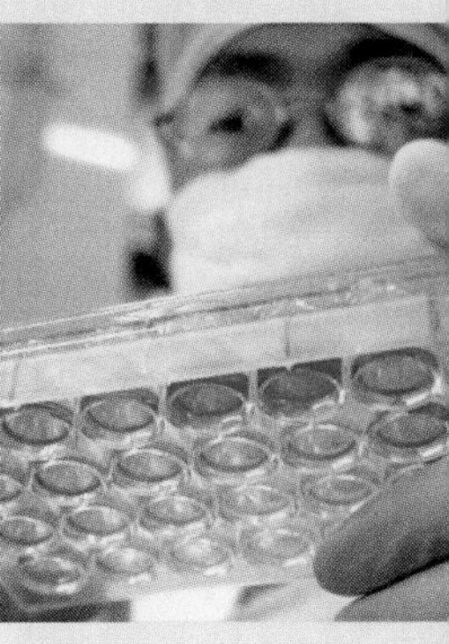

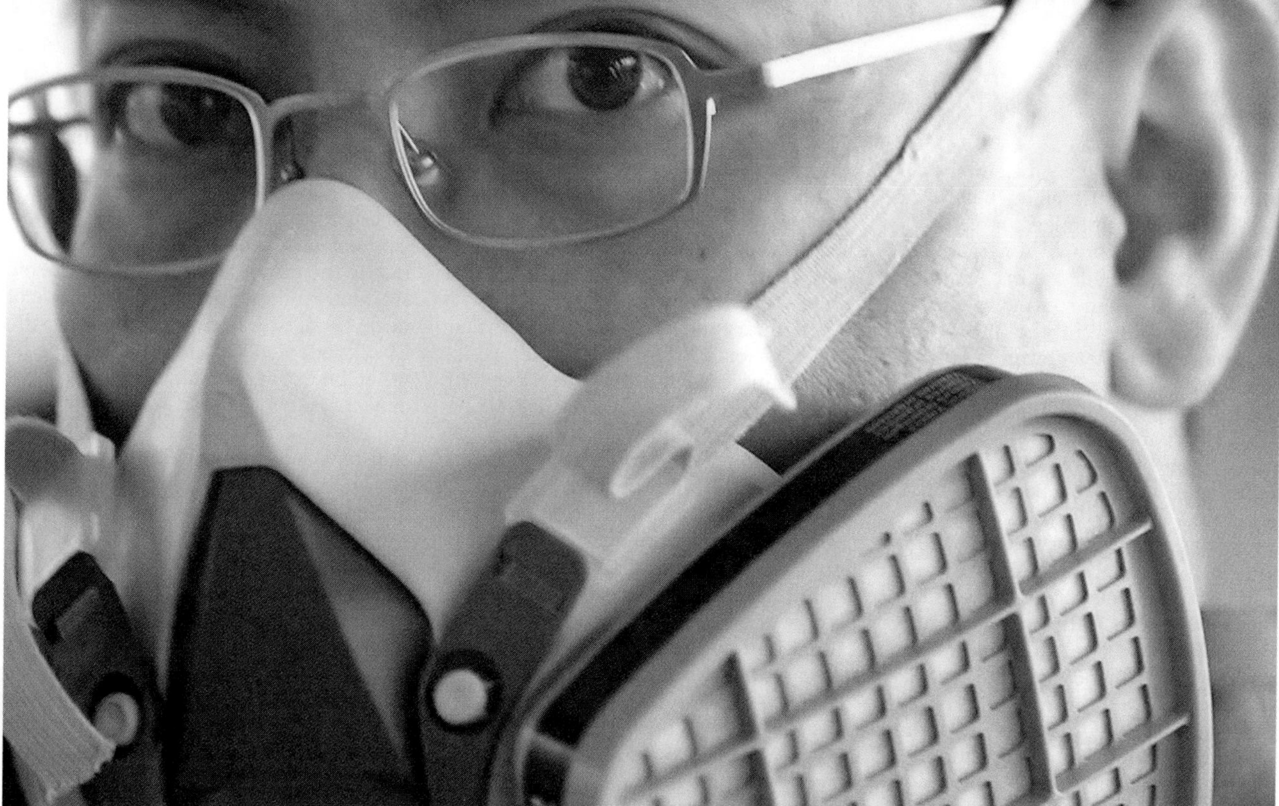

In April a resident of Hong Kong wears a special high-tech mask to prevent the transmission of the SARS virus.

measles carried to them by European explorers. One day Westerners, like the Japanese, may be seen wearing face masks in public places.

Coronaviruses infect many animals (e.g., chickens, pigs, rats, and turkeys, in addition to civets), and in humans they cause about 15% of all colds. Yet a vaccine to prevent the common cold has never been found. In fact, the best preventive measures in the SARS outbreak of 2002–03 were the time-honoured quarantine of contacts and careful personal hygiene. What other diseases are waiting in the wings? How does the disease spread in a modern world?

Waiting in the Wings. In the 19th and early 20th centuries, tuberculosis, or consumption, killed most of the Brontë family as well as John Keats, Frédéric Chopin, Anton Chekhov, and Franz Kafka. Since the introduction of antibiotics in the mid-20th century, tales of consumption and TB sanatoriums have passed from the developed world, but now drug-resistant strains of the tubercle bacillus have been introduced into the West through air travel. Outbreaks of dengue fever, Lyme disease, trench fever, and West Nile virus have occurred far from their places of origin. Korean hemorrhagic fever, caused by the hantavirus and first recognized by Western scientists during the Korean War in the 1950s, has turned up in South America and more recently in the United States, notably California. Finally, monkeypox, a virus related to smallpox that was never before known outside Africa, spread to humans in the United States in 2003 through the importation for pets of exotic animals such as African pouched rats.

Direction for the Future. If viruses are proved to spread through enclosed spaces—such as planes and trains—then new precautions may be needed. We may need to filter and sterilize circulated air, and sensors are already being used to identify passengers with raised temperatures.

Both the Hong Kong and mainland Chinese governments came under criticism from abroad and at home for their lack of openness during the first stages of the SARS outbreak. Other governments were just as reluctant to cause alarm and lose income from tourists. In the future we will have to require a more proactive stance and greater "transparency" on the part of health authorities. In addition, the role of WHO probably will have to become even more important in maintaining the health of the global population.

In any event, massive epidemics are less likely to occur than some people imagine. SARS has largely been contained, even after most commentators suggested it would soon spread worldwide—though of course it has not gone away. One case emerged in Singapore in September 2003; it was managed quickly and with openness by the Singaporean authorities. Such prompt response, along with stricter standards of personal hygiene, higher levels of surveillance, and a readiness to resort to quarantine when necessary, will help us to keep on top of the world's emerging diseases.

Brian J. Ford is a biologist and lecturer and is the author of Future of Food.

April 2
Reported cases of SARS worldwide surpass 2,000.

April 11
The first case of SARS is reported in South Africa.

April 16
The WHO laboratory network identifies the SARS causative agent as an entirely new coronavirus.

April 23
WHO advises only essential travel to Beijing and Shanxi province in China and to Toronto.

April 28
Vietnam is declared to have contained its SARS outbreak.

May 2
Reported cases of SARS worldwide surpass 6,000.

May 22
Reported cases of SARS worldwide surpass 8,000.

The SARS outbreak is contained in
May 31: Singapore
June 23: Hong Kong
June 24: Beijing
July 2: Toronto
July 5: Taiwan (WHO declares SARS epidemic over)

*Source: World Health Organization, "Update 95—SARS," http://www.who.int/csr/don/2003_07_04/en/

(continued from page 203)
longer receive the vaccine. In the end, only about 38,000 civilian health care workers were immunized.

Meanwhile, a study of Americans previously vaccinated against smallpox (before 1972, when routine vaccination was discontinued in the U.S.) found that more than 90%—even people vaccinated as far back as 1928—still had the full range of antibodies to smallpox. The results suggested that a significant proportion of middle-aged and older Americans would be protected in the event of a smallpox attack.

Cardiovascular Disease. For decades, anyone with blood pressure under 140/90 was considered to be in the healthy range. Recently acquired knowledge about the damage done to arteries when blood pressure was even slightly elevated, however, prompted the U.S. National Heart, Lung, and Blood Institute to issue new guidelines, according to which adults with blood-pressure levels previously considered normal (some 45 million in the U.S.) would now be in a category called prehypertension. This group included people with systolic pressure (top number) of 120–139 or diastolic pressure (bottom number) of 80–89. Those in the new category were urged to make lifestyle changes such as losing excess weight, quitting smoking, and consuming less sodium. Those with systolic readings of 140–159 or diastolic readings of 90–99 were in a category called stage 1 hypertension and in most cases would require treatment with blood-pressure-lowering medication. For those with 160/100 and higher—stage 2 hypertension—aggressive treatment with medication to lower blood pressure to at least 140/90 was urged.

Cardiologists had long believed that about half of all heart disease was unrelated to any of the best-known risk factors: high blood pressure, high cholesterol, smoking, and diabetes. Two reports published in the *Journal of the American Medical Association* in August, however, found that 80–90% of people with heart disease had at least one of the four risk factors.

By 2003 most medical scientists had come to appreciate that injury to the arteries resulting from factors such as high blood pressure, high cholesterol, and smoking triggered an inflammatory reaction. A number of biochemical markers of inflammation had been found, but the one for which the most accurate and sensitive test had been devised was C-reactive protein (CRP), a substance found in the blood and produced by the liver in response to inflammation in the body. One study of healthy women found CRP to be a better predictor of cardiovascular disease risk than low-density lipoprotein (the "bad" cholesterol).

In January the CDC and the American Heart Association issued guidelines for physicians on when to order the CRP test (called high sensitivity CRP, or hs-CRP). The guidelines specified that hs-CRP would be useful mainly when it was unclear whether an individual would benefit from preventive treatment (lifestyle changes, medication, or both). A good candidate for the test might be a healthy person with normal blood pressure, cholesterol, and blood sugar but with a family history of heart disease. Most cardiovascular experts believed that considerable further investigation was needed before the implications of elevated CRP in the blood would be fully understood. Moreover, the guidelines emphasized that many things other than damaged arteries could cause inflammation—e.g., infection and autoimmune diseases.

Cancer. Results of a huge American Cancer Society study found that excess body weight significantly increased the risk of death from cancer. The study followed more than 900,000 initially cancer-free American adults for 16 years, during which time slightly more than 57,000 died from cancer. The investigators correlated the volunteers' body-mass index (weight in kilograms divided by the square of height in metres) at the time of entry into the study with the subsequent development of deadly cancers. On the basis of the findings, they estimated that "current patterns of overweight and obesity in the United States could account for 14% of all deaths from cancer in men and 20% of those in women." The study identified several types of cancer that previously had not been associated with excess body weight: cancers of the stomach (in men), liver, pancreas, prostate, cervix, and ovary, as well as non-Hodgkin lymphoma and multiple myeloma.

Cancer treatment specialists were elated about a Canadian-led study's finding that a drug in the class known as aromatase inhibitors significantly prolonged disease-free survival of women who had had breast cancer. The standard, highly effective regimen for women with breast cancer after tumour removal was to take the drug tamoxifen, an antiestrogen, for five years. Beyond that period, however, taking tamoxifen offered no benefit. The new study, which involved more than 5,000 women in Canada, the U.S., and Europe, was stopped early when it became clear that taking the aromatase inhibitor letrozole (Femara) following a five-year course of tamoxifen significantly reduced the likelihood of developing cancer in the other breast and of having the original cancer recur or spread to other sites in the body. Consequently, it was likely that letrozole would be offered to most postmenopausal women with estrogen-receptive breast cancer following tamoxifen treatment, although the optimal length of letrozole therapy was not yet known. (Estrogen stimulates the growth of cancer cells. In postmenopausal women, androgens produced by the adrenal glands are converted to estrogens by the enzyme aromatase. Letrozole works by blocking the action of aromatase and thereby inhibiting the conversion of androgens to estrogens.)

Women's Health. The Women's Health Initiative (WHI) was established by the U.S. National Institutes of Health in the early 1990s as a long-term research program to address the most common causes of death and disability in postmenopausal women. In 2002 a landmark WHI clinical trial was stopped several years early when it became clear that women receiving hormone replacement therapy (HRT) had an increased risk of developing breast cancer, heart disease, stroke, and blood clots and that the risk significantly outweighed any health benefits from HRT. After the study's results were released, the number of women on HRT—i.e., taking estrogen plus progestin—plummeted from an estimated six million to three million in the U.S. alone.

During 2003 more bad news about HRT emerged from additional analyses of the data from the WHI trial. These in-depth studies found that HRT doubled the risk of Alzheimer disease and other dementias in women who began using hormones at age 65 or older. It increased the risk of cognitive decline by a slight but clinically significant amount and increased the risk of stroke. It caused changes in breast tissue that increased the likelihood of abnormal mammograms and impaired the early detection of tumours by mammography. It increased the risk of heart disease by 81% in the first year of therapy. Moreover, HRT failed to improve women's quality of life.

(ELLEN BERNSTEIN)

Law, Crime, and Law Enforcement

Groundbreaking decisions by the SUPREME COURT, questions about the legality of the war in IRAQ, former HEADS OF STATE under indictment for war crimes, prosecutions of alleged TERRORISTS, and other HIGH-PROFILE criminal and civil cases were on the docket in 2003.

INTERNATIONAL LAW

The U.S.-led attack on Iraq in March 2003 raised the question of whether such actions were permitted under international law. The unwillingness of the United Nations Security Council to pass a resolution explicitly authorizing the use of force was cited as evidence of the illegality of the action. (*See* WORLD AFFAIRS: *United Nations:* Special Report.) U.S. Pres. George W. Bush justified the attack as a preemptive strike to ensure American self-defense, a right recognized under international law in certain circumstances. He also defended the action by pointing to UN resolutions passed in 1991 that called for peace and security to be restored in the region, arguing that Iraqi Pres. Saddam Hussein (*see* BIOGRAPHIES) had violated those resolutions and the international community therefore had a right to force him to comply. An additional argument was made that Saddam had refused to adhere to Security Council Resolution 1441 (November 2002), which required him to disarm. The U.S. said that Saddam was a threat to other countries and thus a legitimate target of military action under Chapter VII of the UN Charter, which allows countries to use force to restore international peace and security. Opponents of the U.S. position wanted evidence that Saddam had not complied with Resolution 1441—evidence that arms inspectors had been unable to provide. Another issue relating to international law arising from the U.S.-Iraqi war was the role of the U.S. in the aftermath of the conflict. UN Secretary-General Kofi Annan referred to the U.S. as an "occupying power," angering some American officials. Under international law an "occupying power" has clearly defined responsibilities. The U.S. claimed that it was a "liberating force"—a term that has no meaning in international law—rather than an occupying power but that it would abide by international conventions.

The U.S. continued to hold more than 600 suspected Taliban and al-Qaeda members at the U.S. military base at Guantánamo Bay, Cuba. Six of the prisoners were French citizens, and the French government requested information from the U.S. on the nature of the prisoners' crimes. The U.S. government classified all U.S.-held prisoners as enemy combatants rather than prisoners of war. The international-law community steadfastly objected to this classification, because prisoners of war have more clearly protected rights under international law.

The two International Criminal Tribunals, for Rwanda and for Yugoslavia (ICTR and ICTY, respectively), heard cases throughout 2003. November marked the start of ICTR trials for four former government ministers in Rwanda. Those sentenced at the ICTY included prison guard Predrag Banovic; Milomir Stakic, who was sentenced to life in prison after being acquitted of genocide charges but found guilty of crimes against humanity and war crimes for his role in the occupation of the Prijedor municipality, Bosnia and Herzegovina, in 1992; and Biljana Plavsic, the former president of Republika Srpska, the Serb entity in Bosnia and Herzegovina, who plead guilty and received an 11-year sentence for her role in crimes against humanity. In response to international pressure, Serbia handed over a number of people indicted by the ICTY, but several key figures, including Bosnian Serbs Radovan Karadzic and Ratko Mladic, remained at large. In October the ICTY issued indictments of four more Serbian generals for crimes committed during the Kosovo war.

In April the Council of Europe called for a war crimes tribunal to try Russians accused of war crimes in the suppression of the independence movement in Chechnya, and it was suggested that an international tribunal be set up for East Timor (Timor-Leste).

In October Ethiopia rejected the delineation of its border with Eritrea drawn by the Eritrean-Ethiopian Boundary Commission established by the Permanent Court of Arbitration in The Hague. Cases pending before the International Court of Justice (ICJ) included a border discrepancy between Benin and Niger and disputes over ownership of islands between Malaysia and Singapore and also between Nicaragua and Colombia. In February the ICJ called for a halt to the scheduled executions in the U.S. of three Mexican nationals, pending a hearing on a case brought by Mexico under the 1963 Vienna Convention on Consular Relations. In November the Court issued a judgment in *Iran* v. *U.S.* Both sides alleged that the other had breached the 1955 Treaty of Amity, Economic Relations and Consular Rights—the Americans during attacks on Iranian oil platforms in the Persian Gulf in October 1987 and April 1988, the Iranians during attacks on vessels in the Gulf during the same time period. The ICJ found that neither side had breached the treaty and therefore neither side owed reparations. France allowed the ICJ to have jurisdiction over a case brought by the Republic of the Congo following French attempts to investigate Congolese Pres. Denis Sassou-Nguesso, who the Congo claimed has immunity from French proceedings as a foreign head of state.

Belgium repealed its war crimes law. Relying on the concept of "universal jurisdiction," the 1993 law empowered Belgian courts to hear cases of human rights abuses regardless of the nationality of the offender or the place of the abuse. A new law passed in August limited jurisdiction to cases in which either the defendant or the victim was a Belgian national. Belgium's Supreme Court dismissed cases against foreign

Canadian judge Philippe Kirsch is sworn in as the first president of the International Criminal Court in The Hague on March 11. The court would investigate and prosecute crimes against humanity but had run into some opposition, notably from the U.S.

leaders, including Israeli Prime Minister Ariel Sharon, U.S. Pres. George W. Bush, and Cuban Pres. Fidel Castro.

Spain's government refused to request extradition of 40 Argentines for the purpose of trying them in a Spanish court for crimes against Spanish nationals during the 1976–83 Argentine "Dirty War." In July Argentina stripped the 40 men of immunity from extradition, which led observers to expect that the men would be turned over to Spain. Spain refused to extradite them, however, and Argentina's national congress repealed the amnesty laws that protected military officials from being tried for crimes related to the Dirty War. In a related issue, repeated calls were made for Nigeria to extradite former Liberian president Charles Taylor, who had been forced into exile in August. Taylor was under indictment for war crimes by the Special Court for Sierra Leone for having armed rebels in that country's civil war.

Under the U.S.'s Alien Tort Claims Act, a group of human rights attorneys brought suit against Occidental Petroleum Corp. in a California district court in April. Occidental and its security contractor, Airscan, Inc., were accused of having participated in the murder of nearly 20 civilians in Santo Domingo, Colom., in 1998 during a raid conducted by the Colombian air force but aimed at rebels targeting an Occidental pipeline. Another oil producer, ChevronTexaco, had a suit filed against it in Ecuador, where it was accused of destroying rainforests and polluting land and rivers.

In October the UN General Assembly criticized Israel for violating international law with its construction of a "security barrier" surrounding the Palestinian areas of the West Bank. A similar Security Council resolution was vetoed by the United States.

The first global public-health treaty was signed by unanimous vote at the World Health Organization meeting in May. The Framework Convention on Tobacco Control was designed to reduce the death toll from tobacco. It would go into effect after 40 countries ratified the treaty.

The first judges of the International Criminal Court were seated in March, which enabled the ICC to hold open sessions. The ICC's first chief prosecutor, Luis Moreno Ocampo of Argentina, indicated that the court was "following closely" the situation in the Ituri region of the Democratic Republic of the Congo, and observers speculated that the abuses committed there would be the first cases to be tried before the court. The U.S. continued to work to shield itself from the ICC's reach by persuading countries to sign bilateral immunity agreements (BIAs) under which states promised not to surrender any U.S. nationals or employees to the ICC. Because the U.S. suspended military aid to countries that refused to sign BIAs, some 70 countries had done so as of November 2003. (VICTORIA C. WILLIAMS)

COURT DECISIONS

As chief justice of the United States, William H. Rehnquist had led the Supreme Court, and therefore the nation, down a jurisprudential path of states' rights advocacy. Specifically, in a series of 5–4 rulings questioning state immunity from litigation, he argued for the majorities that federal law does not necessarily penetrate the borders of the states and control public policy. On May 27, 2003, however, the chief justice broke ranks with three of his conservative colleagues and ruled that states can be sued for failing to provide time off for employees experiencing family emergencies. In *Nevada Department of Human Resources* v. *Hibbs,* Rehnquist explained that, unlike previous cases involving broad claims relating to employee disabilities, the Family and Medical Leave Act specifically and successfully sought to remedy pervasive legal, political, and social assumptions about "women's work" and the role of gender in family-care matters. The state's failure to extend unpaid leave privileges to women and men equally constituted a denial of equal protection of law and therefore erased the state's 11th Amendment claim of immunity from suit.

Although the *Nevada* case addressed a core issue in federalism jurisprudence, it was the element of discrimination that decided the case, and in this it comported with a larger civil liberties and civil rights agenda. Just as the court exercised judicial power to establish legal equality according to gender, in a landmark case, *Lawrence* v. *Texas,* it employed the due process clause of the 14th Amendment to protect sexual orientation. Despite Justice Antonin Scalia's scathing dissenting opinion claiming that the court had "signed on to the so-called homosexual agenda" and "taken sides in the culture war," Justice Anthony Kennedy wrote for the majority that gays and lesbians are entitled to the same right to privacy as heterosexuals. In declaring that "the state cannot demean their existence or control their destiny by making their private sexual conduct a crime," the court's ruling invalidated sodomy laws in 13 states. Moreover, in the *Lawrence* decision, for the first time in its history, the court invoked a decision of the European Court of Human Rights. Kennedy's reference to the West's commitment to cultural tolerance prompted Scalia to read from the bench his dissent in which he characterized the court's ruling as "dangerous" to the American legal tradition.

During the final week of the term, in *Gatz* v. *Bollinger* and *Grutter* v. *Bollinger,* the court addressed another salient civil rights issue, affirmative action. The two cases addressed the University of Michigan's policies for undergraduate and law-school admissions, respectively. Although the court invalidated the undergraduate admissions policy because the university's system of awarding points on the basis of race and ethnicity too closely approximated the quotas the court had declared unconstitutional 25 years earlier in *Bakke* v. *Board of Regents,* it upheld the law school's "narrowly tailored" and "holistic" use of race in admissions decisions as a necessary step in furtherance of the compelling interest in establishing racial diversity and educational opportunity. In a manner consistent with her moderate positions on abortion and race-conscious districting, Justice Sandra

Day O'Connor championed tightly fashioned laws designed to protect individual rights as virtual moral imperatives.

The matter of race was central to two other cases in the 2003 term, *Georgia* v. *Ashcroft* and *Virginia* v. *Black.* In the former, O'Connor, whose pivotal vote created a majority in 12 of the 14 cases decided by 5–4 margins in the current term, ruled that racial redistricting designed to enhance African American voting rights through plans that divide black voters among a number of districts rather than being consolidated into fewer, densely populated districts, are constitutionally permissible. In the latter case the court addressed the delicate relationship between race relations, criminal law, and free speech. By a vote of 6–3, the court upheld a Virginia law criminalizing cross burning as a form of intimidation. Although the court had previously ruled in cases such as *Capital Square Review and Advisory Board* v. *Pinette* (1995) that the Ku Klux Klan may participate in seasonal displays involving the cross and in *R.A.V.* v. *St. Paul* (1992) that race-based fighting words may not be treated differently from other fighting words, the court here drew a line between symbolic speech and acts of intimidation. Justice Clarence Thomas, who ordinarily remained silent during oral arguments, argued that a burning cross represents nothing but a "reign of terror" and, as an act of racial intimidation, ought not to be entitled to constitutional protection.

Falling more squarely into the realm of criminal law, the court decided a series of cases that spanned the philosophical continuum. Upholding the rights of the criminally accused, the court decided two death-penalty cases; one, *Miller-El* v. *Cockrell,* required a federal appeals court to grant habeas corpus to a Texas death-row inmate whose sentence allegedly resulted from a racially biased jury-selection process, and the other, *Wiggins* v. *Smith,* resulted in the court's overturning the death sentence on Kevin Wiggins on the grounds of ineffective legal counsel. Less sympathetic to the criminally accused were decisions in two California cases challenging the state's "three-strikes" rule. In *Ewing* v. *California* and *Lockyer* v. *Andrade,* O'Connor once again played a pivotal role, writing 5–4-majority decisions that rejected claims that otherwise-minor third offenses resulting in long mandatory sentences constitute cruel and unusual punishment. The court also rejected a pair of constitutional challenges to "Megan's Law," named for the child victim of sexualized violence. Megan's Law enabled the creation of a sex-offender notification and registration program that had been adopted in every state. Turning away claims of a denial of due process, Rehnquist wrote for the majority in *Connecticut* v. *Doe* that the state did not have to conduct hearings prior to posting photographs and information about offenders on the state's Internet registry. A related case, *Smith* v. *Doe,* involved Alaska's attempt to add to its registry the names of sex offenders convicted before the law was enacted. Arguing that the registry does not impose any punishment on the offender, Kennedy concluded that the ex post facto clause of the Constitution—which prohibits retroactive punishment—is inapplicable to nonpunitive cases.

Among a number of business law cases decided during the 2002–03 Supreme Court term, three stood out as noteworthy: *State Farm Mutual Automobile Insurance Co.* v. *Campbell, Moseley* v. *V Secret Catalogue, Inc.,* and *Eldred* v. *Ashcroft*. In the *State Farm* case, the court decided 6–3 to set new punitive-damages guidelines, scrapping the standing 145:1 ratio of punitive to compensatory damages in favour of an unspecified ratio smaller than 9:1; a settlement above this would almost certainly be regarded by the court as arbitrary and unreasonable. The *V Secret* and *Eldred* cases both pertained to intellectual-property rights. In the former case the court ruled unanimously that economic harm does not have to be demonstrated to prevail in cases under the Federal Trademark Dilution Act. Noneconomic harm, such as discrediting a corporate name or deliberately confusing its identity, are enough to carry forward a successful case under the law. In the latter case the court ruled 7–2 that a congressional act passed in 1998, extending existing copyrights by 20 years, is constitutional. In an opinion that many thought demonstrated a pro-big-business bias, the court noted that the Copyright Term Extension Act is a constitutionally permissible exercise of congressional authority. The validity of the act was expected to prove lucrative to major copyright holders in general and the entertainment industry in particular.

On December 10 in *McConnell* v. *Federal Election Commission,* a divided Supreme Court upheld (5–4) key provisions of the McCain-Feingold campaign finance reform legislation that had passed Congress in 2002. The court ruled that the law's ban on "soft money" (campaign donations not subject to federal regulations) and restrictions on advertisements by interest groups near election day did not violate the First Amendment protection of freedom of speech.

Despite the significance of the decisions reached by the Supreme Court during the term, it was a lower court ruling that proved most salient in the court of public opinion. In *Elk Grove Unified School District* v. *Newdow,* the 9th Circuit Court of Appeals declared unconstitutional the recitation of the Pledge of Allegiance in public schools. On October 14 the U.S. Supreme Court agreed to review the ruling during its 2003–04 term. The central question was whether the phrase "one nation under God" constituted a violation of the Constitution's religious freedom clauses.

(BRIAN SMENTKOWSKI)

CRIME

Terrorism. In 2003 perhaps no single terrorist attack provoked greater universal international outrage than the suicide bombing of the UN's Iraq headquarters in Baghdad on August 19. Some 25 UN officials, Iraqi employees, and others were killed when a truck bomb was detonated near the UN's compound. Among the dead was Brazilian Sérgio Vieira de Mello (*see* OBITUARIES), the UN's special representative in Iraq. U.S. officials focused their investigation on indigenous Iraqi groups who also were suspects in an August 7 car bombing of the Jordanian embassy in Baghdad that killed 17.

According to Ambassador Cofer Black, the U.S. Department of State's coordinator for counterterrorism, al-Qaeda terrorists were on the run, and thousands had been detained. Two of those in custody were captured in Pakistan. Khalid Sheikh Mohammed, a Kuwait-born Pakistani suspected of having been the architect of the Sept. 11, 2001, attacks, was seized on March 1 in Rawalpindi; and on March 16, in Lahore, Pakistani intelligence officers arrested Yassir al-Jazeeri, a Moroccan believed to have been one of Osama bin Laden's principal bodyguards.

Indonesian Riduan Isamuddin, also known as Hambali, was apprehended on August 11 near Bangkok. He was alleged to have instigated the Bali bombings in October 2002, which killed some 200 people, as well as other attacks, including a hotel bombing in

Police burn 500 kg (1,100 lb) of narcotics in Kabul in June. In 2003 Afghanistan was the leading producer of opium, and the country's poppy fields were believed to be the source of three-quarters of the heroin reaching Europe.

Jakarta on August 5 that killed at least 12 people and wounded 150. Hambali had been on the run since 2001 because of his role in a plot on Western embassies in Singapore. He was said to be a key figure in both al-Qaeda and Jemaah Islamiyah, a terrorist network active in Southeast Asia.

On August 7 Amrozi bin Nurhasyim became the first radical Islamist to be convicted and sentenced to death for his involvement in the Bali bombings. Imam Samudra, described as the mastermind of the bombings, met a similar fate on September 10. At a February trial in Hamburg, Ger., a 28-year-old Moroccan student, Mounir al-Motassadeq, who had a "minor but vital" role in the September 11 attacks, was found guilty of belonging to a terrorist group and having aided and abetted 3,066 murders. He was sentenced to 15 years in jail, the maximum penalty permitted under German law.

The September 11 attacks also were the subject of a 900-page U.S. congressional report, issued in July, that was said to allege an indirect flow of funds to al-Qaeda—notably to the 15 hijackers who were Saudi—from the Saudi Arabian government. A crucial part of the report was censored in the interest of national security. The allegation came as the Saudi government cracked down on Islamic extremists following a triple suicide bombing on May 12 that killed 35 people, including the 9 attackers. In August Saudi authorities were said to have seized a truckload of surface-to-air missiles smuggled in from Yemen. The missile seizure underlined a growing concern over the safety of civilian aircraft, especially as several thousand Russian-made surface-to-air missiles known to have been in Iraq were missing.

Drug and Human Trafficking. In June the UN Office on Drugs and Crime (UNODC) announced in its annual report on global illicit drug trends that lands under opium poppy cultivation in Myanmar (Burma) and Laos had been reduced by 40% between 1998 and 2002 and that this downward trend continued in 2003. The Andean region of South America also achieved a significant decline of coca bush cultivation. In March, however, the World Bank warned that opium poppy cultivation in Afghanistan was approaching record levels. Poppy cultivation, banned by the Taliban in 2000, had been reduced to a mere 1,685 ha (4,165 ac) by 2001, according to U.S. Department of State sources. About 18 times that amount of land was under cultivation in 2002, a figure that made Afghanistan the world's leading exporter of heroin.

In April Australian police and military seized a North Korean vessel, the *Pong Su,* in territorial waters after it had transferred 125 kg (275 lb) of heroin to shore. Thirty crew members were charged with aiding and abetting the importation of heroin. At a U.S. Senate subcommittee hearing in May, a former high-ranking North Korean official who had defected to South Korea in 1998 stated that North Korean diplomats and businessmen had trafficked in heroin and other illicit drugs in order to obtain hard currency for the North Korean regime.

In June a Dutch court sentenced Jing Ping Chen, a 37-year-old native of China, to a three-year prison term and fined her $12,800 for human trafficking. Known as Sister Ping, she was said to be one of the most ruthless gang leaders, known as "snake heads," in Europe. Ping's organization was believed to have been involved in the suffocation deaths of 58 Chinese found in a truck at the British port of Dover in June 2000.

Murder and Other Violence. In August the U.S. Bureau of Justice Statistics released figures from its 2002 National Crime Victimization Survey (NCVS). The NCVS collected data from a representative sample of American households on nonfatal crimes, reported or not reported to the police, against those aged 12 or older. It reported that rates were the lowest overall recorded since the survey's inception in 1973. The 23 million criminal victimizations in 2002 continued a downward trend that began in 1994. Between 1993 and 2002 the violent crime rate had decreased by 54% and the property crime rate by 50%.

In January relatives of two victims of the sniper shootings that terrorized the Virginia-Maryland-Washington, D.C., area in October 2002 filed suit against the gun manufacturer and the gun shop linked to the Bushmaster XMI5 assault rifle used in the crimes. In their respective trials, 18-year-old Lee Malvo was sentenced to life imprisonment in December, and 42-year-old John Muhammad was given the death penalty in November for having directed the killings.

In November Gary L. Ridgway, in a plea agreement that would spare his life, confessed to having strangled 48 women, most of them during the 1980s, in what was known as the Green River killing spree in the Seattle, Wash., area.

Serbian Prime Minister Zoran Djindjic (*see* OBITUARIES), known for his reformist and pro-Western policies, was assassinated on March 12 in front of the main government building in Belgrade. The 50-year-old Djindjic had spearheaded the revolt that toppled Slobodan Milosevic in October 2000. As police searched for Milorad Ulemek, a former paramilitary leader and a key suspect, the trial of Milosevic on charges of genocide and crimes against humanity continued in The Hague.

Also murdered was Anna Lindh, Sweden's widely known and respected foreign minister, who on September 10 was attacked and stabbed to death as she shopped. After nine days the Swedish police released the first suspect in the crime, having apprehended a new one.

White Collar Crime, Corruption, and Fraud. The investigation of American corporate scandals involving insider trading, stock manipulation, false accounting, and other such fraud continued at a slow pace. In June Sam Waksal, the 55-year-old founder of drug company ImClone Systems, became the first American corporate chief executive to be imprisoned for the scandals. Waksal, who had pleaded guilty to 6 of 13 charges stemming from his attempt to dump his shares in ImClone before a public announcement caused their value to plunge, was sentenced to more than seven years in prison, the maximum penalty under federal guidelines, and fined $4.3 million. In September Ben Glisan, a former treasurer of Enron, the energy giant that went bankrupt in 2001, was sentenced to five years in jail after he pleaded guilty to criminal conspiracy. Glisan's former boss, Andrew Fastow, former chief financial officer, was scheduled to stand trial in April 2004. Fastow continued to maintain his innocence on each of the charges in his 109-count indictment. Meanwhile, the U.S. Securities and Exchange Commission (SEC) announced in July that two major banking groups, J.P. Morgan Chase and Citigroup, had agreed to pay nearly $300 million to settle SEC allegations regarding their roles in Enron's manipulated financial statements. The SEC said that $236 million would go to defrauded Enron investors.

In South Africa, Winnie Madikizela-Mandela, the former wife of Nelson Mandela, was convicted of 43 counts of fraud and 25 of theft in a bungled banking scam. She was sentenced to four years in jail. In July the former deputy chairman of the British Conservative Party, Lord Jeffrey Archer, was paroled after having served half his four-year sentence for perjury.

British banks announced in September the successful trial of new fraud-busting card technology that utilized a microchip on credit and debit cards and required verification by a personal identification number (PIN) rather than a signature. The new cards were scheduled to debut throughout the U.K. by January 2005. A similar scheme introduced earlier in France had resulted in an 80% decrease in card fraud.

Law Enforcement. The U.S. Department of Justice and the FBI were said to have increased dramatically their use of two little-known powers allowing them to tap telephones, seize records, and obtain other information without immediate oversight by the courts. The FBI, for example, had issued a substantial number of "national security letters" that required businesses to hand over records about finances, phone calls, e-mails, and other personal data. The letters could be issued by FBI field offices and were not subject to judicial review unless a case came to trial. The issuing of these letters was accelerated after the September 11 attacks, when Congress passed the USA PATRIOT Act, a package of sweeping antiterrorism legislation.

Both U.S. civil rights groups and foreign governments decried the George W. Bush administration's decision in July to designate six foreign nationals (including two from the U.K. and one from Australia)—all of whom had been held captive at Guantánamo Bay, Cuba, since the end of the war in Afghanistan—to stand trial before a closed military tribunal that was empowered to order their execution. All had been kept in legal limbo, neither treated as prisoners of war nor charged with a criminal offense. Britain warned that it would not tolerate the imposition of the death penalty on British nationals.

In September Paul Evans, a senior U.S. police commissioner, was appointed to head the British Police Standards Unit. Evans, who was based in Boston, had been chosen because of his impressive record as the architect of Operation Ceasefire, a collaboration between the police and several Boston churches that all but eliminated youth gun crime in Boston and caused the number of homicides to plummet by two-thirds.

In May the interior and justice ministers of the Group of Eight industrialized nations—Britain, Canada, France, Germany, Italy, Japan, the U.S., and Russia—agreed to develop a global system to thwart terrorism, organized crime, illegal immigration, and identity theft. The system would use biometrics such as eye scans, a near-foolproof method of checking identity. A scheme to equip passports with biometric chips capable of storing details of the holder's fingerprints and iris patterns, both of which were extremely difficult to fake, was expected to commence in late 2004 or early 2005.

In Iraq the urgent need to train and equip a police force to replace the security apparatus of Saddam Hussein resulted in a massive program, conducted by the new U.S.-led administration, designed to put in place 75,000 new or retrained police officers by the end of 2004. (DUNCAN CHAPPELL)

Biometric technologies, such as this computerized iris-scanning system, were being developed in 2003 to be used internationally to verify identity.

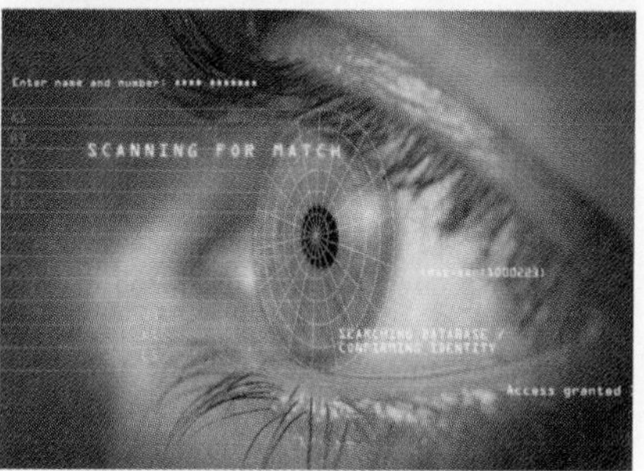

© Varie/Alt/Corbis

DEATH PENALTY

Following the inaugural worldwide Cities Against the Death Penalty observance on Nov. 30, 2002, international pressure for the worldwide abolition of the death penalty continued during 2003. In Europe, Protocol 13 to the European Convention on Human Rights, which banned the death penalty in all circumstances, entered into force on July 1. In line with its commitments as a member of the Council of Europe, the Armenian National Assembly approved a new criminal code that substituted life imprisonment for execution. Kenya continued to move toward abolition as Pres. Mwai Kibaki (*see* BIOGRAPHIES) released 28 prisoners from death row and commuted to life imprisonment the death sentences of 195 others, and Zambian Pres. Levy Mwanawasa appointed a commission to review the nation's constitution and to submit a recommendation regarding the death penalty. In Asia a nonpartisan Japanese parliamentary group drafted legislation to replace the death penalty with life in prison, and the president of Kyrgyzstan announced in January that a countrywide moratorium on executions would continue for another year. In the U.S., Gov. George Ryan of Illinois commuted the death sentences of 167 death-row inmates two days before he left office.

In response to a rise in serious crime, the Sri Lankan minister of interior proposed the reintroduction of the death penalty, more than 26 years after the country's last execution was carried out. In Cuba a three-year de facto moratorium on executions ended when three men who had hijacked a ferry were executed by firing squad. In January, 15 people in the Democratic Republic of the Congo were secretly executed; these were the first executions there in just over two years. (STUART MACDONALD)

Libraries and Museums

The LOSS of priceless books and TREASURES as a result of LOOTING in Iraq, the recovery of some of those objects, the online availability of VIRTUAL COLLECTIONS and manuscripts, and the effect of government policies—all concerned libraries and museums in 2003.

LIBRARIES

When U.S. troops entered Baghdad in April 2003 and Iraqis looted and burned the National Library, many Iraqis recalled the 13th-century sacking of the city by the Mongols. According to legend, the Tigris had turned black from the ink of books thrown into the river.

The *New York Times* reported that "virtually nothing was left of the library" or its contents. Later reports suggested that professional thieves stole priceless documents and unorganized looters burned nearly everything else. Additionally, the city's most important Muslim library was looted, and many priceless Qu'rans were destroyed. U.S. forces were bitterly criticized for their failure to try to limit the looting, and an office of the International Federation of Library Associations and Institutions (IFLA) reported that before the war it had written to Pres. George W. Bush, Prime Minister Tony Blair, and Iraqi leader Saddam Hussein, urging them to protect the country's cultural heritage. Other libraries in the country were also destroyed; in Basra, however, librarian Alia Muhammad Baker spirited away some 30,000 volumes from the city's library, which burned nine days later in a mysterious fire.

Although less epochal than the destruction of a national library, fallout from the war on terror continued to impact American libraries. Section 215 of the USA PATRIOT Act, which Congress had passed in the weeks following 9/11, gave expanded powers to police agencies to obtain library-patron information. Some libraries hung signs and printed bookmarks that warned patrons that what they read was no longer confidential. Other libraries began deleting circulation records. Some 160 communities passed resolutions decrying the law's threat to readers' privacy. At year's end, bills to rescind Section 215 were in both houses of Congress, and Attorney General John Ashcroft was on a 16-state speaking tour to defend the PATRIOT Act.

The 64,000-member American Library Association (ALA) found itself on the losing side in a Supreme Court review of CIPA, the Children's Internet Protection Act. CIPA required school and public libraries that received federal

A stack of books remains in a hallway of the National Library in Baghdad, Iraq. Libraries, museums, and other sites containing the historical, religious, and cultural legacy of the nation were looted and ransacked following the ousting of Saddam Hussein's regime by coalition forces in April.

AP/Wide World Photos

technology funding to install Internet-filtering software. The ALA contended that filters failed to block pornography effectively and blocked legitimate Web sites inadvertently, abridging free speech. In June the court ruled 6–3 that the law did not violate the constitutional guarantee to free speech.

A lagging U.S. economy and financial crises in many states resulted in thousands of libraries cutting service hours, freezing hiring, introducing fees, laying off staff, and even closing branch libraries. Gov. Jeb Bush announced a plan to close the Florida State Library and donate the 350,000-volume collection to a private university. Opposition was immediate and broad, and the plan was killed in the state legislature. Elsewhere, from Massachusetts to Hawaii, library use climbed, as it always did in a poor economy, and library resources dwindled. In South Africa, Pakistan, and China, governments announced initiatives to increase funding levels and build new public libraries.

Libraries of all kinds used serials agents to purchase magazines and journals. In 2003 one of the largest such companies, RoweCom, declared bankruptcy. Tens of millions of dollars disappeared. Publishers were not paid and library subscriptions lapsed. Much of the financial damage was mitigated by an ad hoc committee of publishers and librarians that convinced many publishers to "grace" 2003 subscriptions, and EBSCO Industries, another agent, stepped in to purchase RoweCom. Interestingly, RoweCom filed suit against divine, inc., its parent company, to recover in excess of $70 million that should have gone to publishers; divine, inc., also filed for bankruptcy. Some librarians described the scandal as the "Enron of the library world."

Crime, disease, and censorship confronted libraries worldwide. In Cuba government control of information caused many individuals to open their personal libraries to other readers; in March, however, police arrested some 75 regime critics, many of whom ran libraries, and confiscated thousands of books. Despite international protests, those arrested were quickly sentenced to long prison terms. Among the authors censored were George Orwell and Mario Vargas Llosa. The SARS (severe acute respiratory syndrome) epidemic forced the closing of the Chinese National Library from April 24 until June 9. (*See* HEALTH: Special Report.) Some 1,800 people entered the library during the first hour of service on June 9. In May the Shanghai Library disinfected its 250,000-volume collection; in Toronto a library worker sued Mt. Sinai Hospital for $2.1 million because she was pressed into screening visitors for the disease.

During 2003 Scotland Yard's "Most Wanted List" included a man alleged to be a library thief sought in connection with thefts from the National Library of Wales and libraries in Denmark. In Bath and Bristol, Eng., microfiche containing data on millions of births, deaths, and marriages were stolen. News reports speculated that terrorists might use the records to create false identities. A Hong Kong university asked Japan to return 138 books taken during World War II.

On a positive note, the Massachusetts Institute of Technology made progress in its DSpace initiative to provide digital access to the university's entire research output. The British Library (BL) previewed two exciting new technological services. One was a document-delivery service that offered rapid access to more than a billion items from the BL collections, whether in print, microformat, or digital form. Developers believed that they could offer two-hour delivery to a desktop. Separately, the library unveiled Turning the Pages, a touch-screen system that enabled users to virtually turn the pages of priceless documents such as the Lindisfarne Gospels and Leonardo da Vinci's notebook. (THOMAS M. GAUGHAN)

MUSEUMS

In 2003 museums too felt the impact of recent and past wars, but they also experienced growth and innovation. In April looters plundered Iraqi museums following the invasion of the country by U.S.-led coalition forces, but estimates of damage were reduced after many objects believed to have been stolen were found in safekeeping. The Mesopotamian Warka Vase and the Lady of Warka mask were taken back to the National Museum of Iraq, and about 3,000 other artifacts were returned following an amnesty and a series of raids at airports and border checkpoints. About 10,000 objects from the National Museum of Iraq and the Mosul Museum were still missing, however. The Kuwait National Museum stayed closed, more than a decade after its exhibit halls were burned in fires set by retreating Iraqi forces in 1991. In Afghanistan, however, two rooms reopened at the Kabul Museum, where curators hoped to repair the destruction in 2001 of nearly 2,000 sculptures that the Taliban called offensive to Islam. In New York City, in the area traumatized by the terrorist attacks of Sept. 11, 2001, a new wing that opened at the Museum of Jewish Heritage—A Living Memorial to the Holocaust embodied the museum's theme of rebuilding after tragedy.

A number of museums hosted exhibitions of Iranian, Egyptian, Oriental, and Indian art and antiquities. The British Museum, which aided Iraqi cultural recovery efforts, marked its 250th anniversary with giant red ribbons and special exhibitions, including objects from its founding. In Amsterdam the Van Gogh Museum celebrated the artist's 150th birthday. The 2,000-year-old Dead Sea Scrolls, which rarely traveled, went on display in Michigan at the Public Museum of Grand Rapids in an educational loan from the owners, the Israel Antiquities Authority.

New museums of contemporary art opened their doors in Málaga, Spain; Rovereto, Italy; and Cincinnati, Ohio, where the Contemporary Arts Center showcased performance art. The provocative contemporary art collection of the Saatchi Gallery opened in London, and in Beacon, N.Y., many minimalist works of American artists of the 1960s and '70s filled a new 23,200-sq-m (250,000-sq-ft) exhibition space at Dia Beacon. In Singapore the new Empress Place wing of the Asian Civilizations Museum opened, and the Asian Art Museum of San Francisco reopened with new galleries. The Museum of Immigration and Diversity in London, coinciding with refugee week, opened the exhibit "Suitcases and Sanctuary," recounting stories of three centuries of immigrants to Spitalfields, a traditionally multicultural area of the city.

In a series of setbacks, French ceramics galleries were closed at the Victoria and Albert Museum in London and the Musée des Arts Decoratifs in Paris, and the important 17th- and 18th-century ceramics collection of the chateau of Lunéville, France, was largely lost in a fire.

In August two important appointments were made. The Whitney Museum of American Art selected Adam D. Weinberg as its new director following the resignation in May of embattled director Maxwell L. Anderson, and Ann Little Poulet became the first woman to direct the Frick Collection, after Samuel Sachs II announced in January that he was leaving.

The British Museum in London, the oldest national public museum in the world, celebrates its 250th anniversary on June 6. Museum director Neil MacGregor is joined by 250 schoolchildren for the event.

Furthering efforts by museums to make collections available to researchers on the Internet, the American Museum of Natural History in New York City put photographs and descriptions of its fossils, expedition records, and anthropological and other objects online. The National Museum of Natural History in Washington, D.C., took similar steps, and in the Chicago area the Field Museum, the Morton Arboretum, and the Chicago Botanic Garden created a virtual herbarium online.

In a 2003 survey by the American Association of Museums (AAM), fewer museums reported operating surpluses in 2002 than in 2001, but more reported having broken even financially, perhaps realizing the success of budget cuts. Even in frugal times, a number of museums expanded. In Salem, Mass., a $125 million structure designed by Moshe Safdie incorporated the earlier buildings and mariners' collections of the Peabody Essex Museum and a traveling merchant's 19th-century wood house from China, with goldfish pools in the courtyard. In Fort Worth, Texas, the new home of the Modern Art Museum opened in late 2002. The $65 million glass-and-steel structure surrounded by water was designed by Japanese architect Tadao Ando. In Washington, D.C., several museums planned expansions, including a $22 million project at the Phillips Collection, $1 billion in improvements at the Smithsonian Institution, including a new National Museum of the American Indian, and a new wing designed by Frank Gehry for the Corcoran Gallery of Art. In Qatar a new museum was being built by Sheikh Saud al-Thani to hold Qatari costume, jewelry, Iznikware, and Mamluk glass.

Owing to budget cuts, the Guggenheim Las Vegas (Nev.) closed indefinitely in January, but the Guggenheim agreed to lend its name to a new $130 million museum in Rio de Janeiro, to be funded by the city in a revitalization of its waterfront. In Merion, Pa., the Barnes Foundation, the financially strapped owner of a valuable collection of Post-Impressionist paintings, sought court approval to undo restrictions set by its original donor and move to a more accessible site in Philadelphia.

Art looted by the Nazis continued to haunt museums. In a continuing effort to return to their original owners any Nazi-stolen objects housed in American museums, in September the AAM launched the Nazi-Era Provenance Internet Portal, a searchable registry of American museum objects that had possibly changed hands in Europe in the Nazi era. In a U.S. court the Austrian National Gallery fought a court ruling that the gallery could be sued in California for recovery of six paintings by Gustav Klimt that it possessed. The paintings were sought by the niece of their original owner, a Jew whose vast art collection was stolen by top Nazis after Austria was annexed to Germany in 1938. At the palace of Tsarskoye Selo, Russia, the Amber Room—an 18th-century gift to Tsar Peter the Great that featured 100,000 pieces of carved amber paneling and that had vanished during the German retreat in 1945—was reconstructed, again in amber.

(MARTHA B.G. LUFKIN)

Life Sciences

In 2003, as the world celebrated the 50TH ANNIVERSARY of James Watson and Francis Crick's seminal paper on the DNA DOUBLE HELIX, scientists were just starting to understand how truly DYNAMIC the molecule is. Researchers reported the discovery of a FOSSIL DINOSAUR with FEATHERS on all FOUR LIMBS, observed evidence of CULTURE IN ORANGUTANS, and measured the global effects of CLIMATE CHANGE on PLANT GROWTH.

ZOOLOGY

Primate research in 2003 provided new insight into the evolution of culture—the transmission of socially learned knowledge or tradition to succeeding generations. Humans once had been thought to be the only species in which differences ascribed to culture exist between populations. In 1999, however, observed differences in chimpanzee behaviour in different geographic regions were cited as evidence of culture. During 2003 Carel P. van Schaik of Duke University, Durham, N.C., and colleagues documented geographic variation in the behaviour of another nonhuman primate species, orangutans (*Pongo pygmaeus*), in Borneo and Sumatra. The investigators examined wild orangutan populations at six sites to determine if tool using and other specific behaviours were present in a population at one site but absent in all the others, findings that would support the position that cultural evolution had taken place. Population-specific behaviours that the investigators classified as "very likely cultural variants" included using leaves to wipe the face, poking into tree holes with a tool to obtain insects, using a leafy branch to scoop up water from a tree hole, and making characteristic spluttering sounds when bedding down for the night. The scientists also noted that dissimilarities in the behaviours increased with geographic distance between orangutan populations, which supported the interpretation that the behaviours were culturally based, and that the habitat of a population appeared not to influence whether a given behaviour was present or absent. Further, they suggested that cultures not only can be found currently among the great apes but also may have existed for 14 million years in this group of animals.

As two or more species interact, they can evolve in response to each other, a process called coevolution. In 2000 Ethan J. Temeles and colleagues of Amherst (Mass.) College reported on the dynamics of such a relationship between purple-throated carib hummingbirds (*Eulampis jugularis*) on the island of St. Lucia in the Lesser Antilles and the plants on which the birds feed. The hummingbirds obtain nectar from two heliconia species, *Heliconia caribaea* and *H. bihai,* for which the birds are the only means of pollination. The investigators focused their study on the evolution of sexual dimorphism in the birds—i.e., the differences between males and females in body size or in the proportions and appearance of body parts. Male hummingbirds have larger bodies, longer wings, and shorter, straighter bills than females. They were found to dominate feeding at the more energy-rich plant, *H. caribaea,* which also bears shorter, less-curved floral structures that correspond to the males' bills. In contrast, females were found to feed at *H. bihai,* which bears longer, more curved floral structures corresponding to the females' bills. Temeles and his Amherst colleagues concluded that the differences between the sexes in bill size and shape have an ecological cause involving the birds' specialization on the two flower types. At the same time, they noted that in parts of St. Lucia where *H. caribaea* is rare or absent, *H. bihai* exists in two forms, one with many shorter, straighter flowers matching the bills and energy needs of males and the other with fewer longer, curved flowers matching the bills and energy needs of females. This prompted speculation that *H. bihai* had evolved in response to the birds' sexual dimorphism.

In 2003 Temeles and W. John Kress of the Smithsonian Institution's National Museum of Natural History published a follow-up report on the relationships among carib hummingbirds and heliconias on Dominica, another Lesser Antillean island. In contrast to the situation on St. Lucia, *H. caribaea* was

A female orangutan fashions a tool to probe a tree hole as a youngster watches. In 2003 researchers presented evidence of culture in orangutan populations.

the more abundant plant species. Moreover, analogous to *H. bihai* on St. Lucia, *H. caribaea* was found to have evolved two flower forms, one matching the bills and energy needs of males and the other of females. Together the two studies demonstrated that differences in flower forms drive evolution of sexual dimorphism in the hummingbirds and that hummingbird dimorphisms and partitioning of resources between the sexes drive specialization between and within *Heliconia* species—all in support of the hypothesis that a coevolutionary association indeed exists.

Two research teams independently came to complementary conclusions about the way reproductive success can hinge on a factor that influences a female bird's choice of a mate. The factor in question is a group of organic pigments, called carotenoids, that occur widely in plants and that are the basis for many of the yellow-to-red hues in both plants and animals. Birds and other animals cannot synthesize carotenoids but must obtain them from their diet. In some bird species they are responsible for a secondary sexual trait, the colour of the male's bill, which is used to advertise fitness and influence mate choice and competition between males. In many animal species carotenoids also have important roles in maintaining health. In birds they participate in immune responses, for example, to challenges from foreign invaders such as parasites.

In one study Bruno Faivre of the University of Burgundy, Dijon, France, and colleagues conducted experiments with Old World blackbirds (*Turdus merula*), a species in which males with higher carotenoid levels have brighter orange bills and presumably greater mating success because they are more likely to be chosen by and to mate with healthier females. The investigators tested how carotenoids were allocated between sexual display and immune defenses. They found that bill colour faded in birds that had been injected with foreign cells to stress their immune system, evidence that the sexual signal of bill colour is indeed an indicator of the individual's health. In the second study Jonathan D. Blount of the University of Glasgow, Scot., and colleagues confirmed the phenomenon in experiments with zebra finches (*Taeniopygia* [or *Poephila*] *guttata*) in which each of 10 pairs of sibling males were fed either carotenoids or distilled water (the latter as controls). The bills of birds receiving the carotenoids turned significantly redder than those of the controls, and females spent significantly more time perched next to the males with brighter bills and thereby indicated a preference for them. A plant protein that provokes an immune response in birds then was injected into both the carotenoid-supplemented and the control males. The carotenoid-supplemented birds showed a much stronger immune response, which had already been documented to increase a bird's chances for survival. A significant finding of the studies was that secondary sexual traits used in mate-choice decisions by females can be true indicators of health and presumed fitness of males.

Another study called attention to a different kind of factor that can affect mate choice and reproductive success. Joseph I. Hoffman and William Amos of the University of Cambridge and Ian L. Boyd of the Natural Environment Research Council, Cambridge, correlated details of breeding behaviour in Antarctic fur seals (*Arctocephalus gazella*) with the reproductive success of male seals to assess the importance of male competition and territorial defense on the breeding beach relative to alternative male strategies (e.g., aquatic mating before females reach the beach) and female choice of mates. Classically, in a mammalian breeding colony with male territoriality, the mating system is expected to be polygyny, in which one male mates with multiple females. Successful defense of a territory increases the chances of mating with any females living in the defended area. A successful territorial male thus has a higher probability of reproductive success than one having no territory.

To confirm this expectation for Antarctic fur seals, the investigators determined paternity of seal pups by conducting genetic analyses on 1,800 individuals over a seven-breeding-season period from Bird Island, South Georgia. Of 415 males for which genetic identity could be determined, 22 (about 5%) successfully defended territories. Of 660 seal pups for which paternity could be determined, the 22 territorial males were the fathers of 59%. Although most males had only one successful reproductive season, those returning to the same breeding beach had increasing success in subsequent years. Especially interesting was the observation that the success of territorial males varied among females depending on their maternal status—females that arrived at the breeding beach and did not have pups were more likely to mate with males from other beaches that season. Although the research confirmed that polygyny was the norm in the species, the importance of maternal status in male mating success was unexpected.

(J. WHITFIELD GIBBONS)

BOTANY

British scientists in 2003 reported the results of a large study of the environmental effects of genetically modified (GM) crops. The farm-scale trials, which cost $8.5 million and lasted four years, were designed to test whether weeds and insects, such as butterflies, bees, and beetles, fared better in fields of conventional crops or of crops that had been genetically altered to be resistant to a herbicide for weed control. A major emphasis of the study was on the importance of crop weeds, which were well known to be of benefit to wildlife by providing cover and food for insects (as well as seeds for birds). The experiment found that fields of GM sugar beet and oilseed rape (canola) were worse for insects than fields of conventional varieties of the crops. GM corn (maize), on the other hand, was better for many types of insects than conventional corn. The study attributed the variation to a difference in the weed burdens of the crops. GM beet and rape were associated with fewer weeds than their non-GM equivalents, whereas GM corn actually had more weeds than conventional corn.

It already had been determined that GM crops can crossbreed with wild plants through the spread of their pollen, but new work revealed that the dispersal of seeds carrying modified genetic material also can play an unexpected role in the long-distance spread of the genes. A team headed by Jean-François Arnaud of the University of Lille, France, found that seeds from hybrids of weed beets and GM sugar-beet crops had escaped to more than 1.5 km (about one mile) from the commercial fields in France where they had arisen. These results suggested that seeds carrying GM material may accidentally be spread by humans, most likely in soil caught on vehicle wheels or transported by other agricultural activities. Once the seeds have escaped, the plants can then cross-pollinate with nearby wild relatives and create new and possibly damaging hybrids with modified genes.

Despite the concerns over safety, new and intriguing uses for GM plants were under investigation. The Defense Ad-

Juergen Berger and Javier Palatnik

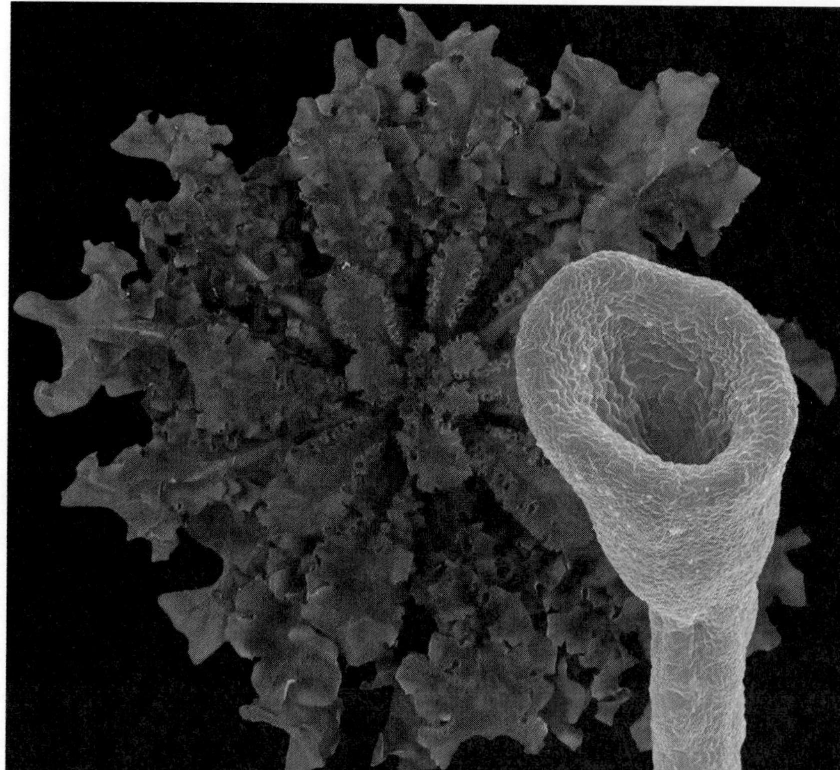

An excess of a gene-regulating microRNA in Arabidopsis *plants (seedling in foreground) was shown to cause leaf crinkling in a mutant variety (background).*

vanced Research Projects Agency, part of the U.S. Department of Defense, awarded a $2 million grant to plant biologist June Medford of Colorado State University for an ingenious plan to genetically engineer plants to detect a chemical or biological attack by changing colour.

Big strides were made in understanding the master controls that plants use to organize their shape and development. A gene dubbed *PHANTASTICA* was found to control whether tomato plants develop their normal featherlike (pinnately compound) leaf arrangement or an umbrella-like (palmately compound) arrangement like clover. "It's a very surprising finding, that modifying one gene in the tomato alters the leaf from one form to another," said Neelima Sinha of the University of California, Davis, who was involved in the research. The same genetic mechanism appeared to be shared by a wide group of flowering plants.

In another breakthrough, for the first time in plants, tiny genetic components called microRNAs were found to switch off the expression of shape-regulating genes. MicroRNA molecules, which were first recognized in the early 1990s, are short strands of RNA that are transcribed from parts of an organism's genetic blueprint that once had been thought to be useless, or "junk," DNA. Rather than being merely the intermediaries between DNA and protein, as are messenger RNA (mRNA) molecules, they have critical roles themselves in the regulation of gene expression. MicroDNAs work by recognizing and binding to specific mRNAs and bringing about their inactivation or destruction at the appropriate time. A team led by Detlef Weigel of the Max Planck Institute for Developmental Biology, Tübingen, Ger., and James Carrington of Oregon State University found overly high levels of one such microRNA in a mutant *Arabidopsis thaliana* plant (a favourite model organism of plant geneticists), which grew unusual crinkled and wrinkly leaves. The researchers showed that this microDNA regulates the expression of a set of genes (named TCP genes) that prevent excess cell division in the growing plant. Too much microDNA in the mutant plant allowed too many cells to proliferate in the leaves and caused the crinkling. By contrast, microDNA in normal plants appears at the right level, time, and place to create flat leaves. As more microRNAs were being discovered, their importance in plant growth and development was becoming clearer. This opened up entirely new and exciting possibilities for the use of these molecules as tools to manipulate the activities of plant genes, with potentially enormous scientific and economic benefits.

With overtones of the movie *Jurassic Park*, the oldest plant DNA found to date was extracted from drilled cores of frozen soil in Siberia by a team led by Eske Willerslev of the University of Copenhagen. The DNA fragments, some from plants that lived as long as 400,000 years ago, were identified as belonging to at least 19 different plant families. This ability to recover specimens of ancient DNA directly from soil samples, which would obviate the need for identifiable fossils, could revolutionize studies that attempt to construct a genetic picture of past ecosystems. Because the extracted DNA was broken up into tiny pieces, however, there seemed little chance of resurrecting any of the species.

The changing world climate was having wide-ranging effects on the productivity of plant life. From 1982 to 1999, climate change resulted in a 6% increase in plant growth over much of the globe, reported Ramakrishna Nemani of the University of Montana and colleagues after they analyzed climatic ground and satellite data. The largest increase occurred in tropical ecosystems and especially in the Amazon rainforests, which accounted for 42% of the global increase, owing mainly to less cloud cover and the resulting increase in sunlight in that region. As trees and other vegetation grow, they take carbon dioxide from the atmosphere and convert it to solid carbon compounds. It was not clear, however, whether or how the observed growth increase would affect the removal of carbon dioxide, a greenhouse gas widely cited as the major driving force behind global warming, and its storage in terrestrial ecosystems over the long term.

The increasingly important role of botanic gardens in understanding and conserving plant life was recognized in July when Kew Gardens in London was added to UNESCO's list of World Heritage Sites. In addition to being known internationally for its historic public gardens and buildings, Kew is a world famous scientific organization, renowned for its living and herbarium collections of plants, research facilities, and contribution on a major scale to conservation and biodiversity.

(PAUL SIMONS)

MOLECULAR BIOLOGY AND GENETICS

DNA at 50. "We wish to suggest a structure for the salt of deoxyribose nucleic acid (D.N.A.). This structure has novel features which are of considerable biological interest."

So began, in the April 25, 1953, issue of *Nature,* the deceptively modest description of DNA that would be hailed a half century later, in 2003, as one of the truly groundbreaking advances in science. In their one-page paper, James Watson and Francis Crick depicted the molecular repository of genetic information as "two helical chains each coiled round the same axis"—a now-iconic image known worldwide. Although these researchers clearly achieved their feat by standing on the shoulders of other giants, perhaps most notably Oswald Avery, Erwin Chargaff, Rosalind Franklin, Linus Pauling, and Maurice Wilkins, their seminal publication has often been cited as the birth of the modern era of molecular genetics. In keeping with that status, the golden anniversary year of the double helix was celebrated with much pomp and ceremony, including an official announcement in April by the Human Genome Project of the completion of its sequencing of the entire human genetic blueprint, or genome, whose rough draft had been announced two years earlier.

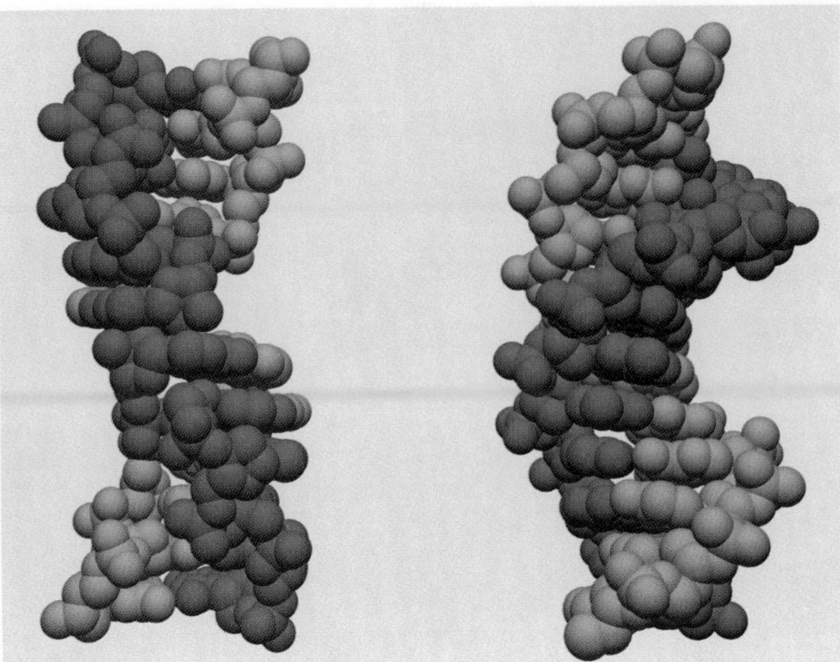

Two molecular models of the DNA double helix, each with its component strands highlighted with separate colours, illustrate structural differences between left-handed Z-DNA (left) and the familiar right-handed form, B-DNA (right).

It was especially fitting in 2003 to ask how far, in real terms, science and medicine have come and what challenges and opportunities lie ahead. Also appropriate were questions about investigators' current views on DNA structure and on the role of structure in defining DNA's biological functions. The answers to these questions are complex and, in most cases, only poorly understood.

In terms of progress, the past five decades have witnessed nothing short of an explosion of new knowledge and new technology. Scientists have come to understand, on a molecular and biochemical level, not only many of the normal workings of living systems, both human and nonhuman, but also the basis of many diseases. Indeed, this new knowledge has revolutionized the ability to diagnose a variety of conditions and has begun to offer novel therapies that previously were unimaginable. Finally, scientists have taken the first steps toward understanding not only the expression and function of individual genes within the genomes of humans and other species but also the anatomy and regulation of the genomes themselves. Thanks to the public availability of the more than 100 genomes, ranging from bacterial to human, that had been sequenced as of 2003, researchers have detected patterns in both the unique and the repeated elements of these genomes that offer tantalizing clues to the evolution of humans and many other species.

Regarding the true structure and function of DNA, appreciation has grown that Watson and Crick's famed right-handed double helical structure is but the tip of the iceberg. Researchers in the field have come to recognize that DNA in living cells is not static in form but continuously moving and changing as it assumes different shapes and associates with different proteins, other macromolecules, or both. For example, in 2001 a research team led by Keji Zhao of the U.S. National Heart, Lung, and Blood Institute, Bethesda, Md., found evidence that part of the regulatory sequence of an immune system gene must transition from its more familiar right-handed form into Z-DNA, a left-handed helical conformation identified in 1979 by Alexander Rich of the Massachusetts Institute of Technology, in order for the gene to be activated. In 2002 Stephen Neidle of the Institute of Cancer Research, London, reported that single-stranded DNA sequences called telomeres, found at the ends of linear chromosomes such as those in humans, can weave themselves into a complex four-stranded loop structure known as a G-quadruplex. Other G-quadruplex forms of DNA were proposed to mediate the regulation of genes, including genes involved in cancer inducement (oncogenes), elsewhere in the genome.

Beyond basic structure, both DNA itself and the proteins with which it associates can be chemically modified—for example, by the addition or removal of simple methyl (CH_3) or acetyl ($COCH_3$) groups. These changes can alter both the structure and the function of DNA. Indeed, some researchers have concluded that the structure, state of modification, and macromolecular associations of DNA may be as important to its function as its sequence of bases.

Although human understanding of DNA may be marking a golden anniversary, those regions of the human genome that have been studied in detail demonstrate a complexity and interdependence that is nothing short of humbling, and clearly the current level of understanding for even these systems is superficial. Perhaps even more humbling is that the vast majority of the human genome has yet to be studied, and despite the declaration of completion in April, many gaps and uncertainties remain in the available human genome sequence database. If the 1953 paper by Watson and Crick was a birth, the status of molecular genetics in 2003 might appropriately be described as a first toddling step.

Killing the Messenger. If genes encode the building blocks of life, the controlled expression of those genes must define the shape and function that the blocks can assume. Gene expression is clearly a highly regulated affair in humans and other living systems, and changes in this regulation underlie both normal processes—such as tissue differentiation, development, and adaptation—and many abnormal conditions, including numerous cancers. A variety of mechanisms are known to mediate gene regulation, and they can operate at almost any of the many steps that must occur for a gene to give rise to a finished protein product. Some of these steps are transcription of the sequence of bases in DNA into the corresponding base sequence in single-stranded messenger RNA (mRNA), processing and stabilization of the mRNA transcript, transport of the mRNA into the cell's cytoplasm, translation of the mRNA into a linear chain of amino acids, processing and folding of the chain into a three-dimensional protein molecule, and binding of additional required atoms or molecular groups called cofactors.

In 1978, a novel mechanism of gene suppression was discovered that involved the activity of short single-stranded RNA or DNA pieces (oligonucleotides) whose sequence is complementary to a specific part of a target mRNA transcript. These bits of sequence, termed antisense oligonucleotides (more specifically, antisense RNA and antisense DNA), appeared to interfere with the manufacture of the gene product at either of two steps: they blocked translation of the target message, or they marked the message for destruction by an enzyme. In both cases they did their work by binding to the mRNA transcript, forming a short stretch of double-stranded RNA similar to the DNA duplex in the double helix.

Later, a second form of oligonucleotide-mediated gene suppression was identified that involves the use of double-stranded RNA sequences. It was called RNA-mediated interference (RNAi), a term coined by Andrew Fire, Craig C. Mello, and colleagues at the Carnegie Institution of Washington (D.C.) and the University of Massachusetts Medical School. These researchers pioneered the field of RNAi in 1998 when they reported that the introduction of minuscule quantities of specific double-stranded RNA sequences into the nematode *Caenorhabditis elegans* (a favourite laboratory animal in molecular genetics research) could effectively silence the expression of a target gene not only in the injected animals but also in their progeny. RNAi subsequently was demonstrated to work in a broad variety of species and cell types. Like antisense oligonucleotides, RNAi also was found to be a naturally occurring method of gene regulation.

Researchers believed that the mechanism of RNAi gene suppression starts with the activity of a specific naturally occurring RNA-cleavage enzyme (RNase) dubbed Dicer. The enzyme recognizes the anomalous double-stranded RNA molecules and cuts them into short pieces that are each about 22 nucleotides long. The fragments, often referred to as siRNA (for short, or small, interfering RNA), are then unwound into their separate strands. One strand associates with a set of specific proteins to form an RNA-induced silencing complex (RISC). Because the RNA portion of the RISC remains exposed near the surface of the complex, it is able to bind with its complementary base sequence in the target mRNA transcript. Once this binding has taken place, an enzyme known as Slicer (which may be part of the RISC complex) recognizes the assembly and cuts the RISC-tagged mRNA in two. The RISC then releases the destroyed mRNA pieces and moves on, ready to bind other complementary targets. In this manner the siRNA-containing RISC acts as an efficient catalyst for the destruction of specific mRNAs in the cell.

By 2003 RNAi already had evolved not only into a useful laboratory tool but also into a promising approach for treating medical conditions in humans, including cancer, neurodegenerative diseases, and viral infections. In each medical application the design involved suppression of the unwanted expression of a gene, with the targets ranging from oncogenes to viral genes from HIV. Although numerous technical hurdles remained, the progress at this point appeared swift and promising.

(JUDITH L. FRIDOVICH-KEIL)

PALEONTOLOGY

Among the more intriguing stories in paleontology during 2003 was the discovery of the dinosaur *Microraptor gui*, a small dromaeosaur from the Early Cretaceous Jiufotang Formation of Liaoning, China. Xing Xu of the Chinese Academy of Sciences and colleagues reported that the 77-cm (2.5-ft)-long animal, which lived between 124 million and 144 million years ago, had fully modern, asymmetrical feathers on all four limbs. Dromaeosaurs belong to the dinosaur subgroup called theropods, which were bipeds (with hind limbs adapted for locomotion) and flesh eaters (ranging from species as small as chickens to the huge *Tyrannosaurus*). Beginning in the late 1990s with the discovery of the first fossils of feathered dinosaurs, it became widely accepted that birds evolved from small light-boned theropod dinosaurs and that feathers originated in nonavian theropods. The question of how flight itself evolved, however, was not settled and continued to be debated. The arguments centred on two hypotheses—the arboreal theory, which suggested that flight arose in tree-dwelling animals through an intermediate gliding stage, and the competing cursorial idea, which suggested that flight evolved in fast-running ground-dwelling animals. If the four feathered limbs on *M. gui* were used for gliding, as the authors proposed, it would strengthen the arboreal theory for the origin of flight.

Over the years many types of evidence have been applied to determine the feeding habits of theropod dinosaurs. A report by Raymond Rogers of Macalester College, St. Paul, Minn., and co-workers on the large Late Cretaceous theropod *Majungatholus atopus* from the Maevarano Formation of Madagascar described heavily tooth-marked fossil bones in support of the idea that the animal defleshed other dinosaur carcasses as it fed. *Majungatholus,* which was as much as 9 m (30 ft) from nose to tail, lived about 70 million years ago. The investigators found well-gnawed bones both of plant-eating sauropods and of *Majungatholus* itself bearing marks that matched the characteristics of the latter animal's teeth, which indicated that the dinosaur was a cannibal.

Paul Sereno of the University of Chicago, Jeff Wilson of the University of Michigan, and colleagues reported that while sifting through fossil remains collected years earlier from deposits along the Narmada River in western India, they found fossil bones belonging to a new species of Late Cretaceous dinosaur. *Rajasaurus narmadensis* was a 9-m (30-ft)-long dinosaur of the theropod family Abelisauridae that lived about 67 million years ago. Abelisaurs

© Sherwin Crasto/Reuters/Corbis

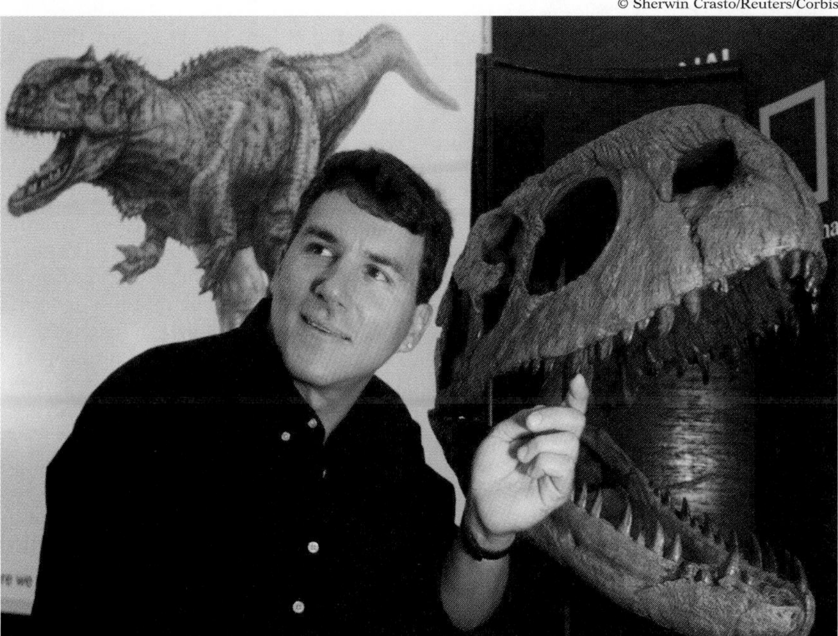

Scientist Paul Sereno fingers a tooth of a skull model of **Rajasaurus narmadensis,** *a new carnivorous dinosaur from India that he helped assemble from remains.*

are Cretaceous theropods with short, high skulls. They were also known from South America and Africa, which like India were part of the ancient supercontinent Gondwanaland.

The caves and deposits at Sterkfontein near Johannesburg, S.Af., are among the richest fossil hominid sites in the world. A report by Timothy Partridge and co-workers from the University of the Witwatersrand, Johannesburg, and Purdue University, West Lafayette, Ind., described recently discovered hominid specimens—possibly of *Australopithecus*—from Jacovec Cavern and elsewhere at Sterkfontein and contended that the specimens are a surprising four million years old. Previous age estimates for the hundreds of hominids from Sterkfontein ranged from 1.5 million to 3.5 million years. The more ancient age values came from a recently developed technique, called cosmogenic burial dating, that was used on the buried sediments associated with the fossils. When sediment is on the surface, its minerals are bombarded by cosmic rays from space. This process continually produces unstable isotopes of beryllium and aluminum that have fairly long half-lives—about a million years. After the sediments are buried, the bombardment stops and the radioactive isotopes decay without further replenishment. By measuring the quantity of the isotopes that remain in a sample, scientists can determine the age at which the sediment and its content of once-living remains were buried.

Since the 1970s the origin of modern primates (euprimates) has been a subject of considerable debate, and a variety of scenarios have been offered to explain how and why their evolution occurred. Jonathan Bloch and Doug Boyer of the University of Michigan presented evidence from a well-preserved 56-million-year-old specimen of *Carpolestes simpsoni* from the Clarks Fork Basin of Wyoming that could resolve this debate. Previous phylogenetic analyses had concluded that the carpolestids are closely related to the euprimates. From their examination of the skull and foot bones of the skeleton, the most complete carpolestid found to date, the investigators inferred that this 30-cm (one-foot)-long animal—and, hence, that the ancestor of modern primates—lacked forward-facing eyes and convergent vision but had an opposable big toe and that it was a grasper adapted for feeding in terminal tree branches. This is in opposition to other hypotheses that suggested the ancestor of the euprimates was either a specialized leaper or a visually directed predator.

The very earliest tetrapods (vertebrates with limbs) date back to the Late Devonian, about 370 million to 354 million years ago. Until 2003 the nine genera described from that age were known only from North America, Europe, and Greenland, apart from a single fragmentary specimen found in Australia. Min Zhu and colleagues from the Chinese Academy of Sciences and the Natural History Museum, London, reported discovery of the first Late Devonian tetrapod fossil from Asia. Their identification of an incomplete left mandible from nonmarine sediments of the Ningxia Hui region of northwestern China indicated that tetrapods became quite widely dispersed in a relatively short time.

A study by Moya Smith of King's College, London, and Zerina Johanson of the Australian Museum, Sydney, concluded that teeth evolved more than once in primitive fish. It formerly had been assumed that teeth evolved only once, in a fish ancestral to all vertebrates with jaws, the gnathostomes. In examining specimens of members of the Arthrodira, an advanced group of extinct predatory jawed fish called placoderms, the investigators found teeth made of dentine. Previously all placoderms had been thought to lack true teeth. If, as speculated, the arthrodires derived from toothless placoderms that were not ancestral to other fish groups, then teeth must have evolved independently in the two lineages.

Samuel Zschokke of the University of Basel, Switz., described an unusual specimen of Early Cretaceous fossil amber from Lebanon in which could be seen an individual thread of viscid (sticky) silk from a spider web. This specimen demonstrated that both the spider superfamily Araneoidea and the use of viscid silk in aerial webs date back at least 130 million years. This silk thread still bore dozens of the glue droplets that typify this type of arachnoid silk.

The gymnosperm ginkgo tree (*Ginkgo biloba*) is in some ways a living fossil, having existed at least since the Middle Jurassic Period 170 million years ago. Previously, there had been a gap of 100 million years in the ginkgo fossil record. In 2003, however, Zhiyan Zhou of the Chinese Academy of Sciences and Shaolin Zheng of the Chinese Ministry of National Land and Resources described a fossil from the Early Cretaceous Yixian Formation of China that fit near the middle of the gap, with an age of 121 million years. The specimen was found to have reproductive structures different from the Jurassic fossils but similar to the modern ginkgo, which showed that the morphology of this ancient tree had changed little over the past 100 million years.

(WILLIAM R. HAMMER)

Literature

South African writer **J.M. COETZEE** took the **NOBEL** for the year, while Australian-born **DBC PIERRE** won the **BOOKER** and American **VALERIE MARTIN** picked up the **ORANGE** Prize. The **JUAN RULFO** Prize for best Latin American and Caribbean literature went to Brazilian **RUBEM FONSECA**. The **INTERNET** played a role in literature from several countries, including **JAPAN** and **TURKEY**. A **YIDDISH** translation of ***THE CAT IN THE HAT*** also was published.

ENGLISH

United Kingdom. Although the Man Booker Prize remained closed to U.S. writers, the winner chosen in 2003 revealed, in the words of one of the judges, "[Britain's] alarm, but also our fascination with modern America." DBC Pierre (pseudonym of Peter Finlay) was widely hailed as the new J.D. Salinger for his debut novel, *Vernon God Little.* Set in a small town known as "the barbecue sauce capital of Texas," the novel is a comic tragedy about the miscarriages of justice and media frenzy that occur when its teenage protagonist is accused of being an accessory to the slaying of 16 of his classmates. Reviewers relished the novel's colourful Texan dialogue, local detail, and "fiendish sense of humour." John Carey, the chairman of the Booker judges, said, "Everybody thought that it was the most imaginative, unusual, exciting, and extraordinary book for a British person to have written." Much media attention was afforded the novel's force as a powerful satire. Liz Fraser echoed the sentiments of many commentators when she described the novel as "a big absurd mix of all that's wrong in American (and Western) society—guns and violence, high-school slayings, teenage alienation, truth and lies, dysfunctional family bonds, the justice system and the frightening power of the media." The *Daily Telegraph* called it "a masterpiece, a scintillating black comedy striking at the very heart of George W. Bush's America."

At the awards ceremony in March, Australian-born Pierre, who was raised in Mexico but currently lived in Ireland, proved to be as colourful a figure as some of his fictional creations. Taking the podium, he confessed to a past tainted by cocaine use, fraud, and gambling debts. (The initials DBC—for "dirty but clean"—referred to his efforts to reform himself after a nine-year drug habit.) He vowed to the audience that he was "not touching a penny" of his £50,000 (£1 = about $1.66) prize, stating, "I am going to pay some debts to see if I can sleep slightly better tonight."

The "literary empress of multicultural Britain," Zadie Smith, picked up a prize for her novel **The Autograph Man.**

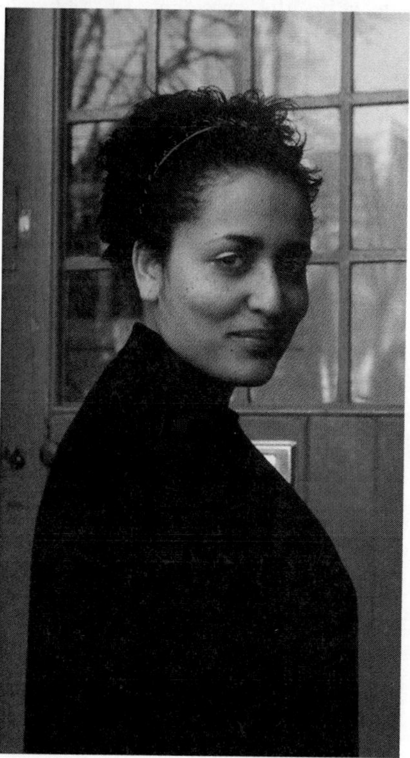

A surprising feature of the 2003 Booker short list, comprising six novels, was the absence of well-known names. Books by Martin Amis, J.M. Coetzee (*see* NOBEL PRIZES), Peter Carey, Graham Swift, and Melvyn Bragg all remained in the discard pile. Margaret Atwood's grim dystopian science fiction *Oryx and Crake* (2002), about the last man alive, was the only novel by a well-established author to make the short list. The bookmakers' favourite was *Brick Lane* by first-time novelist Monica Ali, about a young Bangladeshi woman who moves to London's East End for an arranged marriage. Ali's exploration of the hardships of immigrant life in England won her a place on the *Granta* list of best young novelists. Another newcomer was Clare Morrall, a music teacher in her 50s who had been writing for years before the tiny Birmingham publisher Tindal Street Press showed an interest in her *Astonishing Splashes of Colour.* Taking its name from J.M. Barrie's description of Peter Pan's Never-Never Land, the novel is about a female synesthete who perceives emotions as colours. Also on the list was English novelist Zoë Heller's second work, *Notes on a Scandal,* about an inner-city London pottery teacher and her affair with a precocious male pupil. The one South African writer on the list was Damon Galgut, whose novel *The Good Doctor* described the unraveling of a physician raised in apartheid South Africa when he attempts to carve out a life for himself at a rural hospital. For Julie Wheelwright at *The Independent,* the novel contained "echoes of Doris Lessing, Nadine Gordimer and Joseph Conrad, all of whom have written with an exacting emotional precision about the European's place in Africa."

Mirroring the trend established by the Booker Prize, the Orange Prize for Fiction, worth £30,000 and open only to women, was won by a relatively unknown novelist writing on American themes. American Valerie Martin upset three million-selling authors—Donna Tartt, Zadie Smith (*see* BIOGRAPHIES), and Carol Shields (*see* OBITUARIES)—with her novel *Property,* about slavery in 19th-century Louisiana. Unlike Tartt and Smith, whose works were popular for their wizardry with language, Martin wrote spare prose noted for its universality. The Egyptian novelist Ahdaf Soueif, who headed the judges, said, "Exuberance in a novel is a wonderful quality. *Property* is the opposite of exuberant—but the great quality of this book is its fairness." Discussing Tartt's failure to scoop the prize with her long-awaited second novel, *The Little Friend* (2002), Anita Brookner noted that tastes had changed since Tartt's debut in 1992: "The aftermath of recent and indeed ongoing terrorist attacks has had a strange but observable effect, namely to divert attention from fiction to reality, so that hitherto addictive readers feel a certain impatience with fictional diversions." Brookner credited this trend with creating "a readership less indulgent of extravagant effects" of the sort produced by writers like Tartt. Canadian writer Shields was short-listed for her acclaimed novel *Unless* (2002). Two contenders with distinctly British themes were Anne Donovan and Shena Mackay. Donovan's *Buddha Da* (2002) described the experiences of a Glaswegian housepainter turned Buddhist. Mackay's *Heligoland,* a compassionate take on aging bohemians in the London suburbs, was lauded for its "intense and exotic Englishness, and its delicate, pre-modern feel."

While many were surprised that Smith's *The Autograph Man* (2002) failed to win the Orange Prize, some were critical of its winning the £4,000 *Jewish Quarterly* Wingate Literary Prize for Fiction. Smith's novel portrays an obsessive autograph collector whose Jewish and Chinese roots intermingle with London's multicultural tapestry. Sir Jeremy Isaacs, the chairman of the judging panel, praised Smith for creating an "entertainingly contemporary tale" of a hero who "swims in the swirl of London's multi-racial mix and match, and somehow stays Jewish." Some other panel members, however, showed less enthusiasm, claiming that Smith lacked "real interest or engagement" with Jewish themes. Matthew Reisz, editor of the *Jewish Quarterly,* said, "A lot of people found the Jewish element rather offensive, and felt that she had used the Kabbalah in a rather Madonna-ish, modish way." Boyd Tonkin, literary editory of *The Independent,* noted that despite the criticism, *The Autograph Man* assured Smith's position "as the literary empress of multicultural Britain." Less controversial was the winner of the *Jewish Quarterly* Wingate nonfiction prize, also worth £4,000. This went to *Defying Hitler* (published in English translation in 2002), a memoir of growing up in interwar Germany by the journalist and historian Sebastian Haffner, who died in 1999. Haffner's manuscript was discovered and published by his son.

For the first time in the 14-year history of the British Book Awards, the general public was invited to join members of the publishing industry in choosing the year's winners. The result of a strong telephone vote from across Britain for the award's Book of the Year category suggested the importance of politics in the public's literary taste. A book by Michael Moore (*see* BIOGRAPHIES), *Stupid White Men* (U.K., 2002), a scathing indictment of the Bush administration, beat favourites such as the 2002 Booker Prize winner, Yann Martel's *Life of Pi* (2001), Ian McEwan's *Atonement* (2001), and footballer Roy Keane's autobiography, *Keane* (2002), the top-selling sports book of the year. The award's organizer, Merric Davidson, called Moore's triumph "a very strong anti-war vote." In his acceptance speech Moore claimed that his U.S. publisher, HarperCollins, had shelved the book in the aftermath of the Sept. 11, 2001, attacks when he refused to rewrite large sections that were considered unpatriotic and to tone down his attack on the president. (A lobbying campaign by American librarians eventually persuaded HarperCollins to relent and publish the book.) Penguin, which purchased the book's U.K. rights, published it in paperback in October 2002 and subsequently reported sales of more than one million copies.

The race leading up to the presentation of the Whitbread Book Awards was watched with particular interest, as two of the five finalists for the top prize, Book of the Year, were husband and wife: playwright and novelist Michael Frayn and biographer Claire Tomalin. In the end, judges favoured Tomalin's book, *Samuel Pepys: The Unequalled Self* (2002), about the naval administrator, seducer, and political turncoat whose famous diaries illuminate 1660s London. Tonkin of *The Independent* felt that Tomalin's intimate study of Pepys's personal and professional life had contemporary relevance: "In an age when public life is as confused as ever about the boundaries of personal and political behaviour, Tomalin's account of a full life allows us to understand these contradictions."

In nonfiction, history and biography continued to dominate review pages, if not the best-seller lists. The year 2003 saw the usual proliferation of volumes on British monarchs, politicians, scientists, adventurers, earls, and rogues. David Starkey's *Six Wives: The Queens of Henry VIII* was popular with readers for its high drama and entertainment value, but Kathryn Hughes in the *Literary Review* complained that Starkey was one of many historians suffering from a "tendency to see history as a frock-coated version of the present." Edgar Vincent's *Nelson: Love & Fame* was hailed by the *Daily Telegraph* as "the best modern biography of Britain's greatest admiral." The 20th century, and in particular World War II, also endured as a popular topic. Roy Jenkins's acclaimed volume *Churchill* (2001) was honoured as the Biography of the Year at the 2003 British Book Awards. Russia, whether tsarist or Soviet, similarly remained one of Britain's most fashionable obsessions. Perhaps the weightiest biography to be commended was T.J. Binyon's *Pushkin* (2002), which beat Tomalin's study of Pepys to win the £30,000 Samuel Johnson Prize for nonfiction. The first English-language study of the Russian poet's life in more than 60 years, *Pushkin* was regarded in academic circles as a monumental occasion. Binyon, a 63-year-old Oxford don, was praised by fellow Russianists for having avoided the pitfalls of sensationalism and redressed some of the myths surrounding the life of the great poet. MP Michael Portillo, one of the judges on the Johnson Prize panel, described Binyon's work as "the product of the author's years of dedication to his subject."

In the genre of children's fiction, Madonna stole the media limelight with the simultaneous release of her book *The English Roses* in 30 languages. This was the first of Madonna's projected five children's books, all of which were intended to illustrate some of the moral lessons she claimed to have discovered in the mystical teachings of the Kabbala. Meanwhile, the success of J.K. Rowling's Harry Potter series continued to break publishing-industry records. Rowling's latest installment, *Harry Potter and the Order of the Phoenix,* was published with two different covers, one for children and one for adults not wanting to be seen reading a children's book. At the time of its release, 8.5 million copies had been printed, and international sales of

(continued on page 224)

WORLD LITERARY PRIZES 2003

All prizes are annual and were awarded in 2003 unless otherwise stated. Currency equivalents as of July 1, 2003, were as follows: €1 = $1.158; £1 = $1.663; Can$1 = $0.741; ¥1 = $0.008; SKr 1 = $0.126; and DKr 1 = $0.156.

Nobel Prize for Literature

Awarded since 1901; included in the behest of Alfred Nobel, who specified a prize for those who "shall have produced in the field of literature the most outstanding work in an ideal direction." The prizewinners are selected in October by the Swedish Academy and receive the award on December 10 in Stockholm. Prize: a gold medal and an award that varies from year to year; in 2003 the award was SKr 10,000,000.

J.M. Coetzee (South Africa)

International IMPAC Dublin Literary Award

First awarded in 1996, this is the largest international literary prize; it is open to books written in any language. The award is a joint initiative of Dublin City Council, the Municipal Government of Dublin City, and the productivity-improvement company IMPAC. It is administered by Dublin City Public Libraries. Prize: €100,000, of which 25% goes to the translator if the book was not written in English, and a Waterford crystal trophy. The awards are given at Dublin Castle in May or June.

My Name Is Red by Orhan Pamuk, translated from the Turkish by Erdağ Göknar

Neustadt International Prize for Literature

Established in 1969 and awarded biennially by the University of Oklahoma and *World Literature Today*. Novelists, poets, and dramatists are equally eligible. Prize: $50,000, a replica of an eagle feather cast in silver, and a certificate.

Álvaro Mutis (Colombia), awarded in 2002

Commonwealth Writers Prize

Established in 1987 by the Commonwealth Foundation. In 2003 there was one award of £10,000 for the best book submitted and an award of £3,000 for the best first book. In each of the four regions of the Commonwealth, two prizes of £1,000 are awarded: one for the best book and one for the best first book.

Best Book	*The Polished Hoe* by Austin Clarke (Canada)
Best First Book	*Haweswater* by Sarah Hall (U.K.)
Regional winners—Best Book	
Africa	*The Other Side of Silence* by André Brink (South Africa)
Caribbean & Canada	*The Polished Hoe* by Austin Clarke (Canada)
Eurasia	*Spies* by Michael Frayn (U.K.)
Southeast Asia & South Pacific	*Of a Boy* (U.S. title, *What the Birds See*) by Sonya Hartnett (Australia)

Booker Prize

Established in 1969, sponsored by Booker McConnell Ltd. and, beginning in 2002, the Man Group; administered by the National Book League in the U.K. Awarded to the best full-length novel written by a citizen of the Commonwealth or the Republic of Ireland and published in the U.K. during the 12 months ending September 30. Prize: £50,000.

Vernon God Little by DBC Pierre (Australian-born Irish)

Whitbread Book of the Year

Established in 1971. The winners of the Whitbread Book Awards for Poetry, Biography, Novel, and First Novel as well as the Whitbread Children's Book of the Year each receive £5,000, and the winner of the Whitbread Book of the Year prize receives an additional £25,000. Winners are announced in January of the year following the award.

Samuel Pepys: The Unequalled Self by Claire Tomalin (2002 award)

Orange Prize for Fiction

Established in 1996. Awarded to a work of published fiction written by a woman in English and published in the U.K. during the 12 months ending March 31. Prize: £30,000.

Property by Valerie Martin (U.S.)

PEN/Faulkner Award

The PEN/Faulkner Foundation each year recognizes the best published works of fiction by contemporary American writers. Named for William Faulkner, the PEN/Faulkner Award was founded by writers in 1980 to honour their peers and is now the largest juried award for fiction in the U.S. Prize: $15,000.

The Caprices by Sabina Murray

Pulitzer Prizes in Letters and Drama

Begun in 1917, awarded by Columbia University, New York City, on the recommendation of the Pulitzer Prize Board for books published in the previous year. Five categories in Letters are honoured: Fiction, Biography, and General Non-Fiction (authors of works in these categories must be American citizens); History (the subject must be American history); and Poetry (for original verse by an American author). The Drama prize is for "a distinguished play by an American author, preferably original in its source and dealing with American life." Prize: $10,000 in each category.

Fiction	*Middlesex* by Jeffrey Eugenides
Biography	*Master of the Senate* by Robert A. Caro
Poetry	*Moy Sand & Gravel* by Paul Muldoon
History	*An Army at Dawn: The War in North Africa, 1942–1943* by Rick Atkinson
General Non-Fiction	*"A Problem from Hell": America and the Age of Genocide* by Samantha Power
Drama	*Anna in the Tropics* by Nilo Cruz

National Book Awards

Awarded since 1950 by the National Book Foundation, a consortium of American publishing groups. Categories have varied, beginning with three—Fiction, Nonfiction, and Poetry—swelling to 22 awards in 1983, and returning to four (the initial three plus Young People's Literature) in 2001. Prize: $10,000 and a crystal sculpture.

Fiction	*The Great Fire* by Shirley Hazzard
Nonfiction	*Waiting for Snow in Havana* by Carlos Eire
Poetry	*The Singing* by C.K. Williams

Frost Medal

Awarded annually since 1930 by the Poetry Society of America for distinguished lifetime service to American poetry.

Lawrence Ferlinghetti

Governor General's Literary Awards

Canada's premier literary awards. Prizes are given in 14 categories altogether: Fiction, Poetry, Drama, Translation, Nonfiction, and Children's Literature (Text and Illustration), each in English and French. Established in 1937. Prize: Can$15,000.

Fiction (English)	*Elle* by Douglas Glover
Fiction (French)	*La Maison étrangère* by Élise Turcotte
Poetry (English)	*Kill-Site* by Tim Lilburn
Poetry (French)	*Lignes aériennes* by Pierre Nepveu

Griffin Poetry Prize

Established in 2001 and administered by the Griffin Trust for Excellence in Poetry, the award honours first-edition books of poetry published during the preceding year. Prize: Can$40,000 each for the two awards.

Canadian Award	*Concrete and Wild Carrot* by Margaret Avison
International Award	*Moy Sand and Gravel* by Paul Muldoon (Northern Ireland)

Büchner Prize

Georg-Büchner-Preis. Awarded for a body of literary work in the German language. First awarded in 1923; now administered by the German Academy for Language and Literature. Prize: €40,000.

Alexander Kluge (Germany)

Hooft Prize

P.C. Hooftprijs. The Dutch national prize for literature, established in 1947. Prize: €35,000.

H.H. ter Balkt for poetry

Nordic Council Literary Prize

Established in 1961. Selections are made by a 10-member jury from among original works first published in Danish, Norwegian, or Swedish during the past two years or other Nordic languages (Finnish, Faroese, Sami, etc.) during the past four years. Prize: DKr 350,000.

Revbensstäderna by Eva Ström (Sweden)

Prix Goncourt

Prix de l'Académie Goncourt. First awarded in 1903 from the estate of French literary figure Edmond Huot de Goncourt, to memorialize him and his brother, Jules. Prize: €10.

La Maîtresse de Brecht by Jacques-Pierre Amette

Prix Femina

Established in 1904. The awards for works "of imagination" are announced by an all-women jury in the categories of French fiction, fiction in translation, and nonfiction. Announced in October together with the Prix Médicis. Prize: Not stated (earlier the award was F 5,000 [about $690]).

French Fiction	*Le Complexe de Di* by Dai Sijie

Cervantes Prize for Hispanic Literature

Premio Cervantes. Established in 1976 and awarded for a body of work in the Spanish language. Announced in December and awarded the following April. Prize: €90,000.

Gonzalo Rojas (Chile)

Planeta Prize

Premio Planeta de Novela. Established in 1951 by the Planeta Publishing House for the best unpublished, original novel in Spanish. Awarded in Barcelona in October. Prize: €600,000 and publication by Planeta.

El baile de la Victoria by Antonio Skármeta (Chile)

Camões Prize

Premio Luis da Camões da Literatura. Established in 1988 by the governments of Portugal and Brazil to honour a "representatative" author writing in the Portuguese language. Prize: $100,000.

Rubem Fonseca (Brazil)

Russian Booker Prize

Awarded since 1992, the Russian Booker Prize has sometimes carried the names of various sponsors—e.g., Smirnoff in 1997–2001. In 2002 it was underwritten in part by the Yukos Oil Co. and called the Booker/Open Russia Literary Prize. Awards: $12,500 for the winner; $1,000 for each finalist.

Beloye na chyornom ("White on Black") by Rubén González Gallego

Naguib Mahfouz Medal for Literature

Established in 1996 and awarded for the best contemporary novel published in Arabic. The winning work is translated into English and published in Cairo, London, and New York. Prize: $1,000 and a silver medal.

Wikalat Atiya ("Atiya's Agency") by Khairi Shalabi

Jun'ichirō Tanizaki Prize

Tanizaki Jun'ichirō Shō. Established in 1965 to honour the memory of novelist Jun'ichirō Tanizaki. Awarded annually to a Japanese author for an exemplary literary work. Prize: ¥1,000,000 and a trophy.

Yōko Tawada for *Yōgisha no yakōressha* ("Suspect on the Night Train")

Ryūnosuke Akutagawa Prize

Akutagawa Ryūnosuke Shō. Established in 1935 and now sponsored by the Association for the Promotion of Japanese Literature, the prize is awarded in January and June for the best serious work of fiction by a promising new Japanese writer published in a magazine or journal. Prize: ¥1,000,000 and a commemorative gift.

"Shoppai doraibu" ("Salty Drive") by Tamaki Daidō

"Hariganemushi" ("The Hairworm") by Man'ichi Yoshimura

Mao Dun Literary Award

Established in 1981 to honour contemporary Chinese novels and named after novelist Shen Yanbing (1896–1981), whose nom de plume was Mao Dun; awarded every five years. Latest awards were announced on Oct. 12, 2000 (the same day as the Nobel Prize for Literature).

Jueze ("Hard Choice") by Zhang Ping

Chang hen ge (2000; "Song of Everlasting Sorrow") by Wang Anyi

Chen'ai luo ding (1999; "When Dust Settles") by Ah Lai

Nanfang you jiamu ("Fine Tree Possessed in the Southland") and *Buye zhi hou* ("Delightful Marquis to Break Drowsiness"), from *Charen sanbuqu* ("Trilogy of Tea Men") by Wang Xufeng

(continued from page 222)
the whole series were estimated at more than 200 million. A quieter but no-less-worthy addition to children's fiction was the winner of the *Guardian* Children's Fiction Prize, Mark Haddon's *The Curious Incident of the Dog in the Night-Time,* about a 15-year-old boy with Asperger syndrome (a neurobiological disorder related to autism) who investigates the death of a neighbour's dog. Julia Eccleshare, chair of the prize's judging panel, reported some welcome trends in the genre: "Authors are addressing contemporary family issues realistically but reassuringly, with boys emerging as sensitive characters in their own right rather than as stereotypes in the shadow of more assertive girls." Other books addressing social issues included Michael Morpurgo's latest book, *Cool!* (2002), about a boy in a coma. Morpurgo, the author of more than 90 books, was named Britain's third children's laureate. He said he would spend his time touring teacher-training colleges, schools, and libraries, "simply telling stories."

Chris McManus's *Right Hand, Left Hand* (2002), an exploration into asymmetry as it appears in molecular biology, physics, chemistry, culture, and the cosmos, was suggestive of a trend in which serious scientists tried to reach out to a broader public. McManus, a professor of psychology and medical education at University College London, drew from such diverse sources as anthropology, the notebooks of artist Leonardo da Vinci, and particle physics, to consider questions such as Are left-handed people cognitively different? and Why do tornadoes spin counterclockwise in the Northern Hemisphere? The book won the 2003 Aventis Prize (£10,000) for the best popular-science book. (CAROL PEAKER)

United States. A look at the fiction that appeared in hardcover in 2003 revealed a highly unusual situation. Although a number of fine novels were published, short fiction really took centre stage.

To make things even odder, foremost among short-story collections were a number of reprints that included more than a century of stories. First, there was John Updike's substantial volume titled *The Early Stories, 1953–1975,* with 103 stories. Alongside this stood science-fiction and fantasy master Ray Bradbury's *Bradbury Stories: 100 of His Most Celebrated Tales.* A third collection was *The Stories of Richard Bausch,* an impressive 600-page retrospective by the Virginia story writer—a decade and more younger than either Bradbury or Updike—who (in the eyes of a number of critics) filled the gap left among American realists by the death in 1992 of Richard Yates.

A master of the genre story, Californian Ursula K. Le Guin brought out *Changing Planes,* a collection of whimsical tales that was a charming, but not major, work. Montana writer William Kittredge signed in with a selection of his short fiction, *The Best Short Stories of William Kittredge,* which contained some powerful stories but not enough of them to raise his reputation to more than that of still a contender. The idiosyncratic *Ladies and Gentlemen, the Original Music of the Hebrew Alphabet and Weekend in Mustara* (2002) by New Jersey writer Curt Leviant contained two novellas. With intense, lyrical prose, Stuart Dybek tied together a novel in stories under the title *I Sailed with Magellan.*"Nothing's more natural than sky. . . . From here railroad tracks look like stitching that binds the city together. If shadows can be trusted, the buildings are growing taller. From up here, gliding, it's clear there's a design: the gaps of streets and alleys are for the expansion of shadow the way lines in a sidewalk allow for the expansion of pavement in heat."

From a younger generation came a generous volume, *Collected Stories* by David Leavitt. A still younger group of writers included Montana writer Maile Meloy, with her award-winning story collection *Half in Love* (2002; "If you're white, and you're not rich or poor but somewhere in the middle, it's hard to have worse luck than to be born a girl on a ranch."), and Nell Freudenberger, with her impressive first collection *Lucky Girls.* Midwestern physician John Murray won a number of good notices for his first collection, *A Few Short Notes on Tropical Butterflies.*

"I am an American," Saul Bellow's narrator Augie March announced in 1953, "Chicago-born—Chicago, that somber city—and go at things as I have taught myself, free-style, and will make the record in my own way: first to knock, first admitted." In the kingdom of the novel, reprints also stood out, with a 50th anniversary edition of Saul Bellow's *The Adventures of Augie March* and a new Library of America volume of Bellow's work, *Novels, 1944–1953.* The latter contained Bellow's first two works of fiction, *Dangling Man* (1944) and *The Victim* (1947). Another half-century celebration was held for Ray Bradbury's genre classic *Fahrenheit 451,* also first published in 1953.

Many of the new novels produced by usually heavy hitters did not fare well with the press. Norman Rush's more than 700-page novel *Mortals,* set in Africa and peopled with CIA agents, revolutionaries, and wayward wives, was generally regarded as bloated and not worth the reader's commitment. *Cosmopolis* by Don DeLillo fared even worse, as did Joyce Carol Oates's *The Tattooed Girl.* Nobel laureate Toni Morrison's latest effort, *Love,* drew profoundly mixed responses. *Bay of Souls* by master novelist Robert Stone took a drubbing from reviewers that it probably did not deserve, but it did not go far in extending its author's reputation. Gail Godwin's *Evenings at Five* treated grief with dignity and stateliness—and went without much notice. Louise Erdrich's *The Master Butchers Singing Club* garnered some respectful reviews and some not so respectful.

Novels by writers without enormous reputations received somewhat better notice from reviewers. Kent Nelson's *Land That Moves, Land That Stands Still* was a much-appreciated work. It was set on a farm in South Dakota where a recently widowed woman tries to make a go of the difficult enterprise. In *Drop City* T. Coraghessan Boyle took his cast of characters to Alaska to work on a commune. Nicholson Baker set the reader down in rural New England for an ingenious series of morning meditations in *A Box of Matches.* Moving from the difficult streets of New York City to upstate New York in a major snowstorm, Scott Spencer's wonderfully obsessive *A Ship Made of Paper* entertained a number of reviewers. The domestic drama *Orchard* by Larry Watson won some respect from reviewers, but *King Bongo: A Novel of Havana,* the latest effort from West Coast writer Thomas Sanchez, did not.

Michael Mewshaw's intelligent thriller *Shelter from the Storm,* an engrossing story set in Central Asia, was admired by many. After a long hiatus Stephen Goodwin published *Breaking Her Fall,* an admirable engagement with the problems of contemporary fatherhood, single parenthood, and everyday urban life. Cristina García, author of the well-received novel *The Agüero Sisters* (1997), did not find as much of an audience for her novel *Monkey Hunting. The Namesake,* the first novel by Pulitzer Prize winner Jhumpa Lahiri, was published to faintly positive reviews. Valerie Martin won the British-

American Valerie Martin took Britain's women-only Orange Prize for **Property**, *her powerfully imagined novel set in the antebellum South.*

sponsored Orange Prize for her antebellum *Property.* David Guterson drew some attention for *Our Lady of the Forest,* which concerned a Lourdes-like apparition in a rainforest in the U.S. Northwest.

Among books by serious writers at work on genre fiction, Walter Mosley's *Fear Itself,* a mystery that was set in Los Angeles black districts, was a crowd pleaser, as was *Dragon Bones,* the third of Lisa See's thrillers to be set in China, and Dan Brown's *The Da Vinci Code*. Two reprints of novels originally published in 1966 caught readers' attention: Joseph McElroy's experimental *A Smuggler's Bible* and Charles Wright's *The Wig,* set in the Harlem district of New York City.

Curiously enough, the nonfiction published in 2003 was equal to, if not more compelling than, most of the fiction. In *Reporting the Universe,* the book version of four Harvard lectures by novelist E.L. Doctorow, he stated that "the writer will never know if his work will flash a light from his own time and place across borders and through the ages. His own time and place clutching and pulling at his feet of clay every day of his working life, he will know how faint a light it is, and how easily doused." Norman Mailer offered a similar portrait of the prose artist in *The Spooky Art: Some Thoughts on Writing,* a compilation of lectures, essays, interviews, and notebook entries from the past few decades. Mailer's *Why Are We at War?* on the subject of the U.S. intervention in the Middle East seemed less effective than such narratives as *The Armies of the Night* (1968).

Vietnam veterans played a role in Maxine Hong Kingston's hybrid *The Fifth Book of Peace,* a mixture of fiction (portions of a novel she lost in the Oakland, Calif., fire at the beginning of the 1990s), history, sociology, and memoir, which read more cohesively than one might expect from its description. In *Dark Star Safari: Overland from Cairo to Cape Town* (U.K., 2002), Paul Theroux took the reader on an engrossing road, boat, and airplane trip down the length of Africa. Colson Whitehead, in *The Colossus of New York: A City in Thirteen Parts,* stayed home. In *Local Wonders: Seasons in the Bohemian Alps* (2002), poet Ted Kooser reflected on nature: "Thaw. It starts with the sun's thin breath on the face of a stone that's been trussed in a harness of wire and hung in the tines of a hay rake, the white chalk from the rock's cold face a powder that clouds the glistening film welling up out of the pores."

In *The Case of the Persevering Maltese,* Harry Mathews served up a collection of essays on literary subjects. Writers Flannery O'Connor, Thomas Merton, Dorothy Day, and Walker Percy made up the cast of Paul Elie's *The Life You Save May Be Your Own,* a study of four post-World War II Catholic writers. Psychiatrist and writer Robert Coles took a popular singer as his subject in *Bruce Springsteen's America.* Susan Sontag again addressed the subject of photography in *Regarding the Pain of Others.* Among works of literary criticism, *Reading New York,* John Tytell's mélange of personal history, literary history, and critique, stood out.

Literary figures served as subjects for a number of new biographies, among them Geoffrey Wolff's refreshingly composed *The Art of Burning Bridges: A Life of John O'Hara* and Blake Bailey's *A Tragic Honesty: The Life and Work of Richard Yates.* Brian Herbert wrote about his father, the well-known science-fiction writer, in *Dreamer of Dune: The Biography of Frank Herbert.* Deirdre Bair presented the life of one of the major visionaries of the 20th century in *Jung. Her Dream of Dreams: The Rise and Triumph of Madam C.J. Walker* was novelist Beverly Lowry's portrait of the first black female millionaire businesswoman in the U.S. Scholar Carol Loeb Shloss produced *Lucia Joyce: To Dance in the Wake,* a biography of James Joyce's only daughter.

A number of fiction writers and poets examined their own past. Foremost among these efforts was Joan Didion's treatment of herself and her native California in *Where I Was From.* Poet Gerald Stern treated his life in New Jersey and the Northeast in *What I Can't Bear Losing: Notes from a Life.* In his memoir *First Loves,* Ted Solotaroff wrote about loss and literature. Merrill Joan Gerber produced *Gut Feelings: A Writer's Truths and Minute Inventions.* Sue Miller told about an ailing parent in *The Story of My Father.* In *Do I Owe You Something?* Mewshaw wrote about his encounters as a young writer with the talented and the famous, among them Graham Greene, Robert Penn Warren, James Jones, and Anthony Burgess.

Dan Brown's page-turner **The Da Vinci Code** *involved cryptographers, symbologists, secret religious societies, and, of course, murder.*

"They buried their children and moved on. Gravestones at the foot of Register Cliff in eastern Wyoming give poignant reminder of a scene reenacted many times on the Oregon Trail. . . . It was a common tragedy as pioneers struggled to make new lives for themselves, but it was an old scene in the West. . . . Twelve or thirteen thousand years before the Oregon Trail, parents buried two children on a tributary of the Yellowstone River." Historian Colin G. Calloway in his huge volume *One Vast Winter Count: The Native American West Before Lewis and Clark* illuminated a little-known history of the American West. Novelist Gore Vidal turned in an interesting study of the ideas of the Founding Fathers in *Inventing a Nation.* Former head of the American History Museum at the Smithsonian Roger G. Kennedy focused on *Mr. Jefferson's Lost Cause: Land, Farmers, Slavery, and the Louisiana Purchase.* Stephen W. Sears looked at *Gettysburg.*

American poets in 2003 worked as productively as ever. In *Lay Back the Darkness,* Edward Hirsch used classical motifs to dramatize contemporary emotions: "I listened so the goddess could charm my mind/ against the ravishing sunlight, the lord of noon/ and I could stroll through country unharmed/ toward the prowling straits of Scylla and Charybdis,/ but I was unprepared for the Siren lolling/ on a bed in a dirty room above a tavern." Carol Muske-Dukes, in *Sparrow,* wrote elegiacally about her husband's absence: "After his death I kept an illusion before me: that I would find the key to him, the answer, in the words of a play that he'd put to heart years earlier." *Alabanza: New and Selected Poems, 1982–2002* made the work of Martín Espada available to new audiences.

Carolyn Forché signed in with a new volume of work titled *Blue Hour,* and Gerald Stern contributed *American Sonnets* (2002). *Far Side of the Earth* was Tom Sleigh's offering. Maxine Kumin published *Bringing Together: Uncollected Early Poems, 1958–1988.*

The 2003 PEN/Faulkner Award went to Sabina Murray, for her short-story collection *The Caprices* (2002). The PEN/Malamud Award to honour "excellence in the art of the short story" was divided between veteran short-story writer Barry Hannah and neophyte Maile Meloy. The Pulitzer Prize for fiction went to Jeffrey Eugenides for his novel *Middlesex* (2002); the Pulitzer for poetry was awarded to Paul Muldoon (*see* BIOGRAPHIES) for *Moy Sand and Gravel* (2002); and Robert A. Caro's continuing portrait of Lyndon B. Johnson, *Master of the Senate* (2002), won the award in biography. Shirley Hazzard took the National Book Award for fiction for her novel *The Great Fire,* and C.K. Williams won in poetry for his volume *The Singing.*

The year 2003 also witnessed the passing of three writers, short-story writer Leonard Michaels (*see* OBITUARIES), novelist and essayist Victor Perera, and science-fiction writer Hal Clement (*see* OBITUARIES). (ALAN CHEUSE)

Canada. Growing up in the middle decades of the 20th century, or failing to do so, was a common theme in many English-language Canadian novels in 2003. Ann-Marie MacDonald's *The Way the Crow Flies* presented Madeleine, the youngest daughter of an Ontario military family, coming of age in a milieu tainted by a notorious murder trial; Frances Itani's *Deafening* followed a deaf girl's entrance into maturity, through school, marriage, separation, and war; and the narrator of Barbara Gowdy's *The Romantic* was a girl entering her adult years mesmerized by her infatuation with a childhood sweetheart who no longer loves her. The teenagers depicted in Lynn Coady's *Saints of Big Harbour* (2002) struggled to maintain their dignity in a small-minded rural community, and in a similar vein, Douglas Coupland's *Hey Nostradamus!* burrowed into the many-layered consequences, for students and adults alike, of a high-school shooting. Jack Hodgins transversed the spaces, geographic and psychological, between children and parents in *Distance.*

Barbara Gowdy examined the effects of early experience on adulthood in **The Romantic.**

John Bemrose's *The Island Walkers* tracked the painful descent of the Walkers, an Ontario family that had fallen from grace in the bumptious 1960s. Not falling was the primary concern in Steven Galloway's *Ascension,* which examined the stretch of a high-wire artist's life, culminating with a balancing act above the abyss between the World Trade Center's twin towers; in Lesley Choyce's *Sea of Tranquility,* an island community struggled to preserve its lifeline, the ferry to the mainland. In *Friday Water* Linda Rogers confronted the subtle ambiguities beneath the seemingly perfect surface of one woman's life, and from a different angle Elizabeth Hay, in *Garbo Laughs,* used the black-and-white simplicities of classic movies as foils for the complex actuality of one woman's despair. Douglas Glover's daring *Elle* adventured between the glories of old France and the excitement of the new; M.G. Vassanji's protagonist in *The In-Between World of Vikram Lall* was caught between the jubilation of independence in Kenya and the shame of political corruption; and the young woman in Edeet Ravel's *Ten Thousand Lovers,* a linguistics student in Israel, found herself torn between principles and desire. *Oryx and Crake,* published in the U.S. in 2002, was Margaret Atwood's alternately brooding and humorous, but always inventive, cautionary dystopia.

Many short-story collections explored the nuances of unreality, whether expressed in the conjunction of the minimal and the absurd, as in M.A.C. Farrant's *Darwin Alone in the Universe,* or in the brief, intense tales, innocent and dangerous as kittens at play, in *Kilter: 55 Fictions* by John Gould. Judith McCormack, in *The Rule of Last Clear Chance,* juxtaposed law, luck, and lust and their deceiving talismans; Michael Redhill investigated obscure corners of character, opportunity, and temptation in *Fidelity: Short Fiction,* and Jacqueline Baker, in her first collection, searched for meaning in *A Hard Witching and Other Stories,* set amid the pale, mysterious Sand Hills of Saskatchewan. Delusions of change led exiles from a mining town in Newfoundland back to Black

Rock and the deep pits of their dreams in Michael Crummey's new and expanded edition of *Flesh and Blood,* originally published in 1998.

Poets and their works were as eccentric as ever, ranging from George McWhirter's aptly titled *The Book of Contradictions* (2002) to the long-striding lines of Tim Lilburn's *Kill-Site,* to Di Brandt's impassioned protests against environmental degradation in *Now You Care,* and to Lynn Crosbie's linked poems *Missing Children,* about forbidden relationships and their consequences. In his debut collection, *Nothing Fell Today but Rain,* Evan Jones approached life's vagaries with detached optimism; in *Loop* Anne Simpson carried on creatively around life's many bends; and in *Crowd of Sounds* Adam Sol revealed the infinite beauties of the aural experience. Dennis Lee in *Un* conducted a series of seriously playful excursions into the ambivalences of the universe. Tim Bowling explored a young man's anguished love for his father in *The Witness Ghost,* in counterpoint to Judith Fitzgerald's poignant *Adagios Quartet: Iphigenia's Song,* which traced a daughter's struggle against her own fate and that of her father.

(ELIZABETH RHETT WOODS)

Other Literature in English. In 2003 national, regional, and international award-winning achievement was the norm for writers and writing in English from sub-Saharan Africa, Australia, and New Zealand. Chief among such developments was the announcement in October that the noted South African novelist, essayist, critic, and translator J.M. Coetzee had won the Nobel Prize for Literature. (*See* NOBEL PRIZES.) The Swedish Academy recognized the author, who late in 2003 released a collection of genre pieces entitled *Elizabeth Costello,* for his role as a "scrupulous doubter, ruthless in his criticism of the cruel rationalism and cosmetic morality of Western civilization." Following close behind Coetzee was Australian-born DBC Pierre, who garnered the Man Booker Prize for his first novel, *Vernon God Little.* Prominent veteran author and South African André Brink was a double winner with his latest fiction, *The Other Side of Silence* (2002), receiving both the Alan Paton Award for Fiction and the Commonwealth Writers Prize for the best book (Africa region). Helon Habila won the Commonwealth Writers award in the Africa region for the best first book with *Waiting for an Angel* (2002), the story of a young journalist during the turbulent era of military rule in Nigeria. Similar themes of violence and terror were the subject of South African-born Lewis DeSoto's first novel, *A Blade of Grass.* Nigerian-born Chimamanda Ngozi Adichie made an equally impressive fiction debut with *Purple Hibiscus,* the story of a young woman's awakening at a time when her family and her country are also on the verge of significant change. In *Underground People* (2002), eminent South African critic, novelist, and essayist Lewis Nkosi exposed the underside of a fictional revolutionary movement during the last years of apartheid. Important nonfiction works included Martin Dugard's *Into Africa: The Epic Adventures of Stanley & Livingston;* Aidan Hartley's release *The Zanzibar Chest;* and Es'kia Mphahlele's collected essays and public addresses, *Es'kia* (2002).

Australia made its mark internationally with new fiction from established authors Janette Turner Hospital (*Due Preparations for the Plague,* a timely political thriller and winner of the Queensland Premier's Literary Award) and Peter Carey (*My Life as a Fake*). Other works of note included Patricia Mackintosh's *The Devil's Madness,* a novel set in Australia in the 1960s, and Sonya Hartnett's second novel for adults, *Of a Boy* (2002; also published as *What the Birds See*), winner of the Commonwealth Writers Prize for the best book (Southeast Asia and South Pacific region).

In neighbouring New Zealand, the annual Montana New Zealand Book Awards, the country's most prestigious honours for contemporary literature, recognized authors in several categories representing three genres. The Montana Medal for nonfiction went to Michael Cooper for his *Wine Atlas of New Zealand,* and Auckland writer Stephanie Johnson captured the Deutz Medal for Fiction with her novel *The Shag Incident.* Selected from 10 finalists, poet Glenn Colquhoun received the Montana Readers' Choice Award for *Playing God* (2002); it was the first time a volume of poetry had won the prize. Paula Morris's *Queen of Beauty* (2002) was awarded the New Zealand Society of Authors Hubert Church Best First Book Award for fiction.

(DAVID DRAPER CLARK)

GERMANIC

German. The year 2003 saw the publication of *Jacobs Leiter,* the most ambitious work to date produced by Steffen Mensching, a resident of the former German Democratic Republic (GDR). An autobiographical novel, it ingeniously wove together German, Jewish, and American history and fact and fiction. In the plot sequence around which the novel is structured, the protagonist, a German author visiting New York City, purchases a library of 4,000 German books, most of which once belonged to German Jewish émigrés. The protagonist's curiosity about the books' former owners leads him to a wide-ranging exploration of personal histories. In following this resulting process, the author connected the past and the present and Germany and the U.S. in a complex and surprising textual web.

With Messmers Reisen, *the prolific Martin Walser returned to a protagonist he had introduced in 1985.*

Siegfried Lenz's *Das Fundbüro* concerned an amiable young man working in the lost-and-found office of a major urban train station. The protagonist of the novel befriends a visiting foreign scholar and must decide how to respond when his new friend is attacked by hooligans. The book was a reflection on friendship, human decency, and the simple pleasures of life.

After her remarkably successful debut in *Sommerhaus, später* (1998), Judith Hermann offered *Nichts als Gespenster,* her eagerly awaited second collection of short stories. Like its predecessor, this collection featured stories written in laconic, elegant prose about young Berliners, mostly women, in their 30s and 40s. Hermann examined the problems of contemporary life, which she saw as characterized not so much by heartbreak and sorrow as by the human inability to engage in genuine emotion, particularly love. Georg M. Oswald's satiric novel *Im Himmel* dealt with an even younger group of people coming of age in the rich suburbs of Munich, where financial splendour was accompanied by spiritual squalour.

Two respected older writers published important collections in 2003. Martin Walser's *Messmers Reisen,* a sequel to *Messmers Gedanken* (1985), contained reflections on and aphorisms about contemporary life written with a keen eye for paradox and a sharp ear for language. Christa Wolf's *Ein Tag im Jahr* was a large-scale literary-historical project, featuring a diary that Wolf kept yearly from 1960 to 2000 on September 27. As such, the diary covered most of the history of the former GDR, as well as that state's collapse and the reunification of Germany.

Ulla Hahn's novel *Unscharfe Bilder* and Uwe Timm's *Am Beispiel meines Bruders* were attempts by both writers to come to terms with fictional or real German family histories during the past century. In Hahn's novel the protagonist discovers what she believes to be a picture of her father in an exhibition on the crimes of the German army during World War II. She confronts her father only to discover, after he has told his complicated story, that what had appeared clear and obvious in the black-and-white museum photograph is in fact ambiguous and hard to make out. Timm's memoir dealt with the story of his real-life brother, who at age 16 had volunteered for the SS (the elite corps of the Nazi Party) in World War II and had never returned home. Like Hahn's novel, this memoir dealt with the conflict between family loyalty and love on the one hand and justice and ethics on the other.

Septuagenarian Walter Kempowski's novel *Letzte Grüsse* was a sequel to his *Hundstage* (1988), and it brought back that book's protagonist, writer Alexander Sowtschick, to comment ironically and critically on the German literary world of 1989. The novel presented the German writer's dilemma between pleasing the reading public and pleasing the critical intelligentsia. Sowtschick dies on Nov. 9, 1989, while watching, on American television, pictures of the opening of the Berlin Wall.

Hans Joachim Schädlich's novel *Anders* was a sophisticated and laconic reflection on historical truth and literary fiction. Its protagonist is a researcher examining the lives of people whose real stories do not match the picture they like to present of themselves, including a left-liberal professor and Goethe specialist who as a young man was a member of the SS. The Austrian writer Raoul Schrott's novel *Tristan da Cunha, oder, Die Hälfte der Erde* centred on the tiny remote island of Tristan da Cunha in the South Atlantic and its effect on the lives of four people who land there; the novel addressed eternal issues such as the significance of geography and the concept of utopia.

Durs Grünbein's epic poem *Vom Schnee: oder, Descartes in Deutschland* dealt with the history of the great Enlightenment philosopher and his encounters with Germany. Like many of Grünbein's other poems, this one treated the Enlightenment and its antinomies; it revolved around a dialogue between Descartes, who distinguishes between mind and body, and his unschooled manservant, who resists that distinction. (STEPHEN BROCKMANN)

Netherlandic. In 2003 the Libris Literatuur Prijs went to Abdelkader Benali for his work *De langverwachte* (2002). Benali, who lived in The Netherlands from 1979, was born in 1975 in Ighazzazen, Mor. His humorous and incisive novel, about a family and its generational and cross-cultural differences, was light on its feet and beautifully written. It featured lovingly drawn characters who showed their ties to the past, their struggles with religious tradition, their appreciation for both their North African heritage and their present life in The Netherlands, and their dreams for the future.

The P.C. Hooftprijs for an entire oeuvre was presented to poet H.H. ter Balkt (who previously wrote under the pseudonym Habakuk II de Balker). Ter Balkt's early work had focused on the rewards and exigencies of farm life. He eschewed "poetic" language and academic poetry. His collection *Laaglandse hymnen* (published in three stages, starting in 1991) presented moments in Low Countries history, from the Stone Age to the present. It featured poems about wars and battles, sea voyages, artists, writers, politicians, industrialization, and—continuing a theme from his early work—nature. His tone ranged from deadly serious to light hearted and featured deceptively simple, direct language.

Tomas Ross received a third Golden Noose award for excellence in crime fiction, for his novel *De zesde mei,* which fictionalized the 2002 assassination of Dutch politician Pim Fortuyn. Both its controversial and daring subject matter—the assassination had traumatized the Dutch—and its compelling plot impressed the award's jury.

The Anna Bijns Prize, awarded to a writer with a "uniquely female voice," went to Helga Ruebsamen for her honest and loving portrayals of all sides of life. *Het lied en de waarheid* (1997; *The Song and the Truth,* 2000), told from the often-bewildered perspective of a young girl, described a Jewish family's move from the Dutch East Indies (present-day Indonesia) to The Netherlands at the start of World War II. The narrative offered insights into the role of perception and memory in family relationships.

(JOLANDA VANDERWAL TAYLOR)

Danish. In 2003 Danish writers focused on extraordinary individuals, lost worlds, and forgotten times as well as everyday events. Novelist Charlotte Kornerup's *I spejlet* depicted a young Johanne Luise Heiberg, the 19th-century grande dame of the Royal Theatre. In *Ambrosiuseventyret* Vibeke Arndal recreated the life of the brilliant 18th-century poet and composer Ambrosius Stub. Dorrit Willumsen's *Bruden fra Gent* drew a memorable portrait of Elizabeth of Habsburg, who in 1515, at age 13, made a political marriage to Christian II and eventually won him over. Ib Michael based his *Paven af Indien,* a poignant tale of the suffering of the Inca under colonialism, on an actual 17th-century manuscript in the Royal Library—a lengthy letter from the native Andean chronicler and artist Felipe Guamán Poma de Ayala to Philip III of Spain.

Memorable fictional characters and vivid settings also were evident in Naja Marie Aidt's *Balladen om Bianca* (2002) and in *Unn fra Stjernestene,* Hanne Marie Svendsen's story of two very different women living in hauntingly beautiful medieval Greenland. Iselin C. Hermann's *Der hvor månen ligger ned* (2002) and Jens Christian Grøndahl's *Et andet lys* (2002) dealt with women ending relationships.

In *Den ugudelige farce* (2002), Svend Åge Madsen challenged the reader by offering constant modification of each episode in his brain-damaged protagonist's life. Madsen explored the transcendent power of words in his "double novel," *De gode mennesker i Århus / Læselysten.* The stories in Merete Pryds

Helle's *Ti fingre fra eller til* (2002) ranged in style from straightforward narrative to fantasy. Contemporary life was the subject of both Camilla Christensen's *Jorden under Høje Gladsaxe* (2002) and Jan Sonnergaard's *Jeg er stadig bange for Caspar Michaël Petersen,* the final volume of a trilogy that began with *Radiator* (1997). In *Boks* (2002), John Bang Jensen left readers wondering whether he presented 19 different tales—ranging from brilliant psychoportraits to brief flights of fancy—or 19 scenes from a single work. The veteran writer Jytte Borberg focused on neighbours and strangers in *Alle steder og ingen steder.* Janina Katz offered a collection of poems on love and death, *Det syvende barn* (2002), and established playwright Astrid Saalbach scored a critical success with her rags-to-riches drama *Det kolde hjerte* (2002).

The Danish Booksellers Association awarded the Golden Laurels to Jakob Ejersbo, Hanne-Vibeke Holst claimed the Søren Gyldendal Prize, and Camilla Christensen took the Critics' Prize. Queen Margrethe II received the Hans Christian Andersen Medal for her illustrations of Andersen's *Snedronningen* (2000).

(LANAE HJORTSVANG ISAACSON)

Ib Michael presented the story of Inca suffering under colonial rule. He based his book on a 17th-century manuscript.

© Jerry Bauer

Norwegian. In 2003 the younger generation of up-and-coming authors affirmed its position in the ranks of Norwegian writers. Among those heralded as the *Blindern* (Oslo University) circle were Henrik Langeland, Mattis Øybø, and John Erik Riley. Langeland's best-selling novel *Wonderboy* depicted the hidden power structures of the publishing world. Øybø's thriller *Alle ting skinner,* which delved into deep philosophical questions, was acclaimed as an outstanding debut. Riley's travelogue *San Francisco* ably captured the ambivalence of many Norwegians toward the United States.

Sexual wounds and hang-ups dominated publications by other younger authors. Lars Ramslie's *Fatso,* about a lonely man in his 30s who obsesses about sex, was commended. Selma Lønning Aarø's *Vill ni åka mera?,* about the often-traumatic roots of sexual behaviour patterns, was nominated for the Brage Prize. Ari Behn's *Bakgård,* which concerned a young man's adventures in decadent gay artists' communities in Africa, became a best-seller.

Among several established authors who published well-received novels were Roy Jacobsen, whose *Frost,* a historical novel in the style of an Icelandic saga, was nominated for the Brage Prize and the 2004 Nordic Council Literature Prize; Per Petterson, whose *Ut og stjæle hester,* about a son's struggle to come to terms with his father and himself, was also nominated for the Brage Prize and awarded the Bokhandlerpris; Lars Saaby Christensen, whose *Maskeblomstfamilien* treated the dark dimensions of childhood; and Jostein Gaarder, whose *Appelsinpiken* was a youth novel that raised important existential questions. Critics praised Ingvar Ambjørnsen's bleak short-story collection *Delvis til stede.*

Karsten Alnæs was awarded the Brage Honorary Prize for his enormous contribution to Norwegian letters. His latest book, *Historien om Europa: Oppvåkning, 1300–1600,* the first of four projected volumes on Europe's history, was praised for its broad and well-written coverage. Inger Elisabeth Hansen was awarded the Brage Prize and nominated for the 2004 Nordic Council Literature Prize for *Trask: Forflytninger i tidas skitne fylde,* a politically engaged poetry collection that delved into war-torn areas. Åsne Seierstad published a second best-seller, *Hundre og én dag: en reportasjereise,* this time reporting from the war zone in Baghdad, Iraq, while controversy surrounded her first best-seller, *Bokhandleren i Kabul: et familiedrama* (2002), which was denounced by the bookseller featured in her book. Ingar Sletten Kolloen's momentous biography of Knut Hamsun, *Hamsun: Svermeren,* also instigated debate but was nominated for the Brage Prize.

(ANNE G. SABO)

Swedish. The 700th anniversary of the birth of St. Birgitta, Sweden's only saint and perhaps the best-known Swede of all time, was celebrated in 2003 with the publication of several books that asked: Was she an early feminist or a tough, pragmatic politician? The powerful language in her *Revelations,* which dramatically blended the religious and the worldly, made it possible for modern readers to judge for themselves.

The tension between past and present—as well as between abstract ideas and everyday experiences—also was at the heart of many other Swedish books of various genres. In *Stenmästaren* senior poet Folke Isaksson showed penetrating yet lyrical insight when he compared the contemporary poet's struggles to those of the medieval master stonemason.

In *Imago* Eva-Marie Liffner continued to counterpoise crime story and historical novel, a method she had initiated in her first novel, *Camera* (2001). *Imago* was set on the border between Denmark and Germany. One of its narratives followed a story of mid-20th-century wartime tensions between the two countries, while the other followed a contemporary connection to events revealed in the first story line.

The relationship between the individual and broader human history was a frequently recurring theme. In *Ravensbrück,* a skillful blend of documentary and fiction, Steve Sem-Sandberg depicted the life of Kafka's friend Czech journalist Milena Jesenská, which ended in Ravensbrück concentration camp in 1944. An international perspective reflected in the individual fate was central in works by established writers of Swedish descent, such as Romanian-born Gabriela Melinescu's *Hemma utomlands* and Greek-born Theodor Kallifatides' *En kvinna att älska.*

One of many impressive young authors to debut in 2003, Jonas Hassen Khemiri in *Ett öga rött* detailed a generational conflict in which an immigrant father's ideals of assimilation are not shared by his son, who can speak Swedish but prefers a sort of street slang that marks him as an outcast.

Sweden's relationship to the world at large was also a literary theme in 2003, when Swedes voted against monetary union with the rest of Europe. The questions writers raised concerned the nature of borders and what, in a deeper sense, divided people. (IMMI LUNDIN)

FRENCH

France. In France the literary sensation of 2003 was the proliferation of nonfictional laments for France's decline, testimony to a general malaise after U.S. actions in Iraq underlined France's weakening international clout. Two of these books rocketed to the best-seller list: *Adieu à la France qui s'en va* and *La France qui tombe.* In the former, Jean-Marie Rouart lyrically decried France's loss of faith, honour, and self-sacrifice, the noble qualities that he felt once underpinned France's glory. In the latter book, which was more of an economic analysis, Nicolas Baverez bemoaned France's bloated bureaucracy, failing finances, and loss of international relevance, all of which he saw as eroding France from within. This book's popularity, particularly among politicians, was considered a sign that the ruling class was finally beginning to understand French society's concerns for the future.

Jean-Marie Rouart regretted the fading of France's glory and the values that once distinguished his country.

The sense of loss that these books stressed on the national level also marked more personal nonfiction. This was expressed notably as loss of love in *L'Éclipse,* in which Serge Rezvani movingly described how his wife, afflicted with Alzheimer disease, had been slowly taken from him until he was left with but the shell of the lively, intelligent woman he now had to love from memory. Jérôme Garcin, in *Théâtre intime,* also discussed the loss of his wife but sought to palliate the pain of her death by remembering their first years together, as he followed her through the chaotic world of theatre. A similar attempt to recover a love lost to death was Clémence Boulouque's *Mort d'un silence,* in which the author strove to recapture her father, a famous judge who had committed suicide when accused of corruption. Boulouque tried not so much to prove her father's innocence as to depict the loving man nearly erased during the media's feeding frenzy over his alleged crimes, disgrace, and death.

The theme of loss, so prevalent in nonfiction, also permeated fiction. In Marc J. Bloch's *La Vie fractale,* the absent main character's loss of identity poses the question of what we can ever truly know about another. As the novel attempts to piece together the missing protagonist's personality through fictional interviews with those who knew him, the reader is confronted with contradictory information blurring the picture ever more as those interviewed ultimately reveal nothing but themselves. Régis Jauffret's *Univers, univers* also was experimental in its approach to the loss of identity. Its narrative frame was simple: a woman cooks as she awaits the visit of hated guests. Within this endlessly repeated framework, the woman, overwhelmed by her own meaninglessness, loses herself to assume a series of hypothetical lives as lovers, murderers, objects, animals, only to return unfailingly to the same scene of cooking and waiting.

Yasmina Reza's *Adam Haberberg* dealt with the loss of hope; the protagonist, a failed husband, father, and writer, is contemplating his own futility when he meets a woman whom he has not seen since high school, and she promptly invites him to her home. With Reza's characteristic lightness, this tale of hope for rejuvenation and happiness, flickering one last time before being snuffed, became a touching, even funny, demonstration of human inability to reverse damage wrought by time.

Though built on the same bleak theme of loss, several novels did nonetheless let hope triumph. In Tiphaine Samoyault's *Les Indulgences,* when a woman battered by death, most recently that of her best friend, runs away in an attempt to rediscover life, she learns to treat the living with the same indulgence she had been reserving for the dead.

Love also saved the protagonist of Christine Jordis's *La Chambre blanche;* the successful Camille is barely aware of her life's emptiness until she meets a man with whom she discovers true passion. Through sensuality Camille reaches an unsuspected spirituality within her that remains with her long after love has disappeared.

Unlike the main character in Reza's novel, the protagonist of Andreï Makine's *La Terre et le ciel de Jacques Dorme* does manage to turn back the hands of time when he returns to Siberia in search of traces of a story from his childhood spent in a Russian orphanage, where a woman told him of her love affair with a doomed World War II aviator. As the narrator looks for wreckage from the aviator's plane, the past and present mix with all the beauty of a love story heard long ago.

The Prix Goncourt was awarded to Jacques-Pierre Amette's *La Maîtresse de Brecht,* which was set in communist East Germany in 1948, when the Marxist playwright Bertolt Brecht returned from exile under the suspicious eyes of the secret police. The police provide him with a mistress who reports his every move, pretending to share his love despite her passion for the agent who recruited her. The Prix Femina went to Dai Sijie's *Le Complexe de Di,* the tale of the misadventures of China's first psychoanalyst, who attempts to win his fiancée's freedom by analyzing her neurotic judge. Hubert Mingarelli won the Prix Médicis for *Quatre soldats,* in which four lost soldiers from the Red Army flee Polish forces and learn the value of friendship in the process. Philippe Claudel won the Prix Renaudot for *Les Âmes grises,* which takes place during World War I, when the butchery on the Front is mirrored by the murder of a girl in a small village. Years later the policeman in charge of the investigation searches for the murderer, dredging up the horrors of the past. (VINCENT AURORA)

Canada. In French Canadian literature, 2003 was a fairly lacklustre year, but one phenomenon, Yann Martel, stood out. The globe-trotting Martel, whose parents were Montreal-based Canadian diplomats, won the Man Booker Prize in 2002 for his novel *Life of Pi* (2001). Bilingual French Canadians responded enthusiastically, helping to send the original English version to the top of the best-seller lists. When the French translation (by Martel's parents) appeared in 2003 as *L'Histoire de Pi,* it too was also warmly received.

Nonfiction outsold fiction once again. The publishing firm Éditions Écosociété offered a popular series of books that presented leftist political issues from a populist, ecological point of view. Also popular were two books featuring the French Canadian explorers who were part of the Lewis and Clark Expedition across the western United States: journalist Richard Hétu's historical novel *La Route de l'Ouest* (2002) and historian Denis Vaugeois's *America* (2002), a handsomely illustrated, less-romantic chronicle.

The reputations of some often-overshadowed literary writers were solidified in recent years. Lise Tremblay continued to build a readership with her novel *La Héronnière,* and Rober Racine emerged from his often-experimental style with the surprisingly readable novel *L'Ombre de la terre* (2002). François Gravel, who had known success as a writer for young adults, presented adult readers with a memoir entitled *Adieu, Betty Crocker,* which charmed them with its light touch on serious subjects. Ook Chung, a writer of Korean descent, offered *Contes Butô,* a collection of interrelated short stories.

Poet Gaston Miron, who died in 1996, remained something of a hero in Quebec, and his posthumous book *Poèmes épars* stirred new admiration for his work. Jean-François Chassay, a professor and fiction writer, turned in *Anthologie de l'essai au Québec depuis la révolution tranquille,* a survey of political and cultural writing over the past 40 years. Also noteworthy was the emergence of Marchand de Feuilles, a new publisher that introduced Suzanne Myre's first novel, *Nouvelles d'autres mères.* (DAVID HOMEL)

ITALIAN

Two of the most remarkable novels of 2003, Andrea Camilleri's *Il giro di boa* and Giuseppe Montesano's *Di questa vita menzognera,* offered a critique of contemporary Italian politics. Inspector Salvo Montalbano, the hero of many of Camilleri's works, is so disheartened by recent events (such as the 2001 clashes in Genoa between police and protesters and the 2002 changes in the immigration law) that he contemplates a career change. While swimming, the activity he often relies on to alleviate his discomfort, he discovers a homicide that awakens his inquisitive nature and marks the beginning of a new investigation. Employing a different genre, Montesano's novel described a bold scheme devised by the Negromontes, a wealthy family, to replace the city of Naples with a virtual "Eternapoli." This is only the first step in an even more ambitious plan; with the complicity of political institutions, the Negromontes intend in the long run to privatize all of southern Italy. The novel's many grotesque and visionary scenes culminate in the description of a Gargantuan carnival that envelops all of Naples; the scene juxtaposes the new Naples of the Negromontes with the Naples of the Borbones (House of Bourbon), its victims (such as Eleonora Fonseca Pimentel), and its decadence. The similarities between *Il giro di boa* and *Di questa vita menzognera* extended to the stylistic level, as both authors employed dialect (Sicilian and Neapolitan, respectively) in expressive and effective ways.

Erri De Luca's *Il contrario di uno* was a collection of short stories centred on the theme of human solidarity. Most of the stories examined moments in which a gratuitous act of generosity breaks an individual's isolation or even saves a life. The author's experiences as a volunteer in Africa, a political activist, and a rock climber provided the background for his narratives. The volume also contained a section on the five senses (*I colpi dei sensi*, 1993) and a poem ("Mamm'Emilia") for the author's mother. The success of a completely different type of collection, *Il lato sinistro del cuore,* confirmed Carlo Lucarelli's ongoing popularity as well as Italian readers' passion for mystery stories. The book's 53 pieces constituted, among other things, a perturbing voyage through the deceptively tranquil Italian provincial life of the 1990s. Giorgio Faletti chose a more glamorous setting—the resort of Monte-Carlo—for his novel *Io uccido* (2002), the most successful detective story of 2003. Already known to the Italian public as an actor and singer, the author intermingled musical and cinematic references with his protagonist's investigations.

Between literary divertissement and social commentary, Stefano Benni's *Achille piè veloce* placed characters named after Homeric heroes (Achilles, Ulysses, Circe, Penelope, and so on) in a contemporary urban setting. Paradoxically, Achilles has lost the physical agility to which the title alludes, is confined to a wheelchair, and communicates with the outside world by means of a computer. His heroism lies in the strength with which he confronts not only his disease but also the greed and cynicism of the society around him, as exemplified by his brother Febus. The other central character in the novel, Ulysses, struggles to maintain his love

Erri De Luca's new collection included short stories, a section on the senses, and a poem for his mother.

for literature in spite of his work as a reader in a publishing house, which obliges him to review hundreds of manuscripts and deal with their ambitious and, at times, aggressive authors. The friendship that develops between the two outcasts, united in their heroic resistance to the principles that dominate their times, was at the core of Benni's narration.

Melania G. Mazzucco won the Strega Prize with *Vita,* a story about immigration that traced the cultural displacement, anxiety, and loss such an experience inevitably entailed. The Campiello Literary Award was awarded to Marco Santagata's *Il maestro dei santi pallidi,* a novel set in 15th-century Italy that skillfully blended historical reconstruction with fiction. In the face of death, Cinin, the protagonist, reviews his life and the events that have transformed him from poor servant to famous painter, highlighting the decisive yet uncontrollable power that chance exercises over human destiny. Among the winners of the Grinzane Cavour Prize was Clara Sereni, whose *Passami il sale* (2002) returned to a theme she explored in *Casalinghitudine* (1987). In her latest work the preparation of a meal was presented not as a mere practical necessity but rather as a symbol of a possible reconciliation of mind and body, of public roles and private needs.

Several important literary figures died in 2003, including Giuseppe Pontiggia (author of *Nati due volte* [2000]), literary critic Giacinto Spagnoletti, and Luigi Pintor, cofounder of the daily *Il Manifesto* and its director for more than 20 years. In Pintor's posthumous slim volume, *I luoghi del delitto,* a man diagnosed with a terminal disease muses over the central events of his life and his relationship with death, looking for an answer that remains elusive.

(LAURA BENEDETTI)

SPANISH

Spain. Many of Spain's best-known writers in 2003 invited their readers to look back in order to clarify the present and foresee the future. Rosa Montero, for example, blended fantasy and dreams, madness and passion, and her most secret recollections in *La loca de la casa.* It mixed her own biography with those of other people, but the reader should be cautioned that not all that the writer said about herself was trustworthy; memories do not always reflect reality. Javier Marías's *Tu rostro mañana* (2002) was the first of a projected trilogy. Its protagonist meets an old professor with "too many memories" and also discovers that he has the gift, or curse, of foresight, that he knows in advance who will be a traitor and who will remain loyal.

The Galician Suso de Toro won the National Prize for Narrative for his mystery novel *Trece campanadas* (2002), in which he investigated the past of Santiago de Compostela, Spain, a city for pilgrims that had lost its "secrecy and soul" over the years. Juan Manuel de Prada was awarded the Primavera Prize for the novel for *La vida invisible,* the story of a successful young writer who travels to Chicago after the Sept. 11, 2001, attacks on New York City's World Trade Center. What begins for him as an ordinary journey ends up changing his life forever. The novel explored yearnings, secrets, and the dogged search for happiness. *El caballero del jubón amarillo,* the fifth volume of Arturo Pérez-Reverte's series of adventure novels about Capitán Alatriste, described the clandestine relationship between Alatriste and the funny María de Castro, who is also desired by King Philip IV. The situation is further complicated when conspirators against the king implicate Alatriste in their plot.

Lucía Etxebarría again addressed the topics of women and love in a new collection of stories.

Antonio Gala's highly popular *El dueño de la herida* contained 38 stories about different facets of love. According to the author, "[Love is] infinite, it is the holder of life, and he who has not been wounded by it has never lived." Lucía Etxebarría's *Una historia de amor como otra cualquiera* comprised 15 short stories about women who fought successfully for love. Benjamín Prado published *Jamás saldré vivo de este mundo,* a book of short stories to which he and four renowned authors—Marías, Juan Marsé, Enrique Vila-Matas, and Almudena Grandes—contributed.

In 2003 the two most noted literary prizes offered by Spanish publishers were given to Latin American writers: the Alfaguara Prize to the Mexican Xavier Velasco for his novel *Diablo guardián* and the Planeta Prize to Chilean Antonio Skármeta for his work *El baile de la Victoria.* Julia Uceda, a little-known poet, received the National Prize for Poetry for *En el viento, hacia el mar, 1959–2002,* a selection of her best poems to date. The highest distinction in Spanish letters, the Cervantes Prize, went to Chilean poet Gonzalo Rojas. Readers mourned the death in October of the prolific Manuel Vázquez Montalbán. (*See* OBITUARIES.)

(VERÓNICA ESTEBAN)

Latin America. In 2003 literary news from Latin America centred on the prizes presented by the major publishing houses. Alfaguara granted its sixth prize for the novel to Mexican writer Xavier Velasco for *Diablo guardián.* Seen from the perspective of its female protagonist, the novel examined the clash between Hispanic and U.S. cultures by means of language (especially the mixture known as Spanglish) as well as plot. Casa de las Américas, Cuba's foremost cultural and publishing organization, granted its prize for testimonial literature to Colombian José Alejandro Castaño Hoyos for *La isla de Morgan,* the true account of the author's courageous descent into Medellín's underworld and an extraordinary piece of research. William Ospina, one of Colombia's foremost intellectuals, also received a prize for his book of essays *Los nuevos centros de la esfera.* Fernando Vallejo of Medellín won the Rómulo Gallegos Prize for *El desbarrancadero,* originally published in 2001. Told in first person, the autobiographical novel recounted the main character's voyage to Medellín to witness the shutting down of his childhood home and the death by AIDS of his dissolute but brilliant younger brother.

The Planeta Prize was awarded to Chilean Antonio Skármeta, who also wrote *Ardiente paciencia* (1985), the novel on which the hugely successful film *Il postino* was based. *El baile de la Victoria,* the book for which Skármeta received the Planeta, centred on two ex-convicts who cannot readjust to society outside prison. While both are falling in love with the same woman (the eponymous dancer, Victoria), they plan one last, big heist. Argentine Mariano Dupont won the Emecé 2003 Prize for his novel *Aún,* set in Argentina during the 1970s. Confined to a hospital bed, the novel's narrator recounts the last months of his life—both the good memories, such as those of summer nights and games of dominoes, and the bad ones, such as those of violence and the attenuated atmosphere of fear and tension. During the Guadalajara International Book Fair, Brazilian writer Rubem Fonseca was unanimously awarded the Juan Rulfo Prize. (See *Portuguese Literature: Brazil,* below.) The prize was for Fonseca's entire body of work, which spanned more than 60 years.

Rubem Fonseca, still inventive at age 78, accepted the Juan Rulfo Prize for his large body of work.

© Jerry Bauer

The year 2003 was good for the younger generation of writers who had gained recognition in their own right, far removed from the influence of the so-called literary Boom (represented by the work of writers such as Gabriel García Márquez, Mario Vargas Llosa, and Carlos Fuentes) and "good" Latin American literature that lasted through the late 1980s. Edmundo Paz Soldán of Bolivia published *El delirio de Turing,* which won him his country's Premio Nacional de Novela. Set in Río Fugitivo, Soldán's fictionalized version of his native Cochabamba, the novel featured a computer hacker named Kandinsky, who leads a group of cyberguerrillas intent on avenging the abuses committed by large transnational companies. Although set in the present, the novel evoked an ominous and futuristic atmosphere that seemed closer to that of classic science fiction than to a realistic present-day portrait of a typical Andean town such as Cochabamba. Chilean Alberto Fuguet published *Las películas de mi vida,* which told the story of Beltrán Soler, a Chilean seismologist who obsessively writes a list of the 50 films most important to him and the memories they elicit. Slowly, as the list of movie titles evolves, the novel reveals a life lived in two apparently contradictory worlds: California and Chile. The juxtaposition of the two was potentially unsettling for those who expected just another book of magic realism.

Internationally famous writer Isabel Allende published *Mi país inventado,* a book of memoirs in which she portrayed her native Chile's idiosyncrasies as well as its violent history and indomitable spirit. The book's narrative was framed by two events that occurred on September 11: the death in 1973 of Salvador Allende Gossens, Chile's president and the author's uncle, and the terrorist attack on New York City's World Trade Center in 2001. In the book Allende's readers would encounter characters they had seen throughout her other books: mythical grandparents, uncles, relatives, and friends. The volume was a reflection of the author's struggle to maintain a coherent interior life in a world full of contradictions, and it seemed of particular interest to any immigrant to the United States.

In 2003 Nicaraguan modernist poet Rubén Darío (1867–1916) reappeared in *Rubén Darío y la sacerdotisa de Amón* by Colombian novelist Germán Espinosa. The narrative, which was not biography but fiction, presented Darío as a hard-drinking, erudite, and amorous detective who, while visiting a friend's summer home in Brittany, solves the mysterious murder of another of the guests. The novel successfully re-created the real Darío's character in all its contradictions and complexities. (RICARDO ARMIJO)

PORTUGUESE

Portugal. In 2003 Portuguese literature suffered a grievous loss with the death of Augusto Abelaira in Lisbon on July 4. Abelaira was born on March 18, 1926, in Ançã, near Cantanhede, Port. A distinguished writer and winner of four literary prizes, he started his career during António Salazar's dictatorship. By substituting Florence for Lisbon as the setting of his first novel, *A cidade das flores* (1959), he eluded the censor's watchful eye and voiced the political aspirations of his generation.

Allusion and allegory were effective literary devices in Portuguese fiction and helped the novel to become a sophisticated tool for playing with new ideas. The latest novel by Nobel Prize winner José Saramago moved daringly into the field of science to tackle the question of human cloning. In *O homem duplicado* (2002), Saramago presented a futuristic tale with a precision of detail and an intensity of feeling that made it dramatically convincing. Loving and the sorting out of passions became complex issues when complicated by questions of personal identity.

The fiction prize of the Association of Portuguese Writers was awarded to Lídia Jorge for *O vento assobiando nas gruas* (2002), an ambitious novel that tried to encompass time present and time past. The narrative voice is that of a young woman who tells the story of a large family returning from Africa. On the way she recalls a crime and a love affair—ingredients that make up the stuff of fiction. Torn between two worlds—the contemporary one and that of the immediate past—the main character grows in experience and awakens in others a painful self-awareness. Rich in descriptive detail, the story relied on concrete imagery to evoke inner states of mind, fleeting emotions, and deep-seated convictions. All of these were woven into a discourse that conveyed a sense of change and touched on the degradation of our planet.

The prize for short-story writing, which also was awarded by the Association of Portuguese Writers, went to Teolinda Gersão for *Histórias de ver e andar: contos* (2002). These tales, which examined the contemporary obsession with celebrity, wealth, and the acquisition of material goods, were fine pieces of observation with an ironic twist. The highest distinction in Portuguese letters, the Camões Prize, is awarded to a writer to honour the work of a lifetime; in 2003 it went to Brazilian novelist Rubem Fonseca, whose brutally direct narratives dealt with the world of criminals and outlaws. (L.S. REBELO)

Brazil. The highlight of 2003 for Brazilian letters was the awarding of both the Camões Prize—the equivalent of the Nobel Prize for Literature in Portuguese—and Mexico's Juan Rulfo Prize for Latin American and Caribbean literature to 78-year-old Rubem Fonseca. In 40 years of fiction writing, his main thematic concern was the gritty urban life of Rio de Janeiro: the violence, duplicity, corruption, and social conflicts faced by its beleaguered population. This he presented in an often poetic prose that was tinged with streetwise slang. His notable novels and works of short fiction ranged from *Feliz ano novo* (1975), *O cobrador* (1979), and *Bufo & Spallanzani* (1985) to the 2003 publication *Diário de um fescenino,* a diary presented by a character named Rufus, who was Fonseca's alter ego. Writer Nélida Piñon, currently at the University of Miami, Coral Gables, Fla., was awarded the Spanish Premio Internacional Menéndez Pelayo for her contributions to literature and to teaching.

The American poetry magazine *Rattapallax* dedicated part of an issue to new Brazilian poets, including—among others—Moacir Amâncio, Fabiano Calixto, Ricardo Corona, Chantal Castelli, and Dirceu Villa.

Several important works of criticism appeared during the year. Flora Süssekind was the main author and editor of *Vozes femininas: Gêneros, mediações, e práticas de escrita,* a volume of essays on literature and culture from a feminist perspective. Denilson Lopes's late 2002 publication *O homem que amava rapazes e outros ensaios* considered gay themes in Brazilian literature. Of great note was the 2002 second edition of the three-volume *Intérpretes do Brasil,* compiled and edited by Silviano Santiago. This set, which comprised 4,000 pages, offered both an anthology and a critical appraisal of the fundamental sociocultural analyses produced by 20th-century Brazilian scholars and, consequently, provided an overview of the origins and development of modern Brazilian civilization.

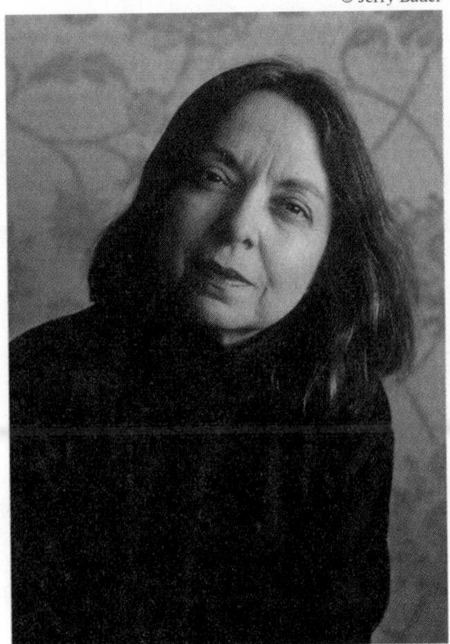

In 2003 Nélida Piñon, whose work was translated into many languages, added yet another prize to her collection of awards.

The Brazilian Academy of Letters elected several important writers to membership, including novelist Moacyr Scliar, literary critic Alfredo Bosi, and children's fiction writer Ana Maria Machado.

The year 2003 was also marked by the deaths of novelist Geraldo França de Lima, *tropicalista* poet Waly Salomão, highly respected poet and literary and cultural critic Haroldo de Campos (*see* OBITUARIES), folklorist Paulo de Carvalho-Neto, and political philosophers Raymundo Faoro and René Dreifuss. Also noteworthy was the passing of Roberto Marinho (*see* OBITUARIES), the journalist and media baron whose omnipresent Organizações Globo media company influenced the direction of modern Brazil. (IRWIN STERN)

RUSSIAN

The central event in Russian literature for the year 2003 was the celebration of the "Russian Year" at the Frankfurt (Ger.) Book Fair. In addition to drawing many Russian publishers and writers, the fair served to publicize German translations of numerous Russian books, primarily fiction from Russia's most popular writers of the 1990s—Viktor Pelevin, Vladimir Sorokin, and Tatyana Tolstaya—but also works from two major writers of an older generation, Yury Mamleyev and Andrey Bitov.

The exciting developments that had been observed at the turn of the century lost steam in 2003, and the outlines of a new era failed to take shape. One thing was clear: the stars of the 1990s attracted fewer readers. For example, the appearance of a new book from Pelevin, Russia's most popular author of the 1990s, sparked no special interest. More attention was drawn to two books by Ilya Stogov, an author whose phantasmagoric and grotesque works, noted for their brutal and laconic confessionalism, were reminiscent of American author Charles Bukowski's output. Stogov's novel *mASIA*—— (2002; with an obscene English word as part of the title) described a trip through the Central Asian republics of the former Soviet Union during and after the Soviet period; his book *Tabloid* (2001), based in part on his own professional experience, was a fierce send-up of journalism. Also popular was Dmitry Bykov's novel *Orfografiya* ("Orthography"). This experiment in "alternative history" imagined the abolition of Russian orthography as a major goal

Tatyana Tolstaya was among the Russian writers honoured at the Frankfurt Book Fair.

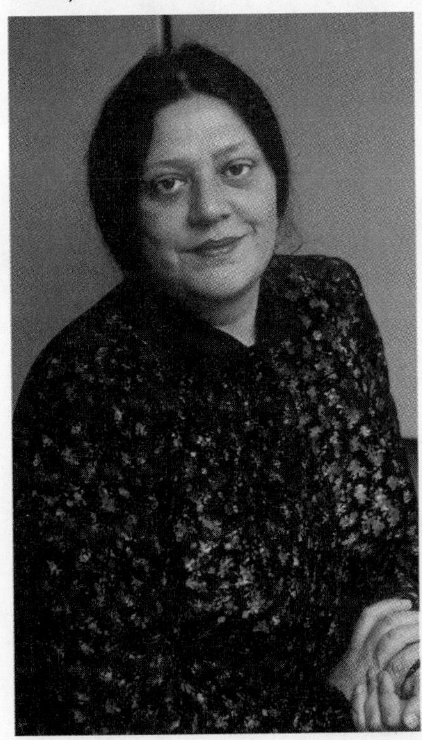

of the Bolsheviks who came to power in 1917. *Leto v Badene* (1999), Leonid Tsypkin's 1970s novel about several events in the life of Fyodor Dostoyevsky, was published in Russian in 2003 and widely discussed in the Russian press. First published in German, the novel was translated into English as *Summer in Baden Baden* (1987).

Although the usual authors—Oleg Pavlov, Marina Vishnevetskaya, and Irina Polyanskaya for the generation of the 1990s and Bitov and Vladimir Makanin for the older generation—were represented in the major literary journals (*Znamya, Novy mir, Oktyabr, Zvezda*), several other works did stand out: Andrey Dmitriyev's novella *Prizrak teatra* ("Phantom of the Theatre"), about a provincial actor; Aleksandr Kabakov's *Opyty chastnoy zhizni* ("Experiments in Personal Life"); Yury Arabov's *Bit-bit*; and *Uchitel bez uchenika* ("Teacher Without a Student"), Mikhail Ayzenberg's memoir about underground prose writer Pavel Ulitin.

The talents of the 30-year-old poet Igor Bulatovsky were on display in his book *Poluostrova* ("The Archipelago"). Also published were two collections by deceased poets of his generation: Anna Gorenko (who lived in Israel) and Boris Ryzhy (from Yekaterinburg). Other well-known poets with new books included Dmitry Bobyshev, Natalya Gorbanevskaya, and Sergey Zavyalov. New poems were also offered by Yelena Shvarts, Olga Martynova, Sergey Volf, Viktor Sosnora, Aleksandr Kushner, Sergey Stratanovsky, Svetlana Kekova, and (after a long silence) Olga Sedakova.

The single most important new theme discussed in the major journals was the rise of a new wave of left-wing political radicalism in the literary milieu. The leading antagonists in this debate were S. Chuprinin and V. Lapenkov. (Some of this discussion can be followed on the Internet at <http://magazines.russ.ru/authors/l/lapenkov>.)

Literary prizes, which had caused several major scandals over the previous few years, produced no sensations in 2003. Vishnevetskaya won the Apollon Grigoryev Prize for her novella *A.K.S. (Opyt lyubvi)* ("A.K.S. (An Experiment in Love)"). The National Best-Seller Prize was awarded to the debut novel *(Golovo)lomka* ("Brain(twister)") by two Russian authors from Riga, Latvia—Aleksandr Garros and Aleksey Yevdokimov. The work was praised for its satiric depiction of the Latvian business world in a style that reminded some of the American filmmakers Joel and Ethan Coen. The Andrey Bely Prize in prose went to Eduard Limonov, for *Kniga vody* ("The Book of Water"), a work he wrote while serving time on a conviction for inciting revolution (he was pardoned in mid-2003). The jury that awarded him the prize, however, noted that it did not share his (neo-Bolshevik) political views. The winner in poetry was Mikhail Gronas and in humanities Vardan Airepetyan. An award for "services to Russian literature" was given to poet Dmitry Kuzmin. The short list for the Russian Booker Prize included the "intellectual detective story" *Kazaroza* by Leonid Yuzefovich; *Iupiter* ("Jupiter") by Leonid Zorin; the autobiographical novel *Beloye na chyornom* ("White On Black") by Rubén David González Gallego (a Russian author of Spanish descent); *Frau Shram* by Afansy Mamedov; *Villa Reno* by Natalya Galkina; and *Lavra* ("The Monastery") by Yelena Chizhova. The relatively low aesthetic level of several nominees did not augur well for the future of this prize. Indeed, the number of literary prizes, which had reached a peak in the mid-1990s, was diminishing noticeably: in 2003 alone both the Anti-Booker and Northern Palmyra prizes were terminated.

Deaths in 2003 included those of Georgy Vladimov, dissident author and 1995 Russian Booker laureate (*see* OBITUARIES); the 92-year-old poet, translator, and memoirist Semyon Lipkin, one of the last Russian Modernists, who personally knew Andrey Bely, Osip Mandelshtam, and Marina Tsvetayeva; and, at age 69, the extremely talented hermetic prose writer Vladimir Gubin.

(VALERY SHUBINSKY)

JEWISH

Hebrew. Perhaps the only interesting phenomenon in Hebrew prose of 2003 was a marked tendency toward rich literary Hebrew, rather than the pedestrian language typical of many 1990s novels. The former was exemplified by Deror Burshṭain's *Avner Brener,* Einat Yakir's *'Iske tivukh* (2002; "A Matter of Negotiation"), and Benny Mer's *Rov ha-lelot* ("Most Nights"). Works by veteran writers included Aharon Appelfeld's *Pit'om ahavah* ("Love, All of a Sudden"), Yoel Hoffmann's *Efrayim*, Gayil Har'even's *Ḥaye mal'akh* ("Life of an Angel"), Mira Magen's *Mal'akheha nirdemu kulam* ("Her Angels Have All Fallen Asleep"), and Beni Barbash's *Hilukh ḥozer* ("Rerun"). First novels included Uri S. Cohen's *'Al meḳomo be-shalom* ("Resting in Peace") and Yossi Avni's *Dodah Farhumah lo hayetah zonah* ("Auntie Farhumah Wasn't a Whore After All").

Agi Mish'ol's *Mivḥar ve-ḥadashim* ("Selected and New Poems") included a critical essay by Dan Miron, and Ramy Ditzanny collected his political poems in *Erets zavah: Shirim 1982–2000* ("Land Oozing: Poems 1982–2000"). Other collections by veteran poets included Yehiel Hazak's *Le-hashiv esh le-esh* ("Flames of Fury"), Meron Ḥ. Izaḳson's *Biṭul ha-liṭuf ha-nashi* ("Banning Her Caress"), and Rachel Gil's *'Akhshav tori lamut* ("My Turn to Die"). The younger generation was represented by Tamir Lahav-Radlmesser's *Temunat maḥazor* ("Year Book"), Yakir Ben-Moshe's *Be-khol boḳer maḳriaḥ le-faḥot adam blondini eḥad* ("Every Morning at Least One Blond Man Goes Bald"), and Liat Kaplan's *Tsel ha-tsipor* ("Shadow of a Bird").

Yafah Berlovits edited an absorbing anthology of stories by women writers in pre-state Israel; *She-ani adamah ve-adam* ("Tender Rib") contradicted the accepted view that there were no Hebrew women writers of note between Devorah Baron, who gained her reputation in the 1920s, and Amalia Kahana-Carmon, prominent during the 1960s and '70s. Another feminist-oriented

In 2003 Aharon Appelfeld produced a book on love, written in his lyrical style.

study was Orli Lubin's *Ishah ḳoret ishah* ("Women Reading Women"). Dan Miron published a comprehensive study of the poetry of Uri Zvi Greenberg, *Aḳdamut le-U.Z.G.* ("Prolegomena to U.Z.G."), and Uzi Shavit interpreted the plague poems of Nathan Alterman (1944) in *Shirah mul ṭoṭaliṭariyut* ("Poetry and Totalitarianism").

(AVRAHAM BALABAN)

Yiddish. Works of Yiddish poetry in 2003 included Russian writer Maks Riant's *Mit di oygn fun mayn harts* ("With the Eyes of My Heart"), a collection of songs, ballads, and poems. *Plutsemdiker regn* ("Sudden Rain") was Gitl Schaechter-Viswanath's poetic debut, and Rivka Basman Ben-Haim's poetic collection *Oyf a strune fun regn* (2002; "On a String of Rain") described a literary pilgrimage from the Vilna (Vilnius) ghetto and German concentration camps to Israel.

From Ukraine came Mikhail Reznikovich's children's book *Ikh hob lib shpiln* ("I Love to Play") and Aleksandr Lizen's reflective *Neviim, emese un falshe* ("Prophets, Real and False").

Zackary Sholem Berger's *Di kats der payats,* a Yiddish translation (in the original rhyme scheme) of Dr. Seuss's *The Cat in the Hat,* joined Leonard Wolf's translation *Vini-der-pu* (A.A. Milne's *Winnie-the-Pooh*) and Shlomo Lerman's translation *Der kleyner prints* (Antoine de Saint-Exupéry's *Le Petit prince*) in the gallery of children's classics available in Yiddish.

Shmuel Gordon's *Yizkor: di farmishpete shrayber* ("Remembrance: The Condemned Writers"), a monumental documentary novel by a participant-observer, recorded the edicts against Jewish cultural activities during the last years of Joseph Stalin's regime and the execution of 13 Soviet Yiddish writers and cultural leaders on Aug. 12, 1952.

In her small lexicon of Vilnius Jewish society, *Mit shraybers, bikher un mit . . . Vilne* ("About Writers, Books, and . . . Vilnius"), Musye Landau provided a rich panorama of the writings and authors she knew.

Based on archival research, Mishe Lev's fictionalized history *Sobibor: ven nit di fraynd mayne . . .* (2002; "Sobibor: If It Were Not My Friends . . .") told the story of the heroic revolt launched on Oct. 14, 1943, by inmates of the Sobibor extermination camp.

The Hebrew University in Jerusalem published *Yidishe dertseylungen 1906–1924* ("Jewish Stories 1906–1924") by Y.D. Berkovitsh, one of Israel's foremost bilingual writers. It provided an arresting portrait of the younger generation of Russian Jews who played an important role in the culture and politics of the early 20th century.

The author of five assemblages of refined poetry, Aleksandr Shpiglblat turned his hand to prose in *Shotns klapn in shoyb* ("Shadows Rap on Glass"), in which he described Jewish life in Romania at the beginning of World War II.

Yiddish literary scholar, poet, and editor Chaim Beyder died in New York City on December 7.

(THOMAS E. BIRD)

TURKISH

The year 2003 was hardly a banner year for Turkish literature; it produced few major novels, few noteworthy collections of poetry, and meagre accomplishments in criticism. For the 30th consecutive year, Turkey's press raised hopes in vain regarding Yashar Kemal's candidacy for a Nobel Prize for Literature. Orhan Pamuk won Ireland's International IMPAC Dublin Literary Award (the world's largest monetary award for a novel) for his book *My Name Is Red* (2001; originally published in Turkish, 1998). Modernist playwright and fiction writer Adalet Ağaoğlu was honoured by a volume of tributes on the occasion of her 55th year as an author.

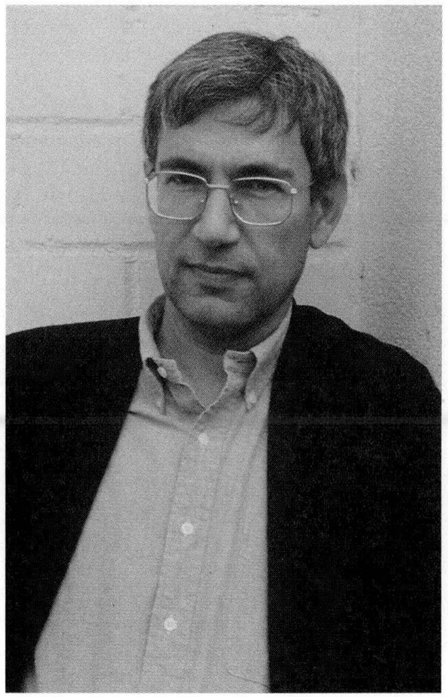

Orhan Pamuk's book My Name Is Red *won the world's largest monetary award for a novel.*

Notable novels of 2003 included Ahmet Ümit's *Beyoğlu rapsodisi* ("Rhapsody of Beyoğlu"), which depicted ordinary lives in Istanbul's European quarter, a once-elegant sector grown seedy and sinful. With this book, the author, who was remarkably successful with his pioneering literary detective fiction, ventured into new territory, portraying Beyoğlu as a vivid character while he explored his central theme of immortality. Another characterization of Istanbul was presented in Tuna Kiremitçi's best-selling *Git kendini çok sevdirmeden* ("Go Away Before You Are Loved Too Much").

Melisa Gürpınar, one of Turkey's prominent woman poets, received the Cevdet Kudret Prize and published an impressive new collection entitled *Ada şiirleri* ("Island Poems"). Already a commanding figure as novelist and playwright, Murathan Mungan produced an attractive new book of poems, *Timsah sokak şiirleri* ("Poems of Alligator Street"). Eminent poet İlhan Berk celebrated his 85th year with an elegant volume of more than 1,900 pages. It contained the entire output of a 65-year career during which he remained at the forefront of poetic experimentation. Also noteworthy was Seyhan Özçelik's *Toplu şiirler* ("Collected Poems"), which included a selection of recent verse.

Among the few exceptional volumes of literary criticism were two by Hilmi Yavuz, *Kara güneş* ("Black Sun") and *Sözün gücü* ("The Power of the Word"), and several stimulating collections of essays, two by Füsun Akatlı—*Kültürsüzlüğümüzün kışı* ("The Winter of Our Culturelessness") and *Felsefe gözüyle edebiyat* ("Literature Through the Vantage Point of Philosophy")—and two by Tahsin Yücel—*Romanımıza neler oldu?* ("What Happened to Our Fiction?") and *Sözcüklerin diliyle konuşmak* ("Speaking in the Language of Words").

(TALAT SAIT HALMAN)

PERSIAN

In 2003 the literary production of all Persian-speaking cultures was driven by certain back-to-basics impulses, as presaged by Iran's 2002 landmark publication of *Farhang-i buzurg-i sukhan* ("Great Speech [or Word] Dictionary"), an eight-volume dictionary of the Persian language. In Afghanistan local reissues of selected expatriate writings of the late 1980s and '90s dominated literary output. Tajikistan's National Assembly made the Cyrillic alphabet the sole official script for Tajiki Persian and thus dealt a final blow to the movement begun in the early 1990s to revive the Perso-Arabic alphabet.

Women continued to play a leading literary role in Iran and within Persian-speaking expatriate communities. Two works, Mahnāz Karīmī's novel *Sinj o sinawbar* ("The Spruce and the Service Tree"), and Jaleh Chegeni's collection of poems, *Sarchishma-yi nigāh* ("Source of Vision"), headed the long list of literary works by younger female writers.

In spring the launch of *Samarkand*, a new literary journal that examined one Western writer per issue, signaled a strong desire to approach the literature of Western cultures in a more systematic way. The first two issues, devoted, respectively, to Virginia Woolf and Marcel Proust, indicated heightened attention to the psychological dimensions of literature. The Fourth Congress of Teachers of Persian Language and Literature, hosted in October by Iran's Ministry of Culture and Islamic Guidance, brought together linguists, language teachers, and literary scholars engaged the world over in the teaching of and research into Persian language and literature. In its resolution the congress issued a plea for the development of a Unicode Standard for the use of the Persian script in cyberspace. Also in October the Mehregān Prize for lifetime achievement went to octogenarian writer Simin Daneshvar, and the prize for works created for young audiences was awarded to Ja'far Tuzandajani's *Mihamnī-yi dīvhā* ("Banquet of the Demons"). The prize for the best novel went unclaimed because, the jurors declared, the year's output did not meet their standards.

In the Iranian diaspora communities, one work stood out in psychological intensity: Partaw Nūrī 'Alā's *Misl-i man* ("Like Me"). This collection of six short stories delved into the private lives of Iranian exiles who, having left behind the traditional modes of meeting potential partners, had yet to be initiated into more Westernized personal and sexual mores. (AHMAD KARIMI-HAKKAK)

ARABIC

In 2003 the Arab world continued to face political and cultural challenges, some resulting from events such as the Second Persian Gulf War and others from the effects of globalization and what is perceived as the West's anti-Islamic crusade. The situation prompted Arab intellectuals to call for a new cultural approach, and in response the Egyptian High Council for Culture hosted a conference on July 1–3 to formulate a new cultural discourse for the future. The Arab representatives stressed the need for an authentic Arab cultural renewal rather than mere conformity with Western culture. They urged a greater freedom of expression for writers, an end to government interference, and the renewal of religious discourse. The number and complexity of the problems at hand, however, made the mood at the conference generally pessimistic.

The Egyptian poet Aḥmad 'Abd al-Mu'ṭī Ḥijāzī invited Arab thinkers to consider the ways in which they might contribute to world culture while protecting their identity and remaining true to themselves without becoming isolated.

Elsewhere, Iraqi writers living in exile responded to the war in Iraq with short stories and poems that took the conflict as their subject. Most were published in Arabic literary journals, and in the May–June issue of one such publication, *Al-Adāb*, Buthayna al-Nāṣirī, an Iraqi living in Egypt, issued a call for Iraqi unity and support.

Poetry also continued to occupy an important place in Arabic literature. On May 29–31, Rabat, Mor., which had been designated the 2003 capital of Arabic culture, hosted an impressive poetry festival—despite the May 16 suicide bombings in Casablanca that had killed 45. The festival was attended by well-known poets such as Palestinian Maḥmūd Darwīsh, Iraqi Sa'dī Yūsuf, and Moroccan Muhammad Bennis, to cite only a few. The festival's main theme was a call for solidarity with the Iraqi and Palestinian peoples.

Two young poets following in their fathers' footsteps published their first books, Tamīm Barghūtī's *Al-Manẓar* (2002; "The View") in colloquial Egyptian and Bahā' Jāhin's *Kūfiyyat ṣūf lī al-ṣhitā'* ("A Woolen Scarf for Winter"). Both were critical of social and political conditions in Egypt. Much of the anger of the younger generation of writers, such as Hudā Ḥusayn (Hoda Hossein) and Rānā 'Abbās Tūnsī (Rana Abbas Tonsi), was expressed in poetry transmitted by means of the Internet.

Three writers used the United States as a location for their books: Muḥammad Sulaymān in his novel *Taḥta samā' ākhar* ("Under Another Sky") addressed its materialism; Aḥmad Mursī wrote of his own experience there in *Brūfah bi al-malābis lī faṣl fī al-jaḥīm* ("Dress Rehearsal for a Season in Hell"), a poetry collection; and Ṣun 'Allāh Ibrāhīm depicted American society during the Bill Clinton–Monica Lewinsky scandal in his novel *Amricanelli* (a combination of the Arabic words *Amrī kāna lī*, "I Decided for Myself" or "My Own Decision"; the Arabic form of the name *America* forms the first part of the word).

Other notable fiction included the work of Jamāl al-Ghīṭānī, Egypt's most prominent and prolific writer, who published an autobiographical trilogy titled *Dafātir al-tadwīn* ("Notebooks"). Central to the trilogy were his encounters with several women he befriends during his travels. His flowing style and concise, evocative phrases were unparalleled. The Egyptian Salwā Bakr took an insightful look at Egyptian morality in her novel *Sawāqī al-waqt* ("The Water Wheels of Time").

New francophone Maghribi literature was represented by Abdelkébir Khatibi's *Pélérinage d'un artiste amoureux*, a mystical journey that examines man's relation to God. Mohamed Taïfi published his first novel, the autobiographical *La Source enragée*, which shed light on colonial rule in Morocco. Siham Ben Chekroun returned to fiction with a collection of short stories, *Les Jours d'ici*. Respected Tunisian writer al-Ḥabīb al-Sālimī paid tribute to women in his novel *'Ushshāq Bayya* ("Bayya's Lovers"), which had a woman as its central character.

A few writers broke their silence after more or less lengthy absences. Fadéla M'rabet returned with *Une Enfance singulière*, an autobiographical novel about her early years in Algeria and her experience with racism in France. Sudanese novelist al-Ṭayyib Ṣāliḥ's *Jabr al-Dār* ("Jabr al-Dar" [a proper name]) was set in The Sudan, like most of his previous novels. Aḥlām Mustaghānimī published her third novel, *'Ābir Sarīr* ("Passing Through a Bed"), and Ḥanān al-Shaykh wrote *Imra'atān 'alā shāṭi' al-baḥr* ("Two Women on the Beach").

Notable deaths in 2003 included those of Palestinian poet Muḥammad al-Qaysī and Algeria's prolific and outstanding francophone novelist and poet, Mohammed Dib. (*See* OBITUARIES.)

(AIDA A. BAMIA)

CHINESE

In 2003 the general situation of Chinese literature in both print and electronic publishing could be described as depressed. One found few new creative literary books in city bookstores; the shelves were occupied almost entirely by popular fiction, including youth *manga*-stories, Korean-style romances, and anticorruption novels.

Among the few books worthy of mention was Yang Xianhui's *Jia bian gou ji shi* ("Accounts of Jia-Bian Valley"), a collection of seven interviews and seven short stories concerning the terrible history of Jia-Bian Valley, where a forced-labour camp (part of the *laogai* system) was established in the mid-1950s. About 3,000 political prisoners were transferred into the camp in 1957–58, but only half that number remained alive in 1961. Yang's stories described in powerful detail the daily lives of the prisoners, especially their fears, hungers, and deaths. Realistic and sharply focused, the book was referred to on the Internet as a Chinese *Gulag Archipelago,* in reference to Aleksandr Solzhenitsyn's exposé of the Soviet system of labour camps for political prisoners.

A noteworthy novel, published in December, was *Shou ji* ("Cell Phone") by Liu Zhenyun. An earlier four-volume novel by Liu, *Gu xiang mian he hua duo* (1998; "Hometown Noodles and Flowers"), had met with a cold reception because of its length. *Shou ji,* by contrast, was short and pithy. It was composed of 42 brief chapters; most of these were under three pages, and some consisted of only one sentence. This stark difference was partly because Liu developed the novel from a film plot by the same name but also partly because he wanted to stress the novel's theme, which was printed on the book's back cover: The useful words in the world make up fewer than 10 sentences a day. Liu brought home this point in his novel by juxtaposing the habits of modern people, who use such high-tech devices as cell phones and communicate little with far too many words, with communication of earlier times. Cell phones, Liu concluded, brought mostly unhappiness. A single sentence transmitted orally 150 years ago could take almost 3 years to reach the intended recipient in distant lands, but it was meaningful enough to reinvigorate a young idler's memories of and feelings for his family and to move him to return home.

Another bright spot of 2003 was the expansion, beginning in October, of the length of the monthly *Shanghai Literature.* This was especially encouraging at a time when many literary journals were being transformed into nonliterary ventures. Chen Sihe, a well-known professor of literature, was named the new editor in chief of the Shanghai-based journal. As one of the leading literary periodicals of mainland China, *Shanghai Literature* continued to play an important role in Chinese literature.

(WANG XIAOMING)

JAPANESE

In May 2003 Nihon Bungaku Shinkokai (Society for the Promotion of Japanese Literature) appointed Eimi Yamada to the screening committee of the Akutagawa Prize—Japan's most prestigious literary award, given semiannually to the most promising new Japanese writers of fiction. Her appointment was unusual because Yamada herself had never won the prize, though in 1987 she won the Naoki Prize (for best work of popular literature). Despite the presence of some other Akutagawa Prize winners among the candidates who had been considered for the position, the society chose Yamada because of her popularity among young readers and for her experience on judging panels for other literary prizes.

In the first half of 2003, the Akutagawa Prize went to Tamaki Daidō's "Shoppai doraibu" ("Salty Drive"), first published in the December 2002 issue of *Bungakukai.* Daidō's story of a love affair between a single 34-year-old woman and a married 66-year-old man created a stir among young Japanese women. Other candidates for the prize included senior high schooler Rio Shimamoto, whose tale "Ritoru bai ritoru" ("Little by Little") was published in the November 2002 issue of *Gunzo* magazine. In the second half of the year, the Akutagawa Prize went to Man'ichi Yoshimura's "Hariganemushi" ("The Hairworm"), originally published in the May 2003 issue of *Bungakukai.* Its narrative involves a high-school ethics teacher who is undone by his increasingly unmanageable sexual obsession with an uneducated married woman.

Perhaps the most significant event for Japanese literature in 2003 was Haruki Murakami's new translation of American author J.D. Salinger's classic novel of adolescence *The Catcher in the Rye* (1951). Published 39 years after Takashi Nozaki's popular and influential version titled *Raimugibatake de tsukamaete* ("Catch Me in the Rye"), Murakami's translation retained a Japanese version of the original English title—*Kyaccha in za rai.* The translations differed in other respects as well; many critics suggested that Murakami's Holden, the teenage narrator of the story, was more pessimistic and more penetrating than Nozaki's Holden, who was seen as wild and uncontrollable.

The subject of older men with young women made Tamaki Daidō's story a hot topic.

Kyōichi Katayama's *Sekai no chūshin de, ai o sakebu* (2001; "Shouting Love in the Centre of the World") remained on the best-seller list throughout 2003. This account of the life and death of a young couple captivated many young Japanese readers.

The Yomiuri Prize for Literature went to Minae Mizumura's *Honkaku shōsetsu* ("Genuine Novel"). Based on the English novelist Emily Brontë's *Wuthering Heights* (1847), it concerns three sisters and their daughters, living in Tokyo. The Kawabata Prize, given to the year's most accomplished work of short fiction, was awarded to Toshiyuki Horie's "Sutansu dotto" ("Stance Dot") and Koji Aoyama's "Wagi moko kanashi" ("Feeling Sorry for My Sister"). Best-selling literary works that appeared in 2003 included Banana Yoshimoto's *Deddo endo no omoide* ("Memory of the Dead End"), Yamada's *Pei dei!!!* ("Pay Day!!!"), Ira Ishida's Naoki Prize-winning fiction *4 teen* ("Fourteen"), and Haruki Murakami's *Shonen kafuka: Kafka on the Shore Official Magazine,* a collection of his Web site dialogues with readers concerning his work *Umibe no Kafuka* (2002; "Kafka on the Shore").

(YOSHIHIKO KAZAMARU)

Media and Publishing

Media network MERGERS came UNGLUED, conglomerates were broken up, and new PLAYERS—in several senses—arrived on the VIDEO scene. In radio, attention focused on a top personality, SATELLITE radio began marketing efforts, and PUBLIC RADIO was riding high.

TELEVISION

Organization and Regulation. In American television much of 2003 was consumed by the bitter and often surprising battle over the attempt by the U.S. Federal Communications Commission (FCC) to relax the rules that tried to minimize concentration of the ownership of television stations. The FCC, led by its conservative chairman, Michael Powell (the son of U.S. Secretary of State Colin Powell), proposed new rules, including ones that would allow one owner to control TV stations reaching 45% of the country, up from 35%, and that would end a ban on a company's owning a newspaper and an over-the-air station in the same city. Protest movements formed, but it was not until after the FCC had voted to change the rules, in June, that the protesters' effectiveness began to be felt. The movement brought together a rare coalition of conservatives and liberals, including the National Rifle Association and the National Organization for Women, who were joined by their fear that increasing media-ownership concentration would squeeze local voices out of the nation's most powerful communications medium. In the September week that the changes were to take effect, however, a federal appeals court issued a stay against their implementation. Both houses of Congress, although led by the Republicans, separately voted to overturn one or more of the new rules. With all of this up in the air at year's end, the rules-change picture was, as Powell said, "muddied." The television networks and big media companies continued to push aggressively for the changes, but what was surprising was the degree to which this seemingly arcane issue eventually caught the attention of average Americans. A compromise was reached on November 24.

Merger-and-acquisition activity continued through 2003. The top story was likely the troubled financial picture at the Vivendi Universal entertainment conglomerate and the signals it sent to NBC, the last American network without a major-studio partner. NBC parent General Electric (GE) reached an agreement to merge Universal, whose TV and movie interests were worth some $13 billion, with the network; GE would own 80% of the new company, which would be named NBC Universal and would be the world's sixth largest media company. In the deal GE acquired Universal's film and TV studios and a 5,000-film library; the USA Network, the SCI FI Channel, and the Trio cable network; the Spanish-language Telemundo network; and an interest in the Universal Studios theme-park chain. The primary benefit of the merger was the protection that it would give NBC from dependency on advertising for its sole revenue stream. All the other major American television networks were already partnered up with or part of more broad-based entertainment companies. FCC and U.S. Department of Justice approval of the NBC-Universal deal was still pending at year's end, but industry analysts saw few likely roadblocks to its completion. In September the New York Supreme Court ordered Vivendi to pay its former CEO Jean-Marie Messier the €20.6 million (about $23.4 million) severance package that had been promised him but had been halted by a French court while stock-market regulators investigated recent Vivendi financial statements.

Another important development in 2003 was the attempt by Rupert Murdoch's News Corp. to gain control of the leading American consumer satellite-subscription service. DirecTV beamed cable and network channels and other programming into more than 12 million American homes. Murdoch had coveted DirecTV for years, and in April News Corp. agreed to spend $6.6 billion to buy a controlling 34% interest in Hughes Electronics Corp., the DirecTV parent and a subsidiary of General Motors Corp. The service would fill a major hole in News Corp.'s worldwide satellite offerings and give the company another outlet for its own programming. Regulatory approval was pending. Murdoch named his youngest son, James, CEO of the British pay-TV company British Sky Broadcasting (BSkyB). News Corp. owned 35% of BSkyB, and Murdoch sat as company chairman.

Liberty Media paid $7.9 billion for a 57% share of the QVC home shopping network, which reached 85 million households. The FCC cleared Liberty's 98% ownership of QVC; the other 2% remained with QVC's management team. Liberty acquired UnitedGlobalCom (UGC), a cable provider to 11 million subscribers in 25 countries. UGC's main subsidiary, Amsterdam-based United Pan-Europe Communications, was reorganizing following bankruptcy.

In October British regulators approved the £4 billion (about $6.7 billion) merger of Granada and Carlton Communications, both of which ran the commercial TV network ITV. American rivals Viacom Inc. and Haim Saban announced interest in the merged company, since new legislation allowed companies outside the European Union to buy into Britain's commercial TV broadcasters. Viacom president Mel Karmazin was looking at ITV competitor Channel Five, which was owned by pan-European broadcaster RTL and Britain's United Business Media. Saban, who had made a fortune in American children's television, closed a long-fought deal to buy Germany's biggest commercial broadcaster, ProSiebenSat.1, from the insolvent KirchMedia.

SBT, Brazil's second largest network, was ostensibly offered in July to Mexican media giant Grupo Televisa by owner Sílvio Santos, who dramatically indicated that he had only six years to live. Santos, who had hosted a 10-hour variety show on Sundays for three decades, also claimed that he was negotiating with José Bonifacio de Oliveira Sobrinho, a former executive of SBT's main rival, Globo TV. In July Microsoft Corp. chairman Bill Gates disclosed ownership of a 7% stake in Grupo Televisa, which clarified the large-scale deployment of Microsoft's channel guide for cable TV by Televisa's subsidiary Cablevision México. Similar deployments in Mexico and Costa Rica were later made by cable companies Cablevision Monterey, Megacable, PCTV, and Cabletica. Refocusing on its television business, TV Azteca, Mexico's number two broadcaster, spun off mobile-phone operator Unefon in October. TV Azteca and the new Azteca Telecom were owned by Mexican tycoon Ricardo Salinas Pliego.

Hong Kong property developer Lai Sun sold its one-third stake in Asia Television Ltd. (HKATV), the smaller of the territory's two free-to-air broadcasters, for HK$230 million (about U.S.$29.6 million). HKATV's CEO Chan Wing-kee bought the shares, increasing his ownership of company shares to half. Television Broadcasts (TVB) launched its Galaxy pay-TV service in Hong Kong in December. Tom.com, the media company of Li Ka-shing, Hong Kong's richest businessman, bought 64% of the Mandarin-language China Entertainment Television (CETV) from AOL Time Warner, which retained 36%. In late October, Metro-Goldwyn-Mayer, in a joint venture with CNBC Asia Pacific, launched an MGM movie channel on satellite and cable TV systems in Asia to broadcast subtitled motion pictures from MGM's 4,000-film library.

Programming. In American television programming, the year's surprise was the initially modest cable makeover show that aimed to bridge the gulf between gay and straight men. *Queer Eye for the Straight Guy* debuted on NBC's Bravo cable outlet in July, featuring a "Fab Five" of gay men, each with special expertise. In each episode they made over a style- or grooming-challenged straight man nominated for the show, usually by his wife or girlfriend. Snappy repartee from the gay men gave it more pungency than most makeover shows, and the program reflected a trend of increasing media acceptance of homosexuality. The audience grew weekly, and the show even proved popular during a few prime-time airings on broadcast network NBC. After a short initial season, a second season of 40 episodes began in November, and the producers were beginning to clone *Queer Eye* to run in other countries.

(From left) Ted Allen, Thom Filicia, Jai Rodriguez, Carson Kressley, and Kyan Douglas—the cast of Queer Eye for the Straight Guy*—arrive at the Emmy Awards ceremony in Los Angeles on September 21.*

The most popular prime-time series, in both the season that ended in May and the early portion of the one that began in September, was again CBS's *CSI: Crime Scene Investigation,* a stylish and carefully detailed drama about a Las Vegas, Nev., forensics team. The most popular comedy was, again, NBC's *Friends,* a series about six young New York City pals that was expected to end its 10-season run with considerable fanfare in May 2004. The Emmy Awards, however, went to NBC's political drama *The West Wing,* which won despite creator and head writer Aaron Sorkin's exit from the show, and to veteran CBS family comedy *Everybody Loves Raymond.* The show's star, Ray Romano, had won an Emmy himself in 2002. (*See* BIOGRAPHIES.) In 2003 James Gandolfini, who played America's favourite bad guy—Tony Soprano on HBO's *The Sopranos*—for a fifth season, took the award for best actor in a drama. (*See* BIOGRAPHIES.)

In the spring the American television networks mostly distinguished themselves with dedicated and costly reporting from the U.S.-led invasion of Iraq. Hundreds of reporters from the U.S. and many other countries were "embedded" with U.S. and British military units, which led to wider coverage of the military action but also increasing possibilities of injury and death. Further, embedded journalists were open to charges that the picture they presented of the war was unbalanced at best, jingoistic at worst. (*See* Special Report.) Australian Psychological Society members urged parents to shield preschool to preteen children from TV's relentless 24-hour coverage of the war.

The 2003–04 American prime-time TV season began in disarray. As the calendar year drew to a close, five of the six broadcast networks, all but CBS, had suffered ratings declines—compared with the beginning of the prior season—among the 18-to-49-year-old viewers advertisers most coveted. Network executives blamed the sharp declines, especially among young men, on a change in the methodology that the Nielsen Media Research audience-measurement service was using to calculate viewership, but Nielsen pointed to other factors—including increased Internet and video-game usage and programming that did not target men—as potential reasons for the dramatic change. With or without young men, none of the nearly 40 new series for the fall television season, including an NBC situation comedy with luminary Whoopi Goldberg, was proving to be especially popular in the beginning months of the season. There were modest successes, such as the CBS drama about a young woman routinely visited by God, *Joan of Arcadia,* but no undeniable breakaway hits.

Although it was the season's clear ratings success, CBS became embroiled in controversy over its movie about former president Ronald Reagan and his wife, Nancy, that it planned to air in November. As conservative groups and the Republican Party raised objections to the portrayal of conservative icon Reagan, who was suffering from Alzheimer disease, CBS declared the program unfair to the president and declined to air it. They sold it to corporate sibling Showtime, a pay-cable channel. Some critics charged that the network's capitulation was politically motivated, in view of its interest in regulatory issues before the Republican-led government, but CBS chief Leslie Moonves insisted that it was merely a matter of the movie that was delivered being different from the one that the network had contracted to buy.

Across the Atlantic, the BBC also was embroiled in a political dispute, this one with Prime Minister Tony Blair over a May 29 report that the government had exaggerated the threat of Iraq's weapons program. A judicial inquiry was set to look into the apparent suicide of British weapons expert David Kelly, which was possibly related to talks he had had with BBC reporter Andrew Gilligan. Also, the BBC was criticized by News Corp. for buying American and other foreign programs that boosted BBC domestic ratings at the expense of commercial broadcasters. It was suggested that the BBC sell some of its more popular programs to other channels.

The Arab satellite station al-Jazeera launched an English-language Web site in September, five months after hackers had brought its temporary Web site down during the Iraq war. Al-Jazeera reporter Tayssir Alouni was arrested and jailed in Spain, accused of being a member of al-Qaeda. In Saudi Arabia an unprecedented TV program, *Saudi Women Speak Out,* allowed eight women to speak openly about subjects such as the right to drive, unemployment, and political participation.

A SARS (severe acute respiratory syndrome) channel was established in May jointly by Singapore Press Holdings, Media Corporation of Singapore, and StarHub to broadcast news and information about the epidemic. (*See* HEALTH AND DISEASE: *Special Report*) Action star Jackie Chan starred in a TV commercial broadcast globally to revive tourism in SARS-hit Hong Kong. A Philippine UNICEF project involving Probe Media Foundation, Asia News Channel, and National Broadcasting Network taught teenagers to search, shoot, and script video news features on topics of interest to the youth for airing as the Kabataan News Network.

A Taiwanese soap opera, or *chinovela* ("Chinese" + "television" + "novella"), made a hit in Asia. *Liow sing hua yen* ("Meteor Garden"), based on the Japanese comic book *Hana yori dango* ("Men Are Better than Flowers"), starred the boy band F4 and Barbie Xu.

News Corp.-owned British subsidiary NDS Ltd. provided China's cable authorities with broadcast encryption technology for distribution nationwide, but News Corp. (and other foreign media) content remained restricted on domestic networks. China's state broadcasting authority disallowed TV commercials for feminine hygiene products and hemorrhoid ointments during mealtimes. Similarly, Vietnam's cultural police disallowed TV ads for condoms and toilet paper at mealtimes. The Ukrainian parliament passed a law banning alcohol and tobacco advertising on TV and radio and restricting ads in print media because of health considerations.

Technology. The flat-screen technology firm Cambridge Display Technology, a University of Cambridge spin-off that was vying with the Eastman Kodak Co. in producing next-generation flat screens from organic LEDs (light-emitting diodes), laid off 20% of its staff to reduce manufacturing costs. South Korea's Samsung Electronics joined with Japan's Sony Corp. to manufacture LCD (liquid crystal display) flat screens, while the largest maker of LCD panels, LG.Philips, a joint venture between South Korea's LG Electronics and Dutch group Philips Electronics, planned to invest $2.6 billion in new flat-screen production. Motorola, Inc., signed with the Hong Kong firm Proview International Holdings to make flat-screen televisions and computer displays. China's TCL International Holdings and the French electronics maker Thomson combined their TV and DVD business to become the world's largest TV maker and produce 18 million TV sets annually, with sales of more than €3 billion (about $3.5 billion).

Télévision Française 1 (TF1) and Canal+, France's two top commercial TV operators and owners of satellite TV services, planned to pipe digital TV over high-speed, high-capacity phone lines. Europe's first high-definition television (HDTV) channel, Euro 1080, made a trial broadcast in September for a planned launch in 2004. Anthony Wood, creator of the ReplayTV digital TV recorder, unveiled his Roku HD1000 media player, which displayed or played digital media such as photos and music on HDTV sets.

AP/Wide World Photos

Flat-screen LCD video displays were all the rage in 2003. Here an array of Samsung flat-panel television monitors is being installed at the Consumer Electronics Show at the Las Vegas (Nev.) Convention Center in January.

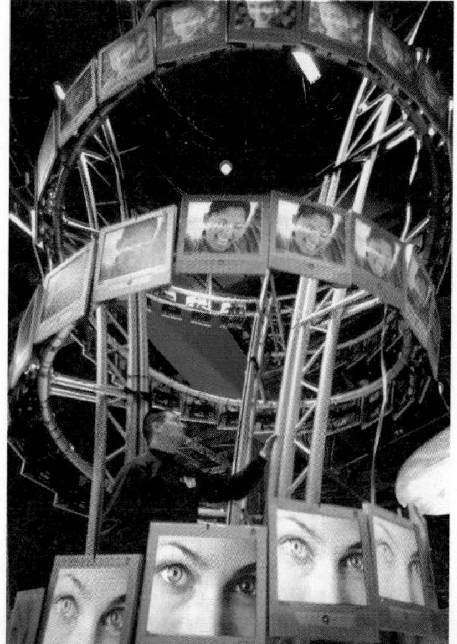

TiVo, a maker of TV-recording devices, introduced a TV-audience-measuring system for advertisers and network programmers. It tracked customer viewing data gathered from TiVo's 700,000 users. J-Phone, a Japanese unit of Britain's Vodafone Group, announced that users could now watch TV programs on mobile phone screens. Personal video players with 20 gigabytes of memory arrived from France. Archos AV320 and Thomson's Lyra RD2780 had 96- and 89-mm (3.8- and 3.5-in) screens, respectively, and could play back digital video from a video camera, the Internet, or TV.

Over the summer India's four biggest cities—Mumbai (Bombay), Delhi, Chennai (Madras), and Kolkata (Calcutta)—began to shift to a set-top-box system for watching cable TV, a move designed to reduce piracy. The box usually cost about $120, however, and so would be out of reach of many potential viewers. India had the third largest cable TV subscriber base in the world (44 million) because of low rates.

RADIO

The big news in American radio was made, not surprisingly, by its biggest star, nationally syndicated right-wing talk-show host Rush Limbaugh, whose show was said to reach some 20 million listeners weekly. First, in early October, Limbaugh lost his side job as a National Football League commentator on the ESPN sports cable TV channel after suggesting that the well-regarded quarterback Donovan McNabb was overrated by media eager for African American quarterbacks to do well. More startling, however, was the admission later that month by Limbaugh that for years following back surgery, he had been addicted to painkillers sometimes prescribed by doctors but also popular with recreational drug users. The admission seemingly was forced by reporting in the *National Enquirer,* a supermarket tabloid often derided for its willingness to pay for information. A former maid of Limbaugh's told the paper that she had been her employer's drug connection and had purchased for him large quantities of OxyContin and other pills. Limbaugh left his show and checked himself into a rehabilitation centre in Arizona. He returned to the air in November after what he called "five intense weeks, probably the most educational and intense five weeks on myself that I have ever spent." He did not try to reconcile the help he received with his frequent on-air calls for harsher punishment for drug use.

The battle to win consumers to the new subscription-based satellite radio technology heated up with aggressive marketing at Christmastime. In December, XM Satellite Radio was the leading player, with over one million subscribers, and Sirius Satellite Radio was a distant second with 200,000. Sirius officials said the service needed two million subscribers to be profitable. Some industry analysts were predicting rapid growth for the services, which broadcast a wide variety of music and other programming with limited or no commercials, as satellite radios began to be included in new-model cars. Sirius launched a broadcast service of 60 types of music into stores and office buildings, hoping to break into the "elevator music" market dominated by Muzak, while XM paired up with Canadian Satellite Radio to sell its services in Canada.

In the meantime, as consolidation elsewhere in the radio business led to homogenization and a loss of local voices, one clear benefit was a gain in listenership for National Public Radio. Moreover, Joan Kroc, the widow of McDonald's restaurant founder Ray Kroc and a devoted public-radio listener, left NPR more than $200 million in her will, an amount NPR said was "believed to be the largest monetary gift ever received by an American cultural institution." NPR officials said that the money would go into an endowment to help create financial stability for the nonprofit organization, which had often scraped for funds. The U.S. Congress approved a budget of $557 million in 2004 for the Broadcasting Board of Governors, overseer of the Voice of America and other overseas radio broadcasters. It also authorized the establishment of a 24-hour Middle East radio and TV network. On November 28 the venerable Radio Free Europe/Radio Liberty announced that it would cease broadcasts to the three Baltic States, Slovakia, Romania, Bulgaria, and Croatia at the end of the year.

U.S. regulators approved Univision Radio, the product of a merger between Univision and Hispanic Broadcasting that brought more than 50 TV stations and 68 radio stations together. Radio Unica Communications, the Miami, Fla.-based Spanish-language broadcaster, filed for bankruptcy to clear the way for its sale to Multicultural Broadcasting for $150 million and the separate sale of its radio network and promotions company. Its AM operations included Radio Unica Network and stations covering Spanish-speaking markets in Florida, New York, Texas, and California.

Former Peruvian president Alberto Fujimori, living in exile in Japan, got his own radio show. Financed by friends in Peru, *The Chino's Hour* (in reference to Fujimori's nickname) offered the disgraced leader's political commentary. *The Voices of Kidnapping,* a call-in program on Radio Caracol, remained a lifeline for Colombians who broadcast messages to their loved ones held hostage by groups of insurgents and criminals. It was the brainchild of Herbin Hoyos, himself a kidnapped-and-escaped radio journalist.

Britain's radio sector seemed ready for mergers and consolidation once the competition commissioners approved. Newly relaxed media ownership laws boosted stocks of Capital Radio, Chrysalis, Emap, and GWR. American companies such as Clear Channel and Viacom showed little interest, however.

(RAMONA MONETTE SARGAN FLORES; STEVE JOHNSON)

NEWSPAPERS

After two years of advertising declines and cost cutting to maintain earnings levels, newspapers in mature Western democracies experienced a financially tepid 2003 with an anxious eye to the end of the worst advertising recession in more than half a century.

The genesis of an economic recovery in North America and Western Europe came without job gains and left newspapers that had become reliant on employment advertising in the past decade struggling to see a turnaround in economic fortunes. Local retail advertising remained strong even as the retail environment continued its strategic shift away from local stores, which promoted themselves on the basis of value, toward national and international megastores that discounted goods and services at the expense of traditional advertising and marketing expenditures. Nevertheless, there were signs of optimism, including the end of double-digit decreases in employment advertising, interest-rate-fueled growth in real-estate and automotive advertising, and sharp growth in nationally focused display advertising and inserts. In some countries the fragmentation of television and radio audiences and the impact of the Internet on television-viewing time helped to better position newspapers in the advertising marketplace.

Paid circulation of daily newspapers had been in decline in North America since 1989 and in Western Europe since 1990. In 2002 circulations in Western countries declined 1.3%—the sharpest one-year decline since 1995. While circulations of daily newspapers had dropped 2.2%, the circulation slide increased to 3.5% in 1997 as the Internet increased in popularity. Significant research in the United States, the United Kingdom, France, Belgium, Norway, and other countries showed that a smaller number of young adults over time were reading newspapers or were reading them with less frequency than previous generations. Not only was the reading habit occurring less in formative teenage years, but new evidence showed that even young adults who had developed the habit were reducing their reading frequency. Rising Internet usage, combined with these long-term trends among young people, continued to impact sales frequency of print daily newspapers.

While regional daily newspapers in the United Kingdom saw circulations decline after the major companies discontinued discounting, newspapers in the United States and elsewhere saw circulations inflated through third-party sales, giveaways to schools, and other marketing offers—blessed by each country's circulation audit bureau. To illustrate the level of gimmickry involved with newspaper subscriptions, a South Korean government commission found that more than 75% of subscription offers since 2000 had come with a discount or gift. Meanwhile, the U.S. became the latest country to create national do-not-call lists that protect consumers from intrusive telemarketers, a move expected to impact those newspapers that relied on telemarketing for more than half of their subscription acquisition.

The launch of free commuter newspapers throughout Europe in the past eight years sparked similar ventures by traditional publishers in Italy, The Netherlands, and the U.S., among others. Led by Metro International, daily newspapers began launching weekly entertainment and youth-oriented newspapers. The Chicago-based Tribune Co. launched a free commuter newspaper in New York City called *amNew York,* and the Washington Post Co. launched a similar venture called *Express.* Other such daily papers were being planned.

Similarly, traditional publishing companies accelerated their creation of Spanish-language daily newspapers in the U.S.—including Belo in southern California and Dallas, Texas; Knight Ridder in Fort Worth, Texas; Tribune in Chicago and Florida; and others.

The lesson learned through the distribution of free commuter newspapers and Spanish-language newspapers was that there were vast numbers of nonreaders and infrequent readers in certain markets that might best be reached through new newspapers instead of traditional ones. That trend extended to newspaper publishing in Latin America, South Africa, and Asia, where down- to midmarket newspapers were aimed at undereducated, nonreading segments of the population.

In recent years Latin American launches had included Epensa's *Correo* in Lima, Peru; Diarios Modernos's *Nuestro Diario* in Guatemala; and La Nación's *Al Día* in San José, Costa Rica. In each case the newspapers were launched in markets that were saturated by existing newspapers, but the new offerings created hundreds of thousands of new daily readers.

Another success story was the national launch in 2002 by South Africa's Media24 of the *Daily Sun.* Similar in style to the Latin American down-market dailies and the Bangkok newspaper *Thai Rath,* the English-language *Daily Sun* captured the imagination of the South African newspaper industry. A decade after the end of apartheid, the majority of South Africa's 34 million blacks, while quickly moving up social and income ladders, remained poor and undereducated. The *Daily Sun* targeted the fast-rising aspirant black population with raucous headlines, many photographs and maps, and short well-written stories in its fixed-page tabloid format. The *Daily Sun* had a 250,000 daily circulation, with a readership that largely had never before read a newspaper. In Nigeria the informal Free Readers Association launched a partnership with vendors to allow people who could not afford to buy newspapers to read them at newsstands.

Perhaps the most significant financial and strategic transaction in 2003 was the purchase by Australia's John Fairfax Holdings of New Zealand's Independent Newspapers Ltd. The largest publishing companies in Denmark, Jyllands-Posten and Politiken, merged. U.S.-based Gannett purchased Scottish Media Group. The New York Times Co. exercised an option to buy out the Washington Post's ownership share in the *International Herald Tribune.* After a dispute between family owners, Freedom Communications put its company up for bid only to reach a settlement that allowed family members who wanted to opt out of ownership to do so. The Seattle (Wash.) Times Co. and the Hearst Corp. tussled over a joint-operating agreement.

In other developments the *San Francisco Examiner,* sold by Hearst three years earlier in a complex exchange sale of assets, laid off most of its staff and switched from paid to free distribution. Even as Axel Springer Verlag went through challenging economic times in Germany, the company launched a 700,000-circulation daily newspaper in Poland called *Fakt.* Hong Kong's popular *Apple Daily* was launched in Taiwan, with an immediate distribution of 750,000. Business-oriented daily newspapers such as the *Financial Times, The Wall Street Journal, De Financieel Economische Tijd,* and others continued to languish in the global business-to-business advertising slump, which thereby prompted rumours of sales and market repositioning.

Size increasingly seemed to be an issue for publishers. In the hypercompetitive London market, the broadsheet *The Independent* launched a same-day tabloid edition in what executives equated to offering toothpaste in different sizes to the marketplace. While Norwegian newspapers continued to move away from broadsheet formats, British editors suggested that even their newspapers could be converted to tabloid format if the market preferred it. In Sweden, *Dagens Nyheter* experimented with a combination of broadsheet and tabloid editions.

Newspapers continued to send mixed signals on whether an industry standard would ever be developed for their popular Web sites. Marketers at newspapers that converted their Web sites to a free-registration basis saw nonreaders of their print titles opt in to digital access at rates of two and three times the print circulation base—names used to sell newspaper-branded products. Other companies, notably CanWest in Canada, declared it irrational for newspaper companies to give away content for free and announced steps to eliminate most free access. In most cases newspapers were implementing strategies somewhere between two extremes—allowing free access to certain content and combinations of pay-per-view and timed access for other content.

The *New York Times* was rocked by a scandal involving a journalist who deceived editors and plagiarized articles. The newspaper's top two editors eventually resigned, and questions were raised about management styles. A new book that alleged close ties between editors of *Le Monde,* France's leading newspaper, and the country's political establishment prompted ethics inquiries. In mid-November Canadian press baron Conrad M. Black resigned as CEO of Hollinger International, whose holdings included major newspapers in Chicago, New York, London, and Jerusalem. Black and his partners were accused of taking $15.6 million in unauthorized payments; he faced the U.S. Securities and Exchange Commission in December.

The never-ending battle over censorship and press freedom continued in many countries. The Jordanian government closed a weekly newspaper and detained three journalists over an article about the Prophet Muhammad's sex life; the Zimbabwean government continued to shutter a number of daily newspapers; and Venezuelan Pres. Hugo Chávez Frías at one point used currency controls to deny newspapers the U.S. dollars they need for importing newsprint. Subtle and not-so-subtle pressure from the government of Pres. Vladimir Putin in Russia prompted the closure of several newspapers there. Meanwhile, the fall of Saddam Hussein's government in Iraq yielded the launch of dozens of new daily newspapers in an array of news and opinions not seen since the collapse of communism in Central and Eastern Europe more than a decade earlier.

The government in China continued its long-term goal of moving the newspaper industry from its subsidized status to being entirely exposed to the free market, and it discontinued the practice of free-subscription offers to households. Analysts expected newspaper closures, but it was unclear whether a private-sector Chinese newspaper industry would be dominated by regional or national dailies. (EARL J. WILKINSON)

MAGAZINES

While the U.S. magazine industry began rebounding in 2003 from its two-year economic slump, its greatest gains came from the electronic sector. The Online Publishers Association, which represented 25 Internet publishers, reported 23% higher advertising revenues among its members during the first nine months of 2003 compared with 2002. During the first quarter of 2003, Meredith Publishing's online advertising revenue increased 80%, and Ziff Davis's online revenue rose 87%. The increases came partly from improved technology that gathered information about online users, which publishers used to sell other products to readers or advertisements to advertisers.

Louis Borders, founder of Borders Books, launched <Keepmedia.com>, a Web venture that allowed users to read content and archives of more than 150 magazines for a $4.95 monthly fee. The site had an intelligent database that tracked what subscribers read and used that information to steer them to additional content. *Folio* magazine reported, "In effect, it creates a second market for magazine stories, not unlike a foreign release for films."

Total advertising revenue for print and online magazines increased 9% during the first nine months of 2003 compared with the same period in 2002. Magazine publishers were worried, however, that as do-it-yourself checkouts spread at grocery and department stores, single-copy sales would continue to fall. In order to distinguish self-checkout areas, many retailers had removed customary magazine racks and other product displays. According to a 2002 supermarket study, only 12% of shoppers who used self-checkout lines bought products that were displayed nearby, compared with 20% in traditional checkouts. Single-copy sales were down in the six months ended June 30 compared with a year earlier; according to the Audit Bureau of Circulations, 54% of titles reported that their sales were off from 2002.

More than 850 publishing delegates gathered at the Carrousel du Louvre in Paris for the 34th Fédération Internationale de la Presse Périodique (FIPP) World Magazine Congress in May. The event was a homecoming in France, where the FIPP had been founded more than 75 years earlier. The record attendance came despite China's last-minute decision to keep its 118 delegates at home owing to the SARS (severe acute respiratory syndrome) scare. The appointment of William T. Kerr, chairman and CEO of Meredith Corp. USA, as FIPP chairman was announced at the closing ceremony. He replaced Gérald de Roquemaurel, chairman and CEO of Hachette Filipacchi Médias, who completed his two-year term.

Everyday Food, *Martha Stewart Living Omnimedia's new magazine, with Stewart's name displayed discreetly on the cover, debuted in September 2003.*

In July the Canadian government announced deep cuts to a fund designed to help protect domestic magazines from American domination. The Canadian Magazine Fund would decrease to $16 million in 2004 from the $32.6 million publishers shared in 2003. Government officials said Canada's magazine industry was on "a solid footing and enjoying healthy growth." A feared saturation of the market by big American magazines after legislative changes in 1999 did not materialize. The government would reallocate some funding to subsidize community newspapers, particularly those catering to ethnic and aboriginal communities.

Wal-Mart's 2,800 stores stopped selling *Maxim, Stuff,* and *FHM* in May because of their racy content and in June added blinders to hide cover lines of *Cosmopolitan, Glamour, Marie Claire,* and *Redbook.* The chain added the family-oriented *American Magazine* to its shelves and gave the June-launched magazine a big boost. According to "Capell's Circulation Report," Wal-Mart accounted for 15% of all single-copy magazine sales. Media buyer Carol McDonald of OMD Chicago told *Folio* magazine, "Let's face it, if you're not in Wal-Mart, you're not doing business in this country."

Another new magazine, *Lucky,* was named *Advertising Age*'s Magazine of the Year in 2003. The women's magazine, which called itself "the magazine about shopping," told readers how and where to buy clothing, beauty items, and household products. It surpassed one million subscribers during its first two years.

Martha Stewart Living cut its rate base from 2.3 million to 1.8 million subscribers in October. Single-copy sales of the magazine fell 18% for the first half of 2003. Martha Stewart Living Omnimedia revenues suffered after insider-trader allegations began swirling around Martha Stewart, the company's founder, in 2002. Stewart resigned as chair and CEO of the company in June 2003. The company began regular publication of *Everyday Food,* a recipe magazine, with the September issue after a six-month test run. It was the first Stewart magazine that did not include her name in the title—a decision she described as a "strategic business move."

(DAVID E. SUMNER)

BOOK PUBLISHING

United States. Toward the end of a seesaw year, many in publishing were hopeful that a third-quarter uptick in book sales in 2003 represented recovery and growth in an industry that had been facing challenging conditions despite increases in both domestic consumer expenditures and publisher net-dollar sales in 2002.

Following a lacklustre 2002 retail holiday season, the new year brought a weak economy, war in the Middle East, and increasing competition from other entertainment media. As a result, in the early months of 2003, trade-book sales fell, and the Census Bureau of the Department of Commerce reported that results for the first five months of the year were 2.6% off the previous year's sales. The publishing industry (including both chain and independent booksellers), however, entered the second half of the year buoyed by more positive sales trends, thanks in large measure to best-selling author J.K. Rowling's fifth Harry Potter title, *Harry Potter and the Order of the Phoenix.*

On June 21 the title—with a record first printing of 6.8 million copies—went on sale, and within days the book's American publisher, Scholastic, estimated that over five million copies had been sold. Quickly, Scholastic went back to press for an additional 1.7 million copy second printing. During the summer consumers also flocked to bookstores to purchase *Living History,* Sen. Hillary Rodham Clinton's memoirs. In addition, the relaunch of TV impresario Oprah Winfrey's book club sent millions out to purchase the backlist classic *East of Eden* by John Steinbeck. As sales of hardcover children's titles led the way, U.S. Census figures showed bookstore sales up over 10% for June, July, and August 2003 (the most recent figures available) over the same period in 2002.

Despite a potential fall recovery, in the minds of many in the industry the prognosis was still guarded. According to the Book Industry Study Group's (BISG's) *2002 Consumer Research Study on Book Purchasing,* trade-publishing growth was flat, and there were no projected changes in the trend. With a sales increase in adult trade titles between 2001 and 2002 of only 1%, consumers purchased 1.63 billion units and spent almost $13 billion in 2002, the last year for which final figures were available. Though publisher revenues were rising, the boost appeared to come from price increases rather than a growth in unit sales. BISG's *Book Industry Trends 2003* projected total consumer expenditures of all book sales in 2003 of $37.6 billion, a rise of 2.8% over 2002. Those sales, however, were projected to be realized on a 0.5% drop in unit sales, and BISG projected only a 0.7% rise in unit sales in 2004. With consumers 50 years or older accounting for 53% of trade books purchased, the industry faced significant challenges in widening and deepening its market.

Many in publishing, however, pointed to several positive signs. One was the phenomenal cultural and consumer event surrounding the publication of the latest Potter title. Nationwide, thousands of bookstores created elaborate events and staged in-store activities for customers that involved the book's settings and characters. For independent booksellers offering such unique experiences, the events helped strengthen ties to customers in a year that saw their market share grow to 15.5%. On the political front, booksellers and librarians in Vermont, Massachusetts, and other states worked during the year with lawmakers on the state and national level to amend the USA PATRIOT Act to preserve the privacy of book-related records. (DAN CULLEN)

International. In a sign that India was finally coming to grips with the issue of piracy, in July Pearson Education successfully pursued Hyderabad publishers through the courts for copyright infringement, and the Delhi High Court published a landmark injunction in August 2003 to stop Indian publisher Pushpa Prakashan from producing illegal translations of J.K. Rowling's Harry Potter titles. Since 2000 some 250,000 titles had been seized. Pirated copies of Rowling books in translation also began to appear in China. Any translations available on the Internet, however, were not subject to copyright laws.

AOL Time Warner put its book division up for sale for at least $400 million but allegedly dropped the price to $300 million when potential bidders, including Bertelsmann subsidiary Random House, failed to make any offers. In May Bertelsmann showed renewed interest after it sold its scientific publishing arm, BertelsmannSpringer, for €1.05 billion (about $1.21 billion) to private equity firms Cinven and Candover.

In July, in the face of fierce opposition by the Bundeskartellamt antitrust body, Bertelsmann subsidiary Random House Deutschland, owner of Goldmann, agreed to drop its controversial takeover of Ullstein Heyne List (Germany's largest trade publisher), which was owned by Axel Springer. It proposed instead to purchase only paperback publisher Heyne.

The European Commission rejected the French government's request to refer the takeover of the European and Latin American businesses of Vivendi Universal Publishing by the Lagardère Group (owner of Hachette Livre) to the competition authorities in France and insisted that the case be kept in Brussels. Its investigation was opened in June, and the final report was due in January 2004.

The U.K.'s Taylor & Francis (T&F) remained active on the takeover front. In January it bought Bios Scientific for £2.7 million (£1 = about $1.61). T&F subsequently paid $95 million for the U.S.-based CRC Press. In July T&F subsidiary Routledge acquired Kogan Page's 200 active higher-education titles. Also in July, after nearly 50 years of independence, Frank Cass & Co accepted a takeover bid worth £11.3 million, with an additional £3.7 million dependent upon future performance, mainly because it was struggling to get space in large high-street booksellers. It claimed that its difficulty in doing so represented a form of "cultural censorship."

In July the merger was completed between Aschehoug Dansk Forlag and Egmont Lademann, both owned by the Egmont Media Group, to create Denmark's second largest publisher, with an output of 1,000 titles annually.

The European Commission announced that printed products would continue to be eligible for reduced rates of value-added tax. Although VAT accordingly remained at 0% in the U.K. and a few other member states, it was expected that a VAT minimum rate of 5% would be established in due course.

The German book industry experienced a 2.7% drop in sales during the first half of the year. Local sensibilities were also offended by the fact that a book in English, Rowling's *Harry Potter and the Order of the Phoenix,* headed the best-seller list for the first time.

The Copyright Amendment (Parallel Importation) Bill 2002 was passed in a much-amended form by the Australian Senate. The final version excluded printed books and thereby effectively upheld the status quo of territorial copyright. (PETER CURWEN)

U.S. Sen. Hillary Rodham Clinton signs copies of her runaway best-selling memoir, Living History, *in a New York City bookstore in June. The first printing's one million copies were sold in a month.*

The Media Go to War

by Peter Kellner

On March 20, 2003, Anglo-American ground forces crossed into Iraq in order to overthrow Pres. Saddam Hussein. The U.S.-led coalition's war against Hussein was an entirely new experience, however, not only for the fighting troops but also for the reporters and crews covering the action. This conflict was the first sustained, conventional land war for many years to be fought by troops from major Western democracies. In the Gulf War of 1991, ground troops were engaged in battle for just four days, while in Kosovo and Afghanistan ground forces from Western countries were not involved to any significant degree. In addition, technology had transformed the way the media worked. By 2003 satellite communications had become compact, mobile, and cheap; 24-hour television and radio news channels had become familiar throughout the world; and the Internet offered the capacity to deliver news around the globe just minutes after it had been written. Live reports could be transmitted from almost every battle zone, so the public could follow the war, or at least some aspects of it, virtually in real time. This resulted in some powerful images and pieces of reporting, both from the front lines of the coalition forces and from inside Iraqi cities, and, for the first time, from Arab as well as Western sources. The Qatar-based Al-Jazeera TV station had access to Basra and parts of Baghdad from which Western journalists were barred until those two cities were occupied by coalition forces.

Photo by Lance Cpl. Jennifer Krusen

A media photographer is himself caught on film by a U.S. servicewoman in a 1st Marine Division convoy in Basra, Iraq, in March.

Journalists who wanted to report on the fighting from the front lines had two options. They could become "embedded" with coalition military units or operate independently as "unilaterals." Some 600 journalists, about 450 of them from the U.S., chose to be "embeds." Each lived with his or her unit and held the honorary rank of major. They witnessed the war firsthand, with almost complete access to the troops. In return, they agreed not to write about imminent attacks, future operations, or classified weapons. Journalists also agreed to report on military actions in only general terms to prevent Iraqi forces from securing vital intelligence. (Geraldo Rivera of Fox News was temporarily removed from his unit for revealing its exact position.)

The embedded journalists produced many dramatic firsthand reports of the fighting as the coalition forces advanced on Baghdad, but doubts surfaced about their ability to assess the wider progress of the war. On March 26 several "embeds" reported that a convoy of up to 120 Iraqi tanks was leaving Basra. The next day a British spokesman admitted that only 14 tanks had left the city. In addition, the very status of these embedded journalists might have compromised their independence. Phillip Knightly, the Australian-born author of *The First Casualty,* one of the standard books on the history of war reporting, said, "I was able to find only one instance of an embedded correspondent who wrote a story highly critical of the behaviour of U.S. troops." This was when William Branigin of the *Washington Post* reported the deaths of Iraqi civilians at a U.S. military checkpoint. The official account said that warning shots had first been fired at a car that refused to stop. Branigin wrote that no such shots were fired.

The "unilaterals" had fewer constraints than their embedded colleagues but also far less access to coalition troops; thus, their ability to report the war proved to be no greater. One of the most significant false stories of the war—that, after 10 days, the U.S. forces were planning a pause in their advance on Baghdad—emanated from a group of unilaterals.

The coalition established an official press centre at its central command in Qatar, where regular briefings were given to the world's media. Many journalists, however, complained that little useful information was provided. The head of communication planning at Britain's Ministry of Defence subsequently admitted severe shortcomings, including the failure to provide adequate "context-setting briefings."

Although the information provided in Qatar was generally accurate, if sparse, there were times when the fog of war obscured the truth. On April 2 reporters were shown military video film of the rescue of U.S. Army Pvt. Jessica

Lynch from an Iraqi military hospital near Nassiriya. According to the official account, which was widely reported around the world, Lynch was part of a maintenance team that had been ambushed on March 23. Nine of the team were killed; Lynch was stabbed and shot but continued to fire back at the Iraqi troops. After she was captured, she was harshly interrogated and slapped about the head. Eight days later U.S. special forces fought their way into the hospital against heavy resistance and rescued her.

Key parts of this account were later found to be untrue. Lynch was wounded but not shot or stabbed, and another soldier in the unit (not Lynch) had fired back. Far from being badly treated in the hospital, she received the best treatment that the Iraqi doctors and their meagre resources could provide. By the time the U.S. special forces arrived, Iraqi troops had left the area. There was no resistance. Moreover, the Iraqi doctors had tried to hand Lynch back to the U.S. Army two days earlier, but when the Iraqi ambulance approached the American lines, U.S. troops opened fire and forced it to turn around.

If the quality of information available to journalists on and behind the coalition lines was variable, it was no better on the other side. Hussein's regime provided no media access to Iraqi troops south of the capital, but it sought to have its side of the arguments—political, diplomatic, and military—conveyed to the outside world via journalists who remained in Baghdad and Basra, notably those working for Al-Jazeera. Although the American TV networks withdrew from Baghdad shortly before the start of the war, the BBC and other British broadcasters remained, as did television teams from many other countries. Some major American newspapers, such as the *New York Times*, had correspondents in Baghdad throughout the war.

Iraqi officials—most notably the perennially optimistic information minister, Muhammad Sa'id al-Sahaf—consistently denied that the coalition forces were gaining ground. As late as April 9, Sahaf was predicting a comprehensive Iraqi victory, even as U.S. tanks could be seen behind him crossing the Tigris River in the heart of Baghdad.

Iraq imposed no formal censorship on foreign journalists, and live reports were a regular feature from the roof of the Palestine Hotel, the de facto Baghdad headquarters of the international press. Some self-censorship, however, was inevitable. Most Western journalists, especially television crews, employed local staff as fixers, interpreters, and support staff and sought to protect them. Only when central Baghdad fell to coalition forces on April 9 did foreign journalists in the city feel able to abandon such restraint and to report without inhibition.

The biggest media winners throughout the world were the television news channels, which saw their audiences increase dramatically. In the U.S., Fox News increased its audience fourfold to a daily average of 3.3 million viewers during the war, overtaking the well-established CNN (with a daily average of 2.65 million viewers). Fox benefited from taking a firmly pro-coalition stance toward the war, while CNN upheld its tradition of striving for objective detachment.

Altogether, 15 journalists lost their lives covering the war, many of them almost certainly victims of "friendly fire." Those dead included NBC TV's David Bloom, Michael Kelly (*see* OBITUARIES) of the *Washington Post*, Terry Lloyd from Britain's Independent Television News, Christian Liebig of the German magazine *Focus*, Julio Anguita Parrado of the Spanish newspaper *El Mundo*, and Argentine television's Mario Podesta. In Baghdad two cameramen, one with Reuters and one with Spanish television, were killed when U.S. tanks fired at the Palestine Hotel, and an Al-Jazeera correspondent died when at least one U.S. bomb hit the station's Baghdad offices. The International Press Institute criticized the U.S. forces for these attacks on civilian targets. Despite high-tech developments, war correspondents in Iraq faced as many challenges and as much danger as those in previous wars ever had.

Peter Kellner is chairman of pollster YouGov Ltd. and the author of The New Mutualism.

Military Affairs

No WMD were used in 2003, but the threat posed by them was enough to initiate a preemptive WAR against IRAQ, create CONFRONTATIONS between the international community and Iran and North Korea, and inspire the creation of a new multinational partnership to combat PROLIFERATION.

IRAQ

After a four-year hiatus, UN weapons inspectors returned to Iraq in November 2002 to verify whether Saddam Hussein's regime had eliminated all of its stockpiles of weapons of mass destruction (WMD; *see* Sidebar) and programs to develop them. By the beginning of March 2003, the United States and the United Kingdom had grown exasperated with the lack of progress and declared the diplomatic process over. Weeks of covert missions by special forces preceded a U.S.-led multinational campaign comprising more than 160,000 troops—dubbed Operation Iraqi Freedom—which began on March 19 when air strikes rocked the capital, Baghdad. U.S. and British ground forces then invaded from Kuwait. British troops concentrated on taking the main southern city of Basra while U.S. troops advanced toward Baghdad in two main thrusts; the marines from the southeast and the 3rd Infantry Division from the southwest. Fierce resistance was encountered in Nasiriyah and other towns. Baghdad fell to U.S. troops on April 9, and the focus of actions then moved to northern Iraq, where U.S.-backed Kurdish forces took control of Kirkuk and Mosul before Saddam's hometown of Tikrit fell to U.S. forces on April 14. U.S. Pres. George W. Bush declared an end to "major combat operations" on May 1. At that point 116 U.S. and 33 U.K. service members had been killed in action, along with 4,000–6,000 Iraqi military personnel and an unknown number of civilians.

Deposed Iraqi strongman Saddam Hussein is shown here in a photograph taken after U.S. military forces captured him on December 13 in a "spider hole" south of his hometown of Tikrit.

Department of Defense

As occupying powers, the U.S. and U.K. established the Coalition Provisional Authority (CPA) under the leadership of retired U.S. Lieut. Gen. Jay Garner. He was removed from office after one month, however, and replaced by Paul Bremer. (*See* BIOGRAPHIES.) Garner later admitted the coalition had made mistakes by not restoring order in Iraq quickly enough. By July a provisional Iraqi Interim Governing Council (IGC) had been established under the direction of the CPA.

In the months following Bush's declaration of an end to hostilities, attacks on coalition forces became bloodier and more frequent, often numbering more than 30 a day. These attacks were typically ambushes involving rocket-propelled grenades and improvised explosive devices. By year's end a total of 480 American military personnel had been killed and more than 2,700 wounded in both combat and noncombat incidents. Civilians and Iraqi police were also increasingly targeted by anti-coalition forces, and the UN and the International Committee of the Red Cross pulled out most of their staffs after fatal bomb attacks. The UN special representative, Sérgio Vieira de Mello, was among the casualties (*see* OBITUARIES), and other coalition members—Bulgaria, Colombia, Denmark, Italy, Japan, Poland, South Korea, Spain, Thailand, and Ukraine—also suffered fatalities.

Saddam was taken into custody without a fight by U.S. forces on December 13. (*See* BIOGRAPHIES.) He was found hiding in a "spider hole" at a farmhouse near his hometown of Tikrit. Despite intense searching by the coalition, no evidence of WMD had been found by year's end.

WMD, ARMS CONTROL, AND DISARMAMENT

France revised its nuclear strategy by targeting nuclear missiles at "rogue states" that had WMD. Previously the French strategy had been founded on the principle of deterrence against declared nuclear powers. The change aligned France with the U.S. and the U.K. In response to a request from the Pentagon, the U.S. Senate voted to lift a decade-old ban on the development of smaller nuclear weapons, referred to as "mininukes," for use in destroying deeply buried or fortified facilities where WMD could be stored by enemy states or terrorists. The U.S.-Russia Strategic Offensive Reductions Treaty, known as the Moscow Treaty, entered into force in June. Both sides pledged to reduce the number of their operationally deployed strategic nuclear warheads to 1,700–2,200 by the end of 2012.

Representatives of more than 150 countries met to assess the global progress toward eliminating all chemical weapons. It was the first review conference of the Organisation for the Prohibition of Chemical Weapons since an international ban on such weapons came into force in 1997. The U.S. met the treaty's deadline for destroying 20% of its chemical weapons ahead of schedule, while Russia barely managed to fulfill its 1% quota (about 400 metric tons) before the conference got under way.

The first international military exercise on intercepting shipments of WMD occurred in September off the

(continued on page 250)

Defining Weapons of Mass Destruction

The continued search in 2003 for weapons of mass destruction (WMD) in Iraq heightened curiosity concerning the definition of WMD. The term has been in use since at least 1937, when newspapers described German bomber aircraft as "weapons of mass destruction" because they were being used to raze Republican-held cities during the Spanish Civil War. During the Cold War, WMD was narrowly defined to include only nuclear weapons because their use threatened the entire planet. By the end of the 1990–91 Gulf War, WMD had been used in United Nations Security Council Resolution 687—which imposed on Iraq strict rules for disarmament—to describe nuclear, biological, and chemical weapons. Since that time others have tried to alter the definition to include any weapon that disperses radioactivity or causes mass panic.

Nuclear Weapons

Nuclear weapons are thus far the most devastating weapon of mass destruction. They inflict their damage by a combination of intense blast, heat, electromagnetic energy, and radioactivity. Within a few minutes the single rudimentary bomb dropped on Hiroshima in August 1945 killed tens of thousands of people and destroyed all the buildings inside a 1.6-km (1-mi) radius of "ground zero" (i.e., the point of impact).

Nuclear weapons get their explosive power from a sustained nuclear chain reaction involving fission (the splitting of atoms) or fusion (the combining of lighter atoms to form new heavier ones). Creating such a chain reaction requires either highly enriched uranium (HEU) or plutonium. Plutonium occurs very rarely in nature and must be made inside a nuclear reactor. Uranium ore contains about 0.7% U-235 (the isotope needed to sustain an explosive chain reaction) and must be refined until the U-235 content is at least 90%. About 50 kg (110 lb) of HEU or 10 kg (22 lb) of plutonium are needed to build a crude nuclear bomb. To acquire even these small amounts, one requires a sophisticated enrichment plant or a nuclear reactor and reprocessing facility to extract plutonium; alternatively, one could acquire HEU or plutonium from someone with such facilities.

The cornerstones of the effort to control the spread of nuclear weapons materials and technologies are the Treaty on the Non-Proliferation of Nuclear Weapons (NPT), which has nearly 200 member states and came into force in 1970, and the Comprehensive Nuclear-Test-Ban Treaty (CTBT), which still requires signature by India, Pakistan, and North Korea. Before it can come into force, nine other countries, including the United States, must ratify the CTBT. The International Atomic Energy Agency (IAEA), established under the auspices of the United Nations in 1957, helps ensure that states live up to their NPT obligations.

Chemical Weapons

During World War I both the German and the Allied armies used chemical weapons (CW) as a means of breaking the deadlock of trench warfare. By war's end in 1918, approximately one million soldiers and civilians had been injured by this type of weapon, and nearly 100,000 had died. More recently, CW were used during the 1980–88 war between Iran and Iraq, most often by the Iraqis, who were trying to overcome the numerical superiority of the Iranian army. CW are divided into four categories:

- Choking agents, such as chlorine and phosgene gas, are the oldest and the easiest to manufacture. These have a corrosive effect on the lining of the lungs, causing fluid buildup, but they can easily be defended against by wearing a gas mask.
- Blood agents, such as hydrogen cyanide and cyanogen chloride gas, work by preventing red blood cells from absorbing oxygen and transmitting it throughout the body.
- Blister agents attack any exposed area of the body, and to defend against them personnel must wear cumbersome protective clothing as well as a gas mask. Mustard gas (sulfur mustard) and lewisite are examples of blister agents.
- Nerve agents were developed in the 1930s to be more lethal and faster acting than previous types of CW. They are absorbed through the skin or lungs and within seconds will disrupt the transmission of nerve signals to and from the brain. These agents include sarin, tabun, and VX.

Controlling the proliferation of CW is difficult because many of the chemicals involved in their production also have nonmilitary uses. For example, thiodiglycol is used to make mustard gas but is also an ingredient in ink for felt-tip pens.

The Chemical Weapons Convention is the first international treaty intended to eliminate an entire category of WMD. The treaty came into force in 1997, and member states have 10 years to eliminate their CW stockpiles and any related infrastructure. The treaty established the Organisation for the Prohibition of Chemical Weapons to monitor and ensure its provisions. This is done through a series of rigorous scheduled and short-notice inspections of known or suspected CW facilities and through the investigation of incidents of alleged use.

Biological Weapons

Biological weapons (BW) encompass pathogens (bacteria, viruses, and fungi) that cause diseases and toxins that are derived from organisms such as plants, snakes, and insects. Anthrax and smallpox are examples of pathogens. An example of a toxin is ricin, which is derived from the seed of the castor bean. Crude forms of biological warfare have been used since ancient times, when the decaying corpses of animals and humans were placed near enemy food and water supplies with the intention of spreading disease. In the 18th century the British distributed blankets contaminated with smallpox to decimate the Indian tribes with which they were warring. During World War II the Japanese used various BW agents against the Chinese. Britain, the Soviet Union, and the U.S. all had significant BW programs during the Cold War.

BW pose a special problem for arms controllers, because most of the equipment and materials used in their production also have peaceful commercial uses. There is very little observable difference between a BW factory and a medical research facility or pharmaceutical plant. The 1975 Biological and Toxin Weapons Convention bans all BW and their production facilities, but its more than 140 member states have been unable to reach an agreement on how to verify the treaty. In 2001 the U.S. pulled out of talks to reach a verification protocol, in part over concerns that the proposed inspections would be so intrusive as to threaten the security of proprietary information owned by pharmaceutical companies. (PETER SARACINO)

(continued from page 248)
northeastern coast of Australia. It was organized by the Proliferation Security Initiative, set up in May by President Bush to counter suspected trade in WMD and related components. Members of the initiative were Australia, France, Germany, Italy, Japan, The Netherlands, Poland, Portugal, Spain, the U.K., and the U.S.

OTHER CONFLICTS

Russia. More than 50 people were killed in the suicide bombing of a government building in the north of the Republic of Chechnya in May. Two days later Akhmad Kadyrov, head of the Russian-appointed administration, narrowly escaped another suicide attack that left more than a dozen dead. Chechen separatists extended their struggle to neighbouring areas as well. Approximately 20 military personnel were killed when a suicide bomber blew up a bus in the North Ossetian Republic. Another suicide bomb attack, this time on a military hospital in the Russian town of Mozdok, near the Chechen border, killed 50 people on August 1.

Latin America. During the year some 800 members of the right-wing United Self-Defense Forces of Colombia (AUC) disarmed. The AUC said all its 13,000 paramilitaries would do so by the end of 2005. Colombia's two most powerful leftist rebel groups—the Revolutionary Armed Forces of Colombia (FARC) and the National Liberation Army (ELN)—announced that they would join forces. In March the Venezuelan army bombed Colombian armed groups operating on its territory. Both countries later agreed to increase security along their common border.

Middle East. Numerous tit-for-tat attacks by Israeli forces and Palestinian militants occurred throughout the year, inflicting hundreds of casualties on both sides and threatening to derail an international plan known as the road map to peace. Israeli jets attacked suspected Hezbollah guerrilla positions in southern Lebanon in response to attacks in Israel and bombed an alleged militant camp in Syria in response to a suicide bomb attack in the city of Haifa that left 19 people dead.

The U.S. accused Iran of trying to build a nuclear weapon and said that it would not preclude the use of a "military option" to deal with such a threat. Following months of international diplomacy, Iran promised total transparency in its nuclear program, which it said was for peaceful purposes only. A November report by the International Atomic Energy Agency said that Iran admitted it had produced plutonium but that there was no evidence the country was trying to build a nuclear bomb. The U.S. dismissed the report.

South and Central Asia. Rivals India and Pakistan continued developing and deploying nuclear-capable ballistic missiles with ranges sufficient to strike each other's capitals. After a lull in the violence over Kashmir's future, conflict in that region flared again. Two bomb blasts killed 52 people and injured 150 in the Indian city of Mumbai (Bombay). India and Pakistan agreed in November to a cease-fire along the Line of Control which separated their forces in Kashmir, as well as on the Siachen glacier in the Himalayas, where fighting had occurred sporadically since 1984.

Clashes between Maoist rebels and Nepal's security forces became regular events following the resumption of violence in August, when rebels broke a seven-month truce. The rebels blamed the collapse on the government's insistence that the monarchy retain its central role in any future constitution for Nepal.

The United Nations suspended humanitarian operations in parts of Afghanistan because of fighting between warlords and attacks on central authorities by a resurgent Taliban. In August NATO took command of the International Security Assistance Force (ISAF), its first deployment of troops outside Europe or North America. The 5,500-strong ISAF was separate from the force of approximately 11,500 U.S.-led troops who were hunting remnants of the al-Qaeda extremist group and the former Taliban regime. ISAF had hoped to extend its influence beyond Kabul but was limited by a shortage of troops and equipment. Operation Avalanche, in the southern and eastern parts of Afghanistan, involved 2,000 U.S. troops in an effort to end a wave of attacks against coalition forces, aid workers, and civilians.

Peace talks to end the 20-year-old civil war in Sri Lanka got under way in Berlin in February. In April the secessionist rebels of the Liberation Tigers of Tamil Eelam suspended their participation, but a cease-fire declared in 2002 continued to hold generally.

East and Southeast Asia. After Indonesia declared martial law in May, it launched an offensive involving 28,000 troops to wipe out the GAM (Free Aceh Movement), which had been fighting for independence since 1976. More than 1,100 guerrillas were reported killed, while another 2,000 surrendered or were arrested. Initial rebel strength was estimated at about 5,000. Foreign analysts and human rights groups questioned whether the military toll for rebel dead might not also have included civilians.

North Korea announced in January that it was withdrawing from the Nuclear Non-proliferation Treaty (NPT). The UN Security Council expressed concern about North Korea's nuclear program but failed to condemn Pyongyang for pulling out of the NPT. In March four North Korean fighter jets intercepted a U.S. reconnaissance aircraft in international air space and shadowed it for 22 minutes. In May North Korea said it was scrapping a 1992 agreement with South Korea to keep the peninsula free from nuclear weapons; this was Pyongyang's last remaining international agreement on nonproliferation. After months of indicating that it had already developed a nuclear weapon, North Korea said in October that it would "physically display" its nuclear deterrent.

The Philippine army mounted an unsuccessful offensive against the country's largest Muslim separatist group, the Moro Islamic Liberation Front (MILF), in February. The government and the MILF signed a cease-fire agreement in July ahead of planned peace talks in Malaysia. Nearly 300 government soldiers mutinied and seized control of a shopping centre in Manila in May to protest working conditions and to accuse the administration of corruption. After negotiations the mutineers surrendered without having fired a shot. A 2,000-strong multinational intervention force led by Australia was sent to the Solomon Islands in July after the government there asked for assistance in ending years of lawlessness and fighting between rival ethnic groups.

Africa. A military coup led by army Gen. Verissimo Correia Seabra ousted the civilian president of Guinea-Bissau in September. A weeklong military coup in São Tomé and Príncipe toppled the government of Pres. Fradique de Menezes in July. He returned to power after an agreement to restore democratic rule was reached with coup leaders.

A 3,000-strong African Union peacekeeping force was deployed to Burundi to oversee a cease-fire agreement and to assist with the demobilization of rebel forces. In July a six-month cease-fire between the government of Burundi

In 2003 France continued to project military power in Africa by sending peacekeeping units to monitor the situation in Côte d'Ivoire and special forces to the Democratic Republic of the Congo, as in this photo taken in the northeastern town of Bunia in June.

and the main Hutu rebel group broke down, which led to renewed fighting and thousands of refugees. South Africa brokered another cease-fire in October.

In June 900 French soldiers arrived in the Democratic Republic of the Congo as the spearhead of a 1,500-strong European Union force to maintain peace between the government and rebels. This was the first EU military operation outside Europe, and it was deployed until the UN's own force (known by its French abbreviation MONUC) could take over in September. In December former government soldiers and troops from the two main rebel groups formed a united military force as part of a power-sharing deal signed earlier in 2003 to end the five-year-old civil war. Some 4,000 French and 1,300 West African soldiers monitored a truce and a no-weapons zone in Côte d'Ivoire after the civil war there was declared over in July.

Fighting intensified in Liberia's civil war after the breakdown of a cease-fire agreement signed in June. Rebels surrounded Monrovia, the capital, and hundreds of people were killed. The Economic Community of West African States (ECOWAS) dispatched a peacekeeping force in August to stabilize the situation until a UN force could arrive. The ECOWAS force was complemented by 2,000 U.S. marines stationed off the coast. Liberian Pres. Charles Taylor left the country in August. U.S. forces withdrew in September and October as the UN Mission in Liberia (UNMIL), comprising approximately 4,500 troops, took over peacekeeping duties. Hundreds of people were killed in the north of Uganda as the Lord's Resistance Army continued its 17-year campaign to overthrow the government. An estimated 1.3 million people had been displaced by the outlaw band. During yearlong negotiations the Muslim government of The Sudan and rebel leaders of the Sudan People's Liberation Army (SPLA) agreed to share oil resources, but differences over territorial and power-sharing issues still precluded an end to Africa's longest civil war.

MILITARY TECHNOLOGY

The U.S. Air Force tested its new 9,500-kg (21,000-lb) Massive Ordnance Air Burst (MOAB) munition. The bomb could spread a flammable mist over its target area and then ignite it, creating a massive blast and fireball 40% more powerful than any other conventional weapon in the U.S. arsenal. The RQ-4A Global Hawk became the first pilotless aircraft allowed to fly routinely in civilian airspace. German shipbuilder Howaldtswerke–Deutsche Werft AG launched the first of a new generation of four extremely quiet submarines that ran on hydrogen fuel cells and were difficult to detect by sonar. Christened U31, the submarine could remain underwater for several weeks, a feat that was previously accomplished only by nuclear-powered submarines.

MILITARY AND SOCIETY

Israel sacked 27 air force pilots for refusing to fly bombing raids on Palestinian cities. The pilots had questioned Israel's policy of "targeted assassinations" that had killed more civilians than the leaders of militant groups it was designed to eliminate. Israel's navy suspended the captain of a patrol boat who refused to conduct missions near the Gaza Strip. In August Sweden announced that its armed forces would operate only during normal office hours for the rest of the year in order to cut costs. Sweden also reduced aircraft patrols, kept navy ships in port, and mothballed armoured vehicles. A senior member of the Kenyan army reported that at least one soldier was dying each day as a result of HIV/AIDS infection. A number of studies showed that HIV/AIDS was the leading cause of death in the military and police forces of several southern African countries.

NATO reduced the number of its regional commands from 20 to 11 and planned to overhaul its command structure to enable deployment of lighter, more flexible forces. Dutch Foreign Minister Jaap de Hoop Scheffer was named to succeed NATO Secretary-General George Robertson with effect from January 2004.

The EU embarked upon its first-ever military mission when it assumed control from NATO of the peacekeeping operation in Macedonia. Approximately 400 troops from 26 EU and non-EU European countries plus Turkey participated. Germany announced the abolition of military conscription and said that the size of its army would be reduced by one-third. The plan was to be phased in over five years and would leave the army with an all-volunteer force of about 200,000 troops.

Kyrgyzstan granted Russia permission to build a military base at Kant to house a new Russian antiterrorism force. It was the first foreign military base established by Russia since the demise of the Soviet Union in 1991.

Environmentalists forced the U.S. Navy to restrict the peacetime use of a powerful new sonar for detecting submarines. A U.S. court issued an injunction against using the sonar after hearing evidence that whales and dolphins had suffered life-threatening injuries as a result of its use.

(PETER SARACINO)

Performing Arts

A new method of music delivery, **iTUNES** Music Store, debuted, and a number of notable CDs were produced—Outkast's ***SPEAKERBOXXX/THE LOVE BELOW***, Mariza's ***FADO CURVO***, and the live World Music recording ***FESTIVAL IN THE DESERT***. Pianist **ALICIA DE LARROCHA** gave her farewell performance, and the last of *The Lord of the Rings* movies, ***THE RETURN OF THE KING***, was released.

MUSIC

Classical Music. On Friday, June 27, 2003, the musicians of the Iraqi National Symphony Orchestra gathered at Baghdad's Ribat Recital Hall to write a new chapter in their country's musical history. Their concert—the orchestra's first of the post-Saddam Hussein era—was more than a mere performance, however. It represented a triumph over years of political censorship, financial adversity, and official neglect. As the musicians played, many in the audience sang along to the song "My Nation," which had been banned by the former dictator: "My nation, my nation, am I going to see you safe, blessed, victorious, and esteemed?" Given the tribulations of 2003, they could just as easily have been singing about classical music in general.

While the Iraqi orchestra's performance was not, arguably, one of the musical high points of 2003, it was emblematic of a year in which classical music was confronted by a range of forces—war, plunging economies, labour strife, a mysterious epidemic—that for the most part overshadowed artistic events and achievements and at times threatened to overwhelm the music and those who made it. In the persons of those Iraqi musicians, whose salaries had been cut to $20 per month, the concert symbolized the way classical music itself somehow managed to persevere and play on.

In North America many classical musicians considered themselves fortunate simply to retain their jobs as orchestras and other musical institutions—their budgets and endowments eviscerated by the ailing economy and flagging sponsorship—plunged into debt. Several orchestras, including the San Antonio (Texas) Symphony, the Colorado Springs (Colo.) Symphony, and the Florida Philharmonic, were forced into bankruptcy, while those in St. Paul (Minn.), Seattle (Wash.), St. Louis (Mo.), and Pittsburgh (Pa.), among others, posted substantial deficits. Philadelphia's Kimmel Center for the Performing Arts announced a deficit of $3.8 million in its first full year of operations.

Elsewhere the economic crunch was felt as well. In Australia, Sydney-based World Orchestras, Ltd., which had brought international ensembles to concert halls Down Under, announced that it was canceling its 2004 season owing to a shortfall of $A 800,000 (about U.S.$580,000). Edinburgh's Scottish Opera contemplated staff cuts and a reduced schedule because of its financial problems, while London's English National Opera threatened at one point to become a part-time company because of its monetary woes.

Musically, France was hardest hit of all. When the government announced that it would cut the benefits offered to the country's entertainment workers, strikes erupted that rocked France's popular and lucrative summer festival season. Prestigious festivals such as those in Aix-en-Provence and Avignon were forced to close, and scores of other events were disrupted or curtailed.

Compounding the economic woes, the outbreak of the SARS (severe acute respiratory syndrome) epidemic in Asia adversely affected musical activities on the Pacific Rim. Taiwan's 2003 Contemporary Festival was canceled because of the outbreak; the Hong Kong Philharmonic postponed several concerts; the third Beijing International Piano Competition was delayed; and the Arts in May series at Singapore's Esplanade performing arts complex was called off.

Amid all of these calamities, of course, there was war. When Australians awoke on a sunny day in March, they were confronted by the sight of their beloved Sydney Opera House defaced by 3-m (10-ft)-high letters spelling out the phrase "No War" on one of its curved white fins. The vandalism was the work of a British scientist and an Australian man who were protesting the U.S.-led invasion of Iraq. In April a concert by Riccardo Muti and La Scala's Philharmonic Orchestra at Rome's La Sapienza University was disrupted by antiwar protesters. A month earlier officials of the Danish Radio Symphony Orchestra had threatened to dismiss conductor Gerd Albrecht for antiwar remarks he made from the podium during a concert. When controversial director Peter Sellars announced in May that he would stage an antiwar production of Mozart's *Idomeneo* at the U.K.'s Glyndebourne Festival, several corporate sponsors of the event threatened to withdraw their support. Public opinion was divided again in the fall when British composer Keith Burstein announced that his opera *Manifest Destiny*—a musical study of the mind and motivations of a terrorist—would premier at London's Cockpit Theatre.

Other voices—less clamorous, more conciliatory—were heard as well. In August the West-Eastern Divan Orchestra—organized by Israeli conductor-pianist Daniel Barenboim and Palestinian American critic Edward Said (*see* OBITUARIES) and comprising Israeli and Arab musicians—gave its first concert in an Arab country, in Rabat, Mor. Two days later the "peace orchestra," whose purpose was to foster an environment of reconciliation between Arabs and Jews, made its French debut in Menton.

Even the daunting spectre of the terrorist attacks of Sept. 11, 2001, was musically addressed in more contemplative ways. At New York's "88 Keys: A Celebration of the Piano" festival in September, composer Daniele Lombardi presented the debut of his tribute to the 9/11 victims with his

Threnodia for 21 pianos. In April composer John Adams's 9/11 commemoration, *On the Transmigration of Souls* (which debuted in 2002), was honoured with the Pulitzer Prize.

Given the tumultuous nature of the musical year, various controversies that came along paled in comparison, like brush fires next to a California wildfire. The most contentious of these flared in June when the New York Philharmonic announced that it would leave its home at Lincoln Center's Avery Fisher Hall and merge with its former musical home, Carnegie Hall. Seemingly left in the lurch, officials at Lincoln Center invoked its lease with the orchestra (which ran through 2011), threatening legal action that later in the year forced a cancellation of the proposed merger. Meanwhile, in France a cellist with the Strasbourg Philharmonic refused to play works by Richard Wagner—sometimes referred to as "Hitler's favourite composer"—because he felt "the presence of the devil" in the music. French pianist François-René Duchable announced that he would perform three final concerts in which he would, respectively, dump a piano into a lake, set fire to his recital suit, and blow up another piano to make the point that "the concert is dead." In Rio de Janeiro opera director Gerald Thomas reacted to boos following his staging of Wagner's *Tristan und Isolde*, which featured explicit sexual scenes and references to Nazis, by dropping his pants and "mooning" the audience.

All of the hoopla was overshadowed at various points during the year by the deaths of several of classical music's esteemed figures. In February the grand old man of the U.S.'s West Coast school, composer Lou Harrison, died at age 85. In Italy provocative avant-garde composer Luciano Berio died in May at age 77, and pianist Eugene Istomin died in October at the same age. (*See* OBITUARIES.) Lithuanian composer Antanas Rekasius, whose works were infused with an irrepressible sense of humour and the absurd, died at age 75.

The musical year, however, was not without its high points as well. Ironically, at a time when many orchestras and institutions were struggling to get by, 2003 was marked by the opening of dazzling new concert halls in various cities. The jewel, by many accounts, was the Frank Gehry-designed Walt Disney Concert Hall in Los Angeles. With its curving, organic design, the hall—the new home of the Los Angeles Philharmonic—was a sonic and visual tour de force. In August the opera-crazed populace of Seattle celebrated the opening of Marion Oliver McCaw Hall to general acclaim; a month later New Yorkers were treated to an intimate new performance space, the Judy and Arthur Zankel Hall, in the lower level of Carnegie Hall. Members of the Detroit Symphony Orchestra were so pleased with their new Max M. Fisher Music Center that they played what was dubbed a "Hard Hat Concert" in October for the construction workers who had built it.

To attract new audiences to their halls, the administrators and marketing departments of various orchestras and opera houses devised imaginative ploys. The Royal Scottish National Orchestra unveiled a series of lively television ads to promote itself, while the London Symphony Orchestra began marketing its recordings—literally—in a chain of U.K. grocery stores. In September, Berlin's Komische Oper staged what it claimed was the world's first "singles party" at an opera performance, in which audience members were encour-

Conductors Play Musical Chairs

In recent years conductors have increasingly become the musical equivalents of professional athletes, parlaying their high-profile public personas and singular skills in a market that is driven by professional excellence and name value. Given that, 2003 was a particularly busy year for conductors, many of whom played their own version of musical chairs at orchestras across the world.

One of the most prominent conductors, Mariss Jansons (*see* BIOGRAPHIES), made his debut as the new music director of the Bavarian Radio Symphony Orchestra at a concert in Munich (Ger.) in October. Jansons, who planned to leave the Pittsburgh (Pa.) Symphony at the end of the 2003–04 season after having taken that orchestra to new critical heights, was also named principal conductor of Amsterdam's Concertgebouw, where he would take over in 2004.

Among those making debuts at the helm of their new orchestras in 2003 were Yakov Kreizberg with the Vienna Symphony, Osmo Vänskä with the Minnesota Orchestra, and Leon Botstein with the Jerusalem Symphony Orchestra. Composer-songwriter Marvin Hamlisch debuted as the principal pops conductor of the Buffalo (N.Y.) Philharmonic Orchestra during the summer, and Claudio Abbado led a new version of the Lucerne (Switz.) Festival Orchestra in August. Abbado re-created the orchestra, which had been founded by the legendary Arturo Toscanini in 1938 and disbanded in 1993.

Other conductors signed contracts during the year that called for them to assume their new posts in 2004. Those included Marek Janowski, who was to take over as the music director of the Orchestre de la Suisse Romande; Andrey Boreyko, who was to become the principal conductor of the Hamburg (Ger.) Symphony; and Edo de Waart, who would take the helm at the Hong Kong Philharmonic. Also in 2004, Christian Thielemann would succeed James Levine as chief conductor of the Munich Philharmonic when the latter left to become the music director of the Boston Symphony Orchestra.

As the year closed, so too did the tenure of Simone Young at Opera Australia. Young's contract was not extended following an acrimonious dispute during which both sides finally agreed that the company could not afford her artistic vision. She was subsequently named the next director of the Hamburg State Opera. Young would be succeeded by British conductor Richard Hickox, who was also the principal conductor of the BBC National Orchestra of Wales and music director of the City of London Sinfonia.

Other agreements concluded in 2003 would also yield results on the horizon. Riccardo Chailly was slated to become the music director of the Leipzig (Ger.) Gewandhaus Orchestra and Leipzig Opera in 2005; and that same year, Ingo Metzmacher would take over as chief conductor of the Netherlands Opera. Kent Nagano, who had become a mainstay of Berlin's music scene as chief conductor and artistic director of the city's Deutsches Symphonie-Orchester, was set to become the general music director of Germany's Bavarian State Opera in 2006.

(HARRY SUMRALL)

The premiere of Deborah Drattell's opera **Nicholas and Alexandra,** *commissioned by the Los Angeles Opera, starred Plácido Domingo as Rasputin.*

aged to write flirtatious notes to each other during intermission. London's Royal Opera House devised a promotional campaign in conjunction with the city's top dance club, the Ministry of Sound, in which a set of promotional DayGlo postcards bearing the words *dance music, soul music,* or *house music* advertised performances of the Royal Ballet and the Royal Opera. Most ingenious of all, perhaps, the Minnesota Orchestra gave away "bobble-head" dolls of its new music director, Osmo Vänskä (one of many new faces on the podiums of major orchestras during the year—*see* Sidebar), featuring a swinging bobble arm that conducted a recorded sample of Sibelius's *Finlandia.*

Performances themselves often lived up to these promotional stratagems. The Washington (D.C.) Opera's September production of Johann Strauss, Jr.'s *Die Fledermaus* featured cameo nonsinging appearances by U.S. Supreme Court Justices Ruth Bader Ginsburg, Anthony Kennedy, and Stephen Breyer. Another legal motif was offered by Reno's Nevada Opera in July when it staged a production of Gilbert and Sullivan's comic opera *Trial by Jury* in a real courtroom, with District Judge Peter Breen presiding. In October the Apartment House theatre in Dresden, Ger., presented the world premiere of Irish composer Jennifer Walshe's *XXX Live Nude Girls,* which featured two naked Barbie dolls (manipulated by a puppeteer and videocast to an onstage screen) backed by a group of offstage musicians and singers. In South Korea a lavish $5.3 million production of Verdi's *Aida* was presented at Seoul's Olympic Stadium with a vast stage set that included a herd of camels.

Along with the onstage antics were sublime moments as well. In December world famous cellist Mstislav Rostropovich performed with the Malaysian Philharmonic Orchestra in the shadow of the 800-year-old Cambodian temple at Angkor Wat in a benefit for a charity that was bringing water to that country's underdeveloped villages. In August legendary pianist Alicia de Larrocha, known as "the first lady of the Mostly Mozart Festival," made her farewell appearance at that Lincoln Center event, capping a tenure that encompassed 80 performances over a 32-year period.

Where it counted most, in the creation and introduction of new works that would ensure the continuation of the classical music tradition itself, 2003 did not disappoint. The year saw the premieres of English composer John Tavener's seven-hour choral work *The Veil of the Temple,* Danish composer Poul Ruders's opera *The Handmaid's Tale,* Chinese American composer Bright Sheng's opera, *Madame Mao,* American composer Deborah Drattell's opera *Nicholas and Alexandra,* and English composer Anthony Payne's new song cycle based on poems by Edward Thomas, among numerous others. Jonathan Mills's opera *The Eternity Man* paid tribute to Arthur Stace, who walked the streets of Sydney for 37 years chalking the word *eternity* on sidewalks.

The year was also endowed with a wide range of new recordings that illuminated the genius of the past while underscoring the vast musical palette that was now a part of the classical music world. Early music was the focus of *The Essential Tallis Scholars* (Gimell), which celebrated 30 years of recordings by the group that was essential in fostering the rebirth of Renaissance music. On *Extempore II* (Harmonia Mundi), an equally important early music ensemble, the Orlando Consort, took a different tack, combining medieval musical motifs with the inspired improvisations of the jazz group Perfect Houseplants. Hilary Hahn delivered a warmly human reading on *Bach Concertos* for Deutsche Grammophon, while violinist Nigel Kennedy teamed with Poland's Kroke Band to explore the myriad forms of Eastern European music. In a touching moment Lang Lang, one of the most promising pianists of his generation, revisited the work that had catapulted him to international acclaim in 1999, recording Tchaikovsky's *Piano Concerto No. 1* with conductor Daniel Barenboim and the Chicago Symphony Orchestra.

Finally, as the tumultuous year drew to a close, a fitting denouement unfolded on December 9 when the Iraqi National Symphony Orchestra—having rehearsed for the grand moment amid bursting bombs and 40.5 °C (105 °F) heat—appeared at the John F. Kennedy Center for the Performing Arts in Washington, D.C., with cellist Yo-Yo Ma. As they played, perhaps the musicians' thoughts turned to that performance in Baghdad earlier in the year when their conductor, Abdel Razak al-Azawi, had said, "Music is great at taking people away from their pain and suffering." (HARRY SUMRALL)

Jazz. In 2003 the collapse of the pop-album market gave the blues to the jazz-record business. The five major record companies—Universal, Sony, BMG, EMI, and Warners—concentrated on issuing popular product and severely scaled down their jazz output; the majority of new jazz CDs were produced by many small independent labels. Hard-pressed retail chain stores that were required to turn over their stock every few months carried few independent-label jazz CDs; they paid their major suppliers' bills first and left small distributors unpaid. CD buyers were forced to frequent jazz specialty stores and search Internet outlets for jazz albums.

The number of jazz albums proliferated, but pressings were typically in small quantities; even important independent labels such as Delmark and Hatology often made first pressings of only 2,000 or fewer copies for new releases. As for reissues, the flow of older jazz packages ground to a near halt, owing to competition from Europe, which had copyright laws that typically protected recordings for only 50 years, compared with 95 years in the U.S. In the 1990s small European labels had begun issuing music that had been recorded by both major and independent labels from the early jazz and swing eras, and in recent years they began issuing those from the bop era as well. These included complete collections of major artists but also those of valuable lesser-known figures. Worst of all, the production of reissues in the U.S. was expensive and time-consuming. Shortly after many reissue sets appeared in the U.S., European "pirates" copied the packages and sold them over the Internet for a fraction of the American price.

Live jazz continued to thrive in clubs, concerts, and festivals. The Lionel Hampton Jazz Festival in Moscow, Idaho, continued despite the death in 2002 of its namesake; Los Angeles hosted the 25th Playboy Jazz Festival; and the San Francisco Jazz Festival, a midautumn event, offered 29 concerts, curated by tenor saxophonist Joshua Redman, who also had directed the San Francisco Spring Season. The 50th anniversary of Delmark Records, which boasted 400 albums in its catalog, was celebrated in Chicago at both the jazz and blues festivals. Ornette Coleman made rare appearances with his swinging trio and quartet at the JVC Jazz Festival in New York City, the New Orleans Jazz & Heritage Festival, and the Umbria Jazz Festival in Perugia, Italy. After a decade's absence saxophonist Joseph Jarman rejoined the Art Ensemble of Chicago and performed on the group's album *The Meeting.* The Big Three Palladium Orchestra, led by Tito Puente, Jr., Tito Rodriguez, Jr. and Mario Grillo, son of Machito—sons of Latin jazz greats—and including musicians from their fathers' historic bands, played a brief concert tour.

The Marsalis Family—a sextet led by pianist Ellis, with his sons Wynton (trumpet), Branford (saxophones), Delfeayo (trombone), and Jason (drums) and bassist Reginald Veal—played an eight-city tour. After he had spent more than 20 years with Columbia Records, Wynton was dropped by that label, and he signed with Blue Note; his Lincoln Center Jazz Orchestra was joined by Spanish pianist Chano Domínguez's combo for a flamenco-jazz fusion concert in February. Branford's Marsalis Music label issued his *Romare Bearden Revealed* CD to coincide with a retrospective of Bearden's paintings that was being held at the National Gallery of Art, Washington, D.C. Marsalis Music also released the CD *Other Hours,* featuring Harry Connick, Jr., who did not sing but played piano. Innovative composer-pianist Toshiko Akiyoshi offered the album *Hiroshima—Rising from the Abyss.* Then, after a farewell concert at Carnegie Hall in New York City, she dissolved her 30-year-old big band. The year's newest jazz vocal star was singer-pianist Peter Cincotti, a 19-year-old college sophomore who offered an eponymous album and toured the U.S. Singer-pianist Norah Jones, the promising new talent of 2002, and her works "Don't Know Why" and *Come Away With Me* picked up eight Grammy Awards in 2003. (*See* BIOGRAPHIES.)

Following two years and $1.6 million in renovations, the home in Queens, New York City, of trumpeter Louis Armstrong and his wife, Lucille, was restored to its condition at the time the couple had lived there. Its opening to the public as a museum was celebrated in October by big and small jazz bands and was accompanied by the publication of the book *Louis Armstrong: The Offstage Story of Satchmo,* written by museum director Michael Cogswell. Executive Producer Martin Scorsese joined six other noted film directors—including, significantly, only one African American—and created *The Blues,* a seven-film PBS series that offered random perspectives on the African American idiom and its effects on rock and jazz.

Spanish flamenco pianist Chano Domínguez and trumpeter Wynton Marsalis, shown here at the Vitoria-Gasteiz (Spain) Jazz Festival, also performed their flamenco-jazz fusion at Lincoln Center, New York City, in 2003.

AP/Wide World Photos

The growing ensemble mastery of Trio 3 (Oliver Lake, alto saxophone; Reggie Workman, bass; Andrew Cyrille, drums) was heard in its CD *Open Ideas.* Other important albums included *Cloth* by Oliver Lake Big Band, the reissue of *Collective Calls* by Evan Parker (saxophone) and Paul Lytton (drums), Cecil Taylor's solo *The Willisau Concert,* and *Nailed* by a quartet that included Taylor and Parker. Hyena Records began issuing recordings from Thelonious Monk's personal collection, beginning with *Monk in Paris: Live at the Olympia* from 1965.

Among the notable deaths during the year were those of alto saxophonist-composer Benny Carter, singer Nina Simone, conguero Mongo Santamaria, flutist Herbie Mann, and salsa star Celia Cruz. (*See* OBITUARIES.) Other losses to jazz included the deaths of saxophonists Allen Eager, Teddy Edwards, Frank Lowe, and Bill Perkins, cornetist Ruby Braff, bassist Chubby Jackson, trombonist Jimmy Knepper, Australian traditional jazz composer David Dallwitz, Dutch bandleader Marcel Thielemans, and *Down Beat* magazine owner Jack Maher.

(JOHN LITWEILER)

Popular. The year 2003 was a classic one for exceptionally varied new music from Mali, which had produced a number of remarkable musicians over the years. In January many of the country's finest singers, along with a handful of supporters from the West, assembled near the city of Timbuktu for a festival in the Sahara. The resulting CD, *Festival in the Desert,* was hailed as one of the best live World Music recordings of all time and featured rousing appearances from Ali Farka Toure and his disciple Afel Bocoum, along with local Tuareg tribesmen, all demonstrating the links that exist between the "desert blues" styles of Mali and the black music of the U.S. The

AP/Wide World Photos

Malian singer Salif Keita entertains at the Paleo Festival in Nyon, Switz. In 2003 he also appeared on an album, Munia: The Tale, *which was released by Cameroonian Richard Bona.*

album included an impressive track from Oumou Sangaré, the country's finest female diva and a champion of women's rights; during the year she also released *Oumou,* a powerful, largely retrospective album. Other stirring performances from the desert concert came from the French band Lo'Jo and from the only visiting Western superstar, Robert Plant, formerly of Led Zeppelin. Accomplished Malian artist Rokia Traoré, who was based in France, had a good year. She used traditional African instruments such as the *n'goni* and *balafon* on her delicate, gently rousing new album *Bowmboi,* in which she set out to "use classical Malian instruments in a new way" and demonstrate a songwriting style that mixed influences from Africa, Europe, and India. She was joined on two tracks by the Kronos Quartet, a highly inventive American string ensemble.

Mali's finest guitarist, Djelimady Tounkara, toured with his legendary group the Super Rail Band, alongside their rivals from the 1960s and '70s, the Guinean band Bembeya Jazz. Meanwhile, Salif Keita, Mali's leading singer, collaborated with the New York-based Cameroonian singer and bass player Richard Bona on his highly eclectic album *Munia,* which mixed African, jazz, and pop influences.

There was another strong Africa-U.S. collaboration on the *Abyssinia Infinite* project, an album in which Ethiopian singer Ejigayehu Shibabaw, better known simply as Gigi, joined the producer and musician Bill Laswell to rework a group of Ethiopian songs, using instrumentation from across Africa, Asia, and the West.

Among the other African female singers producing notable albums were Mauritanian artist Malouma, who mixed Arabic influences with blues as well as rousing rhythm and blues, and French-based Algerian singer Souad Massi, whose album *Deb* ("Heartbroken") showed her moving from North African influences to stirring pop anthems with a Spanish flamenco edge.

Portuguese fado singer Mariza, whose extraordinary looks and even more extraordinary intense and dramatic singing established her position as a global star, produced a fine new album, *Fado Curvo.* (*See* BIOGRAPHIES.) Kristi Stassinopoulou's *The Secret of the Rocks,* a best-selling album in Greece, mixed local folk influences with everything from rock to African styles. In Uzbekistan the young folk singer and pop star Sevara Nazarkhan again mixed traditional styles with Western instrumentation on her charming, gently mournful album *Yol Bolsin.* The success of all of these artists outside their own territories showed the growing interest among European and American audiences for unexpected, different styles of music. Other unlikely outsiders who made an impact included Bic Runga, a part-Chinese, part-Maori singer from New Zealand, and Iraqi singer Ilham al-Madfi. Once known as the "Beatle of Baghdad," he spent much of the Saddam Hussein era living in exile and became a major star in the Arab world. His concert in London in 2003 proved that he was on his way to becoming Iraq's first crossover World Music celebrity.

In the U.K. the music scene was also enlivened by the growth in global-fusion styles. The band Oi Va Voi mixed modern dance beats with Jewish klezmer songs from Eastern Europe. Terry Hall (former lead singer with the Specials) mingled hip-hop, Roma (Gypsy), and Asian influences in his collaboration with Mushtaq on the album *The Hour of Two Lights.* The Mercury Music Prize for 2003, extolling the best in British music, was won by Dizzee Rascal, a 19-year-old garage-style rapper who was praised for his witty, honest lyrics about the everyday lives of young people residing in the east end of London. (ROBIN DENSELOW)

In early October 2003, for the first time in the 45-year history of *Billboard's* Hot 100 chart, all entries in the top 10 were by black artists. Mainstream top 40 radio stations that had featured teen pop groups *NSYNC and the Backstreet Boys on their playlists three years earlier, turned increasingly to rhythm-and-blues and hip-hop tracks. Some observers called the trend a blurring of colour lines and proof that black music had been accepted fully as part of mainstream culture.

Hip-hop artist 50 Cent (Curtis Jackson) sold 1.6 million copies of his CD *Get Rich or Die Tryin'* during the two weeks after its February release. Mentored by the late rapper Jam Master Jay of Run-D.M.C., 50 Cent signed to Eminem's Shady Records and to Dr. Dre's Aftermath Records in a joint venture. The placement of two numbers on Eminem's 2002 movie sound track *8 Mile* helped build anticipation for 50 Cent's 2003 CD release. Hit tracks such as "P.I.M.P.," "In Da Club," "21 Questions," and, with Lil' Kim, "Magic Stick" made the rapper one of the most successful artists of the year. Atlanta, Ga.-based black duo Outkast—Big Boi (Antwan Patton) and Andre 3000 (Andre Benjamin)—drew critical plaudits for a double CD, *Speakerboxxx/The Love Below.* Big Boi created the *Speakerboxxx* disc, closer to Outkast's previous hip-hop style, while Andre 3000 crafted *The Love Below,* on which he sang in a funky style often reminiscent of Prince.

By November the set was certified four-times platinum, for shipments of four million units.

The Love Below included a guest appearance by singer-songwriter Norah Jones (*see* BIOGRAPHIES), who with her works won eight Grammy Awards in February. Bruce Springsteen, who won three Grammys in rock categories, ended his Rising tour in October at Shea Stadium in New York City. Begun in 2002 and traveling to North American and Australian arenas in the spring and European and U.S. stadiums in the summer, the tour grossed $172.7 million during 2003. The Dixie Chicks also won three Grammys, including country album of the year. During their world tour, the trio played to capacity crowds, but they found themselves embroiled in controversy after singer Natalie Maines made a much-publicized negative comment in London about U.S. Pres. George W. Bush. The Chicks also posed nude for the cover of *Entertainment Weekly* magazine and engaged in a public feud with fellow country star Toby Keith. Singer Alan Jackson (*see* BIOGRAPHIES) won three awards at the Country Music Association Awards, including male vocalist of the year and entertainer of the year, and he picked up two Academy of Country Music trophies for album of the year and video of the year for "Drive." Colombian singer-songwriter Juanes had five wins at the fourth annual Latin Grammy Awards in Miami, Fla. His *Un día normal* was named album of the year.

Fox Television's *American Idol* talent-search show brought two pop singers to national prominence, North Carolinian Clay Aiken and Alabaman Ruben Studdard. Aiken's debut CD, *Measure of a Man,* sold 613,000 copies in its first week of release and was placed at number one on the *Billboard* 200 album chart. Studdard's debut, *Soulful,* was released on December 9. Singer Beyoncé Knowles of Destiny's Child released her first solo album, *Dangerously in Love,* which included the radio hits "Baby Boy" and "Crazy in Love." On the former Knowles teamed with dancehall reggae star Sean Paul, and on the latter she worked with rapper Jay-Z.

In late December, album sales for 2003 were down 4.7% compared with 2002. Apple Computer Corp. debuted its iTunes Music Store for the Macintosh in April and sold a million songs within seven days. When Apple made the iTunes Music Store available to Microsoft Windows-based computer users in October, the company sold a million songs in three and a half days. Napster reemerged as an online music store, selling songs and subscriptions for owner Roxio. Bertelsmann AG and Sony Corp. announced in November that they had signed a nonbinding letter of intent to merge their music divisions in a joint venture, to be called Sony BMG. The merger hinged on regulatory approval in the U.S. and the European Union.

Among the deaths during the year were those of icon Johnny Cash; his wife, June Carter Cash; Sun Records founder Sam Phillips; Maurice Gibb of the BeeGees; Bobby Hatfield of the Righteous Brothers; Don Gibson; Barry White; Hank Ballard; and Warren Zevon. (*See* OBITUARIES.) (JAY ORR)

DANCE

North America. The winter, spring, and summer of 2003 had their share of Broadway-inspired ballet offerings, perhaps influenced by the success of Twyla Tharp's *Movin' Out,* which gave Broadway its first thoroughly dance-driven show in quite some time and helped to close out 2002 with a bang. Two of the 2003 offerings were more or less duds. Early in the year New York City Ballet (NYCB) offered Peter Martins's *Thou Swell,* a strung-out suite of nightclub dances-cum-ballet meant to help celebrate the centenary of composer Richard Rodgers's birth. In the early summer Dance Theatre of Harlem (DTH) presented the world premiere of a rather sprawling and jumbled *St. Louis Woman: A Blues Ballet,* with choreography by Michael Smuin, who also reworked the scenario of the 1946 Broadway show to fit his almost-all-dancing scheme (singers appeared onstage). As with Martins's effort, which had set designs by Broadway veteran Robin Wagner and costumes by fashion designer Julius Lumsden, Smuin's collaborators included veterans Tony Walton (sets), Willa Kim (costumes), and Natasha Katz (lighting).

For Broadway-inclined ballet audiences looking for diverting entertainment, in the spring NYCB offered Christopher Wheeldon's enchanting *Carnival of the Animals* (set to the score by Camille Saint-Saëns). Inspired by John Lithgow's charming and poetic libretto concerning a young boy's night alone in a museum of natural history, where his dreams find the displays taking on the personalities of the people in his life, Wheeldon's work presented the visions of a schoolboy's lively imagination. With Lithgow as the ballet's beguiling narrator and precocious School of American Ballet student P.J. Verhoest playing the central figure, *Carnival* unfolded as a smooth sampler of music and moods, wittily designed by Jon Morrell.

Celebrated throughout New York City during the year, postmodernist composer John Adams lent another pervasive theme to dance: NYCB offered Adams's *Guide to Strange Places* in an unmemorable and rather bland ballet by Martins; American Ballet Theatre (ABT) offered a doubleheader of an evening called *HereAfter.* The first act, *Heaven,* used Adams's large-scale choral composition *Harmonium* as a starting point for Natalie Weir's uninspired casual ritualistic romp, in which dancers looked as though they were dressed for a Gap ad. The second act, *Earth,* fared little better; it featured Stanton Welch's often foolishly finicky choreography set to Carl Orff's *Carmina Burana,* which had become wildly popular as music for theatrical accompaniment. ABT's shorter fall season offered a revival of Antony Tudor's *Pillar of Fire* and a restaging of Frederick Ashton's classic *Symphonic Variations,* in preparation for the 2004 centenary of the British ballet master's birth.

Soon after his unimpressive ABT premiere, Welch marked the beginning of his artistic directorship at Houston (Texas) Ballet in the fall season. He took over from Ben Stevenson, who, after being feted for his effective years of service in Houston, moved on to act as artistic adviser to the Texas Ballet Theater (formerly the Fort Worth Dallas Ballet). Welch's opening program for Houston Ballet included his own *A Dance in the Garden of Mirth,* as well as the world premiere of Trey McIntyre's *The Shadow,* inspired by tales of Hans Christian Andersen. Similar changing of the guard marked the activities of Oregon Ballet Theatre. Christopher Stowell took over the position vacated by James Canfield, starting with a *New Beginnings* program that featured works by George Balanchine, Kent Stowell (the director's father), Helgi Tomasson, and Paul Taylor.

After having performed for the earlier part of the year in temporary surroundings, Pacific Northwest Ballet, run by Christopher Stowell's parents (Kent Stowell and Francia Russell), inaugurated its fall season by christening a newly outfitted home theatre, Marion Oliver McCaw Hall, with a new production of *Swan Lake.* The production, choreographed by Kent Stowell, included scenic design by the legendary Ming Cho Lee. San Francisco Ballet offered a new production of the Russian warhorse *Don Quixote* as well as mixed bills featuring ballets by Balanchine and Jerome Robbins. During the late summer the troupe played in Edinburgh with an all-Wheeldon program that proved critically positive for the reputations of both the company and the young choreographer.

At Boston Ballet, where Mikko Nissinen was making his way after having taken over the reins in 2002, the company offered new stagings of Ashton's ever-enchanting *La Fille mal gardée,* Welch's *Madame Butterfly,* and Rudolf Nureyev's *Don Quixote.* Before the fall season got into gear, the company roster changed significantly. Several veteran dancers left, and two of Nissinen's new hires hailed from Ballet Nacional de Cuba—Lorna Feijóo and Havana sensation Rolando Sarabia. The Cuban company made a fall tour of the U.S., including a week at New York City's City Center, with a repertory featuring *Don Quixote* and *Swan Lake* (both productions were supervised by the troupe's legendary director, Alicia Alonso). Pennsylvania Ballet's year included presentation of the East Coast premiere of *The Firebird* by James Kudelka, and by year's end the troupe was kicking off its 40th-anniversary season with a first-time staging of *Fancy Free.* The Joffrey Ballet of Chicago put its art form not only onstage as usual but also on film with the Christmas release of *The Company,* Robert Altman's latest work.

During the renovation of its opera house, the Kennedy Center for the Performing Arts in Washington, D.C., offered a number of dance events in less-usual parts of its complex. Among other events, it held an International Ballet Festival, featuring appearances by ABT, Miami (Fla.) City Ballet, the Bolshoi Ballet, St. Petersburg's Mariinsky Ballet (appearing under its former name, the Kirov Ballet), the Royal Danish Ballet, and Adam Cooper and Company. At year's end, after a U.S. tour that included Las Vegas, Nev., the Mariinsky returned to help reopen the Kennedy Center's opera house with its fantastic version of *The Nutcracker* and its standard staging of *Swan Lake.* The Kennedy Center also presented the Alvin Ailey American Dance Theater and a bill celebrating the legacy of Paul Taylor that featured both the Paul Taylor Dance Company and the Houston Ballet; the latter presented Taylor's now-classic *Company B* and the premiere of his newest creation, *In the Beginning.*

Suzanne Farrell Ballet, anticipating more eagerly than most companies the upcoming centenary of the birth of Balanchine, toured with all-Balanchine programming in the fall, climaxing with a two-program season at the Kennedy Center. The Eifman Ballet of St. Petersburg toured extensively in the U.S., featuring a take on the American movie classic *Some Like It Hot* as a cartoonish dance suite called *Who's Who.*

On other fronts of modern dance, the Merce Cunningham Dance Company helped christen Frank Gehry's shiny and new Richard B. Fisher Center for the Performing Arts at Bard College, Annandale-on-Hudson, N.Y. Later in the year, after wide-ranging touring, the company's continuing celebration of its 50th anniversary wrapped up at the Brooklyn Academy of Music's (BAM's) annual Next Wave Festival with a premiere work specially devised by Cunningham as a collaboration with both Radiohead (*see* BIOGRAPHIES) and Sigur Rós. Mark Morris performed during his annual stint at BAM, near his own headquarters, and gave the West Coast a world premiere, *All Fours* (set to the music of Bela Bartok), in September.

Intriguing entries in New York City's experimental dance scene included John Jasperse's *just two dancers* at Dance Theater Workshop and Sarah Michelson's *Shadowmann,* shown as a two-part miniepic at the Kitchen and PS 122. Susan Marshall's *Sleeping Beauty* and *Other Stories* helped to fill out the Next Wave Festival. The Martha Graham Dance Company was back in business early in the year after litigation over ownership of rights to its namesake's works, but it was back in court by the fall owing to an appeal.

Canada's Royal Winnipeg Ballet made news as a result of its involvement in Guy Maddin's film *Dracula—Pages from a Virgin's Diary,* which was based on Mark Godden's ballet *Dracula,* performed by the Royal Winnipeg. The troupe's fall season kicked off with Godden's latest premiere, *The Magic Flute.* In addition to showcasing a world premiere of *Tristan and Isolde* by John Alleyne, artistic director of Ballet British Columbia, James Kudelka's National Ballet of Canada also offered fall programming featuring innovative work that included the director's own *there, below,* Dominique Dumais's *one hundred words for snow,* and Matjash Mrozewski's *Monument.* Montreal's nearly 20-year-old Gala des Étoiles went forward even as it seemed it might not, thanks to what grateful president Victor Melnikoff called a "rescue operation" headed by Boston Ballet's Nissinen, in which the dancers worked without fees. After a slump in attendance in 2002, Vancouver's third International Dance Festival showcased a wide variety of offerings that included local and well as foreign troupes.

A number of deaths occurred during the year,

CindyMarie Small and Jesús Corrales of the Royal Winnipeg (Man.) Ballet perform as Pamina and Papageno in the premiere of choreographer Mark Godden's ballet set to Mozart's **The Magic Flute.**

David Cooper

including those of Vera Zorina, Cholly Atkins, Bertram Ross, Janet Collins, Howard ("Sandman") Sims, and Gregory Hines. (*See* OBITUARIES.) Other deaths included those of director Anne Belle, choreographers Mel Wong and Amy Sue Rosen, longtime dance educator Thalia Mara, and Muriel Topaz, a prominent figure in the field of dance notation. (ROBERT GRESKOVIC)

Europe. The year 2003 was one of a series of commemorative years for European ballet. The 10th anniversary of the death of Russian dancer Rudolf Nureyev fell in January, and the dance world looked forward to the centenary of the birth in 1904 of British choreographer Sir Frederick Ashton and the bicentenary of the birth in 1805 of Danish dancer and choreographer August Bournonville.

Many of the companies particularly associated with Nureyev gave special performances in tribute. The Paris Opéra Ballet mounted a program featuring several of his protégés and included the company's first performance of Ashton's *Marguerite and Armand,* originally made for Nureyev and Margot Fonteyn. In Vienna the State Opera Ballet performed several extracts from Nureyev's productions of the classics, and the Ballet of the Opéra Nationale de Bordeaux offered two programs of ballets in which Nureyev had danced. In London the National Film Theatre mounted a season of Nureyev's films and television programs, some quite familiar but others rarely seen before. The Royal Ballet also presented an evening of works associated with Nureyev, including a controversial section, arranged by Sylvie Guillem, in which dancers with the company performed some of his greatest roles in front of a large screen while filmed extracts from completely different works were shown simultaneously.

Linda Rich FRPS The Dance Picture Library

Choreographer Christopher Hampson's ballet Trapèze, *created for the English National Ballet, was set to a long-lost ballet score of the same name (commissioned in 1924) by Russian composer Sergey Prokofiev.*

The remainder of the London season included two very successful mixed programs by English National Ballet, which introduced new works by Christopher Hampson, whose ballet *Trapèze* was set to newly discovered music by Sergey Prokofiev, and Michael Corder, who made *Melody on the Move,* a piece evoking the "wireless" age. The Royal Ballet (with Monica Mason confirmed as its director) gave a new production of *The Sleeping Beauty* by Nataliya Makarova—a Russianized version that split both audiences and critics between fervent admiration and passionate disapproval. The Royal Ballet season ended with a new production of Ashton's *Cinderella,* with Sir Anthony Dowell and Wayne Sleep appearing as the Ugly Sisters. Two dancers with the Royal Ballet—Johan Kobborg, a principal dancer, and Carlos Acosta, a guest artist—each launched a program of his own. Company colleagues joined Kobborg in *Out of Denmark,* which showcased classic and contemporary Danish choreography. Acosta's show, *Tocororo—a Cuban Tale,* premiered in Cuba before having its British premiere at Sadler's Wells; it was set in his native Cuba, and he choreographed the piece entirely by himself. The Dance Umbrella festival celebrated its 25th year of presenting contemporary dance with performances by many British companies as well as by such guest companies as those of Merce Cunningham and Stephen Petronio.

Elsewhere in the U.K., the Birmingham Royal Ballet gave the first performance of *Krishna,* a ballet designed to fuse Eastern and Western traditions, with choreography by *kathak* dancer Nahid Siddiqui; the troupe also premiered *Beauty and the Beast,* the latest full-length work by company director David Bintley. Northern Ballet Theatre had a popular success with David Nixon's new work, an evening-long version of *A Midsummer Night's Dream.* A brilliant set by Duncan Hayler featured some spectacular transformation scenes. Scottish Ballet spent the first half of the year working in the studio with new director Ashley Page and then opened the new season with a program that included the revival of *Cheating, Lying and Stealing,* a work originally made by Page for the Royal Ballet. Visitors to England included the National Ballet of China, the Mariinsky Ballet—which gave a week of performances at the Lowry Theatre in Salford in addition to its customary summer season in London—and the company of Boris Eifman.

Brigitte Lefèvre, director of the Paris Opéra Ballet, had a long-established tradition of producing a new full-evening ballet every season, and 2003's work was by Patrice Bart, a former étoile. Bart's *La Petite Danseuse de Degas,* set to specially written music by Denis Levaillant, was based on the real-life story of Degas's model, with Laetitia Pujol in the title role. Other new works during the season included *Air* by Saburo Teshigawara, set to a score by John Cage, and *Phrases de Quatuor* by Maurice Béjart, made for Manuel Legris. Angelin Preljocaj used a score by French rock group Air for a new work, *Near Life Experience,* for the Preljocaj Ballet. Several of the traditional summer festivals in France were curtailed or even canceled altogether as a result of the threat of strikes over changes to welfare payments for workers in the arts who were temporarily unemployed.

In Russia the Mariinsky Ballet revived two works from the Sergey Diaghilev repertoire. Vaslav Nijinsky's *The Rite of Spring,* painstakingly re-created from contemporary source material by Millicent Hodson and Kenneth Archer, had been staged by various other companies in previous years, but this was the first time that it had ever been seen in Russia. Howard Sayette restaged Bronislava Nijinska's most famous work, *Les Noces,* in a reading based on that produced by Nijinska's daughter for the Oakland Ballet, which differed in several respects from the version staged by the choreographer herself for the Royal Ballet. Both ballets looked underrehearsed when they were seen in London; the Mariinsky's very heavy touring program left little time for the preparation of new work. Harald Lander's *Études,* made originally for the Royal Danish Ballet but later adapted for the Paris Opéra Ballet, was also added to the Mariinsky repertory. One of the company's leading ballerinas, Svetlana Zakharova, left at the end of the 2002–03 season to join the Bolshoi Ballet in Moscow. A long series of visiting companies appeared in a festival to celebrate the 300th anniversary of the founding of St. Petersburg.

The ballet of La Scala, Milan, became the first European company to add Balanchine's *A Midsummer Night's Dream* to its repertory, in a new decor by Luisa Spinatelli. Director Frédéric Olivieri was attempting to revitalize the repertory of the company, which had had an unsettled recent history. William Forsythe, with only one more season left as director of the Frankfurt (Ger.) Ballet, made a new work, *Decreation,* a multimedia piece that, owing to its complexity and obscurity, left many of its audiences at a loss. In Switzerland, Davide Bombana staged a ballet based on Vladimir Nabokov's *Lolita* for the Ballet du Grand Théâtre de Genève, and in Germany director Kevin O'Day showed two new works for the Mannheim Ballet.

The Peter Schaufuss Ballet gave the postponed premiere of *Diana—the Princess* at Holstebro in Denmark; as a prologue, Schaufuss used a short piece by Ashton, *Nursery Suite,* which showed imagined scenes from the childhood of Queen Elizabeth II and her sister, Princess Margaret. The Royal Danish Ballet gave the first company performances of Kenneth MacMillan's *Manon,* in a new decor by Mia Stensgaard, and also showed a new production of Bournonville's *La Sylphide,* staged by former Royal Danish dancer Nicolaj Hübbe, currently with NYCB. The Finnish National Ballet mounted a new version of the Marius Petipa classic *Raymonda,* which was jointly produced by Anna-Marie Holmes and ABT director Kevin McKenzie. The work was to be staged by ABT in 2004.

One of the most interesting offstage events was organized by DanceEast in Suffolk, Eng. The company's director, Assis Carreiro, gathered 25 directors of dance companies worldwide to discuss their common problems and plan for the future.

Losses to the dance world in 2003 included British conductor and composer John Lanchbery and Niels Bjørn Larsen, for many years a leading dancer with the Royal Danish Ballet.

(JANE SIMPSON)

THEATRE

Great Britain and Ireland. The National Theatre, formerly the Royal National Theatre, changed its name and changed its style as Nicholas Hytner succeeded Sir Trevor Nunn as artistic director in 2003. By cutting production budgets and attracting more sponsorship, Hytner was able to initiate a season of plays in the largest of the three National auditoriums, the Olivier, for which most seats cost £10 (about $15) each and the rest no more than £25 (about $38).

Whereas the West End theatres around Shaftesbury Avenue suffered one of their worst years in memory, the National was full, buoyant, and offering the best shows in town. The Olivier season began with Hytner's own thrilling production of William Shakespeare's *Henry V,* with a black monarch (Adrian Lester) fighting a war on foreign soil with instant media feedback on a battery of screens and microphones. The play reflected anxieties about the initiative in Iraq while reinventing the king as a modern leader whose justifications for going to war were as important as his military resolve.

Next at the Olivier came *His Girl Friday,* a new stage version by American dramatist John Guare of the Howard Hawks movie, conflated with the play on which it was based, the classic newspaper comedy *The Front Page.* Alex Jennings and Zoë Wanamaker were a scintillating double act. Then Kenneth Branagh returned to the London stage, after an absence of 11 years, as the self-destructive antihero of David Mamet's *Edmond,* a blistering fable of urban dismay and disintegration that Branagh seized upon with an irresistible gusto.

If any one production defined the new era under Hytner, however, it was *Jerry Springer—The Opera,* in the National's second auditorium, the Lyttelton. A scabrous musical setting of the American talk show with sexual deviants and fetishists, it was backed by a full choir (the television studio audience) screaming their obscenities and complaints in the musical language of high, Handelian baroque. Most critics rated this the most sensational new musical theatre event in London in years. It was a sellout success and transferred to the West End in October.

Also in the Lyttelton, there were excellent revivals of Tom Stoppard's *Jumpers* (his first National commission in 1972) starring Simon Russell Beale and Essie Davis, and Anton Chekhov's *Three Sisters,* newly translated by Nicholas Wright and directed by Katie Mitchell. The sisters were played by Lorraine Ashbourne, Eve Best, and Anna Maxwell Martin, a rising new star who finished the year as the young heroine of *His Dark Materials,* a two-play adaptation by the prolific Wright of Philip Pullman's three cult novels.

All the year's best new plays were at the National, in the smallest auditorium, the Cottesloe. Michael Frayn followed up *Copenhagen,* his huge recent hit of friendship and atomic science, with an even more enjoyable and potentially commercial play, *Democracy,* with the unlikely setting of the German chancellor's office during Willy Brandt's tenure in the early 1970s. Roger Allam was a superb, charismatic, and slightly troubled Brandt, partnered by Conleth Hill as the East German spy who infiltrated his office and became both friend and nemesis. Once again, Frayn's regular director Michael Blakemore did a magnificent job.

Other Cottesloe successes were Nick Dear's *Power*—almost a companion piece to *Democracy*—with Robert Lindsay in dazzling form as the unscrupulous financier, Fouquet, at the court of the Sun King, Louis XIV; Kwame Kwei-Armah's *Elmina's Kitchen,* a lively report from the East London front line of small-time crime; and Owen McCafferty's *Scenes from the Big Picture,* a stunning, poetic picture of a day's damage, drinking, and pain on the streets of Belfast, N.Ire., brilliantly directed by Peter Gill.

Not even the Royal Court, once the engine room of new British playwriting, could compete with that roster, although Roy Williams's *Fallout* was a compelling study of violent black teenagers and a policeman from their own environment trying to solve a local murder case. Terry Johnson's *Hitchcock Blonde* was an intriguing but seriously flawed attempt to exploit the great film director's penchant for fair ladies in the overlapping stories of the blonde body double in *Psycho* (a gorgeous Rosamund Pike) and an academic on a Greek island trying to decipher a lost Hitchcock movie while seducing his own assistant.

Hitchcock Blonde transferred to the West End to bolster a weak-looking drama program in the commercial sector. Sir Tom Courtenay gave a lovely performance as the poet Philip Larkin in his solo show, *Pretending to Be Me.* Meanwhile, three leading lights enjoyed varying degrees of success in plays by August Strindberg and Henrik Ibsen: Sir Ian McKellen, partnered by Frances de la Tour, gave a magnificent performance in Strindberg's *The Dance of Death;* Ralph Fiennes was not at his best as Ibsen's gloomy old pastor in *Brand;* and Patrick Stewart was merely stolid as Ibsen's obsessive architect in *The Master Builder.* Dame Joan Plowright led a colourful Luigi Pirandello revival called *Absolutely! (perhaps),* directed by Franco Zeffirelli, and Warren Mitchell scored a triumph as Gregory Solomon, the humorous used-furniture salesman in Arthur Miller's *The Price.*

The musical theatre was in a state of unapologetic nostalgia. *Ragtime* and *Thoroughly Modern Millie* arrived from Broadway, and Denise Van Outen shone gracefully in *Tell Me on a Sunday,* a rewrite of Don Black and Andrew Lloyd Webber's 1982 song cycle. Lloyd Webber and Tim Rice's *Joseph and His Amazing Technicolor Dreamcoat* returned too, with former Boyzone singer Stephen Gately in the lead. Toyah Willcox led a spirited revival of *Calamity Jane,* and the Open Air, Regent's Park, added a jolly version of Cole Porter's *High Society* to its staple diet of summer Shakespeare. To prove that anything goes as long as it went years ago, the 2002 Christmas treat at the National, Nunn's sumptuous revival of Cole Porter's *Anything Goes,* replaced Nunn's other recent National hit, *My Fair Lady,* at the Theatre Royal, Drury Lane, in time for Christmas 2003.

Eve Best's luminous Masha in **Three Sisters** *was but one of the many highlights in director Katie Mitchell's National Theatre production of a new translation of Anton Chekhov's elegiac play.*

Ivan Kyncl

One of the best Shakespeare productions of recent years was also by Nunn, in his farewell season at the National. *Love's Labour's Lost,* with Joseph Fiennes as Berowne, was an amazing show, redefining the romantic comedy as a remembered idyll in the Great War. Nothing at the Royal Shakespeare Company (RSC) came close, though there was a better-than-average *The Taming of the Shrew* at Stratford-upon-Avon, which director Gregory Doran imaginatively paired with John Fletcher's sequel (in which Petruchio's second wife leads a sexual rebellion) *The Tamer Tamed.*

The RSC was eclipsed again by Mark Rylance's Globe on the South Bank. His all-male version of *Richard II* was a huge hit, but nothing compared to the storming brilliance of an all-female reading of *The Taming of the Shrew,* with Janet McTeer's piratical Petruchio exacting all sorts of revenge on the play without the need of the Fletcher sequel. The audiences flocked all summer while the RSC slumped to miserable failure in its Old Vic season; the company remained homeless in London after quitting the Barbican.

Although the RSC rallied at Stratford with a well-received *Titus Andronicus,* directed by former associate director Bill Alexander, the bloody early play of Shakespeare did not beg favourable comparison with previous RSC revivals and seemed old-fashioned next to Julie Taymor's weird and wonderful movie of the play starring Anthony Hopkins and Alan Cumming. David Bradley, for many years one of the most admired supporting actors in Britain, took the leading role and pursued the quiet route. He hardly raised his voice all evening.

Offstage, the RSC confusion continued, with the sudden departure, in quick succession, of the company's managing director, Chris Foy, after just three years in the position, and two other key management figures in the now widely discredited redevelopment scheme. New artistic director Michael Boyd kept a low profile all year but was keen to emphasize a return to the ideal of a permanent company. He also welcomed back Dame Judi Dench at year's end to play the Countess in *All's Well That Ends Well* and Sir Antony Sher to play Iago in *Othello.*

The Donmar Warehouse maintained standards with fine revivals of Albert Camus's *Caligula* (starring Michael Sheen), Stephen Sondheim's *Pacific Overtures,* and one of the year's pleasant surprises, John Osborne's *The Hotel in Amsterdam,* which featured three of Britain's outstanding new young actors. Tom Hollander, Olivia Williams, and Susannah Harker revealed the juicy bile of Osborne's 1968 conversation piece in a luxury hotel, where six media types bitch and moan about an absentee film director. The play opened in the same week as a revival at the Theatre Royal, Haymarket, of Oscar Wilde's *A Woman of No Importance,* starring three more shooting stars—Rupert Graves, Rachael Stirling (Dame Diana

Rigg's daughter), and Julian Ovenden. London theatregoers could clear out their ears for the bracing linguistic vigour of both Osborne and Wilde.

The Almeida Theatre reopened after a £7 million (about $10 million) refurbishment with Natasha Richardson unforgettably claiming a role from her mother, Vanessa Redgrave, in Ibsen's *The Lady from the Sea,* directed by—that man again—Nunn! The new Almeida retained most of the qualities of the old, with its possibility of creating epic intimacy against a bare brick wall, but the building had much-improved front-of-house and backstage facilities. The Ibsen was followed by *I.D.*, a new and first play by Sher, who himself appeared as Demetrios Tsafendas, the parliamentary messenger in Cape Town who in 1966 assassinated South African Prime Minister Hendrik Verwoerd.

In the regions the places to visit were the Sheffield Crucible, the Bristol Old Vic, the Salisbury Playhouse, and the Theatre Royal, Bath, where Sir Peter Hall staged a season of Giuseppe Manfridi, D.H. Lawrence, Noël Coward, Harold Pinter, and Shakespeare to great applause. Hall's own daughter, Rebecca Hall, was a lissome, lovely Rosalind in *As You Like It.* After more than 30 years, Giles Havergal, Philip Prowse, and Robert David MacDonald retired as directors of the Glasgow Citizens. Prowse bowed out with a characteristically brilliant production of Thomas Otway's late 17th-century masterpiece *Venice Preserv'd.*

The new regime at the Chichester Festival Theatre had a marvelous summer, mounting a Venetian season ranging from Gilbert and Sullivan's *The Gondoliers* and Gotthold Lessing's *Nathan the Wise,* with Michael Feast in scintillating form in the title role, to Desmond Barrit as Shylock in *The Merchant of Venice* and a jaunty cabaret entitled *I Caught My Death in Venice.* The Edinburgh International Festival broke all box-office records, Fiona Shaw leading Peter Stein's revival of Chekhov's *The Seagull.* On the Edinburgh Festival Fringe, there was a superb revival of the courtroom classic *Twelve Angry Men* and a breakthrough performance (which later went to London) by the sensational 27-year-old Ross Noble, widely hailed as the best new British stand-up comedian since Eddie Izzard.

The Dublin Theatre Festival hosted two important premieres about artists: Brian Friel's *Performances* at the Gate Theatre boiled over with the obsessive love of Leos Janacek and was performed to the accompaniment of an impassioned Janacek string quartet; and Thomas Kilroy's *The Shape of Metal* at the Abbey explored the life and work of a sculptor and her complex relationship with her two daughters.

(MICHAEL COVENEY)

U.S. and Canada. Playwright Tony Kushner reemerged in 2003 as a force to be reckoned with in the American theatre. During the decade since his precedent-shattering two-part epic *Angels in America* made its unlikely way to a berth on Broadway (where its accolades included a Pulitzer Prize, a raft of Tony Awards, and numerous other theatrical honours), Kushner's new work for the stage had been mostly minor. Although his writing output had continued unabated, and his influence was keenly felt in the often fractious debate about the role of theatre art in politics and society, it was only with the arrival in November 2003 of his first musical, *Caroline, or Change*—a masterful, deeply personal meditation on the civil rights era set in 1963 in his own home town of Lake Charles, La.—and the miniseries-style TV debut a few weeks later of HBO's lavish, star-studded six-hour film of *Angels,* directed by Mike Nichols, that Kushner found himself once again in the full glare of national attention.

Caroline, or Change, which had its premiere at the Public Theatre in New York City in a fluid staging by director George C. Wolfe, was a departure for Kushner in both its chamber-musical form and its near-autobiographical content. Through the lens of the relationship between an eight-year-old Jewish boy and his family's unhappy black maid (the Caroline of the title), Kushner and his collaborator, composer Jeanine Tesori, illuminated a cluster of interlocking themes: the dynamics of dysfunctional families, the corrupting influence of money, the nation's grief over the assassination of Pres. John F. Kennedy, and the promise of social transformation that suffused the early 1960s. At year's end it seemed likely that *Caroline,* buoyed by mostly positive reviews, would follow in the footsteps of *Angels* by transferring to a Broadway house—and that, both in theatre circles and among a wider public exposed to *Angels in America* on television, Kushner's preeminence among American theatre writers would stand confirmed.

In addition to *Caroline*'s Tesori, another member of the post-Stephen Sondheim generation of composers launched a new work destined to have wide impact. Composer-lyricist Adam Guettel, the grandson of Richard Rodgers and author of the critically lauded *Floyd Collins,* joined forces with playwright Craig Lucas to adapt Elizabeth Spencer's short novel *The Light in the Piazza* into a full-scale musical drama. The tale of an innocent young American woman and her wealthy, protective mother on holiday in Florence in 1953 involves psychological intricacies—unbeknownst to her dashing Italian suitor, the 26-year-old daughter's mental development was halted by a childhood accident—as well as large-scale, almost cinematic scenes of Florentine life. Following productions in Seattle (Wash.) and Chicago, *Piazza* was certain to have life in New York City and beyond, thanks particularly to Guettel's radiant, lushly harmonic score.

On the nonmusical front, important premieres included *Gem of the Ocean,* the penultimate entry in August Wilson's decade-by-decade cycle chronicling the African American experience in the 20th-century U.S. The drama, set in 1904 Pittsburgh, Pa., played in Chicago and Los Angeles, where Phylicia Rashad gave a soaring performance as the psychic Aunt Ester. Other Wilson plays—including *Ma Rainey's Black Bottom,* which ran briefly on Broadway with Whoopi Goldberg in the lead—continued to be widely produced across the nation.

The year's Pulitzer Prize for Drama went to a self-consciously poetic and idiosyncratic play by Cuban-born Nilo Cruz called *Anna in the Tropics,* which was first produced at the tiny New Theatre of Coral Gables, Fla., and then widely mounted across the country. By year's end the play, which probed the lives and loves of a family of Depression-era cigar-factory workers, had advanced to Broadway in a somewhat stolid production featuring television actor Jimmy Smits. The other most widely produced works of the year were Canadian writer Michael Healey's *The Drawer Boy,* a three-character play about the theatre's effect on a pair of Ontario farmers; David Auburn's mathematics-flavoured family drama *Proof;* Suzan-Lori Parks's brutal two-hander *Topdog/Underdog;* and Edward Albee's 2002 Tony Award-winning seriocomic foray into bestiality, *The Goat, or Who Is Sylvia?* The biggest winners at the Tony Awards ceremony in June were the campy musical *Hairspray,* which won eight awards, including one for star Harvey Fierstein (*see* BIOGRAPHIES), and Richard Greenberg's gay

Michal Daniel

The premiere of Tony Kushner's chamber musical Caroline, or Change *featured Tonya Pinkins as the eponymous Caroline and Harrison Chad as the boy for whose family she works.*

baseball drama *Take Me Out,* which collected three Tonys.

In some cases what did not happen on American stages seemed as notable as what did. Among the high-visibility cancellations in 2003 were a production at New York's Public Theater of the long-in-development John Kander and Fred Ebb musical *The Visit,* based on the durable Friedrich Dürrenmatt drama, and a New York City engagement of the long-awaited (and frequently renamed) Sondheim musical *Bounce.* The latter work, a vaudeville based on minor historical figures and the first new Sondheim work in nine years, was criticized in its Goodman Theatre of Chicago production for Hal Prince's cartoonish direction and failed to inspire the necessary confidence for a move to New York City.

Not unexpectedly, given the stagnant U.S. economy, funding for the arts in general and nonprofit theatre in particular continued to erode in 2003. Local and city funding (which had dropped by 44% in 2002) declined even further, the number of corporate donors fell, and foundation funding slipped as well. Individual contributions to theatre, by contrast, rallied to cover an increasing percentage of expenses. The overall downturn forced the closure of several organizations, including the highly visible A.S.K. Theater Projects of Los Angeles, which shut its doors in September after 14 years of theatrical-support activities.

Still, under the radar—in storefronts, basements, and makeshift spaces—small-scale alternative and experimental theatre seemed to be thriving. On both coasts, in New York City and Los Angeles, enormous fringe theatre festivals provided outlets for young artists and adventurous projects. *Variety* reported that New York's seventh annual Fringe Festival sold 50,000 tickets to its 200 shows.

In Canada fear of SARS (severe acute respiratory syndrome) took a toll on the country's two major theatre festivals in Ontario. Both the Shaw Festival, which was held in Niagara-on-the-Lake, and the half-century-old Stratford Festival (which relied on American audiences for some 40–50% of their attendance) faced sharp declines in sales at their late-May openings. Montreal's Festival de Théâtre des Amériques fared considerably better the following month, earning international attention for its remounting, 16 years after its premiere, of Robert Lepage's brilliant six-hour epic of Canadian history, *La Trilogie des dragons.* Staged in a disused railway repair shop on the city's outskirts, the production reaffirmed director-actor Lepage's mastery of stage imagery and created a thrilling sense of theatrical event.

Among notable Canadian productions of the year was the commercial restaging, for an extended run, of Djanet Sears's *The Adventures of a Black Girl in Search of God* at Toronto's Harbourfront Centre Theatre. Sears, the highest-profile black theatre artist in Toronto and perhaps in all of Canada, staged her own history-hopping play with a vibrant singing and dancing chorus, who were said to represent the heroine's ancestors.

Those passing from the scene included actor, director, and Open Theatre founder Joseph Chaikin and playwright John Henry Redwood. Others deaths included those of theatre and film director Elia Kazan; dancer-actor Gregory Hines; cartoonist Al Hirschfeld; British stage designer Tanya Moiseiwitsch; actor Hume Cronyn; and playwrights Herb Gardner and Paul Zindel. (*See* OBITUARIES.)

(JIM O'QUINN)

MOTION PICTURES

United States. In terms of box office, the year 2003 was dominated by two concluding trilogies. The 200-minute *The Lord of the Rings: The Return of the King* completed the cycle based on J.R.R. Tolkien's visionary epic. Directed by Peter Jackson (*see* BIOGRAPHIES) and filmed mostly in his native New Zealand, the movie triumphed as a result not only of the careful attention paid to its literary origins but also of the strategy of shooting all the parts together. By contrast, *The Matrix Reloaded* and *The Matrix Revolutions*, which concluded the trilogy devised by the brothers Andy and Larry Wachowski, showed a formula overextended—though still a cunning amalgam of special effects, box-office stars, martial arts, stylish costumes, eroticism, and windy utterances that might be mistaken for mystical philosophy.

Nautical spectacles also won favour at the box office. *Pirates of the Caribbean: The Curse of the Black Pearl,* directed by Gore Verbinski and starring superstars Johnny Depp and Geoffrey Rush, was a lusty, if overlong, pirate yarn based on a ride at Disney World. A shade more serious was Peter Weir's *Master and Commander: The Far Side of the World,* based on the novels of Patrick O'Brian. One of the year's more costly films at upwards of $150 million, it was a painstaking and dramatic evocation of life aboard a British naval vessel during the Napoleonic wars.

Other veteran filmmakers were prominently at work in 2003. In *Anything Else,* Woody Allen returned to his

20th Century Fox/Universal/The Kobal Collection

Costing more than $150 million, **Master and Commander: The Far Side of the World** *featured Russell Crowe as Capt. Jack Aubrey. The story, set during the Napoleonic wars, was adapted from the novels of Patrick O'Brian.*

very distinctive version of life in New York City. *Intolerable Cruelty,* by the Coen brothers, Joel and Ethan, centred on a venomously comic confrontation between an invincible lawyer and a scheming beauty. Both Kevin Costner and Clint Eastwood chose to make films in the classic manner, Costner with the western *Open Range,* and Eastwood with an adaptation of Dennis Lehane's novel *Mystic River.* Robert Altman, always fascinated by the processes of artistic creation, examined the structure of a ballet troupe in *The Company.* Oliver Stone's *Comandante* was a very human and unexpected documentary portrait of Fidel Castro. Stone had less luck in his effort to make a film portrait of Yasir Arafat; the documentary's title *Persona Non Grata* reflected his own failure to get an interview with the Palestinian leader.

The career of the Taiwanese-born Ang Lee took another surprising turn when his *Hulk* transformed a comic-book story into an intelligent and literate investigation of character and identity. Few of the year's other remakes and spin-offs risked any such pretensions. *Terminator 3: Rise of the Machines* followed its old formulas with its original star Arnold Schwarzenegger (*see* BIOGRAPHIES), though with a new director, Jonathan Mostow. Marcus Nispel directed an unnecessary and ineffective remake of *The Texas Chainsaw Massacre.* Occasionally a remake—such as F. Gary Gray's update of the 1969 *The Italian Job* or the sleek and sexy *Charlie's Angels: Full Throttle* from the director known only as McG—outclassed its origins.

The Cannes Palme d'Or garnered by Gus Van Sant's *Elephant* might seem excessive for a film that barely skirted exploitation in its dramatization of the Columbine student shootings. Other films drawn from real events included Roger Spottiswoode's political comedy-drama *Spinning Boris,* based on the true story of the American advisers hired to help with Boris Yeltsin's 1996 reelection campaign.

A number of films revealed Hollywood's growing fascination with East Asia and its flourishing cinema cultures. Quentin Tarantino's *Kill Bill: Vol. 1* was an anthology of memories of old martial arts movies. In Edward Zwick's *The Last Samurai,* Tom Cruise played an American soldier who goes to Japan in 1874 to train the Imperial army in the use of modern weapons. There were amusing cross-cultural references too in *Shanghai Knights,* David Dobkin's sequel to *Shanghai Noon* (2000), in which Jackie Chan, an Imperial guard in the Forbidden City, becomes sheriff of Carson City.

Notable critical successes of the year included Sofia Coppola's *Lost in Translation,* a deft, modish romantic comedy about an encounter between two Americans in Tokyo; and Michael Polish's *Northfork,* scripted by his twin brother, Mark, a richly textured, visionary film about an old frontier town evacuated to make way for a hydroelectric dam. In *The Singing Detective,* directed by Keith Gordon, Robert Downey, Jr., was outstanding as Stephen Potter's tormented, hallucinating hero.

Among the films designed for a younger audience were P.J. Hogan's live-action *Peter Pan* and Bo Welch's *Dr. Seuss' The Cat in the Hat.* As computer techniques made the production process much faster and less dependent on individual artists, animation films proliferated. (*See* Sidebar.) The Disney Studios made *The Jungle Book 2, Piglet's Big Movie,* and *Brother Bear.* Disney's Pixar Studios subsidiary enjoyed success with the computer-made animation feature *Finding Nemo,* and DreamWorks produced *Sinbad: Legend of the Seven Seas.*

Academy Awards were granted to (among others) director-writer Michael Moore, director Roman Polanski, and actress Catherine Zeta-Jones. (*See* BIOGRAPHIES.) For a listing of the winners of major awards, *see* the table *International Film Awards 2003.* Among the notable individuals who died in 2003 were Stan Brakhage, Jeanne Crain, Katharine Hepburn, Dame Wendy Hiller, Bob Hope, Donald O'Connor, Gregory Peck, Leni Riefenstahl, and John Schlesinger. (*See* OBITUARIES.)

United Kingdom. The most spectacular production of 2003 by an English director was Anthony Minghella's *Cold Mountain.* Based on the best-selling 1997 novel by Charles Frazier, it related the odyssey of a wounded Confederate soldier making his way home to Cold Mountain, N.C., and the woman he loves. A more modest spectacle was Kevin Macdonald's *Touching the Void,* an intelligent and superbly photographed reconstruction of a real-life mountain-climbing incident.

The English taste in regional comedy flourished with Nigel Cole's box-office success *Calendar Girls,* featuring a group of senior British actresses (Julie Waters, Helen Mirren) in the real-life account of a women's group that produces a fund-raising calendar featuring them nude. Historical subjects included Mike Barker's study of Oliver Cromwell and the English Commonwealth, *To Kill A King;* Peter Webber's study of the Dutch master Johannes Vermeer, *Girl*

(continued on page 266)

The Reality of Virtual Characters

In 2003 the final film of *The Lord of the Rings* trilogy, *The Return of the King,* further demonstrated what had been realized the year before in the second of the series, *The Two Towers*—how absolutely real a computer-generated (CG) character could seem. From the first appearance of the creature Gollum in *The Two Towers,* it was evident that the day had come when a CG character could play a major acting role in a motion picture and in so doing have as much authenticity—and be as physically and emotionally compelling—as the actual humans on the screen. The performance of Gollum, a once humanlike hobbit whom the power of the ring at the centre of the story had transformed into a slinking, crafty, tormented being obsessed with possessing it, was so striking that there was a campaign to gain him an Academy Award nomination. Indeed, at the MTV Movie Awards in mid-2003, Gollum was the winner twice—for best virtual performance and for being a member, along with actors Elijah Wood and Sean Astin, of the best on-screen team.

Director Peter Jackson (*see* BIOGRAPHIES) wanted the character to be actor-based and arranged for the creation of Gollum to be an elaborate collaboration between a group of animators and actor Andy Serkis. Gollum's computer design had a full skeleton and a system of some 300 muscles and 250 face shapes. Serkis, whose strong interpretation was a major influence on the final realization of the character, voiced Gollum's dialogue, and the actor's facial expressions and body movements were studied by the animators. Further, in a method known as motion capture photography, Serkis's movements, as he acted out the scenes while wearing a special bodysuit covered in small dots, were captured by computer and transformed digitally. Added to this technique were digital sound mixing and the computer generation of imagery, and the result was the first digital character to be the equal of the live actors.

CG characters had been evolving for nearly two decades, since the appearance of what was considered to have been the first one in a film, a knight in a stained-glass window who—during a hallucination sequence in *Young Sherlock Holmes* (1985)—emerges from the window to engage in a fight. Other milestone films included *Who Framed Roger Rabbit* (1988), which pioneered the inclusion of animated characters, complete with three-dimensional shading, in live-action scenes; *The Abyss* (1989), whose seawater being was the first character completely created by computer; *Jurassic Park* (1993), which combined CG techniques with live action and animatronics to create lifelike, textured dinosaurs that moved realistically and could even be seen breathing; *Toy Story* (1995), the first feature film to be entirely computer-animated and to allow the motion of its characters to be independent of background motion within the same sequence; and the video-game-inspired *Final Fantasy: The Spirits Within* (2001), the first animated film to feature human characters who are photo-realistic. CG imagery (CGI) techniques were also used to create realistic-looking people in films for purposes that included enlarging crowds or armies; having dangerous stunts performed by virtual actors; and finishing a film if an actor died before all of his or her scenes had been shot, as was done, for example, for *The Crow* (1994) following the death of Brandon Lee and *Gladiator* (2000) after Oliver Reed died. In *The Matrix Reloaded* (2003), the character Neo engages in a fight scene in which he has to battle scores of identical versions of his archenemy Agent Smith simultaneously. *Star Wars: Episode I—The Phantom Menace* (1999) and *Episode II—Attack of the Clones* (2002) not only made use of CG armies but also had digitally created characters—such as Jar Jar Binks, Watto, and, in *Episode II,* Yoda (a puppet in previous series episodes)—interacting with human actors and seeming just as real. *Harry Potter and the Chamber of Secrets* (2002) did the same with a house elf, Dobby, and in *The Lord of the Rings,* although Gollum was the best-realized and most famous CG creation, virtual characters also appeared elsewhere—such as the walking and talking "living trees" known as Ents.

(Above) Creative director Mark Spanton is pictured with Ananova, a virtual newsreader on the Internet. (Below) Computer-generated Gollum was a major actor in The Lord of the Rings.

The idea of virtual characters was intriguing enough that a 2002 film, *S1m0ne,* posited the substitution of such a creation, named Simone, when the troublesome human star of a film quits; the digital actress fools everyone and becomes a sensation. Not too far removed from this fiction was the actual creation in Japan of a "virtual idol," Kyoko Date, who was given a family and a personal history and released a compact disc; in the U.K. an online virtual newscaster named Ananova, equipped with emotions and facial expressions, was featured on an Internet news service and could be used to deliver customized news broadcasts 24 hours a day—in 16 different languages. Perhaps even closer to real life was the news that a Miss Digital World competition was to be held in 2004, with CG contestants vying to be selected as the virtual embodiment of the ideal contemporary beauty and go on to a career of modeling for advertising, performing in video games, or even starring in virtual-reality films.

(BARBARA WHITNEY)

(continued from page 264)
with a Pearl Earring; and Christine Jeffs's careful but uninvolving portrait of the poet Sylvia Plath in *Sylvia.*

The British predilection for literary adaptation was demonstrated in Tim Fywell's rendering of Dodie Smith's *I Capture The Castle,* Richard Loncraine's elegant adaptation of William Trevor's *My House in Umbria,* and Stephen Fry's directorial debut with *Bright Young Things* from Evelyn Waugh's *Vile Bodies.* David Mackenzie's *Young Adam,* the story of the casual sexual depredations of a 1950s drifter, was adapted from the novel by Alexander Trocchi.

More personal projects were Richard Jobson's *Sixteen Years of Alcohol* (2002), an inventive and cinematic rendering of the director's semiautobiographical novel about a young man's battle with his own violent anger, and Sarah Gavron's *This Little Life,* based on Rosemary Kay's script about parenting a premature baby with little chance of survival. The veteran eccentric of British cinema Peter Greenaway produced two episodes of *The Tulse Luper Suitcases,* a multimedia extravaganza.

Australasia. Few films from Australia made a mark at international festivals in 2003. *Alexandra's Project,* by Rolf de Heer, tells the story of a sadistic punishment devised for an inconsiderate husband. Gregor Jordan's *Ned Kelly* was the sixth screen embodiment of Australia's legendary 19th-century outlaw. From New Zealand the first film entirely shot in Maori was Don Selwyn's *The Maori Merchant of Venice* (2002), a free and imaginative rerendering of Shakespeare. Also noteworthy was Niki Caro's *Whale Rider* (2002), in which a young girl battles ancient patriarchal tradition.

Canada. French-speaking Canada offered *Les Invasions barbares,* in which Denys Arcand continued his tragicomic investigation of family and society begun 17 years earlier with *Le Déclin de l'empire américain.* Many members of the original cast returned in their old roles for a story centred on the fatal illness of one of their number. The ever-inventive Robert Lepage adapted his one-man show into the visually inventive drama *La Face cachée de la lune* (*The Far Side of the Moon*).

Western and Northern Europe. France continued to maintain the highest production levels of any European country and produced more than twice the number of features made in the United Kingdom or Germany. Most were routine genre films, with a predominance of crime dramas and domestic comedies, but the activity and versatility of the most prominent directors remained impressive. The inventive François Ozon's *Swimming Pool* looked at the creative imagination through the confrontation of a disciplined English writer and an out-of-control teenager. The thriller master Claude Chabrol's *La Fleur du mal* (*The Flower of Evil*) depicted a bourgeois French family confronted by a 60-year-old mystery. Patrice Chéreau's *Son frère* (*His Brother*) feelingly recounted the reunion of a man and his terminally ill brother. Alain Corneau's *Stupeur et tremblements* (*Fear and Trembling*) treated with a sharp observant wit the problems of a Belgian interpreter in a Japanese firm. Jean-Pierre Rappeneau's *Bon voyage* followed the fortunes of a group of well-connected but dubious characters evacuated to Bordeaux during the occupation of Paris in 1940. Jacques Rivette's *L'Histoire de Marie et Julien* was a characteristic, exquisitely crafted, quiet anecdote about a couple who meet again after a year apart.

Germany enjoyed a runaway international success with Wolfgang Becker's modest *Good Bye, Lenin!,* an endearing comedy-drama about a devoted son's efforts to hide the reunification of Germany from his ailing mother, a loyal Cold War communist. Margarethe von Trotta's *Rosenstrasse* soberly reconstructed a Holocaust incident and its legacy. In Austria Michael Haneke offered a characteristic apocalyptic vision of contemporary violence in *Le Temps du loup* (*The Time of the Wolf*).

Australian Film Commission/Working Title/The Kobal Collection/Johns, Carolyn

Director Gregor Jordan's Ned Kelly *was based on events in the life of the Australian bushranger (outlaw) named in the title, as traced by Robert Drewe in the novel* Our Sunshine.

Italy's output was mainly genre pictures, but it also continued a tradition of films dealing with contemporary social and political life. Veteran directors in vigorous form included Ermanno Olmi with his exquisite Chinese myth of a lady pirate, *Cantando dietro i paraventi;* Marco Bellocchio with *Buongiorno, notte* (*Good Morning, Night*), a re-creation of the kidnapping and murder of former Italian prime minister Aldo Moro by Red Brigade terrorists; and Pupi Avati with *Il cuore altrove* (*The Heart Is Elsewhere*), an attractive, whimsical story of a virginal classics teacher's encounter with a femme fatale.

From younger directors Gabriele Salvatores's *Io non ho paura* (*I'm Not Scared*) showed visual flair in adapting Niccolò Ammaniti's novel about a Sicilian child who stumbles on his parents' involvement in the abduction of a rich child. Ferzan Ozpetek's *La finestra di fronte* (*The Window Opposite*) ingeniously interwove the mystery of an amnesiac old man and the romantic adventure of a beaten-down working-class wife; Constanza Quatriglio's *L'isola* (*The Island*) skillfully combined fiction with documentary in portraying the life of a small fishing village.

From Spain, with the third largest production in Europe, Miguel Hermoso's *La luz prodigiosa* (*The End of a Mystery*) was an intriguing speculation about the possibility that the poet Federico García Lorca survived execution during the Spanish Civil War to become an amnesiac vagrant. David Trueba's *Soldados de Salamina* (*Soldiers *of Salamina*) also offered a new approach to the recurrent Civil War genre—a young journalist's search for living witnesses. Eloy de la Iglesia's *Los novios búlgaros* (*Bulgarian Lovers*) was a comedy-drama, with social overtones, about a Spaniard's amorous obsession with a Bulgarian immigrant.

The doyen of Scandinavian cinema, Ingmar Bergman, at age 85 declared that *Saraband* (made for television and initially denied theatrical exhibition by its director) was the last film of his long career. This minor but worthy swan song, revisiting the 1973 *Scenes from a Marriage,* chronicled the reunion of wife (Liv Ullmann) and venomously embittered husband (Erland Josephson). Otherwise, films from the Nordic countries were largely crime stories, such as Colin Nutley's *Paradiset,* and light character and genre pieces, such as Icelander Dagur Kári's *Nói albinói* (*Noi the Albino*). The most notable exception was Lars von Trier's multinational co-production *Dogville.* Ingeniously minimalist, the film was a parable of small-town intolerance. Some American critics, offended that it was set in the U.S., deemed it anti-American.

Notable contributions from countries with smaller film industries included the Turkish director Nuri Bilge Ceylan's *Uzak* (2002; *Distant*), an exquisite minimalist study of an everyday relationship between an urban man and his unemployed country cousin; and, from The Netherlands, Ben Sombogaart's *De Tweeling* (2002; *The Twin Sisters*), the historical story of twin sisters, separated in childhood, who grow up in Nazi Germany and Occupied Holland under very different circumstances.

Eastern and Central Europe. Three of the most interesting films from Russia were variations on the theme of fathers and sons. In Andrey Zvyagintsev's *Vozvrashcheniye* (*The Return*), which won the Golden Lion award at the Venice festival, an absent father's return to take his two sons on a trip has a startling outcome. Aleksandr Sokurov's *Otets i syn* (*Father and Son*) explored the mysterious and disturbingly homoerotic depths of a filial relationship. Boris Khlebnikov and Aleksey Popogrebsky's gifted debut film, *Koktebel,* related the odyssey of a widowed father and his 11-year-old son en route to the Crimean city of that name.

The most significant new Hungarian films—notably Benedek Fliegauf's shoestring video piece *Rengeteg* (*Forest*), Péter Gothár's *Magyar szépzég* (*Hungarian Beauty*), and József Pacskovszky's *A Boldogság színe* (*The Colour of Happiness*)—struggled to analyze the contemporary consumerist society and the place of individuals within it. The veteran Károly Makk's *Egy hét Pesten és Budán* (*A Long Weekend in Pest and Buda*) was an echo of his 1971 classic *Szerelem* (*Love*); it concerned an old couple reunited after having been separated by the Revolution of 1956.

Wolfgang Becker's modest **Good Bye, Lenin!**, *a personal take on the meaning of German reunification, was an unexpected international hit.*

WDR/X-Filme/The Kobal Collection

The best films from the Czech Republic contemplated remembered history. Jan Hrebejk's *Pupendo* was a wry look at life in the socialist 1980s and the punishments that the authorities reserved for artists perceived as dissidents. Complementing this, Martin Sulík's *Klíc k urcování trpaslíku aneb poslední cesta Lemuela Gullivera* (2002; *The Key for Determining Dwarfs or the Last Travel of Lemuel Gulliver*) dramatized the diaries of the gifted filmmaker Pavel Juracek (1935–89).

The countries of former Yugoslavia dealt fiercely and fearlessly with recent history and present disorders. From Serbia and Montenegro, Dušan Kovačević's *Profesionalac* (*The Professional*) confronted a former dissident with the policeman who in former years had been his nemesis. From Croatia, Vinko Brešan's well-crafted *Svjedoci* (*Witnesses*) re-created a small segment of the cycle of war crimes through the eyes of a variety of witnesses.

In Romania, Lucian Pintilie's *Niki et Flo* portrayed the breakdown under the pressures of contemporary living of an old army veteran. Nicolae Margineanu's *Binecuvântata fii, închisoare* (2002; *Bless You, Prison*) recorded the prison experiences of intellectual Nicole Valéry in the early socialist era.

Middle East. Despite all cultural obstacles, Iran remained a world centre of creative filmmaking. Foremost among productions in 2003 were Jafar Panahi's *Talaye sorgh* (*Crimson Gold*), scripted by Iran's inspirational master Abbas Kiarostami, the story of a pizza delivery man who finally and fatally rebels against the humiliations heaped upon the have-nots of modern society; and 23-year-old Samira Makhmalbaf's *Panj é asr* (*At Five in the Afternoon*), which related the battle for emancipation of a young Afghan woman, fired with the ambition to become the country's president. A documentary on the making of this film was directed by the director's 15-year-old sister Hana. Modern Iranian youths striving to direct their own destiny was the theme of Parviz Shahbazi's *Nafas-e amigh* (*Deep Breath*), about sophisticated middle-class dropouts; and Mamad Haghighat's *Deux fereshté* (*Two Angels*) was about a boy's persisting in his desire to become a music student despite parental opposition. Abolfazl

(continued on page 269)

INTERNATIONAL FILM AWARDS 2003

Golden Globes, awarded in Beverly Hills, California, in January 2003

Best motion picture drama	*The Hours* (U.S.; director, Stephen Daldry)
Best musical or comedy	*Chicago* (U.S./Canada; director, Rob Marshall)
Best director	Martin Scorsese (*Gangs of New York,* U.S./Germany/ Italy/U.K./Netherlands)
Best actress, drama	Nicole Kidman (*The Hours,* U.S.)
Best actor, drama	Jack Nicholson (*About Schmidt,* U.S.)
Best actress, musical or comedy	Renée Zellweger (*Chicago,* U.S./Canada)
Best actor, musical or comedy	Richard Gere (*Chicago,* U.S./Canada)
Best foreign-language film	*Hable con ella* (*Talk to Her*) (Spain; director, Pedro Almodóvar)

Sundance Film Festival, awarded in Park City, Utah, in January 2003

Grand Jury Prize, dramatic film	*American Splendor* (U.S.; directors, Shari Springer Berman and Robert Pulcini)
Grand Jury Prize, documentary	*Capturing the Friedmans* (U.S.; director, Andrew Jarecki)
Audience Award, dramatic film	*The Station Agent* (U.S.; director, Thomas McCarthy)
Audience Award, documentary	*My Flesh and Blood* (U.S.; director, Jonathan Karsh)
Audience Award, world cinema	*Whale Rider* (New Zealand/Germany; director, Niki Caro)
Best director, dramatic film	Catherine Hardwicke (*Thirteen,* U.S.)
Best director, documentary	Jonathan Karsh (*My Flesh and Blood,* U.S.)
Special Jury Prize, dramatic film	*All the Real Girls* (U.S.; director, David Gordon Green); *What Alice Found* (U.S.; director, A. Dean Bell)
Special Jury Prize, documentary	*A Certain Kind of Death* (U.S.; directors, Grover Babcock and Blue Hadaegh); *The Murder of Emmett Till* (U.S.; director, Stanley Nelson)

Berlin International Film Festival, awarded in February 2003

Golden Bear	*In This World* (U.K.; director, Michael Winterbottom)
Jury Grand Prix, Silver Bear	*Adaptation* (U.S.; director, Spike Jonze)
Best director	Patrice Chéreau (*Son frère* [*His Brother*], France)
Best actress	Meryl Streep, Nicole Kidman, Julianne Moore (*The Hours,* U.S.)
Best actor	Sam Rockwell (*Confessions of a Dangerous Mind,* U.S./Canada/Germany)

Césars (France), awarded in February 2003

Best film	*The Pianist* (U.K./France/Germany/Netherlands/Poland; director, Roman Polanski)
Best director	Roman Polanski (*The Pianist,* U.K./France/Germany/ Netherlands/Poland)
Best actress	Isabelle Carré (*Se souvenir des belles choses,* France)
Best actor	Adrien Brody (*The Pianist,* U.K./France/Germany/ Netherlands/Poland)
Best first film	*Se souvenir des belles choses* (France; director, Zabou Breitman)

Orange British Academy of Film Awards, awarded in London in February 2003

Best film	*The Pianist* (U.K./France/Germany/Netherlands/Poland; director, Roman Polanski)
Best director	Roman Polanski (*The Pianist,* U.K./France/Germany/ Netherlands/Poland)
Best actress	Nicole Kidman (*The Hours,* U.S.)
Best actor	Daniel Day-Lewis (*Gangs of New York,* U.S./Germany/ Italy/U.K./Netherlands)
Best supporting actress	Catherine Zeta-Jones (*Chicago,* U.S./Canada)
Best supporting actor	Christopher Walken (*Catch Me if You Can,* U.S.)
Best foreign-language film	*Hable con ella* (*Talk to Her*) (Spain; director, Pedro Almodóvar)

Academy of Motion Picture Arts and Sciences (Oscars, U.S.), awarded in Hollywood in March 2003

Best film	*Chicago* (U.S./Canada; director, Rob Marshall)
Best director	Roman Polanski (*The Pianist,* U.K./France/Germany/ Netherlands/Poland)
Best actress	Nicole Kidman (*The Hours,* U.S.)
Best actor	Adrien Brody (*The Pianist,* U.K./France/Germany/ Netherlands/Poland)
Best supporting actress	Catherine Zeta-Jones (*Chicago,* U.S./Canada)
Best supporting actor	Chris Cooper (*Adaptation,* U.S.)
Best foreign-language film	*Nirgendwo in Afrika* (*Nowhere in Africa*) (Germany; director, Caroline Link)

Cannes International Film Festival, France, awarded in May 2003

Palme d'Or	*Elephant* (U.S.; director, Gus Van Sant)
Grand Jury Prize	*Uzak* (*Distant*) (Turkey; director, Nuri Bilge Ceylan)
Special Jury Prize	*Panj è asr* (*At Five in the Afternoon*) (Iran/France; director, Samira Makhmalbaf)
Best director	Gus Van Sant (*Elephant,* U.S.)
Best actress	Marie Josée Croze (*Les Invasions barbares* [*Invasion of the Barbarians*], Canada/France)
Best actor	Muzaffer Ozdemir, Emin Toprak (*Uzak* [*Distant*], Turkey)
Caméra d'Or	*Reconstruction* (Denmark; director, Christoffer Boe)

Locarno International Film Festival, Switzerland, awarded in August 2003

Golden Leopard	*Khamosh pani* (*Silent Water*) (Pakistan/France/Germany; director, Sabiha Sumar)
Silver Leopard	*Gori vatra* (Bosnia and Herzegovina/Austria; director, Pjer Zalica); *Thirteen* (U.S.; director, Catherine Hardwicke)

Locarno International Film Festival, Switzerland, awarded in August 2003 (continued)

Best actress	Holly Hunter (*Thirteen,* U.S.); Diana Dumbrava (*Maria,* Romania/Germany/France); Kirron Kher (*Khamosh pani* [*Silent Water*], Pakistan/France/Germany)
Best actor	Serban Ionescu (*Maria,* Romania/Germany/France)

Venice Film Festival, Italy, awarded in September 2003

Golden Lion	*Vozvrashcheniye* (*The Return*) (Russia; director, Andrey Zvyagintsev)
Jury Grand Prix, Silver Lion	*Le Cerf-volant* (Lebanon/France; director, Randa Chahal Sabag)
Volpi Cup, best actress	Katja Riemann (*Rosenstrasse* [*The Women of Rosenstrasse*], Germany/Netherlands)
Volpi Cup, best actor	Sean Penn (*21 Grams,* U.S.)
Silver Lion, best director	Takeshi Kitano (*Zatoichi,* Japan)
Marcello Mastroianni Prize for acting newcomer	Najat Benssallem (*Raja,* France/Morocco)
Prize for outstanding individual contribution	Marco Bellocchio (for screenplay, *Buongiorno, notte* [*Good Morning, Night*], Italy)

Montreal World Film Festival, awarded in September 2003

Best film (Grand Prix of the Americas)	*Kordon* (Serbia and Montenegro; director, Goran Markovic)
Best actress	Marina Glezer (*El polaquito,* Argentina)
Best actor	Silvio Orlando (*Il posto dell'anima,* Italy)
Best director	Antonio Mercero (*Planta 4a,* Spain)
Grand Prix of the Jury	*Gaz Bar Blues* (Canada; director, Louis Bélanger)
Best screenplay	*Profesionalac* (Serbia and Montenegro; writer, Dusan Kovacevic)
International cinema press award	*Profesionalac* (Serbia and Montenegro; director, Dusan Kovacevic)

Toronto International Film Festival, awarded in September 2003

Best Canadian feature film	*Les Invasions barbares* (*Invasion of the Barbarians*) (Canada/France; director, Denys Arcand)
Best Canadian first feature	*Love, Sex and Eating the Bones* (director, David Sutherland)
Best Canadian short film	*Aspiration* (director, Constant Mentzas)
International cinema-tographic press award	*Rhinoceros Eyes* (U.S.; director, Aaron Woodley)
People's Choice Award	*Zatoichi* (Japan; director, Takeshi Kitano)

San Sebastián International Film Festival, Spain, awarded in September 2003

Best film	*Schussangst* (*Gun-Shy*) (Germany; director, Dito Tsintsadze)
Special Jury Prize	*The Station Agent* (U.S.; director, Thomas McCarthy)
Best director	Bong Joon Ho (*Salinui chueok* [*Memories of Murder*], South Korea)
Best actress	Laia Marull (*Te doy mis ojos* [*Take My Eyes*], Spain)
Best actor	Luis Tosar (*Te doy mis ojos* [*Take My Eyes*], Spain)
Best photography	Eduardo Serra (*Girl with a Pearl Earring,* U.K./Luxembourg)
New Directors Prize	Bong Joon Ho (*Salinui chueok* [*Memories of Murder*], South Korea)
International Critics' Award	*Salinui chueok* (*Memories of Murder*) (South Korea; director, Bong Joon Ho)

Vancouver International Film Festival, Canada, awarded in October 2003

Federal Express Award (most popular Canadian film)	*The Corporation* (directors, Mark Achbar and Jennifer Abbott)
Air Canada Award (most popular film)	*Kamchatka* (Argentina/Spain; director, Marcelo Piñeyro)
National Film Board Award (documentary feature)	*Los Angeles Plays Itself* (U.S.; director, Thom Andersen)
Citytv Award for Best Feature Film from Western Canada	*On the Corner* (director, Nathaniel Geary)

Chicago International Film Festival, awarded in October 2003

Best feature film	*Talaye sorgh* (*Crimson Gold*) (Iran; director, Jafar Panahi)
Special Jury Prize	*Uzak* (*Distant*) (Turkey; director, Nuri Bilge Ceylan)
Best actress	Ludivine Sagnier (*La Petite Lili,* France/Canada)
Best actor	Pierre Boulanger (*Monsieur Ibrahim et les fleurs du Coran,* France)
International Film Critics' Prize	*Le Chignon d'Olga* (*Olga's Chignon*) (France/Belgium; director, Jérôme Bonnell)
Best documentary feature	*My Architect: A Son's Journey* (U.S.; director, Nathaniel Kahn)

European Film Awards, awarded in Berlin, December 2003

Best European film of the year	*Good Bye, Lenin!* (Germany; director, Wolfgang Becker)
Best actress	Charlotte Rampling (*Swimming Pool,* France)
Best actor	Daniel Brühl (*Good Bye, Lenin!,* Germany)
Best director	Lars von Trier (*Dogville,* Denmark/Sweden/France/ Norway/Netherlands/Finland/Germany/Italy/Japan/ U.S./U.K.)
Best cinematographer	Anthony Dod Mantle (*Dogville,* Denmark/Sweden/France/ Norway/Netherlands/Finland/Germany/Italy/Japan/ U.S./U.K.; *28 Days Later . . . ,* U.K./U.S./France)
Best screenwriter	Bernd Lichtenberg (*Goodbye, Lenin!,* Germany)
European Discovery of the Year	*Vozvrashcheniye* (*The Return*) (Russia; director, Andrey Zvyagintsev)

(continued from page 267)
Jalili's autobiographical *Abjad* (*The First Letter*)—the story of a sincerely religious young man who is punished for his humanist interpretation of the Qur'an and love of a Jewish young woman—was condemned by the authorities.

Production was revived in Afghanistan and Iraq in 2003. Siddiq Barmak's *Osama,* the first feature film from Afghanistan since the routing of the Taliban, looked at the oppression of women under that misogynist regime through the story of a young girl who secures a job by disguising herself as a boy. The first Iraqi film to be made internationally available in 15 years, Amer Alwan's made-for-television *Zaman, l'homme des roseaux* (*Zaman, the Man from the Reeds*) illuminated Iraq's civilization through the protagonist's journey from an ancient rural world to the terrible modernity of Baghdad, in quest of medicine for his sick wife.

An Israeli film, Ra'anan Alexandrowicz's *Massa'ot James be'eretz hakodesh* (*James' Journey to Jerusalem*) offered a healthily ironic picture of contemporary Israeli society through the travels of a religious young African making a private pilgrimage to Jerusalem.

East Asia. The cinema of China continued to surprise with its interest in private destinies in a fast-changing world. Good examples were Jiang Cheng Ding's Chaplinesque comedy *Xiao ti qing* (*Violin*), about a humble newspaper vendor who discovers his desire to make music; and Guan Hu's *Xi shi yan* (2002; *Eyes of a Beauty*), which intertwined the predicaments of three women. Alongside this a lively subversive cinema brought works such as Hu Ze's *Beijing Suburb* (2002), about an unofficial and repressed artists' colony; and Andrew Cheng's revelation of a defiant sexual subculture in *Mu di di Shanghai* (2002; *Welcome to Destination Shanghai*). In contrast, China's major international film artist Zhang Yimou made his first foray into martial arts films with the epic-scaled *Ying xiong* (*Hero*), mythical in approach but based on the true story of an effort to murder Shihuangdi, the first emperor of unified China, in the 3rd century BC.

The other film industries in the region flourished with an output of formula films—crime, thriller, teen romance, and horror—of varying merit. The rare maverick films of 2003 included, from South Korea, a spectacular adaptation of *Les Liaisons dangereuses* set in 18th-century Korea, *Seukaendeul: Joseon namnyeo sangyeoljisa* (*Untold Scandal*), by E. J-yong (Yi Jae Yong); and most notably Kim Ki Duk's *Bom yeoreum gaeul gyeoul geurigo bom* (*Spring, Summer, Fall, Winter . . . and Spring*), a film of exceptional if sometimes enigmatic aesthetic pleasures: the life—through a cycle of innocence, fall, regeneration, and rebirth—of a young monk at a strange deserted island monastery.

Japanese cinema, outside predictable mainstream production, in 2003 suffered one of the thinnest years in its history. Cult actor-director Takeshi Kitano (*see* BIOGRAPHIES) attracted little attention with his film *Zatōichi,* in which he resurrected the long-popular screen myth of the eponymous blind *yakuza*.

India. Mumbai (Bombay) producers extended the conventions of Indian commercial cinema to embrace new elements of thriller, science fiction (Rakesh Roshan's *Koi . . . mil gaya* [*I Found Someone*]), and gangster movies (Ram Gopal Varma's *Company,* 2002). Outside this mainstream Rituparno Ghosh adapted Rabindranath Tagore's 1902 novel of feminism and colonial resistance, *Chokher bali*. Adoor Gopalakrishnan's *Nizhalkkuthu* (2002; *Shadow Kill*) explored the private agonies of a hangman. Vishal Bharadwaj's *Maqbool* transposed Shakespeare's *Macbeth* to the criminal areas of modern Mumbai. Mahesh Dattani's *Mango Soufflé* (2002), adapted from the director's own play *On a Muggy Night in Mumbai,* was a social breakthrough for India, a sympathetic portrayal of homosexuality in a well-heeled professional society.

Latin America. Few films from the cumulatively prolific Latin American production made an international impact in 2003, though works to note were Argentine Albertina Carri's *Los rubios* (*The Blonds*), a complex, experimental combination of fiction, documentary, and avant-garde filmmaking that explored the disappearance and murder of the writer-director's parents under the military dictatorship; and, from Cuba, Fernando Pérez's *Suite Habana,* a practically wordless mosaic of contemporary Havana characters whose dreams, mostly dashed, provide a subtly subversive critique of Fidel Castro's Cuba.

Africa. While many films, such as Burkina Faso director Idrissa Ouedraogo's *La Colére des dieux* (*Anger of the Gods*), drew on tribal and traditional life, filmmakers in all parts of Africa were consciously using films in the cause of social betterment. One of the most fiercely critical was *Le Silence de la forêt,* a co-production of Cameroon, Gabon, and Central African Republic directed by Didier Ouenangare and Bassek ba Kohbio, about the frustrations of a French-educated idealist who returns to discover the corruption and incorrigibility of society in his (unspecified) native country. From South Africa, David Hickson's *Beat the Drum* was a morality drama on the prevention of AIDS, presented through the journey of a small village boy who becomes briefly an urban street kid. The Tunisian Nouri Bouzid's *Arais al tein* (2002; *Clay Dolls*) looked at the abuse of women and children by those who live by supplying young girls from the poor countryside as maids to rich employers in the city. (DAVID ROBINSON)

Nontheatrical Films. Steven Silver's film *The Last Just Man* (2001) received much favourable attention in 2003. It featured Gen. Roméo Dallaire, who headed the UN troops stationed in Rwanda during the genocidal civil war of 1994. In 2002 the film had won Best of Fest at the Columbus (Ohio) Film Festival and Gold trophies at the Chicago International Television Competition and U.S. International Film and Video Festival, Los Angeles, and in 2003 it continued to garner awards internationally.

A French film made in 2001 won widespread acclaim when it was released in 2003 as *Winged Migration.* Regine Cardin's *Action!* exuded French humour while selling Paris as a good place to do business. Made for the Paris Industrial Chamber of Commerce, the film was Best of Festival at WorldMediaFestival in Hamburg, Ger., and won the Grand Prix at the U.S. International Film and Video Festival.

The merging of tradition and the future, symbolized in the use of Clariant pigments for the creation of a Japanese kite, was the subject of Hagenfilm's *Innovations* for Clariant GmbH. It won top awards at WorldFest in Houston, Texas; INTERCOM, Chicago; and U.S. International Film and Video Festival.

Judy's Time (2000) recounted the life of 57-year-old Judy Flannery, a mother of five, who was also a world champion triathlete in her prime when she was struck and killed by a car. The filmmaker, her daughter Erin, who made the film as a graduate student, received several awards, including CINE's Eagle Award (2000) and Master Series Award (2001) and the International Documentary Association award for Distinguished Short Documentary (2002).

(THOMAS W. HOPE)

Physical Sciences

As human space exploration in 2003 reeled from the CATASTROPHIC LOSS of the shuttle orbiter *COLUMBIA*, several ROBOTIC SPACECRAFT converged on the planet MARS. Chemists synthesized composite FIBRES made of CARBON NANOTUBES that matched the strength of SPIDER SILK. Physicists reported discovery of the first known PENTAQUARK, a particle comprising five quarks.

CHEMISTRY

Nuclear Chemistry. In 2003 the International Union of Pure and Applied Chemistry approved darmstadtium as the official name and Ds as the symbol for element 110 on the periodic table. Scientists working at the Society for Heavy Ion Research, known as GSI, in Darmstadt, Ger., synthesized element 110 for the first time in 1994 and proposed the name. It took some years, however, to verify their work and approve the proposal. Darmstadtium replaced the element's interim name, ununnilium (scientific Latin for *110* with an *-ium* suffix), which had appeared in classroom textbooks and periodic tables.

Carbon Chemistry. All-carbon fullerene molecules, such as the soccer-ball-patterned buckminsterfullerene (C_{60}), have cage structures with open interiors that are ideal for holding metal atoms or small gas molecules. During the year chemists continued to look for ways to trap such substances inside fullerenes in an effort to make new materials that would have scientific or industrial applications.

Koichi Komatsu and colleagues at Kyoto (Japan) University reported synthesis of a fullerene derivative that readily accepts and holds a molecule of hydrogen (H_2). Prepared from C_{60}, the molecule has a tailored "mouth"—an opening in its cage—that is slightly larger than previous versions. Other researchers had made fullerene derivatives that could incorporate hydrogen in as much as 10% yield. Komatsu's derivative, in contrast, can be filled to 100% yield. In laboratory tests no hydrogen leaked from a sample of the filled molecules during more than three months of monitoring at room temperature. The trapped hydrogen was released slowly, however, when the molecules were heated to temperatures above 160 °C (320 °F). Researchers sought to develop materials that could safely hold and release hydrogen, which because of its high flammability poses an explosion hazard, for possible applications in new generations of hydrogen-fueled vehicles. Molecular encapsulation and slow release could solve that problem.

A derivative of the fullerene C_{60} with a tailored "mouth" in its spherical cage encapsulates a molecule of hydrogen (large white spheres) in this computer model. During the year Japanese chemists reported synthesis of the structure.

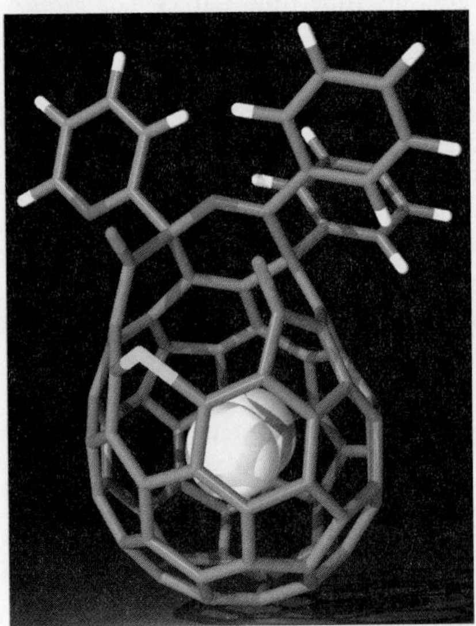

Courtesy of Koichi Komatsu

A strand of spider silk is five times as strong as a strand of steel of identical mass. That strength underpinned ongoing research to make commercial amounts of spider silk for cables, supertough fabrics, and other uses. Ray Baughman of the University of Texas at Dallas and co-workers reported synthesis of long carbon-nanotube composite fibres that match spider silk's strength. Nanotubes consist of carbon atoms bonded into a hexagonal-mesh framework similar to that of graphite; the framework is rolled into a seamless cylinder barely a nanometre in diameter.

Baughman's composite fibres appeared to be tougher than any natural or synthetic organic fibre described to date, and they were able to be woven into textiles. The researchers developed a process for spinning the solid fibres from a gel material consisting of nanotubes and a polymer, polyvinyl alcohol. They produced composite fibres the width of a human hair at a rate of about 70 cm (2.3 ft) per minute and yielded individual strands as long as 100 m (330 ft).

The researchers then used their spun carbon-nanotube fibres to make supercapacitors, electronic devices capable of storing large amounts of electricity. In addition, they wove the supercapacitors, which had the same energy-storage density as large commercial supercapacitors, into conventional fabrics. The fibre capacitors showed no decline in performance during 1,200 charge-discharge cycles. The investigators cited a number of promising electronic-textile applications for the fibres, including electromagnetic shields, sensors, antennae, and batteries.

Inorganic Chemistry. A relatively new group of crystalline ionic compounds, called electrides, was stirring excitement among chemists and materials scientists. The electrons in electrides do not congregate in localized areas of specific atoms or molecules, nor are they delocalized like the electrons in metals. Rather, the electrons are trapped in sites normally occupied by anions, negatively charged atoms or groups such as the chloride ion (Cl^-) and the hydroxyl ion (OH^-).

The trapped electrons act like the smallest possible anions, which opens the door to important practical applications—for example, powerful reducing agents or materials with unusual electrical, magnetic, or optical properties. Scientists had been unable to explore those possibilities because all electrides made in the past were fragile organic complexes. They decomposed at temperatures above –40 °C (–40 °F) and could not withstand exposure to air or water.

Satoru Matsuishi and Hideo Hosono of the Japan Science and Technology Corp., Kawasaki, and colleagues reported an advance that promised to simplify future research on electrides. They synthesized an inorganic electride that is stable at room temperature. The material, having the formula $[Ca_{24}Al_{28}O_{64}]^{4+}(4e^-)$, in which the four electrons (e^-) counterbalance the positively charged (4+) ion, also withstands exposure to air and moisture. Matsuishi's group made it by removing almost all of the oxygen anions (O^{2-}) trapped in cavities in the internal structure of a single crystal of $12CaO \cdot 7Al_2O_3$. The vacant cavities filled with electrons to a density typical of electrides; in the process the colour of the crystal changed from colourless to green and then to black. The researchers believed that the new compound would point the way to other stable electrides with practical applications.

Organic Chemistry. Chemists missed the mark when they picked the original name—inert gases—for a family of six elements that compose group 18 of the periodic table. They thought that helium, neon, argon, krypton, xenon, and radon were inert and never combined with other elements to form chemical compounds. That notion was upset in the 1960s when researchers made the first xenon compounds and the group's preferred name changed to the noble gases. Xenon, for instance, forms a variety of inorganic compounds with oxygen and fluorine.

Leonid Khriyashtchev and co-workers of the University of Helsinki, Fin., reported making the first true organic compound incorporating a noble gas, krypton (Kr). It is the compound HKrCCH, in which a krypton atom is bonded to a carbon atom and a hydrogen atom. They synthesized minute amounts of the compound by focusing ultraviolet light on acetylene (HC≡CH) trapped inside a krypton matrix that had been chilled to within a few degrees of absolute zero. Khriyashtchev believed that the landmark reaction could open a window on a new area of krypton chemistry.

"Green" Chemistry. Catalysts speed up chemical reactions that otherwise would not occur or would occur at a snail's pace. They play an indispensable behind-the-scenes role in the manufacture of hundreds of consumer products, ranging from gasoline to medicines. Chemists face big problems, however, in separating a certain class of catalysts from the products after the reaction is done. Called homogeneous catalysts, they are usually dissolved in the same liquid that contains the reactants. When the reaction finishes, the liquid holds not only the desired products but also the catalyst. Separating the catalyst can be expensive and time-consuming.

During the year R. Morris Bullock and Vladimir K. Dioumaev of Brookhaven National Laboratory, Upton, N.Y., developed a self-separating, reusable catalyst. The catalyst dissolves in the reactants but is insoluble in the product; at the end of the reaction, it precipitates from solution, which makes it easy to recover and reuse. Although the chemists demonstrated the catalyst—an organometallic tungsten-containing complex—in only one specific case, they hoped that the results would lead to a general method for developing self-separating catalysts for a variety of reactions of practical interest.

Bullock and Dioumaev noted that self-precipitating catalysts would be a major advance in "green" chemistry, the effort to replace chemical processes potentially damaging to the environment with friendlier alternatives. Separating homogeneous catalysts from products often requires the use of toxic solvents, which require special disposal methods. Catalysts that automatically separate would reduce or eliminate the need for solvents.

Applied Chemistry. The traditional chemical process for making hydrogen is amenable to industrial-scale production of that clean-burning fuel, but it is far from ideal for small-scale hydrogen production, such as for use in fuel cells in homes or motor vehicles. Termed reforming, the industrial process uses steam and hydrocarbons such as methane as raw materials and requires catalysts and temperatures above 800 °C (1,500 °F).

Zhong L. Wang and Zhenchuan Kang of the Georgia Institute of Technology reported an advance toward a better small-scale hydrogen-production technology. It involved oxides of the rare-earth elements cerium, terbium, and praseodymium. Scientists had long known that these compounds can make hydrogen from water vapour and methane in a continuous "inhale-exhale" cycle. The oxides have a unique internal crystalline structure, which allows up to 20% of their oxygen atoms to leave and return without damaging the crystalline lattice. Integrated into a hydrogen-production system, the oxides would permit oxygen atoms to move out and back in as the oxygen participated in a two-step temperature-governed cycle of oxidation and reduction reactions that produce hydrogen. The built-in oxygen supply would decrease the amount of water vapour needed for the process.

Wang and Kang discovered that doping, or supplementing, the rare-earth oxides with iron atoms lowered the temperatures at which the hydrogen-production cycle could be run. The doped lattice structures "exhale" oxygen atoms at about 700 °C (1,300 °F) and "inhale" them at 375 °C (700 °F). Lowering the latter temperature a little more, to about 350 °C (660 °F), would permit use of solar energy as part of the heat source, Wang noted.

(MICHAEL WOODS)

PHYSICS

Particle Physics. In 2003 independent teams of scientists involved in technically quite different high-energy particle experiments at the Jefferson National Accelerator Facility, Newport News, Va., and the Institute of Theoretical and Experimental Physics, Moscow, reported evidence for a new particle, the theta-plus (Θ^+), made of an unprecedented five quarks. Their findings corroborated evidence for the particle announced the previous year by researchers at the SPring-8 accelerator facility near Osaka, Japan.

It had been known for decades that protons and neutrons, the familiar particles that compose atomic nuclei, are made of still smaller particles called quarks. The standard model, the theory encompassing the fundamental particles and their interactions, does not preclude the existence of five-quark particles, or pentaquarks. Until the latest findings, however, only particles made up of three quarks (e.g., protons and neutrons) or of two quarks (unstable, short-lived particles known as mesons) had ever been observed. The new experiments all pointed to the fleeting existence of a pentaquark with a mass of 1.54 GeV (billion electron volts), which decayed into a neutron and a K-meson (kaon). The results agreed with theoretical predictions of the particle made by Russian physicists in 1997.

Although the existence of quarks was well established, individual "free" quarks—quarks not bound into particles—remained to be observed. Experiments at Brookhaven National Laboratory's Relativistic Heavy Ion Collider (RHIC) in which gold nuclei moving at 99% of the speed of light were collided head-on into one another continued to show intriguing hints of the production of free quarks as part of a so-called quark-gluon plasma. Gluons are the massless field particles that hold quarks together in particles. Physicists expected that at sufficiently high collision energies, the protons and neutrons in the gold nuclei would liberate their quarks and gluons to form an extremely hot, dense "soup" of nuclear matter. Such a quark-gluon plasma was believed to have existed in the first instant after the big-bang birth of the universe.

Condensed-Matter Physics. Experiments that involve cooling a few thousand atoms of a gas to temperatures closely approaching absolute zero (0 K, –273.15 °C, or –459.67 °F) provided fascinating results once again in 2003. When the cooled gas consists of atoms having zero or integral-number intrinsic spins (such atoms are called bosons), the result is a state of matter known as a Bose-Einstein condensate (BEC), which was first created in the laboratory in 1995. Rather than existing as independent particles, the atoms in a BEC become one "superparticle" described by a single set of quantum state functions. In a technological achievement for low-temperature physics, Aaron Leanhardt, Wolfgang Ketterle, and co-workers from the Massachusetts Institute of Technology (MIT)–Harvard University Center for Ultracold Atoms trapped sodium atoms in a "container" of magnetic fields, cooled them to form a BEC, and ultimately brought 2,500 of them to the lowest temperature documented to date—about 500 picokelvins (500 trillionths of a kelvin). The previous low-temperature record had been 3 nanokelvins (3 billionths of a kelvin), six times higher.

Gases consisting of atoms having intrinsic spins that are multiples of half integers (such atoms are known as fermions) also can be cooled similarly, but their properties (as described by the Pauli exclusion principle) do not allow them to fall into the same condensed state. Instead, they fill up all available states starting from the lowest energy. A common example is the stepwise buildup of electrons, which are fermions, in successive orbitals around the nucleus of an atom. At first sight the behaviour of ultracold fermions might seem less interesting than that of bosons but for one possible phenomenon—Cooper pairing. It should be possible for two fermionic atoms to pair in a strongly interacting way. This atom pair would function similarly to the paired electrons called Cooper pairs, which are responsible for superconductivity in some materials when they are cooled to low temperatures. Strongly interacting fermions—not only electrons but also protons, neutrons, and quarks—were involved in some of the most important unanswered questions in science from astrophysics and cosmology to nuclear physics. The controlled production of paired fermionic atoms could give new insight into these questions and lead to novel and useful quantum effects.

By midyear six research teams had succeeded in chilling gases of fermions to their lowest energy states, an important step toward achieving Cooper pairing of atoms. Deborah Jin and colleagues at JILA, Boulder, Colo., worked with potassium atoms, as did Massimo Inguscio and researchers at the University of Florence. Using lithium atoms were Randall Hulet's team at Rice University, Houston, Texas; Christophe Salomon's group at the École Normale Supérieure, Paris; John Thomas's group at Duke University, Durham, N.C.; and Ketterle's team at MIT. No team produced evidence of pairing, but Cindy Regal and co-workers of the JILA group succeeded in forcing fermion atoms to combine into a molecule-like state called a magnetic Feshbach resonance. Some researchers hoped that this fleeting interaction would serve as a stepping-stone from which the atoms could be coaxed further to form Cooper pairs. In terms of fundamental physics, gases of ultracold fermionic atoms might well prove more important than BECs.

Photonics and Optical Physics. A new generation of relatively compact pulsed lasers under development had the potential to produce hitherto undreamed-of power—in the petawatt region (a petawatt is 10^{15} W). A complex system involving compressing, amplifying, stretching, amplifying, and then compressing again converted relatively long-duration low-power laser pulses with energies of hundreds of joules into very short, femtosecond (10^{-15} second), high-power pulses. Many laboratories were working on such devices, which promised to make possible laser-driven fusion reactions and to reproduce in the laboratory the conditions that existed near the birth of the universe. A leader in the field was Victor Yanovsky's group at the University of Michigan, which reported having produced a sharply focused pulse with a power density of 10^{21} W/cm^2. Groups also were working on techniques to use such pulses to control electronic processes.

The refraction of light took on new interest as a number of researchers developed ways of making materials with negative refractive indexes. On entering such a material, electromagnetic radiation such as light would be bent through a negative, rather than a positive, angle; i.e., its change in direction would be opposite that normally observed. C.G. Parazzoli and co-workers of the Boeing Co. and A.A. Houck and colleagues at MIT built systems that exhibited this phenomenon, as did Ertugrul Cubukcu and co-workers from Bilkent University, Ankara, Turkey. In related work Matthew Bigelow and colleagues of the University of Rochester, N.Y., demonstrated the ability to control the propagation of light—slowing it down or speeding it up—as it traveled through a crystalline material at room temperature by altering the material's refractive index.

Quantum Physics. Many research teams continued to investigate the application of quantum phenomena to computing. Operation of quantum computers would involve the storage and transfer of so-called qubits, states of quantum systems that could be used to represent bits of data. The great advantage of such devices was that the transfer of information might not be limited by the speed of light. The bizarre phenomenon of quantum entanglement allows two systems—for example, subatomic particles or atoms—in the same quantum state to be separated by an arbitrary distance but to remain connected in such a way that they reflect each other's condition. Two entangled qubit devices would thus be in contact instantaneously. By 2003 scientists had used entanglement to achieve "quantum teleportation"—the transfer of the quantum state of a particle from point to point (albeit without physical transfer of the particle itself)—on a small scale, but practical systems to store and manipulate qubits without destroying their coupled states remained to be constructed. There were many different candidates on which to base entangled systems, including photons, atoms, trapped ions, and quantum dots, the last being tiny isolated clumps of semiconductor atoms with dimensions measured in nanometres (billionths of a metre).

During the year Markus Aspelmeyer and colleagues of the University of Vienna reported the first long-distance demonstration of quantum entanglement across open space. They showed that photons of light remained coupled and able to communicate their states over a distance of 600 m (more than a third of a mile). The concept of entanglement was now well established, and it appeared increasingly likely that qubit systems would provide the next major leap forward in computing.

(DAVID G.C. JONES)

NASA, ESA and H.E. Bond (STScI)

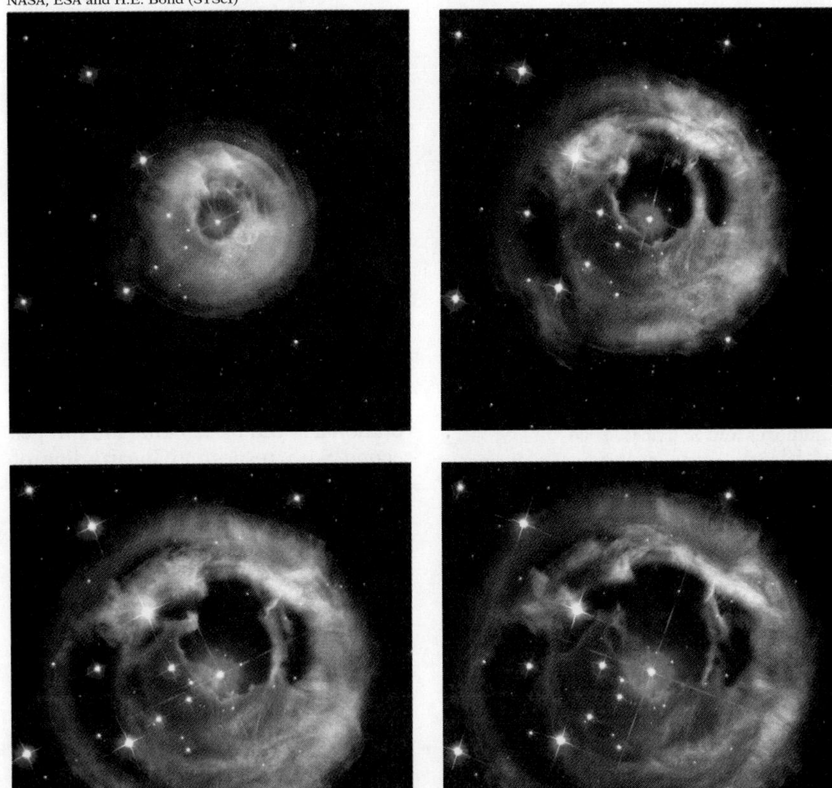

Spectacular dust shells around the star V838 Monocerotis are revealed in a series of images made over a seven-month period by the Hubble Space Telescope. A brief luminous outburst of the star in 2002 illuminated the dust. Differences in the time taken by the reflected light to reach Earth account for the changing details.

ASTRONOMY

Solar System. On the morning of August 27, Mars and Earth made their closest approach in 60,000 years—a "mere" 56 million km (35 million mi) apart. As many people on Earth delighted in the excellent viewing opportunities offered by the event, the exploration of Mars by robotic spacecraft missions continued apace. NASA's Mars Global Surveyor, which had been orbiting Mars since 1997, found more than 500 examples of new types of geologic features on the Red Planet, including evidence of landslides near regions of former volcanic activity and erosion gullies possibly formed by flowing water in the past. It also provided evidence that the planet's core is at least partially liquid iron. NASA's Mars Odyssey spacecraft, which began its observations from orbit in late 2001, continued mapping high levels of hydrogen near the planet's surface, which was suggestive of the presence of large amounts of water ice. Several new spacecraft missions to Mars also were launched during the year. (See *Space Exploration,* below.)

Ever since Galileo pointed his five-centimetre (two-inch)-diameter telescope toward Jupiter in 1610 and discovered four moons of the giant planet, astronomers had sought out heretofore-unseen satellites of the solar system's planets. In 2003 a bevy of new moons were discovered. Using the Keck telescopes in Hawaii, David C. Jewitt and Scott S. Sheppard of the University of Hawaii discovered 21 new satellites of Jupiter. This brought the number of its moons known at year's end to 61. The same astronomers also found another moon of Saturn, which brought its known total to 31. In addition, a group of astronomers led by Matthew J. Holman of the Harvard-Smithsonian Center for Astrophysics, Cambridge, Mass., announced the discovery of three new moons of Neptune, which brought its known total to 11; these were the first new finds for Neptune since 1989, when the Voyager 2 spacecraft discovered several moons during its flyby of the giant planet. All of the moons are small (a few kilometres in diameter) and have orbits suggesting that they were captured by their respective planets rather than being formed with them.

Stars. Since the early 1990s more than 100 extrasolar planets had been discovered revolving around relatively nearby individual stars—stars up to about 100 light-years distant. Astronomers detected most of them indirectly by observing subtle gravitational effects on the parent stars as they were tugged to and fro by the unseen bodies. The year 2003 brought announcements of a variety of new extrasolar planets, some of them comparatively far from Earth. At the start of the year, a Jupiter-mass planet was detected when it passed in front of the star it was orbiting, slightly dimming its light. Called OGLE-TR-56b, it is about 5,000 light-years away and was the first extrasolar planet to be initially detected by its transiting. Another study resulted in the identification of what was likely the oldest planet found to date. This planet orbits a star in a binary system that contains both a radio-emitting pulsar, named PSR B1620-26, and a white dwarf. Furthermore, this stellar-planetary system resides in the globular star cluster M4, which is about 7,000 light-years away and is estimated to be 12.5 billion–13 billion years old. A major implication of the discovery was that at least some planets formed very early in the history of the universe.

Most stars are assumed to be spherical objects. Their shape, nevertheless, is difficult to discern directly because of their relatively small angular diameters as seen from Earth. For a long time only the Sun presented a large-enough target to establish its shape directly. It is spherical to better than one part in 100,000. In 2003 astronomers using the European Southern Observatory's Very Large Telescope Interferometer at Cerro Paranal in Chile found that one of the brightest stars in the night sky, the magnitude-zero Achernar (Alpha Eridani) in the constellation Eridanus, is highly oblate. A team led by Armando Domiciano de Souza of the University Astrophysical Laboratory at Nice, France, found that the star is so flattened by rotation that its radius is 50% larger at its equator than at its poles. The star has a measured surface rotational speed of 225 km (140 mi) per second with respect to Earth's line of sight, too slow to account for the observed oblateness. Astronomers concluded either that the star has its polar axis tipped toward Earth and is actually rotating near its breakup speed of 300 km (186 mi) per second or that it has an interior that rotates much faster than its surface.

Galaxies and Cosmology. Earth's solar system lies in the plane of the Milky Way Galaxy, an average-size spiral galaxy comprising about 100 billion stars plus gas and dust. The Milky Way Galaxy has long been known to be one of several dozen galaxies in the Local Group, which includes the Andromeda Galaxy and the Magellenic Clouds. In 2003 a team of astronomers from France, Italy, Australia, and the U.K. announced the discovery of a new member of the Local Group. It was named the Canis Major Dwarf Galaxy after the constellation in which it appears to lie. Its discovery was made possible by the Two-Micron All Sky Survey (2MASS), a project initiated in the late 1990s in which automated telescopes in Arizona and Chile systematically scanned the entire sky in three infrared wavelengths. 2MASS allowed astronomers to peer through the clouds of dust that pervade the plane of the Milky Way Galaxy. The newly discovered galaxy lies some 25,000 light-years from Earth's solar system and about 42,000 light-years from the centre of the Milky Way, which makes it the closest galaxy to the Milky Way found to date. It contains only about a billion stars, which are being tidally disrupted by the enormous gravitational field of the Milky Way Galaxy.

Another unanticipated aspect of the Milky Way Galaxy was uncovered in studies carried out by the Sloan Digital Sky Survey (SDSS). A detailed mapping project making use of a special-purpose 2.5-m (100-in) telescope at Apache Point Observatory in New Mexico, the SDSS involved observation of the positions and brightnesses of more than 100 million stars and galaxies at five visible and infrared wavelengths. Within the data acquired to date, Brian Yanny of Fermi National Accelerator Laboratory, Batavia, Ill., Heidi Jo Newberg of Rensselaer Polytechnic Institute, Troy, N.Y., and collaborators found evidence for a huge structure containing as many as 500 million stars forming a ring around the Milky Way Galaxy with a radius of about 60,000 light-years. Independent studies by a group of European astronomers led by Annette Ferguson of the University of Groningen, Neth., suggested that the ring may be slightly elliptical. The ring had not been seen in visible light because it lies in the same plane as the dusty disk of the Milky Way. Early studies of stars populating the ring indicated that they were not initially part of the Milky Way Galaxy, which implies that they are debris from another galaxy that collided with the Milky Way Galaxy and then disintegrated. Both the 2MASS and the SDSS galaxy studies underscored the continuing dynamic evolution of the Milky Way Galaxy and its neighbouring galaxies in the Local Group.

Scientists' picture of the origin and evolution of the universe has grown enormously since its expansion was first theorized to exist and subsequently detected in the 1920s. The big-bang model posits that the universe began with a hot, dense explosive phase resulting in the formation of a few elements—mainly hydrogen and helium—and giving rise to galaxies and to radiation detected today primarily at microwave wavelengths with a temperature of about 3 K (–454 °F). Studies of supernovas carried out in the past five years implied that the universe is currently expanding at an accelerating rate, driven by some gravitationally repulsive "dark energy" originally hypothesized in 1917 (for quite different reasons) by Albert Einstein. In 2001 NASA launched the Wilkinson Microwave Anisotropy Probe (WMAP) to study the microwave background radiation with greater precision than had been previously achieved. This radiation was observed to be coming from all directions in the sky. Fluctuations in its overall intensity as small as one part in a million were key to unraveling the origin of both the large- and small-scale structures of the universe. The radiation comes from a time when the

Earth Perihelion and Aphelion, 2004	
Jan. 4	Perihelion, 147,098,250 km (91,402,620 mi) from the Sun
July 5	Aphelion, 152,098,990 km (94,510,000 mi) from the Sun
Equinoxes and Solstices, 2004	
March 20	Vernal equinox, 06:49[1]
June 21	Summer solstice, 00:57[1]
Sept. 22	Autumnal equinox, 16:30[1]
Dec. 21	Winter solstice, 12:42[1]
Eclipses, 2004	
April 19	Sun, partial (begins 11:30[1]), the beginning visible in Coats Land and the Weddell Sea region of Antarctica, the southeastern Atlantic Ocean, the extreme southwestern Indian Ocean, about half of southern Africa, Madagascar; the end visible in the peninsula and Weddell Sea region of Antarctica, the southeastern Atlantic Ocean, part of southern Africa.
May 4	Moon, total (begins 17:51[1]), the beginning visible in Asia (except extreme northeast), Europe (except western region), Africa (except northwestern part), Indonesia, Australia, New Zealand, Antarctica (except part of the peninsula), the eastern South Atlantic Ocean, the Indian Ocean, the western Pacific Ocean; the end visible in Africa, Europe, western Asia, western Australia, Antarctica, South America (except the northwestern part), the eastern North Atlantic Ocean, the South Atlantic Ocean, the Indian Ocean, the extreme southeastern South Pacific Ocean.
Oct. 14	Sun, partial (begins 00:55[1]), the beginning visible in eastern Siberia, Alaska, northeastern China, the Korean peninsula, Japan, the central North Pacific Ocean, Hawaii; the end visible in eastern Siberia, the Korean peninsula, Japan, the west-central North Pacific Ocean.
Oct. 28	Moon, total (begins 00:06[1]), the beginning visible in Africa, Europe, Greenland, the Arctic region, North America (except the extreme northwest), Central America, South America, extreme western Asia, part of Queen Maud Land and the peninsula of Antarctica, the Atlantic Ocean, the eastern South Pacific Ocean, the western Indian Ocean; the end visible in North America, the Arctic region, Greenland, Central America, South America, Europe, western Africa, the Antarctic Peninsula, the eastern Pacific Ocean, the Atlantic Ocean.

[1] Universal time.
Source: *The Astronomical Almanac for the Year 2004* (2003).

universe was only a few thousand years old and when galaxies were just beginning to form.

In February NASA scientists announced the first results from WMAP, which included strong confirmation that the universe is composed of about 4% ordinary (baryonic) matter—such as hydrogen and helium—with the rest being roughly 23% nonbaryonic dark (nonluminous) matter of some kind and 73% dark energy. Other WMAP results suggested that the big bang occurred about 13.7 billion years ago, give or take 200 million years. WMAP also provided the first evidence that the earliest stars formed between 100 million and 400 million years after the big bang.

(KENNETH BRECHER)

SPACE EXPLORATION

Manned Spaceflight. The space community was shattered by the tragic loss on Feb. 1, 2003, of the U.S. space shuttle orbiter *Columbia* and its seven-person crew just minutes before it was to land at the Kennedy Space Center in Florida. The orbiter, which had made the shuttle program's first flight into space in 1981, was concluding its 28th mission (STS-107) when it broke apart over Texas at approximately 9:00 AM Eastern Standard Time at an altitude of 60 km (40 mi), showering debris across southeastern Texas and southern Louisiana. Disintegration of the craft was recorded by television cameras and U.S. Air Force radar. Its major components and the remains of the crew were recovered over the following month.

Destruction of the *Columbia* followed by almost exactly 17 years the loss of the *Challenger* in a launch accident on Jan. 28, 1986. Ironically, the cause of the *Columbia* catastrophe soon was determined to be launch-related as well. Films showed that a piece of insulating foam broke loose from the external propellant tank and struck the leading edge of the left wing approximately 81 seconds after liftoff. Bits of foam had detached in past missions without serious mishap, and at the time of the *Columbia* launch, NASA engineers did not think that the foam carried enough momentum to cause significant damage. In fact, as was demonstrated in post-accident tests, the foam was capable of punching a large hole in the reinforced carbon-carbon insulation tiles that protected the shuttle's nose and wing leading edges from the extreme heat of atmospheric entry. Although some engineers had wanted ground-based cameras to take photos of the orbiting shuttle to look for damage, the request did not get to the right officials.

During *Columbia*'s atmospheric entry, hot gases penetrated the damaged tile section and melted major structural elements of the wing, which eventually collapsed. Data from the vehicle showed rising temperatures within sections of the left wing as early as 8:52 AM, although the crew knew of their situation for perhaps only a minute or so before vehicle breakup. Subsequent investigation by NASA and the independent Columbia Accident Investigation Board uncovered a number of managerial shortcomings, in addition to the immediate technical reason (poor manufacturing control of tank insulation and other defects), that allowed the accident to happen.

The most palpable result of the accident was a grounding of the remaining three shuttles—*Discovery, Atlantis,* and *Endeavour* (the last built to replace *Challenger*)—until NASA and its contractors could develop means to prevent similar accidents, which perhaps would include kits for repairs in orbit. The shuttle Return to Flight mission was STS-114, scheduled for late 2004. At the same time, NASA gave new emphasis to its Orbital Space Plane (OSP) concept, a smaller reusable craft designed to carry as many as four astronauts (but not large cargo) into low Earth orbit. The OSP likely would not be ready until 2008–10, and funding was uncertain.

Assembly of the International Space Station (ISS) in Earth orbit was suspended after the *Columbia* accident until shuttle flights could resume. Limited research was conducted by rotating two-person crews launched in Russian Soyuz spacecraft.

China entered the human spaceflight arena on October 15 with the launch of Shenzhou 5 carrying Yang Liwei, a People's Liberation Army pilot, on a 21-hour, 14-orbit mission. Four unmanned Shenzhou flights over four years had tested the spacecraft in orbital missions. In its general outline the vehicle resembled the Soyuz, but it relied heavily on Chinese-developed technologies and manufacturing. The next Shenzhou mission was expected to have a three-person crew and to last longer. Previously only the U.S. and Russia had had the capability to launch humans into space.

Space Probes. Exploration of Mars and other planets continued apace, with the Red Planet being the target for several new orbiters and landers. Japan's Nozomi, launched in 1998, would have been first to arrive (December 14), but problems with its propulsion system prevented it from being put into Mars orbit. The European Space Agency's (ESA's) Mars Express, which was launched on June 2 from Kazakhstan, went into Mars orbit on December 25. Its lander, named Beagle 2 for the 19th-century ship that carried Charles Darwin, likely reached the Martian surface the same day, but it was not heard from by the end of the year. NASA's twin Spirit and Opportunity rovers were launched on June 10 and July 7, respectively, and were scheduled to land in January 2004.

Mars Express carried a colour stereo camera, an energetic neutral atoms analyzer to study how the solar wind erodes the atmosphere, a mineralogical mapping spectrometer, a radar instru-

Human Spaceflight Launches and Returns, 2003

Country	Flight	Crew[1]	Dates[2]	Mission/payload
U.S.	STS-107, *Columbia*	Rick Husband William McCool Michael Anderson Kalpana Chawla David Brown Laurel Clark Ilan Ramon	January 16–February 1	space experiments in biological and physical sciences; *Columbia* destroyed during return to Earth
Russia	Soyuz TMA-2 (up)	Yury Malenchenko Edward Lu	April 26	transport of replacement crew to ISS
Russia	Soyuz TMA-1 (down)	Ken Bowersox Nikolay Budarin Donald Pettit	May 4	return of departing ISS crew to Earth
China	Shenzhou 5	Yang Liwei	October 15–16	China's first human spaceflight (21.4 hours, 14 orbits)
Russia	Soyuz TMA-3 (up)	Michael Foale Aleksandr Kaleri Pedro Duque	October 18	transport of replacement crew to ISS
Russia	Soyuz TMA-2 (down)	Yury Malenchenko Edward Lu Pedro Duque	October 28	return of departing ISS crew to Earth

[1] For shuttle flight, commander and pilot are listed first; for Soyuz flights, ISS commander is listed first.
[2] Flight dates for shuttle and Shenzhou missions; Soyuz launch or return date for ISS missions.

ment for subsurface and ionospheric sounding, and atmospheric and radio science experiments. Beagle 2 was to have descended by parachute and airbag cushions to a site in Isidis Planitia, a sedimentary basin that may have been formed by water. The 33-kg (73-lb) lander was equipped with a robotic arm to acquire soil and rock samples for X-ray, gamma-ray, and mass spectroscopy analysis.

For landing its Spirit and Opportunity rovers, NASA returned to the parachute-and-enveloping-airbag design successfully used by the Pathfinder/Sojourner mission in 1997. Once deployed, each 18-kg (40-lb), six-wheel, golf-cart-size robot was to range as far as 500 m (0.3 mi) from the landing site. Each rover carried a colour stereo camera, a drill to make small holes for microscopic images of unweathered rock surfaces, and infrared, gamma-ray, and alpha-particle spectrometers to assay the chemistry of rocks and soil.

Japan launched the Hayabusa (MUSES-C) spacecraft on May 9 for a June 2005 rendezvous with the near-Earth asteroid 1998 SF36. It was to orbit the asteroid for several months and then pass near the surface and collect samples vaporized by metal pellets fired into the surface. Hayabusa would return to Earth in 2007 and drop for retrieval a capsule containing the samples. NASA's Galileo spacecraft ended almost eight years of highly successful exploration of Jupiter and its moons with a programmed fiery plunge into the giant planet's atmosphere on September 21.

Unmanned Satellites. The Spitzer Space Telescope, the last of NASA's four Great Observatories for space-based astrophysics, was launched on August 25. The spacecraft, formerly called the Space Infrared Telescope Facility, was renamed Spitzer for the American astrophysicist Lyman Spitzer, Jr., who first proposed the idea of stationing large telescopes in space. To remove the spacecraft from Earth's thermal and radiation effects, it was placed in a solar orbit having a period of revolution that caused it to drift slowly away from Earth as the two orbited the Sun. Spitzer carried an 85-cm (33.5-in) primary mirror that focused infrared light on three instruments—a general-purpose infrared camera, a spectrograph sensitive to mid-infrared wavelengths, and an imaging photometer taking measurements in three far-infrared bands. Together the instruments covered a wavelength range of 3–180 μm (micrometres; the red end of human vision cuts off at about 0.77 μm). To avoid interference from its own heat, the telescope was cooled to 5.5 K (5.5° above absolute zero) and the detectors to 1.5 K, by liquid helium. Spitzer was expected to spend 2.5–5 years gathering information on the origin, evolution, and composition of planets and smaller bodies, stars, galaxies, and the universe as a whole.

The Spitzer Space Telescope, launched into solar orbit on August 25, is shown in space in an artist's rendering. Visible are its cylindrical cryogenic telescope (upper left), flat, Sun-pointing solar array, and high-gain antenna (blunt cone).

Courtesy of NASA/JPL/Caltech

At the other end of the spectrum, ESA's International Gamma-Ray Astrophysics Laboratory (INTEGRAL) started returning science data following its Oct. 17, 2002, launch by Russia. It carried gamma-ray and X-ray imagers and spectrometers to study the most energetic events in the universe. Among several other astronomy-oriented launches in 2003 was Canada's Microvariability and Oscillations of Stars (MOST; June 30), an orbiting telescope for studying physical processes in stars and properties of extrasolar planets.

Launch Vehicles. Brazil's space program suffered a major setback when its VLS-1 launcher exploded on the launchpad at its Alcântara facility on August 22, killing 21 engineers and technicians. One of its four solid-propellant boosters appeared to have ignited prematurely and destroyed the vehicle. Two previous attempts to launch the vehicle, in 1997 and 1999, had ended in failures after liftoff, with no injuries. The first U.S. Delta IV Heavy Evolved Expendable Launch Vehicle moved to the launchpad on December 10, with launch scheduled for July 2004. Equipped with three powerful liquid-fueled (hydrogen-oxygen) engines, it was designed to carry more than 23,000 kg (51,000 lb) into low Earth orbit and more than 13,000 kg (29,000 pounds) into geosynchronous transfer orbit.

Competitors moved closer to the launchpad in the X Prize contest, which was advertised as a $10 million incentive "to jumpstart the space tourism industry through competition." The winning vehicle had to be privately financed and built, to carry at least one person (but be capable of flying three) to the edge of space (100 km, or 62 mi) and back, and to repeat the trip within 14 days. By 2003 the contest, inaugurated in 1996, had registered at least 25 teams, whose designs involved various vertical and horizontal takeoff-and-landing strategies. American aviation pioneer Burt Rutan's company Scaled Composites, for example, was developing SpaceShipOne (SS1), which would be carried to a high launch altitude by a twin-engine jet aircraft, rocket into space, and then glide to a landing. On December 17, SS1 broke the sound barrier at an altitude of nearly 21 km (68,000 ft) during its first powered flight near Mojave, Calif. (DAVE DOOLING)

Religion

Disagreements over SAME-SEX RELATIONSHIPS threw the Anglican Communion into turmoil; violent CLASHES between Muslim groups and other outbursts of RELIGIOUS STRIFE contrasted with efforts to reach interfaith and ecumenical UNDERSTANDING; and courts tackled challenges over displays of RELIGIOUS SYMBOLS in public institutions.

Sexual Issues. The election, confirmation, and consecration as a U.S. Episcopal bishop of the Rev. V. Gene Robinson, a man engaged in an openly homosexual relationship, created an uproar both in his denomination and in the worldwide Anglican Communion during 2003. His confirmation at the church's triennial General Convention in Minneapolis, Minn., in August was denounced by several bishops and primates of other Anglican bodies, as was the convention's declaration that ceremonies to bless same-sex relationships were "an acceptable practice in the church." The unity of the 70-million-member Anglican Communion had already been threatened in May when a homosexual couple was blessed in Vancouver, B.C. The rite had been approved by Bishop Michael Ingham of the Diocese of New Westminster and came just one day after an international gathering of Anglican primates warned that it could lead to schism. In June the openly gay Canon Jeffrey John was nominated as suffragan bishop of Reading, Eng., but an uproar by evangelical parishes in the Church of England led him to withdraw his nomination. After Robinson's election as bishop in New Hampshire was confirmed, Archbishop Rowan Williams of Canterbury (who had been enthroned in February), called an emergency meeting of the primates in October. The 37 Anglican leaders who participated warned that if Robinson's consecration proceeded as scheduled on November 2, "the future of the communion itself will be put in jeopardy." Following the consecration, several Anglican jurisdictions and the Russian Orthodox Church suspended relations with the Episcopal Church. The consecration also led to the cancellation of a meeting of the International Anglican-Roman Catholic Commission for Unity and Mission and the resignation of Episcopal Presiding Bishop Frank Griswold as cochairman of a sister organization, the Anglican–Roman Catholic International Commission.

In October a representative of Outrage!, a gay rights civil disobedience group, demonstrates outside the meeting of the primates of the Anglican Communion in London in favour of a more tolerant attitude within the community.

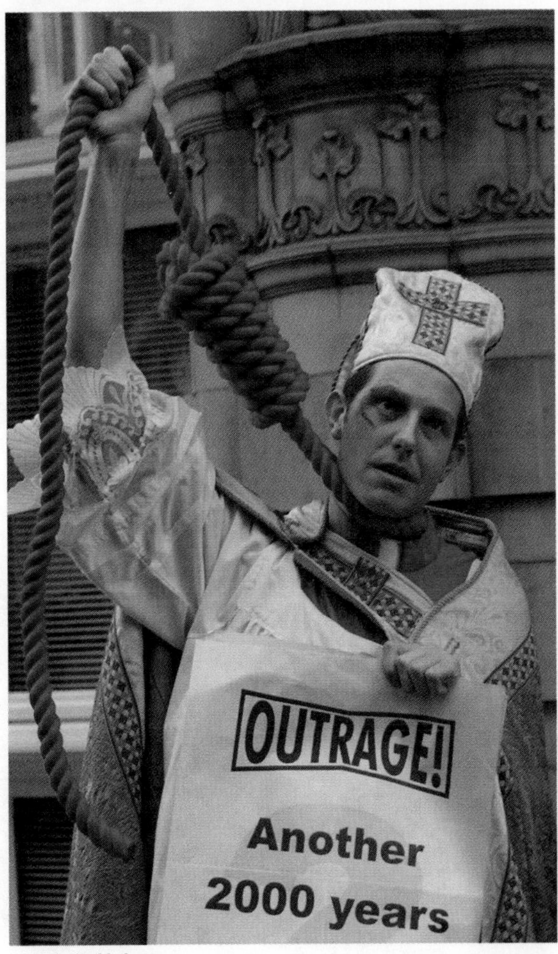

AP/Wide World Photos

The Uniting Church in Australia voted in Melbourne in July to accept gay and lesbian clergy, and the United Church of Canada voted in Wolfville, N.S., in August to urge the Canadian government to recognize same-sex marriages in the same way as heterosexual unions. In response to court rulings in Ontario, British Columbia, and Quebec that bans on gay marriages violated Canada's constitution, the government promised to introduce legislation permitting them. Prime Minister Jean Chrétien said in June that the measure would "protect the right of churches and religious organizations to sanctify marriage as they define it." The Vatican Congregation for the Doctrine of the Faith declared in July that Catholic politicians had a "moral duty" to oppose laws that granted legal rights to gay couples and that non-Catholics should do the same because the issue concerned natural moral law. The 16-million-member Southern Baptist Convention, the largest Protestant denomination in the United States, took a similar stand in June in Phoenix, Ariz., at its annual meeting, and the Coptic Orthodox Church stated its opposition to homosexuality in general in August. In June the Cincinnati (Ohio) Presbytery of the Presbyterian Church (U.S.) voted to remove the Rev. Stephen Van Kuiken from membership in the denomination after he defied a directive from a church court against performing marriages for same-sex couples. The Russian Orthodox Church announced in October that it had defrocked the Rev. Vladimir

Enert, who had conducted the first reported gay wedding in Russia, in the diocese of Nizhny Novgorod. On another issue that involved sexual orientation, the General Synod of the 1.4-million-member United Church of Christ voted in Minneapolis in July to encourage the participation and ministry of transgender persons in the life of the church.

The sex-abuse scandal that had rocked the Roman Catholic Church in 2002 continued to reverberate in 2003. Massachusetts Attorney General Tom Reilly reported in July that there were probably more than 1,000 people in the Boston archdiocese who had been victimized by more than 250 clergy and other church workers over a period spanning six decades. The archdiocese announced in September that it would pay $85 million in settlements to more than 550 people who said that they had been sexually abused by priests. In August John J. Geoghan, the defrocked priest who had been convicted in 2002 of child molestation and whose name was emblematic of the scandal in the Boston archdiocese, was killed by a fellow prisoner at a correctional centre in Massachusetts.

The diocese of San Bernardino, Calif., sued the Boston archdiocese in April for allegedly having concealed the record of sexual molestation by former priest Paul Shanley when he moved to California in 1990. Two Arizona bishops, Manuel Moreno of Tucson and Thomas O'Brien of Phoenix, resigned after they were criticized for allegedly having withheld information on such cases from secular authorities. O'Brien had agreed to relinquish authority over abuse cases in an agreement with prosecutors that enabled him to avoid indictment on obstruction charges. After a fatal hit-and-run accident led to his arrest in June, he resigned. In another resignation in June, former Oklahoma governor Frank Keating gave up his post as chairman of the U.S. church's sexual-abuse review board in the wake of his comparison of the secretive ways of some bishops to those of the Mafia.

Terrorism and Violence. A car bombing at the Imam Ali shrine in the Shi'ite Muslim holy city of Najaf, Iraq, in August claimed the lives of more than 80 people. Among the dead was Ayatollah Muhammad Baqir al-Hakim, leader of the Supreme Council for the Islamic Revolution in Iraq and the most influential Iraqi cleric who had sided openly with the U.S. occupiers of the country; he had returned in May after 23 years in exile. The shrine, the burial place of the son-in-law of the Prophet Muhammad, was also the scene of a riot in April in which two clerics were hacked to death in what appeared to have been a clash between rival Muslim groups. An attack on a mosque in Quetta, Pak., killed more than 40 people and touched off a rampage by Shi'ite Muslims in July. In Mecca, Muhammad's birthplace and Islam's holiest site, Saudi Arabian police killed five people in June who they said had been preparing a terror-

In April, after the fall of the Saddam Hussein regime, a group of Shi'ite Muslim men joyfully make a pilgrimage to the holy city of Kerbala, Iraq, through a desert sandstorm. Access to the site had been denied them for 26 years.

© Yannis Behrakis/Reuters/Corbis

ist attack. Simultaneous car bombings at two synagogues in Istanbul in November killed at least 23 people.

A memorial site in the central Indian state of Madhya Pradesh was opened to Hindus in April after a five-year ban. Both Hindus and Muslims had claimed the 11th-century site in the Bhojshala area of the state's Dhar district. Since 1997 Muslims had been allowed to pray there every Friday, but Hindus were barred except for the worship of the goddess Saraswati inside the complex once a year. The Archaeological Survey of India lifted the restrictions on Hindus after several clashes between Hindus and Muslims. In another development, a report by the government agency on a four-month excavation of the site of the 16th-century Babri Mosque in Ayodhya failed to resolve a dispute between Hindus and Muslims over its history. In 1992 a Hindu mob tore down the mosque, claiming that Muslims had built it after razing a Hindu temple. The government report was not made public, but a lawyer for Hindu groups said it showed that there had been a Hindu temple at the site, while a lawyer for Muslims said that it indicated only that there had been a structure there. In September an Indian court imposed a death sentence on Dara Singh, a Hindu activist who had led a deadly attack on Australian Baptist missionary Graham Staines and his two sons in 1999.

In February a United Nations tribunal convicted a Rwandan Seventh-day Adventist minister and his son of having aided and abetted genocide during the violence in the African country that resulted in 800,000 deaths in 1994. The minister, the Rev. Elizaphan Ntakirutimana, was sentenced to 10 years in prison and became the first clergyman to be convicted of genocide by an international tribunal. In Israel in July a wrecking squad sent by the Interior Ministry tore down a mosque that was being built without a permit next to the Basilica of the Annunciation in Nazareth, where Christians believe the Archangel Gabriel foretold the birth of Jesus.

A joint statement issued in March by officials of the Vatican and Israel's Orthodox Chief Rabbinate denounced religious terrorism and declared that "any attempt to destroy human life must be rejected." In the U.S. the Jewish Council for Public Affairs, meeting in Baltimore, Md., in February, urged Jewish communities to work jointly with evangelical Christians on issues of mutual interest. Evangelicals and Jews found themselves divided, however, in their opinions on *The Passion of the Christ,* a film directed by Mel Gibson that some Jewish leaders feared would reopen accusations that Jews were responsible for the crucifixion of Jesus. A Lutheran Church—Missouri Synod panel reinstated the Rev. David Benke as president of the denomination's Atlantic District and reversed the suspension he had received for having taken part in an interfaith prayer service that was held in New York City in the wake of the Sept. 11, 2001, attacks.

Ecumenism. In an encyclical issued in April, Pope John Paul II said that joint celebrations of the Eucharist between Catholics and Protestants would be an obstacle to full unity by blurring differences between the two Christian groups. In response, the Rev. Ishmael Noko, general secretary of the Lutheran World Federation, said that "an indefinite status quo in this area is clearly not satisfactory" for the Roman Catholic Church or its ecumenical partners. Representatives of 30 denominations meeting in Pasadena, Calif., in January issued a blueprint for an organization that could bring together Roman Catholics, Protestants, and Orthodox Christians in what would be the most broad-based ecumenical organization in the U.S. The group, called Christian Churches Together in the U.S.A., would be formed if 25 denominations formally agreed to participate. Leaders of the Church of England and the Methodist Church of Great Britain signed a covenant in London in November pledging to work toward the organic unity of the two churches, which had been separated for more than two centuries.

Church and State. U.S. courts reached different conclusions over whether the display of the Ten Commandments in public buildings violated the Constitution. In the most publicized case, Chief Justice Roy Moore of the Alabama Supreme Court initially defied the ruling of a federal appeals court in July to remove a 2,400-kg (5,300-lb) granite monument of the Commandments from the rotunda of the state judicial building in Montgomery. Moore later relented after he was suspended for having violated the federal order and all eight associate justices of his court overruled him. He was removed from office by a state disciplinary court in November. Although the federal court that ruled in the Alabama case said that the display was an unconstitutional state establishment of religion, another federal court permitted a small Ten Commandments plaque to remain on a courthouse wall in West Chester, Pa., on the grounds that its historic context outweighed its religious symbolism. Americans United for Separation of Church and State reported in September that a survey it had conducted found that courts had ordered 15 Decalogue displays removed from government buildings while 8 had been allowed to remain. Germany's Federal Constitutional Court ruled in September that the federal constitution did not bar the wearing of Muslim head scarves in classrooms in state-run schools. The court also said, however, that German states could draft laws banning head scarves if the laws also applied to symbols of other religions, such as Christian crosses. French schools grappled with the same issue as Pres. Jacques Chirac endorsed a recommendation of a government-appointed commission calling for a ban on conspicuous religious symbols. A vote by the Israeli cabinet in October to dismantle the Religious Affairs Ministry and transfer authority over rabbinical courts to the Justice Ministry was denounced by the National Religious Party, which threatened to leave the coalition government over the issue if the Knesset (parliament) approved the move.

Religious Liberty. The Saudi Arabian defense minister, Prince Sultan, announced in March that the government would bar the building of Christian churches in the country because their construction "would affect Islam and all Muslims." In February the Cambodian government barred Christian groups from proselytizing in the predominantly Buddhist country. The Vatican criticized the republic of Georgia in September for responding to pressures from Orthodox Christians not to sign an agreement granting religious freedom for Catholics. In a more positive development, Haitian Pres. Jean-Bertrand Aristide issued a decree in April declaring that voodoo was "an essential part of national identity" and allowing the faith's adherents and organizations to register with the Ministry of Foreign Affairs and Religion. In November the 240-member Forn Sidr movement, which worships ancient Norse gods, won approval from the government of Denmark to conduct marriages. Tove Fergo, a Lutheran pastor and the minister for ecclesiastical affairs, described the movement as the country's indigenous religion. The opening of the Great Mosque of Granada in July marked the opening of the first Muslim house of worship in

Spain since Boabdil, the last Moorish king, rode into exile five centuries earlier. A Sikh temple accommodating 3,000 worshipers, believed to be the largest outside India, was opened in March in London. An interfaith group of 33 South African religious leaders met with Pres. Thabo Mbeki in Pretoria for two days in April and said they had agreed on the need for religious groups to be involved in nation building. In contrast, the Zimbabwe Council of Churches apologized in July "for not having done enough at a time when the nation looked to us for guidance" on such issues as political violence, hunger, and economic problems.

A husband-wife team of archaeologists, Jonathan Haas and Winifred Creamer, and their colleague, Alvaro Ruiz, reported in April that they had found a 4,000-year-old Peruvian gourd fragment decorated with the image of a fanged deity. According to Haas, it "appears to be the oldest identifiable religious icon found in the Americas" and "indicates that organized religion began in the Andes more than 1,000 years earlier than previously thought."

Worldwide Adherents of All Religions by Six Continental Areas, Mid-2003

	Africa	Asia	Europe	Latin America	Northern America	Oceania	World	%	Number of Countries
Christians	394,640,000	325,034,000	554,234,000	501,319,000	269,399,000	25,257,000	2,069,883,000	32.9	238
Affiliated Christians	373,110,000	319,090,000	530,451,000	495,550,000	221,060,000	21,454,000	1,960,715,000	31.2	238
Roman Catholics	138,970,000	117,710,000	276,490,000	473,000,000	78,310,000	8,373,000	1,092,853,000	17.4	235
Protestants	105,710,000	54,684,000	74,015,000	51,306,000	70,795,000	8,020,000	364,530,000	5.8	232
Orthodox	36,953,000	13,985,000	158,450,000	477,000	6,426,000	739,000	217,030,000	3.5	134
Anglicans	43,809,000	726,000	26,053,000	950,000	3,121,000	5,329,000	79,988,000	1.3	163
Independents	86,395,000	169,070,000	24,675,000	41,776,000	82,533,000	1,625,000	406,074,000	6.5	221
Marginal Christians	3,108,000	2,776,000	4,071,000	9,201,000	11,344,000	619,000	31,119,000	0.5	215
Multiple affiliation	*–41,835,000*	*–39,861,000*	*–33,303,000*	*–81,160,000*	*–31,469,000*	*–3,251,000*	*–230,879,000*	–3.7	*100*
Unaffiliated Christians	21,530,000	5,944,000	23,783,000	5,769,000	48,339,000	3,803,000	109,168,000	1.7	232
Muslims	344,920,000	869,880,000	32,117,000	1,752,000	4,828,000	725,000	1,254,222,000	19.9	206
Hindus	2,547,000	830,530,000	1,504,000	801,000	1,410,000	470,000	837,262,000	13.3	114
Chinese Universists	34,900	396,720,000	271,000	200,400	695,000	185,000	398,106,300	6.3	91
Buddhists	152,000	366,790,000	1,594,000	698,000	3,086,000	654,000	372,974,000	5.9	129
Ethnoreligionists	100,420,000	132,590,000	1,247,000	2,531,000	1,010,000	298,000	238,096,000	3.8	144
New-Religionists	37,000	103,230,000	191,000	660,000	900,000	88,100	105,106,100	1.7	107
Sikhs	58,700	23,410,000	243,000	0	551,000	32,500	24,295,200	0.4	34
Jews	220,000	4,465,000	2,427,000	1,152,000	6,182,000	105,000	14,551,000	0.2	134
Spiritists	3,100	2,000	137,000	12,426,000	157,000	7,500	12,732,600	0.2	56
Baha'is	1,937,000	3,632,000	146,000	822,000	844,000	122,000	7,503,000	0.1	218
Confucianists	300	6,330,000	17,000	500	0	77,500	6,425,300	0.1	16
Jains	73,000	4,332,000	0	0	7,500	1,200	4,413,700	0.1	11
Zoroastrians	1,000	2,553,000	91,000	0	82,700	6,200	2,733,900	0.0	23
Taoists	0	2,684,000	0	0	11,600	0	2,695,600	0.0	5
Shintoists	0	2,615,000	0	7,100	58,200	0	2,680,300	0.0	8
Other religionists	70,000	65,000	250,000	103,000	620,000	10,000	1,118,000	0.0	78
Nonreligious	5,863,000	620,290,000	107,210,000	16,693,000	30,923,000	3,290,000	784,269,000	12.5	236
Atheists	579,000	120,950,000	22,111,000	2,707,000	1,944,000	369,000	148,660,000	2.4	217
Total population	**851,556,000**	**3,816,102,000**	**723,790,000**	**541,872,000**	**322,709,000**	**31,698,000**	**6,287,732,000**	**100.0**	**238**

Continents. These follow current UN demographic terminology, which now divides the world into the six major areas shown above. *See* United Nations, *World Population Prospects: The 2000 Revision* (New York: UN, 2001), with populations of all continents, regions, and countries covering the period 1950–2050, with 100 variables for every country each year. Note that "Asia" includes the former Soviet Central Asian states and "Europe" includes all of Russia eastward to the Pacific.

Countries. The last column enumerates sovereign and nonsovereign countries in which each religion or religious grouping has a numerically significant and organized following.

Adherents. As defined in the 1948 Universal Declaration of Human Rights, a person's religion is what he or she professes, confesses, or states that it is. Totals are enumerated for each of the world's 238 countries following the methodology of the *World Christian Encyclopedia,* 2nd ed. (2001), and *World Christian Trends* (2001), using recent censuses, polls, surveys, yearbooks, reports, Web sites, literature, and other data. Religions are ranked in order of size in mid-2003.

Christians. Followers of Jesus Christ, enumerated here under **Affiliated Christians,** those affiliated with churches (church members, with names written on church rolls, usually total baptized persons including children baptized, dedicated, or undedicated): total in 2003 being 1,960,715,000, shown above divided among the six standardized ecclesiastical blocs and with (negative and italicized) figures for those with **Multiple affiliation** persons (members of more than one denomination); and **Unaffiliated Christians,** who are persons professing or confessing in censuses or polls to be Christians though not so affiliated.

Independents. This term here denotes members of Christian churches and networks that regard themselves as postdenominationalist and neo-apostolic and thus independent of historic, mainstream, organized, institutionalized, confessional, denominationalist Christianity.

Marginal Christians. Members of denominations who define themselves as Christians but who are on the margins of organized mainstream Christianity (e.g., Unitarians, Mormons, Jehovah's Witnesses, Christian Science, and Religious Science).

Muslims. 83% Sunnites, 16% Shi'ites, 1% other schools.

Hindus. 70% Vaishnavites, 25% Shaivites, 2% neo-Hindus and reform Hindus.

Nonreligious. Persons professing no religion, nonbelievers, agnostics, freethinkers, uninterested, or dereligionized secularists indifferent to all religion but not militantly so.

Chinese Universists. Followers of a unique complex of beliefs and practices that may include: universism (yin/yang cosmology with dualities earth/heaven, evil/good, darkness/light), ancestor cult, Confucian ethics, divination, festivals, folk religion, goddess worship, household gods, local deities, mediums, metaphysics, monasteries, neo-Confucianism, popular religion, sacrifices, shamans, spirit writing, and Taoist and Buddhist elements.

Buddhists. 56% Mahayana, 38% Theravada (Hinayana), 6% Tantrayana (Lamaism).

Ethnoreligionists. Followers of local, tribal, animistic, or shamanistic religions, with members restricted to one ethnic group.

Atheists. Persons professing atheism, skepticism, disbelief, or irreligion, including the militantly antireligious (opposed to all religion).

New-Religionists. Followers of Asian 20th-century New Religions, New Religious movements, radical new crisis religions, and non-Christian syncretistic mass religions, all founded since 1800 and most since 1945.

Jews. Adherents of Judaism. For detailed data on "core" Jewish population, see the annual "World Jewish Populations" article in the American Jewish Committee's American Jewish Year Book.

Confucianists. Non-Chinese followers of Confucius and Confucianism, mostly Koreans in Korea.

Other religionists. Including a handful of religions, quasi-religions, pseudoreligions, parareligions, religious or mystic systems, and religious and semireligious brotherhoods of numerous varieties.

Total population. UN medium variant figures for mid-2003, as given in *World Population Prospects: The 2000 Revision.*

Faith. Issues of belief and nonbelief occupied the attention of religious groups and secularists in 2003. In February the Vatican published what it called *A Christian Reflection on the "New Age,"* in which it said that while such practices as feng shui and yoga were evidences of a "spiritual hunger of contemporary men and women," Christians should respond by highlighting the riches of their own spiritual heritage. More than 40 Southern Baptist Convention missionaries lost their jobs after they refused to sign the denomination's 2000 Baptist Faith and Message statement, which called on wives to "graciously submit" to a subservient role under the leadership of their husbands. The American Humanist Association released Humanist Manifesto III in April, in which it reaffirmed its rejection of religious beliefs and declared that "the responsibility for our lives and the kind of world in which we live is ours and ours alone." The statement was signed by 19 Nobel laureates and 57 other intellectuals.

Personalities. Holmes Rolston III, an American Presbyterian minister and environmental ethicist, was the recipient

Religious Adherents in the United States of America, 1900–2005

	Year 1900	%	mid-1970	%	mid-1990	%	mid-2000	%	mid-2005	%	Annual Change, 1990–2000 Natural	Conversion	Total	Rate (%)
Christians	**73,260,000**	**96.4**	**191,182,000**	**91.0**	**217,623,000**	**85.4**	**238,893,000**	**84.3**	**248,722,000**	**84.0**	**2,429,510**	**−291,013**	**2,138,497**	**0.94**
Affiliated Christians	54,425,000	71.6	153,300,000	73.0	176,030,000	69.1	195,470,000	69.0	203,800,000	68.8	1,977,068	−21,063	1,956,004	1.05
Roman Catholics	10,775,000	14.2	48,305,000	23.0	56,500,000	22.2	62,970,000	22.2	65,655,000	22.2	635,802	15,356	651,157	1.09
Protestants	35,000,000	46.1	58,568,000	27.9	60,216,000	23.6	61,003,000	21.5	62,524,000	21.1	645,109	−566,357	78,752	0.13
Orthodox	400,000	0.5	4,139,000	2.0	5,150,000	2.0	5,638,000	2.0	5,914,000	2.0	57,412	−8,357	49,055	0.91
Anglicans	1,600,000	2.1	3,196,000	1.5	2,450,000	1.0	2,325,000	0.8	2,299,000	0.8	25,412	−37,882	−12,470	−0.52
Multiple affiliation	0	0.0	−2,726,000	−1.3	−24,126,000	−9.5	−24,607,000	−8.7	−26,336,000	−8.9	−259,350	211,201	−48,149	0.20
Independents	5,850,000	7.7	35,691,000	17.0	66,900,000	26.3	77,957,000	27.5	82,423,000	27.8	770,907	345,464	1,116,371	1.54
Marginal Christians	800,000	1.1	6,126,000	2.9	8,940,000	3.5	10,188,000	3.6	11,286,000	3.8	101,796	24,001	125,798	1.32
Evangelicals	*32,068,000*	*42.2*	*33,752,000*	*16.1*	*37,349,000*	*14.7*	*40,735,000*	*14.4*	*41,950,000*	*14.2*	*415,551*	*−75,265*	*340,287*	*0.87*
evangelicals	*11,000,000*	*14.5*	*45,500,000*	*21.7*	*87,656,000*	*34.4*	*97,750,000*	*34.5*	*102,200,000*	*34.5*	*986,703*	*29,222*	*1,015,925*	*1.10*
Unaffiliated Christians	18,835,000	24.8	37,882,000	18.0	41,593,000	16.3	43,423,000	15.3	44,922,000	15.2	452,442	−269,020	183,423	0.43
Jews	1,500,000	2.0	6,700,000	3.2	5,535,000	2.2	5,620,000	2.0	5,700,000	1.9	59,365	−50,859	8,507	0.15
Muslims	10,000	0.0	800,000	0.4	3,500,000	1.4	4,200,000	1.5	4,641,000	1.6	40,978	29,859	70,838	1.84
Black Muslims	0	0.0	200,000	0.1	1,250,000	0.5	1,650,000	0.6	1,850,000	0.6	12,700	17,300	30,000	2.29
Buddhists	30,000	0.0	200,000	0.1	1,880,000	0.7	2,500,000	0.9	2,872,000	1.0	23,310	40,007	63,317	2.89
Hindus	1,000	0.0	100,000	0.1	750,000	0.3	1,050,000	0.4	1,127,000	0.4	9,579	21,218	30,798	3.42
Ethnoreligionists	100,000	0.1	70,000	0.0	780,000	0.3	1,010,000	0.4	1,100,000	0.4	9,526	13,903	23,429	2.62
New-Religionists	10,000	0.0	110,000	0.3	700,000	0.3	850,000	0.3	950,000	0.3	8,249	6,945	15,194	1.96
Baha'is	3,000	0.0	138,000	0.1	600,000	0.2	767,000	0.3	845,000	0.3	7,275	9,717	16,992	2.49
Sikhs	0	0.0	1,000	0.0	160,000	0.1	238,000	0.1	251,000	0.1	2,118	5,943	8,061	4.05
Spiritists	0	0.0	0	0.0	120,000	0.0	141,000	0.0	147,000	0.0	1,389	733	2,122	1.63
Chinese Universists	70,000	0.1	90,000	0.0	76,000	0.0	79,900	0.0	81,000	0.0	830	−439	391	0.50
Shintoists	0	0.0	0	0.0	50,000	0.0	57,200	0.0	59,600	0.0	571	155	726	1.35
Zoroastrians	0	0.0	0	0.0	43,000	0.0	53,600	0.0	58,700	0.0	514	562	1,076	2.23
Taoists	0	0.0	0	0.0	10,000	0.0	11,300	0.0	11,700	0.0	113	18	131	1.23
Jains	0	0.0	0	0.0	5,000	0.0	7,000	0.0	8,000	0.0	64	141	205	3.42
Other religionists	10,000	0.0	450,000	0.2	530,000	0.2	577,000	0.2	602,000	0.2	5,100	−390	4,700	0.85
Nonreligious	1,000,000	1.3	10,070,000	4.8	21,414,000	8.4	25,853,000	9.1	27,500,000	9.3	251,548	197,884	449,432	1.90
Atheists	1,000	0.0	200,000	0.1	1,000,000	0.4	1,319,000	0.5	1,388,000	0.5	12,341	20,211	32,552	2.81
Total population	**75,995,000**	**100.0**	**210,111,000**	**100.0**	**254,776,000**	**100.0**	**283,230,000**	**100.0**	**296,064,000**	**100.0**	**2,845,000**	**0**	**2,845,000**	**1.06**

Methodology. This table extracts and analyzes a microcosm of the world religion table. It depicts the United States, the country with the largest number of adherents to Christianity, the world's largest religion. Statistics at five points in time from 1900 to 2005 are presented. Each religion's Annual Change for 1990–2000 is also analyzed by Natural increase (births minus deaths, plus immigrants minus emigrants) per year and Conversion increase (new converts minus new defectors) per year, which together constitute the Total increase per year. Rate increase is then computed as percentage per year.

Structure. Vertically the table lists 30 major religious categories. The major categories (including nonreligious) in the U.S. are listed with largest (Christians) first. Indented names of groups in the "Adherents" column are subcategories of the groups above them and are also counted in these unindented totals, so they should not be added twice into the column total. Figures in italics draw adherents from all categories of Christians above and so cannot be added together with them. Figures for Christians are built upon detailed head counts by churches, often to the last digit. Totals are then rounded to the nearest 1,000. Because of rounding, the corresponding percentage figures may sometimes not total exactly to 100%.

Christians. All persons who profess publicly to follow Jesus Christ as God and Savior. This category is subdivided into **Affiliated Christians** (church members) and **Unaffiliated** (nominal) **Christians** (professing Christians not affiliated with any church). *See also* the note on Christians to the world religion table.

Evangelicals/evangelicals. These two designations—italicized and enumerated separately here—cut across all of the six Christian traditions or ecclesiastical blocs listed above and should be considered separately from them. **Evangelicals** are mainly Protestant churches, agencies, and individuals that call themselves by this term (for example, members of the National Association of Evangelicals); they usually emphasize 5 or more of 7, 9, or 21 fundamental doctrines (salvation by faith, personal acceptance, verbal inspiration of Scripture, depravity of man, Virgin Birth, miracles of Christ, atonement, evangelism, Second Advent, et al.). The **evangelicals** are Christians of evangelical conviction from all traditions who are committed to the evangel (gospel) and involved in personal witness and mission in the world but who do not belong to specifically Evangelical churches or agencies or give their primary identity as "Evangelical." Alternatively, these are all termed Great Commission Christians.

Jews. Core Jewish population relating to Judaism, excluding Jewish persons professing a different religion.

Other categories. Definitions are as given under the world religion table.

(DAVID B. BARRETT; TODD M. JOHNSON)

On October 16 in St. Peter's Square in Vatican City, Pope John Paul II celebrates mass in commemoration of the 25th anniversary of his accession to the papacy. In 1978 Karol Wojtyla, a Pole, became the first non-Italian pope in 455 years.

AP/Wide World Photos

of the 2003 Templeton Prize for Progress Toward Research or Discoveries About Spiritual Realities. (*See* BIOGRAPHIES.) The Nobel Prize for Peace was awarded to Shirin Ebadi, an Iranian jurist who has asserted that the abuse of women in Islamic countries is based on a misreading of the Qur'an and other Islamic teachings. (*See* NOBEL PRIZES.) Two international ecumenical organizations welcomed new leaders as Presiding Bishop Mark S. Hanson of the Evangelical Lutheran Church in America was elected president of the Lutheran World Federation at the LWF's Tenth Assembly, meeting in Winnipeg, Man., in July, and Kenyan Methodist minister Samuel Kobia was elected general secretary of the World Council of Churches at the WCC's Central Committee meeting in Geneva in August. Pope John Paul II appointed 31 new cardinals in September, including Vatican Foreign Minister Jean-Louis Tauran and the pope's personal theologian, Swiss-born George Marie Cottier. The sole American on the list was Justin Rigali, the new archbishop of Philadelphia. During a visit to Madrid in May, the pope created five new saints, and in October he beatified Mother Teresa, placing her on the first step toward sainthood. Concerns for the pontiff's health were voiced during his four-day visit to Slovakia in September but a month later he celebrated the 25th anniversary of his papacy. Jaime Cardinal Sin, the archbishop of Manila for almost three decades, retired in September.

Rabbi Janet Ross Marder of Los Altos Hills, Calif., became the first female head of a major rabbinical association when she was elected president of the Reform movement's Central Conference of American Rabbis at its meeting in Washington, D.C., in March. In October a 53-member committee chose Alison Eliot of Edinburgh as the first female moderator-designate of the Church of Scotland in the Presbyterian body's 443-year history. An elder, she was also the first non-minister chosen since the 16th century. The Rev. Susan Andrews of Bethesda, Md., became the first woman pastor to serve as moderator of the Presbyterian Church (U.S.) when she was elected at its General Assembly in May in Denver. The Rev. Barry C. Black, a Seventh-day Adventist minister and chief of the U.S. Navy's chaplain corps, became the first black chaplain of the U.S. Senate when he was chosen for the position in June. Bill McCartney, founder of Promise Keepers, resigned the presidency of the evangelical Christian men's movement in October to care for his ailing wife, Lyndi. Imam W. Deen Mohammed, who steered the American Society of Muslims from black separatism to Muslim orthodoxy after the death of his father, Elijah Muhammad, in 1975, resigned as leader of the organization at its national convention in Chicago in September. Dalil Boubakeur, the leader of the Paris Mosque, resigned as president of the national council of Muslims, an agency created in December 2002 to give Islam the same representation before the French government as other religions.

Notable religious figures who died in 2003 included Raphael I Bidawid, patriarch of the Chaldean Catholic Church; Garner Ted Armstrong, longtime voice on *The World Tomorrow* radio and television program and founder of the Intercontinental Church of God; and William Bright, founder of Campus Crusade for Christ and the 1996 Templeton Prize winner. (*See* OBITUARIES.) Others who died during the year were Rabbi Emil Fackenheim, a philosopher who examined the effects of the Holocaust on Jewish theology; Carl F.H. Henry, an influential evangelical theologian and founding editor of *Christianity Today;* and James P. Shannon, former Catholic auxiliary bishop of Minneapolis and St. Paul, Minn., who was excommunicated in 1969 after he submitted his resignation and got married.

(DARRELL J. TURNER)

Social Protection

A final version of MEDICARE WAS PASSED in the U.S. Congress, the number of WORLD REFUGEES DIMINISHED, and antiterrorism measures brought continued concerns about AMERICAN CIVIL LIBERTIES.

BENEFITS AND PROGRAMS

North America. A historic overhaul of Medicare, the health insurance program for 40 million elderly and disabled Americans, was the highlight of social protection activity in the United States in 2003. At the heart of the massive reform, which the government estimated would cost $400 billion over 10 years, were the addition of prescription-drug benefits, a step that had broad bipartisan support, and a much more controversial movement toward a larger role for private health plans.

Starting in 2006, Medicare recipients would be able to obtain federally subsidized prescription drugs by buying a new type of insurance policy or joining a private health plan, with premiums averaging $35 a month plus a $250 yearly deductible. Medicare would cover 75% of drug costs from $251 to $2,250, after which nothing was covered until a person had spent a total of $3,600 out of pocket. From that point on, the government would pay 95% of prescription costs. Low-income beneficiaries would receive additional subsidies to eliminate or reduce premiums and other costs. Until the new benefits went into effect, Medicare recipients would be able to buy a discount card that would reduce prescription costs by an estimated 15%.

Although prescription-drug benefits had widespread support, Democrats and Republicans disagreed vehemently over that part of the legislation that addressed the relationship between government-run Medicare and private health plans. The new law would provide subsidies to private health plans and, starting in 2010, set up a six-year trial program under which traditional Medicare would engage in direct price competition against private health plans in six metropolitan areas. Proponents of greater emphasis on the private sector, including Pres. George W. Bush, argued that this would produce needed cost savings, while foes said it would lead to the end of Medicare as it had been known since its inception in 1965.

In addition to the two major provisions, the reform bill would provide increases in Medicare payments to hospitals, especially those in rural areas, and in fees paid to doctors, and it would offer subsidies to employers to discourage them from dropping drug coverage for their retirees once the new federal benefits became available. The legislation also would offer tax incentives to encourage people to set up health-related savings accounts and for the first time would require wealthier patients to pay more for outpatient care.

While federal lawmakers debated Medicare, state governments struggled with Medicaid, the other vital thread in the U.S. health-care safety net. A joint federal-state program, Medicaid served 50 million poor beneficiaries. It was the fastest-growing item in most state budgets and accounted for about 15% of total state spending.

The Kaiser Commission on Medicaid and the Uninsured reported that financially strapped states slowed their spending on Medicaid for the first time in seven years. They cut benefits, tightened eligibility, increased co-payments, and reduced payments to physicians and hospitals in an effort to combat rising health costs and falling revenues. In the past, many states had allowed residents to take part in Medicaid even though they did not meet the strict federal eligibility rules. More recently, however, several states passed laws or obtained federal permission to disqualify hundreds of thousands of people living near the poverty level.

The cutbacks came despite warnings from some health-policy experts that reductions would lead to large increases in the uninsured and would threaten progress that had been made in covering children. Critics noted a Census Bureau report that revealed that the number of Americans without health insurance rose to 43.6 million in 2002, 2.4 million people more than in

In November senior citizens from Philadelphia listen to politicians addressing the Alliance for Retired Americans on the Medicare reform bill being considered by Congress. Many seniors opposed the Republican-sponsored bill because they believed it would entail higher health care premiums.

2001, an increase of 5.7%. A major reason cited for the increase was the continued decline in employer-sponsored health-insurance programs.

Except for the hard-fought changes in Medicare, partisan disagreements stymied final action in Congress on most key pieces of social protection legislation. One of these was a reauthorization of the 1996 welfare-reform law that was supposed to have expired on Sept. 30, 2002. The landmark law replaced more than 60 years of guaranteed benefits with new work requirements and greater state control of lump-sum federal grants.

The House of Representatives approved a reauthorization in 2002 and again in 2003, but when the Senate did not go along with that version, lawmakers passed a series of temporary extensions. The major disagreements concerned the number of hours recipients would be required to work and the amount that child-care payments should be increased to help offset the longer work schedules.

The House bill, which had the backing of Pres. George W. Bush, would require that by 2008 welfare participants work 40 hours a week and states have at least 70% of their caseloads employed. The 1996 law required states to have half of their caseloads working at least 30 hours a week. The House also added a new program to promote marriage. The Senate's work requirements were not as stringent and left the door open to a greater increase in child-care support.

The 1996 reform was credited with having helped cut welfare rolls in half, but some critics charged that those who left the program later joined the working poor and that the new law increased poverty and created new problems for children. Government studies supported both sides of the issue. A Census Bureau report showed that poverty in the United States was up in 2002 for the second straight year. According to the report, 34.6 million Americans—including 12.1 million children—lived in poverty at the end of the year, an increase of 1.7 million from 2001. The poverty rate was 12.1% in 2002, compared with 11.7% the previous year. The official poverty level varied with family size and the cost of living; in 2002 the level for a family of four was $18,244.

On the other hand, a study financed by the National Institutes of Health found that poor children suffered no psychological damage when their mothers moved from welfare to work. Still another government report showed a marked shift in welfare spending since 1996 from assistance in the form of cash to aid in the form of child care, education, training, and other services intended to help poor people find and keep jobs.

Also facing an uncertain fate in Congress was a watered-down version of Bush's faith-based initiative, which sought to provide federal support for an increase in the involvement of religious organizations in activities for the poor and disabled. The original sticking point in Bush's proposed plan was his insistence that religious groups be allowed to give preference in hiring to members of their own faith. After that provision was dropped, other disagreements arose, such as the need for offsets to pay for the legislation.

Both the House and the Senate passed measures in 2003 that would provide additional tax breaks for charitable donations, although the Senate version scrubbed language that would have allowed groups to retain their religious nature while operating publicly funded social services. As the legislation languished in conference committee, Bush attempted to bypass Congress and jump-start the initiative by using his administrative power to establish regulations that made it easier for religious charities to receive federal money. Critics accused him of undermining the First Amendment separation of church and state.

Reform of the financially shaky Social Security system was complicated by a deep partisan split over the Bush administration's effort to privatize the system by allowing workers to set up individual retirement accounts. Congressional concern about the future of Social Security did not diminish, however, as the baby-boom generation's relentless march toward retirement threatened to overwhelm the system's finances. The Social Security Board of Trustees again warned that the program was not sustainable over the long term. It projected that tax revenues would fall below program costs in 2018 and that trust funds would be exhausted in 2042. The government announced that Social Security benefits would rise 2.1% in 2004, bringing the average payment for the 47 million beneficiaries to $922 a month.

In Canada, as in the United States, government health care efforts stirred concern. Canada's highly touted national health care system, which provided insurance and paid most medical expenses for virtually all citizens, was jolted by reports of long waits for diagnosis and services and "line jumping" by wealthy and influential clients.

According to a government study, 4.3 million Canadian adults, about 18% of those who went to a doctor in 2001, said that they had difficulty seeing the physician or getting tests or surgery done promptly. Several private studies reported that about 3 million persons could not find family physicians. Among the reasons cited for the long waits were overworked technology, a shortage of nurses and health care facilities, and an aging population.

Since its inception in the 1960s, the Canadian health care system had been regarded as politically untouchable. It provided free health insurance at a cost of about $66 billion a year, one of the largest proportions of the total budget of any country.

In another area, Canadian social-service ministers at all levels of government approved $935 million over five years for a national child-care scheme that would provide regulated early-learning and day-care programs. Jane Stewart, human resources development minister, called the action "the beginning of a very solid national day-care program for Canadians." Provinces were to have the final say in how the money was spent.

(DAVID M. MAZIE)

Europe. In an effort to lower administrative costs, Austria merged the pension insurance bodies for blue- and white-collar workers. Traditionally, different provisions such as those pertaining to eligibility criteria and benefit formulas had been applied to manual and nonmanual employees. These differences had been gradually diminished before the establishment in January of the new Pension Insurance Institute. Workers nationwide demonstrated against the government's proposed changes to the state pension system in separate one-day strikes in May and June. Later in June the legislature passed a modified form of the bill that included some concessions. The new law went into effect in August; it included a reduction in benefits and the creation of incentives to work beyond the normal retirement age. Those who did so would see their pensions enhanced by 4.2% annually, rather than 3%. Early-retirement provisions were scheduled to be abolished by 2017.

France's pension reform, approved by Parliament in July, received as little public welcome as Austria's. The decision was made to lengthen progressively the period of contributions necessary to receive a full pension, in both the public and private sectors. In 2008 a full pension would be available only after 40 years of service. Pensions paid to those with less service would be reduced by 5% for each missing year.

Early retirement was also identified as a problem elsewhere. In February the Italian Chamber of Deputies approved a pension-reform bill that would allow employees to work past age 65 with the consent of their employers. The reform proposal also included provisions that would tighten the eligibility criteria for the seniority pension. In April, when the governor of the Bank of Greece presented his annual report, he too called for an increase in the retirement age.

In May the Danish Economic Council, consisting of economic experts and employer, trade union, and government representatives, released a report in which it recommended the abolition of the early-retirement scheme. The council also advised a reform of the unemployment system rules. The existing rules, whereby individuals aged 51 or older could collect unemployment benefits until age 60 (when they became eligible for early retirement), were no longer economically viable. Spain's Toledo Pact Commission, in charge of studying social security reform, agreed that employers should pay the full cost of early retirement if they used these provisions to achieve their restructuring objectives.

Belgium enacted legislation that established a new regulatory framework for complementary (second-pillar) pensions. An occupational pension could be established voluntarily by a single employer or group of employers, or it could be negotiated as part of a collective agreement as a sector plan. Those plans that met specific "social" objectives would be given more favourable tax treatment.

In January the insured of Latvia received the right to select a pension manager of their choice, with analysts expecting about 30% of the second-pillar pension assets eventually to be transferred from the state treasury to private management. In Russia requirements for managers of voluntary pension funds were announced. These funds had been operating for several years in a largely unregulated environment.

The Czech Republic introduced legislation that regulated private pensions in line with European Union principles. In order to approach EU standards more closely, Romania introduced a new labour code with extended employee rights regarding nondiscrimination and employment protection.

A throng of pensioners and their relatives in Baghdad, Iraq, almost overwhelm American soldiers on a tank in mid-May. The crowd of some 5,000 people gathered to receive an emergency payment of $40 from Iraqi authorities to tide them over until the pension records could be sorted out.

AP/Wide World Photos

Germany debated major social reforms: health and long-term care, taxes, and pensions. As a result of lengthy all-party deliberations behind closed doors, a moderate consensus was found, but only in the area of health care. By 2004 a funeral allowance, eyeglass coverage for most adults, and expenses for travel to and from ambulatory treatment would be removed from the benefits package; co-payments would be increased and the principle established that a co-payment for all services was due. Noninsurance services such as maternity benefits would be financed through a higher tobacco tax.

Rising health care costs also caused other European governments to work on reforms and adjustments. As of April, patients in the U.K. had to pay more for medicines and dental treatment when they turned to the National Health Service. The Swiss government announced the introduction in 2004 of a new schedule of deductibles. The standard franchise (amount payable before reimbursement) would be increased from 230 Swiss francs to 300 Swiss francs (U.S.$1 = 1.49 Swiss francs). Switzerland also made it possible for insured people to switch their health insurers without penalty, a move designed to increase competition.

Poland reinstated a centralized approach to health care provision. Legislation that took effect in March abolished the 17 independent (essentially regional) sickness funds and replaced them with a single national health fund. The new law also established a schedule of increases in employee contribution rates for social security health care coverage.

The EU worked on the simplification and modernization of Regulation 1408/71, which provided for the coordination of social security entitlements by those who moved between countries of the European Economic Area (EEA), plus Switzerland. A revised regulation, as proposed by the European Commission, would apply to all persons covered by social security legislation in a member state, including individuals who were not citizens of the EEA or Switzerland, and to people not gainfully employed. Preretirement benefits would come under coordination rules. More rights would be given to unemployed people, frontier workers, and the disabled.

Industrialized Asia and the Pacific. Concern was voiced in the Asia-Pacific region about the viability of social protection programs in aging societies. Australia's Investment and Financial Services Association, in regrouping superannuation (mandatory occupational pensions), investment management, and life-insurance companies, proposed four principles with the acronym SAVE to govern the reform of the retirement system: "simple and secure" (reforms should reduce complexity); "adequate" (reforms should provide incentives for voluntary savings so that retirees were able to maintain an acceptable lifestyle); "viable" (reforms should aim at workable solutions and avoid frequent legislative changes, which lowered trust in the system); and "equitable and efficient" (reforms should maintain generational equity and encourage competition, which would lead to greater efficiency).

The South Korean Ministry of Health and Welfare announced austerity measures, stating that these were needed to save the social protection system from collapse. While the contribution rate (equally divided between employer and employee) would be increased gradually from the existing 9% to 15.9% by 2030, benefits would be lowered. The new benefit formula would provide a pension amounting to 55% of average salary in 2004 and 50% as of 2008—compared with the existing level of 60%.

In Japan the idea of a cut in the normal pension benefit of 59% of final earnings was also circulated. Other proposals for the five-year reform of social security pensions included a change in the rules relating to the division of benefits after divorce and a provision that made it easier for part-timers to join the Employees' Pension Insurance.

Hong Kong's Executive Council approved the introduction of a seven-year residency requirement that restricted entitlement to benefits under the Social Security Allowance and Comprehensive Social Security Assistance programs.

Emerging and Less-Developed Countries. The Chinese government announced in January that workers at state-run institutions could no longer count on employment for life. Some 1.3 million state-financed institutions would be encouraged to sign labour contracts with their employees, paving the way for possible terminations of employment. China's work-injury insurance was reorganized, with the State Council promulgating a decree that required all employers to contribute to workers' compensation funds established by local authorities. China also worked on introducing a health care system for the rural population. Only serious health problems would be covered; participation would be voluntary; and the scheme would be financed by contributions from insured persons, local governments, and the central government. The Indian government launched a new health insurance scheme open to everyone. Previous schemes had had membership restrictions. In July the Turkish parliament passed a social security reform law that gave administrative and financial autonomy to a new social security institution that would feature separate departments for pensions and health care.

Namibia discussed the introduction of a mandatory pension scheme and the implications that it would have for the existing provident fund (a compulsory savings plan to which both employer and employee contributed and which, on termination of employment, provided the employee with a lump sum based on previous contributions) and pension schemes. In Kenya further measures were taken to transform the national provident fund into a social insurance scheme. An advisory group on social security reform in Uganda proposed to set up a system whereby retirement benefits would be provided through the existing National Social Security Fund and through new individual saving accounts managed by private entities.

The pension-reform proposals made by the previous Argentine government were endorsed by the new one. In particular, the optional coverage in a private individual retirement account (AFJP) would be brought to an end; all employees would be covered by the state system and a supplementary personal pension account (AFP).

The Peruvian Congress approved an increase in foreign investments that the administrators of AFPs would be allowed to make, from 10% to 20% of their assets. In Chile the ceiling for foreign investments by AFPs went up from 20% to 25%. Chile also offered better protection for workers upon termination. As of January, the government required employers to prove that pension, health care, and unemployment insurance payments had been made in full before they could lawfully terminate an employee.

(CHRISTIANE KUPTSCH)

HUMAN RIGHTS

Major human rights developments for the year 2003 included ongoing support for the principle of accountability for human rights abuses, growing demands by the less-developed world for recognition of the economic and social aspects of human rights, and the threats to civil liberties posed by antiterrorism measures in the United States and elsewhere. The awarding of the Nobel Prize for Peace to Shirin Ebadi of Iran gave a major boost to women's rights in particular and human rights in general throughout the Muslim world.

New Criminal Courts. A precedent had been set in 2002 with the establishment of the International Criminal Court to prosecute international crimes, including human rights abuses such as genocide and war crimes. Building on that precedent in 2003, additional criminal courts under United Nations auspices dealt with recent major crimes against humanity in Sierra Leone, Cambodia, and East Timor.

The Special Criminal Court for Sierra Leone, along with its companion Truth and Reconciliation Commission, began to investigate those responsible for massive brutalities—including the killing and mutilation of thousands of civilians, widespread rape, the abduction of children for use as soldiers, and the destruction of countless villages—that were committed during the decade-long civil war there. Still in the investigation and indictment stage, the Special Criminal Court was just starting to have a noticeable impact. One of its most important acts was the indictment of Charles Taylor, the former president of Liberia. Because he had supported and trained the insurgents who committed most of the atrocities, Taylor was charged with responsibility for many of the war crimes and crimes against humanity that took place in Sierra Leone. He also was accused of having engineered a similar campaign of atrocities in neighbouring Guinea. Despite the charges against him, Taylor remained at large in Nigeria; under an agreement with Nigerian Pres. Olusegun Obasanjo, Taylor relinquished office and left Liberia in exchange for amnesty from prosecution. Human rights advocates contended, however, that Taylor and others should eventually stand trial.

In June, after years of negotiations, the United Nations signed a landmark agreement with Cambodia to set up special courts to try members of the former Khmer Rouge government, which was responsible for the so-called Killing Fields of the late 1970s, when the ultra-Maoist Pol Pot regime had carried out a campaign that resulted in the death by starvation or execution of nearly two million people.

In August, 18 Indonesian military and civilian officials were tried by the Special Criminal Tribunal for the former East Timor. This tribunal included both international and local judges. Twelve of those indicted were acquitted, and four received minor sentences. The remaining two, Maj. Gen. Adam Damiri, the former military commander of East

Timor (Timor-Leste) and the highest-ranking official indicted, and former East Timor governor Abilio Soares were charged with responsibility for a series of attacks on civilians—including mass murder, arson, and forced expulsions—committed by soldiers and paramilitary groups in 1999. Each was sentenced to three years in jail. The lenient sentences were criticized by the U.S. and others, as was the lack of an indictment against General Wiranto, who was chief of the Indonesian military when the atrocities took place. Fears of new atrocities in Indonesia grew with the crackdown on separatists in Aceh province. Indeed, Damiri missed several court appearances because he was directing military operations in Aceh, which was placed under martial law on May 19.

The Status of War Crimes Trials Elsewhere. The International Criminal Tribunal for Former Yugoslavia continued its groundbreaking work, but progress in the landmark prosecution of former Yugoslav president Slobodan Milosevic was especially slow. Milosevic, the first head of state to have been put on trial for crimes against humanity, insisted on representing himself without help of legal counsel, a circumstance that caused long delays in the trial.

Argentina's Gen. Antonio Domingo Bussi, one of the most despised military commanders during that country's "Dirty War" of the 1970s and '80s, faced trial for crimes against humanity. His indictment was a result of the Argentine Congress's decision to repeal a pair of amnesty laws that had granted immunity to those who had executed (or "caused to disappear") an estimated 30,000 political opponents. Bussi, who in 2003 was elected mayor of San Miguel de Tucumán, was believed responsible for at least 680 "disappearances" in Tucumán province alone.

Elsewhere in Latin America, Chilean Pres. Ricardo Lagos proposed a package of laws that would allow broader prosecution of crimes committed by military and government officials and paramilitary groups during the 17-year military dictatorship of Gen. Augusto Pinochet. In Peru a government-appointed Truth and Reconciliation Commission issued a landmark report documenting the execution of nearly 70,000 people during a 20-year struggle centred in Ayacucho province between the government and members of the Shining Path (Sendero Luminoso) insurgency. Most of the victims were indigenous people, descendants of the Incas.

Economic and Social Rights. In August, over the objection of major drug manufacturers, member governments of the World Trade Organization agreed to make it easier for poor countries to import generic drugs to treat diseases such as AIDS, malaria, and tuberculosis. The agreement allowed the export of patented products as generic drugs for use in those countries unable to make their own medicines and dependent on generic drugs to treat disease. By the terms of the agreement, the poorest nations would be allowed to import and distribute inexpensive lifesaving medicines from manufacturing countries such as India and Brazil without being considered in violation of trade laws that protect patent rights.

In September more general international trade talks were held in Cancún, Mex. These talks were aimed at reducing trade barriers and domestic subsidies for agricultural products in developed nations, programs that made it difficult for poorer nations to export food crops to international markets. Talks broke down when it became apparent that the U.S., Europe, and Japan were unwilling to make sufficient cuts in farm subsidies. These efforts were part of a broader initiative to expand the existing understanding of human rights to include basic economic and social protections, such as health care, education, and the right to work. They were linked to a growing worldwide movement to help the poorest nations by canceling or reducing their debt payments to international lending institutions.

Terrorism and Civil Liberties. In the aftermath of the Sept. 11, 2001, attacks in the U.S., efforts to prevent terrorism produced new threats to human rights in many nations. Antiterrorism laws in the U.S. and Canada resulted in the long-term detention of a large and increasing number of suspected terrorists, who were held without charges. At a military base in Guantánamo Bay, Cuba, the U.S. held more than 600 prisoners captured during the Afghan and Iraq conflicts, and U.S. prisons contained some 1,200 resident aliens believed to have terrorist ties. The U.S. Department of Justice's inspector general found serious violations of law in the handling of detainees, including excessive use of force and ethnic discrimination.

The U.S. government also was accused of "rendition to torture"—that is, sending suspected terrorists to third countries where they could be interrogated with the use of extreme measures that were not tolerated or permitted within the U.S. Another issue was the designation of some suspected terrorists as "enemy combatants." This classification was a first step toward authorizing trial by military (rather than civilian) courts, where normal due process and constitutional protections would not apply. In the past the U.S. had condemned the use of military courts to try civilians in countries such as Greece and Turkey, but the government justified its decision by claiming that normal criminal court proceedings could result in a breach of security or give helpful infor-

In order to dramatize the conditions under which detainees were being held at Camp Delta on the U.S. military base at Guantánamo Bay, Cuba, artist Jai Redman created a mock-up of the facility in Hulme, England. More than 600 suspected terrorists from Afghanistan and Iraq were being held in the camp.

© Howard Walker/Reuters NewMedia Inc./Corbis

mation to those planning terrorist attacks. For this reason the government also decided to drop regular criminal charges against Zacarias Moussaoui in preference for a military trial. In civilian court Moussaoui, whom the government considered to be the 20th September 11 hijacker, had claimed the right to interview other suspected terrorists as part of his defense.

Women's Rights. The removal of the Taliban from power in November 2001 had given hope to Afghan women for the restoration of their rights to leave their homes, hold jobs, attend schools, and be free of oppressive dress codes—rights that had been denied them under the former regime. In 2001 the appointment to the Afghan cabinet of Sima Simar was offered as a sign that "women are free" in Afghanistan, but Afghan women and girls continued to suffer abuse, harassment, and repression at the hands of some of Afghanistan's post-Taliban leaders. They still were harried by religious police, and many restrictions remained. These continuing problems were underscored by the removal of Samar from office by extremists mere months after her appointment.

In Katsina state in Muslim-controlled northern Nigeria, an appeals court revoked a sentence of stoning to death against Amina Lawal, a mother convicted of adultery.

Repression in Myanmar. Myanmar on May 30 returned to centre stage in human rights concerns with the arrest and detention of Nobel Peace Prize winner and political opposition leader Aung San Suu Kyi and a number of her pro-democracy supporters, thus ending a fledgling agreement to move toward democratic reform.

(MORTON SKLAR)

INTERNATIONAL MIGRATION

A defining issue of the 21st century was migration. In 2003 some 175 million people resided outside their home countries. In other words, one of every 35 individuals in the world was a migrant. Migration to developed states made up about 40% of total migration flows. Europe hosted the most international migrants (56.1 million), followed by Asia (49.7 million), North America (40.8 million), Africa (16.2 million), and Oceania (5.8 million).

At the end of 2002, the total number of "persons of concern" to the United Nations High Commissioner for Refugees (UNHCR) was approximately 20.6 million. This included 9.2 million asylum seekers, returned refugees, and certain internally displaced persons and 10.4 million refugees, down from 12 million in 2001 because of the return of nearly 2 million Afghans. The greatest numbers of refugees were in Asia (4.2 million), Africa (3.3 million), and Europe (2.1 million).

Asylum and Refugees. The distinction between voluntary and forced migration was sometimes difficult to discern. With the number of people on the move far outstripping the capacity of existing legal channels for migration—despite a ready market for labour—people who were not in need of protection sometimes used the asylum system. Although the public perception that governments had lost control of asylum provoked anger and sparked outbursts of racism and xenophobia, the necessity remained for some system of safeguarding those who genuinely were in need of protection.

In June UNHCR launched its Convention Plus initiative regarding the status of refugees. The initiative focused on the development of multilateral agreements that would complement the 1951 UN Convention Relating to the Status of Refugees and ensure greater equity between states in the sharing of responsibilities for refugees, notably in the context of mass influxes, mixed migratory flows, and the development of durable solutions. The initiative promoted multilateral commitments that would make the international response to future refugee crises more effective and reliable.

Migration Management. At the turn of the 21st century, public debate on this issue centred on irregular migration and on the migration and asylum nexus. In 2003 the discourse on migration broadened to encompass an increasing recognition that migration was an essential and inevitable component of the economic and social life of states and that managed migration could benefit both individuals and societies.

One topic of expanding interest was the relationship between migration and development, especially the impact of migrant remittances on the economic development of countries of origin. According to the 2003 World Bank report on global development finance, officially recorded worker remittances to less-developed countries amounted to $72.3 billion in 2001, and they were estimated to have risen in 2003 to $90 billion. With the inclusion of transactions

Refugees fleeing the Iraqi city of Basra in March are forced to take cover as militia forces supporting the Saddam Hussein regime fire mortar shells in their direction. In addition to assisting locally displaced persons, UNHCR expected to help a half million Iraqis return to their homeland in the next few years.

effected through informal channels, the total was far higher. In less-developed countries, remittances made up on average 1.3% of GDP, and the proportion was often much higher, as it was in Lesotho (26.5%), Nicaragua (16.2%), and Yemen (16.1%). From this perspective, migrants could be viewed as potential agents of development who strengthened cooperation between home and host countries through the transfer of skills and the development of transnational networks.

Migration's potential impact on national economies became increasingly clear, especially as demographic trends in some developed countries suggested a rising demand for workers that could not be met internally. The concern of countries of origin over the treatment of their workers abroad helped produce the UN Convention on the Protection of the Rights of All Migrant Workers and Members of Their Families, which came into force on July 1. It required states to adhere to human rights standards in their dealings with migrant workers.

The relationship between migration and trade, especially the supply of services via the temporary movement of people across borders, emerged as a major issue in negotiations. The September World Trade Organization meetings in Cancún, Mex., attempted to liberalize trade in agriculture and services to ensure that "world trade works for developing countries." Although barriers for goods were diminishing, most countries retained significant barriers to the movement of people for work.

The Regional Dimension. As individual states came to realize that their endeavours at the national level required multilateral efforts, cooperation on migration at the regional level assumed special importance. Local circumstances dictated the form of regional cooperation that was necessary. On all continents, regional consultative processes on migration were in place; in these, representatives of governments, international organizations, and, where possible, civil society shared information and experiences on migration issues of common concern.

In Asia the rapid growth of a market-led intraregional migration pattern drew attention to the importance of managing labour migration and combating the trafficking in persons. In 2003 ministerial-level consultations for Asian labour-sending countries were held in Colombo, Sri Lanka. There common policy priorities were identified and avenues for cooperation mapped out. In April the second Regional Ministerial Conference on People Smuggling, Trafficking in Persons and Related Transnational Crime was held on the Indonesian island of Bali. Two groups established by the first conference (2002) had developed a framework to strengthen legislation and to improve regional cooperation in law enforcement, information, and intelligence exchange.

In Africa the principal migration concerns included internal displacement caused by conflict, migration health matters (particularly those concerning HIV/AIDS), and the enhancement of development potential while minimizing "brain drain." African countries increased their cooperative efforts to manage migration flows over national borders that often cut across ethnic communities. Consultative regional dialogues, such as the Migration Dialogue for Southern Africa (2000) and the Migration Dialogue for Western Africa, were established to strengthen regional cooperation. In September a Regional Conference on Arab Migration in a Globalized World was held in Cairo. It provided a forum for the discussion of migration issues, in particular the geographic mobility of human resources. Similarly, the Ministerial Conference on Migration in the Western Mediterranean (called the "5+5 Dialogue") furthered an important exchange on migration issues between African and European countries in the western Mediterranean.

In the European Union a major objective in this policy field was the creation of common EU legislation on migration and asylum. Irregular migration remained a major political issue. Although strong controls were in place, complementary measures, including the development of orderly labour migration channels, were necessary.

According to Eurostat, the statistical office of the European Commission, in 2000 some 15 million non-EU migrants lived among the 380 million residents of the 15 EU member states. This included 45% from the rest of Europe, 18% from North Africa, 17% from Asia, and 9% from sub-Saharan Africa. In 2002 some 587,000 foreigners worldwide applied for asylum, including 465,000 in Europe (381,600 in EU countries).

Both the Greek and Italian presidencies of the EU put migration high on the agenda. At the June EU Council meeting in Thessaloniki, Greece, a proposal for more accessible, equitable, and managed asylum systems (including offshore transit centres and zones of protection) was introduced.

Germany's green-card program for the admission and employment of foreigners, launched in August 2000, was extended until the end of 2004, and the 20,000-card limit was removed. EU leaders, including the British and Swedish prime ministers, called for the opening of EU nations to immigration.

Migration patterns in Latin America and the Caribbean were changing significantly. Once of major concern, refugee movements had diminished considerably, and the focus had shifted to migration for work. Since the 1990s agreements and understandings such as the North American Free Trade Agreement and the Southern Cone Common Market agreement between Argentina, Brazil, Paraguay, and Uruguay had demonstrated the benefits of well-managed, safe, and orderly migration. Activities in the area included the regularization of irregular migrants and the harmonization of migration categories and visa policies.

In 2002, according to the Inter-American Development Bank (IDB), remittances to Latin America rose by almost 18% (from 2001 levels) to $32 billion. This equaled roughly 32% of the $103 billion that the IDB estimated were remitted to less-developed countries worldwide (the IMF estimated remittances to less-developed countries at about $70 billion).

The Global Dimension. While there was no normative framework in the field of international migration, governments increasingly recognized the value of international cooperation. Three ongoing processes worked toward this end. The International Dialogue on Migration, launched in 2001 by the International Organization for Migration, encouraged exploration of the links between international migration and other sectors (such as trade, labour, development, and health) by bringing stakeholders together. The Berne Initiative, also launched in 2001, was a consultative process designed to stimulate an exchange of views and promote mutual understanding of different migration realities and stakes. An independent body, the Global Commission on International Migration, was expected to begin its work early in 2004. Its major objective was to raise awareness of the positive contributions of migrants to society. (GERVAIS APPAVE)

Sports and Games

In 2003 **SWITZERLAND** won sailing's **AMERICA'S CUP**, Australia retained the **CRICKET WORLD CUP**, and England captured its first Rugby Union World Cup. Meanwhile, the **SARS OUTBREAK** in Asia **DISRUPTED** the women's **ICE HOCKEY** world championship, the association football (soccer) women's **WORLD CUP**, and other events.

AUTOMOBILE RACING

Grand Prix Racing. By the time the checkered flag fell to mark the end of the 2003 season-ending Japanese Grand Prix at Suzuka, Michael Schumacher (Ferrari) of Germany had finally clinched a record sixth Fédération Internationale de l'Automobile (FIA) world drivers' championship. He had 70 career wins to his credit, and Ferrari, the blue-riband powerhouse of Formula 1 (F1) domination for the previous four seasons, had secured its fifth straight constructors' title, an unparalleled achievement.

Ferrari's new F2003-GA car was better than its predecessor, but Schumacher did not win until the San Marino Grand Prix, the fourth round of the title chase, and even then his success was posted with the old F2002. Two weeks later he gave the new car a triumphant debut at the Spanish Grand Prix in Barcelona, but he freely admitted that he would not have been able to beat Fernando Alonso's Renault R23 if he had had to rely on the old car.

The season began on an uncertain note. FIA Pres. Max Mosley had initiated a raft of rule changes that included one-lap Indy-style qualifying but with a key difference. Beginning in 2003 the second qualifying session on Saturday afternoons would be regarded, in effect, as the first few laps of the race. Cars would be confined to a *parc fermé* area after that session, and no fuel could be added before they took their places on the starting grid the following afternoon. The changes did not please everybody, however. McLaren and Williams had arbitration pending over the manner in which the FIA implemented its revised regulations, which the two teams believed was a clear breach of the governing body's own rules. Mosley claimed that the changes, which included awarding championship points down to eighth place, would still result in the best driver's winning the title, although the task would take a little longer.

Ferrari had an overwhelmingly impressive run. Schumacher never suffered a mechanical failure and retired just once during the course of the season, when he spun off during heavy rain in Brazil. His teammate Rubens Barrichello of Brazil outqualified the world champion in 5 of the season's 16 races, most notably at the British Grand Prix at Silverstone and at Suzuka, where he scored superb wins. In addition, Barrichello clearly had the upper hand during qualifying at the German, Hungarian, and U.S. races, and he could well have added Austria to his tally of victories had it not been for a delay at one refueling stop.

Barrichello's formidable form constituted just one element of the wide-ranging challenge facing Schumacher in 2003. Kimi Räikkönen (McLaren/Mercedes) of Finland and Spain's Fernando Alonso (Renault) both posted their maiden Grand Prix victories during the course of the season, underscoring their eligibility as future title challengers. Williams/BMW drivers Juan Pablo Montoya of Colombia and Ralf Schumacher (Michael's younger brother) each won two races, but neither Williams/BMW nor McLaren/Mercedes had its admittedly competitive machinery consistently honed to the levels required for matching Ferrari.

Concerns about the sport's finances continued to dominate the F1 landscape, in particular the carmakers' challenge with their proposed GPWC racing series, due to start after the expiration of the current Concorde agreement at the end of 2007. The manufacturers, including Fiat (owner of Ferrari), DaimlerChrysler (owner of Mercedes), Renault, BMW, and Ford (owner of Jaguar), founded GPWC Holding BV as a device primarily designed to ensure a more equitable distribution of the sport's commercial rights revenue. The ongoing debate centred around whether F1 racing was best served by power broker Bernie Ecclestone's autocratic management style or whether the sport instead would benefit from a broader-based consensus that would give more scope for the motor industry's voice to be heard. In mid-December Ecclestone and the carmakers agreed to a "memorandum of understanding" that ended the threat of an alternate GPWC racing series. The agreement also brought the two sides closer to reaching a long-term deal that would ensure a fairer spread of the sport's commercial-rights income. This might boost individual team income by about $20 million per season in the future and would represent a lifeline to small teams such as Jordan and Minardi. Elsewhere, the F1 business showed signs of future expansion, with Bahrain and Shanghai both scheduled to hold debut races in 2004. This inevitably put pressure on European events, as the Belgian Grand Prix was canceled and the Austrian was dropped from the calendar at the end of the season. The British Grand Prix was subject to more than its fair share of critical scrutiny from Mosley and Ecclestone, and the rights and wrongs of whether this event should benefit from direct government funding—at a time when just about every other fixture on the world championship calendar enjoyed such luxuries—remained a matter of anxious controversy. (ALAN HENRY)

U.S. Auto Racing. Although he won only one race of the 36-event series, Matt Kenseth, driving a Roush DeWalt Ford Taurus, became the 2003 National Association for Stock Car Auto Racing (NASCAR) Winston Cup champion. After having won at Las Vegas, Nev., Kenseth assumed the points lead in early March by finishing fourth in Atlanta, Ga. Then he took advantage of a race-scoring system that rewarded consistency as he finished 11 times in the top 5 and 25 times in the top 10. Runner-up Jimmie Johnson (Chevrolet) was

90 points behind, and Dale Earnhardt, Jr., in a DEI Chevrolet was third. Ryan Newman, the leading Dodge driver, won eight races. Kenseth clinched the crown with a fourth-place finish at North Carolina Speedway in the season's penultimate event. His title was worth $4,250,000.

During the year NASCAR ended a 32-year relationship with its title sponsor, tobacco company R.J. Reynolds (the maker of Winston cigarettes). Nextel Communications then signed a 10-year sponsorship deal worth approximately $700 million, the largest in the history of any sport. Beginning in 2004 the Winston Cup series would be renamed the Nextel Cup. NASCAR also ended a gasoline sponsorship with Unocal 76, its supplier for 55 years. In 2003 NASCAR, a multibillion-dollar business, controlled 12 of the 23 largest tracks in the nation through its International Speedway Corp.

NASCAR's richest race, the season-opening $14,030,129 Daytona 500, was shortened by rain to 272.5 mi (109 laps). Chevrolet's Michael Waltrip, who earned approximately $1,411,000 for his DEI team, beat Kurt Busch (Ford) and Johnson in that order. Waltrip also won the September restrictor-plate race at Talladega, Ala., while his teammate Earnhardt won at Talladega in April. (The Daytona and Talladega 4-km [2.5-mi] tracks mandated restrictors on the carburetors to limit speed.) Kevin Harvick (Chevrolet) beat Kenseth in the Brickyard 400, and Johnson edged Kenseth in the Coca-Cola 600 at Lowe's Motor Speedway in Charlotte, N.C., in another classic race shortened by rain.

Brian Vickers in a Hendrick Motorsports Chevrolet won the NASCAR Busch Series championship by 14 points over David Green in the finale at Homestead-Miami Speedway. At age 20, Vickers became the youngest driver to capture one of NASCAR's top three titles. The Craftsman Truck Series was equally tight, won by nine points by Travis Kvapil over Dennis Setzer. Both drove Chevrolets.

The Indianapolis 500 continued to be dominated by business magnate Roger Penske. Brazilians Gil de Ferran and defending champion Helio Castroneves ran one-two, respectively, as Team Penske won the Indy 500 for the 13th time. De Ferran in a G-force Toyota edged Castroneves in a Dallara Toyota by 0.299 sec, with Tony Kanaan's Andretti-Green Dallara Honda third. Seven of the first nine finishers were powered by Toyota. The first American engine, Buddy Rice's Dallara Chevrolet, finished 11th. De Ferran won $1,353,265 of the $10,151,830 purse. Castroneves, at 231.725 mph, was the fastest qualifier.

Brazilian teammates Gil de Ferran (left) and Helio Castroneves climb a safety fence to show off for the crowd after finishing one-two, respectively, in the Indianapolis 500 on May 25.

AP/Wide World Photos

The Indy Racing League (IRL) season crown went to New Zealander Scott Dixon in a G-force Toyota. The 14-race IRL series, a single-seater oval-track series in which average speeds often were well over 200 mph, proved a battle between Honda and Toyota because Chevrolet engines, used by many of the best American drivers, were uncompetitive until Chevy engaged Cosworth, a builder associated with rival Ford, to redo its engines. In September, with his car powered by the Cosworth-sourced Chevy Gen IV, series defending champion Sam Hornish, Jr., set a new closed-course world record for an entire race when he won the Toyota 400 at California Speedway at an average speed of 207.151 mph.

The migration of drivers, teams, and manufacturers to the IRL did not prevent the rival Champion Auto Racing Teams (CART) from completing a full season. While CART's financial status was being worked out off the track, president Chris Pook assembled an international schedule and enough teams to make the series viable, even though CART paid $47 million to keep them racing and bought TV time. CART turned itself into a spec series, mandating Ford Cosworth engines, Bridgestone tires, and strict limitations on vehicle configuration. Canadian Paul Tracy in a Lola clinched the title in Australia.

(ROBERT J. FENDELL)

Rallies and Other Races. There were six different winners in the 14-event 2003 world rally championship (WRC), but in the end Petter Solberg (Subaru) of Norway won his first WRC title by only one point (72–71) over his French rival Sébastien Loeb (Citroën). Solberg, whose first victory on the circuit was the 2002 Rally of Great Britain, had already captured three rallies (Cyprus, Australia, and Corsica) in the 2003 season, but he arrived in Wales for the season-ending Rally of Great Britain, held on November 7–9, trailing one point behind Loeb (the winner in Monte Carlo, Germany, and Italy) and his Citroën teammate Carlos Sainz of Spain. Solberg outraced Loeb in Wales to win by 43.6 sec amid accusations that the Citroën team had instructed Loeb to back off so that Citroën could secure the constructors' championship, which it did 160–145 over Peugeot. Defending champion driver Marcus Grönholm fell to sixth place in the final standings. Former champion Richard Burns of Great Britain missed the final rally after he was diagnosed with a brain tumour; he was ruled out of the 2004 season pending treatment.

Team Bentley captured the first two places at the Le Mans 24-hour endurance race in June, anchored by driver Tom Kristensen of Denmark in his fifth Le Mans victory. Bentley had won the event five times between 1924 and 1930 before retiring from racing and had returned to competition only in 2001.

Road racing in the U.S. remained fragmented. In the Rolex 24 Hours of Daytona, sanctioned by the Grand American Road Racing Association on Daytona International Speedway's 5.73-km (3.56-mi) road circuit, a Porsche

GT3 RS won by nine laps over a Ferrari 360 GT, with another GT-class Porsche RS third. Americans Kevin Buckler and Michael Schrom teamed with Germans Timo Bernhard and Jörg Bergmeister for the victorious drive. Finishing fourth was the leading prototype-class car, a Ford Multimatic. The race attracted drivers from Germany, Russia, Belgium, Italy, Canada, England, and the U.S. as the Grand American association began to attempt to simplify road racing by splitting it into two classes, Daytona Prototype and GT.

The rival American LeMans Series was dominated by Audi, which won eight of the nine races, including the Mobil I 12 Hours of Sebring. Frank Biela of Germany, Marco Werner of Germany, and Philipp Peter of Austria won that classic race over another Audi, with two Bentley prototypes finishing third and fourth. Biela and Werner were also the American LeMans season driving champions.

(ROBERT J. FENDELL; MELINDA C. SHEPHERD)

BADMINTON

At the All England Badminton Championships, played in Birmingham in February 2003, Muhammed Hafiz Hashim of Malaysia beat defending champion Chen Hong of China for the men's singles title. It was the first time in 37 years that a Malaysian had won the men's singles event. The Indonesian men's doubles team of Candra Wijaya and Sigit Budiarto won over defending champions Ha Tae Kwon and Kim Dong Moon of South Korea. The three remaining events featured all-Chinese finals. Gao Ling teamed with Huang Sui to win the women's doubles and then with Zhang Jun to capture the mixed doubles. Zhou Mi easily dispatched Xie Xingfang for her first All England women's singles title.

The Sudirman Cup, an international mixed-team event, was contested in Eindhoven, Neth., in March. China had been dominating the biennial competition, winning every time since 1995. After narrowly defeating Denmark in its semifinal, however, South Korea denied the Chinese a fifth straight title with a 3–1 final-round upset. The key match for South Korea came in the men's singles event, when Lee Hyun Il stunned world number one Chen Hong.

The spotlight returned to Birmingham in late July for the world championships. China's Xia Xuanze won the men's singles title, defeating Wong Choong Hann of Malaysia. In the men's doubles final, the young Danish team of Lars Paaske and Jonas Rasmussen had an impressive win over Wijaya and Budiarto. China's Zhang Ning, who had earlier eliminated Danish great Camilla Martin in her last world championships appearance, was too strong for teammate Gong Ruina in the women's singles final. Chinese players earned another gold medal when Gao Ling and Huang Sui beat compatriots Wei Yili and Zhao Tingting for the women's doubles crown. After having lost to them in the 2001 world championships final, the South Korean mixed doubles team of Ra Kyung Min and Kim Dong Moon came through against Gao Ling and Zhang Jun. (DONN GOBBIE)

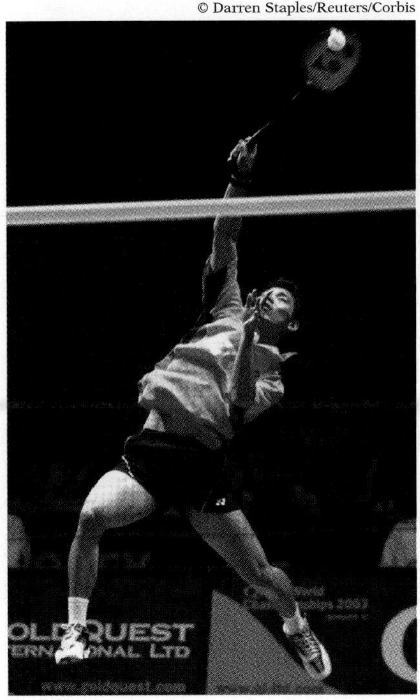

At the men's singles final of the world badminton championships in Birmingham, Eng., in August, China's Xia Xuanze leaps to make a return to Malaysia's Wong Choong Hann.

BASEBALL

North America. Despite a slow start, in part because of inclement weather, the 2003 Major League Baseball season gained momentum during the midsummer months as interleague games in June and a dramatic All-Star Game in July cultivated interest. The second half of the regular season and the playoffs featured a number of story lines that contributed to what some deemed the most appealing postseason in many years. Although overall attendance was flat, especially in the spring, television ratings for marquee events in October indicated a significant upsurge in interest throughout the U.S. and Canada.

World Series. The Florida Marlins defeated the New York Yankees four games to two for their second World Series conquest. The Marlins, a 1993 expansion team, clinched the 2003 championship by beating the Yankees 2–0 in Yankee Stadium on October 25. The triumph completed an unlikely tale for the Marlins, a wild-card entry in the postseason by virtue of having achieved the best record of any second-place team in the National League (NL). (When the Marlins won the title in 1997, they also did so after having secured a wild-card berth.) The Marlins started the 2003 regular season with a 16–22 record, at which point manager Jeff Torborg was dismissed. At age 72, Jack McKeon was lured out of retirement to replace him. The team dipped to 19–29 before it embarked on its startling turnaround.

In the World Series opener at Yankee Stadium on October 18, the Marlins defeated the Yankees 3–2. Brad Penny, who pitched 5⅓ innings, was credited with the victory after the Florida bullpen yielded just two hits during the remainder of the game. The Yankees responded on October 19 to win 6–1 as Hideki Matsui hit a three-run home run in the first inning and Andy Pettitte pitched 8⅔ innings for the Yankees.

With the series tied at one game apiece, the teams moved to Pro Player Stadium in Miami, Fla., for game three on October 21. Matsui's single in the eighth inning broke a 1–1 tie, and Bernie Williams hit a three-run home run in the ninth to bring the Yankees a 6–1 triumph. Williams's home run was the 19th of his career in the postseason, a major league record. The Marlins, however, defeated the Yankees 4–3 in 12 innings on October 22. The Marlins scored three runs in the first inning off 41-year-old star pitcher Roger Clemens, who announced that he was considering retirement. The Yankees tied the game 3–3 in the ninth inning on a two-run pinch-hit triple by Ruben Sierra. That score held until Florida's Alex Gonzalez hit a home run in the 12th inning.

The Marlins won game five 6–4 on October 23 to assume a three games to two lead. That set up game six, in which Josh Beckett, a 23-year-old right-hander who had been the losing pitcher in game three, pitched a complete game, yielding five hits and striking out nine. He was voted the World Series Most Valuable Player (MVP).

Play-offs. The Yankees claimed their 39th American League (AL) pennant by defeating their longtime rivals the Boston Red Sox four games to three in the best-of-seven American League Championship Series (ALCS). In the decisive seventh game, the Yankees, who trailed by three runs as late as the eighth inning, triumphed 6–5 in 11 innings on Aaron Boone's tie-breaking home run. Mariano Rivera of the Yankees was voted MVP of the ALCS. Game three, at Boston's Fenway Park, was marred by an on-field altercation in which 72-year-old Yankee coach Don Zimmer charged Red Sox pitcher Pedro Martinez, who threw Zimmer to the ground. The Yankees had advanced to the ALCS by winning their best-of-five Division Series three games to one over the Minnesota Twins. The Red Sox, the AL wild-card team, had lost the first two games of their Division Series before rallying to eliminate the Oakland A's three games to two.

In the National League Championship Series (NLCS) the Marlins won their second pennant, and the Chicago Cubs, after leading the NLCS three games to one, failed to claim what would have been their first pennant since 1945. The Marlins opened the series by winning game one in Chicago 9–8 in 11 innings but then lost the next three. Beckett struck out 11 and shut out the Cubs 4–0 in game five, after which the Marlins won two games in Chicago. In game six Cubs starting pitcher Mark Prior went into the eighth inning with a 3–0 shutout, but, after a controversial play that many considered fan interference, the Marlins rallied with eight runs in the inning to win 8–3. The Marlins completed a remarkable comeback by beating the Cubs 9–6 in game seven to win the series four games to three. Ivan Rodriguez of Florida was voted the MVP of the NLCS. The Marlins also had rallied to defeat the San Francisco Giants in their best-of-five NL Division Series three games to one. In the other NL Division Series, the Cubs had upset the Atlanta Braves three games to two to win their first postseason series since 1908, their last world-championship season.

Individual Accomplishments. Bill Mueller of the Red Sox won the AL batting title with a .326 average, beating teammate Manny Ramirez, who batted .325. Mueller, a switch hitter, also became the first player in major league history to hit grand slam home runs from both sides of the plate in the same game when he accomplished the feat against Texas. In the NL, Albert Pujols (.359) of the St. Louis Cardinals barely surpassed Todd Helton (.358) of the Colorado Rockies on the final day of the regular season. Before their averages were rounded off, they were separated by only .00022. Jim Thome of the Philadelphia Phillies led the NL in home runs with 47, the same total as that posted by AL MVP Alex Rodriguez of the Texas Rangers. (*See* BIOGRAPHIES.) Preston Wilson of Colorado led the NL in runs batted in with 141; Carlos Delgado of the Toronto Blue Jays set the AL pace with 145. Florida's Juan Pierre collected 65 stolen bases, the most in either league.

Atlanta pitcher Russ Ortiz (21–7) led the NL in victories. Eric Gagne of the Los Angeles Dodgers amassed 55 saves, two short of the major league record, in as many opportunities, and captured the NL Cy Young Award. Toronto's Roy Halliday (22–7), who led the AL in victories, was the other Cy Young winner. Keith Foulke of the A's led the AL in saves with a total of 43. Boston's Martinez achieved the lowest earned run average in either league, 2.22. Kerry Wood of the Cubs led both leagues in strikeouts with 266.

On April 4 Sammy Sosa of the Cubs became the 18th player to reach the 500-home-run benchmark; the Rangers' Rafael Palmeiro joined him on the list in May. Later in the season, however, Sosa was ejected from a game when his broken bat was found to contain cork; he was suspended for seven games. Barry Bonds of the Giants hit 45 home runs—increasing his career total to 658, fourth on the all-time list, behind Hank Aaron (755), Babe Ruth (714), and Willie Mays (660)—and won a record sixth MVP award. Clemens, who had pitched for three different teams—Boston, Toronto, and the Yankees—recorded his 300th victory and his 4,000th strikeout. McKeon and the Kansas City Royals' Tony Peña were named the NL and AL Manager of the Year, respectively. Shortstop Angel Berroa of the Royals was voted AL Rookie of the Year, while Dontrelle Willis of Florida took the NL honour.

In the annual All-Star Game, at U.S. Cellular Field, home of the Chicago White Sox, Hank Blalock of Texas hit a two-run pinch-hit home run in the eighth inning to give the AL a 7–6 victory over the NL. By virtue of the triumph, the AL secured home-field advantage in the World Series. It was the first time that the All-Star Game had been used to determine home-field advantage; previously, the leagues had alternated home-field advantage each season.

Alex Gonzalez of the Florida Marlins slides past New York Yankees catcher Jorge Posada to score in the sixth and final game of the World Series on October 25.

Little League World Series. Musashi-Fuchu Little League of Tokyo defeated a team from East Boynton Beach, Fla., 10–1 to win the Little League World Series in Williamsport, Pa., on August 24. Yuutaro Tanaka struck out 14 batters, and Hokuto Nakahara hit a grand slam home run as Tokyo broke open a scoreless championship game with eight runs in the fourth inning. It was the third time in five years that a Japanese team had won the Little League World Series; East Boynton Beach was the eighth team from Florida to have advanced to the Little League World Series final without claiming the championship.

(ROBERT VERDI)

Latin America. The 2003 Caribbean Series was held in Carolina, P.R., on February 2–8. The Cibao Eagles (Águilas

Cibaeñas), representing the Dominican Republic, defeated the Mayagüez Indians (Indios) of Puerto Rico in a play-off game to win the title. The Dominicans had a 6–1 record, while Mayagüez was 5–2. A second Puerto Rican team, the Caguas Creoles (Criollos) was 2–4, and the Mexican entry, Los Mochis Sugarcane Growers (Cañeros), was 0–6. Puerto Rico had two teams in the series because civil unrest in Venezuela had caused the league there to suspend play midway through the season. This resulted in there being no league champion to send to the series.

In Cuba Industriales defeated Villa Clara four games to none to win the 42nd Serie Nacional (National Series) championship. Industriales, which set a record with 66 wins during the Serie Nacional, defeated Havana in the quarterfinals and Pinar del Río in the semifinals to advance. Las Tunas outfielder Osmani Urrutia hit .421 to win his third consecutive Serie Nacional batting title.

The Cuban national team defeated the United States 3–1 in the title game at the Pan American Games, held in the Dominican Republic in August. It was Cuba's ninth consecutive Pan American gold medal in baseball. Mexico finished in third place.

The Mexico City Red Devils (Diablos Rojas) defeated the Angelopolis Tigers four games to one to win the Mexican League championship series. It was the Red Devils' second consecutive league title and 14th overall. (MILTON JAMAIL)

Japan. The Fukuoka Daiei Hawks won the 2003 Japan Series by defeating the Hanshin Tigers four games to three. The Pacific League (PL) champion Hawks came back after being down three games to two and clinched their first series title since 1999. Daiei starting pitcher Toshiya Sugiuchi, who won games two and six, was named series Most Valuable Player (MVP). Daiei catcher Kenji Jojima tied the series record with four home runs.

Jojima was named the PL's regular-season MVP. He had 34 homers, a .330 batting average, and 119 runs batted in (RBIs); he was second in the league after his teammate Nobuhiko Matsunaka. Hawks pitcher Kazumi Saito led the league in three categories with 20 wins (20–3), a 2.83 earned run average (ERA), and a winning percentage of .870, while pitcher Tsuyoshi Wada was named PL Rookie of the Year. Tuffy Rhodes of the Osaka Kintetsu Buffaloes won his second home run title with 51.

In the Central League (CL), the Tigers, Japan's perennial baseball underdogs, dominated with an impressive 87–51 record and won their first pennant since 1985. Hanshin players also led the league in individual records—left-handed pitcher Kei Igawa, with 20 wins and a 2.80 ERA, was named CL MVP; Makoto Imaoka had a .340 batting average; and Norihiro Akahoshi achieved 61 stolen bases. Tyrone Woods of the Yokohama Bay Stars and Alex Ramirez of the Yakult Swallows led the CL with 40 home runs each. Tigers manager Senichi Hoshino resigned after the Japan Series for health reasons. Yomiuri Giants skipper Tatsunori Hara stepped down to take responsibility for his team's poor performance.

(HIROKI NODA)

Kyodo News

Tadahito Iguchi of the Fukuoka Daiei Hawks celebrates his two-run home run against the Hanshin Tigers in game six of the Japan Series in October; the Hawks won the game and the series.

BASKETBALL

Professional. In 2003 San Antonio's Tim Duncan spelled the end for the Los Angeles Lakers' budding dynasty. Duncan's phenomenal performance propelled the San Antonio Spurs past the Lakers in the National Basketball Association's Western Conference play-offs, but that was just a warm-up for the 2.13-m (7-ft) dynamo who already had powered his team to the Midwest Division title in the 2002–03 regular season. In the end, his brilliance doomed the New Jersey Nets to defeat by four games to two in their second straight NBA finals loss.

New Jersey breezed through early play-off foes to repeat as Eastern Conference champions. When the Nets won game two of the finals 87–85 in San Antonio (after losing game one 101–89), their fans expected guard Jason Kidd to spearhead a breakthrough on his home court. Duncan simply refused to let it happen.

After winning game three 84–79 and then narrowly losing 77–76, the Spurs took the pivotal fifth game on the road by a score of 93–83 and returned home to wrap up the championship on June 15 before an ecstatic throng of 18,797 in the SBC Center. In the decisive sixth game, Duncan strung together 21 points, 20 rebounds, 10 assists, and 8 blocks. With his team trailing 72–63 in the fourth quarter, he turned the game around with a blocked shot. The Spurs went on a 19–0 scoring spree in the next 5 minutes and 10 seconds to seal their 88–77 triumph and the NBA title. The fans joined in savouring this farewell gift to retiring Spurs veteran David ("the Admiral") Robinson.

Duncan was named series Most Valuable Player in addition to garnering his second straight regular-season MVP honour. Amaré Stoudemire of the Phoenix Suns beat out Houston's Chinese phenomenon Yao Ming (*see* BIOGRAPHIES) as Rookie of the Year.

After their play-off ouster, the Lakers signed veteran free agents Karl Malone and Gary Payton to team with superstars Kobe Bryant and Shaquille O'Neal in a lineup many touted as unbeatable. On July 18, however, Bryant was indicted on criminal sexual assault charges, and a pall of gloom was thereby cast over the Los Angeles franchise and the entire world of pro basketball. Bryant, hailed as the NBA's most marketable athlete because of his playing skills and squeaky-clean image, had just signed a $45 million endorsement pact with sportswear giant Nike.

In June the new franchise Charlotte Bobcats, owned by African American business tycoon Robert Johnson (*see* BIOGRAPHIES), was officially unveiled. The team would begin playing in the 2004–05 season.

In the Women's National Basketball Association (WNBA), the Detroit Shock pulled off a courageous comeback to capture the 2002–03 championship. In the opener of the best-of-three final play-offs, the Shock got trounced 75–63 by the Los Angeles Sparks, who were bidding for their third straight league crown. Responding with the same tenacity displayed by their coach, Bill

Laimbeer, in his professional career, the Shock regrouped to take game two 62–61, setting up a winner-take-all showdown in the Palace of Auburn Hills. Thanks to the splendid shooting of 1.96-m (6-ft 5-in) centre Ruth Riley, the Spark prevailed 78–53 before a crowd of 22,076, the largest in WNBA history. Riley, who had led Notre Dame to the 2001 national championship, hit on 11 of 19 shots from the floor for a career-high 27 points. "This was the best basketball game I've ever played," said Riley, while confetti rained down on the celebrating Shock.

College. In 2003 the third time finally proved to be the charm for Coach Jim Boeheim and his Syracuse Orangemen. In the final of the National Collegiate Athletic Association championship in the New Orleans Superdome on April 7, Syracuse repulsed a frantic closing charge by the University of Kansas to prevail 81–78 and present Boeheim with his first NCAA title.

During the tournament, number three seed Syracuse unleashed a giant-killing spree through higher-ranked opponents by blending its seamless 2–3 zone defense with the all-court brilliance of freshmen Carmelo Anthony and Gerry McNamara. The Orangemen upset number one seed Oklahoma 63–47 in the East Regional final. Then they disposed of the South Region's top seed, Texas, 95–84 in their Final Four matchup. Kentucky and Arizona, the tournament favourites, got knocked off by Marquette and Kansas, respectively, in the other regional finals.

In his 27 years at Syracuse, the longest tenure among active Division I head coaches, Boeheim had won 652 games, but his team had been turned back twice on the doorstep of an NCAA crown. Kansas Coach Roy Williams had met with equal frustration in three previous trips to the Final Four. After routing Marquette 94–61 in the semifinal, the second-seeded Jayhawks were equally motivated against Syracuse, with the Superdome crowd of 54,524 anticipating a bitter struggle. Instead, the Orangemen, from the Big East Conference, unleashed a blistering attack to open a 53–42 lead at halftime, the highest-scoring first half in NCAA tournament history. The Jayhawks, from the Big 12 Conference, pulled to within three points of the lead at 81–78 only 14 seconds before the end but failed in two more attempts to score.

San Antonio Spurs superstar Tim Duncan shoots in game six of the NBA finals on June 15; Duncan was named MVP as the Spurs beat the New Jersey Nets four games to two.

© Andrew D. Bernstein/NBAE via Getty Images

Thanks to a combined 38 points from Anthony and McNamara, Syracuse finished with a 30–5 record and gave its coach the 653rd and most rewarding victory of his career. As expected, Anthony elected to drop out after just one college season to enter the NBA draft; he was picked third overall and signed with the Denver Nuggets. Nick Collison paced the Jayhawks (30–8) with 19 points and 21 rebounds. Soon after the tournament ended, Williams departed to take over for Matt Doherty at North Carolina. Kansas quickly lured one of the nation's best young coaches, Bill Self, from Illinois to take over.

In women's basketball, the Connecticut Huskies, under Coach Geno Auriemma, capped an awesome 37–1 season by defeating six-time champion Tennessee (33–5) by a score of 73–68 in the women's NCAA tournament final. It was UConn's second straight national championship and fourth overall, despite having lost four starting players from the 2001–02 team. Diana Taurasi added the Final Four Most Outstanding Player laurels to her national Player of the Year award. In the final she sparked the Huskies with 28 points while shaking off back and ankle injuries.

(ROBERT G. LOGAN)

International. The Fédération Internationale de Basketball (FIBA) national team competitions that dominated the sport in 2003 were played with an eye toward the 2004 Olympic Games in Athens. By October 2003 all 12 qualifiers for the men's Olympic tournament had been decided. Greece, the host country, and Serbia and Montenegro (formerly Yugoslavia), the 2002 world champion, would be joined by the qualifiers from the five continental championships—Angola, Argentina, Australia, Italy, Lithuania, New Zealand, China, Puerto Rico, Spain, and the United States.

After European nations had taken three of the top five places in the 2002 world championships, there was heightened interest in the 2003 European championships. Lithuania won the title for the first time since 1939, defeating defending champion Serbia and Montenegro 98–82 in the quarterfinals and France 74–70 in the semifinals. In the final, guard Arvydas Macijauskas led Lithuania with 21 points in the 93–84 win over Spain. Italy qualified for the Olympics by beating France 69–67 in the bronze-medal game.

Australia swept New Zealand in the three-game Oceania championship series, although both had already qualified for the Olympics. National Basketball Association star Yao Ming (*see* BIOGRAPHIES) led China to a 7–0 sweep in the Asian championships, beating South Korea 106–96 in the final. Angola qualified by defeating Nigeria 85–65 in the African final.

The U.S. responded to its sixth-place finish in the 2002 world championships (which broke a 58–0 winning streak in the FIBA competitions) by cruising through the Tournament of the Americas in San Juan, P.R., with a record of 10–0 to qualify, along with Argentina and Puerto Rico. The U.S. avenged its 87–80 world championship defeat by crushing Argentina 106–73 in the final, while the home crowd roared Puerto Rico to the final Olympic slot with a 79–66 third-place win over Canada.

© Pierre Andrieu/AFP/Getty Images

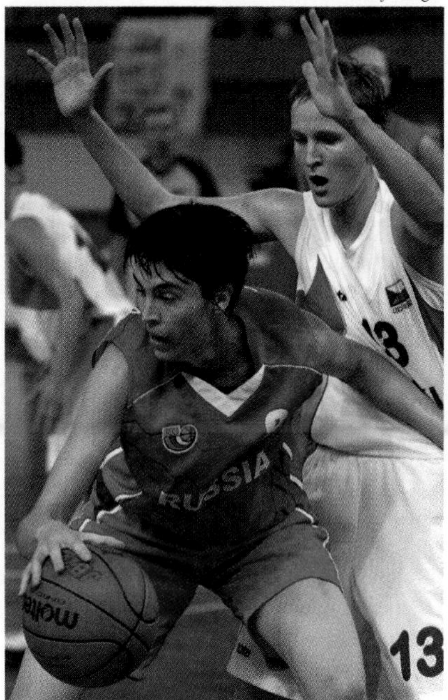

Yelena Baranova of Russia drives the ball past Lucie Blahuskova of the Czech Republic during Russia's 59–56 victory in the women's European basketball championship final.

Greece and the U.S., the 2000 Olympic champion, led the women's qualifiers. By October they had been joined by Australia, Brazil, the Czech Republic, New Zealand, Russia, and Spain. Australia and New Zealand had already qualified, while in the Americas tournament Brazil defeated Cuba 90–81 to qualify. The women's European championships were staged in Greece in September. Russia won its first European title since the breakup of the former Soviet Union by beating the Czechs 59–56, while Spain overcame Poland 87–81 to qualify. This left one African and three Asian qualifiers to be determined. (RICHARD TAYLOR)

BILLIARD GAMES

Carom Billiards. In early 2003 the Billiards Worldcup Association (BWA), the generally recognized professional organization for three-cushion billiards, reorganized, acquired a new board, and announced plans to "relaunch" a new tour with at least three and perhaps as many as five Worldcup tournaments. Two tournaments were held, and a third that was scheduled for Dortmund, Ger., was canceled. Open dates remained to be filled in late fall. On December 6, in Oosterhout, Neth., the BWA board resigned en masse, stating that "irresolvable problems" in negotiations with players to renew their contracts had made it impossible to continue the organization's activities. Administrative activities would continue until a general assembly was held in the first quarter of 2004.

Sweden's Torbjörn Blomdahl defeated Billiard Congress of America (BCA) Hall of Famer Raymond Ceulemans of Belgium 1,512–1,475 to take the BWA Grand Prix Barendrecht (the International Dutch Open) in January. The Las Vegas (Nev.) Worldcup tournament in July went to fan favourite Semih Sayginer of Turkey, who defeated Dick Jaspers of The Netherlands 2,000–1,730. The 10th Crystal Kelly tournament, which featured just eight players, was contested in The Netherlands rather than Monte-Carlo, its customary home. The "home court" advantage might have helped Jaspers, who won with 12 match points. Ceulemans had an impressive high run of 18. At mid season, after the two BWA Worldcup events and the Crystal Kelly Invitational, Blomdahl led the Worldcup rankings with 283 points. Jaspers had 228 points, followed by Marco Zanetti of Italy and Sayginer.

Meanwhile, the Union Mondiale de Billard (UMB) announced plans to launch a competing world cup series of its own. In February Sayginer led Turkey to the title in the UMB world national team championship, held in Viersen, Ger. He followed up with a victory over Filippos Kasidokostas of Greece in the final of the UMB single world championship in Valladolid, Spain, in November. In the semifinals, Sayginer had defeated Blomdahl, while Kasidokostas had overcome Zanetti.

Pocket Billiards. The Women's Professional Billiards Association (WPBA) continued to be the best-organized and most consistent professional tour in an otherwise chaotic pocket billiards world. With its perennial lineup of international players, the WPBA was the de facto world tour for women. With its ongoing ESPN television contract, the WPBA maintained its status as the face of billiards for most enthusiasts, as the men's professional game continued to suffer from disorganization and the lack of a viable governing body.

At the end of 2002, England's Allison Fisher had regained the top spot on the WPBA tour from rival Karen Corr of Northern Ireland, and she parlayed the momentum into 2003. Fisher won three of the first four contests of the 2003 season—the Delta Classic in Robinsonville, Miss., the San Diego (Calif.) Classic, and the Midwest Classic in East Peoria, Ill. At the season's midpoint she was firmly atop the rankings, followed by Corr, Helena Thornfeldt of Sweden, Taiwan's Jennifer Chen, and newcomer Kim Shaw from England. In sixth place was American Jeanette Lee. Corr defeated Fisher in the final of the BCA Open 9-Ball Championship in Las Vegas in May and came within 85 points of her rival in the rankings after winning the WPBA U.S. Open in September and the Canadian Classic in October. In early November Lee won the four-player Tournament of Champions at the Mohegan Sun Casino in Uncasville, Conn., as well as the winner-take-all purse of $25,000. In the season's final contest, the National 9-Ball Championship in Lincoln City, Ore., Fisher beat Lee in the final and kept her top ranking for the season. Corr, who finished in third place, and Thornfeldt held at numbers two and three, respectively, while Lee bettered her final ranking to fourth.

The world nine-ball championships were again sponsored by Matchroom Sport and held in Cardiff, Wales, with the blessing of the World Pool-Billiard Association (WPA). Hours of live TV coverage and high production values marked the contest, which included an uneven mix of WPA-qualified contestants and Matchroom picks. Thorsten Hohmann, a relatively unknown 24-year-old from Germany, defeated Filipino-born Canadian Alex Pagulayan 17–10 in the final to take the WPA world title and $65,000.

With its patchwork of international contests and competing governing bodies, the men's professional game continued to strive for credibility, and the 2003 season comprised a smorgasbord of independent tournaments. A struggling U.S. Professional Poolplayers Association (UPA) sanctioned nine tournaments in 2003. The Mid-Atlantic in January was a $15,000 payday for Efren Reyes of the Philippines. American Johnny Archer won $10,000 at the Brunswick Pro Players Championship in March, and the BCA Open winner on the men's side was Ralf Souquet of Germany. The UPA refused to sanction the U.S. Open, which was won by American Jeremy Jones in Chesapeake, Va., in September. The International Billiard Council (IBC) sponsored 10 events, including the season-ending joint IBC-WPA World Tour Championship in Tokyo. Pagulayan came out on top of an all-Filipino final four, taking the $15,000 top prize.

At the European championships, held in Bialystok, Pol., from March 27 to

April 6, the European Pocket Billiard Federation (EPBF) crowned Denmark's Charlotte Sörensen the women's eight-ball champion and Germany's Sandra Ortner the nine-ball titlist. On the men's side, Oliver Ortmann took the EPBF nine-ball title and Souquet won at eight-ball. Sweden and Germany, respectively, captured the men's and women's team titles.

The BCA remained stalled in its quest to earn pocket billiards a spot in the Olympics. The trade association, which was recognized by the WPA as the North American governing body, made changes to its bylaws to conform more closely to U.S. Olympic Committee requirements. Additional board positions were created for player delegates, and elections were held in conjunction with the BCA's annual open amateur tournament. BCA officials, however, said that they might create a separate, player-oriented entity to pursue their Olympic dream.

Snooker. Welshman Mark Williams used a trio of wins to distance himself from the pack in the world snooker rankings at the close of the 2002–03 season. He became only the third player to sweep the game's three biggest tournaments in one season. (Snooker legends Steve Davis of England and Stephen Hendry of Scotland were the only other players to win a single season's Embassy world championship, U.K. championship, and Benson & Hedges Masters tournament.) Williams ended the season well atop the rankings with 52,600 points. More hotly contested was second place; Hendry had 44,800 points, while Ronnie O'Sullivan of England finished third with 44,750 points.

The first goal of the hat trick occurred at the U.K. championship, where Ken Doherty of Ireland challenged Williams but came away with a 10–9 loss in the final. Williams made his mark in February at the Benson & Hedges Masters, beating Hendry in the final 10–4. In May the world championship at the Crucible Theatre in Sheffield, Eng., was the last jewel in the crown for Williams. He defeated Doherty 18–16. It was the last year of the Benson & Hedges Masters tournament, which was a casualty of the U.K.'s ban on tobacco advertising. Nicknamed "Wembley," the popular tournament ran for 29 years.

In women's snooker, England's Kelly Fisher finished a 69-match, 15-tournament winning streak when she lost in the quarterfinals to Maria Catalano (O'Sullivan's cousin) at the Scottish Open in March. Catalano went on to lose 4–1 in the final to Belgium's Wendy Jans. Despite the loss, Fisher remained atop the rankings, and the next month she won her fifth world championship in six years. (KIRSTIN PIRES)

BOBSLEIGH, SKELETON, AND LUGE

Bobsleigh. The 2002–03 bobsleigh season belonged to the Germans, who dominated the World Cup circuit and the world championships. The men's world championships were held in Lake Placid, N.Y., in February 2003. German drivers André Lange and René Spies battled it out all season, with Lange winning three World Cup four-man events and the overall four-man crown. Lange also drove his crew to gold in the four-man competition at the world championships, where driver Todd Hays of the U.S. took the silver. Lange and Kevin Kuske won the two-man world championship race. Pierre Lueders of Canada won the two-man World Cup season title, just two points ahead of Spies.

German driver Sandra Prokoff dominated the women's circuit, winning five of eight World Cup events during the 2002–03 season and the World Cup title. Teammate Susi Erdmann collected seven medals on the World Cup circuit and finished second in overall standings. Americans Jean Racine, who finished eighth overall, and Jill Bakken battled injuries throughout the season. At the women's world championships in Winterberg, Ger., Erdmann led the Germans to a sweep of the podium, with Prokoff in a close second. Racine and Vonetta Flowers, in sixth place, were the top Americans.

Skeleton. On the skeleton World Cup circuit, Canadian Jeff Pain and American Chris Soule each won two of the six races. Soule proved the overall victor and became only the second American (after Lincoln DeWitt in 2000–01) to win the World Cup season title. Pain finished in second. At the world championships in Nagano, Japan, heavy snow hampered the race, which was shortened from four to three heats. Pain took the gold, with Soule in second place and American Brady Canfield in third.

Canadians Lindsay Alcock and Michelle Kelly dueled throughout the year, with Kelly taking the women's World Cup title by two points. American Tristan Gale finished third. Gale also collected a bronze medal at the 2003 skeleton world championships. Kelly won the event, beating the second-place Yekaterina Mironova of Russia by nearly 1.5 seconds. (JULIE URBANSKY)

Luge. Americans Mark Grimmette and Brian Martin finished in the top two spots in five of seven races to capture the overall luge World Cup title. Patric Leitner and Alexander Resch of Germany finished a close second, with Austrians Tobias Schiegl and Markus Schiegl third. At the 2003 world

Mark Grimmette and Brian Martin of the U.S. show perfect form in the final event of the luge World Cup in February; the Americans clinched their third overall doubles title.

AP/Wide World Photos

championships in Sigulda, Latvia, Austria's Andreas Linger and Wolfgang Linger won the doubles gold, followed by Schiegl and Schiegl. Leitner and Resch battled with Grimmette and Martin for the bronze, eventually winning the medal by three-hundredths of a second.

Markus Kleinheinz of Austria unexpectedly captured the men's singles World Cup title. Germany's Georg Hackl, who won four of the seven season races, finished five points behind. Armin Zöggeler of Italy raced to the bronze medal overall and won his third straight gold at the world championships. American Adam Heidt battled into fourth place at the world championships.

After winning six out of seven World Cup races, Germany's Sylke Otto captured her third straight world championship gold and the overall World Cup title. Her teammates Silke Kraushaar and Barbara Niedernhuber finished second and third, respectively, in both the World Cup and the world championships. (JANELE HINMAN)

BOWLING

World Tenpins. The 2002–03 tenpin-bowling season began with the European Cup in Schiedam, Neth., in the first week of September 2002. In the men's final Jouni Helminen of Finland bested England's Nick Froggatt; Germany's Tanya Petty defeated Mhairi Shaw of Scotland for the women's title. In the last week of October, 83 male and 72 female finalists arrived in Riga, Latvia, for the World Tenpin Bowling Association (WTBA) Bowling World Cup. Mika Luoto of Finland outbowled Remy Ong of Singapore 511–438 in the final, and American Shannon Pluhowsky won the women's championship 426–348 over Nikki Harvey of England.

The first major event of 2003 was the World Tenpin Team Cup, held in Odense, Den., in February. Malaysia surprised the bowling world as the Malaysian men beat Sweden and the women triumphed over England. In April the eight top-ranked bowlers (male or female) from each of the three WTBA geographic zones were invited to Dagenham, Eng., to determine the best tournament bowler of the year. Harvey beat Andrew Frawley of Australia 431–402 and took home the $30,000 first prize. The World Ranking Masters for the top 24 men and women (determined after the 2002 ranking tournaments) took place in Lake Wales, Fla., in July. Anders Öhman of Sweden defeated American Bill Hoffman in the three-game final, while Britt Brönssted of Denmark beat Germany's Patricia Schwarz for the women's title.

The world championships were held at the end of September 2003 in Kuala Lumpur, Malaysia. There were 65 nations represented by 348 men and 234 women. Zara Glover of England won the women's singles, the doubles with her partner, Kirsten Penny, and the all-events with an average of 220.25. Trios gold went to the Philippines, and Malaysia captured the women's team championship. The women's stepladder title went to American Diandra Hyman over Liza Clutario of the Philippines. Luoto won the men's singles. Öhman and Tomas Leandersson took the doubles and led Sweden to the men's team title, while Öhman also won the all-events with an average of 230.58. The U.S. won men's trios. Michael Little of Australia defeated Tim Mack of the U.S. en route to the men's stepladder title. Because of the increasing size of the world championships, the WTBA voted to change the format. In the future, men and women would bowl in separate quadrennial tournaments, with the next women's event scheduled for 2005. (YRJÖ SARAHETE)

U.S. Tenpins. Readers of the summer 2003 issue of *American Bowler,* the official publication of the American Bowling Congress (ABC), were startled by a headline-opening sentence of an editorial by the ABC's executive director, Roger Dalkin: "It's time to dissolve the American Bowling Congress." Dalkin, disappointed that both his organization and the Women's International Bowling Congress (WIBC) had rejected a merger with two smaller bowling groups, was suggesting that it was in the "best interests" of the ABC to be disbanded "in order to create a new organization to serve bowlers of all ages, regardless of gender." At their 2003 conventions a majority of the WIBC delegates did favour the merger, but it did not gain the required two-thirds vote needed for passage, while ABC delegates voted 630–628 against the measure. Officials of both groups said that additional efforts would be made to convince delegates that a merger would be beneficial.

The Professional Bowlers Association (PBA) announced that in 2002–03, its second season as a for-profit institution, it showed a 6% increase in ratings for its ESPN TV broadcasts, a 20% increase in membership, and a 35% increase in tournament entries. In competition six-time PBA Player of the Year Walter Ray Williams, Jr., lost to Byron Smith in the final of the ABC Masters in January but came back to win the U.S. Open on February 2 and the PBA world championship on March 9.

AP/Wide World Photos

Walter Ray Williams, Jr., releases the ball in his 226–205 win over fellow American Brian Kretzer in the final round of the PBA world championship in March.

Significant changes for the 2004–05 PBA tournament tour were announced in August. Sixteen of the 20 nationally televised meets would be limited to 64 entrants, 60 of whom would have exempt status for the full season. Exemptions would be determined by bowlers' performances in the 2003–04 season plus an assortment of qualifying events. For the four major tournaments—the Tournament of Champions, the U.S. Open, the ABC Masters, and the PBA world championship—the old qualifying format would be maintained. The 16 standard meets would consist of best-of-seven matches—except for the televised final round—with losers immediately eliminated. The PBA, however, would award each of the 64 entrants a minimum of $2,000 per week.

(JOHN J. ARCHIBALD)

BOXING

The heavyweight boxing division was in an even greater state of flux than normal in 2003 owing to the reluctance of World Boxing Council (WBC) champion Lennox Lewis (U.K.) to fight on a regular basis. Lewis fought just once, defending his title with a controversial sixth-round technical knockout of Vitali Klitschko (Ukraine) on June 21 in Los Angeles. Klitschko, who replaced Lewis's original opponent, Kirk Johnson (Can.), on two weeks' notice after Johnson was injured in training, staggered the titleholder with hard blows to the head in the first and second rounds. The challenger seemed on his way to an upset victory when Lewis opened a cut over Klitschko's left eye with a legal punch in the third round. The exciting give-and-take match was terminated at the end of the sixth round when the ringside physician ruled that Klitschko's cut was too severe for him to continue. This sparked an animated protest from the Ukrainian and set the stage for a rematch, but Lewis decided that he did not want to fight again in 2003 and said that he was unsure whether he would continue to box. Klitschko strengthened his position by knocking out Johnson in the second round of a bout held at New York City's Madison Square Garden on December 6.

In one of the year's most intriguing contests, Roy Jones, Jr. (*see* BIOGRAPHIES), of the U.S. became only the second light heavyweight champion to win a heavyweight title when he scored a 12-round decision over John Ruiz (U.S.) to capture the World Boxing Association (WBA) title on March 1 in Las Vegas, Nev. Rather than remain a heavyweight, however, Jones dropped back down to the light heavyweight division on November 8 and regained the WBC title with a close and controversial decision over Antonio Tarver (U.S.) in Las Vegas.

International Boxing Federation (IBF) heavyweight champion Chris Byrd (U.S.) defended his title against Fres Oquendo (P.R.) on September 20 in Uncasville, Conn., scoring a hotly debated 12-round decision. IBF cruiserweight titleholder James Toney (U.S.) invaded the heavyweight division and knocked out four-time former champion Evander Holyfield (U.S.) in the ninth round of their bout on October 4 in Las Vegas.

Bernard Hopkins (U.S.), the unified WBA, WBC, and IBF middleweight champion, knocked out Morrade Hakkar (France) in the eighth round on March 29 in Philadelphia and won a 12-round decision over William Joppy (U.S.) on December 13 in Atlantic City, N.J. It was Hopkins's 17th successful defense, a division record.

Oscar de la Hoya (U.S.), the sport's biggest attraction outside the heavyweight division, had a mixed year. On May 3 he defended both the WBC and WBA super welterweight (junior middleweight) titles with a seventh-round knockout of Yory Boy Campas (Mex.) in Las Vegas. Although considered a mismatch, the pay-per-view bout was sold to approximately 350,000 homes. In his next bout, on September 13 in Las Vegas, de la Hoya lost a 12-round decision and both titles to Shane Mosley (U.S.), who had also beaten him in a 2000 welterweight bout. It was a skillful, closely contested fight, and de la Hoya and his promoter, Bob Arum, complained bitterly about the unanimous decision, even though a majority of the media agreed with the three judges, who all scored the bout 115–113 in Mosley's favour. The victory restored Mosley's prestige, which had slumped markedly after he lost two of his three previous bouts. Financially, the Mosley–de la Hoya rematch was the biggest fight of the year. A crowd of 16,268 spectators paid a total of approximately $11 million and filled the MGM Grand Garden Arena to capacity, while almost a million homes purchased the pay-per-view, generating more than $50 million.

Light heavyweight Roy Jones, Jr. (left), of the U.S. punches WBA heavyweight champion John Ruiz of the U.S. in their heavyweight title bout in Las Vegas, Nev., on March 1. Jones won in a decision.

AP/Wide World Photos

One of the biggest upsets of the year came on January 25 in Temecula, Calif., when WBA welterweight titleholder Ricardo Mayorga (Nic.) knocked out WBC titlist Vernon Forrest (U.S.) in the third round to gain a second belt. Going into the bout, the technically proficient Forrest had been widely considered one of the sport's most accomplished craftsmen. The colourful Mayorga, who often lit a victory cigarette in the ring after a bout, beat Forrest again on July 12 in Las Vegas with a 12-round decision in defense of both titles. Mayorga's championship reign came to an end on December 13, when he was outpointed by Cory Spinks (U.S.), the son of former heavyweight champion Leon Spinks.

In the most significant women's bout of the year, Laila Ali (U.S.), the daughter of former heavyweight champion Muhammad Ali, knocked out Christy Martin (U.S.) in the fourth round of a bout held on August 23 in Biloxi, Miss. The match set new highs in live attendance (9,888) and pay-per-view revenue, with more than 100,000 buys.

On May 3 boxing returned to network television for the first time in more than a decade when NBC broadcast the Rocky Juarez–Frankie Archuleta featherweight bout, which Juarez, a silver medal winner in the 2000 Olympics, won via a sixth-round knockout. It was the first of the four Budweiser Boxing Series programs that the network aired in 2003. NBC had made a commitment to broadcast at least five more shows in 2004. (NIGEL COLLINS)

CHESS

Gloom spread in the chess world in 2003 as hopes for a timely reunification of the world-title system, as envisaged in the Prague Agreement of May 2002, were not realized. This deferred further the prospect of having a clear answer to the question Who is world chess champion?

The agreement that had apparently healed the schism dating from Russian Garry Kasparov's 1993 breakaway from the world ruling body, the Fédération Internationale des Échecs (FIDE), envisaged a match in the spring of 2003 between Vladimir Kramnik of Russia and Hungarian Peter Leko, with the winner meeting the victor of a match between Kasparov and the holder of the FIDE world title, Ukrainian teenager Ruslan Ponomaryov.

Chronic underfunding of chess proved to be a stumbling block. FIDE announced that the Kasparov-Ponomaryov match would be in Buenos Aires, Arg., but this proved a chimera. Meanwhile, the Kramnik-Leko match was scheduled to be held in Hungary, but the Hungarian government could not raise the prize money of $1 million. The situation was further bedeviled by financial difficulties for the Einstein Group, which had purchased contractual rights for Kramnik's world-title engagements from the Brain Games organization. The latter had run the 2001 Kasparov-Kramnik match in London. The Einstein Group went into liquidation, and Kramnik officially severed all ties with that organization in September.

Ukraine agreed to host the Kasparov match in the autumn, some six months later than envisaged. This was to be opened by symbolic first moves made on the board by Russian Pres. Vladimir Putin and Pres. Leonid Kuchma of Ukraine. Protocol difficulties arose from the legitimate question of which player was to be regarded as the challenger (traditionally the titleholder needed only a drawn match to be declared winner). At one stage Ponomaryov threatened legal action against FIDE over these difficulties. He finally agreed to waive his rights to ensure that the match took place, but when he failed to sign the required contract in time, FIDE reluctantly canceled the match.

The three traditionally strongest tournaments of the year produced contradictory results that did not cast much light on current form and title-match prospects. At the Wijk aan Zee, Neth., tournament, which was held January 10–26, Viswanathan Anand of India scored 8.5 points (from 13 games), relegating Kramnik (with 7 points) to a shared fourth place. Former child prodigy Judit Polgar (8) of Hungary took second place; Kasparov did not participate.

In the double-round event in Linares, Spain, on February 22–March 9, Leko and Kramnik (both with 7 points out of 12) tied for first place, half a point ahead of Anand and Kasparov. The feature of the event was the sacrificial win by new star Teimour Radjabov of Azerbaijan over Kasparov, who claimed that he had played the worst tournament of his life, blundering in every game. At the closing ceremony Kasparov strongly objected to the awarding of a "beauty prize" to Radjabov for his win against his senior colleague.

Russian Garry Kasparov interacts with a virtual chessboard in his match against the X3D Fritz computer program in November. The four-game match ended with one victory each and two draws.

AP/Wide World Photos

As usual, Kasparov, who had got into a dispute with the organizers 10 years earlier, was absent from the third prestigious tournament of the year, in Dortmund, Ger., on July 31–August 10. Kramnik, Anand, and Leko did take part in the double rounder for six players. Moldova's Viorel Bologan, who was rated 42nd in the world, scored a big upset (6.5 out of 10) to head off Kramnik and Anand (both 5.5).

The British championship, held in Edinburgh in July and August, produced another win for a nonresident of the British Isles, Abhijit Kunte of India. A de facto boycott of the event by most of England's leading players (only 5 of the country's 30 grandmasters entered in 2003) led to a constitutional change: in the future, residence in the British Isles or British dependent territories was to be the sole qualification for the tournament.

At the "FIDE Man–Machine" $1 million match held January 26–February 7 at the New York Athletic Club in New York City, Kasparov gained a munificent prize when he drew 3–3 with the Deep Junior program. Kasparov took an early lead and seemed to be well on top when he slipped back. A short draw in the sixth game brought a disappointing end to a big media event. The live audience even greeted the result with a few boos, probably a first in chess history.

Chess at a lower level continued to flourish on the Internet, though this produced its own casualties as traditional clubs found it harder to attract players from their homes to a central venue. The German-language Swiss weekly *Die Schachwoche*, which for more than 20 years had covered international play and advertised forthcoming tournaments, abruptly closed in May. Many people had looked upon *Die Schachwoche* as a kind of trade paper for the chess professional. The management attributed the closure to catastrophic first-quarter losses to the free replication on the Internet of the publication's paid services.

The book of the year was the first volume of a planned trilogy by Kasparov entitled *Garry Kasparov on My Great Predecessors*, which combined shrewd historical narrative with a fresh look at famous games, revealing new facets of their complexities.

Ludek Pachman, the Czech chess grandmaster, prolific author, and famous dissident who had been jailed for his support of the liberalizing Prague Spring of 1968, died in Passau, Ger., on March 6 at the age of 78. Chess historian Ken Whyld of England, joint author of the standard work *The Oxford Companion to Chess*, died on July 11 at age 77. (BERNARD CAFFERTY)

CRICKET

The World Cup was the highlight of the 2002–03 cricket season, though the tournament was marred by political controversy and the suspension of Australian leg spinner Shane Warne for a drugs offense. (*See* Sidebar.) Australia, the hot pretournament favourite, led by captain Ricky Ponting, ended the year

The 2003 Cricket World Cup

Despite political controversy over games to be played in Zimbabwe and Kenya, the suspension of Australian bowler Shane Warne (one of cricket's leading stars) before a ball had been bowled, and the surprise elimination of host nation South Africa, the 2003 World Cup ended on a high note. After 54 matches spread over 43 days, Australia emerged victorious, beating India by 125 runs in the final, held on March 23 in Johannesburg, S.Af., to retain the trophy it had won in England in 1999. Even without Warne, who was later suspended for a year for having taken a diuretic pill given to him by his mother, Australia was a class apart. Matthew Hayden and captain Ricky Ponting were particularly destructive batsmen, and a posse of high-class bowlers was led by Brett Lee and, until an injury forced him to return home, Jason Gillespie.

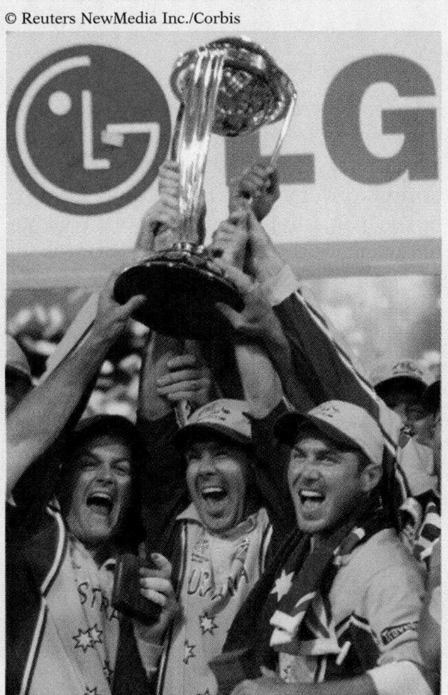

Captain Ricky Ponting (centre) and his teammates raise the trophy commemorating Australia's victory in the cricket World Cup final in Johannesburg, S.Af., on March 23.

England's protracted debate over whether to play in strife-torn Zimbabwe affected the entire mood of the tournament. No one, from the England and Wales Cricket Board to the International Cricket Council (the World Cup organizers), emerged from the wrangling with any credit. When the English team decided to withdraw from its match in Zimbabwe for security reasons, it effectively cost the team a place in the second-round "super six" group of matches. A more effective protest was mounted by two Zimbabwean players, Henry Olonga and Andy Flower, who both wore black armbands in their country's opening match to symbolize the death of democracy in Zimbabwe. Olonga went into hiding after the tournament, and Flower effectively immigrated to England.

New Zealand's similar boycott of its match in Nairobi, Kenya, also skewed the final results, allowing Kenya and Zimbabwe to progress at the expense of more powerful and marketable teams such as West Indies, England, and South Africa. A complex point-scoring system for the second round of matches, which allowed points to be taken forward from first-round games, rendered many of the super six games irrelevant and compounded the growing disinterest in the tournament around the world. Kenya's joy at becoming the first non-Test-playing nation to reach a World Cup semifinal lifted spirits, as did the batting of Canada's John Davison, who scored the fastest century in the tournament's history (in 67 balls against the West Indies), but too many games were one-sided. One match, in which Sri Lanka beat Canada by nine wickets, lasted just 140 balls.

South Africa, one of the pretournament favourites, failed to progress because, in a rain-affected match against Sri Lanka, the batsmen misread the recalculated figures for victory and failed to score off the last ball before rain wiped out play. The South Africans thought that they had won until it became clear that the match had been tied. The extra point put Sri Lanka through at the expense of South Africa. Shaun Pollock, the captain, wept and later was sacked.

India's Sachin Tendulkar, named the Man of the Tournament, scored 673 runs (average 61.18), breaking his own world record for the tournament. Sadly, he failed when it really mattered, in the final, though an unbeaten 140 by Ponting had already effectively sealed the game and the trophy for the defending champions. (ANDREW LONGMORE)

again dominant in both one-day and Test cricket.

Under the leadership of Steve Waugh, Australia won 12 of its 14 Tests through the 2002–03 season, including a 4–1 Ashes series win at home against England; it was the eighth consecutive Ashes victory for Australia, marking the most prolonged period of supremacy by either side in the oldest of all cricketing rivalries. Australia's success, once again, was based on the speed of its run making—with Matthew Hayden, Ponting, and Adam Gilchrist leading the way with some destructive hitting—and the variety of its bowling attack. The sustained pace of Brett Lee and Jason Gillespie, the accurate fast-medium bowling of Glenn McGrath, and the consummate leg spin of Warne sustained a growing belief that the 2003 Australian team was the best of all time.

England did not help its own cause. On the opening morning of the first Test, held in Brisbane, captain Nasser Hussain won the toss and elected to put the Australians in to bat. Australia was 364 for 2 at the close of play on the first day, and, though England fought back, the psychological balance of the series had already swung decisively in favour of the home team. England lost the first Test by 384 runs and after just 11 days of Test cricket had lost the next two Tests and the Ashes urn once again.

England had to console itself with the individual performance of Michael Vaughan, who completed a memorable international season by scoring 633 runs (average 63.3), including three centuries, the highest aggregate total on either side. England won the last Test in Sydney, but the unequal struggle seemed to drain the life out of Hussain. After the drawn first Test against South Africa in the summer, he resigned from the captaincy and was replaced by Vaughan.

In a year of modest Test cricket often played on poorly prepared pitches, one match stood out. Having lost the first three Tests of its series against Australia, a young West Indies side reached

418 for 7 to win the fourth Test in Antigua; this was a record total for a fourth innings in Test cricket. Ramnaresh Sarwan and Shivnarine Chanderpaul both made centuries, which augured well for the recovery of a once-proud cricketing side, but the series was marred by some ugly on-field confrontations between Brian Lara, Sarwan, McGrath, and Hayden. This later led the Australians, the chief culprits in the spread of sledging (systematic verbal abuse of the batsmen), to adopt a written code of conduct for the 2003–04 season.

After its disappointing early exit from the World Cup, South Africa chose 22-year-old Graeme Smith to replace Shaun Pollock as captain, a dramatic move designed to usher South African cricket into a new era after the traumas of the match-fixing allegations and the death in 2002 of disgraced former captain Hansie Cronje. Smith proved a resilient leader and, in the opening two Tests in England, an inspired opening batsman. Strong and unorthodox, the left-hander bludgeoned England for two double centuries (277 and 259) in successive Tests, the latter surpassing Sir Don Bradman as the highest score by an overseas player at Lord's. Makhaya Ntini, the leader of a vibrant new generation of black South African cricketers, took 10 wickets in the second Test to secure England's defeat by an innings, a less-than-auspicious start to Vaughan's captaincy. England fought back to level the series 1–1 and, after losing the fourth match, won the final Test at the Oval with a double century from Marcus Trescothick (219) and 124 from the recalled Graham Thorpe in easily the most enthralling and competitive Test series of the year.

The West Indies showed signs of revival with Lara restored to the captaincy, but Pakistan, India, New Zealand, and Sri Lanka were all in varying stages of transition both on and off the field, while Zimbabwe's cricket reflected the fragility of a country in political turmoil and Bangladesh, the most recent Test-playing nation, lost all 11 of its Test matches, 7 of them by an innings. The one personal feat of note came from Muttiah Muralitharan of Sri Lanka, who took his 450th Test wicket against New Zealand with his unorthodox spin. (*See* BIOGRAPHIES.)

In domestic cricket a new 20-over-a-side floodlit competition was launched in England and proved a great success, particularly among a younger age group. The inaugural competition was won by Surrey. The county championship was won by Sussex for the first time in the county's history, while Gloucestershire won the one-day C&G Trophy. In Australia, New South Wales completed the double, winning the Pura Cup for four-day cricket and the ING one-day tournament.

(ANDREW LONGMORE)

CURLING

The United States won its first women's world curling championship in a 2003 season that was otherwise dominated by the traditional powerhouse Canadians, but it took a Canadian-born skip, Debbie McCormick of Madison, Wis., to turn the trick for the U.S. McCormick, who was born in Saskatoon, Sask., defeated five-time Canadian champion Colleen Jones 5–3 at the world championships in Winnipeg, Man., in April. American women had made it to the final three previous times—in 1992, 1996, and 1999—since the women's event began in 1979, without claiming the gold medal. The defeat was particularly bitter for Jones. The 2001 world champion had gone undefeated in 10 games at the weeklong tournament heading into her showdown with McCormick.

Anette Norberg of Sweden won the women's bronze medal, defeating Dordi Nordby of Norway 7–5. The other women's finishers, in order, were Switzerland, Russia, Scotland, Denmark, Italy, and Japan.

Canadian-born skip Debbie McCormick poses with her gold medal and trophy after guiding the U.S. women's team to victory in the women's world curling championship in April.

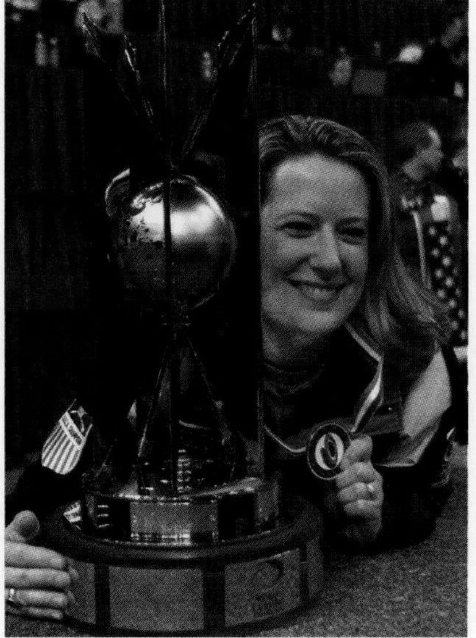

AP/Wide World Photos

Canada's Randy Ferbey defeated Ralph Stöckli of Switzerland 10–6 for the men's world title. Ferbey became the first skip in more than 30 years to win consecutive world championships, matching Canadian Don Duguid's record, and added a record 28th Canadian gold medal to the country's total since the worlds started in 1959.

Olympic champion Pål Trulsen of Norway won the men's bronze with a 9–7 win over Finland's Markku Uusipaavalniemi. The rest of the men's field were, in order, Sweden, Denmark, Scotland, the U.S., Germany, and South Korea, which was making its first appearance at the world curling championships.

At the world junior curling championships, held in Flims, Switz., in March, Canada won both the men's and the women's golds. Steve Laycock defeated Sweden's Eric Carlsen for Canada's sixth consecutive men's junior crown, while Marliese Miller defeated American Cassandra Johnson for the women's title. Miller became the first woman junior to go undefeated at the world championship, with a perfect 11–0 record.

(BRUCE CHEADLE)

CYCLING

Cycling's premier road event, the Tour de France, celebrated its centenary in 2003 and was won for a record-equaling fifth time by American Lance Armstrong, who also joined Miguel Indurain to become one of only two persons to have won in five consecutive years. Armstrong matched the five victories of Jacques Anquetil (1957, 1961–64), Eddy Merckx (1969–72, 1974), Bernard Hinault (1978–79, 1981–82, 1985), and Indurain (1991–95) when he reached the finish line in Paris 1 min 01 sec ahead of Germany's Jan Ullrich on overall time after three weeks and 3,427.5 km (about 2,130 mi) of racing. Joseba Beloki of Spain had crashed in stage nine and was forced to retire while in second place overall, 40 sec behind, and Ullrich had beaten Armstrong by 1 min 36 sec in the 47-km (29-mi) individual time trial from Gaillac to Cap'Découverte (stage 12) to close to within 34 sec. Armstrong had held the lead from the 8th of the 20 stages, but his overall victory was assured only on the penultimate day when Ullrich crashed on wet roads in the final time trial.

Mario Cipollini of Italy claimed two stages of the Tour of Italy (Giro d'Italia) to take his career total to 42, beating Alfredo Binda's record of 41, which had stood since 1933. His countryman

© AFP/Corbis

Cyclist Paolo Bettini of Italy crosses the finish line in the Milan–San Remo road race in March, the first of the three races he won en route to the overall cycling World Cup title.

Gilberto Simoni was the overall winner. Another Italian sprinter, Alessandro Petacchi, secured six stage wins in Italy, four stages in the Tour de France before retiring in the mountains, and five stages of the third major national tour, the Tour of Spain (Vuelta a España), which was won by Spaniard Roberto Heras.

Italy's Paolo Bettini was the overall winner of the World Cup series, decided over 10 road races between March and October, and set a record for the competition with victory in three rounds. The death of Kazakh rider Andrei Kivilev, who suffered fatal head injuries when he crashed on the second stage of the Paris–Nice road race in March, prompted the sport's governing body, the Union Cycliste Internationale (UCI), to make the wearing of hard helmets compulsory in all elite events. Kivilev was not wearing a helmet when he fell.

The UCI world track championships were moved from Shenzen, China, to Stuttgart, Ger., because of concerns over the outbreak of SARS (severe acute respiratory syndrome) in China. Australia broke its own world record by more than two seconds with a time of 3 min 57.280 sec in the final of the 4,000-m team pursuit. Leontien Zijlaard-van Moorsel of The Netherlands won the individual pursuit for her ninth world championship title. In October she set a women's one-hour world record of 46.065 km (about 28.62 mi).

(JOHN R. WILKINSON)

EQUESTRIAN SPORTS

Thoroughbred Racing. *United States.* Thoroughbred horse racing in the U.S., which less than a decade earlier had maintained a hostile stance toward competition from casinos, in 2003 moved closer to forging a partnership with its old adversary. In the eight states that allowed racetracks to have electronic gaming devices, Thoroughbred racing and breeding programs that had been on the brink of extinction were revitalized with an influx of cash from slot-machine revenue. At least a dozen other states were taking "racino" legislation under serious consideration.

The New York Racing Association (NYRA) was the subject of a scathing 64-page report released by New York State Attorney General Eliot Spitzer in June following a three-year investigation that uncovered alleged abuses by employees at NYRA-operated tracks. NYRA president Terry Meyocks resigned his position on September 29.

Funny Cide dominated the racing headlines in the spring by becoming the first New York-bred horse and the first gelding since Clyde Van Dusen in 1929 to win the Kentucky Derby. Almost a week later, scandal was threatened when a controversial photo taken of the finish appeared to show an illegal prodding device in the right hand of winning jockey José Santos. The Churchill Downs board of stewards exonerated Santos of any wrongdoing, however, when they concluded that he was carrying nothing except his whip. Funny Cide scored a convincing victory in the Preakness Stakes two weeks later, but he failed in his bid to become the first Triple Crown winner since Affirmed in 1978 when Empire Maker, which had run second in the Derby and skipped the Preakness, raced to victory in the Belmont Stakes with jockey Jerry D. Bailey on board. Ten Most Wanted, ridden by Pat Day, finished a close second, with Funny Cide third.

The Breeders' Cup World Thoroughbred Championships, held at Santa Anita Park in Arcadia, Calif., on October 25, proved to be entertaining and eventful. A dead heat was recorded for the first time in the 20-year history of the event when Johar and High Chaparral finished on even terms in the Breeders' Cup Turf. Julie Krone became the first female jockey to win a nonsteeplechase Breeders' Cup race when she guided Halfbridled to victory in the Juvenile Fillies. Pleasantly Perfect's win in the $4 million Classic gave trainer Richard Mandella a record fourth win on the program—he had saddled Halfbridled and High Chaparral as well as Action This Day, the winner in the Juvenile. The Ultra Pick 6 wager on Breeders' Cup day raised eyebrows for the second straight year when a lone bettor, in Rapid City, S.D., parlayed an $8 wager into the only ticket in the country with all six winners, worth $2.6 million.

Jockey Gary Stevens, who portrayed George ("The Iceman") Woolf in the 2003 movie *Seabiscuit,* was nearly killed in a bizarre spill in the Arlington Million, at Arlington Park outside Chicago, on August 16. His mount, Storming Home, veered sharply crossing the finish line, unseating Stevens into the path of oncoming horses. Stewards disqualified Storming Home from victory in the $1 million race, and the win was

Empire Maker, with jockey Jerry D. Bailey on board, splashes his way to victory ahead of Ten Most Wanted and jockey Pat Day in the Belmont Stakes on June 7.

AP/Wide World Photos

given to runner-up Sulamani. Stevens suffered a collapsed lung but returned to riding less than three weeks later.

Bobby Frankel set a new single-season North American training record in 2003. Sightseek, which won the Beldame Stakes on October 4 at Belmont Park, was Frankel's 23rd victory in a Grade I stakes, which broke the record set by D. Wayne Lukas in 1987. On October 31 Frankel surpassed Lukas's single-season earnings record of $17,842,358. On November 29 at the NYRA's Aqueduct, Bailey won three stakes races on the program to reach 70 for the year and break Mike Smith's single-season record of 68. Bailey surpassed his own 2002 North American single-season $19.2 million earnings record by pocketing $23,354,960.

Two legendary jockeys died in 2003—Johnny Longden, who at the time of his retirement in 1966 held the record for wins, and Bill Shoemaker, who had broken Longden's record in 1970. (*See* OBITUARIES.) Thoroughbred owner and breeder Henryk de Kwaitkowski, who had purchased famed Calumet Farm for $17 million at auction in 1992, died at age 79 in March. Laffit Pincay, Jr., who had surpassed Shoemaker as racing's all-time leading jockey in 1999 and rode a record 9,531 winners during his long career, announced his retirement at the age of 56 on April 29, 2003, nearly two months after he fractured his neck in a spill at Santa Anita.

Equine deaths in 2003 included Spectacular Bid, which succumbed to a heart attack at age 27. He won 26 of 30 career starts during 1978–80, including the 1979 Kentucky Derby and Preakness Stakes, and was undefeated in nine starts as a four-year-old in 1980, the year he was named Horse of the Year and retired with earnings of $2.7 million. Sunny's Halo, winner of the 1983 Kentucky Derby, was humanely destroyed at age 23. (JOHN G. BROKOPP)

International. In 2003 the introduction of North American-style alternatives to turf courses was accelerating in European Thoroughbred racing. Sweden, Germany, and Belgium had been the first European countries to introduce dirt racing, and Lingfield Park had opened the first British "all-weather" track in October 1989. Cagnes-sur-Mer and Pau, two winter courses located in the south of France, first used fibresand tracks in January 2000. Another French track, Deauville, a year-round training centre as well as the scene of top-class summer racing, opened one in July 2003 and scheduled its first all-dirt meeting for December 2003–January 2004. In Great Britain the greater use of dirt tracks led to an expansion of the fixture list, which would mean racing seven days a week throughout most of 2004. Ireland was the last important European racing country without such a course, but one was planned at Naas.

Ireland staged the race of the year when High Chaparral, ridden by Mick Kinane, narrowly beat Falbrav and Islington in the Irish Champion Stakes at Leopardstown in September. High Chaparral and Islington followed up with victories in Breeders' Cup races at Santa Anita Park in Arcadia, Calif., in October. The fourth- and fifth-place horses at Leopardstown were Alamshar, which won the Irish Derby in June and became the only horse to beat the champion three-year-old Dalakhani, and Moon Ballad, winner of the 2003 Dubai World Cup. Alamshar and Dalakhani, which won the Prix de l'Arc de Triomphe over Mubtaker and High Chaparral at Longchamp in Paris, were both owned by the Aga Khan. He retired Dalakhani to stud in Ireland but sold Alamshar to Japanese breeders.

Falbrav was trained in Italy until after he won the Japan Cup in November 2002. The half-Japanese-owned colt moved to trainer Luca Cumani at Newmarket in England and won four G1 races; he ended his career with a two-length defeat of Rakti in the Hong Kong Cup in December before being retired to stud in Japan. Rakti was also moved to England and won G1 races in Italy and England. Choisir was one of the sensations of the summer in England. The giant Australian-trained sprinter won twice at Royal Ascot in the space of five days, taking the G1 Golden Jubilee Stakes in record time. He put up a heroic fight when beaten by Oasis Dream in the July Cup at Newmarket 19 days later.

Although they won big prizes, Coolmore Stud and Godolphin, the two biggest competitors in European racing, generally had quiet years. Sheikh Muhammad al-Maktoum, the moving spirit behind Godolphin, allowed his trainers a wider range of horse types on both sides of the Atlantic and experienced more success with runners in his own colours. Darley, the sheikh's management company, expanded into Japan with six horses competing in Regional Racing, the lower level of the sport. Darley also built a successful breeding program in Dubai, and Campsie Fells, winner of the Prix Vanteaux at Longchamp in April, became the first Group race winner bred there. She was followed by two more U.A.E.-bred Group winners, Splendid Era and Cairns, at Newmarket in October. Lucky Strike became the first Dutch-trained winner of a Group race when he took the Prix de la Porte Maillot at Longchamp in June.

Coolmore changed its jockey in November, replacing Kinane with Jamie Spencer. Kinane, who captured his 13th Irish championship, had four winners on the last day of the season, including two on his final rides for the Coolmore trainer, Aidan O'Brien. Kinane joined Alamshar's trainer, John Oxx, taking over from Johnny Murtagh, who had struggled with his weight. Kieren Fallon was British champion for the sixth time in seven years. Christophe Soumillon won his first championship in France and became the first jockey to ride 200 winners there since Cash Asmussen in 1988. Pat Eddery, the second most successful jockey ever in Britain, with 4,632 wins and 11 championships, retired in November.

Wando, ridden by Patrick Husbands, was the first Canadian Triple Crown winner since Peteski in 1993, with victories in the Queen's Plate, the Prince of Wales, and the Breeders' Stakes. Trainer Andrew Balding, whose excellent first season in Britain included winning the Epsom Oaks with Casual Look, sent Phoenix Reach to capture the Canadian International. Balding's first horse to run in Australia, Paraca, fared less well, finishing last to Fields of Omagh in the Cox Plate. Northerly, winner of the previous two Cox Plates and Australian Horse of the Year for 2002–03, suffered a serious injury in August. Makybe Diva, bred in Britain by her Australian owner, ran fourth to Mummify in the Caulfield Cup and then beat an international field in the Melbourne Cup 17 days later.

Owner-breeder Jean-Luc Lagardère died in March. He was a major industrialist and had been president of France-Galop, the sport's ruling body in France, since 1995. (*See* OBITUARIES.) (ROBERT W. CARTER)

Harness Racing. No Pan Intended became only the 10th pacer in harness-racing history to sweep the Triple Crown when he won the Cane Pace, Little Brown Jug, and Messenger Stakes in 2003. The bay colt came into the season lightly regarded, but he soon developed an enthusiastic following for his workmanlike way of winning. He captured the Cane Pace at Freehold

Raceway in New Jersey on September 1 and followed with a victory in the Little Brown Jug at the Delaware (Ohio) county fair on September 18. That put strong pressure on No Pan Intended to win the Messenger Stakes on October 18 at The Meadows, a track south of Pittsburgh, Pa. Driver David Miller made a determined bid at the start of the one-mile race and grabbed the lead after a quarter of a mile. Then Miller slowed the tempo and dared anyone to challenge him. When other horses attacked in the final quarter mile, No Pan Intended was ready; he held them off to win by more than a length in his 10th straight victory. "This horse doesn't do anything fancy," said winning owner Bob Glazer after the race. "He just gets the job done." No Pan Intended had originally been named Pacific Wish by his breeder, but Glazer, whose Peter Pan Stable was inspired by a childhood nickname, came up with a new name after paying $150,000 for the colt as a yearling in 2001.

While No Pan Intended was the top three-year-old pacer in harness racing, the three-year-old trotters took turns winning major races. Canadian-owned Amigo Hall pulled an upset at the Meadowlands Racetrack in East Rutherford, N.J., when he won the $1 million Hambletonian at odds of 27–1 on August 2. Sugar Trader won the Yonkers Trot, while Mr. Muscleman won the Canadian Trotting Classic and the Kentucky Futurity.

The dominant older pacer in North America in 2003 was the four-year-old Art Major. In 11 starts he won 8 races and placed second 3 times, banking $1,082,930 for the year. He retired in early October to begin breeding service in New York. The six-year-old pacing mare Eternal Camnation continued to defy time as she raced her way to $3 million in career earnings. Her matches against five-year-old Bunny Lake and four-year-old Worldly Beauty drew loyal and enthusiastic fans, who knew they were watching racing history in the making.

In Europe the German-owned trotter Abano As splashed over a sloppy track at the Vincennes course outside Paris to win the Prix d'Amerique in late January. Driver Jos Verbeeck asked Abano As for every ounce of courage in the final strides to hold off Insert Gede and Gigant Neo in the marathon race over 2,700 m (about 1.7 mi). Four months later five-year-old From Above showed determination and class when he upset cofavourites Victory Tilly and Scarlet Knight to win the prestigious Elitlopp, a one-mile race at the Solvalla racecourse in Stockholm. From Above and driver Orjan Kihlstrom surged past the leaders in the final strides.

In early April, Baltic Eagle came into the Inter-Dominion Pacing Final in Christchurch, N.Z., seemingly unbeatable. Trainer-driver Kim Prentice raced Baltic Eagle with great confidence, sitting on the outside most of the race and winning by a length over fellow Australian pacer Mont Denver Gold. The third-place finisher was Holmes D G, representing New Zealand.

(DEAN A. HOFFMAN)

Steeplechasing. Best Mate, ridden by Jim Culloty, was the champion steeplechaser in Britain in 2003, winning his second consecutive Cheltenham Gold Cup by 10 lengths. Monty's Pass, with Barry Geraghty on board, became the third Irish-trained winner of the Grand National in five years, with a 12-length triumph on April 5. Two weeks later Culloty guided Timbera to victory in the Irish Grand National. Rooster Booster won the Champion Hurdle at Cheltenham, and the Irish-trained mare Nobody Told Me won the French equivalent, the Grande Course de Haies d'Auteuil. Line Marine, another mare, defeated the English-trained Batman Senora in the Grand Steeple-Chase de Paris in May. (ROBERT W. CARTER)

FENCING

With the previous year's problems regarding the fencing quotas for the 2004 Olympic Games behind it, the Fédération Internationale d'Escrime (FIE) in 2003 returned to its program of modernization and, in particular, the rules and refereeing problems associated with foil. The target at foil was restricted, and a white light was used to indicate off-target hits. In addition, the classical definition of an attack had little in common with current practice. The result was a messy spectacle that was difficult for the nonexpert to follow. Several solutions to the problem had been proposed, but the most promising strategy was to require longer contact time between the weapon point and the target to register a hit (thus removing the flick hit) and to dispense with the white light and ignore the off-target hits. This would allow the use of wireless apparatus, render the metallic piste (the strip on which play takes place) redundant and thus reduce costs, and allow for continuous and comprehensible play with fewer interruptions.

During 2003 the Western and Central European monopoly of individual junior and cadet world championship medals was breached as the U.S. took two gold medals and China captured three. The U.S. also topped the world rankings in women's sabre after the junior/cadet world championships, while Israel took third place in men's épée. In the senior world championships, held in Havana in October, Italy and Russia dominated the medals. France slipped to fifth place, and China rose to eighth.

Doping had always been unusual in fencing, but in 2003 one French fencer was found to be exceeding the limits of 19-Norandrosterone (a banned substance) and after a series of FIE Commission meetings and appeals was duly penalized. Some matters on the periphery of the case continued at year's end.

(GRAHAM MORRISON)

AP/Wide World Photos

At the fencing world championships, which were held in Havana in October, Viktoriya Nikishina of Russia lunges at her Polish opponent, Magdalena Mroczkiewicz, in the women's team foil final; Poland defeated Russia for its first gold medal in the event.

FOOTBALL

Association Football (Soccer). *Europe.* In 2003 national teams were occupied with qualifying for the final stages of Euro 2004, the European association football (soccer) championship to be held in Portugal in 2004, but the continuing conflict of club against country dominated the region.

While fan violence had not vanished from the soccer scene, another worrying trend was the increase in racist abuse, particularly against black players. Some of the worst instances of abuse involved countries of the former Yugoslavia against players from Western Europe. The English Football Association (FA) was fined £99,000 (£1 = about $1.67) in May for two pitch invasions and racist chanting by spectators at England's match with Turkey in Sunderland, Eng., the previous month. The Union des Associations Européennes de Football (UEFA) also warned the FA that further misconduct would result in expulsion from the Euro 2004 competition.

While there was a consensus of opinion concerning the extensive demands on the physical fitness of leading players, there were differing views on a solution. The Fédération Internationale de Football Association (FIFA) wanted fewer domestic matches, while clubs, which paid the players' wages, considered that there were too many international matches. The situation was brought into sharp focus by the untimely death of Marc-Vivien Foé, the 28-year-old international player (for the Cameroon national team) who collapsed during the Confederations Cup match with Colombia on June 26. As an example of the punishing schedule faced by some players, Gilberto Silva, a Brazilian international midfielder, was due to travel more than 28,900 km (about 18,000 mi) in a round trip from England, where he played for Arsenal, to Brazil in order to compete for his country in two World Cup qualifying matches. This included 36 hours of air travel in 10 days.

FIFA was also keen to restrict the number of international noncompetitive games (friendlies) and replace them with more competitive matches, in which substitutions were restricted to three per team. This would prevent national team managers and coaches from fielding unlimited numbers of substitutes. As an example, when England met Australia in February, it used one team in the first half and another 11 players in the second half. Increasing the number of competitive international games in which clubs would be forced to release star players could provide another collision course between FIFA and the clubs.

Germany's Maren Meinert (right) and Frida Oestberg of Sweden jostle for possession of the ball in the women's FIFA World Cup final in Carson, Calif., in October. Meinert scored the first of Germany's goals in its 2–1 victory.

AP/Wide World Photos

Though transfer fees (the money involved in player trades) and the number of transfers had been reduced somewhat since the introduction of the so-called Bosman ruling in 1995, which allowed more freedom of contract for players, the purchase by Russian oil billionaire Roman Abramovich of the English club Chelsea in July saw unprecedented spending on 13 players for a total of £111 million. The arrivals included Juan Sebastián Verón, the Argentine international midfield player who had been, for a year, the most expensive player in England when he was signed by Manchester United from Italy's Lazio in 2001 for £28.1 million. Chelsea paid United only £15.2 million for Verón, while its most expensive recruit was Ireland international playmaker Damien Duff, who was acquired from Blackburn Rovers for £17 million. Chelsea also pulled off another coup with the capture of Manchester United chief executive Peter Kenyon, who was thought to have been the architect over the previous three years of extending the Old Trafford club's global popularity and wealth.

David Beckham, the Manchester United and England midfielder and the most celebrated soccer player in the world, was transferred to Spain's Real Madrid in a complicated financial deal disclosed at £23.5 million. As part of the deal, United decided to take £11.1 million of the transfer fee up front instead of waiting for staggered payments totalling £12 million over four years because it wanted to balance its accounts, despite being considered one of the richest clubs in the world. Beckham was said to be earning £100,000 a week plus £20 million a year in commercial contracts.

On May 28 the UEFA Champions League final, played at United's Old Trafford ground, was decided by a penalty shoot-out after a defense-dominated goalless draw. It was an all-Italian affair, with AC Milan edging Juventus 3–2 on penalties. Milan's Clarence Seedorf made history as the first player to have appeared on the winning team for three different clubs in the competition—he had previously appeared with Amsterdam's Ajax in 1995 and Real Madrid in 1998. Milan's captain, Paolo Maldini, tied with Beckham with 81 Champions League appearances, the most in qualifying and group games over the 11 seasons since the former European Cup of the Champions changed its name. Maldini also equaled the feat of his father, Cesare Maldini, who had led Milan to European Cup success in 1963.

In the 2003 final Milan probably deserved ultimate victory for its enterprise over the first 90 minutes. Both teams employed a 4–4–2 formation, and neither yielded any ground. It was appropriate that Milan's standout player, Ukrainian Andrey Shevchenko, scored the crucial goal in the shoot-out. He had come closest to scoring in the ninth minute of play when his effort was ruled out for being offside. Eight minutes later Juventus goalkeeper Gianluigi Buffon had made the save of the match from Filippo Inzaghi. Juventus, which missed the influence of suspended playmaker Pavel Nedved, the Czech Republic international, had additional problems when five members of the team refused to take penalties in the shoot-out. Dida Silva Nelson, Milan's Brazilian goalkeeper, made three penalty saves, but—in a clear violation of the rules—moved before the kick was taken on each occasion.

Barcelona enjoyed a record 11 successive victories in Champions League matches. Rosenborg of Norway's ninth consecutive qualification in the 2003–04 series was another milestone, with captain Roar Strand having appeared in each season. Another Norwegian team, Lyn, produced an outstanding individual feat when Eldar Hadzhimemedovic, an 18-year-old Bosnian, scored not only his first goals for the club but also all six goals in a qualifying match against Runavik of the Faroe Islands.

On May 21 the final of the UEFA Cup between Scotland's Glasgow Celtic and Portugal's FC Porto in a baking-hot Sevilla, Spain, also needed overtime and produced five goals from open play. The traditional formula with a clash of styles made for an absorbing contest as Porto revealed patience, technical skill, and enough gamesmanship to upset the opposition but not the referee. Celtic used a more direct, physical approach but went behind in first-half injury time when Brazilian Anderson de Souza Deco crossed the ball for Russian Dmitry Alenichev to shoot. Celtic goalkeeper Robert Douglas parried the effort, but Deco's Brazilian colleague Vanderlei Fernandes Derlei followed up to open the score.

It took only two minutes after the break for Celtic to level the scoring when Swedish international Henrik Larsson, unchallenged, headed a centre by Didier Agathe. In 54 minutes Porto restored its lead. Derlei set up Alenichev only for Larsson to head the second and Celtic's equalizer three minutes later. In case of overtime UEFA had decided to use its new "silver goal" ruling: if a goal was scored in either of the two halves of extra time, the match would conclude at the next break, in contrast to a golden goal, which would instantly signal the end of play. Crucially for Celtic it had had defender Bobo Balde sent off for his second yellow card in the 95th minute, and 10 minutes later Derlei settled the issue when Celtic defenders were slow to clear after Douglas had made a partial save.

Domestically the most serious problems surrounded Azerbaijan, where the dispute between leading clubs and the Football Association prevented the championship from being held. This was followed by a ban from FIFA on international matches, which threatened Azerbaijan's involvement in Euro 2004 until a settlement was reached. In Bulgaria, CSKA Sofia broke all local records by winning its first 13 league games and recaptured the title from rival Levski. League and Cup double winners included Bayern Munich, Germany's most successful club in both competitions, while in Scotland, Glasgow Rangers won all three senior trophies.

Because of the Middle East crisis, Israel was forced to play all international and club matches against foreign teams in a neutral European country.

(JACK ROLLIN)

The Americas. Brazil, winner of the 2002 FIFA World Cup, finished 2003 as the champion in all men's categories after having defeated Spain for the under-20 and under-17 titles. In both events three of the four semifinalists (Brazil, Argentina, and Colombia) were from South America. The only tournaments Brazil did not win in 2003 were the CONFUT (formerly CONCACAF) Gold Cup, in which it lost to Mexico 1–0 in the final, and FIFA's Confederations Cup, but on both occasions Brazil sent below-strength teams.

Boca Juniors was South America's most successful club, winning its fifth Libertadores de América Cup by beating Brazil's Santos 5–1 on aggregate in home and away finals and its third Intercontinental Cup with a 3–1 victory on penalties, after a 1–1 draw on goals, over Italy's European Cup champion AC Milan in Yokohama, Japan. The South American Cup, in its second season, had a surprise winner in Cienciano from Cuzco, Peru, which beat Argentina's River Plate 4–3 on aggregate in the final. Two Mexican clubs played the final of the CONFUT club tournament, with Toluca defeating Morelia 5–4 on aggregate at home and away.

On the domestic scene, Brazil's Cruzeiro captured the Minas Gerais state championship, the Brazilian Cup (knockout), and the national championship. Cruzeiro also had a 36-match unbeaten run, but the club did not take part in international cups. In Argentina the opening championship was stopped for almost a month after serious hooligan trouble, while in Peru the closing championship was suspended when players went on strike for lack of payment and no agreement could be reached. Serious financial difficulties continued at many of the continent's clubs, despite an influx of cash from the transfer of South America's top players to Europe. In the U.S. the San Jose Earthquakes won their second Major League Soccer championship when they defeated the Chicago Fire 4–2 in the MLS Cup final.

The women's FIFA World Cup, which had been scheduled to be held in China, was moved to the U.S. because of the outbreak of SARS (severe acute respiratory syndrome) in Asia. Germany defeated Sweden 2–1 in the final, held in Carson, Calif., on October 12. The top-ranked U.S. finished in third place. In the Women's United Soccer Association, the Washington Freedom beat the Atlanta Beat 2–1 in overtime for the Founders Cup in August, but the U.S. professional organization was shut down just days before the World Cup began.

(ERIC WEIL)

Africa and Asia. On Nov. 30, 2003, in Aba, Nigeria, Enyimba established a 2–0 lead on its home leg of the African Champions League final against the Egyptian team Ismaili. In the second leg, played in Ismailia, Egypt, on December 12, Ismaili won 1–0, but it was beaten 2–1 on aggregate scores for the title. In the African Cup Winners' Cup, Étoile du Sahel from Tunisia achieved a dramatic victory over the Nigerian team Julius Berger on December 6 in Sousse, Tun., having lost its away leg 2–0 in Abeokuta, Nigeria, on November

15. The Tunisian team scored three times for a 3–2 aggregate win.

The Asian Football Confederation Champions League saw the U.A.E. team Al-Ain defeat BEC Tero Sasana of Thailand 2–0, 0–1 in the two-leg final. The inaugural East Asian Cup was won by South Korea, which drew 0–0 with Japan but was victorious because the team had scored more goals in the tournament. A crowd of 62,633 fans watched the final in the Yokohama (Japan) International Stadium on December 10. (JACK ROLLIN)

U.S. Football. *College.* For the 2003–04 season, the University of Southern California (USC) and Louisiana State University (LSU) shared the national championship of college football in the first split decision since 1997, despite a six-year-old process designed to crown an undisputed champion in the big budget teams' Division I-A of the National Collegiate Athletic Association (NCAA). Pacific-10 Conference winner USC (12–1) defeated Big Ten champion Michigan (10–3) by a score of 28–14 in the Rose Bowl on Jan. 1, 2004, and Southeastern Conference winner LSU (13–1) defeated Oklahoma (12–2) 21–14 in the Sugar Bowl, the Bowl Championship Series (BCS) nominal national championship game, three days later. USC won its first national title since 1978 in the media members' poll, while LSU won its first title since 1958 in the coaches' poll, which was obligated to select the Sugar Bowl winner. The computerized selection of the teams to play in the BCS championship game was controversial for the fourth time in six years, and there was pressure to change the process after USC was left out of the Sugar Bowl despite ranking first in both the coaches' and media polls before the bowl games.

The polls agreed on the third through fifth rankings of Oklahoma (12–2), Fiesta Bowl winner Ohio State (11–2), and Big East champion Miami of Florida (11–2), which defeated Atlantic Coast Conference champion Florida State (10–3) in the Orange Bowl. Other conference champions were Fiesta Bowl loser Kansas State (11–4) in the Big 12, Utah (10–2) in the Mountain West, Boise State (13–1) in the Western Athletic, North Texas (9–4) in the Sun Belt, and Southern Mississippi (9–4) in Conference U.S.A.

Oklahoma dominated individual awards, led by Jason White, who won the Heisman Trophy as the top player and the Davey O'Brien Award as the top quarterback. Teddy Lehman won both the Chuck Bednarik Award (for defensive players) and the Dick Butkus Award for linebackers, while Derrick Strait gained both the Bronko Nagurski Trophy (for defenders) and the Jim Thorpe Award for cornerbacks. Defensive tackle Tommie Harris was awarded the Vince Lombardi Award for linemen. Oklahoma led Division I-A with 45.2 points per regular-season game and defensive averages of 145.9 yd passing and 255.6 total yards allowed.

Also winning recognition as top players were Maxwell Award-winning quarterback Eli Manning of Mississippi (Indianapolis Colts quarterback Peyton Manning's younger brother) and Walter Camp Award-winning wide receiver Larry Fitzgerald of Pittsburgh, who received the top receiver's award with 1,672 yd and 22 touchdowns, both of which led Division 1-A. Offensive tackle Robert Gallery of Iowa won the Outland Trophy for interior linemen, while other position awards went to Michigan's Chris Perry for running backs, Miami's Kellen Winslow II for tight ends, Mississippi's Jonathan Nichols for kickers, and Ohio State's B.J. Sander for punters. B.J. Symons was the I-A leader with 5,336 yd passing, 48 touchdown passes, and 456.3 yd total offense per game for Texas Tech, which was also the team leader with 473.5 yd passing and 584.6 total yards per game. Patrick Cobbs's 152.7 yd rushing per game for North Texas and DeAngelo Williams's 192.1 all-purpose yards per game for Memphis were designated the best (Kansas State's Darren Sproles exceeded both totals but played in more games). Other individual highs were Lance Moore's 103 catches for Toledo, Bradlee Van Pelt's 9.9 yd per pass for Colorado State, and Philip Rivers's 170.5 passer rating points and .720 completion percentage for North Carolina State. LSU allowed the fewest points, 10.8 per game, while the team rushing leaders per game were Navy with 326.1 yd on offense and Ohio State with 60.5 yd allowed per game.

Delaware (15–1) was the champion in Division I-AA, Grand Valley State of Michigan (14–1) topped Division II, St. John's of Minnesota (14–0) headed Division III, and Carroll of Montana (15–0) won the National Association of Intercollegiate Athletics (NAIA) championship. St. John's ended the NCAA-record 55-game winning streak of Mount Union of Ohio and gave coach John Gagliardi a record 414 wins, while Blake Elliott of St. John's won the Gagliardi Trophy as the best Division III player. Other divisions' top-player awards went to North Alabama's Will Hall in Division II, Colgate's Jamaal Branch for I-AA offense, Idaho State's Jared Allen for I-AA defense, and Carroll's Tyler Emmert in the NAIA.

AP/Wide World Photos

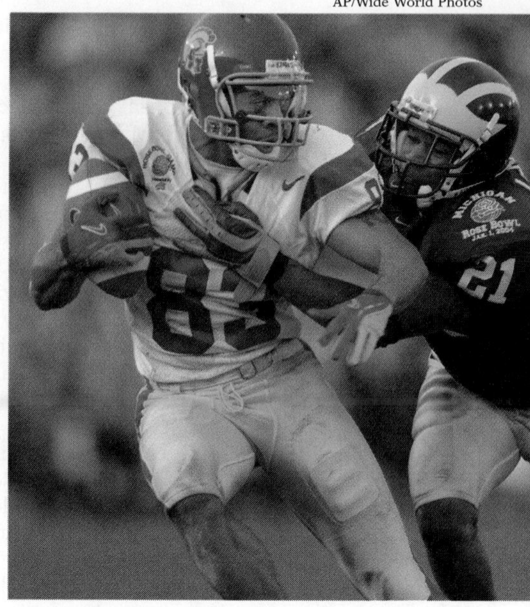

Wide receiver Keary Colbert of Southern California evades a tackle to score in the Rose Bowl on Jan. 1, 2004. USC's 28–14 victory over the University of Michigan gave it a claim to the college football 2003–04 national title.

Professional. It was the "Pats" versus the "Cats" in Super Bowl XXXVIII, held in Reliant Stadium in Houston, Texas, on Feb. 1, 2004, and the game proved to be a real nail-biter. With only four seconds on the clock and the score tied, the American Football Conference (AFC) New England Patriots defeated the National Football Conference (NFC) Carolina Panthers 32–29 on a 41-yd field goal by Adam Vinatieri to win their second National Football League (NFL) title in three years. Patriots quarterback Tom Brady threw for 354 yd and three touchdowns and was named the Super Bowl Most Valuable Player (MVP) for the second time. New England, led by coach Bill Belichick, had come into the Super Bowl with an impressive 14-game winning streak, including a 17–14 win over Tennessee in the divisional play-offs and a 24–14 triumph over Indianapolis for the AFC title. Carolina, which had made an astonishing comeback in 2003–04 under coach John Fox after a 1–15 season just two years earlier, had overcome Dallas 29–10 in the wild-card game, St. Louis 29–23 in the divisional play-offs, and Philadelphia 14–3 in the NFC championship game.

Eight of the previous year's 12 play-off teams finished the season with losing records, including both defending conference champions for only the second time in 37 years. Tampa Bay, the 2002–03 Super Bowl champion under first-year coach Jon Gruden (*see* BIOGRAPHIES), was one of seven teams whose won-lost records dropped by at least four games, led by defending AFC champion Oakland's seven-game decline. Cincinnati made the biggest improvement, six games, as six teams added at least four wins to their previous year's total.

NFC South champion Carolina won its first division title in seven years, AFC West leader Kansas City gained its first in six years, and AFC North champion Baltimore captured its first since 1989, when it played in Cleveland (Baltimore had won the 2000–01 Super Bowl as a wild-card play-off team as one of the best division runners-up). The only repeating division champions were Philadelphia of the NFC East for the third consecutive year and Green Bay of the NFC North for the second. The other division winners were St. Louis in the NFC West, New England in the AFC East, and Indianapolis in the AFC South. The wild-card teams were Tennessee and Denver in the AFC and Dallas and Seattle in the NFC.

Kansas City had the league's most potent offense, with 30.3 points per game as Priest Holmes scored a record 27 touchdowns. Jamal Lewis of Baltimore led all rushers with 2,066 yd, and his team's 167.1 yd rushing per game was the league's best. Indianapolis led with 261.2 yd passing per game behind Manning's league-best 4,267 yd and .670 completion percentage. Overall passing leader Steve McNair of Tennessee had 100.4 rating points with 8.0 yd per attempt, the league's most. Brett Favre's 32 touchdown passes for Green Bay and Aaron Brooks's .154 interception percentage for New Orleans also led the NFL. Manning and McNair shared the regular-season MVP award.

Torry Holt of St. Louis made 117 pass receptions and gained 1,696 yd, both league highs. Randy Moss, the receptions runner-up, led the league with 17 touchdowns receiving for Minnesota, the total offense leader with 393.4 yd per game. LaDainian Tomlinson of San Diego gained the most yards from scrimmage with 2,370. Kansas City's Dante Hall scored four times on kick returns and led with 16.3 yd per punt return, while Chicago's Jerry Azumah had the best kickoff-return average with 29.0 yd. Scoring leader Jeff Wilkins of St. Louis made a league-high 39 field goals among his 163 points, and Indianapolis's Mike Vanderjagt made all 37 field goal attempts, setting a record of 41 consecutive field goals over more than one season. The punting leaders were Oakland's Shane Lechler with 46.9 yd per punt and New Orleans's Mitch Berger with 38.2 net yards per punting play. New England allowed the fewest points, 14.9 per game, and the defensive yardage leaders were Dallas with 253.5 total yards and 164.4 yd passing per game and Tennessee with 80.9 yd rushing per game. Individually, Michael Strahan of the New York Giants had a league-high 18.5 sacks, and Minnesota's Brian Russell and San Francisco's Tony Parrish each made nine interceptions.

In the springtime leagues, the Tampa Bay Storm (15–4) won the indoor Arena Football League championship with a 43–29 victory over the Arizona Rattlers (13–7) on June 22, and the Frankfurt Galaxy (7–4) won the developmental NFL Europe League by prevailing 35–16 over its German rival, the Rhein Fire (6–5), in the World Bowl on June 14. (KEVIN M. LAMB)

Canadian Football. The Edmonton Eskimos won the 2003 Canadian Football League (CFL) championship by defeating the Montreal Alouettes 34–22 in the Grey Cup on November 16 at Regina, Sask., avenging their 2002 loss to Montreal. Eskimos receiver Jason Tucker was named the game's Most Outstanding Player. West Division winner Edmonton (13–5) led the league both offensively and defensively, having scored an average of 29.1 points per game and allowed an average of 20.4, while Mike Pringle's 15 touchdowns gave him a career record of 128 and tied him for the league lead with Montreal's Ben Cahoon and Milt Stegall of the Winnipeg Blue Bombers (11–7). Cahoon also led the league with 112 catches and was named the Outstanding Canadian.

Quarterback Anthony Calvillo of East Division winner Montreal (13–5) was the regular-season Most Outstanding Player. He led the league with 37 touchdown passes and 5,891 yd passing, while his teammate Jermaine Copeland led with 1,757 yd on receptions. Dave Dickenson's 112.7 passer rating and 10.0 yd per pass led the league for the B.C. Lions (11–7), as did Ricky Ray's .676 completion percentage for Edmonton. Winnipeg's Charles Roberts gained a league-leading 1,554 yd rushing, 2,102 yd from scrimmage, and 3,147 yd combined on run, pass, and return plays. Other outstanding-player awards went to Joe Fleming of the Calgary Stampeders (5–13) for defensive players, Andrew Greene of the Saskatchewan Roughriders (11–7) for linemen, B.C.'s Frank Cutolo for rookies, and Bashir Levingston, who scored a record five special-teams touchdowns for the Toronto Argonauts (9–9), for special teams. Eric England made a league-leading 14 sacks for Toronto, while kickers Lawrence Tynes of the Ottawa Renegades (7–11) and Winnipeg's Troy Westwood were the scoring coleaders, with 198 points each. Montreal, with 343.3 yd passing, 240.9 yd allowed on passes, and 302.0 total yards allowed, had the league's best per-game averages. B.C.'s 421.8 total yards, Saskatchewan's 144.7 yd rushing, and Winnipeg's 72.8 yd allowed rushing also were per-game bests. (KEVIN M. LAMB)

Australian Football. The Brisbane Lions won their third successive Australian Football League (AFL) premiership on Sept. 27, 2003, and for the second year in a row Collingwood was the victim. The Lions won the Grand Final by 50 points for a final score of 20.14 (134) to 12.12 (84), a far bigger winning margin than in 2002, when they had defeated the Magpies by only 9 points. A crowd of 79,451 attended the game at the Melbourne Cricket Ground, although attendance was down from previous years because a huge new grandstand was still under construction. The star of the match was Brisbane's Simon Black, who won the Norm Smith Medal as the game's best player.

At the completion of the 22 home-and-away matches leading up to the finals, Port Adelaide had topped the ladder, with Collingwood second and Brisbane third in the 16-club AFL competition. Three players—Adam Goodes of Sydney, Mark Ricciuto of Adelaide, and Collingwood's Nathan Buckley—tied for the Brownlow Medal, awarded to the regular season's fairest and best player. Other leading medalists in the regular season included the Coleman Medal winner, Matthew Lloyd of Essendon, and Hawthorn's Sam Mitchell, who won the Rising Star Award. Michael Voss of Brisbane was selected captain of the All-Australian team. (GREG HOBBS)

Rugby Football. The 2003 Rugby Union World Cup included 48 games, played in 10 Australian towns and cities, and almost two million fans, but just one winner emerged—England, the first Rugby Union champion from the Northern Hemisphere. In a fitting climax to what observers called the biggest and best Rugby World Cup to date, the final on November 22 between England and Australia, the defending champion, was one of the greatest spectacles the sport had ever seen. Sydney's Olympic Stadium was packed with 83,000 fans, about 35,000 of them from England, and in the end the result came down to one drop kick, with just 25 seconds left. With the score tied at 17–17 (and the end of extra time looming), England's outside-half Jonny Wilkinson produced the winning kick, off his weaker right foot. The foundation of England's victory was the team's inspirational captain, Martin Johnson.

The Australians emerged from the tournament with their heads held high, and both team captain George Gregan and coach Eddie Jones were dignified in their praise of England. The fallout from the near miss in Australia, where rugby was not the biggest sport, would not be huge. In New Zealand, however, where rugby was regarded as the national sport, it could take some time to recover from the team's semifinal exit in a 22–10 loss to Australia. It was the second World Cup in a row in which the All Blacks had been knocked out in the last four, and within days applications were being accepted for a new New Zealand coach. In December respected coach Graham Henry was named to fill the post with the All Blacks.

Australia, which had originally expected to share the competition with cohost New Zealand, gave the event 100% support. In Tasmania, where one game between Romania and Namibia took place, the mayor of Launceston suggested that all citizens born on even days back Namibia and those born on odd days support Romania.

A team of young players restored some pride to the Welsh nation with spectacular displays against England in the Welsh 28–17 quarterfinal loss and in an earlier match against New Zealand. A new breed of rugby nations also emerged. Georgia appeared for the first time, Uruguay had its one and only victory of the tournament, and Japan overachieved with four great matches. With a one-point victory over Argentina, Ireland moved back into the world's top eight nations.

As usual in a World Cup year, other domestic and international competitions were overshadowed. New Zealand's victory in the Tri-Nations tournament did not help it in the World Cup, while England's Six Nations grand slam set it up for a tilt at the World Cup. Domestically, the Wasps were the champions of England, beating Gloucester in a new play-off format. Toulouse was crowned the European champion, and the Auckland Blues emerged triumphant from the Super 12.

In Rugby League the Bradford Bulls won the English Super League grand final 25–12 over the Wigan Warriors. In Australia the Penrith Panthers upset the defending National Rugby League champion Sydney Roosters 18–6 in the NRL grand final. Meanwhile, Australia swept the three-Test-match Ashes series against England. (PAUL MORGAN)

GOLF

With Eldrick ("Tiger") Woods for once unable to add to his collection of major championship golf titles during 2003, his main rivals had a chance to make their mark, but it was not to be. For the first time since 1969, the four majors—the Masters, the U.S. Open, the British Open, and the Professional Golfers' Association of America (PGA) championship—were won by players who had not tasted success in them before, and two majors were captured by complete outsiders. Following knee surgery, however, Woods won five other tournaments to remain unchallenged as world number one throughout yet another season.

American Ben Curtis began the year ranked 1,269th in the world. By the time he teed off on July 17 in the British Open at Royal St. George's Golf Club in Sandwich, Kent, Eng., the 26-year-old PGA Tour rookie was still only 396th and chasing his first top 10 finish in a Tour event. By the end of the tournament, Curtis had achieved one of the biggest upsets in major golf history. Although records were hard to find, it was believed that not since Francis Ouimet at the 1913 U.S. Open had a golfer won the very first major in which he competed. After bursting clear on the final afternoon, Curtis had four bogeys in the last seven holes to finish with a one-under-par aggregate score of 283. Thomas Björn of Denmark stood on the 15th tee three strokes in the lead, but he bogeyed the 15th hole, needed three attempts to get out of a bunker for a double-bogey five at the par-three 16th, and had another bogey

Little-known American golfer Ben Curtis concentrates on his bunker shot on the final day of the British Open in July; Curtis went on to win his first major tournament by one stroke.

on the 17th to finish tied with Fiji's Vijay Singh one stroke behind Curtis.

England's Mark Roe would remember the tournament for a very different reason. A third-round score of 67 should have left Roe in joint third place, but he and playing partner Jesper Parnevik had forgotten to exchange scorecards on the first tee, and the error was not spotted by officials until it was too late. They both were disqualified for signing incorrect scores.

Four weeks later 34-year-old Shaun Micheel, playing in only the third major of his career, scored his own upset in the PGA championship at Oak Hill Country Club in Rochester, N.Y. He was ranked 169th in the world, had not won on the PGA Tour, and was best known for having received a 1994 bravery award for diving into a river and rescuing an elderly couple from a sinking car. Playing in the final group with fellow American Chad Campbell and holding a one-shot lead with one hole to play, Micheel hit a stunning 159-m

(174-yd) seven-iron shot that settled just short of the hole. The tap-in birdie for a four-under-par 276 gave him a two-stroke triumph.

The victors of the Masters at the Augusta (Ga.) National Golf Club in April and the U.S. Open at Olympia Fields near Chicago in June were less surprising, but Canadian Mike Weir and American Jim Furyk, respectively, were first-time major winners nonetheless. Weir had won twice on the PGA Tour earlier in the season when he became the first Canadian and second left-hander to win a major (left-handed New Zealander Bob Charles won the 1963 British Open). A brilliant putting display at Augusta enabled Weir to tie American Len Mattiace at a seven-under-par 281; Mattiace, who had shot a spectacular final round of 65, then ran up a double-bogey six at the first hole of a sudden-death play-off.

The buildup to the tournament had been dominated by controversy. Martha Burk, head of the National Council of Women's Organizations, wrote to Augusta National urging a change to the club's all-male membership, and club chairman Hootie Johnson responded with a public statement: "We will not be bullied, threatened or intimidated. There may well come a day when women will be invited to join our membership, but that timetable will be ours and not at the point of a bayonet." The row escalated to the point where Augusta National broadcast the tournament without television advertising so that companies associated with the event would not come under pressure. A protest took place during the week of the tournament, but the club maintained its stance.

The U.S. Open had no such controversy—just record scoring. Furyk and Singh each set a new 36-hole record of 133. Singh equaled the lowest round ever in a major event with his second-round 63. Furyk added a 67 for a 54-hole record of 200, and his final-round 72 earned him a three-stroke victory over Australian Stephen Leaney. Furyk's eight-under-par 272 tied the championship record.

South Africa's Ernie Els had seven wins around the globe, finishing the year as the leading money winner (€2,975,374 [about $3,500,000]) on the European tour and equaling the record of Gary Player and Severiano Ballesteros with a fifth victory in the HSBC World Match Play Championship at the Wentworth Club in Surrey, Eng. Els, however, lost the world number two position to Singh, whose four PGA Tour titles and $7,611,995 in winnings helped him deny Woods what would have been a record fifth successive money-list crown.

A player who finished 96th out of 114 in a tournament would not normally be worthy of mention, but there was huge interest when Sweden's Annika Sörenstam agreed to become the first woman to play a PGA Tour event since 1945. Sörenstam, the women's world number one, captured two of the Ladies Professional Golf Association's (LPGA's) four majors during the season, but it was her appearance at the PGA's Bank of America Colonial Classic tournament at the Colonial Country Club in Fort Worth, Texas, that captured the imagination of the sporting public. Under the biggest scrutiny of her career (for what she insisted was a one-off appearance in a men's event), Sörenstam held her head high, scoring a one-over-par 71 in the first round before slipping to a second-round 74 and missing the halfway cut by four strokes.

It set the ball rolling for other appearances by women in previously men-only tournaments. American Suzy Whaley finished 148th out of 156 in the Greater Hartford Open event for which she had qualified; Australian Jan Stephenson played on the U.S. Champions Tour for golfers over age 50 (she tied for last place); teenage Hawaiian amateur Michelle Wie missed the cut on both the PGA Tour's second-string Nationwide Tour and the Canadian circuit; England's Laura Davies competed in the Korean Open (also missing the cut); and Pak Se Ri, the women's world number two, finished a notable 10th in the SBS Super Tournament in her native South Korea.

The phenomenal Wie was only 13 when she finished ninth in the Kraft Nabisco championship, the first of the women's majors, at Rancho Mirage, Calif., in March. The title went to Patricia Meunier-Lebouc of France one stroke ahead of Sörenstam, who went on to win the McDonald's LPGA championship at DuPont Country Club in Wilmington, Del., in June after a one-hole play-off with South Korea's Grace Park, and the Weetabix Women's British Open at Royal Lytham and St. Annes Golf Club in Lancashire, Eng., by one stroke from Pak in July and August. That win completed a career Grand Slam for the 32-year-old Sörenstam, but the U.S. Women's Open at Pumpkin Ridge Golf Club in North Plains, Ore., produced another huge shock, with Hilary Lunke coming through sectional and final qualifying to beat fellow Americans Kelly Robbins and Angela Stanford in an 18-hole play-off. Sörenstam finished atop the LPGA money list with $2,029,506.

The President's Cup match between the U.S. holders and the international side, held in George, S.Af., ended in a 17–17 tie after Woods and Els halved three holes in a sudden death play-off and it was agreed that the trophy be shared. The World Cup, at Kiawah, S.C., was won by South Africa's Rory Sabbatini and Trevor Immelman. They were standing in for Els and Retief Goosen, both of whom chose not to play. In the Solheim Cup at Barseback Golf and Country Club near Malmö, Swed., Europe's women beat the U.S. 17½–10½, while Britain and Ireland's men amateurs achieved a third successive victory over the U.S. in the Walker Cup, winning 12½–11½ at Ganton, North Yorkshire, Eng. Gary Wolstenholme, a member of the Britain and Ireland side, won his second British amateur title at Royal Troon in Scotland, while the American amateur championship at Oakmont (Pa.) Country Club saw 19-year-old Nick Flanagan become not only the second youngest winner (after Woods) but also the first Australian to win in 100 years. (MARK GARROD)

GYMNASTICS

The 100th anniversary of the world gymnastics championships took place in Anaheim, Calif., during Aug. 16–24, 2003. Despite losing three members of its team to injury and/or illness, the United States captured its first women's team gold medal. Romania, the team that had won every women's world team title since 1991, finished a distant second, and Australia earned its first team medal, taking the bronze. Russia's Svetlana Khorkina came from behind to win her third world championships all-around title. Carly Patterson of the U.S. finished a close second, and China's Zhang Nan was third. During the event finals, Uzbekistan's Oksana Chusovitina, competing in her seventh world championships at age 28, took the gold medal on vault. There was a tie for the gold on the uneven bars between Americans Hollie Vise and Chellsie Memmel. Fan Ye of China took first place on the beam, and Daiane Dos Santos was the top scoring gymnast on floor exercise, becoming Brazil's first gymnastics world champion.

© Reuters NewMedia Inc./Corbis

Hollie Vise of the gold medal-winning United States team performs on the balance beam during the team finals at the artistic gymnastics world championships in August.

On the men's side, the ever-powerful Chinese maintained their dominance, winning the team title. China had won five of the last six men's world team titles; in 2001 China had finished fifth when its top gymnasts stayed home to compete in the Chinese national games. The U.S., which had led after the preliminary round of competition, won its second consecutive team silver medal. Japan, which had stayed home from the world championships in 2001, finished third. Paul Hamm won the all-around title, the first male gymnast from the U.S. to accomplish this feat. China's Yang Wei finished second, and Japan's Hiroyuki Tomita was third. In three of the six event finals, gold medals were won by athletes from China: Teng Haibin on the pommel horse (tied with Japan's Takehiro Kashima) and Li Xiaopeng in both the vault and the parallel bars. Hamm and Bulgaria's Iordan Iovchev tied for the gold medal on floor exercise, and Iovchev and Greece's Dimosthenis Tampakos tied for top honours on the still rings. Kashima had the highest score on the horizontal bar.

The rhythmic gymnastics world championships took place September 24–28 in Budapest. Russia won the world team title. With a comfortable lead after day one, the Russian team held strong during day two of competition. Ukraine, the defending world champion, could achieve only second place. The fight for third place was intense between Belarus and Greece, but Belarus finally managed to take the bronze medal. In the all-around competition, Russia's Alina Kabayeva won the title. Ukraine's Anna Bessonova, who was the crowd favourite, trailed slightly to earn the silver medal. Irina Chashina of Russia took home the bronze. During the event finals, Bessonova won the hoop and the clubs events, while Kabayeva won the ball and the ribbon competitions. Russia won the group event, followed by Bulgaria and Belarus. (LUAN PESZEK)

ICE HOCKEY

North America. The National Hockey League (NHL) experienced a season troubled by operating losses, labour uncertainty, and diminished television ratings during 2002–03. The game on the ice also lost some of its offensive excitement, speed, and scoring, despite the addition of a second referee to NHL officiating crews and an extensive, if futile, attempt to eliminate hooking and holding violations.

Some observers blamed the decline in the number of goals scored on talent that had been diluted through expansion of the number of teams. A decade earlier, when the NHL was composed of 24 teams, the league could count on its rosters 14 players who scored 50 goals or more per season. In the 30-team NHL of 2002–03, only Milan Hejduk, the Czech right wing who played for Colorado, reached the 50-goal mark. Critics also pointed to NHL goalies outfitted in huge uniforms and bulky pads that left little space in goal for even the best shot makers.

Given the defense-dominated games that caused TV ratings to plummet even in Canada, the NHL got a surprisingly dramatic windup to its season on June 9, 2003, when the New Jersey Devils beat the Anaheim Mighty Ducks 3–0 to win the Stanley Cup four games to three.

The Devils' third NHL championship since 1995 owed much to a superb performance by goalie Martin Brodeur, who blocked 24 shots and broke Dominik Hasek's NHL record with his seventh shutout of the play-offs. Brodeur also held the Ducks scoreless in the first two games of the final series, each of which ended in a 3–0 Devils victory. The second game, on May 29, saw Brodeur become the first goalkeeper since Detroit's Terry Sawchuk in 1952 to record back-to-back shutouts in the Stanley Cup finals.

Anaheim, the seventh-seeded team in the NHL Western Conference play-offs, had never previously survived the postseason competition beyond the second round. The Ducks refused to bow out quietly and took a page from the Devils' approach for a 3–2 victory in game three at Anaheim, Calif., on May 31. The Ducks got back into contention on the sterling effort of goalie Jean-Sébastien Giguère, who stopped 29 New Jersey shots and extended his streak of scoreless overtime to 166 minutes 4 seconds, an NHL record.

The Ducks squared the series at two games each with another overtime triumph on June 2, when Steve Thomas, playing the first Stanley Cup series of his 19-season career, beat Brodeur with a rebound shot for the game's only goal. Giguère improved his scoreless overtime record to 168 minutes 27 seconds.

The Devils rebounded on June 5 with a 6–3 victory that raised their record to 11–1 for play-off games on home ice. It was the Ducks' ninth consecutive loss at New Jersey's Continental Arena. Two nights later in Anaheim, the Ducks scored a 5–2 victory that left both teams battered, weary, and deadlocked at three games each.

The decisive seventh game delivered the title to the Devils before an ecstatic sellout crowd of 19,040 at Continental Arena and completed a series in which the home team won every game. The Devils got their first goal from Mike Rupp, a 23-year-old rookie who had spent most of his season with Albany of the American Hockey League. Jeff Friesen, a former member of the Mighty Ducks who had gone to New Jersey in a 2002 trade, scored the other two goals. The Devils finished as the first team in 29 seasons to win the championship despite having had an overall losing record (4–7) for play-off games on the road.

The Conn Smythe Trophy went to Giguère as the most valuable player (MVP) of the play-offs. The Ducks' goalie thus became only the fifth player from the losing team to win the award. Brodeur won the Vezina Trophy as the league's best goalie.

Among the 30 teams that contested the 82-game regular season, Ottawa topped the NHL with 52 victories and 113 points and won its division by a 15-point margin over runner-up Toronto (44 victories). Dallas (111 points), Detroit (110), New Jersey (108), Colorado (105), and Tampa Bay (93) were the other division champions that moved on to the 16-team play-offs. New Jersey reached the Stanley Cup finals by beating Boston and Tampa Bay, each by four games to one, as a prelude to defeating Ottawa four games to three for the Eastern Conference championship. Anaheim made the Stanley Cup final series for the first time in NHL history, beating Detroit four games to none and Dallas four games to two before taking the Western Conference title four games to none over Minnesota.

In the 53rd NHL All-Star game, played in Sunrise, Fla., on Feb. 2, 2003, the Western Conference players beat their rivals from the Eastern Conference 6–5 in overtime. Dany Heatley, the Atlanta rookie right wing, made a brilliant All-Star-game debut by scoring four goals for the East. He was named MVP after the game ended in a first-time Olympics-style shootout, which was won by the West 3–1.

International. Canada added another major conquest to its storied ice hockey history on May 11, 2003, in Helsinki, Fin., where the Canadian men's team scored a 3–2 overtime victory over Sweden for the 2003 International Ice Hockey Federation (IIHF) world championship. The Canadian triumph came after a lengthy video-replay review of a goal scored by Anson Carter at 13 minutes 49 seconds of four-on-four overtime. It ended a spectacular game and brought the Canadians their 18th gold medal in world championship play since 1930.

Sweden took a 2–0 lead on first-period goals by Mattias Tjarnqvist and Per-Johan Axelsson, but Canada responded with a first-period goal by Shawn Horcoff and another in the third period from Shane Doan to set up Carter's closing act. The thrilling finish to the extraordinary overtime period began when Carter skated down the right side of the ice and sent a powerful slap shot sailing toward Mikael Tellqvist, the Swedish goalkeeper. Tellqvist partially blocked the shot with his glove, but when the puck fell to the side of the net, Carter got his rebound, spun to the left side of the cage, and fired the puck into the goal between Tellqvist's right pad and the goalpost. Carter raised both arms in the traditional sign of celebration, but the goal light did not go on until seven or eight minutes after the score. Referee Vladimir Sindler, who was not in position to make the call when Carter made his shot, signaled Canada's victory only after conferring with the video goal judge, who reviewed the play from seven different angles.

Team Canada finished the tournament unbeaten, having compiled an 8–0–1 record. The Canadians profited from strong defensive play and the goaltending of Roberto Luongo, who was beaten for a power-play goal only once.

Sweden was left with the silver medal, and Slovakia beat the Czech Republic 4–2 in the bronze-medal game. The United States was knocked out of medal contention and finished 13th. The 16-team tournament drew 454,693 fans.

Canada also captured the under-18 world championship with a 3–0 victory over Slovakia on April 22 at Yaroslavl, Russia. Goalie Ryan Munce led the Canadian shutout victory with 25 saves. Canada reached the gold-medal game by beating the defending champion U.S. 2–1 in overtime on April 20.

In Europe the Continental Cup produced one of the season's most thrilling games on January 12 when Jokerit Helsinki of Finland beat Lokomotiv Yaroslavl of Russia 2–1 in Lugano, Switz. The hard-fought game was ultimately decided by a shootout that followed an overtime period. The Finns' Jukka Voutilainen feinted Russian goalie Egor Podomatsky out of position to make the game-winning goal that gave his team the Cup and $53,344 in prize money. Earlier, first-period goals had been scored by Yury Butsayev of

Anson Carter of Canada (22) sets up the winning goal in the final of the world ice hockey championship in May; Canada defeated Sweden 3–2 in overtime.

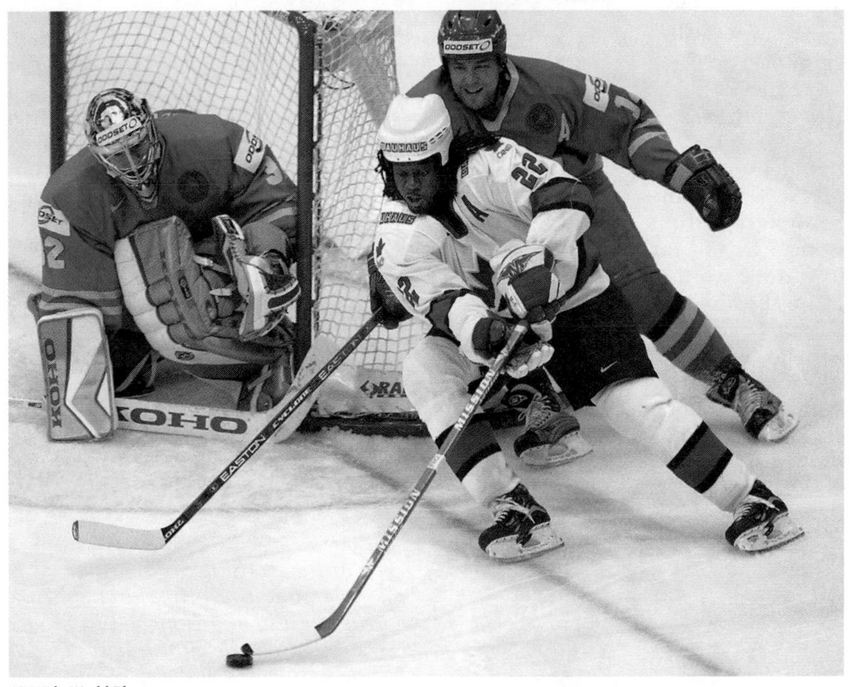

AP/Wide World Photos

Lokomotiv, after 8 minutes 49 seconds, and Petri Pakaslahti of Jokerit, after 17 minutes 20 seconds.

The 2003 IIHF world championship for women, scheduled to be contested in Beijing in April, was canceled because of the SARS (severe acute respiratory syndrome) epidemic in China. (*See* HEALTH AND DISEASE: *Special Report*.)

(RON REID)

ICE SKATING

Figure Skating. In 2003 the International Skating Union, still smarting from its judging scandal at the 2002 Winter Olympics, launched a controversial new computerized system to determine a skater's marks. The chief element of the new system was anonymity for 10 judges, only 7 of whom had their votes counted. On the ice, Michelle Kwan of the United States and Yevgeny Plushchenko of Russia each captured a world championship gold medal, just as they had in 2001.

Making her 10th appearance in the world competition, Kwan captivated a crowd of 16,000 spectators at the MCI Center in Washington, D.C., matching athleticism with artistry and an assuredness that had abandoned her in the 2002 Winter Olympics, where she settled for a bronze medal. Kwan landed six triple jumps in the error-free long program she skated on March 29. Her performance ended to thunderous applause as Kwan became the first woman in 43 years to win the world title for the fifth time. Yelena Sokolova of Russia won the silver medal, and Fumie Suguri of Japan took the bronze for the second year in a row.

The 22-year-old Kwan started the 2003 season on a note of uncertainty, but in taking an uncustomary easygoing approach to her skating, Kwan soon found success. In January she won her seventh U.S. championship (and sixth in a row), in Dallas, Texas, skating a clean program that included six triple jumps and her trademark change-edge spiral. All nine judges ranked Kwan first, while 17-year-old Sarah Hughes, the 2002 Olympic champion, won the silver medal and Sasha Cohen took the bronze. Michael Weiss captured the U.S. men's title by outskating Timothy Goebel, the first man to land three quadruple jumps in a single performance (at Skate America in 1999). Ryan Jahnke was the bronze medalist.

Russian Aleksey Yagudin, the defending champion and 2002 Olympic gold medalist, was forced out of the world championships by a hip injury, but Plushchenko, who had captured the European championship in January at Malmö, Swed., returned to the worlds after a year's absence to win his second gold medal. In the qualifying round Plushchenko landed the first quad toe/triple toe/triple loop combination ever achieved in world competition. In the free skate Plushchenko excelled in a program that included a quad toe/triple toe/double toe, two triple axels, and four more triples. Goebel took the silver medal, while the bronze went to Takeshi Honda of Japan.

The Chinese duo of Shen Xue and Zhao Hongbo received a standing ovation after a thrilling performance that brought them the pairs gold medal for the second year in a row. Canada's Shae-Lynn Bourne and Victor Kraatz topped their rivals to win the ice-dancing gold medal.

At the world figure-skating championships in March, Shen Xue (left) and Zhao Hongbo of China successfully defended their pairs title with grace and elegance.

AP/Wide World Photos

Speed Skating. The Dutch men and the German women were the most successful skaters at the 2003 world single-distance speed-skating championships, held in Berlin. Jochem Uytdehaage and his Dutch teammates Bob de Jong and Carl Verheijen skated to a 1–2–3 finish in the men's 5,000-m final on March 14, two days before de Jong took the 10,000 m by a 10.2-sec margin over Verheijen. The Netherlands earned two more gold medals from Erben Wennemars, who won his first world title in the 1,500 m the day before he won the 1,000 m.

Germany's Anni Friesinger, the 2002 Olympic champion, struck gold in the women's 1,500-, 3,000- and 1,000-m finals. In the 3,000 m Friesinger sped to the finish line 1.92 sec faster than teammate Claudia Pechstein, who captured the 5,000-m gold.

On March 7 in Heerenveen, Neth., Canada's Cindy Klassen won the final women's 1,500-m race of the World Cup long-track season, edging out American Jennifer Rodriguez by 1.08 sec. Rodriguez came back to win the 1,000-m final a day later, collecting her sixth medal of the World Cup season. Klassen ranked number one in the World Cup season's 1,500-m standings, with four gold medals and one silver.

In the men's competition Wennemars took the 500-m final in 35.25 sec and the 1,000 m in 1 min 9.11 sec. Russia's Yevgeny Lalenkov won the 1,500 m with a time of 1 min 47.77 sec to finish first in the World Cup 1,500-m rankings with three gold medals and two silver medals. The Netherlands scored again when Uytdehaage, a double gold medalist at the 2002 Olympics, captured the men's 5,000-m final in 6 min 27.42 sec on the last day of the competition.

In short-track competition Apolo Anton Ohno of the U.S. won his second career World Cup title in February. Scoring 196 points out of a possible 200, Ohno edged South Korean Ahn Hyun Soo by two points. Ahn took revenge a month later when he won the men's overall title in the short-track world championships, held in Warsaw, where Ohno won only one medal. South Korea's Choi Eun Kyung won the women's overall title at the worlds.

In the world short-track team championships, contested March 15–16 in Sofia, Bulg., Canada won the men's team title for the sixth time in 12 years. China took the women's team title, despite the fact that South Korea finished first at every distance except the relay, which was won by Italy.

(RON REID)

RODEO

In December 2003 calf roper Cody Ohl of Stephenville, Texas, was back in action and roping for the world title after a career-threatening injury. Two years earlier Ohl had been writhing in pain on the floor of the Thomas & Mack Center in Las Vegas, Nev., with the ligaments in his right knee shredded. Although he had just secured the 2001 Professional Rodeo Cowboy Association (PRCA) all-around cowboy world championship, his immediate thought was that he would never walk again properly, much less compete at the elite level of professional rodeo. In the 10th and final round of the 2003 National Finals Rodeo (NFR), however, Ohl and 2002 champ Fred Whitfield of Hockley, Texas, were vying for the tie-down championship. Ohl, whose knee had been repaired through a succession of three surgeries, nodded for his calf and tied it down in 6.5 seconds—the fastest time in the history of professional rodeo. With $222,025 in season earnings, Ohl earned his fifth PRCA world championship. (Rodeo world championships are decided by money won over the yearlong rodeo season plus the championship-determining NFR.)

The 2003 NFR, held December 5–14, paid a record $5 million. Ohl's win highlighted several record-breaking and record-tying moments at the national finals. Texas team ropers Rich Skelton of Llano and Speed Williams of Amarillo earned a record seventh consecutive world title with $180,305. The duo also tied the all-time record for world championships set by Jake Barnes and Clay O'Brien Cooper, who had captured the team roping title seven times between 1985 and 1994. Saddle bronc rider Dan Mortensen of Billings, Mont., earned his sixth world championship with $219,999 to draw even with Casey Tibbs, who had established the mark for saddle bronc titles in the 1950s. Other champions for 2003 included Will Lowe of Canyon, Texas, in bareback riding ($188,247); Teddy Johnson of Checotah, Okla., in steer wrestling ($149,499); Janae Ward of Addington, Okla., in barrel racing ($155,792); and Terry Don West of Henryetta, Okla., in bull riding ($211,879).

Multievent cowboy Trevor Brazile of Decatur, Texas, successfully defended his 2002 world champion all-around cowboy title with $294,839 in earnings in three events—steer roping, team roping, and tie-down. At the National Finals Steer Roping, held in Amarillo in November, Guy Allen of Santa Anna, Texas, earned his 17th world championship, surpassing the all-time record for rodeo world titles established by Jim Shoulders in 1959.

(GAVIN FORBES EHRINGER)

ROWING

In 2003 Germany continued its overall supremacy in world rowing events, with the United States, Italy, Canada, Australia, Great Britain, and Romania prominent in its wake. Germany again dominated the World Cup, the seventh series of which was held in Milan; Munich, Ger.; and Lucerne, Switz., in 2003. Germany finished with 198 points, well ahead of Great Britain (97) and Italy (87). Overall, Germany (with 407 points) led Great Britain (206) and Italy (161).

At the Fédération Internationale des Sociétés d'Aviron (FISA) world championships, hosted for the first time by Italy (in Milan), half of the 47 competing nations contested the two dozen finals. Germany was the only country to reach double figures in the medal tables and finished with four championship titles. Canada, Italy, and the U.S. each scored three victories, while Australia and Denmark each won twice. The seven other gold medals went to Bulgaria, China, France, Great Britain, New Zealand, Norway, and Romania. The honours were evenly spread in women's events, with only Germany winning two golds.

The world junior championships, which were rowed August 6–9 on the new Olympic course at Schinias, Greece, provided an unexpected foretaste of what could happen in 2004. A prevailing tailwind blew straight down the centre of the shallow course, which caused buoyancy difficulties on the opening day and swamped some of the slender racing shells after 1,250 m. Disorder turned to delay with the loss of the next day's racing, as the prevailing coastal breeze did not abate. Ultimately, the 14 finals were halved to 1,000 m to avoid the roughest water. Australia, Italy, and Romania each won two gold medals; the others went to Great Britain, The Netherlands, Latvia, Lithuania, Poland, Russia, Serbia and Montenegro, and Slovenia. Subsequently, the Olympic organizers and FISA considered the possibility of introducing night rowing at the Olympics in the event of a repetition of the extreme conditions experienced by the juniors. Australia and Germany each captured four titles at the World Under 23 Regatta in Belgrade, Serbia and Montenegro, in July. Romania, Italy, and China won two gold medals, with Canada, Hungary, Poland, and Slovenia the other winners.

At the 154th Henley Royal Regatta in England, overseas entries from seven countries won a dozen trophies. Canada retained the Grand Challenge Cup (eights) and won both the Remenham Cup (women's eights) and the Stewards' Cup (coxless fours). Germany took the Thames Cup (eights) and the Double Sculls cup. There was also a double triumph in eights for the U.S. in the Ladies' Plate and Temple Cup, while Ireland claimed the Men's Quadruple Sculls cup and the Visitors' Cup (coxless fours). The Queen Mother Cup (quadruple sculls) went to Poland, and Ukraine won the new Princess Grace Cup (women's quad sculls). Australian Catriona Oliver triumphed in the Princess Royal Cup (women's single sculls). The British were not shut out, as Alan Campbell won the Diamond Challenge Sculls (men's single sculls) and Matthew Pinsent and James Cracknell captured two gold medals, their third consecutive (Pinsent's seventh) Silver Goblets & Nickalls Cup (coxless pairs) and the Prince Philip Cup (coxed fours).

The 149th University Boat Race was the closest since the 1877 dead heat, with the crews overlapping all the way for 6.4 km (4 mi). Oxford gained a third of a length in the first mile before Cambridge took control and led by one second at the halfway point. Oxford regained the lead by two-thirds of a length with three minutes to go. Cambridge responded strongly with a storming last minute, closing rapidly with every stroke to finish almost level. In the end, however, Oxford won by 30 cm (one foot) to reduce Cambridge's lead in the series to 77–71.

(KEITH L. OSBORNE)

SAILING (YACHTING)

The major sailing drama of 2003 was played out in the Hauraki Gulf off Auckland, N.Z., early in the year. *Alinghi* of Switzerland completed its victory in a tightly contested challenger series in January and then went on to trounce the New Zealand defender of the America's Cup. The victory by the Swiss team, headed by Ernesto Bertarelli but with New Zealander Russell Coutts as skipper, took the cup to Europe for the first time. In November it was announced that the next cup would be held off Valencia, Spain, in 2007.

Offshore racing's premier event, the Admiral's Cup, took place in July in The Solent, off the Isle of Wight, and surrounding waters. The event was sailed for the first time under the Royal Ocean Racing Club's own handicap rule, the IRM. Australia's Royal Prince Alfred team (comprising *Wild Oats* and *Aftershock*) won, with the Spanish team second and Britain third. The other major international handicapping system, IMS, held its world championship in Italy's Gulf of Naples, where *Italtel* earned the IMS 600 title. Off Porto Cervo, Sardinia, Italy, *Nerone* won the world championship for the most competitive of the offshore one-design boats, the Farr 40.

The Around Alone event finished off Newport, R.I., in the spring. Bernard Stamm in *Bobst Group Armor Lux* won Class 1 with 49 of 50 possible points, while Brad Van Liew in *Tommy Hilfiger Spirit of America* won Class 2 with a perfect score of 50. The Volvo Ocean Race for fully crewed monohulls, scheduled for 2005, announced parameters for a new class of high-tech 21.5-m (70.5-ft) boats for the race. On December 30 *First National,* skippered by Michael Spies and Peter Johnson, was named the overall winner in Australia's 59th Rolex Sydney–Hobart race, almost 90 minutes ahead of Thorry Gunnerson's wooden-hulled *Tilting at Windmills*.

The International Sailing Federation (ISAF) reported the implementation of a Competitor Classification scheme, which would provide event organizers with the means of controlling competitors in terms of their employment in the sailing industry. The application of the scheme was voluntary. Some events might be completely amateur, while others would have limited professional involvement; if the scheme was not invoked, the event would be open to all competitors. US Sailing declared almost immediately that its similar scheme would be shelved in favour of the ISAF program. The ISAF match racing world championship was won by Ed Baird (U.S.); an American team also won the ISAF team racing honours.

Several new records were established in 2003. The British 42.7-m (140-ft) high-tech "super maxi" *Mari Cha IV* established a new speed record for monohulls in September, achieving 525 nm (nautical miles; 1 nm = 1.85 km) in 24 hours—an average speed of nearly 22 knots under sail. The boat went on to complete a transatlantic passage in 6 days 17 hr—another new record. Steve Fossett's giant catamaran *Playstation* established a new record for the "Discovery Route" from Cádiz, Spain, to San Salvador, El Salvador, in 9 days 13 hr, cutting a full day off the previous record for the trip that took Christopher Columbus 45 days. The trimaran *Great American II* eclipsed a record for Hong Kong–New York City set by the extreme clipper *Sea Witch* in 1849, by completing the voyage in just 74 days. *Windward Passage's* long-held record for the race from Ft. Lauderdale, Fla., to Montego Bay, Jamaica, fell to Bob McNeil's super-sled, *Zephyrus V,* which trimmed 4½ hours off the record. The Route du Rhum, a single-handed race in 18.3-m (60-ft) trimarans from Saint-Malo, France, to Guadeloupe set another sort of record when 15 of the 18 entries failed to complete the race after a fierce storm. (JOHN B. BONDS)

Wild Oats, *one of the two yachts representing Australia, catches the wind in the Admiral's Cup off the English coast in July.* **Wild Oats** *won the final race in the nine-race series to clinch the trophy for Australia.*

© Martyn Hayhow/AFP/Getty Images

SKIING

Alpine Skiing. In 2003 Austrian Stephan Eberharter collected three World Cup titles for the second straight season, but it was American Bode Miller who lit up race courses and race crowds worldwide. Eberharter, who seldom skied slalom, took command at the start of the season, winning the opening race, but he missed three weeks with a knee injury. Miller started skiing in speed events—downhill and supergiant slalom (super G)—regularly, and in January he pulled ahead briefly. Eberharter surged to the overall title with 1,333 points, 233 points ahead of Miller, who faltered in the final month. Eberharter had nine wins and was first or second in four of the final six races. For the second winter in a row, Miller had the best season for an American man since Phil Mahre won the overall and giant slalom (GS) titles in 1983. Miller also won two gold medals and a silver at the world championships in St. Moritz, Switz., the best showing ever by an American man.

Michael von Grünigen of Switzerland retired at season's end after winning the World Cup GS title. The slalom championship, the first Alpine World Cup title won by a Finn, went to Kalle Palander. Austrian icon Hermann Maier, who missed the Olympic season following a motorcycle accident, returned in mid-January 2003 with a rod stabilizing his leg. He won a super-G World Cup event and a silver medal at the world championships before quitting to give his leg more time to heal.

Croatian Janica Kostelic did not win until the third World Cup race of the 2002–03 season. Thereafter, she won six races and her second overall title, as well as the slalom title. At the world championships she captured the combined and the slalom; when her older brother, Ivica, won the men's slalom, it marked the first brother-sister champions at a single championship.

Stephan Eberharter of Austria charges down the slope in the final World Cup downhill race on February 22; he won the downhill and overall World Cup titles.

Austrian Michaela Dorfmeister won the World Cup downhill championship and took super-G gold at the world championships. Carole Montillet of France was the World Cup super-G champion, while Sweden's Anja Pärson edged Italy's Karen Putzer in the GS.

Nordic Skiing. Norway's Bente Skari stormed to 14 World Cup victories en route to her second straight cross-country championship. She won the two races she entered at the world championships in Val di Fiemme, Italy, before withdrawing due to illness. Then she retired. (*See* BIOGRAPHIES.)

Mathias Fredriksson gave Sweden its first cross-country World Cup king since Gunde Svan in 1989. Not quite as big a surprise was the announcement by Olympic and World Cup champion Thomas Alsgaard that he was retiring.

Poland's Adam Malysz cruised to his third consecutive ski-jumping title and won both gold medals at the world championships. After Ronny Ackermann of Germany won the individual Nordic combined event and Felix Gottwald lifted Austria in the team event, American Johnny Spillane outskied Gottwald and Ackermann to win the Nordic combined sprint—the first Nordic gold at an Olympics or a world championship by an American skier.

In June, because of a failed drug test, Russian Larisa Lazutina was stripped of the two silver medals she won at the 2002 Winter Olympics. Bronze medalists Beckie Scott of Canada (in the 5-km event) and Katerina Neumannova of the Czech Republic (15 km) were moved up to silver. In December, Russian Olga Danilova's 5-km gold medal was taken away also, and Scott was catapulted into the top slot. In the same ruling, Johann Mühlegg of Spain lost two other gold medals, for the 10-km pursuit and the 30-km mass start races (both he and Lazutina had already been forced to give up medals during the Games).

Freestyle Skiing. Former gymnast Alisa Camplin of Australia, who gained an Olympic gold medal in 2002 before she had won a World Cup aerials event, filled in her résumé during 2002–03. She won three World Cup contests, the World Cup aerial title, and the gold medal at the world championships in Deer Valley, Utah. Dmitry Arkhipov of Russia, who entered the season with one victory in his career, won three events, the World Cup overall and aerial titles, and aerial gold at the world championships.

In moguls Americans Travis Cabral and Shannon ("Sparky") Bahrke captured the World Cup titles. Finland's Janne Lahtela and Austrian Margarita Marbler, respectively, took the men's and women's dual moguls titles. Skier-cross ("roller derby on skis") debuted in 2003; Japan's Hiroomi Takizawa won the men's title, and Valentine Scuotto of France was the women's champion. Mogul specialist Kari Traa of Norway earned her second consecutive overall title.

American skiers collected six medals at the 2003 world championships—most notably, Jeremy Bloom, who played football and joined the World Cup with minimal on-snow training, won gold in the men's dual moguls and silver in moguls. Traa captured both women's moguls titles, while Mikko Ronkainen of Finland was the men's moguls champion.

Snowboarding. Things cooled in the 2002–03 snowboarding season, as most American 2002 Olympic medalists took a low-key approach—Olympic halfpipe champion Ross Powers got married and became a father, although he won the heralded U.S. Open superpipe contest again in 2003, and women's halfpipe gold medalist Kelly Clark had preseason knee surgery and competed sparingly. Karine Ruby of France won a third straight overall World Cup championship, as did Canadian Jasey Jay Anderson. World Cup titles in parallel went to Ursula Bruhin of Switzerland and Mathieu Bozzetto of France. Halfpipe titles were won by Germany's Xavier Hoffmann and Manuela Laura Pesko of Switzerland, while Xavier Delerue of France and Ruby won the snowboard-cross titles. The men-only big air World Cup championship went to Jukka Eratuli of Finland. (PAUL ROBBINS)

SQUASH

At the start of 2003, Australian five-time world champion Sarah Fitz-Gerald (*see* BIOGRAPHIES) retired from the Women's International Squash Players Association (WISPA) Tour, leaving the field clear for New Zealander Carol Owens. For the first half of the season, Owens was unbeaten. She collected six WISPA titles, including the Grand Prix in Qatar in May, but her preeminence was not to last. Australian Rachael Grinham beat Owens in the quarterfinals of the British Open before claiming her maiden title with a victory over England's Cassie Jackman in the final. Jackman beat Owens in the final of the U.S. Open, and Natalie Grainger of the U.S. took the prestigious Qatar Classic title in yet another final-match victory over Owens. In mid-December the action moved to Hong Kong, host of the imaginatively staged World Open, which featured final rounds played on an outdoor court set up next to the harbour. Owens was not to be denied this time, taking her second World Open title with a final victory over Jackman.

The men's tour was wide open during the year. David Palmer of Australia, the 2002 World Open champion, won the

2003 British Open, beating England's Peter Nicol in the final after Nicol had come back from near defeat against Canadian Jonathon Power in the semifinal. Lee Beachill of England moved through the field to take the Qatar Classic surprisingly ahead of Scotland's John White. At the World Open in Lahore, Pak., in December, all of the top-ranked players went out early, which left Frenchman Thierry Lincou as the favourite to take the title and become world number one. In an upset, Lincou was beaten by ninth seed Amr Shabana of Egypt in the final, but reaching the final was enough to propel Lincou to the top of the world rankings. Australia won the men's world team title in Vienna, beating France in the final after the French had toppled England in the semifinals. (ANDREW SHELLEY)

SWIMMING

The 10th Fédération Internationale de Natation (FINA) world swimming championships, held in Barcelona, Spain, in July 2003, provided a showcase for talent one year before the Olympic Games in Athens. A record 2,015 competitors, representing 157 nations, took part. The U.S. (with 28 medals, including 11 gold) and Australia (22 medals, 6 gold) dominated the proceedings in the pool, but swimmers from 11 other nations won gold medals, and athletes from another 11 took silver or bronze. World records were broken 14 times in 11 events, and championship records were bettered 38 times.

One individual, however, dominated the event: 18-year-old American Michael Phelps, who broke a world record five times and won five medals—three gold and two silver. Phelps won the 200-m butterfly in 1 min 54.35 sec after having reduced his own world record to 1 min 53.93 sec in the semifinals. He also lowered his own record to 1 min 57.52 sec in the semifinals of the 200-m individual medley and then swam even faster (1 min 56.04 sec) in the final. (A week later, at the U.S. national championships, he lowered that time to 1 min 55.94 sec.) After Ukraine's Andrey Serdinov (51.76 sec) broke Australian Michael Klim's four-year-old 100-m butterfly record in the first semifinal, Phelps won his semifinal in 51.47 sec. He swam the final in 51.10 sec but, in the biggest upset of the meet, was beaten by teammate Ian Crocker (50.98 sec). Phelps also smashed his own world record in the 400-m individual medley with a 4-min 9.09-sec final and led off the American team's silver-medal-winning 4 × 200-m freestyle relay. At year's end he was named the male World Swimmer of the Year by *Swimming World* magazine, replacing Australia's Ian Thorpe, who had won the honour two years in a row and four of the previous five years.

Japan's Kosuke Kitajima set breaststroke world records in both the 100-m (59.78 sec) and 200-m (2 min 9.42 sec) events. Russia's 31-year-old Aleksandr Popov won the 50-m freestyle in 21.92 sec (a championship record), upset favourite Pieter van den Hoogenband of The Netherlands in the 100-m freestyle, and swam the anchor leg in Russia's unexpected triumph over the U.S. in the 4 × 100-m freestyle relay. Thorpe was victorious in the 200-m freestyle and easily vanquished teammate Grant Hackett in the 400-m freestyle race. Hackett won the 1,500 m for the third straight time, finishing almost a full pool length ahead of Ukraine's Igor Chervynsky. Hackett also triumphed in the 800-m freestyle and led off Australia's gold medal 4 × 200-m freestyle relay. American Aaron Peirsol swept the 100-m and 200-m backstroke events. Germany's Thomas Rupprath (24.80-sec) smashed the 50-m backstroke world record, and Australian backstroker Matt Welsh set a new standard in the 50-m butterfly with his 23.43-sec victory. Peirsol, Brendan Hansen, Crocker, and Jason Lezak broke the world record in the final of the 4 × 100-m medley relay (3 min 31.54 sec). James Gibson won the 50-m breaststroke, becoming the first British man to win a global title in more than a quarter of a century.

In the women's competition Germany's Hannah Stockbauer was the only other swimmer besides Phelps to win three individual gold medals in Barcelona—in the 400-m, 800-m, and 1,500-m freestyle. The feat earned her *Swimming World*'s female World Swimmer of the Year honours. Three other women won two gold medals each. Inge de Bruijn of The Netherlands was victorious in the 50-m freestyle and the 50-m butterfly. China's Luo Xuejuan won the 50-m breaststroke and captured the 100-m breaststroke gold medal with a time of 1 min 6.80 sec after Australia's Leisel Jones had set a world record (1 min 6.37 sec) in the semifinals. (In Melbourne in November, Jones set more new records: 2 min 17.75 sec in the 200 m and 1 min 5.09 sec in the 100 m. Yana Klochkova of Ukraine repeated her 2000 Olympic triumphs in both individual medleys.

Amanda Beard of the U.S. swam a brilliant 200-m final, equaling the world record (2 min 22.99 sec). American Jenny Thompson captured another

At the U.S. national swimming championships on August 9, Michael Phelps swims the butterfly en route to breaking his own world record in the individual medley, one of seven world records the 18-year-old American set in 2003.

AP/Wide World Photos

world title—this time in the 100-m butterfly. The 30-year-old second-year medical school student also anchored the U.S.'s winning 4 × 100-m freestyle relay and garnered silver in the 50-m butterfly and the medley relay, in which she swam the butterfly leg. By the end of the meet, Thompson had a record 15 world championship medals. The 100-m and 200-m freestyle gold medals went to Finland's Hanna-Maria Seppälä and Belarus's Alena Popchanka, respectively. Nina Zhivanevskaya of Spain won the 50-m backstroke, with Germany's Antje Buschschulte triumphant in the 100-m backstroke and Britain's Katy Sexton in the 200 m. Poland's Otylia Jedrzejczak, who finished second behind Thompson in the 100-m butterfly, won the 200 m. The U.S. triumphed in both freestyle relays but finished second behind China in the medley relay. World record holder Natalie Coughlin of the U.S. saw limited action after being stricken with the flu.

World records were set in five short-course events in 2003. American Lindsay Benko broke the four-minute barrier for 400-m freestyle when she clocked 3 min 59.53 sec at a World Cup meet in Berlin. Sweden's Emma Igelström took the 100-m breaststroke mark down twice to 1 min 5.11 sec, but Jones lowered it again in November to 1 min 5.09 sec. Jones also set a new 200-m breaststroke record (2 min 17.75 sec). Rupprath lowered the men's 100-m individual medley standard to 52.58 sec, while Canada's Brian Johns clocked 4 min 2.72 sec for the 400-m individual medley.

Diving. China again dominated the world diving scene in 2003, gaining 12 medals—including 4 gold—at the FINA world championships. In the men's 1-m springboard, China's Xu Xiang and Wang Kenan took gold and silver, respectively. Joona Puhakka was third, earning Finland's first diving medal. Unheralded Aleksandr Dobrosok of Russia pulled off a stunning upset in the 3-m springboard, nipping China's Peng Bo and the favourite, his Russian teammate Dmitry Sautin. (An unprecedented 33 top scores of 10 were awarded by the judges, 13 of them going to Sautin.) The 10-m platform saw another upset, with Alexandre Despatie, 18, becoming Canada's first male world champion diver. In synchronized diving Sautin and Dobrosok breezed to victory in the 3-m springboard, while Australia's Mathew Helm and Robert Newberry came from behind to win the 10-m platform.

Irina Lashko, who had won gold for Russia in the women's 1-m springboard competition at the 1998 world championships, repeated her triumph for her adopted country, Australia. China was shut out of the medals. It was a different story, however, on the 3-m springboard, with China's Guo Jingjing and Wu Minxia taking first and third; Russia's Yuliya Pakhalina snatched second place. In an astonishing upset, Canada's Emilie Heymans scored 9s and 10s on her final dive to win the 10-m platform event. China swept both women's synchronized diving events as Wu and Guo won the 3-m springboard and Lao Lishi and Li Ting triumphed on the 10-m platform.

Synchronized Swimming. Russia (with two gold medals and a silver) and Japan (one gold and two silvers) dominated the synchronized swimming competition at the world championships. France's Virginie Dedieu gained the top solo honours, ahead of Russia's Anastasiya Yermakova. In the duet competition Yermakova and Anastasiya Davydova dethroned defending champions Miya Tachibana and Miho Takeda of Japan. Russia and Japan earned the top two spots in the team competition, respectively, and the U.S. edged Spain for the bronze medal. Japan easily won the first world championship in the dramatic free-routine combination; the U.S. and Spain tied for second. (PHILLIP WHITTEN)

TENNIS

A pair of talented, purposeful, and tenacious individuals made immense strides across the 2003 season, moving past all of their chief adversaries to the top of the tennis world. American Andy Roddick—blessed with one of the game's most explosive serves, a maturing match-playing temperament, and a growing awareness of his potential—garnered the number one world ranking among the men, capping a brilliant campaign by securing his first major at the U.S. Open. Belgium's Justine Henin-Hardenne was victorious at the French Open and the U.S. Open, establishing herself unequivocally as the best in the world.

The rise of Roddick and Henin-Hardenne overshadowed nearly everything and everyone else during a riveting year on the courts. Before she was forced away from the game by knee surgery in August, however, American Serena Williams won the Australian Open and All-England (Wimbledon) championships to lift her total of career Grand Slam tournament triumphs to six. Spain's Juan Carlos Ferrero and Switzerland's Roger Federer came through to take their first major singles titles at the French Open and Wimbledon, respectively. At age 32 the evergreen Andre Agassi of the U.S. raised his historical stock by collecting an eighth Grand Slam title with his Australian Open victory. Henin-Hardenne's

Belgian tennis player Justine Henin-Hardenne (right) beams after defeating her countrywoman Kim Clijsters (left) in the final of the U.S. Open in September.

AP/Wide World Photos

countrywoman Kim Clijsters was the highest-paid woman with record prize-money earnings of $4,091,594. Leading the way among the men was Federer with $4,000,680. This was the first time the top woman earned more than the highest-paid man.

Australian Open. Meeting in their fourth consecutive major final, Serena Williams and her sister Venus went full force after a title neither had ever won. Serena again was the superior player, but not by much. In perhaps their highest-quality confrontation, Serena beat Venus 7–6 (4), 3–6, 6–4 and became only the fifth woman to have won four consecutive major championships. With the temperature soaring to 43.9 °C (111 °F), the all-Williams final was contested indoors under a retractable roof. In the semifinals Clijsters had led Serena 5–1 in the third and final set and twice reached match point before Williams collected six games in a row to close out an arduous battle 4–6, 6–3, 7–5.

Agassi continued his impressive hard-court mastery "Down Under" and dropped only one set in seven nearly impeccable matches. The number two seed American crushed number 31 seed Rainer Schüttler of Germany 6–2, 6–2, 6–1 in the final to record his fourth triumph at the season's first Grand Slam championship. Schüttler had upset a debilitated Roddick in a four-set semifinal after Roddick had stopped Morocco's captivating Younes El Aynaoui 4–6, 7–6 (5), 4–6, 6–4, 21–19. In this five-hour quarterfinal, Roddick saved a match point in the fifth set, which lasted 2 hours 23 minutes. El Aynaoui had ousted top-seeded Lleyton Hewitt of Australia 6–7 (4), 7–6 (4), 7–6 (5), 6–4 in the fourth round without conceding a single service game.

French Open. Ferrero lost in the French semifinal in 2000 and 2001 and was the runner-up in 2002, but in 2003 the time had come for the stylish Spaniard to rule on the red clay courts at Roland Garros. The 23-year-old number three seed took the world's premier clay-court championship emphatically, casting aside the big Dutchman Martin Verkerk 6–1, 6–3, 6–2 in a lopsided final. Verkerk had never won a match in a major before and had appeared in only two Grand Slam events prior to his astonishing showing in Paris.

Henin-Hardenne and Clijsters collided in an all-Belgian women's final, with a poised Henin-Hardenne rolling comfortably to a 6–0, 6–4 triumph. Clijsters, who had been beaten 1–6, 6–4, 12–10 by American Jennifer Capriati in the 2001 Roland Garros final, could not find her range off the ground, while Henin-Hardenne sparkled in all facets of her game. In a riveting semifinal the number four seed Henin-Hardenne had stopped number one seed Serena Williams 6–2, 4–6, 7–5. Williams had led 4–2, 30–0 in the final set but could not close the account.

Wimbledon. The surging Federer had already secured five tournament victories by the time he arrived at Wimbledon as the number four seed. On the All-England Club's fabled Centre Court, the Swiss all-court stylist was dazzling—serving and volleying majestically on the grass, returning serve adroitly, carrying himself confidently, and sweeping 21 of 22 sets. Federer did not lose his serve in his last two matches and defeated number five seed Roddick 7–6 (6), 6–3, 6–3 in the semifinals and unseeded Australian Mark Philippoussis 7–6 (5), 6–2, 7–6 (3) for the title. Philippoussis had released an astounding 46 aces in a five-set win over number two seed Agassi in the fourth round. For the first time since 1967, the defending men's champion lost in the opening round as an out-of-sorts Hewitt was struck down by Croatian qualifier Ivo Karlovic 1–6, 7–6 (5), 6–3, 6–4.

The Williams sisters made it to the women's final for the second year in a row. Serena, the top seed, battled back gamely to beat an ailing Venus 4–6, 6–4, 6–2, garnering her sixth career Grand Slam title and preventing Venus from taking her fifth. Neither woman competed again for the rest of the year; Venus never fully recovered from an abdominal stomach strain, and Serena had knee surgery. Serena had overwhelmed Henin-Hardenne 6–3, 6–2 in their semifinal. Venus was hurting badly during her semifinal battle with Clijsters, but in a spectacular turnaround she rallied to win 10 of the last 11 games in a 4–6, 6–3, 6–1 victory.

U.S. Open. Roddick became the first player since Pete Sampras in 1996 to capture a major championship from match point down during the course of the event. In his semifinal showdown with Argentina's David Nalbandian at Flushing Meadows, N.Y., the number four seed lost the first two sets and was one point away from elimination in the third set, but he rallied valiantly for a 6–7 (4), 3–6, 7–6 (7), 6–1, 6–3 triumph. Buoyant after that close call, Roddick dismantled number three seed Ferrero 6–3, 7–6 (2), 6–3. The 21-year-old American won 68 of 87 points on his potent delivery, produced 23 aces, and did not lose his serve. Agassi had fallen to Ferrero in a four-set semifinal.

The top-seeded Clijsters and second seed Henin-Hardenne met in their second major final of the season, and Henin-Hardenne was once more the player with the upper hand. Clijsters served for the first set at 5–4, but she lost 9 of the last 10 games as Henin-Hardenne pulled away for a 7–5, 6–1 win. In a stirring semifinal Henin-Hardenne was two points from defeat against Capriati no fewer than 10 times, but she somehow escaped 4–6, 7–5, 7–6 (4) in what was arguably the match of the year for the women.

Other Events. Federer routed Agassi 6–3, 6–0, 6–4 in the final of the season-ending Tennis Masters Cup in Houston, Texas, for his seventh title of the year; he finished the season at number two in the world behind Roddick. Henin-Hardenne ended 2003 ranked at the top, with Clijsters close behind at number two.

Led by Amélie Mauresmo and Mary Pierce, France defeated the U.S. 4–1 in the Fed Cup final in Moscow in November for that country's second women's team championship. A week later Australia captured its 28th Davis Cup in Melbourne, Australia, with a 3–1 win over Spain. Both Hewitt and Philippoussis produced upset victories over Ferrero on the grass courts.

Sampras—the men's record holder with 14 Grand Slam titles and the man many considered the greatest player of all time—officially announced his retirement at an emotional ceremony on opening night of the U.S. Open. American Michael Chang also retired during the Open. Former women's number one Martina Hingis of Switzerland left the game—almost certainly for good—in March following leg surgery.

(STEVE FLINK)

TRACK AND FIELD SPORTS (ATHLETICS)

The 2003 track and field (athletics) season featured both indoor and outdoor world championships and was noteworthy for spectacular distance races and the emergence of new young champions in many events.

World Indoor Championships. At the International Association of Athletics Federations (IAAF) world indoor championships, held in Birmingham, Eng., on March 14–16, Svetlana Feofanova cleared a world record 4.80 m (15 ft 9 in) in the women's pole vault. The 22-year-old Russian had set world indoor records five times before, but this win marked a decisive turning point in her rivalry with American Stacy Dragila, who failed to clear a height to qualify for the final. Mozambican Maria Mutola became the first woman to earn five world indoor gold medals as she won the 800-m final in 1 min 58.94 sec. Ethiopian Haile Gebrselassie, shortly before his 30th birthday, won the 3,000-m race for an event-record third time in 7 min 40.97 sec.

Swedish high jumpers repeated as champions when Stefan Holm took the men's gold at 2.35 m (7 ft 8½ in) and Kajsa Bergqvist captured the women's title at 2.01 m (6 ft 7 in). Other victorious Swedes included triple jumper Christian Olsson, who won with a jump of 17.70 m (58 ft 1 in), and Carolina Klüft, who set a meet-record 4,933 points in the women's pentathlon. Klüft, 20, was part of a youth movement that also included 21-year-old American Justin Gatlin, who won the men's 60 m (6.46 sec) by the largest margin in meet history (0.07 sec). Meet records also went to a pair of veteran women as 39-year-old American Regina Jacobs took the 1,500 m in 4 min 1.67 sec and 28-year-old Russian Irina Korzhanenko won the shot put with a distance of 20.55 m (67 ft 5½ in).

World Outdoor Championships. On August 23–31 the Parisian suburb of St. Denis hosted the world outdoor championships. In the men's 10,000 m, world record holder Gebrselassie met 20-year-old Ethiopian teammate Kenenisa Bekele (*see* BIOGRAPHIES), who had beaten him once in June. After a slow first half, Gebrselassie began to push the pace, a tactic he had never before used in six world championship and Olympic 10,000-m wins. He dropped four Kenyan challengers and controlled the race until Bekele sprinted past to lead an Ethiopian medal sweep, with Sileshi Sihine third. Not only was Bekele's time of 27 min 49.57 sec a meet record, but he also ran the second half (12 min 57.24 sec) faster than the meet record for the 5,000 m. In the women's 10,000 m, Ethiopian Berhane Adere's win in 30 min 4.18 sec led a race that produced 7 of the 20 fastest times in history.

Miler Hicham El Guerrouj of Morocco wanted to distance himself from the notion that pacemakers had aided his three previous world championship 1,500-m wins. With no teammate to assist, El Guerrouj took the lead at 600 m and won by 0.54 sec over France's Mehdi Baala in 3 min 31.77 sec. Four days later, eager to become the first global 1,500-m/5,000-m double gold medalist since Finland's Paavo Nurmi at the 1924 Olympics, El Guerrouj faced Bekele in the 5,000-m final. Bekele set a hard early pace but slowed at halfway. The victory appeared to be El Guerrouj's until 18-year-old Kenyan Eliud Kipchoge outleaned him by 0.04 sec in a meet-record finish in 12 min 52.79 sec.

Steeplechase champion Saif Saaeed Shaheen was actually a Kenyan athlete named Stephen Cherono who had switched his citizenship to Qatar (and changed his name) earlier in the summer for a sum alternately reported as $1,000,000 and $1,000 per month for life. Shaheen, whose brother Christopher Kosgei had won the 1999 steeplechase world title, set a blistering pace

Felix Sánchez sails over the last hurdle on his way to winning the gold medal in the 400-m hurdles at the Pan American Games, held in his native Dominican Republic in August.

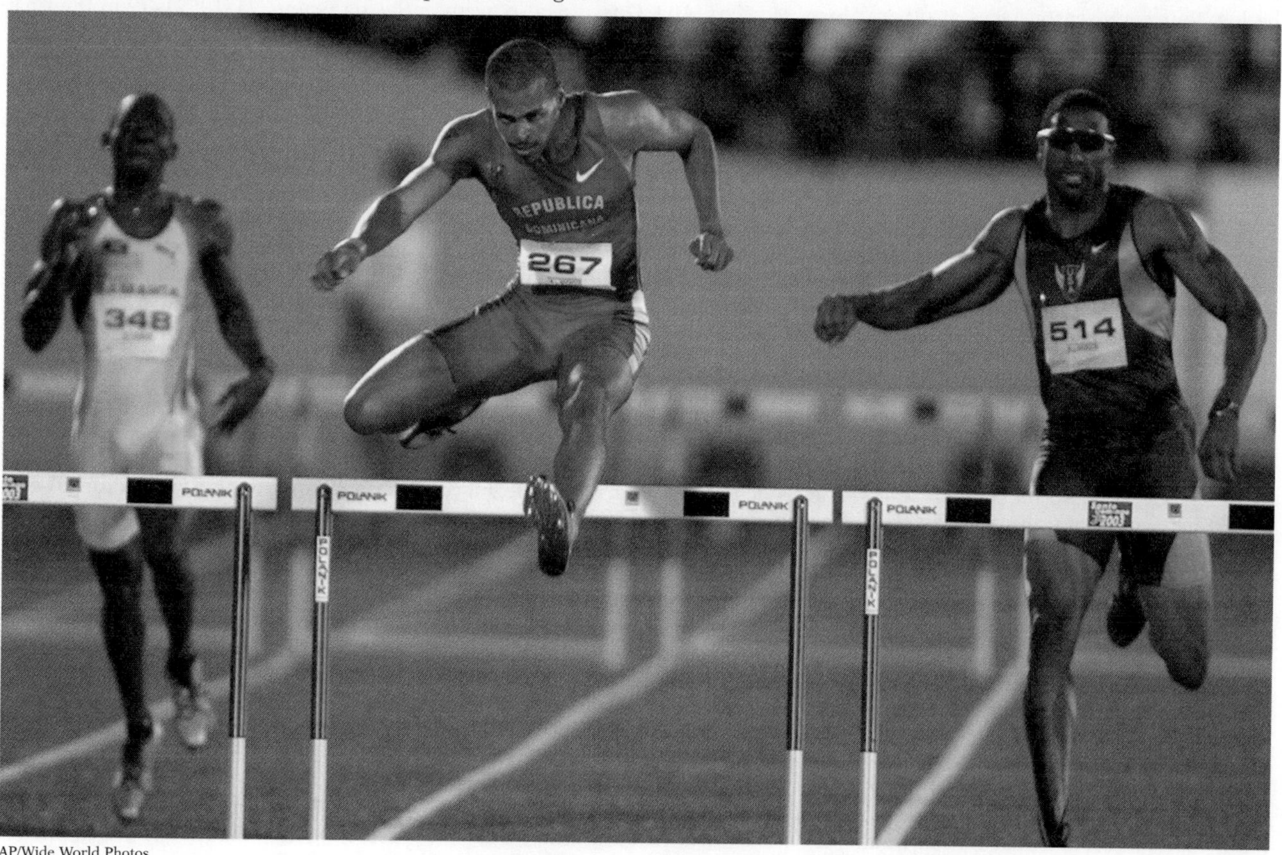

AP/Wide World Photos

and then inexplicably slowed and let the field catch up before exploding past Kenyan champion Ezekiel Kemboi 50 m (164 ft) before the finish to win.

The championships also had controversy in the sprints. American Jon Drummond refused to leave the track after a questionable false-start disqualification during the 100-m quarterfinals. He argued, lay down in his lane, and delayed the competition for more than 20 minutes. Drummond eventually gave up, but he was charged by the IAAF with having brought the sport into disrepute and voluntarily ended his season in an attempt to forestall further disciplinary action. Kim Collins of tiny Saint Kitts and Nevis won the 100-m final in 10.07 sec. American Kelli White won the women's 100 m and 200 m, but she tested positive for a mild stimulant, modafinil. White argued that the drug, which she claimed to take for narcolepsy, was not on the IAAF's banned list, but at season's end, as reports that other athletes were testing positive for the same drug began to mount, it appeared likely that she would be stripped of her medals.

Men's International Competition. Felix Sánchez of the Dominican Republic went undefeated in all 11 of his 400-m hurdle races during the year, although he lost four early-season races at other distances. Sánchez, whose 47.25-sec winning time at the world championships strengthened his position as the sixth-fastest 400-m hurdler in history, extended his winning streak since July 2001 to 28 meets. El Guerrouj won seven 1,500-m and mile finals, retaining a perfect record in those events since the 2000 Olympics. The IAAF changed the name of its annual Grand Prix Final meet to the World Athletics Final and expanded the competition to include all the standard Olympic events except the road races, 10,000 m, and multidiscipline events. El Guerrouj, citing fatigue, skipped the meet, but he still won the $100,000 IAAF men's Athlete of the Year title, which was based for the first time on points earned in the IAAF world rankings. Shaheen never lost in eight steeplechases and beat El Guerrouj in a 5,000-m race, where his winning time of 12 min 48.81 sec made him the third fastest ever. For a 10.05-sec 100-m win in Moscow in September, Gatlin won $500,000, the largest prize purse ever at a standard track meet.

A drug scandal surfaced late in the year when the U.S. Anti-Doping Agency (USADA) revealed that an anonymous informant had turned in a sample of a previously undetectable anabolic steroid, tetrahydrogestrinone (THG), for which it had developed a test. USADA and international doping officials said that several men and women athletes had tested positive for the substance and were likely to be suspended for two years. British sprinter Dwain Chambers became the first to admit taking THG and claimed that he had believed it was not banned. Kenyan Bernard Lagat, an Olympic and 2001 world championships 1,500-m medalist, suffered an emotional blow as well as one to his career when the news was leaked that he had tested positive for banned synthetic erythropoietin in August. A test of the second part of Lagat's sample exonerated him, but not before he had missed the world championships and other meets.

Women's International Competition. Mutola won the Golden League, a series that offered shares of a $1 million prize to athletes who won their events at all six Golden League meets. Her last challenger, sprinter Chandra Sturrup of The Bahamas, lost at the penultimate meet in Berlin, which allowed Mutola to collect the entire jackpot when she won at the last Golden League meet in Brussels. Mutola ran 19 finals, indoors and out, at 800 m and 1,000 m without a loss. Mexico's Ana Guevara also went undefeated in seven races at 400 m plus a race at the rarely run 300-m distance in Mexico City, where she ran the fastest time ever (35.30 sec). Feofanova won 9 of 16 pole vaults, losing once to Dragila and six times to other Russians. At the London Grand Prix in July, Yelena Isinbayeva of Russia lifted Dragila's outdoor world record to 4.82 m (15 ft 9¾ in). South African high jumper Hestrie Cloete, victorious in 22 of 26 meets, won the IAAF women's Athlete of the Year title.

Cross Country and Marathon Running. Men's and women's marathon world records set by Kenyan Paul Tergat and Briton Paula Radcliffe were the performances of the year. Radcliffe raced through the London Marathon in April in 2 hours 15 min 25 sec to clip a stunning 1 min 53 sec from her own standard set in Chicago in 2002. The magnitude of the achievement was underscored by Radcliffe's victory margin of 4 min 30 sec over former world record holder Catherine Ndereba of Kenya. In the fall Radcliffe ran the fastest half-marathon ever, over a slightly downhill course that was ineligible for record consideration, and won her third world half-marathon title.

At the Berlin Marathon in September, former track 10,000-m world-record holder Tergat got his first marathon win and the record. Even Tergat was surprised by the time—2 hours 4 min 55 sec, a 43-sec reduction of the standard set by Khalid Khannouchi of the U.S. in London in 2002. Within sight of the finish, Tergat paused momentarily, unsure of which portal of the famed Brandenburg Gate he should run through. Sammy Korir, Tergat's pacemaker who had elected to finish the race, caught up and forced Tergat to sprint at the end. Korir finished just one second behind.

At the world cross country championships in Avenches, Switz., Bekele repeated as double champion in the men's long- and short-course races. Kenya's Edith Masai defended her short-course title, and Ethiopian Worknesh Kidane took the women's long-course crown. Kenya won four of the six team battles, and Ethiopia took the women's long-course and junior women's team titles.

(SIEG LINDSTROM)

VOLLEYBALL

Misty May and Kerri Walsh of the United States upset the Brazilian defending champions, Adriana Behar and Shelda Bruno, 21–19, 21–19 in the final of the Fédération Internationale de Volleyball (FIVB) 2003 beach volleyball world championships, held in Rio de Janeiro in October. Australia's Natalie Cook and Nicole Sanderson collected the bronze medal with a 21–16, 21–17 win over Americans Jenny Jordan and Annett Davis. May and Walsh had captured five titles in the 2003 FIVB World Tour and had finished no lower than fourth in 8 of the 12 tour's events. They took second place in the FIVB overall rankings behind Ana Paula Connelly and Sandra Pires Tavares of Brazil.

One week later Brazil's Ricardo Alex Costa Santos and Emanuel Rego, the world number one ranked duo, defeated Americans Dax Holdren and Stein Metzger 21–18, 21–15 in the final of the men's beach volleyball world championships. The bronze medal was awarded to Benjamin Insfran and Marcio Henrique Araujo of Brazil after Portugal's Luis Miguel Maia and João Carlos Brenha were unable to play because of an injury.

In the $15 million men's World League finals, held in Madrid in July, Brazil triumphed 3–2 over Serbia and Montenegro. Italy finished third after defeating the Czech Republic. Martin

Lebl of the Czech Republic was crowned the top spiker, while the top server and blocker was Andrija Geric of Serbia and Montenegro.

China captured the 2003 women's World Grand Prix following a 3–0 victory over defending champions Russia in the final in Andria, Italy. The U.S. placed third overall in the 12-team competition. Russian players dominated the individual awards, with Yekaterina Gamova (top scorer), Yelizaveta Tishchenko (top spiker), and Anastasiya Belikova (top blocker) each earning honours.

Brazil, Italy, and Serbia and Montenegro earned spots in the 2004 Olympic Games following top-three finishes in the men's World Cup, while Brazil, China, and the U.S. qualified for the Olympics via top-three finishes at the women's World Cup.

(RICHARD S. WANNINGER)

WEIGHT LIFTING

The 2003 International Weightlifting Federation world championships took place in Vancouver, B.C., on November 14–22. It was also the main qualification event for the 2004 Olympic Games in Athens, as the teams that finished in the top 28 places in the men's division and the top 17 positions in the women's earned spots for the Olympics. A total of 505 athletes entered the competition, 297 men representing 59 countries in eight body-weight classes and 208 women representing 47 countries in seven body-weight classes.

China topped the women's medal rankings with 19 medals (15 gold, 2 silver, and 2 bronze), followed by Thailand (8), Ukraine (5), North Korea (3), and Belarus (2). China's Ding Meiyuan, the 2000 Olympic champion, won the women's superheavyweight category with a 300-kg (661.4-lb) overall total. In the women's competition 23 world records—12 senior and 11 junior—were broken. Chinese athletes broke 10 world records, and competitors from Thailand broke 5.

In the men's division China topped the medal rankings with 13 (6 gold, 5 silver, and 2 bronze), followed by Iran (5, including 4 gold), Turkey (12), Bulgaria (6), and Russia (7). Iran's superheavyweight Hossein Rezazadeh, the reigning Olympic and world champion, won the 2003 title with a 457.5-kg (1,008.6-lb) total result. Two junior men's world records were broken, both by Vladislav Lukanin of Russia.

(DRAGOMIR CIOROSLAN)

AP/Wide World Photos

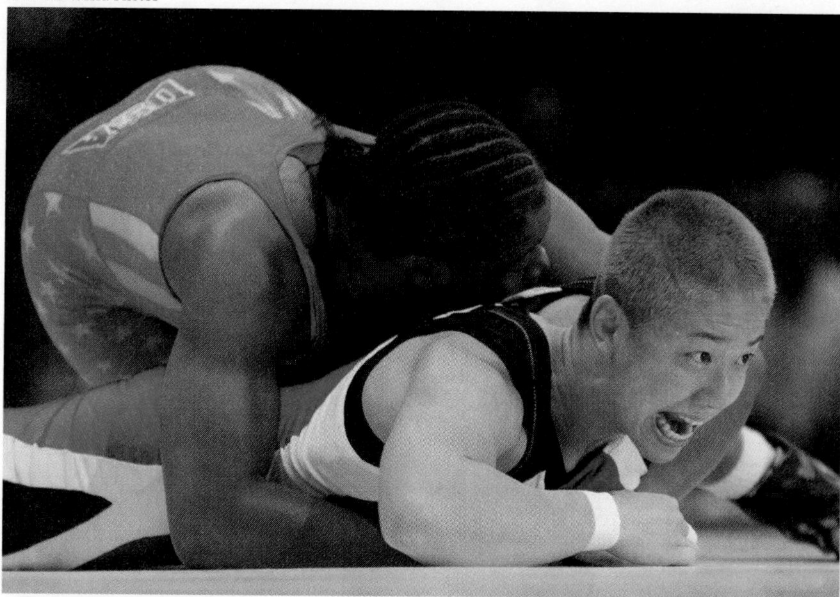

American Toccara Montgomery holds down Kyoko Hamaguchi of Japan in the final of the 72-kg weight class at the women's world freestyle wrestling championships in September; Hamaguchi recovered to win the gold medal.

WRESTLING

Freestyle and Greco-Roman. In September 2003 Georgia triumphed by one point in the Fédération Internationale de Lutte Amateur (FILA) men's world freestyle wrestling championships at Madison Square Garden in New York City. The U.S. beat Iran for second place via a tiebreaker because Americans had gained the most silver medals. Top wrestlers from more than 70 countries took part in the event, which set a record for attendance for a non-Olympic international wrestling event, drawing a total of 53,665 spectators.

At the women's freestyle championships, which were held in conjunction with the men's, Japan tied with the U.S. but won the tiebreaker by earning more gold medals. Japanese women swept all five of their finals, beating Americans in three of those bouts. The U.S. qualified for all four women's Olympic weight classes for the 2004 Olympic Games in Athens.

At the Greco-Roman world championships, held in Créteil, France, in October, Georgia also took the team gold medal (its second), scoring 29 points to beat the runner-up and reigning world champion, Russia (25 points), and Ukraine (25).

FILA announced that it would induct its first class of honorees for the new FILA International Wrestling Hall of Fame. The FILA Hall of Fame would be housed at the National Wrestling Hall of Fame and Museum in Stillwater, Okla.

In March Oklahoma State University won its 31st National Collegiate Athletic Association wrestling championship with a 38.5 margin of victory over the University of Minnesota.

(ANDRÉ REDDINGTON)

Sumo. *Yokozuna* (grand champion) Takanohana, who had dominated professional sumo for the past decade, retired in January 2003. This event almost overshadowed the performance of Asashoryu, who won promotion to *yokozuna* after his second consecutive *yusho* (championship). For the rest of 2003, Mongolian-born Asashoryu stood with the U.S.-born *yokozuna* Musashimaru at the top rank of the sumo world, the first time two foreigners had done so.

Asashoryu had the most victories of any *rikishi* ("strong man") for the year, adding championships at the Natsu Basho in May and the Aki Basho in September. Three men at *ozeki* (champion) rank won the events staged outside Tokyo. Chiyotaikai and Kaio seized the Emperor's Cup in Osaka's Haru Basho in March and July's Nagoya Basho, respectively, while Tochiazuma won the Kyushu Basho in Fukuoka in November.

At the end of the year, former *yokozuna* Akebono abruptly left the Japan Sumo Association, dashing hopes that he would succeed his coach. Musashimaru retired, as did former *maegashira* (rank-and-file) Sentoryu (Henry Armstrong Miller) of St. Louis, Mo.

(KEN COLLER)

Sporting Record

ARCHERY

FITA Outdoor World Target Archery Championships*

Year	Men's individual Winner	Points	Men's team Winner	Points
1999	Hong Sung Chil (S.Kor.)	115	Italy	252
2001	Yeon Jung Ki (S.Kor.)	115	South Korea	247
2003	**M. Frangilli (Italy)**	**113**	**South Korea**	**238**

Year	Women's individual Winner	Points	Women's team Winner	Points
1999	Lee Eun Kyung (S.Kor.)	115	Italy	240
2001	Park Sung Hyun (S.Kor.)	111	China	232
2003	**Yun Mi Jin (S.Kor.)**	**116**	**South Korea**	**252**

*Olympic (recurve) division.

AUTOMOBILE RACING

Formula One Grand Prix Race Results, 2003

Race	Driver	Winner's time (hr:min:sec)
Australian GP	D. Coulthard (U.K.)	1:34:42.124
Malaysian GP	K. Räikkönen (Fin.)	1:32:22.195
Brazilian GP	G. Fisichella* (Italy)	1:31:17.748
San Marino GP	M. Schumacher (Ger.)	1:28:12.058
Spanish GP	M. Schumacher (Ger.)	1:33:46.933
Austrian GP	M. Schumacher (Ger.)	1:28:04.888
Monaco GP	J.P. Montoya (Colom.)	1:42:19.012
Canadian GP	M. Schumacher (Ger.)	1:31:13.591
European GP	R. Schumacher (Ger.)	1:34:43.622
British GP	R. Barrichello (Braz.)	1:28:34.554
French GP	R. Schumacher (Ger.)	1:30:49.213
German GP	J.P. Montoya (Colom.)	1:28:48.769
Hungarian GP	F. Alonso (Spain)	1:39:01.460
Belgian GP	*canceled*	
Italian GP	M. Schumacher (Ger.)	1:14:19.838
United States GP	M. Schumacher (Ger.)	1:33:35.997
Japanese GP	R. Barrichello (Braz.)	1:25:11.743

WORLD DRIVERS' CHAMPIONSHIP: M. Schumacher 93 points, Räikkönen 91 points, Montoya 82 points. CONSTRUCTORS' CHAMPIONSHIP: Ferrari 158 points, Williams/BMW 144 points, McLaren/Mercedes 142 points.

*Race stopped; Fisichella declared winner after stewards' review.

National Association for Stock Car Auto Racing (NASCAR) Winston Cup Champions

Year	Winner
2001	J. Gordon
2002	T. Stewart
2003	**M. Kenseth**

Indy Car Champions*

Year	Driver
2001	G. de Ferran (Braz.)
2002	C. da Matta (Braz.)
2003	**P. Tracy (Can.)**

*CART champion.

AP/Wide World Photos

Formula One Grand Prix drivers' champion Michael Schumacher.

Daytona 500

Year	Winner	Avg. speed in mph
2001	M. Waltrip	161.783
2002	W. Burton	142.971
2003	**M. Waltrip**	**133.870**

Indianapolis 500

Year	Winner	Avg. speed in mph
2001	H. Castroneves	153.601
2002	H. Castroneves	166.499
2003	**G. de Ferran**	**156.291**

Le Mans 24-Hour Grand Prix d'Endurance

Year	Car	Drivers
2001	Audi R8	F. Biela, T. Kristensen, E. Pirro
2002	Audi R8	F. Biela, T. Kristensen, E. Pirro
2003	**Bentley**	**T. Kristensen, R. Capello, G. Smith**

Monte-Carlo Rally

Year	Car	Driver
2001	Mitsubishi Lancer	T. Mäkinen (Fin.)
2002	Subaru	T. Mäkinen (Fin.)
2003	**Citroën**	**S. Loeb (Fr.)**

BADMINTON

All-England Championships—Singles

Year	Men	Women
2001	P. Gopichand (India)	Gong Zhichao (China)
2002	Chen Hong (China)	C. Martin (Den.)
2003	**Muhammad Hafiz Hashim (Malay.)**	**Zhou Mi (China)**

Uber Cup (women)

Year	Winner	Runner-up
1997–98	China	Indonesia
1999–2000	China	Denmark
2001–02	China	South Korea

Thomas Cup (men)

Year	Winner	Runner-up
1997–98	Indonesia	Malaysia
1999–2000	Indonesia	China
2001–02	Indonesia	Malaysia

World Badminton Championships

Year	Men's singles	Women's singles	Men's doubles	Women's doubles
1999	Sun Jun (China)	C. Martin (Den.)	Kim Dong Moon, Ha Tae Kwon (S.Kor.)	Ge Fei, Gu Jun (China)
2001	Hendrawan (Indon.)	Gong Ruina (China)	T. Gunawan, H. Haryanto (Indon.)	Gao Ling, Huang Sui (China)
2003	**Xia Xuanze (China)**	**Zhang Ning (China)**	**L. Paaske, J. Rasmussen (Den.)**	**Gao Ling, Huang Sui (China)**

BASEBALL

Final Major League Standings, 2003

AMERICAN LEAGUE

East Division				Central Division				West Division			
Club	W.	L.	G.B.	Club	W.	L.	G.B.	Club	W.	L.	G.B.
*New York	101	61	—	*Minnesota	90	72	—	*Oakland	96	66	—
*Boston	95	67	6	Chicago	86	76	4	Seattle	93	69	3
Toronto	86	76	15	Kansas City	83	79	7	Anaheim	77	85	19
Baltimore	71	91	30	Cleveland	68	94	22	Texas	71	91	25
Tampa Bay	63	99	38	Detroit	43	119	47				

NATIONAL LEAGUE

East Division				Central Division				West Division			
Club	W.	L.	G.B.	Club	W.	L.	G.B.	Club	W.	L.	G.B.
*Atlanta	101	61	—	*Chicago	88	74	—	*San Francisco	100	61	—
*Florida	91	71	10	Houston	87	75	1	Los Angeles	85	77	15½
Philadelphia	86	76	15	St. Louis	85	77	3	Arizona	84	78	16½
Montreal	83	79	18	Pittsburgh	75	87	13	Colorado	74	88	26½
New York	66	95	34½	Cincinnati	69	93	19	San Diego	64	98	36½
				Milwaukee	68	94	20				

*Gained play-off berth.

Caribbean Series

Year	Winning team	Country
2001	Cibao Eagles	Dominican Republic
2002	Culiacán Tomato Growers	Mexico
2003	**Cibao Eagles**	**Dominican Republic**

World Series*

Year	Winning team	Losing team	Results
2001	Arizona Diamondbacks (NL)	New York Yankees (AL)	4–3
2002	Anaheim Angels (AL)	San Francisco Giants (NL)	4–3
2003	**Florida Marlins (NL)**	**New York Yankees (AL)**	**4–2**

*AL—American League; NL—National League.

Japan Series*

Year	Winning team	Losing team	Results
2001	Yakult Swallows (CL)	Osaka Kintetsu Buffaloes (PL)	4–1
2002	Yomiuri Giants (CL)	Seibu Lions (PL)	4–0
2003	**Fukuoka Daiei Hawks (PL)**	**Hanshin Tigers (CL)**	**4–2**

*CL—Central League; PL—Pacific League.

BASKETBALL

NBA Final Standings, 2002–03

EASTERN CONFERENCE

Team	Won	Lost	G.B.	Team	Won	Lost	G.B.
Atlantic Division				Central Division			
*New Jersey	49	33	—	*Detroit	50	32	—
*Philadelphia	48	34	1	*Indiana	48	34	2
*Boston	44	38	5	*New Orleans	47	35	3
*Orlando	42	40	7	*Milwaukee	42	40	8
Washington	37	45	12	Atlanta	35	47	15
New York	37	45	12	Chicago	30	52	20
Miami	25	57	24	Toronto	24	58	26
				Cleveland	17	65	33

WESTERN CONFERENCE

Team	Won	Lost	G.B.	Team	Won	Lost	G.B.
Midwest Division				Pacific Division			
*San Antonio	60	22	—	*Sacramento	59	23	—
*Dallas	60	22	0	*L.A. Lakers	50	32	9
*Minnesota	51	31	9	*Portland	50	32	9
*Utah	47	35	13	*Phoenix	44	38	15
Houston	43	39	17	Seattle	40	42	19
Memphis	28	54	32	Golden State	38	44	21
Denver	17	65	43	L.A. Clippers	27	55	32

*Gained play-off berth.

National Basketball Association (NBA) Championship

Season	Winner	Runner-up	Results
2000–01	Los Angeles Lakers	Philadelphia 76ers	4–1
2001–02	Los Angeles Lakers	New Jersey Nets	4–0
2002–03	**San Antonio Spurs**	**New Jersey Nets**	**4–2**

Women's National Basketball Association (WNBA) Championship

Season	Winner	Runner-up	Results
2001	Los Angeles Sparks	Charlotte Sting	2–0
2002	Los Angeles Sparks	New York Liberty	2–0
2003	**Detroit Shock**	**Los Angeles Sparks**	**2–1**

Division I National Collegiate Athletic Association (NCAA) Championship—Men

Year	Winner	Runner-up	Score
2001	Duke	Arizona	82–72
2002	Maryland	Indiana	64–52
2003	**Syracuse**	**Kansas**	**81–78**

Division I National Collegiate Athletic Association (NCAA) Championship—Women

Year	Winner	Runner-up	Score
2001	Notre Dame	Purdue	68–66
2002	Connecticut	Oklahoma	82–70
2003	**Connecticut**	**Tennessee**	**73–68**

World Basketball Championship—Men

Year	Winner	Runner-up
1998	Yugoslavia	Russia
2000	United States	France
2002	Yugoslavia	Argentina

World Basketball Championship—Women

Year	Winner	Runner-up
1998	United States	Russia
2000	United States	Australia
2002	United States	Russia

BILLIARD GAMES

World Three-Cushion Championship*

Year	Winner
2001	R. Ceulemans (Belg.)
2002	M. Zanetti (Italy)
2003	**S. Sayginer (Tur.)**

*Union Mondiale de Billard champion.

WPA World Nine-Ball Championships

Year	Men's champion
2001	M. Immonen (Fin.)
2002	E. Strickland (U.S.)
2003	**T. Hohmann (Ger.)**

Year	Women's champion
2001	A. Fisher (U.K.)
2002	Liu Shin-Mei (Taiwan)
2003	**not held**

World Professional Snooker Championship

Year	Winner
2001	R. O'Sullivan
2002	P. Ebdon
2003	**M. Williams**

BOBSLEIGH AND LUGE

Bobsleigh and Skeleton World Championships

Year	Two-man bobsleigh	Four-man	Women's bobsleigh	Men's skeleton	Women's skeleton
2001	C. Langen, M. Jakobs (Ger.)	Germany	F. Burdet, K. Sutter (Switz.)	M. Rettl (Austria)	M. Pedersen (Switz.)
2002*	C. Langen, M. Zimmermann (Ger.)	Germany	J. Bakken, V. Flowers (U.S.)	J. Shea, Jr. (U.S.)	T. Gale (U.S.)
2003	**A. Lange, K. Kuske (Ger.)**	**Germany**	**S. Erdmann, A. Dietrich (Ger.)**	**J. Pain (Can.)**	**M. Kelly (Can.)**

*Olympic champions.

Luge World Championships*

Year	Men	Women	Doubles	Team
2001	A. Zöggeler (Italy)	S. Otto (Ger.)	A. Florschütz, T. Wustlich (Ger.)	Germany
2002†	A. Zöggeler (Italy)	S. Otto (Ger.)	P. Leitner, A. Resch (Ger.)	
2003	**A. Zöggeler (Italy)**	**S. Otto (Ger.)**	**A. Linger, W. Linger (Austria)**	**Germany**

*Artificial track. †Olympic champions.

BOWLING

ABC Bowling Championships—Regular Divisions

Year	Singles	Score	All-events	Score
2001	N. Hoagland	798	D.J. Archer	2,219
2002	M. Millsap	823	S.A. Hardy	2,279
2003	**R. Bahr**	**837**	**S. Kloempken**	**2,215**

WIBC Bowling Championships—Classic Division

Year	Singles	Score	All-events	Score
2001	L. Wagner	756	J. Armon	2,044
2002	T. Smith	752	C. Honeychurch	2,150
2003	**M. Feldman**	**764**	**M. Feldman**	**2,048**

World Tenpin Bowling Championships—Men

Year	Singles	Pairs	Triples	Team (fives)
1995	M. Doi (Can.)	Sweden	Netherlands	Netherlands
1999	G. Verbruggen (Belg.)	Sweden	Finland	Sweden
2003	**M. Luoto (Fin.)**	**Sweden**	**United States**	**Sweden**

World Tenpin Bowling Championships—Women

Year	Singles	Pairs	Triples	Team (fives)
1995	D. Ship (Can.)	Thailand	Australia	Finland
1999	K. Kulick (U.S.)	Australia	South Korea	South Korea
2003	**Z. Glover (Eng.)**	**England**	**Philippines**	**Malaysia**

PBA Tournament of Champions

Year	Champion
2000	J. Couch
2001	not held
2002–03	**J. Couch**

PBA World Championship*

Year	Winner
2001	W.R. Williams, Jr.
2001–02	D. Kent
2002–03	**W.R. Williams, Jr.**

*PBA National Championship until 2002.

BOXING

World Heavyweight Champions No Weight Limit

WBA

John Ruiz (U.S.; 3/3/01)
Roy Jones, Jr. (U.S.; 3/1/03)

WBC

Lennox Lewis (U.K.; 11/17/01)

IBF

Chris Byrd (U.S.; 12/14/02)

World Cruiserweight Champions Top Weight 195 Pounds (WBC 200 Pounds)

WBA

Jean-Marc Mormeck (Fr.; 2/23/02)

WBC

Wayne Braithwaite (Guyana; 10/11/02)

IBF

Vassily Jirov (Vasily Zhirov) (Kazakh.; 6/5/99)
James Toney (U.S.; 4/26/03)

AP/Wide World Photos

Kostya Tszyu, the undisputed world junior welterweight champion.

BOXING (continued)

World Light Heavyweight Champions
Top Weight 175 Pounds

WBA

Roy Jones, Jr. (U.S.; 7/18/98)
declared super champion in 2001
gave up super title in 2003

Bruno Girard (Fr.; 12/22/01)

Mehdi Sahnoune (Fr.; 3/8/03, defeated Girard)

Silvio Branco (Italy; 10/10/03)

WBC

Roy Jones, Jr. (U.S.; 8/7/97)
gave up title in 2003

Antonio Tarver (U.S.; 4/26/03)

Roy Jones, Jr. (U.S.; 11/8/03)

IBF

Roy Jones, Jr. (U.S.; 6/5/99)
stripped of title in 2002

Antonio Tarver (U.S.; 4/26/03)
gave up title in 2003

World Super Middleweight Champions
Top Weight 168 Pounds

WBA

Byron Mitchell (U.S.; 3/3/01)

Sven Ottke (Ger.; 3/15/03)
declared super champion in 2003

Anthony Mundine (Austl.; 9/3/03)

WBC

Eric Lucas (Can.; 7/10/01)

Markus Beyer (Ger.; 4/5/03)

IBF

Sven Ottke (Ger.; 10/24/98)

World Middleweight Champions
Top Weight 160 Pounds

WBA

Bernard Hopkins (U.S.; 9/29/01)
declared super champion in 2001

William Joppy (U.S.; 11/17/01)

Bernard Hopkins (U.S.; 12/13/03)
declared undisputed champion

WBC

Bernard Hopkins (U.S.; 4/14/01)

IBF

Bernard Hopkins (U.S.; 4/29/95)

World Junior Middleweight Champions
Top Weight 154 Pounds
(also called super welterweight)

WBA

Oscar de la Hoya (U.S.; 9/14/02)
declared super champion in 2002

Santiago Samaniego (Pan.; 8/10/02)

Alejandro García (Mex.; 3/1/03, defeated Samaniego)

Shane Mosley (U.S.; 9/13/03, defeated de la Hoya)
declared super champion

Travis Simms (U.S.; 12/13/03, defeated García)

WBC

Oscar de la Hoya (U.S.; 6/23/01)

Shane Mosley (U.S.; 9/13/03)

IBF

Ronald Wright (U.S.; 10/12/01)

World Welterweight Champions
Top Weight 147 Pounds

WBA

Ricardo Mayorga (Nic.; 3/30/02)
declared super champion in 2003

Jose Rivera (U.S.; 9/13/03)

Cory Spinks (U.S.; 12/13/03, defeated Mayorga)
declared undisputed champion

WBC

Vernon Forrest (U.S.; 1/26/02)

Ricardo Mayorga (Nic.; 1/25/03)

Cory Spinks (U.S.; 12/13/03)

IBF

Michele Piccirillo (Italy; 4/13/02)

Cory Spinks (U.S.; 3/22/03)

World Junior Welterweight Champions
Top Weight 140 Pounds
(also called super lightweight)

WBA

Kostya Tszyu (Austl.; 2/3/01)
declared super champion in 2001
declared undisputed champion in 2003

Diobelys Hurtado (Cuba; 5/11/02)

Vivian Harris (Guyana; 10/19/02)

WBC

Kostya Tszyu (Austl.; 8/21/99)
declared emeritus champion in 2003

IBF

Kostya Tszyu (Austl.; 11/3/01)

World Lightweight Champions
Top Weight 135 Pounds

WBA

Leonard Dorin (Can.; 1/5/02)
stripped of title in 2003

WBC

Floyd Mayweather, Jr. (U.S.; 4/20/02)

IBF

Paul Spadafora (U.S.; 8/20/99)
gave up title in 2003

Javier Jauregui (Mex.; 11/22/03)

World Junior Lightweight Champions
Top Weight 130 Pounds
(also called super featherweight)

WBA

Acelino Freitas (Braz.; 1/12/02)
declared super champion in 2002

Yodsanan Nanthachai (Thai.; 4/13/02)

WBC

Sirimongkol Singmanassuk (Thai.; 8/24/02)

Jesús Chávez (Mex.; 8/15/03)

IBF

Steve Forbes (U.S.; 12/3/00)
stripped of title in 2002

Carlos Hernández (El Sal.; 2/1/03)

World Featherweight Champions
Top Weight 126 Pounds

WBA

Derrick Gainer (U.S.; 9/9/00)

Juan Manuel Márquez (Mex.; 11/1/03)

WBC

Erik Morales (Mex.; 11/16/02)
declared emeritus champion in 2003

IBF

Johnny Tapia (U.S.; 4/27/02)
stripped of title in 2002

Juan Manuel Márquez (Mex.; 2/1/03)

World Junior Featherweight Champions
Top Weight 122 Pounds
(also called super bantamweight)

WBA

Salim Medjkoune (Fr.; 10/9/02)

Mahyar Monshipour (Fr.; 7/4/03)

WBC

Oscar Larios (Mex.; 11/1/02)

IBF

Manny Pacquiao (Phil.; 6/23/01)

World Bantamweight Champions
Top Weight 118 Pounds

WBA

Johnny Bredahl (Den.; 4/19/02)

WBC

Veeraphol Sahaprom (Thai.; 12/29/98)

IBF

Tim Austin (U.S.; 7/19/97)

Rafael Márquez (Mex.; 2/15/03)

World Junior Bantamweight Champions
Top Weight 115 Pounds
(also called super flyweight)

WBA

Alexander Muñoz (Venez.; 3/9/02)

WBC

Masanori Tokuyama (Japan; 8/27/00)

IBF

Félix Machado (Venez.; 7/22/00)

Luis Pérez (Nic.; 1/4/03)

BOXING (continued)

World Flyweight Champions
Top Weight 112 Pounds

WBA

Eric Morel (P.R.; 8/5/00)
Lorenzo Parra (Venez.; 12/6/03)

WBC

Pongsaklek Wongjongkam (Thai.; 3/2/01)

IBF

Irene Pacheco (Colom.; 4/10/99)

World Junior Flyweight Champions
Top Weight 108 Pounds

WBA

Rosendo Álvarez (Nic.; 3/3/01)

WBC

Jorge Arce (Mex.; 7/6/02)

IBF

Ricardo López (Mex.; 10/2/99)
gave up title in 2002
José Víctor Burgos (Mex.; 2/15/03)

World Mini-flyweight Champions
Top Weight 105 Pounds
(also called strawweight)

WBA

Noel Arambulet (Venez.; 7/29/02)

WBC

José Antonio Aguirre (Mex.; 2/11/00)

IBF

Miguel Barrera (Colom.; 8/9/02)
Edgar Cárdenas (Mex.; 5/31/03)
Daniel Reyes (Colom.; 10/4/03)

CHESS

FIDE Chess Championship—Men

Year	Winner	Runner-up
1999	A. Khalifman (Russia)	V. Akopyan (Arm.)
2000	V. Anand (India)	A. Shirov (Spain)
2002	R. Ponomaryov (Ukr.)	V. Ivanchuk (Ukr.)

FIDE Chess Championship—Women

Year	Winner	Runner-up
1999	Xie Jun (China)	A. Galyamova (Russia)
2000	Xie Jun (China)	Qin Karying (China)
2001	Zhu Chen (China)	A. Kostenyuk (Russia)

FIDE Olympiad—Open

Year	Winner	Runner-up
1998	Russia	United States
2000	Russia	Germany
2002	Russia	Hungary

FIDE Olympiad—Women

Year	Winner	Runner-up
1998	China	Russia
2000	China	Georgia
2002	China	Russia

CRICKET

Cricket World Cup

Year	Result			
1996	Sri Lanka	245 for 3	Australia	241
1999	Australia	133 for 2	Pakistan	132
2003	**Australia**	**359 for 2**	**India**	**234**

Test Match Results, October 2002–September 2003

Host/Ground	Date	Scores	Result
Pakistan/Colombo (Sri Lanka)*	Oct. 3–7	Austl. 467 and 127; Pak. 279 and 274	Austl. won by 41 runs
Pakistan/Sharjah (U.A.E.)*	Oct. 11–12	Pak. 59 and 53; Austl. 310	Austl. won by an innings and 198 runs
Pakistan/Sharjah (U.A.E.)*	Oct. 19–22	Austl. 444; Pak. 221 and 203	Austl. won by an innings and 20 runs; Austl. won series 3–0
India/Mumbai	Oct. 9–12	India 457; W.Ind. 157 and 188	India won by an innings and 112 runs
India/Chennai	Oct. 17–20	W.Ind. 167 and 229; India 316 and 81 for 2	India won by 8 wickets
India/Kolkata	Oct. 30–Nov. 3	India 358 and 471 for 8; W.Ind. 497	Match drawn; India won series 2–0
South Africa/East London	Oct. 18–21	S.Af. 529 for 4 dec; Bangl. 170 and 252	S.Af. won by an innings and 107 runs
South Africa/Potchefstroom	Oct. 25–27	Bangl. 215 and 107; S.Af. 482 for 5 dec	S.Af. won by an innings and 160 runs; S.Af. won series 2–0
Australia/Brisbane	Nov. 7–10	Austl. 492 and 296 for 5 dec; Eng. 325 and 79	Austl. won by 384 runs
Australia/Adelaide	Nov. 21–24	Eng. 342 and 159; Austl. 552 for 9 dec	Austl. won by an innings and 51 runs
Australia/Perth	Nov. 29–Dec. 1	Eng. 185 and 223; Austl. 456	Austl. won by an innings and 48 runs
Australia/Melbourne	Dec. 26–30	Austl. 551 for 6 dec and 107 for 5; Eng. 270 and 387	Austl. won by 5 wickets
Australia/Sydney	Jan. 2–6	Eng. 362 and 452 for 9 dec; Austl. 363 and 226	Eng. won by 225 runs; Austl. won series 4–1
South Africa/Johannesburg	Nov. 8–10	SriL. 192 and 130; S.Af. 386	S.Af. won by an innings and 64 runs
South Africa/Centurion	Nov. 15–19	SriL. 323 and 245; S.Af. 448 and 124 for 7	S.Af. won by 3 wickets; S.Af. won series 2–0
Zimbabwe/Harare	Nov. 9–12	Pak. 285 and 369; Zimb. 225 and 310	Pak. won by 119 runs
Zimbabwe/Bulawayo	Nov. 16–19	Zimb. 178 and 281; Pak. 403 and 57 for 0	Pak. won by 10 wickets; Pak. won series 2–0
Bangladesh/Dhaka	Dec. 8–10	Bangl. 139 and 87; W.Ind. 536	W.Ind. won by an innings and 310 runs
Bangladesh/Chittagong	Dec. 16–18	Bangl. 194 and 212; W.Ind. 296 and 111 for 3	W.Ind. won by 7 wickets; W.Ind. won series 2–0
South Africa/Durban	Dec. 26–29	S.Af. 368 and 45 for 0; Pak. 161 and 250	S.Af. won by 10 wickets
South Africa/Cape Town	Jan. 2–5	S.Af. 620 for 7 dec; Pak. 252 and 226	S.Af. won by an innings and 142 runs; S.Af. won series 2–0
New Zealand/Wellington	Dec. 12–14	India 161 and 121; N.Z. 247 and 36 for 0	N.Z. won by 10 wickets
New Zealand/Hamilton	Dec. 19–22	India 99 and 154; N.Z. 94 and 160 for 6	N.Z. won by 4 wickets; N.Z. won series 2–0

CRICKET (continued)

Test Match Results, October 2002–September 2003 (continued)

Host/Ground	Date	Scores	Result
West Indies/Guyana	April 10–13	W.Ind. 237 and 398; Austl. 489 and 147 for 1	Austl. won by 9 wickets
West Indies/Trinidad	April 19–23	Austl. 576 for 4 dec and 238 for 3 dec; W.Ind. 408 and 288	Austl. won by 118 runs
West Indies/Barbados	May 1–5	Austl. 605 for 9 dec and 8 for 1; W.Ind. 328 and 284	Austl. won by 9 wickets
West Indies/Antigua	May 9–13	Austl. 240 and 417; W.Ind. 240 and 418 for 7	W.Ind. won by 3 wickets; Austl. won series 3–1
Bangladesh/Chittagong	April 24–27	Bangl. 173 and 237; S.Af. 470 for 2 dec	S.Af. won by an innings and 60 runs
Bangladesh/Dhaka	May 1–4	S.Af. 330; Bangl. 102 and 210	S.Af. won by an innings and 18 runs; S.Af. won series 2–0
Sri Lanka/Colombo	April 25–29	N.Z. 515 for 7 dec and 161 for 5 dec; SriL. 483	Match drawn
Sri Lanka/Kandy	May 3–7	N.Z. 305 and 183; SriL. 298 and 72 for 1	Match drawn; series drawn 0–0
England/London (Lord's)	May 22–24	Eng. 472; Zimb. 147 and 233	Eng. won by an innings and 92 runs
England/Durham (Chester-le-Street)	June 5–7	Eng. 416; Zimb. 94 and 253	Eng. won by an innings and 69 runs; Eng. won series 2–0
West Indies/St. Lucia	June 20–24	SriL. 354 and 126 for 0; W.Ind. 477 for 9 dec	Match drawn
West Indies/Jamaica	June 27–29	SriL. 208 and 194; W.Ind. 191 and 212 for 3	W.Ind. won by 7 wickets; W.Ind. won series 1–0
Australia/Darwin	July 18–20	Bangl. 97 and 178; Austl. 407 for 7 dec	Austl. won by an innings and 132 runs
Australia/Cairns	July 25–28	Bangl. 295 and 163; Austl. 556 for 4 dec	Austl. won by an innings and 98 runs; Austl. won series 2–0
England/Birmingham	July 24–28	S.Af. 594 for 5 dec and 134 for 4 dec; Eng. 408 and 110 for 1	Match drawn
England/London (Lord's)	July 31–Aug. 3	Eng. 173 and 417; S.Af. 682 for 6 dec	S.Af. won by an innings and 92 runs
England/Nottingham	Aug. 14–18	Eng. 445 and 118; S.Af. 362 and 131	Eng. won by 70 runs
England/Leeds	Aug. 21–25	S.Af. 342 and 365; Eng. 307 and 209	S.Af. won by 191 runs
England/London (The Oval)	Sept. 4–8	S.Af. 484 and 229; Eng. 604 for 9 dec and 110 for 1	Eng. won by 9 wickets; series drawn 2–2
Pakistan/Karachi	Aug. 20–24	Bangl. 288 and 274; Pak. 346 and 217 for 3	Pak. won by 7 wickets
Pakistan/Peshawar	Aug. 27–31	Bangl. 361 and 96; Pak. 295 and 165 for 1	Pak. won by 9 wickets
Pakistan/Multan	Sept. 3–7	Bangl. 281 and 154; Pak. 175 and 262 for 9	Pak. won by 1 wicket; Pak. won series 3–0

*Played on independent grounds for security reasons.

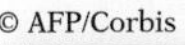

Australia's Adam Gilchrist scores against Sri Lanka in the semifinal of the cricket World Cup; Australia defeated India in the final.

CURLING

World Curling Championship—Men

Year	Winner	Runner-up
2001	Sweden	Switzerland
2002	Canada	Norway
2003	**Canada**	**Switzerland**

World Curling Championship—Women

Year	Winner	Runner-up
2001	Canada	Sweden
2002	Scotland	Sweden
2003	**United States**	**Canada**

CYCLING

Cycling Champions, 2003

Event	Winner	Country
WORLD CHAMPIONS—TRACK		
Men		
Sprint	L. Gané	France
Individual pursuit	B. Wiggins	Great Britain
Kilometre time trial	S. Nimke	Germany
40-km points	F. Stocher	Austria
Team pursuit	G. Brown, P. Dawson, B. Lancaster, L. Roberts	Australia
Keirin	L. Gané	France
Team sprint	C. Bergemann, J. Fiedler, R. Wolff	Germany
50-km Madison	F. Marvulli, B. Risi	Switzerland
15-km scratch	F. Marvulli	Switzerland
Women		
Sprint	S. Grankovskaya	Russia
Individual pursuit	L. Zijlaard-van Moorsel	Netherlands
500-m time trial	N. Tsylinskaya	Belarus
24-km points	O. Slyusareva	Russia
10-km scratch	O. Slyusareva	Russia
Keirin	S. Grankovskaya	Russia
WORLD CHAMPIONS—ROAD		
Men		
Individual road race	I. Astarloa	Spain
Individual time trial	D. Millar	Great Britain
Women		
Individual road race	S. Ljungskog	Sweden
Individual time trial	J. Somarriba Arrola	Spain
WORLD CHAMPION—CYCLO-CROSS		
Men	B. Wellens	Belgium
Women	D. Van den Brand	Netherlands
WORLD CHAMPIONS—MOUNTAIN BIKES		
Men		
Cross-country	F. Meirhaeghe	Belgium
Downhill	G. Minnaar	South Africa
Women		
Cross-country	S. Spitz	Germany
Downhill	A.-C. Chausson	France
MAJOR ELITE ROAD-RACE WINNERS		
Tour de France	L. Armstrong	United States
Tour of Italy	G. Simoni	Italy
Tour of Spain	R. Heras	Spain
Tour of Switzerland	A. Vinokurov	Kazakhstan
Milan–San Remo	P. Bettini	Italy
Tour of Flanders	P. Van Petegem	Belgium
Paris–Roubaix	P. Van Petegem	Belgium
Liège–Bastogne–Liège	T. Hamilton	United States
Amstel Gold	A. Vinokurov	Kazakhstan
HEW–Cyclassics Cup	P. Bettini	Italy
San Sebastian Classic	P. Bettini	Italy
Zürich Championship	D. Nardello	Italy
Paris–Tours	E. Zabel	Germany
Tour of Lombardy	M. Bartoli	Italy
Paris–Nice	A. Vinokurov	Kazakhstan
Ghent–Wevelgem	A. Klier	Germany
Flèche Wallonne	I. Astarloa	Spain
Tour of Romandie	T. Hamilton	United States
Dauphiné Libéré	L. Armstrong	United States
Tirreno–Adriatico	F. Pozzato	Italy

EQUESTRIAN SPORTS

The Kentucky Derby

Year	Horse	Jockey
2001	Monarchos	J. Chavez
2002	War Emblem	V. Espinoza
2003	**Funny Cide**	**J. Santos**

The Preakness Stakes

Year	Horse	Jockey
2001	Point Given	G. Stevens
2002	War Emblem	V. Espinoza
2003	**Funny Cide**	**J. Santos**

The Belmont Stakes

Year	Horse	Jockey
2001	Point Given	G. Stevens
2002	Sarava	E. Prado
2003	**Empire Maker**	**J. Bailey**

2,000 Guineas

Year	Horse	Jockey
2001	Golan	K. Fallon
2002	Rock of Gibraltar	J. Murtagh
2003	**Refuse To Bend**	**P. Smullen**

The Derby

Year	Horse	Jockey
2001	Galileo	M. Kinane
2002	High Chaparral	J. Murtagh
2003	**Kris Kin**	**K. Fallon**

The St. Leger

Year	Horse	Jockey
2001	Milan	M. Kinane
2002	Bollin Eric	K. Darley
2003	**Brian Boru**	**J. Spencer**

Triple Crown Champions—U.S.

Year	Horse
1973	Secretariat
1977	Seattle Slew
1978	Affirmed

Triple Crown Champions—British

Year	Winner
1918	Gainsborough
1935	Bahram
1970	Nijinsky

Melbourne Cup

Year	Horse	Jockey
2001	Ethereal	S. Seamer
2002	Media Puzzle	D. Oliver
2003	**Makybe Diva**	**G. Boss**

The Hambletonian Trot

Year	Horse	Driver
2001	Scarlet Knight	S. Melander
2002	Chip Chip Hooray	E. Ledford
2003	**Amigo Hall**	**M. Lachance**

EQUESTRIAN SPORTS (continued)

Major Thoroughbred Race Winners, 2003

Race	Won by	Jockey
United States		
Acorn	Bird Town	E. Prado
Alabama Stakes	Island Fashion	J. Velazquez
Apple Blossom	Azeri	M. Smith
Arlington Million	Sulamani	D. Flores
Ashland Stakes	Elloluv	R. Albarado
Beldame	Sightseek	J. Bailey
Belmont	Empire Maker	J. Bailey
Beverly D.	Heat Haze	J. Valdivia, Jr.
Blue Grass Stakes	Peace Rules	E. Prado
Breeders' Cup Juvenile	Action This Day	D. Flores
Breeders' Cup Juvenile Fillies	Halfbridled	J. Krone
Breeders' Cup Sprint	Cajun Beat	C. Velasquez
Breeders' Cup Mile	Six Perfections	J. Bailey
Breeders' Cup Distaff	Adoration	P. Valenzuela
Breeders' Cup Turf	High Chaparral*	M. Kinane
	Johar*	A. Solis
Breeders' Cup Filly and Mare Turf	Islington	K. Fallon
Breeders' Cup Classic	Pleasantly Perfect	A. Solis
Carter Handicap	Congaree	G. Stevens
Champagne	Birdstone	J. Bailey
Charles Wittingham Memorial	Storming Home	G. Stevens
Cigar Mile Handicap	Congaree	J. Bailey
Coaching Club American Oaks	Spoken Fur	J. Bailey
Donn Handicap	Harlan's Holiday	J. Velazquez
Eddie Read	Special Ring	D. Flores
Florida Derby	Empire Maker	J. Bailey
Flower Bowl Invitational	Dimitrova	J. Bailey
Fountain of Youth	Trust N Luck	C. Velasquez
Futurity Stakes	Cuvee	J. Bailey
Gulfstream Park Breeders' Cup Handicap	Man From Wicklow	J. Bailey
Haskell Invitational Handicap	Peace Rules	E. Prado
Hollywood Derby	Sweet Return	J. Krone
Hollywood Futurity	Lion Heart	M. Smith
Hollywood Gold Cup	Congaree	J. Bailey
Hollywood Starlet	Hollywood Story	P. Valenzuela
Hollywood Turf Cup	Continuously	A. Solis
Hopeful Stakes	Silver Wagon	J. Bailey
Jockey Club Gold Cup	Mineshaft	R. Albarado
Kentucky Derby	Funny Cide	J. Santos
Kentucky Oaks	Bird Town	E. Prado
Man o' War	Lunar Sovereign	R. Migliore
Matriarch Stakes	Heat Haze	J. Velazquez
Metropolitan	Aldebaran	J. Bailey
Mother Goose	Spoken Fur	J. Bailey
Pacific Classic	Candy Ride	J. Krone
Pimlico Special	Mineshaft	R. Albarado
Preakness	Funny Cide	J. Santos
Queen Elizabeth II Challenge Cup	Film Maker	E. Prado
San Juan Capistrano	Passinetti	B. Blanc
Santa Anita Derby	Buddy Gil	G. Stevens
Santa Anita Handicap	Milwaukee Brew	E. Prado
Secretariat Stakes	Kicken Kris	J. Castellano
Spinaway Stakes	Ashado	E. Prado
Spinster Stakes	Take Charge Lady	E. Prado
Stephen Foster Handicap	Perfect Drift	P. Day
Suburban Handicap	Mineshaft	R. Albarado
Travers	Ten Most Wanted	P. Day
Turf Classic	Sulamani	J. Bailey
United Nations Handicap	Balto Star	J. Velez Jr.
Whitney	Medaglia d'Oro	J. Bailey
Wood Memorial	Empire Maker	J. Bailey
Woodward	Mineshaft	R. Albarado
Yellow Ribbon Stakes	Tates Creek	P. Valenzuela

*Dead heat.

Race	Won by	Jockey
England		
One Thousand Guineas	Russian Rhythm	K. Fallon
Two Thousand Guineas	Refuse To Bend	P. Smullen
Derby	Kris Kin	K. Fallon
Oaks	Casual Look	M. Dwyer
St. Leger	Brian Boru	J. Spencer
Coronation Cup	Warrsan	P. Robinson
Ascot Gold Cup	Mr. Dinos	K. Fallon
Coral-Eclipse Stakes	Falbrav	D. Holland
King George VI and Queen Elizabeth Diamond Stakes	Alamshar	J. Murtagh
Sussex Stakes	Reel Buddy	P. Eddery
Juddmonte International Stakes	Falbrav	D. Holland
Dubai Champion Stakes	Rakti	P. Robinson
France		
Poule d'Essai des Poulains	Clodovil	C. Soumillon
Poule d'Essai des Pouliches	Musical Chimes	C. Soumillon
Prix du Jockey-Club	Dalakhani	C. Soumillon
Prix de Diane	Nebraska Tornado	R. Hughes
Prix Royal-Oak	Westerner	D. Boeuf
Prix Ganay	Fair Mix	O. Peslier
Prix Jacques Le Marois	Six Perfections	T. Thulliez
Grand Prix de Paris	Vespone	C.-P. Lemaire
Grand Prix de Saint-Cloud	Ange Gabriel	T. Jarnet
Prix Vermeille	Mezzo Soprano	L. Dettori
Prix de l'Arc de Triomphe	Dalakhani	C. Soumillon
Grand Criterium	American Post	R. Hughes
Ireland		
Irish Two Thousand Guineas	Indian Haven	J. Egan
Irish One Thousand Guineas	Yesterday	M. Kinane
Irish Derby	Alamshar	J. Murtagh
Irish Oaks	Vintage Tipple	L. Dettori
Irish St. Leger	Vinnie Roe	P. Smullen
Irish Champion Stakes	High Chaparral	M. Kinane
Italy		
Derby Italiano	Osorio	M. Esposito
Gran Premio del Jockey Club	Ekraar	R. Hills
Germany		
Deutsches Derby	Dai Jin	O. Peslier
Grosser Preis von Baden	Mamool	L. Dettori
Preis von Europa	Mamool	L. Dettori
Australia		
Melbourne Cup	Makybe Diva	G. Boss
Cox Plate	Fields Of Omagh	S. King
Caulfield Cup	Mummify	D. Nikolic
United Arab Emirates		
Dubai World Cup	Moon Ballad	L. Dettori
Asia		
Japan Cup	Tap Dance City	T. Sato
Singapore Cup	*canceled*	
Canada		
Queen's Plate Stakes	Wando	P. Husbands
Prince of Wales Stakes	Wando	P. Husbands
Breeders' Stakes	Wando	P. Husbands

FENCING

World Fencing Championships—Men

Year	Individual Foil	Individual Épée	Individual Sabre	Team Foil	Team Épée	Team Sabre
2001	S. Sanzo (Italy)	P. Milanoli (Italy)	S. Pozdnyakov (Russia)	France	Hungary	Russia
2002	S. Vanni (Italy)	P. Kolobkov (Russia)	S. Pozdnyakov (Russia)	Germany	France	Russia
2003	**P. Joppich (Ger.)**	**F. Jeannet (Fr.)**	**V. Lukashenko (Ukr.)**	**Italy**	**Russia**	**Russia**

World Fencing Championships—Women

Year	Individual Foil	Individual Épée	Individual Sabre	Team Foil	Team Épée	Team Sabre
2001	V. Vezzali (Italy)	C. Bokel (Ger.)	A.-L. Touya (Fr.)	Italy	Russia	Russia
2002	S. Boyko (Russia)	Hyun Hee (S.Kor.)	Tan Xue (China)	Russia	Hungary	Russia
2003	**V. Vezzali (Italy)**	**N. Conrad (Ukr.)**	**D. Mihai (Rom.)**	**Poland**	**Russia**	**Italy**

FIELD HOCKEY

World Cup Field Hockey Championship—Men

Year	Winner	Runner-up
1994	Pakistan	Netherlands
1998	Netherlands	Spain
2002	Germany	Australia

World Cup Field Hockey Championship—Women

Year	Winner	Runner-up
1994	Australia	Argentina
1998	Australia	Netherlands
2002	Argentina	Netherlands

FOOTBALL

FIFA World Cup—Men

Year	Result			
1994	Brazil*	0	Italy	0
1998	France	3	Brazil	0
2002	Brazil	2	Germany	0

*Won on penalty kicks.

FIFA World Cup—Women

Year	Result			
1995	Norway	2	Germany	0
1999	United States*	0	China	0
2003	**Germany**	**2**	**Sweden**	**1**

*Won on penalty kicks.

Association Football National Champions, 2003

Nation	League Champions	Cup Winners
Argentina	Independiente (Opening)	River Plate (Closing)
Australia	Perth Glory	
Austria	FK Austria	FK Austria
Belgium	La Louviere	FC Brugge
Bolivia	Bolívar	
Brazil	Santos	Corinthians
Bulgaria	CSKA Sofia	Levski
Cameroon	Cotonsport	Mount Cameroon
Chile	Universidad Catolica (Opening)	Colo Colo (Closing)
China	Dalian Shide	Dalian Shide
Colombia	América Cali (Opening)	Independiente Medellin (Closing)
Costa Rica	Alajuelense	
Croatia	Dynamo Zagreb	Hajduk Split
Czech Republic	Sparta Prague	Teplice
Denmark	FC Copenhagen	Brondby
Ecuador	Emelec	
England	Manchester United	Arsenal
Finland	HJK Helsinki	Haka
France	Lyon	Auxerre
Georgia	Dynamo Tbilisi	Dynamo Tbilisi
Germany	Bayern Munich	Bayern Munich
Greece	Olympiakos	PAOK Salonika
Holland	PSV Eindhoven	Utrecht
Hungary	MTK Budapest	Ferencvaros
Ireland	Bohemians	Derry City
Israel	Maccabi Tel Aviv	Hapoel Ramat Gan
Italy	Juventus	AC Milan
Japan	Jubilo Iwata	Kyoto Purple
Mexico	Toluca	
Morocco	HUSA	
Nigeria	Enyimba	Julius Berger
Northern Ireland	Glentoran	Coleraine
Norway	Rosenborg	Valerenga
Paraguay	Libertad	
Peru	Sporting Cristal	
Poland	Wisla (Krakow)	Wisla (Krakow)
Portugal	Porto	Porto
Romania	Rapid	Dinamo
Russia	Lokomotiv Moscow	Spartak Moscow
Saudi Arabia	Al-Ittihad	Al-Hilal
Scotland	Rangers	Rangers
Senegal	Jeanne d'Arc	AS Douanes
Serbia & Montenegro	Partizan Belgrade	Sartid
Slovakia	Zilina	Matador
Slovenia	Maribor	Olimpija
South Africa	Orlando Pirates	
South Korea	Songnam	Suwon Samsung
Spain	Real Madrid	Mallorca
Sweden	Djurgaarden	Djurgaarden
Switzerland	Grasshoppers	Basle
Tunisia	Esperance	Stade Tunisien
Turkey	Besiktas	Trabzonspor
Ukraine	Dynamo Kiev	Dynamo Kiev
Uruguay	Nacional	
United States (MLS)	Los Angeles Galaxy	San Jose Earthquakes
Venezuela	Caracas	

UEFA Champions League

Season	Result			
2000–01	Bayern Munich (Ger.)*	1	Valencia (Spain)	1
2001–02	Real Madrid (Spain)	2	Bayer 04 Leverkusen (Ger.)	1
2002–03	**AC Milan (Italy)***	**0**	**Juventus (Italy)**	**0**

*Won on penalty kicks.

UEFA Cup

Season	Result			
2000–01	Liverpool (Eng.)	5	Alavés (Spain)	4
2001–02	Feyenoord (Neth.)	3	Borussia Dortmund (Ger.)	2
2002–03	**Porto (Port.)***	**3**	**Celtic (Scot.)**	**2**

*Won on "Silver Goal" in overtime.

FOOTBALL (continued)

Libertadores de América Cup

Year	Winner (country)	Runner-up (country)	Scores
2001	Boca Juniors (Arg.)	Cruz Azul (Mex.)	1–0, 0–1, 3–1*
2002	Olímpia (Par.)	São Caetano (Braz.)	0–1, 2–1, 4–2*
2003	**Boca Juniors (Arg.)**	**Santos FC (Braz.)**	**2–0, 3–1**

*Winner determined in penalty shoot-out.

Copa América

Year	Result			
1997	Brazil	3	Bolivia	1
1999	Brazil	3	Uruguay	1
2001	Colombia	1	Mexico	0

MLS Cup

Year	Result			
2001	San Jose Earthquakes	2	Los Angeles Galaxy	1
2002	Los Angeles Galaxy	1	New England Revolution	0
2003	**San Jose Earthquakes**	**4**	**Chicago Fire**	**2**

U.S. College Football National Champions

Season	Champion
2001–02	Miami
2002–03	Ohio State
2003–04	**Louisiana State*** **Southern California†**

*BCS champion. †AP champion.

Rose Bowl

Season	Result			
2001–02	Miami	37	Nebraska	14
2002–03	Oklahoma	34	Washington State	14
2003–04	**Southern California**	**28**	**Michigan**	**14**

Orange Bowl

Season	Result			
2001–02	Florida	56	Maryland	23
2002–03	Southern California	38	Iowa	17
2003–04	**Miami**	**16**	**Florida State**	**14**

Fiesta Bowl

Season	Result			
2001–02	Oregon	38	Colorado	16
2002–03	Ohio State	31	Miami	24
2003–04	**Ohio State**	**35**	**Kansas State**	**28**

Sugar Bowl

Season	Result			
2001–02	Louisiana State	47	Illinois	34
2002–03	Georgia	26	Florida State	13
2003–04	**Louisiana State**	**21**	**Oklahoma**	**14**

NFL Final Standings, 2003–04

AMERICAN CONFERENCE

East Division	W	L	T
*New England	14	2	0
Miami	10	6	0
Buffalo	6	10	0
New York Jets	6	10	0

North Division	W	L	T
*Baltimore	10	6	0
Cincinnati	8	8	0
Pittsburgh	6	10	0
Cleveland	5	11	0

South Division	W	L	T
*Indianapolis	12	4	0
*Tennessee	12	4	0
Jacksonville	5	11	0
Houston	5	11	0

West Division	W	L	T
*Kansas City	13	3	0
*Denver	10	6	0
Oakland	4	12	0
San Diego	4	12	0

NATIONAL CONFERENCE

East Division	W	L	T
*Philadelphia	12	4	0
*Dallas	10	6	0
Washington	5	11	0
New York Giants	4	12	0

North Division	W	L	T
*Green Bay	10	6	0
Minnesota	9	7	0
Chicago	7	9	0
Detroit	5	11	0

South Division	W	L	T
*Carolina	11	5	0
New Orleans	8	8	0
Tampa Bay	7	9	0
Atlanta	5	11	0

West Division	W	L	T
*St. Louis	12	4	0
*Seattle	10	6	0
San Francisco	7	9	0
Arizona	4	12	0

*Qualified for play-offs.

Super Bowl

	Season	Result			
XXXVI	2001–02	New England Patriots (AFC)	20	St. Louis Rams (NFC)	17
XXXVII	2002–03	Tampa Bay Buccaneers (NFC)	48	Oakland Raiders (AFC)	21
XXXVIII	**2003–04**	**New England Patriots (AFC)**	**32**	**Carolina Panthers (NFC)**	**29**

CFL Grey Cup*

Year	Result			
2001	Calgary Stampeders (WD)	27	Winnipeg Blue Bombers (ED)	19
2002	Montreal Alouettes (ED)	25	Edmonton Eskimos (WD)	16
2003	**Edmonton Eskimos (WD)**	**34**	**Montreal Alouettes (ED)**	**22**

*ED—Eastern Division; WD—Western Division.

FOOTBALL (continued)

AFL Grand Final

Year	Result			
2001	Brisbane Lions	15.18 (108)	Essendon	12.10 (82)
2002	Brisbane Lions	10.15 (75)	Collingwood	9.12 (66)
2003	**Brisbane Lions**	**20.14 (134)**	**Collingwood**	**12.12 (84)**

Rugby League World Cup

Year	Result			
1992	Australia	10	Great Britain	6
1995	Australia	16	England	8
2000	Australia	40	New Zealand	12

Rugby Union World Cup

Year	Result			
1995	South Africa	15	New Zealand	12
1999	Australia	35	France	12
2003	**England**	**20**	**Australia**	**17**

Six Nations Championship*

Year	Result
2001	England
2002	France†
2003	**England†**

*Five Nations until 2000. †Grand Slam winner.

GOLF

Masters Tournament

Year	Winner
2001	T. Woods (U.S.)
2002	T. Woods (U.S.)
2003	**M. Weir (Can.)**

United States Open Championship (men)

Year	Winner
2001	R. Goosen (S.Af.)
2002	T. Woods (U.S.)
2003	**J. Furyk (U.S.)**

British Open Tournament (men)

Year	Winner
2001	D. Duval (U.S.)
2002	E. Els (S.Af.)
2003	**B. Curtis (U.S.)**

U.S. Professional Golfers' Association (PGA) Championship

Year	Winner
2001	D. Toms (U.S.)
2002	R. Beem (U.S.)
2003	**S. Micheel (U.S.)**

United States Amateur Championship (men)

Year	Winner
2001	B. Dickerson (U.S.)
2002	R. Barnes (U.S.)
2003	**N. Flanagan (Austl.)**

British Amateur Championship (men)

Year	Winner
2001	M. Hoey (Ire.)
2002	A. Larrazabal (Spain)
2003	**G. Wolstenholme (U.K.)**

United States Women's Open Championship

Year	Winner
2001	K. Webb (Austl.)
2002	J. Inkster (U.S.)
2003	**H. Lunke (U.S.)**

Women's British Open Championship

Year	Winner
2001	Pak Se Ri (S.Kor.)
2002	K. Webb (Austl.)
2003	**A. Sörenstam (Swed.)**

Ladies Professional Golf Association (LPGA) Championship

Year	Winner
2001	K. Webb (Austl.)
2002	Pak Se Ri (S.Kor.)
2003	**A. Sörenstam (Swed.)**

United States Women's Amateur Championship

Year	Winner
2001	M. Duncan (U.S.)
2002	B. Lucidi (U.S.)
2003	**V. Nirapathpongporn (Thai.)**

England's Martin Johnson (left) attempts to reach past Australian David Lyons for possession of the ball in the Rugby Union World Cup final on November 22.

Ladies' British Amateur Championship

Year	Winner
2001	M. Prieto (Spain)
2002	R. Hudson (U.K.)
2003	**E. Serramia (Spain)**

World Cup (men; professional)

Year	Winner
2001	South Africa (E. Els and R. Goosen)
2002	Japan (T. Izawa and S. Maruyama)
2003	**South Africa (T. Immelman and R. Sabbatini)**

Solheim Cup (women; professional)

Year	Result
2000	Europe 14½, United States 11½
2002	United States 15½, Europe 12½
2003	**Europe 17½, United States 10½**

Ryder Cup (men; professional)

Year	Result
1997	Europe 14½, United States 13½
1999	United States 14½, Europe 13½
2002	Europe 15½, United States 12½

GYMNASTICS

World Gymnastics Championships—Men

Year	All-around team	All-around individual	Horizontal bar	Parallel bars
2001	Belarus	Feng Jing (China)	V. Maras (Greece)	S. Townsend (U.S.)
2002	not held	not held	V. Maras (Greece)	Li Xiaopeng (China)
2003	**China**	**P. Hamm (U.S.)**	**T. Kashima (Japan)**	**Li Xiaopeng (China)**

Year	Pommel horse	Rings	Vault	Floor exercise
2001	M. Urzica (Rom.)	I. Iovchev (Bulg.)	M. Dragulescu (Rom.)	I. Iovchev (Bulg.)* M. Dragulescu (Rom.)*
2002	M. Urzica (Rom.)	S. Csollany (Hung.)	Li Xiaopeng (China)	M. Dragulescu (Rom.)
2003	**Teng Haibin (China)*** **T. Kashima (Japan)***	**I. Iovchev (Bulg.)*** **D. Tampakos (Greece)***	**Li Xiaopeng (China)**	**P. Hamm (U.S.)*** **I. Iovchev (Bulg.)***

* Tied.

World Gymnastics Championships—Women

Year	All-around team	All-around individual	Balance beam
2001	Romania	S. Khorkina (Russia)	A. Raducan (Rom.)
2002	not held	not held	A. Postell (U.S.)
2003	**United States**	**S. Khorkina (Russia)**	**Fan Ye (China)**

Year	Uneven parallel bars	Vault	Floor exercise
2001	S. Khorkina (Russia)	S. Khorkina (Russia)	A. Raducan (Rom.)
2002	C. Kupets (U.S.)	Ye. Zamolodchikova (Russia)	E. Gómez (Spain)
2003	**C. Memmel (U.S.)*** **H. Vise (U.S.)***	**O. Chusovitina (Uzbek.)**	**D. Dos Santos (Braz.)**

* Tied.

Gymnastics all-around gold medalist Paul Hamm competes on the rings.

ICE HOCKEY

NHL Final Standings, 2003

EASTERN CONFERENCE

Northeast Division	W	L	T	OTL*
†Ottawa	52	21	8	1
†Toronto	44	28	7	3
†Boston	36	31	11	4
Montreal	30	35	8	9
Buffalo	27	37	10	8

Atlantic Division	W	L	T	OTL*
†New Jersey	46	20	10	6
†Philadelphia	45	20	13	4
†New York Islanders	35	34	11	2
New York Rangers	32	36	10	4
Pittsburgh	27	44	6	5

Southeast Division	W	L	T	OTL*
†Tampa Bay	36	25	16	5
†Washington	39	29	8	6
Atlanta	31	39	7	5
Florida	24	36	13	9
Carolina	22	43	11	6

WESTERN CONFERENCE

Central Division	W	L	T	OTL*
†Detroit	48	20	10	4
†St. Louis	41	24	11	6
Chicago	30	33	13	6
Nashville	27	35	13	7
Columbus	29	42	8	3

Northwest Division	W	L	T	OTL*
†Colorado	42	19	13	8
†Vancouver	45	23	13	1
†Minnesota	42	29	10	1
†Edmonton	36	26	11	9
Calgary	29	36	13	4

Pacific Division	W	L	T	OTL*
†Dallas	46	17	15	4
†Anaheim	40	27	9	6
Los Angeles	33	37	6	6
Phoenix	31	35	11	5
San Jose	28	37	9	8

*Overtime losses, worth one point. †Qualified for play-offs.

The Stanley Cup

Season	Winner	Runner-up	Games
2000–01	Colorado Avalanche	New Jersey Devils	4–3
2001–02	Detroit Red Wings	Carolina Hurricanes	4–1
2002–03	**New Jersey Devils**	**Anaheim Mighty Ducks**	**4–3**

World Ice Hockey Championship—Men

Year	Winner
2001	Czech Republic
2002	Slovakia
2003	**Canada**

World Ice Hockey Championship—Women

Year	Winner
2001	Canada
2002	not held
2003	**canceled**

ICE SKATING

World Figure Skating Champions—Men

Year	Winner
2001	Ye. Plushchenko (Russia)
2002	A. Yagudin (Russia)
2003	**Ye. Plushchenko (Russia)**

World Figure Skating Champions—Women

Year	Winner
2001	M. Kwan (U.S.)
2002	I. Slutskaya (Russia)
2003	**M. Kwan (U.S.)**

World Figure Skating Champions—Pairs

Year	Winners
2001	J. Salé, D. Pelletier (Can.)
2002	Shen Xue, Zhao Hongbo (China)
2003	**Shen Xue, Zhao Hongbo (China)**

World Ice Dancing Champions

Year	Winners
2001	B. Fusar Poli, M. Margaglio (Italy)
2002	I. Lobachyova, I. Averbukh (Russia)
2003	**S. Bourne, V. Kraatz (Can.)**

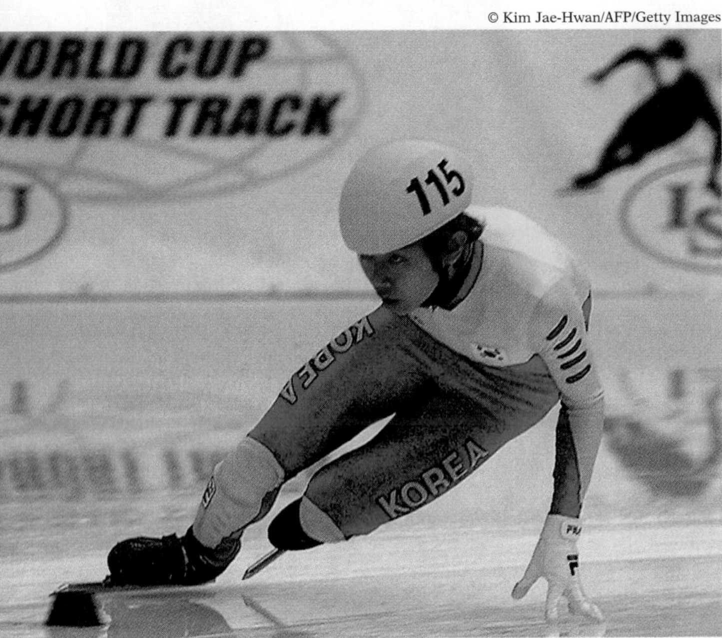

Short-track speed-skating overall world champion Ahn Hyun Soo.

ICE SKATING (continued)

World Ice Speed-Skating Records Set in 2003 on Major Tracks*

Event	Name	Country	Result
MEN			
100 m	Hiroyasu Shimizu	Japan	9.43 sec
sprint	Jeremy Wotherspoon	Canada	137.270 points
	Jeremy Wotherspoon	Canada	137.230 points
WOMEN			
sprint	Monique Garbrecht-Enfeldt	Germany	149.305 points

*May include records awaiting ISU ratification at year's end.

World Ice Speed-Skating Records Set in 2003 on Short Tracks*

Event	Name	Country	Time
MEN			
500 m	Jeffrey Scholten	Canada	41.289 sec
	Jean-François Monette	Canada	41.184 sec
1,000 m	Jean-François Monette	Canada	1 min 25.662 sec
1,500 m	Ahn Hyun Soo	South Korea	2 min 10.639 sec
3,000 m	Ahn Hyun Soo	South Korea	4 min 32.646 sec
5,000-m relay	Canada National Team	Canada	6 min 43.667 sec
	South Korea National Team	South Korea	6 min 42.893 sec
WOMEN			
1,000 m	Byun Chun Sa	South Korea	1 min 30.483 sec
3,000-m relay	South Korea National Team	South Korea	4 min 11.742 sec

*May include records awaiting ISU ratification at year's end.

World Speed-Skating Sprint Champions

Year	Men	Women
2001	M. Ireland (Can.)	M. Garbrecht-Enfeldt (Ger.)
2002	J. Wotherspoon (Can.)	C. LeMay Doan (Can.)
2003	**J. Wotherspoon (Can.)**	**M. Garbrecht-Enfeldt (Ger.)**

World All-Around Speed-Skating Champions

Year	Men	Women
2001	R. Ritsma (Neth.)	A. Friesinger (Ger.)
2002	J. Uytdehaage (Neth.)	A. Friesinger (Ger.)
2003	**G. Romme (Neth.)**	**C. Klassen (Can.)**

World Short-Track Speed-Skating Championships—Overall Winners

Year	Men	Women
2001	Li Jianjun (China)	Yang Yang (A) (China)
2002	Kim Dong Sung (S.Kor.)	Yang Yang (A) (China)
2003	**Ahn Hyun Soo (S.Kor.)**	**Choi Eun Kyung (S.Kor.)**

JUDO

World Judo Championships—Men

Year	Open weights	60 kg	66 kg	73 kg
1999	S. Shinohara (Japan)	M. Poulot (Cuba)	L. Benboudaoud (Fr.)	J. Pedro (U.S.)
2001	A. Mikhaylin (Russia)	A. Lounifi (Tun.)	A. Miresmaeili (Iran)	V. Makarov (Russia)
2003	**K. Suzuki (Japan)**	**Choi Min Ho (S.Kor.)**	**A. Miresmaeili (Iran)**	**Lee Won Hee (S.Kor.)**
Year	**81 kg**	**90 kg**	**100 kg**	**+100 kg**
1999	G. Randall (U.K.)	H. Yoshida (Japan)	K. Inoue (Japan)	S. Shinohara (Japan)
2001	Cho In Chul (S.Kor.)	F. Demontfaucon (Fr.)	K. Inoue (Japan)	A. Mikhaylin (Russia)
2003	**F. Wanner (Ger.)**	**Hwang Hee Tae (S.Kor.)**	**K. Inoue (Japan)**	**Y. Muneta (Japan)**

World Judo Championships—Women

Year	Open weights	48 kg	52 kg	57 kg
1999	D. Beltran (Cuba)	R. Tamura (Japan)	N. Narasaki (Japan)	D. González (Cuba)
2001	C. Lebrun (Fr.)	R. Tamura (Japan)	Kye Sun Hui (N.Kor.)	Y. Lupetey (Cuba)
2003	**Tong Wen (China)**	**R. Tamura (Japan)**	**A. Savon (Cuba)**	**Kye Sun Hui (N.Kor.)**
Year	**63 kg**	**70 kg**	**78 kg**	**+78 kg**
1999	K. Maeda (Japan)	S. Veranes (Cuba)	N. Anno (Japan)	B. Maksymow (Pol.)
2001	G. Vandecaveye (Belg.)	M. Ueno (Japan)	N. Anno (Japan)	Yuan Hua (China)
2003	**D. Krukower (Arg.)**	**M. Ueno (Japan)**	**N. Anno (Japan)**	**Sun Fuming (China)**

ROWING

World Rowing Championships—Men

Year	Single sculls	Min:sec	Double sculls	Min:sec	Quadruple sculls	Min:sec	Coxed pairs	Min:sec
2001	O. Tufte (Nor.)	6:43.04	A. Haller, T. Peto (Hung.)	6:14.16	Germany	5:40.89	J. Cracknell, M. Pinsent (Gr.Brit.)	6:49.33
2002	M. Hacker (Ger.)	6:36.33	A. Haller, T. Peto (Hung.)	6:05.74	Germany	5:39.57	L. Krisch, A. Werner (Ger.)	6:47.93
2003	**O. Tufte (Nor.)**	**6:46.15**	**A. Hardy, S. Vielledent (Fr.)**	**6:13.93**	**Germany**	**6:12.26**	**D. Berry, M. Rich (U.S.)**	**7:10.11**

Year	Coxless pairs	Min:sec	Coxed fours	Min:sec	Coxless fours	Min:sec	Eights	Min:sec
2001	J. Cracknell, M. Pinsent (Gr.Brit.)	6:27.57	France	6:08.25	Great Britain	5:48.98	Romania	5:27.48
2002	J. Cracknell, M. Pinsent (Gr.Brit.)	6:14.27	Great Britain	6:06.70	Germany	5:41.35	Canada	5:26.92
2003	**D. Ginn, J. Tomkins (Austl.)**	**6:19.31**	**United States**	**6:04.68**	**Canada**	**5:52.91**	**Canada**	**6:00.44**

World Rowing Championships—Women

Year	Single sculls	Min:sec	Coxless pairs	Min:sec
2001	K. Rutschow-Stomporowski (Ger.)	7:19.25	G. Damian, V. Susanu (Rom.)	7:01.27
2002	R. Neykova (Bulg.)	7:07.71	G. Andrunache, V. Susanu (Rom.)	6:53.80
2003	**R. Neykova (Bulg.)**	**7:18.12**	**C. Bishop, K. Grainger (Gt.Brit.)**	**7:04.88**

Year	Double sculls	Min:sec	Coxless fours	Min:sec
2001	K. Boron, K. Kowalski (Ger.)	6:50.20	Australia	6:27.23
2002	G. Evers-Swindell, C. Evers-Swindell (N.Z.)	6:38.78	Australia	6:26.11
2003	**G. Evers-Swindell, C. Evers-Swindell (N.Z.)**	**6:45.79**	**United States**	**6:53.08**

Year	Quadruple sculls	Min:sec	Eights	Min:sec
2001	Germany	6:12.95	Australia	6:03.66
2002	Germany	6:15.66	United States	6:04.25
2003	**Australia**	**6:46.52**	**Germany**	**6:41.23**

Twin sisters Georgina (left) and Caroline Evers-Swindell display their double sculls rowing gold medals.

AP/Wide World Photos

SAILING (YACHTING)

America's Cup

Year	Winning yacht	Owner	Skipper	Losing yacht	Owner
1995	*Black Magic* (N.Z.)	P. Blake and Team New Zealand	R. Coutts	*Young America* (U.S.)	Pact 95 syndicate
2000	*Black Magic* (N.Z.)	Team New Zealand	R. Coutts	*Luna Rossa* (Italy)	Prada Challenge
2003	***Alinghi* (Switz.)**	**Alinghi Swiss Challenge**	**R. Coutts**	***New Zealand* (N.Z.)**	**Team New Zealand**

World Class Boat Champions, 2003

Class	Winner	Country
Etchells 22	K. Read	United States
Europe dinghy	S. Sundby	Norway
Finn dinghy	B. Ainslie	Great Britain
2.4 Metre	M. Dahlberg	Finland
470 (men)	G. Zandona/A. Traini	Italy
470 (women)	S. Bekatorou/E. Tsoulfa	Greece
49er	C. Draper/S. Hiscocks	Great Britain
Laser	G. Lima	Portugal
Mistral (men)	P. Miarczyski	Poland
Mistral (women)	L. Korsitz	Israel
J/24	L. Bressani	Italy
Optimist	F. Matika	Croatia
Star	X. Rohart/P. Rambeau	France
Tornado	D. Bundock/J. Forbes	Australia
Yngling (open)	B. Alison	United States
Yngling (women)	H. Swett	United States

Admiral's Cup

Year	Winning team
1999	Netherlands
2001	canceled
2003	**Australia**

Transpacific Race

Year	Winning yacht	Owner
1999	*Grand Illusion*	J. McDowell
2001	*Bull*	S. Radow
2003	***Alta Vita***	**B. Turpin**

Bermuda Race

Year	Winning yacht	Owner
1998	*Kodiak*	L. Ecclestone
2000	*Restless*	E. Crawford
2002	*Zaraffa*	S. Sheldon

SKIING

World Alpine Skiing Championships—Slalom

Year	Men's slalom	Men's giant slalom	Men's supergiant	Women's slalom	Women's giant slalom	Women's supergiant
2001	M. Matt (Austria)	M. von Grünigen (Switz.)	D. Rahlves (U.S.)	A. Pärson (Swed.)	S. Nef (Switz.)	R. Cavagnoud (Fr.)
2002*	J.-P. Vidal (Fr.)	S. Eberharter (Austria)	K.A. Aamodt (Nor.)	J. Kostelic (Cro.)	J. Kostelic (Cro)	D. Ceccarelli (Italy)
2003	**I. Kostelic (Cro.)**	**B. Miller (U.S.)**	**S. Eberharter (Austria)**	**J. Kostelic (Cro.)**	**A. Pärson (Swed.)**	**M. Dorfmeister (Austria)**

*Olympic champions.

World Alpine Skiing Championships—Downhill

Year	Men	Women
2001	H. Trinkl (Austria)	M. Dorfmeister (Austria)
2002*	F. Strobl (Austria)	C. Montillet (Fr.)
2003	**M. Walchhofer (Austria)**	**M. Turgeon (Can.)**

*Olympic champions.

World Alpine Skiing Championships—Combined

Year	Men	Women
2001	K.A. Aamodt (Nor.)	M. Ertl (Ger.)
2002*	K.A. Aamodt (Nor.)	J. Kostelic (Cro.)
2003	**B. Miller (U.S.)**	**J. Kostelic (Cro.)**

*Olympic champions.

World Nordic Skiing Championships—Men

Year	Sprint	Double pursuit	10-km	15-km	30-km	50-km	Relay
2001	T.A. Hetland (Nor.)		P. Elofsson (Swed.)	P. Elofsson (Swed.)	A. Veerpalu (Est.)	J. Mühlegg (Spain)	Norway
2002*	T.A. Hetland (Nor.)		J. Mühlegg (Spain)	A. Veerpalu (Est.)	J. Mühlegg (Spain)	M. Ivanov (Russia)	Norway
2003	**T. Fredriksson (Swed.)**	**P. Elofsson (Swed.)**		**A. Teichmann (Ger.)**	**T. Alsgaard (Nor.)**	**M. Koukal (Cz.Rep.)**	**Norway**

*Olympic champions.

World Nordic Skiing Championships—Women

Year	Sprint	Double pursuit	5-km	10-km	15-km	30-km	Relay
2001	P. Manninen (Fin.)		V. Kuitunen (Fin.)	B. Martinsen Skari (Nor.)	B. Martinsen Skari (Nor.)	canceled	Russia
2002*	Yu. Chepalova (Russia)		O. Danilova (Russia)	B. Skari (Nor.)	S. Belmondo (Italy)	G. Paruzzi (Italy)	Germany
2003	**M. Bjørgen (Nor.)**	**K. Smigun (Est.)**		**B. Skari (Nor.)**	**B. Skari (Nor.)**	**O. Savyalova (Russia)**	**Germany**

*Olympic champions.

World Nordic Skiing Championships—Ski Jump

Year	Normal hill (90 m)*	Large hill (120 m)†	Team jump (normal hill)	Team jump (large hill)	Nordic Combined (7.5-km)	Nordic Combined (15-km)	Nordic Combined Team
2001	A. Malysz (Pol.)	M. Schmitt (Ger.)	Austria	Germany	M. Baacke (Ger.)	B.E. Vik (Nor.)	Norway
2002‡	S. Ammann (Switz.)	S. Ammann (Switz.)		Germany	S. Lajunen (Fin.)	S. Lajunen (Fin.)	Finland
2003	**A. Malysz (Pol.)**	**A. Malysz (Pol.)**		**Finland**	**J. Spillane (U.S.)**	**R. Ackermann (Ger.)**	**Austria**

*95-m in 2003. †116 m in 2001. ‡Olympic champions.

Alpine World Cup

Year	Men	Women
2001	H. Maier (Austria)	J. Kostelic (Cro.)
2002	S. Eberharter (Austria)	M. Dorfmeister (Austria)
2003	**S. Eberharter (Austria)**	**J. Kostelic (Cro.)**

Nordic World Cup

Year	Men	Women
2001	P. Elofsson (Swed.)	Yu. Chepalova (Russia)
2002	P. Elofsson (Swed.)	B. Martinsen Skari (Nor.)
2003	**M. Fredriksson (Swed.)**	**B. Skari (Nor.)**

Freestyle Skiing World Cup

Year	Men	Women
2001	M. Ronkainen (Fin.)	J. Cooper (Austl.)
2002	E. Bergoust (U.S.)	K. Traa (Nor.)
2003	**D. Arkhipov (Russia)**	**K. Traa (Nor.)**

Snowboard World Cup

Year	Men	Women
2001	J.J. Anderson (Can.)	K. Ruby (Fr.)
2002	J.J. Anderson (Can.)	K. Ruby (Fr.)
2003	**J.J. Anderson (Can.)**	**K. Ruby (Fr.)**

Gold medalist Adam Malysz soars in the large hill (120-m) individual ski jumping world championship.

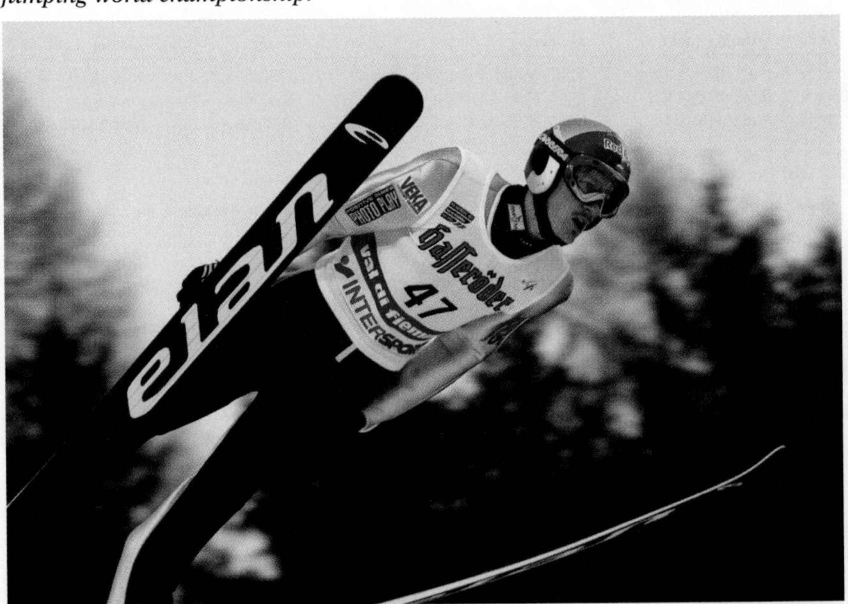

SQUASH

British Open Championship—Men

Year	Winner
2000–01	D. Palmer (Austl.)
2001–02	P. Nicol (Eng.)
2002–03	**D. Palmer (Austl.)**

British Open Championship—Women

Year	Winner
2000–01	S. Fitz-Gerald (Austl.)
2001–02	S. Fitz-Gerald (Austl.)
2002–03	**R. Grinham (Austl.)**

World Open Championship—Men

Year	Winner
2001	canceled
2002	D. Palmer (Austl.)
2003	**A. Shabana (Egypt)**

World Open Championship—Women

Year	Winner
2001	S. Fitz-Gerald (Austl.)
2002	S. Fitz-Gerald (Austl.)
2003	**C. Owens (N.Z.)**

SWIMMING

World Swimming Records Set in 2003 in 25-m Pools*

Event	Name	Country	Time
MEN			
100-m butterfly	Milorad Cavic	Serbia and Montenegro	50.02 sec
100-m individual medley	Thomas Rupprath	Germany	52.58 sec
400-m individual medley	Brian Johns	Canada	4 min 2.72 sec
4 × 50-m medley relay†	German National Team	Germany	1 min 34.46 sec
4 × 50-m freestyle relay†	Netherlands National Team	Netherlands	1 min 25.55 sec
WOMEN			
400-m freestyle	Lindsay Benko	United States	3 min 59.53 sec
100-m breaststroke	Emma Igelström	Sweden	1 min 5.29 sec
	Emma Igelström	Sweden	1 min 5.11 sec
	Leisel Jones	Australia	1 min 5.09 sec
200-m breaststroke	Leisel Jones	Australia	2 min 17.75 sec
4 × 50-m freestyle relay†	Netherlands National Team	Netherlands	1 min 38.13 sec
	Netherlands National Team	Netherlands	1 min 37.52 sec

*May include records awaiting FINA ratification at year's end. †Not an officially ratified event; best performance on record.

World Swimming Records Set in 2003 in 50-m Pools*

Event	Name	Country	Time
MEN			
50-m backstroke	Thomas Rupprath	Germany	24.80 sec
100-m breaststroke	Kosuke Kitajima	Japan	59.78 sec
200-m breaststroke	Dmitry Komornikov	Russia	2 min 9.52 sec
	Kosuke Kitajima	Japan	2 min 9.42 sec
50-m butterfly	Matthew Welsh	Australia	23.43 sec
100-m butterfly	Andrey Serdinov	Ukraine	51.76 sec
	Michael Phelps	United States	51.47 sec
	Ian Crocker	United States	50.98 sec
200-m butterfly	Michael Phelps	United States	1 min 53.93 sec
200-m individual medley	Michael Phelps	United States	1 min 57.94 sec
	Michael Phelps	United States	1 min 57.52 sec
	Michael Phelps	United States	1 min 56.04 sec
	Michael Phelps	United States	1 min 55.94 sec
400-m individual medley	Michael Phelps	United States	4 min 10.73 sec
	Michael Phelps	United States	4 min 9.09 sec
4 × 100-m medley relay	United States National Team	United States	3 min 31.54 sec
WOMEN			
100-m breaststroke	Leisel Jones	Australia	1 min 6.37 sec
200-m breaststroke	Amanda Beard	United States	2 min 22.99 sec†

*May include records awaiting FINA ratification at year's end. †Equals world record.

World Swimming and Diving Championships—Men

	Freestyle					
Year	50 m	100 m	200 m	400 m	800 m	1,500 m
1998	B. Pilczuk (U.S.)	A. Popov (Russia)	M. Klim (Austl.)	I. Thorpe (Austl.)		G. Hackett (Austl.)
2001	A. Ervin (U.S.)	A. Ervin (U.S.)	I. Thorpe (Austl.)	I. Thorpe (Austl.)	I. Thorpe (Austl.)	G. Hackett (Austl.)
2003	**A. Popov (Russia)**	**A. Popov (Russia)**	**I. Thorpe (Austl.)**	**I. Thorpe (Austl.)**	**G. Hackett (Austl.)**	**G. Hackett (Austl.)**

	Backstroke			Breaststroke		
	50 m	100 m	200 m	50 m	100 m	200 m
1998		L. Krayzelburg (U.S.)	L. Krayzelburg (U.S.)		F. De Burghgraeve (Belg.)	K. Grote (U.S.)
2001	R. Bal (U.S.)	M. Welsh (Austl.)	A. Peirsol (U.S.)	O. Lisogor (Ukr.)	R. Sludnov (Russia)	B. Hansen (U.S.)
2003	**T. Rupprath (Ger.)**	**A. Peirsol (U.S.)**	**A. Peirsol (U.S.)**	**J. Gibson (U.K.)**	**K. Kitajima (Japan)**	**K. Kitajima (Japan)**

	Butterfly			Individual medley		Team relays
	50 m	100 m	200 m	200 m	400 m	4 × 100-m freestyle
1998		M. Klim (Austl.)	D. Silantyev (Ukr.)	M. Wouda (Neth.)	T. Dolan (U.S.)	United States
2001	G. Huegill (Austl.)	L. Frölander (Swed.)	M. Phelps (U.S.)	M. Rosolino (Italy)	A. Boggiatto (Italy)	Australia
2003	**M. Welsh (Austl.)**	**I. Crocker (U.S.)**	**M. Phelps (U.S.)**	**M. Phelps (U.S.)**	**M. Phelps (U.S.)**	**Russia**

			Diving				
	4 × 200-m freestyle	4 × 100-m medley	1-m springboard	3-m springboard	Platform	3-m synchronized	10-m synchronized
1998	Australia	Australia	Yu Zhuocheng (China)	D. Sautin (Russia)	D. Sautin (Russia)	China	China
2001	Australia	Australia	Wang Feng (China)	D. Sautin (Russia)	Tian Liang (China)	China	China
2003	**Australia**	**United States**	**Xu Xiang (China)**	**A. Dobrosok (Russia)**	**A. Despatie (Can.)**	**Russia**	**Australia**

SWIMMING (continued)

World Swimming and Diving Championships—Women

	Freestyle					
Year	50 m	100 m	200 m	400 m	800 m	1,500 m
1998	A. Van Dyken (U.S.)	J. Thompson (U.S.)	C. Poll (C.Rica)	Chen Yan (China)	B. Bennett (U.S.)	
2001	I. de Bruijn (Neth.)	I. de Bruijn (Neth.)	G. Rooney (Austl.)	Ya. Klochkova (Ukr.)	H. Stockbauer (Ger.)	H. Stockbauer (Ger.)
2003	**I. de Bruijn (Neth.)**	**H.-M. Seppälä (Fin.)**	**A. Popchanka (Bela.)**	**H. Stockbauer (Ger.)**	**H. Stockbauer (Ger.)**	**H. Stockbauer (Ger.)**

	Backstroke			Breaststroke		
	50 m	100 m	200 m	50 m	100 m	200 m
1998		L. Maurer (U.S.)	R. Maracineanu (Fr.)		K. Kowal (U.S.)	A. Kovacs (Hung.)
2001	H. Cope (U.S.)	N. Coughlin (U.S.)	D. Mocanu (Rom.)	Luo Xuejuan (China)	Luo Xuejuan (China)	A. Kovacs (Hung.)
2003	**N. Zhivanevskaya (Spain)**	**A. Buschschulte (Ger.)**	**K. Sexton (U.K.)**	**Luo Xuejuan (China)**	**Luo Xuejuan (China)**	**A. Beard (U.S.)**

	Butterfly			Individual medley		Team relays
	50 m	100 m	200 m	200 m	400 m	4 × 100-m freestyle
1998		J. Thompson (U.S.)	S. O'Neill (Austl.)	Wu Yanyan (China)	Chen Yan (China)	United States
2001	I. de Bruijn (Neth.)	P. Thomas (Austl.)	P. Thomas (Austl.)	M. Bowen (U.S.)	Ya. Klochkova (Ukr.)	Germany
2003	**I. de Bruijn (Neth.)**	**J. Thompson (U.S.)**	**O. Jedrzejczak (Pol.)**	**Ya. Klochkova (Ukr.)**	**Ya. Klochkova (Ukr.)**	**United States**

			Diving				
	4 × 200-m freestyle	4 × 100-m medley	1-m springboard	3-m springboard	Platform	3-m synchronized	10-m synchronized
1998	Germany	United States	I. Lashko (Russia)	Y. Pakhalina (Russia)	O. Zhupina (Ukr.)	Russia	Ukraine
2001	United Kingdom	Australia	B. Hartley (Can.)	Guo Jingjing (China)	Xu Mian (China)	China	China
2003	**United States**	**China**	**I. Lashko (Austl.)**	**Guo Jingjing (China)**	**E. Heymans (Can.)**	**China**	**China**

Guo Jingjing en route to victory in the 3-m springboard event at the world swimming and diving championships in July.

TABLE TENNIS

World Table Tennis Championships—Men

Year	St. Bride's Vase (singles)	Iran Cup (doubles)
1999	Liu Guoliang (China)	Kong Linghui, Liu Guoliang (China)
2001	Wang Liqin (China)	Wang Liqin, Yan Sen (China)
2003	**W. Schlager (Austria)**	**Wang Liqin, Yan Sen (China)**

World Table Tennis Championships—Women

Year	G. Geist Prize (singles)	W.J. Pope Trophy (doubles)
1999	Wang Nan (China)	Wang Nan, Li Ju (China)
2001	Wang Nan (China)	Wang Nan, Li Ju (China)
2003	**Wang Nan (China)**	**Wang Nan, Zhang Yining (China)**

World Table Tennis Championships—Mixed

Year	Heydusek Prize
1999	Ma Lin, Zhang Yingying (China)
2001	Qin Zhijian, Yang Ying (China)
2003	**Ma Lin, Wang Nan (China)**

World Table Tennis Championships—Team

Year	Swaythling Cup (men)	Corbillon Cup (women)
1997	China	China
2000	Sweden	China
2001	China	China

Table Tennis World Cup

Year	Men
2001	V. Samsonov (Bela.)
2002	T. Boll (Ger.)
2003	**Ma Lin (China)**

Year	Women
2001	Zhang Yining (China)
2002	Zhang Yining (China)
2003	**Wang Nan (China)**

TENNIS

Australian Open Tennis Championships—Singles

Year	Men	Women
2001	A. Agassi (U.S.)	J. Capriati (U.S.)
2002	T. Johansson (Swed.)	J. Capriati (U.S.)
2003	**A. Agassi (U.S.)**	**S. Williams (U.S.)**

Australian Open Tennis Championships—Doubles

Year	Men	Women
2001	J. Bjorkman, T. Woodbridge	S. Williams, V. Williams
2002	M. Knowles, D. Nestor	M. Hingis, A. Kournikova
2003	**M. Llodra, F. Santoro**	**S. Williams, V. Williams**

French Open Tennis Championships—Singles

Year	Men	Women
2001	G. Kuerten (Braz.)	J. Capriati (U.S.)
2002	A. Costa (Spain)	S. Williams (U.S.)
2003	**J.C. Ferrero (Spain)**	**J. Henin-Hardenne (Belg.)**

French Open Tennis Championships—Doubles

Year	Men	Women
2001	M. Bhupathi, L. Paes	V. Ruano Pascual, P. Suarez
2002	P. Haarhuis, Ye. Kafelnikov	V. Ruano Pascual, P. Suarez
2003	**B. Bryan, M. Bryan**	**K. Clijsters, A. Sugiyama**

All-England (Wimbledon) Tennis Championships—Singles

Year	Men	Women
2001	G. Ivanisevic (Cro.)	V. Williams (U.S.)
2002	L. Hewitt (Austl.)	S. Williams (U.S.)
2003	**R. Federer (Switz.)**	**S. Williams (U.S.)**

All-England (Wimbledon) Tennis Championships—Doubles

Year	Men	Women
2001	D. Johnson, J. Palmer	L. Raymond, R. Stubbs
2002	J. Bjorkman, T. Woodbridge	S. Williams, V. Williams
2003	**J. Bjorkman, T. Woodbridge**	**K. Clijsters, A. Sugiyama**

United States Open Tennis Championships—Singles

Year	Men	Women
2001	L. Hewitt (Austl.)	V. Williams (U.S.)
2002	P. Sampras (U.S.)	S. Williams (U.S.)
2003	**A. Roddick (U.S.)**	**J. Henin-Hardenne (Belg.)**

United States Open Tennis Championships—Doubles

Year	Men	Women
2001	W. Black, K. Ullyet	L. Raymond, R. Stubbs
2002	M. Bhupathi, M. Mirnyi	V. Ruano Pascual, P. Suarez
2003	**J. Bjorkman, T. Woodbridge**	**V. Ruano Pascual, P. Suarez**

Davis Cup (men)

Year	Winner	Runner-up	Results
2001	France	Australia	3–2
2002	Russia	France	3–2
2003	**Australia**	**Spain**	**3–1**

Fed Cup (women)

Year	Winner	Runner-up	Results
2001	Belgium	Russia	2–1
2002	Slovakia	Spain	3–1
2003	**France**	**United States**	**4–1**

TRACK AND FIELD SPORTS (ATHLETICS)

World Outdoor Track and Field Championships—Men

Event	2001	2003
100 m	M. Greene (U.S.)	K. Collins (S.Kitts)
200 m	K. Kederis (Greece)	J. Capel (U.S.)
400 m	A. Moncur (Bahamas)	J. Young (U.S.)
800 m	A. Bucher (Switz.)	D. Saïd-Guerni (Alg.)
1,500 m	H. El Guerrouj (Mor.)	H. El Guerrouj (Mor.)
5,000 m	R. Limo (Kenya)	E. Kipchoge (Kenya)
10,000 m	C. Kamathi (Kenya)	K. Bekele (Eth.)
steeplechase	R. Kosgei (Kenya)	S.S. Shaheen (Qatar)
110-m hurdles	A. Johnson (U.S.)	A. Johnson (U.S.)
400-m hurdles	F. Sánchez (Dom.Rep.)	F. Sánchez (Dom.Rep.)
marathon	G. Abera (Eth.)	J. Gharib (Mor.)
20-km walk	R. Rasskazov (Russia)	J. Pérez (Ecua.)
50-km walk	R. Korzeniowski (Pol.)	R. Korzeniowski (Pol.)
4 × 100-m relay	United States (M. Grimes, B. Williams, D. Mitchell, T. Montgomery)	United States (J. Capel, B. Williams, D. Patton, J.J. Johnson)
4 × 400-m relay	United States (L. Byrd, A. Pettigrew, D. Brew, A. Taylor)	United States (C. Harrison, T. Washington, D. Brew, J. Young)
high jump	M. Buss (Ger.)	J. Freitag (S.Af.)
pole vault	D. Markov (Austl.)	G. Gibilisco (Italy)
long jump	I. Pedroso (Cuba)	D. Phillips (U.S.)
triple jump	J. Edwards (U.K.)	C. Olsson (Swed.)
shot put	J. Godina (U.S.)	A. Mikhnevich (Bela.)
discus throw	L. Riedel (Ger.)	V. Alekna (Lith.)
hammer throw	S. Ziolkowski (Pol.)	I. Tikhon (Bela.)
javelin throw	J. Zelezny (Cz.Rep.)	S. Makarov (Russia)
decathlon	T. Dvorak (Cz.Rep.)	T. Pappas (U.S.)

World Outdoor Track and Field Championships—Women

Event	2001	2003
100 m	Z. Pintusevich-Block (Ukr.)	K. White (U.S.)
200 m	M. Jones (U.S.)	K. White (U.S.)
400 m	A. Mbacke Thiam (Seneg.)	A. Guevara (Mex.)
800 m	M. Mutola (Mozam.)	M. Mutola (Mozam.)
1,500 m	G. Szabo (Rom.)	T. Tomashova (Russia)
5,000 m	O. Yegorova (Russia)	T. Dibaba (Eth.)
10,000 m	D. Tulu (Eth.)	B. Adere (Eth.)
100-m hurdles	A. Kirkland (U.S.)	P. Felicien (Can.)
400-m hurdles	N. Bidouane (Mor.)	J. Pittman (Austl.)
marathon	L. Simon (Rom.)	C. Ndereba (Kenya)
20-km walk	O. Ivanova (Russia)	Ye. Nikolayeva (Russia)
4 × 100-m relay	United States (K. White, C. Gaines, I. Miller, M. Jones)	France (P. Girard, M. Hurtis, S. Félix, C. Arron)
4 × 400-m relay	Jamaica (S. Richards, C. Scott, D.-A. Parris, L. Fenton)	United States (M. Barber, D. Washington, J. Miles Clark, S. Richards)
high jump	H. Cloete (S.Afr.)	H. Cloete (S.Af.)
pole vault	S. Dragila (U.S.)	S. Feofanova (Russia)
long jump	F. May (Italy)	E. Barber (Fr.)
triple jump	T. Lebedeva (Russia)	T. Lebedeva (Russia)
shot put	Ya. Korolchik (Bela.)	S. Krivelyova (Russia)
discus throw	N. Sadova (Russia)	I. Yatchenko (Bela.)
hammer throw	Y. Moreno (Cuba)	Y. Moreno (Cuba)
javelin throw	O. Menéndez (Cuba)	M. Manjani (Greece)
heptathlon	Ye. Prokhorova (Russia)	C. Klüft (Swed.)

TRACK AND FIELD SPORTS (ATHLETICS) (continued)

World Indoor Track and Field Championships—Men

Event	2001	2003
60 m	T. Harden (U.S.)	J. Gatlin (U.S.)
200 m	S. Crawford (U.S.)	M. Devonish (Gr.Brit.)
400 m	D. Caines (Gr.Brit.)	T. Washington (U.S.)
800 m	Yu. Borzakovskiy (Russia)	D. Krummenacker (U.S.)
1,500 m	R. Silva (Port.)	D. Maazouzi (Fr.)
3,000 m	H. El Guerrouj (Mor.)	H. Gebrselassie (Eth.)
60-m hurdles	T. Trammell (U.S.)	A. Johnson (U.S.)
4 × 400-m relay	Poland (P. Rysiukiewicz, P. Haczek, J. Bocian, R. Mackowiak)	United States (J. Davis, J. Young, M. Campbell, T. Washington)
high jump	S. Holm (Swed.)	S. Holm (Swed.)
pole vault	L. Johnson (U.S.)	T. Lobinger (Ger.)
long jump	I. Pedroso (Cuba)	D. Phillips (U.S.)
triple jump	P. Camossi (Italy)	C. Olsson (Swed.)
shot put	J. Godina (U.S.)	M. Martínez (Spain)
heptathon	R. Sebrle (Cz.Rep.)	T. Pappas (U.S.)

World Indoor Track and Field Championships—Women

Event	2001	2003
60 m	C. Sturrup (Bah.)	Z. Block (Ukr.)
200 m	J. Campbell (Jam.)	M. Collins (U.S.)
400 m	S. Richards (Jam.)	N. Nazarova (Russia)
800 m	M. Mutola (Mozam.)	M. Mutola (Mozam.)
1,500 m	H. Benhassi (Mor.)	R. Jacobs (U.S.)
3,000 m	O. Yegorova (Russia)	B. Adere (Eth.)
60-m hurdles	A. Kirkland (U.S.)	G. Devers (U.S.)
4 × 400-m relay	Russia (Yu. Nosova, O. Zykina, Yu. Sotnikova, O. Kotlyarova)	Russia (N. Antyukh, Yu. Pechonkina, O. Zykina, N. Nazarova)
high jump	K. Bergqvist (Swed.)	K. Bergqvist (Swed.)
pole vault	P. Hamackova (Cz.Rep.)	S. Feofanova (Russia)
long jump	D. Burrell (U.S.)	T. Kotova (Russia)
triple jump	T. Marinova (Bulg.)	A. Hansen (Gr.Brit.)
shot put	L. Peleshenko (Russia)	I. Korzhanenko (Russia)
pentathlon	N. Sazanovich (Bela.)	C. Klüft (Swed.)

2003 World Indoor Records—Men*

Event	Competitor and country	Performance
2 mi†	Haile Gebrselassie (Eth.)	8 min 4.69 sec

*May include records awaiting IAAF ratification at year's end. †Not an officially ratified event; best performance on record.

2003 World Indoor Records—Women*

Event	Competitor and country	Performance
150 m†	Birgit Rockmeier (Ger.)	17.84 sec
1,500 m	Regina Jacobs (U.S.)	3 min 59.98 sec
Pole vault	Svetlana Feofanova (Russia)	4.76 m (15 ft 7¼ in)
	Svetlana Feofanova (Russia)	4.77 m (15 ft 7¾ in)
	Stacy Dragila (U.S.)	4.78 m (15 ft 8¼ in)
	Svetlana Feofanova (Russia)	4.80 m (15 ft 9 in)

*May include records awaiting IAAF ratification at year's end. †Not an officially ratified event; best performance on record.

2003 World Outdoor Records—Men*

Event	Competitor and country	Performance
30-km road race	Takayuki Matsumiya (Japan)	1 hr 28 min 36 sec
marathon	Paul Tergat (Kenya)	2 hr 4 min 55 sec
20-km walking	Jefferson Pérez (Ecua.)	1 hr 17 min 21 sec
50-km walking	Robert Korzeniowski (Pol.)	3 hr 36 min 3 sec

*May include records awaiting IAAF ratification at year's end.

2003 World Outdoor Records—Women*

Event	Competitor and country	Performance
300 m†	Ana Gabriela Guevara (Mex.)	35.30 sec
400-m hurdles	Yuliya Pechonkina (Russia)	52.34 sec
30,000 m	Tegla Loroupe (Kenya)	1 hr 45 min 50 sec
steeplechase	Gulnara Samitova (Russia)	9 min 8.33 sec
pole vault	Yelena Isinbayeva (Russia)	4.82 m (15 ft 9¾ in)
5-km road race†	Berhane Adere (Eth.)	14 min 54 sec‡
	Paula Radcliffe (U.K.)	14 min 51 sec
10-km road race†	Paula Radcliffe (U.K.)	30 min 21 sec
marathon	Paula Radcliffe (U.K.)	2 hr 15 min 25 sec

*May include records awaiting IAAF ratification at year's end. †Not an officially ratified event; best performance on record. ‡Equals world record.

World Cross Country Championships—Men

Year	Individual	Team
2001	M. Mourhit (Belg.)	Kenya
2002	K. Bekele (Eth.)	Kenya
2003	**K. Bekele (Eth.)**	**Kenya**

World Cross Country Championships—Women

Year	Individual	Team
2001	P. Radcliffe (U.K.)	Kenya
2002	P. Radcliffe (U.K.)	Ethiopia
2003	**W. Kidane (Eth.)**	**Ethiopia**

Boston Marathon

Year	Men	hr:min:sec
2001	Lee Bong Ju (S.Kor.)	2:09:43
2002	R. Rop (Kenya)	2:09:02
2003	**R.K. Cheruiyot (Kenya)**	**2:10:11**

Year	Women	hr:min:sec
2001	C. Ndereba (Kenya)	2:23:53
2002	M. Okayo (Kenya)	2:20:43
2003	**S. Zakharova (Russia)**	**2:25:20**

Chicago Marathon

Year	Men	hr:min:sec
2001	B. Kimondiu (Kenya)	2:08:52
2002	K. Khannouchi (U.S.)	2:05:56
2003	**E. Rutto (Kenya)**	**2:05:50**

Year	Women	hr:min:sec
2001	C. Ndereba (Kenya)	2:18:47
2002	P. Radcliffe (U.K.)	2:17:18
2003	**S. Zakharova (Russia)**	**2:23:07**

London Marathon

Year	Men	hr:min:sec
2001	A. El Mouaziz (Mor.)	2:07:11
2002	K. Khannouchi (U.S.)	2:05:38
2003	**G. Abera (Eth.)**	**2:07:56**

Year	Women	hr:min:sec
2001	D. Tulu (Eth.)	2:23:57
2002	P. Radcliffe (U.K.)	2:18:56
2003	**P. Radcliffe (U.K.)**	**2:15:25**

New York City Marathon

Year	Men	hr:min:sec
2001	T. Jifar (Eth.)	2:07:43
2002	R. Rop (Kenya)	2:08:07
2003	**M. Lel (Kenya)**	**2:10:30**

Year	Women	hr:min:sec
2001	M. Okayo (Kenya)	2:24:21
2002	J. Chepchumba (Kenya)	2:25:56
2003	**M. Okayo (Kenya)**	**2:22:31**

AP/Wide World Photos

Saif Assad Assad, winner of the 105 kg (231 lb) weight class at the world weight lifting championships in November.

VOLLEYBALL

Beach Volleyball World Championships

Year	Men	Women
1999	J. Loiola, E. Rego (Braz.)	A. Behar, Shelda (Braz.)
2001	M. Baracetti, M. Conde (Arg.)	A. Behar, Shelda (Braz.)
2003	**R. Santos, E. Rego (Braz.)**	**M. May, K. Walsh (U.S.)**

World Volleyball Championships

Year	Men	Women
1998	Italy	Cuba
2000	Yugoslavia	Cuba
2002	Brazil	Italy

WEIGHT LIFTING

World Weight Lifting Champions, 2003

MEN

Weight class	Winner and country	Performance
56 kg (123 lb)	Wu Meijin (China)	287.5 kg (633.8 lb)
62 kg (136.5 lb)	Halil Mutlu (Tur.)	322.5 kg (711 lb)
69 kg (152 lb)	Zhang Gouzheng (China)	345 kg (760.6 lb)
77 kg (169.5 lb)	Falahati Mohammad Nejad (Iran)	357.5 kg (788.1 lb)
85 kg (187 lb)	Valeriu Calancea (Rom.)	382.5 kg (843.3 lb)
94 kg (207 lb)	Milen Dobrev (Bulg.)	405 kg (892.9 lb)
105 kg (231 lb)	Saif Assad Assad (Qatar)	422.5 kg (931.4 lb)
+105 kg (+231 lb)	Hossein Rezazadeh (Iran)	457.5 kg (1,008.6 lb)

WOMEN

Weight class	Winner and country	Performance
48 kg (105.5 lb)	Wang Mingjuan (China)	200 kg (440.9 lb)
53 kg (116.5 lb)	Polsak Udomporn (Thai.)	222.5 kg (490.5 lb)
58 kg (127.5 lb)	Sun Caiyan (China)	225 kg (496 lb)
63 kg (138.5 lb)	Natalya Skakun (Ukr.)	247.5 kg (545.6 lb)
69 kg (152 lb)	Liu Chunhong (China)	270 kg (595.2 lb)
75 kg (165 lb)	Shang Shichun (China)	272.5 kg (600.7 lb)
+75 kg (+165 lb)	Ding Meiyuan (China)	300 kg (661.4 lb)

WRESTLING

World Wrestling Championships—Freestyle*

Year	54 kg (55 kg)	58 kg (60 kg)	63 kg (66 kg)	69 kg
2001	H. Kantoyeu (Bela.)	G. Sissaouri (Can.)	S. Barzakov (Bulg.)	N. Paslar (Bulg.)
2002	R. Montero (Cuba)	A. Margaryan (Arm.)	E. Tedeyev (Ukr.)	
2003	**D. Mansurov (Uzbek.)**	**A.A. Yadulla (Azer.)**	**I. Farniyev (Russia)**	
Year	**76 kg (74 kg)**	**85 kg (84 kg)**	**97 kg (96 kg)**	**130 kg (120 kg)**
2001	B. Saytyev (Russia)	K. Magomedov (Russia)	G. Gogchelidze (Russia)	D. Musulbes (Russia)
2002	M. Hajizadeh (Iran)	A. Saytyev (Russia)	E. Kurtanidze (Georgia)	D. Musulbes (Russia)
2003	**B. Saytyev (Russia)**	**S. Sazhidov (Russia)**	**E. Kurtanidze (Georgia)**	**A. Taymazov (Uzbek.)**

*Figures in parentheses represent new weight classes established in 2002.

World Wrestling Championships—Greco-Roman Style*

Year	54 kg (55 kg)	58 kg (60 kg)	63 kg (66 kg)	69 kg
2001	H. Rangraz (Iran)	D. Aripov (Uzbek.)	V. Galustyan (Arm.)	F. Azcuy (Cuba)
2002	G. Mamedaliyev (Russia)	A. Nazaryan (Bulg.)	J. Samuelsson (Swed.)	
2003	**D. Jablonski (Pol.)**	**A. Nazaryan (Bulg.)**	**M. Kvirkvelia (Georgia)**	
Year	**76 kg (74 kg)**	**85 kg (84 kg)**	**97 kg (96 kg)**	**130 kg (120 kg)**
2001	A. Abrahamian (Swed.)	M. Vakhrangadze (Georgia)	A. Bezruchkin (Russia)	R. Gardner (U.S.)
2002	V. Samurgashev (Russia)	A. Abrahamian (Swed.)	M. Ozal (Tur.)	D. Byers (U.S.)
2003	**A. Glushkov (Russia)**	**G. Ziziashvilly (Israel)**	**M. Lidberg (Swed.)**	**K. Baroyev (Russia)**

*Figures in parentheses represent new weight classes established in 2002.

Sumo Tournament Champions, 2003

Tournament	Location	Winner	Winner's record
Hatsu Basho (New Year's tournament)	Tokyo	Asashoryu	14–1
Haru Basho (spring tournament)	Osaka	Chiyotaikai	12–3
Natsu Basho (summer tournament)	Tokyo	Asashoryu	13–2
Nagoya Basho (Nagoya tournament)	Nagoya	Kaio	12–3
Aki Basho (autumn tournament)	Tokyo	Asashoryu	13–2
Kyushu Basho (Kyushu tournament)	Fukuoka	Tochiazuma	13–2

The World in 2003

Afghan girls, some of the 2.2 million refugees who have returned from Pakistan since 2001, gather in a camp in Kabul in August.

AP/Wide World Photos

World Affairs

Dominating the international scene in 2003 were the U.S.-led war in IRAQ and the worldwide reaction to the invasion, which occurred without UN SECURITY COUNCIL sanction; the ouster of CHARLES TAYLOR in Liberia; the introduction of a "ROAD MAP" for peace in the Middle East; the SARS outbreak and the rampant increase in HIV/AIDS infections and deaths; and the continued search for former Iraqi leader SADDAM HUSSEIN and terrorist OSAMA BIN LADEN.

UNITED NATIONS

Although the occasion passed largely unnoticed, 2003 marked the 60th anniversary of the actual launching of the United Nations system. Meeting in Hot Springs, Va., in May 1943, the 44-member states of the United Nations alliance founded the United Nations Interim Commission on Food and Agriculture—later to be christened the Food and Agriculture Organization. Even though this anniversary of sorts passed without fanfare, the UN system occupied centre stage on the international scene during much of 2003. The UN Security Council served as the forum of choice for debates over the situation in Iraq and the subsequent U.S.-led invasion and occupation of that country. Concern voiced by the administration of U.S. Pres. George W. Bush about the irrelevance of the UN proved to be greatly overstated, as subsequent events demonstrated that the UN continued to be the world's most widely accepted source of international legitimacy. Even the Bush administration came to realize that building permanent peace and stability in Iraq was not possible without the assistance of the world body. (*See* Special Report.) On another important front, the World Health Organization (WHO) quickly responded to the outbreak of SARS (severe acute respiratory syndrome) and successfully coordinated an effective global response. (*See* HEALTH AND DISEASE: *Special Report.*)

The U.S.-Led Invasion of Iraq. The year 2003 was a defining moment in U.S.-UN relations. The Bush administration disregarded the UN and the international legal norms on which it is based and on March 19 launched a preemptive war on Iraq. With the stated purpose of countering an Iraqi buildup of weapons of mass destruction and Iraqi support for al-Qaeda and other terrorist networks, the U.S. and the U.K. attempted to pressure other members of the UN Security Council into legitimizing the invasion. The sole superpower and its several allies in the action argued that since Iraq was in material breach of several previous Security Council resolutions, they had the implicit authority to go to war and even to launch a cruise-missile attack in an attempt to assassinate the Iraqi head of state—despite the fact that this action itself was in violation of the UN Charter and international law.

Although Bush declared the official end to the U.S.-led war on May 1, violence and insecurity continued to persist. The Security Council voted on May 22 to lift economic sanctions against Iraq, cede wide-ranging authority to the U.S. and the U.K. over governing Iraq, and authorize a new role for the UN in rebuilding the war-ravaged nation. As instructed by the Council, Secretary-General Kofi Annan shortly thereafter appointed UN High Commissioner for Human Rights Sérgio Vieira de Mello as a special representative for Iraq with independent responsibilities for coordinating UN activities and assisting the Iraqi people. On August 19 Vieira de Mello (*see* OBITUARIES) and at least 21 other UN staff members were killed in the bombing of the UN headquarters in Baghdad.

After intensive negotiations, on October 16 the members of the Security Council unanimously adopted Resolution 1511, which expanded the UN role in the transition process to self-governance in Iraq and authorized a U.S.-led multinational force "to take all necessary measures to contribute to the maintenance of security and stability in Iraq, including for the purpose of ensuring necessary conditions for the implementation of the timetable and programme as well as to contribute to the security of the United Nations Assistance Mission for Iraq, the Governing Council of Iraq and other institutions of the Iraqi interim administration, and key humanitarian and economic infrastructure." Furthermore, the resolution underscored the temporary nature of the U.S.-occupation Coalition Provisional Authority and asked the Iraqi Governing Council to provide the Security Council with a timetable and work program for drafting a new constitution for Iraq and for holding democratic elections.

The administration of the "oil-for-food" program, which had been established in 1995 to permit the Iraqi government to sell oil under UN supervision in order to purchase food and humanitarian supplies while the country was under sanctions, was officially transferred to the Coalition Provisional Authority and U.S.-appointed Iraqi officials on November 22.

After having successfully eluded U.S.-led occupation forces for many months, former Iraqi leader Saddam Hussein (*see* BIOGRAPHIES) was captured on December 13 outside his ancestral hometown of Tikrit.

Health. After the first confirmed cases of SARS were reported in Vietnam and China in February, WHO quickly moved into action, issuing a global health alert on March 12 and later a number of travel advisories. Underpinning this rapid response was the newly established Global Outbreak Alert and Response Network, which electronically linked 112 existing public-health networks worldwide. This capability was buttressed in May when WHO launched an initiative to build more effective linkages between local and global public-health surveillance, epidemiology, and response systems. Also, in partnership with the World Economic Forum's Global Health Initiative, WHO moved to mobilize the financial and other resources needed for the SARS campaign. WHO member states voted unanimously in May at their annual World Health Assembly (WHA) to expand WHO's powers, permitting WHO officials to take certain kinds of actions to respond to global health crises even if individual states did not approve or invite the action. In November WHO hosted the Consultation on SARS Vaccine Research and Development in Geneva to review progress and identify ways to hasten the development of a SARS vaccine.

On November 18 the UN Security Council convened a special meeting to focus on the impact of HIV/AIDS, the fourth leading cause of death in the world. A record three million people reportedly died of AIDS during the year, and an estimated five million people were thought to have newly acquired the HIV syndrome. On December 1, World AIDS Day, WHO and UNAIDS (the Joint United Nations Programme on HIV/AIDS) announced an initiative to help three million people get access to AIDS medicines and antiretroviral treatment by the end of 2005. The "3 by 5 initiative" sought to develop standardized approaches to delivering antiretroviral therapy; ensure effective and reliable supplies of medicines and diagnostic equipment; identify, disseminate, and apply new knowledge and successful strategies; provide rapid and sustained support for countries in need; and promote more effective global leadership, strong partnerships, and advocacy.

On May 13 WHO, UNICEF, the U.S. Centers for Disease Control and Prevention, and Rotary International announced a new Global Polio Eradication Initiative to wipe out the disease by 2005. Finally, the WHA voted unanimously on May 21 to adopt WHO's first international treaty, the Framework Convention on Tobacco Control. The purpose of the convention was to curb cigarette smuggling, regulate tobacco advertising, and reduce secondhand-smoke-related health problems. The leaders of 79 states and the EU signed the convention, and, as of December 1, five countries had ratified and become full parties to the accord.

AP/Wide World Photos

Little remains of the UN headquarters in Baghdad, Iraq, on August 19, following a bomb explosion. At least 22 UN staff members, including Special Representative Sérgio Vieira de Mello, were killed.

International Law. The United Nations Convention Against Transnational Organized Crime entered into force on September 29 and became the first international legal instrument against this type of crime. It dealt with a broad range of issues, including corruption, money laundering, extradition laws, obstruction of justice, and crime prevention. More than 140 countries signed the convention, and, as of the date of entry into force, more than 50 countries had ratified the agreement.

Refugees. As of January 1, there were more than 20.6 million "persons of concern" who fell under the mandate of the UN High Commission for Refugees, as compared with some 19.8 million the previous year. Half of these persons of concern were officially classified as refugees. (*See* SOCIAL PROTECTION: *International Migration.*)

Digital Divide. In an effort to address concerns regarding cultural norms, linguistic diversity, local governance capacity, and numerous other dimensions of basic human security, the UN initiated the two-stage World Summit on the Information Society. The first phase was convened on December 10–12 in Geneva, and the second phase was to be held in Tunis, Tun., in 2005.

Trade. The World Trade Organization's (WTO's) negotiating round in Cancún, Mex., abruptly ended on September 14 as ministers from rich and poor countries failed to reach agreement on proposals for facilitating trade, governing investment, and bringing about greater transparency in government procurement. Although some progress seemed to have been made in negotiations over certain specific agricultural subsidies, such as those for cotton, the overall negotiations floundered. On a more positive note, in August an agreement was reached in the WTO that authorized approval for the countries most affected by life-threatening diseases, such as HIV/AIDS and malaria, to import generic versions of patented medications made in other countries while paying a small royalty to the patent holder.

The WTO moved closer to universality on September 11 when WTO ministers meeting in Cancún approved membership for Cambodia and Nepal, the first less-developed countries to join the organization through the full working-party negotiating process. Once the two respective governments ratified the terms of the agreement, the WTO membership would stand at 148.

(continued on page 350)

What Ails the UN Security Council?

by Edward C. Luck

The UN Security Council's irresolute wrangling in 2003 over whether to use force in Iraq spurred pointed questioning by many observers about its relevance and even its future. Continuing differences over the course of postwar reconstruction only added to the chorus of doubts. On one point the world body's most fervent admirers and detractors seemed to agree: the Security Council was in serious, perhaps critical, condition. "Events have shaken the international system," warned UN Secretary-General Kofi Annan. If the UN's principal organs—beginning with the Security Council—"are to regain their authority, they may need radical reform."

Perhaps, as Annan warned, the world body is—once again—at a crossroads. Before sharpening their scalpels in preparation for radical reform, however, the member states should ask whether the diagnosis of the malady is, in fact, correct. A second opinion, or at least a quick historical review, would be in order before reserving the operating room.

The United Nations was established in 1945, largely on U.S. initiative, to maintain international peace and security. The key Security Council was granted unprecedented legal and enforcement powers under Chapter VII of the UN Charter to ensure that its decisions would be respected and implemented by all member states. On the other hand, the charter granted the leaders of the victorious World War II coalition—the United States, the Soviet Union, the United Kingdom, China, and France—veto power over the Council's substantive decisions. This was seen as a way to both protect their individual interests and help perpetuate the wartime alliance, a key goal. These provisions were soon put to a severe test.

When the alliance gave way to the Cold War just a few years after the UN's founding conference in San Francisco, Moscow began to cast veto after veto, and the Council was paralyzed for much of the next four decades. Critics, particularly from the U.S. Congress, questioned the utility of a Council that was so fundamentally divided. Many called for the elimination of the veto, but the founders had placed the bar for amending the charter—ratification by all five permanent members and two-thirds of the membership as a whole—very high so that their original architecture could withstand shifts in political fortunes. As large numbers of newly independent states from Africa and Asia joined the world body it was the United States that came to rely on its right to block disagreeable Council actions. Over the UN's first quarter century, the U.S. did not exercise a single veto, but after 1970 it exercised its veto power substantially more often than any of the other four permanent members.

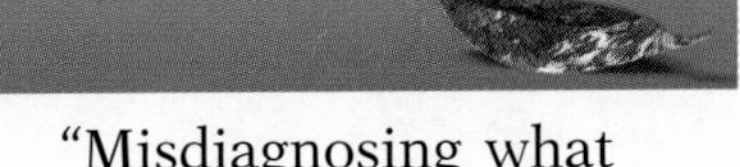

"Misdiagnosing what ails the Council could well risk transforming the claim of its irrelevance into a self-fulfilling prophecy."

Following the end of the Cold War, the Council rediscovered Chapter VII and began to act more decisively to protect world security. During the 1990s it passed a record number of enforcement, peacekeeping, and nation-building measures. For example, the Council authorized a U.S.-led military coalition to expel Iraqi forces that had invaded Kuwait in 1991, imposed damaging economic sanctions on Baghdad, and mandated unusually intrusive inspections of Iraqi weapons development. For more than a decade, Iraqi Pres. Saddam Hussein responded with islands of cooperation amid a sea of defiance, a policy that time and again left the Council members divided about how to proceed.

It was thus hardly surprising that the Council members were unable to endorse the use of force against Iraq in 2002–03, despite Pres. George W. Bush's repeated contention that the very credibility of the Council was at stake. To the president's critics, the U.S.-U.K. decision to intervene militarily without the explicit authorization of the Council represented what Annan called "a fundamental challenge to the principles on which, however imperfectly, world peace and stability have rested for the last 58 years." Clearly the rift over the Council's proper role in international security matters remained as wide as ever.

The United States had never accepted that it could use force only with the Council's approval. By their actions over the decades, other countries had made it clear that they too reserved this prerogative for themselves. Prior Council approval of military action had rarely been sought and had infrequently been granted. Of the hundreds of uses of force by various member states since 1945, only a handful had been graced with Council sanction. Even Annan had argued that when the Council is deadlocked over the use of force to relieve a humanitarian calamity, as in the case of Kosovo in 1999, it may be morally, if not legally, justifiable to act outside the UN Charter.

The member states, it seemed, had some significant differences of perspective and values to sort out. But is the nature of the Council's current malaise primarily institutional or political? Would the cure lie in reshaping the composition and rules of the Council or in addressing the evident political differences between the member states? Should the locus of the surgery, in other words, be within the walls of the Security Council chamber or in national capitals? At this juncture, misdiagnosing what ails the Council could well risk transforming the claim of its irrelevance into a self-fulfilling prophecy.

For a decade now the UN member states—now numbering 191—have been engaged in a vigourous and inconclusive debate about what a reformed Security Council should look like. It is widely accepted that the

Council should be enlarged from 15 to 20–25 members, in part to correct a perceived underrepresentation of less-developed countries. Perhaps five of these seats would go to new permanent members. Most observers call for greater transparency and accountability in the Council's decision making and either constraints on or the elimination of the veto. Yet these same voices insist that, in the name of equity, any new permanent members should have the same veto powers as the original five. Under this recipe for gridlock, any one of as many as 10 countries could block, or threaten to block, Council action.

All of this is moot, of course, as long as the member states remain divided over which states should be named to the Council. Indeed, the very factor that prompted Annan's plea for radical reform—the political crisis within the Council—suggested that the prospects for reaching agreement were even worse today than they were in the mid-1990s, when the last reform push took place. Perversely, for this we should be thankful; the core problem is strategic, not institutional. It hinges on Security Council relations with the U.S., not with the less-developed world. As the 2003 war in Iraq demonstrated, U.S. military capacities far surpass those of other Council members, and the gap is widening. Since 9/11 Americans have also felt far more vulnerable to terrorist attacks and, hence, are less inclined to place their national defense in the hands of non-Americans. This combination foreshadows both future splits within the Council and the likelihood that the U.S. would consider military options outside the framework of a deadlocked Security Council.

The good news is that a Security Council that could survive the ideological struggles of the Cold War is likely to find ways of adapting to these new political challenges. Even in the midst of the bitter debate over Iraq, the Council members managed to find common ground on acute crises in other parts of the world. The bad news is that those who pressed for an enlargement of the Council and limitations on the veto, in part to counterbalance American influence, were running the risk of creating an organ that was even less reflective of the balance of power outside the organization. This would likely encourage the very trends toward unilateralism in Washington that could eventually undermine the political and strategic foundation of the world body. Part of this foundation from the outset, it should be recalled, was the centrality of American power and vision for the global enterprise. Building a stronger bridge between Washington and Turtle Bay is where reform should begin.

Edward C. Luck is Professor of Practice in International and Public Affairs and Director of the Center on International Organization at the School of International and Public Affairs at Columbia University, New York City. He is the author of Mixed Messages: American Politics and International Organization, 1919–1999 *(1999).*

Illustration by Mirko Ilić Corp.

(continued from page 347)

Peace Operations. In mid-2003 there were more than 42,000 military and civilian police serving in 11 active United Nations peace operations—in Georgia, Kosovo, Cyprus, Lebanon, Western Sahara, Sierra Leone, the Democratic Republic of the Congo, Ethiopia and Eritrea, Iraq and Kuwait, Syria, and East Timor (Timor-Leste). The UN Mission of Support in East Timor, generally viewed as one of the UN's most successful peace operations, continued to train police and strengthen the judicial system in the UN's newest member state.

Africa, where two-thirds of all UN peacekeeping troops were based, again dominated the agenda of the Security Council, which on September 19 adopted Resolution 1509, establishing UNMIL (UN Mission in Liberia). This operation was designed to support the implementation of a cease-fire agreement; protect UN staff, facilities, and civilians; support humanitarian and human rights activities; and assist in police training and the formation of a new, restructured military. Reviewing the situation in early December, the Security Council decided to continue its arms and trade embargo against Liberia.

In regard to the Israeli-Palestinian conflict, on November 19 the Security Council unanimously adopted a resolution endorsing the "road map" to peace in the Middle East and calling for "an immediate cessation of all acts of violence, including all acts of terrorism, provocation, incitement and destruction."

Personnel, Budget, and Membership. The United Nations continued to experience strained financial circumstances. As of late November, the organization's main budgets were all projected to end the year in deficit. It was estimated that the regular budget would end the year $12 million in debt and the peacekeeping budget $1.18 billion in debt unless member states paid their overdue legal assessments by year's end. Nearly one-third of the UN member states had not paid their dues in full. The United States was the largest single debtor, owing near year's end $280 million to the regular budget. Fortunately, several other large member states were willing to make payment in advance for their own annual assessments for the forthcoming year. In the context of a decade of no-growth budgets and growing pressures on the UN's modest resources, Annan submitted the 2004–05 biennial budget, requesting a slight increase to $3.06 billion. The new budget contained additional resources for development financing, the special needs of Africa, drug control, human rights, and crime prevention. On the other hand, the 2003–04 peacekeeping budget adopted by the General Assembly in June represented a significant reduction from the previous year—$2.17 billion compared with $2.6 billion—mostly owing to the termination of the UN Mission in Bosnia and Herzegovina and the downsizing of operations in Kosovo, East Timor, Sierra Leone, and Lebanon.

Interestingly, the 2004–05 biennial budget proposed by the secretary-general did not include funds for increasing the security of UN mission-staff personnel. In addition to the at least 22 UN civilian staff members killed in the August terrorist bombing in Baghdad, 5 other UN mission staffers were killed during the period from July 1, 2002, to June 30, 2003. Other forms of violence against UN staff were also on the rise. During that same period, 14 mission staff were victims of hostage taking, kidnapping, and sexual assault, and there were 258 reported cases of assault, 168 incidents of harassment, and 83 incursions into UN compounds, as well as 270 violent attacks on UN and nongovernmental-organization compounds and convoys, and 550 incidents of theft.

Having withdrawn from the international agency in 1984 over ideological and substantive differences, the U.S. officially rejoined UNESCO on October 1. The U.S. action, combined with the entrance of East Timor, brought the total number of member states in the world body to 190.

Although no new member states were admitted to the UN during 2003, Switzerland and East Timor settled into their newly occupied seats, and the Vatican, an independent state since 1929, made public that it was contemplating officially joining the world body. For the 11th time, Taiwan was rebuffed in its bid for membership.

Reform. The crisis in Iraq not only thrust the United Nations into the global spotlight but also highlighted the need to bolster the UN's credibility, make its structures more representative of the international community, and reform the Security Council to reflect more closely the geopolitical realities of the contemporary world. A panel of high-level experts was appointed with the mandated task of presenting recommendations for reform to the 59th General Assembly in 2004.

(ROGER A. COATE)

EUROPEAN UNION

The year 2003 would be remembered as the last in which the European Union was a uniquely Western club. It was a year of preparation for historic change that would see 10 new member states—8 of them from former communist Eastern Europe—join the community in May 2004. (*See* Map.) On a continent split for so long by the Iron Curtain, hopes were high that expansion would mark the final healing of its post-World War II divisions. Though preparations for enlargement brought EU nations together in a common purpose, profound differences were also exposed about the kind of union that the future membership of 25 countries wanted to create for the 21st century.

Tensions were bought into focus most sharply by the war in Iraq. As British Prime Minister Tony Blair, backed by Spanish Prime Minister José María Aznar López, supported U.S. Pres. George W. Bush's war with Saddam Hussein in the early months of the year, France and Germany—the most powerful axis in EU politics—led opposition to armed conflict to the last.

The war begged a series of key questions about the EU and its future direction. Was it sensible for the community to push forward in the creation of a common foreign policy—as it was trying to do—when big international issues such as Iraq merely highlighted profound differences between its member states? Was it a good idea for the bloc to create its own defense force with a measure of independence from NATO, as the French, Germans, Belgians, and Luxembourgers suggested, if this risked further upsetting the Americans and dividing the two continents? Indeed, what should the EU's relationship be with the superpower U.S. in the era of global markets, global diplomacy, and global terrorism? Should it be a rival, preaching its alternative economic philosophy and foreign-policy priorities, or a superpower partner?

The year opened amid much economic and diplomatic uncertainty. The euro was finally moving upward against the U.S. dollar and British sterling after four years on the slide since the currency's birth. Its climb was less a sign of the euro zone's economic health than of uncertainties in the U.S. Germany, the EU's economic powerhouse, was in the doldrums with barely any economic growth as it struggled with inflexible labour markets and resulting high unemployment. The stronger euro merely added to the pain and made exports from Europe's manufacturing areas more expensive.

Britain, which remained outside the euro zone, was the notable exception, and it fared far better than most other EU member states. The U.K.'s relative success begged another question. Was the EU's five-year-old monetary union—from which Britain, Denmark, and Sweden had been the only three nations to stand apart—doing mainland Europe more harm than good? Many believed that the one-size-fits-all interest rate for 12 nations was not delivering success. In June the British government, as expected, put off a decision to join the euro yet again, in effect for several years, in a further sign of its flagging confidence in the European economic system.

Worse was to come for the EU integrationists, however, when the Swedes rejected the euro by a substantial margin in a referendum in September, despite a strong campaign by government and business for a vote in favour. The campaign was marred by the murder of Anna Lindh, the popular pro-euro foreign minister, just days before the vote. While she was shopping, she was stabbed in what appeared at first to be an attack by an anti-EU fanatic. Investigators later ruled this out as a motive after they arrested a man with Serbian links and strong political views about the Balkan wars.

On the diplomatic front, it was Paris that was to set the tone for a year of rancorous exchanges between Europe and Washington—and bitter squabbling between the EU member states over the wisdom of the war in Iraq. In February the row between the Europeans became so serious that it threatened to throw enlargement off course. In that month French Pres. Jacques Chirac suggested that nations that were due to join the EU were putting their chances of admission at risk by supporting the Iraq war in defiance of Berlin and Paris. "These countries are very rude and rather reckless of the danger of aligning themselves too quickly with the Americans," said Chirac. "Their situation is very delicate. If they wanted to diminish their chances of joining the EU, they couldn't have chosen a better way." The accession nations were furious, as was London, which had always seen itself as the number one supporter of enlargement to the east.

As the Iraqi conflict neared, Blair made no attempt to hide the rift with Paris and Berlin. His hopes of acting as a diplomatic bridge linking Europe and the U.S. lay in ruins. The French, Germans, Belgians, and Luxembourgers seemed determined to add to Blair's discomfort as they hatched plans for a European defense force that went well beyond ideas envisaged by Blair. The four powers were plotting the creation of what would in effect be a new European army with its own command headquarters, rather than a mere peacekeeping force that could draw its recruits from national armies as before. In London and Washington there were worries that such a scheme would challenge the supremacy of NATO.

Though the Iraqi crisis was dominating world affairs, EU leaders still had to agree on how a community that was about to expand from 15 to 25 members would work. Poland, Hungary, the Czech Republic, Slovenia, Slovakia, Estonia, Lithuania, and Latvia—all from the former communist bloc—were due to join the following May, along with Malta and the Greek section of Cyprus.

For the first time, EU leaders decided to formulate a constitution that would lay down the rules about how an enlarged community would function and what its objectives and values would be. They had to decide how powers would be distributed between big and small member states and how to adapt Europe's institutions that had originally been built for just six founding members in the 1950s.

Among the accession nations, the whole process was causing a mixture of excitement and alarm. In staunchly Roman Catholic Poland, the biggest in area and population of the accession nations, there were fears that its traditions would be swept away on a tide of EU conformity. There was to be no mention of God in the constitution, an omission that offended Poland's Roman Catholic traditionalists. Fears grew that the Poles might reject entry in a referendum that was supposed merely to confirm the people's will to join. In June, however, the Poles voted overwhelmingly in favour of entry, sending a positive, upbeat signal that encouraged many of their Eastern neighbours to do the same in national votes. Pope John Paul II did the "yes" cause enormous good when he publicly exhorted his Polish countrymen to support membership.

In June former French president Valéry Giscard d'Estaing, who had been placed in charge of drawing up the initial draft of the EU constitution, handed over a copy of the draft to EU heads of government. The document laid out plans to create a new full-time European president, a foreign minister, and a European public prosecutor. The powers of the European Parliament would be doubled and those of the European Commission (EC) greatly increased. Also important, the constitution would give the EU "legal personality" for the first time, granting it in effect the sole right to negotiate most treaties.

By mid-year, however, fraud had been uncovered inside the institutions. Romano Prodi, the EC president, had promised to root out financial mismanagement and corruption after a series of scandals under his predecessor, Jacques Santer, but it appeared that little progress had been made when secret bank accounts were found at Eurostat, the community's statistical wing. The suspension of three senior officials followed allegations that millions of dollars had been siphoned into secret bank accounts over several years. Officials were also accused of having wrongly awarded contracts to the same outside companies over which they themselves presided. Slush funds, it was alleged, were used to pay for dinners, travel under false pretenses, and perks for high-ranking officials. In October insider-trading claims surfaced in the EU's agriculture fiefdom.

The last quarter of the year saw the French and Germans trying to rebuild diplomatic bridges with the U.S., but the niggling arguments about European defense continued to anger the Americans, so much so that in October they called a special meeting of NATO to discuss the threat to the alliance. Blair reassured the Americans that he would agree to nothing that would harm NATO, but Washington's suspicions remained.

In November the EC published a report on the accession nations that claimed that in many ways they were not yet ready to be members. Corruption, the report said, was rife in public life, and legal systems were inadequate. Though arguments ensued over the constitution and the widespread belief that accession nations were not yet ready to be full members, it was made clear that they would join nonetheless the following May. In December the community failed to agree on a new draft constitution backed by Germany and France but objected to by Spain and Poland because of its changes in voting weights allocated between large and small EU members. (TOBY HELM)

MULTINATIONAL AND REGIONAL ORGANIZATIONS

Nontraditional threats to security and terrorism again dominated the agendas of many multinational and regional organizations in 2003, and the U.S.-led war in Iraq was also a matter of major concern. In Africa and Latin America, efforts continued to strengthen support for democratic governments, economic growth, and social equity. Iraq dominated the agenda of the March 1 Arab League Summit in Sharm el-Sheikh, Egypt. A proposal to call on Iraqi Pres. Saddam Hussein to resign led to a shouting match between Libyan leader Muammar al-Qaddafi and Saudi Crown Prince Abdullah. The summit concluded with a declaration rejecting any military action against Iraq and calling for a team of foreign ministers to meet with Saddam and the permanent members of the UN Security Council in an effort to avert war. On September 9 the Arab League unanimously recognized the Iraqi Governing Council and its ability to operate until a legitimate government was formed and a new constitution written. Subsequently, the league condemned the bombings in Baghdad, Iraq, in Riyadh, Saudi Arabia, and in Istanbul, as well as Israel's construction of a security fence in the West Bank. It hailed the UN Security Council's endorsement of the so-called road map for peace between Israel and the Palestinians.

Stability of oil supplies and markets preoccupied OPEC. On March 8 it announced that the looming conflict in Iraq would not influence global petroleum supplies. At the annual meeting on September 24, it was noted that increased production in Iraq coupled with improved production in non-OPEC countries could create destabilizing effects on the market.

The October summit meeting of Asia-Pacific Economic Cooperation (APEC) focused on promoting international trade and continued steps toward investment liberalization. Mindful of the collapse of World Trade Organization talks in September, leaders agreed that the WTO Doha Development Agenda still provided growth potential for all economies. APEC leaders promised to work toward ending agricultural subsidies. Much of the discussion, however, focused on security issues; leaders declared that global terrorism and the proliferation of weapons of mass destruction (WMD) posed the greatest threats to economic prosperity.

Iraq, terrorism, the situation in North Korea, and expanding cooperation were major concerns for members of the Association of Southeast Asian Nations (ASEAN). At a special meeting on March 19, ministers denounced the imminent war with Iraq and expressed concern over the situation on the Korean peninsula. At the ninth summit, held on October 7–8 on the Indonesian island of Bali, ASEAN leaders agreed on a comprehensive framework for economic cooperation with India. In the Bali Concord II, they pledged to achieve an ASEAN community by 2020 based on three pillars of cooperation: political and security, economic, and sociocultural.

The Group of Eight summit held on June 1–3 in Évian, France, included leaders from 11 less-developed countries as well as representatives from the UN, the World Bank, the IMF, and the WTO. The G-8 meeting focused on strengthening growth and the global economy through continued structural reform on several fronts, on assistance to Africa in combating famine and AIDS, and on a further commitment to speedy debt reduction for Heavily Indebted Poor Countries. A Counter-Terrorism Action Group was created to work with the UN Counter-Terrorism Committee, and leaders affirmed their

Zimbabwean Pres. Robert Mugabe speaks at a political rally on December 5. Zimbabwe was suspended for a second year at the Commonwealth Ministerial Action Group meeting held in Abuja, Nigeria. On December 8 Mugabe took his country out of the 54-member Commonwealth of Nations.

AP/Wide World Photos

commitment to stopping the flow of financing that supported terrorism and the spread of WMD. The group endorsed the road map for Middle East peace and called for a peaceful, comprehensive solution to the North Korean nuclear issue.

In June the General Assembly of the Organization of American States (OAS) declared support for good governance throughout the region and proposed strengthening political parties, citizen participation, judicial reform, and rule-of-law standards. In addition, the OAS endorsed the Rio Group declaration calling upon UN Secretary-General Kofi Annan to use his good offices to promote peace in Colombia.

In November negotiations resumed on the proposed Free Trade Area of the Americas. Facing some of the same problems that stalled WTO talks, notably the reluctance of Brazil and some others to open their economies to competition unless the United States reduced its farm subsidies and antidumping rules, ministers scaled back the scope of the proposed accord to a limited number of tariff cuts and common standards. This fueled a trend toward separate bilateral free-trade agreements with the U.S.

The second session of the African Union (AU) in Maputo, Mozambique, on July 10–12 focused on concerns about WTO decision-making procedures, the spread of HIV/AIDS, and implementation of the New Partnership for Africa's Development. Also in July, the Executive Council welcomed progress toward peace in Côte d'Ivoire and the efforts of the Economic Community of West African States to end the violence in Liberia. The council reiterated its position that the AU would not recognize an illegitimate change in government and called on AU members and the international community for humanitarian assistance and an interposition force to end the fighting.

The Commonwealth of Nations announced in March that it would continue Zimbabwe's suspension because of questionable election practices. At the December Commonwealth Ministerial Action Group (CMAG) meeting, members upheld the suspension. In response, Zimbabwe withdrew from the Commonwealth. The CMAG continued to monitor the progress of democratic reform in Pakistan, which also remained suspended from the Commonwealth because of concerns regarding its legal framework.

(MARGARET P. KARNS)

DEPENDENT STATES

Europe and the Atlantic. On Jan. 15, 2003, Greenland's government, formed after the December 2002 election, collapsed when the pro-independence Inuit Ataqatigiit (IA), with 8 seats in Parliament, withdrew from its coalition with Siumut (the largest party, with 10 seats), in protest against the handling of alleged cronyism. Jens Lyberth, the government's administrative manager and a friend of Prime Minister Hans Enoksen, drew criticism when he hired a spiritual healer to drive out "negative energy" from government offices. Enoksen fired Lyberth, and on January 17 Siumut and the conservative Atassut (seven seats) formed a new coalition. In September Finance Minister Augusta Salling, of Atassut, refused to resign after a €13 million (about $14 million) budget error. The prime minister dissolved the government and agreed on a new coalition with IA.

In May Enoksen and Danish Foreign Minister Per Stig Møller signed an agreement that would give Greenland a greater say in negotiations on the status of Thule Air Base, which the U.S. wanted to enlarge as part of an expanded missile defense system. Inuit continued to protest their 1953 eviction from the region, but in November the Danish Supreme Court ruled against additional compensation for a group of Inuit hunters and their families. The Nalunaq gold mine, the first new such mine in 25 years, opened in southern Greenland; it was expected to yield an initial annual gold production of at least 130,000 oz (3,685,000 g).

Also in May, Gibraltar's new British governor, Sir Francis Richards, was sworn in. In June Denis MacShane, the U.K.'s minister for Europe, reiterated that Britain would not share sovereignty over the territory with Spain without the consent of the local population. In September the European Court of Justice ruled that the EU's single-market directives did not apply to Gibraltar. The arrival in November of a British cruise ship on which more than 430 passengers had been taken ill caused Spain to close down the border with the territory temporarily, stranding thousands of workers and tourists for hours and triggering British protests. In the election to the House of Assembly on November 28, the ruling Gibraltar Social Democrats won 8 of the 15 seats.

In August Gov. Howard Pearce of the Falkland Islands/Islas Malvinas returned to the U.K.; Harriet Hall was sworn in as acting governor, the first woman to hold the post.

(MELINDA C. SHEPHERD)

Caribbean and Bermuda. Puerto Rico's largest bank was fined $21.6 million in January 2003 by the U.S. Department of Justice for allegedly having allowed millions of dollars in drug money to be laundered because of a failure to report suspicious activities to the authorities. The head of the Cayman Islands' Financial Reporting Unit, Brian Gibbs, resigned and left the region following the collapse of a high-profile money-laundering case involving four officials of the offshore Euro Bank Corp., which later closed. Gibbs admitted having shredded vital evidence in the case, which damaged the prosecution's arguments and led to not-guilty verdicts. The Cayman Islands' legislature in February unanimously voted to censure Attorney General David Ballantyne, who was subsequently removed from office by the British government.

The British Virgin Islands' Parliament voted in April to curtail the level of secrecy afforded to international business companies (IBCs) resident in the islands. In the future, IBCs would have to reveal the identities of their directors and shareholders to regulators

Dependent States[1]

Australia

- Christmas Island
- Cocos (Keeling) Islands
- Norfolk Island

Denmark

- Faroe Islands
- Greenland

France

- French Guiana
- French Polynesia
- Guadeloupe
- Martinique
- Mayotte
- New Caledonia
- Réunion
- Saint Pierre and Miquelon
- Wallis and Futuna

Netherlands, The

- Aruba
- Netherlands Antilles

New Zealand

- Cook Islands
- Niue
- Tokelau

United Kingdom

- Anguilla
- Bermuda
- British Virgin Islands
- Cayman Islands
- Falkland Islands
- Gibraltar
- Guernsey
- Isle of Man
- Jersey
- Montserrat
- Pitcairn Island
- Saint Helena
  Tristan da Cunha
- Turks and Caicos Islands

United States

- American Samoa
- Guam
- Northern Mariana Islands
- Puerto Rico
- Virgin Islands (of the U.S.)

[1]Excludes territories (1) to which Antarctic Treaty is applicable in whole or in part, (2) without permanent civilian population, (3) without internationally recognized civilian government (Western Sahara), or (4) representing unadjudicated unilateral or multilateral territorial claims.

Diego Garcia: A Strategic Base

When the U.S. and its allies launched their attack on Iraq in 2003, Diego Garcia—home to U.S. long-range bombers, patrol planes, and cargo ships as well as refueling and other support personnel—once again proved its logistic value as what many considered one of the top three U.S. military bases in the world. The Persian Gulf War of 1990–91 and the war in Afghanistan had already demonstrated the military importance of the Indian Ocean atoll as a naval and air force base and observatory (both satellite and communications). From a geostrategic point of view, the Diego Garcia atoll, located in the Chagos Archipelago, or British Indian Ocean Territory (BIOT), boasts undeniable advantages—a lagoon of considerable size and depth; a natural port able to accommodate ships, aircraft carriers, and both classic and nuclear submarines; and an ideal location in a cyclone-free zone in close proximity to international shipping lanes. (*See* Map.) Such advantages made a military stronghold of Diego Garcia, and during the 1970s and '80s it became the largest British-American naval support base in the Indian Ocean.

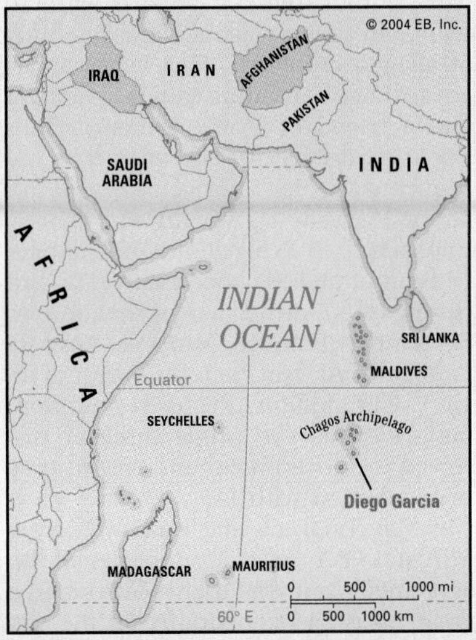

The U.K. had bought the Chagos Archipelago in November 1965 from Mauritius, then a British crown colony. The deal was accepted without much negotiation by Mauritius Chief Minister Sir Seewoosagur Ramgoolam, whose primary objective was to achieve independence (obtained in 1968). The strategically placed BIOT initially comprised the Chagos Archipelago and three other islands belonging to the Seychelles. After the Seychelles gained independence in 1976–77, London returned the three islands.

The militarization of Diego Garcia was the result of three successive bilateral treaties between the U.K. and the U.S. between 1966 and 1976. In the treaty of Dec. 12, 1966, control of Diego Garcia was handed over to the U.S. for 50 years, renegotiable for an additional 20 years. Although the British retained sovereignty with an on-site flagship, the administration was American. Thanks to the treaty of Feb. 25, 1976, a naval support base was officially installed, which allowed the U.S. Navy a permanent outpost in the Indian Ocean. This new development elicited protests, notably from the U.S.S.R.; the UN, which in 1971 had approved a resolution by Sri Lanka and India declaring the Indian Ocean a "peace zone"; and Mauritius, which initiated an annual debate in parliamentary hearings and international forums regarding the retrocession of the Chagos islands.

Between 1967 and 1973 some 1,400 (estimates varied) Chagos islanders, called Ilois, were expelled to live in Mauritius and Seychelles. In 1976 the U.S. ordered the systematic displacement of the remaining local people on Diego Garcia and replaced them with a temporary staff brought in from Mauritius and Seychelles.

(CHARLES CADOUX)

and law-enforcement officers. In 2003 the British Virgin Islands had more than 500,000 IBCs, with about 380,000 regarded as "active." In June the Virgin Islands Party, led by Ralph O'Neal, lost office after 17 years when the National Democratic Party won the general election by eight seats to five. NDP leader D. Orlando Smith became the new chief minister.

Political parties in Sint Maarten, in the Netherlands Antilles group, reemphasized in February that they wished greater autonomy on the model of Aruba. In a referendum on December 7, French Saint Martin, which shared the island with Sint Maarten, and Saint-Barthélemy voted in favour of separate status with France, as distinct from being subprefectures of Guadeloupe. Meanwhile, Guadeloupe and Martinique rejected Paris's proposed merger of their regional and general councils.

The People's Democratic Movement (PDM), led by Derek Taylor, won an unprecedented third straight term in the April general election in Turks and Caicos Islands but remained in office for only four months because the Supreme Court ruled that the results in two constituencies had been influenced by "errors" and "irregularities." By-elections in August reversed the April result by adding the two contested seats to the six the Progressive National Party (PNP) had obtained earlier, which left the PDM with five. PNP leader Michael Misick was appointed chief minister.

Montserrat's Chances Peak volcano erupted again in July as part of the dome collapsed and ash was spewed up to 12,200 m (about 40,000 ft). The southern half of the island continued to be uninhabitable, and some 4,000 residents remained squeezed into the northern half. Britain extended $1.5 million in emergency assistance following the eruption.

In early September Bermuda suffered massive damage from Hurricane Fabian, the worst storm to hit the island in some 50 years. Prime Minister Alex Scott's pro-independence government, which had won reelection in July, refused British assistance in the cleanup.

(DAVID RENWICK)

Pacific Ocean. There was a focus on the French Pacific territories in 2003, with French Pres. Jacques Chirac's first visit to the region and constitutional changes that would increase French Polynesia's representation in the French Senate and open the way to greater autonomy. In July Chirac met Pacific islands leaders in Papeete, on Tahiti, and announced a 50% increase in French aid to the region during 2004–07. A November 2002 census had counted the population of French Polynesia at some 245,000, 75% of whom lived in Tahiti and Moorea. There remained political tensions in New Caledonia, with some groups demanding greater recognition of indigenous rights and even independence. The debate was sharpened when the planned census there was dropped after Chirac criticized the inclusion of questions concerning ethnic origin. In March Cyclone Erica caused widespread damage and two deaths.

American Samoa's governor, Tauese Pita Fiti Sunia, died in March while traveling to Hawaii for medical treatment. He was succeeded by Lieut. Gov. Togiola Tulafono. In May, American Samoa experienced heavy rain, which caused floods, landslides, and four deaths. A census in the Commonwealth of the Northern Marianas showed that less than half of the 80,000 population had been born there; more than 35,000 guest workers laboured in the garment industry, which enjoyed preferential trade with the U.S. but could operate outside the U.S. minimum-wage laws. Guam continued to suffer the effects of Typhoon Pongsana, which had hit the island in December 2002. The government sought compensatory funds from the U.S. for the collateral effects of new Compacts of Free Association reached between the U.S. and the former Trust Territories, especially in regard to costs incurred by migrants to Guam from those countries.

In the Cook Islands the formerly estranged factions of the Democratic and Democratic-Alliance parties reunited, ousting the Cook Islands Party from power early in the year and installing Terepai Maoate as deputy prime minster. In November, after divisions within the cabinet, Maoate presented a vote of no confidence in Prime Minister Robert Woonton, which led to the suspension of House proceedings. An MP for Aitutaki resigned over budget allocations to his island but then returned victorious as the only candidate standing in the by-election. The government abolished the parliamentary seat for Cook Islanders living overseas and opened the way to reducing the parliamentary term from five years to four. The government also took steps to reduce its offshore banking business and increase the transparency of its financial arrangements in order to ensure the removal of the Cook Islands from an Organisation of Economic Cooperation and Development blacklist of money-laundering states. Niue had taken similar steps in 2002, and it sought to build its economy by increasing vanilla production, tourism, and fisheries output.

(BARRIE MACDONALD)

Indian Ocean. The French government's policy regarding economic decentralization and privatization had notable repercussions for Réunion in 2003. The Overseas Act passed on June 30 introduced a set of economic and fiscal measures with the objective of encouraging private initiative, above all in small and medium-sized companies in such areas as hospitality and tourism. In the media sector a new private television station was launched. In spite of occasional reforms, for some 20 years the Réunion station RFO had represented the voice of metropolitan France. In the future the competition between public and private sectors would force the station to reposition itself within the Indian Ocean zone.

The year's most important sociopolitical event was the unexpectedly widespread and violent response against the French government's planned education reforms. Unrest during April–June (including teachers' strikes, demonstrations, class closings, and the postponement of exams) was particularly virulent in Réunion. Baccalaureat (secondary-school senior exams) results in Réunion showed a higher rate of success in 2003 (82.07%) than in 2002 (72.73%), and for the first time Réunion surpassed the national average rate for metropolitan France (80.1%).

The Mayotte assembly's vote to amend the "personal status" code in 2003 sparked a debate between religious conservatives and reformers. The amendment aimed to abolish polygamy and the repudiation of women by their husbands, as well as to establish sexual equality in matters of inheritance and the settling of estates. It was expected to be a difficult adjustment for the predominantly Muslim population.

In October a British High Court justice ruled that the Ilois, who had been displaced from the Chagos Archipelago, or British Indian Ocean Territory, more than 30 years earlier, could not claim additional compensation. The archipelago's Diego Garcia atoll was the site of a strategically important U.S. naval support base. (*See* Sidebar.)

(CHARLES CADOUX)

ANTARCTICA

Ice averaging 2,160 m (7,085 ft) in thickness covers more than about 98% of the continent of Antarctica, which has an area of 14 million sq km (5.4 million sq mi). There is no indigenous human population, and there is no land-based industry. Human activity consists mainly of scientific research. The 45-nation Antarctic Treaty is the managerial mechanism for the region south of latitude 60° S, which includes all of Antarctica. The treaty reserves the area for peaceful purposes, encourages cooperation in science, prescribes environmental protection, allows inspections to verify adherence, and defers the issue of territorial sovereignty.

In 2003 representatives of the Antarctic Treaty nations finally reached consensus on creating a permanent secretariat in Argentina. The measure was to take legal effect after all the parties ratified it. Because of the immediate need, the representatives agreed to get the secretariat working, using voluntary contributions after the selection of an executive secretary in 2004. Membership in the Antarctic Treaty had grown from the original 12 nations to 45, and Malaysia expressed interest in achieving membership and sent investigators to Antarctica and observers to the 2003 consultative meeting, which was held June 9–20 in Madrid.

The International Association of Antarctica Tour Operators reported that 13,571 tourists landed in the Antarctic in the 2002–03 summer on privately organized expeditions—most of them aboard commercial ships. Four nations—the U.S., Germany, Great Britain, and Australia—accounted for 73% of the travelers. This was a big increase over the 2001–02 season, which had had 11,588 tourists. The association expected tourism to increase again in 2003–04.

In August an Australian military ship, after a chase that lasted 21 days, seized a Uruguayan-flagged boat on suspicion of poaching Patagonian toothfish (usually marketed as Chilean sea bass), which were protected in Antarctic waters by an international convention. Australian customs officials said that the boat was carrying 85 metric tons of the fish, which can grow to 2.2 m (7 ft) in length. The crew members were taken to Fremantle, Australia, where they faced fines and jail. Harvesting the fish remained legal under a permit system, but illegal, unreported fishing was thought to exceed the allowed limit severalfold and to threaten depletion of the stock in a few years if it was not stopped.

The ozone hole covered much of Antarctica (and beyond) in the austral spring of 2003 and thus permitted ultraviolet radiation from the Sun to reach the Earth's surface in increased amounts. At 28.75 million sq km (about 11.1 million sq mi), the 2003 ozone hole was the second largest on record. The World Bank reported that global consumption of chlorinated fluorocarbons had dropped from 1,100,000 tons in 1986 to 150,000 tons in 1999. The international decision to cut the production of man-made chemicals that cause the ozone hole and lesser stratospheric ozone depletions worldwide had been made in 1987, when stratospheric chemists based at McMurdo Sound showed that the chemicals caused the ozone hole. The Bank said that without the changes dictated by the Montreal Protocol on Substances That Deplete the Ozone Layer (1987), consumption would have reached 3,000,000 tons by 2010.

Scientists from Canada and the U.S. reported that their modeling studies found the Antarctic ozone hole to be responsible for the observed spring and summertime warming in the Southern Hemisphere over the past 40 years. The work helped to quantify the possible influence of the stratosphere (where the ozone hole occurs) on weather and climate. Increased circumpolar westerly winds also were blamed on the ozone hole. The scientists said that their work showed that human emissions of ozone-depleting gases had affected surface climate over the past few decades.

According to a 2003 report based on a study of rock samples collected at Graphite Peak, the collision of a meteorite with the Earth was the cause of a global mass extinction 251 million years ago that exterminated more than 90% of the world's living things. The event was the biggest of Earth's so-called Big Five mass extinctions documented in the geologic record. The finding was based on samples collected in the Antarctic in the mid-1990s, and some scientists considered it controversial because they believed that weathering during the 251 million years since the meteorite struck would have made the rock samples unreliable. Scientists returned to the Antarctic in late 2003 to search for more samples that might help resolve the criticism.

Australian researchers studying chemical evidence from ice cores taken at Law Dome reported that Antarctic sea ice, which was stable from 1840 to 1950, had decreased sharply in area since then. The decline of about 20% was not uniform, and the data were focused on the area of the Southern Ocean south of Australia, but the investigators said that their findings lengthened the history represented by the short period that had been monitored by satellite imagers and strongly suggested that the total sea-ice extent around Antarctica had been in decline since the 1950s.

Argentine and British scientists published a report in 2003 in which they suggested that the Larsen Ice Shelf on the east coast of the Antarctic Peninsula, which had lost massive sections in 1995 and 2002, was a model for what could happen to larger ice shelves farther south. Earlier work had indicated that regional warming and surface melting over the past several decades were the main causes; the new report gave more weight to ocean warming. A report by American and British investigators on the complex science of ice dynamics found that "a major West Antarctic ice stream discharges by sudden and brief periods of very rapid motion paced by oceanic tidal oscillations of about 1 metre" per hour.

Ancient Antarctic life was the subject of two unusual studies reported in 2003. According to a report in the *New York Times,* Lake Vida in the McMurdo Dry Valleys, which was covered by 18.3 m (about 60 ft) of ice, yielded bacteria that froze at about the time that Rome was founded and were successfully brought back to life. Scientists reported in *Nature* magazine that they had discovered the fossil of a fly 500 km (about 310 mi) from the South Pole, which went against the long-held belief that these insects never inhabited the continent. The fly had lived there between 3 million and 17 million years ago.

(GUY G. GUTHRIDGE)

ARCTIC REGIONS

The Arctic regions may be defined in physical terms (astronomical [north of the Arctic Circle, latitude 66° 30′ N], climatic [above the 10 °C (50 °F) July isotherm], or vegetational [above the northern limit of the tree line]) or in human terms (the territory inhabited by the circumpolar cultures—Inuit [Eskimo] and Aleut in North America and Russia, Sami [Lapp] in northern Scandinavia and Russia, and 29 other peoples of the Russian North, Siberia, and East Asia). No single national sovereignty or treaty regime governs the region, which includes portions of eight countries: Canada, the United States, Russia, Finland, Sweden, Norway, Iceland, and Greenland (part of Denmark). The Arctic Ocean, 14.09 million sq km (5.44 million sq mi) in area, constitutes about two-thirds of the region. The land area consists of permanent ice cap, tundra, or taiga. The population (2003 est.) of peoples belonging to the circumpolar cultures is about 375,000. International organizations concerned with the Arctic include the Arctic Council, institutions of the Barents Region, the Inuit Circumpolar Conference, and the Indigenous Peoples' Secretariat. International scientific cooperation in the Arctic is the focus of the International Arctic Research Center of the University of Alaska at Fairbanks.

As 2003 ended, a dispute between U.S. Pres. George W. Bush's administration and key congressional leaders had stalled the 25-year-old plan to build a $20 billion, 5,800-km (1 km = about 0.62 mi) Alaskan natural gas pipeline from Alaska through Canada to the lower 48 states. Bush's energy bill mandated that the proposed pipeline stretch from Prudhoe Bay in northern Alaska to near Fairbanks and then along the Alaska Highway to Alberta, where it would connect to existing pipelines to Chicago. Passage of the energy bill through the U.S. House and Senate was delayed in part because representatives from Alaska had insisted that financial incentives for gas producers be part of the sweeping energy bill, including a floor price of $3.25 per thousand cubic feet delivered to key distribution points in Alberta for Alaskan gas. The proposed floor price reflected the high costs of transportation from Alaska to Alberta. The gas prices in September were more than twice the proposed floor price. The pipeline's proponents maintained that tax breaks were essential to making the pipeline economical.

Canada's oil and gas industry was concerned that U.S. government incentives for the Alaska project could jeopardize a rival natural gas pipeline project in the Mackenzie Delta, as well as natural gas produced in Canada, where government incentives were not available to natural gas producers. Because the energy bill was designed to reduce American dependence on foreign energy sources, and because American gas inventories were 29% lower than the previous five-year inventory average, U.S. legislators were under increasing pressure to find ways to increase natural gas supplies by supporting the Alaska pipeline project. The prospects of the U.S. gas subsidy and approval of the energy bill received a boost after a power blackout in August left an estimated 50 million people in Canada and the U.S. in the dark. Proponents of the bill expected that the power blackout would spur a compromise with opponents. The bill passed in the House in November, but a Democratic filibuster blocked it in the Senate.

Development of the estimated 5.7 billion–16 billion bbl of oil under the 160-km coastal plain of the 7.7-million-ha (19-million-ac) Arctic National Wildlife Refuge (ANWR) also was a key part of the president's bill, but the ANWR drilling program had been rejected by the Senate in March.

In June an agreement was announced between the Inuvik, N.W.Terr.-based Aboriginal Pipeline Group, which owned 33.3% of the project, and Canadian and American energy producers and pipeline builders for the Can$5 billion (US$3.75 billion) Mackenzie Delta natural gas pipeline. The announcement cleared the way for the preliminary information package to be sent to the relevant regulatory authorities. Supporters of the pipeline had proposed building twin pipelines from the Mackenzie Delta to northern Alberta. One pipeline would transport natural gas along the complete 1,300-km route. A shorter, 500-km, pipeline would carry natural gas liquids (NGLs) to Norman Wells, N.W.Terr. The construction of a separate line for NGLs would allay criticism that natural gas from Canada's Arctic could be shipped to the U.S. without having that gas stripped of its value-added petrochemical-related content, such as ethane and propane. Most of the natural gas would most likely initially fuel refineries in the oil sands of northern Alberta.

In September it was reported that Royal Dutch Shell had approved a $1 billion plan for a 600-million-bbl Siberian reserve oil project in a 50–50 partnership with Evikhon, a Russian company. Russia was the world's second biggest oil producer, and its vast energy reserves were among the few available for purchase outside the Middle East.

According to federal wildlife biologists in the U.S., 200–400 polar bears that crossed over the floating ice between Alaska and Russia were being shot each year by Russian poachers. The findings were reported as part of negotiations to ratify a 2000 treaty between the U.S. and Russia to protect the shared population of bears. If that level of hunting persisted, the estimated population of 4,000 bears could be cut in half by 2020. The treaty would allow limited subsistence hunting by indigenous peoples.

The Inuit Circumpolar Conference (ICC) launched a potentially groundbreaking legal action on global warming through a petition to the Inter-American Commission on Human Rights. The ICC's petition addressed man-made global warming and the threat that it posed to the Inuit homeland and culture. Climate-change experts had predicted that most of the permanent ice in the Arctic Ocean would disappear between 2050 and 2070 and that the Arctic would become ice-free in the summer. These changes would have a negative impact on the Inuit's traditional wildlife harvesting and would open up the Northwest Passage to commercial ships, which would thus create new environmental dangers to Arctic offshore areas.

In September the 3,000-year-old Ward Hunt Ice Shelf, located on the north coast of Ellesmere Island, was reported to have split in half and started to break up into icebergs. At 443 sq km (about 171 sq mi), the shelf was the largest in the Arctic, and according to University of Alaska experts, its breakup was a clear sign of global warming's impact on the Arctic Ocean.

In July a team of European scientists completed the deepest hole—more than three kilometers—ever drilled through ice in the Northern Hemisphere. The objective of the North Greenland Ice Core Project was to extract a core sample of ice that would enable the scientists to explore the history of the world's changing climate. The research was expected to help predict future climate changes, including the possibility that recent indications of global warming would be replaced by a rapid cooling of the Earth.

(KENNETH DE LA BARRE)

Scientists observe a crack in the Ward Hunt Ice Shelf on the northern coast of Ellesmere Island, Nunavut. The ice shelf was reported in September as having broken in two, probably because of climate change in the north polar region, after having been in place for 3,000 years.

V. Sahanatien, Parks Canada

AFGHANISTAN

Area: 645,807 sq km (249,347 sq mi)
Population (2003 est.): 28,717,000 (including Afghan refugees estimated to number about 1,100,000 in Pakistan and about 1,000,000 in Iran, many of whom have returned home)
Capital: Kabul
Chief of state and head of government: President Hamid Karzai

Afghanistan continued to work toward stabilization and reconstruction in 2003, but uneven progress and fears over security throughout the country left the precarious transitional administration of Hamid Karzai vulnerable to charges of impotence and a target for groups hostile to its U.S. and other international supporters. Well-wishers of the administration could point to a number of positive developments, but most of them were balanced by negative or uncertain realities.

Following the timetable fixed by the 2001 Bonn Agreement for establishing a fully representative government, preparations were made to register Afghans for a general election in June 2004. In November the government announced the draft of a new constitution that was submitted to a special *loya jirga* ("grand council") in December. Some Afghans criticized the government for having invited public debate only after the constitution was drafted, and many, both in and out of the government, advocated strict accordance with Shari'ah, Islam's traditional legal framework. Lack of countrywide security caused some, including UN special representative Lakhdar Brahimi, to doubt the possibility of conducting fair elections on schedule.

Kabul experienced something of a boom with the increase of reconstruction projects paid for with international assistance. Much of the $4.5 billion previously pledged to Afghanistan's reconstruction, however, had not arrived or had already been consumed as humanitarian aid. In the summer the U.S. said it would increase its reconstruction aid by $900 million.

The currency reform of 2002 appeared to have been successful, creating a foundation for economic growth, yet the economy remained much smaller that it had been before the Soviet invasion in 1979. Economic hardship as well as unsettled politics motivated increased opium production even while relief from years of drought allowed a 2003 cereal harvest 50% higher than that of the previous year.

More than 2.5 million refugees and internally displaced persons had returned voluntarily to their homes, but food shortages and an increased cost of living threatened some, especially landless returnees and households headed by women. Many refugees, even those who had been living for years in camps in Iran or Pakistan, had become accustomed to electricity and schools. When the country's school system reopened in March, five million students, boys and girls, enrolled. Construction on the Kabul–Kandahar–Herat highway reached Kandahar, restoring a vital part of the overland route linking Europe and the Middle East with South Asia.

The most serious worry to those who were working for a stable, democratic Afghanistan was the general deterioration of security in parts of the country beyond the reach of the central government. U.S. Defense Secretary Donald Rumsfeld visited Kabul in May and declared that major combat activity by U.S. forces there was over. Still, Operation Enduring Freedom, a U.S.-led coalition of 12,500 soldiers, battled throughout the year against terrorist opposition thought to be grouped around al-Qaeda loyalists of Osama bin Laden, followers of ousted Taliban leader Mohammad Omar, and Hezbi Islami forces of Gulbuddin Hekmatyar. All three leaders continued to elude capture.

© Reuters NewMedia Inc./Corbis

On the first day of school in Kabul, March 23, pupils peer through a fence at Ferdosi High School. This school, like many others in Afghanistan, was running three shifts a day to take care of the demand.

A separate International Security Assistance Force (ISAF)—5,000 troops contributed by 31 countries—was the security guarantor for areas directly under the control of the central government. In August NATO assumed responsibility for ISAF, and in October the UN Security Council authorized NATO to send ISAF troops anywhere in Afghanistan. This was intended as support for President Karzai. Pakistan's Pres. Pervez Musharraf had called for ISAF to end what he called a power vacuum in Afghanistan. In July an exchange of fire between Pakistani troops and Afghans had led to charges that Pakistan had violated the Afghan border. After a mob ransacked Pakistan's embassy in Kabul, relations between the two countries became tense.

Reports of raids and bomb attacks by Taliban fighters increased throughout the year, although the degree to which they were coordinated was uncertain. In the summer the Taliban reportedly set up a new command structure for southern Afghanistan, its traditional base of support, and weeks later establishment of another Taliban command for northern Afghanistan was claimed.

International forces began a new tactic in 2003 for winning support outside Kabul, the capital. The U.S., the U.K., New Zealand, and Germany formed provincial reconstruction teams, small lightly armed groups whose task was to assist in reconstruction projects across the country. (STEPHEN SEGO)

Albanian soldiers train in land-mine-removal techniques at a base near Tirana in March. They were part of a 70-member elite force that was deployed to Iraq in April to join peacekeeping operations.

AP/Wide World Photos

ALBANIA

Area: 28,703 sq km (11,082 sq mi)
Population (2003 est.): 3,166,000 (not including Albanians living abroad)
Capital: Tirana
Chief of state: President Alfred Moisiu
Head of government: Prime Minister Fatos Nano

Politics in Albania in 2003 focused largely on local elections that took place on October 12. The governing Socialist Party claimed victory in 36 of the country's 65 largest towns, including the capital, Tirana. Final results could not be published, since the opposition refused to sign the ballot protocols, charging the Socialists with "fixing the results." After the ballot, the Organization for Security and Cooperation in Europe (OSCE) mission chief Robert Barry noted "progress toward compliance with OSCE, Council of Europe, and other international standards," however. In the run-up to the voting, Prime Minister Fatos Nano strengthened the influence of his conservative wing of the Socialist Party through a government reshuffle on July 23 following the resignation of his rival, the foreign minister and former prime minister Ilir Meta, from office. On July 28, however, the Assembly rejected Nano's nomination of Marko Bello to succeed Meta, showing that support for Meta, who belonged to the reform wing of the party, was still strong among the majority of the Socialist legislators.

On February 13 in Tirana, the integration minister, Sokol Nako, and European Union representatives held the first round of talks on the Stabilization and Association Agreement. In March, in its second annual report on the stabilization and association process, the European Commission warned Albania to speed up legal and administrative reforms, fight corruption and organized crime, and start the restitution of or compensation for land expropriated during the communist regime. On August 7 Nano announced the return of property to the family of Leka Zogu, the son of the late King Zog. At the same time, the Assembly began debating a law on restitution sponsored by the OSCE.

Albania sent a contingent of 70 soldiers in April to join the U.S.-led coalition in the Iraq war. The foreign ministers of Albania, Croatia, and Macedonia signed the U.S.-Adriatic Charter with the U.S. secretary of state in Tirana on May 2 to promote mutual cooperation.

Albania's relations with neighbouring countries and regions generally improved in 2003. Following an outbreak of ethnic Albanian separatist violence in northern Macedonia in late August, Albanian Pres. Alfred Moisiu expressed his full support of the Macedonian authorities' fight against "extremist groups." On September 12 the defense ministers of Albania, Croatia, and Macedonia signed a declaration stressing the need for a joint fight against organized crime and terrorism. In mid-July the presidents of Albania, Bulgaria, and Macedonia held a series of meetings on infrastructure cooperation, focusing on the east-west transport Corridor VIII and a joint pipeline project. Albania also opened new border crossings with Macedonia and Montenegro. A free-trade agreement between Albania and Kosovo was signed in Pristina, the capital of the Serbian province, on July 7.

Relations with the newly renamed Serbia and Montenegro deteriorated, however, after the Serbian parliament approved a declaration on August 27 reaffirming its claim to Kosovo and a draft constitution for Serbia and Montenegro referred to Kosovo as a part of Serbia. The Albanian parliament declared that this resembled "a dangerous return . . . to nationalist policies."

Unemployment was on the decline in Albania and was about 15% in 2003. GDP growth remained about 5% in 2003, while the budget deficit decreased to about 6% of GDP.

(FABIAN SCHMIDT)

ALGERIA

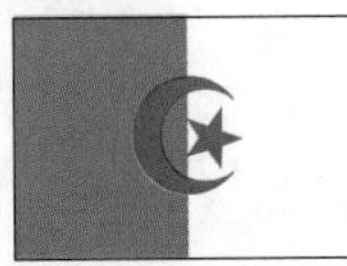

Area: 2,381,741 sq km (919,595 sq mi)
Population (2003 est.): 31,800,000
Capital: Algiers
Chief of state: President Abdelaziz Bouteflika
Head of government: Prime Ministers Ali Benflis and, from May 5, Ahmed Ouyahia

During 2003 Algeria experienced a lessening in the violence that had plagued the country for 12 years, and the death toll dropped to below 100 persons a month. The Armed Islamic Group (GIA) appeared fragmented by midyear, even though the Salafist Group for Preaching and Combat (GSPC) continued to threaten the east of the country. In one bizarre episode the GSPC took hostage 32 European tourists traveling in the Sahara, holding some of them for up to five months. Although 17 were released by the Algerian army in May, the remainder had to be ransomed from Mali in August at a cost, it was believed, of about $5 million, apparently paid by Libya or Germany. Abassi Madani and Ali Ben Hadj, the two former paramount Islamic Salvation Front (FIS) leaders, ended their sentences in July and were set free.

The Kabyle crisis quieted down as first the prime minister and then Pres. Abdelaziz Bouteflika himself indicated that the government would engage in dialogue with the *aarchs* (informal tribal and village councils) without preconditions. After considerable hesitation, the *aarch* movement agreed to enter into dialogue provided that the demands of the El Kseur Platform, which included regional autonomy, were first stipulated. At the same time, the *aarch* movement was weakened by the Rally for Culture and Democracy (RCD), one of the two Berberist political parties, alongside the FFS, that tried to force it to engage in a wider national debate about political decentralization, and by the emergence of a new political party clearly designed to undermine the movement.

Overshadowing all of this, however, was the run-up to the presidential elections to be held in April 2004. President Bouteflika intended to stand again despite hostility from the army, and he organized a massive electioneering campaign around the country during the year. When the National Liberation Front (FLN) refused to endorse him formally, the Ali Benflis government was removed in June and Ahmed Ouyahia, the National Democratic Rally leader, was installed in his place. Benflis was also the FLN leader and became the party's candidate at a special congress in October. Faced with a threat that the National Popular Assembly might refuse to endorse decrees he had issued during its summer recess, the president threatened to dissolve the body, although in October the measures were passed without FLN opposition.

Bouteflika also turned on the press as revelations of scandals began to touch the presidential entourage. Two close presidential supporters, Interior Minister Yazid Zerhouni and Energy Minister Chakib Khelil, were the prime targets. Six newspapers were temporarily closed down, allegedly for financial irregularities, and the directors of two of them faced defamation charges. The government's proposed privatization program was delayed yet again by determined trade-union opposition. A new hydrocarbons law that would have opened Algeria up to greater foreign investment had to be scrapped for the same reason. In April Algeria signed the European Union's Euro-Mediterranean Partnership association agreement for free trade in industrial goods and subsequently applied to join the World Trade Organization. Despite increased oil-production capacity, Algeria agreed to abide by OPEC's quota reductions in September in order to keep world oil prices high. (GEORGE JOFFÉ)

ANDORRA

Area: 464 sq km (179 sq mi)
Population (2003 est.): 66,900
Capital: Andorra la Vella
Chiefs of state: Co-princes of Andorra, the president of France and the bishop of Urgell, Spain
Head of government: Chief Executive Marc Forné Molné

In a year dominated by wars, violence, and terrorist attacks in much of the world, Andorra remained serene during 2003 in its nest in the Pyrenees. The country responded to the European Union's request to modify its banking secrecy laws to help in the search for terrorist funds.

After having served since 1971 as bishop of Urgell, an honorary position that made him ex officio co-prince of Andorra, Mgr. Joan Marti Alanis retired and was succeeded by Mgr. Joan Enric Vives Sicilia on May 12.

Andorra's economy, based primarily on the country's attraction to visitors, continued to thrive. Tourism made up approximately 80% of gross domestic product, and Andorra welcomed about 11 million visitors annually. The banking sector, the second largest component of the economy, continued to prosper as it worked to expand its financial services. (ANNE ROBY)

In September French tobacco shop owners block the road leading into Andorra to protest a tax raise of up to 20% that would make it even more beneficial for the French to buy contraband cigarettes in Andorra, where tobacco, alcohol, and perfume had long been tax-free.

A woman walks under a fallen building in Kuito, Angola, evidence of the devastation wrought by a quarter of a century of civil war. With its great mineral and oil resources, Angola could be one of the richest countries in Africa.

AP/Wide World Photos

ANGOLA

Area: 1,246,700 sq km (481,354 sq mi)
Population (2003 est.): 10,766,000
Capital: Luanda
Chief of state and head of government: President José Eduardo dos Santos, assisted by Prime Minister Fernando da Piedade Dias dos Santos

In approving a budget for 2003 of almost 359 billion kwanzas (about $6.3 billion), the Angolan National Assembly urged the government to introduce incentives to attract external investment. This was needed, the Assembly felt, to reduce the hardships that the majority of the population was still suffering in the aftermath of Angola's 27-year civil war. Virtually the only immediate resource available was oil, although diamond mining showed signs of recovery. Coffee, which had been exported before the civil war, now commanded so low a price on the world market that there was little point in trying to revive production. With oil output reaching 900,000 bbl a day by midyear (of which 70% was exported to the U.S.) and with no restrictions on production similar to the quota system that operated among OPEC countries, the prospects for Angola's economic recovery seemed reasonably good.

One potential snag was the fact that 60% of the country's known oil reserves were located in Cabinda, a region that was detached from the body of the country but had been declared a province of Angola upon independence in 1975. The inhabitants of Cabinda still questioned their status, although in April representatives of the province offered to negotiate.

Accusations of corruption were leveled against Angola's government, and these aroused fears among international aid agencies that profits from oil exports might not be used to benefit the citizenry. While admitting that some of the income from oil sales was missing, the government maintained that accounting problems, rather than corruption, were responsible. A mission was sent by the International Monetary Fund in April–May to seek clarification of the issue.

Although it was claimed in April that 1.7 million people displaced during the civil war had returned to their homes, some 110,000 former rebel fighters and their families were still living in camps, where food shortages remained an acute problem. Thousands of others in an equally parlous condition were still trying to make their way home. Early in the year the World Bank provided more than $100 million to assist these displaced persons but, ignoring the government's protestations, warned that further help would depend upon corruption's being dealt with urgently. Pres. José Eduardo dos Santos's response was to appoint a number of reform-minded ministers to his cabinet, including a former executive director of the IMF.

Shedding its military garb, the National Union for the Total Independence of Angola (UNITA) emerged as a political force. In June a party congress elected Isaias Samakuva as its leader. He immediately took advantage of UNITA's debut in the Council of the Republic, a consultative body created to make recommendations regarding elections, to call for both presidential and parliamentary elections to be held early in 2004, in advance of the date previously suggested by the president. Dos Santos said he would not seek reelection, but his party made no apparent effort to nominate an alternative candidate. (KENNETH INGHAM)

ANTIGUA AND BARBUDA

Area: 442 sq km (171 sq mi)
Population (2003 est.): 76,800
Capital: Saint John's
Chief of state: Queen Elizabeth II, represented by Governor-General Sir James Carlisle
Head of government: Prime Minister Lester Bird

Prime Minister Lester Bird lost his Antigua Labour Party (ALP) majority in the House of Representatives for three days in June 2003 following the resignation of four ALP MPs. ALP's nine-member majority was swiftly restored, however, when one MP changed his mind and reaccepted the party whip. Nevertheless, Bird signaled that he would call a general election prior to June 2004, the constitutional deadline for the event.

The World Trade Organization agreed to appoint a three-member disputes panel in late July to adjudicate on Antigua and Barbuda's claim that the U.S. government breached its commitments under the General Agreement on Trade in Services by banning U.S. residents from using credit cards, checks, or electronic bank transfers when placing bets with Internet-based gambling operations on the islands. As a result of the action, Antigua and Barbuda suffered an estimated $33.3 million in lost license fees, the number of gaming operations was reduced from 100 to fewer than 36, and employment in the gambling industry shrank from 5,000 to 2,500. (DAVID RENWICK)

ARGENTINA

Area: 2,780,092 sq km (1,073,400 sq mi)
Population (2003 est.): 36,846,000
Capital: Buenos Aires
Head of state: Presidents Eduardo Duhalde and, from May 25, Néstor Kirchner

Following the political, economic, and social chaos experienced in 2002, the year 2003 was one of relative stabilization and normalization in Argentina. Néstor Kirchner (*see* BIOGRAPHIES) was elected president; the economy began to grow again; and the level of social tension dropped.

In the political arena, the first round of presidential elections was held on April 27. The election date had been switched several times by interim president Eduardo Duhalde as part of his master plan to impede the election of former president Carlos Menem (1989–99); both Duhalde and Menem belonged to the Justicialist (Peronist) Party (PJ). Certain that Menem would win if the party held a primary, the PJ did not select one presidential candidate as originally planned. Instead, three different candidates ran under the PJ label: Menem, Santa Cruz governor Kirchner (Duhalde's handpicked candidate), and former interim president Adolfo Rodríguez Saá.

Two former members of the country's second largest party, the Radical Civic Union (UCR), ran as candidates of their own personal parties, Elisa Carrió (a national deputy from Chaco) and Ricardo López Murphy (a cabinet minister in the government of Pres. Fernando de la Rúa, 1999–2001). Thirteen other candidates, including the official UCR candidate, Leopoldo Moreau, also competed.

On April 27 Menem finished first with 24.5% of the valid vote, followed by Kirchner (22.2%), López Murphy (16.4%), Rodríguez Saá (14.1%), Carrió (14.1%), and Moreau (2.3%). Since no candidate surpassed the threshold needed to win in the first round, a second-round runoff between Menem and Kirchner was scheduled for May 18. The week prior to this election, however, Menem—under pressure from many of his supporters who realized that he had little chance of victory—withdrew from the runoff, which resulted in Kirchner's victory by default. On May 25 Kirchner assumed the presidency; his term in office was to run until Dec. 10, 2007.

Every two years Argentina renewed one-half of its Chamber of Deputies and one-third of its Senate. Though the presidential election was held on April 27, only 7 of the 130 Chamber seats (out of 257) and none of the 24 Senate seats (out of 72) were determined on April 27. As a result, the elections for the remaining seats (as well as 20 of the 24 governorships) were held between June 8 and November 23, with every province responsible for scheduling its own elections. By the end of this period, the PJ had increased its dominance in the Chamber of Deputies (131 seats) and the Senate (41 seats) as well as at the provincial level (16 governorships). A weakened UCR remained the country's only other relevant political force, with 47 deputies, 16 senators, and 6 governors.

President Kirchner spent the first seven months of his administration attempting to consolidate his power by taking actions that were popular with the general public. These measures included annulling restrictions on the extradition of military officers accused of having committed human rights abuses during the 1976–83 military dictatorship, attacking unpopular institutions such as the Supreme Court and the privately run utility companies, and resisting IMF pressure on Argentina to implement fiscally sound policies, policies that nonetheless would entail significant short-term costs for much of the Argentine citizenry.

In the economic arena, the free fall Argentina had experienced since 2001 finally stopped, and the economy began to stabilize and grow again. During 2003 GDP increased by 6%, and the inflation rate was a mere 3%. In spite of these positive indicators, serious unresolved issues such as reform in the banking sector, utility price increases, a lack of governmental respect for the rule of law, and Argentina's considerable foreign and domestic debt (much of which was in default) continued to represent serious obstacles to increased growth and development. These issues exercised a chilling effect on most forms of foreign and domestic investment (except in a few select areas) as well as on consumer spending.

In the social arena, the number and intensity of popular protests dropped significantly in 2003. In particular, following Kirchner's assumption of office in May, Argentines became much more positive about their personal situation as well as more optimistic about the country's future. This positive national mood was reflected in the reduced level of protest as well as in the very high public approval ratings (generally above 75%) enjoyed by President Kirchner.

Kirchner's foreign-policy agenda marked a break with that in place during the previous dozen years. It involved a greater level of coordination and stronger ties with neighbour Brazil and attempts to revitalize Mercosur (the Common Market of the South). President Kirchner also fostered improved diplomatic relations with Latin America's more radical leaders: Presidents Fidel Castro of Cuba and Hugo Chávez of Venezuela. In contrast, relations with the United States and traditional European allies Italy and Spain became much cooler than in the recent past. (MARK P. JONES)

ARMENIA

Area: 29,743 sq km (11,484 sq mi). About 16% of neighbouring Azerbaijan (including the 4,400-sq-km [1,700-sq-mi] disputed region of Nagorno-Karabakh [Armenian: Artsakh]) has been under Armenian control since 1993.
Population (2003 est.): 3,061,000 (plus 130,000 in Nagorno-Karabakh)
Capital: Yerevan
Chief of state: President Robert Kocharyan
Head of government: Prime Minister Andranik Markaryan

On March 5, 2003, Robert Kocharyan was reelected as Armenian president in a fiercely fought ballot. In the first round on February 19, Kocharyan polled 49.5% of the vote, less than the 50% needed for an outright win, while the People's Party of Armenia chairman, Stepan Demirchyan, placed second of eight rival candidates with 28.2%. Demirchyan's supporters staged daily protests against alleged voter fraud both before and after the runoff, which Kocharyan won handily, with 67.4% of the vote.

Demirchyan's opposition Justice bloc suffered a further defeat in the May 25 parliamentary election, winning only 15 of the 131 mandates. The Organization for Security and Co-operation in Europe and the Council of Europe criticized both the presidential and the parliamentary ballots as having fallen short of international standards for free elections.

The Justice bloc and the National Unity Party boycotted parliamentary sessions until September to protest the alleged falsification of the parliamentary election results.

Prime Minister Andranik Markaryan's Republican Party, the largest faction, with 40 parliamentary seats, formed a new coalition government with the Law-Based State Party (20 seats) and the Armenian Revolutionary Federation–Dashnaktsutyun (11 seats). Markaryan remained prime minister, while the Law-Based State Party chairman, Artur Baghdasaryan, was named Chairman of the National Assembly. Disagreements swiftly arose between the three coalition parties, however, over the distribution of deputy minister posts, relations with Turkey, and proposed anticorruption measures.

Having failed to meet a June deadline to do so, on September 9 the National Assembly voted under pressure from the Council of Europe unconditionally to abolish the death penalty. On November 18 Armen Sargsyan, a brother of former prime minister and opposition Republican Party leader Aram Sargsyan, was jailed for 15 years for plotting the murder in 2002 of Public Radio and Television head Tigran Naghdalyan. The five gunmen who killed eight senior officials in the parliament building in 1999 were sentenced to life imprisonment on December 2.

Armenia registered double-digit economic growth for the second consecutive year, with a 15.7% increase in GDP during the first 10 months. In August the government adopted a 12-year antipoverty program. In September the government ceded control of the Medzamor nuclear power station for five years to Russia's Unified Energy Systems in payment of debts for supplies of nuclear fuel.

In June Armenia served as host of NATO war games in which 19 countries, including Turkey, participated. The country's annual joint maneuvers with Russia took place in early August.

(ELIZABETH FULLER)

AUSTRALIA

Area: 7,692,208 sq km (2,969,978 sq mi)
Population (2003 est.): 19,880,000
Capital: Canberra
Chief of state: Queen Elizabeth II, represented by Governors-General the Right Rev. Peter Hollingworth until May 29, Sir Guy Green (acting) from May 15 to August 11, and, from August 11, Michael Jeffery
Head of government: Prime Minister John Howard

Domestic Affairs. Prime Minister John Howard dominated the Australian political scene in 2003. His controversial decision to commit troops to the war in Iraq eventually was accepted by the public. Although no weapons of mass destruction were found and the Office of National Assessments admitted that it had not passed on its awareness of the U.S. State Department's doubts regarding whether Iraq was trying to obtain uranium from Niger, Howard remained overwhelmingly popular with the electorate. This was in part due to divisions within the opposition Australian Labor Party (ALP), where former ALP leader Kim Beazley challenged party head Simon Crean for the top job only to be defeated in the ALP caucus. In late November, however, amid flag-

Maj. Gen. Michael Jeffery inspects an honour guard during ceremonies after he was sworn in as Australia's new governor-general. The governor-general represents Queen Elizabeth II, the official chief of state of the Commonwealth of Australia.

ging support from ALP colleagues, Crean stepped down. When the party selected a new leader in December, treasury spokesman Mark Latham emerged victorious over Beazley, who had been favoured to win. Howard's stature as a world statesman grew to such an extent that he decided not to retire at 65 but rather to continue as prime minister for the foreseeable future. Treasurer Peter Costello, Howard's heir apparent, said that the prime minister's decision was not the "happiest day" for him.

Howard's first major domestic difficulty in 2003 came after an inquiry by the Anglican Church in Brisbane found that Gov.-Gen. Peter Hollingworth, who had been an archbishop before he accepted his viceregal post, had acted inappropriately in his handling of cases of sexual abuse in his diocese. Further damaging controversy followed as Hollingworth faced a rape charge in court. The case collapsed, but the governor-general resigned for the good of the office. After naming Sir Guy Green to fill in temporarily for Hollingworth, Howard chose Maj.-Gen. Michael Jeffery as the new governor-general. Jeffery was a former commander of the Special Air Service Regiment, a retired governor of Western Australia, and the recipient of the Military Cross for courageous action as an infantry company commander in Vietnam.

Divisions remained in the Australian community over how to treat refugees. Some Vietnamese asylum seekers managed to reach Port Hedland in July, but they were immediately removed to Christmas Island for processing. Howard continued his successful hardline policy and said that whatever it cost to transfer the illegal immigrants out of Australian inshore waters, it was worth it to get the message through that boat people would never make it to the mainland. A decision by the family court in Melbourne set an important precedent for holding asylum seekers' children in immigration centres when it ordered the release of five children being held in a South Australian detention centre while their parents sought asylum. Jeremy Moore, the lawyer representing the children, described the decision as "wonderful" and "amazing" because it meant that the courts would in future have to consider releasing all children from detention centres.

Pauline Hanson, the former One Nation leader, was jailed for three years after being convicted for having fraudulently registered her party. Hanson and One Nation cofounder David Ettridge were released in November after their convictions were overturned on appeal.

The Economy. Opinions were divided about the strength of the Australian economy in 2003. Costello described Australian economic performance in the second quarter of 2003 as being one of the worst the country had ever experienced. Australia recorded its biggest-ever quarterly current-account deficit of $A 12.7 billion ($A 1 = about U.S.$0.66) in August; the figures reflected a slump in the nation's export performance. Ian Macfarlane, governor of the Reserve Bank of Australia, warned that trouble for the economy was looming if housing prices continued to increase in the wake of a weak global economy. By August the housing boom had become so strong that Macfarlane expressed concern that many Australians were dangerously stretched beyond their means in their borrowings from lending institutions. The prime minister called a summit meeting to investigate ways to make housing more affordable in Australia, especially for first-time buyers. Nevertheless, the Reserve Bank held the cash interest rates at 4.75% in September, making it the 15th month in a row with no change to interest rates. Macfarlane defended his decision to hold interest rates, when other countries were cutting rates, because he believed Australia was in a healthier position. Nevertheless, he warned that if the world economy failed to recover or the Australian dollar continued to climb, interest rates would be lowered.

High defense expenditure put extra pressure on the Australian economy, which was already weakened by drought, the outbreak of SARS (severe acute respiratory syndrome) in Asia, and a sluggish global economy. At 2003 estimates, the government did not have the money to fund its 10-year, $A 50 billion defense-capability plan. While the government accepted strategic advice that Australia faced no conventional military threat for the next 15 years, the treasury nevertheless sought the funds necessary to place greater emphasis on overseas coalition operations. To reduce costs the Defence Department suggested that the Royal Australian Air Force's 35 F-111 warplanes should retire in 2006, about 10 years earlier than previously planned.

Foreign Affairs. The prime minister continued his high-profile international activities in 2003, making more trips overseas than ever before and overshadowing Foreign Minister Alexander Downer as the principal spokesman on diplomatic matters. In July Howard visited the Philippines to discuss international terrorism. He followed these talks with meetings in Japan and South Korea, where the growing crisis involving North Korea's weapons of mass destruction program was high on the agenda. Howard also committed Australian police and troops to the Solomon Islands as part of a multinational group (which included New Zealand and Papua New Guinea) intent on restoring law and order. (See *Solomon Islands*, below.) Howard chose a civilian, Nick Warner, to lead the police action. Warner was immediately successful in collecting and destroying illegal weapon supplies in the Weathercoast region of one of the Solomon Islands, Guadalcanal, where many hostages had been taken and killed. Rebel leader Harold Keke surrendered to Warner, and public opinion in both the Solomons and Australia saw Canberra's intervention as justified by the increased local security.

Many Australians took a keen interest in the trial in Denpasar, Indon., of the alleged bombers who had destroyed a nightclub on the Indonesian island of Bali in October 2002 with great loss of Australian life. When the first Indonesian defendant was sentenced to death, Howard declared that he would not oppose the death penalty because to do so would interfere with the internal affairs of another country. Although some relatives of the 88 Australians who died in the bombing warned that executing the terrorists would increase the likelihood of more attacks on Australians, public opinion in Australia was generally in favour of bringing back the death penalty for terrorist offenses. Australia and Indonesia drew into an even closer partnership after a terrorist bomb attack occurred near the entrance of the JW Marriott Hotel in Jakarta on August 5. Counterterrorism cooperation and political support for Indonesian Pres. Megawati Sukarnoputri was underlined as Howard scheduled eight visits to Indonesia by October. The ALP opposed cooperating with Indonesia when it came to working with the Indonesian special forces unit, Kopassus. Australia's military chief, Gen. Peter Cosgrove, however, confirmed that the Howard government had decided to renew ties with Kopassus as a strategy for dealing with terrorists and hostage situations in the region. (A.R.G. GRIFFITHS)

AUSTRIA

Area: 83,871 sq km (32,383 sq mi)
Population (2003 est.): 8,054,000
Capital: Vienna
Chief of state: President Thomas Klestil
Head of government: Chancellor Wolfgang Schüssel

Following the collapse in September 2002 of the coalition that comprised the centre-right Austrian People's Party (ÖVP) and the far-right populist Freedom Party (FPÖ), the opening months of 2003 saw the four main political parties in Austria involved in negotiations on the formation of a new government. The ÖVP was in the box seat, having emerged from the November 2002 general election as the largest party in Austria for the first time in 36 years, gaining 42% of the vote.

The expectation was that the ÖVP would once again join forces with its nearest rival, the Social Democratic Party (SPÖ), to form a "grand coalition," an arrangement that had cornered power in Austria for decades prior to the FPÖ's entering government in 2000. This development appeared to be the preferred outcome for the majority of Austrians, including the business community, which hoped that such a coalition would be able to build a more broad-based consensus (including the trade unions) in support of the program of structural reforms required in the Austrian economy. The talks eventually broke down, however, when the parties were unable to reach agreement on a range of issues.

The ÖVP then turned its attention to the Greens, a party that was looking to enter government for the first time. Initially this alliance appeared an attractive proposition to both sides, but it soon became clear that significant differences of opinion again existed between the parties over proposed pension reforms and the costly purchase of a fleet of Eurofighter aircraft. Thus, the ÖVP leader and chancellor, Wolfgang Schüssel, looked instead to reviving the coalition with the FPÖ. Not surprisingly, large sections of the ÖVP were highly skeptical about the merits of working alongside the far-right party for a second time, given that the FPÖ had made heavy weather of reconciling its brand of protest politics to the responsibilities of high office in the previous legislative term, when the significant internal divisions within the party had often been exposed. Nevertheless, amid signs of increasing impatience among the electorate over the length of the postelection talks, as well as the desire to have a government in place before the onset of any military action in Iraq, the two parties reached agreement, and the new coalition was sworn in on February 28.

AP/Wide World Photos

Hospital workers in Rahmen, Austria, protest pension reforms proposed by the rightist government that would reduce benefits by an average of 10–15%. The sign front and centre reads, "Finally on Pension."

The decision was greeted with widespread dissatisfaction across Austria, which was hardly tempered by the announcement of the government's program for the legislative term, which included proposals for a wide-ranging reform of the generous state pension scheme and the country's health care system. Tensions also quickly emerged between the coalition partners, owing largely to the destabilizing influence of the FPÖ's erstwhile leader Jörg Haider (still widely regarded as the dominant figure in the party). In May, Austria's largest public- and private-sector strikes in more than 50 years were held to protest the package of pension-reform measures, which envisaged a reduction in benefits by an average of 10–15%. The strikes provided Haider with a perfect opportunity to boost both his own profile and the flagging fortunes of the FPÖ. His headline-grabbing campaigns—often contrasting sharply with the government's positions—served to underscore the sharp divisions between moderates in the party and more extreme elements. In September the FPÖ performed disastrously at the polls in two provincial (state) elections, raising further doubts over the future of the ruling coalition.

The sluggish performance of the Austrian economy in 2003 mirrored the situation in most European countries. Foreign demand remained weak, negating any stimulus from the export sector, while businesses continued to hold back on their investment plans, given the uncertain economic climate. Households recorded a modest increase in spending despite a rise in unemployment, but this could not prevent the economy from recording its third consecutive year of below-average growth.

(NEIL PROTHERO)

AZERBAIJAN

Area: 86,600 sq km (33,400 sq mi), including the 5,500-sq-km (2,100-sq-mi) exclave of Nakhichevan and the 4,400-sq-km (1,700-sq-mi) disputed region (with Armenia) of Nagorno-Karabakh
Population (2003 est.): 8,235,000
Capital: Baku
Head of state and government: Presidents Heydar Aliyev, assisted by Prime Minister Artur Rasizade (Ilham Aliyev served as prime minister August 4–6 before Rasizade returned in an acting capacity), and, from October 31, Ilham Aliyev, assisted by Prime Minister Rasizade (acting until November 4)

The long-awaited transition of power from Pres. Heydar Aliyev to his son, Ilham, took place in 2003. The elder Aliyev collapsed twice during a televised speech on April 21 and underwent medical treatment in Turkey May 3–11. He was again hospitalized in Turkey on July 8 and was then flown on August 6 to the U.S. for further treatment. He died on December 12. (*See* OBITUARIES.) On August 4 he appointed Ilham prime minister.

Both Heydar and Ilham Aliyev were among the 12 candidates, of a total of 29 applicants, who succeeded in registering to contest the presidential elec-

Protesters turn out in force—and are countered by riot police—in Baku in October after the presidential election was won by Ilham Aliyev, the son of longtime president Heydar Aliyev, in a ballot that outside observers found to be flawed.

tions on October 15. For several months leaders of the four main opposition parties discussed fielding a single opposition presidential candidate but finally failed to agree on anyone. Heydar Aliyev withdrew his candidacy on October 2, calling on the citizens to vote for his son.

The election campaign was marred by police violence against opposition supporters. International observers registered widespread fraud during the October 15 ballot, which they and the U.S. government described as having fallen short of democratic standards. Supporters of opposition candidate and Musavat Party chairman Isa Gambar clashed with police late on October 15 and again on October 16 after it was announced that Aliyev had won the ballot with 79% of the vote. Hundreds of demonstrators and journalists were arrested, together with numerous local election officials who refused to endorse fraudulent election returns. Musavat and several other opposition parties refused to accept the final results, which gave Aliyev 77% of the vote and Gambar 14%.

Azerbaijan's GDP grew by 10.1% during the first seven months of 2003. In November the World Bank and the European Bank for Reconstruction and Development each pledged a $250-million loan toward the cost of the strategic Baku-Ceyhan oil-export pipeline. In March, Pres. Heydar Aliyev said that Azerbaijan hoped to join NATO, but on October 19 the younger Aliyev dismissed as premature any speculation that Azerbaijan would host a NATO military base. Officials of the Organization for Security and Co-operation in Europe tasked with mediating a solution of the Nagorno-Karabakh conflict visited Baku and the Armenian capital, Yerevan, on December 5-6 but failed to present a new peace plan.

(ELIZABETH FULLER)

BAHAMAS, THE

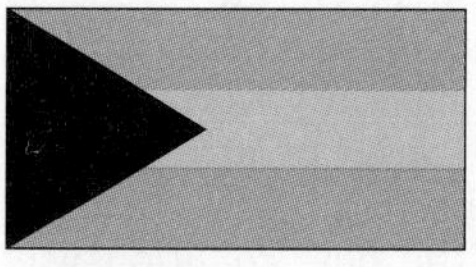

Area: 13,939 sq km (5,382 sq mi)
Population (2003 est.): 314,000
Capital: Nassau
Chief of state: Queen Elizabeth II, represented by Governor-General Ivy Dumont
Head of government: Prime Minister Perry Christie

In a report published in February 2003, the U.S. Department of State identified The Bahamas as a "major" Caribbean transit route for Colombian cocaine headed for the U.S.; an estimated 10–15% of cocaine shipments passed through the islands, and about a dozen trafficking organizations were allegedly based in the scattered Bahamian archipelago.

Plans moved ahead for the delivery of liquefied natural gas from a regasification facility in Freeport, Grand Bahama, to Florida when the Federal Energy Regulation Commission gave preliminary approval to Tractebel Electricity and Gas to complete the $585 million 145-km (90-mi)-long Calypso pipeline. Applied Energy Services and the El Paso (Texas) Corp. were also interested in supplying gas to Florida via The Bahamas. American oil company Kerr McGee agreed in June to explore for oil offshore The Bahamas in a 2.6-million-ha (6.5-million-ac) licensed area in the Blake Plateau Basin, 160 km (100 mi) north of Freeport.

Hotel expansion in The Bahamas took a major leap forward in May when Kerzner International signed an agreement with the government for a $600 million expansion of the Atlantis complex on Paradise Island.

In July, The Bahamas went to the international bond market for the first time in six years to raise $200 million, partly to refinance an existing loan. The country had an A3 rating from Moody's.

(DAVID RENWICK)

BAHRAIN

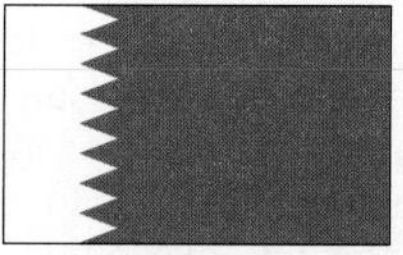

Area: 716 sq km (276 sq mi)
Population (2003 est.): 674,000
Capital: Manama
Chief of state: King Hamad ibn Isa al-Khalifah
Head of government: Prime Minister Khalifah ibn Sulman al-Khalifah

The Bahraini economy was continuing to show strength at the beginning of 2003. The country's gross domestic product had risen from $7.2 billion in 2001 to $7.6 billion in 2002, an increase of 5.1%. Early in the year the government announced a multimillion-dollar plan for the complete renovation of the old port of Manama to enable it to compete with modern Persian Gulf ports, notably that of Dubai.

Constitutional changes continued to affect the country's political life. Elections to the lower house of the National Assembly were held in October 2002; they marked the first time that women in the Arab Gulf countries could vote and run for the legislature.

A proposal to award Bahraini citizenship to Sunni Arabs from the Arabian Peninsula led to strong protests from the Shi'ite community; it accused the government of trying to change the demographic balance in Bahrain, which had a Shi'ite majority. In mid-May Iranian Pres. Mohammad Khatami made an official visit to Bahrain. Bilateral relations had been strained, in part because Bahrain accused Iran of interfering in its internal affairs and encouraging Shi'ite antigovernment activism.

As the headquarters for the U.S. Fifth Fleet, Bahrain was one of the most important U.S. allies in the Gulf region. Before and during the military campaign that led to the occupation of Iraq in April 2003, the country suffered civilian attacks on U.S. interests.

(LOUAY BAHRY)

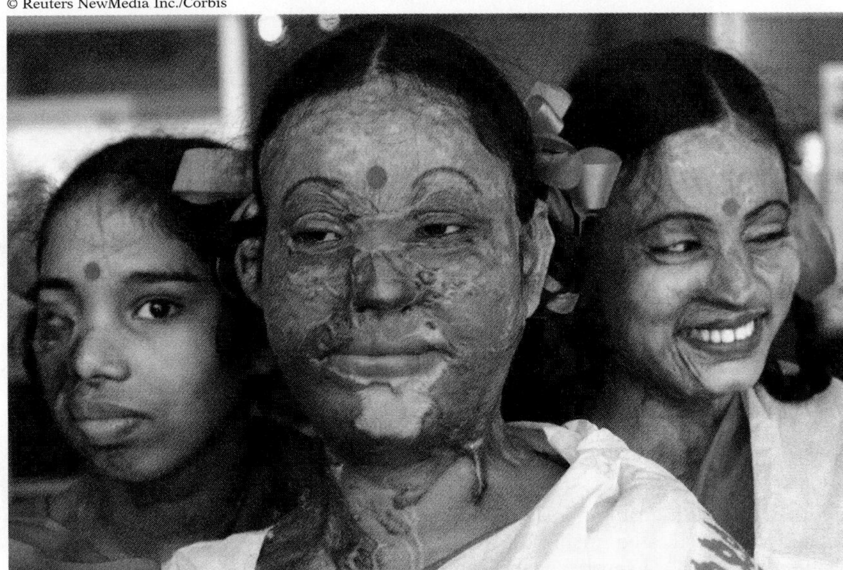

Three young Bangladeshi women whose faces were deformed by acid thrown on them by men whose romantic attentions they refused join a rally to celebrate International Women's Day on March 8. Hundreds of such attacks occurred yearly in Bangladesh, which was striving to improve the status of women.

BANGLADESH

Area: 147,570 sq km (56,977 sq mi)
Population (2003 est.): 133,107,000
Capital: Dhaka
Chief of state: President Iajuddin Ahmed
Head of government: Prime Minister Khaleda Zia

The year 2003 began in Bangladesh with a controversial bill proposed by the government indemnifying the members of the armed forces who had taken part in the anticrime drive known as Operation Clean Heart. This drive consisted of house raids, severe interrogation, and arrests without warrants, and at least 40 suspects died in the hands of the authorities. The indemnity law was intended to prevent any legal action by the victims' families.

Important laws passed during 2003 included those promising speedy trials and tribunals, a ban on money laundering, and improvement in the status of women. The independent judiciary mandated by an earlier Supreme Court judgment experienced more delays as the government bargained for more time to prepare an appropriate law. The government submitted a draft of the long-awaited independent-anticorruption-commission bill to Parliament in July but withdrew it for further modification after discussions with experts and the public. For the third year in a row, Bangladesh was ranked at the top of Transparency International's list of most corrupt countries.

The general political atmosphere of the country continued to worsen, with the relationship between ruling and opposition parties deteriorating further. More *hartals* (general strikes) were called, and more boycotts of the parliamentary sessions took place, with increasing indications that the opposition might stage more street protests and stir up agitation. It had already called upon the government several times to quit power. The situation became more confrontational when corruption charges were filed against the leader of the opposition in connection with the purchase of a navy frigate from South Korea.

The higher judiciary, which had been known in Bangladesh for its independence, became the subject of controversy regarding the appointment of some judges, including that of the chief justice. The Supreme Court Bar Association observed two days of work stoppage as a mark of protest.

On the financial front, Bangladesh boldly and surprisingly opted for a free-floating foreign-exchange rate. The fact that the taka did not suffer any significant erosion of value following this move boosted the confidence of investors, both local and foreign. The government also suspended 45,000 employees of state-owned enterprises, with a target of 94,000 over the following two years.

The export sector, after a miserable performance the previous year, regained its position and recorded a positive growth rate of 9.39%, compared with −7.44% in 2002. Foreign-exchange reserves stood at $2.49 billion in September 2003, up from $1.73 billion over the previous year. Remittances from abroad, which were one of the main sources of Bangladesh's foreign-exchange earnings, took a dive to −0.8% in the third quarter, compared with 34.15% in the same period in 2002. Inflation stood at 5.14% in July 2003, compared with 3.55% the previous year.

(MAHFUZ ANAM)

BARBADOS

Area: 430 sq km (166 sq mi)
Population (2003 est.): 272,000
Capital: Bridgetown
Chief of state: Queen Elizabeth II, represented by Governor-General Sir Clifford Husbands
Head of government: Prime Minister Owen Arthur

The Barbados Labour Party (BLP), led by Owen Arthur, won a third successive term in office in the May 2003 general election, capturing 23 seats in the House of Assembly, compared with 7 for the Democratic Labour Party (DLP). The latter did better than expected, however; prior to the election, the DLP had held only two seats in the Assembly.

During the election campaign, Arthur promised to replace the country's existing monarchical constitution with a republican one. This would result in the replacement of the governor-general (who represented the queen of England) with a nonexecutive president as head of state.

One of the main tasks facing the new BLP administration was the restoration of economic growth. The Barbados economy had contracted by 0.6% in 2002 and 2.8% in 2001, owing to the reduction in Caribbean tourism following 9/11 and the general world economic decline. As the result of a poor crop, Barbados signaled that it was unlikely to meet its annual European Union sugar quota of 54,000 metric tons. The search for oil was accelerated during the year; drilling began on a 13-well development program, mainly in known fields. Barbados produced about 1,300 bbl a day of oil on average. (DAVID RENWICK)

A national outpouring of grief is demonstrated at a funeral procession that accompanies the open coffin in which lies the body of Belarusian author Vasil Bykau (Vasily Bykov) in Minsk on June 25. Bykau's popularity as a writer was enhanced by his opposition to the country's authoritarian regime.

BELARUS

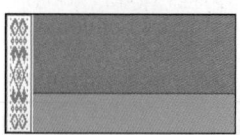

Area: 207,595 sq km (80,153 sq mi)
Population (2003 est.): 9,881,000
Capital: Minsk
Head of state and government: President Alyaksandr G. Lukashenka, assisted by Prime Ministers Henadz Navitski and, from July 10 (acting until December 19), Syarhey Sidorski

The year 2003 began promisingly in Belarus. The reopening in January of the Minsk office of the Organization for Security and Co-operation in Europe led to the lifting of visa bans on Pres. Alyaksandr Lukashenka and seven cabinet members by the United States and the European Union in mid-April.

Politics centred on the possibility of President Lukashenka's running for a third term in office and holding a referendum to amend the constitution to permit him to do so. Almost 60% of Belarusians polled reportedly opposed this proposal. Lukashenka rearranged the cabinet in July, blaming Prime Minister Henadz Navitski for the lamentable state of agriculture and food supply and replacing him and two other ministers. Though GDP rose by 5.3% between January and August (as compared with the levels of 2002) and industrial output by 6.5%, the figure for agriculture was –5.1%. Inflation, though falling, remained the highest among the former Soviet states, at as much as 25%.

Internally, the regime remained repressive. There was a severe clampdown on the demonstrations of the activist opposition group For a Better Life and for the commemoration on March 25 of the Republic of Belarus's 85th anniversary. On July 7 the Foreign Ministry informed the American academic-exchange organization IREX that it would be shut down, allegedly for financial violations. The reputable business newspaper *Belaruskaya Delovaya Gazeta* was closed on May 28 for three months, also for having transgressed the law, and numerous smaller newspapers and NGOs ceased to exist as a result of government actions.

In March, Belarus and Russia produced a draft Constitutional Act for a Russia-Belarus Union, which would feature a rotating chairmanship of the Supreme State Council and a single flag, emblem, and state currency. In June, however, Lukashenka distanced himself from the concept of a state currency that would be issued in Moscow under Russian supervision. He also shied away from selling Belarusian assets to Russian companies. The Russian giant Gazprom offered a sum of $600 million–$800 million for Beltransgaz, Belarus's main gas pipeline operator, whereas Lukashenka was hoping for a figure closer to "market prices" at $2.5 billion–$5 billion.

Relations with the U.S. were also complex, particularly after the U.S.-led war in Iraq (with accusations against Belarus of low-level military support for Saddam Hussein) and the passage by the U.S. House of Representatives on July 16 of the Foreign Relations Authorization Act for 2004 and 2005, which anticipated the issuance of $40 million for NGOs and the independent media to help promote democracy in Belarus. If signed into law, the act would also reintroduce a travel ban on Belarusian officials and cut off all official assistance to the government.

The death of internationally renowned writer Vasil Bykau (Vasily Bykov) on June 22 provided a moment of poignancy and controversy. (*See* OBITUARIES.) Thousands attended the funeral, but the government refused to acknowledge a writer who had spent his final years abroad rather than live under an authoritarian regime.

(DAVID R. MARPLES)

BELGIUM

Area: 30,528 sq km (11,787 sq mi)
Population (2003 est.): 10,341,000
Capital: Brussels
Chief of state: King Albert II
Head of government: Prime Minister Guy Verhofstadt

Flemish Liberal Guy Verhofstadt began his second term as prime minister of Belgium in early summer after having won a resounding victory in the country's general election on May 18, 2003. Instead of leading a six-party rainbow coalition of French and Dutch-speaking Liberals, Socialists, and Greens, as he had done for the previous four years, his new government had a more violet hue, blending the blue of liberalism with the red of socialism.

The election confirmed the changes taking place in the modern Belgian political landscape. Liberals and Socialists were consolidating their position as the major political forces in both Flanders and Wallonia. Christian Democrats, who had been a traditional feature of Belgian governments for four decades, continued their decline. The Greens, who had clashed with Verhofstadt in the final days of the outgoing government, suffered major losses across the country, while the far-right Vlaams Blok made noticeable gains in Flanders.

The coalition's program included a pledge to create 200,000 new jobs, support small and medium-sized businesses, set aside extra finances for public services such as railways and post offices, and increase health expenditure. The government was also looking to woo back the billions of dollars Belgians held in foreign accounts by offering an amnesty that would apply low taxes on repatriated funds.

Belgium's relationship with the U.S. went through a particularly difficult period during the year. The government, especially Foreign Minister Louis Michel, was openly hostile to the war in Iraq. More significantly, Washington was outraged by efforts to use Belgium's law on universal competence, which gave its courts jurisdiction over genocide and war crimes irrespective of the location of the alleged offenses or the nationalities of those involved, to try both U.S. Pres. George W. Bush and Gen. Tommy Franks. (*See* BIOGRAPHIES.) Although the legal challenges were rejected and the outgoing government amended the law, Verhofstadt continued to come under strong U.S. pressure with suggestions that NATO and Supreme Headquarters Allied Powers Europe headquarters might be moved from Belgian soil. After the elections the Belgian government decided to revise the controversial law further so that it could be applied only to Belgians or long-term foreign residents.

After having legalized euthanasia and decriminalized the private use of cannabis in 2002, Belgium continued to relax societal rules. In June legislation entered into force allowing people of the same sex to marry. Belgium continued to stamp its mark on the world of women's tennis. At one moment Kim Clijsters was ranked number one in the world—the first time a Belgian had ever held that rank—while her compatriot Justine Henin-Hardenne won her first grand-slam final, the Roland Garros (French Open) in Paris, against Clijsters. Henin-Hardenne followed this up by winning the U.S. Open a few months later.

In August Princess Mathilde gave birth to a son, Prince Gabriel, who became third in line to the throne after his father, Prince Philippe, and sister, Elisabeth, born in 2001. Earlier, in April, Prince Philippe's younger brother, Prince Laurent, had married Claire Coombs, whose father was British and mother Belgian. Ilya Prigogine, the winner of the 1977 Nobel Prize for Chemistry and a Belgian citizen since 1949, died in May. (*See* OBITUARIES.)

(RORY WATSON)

Belgium's Prince Laurent, who is the younger son of King Albert II, and Princess Claire wave to the crowd after their wedding in April. The flower girl on the right is Laurent's niece, Princess Louisa Maria.

BELIZE

Area: 22,965 sq km (8,867 sq mi)
Population (2003 est.): 269,000
Capital: Belmopan
Chief of state: Queen Elizabeth II, represented by Governor-General Colville Young
Head of government: Prime Minister Said Musa

In March 2003 the People's United Party (PUP) was reelected as head of Belize's national government, and it also captured a majority in the municipal elections. The PUP's resounding victory was attributed to the fact that it had increased jobs and kept inflation down. Continued economic growth came from increases in production in citrus, sugar, and bananas, together with expansion in the nontraditional industries of shrimp farming, tourism, and papaya and soybean production.

The government faced a number of challenges, however. The rate of violent crime involving firearms reached alarming levels, and the ability of the police and the justice system to respond was hampered by a shortage of technical and human resources. The incidence rate of HIV/AIDS in Belize was the highest in Central America and sixth in the Caribbean. An experimental National Health Insurance system designed to meet health care costs in parts of Belize City ended, and expectations that it would be extended to other parts of the country were thus deflated.

The government also faced a continued campaign by environmentalists to thwart its efforts to proceed with the construction of the Chalillo Dam. The case was awaiting appeal in the Privy Council in the U.K.; a decision was due in December. The U.S., Belize's largest trade partner, placed a number of restrictions on Belize aimed at thwarting terrorism and regional drug trafficking.

(JOSEPH O. PALACIO)

BENIN

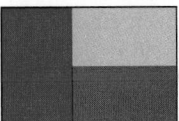

Area: 112,622 sq km (43,484 sq mi)
Population (2003 est.): 7,041,000
Capital: Porto-Novo (executive and ministerial offices remain in Cotonou)
Head of state and government: President Mathieu Kérékou

Under their coalition banner, the Union for the Future of Benin (UBF), parties supporting Pres. Mathieu Kérékou were victorious in the municipal elections of December 2002 and January 2003. In the March 30 legislative elections, the UBF again triumphed, taking 52 of the 83 legislative seats. The polls marked the first time since multiparty democracy was restored in 1990 that a president was able to work with an absolute majority in the National Assembly.

Protesting an unacceptable increase in armed robbery and smuggling, Nigeria closed its border with Benin on August 10. Talks were held between the two presidents, and Nigeria agreed to reopen the border. In return, Benin prepared to extradite 44 persons wanted in Nigeria. On August 27 the National Assembly announced the creation of a parliamentary commission to investigate cross-border crime.

Benin, Ghana, Nigeria, and Togo signed a treaty in February establishing the framework for a 1,033-km (620-mi) gas pipeline budgeted at $500 million and expected to begin operation in June 2005. Later that month the government authorized the launching of 4 television channels and 35 radio stations, all of which were to be privately owned and operated. Signaling its approval of the nation's economic growth and policies, on March 25 the International Monetary Fund released $5.5 million of Benin's line of credit and forgave $460 million of its external debt.

(NANCY ELLEN LAWLER)

BHUTAN

Area: 47,000 sq km (18,150 sq mi)
Population (2003 est.): 685,000 (excluding more than 100,000 refugees in Nepal)
Capital: Thimphu
Head of state: Druk Gyalpo (King) Jigme Singye Wangchuk
Head of government: Prime Ministers Lyonpo Kinzang Dorji and, from August 30, Lyonpo Jigme Y. Thinley

On June 28, 2003, Bhutan's National Assembly elected a 10-member Council of Ministers consisting of 6 ministers from the old cabinet and 4 new members from a list nominated by the king. The new cabinet took office in mid-July, and on August 30 the Assembly elected Lyonpo Jigme Y. Thinley prime minister. The primary duty of the Assembly was to approve the final draft of the new constitution submitted to the king in June by the Constitution Drafting Committee.

The government continued to be concerned primarily with the problem of bases established on Bhutanese territory by three Indian "terrorist" organizations to support their revolutionary activities against the Indian state governments of Assam and West Bengal. More than 2,000 militants were believed to be operating out of these camps. Bhutan had long sought to negotiate the closure of the bases. Discussions with Nepal over Bhutanese refugees living in camps in eastern Nepal showed some progress.

Bhutan's economy continued to prosper both internally and externally. One positive achievement was the decision to redistribute 50,000 ha (about 122,000 ac) of excess land to landless families.

(LEO E. ROSE)

BOLIVIA

Area: 1,098,581 sq km (424,164 sq mi)
Population (2003 est.): 8,586,000
Capitals: La Paz (administrative) and Sucre (judicial)
Head of state and government: Presidents Gonzalo Sánchez de Lozada and, from October 17, Carlos Mesa Gisbert

The worst social unrest in more than two decades forced Bolivian Pres. Gonzalo Sánchez de Lozada to step down on Oct. 17, 2003, after having served less than 15 months in office. His governing coalition collapsed after a month of clashes between mainly Indian protesters and the security forces, in which more than 70 people were killed. Without majority support in Congress, Sánchez de Lozada resigned and boarded a plane for Miami, Fla. Vice Pres. Carlos Mesa Gisbert, a 50-year-old historian and television journalist with little political experience, was sworn in as president.

Various grievances underlay the protests, but the main cause was Sánchez de Lozada's advocacy of the Pacific LNG (liquefied natural gas) project, led by a consortium of foreign-owned companies that planned to liquefy natural gas from Bolivia's vast reserves and export it to Mexico and the U.S. The president had hoped that LNG revenues would help overhaul the education system and lower the poverty rate. His opponents denounced the project as a sellout, saying Bolivians would not benefit from it. Nationalist sentiment was also aroused, because Pacific LNG promoters wanted to export the gas through Chile, whose conquest of Bolivia's Pacific coast in 1879 had left a legacy of bitterness.

The protesters focused their anger on Sánchez de Lozada, a wealthy mining magnate whose years of living in the U.S. had left him speaking Spanish with an American accent. In February he had been forced to vacate the presidential palace in La Paz briefly after bullets were fired into the building during a gun battle between soldiers and striking policemen. Protests had erupted over a government income tax proposal aimed at reducing the fiscal deficit—a key demand of the International Monetary Fund in return for a $4 billion loan package. Elite police units in La Paz took advantage of the protests to walk off the job in support of demands for a wage increase. Their absence encouraged looters, and soldiers were deployed to restore order. At least 29 people died in the violence.

The upheavals highlighted the growing political importance of Aymara- and Quechua-speaking Indians, who made up two-thirds of Bolivia's population. In a speech to business leaders in November, President Mesa said, "For the first time the Quechua and Aymara world is thinking for itself." He appointed a nonpartisan cabinet that included a minister of indigenous affairs. Coca farmers' leader Evo Morales Ayma said that he would give Mesa some breathing room, and Mesa said that he would consider making changes to the highly unpopular U.S.-backed campaign to eradicate illegal coca-leaf plantations. Another powerful Indian leader, Felipe Quispe Huanca, said he was suspicious of the new president, however.

Mesa warned that all Bolivians would have to make further sacrifices if the country was to avoid disaster. He promised to hold a referendum on the Pacific LNG project and to convene a constituent assembly to consider reforms to natural-resources laws. Nevertheless, some industry observers believed that Bolivia had missed its chance to crack the offshore natural-gas market as projects to ship gas from more stable countries forged ahead.

(PAUL KNOX)

BOSNIA AND HERZEGOVINA

Area: 51,197 sq km (19,767 sq mi)
Population (2003 est.): 3,720,000
Capital: Sarajevo
Heads of state: Nominally a tripartite presidency chaired by Mirko Sarovic, Borislav Paravac, from April 10, and, from June 27, Dragan Covic; final authority resides in the Office of the High Representative, Paddy Ashdown, Baron Ashdown (U.K.)
Head of government: Prime Minister Adnan Terzic

Bosnia and Herzegovina and its two entities, the Muslim-Croat Federation and the Serb Republika Srpska, experienced a relatively uneventful year in 2003. Since the end of the civil war in 1995, the ethnic-based entities had operated with parallel political, economic, and social infrastructures. The few steps toward integration in recent years had been taken only through international pressure.

Nationalist parties continued to obstruct and hinder both the implementation of the 1995 Dayton Peace Agreement and the process of reconstruction. A vast majority of Croats were seeking either their own republic or union with Croatia. Similarly, the majority of Bosnian Serbs still believed their future lay with Serbia and not in union with the federation. Borislav Paravac, a hard-line nationalist member of the ruling Serbian Democratic Party, was elected in April to represent the Bosnian Serbs in Bosnia's multiethnic presidency. Paravac replaced Mirko Sarovic, who resigned under international pressure for having allowed a Bosnian Serb company to sell arms to Iraq. The Bosnian Serb constitution was redrafted to place the army under full civilian control and remove all references to statehood and sovereignty. Alija Izetbegovic, the first president of Bosnia and Herzegovina, died on October 19. (*See* OBITUARIES.) Shortly after his death the International Criminal Tribunal for the Former Yugoslavia announced that he had been under investigation as a war-crimes suspect.

In September the Muslim-Croat Federation and the Republika Srpska signed an agreement that established a new locally administered Human Rights Commission. The body became part of each entity's constitutional court system and replaced the Human Rights Chamber, an internationally sponsored court set up under the Dayton accord. The commission was dealing with some 10,000 cases, most of which had to do with property disputes. Under international pressure to reform the armed forces and intelligence services, the two entities agreed to set up their first joint intelligence agency in 2004 and began negotiations toward the formation of a unified force of about 15,000 troops, which was a prerequisite for Bosnia to qualify for full entry into NATO's Partnership for Peace program.

The economy steadily declined in 2003. Social unrest escalated as thousands of workers mounted strikes in October and November to demand overdue wages and contributions to pension and health-insurance plans. Labour union officials threatened a nationwide general strike in early 2004. The European Bank for Reconstruction and Development reported some reduction in the rate of inflation and improvements in fiscal discipline but warned of weak economic growth due to the lack of new sources of investment to replace the loss of aid through foreign investment and private-sector activity. According to the Office of the High Representative, there was no substantial progress in the private sector of the economy in either entity during the first half of 2003. Unemployment was officially set at 40%. International organizations warned of a dramatic rise of AIDS throughout the region amid reports of alarming increases in drug abuse and prostitution.

(MILAN ANDREJEVICH)

BOTSWANA

Area: 582,356 sq km (224,848 sq mi)
Population (2003 est.): 1,663,000
Capital: Gaborone
Head of state and government: President Festus Mogae

AP/Wide World Photos

Mosadi Seboko proudly wears the leopard skin that symbolizes her authority as leader of the Balete people, the first woman ever to hold such a position in Botswana. Her appointment in August made her one of the most powerful women in African traditional affairs.

In a country noted for peaceful continuity, 2003 was notable for the passing from power of old-guard politicians. After some public acrimony, Ponatshego Kedikilwe, back-bench parliamentary critic of Pres. Festus Mogae, lost the chairmanship of the ruling Botswana Democratic Party to Vice Pres. Ian Khama. Kenneth Koma, founder of the opposition Botswana National Front in 1965, was ousted from his party in February after refusing to retire as leader. In August Mosadi Seboko, a single mother and former bank manager, was installed as chief of the Balete, becoming the only woman among the country's eight hereditary paramount chiefs.

The Swiss-based World Economic Forum credited Botswana with the best governance in Africa, even though government budgets had been in deficit for two years running, with a resulting consumer boom. The year was marked by the opening of large new shopping malls in Gaborone and other towns; the malls featured South African chain stores selling goods with price markups exceeding exchange-rate differences. Privatization of state assets was pushed ahead when the national airline, Air Botswana, was offered to international bidders.

Relations with crisis-stricken Zimbabwe continued to be tense. Zimbabwe took exception to Botswana's construction of new border fencing to keep out cattle that might have foot-and-mouth disease. It was also reported that large numbers of Zimbabwean refugees were being deported from Botswana daily. Within Botswana, political controversy was set off when the government granted immunity from International Criminal Court jurisdiction to U.S. citizens at the behest of U.S. Pres. George W. Bush, who visited Gaborone in July. (NEIL PARSONS)

BRAZIL

Area: 8,514,047 sq km (3,287,292 sq mi)
Population (2003 est.): 178,470,000
Capital: Brasília
Head of state and government: President Luiz Inácio Lula da Silva

After winning the 2002 election with 61% of the vote, Luiz Inácio Lula da Silva of the Workers' Party (PT) was sworn in on Jan. 1, 2003, as president of Brazil before a crowd of 100,000 people. The inauguration ceremony marked the first time in more than 40 years that a democratically elected incumbent president had transferred power to a democratically elected successor.

Though he had campaigned on a leftist platform, President Lula immediately instituted austerity measures. After having raised the overnight bank rate for government bonds from 25% to 25.5% on January 22, the central bank's monetary policy committee (Copom) raised the rate to 26.5% on February 19. That same day the central bank increased the compulsory deposits held by banks from 45% to 60%. In the face of market uncertainty after a political change, these moves were intended to keep inflation in check, pull money from circulation, and send a signal to the international financial community that the new administration would continue to prioritize macroeconomic stability. Responding to the success of its inflation-targeting program, Copom reduced the overnight rate for government bonds throughout the year, finally taking it to 16.5% on December 17.

More than 100,000 participants gathered January 23–28 at the World Social Forum (WSF) in Pôrto Alegre, Rio Grande do Sul. WSF participants organized in opposition to the annual World Economic Forum, held in Davos, Switz. At the WSF, 126 countries, 30,000 delegations, and 5,480 organizations were represented. Lula, a former labour militant, addressed the WSF before traveling to Davos, where he called for "globalization with solidarity." The two visits encapsulated much of the new administration's challenge in governing Brazil.

The Brazilian Congress opened on February 1, and the 508 deputies and 54 senators who had been elected in 2002 were sworn in to the Chamber of Deputies and Senate, respectively. Fresh from winning the presidency, the PT won the presidency of the Chamber with the election of João Paulo of São Paulo. José Sarney of Amapá state was elected leader of the Senate; he was a former president of Brazil and represented the Party of the Brazilian Democratic Movement (PMDB).

The judiciary faced allegations of corruption and nepotism throughout the year. Federal investigations involving wiretaps uncovered a corruption scheme whereby members of the judiciary sold habeas corpus decisions to organized-crime interests. Federal wiretaps implicated members of the Superior Court of Justice (STJ), including Minister Vicente Leal and Ceará Federal Deputy Pinheiro Landim, and caused a split among jurists. Further investigations found clear links to STJ judges' family members and organized crime. On February 25 Landim resigned, and the STJ voted to suspend Leal on April 4.

A crime wave, linked to organized crime and drug trafficking, spread throughout Rio de Janeiro in February and March; supermarkets were looted and vehicles demolished, partly in protest against the transfer of drug kingpin Fernandinho Beira-Mar from Bangu penitentiary in Rio de Janeiro to a maximum-security prison in Presidente Bernardes, São Paulo. With "shoot to kill" orders, the federal government sent 3,000 army troops into the streets of Rio on February 27 in order to maintain law and order during the Carnival period. The army maintained its presence until March 14, the same day that Judge Antonio Machado Dias, who was responsible for authorizing Beira-Mar's transfer, was assassinated. The assassination forced changes in the courts; judges were granted anonymity in their prison-transfer decisions and were provided with escort guards.

During May, Lula named three judges to the 11-member Supreme Court to replace jurists who had reached the mandatory retirement age of 70. The Senate confirmed all three nominees, including Joaquim Benedito Barbosa Gomes, the first self-proclaimed Afro-Brazilian to sit on the court.

Lula pressed forward on his earlier promises of reform, and social security and tax-reform legislation worked its way through Congress. In order to win the support of Congress, Lula held a series of meetings with state governors who were seeking assurances that the reforms would not affect their already-limited fiscal capacities adversely. In return for their support in influencing their congressional delegations, the governors, led by Minas Gerais Gov. Aécio Neves, lobbied for benefits ceilings on social security and the discretion to redirect earmarked federal transfers. The debates on social security caused controversy among privileged classes, such as civil servants and the judiciary, giving rise on June 11 to the first large protest movements of the Lula administration. Protests took place in Brasília, São Paulo, and Belo Horizonte.

The PT's governing coalition was bolstered when the PMDB joined the coalition on May 27. It was expected that once tax and social security reforms had been passed at the end of 2003, Lula would reshuffle his cabinet to reflect the inclusion of the PMDB. The governing coalition also attracted a number of individuals who switched parties in time to meet the October deadline for establishing party identity on the side of the government to contest the 2004 municipal elections.

On October 20 Lula announced the unification of several social programs, including Zero Hunger, his first policy initiative, into the Family Stipend, which included government efforts to bolster education and help the poorest families combat hunger, poverty, and child labour. Other social initiatives taken by Lula included in November a pledge to redistribute land for the benefit of some 400,000 landless peasants and in December a strict new law that prohibited the carrying of guns and set up a national firearms registry.

According to the Brazilian Institute for Geography and Statistics, Brazil's GDP grew 1.9% in 2002. The poor domestic performance continued in 2003 as national retail sales from January to July fell 5.4% year-on-year. Unemployment in the country's six major metropolitan regions registered 12.8% in July, and the broad consumer price index (IPCA) recorded 11.02% inflation for the 12 months ended in November. A favourable exchange rate for exports permitted increases across all sectors, which led to record trade surpluses of $17.8 billion from January through August and $23.1 billion for the12 months ended in August. In percentage terms exports grew 22% from January to September year-on-year, and imports fell 1.4% during that same period.

(JOHN CHARLES CUTTINO)

BRUNEI

Area: 5,765 sq km (2,226 sq mi)
Population (2003 est.): 344,000
Capital: Bandar Seri Begawan
Head of state and government: Sultan and Prime Minister Haji Hassanal Bolkiah Mu'izzaddin Waddaulah

Although there were no cases of SARS (severe acute respiratory syndrome) in Brunei, the 2003 SARS outbreak in Asia—as well as the war in Iraq—contributed to further economic slowdown. The oil- and gas-rich sultanate continued to strive for economic diversification amid growing youth unemployment. The government injected $1 billion into the Eighth National Development Plan (2001–2005), but the multimillion-dollar Muara port project and an aluminum smelting plant in Sungai Liang were still in the planning stage.

Talks continued with Malaysia to demarcate economic and territorial zones for deepwater oil prospecting off Sabah. Efforts also continued to resolve the long-standing border issue of Limbang, a strip of land on the island of Borneo claimed by Brunei but annexed in 1890 by the raja of Sarawak.

Two important international meetings were held in Brunei in September. At the 15th meeting of the Pacific Economic Cooperation Council, officials from the Philippines, Malaysia, and Thailand discussed terrorism and economic-cooperation issues. Later in the month finance ministers from 52 Commonwealth countries met in the capital, Bandar Seri Begawan.

Prince Jeffri, the sultan's younger brother and the former minister of finance, returned to Brunei's public eye in July after a five-year absence. He had been stripped of his official positions because of his alleged responsibility for the disappearance of billions of dollars from state coffers. In February Sultan Haji Hassanal Bolkiah divorced his second wife, Pengiran Isteri Hajah Mariam binte Abdul Aziz. (B.A. HUSSAINMIYA)

BULGARIA

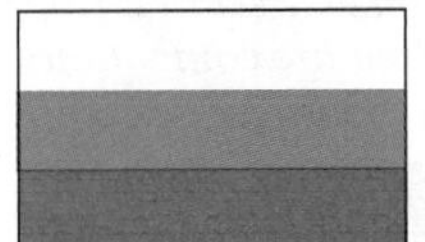

Area: 110,971 sq km (42,846 sq mi)
Population (2003 est.): 7,786,000
Capital: Sofia
Chief of state: President Georgi Purvanov
Head of government: Prime Minister Simeon Saxecoburggotski

Having a seat on the UN Security Council in 2003 made Bulgaria an important factor in the crisis over Iraq. The government adopted a pro-U.S. stance that was not, however, shared by the president or his opposition Bulgarian Socialist Party. It also caused embarrassment with France, whose ambassador warned on February 12 that Bulgaria's position on the Iraq question could pose problems for Bulgaria's integration into the European Union. Still, Bulgaria lent its support to the coalition and allowed U.S. airplanes to use the airport at Sarafovo on the Black Sea coast. After the war Bulgaria agreed to send a military contingent, and by mid-August some 500 Bulgarian troops were in Karbala', Iraq. In August Bulgaria cosponsored with Britain a draft UN resolution proposing that sanctions on Libya be lifted. Many assumed that this action was dictated by a desire to help the six Bulgarian medics who were on trial in Libya charged with having deliberately infected 393 Libyan children with HIV. Bulgaria continued its progress toward membership in NATO when the National Assembly agreed on March 28 to accept the protocols of accession stipulated by the organization's member states.

On the domestic front in Bulgaria, there was considerable instability. The judiciary disliked reform proposals that would limit its power, notably an amendment to the Privatization Act making the National Assembly and the government, rather than the courts, the final arbiters in the privatization process. The judiciary responded to the attempted reforms by complicating important privatization processes, particularly with regard to the sale of the state tobacco and telephone companies. In the latter case an agreement reached in December 2002 was nullified, only to be accepted finally in September 2003. In local elections in late October, the Socialist Party (former communists) showed strongly with 33% of the vote.

The country continued to be troubled by violence and organized crime. On March 25 a bomb shattered windows at the Sofia District Prosecutor's Office, and in the following months a number of prominent businessmen, some of them believed to have been connected with illegal groups, fell to assassins' bullets.

The spectre of corruption also continued to haunt Bulgarian public life. In April a report from the Ministry of the Interior spoke of connections of politicians and members of the judiciary with organized crime. Particularly embarrassing for the government were allegations that the minister of finance, Milen Velchev, had had contacts with a businessman suspected of large-scale smuggling. Velchev resigned in August, only to withdraw his resignation two weeks later. (RICHARD J. CRAMPTON)

BURKINA FASO

Area: 267,950 sq km (103,456 sq mi)
Population (2003 est.): 13,228,000
Capital: Ouagadougou
Chief of state: President Blaise Compaoré
Head of government: Prime Minister Ernest Paramanga Yonli

An estimated 350,000 Burkinabes fled the civil war in neighbouring Côte d'Ivoire during 2003, escaping the rising tide of violence and xenophobia directed against them. Burkina Faso's economy received some aid from international donors to assist in the resettlement of the refugees. The virtual cessation of trade until the border was reopened in September severely damaged the economy, particularly in the livestock and transport sectors. Despite these difficulties, the IMF predicted that the country's GDP would achieve a modest growth in 2003 of 2.6%.

In April donors agreed to provide $123 million to fund the first phase of Burkina Faso's National Health Development Plan, which was designed to modernize the health sector and fight the spread of endemic disease. Although a meningitis epidemic took more than 900 lives in 2003 and malaria remained the major cause of death in the country, with 5,000 dying annually, the plan particularly focused on the rising incidence of HIV/AIDS.

Conservation measures introduced on May 22 to deal with a severe water shortage in Ouagadougou were eased following unusually heavy summer rainfall. Burkina Faso became the first West African country to test genetically modified cotton. In October at least 16 people were arrested in connection with an alleged military coup conspiracy against Pres. Blaise Compaoré. Those being detained at year's end included a political opposition leader.

(NANCY ELLEN LAWLER)

BURUNDI

Area: 27,816 sq km (10,740 sq mi)
Population (2003 est.): 6,096,000 (excluding more than 500,000 refugees in Tanzania)
Capital: Bujumbura
Head of state and government: Presidents Pierre Buyoya and, from April 30, Domitien Ndayizeye

Stability in the ongoing peace process between the Burundi government and rebel forces spiraled downward during most of 2003. A cease-fire agreement signed in December 2002 by Pres. Pierre Buyoya and leaders of three insurgency groups, including the largest, the Forces for Defense of Democracy (FDD), was soon violated when government soldiers and FDD rebels engaged in combat in early January 2003. Fighting between the army, the FDD, and the second largest rebel force, the National Liberation Front (FNL), which had refused to sign any cease-fire agreements with the government, was sustained throughout the year. In April the United Nations estimated that at least 440 people had been killed and more than 260,000 civilians had been displaced since the start of the year. More than 800,000 people were displaced either within Burundi or in neighbouring countries.

In February two army officers received suspended sentences for their roles in a massacre of 173 people by government forces in September 2002. Some 3,500 peacekeepers from African Union member states began to arrive in Burundi at the end of April. In accordance with the Arusha accords signed in August 2000, President Buyoya, a minority Tutsi, stepped down from the presidency of the power-sharing transitional government and handed power over to his vice president, Domitien Ndayizeye, a majority Hutu, on April 30.

The progress that had been gained in the June peace meetings was rolled back on July 7 when FNL troops launched an assault on the capital. The weeklong attack was the fiercest battle since the war began in 1993, and foreign aid workers were evacuated from the capital. In an effort to revitalize the peace process, South African Deputy Pres. Jacob Zuma facilitated a three-day meeting in Pretoria between President Ndayizeye and the head of the FDD, Pierre Nkurunziza, in August. Heavy fighting resumed in early September between FDD and FNL forces. The FDD canceled a September 15 summit in Dar es Salaam, Tanz., but on October 8 the government signed a peace accord with the FDD that gave the rebels a greater power-sharing role. The FNL rejected the agreement, however, and fighting continued. On December 29 the papal envoy to Burundi was assassinated. (MARY F.E. EBELING)

The body of a young rebel of the National Liberation Front lies on a street in an upscale district of Burundi's capital, Bujumbura, in July. Children are combatants in the decade-long civil war here and in many other conflicts in Africa.

CAMBODIA

Area: 181,035 sq km (69,898 sq mi)
Population (2003 est.): 13,125,000
Capital: Phnom Penh
Chief of state: King Norodom Sihanouk
Head of government: Prime Minister Hun Sen

On July 25, two days before Cambodia's national elections, supporters of the Sam Rainsy Party hold a candlelight rally in front of a monument in Phnom Penh, the capital.

Parliamentary elections in July 2003, the third under the UN-brokered constitution of 1993, were won as expected by Prime Minister Hun Sen's Cambodian People's Party (CPP) with 73 of the 123 seats, a gain of 9 seats but still less than the two-thirds majority necessary to govern without a coalition. Under Cambodia's complex proportional representation system, the royalist Funcinpec Party, junior partner in the outgoing government, won 26 seats, a dramatic loss of 17 seats from the 1998 polls. The Sam Rainsy Party (SRP), with 24 seats, also gained 9 seats. Funcinpec, led by Prince Norodom Ranariddh, a son of the king, and the SRP commanded mainly urban constituencies, while the CPP was strongest in the rural base of 80% of the 6.3 million electorate.

In the ensuing stalemate, Funcinpec and the SRP formed an alliance and then demanded a tripartite government without Hun Sen at its head. The swearing-in ceremony to inaugurate the new National Assembly, required by law within 60 days of elections, was boycotted by both minority parties and King Norodom Sihanouk in September but later was held at the royal palace. On October 17 the king invited all parties to talks "as one Cambodian family," but the minority parties pulled out after violence against Funcinpec-linked personalities. On November 5 the ailing 81-year-old king mediated a three-way agreement. The deal fell apart, however, amid legal wrangling between Hun Sen and Norodom Ranariddh, and the stalemate continued. At year's end no government had yet been formed.

The election year passed peacefully compared with earlier polls, after a violent start on January 29 when rioters in Phnom Penh destroyed the Thai embassy and several Thai businesses, including one belonging to the Thai prime minister's family. A local newspaper had erroneously quoted a Thai TV actress as claiming that Angkor Wat, the ancient Buddhist temple complex and icon of the Cambodian nation, had been stolen from Thailand. Many observers suspected that the ruling party was behind an attempt to ignite preelection nationalist fervour against the heavy presence of Thai business. Though Cambodia agreed to provide compensation for the embassy and business losses, relations between the two neighbours remained cold until joint cabinet meetings were held in late May.

In June the UN and Cambodia signed a long-delayed agreement paving the way for a tribunal to bring former Khmer Rouge leaders to justice; the UN warned, however, that it was too early to say when trials would begin. Internationally, Hun Sen found favour siding with the U.S.-led war on terrorism; arrests were made of suspects said to be linked to Jemaah Islamiyah, a group thought to be behind the 2002 bombings on the Indonesian island of Bali. Tourism, which generated 20% of GDP in 2002, suffered from the regional downturn caused by SARS (severe acute respiratory syndrome) and security fears, but it was expected to pick up in late 2003. In September Cambodia was invited to join the World Trade Organization; membership still required national ratification and would entail tougher global competition, especially in the vital garments sector, which was responsible for 12.5% of GDP. International agencies expected growth of 5% in 2003 and 5.5% in 2004, dependent on still-elusive political stability. (JOHN BEAUMONT ASH)

CAMEROON

Area: 475,442 sq km (183,569 sq mi)
Population (2003 est.): 15,746,000
Capital: Yaoundé
Chief of state: President Paul Biya
Head of government: Prime Minister Peter Mafany Musonge

Late in 2002 the International Court of Justice ruled in favour of Cameroon in the territorial dispute over possession of the Bakassi peninsula. Nigeria, which had been contesting the ownership of the oil-rich area since 1993, initially refused to accept the judgment. Several bilateral meetings were held to find a peaceful solution, and in December, Nigeria relinquished 32 disputed border villages, but it was uncertain when Nigeria would cede the peninsula to Cameroon. Charges had been leveled on May 21 that Nigeria was financing dissidents in northern Cameroon opposed to the policies of Pres. Paul Biya.

Sixteen leaders of Cameroon's opposition parties protested after the government prohibited them from holding a press conference on February 5. The government shut down two privately owned television stations on February 19 following their broadcast of a political debate critical of the president. Similar action was taken against a private radio station on March 19; another radio station was closed on May 23. On April 16 the U.S. State Department published a stinging report on the government's record on human rights in general and prison conditions in particular. At least five people were killed in Douala on July 9 when a demonstration against police corruption and harassment turned violent.

The government pledged on April 24 to launch an initiative designed to facilitate especially the growth of the private sector of the economy. On April 28 Prime Minister Peter Mafany Musonge announced the opening of the Douala Stock Exchange, the first to be set up in Central Africa and a project more than three years in the making. The World Bank announced a loan of $49.7 million to assist Cameroon in reducing its commercial debt. A $200 million shipyard for the repair of deep-sea oil platforms was to be built in Limbé, on the southwest coast. (NANCY ELLEN LAWLER)

CANADA

Area: 9,984,670 sq km (3,855,103 sq mi)
Population (2003 est.): 31,590,000
Capital: Ottawa
Chief of state: Queen Elizabeth II, represented by Governor-General Adrienne Clarkson
Head of government: Prime Ministers Jean Chrétien and, from December 12, Paul Martin

Domestic Affairs. Canadians in 2003 grappled with the unforeseen consequences of disease affecting both humans and animals. SARS (severe acute respiratory syndrome), imported from Asia, caused over 40 deaths in Toronto, the country's financial centre. (*See* HEALTH AND DISEASE: *Special Report.*) In Alberta an outbreak of "mad cow" disease (bovine spongiform encephalopathy [BSE]) closed international markets to Canadian beef.

On the political front, the major parties moved to select new leaders. The governing Liberal Party replaced its leader, Prime Minister Jean Chrétien, who initially had announced that he would step down in February 2004. He spent the year shepherding new legislation, intended to define his "legacy." The contest to succeed him proved to be a tepid affair. Paul Martin (*see* BIOGRAPHIES), former minister of finance, had worked relentlessly to build up support within the party. One by one, cabinet colleagues who had been expected to challenge him dropped from the race. The last to withdraw was Deputy Prime Minister and Minister of Finance John Manley, Chrétien's favoured successor. Sheila Copps, minister of Canadian heritage, representing the left-of-centre wing of the party, remained Martin's only opponent. A public opinion poll in late August showed that 49% of Canadians favoured Martin as the country's next prime minister. At the leadership convention held in Toronto on November 14, Martin gained the support of 94% of the delegates. Chrétien stepped down as prime minister on December 12, following his attendance at a Commonwealth heads of government conference in Nigeria. In the 301-seat House of Commons, the Liberals held 171 seats, a comfortable majority.

The Liberal Party's historic rival, the Progressive Conservative Party (PCP), changed its leader at the end of May, replacing former prime minister Joe Clark with a younger figure. Peter MacKay, 37, an MP from Nova Scotia, won the leadership on the fourth ballot. Although the PCP held only 15 seats in the Commons, MacKay vacillated on cooperation with the Western-based conservative party, the Canadian Alliance, which held 63 seats. During the summer, discussions began between MacKay and Stephen Harper, leader of the Alliance. On October 14 the two struck a deal for the merger of their parties, which took place in December after delegates of both parties had voted to approve the merger. Canada's socialist party, the New Democratic Party (NDP), also chose a new leader—Jack Layton, a community activist from Toronto. Although not an MP, Layton had served since 1982 on the Toronto City Council. He was expected to appeal to urban voters, once a strong constituency for the NDP, which held only 14 seats in the Commons. The separatist Bloc Québécois lost ground in Quebec. At the end of 2003 it held 34 seats from the province, but it was expected to suffer losses at the next general election. There were also four independents in the Commons.

Canada's prized system of public health care received new impetus in 2003. In operation for almost 40 years, the plan was funded jointly by the provincial and federal governments. Delivery, however, was in the hands of the provinces. It was universally accessible, portable across Canada, and comprehensive in scope. In November 2002 a commission of inquiry headed by Roy Romanow, a former premier of Saskatchewan, had issued a report in which it recommended changes to strengthen the health system and enlarge the system's reach. Romanow urged a massive transfer of additional funds from Ottawa to the provinces, designed to replace cutbacks carried out by the Liberal government. The commission recommended increased assistance for home care, expansion of the existing drug plan, and the purchase of additional diagnostic equipment. Romanow advocated a federal-provincial health council as a watchdog to report to Canadians. Above all, he insisted that the system remain the responsibility of the state and that the intrusion of private medicine, favourably considered in some provinces, be denied. During 12 hours of bargaining in the capital on Feb. 5, 2003, Prime Minister Chrétien and the premiers of the 10 provinces and 3 territories closely examined the Romanow report. The premiers established a united front and insisted that large amounts of additional funds be transferred to the political units actually delivering health services. The federal government offered funding of Can$34.8 billion (Can$1 = about U.S $1.35) over the next five years. Priorities for the use of this money would be primary health care, drug coverage, and diagnostic equipment. The provinces complained that much of this money was already in the system and that new

Dozens of houses on a hillside above the town of Kelowna, northeast of Vancouver, B.C., are consumed by a forest fire driven by high winds on August 22. Wildfires in British Columbia and Alberta were the worst in many decades.

funding would not be at the levels recommended by Romanow. In the end the federal offer was grudgingly accepted. Meanwhile, Americans were buying prescription drugs in Canada at lower prices than they would pay at home (*see* SIDEBAR).

Prime Minister Chrétien introduced a measure in January banning contributions to political parties from corporations and unions. Donations could still be made, up to a maximum of Can$1,000, to individual candidates. Corporation and union funding would be replaced by government subsidies. These grants were to be based on the success of parties in past elections. The subsidy would amount to about Can$1.75 for each vote cast. The bill passed easily, 172–62, on June 11. The Chrétien government brought forward another controversial subject for legislation—a change in the definition of marriage. On June 10 the Ontario Court of Appeal ruled that the current definition, a union between a man and a woman, contravened the Charter of Rights and Freedoms and that same-sex marriages should be permitted immediately. On June 17 the government announced that it would introduce a new marriage law while at the same time asking the Supreme Court to review its constitutionality. Churches would be free to retain their own practices. The Supreme Court decision was not expected before April 2004, at which time official debate could begin.

Marijuana was another subject of debate. In May the government introduced a measure to decriminalize the possession of small amounts of marijuana. U.S. officials expressed concern over this initiative, fearing that it would hinder antidrug measures in their country. Later the bill was withdrawn, though the government indicated that it would be reintroduced in 2004. In July the government announced a plan to make marijuana available to about 600 registered individuals to relieve pain. The drug would be distributed by physicians. The marijuana was supplied by a government facility in an abandoned mine in northern Manitoba. U.S. authorities and many Canadian physicians were unhappy with the distribution scheme. On December 23 the Canadian Supreme Court ruled that "it is open to Parliament to decriminalize or otherwise modify any aspect of the marijuana laws that it no longer considers to be good public policy."

The Economy. The Canadian economy, after several years of leading the Group of Eight industrialized nations in economic performance, faltered in the second quarter of 2003. A growth rate that had been predicted at 3.2% for the year was revised downward at the end of June to 2.2%. A range of economic indicators showed signs of trouble. A principal contributor to the decline was the continued weakness of the U.S. economy, Canada's main export market. Another was the rising value of the Canadian dollar in relation to its U.S. counterpart, which impacted the trade in automobiles and parts moving from Canada to the U.S.

Two causes for the contraction in economic activity could not have been anticipated. One was the outbreak of SARS, which had an adverse economic impact on many parts of the country and especially on Toronto. On April 23 the World Health Organization issued a travel advisory for Toronto, but the city's officer of medical health, Sheela Basrur (*see* BIOGRAPHIES), was instrumental in having the advisory lifted a week later. The other was the appearance of BSE in North America, which created havoc in the beef industry.

On February 18 Manley delivered the Chrétien administration's final budget. Since the Chrétien government as-

Filling Prescriptions for Americans—Big Business in Canada

On a chilly September morning in Duluth, Minn., 20 or so Minnesotans boarded the "Rx Express" bus bound for Winnipeg, Man. The passengers, senior citizens on fixed incomes, were on a quest for prescription drugs at prices they could afford. Their tab, including appointments with physicians, hotel stays, and meals, would be picked up by U.S. Sen. Mark Dayton, who had been using his government salary to finance Rx Express trips since 2000. The fact that the seniors would save up to 80% by buying their drugs in Canada rather than in the U.S. made the 10-hour, 685-km (425-mi) bus ride well worth it.

Trips to Canada were one way Americans were seeking more reasonably priced medications. Another, more convenient way was via the Internet, and in 2003 well over one million American consumers—not just seniors—took advantage of savings they could get by forwarding prescriptions from their American doctors to an ever-growing number of Canadian mail-order "e-pharmacies." Still another way was through local government initiatives. In July Springfield, Mass., became the first American city to establish a "drug reimportation" program—so named because many of the drugs dispensed in Canada were American-made—for its 9,000 employees and retirees. Governors from Illinois, Minnesota, Wisconsin, Massachusetts, Iowa, and West Virginia were looking into implementing similar programs, as was New York City Mayor Michael Bloomberg.

Drugs in Canada were generally less expensive because the national government negotiated prices, capped subsequent price increases, and granted pharmaceutical companies extended patent rights. In the U.S. unregulated drug prices were among the highest in the world. The booming business that Americans were bringing to Canadian pharmacies was evidence that the U.S. was not doing enough to make drugs affordable to all of its citizens. Even though Pres. George W. Bush said the new Medicare legislation, which he signed into law on December 8, was "finally bringing prescription drug coverage to the seniors of America," the savings it would offer them—at least in the short term—would remain far less than the savings from their northern neighbour.

Technically, it was illegal for Americans to import or reimport prescription drugs from a foreign country. The U.S. Food and Drug Administration (FDA) was strongly opposed to the cross-border pharmaceutical trade, citing mainly safety reasons. Although the regulatory agency had exercised "enforcement discretion" with individuals who obtained small quantities of medications for personal use, it began cracking down on profit-making storefront businesses that were facilitating transactions with Canadian pharmacies. In March the FDA warned one of the biggest commercial ventures, Rx Depot, Inc., that its actions violated the law; a U.S. district court subsequently ordered Rx Depot to shut down its 85 storefronts in 26 states.

(ELLEN BERNSTEIN)

sumed office in 1993, the budgets had contained a spate of cost-cutting measures, but his 2003 budget was dominated by spending. Expenditures rose 11% over those in the 2002 budget. Federal contributions to health care, some already announced, were scheduled to increase by Can$35 billion over the next five years. Foreign aid, half to Africa, was markedly increased, as was assistance to improve the health of Aboriginals. Funding was also put aside to fulfill pledges made under the Kyoto Protocol to limit the emission of greenhouse gases. Defense spending was given its largest increase of the Chrétien years. There were no new taxes, however, and tax cuts were limited to small businesses. Despite high expenditures, the budget remained balanced for the sixth year in succession. A surplus of Can$4 billion was predicted for fiscal year 2003–04, and reduction of the debt continued.

Foreign Affairs. Strains appeared in the close relationship with the U.S. as Canada made it clear that it would not participate in the war against Iraq without prior UN approval. On February 12 the minister of defense, John McCallum, stated that Canada would provide a force to help maintain internal security in Afghanistan, which, in view of Ottawa's limited military capacity, meant that there would be no combat force available for a war in Iraq. At the UN, Canada sought support for a resolution that would set a deadline for the UN inspectors' report on the status of Iraq's alleged possession of weapons of mass destruction. (*See* MILITARY AFFAIRS: *Sidebar.*) Canada's efforts at compromise failed when Pres. George W. Bush launched a military strike against Iraq without UN authorization. (See *United Nations:* Special Report, above.) Canada continued to maintain a small force of ships and airplanes in the Persian Gulf as part of the ongoing international campaign against terrorism.

Canada's doubts about the wisdom of President Bush's action led to critical comments, made both privately and publicly, from Canadians. On April 13 an announcement was made that President Bush would postpone a visit to Ottawa planned for May 5. Cool personal relations between Bush and Chrétien were believed to have been a factor in the decision.

Although Canadians questioned the justification for the attack on Iraq, they were prepared to see a military force sent to Afghanistan. A force of about 1,900 troops arrived in Kabul, the Afghan capital, in early August. The force became part of a new UN structure intended to bring stability to Afghanistan. The Canadian mission would last one year.

Although Canada refused to take part in the Iraq war, it was willing to cooperate with the U.S. on defense measures. The government announced on May 29 that Canada would join talks on President Bush's plan for a missile shield to defend North America against possible attacks by rogue states. Canada did not favour the deployment of weapons in outer space, however. During the summer Canadian and American negotiators began discussing the project. Canada wished to see the system under joint control, an arrangement used in the NORAD command, founded in 1957.

With such a massive flow of trade streaming between closely connected economies, it was inevitable that commercial disputes would emerge. U.S. duties on construction lumber from Canada, imposed in 2001, continued to have an impact on an export trade valued in Canada at Can$10 billion a year. Several trade-dispute panels, drawn from both the World Trade Organization and the North American Free Trade Agreement, ruled on the case during the year. Their conclusions provided mixed signals. Provincial systems for granting timber licenses could, under certain conditions, represent a subsidy. The U.S. erred, however, in comparing cross-border timber prices. The dispute dragged on, damaging the forest economy in British Columbia, the largest timber-exporting province.

The U.S. ban on beef cattle from Canada, a trade valued at nearly $3 billion a year, was complicated by the action of Japan in denying entrance to American beef unless it could be clearly differentiated from Canadian. This distinction was virtually impossible, because animals traveled constantly back and forth across the North American border before going to market. Canadian safety regulations were changed to conform almost identically with those of the U.S., but the Japanese remained adamant. The beef ban was eased slightly in October when U.S. sanctions on animals under 30 months of age were lifted. In December, however, the U.S. Department of Agriculture identified Canada as a possible source of a BSE-infected cow found in Washington state.

(DAVID M.L. FARR)

CAPE VERDE

Area: 4,033 sq km (1,557 sq mi)
Population (2003 est.): 438,000
Capital: Praia
Chief of state: President Pedro Pires
Head of government: Prime Minister José Maria Neves

Cape Verde suffered in 2003 from the consequences of a failed harvest in 2002. The country had long been heavily dependent on food imports, and the World Food Programme had to begin to supply food aid. The IMF had granted the country a loan in 2002. Working closely with the IMF, the government tried to reduce the deficit by cutting expenditure, keeping down inflation, and strengthening its reserves. A value-added tax was implemented in 2003, and two money-losing public enterprises were liquidated. Further privatization was planned, and in May 2003 the World Bank approved a loan to help promote the private sector by reducing government red tape and providing support to private companies.

The visit of Pres. Pedro Pires to the U.S. in mid-2002 had been intended in part to persuade the many Cape Verdeans resident there—especially in New England—to assist their country. Cape Verde was a member of the organization of African Portuguese-speaking countries known as PALOP and in September 2003 participated in a meeting in Lisbon, where members decided to strengthen cooperation between PALOP and Portugal itself. At the same time a bilateral commission worked to promote relations with Angola.

(CHRISTOPHER SAUNDERS)

CENTRAL AFRICAN REPUBLIC

Area: 622,436 sq km (240,324 sq mi)
Population (2003 est.): 3,684,000
Capital: Bangui
Chief of state: Presidents Ange-Félix Patassé and, from March 15, François Bozizé
Head of government: Prime Ministers Martin Ziguélé and, from March 23, Abel Goumba

On March 15, 2003, rebels backing Gen. François Bozizé, the ousted army chief, stormed into the capital of the Central African Republic. Government troops, unpaid for months, offered little resistance. Pres. Ange-Félix Patassé, returning from a conference in Niamey, Niger, flew instead to Cameroon and then on to Lomé, Togo. As if to echo the troubled history of the CAR, the country's first president, David Dacko, who was twice ousted from power, died in November. (*See* OBITUARIES.)

Declaring himself head of state, Bozizé suspended the constitution but announced plans for a National Transitional Council to draw up a new electoral code and to plan for elections that he promised would be held within 18 to 30 months. The new president appeared to have won considerable support throughout the country, not least for his promises to stamp out corruption and to restore internal security. On September 15 the first session of the oft-postponed national reconciliation talks was held.

On April 1 the newly appointed prime minister, Abel Goumba, named a 28-member cabinet that included two members of Patassé's former government, although key portfolios were in the hands of Bozizé's allies. All incoming ministers had to declare their wealth before taking office. On July 17 soldiers were sent to reestablish order in six important towns in the north and west, where armed bands had terrorized the population and paralyzed the economy. (NANCY ELLEN LAWLER)

AP/Wide World Photos

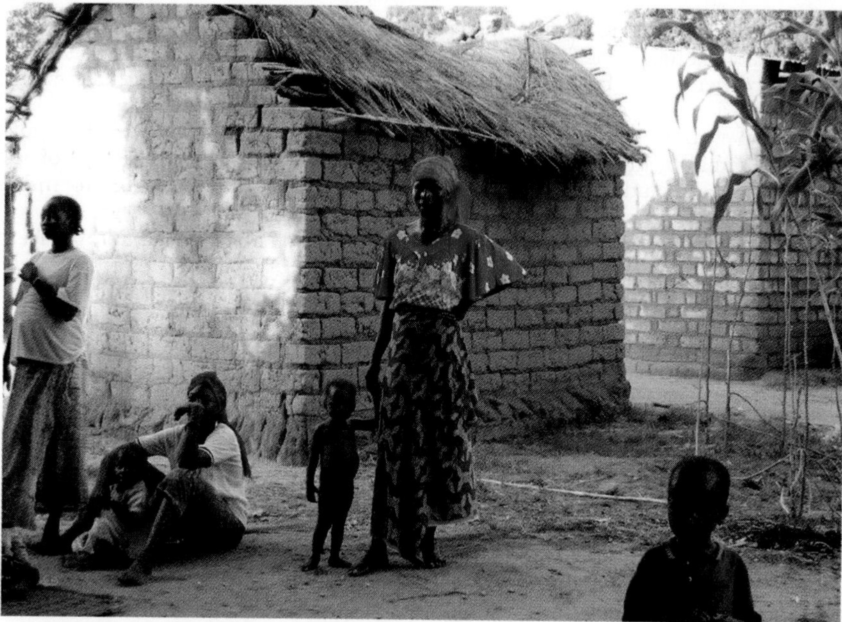

Funds from oil production in Doba basin enabled the construction in Bonia, Chad, of the new house, right rear, of laterite-cement block with a corrugated iron roof. A traditional mud-brick and thatch house is pictured in the foreground.

CHAD

Area: 1,284,000 sq km (495,755 sq mi)
Population (2003 est.): 9,253,000
Capital: N'Djamena
Chief of state: President Lieut. Gen. Idriss Déby
Head of government: Prime Ministers Haroun Kabadi and, from June 24, Moussa Faki

In 2003, after years of effort and $3.7 billion in expenditures, oil began to flow from southern Chad's Doba basin to the port of Kribi in Cameroon. Though Chad remained one of the poorest countries in the world, it hoped to receive $80 million annually from oil exports. Plans had been laid for the oil revenues to be spent on social improvements in Chad, especially the Doba basin, but by mid-2003 there were already signs that benefits would mainly accrue to the ruling elite.

In January 2003 it was announced that the government had signed a peace agreement with a major rebel group, the National Resistance Army (ANR), which had been active near the border with The Sudan and the Central African Republic (CAR). The agreement provided for a cease-fire and amnesty and the integration of the rebels into the national army or their return to civilian life. Unrest continued on the border with the CAR, however, and from late 2002 Chad became increasingly involved in fighting between the CAR government and rebels seeking to overthrow it. Each country accused the other of supporting opposition groups. Tens of thousands of people, many of them Chadians who had been living in the northern CAR, fled into southern Chad to escape the fighting. Pres. Idriss Déby visited the CAR in February 2003 in an attempt to improve relations, but in March the rebels overthrew CAR Pres. Ange-Félix Patassé, and the self-declared president, Gen. François Bozizé, immediately called upon Chad to send troops to help. A Chadian contingent of 400 soldiers was dispatched and stabilized the situation in Bangui. Bozizé's visit to Chad in May reflected the new friendship between the governments.

(CHRISTOPHER SAUNDERS)

CHILE

Area: 756,096 sq km (291,930 sq mi)
Population (2003 est.): 15,326000
Capitals: Santiago (national) and Valparaíso (legislative)
Head of state and government: President Ricardo Lagos Escobar

Sept. 11, 2003, marked the 30th anniversary of the military coup that resulted in the overthrow of the democratic government of Socialist Pres. Salvador Allende Gossens and the installation of Gen. Augusto Pinochet Ugarte as president of Chile; the event remained a lightning rod for the many relatives of the estimated 4,000 people who were killed or went missing during the Pinochet era. Events that harked back to that period, such as the erection of a statue of Allende near the presidential palace, still elicited strong public debates and protests and laid bare the polarized political camps that continued to exist.

The year began with political scandals that threatened the ruling Concertación coalition when major coalition figures were placed under judicial investigation. Former public works minister Carlos Cruz had allegedly been involved in activities that included irregular payments and kickbacks to ministerial staff members, and five Concertación congressional deputies were accused of having taken bribes to influence congressional votes. In mid-January the five deputies were barred from exercising their congressional responsibilities while under investigation; as a result, for several months the Concertación had the slimmest of majorities—one vote—in the Chamber of Deputies. One of the five, Socialist Deputy Juan Pablo Letelier, the son of murdered diplomat Orlando Letelier, was cleared of all charges in August. These events brought to light serious underlying problems, such as the lack of regulations and public financing for campaigns—a particularly acute problem for Concertación candidates who did not have the same easy access to financing as did right-wing candidates—and the difficulty government officials had in hiring highly qualified people to staff ministries, given historically low salaries. The scale of the scandals and especially the involvement of Cruz hurt the government's image. Scandals also touched the right; among them was an allegation in October by a right-wing deputy that three Chilean politicians had been involved in sex parties with Claudio Spiniak, who had been arrested in September for serious sex-related crimes.

On the positive side, there were important gains in the area of human rights. Judicial investigations continued to mount against members of the armed forces for violations during military rule (1973–90). Among those brought to trial was retired general Manuel Contreras—former head of the Pinochet secret police force, the DINA—who had already served time for the car-bomb murder of Orlando Letelier. Contreras was convicted in April and sentenced to 15 years in prison for the 1975 killing of Miguel Sandoval. In June, Army Commander in Chief Gen. Juan Emilio Cheyre acknowledged the military's lamentable role in the human rights abuses during the Pinochet years and pledged "never again" to resort to military intervention.

Despite increasing opposition to the cost of the government's Plan AUGE, which was designed to provide coverage for 56 common illnesses, the administration of Pres. Ricardo Lagos Escobar remained committed to its major health initiative.

On the economic front, Chile appeared to be working its way out of recession. Although unemployment remained high, economic growth for 2003 was 3.5%, while inflation stayed low, at 3%. Chile's balance of trade was positive and growing. The price of copper, a prime export, also increased during the year. Lagos's team also finalized free-trade agreements with South Korea and Singapore and, most important, one with the U.S. that would become effective in January 2004. In October, Chile assumed the chair of Asia-Pacific Economic Cooperation.

Chile's close relationship with the U.S. was tested during the year when Chile voted against a U.S. invasion of Iraq at the UN Security Council. This occurred at precisely the same time that the two countries were in the process of approving the free-trade agreement.

(LOIS HECHT OPPENHEIM)

CHINA

Area: 9,572,900 sq km (3,696,100 sq mi), including Tibet and excluding Taiwan and the special autonomous regions of Hong Kong and Macau

Population (2003 est., excluding Taiwan, Hong Kong, and Macau): 1,288,892,000

Capital: Beijing

Chief of state: Presidents Jiang Zemin and, from March 15, Hu Jintao

Head of government: Premiers Zhu Rongji and, from March 16, Wen Jiabao

A new era in Chinese politics and economic development began in 2003. Three major domestic events highlighted the rough beginning of the leadership turnover. First, at the 10th National People's Congress in March, former Communist Party of China (CPC) general secretary Jiang Zemin passed the post of state presidency to CPC General Secretary Hu Jintao but retained the top military post. Second, the SARS (severe acute respiratory syndrome) epidemic originated in China and quickly spread out of control, not only threatening public health worldwide but also wreaking political and economic havoc in China. Third Zhou Zhengyi, a business tycoon who had close ties with senior Shanghai officials, was arrested and placed under investigation for economic crimes. Internationally, the new leaders engaged in a fresh round of diplomatic visits and generally showed more involvement in international affairs.

Domestic Politics. As expected, Jiang Zemin stepped down from the Chinese presidency at the 10th National People's Congress in March 2003, although he kept control over the country's military authority and maneuvered to keep or put his protégés in key positions. Five men on the nine-member Political Bureau Standing Committee were close Jiang associates: Vice Pres. Zeng Qinghong, Chairman of the National People's Congress Wu Bangguo, State Council Vice-Premier Huang Ju, Chairman of the Chinese People's Political Consultative Conference Jia Qinglin, and Li Changchun, the former CPC secretary of Guangdong province.

Accordingly, the political events for much of the year were interpreted as a postsuccession struggle between Hu and Jiang and their respective protégés. Hu was typically cast as a progressive and a reformer, while Jiang's forces were seen as opposed to any political change. Hu and new Premier Wen Jiabao were believed to be practical men who favoured economic reforms to better the people's standard of living, while Jiang and his allies were viewed as doctrinaires who sought economic reforms that favoured the business elite.

Hu worked to set his policy line apart from Jiang's. In December 2002 he took

The new Chinese president, Hu Jintao (right), is congratulated by his predecessor, Jiang Zemin, at the National People's Congress on March 12. Though he gave up the presidency, Jiang kept control of China's military forces.

AP/Wide World Photos

three opportunities to address issues that had been much neglected by his predecessor. During Hu's participation in the celebration of the 20th anniversary of China's constitution, he emphasized the authoritativeness of the constitution and the rule of law. In the following two days, Hu sought to establish his credentials as the champion of the poor when he paid a visit to Xibaipo, the site of a historical 1949 speech to the party faithful by Mao Zedong on the importance of serving the masses. Later in the month, he hosted the first study session of the Political Bureau to study the constitution. Hu reinterpreted Jiang's policy of "three represents"—that the CPC should represent the interests of all the people, including the business class, rather than just the working class—by emphasizing Mao's dictum "to be close to the masses." For such public gestures intended to identify him with the old-time communist virtues of self-sacrifice and devotion to the downtrodden, Hu won praise from the party faithful and the public as well as from many intellectuals.

The significance of the arrest of Shanghai business tycoon Zhou Zhengyi was multifaceted. It signaled that Shanghai upstarts were not immune from criminal prosecution and that the Shanghai proteges of former president Jiang might no longer be exempt from investigations into corruption and criminal misdeeds. The new administration sought to portray itself as a government for the masses. During the year the CPC Central Discipline and Inspection Commission sentenced or removed 10 senior government and party officials, ranging from governors to ministers. Two of them were sentenced to death and two others to life in prison.

At midyear a senior labour-union official called for direct elections of local union bosses by factory workers, an arrangement that had not been seriously discussed for years. Moreover, a group of senior party officials wrote letters that urged Jiang to step down from all his positions. In June the main CPC publication, *Seeking Truth,* included an article calling for more democracy within the party. This would mean more transparency in decision making and more leeway for CPC cadres to pick leaders such as provincial and municipal party bosses. It was also regarded as a first step toward democracy for the whole country. In late July the same periodical carried another piece calling for democratic reform within the party through the setting up of standing committees at municipal and county levels to which CPC secretaries would report between annual party congresses. A few cities in Sichuan province experimented with regular meetings of party congresses, where deputies could exercise some form of supervision over party authorities.

At about the same time, six articles that called for political reform ran in *Study Times,* a CPC publication put out by the Central Party School, and in early August an article appeared that called for party committees to stop influencing government agencies, an idea that had last been promoted before Jiang came to power.

Wu Bangguo, the chairman of the National People's Congress, chaired a special committee on constitutional reform that considered two main additions to the current constitution—one a provision protecting private property and the other an enshrining of Jiang's "three represents." If the "three represents" were to be written into the constitution, Jiang's legacy (and the influence of his group) would be secured, and he would be accorded a status almost equivalent to that of the other two paramount Chinese leaders, Mao and Deng Xiaoping. In late June leading academics and a few government officials held a conference on constitutional reform, openly criticizing the "three represents." In late summer, after having given the intellectuals some latitude in discussing these reforms, the CPC ordered a cessation of the discussions. At the end of the year the CPC formally called for protection of private property and the theory of the "three represents" to be included in the constitution.

In September the authorities announced cuts of 200,000 troops, including 200 generals, within the next two years in order to reduce the size of the army to about 2.3 million. The reform was said to be needed in order to accelerate the modernization of the army. As chairman of the Central Military Commission, Jiang described the move as part of a worldwide trend in military reform in which the focus was shifting from mechanized warfare to information warfare. On December 15 China issued a terrorist list that included 4 Muslim separatist groups in Xinjiang province and 11 individuals.

Hong Kong. Political turmoil engulfed Hong Kong in 2003 when the territory's chief executive had to postpone a vote in the legislature over a controversial security bill. The most objectionable provision would have allowed the government to ban in Hong Kong groups that had links to any organization that for national security reasons Beijing had prohibited from operating in the rest of China. Mass popular demonstrations, the resignation from the cabinet of the leader of a pro-government political party, and the big victory for pro-democracy candidates in the November local elections underlined the seriousness of the issues.

SARS and the Economy. The new leaders faced their first major test when SARS broke out, first in Guangdong and Hong Kong and later spreading to the entire country and many parts of the world. The first cases of SARS were detected at the end of 2002, but the Chinese government underestimated the severity of the disease and then, during the national political conferences, tried to cover up its own inaction. Hu and Wen were forced to take up the challenge by themselves. Partially as a result of the initial cover-up, the total death toll in China reached 349. (*See* HEALTH AND DISEASE: *Special Report.*)

SARS caused political and economic casualties as well. Zhang Wenkang, the minister of health and Jiang's longtime personal physician, and Meng Xuenong, the newly elected mayor of Beijing, were sacked. By the end of May, some 1,000 officials nationwide had been removed from their posts for negligence or incompetence. The economic effects of SARS were devastating; airline earnings were in free fall, with April–June earnings only 20% of second-quarter 2002 figures. According to estimates by the Ministry of Labour and Social Security in early June, more than one million jobs were lost, especially in transportation, wholesale and retail trade, and food services. The national tourist bureau reported the first decrease in tourism since 1989 and estimated that in 2003 China would lose $33.3 billion in tourism revenue. One additional suspected SARS case in late December elicited a quick response from Chinese officials.

Recurring natural disasters added to Beijing's economic woes. The flooding of the Huai River, traditionally one of China's problem waterways, affected the lives of 100 million people in 16 provinces and caused the death of more than 300 people as well as some $2.2 billion in damages.

At the national level, for the first time the Chinese government openly acknowledged the problem of the disparity in the population's income distribution. It was reported that the Gini

Yang Liwei, the first Chinese astronaut, waves to the cameras on October 16 after 21 hours in orbit and a landing on the Inner Mongolian grasslands of northern China.

AP/Wide World Photos

coefficient (a measure of income distribution in a society by which 0 = perfect equality and 1 = perfect inequality) in China was 0.282 in 1991, 0.456 in 1998, 0.457 in 1999, and 0.458 in 2000; the ratio had increased 1.62 times within a decade and seemed to be steadily rising.

Facing the economic slowdown caused by the outbreak of SARS and other potentially explosive economic problems, the State Council took five new measures to advance economic development. These focused on troubled industries, smaller enterprises, and the less-privileged population and sought to stimulate domestic demand, expand exports, and revitalize the traditional industrial base. The proclamation of a new ordinance regarding asset management in state-owned enterprises set the stage for a new round of economic reform.

In early July the Chinese Academy of Social Sciences, a leading research institution, reported that a GDP growth rate of 8% was still possible. It predicted a 14.5% increase in fixed-assets investment, a 7.9% rise in urban personal income, and a 3.7% increase in rural personal income. The consumer price index was expected to rise only 0.3%, with exports up 14.1% and revenue growth of 15.8%. The academy's optimism was confirmed in November by the IMF, which predicted GDP growth of 8.5%. In addition, the successful launch of the *Shenzhou V* manned spaceship marked a new era of progress and self-confidence for China.

Foreign Relations. Active diplomacy characterized Chinese foreign relations during the year. Hu and U.S. Pres. George W. Bush met at international events in France (June 1) and Thailand (October 19), and they exchanged views on northeastern Asian security, the war on terrorism, bilateral trade, and the Taiwan issue. Much to the satisfaction of China, during both meetings Bush upheld the "one-China" policy of the U.S. government, although he also reiterated the U.S. commitment to defend Taiwan. Amid Taiwan's call for a "defensive referendum" against the mainland's display of missiles, Prime Minister Wen's visit to the U.S. in December reconfirmed Bush's support of mainland China's position. Both governments seemed satisfied that bilateral political relations were as good as they had been in 30 years.

China-U.S. trade relations were not so rosy, however. China received a frontal attack from the U.S. on its rigid foreign-currency exchange rates, which the U.S. considered unfair terms of trade. Washington first insisted that Beijing float its exchange rates but later softened its demands. There were some indications that not all American businesses supported an inflexible U.S. trade policy toward China. In accordance with World Trade Organization regulations, China lowered its wall against American cars and car parts; imports of 15,000 cars and trucks as well as more than $1 billion in parts from Big-Three American automakers were to be allowed. In addition, China dispatched three "shopping" delegations to the U.S. and purchased American products worth more than $6 billion, including Boeing planes, airplane engines, and automobiles. At the end of the year, however, after the U.S. imposed more trade restrictions on Chinese textiles, a planned fourth shopping spree, which was to include the purchase of soybeans, cotton, fertilizers, and electronics, was canceled.

As the nuclear crisis in North Korea intensified in the spring, China offered assistance in resolving the skirmish between the U.S. and North Korea. China suspended crucial oil shipments to North Korea, sent high-level envoys to Pyongyang, and arranged tripartite talks in Beijing. Amid deepening pessimism, Beijing took the further step of hosting high-level six-party talks involving a dialogue between North Korea and the U.S., Russia, Japan, South Korea, and China. China's worries included both a nuclear North Korea and hawks in Washington, but it wanted to play "honest broker" in the crisis. After the first rounds of talks, Chinese officials shuttled between Pyongyang and Washington to guarantee that the dialogue would continue.

The two largest Asian states, historical adversaries, took steps to put 40 years of distrust and diplomatic stalemate behind them. In June, Indian Prime Minister Atal Bihari Vajpayee visited China. India officially accepted China's definition of Tibet as a part of China and agreed not to permit "anti-China activities" by Tibetans who were living in India (notably the Dalai Lama, who resided with his entourage at Dharamsala, India). China in turn agreed to open trade with India's northeastern region via Sikkim, a development that India viewed as an affirmation of its sovereignty over the mountainous border state. Later that month Vajpayee called for India to form a partnership with China in the information-technology industry. Trade between India and China had grown apace in recent years but remained at modest levels in comparison with China's trade with the U.S., Japan, and the European Union. Finally, the two countries made naval history in 2003 by launching their first-ever joint naval exercises, off the coast of Shanghai.

China continued to craft good relationships with all five former Soviet Central Asian countries—Kazakhstan, Kyrgyzstan, Tajikistan, Uzbekistan, and Turkmenistan. The Shanghai Group forum, comprising Russia and all of those countries except Turkmenistan, met in China, and all but Uzbekistan participated in joint military exercises on the China-Kazakhstan border.

(XIAOBO HU)

COLOMBIA

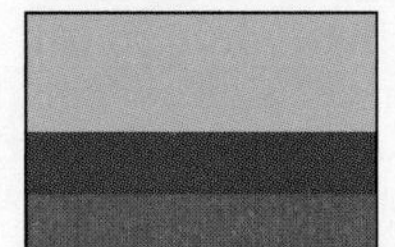

Area: 1,141,568 sq km (440,762 sq mi)
Population (2003 est.): 41,662,000
Capital: Bogotá
Head of state and government: President Álvaro Uribe Vélez

The new government of Pres. Álvaro Uribe completed its first year in office in August 2003 and continued to face the challenges of reforming a political system with little public support and responding to the long-standing and violent conflict with guerrilla groups. Uribe's promised tough stand against guerrillas was very popular at home (and in the U.S. Congress). In the war on drugs, fumigation efforts cut coca exports by approximately one-third. President Uribe boosted military spending, promised a police presence in all parts of the country, helped arm peasants in already-violent areas, and proposed wider powers of arrest and detention for the military.

The government's advances seemed only to enhance the resolve of the largest guerrilla group—the Revolutionary Armed Forces of Colombia (FARC). In a particularly potent attack, 36 people were killed and 160 were injured when a bomb exploded at Club El Nogal in northern Bogotá in February. A military rescue attempt gone awry in May resulted in the killing by the guerrillas of 10 hostages—including a governor and a former defense minister who had been taken hostage while leading a peace march in 2002. Kidnappings and bombings continued apace throughout the year and were expected to intensify around local, state, and national referendum elections in late October. The wisdom of prisoner exchanges was debated repeatedly, especially after the FARC released a tape of a former presidential candidate and senator, Ingrid Betancourt, calling on President Uribe to negotiate her release.

The government continued to discuss a peace accord with the United Self-Defense Forces of Colombia (AUC)—an extremely violent right-wing paramilitary group. The government's decision to submit an amnesty bill to Congress and to consider alternative punishments for guerrillas released from jail to participate in peace talks resulted in sharp criticism from members of the U.S. Congress and human rights organizations that had reported AUC atrocities. The government claimed that without this tool in its repertoire, it could not expect armed groups seriously to consider laying down their weapons.

While relations between the new administration and the U.S. president remained generally positive, relations with the U.S. Congress (and the United Nations) were occasionally strained by seemingly contradictory moves—stepping up arrests and detentions of suspected guerrilla supporters and criticizing human rights organizations while asking for the power to grant amnesty to those already convicted of violent acts. U.S. Special Forces troops were sent to the country early in the year, however, and it seemed unlikely that any small rifts with the U.S. or even the shooting down of an American fumigation plane by guerrillas would jeopardize the continued disbursement of funds under Plan Colombia.

A funeral procession for peasants killed in an incident in January, reportedly by the Revolutionary Armed Forces of Colombia (FARC) rebel group, wends through the streets of San Carlos, Colom., northwest of Bogotá.

© AFP/Corbis

The government used a great deal of its capital at home in the pursuit of political reform. The executive branch initially announced its intent to put a referendum before the voters that included a wide-ranging series of reforms, but several parts of the package were dropped along the way owing to pressure from Congress and a Supreme Court ruling that declared parts of the proposal unconstitutional. In an effort to undercut the president's momentum, Congress adopted its own more limited but still substantial set of political reforms related primarily to elections. The pared-down version of Uribe's package was defeated in the referendum on October 25. Congress was divided between the internally diverse Liberal Party (the president's former party), the Conservative Party, and a loose group of members claiming allegiance to the government. There were several important pieces of legislation on the agenda, and it was unclear as to the extent to which the government would be able to hold together support for its preferences during 2004. (BRIAN F. CRISP)

COMOROS

Area: 1,862 sq km (719 sq mi), excluding the 374-sq-km (144-sq-mi) island of Mayotte, a de facto dependency of France since 1976
Population (2003 est.): 584,000 (excluding 165,000 on Mayotte)
Capital: Moroni
Chief of state and head of government: President Col. Azali Assoumani

Parliamentary elections for each autonomous island—Anjouan, Grande Comore, and Mohéli—as well as elections for the Comoros Union scheduled for March 2003 were postponed indefinitely owing to disagreements between the four governments. The ongoing constitutional crisis deepened in February when plans for an alleged coup to overthrow union Pres. Azali Assoumani were revealed. Two ministers in the Grande Comore government along with a dozen gendarmes were arrested. In March a senior union official was arrested for alleged plans to hire mercenaries to destabilize the autonomous islands.

Heavy floods in April displaced 300 people on Mohéli. A one-day strike, also in April, by the commercial sector on Grande Comore protested the double taxation by the autonomous and union governments and highlighted the legislative crisis. A meeting in August hosted in Pretoria, S.Af., by the South African foreign affairs minister, Nkosazana Dlamini Zuma, to reconcile the Comoros governments resulted in a draft agreement that addressed the disputes over customs management, internal security, and the 2003 budget, prepared previously in consultation with the International Monetary Fund and the World Bank. In early September, however, President Assoumani reversed his position and rejected the agreement. (MARY F.E. EBELING)

CONGO, DEMOCRATIC REPUBLIC OF THE

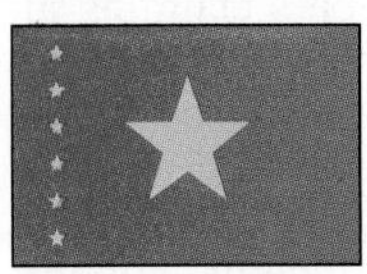

Area: 2,344,858 sq km (905,354 sq mi)
Population (2003 est.): 52,771,000 (adjusted for 1998–2003 war-related deaths of 3,000,000 in eastern DRC [mostly from starvation, disease, and deprivation])
Capital: Kinshasa
Head of state and government: President Joseph Kabila

Throughout 2003 measures were taken aimed at setting up a stable government and at putting an end to the armed conflict that continued to ravage the whole of the eastern region. At each stage, however, new outbreaks of violence bedeviled the process. Also unhelpful were the supplies of aid and even arms to the different factions by foreign powers and businessmen eager to lay hands on the rich mineral resources of the eastern Congo.

In December 2002 the government had signed a peace treaty with the leaders of the two main rebel groups and of the political opposition parties. None of these had been a signatory to the earlier peace agreements with Uganda and Rwanda, whose armed forces had invaded Congo. Under the terms of the new agreement, Joseph Kabila would head a transitional government for two years. Within a week, however, the Rwandan-backed Congolese Rally for Democracy (RCD) claimed to have captured the port of Uvira on Lake Tanganyika, while on January 15 UN investigators accused members of another rebel group, the Uganda-backed Movement for the Liberation of Congo, of the kidnapping, rape, and cannibalism of pygmies in the Ituri region.

On February 10 Uganda agreed to withdraw all its troops from Congo, but when it failed to fulfill its promise, Rwanda, which had already withdrawn its own forces, threatened to reinvade. Uganda claimed that Kabila had asked for its soldiers to remain in the country until adequate Congolese government forces were available to maintain order. Under pressure from the UN, Ugandan troops were finally withdrawn by May 6.

Meanwhile, on March 6, the government and the two main rebel groups had agreed on a draft transitional constitution that would create a democratic all-party government and guarantee individual rights. There would also be a unified army. On that basis Kabila was sworn in as head of a transitional administration on April 7. These hopeful developments, however, took place against a background of extreme violence between the Lendu and Hema ethnic groups in the east led by power-seeking warlords. Through the intervention of Tanzania and Uganda, Kabila was able to meet leaders of several rebel groups in Dar es Salaam, Tanz., on May 15 to try to put an end to the fighting, and on May 30 the UN Security Council agreed to send in an international force. The French-led force, consisting of only 1,400 troops, was on the ground within two weeks and was able to establish order in Bunia, a town near the border with Uganda. Conflict continued in the surrounding countryside and further south in the region immediately to the west of Lake Kivu.

On July 17 the first power-sharing government was sworn in, but a single military hierarchy was not set up until September. Even then, three leading generals of the RCD failed to cooperate, and recruitment to both of the main rebel groups continued. On a visit to Washington D.C., in November, Kabila sought U.S. support for his government and spoke out against U.S. farm subsidies. (KENNETH INGHAM)

AP/Wide World Photos

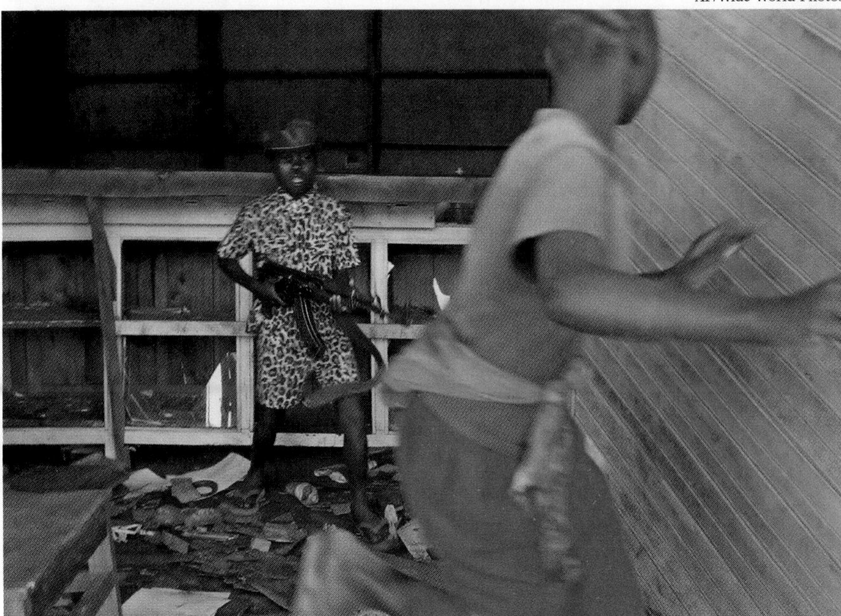

The Hema militia, including this 10-year-old soldier, who is chasing a woman from a house at gunpoint, held sway in the town of Bunia in northeastern Democratic Republic of the Congo in May.

CONGO, REPUBLIC OF THE

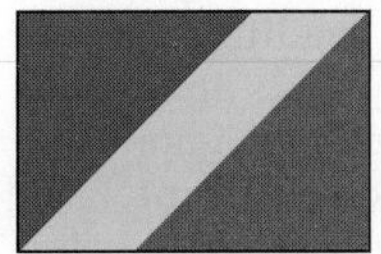

Area: 342,000 sq km (132,047 sq mi)
Population (2003 est.): 3,724,000
Capital: Brazzaville
Head of state and government: President Denis Sassou-Nguesso

The government and representatives of Pastor Frédéric Bitsangou, leader of the rebel "Ninja" militia, signed a peace agreement on March 17, 2003, ending a year of civil war. Thousands of displaced persons in the Pool region began returning home. The government promised to grant an amnesty to the rebels and to reintegrate them into the army. By the end of April, more than 1,000 Ninjas had turned in their arms and gone back to their villages and farms. By June the opening of road traffic from the capital to the Pool region had greatly alleviated the desperate food shortages resulting from the rebellion.

The government renewed its truce with major trade unions for another two years on August 10. In return for the no-strike agreement, salary arrears were to be paid in full and pensions increased. On August 12, 35 members of the High Court of Justice, established under the January 2002 constitutional referendum, were sworn in. Justin Koumba, formerly president of the National Transition Council, was appointed president of the new National Commission for Human Rights.

In the north an outbreak of the Ebola virus took at least 100 lives between February and April, and another outbreak was reported on October 31. The disease was estimated to have also killed 600 to 800 lowland gorillas, an endangered species. On July 4 the government launched a vaccination program aimed at protecting 100,000 children from contracting measles and polio.

The World Bank announced on June 24 that a credit of $41 million would be given to the country to facilitate its stabilization and recovery process. The national railway, severely damaged during the civil war, announced in July the receipt of a large shipment of construction materials as part of a second World Bank $16 million rehabilitation project. (NANCY ELLEN LAWLER)

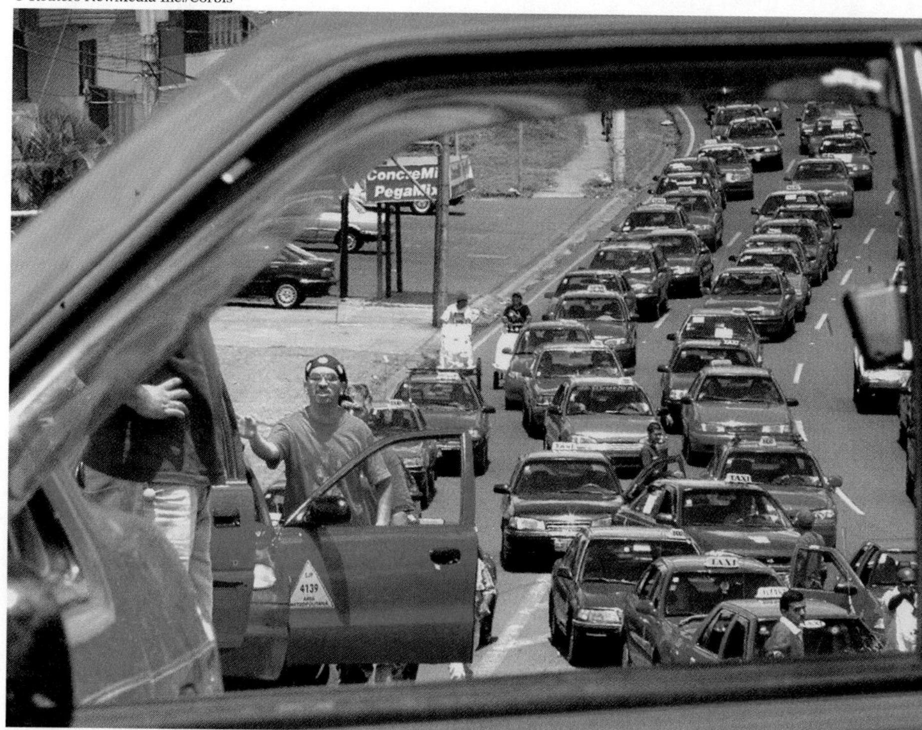

In San José, Costa Rica, on March 18, a street near the presidential residence is blocked by hundreds of taxi drivers demonstrating in support of a 20% taxicab fare increase to offset the gasoline price hikes caused by the uncertain situation in Iraq.

COSTA RICA

Area: 51,100 sq km (19,730 sq mi)
Population (2003 est.): 4,171,000
Capital: San José
Head of state and government: President Abel Pacheco de la Espriella

Public attention remained riveted during 2003 on the changing fate of Pres. Abel Pacheco de la Espriella, who had been elected in April 2002 after soundly defeating his rival in the first-ever runoff election in Costa Rica. Though Pacheco largely retained his preelection personal popularity, his job-performance rating slipped dramatically, falling to about half of what it had been at the beginning of his term. Contributing to the slide was the growing government budget deficit of more than 5% and Pacheco's inability to reign in government spending fully. In response, by the spring of 2003 international credit agencies were lowering their outlook for the Costa Rican economy. Optimists pointed to the promise of the proposed U.S.–Central American Free Trade Area as well as Costa Rica's recent success in expanding exports to the U.S., the destination of about 50% of its exports. On the other hand, Pacheco's administration was in disarray; several ministers had left the cabinet. Perhaps his most serious problem was the discovery of apparently illegal campaign contribution funds hidden in Panamanian banks; the discovery sparked a series of hearings in the Legislative Assembly and shook the confidence of Costa Ricans. Traditionally, elections in Costa Rica were extremely clean by any standard.

In some ways the troubling news about President Pacheco was overshadowed by the revitalization of the prospects for veteran politician and Nobel Peace Prize winner Óscar Arias Sánchez, who in polls regularly ranked as Costa Rica's most popular political figure. Though he had held the presidency from 1986 to 1990, during which time he used his position to help negotiate peace agreements in both Nicaragua and El Salvador, Arias had been prevented from running for office again as a result of a 1969 reform of Article 132 of the Costa Rican constitution. Arias had unsuccessfully challenged that reform before the Supreme Court (Sala IV) on two prior occasions, but on April 4, 2003, the court reversed itself and ruled that restricting the right to reelection was a limitation of constitutional rights. It was widely expected that Arias would run for office again in 2006.

(MITCHELL A. SELIGSON)

CÔTE D'IVOIRE

Area: 320,803 sq km (123,863 sq mi)
Population (2003 est.): 16,631,000
De facto capital: Abidjan
Chief of state: President Laurent Gbagbo
Head of government: Prime Ministers Affi N'Guessan and, from February 10, Seydou Diarra

Attempts to end the civil war in what was once one of West Africa's most stable nations met with limited success by the end 2003. The troubles had begun on Sept. 19, 2002, when 700 soldiers, supporters of former military strongman Robert Gueï who refused to be demobilized, mutinied. Forced from Abidjan, they quickly reassembled and designated themselves the Ivory Coast Patriotic Movement (MPCI). They rapidly gained support in the heavily Muslim north, where residents had long felt marginalized by the more prosperous and mainly Christian south. A cease-fire was signed between the government and the MPCI, but two other rebel groups, the Movement for Justice and Peace and the Ivorian Popular Movement of the Great West, emerged and seized control of much of the west and southwest of the country. The signing of a power-sharing peace accord between the government and the rebels on January 25 led to furious protests by supporters of Pres. Laurent Gbagbo (*see* BIOGRAPHIES), backed by army leaders. Riots broke out in the capital. In February the UN accused the government of condoning death squads that had killed hundreds of northerners and migrant workers in Abidjan. The government denied the charges, retorting that the rebels were carrying out executions in areas they controlled.

Seydou Diarra, who had been named as prime minister by consensus at the January peace talks, was officially appointed by Gbagbo on February 10 and was finally sworn in as head of a new government of national unity on March 11. Details of a 41-member coalition cabinet, approved by all parties to the peace treaty, were announced a week later. All nine ministers appointed from the three rebel groups took their seats in the government by April 16 after a boycott over fears for their security and the delay in naming the key ministers of defense and interior. On May 4 a new cease-fire was declared, and nearly 4,000 French troops were deployed to enforce the truce in the central Bouaké area. Although a nighttime curfew was lifted on May 10 and an amnesty law passed overwhelmingly by the parliament on August 6, tensions remained high. Authorities arrested about 100 people, including three generals, for plotting a coup and the assassination of President Gbagbo. Gen. Abdoulaye Coulibaly, a high-ranking member of the junta that seized power in 1999, was released in September, but nearly two dozen others remained in custody.

By late September, attempts to achieve a permanent peace faltered, and economic and diplomatic activity virtually ground to a halt. At year's end the country remained divided in half by a "confidence zone," representatives of most international agencies and firms were evacuated, and sporadic violence continued. (NANCY ELLEN LAWLER)

CROATIA

Area: 56,542 sq km (21,831 sq mi)
Population (2003 est.): 4,428,000
Capital: Zagreb
Chief of state: President Stipe Mesic
Head of government: Prime Ministers Ivica Racan and, from December 9, Ivo Sanader

Croatia's hopes for accession into the European Union by 2007, a centrepiece of the centre-left coalition government's foreign policy, were dashed at the May 6, 2003, EU Enlargement Summit when Brussels announced it was premature to discuss any date for Croatian admission. Early accession was to have been a key achievement in the run-up to national elections held at year's end. The decision highlighted the government's inability to free the country from what it felt were Balkan problems.

Dealings with the International Criminal Tribunal for the Former Yugoslavia (ICTY) dominated Croatia's international relations. The death of war hero Gen. Janko Bobetko ended a bitter row with the Hague court; his funeral on May 2 drew 25,000 mourners. Bobetko's indictment the year before was considered unjustified and reflective of the court's moral ambiguity concerning the Yugoslav wars. The Bobetko affair and public opposition to ICTY indictments of other Croatian military leaders resurrected old political divisions regarding the role of Croatian nationalism since World War II. Pres. Stipe Mesic and coalition leaders boycotted the annual Alka games, a traditional equestrian event held in August, after organizers publicly supported the indicted Croatian generals.

Relations with Serbia and Montenegro improved, as was marked by President Mesic's trip to Belgrade on September 10, the first presidential visit between the former warring countries. Relations with Slovenia soured, however. On August 31 Ljubljana recalled its ambassador after Zagreb announced it would establish an exclusive economic zone in the Adriatic Sea that would restrict its neighbour's access to international waters. The unexpected failure to secure EU backing in its dispute sharpened perceptions that foreign policy under Foreign Minister Tonino Picula was in disarray. The signing of the U.S.-Adriatic Charter on May 2 with the United States, Albania, and Macedonia did little to quell pervasive public fears that international powers were bent on relegating Croatia to the Balkans. The decision of Pope John Paul II to mark the 100th trip of his 25-year papacy by visiting Croatia for a third time, starting June 5, gave this mostly Roman Catholic country a rare opportunity for national pride.

On the economic front, concerns mounted that positive trends—a growth rate of 3.5% and inflation at a low 2.5%—had been achieved at the cost of accelerating debt. The government budget deficit swelled to over 8% of gross domestic product, while foreign debt reached $21 billion, having more than doubled since the coalition took power four years earlier. The government's financial woes reflected increasing wage pressures by unions, which earlier in the year had led widespread strikes of publicly employed doctors and teachers demanding higher salaries. It also revealed lower-than-expected foreign investment revenues.

On July 17 the parliament approved the sale of a 25% share of national oil giant INA to the Hungarian oil company MOL, bringing $505 million to state coffers. Tourism, bucking world trends, increased by 6% and generated over $4 billion in revenues, reaching record levels. Nevertheless, clashing political views within the coalition on whether to privatize by selling to foreigners some remaining nonperforming state assets set back planned privatizations of the state insurance and electricity companies. The Croatian Peasant Party (HSS), the second largest coalition partner, advocated a more state-centred economic model, while the coalition leader Socialist Democratic Party (SDP) favoured foreign investment as a way to stimulate economic growth and cut into the stubbornly high unemployment rate of 20%. This clash of views came to a head in February when the HSS forced the SDP to overturn a decision by the State Privatization Fund to sell the state-owned tourism company Suncani Hvar to a Slovenian investor.

The centre-right Croatian Democratic Union (HDZ) registered a convincing victory (66 of 152 seats) in the November parliamentary elections. HDZ leader Ivo Sanader was named prime minister on December 9, and his cabinet was approved on December 23. (MAX PRIMORAC)

CUBA

Area: 110,861 sq km (42,804 sq mi)
Population (2003 est.): 11,295,000
Capital: Havana
Head of state and government: President of the Council of State and President of the Council of Ministers Fidel Castro Ruz

In 2003 Cuba commemorated the 50th anniversary of the assault on the Moncada Barracks that launched the Cuban Revolution in 1953. In an uncontested election the National Assembly unanimously confirmed Pres. Fidel Castro as the country's leader for another five-year term. The Cuban government replaced several high-level officials, including the head of ideology and the ministers of transportation and finance, but failed to hold the overdue (sixth) Party Congress, the event at which major personnel and policy changes were to be charted. Cuba continued to campaign for the return of the "Miami 5," five Cuban agents arrested for spying on exile groups in the United States, but the cause received little attention outside the island.

In March and April the Cuban government orchestrated the largest crackdown on internal dissent in recent years, arresting dozens of independent journalists and pro-democracy activists. Timed to coincide with the U.S.-led war on Iraq, Cuba tried and convicted at least 75 peaceful activists on charges of having conspired with the U.S. to subvert the Cuban revolution. The trials revealed that Cuban security agents had penetrated the main dissident groups, and the severe sentences ranged up to 28 years in prison. The government also continued to harass two leading opposition figures who escaped arrest: Osvaldo Payá, leader of the Varela Project, a movement for democratic reform, and Elizardo Sánchez, head of the Cuban Commission for Human Rights and National Reconciliation. During the same period, Cuba summarily tried and executed three hijackers who had attempted to escape the island by seizing control of a Havana Bay passenger ferry, and an informal moratorium on the death penalty that had been in place for several years was thus effectively ended.

Cuba's wave of repression provoked widespread international consternation but few serious consequences. The Bush administration condemned the crackdown but took no steps to reduce Cuban-American remittance flows or restrict the sale of American agricultural products, which were projected to total $166 million in 2003, almost a 20% increase over 2002. The U.S. Congress protested the arrests in a vote of 414 to 0, but it later challenged new limits on educational travel and voted to lift the travel ban for the third consecutive year. Diplomatic tensions between the U.S. and Cuba reached new levels, however. Castro threatened to close the U.S. interests section in Havana because of its contacts with dissidents, while the U.S. ejected 14 Cuban diplomats for possible espionage and imposed new limits on travel and vehicle ownership. The Bush administration continued to oppose further loosening of the U.S. embargo of Cuba.

Several Latin American countries sponsored a UN resolution criticizing Cuba's human rights record, but a similar effort stalled in the Organization of American States because of resistance from the Caribbean countries. Cuba remained closely allied with Venezuela and hosted a state visit by Brazilian Pres. Luiz Inácio Lula da Silva. Castro received a standing ovation when attending the inauguration of Néstor Kirschner in Argentina and later caused a similar stir in Paraguay. Cuba's relations with other socialist countries remained warm following official visits by Castro to China and Vietnam. The worst diplomatic row broke out between Cuba and the European Union; Castro described Spanish Prime Minister José María Aznar as "fascist," likened Italy's Prime Minister Silvio Berlusconi to the dictator Benito Mussolini, and denounced European aid as a "Trojan horse" for the United States. The EU responded by stepping up support for Cuban opposition groups, but for the most part European tourism, trade, and official aid programs continued unimpeded.

The Cuban economy's recovery from the post-9/11 decline appeared slower than initially forecast, with only minor gains in tourism after a 5% drop in 2002. Cuba projected that 2003 would be a difficult year with GDP growth of no more than 1.5%, and official hard currency foreign debt reached a high of $12.2 billion. The sugar harvest of about two million tons was the worst since 1933. On the basis of Cuba's accumulating arrears and dim immediate prospects, international credit agencies lowered the island's rating to "speculative grade, very poor." Perhaps in response to the deteriorating economic condition, the government fired four of six vice-ministers of the economy. The minister of economy, José Luis Rodríguez, retained his position but was removed from the Council of State, Cuba's highest governing body.

(DANIEL P. ERIKSON)

CYPRUS

Area: 9,251 sq km (3,572 sq mi) for the entire island; the area of the Turkish Republic of Northern Cyprus (TRNC), proclaimed unilaterally (1983) in the occupied northern third of the island, 3,355 sq km (1,295 sq mi)
Population (2003 est.): island 921,000; TRNC only, 207,000 (including Turkish settlers and Turkish military)
Capital: Lefkosia/Lefkosa (also known as Nicosia)
Head(s) of state and government: Presidents Glafcos Clerides and, from February 28, Tassos Papadopoulos; of the TRNC, President Rauf Denktash

In Cyprus 2003 was dominated by impending European Union membership. Greek Cyprus signed the accession treaty in April, effective May 1, 2004, with the understanding that Turkish Cyprus would come in upon reunification of the island. Direct talks between the two presidents continued as the year began, and UN Secretary-General Kofi Annan submitted a plan for a federal state. The UN plan included a deadline to allow a referendum and reunification before EU accession. Loss of sovereignty was too much of a price for Turkish Cypriot Pres. Rauf Denktash to pay, however, and he ended all talks.

Thousands of Turkish Cypriots demonstrated in favour of EU membership, but Denktash stood firm and prevailed. On the other hand, Glafkos Clerides, president of Greek Cyprus, was defeated at the polls in February by Tassos Papadopoulos (*see* BIOGRAPHIES), who had voiced doubts on the UN plan in his campaign. Results of the late December parliamentary elections in Turkish Cyprus were dead even on the EU issue.

Day-to-day Greek-Turkish tensions eased dramatically, with moves to clear mines, account for the missing, and ease trade restrictions. Turkish classes were given in Greek Cypriot universities, and a compensation commission in Turkish Cyprus was set up to handle Greek Cypriot claims against the north. Probably the images that most Cypriots would retain from 2003, however, were the dramatic traffic jams after Turkish Cyprus opened the border-crossing points. There were problems too, of course. In one ugly incident, Turkish Cypriots were assaulted when they visited their former homes on the Greek side. The Greek Cyprus government deplored the incident.

(GEORGE H. KELLING)

CZECH REPUBLIC

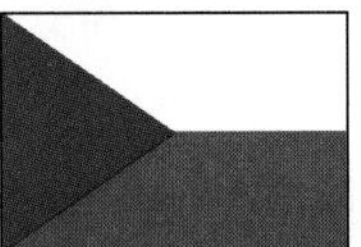

Area: 78,866 sq km (30,450 sq mi)
Population (2003 est.): 10,202,000
Capital: Prague
Chief of state: Presidents Vaclav Havel, Vladimir Spidla (acting) from February 2, and, from March 7, Vaclav Klaus
Head of government: Prime Minister Vladimir Spidla

The Czech Republic slipped backward somewhat in 2003 amid political uncertainty and economic sluggishness. The key political events for the Czechs in 2003 were the parliament's election of the new president in February and the referendum on European Union membership, held on June 13–14. The presidential elections were considered the first major failure for the government—the ruling parties' candidate lost. Meanwhile, the EU referendum was a key success; a total of 55.2% of the Czech electorate participated in the country's first-ever referendum, with 77.3% voting in favour of joining the EU. The country was scheduled to join the EU on May 1, 2004.

The conclusion of Pres. Vaclav Havel's final term in office in February (he was ineligible to run for another term) represented the end of an era for the Czechs. That was particularly true, given that his successor was Vaclav Klaus, who in many ways represented the antithesis of Havel. Klaus, the former chairman of the opposition Civic Democratic Party (ODS), won the presidency despite the fact that the three ruling parties had vowed to support an alternative candidate, former dissident Jan Sokol. From the start, Klaus's victory promised to be a thorn in the side of the ruling coalition, since he was a self-proclaimed "Thatcherite" and an outspoken conservative and Euroskeptic. In contrast, the Social Democrats (CSSD), the biggest party in the ruling coalition, leaned to the left and was strongly pro-EU.

The presidential vote revealed growing tensions within the CSSD, as some party representatives reportedly voted for Klaus rather than Sokol. From the start, maintenance of the new government was expected to be difficult, since the ruling parties had won just 101 seats in the 200-member parliament in the June 2002 elections, barely enough for a majority. Initially it was expected that the CSSD's two centre-right junior coalition partners, rather than the CSSD itself, would provide the impetus to provoke instability within the cabinet. Following Klaus's election as president, Prime Minister Vladimir Spidla called a vote of confidence in his government for March 11, and the measure passed by the narrowest-possible majority. Nonetheless, internal strife within the CSSD continued. The cabinet suffered a major blow on July 22 when it lost its parliamentary majority owing to the resignation of Josef Hojdar from the CSSD's parliamentary caucus. Although CSSD representatives played down the importance of his departure, Hojdar's support was particularly important, given the need for an absolute majority of all deputies (101 votes) to override a veto by the president or the Senate, where the ruling coalition also lacked a majority.

In late September political tensions heated up considerably as the parliament discussed a package of 11 bills related to public finance reform and the opposition called a no-confidence vote in the cabinet. Many observers believed the fiscal-reform legislation would fail to gain approval after Hojdar's departure, especially given the complaints of many other CSSD representatives that the bills ran contrary to party principles. Nonetheless, all 11 of the bills were approved, while the government won the confidence vote by a narrow margin of 100–98, with Hojdar abstaining. Despite those successes, the government's position remained unstable, as the reform measures still needed to be approved by the Senate and signed by President Klaus. If rejected by either the Senate or the president, the bills would return to the parliament, where they would require the support of 101 of the 200 deputies. The Senate was expected to discuss the remaining finance-reform bills at a later time.

The Czech economic performance was somewhat disappointing in 2003; GDP growth was sluggish, and the unemployment rate rose above 10% for the first time. Exports recorded a recovery despite the difficult external sit-

Vaclav Klaus, former leader of the Civic Democratic Party and former prime minister, led his conservative faction in the Czech legislature in the struggle to elect a new president to replace Vaclav Havel. Finally, on February 28, Klaus was elected over the Social Democrat Jan Sokol.

uation, and industry performed well. Imports also rose steadily as strong wage growth and disinflation contributed to a rise in household consumption. The government's biggest economic challenge in 2003 was to put the country's fiscal house in order. Although the cabinet's reform bills would move the Czech Republic partly in that direction, the changes were generally seen as haphazard and insufficient.

(SHARON FISHER)

DENMARK

Area: 43,098 sq km (16,640 sq mi)
Population (2003 est.): 5,387,000
Capital: Copenhagen
Chief of state: Queen Margrethe II
Head of government: Prime Minister Anders Fogh Rasmussen

AP/Wide World Photos

Crown Prince Frederik and Australian Mary Elizabeth Donaldson received formal approval from Frederik's mother, Queen Margrethe II of Denmark, to marry in May 2004.

The political debate in late 2003 focused on Denmark's future as a member of the European Union—a thorny issue for a country known for its profound skepticism about Brussels. The failure of the mid-December summit to agree on an EU constitution would delay Denmark's plans to hold a referendum on the issue, possibly in 2004. A "no" vote would in all likelihood signal the end of Denmark's membership in the bloc. In 1993 Danes had voted "yes" to the Maastricht Treaty on the formation of the European Union but had secured clauses that allowed Denmark to opt out of participation in the single European currency (the euro), joint defense, justice cooperation, and union citizenship. These exemptions, supported by most of the Danish people but anathema to almost the entire political establishment, deeply split the country on the European question and condemned Denmark to a marginal role in the EU. The main political parties had long wanted to eradicate the exemptions; Prime Minister Anders Fogh Rasmussen hatched a plan to attach an amended version of the justice-cooperation exemption to the referendum on the EU constitution. The model would allow Denmark to maintain its notoriously stringent immigration policy, but the Folketing (parliament) would be empowered to decide on legal issues on a case-by-case basis.

Opinion polls showed that Danes seemed willing to forgo the other exemptions, but they remained adamant on tight immigration controls. The Liberal-Conservative government's stringent immigration controls—worked out in close cooperation with the far-right, nationalist Danish People's Party and therefore supported by a parliamentary majority—continued to draw criticism from human rights organizations. The infamous family-reunifications stipulation—preventing young people from marrying or bringing in foreigners under the age of 24—achieved its aim; the number of asylum seekers and mixed marriages was slashed by two-thirds, although an amendment was made to allow Danes to bring their foreign-born spouses back with them to live in Denmark. Hundreds of couples had been forced to live in exile in south Sweden.

On the international front, Denmark, one of the few EU nations to actively support the U.S.-led war in Iraq, made the symbolic contribution of a warship and a submarine to the conflict. A Danish soldier, one of 500 who had been sent to support British troops in southern Iraq, was killed in an exchange of gunfire near Basra in August, becoming the first fatality from forces other than those of the Americans and British. Mystery shrouded the disappearance from house arrest near Copenhagen of Iraqi Gen. Nizar al-Khazraji, Saddam Hussein's former chief of staff and the most senior officer to have defected from Baghdad prior to the war. Khazraji was being held in Denmark on war-crime charges for alleged chemical-weapon attacks on Iraqi Kurds in the 1980s; he had applied for political asylum in 1999, and he vanished in March 2003.

In September the royal palace announced the engagement of Crown Prince Frederik, heir to the Danish throne, to Australian Mary Donaldson. The wedding was to take place on May 14, 2004, in Copenhagen Cathedral.

(CHRISTOPHER FOLLETT)

DJIBOUTI

Area: 23,200 sq km (8,950 sq mi)
Population (2003 est.): 457,000 (excluding 25,000 refugees)
Capital: Djibouti
Chief of state and head of government: President Ismail Omar Guelleh, assisted by Prime Minister Dileita Muhammad Dileita

In January 2003 the Union for the Presidential Majority (UMP), a coalition supporting Pres. Ismail Omar Guelleh, took all 65 parliamentary seats in Djibouti's first full multiparty election. Opposition leader Ahmed Dini alleged fraud, but he was unsuccessful in challenging the election results. Seven women entered the new National Assembly, following a new law mandating such an inclusion.

Despite a serious drought and food shortage, the presence of U.S. troops emerged as the major campaign issue in the parliamentary election. The opposition maintained that the presence of U.S. soldiers could incite terrorist attacks. After the election President Guelleh continued to foster diplomatic ties with the U.S.; however, the U.S. was not given permission to launch attacks from Djibouti during the 2003 Iraq war. Guelleh criticized the war effort, citing the lack of UN approval for the operation. During the course of the war, there were two large antiwar demonstrations on the streets of Djibouti.

In September Djibouti's military began forcefully deporting thousands of illegal Somali, Ethiopian, and Eritrean immigrants who had ignored a late-July call to leave voluntarily. Djibouti's high unemployment rate and security concerns were given as primary reasons for the expulsion of an estimated 100,000 illegal immigrants who had been living in the country.

(ANDREW EISENBERG)

DOMINICA

Area: 750 sq km (290 sq mi)
Population (2003 est.): 69,700
Capital: Roseau
Chief of state: Presidents Vernon Shaw and, from October 2, Nicholas Liverpool
Head of government: Prime Minister Pierre Charles

Dominica exited the controversial offshore-banking business in February 2003 when the last such institution operating in the country, Bank Caribe, was closed. The government then moved against terrorism-related money laundering in April, piloting through the House of Assembly the Suppression of Financing of Terrorism Act, which was designed to cut off such funding and carried jail terms of up to 25 years for offenders.

A $123.4 million austerity budget was presented in June, with the aim of getting Dominica's shaky public finances back on track. Measures included a 5% pay cut for civil servants, a 10% reduction in travel and other allowances, an increase in the sales tax to 7.5%, and the withdrawal of duty and tax allowances to companies. The fiscal gap would be covered by financial assistance from the European Union, the World Bank, and the Caribbean Development Bank. The International Monetary Fund also extended assistance in the form of a one-year stand-by credit arrangement. Prime Minister Pierre Charles's government committed itself to public-sector reform, which included divestiture of the state's share in the National Commercial Bank.

In July, Dominica reaffirmed its decision to maintain diplomatic relations with Taiwan, its single largest aid donor, in preference to forging diplomatic ties with China.

(DAVID RENWICK)

DOMINICAN REPUBLIC

Area: 48,671 sq km (18,792 sq mi)
Population (2003 est.): 8,716,000
Capital: Santo Domingo
Head of state and government: President Hipólito Mejía Domínguez

The year 2003 was not a good one for the Dominican Republic. The long surge of growth, unparalleled in the Caribbean, reversed as the economy shrank by 2.8%. Investment confidence was badly shaken by the massive $2.2 billion scandal and collapse of Banco Intercontinental (Baninter), the country's second largest commercial bank. The resulting deficit and acceleration in inflation precipitated negotiations with the International Monetary Fund. A standby agreement of $618 million was reached in August but came with politically unwelcome conditions—fiscal reform and cutbacks in the public sector. The government was also criticized for its failure to address chronic deficiencies in the electricity grid and generating capacity.

The economic downturn, including the sharp fall in the value of the peso, impacted the poor in particular and contributed to Pres. Hipólito Mejía's drop in popularity. Both Mejía and Leonel Fernández, a former president and the candidate of the principal opposition party, had been tarred by the Baninter scandal for accepting bank favours. Mejía's decision to break with party policy and run for reelection split his party as the country moved abrasively toward elections in 2004. Lightening this gloom was the tourist industry's continued success. The country's revenues had improved steadily following the Sept. 11, 2001, terrorist attacks in the United States.

Mejía continued to implement his policy of bettering relations with his impoverished neighbour by opening a free-trade zone on the Haitian side of the frontier. The initiative was also intended to slow the movement of illegal Haitian migrants to the Dominican Republic by generating jobs and to reward Dominican investors with cheap labour. In other foreign-policy matters, Mejía endorsed the U.S.-led war in Iraq, a position contrary to that of the majority of his Latin American colleagues and one that led to the resignation of his foreign minister. Mejía also approved in principle a free-trade agreement with Canada.

(JOHN W. GRAHAM)

EAST TIMOR (TIMOR-LESTE)

Area: 14,604 sq km (5,639 sq mi)
Population (2003 est.) 778,000
Capital: Dili
Chief of state: President Xanana Gusmão
Head of government: Prime Minister Mari Alkatiri

In 2003 Pres. Xanana Gusmão's government's efforts to set up the public institutions that had been established by East Timor's 2002 constitution proceeded without encountering any particular difficulties on the political level, despite existing rivalries between political parties.

The terrorist attack on the UN mission in Baghdad, Iraq, on August 19 provoked a widespread emotional response throughout East Timor. Among the victims of this attack was Sérgio Vieira de Mello (*see* OBITUARIES), the Brazilian diplomat who was well known and respected in East Timor when he headed the task force responsible for the reconstruction of East Timor after Indonesian occupation.

UN and East Timorese prosecutors indicted numerous former Indonesian administrators and military personnel, but Jakarta refused to extradite those charged. Meanwhile, though, Indonesia convicted Brig. Gen. Noer Moeis, the former head of Indonesia's troops in East Timor, of "crimes against humanity."

Economic development remained a priority, but considerable constraints still existed, notably the lack of reliable information. Most of the important socioeconomic indicators, such as the Human Development Index, were still unknown for East Timor, while the country's estimated GDP of $528 per capita lagged far behind that of Indonesia and the Philippines.

In August, at the International Association of Athletics Federations Congress in Paris, East Timor was voted in by near-unanimous approval as the 211th IAAF member state.

(CHARLES CADOUX)

ECUADOR

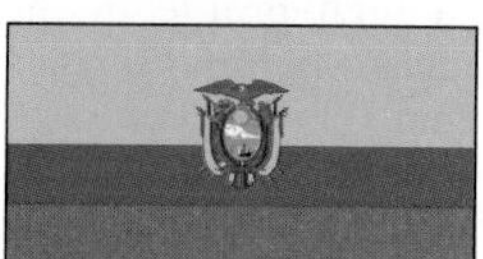

Area: 272,045 sq km (105,037 sq mi), including the 8,010-sq-km (3,093-sq-mi) Galápagos Islands
Population (2003 est.): 13,003,000 (Galápagos Islands, about 20,000)
Capital: Quito
Chief of state and head of government: Presidents Gustavo Noboa Bejarano and, from January 15, Lucio Gutiérrez Borbúa

Pres. Lucio Gutiérrez's (*see* BIOGRAPHIES) political honeymoon ended in August 2003 when his alliance with the Indian movement Pachakutik was dissolved. Gutiérrez was inaugurated on January 15 after having won election in November 2002 with the support of Pachakutik and his own January 21 Patriotic Society Party (PSP). He had difficulty, however, striking a balance between satisfying long-standing demands for social reform and demonstrating fiscal austerity to foreign creditors. The latter goal appeared to be Gutiérrez's priority. He chose former banker Mauricio Pozo Crespo as economy minister and reached an agreement with the International Monetary Fund in March that required him to trim the government deficit and raise taxes. After Pachakutik deputies helped defeat a law limiting benefits to state workers, which was part of the IMF program, Gutiérrez dismissed the three cabinet ministers who belonged to the movement. Since the PSP held only a handful of congressional seats, the president was under pressure to form another coalition to improve prospects for getting legislation passed during the rest of his four-year term. Gutiérrez, who had harshly criticized corruption under previous governments, came under fire himself for naming relatives and former military associates to senior positions. Former president Gustavo Noboa Bejarano, who claimed to be the victim of political persecution when his financial dealings were investigated, was granted asylum in the Dominican Republic.

Gutiérrez asserted that the armed conflict in neighbouring Colombia was responsible for rising crime in his own country, and he called for a greater role for the United Nations and countries of the Andean region in seeking peace between the Colombian government and leftist guerrillas. The replacement of

AP/Wide World Photos

Indigenous peoples in Ecuador, including this Huaorani woman and her infant, demonstrate in October at the trial of the petroleum-extraction company ChevronTexaco on charges of having damaged the environment in the Amazon region.

Foreign Minister Nina Pacari, a Pachakutik member, with Patricio Zuquilanda Duque was believed to have given Gutiérrez a freer hand in dealing with Colombia. Meanwhile, the Ecuadoran armed forces acknowledged that large quantities of firearms and other munitions had gone missing. It was strongly suspected that the weapons had been sold to the Colombian guerrillas. Unlike Colombia, Ecuador declined to exempt American citizens from being extradited for prosecution at the International Criminal Court, and U.S. military aid was suspended as a result.

Oil workers staged a nine-day strike in June, forcing postponement of plans to allow foreign companies to develop new Amazon basin petroleum deposits. Nevertheless, export earnings grew by 13.5% from January to May over the same period in 2002, largely owing to higher oil prices. The new foreign-operated OCP (Oleoducto de Crudos Pesados) pipeline began operations but was pumping less crude oil than had been expected. (PAUL KNOX)

EGYPT

Area: 997,690 sq km (385,210 sq mi)
Population (2003 est.): 68,185,000
Capital: Cairo
Chief of state: President Hosni Mubarak
Head of government: Prime Minister Atef Ebeid

On March 18, 2003, Sa'd al-Din Ibrahim, a professor of sociology and prominent human rights activist, was exonerated and declared innocent by the highest court of appeals, the Court of Cassation, of having illegally received funds from the European Union, embezzled the funds, and tarnished Egypt's image abroad. In 2001 he had been sentenced to seven years' hard labour, but he was granted a retrial in 2002. Ibrahim, a particularly harsh government critic, had spent 14 months in prison.

In September Pres. Hosni Mubarak's ruling National Democratic Party (NDP) convened its first annual conference (hitherto its general conferences were held every few years). Mubarak's 40-year-old son, Gamal Mubarak, head of the NDP's Policies Secretariat, had a high profile in the conference—perceived by many as a clear indication that the president was preparing him for succession.

Economic issues loomed large at the NDP conference. Since the Egyptian pound was floated in January, the prices of basic goods had risen by 40%. To remedy the situation, the chairman of the NDP's economics committee proposed to introduce to the parliament a number of legislative bills, including ones addressing consumer protection, tax reform, and monopolies. Following the conference, the Egyptian Organization for Human Rights issued a statement demanding that the president be chosen not in a single-candidate referendum, the current system, but in a multicandidate election.

© AFP/Corbis

Cultural authorities in Cairo were upset when the director of the Egyptian Museum and Papyrus Collection in Berlin allowed the 3,300-year-old bust of Egyptian Queen Nefertiti to be placed briefly in May atop a near-nude statue.

The opposition political parties were skeptical of the promised reforms by the NDP, and opposition leaders called for the abolition of the state of emergency that had granted the government a wide scope of powers. Ibrahim Dusuqi Abaza, a prominent member of the liberal opposition New Wafd Party, expressed succinctly: "Nothing will be done in this country if we don't advance political reform. We need democracy to control the economy and to guide the economy so it can take off."

On the foreign-affairs front, Mubarak accepted the invitation of French Pres. Jacques Chirac to attend—along with other heads of state from Africa, Latin America, and Asia—the Group of Eight summit of industrialized nations in Évian. The subject matter at the June 1 summit ranged from problems pertaining to economic and social development to public health issues, particularly AIDS.

In an effort to prepare the groundwork for the resumption of peace talks between the Israelis and the Palestinians, President Mubarak hosted an Arab-U.S. summit in Sharm al-Shaykh on June 3. Crown Prince Abdullah of Saudi Arabia, King Abdullah II of Jordan, King Hamad ibn Isa al-Khalifah of Bahrain, and Palestinian Prime Minister Mahmoud Abbas (*see* BIOGRAPHIES) met with U.S. Pres. George W. Bush to show their support for the road map for peace.

After a hiatus of two years, the only peace movement that united the Israelis and the Arabs, the International Alliance for Arab-Israeli Peace, had its third meeting on May 8–9 in Copenhagen. One hundred Israelis, Palestinians, Jordanians, and Egyptians met. In a statement issued by the group, the declaration was made that "peace in the Middle East is not only possible but inevitable." The head of the Egyptian delegation, former ambassador Adel al-Adawi, explained the reason for the resumption of the group's activities: "We can't leave those who are against peace to talk freely and loudly, while we just wait and do nothing."

The Egyptian minister of culture on June 8 denounced the placing of a sculpture of the head of Queen Nefertiti on an almost-naked statue in the Egyptian Museum and Papyrus Collection in Berlin-Charlottenburg, Ger. He called it a "shameful" act and asked for the return of this unique artifact to its home country. (MARIUS K. DEEB)

EL SALVADOR

Area: 21,041 sq km (8,124 sq mi)
Population (2003 est.): 6,515,000
Capital: San Salvador
Head of state and government: President Francisco Flores Pérez

Throughout 2003 El Salvador negotiated with four other Central American countries and the United States to form a Central American Free Trade Agreement (CAFTA) and sought preferential treatment for its coffee within that agreement. Fear of U.S. dominance, however, increased popular opposition to CAFTA in El Salvador. There was also widespread popular opposition, led by the leftist Farabundo Martí Front for National Liberation (FMLN), to the U.S.-led invasion of Iraq. Nonetheless, the Salvadoran government agreed to send troops to join the peacekeeping brigade that was organized by Spain. U.S. pressure for consolidation of Central America's armed forces, however, met with sharp resistance from El Salvador. Spanish Pres. José María Aznar visited El Salvador in July in an attempt to develop closer economic relations between El Salvador and the European Union and to increase Spanish private investment in Central America.

Two youngsters in El Salvador eat a meal provided by the St. Anthony Roman Catholic Church in June. From a program called "Hope for Children" they received food, education, assistance in getting over drug addiction, and other social aid.

The FMLN made gains in March elections and won the mayorship of San Salvador as well as a plurality of seats (31) in the National Assembly, compared with 27 seats for the ruling National Republican Alliance (ARENA); 26 other seats were divided among four other parties. Cementing its coalition with the National Conciliation Party (PCN), ARENA continued to rule the country with 43 of the 84 seats in the unicameral legislature. As in the past, voters continued to ignore the polls, and there appeared to be widespread irregularities in the voting. The election was waged against the backdrop of a national strike by health care workers, who shut down public medical services to prevent privatization of health care services. Following its defeat, ARENA went through a major shake-up of its leadership, with coffee magnate José Antonio Salaverria Borja emerging as the new party leader. The FMLN was favoured to win the March 2004 national elections; Pres. Francisco Flores was suffering the lowest approval ratings of his administration. The U.S. ambassador warned that an FMLN victory would be harmful to U.S.-Salvadoran relations.

Salvadoran activists in Los Angeles campaigned to protect Salvadoran citizens in the U.S. in the face of a hardening U.S. policy against illegal immigrants. Remittances of approximately $2 billion annually from an estimated 280,000 Salvadorans who lived in the U.S. under the provisions of the Temporary Protected Status, a section of the Immigration and Naturalization Act, were a vital source of foreign exchange for El Salvador.

(RALPH LEE WOODWARD, JR.)

EQUATORIAL GUINEA

Area: 28,051 sq km (10,831 sq mi)
Population (2003 est.): 494,000
Capital: Malabo
Chief of state: President Brig. Gen. Teodoro Obiang Nguema Mbasogo
Head of government: Prime Minister Cándido Muatetema Rivas

Equatorial Guinea saw nearly 25% growth in the economy in 2002, the best economic performance of any African country; the rise was attributed to oil, which accounted for 90% of all wealth produced. Relations with the U.S. administration of George W. Bush, keen to reduce American dependence on Middle Eastern oil, grew more cordial in 2003. Pres. Teodoro Obiang Nguema Mbasogo had met with Bush in September 2002, and the U.S. reopened its embassy in the capital, Malabo, which had been closed in 1995, before oil was discovered off Bioko island.

The U.S. claimed that it could engage with Obiang's government and persuade it to improve its notorious political and human rights record. President Obiang, in power since 1979 and reelected in December 2002 in a poll rejected by the opposition as fraudulent, remained head of a highly corrupt administration, however. There was no proper accounting for the oil revenues that went to the state, and there was much evidence that most of the new oil wealth was being siphoned off by the ruling elite. A new airport opened in August, and construction began late in the year for a new capital city, Malabo 2. Meanwhile, new discoveries of oil and gas reserves were made, and in May the government approved the construction by Marathon of a natural-gas plant on Bioko. (CHRISTOPHER SAUNDERS)

ERITREA

Area: 121,144 sq km (46,774 sq mi)
Population (2003 est.): 4,141,000
Capital: Asmara
Head of state and government: President Isaias Afwerki

In 2003 Eritrea continued its campaign of national development—*Wefri Warsay Yi'Kaalo* (*WWY*). Dubbed the "Eritrean Marshall Plan" by Pres. Isaias Afwerki, *WWY* included the establishment of a preparatory school located at Sawa, the nation's military training centre. The Warsay Yi'Kaalo School opened its doors to 5,200 students in February, signaling the start of the long-awaited demobilization and reintegration of soldiers. *WWY* continued to focus on infrastructure development and export-oriented joint ventures with foreign companies interested in the exportation of gold, copper, oil, natural gas, and quarried marble. By March Ethiopia's belated misgivings over the placement of the town of Badme within Eritrea's borders had resuscitated a sense of mistrust and insecurity over the future of normalization.

In the second quarter of 2003, the discovery of gold and copper deposits in the Gash-Barka region was overshadowed by the gruesome murder of a British geologist. The government blamed "terrorists sponsored by The Sudan," a claim refuted by the Khartoum government. Citing security reasons, members of the Kunama people along the Gash River were quietly removed from their traditional enclaves and relocated to designated villages. At a comfortable distance from the sites of mines and security hamlets, the government in Asmara announced the inauguration of Eritrean Airlines and the attainment of observer status in the Arab League. Pres. Afwerki publicly endorsed the U.S. occupation of Iraq, presided over the 10th anniversary of national independence, belatedly authorized the announcement of the list of Eritreans who perished in the 1998–2000 border war, and declared the completion of village- and district-level elections. Following the June 20 Martyrs Day commemorations, the nation plunged into a period of mourning, despite official exhortations intended to dispel the sombre mood.

The third quarter was dominated by anxiety and irritation at Ethiopia's continued obstruction of the demarcation of borders. Diplomatic exchanges between the two countries became more strident, with the Eritrean side demanding immediate demarcation and the Ethiopians insisting on revisions of the April 2002 international adjudication—which it had earlier accepted without reservation. In September the work of UNMEE, the United Nations peacekeeping mission, was extended to preempt a return to hostilities.

The last quarter of the year witnessed a further rise in tensions over the Ethiopian border as well as a tightening of internal controls over a population made even more vulnerable by five years of drought-triggered food insecurity. As the year came to a close, Eritreans faced the prospect of dwindling food reserves and had little hope for the normalization of relations with their southern neighbour. (RUTH IYOB)

ESTONIA

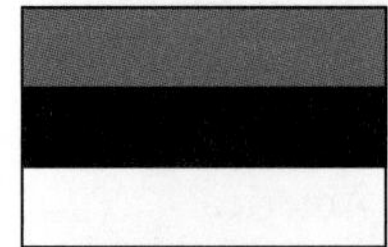

Area: 45,227 sq km (17,462 sq mi)
Population (2003 est.): 1,353,000
Capital: Tallinn
Chief of state: President Arnold Rüütel
Head of government: Prime Ministers Siim Kallas and, from April 10, Juhan Parts

On March 2, 2003, voters in Estonia went to the polls for the country's fourth parliamentary elections since 1992. For the first time in the postcommunist era, the ruling coalition (Prime Minister Siim Kallas's Reform Party and the Centre Party) held its own in the vote, but policy differences between the two parties precluded any renewal of their governing agreement. Instead Juhan Parts led a new centre-right coalition—consisting of his Res Publica party, the Reform Party, and the People's Union—that pledged to lower taxes gradually over the next four years. The new government held a solid 60 seats in the 101-member parliament. In its first national campaign, Res Publica burst onto the scene and tied the Centre Party for the most seats (28) by drawing voters away from several established parties. At 58%, voter turnout remained at the same level as that of the 1999 parliamentary elections.

On a poster in the Estonian capital, Tallinn, in September, Prime Minister Juhan Parts urges his fellow citizens to vote "yes" in a referendum on joining the European Union. They did so with a 66.9% majority.

AP/Wide World Photos

The Estonian economy continued its robust performance, with a fourth straight year of substantial growth in gross domestic product. In 2003 inflation fell to record low levels for the period since renewed independence in 1991. Finland and Sweden remained Estonia's main trading partners and foreign investors. The major cause for concern in the economy was a growing trade deficit.

After months of at times highly emotional debate, the citizens of Estonia accepted the European Union's invitation for membership by a majority of 66.9% on September 14. Polls showed that support for the EU had dipped below 50% in June, but in the end arguments based on security issues—especially fear of renewed Russian dominance—and economic benefits carried the day. Estonia's impending membership in NATO received a strong boost in May when the U.S. Senate unanimously ratified the current round of expansion. (TOIVO U. RAUN)

ETHIOPIA

Area: 1,133,882 sq km (437,794 sq mi)
Population (2003 est.): 66,558,000
Capital: Addis Ababa
Chief of state: President Girma Wolde-Giyorgis
Head of government: Prime Minister Meles Zenawi

Several natural disasters beset Ethiopia in 2003, the most notable of which was a drought, the worst in decades. The ensuing famine affected more than 15 million people in Ethiopia, most severely those living in the southeast and the northern highlands. The famine was expected to worsen if the drought continued. The government began a voluntary resettlement program, moving some peasants from the worst-affected regions in the north to areas in the south, and substantial international humanitarian contributions were received. A malaria epidemic and widespread incidence of waterborne illnesses compounded the suffering. Flooding in the south in May forced thousands to leave

On a trip to Ethiopia in May to highlight the food and health crisis in the Horn of Africa, Irish rock star and humanitarian Bob Geldof visits with an AIDS-stricken boy and his mother in a hospital in the town of Dilla.

their homes and resulted in the deaths of more than 100 people.

The border demarcation that had been agreed upon at the conclusion of the border war with Eritrea in 2000 was delayed twice during 2003 as Ethiopian Prime Minister Meles Zenawi protested the decision to place the town of Badme within Eritrea. It was expected that the border would not be formally established until sometime in 2004. A UN peacekeeping force numbering 1,500 troops remained deployed in the border area, and its mandate was extended until the border demarcation was completed. Relations with Eritrea remained strained; the two countries had not had face-to-face meetings over the border issue since the 2000 cessation of hostilities. Ethiopia's relations with Somalia also continued to be tense, as the transitional government of Somalia accused Ethiopian troops of border violations. The U.S. forgave Ethiopia's bilateral debt and was providing Ethiopian troops with antiterrorist and counterterrorist training. U.S. Special Forces set up a base in nearby Djibouti through which all counterterrorism efforts in the Horn of Africa were being channeled. Ethiopia joined the U.S.-U.K. coalition in the war in Iraq.

The International Monetary Fund forecast Ethiopia's 2003 economic growth rate at 6.7%, but the final figure would depend on the course of the drought. International coffee prices remained low, and it was likely that the drought would drive Ethiopia's important coffee revenues lower still. In some areas farmers started to pull up their coffee plants and replace them with khat, a mildly narcotic, drought-resistant plant.

In domestic politics, the opposition focused on a new law that would allow the government to intervene in regional affairs in times of emergency and on a controversial new press law that was criticized as imposing excessive restrictions on media content. In both cases the opposition parties decried government attempts to centralize power. The United Ethiopian Democratic Forces, led by Beyene Petros, was formed in September and was the largest opposition coalition.

An important fossil discovery in the Afar region in June provided exciting new evidence concerning the origins of *Homo sapiens*. The fossils, called Idaltu—"elder" in the Afar language—were estimated to be 160,000 years old and provided further evidence of man's having evolved in Africa before migrating into Europe and Asia. (*See* ANTHROPOLOGY AND ARCHAEOLOGY: *Anthropology*.) (SANDRA F. JOIREMAN)

FIJI

Area: 18,272 sq km (7,055 sq mi)
Population (2003 est.): 827,000
Capital: Suva
Chief of state: President Ratu Josefa Iloilo
Head of government: Prime Minister Laisenia Qarase

A Fiji Supreme Court ruling in 2003 obliged Prime Minister Laisenia Qarase to include members of the Fiji Labour Party (FLP) in his cabinet, but there was disagreement over the number of places to be allocated and the overall size of the cabinet. Qarase also excluded FLP leader Mahendra Chaudhry. The issue was referred back to the court. During the year there were treason convictions for participants in the failed coup of 2000, including prominent politicians, and charges were filed against leaders of a related mutiny within the army.

In January Cyclone Ami ripped through the northern and eastern districts, causing at least 14 deaths and an estimated $35 million in damage. Continuing drought, especially in western districts, affected agricultural and domestic water supplies, led to the loss of pine forests through fire, and compromised the hydroelectricity system. There was a slow recovery of tourism after SARS (severe acute respiratory syndrome) and security scares. The sugar industry remained dependent on EU subsidies, though an Asian Development Bank loan of $25 million was to be used to support alternative projects for farmers. The Fiji Sugar Corp. had been unable to handle all of the sugar produced in 2002, and its attempts to reduce the harvest for 2003 were thwarted by farmers. Remittances from workers and migrants living overseas reached a record $116 million, reflecting recent out-migration and the number of Fijian servicemen on peacekeeping missions.

(BARRIE MACDONALD)

FINLAND

Area: 338,145 sq km (130,559 sq mi)
Population (2003 est.): 5,212,000
Capital: Helsinki
Chief of state: President Tarja Halonen
Head of government: Prime Ministers Paavo Lipponen, Anneli Jäätteenmäki from April 17, Antii Kalliomäki (acting) from June 18, and, from June 24, Matti Vanhanen

Following the general elections in March 2003, opposition leader Anneli Jäätteenmäki became prime minister in April, but she resigned in June after confessing that she did not have the confidence of Parliament. Jäätteenmäki had come under intense pressure after it became known that she had acquired secret minutes of talks on Iraq held in Washington, D.C., in December 2002 between former prime minister Paavo Lipponen and U.S. Pres. George W. Bush. In her election campaign she had made use of her personal knowledge of the talks to assert that during those talks Lipponen had taken Finland closer to the U.S. position on Iraq than Finland's traditionally pro-UN policy warranted. Though critics did not dispute her right to the information, they blamed her for the underhanded way in which she had obtained the minutes from a top official. In December Jäätteenmäki was charged with having incited or helped a former presidential aide, Martti Manninen (who was also charged), to leak official secrets. The premiership went to Matti Vanhanen, also a member of the Centre Party, which formed a new government together with the Social Democratic and Swedish People's parties after the elections.

The government reiterated its support for the UN but refrained from any overt criticism of the U.S. military action in Iraq. Former president Martti Ahtisaari—appointed in September to head a panel to report to the UN on the August bombing of its headquarters in Baghdad—compared the attack to those of 9/11 in the United States.

Defense forces chief Juhani Kaskeala remarked in a speech in September that European Union defense and NATO were indivisible and that the transatlantic link was vital. His comments were broadly interpreted as suggesting that nonallied Finland should join NATO. In reviewing the national-security policy, the government considered a number of options, including cooperation with the EU and the possibility of joining the Atlantic alliance.

Alpo Rusi, an aide to Ahtisaari who was under investigation by police for having spied for East Germany, would not face charges, a prosecutor said; there was no proof of gross espionage, and any lesser offense was barred owing to the passage of time. In addition, the prosecutor declared that the large number of unnamed Finns whom the news media had accused in 2002 of having passed information to East Germany would not be tried.

Authorities, fearing the spread of crime, decided not to relax visa controls with neighbouring Russia.

(EDWARD SUMMERHILL)

FRANCE

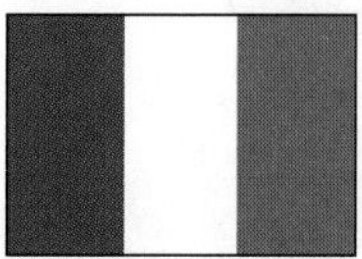

Area: 543,965 sq km (210,026 sq mi)
Population (2003 est.): 59,773,000
Capital: Paris
Chief of state: President Jacques Chirac
Head of government: Prime Minister Jean-Pierre Raffarin

The big event of 2003 for France was its clash with the administration of U.S. Pres. George W. Bush over Iraq. France failed to block what it considered an ill-judged Anglo-American rush to topple Iraqi Pres. Saddam Hussein's regime as Bush and British Prime Minister Tony Blair simply decided to do without the UN authorization for war that Paris had promised to veto. French Pres. Jacques Chirac's firm opposition to the war, for which he won widespread support, helped widen the split between the Bush administration and much of Europe. Iraq had long been a specific bone of contention between France and its English-speaking allies, but this confrontation went wider, with France claiming to be acting in defense of the international system represented by the United Nations and insisting that only UN approval could legitimize the U.S.-led invasion of Iraq. (See *United Nations:* Special Report.)

Foreign Policy. In the protracted crisis over Iraq, initial Franco-American cooperation dissolved rapidly at the start of 2003 as it became clear that the U.S. intended to disarm Hussein by force and that Paris intended to thwart such moves at the UN. On January 20 French Foreign Minister Dominique de Villepin (*see* BIOGRAPHIES) turned a UN discussion of the general scourge of terrorism into a sharp attack on the U.S. rush to war against Baghdad. Two weeks later the confrontation at the UN became even more public when de Villepin passionately rebuked U.S. Secretary of State Colin Powell for justifying war.

In January, during celebrations in Paris to mark the 40th anniversary of the Élysée Treaty between France and Germany, Chirac declared his total solidarity with German Chancellor Gerhard Schröder, who had included opposition to war in Iraq as a plank of his 2002 reelection campaign. U.S. Secretary of Defense Donald Rumsfeld had already dismissed the views of France and Germany as representing "old Europe," in contrast to the more pro-U.S. sentiments of the "new Europe," primarily countries in the process of joining the European Union and NATO. Chirac used an emergency EU summit on Iraq on February 17 to tell the leaders of the applicant countries, who were present at the meeting as observers, that they had "missed a good opportunity to remain silent" and had a lot to learn about their incipient EU obligations. On March 10 Chirac made clear his intention to veto the resolution proposed by the U.S. and the U.K. for the UN Security Council to specifically authorize military intervention when he said on television that "whatever the circumstances, France will vote no."

Further division came within NATO over the provision of alliance protection for Turkey if it got caught up in a war in Iraq. Both the U.S. and Turkey had requested such aid in January, but France, together with Belgium and Germany, formally blocked the request on the grounds that it assumed the possibility of war and therefore made it more likely. On February 19 the request was approved by NATO's defense planning committee, of which France was not a member.

France's stand on Iraq infuriated many Americans, some of whom boycotted French wine and renamed French fries "freedom fries," while the

French Pres. Jacques Chirac greets U.S. Pres. George W. Bush, who has arrived in the resort town of Évian, France, for the Group of Eight summit in June. The two leaders met again in New York City in September.

U.S. government muttered darkly about France's behaviour having "consequences." In fact, the only obvious reprisal was the absence of American aerospace companies and the U.S. Air Force from the Paris air show in June.

Modest efforts to patch up relations were made at the Group of Eight summit hosted by Chirac at Évian in early June. Bush commented that "just because we have disagreements does not mean we have to be disagreeable to each other," and Chirac ensured that the summit communiqué amply reflected U.S. concerns about weapons of mass destruction and terrorism. The French and U.S. presidents met again in New York City in September. France eventually joined all other countries on the Security Council to vote on October 16 for a U.S.-sponsored UN resolution to internationalize peacekeeping and postwar reconstruction in Iraq, though at the same time Paris said it would not contribute troops or money because the resolution did not go far enough to transfer political power to the Iraqis.

The conflict over Iraq did not dampen French foreign policy ambitions elsewhere. Paris continued efforts to end the civil war in Côte d'Ivoire and in June led an EU peacekeeping contingent into the Democratic Republic of the Congo, the first such mission by the EU.

The Economy. The French government fought with its EU partners over the stability pact rules that euro-zone deficits had to be kept within 3% of national income. The French deficit breached this in 2002 and looked certain to do so again in 2003. This was partly a consequence of growth's dipping below 1%, but it also reflected Chirac's insistence on carrying out income tax cuts he had pledged in his 2002 reelection campaign.

A pension reform aimed at making people contribute to plans longer before they can become eligible to draw out full retirement benefits also created problems. Public-sector unions opposed the reform because it involved raising their pension contributions to the level required of private-sector employees. Though Prime Minister Jean-Pierre Raffarin's government weathered transport strikes in May and June, as well as the filibustering of parliamentary amendments by the Socialist opposition, the reform passed through Parliament in July.

Domestic Affairs. Corsican autonomy received a setback on July 6 when a referendum on the creation of a single electoral district on that Mediterranean island was narrowly voted down. The measure had been intended to make future regional polls easier.

In response to the growing tendency of Muslim girls to wear Islamic headscarves to school, a government-appointed commission recommended in December that all such conspicuous religious symbols, including Jewish skullcaps and outsize Christian crucifixes, be banned from public schools in order to preserve France's long-standing separation of church and state. On December 17 President Chirac publicly supported such a ban.

As a heat wave blisters Europe in August, these women cool off in a fountain in the Place de la Concorde in Paris. There were some 14,800 deaths in France.

The biggest shock to the country's vaunted social solidarity came in the August heat wave, which caused some 14,800 deaths, mainly of the elderly. This toll, which was far higher than elsewhere in Europe, was partly due to air pollution and the lack of air conditioning in private homes. The public health system was also blamed for not coping well, and its top official resigned. Most shocking was the evidently large number of elderly people abandoned by their vacationing families and the slowness of the latter to reclaim their relatives' corpses. Refrigerated trucks were used as makeshift morgues, and on September 3 the state buried, in paupers' graves, 57 unclaimed bodies.

(DAVID BUCHAN)

GABON

Area: 267,667 sq km (103,347 sq mi)
Population (2003 est.): 1,329,000
Capital: Libreville
Chief of state: President Omar Bongo
Head of government: Prime Minister Jean-François Ntoutoume-Emane

In February 2003, Gérard Nguema Mitoghe, president of Gabon's opposition National Rally of Republicans, demanded the dissolution of Parliament and municipal councils, citing the high level of voter abstention in the December 2001 elections. Condemning the conduct of the Omar Bongo regime and accusing unnamed high government officials of enriching themselves with public funds, he announced the formation of a shadow cabinet on March 22. On May 12 two privately owned magazines were shut down following the publication of articles critical of the government. Despite opposition protests, the ruling party pushed through constitutional changes in July that removed term restrictions. This move effectively allowed Bongo, whose term was to expire in 2005, to stand for reelection indefinitely. He had ruled for 36 years.

In March Gabon rebuffed demands by Equatorial Guinea that Gabonese troops be removed from Mbagne, an island in the oil-rich Corisco Bay claimed by both nations. Although the dispute remained unresolved, plans were announced in August for the construction of two bridges over the Ntem River to link Gabon with both Equatorial Guinea and Cameroon. This project, to be launched in 2005, also included the construction of an all-weather road in the "Three Frontiers" area. Oil production, the backbone of Gabon's economy, declined during the year, and this created severe financial problems. (NANCY ELLEN LAWLER)

GAMBIA, THE

Area: 10,689 sq km (4,127 sq mi)
Population (2003 est.): 1,426,000
Capital: Banjul
Head of state and government: President Col. Yahya Jammeh

In 2003 the regime of Pres. Yahya Jammeh continued to be eccentric and semiautocratic, and the country, which lived off tourism, groundnuts, and aid remained extremely poor. Jammeh kept close ties with Liberia's notorious Pres. Charles Taylor before Taylor was forced into exile in Nigeria.

A tough media law that took effect in August 2002 gave a national media commission, appointed by the president, the powers of a court of law to examine complaints against media outlets and their employees, including the ability to bring them to trial. International media groups were especially critical of the powers given the commission to suspend or retract authorization for journalists to work. In September 2003 the editor in chief of the country's twice-weekly the *Independent* newspaper was arrested in Banjul by the National Intelligence Agency after the paper published an article critical of the president. He was released a few days later after an international outcry.

International human rights bodies were also critical of the female genital mutilation that continued to be practiced widely in the country, but President Jammeh publicly opposed banning it on the grounds that it was part of the country's culture. Meanwhile, a group of Gambians living in the U.S. formed a Save the Gambia Fund to promote democratic change in their country of origin and prepare for the 2006 presidential election. (CHRISTOPHER SAUNDERS)

GEORGIA

Area: 69,700 sq km (26,911 sq mi)
Population (2003 est.): 4,934,000
Capital: Tbilisi
Head of state and government: Presidents Eduard Shevardnadze and, from November 23, Nino Burdjanadze (acting), assisted by Ministers of State Avtandil Djorbenadze and, from November 27, Zurab Zhvania

Following disagreements among the Georgian leadership in January 2003 over the optimum approach to resolving the Abkhaz conflict, the opposition National Movement and New Rights Party claimed in early February that senior government officials were planning to oust Pres. Eduard Shevardnadze, who rejected those allegations as implausible.

In early April the pro-Shevardnadze Citizens' Union of Georgia and the Socialist Party formed the For a New Georgia (AS) bloc to contest the parliamentary elections scheduled for November 2. In August Chairman of the Parliament Nino Burdjanadze and her predecessor Zurab Zhvania aligned to form the Burdjanadze-Democrats election bloc.

Nine blocs and 12 political parties registered to contest the election, which international observers condemned as marred by falsification and the exclusion of tens of thousands of names from voter lists. Preliminary official returns showed AS in the lead with 27.8% of the vote, followed next by the Saakashvili–National Movement bloc, headed by former justice minister Mikhail Saakashvili, with 23.1%, while informal exit polls showed Saakashvili the winner with 20–27%. Beginning on November 4, Burdjanadze, Zhvania, and Saakashvili convened repeated demonstrations in Tbilisi to demand that the election results be annulled; Saakashvili also demanded Shevardnadze's resignation. On November 20 the U.S. condemned as falsified the final returns that gave AS 21.39% of the vote, followed by Adjar leader Aslan Abashidze's Democratic Revival Union's 18.84% and the Saakashvili bloc's 18.8%.

On November 22 Saakashvili and thousands of unarmed supporters occupied the Parliament building, where Shevardnadze was addressing the first session of the new legislature. Shevardnadze fled and declared a state of emergency but then announced his resignation late on November 23 following talks with the three opposition leaders mediated by Russian Foreign Minister Igor Ivanov.

The outgoing Parliament confirmed Burdjanadze as acting president and on November 25 scheduled a preterm presidential ballot for Jan. 4, 2004, in which Saakashvili and five other candidates registered.

The International Monetary Fund suspended cooperation with Georgia in August, citing tax-collection shortfalls and lagging systemic reform. The new

Joyous Georgian opposition supporters, who had demanded the resignation of Pres. Eduard Shevardnadze, wave flags atop a tank as they celebrate his decision to step down in order to avoid a bloody confrontation.

leadership appealed in late November for emergency international aid.

President Shevardnadze and his Russian counterpart, Vladimir Putin, signed an agreement on March 7 on a number of confidence-building measures to promote a settlement of the Abkhaz conflict, including the resumption of rail transport through Abkhazia and the return of Georgian displaced persons. The planned deployment of a UN police force to Abkhazia was delayed.

(ELIZABETH FULLER)

GERMANY

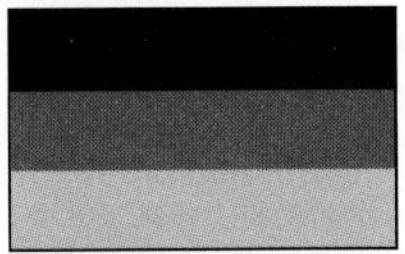

Area: 357,021 sq km (137,847 sq mi)
Population (2003 est.): 82,604,000
Capital: Berlin; some ministries remain in Bonn
Chief of state: President Johannes Rau
Head of government: Chancellor Gerhard Schröder

For Germany 2003 marked the cautious beginning of an economic-reform process that the country had debated for two decades. The momentum of Chancellor Gerhard Schröder's 2002 reelection victory quickly evaporated, however, as Germans entered the new year in a deep economic crisis, with spiraling public debt and stubbornly high unemployment that was eating its way into the middle class. In the past, German governments had blamed the country's economic weakness on outside influences, but by early 2003 there was a growing public understanding that what some Europeans called "the German disease" was homemade. Even a healthier world economy, an increasing number of Germans realized, would not lift the economic fortunes of their country, whose problems were structural rather than cyclic. Internationally Germany at first stood alone after it categorically rejected any participation in a possible U.S. military campaign against Iraq. The move not only angered Germany's U.S. allies but also isolated the country from fellow Europeans, including the French, who had so far not ruled out their support for military action. In foreign affairs most of the year was therefore consumed by damage control. First, Germany lobbied France, Russia, and other nations to join its antiwar stance, and later in the year it worked on mending fences with the Americans.

Domestic Affairs. The German government suffered a serious setback on February 2 when its bigger component, the Social Democratic Party (SPD), lost elections in two of Germany's 16 federal states. In both Hesse and Lower Saxony, which held elections on the same day, the party suffered double-digit percentage losses. The ballot marked a triumph for the country's centre-right opposition, which also emerged strengthened in the upper house of the national parliament, the Bundesrat. With a majority in the Bundesrat, where the states were represented, the opposition could block government moves. The defeat in Lower Saxony was an additional embarrassment to Chancellor Schröder because it prompted a change to a conservative government in his home state. In both regions voters said their decision had been influenced by frustration with the federal government. Opinion polls revealed that to many the primary bones of contention were education and the economy. In preelection rallies Schröder and other leaders of the SPD and Greens had tried to shift the campaign's focus to the looming war in Iraq. While the government's pacifist stance had helped it to win the national election four months earlier, it did not score many votes this time around.

Along with Germany's pressing economic problems, the sorry state of its schools and universities was an issue of public concern in 2003. Germany's education system, like its economy, was once considered one of the best in Europe, but in recent years educational standards had continuously slipped. A growing number of elite students left for foreign universities, often in the U.S., and many never returned, which created a harmful brain drain. Germans also realized that the quality of their primary and secondary schools had worsened. At German schools classes were held only in the morning. Students were generally home by lunchtime, after an average of three hours of classes in elementary school and less than five in high schools. A shortage of teachers caused frequent cancellations of classes.

A state election on September 21 in Bavaria was another disappointment for the SPD. The Socialists were never expected to win in the deeply conservative region. With good schools, economic growth, and a jobless rate of 6.6%—well below the national average of 10.4%—Bavaria had also retained an image of success that had eluded the rest of the country. Even so, the SPD suffered its worst defeat since World War II, scoring less than 20% of the vote while the ruling Christian Social Union (CSU) was supported by nearly 60.7% of voters. It was a day of sweet revenge for the conservative state governor Edmund Stoiber, who had lost to Schröder in the national vote a year earlier. The CSU comeback bolstered Stoiber's claim to challenge Schröder again in the next federal election.

While giving Germany's conservatives a boost, the state ballots also revealed the deep divisions among them. Stoiber's leadership claim was rivaled by national party chair Angela Merkel, who also reserved for herself the right to stand in the next election. Although the next national vote was not to be held until 2006, the chancellor and Foreign Minister Joschka Fischer had already announced that they would run again.

In addition, the Christian Democratic Union (CDU) and its Bavarian sister party, Stoiber's CSU, fought about

Fereshta Ludin, an Afghan-born teacher in Stuttgart, Ger., faces the Constitutional Court after its ruling that Muslim women may wear headscarves in classrooms. The right to wear religious clothing in public was an issue in several European countries.

whether they should block or support the government's economic reforms. In September a prominent party official, Friedrich Merz, threatened to step down as deputy parliamentary leader in protest against a compromise on health reforms agreed to by the CDU with the government. Merz's threat was later withdrawn, but it showed the leadership disputes that had plagued the opposition since its longtime leader, former chancellor Helmut Kohl, was ousted by Schröder in 1998. Worse, it cast uncertainty over Schröder's chances of reforming the economy, which depended on the opposition's cooperation.

On March 29 some 40,000 people formed a human chain at Berlin's Brandenburg Gate to protest the U.S.-led war in Iraq, while another 50,000 demonstrators packed into the German capital.

© AFP/Corbis

The Economy. In 2003 the German government proposed a series of economic reforms. Europe's biggest economy was in a sorry state. Unemployment stubbornly hovered around 10%, growth was anemic, and social spending had reached close to 30% of GDP, the highest rate of any country in the world except Sweden. The growing struggle to finance this generous welfare system continuously threatened to send public deficits past the European Union's budget-deficit limits for members of the euro zone. In March unemployment jumped to a five-year high of 11.3%. The government blamed the weak world economy and the war in Iraq. Still, in a widely anticipated speech on March 14, Schröder unveiled his so-called Agenda 2010, a sweeping package of economic and welfare reforms.

"We must find the courage to expect of ourselves and our country the changes that are needed to bring it back to the peak of economic and social development in Europe," Schröder told Parliament in the address. Among other things, he proposed cuts in jobless benefits, a loosening of labour market restrictions, a simpler tax code for small companies, more flexibility from industrywide wage agreements, an adjustment of the pension formula to reduce benefits, more competition between health care providers, and a reduction of benefits covered by the state medical insurance scheme. In the area of fiscal policy, Schröder's plans included supporting municipalities and the construction sector with subsidized loans worth €15 billion (about $17 million), boosting the revenues of municipalities, and reforming local taxes, as well as reducing interest income and introducing a capital-gains tax. German industry welcomed the plan as a step in the right direction but charged that Schröder's proposals did not go far enough. Keenly aware that some of his plans would anger the unions and raise questions about his credentials as a Social Democrat, Schröder had not touched two key parts of Germany's economic system: sectorwide wage agreements and workers' co-determination. This omission was harmful, some critics said, because both practices were leading obstacles to higher growth and employment.

Party traditionalists also attacked Schröder's reform plan. A dozen SPD deputies signed a petition calling for an inner-party referendum on Agenda 2010, which they saw as a betrayal of the SPD's long-standing commitment to social justice. Schröder, who was both chancellor and SPD chairman, responded with a "back me or sack me" strategy. He rejected major changes to the reform plan and scheduled a series of regional party meetings, as well as a special SPD congress on June 1. After repeated threats to resign, Schröder won an overwhelming endorsement for the changes from the party conference. The SPD's coalition partner, the Greens, approved the reform plan two weeks later, and the German cabinet formalized Agenda 2010 in August.

Germany's powerful unions rejected the reforms as well. Addressing traditional May Day rallies, Schröder faced booing and whistling. The unions had another battle to fight, however. A labour strike in June for a shorter workweek in eastern Germany drew sharp public criticism, as Germans felt that the action could damage their already feeble economy. IG Metall, the country's largest industrial union, insisted that the strikes were necessary to put eastern workers on par with their western counterparts by shortening their workweek from 38 to 35 hours, which was standard in much of western Germany. In addition, the union said, a shorter workweek would create some 15,000 jobs.

The walkouts forced automakers across the country, such as BMW, Volkswagen, and DaimlerChrysler, to shut down assembly lines for lack of parts. The strike hit car companies at a time when they were already struggling with a stagnant economy and a stronger euro. In opinion polls a majority of Germans said that they had no sympathy for the strikers. Even most Social Democrats, many of whom were card-carrying unionists, agreed. After four weeks of strikes, IG Metall gave up. The defeat was one of the worst setbacks since the 1950s for Germany's organized labour, which was already reeling from a steady loss of members. In July IG Metall's longtime chairman Klaus Zwickel stepped down earlier than expected out of protest that his deputy, who was responsible for the failed strike, was to become his successor.

The end of the strike coincided with another market-friendly move by the government. In late June Schröder announced that he would accelerate a sweeping tax cut to accelerate lacklustre consumption in Germany. The government said that it would bring the tax cuts, worth €18 billion (about $20.5 billion), forward by a year. They had originally been scheduled for 2005 and came on top of tax cuts planned to go in effect in 2004. Together their two rounds of tax cuts would bring the top income-tax rate down to 42% from 48.5% and the bottom rate to 15% from 19%.

The cuts presented a fresh challenge to Germany's already-strapped state budget. By the summer the country was on track to exceed the EU's deficit limit for the third year in a row. Schröder, along with his French counterparts, increasingly challenged that limit. He repeatedly warned the EU against becoming fixated on curbing deficits and ignoring member countries' need for economic growth. In August Germany tipped into recession after having recorded two consecutive quarters of economic contraction. In September Schröder and French Pres. Jacques Chirac proposed a multibillion-euro spending plan to beef up Europe's infrastructure and spur their flailing economies.

In the fall the government worked on pushing Agenda 2010 through Parliament. In mid-December, however, opposition leaders forced Schröder to modify his plan. Under the new agreement, the tax cuts would be distributed evenly over 2004 and 2005. Compromises were also reached on a number of other provisions of Agenda 2010.

Foreign Relations. In international relations 2003 was largely consumed by German efforts to come in from the cold after Berlin's lone rejection of military action against Iraq. The move had angered the U.S. and isolated Germany from its European allies at a time when the European Union was working on a common foreign policy.

Help came on January 22 during a trip Schröder took to Paris to celebrate 40 years of Franco-German cooperation. For months France had left open the option to join the U.S. in a military campaign. It had also backed an initial resolution of the UN Security Council authorizing a possible war on Iraq. Now France joined Germany in an outright rejection of a military campaign. The agreement was a historic turning point; over the years the U.S. had had periodic spats with its European allies, but never before had Europe's two most powerful countries teamed up to challenge Washington's top foreign priority, in this case the removal of Iraqi dictator Saddam Hussein. (*See* BIOGRAPHIES.) The German-French understanding also split European nations between those that embraced the U.S. plans and those that opposed them. The U.S. was dismayed. In January, U.S. Secretary of Defense Donald Rumsfeld dismissed Germany and France as part of an "old Europe" that was losing in importance to a "new Europe," consisting of the new Western-allied countries such as Poland and Hungary, which supported the Iraq invasion. Foreign Minister Fischer returned the insult by telling Rumsfeld at a security conference in Munich that he was "not convinced" by U.S. reasoning for intervention. France and Germany actively lobbied other nations to join the antiwar camp. In February Russia's foreign minister began to echo France in threatening to veto a second UN resolution. Late that month Schröder traveled to Moscow to lobby Russian Pres. Vladimir Putin to side with the Franco-German alliance. Russia eventually did so, boosting the international opposition to U.S. plans. Also in February Merkel went to Washington. U.S. leaders expressed their bitterness about Germany's stance and talked about moving U.S. military bases from Germany to friendlier and cheaper countries in Eastern Europe.

When hostilities began in Iraq in late March, Germany was awash in peace demonstrations. Tens of thousands protested what they saw as an American violation of international law and demanded that Schröder deny the U.S. overflight rights and use of its military installations in Germany.

In April the leaders of France, Germany, Belgium, and Luxembourg held talks on boosting defense cooperation and reducing Europe's military reliance on the U.S. Participants said the plans were not directed against NATO but aimed to strengthen the European pillar in the transatlantic alliance. Also in April Schröder made his first attempt to patch up differences within Europe and with the U.S. by speaking out in support of the removal of Iraqi leader Saddam Hussein. In a speech to Parliament, the German leader said he hoped the war would end swiftly with "a victory for the allies." A month later, during a visit to Berlin by U.S. Secretary of State Colin Powell, he backed a U.S. push to lift sanctions against Iraq. Soon afterward Schröder shook hands with U.S. Pres. George W. Bush at a meeting of the Group of Eight in Évian, France. A more formal meeting of the two leaders came in September in New York, where Bush lobbied UN member states for financial and military help in Iraq. Yet differences continued about Iraq's postwar affairs. Germany, along with France and Russia, rejected U.S. pleas to share among states the burden of Iraqi reconstruction. An American draft resolution before the UN called for a multinational force to help bring order to Iraq. Germany and others wanted the UN to play a greater role than foreseen in the U.S. proposal. They also argued that Washington should hand over political authority to Iraqis as soon as possible.

(CECILIE ROHWEDDER)

GHANA

Area: 238,533 sq km (92,098 sq mi)
Population (2003 est.): 20,468,000
Capital: Accra
Head of state and government: President John Agyekum Kufuor

On Jan. 14, 2003, Ghana's National Reconciliation Commission, which had been established to find means of redressing the past abuses of Ghanaian citizens, began hearing petitions from alleged victims of the human rights abuses under former military regimes. Most complaints lodged throughout 2003 focused on events during the years that Jerry Rawlings was in power (1979 and 1981–2000).

On January 17 the government raised fuel prices by 90.4% to aid its ailing state refinery, an action that put a new strain on citizens of all economic classes. Nevertheless, the ruling party won control of Parliament by a slim margin in a decisive by-election. Ghana was faced with weighty issues of international investment as well. On February 10, Telekom Malaysia filed for international arbitration in its dispute with the Ghanaian government over the fate of approximately $100 million of investments and services. In October the government approved Ashanti Goldfields' merger with South African Anglogold to create a new gold-mining giant.

From June through August Ghana played host to high-profile peace talks aimed at ending a violent rebellion in Liberia. The United Nations-sponsored Special Court for Sierra Leone indicted Liberian Pres. Charles Taylor upon his arrival in Ghana and attempted to capture him while he was traveling outside Liberia. The Ghanaian government, however, quickly spirited Taylor back to his home country instead of detaining him, which prompted harsh criticism by the UN. The Liberian peace talks resulted in a power-sharing agreement after Taylor went into exile in Nigeria.

(ANDREW EISENBERG)

GREECE

Area: 131,957 sq km (50,949 sq mi)
Population (2003 est.): 11,001,000
Capital: Athens
Chief of state: President Konstantinos Stephanopoulos
Head of government: Prime Minister Konstantinos Simitis

In a Greek prison four men accused of being members of the terrorist organization November 17 are photographed during a break in their trial in June. The government was eager to neutralize terrorist threats well in advance of the Olympic Summer Games scheduled to open in Athens on Aug. 13, 2004.

During the first half of 2003, when Greece held the rotating European Union presidency, a number of notable events took place. The accession treaty for the 10 countries that would join the EU in 2004 was signed in Athens on April 16, and the draft EU constitution was presented to the leaders of the member states at the EU summit in Thessaloniki on June 19–20. Meanwhile, the war in Iraq put the Greek government in the position of trying to reconcile diverging views among EU member states while at the same time attempting to take a balanced approach to the conflict, despite overwhelmingly negative public opinion at home against the war; there were mass protests throughout the spring.

On March 3 in Athens, amid great public interest and tight security measures, the trial began for the 19 persons accused of membership in the terrorist organization November 17. The trial ended in December with the conviction of 15 of the defendants. While many of the defendants had admitted membership in November 17 and confessed to the individual crimes with which they were charged, the group's alleged mastermind, Alexandros Giotopoulos, had denied any involvement. Giotopoulos was among five defendants who received multiple life sentences. In early February police also arrested five suspected members of the Revolutionary People's Struggle (ELA), a terrorist group that claimed responsibility for two killings and numerous bomb attacks in 1975–95.

Throughout the year political parties tried to position themselves for the parliamentary elections due in April 2004 at the latest. Clearly leading in opinion polls, the conservative New Democracy party demanded early elections, but Prime Minister Konstantinos ("Kostas") Simitis insisted that the polls would not take place until the end of the parliament's four-year term.

On July 2 Simitis announced that government ministers could no longer be members of the ruling Panhellenic Socialist Movement's (PASOK) Executive Bureau and that those who were both would have to choose between posts. At the same time, he asked PASOK's general secretary, Konstantinos ("Kostas") Laliotis, to give up his party post and return to government. Laliotis turned down the request and resigned. On July 3 PASOK's Central Committee approved a new Executive Bureau and Simitis's choice as party general secretary, Michalis Chrysochoidis. After Chrysochoidis gave up his position as minister of public order, Simitis carried out a minor government reshuffle on July 4, but most government ministers kept their jobs.

On September 2 Simitis unveiled a €1.7 billion (about $1.85 billion) "social package" of measures aimed at supporting farmers, families, and small- and medium-sized enterprises, a move that would increase PASOK's chances in the upcoming elections. This announcement was followed by another on September 10 that introduced a "social charter" for the period 2004–08 that was aimed at reducing unemployment and bringing average income closer to the EU average.

Outside the EU presidency, Greek foreign policy was dominated by attempts to find a solution to the Cyprus problem before the divided island joined the EU in 2004. Despite the failure to reach a breakthrough and despite frequent violations of Greek airspace by Turkish fighter places, relations with Ankara remained stable. As in previous years, no compromise was found on Macedonia's name, but the Greek government took a positive step in August when it allowed several hundred refugees of the Greek Civil War living in Macedonia to enter Greece to visit their hometowns.

As a result of previous delays, preparations for the 2004 Olympic Games continued under a very tight schedule. In August a series of test events took place, and most of them were successfully executed. The rowing event, however, was marred by strong winds, and several boats sank. (*See* SPORTS AND GAMES: *Rowing.*) A *Washington Post* article criticizing security arrangements for the Olympics was dismissed by the organizing committee on September 28.

The Greek economy was expected to grow by 3.5% in 2003, while unemployment decreased from 9.6% to 8.9% in the second quarter, compared with 2002. Year-on-year inflation was 3.3% in August; prices of some goods, however, in particular foodstuff, increased substantially, in some cases doubling. The Athens Stock Exchange closed at 2,203.56 points on December 23, up from 1,748.42 points at the end of the previous year.

On August 29 the government presented a draft law for the creation of a new national carrier, Olympic Airlines. Under the draft debt-ridden Olympic Airways would be broken up into separate companies to be put up for privatization, with Olympic Airlines retaining only the flight operations and a significantly reduced staff. On June 26 a new private carrier, Hellas Jet, began operations. (STEFAN KRAUSE)

GRENADA

Area: 344 sq km (133 sq mi)
Population (2003 est.): 102,000
Capital: Saint George's
Chief of state: Queen Elizabeth II, represented by Governor-General Sir Daniel Williams
Head of government: Prime Minister Keith Mitchell

The International Monetary Fund approved an emergency $4 million loan for Grenada in January 2003 to help cover the foreign- exchange costs associated with the restoration of physical assets that had been destroyed by a tropical storm in September 2002. Damage caused to the country's economic infrastructure, commercial and private property, and agriculture amounted to almost 2% of gross domestic product. Almost a third of agricultural export income was lost.

After having passed the necessary anti-money-laundering laws, Grenada was removed in February and May, respectively, from the "blacklists" imposed by the Paris-based Financial Action Task Force and the U.S. Department of the Treasury's Financial Crimes Enforcement Network. By midyear only five offshore banks were still operating locally.

Grenada was added to the list of Caribbean territories enjoying a competitive telecommunications environment; the Irish company Digicel began operating a cellular service alongside traditional provider Cable & Wireless.

In the general election in November, the governing New National Party (NNP) barely held onto office, winning 8 seats in the House of Representatives to the 7 seats secured by the National Democratic Congress. NNP leader Keith Mitchell thus retained the prime ministership for a third consecutive term. (DAVID RENWICK)

GUATEMALA

Area: 109,117 sq km (42,130 sq mi)
Population (2003 est.): 12,347,000
Capital: Guatemala City
Head of state and government: President Alfonso Portillo Cabrera

Political violence and disruption characterized Guatemala during 2003. Opponents of Pres. Alfonso Portillo accused his administration of corruption, fraud, and incompetence. Overshadowing the president in the public eye, however, was Efraín Ríos Montt, head of the ruling Guatemalan Republican Front and the leading contender to succeed Portillo as president. Ríos Montt had previously been deemed ineligible for the presidency, but in July the Court of Constitutionality ruled that he could run in the November election. Though there was widespread criticism of this decision, Ríos Montt withstood all legal challenges. Oscar Berger of the Grand National Alliance and Alvaro Colom of the National Unity of Hope party were Ríos Montt's principal challengers in the election. In the first round of voting, held on November 9, Ríos Montt finished well behind both Berger and Colom, and in the December 28 runoff, Berger claimed the presidency with 54% of the vote to Colom's 46%. Berger was set to take office on Jan. 14, 2004.

Negotiations for a U.S.–Central American Free Trade Agreement (CAFTA) continued throughout the year, but serious disagreements delayed conclusion of a treaty. After Pres. George W. Bush met with the Central American presidents in April, Guatemala unilaterally proposed to allow most U.S. goods to enter the country duty-free, but this angered the other Central American states. In January the U.S. decertified Guatemala as an ally in its war on drugs; it did not implement penalties, however, and the decertification was thus rendered largely symbolic. The U.S. Drug Enforcement Agency repeatedly charged that Guatemala was a transshipment point for Colombian cocaine and heroin. Guatemala's refusal to support the U.S.-led war in Iraq brought the Portillo government considerable popular support but contributed to a cooling in U.S. relations.

Human rights violations continued to haunt Guatemala, and thousands of Guatemalans fled their country for Mexico and the U.S. In 2003 the Bush administration's policy against illegal immigration led to the forcible repatriation of many. The Inter-American Press Association cited Guatemala for restraints on press freedom after President Portillo allegedly threatened and intimidated editors. Press credibility, however, increased, as did newspaper circulation. When a Guatemalan appeals court on May 7 reversed the conviction of a military officer who had allegedly ordered the 1990 assassination of sociologist Myrna Mack, international criticism of the Guatemalan judicial system soared. Strikes and labour unrest were also on the rise.

Archbishop Rodolfo Quezada Toruno was among 31 new cardinals named by Pope John Paul II in September. (RALPH LEE WOODWARD, JR.)

AP/Wide World Photos

A young supporter of Guatemalan presidential candidate Oscar Berger participates in a rally near Guatemala City on October 12.

GUINEA

Area: 245,857 sq km (94,926 sq mi)
Population (2003 est.): 8,480,000
Capital: Conakry
Head of state and government: President Gen. Lansana Conté, assisted by Prime Minister Lamine Sidimé

A series of protests in both the capital and rural areas led to numerous confrontations with security forces in 2003. In Conakry hundreds of young people took to the streets on January 31 to demonstrate against water shortages and daily power outages. Electricity cuts resulted in blackouts in most of the city from 7 AM until midnight. Only the areas containing government buildings and official residences were getting power 24 hours a day. The government blamed the low rainfall in 2002 for the problem, but many Guineans attributed it to poor management and the failure to complete a merger with a French power company. The police killed a student on March 13 during violent protests against fuel price increases. On June 10 in the Koya district, 50 km (30 mi) from the capital, police killed a local man suspected of drug dealing. In the demonstrations that followed, furious residents set fire to the police station and the prefect's house, and security forces killed a protester.

On June 8 Alpha Condé, leader of the opposition Rally of the Guinean People (RPG), accompanied by several politicians from other West African nations, flew into Conakry to attend a conference on the role of political parties in a democracy. Although the foreign dignitaries had visas, immigration officials refused to let them enter the country. When the police attempted to disperse the large crowd of waiting RPG supporters, riots broke out. Forty RPG members were arrested. The government defended its actions on the grounds that the conference was unauthorized and that the presence of Condé's guests would lead to public unrest. On July 25 six opposition parties declined a government offer to attend talks on the conduct of the upcoming presidential election, and they demanded that an independent electoral commission be established and privately owned radio and TV stations be allowed to operate in the country. By the end of September, however, talks were set to resume. Pres. Lansana Conté, despite increasingly bad health, announced that he would stand for reelection. He had ruled the country since the 1984 coup.

(NANCY ELLEN LAWLER)

GUINEA-BISSAU

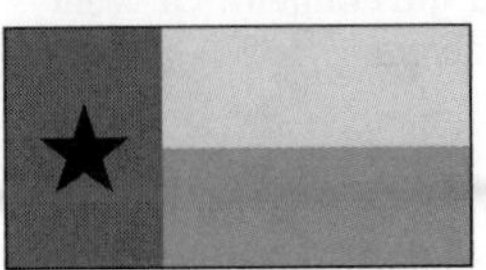

Area: 36,125 sq km (13,948 sq mi)
Population (2003 est.): 1,361,000
Capital: Bissau
Chief of state: Presidents Kumba Ialá (Yalla), Gen. Verissimo Correia Seabra (acting) from September 14, and, from September 28, Henrique Pereira Rosa (acting).
Head of government: Prime Ministers Mario Pires and, from September 28, Antonio Artur Sanhá

Guinea-Bissau remained one of the poorest countries in the world and was beset with political upheaval in 2003. Alleging various coup plots against him, Pres. Kumba Ialá frequently dismissed ministers, resorted to attacks on the judiciary and the independent media, and summarily arrested opponents. In November 2002, after the parliament passed a motion of no confidence in him, he dissolved it and called for a legislative election within 90 days.

The election was postponed three times in 2003, but before it could take place, on September 14 Ialá was deposed in a coup led by Gen. Verissimo Correia Seabra and placed under house arrest. Other African countries condemned the coup, but most political and civic leaders in Guinea-Bissau welcomed it. The junta's choice of businessman Henrique Pereira Rosa as interim president met general acceptance, but most political leaders were unhappy with its installation of Antonio Artur Sanhá, the secretary-general of the Social Renovation Party, as prime minister of an interim government. At the end of September the military junta signed an agreement with political and civil groups to form a National Transition Council, which met under Seabra's chairmanship, to act in place of parliament until legislative elections could be held.

(CHRISTOPHER SAUNDERS)

GUYANA

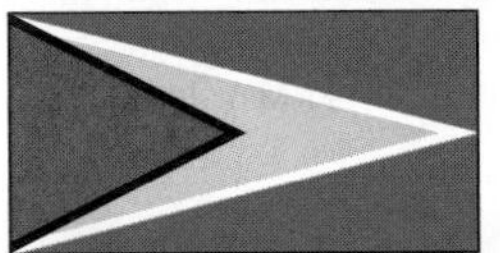

Area: 215,083 sq km (83,044 sq mi)
Population (2003 est.): 778,000
Capital: Georgetown
Chief of state: President Bharrat Jagdeo
Head of government: Prime Minister Sam Hinds

The opposition People's National Congress (PNC) acquired a new leader in February 2003, when attorney Robert Corbin succeeded Desmond Hoyte, who had died in December 2002. Corbin promptly led the PNC back into the National Assembly; the party had refused to take up its 27 seats in 2002.

American diplomat Stephen Lesniak was kidnapped in April while playing

Verissimo Correia Seabra (on left) and an army colleague make an appearance a few days after the bloodless coup Seabra led in Guinea-Bissau on September 14. Two weeks later Seabra turned over the interim presidency to Henrique Rosa.

AP/Wide World Photos

golf and was held for 10 hours. A ransom for his release was reportedly paid by a female friend. He was the 18th kidnap victim in Guyana in a year. Washington sent a special team to Georgetown to investigate the incident.

Guyana began to pursue two transcontinental infrastructure projects that could, according to Foreign Affairs Minister Rudy Insanally, position the country as a gateway to Latin America. Plans progressed for the upgrading of the Guyana-Brazil highway and a new road project linking Georgetown with Caracas, Venez.

Following pressure from the U.S. government, Guyana agreed in July to exempt U.S. citizens from prosecution at the International Criminal Court (ICC) in The Hague. The administration in Washington was a strong opponent of the ICC and suspended military aid during the year to six Caribbean countries that had declined to follow Guyana's example. In September Guyanese Pres. Bharrat Jagdeo was among an exclusive group of Caribbean leaders invited to a breakfast meeting with U.S. Pres. George W. Bush in New York City. (DAVID RENWICK)

HAITI

Area: 27,700 sq km (10,695 sq mi)
Population (2003 est.): 7,528,000
Capital: Port-au-Prince
Chief of state and government: President Jean-Bertrand Aristide, assisted by Prime Minister Yvon Neptune

The political crisis emanating from the disputed May 2000 parliamentary elections continued to cast a pall over Haiti in 2003. In September 2002 the Organization of American States (OAS) had adopted Permanent Council Resolution 822 (CP Res. 822) as a framework for negotiating a solution to the crisis. The OAS struggled, however, in the creation of a multisectoral Provisional Electoral Council (CEP) to organize a new round of parliamentary elections. The principle opposition group, Democratic Convergence (CD), refused to name representatives to the council, citing the government's unwillingness to ensure electoral security. In August the government of Pres. Bertrand Aristide announced plans to hold elections in November 2003, with or without CD participation, citing the constitutionally mandated necessity to renew parliamentary seats that were due to expire in early 2004. By year's end, however, elections had not been held.

A provision of CP Res. 822—the separation of Haiti's political crisis from the ongoing suspension of international financial assistance to the government—facilitated several important economic developments. Following negotiation of a stand-by agreement with the International Monetary Fund, in July the government settled its $32 million arrears with the Inter-American Development Bank, opening the door to the resumption of disbursements of about $200 million in development loans that were suspended after the disputed 2000 elections. These loans—earmarked for infrastructure, health, and education projects—were significant, given the continuing deterioration of the country's economy and the lack of investment in its physical and human infrastructure. The approximately $800 million in remittances sent home by Haitians living overseas, an estimated 20% of Haiti's gross national product, served as an economic lifeline for millions of Haitians who struggled to make ends meet following a 60% depreciation of the national currency (gourde) between September 2002 and March 2003.

Buffeting Haiti were continuing trends toward lawlessness, politically inspired street violence, and an overall growing climate of insecurity. The Haitian National Police, with fewer than 4,000 members, struggled throughout the year with increased politicization and its inability to respond consistently to street and gang violence. A national civil society organization, the Group of 184, formed in 2002 as a potential moderating political force, evolved toward staunch opposition of the government, leading confrontational demonstrations that called for the resignation of President Aristide. As the Jan. 1, 2004, bicentennial of Haiti's independence neared, most Haitians had little to celebrate. (ROBERT MAGUIRE)

HONDURAS

Area: 112,492 sq km (43,433 sq mi)
Population (2003 est.): 6,803,000
Capital: Tegucigalpa
Head of state and government: President Ricardo Maduro

Crime issues dominated Honduran politics in 2003. Pres. Ricardo Maduro continued his "zero tolerance" policy and targeted gang violence. The Congress passed two major laws as part of the government's efforts to combat crime; in July citizens were required to surrender all firearms, and in August

Despite the fact that maras, *or youth gangs, were outlawed in Honduras in 2003, as many as 100,000 gang members were still terrorizing the country. Here, members of two* maras *are processed by police officers in Tegucigalpa in September.*

AP/Wide World Photos

membership in a gang became illegal. Despite Maduro's aggressive tactics, detractors claimed that his programs were not yet a success and that the only solution to the crime problem was to address its root causes: poverty and the lack of education and jobs. International attention was drawn to the crime problem on April 5 when a gang fight in the El Porvenir prison left 69 inmates dead and approximately 33 injured. The riot caused a government scandal when investigations showed that prison guards had shot many inmates.

Government efforts to bring economic indicators in line with International Monetary Fund requirements created much popular unrest. Honduras's three-year loan agreement with the IMF had expired at the end of 2002, and by September 2003 the country still had not reached an agreement with the IMF for new loans, which severely constrained public finance. To appease the IMF, the government tried to broaden the tax base and reduce spending by cutting government jobs and freezing public-sector wages. These policies met with repeated strikes, particularly in the health, education, and transportation sectors.

In international affairs Honduras participated with the other four Central American countries in negotiations with the United States to establish a Central American Free Trade Agreement. Honduras was also part of the "coalition of the willing"—countries that supported the U.S.-led war to oust Saddam Hussein—and in July Honduras sent a contingent of 370 troops to Iraq to serve under Polish command in an effort to internationalize the forces occupying Iraq.

(MICHELLE M. TAYLOR-ROBINSON)

HUNGARY

Area: 93,030 sq km (35,919 sq mi)
Population (2003 est.): 10,136,000
Capital: Budapest
Chief of state: President Ferenc Madl
Head of government: Prime Minister Peter Medgyessy

The year 2003 would be remembered for the signing by Prime Minister Peter Medgyessy of the EU accession treaty and also for emerging rifts between Hungary and core EU states France and Germany. In January Medgyessy joined several EU countries as well as the Czech Republic and Poland in signing an open letter in support of the U.S.-led intervention in Iraq. The endorsement of the war by Hungary, and other EU candidate states, sparked a major controversy within the EU. Within Hungary too the EU was seen as an increasingly problematic goal. In an April referendum, 84% of Hungarian voters approved EU membership, but the 45.6% turnout, the lowest among the eight former communist candidate countries, sent confusing signals to both Budapest and Brussels. The apathy and uncertainty among the public were rooted in the lacklustre government information campaign and the absence of societal debate on the conditions and implications of membership.

In response to a U.S. request, the National Assembly voted in June to send a 233-strong peacekeeping contingent to Iraq. It later also began negotiations with Washington on the use of a military base in southern Hungary to train an Iraqi police force.

The country continued to be run by the ex-communist Hungarian Socialist Party, which in 2002 had scored a narrow victory over the conservative government led by the Fidesz-Hungarian Civic Alliance (then known as the Fidesz-Hungarian Civic Party). In May the National Assembly amended the "status law," which had caused controversy in neighbouring countries and was even criticized by the EU and the Council of Europe for noncompliance with European rules on nondiscrimination. Passed during the tenure of the previous, Fidesz-led government, the law had extended employment, education, health, and travel benefits to ethnic Hungarians living abroad. The new text no longer included the claim that Hungarians abroad form part of a "single

Wearing native costumes, women from a village east of Budapest vote in April in a referendum on Hungary's joining the European Union. Voter turnout was low, but 84% voted in favour of accession.

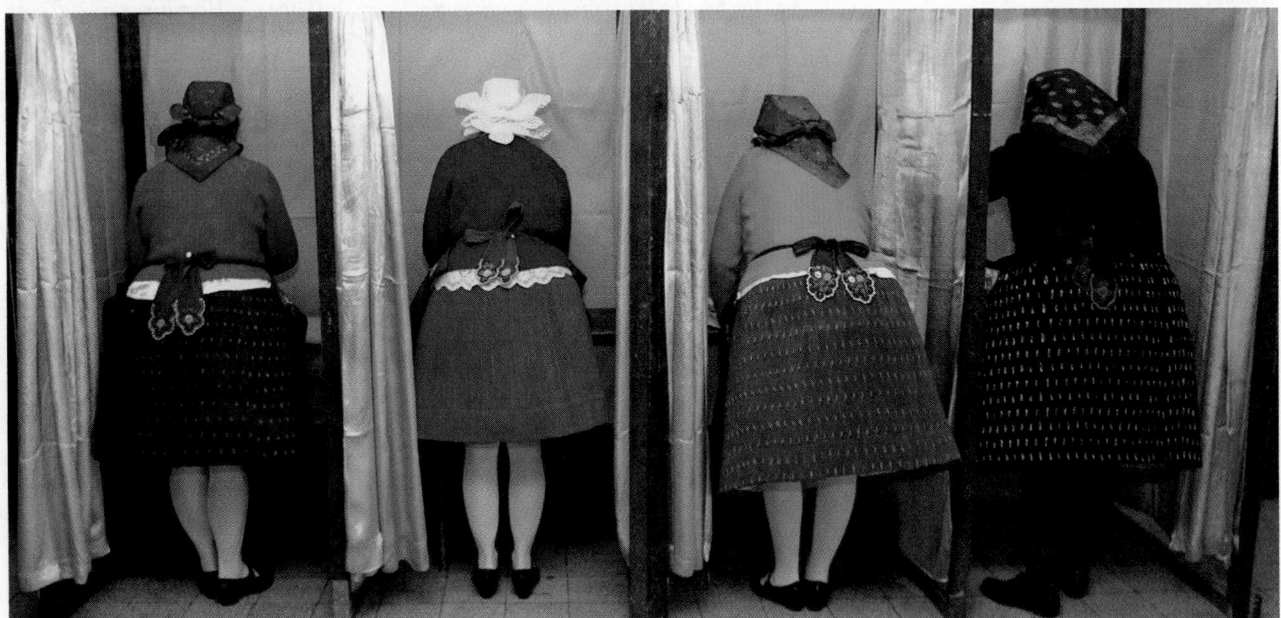

Hungarian nation"—an assertion that had angered Romania and Slovakia. Deleted too was the promise of work permits and social-security benefits for ethnic Magyars living outside Hungary.

In what was described as the "social paradigm of the century," the National Assembly in July passed a fundamental law reforming the operation of health care institutions. Strongly criticized by the opposition, the new legislation allowed the system's current owners—local and state governments—to sell up to 49% of the health care institutions to private investors and to run them as profit-oriented companies. The health minister soon resigned amid debates over the 2004 state budget and likely cuts in health spending.

The year also witnessed the unfolding of a large fraud scandal at K&H Equities, the stockbroker arm of K&H Bank, the country's second largest. The chief executive of the Belgian-Dutch-owned bank was arrested for mismanagement, and the police found links to Syrian businessmen suspected of money laundering. The investigation suggested that all questionable transactions had been executed by one investment adviser, but his so-called VIP-list included the names of several leading politicians and public personalities.

In synch with the European economic malaise, Hungary's GDP growth dropped from 3.3% in 2002 to 2.7% in 2003. Meanwhile, annual inflation soared to 5.2%, up from 4.6% the year before. The Hungarian National Bank repeatedly warned that the country would not meet the EU's convergence criteria for adopting the euro in 2008 unless the government took steps to tighten fiscal policy and reduce inflation.

(ZSOFIA SZILAGYI)

ICELAND

Area: 102,928 sq km (39,741 sq mi)
Population (2003 est.): 290,000
Capital: Reykjavík
Chief of state: President Ólafur Ragnar Grímsson
Head of government: Prime Minister Davíd Oddsson

Elections to Iceland's Althingi (parliament) took place on May 10, 2003. The incumbent coalition of the Independence and Progressive parties received 34 seats in the 63-member legislative body and continued in office. Prime Minister Davíd Oddsson, leader of the Independence Party, announced that he would step down on Sept. 1, 2004, to be succeeded by the foreign minister and Progressive Party leader, Halldór Ásgrímsson.

Iceland concluded a firm contract in March to build a hydroelectric-power facility at Kárahnjúkar and to sell the power to Alcoa Inc., which would build a 320,000-ton-per-year aluminum plant at Reyðarfjörður on the sparsely populated northeastern coast. The combined construction cost was estimated at $2.5 billion. The plant was expected to enter into production in 2007 and to create about 400 jobs in the depressed area.

The government also pursued the possibility of creating a controversial water reservoir at Nordlingaalda, in the southwestern part of the country. The reservoir would feed into a series of nearby hydroelectric-power stations and make it possible to sell power for the expansion of another aluminum plant near Reykjavík. In September the project was indefinitely shelved because of environmental objections.

In August the government decided to resume whaling, allowing a catch of 250 whales in 2003–04, of which 38 minke whales could be caught in 2003, all for scientific research. There were widespread protests from abroad but few from Icelanders.

The economy revived in 2003, following a shallow recession. Growth in GDP was estimated at 1½–2%, after a decline of ½% in 2002. The economy was expected to accelerate in 2004–06 because of the ongoing construction of the Kárahnjúkar power facility and the Alcoa aluminum plant, which would create up to 2,000 additional jobs during the peak period of construction activity in 2005–06. (BJÖRN MATTHÍASSON)

INDIA

Area: 3,166,414 sq km (1,222,559 sq mi)
Population (2003 est.): 1,065,462,000
Capital: New Delhi
Chief of state: President A.P.J. Abdul Kalam
Head of government: Prime Minister Atal Bihari Vajpayee

The monsoons make all the difference to life on the Indian subcontinent. The year 2003 would be remembered in India for the above-normal rainfall and the good feelings that it helped induce among citizens and investors.

Domestic Affairs. Politically, the year was one of anticipation. The Bharatiya Janata Party (BJP), the principal constituent of the ruling National Democratic Alliance, had been reduced to leading governments in only a handful of states, and it remained preoccupied with provincial elections scheduled for the end of the year in four northern states. Among other problems, because of the divisions and dissension among the BJP leadership, Prime Minister Atal Bihari Vajpayee's attempt to find a solution to the long-standing dispute over the Muslim Babri Masjid complex in Ayodhya and plans to build a Hindu temple there came to nought.

Given the persistent dissension within the BJP between the political moderates, best represented by the prime minister himself, and the *hindutva* hard-liners rallying around Narendra Modi, the chief minister of Gujarat state, political attention focused on the sharp communal divide within the country and, more important, within the BJP itself. Meanwhile, the Congress (I), the main opposition party at the centre (central government) but in power in a dozen states, quietly consolidated its position.

In the states Kerala mounted a new economic-reform campaign and sought foreign investment for its information technology and tourism sectors. In Tamil Nadu state Jayalalitha, the tough-minded chief minister and former actress, fought hard against the state's government employees' unions and succeeded in getting their strikes banned. Tamil Nadu's automobile industry acquired new lustre when South Korea's Hyundai began exporting cars to Europe from its Chennai (Madras) plant. In Karnataka and Andhra Pradesh, the boom in call centres and business process outsourcing continued, with thousands of new jobs being created.

In the north, elections were due in Rajasthan, Madhya Pradesh, and Delhi. The constant jockeying for power between various minority groups in Uttar Pradesh led to the ouster of the government headed by Chief Minister Mayawati of the BJP-supported Bahujan Samaj Party and the installation of Mulayam Singh Yadav and the Samajwadi Party. Chief Minister Mufti Mohammad Sayeed succeeded in restoring

Business process outsourcing continued to fuel bullish growth in India's computer software industry. Located in Bangalore's Electronics City, Infosys Technologies, whose server room is pictured here, was India's number one software exporter.

normalcy to Jammu and Kashmir by the summer months, and the state witnessed a welcome surge in tourist arrivals. These signs of stability, however, stirred terrorists groups to renewed action in August and September with bomb blasts in Srinagar.

The Economy. After five years of national income growth hovering around 5%, in 2003 India's economy registered a rate over 6%. A spurt in agricultural production due to a good monsoon revived market sentiment, and the Mumbai (Bombay) Stock Exchange witnessed a sustained rise in the stock market indexes, notwithstanding bomb blasts in Mumbai in August that were aimed at spreading nervousness in India's financial capital. Apart from an expected 7% growth in agricultural production that followed a year of a 3.5% decline, a 6% growth in industrial production and a 7% growth in services-sector income were expected to contribute to an overall 6.5% growth of national income. Increased investment demand in automobiles and related products, pharmaceuticals, steel, cement, and engineering goods boosted industrial growth. Part of the growth was fueled by public investment in infrastructure. The National Highways Authority was on course to implement a nationwide road-building program that would link the metropolitan areas of New Delhi, Mumbai, Kolkata (Calcutta), and Chennai with four-lane highways.

Despite a slowdown in global economic growth and an appreciation of the Indian rupee against the dollar, India's exports continued to grow in 2003 at double-digit rates, contributing to the sustained increase in the country's foreign-exchange reserves. The rupee appreciated by more than 5% against the dollar, mainly because of continued foreign-exchange inflows. Foreign-exchange reserves were expected to reach $95 billion by the end of 2003, and $100 billion by the end of fiscal 2003–04—that is, March 31, 2004. All these elements on the economic front generated what union Finance Minister Jaswant Singh termed a "feel-good feeling."

Responding to this robust external economic performance, the government enunciated a new policy on external aid and further liberalized economic transactions on current and capital accounts. New Delhi announced that India would stop accepting official development assistance from all but five countries—the U.S., the U.K., Germany, Russia, and Japan. India also prepaid some of its external debt, rescheduled a portion by replacing higher-cost debt with lower-cost debt, and increased its contribution to the International Monetary Fund. In his budget speech in February 2003, the finance minister announced the creation of a special fund to extend bilateral aid to less-developed countries in Southeast Asia and sub-Saharan Africa.

In the services sector the growth of business process outsourcing and information technology-enabled services helped generate new jobs in centres around New Delhi, Bangalore, and Hyderabad. India's software exports continued to grow, contributing to a 9% growth in services-sector income during the year.

Foreign Relations. The year began on a hopeful note with tensions between India and Pakistan winding down and New Delhi making a decision to demobilize troops from its western borders. On May 2 Prime Minister Vajpayee announced the restoration of diplomatic relations with Pakistan. The major foreign-policy challenge India had to grapple with in 2003, however, was whether to send its security forces to Iraq in response to a U.S. request. The matter was debated both within government and in public. The government took the view that it would consider the request only if Indian troops were sought as part of a United Nations peacekeeping force and would function under UN command. The government was restrained in its options by a parliamentary resolution critical of U.S. unilateral action in Iraq. Later, on a visit to UN headquarters in September, Vajpayee met with U.S. Pres. George W. Bush and reiterated India's official view on the need for a UN cover for sending troops to Iraq.

India also sought to improve bilateral relations with China. During the prime minister's visit to Beijing in June, it was agreed that border trade via Sikkim would resume. This was considered a major diplomatic win for India because China had not yet officially accepted Sikkim's accession to India. Bilateral trade with China grew at close to 90% in 2003, and China emerged as a major destination for Indian exports. Another important milestone in India's "Look East" policy was marked when talks began with Thailand on a free-trade agreement and a comprehensive economic-cooperation agreement was negotiated with Singapore. Together with other large less-developed economies, India was invited to the Group of Eight meeting at Evian, France, in June.

(SANJAYA BARU)

INDONESIA

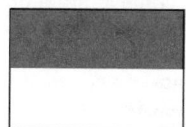

Area: 1,922,570 sq km (742,308 sq mi)
Population (2003 est.): 219,883,000
Capital: Jakarta
Head of state and government: President Megawati Sukarnoputri

Terrorism, separatism, economic growth, and the approaching 2004 general and presidential elections dominated Indonesian affairs during 2003. International attention had focused on the terrorism issue since the bombing of two nightclubs in Bali on Oct. 12, 2002, in which 202 people died.

The response of Pres. Megawati Sukarnoputri and her government to terrorism was mixed. Immediately after the Bali attack, the government took the unprecedented step of allowing in foreign police and intelligence services to assist Indonesian police with their investigations. It also introduced retroactive antiterrorism laws that gave the police and judiciary wider powers to deal with extremism. These measures met with considerable success. The clandestine al-Qaeda–linked Jemaah Islamiyah movement was quickly identified as having carried out the bombing, and more than 80 JI members were subsequently arrested. Several of the key figures were tried and sentenced to death. Indonesia's police and judicial systems, regarded in the past as among Asia's most corrupt and ineffective, won high praise on this occasion. The government, however, gave little leadership in the public debate over Islamic radicalism. Megawati repeatedly maintained that responsibility for combating terrorist ideology rested with Islamic leaders rather than with the government.

Despite the government's antiterrorism successes, JI and other extremist groups remained a significant threat. The car bombing of the J.W. Marriott hotel in Jakarta on Aug. 5, 2003, which killed 12 people, was almost certainly the work of JI; another attack in South Sulawesi was carried out by a JI-linked militant group. Recent information suggested that JI was more widespread and deeply entrenched than had been originally suspected and that the group was likely to continue to pose a threat for many years.

While terrorism captured the international community's attention, Indonesians were more preoccupied with the spectre of separatism, particularly in Aceh and Papua provinces. Aceh proved to be the government's most pressing domestic problem. A fragile cessation-of-hostilities agreement, which had been signed in December 2002 by the government and the Free Aceh Movement (GAM), collapsed in early 2003; both the GAM and the Indonesian military (TNI) had repeatedly breached the spirit and letter of the accord. In May the government declared a state of emergency in the province and mobilized some 35,000 troops as part of a sweeping campaign to destroy the GAM. In the first four months of fighting, the TNI claimed that about 700 GAM soldiers, of a military force estimated at 5,000, had been killed. Human rights groups strongly criticized the TNI's actions, claiming that there had been extensive depredations against the civilian population. The military's effective closure of the province to external observers and clampdown on media coverage made it difficult to confirm the extent of abuses by both the TNI and the GAM, though the TNI had admitted that almost 300 civilians had been killed in the fighting.

Papua also remained troublesome for the government. Having supported special autonomy laws for the province in 2001, the Megawati government backed away from key elements of the package. Much to the chagrin of the Papuan elite, the government failed to establish the special Papuan assembly stipulated in the legislation, seemingly for fear that it would strengthen pro-independence sentiment. The government then embarked on a controversial partition of Papua into three new provinces, hoping that the division of the territory would cause splits in the separatist movement. The creation of new provinces sparked violence in several areas and forced the government to postpone further implementation.

Elsewhere in Indonesia, levels of social conflict appeared to have abated. Government-brokered peace accords in Maluku and Central Sulawesi, both of which had experienced bloody Christian-Muslim violence in recent years, helped to greatly reduce intracommunal attacks, and some progress was made in restoring social harmony.

Opinion polls suggested that there was mounting public dissatisfaction with the performance of President Megawati and her government during the year. Megawati was widely criticized for poor management of her cabinet and for failing to carry out political and economic reforms. Attempts to halt corruption were halfhearted at best, and Megawati was attacked for not sacking her attorney general after it was revealed that he had provided a false statement of his assets. She also failed to discipline several of her economic ministers for openly criticizing cabinet decisions. The president's handling of controversies within her own Indonesian Democratic Party of Struggle (PDI-P) proved especially

Sarjiyo, an Indonesian linked to the terrorist Jemaah Islamiyah group, is shown on October 30 at his trial for involvement in the making of the bombs that killed 202 people in a club in Bali in 2002.

damaging. She sparked dissent by nominating candidates in gubernatorial and district-head elections who were not supported by local PDI-P branches, and key party figures were increasingly vocal in their criticism of her leadership.

Megawati's political setbacks gave hope to her rivals in the 2004 general and presidential elections. Though she was still seen as the front-runner in the presidential race, her opponents regarded her as vulnerable on matters pertaining to economic management, Islam, the fight against corruption, and national security. Her main rivals were likely to be Amien Rais, the chairman of the People's Consultative Assembly, and Akbar Tanjung, the parliamentary speaker. Megawati's PDI-P was also likely to suffer a significant drop in support.

Although there was criticism of Megawati's economic policies, the Indonesian economy performed better than many of its regional counterparts. Gross domestic product grew 3.8% over the year to June 2003; inflation was reduced to 6% (from 14% in early 2002); and the exchange rate remained steady (8,400 Indonesian rupiah = about $1). Domestic consumption continued to drive economic growth. Though investment remained at about two-thirds the level preceding the 1997 financial crisis, international investors were reluctant to commit capital to Indonesia.

(GREG FEALY)

IRAN

Area: 1,629,918 sq km (629,315 sq mi)
Population (2003 est.): 66,255,000 (excluding roughly 1,000,000 Afghan refugees)
Capital: Tehran
Supreme political and religious authority: *Rahbar* **(Spiritual Leader) Ayatollah Sayyed Ali Khamenei**
Head of state and government: President Mohammad Khatami

The deep divisions between the array of factions within Iran, principally those with conservative and reformist tendencies, persisted in 2003, and the clerical opponents of modernization grew in strength. Pres. Mohammad Khatami suffered reverses following the dissolution of the Tehran City Council on January 14 and a poor performance in subsequent local elections on February 28, when there was a low turnout at the polls (12% in Tehran and 25% elsewhere) that was a humiliation for the reform groups. In March the Expediency Council ratified, in defiance of the president, a sizable increase in the budget of the Council of Guardians to fund that group's operations vetting nominations for the 2004 elections, which thereby ensured the Council of Guardians' control over the selection of candidates. Khatami appeared to give up his program of modernization; he refused to stand again in the upcoming presidential election and offered to accept a call in June from reformists for his resignation.

There was little respite in the crackdown on freedom of speech. In January two newspapers were suspended by the conservative-controlled judiciary, and legal proceedings were instituted against the managers of opinion polls when the results offended hard-liners. The reprieve granted to Hashem Aghajari, a history professor sentenced to death for apostasy in 2002, was commuted to a four-year jail sentence in July but was offset by continuing arrests of lawyers and newsmen. Fifteen members of the Freedom Movement of Iran were sent to prison in May. Internet access to foreign news on 15,000 Web sites also was cut off, and the systematic jamming of satellite television channels began. Zahra Kazemi, a Canadian-Iranian journalist who was arrested for taking photographs outside a prison, died of head injuries while in custody in July. Canada condemned her death, and several members of the Iranian security services were arrested. In October Shirin Ebadi, an outspoken Iranian lawyer and human rights activist, was announced as the winner of the 2003 Nobel Prize for Peace. (*See* NOBEL PRIZES.)

The fighting forces of the Mujahed-din-e Khalq Organization (MKO) were disarmed by the U.S.-led coalition after the fall of Iraq. The MKO profile was sustained by the trial of activists following violence against the Iranian embassies in Paris and Oslo. Student opposition to the regime erupted in Tehran in July.

Iranian foreign policy was dominated by relations with the U.S. and events surrounding the U.S.-led coalition's invasion of Iraq. Iran accepted the fall of Iraqi Pres. Saddam Hussein and supported the liberation of the Shi'ite communities in Iraq but was disturbed by the U.S. occupation. There were fears that Iran could become a target of U.S. action, and Iranian authorities responded with a mixture of threats and conciliation. The situation was made more difficult by increasing evidence that the Iranian nuclear-development program included the creation of weapons of mass destruction (WMD). In March President Khatami announced that a uranium-enrichment plant would be constructed near Esfahan to process local raw materials. Visits by the International Atomic Energy Agency (IAEA) later in the year confirmed that highly enriched uranium was present at two other locations. The IAEA called on Iran to prove by October 31 that it had not diverted materials to weapons use or face referral to the UN Security Council. Conservative factions opposed foreign intervention on this issue, but Foreign Minister Kamal Kharrazi offered in September to sign the additional safeguards to the Nuclear Non-proliferation Treaty, provided that the nuclear-enrichment program would be allowed to proceed. The Iran-Libya Sanctions Act remained in effect in view of U.S. concerns over Iranian involvement in the acquisition of WMD and continuing participation in terrorism.

The U.S. accused Iran of harbouring al-Qaeda members suspected of involvement in the May attack on U.S. interests in Riyadh, Saudi Arabia. Iran acknowledged the activities of al-Qaeda personnel in the country but denied their connection with the terrorist incident in Riyadh. Russia adhered to its policy expanding commercial links with Iran and of aiding in the construction of an Iranian nuclear station at Bushehr but concurred with the U.S. in opposing the station's use for military ends.

On December 26 a massive earthquake flattened the city of Bam in southeastern Iran, killing and injuring thousands. (*See* DISASTERS.) More than 20 countries sent aid workers to help in the relief effort. The U.S. temporarily eased restrictions on sending assistance to Iran, though an American offer for an official aid mission was declined.

Economic growth was strong at 6.5% in real terms in 2003, supported by an 18% rise in oil and gas exports to $22.8 billion. Problems persisted, however, with unemployment (16%), the foreign debt ($24 billion), and inflation (16%). The governor of the central bank, Mohsen Nourbakhsh, died on March 22 at age 54; his replacement was Ebrahim Sheibani. (KEITH S. MCLACHLAN)

IRAQ

Area: 434,128 sq km (167,618 sq mi)
Population (2003 est.): 24,683,000
Capital: Baghdad
Head of state and government: President and Prime Minister Saddam Hussein until April 9; thereafter, coalition occupation regimes headed by Director of the Office of Reconstruction and Humanitarian Assistance Jay M. Garner (April 21–May 12) and Director of the Coalition Provisional Authority L. Paul Bremer III (from May 12); a Governing Council of Iraqi leaders with a rotating presidency was established on July 13

By the end of 2002, Iraq had announced that it would cooperate with the inspectors on the United Nations Monitoring, Verification, and Inspection Commission (UNMOVIC) on weapons of mass destruction (WMD). (*See* MILITARY AFFAIRS: Sidebar.) Thereafter, UN inspection teams worked for several weeks in Iraq, but their final report was inconclusive. Meanwhile, the U.S. and the U.K. continued to build up military forces around Iraq (mainly in Kuwait, Qatar, and Bahrain). They claimed that Iraq was still concealing some WMD and threatened military action if Iraq did not disarm. Other countries, notably France, Germany, and Russia, demanded that UN inspectors be allowed more time to reach conclusive results. The U.S. and the U.K., however, decided to act on the authority of UN Resolution 1441. This resolution, adopted unanimously by the Security Council on Nov. 8, 2002, demanded that Iraq accept rigorous arms inspection.

On March 17, 2003, U.S. Pres. George W. Bush issued an ultimatum demanding that Iraqi Pres. Saddam Hussein (*see* BIOGRAPHIES) and his cohorts leave the country within 48 hours. The U.S. ultimatum was rejected, and the UN inspection team left Iraq. On March 20 the first air attacks on Baghdad began, and soon afterward U.S. and British ground forces invaded southern Iraq from Kuwait. Turkey rejected U.S. requests that it allow U.S. troops to traverse its territory and open a second front in northern Iraq.

Coalition (mainly U.S. and British) forces met stiff resistance before taking the southern city of Basra, but coalition troops thereafter advanced steadily toward Baghdad with less resistance, except around Nasiriyah and Najaf. By April 6 Baghdad was under siege, with defenders digging trenches in urban neighbourhoods filled with elite Republican Guards, regular army troops, and militiamen. On April 9 Iraqi resistance melted, and Baghdad fell to the coalition; by April 18 most of the country was under the control of U.S. forces. On May 1 President Bush officially declared that major combat had ended.

Even while military operations were taking place, the U.S. began airlifting hundreds of members of an exile group, the Iraq National Congress, meant to be the vanguard of a new Iraqi army. The Pentagon appointed a retired army lieutenant general, Jay M. Garner, as Iraq's new administrator. He was soon replaced, however, by L. Paul Bremer III, a diplomat. (*See* BIOGRAPHIES.)

The fall of Baghdad was followed by widespread acts of looting, vandalism, sabotage, and burning of public buildings and residences, especially those belonging to leading members of the fallen regime. The National Museum of Iraq, which held some of the finest treasures of ancient Mesopotamia, was looted; however, many of the artifacts that were feared lost were later found or returned to the museum. Iraq entered a cycle of violence and instability combined with a breakdown of the electrical-power grid and telephone services, especially in Baghdad.

Almost immediately after the occupation, various forms of Iraqi resistance arose. U.S. forces and Iraqis who were cooperating with the coalition forces became targets of attacks in an increasingly focused and organized guerrilla campaign. On the whole, the Iraqi Shi'ite community remained relatively calm, as did the areas in the north that were under control of Kurdish opposition parties. Anti-American sentiments and daily attacks against U.S. forces were concentrated in areas of Baghdad and in the Arab Sunnite cities in the centre and west of the country, an area that came to be known as the "Sunni triangle." By November the number of U.S. forces killed after Bush announced the end of major combat exceeded the number of those killed in the war.

The resistance increasingly undertook spectacular acts of violence, including suicide bomb attacks. On August 29 in the religious city of Najaf, a bomb attack killed some 80 people, among them Ayatollah Muhammad Baqir al-Hakim, an important Shi'ite cleric. On August 19 a blast caused by a suicide bomber devastated the Baghdad headquarters of

ETHNIC AND RELIGIOUS GROUPS IN IRAQ AND VICINITY

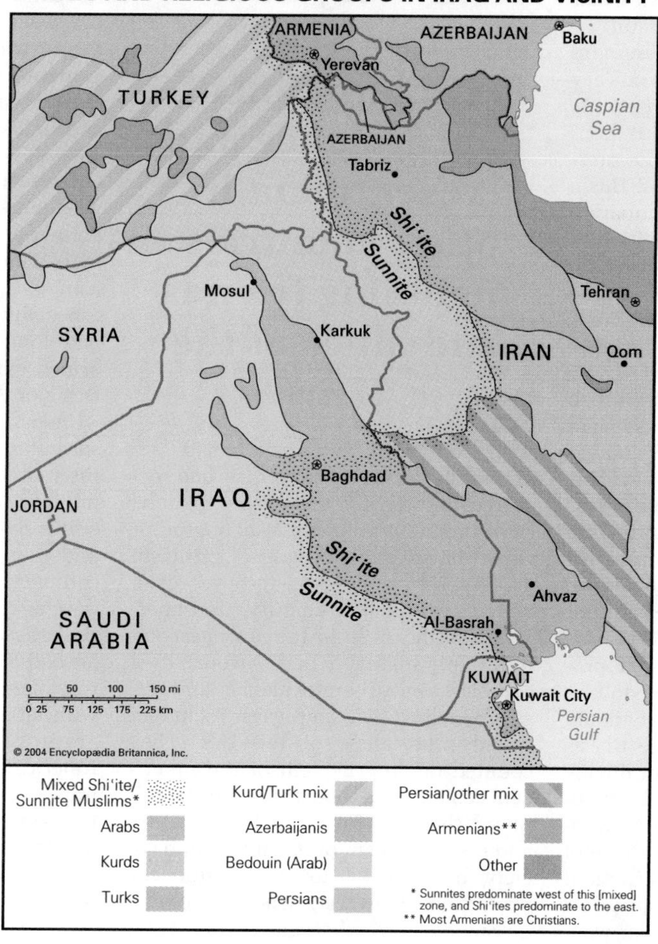

(continued on page 416)

Bush, Iraq, and the World

by Strobe Talbott

From the moment that the first explosions lit up the night sky over Baghdad, this war was personal. Four huge bombs and about 40 cruise missiles slammed into a heavily fortified VIP compound near the Tigris River. The opening salvo was intended not just to inspire "shock and awe" among the Iraqi people but to kill their leader, Saddam Hussein. "Selected targets of military importance," said Pres. George W. Bush when he went on national television half an hour later. "A target of opportunity," added White House and Pentagon sources in the hours that followed. They left no doubt who was in the crosshairs.

Bush had come by his animus honestly. The greatest triumph of the presidency of his father, George H.W. Bush, had been to end Saddam's occupation of Kuwait in the Gulf War of 1991. But that victory had been incomplete. Saddam survived, and two years later he plotted to assassinate the senior Bush, who was then out of office, during a visit to Kuwait.

No wonder the second President Bush felt he had a score to settle. He also had objective reasons to wish for Saddam's demise, as did the whole world. The Iraqi dictator was an affront to the very idea of an international community. He had spent the 1990s intimidating his neighbours, brutalizing his own people, engaging in genocidal repression of Iraq's Marsh Arabs and Kurds, and systematically flouting the terms of probation that the UN had imposed on him after his eviction from Kuwait. Saddam played cat and mouse with the UN as it tried to make sure he was not illicitly developing chemical, biological, or nuclear weapons. In 1998 the UN withdrew its arms inspectors in the face of Iraqi deceit, defiance, and obstruction.

So, in addition to its being personal for President Bush, this was a war waiting to happen. Whenever it had occurred and however it was explained from the bully pulpit in Washington, it would have set off a wave of criticism and second-guessing around the world. For at least half a century, the emergence of the U.S. as the strongest nation in history had aroused a combination of ambivalence and resentment in other countries, including friends and allies of the U.S. They counted on the strength of the American economy to boost their own, admired the U.S. for its political values and the dynamism of its culture and society, and looked to Washington for protection. However, when American presidents—in disregard of John Quincy Adams's famous advice—went abroad in search of monsters to destroy, the foreign reaction to success was two cheers, not three, and the reaction to failure was varying degrees of schadenfreude.

> **"For at least half a century, the emergence of the U.S. as the strongest nation in history had aroused a combination of ambivalence and resentment in other countries, including friends and allies of the U.S."**

Pres. John F. Kennedy took his lumps abroad as well as at home for botching an attempt to eliminate Fidel Castro in Cuba. Lyndon Johnson's debacle in Vietnam was widely seen as Goliath meeting his match. Ronald Reagan made quick work of tiny Grenada in 1983, but the pretext for the invasion—the rescue of American students at a beachfront medical school—struck many as implausible and unjustified. In addition to his own showdown with Saddam Hussein, George H.W. Bush went into Panama with guns blazing, kicked down the door, and dragged the country's strongman, Manuel Noriega, off to an American jail. By what right? asked many, especially in Latin America, which has had long experience with "Tio Sam" armed with a pistol and a "Wanted Dead or Alive" poster.

Under Pres. Bill Clinton, the U.S. resorted to force on a significant scale three times: in 1994, when it replaced a military junta in Haiti with the democratically elected president, and in 1995 and 1999, when it conducted bombing campaigns to stop Slobodan Milosevic's rampages of ethnic cleansing in the Balkans. Once again the reaction abroad to the U.S.'s actions was a mixture of astonishment (sometimes tinged with anxiety) at U.S. military prowess, gratitude (sometimes grudging) for American leadership, and unease at the unprecedented, unrivaled, and unregulated extent of American power. When in 1999 French Foreign Minister Hubert Védrine labeled the U.S. *l'hyperpuissance*, or "the hyperpower," he did not mean it as a compliment, and he

Photo credits page 413 (clockwise from bottom): © Reuters NewMedia Inc./Corbis; © AFP/Corbis; © Patrick Robert/Corbis; © Reuters NewMedia Inc./Corbis; AP/Wide World Photos; © Brooks Kraft/Corbis

had in mind the foreign policy of the archmultilateralist Clinton.

It was against this backdrop that George W. Bush became the custodian of all that power in January 2001. Yes, he had a glint of vengeance in his eye on the subject of Saddam, and yes, he slipped naturally into the Gary Cooper role as the marshal in *High Noon*—facing down the bad guys while the frightened townspeople disappear from the streets, duck behind closed doors, and peek out through drawn blinds. But he also had a strong case, and plenty of precedent, for making the downfall of an international outlaw a priority of his foreign policy.

However, the second Gulf War as waged by the second President Bush proved to be more controversial abroad than any other American military adventure since Vietnam—which is all the more extraordinary in that it took only six weeks and relatively little death and destruction for the U.S. to accomplish its immediate objectives. The war was seen as dramatic evidence of what many had feared for over two years. From virtually the day he took office, Bush had put the world on notice that the executive branch of the U.S. government was operating under a new concept of the American mission and how to accomplish it. Previously, the assumption had been: "Together if we can, alone if we must." "Together" meant a preference for working with allies, with regional security organizations, and with the authorization of UN Security Council resolutions. The Bush administration stood the formula on its head: "Alone if we can, together if we must."

In one respect this shift was unabashedly political. Spokesmen for the new administration claimed that Democrats—particularly the one who occupied the presidency between the two Bushes—had diluted the U.S.'s power, squandered the nation's resources, and emboldened its enemies. They had done so through misplaced idealism about the nature of the world, a naive belief in the illusory if not oxymoronic concept of international law, excessive deference to the sensibilities of other countries (notably including allies), a foolish reliance on feckless international organizations, and a timidity about the decisive use of U.S. force.

While this critique was directed primarily against Clinton, it was, ironically though inescapably, also a tacit put-down of the elder Bush's concept, enunciated in 1991, that the end of the Cold War made possible a "new world order," led by the U.S. but based on collaboration with old friends and new partners and the strengthening of international institutions.

During the first nine months of 2001, the administration made statements and took actions intended to demonstrate a new self-reliance and assertiveness and, accordingly, a new resistance to agreements and arrangements that limited the U.S.'s freedom of action. The U.S. renounced, "unsigned," weakened, disdained, or ignored more than a dozen treaties and diplomatic works in progress that it had inherited from its predecessors, Republican as well as Democratic. These included the Kyoto Protocol on

U.S. Pres. George W. Bush and a few of the world leaders with whom he interacted in 2003 (clockwise from 9:00): British Prime Minister Tony Blair, French Pres. Jacques Chirac, North Korean leader Kim Jong Il, UN Secretary-General Kofi Annan, and Afghan Pres. Hamid Karzai.

A major goal of the U.S.-led invasion of Iraq was the extirpation of the dictatorship of Pres. Saddam Hussein, shown here in a 1996 photograph with his sons Uday (left) and Qusay, who also held positions of great power and influence in the regime.

climate change, the International Criminal Court, the Treaty on Anti-Ballistic Missile Systems, the land-mine-ban treaty, and an array of conventions designed to protect the rights of children, stop torture, curb discrimination by race and gender, end the production of biological weapons, prevent money laundering, and limit trafficking in small arms. Earlier administrations had had objections to some features of many of these accords but had sought to improve them; the Bush administration seemed to want nothing to do with agreements of this kind.

The new U.S. leadership also downgraded the importance it attached to diplomacy, since that is an exercise in compromise and the Bush team was not in a compromising mood. The U.S. suspended the Middle East peace process and the dialogue with North Korea.

By the late summer of 2001, there was more grumbling than ever before from those around the world who were prepared to follow the U.S. president as a leader but were less inclined to take orders from him as a boss. Vice Pres. Richard Cheney and Secretary of Defense Donald Rumsfeld quickly established themselves as the advocates, in public and in the councils of the administration, of unilateralism without apologies. Secretary of State Colin Powell seemed to be standing alone in voicing a more traditional, cooperative, and institutional approach. He lost one battle after another, and his imminent resignation was frequently rumoured.

"The willingness of the American people to support military action in Iraq increased because of September 11."

Then came September 11. The immediate effect of the attacks was to galvanize international sympathy for the U.S. There was a sudden burst of approval for President Bush as a righteous lawman, and the world became one big posse. The normally hyperpuissance-bashing Paris daily *Le Monde* ran a banner headline proclaiming, "We are all Americans now."

Secretary Powell went from being the odd man out to being the man of the hour. He assembled an international coalition of unprecedented breadth to back the U.S. as it prepared for retribution against Afghanistan, which had become a breeding ground for radical Islamists and a sanctuary for Osama bin Laden and his al-Qaeda terrorist network.

The Bush administration was glad to have good wishes and political support from abroad. But when NATO, for the first time in its history, invoked Article V of its charter, proclaiming that the assaults against the World Trade Center and the Pentagon constituted an attack on all member states, the U.S. said, in effect, "Thanks very much; now please stay out of the way while we take care of this." As a result, the alliance was largely sidelined during the military action in Afghanistan.

Only when the Afghan Taliban had been driven from power and the U.S. turned to the hard work of reconstruction did it welcome international participation. One reason was that the Bush administration saw itself as doing regime change but not nation building. Another was that it wanted, as quickly as possible, to get on with changing another regime—in Iraq. The day after September 11, Paul Wolfowitz, Rumsfeld's intellectually formidable and politically powerful deputy, made the case in a meeting with the president that once the U.S. had taken care of Target Kabul, it should turn to Target Baghdad.

The willingness of the American people to support military action in Iraq increased because of September 11. Before the terror attacks, the term *national security* had been an abstraction for many Americans. Afterward it had new, concrete meaning virtually synonymous with personal safety. The world was a place where bad people—"evildoers," as the president put it—were looking for ways to kill Americans on their own territory. It was easier than it would have been otherwise for the administration to convince Americans that Saddam too was an evildoer who would kill Americans if he could and that the U.S. therefore had to kill him first. That was the subtext of the doctrine that the administration promulgated a year after September 11 in a presidential document identifying preemptive and preventive war as vital tools for the defense of the homeland.

In a speech to the Veterans of Foreign Wars in August 2002, Vice President Cheney set the stage for applying the new doctrine to Iraq. "We must take the battle to the enemy," he said. "We" meant the U.S.; the United Nations, Cheney made clear, had disqualified itself and should step aside.

In a phrase that had gained currency since September 11, the administration set about "connecting the dots" between Saddam on the one hand and weapons of mass destruction (WMD) and the forces of international terrorism on the other. Since Saddam was trying to acquire WMD and might give them to terrorists, the U.S. should bring him down. Embedded in this syllogism was a major weakness in the administration's case for war. In his effort to build domestic and international support for military action, Bush was driven to assert—and, as it turned out, exaggerate—the extent of Saddam's WMD programs and his ties to terrorists.

The most vocal skeptics about the logic of the administration's argument were Republicans associated with the first President Bush, particularly former national security adviser Brent Scowcroft and former secretary of state James Baker. Whatever the misgivings of prominent Democrats, they were reluctant to tackle a president who was riding high largely because of his robust response to September 11. Within the administration, Powell continued to be a force for moderation. He persuaded Bush to address the UN and give multilateralism one more chance. The president dared the UN to prove itself relevant but, unlike Cheney, did not dismiss its ability to do so. The challenge led directly to the unanimous passage of Security Council Resolution 1441, which warned of "serious consequences" if Iraq did not comply with tough new inspections. Saddam immediately adopted his familiar practice of dodging and weaving, but it looked as though the U.S. might finally have laid the basis for a UN-authorized, U.S.-led military action.

Had it worked out that way, Gulf War II would have been part of the continuum going back to Gulf War I and the Clinton administration's use of force in Haiti and the Balkans. Not only would Bush have prevailed over Saddam, but he would have had the much-vaunted international community largely behind him—and, indeed, with him on the ground in large and diverse numbers.

Instead, the juggernaut that Bush and Powell had put in motion turned into a train wreck, primarily between the U.S. and France. Pres. Jacques Chirac shares the blame. In an interview on March 10, 2003, he warned that France would veto a new resolution authorizing force under any circumstances. Russia and China, which were prepared to go along with France in either direction, took a similar position. Chirac's obstinacy and grandstanding cut the legs out from under Powell and strengthened those in the administration who had warned that by going to the UN in the first place, the president had fallen into a trap. Now the U.S. was, in the eyes of the unilateralists, free to do the job right, with a "coalition" that included, in its military dimension, Great Britain, Australia, and Poland, as well as some crucial logistic support from the smaller Gulf states.

Operation Iraqi Freedom produced two positive results. First, it rid Iraq, the region, and the world of a scourge; and second, in part because of an understanding he had with British Prime Minister Tony Blair, his staunchest ally, Bush relaunched the Middle East peace process.

On the other hand, the war did profound damage to American relations with a wide array of countries and several international institutions, principally the UN and NATO, which were further marginalized. More generally, it heightened anxieties that American power, benevolent though its motivations might be, was a problem for virtually every other country on Earth, especially if the victory in Iraq vindicated the unilateralists and ensured their continued ascendancy in the U.S. As American and British troops were tearing down Saddam's statues and scouring the country for the man himself, many around the world (and in the U.S. as well) feared that the "Iraq model" would serve as a template for changing two other regimes that Bush had named as part of the "axis of evil," Iran and North Korea, since both had nuclear-weapons programs far more advanced than Iraq's.

It was not that simple, however. In the second half of 2003, the United States military had its hands full in Iraq and Afghanistan, both of which were far from stabilized. Partly for that reason, and also because the U.S. needed as much international help as possible for the jobs ahead in those two countries, the administration put its six-shooter back in its holster and resorted to multilateral diplomacy in trying to deal with Iran and North Korea. Just as it quickly became apparent that the Iraq war would have a long, messy, and uncertain aftermath, so the struggle to define the future of American foreign policy was far from over. What was already being called the "Bush revolution" in U.S. foreign policy might yet give way to at least a partial restoration of traditional American internationalism.

Strobe Talbott is a former journalist for Time *and deputy secretary of state (1994–2001) and now president of the Brookings Institution, Washington, D.C. His latest book is* The Russia Hand: A Memoir of Presidential Diplomacy *(Random House, 2002).*

(continued from page 411)

the UN, killing at least 22 people, among them the top UN envoy to Iraq, Sérgio Vieira de Mello. (*See* OBITUARIES.)

Saddam's two sons, Uday and Qusay, were killed on July 22 in a firefight with U.S. troops in Mosul. (*See* OBITUARIES.) The two men were among those on a U.S. list of 55 persons described as the "most wanted" personalities of the former regime. By the end of the year, 42 people on that list had been either captured or killed. On December 13, U.S. forces tracked Saddam to a farm outside Tikrit, where he was found hiding in a "spider hole"; he surrendered without a fight.

Several countries responded favourably to U.S. requests for troops to be sent to Iraq to help provide peace and security. Others insisted that the UN had to be given more authority for the administration of Iraq before they would consider sending troops.

Months after the U.S. occupation of Iraq, and despite intensive searching, no chemical or biological WMD had been found. Some people accused the U.S. and British governments of having gone to war in Iraq on the basis of outdated and inconclusive intelligence—or worse.

On July 13, U.S. authorities in Iraq nominated a 25-member body, called the Iraqi Interim Governing Council. Its members included 13 Shi'ites, 5 Arab Sunnites, 5 Kurds, 1 Turkmen, and 1 Assyrian Christian. The council was given limited powers but was asked to come up with a process for drafting a constitution and holding a general election in Iraq before the end of 2004. The Governing Council was able to meet some important challenges. In the first week of October, all schools and universities were reopened for a new school year, and in mid-October a new Iraqi currency was introduced to replace the old one that bore Saddam's picture.

The economic situation in Iraq deteriorated after the occupation of the country. Unemployment was high, anywhere between 50% and 80% of the adult population. Foreign companies were reluctant to invest or work in Iraq because of a lack of security. On May 22 the UN voted to lift sanctions, and an international donors conference in Madrid on October 24 promised more than $33 billion for Iraq's reconstruction over a four-year period. By year's end several creditor countries were contemplating restructuring or forgiving portions of Iraq's massive foreign debt. (LOUAY BAHRY)

IRELAND

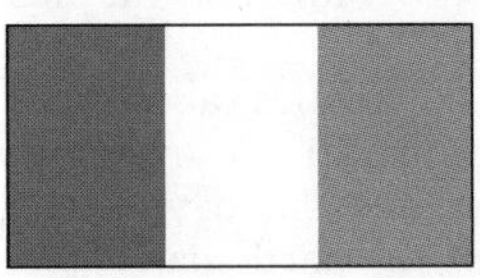

Area: 70,273 sq km (27,133 sq mi)
Population (2003 est.): 3,969,000
Capital: Dublin
Chief of state: President Mary McAleese
Head of government: Prime Minister Bertie Ahern

Most of Ireland's economic indicators, which had begun to turn down in 2001 after five years of unprecedented growth, continued to drop in 2003. Growth of 3.5% in GDP had been predicted for 2003. By August, however, the Department of Finance (DOF) had revised that to 1.5%. Although inflation came down from 2002 levels, it remained among the highest in the European Union (EU), at 3.3%. Unemployment reached 4.6%, but this began to drop a little in the second half of the year. In June the DOF said that taxation revenue would be €500 million (about $590 million) below the budget projection for the year. A boost in tax revenues in the last quarter of the year offered more flexibility to Finance Minister Charles McCreevey in framing a budget for 2004. Ministers insisted that the economic fundamentals were sound, and they were cautiously optimistic that the 2004 budget could be constructed without significant borrowing.

The coalition government of Fianna Fail and the Progressive Democrats, which had been returned to office in May 2002, found itself under much criticism. The opposition accused it of downplaying the realities of a deteriorating economic landscape. Government ministers argued that Ireland's economic performance, however, was still close to the top rank of both the EU and the Organisation for Economic Co-operation and Development.

Opinion polls showed a steady drop in satisfaction ratings with the government and with Prime Minister Bertie Ahern. Despite the enduring benefits of the Celtic Tiger boom of the late 1990s, Ahern and his ministers were criticized for the slowdown that had begun in 2001 and for a range of administrative failures.

Principal among these perceived failures was a continuing crisis in the public-health services, which had not been significantly alleviated by heavy investment. There were long waiting lists for medical treatment. Accident and emergency centres were frequently in crisis, with patients being turned away or forced to remain on ambulance trolleys. The death of a young child in Dublin, after a heart operation

Accompanied by Chinese Pres. Hu Jintao, Ireland's Pres. Mary McAleese reviews the honour guard that was assembled at the Great Hall of the People in Beijing to welcome her for a 10-day state visit in October.

was deferred, caused a public outcry. A shortage of housing had raised prices, and many first-time buyers were thus unable to acquire a home, although the rate of increase in housing prices was slowing. Meanwhile, inadequate public-transport systems struggled to handle commuters on clogged roads and outdated railways. Many important infrastructure projects, such as a light-rail system for Dublin and an orbital highway around the city, were behind schedule, over budget, or both.

Not all of the factors contributing to a downbeat public mood were economic. A number of judicial tribunals that had been established to investigate allegations of political corruption revealed the seamier sides of Irish public life. Liam Lawlor, a Fianna Fail member of the Dail (parliament), went to prison three times for failure to cooperate with a tribunal investigating land rezoning. Public disquiet grew over the performance of the national police, and the justice minister, Michael McDowell, promised police-reform legislation. There also was widespread anger over the collapse in September of the commission investigating the abuse of children in residential institutions. The head of the commission, High Court Judge Mary Laffoy, resigned, stating that she had not been given the resources to do the job properly.

It was a problematic year for the Northern Ireland peace process, although the cease-fires by the main paramilitary groups generally held firm. The leadership of Sinn Fein, which had supported the process, remained in control. David Trimble, the moderate Ulster Unionist Party (UUP) leader and former first minister of Northern Ireland, had to grapple with repeated attempts by internal party opponents to overthrow him.

The British and Irish governments attempted to restore the Northern Ireland Executive and Assembly, which had been set up under the 1998 Belfast Agreement. These institutions, operating under authority devolved from the British Parliament, had been suspended in October 2002. Unionists had refused to share power with Sinn Fein as long as the Irish Republican Army (IRA), Sinn Fein's paramilitary arm, remained mobilized. In fresh elections held at the end of November, Sinn Fein (24 seats) made significant gains at the expense of the moderate Social Democratic and Labour Party (18). Ian Paisley's Democratic Unionist Party took 30 seats, more than the UUP's 27. It was unclear at year's end whether an executive could be formed against a background of gains by extremists and losses by moderates.

The security forces in both parts of Ireland were pleased with the conviction and sentencing in Dublin of Michael McKevitt for directing the self-styled Real Irish Republican Army. In August 1998 this extremist splinter group had bombed the market town of Omagh, N.Ire., with the loss of 29 lives.

Ireland's historically strong relationship with the United States came under strain in the buildup to the U.S.-led war in Iraq. A vigorous antiwar movement took to the streets and challenged the use of Shannon Airport by U.S. military aircraft. The government held firm, arguing that it was in accord with UN resolutions. (CONOR BRADY)

ISRAEL

Area: 21,671 sq km (8,367 sq mi), including the Golan Heights and disputed East Jerusalem, excluding the Emerging Palestinian Autonomous Areas
Population (2003 est.): 6,473,000
Capital: Jerusalem is the proclaimed capital of Israel (since Jan. 23, 1950) and the actual seat of government, but recognition has generally been withheld by the international community
Chief of state: President Moshe Katzav
Head of government: Prime Minister Ariel Sharon

The Emerging Palestinian Autonomous Areas (the West Bank and the Gaza Strip)
Total area under disputed administration: West Bank 5,900 sq km (2,270 sq mi); Gaza Strip 363 sq km (140 sq mi)
Population (2003 est.): West Bank 2,467,000, including 2,237,000 Arabs and 230,000 Jews; Gaza Strip 1,304,000, including 1,297,000 Arabs and 7,000 Jews
Principal administrative centres: Ram Allah and Gaza
Head of government: President Yasir Arafat, assisted by Prime Ministers Mahmoud Abbas from April 30 and, from September 9, Ahmad Qurei

After nearly three years of relentless bloodletting, Israel and the Palestinians responded in mid-2003 to international efforts to promote peace. The early promise of a breakthrough proved illusory, however, and the cycle of violence continued. Intense Israeli military pressure, following reoccupation of Palestinian cities in the West Bank and a determined hands-on American approach in the wake of a victorious spring campaign in Iraq, had led to the emergence of a more pragmatic Palestinian leadership that was willing to consider ending terrorism in order to achieve Palestinian goals through international—especially U.S.—pressure on Israel.

On April 30, after Mahmoud Abbas (*see* BIOGRAPHIES) was installed as the Palestinian prime minister, representatives of the U.S., the European Union, Russia, and the UN formally presented the American-initiated peace plan, known as the "road map for peace in the Middle East," which outlined steps for the establishment of a Palestinian state that would coexist peacefully with Israel. The Palestinians accepted the plan immediately. The Israeli cabinet approved it on May 25, with 14 reservations. By pushing the decision through over strong right-wing opposition, Prime Minister Ariel Sharon struck a new conciliatory chord: "It's not right for Israel to rule over 3.5 million Palestinians," he declared.

Sharon, who had consistently refused to meet with Palestinian Pres. Yasir Arafat because of Arafat's alleged ties to terrorism, emphasized the changed diplomatic climate by hosting Abbas in his Jerusalem office on May 29. In an effort to invigorate the peace process, Sharon, Abbas, and U.S. Pres. George W. Bush held a high-profile summit on June 4 at the Red Sea port of Al-'Aqabah, Jordan. Abbas declared an end to the armed uprising against Israel, renounced terrorism against Israelis "wherever they might be," and acknowledged "Jewish suffering through the ages." Sharon asserted that it was in Israel's interest "for the Palestinians to govern themselves in their own state." Bush affirmed the U.S. commitment to "Israel's security as a vibrant Jewish state" and to "freedom and statehood for the Palestinian people."

On June 29, Palestinian militias, including the radical Islamicist Hamas and Islamic Jihad, declared an initial three-month cease-fire. On the next day, Israel withdrew troops from the Gaza Strip and handed over security control to the Palestinian Authority. On July 2 Israel ceded security control in Bethlehem and declared that the handover of additional cities would be contingent

The town of Tol Karem is visible beyond a section of the separation fence, a part of the "Green Line" being constructed by Israeli authorities to restrict the movement of people between Palestinian areas and the Israeli-administered West Bank.

on the Palestinians' fulfillment of their obligations under the road map.

Although the road map's main demand required that the Palestinians preempt future terrorist attacks by disbanding terrorist groups and collecting their weapons, the Palestinians maintained that any attempt to do so would lead to civil war. Instead, they focused on Israel's obligation to dismantle "unauthorized" West Bank settlement outposts and called for the release of more than 6,000 Palestinian prisoners in Israeli jails; Israel's removal of a handful of settlements and the release of a few hundred prisoners was viewed as inadequate.

The Palestinians also complained about a security barrier Israel was building to keep terrorists from crossing from the West Bank into Israel proper. After a White House meeting with Abbas in late July, Bush urged Israel to erect the barrier as closely as possible to the pre-1967 war border between Israel and the West Bank. The barrier's route became a major bone of contention between Israel and the U.S. Israel insisted on building part of it around the large settlement of Ari'el, 19 km (12 mi) inside the West Bank. The Americans threatened to reduce aid to Israel by the amount spent on the barrier in Palestinian territory and charged that the barrier prejudiced the outcome of peace talks and encroached on everyday Palestinian life.

When the Abbas government failed to take action to dismantle the terrorist militias, as required by the road map, Israel launched a series of targeted assassinations against Hamas military and political leaders, and the cease-fire collapsed. Abbas, unable to stop work on the fence or to ameliorate Palestinian living conditions, lost the last vestiges of support he had had among the Palestinian public. He charged that his policy of moderation had been undercut by the U.S., Israel, and Arafat. Abbas resigned on September 6, following an angry demonstration outside the Legislative Council building in Ram Allah, where he had gone to seek a renewed vote of confidence after just 100 days in office. His departure threw the nascent peace process into deep disarray. Arafat nominated Ahmad Qurei, speaker of the Palestinian Legislative Council and a close confidant, to replace Abbas.

Israel placed the blame for Abbas's failure squarely on Arafat. Defining him as an "obstacle" that had to be "removed," the government decided "in principle" on September 11 to expel the Palestinian president. The decision sparked a wave of international and Palestinian protest.

Failure to take the process forward through official channels spawned two significant private peace initiatives. In June, Ami Ayalon, a former head of Israel's Shin Bet General Security Service, and Sari Nusseibeh, president of al-Quds University, launched the "People's Voice" petition in support of their six principles for a final peace deal. In mid-October other Israeli and Palestinian moderates produced a fully articulated model peace treaty, known as the "Geneva Agreement" in deference to logistic support provided by the Swiss authorities. The fact that such accords were possible put pressure on the Sharon government to come out with an initiative of its own, and in late November the prime minister reiterated his readiness to make "painful concessions" for peace but warned that if the Palestinians failed to seize the opportunity, Israel would take unspecified "unilateral steps."

Despite Sharon's failure to end the violence or right the depressed Israeli economy, his leadership position remained strong. Although a rash of corruption scandals had touched him, his family, and his party, he led the Likud to a landslide victory in early elections on January 28, winning 38 seats in the 120-member Knesset; the Labor Party won 19. The staunchly secular Shinui emerged as Israel's third largest party with 15 seats, ahead of the ultra-Orthodox Shas with 11. Shinui's inclusion in the government promised to shake up criteria for citizenship in Israel and to challenge the Orthodox hegemony over religion, but little change actually occurred.

Much of Shinui's electoral success came at the expense of the Labor Party, which suffered a disastrous year. Its election debacle was followed by bitter party infighting, which led to the resignation on May 4 of its newly elected leader, former Haifa mayor Amram Mitzna. To defer another potentially divisive leadership struggle, 79-year-old Shimon Peres, a former prime minister and party leader, took over as Labor's temporary chairman.

The three-year-long economic recession continued through 2003, although the relative quiet of the brief cease-fire helped spark a minor upturn in the summer as Israelis, less concerned for their safety, flocked to the shops. Earlier, Finance Minister Benjamin Netanyahu had taken steps to boost international confidence by slashing nearly $2.5 billion from the national budget of $67.5 billion. The cuts deepened unemployment, however, which reached nearly 11%; a record 300,000 Israelis were out of work. The cuts also hit poorer Israelis who relied on social security payments to raise their incomes.

In early July Vicki Knafo, a 43-year-old woman from the Negev desert town of Mitzpe Ramon, captured the national imagination when, draped in a large Israeli flag, she walked more than 200 km (125 mi) to Jerusalem and set up a camp outside the Finance Ministry to protest cuts in supplementary benefits to single mothers. Three months later, after having failed to extract any concessions from Netanyahu, she was forced to admit defeat.

The standoff between Netanyahu and the demonstrators raised fundamental questions about the nature of the Israeli state. Netanyahu claimed that he was weaning poor Israelis from a culture of handouts to a culture of work. His critics, however, pointed to the dearth of available jobs and argued that the finance minister was destroying Israel's welfare state and widening already-large gaps between Israel's rich and poor. (LESLIE D. SUSSER)

ITALY

Area: 301,333 sq km (116,345 sq mi)
Population (2003 est.): 57,033,000
Capital: Rome
Chief of state: President Carlo Azeglio Ciampi
Head of government: Prime Minister Silvio Berlusconi

Shock waves shook Italy in 2003 when 19 Italians were killed in a suicide-bomb attack against a military base in southern Iraq in November. The incident was described as one of the deadliest blows suffered by Italian armed forces since World War II. Dismay in Italy was all the greater because the dead belonged to a contingent of some 2,500 men dispatched to Iraq, after parliamentary approval, on a peace mission, to be involved in "reconstruction tasks."

When the Iraq crisis erupted, Italy's right-wing prime minister, media magnate Silvio Berlusconi, faced widespread domestic hostility to the U.S.-led war. This was highlighted in February by a massive protest demonstration in Rome, with—according to the organizers—some two million people from all over Italy descending upon the city. Protesters also blocked trains moving military matériel from some of the seven U.S. military bases in Italy to the main U.S. supply depot in Tuscany.

Berlusconi explained to Parliament that his government wanted to avoid war, but his constant theme during the run-up to the Anglo-American attack on Iraq was Italy's debt and loyalty to the United States, partly as Europe's "saviour" during and after World War II. He initially insisted on a UN solution to the Iraq issue, including a UN go-ahead to the use of force if necessary, and called on Europe to repair its already-shattered unity. The issue of Iraq split Parliament in two; a government motion that echoed Berlusconi was carried 302–236, and an opposition centre-left call for Italy to act instead in concert with the European Union (EU) and deny any form of support for military action was defeated 227–311.

At one point Berlusconi predicted that any U.S. unilateral initiative in Iraq would be a "disaster," but he later remarked that Italy would not break with the U.S. if it went to war alone. Former left-wing prime minister Massimo D'Alema accused Berlusconi of ambiguity over how to deal with Iraq. It was from the U.S. Pres. George W. Bush's White House in March that Italians first learned officially that they were to be among the U.S.'s 30 allies in the conflict. Berlusconi finally announced that Italy would play no direct part in combat operations. In April Parliament approved the dispatch to Iraq of a military force earmarked for reconstruction tasks. This force was to be placed under British command and stationed at Nasiriyah in southern Iraq.

The opposition centre-left "Olive Tree" alliance proclaimed a turning point on the domestic political scene after successes against the Berlusconi-led centre-right House of Freedoms coalition in regional, provincial, and town-council elections in May and June, in which more than 11 million Italians voted. The centre-left won seven provinces versus five captured by the centre-right, but commentators saw the Olive Tree victories in the province of Rome and the strategic region of Friuli–Venezia Giulia in the northeast as the alliance's most significant gains. Berlusconi assured his Forza Italia party that his team had accomplished much, although the results had not yet become perceptible to the general public. Signs of internal friction emerged during the year within the ruling coalition.

The opposition stalked out of Parliament in June over the passage of the latest in a series of new laws. This legislation exempted Italy's five most senior holders of office from prosecution and from pending trials; the result was the suspension of a Milan trial in which Berlusconi was accused of having bribed Roman judges in a scandal over the privatization of a major food concern, SME, in 1985. A co-defendant, former defense minister Cesare Previti, had already been sentenced to an 11-year jail term.

Italy assumed the rotating EU presidency in July. Addressing the European Parliament in Strasbourg, France, Berlusconi retorted to remarks by a German MEP by likening the man to a Nazi concentration camp guard. This assertion was the first of what was seen as a succession of resounding gaffes by the prime minister. German Chancellor Gerhard Schröder called off a vacation in Italy. The two leaders then agreed to a night at the opera together in Verona, but Berlusconi canceled at the last minute (apparently out of fear that hecklers would ruin the performance). They met the next day instead. Berlusconi said that he had meant his Strasbourg remarks as a joke.

He created further uproar in September in the latest episode in his periodic broadsides against the judiciary. Next, the entire political spectrum disassociated itself from his portrayal of Mussolini as a "benign" dictator who "never killed anyone." He later apologized in person to leaders of Italy's Jewish community, which had suffered persecution under Mussolini, but his excuses were reported to have made scant impression. In October, as Berlusconi chaired the opening conference in Rome of EU negotiations aimed at a pan-European convention, eyebrows were raised when he designated Romano Prodi, head of the EU Commission and no close friend, as the platform's last speaker instead of the third, as normally required by protocol. The Italian press called it a snub, but the prime minister said that placing Prodi last had been meant to do him honour.

A gun battle on a train between Rome and Florence produced a flicker of domestic terrorism in March as three police officers checked the false identity cards of two wanted militants belonging to an allegedly reactivated band of Red Brigades, which had been active in the 1970s. One policeman and a 37-year-old gunman died and another policeman was wounded before the gunman's female companion was arrested.

Throughout the year clandestine immigrants continued to be smuggled toward Italy by sea. The dangers facing them were highlighted in June when, within three days, two crowded and rusting vessels sank in rough seas between Tunisia and the island of Lampedusa off Sicily, drowning an estimated 270 would-be refugees, thought to include Africans, Kurds, Iraqis, and Indians.

In September most of Italy was plunged into darkness during a weekend power failure that lasted variously from 4 to 13 hours. Worst hit were the railways, with an estimated 30,000 passengers stranded in 110 trains. Initial fears echoed the early reaction to the widespread North American blackout in August, but the government ruled out terrorism. The accident was attributed to a tree's having fallen and knocked out a high-tension line in Switzerland, which supplied some of Italy's power.

In December the dairy and food conglomerate Parmalat imploded as many of the company's assets were found to be fictional. The resignation of Parmalat's founder and chairman, Calisto Tanzi, was insufficient to prevent his arrest or the bankruptcy of the company.

Two quintessential Italian figures died in 2003. Gianni Agnelli, for 30 years head of the Fiat car firm in Turin, was the emblem of Italy's economic evolution and attendant conflicts in the post-World War II period. His brother, Umberto, took over as Fiat chairman. Exactly a month later, Alberto Sordi, the exuberant "Signor Rossi" of the Italian cinema, died. (*See* OBITUARIES.)

(DEREK WILSON)

JAMAICA

Area: 10,991 sq km (4,244 sq mi)
Population (2003 est.): 2,644,000
Capital: Kingston
Chief of state: Queen Elizabeth II, represented by Governor-General Sir Howard Cooke
Head of government: Prime Minister Percival J. Patterson

The UN Commission on Human Rights took Jamaica to task in February 2003 for what was described as "too many questionable police shootings." A commission official stressed that there were "strong indications" that allegations of police contract killings "might be accurate." In 2002, 133 people in Jamaica had died after being shot by police. Amnesty International and the U.S. State Department were also continuous critics of police killings in the Caribbean island nation.

The People's National Party's run of electoral successes—it had won its fourth straight general election in 2002—was abruptly halted in June when the opposition Jamaica Labour Party (JLP) captured 12 out of 13 parish councils in the local government elections. Notwithstanding a low voter turnout (37%), the JLP took 126 out of 227 seats at stake, bolstering its chances of a possible comeback in the next general election, due in 2007.

Jamaica confirmed its position as one of the Caribbean's top cruise ship destinations in 2003 by attracting more than one million cruise visitors for the first time, despite the economic problems in the U.S., the main source of cruise visitors. Cruise ship visitor growth was 20% over the previous year.

In September Prime Minister Percival Patterson said that he wanted Jamaica to adopt a republican form of government by 2007. The JLP, however, declared that it might not support the government in the required constitutional amendments. (DAVID RENWICK)

JAPAN

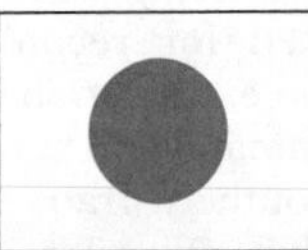

Area: 377,873 sq km (145,898 sq mi)
Population (2003 est.): 127,546,000
Capital: Tokyo
Symbol of state: Emperor Akihito
Head of government: Prime Minister Junichiro Koizumi

Domestic Affairs. On Sept. 20, 2003, Prime Minister Junichiro Koizumi, who had begun his third year in office in April, was reelected president of the majority Liberal Democratic Party (LDP), which had, often with small parties in coalition, governed Japan for almost 50 years. On November 9 an LDP-led conservative coalition took 275 of 480 lower-house seats in the parliamentary elections. This victory assured Koizumi a second term as prime minister. The opposition coalition, led by the new Democratic Party of Japan (DPJ), made a strong showing, however, by winning 202 seats (a gain from 193). The DPJ strongly appealed for reform and inspired widespread talk of the appearance of a true two-party system.

In January Koizumi made his third official visit to the Yasukuni Shrine in Tokyo "to meditate on peace," but the action caused strong controversy between the dwindling number of relatives of the more than two million Japanese enshrined at Yasukuni and the increasing number of younger citizens who simply did not identify with the shrine or who, embracing "progressive" politics, were opposed to Koizumi and his "reactionary" ruling party. The opposition denounced the shrine for recalling memories of Japanese imperialism. Perhaps more important, the shrine and official visits triggered diplomatic protests from Japan's neighbours—China and the two Koreas, past victims of Japanese aggression. Their governments pointed out that buried with the veterans were 14 convicted Class A war criminals who were linked to atrocities committed during World War II.

Already the most heavily indebted nation in the developed world, Japan increasingly felt the effects of a decade of recession. Traditionally famous for their high household savings rate—14% in 1990 and 11% in 1999—the Japanese saw their rate of savings fall to a postwar low of 6.9% in 2001 before declining further in 2002. The number of individual bankruptcies had increased by more than 30% over the previous year.

These trends, however, were related to the fact that the Japanese had become the fastest-aging population in the world. It was expected that by 2010 more than 22% of Japanese would be 65 years of age or older (up from 17% in 2000). With interest rates near zero and pensions falling, elders were feeling the financial pinch.

Japanese Prime Minister Junichiro Koizumi signals his pleasure at being reelected president of the Liberal Democratic Party by a landslide vote on September 20 in Tokyo.

Twin problems—an aging population and declining fertility—were compounded by two others. As was the case with most advanced nations, Japan needed to allow more immigration, but, owing to outdated concepts of racial purity, most of its citizens refused to make non-Japanese feel welcome. According to a United Nations estimate, the country would need 17 million additional immigrants by 2050. This would bring the proportion of immigrants to 18% of the population (in 2003 it was 1%). Entrenched attitudes also put a ceiling on the hopes of existing immigrants (a majority of them from the Koreas and China) to rise to better positions in the business world.

Another example of the ineffective use of human resources was the underutilization of Japanese women in managerial positions. About 40% of the country's women worked, usually while they remained single and before they bore children, but only about 9% of Japanese females held managerial positions (compared with 45% of American women).

AP/Wide World Photos

Workers repair a section of a road on the island of Hokkaido that was severely damaged in the September 25 earthquake. The magnitude-8 quake injured more than 500 people in northern Japan, but most injuries were minor.

Economy. Despite having called for the appointment of a dedicated reformer to become governor of the Bank of Japan (BOJ), in February Prime Minister Koizumi instead selected Toshihiko Fukui, a career bureaucrat and veteran of the conservative establishment. When Fukui took office, the government's assessment of Japan's economic status remained unchanged; gains were listed in some business sectors, but they were offset by concerns pertaining to Iraq, SARS (severe acute respiratory syndrome), and economic weakness in the U.S.

For more than four years, the BOJ had maintained short-term interest rates effectively at zero in order to stem deflation but without success. Negative interest—whereby one bank paid another to borrow its money—subsequently appeared in Japan. Most often the procedure involved financial institutions' swapping yen for dollars in forward contracts written in a third nation. On March 6 the BOJ again left monetary policy unchanged, announcing that ¥20 trillion (about $165 billion) would remain in the market, matching maintenance of the zero-interest policy. The BOJ noted that during the fiscal year ended March 31, 2003, assets had risen 1.9%.

In May the BOJ lowered its assessment of the economy, partly because of the yen's rising value, which increased the costs of Japan's exports. Governor Fukui warned that the economy was weak and called for moves to head off a crisis. The nation's GDP had risen only 0.1% in the first quarter. On May 21 the BOJ once again set the interest rate near zero. In its report for July, the BOJ raised its annual assessment of the economy for the first time in a year. The BOJ's October report was also positive. Deflation, however, continued to deepen and provided banking problems in the form of nonperforming loans. On July 24 Fukui defended zero-interest policy and its continuation until the consumer price index started to rise.

Prices continued to fall, however, and the consumer price index set a record low for some 40 months. In July the deflation rate paused at 0.2%, the lowest figure in more than two years. In the third quarter, however, exceptionally cool weather and an extended rainy season cramped sales and reduced travel. Increased social security premiums were taking a larger share of standard summer bonuses.

Meanwhile, in February industrial production, an indicator of economic status, had also fallen an unexpected 1.7% in one month. In March it dropped an additional 0.2% as the war in Iraq reduced Japanese exports. Production fell further in June and pushed stock prices down a little more than 2%.

Earlier, in May, Fukui had begun to face a related problem. Resona Holdings, one of Japan's five largest bank groups, asked for a grant of more than ¥2 trillion (more than $17 billion) in public funds to cover nonperforming loans. The situation echoed that of almost two dozen banks the government bailed out in 1998–99. A transfer was made, but the government delayed in taking control of two-thirds of the company's voting stock in order to make certain funds were used properly. By delaying action, the government sought to avoid widening the recession. Critics complained that inaction simply spread losses across the entire population, and within a week's time four other large conglomerates—Mizuho, Sumitomo-Mitsui, Mitsubishi-Tokyo, and UFJ Holdings—revealed combined losses of ¥3.6 trillion ($31 billion).

Despite such problems, it was clear that a competitive export business represented about 10% of the Japanese economy. As a result, it was possible for the country to enjoy some growth while experiencing deflation at home. In the second quarter the economy grew at an annual rate of 3.9%. Exports of digital cameras, cellular phones, and television equipment attracted foreign investors, and the Nikkei stock index, after dropping to a 20-year low in April, rose more than 36% by August and to a 14-month high (10,922) in September.

Many of these economic trends were reflected in a statistic regularly cited by the government, the current-account surplus (since the 1980s, an excess in the value of exports over imports). In January the surplus stood at ¥105 billion (about $890 million), 42.8% lower than in January 2002. In February it began to expand again, aided by an increase in exports to China. In April total exports rose almost 5%, despite a decline in the surplus with the U.S., and in May the total current account (exports and imports) reached ¥1.35 trillion ($11.2 billion). The surplus swelled 4.8% in September compared with the same period in 2002.

Foreign Affairs. During the year the Japanese had occasion to recall that they had been engaged with Americans for 150 years. In early August they mounted a parade in Yokosuka to recognize the 150th anniversary of the first formal contact with Americans. On July 8, 1853, Commodore Matthew C. Perry had arrived in the port with his "black ships." A year later he returned with overwhelming force to open Japan to international trade, after the country had experienced 200 years of isolation under the feudal Tokugawa regime.

At times the Japanese were proud of their close relationship with Americans, but sometimes they reacted with despair. On August 1 in Washington, delegates of the two nations completed over 40 days of exhausting negotiations on the status of U.S. military personnel stationed in Japan, without complete success. Decades after the 1952 peace treaty, the U.S. still kept about 50,000 troops in the country; of these some 24,000 were based on relatively poor Okinawa. There "base pollution" had resulted in local protests. The two delegations were able to agree only on an American pledge to give "favourable consideration" to any Tokyo request for transfer of U.S. service personnel charged with a serious crime to Japan's custody before indictment.

On May 25 in Okinawa a U.S. marine was accused of having raped a village woman. The local police issued an arrest warrant, but the suspect remained in U.S. military custody. On June 18 he was turned over to the Japanese police and pleaded guilty, and the local uproar quieted. On September 12 he was sentenced to three and a half years in prison.

Meanwhile, Iraq provided yet another challenge to the uneasy alliance. U.S. Secretary of State Colin Powell was in Tokyo on February 23, urging Japan's support for a U.S. resolution on Iraq in the UN Security Council. On March 8 Foreign Minister Yoriko Kawaguchi announced that Tokyo would back the U.S. position. Ten days later Prime Minister Koizumi strongly supported a U.S. ultimatum to Pres. Saddam Hussein to resign and leave Iraq. Late in March, however, a crowd of Japanese demonstrated near the U.S. Navy base at Yokosuka to protest against Washington's Iraq campaign.

Nevertheless, on July 26 the Diet (parliament) passed a law providing for the dispatch of Japanese troops to Iraq to aid the American occupation (their exact role was to be defined later). This was the first deployment of Japan's military units into a war zone since the end of World War II. According to a newspaper poll, only 33% of respondents supported the legislation, while 55% opposed the measure. It was a supreme historical irony that the step doubtless violated Japan's postwar constitution, which the U.S. had helped Japan to draft. The organic law indicated why the present-day Japanese military had been called the Self Defense Forces.

Tokyo was less reluctant to help on another front. In late March the Japanese launched a low-orbit spy satellite from Tanegashima (south of Kyushu), ignoring immediate threats by North Korea. The long-run danger was, however, taken seriously; in 1998 a missile had been fired from North Korea over Japan into the sea. On April 16 Defense Minister Shigeru Ishiba urged an expansion of defenses and later asked the Diet to appropriate funds to support a missile shield designed by Americans.

On May 23, speaking during a visit to U.S. Pres. George W. Bush's ranch in Texas, Prime Minister Koizumi cautioned North Korea that any development of nuclear weapons would be opposed by Japan and the U.S. He stressed that the issue should be settled through diplomacy. In Beijing in over three days of intensive talks that ended on August 29, Tokyo's diplomats had an opportunity to size up Pyongyang's representatives and to hear their arguments. Then Japan joined four other nations—South Korea, the U.S., Russia, and China—to warn North Korea that it had no alternative but to abandon further nuclear activity. In the month that followed, the North Koreans vacillated between agreeing to talks and offering threats.

During the year Japan enjoyed quieter relations with China, its largest neighbour. In 2002 China had surpassed the U.S. as the leading exporter to Japan; imports from China totaled more than $60 billion, accounting for about 18% of all Japanese imports.

Moreover, Tokyo moved promptly when on August 4 three dozen Chinese workers became ill in Qiqihar, northeastern China, where they had dug up five drums that apparently contained mustard gas and had been left there by Japanese troops at the end of World War II. Japan's Foreign Ministry quickly investigated and issued an apology, stating that the sickness "was caused by abandoned chemical weapons of the former Japanese Army." That same week the Japanese were mounting ceremonies to mark the 25th anniversary of the normalization of relations with China.

Japan also welcomed improved relations with Russia. On January 10, when Prime Minister Koizumi conferred with Pres. Vladimir Putin in Moscow, the two agreed to speed up settlement of a territorial dispute over a chain of tiny islands (the Japanese called them the Northern Territories; the Russians referred to them as the southern Kurils). The islands were occupied by Russia in 1945. As a result, the two nations legally remained in a state of war. In typical fashion the agreement was called an "action plan" and did not establish how or when the dispute should be settled.

The Russians were motivated, however, by the possibility of Japanese support for two construction and trade projects. Two days after the meeting in Moscow, Koizumi was in Khabarovsk. It was the first visit by a Japanese leader to Russia's Far East. He was lobbying for the building of a 4,000-km (2,500-mi) oil pipeline from Angarsk (near Lake Baikal) to Nakhodka (a port on the Sea of Japan just east of Vladivostok). The line would cost $5 billion, but it would carry one million barrels a day and thus aid Japan, the second largest consumer of oil in the world.

The second plan involved a Russian-Japanese partnership on the construction of a $10 billion liquefied-natural-gas facility, the first in Russia. The drilling of a series of wells tapping an offshore area off Sakhalin Island would begin in June. An official of the Sakhalin Energy Investment Co. predicted that in 10 years liquefied gas would supply 15% of Tokyo's electricity needs.

On February 14, 22 of the world's largest economies sent ministers to Tokyo for a three-day World Trade Organization (WTO) conference on agricultural tariffs and subsidies. The U.S., Japan, and other developed nations were pressed by less-developed nations to reduce barriers on agricultural products. Eventually the developed group proposed a reduction in its tariffs, but only to 25% of the value of, for example, grain, fruit, and meat products. South Korea and nations in the European Union also advocated only limited reductions. At work in Japan and in the U.S. was the relatively powerful political clout of agricultural sectors of the economies seeking to continue protection. Japanese rice farmers, for example, had been a vital source of support for the LDP. At the WTO meeting in Tokyo, the only agreement was to continue talks at an interim conference in Cancún, Mex., in September. The gathering there, however, also fell into deadlock and adjourned, and a final session in 2005 was quite uncertain.

Meanwhile, late in January Tokyo announced that it planned a 25% reduction in Japan's support of the UN. Spokesmen pointed out that although the country's GDP had accounted for slightly more than 14% of the world economy, Japan had covered nearly 20% of the UN budget. (ARDATH W. BURKS)

JORDAN

Area: 89,342 sq km (34,495 sq mi)
Population (2003 est.): 5,395,000 (including nearly 1,725,000 Palestinian refugees, most of whom hold Jordanian citizenship)
Capital: Amman
Head of state and government: King Abdullah II, assisted by Prime Ministers 'Ali Abu al-Raghib and, from October 25, Faisal al-Fayez

The World Economic Forum (WEF) convened its extraordinary meeting, held June 21–23, 2003, on the Jordanian shores of the Dead Sea. Klaus Schwab, president of the WEF, justified the meeting place by stating that "the world and, above all, the [Middle Eastern] region were in urgent need of healing processes." Policy makers, political leaders, academicians, intellectuals, and religious leaders, representing 65 countries, attended the gathering, which was hosted by King Abdullah II. The conference addressed such issues as peace, combating terrorism in the Middle East, trade, and economic reforms.

Since the majority of the citizens of Jordan were of Palestinian origin, King Abdullah II was keenly interested in reviving the stalled Israeli-Palestinian peace process. On June 4 Abdullah II hosted a summit at the Red Sea resort of Al-ʿAqabah, where Israeli Prime Minister Ariel Sharon, Palestinian Prime Minister Mahmoud Abbas (*see* BIOGRAPHIES), and U.S. Pres. George W. Bush met to discuss the road map for peace.

At her home near Amman, together with her supporters, Hayat al-Massimi (front left), a female activist, celebrates her election to the Jordanian parliament in June.

It was the first meeting between top Israeli and Palestinian leaders since the second *intifadah* (uprising) erupted on Sept. 28, 2000.

Despite the efforts of the Jordanian authorities to stem the power of the Islamists, the latter made an alliance with Pan-Arabists and won the elections in May for the powerful Jordan Engineers Association (JEA), which had more than 50,000 active members. As a leading civil-society organization, the JEA had been used by its leaders as a vehicle for championing the antinormalization movement with Israel.

On June 17, 1.3 million Jordanians (58.8% of registered voters) participated in parliamentary elections. The Jordanian authorities had redrawn the electoral constituencies in a manner that favoured the election of tribal and independent candidates. It came as no surprise then when the vast majority of the seats (85 out of 110) were won by these groups. The representation of political parties was meagre, with the exception of the Islamic Action Front, the political arm of the Muslim Brothers, which won 17 seats and became the leading opposition bloc in the parliament.

Members of the council of the Jordan Farmers Union (JFU), which represented 7,000 members, threatened on June 25 to submit their resignations if the government "continued ignoring the plight of the union and the farmers." The JFU asked for the cancellation of recently imposed taxes on agricultural inputs and products.

On July 31 two daughters of Saddam Hussein, Rana and Raghad, were permitted to enter Jordan together with their nine children and were given refuge by the Jordanian authorities. Shortly thereafter, the embassy of Jordan in Iraq was the target of a terrorist attack involving a truck bomb that exploded on August 7; 11 persons were killed and more than 50 were wounded in the incident. (MARIUS DEEB)

KAZAKHSTAN

Area: 2,724,900 sq km (1,052,090 sq mi)
Population (2003 est.): 14,790,000
Capital: Astana
Head of state and government: President Nursultan Nazarbayev, assisted by Prime Ministers Imangali Tasmagambetov and, from June 13, Daniyal Akhmetov

Kazakhstan joined with Russia, Belarus, and Ukraine at the Commonwealth of Independent States summit in Yalta, Ukraine, in September 2003 to create the Common Economic Space, an integration mechanism for the four strongest economies in the CIS. The concept had been proposed by Kazakh Pres. Nursultan Nazarbayev in the early 1990s, and its realization was a tribute to Kazakhstan's success in the transition to a modern market economy. The U.S. had already announced in June that aid to Kazakhstan would be reduced because of the country's economic achievements, and Kazakhstan was generally acknowledged to be the richest state in Central Asia because of its oil and mineral wealth. Economics Minister Kairat Kelimbetov warned the Cabinet of Ministers in June, however, that significant sections of the population—pensioners, the unemployed, and the handicapped—were not benefiting from the improvement in the economy.

Prime Minister Imangali Tasmagambetov resigned on June 11 after losing a struggle with Parliament over a new land code that introduced private ownership of agricultural land. Many politicians argued that the terms of the code meant that only the wealthy would be able to buy land. The code was finally adopted by Parliament in late June after the president himself had made corrections to the draft. The new prime minister, Daniyal Akhmetov, presented an action plan at the end of

June that was intended to triple gross domestic product by 2015; he also promised to raise taxes on the oil and gas industries and then had to reassure foreign investors that existing contracts in these industries would not be altered.

The domestic opposition and the international community complained that Kazakhstan's ruling elite was becoming increasingly authoritarian. The independent media were sharply critical of a draft media law that it said would attempt to curb the reporting of stories that upset the government, such as the so-called Kazakhgate affair, in which American businessmen were accused of having paid bribes to high-ranking Kazakh government officials.

The government also came under international criticism over the sentencing of independent journalist Sergey Duvanov in January to three and a half years in prison on a rape charge that the opposition insisted was fabricated in retaliation for his stories about high-level corruption. In February the European Parliament adopted a resolution expressing concern over the course of democratic reform and the situation of the independent media in Kazakhstan that worried the government and inspired the opposition. (BESS BROWN)

KENYA

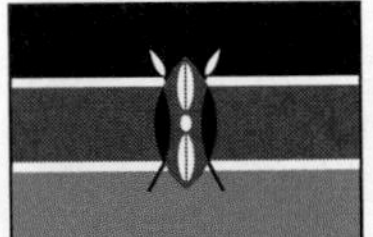

Area: 582,646 sq km (224,961 sq mi)
Population (2003 est.): 31,639,000
Capital: Nairobi
Head of state and government: President Mwai Kibaki

The overwhelming victory of Mwai Kibaki (*see* BIOGRAPHIES) and the National Rainbow Coalition in the presidential and parliamentary elections in December 2002 encouraged aid agencies to renew their offers of assistance in 2003. The new government immediately implemented its election promise to offer free primary education to all (the cost would be paid from tax income). The gesture met with such an enthusiastic response, however, that classrooms were overcrowded and there were not enough teachers to cope with the influx of students. Nor was the government able to fulfill its promise to respond to the teachers' demand for higher salaries within the previously agreed-upon 100-day time frame.

Eager to take advantage of the free primary education promised by Kenya's new president, Mwai Kibaki, parents and children line up to register at a school in Nairobi on the first day of school, January 6.

AP/Wide World Photos

Kibaki was also determined to tackle the corruption that had ruined the country's economy and had resulted in the withdrawal of foreign aid. Early in January two anticorruption courts were established, and two anticorruption bills were prepared for parliamentary debate. In February Kibaki suspended Chief Justice Bernard Chunga and appointed a tribunal to investigate Chunga's conduct while in office, and on March 19 a committee was appointed to investigate the integrity of the judiciary as a whole.

The government's good intentions were met with obstacles, however. The anticorruption bills had to be withdrawn when MPs threatened to vote against them. MPs also demanded a 20% increase in their salaries and substantial grants to enable them to purchase cars—as a disincentive, they maintained, to corruption and the taking of bribes.

In addition, there were complaints that measures proposed by a commission in 2002 to introduce the new constitution had been slow to materialize. There was also pressure to appoint an executive prime minister to serve as a check on the power of the president. Much of this discontent sprang from personal ambition and ethnic rivalry between members of the coalition, some of whom claimed that too many important offices were being awarded to the Kikuyu inhabitants of the Mount Kenya district, who were closely linked with President Kibaki.

The problem of cabinet appointments was exacerbated when Vice Pres. Michael Kijana Wamalwa died in August. The appointment of Wamalwa, a Luhya from western Kenya, had symbolized the interethnic character of the government, and some feared that the balance might not be maintained. The murder in September of Crispin Odhiambo Mbai, a leading figure in the campaign for a new constitution, then gave rise to additional fears over the revival of the government practice of forcibly silencing critics, as had been witnessed during the presidency of Daniel arap Moi. In September Moi resigned as chairman of the Kenya African National Union.

Despite these difficulties and criticism from opposition parties, Kibaki continued to pursue his anticorruption campaign. He suspended 6 of the 9 Appeal Court judges and 17 of the 36 High Court judges for alleged corruption, and in October two tribunals began investigating them.

Political rivalries were not the government's only problem. The agricultural sector of the economy remained depressed; world prices for primary produce remained at a low level. At the same time, the euphoria that had greeted the early actions of the new government resulted in a marked appreciation in the value of the Kenya shilling, a development that added to the problems of exporters. Fears of terrorist action also seriously affected income from tourism when in May both the U.K. and the U.S. governments temporarily discouraged their citizens from traveling to Kenya. To this catalog of difficulties, nature added its quota when heavy rains in western Kenya in May caused flooding that killed more than 40 people and displaced 60,000.

(KENNETH INGHAM)

KIRIBATI

Area: 811 sq km (313 sq mi)
Population (2003 est.): 87,900
Capital: Bairiki, on Tarawa
Head of state and government: Presidents Teburoro Tito and, from July 10, Anote Tong

A period of political instability and a series of elections dominated Kiribati in 2003. Political parties followed tradition by reflecting personal political allegiance and local issues rather than philosophical differences or widespread popular support. Apart from personal and local issues, the main election debates were over the economy, the government's leasing of aircraft, and the presence of a Chinese spy satellite base on Tarawa Atoll.

In November 2002 Pres. Teburoro Tito's Maneaba Te Mauri (MTM) party had been heavily defeated at the polls, but a subsequent split within the opposition Boutokaan Te Koaua (BTK) party helped him secure his third (and final, under the constitution) term in the March 2003 presidential elections. When the House of Assembly met, however, the government was brought down in a no-confidence vote, which led to the establishment of an interim administration under the Council of State. Another general election in May was followed by a remarkable presidential election on July 4. Harry Tong, a former leading opposition figure, represented the ruling MTM, while his younger brother, Anote, represented the opposition. Anote Tong was successful by a margin of about 1,100 votes (47.4–43.5%). The new government's recognition of Taiwan led China to withdraw diplomatic ties and close its satellite station and embassy. President Tong announced that Taiwan had promised development assistance of $A 10 million (about U.S.$7.2 million) a year.

(BARRIE MACDONALD)

KOREA, DEMOCRATIC PEOPLE'S REPUBLIC OF

Area: 122,762 sq km (47,399 sq mi)
Population (2003 est.): 22,466,000
Capital: Pyongyang
Head of state and government: Chairman of the National Defense Commission Kim Jong Il

North Korea began the year 2003 with a confrontation with the United States over the development of nuclear weapons. North Korea charged that the U.S. had not fulfilled its part of the 1994 agreements to supply aid in exchange for cessation of its nuclear weapons development program. North Korea had changed its position. Rather than continuing adherence to the Nuclear Non-proliferation Treaty, North Korea announced that it was pulling out and would proceed to develop nuclear weapons. Talks between North and South Korea, the U.S., China, Russia, and Japan were held in Beijing in August but ended without agreement. Disputes over what compensation could be offered if North Korea did not develop nuclear arms caused postponement of the multilateral talks past the end of the year.

In February, North Korea tested an antiship missile by firing it into the East Sea (Sea of Japan). The timing was significant; it happened on the day before South Korea inaugurated its new president, Roh Moo Hyun. The 53rd anniversary of the outbreak of the Korean War was commemorated in June with an anti-American demonstration in the streets of Pyongyang reportedly attended by over one million people. Even so, relations with South Korea were not universally bad. Several high-level meetings took place between officials of the two countries at which agreement was reached to develop a combined economic development zone in Kaesong, just across the demilitarized zone from South Korea. The year also saw more reunions of separated families, exchanges of letters, and sports competitions between the two rival countries.

The North Korean economy improved at a modest rate, but help was still needed from the international community to provide the population with food and grains. Exports picked up, and for the first time in the history of the two countries, North Korea's exports to South Korea surpassed those to its longtime ally, China. Russia was quick to take advantage of the situation when North Korea's trade opportunities with many states were effectively closed off by the U.S. and Japan.

(MARK PETERSON)

AP/Wide World Photos

Brothers Choe Soon Bo (right) of North Korea and Choe Soon Nam are overcome with emotion when Soon Nam, one of the several hundred South Koreans permitted to make a three-day visit to the north, arrives in September.

KOREA, REPUBLIC OF

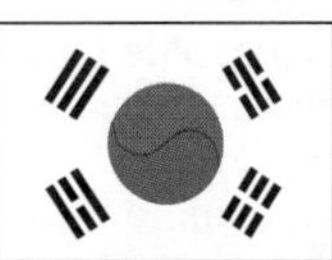

Area: 99,538 sq km (38,432 sq mi)
Population (2003 est.): 47,925,000
Capital: Seoul
Head of state and government: Presidents Kim Dae Jung and, from February 25, Roh Moo Hyun, assisted by Prime Minister Kim Suk Soo and, from February 26, Goh Kun

On Feb. 25, 2003, South Korea began a new political era with the inauguration

AP/Wide World Photos

South Korean Pres. Roh Moo Hyun and his wife, Kwon Yang Sook, walk on the Great Wall during a visit to China in July. China was especially helpful in the struggle to improve relations between the regimes in the north and the south.

of a new president, Roh Moo Hyun. Roh had been an opposition leader during the time of the military governments in the past and had established a reputation as a defender of unpopular and leftist demonstrators. His campaign attracted young people and many who were openly anti-American. For the first time since South Korea developed a truly democratic system in the late 1980s, a political newcomer was elected president. Roh succeeded Kim Dae Jung, who had been an advocate of democracy in his country and who had succeeded Kim Young Sam, another opposition leader, who was elected president when he joined the party set up by the last military government. The two Kims had been active in politics since the 1960s, so Roh's election therefore represented a transition of leadership from an older generation. The new breed of politician was supported by a younger electorate—a generation that had not known the Korean War, the poverty and social strains of rebuilding after the war, or the great economic boom that had made South Korea a strong country. Roh's election symbolized South Korea's coming of age as a modern developed country.

The new administration enjoyed only a brief celebration before the problems of a divided country began to weigh down on it. Soon after his inauguration Roh visited Washington, D.C., in what should have been a joyful celebration and a chance to coordinate efforts on many fronts with South Korea's closest ally. The meeting was not harmonious, however, and unfavourable press reports led to even greater disappointment when Roh returned home. Whereas Roh had campaigned on a promise of engagement with North Korea, in continuation of the policy established by his predecessor and party-mate Kim, the White House was embarking on a policy of confrontation with Pyongyang. North Korea's announcement that it was moving forward with the development of nuclear weapons had greatly disturbed the U.S. administration, which took the position that it would not reward bad behaviour. The South Korean media, meanwhile, took pains to remind Roh that he had pledged not to visit the United States, and the president's level of popular support began to erode. The situation reached such a pass that by October Roh had offered to hold a referendum on his policies and to step down if the public voted against him. The referendum was not held, however, and Roh's approval ratings began to rise somewhat as the year came to a close.

Roh's policies toward North Korea were largely tailored to fit Washington's concerns about Pyongyang's development of nuclear weapons. On other issues, however, South Korea was able to interact with North Korea, and gradually progress was made in joint economic ventures, exchanges of letters, and reunions of separated families.

On the economic front there was good news in 2003. The economy continued its growth and recovery from the crash of 1997. At midyear median personal income regained the $10,000 level that it had reached just before the crash, and industrial output and exports continued to grow. As an example, led by the Hyundai shipyard, South Korea took over the position as the number one shipbuilding country in the world. It was a world leader in personal electronics as well; the country moved into the top five in both cellphone usage per capita and availability of Internet access. Extremely fast broadband connections were available to a higher percentage of people in South Korea than in any other country in the world. (MARK PETERSON)

KUWAIT

Area: 17,818 sq km (6,880 sq mi)
Population (2003 est.): 2,439,000
Capital: Kuwait
Head of state and government: Emir Sheikh Jabir al-Ahmad al-Jabir al-Sabah, assisted by Prime Ministers Crown Prince Sheikh Saad al-Abdullah al-Salim al-Sabah and, from July 13, Sheikh Sabah al-Ahmad al-Jabir al-Sabah

In 2003 the Kuwaiti government supported international efforts to induce Iraqi Pres. Saddam Hussein to resign and leave Iraq voluntarily. When those failed, Kuwait supported the U.S.-led campaign against Iraq and allowed a massive military buildup by U.S. and

Kuwaiti Sheikh Saad al-Abdullah al-Salim al-Sabah is assisted by his aides onto an airplane to the U.K. for a medical checkup in September. Sheikh Saad was replaced as prime minister in 2003 but retained his position as crown prince.

© Stephanie McGehee/Reuters NewMedia Inc./Corbis

British troops on its territory. These forces finally invaded and occupied Iraq in March and April. Afterward, Kuwait was the first Arab country to help the Iraqi people with supplies of fresh water and emergency materials.

A general election was held in Kuwait on July 5. The liberals sustained heavy losses, and the new 50-member National Assembly came under the control of Islamist, conservative, and pro-government elements. The election results stunned liberal Kuwaitis, who had thought that important changes in the region, particularly in Iraq, would set the stage for long-awaited internal reforms, including giving women the right to vote and to be candidates in general elections. Kuwait and Saudi Arabia remained the only two members of the six Gulf Cooperation Council (GCC) states in which women did not have such political rights.

After the election, the emir of Kuwait met a long-standing demand of political activists to separate the position of crown prince from the office of prime minister. On July 13 Sheikh Sabah al-Ahmad al-Jabir al-Sabah (the former foreign minister) was appointed prime minister, while Sheikh Saad al-Abdullah al-Salim al-Sabah, who belonged to a different branch of the ruling family, remained crown prince. The change meant that the prime minister could be subjected to questioning by the National Assembly.

The problem of stateless people (*biduns*) remained unsolved. These immigrants, numbering 100,000 to 250,000, were mainly of Iraqi or Iranian origin and had lived for decades in the country without obtaining Kuwaiti nationality. The Kuwaiti government was awarding them citizenship at the rate of about 5,000 a year, but the process was too slow to solve the problem.

(LOUAY BAHRY)

KYRGYZSTAN

Area: 199,945 sq km (77,199 sq mi), including about 1,250 sq km (480 sq mi) ceded to China in May 2002
Population (2003 est.): 5,059,000
Capital: Bishkek
Head of state and government: President Askar Akayev, assisted by Prime Minister Nikolay Tanayev

Kyrgyzstan's reputation as the Central Asian state that had moved farthest on the road to democracy suffered in 2003 from the increasing authoritarianism of Pres. Askar Akayev and his government. Among opposition demands that the government was unwilling to meet were prosecution of the officials responsible for the killing of five antigovernment demonstrators by police in 2002 and the release from prison of former vice president Feliks Kulov, who was serving a 10-year sentence for crimes allegedly committed during his government service—a sentence widely believed to have been politically motivated because of his opposition to Akayev.

In a report published in April, the World Bank, the International Monetary Fund, the European Bank for Reconstruction and Development, and the Asian Development Bank—all of which had provided financial support to the country since its independence—declared that Kyrgyzstan was the most corrupt of the seven poorest members of the Commonwealth of Independent States (CIS) and the only one where corruption had worsened since 1999. The previous month Akayev had told his National Security Council that many citizens considered corruption to be the reason for Kyrgyzstan's economic ills, a point many opposition figures had been making for years. A National Council for Good Governance was set up in April, but the opposition jeered that the government was the source of the corruption. In September the National Statistical Committee reported that 54% of the population was living below the poverty line.

Official figures continued their practice of trying to silence criticism in the independent media by suing journalists and publications for criminal libel and demanding huge monetary damages, which caused the bankruptcy of a number of publications, including the popular newspaper *Moya Stolitsa,* which was forced to cease publication after Prime Minister Nikolay Tanayev won a libel case against it in June.

Kyrgyzstan continued to host the U.S.-led international antiterrorism coalition air base near Bishkek, from which coalition forces supported military action in Afghanistan. After months of negotiations, the Kyrgyz government agreed to the establishment of a Russian air base some 30 km (18 mi) from the coalition base. The Russian base was ostensibly part of the CIS rapid reaction force, but some

AP/Wide World Photos

On October 23, upon his arrival at Bishkek airport, Russian Pres. Vladimir Putin (left) is greeted by Kyrgyz Pres. Askar Akayev; later in the day Putin opened a Russian military base in the town of Kant, not far from an airbase of the U.S.-led coalition forces.

Kyrgyz observers suggested that it was intended to keep an eye on coalition forces, particularly the Americans.

(BESS BROWN)

LAOS

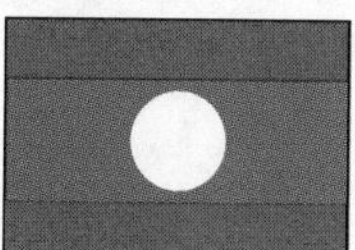

Area: 236,800 sq km (91,429 sq mi)
Population (2003 est.): 5,657,000
Capital: Vientiane
Chief of state: President Khamtay Siphandone
Head of government: Prime Minister Bounngang Vorachith

Laos made headlines in 2003 when a Belgian reporter, a French photographer, and their interpreter (an ethnic Hmong U.S. citizen) were given 15-year prison sentences after a two-hour trial in late June; they were deported two weeks later following intense diplomatic pressure. While reporting on the remaining members of a Hmong hill-tribe army who had been resisting the government since 1975, the trio had been caught in a skirmish in which a village official was killed. Support for the insurgents by U.S.-based Hmong exiles gained sharper focus during the year as the U.S. and Laos moved toward "normal trade relations."

In February, 2 European cyclists and 10 bus travelers died in an ambush on Highway 13, which links Vientiane with the ancient capital, Luang Prabang. Another bus attack in February was followed by an ambush in April in which 12 were killed, a bomb explosion on a bus in the south in June, a border-post gunfight in July, a bomb explosion at a Vientiane bus station and reported clashes in the northwest in August, and grenade attacks in two markets in late October. Dismissed by the government as "bandits," the shadowy perpetrators nevertheless caused embassies to renew travel warnings. In September two men were sentenced to life imprisonment for bombings in 2000 and 2001, and a third was sentenced to 14 months for not having reported the crimes. In October Bouasone Bouphavanh, a close aide to Pres. Khamtay Siphandone, was appointed deputy prime minister responsible for home affairs, which included tackling insurgency.

Aid-dependent Laos, battered by "donor fatigue," security concerns, a weakening currency, and a regional downturn in tourism, was shaken in July by the withdrawal from the Nam Theun-2 hydroelectric power plant project of its largest shareholder, EdF International, a subsidiary of state-owned Electricité de France, one day before a power purchase contract was to be signed with the Electricity Generating Authority of Thailand. In October the French reversed course and Lao officials insisted that the project would be completed in 2009. Prime Minister Bounngang Vorachith told the Fourth National Assembly that GDP growth for 2002–03 was 5.9%, higher than the 5.5% estimated by international agencies but close to projections for 2004.

Thailand approved assistance for a 3.5-km (2.2-mi) railway from its Nong Khai border to Tha Na Lueng in Laos; a 49-km (30-mi) road into northern Laos; cooperation on border security, drugs, and human trafficking; and a tourism tie-up in the Emerald Triangle, which links Laos, Thailand, and Cambodia. The national carrier changed its name to Lao Airlines and leased its first Airbus. In October Foreign Minister Somsavat Lengsavad assured colleagues at the Association of Southeast Asian Nations that Laos, which still lacked a completed five-star hotel or convention centre, would be ready to host their 10th summit in 2004.

(JOHN BEAUMONT ASH)

Annie-Jeanne Reynaud, the mother of French photographer Vincent Reynaud, who with a journalist and an interpreter was arrested by Laotian authorities and sentenced to a long prison term, demonstrates in front of the European Parliament in Strasbourg, France.

LATVIA

Area: 64,589 sq km (24,938 sq mi)
Population (2003 est.): 2,324,000
Capital: Riga
Chief of state: President Vaira Vike-Freiberga
Head of government: Prime Minister Einars Repse

In March 2003 the protocol for Latvia's admission into NATO was signed, as was, a month later, the treaty of accession to the European Union. Latvia was set to become a full-fledged member of both in 2004. Despite an upsurge of "Euroskepticism" earlier in 2003, in the referendum in September 67% of the Latvian electorate endorsed EU membership.

Contributing to peacekeeping efforts in Iraq, Afghanistan, and the Balkans, Latvia enjoyed good relations with international organizations and countries throughout the world. Relations with Russia cooled, however, as Latvia's membership in the EU and NATO drew nearer. Despite complaints from Riga and protests from Russia's largest oil producers, Moscow stuck to the order issued in 2002 to stop the flow of Russian petroleum to the Latvian port of Ventspils for transshipment abroad. Disregarding Moscow's accusations that it was violating the rights of its Russian-speaking population, Latvia continued to prosecute former Soviet officials for crimes against humanity committed during and after World War II. The rhetoric escalated in autumn when, after years of preparation, an education reform was launched in national minority schools; it stipulated instruction in Latvian of 60% of the curriculum of public secondary schools. Formerly teaching was conducted overwhelmingly in Russian.

Despite the disastrous grain harvest and plummeting revenues from Ventspils, the country's economy grew, which enabled raising pensions and wages in 2003 and increasing the minimum wage on Jan. 1, 2004. Growth of GDP in 2003 was expected to reach the 2002 figure of 6.1%.

Prime Minister Einars Repse's government was buffeted by tensions derived from its inexperience and inconsistencies, strong-handed leadership, inherent difficulties of harmonizing coalition interests, and sharp criticism from the more experienced opposition parties. Public support for the government and Repse's New Era party faltered but resumed, owing especially to the government's fight against corruption. The reelection in 2003 of the widely respected Vaira Vike-Freiberga to another four-year term as president ensured political stability. (DZINTRA BUNGS)

LEBANON

Area: 10,400 sq km (4,016 sq mi)
Population (2003 est.): 3,728,000 (excluding Palestinian refugees estimated to number nearly 400,000)
Capital: Beirut
Chief of state: President Gen. Émile Lahoud
Head of government: Prime Minister Rafiq al-Hariri

The dominant issue in Lebanese politics in 2003 was the polarization between Pres. Gen. Émile Lahoud and Prime Minister Rafiq al-Hariri. The main thrust of the discord was al-Hariri's concern over the possibility of the renewal of the president's term in office for another six years or the extension of his term for an additional three years starting in late 2004, when Lahoud's term was due to expire. Their differences probably accounted for Lahoud heading the duties of the ministerial council, an activity that was usually presided over by the prime minister. The latter's position was strengthened by the highest Maronite Christian authority in the country, Patriarch Nasrallah Sfeir, who openly expressed opposition to constitutional amendments and to renewal, though not necessarily extension, of the presidential term.

Tension surfaced between Beirut and Washington in September when anti-Syrian former prime minister Gen. Michel Aoun spoke out against the Syrian military and political presence in Lebanon in an open session of the U.S. Congress. The Lebanese authorities considered Aoun's testimony an act of treason and started legal proceedings against him. This led to an unfriendly debate between Vincent Battle, the U.S. ambassador to Beirut, and a number of Lebanese parliamentarians. Prior to this development Aoun, who lived in France and headed the anti-Syrian Free Patriotic Movement, had proclaimed that he intended to run in the next Lebanese parliamentary elections. He was heartened in August when his candidate won in the by-election in Baabda-Aley.

Strain in the regional political atmosphere also affected Lebanon. An Israeli bombing raid on Syrian territory near Damascus in early October, the first such military act in three decades, and the approval by the U.S. Congress of the Syria Accountability and Lebanese Sovereignty Restoration Act made it necessary for Lebanon to send troops to the southern borders with Israel. In addition, the act classified Hezbollah, the main Lebanese resistance force in the south, as a Syrian-backed terrorist group. The act also called for the Syrian army to evacuate its troops (numbering about 20,000) from Lebanon or face sanctions. In July, Syria had withdrawn its troops from Beirut, ending almost 25 years of its military presence in that city.

Economically, the government had promised in 2002 to lower the budget deficit to 25% of spending, but the deficit remained as high as 38%. The privatization of state assets proved much more difficult than expected, and political factors hindered the downsizing of the bureaucracy. Tourism rose by 4%, however, and the national flag carrier, Middle East Airlines, made $3 million in profit, registering positive revenues for the first time in 26 years. On a negative note, rampant corruption earned Lebanon a ranking of 78 on the list of 133 countries that were perceived as corrupt in the 2003 index released by Transparency International. (MAHMOUD HADDAD)

LESOTHO

Area: 30,355 sq km (11,720 sq mi)
Population (2003 est.): 1,802,000
Capital: Maseru
Chief of state: King Letsie III
Head of government: Prime Minister Bethuel Pakalitha Mosisili

After years of political crisis, Lesotho enjoyed relative stability in 2003, with the military back in its barracks and the king performing only honorific duties. The first mixed member proportional representation Parliament convened in July and met sporadically thereafter. The government took the lead in trying to grapple with the country's serious socioeconomic problems.

A harsh winter drought cut cereal production to less than 60% of normal levels. Agricultural production was further reduced as HIV spread among the rural population, many of whom were landless and had no income; considerable quantities of food aid were needed to prevent mass starvation.

By 2003 Lesotho had one of the highest HIV prevalence rates in the world. An estimated 31% of the adults were infected, and more than 80% of those dying of AIDS-related illnesses were in the productive age group (ages 15–49). Half of all hospital patients were HIV infected, and large numbers of children had been orphaned. Though the government committed about $5.6 million to programs to improve knowledge of the disease and boost prevention efforts and donors and civil society organizations matched that amount, these sums fell far short of what was required. Factors contributing to the spread of the disease were the long periods of time that some 60,000 Basotho men spent away from home working on the mines and farms of South Africa, the belief that having sex with a virgin would cure HIV, and the use of shared knives in circumcision rituals.

Meanwhile, following the 2002 conviction and sentencing of Masupha Sole—the former chief executive officer of the Lesotho Highlands Development Authority—a Canadian engineering company, Acres International, and a German engineering company were convicted of having paid bribes and were fined large sums. (CHRISTOPHER SAUNDERS)

LIBERIA

Area: 97,754 sq km (37,743 sq mi)
Population (2003 est.): 3,317,000 (including about 300,000 refugees in neighbouring countries)
Capital: Monrovia
Head of state and government: Presidents Charles Taylor and, from August 11, Moses Blah; and, from October 14, Chairman of the National Transitional Government Charles Gyude Bryant

AP/Wide World Photos

Pres. Charles Taylor of Liberia is pictured on August 11, shortly before he handed over power to his vice president and fled the country. By year's end Taylor had been declared a war criminal, and officials were seeking his extradition from Nigeria.

The three-year-old civil war that had gripped Liberia, killing or displacing thousands of citizens and contributing to the destabilization of the entire region, finally came to an end in 2003. In early February, Defense Minister Daniel Chea admitted that the armed forces were facing difficulties against the rebels because of an international weapons embargo. While government troops faced major shortages, rebels were apparently being supplied by neighbouring Guinea, which had ongoing border disputes with Liberia. In May the UN imposed an export ban on Liberian unsawn timber, further crippling the government's ability to fund military actions.

In June, as rebel forces began closing around the capital, a UN-sponsored war-crimes tribunal indicted Pres. Charles Taylor for his part in sponsoring a bloody rebellion in neighbouring Sierra Leone. The indictment came while Taylor was in Ghana attending peace talks between his government and rebel groups. The Ghanaian government ignored the well-publicized indictment long enough for Taylor to attend a ceremony with other African leaders before traveling back to Liberia. Taylor's indictment emboldened Liberians and foreign leaders to call for his removal.

On August 11 Taylor went into exile in Nigeria, leaving Vice Pres. Moses Blah in charge. Nigerian peacekeeping troops representing ECOWAS (the Economic Community of West African States) began to enter Monrovia in early August. In October, as occasional gun battles still flared up in Monrovia, the UN took charge of Liberian peacekeeping. On October 14 Christian leader and businessman Charles Gyude Bryant was sworn in to head a new transitional government.

In December the UN launched a disarmament program, offering money and vocational training to an estimated 40,000 former soldiers if they surrendered their weapons. After fighting and rioting had broken out among people desperate for the promised remuneration, the UN paused the program after less than two weeks. As 2003 came to a close, UN peacekeepers began to move beyond the capital in an attempt to make the country safe for the return of refugees. (ANDREW EISENBERG)

LIBYA

Area: 1,759,540 sq km (679,362 sq mi)
Population (2003 est.): 5,551,000
Capital: Tripoli (policy-making body intermittently meets in Surt)
Chief of state: (de facto) Col. Muammar al-Qaddafi; (nominal) Secretary of the General People's Congress Zentani Muhammad al-Zentani
Head of government: Secretaries of the General People's Committee (Prime Ministers) Mubarak Abdallah al-Shamikh and, from June 14, Shokri Ghanem

In August 2003 Libya finally reached a deal that would end 11 years of UN sanctions that had been imposed for the bombing of Pan Am Flight 103, which killed 270 people at Lockerbie, Scot., in December 1988. After years of negotiation (most recently and intensely by British diplomats), Libya agreed to pay $2.7 billion to the families of the victims. On September 12 the UN Security Council lifted its sanctions; the U.S. abstained in the vote. (The sanctions had actually been suspended in 1999 when Libya agreed to give up two agents for trial in a Dutch court.) Libya officially recognized the possibility that a Libyan had planted the bomb, but the blame did not extend to the government or to its leader, Muammar al-Qaddafi. The Security Council action was stalled for several weeks because France had threatened to exercise a veto unless the victims of the French UTA Flight 772, downed over the Sahara in 1989, received the same level of compensation—$10 million per victim rather than the previously agreed-upon $194,000. (In 1999 a French court had ordered Libya in absentia to pay a total of $33 million.) After initial hesitation, Libya said that it would pay the additional higher sum. As a result, France also abstained in the Security Council vote.

The U.S. government was not convinced that the Libyan leadership had renounced terrorism. Therefore, U.S. trade sanctions remained in place. Meanwhile, American companies were eager to get a share of the expanding Libyan market. Months of secret diplomacy bore fruit late in December when Libya agreed to jettison its unconventional weapons under international supervision, which was expected to lead to the lifting of U.S. sanctions.

Radical economic reforms were being contemplated. For three decades Libya had been a principled socialist state enduring uncomfortably variable levels of oil revenues. It had a low-wage policy, and food and public-utility prices were heavily subsidized. In 2003, however, newly appointed Prime Minister Shokri Ghanem, an economist with wide international experience, launched, with Qaddafi's public blessing, a program to introduce market incentives, privatization, and the reform of economic regulation. (J.A. ALLAN)

LIECHTENSTEIN

Area: 160 sq km (62 sq mi)
Population (2003 est.): 34,100
Capital: Vaduz
Chief of state: Prince Hans Adam II
Head of government: Otmar Hasler

In 2003 Prince Hans Adam II won his long-standing battle for constitutional changes that would greatly increase his powers in Liechtenstein. A referendum held on March 16 granted the prince sweeping powers to veto parliamentary legislation, dismiss the entire government, and implement emergency powers. With a voter turnout of 87.7%, a huge majority of 64.3% voted for the prince's changes, while only 35.7% voted against. The 44-nation Council of Europe opposed the referendum and called the changes "a serious step backward" that might easily "lead to the isolation of Liechtenstein within the European community of states." Opposition within the country had been led by former prime minister Mario Frick. In August Hans Adam announced that he would cede power to his son Alois in 2004.

An initiative by the Organisation for Economic Co-operation and Development (OECD) in January introduced new rules to ensure that European Union citizens would be taxed on income from savings accounts they had established abroad. Liechtenstein, which was not an EU member and opposed the directives, had been cited by the OECD as one of the world's few remaining real tax havens. In July two former U.S. Pentagon officials were convicted of extortion, fraud, and money laundering in a scheme to profit from minority contracts; the money-laundering scheme had involved bank accounts in Liechtenstein.

(ANNE ROBY)

Liechtenstein's Prince Hans Adam II won a big victory in a referendum in March, gaining powers over the citizens of his mountainous principality that no other royal in Europe could rival.

AP/Wide World Photos

LITHUANIA

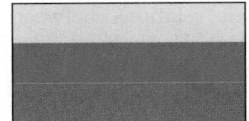

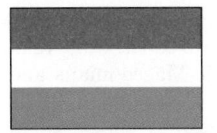

Area: 65,300 sq km (25,212 sq mi)
Population (2003 est.): 3,454,000
Capital: Vilnius
Chief of state: Presidents Valdas Adamkus and, from February 26, Rolandas Paksas
Head of government: Prime Minister Algirdas Brazauskas

In the second round of voting in the presidential elections on Jan. 5, 2003, Rolandas Paksas (*see* BIOGRAPHIES), the leader of Lithuania's new populist Liberal Democratic Party, emerged the victor. The young and aggressive Paksas received 54.7% of votes, defeating the much more experienced centre-right incumbent, Pres. Valdas Adamkus, with 45.3%. Voter turnout was 52.6%. Late in the year, though, allegations arose that Paksas's top administration had ties to Russian mobsters, and the parliament began impeachment proceedings on December 18.

Lithuania's economy registered a GDP growth rate of 9.4% and a 25.9% rise in exports in the first quarter of the year, while the unemployment rate decreased to 9.7%. Lithuania was dubbed "the Baltic Tiger" by *The Economist.* Nonetheless, one-fifth of the population was living in poverty, and salaries of academics and physicians had been frozen for six years.

In international affairs, on May 8 the U.S. Senate unanimously ratified the enlargement of NATO, including the Baltic States. On May 10–11 Lithuania voted to join the EU and became the first Baltic candidate country to hold a referendum on the issue (89.95% voted "for," with 63.4% turnout).

The centre-right Homeland Union (Conservatives) organized a 10-day demonstration in September near (Russian-owned) Lukoil service stations in Lithuania to protest Russia's plans to extract oil in the Baltic Sea five kilometres (three miles) off Lithuania's coast. It feared ecological disaster for the Curonian Spit, a Lithuanian national park and UNESCO World Natural Heritage site.

Lithuania celebrated its 750th anniversary, dated to the coronation of King Mindaugas, on July 6. The largest-ever World Lithuanian Song and Dance Festival took place in Vilnius, and national pride surged again in September when the national team won gold in the European basketball championship in Stockholm.

(DARIUS FURMONAVIČIUS)

LUXEMBOURG

Area: 2,586 sq km (999 sq mi)
Population (2003 est.): 453,000
Capital: Luxembourg
Chief of state: Grand Duke Henri
Head of government: Prime Minister Jean-Claude Juncker

In 2003 Luxembourg actively pursued its commitment to the integration of Europe. Prime Minister Jean-Claude Juncker represented Luxembourg at the European Council meeting held in Brussels on October 16–17. EU foreign ministers met in Luxembourg on October 13 and approved an aid plan for the reconstruction of Iraq. The pledge of €200 million (about $235.5 million) required approval by the European Parliament.

In the ongoing battle against tax evasion, 12 of the 15 EU countries agreed to share information on savings accounts of EU citizens abroad. Luxembourg, Austria, and Belgium held out for their banking secrecy laws, and they (along with nonmember Switzerland) were allowed instead to impose a withholding tax on the accounts. Meanwhile, Luxembourg maintained its status as one of the world's richest countries per capita.

A ceremony on October 15 marked the return of archives from World War II. The files of the Grande Loge organization had been hidden during the Nazi occupation, but they had been seized by the Red Army in the last months of the war and removed to the Soviet Union. The director of Luxembourg's national archives received the eight cartons of historical files.

(ANNE ROBY)

MACEDONIA

Area: 25,713 sq km (9,928 sq mi)
Population (2003 est.): 2,056,000
Capital: Skopje
Chief of state: President Boris Trajkovski
Head of government: Prime Minister Branko Crvenkovski

In 2003, two years after Macedonia almost descended into civil war, relations between ethnic Macedonians and the sizable ethnic Albanian minority were again put to the test. A series of bomb explosions—in Struga in February, in Skopje and Kumanovo in June, and again in Skopje in August—a shoot-out in Skopje on July 9 that left five people dead, and the abduction of two policemen near Kumanovo the same month were the main incidents. The shadowy separatist Albanian National Army claimed responsibility for many of these acts. In addition, there were violent clashes between ethnic Albanian and ethnic Macedonian youths in Tetovo and elsewhere. These incidents strained relations between the ruling parties. There were also positive developments in the field of interethnic relations as well, however, including the legalization of the Albanian-language Tetovo University, further moves to increase the official use of Albanian, and attempts to boost the percentage of ethnic Albanian army officers. On May 28 the parliament passed a law granting amnesties to those who handed over guns within the framework of a 45-day nationwide weapons-collection program that was started on November 1.

Macedonia promised amnesty to ethnic Albanian oppositionists who gave up their arms and ammunition. Here, at an army training base in Krivolak in late December, Macedonian soldiers destroy shells turned in under the program.

AP/Wide World Photos

Pres. Boris Trajkovski on April 7 pardoned former interior minister Dosta Dimovska and a former high-ranking Interior Ministry official, both of whom had been implicated in a 2001 wiretapping scandal. While Trajkovski defended his controversial pardons, Dimovska resigned as head of the Macedonian Intelligence Agency in an attempt to defuse tensions between Trajkovski and the government. In early November Prime Minister Branko Crvenkovski replaced the ministers of finance, economy, justice, and transport and communications.

On March 31 the European Union launched Operation Concordia, which replaced NATO's Allied Harmony peacekeeping mission. In July the six-month mandate of the 400-strong mission was extended to December 15, and then on September 29 EU foreign ministers agreed to replace Concordia with a 200-strong police mission. Relations between Macedonia and its neighbours remained stable, although pending issues such as the dispute between Skopje and Athens over Macedonia's name remained unresolved. Macedonia strengthened cooperation with Albania and Croatia, particularly in the fields of security, defense, and infrastructure projects.

After the government supported the United States in the war against Iraq and granted U.S. troops use of Macedonian military facilities, the parliament on April 22 approved the deployment of a small military contingent to Iraq, which embarked in early June. On June 30 Macedonia and the U.S. signed a bilateral agreement prohibiting the handover of each other's citizens to the International Criminal Court; the agreement was ratified by the Macedonian parliament on October 16. On April 4 Macedonia became the 146th member of the World Trade Organization.

Macedonia's economy was expected to grow by about 3% in 2003, with low inflation and a target budget deficit of 2.5% of GDP. Unemployment of around 30% and social problems led to a series of strikes throughout the year, however. In late July the German WAZ media group announced that it had purchased majority stakes in three major Macedonian-language daily newspapers, giving it a near monopoly, especially as the state-owned publishing house Nova Makedonija went into liquidation in October. (STEFAN KRAUSE)

MADAGASCAR

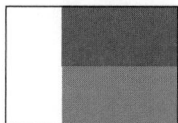

Area: 587,041 sq km (226,658 sq mi)
Population (2003 est.): 16,606,000
Capital: Antananarivo
Chief of state and head of government: President Marc Ravalomanana

In 2003 Madagascar was trying to recover from the political crisis that in 2002 had left 70 people dead and hundreds of thousands without work. After having his TIM ("I Love Madagascar") party score a landslide in the parliamentary elections in December 2002, Pres. Marc Ravalomanana began in 2003 to implement a program designed to boost economic growth and recovery; the AREMA party of former president Didier Ratsiraka had won only three seats. After the 2002 election, Ravalomanana, who had disputed the 2001 election results and had himself sworn in as president, was accepted by the African Union as the country's legitimate president. Representatives of the World Bank and the IMF visited Madagascar, and investment began to pick up. In September the African Development Fund approved a loan of $34.4 million to Madagascar to assist humanitarian and economic-recovery programs. Some of the factories that had closed during the unrest began to reopen. On the other hand, much of the country's infrastructure had been damaged, and the population largely remained in dire poverty. Malnutrition was rife, and many people in urban areas lived on the streets.

Madagascar, which produced half the world supply of vanilla, saw the price rise to an all-time high, but this was partly due to scarcity; more than 20% of the crop had been destroyed in a cyclone in 2000.

Some 200 political prisoners, including a former prime minister, remained in jail and faced charges ranging from corruption to endangering the state. Ratsiraka, having lived in exile in France since July 2002, seemed beyond the reach of attempts to bring him to trial. In December former prime minister Tantely Andrianarivo, who had led Ratsiraka's government, was sentenced to 12 years' hard labour and fined $7 million.

In September Ravalomanana told the fifth World Parks Congress in Durban, S.Af., that his government would more than triple the size of the areas under protection over the next five years, create wildlife corridors that would connect existing parks, preserve rare habitats, and protect watersheds.
(CHRISTOPHER SAUNDERS)

MALAWI

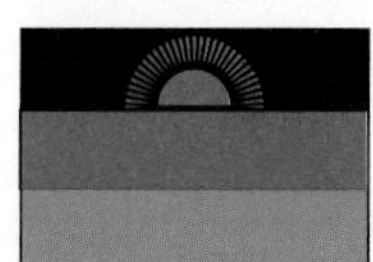

Area: 118,484 sq km (45,747 sq mi)
Population (2003 est.): 11,651,000
Capital: Lilongwe; judiciary meets in Blantyre
Head of state and government: President Bakili Muluzi

After Pres. Bakili Muluzi decided in March 2003 to abandon his plan to change the constitution so that he could stand for a third term of office in the May 2004 presidential election, there was an immediate offer from donors to finance half the cost of the election process. Muluzi insisted that he had taken the decision to encourage the renewal of aid by external agencies that, wrongly in his view, were trying to impose an alien form of democracy on his country. He also said that he was trying to avoid internal discord and to maintain the peace and stability that had characterized Malawi since it became independent.

Suspicions were aroused when Bingu wa Mutharika, an economist who had worked for the UN and the World Bank, was nominated as the ruling party's candidate for the presidency. Mutharika had no political power base inside Malawi, and since Muluzi intended to remain as chairman of the party, there were fears that the president planned to control affairs from the wings. Muluzi maintained that he had endorsed Mutharika only after his name had emerged from cabinet discussions. Nevertheless, on April 2 Muluzi dissolved his cabinet but denied that the action was in answer to dissent over Mutharika's nomination among its members. (KENNETH INGHAM)

MALAYSIA

Area: 329,847 sq km (127,355 sq mi)
Population (2003 est.): 25,225,000
Capital: Kuala Lumpur; head of government office in Putrajaya (the future planned capital) from 1999
Chief of state: *Yang di-Pertuan Agong* (Paramount Ruler) Tuanku Syed Sirajuddin ibni al-Marhum Tuanku Syed Putra Jamalullail
Head of government: Prime Ministers Datuk Seri Mahathir bin Mohamad and, from October 31, Datuk Seri Abdullah Ahmad Badawi

On Oct. 31, 2003, Prime Minister Datuk Seri Mahathir bin Mohamad stepped down after 22 years in office. The early part of the year had had all the hallmarks of Mahathir's tumultuous rule. In April he accused educators in the country's Muslim religious schools of teaching hate and ended government subsidies to the schools, where more than 125,000 children were enrolled. Earlier, in March, Mahathir's former deputy, Anwar Ibrahim, had appealed his 2000 conviction on what his supporters had long claimed were trumped-up charges of sodomy. To no one's surprise the Court of Appeal upheld the original ruling, and in October Anwar filed an appeal with the country's highest court.

The Malaysian economy performed strongly in 2003, with GDP growth at 4.5%, though challenges to future growth became increasingly apparent. Foreign investment in Malaysia was down, and the emergence of China as the region's preferred manufacturing destination was largely to blame. Malaysia, having earlier diversified its economy—at Mahathir's insistence—to become a world leader in electronics manufacturing and assembly, turned in its new search for growth to the development of service industries, including tourism and health care. In his final budget, which was released in mid-September, Mahathir incorporated tax breaks for small and medium-sized companies as well as special incentives for hotel and tourism operators.

On October 31 Datuk Seri Abdullah Ahmad Badawi, Mahathir's handpicked successor, was sworn in as the country's new prime minister and assumed the leadership of the United Malays National Organization (the party of which

The new Malaysian Prime Minister Abdullah Ahmad Badawi is greeted by well-wishers as he goes to his office in Putrajaya, south of Kuala Lumpur, on October 31. Abdullah's predecessor had been in office for 22 years.

his father was a founding member). The soft-spoken Abdullah had served as Malaysia's foreign minister and minister of education and defense before being named deputy prime minister in 1999. In November he moved quickly to set a new tone, and in his first parliamentary address as prime minister, he pledged to strengthen Malaysia's democratic culture, honour the system of checks and balances on power that Mahathir was widely considered to have undermined, and root out corruption.

Internationally, Malaysia continued to assert its economic and political influence in Southeast Asia and, increasingly, the world. Mahathir was one of the most vociferous critics of the U.S.-led war in Iraq and of Western countries' treatment of Muslim countries and Muslims in general, despite his own intolerance toward Muslim fundamentalism and his role as a prominent U.S. ally in the international war on terrorism. Though Malaysia was among the top U.S. trading partners, it openly sought to strengthen its ties with other nations. Mahathir negotiated with the sultan of Brunei in May to end the dispute over a huge oil field off the coast of Borneo; Malaysia proposed to develop the oil field jointly with Brunei. In August Mahathir met Russian Pres. Vladimir Putin, who initialed a $900 million deal for Malaysia's purchase of 18 Sukhoy warplanes. In December 2002 the International Court of Justice had recognized Malaysia's claim to the disputed islands of Ligitan and Sipadan; the ruling allowed the country to continue development of Sipadan as one of the world's most popular scuba-diving destinations.

(JANET MOREDOCK)

MALDIVES

Area: 298 sq km (115 sq mi)
Population (2003 est.): 285,000
Capital: Male
Head of state and government: President Maumoon Abdul Gayoom

On Sept. 25, 2003, Maldives's 50-member Majlis (parliament) nominated, by a unanimous vote, Pres. Maumoon Abdul Gayoom to seek reelection for a sixth consecutive five-year term. A public referendum on October 17 gave him overwhelming support. The voting was overshadowed, however, by riots in Male on September 19–21. These were triggered by the death of a prisoner (allegedly from being beaten by guards) at Maafushi prison on September 19 and a shooting incident the next day against prisoners who had attacked the guards and tried to break into the armory. The rioters in Male caused damage to public property and committed arson, but government security forces quickly brought the situation under control. Gayoom appointed a five-member commission to inquire into the custodial death and arrested 11 National Security Service personnel in connection with the incident.

On the economic front, the government pursued greater diversification and sought to develop the tourism, fisheries, and agricultural sectors. In the budget for 2003, the biggest outlays were for social development and the improvement of general services. During President Gayoom's four-day visit to Sri Lanka in May, Maldives and Sri Lanka signed a memorandum of understanding to cooperate on tourism development through joint marketing and investment. (PONMONI SAHADEVAN)

MALI

Area: 1,248,574 sq km (482,077 sq mi)
Population (2003 est.): 11,626,000
Capital: Bamako
Chief of state: President Amadou Toumani Touré
Head of government: Prime Minister Ahmed Mohamed Ag Hamani

A poor rainfall in 2002 and the effects of the civil war in Côte d'Ivoire shook Mali's fragile economy in 2003. Border closures and banditry on the Ivorian roads brought much of Mali's commerce to a standstill. Transport costs increased dramatically in the food and cotton sectors, and the government began distributing free grain and rice to villages in the western regions. Revenues from cotton tumbled, and hundreds of employees were laid off in the textile industry. Blaming the record-low world prices on subsidies paid by the U.S. and Europe to their own cotton growers, the government joined Brazil in filing an official protest with the World Trade Organization. On March 7 the IMF and the World Bank announced that Mali would be granted $675 million in debt relief; the bank later released an additional $8.5 million to help reduce poverty and promote growth.

On May 22 South Africa and Mali agreed to work together to preserve Timbuktu's collections of manuscripts in Arabic, many of them written by Malian scholars half a millennium ago or more. A trust fund was also being created for a purpose-built library to house them.

The death of Bakari Soumano, chief of the Malian griot association, was announced on July 24. Wahhabi Sunni Muslims, building a mosque in the village of Yéréré in western Mali, were attacked on August 25 by followers of a more traditional affiliation; at least 10 people were killed in the violence. After months of negotiations, 14 Europeans taken hostage in March by Algerian Islamic militants were released in northern Mali on August 18.

(NANCY ELLEN LAWLER)

MALTA

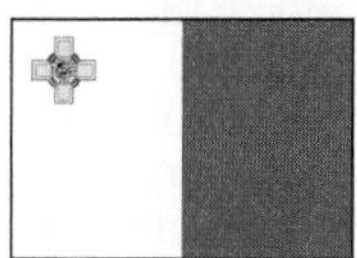

Area: 316 sq km (122 sq mi)
Population (2003 est.): 399,000
Capital: Valletta
Chief of state: President Guido de Marco
Head of government: Prime Minister Eddie Fenech Adami

The year 2003 decided Malta's destiny. A referendum was held on March 8 to determine whether the country should form part of the next European Union enlargement. At the same time, a third of the electorate voted in local council elections, avoiding a boycott of the referendum by the opposition Labour Party (LP). The turnout was 91% of the electorate, the highest ever recorded in Europe; 53.6% voted in favour of EU membership, while 46.4% voted against. The result was hailed by Prime Minister Eddie Fenech Adami as a victory for the "yes" camp. The Labour leader, former prime minister Alfred Sant, however, insisted that the issue should be decided by a general election.

The prime minister advised Pres. Guido de Marco to dissolve the parliament, and a general election was called for April 12. On a turnout of 96% of the voters, the ruling Nationalist Party obtained an absolute majority with 51.8% of the votes and thus secured Malta's future in the EU. In Athens on April 16, Fenech Adami joined the leaders of the other candidate countries in signing the EU accession treaty.

Sant declared that he did not intend to contest the LP leadership at the next party general conference, but he later decided otherwise. He told his supporters that the LP had a duty to accept the people's decision in favour of EU membership. (ALBERT GANADO)

Maltese Prime Minister Eddie Fenech Adami, fresh from a victory in a referendum on Malta's joining the EU, campaigns for reelection in a suburb of the capital, Valletta, in April. His Nationalist Party won an impressive 51.8% majority.

MARSHALL ISLANDS

Area: 181 sq km (70 sq mi)
Population (2003 est.): 56,400
Capital: Majuro
Head of state and government: President Kessai Note

After four years of negotiation, a renewed Compact of Free Association between the Marshall Islands and the U.S. was signed on April 30, 2003. The compact provided for payments by the U.S. of $3.1 billion over 20 years—$800 million for annual grants and the building of a trust fund for long-term sustainability and $2.3 billion for land leased on Kwajalein Atoll, where the U.S. continued to maintain a missile-testing facility. Conditions on Ebeye, the dormitory settlement for local workers at Kwajalein, were expected to improve, and Marshall Islands citizens would have unfettered access to the U.S. for education and employment. The U.S. would maintain its effective control over defense and security. Kwajalein landholders protested the level of lease payments, however, and those affected by past U.S. nuclear tests on Bikini, Enewetak, Rongelap, and Utrik atolls wanted a stronger commitment to ongoing health costs. There also were objections to tighter controls on immigration and adoption.

The government continued its program of structural reform, but the economy remained heavily dependent on U.S. aid, and unemployment was 31%. Drought also caused water rationing in parts of the country and affected copra production. The government suffered a 30% fall in revenue in the nine months to June, with contributions from fishing, ship registration, and business taxes all down. (BARRIE MACDONALD)

MAURITANIA

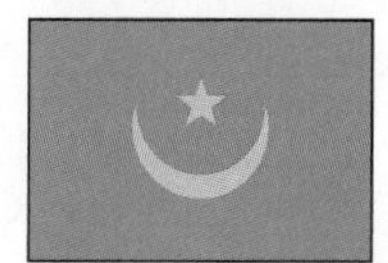

Area: 1,030,700 sq km (398,000 sq mi)
Population (2003 est.): 2,696,000
Capital: Nouakchott
Chief of state: President Col. Maaouya Ould Sid'Ahmed Taya
Head of government: Prime Ministers Cheikh El Avia Ould Mohamed Khouna and, from July 6, Sghair Ould M'Barek

As a result of the U.S.-led invasion of Iraq, Mauritanian Pres. Maaouya Ould Sid'Ahmed Taya in May 2003 ordered a crackdown on Islamic militants, opposition party members, and other critics of his regime. Dozens were arrested, and the Arabic-language newspaper *Erraya* was charged with subversion and shut down. On June 8 rebels led by former army colonel Saleh Ould Hannena attacked the presidential palace with tanks and machine guns, drove Taya into hiding, shut down television and radio broadcasts for 24 hours, and released all prisoners from the capital's jail. The coup failed when the bulk of the army remained loyal to the government, but in two days of intense fighting at least 30 people were killed. Among them was the army chief of staff, Mohamed Lemine Ould N'Deyane, one of the president's closest advisers. The reasons behind the coup remained unclear. On August 6 the 90 soldiers who had been taken into custody following the coup were released, and on August 22 the clerics and political opponents jailed in May were freed. In the November 7 presidential election, Taya was returned to power with 67% of the vote.

Although torrential rains finally unleashed in August, hundreds of thousands of people were still suffering from the 2002 drought. On February 18 OPEC contributed $300,000 to the emergency food operation organized by the World Food Programme. In early July the World Bank approved $39 million in grants and credits to finance improvements in mining operations and to fight the spread of HIV/AIDS.

Supporters of Mauritania's incumbent Pres. Maaouya Ould Sid'Ahmed Taya gather at his final rally in Nouakchott, the capital, on November 5 before the presidential elections. Taya scored a comfortable win with 67% of the vote.

On a more positive note, Mauritanian director Abderrahmane Sissako's film *Heremakono* won the top prize at Fespaco, the pan-African film and television festival. (NANCY ELLEN LAWLER)

MAURITIUS

Area: 2,040 sq km (788 sq mi)
Population (2003 est.): 1,221,000
Capital: Port Louis
Chief of state: Presidents Karl Offmann, Raouf Bundhun (acting) from October 1, and, from October 7, Sir Anerood Jugnauth
Head of government: Prime Ministers Sir Anerood Jugnauth and, from September 30, Paul Bérenger

In 2003 the Mauritian government continued to focus on developing the high-tech sector of its economy. The construction of a state-of-the-art business facility, or "Cyber City," outside the capital received international media attention.

The government also continued its cooperation with the U.S.-led campaign against international terrorism. In August the parliament passed a bill ratifying a UN convention on the blocking of terrorist assets. In April, however, there were demonstrations by various Muslim groups, students, and political parties against the U.S.-led war in Iraq.

On September 30 Paul Bérenger, a Mauritian of French descent, was sworn in as the first non-Indian prime minister of Mauritius. For three years Bérenger had served as deputy prime minister and finance minister under Sir Anerood Jugnauth, who had been widely credited with effecting the country's exceptional economic expansion of the 1980s through neoliberal trade policies while serving as prime minister (1982–95 and 2000–03).

In accordance with the terms of a power-sharing agreement that was drawn up between Bérenger's Mauritian Militant Movement and Jugnauth's Militant Socialist Movement (MSM) prior to the 2000 parliamentary election, Bérenger succeeded Jugnauth as prime minister, and the latter was appointed to the largely ceremonial post of president. Jugnauth's son, Pravind Jugnauth, who had replaced his father as the new leader of the MSM in April, became the new deputy prime minister and finance minister.

(ANDREW EISENBERG)

MEXICO

Area: 1,964,375 sq km (758,449 sq mi)
Population (2003 est.): 100,588,000
Capital: Mexico City
Head of state and government: President Vicente Fox Quesada

The year 2003 saw important developments in Mexico's economy, domestic politics, and international affairs. The economy, burdened by the recession in the United States (Mexico's largest export market), had grown by only 0.9% in inflation-adjusted terms in 2002. As the U.S. recovery began, analysts predicted real growth of 1.3% in Mexico for 2003. Growth at this pace, however, was insufficient to generate the volume of jobs required by Mexico's expanding workforce or to reduce severe socioeconomic and regional inequalities. The combination of economic downturn during 2001–02 and gradually rising labour costs continued to encourage some employers to move production facilities from Mexico to lower-wage competitors such as China. Nevertheless, macroeconomic trends (including an inflation rate in the single digits) were generally more positive during 2003.

The agricultural sector was a major exception. As the North American Free Trade Agreement (NAFTA) entered its 10th year, a further round of scheduled tariff reductions on trade in agricultural products posed new challenges to Mexican farmers, who already had long suffered from shortfalls in financial credits, technological inputs, and transportation and marketing arrangements. These concerns sparked widespread protests and demands (fueled by U.S. criticism of Mexican government subsidies for agricultural producers at a time when U.S. farm supports had increased rapidly) that the NAFTA provisions on trade in agricultural products be rejected or renegotiated. The protests forced Pres. Vicente Fox's administration to undertake protracted negotiations with agricultural producers. The government's announcement of an expanded package of rural-development measures (including higher price supports for certain grains) temporarily eased the domestic political problem, but the long-term crisis of the Mexican countryside remained unresolved.

Political news was dominated by the hotly contested midterm congressional and state-level elections held on July 6. Many observers were inclined to view the elections as a referendum on the Fox administration, and from that perspective the results were indeed disappointing for Fox. Although his personal popularity remained in the 60% range, his centre-right National Action Party (PAN) won just 30.5% of the valid congressional vote. This compared with 34.4% for the long-dominant Institutional Revolutionary Party (PRI), 17.1% for the centre-left Party of the Democratic Revolution (PRD), 6.2% for the Mexican Ecological Green Party (PVEM), 2.4% for the Labour Party (PT), and 2.3% for the Democratic Convergence Party (PCD).

The PRI was reinvigorated by its results in the national election and by its victory in the Nuevo León gubernatorial race. More generally, some analysts interpreted the outcome as voters' rejection of Fox's economic-reform agenda, especially his continued advocacy of unpopular efforts to promote foreign private investment in the petroleum and electrical-power industries. Others wondered whether the comparatively low turnout rate in the July elections (just 41% of registered voters went to the polls) signaled growing disillusionment with the slow pace of further democratic reform since Fox's election. Nevertheless, the PAN's showing in July—although well below the share of the vote that it had received in 2000 when the charismatic Fox was its presidential candidate and the electorate embraced his call for "Change Now!"—was substantially higher than its historical average and indicated further organizational consolidation at the national level. The PRD also recovered somewhat from its especially poor performance in 2000; on the basis of the popularity of Mayor Andrés Manuel López Obrador, it scored an overwhelming victory in Federal District local elections.

Ten years after the adoption of NAFTA, many Mexicans, such as this farmer brandishing a machete in a demonstration in Mexico City on January 31, were finding themselves increasingly disadvantaged economically because of the trade pact.

The most immediate result of the elections was the continuation of divided government. The PAN held only the second largest bloc of representatives (151) in the federal Chamber of Deputies; the other seats were distributed between the PRI (224), PRD (96), PVEM (17), PT (6), and PCD (5), with a final seat to be given to either the PAN or the PT. The PAN's failure to win a majority in the Chamber promised to complicate even further such Fox legislative initiatives as reform of the federal labour law.

In January Secretary of Foreign Relations Jorge G. Castañeda—the architect of many significant departures in Mexican foreign policy—resigned his position, citing frustration with Mexico's inability to conclude a historic agreement on migration issues with the United States. He was replaced by Luis Ernesto Derbez, formerly secretary of the economy (whose position was, in turn, taken by Fernando Canales Clariond, until then governor of Nuevo León). Between April and September cabinet officials changed at the comptroller general's office and at the Secretariats of Agrarian Reform, Energy, Environment and Natural Resources, and Tourism. Some shifts were part of Fox's efforts to reinvigorate his administration after the July elections; many of these appointments brought experienced PAN leaders into national office.

In international affairs the failure of Mexican and U.S. negotiators to reach agreement over migration reform and the significant domestic political opposition to the Fox administration's high-profile engagement with the United States contributed to a cooling in bilateral relations. Perhaps partly to signal its displeasure over the failure to conclude an agreement on migration issues, the Fox government aggressively criticized the use of the death penalty in the U.S. In January Mexico petitioned the International Court of Justice to block the executions of 51 Mexican nationals held on death row in the U.S. The action was taken on the grounds that state and local U.S. officials had violated the 1963 Vienna Convention by failing to notify Mexican prisoners of their right to communicate with their consulates.

The U.S.-led invasion of Iraq also raised tensions. In 2001 Mexico had assumed one of the nonpermanent seats on the UN Security Council for only the third time in history. As international tensions over Iraq mounted, the Fox administration was squeezed between vocal domestic opposition to the immediate use of force against Iraq and escalating pressure from the United States for Mexico to support the U.S. position. In the end the U.S. decision to invade Iraq without a Security Council resolution specifically authorizing the use of force saved the Fox administration from making a difficult choice (Fox had indicated opposition to a proposed U.S. resolution), but not before the Iraq crisis introduced new strains in Mexico-U.S. relations.

(KEVIN J. MIDDLEBROOK)

MICRONESIA, FEDERATED STATES OF

Area: 701 sq km (271 sq mi)
Population (2003 est.): 112,000
Capital: Palikir, on Pohnpei
Head of state and government: Presidents Leo A. Falcam and, from May 11, Joseph J. Urusemal

After four years of negotiations, the Federated States of Micronesia (FSM) signed a renewed Compact of Free Association with the United States in May 2003. The previous compact had expired in 2001. The new compact would run for 20 years, with financial assistance set at $1.8 billion over the period—$92 million a year to support the FSM economy and to establish an investment fund, the returns on which were expected to provide for long-term economic sustainability. The FSM would retain its economic privileges, and its citizens would continue to enjoy visa-free entry to the U.S. The U.S. would retain protection of its strategic and military interests.

In congressional elections in March, Pres. Leo A. Falcam lost his constituency in Pohnpei state to rival Resio Moses; in Kosrae state former president Jacob Nena was heavily defeated. The new president, elected in May, was Joseph J. Urusemal from Yap state. The new vice president, Redley Killion, was from Chuuk state, where leaders of the Faichuk district, in an attempt to address issues of economic underdevelopment and significant outmigration, continued to seek separation from the FSM and republican status in close association with the U.S.

(BARRIE MACDONALD)

MOLDOVA

Area: 33,843 sq km (13,066 sq mi)
Population (2003 est.): 4,267,000 (including some 600,000 persons working abroad)
Capital: Chisinau
Chief of state: President Vladimir Voronin
Head of government: Prime Minister Vasile Tarlev

International efforts to resolve the 12-year dispute between Moldova and the breakaway Transnistria territory dominated politics for much of 2003. In February, Pres. Vladimir Voronin announced plans for a federation in which Transnistria would be granted substantial autonomy. Voronin unveiled these plans shortly after a meeting in the White House with Pres. George W. Bush, for whom stability in the Black Sea region was of paramount concern, as countries adjacent to Moldova provided military facilities for U.S. operations in the Middle East. In July the European Union expressed its willingness to send a peacekeeping mission to Moldova. The Organization for Security and Co-operation in Europe (OSCE), long involved as a mediator, hoped that rapid federalization could be accompanied by the withdrawal of Russian troops that had buttressed the Transnistrian regime. The OSCE requested their pullout by the end of 2003, but Moscow was unresponsive.

These international initiatives encountered withering criticism from a range of international and local analysts and Moldovan nongovernmental organizations fearful that the OSCE plan would turn Moldova into a satellite of Russia. Prospects for a breakthrough appeared slim. The Transnistrian authorities were reluctant to lift their authoritarian controls or abandon lucrative smuggling activities that left Transnistria isolated but for its lifeline to Russia and its leaders banned from traveling to Western countries. Meanwhile, a significant exodus of adult Moldovans was taking place owing to endemic corruption at the elite level and the contraction of the economy; the country's population was a scant 39.5% of the size it was in 1990. Many people swapped professional jobs at home for menial ones in Western Europe in order to earn enough to support their families. (TOM GALLAGHER)

MONACO

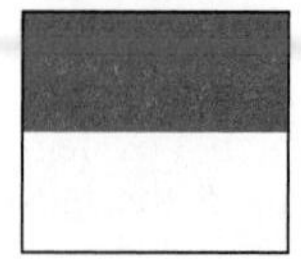

Area: 1.95 sq km (0.75 sq mi)
Population (2003 est.): 32,400
Chief of state: Prince Rainier III
Head of government: Minister of State Patrick Leclercq

In the Feb. 9, 2003, election for Monaco's National Council, the opposition party, Union for Monaco (UNAM), swept to power. Led by Stéphane Valéri, the UNAM gained 21 of the 24 seats, and the former ruling party, the National and Democratic Union (UND), won only 3. With a high turnout of approximately 80% of the 5,800 eligible voters, the UNAM won 58.5% of the ballots and the UND 41.5%. (Eight of the seats were reserved for a system of proportional representation to ensure pluralism in the Council.) The defeat of the UND, which had led the Council for more than three decades, was attributed to the UND's lack of support for Monaco's bid to join the Council of Europe—a move supported "with fervour" by the UNAM and by Prince Rainier III.

In October 2002, after more than two years of negotiations, Monaco and France had signed a new treaty to replace the Treaty of 1918. The new accord affirmed Monaco's status as an independent state, clarified the right of succession, and confirmed Monaco's right to establish its own diplomatic relations with other countries. In light of these changes, Prince Albert made several official overseas trips in 2003, including a visit to Russia, where he installed an honorary consul for Monaco in St. Petersburg. He also hosted the inaugural International Association of Athletics Federations World Athletics Finals, which were held in Monte-Carlo on September 13–14. (ANNE ROBY)

MONGOLIA

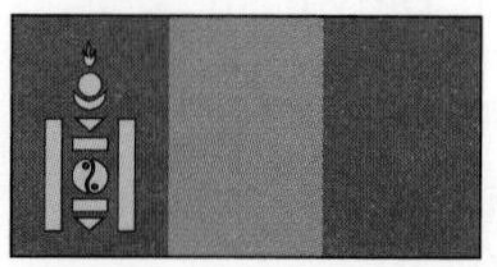

Area: 1,564,116 sq km (603,909 sq mi)
Population (2003 est.): 2,493,000
Capital: Ulaanbaatar
Chief of state: President Natsagiyn Bagabandi
Head of government: Prime Minister Nambaryn Enhbayar

With the June 2004 general elections to the Great Hural (parliament) on the horizon, a key achievement of the political opposition to the ruling Mongolian People's Revolutionary Party (MPRP) was the formation in 2003 of the "Motherland-Democracy" coalition of the Democratic Party (DP), led by former prime minister Mendsayhany Enhsayhan, and the "Motherland"–Mongolian Democratic New Socialist Party, headed by businessman Badarchiyn Erdenebat. The other main opposition force, the Civil Courage–Republican Party (CCRP)—amalgamated in February 2002 under Sanjaasürengiyn Oyuun—was negotiating to join the "Motherland-Democracy" coalition after expelling its deputy president, Bazarsadyn Jargalsayhan, who pledged to rebuild the Republican Party he had led and, it was rumoured, form an alliance with the MPRP.

Protests by DP Deputy Chairman Lamjavyn Gündalay against MPRP government "gagging" of the opposition in the Great Hural continued at the spring and autumn 2003 opening sessions. He again interrupted the prime minister's televised speech, displaying to the cameras such slogans as "Free land for farmers!" and "National Radio and TV are not MPRP property!" Another DP leader protested that poor farmers were denied land under the new Law on Land Privatization. In July Pres. Natsagiyn Bagabandi vetoed a government resolution obliging daily newspapers to publish government decisions. According to a Freedom House survey in April, the Mongolian press was "half-free."

In May Gündalay accused Minister of Justice and Home Affairs Tsendiyn Nyamdorj of being a Chinese spy. On his way to a conference in Singapore in July, Gündalay was detained at Ulaanbaatar airport and, amid violent scenes, arrested at DP headquarters. Charges were dropped, but his arrest provoked an uproar about the violation of Gündalay's parliamentary immunity.

In Moscow in July, the Mongolian and Russian prime ministers met to renew agreement on the Erdenet copper enterprise that preserved Mongolia's 51% ownership. In Tokyo in November, the Mongolia Consultative Group of aid donors pledged aid worth $336 million over 12 months. (ALAN J.K. SANDERS)

MOROCCO

Area: 710,850 sq km (274,461 sq mi), including the 252,120-sq-km (97,344-sq-mi) area of the disputed Western Sahara annexation
Population (2003 est.): 30,097,000, of which Western Sahara 262,000
Capital: Rabat
Head of state and government: King Muhammad VI, assisted by Prime Minister Driss Jettou

Morocco was forced into the spotlight of global terrorism in 2003 when on May 16 a group of 12 suicide bombers struck at 5 locations in Casablanca, killing 45 persons including the bombers and injuring 100. According to government sources, all were members of as-Sirat al-Mustaqim, part of the Salafiya-Jihadiya movement, and all were from the poverty-stricken Casablanca district of Sidi Moumin. Other observers, however, claimed links with al-Qaeda, especially as the attacks came four days after similar suicide attacks in Riyadh, Saudi Arabia.

In the wake of the incidents, the Moroccan parliament passed a ferocious antiterrorism law, and 16 persons allegedly involved in the incidents were arrested. They went on trial in late May, but the alleged ringleader, Moul Sebbat, died in police custody shortly after his arrest in Fez—from chronic liver damage while being transferred to the hospital, according to the police. At the start of June, a French national was also arrested in connection with the incidents and was sentenced to life in prison at his trial.

The Moroccan political spring also seemed to have come to an end with the arrest and condemnation to four years' imprisonment of Ali Lmrabet, the editor of *Demain* and *Doumane,* for having insulted the king—the first time this offense had been prosecuted in 30 years. On appeal his sentence was reduced to three years, but Lmrabet went on a hunger strike to protest his condemnation. In mid-October at the opening of the parliamentary session, King Muhammad VI announced radical changes to Morocco's family law, the Mudawwanah, which dramatically improved the position of women without outraging Islamist sentiment.

Morocco had to deal with an unexpected turn in the Western Sahara independence issue in August when the Algerian government persuaded the Polisario Front, the Western Saharan national liberation movement, to accept the Baker Plan. The plan anticipated a referendum for self-determination after five years of autonomy under Moroccan suzerainty, but Moroccans feared that if the plan was enacted, Morocco's claim to sovereignty in the region would eventually be sapped. The Polisario Front also accelerated prisoner releases during the year. At the start of 2003, Morocco began negotiations with the United States over a free-trade-area agreement and renewed diplomatic relations with Spain, which had been broken off in October 2001.

(GEORGE JOFFÉ)

The Hotel Safir, one of five targets of suicide bombers in Casablanca, Mor., on May 16, received extensive damage. The coordinated attacks, conducted by 12 members of a subgroup of the underground Islamist Salafiya-Jihadiya movement, killed 45 people.

MOZAMBIQUE

Area: 812,379 sq km (313,661 sq mi)
Population (2003 est.): 18,568,000
Capital: Maputo
Head of state and government: President Joaquim Chissano, assisted by Prime Minister Pascoal Mocumbi

In 2003 external investors continued to respond favourably to the Mozambican government's liberal trade policy. The Mozal aluminum smelter began exporting in April, ahead of schedule, and additional investments to expand operations promised a doubling of output by 2004. Also contributing greatly to the country's economic growth were other projects funded by external investors and the progress made by the South African company SASOL in the construction of a pipeline that would carry natural gas from Mozambique to South Africa when completed in 2004. These initiatives, however, did not benefit the vast majority of the population, who relied exclusively on agriculture for their subsistence and for additional income. As a result of alternating drought and flooding in recent years, the UN World Food Programme estimated that 788,000 people would need food assistance at least until September and that the number of needy might rise in subsequent months owing to a lack of seed for planting.

The second summit meeting of the African Union took place in Maputo during July 4–12. As the AU's new chairman, Pres. Joaquim Chissano presided over its deliberations with great skill; his fluency in English, French, and Portuguese enabled him to speak to all the other heads of state in their own official languages. On August 27 he met again with South African Pres. Thabo Mbeki in Pemba, Mozambique, to discuss a number of issues, including bilateral cooperation for migrant labour as well as transport and communication. Prominent among the projects they considered was one to which the World Bank had already given its support in principle—South Africa's role in rehabilitating the Sena Railway linking the Mozambican port of Beira with the interior and with neighbouring Malawi. In October the World Bank Consultative Group pledged $790 million in assistance for the project.

The local government elections, scheduled for October, were postponed until November owing to a lack of funds. A grant of $3.7 million pledged by the UN Development Programme failed to arrive in time for the registration process, but Antonio Carasco, director general of the electoral administration secretariat, was unfazed by the delay. Presidential and party elections were to be held in 2004, and Chissano would be stepping down after having served two consecutive terms in office. The ruling Frelimo party had selected its secretary-general, Armando Guebuza, as its presidential candidate to run against Afonso Dhlakama, the leader of the Mozambique National Resistance (Renamo) opposition movement.

(KENNETH INGHAM)

MYANMAR (BURMA)

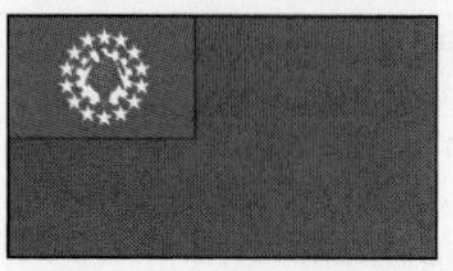

Area: 676,577 sq km (261,228 sq mi)
Population (2003 est.): 42,511,000
Capital: Yangon (Rangoon)
Head of state and government: Chairman of the State Peace and Development Council Gen. Than Shwe; on August 25 Gen. Khin Nyunt became prime minister

In 2003 Myanmar became even more isolated owing to international outrage over the rearrest of opposition leader Aung San Suu Kyi on May 30. The Association of Southeast Asian Nations (ASEAN) broke from its traditional stance of noninterference in internal affairs when Malaysian Prime Minister Datuk Seri Mahathir bin Mohamad publicly threatened Myanmar's expulsion from the regional organization if Yangon did not release Suu Kyi and 1,400 other political prisoners. Myanmar had become a major embarrassment that tarnished ASEAN's reputation internationally.

As part of a large-scale government reshuffle on August 25, Gen. Than Shwe gave up the prime ministership but retained the chairmanship of the military-dominated State Peace and Development Council. Gen. Khin Nyunt, hitherto the chief of military intelligence, replaced Than Shwe as prime minister.

The United States imposed new sanctions, including a ban on all imports from Myanmar, a freeze of the assets in U.S. banks of Myanmar's rulers, and an expansion of the U.S. visa blacklist. In addition, the U.S. opposed IMF and World Bank loans to Myanmar. The U.S. bans on imports, mainly textiles and footwear, could result in the loss of some 350,000 jobs and substantial revenue, which had totaled $356 million in 2002. Japan, Myanmar's top donor, stopped all new humanitarian and developmental aid, and the European Union extended and intensified sanctions for another year. The International Labour Organization expelled Myanmar because of its flagrant use of forced labour; it was the only nation ever to experience such censure.

The kyat was trading at a record low 1,000 to the U.S. dollar, inflation was running high, and the banking system was in deep crisis. In November the UN human rights envoy, Paulo Sergio Pinheiro, met Suu Kyi in Yangon before submitting his report to the UN secretary-general.

Yangon relied on its Asian neighbours, especially its main trading partner, China—which controlled 60% of the Myanmar economy—for diplomatic, military, and economic support. Exploiting India's rivalry with China, Yangon welcomed New Delhi's plans to build a modern highway linking India's Nagaland to Myanmar's Mandalay and Yangon and on to Bangkok. Indian Vice Pres. B.S. Shekhawat visited Myanmar in November. ASEAN's, Australia's, and India's policies of "constructive engagement" of the military junta not only undermined sanctions imposed by the U.S. and the EU but also failed to prevent Myanmar's rapid slide into China's orbit.

(MOHAN MALIK)

NAMIBIA

Area: 825,118 sq km (318,580 sq mi)
Population (2003 est.): 1,927,000
Capital: Windhoek
Chief of state and head of government: President Sam Nujoma, assisted by Prime Minister Theo-Ben Gurirab

In February 2003 Pres. Sam Nujoma again declared that he would not stand for a fourth five-year term in office. The man most likely to succeed him was Minister for Foreign Affairs Hidipo Hamutenya, who could count on the backing of the Kwanyama, the largest subgroup of the majority Ovambo-speaking people. The other main contenders were Prime Minister Theo-Ben Gurirab, a Damara, and Hifikepunye Pohamba, the South West Africa People's Organization (SWAPO) vice president. Hage Geingob, ousted as prime minister in 2002, was unable to find a role for himself in Namibia and left to become executive secretary of the Global Coalition for Africa in Washington, D.C.

The issue of land reform and redistribution, raised in 2002, was reopened when the *Namibian* newspaper announced that a government list compiled in April 2003 contained the names of 300 commercial farms owned by non-Namibians, farms that were earmarked for resettling landless people. Though some landowners feared a Zimbabwean-style landgrab, the government said that it remained committed to working within the constitution and that there were no immediate plans for land seizures. Critics of the SWAPO government continued to complain of a lack of transparency and accountability. The president and a number of his ministers attacked the media, especially the *Namibian* newspaper, from time to time. The construction of a vast and very costly new statehouse went ahead in Windhoek. An estimated 260,000 Namibians were living with HIV/AIDS, and almost 400,000 cases of malaria were reported annually.

With peace restored to Angola, unrest on Namibia's northern border ceased, and the Angolan refugees in Namibia began to be repatriated. Despite the suspension of U.S. military aid, Namibia rejected a U.S. request that American soldiers be given blanket immunity from prosecution in the International Criminal Court.

(CHRISTOPHER SAUNDERS)

NAURU

Area: 21.2 sq km (8.2 sq mi)
Population (2003 est.): 12,600, excluding asylum seekers
Capital: Government offices in Yaren district
Head of state and government: Presidents René Harris, Bernard Dowiyogo from January 9, Harris from January 17, Dowiyogo from January 18, Derog Gioura (acting) from March 10, Ludwig Scotty from May 29, and, from August 8, Harris

There were many leadership changes in Nauru in 2003. The crises began when opposition members of Parliament passed a no-confidence motion against Pres. René Harris and sought to reinstall former president Bernard Dowiyogo. (*See* OBITUARIES.) Chief Justice Barry Connell ruled that since nine votes were needed to pass the motion of no-confidence and only eight MPs had voted, the vote was unconstitutional. Nevertheless, Harris was replaced as president in mid-January by Dowiyogo, who subsequently died in Washington, D.C. Derog Gioura served as acting president until an election was held in May; Ludwig Scotty was elected president, but he was unable to command Parliament's confidence. In August Harris returned to office.

Harris continued to help Australia administer the "Pacific solution," under which about 600 asylum seekers were camped on Nauru at Australia's expense while their refugee status was determined. Australia provided A$41 million (about $28 million) annually to cover the costs of the detention. The *Weekend Australian* revealed that Nauru was asked to use its diplomatic resources in Beijing to help smuggle senior North Korean scientists and military officers to Western countries in an intelligence mission that was code-named Operation Weasel.

(A.R.G. GRIFFITHS)

NEPAL

Area: 147,181 sq km (56,827 sq mi)
Population (2003 est.): 24,172,000
Capital: Kathmandu
Head of state: King Gyanendra Bir Bikram Shah Dev
Head of government: Prime Ministers Lokendra Bahadur Chand and, from June 5, Surya Bahadur Thapa

Political chaos continued to be the norm in Nepal through September 2003, owing to the division between the major contenders for power—King Gyanendra and the cabinet he appointed, headed by Surya Bahadur Thapa; the Communist Party of Nepal (Maoist); and the coalition of the five major political parties, including the Nepali Congress Party and the Communist Party of Nepal (Unified Marxist-Leninist). Negotiations between these different factions were held, but the most important occurred on August 17–27 between the Maoists and the government at a conference in Nepalganj. The talks ended without any progress made, primarily because of the government's refusal to accept the Maoists' demand for the election of a new constituent assembly. The Maoists ended the cease-fire in late August, and deadly clashes with police intensified in October. The five-party coalition decided on September 1 to "postpone" the political movement that it had slated to begin on that date.

National joy and pride attend the wedding on January 22 in Kathmandu of Nepal's Princess Prearana Rajya Laxmi Devi Shah and commoner Kumar Raj Bahadur Singh, a University of California-trained computer scientist.

© John Van Hasselt/Corbis

Nepal's relations with its two neighbours, India and China, were not a critical issue in 2003. Talks with India were held in August about the construction by India of bunds (embankments) on waterways along the border; the action had led to flooding in some Nepali lands in the area. The dispute remained unresolved, however. In September the U.S., Indian, Chinese, and Pakistani ambassadors met separately with Nepali political party leaders and urged them "to build a consensus with the king to settle the current political crisis."

(LEO E. ROSE)

NETHERLANDS, THE

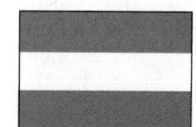

Area: 41,528 sq km (16,034 sq mi)
Population (2003 est.): 16,238,000
Capital: Amsterdam; seat of government, The Hague
Chief of state: Queen Beatrix
Head of government: Prime Minister Jan Peter Balkenende

The Netherlands went to the polls on Jan. 22, 2003, to elect a new parliament. With nearly 80% of eligible voters participating, the Labour Party (PvdA) made the most dramatic gains, increasing from 23 to 42 seats (out of 150), while the Christian Democrats (CDA) won the greatest number of seats (44). The Socialist Party, which had been polling at 20 or more seats just two months previously, received only 9. The CDA and PvdA attempted to form a government, but this effort was abandoned after weeks of negotiations. In the end, a centre-right coalition was formed, and Prime Minister Jan Peter Balkenende's second cabinet within a year was sworn in on May 27.

The U.S.-led war in Iraq highlighted dissent among the Dutch, as well as concern for the responses of the country's Islamic residents and citizens. A lively debate continued in The Netherlands about the value, meaning, and appropriate methods of integration of foreign residents and citizens of foreign descent. Fewer refugees arrived in 2003, apparently in response to tightened entrance policies. The government promised that it would soon settle on clear criteria with which finally to decide the fate of asylum seekers who had been in residence for many years.

In February Royal Ahold, a Dutch food retailer that ranked third in the world, found that it had overstated its earnings for two years, which caused the value of the company's stock to decline dramatically (by over 60% the first day).

The 18-year prison sentence of Volkert van der Graaf, who assassinated politician Pim Fortuyn in 2002, was confirmed upon appeal. Considerations in favour of a heavy sentence included concern that van der Graaf might reoffend in the future and that his act had harmed the democratic process significantly.

Reports indicated that some 1,400 people died in The Netherlands during Europe's summer heat crisis. Historically high temperatures and drought also caused dikes to break in the province of Utrecht and in Rotterdam. These dikes contained peat, which had dried out so thoroughly that the dikes lost their structural integrity, sagged, and slid from their normal positions, causing local flooding. The government began an additional inspection of some 14,000 km (about 8,700 mi) of regional and local dikes.

On June 30 Prince Johan Friso, the second son of Queen Beatrix, announced his engagement to Mabel Wisse Smit, with the wedding scheduled to take place in 2004. Amid revelations that the prince and his fiancée had initially been less than forthcoming with information about her connections to an alleged gangster (who was murdered in 1991), the prince decided not to pursue a request for the States-General's approval of his marriage. This action effectively removed Johan Friso from his right of succession as second in line to the throne, after his older brother, Crown Prince Willem-Alexander, whose daughter, Amalia, born in December, assumed the second position in the succession.

(JOLANDA VANDERWAL TAYLOR)

NEW ZEALAND

Area: 270,534 sq km (104,454 sq mi)
Population (2003 est.): 4,001,000
Capital: Wellington
Chief of state: Queen Elizabeth II, represented by Governor-General Dame Silvia Cartwright
Head of government: Prime Minister Helen Clark

Historic links with the U.K. and the British monarchy were loosened in 2003 by constitutional changes enacted by New Zealand Prime Minister Helen Clark's reform-minded government. The House of Representatives controversially established a new Supreme Court to replace the London-based judicial committee of the Privy Council as New Zealand's court of final appeal and scrapped the prestigious designation of queen's counsel for senior barristers. This action followed the abolition of knighthoods and damehoods in the biannual honours list. Opposition National Party leader Bill English accused Clark of "Trojan horse" motives aimed at converting New Zealand to a republic.

Long-standing Maori grievances over land claims were revived when the government denied Maori title to the nation's foreshore and seabed and designated the area as public domain. Opposition parties announced policies to abolish separate Maori representation in Parliament. Clark not only endorsed retention of Maori seats—all seven of which were held by her ruling Labour Party—but also gave regional, district, and city councils the option of creating Maori-only constituencies. Local governments were empowered to engage freely in commercial trading activity.

In March Team New Zealand lost sailing's America's Cup to the Swiss challenger, *Alinghi,* led by former New Zealand skipper Russell Coutts. *Alinghi* won five consecutive races out of a possible nine. Ceremonies in May honoured the 50th anniversary of the first ascent of Mt. Everest, by Sir Edmund Hillary and Tenzing Norgay. Wellington also commemorated the 20th anniversary of the Australia–New Zealand Closer Economic Relations agreement, which achieved total free trade in goods between both nations and harmonized trade in most service sectors.

Relations with the U.S. were strained as New Zealand refused to commit militarily in Iraq without UN sanction and retained the embargo on visits by nuclear-powered naval vessels. Charles Swindells, the U.S. ambassador to New Zealand, stated that Washington was not prepared to schedule bilateral free-trade negotiations "at this time" and suggested that a reexamination of New Zealand's antinuclear stance could be beneficial to both countries.

Michael Cullen, deputy prime minister and finance minister, announced a "careful Budget for uncertain times," attributable to weaker commodity prices, a strong New Zealand dollar, and a sharp decline in farm incomes weighing upon business confidence and activity. He predicted 2003–04 revenue at $NZ 58,798,000,000 (about U.S.$33,290,000,000) and spending at $NZ 55,037,000,000 (about U.S.$32,830,000,000). Gross debt was projected to decline to about 23% of GDP by 2006-07. Australian interests bought New Zealand's national railways and the ancillary road-rail interisland ferries, with the state assuming ownership of the rail-track network and committing to its upgrade.

Strategies were defined to reduce greenhouse-gas emissions in line with New Zealand's obligations as a signatory to the Kyoto Protocol on global warming. Hundreds of farmers converged on Wellington to protest a proposed levy on the flatulence emitted by their livestock, notably dairy cows and sheep; National Party MP Shane Ardern was prosecuted for driving a vintage tractor up the main steps of Parliament. A moratorium on the release of genetically modified (GM) organisms expired in October; the government overruled demands by the Green Party, lobby groups, and public-opinion polls to extend the GM ban another five years.

During the year New Zealand also decriminalized prostitution; established a new regime to control gambling; announced a ban on smoking in restaurants, bars, casinos, and public transport; and set up a government-sponsored Families Commission (from mid-2004) to advocate family-friendly policies.

Tightened security measures caused a moment of embarrassment when Clark was selected for extra screening at Sydney (Australia) Airport in October.

(NEALE MCMILLAN)

NICARAGUA

Area: 130,373 sq km (50,337 sq mi)
Population (2003 est.): 5,482,000
Capital: Managua
Head of state and government: President Enrique Bolaños Geyer

Former president Arnoldo Alemán Lacayo—who had been under house arrest in Nicaragua since December 2002 awaiting trial for corruption—was transferred to prison in August 2003. In December he received a 20-year prison sentence and a $17 million fine. His former tax director, Byron Jerez, was convicted in June and sentenced to eight years in jail for having fraudulently diverted state funds. Pres. Enrique Bolaños's anticorruption campaign stalled, and in May he broke with pro-Alemán "Arnoldistas" dominating the Constitutionalist Liberal Party (PLC) and joined a new coalition of small non-Arnoldista Liberal parties, the Movement of Liberal Unity (MUL).

In January the Supreme Electoral Council restored legal status to 26 parties after the Supreme Court had overturned portions of the 2000 electoral reforms forged by the Sandinista Front (FSLN) and the PLC that disadvantaged other parties. In June the legislature, in partisan voting to fill 9 openings on the 16-member Supreme Court, elected 4 members each from the FSLN and the PLC-Arnoldista parties; both parties agreed on the remaining member. In the July 19 commemoration of the Sandinista revolution, FSLN leader Daniel Ortega Saavedra publicly apologized for government tensions with the Roman Catholic Church hierarchy in the 1980s.

Low coffee prices kept per capita economic growth negative. In July 5,000 unemployed coffee workers marched from Matagalpa to Managua in protest against government failure to fulfill September 2002 accords promising assistance. Implementation of a December 2002 three-year, $1.1 billion International Monetary Fund (IMF) loan agreement sparked protests against privatization of communication and hydroelectric enterprises as well as user fees for education. Budget battles jeopardized compliance with IMF terms, but fiscal reforms kept Nicaragua eligible for foreign-debt forgiveness.

Thousands of Nicaraguan coffee workers return to Matagalpa on August 1 following a march to the capital, Managua, in July to demand more land and social benefits from the government.

U.S.–Central American Free Trade Agreement negotiations were successfully concluded with the signing of a pact in December. Nicaragua expressed strong support in the United Nations for military action in Iraq and contributed troops to the U.S.-led occupation despite heavy public opposition. Nicaragua asked the International Court of Justice in April to rule on a maritime rights conflict with Colombia over the San Andrés archipelago and nearby keys. In May four American firms received concessions for oil exploration off the Pacific and Caribbean coasts. The National Assembly unanimously approved legislation in July codifying the 1987 Autonomy Law for the Caribbean region. (RICHARD STAHLER-SHOLK)

NIGER

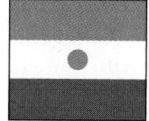

Area: 1,267,000 sq km (489,000 sq mi)
Population (2003 est.): 11,380,000
Capital: Niamey
Head of state and government: President Tandja Mamadou, assisted by Prime Minister Hama Amadou

The accusation by U.S. Pres. George W. Bush in January 2003 that Niger had exported uranium to Iraq for its nuclear program was met by Niger's government with angry denials and demands for an apology. The International Atomic Energy Agency declared in March that the U.S. report had been based on forged documents, and in July the White House admitted that the charge was baseless.

Although opposition deputies had charged that the military tribunals called for in the country's new military justice code (passed by the National Assembly in December 2002) violated the constitution by creating a situation of double jeopardy, in late February 2003 the Constitutional Court upheld their legality. On March 13 police broke up a demonstration in Niamey by families and supporters of the more than 200 soldiers who had been imprisoned after a series of mutinies in July 2002. The protesters demanded the immediate release of the men, who had been held without official charges in military camps 1,500 km (930 mi) southeast of Niamey. Pres. Tandja Mamadou pledged on April 16 to root out corruption in the country's judicial system.

In January 170 Niger soldiers arrived in Côte d'Ivoire to join the West African peacekeeping force that had been sent to help reestablish order there. More than 10,000 Nigerois had returned home from Côte d'Ivoire as a result of the violence directed against them and other expatriate residents during the Ivorian civil war.

Abundant rainfall and a 15% increase in land under cultivation in the 2002–03 farming season resulted in a larger-than-estimated harvest of foodstuffs. Budgetary constraints imposed by international donors prompted two strikes by civil servants demanding higher wages and lower taxes. The Democratic Confederation of the Workers of Niger walked out for five days on May 1 and again on May 27.

(NANCY ELLEN LAWLER)

NIGERIA

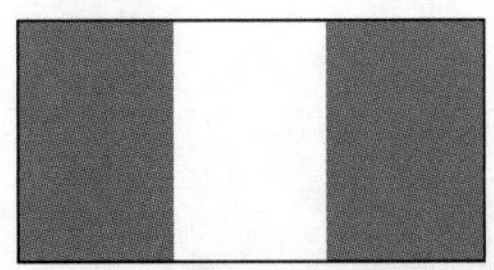

Area: 923,768 sq km (356,669 sq mi)
Population (2003 est.): 125,275,000
Capital: Abuja
Head of state and government: President Olusegun Obasanjo

With the reelection of Pres. Olusegun Obasanjo in April 2003, Nigeria saw its first civilian transition of power since the country achieved independence in 1960. The polling for the presidential election was generally peaceful, despite fears of violence fueled by the March killing of Marshall Harry, one of Obasanjo's rivals. (In April Nigerian police determined that Marshall's murder was not a political assassination.) Numerous sources cited inconsistencies in the results of certain polling districts; however, European Union monitors later conceded that the end result was likely accurate. The main opposition candidate, former military leader Muhammadu Buhari, called the election "a joke" and immediately petitioned the Court of Appeal to nullify the results. Legal wrangling over the election continued throughout the rest of the year. President Obasanjo's People's Democratic Party (PDP) also gained eight governorships in the April elections. The only state lost by the PDP was the northern state of Kano, which, as per the general political trend in the north, elected a governor more willing to enforce Islamic Shari'ah law.

At the outset of his second term, Obasanjo reduced petroleum subsidies, which led to a 54% rise in fuel prices for ordinary citizens. Trade unions responded with a general strike, crippling commerce in urban areas. The strike lasted nine days, until the government agreed to reduce the amount of the subsidy cut.

The increasing role of conservative Islam in northern Nigerian politics continued to spawn controversy in 2003. In September governments and human rights organizations welcomed the news that Amina Lawal, a woman convicted of adultery in a Shari'ah court in 2002 and sentenced to death by stoning, had been acquitted by a court of appeals. In October three northern states halted a World Health Organization polio vaccination drive on the advice of influential Muslims. Some religious leaders claimed that vaccines from Western nations might be used to kill or sterilize Nigeria's Muslim population. The Nigerian government had the vaccine analyzed in November by a committee within the country and thereby set the stage for the resumption of inoculations.

Nigeria's oil industry continued to be the centre of strife. The oil-rich Niger Delta region, a site of much turmoil since the mid-1990s, erupted into violence in the weeks before the April elections and again in August. The deadly clashes involved militias of Ijo and Itsekiri ethnic communities as well as Nigerian navy forces. Ijo youths targeted Itsekiri communities and petroleum industry installations in support of their struggle to obtain greater political representation. The Nigerian military intervened to restore calm and protect the region's oil interests. Certain armed groups targeted oil facilities directly, rupturing a major pipeline with explosives in April. In response to the violence, ChevronTexaco and Shell cut production dramatically in late March, which contributed to a worldwide rise in oil prices. In April striking oil workers held 97 American and British workers, along with 170 Nigerian workers, on offshore oil rigs for nearly two weeks. In June an accidental pipeline explosion in the state of Abia killed more than 100 residents.

In August Nigerian peacekeeping troops took to the streets of Monrovia, Liberia, to enforce a cease-fire in the civil war in that country. On August 11 Liberian Pres. Charles Taylor went into exile in the southern Nigerian city of Calabar, effectively ending the three-year-old Liberian civil war. In September and October the Nigerian government issued Taylor warnings amid allegations that he was ignoring the conditions of his asylum by remaining in contact with Liberian politicians. Meanwhile, Nigeria rejected UN and Interpol calls for the arrest of Taylor on charges of war crimes and crimes against humanity.

On September 27 Nigeria became the first sub-Saharan African nation after South Africa to have its own satellite in orbit. Developed for the purpose of monitoring regional disasters, NigeriaSat-1 was built by 15 Nigerian engineers, with technical input from Surrey Satellite Technology in England. (ANDREW EISENBERG)

NORWAY

Area: 323,758 sq km (125,004 sq mi)
Population (2003 est.): 4,569,000
Capital: Oslo
Chief of state: King Harald V
Head of government: Prime Minister Kjell Magne Bondevik

During 2003 the Bank of Norway, in an effort to strengthen the labour market and favour exports, reduced its interest rate, designed to prevent inflation, from 6.5% to 2.25%. The effect was slow to be seen. Exports declined continuously, but the feared inflation did not appear. Norwegians, who had enjoyed higher wages since 2000 and were taking advantage of low interest rates, continued to furnish and improve their residences and summer homes, and rising numbers crossed the border to buy high-quality Swedish wares and inexpensive spirits. The Norwegian krone remained strong, from 20% "above" the Swedish krona in January to 10% in July, or—in a wider view—about 8 kroner to the euro and 7 kroner to a weakening U.S. dollar.

A strong currency, however, resulted in a weak market for expensive Norwegian exports. In recent years Norwegian companies had moved their production to cheap labour markets in Eastern Europe and East Asia. This led to declining industrial production in Norway, the loss of skilled labour, and unemployment (hitherto unknown) even among scientists and highly educated engineers. In the autumn the unemployment rate stood at about 4.3%.

Norway's prosperity was attributed to its rich offshore oil and gas deposits. The Norwegian companies Hydro, Statoil, and Norske Shell showed declining or no mainland investments and rising offshore investments (15% since 2002), even north of the Arctic Circle, notably off the coast of Lofoten Islands, and the town of Hammerfest, the future "liquefied natural gas centre" of northern Norway. In December the government stated that the Barents Sea would be opened for oil exploration, despite opposition from environmentalists.

The centre-right coalition government of Prime Minister Kjell Magne Bondevik, which had been weak from its formation in October 2001, lost support in

Keiko, the orca that was featured in the Free Willy *films, died in Norway on December 12. Shown here with his trainer in Taksnes Bay, Norway, in July, Keiko had been released into the wild in Iceland in 2002 but promptly swam directly to Norway.*

AP/Wide World Photos

2003 in the press, among employer federations, in the Confederation of Trade Unions, and in professional organizations. In an October Gallup poll the Labour Party, the Socialist Left, and the populist Progress Party scored almost 25% approval each, but the latter had never been considered trustworthy by any other party. The standing problem was the conflicting attitudes toward membership in the European Union. Though the Christian Democrats did not openly decide on the question, the agrarian Centre Party saw the EU as a devastating threat to agriculture in Norway. The general population was divided almost evenly. Having lost two referenda (1972 and 1994) on the issue of EU membership, the government would not apply for membership unless it was certain that the measure would pass a referendum.

At the end of November, the Storting (parliament) accepted the government's draft budget of 580 billion kroner, an increase of 2% over 2002; a deficit was covered by taking 70 billion kroner from the Government Petroleum Fund, which totaled about 700 billion kroner near year's end.

Princess Märtha Louise gave birth in April to a girl, Maud Angelica Behn; it was the country's first royal birth in nearly 30 years. Crown Prince Haakon and his wife, Crown Princess Mette-Marit, were expecting a baby in January 2004; regardless of its sex, the child would be second in line to the throne behind its father. (GUDMUND SANDVIK)

OMAN

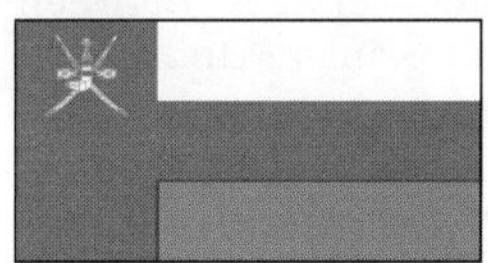

Area: 309,500 sq km (119,500 sq mi)
Population (2003 est.): 2,621,000
Capital: Muscat
Head of state and government: Sultan and Prime Minister Qabus ibn Sa'id

In 2003 Oman faced near-term uncertainties regarding its petroleum and liquefied natural gas (LNG) industries, income from which continued to constitute nearly three-quarters of the government's revenues and nearly half of the country's GNP. In addition, privatization of state-owned enterprises in the fields of power generation, transmission, and distribution, as well as waste-water management and telecommunications, remained stalled.

On the other hand, Oman succeeded in securing a major international agreement intended to increase the levels of its LNG production and exports by as much as a third in the coming two years. Oman continued to benefit from having successfully outsourced to a British firm the management of and investment in the country's two largest airports, at Seeb and Salalah, with plans to more than double passenger throughput at the two airports by 2006.

Oman conducted its first-ever maneuvers with the navies of India, the U.S., and Russia off India's west coast. In addition, the sultanate explored further opportunities to link its economic infrastructure with that of the neighbouring United Arab Emirates.

The Oman–United States bilateral relationship suffered. In March, following a series of official U.S. travel advisories that discouraged Americans from visiting various Arabian Peninsula countries, Oman issued an advisory to its citizens against travel to the United States. Oman also opposed the U.S. decision to use armed force against Iraq.

On October 4 a new 83-member consultative assembly was chosen in the first Omani election open to all adult citizens. In previous elections only a select 25% of the population voted.

(JOHN DUKE ANTHONY)

PAKISTAN

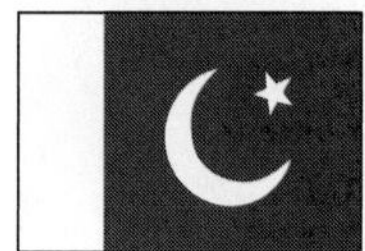

Area: 796,096 sq km (307,374 sq mi), excluding the 84,159-sq-km Pakistani-administered portion of Jammu and Kashmir
Population (2003 est.): 149,030,000 (excluding 4,150,000 residents of Pakistani-administered Jammu and Kashmir as well as 1,500,000 Afghan refugees)
Capital: Islamabad
Head of state and government: President and Chief Executive Gen. Pervez Musharraf, assisted by Prime Minister Mir Zafarullah Khan Jamali

With substantial victories in the October 2002 elections, the Muttahida Majlis-i-Amal (MMA), the major coalition of Islamist parties, brought Pakistan's clerics into the political arena in 2003 as never before. From its inside position in the National Assembly and as the government in the North-West Frontier Province, the MMA became a major political force. The MMA called for the creation of an Islamic state and was relentless in its criticism of Pres. Pervez Musharraf. Arguing that Musharraf could not serve as both president and commander of the army, the MMA demanded the rescinding of his Legal Framework Order, the source of his constitutional power. The MMA also intensified its demand that Musharraf retire from the army.

When the threat of terrorist strikes rose in the Pakistani city of Karachi in October, extra police were called to duty to guard diplomatic missions, businesses, and places of worship—such as this Shi'ite mosque.

The MMA's power stemmed from Pakistan's "war on terrorism," especially Musharraf's support for U.S. actions in Afghanistan that continued to be directed at eliminating Taliban and al-Qaeda operatives. While sustaining its attack on the U.S., the MMA remained highly critical of Pakistani army operations, especially in South Waziristan (an area along the Afghan border not subject to the Pakistani legal code). The MMA also exploited public sentiment opposing the U.S. occupation of Iraq. Insisting "no American will be safe here," an MMA leader declared that Muslims were obligated to wage "holy war" against the U.S. Reports that U.S. special forces had entered Pakistan's frontier region in pursuit of al-Qaeda and Taliban further elevated anti-Americanism and intensified the criticism directed against the Musharraf administration.

Musharraf tried to deflect adverse opinion by sustaining a hard line with India. Pakistan test-fired improved short- and medium-range missiles and sought an enlarged military capability. Pakistani and Indian forces continued to clash in Kashmir, and the guerrilla war in the territory was unabated. Reported daily acts of terror and skirmishes between jihad groups and Indian security forces brought mounting casualties. Musharraf denied any connection with terrorist organizations operating in Kashmir, but he continued to endorse Kashmir's right to self-determination. Toward the end of the year, in a surprise maneuver and over MMA opposition, Musharraf banned three militant groups outlawed in 2002 under different names and placed a fourth on a "watch list." Several days later he declared his intention to merge Pakistan's tribal areas with the country's settled regions and warned terrorists and extremists taking refuge in the tribal belt along the frontier with Afghanistan that they would be forcibly expelled. Then, on November 23 the Pakistani government declared a unilateral cease-fire along the Line of Control in Kashmir and indicated its willingness to commence bus services between Muzaffarabad and Srinigar, India, and ferry service from Karachi to Mumbai (Bombay). India's response to the declaration was immediate and positive. On November 25 the cease-fire became effective, and on December 1 New Delhi and Islamabad agreed to resume air links and overflights from Jan. 1, 2004, and prepared the ground for India's prime minister to travel to Pakistan that month. Citing this as a "significant watershed" in the peace process, Pakistan called for a pullout of Pakistani and Indian forces from Kashmir.

On December 14 a high-intensity bomb seriously damaged the bridge near 10th Corps headquarters (near Islamabad) just seconds after the last vehicle in President Musharraf's motorcade passed over it. Judging it to be an assassination attempt, the government announced the arrest of several individuals thought to be opposed to the general's effort at normalizing relations with India as well as his intimacy with the U.S. in its war on terrorism. A defiant Musharraf declared afterward that he would not be deterred by the terrorist act. On December 24, immediately after the signing of an agreement between the governing Pakistan Muslim League (Q) and the opposition MMA on the validity of the Legal Framework Order (LFO), Musharraf announced to the nation that he would retire from the army before Dec. 31, 2004. The very next day, however, an even more serious attempt was made to assassinate the president when two suicide car bombers made a direct assault on his motorcade. Although the president was not a victim, 14 people died and 46 were wounded. Appearing later on Pakistani television, Musharraf pledged to sustain the effort at blotting out terrorism from the country.

On December 28 Musharraf announced that he would start 2004 by seeking a confidence vote from his electoral college on January 1, three days before the beginning of the South Asian leaders summit in Islamabad. Although an extraconstitutional issue, the vote was deemed necessary to ensure that the president functioned from a position of strength when he met with the Indian prime minister. The next day the Pakistan National Assembly passed the 17th Amendment Bill by a vote of 248–0 (with more than 100 members not voting) and appointed a 12-member committee to review all constitutional amendments brought in the statutory document since 1973. Supported by the MMA, the combined actions appeared to divide the MMA from the Alliance for the Restoration of Democracy, the other main opposition group in the parliament. The 17th amendment's passage meant that Musharraf's LFO powers (as altered by the deal with the MMA) had become part of the constitution. Despite some restrictions, the amendment allowed Musharraf to retain presidential power to dismiss a prime minister, to dissolve the National Assembly, and to appoint armed forces chiefs and provincial governors. It also permitted Musharraf to retain his army post through 2004 and serve out his presidential term through 2007. (LAWRENCE ZIRING)

PALAU

Area: 488 sq km (188 sq mi)
Population (2003 est.): 20,200
Provisional capital: Koror; new capital buildings at Melekeok (on Babelthuap) had not been completed as of late 2003
Head of state and government: President Tommy Remengesau, Jr.

Palau joined the "coalition of the willing" in March 2003 and supported the U.S.-led war on Iraq. Acting under Palau's Compact of Free Association with the U.S., Pres. Tommy Remengesau, Jr., offered the use of Palau's facilities as an additional staging area for American military operations. Remengesau visited Washington, D.C., when U.S. forces began their military strike on Iraq and told Pres. George W. Bush that he prayed for the young men and women who were "defending freedom and democracy in America's military." Vice Pres. Sandra Pierantozzi convened both the National Emergency Committee and the National Emergency Management Office to tighten all points of entry into the country and to enhance security at power plants and embassies. Pierantozzi also took steps to prevent opportunistic increases in the cost of such basic commodities as fuel and oil.

Remengesau vowed to push for a bill to permit dual citizenship for Palauans in the U.S. in an effort to help the many Palauans serving in the U.S. military gain promotions yet retain voting and property rights in Palau. Remengesau also gave his support to 10 Palauan policemen who volunteered to join the Solomon Islands peacekeeping mission, and he pledged Palau's assistance to help restore law and order there.

(A.R.G. GRIFFITHS)

PANAMA

Area: 74,979 sq km (28,950 sq mi)
Population (2003 est.): 3,116,000
Capital: Panama City
Head of state and government: President Mireya Moscoso

The year 2003 marked the 100th anniversary of Panama's independence from Colombia. The event was celebrated throughout the year with musical concerts, academic conferences, and a massive parade in Panama City on November 3.

Electoral campaigning began in preparation for the May 2004 general elections. Three candidates emerged as the leading contenders: Martin Torrijos, who represented the Democratic Revolutionary Party, the main opposition force; former president Guillermo Endara, who would run under the banner of the Solidarity Party; and José Miguel Alemán, the ruling-party candidate.

Corruption continued to plague the government. One of the most notorious cases involved the legislative assembly and accusations that votes had been bought both in the approval of Supreme Court justices and in a multimodal transportation and industrial development project. An investigation into the matter was stalled. The Transparency International corruption index listed Panama as the 67th most corrupt country of 133 surveyed. To complicate matters, Pres. Mireya Moscoso vetoed legislation to stiffen penalties for embezzlement, bankruptcy fraud, the destruction of certain business records, and a host of other financial crimes. Given the continued charges of corruption and a weak economy, it was not surprising that Moscoso's approval rating was the lowest for any national leader since the 1989 U.S. invasion that ousted Manuel Noriega.

Panama agreed to move four police border outposts that the Colombian government said encroached on its territory. Problems concerning the movement of the Revolutionary Armed Forces of Colombia guerrillas and right-wing paramilitary forces across the Colombian–Panamanian border continued to be a source of contention.

On June 24–26 President Moscoso met with U.S. Pres. George W. Bush in Washington, D.C., where discussions centred on the establishment of a free-trade area, the situation in Colombia, and the possibilities of seaborne terrorist attacks on U.S. ports by ship bombs passing through the Panama Canal. Moscoso signed legislation that provided a 20-year prison term for any person who participated in, financed, or otherwise materially supported acts of terrorism. Panama also agreed to send Americans accused of genocide or war crimes to the U.S. rather than handing them over to the International Criminal Court in The Hague. (ORLANDO J. PÉREZ)

PAPUA NEW GUINEA

Area: 462,840 sq km (178,704 sq mi)
Population (2003 est.): 5,426,000
Capital: Port Moresby
Chief of state: Queen Elizabeth II, represented by Governor-General Sir Silas Atopare
Head of government: Prime Minister Sir Michael Somare

Prime Minister Sir Michael Somare, who had served as Papua New Guinea's first prime minister, brought more than 25 years of experience and a highly regarded regional stature to the difficult task of managing the country's key relationship with Australia, its neighbour and patron. Relations between the two countries became tense in 2003 when Australia decided to tie its vital annual aid of A$350 million (about $250 million) to a proposal to insert Australian police and civil-service bureaucrats into the administration of its former colony. Initially, Somare canceled arrangements for Australian Foreign Minister Alexander Downer's visit to discuss the proposal. Somare maintained that he would not abide interference in the sovereignty of Papua New Guinea and described Australia's perception that Papua New Guinea's law and order and financial management had gone wrong as "absolute rubbish." He was also disappointed that Papua New Guinea had been branded a weak nation. In addition, Somare was put under pressure by the World Bank, which threatened to pull out of the country over the government's logging policy. Somare said that he could not understand the hard-line approach taken by the World Bank over logging rights given to local and foreign companies. (A.R.G. GRIFFITHS)

PARAGUAY

Area: 406,752 sq km (157,048 sq mi)
Population (2003 est.): 5,642,000
Capital: Asunción
Head of state and government: Presidents Luis Ángel González Macchi and, from August 15, Nicanor Duarte Frutos

Paraguay's Senate began formal impeachment proceedings against Pres. Luis Ángel González in January 2003 as the ruling Colorado Party nominated its candidate for the April 27 presidential election. The president was accused of five counts of corruption, including the embezzlement of $16 million from the central bank. After six extraordinary sessions and much negotiation, González, who had survived impeachment proceedings in 2002, once again eluded indictment when in February

AP/Wide World Photos

On August 15, the day of his inauguration as Paraguay's new president, Nicanor Duarte Frutos, accompanied by his wife, parades through the streets of Asunción, the capital. He faced enormous political and economic problems.

the Senate fell 5 votes short of the 30 needed to dismiss him.

Colorado Party leader Nicanor Duarte won the election with over 37% of the vote, followed by former vice president Julio Cesar Franco of the Authentic Radical Liberal Party (23%) and businessman Pedro Fadul, representing a new party, Patria Querida (22%). When Duarte took office on August 15, he faced many challenges, including a Congress controlled by the opposition; the Colorado Party had won 37 of the 80 seats in the Chamber of Deputies and 16 of the 45 Senate seats.

Duarte inherited a country in the throes of financial and social meltdown. Several private and state banks were seized by the central bank owing to mismanagement and fraud, and the government faced growing pressures from protesting peasant farmers who demanded land and credit.

Paraguay was unable to pay some of its debt-servicing obligations and salaries of state employees as a result of bankrupt accounts. Corruption and tax evasion were rampant and contributed to the lack of funds. The World Bank reported that 64% of Paraguayans lived below the poverty level, a 15% increase over 2002. Unemployment was expected to reach 18–20% and inflation about 15%.

President Duarte launched his campaign against corruption by attempting to reform the judiciary, specifically drafting a bill to retire up to six of the nine Supreme Court justices. Other efforts were under way to reform and streamline the state, but Duarte insisted that there would be no privatization or effort to implement other neoliberal reforms that "deny and subjugate human dignity." Former president González was indicted on fraud charges in September. (FRANK O. MORA)

PERU

Area: 1,285,216 sq km (496,225 sq mi)
Population (2003 est.): 27,148,000
Capital: Lima
Head of state and government: President Alejandro Toledo

Although Peru's overall economic picture was healthy in 2003, with gross national product growth and minimal inflation, Pres. Alejandro Toledo's approval ratings ran between 10% and 15%. Contributing to his abysmal ratings were persistent low levels of job growth and the implementation in midyear of a state of emergency in response to farmer strikes, which resulted in a disruption in the flow of goods throughout the country.

Toledo also had difficulties with the Peruvian Congress. A variety of issues produced wrangling between the two bodies of government, and Toledo found himself repeatedly forced to juggle his cabinet and replace ministers. Although cabinet reshuffles were not infrequent in Peru, Toledo was publicly embarrassed when in the run-up to the July 28 Independence Day celebrations (when the president delivered the state of the union address) he was turned down repeatedly after asking various individuals to take over as head of the cabinet. He eventually selected Beatriz Merino, Peru's first female head of cabinet, but on December 15 she resigned and was replaced by Carlos Ferrero Costa, a former congressional speaker.

Another source of unrest emerged with the suspected reappearance of the Sendero Luminoso (Shining Path), an insurgent group that had brought widespread damage and intimidation to Peru during the 1980s and early '90s. A group claiming to be a reborn Shining Path seized several dozen people working on a gas pipeline in June and in July ambushed a military patrol, killing five soldiers and two civilian guides. Jaime Zuniga (aka "Cirilo" and "Dalton"), a prominent leader of the Shining Path, was captured in November.

The Truth and Reconciliation Commission—appointed in 2001 to inquire into the breadth and depth of killings, assassinations, and human rights abuses that occurred between 1980 and 2000 when the Shining Path was terrorizing the nation—released its nine-volume report. Most startlingly, the commission found that the number of dead was approximately 70,000—twice the figure usually quoted. The commission also cast wide blame when it noted that it had uncovered "murder, disappearance, and torture on a grand scale and indolence, ineptitude, and indifference on the part of those who might have stopped this human catastrophe but did not." The Shining Path was blamed for more than half of the deaths, while security forces were culpable for about one-third. The sweeping magnitude of the report generated protest from all sides. Some saw the findings as sympathetic to the insurgents; others, especially military officers and politicians in office at that time, feared that they would be charged with human rights abuses.

Peru captured a degree of international attention because of a high-pro-

AP/Wide World Photos

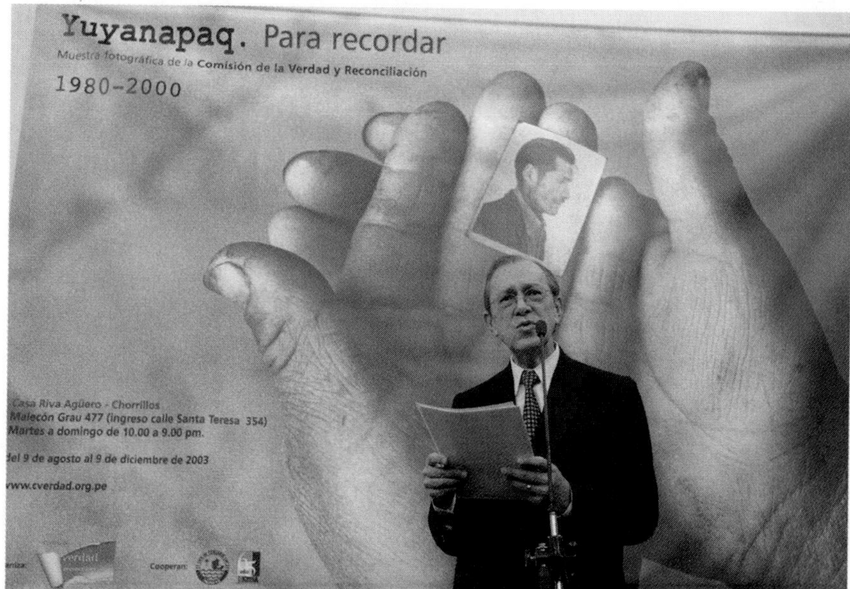

Salomon Lerner, the chairman of Peru's Truth and Reconciliation Commission, which was constituted to report on two decades of civil violence, opens a photo exhibit titled Yuyanapaq. Para recordar *("Reminder" in Quechua and Spanish) on August 9.*

file project to tap into the immense natural-gas deposits in a jungle area known as Camisea. A multinational consortium headed by Argentina was building a pipeline from the jungle to the coast, and numerous environmental and indigenous watchdog groups protested that the project would do harm to local tribes living in the area and to the environment. Despite such protests, funding was approved, and the project moved ahead.

Though President Toledo was scheduled to complete his term in 2006, his lack of popularity coupled with the inchoate state of Peru's political parties made the country's future unpredictable, a situation that was likely to persist. (HENRY A. DIETZ)

PHILIPPINES

Area: 300,076 sq km (115,860 sq mi)
Population (2003 est.): 81,161,000
Capital: Quezon City (designated national government centre and the location of the lower house of the legislature and some ministries); many government offices are in Manila or other suburbs
Head of state and government: President Gloria Macapagal Arroyo

Political turmoil marked by accusations and coup rumours gripped the Philippines during 2003. Pres. Gloria Macapagal Arroyo blamed the trouble on desperate politicians preparing for elections in May 2004; she reversed her earlier decision and said that she would seek a new presidential term.

After rumours of a military coup, Arroyo ordered the arrest on July 26 of "a small band of rogue junior officers." On the following day, that action apparently triggered the seizure by 320 junior officers and soldiers of an apartment building in Manila that they then booby-trapped. They accused Arroyo and Defense Secretary Angelo Reyes of heading a corrupt and inefficient system, demanded their resignations, and requested better military equipment for soldiers fighting guerrillas. The group surrendered peacefully 20 hours later.

Arroyo announced the creation of commissions to investigate the origins of the uprising and the soldiers' accusations. Officials said that the episode was the remnant of a foiled plot to overthrow Arroyo's government and possibly assassinate her. In addition, they believed that the objective of the coup was to install former president Joseph Estrada, who had been forced out by a corruption scandal in 2001, and then have him yield power to a military dictatorship. Estrada had been imprisoned while on trial for the charges. Sen. Gregorio Honasan and six associates were accused of having organized the coup plot. He had led three unsuccessful coup attempts between 1986 and 1989 while an army colonel. Honasan denied any involvement in the recent attempt and went into hiding.

Defense Secretary Reyes resigned in August and warned of a "well-organized and well-funded effort by certain forces to bring down our democracy through massive disinformation and political agitation." The armed forces chief of staff said on September 4 that Arroyo's opponents had offered generals $185,000 and soldiers $950 each to join a coup attempt.

Amid new coup fears, Arroyo ordered a presidential antigraft commission to investigate whether top military and defense officials were living beyond their means. She also formed a task force to revamp armed-forces procurement. She promised to shake up the national police after a reputed leader and bomb-making expert of Jemaah Islamiyah (JI) escaped from a cell at police intelligence headquarters in Manila on July 14; he was tracked down and killed in October. Arroyo attributed the escape to police corruption. Reform efforts were complicated by accusations that her husband had improperly handled her political campaign funds.

Government officials asserted that the turmoil could damage business confidence and drive off badly needed foreign investment. The finance secretary, however, predicted that economic growth in 2003 would be higher than in some other Southeast Asian nations, although a bit lower than the 4.4% of 2002.

Despite sporadic peace talks, guerrilla warfare flared in the southern islands during 2003. The government fought two Islamic groups, the separatist Moro Islamic Liberation Front (MILF) and the piratical Abu Sayyaf. The head of the 12,000-strong MILF, Hashim Salamat, died of a heart attack on July 13. His successor, Al Haj Murad, was a military commander who headed the MILF team for peace talks held in Malaysia. The MILF was blamed for the March 4 and April 2 bombings in the southern city of Davao that killed 39 people. Investigators also suspected that the bombings were connected with JI, which had ties to al-Qaeda terrorists.

United States special forces in 2003 continued to train Filipino soldiers to fight rebels. Washington offered to send 1,700 troops to participate in the fight, but the Philippine constitution barred foreign soldiers from combat there. (HENRY S. BRADSHER)

POLAND

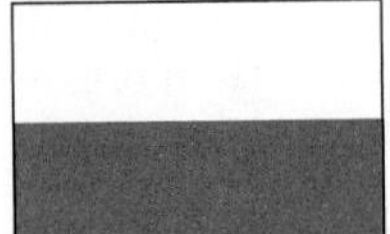

Area: 312,685 sq km (120,728 sq mi)
Population (2003 est.): 38,623,000
Capital: Warsaw
Chief of state: President Aleksander Kwasniewski
Head of government: Prime Minister Leszek Miller

In September Polish police try to control a demonstration by coal miners in front of a government ministry in Warsaw after it has turned into a riot. The miners were protesting planned job cuts and pit closings.

Poland was invited to join the European Union on Dec. 13, 2002, exactly 21 years after the declaration of martial law in Poland that had abruptly ended Solidarity's attempts to break away from the communist system. The accession treaty was signed in April 2003, and the preparation for a referendum in June on EU membership was a preoccupation from the beginning of the year. This "act of historic justice," as Pope John Paul II called EU membership, could be seen as a symbolic end to the years of political, economic, and cultural isolation, sealing Poland's return to the community of European states. Yet opinions were divided on membership issues among the main parties and within the government itself.

Declining support for the ruling SLD-UP (Democratic Left Alliance–Union of Labour) and PSL (Polish Peasant Party) coalition formed in 2001 had manifested itself in the results of the local elections in October 2002. A series of dismissals began in January 2003, including the long-awaited removal of the health minister who had been criticized for having liquidated regional patient funds and pushed through a costly but ineffective centralized health-fund system. In February the coalition collapsed, leaving the SLD-UP as a minority government. The economic recession continued, unemployment remained high (18.7% in January), and instances of mismanagement of public money were increasingly made public.

A hot issue throughout the year was the disclosure of an attempt to solicit a bribe from the largest daily newspaper, allegedly on behalf of the ruling party, for changes to a proposed media law that would secure its private owner rights to expand. A televised parliamentary investigation revealed frequent abuses of power and manipulations in the lawmaking process. A political crisis seemed imminent.

Many ordinary Poles who supported EU entry feared that a vote in favour would give unintended credit to Prime Minister Leszek Miller and his government, during whose term corruption in public administration reached its peak; they therefore might have boycotted the referendum or voted against accession. Poland was by far the largest EU candidate state, and concerns were voiced that a negative Polish vote might prejudice the referenda on the issue in other candidate states.

These emotions were played upon by the populist groups and strongest EU opponents Samoobrona (Self-defense) and the League of Polish Families; their scaremongering tactics also pointed to the loss of sovereignty, Christian values, or national identity and the likely buy-out of land should Poland join the EU. Reason and pragmatism won out, however, and the referendum gave 77.45% support for entry, with a voter turnout of 58.85%. Prime Minister Miller immediately seized the opportunity to regain support for his government and called for and won a vote of confidence. He shifted control of overall economic policy to the economy and labour minister and made promises that prompted Finance Minister Grzegorz Kolodko to resign.

Unexpectedly, the third-quarter growth rate reached 3.9%, and now a 2003 GDP of 3.5% seemed possible. The recession apparently had been derailed. Once the Sejm (lower house of parliament) had accepted the 2004 budget deficit of 45.5 billion zlotys (about $11.3 billion), however, drastic cuts in public spending and a thorough reform of public finances had to follow. These actions, although unpopular, were unavoidable, because the public debt was teetering near the constitutionally permissible threshold level of 60% of GDP and now posed a serious threat to the health of the economy.

Poland was also active internationally. Its choice to buy American F-16 fighters for the air force and the strategic decision (made on the eve of Poland's entrance into the EU in 2004) to support, even if only symbolically, the U.S. in the Iraq war stirred criticism, even rebuke, in "Old Europe." Poland was proud to have made a sovereign, independent decision and garnered respect for its foreign policy; it secured a Polish-led peacekeeping sector in Iraq. Later in the year, however, public enthusiasm for Poland's involvement in the war and its participation in the

Iraqi stabilization mission significantly declined.

Prime Minister Miller visited Polish troops in Iraq on November 11, and Pres. Aleksander Kwasniewski followed suit on December 22. (IWONA GRENDA)

PORTUGAL

Area: 92,152 sq km (35,580 sq mi)
Population (2003 est.): 10,181,000
Capital: Lisbon
Chief of state: President Jorge Sampaio
Head of government: Prime Minister José Manuel Durão Barroso

In 2003 the Portuguese government was determined to comply with the rigours of the European Union's stability and growth pact and to keep its budget deficit under 3% of gross domestic product, although unemployment crept higher and the economy was still struggling. The first half of the year showed the country suffering from recession, and it was not until late in the third quarter that the first tentative signs of recovery appeared. This gloomy backdrop kept pressure on Prime Minister José Manuel Durão Barroso's centre-right coalition government, especially as it made other unpopular decisions, such as supporting the U.S.-led war in Iraq. Even as Portuguese citizens—like many other Europeans—expressed their opposition to the impending conflict, Portugal's Azores archipelago was the scene of a prewar summit with U.S. Pres. George W. Bush, Spain's Prime Minister José María Aznar, U.K. Prime Minister Tony Blair, and Durão Barroso just days before Operation Iraqi Freedom began.

Durão Barroso stressed the business-friendly side of his administration and insisted on plans to cut the corporate tax rate in 2004, despite warnings from the central bank and opposition political parties. At year's end the spending cuts and increased efforts to fight tax evasion brought the 2003 budget in under the 3% limit without having to resort to major one-time asset sales, as had been necessary in 2002.

Another shadow throughout the year was the long-running investigation into an alleged pedophilia and child-pornography ring that centred on the state-run Casa Pia orphanage. More than 10 people were detained as the inquiry into what was allegedly decades of abuse of young children continued; those detained included a popular television personality, a former diplomat, and the Socialist Party spokesman. The high-profile case sparked national soul-searching as people questioned everything from the sluggish judicial system to the rules for the preventive detention of suspects and the duties of journalists to protect underage or threatened sources. Though the Socialist Party spokesman was released, most of the suspects remained in custody, and in late December prosecutors brought pedophile charges against 10 people, including a lawmaker and 2 TV personalities.

Extreme heat was blamed for a large number of deaths during the summer, though fewer than in Italy and France. The hot, dry air also contributed to Portugal's worst forest fires in living memory, with some 400,000 ha (almost one million acres)—around 8% of the country's total forests—burned and damages estimated at more than €1 billion (about $1.12 billion). At least 18 people died in the blazes, most of which stemmed from carelessness or lightning strikes, though some were thought to have been caused by arson.

In the autumn the government suffered its first major setbacks when two ministers were forced to resign over allegations of favouritism. Foreign Minister António Martins da Cruz was considered a key ally of the prime minister and was in the middle of complex negotiations over Europe's planned constitution when he resigned. Education Minister Pedro Lynce, meanwhile, had been working on one of the government's key programs, a long-awaited overhaul of the university system. While the cabinet shuffle was a blow to Durão Barroso's government, the coalition with the right-leaning Partido Popular remained strong, and the 2004 budget—which continued to tighten the belt on spending in an effort to keep the deficit below 3% of GDP—passed in its parliamentary vote in November. (ERIK T. BURNS)

AP/Wide World Photos

An airplane releases water to help fight a forest fire near Partida, Port., in July. The summer heat wave and drought were especially devastating in southwestern Europe and contributed to a large number of wildfires.

QATAR

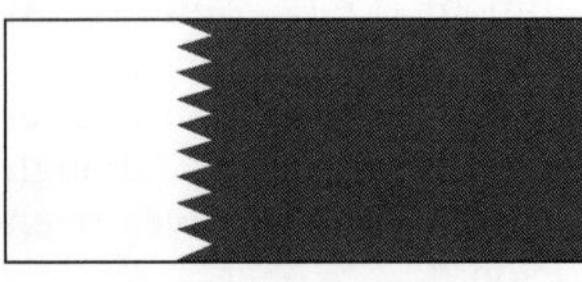

Area: 11,427 sq km (4,412 sq mi)
Population (2003 est.): 626,000
Capital: Doha
Head of state and government: Emir Sheikh Hamad ibn Khalifah al-Thani, assisted by Prime Minister Sheikh Abdullah ibn Khalifah al-Thani

In late March 2003, Qatar served as regional headquarters for the U.S.-led allied coalition that invaded Iraq, and Qatar became the principal centre for the U.S. Central Command's air command and control operations in the Persian Gulf.

Sheikh Jassim ibn Hamad al-Thani, the emir's son, relinquished the post of crown prince to his younger brother Sheikh Tamim, who was later named deputy commander in chief of the country's armed forces. In a referendum in April, voters elected to make permanent a draft constitution that provided for universal suffrage and a 45-member advisory assembly, which paved the way for parliamentary elections in 2004.

In October Qatar relinquished leadership to Malaysia of the Organization of the Islamic Conference, and in December it completed its year of holding the presidency of the Supreme Council and chairmanship of the Ministerial Council of the Gulf Cooperation Council (GCC). Qatar remained first among GCC countries in annual GDP growth rate. Qatar continued to develop the offshore North Field, the world's largest nonassociated natural-gas reservoir, while revenue from liquefied natural gas (LNG), whose infrastructure had long received the country's greatest investment, approached that from oil. It was announced that Qatar would become the Middle East's first and, soon thereafter, premier producer of gas-to-liquids, including an environmentally cleaner and reduced-emissions version of conventional diesel fuel.

(JOHN DUKE ANTHONY)

Doha, Qatar, was the headquarters for the U.S. Central Command (CENTCOM) and as such became a focal point of the U.S.-led invasion of Iraq in March. The System Control Room at Camp Doha is pictured here on April 1.

ROMANIA

Area: 237,500 sq km (91,699 sq mi)
Population (2003 est.): 21,616,000
Capital: Bucharest
Chief of state: President Ion Iliescu
Head of government: Prime Minister Adrian Nastase

Romania's forthright support for the U.S.-led coalition that occupied Iraq in the spring of 2003 boosted the influence of the former communists who had largely controlled the country since 1989. In May, U.S. Deputy Defense Secretary Paul Wolfowitz said he was relying on Romanian officials (in light of their own experience of totalitarianism) to give him advice about how to neutralize the legacy of Saddam Hussein in Iraq. Washington's allies in the European Union—the U.K., Spain, and Italy—also strongly pushed for Romania to join the EU by the 2007 target date. Romania was the beneficiary of flexible entry terms as it became increasingly clear that it would take many years before it could fit and cooperate effectively with existing EU members.

Ana-Maria Cioaba, 12, of Romania is comforted by a photographer as her 15-year-old groom, Mihai Birita, looks on. Marriages at such a young age were common among the Roma (Gypsy) people, but this wedding caused an international outcry.

The government of Adrian Nastase continued to resist EU calls to strengthen the rule of law, modernize public services, and reduce the influence of the ruling Social Democratic Party (PSD) over public appointments. An anticorruption agency set up in 2002 instead targeted officials who tried to preserve their political independence. An outcry ensued in June when Andreea Ciuca, a judge widely respected for her impartiality, was jailed on the orders of this agency (only to be set free by a higher court). This incident was widely seen as a warning from the PSD to Romanians prepared to challenge its monopolistic approach to power that serious reprisals were bound to follow. The PSD had been trying to drive its most effective challenger, Traian Basescu, the mayor of Bucharest, from public life by opening up an old case implicating him in the sell-off of the merchant fleet on terms disadvantageous to Romania. On September 28 Basescu's party and the Liberals formed the Truth and Justice

Alliance, which some observers believed was capable of challenging the PSD's hold on power in the future.

Pres. Ion Iliescu again assumed leadership of the PSD as the last term in office that he could serve approached its end. In 2003 he made a number of controversial decisions that suggested that he would appeal to nationalism in order to prevent his nominally left-wing party from losing ground electorally because of its pro-business orientation. In May Iliescu attacked foreign ambassadors for having complained about widespread corruption, which he described as an interference in internal affairs. In July he bestowed a top honour on Adrian Paunescu, formerly the court poet of communist dictator Nicolae Ceausescu. Most controversially of all, on July 25 he declared that "the Holocaust was not unique to the Jewish people in Europe," comparing the suffering of prewar Romanian communists (including his father) with that of the Jews.

The event that undoubtedly received the most international attention in 2003, however, was the arranged marriage in the town of Sibiu on September 27 of 12-year-old Ana-Maria, the daughter of the self-proclaimed Roma (Gypsy) king, Florin Cioaba. EU officials and human rights activists expressed horror at an arranged marriage involving a minor in an EU candidate country, but the practice remained common among the Gypsies of Romania. (TOM GALLAGHER)

RUSSIA

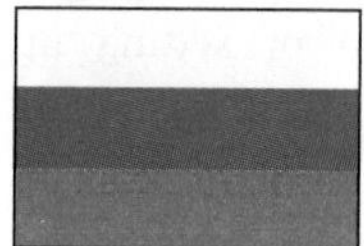

Area: 17,075,400 sq km (6,592,800 sq mi)
Population (2003 est.): 144,893,000
Capital: Moscow
Chief of state: President Vladimir Putin
Head of government: Prime Minister Mikhail Kasyanov

Domestic Politics. A general election to the State Duma, the 450-member lower house of the Russian parliament, was held on Dec. 7, 2003. The result was an overwhelming victory for parties supporting the policies of Pres. Vladimir Putin and a crushing defeat for the opposition. First place went to the pro-presidential United Russia, commonly known as the "party of power," which took 37.6% of the national vote. The Communist Party (CPRF) came in second with 12.6%—half the size of its vote in the preceding election of 1999. The maverick Liberal Democratic Party came in third with 11.5%, while the nationalistic Motherland bloc won 9%. Neither of Russia's liberal right-wing parties, Yabloko and the Union of Right Forces (SPS), cleared the 5% hurdle to win seats. No one doubted that these results accurately reflected the wishes of the voters, but the Organization for Security and Co-operation in Europe, which observed the election, criticized the misuse of "administrative resources" (state infrastructure and personnel on the public payroll) to campaign for United Russia and media coverage excessively favourable to the pro-presidential parties.

While the parliamentary election was the major formal political event of 2003, the strong executive and legislative powers that the Russian constitution vested in the office of the president meant that the main issue preoccupying the political elite was the presidential election scheduled for March 2004. Opinion polls indicated that Putin's popularity remained high and he was virtually certain to win a second term. Following the general election, Putin publicly confirmed that he would run for reelection. Throughout the year, however, observers detected increasingly bitter signs of rivalry within the presidential administration, divided as it was commonly believed to be into opposing factions, each determined to ensure that it, not its rivals, would have the president's ear during his anticipated second term. These groups were popularly nicknamed the "Family" and the *Siloviki*. The Family represented the interests of those who came to power under former president Boris Yeltsin and benefited (sometimes by dubious means) from the privatization of formerly state-owned assets in the 1990s; they were seen as liberal, pro-market, and Western-oriented. The second group was known both as *Siloviki* (denoting their roots in state institutions with the right to wield force) and as *Gosudarstvenniki* ("Statists"). They favoured a strong state role in the economy; they were seen as opposing foreign investment in key areas of the Russian economy and wary of Russia's rapprochement with the West, especially the U.S. They included the leaders of state-owned industries, the military, and the intelligence and security agencies. Their status had risen sharply since Putin became president, with many of their number having been promoted to top posts in all branches of government and administration. Having missed out during the privatization of the 1990s, they were believed to want both to secure their slice of the pie and to ensure that key sectors of the economy remained under state control. They also called for state intervention to tax the "superprofits" accruing from high world prices and the redistribution of the funds to foster social welfare and Russia's technological advancement.

The Yukos affair brought the clash between these two groups into the open. It began in early July, when the prosecutor general's office launched an investigation into the activities of Yukos, Russia's leading oil company. A Yukos shareholder, billionaire Platon Lebedev, was arrested and imprisoned on suspicion of financial wrongdoing during the privatization of a fertilizer company in the 1990s. Alarm bells rang because similar charges could have been leveled against most, if not all, Russian businesses established at that time. Prosecutors announced that they were also investigating allegations of tax evasion, fraud, and even murder. Police conducted numerous searches of offices belonging to or associated with Yukos.

In October, Mikhail Khodorkovsky, chairman of Yukos and the richest man in Russia, was arrested and imprisoned on suspicion of tax evasion. Many commentators believed the case to be politically motivated. Khodorkovsky, they argued, had run afoul of the so-called historic compromise that Putin had struck with Russia's business tycoons (commonly known as "oligarchs") after becoming president in 2000; as long as the oligarchs stayed out of politics, they would be allowed to keep the properties they had acquired under privatization, regardless of how these had been obtained, but they were not to use their billions to interfere in the political process.

One of seven bankers who built huge fortunes during the controversial "loans-for-shares" scheme of 1995, Khodorkovsky had had a typically controversial rise to the top of the business world. Latterly, however, he had tried to turn Yukos into a model of transparency. In so doing, he had won the admiration of Western business circles. At the same time, Khodorkovsky began to take an interest in politics. He established a charitable foundation that contributed large sums of money to universities and the arts, sponsored the use of the Internet in the regions, and made financial contributions to

AP/Wide World Photos

Mikhail Khodorkovsky, who faced government charges of fraud and extortion, resigned as head of his giant Yukos oil company on November 3. His tribulations were part of an official crackdown on Russia's "oligarchs."

Russian political parties such as Yabloko, the SPS, and even, reportedly, the CPRF. According to some reports, Khodorkovsky hoped to ensure that smaller political parties would be represented in the Duma elected in December, which thereby would reduce the chances that the "party of power" would dominate the new parliament. According to more hostile reports, he had been planning to "buy" the Duma and turn Russia into a parliamentary republic in which the prime minister, not the president, played the dominant role. There was general agreement that whatever his aim, Khodorkovsky had violated the terms of Putin's historic compromise. The affair took a fresh turn in October when prosecutors froze the controlling stake in Yukos owned by Khodorkovsky and his partners. Alarmed, other businessmen called on the Kremlin for assurances that the Yukos investigation did not signal the beginning of a witch hunt against Russian business as a whole. Putin assured them that he was committed to a market economy and that the privatization process would not be reversed.

Human rights activists accused the Putin administration of curtailing democracy at home, especially as regards press freedom. The U.S.-based civil rights monitor Freedom House downgraded Russia's media status to "Not Free" after Boris Jordan was forced out of his post as the last independent head of the state-owned television station NTV in January. In June, TVS, Russia's last private television station with a nationwide audience, was closed on orders of the Press Ministry.

June saw the refurbished city of St. Petersburg celebrate the 300th anniversary of its foundation by Peter the Great as his "window on the West." This was seen as symbolic of Russia's post-Soviet opening to the outside world. Symbolic also of the Russian people's reconciliation with its troubled past was the consecration in July of the Cathedral on the Blood in Yekaterinburg, built on the spot where the last tsar and his family were assassinated in 1918.

The Economy. The economy recorded its fifth consecutive year of growth since the prolonged output collapse of 1989–98. For 2003 as a whole, GDP was projected to grow at a rate of over 6.5%. Kick-started by the ruble devaluation of 1998, growth was maintained by high world oil prices. Russia maintained a high trade surplus and met its external-debt repayments ahead of schedule. The government won praise for its decision to establish a budgetary-stabilization fund from revenue arising from oil prices higher than that on which the budget had been based; this would give the economy some protection for debt-service commitments in the event of sharp fluctuations in the oil price. Growth did not depend solely on high oil prices, however, or even on the substantial volume of Russian oil exports. It also reflected—at least, until the eruption of the Yukos case in July—increasing business confidence in the Russian economy, boosted by the fact that the Putin administration was continuing to follow a path of liberalizing institutional reform.

Consumer price inflation declined slowly and reached 12% by year's end. Unemployment remained low by international standards. Living standards rose. In the first half of 2003, both average real wages and retail sales in real terms (that is, adjusted for inflation) rose some 8% over the first half of 2002. The immediate effects of the economic boom, however, were largely confined to Moscow and other big cities, and many people in the countryside and small towns remained mired in poverty.

Rising confidence encouraged foreign investment. Foreign direct investment (FDI) totaled $3.9 billion in January–September, against $2.1 billion in the first nine months of 2002. Particularly notable was the decision of British Petroleum (BP) to invest in the creation of a new oil and gas holding company, TNK-BP Ltd., formed through the merger of the oil and gas assets of Russia's Tyumen Oil Co. (TNK) and those of BP in Russia. The deal represented the largest overseas investment in the Russian economy to date and made the U.K. the largest source of FDI in Russia. Russia's economic achievements were recognized in October when the international ratings agency, Moody's, raised its rating of Russian sovereign debt to the investment-grade category.

At the same time, however, some of Russia's richest businessmen began to remove their capital from the country. The first sign came in the spring when Family member Boris Abramovich sold his Russian assets, bought Britain's prestigious Chelsea Football Club, and declared his intention of setting up home in the U.K.

Military and Security Policy. Military reform remained stalled. In March, Putin announced a major reorganization of Russia's security and intelligence agencies. Whereas former president Yeltsin had clipped the wings of the security apparatus, dividing the Soviet-era Committee for State Security (KGB) into several smaller organizations, Putin's changes consolidated and strengthened the apparatus. The main beneficiary of his reorganization was the domestic-security agency, the Federal Security Service (FSB), which regained nearly all of the functions lost when the KGB, its parent organization, was disbanded in 1991. Under Putin's reorganization the only KGB functions left outside the control of the FSB were foreign intelligence—which remained the responsibility of the Foreign Intelligence Service (SVR)—and the physical protection of state officials—the preserve of the small Federal Protection Service (FSO). Meanwhile, the Federal Agency for Government Communications and Information (FAPSI) was disbanded; its functions, which included monitoring radio and other communications both at home and abroad, were distributed between the FSB, SVR, and FSO. The Federal Border Guards were resubordinated to the FSB, the aim being to tighten control over Russia's borders and combat illegal immigration, people trafficking, and weapons smuggling. In a move expected to benefit small and medium-size businesses, the notoriously corrupt Federal Tax Police was downsized and subordinated to the Interior Ministry. A new body was created to combat Russia's growing drug problem. If successful this could help to alleviate the threat of HIV/AIDS infection; in 2003 Russia and neighbouring Ukraine reported the world's fastest-growing infection rates.

Chechnya. Following the terrorist attacks of Sept. 11, 2001, in the United States, the Kremlin redefined Russia's conflict with its secessionist republic as an integral part of the international terrorist threat. This deflected international criticism of Russia's handling of the conflict and enabled the Kremlin to maintain its refusal to negotiate with the rebels, who in turn became more radicalized. Until 2003, suicide bombings were a rare occurrence in Russia. In 2003 they became the rebels' weapon of choice, enabling them to shift the conflict to the Russian heartland. In July, 17 people were killed when two women blew themselves up at the entrance to a rock festival in Moscow. By year's end well over 150 people had been killed by suicide bombings.

In March the Russian authorities organized a referendum in Chechnya. Voter turnout was put at 88%, and what some thought an improbably high 96% of those who voted supported a new constitution defining Chechnya as an integral part of the Russian Federation. Moscow declared that the "counterterrorism operation" in Chechnya, which had been conducted by the FSB, was complete; in September command and control passed to the Interior Ministry. In October an election was held for president of the republic. Turnout was put at 81%, and the election was won—with 80% of the votes cast—by Akhmad Kadyrov, who had since June 2000 been acting head of Chechnya's pro-Kremlin administration. The presidential election was to be followed by the negotiation of a bilateral treaty on the division of powers between Chechnya and the Russian Federation.

Foreign Policy. President Putin steered Russia through a difficult year in international relations, and, on the whole, Russia's relations with the outside world remained good. Relations with the U.S. hit a rocky patch in the spring following Russia's decision to side with France and Germany in refusing to support the U.S.-led military operation in Iraq. The administration of Pres. George W. Bush declared in the aftermath of the Iraq war, however, that while it intended to punish France and ignore Germany, Russia was to be forgiven. France, Germany, and Italy made efforts to maintain good relations with Moscow, while in June the U.K. welcomed Putin on the first state visit to Britain by a Russian leader since 1874. A continuing irritant in U.S.-Russian relations was Moscow's refusal to slow down or halt its nuclear cooperation with Iran. At first Russia brushed aside U.S. fears that Iran might use the technology to develop a secret nuclear-weapons program. Later, however, Moscow pressed Iran to agree to return to Russia all spent nuclear fuel and to accept short-notice inspections by the International Atomic Energy Agency.

Russia's relations with its post-Soviet neighbours were more stormy. During his first two years in office, Putin had seemed to switch Russia's focus from the (often ineffectual) framework of multilateral relations within the Commonwealth of Independent States (CIS) and concentrate instead on building effective bilateral relations. In 2003, however, Russia's increasing self-confidence on the international stage translated into a more assertive attitude toward its neighbours. Russia opened an air base in Kyrgyzstan; the move appeared designed to reassert Russia's military influence in Central Asia, where in the period after 9/11 the United States had established its own semipermanent military presence. Russia failed, however, to persuade Moldova to accept a constitutional settlement with its breakaway Transnistria region that would have sanctioned the continuing presence of Russian troops on Moldovan territory. Border frictions erupted with Ukraine, and Moscow was alarmed by the change of regime in Georgia.

Finally, the year saw hints that a two- or even three-speed CIS was beginning to evolve. In September the most economically developed of the CIS states—Russia, Ukraine, Kazakhstan, and Belarus—signed an agreement on the creation of a Single Economic Space, intended to lead eventually to the establishment of full economic union and even a single currency. In December a new Collective Security Treaty Organization, bringing together Armenia, Belarus, Kazakhstan, Kyrgyzstan, Russia, and Tajikistan, was officially recognized by the UN as a regional international organization. (ELIZABETH TEAGUE)

Akhmad Kadyrov, shown here at his inauguration in the city of Gudermes, Chechnya, on October 19, was elected president of this Russian republic with some 80% of the vote, although local rebels and international rights groups faulted the balloting.

RWANDA

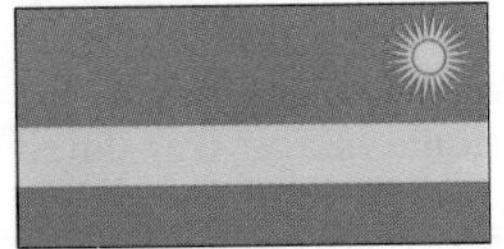

Area: 26,338 sq km (10,169 sq mi)
Population (2003 est.): 8,387,000
Capital: Kigali
Head of state and government: President Maj. Gen. Paul Kagame, assisted by Prime Minister Bernard Makuza

On September 12 Paul Kagame is sworn in as president of Rwanda in ceremonies in Kigali, the capital. Kagame received 95% of the vote in the first presidential elections since the genocidal civil war was ended in 1994.

AP/Wide World Photos

By early January 2003, most of the estimated 23,000 Rwandan refugees living in camps in Tanzania had been repatriated. The U.S. Committee for Refugees reported that the repatriation effort was unorganized, which caused close to 3,000 refugees to flee to Uganda seeking asylum and deepened the mistrust between the Rwandan and Ugandan governments. Tensions between the two countries heightened in January when Jean Bosco Barihima, leader of a Congolese rebel force, alleged that the Ugandan government was allowing Hutu dissidents to use Ugandan-controlled parts of the Democratic Republic of the Congo (DRC) to execute cross-border attacks on Rwanda. Uganda flatly denied the allegations. Relations cooled significantly in March when accusations were lobbed between the two countries; each blamed the other for supporting rebels in the DRC. The crisis intensified later that month when the Rwandan parliament voted to redeploy troops to the DRC and when former Rwandan defense minister Emmanuel Habyarimana, accused of engaging in subversive activities and of holding Hutu-extremist views, was granted temporary asylum by Uganda. A London meeting in early May between Presidents Kagame and Yoweri Museveni, hosted by British cabinet minister Clare Short (*see* BIOGRAPHIES), eased tensions ahead of the installation of a transitional government in the DRC.

In August, UN Secretary-General Kofi Annan asked Carla Del Ponte, chief prosecutor for the International Criminal Tribunal for Rwanda (ICTR), to step down amid complaints by the Rwandan government that she had not been spending enough time prosecuting cases of accused war criminals from the 1994 genocide and following tensions over the ICTR's attempt to prosecute crimes committed by Kagame's Rwanda Patriotic Front (FPR) in 1994, when it quelled the genocide. In September Gambian Hassan Jallow took over as the ICTR's chief prosecutor. Broadcaster Ferdinand Nahimana of radio station RTLM and Hassan Ngeze, editor of the newspaper *Kangura,* were sentenced to life imprisonment on December 3. A third person, also from RTLM, received a 35-year sentence. Both media outlets were accused of having encouraged the 1994 genocide by publicizing names of those to be killed.

On August 25, in the first multiparty election held since Rwanda gained independence in 1962, Kagame won 95% of the vote. Many campaign tactics were found to have been irregular, including harassment and intimidation of opposition party members and supporters. On October 10 the first democratically elected parliament was sworn in, and the nine-year transitional government installed by the Tutsi-led FPR ended. (MARY F.E. EBELING)

SAINT KITTS AND NEVIS

Area: 269 sq km (104 sq mi)
Population (2003 est.): 46,400
Capital: Basseterre
Chief of state: Queen Elizabeth II, represented by Governor-General Sir Cuthbert Montraville Sebastian
Head of government: Prime Minister Denzil Douglas

The potential breakup of the twin-island state of Saint Kitts and Nevis became an issue once more in February 2003 when Nevis's two political parties—the governing Concerned Citizens Movement and the opposition Nevis Reformation Party—said that they would revive an initiative to seek autonomy for the island. In 1998 Nevis residents had voted 62% in favour of independence, but the measure needed 67% approval in order to pass. The two territories had been united since independence from Britain in 1983, but Nevis had its own Island Assembly that looked after local matters.

In June the Assembly took the matter a step farther when it unanimously accepted Nevis Premier Vance Amory's resolution to seek full independence for the island. The rest of the Caribbean Community and Common Market (Caricom) bloc expressed its strong opposition to the move at the annual Caricom meeting in July.

In September Prime Minister Denzil Douglas was appointed chairman of the Small States Forum, which addressed issues of concern to microstates worldwide. (DAVID RENWICK)

SAINT LUCIA

Area: 617 sq km (238 sq mi)
Population (2003 est.): 162,000
Capital: Castries
Chief of state: Queen Elizabeth II, represented by Governor-General Dame Pearlette Louisy
Head of government: Prime Minister Kenny Anthony

In the annual budget presented in April 2003 by Saint Lucia Prime Minister and Minister of Finance Kenny Anthony, $325 million was devoted to capital and recurrent expenditure in the 2003–04 fiscal year. The amount had risen 10.3% above that of the previous year and was designed to advance infrastructure development and keep the country on the path of economic recovery.

In September Anthony accused some Saint Lucia citizens of having made outrageously false refugee claims in order to gain admittance into Canada. This strategy had been employed over the years by people from other Caribbean territories who apparently considered their chances of migrating by normal channels slim.

George Odlum, one of Saint Lucia's most renowned politicians, died of cancer in September. Although Odlum was noted most of his career for his left-wing views, for a time he had moderated his beliefs sufficiently to be able to serve as Saint Lucia's foreign minister. That same month Anthony met U.S. Pres. George W. Bush in New York City for discussions on Caribbean affairs.

(DAVID RENWICK)

SAINT VINCENT AND THE GRENADINES

Area: 389 sq km (150 sq mi)
Population (2003 est.): 113,000
Capital: Kingstown
Chief of state: Queen Elizabeth II, represented by Governor-General Sir Frederick Ballantyne
Head of government: Prime Minister Ralph Gonsalves

Saint Vincent and the Grenadines was finally removed in June 2003 from the money-laundering blacklist drawn up by the Paris-based Financial Action Task Force. Prime Minister Ralph Gonsalves announced that the FATF was satisfied that the 25 conditions had been met to allow delisting. By midyear the names of all of the Caribbean countries had been removed from the list.

Saint Vincent and the Grenadines found itself among five Caribbean states on an entirely different list in July; the group was cut off from U.S. military aid after it declined to exempt U.S. citizens from prosecution before the International Criminal Court. The cut in aid did not include U.S. assistance in such areas as economic development and anti-AIDS programs, however.

Education Minister Mike Browne reported in August that the territory was likely to achieve its goal of free high-school education for all students by 2005—five years ahead of the target date.

Saint Vincent and the Grenadines, one of only three Caribbean states to recognize Taiwan rather than mainland China, solidified its relationship with Taiwan when Gonsalves visited the country in September. He came away with a promise of $27 million for a new cross-island highway.

(DAVID RENWICK)

SAMOA

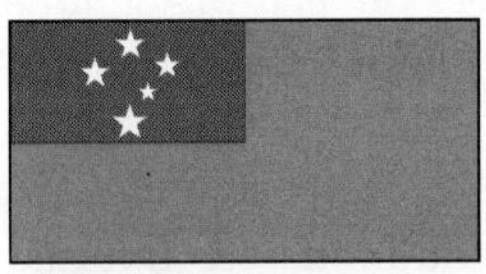

Area: 2,831 sq km (1,093 sq mi)
Population (2003 est.): 179,000
Capital: Apia
Chief of state: *O le Ao o le Malo* (Head of State) Malietoa Tanumafili II
Head of government: Prime Minister Tuila'epa Sa'ilele Malielegaoi

In May 2003 the Samoan government took steps to address transnational crimes, focusing on immigration, human and drug trafficking, money laundering, and Internet-based pornography and crime. In August Prime Minister Tuila'epa Sa'ilele Malielegaoi reshuffled his cabinet and redistributed portfolios that had been held in the prime minister's office.

Samoa had applied to join the World Trade Organization in 1998 but met with resistance at home from activists opposed to the local impact of globalization and abroad from WTO members suggesting that utilities and public services in Samoa should be privatized rather than provided by the government. The trade deficit worsened, and in March the government reduced the tax on fish landed from large vessels in order to encourage the fishing industry. The economy remained heavily dependent on remittances from Samoans living abroad.

In March petitioners demonstrated for the repeal of the 1982 New Zealand legislation that had removed New Zealand citizenship from Samoans born before 1948. (Samoa was administered by New Zealand under UN trusteeship until 1962.) The appeal was rejected by the New Zealand government, which noted that the Citizenship (Western Samoa) Act had also bestowed New Zealand citizenship on many Samoans living in New Zealand at the time.

(BARRIE MACDONALD)

SAN MARINO

Area: 61.2 sq km (23.6 sq mi)
Population (2003 est.): 29,200
Capital: San Marino
Heads of state and government: The republic is governed by two capitani reggenti, or coregents, appointed every six months by a popularly elected Great and General Council.

On July 3–4, 2003, Walter Schwimmer, secretary-general of the Council of Europe, made an official visit to San Marino. Schwimmer met with the two coregents, as well as Fiorenzo Stolfi, secretary of state for foreign and political affairs, and addressed the Great and General Council. In keeping with a Council of Europe conference on gender equality in January, San Marino had signed international agreements requiring respect for the principle of gender equality, and the country was moving ahead in order to turn the principle into a reality. One area of concern was the fact that Sammarinese men automatically transmitted citizenship to their lawful offspring, but there still were restrictions on children of women nationals married to foreigners.

San Marino made headlines when it appointed German Formula One driver Michael Schumacher as "ambassador of the republic." This followed Schumacher's victory at the San Marino Grand Prix and was intended not only to help him in his many humanitarian activities but also to gain international visibility for San Marino in a period of declining tourism revenues. It was hoped that a racy new image might help bolster a segment of the economy that accounted for 30% of GDP.

(GREGORY O. SMITH)

SÃO TOMÉ AND PRÍNCIPE

Area: 1,001 sq km (386 sq mi)
Population (2003 est.): 161,000
Capital: São Tomé
Chief of state: Presidents Fradique de Menezes, Fernando Pereira (de facto) from July 16, and, from July 23, Fradique de Menezes
Head of government: Prime Minister Maria das Neves

During 2003 São Tomé and Príncipe and Nigeria agreed to share (40% and 60%, respectively) the proceeds of the oil found in the offshore waters between them. A Joint High Authority was established to manage offshore oil exploration in the disputed Gulf of Guinea, though the exact border demarcation between the two countries remained unresolved. Nigeria released $8 million for the management of São Tomé and Príncipe's oil industry and promised to build an oil refinery and deepwater port. Prospecting contracts with three oil companies were renegotiated, and in April São Tomé and Príncipe and Nigeria began the auction of nine exploration blocs in their joint maritime zone. These deals were expected to bring about $100 million to the archipelago, double its annual budget.

In July, when de Menezes was visiting Abuja, Nigeria, a group of soldiers led by Maj. Fernando Pereira seized power in a bloodless coup. Prime Minister Maria das Nevas was locked up, and the parliament was dissolved. After a few days of negotiations, brokered by Portuguese, Nigerian, and U.S. diplomats, the leaders of the coup agreed to the return of de Menezes on the condition that they would not be punished for their actions.

(CHRISTOPHER SAUNDERS)

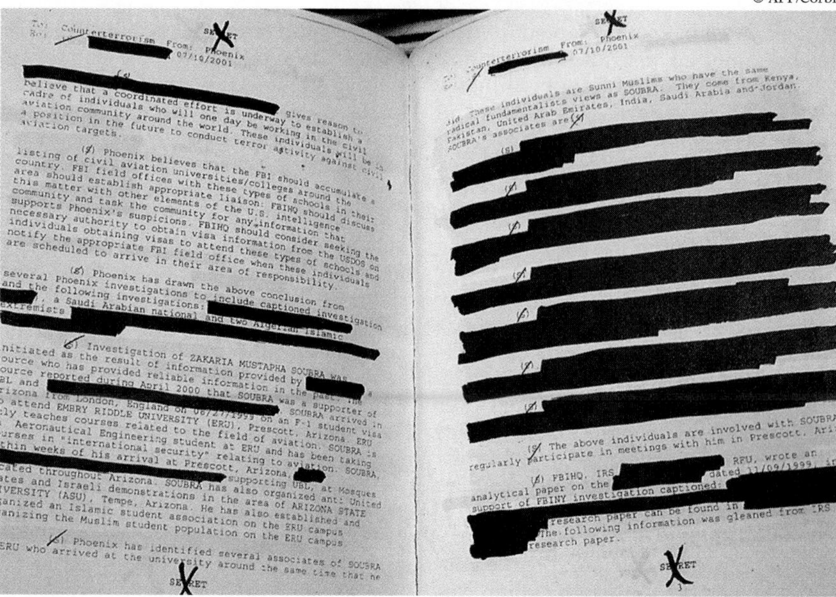

In July the U.S. Congress released a report on the 9/11 terrorist strikes that contained passages implicating Saudi Arabia in the attacks on the U.S. Because the allegations could not be substantiated, however, these passages were blacked out in the public version of the report.

SAUDI ARABIA

Area: 2,149,690 sq km (830,000 sq mi)
Population (2003 est.): 24,008,000
Capital: Riyadh
Head of state and government: King Fahd, assisted by Crown Prince Abdullah

The issue that dominated internal Saudi Arabian affairs in 2003 was the intensification of the official campaign against anti-Western Islamic groups accused of involvement in acts of sabotage. During the year the latter clashed with security forces, and there were casualties on both sides. According to official sources, 600 people were arrested. The Saudi political and religious authorities emphasized detachment from any views that called for military actions against non-Muslims in the name of Islam. Crown Prince Abdullah, the unofficial de facto ruler, vowed to uproot extremism in the country, and Prince Naif, the minister of the interior, took an unexpected step in March by attacking the Muslim Brothers, a largely Egyptian party that had not been accused of any extremist actions and that for decades had enjoyed very good relations with the Saudi establishment. Concurrently, the Saudi highest cleric, Sheikh Abdul-Aziz al-Sheikh, told the Saudis in August to ignore fanatic interpretations of Islam or risk "banning God's bounty." That same month the U.S. military shut down the largest remaining air force unit at Prince Sultan Air Base, which brought the American military presence in the kingdom to a very low level. The move helped to diffuse resentment over the military's close proximity to Islam's holiest sites.

Saudi officials criticized a U.S. congressional report that implied the country's complicity in the Sept. 11, 2001, attacks in the U.S. Foreign Minister Saud al-Faisal remarked that the report was "illogical and unacceptable," and he offered to cooperate with the FBI in providing information on any Saudi found to be linked to the attacks. At the same time, King Fahd issued a special pardon releasing five British nationals and one Canadian who had been jailed for their alleged involvement in explosions related to alcohol trafficking in 2000 and 2001.

Calls for political and social reform were expressed in both official and unofficial circles. In June more than 500 intellectuals and clerics representing the country's Sunni majority and Shi'ite and Isma'ili minorities, together with liberals and technocrats, gathered for a four-day meeting. The unprecedented event ended with a list of recommendations being submitted to the crown prince. The document called for greater participation by women in Saudi affairs, expansion of democratic-type freedoms, and the restriction to capable clerics of the right to issue religious fatwas. Similar requests came from other Saudi groups abroad. In response, in October the government announced that the first-ever political elections would be held in 2004, in which half the members of the municipal council would be elected. In addition, the country held a human rights conference that month, and the first woman dean was appointed to a Saudi university. Nevertheless, in late October nationwide protests were staged twice by the Movement for Islamic Reform.

On the economic front, the two-year-long negotiations collapsed between the Saudi government and major American oil companies to finance a $25 billion natural-gas scheme. A smaller agreement was signed, however, between Dutch Shell (40%), French Total (30%), and Saudi Aramco (30%), for a $5 billion project to extract natural gas from an area south of the Rubʿ al-Khali desert.

The Saudi balance of payments registered another surplus in 2003, owing to the relatively high price of exported crude oil. Nevertheless, the government pursued plans to privatize certain sectors of the economy, especially electricity and transportation.

(MAHMOUD HADDAD)

SENEGAL

Area: 196,722 sq km (75,955 sq mi)
Population (2003 est.): 10,095,000
Capital: Dakar
Chief of state: President Abdoulaye Wade, assisted by Prime Minister Idrissa Seck

After a six-month truce, fighting broke out in early January 2003 in Casamance between the Senegalese army and breakaway hard-line members of the Movement of Democratic Forces of Casamance (MFDC); the MFDC was seeking independence for the region. At least 30 rebels and 4 soldiers died in clashes near Ziguinchor, the Casamance regional capital, and the resorts of Cap Skirring. On April 3 Pres. Abdoulaye Wade ordered the government to find means for the rebuilding of the southern province and the repatriation and resettlement of the more than 28,000 people who had fled the area during the 21-year rebellion. In an attack on May 7 in the village of Bofa, 23 km (14 mi) from Ziguinchor, one soldier was killed and another wounded. The mainstream and moderate faction of the MFDC, led by former priest Augustin Diamacoune Senghor, denied responsibility for the raid. On May 26 the MFDC announced the death of Sidi Badji, the 83-year-old leader of the militant faction. Following a rebel attack on another southern village, the army launched a new security operation on August 6.

Amid continued inquiries into the cause of the sinking of the ferry *Le Joola* in September 2002, a Senegalese cargo ship sank off the coast of Mauritania on Jan. 20, 2003; 11 of the 19 crewmen were rescued. Wade laid the blame for the ferry disaster squarely on the military and the feeble and chaotic rescue operation that followed. After months of dispute over the level of compensation to be paid to families of the 1,863 victims, the amount was finally fixed at 5 million CFA francs (about $9,000) each, and payments began on September 29.

(NANCY ELLEN LAWLER)

Boys study the Qu'ran, using prayer boards inscribed with scripture, in a makeshift Muslim school in an unfinished house outside Dakar, Senegal. About 92% of the citizens of the West African country followed Sunni Islam.

SERBIA AND MONTENEGRO

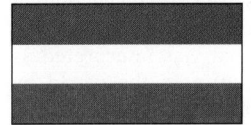

Area: 102,173 sq km (39,449 sq mi)
Population (2003 est.): 10,527,000
Administrative centres: Belgrade (Serbia) and Podgorica (Montenegro)
Chief of state: Presidents Vojislav Kostunica and, from March 7, Svetozar Marovic. The name of the state was changed from the Federal Republic of Yugoslavia to Serbia and Montenegro on February 4.
Head of government: Prime Minister (of Yugoslavia) Dragisa Pesic to March 27; after that date the two constituent governments were led by Prime Minister Zoran Zivkovic (Serbia, elected by Parliament on March 18) and Milo Djukanovic (Montenegro, elected by Parliament on January 8)

On Feb. 4, 2003, a new entity, dubbed a "state union" (*drzavna zajednica* in Serbian) and named Serbia and Montenegro, replaced the Federal Republic of Yugoslavia. The union was very loose; each republic maintained its own foreign policy, budget and fiscal system, trade and customs arrangements, and currency. The instrument of formation of the union, due to expire in 2006, was a prerequisite for the country's joining the Council of Europe and NATO's Partnership for Peace program. From the outset, however, the ongoing political crisis in Serbia and Montenegro's halfhearted support for union with Serbia threatened to disrupt the country's bid to join these organizations.

The assassination of Serbian Prime Minister Zoran Djindjic in March resulted in an extensive crackdown on crime. (*See* OBITUARIES.) Among the estimated 10,000 individuals who were either detained or charged were former police, government, and military officials, many of whom had links to organized crime and to paramilitary groups reported to have committed war crimes in Croatia, Bosnia and Herzegovina, and Kosovo during the 1990s.

Djindjic's successor, Zoran Zivkovic, was unable to jump-start the reform process. (*See* BIOGRAPHIES.) Serbia failed in three attempts to elect a president, and the republic remained without a leader for more than a year; another attempt was to be made in January 2004. A draft republican constitution was not adopted, and the coalition government headed by the Democratic Opposition of Serbia dissolved, which forced parliamentary elections on December 28. In what was interpreted as a "hands-off" gesture to the world by the Serbian populace, two men sitting in jail in The Hague under indictment for war crimes, Slobodan Milosevic and Vojislav Seselj, won seats, and Seselj's ultranationalist Serbian Radical Party received the most votes, though not a clear majority. Observers expected a weak coalition government to be formed in early 2004.

Seselj's victory and that of his party were emblematic of increasing disillusionment over the political stagnation in Serbia. Support for Montenegrin Pres. Milo Djukanovic also waned as he faced allegations of corruption, involvement in organized crime, conspiracy in a high-profile case involving human trafficking and prostitution, and complicity in war crimes. Even Djindjic was accused by his rivals of having been involved with criminal groups, and it was pointed out that his murder was masterminded by one such group after he vowed to crack down on crime.

In June Serbia's parliament passed legislation allowing local courts to prosecute war crimes committed anywhere in the former Yugoslavia. More indictments were served by the International Criminal Tribunal for the Former Yugoslavia (ICTY) for atrocities allegedly committed by Serbian generals during the war in Kosovo. Zivkovic refused to accept the sealed indictments from ICTY chief prosecutor Carla del Ponte, stating that the matter was not a priority for the government. In October del Ponte gave the UN Security Council a negative assessment of Serbia and Montenegro's cooperation with the tribunal.

The economy showed little sign of improvement. GDP growth was less than 1%—well below expectations and down 3% from the previous year. The trade deficit was $2.8 billion for the first eight months of 2003—a 35% increase over the same period in 2002—and Belgrade anted up only 10% of the $450 million it was scheduled to pay to service its $13 billion foreign debt. According to government figures, the unemployment rate was 30%, though independent economists estimated it at nearer 45%. On the positive side, the federal government ended with budget surpluses of $100 million in 2002 and about $55 million in 2003.

Negotiations began between ethnic Serbs and Albanians over the status of Kosovo. Kosovo's Albanian leaders held steadfast to their aspirations of independence, while the Serbian government and parliament ruled it out. Kosovo Serbs called for the ethnic partition of the region, a move supported by Djindjic and Zivkovic. The first-ever formal talks between the two communities dealt with issues such as identity cards, vehicle registration, electric energy supplies, and the return of people displaced by the 1999 conflict. The international community pressured Kosovo's Albanian leaders to issue a statement urging displaced Serbs to return to their homes in the province.

(MILAN ANDREJEVICH)

SEYCHELLES

Area: 455 sq km (176 sq mi)
Population (2003 est.): 81,500
Capital: Victoria
Head of state and government: President France-Albert René

In July 2003 the state-run Macro-Economic Reform Programme implemented economic measures to shrink Seychelles's 16% budget deficit. A new trade tax was placed on imports as well as on local goods and services. Three overseas embassies were closed (an estimated savings of about $1.7 million), and the island nation pulled out of the Southern African Development Community (an additional savings of $500,000). Later in the month police arrested four members of the opposition

The streets of Belgrade overflow with hundreds of thousands of people who have gathered to pay their last respects to the assassinated prime minister of Serbia, Zoran Djindjic, on March 15.

Seychelles National Party (SNP), including its leader, Jean-François Ferrari, the publisher of the independent weekly *Regar.* The members were arrested as they were collecting signatures for a petition against the new tax. In December 2002 elections, the SNP had increased its share in the 34-member parliament from 1 to 11 seats; the ruling Seychelles People's Progressive Front captured the remaining 23 seats.

The body of French citizen Therese Blanc, a relative of Ferrari, was discovered on a beach in early September. The event prompted the European Parliament's Committee on Cooperation and Development to ask the government of Pres. France-Albert René for a report on the political and human rights climate in the country. The committee also decided to present an emergency resolution concerning the Seychelles at the European Parliament's October session.

(MARY F.E. EBELING)

SIERRA LEONE

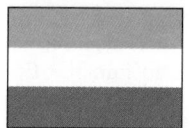

Area: 71,740 sq km (27,699 sq mi)
Population (2003 est.): 4,971,000
Capital: Freetown
Head of state and government: President Ahmad Tejan Kabbah

In 2003 survivors of Sierra Leone's horrific and devastating 1991–2002 civil war embarked on a particular kind of healing process involving intensive fact-finding and public disclosure of information. In January, Human Rights Watch released a 75-page report exploring the widespread instances of girls and women being raped by rebels, government troops, and international peacekeeping forces. In March police began arresting high-profile war-crimes suspects to be put on trial before a UN-sponsored war-crimes tribunal, the Special Court for Sierra Leone (SCSL). Some notorious figures died before their cases could be heard. Foday Sankoh, the founding leader of the Revolutionary United Front (RUF), died on July 29 of complications from an earlier stroke. Sankoh was set to stand trial for having ordered the RUF to terrorize Sierra Leoneans through dismemberments, killings, and rape. Later

AP/Wide World Photos

Workers search for diamonds in a mine in the town of Koidu, Sierra Leone, in May. Revenues from diamonds financed the brutal civil war from 1991 to 2002 but could also help pay for reconstruction in the exhausted country.

in the year Sam Bockarie, another infamous former RUF leader, turned up dead in Liberia, apparently killed by Liberian Pres. Charles Taylor's forces in May. Johnny Paul Koroma, former leader of an RUF-allied military junta that seized power in 1997, was reported to have suffered a similar fate in June, but the questions of his status or whereabouts remained unanswered at the end of 2003. Both Bockarie and Koroma had been allied with Taylor in the past, and the SCSL warned Taylor not to offer them safe haven. In early June the SCSL indicted Taylor himself and accused him of supporting Sankoh and the RUF in order to get a share of Sierra Leone's considerable diamond wealth. His indictment was kept secret until he arrived in Ghana for peace talks aimed at ending Liberia's civil war. The Ghanaians frustrated the SCSL and incurred the rancour of the UN by allowing Taylor to return to Liberia instead of detaining him. In August, Taylor entered into exile in Nigeria, formally out of reach of the SCSL.

In April, Sierra Leone's Truth and Reconciliation Commission (TRC) began holding public hearings. Pres. Ahmad Tejan Kabbah appeared before the TRC in August. He claimed to have had no say over the controversial activities of the militias supporting his government during the 10-year civil war. Sam Hinga Norman, the man who had been more directly in charge of Kabbah's Civil Defense Forces, was indicted by the SCSL for war crimes and crimes against humanity. British Prime Minister Tony Blair remarked that Kabbah should have been indicted as well.

(ANDREW EISENBERG)

SINGAPORE

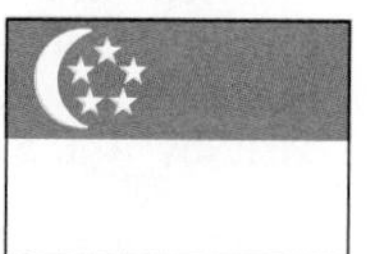

Area: 685 sq km (265 sq mi)
Population (2003 est.): 4,233,000
Head of state: President S.R. Nathan
Head of government: Prime Minister Goh Chok Tong

The year 2003 was an unusually eventful one for Singapore. For the first time in the 38 years since it gained independence, the country went on a nationwide health alert as the pneumonia-like SARS (severe acute respiratory syndrome) reached its shores in late February, carried by three Singaporeans returning from a holiday in Hong Kong. Daily fever checks, stringent quarantine measures—enforced upon pain of jail—and temperature screening in schools, in workplaces, and at immigration entry points became de rigueur. Thanks to these measures, the outbreak was brought under control three months later. Meanwhile, research into the virus intensified at various laboratories, including the Genome Institute of Singapore. (*See* HEALTH AND DISEASE: *Special Report.*)

The bigger battle of the year for Singapore was economic. The country sought to enhance its competitiveness relative to other rival destinations for foreign investments. With an increasing number of both blue- and white-collar jobs having been lost to countries in Asia with lower labour costs, the government moved swiftly to cut wage costs by reducing the employer contribution rates to the Central Provident Fund, a compulsory worker-savings scheme. Corporate taxes were also slashed and government rentals and fees reduced.

Accompanying these measures was a parallel effort to spur homegrown entrepreneurship in the hopes that this would reduce the country's dependence on multinationals for job creation. Another push was for new bilateral free-trade agreements with Canada, India, Chile, Mexico, South Korea, Jordan, and Sri Lanka, in addition to those already established with Japan, Australia, New Zealand, and the European Free Trade Association.

On the diplomatic front, 2003 marked a high point in Singapore's relations with the United States, thanks to Singapore's support for the U.S.-led war in Iraq. The Singapore-U.S. free-trade agreement was signed in September, capping almost three years of negotiations. Pres. George W. Bush arrived in late October, the first visit by a U.S. president in 11 years.

Singapore's relations with Malaysia, its nearest neighbour, sank to a new low, however, as bilateral disputes over the pricing of water Malaysia sold to Singapore mushroomed into rival ad campaigns. A territorial dispute was referred to the International Court of Justice, and another over the effects of land reclamation ended up before the International Tribunal for the Law of the Sea.

The domestic political front was far more placid. Prime Minister Goh Chok Tong announced for the first time that he would step down by 2005 and hand over power to Deputy Prime Minister Lee Hsien Loong. The next general election was not due until 2007.

(CHUA LEE HOONG)

SLOVAKIA

Area: 49,035 sq km (18,933 sq mi)
Population (2003 est.): 5,402,000
Capital: Bratislava
Chief of state: President Rudolf Schuster
Head of government: Prime Minister Mikulas Dzurinda

Slovakia achieved considerable success in economic policy and foreign affairs in 2003, but the year was disappointing politically. Probably the most important event was the referendum on accession to the European Union, held on May 16–17. It was Slovakia's first successful referendum; all previous attempts had failed to attract the required 50% turnout. This time the threshold was just barely achieved, with a turnout of 52.2%, and politicians from across the political spectrum showed unprecedented unity in encouraging voters to participate. Voters gave a resounding "yes" to accession, with 92.5% in favour, the highest of any EU candidate country. Despite the strong "yes" vote, Pal Csaky, deputy prime minister for European integration, was criticized for the lower-than-expected turnout as well as Slovakia's relatively poor preparations for joining the union.

In economic policy the centre-right ruling coalition showed courage in approving wide-ranging fiscal reforms that seemed likely to lower the budget deficit substantially over the coming years. In addition to pension, social welfare, and health care reforms, legislation providing for a flat income tax for both individuals and corporations, as well as a unified value-added tax rate, all at 19%, was approved. The government's progressive economic policies made Slovakia more attractive to foreign investors, as demonstrated by the January decision of PSA Peugeot Citroën to build a plant in the town of Trnava. Although GDP growth decelerated somewhat in 2003 owing to slowing domestic demand, the country was still one of the fastest-growing economies in Central Europe.

Politically, the situation was not so promising, as the ruling coalition began to experience serious conflicts less than a year after the September 2002 parliamentary elections, and some of the sheen was thereby taken off the government's image both at home and abroad. Although all four ruling parties easily agreed on economic policy, the conservative Christian Democrats (KDH) and the liberal Alliance of the New Citizen (ANO) were at odds over social policy, particularly over the question of abortion. Moreover, conflicts within both the ANO and Prime Minister Mikulas Dzurinda's party, the Slovak Democratic and Christian Union (SDKU), led to changes in the government lineup, with the replacement of two well-respected ministers and the dismissal of the head of the National Security Office. After three deputies left the ANO's parliamentary caucus in the autumn, the ruling coalition lost its parliamentary majority, with 75 of 150 seats, but the government managed to remain intact.

(SHARON FISHER)

SLOVENIA

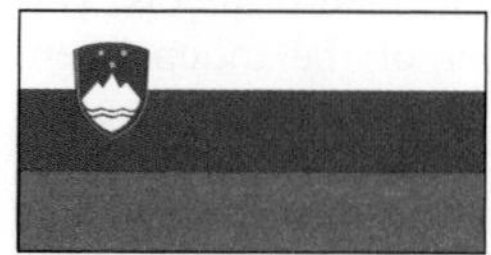

Area: 20,273 sq km (7,827 sq mi)
Population (2003 est.): 1,971,000
Capital: Ljubljana
Chief of state: President Janez Drnovsek
Head of government: Prime Minister Anton Rop

Slovenia began 2003 with a new president, Janez Drnovsek, who was elected on Dec. 1, 2002, to a five-year term. Drnovsek had served as prime minister for most of Slovenia's 12 years as an independent country. Anton Rop was chosen to succeed Drnovsek as prime minister and head of a four-party centre-left coalition. Rop also succeeded Drnovsek as president of Liberal Democracy of Slovenia, the country's largest party. The change in leadership did not result in any basic internal or foreign-policy changes during the year.

On March 23 a national referendum asked voters to confirm Slovenia's acceptance of invitations to join the European Union and NATO. Formal accession to both was slated for May 2004. With 60% participation, the vote in favour of EU membership was 89.6%,

AP/Wide World Photos

In Brdo, Slovenia, in November, Prime Minister Anton Rop (left) greets his counterpart, Mikulas Dzurinda of Slovakia, at a summit of the Central European Free Trade Agreement. Five of the eight CEFTA members were to join the EU in May 2004.

while NATO membership received a 66% favourable vote.

Slovenia declined to support or participate in the U.S.-led war in Iraq. The government asserted that a specific United Nations Security Council resolution authorizing such a conflict was lacking. By year's end, with a unanimously adopted Security Council resolution authorizing assistance in reconstruction efforts in Iraq, Slovenia's government was considering how to participate. In another unsettled region, Afghanistan, Slovenia sent a 17-member military unit to assist in peacekeeping efforts.

Slovenia was one of the founding members of the new International Criminal Court. It declined a request by the U.S. to sign a separate agreement that would preclude the extradition by Slovenia of American citizens to the jurisdiction of this court.

Slovenia's Supreme Court continued to hold in abeyance a ruling on the constitutionality of an agreement signed in 2001 between Slovenia and the Vatican delineating the legal status of the Roman Catholic Church. Church leaders frequently criticized the slowness of the denationalization process involving seized church property and especially the failure to reach agreement allowing religious instruction in public schools.

Slovenia's relations with its neighbours remained uneventful, except for Croatia, which angered Slovenia by declaring an exclusive economic zone in the Adriatic Sea. The sea and land border between Slovenia and Croatia remained unresolved, with the main issues for Slovenia being independent access to the open sea and fishing rights. Efforts to negotiate an agreement failed.

As part of a basic reform of its military system, Slovenia abolished compulsory military service. In October the last class of draftees returned to civilian life. (RUDOLPH M. SUSEL)

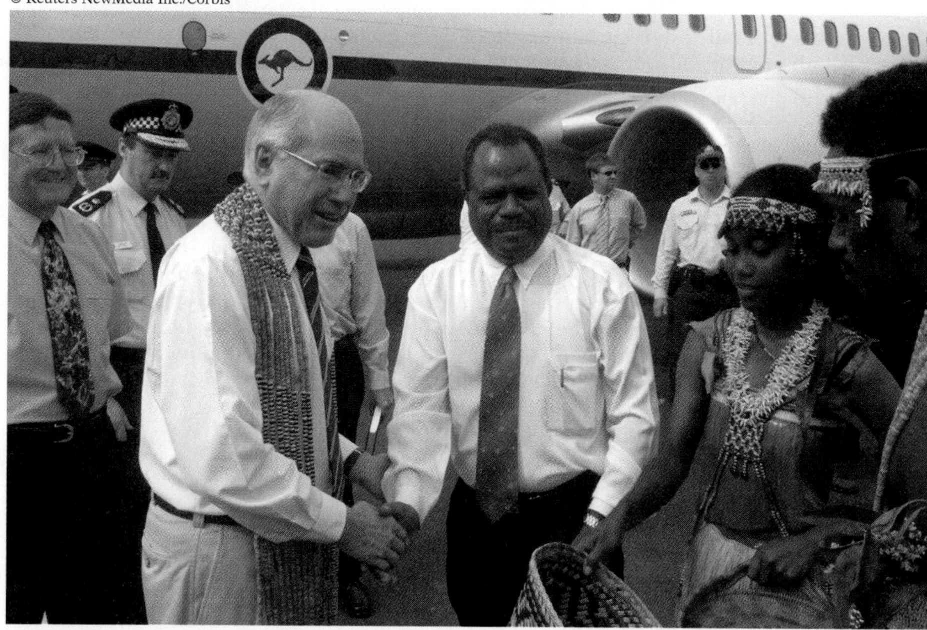

Solomon Islands Prime Minister Sir Allan Kemakeza (centre) welcomes Australian Prime Minister John Howard on his visit to Honiara in August. Australia led a multinational mission to help restore and maintain order that had been disrupted by insurgent militia groups.

SOLOMON ISLANDS

Area: 28,370 sq km (10,954 sq mi)
Population (2003 est.): 450,000
Capital: Honiara
Chief of state: Queen Elizabeth II, represented by Governor-General Sir John Lapli
Head of government: Prime Minister Sir Allan Kemakeza

For the first part of 2003, Solomon Islands remained in crisis—the government was effectively bankrupt and unable to provide services or ensure public safety, and armed militias remained a disruptive force. Sir Frederick Soaki, a leading member of the National Peace Council, was murdered in February. The economy had declined by 25% in three years.

In midyear and at the invitation of Solomon Islands, the 16 governments of the Pacific Islands Forum formed an Australian-led Regional Assistance Mission (RAM), which comprised a multinational police force supported by armed troops, to disarm militias and restore public order. The RAM had an early success with the surrender and arrest of Harold Keke, a self-styled general of the Guadalcanal Liberation Army, who had terrorized the Weather Coast of Guadalcanal and was believed to have been responsible for a number of murders and kidnappings. By October, Australia and New Zealand were able to reduce their military presence, but the police remained.

With order restored, aid donors—notably Australia, New Zealand, and the EU—again released funds that would provide assistance for trade and development. A major donors conference took place in Honiara in November, and the cost of a recovery package was estimated at $700 million. The government was developing a new draft constitution that would attempt to address provincial and ethnic tensions through a federal structure.

(BARRIE MACDONALD)

SOMALIA

Area: 637,000 sq km (246,000 sq mi), including the 176,000-sq-km (68,000-sq-mi) area of the unilaterally declared (in 1991) and unrecognized Republic of Somaliland
Population (2003 est.): 8,025,000 (including Somaliland); about 425,000 refugees are in neighbouring countries, of which about 300,000 are registered
Capital: Mogadishu; Hargeysa is the capital of Somaliland
Head of state and government: Somalia's government under President Abdiqassim Salad Hassan was barely functioning in 2003, with opposition forces controlling parts of the country.

In 2003 Somalia still had no national government. The Transitional National Government (TNG) of Pres. Abdiqassim Salad Hassan suffered from internal splits and failed to control more than a small area of Mogadishu and southern Somalia. The remainder of the country was divided between clan-based factions. In August the TNG came to the end of its three-year term, but Hassan said that it would continue until new institutions had been formed.

The peace talks that had been launched in October 2002 in Eldoret, Kenya, with the objective of setting up a federal government lurched from one crisis to another. The more than 350 delegates represented the TNG, a group of TNG opposition factions called the Somali Reconciliation and Restoration Council, a group of factions known as the G8, and a number of civil-society organizations. The conference was boycotted by the self-proclaimed Republic of Somaliland and the autonomous region of Puntland in the northeast. The Intergovernmental Authority on Development (made up of Somalia, Djibouti, Ethiopia, Kenya, Eritrea, The Sudan, and Uganda) served as the mediator, but the refusal of the delegates to recognize one another's legitimacy interfered with progress. In February 2003 the venue was moved from Eldoret to Nairobi, Kenya. An agreement was reached on July 5 to set up a federal government, but it was immediately denounced by the TNG and several other groups. The talks continued, however.

Meanwhile, despite a cease-fire declaration that had been signed by the Mogadishu-based factions in December 2002, street violence and spasmodic faction fighting continued throughout the south. In Mogadishu, however, the principal danger came from kidnapping for ransom by armed gangs. The violence was fueled by the continued flow of arms into the country, despite attempts by the UN to enforce an embargo. In the southwestern town of Baidoa, a power struggle continued between two rival factions of the Rahanweyn Resistance Army (RRA) under its chairman Hassan Muhammad Nur Shatigadud and his rival Sheikh Adan Madobe. Nonetheless, the economy thrived, but there was heavy dependence on remittances from Somalis abroad. Despite an exceptionally good harvest in the south in March–April, food shortages continued in parts of the country. In June a new medical college opened in Mogadishu.

Separate peace talks were held in Puntland between Pres. Col. Abdullahi Yusuf Ahmed and the armed opposition led by Gen. Ade Muse Hersi, an ally of Jama Ali Jama, a rival claimant; the talks remained inconclusive.

Somaliland remained stable, although it had not attained international recognition. Its economy, which depended on livestock, remained crippled by Saudia Arabia's ban on imports. Pres. Dahir Riyale Kahin—who had been elevated from vice president to president following the death in 2002 of Muhammad Ibrahim Egal—had his position confirmed in the presidential elections in April. His main opponent, Ahmed Mohamed Silanyo, initially challenged the result but finally accepted it in June. (VIRGINIA LULING)

SOUTH AFRICA

Area: 1,219,090 sq km (470,693 sq mi)
Population (2003 est.): 45,349,000
Capitals (de facto): Pretoria/Tshwane (executive); Bloemfontein/Mangaung (judicial); Cape Town (legislative)
Head of state and government: President Thabo Mbeki

Domestic Affairs. In January 2003 South African Pres. Thabo Mbeki praised his African National Congress (ANC) government's ensuring of fiscal discipline and macroeconomic stability. Speaking at the opening of Parliament in February, he identified unemployment as a major challenge and called for economic growth and job creation based on black empowerment. In June a growth and development summit attended by representatives of government, business, and labour agreed on public-works programs—particularly in the development of transport infrastructure—together with investment of 145 billion rands (1 rand = about $0.14) of private capital.

At an international conference on AIDS in Paris in July, former president Nelson Mandela spoke of HIV/AIDS as "the greatest health crisis in human history." At the same time, the Treatment Action Campaign (TAC) leaked a government report that concluded that 733,000 deaths could be prevented by 2010 if only half the people needing antiretrovirals were given them. On the other hand, President Mbeki continued to be criticized for the government's lack of attention to HIV/AIDS. Health Minister Manto Tshabalala-Msimang was likewise criticized for her view that nutrition alone was the solution to AIDS. Thousands of AIDS activists organized by the TAC marched at the opening of Parliament to demand provision of antiretroviral drugs to HIV/AIDS victims, and in March the TAC launched a campaign of civil disobedience to the same end. After months of delay, the government late in the year announced a detailed operational plan for the provision of antiretrovirals.

The Inkatha Freedom Party (IFP) came to terms with the Truth and Reconciliation Commission (TRC) at the end of January, clearing the way for publication of the final two volumes of the TRC's report. In this the TRC continued to accuse the IFP of human rights violations, but the IFP's defense against the charges was included. The report contained a recommendation that foreign and South African companies be taxed on a one-off basis for reparations. Victims of apartheid launched several lawsuits against foreign and South African firms in American courts during the year. President Mbeki opposed these suits and the idea of a wealth tax. At the same time, he stated that there would be no blanket amnesty for perpetrators of human rights violations and that victims would receive one-time payments of 30,000 rands.

In KwaZulu-Natal sniping between the IFP and the ANC over the composition of the provincial government continued throughout the year. The IFP was particularly concerned about the forthcoming "window period," when elected representatives would be allowed to defect to other parties, fearing this would lead to the loss of their majority in the provincial legislature, and welcomed the ANC's cancellation plans to make the legislation retroactive. When the two-week "window period" opened in March, considerable "floor crossing" took place. The effect was, first of all, to weaken the New National Party (NNP) considerably, with defections both to the Democratic Alliance (DA) and to the ANC. As a result of the floor crossing the ANC gained an absolute majority in the Western Cape legislature, and the balance in KwaZulu-Natal passed to minority parties. In the Cape, however, the ANC retained its coalition with the NNP and allowed an NNP premier to remain. Seven new parties were formed, including former Pan Africanist Congress (PAC) MP Patricia de Lille's Independent Democrats and Peter Marais's New Labour Party. In the latter part of the year IFP Pres. Mangosutho Buthelezi

Men seeking day jobs greet the dawn along a street serving as an informal labour market in Cape Town. South Africa's rates of unemployment were stubbornly high, ranging from 30% to 40%.

called for a coalition of opposition parties, notably the DA, to unseat the ANC in the 2004 elections.

The congress of the PAC in December 2002 was aborted owing to alleged fraud in leadership elections. In June 2003 a resumed congress elected Motsoko Pheko president. The unsuccessful candidate, former secretary-general Thami Ka Plaatjie, was subsequently expelled, which foreshadowed a split in the organization. From May, although with frequent delays, 22 members of the ultraright-wing white racist Boeremag were tried on charges of treason, terrorism, and murder.

The second part of the year became increasingly dominated by crisis in the upper echelons of the ANC that resulted from continual fallout from a controversial arms deal signed in 1999. The most significant of these developments were the allegations that Deputy Pres. Jacob Zuma had tried to solicit a 500,000-rand bribe from the former South African head of a French arms company through his financial adviser, Schabir Shaik, and had received money from Shaik. Shaik was also alleged to have provided irregular payments to former minister of transport Mac Maharaj. On August 23 Bulelani Ngcuka, national director of prosecutions, stated that Zuma would not be charged because, while there was a prima facie case of corruption, the prospects of successful prosecution were slim. The consequence was a newspaper's publication in September of allegations that Ngcuka had been an apartheid-era spy. The government established a commission under retired judge Joos Hefer to investigate these claims; it completed its investigation but had not reported by the end of the year.

Also as a result of the arms deal, Tony Yengeni (former ANC chief whip), pleaded guilty to fraud in February, was sentenced to a four-year jail term, which he appealed, and resigned from Parliament. In April, Winnie Madikizela-Mandela, former wife of Nelson Mandela, was convicted on fraud and theft charges (unrelated to the arms deal) and resigned from Parliament and as president of the ANC Women's League. Nelson Mandela's 85th birthday on July 18 was celebrated by a party of 1,600 international guests, including former U.S. president Bill Clinton and his wife, Hillary. Walter Sisulu, a close comrade of Nelson Mandela, died in May at the age of 90. (*See* OBITUARIES.)

Economy. The South African economy grew by 3% during 2002 but slowed down from the third quarter (2.9%). Growth in the fourth quarter of 2002 was 2.4%, but it fell to 0.9% in the first quarter of 2003 and to 0.5% in the second quarter before a slight pickup to 1.1% in the third quarter. The manufacturing sector contracted during the first half of 2003. The slowdown was attributed to sluggish global demand, increased interest rates, and the strengthening of the rand. Unemployment in the country remained high, with the official rate 30.5% in September 2002.

The budget boosted social services and grants to the poor and relaxed foreign-exchange controls. A cut of 13.3 billion rands was made from personal income tax, while real spending increased by 6.8%. The deficit was thus expected to be 2.4% of GDP (1.4% in 2002–03). The child-support grant increased to 160 rands, and an additional 3.3-billion-rand allocation would go to fight AIDS; 10 billion rands were provided over five years to assist black-empowerment ventures. In the only major privatization of the year, 25% of the shares of the telephone company Telkom were sold off, in addition to the 30% stake privatized in 1997.

Foreign Relations. President Mbeki traveled frequently during the year in his capacity as chairman of the African Union, as a guider of the New Partnership for African Development (NEPAD), and as a mediator of conflicts in Africa in the Democratic Republic of the Congo, Burundi, and Liberia.

Mandela criticized U.S. Pres. George W. Bush harshly for going to war in Iraq, saying that Bush could not "think properly" and wanted "to plunge the world into a holocaust." South Africa led a last-minute unavailing attempt to prevent the war. Bush, however, visited South Africa in July in the course of a trip to several African countries. He said he saw Mbeki as the "point man" on troubles in Zimbabwe and added that "we share the same objective." (MARTIN LEGASSICK)

SPAIN

Area: 506,030 sq km (195,379 sq mi)
Population (2003 est.): 42,600,000
Capital: Madrid
Chief of state: King Juan Carlos I
Head of government: Prime Minister José María Aznar López

Amid the stagnant European economies, estimated GDP growth of 2.3% made Spain the second fastest-growing economy in the European Union in 2003. Continued expansion enabled the Spanish government to proclaim proudly that it would end the year with a budget surplus for the first time in recent history. There was little cause for complacency, however; inflation was running at 2.7% (compared with the EU's 1.7%) in November, unemployment stood at more than 10%, almost one-third of the workforce had temporary contracts, and housing prices were spiraling. The European Commission shared analysts' concerns that a hike in interest rates or unemployment could send housing prices tumbling, with disastrous consequences for families that were burdened with unprecedented levels of debt and for the financial institutions that had given them loans.

The war in Iraq inevitably dominated Spain's international agenda. Prime Minister José María Aznar and his centre-right Popular Party (PP) unequivocally backed Washington. Aznar defended the legitimacy of armed intervention even without a UN mandate, sent Spanish medical units to the war zone, and, once Saddam Hussein had fallen, dispatched some 1,300 troops to reinforce the U.S.-led occupying forces. In October Aznar suggested a fundamental redefinition of Spain's defense policy and adhered to the doctrine of preventive attacks put forth by the administration of U.S. Pres. George W. Bush. Aznar was rewarded with a series of well-publicized meetings with Bush, an invitation to the U.S.-British-Spanish summit held in the Azores on the eve of the war, and the choice of Madrid to host the Iraq donors conference in October. Days earlier he had visited New York City to collect the Appeal of Conscience Foundation's World Statesman Award "for his courageous leadership and as an indefatigable champion of democracy."

At home Aznar's uncritical pro-American stance was highly unpopular. In the parliament all the main opposition parties were against the war, as were no fewer than two-thirds of voters, which made Spain one of the least pro-war of all European countries. Over two million people took to the streets on February 15 for the international day of protest, an event followed by additional smaller demonstrations against government and U.S. policies later in the year. Aznar, a Roman Catholic, was lucky to escape a public reprimand for his pro-war stance from Pope John Paul II, who was in Madrid in early May to canonize five 20th-century Spanish saints.

The official explanations for this break with Spain's traditionally more European- and UN-oriented foreign policy wavered erratically between a principled commitment to the war on terrorism and more pragmatic considerations such as the need to ensure U.S. support in Spain's struggle against the armed Euskadi Ta Askatasuna (ETA) Basque separatists. Some

As Prime Minister José María Aznar addresses Spain's parliament on April 9, Spanish photojournalists display pictures of José Couso, a colleague killed by "friendly fire" in Iraq. Aznar's support of the U.S.-led war was highly unpopular in Spain.

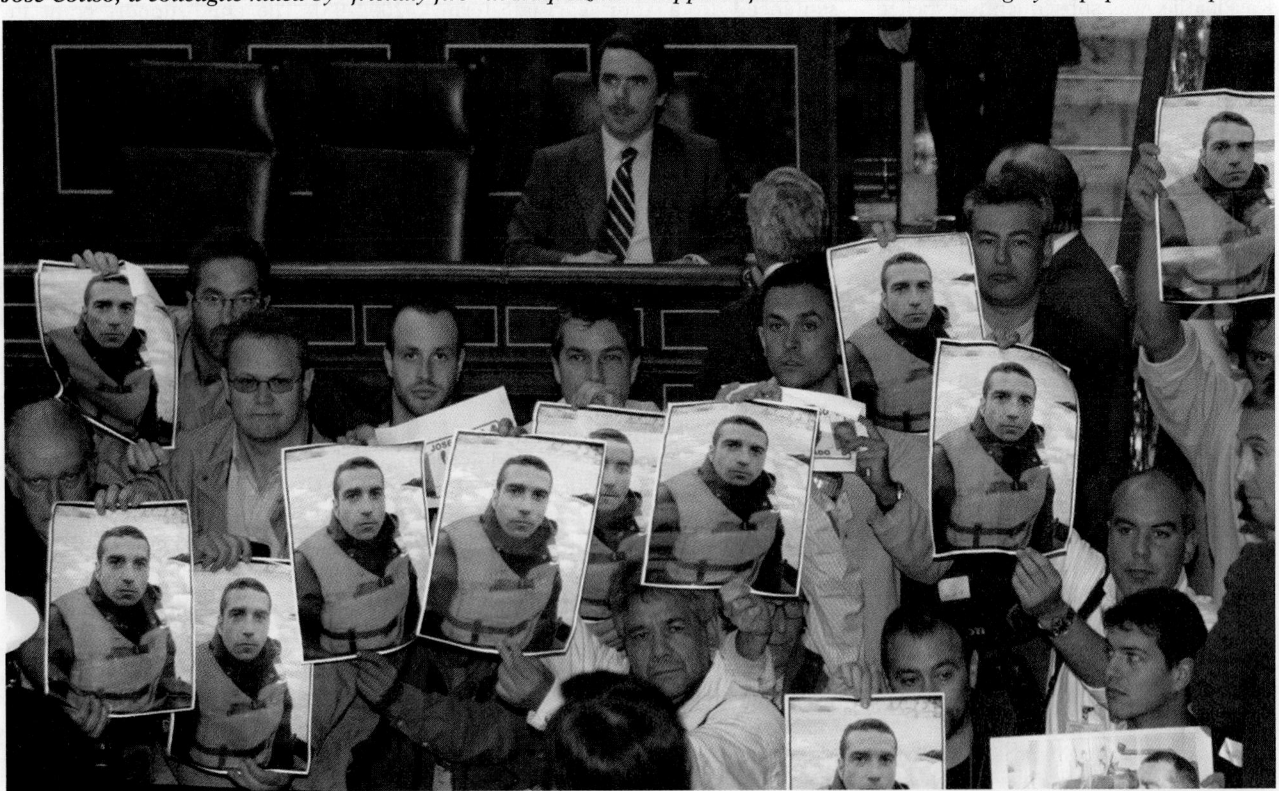

analysts also pointed to a strategic realignment toward a North Atlantic axis with Britain and the U.S., founded on ideological affinities and the shift in the balance of power in the EU toward Germany and the East, as well as the desire to strengthen ties with the world's only superpower.

Despite the government's inept handling of the *Prestige* oil-tanker disaster in November 2002 and the public opposition to the war, the PP did better than expected in municipal and regional elections in May; the PP polled just 1% fewer votes than the Spanish Socialist Workers' Party (PSOE). A scandal reeking of sleaze and corruption robbed the Socialists of their star prize, the Madrid regional government, which went to the PP after a rerun of the elections in October. All this did nothing to favour the PSOE's prospects in the 2004 general elections.

In September the PP's National Committee, by a vote of 503–0, with just one abstention, elected Aznar's chosen successor, Deputy Prime Minister Mariano Rajoy, party leader and candidate for the premiership. Though Rajoy promised to maintain Aznar's policies, some observers predicted that he would bring a less-aggressive and less-autocratic style to politics.

Once again the most conflictive issue in Spanish domestic politics was the Basque question. The relative lull in terrorist activity was offset by the heightened tension between Madrid and the Basque Nationalist Party (PNV)-controlled regional government. In rare agreement, all the parliamentary statewide parties rejected the proposal of the regional premier, Juan José Ibarretxe, to take the Basque Country, if necessarily unilaterally, toward "freely associated state" status with Spain. The PNV disingenuously maintained that this merely required the amendment of the region's existing autonomy statute. In accord with most constitutional experts, the government disagreed and considered the so-called Plan Ibarretxe the greatest challenge yet to the 1978 constitutional settlement. When in October the regional assembly agreed to consider a bill to this effect, the government immediately announced an appeal to the Constitutional Tribunal to block discussion of the proposal.

In November the announcement of the engagement of 35-year-old Crown Prince Felipe to TV journalist Leticia Ortiz Rocasolano brought a lighter note to a tense 12 months. (JUSTIN BYRNE)

SRI LANKA

Area: 65,610 sq km (25,332 sq mi)
Population (2003 est.): 19,065,000
Capitals: Sri Jayawardenepura Kotte (legislative and judicial); Colombo (executive)
Head of state and government: President Chandrika Kumaratunga, assisted by Prime Minister Ranil Wickremesinghe

Negotiations to end Sri Lanka's 20-year civil war continued in early 2003 between the United National Party (UNP) government (headed by Prime Minister Ranil Wickremesinghe) and the Liberation Tigers of Tamil Eelam (LTTE), led by Vellupillai Prabhakaran. Foreign-aid discussions held in April in Washington, D.C., produced pledges totaling $4.5 billion, which would be disbursed only after the two sides agreed on a peace plan.

Since the UNP gained control of Parliament in the general election of December 2001, there had been tension between Prime Minister Wickremesinghe and Pres. Chandrika Kumaratunga, who led the rival People's Alliance (PA). This tension boiled over in early November 2003, after the LTTE presented a proposal for regional autonomy. Saying that the UNP government threatened national security, President Kumaratunga dismissed three ministers with security-related portfolios and declared a short-lived state of emergency. Negotiations between the president and the prime minister led to a deadlock that persisted to the end of the year. Peace talks stalled, and Norway pulled back from its mediating role, declaring that it would resume its efforts to bring peace to Sri Lanka only when the power struggle among the leadership had ended.

Military conflict, terrorism, and assassinations diminished in 2003 compared with previous years. Several minor incidents involved the Sri Lankan navy and LTTE vessels bringing in arms and ammunition. Two anti-LTTE Tamil politicians were assassinated in Jaffna in June.

Trade, foreign investment, and tourism all rebounded before the crisis hit. GDP, which had contracted in 2001 and grown by 4% in 2002, had been expected to rise by 5.5%. In April the IMF approved a $567 million support package, to be disbursed semiannually through February 2006. Financial reforms would be introduced as part of the IMF agreement. Also promised were reforms in civil service, trade, taxes, and the labour market as well as additional privatization. Investors remained reluctant, however, and became even more hesitant following the November crisis.

Though life expectancy was close to 75 years and fertility was near the replacement level, the quality of education declined and access to university was severely restricted. Unemployment was high, especially among educated youth, and labour emigration continued, mostly to the Middle East.

In May floods and landslides struck Ratnapura district and other southern regions. Estimates varied, but as many as 300 people were thought to have been killed and 350,000 rendered homeless. (DONALD SNODGRASS)

SUDAN, THE

Area: 2,503,890 sq km (966,757 sq mi)
Population (2003 est.): 38,114,000
Capitals: Khartoum (executive and ministerial) and Omdurman (legislative)
Head of state and government: President and Prime Minister Lieut. Gen. Omar Hassan Ahmad al-Bashir

Peace talks between the Sudanese government and the rebel Southern Peoples Liberation Movement/Army (SPLM/A) resumed in late January 2003 in Nairobi, Kenya, amid a background of each accusing the other of having broken the cease-fire. Their discussions centred on the Machakos Protocol of July 2002, to which both parties had agreed in principle.

In the hopes of a successful outcome to the talks, the U.S. and other donor agencies were poised to renew the flow of aid. Charitable bodies, however, protested that the government had used money derived from the oil fields in the border region between the north and the south to fund its military activities against the rebels and that oil exploitation was rendering thousands of people homeless. Awad Ahmad al-Jaz, minister of energy and mines, denied

AP/Wide World Photos

A Sudanese boy watches as workers prepare to unload food aid from a United Nations plane in November. A cease-fire in The Sudan's 20-year civil war had helped to restore the flow of international aid.

all knowledge of these problems and was supported by Muhammad al-Mubarak, general manager of Sudapet, the Sudanese member of the international consortium developing the oil fields. Nevertheless, the Canadian company Talisman, another member of the consortium, continued to sell off its holdings to an Indian-owned company in response to these concerns. The other two members, Chinese and Malaysian, did not follow suit.

Among the areas of dispute between the government and the SPLM/A was Pres. Omar al-Bashir's refusal to grant self-determination to three predominantly non-Arab areas located in the northern half of the country. There were also divisions between the various ethnic groups in the south.

Early in August a crisis arose when floodwaters in the east reached their highest level in 70 years, leaving thousands of people homeless. The government was forced to declare the town of Kassala a disaster area and to fly in food.

Later that month political discussions stalled briefly. Under considerable international pressure, not least from the U.S., they resumed on September 4 in Naivasha, Kenya. The parties agreed to extend their cease-fire for an additional two months, and on September 25 it was agreed that the SPLM/A would retain its forces in the south but that the armies would be integrated in Khartoum and in the three non-Arab northern areas. Talks resumed in a spirit of optimism, and on December 20 the two sides agreed to share oil wealth on a 50-50 basis. With the greatest obstacle to peace overcome, at year's end the prospects seemed good for an overall accord, including sharing of other wealth and a political settlement, early in 2004.

Under external pressure to end political oppression, the government took the risky step in October of releasing from detention Islamist leader Hassan al-Turabi and lifting the ban on his party's activities. (KENNETH INGHAM)

SURINAME

Area: 163,820 sq km (63,251 sq mi)
Population (2003 est.): 435,000
Capital: Paramaribo
Head of state and government: President Ronald Venetiaan, assisted by Prime Minister Jules Rattankoemar Ajodhia

Showing resolve and unusual fiscal discipline, Pres. Ronald Venetiaan in 2003 lifted Suriname out of the largely self-inflicted slump of 2002. Holding the line on civil-service wages was a key factor in an environment in which pressures from the public sector had traditionally led to destabilization. This policy was reinforced by measures to raise taxes and introduce rules to strengthen the regulatory framework of the country's banks. Continued support was provided by the principal donors, the Inter-American Development Bank and the government of The Netherlands. Moreover, Venetiaan's loose four-party coalition continued to hold together. A contract for the industrialized extraction of gold was expected to divert income to the government from a largely informal and tax-resistant sector.

Other sectors were less resilient. Bauxite production was down, and the public-service sector remained extravagantly bloated. In addition, the government supported more than a hundred parastatal corporations, of which only four showed a profit.

Of equal long-term concern was the political ambition of former dictator Dési Bouterse, who, although convicted by a Dutch court on narcotics charges and facing charges for crimes against humanity, demonstrated that he was Suriname's only charismatic leader and that he had retained widespread political support. (JOHN W. GRAHAM)

SWAZILAND

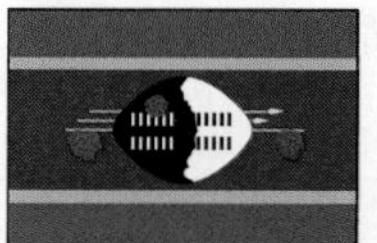

Area: 17,364 sq km (6,704 sq mi)
Population (2003 est.): 1,077,000
Capitals: Mbabane (administrative and judicial); Lozitha and Ludzidzini (royal); Lobamba (legislative)
Chief of state: King Mswati III, with much power shared by his mother, Queen Mother Ntombi Latfwala
Head of government: Prime Ministers Barnabas Sibusiso Dlamini, Paul Shabangu (acting) from September 29, and, from November 14, Absalom Themba Dlamini

The draft constitution that had been presented to King Mswati III in October 2002 dominated the Swazi political agenda in 2003, followed closely by HIV/AIDS, which touched 38.6% of the population, and poverty, which affected about two-thirds of the people. On May 31 King Mswati presented the draft constitution to the Swazi nation and launched a public debate as the final

AP/Wide World Photos

King Mswati III of Swaziland enters the royal kraal (cattle enclosure) on November 14 to accept the ceremonial presentation of the country's new draft constitution.

stage of national consultations. Although he had indicated that he wanted a new constitution finalized before the end of October, the Constitutional Drafting Committee, which had been touring the country to gauge public opinion, did not complete its travels until mid-October. In addition, King Mswati went into ritual seclusion in mid-November for the Incwala (kingship) ceremony. The delay gave prodemocracy groups more time to review the draft constitution. Meanwhile, primary elections were held in September, and secondary and final elections were completed in October.

King Mswati accepted the decision of the parliament not to buy him the jet that he had requested; the issue had aroused much domestic and international criticism. In June he organized and chaired a National Dialogue, an unusual and extraordinary event that received loud applause and was boycotted only by the Swaziland Federation of Trade Unions. In mid-August the king hosted Global 2003, a Smart Partnership International Dialogue, amid some protests. Pro-democracy groups continued to protest and put pressure on the government throughout the year. (ACKSON M. KANDUZA)

SWEDEN

Area: 449,964 sq km (173,732 sq mi)
Population (2003 est.): 8,958,000
Capital: Stockholm
Chief of state: King Carl XVI Gustaf
Head of government: Prime Minister Göran Persson

One week in September defined 2003 for most Swedes. Foreign Minister Anna Lindh, 46, was murdered only days before a referendum in which the country decisively rejected membership of the euro, the single European currency. Lindh, who had been a fervent campaigner for the euro, was attacked on September 10 while on a private shopping trip to a department store in central Stockholm. She was stabbed repeatedly and died the following day of her injuries. Lindh, a popular politician who managed to combine outspoken views with charm, was seen as the natural successor to Social Democratic Prime Minister Göran Persson. The killing shocked a nation that had continued to cherish its open democracy, which allowed citizens easy access to their leaders.

Lindh's death led to an outpouring of public grief in the traditionally restrained country and brought to a halt all campaigning in the euro referendum, which took place three days later. At year's end a case was being prepared against a Swedish-born Serb with a history of mental instability and violence. Prosecutors believed that there was no political motive in the attack, in connection with either the euro referendum or other European issues.

Despite fears that the vote would be influenced by a sympathy vote for Lindh, Swedes voted by an overwhelming majority of 56% to 42% to stay outside the euro zone. The size of the defeat was surprising, considering that the "yes" side had the backing of the Social Democratic government, the largest opposition parties, and a majority of the Riksdag (parliament), as well as the financial resources of the business community. Supporters of the euro said that membership would make trade easier, increase the pace of economic growth, and give the country more influence in the European Union. Moreover, unlike the U.K. and Denmark, the other two EU members outside the euro zone, Sweden did not formally have the right to opt out of the currency.

Swedish Foreign Minister Anna Lindh was stabbed on September 10 while out shopping in Stockholm. The popular politician's death sent shock waves through the nation, where the level of civil violence traditionally was low.

AP/Wide World Photos

Those against adopting the euro said it would mean a loss of sovereignty and was a step toward a federal Europe. They claimed that it would threaten the Swedish economic model of high taxes and generous welfare spending. Persson campaigned vigorously for a "yes," but with key members of his own cabinet openly opposed to membership and the Swedish economy outperforming the euro zone, he struggled to convince a skeptical population. The decisive majority against meant that Sweden would be unlikely to vote again on the issue for several years.

Despite the scale of Persson's defeat and his close association with the campaign, there were few calls for his resignation. Lindh's death deprived him of an obvious successor, and in the wake of her murder, the emphasis was on political stability.

In 2004 Persson would have to cope with the consequences of standing outside the euro and with a reinvigorated opposition. The Moderates, the main conservative party, appointed 38-year-old Fredrik Reinfeldt its new leader and saw a surge in its popularity. Reinfeldt was expected to take the Moderates toward the political centre.

Outside politics the news was dominated by a string of scandals in both the public and the private sector. The most spectacular was at Skandia, the financial services group, which in 2000 was Sweden's second most valuable company. Revelations of poor corporate governance, management perks, and huge bonus payments led to criminal investigations and the dismissal of senior executives. The repercussions of the scandal would continue to preoccupy the nation in 2004 as the government and business community attempted to restore investors' and consumers' confidence in their political and business leadership.

(NICHOLAS GEORGE)

SWITZERLAND

Area: 41,284 sq km (15,940 sq mi)
Population (2003 est.): 7,336,000
Capitals: Bern (administrative) and Lausanne (judicial)
Head of state and government: President Pascal Couchepin

Switzerland's 44-year-old "magic formula" system of government was thrown into disarray following sweeping gains by the nationalist Swiss People's Party (SVP) in the Oct. 19, 2003, general elections. With its anti-immigration, anti-European Union campaign, the SVP won 26.6% of the vote to become the largest force in the Federal Assembly. The left-of-centre Social Democrats were in second place with 23.3%, while the centrist Radical Democrats and Christian Democrats trailed with 17.3% and 14.4%, respectively. The SVP—the junior member of the governing coalition since 1959, with one seat on the seven-member federal executive—immediately staked its claim to an extra cabinet seat for party leader Christoph Blocher. The billionaire industrialist's penchant for populist and inflammatory rhetoric looked set to spell the end of Switzerland's polite consensus politics and of any lingering hopes that the country would join the EU.

Turnout at the general election was just 44.5%—an increase from 1999 but still below the European average. Many Swiss attributed their apathy to the sheer number of elections and referendums held under the nation's direct-democracy system, whereby 50,000 signatures could force a national vote. In a marathon day at the ballot box in May, the 4.7-million-strong electorate had been called to decide on nine different proposals—the highest number in 137 years. Voters had endorsed government plans to modernize the armed forces and to overhaul the country's civil-defense system, notably ending the Cold War-era requirement that all new buildings contain nuclear bunkers. They had rejected two proposals to scrap or freeze nuclear energy, a plan to designate four automobile-free Sundays per year, universal access to public buildings for the disabled, planned changes in health-insurance funding, a tenants' rights scheme, and an increase in apprenticeships.

The SVP threatened to force a referendum to frustrate government plans to make it easier for foreign nationals to become citizens. The party vowed to fight a Supreme Court ruling that public votes on citizenship applications were unconstitutional. The Supreme Court judgment in July came in the wake of a notorious decision in 2000 by natives of the town of Emmen, who rejected citizenship applications by 48 people, mostly from former Yugoslavia and Turkey, while accepting those from Italians. About one-fifth of Switzerland's residents were foreigners—one of the highest proportions in Europe—partly because of restrictions on naturalization.

Fearing castigation from neighbouring countries, the National Council in September blocked the government's proposed narcotics-law revision. This change would have decriminalized the consumption and, under certain conditions, the production and sale of cannabis and would have provided a permanent legal basis for the state prescription of heroin to some 1,300 severe addicts.

Swiss tolerance of assisted suicide came under increasing scrutiny because of the activities of Dignitas, an organization that helped a steady stream of terminally ill foreigners die with an overdose of barbiturates at its Zürich headquarters. Dignitas insisted that it was acting out of compassion for the terminally ill who had been denied the right to die with dignity in their home countries. Although Swiss authorities were unhappy with headlines likening Zürich to a city of death, their powers were limited by a Swiss law that allowed trained counselors to help with suicide.

The Swiss economy limped through the year, shrinking slightly by 0.3% according to government figures, but unemployment remained below 4% and inflation was about 0.5%. Fears concerning the bankruptcy of the national airline, swiss, were eased when it was admitted to the protective umbrella of the OneWorld alliance, dominated by British Airways.

(CLARE KAPP)

SYRIA

Area: 185,180 sq km (71,498 sq mi)
Population (2003 est.): 17,586,000
Capital: Damascus
Head of state and government: President Bashar al-Assad, assisted by Prime Ministers Muhammad Mustafa Mero and, from September 10, Muhammad Naji al-Otari

Parliamentary elections in March 2003 brought 178 new faces to Syria's 250-member People's Assembly. Among the winners were four representatives of the Syrian Social Nationalist Party, a long-time rival of the ruling Ba'th Party, and seven prominent businessmen who ran as independents. All 167 candidates put forward by the Front were elected, including 135 from the Ba'th Party. Most significant was the large number of seats (125) captured by delegates under the age of 50. Five parties banned by the government urged their supporters to boycott the elections. The Yekiti Party, which had a constituency that consisted primarily of Kurds in the northeastern provinces, also boycotted the voting.

The U.S.-led war in Iraq beginning in mid-March disrupted Syria's extensive, but largely illicit, commercial relations with Iraq and deprived Syrian companies of preferential markets for a wide range of consumer goods. More important, it cut off the flow of some 200,000 bbl per day of Iraqi crude oil through the pipeline linking Kirkuk, Iraq, to Syria's Mediterranean port of Banyas. This supply line had provided Damascus with handsome transit fees while enabling Syria to export its own oil at prevailing world prices and divert Iraqi supplies for domestic use. Faced with the prospect of a sharp economic downturn, the government issued licenses to set up four private radio stations, two private universities, and the first three private banks since the nationalizations of 1963. Nevertheless, after persistent harassment by the authorities, Syria's only private newspaper shut down in May. When it failed to resume publication after three months, its license was revoked according to the Press Law.

Damascus openly opposed the U.S.-led military operations in Iraq, and Vice Pres. 'Abd al-Halim Khaddam, Pres. Bashar al-Assad, and the country's grand mufti strongly denounced the action. Such statements soured relations with Washington, and U.S. officials repeatedly charged that Syria was permitting combatants and military supplies to cross into Iraq. In mid-June U.S. forces attacked a convoy of Iraqi vehicles inside Syrian territory. In mid-October, however, Syria voted in favour of a UN Security Council resolution that endorsed Washington's efforts to stabilize Iraq. On December 12 U.S. Pres. George W. Bush signed a bill that imposed economic sanctions on Syria because of its support of terrorism, occupation of Lebanon, development of weapons of mass destruction, and trade in military and economic commodities with Iraq.

Meanwhile, tensions steadily escalated with Israel. In early January Israeli forces opened fire on Syrian troops in the demilitarized zone along the Golan border. On October 5, Israeli warplanes bombed a site on the outskirts of Damascus that was suspected of housing guerrillas of the Popular Front for the Liberation of Palestine—General Command. The attack represented the first violation by either side of the Second Disengagement Agreement, signed by the two governments in 1974. (FRED H. LAWSON)

TAIWAN

Area: 36,188 sq km (13,972 sq mi)
Population (2003 est.): 22,569,000
Capital: Taipei
Chief of state: President Chen Shui-bian
Head of government: President of the Executive Yuan (Premier) Yu Shyi-kun

Throughout 2003, as the political frenzy in Taiwan mounted in the run-up to the March 2004 elections, political forces appeared to be polarizing between independence for the island and unification with China, although scholarly studies suggested there was little change in voter alignment. Two former presidential candidates now in opposition parties, Lien Chan of the Nationalist Party (KMT) and James Soong of the People's First Party (PFP), joined forces for the 2004 presidential election, with Lien in the top slot and Soong as his vice presidential running mate. The KMT-PFP alliance gave the nationalist pan-blue (so-called because blue is the colour of the KMT) parties some hope of winning the election. Soong, a former KMT member, had run as an independent candidate three years earlier, which split the pan-blue vote and likely cost the KMT the presidency.

Chen prepared for his reelection bid by making radical moves in the direction of independence. He reiterated his pro-independence catchphrase of "one country on each side" of the Taiwan Strait. The minister of education proposed controversial changes in high-school textbooks, including moving the discussion of China's post-1911 period to the section on world history. A new design for the passport added the word *Taiwan* to its cover.

Newspapers, meanwhile, were filled with political scandals, including news of two high-profile investigations. First, the KMT accused Pres. Chen Shui-bian of having accrued $1.7 billion within the past year, but Chen's Democratic Progressive Party (DPP) and the government countered that his assets were $56,000 less in 2002 than in the year

At an October 25 rally in Kao-hsiung, Taiwan, demonstrators carry a giant banner that reads "referendum." The rally, which drew an estimated 200,000 people, was in support of Taiwanese Pres. Chen Shui-bian's call for a national plebiscite.

before. In a second case, former president Lee Teng-hui's financial director, Liu Tai-ying, was rearrested three days after he was released on bail, accused of having taken bribes of nearly $10 million.

The legislature passed a historic proposal that would give the president the power to hold a national "defensive referendum" on independence should China try to force reunification with the mainland. The 108–82 vote was a major show of defiance to Beijing insofar as China had warned Taiwan that such moves could lead to a devastating war across the Taiwan Strait. At the same time, however, the legislators carefully rejected different radical versions, including one by the ruling party, that would place no restrictions on holding referenda on such issues as independence and sovereignty that worried China most. Rather, the legislature retained the power to screen potential referendum issues that might involve changes to the constitution. The version passed was written by KMT members who held a majority in the legislature and opposed changes to the status quo across the Taiwan Strait. According to the law, only the public and the legislature were given the power to initiate a vote—except for a referendum defending the nation in case of war, the so-called "defensive referendum." President Chen had long said that he would not hold a referendum on sovereignty issues as long as China did not attack Taiwan. Only three days after the referendum law was passed, however, he proposed to hold the "defensive referendum" on the next presidential election day, demanding that China remove its missiles from its coastlines. Such a move exacerbated the already strained relationship between the island and the mainland as well as that between Taiwan and the U.S., which preferred the status quo.

The completion of President Chen's first term in office was occasion for a public review of his performance. It was reported that during his three years in office the government had accumulated debts of about $100 billion, the equivalent of $16,000 per family, a year's wages of a salaried worker in Taiwan. By mid-2003 the government had already issued about $8 billion in government bonds in an effort to raise funds for its operations. Economists were predicting that Taiwan might face four major fiscal problems: a growing imbalance in government revenue and expenditure; a high budget deficit, which was estimated to reach 34% of GDP by 2006; use of more government bonds to cover the deficit; and continued tax reductions, which added salt to the fiscal wounds. Partly as a result of the economic stagnation at home, Taiwanese investment continued to flow into China's market—which further aggravated the pro-independence alliance. SinoPac Holdings became the first Taiwanese financial institution to offer local currency financing in China, the boldest move so far by a Taiwanese bank to flout the official ban and enter the Chinese market. (XIAOBO HU)

TAJIKISTAN

Area: 143,100 sq km (55,300 sq mi)
Population (2003 est.): 6,535,000
Capital: Dushanbe
Chief of state: President Imomali Rakhmonov
Head of government: Prime Minister Akil Akilov

A delegation of the European Parliament that arrived in Dushanbe in October 2003 summed up Tajikistan's situation very well: a country on the road to democracy but suffering from acute economic problems. One of the points on which the entire Tajik political spectrum agreed was the urgent need to reduce a level of poverty in the country that was forcing up to 800,000 Tajik citizens to go abroad, mostly to Russia, every summer in search of work. The Tajik leadership made it a top priority to seek foreign investment that would create jobs at home.

Another top priority for Tajikistan was to try to stop the flow of contraband drugs from Afghanistan that were intended ultimately for Russia. In the first nine months of 2003, Russian border guards stationed on the Tajik-Afghan frontier and Tajik law-enforcement officers together seized almost 7 metric tons of illegal drugs, of which 4.5 tons were heroin. The comparable figures for 2002 were 4.3 tons of drugs, including 2.7 tons of heroin. These figures gave emphasis to Tajik Pres. Imomali Rakhmonov's plea to the UN General Assembly in September for the creation of an international antidrug coalition.

President Rakhmonov precipitated a political crisis in the first half of the year with his request that the parliament submit to national referendum a series of constitutional amendments that he said were necessary to modernize the country. The most controversial amendment lifted a restriction on the number of presidential terms, and would thus make it possible for Rakhmonov to remain in office for 14 more years. Other changes included dropping constitutional guarantees of free health care and free higher education. Some opposition parties predicted that social instability would result if the amendments were adopted in the June 22 referendum. The amendments were adopted, but there was no evidence of massive social discontent over the changes.

The most visible evidence of popular discontent over the situation in the country, in addition to the large-scale labour migration, was a growing presence of the international extremist Muslim party Hizb ut-Tahrir. According to sources in Tajik law enforcement, more than 200 party activists were arrested in 2002 and 2003, and "tons" of subversive literature calling for the establishment of an Islamic caliphate in Central Asia were confiscated. The authorities were particularly disturbed in 2003 by increasing evidence that Hizb ut-Tahrir was spreading its influence in Tajikistan beyond the Tajik portion of the Fergana Valley. (BESS BROWN)

TANZANIA

Area: 945,090 sq km (364,901 sq mi)
Population (2003 est.): 35,078,000
De facto capital: Dar es Salaam; the legislature meets in Dodoma, the pending capital
Chief of state and head of government: President Benjamin William Mkapa, assisted by Prime Minister Frederick Tulway Sumaye

In May 2003, by-elections were held in all the constituencies of Tanzania that had had no parliamentary representatives since the opposition Civic United Front (CUF) in Zanzibar and Pemba had refused to recognize the elections of 2000. On Pemba the CUF won all 15 contested seats for the Union Parliament and 11 for the Zanzibar House of Representatives. To build on this successful outcome (following earlier disagreements), in October the Commonwealth urged the government to reform the

Zanzibar judiciary and the Zanzibar Electoral Commission.

The economic situation was less buoyant. CDC Globeleq, a subsidiary of the CDC Group owned by the British government through its Department for International Development, took a controlling interest in the Songas project. The project aimed to bring gas to Dar-es-Salaam by means of a 225-km (140-mi) pipeline from Songo Island and thus gave an important boost to Tanzania's economic potential. The fishing industry based on Lake Victoria was thriving as a result of the increased demand from the EU. Fish became Tanzania's biggest export, accounting for 25% of the country's export earnings. The boom had its downside, however, and overfishing by all the countries around Lake Victoria threatened to deplete the stocks of fish seriously.

In January, fears of a possible terrorist attack on Zanzibar caused the U.S. and other Western countries to issue a warning to their nationals of the danger of visiting the island. Although no attack took place, Tanzanian economic planners who were hoping to make tourism their country's largest foreign currency earner were given a brief setback. Others were less concerned, fearing that the main beneficiaries of tourism would be foreign tourist operators and hoteliers rather than the population as a whole. They were particularly worried by the future availability of land for smallholdings and cattle herding, upon which the majority of the population depended and to which there appeared no visible alternative form of employment for the numbers of people involved. The setting aside of large areas of land as wildlife conservation parks to attract tourists was already depriving herdsmen such as the Masai of land they needed for their cattle. At the same time, leading politicians and successful businessmen were acquiring large pieces of land, and the arrival of numbers of white Zimbabweans fleeing from Pres. Robert Mugabe's land reforms was further increasing the demand. Of still greater concern was the fear that the government appeared ready to acquiesce in the call from the president of the World Bank, James Wolfensohn, for a change in the land law to encourage foreign enterprises.

In August Pres. Benjamin Mkapa highlighted a further problem when he destroyed 1,000 guns as part of his plan to rid the country of illegal arms seized by the police. The flow of small arms into the lake region was, he maintained, an important factor contributing to the unrest in the area and thus to the influx of refugees into Tanzania, which was imposing a serious burden on the country's administrative resources. In October the UN World Food Programme appealed to the international community for $17 million to assist 2 million people in the centre and north of the country who were suffering severe food shortages as a result of adverse weather conditions. (KENNETH INGHAM)

THAILAND

Area: 513,115 sq km (198,115 sq mi)
Population (2003 est.): 64,022,000
Capital: Bangkok
Chief of state: King Bhumibol Adulyadej
Head of government: Prime Minister Thaksin Shinawatra

Gilded mythical creatures on the River of Kings crowned a boom year for Thailand in 2003 with a Royal Barge Procession witnessed by leaders of China, Russia, the U.S., and 18 other states in Bangkok for the October summit of APEC (Asia-Pacific Economic Cooperation). In July IMF loans were repaid two years early. Consumer spending and construction surged, led by massive investment in a new Bangkok airport named Suvarnabhumi ("Golden Land"), scheduled to open in 2005.

On January 29, Cambodian rioters in Phnom Penh razed the Thai embassy and several businesses, one of which belonged to the family of Thai Prime Minister Thaksin Shinawatra, after a newspaper erroneously quoted a Thai TV actress as having claimed that Angkor Wat, the iconic Khmer Buddhist temple complex, had been stolen from Thailand. Relations remained icy until joint cabinet meetings were held in May. In February Thaksin launched a "war on drugs," which in three months resulted in the deaths of some 2,500 suspected dealers; critics claimed that there were many more extrajudicial killings. Former interior minister Purachai Piumsombun lost his post at the Justice Ministry, where Thaksin's brother-in-law was permanent secretary. Purachai became a deputy prime minister charged with overseeing a new crusade against vice. A campaign against "influential figures," a euphemism for high-ranking corrupt officials, politicians, and well-connected gangsters, began in June. Massage tycoon Chuwit Kamolvisit oiled the anticorruption drive by claiming he had paid huge bribes to police. Former health minister Rakkiat Sukthana had his assets seized and vanished ahead of a bribery verdict and 15-year prison sentence. Thaksin's cousin Chaiyasit Shinawatra became army

Thai Prime Minister Thaksin Shinawatra (front, third from left) launches the Thailand Elite Card, which granted a wide range of privileges to people who paid $25,000 to become members, in an effort to attract well-heeled tourists to Thailand.

AP/Wide World Photos

commander. In November Thaksin announced a major cabinet reshuffle, dropping the minority Chart Pattana Party from the ruling coalition and moving former businessman Adisai Bodharamik from commerce to education, the fifth incumbent in three years at the reform-resistant ministry. Though critics deplored the government's lack of transparency, public support for Thaksin was strong. The opposition Democrat Party was weakened when Banyat Bantadtan was elected over the youthful Abhisit Vejjajiva to replace retiring party leader Chuan Leekpai.

Though Thaksin initially scorned reports of Thailand as a terrorists' haven and was cool to the U.S.-led Iraq invasion, he switched track in midyear, bypassing the parliament with an antiterrorism decree. In June three Thai Muslims were arrested, suspected of plots involving Jemaah Islamiyah (JI), the al-Qaeda-associated group linked to the 2002 bombings on the Indonesian island of Bali. On August 11 Indonesian Riduan Isamuddin, alias Hambali, Southeast Asia's most-wanted man and alleged JI mastermind, was captured in Ayutthaya and handed over to U.S. authorities. Thailand received a $10 million reward and, with troops in Afghanistan and postinvasion Iraq, was named a "major non-NATO ally."

Tourism, which contributed 6% of GDP, suffered during the outbreak of SARS (severe acute respiratory syndrome). Thailand registered only nine cases, but arrivals dropped more than 40% in April and 30% in May, which caused GDP forecasts to dip to a still-bullish 5.8%. Confidence was jolted in April when the Central Bankruptcy Court returned Thai Petrochemical Industry, Thailand's biggest corporate debtor, to its owner. Thaksin, redefining his populist economics as "social capitalism," continued high-spending policies focused on rural small- and medium-scale business. Interest rates and inflation remained low. Infrastructure support was promised to Cambodia, Laos, and Myanmar (Burma), and free-trade agreements were signed with China, India, Australia, and Singapore.

(JOHN BEAUMONT ASH)

TOGO

Area: 56,785 sq km (21,925 sq mi)
Population (2003 est.): 5,429,000
Capital: Lomé
Chief of state: President Gen. Gnassingbé Eyadéma
Head of government: Prime Minister Koffi Sama

After having paved the way on Dec. 30, 2002, for Pres. Gnassingbé Eyadéma (Africa's longest-serving ruler) to seek a third five-year presidential mandate, Togo's parliament further strengthened Eyadéma's position in February 2003 by shifting the responsibility for organizing and conducting elections from the Independent National Elections Commission to the Ministry of the Interior. Eyadéma's party, the Rally of the Togolese People, held 72 of the 81 legislative seats. After Gilchrist Olympio, leader of the opposition Union for the Forces of Change (UFC), was barred from standing as a presidential candidate on the grounds that he did not possess a residency certificate or pay Togolese taxes, Eyadéma won reelection easily in the June 1 poll. Two UFC leaders were jailed on charges of having encouraged rebellion when, amid widespread allegations of fraud, violent protests broke out in the capital after the elections. Three journalists who had been investigating the conduct of the poll were arrested on June 14 and 15. Their hunger strike led to their release in July. Though Eyadéma pledged on July 9 to form a united national government, only two opposition deputies were given posts in the cabinet announced on July 29.

Togo was to receive $2 million from CARE International to provide schooling both for potential victims of child trafficking in West Africa and for those children who had been rescued from servitude in neighbouring countries. On July 3 France agreed to provide more than 4 billion CFA francs (about $7 million) for education in the northern Kara region, the region of Eyadéma's home district.

(NANCY ELLEN LAWLER)

Supporters of Togolese Pres. Gnassingbé Eyadéma dance at a rally on May 31, the day before Eyadéma easily won reelection after a number of legal maneuvers to ensure that outcome.

AP/Wide World Photos

TONGA

Area: 750 sq km (290 sq mi)
Population (2003 est.): 102,000
Capital: Nuku'alofa
Head of state and government: King Taufa'ahau Tupou IV, assisted by Prime Minister of Privy Council Prince 'Ulukalala Lavaka Ata

In 2003 in Tonga focus was on freedom of speech and the government's attempts to muzzle its critics and control the media. Several unsuccessful attempts were made to ban *Taimi 'o Tonga* ("Times of Tonga"), which was published in New Zealand but was distributed in Tonga. The Supreme Court declared as unconstitutional related law changes made by King Taufa'ahau Tupou IV in Privy Council. The government's response was to legislate general media controls in July and in October to amend Clause 7 of the constitution, which guaranteed freedom of speech. Legislation was passed to regulate newspapers and, potentially, control their content. The constitutional change was opposed by the representatives elected by the people, who formed a minority of the legislature. Unusually, they were joined by three of the nine nobles' representatives (the balance of the legislature comprised ministers who had been appointed for life by the king). There were large antigovernment demonstrations and complaints that members of the Police Special Branch were attending political meetings.

In October proposed changes that would reduce income tax for low-wage workers and reduce other taxes and duties in favour of a broad-based consumption tax were introduced to the legislature. The economy remained heavily dependent on remittances from Tongans living abroad. Tourism grew by 14% in 2002 over 2001; tourism interests, in an effort to boost the number of visitors, strongly advocated an official declaration designating Tonga's waters a whale sanctuary. (BARRIE MACDONALD)

TRINIDAD AND TOBAGO

Area: 5,128 sq km (1,980 sq mi)
Population (2003 est.): 1,279,000
Capital: Port of Spain
Chief of state: Presidents Arthur Napoleon Raymond Robinson and, from March 17, Maxwell Richards
Head of government: Prime Minister Patrick Manning

Parliament, sitting as an electoral college, voted Max Richards, former principal of the Trinidad and Tobago campus of the University of the West Indies, into office in February 2003 as the country's new president; he was sworn in the next month.

The government made the long-expected move in midyear to downsize the sugar industry, which had once been the backbone of the Trinidad and Tobago economy but had fallen on hard times in recent decades as production costs outran prices available even in the protected European Union market. The entire 9,000-member workforce at the state-owned sugar producer and refiner, Caroni Ltd., was laid off, and the workers received $16.6 million in compensation. In the future, sugar would be produced mainly to meet local demand.

The People's National Movement party, which won the general election in 2002, also emerged victorious in the local government election in July 2003 and won control of 9 of the 14 municipalities and regional corporations. The United National Congress took four of the local government bodies, and there was a dead heat in one.

In August the London-based World Markets Research Centre ranked Trinidad and Tobago as the Caribbean country most vulnerable to targeting for terrorism. (DAVID RENWICK)

TUNISIA

Area: 163,610 sq km (63,170 sq mi)
Population (2003 est.): 9,764,000
Capital: Tunis
Chief of state: President Gen. Zine al-Abidine Ben Ali
Head of government: Prime Minister Mohamed Ghannouchi

The Tunisian government continued to improve its economic performance in 2003, earning plaudits from the IMF, which also warned, however, that there was still considerable progress to be made before the Tunisian economy would have completely liberalized its structures. Like Morocco, Tunisia was seeking a free-trade agreement with the United States, over French objections and despite the dominance of the European Union in its foreign trade. The drought underlined the country's continued dependence on the agricultural sector, and the abundant rainfall in September was hailed as a harbinger of a better year in 2004.

Tourism appeared to have recovered from the shock of the events of Sept. 11, 2001, and avoided a further recession as a result of the war against Iraq in March and April. In July the sector showed a 7% growth over the levels of the previous year. In recognition of the importance of tourism, no doubt, TunisAir, the national airline, and Morocco's Royal Air Maroc signed a cooperation agreement in midyear to code-share, which thus expanded each airline's potential for attracting tourists to the region.

Tunisia also continued to attract foreign investment during the year because of prudent economic management. Late in 2002 France's Société Générale Group purchased a majority holding in the Tunisian company Union Internationale des Banques. A further vote of confidence was provided by the American-based investors service Moody's, which raised Tunisia's investment rating from Baa3 to Baa2.

Domestic politics continued in a repressive atmosphere. The decree banning the wearing of the *hijab* (veil), first passed in 1981, was renewed in June 2003. Gen. Zine al-Abidine Ben Ali planned to stand for a further presidential term in 2004, and the political institutions he controlled were being rallied to call for him to stand again. At the same time, opponents and dissidents faced continued repression. In late summer the New York-based organization Human Rights Watch highlighted the plight of Abdullah Zouari, who had completed an 11-year sentence in 2002 but who was continuously harassed after his release and was now being held in Harboub prison. Amnesty International claimed that there were 1,000 prisoners of conscience in Tunisia. Radia Nasraoui, a well-known human-rights lawyer, began a hunger strike on October 15 because of continued harassment of her family. (GEORGE JOFFÉ)

TURKEY

Area: 774,815 sq km (299,158 sq mi)
Population (2003 est.): 70,597,000
Capital: Ankara
Chief of state: President Ahmet Necdet Sezer
Head of government: Prime Ministers Abdullah Gul and, from March 14, Recep Tayyip Erdogan

Emergency workers and survivors sift through the wreckage of one of two large synagogues in Istanbul that were destroyed by truck bombs nearly simultaneously on November 15.

Turkey's Justice and Development Party (AKP) had a trying first year in office in 2003. On February 6 Prime Minister Abdullah Gul, acting as a proxy for party leader Recep Tayyip Erdogan, who had been prevented from standing for the parliament in the elections in November 2002 (*see* BIOGRAPHIES), secured parliamentary approval of a resolution allowing the U.S. to upgrade air bases and harbours in Turkey for use against the regime of Saddam Hussein in Iraq. The party was divided, however, and the country overwhelmingly antagonistic when Gul presented a second resolution asking the Grand National Assembly for permission to allow foreign troops to transit through Turkish territory and Turkish troops to be sent abroad. The vote on March 1 failed by three votes. When Erdogan won a by-election on March 9, Gul resigned. Erdogan formed a new government on March 14 in which Gul became deputy prime minister and foreign minister.

A decision by the Grand National Assembly on March 20 to open Turkish airspace to coalition aircraft helped soothe U.S.-Turkish relations and allowed Erdogan to concentrate on internal reforms in an effort to meet the criteria for Turkey's membership in the European Union. On August 7 the parliament approved the seventh "harmonization package," which reduced the powers of the National Security Council. This body, which brought together the government and the top military commanders, was assigned a purely consultative function. Erdogan declared that the legislative changes demanded by the EU had been completed, which left a year for implementation, and that a special ministerial committee would make sure that the European Council, which had promised a decision in December 2004, would have no grounds for delaying further the beginning of accession negotiations.

In the meantime, the Turkish government continued to proclaim its determination to promote a settlement in Cyprus. This process was set back when, at a meeting at The Hague on March 10–11, UN Secretary-General Kofi Annan failed to persuade Turkish Cypriot leader Rauf Denktash to submit to a referendum the plan prepared under UN auspices for the reunification of the island prior to its accession to the EU, planned for May 2004.

After lengthy negotiations with the U.S., the Turkish government decided to meet the American request for Turkish troops to help keep the peace in Iraq. A resolution allowing the government to send troops abroad for one year was approved by the parliament on October 7 by 358 votes to 183. The parliamentary vote was followed by more talks with the U.S., but they were suspended after the Iraqi Governing Council expressed its opposition, and on November 7 it was announced that Turkey had withdrawn its offer to send peacekeepers. Throughout, Turkey had insisted on U.S. action to eliminate from northern Iraq the estimated 5,000 fighters of the Kurdistan Workers Party (PKK, renamed KADEK/Congress for Freedom and Democracy in Kurdistan). The Kurds announced on September 1 that they had ended the unilateral cease-fire that, they claimed, they had observed for four years in their struggle with Turkish security forces. The PKK declaration followed the approval by the Turkish parliament on July 29 of a law granting a limited amnesty to those who had been incarcerated for terrorism. Only a handful of PKK militants in Iraq returned home as a result. On November 11 KADEK announced that it was dissolving itself and that a new group would be formed to pursue Kurdish rights through negotiations.

Also in November, two terrorist incidents perpetrated by an al-Qaeda cell in Istanbul caused great carnage. On November 15, truck bombs destroyed the largest synagogue in Istanbul and another synagogue as well, killing at least 20 people. Five days later two more truck bombs blew up the British consulate and a British-owned bank, killing some 30 people. In late December, Istanbul's governor declared that the terrorist cell had been broken up.

The economy continued to improve after the 2001 financial crisis. Growth continued at a slower rate than in 2002, but, at 7.4% in the first quarter and 3.7% in the second, it was still high. November's terrorist attacks, however, threatened to scuttle the recovery. Inflation was nearly halved, as was the yield on government bonds. The unemployment rate, at 10%, remained the biggest cause of discontent in the country. (ANDREW MANGO)

TURKMENISTAN

Area: 488,100 sq km (188,500 sq mi)
Population (2003 est.): 4,867,000
Capital: Ashgabat
Head of state and government: President Saparmurad Niyazov

Political life in Turkmenistan continued to be dominated by the reaction of Pres. Saparmurad Niyazov (*see* BIOGRAPHIES) to the alleged attempt on his life in November 2002. Some opposition sympathizers described the incident simply as a coup attempt to remove a dictator from power. Nonetheless, Niyazov used the purported attack as a justification for crushing any suspected internal opposition and called on foreign countries to hand over members of the opposition in exile. Even extended families of suspected plotters were arrested and tortured, and those considered by Niyazov to have been the ringleaders were sentenced to life in prison. By late autumn opposition members in exile had reported that one alleged plotter—Amanmuhammed Yklymov—had died of torture, imprisoned former foreign minister Batyr Berdiyev was either seriously ill or had died, and Boris Shikhmuradov, also a former foreign minister, was near death in prison. Sharp criticism from the international community—including censure by the UN Commission on Human Rights—of such methods was largely ignored by the Turkmen leader, although he attempted to persuade Dutch Foreign Minister Jaap de Hoop Scheffer, on a visit to Ashgabat in March for the Organization for Security and Co-operation in Europe to try to investigate reports of massive human rights violations in the treatment of the alleged plotters, to accept Niyazov's definition of the opposition as terrorists who were beyond the law.

In April Niyazov traveled to Moscow to sign a 25-year deal with the Russian state gas firm Gazprom for the sale of Turkmen natural gas. The Turkmen president persuaded his Russian counterpart to agree to revoke a 1993 Russian-Turkmen agreement recognizing dual citizenship. Shortly after his return home, Niyazov unilaterally decreed that some 100,000 holders of dual Russian-Turkmen citizenship had two months to decide which citizenship they wanted to retain and to leave the country if they chose to keep their Russian passports. The result was a sharp reaction in the Russian State Duma and the Russian media, and Russian Pres. Vladimir Putin was accused of selling out Russian citizens in return for Turkmen gas. An attempt by the two Foreign Ministries to resolve the issue of dual citizenship failed, and it was generally believed that Russian Defense Minister Sergey Ivanov's assertion in October that Russia was prepared to intervene abroad to protect its citizens was aimed primarily at Turkmenistan. (BESS BROWN)

TUVALU

Area: 25.6 sq km (9.9 sq mi)
Population (2003 est.): 10,200
Capital: Government offices in Vaiaku, Fongafale islet, of Funafuti atoll
Chief of state: Queen Elizabeth II, represented by Governor-General Sir Tomasi Puapua and, from September 9, Faimalaga Luka
Head of government: Prime Minister Saufatu Sopoaga

Tuvalu spent much of 2003 in political stalemate. After the government of Prime Minister Saufatu Sopoaga lost its majority in the 15-member legislature in two by-elections in May, it sought to attract opposition members to ensure a majority before calling for Parliament to convene. The governor-general then called for Parliament to meet for the purpose of electing a speaker. After this was done, Sopoaga again adjourned Parliament, and opposition members took legal action. There was further confusion when Faimalaga Luka, the recently elected speaker, was confirmed as the new governor-general; his predecessor had completed a five-year term. With a government supporter victorious in the consequent by-election and an opposition member who had defected to the government, Sopoaga had an assured majority and called Parliament in early November.

Tuvalu was one of the Pacific islands countries scheduled to receive planning assistance under an Asian Development Bank project to develop rules to cope with anticipated rising sea levels to be caused by expected climate change over the next 50 years. A rise in sea level of 50 cm (20 in) would submerge more than half of the area of Tuvalu's low-lying islands, and the accompanying higher sea temperatures would increase Tuvalu's vulnerability to cyclonic storms. As part of its planning efforts, Tuvalu continued to seek emigration opportunities for its population.

(BARRIE MACDONALD)

UGANDA

Area: 241,038 sq km (93,065 sq mi)
Population (2003 est.): 25,437,000
Capital: Kampala
Head of state and government: President Yoweri Museveni, assisted by Prime Minister Apolo Nsibambi

Throughout 2003 Pres. Yoweri Museveni's Uganda remained the darling of the Western powers, drawing half its revenue from external aid. The World Bank continued to call Uganda Africa's most consistently good performer. The immediate economic outlook was less favourable, however. The world price for unprocessed coffee, at about 34% of total export income Uganda's best foreign-currency earner, remained at a very low level, and vigorous attempts to diversify exports were slow to make an impact.

There was also some muted criticism from international financial institutions that saw that money intended for social services had been diverted to the defense budget. Most of it had been spent on the lengthy invasion of the Democratic Republic of the Congo, from which Ugandan troops were finally withdrawn only on May 6. Meanwhile, in the north more than a quarter of Uganda itself was being ravaged by Joseph Kony's anarchic Lord's Resistance Army (LRA), and such military forces as were made available proved incapable of halting the devastation. So long as the rebels remained at a distance from the more affluent south, international observers seemed prepared to turn a blind eye.

When it was learned that U.S. Pres. George W. Bush was to visit the country on July 11, Ugandan religious leaders urged him to raise with President Museveni their concern over the huge numbers of children being kidnapped by the LRA. President Bush, however, praised both Uganda's free-trade policy and the remarkable success that it had achieved in its campaign to combat HIV/AIDS. As a further boost to that success, trials had been started in February on a vaccine specially designed to resist the A strain of the HIV virus, the type most common in East Africa.

Uncertainty continued regarding the country's political future. A number of supporters of opposition leader Kizza Besigye were arrested early in the year. Besigye himself had fled the country, and two senior army officers who were Besigye sympathizers had taken refuge in Rwanda. There, it was claimed, they were training a force to try to overthrow Museveni. Both the officers and Rwandan Pres. Paul Kagame denied the accusations.

In March in response to a petition by Paul Ssemogerere, the leader of the Democratic Party, the country's constitutional court ruled that parts of the Political Parties and Organisations Act of 2002 had imposed unjustifiable restrictions on the activities of political parties. On a number of occasions, Museveni himself raised the idea of removing the ban on all political party activities that he had imposed in 1986, but he linked it with the proposal to amend the constitution so as to allow the president to serve an unlimited number of terms in office.

The death of former president Idi Amin in Saudi Arabia in August (*see* OBITUARIES) caused little reaction in Uganda, although one of his sons, Taban Amin, who had for some time been trying to recruit fighters from the Congo to invade the northwest of Uganda, showed no sign of abandoning his efforts. In November, following a complaint from President Musaveni, the government of the Congo rejected any suggestion that Ugandan troops should be allowed to pursue rebels said to be operating from within the Congo.

(KENNETH INGHAM)

UKRAINE

Area: 603,700 sq km (233,100 sq mi)
Population (2003 est.): 47,856,000
Capital: Kiev
Chief of state: President Leonid Kuchma
Head of government: Prime Minister Viktor Yanukovich

Ukraine was dominated in 2003 by two issues: relations with Russia and the proposals to make constitutional changes to the way the parliament and president were elected. On January 28 Pres. Leonid Kuchma and Russian Pres. Vladimir Putin signed a number of bilateral documents, including one on border issues. Proposals to establish a "joint economic space" with Russia, Belarus, and Kazakhstan were accepted in principle by the parliament in May and signed by the leaders of the four countries in Yalta on September 19. Relations with Russia suddenly deteriorated in October following Russia's commencement of construction on a dam between the Taman Peninsula (on Russian soil) and Tuzla Island on the Kerch Strait of Crimea. Ostensibly Russia wished to lay claims to the area between the Kerch Strait and the Sea of Azov and to redraw existing borders. On October 16 Ukraine sent border guards to halt construction, and the parliament issued a resolution to end the threat to Ukrainian "territorial integrity." The prime ministers of the two countries met on October 24 and agreed that Ukraine would remove its border guards and Russia would stop construction of the dam pending further discussions.

Ukraine's attitude toward the U.S.-led invasion of Iraq was ambivalent. It agreed to send a chemical defense battalion to Kuwait at the request of the U.S., but the legislature condemned the attack on Iraq by a vote of 229 to 5.

At home the Kuchma regime encountered increasingly strong opposition from the Our Ukraine faction in the Supreme Council, led by former prime minister Viktor Yushchenko. In late February Yushchenko demanded an end to political terror in the country, and an antipresidential rally of some 50,000 people followed on March 9. At a forum of democratic forces later in the month in Kiev, Yushchenko anticipated that his bloc would form a new political party with a broad base in alliance with the Yuliya Tymoshenko Bloc. The authorities blocked another Our Ukraine forum in November in Donetsk.

Behind the conflict lay the prospect of the 2004 presidential election and the president's proposals to change the political system. In March Kuchma suggested that the president should have the power to dissolve the parliament should it fail to acquire a working majority and that the parliament should be elected according to a party list for a five-year term and that there should be an upper and a lower assembly.

Kuchma's proposals encountered bitter resistance, and he was forced to back off. The opposition supported elections according to a system of proportional representation and the election of the president directly by the parliament, although the 2004 election would still be held by direct ballot, and requiring a two-thirds majority of parliamentary deputies for ratification. In October deputies from the Socialist Party (Oleksander Moroz), the Yuliya Tymoshenko Bloc, and Our Ukraine prevented access to the rostrum of the Supreme Council and demanded that a vote be held at once on the question of a system of full proportional representation. In December the Constitutional Court ruled that the parliament could legally elect the president in 2004 and that Kuchma could be a candidate in that election, as his first term had begun before the enactment of the constitution.

The economy continued to improve. GDP rose by 4.1% in 2002 and was projected to increase by 5–6% in 2003. Meanwhile, a government economic plan foresaw a rise in the monthly wage to reach 342 hryvnyas (about $65) by 2007. From Jan. 1, 2004, Ukrainian residents would pay a flat tax of 13%, which was expected to boost the consumer market.

Not all sectors of society were satisfied with the economic situation, however. Coal miners went on strike in March for higher wages. The 2003 harvest was anticipated to be so poor that the government imposed food price hikes, which led to protests outside the parliament in early July. The government reacted furiously, dismissing the head of the State Food Department and numerous other officials. Up to seven million Ukrainians were reportedly working abroad because of the difficult situation within the country.

Two important anniversaries received very different commemoration in 2003. The 60th anniversary of the "Volyn massacre" of Poles by Ukrainian insurgents in 1943 was combined with acknowledgement of the repression of Ukrainians by Poles during postwar resettlement. The 70th anniversary of the Ukrainian famine (known in Ukraine as the Holodomor) resulted in a resolution by the Supreme Council on May 15 that stated that the famine had been "an act of genocide" and political terrorism carried out by the Stalinist regime against the people of Ukraine. Ukrainian historians estimated that the famine cost the country between five million and seven million lives.

(DAVID R. MARPLES)

UNITED ARAB EMIRATES

Area: 83,600 sq km (32,280 sq mi)
Population (2003 est.): 3,818,000, of which about 1,600,000 are citizens
Capital: Abu Dhabi
Chief of state: President Sheikh Zayid ibn Sultan Al Nahyan
Head of government: Prime Minister Sheikh Maktum ibn Rashid al-Maktum

The economy of the United Arab Emirates showed signs of even greater strength in 2003. GDP grew an estimated 4.6%, compared with 1.8% in 2002. A major reason for the growth was strong oil prices, which reached levels substantially higher than in recent years. Since oil accounted for 60%

of government revenues, high prices also benefited the national budget, and the government was able to continue to provide good subsidies and benefits, which had grown by 35% over the previous five years. With a native population of only 1.6 million, the more than $70 billion GDP supported a comfortable life for the country's citizens. The private sector also continued to grow and contributed about 47% of GDP. The companies and banks in the U.A.E. stock market showed gains. In addition, Dolphin Energy announced plans to build a pipeline to Oman designed to import Omani natural gas, a move that would extend the project's scope beyond Qatar.

In 2003 the U.A.E. and Oman signed and ratified a comprehensive agreement to delimit their long common border. The agreement included resolution of the status of the Musandam Peninsula and the Madhah enclave, which belonged to Oman but were not contiguous to other Omani sovereign territory.

Prior to the U.S.-led war in Iraq, the U.A.E. called for Saddam Hussein to step down to avoid the use of force. Later the U.A.E. provided humanitarian assistance to the Iraqi people and urged that they be given control over their own lives as soon as possible. Reconciliation with Iran continued its slow pace. (WILLIAM A. RUGH)

UNITED KINGDOM

Area: 244,101 sq km (94,248 sq mi)
Population (2003 est.): 59,164,000
Capital: London
Chief of state: Queen Elizabeth II
Head of government: Prime Minister Tony Blair

Domestic Affairs. British politics in 2003 was dominated by the domestic repercussions of the Iraq war. Two cabinet members resigned: Robin Cook, the leader of the House of Commons (and previously foreign secretary), on March 17 in protest against "the decision to commit Britain now to military action in Iraq without international agreement or domestic support," and Clare Short (*see* BIOGRAPHIES), the international development secretary, on May 12, saying that Prime Minister Tony Blair had reneged on a pledge to work through the United Nations to rebuild Iraq following the war.

These events took place against a backdrop of public opinion that until mid-March was hostile to military action outside the UN, then was broadly supportive of the war while it lasted and during its immediate aftermath, and after that, from June onward, was increasingly skeptical about the case that Blair and other ministers had made for regarding Iraqi Pres. Saddam Hussein as a dangerous threat.

These controversies were heightened by accusations by British Broadcasting Corporation reporter Andrew Gilligan that Blair had knowingly misled the public in September 2002 when a government report stated that Saddam was able to deploy weapons of mass destruction (WMD) at 45 minutes' notice. Alastair Campbell, Blair's press secretary, accused the BBC and Gilligan of having made serious allegations that were untrue and that were not checked prior to being published. (Gilligan's reports appeared both on the BBC and in the newspaper *Mail on Sunday.*)

Much turned on the reliability of Gilligan's source. On July 4 David Kelly, a WMD expert who worked for the Ministry of Defence, admitted to his line manager that he had spoken to Gilligan. Kelly's name was confirmed to journalists on July 9. On July 15–16 Kelly gave evidence to two different committees of MPs inquiring into the buildup to war. Clearly under strain, he denied he was the source of Gilligan's most controversial allegations. Kelly left his Oxfordshire home on July 17, telling his wife that he was going for a walk. The following morning he was found dead, with one of his wrists severely slashed.

Blair immediately announced a public inquiry into the circumstances of Kelly's death. The immediate cause was not disputed; Kelly had committed suicide. The inquiry, however, which was conducted by Lord Hutton, a senior judge, effectively turned into an inquiry into the conduct of the government in the build-up to war. Many of the principal politicians and officials gave evidence, ranging from Blair to Sir Richard Dearlove, the chief of Britain's Secret Intelligence Service, MI-6. This was the first time a chief of MI-6 had ever been questioned in public. Like all the officials and politicians questioned, he denied that either ministers or the intelligence services had deliberately exaggerated the threat from Saddam. Nevertheless, the inquiry (whose report was expected to be published in January 2004) uncovered evidence of doubts within the middle ranks of the intelligence community about some of the statements made before the war. It also transpired that Saddam's capacity to unleash WMD within 45 minutes of an order's being given related solely to battlefield weapons and not—in contradiction to many reports at the time—to any capacity to attack British or other Western targets outside Iraq.

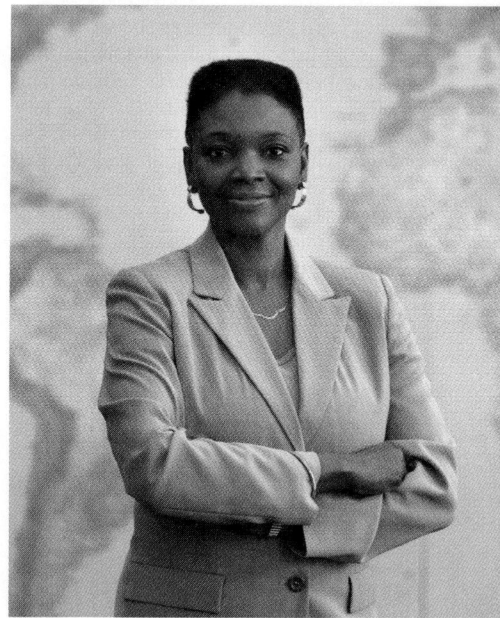

Baroness Amos poses in her office in May after being named to replace Clare Short as Great Britain's secretary of state for international development.

Short's resignation led to the appointment of the first black woman member of a British cabinet. Baroness Amos succeeded Short in May as secretary of state for international development. Five months later she was promoted to become leader of the House of Lords. One of her tasks was to secure the next stage of reform of the Lords. Following the failure on February 4 of the House of Commons to construct a majority for any specific proposal for long-term reform, the government announced that as an interim measure it would prepare a bill to abolish the rights of the remaining 92 hereditary members to sit in the Lords. This would leave the Lords as a wholly appointed chamber. One additional reform was announced in June: the abolition of the post of lord chancellor, which had existed for almost 1,400 years. Lord Falconer (*see* BIOGRAPHIES) was appointed in June 2003 as its final holder, pending the post's replacement in due course by a minister of a new Department for Constitutional Affairs.

Meanwhile, opinion polls were recording widespread disillusion with the Blair government—and not simply because of controversies concerning the Iraq war. Despite presiding over a reasonably strong economy, the government was widely perceived to be failing to improve public services such as health, education, and transport. On September 18 Labour lost one of its safest seats, the north London constituency of Brent East, in a by-election necessitated by the death of the sitting MP. This was the first seat that Labour had lost in a by-election since Blair became party leader in 1994. The seat was taken by the Liberal Democrats, the third largest party in the House of Commons.

The Brent result was bad not only for Labour but also for the Conservative Party, which came in a poor third. This added to pressure on Conservative leader Iain Duncan Smith. Even though the Conservatives made widespread gains in local elections held in May, he failed to establish the command over the political terrain that opposition leaders historically needed in the midterm of a Parliament in order to win the following general election. The party's annual conference, held October 6–9, was marked by bitter factional infighting. Duncan Smith, who had been elected party leader two years earlier, pleaded for party unity; however, on October 29 Conservative MPs voted 90–75 to eject him and hold a new election for party leader. Only one person put his name forward: Michael Howard, an experienced right-wing politician who had served as home secretary in the previous Conservative government. He duly succeeded Duncan Smith on November 6.

In May the second round of elections took place for the Scottish Parliament and the Welsh Assembly. In Scotland the ruling Labour–Liberal Democrat coalition remained in power in the 129-seat Parliament, although Labour lost 6 seats to finish with 50, while the Liberal Democrats remained at 17. The Scottish Nationalists won 27 seats, a loss of 8, while the Conservatives held steady with 18. The Greens won 7 seats, while the left-wing Scottish Socialist Party took 6; each party had previously held only one seat. The remaining four seats were won by three independents and one candidate standing for the Scottish Senior Citizens' Unity Party.

In Wales Labour gained two seats, to end up with 30 out of a total of 60 seats in the Assembly. The Welsh nationalist party Plaid Cymru won 12 (down from 17), while the Conservatives won 11 (an increase of 2) and the Liberal Democrats were unchanged with 6. The final seat was won by an independent. With exactly half the seats, Labour decided to govern on its own, rather than continue the Labour–Liberal Democrat administration that had been in power before the election.

London saw a radical innovation: the introduction on February 17 of a daily £5 ($8) "congestion charge" on all cars entering the centre of the capital between 7 AM and 6:30 PM, Monday to Friday. The aim of this, the first "road tax" of any large city in a major industrialized country, was both to reduce congestion and to raise money to invest in improvements in public transport. Fears that the new system would fail did not materialize. Despite some initial hiccups, the technology worked well. This involved cameras at each entry point photographing auto license plates, and penalty notices being sent to cars whose owners failed to pay the charge by 10 PM. Once the new system had settled down, traffic levels in central London were reduced 16%, and the average speed of traffic during the day was up by 37%, from 13 km/hr (8 mph) to 17 km/hr (11 mph).

The letter "C" painted on the street marks the beginning of London's "congestion charge" zone; motorists who use the zone from morning to evening rush hour on weekdays must pay £5 ($8) for the privilege, an initiative intended to raise revenue and decrease traffic congestion.

© Scott Barbour/Getty Images

Economic Affairs. Economic growth remained below trend in 2003, at about 2% a year, but this was a higher growth rate than in most major economies and was sufficient to prevent any significant rise in the U.K.'s low levels of unemployment. Against this, the slow growth meant that government borrowing rose faster than Gordon Brown, the chancellor of the Exchequer, had predicted. By December, Brown had admitted that borrowing in the 2003–04 fiscal year would climb to £37 billion ($62 billion). In the short run he was under no pressure to raise taxes, but many economists predicted that within two or three years the government would have to either raise taxes further or reduce its ambitious plans to increase spending on public services. In July the Bank of England reduced its benchmark "repo" interest rate to 3.5%, the lowest level since January 1955. This lasted until November, when the Bank announced the first increase in almost four years, to 3.75%, in response to evidence that economic growth had started to recover.

On June 9 Brown announced the results of five tests he had originally said, in October 1997, had to be passed if the government was to call a referendum to recommend that the U.K. enter the European Union's single currency. He reported that despite considerable progress, only one of the tests—that joining the euro would be good for the U.K.'s financial services industry—had been unambiguously passed. In particular, recent signs of convergence in the economic cycles of the U.K. and the euro zone were too fragile for the government to be certain that convergence would last. Although Blair wanted to keep open the option of a referendum before the next general election, which was due in 2005 or 2006, Brown's announcement made it all but certain that any referendum would have to wait.

Foreign Affairs. In the early months of 2003, the U.K. worked with the United States to secure a UN resolution explicitly authorizing military action against Iraq. This led to tensions inside the EU, especially with France (like the U.K., a veto-wielding member of the UN Security Council), which opposed any such resolution. On March 18, following the breakdown of negotiations at the UN, the House of Commons voted to commit British troops to a U.S.-led military action to remove Hussein from power. (See *United Nations:* Special Report, above.)

Altogether, 45,000 British service personnel took part in the invasion, including 26,000 ground troops. Britain deployed 116 Challenger 2 tanks and 100 aircraft (including helicopters). The main function of the British contingent was to liberate southern Iraq, especially Basra. (Smaller numbers of British special forces were engaged in particular missions behind the lines in western and northern Iraq.) Following the war British troops continued to occupy Basra, seeking to restore civil society to the city. They adopted a "soft-hat" strategy, in which soldiers, wherever possible, patrolled the streets with only light arms and wore berets rather than hard hats. Postwar Iraqi resistance actions against the British troops in Basra were far fewer than U.S. troops faced in Baghdad, but sporadic assaults still took place.

Closer to home, on July 8 Blair welcomed the draft EU constitution, which had been drawn up by a group chaired by former French president Valéry Giscard d'Estaing, as "a pretty good outcome for Britain." The prime minister argued that it largely involved a tidying up of existing arrangements, in contrast to the Conservative Party and other critics, who said that the new constitution would take more powers from member states and transfer them to the EU. In negotiations over the new constitution, the U.K. had resisted attempts by some other EU members to extend majority voting to matters of foreign affairs and taxation. Nevertheless, polls showed widespread public hostility within the U.K. to the new constitution; when negotiations collapsed at the EU summit in Brussels on December 13, Foreign Secretary Jack Straw expressed only mild disappointment.

British Prime Minister Tony Blair (left) and U.S. Pres. George W. Bush conclude a press conference at Camp David, Maryland, after discussions on the progress of the war and reconstruction in Iraq.

Northern Ireland. At the start of 2003, Northern Ireland was ruled directly from London, following the suspension of the Northern Ireland Assembly and Executive in October 2002. Negotiations aimed at paving the way for new Assembly elections were slow and faltering. The elections, due to be held on May 1, were twice postponed—initially until May 29, and then until the autumn. Following the announcement on May 1 of the second suspension, Britain promised to reduce the number of troops in the province and to give up its power to suspend the Assembly in return for a complete end to all paramilitary violence and the establishment of an independent monitoring body that would have the power to punish organizations, including political parties, associated with any outbreak of future paramilitary violence.

David Trimble, Northern Ireland's first minister, made it clear, however, that he would resume his position only if the IRA went farther than it had before to declare a complete end to its war against Northern Ireland's status as part of the U.K. For some hours on October 21, the deadlock appeared to have been broken. Britain announced that the Assembly elections would take place on November 26; Gerry Adams, the president of Sinn Fein, went farther than ever before to embrace purely political means for advancing the republican cause and opposing "any use or threat of force for any political purpose"; the IRA issued a statement endorsing Adams's words; and Gen. John de Chastelain, the Canadian head of the independent body overseeing arms decommissioning, announced that the IRA had "put beyond use" a substantial quantity of arms. Optimism that the peace process was back on track was punctured hours later by Trimble, who said that not enough had been done for the Ulster Unionists to reenter power sharing with the republicans.

Nevertheless, fresh elections for the 108-seat Northern Ireland Assembly were held on November 26. The outcome was a setback for the two moderate parties that had championed the peace process—the Ulster Unionists and the mainly Catholic Social Democratic and Labour Party. The Ulster Unionists were overtaken as the largest party by the Democratic Unionists, which had consistently opposed the 1998 Good Friday Agreement. The SDLP was overtaken by Sinn Fein. Blair decided not to revive the Northern Ireland executive for the time being, as it was clear that the two largest parties, the Democratic Unionists and Sinn Fein, would be unable to work together as required by the Good Friday Agreement.

Meanwhile, additional evidence had come to light about the conflict in 1969–97 between the IRA and the British army. On April 17 Sir John Stevens, the head of London's Metropolitan Police, published the results of an official inquiry into allegations of collusion between the British army and antirepublican "loyalist" (i.e., Protestant) terrorist groups. Stevens reported that his inquiries had been obstructed by the army and local police officials. His own incident room had been destroyed by fire, which in his view was "a deliberate act of arson." Nevertheless, he stated: "My enquiries have highlighted collusion, the willful failure to keep records, the absence of accountability, the withholding of intelligence and evidence, and the extreme of agents being involved in murder. These serious acts and omissions have meant that people have been killed or seriously injured." (PETER KELLNER)

UNITED STATES

Area: 9,363,364 sq km (3,615,215 sq mi), including 204,446 sq km of inland water but excluding the 155,534 sq km of the Great Lakes that lie within U.S. boundaries
Population (2003 est.): 291,587,000; based on 2000 unadjusted census results
Capital: Washington, D.C.
Head of state and government: President George W. Bush

Even as the U.S. struggled for months during 2003 with a sluggish economy and the multiple burdens of an unprecedented war on terrorism, overextension of unrivaled U.S. military and economic power seemed a remote prospect. In March, however, the United States initiated its second major military incursion in a Muslim country in 18 months when it led an invasion into Iraq. (U.S. troops were still committed to Afghanistan.) While staged combat was over quickly, an untidy aftermath in Iraq seriously strained both American resources and the national will. The aggressive U.S. action, grounded in a new assertion of the right to wage "preemptive war" against terrorists, badly divided the country's traditional allies and energized a long-dormant antiwar faction in the domestic American body politic. By year's end, although there were signs of stabilization in Iraq, the U.S. was scaling back ambitious plans to transition Iraq into a Western-style democracy, and the ultimate outcome of the U.S. commitment was very much in doubt.

Backed by a handful of major countries, dubbed the "coalition of the willing" by Pres. George W. Bush, the U.S. in early spring overran Iraq in a little over three weeks. The invasion was at least partially justified on the basis of fears, fueled by reports compiled by Western intelligence agencies, about Iraq's possession of weapons of mass destruction, which by year's end had not been found. The liberation of Iraq was a clear humanitarian triumph, however, and a tonic for the U.S. economy as well. By coincidence or not, U.S. business expansion resumed with a vengeance in the weeks following the war, emphatically ending a 30-month economic malaise.

War in Iraq. During January and February some 300,000 U.S. and British troops and 1,150 coalition aircraft were deployed near Iraq—even while 200 newly admitted United Nations inspectors under Hans Blix scoured suspected Iraqi sites, looking for evidence of nuclear, chemical, and biological weaponry and banned missile systems. (*See* MILITARY AFFAIRS: *Sidebar.*) The inspection team had limited success; they located and began arranging destruction of 120 al-Samoud 2 missiles but found no evidence of an active nuclear-weapons program. Additionally, Iraq could not account for chemical and biological agents, including anthrax, that had been in its possession in the late 1990s.

Several influential countries, including France, Germany, and Russia, viewed the inspections as a major step forward in disarming Iraq; they counseled patience and additional diplomacy. Bush and British Prime Minister Tony Blair, however—their armed forces extended on combat readiness—declared the Iraqis to be stalling and continued the allied military buildup. The coalition suffered a major setback on March 1 when the Turkish parliament narrowly rejected a plan to allow U.S. troops to use Turkey, on Iraq's northern border, as a staging area.

On March 17 President Bush gave Iraqi Pres. Saddam Hussein (*see* BIOGRAPHIES) and his family 48 hours to leave the country so that all UN weapons-disarmament decrees could be fully enforced. Two days later, with no explicit UN approval, the U.S. began launching Tomahawk missile strikes on suspected Iraqi leadership sites. Coalition troops began crossing the Iraqi border from Kuwait on March 20. The attack moved quickly toward Baghdad from the west and southwest, covering 300 km (186 mi) in less than a week. Direct resistance was light, although guerrilla attacks behind supply lines inflicted some casualties on coalition forces. A week later U.S. airborne forces opened a third front from the north.

By April 4 the U.S. expeditionary force had captured Saddam International Airport near Baghdad. Threats of block-by-block Iraqi resistance in crowded urban areas of Baghdad proved illusory. Repeated armoured probes of the capital failed to encounter major resistance, and the city was largely under coalition control by April 9. By the middle of the month, the final remnants of Iraqi military forces had been dispersed. That led to the toppling of statues of Saddam all over Iraq even while looters ravaged government offices and cultural centres that occupation troops had left unprotected. Fewer than 200 allied service personnel, including 138 Americans,

On the morning of his state of the union address, Jan. 28, 2003, Pres. George W. Bush (centre, flanked by Secretary of State Colin Powell [on his right] and Secretary of Defense Donald Rumsfeld, opens a cabinet meeting, as he traditionally does, with a prayer.

A U.S. Navy hospital corpsman holds a young child who was wounded in central Iraq on March 29 when a group of civilians, apparently forced by Iraqi soldiers to advance toward U.S. Marine Corps positions, were caught in a cross fire.

died from hostile action during the invasion period.

Almost immediately, however, hit-and-run attacks began on coalition forces even as the allies appointed an Iraqi Governing Council to oversee the transition to Iraqi civilian rule. The death of Saddam's sons Uday and Qusay on July 22 did little to stop sabotage and resistance. (*See* OBITUARIES.) The attacks reached a crescendo in November when a series of bombing and missile attacks on helicopters, planes, and military vehicles left 81 Americans dead. On December 13, however, U.S. forces discovered Saddam hiding in an underground "spider hole" near his hometown, Tikrit. He was captured and held for trial. Even so, by year's end U.S. casualties had reached 480, and attacks on U.S. troops were continuing daily.

The war on terrorism, including the Iraq invasion, dominated both U.S. domestic policy and foreign politics throughout the year. The war split Democrats and roiled the Democratic presidential campaign, leading directly to the emergence of former Vermont governor Howard Dean as the front-runner for the 2004 nomination. Traditional allies of the U.S., led by France, declined to share in the costs of putting Iraq back on its feet. In September the Bush administration acknowledged reluctantly that reconstruction costs in Iraq and Afghanistan would require $86 billion in additional U.S. funds. After extended controversy, Congress eventually approved the outlay.

Domestic Issues. Although Bush had vowed to bring a bipartisan civility to Washington, partisan divisions in Congress deepened during the year as the country prepared for the 2004 elections. In the U.S. Senate, Democrats expanded a campaign to block administration judicial nominees they considered excessively conservative from being confirmed to circuit courts of appeal. By the end of the year, an unprecedented six nominations were being stalled by threat of filibuster. The Congress also again failed, owing to regional and partisan differences, to approve long-considered legislation to stimulate U.S. energy supplies.

After 15 years of discussion, however, legislators approved reform of the national Medicare system for older Americans, adding a controversial prescription-drug benefit and introducing private-sector competition to the plan. The price tag for the new drug-benefit entitlement was $400 billion over 10 years, an amount deemed inadequate by liberals and excessive by fiscal conservatives. Republicans were not keen to expand Medicare, but with medical costs rising rapidly and shifting heavily toward drug therapy, public support for a drug benefit was rising. In his 2000 campaign, candidate Bush had promised action on the measure, and in 2003 he pushed aggressively for its passage prior to the 2004 election year. The bill was approved only after it was endorsed by AARP (formerly the American Association of Retired Persons), an influential lobbying group for seniors, which vowed to seek improvements, including expansion of benefits, in future years.

The Federal Trade Commission established a national "do not call" registry for persons wishing to avoid unsolicited sales calls over the telephone. More than 60 million telephone numbers were quickly registered, and Congress endorsed the registry in later legislation. Adopting an idea pioneered by state governments, Congress also approved a bill that permitted consumers free access to their credit reports. After a series of forest fires in California killed 22, destroyed 4,800 buildings, and burned nearly 400,000 ha (1 million ac) of land, Congress approved the Bush administration's Healthy Forests initiative. The measure, which was signed into law in December, provided for active federal land management, including thinning of undergrowth and planned burns, to reduce fire damage.

Following an adverse ruling from the World Trade Organization, the Bush administration moved to rescind protective tariffs on steel imports first imposed in 2002. The tariffs followed another Bush campaign promise, this time to steel-manufacturing areas, but they were wildly unpopular among consumers of steel, including automobile manufacturers.

The U.S. Supreme Court, in a 5–4 decision, upheld most of the 2002 McCain-Feingold campaign-finance law designed to reduce the influence of special-interest money in federal elections. The high court approved the law's ban on national "soft money" donations by corporations and labour unions and endorsed curbs on advertising by third-party groups that benefited individual candidates. In another landmark decision, also by a 5–4 vote, the high court approved limited use of affirmative-action policies to benefit minority candidates for admission to institutions of higher learning. (*See* LAW, CRIME, AND LAW ENFORCEMENT: *Court Decisions*.)

The struggling national economy and controversy over President Bush's handling of Iraq drew a large field for the

Nine Democratic presidential hopefuls line up before their debate in Phoenix, Ariz., on October 9: (from left) former senator Carol Moseley Braun, Gen. Wesley Clark, the Rev. Al Sharpton, Sen. John Edwards, Rep. Richard Gephardt, Sen. John Kerry, Rep. Dennis Kucinich, former governor Howard Dean, and Sen. Joseph Lieberman.

2004 Democratic presidential nomination—10 candidates at one point, before their ranks were reduced to 9. The 10 were Dean; Rep. Richard Gephardt of Missouri, the former U.S. House leader; Rep. Dennis Kucinich of Ohio; North Carolina Sen. John Edwards; Florida Sen. Bob Graham (who dropped out after five months); Massachusetts Sen. John Kerry; Connecticut Sen. Joseph Lieberman; former Illinois senator Carol Moseley Braun; U.S. Army Gen. Wesley Clark; and African American leader Al Sharpton. Washington outsiders soon established themselves as the front-runners, however. Dean distinguished himself with a strong antiwar stance and savvy use of the Internet for fund-raising and organization; by year's end he was ahead in public-opinion polls but under assault from other contenders as excessively liberal and unelectable against Bush. Late entry Clark was viewed by some Democrats as best positioned to challenge Bush; he received backing from party moderates and aides to former president Bill Clinton.

The U.S. space program sustained a catastrophic loss on February 1 when the space shuttle *Columbia* orbiter disintegrated on reentry over Texas, killing all seven astronauts on board. (*See* OBITUARIES: *Sidebar.*) The tragedy was eventually traced to a 680-g (24-oz) section of foam insulation that had broken away from an external fuel tank on liftoff, damaging *Columbia*'s left wing and dooming the mission. A commission of inquiry later criticized NASA for having a culture that allowed schedule requirements to dominate safety concerns. (*See* PHYSICAL SCIENCES: *Space Exploration.*)

The Economy. With the world watching its main economic engine nervously, the U.S. economy finally shrugged off a lingering hangover from dot-com overexuberance and resumed serious growth during 2003. The revival ended two agonizing years of national economic drift and arrived even as the business community was wrestling with new allegations of wrongdoing in financial markets.

The year started sluggishly, with the economy technically expanding but at such an anemic rate that jobs continued to disappear overall. Economic growth averaged only about 2% for the first six months, and unemployment rose from 5.7% in January to 6.4% by midyear. Government officials appeared to have exhausted their ability to recharge the economy. The Federal Reserve System reduced the already-nominal federal funds interest rate by one-quarter point to 1% in June.

A coalition victory in Iraq, however, appeared to inspire an early spring revival in the equity markets, and by the third quarter the national economy was growing at an 8.2% rate, the fastest clip in two decades. The brisk expansion was fully under way by summer, spurred by low interest rates and inflation and the stimulus of major tax cuts and government spending flowing through the economy. Growth was also aided by a sizable jump in worker productivity, reflecting business economizing and efficiencies.

Another stimulative factor was a record federal budget deficit. The shortfall was estimated at $455 billion in July, but rapid second-half growth lowered the actual deficit to $374 billion by October. Reversing their historic role, Democrats criticized the Bush administration for fiscal irresponsibility, alleging that Republican tax cuts mostly benefited the wealthy and were creating debt to be paid by future generations. Republicans attributed most of the shortfall to temporary costs associated with the moribund economy and the war on terrorism. Even so, the deficit and the rapid growth failed to produce any revival of inflation, with consumer prices growing less than 2% for the year. Though unemployment fell back to 5.7% in December, only 1,000 jobs were created that month, and about 309,000 people stopped looking for work.

By year's end the equity markets had posted substantial gains, their first in three years. The Dow Jones Industrial Average finished the year at 10,453.92, more than 3,000 points higher than the March low, and the technology-heavy Nasdaq average rose from 1253.22 in March to above 2000 at year's end. Even so, both averages remained well under their record highs, established in 2000.

Incidence of corporate wrongdoing and accounting irregularities, widespread during 2002, subsided during the year, but the national system of market regulation sustained major strains. Richard Grasso, chairman of the New York Stock Exchange, was forced to step down after his $187.5 million compensation package was revealed. The nation's $7 trillion mutual-fund industry was rocked by allegations of misconduct, including after-hours and insider trading. The mutual-fund investigation was spearheaded not by the federal Securities and Exchange Commission, which normally took the lead role in market regulation, but by Eliot Spitzer, the controversial and aggressive New York state attorney general.

Foreign Policy. The new U.S. preemptive-war policy, and particularly U.S. action in Iraq, threatened to fracture U.S. relations with several European powers.

In March, France, Germany, and Russia refused to allow a United Nations vote authorizing the Iraq incursion. After the U.S.-led coalition victory, France was among the countries refusing to contribute security forces to restore law and order in Iraq and declining to assist in that country's economic reconstruction.

With costs rising, including financial outlays and U.S. troop casualties, diplomacy came close to a breakdown. At one point U.S. Defense Secretary Donald Rumsfeld derisively dismissed recalcitrant major powers as "Old Europe," contrasting their foot dragging with the actions of new democracies such as Poland, Romania, and Bulgaria, as well as other countries that wholeheartedly supported the coalition effort. The Pentagon then explicitly refused to consider corporate construction and supply bids for Iraq from countries that had failed to support the war effort, which further angered French, German, and Russian interests. At year's end, however, President Bush dispatched former secretary of state James Baker to negotiate a reduction of the $120 billion external debt left by the Saddam regime. Baker was largely successful, and U.S. diplomatic relations with its estranged allies improved.

Another major effort to resolve the long-standing Israeli-Palestinian standoff foundered during the year. The European Union, Russia, the United States, and the United Nations devised a "road map to peace" and obtained nominal agreement to it from both sides. To aid in breaking the deadlock, Palestinian leader Yasir Arafat was forced to share power by appointing a prime minister. The new official, Mahmoud Abbas (*see* BIOGRAPHIES), was not able to assert his authority, however, and he resigned his post, leaving the Middle East peace process with no significant progress for the year.

Concerns over nuclear proliferation in Third World countries continued to preoccupy U.S. diplomats. As the year began, North Korea withdrew from the Nuclear Non-proliferation Treaty, the first signatory ever to do so, and threatened concerted efforts toward building up its nuclear-weapons program. North Korea insisted on direct negotiations with the U.S., preceded by a U.S. nonaggression guarantee. Six-country talks, including North Korea's ally China, were held at midyear, without apparent progress, but after the U.S. offered limited security promises, negotiations were again resumed at year's end.

Iran and Libya, under international pressure, promised to open their long-running and secretive nuclear programs to inspection during the year. Iran revealed that its efforts had been under way for 18 years, which prompted U.S. calls for punitive measures, but UN authorities elected instead to push only for more effective future inspections. Libya, struggling to escape UN economic sanctions, agreed to pay $2.7 billion to families of victims of the 1988 airline tragedy in Lockerbie, Scot. Later in the year a shipment of centrifuge equipment heading to Libya was intercepted at an Italian port, the first action under a U.S.-led 11-nation Proliferation Security Initiative. Within weeks the Libyan regime publicly disclosed its own nuclear-weapons-development program and promised to dismantle it. Bush administration backers attributed progress on nuclear nonproliferation to the U.S. hard line on Iraq.

U.S. relations with China continued to warm despite concerns over a major trade imbalance and Taiwan. As the Chinese economy expanded rapidly, creating a massive trade surplus with the U.S., the Bush administration suggested that China was manipulating its currency to make the trade imbalance even more one-sided. Later, however, as Taiwan politicians talked of independence, the U.S. forcefully reminded them that the U.S. "one China" policy opposed any complete and permanent Taiwan-China break. (DAVID C. BECKWITH)

DEVELOPMENTS IN THE STATES

A roller-coaster national economy and unsettled relations with the federal government made 2003 a turbulent year for U.S. state governments. Severe budget problems deteriorated further early in the year, which prompted a variety of measures to balance revenue and spending. The national economy leveled off and began growing rapidly at midyear, which eased financial pressures on state governments but not before the tumult helped produce a rare event, the recall of a state governor.

Party Strengths. Democrats made modest gains overall in limited state legislative balloting in 2003; though they lost seats in Mississippi, they made gains in New Jersey and Virginia. Those results left the two major parties at virtually equal strength across the country, with Republicans holding a slight advantage of fewer than 1% of overall legislative seats.

For 2004, Republicans would continue to control both state legislative chambers in 21 states. Democrats would dominate both bodies in 17 states, up from 16 in 2003. Eleven states were split, with neither party organizing both chambers. Nebraska has a nonpartisan legislature.

The Ten Commandments monument is removed from the rotunda of the Alabama Judicial Building in Montgomery on August 27 following a U.S. district judge's ruling that the public display of the monument was unconstitutional.

AP/Wide World Photos

For most of the year, Republicans had a 26–24 advantage in governorships. In October voters in California recalled Democratic Gov. Gray Davis and replaced him with Austrian-born actor Arnold Schwarzenegger (*see* BIOGRAPHIES), a Republican (*see* below). The next month Republicans won two of three gubernatorial elections, prevailing in Kentucky and Mississippi but losing in Louisiana. The gubernatorial lineup for 2004 would thus include 28 Republicans and 22 Democrats.

Structure, Powers. The chief justice of Alabama, Roy Moore, was removed from office after a judicial evaluation commission determined that he had failed to heed a federal court order. In 2001 Moore had installed a 2,400-kg (5,300-lb) granite monument to the Ten Commandments in the state judicial building lobby, and Moore later ignored a federal court order that it be removed.

The Colorado Supreme Court, in a controversial ruling, declared that the state constitution prohibits mid-decade redistricting. Following the 2000 census, the legislature defaulted to the courts in its duty to draw a new district map. With Republicans in full control in 2003, the legislature attempted to strengthen its hold on seven of nine seats, but the state high court said that no further redistricting could be done until after the 2010 census.

Republicans were more successful in Texas. After having taken majority control of the legislature in 2002 elections, Republicans started redrawing U.S. House of Representatives district lines. Democrat House members fled to Ardmore, Okla., for four days and thereby prevented a quorum from assembling during regular session. During a subsequent special session, Senate Democrats flew to Albuquerque, N.M., and stayed out of state for more than a month, which also prevented a quorum. In a third special session, however, a new map was approved that promised to add at least five new Republicans to a delegation previously controlled 17–15 by Democrats.

Government Relations. Relations between states and the federal government, always contentious, were uneven during 2003. After having mandated improvements in public education, homeland security, election procedures, and other local concerns, the U.S. government made only partial reimbursement for costs, and this had an adverse impact on deteriorating state budgets. With some state taxes tied to federal levies, administration-backed tax cuts eroded state revenue collections. Congress extended a ban on taxation of some Internet service providers, depriving states of a needed, growing revenue source.

AP/Wide World Photos

Film star Arnold Schwarzenegger gives a thumbs-up sign as he boards his campaign bus on October 2 during his (successful) campaign to replace California Gov. Gray Davis if voters chose to recall him.

The administration of U.S. Pres. George W. Bush at midyear proposed converting six existing federal programs—Medicaid, low-income housing, workforce development, child protection, transportation, and Head Start—into block grants administered by the states. Backers suggested that local control would eliminate overhead and provide needed flexibility in the administration of social programs. No action was taken on the proposal during 2003.

Citing excessive expense, legislators in Colorado, Kansas, Maine, New Mexico, North Dakota, Washington, and Utah canceled their states' presidential primaries, which had been scheduled for 2004. Governors in Arizona and Missouri vetoed similar bills and restored primary-election funding.

Finances. An underperforming national economy continued to limit state revenue growth and increase social-service costs, and many relatively painless budget adjustments were quickly exhausted. At one point 45 states faced budget shortfalls, and the cumulative state deficit nationwide was estimated at a record $70 billion. More than half of that, $38.2 billion, was the responsibility of California.

States responded with a wide variety of measures. Nearly 30 states raised taxes, 8 of them by more than 5%. Alabama attempted to raise taxes by nearly 10%, but the measure was rejected by voters. Although 20 states were able to avoid significant tax increases, only Hawaii was able to reduce overall taxation levels during the year. Most states increased user fees on everything from health care and motor-vehicle licensing to court costs. Many states showed creativity in finding new revenue sources; Massachusetts, for example, increased fees for skating-rink licenses and for taking the bar exam. Fifteen states increased tuition at public colleges. Eight states raised revenue by expanding state-sponsored gambling, but Maine voters rejected a referendum that would have allowed Indian-owned casinos. Other revenue measures included exhausting rainy-day savings, diverting other appropriated money, and enacting tax-amnesty or tax-enforcement programs.

Some 35 states slashed spending, usually by a reduction in workforce. The cuts even extended to previously sacrosanct areas such as public-school funding and safety-net expenditures. With health costs rising rapidly, many states trimmed Medicaid and children's health insurance, usually eliminating some coverage, reducing benefits, or establishing waiting periods.

For months the Bush administration opposed federal assistance to hard-pressed state treasuries, urging states instead to reduce spending. In May, however, as part of a tax-cut compromise, Washington agreed to send $20 billion to state governments, roughly half in flexible grants and half in additional Medicaid funding. Those payments coincided with a midyear economic pickup that dramatically improved the outlook for state budgets. By year's end a majority of states were running ahead of budget projections, most states were recovering, and only California among major states was still projecting a significant deficit.

California Recall. Prior to 2003, citizens of only a single U.S. state—North Dakota in 1921—had ever recalled their governor by popular election. "A perfect storm" of economic and political maelstroms had enveloped California Governor Davis only months after his November 2002 reelection, however, and it prompted his recall and replacement by a political newcomer.

Davis, faulted for a relatively colourless personal style, was weakened by his handling of California's electricity crisis in 2001 and his perceived failure to reign in state spending after the "dot-com boom" ended and government revenues plunged. After his reelection Davis boosted state-deficit estimates and then encountered gridlock in budget negotiations—Republicans refused to raise taxes, and Democrats resisted major cuts in spending. By midyear, after the state had tripled an unpopular automobile tax, opinion polls showed Davis's approval ratings hitting record lows.

Recall advocates needed 897,000 voter signatures to force a recall election. Aided by funding from a wealthy Republican gubernatorial hopeful who later dropped out, anti-Davis forces gathered more than 1.3 million valid signatures. The election was eventually set for October 7 to decide two questions: should Davis be recalled, and, if so, who should replace him?

During the campaign, Democrats were badly split; some concentrated on retaining Davis, but others backed Lieut. Gov. Cruz Bustamante in case Davis was recalled. On October 7 Davis was ousted by a margin of 55.4% to 44.6%. On the second question, voters chose from among 135 candidates of wildly varying backgrounds. The winner was Schwarzenegger, with a plurality of 48.7%; Bustamante was second with 31.6%. Schwarzenegger was sworn in after the results were certified on November 14.

Laws and Justice. With business groups warning of potential job losses, Washington voters overturned a legislature-approved ergonomics law that provided workers with strong protection against repetitive-motion injuries. Maryland joined 13 states providing protection to users of marijuana for medical purposes.

Budget pressure spurred review of state corrections policies, and a recent prison-construction boom slowed. States executed 65 death-row inmates during the year, 24 of them in Texas. Illinois Gov. George Ryan, two days before leaving office in January, issued a blanket statewide clemency to all 167 convicts on death row. Ryan had suspended the imposition of capital punishment in 2000, saying it was applied arbitrarily. At year's end, Ryan was indicted on federal corruption charges, which were unrelated to his death-penalty actions.

Health and Welfare. States struggled to contain medical costs, particularly for expensive prescription drugs. Some states attempted to negotiate prices directly with pharmaceutical companies on behalf of low-income or elderly users, and the U.S. Supreme Court approved a closely watched Maine plan that drug companies alleged was coercive. Other states formed pools to facilitate bulk purchases of popular medications. Officials in several states moved to reimport American drugs from Canada, where prices were often cheaper, but the federal Food and Drug Administration rejected the idea. (See *Canada:* Sidebar, above.)

New York and Massachusetts joined California, Connecticut, Delaware, and Maine in banning smoking in virtually all workplaces, including taverns and restaurants.

Education. A trend toward more competition in K–12 education expanded during 2003. Colorado's legislature approved a school-voucher plan, although a federal judge later struck it down as an unconstitutional interference in the local control of education. Officials in Arkansas, California, and Texas banned the sale of candy, gum, and soft drinks in public elementary and secondary schools. Tuition savings plans that guaranteed future state-university enrollment at current fees were a budget casualty in several states; Kentucky, Ohio, Texas, and West Virginia suspended new enrollments, and Colorado terminated its plan.

States struggled with mandates of the federal No Child Left Behind Act, which required "high stakes" testing, upgraded teacher-qualification requirements, and prescribed penalties for lagging schools. The Bush administration said the tumult was an expected product of significant reform of public education, however, and state requests for waivers from or amendments to the act were postponed until after the 2004 election.

Equal Rights. At the urging of embattled Governor Davis, the California legislature approved a law allowing illegal aliens to obtain state drivers' licenses. The measure was widely viewed as having facilitated Davis's recall, and at year's end legislators repealed it by a near-unanimous vote. In a widely anticipated ruling based on two cases from the University of Michigan, the U.S. Supreme Court permitted affirmative action benefiting minorities in university admissions. The ruling had no effect in California and Washington, where voters had banned race-conscious state policies, but it allowed the resumption of affirmative action in Texas, Louisiana, and Alabama, where lower federal courts had ruled it unconstitutional.

Supporters of homosexual rights made major gains during the year. The U.S. Supreme Court, in a Texas case, invalidated state sodomy statutes on privacy grounds. Critics charged that the ruling would inevitably lead to judicial sanction of same-sex marriage. Later in the year, in a 4–3 decision, the Massachusetts Supreme Judicial Court ruled that the state constitution forbade denying homosexual couples the right to marry. Similar rulings had been overturned by state constitutional amendments in Hawaii and Alaska and by a "civil unions" law in Vermont that granted only marriagelike rights. Though amendments to the Massachusetts constitution required at least two years for passage, the state high court gave the legislature only six months to comply. Supporters cheered the ruling as providing equality for homosexuals in hospital visits, inheritance rights, and even Social Security entitlements.

The decision also created uncertainty nationwide on both state and federal levels. Reacting to the Hawaii decision, 37 states had approved laws defining marriage as a union between a man and a woman. The U.S. Constitution, however, requires states to give "full faith and credit" to laws of other states, and it was thus inferred that a homosexual marriage in Massachusetts had to be recognized universally, so the validity of those 37 state laws was in doubt. At year's end, traditional-family proponents vowed support for a U.S. constitutional amendment that would overturn the Massachusetts ruling, which they predicted would undermine traditional marriage, harm children, and threaten social stability.

(DAVID C. BECKWITH)

URUGUAY

Area: 176,215 sq km (68,037 sq mi)
Population (2003 est.): 3,380,000
Capital: Montevideo
Head of state and government: President Jorge Batlle Ibáñez

The year 2003 was another difficult one for the Uruguayan economy, but it was not as disastrous as the previous year. After a fall in GDP of more than 10% in 2002 and an additional decline of 6% in the first half of 2003, data for the second half showed that there was enough economic strengthening for Uruguay to record no growth or a modest decline for 2003. In May, Uruguay successfully renegotiated its private debt with an innovative bond exchange that stretched out the repayment schedule and thereby gave some breathing room for the last two years of the administration of Pres. Jorge Batlle Ibáñez and the first year of the next government. The banking system remained deeply depressed; 25% of loans at private banks were nonperforming, and such key public institutions as the Banco de la República and the Mortgage Bank (Banco Hipotecario) saw a staggering nonperforming-loan rate of 50%. The latter institution lost $1.1 billion in 2002. The sudden resignation of Finance Minister Alejandro Atchugarry did not inspire confidence, although his replacement, Isaac Alfie, was generally well received by key financial, diplomatic, and political players. A major strike in the hospital and health care system ended only after strenuous negotiations and concessions from the government.

Politically, the presidential candidates began positioning for the October 2004 elections. Former presidents—Julio María Sanguinetti of the ruling Colorado Party and Luis Alberto Lacalle of the Blanco Party—expressed interest in running, but both faced a daunting task in light of polls that showed the leftist Broad Front–Progressive Encounter coalition obtaining a majority or near majority behind its leader, Tabaré Vázquez. The December 7 national referendum on whether to break up the state-owned oil refinery monopoly or allow it to take on private partners was seen as a test of political strength prior to the upcoming elections.

(MARTIN WEINSTEIN)

Supporters of a "yes" vote in a Uruguayan national referendum on whether to break up the state-owned petroleum monopoly demonstrate in Montevideo on December 7. More than half voted "yes," a sign of a lack of popular support for the government of Pres. Jorge Batlle Ibáñez.

UZBEKISTAN

Area: 447,400 sq km (172,700 sq mi)
Population (2003 est.): 25,640,000
Capital: Tashkent
Chief of state and head of government: President Islam Karimov, assisted by Prime Minister Otkir Sultonov

Uzbekistan's economy in 2003 showed little of the dynamism needed to lift the country out of the ranks of the poorer successor states to the U.S.S.R. In April the independent newspaper *Hurriyat* reported that between 500,000 and 700,000 Uzbek citizens had gone abroad to find work. A World Bank assessment of living standards that was published in July found that over a quarter of the population was living below the poverty line. After a reported drop of 22% in foreign investment in 2002, which made Uzbekistan the state with the lowest rate of foreign investment in the Commonwealth of Independent States, Pres. Islam Karimov issued a series of decrees that were ostensibly intended to liberalize the country's economy and make it more attractive to foreign investors. Karimov announced that small business would be the engine for economic development, but small businessmen reported that they were being discouraged by widespread corruption. A decree in March was supposed to loosen state control over private farmers, but at the end of October a nationwide organization of farmers said its members were still being told what to plant by local government officials.

Karimov regarded as a major triumph for his policy of gradual economic liberalization and minimal democratization the decision of the European Bank for Reconstruction and Development (EBRD) to hold the annual meeting of its board in Tashkent in May. The EBRD explained the choice as a means of encouraging Uzbekistan to improve its performance. Before the meeting international human rights groups soundly criticized the bank for appearing to ignore the human rights abuses committed by the Uzbek authorities; during the meeting some foreign participants lectured their Uzbek hosts on this issue, but critics complained that little was achieved beyond the setting of specific "benchmarks" that Uzbekistan had to meet in order for EBRD programs to continue. As the year continued, however, more and more citizens' groups picketed government institutions and demonstrated publicly in support of their specific demands.

Many of the popular protests involved demands for a stop to the imprisonment of practicing Muslims who were arrested on charges of seeking to overthrow the country's constitutional order by spreading the ideas of the international Islamic extremist party Hizb ut-Tahrir. There were also protests against the continuing use of torture by law-enforcement and prison officials, despite official Uzbek promises to stop the practice after the country was censured by the UN Commission on Human Rights in March. (BESS BROWN)

VANUATU

Area: 12,190 sq km (4,707 sq mi)
Population (2003 est.): 204,000
Capital: Vila
Chief of state: President John Bernard Bani
Head of government: Prime Minister Edward Natapei

The coalition government led by Prime Minister Edward Natapei remained in office during 2003 and, unusual for Vanuatu, seemed destined to complete its four-year term. Veteran politician and former prime minister Barak Sopé remained a controversial figure. Having been convicted of fraud and sentenced to a term of imprisonment of three years in 2002, Sopé was pardoned by Pres. John Bernard Bani on health grounds after having served only a few months of his sentence. The chief electoral officer then ruled that because of the pardon Sopé was eligible to stand as a candidate in the November 2003 by-election. In late November the government was challenged by a parliamentary motion of censure but survived with the assistance of a cabinet reshuffle. The sense of instability was exacerbated when Sopé was victorious in the by-election and returned to Parliament.

Under pressure from the Organisation for Economic Co-operation and Development, Vanuatu agreed to change some of its tax-haven laws and to ensure greater transparency and information sharing with other jurisdictions. These concessions were sufficient for Vanuatu's removal in May from the OECD list of uncooperative nations. In another move that threatened Vanuatu's tax-haven business, Canberra announced that it was investigating a number of Vanuatu tax-avoidance schemes used by Australian citizens.

Vanuatu contributed to the multinational Pacific police force sent to restore order in neighbouring Solomon Islands. Prime Minister Natapei attended the Japan-sponsored Pacific leaders meeting in Okinawa, visited New Caledonia on trade matters, and led a delegation to Paris. In May Vanuatu opened the world's first underwater post office, an event that provided an opportunity for divers to post waterproof postcards; a commemorative stamp was issued for the occasion. (BARRIE MACDONALD)

A postal worker in scuba gear mans the world's first underwater post office 3 m (10 ft) deep off Hideaway Island, Vanuatu, while a snorkeling customer uses the aquatic postbox.

VATICAN CITY STATE

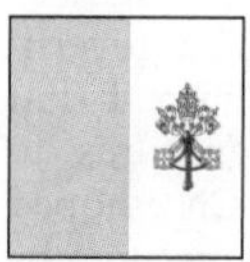

Area: 44 ha (109 ac)
Population (2003 est.): 900
Chief of state: (sovereign pontiff) Pope John Paul II
Head of administration: Secretary of State Angelo Cardinal Sodano, who heads a pontifical commission of five cardinals

On Oct. 16, 2003, 83-year-old Pope John Paul II celebrated the 25th anniversary of his papacy. Age and infirmity caused the press to speculate that he might step down soon, but the pope pledged to carry on through his lifelong term, and he continued to make pastoral visits. His journey to Croatia in June was his 100th visit outside Italian borders. During his pontificate the pope had seen the number of Roman Catholics increase from 775 million to more than 1 billion. In addition, the number of ordained priests was also rising.

The greatest rise in the number of Roman Catholics was in Africa. In addition to contributing directly to health care and education in some of Africa's poorest countries, the Vatican had lobbied successfully so that lifesaving pharmaceutical products could be made available to the world's poor at a low cost. This initiative was particularly beneficial to many African nations. The smallest percentage of the faithful were found in Asia, an area in which the Vatican continued to show a keen interest; during the year the pope appointed the first bishop ever to Mongolia. In Europe the Roman Catholic population in terms of percentages continued to decline. The long wave of secularization prompted the Vatican to push for the European Union to mention the Christian roots of Europe in the future EU constitution. The Roman Catholic Church was still very European, and though the College of Cardinals had experienced progressive internationalization from the 1960s onward, it was still dominated by Europeans. Indeed, many observers speculated that the next pope would be Italian, just as the majority of others had been.

(GREGORY O. SMITH)

VENEZUELA

Area: 916,445 sq km (353,841 sq mi)
Population (2003 est.): 25,699,000
Capital: Caracas
Head of state and government: President Hugo Chávez Frías

The general strike in Venezuela that began on Dec. 2, 2002, continued into early February 2003. Hundreds of thousands of middle- and working-class opponents of the government paraded through eastern Caracas day after day demanding the resignation of Pres. Hugo Chávez Frías. In the city's western zone, counterdemonstrators composed largely of the urban underclass marched in support of Chávez. While the two camps exchanged gunshots, there were few casualties, owing largely to the professionalism of the police and the National Guard. Similar

© Reuters NewMedia Inc./Corbis

Opinions about Venezuelan Pres. Hugo Chávez Frías further polarized in 2003. Here members of the armed women's group Carapaicas, which supports Chávez and a six-year presidential term, address the press at a clandestine location in Caracas in February.

demonstrations and counterdemonstrations occurred in Maracaibo (the second largest city) and in Puerto La Cruz (a city in northeastern Venezuela), but the interior cities generally remained calm. The failure by government opponents to mount their demonstrations outside the capital was critical to the government's survival.

Normalcy began to return in the second week of February, but the opposition continued to demand that Chávez step down. The president, however, was adamant that he would remain in office unless the opposition could obtain the number of signatures required—20% of voters—for forcing a recall election. From March through December politics in Venezuela revolved around determining the conditions under which valid signatures could be obtained.

The 1999 constitution states that an elected official can be removed by means of a recall election. In such an election those seeking to remove the official must obtain the same number of votes (plus one) as the number of votes that the official had received in the election that placed him in office (unless even more voters said no). There were no rules or regulations governing the collection of valid signatures to initiate recall elections until they were issued by the National Electoral Council (CNE) on September 25. The CNE gave opponents a relatively short period during which they could seek the 2.4 million signatures required for forcing the recall election.

The recall-signature-gathering event occurred in two phases. During the first, November 21–24, government supporters collected signatures that would authorize a recall election to replace 30 opposition deputies in the National Assembly. A week later, the opposition solicited signatures for the same purpose against 30 government deputies and President Chávez. International observers from the Organization of American States and the Carter Center confirmed that the signature-solicitation process in both instances was free and transparent. The government and the opposition claimed that they received sufficient signatures to justify a recall election. The CNE hoped to finish its review of the signatures by mid-January 2004.

The general strike and the recall efforts destabilized the economy as well as the polity. Venezuela's GDP contracted 29% in the first quarter of 2003, and even in the wake of normalization in the second and third quarters, economic contraction remained an abysmal 19%. Inflation for the same period topped 20%, the highest rate in Latin America. It was acknowledged that the general strike had cost the government $7 billion in lost revenue. Extreme poverty remained at about the same level that it had been during the administration of Rafael Caldera (1994–99), roughly 40%; and 70% of all Venezuelan households had incomes below the poverty line. The likely consequences of this dismal state of affairs for the government were disastrous. Therefore, in the fourth quarter Chávez increased fiscal expenditures, most of which went directly into salaries rather than into repairing or expanding the public infrastructure, which was deteriorating at an alarming rate.

The Chávez government continued to strengthen relations with Third World countries viewed as supportive of a multipolar world. At the Cancún, Mex., economic summit in September, Víctor Álvarez, Venezuela's chief trade negotiator, attacked the globalization agenda of the World Trade Organization. Relations with the U.S. government remained frosty, a reflection of Chávez's suspicion that Washington had encouraged the coup of April 11–13, 2002, that briefly removed him from power. Nevertheless, Venezuela continued to supply the U.S. with 1.5 million bbl of petroleum daily. Caracas even offered to increase production to 6 million bbl per day if the U.S. would provide Venezuela loan guarantees of $8 billion annually for five years. The administration of U.S. Pres. George W. Bush refused, having viewed the offer as a ploy to take advantage of uncertainties in the global petroleum market following the Iraq war. (DAVID J. MYERS)

VIETNAM

Area: 332,501 sq km (128,379 sq mi)
Population (2003 est.): 81,377,000
Capital: Hanoi
Chief of state: President Tran Duc Luong
Head of government: Prime Minister Phan Van Khai

Domestic affairs were dominated in 2003 by the largest corruption trial in postunification Vietnam. Court proceedings revealed that organized crime had infiltrated the Ho Chi Minh City police force and spread its influence to senior state and party officials. The scandal, known as the "Nam Cam" affair, took its name from the nickname of crime boss Truong Van Cam, its central figure.

In January the Vietnam Communist Party (VCP) Central Committee held its seventh plenum (second session). At the meeting Politburo member Truong Tan Sang was disciplined in connection with the Nam Cam affair, and Minister of Public Security Le Hong Anh was dismissed as director of the Inspection Commission. The plenum adopted four resolutions pertaining to strengthening national unity, ethnic minorities, religion, and legislative land reform.

In February Nam Cam and 154 of his associates went to trial on a range of charges including gambling, bribery, and murder. The proceedings were given wide coverage in the local media. In June Nam Cam and five associates were found guilty and sentenced to death by firing squad. Two others, expelled VCP Central Committee members Bui Quoc Huy and Tran Mai Hanh, were given prison terms of 4 and 10 years, respectively.

Sixty-nine defendants, including Nam Cam, appealed. The judges upheld five of the six death sentences, including that of Nam Cam. The court upheld the sentences of all former senior officials except for Tran Mai Hanh, whose 10-year sentence was reduced by one year.

In April the VCP reaffirmed its commitment to a policy that called for the rotation of officials after they had served three years in a post. Deputy ministers and their party equivalents were to be sent to provincial posts, and lower-level officials would be given assignments at district level. The purpose of this policy was to increase practical experience and to prevent cliques from forming. In October, in a move to clear deadwood from the VCP, it was announced that all party membership cards would have to be renewed. The eighth plenum of the Central Committee met in July and adopted a national-defense strategy and a salary-reform package.

During the year Vietnamese security forces continued their crackdown on political dissidents. Tran Dung Tien was arrested in January after urging the release of political prisoners. Nguyen Dan Que, a leading pro-democracy activist, and Pham Hong Son were arrested in March and June, respectively, for using the Internet to propagate their ideas. Son was later convicted on charges of espionage and sentenced to 13 years in prison, but an appeals court reduced the term to 5 years.

In April, as a conciliatory gesture, Prime Minister Phan Van Khai publicly met with Thich Huyen Quang, the aged leader of the banned Unified Buddhist Church of Vietnam (UBCV). In midyear the regime released from house arrest Thich Quang Do, the head of the Institute for the Propagation of the Dharma. Government officials approached Quang with an offer of a position in the state-sponsored Vietnam Buddhist Church, but Quang turned it down.

In October Quang convened a public meeting of the UBCV and announced plans to restructure the organization to include representatives from the overseas Vietnamese community. These resolutions were conveyed to UBCV supporters meeting in Australia. When Quang and a group of monks attempted to travel from Binh Dinh province to Ho Chi Minh City, provincial security police intervened. Quang was returned to exile, and Do was again placed under house arrest. Police officials charged them with undermining national unity and illegally seeking assistance from abroad.

Relations with the United States took an unexpected turn during the year when Vietnam signaled its interest in expanding military relations. Gen. Pham Van Tra, the minister of national defense, visited Washington in November to discuss future cooperation with his U.S. counterpart, Secretary of Defense Donald Rumsfeld.

(CARLYLE A. THAYER)

YEMEN

Area: 555,000 sq km (214,300 sq mi)
Population (2003 est.): 20,010,000
Capital: Sanaa
Chief of state: President Maj. Gen. ʿAli ʿAbdallah Salih
Head of government: Prime Minister ʿAbd al-Qadir al-Ba Jamal

On April 27, 2003, Yemen held its third national parliamentary election since the introduction in 1990 of a multiparty democratic system. Though the Yemeni Socialist Party (YSP), which represented southern constituents, had boycotted the 1997 election, it participated this time. Nevertheless, the election gave the General People's Congress (GPC) of Pres. Maj. Gen. ʿAli ʿAbdallah Salih an increase in its legislative majority to 238 of the 301 seats. The GPC was helped in part by competition between the 21 opposition parties and independents. The YSP won only eight seats. It was noteworthy that 40% of the registered voters were women, one of the highest percentages in the Arab world.

In May, President Salih pardoned four politicians who had led an attempted southern secession in 1994; the four had been condemned to death for treason after the 1994 civil war and had been living in exile. As a symbol of north-south reconciliation, Salih named one of them his special adviser.

The economy was bolstered by the $2.3 billion in economic support that had been pledged for Yemen at a 2002 meeting in Paris between Yemeni government officials and donor countries. Yemen was attempting to hold down spending and comply with IMF recommendations.

(WILLIAM A. RUGH)

ZAMBIA

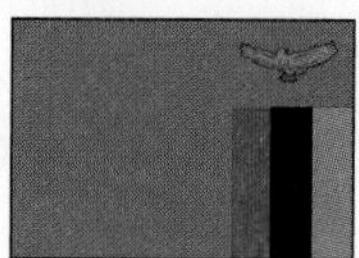

Area: 752,612 sq km (290,585 sq mi)
Population (2003 est.): 10,812,000
Capital: Lusaka
Head of state and government: President Levy Mwanawasa

Zambia's Pres. Levy Mwanawasa continued to pursue his individual political agenda in 2003. In February he took the unusual step of appointing a number of opposition party members to his cabinet, claiming that this would be an important development in Zambia's history. His equally controversial appointment of Nevers Mumba as vice president in May was immediately challenged on the ground that the appointment was unconstitutional. Meanwhile, the challenge to Mwanawasa's own election to the presidency was still before the Supreme Court. Criticism of the president and his methods persisted throughout the year, and a conference organized by Mwanawasa in October to try to ease the situation was boycotted by opposition parties.

The door was opened for charges of corruption to be brought against former president Frederick Chiluba in February when his appeal against the lifting of his presidential immunity from prosecution was rejected. At once he was charged with 59 counts of "theft by public servant," and in August more counts were added as he was accused of having misappropriated $26.7 million of public money. Chiluba denied the allegations. On the other hand, the moral standing of Zambia's respected first

With inflation steeply rising—and having reached well over 400% a year—even the new Z$1,000 bill (worth about U.S.$1.23 on October 1), the largest note available, was not enough to pay for a standard loaf of bread.

president (1964–91), Kenneth Kaunda, was further enhanced in January when President Mwanawasa awarded him the Grand Order of the Eagle.

The strength of public feeling, together with the mixed fortunes that the country had experienced when attempting to privatize government assets, made Mwanawasa determined to keep banking, electricity, and telephone companies in government hands. The uneven results of copper privatization reinforced his decision. The sale of the Chambishi Copper Mines had been a success, with the mines coming into full production in June. By contrast, negotiations leading to the sale of the bankrupt Roan Antelope Mining Corp. and the Konkola Copper Mines proved to be lengthy affairs.

An acute shortage of petroleum presented a serious obstacle to all development. In March the war in Iraq put an end to hopes of a deal to improve the situation, and approaches to South Africa met with a cool reception because of Zambia's lack of funds.

In June the announcement that the president, vice president, and members of the cabinet were to take a 30% pay cut met with the approval of the IMF and World Bank. On August 11, however, civil servants went on strike to demand the payment of the 40% increase in their housing allowance that they believed had been agreed earlier in the year.

There was a little movement in the agricultural sector. Coffee exports were rising, and white farmers, refugees from Zimbabwe, were beginning to produce quantities of tobacco. A new project to grow sugar was launched in August. In April the U.S. Department of State made a welcome grant of $42.6 million to help in the fight against AIDS and tuberculosis. (KENNETH INGHAM)

ZIMBABWE

Area: 390,757 sq km (150,872 sq mi)
Population (2003 est.): 11,719,000
Capital: Harare
Head of state and government: President Robert Mugabe

Events in Zimbabwe in 2003 echoed those of the previous year. In February both Pres. Robert Mugabe and opposition leader Morgan Tsvangirai rejected a deal approved by both the British and the South African governments that called for Mugabe to resign and for a government of unity to be instituted, with Emmerson Mnangagwa, the speaker of the House of Assembly, as president.

On February 3 the hearing of a treason charge against Tsvangirai opened in court but was overshadowed when French Pres. Jacques Chirac flouted the EU ban on travel to Europe by members of the Zimbabwean government by inviting Mugabe to attend a Franco-African summit in Paris. Only a few days later, South African Pres. Thabo Mbeki accused Britain of waging an international campaign against Zimbabwe and urged that the suspension of the country from membership of the Commonwealth be lifted so that Mugabe could attend a summit meeting in Nigeria in December. Pres. Olusegun Obasanjo of Nigeria, who would host the meeting, echoed Mbeki's appeal. These actions won approval in many African countries, which resented what they saw as British neocolonialism, but a majority of Commonwealth countries upheld the suspension.

Violent protests by supporters of the opposition Movement for Democratic Change (MDC) in March were harshly suppressed by security forces. The MDC vice president, Gibson Sibanda, was arrested, as was Paul Themba Nyathi, another leading member of the party. In April the Roman Catholic Church in Zimbabwe condemned the government's abuse of power. In May another British mediation initiative, working through the presidents of Malawi, Nigeria, and South Africa, was as unsuccessful as earlier attempts had been.

What Tsvangirai described as a "final push" to oust Mugabe in June resulted in a widely observed five-day stay-at-home. The large-scale marches that had been planned to coincide with the strike failed, however, because of overwhelming security forces, which acted with great severity against the few protesters who appeared. A further charge of treason was brought against Tsvangirai for having disregarded an order banning the demonstration.

On June 6 the IMF suspended Zimbabwe's membership on the grounds of noncooperation. The price of fuel, which had risen by more than 300% in April, increased by a further 160% in August and another 70% in October. In July the price of corn (maize) meal, the staple diet of most Zimbabweans, rose by 500%. In August the government ordered the UN to hand over its famine-relief operations, and when the order was ignored, UN food-distribution offices in the provinces were closed.

The government received a shock in September when the MDC won a resounding victory in urban local elections. In spite of the efforts of a number of judges who refused to submit to government intervention, the *Daily News,* the only remaining independent newspaper, was closed by police. In November, however, Tsvangirai's challenge of Mugabe's election as president opened in court. In December, after the Commonwealth extended Zimbabwe's suspension, Mugabe responded by canceling the country's membership. (KENNETH INGHAM)

Alexander, Steve. Freelance Technology Writer. •COMPUTERS AND INFORMATION SYSTEMS

Allaby, Michael. Freelance Writer. Author of *Encyclopedia of Weather and Climate* and *Basics of Environmental Science.* •BIOGRAPHIES *(in part);* THE ENVIRONMENT: *Environmental Issues; International Activities*

Allan, J.A. Professor of Geography, School of Oriental and African Studies, University of London. Author of *The Middle East Water Question: Hydropolitics and the Global Economy.* •WORLD AFFAIRS: *Libya*

Anam, Mahfuz. Editor and Publisher, *The Daily Star,* Bangladesh. •WORLD AFFAIRS: *Bangladesh*

Andrejevich, Milan. Adjunct Professor of Communications and History, Valparaiso University and Indiana University Northwest; Team Leader, Scholars Initiative on the Former Yugoslavia. Author of *The Sandžak: A Perspective of Serb-Muslim Relations.* •BIOGRAPHIES *(in part);* WORLD AFFAIRS: *Bosnia and Herzegovina; Serbia and Montenegro*

Anthony, John Duke. President and CEO, National Council on U.S.-Arab Relations; Secretary, U.S. Gulf Cooperation Council Corporate Cooperation Committee; Consultant to U.S. Departments of Defense and State. •WORLD AFFAIRS: *Oman; Qatar*

Appave, Gervais. Director, Migration Policy and Research Programme, International Organization for Migration. •SOCIAL PROTECTION: *International Migration*

Archibald, John J. Retired Feature Writer, *St. Louis* (Mo.) *Post-Dispatch.* Member of the American Bowling Congress Hall of Fame. •SPORTS AND GAMES: *Bowling:* U.S. Tenpins

Armijo, Ricardo. Freelance Editor and Writer; Contributor to *Contratiempo Magazine.* •LITERATURE: *Spanish:* Latin America

Ash, John Beaumont. Independent Writer on South and Southeast Asia. •WORLD AFFAIRS: *Cambodia; Laos; Thailand*

Aurora, Vincent. Lecturer in French and Romance Philology, Columbia University, New York City. Author of *Michel Leiris' Failles: immobile in mobili.* •LITERATURE: *French:* France

Bahry, Louay. Adjunct Professor of Political Science, University of Tennessee. Author of *The Baghdad Bahn.* •BIOGRAPHIES *(in part);* WORLD AFFAIRS: *Bahrain; Iraq; Kuwait*

Balaban, Avraham. Professor of Modern Hebrew Literature, University of Florida. Author of *Shiv'ah* ("Mourning"). •LITERATURE: *Jewish:* Hebrew

Bamia, Aida A. Professor of Arabic Language and Literature, University of Florida. Author of *The Graying of the Raven: Cultural and Sociopolitical Significance of Algerian Folk Poetry.* Associate Editor of *Encyclopedia of African Literature, 2003.* •LITERATURE: *Arabic*

Barrett, David B. Research Professor of Missiometrics, Regent University, Virginia Beach, Va. Author of *World Christian Encyclopedia* and *Schism and Renewal in Africa.* Coauthor of *World Christian Trends, AD* 30–*AD* 2200: Interpreting the Annual Christian Megacensus. •RELIGION: *Tables (in part)*

Baru, Sanjaya. Chief Editor, *The Financial Express,* India. Author of *The Political Economy of Indian Sugar: State Intervention and Structural Change.* •WORLD AFFAIRS: *India*

Bauer, Patricia. Assistant Editor, Encyclopædia Britannica. •CALENDAR; DISASTERS; OBITUARIES *(in part)*

Beckwith, David C. Vice President, National Cable Television Association. •WORLD AFFAIRS: *United States; United States:* State and Local Affairs

Benedetti, Laura. Laura and Gaetano De Sole Associate Professor of Contemporary Italian Culture, Georgetown University, Washington, D.C. Author of *La sconfitta di Diana: un percorso per la Gerusalemme liberata.* •LITERATURE: *Italian*

Bernstein, Ellen. Freelance Writer and Editor, specializing in health and medicine, Chicago. •HEALTH AND DISEASE; WORLD AFFAIRS: *Canada:* Sidebar

Bird, Thomas E. Professor of European Languages, the Jewish Studies Program, Queens College, City University of New York. Coeditor of *Hryhorij Savyč Skovoroda: An Anthology of Critical Articles.* •LITERATURE: *Jewish:* Yiddish

Bonds, John B. Visiting Assistant Professor of History, The Citadel, Charleston, S.C. Author of *Bipartisan Strategy: Selling the Marshall Plan.* •SPORTS AND GAMES: *Sailing (Yachting)*

Bradsher, Henry S. Foreign Affairs Analyst, Author, and Lecturer. •WORLD AFFAIRS: *Philippines*

Brady, Conor. Editor Emeritus, *The Irish Times,* Dublin. •WORLD AFFAIRS: *Ireland*

Brecher, Kenneth. Professor of Astronomy and Physics; Director, Science and Mathematics Education Center, Boston University. •PHYSICAL SCIENCES: *Astronomy*

Brockmann, Stephen. Associate Professor of German, Carnegie Mellon University, Pittsburgh, Pa. Editor of *The Brecht Yearbook.* Author of *Literature and German Reunification.* •LITERATURE: *German*

Brokopp, John G. Media Relations Consultant, National Jockey Club; Syndicated casino gambling columnist. Author of *Thrifty Gambling* and *Insider's Guide to Internet Gambling: Your Sourcebook for Safe and Profitable Gambling.* •SPORTS AND GAMES: *Equestrian Sports:* Thoroughbred Racing: *United States*

Brown, Bess. Consultant on Central Asia, Munich, Ger. Author of *Authoritarianism in the New States of Central Asia.* •BIOGRAPHIES *(in part);* WORLD AFFAIRS: *Kazakhstan; Kyrgyzstan; Tajikistan; Turkmenistan; Uzbekistan*

Buchan, David. Foreign Editorial Writer, *Financial Times,* London. Author of *The Single Market and Tomorrow's Europe: A Progress Report from the European Commission.* •BIOGRAPHIES *(in part);* WORLD AFFAIRS: *France*

Bungs, Dzintra. Senior Research Fellow, Latvian Institute of International Affairs, Riga. Author of *The Baltic States: Problems and Prospects of Membership in the European Union.* •WORLD AFFAIRS: *Latvia*

Burks, Ardath W. Professor Emeritus of Asian Studies, Rutgers University, New Brunswick, N.J. Author of *Japan: A Postindustrial Power.* •WORLD AFFAIRS: *Japan*

Burns, Erik T. Bureau Chief, Dow Jones Newswires, Lisbon. •WORLD AFFAIRS: *Portugal*

Byrne, Justin. Researcher, Center for Advanced Study in the Social Sciences, Instituto Juan March de Estudios e Investigaciones, Madrid. •WORLD AFFAIRS: *Spain*

Cadoux, Charles. Professor of Public Law, University of Aix-Marseille III, Aix-en-Provence, France. •WORLD AFFAIRS: *Dependent States:* Indian Ocean and Southeast Asia; Sidebar; *East Timor*

Cafferty, Bernard. Associate Editor, *British Chess Magazine.* Author of *The Soviet Championships.* •SPORTS AND GAMES: *Chess*

Calhoun, David R. Freelance Editor and Writer. •*Architecture:* Sidebar; BIOGRAPHIES *(in part)*

Campbell, Robert. Architect and Architecture Critic. Author of *Cityscapes of Boston: An American City Through Time.* •ARCHITECTURE AND CIVIL ENGINEERING: *Architecture*

Caplan, Marla. Graduate Assistant, International Center of Photography, New York City. • ART AND ART EXHIBITIONS: *Photography*

Carter, Robert W. Journalist. •SPORTS AND GAMES: *Equestrian Sports:* Steeplechasing; Thoroughbred Racing: *International*

Chappell, Duncan. President, Mental Health Review Tribunal, Sydney, Australia. Author of *Violence at Work.* •LAW, CRIME, AND LAW ENFORCEMENT: *Crime*

Cheadle, Bruce. Journalist, Canadian Press news agency. •SPORTS AND GAMES: *Curling*

Cheuse, Alan. Writing Faculty, English Department, George Mason University, Fairfax, Va.; Book Commentator, National Public Radio. Author of *The Light Possessed* and *Listening to the Page: Adventures in Reading and Writing.* •LITERATURE: *English:* United States

Chua, Lee Hoong. Features Editor, *The Straits Times,* Singapore. •WORLD AFFAIRS: *Singapore*

Cioroslan, Dragomir. National Team Coach, U.S.A. Weightlifting, Inc.; Executive Board Member, International Weightlifting Federation. Coauthor of *Banish Your Belly.* •SPORTS AND GAMES: *Weight Lifting*

Clark, David Draper. Editor in Chief, *World Literature Today.* •LITERATURE: *English:* Other Literature in English

Clark, Janet H. Editor, Independent Analyst, and Writer on economic and financial topics. •NOBEL PRIZES *(in part)*

Coate, Roger A. Professor of International Organization; Director, Walker Institute of International Studies, University of South Carolina. Coauthor of *The United Nations and Changing World Politics.* •WORLD AFFAIRS: *United Nations*

Coller, Ken. President, West Seattle Productions. •SPORTS AND GAMES: *Wrestling:* Sumo

Collins, Nigel. Editor in Chief, *The Ring, KO, World Boxing,* and *Boxing 2003.* •BIOGRAPHIES *(in part);* SPORTS AND GAMES: *Boxing*

Cosgrave, Bronwyn. Author, Journalist. Author of *Costume and Fashion: A Complete History.* •BIOGRAPHIES *(in part);* FASHIONS

Coveney, Michael. Theatre Critic, *The Daily Mail.* Author of *The Andrew Lloyd Webber Story* and others. •PERFORMING ARTS: *Theatre:* Great Britain and Ireland

Craine, Anthony G. Writer. •BIOGRAPHIES *(in part)*

Crampton, Richard J. Professor of East European History, University of Oxford. Author of *A Concise History of Bulgaria* and *The Balkans Since the Second World War.* •WORLD AFFAIRS: *Bulgaria*

Crisp, Brian F. Associate Professor of Political Science, University of Arizona. Author of *Democratic Institutional Design.* •WORLD AFFAIRS: *Colombia*

Cullen, Dan. Director, American Booksellers Association, Information Department. •MEDIA AND PUBLISHING: *Book Publishing* (U.S.)

Curwen, Peter. Professor of Telecommunications, Strathclyde University, Glasgow, Scot. Author of *The U.K. Publishing Industry* and others. •MEDIA AND PUBLISHING: *Book Publishing* (international)

Cuttino, John Charles. Lyndon B. Johnson School of Public Affairs, University of Texas at Austin. Coauthor of *The Impacts of U.S.–Latin American Trade on the Southwest's Economy and Transportation System: An Assessment of Impact Methodologies.* •WORLD AFFAIRS: *Brazil*

Dailey, Meghan. Art Historian and Critic, New York City. •ART AND ART EXHIBITIONS: *Art; Art Exhibitions*

Deeb, Marius K. Professor of Middle East Studies, SAIS, Johns Hopkins University, Washington, D.C. Author of *Syria's Terrorist War on Lebanon and the Peace Process* and others. •WORLD AFFAIRS: *Egypt; Jordan*

de la Barre, Kenneth. Fellow, Arctic Institute of North America; Research Associate, Yukon College, Northern Research Institute. •WORLD AFFAIRS: *Arctic Regions*

Denselow, Robin. Correspondent, BBC Television's *Newsnight.* Author of *When the Music's Over: The Story of Political Pop.* •PERFORMING ARTS: *Music:* Popular (international)

Dietz, Henry A. Professor, Department of Government, University of Texas at Austin. •WORLD AFFAIRS: *Peru*

Dooling, Dave. Outreach Education Officer, National Solar Observatory, Sacramento Peak, New Mexico. Coauthor of *Engineering Tomorrow.* •PHYSICAL SCIENCES: *Space Exploration*

Dowd, Siobhan. Columnist, *Literary Review* (London); *Glimmer Train* (U.S.). Author of *This Prison Where I Live* and *Roads of the Roma.* •BIOGRAPHIES *(in part)*

Ebeling, Mary F.E. Department of Sociology, University of Surrey, Guildford, Eng. •WORLD AFFAIRS: *Burundi; Comoros; Rwanda; Seychelles*

Ehringer, Gavin Forbes. Sports Columnist, *Rocky Mountain News* and *Western Horseman.* Author of *Rodeo Legends.* •SPORTS AND GAMES: *Rodeo*

Eisenberg, Andrew. Department of Music, Ethnomusicology Program, Columbia University, New York City. •WORLD AFFAIRS: *Djibouti; Ghana; Liberia; Mauritius; Nigeria; Sierra Leone*

Erikson, Daniel P. Director, the Cuba Program, Inter-American Dialogue, Washington, D.C. •WORLD AFFAIRS: *Cuba*

Esteban, Verónica. Journalist and Bilingual Editor. •LITERATURE: *Spanish:* Spain

Fagan, Brian. Professor of Anthropology, University of California, Santa Barbara. Author of *The Little Ice Age: How Climate Made History, 1300–1850; Floods, Famines, and Emperors: El Niño and the Fate of Civilizations; The Long Summer: How Climate Changed Civilization.* •ANTHROPOLOGY AND ARCHAEOLOGY: *Archaeology:* Western Hemisphere

Farr, David M.L. Professor Emeritus of History, Carleton University, Ottawa. •BIOGRAPHIES *(in part);* WORLD AFFAIRS: *Canada*

Fealy, Greg. Research Fellow in Indonesian Politics, Research School of Pacific and Asian Studies, Australian National University, Canberra. Author of *The Release of Indonesia's Political Prisoners: Domestic Versus Foreign Policy, 1975–1979.* •WORLD AFFAIRS: *Indonesia*

Fendell, Robert J. Freelance Writer on automobiles and racing. Author of *The Encyclopedia of Auto Racing Greats.* •SPORTS AND GAMES: *Automobile Racing:* U.S. Auto Racing *(in part)*

Fisher, Martin. Editor, *Oryx;* Coeditor, *The Natural History of Oman: A Festschrift for Michael Gallagher.* •THE ENVIRONMENT: *Wildlife Conservation*

Fisher, Sharon. Central European Specialist, Global Insight, Inc., Washington, D.C. •WORLD AFFAIRS: *Czech Republic; Slovakia*

Flink, Steve. Senior Correspondent, *Tennis Week.* Author of *The Greatest Tennis Matches of the Twentieth Century.* •SPORTS AND GAMES: *Tennis*

Flores, Ramona Monette Sargan. Professor, Department of Speech Communication and Theatre Arts, University of the Philippines, Quezon City; Freelance Journalist. •MEDIA AND PUBLISHING: *Radio* (international); *Television* (international)

Follett, Christopher. Denmark Correspondent, *The Times;* Editor, *Copenhagen This Week.* Author of *Fodspor paa Cypern.* •WORLD AFFAIRS: *Denmark*

Ford, Brian J. Biologist, Author, and Lecturer. Author of *The Future of Food.* •HEALTH AND DISEASE: *Special Report:* What's Next After SARS?

Fridovich-Keil, Judith L. Associate Professor, Department of Human Genetics, Emory University School of Medicine, Atlanta, Ga. •LIFE SCIENCES: *Molecular Biology and Genetics*

Fuller, Elizabeth. Editor, *Newsline,* Radio Free Europe/Radio Liberty, Prague. •WORLD AFFAIRS: *Armenia; Azerbaijan; Georgia*

Furmonavičius, Darius. Postdoctoral Research Fellow, Baltic Research Unit, Department of European Studies, University of Bradford, Eng. •BIOGRAPHIES *(in part);* WORLD AFFAIRS: *Lithuania*

Gallagher, Tom. Professor of Ethnic Peace and Conflict, University of Bradford, Eng. Author of *The Balkans After the Cold War: From Tyranny to Tragedy* and others. •WORLD AFFAIRS: *Moldova; Romania*

Ganado, Albert. Lawyer; Chairman, Malta National Archives Advisory Committee; Vice President, Malta Historical Society. Coauthor of *A Study in Depth of 143 Maps Representing the Great Siege of Malta of 1565.* •WORLD AFFAIRS: *Malta*

Garrod, Mark. Golf Correspondent, PA Sport, U.K. •SPORTS AND GAMES: *Golf*

Gaughan, Thomas. Library Director, Muhlenberg College, Allentown, Pa. •LIBRARIES AND MUSEUMS: *Libraries*

George, Nicholas. Stockholm Correspondent, *Financial Times.* •WORLD AFFAIRS: *Sweden*

Gibbons, J. Whitfield. Professor of Ecology, Savannah River Ecology Laboratory, University of Georgia. Coauthor of *Ecoviews: Snakes, Snails and Environmental Tales.* •LIFE SCIENCES: *Zoology*

Gill, Martin J. Executive Director, Food Certification (Scotland) Ltd. •AGRICULTURE AND FOOD SUPPLIES: *Fisheries*

Gobbie, Donn. CEO, American Badminton League. •SPORTS AND GAMES: *Badminton*

Graham, John W. Chair, Canadian Foundation for the Americas; Former Canadian Ambassador. •WORLD AFFAIRS: *Dominican Republic; Suriname*

Grenda, Iwona. Senior Lecturer in English, the Faculty of Law and Administration, Adam Mickiewicz University, Poznan, Pol. •WORLD AFFAIRS: *Poland*

Greskovic, Robert. Dance Writer, *The Wall Street Journal.* Author of *Ballet 101.* •PERFORMING ARTS: *Dance:* North America

Griffiths, A.R.G. Associate Professor in History, Flinders University of South Australia. Author of *Contemporary Australia* and *Beautiful Lies.* •WORLD AFFAIRS: *Australia; Nauru; Palau; Papua New Guinea*

Guthridge, Guy G. Manager, Antarctic Information Program, U.S. National Science Foundation. •WORLD AFFAIRS: *Antarctica*

Haddad, Mahmoud. Associate Professor of History, the University of Balamand, Lebanon. Contributor to *Altruism and Imperialism: Western Cultural and Religious Missions in the Middle East.* •WORLD AFFAIRS: *Lebanon; Saudi Arabia*

Halman, Talat Sait. Professor and Chairman, Department of Turkish Literature, Bilkent University, Ankara, Turkey. Author of *Aklın Yolu Bindir.* •LITERATURE: *Turkish*

Hammer, William R. Professor and Chair, Department of Geology, Augustana College, Rock Island, Ill. Author of *Gondwana Dinosaurs from the Jurassic of Antarctica.* •LIFE SCIENCES: *Paleontology*

Helm, Toby. Chief Political Correspondent, *The Daily Telegraph.* •WORLD AFFAIRS: *European Union*

Henry, Alan. Grand Prix Editor, *Autocar* (London); Motor Racing Correspondent, *The Guardian.* Author of *50 Years of World Championship Grand Prix Motor Racing* and *Four Seasons at Ferrari: The Lauda Years.* •SPORTS AND GAMES: *Automobile Racing:* Grand Prix Racing

Hinman, Janele M. Assistant Account Executive, Crowley Webb & Associates. •SPORTS AND GAMES: *Bobsleigh, Skeleton, and Luge:* Luge

Hobbs, Greg. Senior Writer, *AFL Record.* Author of *One Hundred and Twenty-Five Years of the Melbourne Demons.* •SPORTS AND GAMES: *Football:* Australian

Hoffman, Dean A. Executive Editor, *Hoof Beats.* Author of *The Hambletonian: America's Trotting Classic.* •SPORTS AND GAMES: *Equestrian Sports:* Harness Racing

Hollar, Sherman. Associate Editor, Encyclopædia Britannica. •BIOGRAPHIES *(in part);* OBITUARIES *(in part)*

Homel, David. Freelance Writer; Lecturer, Concordia University, Montreal. Author of *The Speaking Cure: A Novel* and others. •LITERATURE: *French:* Canada

Hope, Thomas W. Owner, Hope Reports, Inc.; Former Film Producer. Contributor to *Encyclopedia of Imaging Science and Technology.* •PERFORMING ARTS: *Motion Pictures:* Nontheatrical Films

Hosch, William L. Editor, Encyclopædia Britannica. •BIOGRAPHIES: *(in part)*

Hu, Xiaobo. Associate Professor of Political Science, Clemson (S.C.) University. Coeditor of *China After Jiang.* •WORLD AFFAIRS: *China; Taiwan*

Hussainmiya, B.A. Senior Lecturer, Department of History, University of Brunei Darussalam. Author of *The Brunei Constitution of 1959: An Inside History.* •WORLD AFFAIRS: *Brunei*

IEIS. International Economic Information Services. •ECONOMIC AFFAIRS: *World Economy; Stock Markets* (international)

Ingham, Kenneth. Emeritus Professor of History, University of Bristol, Eng. Author of *Politics in Modern Africa: The Uneven Tribal Dimension* and others. •WORLD AFFAIRS: *Angola; Congo, Democratic Republic of the; Kenya; Malawi; Mozambique; Sudan, The; Tanzania; Uganda; Zambia; Zimbabwe*

Isaacson, Lanae Hjortsvang. Editor, *Nordic Women Writers.* •LITERATURE: *Danish*

Iyob, Ruth. Associate Professor of Political Science, University of Missouri at St. Louis; Fellow, Center for International Studies. Contributor to *African Foreign Policies: Power and Process.* •WORLD AFFAIRS: *Eritrea*

Jamail, Milton. Lecturer, Department of Government, University of Texas at Austin. Author of *Full Count: Inside Cuban Baseball.* •SPORTS AND GAMES: *Baseball:* Latin America

Joffé, George. Research Fellow, Centre of International Studies, University of Cambridge; Visiting Professor, Department of Geography, King's College, University of London. Editor, *Jordan in Transition.* •WORLD AFFAIRS: *Algeria; Morocco; Tunisia*

Johnson, Steve. Television Critic, *Chicago Tribune.* •MEDIA AND PUBLISHING: *Radio* (U.S.); *Television* (U.S.)

Johnson, Todd M. Director, Center for the Study of Global Christianity. Coauthor of *World Christian Encyclopedia.* •RELIGION: *Tables (in part)*

Joireman, Sandra F. Associate Professor of Politics and International Relations, Wheaton (Ill.) College. Author of *Property Rights and Political Development in Ethiopia and Eritrea.* •WORLD AFFAIRS: *Ethiopia*

Jones, David G.C. Tutor, Department of Continuing Education, University of Aberystwyth, Wales. Author of *Atomic Physics.* •PHYSICAL SCIENCES: *Physics*

Jones, Mark P. Associate Professor of Political Science, Michigan State University. Author of *Electoral Laws and the Survival of Presidential Democracies.* •BIOGRAPHIES *(in part);* WORLD AFFAIRS: *Argentina*

Kanduza, Ackson M. Associate Professor, Department of History, University of Swaziland. Author of *Political Economy of Democratisation in Swaziland.* •WORLD AFFAIRS: *Swaziland*

Kapp, Clare. Freelance Journalist; Contributor to *The Lancet.* •WORLD AFFAIRS: *Switzerland*

Karimi-Hakkak, Ahmad. Professor of Persian Languages and Literature, University of Washington. Author of *Recasting Persian Poetry: Scenarios of Poetic Modernity in Iran.* •LITERATURE: *Persian*

Karns, Margaret P. Professor of Political Science, University of Dayton, Ohio. Coauthor of *The United Nations in the Post-Cold War Era.* •WORLD AFFAIRS: *Multinational and Regional Organizations*

Kazamaru, Yoshihiko. Literary Critic. •LITERATURE: *Japanese*

Kelling, George H. Lieutenant Colonel, U.S. Army (ret.). Author of *Countdown to Rebellion: British Policy in Cyprus 1939–1955.* •BIOGRAPHIES *(in part);* WORLD AFFAIRS: *Cyprus*

Kellner, Peter. Chairman, YouGov Ltd. Author of *The New Mutualism* and others. •BIOGRAPHIES *(in part);* MEDIA AND PUBLISHING: *Special Report:* The Media Go to War; WORLD AFFAIRS: *United Kingdom*

Knox, Paul. International Affairs Columnist, *The Globe and Mail,* Toronto. •BIOGRAPHIES *(in part);* WORLD AFFAIRS: *Bolivia; Ecuador*

Kobliner, Beth. Journalist. Author of *Get a Financial Life.* •ECONOMIC AFFAIRS: *Stock Markets:* Canada, U.S.

Krause, Stefan. Freelance Political Analyst, Athens. •WORLD AFFAIRS: *Greece; Macedonia*

Kuiper, Kathleen. Senior Editor, Encyclopædia Britannica. Editor, *Merriam-Webster's Encyclopedia of Literature.* •OBITUARIES *(in part)*

Kuptsch, Christiane. Research Officer, International Institute for Labour Studies, International Labour Office. Coeditor of *Social Security at the Dawn of the 21st Century.* •SOCIAL PROTECTION (international)

Lamb, Kevin M. Health and Medical Writer, *Dayton* (Ohio) *Daily News.* Author of *Quarterbacks, Nickelbacks & Other Loose Change.* •SPORTS AND GAMES: *Football:* Canadian, U.S.

Lawler, Nancy Ellen. Professor Emeritus, Oakton Community College, Des Plaines, Ill. Author of *Soldiers, Airmen, Spies, and Whisperers: The Gold Coast in World War II* and others. •WORLD AFFAIRS: *Benin; Burkina Faso; Cameroon; Central African Republic; Congo, Republic of the; Côte d'Ivoire; Gabon; Guinea; Mali; Mauritania; Niger; Senegal; Togo*

Lawson, Fred H. Professor of Government, Mills College, Oakland, Calif. Author of *Why Syria Goes to War.* •WORLD AFFAIRS: *Syria*

Le Comte, Douglas. Meteorologist, Climate Prediction Center, National Oceanic and Atmospheric Administration. •EARTH SCIENCES: *Meteorology and Climate*

Legassick, Martin. Professor of History, University of the Western Cape, Bellville, S.Af. Author of *Skeletons in the Cupboard: South African Museums and the Trade in Human Remains 1907–1917.* •WORLD AFFAIRS: *South Africa*

Levy, Michael I. Associate Editor, Encyclopædia Britannica. •BIOGRAPHIES *(in part)*

Lindstrom, Sieg. Managing Editor, *Track & Field News.* •BIOGRAPHIES *(in part);* SPORTS AND GAMES: *Track and Field Sports (Athletics)*

Litweiler, John. Jazz Critic. Author of *The Freedom Principle: Jazz After 1958* and *Ornette Coleman: A Harmolodic Life.* •BIOGRAPHIES *(in part);* OBITUARIES *(in part);* PERFORMING ARTS: *Music:* Jazz

Logan, Robert G. Sports Journalist. Author of *Bob Logan's Tales from Chicago Sports: Cubs, Bulls, Bears, and Other Animals* and others. •SPORTS AND GAMES: *Basketball:* United States

Longmore, Andrew. Senior Sports Writer, *Sunday Times;* Former Assistant Editor, *The Cricketer.* Author of *The Complete Guide to Cycling.* •BIOGRAPHIES *(in part);* SPORTS AND GAMES: *Cricket; Cricket:* Sidebar

Luck, Edward C. Professor of Practice in International and Public Affairs and Director, Center on International Organization, School of International and Public Affairs, Columbia University, New York City. Author of *Mixed Messages: American Politics and International Organization, 1919–1999.* •WORLD AFFAIRS: *Special Report:* What Ails the UN Security Council?

Lufkin, Martha B.G. Legal Correspondent, *The Art Newspaper;* Attorney at Law, Lincoln, Mass. •LIBRARIES AND MUSEUMS: *Museums*

Luling, Virginia. Independent Researcher. Author of *Somali Sultanate: The Geledi City-State over 150 Years.* •WORLD AFFAIRS: *Somalia*

Lundin, Immi. Freelance Journalist and Literary Critic. •LITERATURE: *Swedish*

Macdonald, Barrie. Professor of History, Massey University, Palmerston, N.Z. •WORLD AFFAIRS: *Dependent States:* Pacific; *Fiji; Kiribati; Marshall Islands; Micronesia, Federated States of; Samoa; Solomon Islands; Tonga; Tuvalu; Vanuatu*

Macdonald, Stuart. Lecturer in Law, University of Southampton, Eng. •LAW, CRIME, AND LAW ENFORCEMENT: *Death Penalty*

Maguire, Robert. Director, Trinity College Haiti Program, Washington, D.C. •WORLD AFFAIRS: *Haiti*

Malik, Mohan. Professor, Asia-Pacific Center for Security Studies, Honolulu. •WORLD AFFAIRS: *Myanmar (Burma)*

Manghnani, Murli H. Professor of Geophysics, University of Hawaii at Manoa, Honolulu. •EARTH SCIENCES: *Geophysics*

Mango, Andrew. Foreign Affairs Analyst. Author of *Atatürk: The Biography of the Founder of Modern Turkey* and *Turkey: The Challenge of a New Role.* •BIOGRAPHIES *(in part);* WORLD AFFAIRS: *Turkey*

Marples, David R. Professor of History, University of Alberta. Author of *Belarus: A Denationalized Nation* and *Lenin's Revolution: Russia, 1917–1921.* •WORLD AFFAIRS: *Belarus; Ukraine*

Matthíasson, Björn. Economist, Ministry of Finance, Iceland. •WORLD AFFAIRS: *Iceland*

Mazie, David M. Freelance Journalist. •SOCIAL PROTECTION (U.S.)

McLachlan, Keith S. Professor Emeritus, School of Oriental and African Studies, University of London. Coeditor of *Landlocked States of Africa and Asia.* Author of *Boundaries of Modern Iran.* •WORLD AFFAIRS: *Iran*

McMillan, Neale. Managing Editor, *South Pacific News Service.* Author of *Top of the Greasy Pole: New Zealand Prime Ministers of Recent Times.* •WORLD AFFAIRS: *New Zealand*

Michael, Tom. Editor, Encyclopædia Britannica. •BIOGRAPHIES *(in part)*

Middlebrook, Kevin J. Reader in Latin American Politics, Institute of Latin American Studies, University of London. Coeditor of *Confronting Development: Assessing Mexico's Economic and Social Policy Challenges.* •WORLD AFFAIRS: *Mexico*

Mora, Frank O. Associate Professor of International Studies and Senior Latin American Studies Fellow, Rhodes College, Memphis, Tenn. •WORLD AFFAIRS: *Paraguay*

Moredock, Janet. Freelance Writer and Editor. •BIOGRAPHIES *(in part);* OBITUARIES *(in part);* WORLD AFFAIRS: *Malaysia*

Morgan, Paul. Editor, *Rugby World.* •SPORTS AND GAMES: *Football:* Rugby Football

Morrison, Graham. Press Officer, British Fencing Association; Correspondent, *Daily Telegraph; Country Life.* •SPORTS AND GAMES: *Fencing*

Myers, David J. Professor of Political Science, Pennsylvania State University. Coauthor of *Capital City Politics in Latin America: Democratization and Empowerment.* •WORLD AFFAIRS: *Venezuela*

Noda, Hiroki. Staff Reporter, *Jiji Press Ltd.,* Japan. •SPORTS AND GAMES: *Baseball:* Japan

O'Leary, Christopher. Assistant Managing Editor, *Investment Dealers Digest.* •ECONOMIC AFFAIRS: *Business Overview*

Oppenheim, Lois Hecht. Professor of Political Science and Vice President for Academic Affairs, University of Judaism, Los Angeles. Author of *Politics in Chile: Democracy, Authoritarianism and the Search for Development.* •WORLD AFFAIRS: *Chile*

O'Quinn, Jim. Editor in Chief, *American Theatre.* •BIOGRAPHIES *(in part);* PERFORMING ARTS: *Theatre:* U.S. and Canada

Orr, Jay. Senior Museum Editor, Country Music Hall of Fame. •BIOGRAPHIES *(in part);* PERFORMING ARTS: *Music:* Popular (U.S.)

Orwig, Sarah Forbes. Associate Editor, Encyclopædia Britannica. Contributor to *The Next Phase of Business Ethics: Integrating Psychology and Ethics.* •BIOGRAPHIES *(in part)*

Osborne, Keith L. Editor, *British Rowing Almanack.* Author of *Berlin or Bust; Boat Racing in Britain, 1715–1975;* and *One Man Went to Row.* •SPORTS AND GAMES: *Rowing*

Paarlberg, Philip L. Professor of Agricultural Economics, Purdue University, West Lafayette, Ind. •AGRICULTURE AND FOOD SUPPLIES: *Agriculture*

Palacio, Joseph O. Resident Tutor and Head, University Centre, University of the West Indies School of Continuing Studies. Author of *Development in Belize, 1960–1980: Initiatives at the State and Community Levels.* •WORLD AFFAIRS: *Belize*

Parsons, Neil. Professor of History, University of Botswana. Author of *King Khama, Emperor Joe, and the Great White Queen.* •WORLD AFFAIRS: *Botswana*

Peaker, Carol. D.Phil. Candidate, Wolfson College, University of Oxford. Author of *The Penguin Modern Painters: A History.* •LITERATURE: *English:* United Kingdom

Pérez, Orlando J. Associate Professor of Political Science, Central Michigan University. Editor of *Post-Invasion Panama: The Challenges of Democratization in the New World Order* and others. •WORLD AFFAIRS: *Panama*

Peszek, Luan. Publications Director and Editor, *U.S.A. Gymnastics.* Author of *Gymnastics Almanac.* •SPORTS AND GAMES: *Gymnastics*

Peterson, Mark. Associate Professor of Korean Studies, Brigham Young University, Provo, Utah. Author of *Korean Adoption and Inheritance* and others. •WORLD AFFAIRS: *Korea, Democratic People's Republic of; Korea, Republic of*

Pires, Kirstin. Former Editor, *Billiards Digest.* •SPORTS AND GAMES: *Billiard Games*

Ponmoni Sahadevan. Associate Professor, Jawaharlal Nehru University, New Delhi. Author of *Conflict and Peacemaking in South Asia.* •WORLD AFFAIRS: *Maldives*

Primorac, Max. Executive Director, Institute of World Affairs, Zagreb, Croatia. •WORLD AFFAIRS: *Croatia*

Prothero, Neil. Editor and Economist, Economist Intelligence Unit, Europe. •WORLD AFFAIRS: *Austria*

Rauch, Robert. Freelance Editor and Writer. •BIOGRAPHIES *(in part);* NOBEL PRIZES *(in part);* OBITUARIES *(in part)*

Raun, Toivo U. Professor of Central Eurasian Studies, Indiana University. Author of *Estonia and the Estonians.* Contributor to *Nations and Nationalism.* •WORLD AFFAIRS: *Estonia*

Ray, Michael. Copy Editor, Encyclopædia Britannica; Contributor to *Trimtab* (the newsletter of the Buckminster Fuller Institute). •OBITUARIES *(in part)*

Rebelo, L.S. Professor Emeritus, Department of Portuguese Studies, King's College, University of London. Author of *Lilia Pegado: Painter of the Future.* •LITERATURE: *Portuguese:* Portugal

Reddington, André. Assistant Editor, *Amateur Wrestling News.* •SPORTS AND GAMES: *Wrestling:* Freestyle and Greco-Roman

Reid, Ron. Staff Writer, *Philadelphia Inquirer.* •SPORTS AND GAMES: *Ice Hockey; Ice Skating*

Renwick, David. Freelance Journalist. •WORLD AFFAIRS: *Antigua and Barbuda; Bahamas, The; Barbados; Dependent States:* Caribbean and Bermuda; *Dominica; Grenada; Guyana; Jamaica; Saint Kitts and Nevis; Saint Lucia; Saint Vincent and the Grenadines; Trinidad and Tobago*

Robbins, Paul. Freelance Writer; Correspondent, *Ski Trax* and *Ski Racing.* •BIOGRAPHIES *(in part);* SPORTS AND GAMES: *Skiing*

Robinson, David. Film Critic and Historian. Author of *A History of World Cinema* and others. •PERFORMING ARTS: *Motion Pictures*

Roby, Anne. Freelance Journalist; Program Associate, Institute for Mathematics and Science Education, University of Illinois at Chicago. •WORLD AFFAIRS: *Andorra; Liechtenstein; Luxembourg; Monaco*

Rogers, Peter. Gordon McKay Professor of Environmental Engineering and Professor of City Planning, Harvard University. Contributor to *Transportation Research Record.* •THE ENVIRONMENT: *Special Report:* World Water Crisis: Is There a Way Out?

Rohwedder, Cecilie. Staff Reporter, *The Wall Street Journal Europe.* •WORLD AFFAIRS: *Germany*

Rollin, Jack. Editor, *Sky Sports Football Yearbook* and *Playfair Football Annual.* Author of *The World Cup 1930–1990: Sixty Glorious Years of Soccer's Premier Event* and others. •BIOGRAPHIES *(in part);* SPORTS AND GAMES: *Football:* Association Football (Soccer): *Africa and Asia; Europe*

Rose, Leo E. Professor Emeritus of Political Science, University of California, Berkeley. •WORLD AFFAIRS: *Bhutan; Nepal*

Rugh, William A. President and CEO, AMIDEAST; Former U.S. Ambassador to Yemen and the United Arab Emirates. Author of *The Arab Press.* •WORLD AFFAIRS: *United Arab Emirates; Yemen*

Sabo, Anne G. Assistant Professor of Norwegian, St. Olaf College, Northfield, Minn.; Contributor to *Scandinavian Studies.* •LITERATURE: *Norwegian*

Sanders, Alan J.K. Former Lecturer in Mongolian Studies, School of Oriental and African Studies, University of London. Author of *Historical Dictionary of Mongolia;* Coauthor of *Colloquial Mongolian.* •WORLD AFFAIRS: *Mongolia*

Sandvik, Gudmund. Professor Emeritus of Legal History, Faculty of Law, University of Oslo. •WORLD AFFAIRS: *Norway*

Saracino, Peter. Freelance Defense Journalist; Contributor to *PEJ News,* Victoria, B.C. •BIOGRAPHIES *(in part);* MILITARY AFFAIRS; MILITARY AFFAIRS: Sidebar

Sarahete, Yrjö. Secretary Emeritus, Fédération Internationale des Quilleurs. •SPORTS AND GAMES: *Bowling:* World Tenpins

Saunders, Christopher. Professor of Historical Studies, University of Cape Town. Coauthor of *Historical Dictionary of South Africa* and *South Africa: A Modern History.* •WORLD AFFAIRS: *Cape Verde; Chad; Equatorial Guinea; Gambia, The; Guinea-Bissau; Lesotho; Madagascar; Namibia; São Tomé and Príncipe*

Schmidt, Fabian. Head of the Bosnian Program, Deutsche Welle. •WORLD AFFAIRS: *Albania*

Schuster, Angela M.H. Editor in Chief, *ICON;* Editor, *The Explorers Journal;* Contributing Editor, *Archaeology;* Science Correspondent, *Corriere della Sera* (Italy); Contributor, *New York Times.* •ANTHROPOLOGY AND ARCHAEOLOGY: *Archaeology:* Eastern Hemisphere

Sego, Stephen. Freelance Journalist; Former Director, Radio Free Afghanistan. •WORLD AFFAIRS: *Afghanistan*

Seligson, Mitchell A. Daniel H. Wallace Professor of Political Science, University of Pittsburgh, Pa. Editor of *Elections and Democracy in Central America, Revisited.* •WORLD AFFAIRS: *Costa Rica*

Serafin, Steven R. Director, Writing Center, Hunter College, City University of New York. Coeditor of *The Continuum Encyclopedia of American Literature* and *The Continuum Encyclopedia of British Literature.* •NOBEL PRIZES *(in part)*

Shelley, Andrew. Director, Women's International Squash Players Association; Technical Director, World Squash Federation. Author of *Squash Rules: A Players Guide.* •BIOGRAPHIES *(in part);* SPORTS AND GAMES: *Squash*

Shepherd, Melinda C. Associate Editor, Encyclopædia Britannica. •OBITUARIES *(in part);* SPORTS AND GAMES: *Automobile Racing:* Rallies and Other Races *(in part);* WORLD AFFAIRS: *Dependent States:* Europe and the Atlantic

Shubinsky, Valery. Freelance Critic and Journalist. •LITERATURE: *Russian*

Siler, Shanda. Editorial Assistant, Encyclopædia Britannica. •BIOGRAPHIES *(in part)*

Simons, Paul. Freelance Journalist. Author of *The Action Plant.* •LIFE SCIENCES: *Botany*

Simpson, Jane. Freelance Writer. •PERFORMING ARTS: *Dance:* European

Sklar, Morton. Executive Director, World Organization Against Torture USA; Judge, Administrative Labor Tribunal, Organization of American States; Member of the Board of Directors, Amnesty International USA. Editor, *The Status of Human Rights in the United States* and *Torture in the U.S.* Author of *The Right to Travel* and others. •SOCIAL PROTECTION: *Human Rights*

Smentkowski, Brian. Associate Professor of Political Science and Associate Dean, College of Liberal Arts, Southeast Missouri State University. •LAW, CRIME, AND LAW ENFORCEMENT: *Court Decisions*

Smith, Gregory O. Academic Director, European School of Economics. •WORLD AFFAIRS: *San Marino; Vatican City State*

Smith-Irowa, Pamela. Adjunct, Saint Xavier University, Chicago. •BIOGRAPHIES *(in part)*

Snodgrass, Donald. Institute Fellow Emeritus, Harvard University. Coauthor of *Economics of Development,* 5th ed. •WORLD AFFAIRS: *Sri Lanka*

Sparks, Karen J. Editor, Encyclopædia Britannica. •OBITUARIES *(in part)*

Stahler-Sholk, Richard. Associate Professor of Political Science, Eastern Michigan University. •WORLD AFFAIRS: *Nicaragua*

Stern, Irwin. Lecturer in Foreign Languages, North Carolina State University. Editor of *Dictionary of Brazilian Literature.* Coauthor of *Paso a Paso: Spanish for Health Professionals.* •LITERATURE: *Portuguese:* Brazil

Stewart, Alan. Freelance Journalist. Author of *How to Make It in IT.* •BIOGRAPHIES *(in part);* COMPUTERS AND INFORMATION SYSTEMS: Sidebar; OBITUARIES (IN PART)

Summerhill, Edward M. Lead Editor of the News Bulletin, Finnish News Agency. •WORLD AFFAIRS: *Finland*

Sumner, David E. Professor of Journalism and Head of the Magazine Program, Ball State University, Muncie, Ind. Contributor to *Encyclopedia of International Media and Communications.* •MEDIA AND PUBLISHING: *Magazines*

Sumrall, Harry. Editor in Chief, RedLudwig.com. •BIOGRAPHIES *(in part);* PERFORMING ARTS: *Music:* Classical; *Music:* Sidebar

Susel, Rudolph M. Editor, *American Home.* •WORLD AFFAIRS: *Slovenia*

Susser, Leslie D. Diplomatic Correspondent, *The Jerusalem Report.* Coauthor of *Shalom Friend: The Life and Legacy of Yitzhak Rabin.* •BIOGRAPHIES *(in part);* WORLD AFFAIRS: *Israel*

Szilagyi, Zsofia. Freelance Writer. •WORLD AFFAIRS: *Hungary*

Talbott, Strobe. President, The Brookings Institution. Author of *The Russia Hand: A Memoir of Presidential Diplomacy.* •WORLD AFFAIRS: *Special Report:* Bush, Iraq, and the World

Taylor, Jolanda Vanderwal. Associate Professor of Dutch and German, University of Wisconsin at Madison. Author of *A Family Occupation: Children of the War and the Memory of World War II in Dutch Literature of the 1980s.* •LITERATURE: *Netherlandic;* WORLD AFFAIRS: *The Netherlands*

Taylor, Richard. Basketball Correspondent, *The Independent;* Production Editor, Midland Weekly Media (Trinity Mirror). •SPORTS AND GAMES: *Basketball:* International

Taylor-Robinson, Michelle M. Associate Professor of Political Science, Texas A&M University. Coauthor of *Negotiating Democracy: Transitions from Authoritarian Rule.* •WORLD AFFAIRS: *Honduras*

Teague, Elizabeth. Ministry of Defence, London. (The opinions expressed are personal and do not necessarily represent those of the British government.) •WORLD AFFAIRS: *Russia*

Thayer, Carlyle A. Professor of Politics, Australian Defence Force Academy, Canberra. Author of *The Vietnam People's Army Under Doi Moi.* •WORLD AFFAIRS: *Vietnam*

Thomas, R. Murray. Professor Emeritus of Education, University of California, Santa Barbara. Author of *Recent Theories of Human Development* and *Folk Psychologies Across Cultures.* •BIOGRAPHIES *(in part);* EDUCATION; EDUCATION: Sidebar

Tikkanen, Amy. Freelance Writer and Editor. •BIOGRAPHIES *(in part);* OBITUARIES *(in part)*

Turner, Darrell J. Freelance Writer; Former Religion Writer, *Fort Wayne* (Ind.) *Journal Gazette;* Former Associate Editor, Religion News Service. •BIOGRAPHIES *(in part);* RELIGION

Urbansky, Julie. Communications and Promotions Coordinator, Hersheypark Sports and Entertainment. •SPORTS AND GAMES: *Bobsleigh, Skeleton, and Luge:* Bobsleigh; Skeleton

Verdi, Robert. Senior Writer, *Golf Digest, Golf World;* Contributing Columnist, *Chicago Tribune.* •BIOGRAPHIES *(in part);* SPORTS AND GAMES: *Baseball* (U.S. and Canada)

Wallenfeldt, Jeff. Senior Editor, Encyclopædia Britannica. •BIOGRAPHIES *(in part);* OBITUARIES *(in part)*

Wang Xiaoming. Professor of Modern Chinese Literature; Director, Center for Contemporary Culture Studies, Shanghai University. Author of *The Cold Face of Reality: A Biography of Lu Xun.* •LITERATURE: *Chinese*

Wanninger, Richard S. Freelance Journalist. •SPORTS AND GAMES: *Volleyball*

Watson, Rory. Freelance Journalist specializing in European Union affairs. Coauthor of *The American Express Guide to Brussels* and Contributor to *The European Union: How Does It Work?* Brussels Correspondent, *The Times.* •WORLD AFFAIRS: *Belgium*

Weil, Eric. Columnist and Contributor, *Buenos Aires* (Arg.) *Herald;* South America Correspondent, *World Soccer Magazine;* Contributor to *FIFA Magazine.* •SPORTS AND GAMES: *Football:* Association Football (Soccer): *The Americas*

Weinstein, Martin. Professor of Political Science, William Paterson University of New Jersey. Author of *Uruguay: Democracy at the Crossroads.* •WORLD AFFAIRS: *Uruguay*

White, Martin L. Freelance Writer, Chicago. •OBITUARIES *(in part)*

Whitney, Barbara. Copy Supervisor, Encyclopædia Britannica. •BIOGRAPHIES *(in part);* OBITUARIES *(in part);* PERFORMING ARTS: *Motion Pictures:* Sidebar

Whitten, Phillip. Editor in Chief, Swiminfo.com, *Swimming World, Swim,* and *Swimming Technique* magazines. Author of *The Complete Book of Swimming* and others. •SPORTS AND GAMES: *Swimming*

Wiggins, David J. Freelance Cartographer. •MAPS: *Ethnic and Religious Groups in Iraq and Vicinity; The European Union; Freshwater Stress; SARS Epidemic, 2002–2003*

Wilkinson, Earl J. Executive Director and Chief Executive Officer, International Newspaper Marketing Association. Author of *Branding and the Newspaper Consumer.* •MEDIA AND PUBLISHING: *Newspapers*

Wilkinson, John R. Sportswriter, Coventry Newspapers. •SPORTS AND GAMES: *Cycling*

Williams, Victoria C. Assistant Professor of the Humanities, Alvernia College, Reading, Pa.; Independent Consultant on international affairs. •LAW, CRIME, AND LAW ENFORCEMENT: *International Law*

Wilson, Derek. Former Correspondent, BBC. Author of *Rome, Umbria and Tuscany.* •WORLD AFFAIRS: *Italy*

Woods, Elizabeth Rhett. Writer. Author of *Family Fictions; If Only Things Were Different (I): A Model for a Sustainable Society; Bird Salad;* and others. •BIOGRAPHIES *(in part);* LITERATURE: *English:* Canada; OBITUARIES *(in part)*

Woods, Michael. Science Editor, *Toledo* (Ohio) *Blade.* Author of *Ancient Technology.* •PHYSICAL SCIENCES: *Chemistry;* NOBEL PRIZES *(in part)*

Woodward, Ralph Lee, Jr. Emeritus Professor of Latin American History, Tulane University, New Orleans. Author of *Central America, a Nation Divided.* •WORLD AFFAIRS: *El Salvador; Guatemala*

Wyllie, Peter J. Emeritus Professor of Geology, California Institute of Technology. Author of *The Dynamic Earth* and *The Way the Earth Works.* •EARTH SCIENCES: *Geology and Geochemistry*

Zegura, Stephen L. Professor of Anthropology, University of Arizona. •ANTHROPOLOGY AND ARCHAEOLOGY: *Anthropology*

Ziring, Lawrence. Arnold E. Schnieder Professor of Political Science, Western Michigan University. Author of *Pakistan in the Twentieth Century: A Political History* and *Pakistan: At the Crosscurrent of History.* •WORLD AFFAIRS: *Pakistan*

World Data

Rolls of coiled steel being unloaded at the Poland Street Wharf in New Orleans. Steel usually accounts for 40% of general cargo imports to the port; however, after United States Pres. George W. Bush enacted steel tariffs in 2002, that number dropped to nearly 25%. He rescinded the tariffs in December 2003.

Manager, World Data Rosaline Jackson Keys
Senior Editor Stephen Neher
Research Editors Lyudmila Skoropistsev, DeAudray Brown

Contributors M.C. MacDonald, Susana Darwin

Director, Copy Department Sylvia Wallace
Supervisor, Copy Department Dennis Skord

Compositor Carol A. Gaines

Senior Coordinator, Production Control Marilyn L. Barton

Cartographer Michael Nutter

Director, Information Management Carmen-Maria Hetrea

Director, Editorial Technologies Steven Bosco
Editorial Technologies Staff Gavin Chiu, Bruce Walters, Mark Wiechec

Design Director Nancy Donahue Canfield
Senior Designer Steven N. Kapusta
Manager, Art Department Kathy Nakamura
Senior Photography Editor Kristine Strom
Director, Composition Technology Melvin Stagner
Director, Manufacturing Dennis Flaherty

Head Librarian Henry Bolzon
Curator, Geography Lars Mahinske

ENCYCLOPÆDIA BRITANNICA, INC.

Chairman of the Board Jacob E. Safra
President Jorge Aguilar-Cauz
Senior Vice President and Editor Dale H. Hoiberg
Director of Yearbooks Charles P. Trumbull
Director of Production Marsha Mackenzie

CONTENTS

INTRODUCTION

Britannica World Data provides a statistical portrait of some 217 countries and dependencies of the world, at a level appropriate to the significance of each. It contains 214 country statements (the "Nations of the World" section), ranging in length from one to six pages, and permits, in the 20 major thematic tables (the "Comparative National Statistics" [CNS] section), comparisons among these larger countries and 4 other states.

Updated annually, *Britannica World Data* is particularly intended as direct, structured support for many of Britannica's other reference works—encyclopaedias, yearbooks, atlases—at a level of detail that their editorial style or design do not permit.

Like the textual, graphic, or cartographic modes of expression of these other products, statistics possess their own inherent editorial virtues and weaknesses. Two principal goals in the creation of *Britannica World Data* were up-to-dateness and comparability, each possible to maximize separately, but not always possible to combine. If, for example, research on some subject is completed during a particular year (x), figures may be available for 100 countries for the preceding year ($x - 1$), for 140 countries for the year before that ($x - 2$), and for 180 countries for the year before that ($x - 3$).

Which year should be the basis of a thematic compilation for 217 countries so as to give the best combination of up-to-dateness and comparability? And, should $x - 1$ be adopted for the thematic table, ought up-to-dateness in the country table (for which year x is already available) be sacrificed for agreement with the thematic table? In general, the editors have opted for maximum up-to-dateness in the country statistical boxes and maximum comparability in the thematic tables.

Comparability, however, also resides in the meaning of the numbers compiled, which may differ greatly from country to country. The headnotes to the thematic tables explain many of these methodological problems; the Glossary serves the same purpose for the country statistical pages. Published data do not always provide the researcher or editor with a neat, unambiguous choice between a datum compiled on two different bases (say, railroad track length, or route length), one of which is wanted and the other not. More often a choice must be made among a variety of official, private, and external intergovernmental (UN, FAO, IMF) sources, each reporting its best data but each representing a set of problems: (1) of methodological variance from (or among) international conventions; (2) of analytical completeness (data for a single year may, successively, be projected [based on 10 months' data], preliminary [for 12 months], final, revised or adjusted, etc.); (3) of time frame, or accounting interval (data may represent a full Gregorian calendar year [preferred], a fiscal year, an Islamic or other national or religious year, a multiyear period or average [when a one-year statement would contain unrepresentative results]); (4) of continuity with previous data; and the like. Finally, published data on a particular subject may be complete and final but impossible to summarize in a simple manner. The education system of a single country may include, for example, public and private sectors; local, state, or national systems; varying grades, tracks, or forms within a single system; or opportunities for double-counting or fractional counting of a student, teacher, or institution. When no recent official data exist, or they exist, but may be suspect, the tables may show unofficial estimates, a range (of published opinion), analogous data, or no data at all.

The published basis of the information compiled is the statistical collections of Encyclopædia Britannica, Inc., some of the principal elements of which are enumerated in the Bibliography. Holdings for a given country may include any of the following: the national statistical abstract; the constitution; the most recent censuses of population; periodic or occasional reports on vital statistics, social indicators, agriculture, mining, labour, manufacturing, domestic and foreign trade, finance and banking, transportation, and communications. Further information is received in a variety of formats—telephone, letter, fax, microfilm and microfiche, and most recently, in electronic formats such as computer disks, CD-ROMs, and the Internet. So substantial has the resources of the Internet become that it was decided to add uniform resource locators (URLs) to the great majority of country pages and a number of the CNS tables (summary world sites with data on all countries still being somewhat of a rarity) so as to apprise the reader of the possibility and means to access current information on these subjects year-round.

The recommendations offered are usually to official sites (national statistical offices, general national governments, central banks, embassies, intergovernmental organizations [especially the UN Development Programme], and the like). Though often dissimilar in content, they will usually be updated year-round, expanded as opportunity permits, and lead on to related sites, such as parliamentary offices, information offices, diplomatic and consular sites, news agencies and newspapers, and, beyond, to the myriad academic, commercial, and private sites now accessible from the personal computer. While these URLs were correct and current at the time of writing, they may be subject to change.

The great majority of the social, economic, and financial data contained in this work should not be interpreted in isolation. Interpretive text of long perspective, such as that of the *Encyclopædia Britannica* itself; political, geographic, and topical maps, such as those in the *Britannica Atlas;* and recent analysis of political events and economic trends, such as that contained in the articles of the *Book of the Year,* will all help to supply analytic focus that numbers alone cannot. By the same token, study of those sources will be made more concrete by use of *Britannica World Data* to supply up-to-date geographic, demographic, and economic detail.

GLOSSARY

A number of terms that are used to classify and report data in the "Nations of the World" section require some explanation.

Those italicized terms that are used regularly in the country compilations to introduce specific categories of information (*e.g., birth rate, budget*) appear in this glossary in italic boldface type, followed by a description of the precise kind of information being offered and how it has been edited and presented.

All other terms are printed here in roman boldface type. Many terms have quite specific meanings in statistical reporting, and they are so defined here. Other terms have less specific application as they are used by different countries or organizations. Data in the country compilations based on definitions markedly different from those below will usually be footnoted.

Terms that appear in small capitals in certain definitions are themselves defined at their respective alphabetical locations.

Terms whose definitions are marked by an asterisk (*) refer to data supplied only in the larger two- to four-page country compilations.

access to services, a group of measures indicating a population's level of access to public services, including electrical power, treated public drinking water, sewage removal, and fire protection.*

activity rate, *see* participation/activity rates.

age breakdown, the distribution of a given population by age, usually reported here as percentages of total population in 15-year age brackets. When substantial numbers of persons do not know, or state, their exact age, distributions may not total 100.0%.

area, the total surface area of a country or its administrative subdivisions, including both land and inland (nontidal) water area. Land area is usually calculated from "mean low water" on a "plane table," or flat, basis.

area and population, a tabulation usually including the first-order administrative subdivisions of the country (such as the states of the United States), with capital (headquarters, or administrative seat), area, and population. When these subdivisions are especially numerous or, occasionally, nonexistent, a planning, electoral, census, or other nonadministrative scheme of regional subdivisions has been substituted.

associated state, *see* state.

atheist, in statements of religious affiliation, one who professes active opposition to religion; "nonreligious" refers to those professing only no religion, nonbelief, or doubt.

balance of payments, a financial statement for a country for a given period showing the balance among: (1) transactions in goods, services, and income between that country and the rest of the world, (2) changes in ownership or valuation of that country's monetary gold, SPECIAL DRAWING RIGHTS, and claims on and liabilities to the rest of the world, and (3) unrequited transfers and counterpart entries needed (in an accounting sense) to balance transactions and changes among any of the foregoing types of exchange that are not mutually offsetting. Detail of national law as to what constitutes a transaction, the basis of its valuation, and the size of a transaction visible to fiscal authorities all result in differences in the meaning of a particular national statement.*

balance of trade, the net value of all international goods trade of a country, usually excluding reexports (goods received only for transshipment), and the percentage that this net represents of total trade.

Balance of trade refers only to the "visible" international trade of goods as recorded by customs authorities and is thus a segment of a country's BALANCE OF PAYMENTS, which takes all visible and invisible trade with other countries into account. (Invisible trade refers to imports and exports of money, financial instruments, and services such as transport, tourism, and insurance.) A country has a favourable, or positive (+), balance of trade when the value of exports exceeds that of imports and negative (–) when imports exceed exports.

barrel (bbl), a unit of liquid measure. The barrel conventionally used for reporting crude petroleum and petroleum products is equal to 42 U.S. gallons, or 159 litres. The number of barrels of crude petroleum per metric ton, ranging typically from 6.20 to 8.13, depends upon the specific gravity of the petroleum. The world average is roughly 7.33 barrels per ton.

birth rate, the number of live births annually per 1,000 of midyear population. Birth rates for individual countries may be compared with the estimated world annual average of 22.5 births per 1,000 population in 2000.

budget, the annual receipts and expenditures—of a central government for its activities only;

Abbreviations

Measurements

cu m	cubic metre(s)
kg	kilograms(s)
km	kilometre(s)
kW	kilowatt(s)
kW-hr	kilowatt-hour(s)
metric ton-km	metric ton-kilometre(s)
mi	mile(s)
passenger-km	passenger-kilometre(s)
passenger-mi	passenger-mile(s)
short ton-mi	short ton-mile(s)
sq km	square kilometre(s)
sq m	square metre(s)
sq mi	square mile(s)
troy oz	troy ounce(s)
yr	year(s)

Political Units and International Organizations

CACM	Central American Common Market
Caricom	Caribbean Community and Common Market
CFA	Communauté Financière Africaine
CFP	Comptoirs Françaises du Pacifique
CIS	Commonwealth of Independent States
CUSA	Customs Union of Southern Africa
EC	European Communities
ESCWA	Economic and Social Commission for Western Asia
EU	European Union
FAO	United Nations Food and Agriculture Organization
IMF	International Monetary Fund
OECD	Organization for Economic Cooperation and Development
OECS	Organization of Eastern Caribbean States
U.A.E.	United Arab Emirates
U.K.	United Kingdom
UNDP	United Nations Development Programme
U.S.	United States
U.S.S.R.	Union of Soviet Socialist Republics

Months

Jan.	January	Oct.	October
Feb.	February	Nov.	November
Aug.	August	Dec.	December
Sept.	September		

Miscellaneous

AIDS	Acquired Immune Deficiency Syndrome
avg.	average
c.i.f.	cost, insurance, and freight
commun.	communications
CPI	consumer price index
est.	estimate(d)
excl.	excluding
f.o.b.	free on board
GDP	gross domestic product
GNP	gross national product
govt.	government
incl.	including
mo.	month(s)
n.a.	not available (in text)
n.e.s.	not elsewhere specified
no.	number
pl.	plural
pos.	position
pub. admin.	public administration
SDR	Special Drawing Right
SITC	Standard International Trade Classification
svcs.	services
teacher tr.	teacher training
transp.	transportation
VAT	value-added taxes
voc.	vocational
$	dollar (of any currency area)
£	pound (of any currency area)
...	not available (in tables)
—	none, less than half the smallest unit shown, or not applicable (in tables)

does not include state, provincial, or local governments or semipublic (parastatal, quasi-nongovernmental) corporations unless otherwise specified. Figures for budgets are limited to ordinary (recurrent) receipts and expenditures, wherever possible, and exclude capital expenditures—*i.e.,* funds for development and other special projects originating as foreign-aid grants or loans.

When both a recurrent and a capital budget exist for a single country, the former is the budget funded entirely from national resources (taxes, duties, excises, etc.) that would recur (be generated by economic activity) every year. It funds the most basic governmental services, those least able to suffer interruption. The capital budget is usually funded by external aid and may change its size considerably from year to year.

capital, usually, the actual seat of government and administration of a state. When more than one capital exists, each is identified by kind; when interim arrangements exist during the creation or movement of a national capital, the de facto situation is described.

Anomalous cases are annotated, such as those in which (1) the de jure designation under the country's laws differs from actual local practice (*e.g.,* Benin's designation of one capital in constitutional law, but another in actual practice), (2) international recognition does not validate a country's claim (as with the proclamation by Israel of a capital on territory not internationally recognized as part of Israel), or (3) both a state and a capital have been proclaimed on territory recognized as part of another state (as with the Turkish Republic of Northern Cyprus).

capital budget, *see* budget.

causes of death, as defined by the World Health Organization (WHO), "the disease or injury which initiated the train of morbid events leading directly to death, or the circumstances of accident or violence which produced the fatal injury." This principle, the "underlying cause of death," is the basis of the medical judgment as to cause; the statistical classification system according to which these causes are grouped and named is the *International List of Causes of Death,* the latest revision of which is the Tenth. Reporting is usually in terms of events per 100,000 population. When data on actual causes of death are unavailable, information on morbidity, or illness rate, usually given as reported cases per 100,000 of infectious diseases (notifiable to WHO as a matter of international agreement), may be substituted.

chief of state/head of government, paramount national governmental officer(s) exercising the highest executive and/or ceremonial roles of a country's government. In general usage, the chief of state is the formal head of a national state. The primary responsibilities of the chief of state may range from the purely ceremonial—convening legislatures and greeting foreign officials—to the exercise of complete national executive authority. The head of government, when this function exists separately, is the officer nominally charged (by the constitution) with the majority of actual executive powers, though they may not in practice be exercised, especially in military or single-party regimes in which effective power may reside entirely outside the executive governmental machinery provided by the constitution. A prime minister, for example, usually the actual head of government, may in practice exercise only Cabinet-level authority.

In communist countries an official identified as the chief of state may be the chairman of the policy-making organ, and the official given as the head of government the chairman of the nominal administrative/executive organ.

c.i.f. (trade valuation): *see* imports.

colony, an area annexed to, or controlled by, an independent state but not an integral part of it; a non-self-governing territory. A colony has a charter and may have a degree of self-government. A crown colony is a colony originally chartered by the British government.

commonwealth (U.K. and U.S.), a self-governing political entity that has regard to the common weal, or good; usually associated with the United Kingdom or United States. Examples include the Commonwealth (composed of independent states [from 1931 onward]), Puerto Rico since 1952, and the Northern Marianas since 1979.

communications, collectively, the means available for the public transmission of information within a country. Data are tabulated for: daily newspapers and their total circulation; radio and television as total numbers of receivers; telephone data as "main lines," or the number of subscriber lines (not receivers) having access to the public switched network; cellular telephones as number of subscribers; and facsimile machines and personal computers as number of units. For each, a rate per 1,000 persons is given.

constant prices, an adjustment to the members of a financial time series to eliminate the effect of inflation year by year. It consists of referring all data in the series to a single year so that "real" change may be seen.

constitutional monarchy, *see* monarchy.

consumer price index (CPI), also known as the retail price index, or the cost-of-living index, a series of index numbers assigned to the price of a selected "basket," or assortment, of basic consumer goods and services in a country, region, city, or type of household in order to measure changes over time in prices paid by a typical household for those goods and services. Items included in the CPI are ordinarily determined by governmental surveys of typical household expenditures and are assigned weights relative to their proportion of those expenditures. Index values are period averages unless otherwise noted.

coprincipality, *see* monarchy.

current prices, the valuation of a financial aggregate as of the year reported.

daily per capita caloric intake (supply), the calories equivalent to the known average daily supply of foodstuffs for human consumption in a given country divided by the population of the country (and the proportion of that supply provided, respectively, by vegetable and animal sources). The daily per capita caloric intake of a country may be compared with the corresponding recommended minimum daily requirement. The latter is calculated by the Food and Agriculture Organization of the United Nations from the age and sex distributions, average body weights, and environmental temperatures in a given region to determine the calories needed to sustain a person there at normal levels of activity and health. The daily per capita caloric requirement ranges from 2,200 to 2,500.

de facto population, for a given area, the population composed of those actually present at a particular time, including temporary residents and visitors (such as immigrants not yet granted permanent status, "guest" or expatriate workers, refugees, or tourists), but excluding legal residents temporarily absent.

de jure population, for a given area, the population composed only of those legally resident at a particular time, excluding temporary residents and visitors (such as "guest" or expatriate workers, refugees, or tourists), but including legal residents temporarily absent.

deadweight tonnage, the maximum weight of cargo, fuel, fresh water, stores, and persons that may safely by carried by a ship. It is customarily measured in long tons of 2,240 pounds each, equivalent to 1.016 metric tons. Deadweight tonnage is the difference between the tonnage of a fully loaded ship and the fully unloaded tonnage of that ship.

See also gross ton.

death rate, the number of deaths annually per 1,000 of midyear population. Death rates for individual countries may be compared with the estimated world annual average of 9.0 deaths per 1,000 population in 2000.

density (of population), usually, the DE FACTO POPULATION of a country divided by its total area. Special adjustment is made for large areas of inland water, desert, or other uninhabitable areas—*e.g.,* excluding the ice cap of Greenland.

dependent state, constitutionally or statutorily organized political entity outside of and under the jurisdiction of an independent state (or a federal element of such a state) but not formally annexed to it (*see* Table).

Dependent states[1]

Australia
Christmas Island
Cocos (Keeling) Islands
Norfolk Island

Denmark
Faroe Islands
Greenland

France
French Guiana
French Polynesia
Guadeloupe
Martinique
Mayotte
New Caledonia
Réunion
Saint Pierre and Miquelon
Wallis and Futuna

Netherlands, The
Aruba
Netherlands Antilles

New Zealand
Cook Islands
Niue
Tokelau

United Kingdom
Anguilla
Bermuda
British Virgin Islands
Cayman Islands
Falkland Islands
Gibraltar
Guernsey
Isle of Man
Jersey
Montserrat
Pitcairn Island
Saint Helena and Dependencies
Turks and Caicos Islands

United States
American Samoa
Guam
Northern Mariana Islands
Puerto Rico
Virgin Islands (of the U.S.)

[1]Excludes territories (1) to which Antarctic Treaty is applicable in whole or in part, (2) without permanent civilian population, (3) without internationally recognized civilian government (Western Sahara, Gaza Strip), or (4) representing unadjudicated unilateral or multilateral territorial claims.

direct taxes, taxes levied directly on firms and individuals, such as taxes on income, profits, and capital gains. The *immediate* incidence, or burden, of direct taxes is on the firms and individuals thus taxed; direct taxes on firms may, however, be passed on to consumers and other economic units in the form of higher prices for goods and services, blurring the distinction between direct and indirect taxation.

distribution of income/wealth, the portion of personal income or wealth accruing to households or individuals constituting each respective decile (tenth) or quintile (fifth) of a country's households or individuals.*

divorce rate, the number of legal, civilly recognized divorces annually per 1,000 population.

doubling time, the number of complete years required for a country to double its population at its current rate of natural increase.

earnings index, a series of index numbers comparing average wages in a collective industrial sample for a country or region with the same industries at a previous period to measure changes over time in those wages. It is most commonly reported for wages paid on a daily, weekly, or monthly basis; annual figures may represent total income or averages of these shorter periods. The scope of the earnings index varies from country to country. The index is often limited to earnings in manufacturing industries. The index for each country applies to all wage earners in a designated group and ordinarily takes into account basic wages (overtime is normally distinguished), bonuses, cost-of-living allowances, and contributions toward social security. Some countries include payments in kind. Contributions toward social security by employers are usually excluded, as are social security benefits received by wage earners.

economically active population, *see* population economically active.

education, tabulation of the principal elements of a country's educational establishment, classified as far as possible according to the country's own system of primary, secondary, and higher levels (the usual age limits for these levels being identified in parentheses), with total number of schools (physical facilities) and of teachers and students (whether full- or part-time). The student-teacher ratio is calculated whenever available data permit.

educational attainment, the distribution of the population age 25 and over with completed educations by the highest level of formal education attained or completed; it must sometimes be reported, however, for age groups still in school or for the economically active only.

emirate, *see* monarchy.

enterprise, a legal entity formed to conduct a business, which it may do from more than one establishment (place of business or service point).

ethnic/linguistic composition, ethnic, racial, or linguistic composition of a national population, reported here according to the most reliable breakdown available, whether published in official sources (such as a census) or in external analysis (when the subject is not addressed in national sources).

exchange rate, the value of one currency compared with another, or with a standardized unit of account such as the SPECIAL DRAWING RIGHT, or as mandated by local statute when one currency is "tied" by a par value to another. Rates given usually refer to free market values when the currency has no, or very limited, restrictions on its convertibility into other currencies.

exports, material goods legally leaving a country (or customs area) and subject to customs regulations. The total value and distribution by percentage of the major items (in preference to groups of goods) exported are given, together with the distribution of trade among major trading partners (usually single countries or trading blocs). Valuation of goods exported is free on board (f.o.b.) unless otherwise specified. The value of goods exported and imported f.o.b. is calculated from the cost of production and excludes the cost of transport.

external debt, public and publicly guaranteed debt with a maturity of more than one year owed to nonnationals of a country and repayable in foreign currency, goods, or services. The debt may be an obligation of a national or subnational governmental body (or an agency of either), of an autonomous public body, or of a private debtor that is guaranteed by a public entity. The debt is usually either outstanding (contracted) or disbursed (drawn).

external territory (Australia), *see* territory.

federal, consisting of first-order political subdivisions that are prior to and independent of the central government in certain functions.

federal republic, *see* republic.

federation, union of coequal, preexisting political entities that retain some degree of autonomy and (usually) right of secession within the union.

fertility rate, *see* total fertility rate.

financial aggregates, tabulation of seven-year time series, providing principal measures of the financial condition of a country, including: (1) the exchange rate of the national crurency against the U.S. dollar, the pound sterling, and the International Monetary Fund's SPECIAL DRAWING RIGHT (SDR), (2) the amount and kind of international reserves (holdings of SDRs, gold, and foreign currencies) and reserve position of the country in the IMF, and (3) principal economic rates and prices (central bank discount rate, government bond yields, and industrial stock [share] prices). For BALANCE OF PAYMENTS, the origin in terms of component balance of trade items and balance of invisibles (net) is given.*

fish catch, the live-weight equivalent of the aquatic animals (including fish, crustaceans, mollusks, etc., but excluding whales, seals, and other aquatic mammals) caught in freshwater or marine areas by national fleets and landed in domestic or foreign harbours for commercial, industrial, or subsistence purposes.

f.o.b. (trade valuation), *see* exports.

food, *see* daily per capita caloric intake.

form of government/political status, the type of administration provided for by a country's constitution—whether or not suspended by extralegal military or civil action, although such de facto administrations are identified—together with the number of members (elected, appointed, and ex officio) for each legislative house, named according to its English rendering. Dependent states (*see* Table) are classified according to the status of their political association with the administering country.

gross domestic product (GDP), the total value of the final goods and services produced by residents and nonresidents within a given country during a given accounting period, usually a year. Unless otherwise noted, the value is given in current prices of the year indicated. The *System of National Accounts* (SNA, published under the joint auspices of the UN, IMF, OECD, EC, and World Bank) provides a framework for international comparability in classifying domestic accounting aggregates and international transactions comprising "net factor income from abroad," the measure that distinguishes GDP and GNP.

gross national product (GNP), the total value of final goods and services produced both from within a given country *and* from external (foreign) transactions in a given accounting period, usually a year. Unless otherwise noted, the value is given in current prices of the year indicated. GNP is equal to GROSS DOMESTIC PRODUCT (*q.v.*) adjusted by net factor income from abroad, which is the income residents receive from abroad for factor services (labour, investment, and interest) less similar payments made to nonresidents who contribute to the domestic economy.

gross ton, volumetric unit of measure (equaling 100 cubic feet [2.83 cu m]) of the permanently enclosed volume of a ship, above and below decks available for cargo, stores, or passenger accommodation. Net, or register, tonnage exempts certain nonrevenue spaces—such as those devoted to machinery, bunkers, crew accommodations, and ballast—from the gross tonnage. *See also* deadweight tonnage.

head of government, *see* chief of state/head of government.

health, a group of measures including number of accredited physicians currently practicing or employed and their ratio to the total population; total hospital beds and their ratio; and INFANT MORTALITY RATE.

household, economically autonomous individual or group of individuals living in a single dwelling unit. A family household is one composed principally of individuals related by blood or marriage.

household income and expenditure, data for average size of a HOUSEHOLD (by number of individuals) and median household income. Sources of income and expenditures for major items of consumption are given as percentages.

In general, household income is the amount of funds, usually measured in monetary units, received by the members (generally those 14 years old and over) of a household in a given time period. The income can be derived from (1) wages or salaries, (2) nonfarm or farm SELF-EMPLOYMENT, (3) transfer payments, such as pensions, public assistance, unemployment benefits, etc., and (4) other income, including interest and dividends, rent, royalties, etc. The income of a household is expressed as a gross amount before deductions for taxes. Data on expenditure refer to consumption of personal or household goods and services; they normally exclude savings, taxes, and insurance; practice with regard to inclusion of credit purchases differs markedly.

immigration, usually, the number and origin of those immigrants admitted to a nation in a legal status that would eventually permit the granting of the right to settle permanently or to acquire citizenship.*

imports, material goods legally entering a country (or customs area) and subject to customs regulations; excludes financial movements. The total value and distribution by percentage of the major items (in preference to groups of goods) imported are given, together with the direction of trade among major trading partners (usually single countries), trading blocs (such as the European Union), or customs areas (such as Belgium-Luxembourg). The value of goods imported is given free on board (f.o.b.) unless otherwise specified; f.o.b. is defined above under EXPORTS.

The principal alternate basis for valuation of goods in international trade is that of cost, insurance, and freight (c.i.f.); its use is restricted to imports, as it comprises the principal charges needed to bring the goods to the customs house in the country of destination. Because it inflates the value of imports relative to exports, more countries have, latterly, been estimating imports on an f.o.b. basis as well.

incorporated territory (U.S.), *see* territory.

independent, of a state, autonomous and controlling both its internal and external affairs. Its date usually refers to the date from which the country was in effective control of these affairs within its present boundaries, rather than the date independence was proclaimed or the date recognized as a de jure act by the former administering power.

indirect taxes, taxes levied on sales or transfers of selected intermediate goods and services, including excises, value-added taxes, and tariffs, that are ordinarily passed on to the ultimate consumers of the goods and services. Figures given for individual countries are limited to indirect taxes levied by their respective central governments unless otherwise specified.

infant mortality rate, the number of children per 1,000 live births who die before their first birthday. Total infant mortality includes neonatal mortality, which is deaths of children within one month of birth.

invisibles (invisible trade), *see* balance of trade.

kingdom, *see* monarchy.

labour force, portion of the POPULATION ECONOMICALLY ACTIVE (PEA) comprising those most fully employed or attached to the labour market (the unemployed are considered to be "attached" in that they usually represent persons previously employed seeking to be reemployed), particularly as viewed from a short-term perspective. It normally includes those who are self-employed, employed by others (whether full-time, part-time, seasonally, or on some other less than full-time, basis), and, as noted above, the unemployed (both those previously employed and those seeking work for the first time). In the "gross domestic product and labour force" table, the majority of the labour data provided refer to population economically active, since PEA represents the longer-term view of working population and, thus, subsumes more of the marginal workers who are often missed by shorter-term surveys.

land use, distribution by classes of vegetational cover or economic use of the land area only (excluding inland water, for example, but not marshland), reported as percentages. The principal categories utilized include: (1) forest, which includes natural and planted tracts, (2) meadows and pastures, which includes land in temporary or permanent use whose principal purpose is the growing of animal fodder, (3) agricultural and under permanent cultivation, which includes temporary and permanent cropland, as well as land left fallow less than five years, but capable of being returned to production without special preparation, and (4) other, which includes built-up, wasteland, watercourses, and the like.

leisure, the principal monetary expenditures, uses, or reported preferences in the use of the individual's free time for recreation, rest, or self-improvement.*

life expectancy, the number of years a person born within a particular population group (age cohort) would be expected to live, based on actuarial calculations.

literacy, the ability to read and write a language with some degree of competence; the precise degree constituting the basis of a particular national statement is usually defined by the national census and is often tested by the census enumerator. Elsewhere, particularly where much adult literacy may be the result of literacy campaigns rather than passage through a formal educational system, definition and testing of literacy may be better standardized.

major cities, usually the five largest cities proper (national capitals are always given, regardless of size); fewer cities may be listed if there are fewer urban localities in the country. For multipage tables, 10 or more may be listed.* Populations for cities will usually refer to the city proper—*i.e.,* the legally bounded corporate entity, or the most compact, contiguous, demographically urban portion of the entity defined by the local authorities. Occasionally figures for METROPOLITAN AREAS are cited when the relevant civil entity at the core of a major agglomeration had an unrepresentatively small population.

manufacturing, mining, and construction enterprises/retail sales and service enterprises, a detailed tabulation of the principal industries in these sectors, showing for each industry the number of enterprises and employees, wages in that industry as a percentage of the general average wage, and the value of that industry's output in terms of value added or turnover.*

marriage rate, the number of legal, civilly recognized marriages annually per 1,000 population.

material well-being, a group of measures indicating the percentage of households or dwellings possessing certain goods or appliances, including automobiles, telephones, television receivers, refrigerators, air conditioners, and washing machines.*

merchant marine, the privately or publicly owned ships registered with the maritime authority of a nation (limited to those in Lloyd's of London statistical reporting of 100 or more GROSS TONS) that are employed in commerce, whether or not owned or operated by nationals of the country.

metropolitan area, a city and the region of dense, predominantly urban, settlement around the city; the population of the whole usually has strong economic and cultural affinities with the central city.

military expenditure, the apparent value of all identifiable military expenditure by the central government on hardware, personnel, pensions, research and development, etc., reported here both as a percentage of the GNP, with a comparison to the world average, and as a per capita value in U.S. dollars.

military personnel, *see* total active duty personnel.

mobility, the rate at which individuals or households change dwellings, usually measured between censuses and including international as well as domestic migration.*

monarchy, a government in which the CHIEF OF STATE holds office, usually hereditarily and for life, but sometimes electively for a term. The state may be a coprincipality, emirate, kingdom, principality, sheikhdom, or sultanate. The powers of the monarch may range from absolute (*i.e.,* the monarch both reigns and rules) through various degrees of limitation of authority to nominal, as in a constitutional monarchy, in which the titular monarch reigns but others, as elected officials, effectively rule.

monetary unit, currency of issue, or that in official use in a given country; name, spelling, and abbreviation in English according to International Monetary Fund recommendations or local practice; name of the lesser, usually decimal, monetary unit constituting the main currency; and valuation in U.S. dollars and U.K. pounds sterling, usually according to free-market or commercial rates.

See also exchange rate.

natural increase, also called natural growth, or the balance of births and deaths, the excess of births over deaths in a population; the rate of natural increase is the difference between the BIRTH RATE and the DEATH RATE of a given population. The estimated world average during 2000 was 13.5 per 1,000 population, or 1.35% annually. Natural increase is added to the balance of migration to calculate the total growth of that population.

net material product, *see* material product.

nonreligious, *see* atheist.

official language(s), that (or those) prescribed by the national constitution for day-to-day conduct and publication of a country's official business or, when no explicit constitutional provision exists, that of the constitution itself, the national gazette (record of legislative activity), or like official documents. Other languages may have local protection, may be permitted in parliamentary debate or legal action (such as a trial), or may be "national languages," for the protection of which special provisions have been made, but these are not deemed official. The United States, for example, does not yet formally identify English as "official," though it uses it for virtually all official purposes.

official name, the local official form(s), short or long, of a country's legal name(s) taken from the country's constitution or from other official documents. The English-language form is usually the protocol form in use by the country, the U.S. Department of State, and the United Nations.

official religion, generally, any religion prescribed or given special status or protection by the constitution or legal system of a country. Identification as such is not confined to constitutional documents utilizing the term explicitly.

organized territory (U.S.), *see* territory.

overseas department (France), *see* department.

overseas territory (France), *see* territory.

parliamentary state, *see* state.

part of a realm, a dependent Dutch political entity with some degree of self-government and having a special status above that of a colony (*e.g.,* the prerogative of rejecting for local application any law enacted by The Netherlands).

participation/activity rates, measures defining differential rates of economic activity within a population. Participation rate refers to the percentage of those employed or economically active who possess a particular characteristic (sex, age, etc.); activity rate refers to the fraction of the total population who *are* economically active.

passenger-miles, or **passenger-kilometres,** aggregate measure of passenger carriage by a specified means of transportation, equal to the number of passengers carried multiplied by the number of miles (or kilometres) each is transported. Figures given for countries are often calculated from ticket sales and ordinarily exclude passengers carried free of charge.

people's republic, *see* republic.

place of birth/national origin, if the former, numbers of native- and foreign-born population of a country by actual place of birth; if the latter, any of several classifications, including those based on origin of passport at original admission to country, on cultural heritage of family name, on self-designated (often multiple) origin of (some) ancestors, and on other systems for assigning national origin.*

political status, *see* form of government/political status.

population, the number of persons present within a country, city, or other civil entity at the date of a census of population, survey, cumulation of a civil register, or other enumeration. Unless otherwise specified, populations given are DE FACTO, referring to those actually present, rather than DE JURE, those legally resident but not necessarily present on the referent date. If a time series, noncensus year, or per capita ratio referring to a country's total population is cited, it will usually refer to midyear of the calendar year indicated.

population economically active, the total number of persons (above a set age for economic labour, usually 10–15 years) in all employment statuses—self-employed, wage- or salary-earning, part-time, seasonal, unemployed, etc. The International Labour Organisation defines the economically active as "all persons of either sex who furnish the supply of labour for the production of economic goods and services." National practices vary as regards the treatment of such groups as armed forces, inmates of institutions, persons seeking their first job, unpaid family workers, seasonal workers and persons engaged in part-time economic activities. In some countries, all or part of these groups may be included among the economically active, while in other countries the same groups may be treated as inactive. In general, however, the data on economically active population do not include students, persons occupied solely in family or household work, retired persons, persons living entirely on their own means, and persons wholly dependent upon others.

See also labour force.

population projection, the expected population in the years 2010 and 2020, embodying the country's own projections wherever possible. Estimates of the future size of a population are usually based on assumed levels of fertility, mortality, and migration. Projections in the tables, unless otherwise specified, are medium (*i.e.,* most likely) variants, whether based on external estimates by the United Nations, World Bank, or U.S. Department of Commerce or on those of the country itself.

price and earnings indexes, tabulation comparing the change in the CONSUMER PRICE INDEX over a period of seven years with the change in the general labour force's EARNINGS INDEX for the same period.

principality, *see* monarchy.

production, the physical quantity or monetary value of the output of an industry, usually tabulated here as the most important items or groups of items (depending on the available detail) of primary (extractive) and secondary (manufactured) production, including construction. When a single consistent measure of value, such as VALUE ADDED, can be obtained, this is given, ranked by value; otherwise, and more usually, quantity of production is given.

public debt, the current outstanding debt of all periods of maturity for which the central government and its organs are obligated. Publicly guaranteed private debt is excluded. For countries that report debt under the World Bank Debtor Reporting System (DRS), figures for outstanding, long-term EXTERNAL DEBT are given.

quality of working life, a group of measures including weekly hours of work (including overtime); rates per 100,000 for job-connected injury, illness, and mortality; coverage of labour force by insurance for injury, permanent disability, and death; workdays lost to labour strikes and stoppages; and commuting patterns (length of journey to work in minutes and usual method of transportation).*

railroads, mode of transportation by self-driven or locomotive-drawn cars over fixed rails. Length-of-track figures include all mainline and spurline running track but exclude switching sidings and yard track. Route length, when given, does not compound multiple running tracks laid on the same trackbed.

recurrent budget, *see* budget.

religious affiliation, distribution of nominal religionists, whether practicing or not, as a percentage of total population. This usually assigns to children the religion of their parents.

republic, a state with elected leaders and a centralized presidential form of government, local subdivisions being subordinate to the national government. A *federal republic* (as distinguished from a unitary republic) is a republic in which power is divided between the central government and the constituent subnational administrative divisions (*e.g.,* states, provinces, or cantons) in whom the central government itself is held to originate, the division of power being defined in a written constitution and jurisdictional disputes usually being settled in a court; sovereignty usually rests with the authority that has the power to amend the constitution. A *unitary republic* (as distinguished from a federal republic) is a republic in which power originates in a central authority and is not derived from constituent subdivisions. A *people's republic,* in the dialectics of Communism, is the first stage of development toward a communist state, the second stage being a *socialist republic.* An *Islamic republic* is structured around social, ethical, legal, and religious precepts central to the Islamic faith.

retail price index, *see* consumer price index.

retail sales and service enterprises, *see* manufacturing, mining, and construction enterprises/retail sales and service enterprises.

roundwood, wood obtained from removals from forests, felled or harvested (with or without bark), in all forms.

rural, *see* urban-rural.

self-employment, work in which income derives from direct employment in one's own business, trade, or profession, as opposed to work in which salary or wages are earned from an employer.

self-governing, of a state, in control of its internal affairs in degrees ranging from control of most internal affairs (though perhaps not of public order or of internal security) to complete control of all internal affairs (*i.e.,* the state is autonomous) but having no control of external affairs or defense. In this work the term self-governing refers to the final stage in the successive stages of increasing self-government that generally precede independence.

service/trade enterprises, *see* manufacturing, mining, and construction enterprises/retail sales and service enterprises.

sex distribution, ratios, calculated as percentages, of male and female population to total population.

sheikhdom, *see* monarchy.

social deviance, a group of measures, usually reported as rates per 100,000 for principal categories of socially deviant behaviour, including specified crimes, alcoholism, drug abuse, and suicide.*

social participation, a group of measures indicative of the degree of social engagement displayed by a particular population, including rates of participation in such activities as elections, voluntary work or memberships, trade unions, and religion.*

social security, public programs designed to protect individuals and families from loss of income owing to unemployment, old age, sickness or disability, or death and to provide other services such as medical care, health and welfare programs, or income maintenance.

socialist republic, *see* republic.

sources of income, *see* household income and expenditure.

Special Drawing Right (SDR), a unit of account utilized by the International Monetary Fund (IMF) to denominate monetary reserves available under a quota system to IMF members to maintain the value of their national currency unit in international transactions.*

state, in international law, a political entity possessing the attributes of: territory, permanent civilian population, government, and the capacity to conduct relations with other states. Though the term is sometimes limited in meaning to fully independent and internationally recognized states, the more general sense of an entity possessing a *preponderance* of these characteristics is intended here. It is, thus, also a first-order civil administrative subdivision, especially of a federated union. An associated state is an autonomous state in free association with another that conducts its external affairs and defense; the association may be terminated in full independence at the instance of the autonomous state in consultation with the administering power. A *parliamentary state* is an independent state of the Commonwealth that is governed by a parliament and that may recognize the British monarch as its titular head.

structure of gross domestic product and labour force, tabulation of the principal elements of the national economy, according to standard industrial categories, together with the corresponding distribution of the labour force (when possible POPULATION ECONOMICALLY ACTIVE) that generates the GROSS DOMESTIC PRODUCT.

sultanate, *see* monarchy.

territory, a noncategorized political dependency; a first-order administrative subdivision; a dependent political entity with some degree of self-government, but with fewer rights and less autonomy than a colony because there is no charter. An *external territory* (Australia) is a territory situated outside the area of the country. An *organized territory* (U.S.) is a territory for which a system of laws and a settled government have been provided by an act of the United States Congress. An *overseas territory* (France) is an overseas subdivision of the French Republic with elected representation in the French Parliament, having individual statutes, laws, and internal organization adapted to local conditions.

ton-miles, or **ton-kilometres,** aggregate measure of freight hauled by a specified means of transportation, equal to tons of freight multiplied by the miles (or kilometres) each ton is transported. Figures are compiled from waybills (nationally) and ordinarily exclude mail, specie, passengers' baggage, the fuel and stores of the conveyance, and goods carried free.

total active duty personnel, full-time active duty military personnel (excluding militias and part-time, informal, or other paramilitary elements), with their distribution by percentages among the major services.

total fertility rate, the sum of the current age-specific birth rates for each of the child-bearing years (usually 15–49). It is the probable number of births, given present fertility data, that would occur during the lifetime of each woman should she live to the end of her child-bearing years.

tourism, service industry comprising activities connected with domestic and international travel for pleasure or recreation; confined here to international travel and reported as expenditures in U.S. dollars by tourists of all nationalities visiting a particular country and, conversely, the estimated expenditures of that country's nationals in all countries of destination.

transfer payments, *see* household income and expenditure.

transport, all mechanical methods of moving persons or goods. Data reported for national establishments include: for railroads, length of track and volume of traffic for passengers and cargo (but excluding mail, etc.); for roads, length of network and numbers of passenger cars and of commercial vehicles (*i.e.,* trucks and buses); for merchant marine, the number of vessels of more than 100 gross tons and their total deadweight tonnage; for air transport, traffic data for passengers and cargo and the number of airports with scheduled flights.

unincorporated territory (U.S.), *see* territory.

unitary republic, *see* republic.

urban-rural, social characteristic of local or national populations, defined by predominant economic activities, "urban" referring to a group of largely nonagricultural pursuits, "rural" to agriculturally oriented employment patterns. The distinction is usually based on the country's own definition of urban, which may depend only upon the size (population) of a place or upon factors like employment, administrative status, density of housing, etc.

value added, also called value added by manufacture, the gross output value of a firm or industry minus the cost of inputs—raw materials, supplies, and payments to other firms—required to produce it. Value added is the portion of the sales value or gross output value that is actually created by the firm or industry. Value added generally includes labour costs, administrative costs, and operating profits.

The Nations of the World

Afghanistan

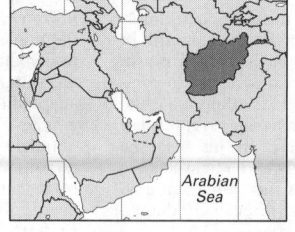

Official name: Islamic State of Afghanistan[1] (Dowlat-e Eslāmī-ye Afghānestān [Persian]).
Form of government: transitional government[2].
Head of state and government: President.
Capital: Kabul.
Official languages: Dari (Persian); Pashto.
Official religion: Islam.
Monetary unit: 1 (new) afghani (Af) = 100 puls (puli); valuation (Sept. 8, 2003) 1 U.S.$ = Af 43.00; 1 £ = Af 68.18[3].

Arabian Sea

Area and population		area		population
Geographic regions	**Principal cities**	sq mi	sq km	2000 estimate[4]
Central	Kabul	11,083	28,706	5,441,943
East	Jalālābād	9,937	25,737	2,572,929[5]
East-central	Bāmiān	19,558	50,654	1,285,963
North	Mazār-e Sharīf	29,576	76,601	3,972,086[5]
North-east	Kondūz	33,031	85,550	3,966,509
South	Gardeyz	20,456	52,980	2,670,048[5]
South-west	Kandahār (Qandahār)	77,892	201,739	3,480,108
West	Herāt	47,815	123,840	2,417,027
TOTAL		249,347	645,807	25,806,613

Demography

Population (2003): 28,717,000[6].
Density (2003): persons per sq mi 115.2, persons per sq km 44.5.
Urban-rural (2001): urban 22.3%; rural 77.7%.
Sex distribution (2002): male 51.51%; female 48.49%.
Age breakdown (2002): under 15, 42.0%; 15–29, 27.7%; 30–44, 16.6%; 45–59, 9.1%; 60–74, 3.9%; 75 and over, 0.7%.
Population projection: (2010) 33,864,000; (2020) 41,735,000.
Doubling time: 29 years.
Ethnolinguistic composition (early 1990s[6]): Pashtun 52.4%; Tajik 20.4%; Ḥazāra 8.8%; Uzbek 8.8%; Chahar Aimak 2.8%; Turkmen 1.9%; other 4.9%.
Religious affiliation (2000): Sunnī Muslim 89.2%; Shīʿī Muslim 8.9%; Zoroastrian 1.4%; Hindu 0.4%; other 0.1%.
Major cities (1988): Kabul 2,602,000[7]; Kandahār (Qandahār) 225,500; Herāt 177,300; Mazār-e Sharīf 130,600; Jalālābād 55,000.

Vital statistics

Birth rate per 1,000 population (2002): 41.0 (world avg. 21.3).
Death rate per 1,000 population (2002): 17.4 (world avg. 9.1).
Natural increase rate per 1,000 population (2002): 23.6 (world avg. 12.2).
Total fertility rate (avg. births per childbearing woman; 2002): 5.7.
Life expectancy at birth (2002): male 47.3 years; female 45.9 years.

National economy

Budget (2002–03). Revenue: U.S.$221,200,000 (foreign grants 62.5%, local revenue 37.5%). Expenditures: U.S.$460,300,000 (defense and public safety 43.2%, wages 22.7%, goods and services 13.2%, other 20.9%).
Gross national product (2000): U.S.$21,000,000,000 (U.S.$800 per capita).

Structure of gross domestic product and labour force	1992–93			
	in value Af '000,000[8]	% of total value	labour force	% of labour force
Agriculture	61,400	48.5	4,276,100	67.2
Manufacturing; Mining and public utilities	32,800	25.9	298,900	4.7
Construction	12,400	9.8	81,400	1.3
Transp. and commun.	5,300	4.2	139,900	2.2
Trade	12,400	9.8	420,600	6.6
Pub. admin., services	2,400	1.9	929,300	14.6
Other			214,300	3.4
TOTAL	126,700	100.0[9]	6,360,500	100.0

Public debt (external, outstanding; 1999): U.S.$5,800,000,000.
Production (metric tons except as noted). Agriculture, forestry, fishing (2002): wheat 2,686,000, rice 388,000, grapes 365,000, barley 345,000, corn (maize) 298,000, potatoes 240,000, apricots 38,000, opium poppy 4,600[10]; livestock (number of live animals) 11,000,000 sheep, 5,000,000 goats, 2,000,000 cattle, 920,000 asses; roundwood (2001) 3,074,150 cu m; fish catch (2000) 2,000. Mining and quarrying (2000): salt 13,000; copper (metal content) 5,000. Manufacturing (by production value in Af '000,000; 1988–89): food products 4,019; leather and fur products 2,678; textiles 1,760; printing and publishing 1,070; industrial chemicals (including fertilizers) 1,053; footwear 999. Energy production (consumption): electricity (kW-hr; 1999) 485,000,000 (580,000,000); coal (metric tons; 1999) 1,000 (1,000); petroleum products (metric tons; 1999) none (208,000); natural gas (cu m; 1999) 126,900,000 (126,900,000).
Population economically active (1994)[11]: total 5,557,000; activity rate of total population 29.4% (participation rates: female 9.0%; unemployed [1995] *c.* 8%).

Consumer price index (1990 = 100)	1988	1989	1990	1991	1992	1993	1994
Consumer price index	64.3	83.1	100.0	266.0	420.8	563.9	676.7

Tourism: receipts (1997) U.S.$1,000,000; expenditures (1997) U.S.$1,000,000.
Land use (1994): forested 2.9%; meadows and pastures 46.0%; agricultural and under permanent cultivation 12.4%; other 38.7%.

Foreign trade[12]

Balance of trade (current prices)	1994	1995	1996	1997	1998	1999
U.S.$'000,000	−245	−193	−494	−424	−356	−450
% of total	54.6%	36.8%	66.0%	59.2%	55.6%	60.0%

Imports (1999): U.S.$600,000,000 (agricultural products *c.* 38%, of which cereals *c.* 10%; unspecified commodities *c.* 62%). *Major import sources:* Pakistan *c.* 19%; Japan *c.* 16%; South Korea *c.* 7%; Turkmenistan *c.* 6%; India *c.* 6%.
Exports (1999): U.S.$150,000,000 (1995; carpets and rugs 54.3%, dried fruits and nuts 15.6%). *Major export destinations:* Pakistan *c.* 32%; India *c.* 8%; United States *c.* 7%; Russia *c.* 5%.

Transport and communications

Transport. Railroads (2003): none operational. Roads (2001): total length 20,720 km (paved 12%). Vehicles (1996): passenger cars 31,000; trucks and buses 25,000. Air transport[13]: passenger-km (1998) 88,000,000; metric ton-km cargo 24,000,000; airports (2002) 2.

Communications				units
Medium	date	unit	number	per 1,000 persons
Daily newspapers	2000	circulation	129,000	5.0
Radio	2000	receivers	2,950,000	114
Television[14]	2000	receivers	362,000	14
Telephones	2000	main lines	29,000	1.3

Education and health

Educational attainment: n.a. *Literacy* (1995): total population age 15 and over literate 31.5%; males 47.2%; females 15.1%.

Education (1995–96)	schools	teachers	students	student/ teacher ratio
Primary	2,146	21,869	1,312,197	60.0
Secondary	...	19,085	512,851	26.9
Higher	...	...	12,800	...

Health: physicians (1997) 2,555[6] (1 per 9,091 persons); hospital beds, n.a.; infant mortality rate (2002) 144.8.
Food (1999): daily per capita caloric intake 1,755 (vegetable products 79%, animal products 21%); 72% of FAO recommended minimum requirement.

Military

Total active duty personnel (July 2003): 5,000 (army 100%); size of planned army is 70,000[15].

[1]Long-form name of transitional government. [2]Replaced interim government in June 2002; to be the governmental authority until early 2004. [3]The afghani was re-denominated on Oct. 7, 2002; from that date 100 (old) afghanis equalled 1 (new) afghani. The Pakistan rupee and U.S. dollar are also commonly used as of mid-2003. [4]Estimate of LandScan Global Population 2000 Database. [5]Includes population of administrative subdivisions created after 1990. [6]Includes Afghan refugees (estimated to number about 1.1 million in Pakistan and about 1.0 million in Iran in June 2003). [7]2001 estimate for urban agglomeration. [8]At prices of 1978–79. [9]Detail does not add to total given because of rounding. [10]Represents 75% of world production; production declined significantly in 2001. [11]Based on settled population only. [12]Exports are f.o.b. and imports are c.i.f. [13]Ariana Afghan Airlines only. [14]Officially outlawed in 1998–2001. [15]Foreign troops (August 2003): 5,500-member, NATO-controlled, 31-nation International Security Assistance Force (ISAF) and 9,000-member, non-ISAF U.S. troops searching for al-Qaeda and Taliban fighters.

Albania

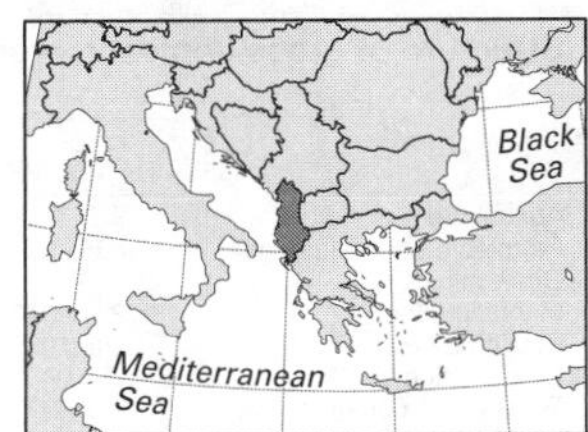

Official name: Republika e Shqipërisë (Republic of Albania).
Form of government: unitary multiparty republic with one legislative house (Assembly [140]).
Chief of state: President.
Head of government: Prime Minister.
Capital: Tirana (Tiranë).
Official language: Albanian.
Official religion: none.
Monetary unit: 1 lek = 100 qindars; valuation (Sept. 8, 2003) 1 U.S.$ = 122.89 leks; 1 £ = 194.84 leks.

Area and population

		area		population
Provinces	**Capitals**	sq mi	sq km	2001 census
Berat	Berat	353	915	128,410
Bulqizë	Bulqizë	277	718	42,985
Delvinë	Delvinë	142	367	10,859
Devoll	Bilisht	166	429	34,744
Dibër	Peshkopi	294	761	86,144
Durrës	Durrës	176	455	182,988
Elbasan	Elbasan	498	1,290	224,974
Fier	Fier	328	850	200,154
Gjirokastër	Gjirokastër	439	1,137	55,991
Gramsh	Gramsh	268	695	35,723
Has	Krumë	144	374	19,842
Kavajë	Kavajë	152	393	78,415
Kolonjë	Ersekë	311	805	17,179
Korçë	Korçë	676	1,752	143,499
Krujë	Krujë	144	372	64,357
Kuçovë	Kuçovë	43	112	35,571
Kukës	Kukës	369	956	64,054
Kurbin[1]	Laç	91	235	54,519
Lezhë	Lezhë	185	479	68,218
Librazhd	Librazhd	425	1,102	72,520
Lushnjë	Lushnjë	275	712	144,351
Malësi e Madhe	Koplic	346	897	36,770
Mallakastër	Ballsh	125	325	39,881
Mat	Burrel	397	1,028	61,906
Mirditë	Rrëshen	335	867	37,055
Peqin	Peqin	74	191	32,920
Përmet	Përmet	359	929	25,837
Pogradec	Pogradec	280	725	70,900
Pukë	Pukë	399	1,034	34,454
Sarandë	Sarandë	282	730	35,235
Shkodër	Shkodër	630	1,631	185,794
Skrapar	Çorovoda	299	775	29,874
Tepelenë	Tepelenë	315	817	32,465
Tiranë	Tirana (Tiranë)	461	1,193	523,150
Tropojë	Bajram	403	1,043	28,154
Vlorë	Vlorë	621	1,609	147,267
TOTAL		11,082	28,703	3,087,159

Demography

Population (2003): 3,166,000.
Density (2003): persons per sq mi 285.7, persons per sq km 110.3.
Urban-rural (2002): urban 43.0%; rural 57.0%.
Sex distribution (2002): male 48.92%; female 51.08%.
Age breakdown (2002): under 15, 28.8%; 15–29, 27.2%; 30–44, 19.6%; 45–59, 13.7%; 60–74, 8.3%; 75 and over, 2.4%.
Population projection: (2010) 3,335,000; (2020) 3,548,000.
Doubling time: 58 years.
Ethnic composition (2000): Albanian 91.7%; Vlach (Aromanian) 3.6%; Greek 2.3%; other 2.4%.
Religious affiliation (2000): Muslim 38.8%; Roman Catholic 16.7%; nonreligious 16.6%; Albanian Orthodox 10.4%; other Orthodox 5.7%; other 11.8%.
Major cities (1991): Tirana (Tiranë) 279,000 (1999); Durrës 86,900; Shkodër 83,700; Elbasan 83,200.

Vital statistics

Birth rate per 1,000 population (2002): 18.6 (world avg. 21.3).
Death rate per 1,000 population (2002): 6.5 (world avg. 9.1).
Natural increase rate per 1,000 population (2002): 12.1 (world avg. 12.2).
Total fertility rate (avg. births per childbearing woman; 2002): 2.3.
Marriage rate per 1,000 population (1998): 7.4.
Life expectancy at birth (2002): male 69.3 years; female 75.1 years.

National economy

Budget (2001). Revenue: 135,484,000,000 leks (taxes 84.4%, of which value-added tax 30.4%, social security contributions 16.6%, import duties and export taxes 15.4%, income tax 13.7%, other 8.3%; nontax revenue 15.6%). Expenditures: 186,050,000,000 leks (current expenditure 76.7%, of which social security 23.4%, wages 23.1%, interest on debt 12.7%, government operations 8.5%, other 9.0%; capital expenditure 23.3%).
Public debt (2001): U.S.$970,000,000.
Production (metric tons except as noted). Agriculture, forestry, fishing (2002): vegetables and melons 650,000 (mainly beans, peas, onions, tomatoes, cabbage, eggplants, and carrots), cereals 472,500, watermelons 293,000, potatoes 163,100; livestock (number of live animals) 1,844,000 sheep, 929,000 goats, 690,000 cattle, 4,446,000 poultry; roundwood (2001) 459,000 cu m; fish catch (2000) 3,627. Mining and quarrying (2001): chromium ore 165,000; copper ore 45,000. Manufacturing (2000): cement 180,000; bread 67,000; cheese 7,000; rolled steel 6,000; beer 91,000 hectolitres; wine 29,000 hectolitres. Energy production (consumption): electricity (kW-hr; 2001) 3,584,000,000 (3,584,000,000); lignite (metric tons; 2001) 17,300 (17,300); crude petroleum (barrels; 1999) 2,368,000 (2,413,000 [1997]); petroleum products (metric tons; 1999) 263,000 (406,000); natural gas (cu m; 2001) 10,000,000 (10,000,000).
Gross national product (2001): U.S.$4,236,000,000 (U.S.$1,370 per capita).

Structure of gross domestic product and labour force

	2001			
	in value '000,000 leks	% of total value	labour force	% of labour force
Agriculture	201,777	34.2	767,000	61.7
Manufacturing, mining, public utilities	77,648	13.2	55,000	4.4
Construction	61,058	10.3	13,000	1.0
Transp. and commun. }	59,631	10.1	24,000	1.9
Trade }			56,000	4.5
Pub. admin., defense }		}	148,000	11.9
Services }	190,124	32.2 }		
Other }			181,000[2]	14.5[2]
TOTAL	590,238	100.0	1,244,000	100.0[3]

Population economically active (2001): total 1,244,000; activity rate of total population 40.3% (participation rates: ages 15–64, 55.4%; female 49.8%; unemployed 14.5%).

Price index (1995 = 100)

	1996	1997	1998	1999	2000	2001	2002
Consumer price index	112.7	150.1	181.1	181.8	187.0	183.2	196.0

Household income and expenditure. Average household size (2000): 4.0; annual income per rural household (1989) 80,835 leks (U.S.$ value, n.a.); sources of income: wages 53.0%, transfers from relatives abroad 21.5%, social insurance 11.4%; expenditure: n.a.
Tourism (2001): receipts U.S.$446,000,000; expenditures U.S.$258,000,000.

Foreign trade

Balance of trade (current prices)

	1996	1997	1998	1999	2000	2001
U.S.$'000,000	–678	–535	–604	–663	–814	–1,033
% of total	58.2%	62.8%	59.2%	54.6%	61.4%	62.9%

Imports (2001): U.S.$1,337,000,000 (food and beverages 19.4%; nonelectrical and electrical machinery 18.4%; mineral fuels 13.8%; textiles and clothing 10.4%; base and fabricated metals 8.8%). *Major import sources:* Italy 36.5%; Greece 31.5%; Turkey 6.7%; Germany 5.3%; United Kingdom 3.8%.
Exports (2001): U.S.$304,000,000 (textiles and clothing 37.4%; footwear and related products 28.6%; base and fabricated metals 8.0%). *Major export destinations:* Italy 71.6%; Greece 13.1%; Germany 5.6%; Yugoslavia 3.1%.

Transport and communications

Transport. Railroads (2001): length 670 km; passenger-km 138,000,000; metric ton-km cargo 19,000. Roads (2000): total length 18,000 km (paved 30%). Vehicles (2001): passenger cars 133,533; trucks and buses 70,413. Merchant marine (1992): vessels (100 gross tons and over) 24; total deadweight tonnage 80,954. Air transport (2001)[4]: passenger-km 82,298,000, passenger-mi 56,370,000; short ton-mi, none, metric ton-km, none; airports (2001) 1.

Communications

Medium	date	unit	number	units per 1,000 persons
Daily newspapers	2000	circulation	109,000	35
Radio	2000	receivers	756,000	243
Television	2000	receivers	383,000	123
Telephones	2002	main lines	220,000	55
Cellular telephones	2002	subscribers	800,000	199
Internet	2001	users	10,000	2.5

Education and health

Educational attainment (1989). Population age 10 and over having: primary education 65.3%; secondary 29.1%; higher 5.6%. *Literacy* (1999): total population age 10 and over literate 84.0%; males 90.9%; females 76.9%.

Education (2000–01)

	schools	teachers	students	student/ teacher ratio
Primary (age 6–13)	1,782[5]	28,293	535,238	18.9
Secondary (age 14–17)	162[6]	5,760	108,173	18.8
Voc., teacher tr.	259[6]	2,174[7]	18,504[7]	8.5[7]
Higher	10	1,683	40,859	24.3

Health (1999): physicians 4,325 (1 per 724 persons); hospital beds 10,237 (1 per 306 persons); infant mortality rate per 1,000 live births (2002) 38.6.
Food (2001): daily per capita caloric intake 2,900 (vegetable products 72%, animal products 28%); 110% of FAO recommended minimum requirement.

Military

Total active duty personnel (2002): 27,000 (army 74.1%, navy 9.3%, air force 16.7%). *Military expenditure as percentage of GNP* (1999): 1.3% (world 2.4%); per capita expenditure U.S.$21.

[1]Name changed from Laç to Kurbin in 1999. [2]Unemployed. [3]Detail does not add to total given because of rounding. [4]Albanian Air only. [5]1995. [6]1990. [7]1996.

Internet resources for further information:
- **Albanian Economic Development Agency http://www.aeda.gov.al**
- **Instituti i Statistikës http://www.instat.gov.al**

Algeria

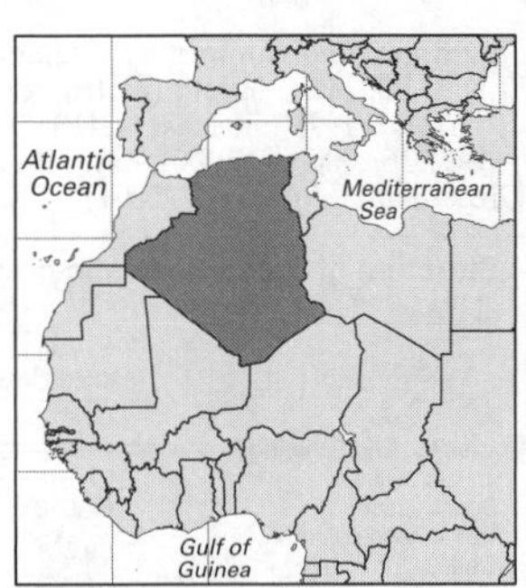

Official name: Al-Jumhūrīyah al-Jazāʾirīyah ad-Dīmuqrāṭīyah ash-Shaʿbīyah (Arabic) (People's Democratic Republic of Algeria).
Form of government: multiparty republic with two legislative bodies (Council of the Nation [144][1]; National People's Assembly [389]).
Chief of state: President.
Head of government: Prime Minister.
Capital: Algiers.
Official language: Arabic[2].
Official religion: Islam.
Monetary unit: 1 Algerian dinar (DA) = 100 centimes; valuation (Sept. 8, 2003) 1 U.S.$ = DA 77.97; 1 £ = DA 123.63.

Population (1998 census)

Provinces	population	Provinces	population	Provinces	population
Adrar	313,417	El-Bayadh	172,957	Ouargla	444,683
Aïn Defla	658,897	El-Oued	525,083	Oum el-Bouaghi	529,540
Aïn Temouchent	337,570	Et-Tarf	350,789	Relizane	646,175
Alger	2,423,694	Ghardaïa	311,678	Saïda	313,351
Annaba	559,898	Guelma	444,231	Sétif	1,299,116
Batna	987,475	Illizi	34,189	Sidi bel-Abbès	535,634
Béchar	232,012	Jijel	582,865	Skikda	793,146
Bejaïa	836,301	Khenchela	345,009	Souk Ahras	365,106
Biskra	568,701	Laghouat	326,862	Tamanrasset	138,704
Blida	796,616	Mascara	651,239	Tébessa	565,125
Bordj Bou Arreridj	561,471	Médéa	859,273	Tiaret	770,194
Bouira	637,042	Mila	663,578	Tindouf	27,053
Boumerdes	608,806	Mostaganem	636,884	Tipaza	507,959
Constantine	807,371	M'Sila	835,701	Tissemsilt	274,380
Djelfa	805,298	Naâma	131,846	Tizi Ouzou	1,100,297
Ech-Cheliff	874,917	Oran	1,208,171	Tlemcen	873,039
				TOTAL	29,273,343

Demography

Area: 919,595 sq mi, 2,381,741 sq km.
Population (2003): 31,800,000.
Density (2003): persons per sq mi 34.6, persons per sq km 13.4.
Urban-rural (1998): urban 80.8%; rural 19.2%.
Sex distribution (1998): male 50.56%; female 49.44%.
Age breakdown (1998): under 15, 36.2%; 15–29, 30.6%; 30–44, 17.7%; 45–59, 8.9%; 60–74, 5.1%; 75 and over, 1.5%.
Population projection: (2010) 35,549,000; (2020) 40,479,000.
Doubling time: 41 years.
Ethnic composition (2000): Algerian Arab 59.1%; Berber 26.2%, of which Arabized Berber 3.0%; Bedouin Arab 14.5%; other 0.2%.
Religious affiliation (2000): Muslim 99.7%, of which Sunnī 99.1%, Ibāḍīyah 0.6%; Christian 0.3%.
Major cities (1998): Algiers 1,519,570; Oran 692,516; Constantine 462,187; Annaba 348,554; Batna 242,514; Blida 226,512; Sétif 211,859.

Vital statistics

Birth rate per 1,000 population (2002): 22.3 (world avg. 21.3).
Death rate per 1,000 population (2002): 5.2 (world avg. 9.1).
Natural increase rate per 1,000 population (2002): 17.1 (world avg. 12.2).
Total fertility rate (avg. births per childbearing woman; 2002): 2.6.
Marriage rate per 1,000 population (2000): 5.8.
Life expectancy at birth (2002): male 68.9 years; female 71.7 years.
Notified cases of infectious diseases per 100,000 population (1996): measles 67.8; typhoid fever 15.2; hepatitis 11.3; dysentery 10.1; meningitis 9.4.

National economy

Budget (2001). Revenue: DA 1,478,500,000,000 (taxes on hydrocarbons 68.7%, value-added taxes 7.0%, other 24.3%). Expenditures: DA 1,321,000,000,000 (current expenditure 72.9%, development expenditure 27.1%).
Land use (1994): forested 1.6%; meadows and pastures 13.3%; agricultural and under permanent cultivation 3.4%; other (mostly desert) 81.7%.
Production (metric tons except as noted). Agriculture, forestry, fishing (2002): wheat 1,502,000, potatoes 1,000,000, tomatoes 830,000, barley 550,000, dates 437,000, onions 430,000, oranges 330,000, olives 200,000, grapes 196,000; livestock (number of live animals) 17,300,000 sheep, 3,200,000 goats; roundwood (2001) 7,396,295 cu m; fish catch (2000) 100,275. Mining and quarrying (2001): iron ore 1,271,000; phosphate rock 901,000; mercury 306. Manufacturing (value added in U.S.$'000,000; 1997): food products 463; cement, bricks, and tiles 393; iron and steel 118; tobacco products 114; paints, soaps, and related products 105; electrical machinery 79. Energy production (consumption): electricity (kW-hr; 2000) 25,412,000,000 (21,212,000,000); coal (metric tons; 1999) 24,000 (656,000); crude petroleum (barrels; 2000) 307,091,000 ([1999] 131,500,000); petroleum products (metric tons; 1999) 45,455,000 (11,212,000); natural gas (cu m; 2000) 79,762,000,000 (28,074,000,000).
Household income and expenditure. Average household size (2000) 6.3; income per household (2001) *c.* U.S.$6,700; sources of income (2001): wages and salaries 39.9%, self-employment 39.2%, transfers 20.9%; expenditure (2001): food and beverages 44.1%, clothing and footwear 11.6%, transportation and communications 11.5%, furniture 6.8%, education 6.5%, housing 5.6%, health 3.4%, other 10.5%.
Gross national product (2001): U.S.$50,355,000,000 (U.S.$1,635 per capita).

Structure of gross domestic product and labour force

	2000			
	in value DA '000,000	% of total value	labour force	% of labour force
Agriculture	325,751	8.0	897,984	11.0
Petroleum and natural gas	1,666,236[3]	40.9[3]	720,940	8.8
Other mining	5,022	0.1		
Manufacturing	234,624[3]	5.8[3]		
Public utilities	44,108	1.0		
Construction	292,046	7.2	669,826	8.2
Transp. and commun.	272,697	6.7	731,446	9.0
Trade, restaurants	478,840	11.7		
Pub. admin., defense	359,744	8.8	1,773,156	21.7
Services[4]	194,698	4.8	932,569	11.4
Other	204,909[5]	5.0[5]	2,427,700[6]	29.8[6]
TOTAL	4,078,675	100.0	8,153,621	100.0[7]

Population economically active (2001): total 9,074,000; activity rate of population 29.5% (participation rates: ages 15–64 [1998] 52.6%; female [1987] 9.2%; unemployed [2001] 27.3%).

Price and earnings indexes (1995 = 100)

	1996	1997	1998	1999	2000	2001	2002
Consumer price index	118.7	128.7	131.7	135.2	134.4	139.1	143.4
Earnings index	…	…	…	…	…	…	…

Public debt (external, outstanding; 2001): U.S.$20,786,000,000.
Tourism: receipts from visitors (2001) U.S.$100,000,000; expenditures by nationals abroad (2000) U.S.$193,000,000.

Foreign trade[8]

Balance of trade (current prices)

	1996	1997	1998	1999	2000	2001
U.S.$'000,000	+1,994	+5,206	+435	+3,363	+12,879	+9,610
% of total	9.9%	23.1%	2.4%	15.5%	41.3%	33.6%

Imports (2000): U.S.$9,152,000,000 (food 25.8%, of which wheat 8.8%; nonelectrical machinery 16.7%; transport equipment 9.6%). *Major import sources:* France 23.6%; U.S. 11.4%; Italy 8.9%; Germany 7.8%; Spain 6.0%.
Exports (2000): U.S.$22,031,000,000 (crude petroleum 42.0%, natural and manufactured gas 40.9%, refined petroleum 14.3%). *Major export destinations:* Italy 20.1%; U.S. 15.5%; France 13.3%; Spain 10.6%; The Netherlands 7.5%.

Transport and communications

Transport. Railroads (2000): route length 2,451 mi, 3,945 km; passenger-km 1,142,000,000; metric ton-km cargo 2,029,000,000. Roads (1995): total length 63,643 mi, 102,424 km (paved 69%). Vehicles (2001): passenger cars 1,692,148; trucks and buses 948,553. Air transport (2001)[9]: passenger-km 2,944,681,000; metric ton-km cargo 18,050,000; airports (1996) 28.

Communications

Medium	date	unit	number	units per 1,000 persons
Daily newspapers	2000	circulation	817,000	27
Radio	2000	receivers	7,380,000	244
Television	2000	receivers	3,300,000	110
Telephones	2001	main lines	1,880,000	61
Cellular telephones	2002	subscribers	300,000	9.6
Personal computers	2001	units	220,000	7.1
Internet	2002	users	300,000	16.0

Education and health

Educational attainment (1998). Percentage of economically active population age 6 and over having: no formal schooling 30.1%; primary education 29.9%; lower secondary 20.7%; upper secondary 13.4%; higher 4.3%; other 1.6%.
Literacy (1998): total population age 10 and over literate 15,314,109 (68.1%); males literate 8,650,719 (76.3%); females literate 6,663,392 (59.7%).

Education (1996–97)

	schools	teachers	students	student/ teacher ratio
Primary (age 6–11)	15,426	170,956	4,674,947	27.3
Secondary (age 12–17)	3,954[10]	151,948	2,618,242	17.2
Higher[10]	…	19,910	347,410	17.4

Health (1996): physicians 27,650 (1 per 1,015 persons); hospital beds 34,544 (1 per 812 persons); infant mortality rate per 1,000 live births (2002) 39.2.
Food (2000): daily per capita caloric intake 2,987 (vegetable products 90%, animal products 10%); 124% of FAO recommended minimum requirement.

Military

Total active duty personnel (2002): 136,700 (army 87.8%, navy 4.9%, air force 7.3%). *Military expenditure as percentage of GNP* (1999): 4.0% (world 2.4%); per capita expenditure U.S.$60.

[1]Includes 48 nonelected seats appointed by the president. [2]The Berber language, Tamazight, became a national language in April 2002. [3]Petroleum and natural gas includes (and Manufacturing excludes) refined petroleum and manufacture of hydrocarbons. [4]Includes finance and real estate. [5]Import taxes and duties. [6]Unemployed. [7]Detail does not add to total given because of rounding. [8]Imports c.i.f.; exports f.o.b. [9]Air Algérie. [10]1995–96.

Internet resources for further information:

- **Statistiques Algérie http://www.ons.dz/them_sta.htm**

American Samoa

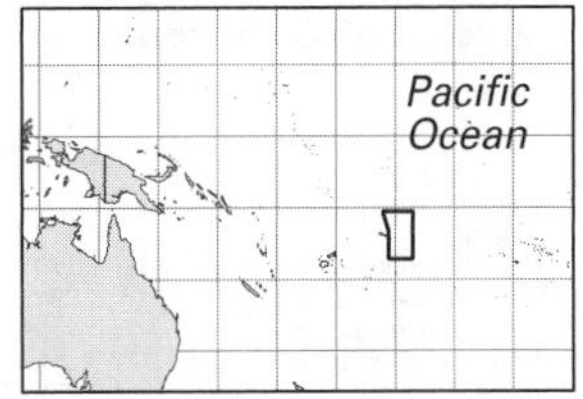

Official name: American Samoa (English); Amerika Samoa (Samoan).
Political status: unincorporated and unorganized territory of the United States with two legislative houses (Senate [18]; House of Representatives [20])[1].
Chief of state: President of the United States.
Head of government: Governor.
Capital: Fagatogo[2] (legislative and judicial) and Utulei (executive).
Official languages: English; Samoan.
Official religion: none.
Monetary unit: 1 dollar (U.S.$) = 100 cents; valuation (Sept. 8, 2003) 1 U.S.$ = £0.63.

Area and population

Districts and islands	area sq mi	area sq km	population 2000 census
Eastern District	25.9	67.1	23,441
Tutuila Island (part)	25.3	65.5	21,673
Aunu'u Island	0.6	1.6	1,768
Western District	28.8	74.6	32,435
Tutuila Island (part)	28.8	74.6	32,435
Manu'a District (Manu'a Islands)	21.9	56.7	1,378
Ofu Island	2.8	7.2	289
Olosega Island	2.0	5.2	216
Ta'u Island	17.1	44.3	873
Rose Island[3]	0.1	0.3	0
Swains Island[3]	0.6	1.5	37
LAND AREA	77.3	200.2	—
INLAND WATER (HARBOUR) AREAS	7.1	18.4	—
TOTAL AREA	84.4	218.6	57,291

Demography

Population (2003): 61,200.
Density (2002)[4]: persons per sq mi 791.7, persons per sq km 305.7.
Urban-rural (2001): urban 53.2%; rural 46.8%.
Sex distribution (2000): male 48.50%; female 51.50%.
Age breakdown (2000): under 15, 38.7%; 15–29, 24.5%; 30–44, 20.5%; 45–59, 10.9%; 60–74, 4.4%; 75 and over, 1.0%.
Population projection: (2010) 70,000; (2020) 86,000.
Doubling time: 35 years.
Ethnic composition (2000): Samoan 88.2%; Tongan 2.8%; Asian 2.8%; Caucasian 1.1%; other 5.1%.
Religious affiliation (1995): 4 major Protestant groups 60.1%; Roman Catholic 19.4%; Mormon 12.5%; other 8.0%.
Major villages (2000): Tafuna 8,406; Nu'uuli 5,154; Pago Pago 4,278 (urban agglomeration [2001] 15,000); Leone 3,568; Fagatogo 2,096[2].

Vital statistics

Birth rate per 1,000 population (2002): 24.0 (world avg. 21.3); legitimate, n.a.; illegitimate, n.a.
Death rate per 1,000 population (2002): 4.3 (world avg. 9.1).
Natural increase rate per 1,000 population (2002): 19.7 (world avg. 12.2).
Total fertility rate (avg. births per childbearing woman; 2000): 3.6.
Marriage rate per 1,000 population (2000): 4.7.
Divorce rate per 1,000 population (1993): 0.5.
Life expectancy at birth (2002): male 71.1 years; female 80.2 years.
Major causes of death per 100,000 population (2000): heart diseases 89; malignant neoplasms (cancers) 61; cerebrovascular diseases 31; accidents 28; other causes 72.

National economy

Budget (1997). Revenue: U.S.$144,438,095 (U.S. government grants 67.4%; taxes 23.6%; insurance claims 4.9%; other 4.1%). Expenditures: U.S.$152,912,308 (education and culture 28.5%; health and welfare 27.3%; general government 14.1%; public works and parks 12.8%; public safety 6.9%; economic development 6.1%; capital projects 3.4%; debt 0.9%).
Gross national product (1997): U.S.$253,000,000 (U.S.$4,300 per capita).

Structure of labour force

	2000 labour force	2000 % of labour force
Agriculture, forestry, and fishing	517	2.9
Manufacturing	5,900	33.4
Construction	1,066	6.0
Transp. and commun.	1,036	5.9
Trade	1,790	10.1
Finance, real estate	311	1.8
Public administration	1,550	8.8
Services	4,548	25.7
Other	946[5]	5.4
TOTAL	17,664	100.0

Production (metric tons except as noted). Agriculture, forestry, fishing (2002): coconuts 4,700, taros 1,500, fruits (excluding melons) 1,200, bananas 750, vegetables and melons 470; livestock (number of live animals; 2002) 10,700 pigs, 37,000 chickens; forestry, n.a.; fish catch (2000) 866, of which tunas, bonitos, and billfish 820. Mining and quarrying: n.a. Manufacturing (value of export in U.S.$; 2000): canned tuna 333,487,000; pet food 9,696,000; other manufactures include garments, handicrafts, soap, and alcoholic beverages. Construction (value of building permits in U.S.$; 2000) 12,801,000. Energy production (consumption): electricity (kW-hr; 2000) 169,082,000 (154,167,000); coal, none (n.a.); crude petroleum, none (n.a.); petroleum products (metric tons; 1998) none (94,000); natural gas, none (n.a.).
Public debt: n.a.
Population economically active (2000): total 17,664, activity rate of total population 30.8% (participation rates: ages 16 and over 52.0%; female 41.5%; unemployed 5.3%).

Price index (1990 = 100)

	1990	1991	1992	1993	1994	1995	1996
Consumer price index	100.0	104.0	109.0	109.0	111.0	113.0	118.0

Household income and expenditure. Average household size (2000) 6.0; income per household (2000): U.S.$24,000; sources of income: n.a.; expenditure (1995): food and beverages 30.9%, housing and furnishings 25.8%, church donations 20.7%, transportation and communications 9.4%, clothing 2.9%, other 10.3%.
Tourism: receipts from visitors (1997) U.S.$10,000,000; expenditures by nationals abroad (1996) U.S.$2,000,000.
Land use (1994): forested 70%; agricultural and under permanent cultivation 15%; other 15%.

Foreign trade[6]

Balance of trade (current prices)

	1995	1996	1997	1998	1999	2000
U.S.$'000,000	–144.2	–157.8	–104.3	–83.4	–107.5	–159.6
% of total	21.0%	20.1%	10.9%	9.1%	13.5%	18.7%

Imports (2000): U.S.$505,900,000 (fish for cannery 53.5%, other food 12.8%, tinplate 10.7%, mineral fuels 7.0%). *Major import sources:* United States 56.7%; Australia 14.9%; New Zealand 11.1%; Fiji 5.7%; Samoa 3.1%.
Exports (2000)[6]: U.S.$346,300,000 (tuna in airtight containers 96.3%, pet food 2.8%, fish meal 0.7%). *Major export destinations:* United States 99.6%.

Transport and communications

Transport. Railroads: none. Roads (1991): total length 217 mi, 350 km (paved, 43%). Vehicles (2000): passenger cars 6,394; trucks and buses 765. Merchant marine (1990): vessels (100 gross tons and over) 3; total deadweight tonnage 143. Air transport (2000): incoming flights 7,899; incoming passengers 91,826; incoming cargo 677 metric tons; airports (2000) with scheduled flights 3.

Communications

Medium	date	unit	number	units per 1,000 persons
Daily newspapers	1996	circulation	5,000	85
Radio	1997	receivers	57,000	929
Television	2000	receivers	13,200	211
Telephones	2000	main lines	10,252	178
Cellular telephones	2000	subscribers	3,304	57

Education and health

Educational attainment (2000). Percentage of population age 25 and over having: no formal schooling to some secondary education 33.9%; completed secondary 39.3%; some college 19.4%; undergraduate degree 4.8%; graduate degree 2.6%. *Literacy* (2000): total population age 10 and over literate 33,993 (99.4%); males literate 17,704 (99.4%); females literate 16,589 (99.5%).

Education (2000–01)

	schools[7]	teachers	students	student/teacher ratio
Primary (age 6–14)	32	...	11,396	...
Secondary (age 14–18)	9	...	4,075	...
Vocational	...	21[8]	160[8]	7.6[8]
Higher[9]	1	77	1,428	18.5

Health (1991): physicians 26 (1 per 1,888 persons); hospital beds (1995) 140 (1 per 4.7 persons); infant mortality rate per 1,000 live births (2001) 10.4.
Food: daily per capita caloric intake, n.a.

Military

Military defense is the responsibility of the United States.

[1]Excludes nonvoting delegate representing Swains Island. [2]The seat of the legislature, as defined by the Constitution of American Samoa, is at Fagatogo, one of a number of villages within an urban agglomeration collectively known as Pago Pago. [3]Not within district administrative structure. Swains Island is administered by a village government and a representative of the governor. [4]Based on land area. [5]Includes 909 unemployed and 37 in military. [6]Based on exports to United States only. [7]1999–2000. [8]1997–98. [9]American Samoa Community College at Mapusaga.

Internet resources for further information:
- **U.S. Department of the Interior: Pacific Web http://www.pacificweb.org**
- **Bank of Hawaii: Economics Research Center http://www.boh.com/econ/pacific**
- **American Samoa Government Department of Commerce http://www.amsamoa.com**

Andorra

Official name: Principat d'Andorra (Principality of Andorra).
Form of government: parliamentary coprincipality with one legislative house (General Council [28]).
Chiefs of state: President of France; Bishop of Urgell, Spain.
Head of government: Head of Government.
Capital: Andorra la Vella.
Official language: Catalan.
Official religion: none[1].
Monetary unit[2]: 1 euro (€) = 100 cents; valuation (Sept. 8, 2003) 1 U.S.$ = €0.90; 1 £ = €1.43.

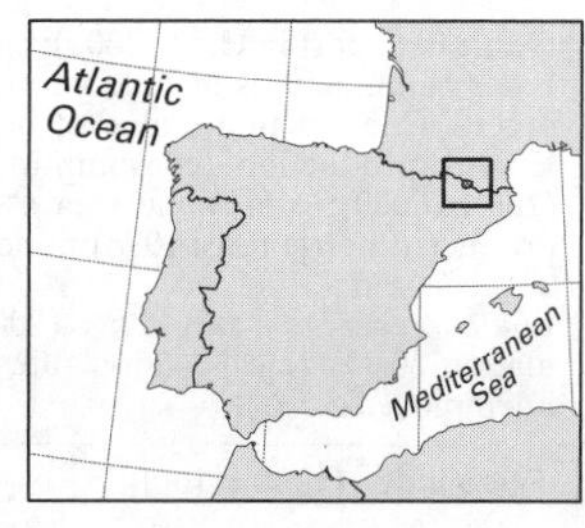

Area and population

Parishes	Capitals	area sq mi	area sq km	population 2002[3] estimate
Andorra la Vella	Andorra la Vella	23[4]	59[4]	20,787
Canillo	Canillo	47	121	3,014
Encamp	Encamp	29	74	10,627
La Massana	La Massana	23	61	6,375
Les Escaldes–Engordany	—	4	4	15,519
Ordino	Ordino	34	89	2,366
Sant Julià de Lòria	Sant Julià de Lòria	23	60	7,656
TOTAL		179	464	66,334[5]

Demography

Population (2003): 66,900.
Density (2003): persons per sq mi 373.7, persons per sq km 144.2.
Urban-rural (2002): urban 93%; rural 7%.
Sex distribution (2000): male 52.04%; female 47.96%.
Age breakdown (2000): under 15, 15.3%; 15–29, 19.8%; 30–44, 29.1%; 45–59, 19.2%; 60–74, 10.9%; 75 and over, 5.7%.
Population projection: (2010) 70,000; (2020) 74,000.
Doubling time: 94 years.
Ethnic composition (by nationality; 2000): Spanish 40.6%; Andorran 36.0%; Portuguese 10.2%; French 6.5%; British 1.4%; Moroccan 0.7%; German 0.5%; other 4.1%.
Religious affiliation (2000): Roman Catholic 89.1%; other Christian 4.3%; Muslim 0.6%; Hindu 0.5%; nonreligious 5.0%; other 0.5%.
Major urban areas (2002[3]): Andorra la Vella 20,787; Les Escaldes–Engordany 15,519; Encamp 10,627.

Vital statistics

Birth rate per 1,000 population (2000): 11.3[6] (world avg. 21.3).
Death rate per 1,000 population (2000): 3.9[6] (world avg. 9.1).
Natural increase rate per 1,000 population (2000): 7.4[6] (world avg. 12.2).
Total fertility rate (avg. births per childbearing woman; 2002): 1.2.
Marriage rate per 1,000 population (2000): 3.4.
Life expectancy at birth (2001): male 80.6 years; female 86.6 years.
Major causes of death per 100,000 population (1996–2000 avg.): cancers (neoplasms) 103.2; diseases of the circulatory system 90.0; diseases of the respiratory system 28.6; accidents and violence 24.3; diseases of the digestive system 16.9.

National economy

Budget (2001). Revenue: €234,705,780 (indirect taxes 75.2%, taxes from government enterprises 17.8%, revenue from capital 7.0%). Expenditures: €250,775,790 (current expenditures 51.5%, development expenditures 48.5%).
Public debt (1995): about U.S.$500,000,000.
Production. Agriculture (2000): tobacco 324 metric tons; other traditional crops include hay, potatoes, and grapes; livestock (number of live animals; 2000) 1,586 sheep[7], 1,181 cattle, 850 horses. Quarrying: small amounts of marble are quarried. Manufacturing (value of recorded exports in €'000; 2000): electrical machinery and apparatus 11,090; motor vehicles and parts 8,500; newspapers and periodicals 4,690; clothing 2,180; other products include furniture, cigarettes, and liqueurs. Construction (approved new building construction; 2000): 233,940 sq m. Energy production (consumption): electricity (kW-hr; 1997) 116,000,000 ([2000] 412,143,000); coal, none (n.a.); crude petroleum, none (n.a.); petroleum products, none ([2000] 201,677,000 litres); natural gas, none (n.a.).
Household expenditure (1997)[8]: food, beverages, and tobacco 25.5%, housing and energy 19.4%, transportation 17.7%, clothing and footwear 9.2%.
Land use (1994): forested 22.0%; meadows and pastures 56.0%; agricultural and under permanent cultivation 2.0%; other 20.0%.
Population economically active (2000)[9]: total 34,494; activity rate of total population 52.4% (participation rates: ages 15–64, 72.6%; female, n.a.; unemployed [2000] unofficially, none[10]).

Price and earnings indexes (1997 = 100)[11]

	1994	1995	1996	1997	1998	1999	2000
Consumer price index	...	...	...	100.0	101.6	104.3	108.8
Annual earnings index	91.2	95.5	98.6	100.0	101.6	103.7	105.8

Gross national product (at current market prices; 1998): U.S.$1,110,000,000 (U.S.$16,930 per capita)[12].

Structure of labour force[9]

	2000 labour force	2000 % of labour force
Agriculture, Mining	161	0.5
Manufacturing	1,170	3.4
Construction	5,791	16.8
Public utilities	...	...
Transp. and commun.	...	...
Trade	6,673	19.3
Restaurants, hotels	6,434	18.7
Finance, real estate, insurance	1,416	4.1
Pub. admin., defense	4,275	12.4
Services	6,533	18.9
Other	2,041	5.9
TOTAL	34,494	100.0

Tourism (2001): 11,351,000 visitors; number of hotels 271.

Foreign trade

Balance of trade (current prices)

	1995	1996	1997	1998	1999	2000
€'000,000	–754	–779	–902	–918	–989	–1,057
% of total	88.0%	91.7%	91.4%	89.8%	92.4%	91.4%

Imports (2000): €1,106,006,000 (food, beverages, and tobacco 20.0%; machinery and apparatus 16.2%; chemicals and chemical products 10.1%; transport equipment 9.1%; textiles and wearing apparel 9.1%; photographic and optical goods and watches and clocks 5.0%). *Major import sources:* Spain 48.5%; France 26.6%; Germany 4.4%; Italy 4.1%; Japan 3.1%.
Exports (2000): €49,491,000 (electrical machinery and apparatus 17.2%; motor vehicles and parts 15.2%; newspapers, books, and periodicals 9.5%; chemicals and chemical products 7.4%; optical and photo equipment 7.2%; tobacco 6.9%; clothing 4.4%). *Major export destinations:* Spain 60.9%; France 26.1%; Hong Kong 2.4%; Greece 1.7%; Germany 1.5%.

Transport and communications

Transport. Railroads: none; however, both French and Spanish railways stop near the border. Roads (1999): total length 167 mi, 269 km (paved 74%). Vehicles (2000): passenger cars 60,287; trucks and buses 4,400. Airports with scheduled flights: none.

Communications

Medium	date	unit	number	units per 1,000 persons
Daily newspapers	1996	circulation	4,000	62
Radio	1997	receivers	16,000	247
Television	2000	receivers	30,400	458
Telephones	2001	main lines	35,000	438
Cellular telephones	2001	subscribers	23,543	302
Internet	2001	users	7,000	88

Education and health

Educational attainment (mid-1980s). Percentage of population age 15 and over having: no formal schooling 5.5%; primary education 47.3%; secondary education 21.6%; postsecondary education 24.9%; unknown 0.7%. *Literacy:* resident population is virtually 100% literate.

Education (1998–99)

	schools	teachers	students	student/ teacher ratio
Primary/lower secondary (age 7–15)	12	...	5,960	...
Upper secondary	6	...	1,164	...
Higher	1	...	1,405	...

Health (1999): physicians 218 (1 per 303 persons); hospital beds 203 (1 per 323 persons); infant mortality rate per 1,000 live births (1999–2001 avg.) 4.1.
Food: n.a.

Military

Total active duty personnel: none. France and Spain are responsible for Andorra's external security; the police force is assisted in alternate years by either French gendarmerie or Barcelona police.

[1]Roman Catholicism enjoys special recognition in accordance with Andorran tradition. [2]The French franc and Spanish peseta were the former monetary units; on Jan. 1, 2002, F 6.56 = €1 and Pta 166.39 = €1. [3]January 1. [4]Andorra la Vella includes Les Escaldes–Engordany. [5]Detail does not add to total given because of statistical discrepancy. [6]Official government figures. [7]Large herds of sheep and goats from Spain and France feed in Andorra in the summer. [8]Weights of consumer price index components. [9]Labour force receiving wages only; total population economically active equals 39,895. [10]The restricted size of the indigenous labour force has in the near past necessitated immigration to serve the tourist trade. [11]All indexes are end of year. [12]Tourism (including winter-season sports, fairs, festivals, and income earned from low-duty imported manufactured items) and the banking system are the primary sources of GNP.

Internet resources for further information:
- **Andorra National Information Centre http://www.andorra.ad**
- **Department d'Estudis i d'Estadística http://www.finances.ad**

Angola

Official name: República de Angola (Republic of Angola).
Form of government: unitary multiparty republic with one legislative house (National Assembly [220])[1].
Head of state and government: President assisted by Prime Minister[2].
Capital: Luanda.
Official language: Portuguese.
Official religion: none.
Monetary unit: 1 refloated kwanza = 100 lwei; valuation (Sept. 8, 2003) 1 U.S.$ = refloated kwanza 79.83; 1 £ = refloated kwanza 126.57.

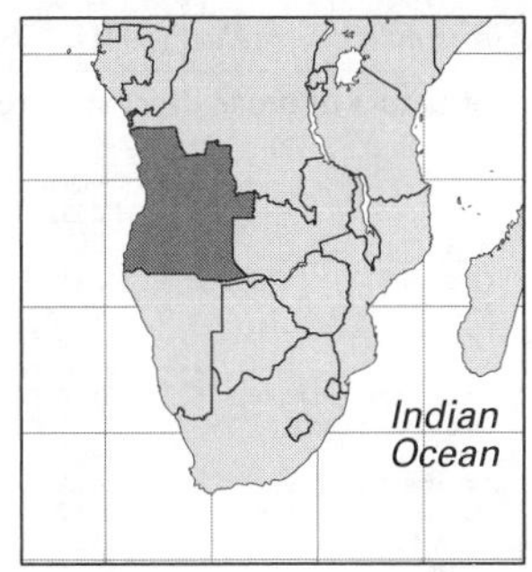

Area and population

Provinces	Capitals	area sq mi	area sq km	population 2001 estimate
Bengo	Caxito	12,112	31,371	...
Benguela	Benguela	12,273	31,788	...
Bié	Kuito	27,148	70,314	...
Cabinda	Cabinda	2,807	7,270	...
Cunene	N'Giva	34,495	89,342	...
Huambo	Huambo	13,233	34,274	...
Huíla	Lubango	28,958	75,002	...
Kuando Kubango	Menongue	76,853	199,049	...
Kuanza Norte	N'Dalatando	9,340	24,190	...
Kuanza Sul	Sumbe	21,490	55,660	...
Luanda	Luanda	934	2,418	...
Lunda Norte	Lucapa	39,685	102,783	...
Lunda Sul	Saurimo	17,625	45,649	...
Malanje	Malanje	37,684	97,602	...
Moxico	Lwena	86,110	223,023	...
Namibe	Namibe	22,447	58,137	...
Uíge	Uíge	22,663	58,698	...
Zaire	M'Banza Kongo	15,494	40,130	...
TOTAL		481,354[3]	1,246,700	10,342,000

Demography

Population (2003): 10,776,000.
Density (2003): persons per sq mi 22.4, persons per sq km 8.6.
Urban-rural (2001): urban 34.9%; rural 65.1%.
Sex distribution (2002): male 50.54%; female 49.46%.
Age breakdown (2002): under 15, 43.5%; 15–29, 26.5%; 30–44, 16.8%; 45–59, 8.6%; 60–74, 4.1%; 75 and over, 0.5%.
Population projection: (2010) 12,250,000; (2020) 14,473,000.
Doubling time: 35 years.
Ethnic composition (2000): Ovimbundu 25.2%; Kimbundu 23.1%; Kongo 12.6%; Lwena (Luvale) 8.2%; Chokwe 5.0%; Kwanyama 4.1%; Nyaneka 3.9%; Luchazi 2.3%; Ambo (Ovambo) 2.0%; Mbwela 1.7%; Nyemba 1.7%; other 10.2%.
Religious affiliation (2001): Christian 94.1%, of which Roman Catholic 62.1%, Protestant 15.0%; traditional beliefs 5.0%; other 0.9%.
Major cities (1999): Luanda 2,555,000; Huambo 400,000[4]; Benguela 155,000[5]; Lobito 150,000[5]; Lubango 105,000[6].

Vital statistics

Birth rate per 1,000 population (2002): 46.0 (world avg. 21.3).
Death rate per 1,000 population (2002): 25.8 (world avg. 9.1).
Natural increase rate per 1,000 population (2002): 20.2 (world avg. 12.2).
Total fertility rate (avg. births per childbearing woman; 2002): 6.4.
Life expectancy at birth (2002): male 36.2 years; female 38.1 years.
Major causes of death (percentage of total deaths; 1990): diarrheal diseases 25.8%; malaria 19.4%; cholera 7.3%; acute respiratory infections 6.8%.

National economy

Budget (2002). Revenue: U.S.$4,367,000,000 (oil revenue 76.7%, non-oil revenue 23.3%, of which tax on goods 7.7%, income tax 6.6%, import duties 5.6%, other 3.4%). Expenditure: U.S.$5,370,000,000 (defense and internal security 15.0%, social security 7.0%, education 6.0%, economic services 5.2%, health 4.0%, interest payment 2.1%, other 60.7%).
Public debt (external, outstanding; 2001): U.S.$7,443,000,000.
Household income and expenditure. Average household size (2000) 4.7; annual income per household: n.a.; sources of income: n.a.; expenditure: n.a.
Production (metric tons except as noted). Agriculture, forestry, fishing (2002): cassava 5,400,000, corn (maize) 430,000, sugarcane 360,000, sweet potatoes 355,000, bananas 300,000, oil palm fruit 280,000, millet 100,000, dry beans 89,000, pineapples 40,000, peanuts (groundnuts) 27,000, coffee 2,160; livestock (number of live animals) 4,150,000 cattle, 2,050,000 goats, 780,000 pigs, 340,000 sheep, 6,800,000 chickens; roundwood (2001) 4,356,600 cu m; fish catch (2001) 252,518. Mining and quarrying (2000): diamonds 4,349,000 carats. Manufacturing (1999): bread 87,500; frozen fish 57,700; wheat flour 57,500; soap 8,565; salt 7,803; leather shoes 25,000 pairs; beer 160,900 hectolitres; fabric 316,000 sq m. Energy production (consumption): electricity (kW-hr; 2000) 1,445,000,000 (1,235,000,000); coal, none (none); crude petroleum (barrels; 2001) 270,800,000 ([1999] 25,200,000); petroleum products (metric tons; 1999) 1,760,000 (922,000); natural gas (cu m; 1999) 545,300,000 (545,300,000).
Tourism: receipts from visitors (2001) U.S.$22,000,000; expenditures by nationals abroad (2000) U.S.$136,000,000.
Gross national product (at current market prices; 2001): U.S.$6,700,000,000 (U.S.$500 per capita).

Structure of gross domestic product and labour force

	2002 in value Kz '000,000,000	2002 % of total value	1999 labour force	1999 % of labour force
Agriculture	38.3	7.8	4,132,000	72.1
Mining	298.8	61.0		
Manufacturing	18.2	3.7	1,597,000	27.9
Construction	16.5	3.4		
Finance, Trade, Public utilities, Transp. and commun.	74.9	15.3		
Pub. admin., defense, Services, Other	42.9	8.8		
Other			...	...
TOTAL	489.6	100.0	5,729,000	100.0

Population economically active (1999): total 5,729,000; activity rate of total population 57.7% (participation rates over age 10 [1991] 60.1%; female 38.4%; unemployed [2002] 70%).

Price and earnings indexes (1995 = 100)

	1996	1997	1998	1999	2000	2001
Consumer price index	4,245.2	13,550.1	25,327.3	43,661	61,311	64,811
Monthly earnings index	...	...	...	...	...	...

Land use (1995): forested 18.5%; meadows and pastures 43.3%; agricultural and under permanent cultivation 2.8%; other 35.4%.

Foreign trade

Balance of trade (current prices)

	1996	1997	1998	1999	2000	2001
U.S.$'000,000	+3,055	+2,410	+1,464	+2,077	+4,881	+3,355
% of total	42.8%	31.7%	26.0%	24.1%	44.5%	34.6%

Imports (2001): U.S.$3,179,000,000 (consumer goods 68.4%, capital goods 22.1%, intermediate goods 9.5%). *Major import sources* (2001): South Korea 22.4%; Portugal 14.5%; South Africa 12.3%; U.S. 8.9%; France 4.8%.
Exports (2001): U.S.$6,534,000,000 (crude petroleum 90.5%, diamonds 7.6%, refined petroleum 1.4%, coffee 0.1%). *Major export destinations* (2001): U.S. 44.3%; China 18.7%; France 9.0%; Belgium 8.8%; Taiwan 6.8%.

Transport and communications

Transport. Railroads (2001): route length 1,722 mi, 2,771 km; (1991) passenger-mi 153,000,000, passenger-km 246,200,000; short ton-mi cargo 28,100,000, metric ton-km cargo 45,300,000. Roads (1998): total length 45,128 mi, 72,626 km (paved 25%). Vehicles (1997): passenger cars 207,000; trucks and buses 25,000. Merchant marine (1998): vessels (100 gross tons and over) 123; total deadweight tonnage 73,907. Air transport (2001)[7]: passenger-mi 455,400,000, passenger-km 732,968,000; short ton-mi cargo 35,800,000, metric ton-km cargo 57,662,000; airports (1999) with scheduled flights 17.

Communications

Medium	date	unit	number	units per 1,000 persons
Daily newspapers	2000	circulation	111,000	11
Television	2000	receivers	193,000	19
Telephones	2000	main lines	85,000	6.1
Cellular telephones	2002	subscribers	130,000	9.3
Personal computers	2002	units	27,000	1.9
Internet	2002	users	41,000	2.9

Education and health

Educational attainment: n.a. *Literacy* (1998): percentage of population age 15 and over literate 41.7%; males literate 55.6%; females literate 28.5%.

Education (1997–98)

	schools[8]	teachers	students	student/ teacher ratio
Primary (age 7–10)	6,308	31,062[9]	1,342,116	...
Secondary (age 11–16)	5,276	5,138[10]	267,399	...
Voc., teacher tr.	...	566[10]	22,888[12]	...
Higher	1	776	8,337	10.7

Health (1997): physicians 736 (1 per 12,985 persons); hospital beds (1990) 11,857 (1 per 845 persons); infant mortality rate per 1,000 live births (2002) 195.2.
Food (2000): daily per capita caloric intake 1,953 (vegetable products 92%, animal products 8%); 81% of FAO recommended minimum requirement.

Military

Total active duty personnel (2002): 100,000 (army 90.0%, navy 4.0%, air force 6.0%). *Military expenditure as percentage of GNP* (1999): 21.2% (world 2.4%); per capita expenditure U.S.$248.

[1]Civil war begun in 1975 was officially declared over on Aug. 2, 2002. A cease-fire agreement had been signed earlier in April 2002. [2]Post of Prime Minister abolished in January 1999 and reinstated in December 2002. [3]Detail does not add to total given because of rounding. [4]1995. [5]1983. [6]1984. [7]TAAG airline. [8]1985–86. [9]1991–92. [10]1989–90.

Internet resources for further information:

- **Official Home Page of the Republic of Angola http://www.angola.org**
- **Bank of Angola http://www.ebonet.net/bna/bna_blind.htm**

Antigua and Barbuda

Official name: Antigua and Barbuda.
Form of government: constitutional monarchy with two legislative houses (Senate [17]; House of Representatives [17[1]]).
Chief of state: British Monarch represented by Governor-General.
Head of government: Prime Minister.
Capital: Saint John's.
Official language: English.
Official religion: none.
Monetary unit: 1 Eastern Caribbean dollar (EC$) = 100 cents; valuation (Sept. 8, 2003) 1 U.S.$ = EC$2.70; 1 £ = EC$4.28.

Area and population	area		population
			2001
Parishes (of Antigua)[2]	sq mi	sq km	census[3]
Saint George	9.3	24.1	
Saint John's	28.5	73.8	
Saint Mary	22.0	57.0	74,324
Saint Paul	18.5	47.9	
Saint Peter	12.7	32.9	
Saint Phillip	17.0	44.0	
Other islands[2]			
Barbuda	62.0	160.6	1,417
Redonda	0.5	1.3	0
TOTAL	170.5	441.6	75,741

Demography

Population (2003): 76,800.
Density (2003): persons per sq mi 450.4, persons per sq km 173.9.
Urban-rural (2001): urban 36.9%; rural 63.1%.
Sex distribution (2001): male 47.55%; female 52.45%.
Age breakdown (1991): under 15, 30.4%; 15–29, 27.8%; 30–44, 20.5%; 45–59, 10.2%; 60–74, 7.7%; 75 and over, 3.4%.
Population projection: (2010) 80,000; (2020) 84,000.
Doubling time: 56 years.
Ethnic composition (2000): black 82.4%; U.S. white 12.0%; mulatto 3.5%; British 1.3%; other 0.8%.
Religious affiliation (1991): Protestant 73.7%, of which Anglican 32.1%, Moravian 12.0%, Methodist 9.1%, Seventh-day Adventist 8.8%; Roman Catholic 10.8%; Jehovah's Witness 1.2%; Rastafarian 0.8%[4]; other religion/no religion/not stated 13.5%.
Major city (2001): Saint John's 24,000[5].

Vital statistics

Birth rate per 1,000 population (2002): 18.4 (world avg. 21.3); (1988) legitimate 23.4%; illegitimate 76.6%.
Death rate per 1,000 population (2002): 5.8 (world avg. 9.1).
Natural increase rate per 1,000 population (2002): 12.6 (world avg. 12.2).
Total fertility rate (avg. births per childbearing woman; 2001): 2.3.
Marriage rate per 1,000 population (1995): 22.1.
Divorce rate per 1,000 population (1988): 0.2.
Life expectancy at birth (2002): male 68.7 years; female 73.5 years.
Major causes of death per 100,000 population (1993–95): diseases of the circulatory system 258.1, of which cerebrovascular disease 103.3, diseases of pulmonary circulation and other forms of heart disease 76.9; malignant neoplasms (cancers) 104.9; endocrine and metabolic disorders 73.7.

National economy

Budget (2001). Revenue: EC$364,900,000 (tax revenue 89.0%, of which taxes on international transactions 55.0%, consumption taxes 18.9%, corporate income taxes 13.4%; nontax revenue 11.0%). Expenditures: EC$410,300,000 (current expenditures 82.2%; development expenditures 17.8%).
Public debt (external, outstanding; end of 1998): U.S.$406,400,000.
Production (metric tons except as noted). Agriculture, forestry, fishing (2002): tropical fruit (including papayas, guavas, soursops, and oranges) 6,750, mangoes 1,400, eggplants 270, lemons and limes 230, carrots 220, "Antiguan Black" pineapples 150; livestock (number of live animals) 18,500 sheep, 13,800 cattle; roundwood, n.a.; fish catch (2000) 1,481. Mining and quarrying: crushed stone for local use. Manufacturing (1994): beer and malt 166,000 cases; T-shirts 179,000 units; other manufactures include cement, handicrafts, and furniture, as well as electronic components for export. Construction (1998): gross value of building applications EC$323,000,000. Energy production (consumption): electricity (kW-hr; 1999) 99,000,000 (99,000,000); coal, none (none); crude petroleum, none (none); petroleum products (metric tons; 1999) negligible (114,000); natural gas, none (none).
Population economically active (1991): total 26,753; activity rate of total population 45.1% (participation rates: ages 15–64, 69.7%; female 45.6%; unemployed [2000] 11.0%).

Price and earnings indexes (1996 = 100)	1996	1997	1998	1999	2000	2001
Consumer price index	100.0	98.9	103.6	104.4	104.6	106.3
Annual earnings index[6]	100.0	100.0	106.0	106.0	106.0	106.0

Household income and expenditure. Average household size (2001) 3.1; income per household: n.a.; sources of income: n.a.; expenditure: n.a.

Gross national product (2001): U.S.$621,000,000 (U.S.$8,200 per capita).

Structure of gross domestic product and labour force	2000		1991	
	in value EC$'000,000	% of total value	labour force	% of labour force
Agriculture, fishing	61.1	4.0	1,040	3.9
Quarrying	26.8	1.7	64	0.2
Manufacturing	35.2	2.3	1,444	5.4
Construction	199.2	12.9	3,109	11.6
Public utilities	52.4	3.4	435	1.6
Transp. and commun.	311.6	20.1	2,395	9.0
Trade, restaurants, and hotels	348.5	22.5	8,524	31.9
Finance, real estate	248.2	16.1	1,454	5.4
Pub. admin., defense	269.2	17.4	2,572	9.6
Services	118.0	7.6	5,207	19.5
Other	–124.2[7]	–8.0[7]	509	1.9
TOTAL	1,546.2	100.0	26,753	100.0

Land use (1994): forested 11.0%; meadows and pastures 9.0%; agricultural and under permanent cultivation 18.0%; other 62.0%.
Tourism: receipts from visitors (2001) U.S.$272,000,000; expenditures by nationals abroad U.S.$31,000,000.

Foreign trade[8]

Balance of trade (current prices)	1996	1997	1998	1999	2000	2001
U.S.$'000,000	–302	–297	–304	–335	–322	–318
% of total	90.0%	91.9%	91.1%	91.4%	90.8%	90.4%

Imports (1998): U.S.$357,500,000 ([9]agricultural products 11%, other [including petroleum products for reexport] 89%). *Major import sources:* United States 26.6%; United Kingdom 10.0%; Trinidad and Tobago 3.1%; Canada 3.0%.
Exports (1998): U.S.$36,200,000 (reexports [significantly, petroleum products reexported to neighbouring islands] 59.1%, domestic exports 40.9%). *Major export destinations:* Barbados 9.5%; Trinidad and Tobago 7.3%; St. Lucia 7.3%; United Kingdom 6.1%; unspecified 52.5%.

Transport and communications

Transport. Railroad[10]. Roads (1998): total length 155 mi, 250 km (paved, n.a.). Vehicles (1995): passenger cars 13,588; trucks and buses 1,342. Merchant marine (1992): vessels (100 gross tons and over) 292; total deadweight tonnage 997,381. Air transport (1999): passenger-mi 172,000,000, passenger-km 276,300,000; short ton-mi cargo 205,000, metric ton-km cargo 300,000; airports (2001) with scheduled flights 2.

Communications Medium	date	unit	number	units per 1,000 persons
Daily newspapers	1996	circulation	6,000	87
Radio	1997	receivers	36,000	523
Television	1997	receivers	31,000	451
Telephones	2001	main lines	37,300	474
Cellular telephones	2001	subscribers	25,000	318
Internet	2001	users	7,000	90

Education and health

Educational attainment (1991). Percentage of population age 25 and over having: no formal schooling 1.1%; primary education 50.5%; secondary 33.4%; higher (not university) 5.4%; university 6.2%; other/unknown 3.4%. *Literacy* (1995): percentage of total population age 15 and over literate 90.0%.

Education (1996–97)	schools	teachers	students	student/ teacher ratio
Primary (age 5–11)	58	559	12,229	21.9
Secondary (age 12–16)	13	389	4,260	11.0
Higher[11]	1	16	46	2.9

Health (1996): physicians 75 (1 per 915 persons); hospital beds 255 (1 per 269 persons); infant mortality rate per 1,000 live births (2002) 21.6.
Food (2000): daily per capita caloric intake 2,381 (vegetable products 67%, animal products 33%); 102% of FAO recommended minimum requirement.

Military

Total active duty personnel (2001): a 170-member defense force (army 73.5%, navy 26.5%) is part of the Eastern Caribbean regional security system. *Military expenditure as percentage of GNP* (1998): 0.7%[9] (world 2.5%); per capita expenditure U.S.$57.

[1]Directly elected seats only; attorney general and speaker may serve ex officio if they are not elected to House of Representatives. [2]Community councils on Antigua and the local government council on Barbuda are the organs of local government. [3]Preliminary figures. [4]Increased to more than 3% of population by 2000. [5]Large settlements include (1991): All Saints 2,230; Liberta 1,473; Codrington 814. [6]Public sector only. [7]Net indirect taxes less imputed bank service charges. [8]Balance of trade excludes reexports; data for commodities and destinations includes reexports. [9]Estimated percentages. [10]Mostly nonoperative privately owned tracks. [11]1994–95.

Internet resources for further information:
- **Eastern Caribbean Central Bank http://www.eccb-centralbank.org**
- **Ministry of Foreign Affairs http://www.foreignaffairs.gov.ag**

Argentina

Official name: República Argentina (Argentine Republic).
Form of government: federal republic with two legislative houses (Senate [72]; Chamber of Deputies [257]).
Head of state and government: President[1].
Capital: Buenos Aires.
Official language: Spanish.
Official religion: Roman Catholicism.
Monetary unit: 1 peso (pl. pesos) (Arg$) = 100 centavos; valuation (Sept. 8, 2003) 1 U.S.$ = Arg$2.95; 1 £ = Arg$4.67.

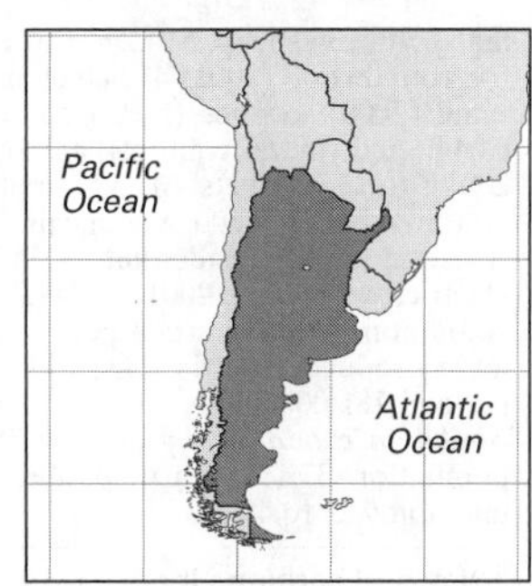

Area and population

Provinces	Capitals	area sq mi	area sq km	population 2001 census[2]
Buenos Aires	La Plata	118,754	307,571	13,818,677
Catamarca	Catamarca	39,615	102,602	333,661
Chaco	Resistencia	38,469	99,633	983,087
Chubut	Rawson	86,752	224,686	413,240
Córdoba	Córdoba	63,831	165,321	3,061,611
Corrientes	Corrientes	34,054	88,199	929,236
Entre Ríos	Paraná	30,418	78,781	1,156,799
Formosa	Formosa	27,825	72,066	485,700
Jujuy	San Salvador de Jujuy	20,548	53,219	611,484
La Pampa	Santa Rosa	55,382	143,440	298,460
La Rioja	La Rioja	34,626	89,680	289,820
Mendoza	Mendoza	57,462	148,827	1,576,585
Misiones	Posadas	11,506	29,801	963,869
Neuquén	Neuquén	36,324	94,078	473,315
Río Negro	Viedma	78,384	203,013	552,677
Salta	Salta	60,034	155,488	1,079,422
San Juan	San Juan	34,614	89,651	622,094
San Luis	San Luis	29,633	76,748	366,900
Santa Cruz	Río Gallegos	94,187	243,943	197,191
Santa Fe	Santa Fe	51,354	133,007	2,997,376
Santiago del Estero	Santiago del Estero	52,645	136,351	806,347
Tierra del Fuego[3]	Ushuaia	8,210	21,263	100,960
Tucumán	San Miguel de Tucumán	8,697	22,524	1,336,664
Autonomous city				
Buenos Aires	—	77	200	2,768,772
TOTAL		1,073,400[4]	2,780,092	36,223,947

Demography

Population (2003): 36,846,000.
Density (2002): persons per sq mi 34.3, persons per sq km 13.3.
Urban-rural (2000): urban 89.6%; rural 10.4%.
Sex distribution (2002): male 49.35%; female 50.65%.
Age breakdown (2002): under 15, 26.5%; 15–29, 25.4%; 30–44, 18.9%; 45–59, 15.1%; 60–74, 9.5%; 75 and over, 4.6%.
Population projection: (2010) 39,769,000; (2020) 43,486,000.
Ethnic composition (2000): European extraction 86.4%; mestizo 6.5%; Amerindian 3.4%; Arab 3.3%; other 0.4%.
Religious affiliation (2000): Roman Catholic 79.8%; Protestant 5.4%; Muslim 1.9%; Jewish 1.3%; other 11.6%.
Major cities (2001): Buenos Aires 2,768,772 (13,818,677[5]); Córdoba 1,261,000; San Justo 1,257,000; Rosario 943,000; La Plata 550,000; Mar del Plata 542,000.

Vital statistics

Birth rate per 1,000 population (2002): 17.7 (world avg. 21.3).
Death rate per 1,000 population (2002): 7.6 (world avg. 9.1).
Natural increase rate per 1,000 population (2002): 10.1 (world avg. 12.2).
Total fertility rate (avg. births per childbearing woman; 2002): 2.3.
Life expectancy at birth (2002): male 71.5 years; female 79.2 years.
Major causes of death per 100,000 population (1998): diseases of the circulatory system 265.8; neoplasms (cancers) 146.3; diseases of the respiratory system 91.0; accidents 30.5.

National economy

Budget (2000). Revenue: Arg$40,346,000,000 (current revenue 99.9%, of which tax revenue 91.2%, nontax revenue 8.7%; capital revenue 0.1%). Expenditure: Arg$48,225,000,000 (social security 48.5%; debt service 14.0%; general public services 9.2%; education 6.3%; economic services 4.7%; defense 4.0%; health 1.9%; other 11.4%).
Public debt (external, outstanding; 2001): U.S.$85,337,000,000.
Gross national product (2002): U.S.$276,228,000,000 (U.S.$7,460 per capita).

Structure of gross domestic product and labour force

	2000		1996	
	in value Arg$'000,000	% of total value	labour force	% of labour force
Agriculture	12,785	4.5	190,300[6]	1.5[6]
Mining	7,112	2.5		
Manufacturing	47,327	16.6	1,999,600	15.9
Construction	12,926	4.5	1,217,400	9.7
Public utilities	6,573	2.3	115,700	0.9
Transp. and commun.	23,957	8.4	873,300	6.9
Trade, restaurants	44,599	15.7	2,523,800	20.0
Finance, real estate	56,762	19.9	1,021,800	8.1
Pub. admin., defense	56,291	19.8	1,010,500	8.0
Services			3,573,000	28.4
Other	16,628	5.8	63,500	0.5
TOTAL	284,960	100.0	12,588,900[6]	100.0[4]

Production (metric tons except as noted). Agriculture, forestry, fishing (2002): soybeans 30,000,000, sugarcane 16,500,000, corn (maize) 14,710,000, wheat 12,500,000, sunflower seeds 3,843,600, grapes 2,460,000, potatoes 2,132,500; livestock (number of live animals) 50,669,000 cattle, 14,000,000 sheep; roundwood (2001) 9,970,000 cu m; fish catch (2000) 919,509. Mining and quarrying (2000): silver 78,271 kg; gold 25,924 kg. Manufacturing (2000): cement 6,114,000; crude steel 4,472,000; crude iron 3,605,000; sugar 1,462,000; paper 1,214,000; polyethylene 286,500; wine 14,500,000 hectolitres; beer 13,700,000 hectolitres. Energy production (consumption): electricity (kW-hr; 2001) 84,540,000,000 ([1999] 86,134,000,000); coal (1999) 336,000 (1,250,000); crude petroleum (barrels; 2001) 277,000,000 ([1999] 202,900,000); petroleum products (metric tons; 1999) 23,517,000 (20,594,000); natural gas (cu m; 2001) 53,298,000,000 ([1999] 35,719,700,000).
Tourism (2001): receipts U.S.$2,547,000,000; expenditures U.S.$3,800,000,000.
Population economically active (2000): total 15,846,000; activity rate of total population 44.4% (participation rates [1995]: ages 15–64, 64.5%; female 40.2%; unemployed 15.0%).

Price and earnings indexes (1995 = 100)

	1995	1996	1997	1998	1999	2000	2001
Consumer price index	100.0	100.2	100.7	101.6	100.4	99.5	98.4
Monthly earnings index[7]	100.0	100.7	...	...	...	...	...

Household size and expenditure. Average household size (2000) 3.7; expenditure (1985–86): food 38.2%, transportation 11.6%, housing 9.3%, energy 9.0%, clothing 8.0%, health 7.9%, recreation 7.5%, other 8.5%.

Foreign trade[8]

Balance of trade (current prices)

	1996	1997	1998	1999	2000	2001
U.S.$'000,000	+1,760	−2,123	−3,097	−794	+2,558	+7,451
% of total	3.8%	3.9%	5.5%	1.7%	5.1%	16.3%

Imports (2000): U.S.$25,243,000,000 (nonelectrical machinery 16.5%, electrical machinery 15.8%, chemicals and chemical products 15.6%, transport equipment 12.4%). *Major import sources:* Brazil 25.5%; U.S. 18.7%; Germany 5.0%; China 4.6%; Italy 4.0%; Japan 4.0%.
Exports (2000): U.S.$26,409,000,000 (food products and live animals 32.1%, of which soybean oil cake 8.2%, wheat 4.6%, corn (maize) 3.8%; crude petroleum 10.8%; road vehicles 7.4%; fixed vegetable oils 6.0%; refined petroleum 4.5%; nonelectrical machinery 4.5%). *Major export destinations:* Brazil 26.5%; U.S. 11.9%; Chile 10.1%; Spain 3.5%; Uruguay 3.1%; China 3.0%.

Transport and communications

Transport. Railroads (2000): route length 35,753 km; (1999) passenger-km 9,102,000,000; (1999) metric ton-km cargo 9,120,000,000. Roads (1999): total length 133,890 mi, 215,471 km (paved 29%). Vehicles (1998): passenger cars 5,047,630; commercial vehicles and buses 1,496,567. Air transport (2001): passenger-km 4,575,000,000; metric ton-km cargo 105,342,000; airports (1997) 39.

Communications

Medium	date	unit	number	units per 1,000 persons
Daily newspapers	2000	circulation	1,320,000	37
Radio	2000	receivers	24,300,000	681
Television	2000	receivers	10,500,000	293
Telephones	2002	main lines	8,009,400	219
Cellular telephones	2002	subscribers	6,500,000	178
Personal computers	2002	units	3,000,000	82
Internet	2002	users	4,100,000	112

Education and health

Educational attainment (1991). Percentage of population age 25 and over having: no formal schooling 5.7%; less than primary education 22.3%; primary 34.6%; incomplete secondary 12.5%; complete secondary 12.8%; higher 12.0%. *Literacy* (1999): percentage of total population age 15 and over literate 96.7%; males literate 96.8%; females literate 96.7%.

Education (1999–2000)

	schools	teachers	students	student/ teacher ratio
Primary (age 6–12)	22,283	307,874	4,609,077	15.0
Secondary (age 13–17)[9]	21,492	127,718	3,281,512	25.7
Higher	1,744	126,224	1,336,800	10.6

Health: physicians (1992) 88,800 (1 per 376 persons); hospital beds (1996) 115,803 (1 per 304 persons); infant mortality rate (2002) 16.7.
Food (2001): daily per capita caloric intake 3,171 (vegetable products 70%, animal products 30%); 135% of FAO recommended minimum requirement.

Military

Total active duty personnel (2002): 69,900 (army 59.2%, navy 22.9%, air force 17.9%). *Military expenditure as percentage of GNP* (1999): 1.6% (world 2.4%); per capita expenditure U.S.$118.

[1]Assisted by a ministerial coordinator who exercises general administration of the country. [2]Preliminary. [3]Area of Tierra del Fuego (province since 1991) excludes claims to British-held islands in the South Atlantic Ocean. [4]Detail does not add to total given because of rounding. [5]Urban agglomeration. [6]Based on October survey; data for agriculture and mining sectors are incomplete. [7]Manufacturing sector only. [8]Import figures are f.o.b. in balance of trade and c.i.f. in commodities and trading partners. [9]Secondary includes vocational and teacher training.

Internet resources for further information:
- **National Institute of Statistics and Censuses http://www.indec.mecon.ar**

Armenia

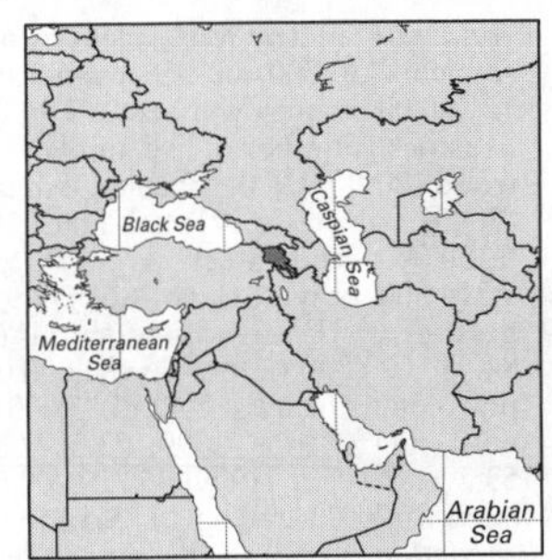

Official name: Hayastani Hanrapetut'yun (Republic of Armenia).
Form of government: unitary multiparty republic with a single legislative body (National Assembly [131]).
Head of state: President.
Head of government: Prime Minister.
Capital: Yerevan.
Official language: Armenian.
Official religion: none[1].
Monetary unit: 1 dram = 100 lumas; valuation (Sept. 8, 2003) official, 1 U.S.$ = 558.14 drams; 1 £ = 884.96 drams.

Area and population		area		population
				2002
Districts	**Centres**	sq mi	sq km	estimate
Aragatsotn	Ashtarak	1,063	2,753	168,100
Ararat	Artashat	809	2,096	311,400
Armavir	Armavir	480	1,242	323,300
Gegharkunik	Gavar	2,065[2]	5,348[2]	278,600
Lori	Vanadzor	1,463	3,789	392,300
Kotayk	Hrazdan	807	2,089	328,900
Shirak	Gyumri	1,035	2,681	361,400
Syunik	Kapan	1,740	4,506	164,000
Vayots-Dzor	Yeghegnadzor	891	2,308	69,400
Tavush	Ijevan	1,044	2,704	156,500
City				
Yerevan	—	88	227	1,246,100
TOTAL		11,484[3, 4]	29,743[3]	3,800,000[5]

Demography

Population (2003): 3,061,000.
Density (2003): persons per sq mi 266.5, persons per sq km 102.9.
Urban-rural (2002): urban 66.6%; rural 33.4%.
Sex distribution (2001): male 48.68%; female 51.32%.
Age breakdown (2001): under 15, 23.2%; 15–29, 24.6%; 30–44, 23.3%; 45–59, 14.5%; 60–74, 11.6%; 75 and over, 2.8%.
Population projection: (2010) 2,991,000; (2020) 2,926,000.
Doubling time: n.a.; doubling time exceeds 100 years.
Ethnic composition (2000): Armenian 94.6%; Kurdish 1.7%; Russian 1.5%; Azerbaijani 0.5%; other 1.7%.
Religious affiliation (1995): Armenian Apostolic 64.5%; other Christian 1.3%; other (mostly nonreligious) 34.2%.
Major cities (2001[5]): Yerevan 1,246,100; Gyumri 210,100; Vanadzor (Kirovakan) 170,800.

Vital statistics

Birth rate per 1,000 population (2001): 9.4 (world avg. 21.3); (1993) legitimate 86.0%; illegitimate 14.0%.
Death rate per 1,000 population (2001): 6.7 (world avg. 9.1).
Natural increase rate per 1,000 population (2001): 2.7 (world avg. 12.2).
Total fertility rate (avg. births per childbearing woman; 2001): 1.1.
Marriage rate per 1,000 population (2001): 3.2.
Divorce rate per 1,000 population (2001): 0.5.
Life expectancy at birth (2001): male 62.1 years; female 71.1 years.
Major causes of death per 100,000 population (1999): circulatory diseases 342.1; cancers 106.0; respiratory diseases 36.2; accidents and violence 33.2.

National economy

Budget (2001). Revenue: 200,800,000,000 drams (revenue 90.8%, of which value-added tax 39.6%, excise tax 15.4%, enterprise profit tax 8.1%, stamp duties 6.9%, income tax 5.6%; grants 9.2%). Expenditures: 247,200,000,000 drams (current expenditures 74.9%, of which pensions and social welfare 20.9%, defense 14.9%, wages 13.0%, education 11.0%, health 6.4%, interest 5.9%, other 2.8%; capital expenditure and net lending 25.1%).
Public debt (external, outstanding; 2001): U.S.$766,000,000.
Tourism (2001): receipts from visitors U.S.$123,000,000; expenditures by nationals abroad U.S.$40,000,000.
Land use (1994): forest 13.4%; pasture 23.1%; agriculture 20.1%; other 43.4%.
Gross national product (2001): U.S.$2,200,000,000 (U.S.$570 per capita).

Structure of net material product and labour force	2001			
	in value '000,000 drams	% of total value	labour force	% of labour force
Agriculture	293,872	25.0	570,000	40.4
Manufacturing, mining } Public utilities }	237,668	20.2	169,600	12.0
Construction	125,777	10.7	41,200	2.9
Transp. and commun.	88,162	7.5	44,200	3.1
Trade	115,198	9.8	110,500	7.8
Finance	...	...	25,200	1.8
Pub. admin., defense Services	... ...	... } ... }	267,200	18.9
Other	314,810	26.8	183,800[6]	13.0[6]
TOTAL	1,175,487	100.0	1,411,700	100.0[4]

Production (metric tons except as noted). Agriculture, forestry, fishing (2002): potatoes 374,263, wheat 280,477, tomatoes 171,000, barley 113,332, grapes 103,962, watermelons 89,727, apples 35,200; livestock (number of live animals) 546,136 sheep, 514,244 cattle, 97,884 pigs, 45,950 goats, 4,400,000 poultry; roundwood (2001) 41,800 cu m; fish catch (2000) 2,007. Mining and quarrying (2000): copper (metal content) 14,000; molybdenum (metal content) 6,044; gold (metal content) 400 kg. Manufacturing (value in '000,000 drams; 2001): food products 109,300; metals 24,600; jewelry 16,600; machinery and motor vehicles 9,600; chemicals 9,300; tobacco 8,600; textiles 4,100. Construction (2000): residential 195,000 sq m. Energy production (consumption): electricity (kW-hr; 2001) 5,744,000,000 (5,744,000,000); coal (metric tons; 2001) none (5,000); crude petroleum (barrels; 1998) none (1,035,000); petroleum products (metric tons; 1999) none (212,000); natural gas (cu m; 1999) none (1,185,000,000).
Population economically active (2001): total 1,411,700; activity rate of total population 37.1% (participation rates: ages 16–60, 77.4%; female 48.0%; unemployed 10.4%).

Price and earnings indexes (1995 = 100)						
	1997	1998	1999	2000	2001	2002
Consumer price index	135	147	147.9	146.7	151.3	153.0
Earnings index	...	...	...	...	...	...

Household income and expenditure. Average household size (2000) 4.2; income per household (1999) 664,700 drams (U.S.$1,200); sources of income (1999): agricultural income 32.1%, wages and salaries 24.6%, transfers 19.3%, help from abroad 12.8%, self-employment 10.6%, other 0.6%; expenditure (1999): food 67.0%, beverages and tobacco 19.2%, services 12.4%, other 1.4%.

Foreign trade[7]

Balance of trade (current prices)						
	1996	1997	1998	1999	2000	2001
U.S.$'000,000	–467	–547	–574	–471	–482	–536
% of total	44.6%	54.0%	56.5%	50.4%	45.0%	44.0%

Imports (2001): U.S.$877,434,000 (2000: mineral fuels 20.8%; food 20.6%, of which cereals 9.8%; rough diamonds 11.0%; nonelectrical machinery 10.9%). *Major import sources* (2001): Russia 19.5%; U.K. 10.4%; U.S. 9.6%; Iran 8.9%; U.A.E. 5.4%; Belgium 4.8%.
Exports (2001): U.S.$341,836,000 (2000: cut diamonds 33.5%; alcoholic beverages 7.5%; electric current 7.0%; metal scrap 6.8%; nonelectrical machinery 6.4%). *Major export destinations* (2001): Russia 17.7%; U.S. 15.3%; Belgium 13.6%; Iran 9.5%; U.K. 5.9%.

Transport and communications

Transport. Railroads (2002): length 529 mi, 852 km; (1999) passenger-mi 28,832,000, passenger-km 46,400,000; ton-mi cargo 201,262,000, metric ton-km cargo 323,900,000. Roads (2000): length 4,677 mi, 7,527 km (paved 100%). Vehicles (1996): passenger cars 1,300; trucks and buses 4,460. Air transport (2001): passenger-mi 438,900,000, passenger-km 706,300,000; short ton-mi cargo 5,659,000, metric ton-km cargo 8,262,000; airports (2001) 1.

Communications				units
				per 1,000
Medium	date	unit	number	persons
Daily newspapers	2000	circulation	18,700	6.2
Radio	2000	receivers	700,000	225
Television	2000	receivers	759,000	244
Telephones	2001	main lines	531,500	155
Cellular telephones	2002	subscribers	44,000	12
Personal computers	2001	units	35,000	9.2
Internet	2002	users	70,000	18

Education and health

Educational attainment (1999). Percentage of population age 15 and over having: primary education or no formal schooling 5.9%; some secondary 15.2%; completed secondary and some postsecondary 60.2%; higher 15.0%. *Literacy* (2001): total population age 15 and over literate 98.8%.

Education (2000–01)				student/
	schools	teachers	students	teacher ratio
Primary (age 6–13) } Secondary (age 14–17) }	1,407	56,061	564,600	10.0
Voc., teacher tr.[8]	63	1,809	28,048	15.5
Higher	20	4,020	47,000	11.7

Health (2001): physicians 10,029 (1 per 303 persons); hospital beds 16,170 (1 per 235 persons); infant mortality rate (2001) 15.4.
Food (2001): daily per capita caloric intake 1,991 (vegetable products 84%, animal products 16%); 80% of FAO recommended minimum requirement.

Military

Total active duty personnel (2002): 44,610 (army 87%, air force 13%). *Military expenditure as percentage of GNP* (1999): 5.8% (world 2.4%); per capita expenditure U.S.$170.

[1]The Armenian Apostolic Church (Armenian Orthodox Church) has special status per 1991 religious law. [2]Includes area of Lake Sevan. [3]In addition, about 16% of neighbouring Azerbaijan (including the 4,400-sq km geographic region of Nagorno-Karabakh [Armenian: Artsakh]) has been occupied by Armenian forces since 1993. [4]Detail does not add to total given because of rounding. [5]Beginning of year de jure figure (about 1/4 of Armenia's population has migrated since the demise of the Soviet Union in 1991). [6]Includes 146,800 unemployed. [7]Imports f.o.b. in balance of trade and c.i.f. in commodities and trading partners. [8]1999–2000.

Internet resources for further information:
- **The Embassy of the Republic of Armenia http://www.armeniaemb.org**

Aruba

Official name: Aruba.
Political status: nonmetropolitan territory of The Netherlands with one legislative house (States of Aruba [21]).
Chief of state: Dutch Monarch represented by Governor.
Head of government: Prime Minister.
Capital: Oranjestad.
Official language: Dutch.
Official religion: none.
Monetary unit: 1 Aruban florin[1] (Af.) = 100 cents; valuation (Sept. 8, 2003) 1 U.S.$ = Af. 1.79; 1 £ = Af. 2.84.

Area and population

	area[2]		population
Census region	sq mi	sq km	2000 census
Noord/Tanki Leendert	14	37	16,944
Oranjestad East	5	13	14,224
Oranjestad West	4	10	12,131
Paradera	10	25	9,037
San Nicolas North	9	23	10,118
San Nicolas South	4	10	5,730
Santa Cruz	18	47	12,326
Savaneta	11	28	9,996
TOTAL	75	193	90,506

Demography

Population (2003): 92,700.
Density (2003): persons per sq mi 1,236.0, persons per sq km 480.3.
Urban-rural (2001): urban 67.0%; rural 33.0%.
Sex distribution (2002): male 47.81%; female 52.19%.
Age breakdown (2002): under 15, 22.9%; 15–29, 19.4%; 30–44, 27.5%; 45–59, 18.7%; 60–74, 8.7%; 75 and over, 2.7%; unknown 0.1%.
Population projection: (2010) 96,000; (2020) 98,000.
Linguistic composition (2000): Papiamento 69.4%; Spanish 13.2%; English 8.1%; Dutch 6.1%; Portuguese 0.3%; other 2.0%; unknown 0.9%.[3]
Religious affiliation (2000): Christian 96.2%, of which Roman Catholic 81.9%, Protestant 7.3%, other Christian (Jehovah's Witness) 1.3%; Spiritist 1.0%; nonreligious 1.4%; other 1.4%.
Major urban areas (2000): Oranjestad 26,355[4]; San Nicolas 15,848[5].

Vital statistics

Birth rate per 1,000 population (2002): 14.6 (world avg. 21.3); legitimate 52.5%; illegitimate 47.5%.
Death rate per 1,000 population (2002): 5.2 (world avg. 9.1).
Natural increase rate per 1,000 population (2002): 9.4 (world avg. 12.2).
Total fertility rate (avg. births per childbearing woman; 2002): 1.8.
Marriage rate per 1,000 population (2002): 6.9.
Divorce rate per 1,000 population (2002): 5.2.
Life expectancy at birth (2002): male 70.0 years; female 76.0 years.
Major causes of death per 100,000 population (2001): diseases of the circulatory system 151.9, malignant neoplasms (cancers) 109.1, infectious and parasitic diseases/diseases of the respiratory system 48.1.

National economy

Budget (2001). Revenue: Af. 731,800,000 (tax revenue 82.9%, of which taxes on wages and income 28.7%, excise taxes on gasoline 14.3%, import duties 13.4%, taxes on profits 12.3%; nontax revenue 17.1%). Expenditures: Af. 818,900,000.
Production (metric tons except as noted). Agriculture, forestry, fishing: aloes are cultivated for export; small amounts of tomatoes, beans, cucumbers, gherkins, watermelons, and lettuce are grown on hydroponic farms; divi-divi pods, sour orange fruit, sorghum, and peanuts (groundnuts) are nonhydroponic crops of limited value; livestock (number of live animals) Aruba has very few livestock; roundwood, n.a.; fish catch (1997) 205. Mining and quarrying: excavation of sand for local use. Manufacturing[6]: rum, cigarettes, aloe products, and soaps. Construction (value of residential and nonresidential construction permits; 2000): Af. 183,300,000. Energy production (consumption): electricity (kW-hr; 2002) 824,649,000 (690,129,000); coal, none (none); crude petroleum (barrels; 1999) none (2,400,000); petroleum products (metric tons; 1999) none (296,000); natural gas, none (none).
Gross domestic product (2002): U.S.$1,875,000,000 (U.S.$20,100 per capita).

Structure of gross domestic product and labour force

	1998		2000	
	in value Af. '000,000	% of total value	labour force	% of labour force
Agriculture Mining	11	0.4	212 38	0.5 0.1
Manufacturing	77	2.6	2,440	5.4
Construction	218	7.5	3,892	8.6
Public utilities	193	6.6	500	1.1
Transp. and commun.	234	8.0	2,905	6.5
Trade, restaurants	692	23.7	14,763	32.8
Finance, real estate	772	26.4	5,206	11.6
Pub. admin., defense	364	12.5	3,528	7.8
Services	285	9.8	8,129	18.1
Other	77	2.6	3,423[7]	7.6[7]
TOTAL	2,923	100.0[8]	45,036	100.0[8]

Population economically active (2000): total 45,036; activity rate of total population 49.5% (participation rates: ages 15–64, 71.9%; female 46.6%; unemployed 6.9%).

Price and earnings indexes (1995 = 100)

	1996	1997	1998	1999	2000	2001	2002
Consumer price index	103.0	106.0	108.0	111.0	115.0	119.0	120.0[9]
Earnings index[10]	103.1	106.6	109.5	111.9	...	...	...

Public debt (external, outstanding; 2001): U.S.$393,300,000.
Household income and expenditure (1999): average household size 3.6; average annual income per household: Af. 39,000 (U.S.$21,800); sources of income: n.a.; expenditure (1994)[11]: transportation and communications 20.7%, food and beverages 18.4%, clothing and footwear 11.3%, household furnishings 10.4%, housing 9.8%.
Tourism: receipts from visitors (2001) U.S.$890,000,000; expenditures by nationals abroad (2000) U.S.$158,000,000.
Land use (1998): forest, negligible; meadows and pastures, negligible; agricultural and under permanent cultivation 11.0%; other (dry savanna and built-up) 89.0%.

Foreign trade

Balance of trade (current prices)

	1996	1997	1998	1999	2000	2001
U.S.$'000,000	–308	–391	–354	–594	–35	+77
% of total	8.1%	10.2%	13.2%	17.3%	0.7%	1.6%

Imports (2001): U.S.$2,362,000,000 (petroleum [all forms] and free-zone imports 68.8%, food and beverages 7.1%, electrical and nonelectrical machinery 5.5%). *Major import sources*[12]: United States 61.9%; The Netherlands 11.6%; Netherlands Antilles 3.6%; Venezuela 3.1%.
Exports (2001): U.S.$2,439,000,000 (petroleum [all forms] and free-zone exports 98.8%, food and beverages 0.5%). *Major export destinations*[12]: United States 25.9%; Venezuela 21.3%; Netherlands Antilles 19.8%; The Netherlands 14.5%.

Transport and communications

Transport. Railroads: none. Roads (1995): total length 497 mi, 800 km (paved 64%). Vehicles (2002): passenger cars 42,802; trucks and buses 1,072. Air transport (2001)[13]: passenger-mi 497,000,000, passenger-km 800,000,000; metric ton-mi cargo, n.a.; airports (2001) with scheduled flights 1.

Communications

Medium	date	unit	number	units per 1,000 persons
Daily newspapers	1996	circulation	73,000	851
Radio	2000	receivers	51,000	562
Television	2000	receivers	20,000	224
Telephones	2001	main lines	37,100	350
Cellular telephones	2001	subscribers	53,000	500
Internet	2001	users	24,000	226

Education and health

Educational attainment (2000). Percentage of population age 25 and over having: no formal schooling or incomplete primary education 9.7%; primary education 33.9%; secondary/vocational 39.2%; advanced vocational/higher 16.2%; unknown status 1.0%. *Literacy* (2000): percentage of total population age 13 and over literate 97.3%.

Education (2001)

	schools	teachers	students	student/ teacher ratio
Primary (age 6–12)	33	437	9,245	21.2
Secondary (age 12–17) Voc., teacher tr.	12	533	7,924	14.9
Higher	2	49	437	8.9

Health (2002): physicians 99 (1 per 944 persons); hospital beds 305 (1 per 306 persons); infant mortality rate per 1,000 live births (2000) 6.5.

Military

Total active duty personnel (1999): a 45-member Dutch naval/air force contingent is stationed in Aruba and the Netherlands Antilles.

[1]The Aruban florin (Af.) is pegged to the U.S. dollar at a fixed rate of Af. 1.79 = 1 U.S.$. [2]Areas for census regions are approximate. [3]Most Arubans are racially and ethnically mixed; ethnic composition (1998): Amerindian/other 80%; other (primarily Dutch, Spanish and/or black) 20%. [4]Combined population of Oranjestad East and Oranjestad West. [5]Combined population of San Nicolas North and San Nicolas South. [6]Service facilities include a free zone, offshore corporate banking facilities, casino/resort complexes, a petroleum transshipment terminal, a cruise ship terminal, and ship repair and bunkering facilities. [7]Includes 3,118 unemployed. [8]Detail does not add to total given because of rounding. [9]March. [10]Minimum wage in construction and manufacturing. [11]Weights of consumer price index components. [12]Excludes petroleum (all forms) and free-zone trade. [13]Air Aruba only.

Internet resources for further information:
- **Centrale Bank van Aruba**
  http://www.cbaruba.org

Australia

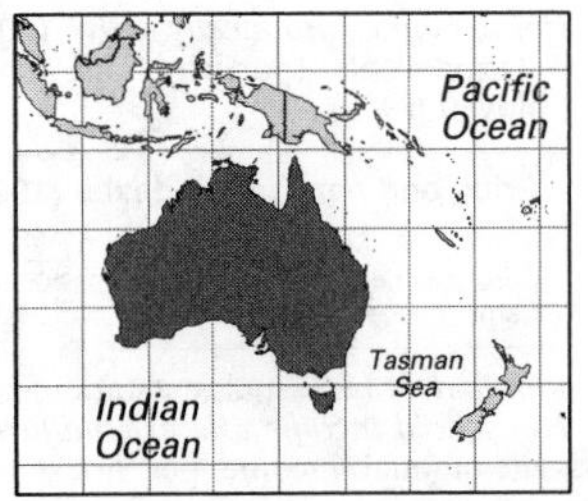

Official name: Commonwealth of Australia.
Form of government: federal parliamentary state (formally a constitutional monarchy) with two legislative houses (Senate [76]; House of Representatives [150]).
Chief of state: British Monarch represented by Governor-General.
Head of government: Prime Minister.
Capital: Canberra.
Official language: English.
Official religion: none.
Monetary unit: 1 Australian dollar ($A) = 100 cents; valuation (Sept. 8, 2003) 1 U.S.$ = $A 1.55; 1 £ = $A 2.46.

Area and population

		area[1]		population
States	**Capitals**	sq mi	sq km	2001 census[2]
New South Wales	Sydney	309,130	800,642	6,609,304
Queensland	Brisbane	668,207	1,730,648	3,635,121
South Australia	Adelaide	379,725	983,482	1,514,854
Tasmania	Hobart	26,410	68,401	472,931
Victoria	Melbourne	87,806	227,416	4,822,663
Western Australia	Perth	976,790	2,529,875	1,906,114
Territories[3]				
Australian Capital Territory	Canberra	910	2,358	321,680
Christmas Island	The Settlement	52	135	} 2,592
Cocos (Keeling) Islands	West Island	5	14	
Jervis Bay	—	28	73	
Norfolk Island[4]	Kingston	13	35	2,037
Northern Territory	Darwin	520,902	1,349,129	200,019
TOTAL		2,969,978	7,692,208	19,487,315

Demography

Population (2003): 19,880,000.
Density (2003): persons per sq mi 6.7, persons per sq km 2.6.
Urban-rural (2002): urban 85.0%; rural 15.0%.
Sex distribution (2001): male 49.35%; female 50.65%.
Age breakdown (2001): under 15, 20.8%; 15–24, 13.7%; 25–44, 29.8%; 45–64, 23.1%; 65 and over, 12.6%.
Population projection: (2010) 21,082,000; (2020) 22,577,000.
Doubling time: over 100 years.
Ethnic composition (2001): white *c.* 92%; Asian *c.* 6%; aboriginal *c.* 2%.
Religious affiliation (2001): Christian 68.0%, of which Roman Catholic 26.6%, Anglican Church of Australia 20.7%, other Protestant 15.8% (Uniting Church 6.7%, Presbyterian 3.4%), Orthodox 2.8%, other Christian 2.1%; Buddhist 1.9%; Muslim 1.5%; Hindu 0.5%; Jewish 0.4%; no religion 15.5%; other 12.2%.
Metropolitan areas (2001): Sydney 3,997,321; Melbourne 3,366,542; Brisbane 1,627,535; Perth 1,339,993; Adelaide 1,072,585; Newcastle 470,610; Gold Coast 444,077; Canberra 353,149; Wollongong 257,510; Caloundra 192,397; Hobart 191,169.
Place of birth (2001): 76.9% native-born; 23.1% foreign-born, of which Europe 9.7% (United Kingdom and Republic of Ireland 5.5%, Italy 1.2%, Greece 0.7%, Germany 0.7%, The Netherlands 0.5%, other Europe 1.1%), Asia and Middle East 3.9%, New Zealand 1.9%, Africa, the Americas, and other 7.6%.
Mobility (1995–96). Population age 15 and over living in the same residence as in 1994: 81.6%; different residence between states, regions, and neighbourhoods 18.4%.
Households (2000). Total number of households 7,510,000. Average household size 3.0; 1 person 25.1%, 2 persons 33.4%, 3 or more persons 41.5%. Family households 5,367,000 (71.5%), nonfamily 2,143,000 (28.5%), of which 1-person 25.1%.
Immigration (2001–02): permanent immigrants admitted 88,900, from New Zealand 17.6%, United Kingdom and Ireland 10.4%, China 7.5%, India 5.7%, Indonesia 4.7%, South Africa 4.0%, Vietnam 2.3%, Philippines 2.3%, former Yugoslavia 2.3%, Sri Lanka 2.3%. Refugee arrivals (2001–02): 12,349. Emigration (2001–02): 48,241.

Vital statistics

Birth rate per 1,000 population (2002): 12.8 (world avg. 21.3); (2000) legitimate 69.3%; illegitimate 30.7%.
Death rate per 1,000 population (2002): 7.4 (world avg. 9.1).
Natural increase rate per 1,000 population (2002): 5.4 (world avg. 12.2).
Total fertility rate (avg. births per childbearing woman; 2002): 1.8.
Marriage rate per 1,000 population (2001): 5.3.
Divorce rate per 1,000 population (2001): 2.8.
Life expectancy at birth (2001): male 77.0 years; female 82.4 years.
Major causes of death per 100,000 population (2001): diseases of the circulatory system 219.0; cancers 162.0; respiratory diseases 48.0; accidents, poisoning, and violence 27.0; diabetes 13.0; suicides 13.0.

Social indicators

Educational attainment (1999). Percentage of population age 15 to 64 having: no formal schooling and incomplete secondary education 38.0%; completed secondary 18.3%; postsecondary, technical, or other certificate/diploma 28.3%; university 15.4%.
Quality of working life (2003). Average workweek: 34.7 hours. Working 50 hours a week or more 28.8%. Annual rate per 100,000 workers for: accidental injury and industrial disease, 3,200[5]; death, n.a. Proportion of employed persons insured for damages or income loss resulting from: injury 100%; permanent disability 100%; death 100%. Working days lost to industrial disputes per 1,000 employees (2000): 52. Means of transportation to work (2000): private automobile 76.0%; public transportation 12.0%; motorcycle, bicycle, and foot 12.0%. Discouraged job seekers (2002): 78,000 (0.8% of labour force).

Distribution of household income (1999–2000)

percentage of household income by quintile

lowest	second	third	fourth	highest
3.8%	9.0%	15.0%	23.8%	48.4%

Social participation. Eligible voters participating in last national election (2001): 95.0%; voting is compulsory. Trade union membership in total workforce (2002): 23.1%.
Social deviance (2002). Offense rate per 100,000 population for: murder 1.6; sexual assault 90.6; assault 809.7; auto theft 575.4; burglary and housebreaking 2,001.4; armed robbery 106.4. Incidence per 100,000 in general population of (2001): prisoners 139; suicide 13.0.
Material well-being (1995). Households possessing: automobile 85%; telephone 95%; refrigerator 99.7%; personal computer 54.0%[6]; washing machine 90.0%.

National economy

Gross national product (at current market prices; 2001): U.S.$385,900,000,000 (U.S.$19,900 per capita).

Structure of gross domestic product and labour force

	2001			
	in value $A '000,000[7]	% of total value	labour force	% of labour force
Agriculture	19,005	3.1	433,500	4.4
Mining	26,183	4.2	68,300	0.8
Manufacturing	75,560	12.2	1,109,100	11.3
Construction	34,434	5.5	678,300	6.9
Public utilities	11,314	1.8	67,400	0.7
Transportation and communications	54,049	8.7	600,900	6.1
Trade[8]	122,282	19.7	2,254,200	23.0
Finance, real estate	114,389	18.4	1,433,300	14.6
Pub. admin., defense	22,702	3.7	480,400	4.9
Services	95,079	15.3	1,998,500	20.4
Other	45,966[9]	7.4[9]	666,700[10]	6.8[10]
TOTAL	620,963	100.0	9,790,600	100.0[11]

Budget (2001–02). Revenue: $A 162,388,000,000 (tax revenue 92.3%, of which individual 53.2%, corporate 16.7%, excise duties and sales tax 15.8%; nontax revenue 7.7%). Expenditures: $A 166,482,000,000 (social security and welfare 41.5%; health 16.6%; defense 7.2%; education 7.1%; economic services 6.8%; interest on public debt 3.0%).
Public debt (2000–01): $A 69,226,000,000.
Tourism (2001): receipts from visitors U.S.$7,625,000,000; expenditures by nationals abroad U.S.$5,812,000,000.

Manufacturing, mining, and construction enterprises (2000–01)

	no. of establishments[12]	no. of employees	value added per person employed ($A '000)	value added ($A '000,000)
Manufacturing				
Food, beverages, and tobacco	3,984	189,603	77.6	14,708.9
Metal products	9,348[13]	147,045	92.9	13,665.2
Machinery and equipment	7,448	202,170	66.7	13,487.3
Chemical, petroleum, and coal products	4,581	101,256	98.4	9,959.6
Printing and publishing	5,265[14]	91,630	72.0	6,599.2
Miscellaneous manufacturing	7,410	54,241	44.6	2,416.7
Wood and paper products	4,956[15]	65,008	75.8	4,929.4
Nonmetallic mineral products	4,801	37,166	97.0	3,606.1
Textile, clothing, footwear, and leather	8,326	57,764	44.7	2,583.3
Mining[16]				
Coal, oil, and gas	...	26,769	...	...
Metallic minerals	...	24,106	...	...
Nonmetallic minerals[17]	699	8,799	...	...
Construction[18]	194,300	484,100	...	...

Production (gross value in $A '000 except as noted). Agriculture, forestry, fishing (1999–2000): livestock[19] 7,946,900 (cattle 5,050,900, sheep and lambs 1,053,900, poultry 1,031,000, pigs 791,700); wheat 4,831,200, wool 2,149,000, vegetables 1,861,900, fruits and nuts 1,761,100, seed cotton 1,400,000, grapes 1,118,200, sugarcane 881,900, barley 864,800, canola 638,000, oats 118,400, sunflower seeds 74,000, corn (maize) 60,000, tobacco 40,000, other cereal crops 4,735,100; livestock (number of live animals; 2002) 113,000,000 sheep, 30,500,000 cattle, 2,912,000 pigs, 93,000,000 poultry; roundwood (2001) 30,915,306 cu m; fish catch (2000) 251,300 metric tons. Mining and quarrying (metric tons [tons of contained metal]; 2000): iron ore 170,999,000; bauxite 53,802,000; zinc 1,410,000; copper 830,000; lead 678,000; uranium oxide 4,910; gold 296,410 kg; diamonds 26,648,000 carats. Manufacturing (value added in U.S.$'000,000 except as noted; 1998): food products 13,216; machinery and transport equipment 12,956; printing and publishing 6,458; nonferrous metals 3,605; metal products 3,604; electrical machinery 1,809. Construction (buildings completed, by value in $A '000; 2002): new dwellings 15,043,000; alterations and additions to dwellings 4,081,000; nonresidential (1998–99) 14,016,000.

Retail and service enterprises

	no. of establishments	no. of employees	total wages and salaries ($A '000,000)	annual turnover ($A '000,000)
Retail[20]				
Motor vehicle dealers, gasoline and tire dealers	37,305	220,661	...	44,954
Food stores	53,166	406,299	...	63,340[21]
Department and general stores	459	87,148	...	13,714[21]
Clothing, fabric, and furniture stores	21,688	91,138	...	11,005[21]
Household appliances and hardware stores	14,268	75,355	629	20,554[21]
Recreational goods	...	...	...	7,393[21]
Services				
Real estate agents[22]	7,589	52,079	1,847.5	3,902.7
Pubs, taverns, and bars	4,792[16]	81,724[16]	...	9,007.2[21]
Dental services[16]	5,257	24,108	568.4	1,685.2
Consulting engineering services[23]	5,514	30,736	1,242	3,233.3
Legal services[22]	10,819	73,186	2,181.0	7,034.3
Accounting services[23]	8,389	66,792	...	4,939.1
Computing services[22]	14,731	74,395	4,065.0	10,474.0
Travel agency services[18]	3,266	24,451	647.9	1,979.5
Market research services[22]	272	10,744	203.4	455.8
Private security services[22]	1,714	31,752	756.2	1,394.8

Energy production (consumption): electricity (kW-hr; 1999) 203,380,000,000 (203,380,000,000); hard coal (metric tons; 1999) 223,721,000 (60,643,000); lignite (metric tons; 1999) 67,281,000 (67,281,000); crude petroleum (barrels; 1999) 123,800,000 (225,200,000); petroleum products (metric tons; 1999) 33,854,000 (32,597,000); natural gas (cu m; 2000) 30,794,000,000 ([1999] 22,738,000,000).

Population economically active (2003): total 9,517,500; activity rate of total population 48.8% (participation rates: over age 15, 63.9%; female 44.0%; unemployed [June 2003] 6.1%).

Price and earnings indexes (1995 = 100)

	1996	1997	1998	1999	2000	2001	2002
Consumer price index	102.6	102.9	103.7	105.3	110.0	114.8	118.2
Weekly earnings index	104.0	108.3	112.7	115.7	121.4	127.4	128.4

Household income and expenditure (1999–2000). Average household size (2002) 3.0; average annual income per household $A 37,752 (U.S.$20,600); sources of income: wages and salaries 56.7%, transfer payments 28.0%, self-employment 6.0%, other 9.3%; expenditure (1998–99): food and nonbeverages 18.2%, transportation and communications 16.9%, housing 13.9%, recreation 12.7%, household durable goods 6.0%, household services and operation 5.9%, clothing and footwear 4.6%, health 4.6%, alcoholic beverages 2.9%, energy 2.6%, other 11.7%.

Financial aggregates

	1996	1997	1998	1999	2000	2001	2002
Exchange rate, $A 1.00 per:							
U.S. dollar	0.78	0.74	0.63	0.65	0.58	0.51	0.57
£	0.50	0.45	0.38	0.40	0.38	0.35	0.38
SDR	0.55	0.48	0.44	0.48	0.43	0.41	0.42
International reserves (U.S.$)							
Total (excl. gold; '000,000)	14,485	16,845	14,641	21,212	18,118	17,955	20,689
SDRs ('000,000)	37	19	18	72	94	109	136
Reserve pos. in IMF ('000,000)	482	727	1,256	1,633	1,243	1,412	1,934
Foreign exchange ('000,000)	13,967	16,099	13,366	19,507	16,782	16,434	18,618
Gold ('000,000 fine troy oz)	7.90	2.56	2.56	2.56	2.56	2.56	2.56
% world reserves	0.9	0.3	0.3	0.3	0.3	0.3	0.3
Interest and prices							
Central bank discount (%)	5.75	...	...	...	...	...	...
Govt. bond yield (short-term; %)	7.53	6.00	5.02	5.55	6.18	4.97	5.30
Industrial share prices (1995 = 100)	112.1	125.2	131.3	145.1	156.6	161.5	156.8
Balance of payments (U.S.$'000,000)							
Balance of visible trade	–635	1,849	–5,367	–9,767	–4,700	+1,874	–5,428
Imports, f.o.b.	61,032	63,044	61,215	65,826	68,752	61,802	70,501
Exports, f.o.b.	60,397	64,893	55,848	56,059	64,052	63,676	65,073
Balance of invisibles	–15,380	–14,580	–12,878	–13,408	–13,249	–6,804	–23,307
Balance of payments, current account	–16,015	–12,731	–18,245	–23,012	–15,123	–8,678	–17,879

Land use (2000): agricultural and under permanent cultivation 7.0%; other 93.0% (of which, meadows and pastures 54.0%).

Foreign trade[24]

Balance of trade (current prices)

	1996	1997	1998	1999	2000	2001
$A '000,000	–1,424	+1,422	–7,746	–14,551	–6,376	+5,307
% of total	0.9%	0.8%	4.2%	7.7%	2.8%	2.2%

Imports (2000–01): $A 118,264,000,000 (machinery and transport equipment 45.2%, of which road motor vehicles 12.1%, office machines and automatic data-processing equipment 7.0%, telecommunications equipment 6.7%; chemicals and related products 12.0%, of which medicines and pharmaceuticals 3.7%; mineral fuels and lubricants 8.9%; food and live animals 3.6%). *Major import sources:* U.S. 18.9%; Japan 13.0%; China 8.4%; U.K. 5.3%; Germany 5.2%; South Korea 4.0%; New Zealand 3.9%; Malaysia 3.5%; Singapore 3.3%; Taiwan 2.8%.

Exports (2000–01): $A 119,602,000,000 (mineral fuels 21.1%, of which coal [all forms] 9.1%, petroleum products and natural gas 9.1%; crude materials excluding fuels 19.7%, of which metalliferous ores and metal scrap [mostly iron ore and alumina] 12.3%, textile fibres 4.7%; food 16.8%, of which meat and meat preparations 4.8%, cereals and cereal preparations 4.5%; nonferrous metals 7.9%). *Major export destinations:* Japan 19.6%; U.S. 9.7%; South Korea 7.7%; New Zealand 5.7%; China 5.7%; Singapore 5.0%; Taiwan 4.9%; U.K. 3.9%; Hong Kong 3.3%; Indonesia 2.6%.

Trade by commodity group (1999–2000)

SITC Group	imports U.S.$'000,000	imports %	exports U.S.$'000,000	exports %
00 Food and live animals	2,488	3.6	10,570	17.3
01 Beverages and tobacco	445	0.6	988	1.6
02 Crude materials, excluding fuels	1,162	1.7	11,556	18.9
03 Mineral fuels, lubricants, and related materials	4,832	7.0	11,366	18.6
04 Animal and vegetable oils, fat, and waxes	174	0.3	190	0.3
05 Chemicals and related products, n.e.s.	7,863	11.4	2,638	4.3
06 Basic manufactures	8,614	12.4	7,746	12.7
07 Machinery and transport equipment	32,305	46.6	7,302	11.9
08 Miscellaneous manufactured articles	9,759	14.1	2,409	3.9
09 Goods not classified by kind	1,614	2.3	6,421	10.5
TOTAL	69,256	100.0	61,186	100.0

Direction of trade (1999–2000)

	imports U.S.$'000,000	imports %	exports U.S.$'000,000	exports %
Africa	627	0.9	1,363	2.2
Asia	31,198	45.1	37,117	60.7
Japan	8,895	12.8	11,828	19.3
South America	403	0.6	498	0.8
North and Central America	16,018	23.1	7,020	11.5
United States	14,462	20.9	6,025	9.8
Europe	16,512	23.8	8,254	13.5
European Union	15,321	22.1	7,573	12.4
Russia	37	—	119	0.2
Other Europe	1,154	1.7	562	0.9
Oceania	4,220	6.1	5,663	9.2
New Zealand	2,750	4.0	4,235	6.9
Other	278	0.4	1,271	2.1
TOTAL	69,256	100.0	61,186	100.0

Transport and communications

Transport. Railroads (1998–99)[25]: route length 22,233 mi, 35,780 km; passengers carried 595,200,000; short ton-mi cargo 87,262,000,000, metric ton-km cargo 127,400,000,000. Roads (2000): total length 502,356 mi, 808,465 km (paved 40%). Vehicles (1999): passenger cars 9,719,900; trucks and buses 2,214,900. Merchant marine (1999): vessels (150 gross tons and over) 77; total deadweight tonnage 2,505,369. Air transport (1999)[26]: passenger-mi 46,646,591,000, passenger-km 75,070,556,000; short ton-mi cargo 1,156,331,000, metric ton-km cargo 1,688,215,000; airports (1996) with scheduled flights 400.

Communications

Medium	date	unit	number	units per 1,000 persons
Daily newspapers	2000	circulation	5,630,000	293
Radio	2000	receivers	36,700,000	1,908
Television	2000	receivers	14,200,000	738
Telephones	2002	main lines	10,590,000	539
Cellular telephones	2002	subscribers	12,579,000	640
Personal computers	2001	units	10,000,000	517
Internet	2002	users	8,400,000	427

Education and health

Literacy (1996): total population literate, virtually 100%[27].

Education (2001)

	schools	teachers	students	student/ teacher ratio
Primary (age 6–12)	9,596	114,400	1,384,866	16.9
Secondary (age 13–17)		110,900	863,353	12.5
Vocational[28]	541[15]	26,345[15]	1,757,000	...
Higher	43	78,228	795,000	18.3

Health: physicians (2001) 48,211 (1 per 404 persons); hospital beds (2001) 79,900 (1 per 244 persons); infant mortality rate (2001) 5.3.

Food (2001): daily per capita caloric intake 3,126 (vegetable products 66%, animal products 34%); 117% of FAO recommended minimum requirement.

Military

Total active duty personnel (2002): 50,920 (army 49.4%, navy 24.7%, air force 25.9%). *Military expenditure as percentage of GNP* (1999): 1.8% (world 2.4%); per capita expenditure U.S.$372.

[1]Mainland and island areas only; excludes coastal water. [2]Adjusted for underenumeration. [3]With permanent civilian population only. [4]Has greater degree of self-government than other territories. [5]1992–93. [6]1994. [7]At 1996–97 prices. [8]Trade includes hotels and restaurants. [9]Import duties less imputed bank service charges. [10]Mostly unemployed. [11]Detail does not add to total given because of rounding. [12]1997. [13]1994–95. [14]1993–94. [15]1996. [16]1997–98. [17]1990–91. [18]1996–97. [19]Slaughtered value. [20]1991–92. [21]2001–02. [22]1998–99. [23]1995–96. [24]Imports f.o.b.; exports c.i.f. [25]Government railways only. [26]Includes Qantas and Ansett Australia. [27]A national survey conducted in 1996 put the number of persons who had very poor literacy and numeracy skills at about 17% of the total population (age 15 to 64). [28]Includes special education.

Internet resources for further information:

- **Australian Bureau of Statistics http://www.abs.gov.au**

Austria

Official name: Republik Österreich (Republic of Austria).
Form of government: federal state with two legislative houses (Federal Council [64]; National Council [183]).
Chief of state: President.
Head of government: Chancellor.
Capital: Vienna.
Official language: German.
Official religion: none.
Monetary unit: 1 euro (€) = 100 cents; valuation (Sept. 8, 2003) 1 U.S.$ = €0.90; 1 £ = €1.43[1].

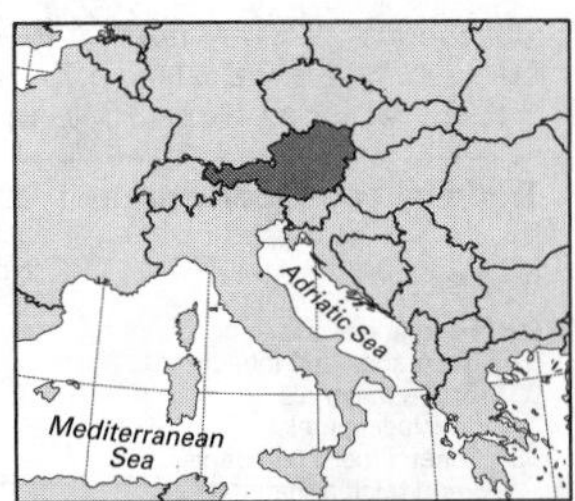

Area and population

States	Capitals	area sq mi	area sq km	population 2001 census
Burgenland	Eisenstadt	1,531	3,965	277,569
Kärnten	Klagenfurt	3,682	9,536	559,404
Niederösterreich	Sankt Pölten	7,404	19,178	1,545,804
Oberösterreich	Linz	4,626	11,982	1,376,797
Salzburg	Salzburg	2,762	7,154	515,327
Steiermark	Graz	6,329	16,392	1,183,303
Tirol	Innsbruck	4,883	12,648	673,504
Vorarlberg	Bregenz	1,004	2,601	351,095
Wien (Vienna)	—	160	415	1,550,123
TOTAL		32,383[2]	83,871	8,032,926

Demography

Population (2003): 8,054,000.
Density (2003): persons per sq mi 248.7, persons per sq km 96.0.
Urban-rural (2001): urban 67.4%; rural 32.6%.
Sex distribution (2001): male 48.44%; female 51.56%.
Age breakdown (2001): under 15, 16.8%; 15–29, 18.7%; 30–44, 24.9%; 45–59, 18.6%; 60–74, 13.8%; 75 and over, 7.2%.
Population projection: (2010) 8,130,000; (2020) 8,225,000.
Doubling time: not applicable; population is stable.
Ethnic composition (national origin; 1998): Austrian 91.2%; citizens of former Yugoslavia 4.0%; Turkish 1.6%; other 3.2%.
Religious affiliation (1995): Roman Catholic 75.1%; nonreligious and atheist 8.6%; Protestant (mostly Lutheran) 5.4%; Muslim 2.1%; Eastern Orthodox 0.7%; Jewish 0.1%; other 1.9%; unknown 6.1%.
Major cities (2001): Vienna 1,550,123; Graz 226,244; Linz 183,504; Salzburg 142,662; Innsbruck 113,392; Klagenfurt 90,141.

Vital statistics

Birth rate per 1,000 population (2001): 9.3 (world avg. 21.3); (2000) legitimate 71.7%; illegitimate 28.3%.
Death rate per 1,000 population (2001): 9.2 (world avg. 9.1).
Natural increase rate per 1,000 population (2001): 0.1 (world avg. 12.2).
Total fertility rate (avg. births per childbearing woman; 2001): 1.3.
Marriage rate per 1,000 population (2001): 4.8.
Divorce rate per 1,000 population (2001): 2.5.
Life expectancy at birth (2001): male 75.9 years; female 81.7 years.
Major causes of death per 100,000 population (2001): diseases of the circulatory system 526.6; malignant neoplasms (cancers) 235.4.

National economy

Budget (1997). Revenue: S 950,820,000,000 (tax revenue 92.0%, of which social security contributions 37.7%, individual income taxes 17.3%, value-added taxes 16.2%). Expenditures: S 1,017,870,000 (social security and welfare 42.0%; health 14.4%; education 9.2%; interest 9.2%; defense 2.0%).
National debt (end of year 2001): U.S.$161,700,000,000.
Production (metric tons except as noted). Agriculture, forestry, fishing (2002): sugar beets 3,005,000, corn (maize) 2,000,000, wheat 1,460,000, barley 946,000, potatoes 684,000, apples 480,844, grapes 350,000, rye 200,000, triticale 190,000, rapeseed 150,000; livestock (number of live animals) 3,440,405 pigs, 2,118,454 cattle, 11,000,000 chickens; roundwood (2001) 13,467,000 cu m; fish catch (2000) 3,706. Mining and quarrying (1999): iron ore 1,747,000; magnesite 748,600; talc 129,600. Manufacturing (value added in U.S.$'000,000; 1998): electrical machinery and apparatus 4,106; nonelectrical machinery and apparatus 4,030; food and beverages 3,350; fabricated metals 3,300; base metals 2,340; chemicals and chemical products 2,149. Energy production (consumption): electricity (kW-hr; 2001) 62,426,000,000 ([1999] 64,214,000,000); hard coal (metric tons; 2001) negligible ([1999] 3,832,000); lignite (metric tons; 1999) 1,138,000 (1,535,000); crude petroleum (barrels; 2001) 7,139,000 ([1999] 62,600,000); petroleum products (metric tons; 1999) 8,095,000 (10,900,000); natural gas (cu m; 1999) 1,808,200,000 (8,058,300,000).
Tourism (U.S.$'000,000; 2001): receipts U.S.$10,118; expenditures U.S.$8,886.
Population economically active (2001): total 3,940,300; activity rate of total population 48.3% (participation rates: ages 15–64, 72.0%; female 43.3%; unemployed 5.5%).

Price and earnings indexes (1996 = 100)

	1997	1998	1999	2000	2001	2002	2003[3]
Consumer price index	101.8	103.0	103.6	106.1	108.9	118.2	121.0
Annual earnings index	100.5	104.0	104.6	...	...	...	...

Gross national product (at current market prices; 2001): U.S.$194,463,000,000 (U.S.$24,200 per capita).

Structure of gross domestic product and labour force

	1999 in value S '000,000	1999 % of total value	2001 labour force	2001 % of labour force
Agriculture, forestry	53,920	2.0	219,000	5.6
Mining	9,170	0.3	9,700	0.2
Manufacturing	508,910	18.8	773,600	19.6
Construction	212,830	7.8	381,100	9.9
Public utilities	63,430	2.3	31,700	0.8
Transp. and commun.	179,260	6.6	262,700	6.7
Trade, restaurants	424,920	15.7	852,200	21.6
Finance, real estate	560,460	20.7	440,400	11.1
Pub. admin., defense	168,170	6.2	260,200	6.6
Services	349,240	12.9	709,700	18.0
Other	181,820[4]	6.7[4]	—	—
TOTAL	2,712,030	100.0	3,940,300	100.0[2]

Household income and expenditure. Average household size (2001) 2.4; sources of income (1995): wages and salaries 54.8%, transfer payments 25.9%; expenditure (2000): utilities 24.5%, transportation and communications 17.5%, food and beverages 15.2%, entertainment and sport 12.4%, housing 7.0%, clothing 6.4%, cafe and hotel expenditures 5.9%, health 2.4%.
Land use (1994): forested 39.2%; meadows and pastures 24.3%; agricultural and under permanent cultivation 18.3%; other 18.2%.

Foreign trade[5]

Balance of trade (current prices)

	1996	1997	1998	1999	2000	2001
€'000,000,000	−100.6[6]	−75.3[6]	−67.4[6]	−5.05	−5.25	−4.44
% of total	7.6%	5.0%	4.2%	4.0%	3.6%	2.9%

Imports (2001): €78,692,000,000 (machinery and transport equipment 40.2%, of which road vehicles 11.5%, electrical machinery and apparatus 7.9%; chemicals and related products 10.5%; food products 5.0%; fabricated metals 4.1%). *Major import sources:* Germany 40.5%; Italy 7.2%; United States 5.3%; France 4.1%; Hungary 3.4%; Switzerland 3.2%.
Exports (2001): €74,251,000,000 (machinery and apparatus 31.3%; transportation equipment 12.0%; chemical products 9.5%; paper and paper products 4.6%; fabricated metals 4.5%; iron and steel 4.3%). *Major export destinations:* Germany 32.5%; Italy 8.5%; United States 5.3%; Switzerland 5.2%; United Kingdom 4.7%; France 4.6%.

Transport and communications

Transport. Railroads[7]: (2000) length 5,643 km; (1998) passenger-km 7,971,000,000; (1998) metric ton-km cargo 15,348,000,000. Roads (1997): total length 200,000 km (paved 100%). Vehicles (2000): passenger cars 4,009,604; trucks and buses 328,591. Air transport (2001)[8]: passenger-km 12,832,000,000; metric ton-km cargo 355,923,000; airports (2000) with scheduled flights 6.

Communications

Medium	date	unit	number	units per 1,000 persons
Daily newspapers	2000	circulation	2,380,000	296
Radio	2000	receivers	6,050,000	753
Television	2000	receivers	4,310,000	536
Telephones	2001	main lines	3,810,000	468
Cellular telephones	2002	subscribers	6,760,000	829
Personal computers	2001	units	2,730,000	335
Internet	2002	users	3,340,000	409

Education and health

Educational attainment (1993). Percentage of population age 25 and over having: lower-secondary education 37.5%; vocational education ending at secondary level 44.6%; completed upper secondary 6.1%; higher vocational 5.5%; higher 6.3%. *Literacy:* virtually 100%.

Education (2000–01)

	schools	teachers	students	student/ teacher ratio
Primary/lower secondary (age 6–13)	4,985	75,748	686,276	9.1
Upper secondary/voc. (age 14–17)	717	41,884	325,768	7.8
Higher[9]	19	16,099	239,691	14.9

Health: physicians (2002) 35,400[10] (1 per 227 persons); hospital beds (2001) 66,395[10] (1 per 121 persons); infant mortality rate per 1,000 live births (2001) 4.8.
Food (2001): daily per capita caloric intake 3,799 (vegetable products 67%; animal products 33%); 144% of FAO recommended minimum requirement.

Military

Total active duty personnel (2002): 34,600 (army 80.2%; air force 19.8%). *Military expenditure as percentage of GNP* (1999): 0.8% (world 2.4%); per capita expenditure U.S.$208.

[1]The Austrian Schilling (S) was the former monetary unit; on Jan. 1, 2002, S 13.76 = €1. [2]Detail does not add to total given because of rounding. [3]First quarter. [4]Value-added tax less imputed bank service charges and subsidies. [5]Imports c.i.f., exports f.o.b. [6]In Austrian Schillings. [7]Federal railways only. [8]Austrian Airlines and Lauda Air. [9]Universities only. [10]January 1.

Internet resources for further information:
- **Austrian Central Office of Statistics http://www.statistik.at**
- **Austrian Press and Information Service (Washington, D.C.) http://www.austria.org/index.html**

Azerbaijan

Official name: Azərbaycan Respublikası (Republic of Azerbaijan).
Form of government: unitary multiparty republic with a single legislative body (National Assembly [124[1]]).
Head of state and government: President assisted by Prime Minister.
Capital: Baku (Azerbaijani: Bakı).
Official language: Azerbaijani.
Official religion: none.
Monetary unit: 1 manat (A.M.) = 100 gopik; valuation (Sept. 8, 2003) free rate, 1 U.S.$ = A.M. 4,912; 1 £ = A.M. 7,788.

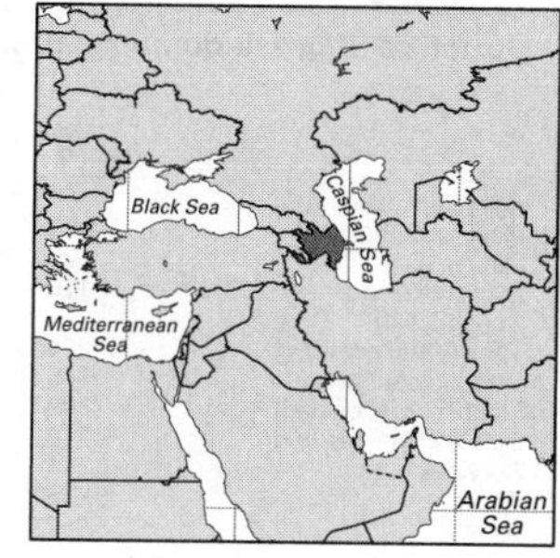

Area and population

	area	population
		2000
Economic regions	sq km	estimate
Absheron	5,400	2,182,000
Gyadza	5,400	529,000
Kazakh	7,100	568,000
Kelbadjar	7,400	259,000
Khachmas	7,000	455,000
Lenkoran	6,100	744,000
Mil-Karabakh	6,500	696,000
Mugan-Salyan	9,000	621,000
Priarak	4,300	323,000
Sheki	9,000	531,000
Shirvan	11,200	661,000
Upper-Karabakh[2]	2,700	143,000
Autonomous regions		
Nakhchivan	5,500	363,000
TOTAL	86,600	8,075,000[3]

Demography

Population (2003): 8,235,000.
Density (2003): persons per sq mi 246.6, persons per sq km 95.1.
Urban-rural (2001): urban 50.8%; rural 49.2%.
Sex distribution (2001): male 48.94%; female 51.06%.
Age breakdown (2001): under 15, 31.8%; 15–29, 25.6%; 30–44, 24.1%; 45–59, 9.5%; 60–69, 7.6%; 70 and over, 1.4%.
Population projection: (2010) 8,839,000; (2020) 9,717,000.
Doubling time: 77 years.
Ethnic composition (1995): Azerbaijani 89.0%; Russian 3.0%; Lezgian 2.2%; Armenian 2.0%; other 3.8%.
Religious affiliation (1995): Muslim 93.4%, of which Shīʿī 65.4%, Sunnī 28.0%; Russian Orthodox 1.1%; Armenian Apostolic (Orthodox) 1.1%; other 4.4%.
Major cities (2002): Baku 1,817,900; Gäncä (formerly Kirovabad) 300,900; Sumqayıt (Sumgait) 261,200; Mingäçevir (Mingechaur) 94,600.

Vital statistics

Birth rate per 1,000 population (2001): 14.8 (world avg. 21.3); (2000) legitimate 94.6%; illegitimate 5.4%.
Death rate per 1,000 population (2001): 5.9 (world avg. 9.1).
Natural increase rate per 1,000 population (2001): 8.9 (world avg. 12.2).
Total fertility rate (avg. births per childbearing woman; 2001): 1.6.
Life expectancy at birth (2001): male 68.1 years; female 75.1 years.
Major causes of death per 100,000 population (2000): diseases of the circulatory system 330.5; malignant neoplasms (cancers) 64.1; diseases of the respiratory system 53.1; diseases of the digestive system 28.1; infectious and parasitic diseases 27.0; accidents, poisoning, and violence 26.4.

National economy

Budget (2002). Revenue: A.M. 8,219,000,000,000 (tax revenue 55.7%, of which value-added tax 20.4%, enterprise profits tax 9.0%, social security contributions 7.8%, personal income tax 6.7%, excise taxes 5.3%; nontax revenue 44.3%, of which petroleum fund 14.0%). Expenditures: A.M. 8,384,000,000,000 (national economy 20.9%; education 20.4%; social security 20.4%; defense 13.0%; health 4.8%).
Public debt (external, outstanding; 2001): U.S.$726,000,000.
Production (metric tons except as noted). Agriculture, forestry, fishing (2002): cereals 1,970,300, vegetables (except potatoes) 916,400, potatoes 694,900, fruit (except grapes) 390,600, cotton 80,400, grapes 61,965, sugar beets 38,900, tobacco leaves 12,700, tea 1,100; livestock (number of live animals) 6,559,000 sheep and goats, 2,098,000 cattle, 15,351,000 poultry; roundwood (2001) 13,500 cu m; fish catch (2000) 18,917. Mining and quarrying (2000): alumina 200,000; gypsum 60,000. Manufacturing (gross value of production in U.S.$'000,000; 2001): oil refinery products 504.5; food products 450.2; electricity and gas 362.2; chemicals 124.1; machinery and equipment 81.6. Construction (2001): residential 559,000 sq m. Energy production (consumption): electricity (kW-hr; 2001) 18,699,000,000 (19,193,000,000); coal (metric tons; 2001) none (1,000); crude petroleum (barrels; 2000) 102,200,000 (47,200,000); petroleum products (metric tons; 2000) 7,520,000 ([1999] 5,030,000); natural gas (cu m; 2002) 5,500,000,000 (5,500,000,000).
Household income and expenditure. Average household size (2000) 5.3; income per household (2000) U.S.$460; sources of income: wages and salaries 35.7%, other 64.3%; expenditure: food 66.1%, other 33.9%.
Tourism (2001): receipts U.S.$43,000,000; expenditures U.S.$109,000,000.
Gross national product (2001): U.S.$5,300,000,000 (U.S.$650 per capita).

Structure of gross domestic product and labour force

	2002		2000	
	in value A.M. '000,000	% of total value	labour force	% of labour force
Agriculture	4,195,000	14.2	1,567,000	42.3
Petroleum and natural gas	8,121,000	27.4	39,600	1.1
Manufacturing	1,817,000	6.1	180,700	4.9
Public utilities	383,000	1.3	38,800	1.0
Construction	3,185,000	10.8	155,000	4.2
Transp. and commun.	2,903,000	9.8	168,600	4.6
Trade	2,354,000	8.0	685,500	18.5
Finance	} 4,350,000	} 14.7	15,200	0.4
Pub. admin., defense			260,200	7.0
Services			593,900	16.0
Other	2,294,000[4]	7.7[4]	—	—
TOTAL	29,602,000	100.0	3,704,500	100.0

Population economically active (2002): total 3,778,000, activity rate 46.1% (participation rates: ages 15–64, 77.2%; female 47.7%; unemployed 1.3%).

Price and earnings indexes (1995 = 100)

	1996	1997	1998	1999	2000	2001
Consumer price index	119.9	124.3	123.3	112.8	114.9	116.6
Earnings index	...	...	...	...	...	...

Land use (2000): forest 11.5%; pasture 25.4%; agriculture 50.0%; other 12.6%.

Foreign trade

Balance of trade (current prices)

	1997	1998	1999	2000	2001	2002
U.S.$'000,000	−567	−470	−106	+573	+883	+482
% of total	26.0%	28.0%	5.4%	19.6%	23.6%	11.7%

Imports (2001): U.S.$1,465,000,000 (machinery and equipment 23.7%, food 23.2%, metals 7.2%, chemicals 4.4%). *Major import sources* (2001): U.S. 16.1%; Russia 10.7%; Turkey 10.4%; Turkmenistan 9.4%; Kazakhstan 7.0%; Germany 5.1%.
Exports (2002): U.S.$2,046,000,000 (crude petroleum 56.5%, refined petroleum 27.5%, cotton 2.1%, food 1.9%). *Major export destinations* (2001): Italy 57.2%; Israel 7.1%; Georgia 4.5%; Spain 4.4%; Russia 3.4%.

Transport and communications

Transport. Railroads (2001): length 2,120 km; passenger-km 537,000,000; metric ton-km cargo 6,141,000. Roads (2002): total length 45,870 km (paved 94%). Vehicles (2000): passenger cars 332,100; trucks and buses 78,300. Merchant marine (2000): vessels (100 gross tons and over) 68; total deadweight tonnage, n.a. Air transport (2001): passenger-km 827,000,000; metric ton-km cargo 76,000,000; airports (2001) 3.

Communications

Medium	date	unit	number	units per 1,000 persons
Daily newspapers	2000	circulation	217,000	27
Radio	2000	receivers	177,000	22
Television	2000	receivers	2,080,000	259
Telephones	2002	main lines	989,200	121
Cellular telephones	2002	subscribers	870,000	107
Internet	2002	users	300,000	37

Education and health

Educational attainment (1995). Percentage of population age 15 and over having: primary education or no formal schooling 12.1%, some secondary 9.1%; completed secondary and some postsecondary 27.5%; higher 7.6%. *Literacy* (1989): percentage of total population 15 and over literate 97.3%; males literate 98.9%; females 95.9%.

Education (2000–01)

	schools	teachers	students	student/ teacher ratio
Primary (age 6–13)	} 4,548	} 165,000	689,000	...
Secondary (age 14–17)			960,000	...
Voc., teacher tr.	71	...	34,300	...
Higher	43	18,184[5]	119,700	...

Health (2000): physicians 28,600 (1 per 281 persons); hospital beds 70,000 (1 per 115 persons); infant mortality rate per 1,000 live births (2001) 30.0.
Food (2001): daily per capita caloric intake 2,474 (vegetable products 86%, animal products 14%); 96% of FAO recommended minimum requirement.

Military

Total active duty personnel (2002): 72,100 (army 86.0%, navy 3.0%, air force 11.0%). *Military expenditure as percentage of GNP* (1999): 6.6% (world 2.4%); per capita expenditure U.S.$120.

[1]Excludes one vacant seat reserved for Nagorno-Karabakh representative. [2]Controlled in part by Armenian forces from 1993. [3]Sum of grossly rounded parts; beginning of year 2001 population estimate is 8,081,000. [4]Taxes and subsidies on goods and services. [5]1994–95.

Internet resources for further information:
- **The National Bank of Azerbaijan Republic http://www.nba.az/eng**

Bahamas, The

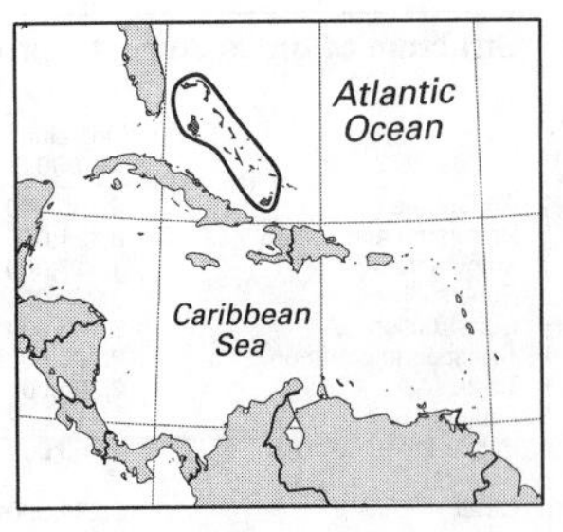

Official name: The Commonwealth of The Bahamas.
Form of government: constitutional monarchy with two legislative houses (Senate [16]; House of Assembly [40]).
Chief of state: British Monarch represented by Governor-General.
Head of government: Prime Minister.
Capital: Nassau.
Official language: English.
Official religion: none.
Monetary unit: 1 Bahamian dollar (B$) = 100 cents; valuation (Sept. 8, 2003) 1 U.S.$ = B$1.00; 1 £ = B$1.59.

Area and population

Islands and Island Groups[2]	area[1] sq mi	area[1] sq km	population 2000 census
Abaco, Great and Little	649	1,681	13,170
Acklins	192	497	428
Andros	2,300	5,957	7,686
Berry Islands	12	31	709
Bimini Islands	9	23	1,717
Cat Island	150	388	1,647
Crooked and Long Cay	93	241	350
Eleuthera	187	484	7,999
Exuma, Great, and Exuma Cays	112	290	3,571
Grand Bahama	530	1,373	46,994
Harbour Island	3	8	1,639
Inagua, Great and Little	599	1,551	969
Long Island	230	596	2,992
Mayaguana	110	285	259
New Providence	80	207	210,832
Ragged Island	14	36	72
Rum Cay	30	78	80
San Salvador	63	163	970
Spanish Wells	10	26	1,527
Other uninhabited cays and rocks	9	23	—
TOTAL	5,382	13,939[3]	303,611

Demography

Population (2003): 314,000.
Density (2003)[4]: persons per sq mi 80.7, persons per sq km 31.2.
Urban-rural (2000): urban 88.3%; rural 11.7%.
Sex distribution (2000): male 49.34%; female 50.66%.
Age breakdown (2000): under 15, 29.5%; 15–29, 27.2%; 30–44, 23.3%; 45–59, 12.1%; 60–74, 5.9%; 75 and over, 2.0%.
Population projection: (2010) 336,000; (2020) 363,000.
Doubling time: 55 years.
Ethnic composition (2000): local black 67.5%; mulatto 14.2%; British 12.0%; Haitian black 3.0%; U.S. white 2.4%; other 0.9%.
Religious affiliation (1995): non-Anglican Protestant 45.4%, of which Baptist 17.5%; Roman Catholic 16.8%; Anglican 10.8%; nonreligious 5.3%; Spiritist 1.5%; other (mostly independent and unaffiliated Christian) 20.2%.
Major cities (2000): Nassau 210,832[5]; Freeport 26,910; Marsh Harbour 3,611[6]; Bailey Town 1,490[6].

Vital statistics

Birth rate per 1,000 population (2000): 19.5 (world avg. 21.3); legitimate 43.2%; illegitimate 56.8%.
Death rate per 1,000 population (2000): 6.8 (world avg. 9.1).
Natural increase rate per 1,000 population (2000): 12.7 (world avg. 12.2).
Total fertility rate (avg. births per childbearing woman; 2000): 2.3.
Marriage rate per 1,000 population (2000): 7.8.
Life expectancy at birth (2000): male 68.3 years; female 73.9 years.
Major causes of death per 100,000 population (2000): diseases of the circulatory system 145.0; HIV/AIDS 80.7; malignant neoplasms (cancers) 73.8; accidents and violence 71.8; diabetes 34.6.

National economy

Budget (2001). Revenue: B$957,400,000 (import taxes 43.0%, stamp taxes from imports 10.8%, business and professional licenses 8.2%, departure taxes 5.8%). Expenditures: B$957,400,000 (education 20.1%, health 16.5%, public order 11.8%, interest on public debt 10.5%, defense 2.8%).
National debt (2001): U.S.$1,483,800,000.
Production (value of production in B$'000 except as noted). Agriculture, forestry, fishing (2001): crayfish 56,500, poultry products 28,300[7], citrus and other fruit 21,300[7], conch 4,300; roundwood (2001) 17,000 cu m. Mining and quarrying (value of export production; 2000): aragonite 26,086; salt 12,447. Manufacturing (value of export production; 2000): chemical products 42,787; rum 18,856. Construction (2001): residential 210,000, nonresidential 103,400. Energy production (consumption): electricity (kW-hr; 2002) 1,826,000,000 (1,566,000,000); petroleum products (metric tons; 1999) none (583,000).
Tourism (U.S.$'000,000; 2001): receipts 1,665; expenditures 297.
Household income and expenditure. Average household size (2000) 3.5; income per household (1996) B$27,252 (U.S.$27,252); sources of income: n.a.; expenditure (1995)[8]: housing 32.8%, transportation and communications 14.8%, food and beverages 13.8%, household furnishings 8.9%.
Gross national product (at current market prices; 2001): U.S.$4,500,000,000 (U.S.$14,860 per capita).

Structure of gross domestic product and labour force

	1995 in value B$'000,000	1995 % of total value	2000 labour force	2000 % of labour force
Agriculture, fishing	100	3.3	5,058	3.3
Manufacturing	80	2.6	6,108	4.0
Mining	26	0.8	2,225	1.4
Public utilities	116	3.8		
Construction	71	2.3	16,980	11.0
Transp. and commun.	295	9.6	10,776	7.0
Trade, restaurants	705	23.0	46,908	30.4
Finance, real estate	599	19.5	15,900	10.3
Pub. admin., defense	210	6.8	13,069	8.5
Services	301	9.8	29,630	19.2
Other	568[9]	18.5[9]	7,742[10]	5.0[10]
TOTAL	3,069[3]	100.0	154,396	100.0[3]

Population economically active (2000): total 154,396; activity rate of total population 50.9% (participation rates: ages 15–64, 72.1%; female 47.5%; unemployed [2001] 6.9%).

Price and earnings indexes (1995 = 100)

	1996	1997	1998	1999	2000	2001	2002
Consumer price index	101.4	101.9	103.3	104.6	106.3	108.4	110.8
Annual earnings index	...	...	...	...	...	...	...

Land use (1994): forest 32.4%; pasture 0.2%; agriculture 1.0%; other 66.4%.

Foreign trade[11]

Balance of trade (current prices)

	1996	1997	1998	1999	2000
B$'000,000	–1,185	–1,441	–1,516	–1,479	–1,669
% of total	76.7%	79.9%	71.6%	63.3%	57.9%

Imports (2000): B$2,276,000,000 (machinery and transport equipment 25.9%; food products 14.8%; mineral fuels 10.2%; chemicals and chemical products 9.4%). *Major import sources*[12]: U.S. 91.8%; EC 1.5%.
Exports (2000): B$607,000,000 (domestic exports 52.8%, of which crayfish 14.0%, pharmaceuticals and other chemical products 7.1%; reexports 33.5%; mineral fuels 13.7%). *Major export destinations*[12]: U.S. 82.1%; EC 8.3%; Canada 1.5%.

Transport and communications

Transport. Railroads: none. Roads (2000): total length 1,673 mi, 2,693 km (paved 57%). Vehicles (1996)[13]: passenger cars 89,263; trucks and buses 17,228. Air transport (2001)[14]: passenger-mi 232,000,000, passenger-km 374,000,000; short ton-mi cargo 1,208,000, metric ton-km cargo 1,764,000; airports (1997) with scheduled flights 22.

Communications

Medium	date	unit	number	units per 1,000 persons
Daily newspapers	1996	circulation	28,000	99
Radio	1997	receivers	215,000	744
Television	2000	receivers	75,200	247
Telephones	2002	main lines	126,600	405
Cellular telephones	2002	subscribers	121,800	390
Internet	2002	users	21,200	68

Education and health

Educational attainment (2000). Percentage of population age 15 and over having: no formal schooling 1.5%; primary education 8.7%; incomplete secondary 19.9%; complete secondary 53.7%; incomplete higher 8.1%; complete higher 7.1%; not stated 1.0%. *Literacy* (2000): total percentage age 15 and over literate 98.5%.

Education (1996–97)

	schools	teachers	students	student/teacher ratio
Primary (age 5–10)	113	1,540	34,199	22.2
Secondary (age 11–16)[15]	...	1,352	27,970	20.7
Higher[16]	1	160	3,463	21.6

Health: physicians (1996) 419 (1 per 678 persons); hospital beds (1997) 1,119 (1 per 258 persons); infant mortality rate per 1,000 live births (2000) 17.0.
Food (2001): daily per capita caloric intake 2,777 (vegetable products 67%, animal products 33%); 104% of FAO recommended minimum requirement.

Military

Total active duty personnel (2002): 860 (paramilitary coast guard 100%). *Military expenditure as percentage of GNP* (2000): 0.6% (world, n.a.); per capita expenditure U.S.$85.

[1]Includes areas of lakes and ponds, as well as lagoons and sounds almost entirely surrounded by land; area of land only is about 3,890 sq mi (10,070 sq km). [2]For local administrative purposes, The Out Islands of the Bahamas are divided into 31 districts; New Providence Island is administered directly by the national government. [3]Detail does not add to total given because of rounding. [4]Land area only. [5]Population cited is for New Providence Island. [6]1990. [7]1998. [8]Weights of retail price index components. [9]Includes net indirect taxes (B$503,000,000) and statistical discrepancy (B$65,000,000). [10]Includes 552 not adequately defined and 7,190 unemployed. [11]Imports c.i.f.; exports f.o.b. [12]Excludes all petroleum imports/exports. [13]New Providence and Grand Bahama only. [14]Bahamasair only. [15]Public sector only. [16]College of The Bahamas only; 1997–98.

Internet resources for further information:
- **The Central Bank of The Bahamas http://www.bahamascentralbank.com**

Bahrain

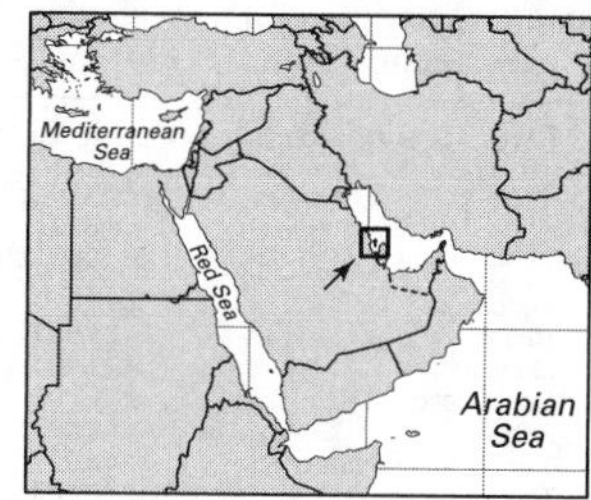

Official name: Mamlakat al-Baḥrayn (Kingdom of Bahrain).
Form of government: constitutional monarchy with a parliament comprising two bodies (Chamber of Deputies [40]; Consultative Council [40])[1].
Chief of state: Monarch.
Head of government: Prime Minister.
Capital: Manama.
Official language: Arabic.
Official religion: Islam.
Monetary unit: 1 Bahrain dinar (BD) = 1,000 fils; valuation (Sept. 8, 2003) 1 BD = U.S.$2.66 = £1.68.

Area and population

	area		population
Regions[2]	sq mi	sq km	2001 census
Al-Gharbīyah (Western)	60.7	157.2	26,149
Al-Ḥadd	4.2	10.9	11,637
Jidd (Judd) Ḥafṣ	9.4	24.3	52,450
Al-Manāmah (Manama)	10.6	27.5	153,395
Al-Muḥarraq	8.9	23.1	91,939
Ar-Rifāʿ	112.9	292.4	79,985
Ash-Shamālīyah (Northern)	14.4	37.4	43,691
Ash-Sharqīyah (Eastern)[3, 4]	20.1	52.1	3,875
Sitrah	11.6	30.0	43,910
Al-Wusṭā (Central)	13.7	35.4	49,969
Towns with special status			
Ḥammād	5.1	13.1	52,718
Madīnat ʿĪsā	4.8	12.4	36,833
TOTAL	276.4	715.8	650,604[5]

Demography

Population (2003): 674,000.
Density (2003): persons per sq mi 2,438.5, persons per sq km 941.5.
Urban-rural (2001): urban 90.3%; rural 9.7%.
Sex distribution (2001): male 57.43%; female 42.57%.
Age breakdown (2001): under 15, 27.9%; 15–29, 27.5%; 30–44, 29.7%; 45–59, 11.0%; 60–74, 3.2%; 75 and over, 0.7%.
Population projection: (2010) 748,000; (2020) 838,000.
Doubling time: 43 years.
Ethnic composition (2000): Bahraini Arab 63.9%; Indo-Pakistani 14.8%, of which Urdu 4.5%, Malayali 3.5%; Persian 13.0%; Filipino 4.5%; British 2.1%; other 1.7%.
Religious affiliation (2000): Muslim 82.4%, of which Shīʿī *c.* 41%, Sunnī *c.* 41%; Christian 10.5%; Hindu 6.3%; other 0.8%.
Major urban areas (2001): Manama 143,035; Al-Muḥarraq 91,307; Ar-Rifāʿ 79,550; Ḥammād 52,718; Madīnat ʿĪsā 36,833.

Vital statistics

Birth rate per 1,000 population (2001): 20.1 (world avg. 21.3).
Death rate per 1,000 population (2001): 3.9 (world avg. 9.1).
Natural increase rate per 1,000 population (2001): 16.2 (world avg. 12.2).
Total fertility rate (avg. births per childbearing woman; 2001): 3.0.
Marriage rate per 1,000 population (2001): 6.9.
Divorce rate per 1,000 population (2001): 1.2.
Life expectancy at birth (2001): male 73.2 years; female 76.2 years.
Major causes of death per 100,000 population (2000): diseases of the circulatory system 77.6; injury and poisoning 44.9; malignant neoplasms (cancers) 35.8; metabolic and immunity diseases 20.3; diseases of the respiratory system 12.2; diseases of the digestive system 10.6; congenital anomalies 7.2.

National economy

Budget (2001). Revenue: BD 980,900,000 (petroleum revenue 68.5%, nonpetroleum revenue 31.5%). Expenditures: BD 911,300,000 (infrastructure 30.1%, general administration and public order 29.3%, social services 21.6%, transfers 13.6%, economic services 3.5%).
Production (metric tons except as noted). Agriculture, forestry, fishing (2001): fruit (excluding melons) 21,518, dates 16,508, cow's milk 16,000, tomatoes 3,397, hen's eggs 3,200; livestock (number of live animals) 17,500 sheep, 16,300 goats, 11,000 cattle; fish catch (2001) 11,230. Manufacturing (barrels; 2001): gas oil 30,673,000; kerosene and jet fuel 18,274,000; fuel oil 17,188,000; naphtha 13,024,000; gasoline 6,182,000; aluminum (2001) 800,000 metric tons. Construction (permits issued; 2001): residential 6,337, nonresidential 929. Energy production (consumption): electricity (kW-hr; 2001) 6,779,000,000 (5,951,000,000); crude petroleum (barrels; 2001) 13,656,000 ([1999] 96,100,000); petroleum products (metric tons; 1999) 11,283,000 (861,000); natural gas (cu m; 2001) 9,285,000,000 (9,285,000,000).
Public debt (1999): BD 589,800,000 (U.S.$1,568,632,000).
Population economically active (2001): total 308,341; activity rate of total population 47.4% (participation rates: ages 15 and over 63.3%; female 21.7%; unemployed 5.5%).

Price and earnings indexes (1995 = 100)

	1995	1996	1997	1998	1999	2000	2001
Consumer price index	100.0	99.5	102.0	101.6	96.4	99.8	101.0
Earnings index	...	...	...	...	...	...	...

Tourism (2001): receipts from visitors U.S.$630,000,000; expenditures by nationals abroad U.S.$250,000,000.

Gross national product (2001): U.S.$7,200,000,000 (U.S.$11,130 per capita).

Structure of gross domestic product and labour force

	2001			
	value in BD '000,000	% of total value	labour force[6]	% of labour force[6]
Agriculture, fishing	21.7	0.7	4,483	1.5
Mining	740.0	24.8	2,780	0.9
Manufacturing	358.1	12.0	49,979	16.2
Construction	119.4	4.0	26,416	8.6
Public utilities	42.8	1.4	2,515	0.8
Transp. and commun.	224.2	7.5	13,769	4.5
Trade, restaurants	252.4	8.5	47,570	15.5
Finance[7]	842.2	28.3	24,797	8.1
Pub. admin., defense	321.3	10.8	52,389	17.0
Services[7]			61,256	19.9
Other	59.1[8]	2.0[8]	21,560[9]	7.0[9]
TOTAL	2,981.2	100.0	307,514	100.0[10]

Household income and expenditure. Average household size (2001) 6.2; expenditure (1984): food and tobacco 33.3%, housing 21.2%, household durable goods 9.8%, transportation and communications 8.5%, recreation 6.4%, clothing and footwear 5.9%.
Land use (1994): meadows and pastures 5.8%; agricultural and under permanent cultivation 2.9%; built-on and wasteland 91.3%.

Foreign trade[11]

Balance of trade (current prices)

	1996	1997	1998	1999	2000	2001
BD '000,000	+160.5	+134.6	–111.3	+166.5	+420.0	+482.0
% of total	4.8%	4.3%	4.3%	5.6%	10.8%	13.1%

Imports (2001): BD 1,602,800,000 (petroleum products 36.6%, machinery and transport equipment 11.8%, food, beverages, and tobacco products 11.2%). *Major import sources*[12]: Australia 10.0%; Saudi Arabia 9.0%; Japan 8.3%; U.S. 7.8%; U.K. 6.4%; Germany 6.0%.
Exports (2001): BD 2,084,800,000 (petroleum products 66.9%, aluminum [all forms] 15.0%, textiles and clothing 7.6%). *Major export destinations*[12]: U.S. 23.8%; Saudi Arabia 14.2%; Taiwan 9.8%; Malaysia 4.3%; India 4.2%.

Transport and communications

Transport. Railroads: none. Roads (2001): total length 3,583 km (paved 80%). Vehicles (2002): passenger cars 176,261; trucks and buses 36,231. Merchant marine (2002): registered vessels 121; total displacement tonnage 338,091. Air transport (2001)[13]: passenger-km 3,076,180,000; metric ton-km cargo 135,000,000; airports (2001) with scheduled flights 1.

Communications

Medium	date	unit	number	units per 1,000 persons
Daily newspapers	1996	circulation	67,000	117
Radio	2000	receivers	48,500	76
Television	2000	receivers	256,000	402
Telephones	2002	main lines	175,400	263
Cellular telephones	2002	subscribers	389,000	583
Personal computers	2002	units	107,000	160
Internet	2002	users	165,000	24,750

Education and health

Educational attainment (2001). Percentage of population age 15 and over having: no formal education 24.0%; primary education 37.1%; secondary 26.4%; higher 12.5%. *Literacy* (2001): percentage of population age 15 and over literate 87.7%; males literate 92.5%; females literate 83.0%.

Education (2000–01)

	schools	teachers	students	student/teacher ratio
Primary (age 6–11) / Secondary (age 12–17)	235	8,961	140,946	15.7
Voc., teacher tr.	5	718[14]	11,392	...
Higher[15]	2	582	13,439	23.1

Health (2001): physicians 1,101 (1 per 591 persons); hospital beds 1,836 (1 per 354 persons); infant mortality rate per 1,000 live births (2001) 8.7.

Military

Total active duty personnel (2002): 10,700 (army 79.4%, navy 9.3%, air force 11.3%)[16]. *Military expenditure as percentage of GNP* (1999): 8.1% (world 2.4%); per capita expenditure U.S.$666.

[1]Constitutional monarchy declared Feb. 14, 2002. Seats of Chamber of Deputies are elected, and seats of the Consultative Council are appointed by the monarch. [2]Official reorganization into 5 governorates announced July 2002. [3]Ash-Sharqīyah (Eastern) is regional name of Ḥawār Island and other nearby islets. [4]The International Court of Justice awarded the jurisdiction of Ḥawār to Bahrain in early 2001; jurisdiction of islets nearby to Ḥawār was split between Bahrain and Qatar. [5]Includes 4,053 living abroad. [6]Excludes small number of unemployed non-Bahrainis. [7]Finance includes Services. [8]Import duties. [9]Includes 5,424 inadequately defined and 16,136 unemployed Bahrainis. [10]Of which *c.* 59% non-Bahrainis. [11]Imports c.i.f. [12]Excludes trade in petroleum. [13]One-fourth apportionment of international flights of Gulf Air (jointly administered by the governments of Bahrain, Oman, Qatar, and the United Arab Emirates). [14]1998–99. [15]Bahrain and Arabian Gulf universities only. [16]U.S. troops in Bahrain (2003): 4,000.

Internet resources for further information:
- **Bahrain Government Homepage http://www.bahrain.gov.bh/english/index.asp**
- **Bahrain Monetary Agency http://www.bma.gov.bh**

Bangladesh

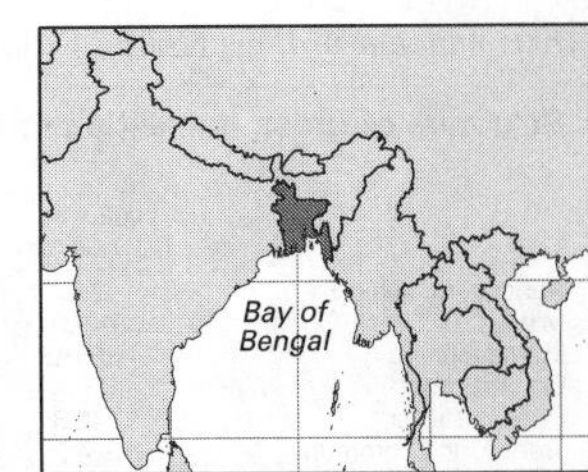

Official name: Gana Prajatantri Bangladesh (People's Republic of Bangladesh).
Form of government: unitary multiparty republic with one legislative house (Parliament [330[1]).
Chief of state: President.
Head of government: Prime Minister.
Capital: Dhaka.
Official language: Bengali (Bangla).
Official religion: Islam.
Monetary unit: 1 Bangladesh taka (Tk) = 100 paisa; valuation (Sept. 8, 2003) 1 U.S.$ = Tk 58.42; 1 £ = Tk 92.63.

Area and population

Divisions	Administrative centres	area sq mi	area sq km	population 2001 census[2]
Barisal	Barisal	5,134	13,297	8,514,000
Chittagong	Chittagong	7,906	20,476	23,796,682
Dhaka	Dhaka	12,015	31,119	40,592,431
Khulna	Khulna	8,600	22,274	15,185,026
Rajshahi	Rajshahi	13,326	34,513	31,477,606
Sylhet	Sylhet	4,863	12,596	8,290,857
Tribal region				
Chittagong Hill Tracts[3]	Rangamati	5,133	13,295	1,390,631
TOTAL		56,977[4]	147,570[4]	129,247,233

Demography

Population (2003): 133,107,000.
Density (2002)[5]: persons per sq mi 2,474.2, persons per sq km 955.3.
Urban-rural (2001): urban 23.4%; rural 76.6%.
Sex distribution (2001): male 50.94%; female 49.06%.
Age breakdown (2001): under 15, 35.9%; 15–29, 31.5%; 30–44, 17.6%; 45–59, 9.9%; 60–74, 4.0%; 75 and over, 1.1%.
Population projection: (2010) 147,253,000; (2020) 170,108,000.
Doubling time: 33 years.
Ethnic composition (1997): Bengali 97.7%; tribal 1.9%, of which Chakma 0.4%, Saontal 0.2%, Marma 0.1%; other 0.4%.
Religious affiliation (2000): Muslim 85.8%; Hindu 12.4%; Christian 0.7%; Buddhist 0.6%; other 0.5%.
Major cities/urban agglomerations (2001): Dhaka 5,644,235/10,403,597; Chittagong 2,199,590/3,361,244; Khulna 811,490/1,287,987; Rajshahi 402,646/678,728.

Vital statistics

Birth rate per 1,000 population (2002): 30.1 (world avg. 21.3).
Death rate per 1,000 population (2002): 8.8 (world avg. 9.1).
Natural increase rate per 1,000 population (2002): 21.3 (world avg. 12.2).
Total fertility rate (avg. births per childbearing woman; 2002): 3.6.
Marriage rate per 1,000 population (1998): 9.2.
Life expectancy at birth (2002): male 60.0 years; female 61.0 years.
Major causes of death (1990; percentage of recorded deaths): typhoid fever 19.8%; old age 14.8%; tetanus 10.1%; tuberculosis and other respiratory diseases 8.7%; diarrhea 6.4%; suicide, accidents, and poisoning 5.1%; high blood pressure and heart diseases 5.0%.

National economy

Budget (2002–03). Revenue: Tk 326,000,000,000 (value-added tax 39.3%, international trade 36.2%; income taxes 14.7%; other 9.8%). Expenditures: Tk 448,000,000,000 (development program 42.4%, wages 16.5%, subsidies 14.7%; interest payments 10.3%, goods and services 8.3%, other 7.8%).
Production (metric tons except as noted). Agriculture, forestry, fishing (2002): paddy rice 38,134,000, sugarcane 6,502,000, potatoes 3,216,000, wheat 1,606,000, jute 858,740, bananas 606,000, sweet potatoes 346,000, oilseeds 279,100, mangoes 188,000, tea 52,000; livestock (number of live animals) 34,400,000 goats, 24,000,000 cattle, 1,143,000 sheep, 830,000 water buffalo, 140,000,000 chickens, 13,000,000 ducks; roundwood (2001) 28,421,728 cu m; fish catch (2000) 1,661,385. Mining and quarrying (1997–98): marine salt 350,000; industrial limestone 32,324. Manufacturing (value added in U.S.$'000,000; 1995): textiles 651; industrial chemicals 441; food products 331; wearing apparel 242; tobacco products 347; transport equipment 128; iron and steel 108. Energy production (consumption): electricity (kW-hr; 2002) 17,021,000,000 (17,021,000,000); coal (metric tons; 1999) none (92,000); crude petroleum (barrels; 1999) 7,000 (7,500,000); petroleum products (metric tons; 2002) 1,323,000 (3,769,000); natural gas (cu m; 2002) 6,568,000,000 (3,096,000,000).
Household income. Average household size (2000) 5.7; average annual income per household Tk 52,389 (U.S.$1,277); sources of income: self-employment 56.9%, wages and salaries 28.1%, transfer payments 9.1%, other 5.9%; expenditure (2002–03): food and drink 64.5%, housing and energy 15.0%, clothing and footwear 5.9%, transport 3.3%, other 11.3%.
Population economically active (2000): total 52,847,000; activity rate of total population 47.3% (participation rates: over age 15, 58.8%; female 37.5%; unemployed 2.0%[6]).

Price and earnings indexes (1995 = 100)

	1995	1996	1997	1998	1999	2000	2001
Consumer price index	100.0	104.1	109.5	118.6	125.9	128.9	131.4
Earnings index[7]	100.0	106.0	111.0	123.0	129.5	...	...

Public debt (external, outstanding; 2002): U.S.$15,970,000,000.
Gross national product (2001): U.S.$48,600,000,000 (U.S.$360 per capita).

Structure of gross domestic product and labour force

	2001–02 in value Tk '000,000	2001–02 % of total value	2000 labour force	2000 % of labour force
Agriculture	595,000	21.9	32,171,000	60.9
Mining	29,000	1.1	295,000	0.6
Manufacturing	422,000	15.4	3,783,000	7.1
Construction	211,000	7.8	1,099,000	2.1
Public utilities	37,000	1.4	134,000	0.3
Transp. and commun.	242,000	8.9	2,509,000	4.7
Trade	370,000	13.6	6,276,000	11.9
Finance	282,000	10.4	403,000	0.8
Public admin., defense, and services	529,000	19.5	5,095,000	9.6
Other	—	—	1,084,000[8]	2.0[8]
TOTAL	2,717,000	100.0	52,847,000	100.0

Land use (1998): pasture 4.6%; agriculture 68.6%; forest and other 26.8%.
Tourism (2001): receipts U.S.$48,000,000; expenditures U.S.$166,000,000.

Foreign trade[9]

Balance of trade (current prices)

	1996	1997	1998	1999	2000	2001
Tk '000,000	−110,988	−99,478	−118,772	−149,493	−144,480	−152,265
% of total	28.7%	23.0%	24.8%	28.0%	22.4%	22.0%

Imports (2001–02): Tk 460,700,000,000 (capital goods 30.6%; textile yarn, fabrics, and made-up articles 19.4%; consumer durables and motor cars 15.0%; imports for export processing zone 7.3%; iron and steel 4.8%). *Major import sources* (2000–01): India 16.8%; Western Europe 12.7%; Singapore 11.8%; China 9.5%; Hong Kong 6.9%; South Korea 5.6%.
Exports (2001–02): Tk 322,900,000,000 (ready-made garments 52.2%; hosiery and knitwear 24.4%; frozen fish and shrimp 4.6%; jute manufactures 4.0%). *Major export destinations* (2001–01): Western Europe 48.8%; U.S. 36.2%; Hong Kong 2.0%; Canada 2.0%.

Transport and communications

Transport. Railroads (1998–99): route length 1,699 mi, 2,734 km; passenger-mi 3,094,000,000, passenger-km 4,980,000,000; short ton-mi cargo 567,000,000, metric ton-km cargo 828,000,000. Roads (1999): total length 128,925 mi, 207,486 km (paved 10%). Vehicles (1999): passenger cars 66,723; trucks and buses 82,025. Merchant marine (1992): vessels (100 gross tons and over) 301; total deadweight tonnage 566,775. Air transport (2001)[10]: passenger-mi 2,763,175,000, passenger-km 4,446,908,000; short ton-mi cargo 117,478,000, metric ton-km cargo 171,515,000; airports with scheduled flights (2001) 8.

Communications

Medium	date	unit	number	units per 1,000 persons
Daily newspapers	2000	circulation	6,880,000	53
Radio	2000	receivers	6,360,000	49
Television	2000	receivers	909,000	7.0
Telephones	2002	main lines	682,000	5.1
Cellular telephones	2002	subscribers	1,075,000	8.1
Personal computers	2002	units	450,000	3.0
Internet	2002	users	204,000	1.5

Education and health

Educational attainment (1991). Percentage of population age 25 and over having: no formal schooling 65.4%; primary education 17.1%; secondary 13.8%; postsecondary 3.7%. *Literacy* (2000): total population age 15 and over literate 41.3%; males literate 52.3%; females literate 29.9%.

Education (1997–98)

	schools	teachers	students	student/ teacher ratio
Primary (age 6–10)	66,235	250,990	17,627,000	70.2
Secondary (age 11–17)	13,419	161,141	6,289,000	39.0
Voc., teacher tr.[11]	165	1,896[12]	41,650	16.1[12]
Higher[11, 13]	3,123	77,644	2,573,439	33.1

Health (1999): physicians 30,864 (1 per 4,150 persons); hospital beds 44,374 (1 per 2,886 persons); infant mortality rate (2002) 68.0.
Food (2001): daily per capita caloric intake 2,187 (vegetable products 97%, animal products 3%); 95% of FAO recommended minimum requirement.

Military

Total active duty personnel (2002): 137,000 (army 87.6%, navy 7.7%, air force 4.7%). *Military expenditure as percentage of GNP* (1999): 1.4% (world 2.4%); per capita expenditure U.S.$5.

[1]Includes 30 seats reserved for women. [2]Preliminary figure. [3]Autonomous region for non-Bengali tribal people was created by accord signed in December 1997 and formally established in May 1999. [4]The total area excluding the river area equals 53,797 sq mi (139,334 sq km). [5]Based on the total area excluding the river area. [6]Excluding underemployment. [7]Wage earnings in manufacturing. [8]Unemployed. [9]Import figures are f.o.b. in balance of trade and c.i.f. in commodities and trading partners. [10]Bangladesh Biman only. [11]1996–97. [12]Excludes teachers' training school data. [13]Excludes professional and technical colleges.

Internet resources for further information:
- **Government of the People's Republic of Bangladesh http://www.bangladeshgov.org**
- **National Data Bank http://www.bbsgov.org**

Barbados

Official name: Barbados.
Form of government: constitutional monarchy with two legislative houses (Senate [21]; House of Assembly [30]).
Chief of state: British Monarch represented by Governor-General.
Head of government: Prime Minister.
Capital: Bridgetown.
Official language: English.
Official religion: none.
Monetary unit: 1 Barbados dollar (BDS$) = 100 cents; valuation (Sept. 8, 2003) 1 U.S.$ = BDS$2.00; 1 £ = BDS$3.17.

Area and population

	area		population
			1990
Parishes[1]	sq mi	sq km	census
Christ Church	22	57	47,050
St. Andrew	14	36	6,346
St. George	17	44	17,905
St. James	12	31	21,001
St. John	13	34	10,206
St. Joseph	10	26	7,619
St. Lucy	14	36	9,455
St. Michael[2]	15	39	97,516
St. Peter	13	34	11,263
St. Philip	23	60	20,540
St. Thomas	13	34	11,590
TOTAL	166	430[3]	260,491

Demography

Population (2003): 272,000.
Density (2003): persons per sq mi 1,638.6, persons per sq km 632.6.
Urban-rural (2001): urban 50.5%; rural 49.5%.
Sex distribution (2002): male 48.17%; female 51.83%.
Age breakdown (2000): under 15, 22.0%; 15–29, 24.2%; 30–44, 26.1%; 45–59, 15.7%; 60–74, 7.9%; 75 and over, 4.1%.
Population projection: (2010) 278,000; (2020) 283,000.
Ethnic composition (2000): local black 87.1%; mulatto 6.0%; British expatriates 4.3%; U.S. white 1.2%; Indo-Pakistani 1.1%; other 0.3%.
Religious affiliation (1995): Protestant 63.0%, of which Anglican 26.3%, Pentecostal 10.6%, Methodist 5.7%; Roman Catholic 4.8%; other Christian 2.0%; nonreligious/other 30.2%.
Major cities (1990): Bridgetown 6,070 (urban agglomeration [2001] 136,000); Speightstown, *c.* 3,500.

Vital statistics

Birth rate per 1,000 population (2000): 13.6 (world avg. 21.3).
Death rate per 1,000 population (2000): 8.7 (world avg. 9.1).
Natural increase rate per 1,000 population (2000): 4.9 (world avg. 12.2).
Total fertility rate (avg. births per childbearing woman; 2000): 1.6.
Marriage rate per 1,000 population (1995): 13.5.
Divorce rate per 1,000 population (1995): 1.5.
Life expectancy at birth (2000): male 70.4 years; female 75.6 years.
Major causes of death per 100,000 population (1995): diseases of the circulatory system 369.7; malignant neoplasms (cancers) 163.6; endocrine and metabolic disorders 151.3; diseases of the respiratory system 56.3; accidents, poisonings, and violence 36.4; diseases of the digestive system 34.5; infectious and parasitic diseases 27.6; diseases of the nervous system 23.0.

National economy

Budget (2000–01). Revenue: BDS$1,703,000,000[4] (tax revenue 94.7%, of which goods and services taxes 44.0%, personal income and company taxes 34.7%, import duties 8.0%; nontax revenue 5.3%). Expenditures: BDS$1,802,600,000 (current expenditure 83.3%, of which education 19.6%, debt payment 12.5%, health 11.3%, economic services 11.0%, social security and welfare 8.4%; capital expenditure 16.7%).
Production (metric tons except as noted). Agriculture, forestry, fishing (2002): raw sugar 50,000, sweet potatoes 5,300, yams 1,450, cucumbers and gherkins 1,350, cabbage 1,275, pumpkins, squash, and gourds 1,050, cassava 830, carrots 810, tomatoes 720; livestock (number of live animals) 41,300 sheep, 35,000 pigs, 21,000 cattle; roundwood (2001) 5,000; fish catch (2000) 3,100. Manufacturing (value added in BDS$'000; 1995): food, beverages, and tobacco (mostly sugar, molasses, rum, beer, and cigarettes) 108,000; paper products, printing, and publishing 33,400; metal products and assembly-type goods (mostly electronic components) 28,000; textiles and wearing apparel 11,700. Energy production (consumption): electricity (kW-hr; 2000) 737,100,000 (737,100,000); crude petroleum (barrels; 2001) 463,700 ([1999] 1,900,000); petroleum products (metric tons; 1999) 4,000 (335,000); natural gas (cu m; 2001) 34,900,000 (34,900,000).
Household income and expenditure. Average household size (2000) 2.8; income per household (1988) BDS$13,455 (U.S.$6,690); sources of income: n.a.; expenditure (1994): food 39.4%, housing 16.8%, transportation 10.5%, household operations 8.1%, alcohol and tobacco 6.4%, fuel and light 5.2%, clothing and footwear 5.0%, other 8.6%.
Population economically active (2001): total 145,100; activity rate of total population 53.1% (participation rates: ages 15 and over, 69.5%; female 47.3%; unemployed 9.9%).

Price and earnings indexes (1995 = 100)

	1996	1997	1998	1999	2000	2001	2002
Consumer price index	102.4	110.3	108.9	110.6	113.3	116.2	116.3
Earnings index	...	...	...	...	...	...	...

Gross national product (2000): U.S.$2,600,000,000 (U.S.$9,750 per capita).

Structure of gross domestic product and labour force

	1999		2001	
	in value BDS$'000,000	% of total value	labour force	% of labour force
Agriculture, fishing	202.3	4.9	6,100	4.2
Mining	27.8[5]	0.7[5]	...	...
Manufacturing	260.8	6.3	10,160	7.0
Construction	241.8	5.8	15,960	11.0
Public utilities	134.0[5]	3.2[5]	2,180	1.5
Transp. and commun.	429.0	10.4	6,400	4.4
Trade, restaurants	1,205.0	29.1	37,000	25.5
Finance, real estate	739.2	17.8	11,600	8.0
Pub. admin., defense	713.5	17.2	55,700	38.4
Services	191.3	4.6		
TOTAL	4,144.7	100.0	145,100	100.0

Public debt (external, outstanding; 2001): U.S.$700,700,000.
Tourism: receipts from visitors (2001) U.S.$687,000,000; expenditures by nationals abroad (2000) U.S.$94,000,000.

Foreign trade[6]

Balance of trade (current prices)

	1996	1997	1998	1999	2000	2001
BDS$'000,000	–1,106	–1,425	–1,541	–1,689	–1,767	–1,619
% of total	49.6%	55.7%	59.6%	61.5%	61.9%	60.9%

Imports (2001): BDS$2,137,000,000 (retained imports 92.2%, of which machinery 17.9%, food and beverages 15.4%, mineral fuels 7.6%, construction materials 7.1%; reexported imports 7.8%). *Major import sources* (2000): U.S. 41.6%[7]; Trinidad and Tobago 16.5%; U.K. 8.1%; Japan 5.2%.
Exports (2001): BDS$519,000,000 (domestic exports 68.0%, of which food and beverages 27.7% (including sugar 8.5%, rum 6.9%), chemical products 8.4%, electrical components 7.1%; reexports 32.0%). *Major export destinations* (2000): U.S. 15.8%[7]; Trinidad and Tobago 13.2%; U.K. 13.2%; Jamaica 7.0%; bunkers and ships' stores 16.3%.

Transport and communications

Transport. Railroads: none. Roads (2000): total length 9,942 mi, 1,600 km (paved 99%). Vehicles (2001): passenger cars 64,900; trucks and buses 11,400. Merchant marine (1992): vessels (100 gross tons and over) 37; total deadweight tonnage 84,000. Air transport: (2001) passenger arrivals and departures 1,760,000; (2000) cargo unloaded and loaded 14,000 metric tons; airports (2001) with scheduled flights 1.

Communications

Medium	date	unit	number	units per 1,000 persons
Daily newspapers	1996	circulation	53,000	199
Radio	2001	receivers	202,000	749
Television	2001	receivers	83,700	310
Telephones	2001	main lines	123,800	460
Cellular telephones	2001	subscribers	53,100	198
Personal computers	2001	units	25,000	93
Internet	2001	users	15,000	56

Education and health

Educational attainment (1990). Percentage of population age 25 and over having: no formal schooling 0.4%; primary education 23.7%; secondary 60.3%[8]; higher 11.2%; other 4.4%. *Literacy* (1995): total population age 15 and over literate 97.4%; males literate 98.0%; females literate 96.8%.

Education (1995–96)

	schools	teachers	students	student/ teacher ratio
Primary (age 3–11)	79	994	18,513	18.6
Secondary (age 12–16)	21	1,263	21,455	17.0
Vocational[9]	8	79	996	12.6
Higher	4	544[10]	6,622	...

Health: physicians (2002) 376 (1 per 721 persons); hospital beds (1992) 1,966 (1 per 134 persons); infant mortality rate per 1,000 live births (2002) 12.6.
Food (2001): daily per capita caloric intake 2,992 (vegetable products 75%, animal products 25%); 124% of FAO recommended minimum requirement.

Military

Total active duty personnel (2002): 610 (army 82.0%, navy 18.0%). *Military expenditure as percentage of GNP* (1999): 0.5% (world 2.4%); per capita expenditure U.S.$44.

[1]Parishes and city of Bridgetown have no local administrative function. [2]Includes city of Bridgetown. [3]Detail does not add to total given because of rounding. [4]Current revenue only. [5]Mining excludes natural gas; Public utilities includes natural gas. [6]Import figures are c.i.f. [7]Includes Puerto Rico. [8]Includes composite senior. [9]1987–88. [10]1984.

Internet resources for further information:
- **Central Bank of Barbados http://www.centralbank.org.bb**

Belarus

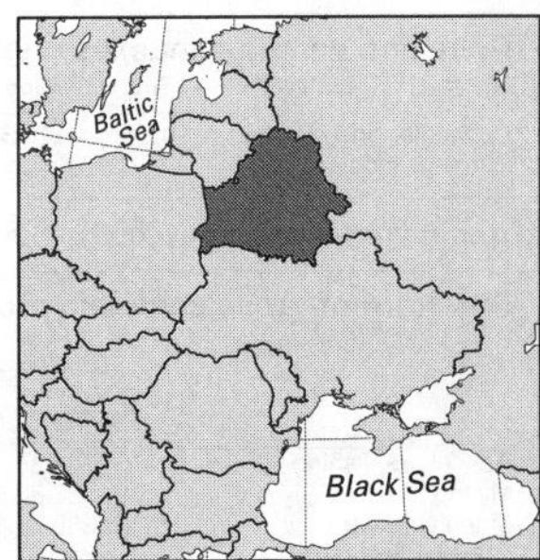

Official name: Respublika Belarus (Republic of Belarus).
Form of government: republic with two legislative bodies (Council of the Republic [62[1]]; House of Representatives [110[1]]).
Head of state and government: President assisted by Prime Minister.
Capital: Minsk.
Official languages: Belarusian; Russian.
Official religion: none.
Monetary unit: rubel[2] (Rbl; plural rubli); valuation (Sept. 8, 2003), 1 U.S.$ = (new) Rbl 2,103; 1 £ = (new) Rbl 3,334.

Area and population		area		population
				2002
Provinces	**Capitals**	sq mi	sq km	estimate
Brest	Brest	12,700	32,800	1,477,200
Homel (Gomel)	Homel	15,600	40,400	1,527,500
Hrodno (Grodno)	Hrodno	9,700	25,100	1,166,200
Mahilyoŭ (Mogilyov)	Mahilyoŭ	11,200	29,100	1,191,800
Minsk (Mensk)	Minsk	15,500[3]	40,200[3]	1,527,300
Vitebsk	Vitebsk	15,500	40,000	1,348,300
City				
Minsk (Mensk)	—	[3]	[3]	1,712,600
TOTAL		80,200[4]	207,600[4]	8,950,900

Demography

Population (2003): 9,881,000.
Density (2003): persons per sq mi 123.3, persons per sq km 47.6.
Urban-rural (2002): urban 71.1%; rural 28.9%.
Sex distribution (2002): male 46.89%; female 53.11%.
Age breakdown (2001): under 15, 18.3%; 15–29, 22.5%; 30–44, 23.2%; 45–59, 16.9%; 60–69, 10.2%; 70 and over, 8.9%.
Population projection: (2010) 9,598,000; (2020) 9,195,000.
Doubling time: not applicable; population is declining.
Ethnic composition (1999): Belarusian 81.2%; Russian 11.4%; Polish 3.9%; Ukrainian 2.4%; Jewish 0.3%; other 0.8%.
Religious affiliation (1995): Belarusian Orthodox 31.6%; Roman Catholic 17.7%; other (mostly nonreligious) 50.7%.
Major cities (2001): Minsk 1,699,000; Homel 490,000; Mahilyoŭ 361,000; Vitebsk 349,000; Hrodno 307,000.

Vital statistics

Birth rate per 1,000 population (2000): 9.4 (world avg. 21.3); legitimate 81.4%; illegitimate 18.6%.
Death rate per 1,000 population (2000): 13.5 (world avg. 9.1).
Natural increase rate per 1,000 population (2000): –4.1 (world avg. 12.2).
Total fertility rate (avg. births per childbearing woman; 2000): 1.3.
Marriage rate per 1,000 population (2000): 6.2.
Divorce rate per 1,000 population (2000): 4.3.
Life expectancy at birth (2000): male 63.4 years; female 74.7 years.
Major causes of death per 100,000 population (2000): diseases of the circulatory system 722.6; malignant neoplasms (cancers) 195.3; accidents and violence 157.8; diseases of the respiratory system 66.7.

National economy

Budget (2000). Revenue: Rbl 3,181,000,000,000 (tax revenue 76.5%, of which value-added tax 25.7%, taxes on profits 13.8%, taxes on income 8.7%, excise taxes 8.0%, taxes on international trade 4.5%, other 15.8%; nontax revenue 23.5%). Expenditures: Rbl 3,236,000,000,000 (target budgetary fund 17.6%, education 17.4%, health 14.1%, subsidies 7.7%, capital expenditure 6.9%, other 36.3%).
Public debt (external, outstanding; 2001): U.S.$640,900,000.
Household income and expenditure. Average household size (2000) 3.4; income per household (1995) (old) Rbl 2,400,000[2]; sources of income (2000): wages and salaries 51.9%, business activities 28.3%, transfers 18.0%, property income 1.8%; expenditure (2000): food, beverages, and tobacco 64.9%; clothing 11.7%; transport 6.9%; household appliances 4.1%; rent 3.0%; health 2.2%; education 2.2%; other 5.0%.
Population economically active (2002): 4,459,000; activity rate of total population 45.0% (participation rate: ages 16–59 [male], 16–54 [female] 75.7%; female 53.2%; unemployed 3.0%).

Price and earnings indexes (1995 = 100)

	1997	1998	1999	2000	2001	2002
Consumer price index	250.3	432.7	1,703.6	4,576.0	7,371.9	10,505.0
Annual earnings index	300.6	613.9	2,592.9	7,802.2	16,290.9	25,055.4

Production (metric tons except as noted). Agriculture, forestry, fishing (2002): potatoes 7,420,000, cereal 5,194,000, vegetables 1,420,000, sugar beets 1,149,000, fruit 340,000; livestock (number of live animals) 4,084,500 cattle, 3,372,600 pigs, 209,400 horses, 144,600 sheep and goats, 33,600,000 poultry; roundwood (2001) 6,273,200 cu m; fish catch (2000) 7,269. Mining and quarrying (2000): potash 3,400,000; peat 2,211,000. Manufacturing (value of production in [old] Rbl '000,000; 1994): machine-building equipment 1,086,650; chemical products 659,438; food products 562,438; construction materials 142,555. Construction (2000): 3,528,000 sq m. Energy production (consumption): electricity (kW-hr; 1999) 26,516,000,000 (33,680,000,000); coal (1999) none (678,000); crude petroleum (barrels; 1999) 13,500,000 (83,800,000); petroleum products (1999) 10,181,000 (6,375,000); natural gas (cu m; 2000) 257,000,000 (16,402,000,000).
Gross national product (2001): U.S.$12,900,000,000 (U.S.$1,290 per capita).

Structure of gross domestic product and labour force

	2000			
	in value Rbl '000,000,000[5]	% of total value[5]	labour force	% of labour force
Agriculture	1,197.5	15.3	657,600	14.5
Mining Manufacturing	2,354.9	30.1	1,226,700	27.0
Public utilities	153.4	2.0	208,100	4.6
Construction	516.3	6.6	312,300	6.9
Transp. and commun.	1,078.1	13.8	318,300	7.0
Trade	967.3	12.4	532,300	11.7
Finance	500.3	6.4	58,400	1.3
Public admin., defense	276.2	3.5	912,200	20.1
Services	952.2	12.2		
Other	–177.3[6]	–2.3[6]	311,100[7]	6.9[7]
TOTAL	7,818.9	100.0	4,537,000	100.0

Tourism (2001): receipts U.S.$82,000,000; expenditures U.S.$263,000,000.
Land use (1994)[8]: forested 33.7%; meadows and pastures 14.1%; agricultural and under permanent cultivation 30.5%; other 21.7%.

Foreign trade[9]

Balance of trade (current prices)

	1996	1997	1998	1999	2000	2001
U.S.$'000,000	–1,287	–1,388	–1,479	–765	–1,161	–656
% of total	10.2%	8.7%	9.5%	6.1%	7.3%	4.2%

Imports (2000): U.S.$8,492,000,000 (crude petroleum 19.2%, machinery and apparatus 13.5%, chemicals and chemical products 11.5%, food and beverages 9.6%, iron and steel 6.8%, natural and manufactured gas 6.7%). *Major import sources:* Russia 65.3%; Germany 6.9%; Ukraine 4.0%; Poland 2.5%; Italy 1.9%.
Exports (2000): U.S.$7,331,000,000 (refined petroleum 18.5%, road vehicles 10.2%, nonelectrical machinery 8.0%, food 6.1%, potassium chloride 5.6%, textile yarn, fabrics, and made-up articles 5.5%). *Major export destinations:* Russia 50.7%; Ukraine 7.6%; Latvia 6.4%; Lithuania 4.8%; Poland 3.8%.

Transport and communications

Transport. Railroads (2002): length 5,533 km; passenger-km 14,349,000,000; metric ton-km cargo (2000) 31,425,000,000. Roads (2000): total length 74,400 km (paved 89.0%). Vehicles (2000): passenger cars 1,448,461; trucks and buses 85,791. Air transport (2000): passenger-km 513,000,000; metric ton-km cargo 18,000,000; airports 1.

Communications

Medium	date	unit	number	units per 1,000 persons
Daily newspapers	2000	circulation	1,550,000	155
Radio	2000	receivers	2,990,000	299
Television	2000	receivers	3,420,000	342
Telephones	2002	main lines	2,967,200	299
Cellular telephones	2002	subscribers	465,200	47
Internet	2002	users	808,700	82

Education and health

Educational attainment: n.a.

Education (2002–03)

	schools	teachers	students	student/ teacher ratio
Primary (age 6–13) Secondary (age 14–17)	4,543	151,100[10]	1,430,000	...
Voc., teacher tr.	150	8,800[11]	160,900	...
Higher	58	16,300[11]	320,700	...

Literacy (1999): total population age 15 and over literate 99.5%; males literate 99.7%; females literate 99.4%.
Health (2000): physicians (2002) 44,800 (1 per 221 persons); hospital beds 126,209 (1 per 79 persons); infant mortality rate per 1,000 live births 9.3.
Food (2001): daily per capita caloric intake 2,925 (vegetable products 72%, animal products 28%); 113% of FAO recommended minimum requirement.

Military

Total active duty personnel (2002): 79,800 (army 51.8%, air force and air defense 27.6%, other 20.6%). *Military expenditure as percentage of GNP* (1999): 1.3% (world 2.4%); per capita expenditure U.S.$89.

[1]Statutory number. [2]Rubel re-denominated Jan. 1, 2000; 1,000 (old) rubli = 1 (new) rubel. [3]Minsk province includes Minsk city. [4]Rounded area figures; exact area figures are 80,153 sq mi (207,595 sq km). [5]At factor cost. [6]Less imputed bank service charge. [7]Includes 96,000 unemployed and 215,100 undistributed employed. [8]25% of Belarusian territory severely affected by radioactive fallout from Chernobyl. [9]Imports c.i.f.; exports f.o.b. [10]2000–01. [11]1997–98.

Internet resources for further information:
- **Ministry of Statistics and Analysis**
http://president.gov.by/Minstat/en/main.html
- **The Belarusian WWW-server for Businessmen**
http://www.belarus.net

Belgium

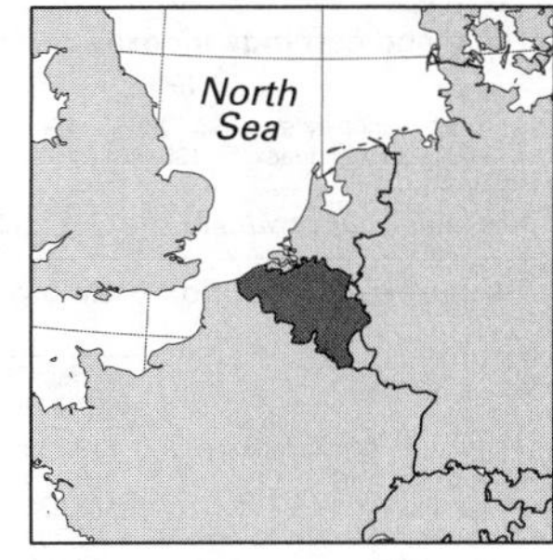

Official name: Koninkrijk België (Dutch); Royaume de Belgique (French) (Kingdom of Belgium).
Form of government: federal constitutional monarchy with a Parliament composed of two legislative chambers (Senate [71[1]]; House of Representatives [150]).
Chief of state: Monarch.
Head of government: Prime Minister.
Capital: Brussels.
Official languages: Dutch; French; German.
Official religion: none.
Monetary unit: 1 euro (€) = 100 cents; valuation (Sept. 8, 2003) 1 U.S.$ = €0.90; 1£ = €1.43[2].

Area and population

Regions[3] Provinces	Capitals	area sq mi	area sq km	population 2002[4] estimate
Brussels[5]	—	62	161	978,384
Flanders	—	5,221[6]	13,522	5,972,781
Antwerp	Antwerp	1,107	2,867	1,652,450
East Flanders	Ghent	1,151	2,982	1,366,652
Flemish Brabant	Leuven	813	2,106	1,022,821
Limburg	Hasselt	935	2,422	798,583
West Flanders	Brugge	1,214	3,145	1,132,275
Wallonia	—	6,504[6]	16,844	3,358,560
Hainaut	Mons	1,462	3,786	1,281,042
Liège	Liège	1,491	3,862	1,024,130
Luxembourg	Arlon	1,714	4,440	250,406
Namur	Namur	1,415	3,666	447,775
Walloon Brabant	Wavre	421	1,091	355,207
TOTAL		11,787	30,528[6]	10,309,725

Demography

Population (2003): 10,341,000.
Density (2003): persons per sq mi 877.3, persons per sq km 338.7.
Urban-rural (2001)[7]: urban 97.4%; rural 2.6%.
Sex distribution (2002): male 48.94%; female 51.06%.
Age breakdown (2002): under 15, 17.3%; 15–29, 18.4%; 30–44, 22.7%; 45–59, 19.7%; 60–74, 14.2%; 75 and over, 7.7%.
Population projection: (2010) 10,458,000; (2020) 10,529,000.
Ethnic composition (2000): Flemish 53.7%; Walloon (French) 31.6%; Italian 2.6%; French 2.0%; Arab 1.8%; German 1.5%; Berber 0.9%; other 5.9%.
Religious affiliation (1995): Roman Catholic 87.9%; Muslim 2.5%; other Christian 2.4%, of which Protestant 1.0%; Jewish 0.3%; other 6.9%.
Major cities (2002[4]): Brussels 978,384[5]; Antwerp 448,709; Ghent 226,220; Charleroi 200,578; Liège 185,131.

Vital statistics

Birth rate per 1,000 population (2002): 10.9 (world avg. 21.3).
Death rate per 1,000 population (2002): 10.2 (world avg. 9.1).
Natural increase rate per 1,000 population (2002): 0.7 (world avg. 12.2).
Total fertility rate (avg. births per childbearing woman; 2002): 1.6.
Marriage rate per 1,000 population (2000): 4.4.
Divorce rate per 1,000 population (2000): 2.6.
Life expectancy at birth (2002): male 74.9 years; female 81.4 years.
Major causes of death per 100,000 population (1992): diseases of the circulatory system 383.3; malignant neoplasms (cancers) 272.6; diseases of the respiratory system 90.6; accidents and violence 40.9.

National economy

Budget (2002). Revenue: €130,589,000,000 (social security contributions 29.4%, income tax 25.5%, taxes on goods and services 22.3%, property tax 6.8%, other 16.0%). Expenditures: €114,809,000,000 (social security payments 29.2%, wages 27.2%, interest on debt 13.8%, health 13.5%, capital expenditure 5.7%, other 10.6%).
Public debt (1999): U.S.$250,459,000,000.
Production (metric tons except as noted). Agriculture, forestry, fishing (2002)[7]: sugar beets 5,898,000, potatoes 2,796,000, wheat 1,708,000, barley 381,000, apples 313,960, tomatoes 250,000; livestock (number of live animals) 6,851,000 pigs, 3,106,000 cattle, 160,000 sheep, 75,000 horses; roundwood (2001)[7] 4,190,000 cu m; fish catch (2000) 31,441. Mining and quarrying (2002): limestone 30,000,000; granite (Belgium bluestone) 1,200,000 cu m. Manufacturing (value added in BF '000,000; 1996): metal products 468,894; food 263,382; chemicals 243,787; printing 69,991; textiles 66,524; furniture 58,115; value of traded diamonds handled in Antwerp (2002) U.S.$26,000,000,000. Energy production (consumption): electricity (kW-hr; 1999) 84,465,000,000 (85,317,000,000); coal (metric tons; 1999) 364,000 (10,033,000); crude petroleum (barrels; 1999) none (235,600,000); petroleum products (metric tons; 1999) 27,961,000 (17,150,000); natural gas (cu m; 1999) 534,000 (15,903,700,000).
Household income and expenditure. Avg. household size (2000) 2.5; sources of income (2002): wages and transfer payments 69.4%, property income 11.0%, mixed income 24.1%; expenditure (1992): food 18.0%, housing 17.0%, transportation 13.3%, health 11.8%, durable goods 10.7%, clothing 7.7%.
Tourism (2001): receipts U.S.$6,917,000,000; expenditures U.S.$9,766,000,000.
Population economically active (2000): total 4,332,400; activity rate 42.3% (participation rates: ages 15–64, 69.2%; female 43.1%; unemployed 3.5%).

Price and earnings indexes (1995 = 100)

	1994	1995	1996	1997	1998	1999	2000
Consumer price index	98.6	100.0	102.1	103.7	104.7	105.9	108.6
Earnings index	...	...	...	...	...	...	...

Gross national product (2001): U.S.$245,300,000,000 (U.S.$23,850 per capita).

Structure of gross domestic product and labour force

	2000			
	in value BF '000,000	% of total value	labour force	% of labour force
Agriculture	125,771	1.3	79,100	1.8
Mining	14,437	0.1	4,200	0.1
Manufacturing	1,747,195	17.4	652,400	15.1
Construction	463,796	4.6	232,500	5.4
Public utilities	240,897	2.4	27,100	0.6
Transp. and commun.	628,840	6.3	272,200	6.3
Trade	1,246,148	12.4	615,400	14.2
Finance	2,622,550	26.2	592,300	13.6
Pub. admin., defense	734,335	7.3	426,700	9.8
Services	1,443,340	14.4	1,015,600	23.4
Other	750,625[8]	7.5[8]	414,900[9]	9.6[9]
TOTAL	10,017,934	100.0[6]	4,332,400	100.0[6]

Land use (1994)[7]: forest 21.3%; pasture 21.0%; agriculture 24.2%; other 33.5%.

Foreign trade[10]

Balance of trade (current prices)

	1996	1997	1998	1999	2000	2001
€'000,000	+7,500	+11,100	+11,600	+13,500	+14,600	+12,500
% of total	2.8%	3.7%	3.7%	4.2%	3.8%	3.1%

Imports (2000): €183,700,000,000 (machinery and apparatus 18.3%, road vehicles 11.3%, diamonds 7.7%, food 6.8%, petroleum products 6.6%, organic chemicals 4.9%). *Major import sources* (2001): The Netherlands 16.9%; Germany 16.2%; France 13.4%; U.K. 7.7%; U.S. 6.9%.
Exports (2000): €198,300,000,000 (machinery and apparatus 15.4%, road vehicles 13.3%, food 7.8%, resins and plastic materials 5.6%, organic chemicals 4.6%, iron and steel 4.3%). *Major export destinations* (2001): Germany 18.2%; France 17.4%; The Netherlands 12.1%; U.K. 10.1%; Italy 5.8%.

Transport and communications

Transport. Railroads (2000): route length 3,380 km; passenger-km 7,755,000,000; metric ton-km cargo 7,674,000,000. Roads (1997): total length 143,800 km (paved 97%). Vehicles (1998): passenger cars 4,491,734; trucks and buses 453,122. Air transport (2000)[11]: passenger-km 19,378,689,000; metric ton-km cargo 568,244,000; airports (2000) 2.

Communications

Medium	date	unit	number	units per 1,000 persons
Daily newspapers	2000	circulation	1,640,000	160
Radio	2000	receivers	8,130,000	793
Television	2000	receivers	5,550,000	541
Telephones	2002	main lines	5,132,400	496
Cellular telephones	2002	subscribers	8,135,500	786
Personal computers	2002	units	2,500,000	242
Internet	2002	users	3,400,000	329

Education and health

Educational attainment (1991). Percentage of population age 18 and over having: less than secondary education 46.8%; lower secondary 16.6%; upper secondary 21.6%; teacher's college 3.7%; university 11.3%.

Education (1999–2000)

	schools[12]	teachers	students	student/ teacher ratio
Primary (age 6–12)	4,401	82,168[13]	778,000	...
Secondary (age 12–18)	1,727	115,262	779,000	...
Voc., teacher tr.[14]	304	...	155,192[12]	...
Higher	151	38,014[12]	298,000	...

Health: physicians (1999) 36,682 (1 per 279 persons); hospital beds (1998) 75,360 (1 per 135 persons); infant mortality rate (2000) 4.8.
Food (2001)[7]: daily per capita caloric intake 3,682 (vegetable products 69%, animal products 31%); 140% of FAO recommended minimum requirement.

Military

Total active duty personnel (2002): 39,260 (army 67.0%, navy 6.5%, air force 21.8%, medical service 4.7%). *Military expenditure as percentage of GNP* (1999): 1.4% (world 2.4%); per capita expenditure U.S.$352.

[1]Excludes children of the monarch serving ex officio from age 18. [2]The Belgian franc (BF) was the former monetary unit; on Jan. 1, 2002, BF 40.34 = €1. [3]Corresponding to three language-based federal community councils: Dutch (Flanders), French (Wallonia), and bilingual (Brussels) having authority in cultural affairs; a fourth (German) community council (within Wallonia; 2002 population 71,287) lacks expression as an administrative region. [4]January 1. [5]Officially, Brussels Capital Region. [6]Detail does not add to total given because of rounding. [7]Includes Luxembourg. [8]Taxes on products less subsidies on products. [9]Includes 362,000 unemployed, and 52,900 employed abroad. [10]Imports c.i.f.; exports f.o.b. [11]Sabena airlines only; shut down November 2001. [12]1996–97. [13]Includes preschool teachers. [14]1991–92.

Internet resources for further information:
- **Belgian Federal Government On Line http://belgium.fgov.be**
- **National Bank of Belgium http://www.bnb.be/sg/index.htm**

Belize

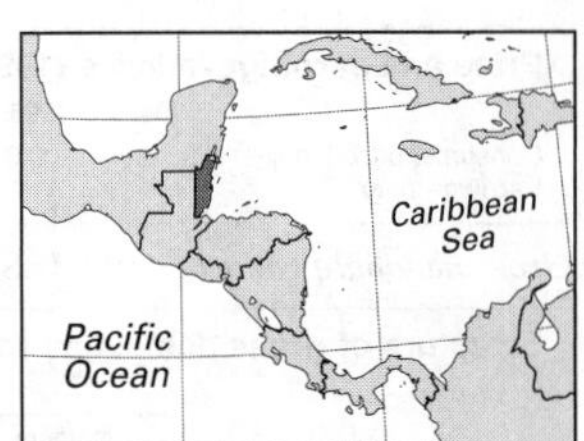

Official name: Belize.
Form of government: constitutional monarchy with two legislative houses (Senate [8[1]]; House of Representatives [29[2]]).
Chief of state: British Monarch represented by Governor-General.
Head of government: Prime Minister.
Capital: Belmopan.
Official language: English.
Official religion: none.
Monetary unit: 1 Belize dollar (BZ$) = 100 cents; valuation (Sept. 8, 2003) 1 U.S.$ = BZ$2.00; 1 £ = BZ$3.17.

Area and population

		area		population
				2000
Districts	**Capitals**	sq mi	sq km	census
Belize	Belize City	1,663	4,307	68,197
Cayo	San Ignacio/Santa Elena	2,006	5,196	52,564
Corozal	Corozal	718	1,860	32,708
Orange Walk	Orange Walk	1,790	4,636	38,890
Stann Creek	Dangriga	986	2,554	24,548
Toledo	Punta Gorda	1,704	4,413	23,297
TOTAL		8,867[3]	22,965[3, 4]	240,204[5]

Demography

Population (2003): 269,000.
Density (2003): persons per sq mi 30.3, persons per sq km 11.7.
Urban-rural (2000): urban 45.4%; rural 54.6%.
Sex distribution (2000): male 50.26%; female 49.74%.
Age breakdown (2000): under 15, 41.0%; 15–29, 26.3%; 30–44, 16.8%; 45–59, 8.9%; 60–74, 4.9%; 75 and over, 2.1%.
Population projection: (2010) 316,000; (2020) 383,000.
Doubling time: 26 years.
Ethnic composition (2000): mestizo (Spanish-Indian) 48.7%; Creole (predominantly black) 24.9%; Mayan Indian 10.6%; Garifuna (black-Carib Indian) 6.1%; white 4.3%; East Indian 3.0%; other or not stated 2.4%.
Religious affiliation (2000): Roman Catholic 49.6%; Protestant 31.8%, of which Pentecostal 7.4%, Anglican 5.3%, Seventh-day Adventist 5.2%, Mennonite 4.1%; other Christian 1.9%; nonreligious 9.4%; other 7.3%.
Major cities (2000): Belize City 49,050; Orange Walk 13,483; San Ignacio/Santa Elena 13,260; Dangriga 8,814; Belmopan 8,130.

Vital statistics

Birth rate per 1,000 population (2000): 32.3 (world avg. 21.3); (1997) legitimate 40.3%; illegitimate 59.7%.
Death rate per 1,000 population (2000): 4.8 (world avg. 9.1).
Natural increase rate per 1,000 population (2000): 27.5 (world avg. 12.2).
Total fertility rate (avg. births per childbearing woman; 2000): 4.1.
Marriage rate per 1,000 population (1998): 5.8.
Divorce rate per 1,000 population (1998): 0.2.
Life expectancy at birth (2000): male 68.7 years; female 73.3 years.
Major causes of death per 100,000 population (1995): diseases of the circulatory system 119.8; accidents and violence 57.1; diseases of the respiratory system 47.8; malignant neoplasms 38.1; infectious and parasitic diseases 23.7.

National economy

Budget (2001). Revenue: BZ$450,852,000 (tax revenue 71.5%, of which import duties 30.5%, general sales taxes 23.8%; income and profit 17.2%; capital revenue 16.4%; nontax revenue 9.3%; grants 2.8%). Expenditures: BZ$581,132,000 (current expenditure 57.4%; capital expenditure 42.6%).
Production (metric tons except as noted). Agriculture, forestry, fishing (2002): sugarcane 1,150,656, oranges 168,652, grapefruits 44,762, bananas 43,030, corn (maize) 33,459, plantain 28,000, sorghum 12,144; livestock (number of live animals; 2002) 56,949 cattle, 22,874 pigs, 1,400,000 chickens; roundwood (2001) 187,600 cu m; fish catch (1999) 43,103, of which marine fish 25,679, cephalopods 11,974, crustaceans 5,310. Mining and quarrying (1997): sand and gravel 350,000; limestone 310,000. Manufacturing (2000–01): sugar 105,500; molasses 35,000; flour 11,800; orange concentrate 187,000 hectolitres; beer 110,000 hectolitres; grapefruit concentrate 29,000 hectolitres; cigarettes 88,000,000 units; garments 1,507,000 units. Energy production (consumption): electricity (kW-hr; 1999) 124,000,000 (149,000,000); coal, none (none); crude petroleum, none (none); petroleum products (metric tons; 1999) none (202,000); natural gas, none (none).
Household income and expenditure. Average household size (2000) 4.5; average annual income of employed head of household (1993) BZ$6,450[6] (U.S.$3,225[6]); sources of income, n.a.; expenditure (1990): food, beverages, and tobacco 34.0%, transportation 13.7%, energy and water 9.1%, housing 9.0%, clothing and footwear 8.8%, household furnishings 8.0%.
Tourism (2001): receipts from visitors U.S.$121,000,000; expenditures by nationals abroad U.S.$24,000,000.
Land use (1994): forested 92.1%; meadows and pastures 2.2%; agricultural and under permanent cultivation 3.6%; other 2.1%.
Population economically active (2001): total 95,690; activity rate of total population 37.3% (participation rates [2000]: ages 14 and over 67.1%; female 29.6%; unemployed 9.3%).

Price and earnings indexes (1995 = 100)

	1995	1996	1997	1998	1999	2000	2001
Consumer price index	100.0	106.4	107.5	106.6	105.3	105.9	107.2
Monthly earnings index[7]	100.0	102.5	98.8	…	…	…	…

Gross national product (2001): U.S.$700,000,000 (U.S.$2,940 per capita).

Structure of gross domestic product and labour force

	2001			
	in value BZ$'000[8]	% of total value[8]	labour force	% of labour force
Agriculture, fishing, forestry	219,130	16.1	23,610	24.7
Mining	9,429	0.7	315	0.3
Manufacturing	183,236	13.4	8,170	8.5
Construction	96,789	7.1	5,055	5.3
Public utilities	43,560	3.2	1,135	1.2
Transp. and commun.	143,434	10.5	4,685	4.9
Trade, restaurants	291,401	21.4	19,965	20.9
Finance, real estate, insurance	180,060	13.2	3,285	3.4
Pub. admin., defense	168,208	12.3	20,315	21.2
Services	76,008	5.6		
Other	–47,458[9]	–3.5[9]	9,155[10]	9.6[10]
TOTAL	1,363,797	100.0	95,690	100.0

Public debt (external, outstanding; 2001): U.S.$657,600,000.

Foreign trade[11]

Balance of trade (current prices)

	1996	1997	1998	1999	2000	2001
BZ$'000,000	–175.7	–219.7	–257.4	–379.3	–480.0	–382.9
% of total	20.8%	23.8%	27.6%	33.9%	39.1%	26.2%

Imports (2001): BZ$921,100,000 (machinery and transport equipment 27.7%; food 13.5%; mineral fuels and lubricants 18.2%; chemicals and chemical products 8.0%). *Major import sources:* U.S. 47.2%; Mexico 11.2%; Caricom 5.0%; U.K. 2.7%; other EU 3.8%.
Exports (2001): BZ$538,200,000 (domestic exports 61.8%, of which citrus concentrate 16.5%, raw sugar 11.0%, shrimp 8.7%, bananas 8.0%, garments 5.6%; reexports [principally to Mexico] 38.2%). *Major export destinations*[12]: U.S. 53.8%; U.K. 23.0%; other EU 6.7%; Caricom 6.4%.

Transport and communications

Transport. Railroads: none. Roads (1999): total length 1,785 mi, 2,872 km (paved 18%). Vehicles (1998): passenger cars 9,929; trucks and buses 11,755. Merchant marine (1992): vessels (100 gross tons and over) 32; total deadweight tonnage 45,706. Air transport (1998)[13]: passenger arrivals 199,475, passenger departures 193,620; cargo loaded 166 metric tons, cargo unloaded 1,082 metric tons. Airports (1997) with scheduled flights 9.

Communications

Medium	date	unit	number	units per 1,000 persons
Radio	1997	receivers	133,000	571
Television	1998	receivers	42,000	183
Telephones	2002	main lines	31,600	125
Cellular telephones	2002	subscribers	52,500	207
Personal computers	2002	units	35,000	138
Internet	2002	users	22,000	87

Education and health

Educational attainment (2000). Percentage of population age 25 and over having: no formal schooling 36.6%; primary education 40.9%; secondary 11.7%; postsecondary/advanced vocational 6.4%; university 3.8%; other/unknown 0.6%. *Literacy* (1999): total population age 14 and over literate 93.1%; males 93.2%; female 92.9%.

Education (1998–99)

	schools	teachers	students	student/ teacher ratio
Primary (age 5–12)	284	2,064	54,616	26.5
Secondary (age 13–16)	34	754	11,724	15.5
Higher	12[14]	228[14]	2,853	12.1[14]

Health (1998): physicians 155 (1 per 1,558 persons); hospital beds 554 (1 per 435 persons); infant mortality rate per 1,000 live births (2000) 26.0.
Food (2001): daily per capita caloric intake 2,885 (vegetable products 79%, animal products 21%); 128% of FAO recommended minimum requirement.

Military

Total active duty personnel (2002): 1,050 (army 100%).[15] *Military expenditure as percentage of GNP* (1999): 1.6% (world 2.4%); per capita expenditure U.S.$47.

[1]Excludes president of the Senate, who may be elected by the Senate from outside its appointed membership. [2]Excludes speaker of the House of Representatives, who may be elected by the House from outside its elected membership. [3]Includes offshore cays totaling 266 sq mi (689 sq km). [4]Detail does not add to total given because of rounding. [5]Unadjusted figure; final adjusted figure equals 248,916. [6]Estimated figure for about 33,000 employed heads of household. [7]In manufacturing, transportation, trade, and finance. [8]At factor cost. [9]Less imputed bank service charges. [10]Includes 245 not adequately defined and 8,910 unemployed. [11]Imports c.i.f.; exports f.o.b. [12]Domestic exports only. [13]Belize international airport only. [14]1997–98. [15]Foreign forces (2002): British army 30.

Internet resources for further information:
- **Government of Belize http://www.belize.gov.bz**

Benin

Official name: République du Bénin (Republic of Benin).
Form of government: multiparty republic with one legislative house (National Assembly [83]).
Head of state and government: President, assisted by Prime Minister[1].
Capital[2]: Porto-Novo.
Official language: French.
Official religion: none.
Monetary unit: 1 CFA franc (CFAF) = 100 centimes; valuation (Sept. 8, 2003) 1 U.S.$ = CFAF 594.70; 1 £ = CFAF 942.93[3].

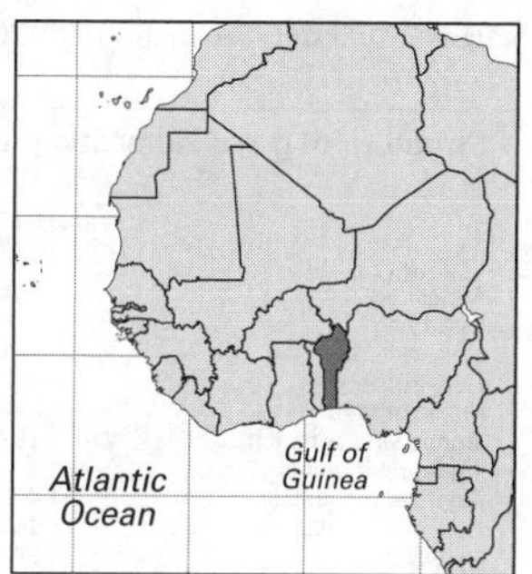

Area and population

Departments	Capitals	area sq mi	area sq km	population 1992 census
Alibori	Kandi	9,916	25,683	355,950
Atacora	Natitingou	7,899	20,459	400,613
Atlantique	Ouidah	1,248	3,233	530,246
Borgou	Parakou	9,772	25,310	471,975
Collines	Savalou	5,236	13,561	340,284
Couffo	Dogbo	928	2,404	403,132
Donga	Djougou	4,128	10,691	248,693
Littoral	Cotonou	31	79	536,827
Mono	Lokossa	539	1,396	281,245
Ouémé	Porto-Novo	1,095	2,835	568,898
Plateau	Sakété	720	1,865	307,676
Zou	Abomey	1,971	5,106	478,714
TOTAL		43,483	112,622	4,924,253[4]

Demography

Population (2003): 7,041,000.
Density (2003): persons per sq mi 161.9, persons per sq km 62.5.
Urban-rural (2002): urban 43.0%; rural 57%.
Sex distribution (2002): male 49.31%; female 50.69%.
Age breakdown (2002): under 15, 47.1%; 15–29, 27.7%; 30–44, 14.3%; 45–59, 7.1%; 60–74, 3.0%; 75 and over, 0.8%.
Population projection: (2010) 8,504,000; (2020) 10,647,000.
Doubling time: 23 years.
Ethnic composition (1992): Fon 39.7%; Yoruba (Nago) 12.1%; Adjara 11.1%; Bariba 8.6%; Aizo 8.6%; Somba (Otomary) 6.6%; Fulani 5.6%; other 7.7%.
Religious affiliation (1992): Christian 35.4%, of which Roman Catholic 25.9%, Protestant 9.5%; traditional beliefs, including voodoo 35.0%; Muslim 20.6%; other 9.0%.
Major cities (1998): Cotonou 649,580; Porto-Novo 218,241; Djougou 132,000[5]; Parakou 128,277; Abomey 80,000.

Vital statistics

Birth rate per 1,000 population (2002): 43.7 (world avg. 21.3).
Death rate per 1,000 population (2002): 13.6 (world avg. 9.1).
Natural increase rate per 1,000 population (2001): 30.1 (world avg. 12.2).
Total fertility rate (avg. births per childbearing woman; 2002): 6.1.
Life expectancy at birth (2002): male 50.4 years; female 52.2 years.

National economy

Budget (2001). Revenue: CFAF 281,000,000,000 (tax revenue 87.9%, of which tax on international trade 47.4%, direct and indirect taxes 40.5%; nontax revenue 12.1%). Expenditures: CFAF 353,200,000,000 (current expenditures 61.7%; development expenditure 38.3%).
Production (metric tons except as noted). Agriculture, forestry, fishing (2002): cassava 2,452,050, yams 1,785,000, corn (maize) 622,136, seed cotton 485,522, oil palm fruit 220,000, sorghum 195,468, peanuts (groundnuts) 146,214, tomatoes 141,301, dry beans 100,462, pineapples 86,700, karité nuts (shea nuts) 21,000; livestock (number of live animals; 2002) 1,550,000 cattle, 1,270,000 goats, 670,000 sheep, 550,000 pigs, 10,000,000 chickens; roundwood (2001) 6,269,375 cu m; fish catch (2000) 32,324. Manufacturing (1998): cement 350,000; cotton fibre 175,000; meat 70,000; wheat flour 12,500; palm oil 11,000. Energy production (consumption): electricity (kW-hr; 2001) 55,888,000 (413,587,000); coal, none (none); crude petroleum (barrels; 2001) none (negligible); petroleum products (metric tons; 2001) none (150,000); natural gas, none (none).
Public debt (external, outstanding; 2001): U.S.$1,503,000,000.
Gross national product (2001): U.S.$2,400,000,000 (U.S.$380 per capita).

Structure of gross domestic product and labour force

	2001 in value CFAF '000,000,000	2001 % of total value	1992 labour force[6]	1992 % of labour force[6]
Agriculture	617.7	35.5	1,147,746	55.0
Mining	4.0	0.2	661	0.0
Manufacturing	159.7	9.2	160,406	7.7
Public utilities	16.6	1.0	1,176	0.1
Construction	70.7	4.1	51,655	2.5
Transp. and commun.	139.8	8.0	52,837	2.5
Trade	318.0	18.3	432,501	20.7
Finance	167.5	9.6	3,106	0.1
Pub. admin., defense } Services }	106.8	6.1	164,544	7.9
Other	137.8[7]	7.9[7]	70,814	3.4
TOTAL	1,738.6	100.0[8]	2,085,446	100.0[8]

Population economically active (1997): total 2,608,000; activity rate of total population 44.2% (participation rates: ages 15–64, 84.3%; female 48.3%; unemployed, n.a.).

Price and earnings indexes (1995 = 100)

	1995	1996	1997	1998	1999	2000	2001
Consumer price index	100.0	104.9	108.6	114.8	115.2	120.0	124.3
Hourly earnings index	...	...	...	...	...	...	...

Household income and expenditure. Average household size (2000) 6.1; income per household: n.a.; sources of income: n.a.; expenditure: n.a.
Land use (1995): agricultural and under permanent cultivation 17.0%; other 83.0% (of which [1994] forested 30.7%, meadows and pastures 4.0%).
Tourism (2000): receipts from visitors U.S.$77,000,000; expenditures by nationals abroad U.S.$12,000,000.

Foreign trade[9]

Balance of trade (current prices)

	1996	1997	1998	1999	2000	2001
CFAF '000,000,000	–16.4	–89.2	–93.4	–131.6	–88.1	–122.8
% of total	2.9%	15.3%	16.0%	20.2%	13.6%	18.5%

Imports (2001): CFAF 393,000,000,000 (food products 26.2%; machinery and transport equipment 20.0%; petroleum products 11.9%). *Major import sources* (1999): France 22.0%; Côte d'Ivoire 10.5%; Togo 5.6%; China 5.1%; United States 5.1%; The Netherlands 4.8%.
Exports (2001): CFAF 270,200,000,000 (domestic exports 55.0%, of which cotton yarn 43.5%, cotton seed 1.4%; reexports 45.0%). *Major export destinations* (1999): Brazil 19.8%; India 15.5%; Indonesia 10.0%; Thailand 5.3%; Bangladesh 4.7%.

Transport and communications

Transport. Railroads (2000): length 359 mi, 578 km; passenger-mi 97,306,000, passenger-km 156,600,000; short ton-mi cargo 95,194,000, metric ton-km cargo 153,200,000. Roads (1999): total length 4,217 mi, 6,787 km (paved 20.0%). Vehicles (1996): passenger cars 37,772; trucks and buses 8,058. Merchant marine (1992): vessels (100 gross tons and over) 12; total deadweight tonnage 210. Air transport[10]: n.a.; airports (2002) with scheduled flights 1.

Communications

Medium	date	unit	number	units per 1,000 persons
Daily newspapers	2000	circulation	12,900	2
Radio	2000	receivers	2,820,000	439
Television	2000	receivers	289,000	45
Telephones	2001	main lines	59,300	9.2
Cellular telephones	2001	subscribers	125,000	19.4
Personal computers	2001	units	11,000	1.7
Internet	2001	users	25,000	3.8

Education and health

Educational attainment (1992). Percentage of population age 25 and over having: no formal schooling 78.5%; primary education 10.8%; some secondary 8.2%; secondary 1.2%; postsecondary 1.3%. *Literacy* (1998): total percentage of population age 15 and over literate 37.7%; males literate 53.8%; females literate 22.6%.

Education (1996–97)

	schools	teachers	students	student/ teacher ratio
Primary	3,072	13,957	779,329	55.8
Secondary	145[11]	5,352	146,135	27.3
Voc., teacher tr.[11]	14	283	4,873	17.2
Higher	16[11]	962	14,085	14.6

Health: physicians (1995) 313 (1 per 17,520 persons); hospital beds (1993) 1,235 (1 per 4,182 persons); infant mortality rate (2002) 87.6.
Food (2001): daily per capita caloric intake 2,455 (vegetable products 96%, animal products 4%); 107% of FAO recommended minimum requirement.

Military

Total active duty personnel (2002): 4,550 (army 95.2%, navy 2.2%, air force 2.6%). *Military expenditure as percentage of GNP* (1999): 1.4% (world 2.4%); per capita expenditure U.S.$5.

[1]Office of Prime Minister vacant from May 1998. [2]Porto-Novo, the official capital established under the constitution, is the seat of the legislature, but the president and most government ministers reside in Cotonou. [3]Formerly pegged to the French franc and since Jan. 1, 2002, to the euro at the rate of €1 = CFAF 655.96. [4]Represents sum of departments' populations; reported census total is 4,915,555. [5]1994. [6]Age 10 years and over. [7]Indirect taxes. [8]Detail does not add to total given because of rounding. [9]Import figures are f.o.b. in balance of trade and commodities and c.i.f. in trading partners. [10]Air Afrique, an airline jointly owned by 11 African countries (including Benin) was declared bankrupt in February 2002. [11]1993–94.

Internet resources for further information:
- **Embassy of Benin in Paris, France**
  http://www.ambassade-benin.org
- **Investir en Zone Franc**
  http://www.izf.net/Index.htm

Bermuda

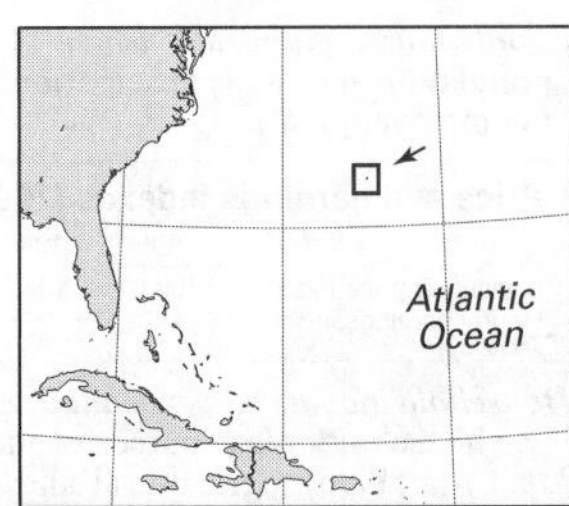

Official name: Bermuda.
Political status: colony (United Kingdom) with two legislative houses (Senate [11]; House of Assembly [36]).
Chief of state: British Monarch, represented by Governor.
Head of government: Premier.
Capital: Hamilton.
Official language: English.
Official religion: none.
Monetary unit: 1 Bermuda dollar (Bd$) = 100 cents; valuation (Sept. 8, 2003) 1 U.S.$ = Bd$1.00[1]; 1 £ = Bd$1.59.

Area and population	area		population
			2000
Municipalities	sq mi	sq km	census
Hamilton	0.3	0.8	969
St. George	0.5	1.3	1,752
Parishes			
Devonshire	2.0	5.1	7,307
Hamilton	2.0	5.1	5,270
Paget	2.1	5.3	5,088
Pembroke[2]	1.8	4.6	10,337
St. George's[3, 4]	3.5	8.0	3,699
Sandys	2.1	5.4	7,275
Smith's	1.8	4.7	5,658
Southampton	2.2	5.6	6,117
Warwick	2.0	5.1	8,587
TOTAL	20.5[5, 6]	53.1[5, 6]	62,059[7]

Demography

Population (2003): 64,000.
Density (2003): persons per sq mi 3,048, persons per sq km 1,185.
Urban-rural (2002): urban 100.0%; rural, none.
Sex distribution (2000): male 48.03%; female 51.97%.
Age breakdown (2000): under 15, 19.1%; 15–29, 18.4%; 30–44, 27.9%; 45–59, 19.6%; 60–74, 10.9%; 75 and over, 4.1%.
Population projection: (2010) 67,000; (2020) 69,000.
Ethnic composition (2000): black 50.4%; British expatriates 29.0%; mulatto 10.0%; U.S. white 6.0%; Portuguese 4.5%; other 0.1%.
Religious affiliation (2000): Protestant 64.3%, of which Anglican 22.6%, Methodist 14.9%; Roman Catholic 14.9%; nonreligious 13.8%; other 6.0%; unknown 1.0%.
Major cities (2000): St. George 1,752; Hamilton 969.

Vital statistics

Birth rate per 1,000 population (2001): 13.2 (world avg. 21.3); legitimate 62.3%; illegitimate 37.7%.
Death rate per 1,000 population (2001): 7.0 (world avg. 9.1).
Natural increase rate per 1,000 population (2001): 6.2 (world avg. 12.2).
Total fertility rate (avg. births per childbearing woman; 2000): 1.8.
Marriage rate per 1,000 population (2001): 14.6.
Divorce rate per 1,000 population (2000): 3.5.
Life expectancy at birth (2000): male 74.9 years; female 78.9 years.
Major causes of death per 100,000 population (1998): diseases of the circulatory system 313.9; malignant neoplasms (cancers) 252.7; accidents and violence 38.6; AIDS 27.4.

National economy

Budget (2001). Revenue: Bd$615,200,000 (payroll tax 29.8%; customs duty 28.5%; tax on international companies 7.3%; land tax 6.1%; stamp duties 4.4%; other 23.9%). Expenditures: Bd$599,700,000 (current expenditure 88.4%, of which wages 43.2%, goods and services 23.1%, grants and contributions 20.0%; development expenditure 11.6%).
Production (value in Bd$'000 except as noted). Agriculture, forestry, fishing (1999): vegetables 3,000, milk 1,657, fruits 900, eggs 435, honey 160; livestock number of live animals; 2002) 900 horses, 600 cattle, 45,000 chickens; roundwood, n.a.; fish catch (metric tons; 2000) 286, of which crustaceans and mollusks 21. Mining and quarrying: crushed stone for local use. Manufacturing: industries include pharmaceuticals, cosmetics, electronics, fish processing, handicrafts, and small boat building[8]. Construction (2001): residential 47,700,000; nonresidential 128,700,000. Energy production (consumption): electricity (kW-hr; 1999) 550,000,000 (550,000,000); coal, none (none); crude petroleum, none (none); petroleum products (metric tons; 1999) none (151,000); natural gas, none (none).
Land use (1988): forested 20.0%; meadows and pastures 0.9%; agricultural and under permanent cultivation 3.1%; built-on, wasteland, and other 76.0%.
Tourism: receipts from visitors (2001) U.S.$351,000,000; expenditures by nationals abroad (1997) U.S.$148,000,000.
Population economically active (2000): total 37,878; activity rate of total population 61.0% (participation rates: ages 15–64, 88.1%; female 48.5%; unemployed 2.9%).

Price and earnings indexes (1995 = 100)	1995	1996	1997	1998	1999	2000	2001
Consumer price index	100.0	102.5	104.6	106.7	109.3	112.3	115.1
Weekly earnings index[9]	100.0	103.2	106.5	109.8	113.1	…	…

Gross domestic product (1999–2000): U.S.$2,624,000,000 (U.S.$41,690 per capita).

Structure of gross domestic product and labour force	2000			
	in value BD$'000,000	% of total value	labour force	% of labour force
Agriculture, fishing	24	0.8	573	1.5
Quarrying	6	0.2		
Manufacturing	71	2.3	1,176	3.1
Construction	178	5.9	3,792	10.0
Public utilities	73	2.4	425	1.1
Transp. and commun.	207	6.8	2,843	7.5
Trade, restaurants	465	15.4	9,070	23.9
Finance, real estate	1,489	49.3	3,245	8.6
Pub. admin., defense	164	5.4	2,510	6.6
Services	346	11.4	13,153	34.7
Other	…	…	1,091[9]	2.9[9]
TOTAL	3,023	100.0[6]	37,878	100.0[6]

Public debt (external, outstanding): n.a.
Household income and expenditure. Average household size (2000) 2.4; average annual income per household (2001) Bd$72,500 (U.S.$72,500); sources of income (1993): wages and salaries 65.3%, imputed income from owner occupancy 10.6%, self-employment 9.0%, net rental income 4.8%, other 10.4%; expenditure (1993): housing 27.7%, household furnishings 16.6%, food and nonalcoholic beverages 14.6%, health care 7.6%, transportation 7.3%, foreign travel 6.0%, clothing and footwear 4.9%, recreation 4.8%.

Foreign trade

Balance of trade (current prices)	1994	1995	1996	1997	1998	1999
Bd$'000,000	–514	–496	–514	–554	–564	–661
% of total	87.4%	82.1%	82.4%	81.0%	80.3%	86.6%

Imports (2001–02): Bd$760,000,000 (food, beverages, and tobacco 20.2%; machinery 16.5%; chemicals and chemical products 13.9%; mineral fuels 7.8%; transport equipment 6.0%). *Major import sources:* United States 73.6%; Canada 4.5%; United Kingdom 3.9%; Caribbean countries (mostly Netherlands Antilles) 3.7%.
Exports (1999): Bd$51,000,000 (nearly all reexports; diamond market was established in 1990s). *Major export destinations* (2000): mostly United States, United Kingdom, Norway, and Spain.

Transport and communications

Transport. Railroads: none. Roads (1997): total length 140 mi, 225 km (paved 100%)[10]. Vehicles (1999): passenger cars 22,567; trucks and buses 4,215. Air transport (2000): passenger arrivals 913,000, passenger departures 913,000; cargo loaded and unloaded 5,600 metric tons; airports (2002) with scheduled flights 1.

Communications				units
Medium	date	unit	number	per 1,000 persons
Daily newspapers	1996	circulation	17,000	277
Radio	1997	receivers	82,000	1,328
Television	1997	receivers	66,000	1,069
Telephones	2001	main lines	56,300	872
Cellular telephones	2001	subscribers	13,300	206
Personal computers	2001	units	32,000	495
Internet	2001	users	30,000	464

Education and health

Educational attainment (2000). Percentage of total population age 16 and over having: no formal schooling 0.4%; primary education 7.0%; secondary 39.3%; post-secondary technical 25.7%; higher 26.8%; not stated 0.8%. *Literacy* (1997): total population age 15 and over literate, 98%.

Education (1999)	schools	teachers[11]	students	student/ teacher ratio
Primary (age 5–11)	26[11]	306	7,353	…
Secondary (age 12–16)	…	199	2,335	…
Higher	1	…	628	…

Health (1999): physicians 116 (1 per 539 persons); hospital beds 251[12] (1 per 249 persons); infant mortality rate per 1,000 live births (2001) 3.6.
Food (2001): daily per capita caloric intake 2,904 (vegetable products 74%, animal products 26%); 115% of FAO recommended minimum requirement.

Military

Total active duty personnel (1997): 700; part-time defense force assists police and is drawn from Bermudian conscripts.

[1]The Bermuda dollar is at par with the U.S. dollar. [2]Excludes the area and population of the city of Hamilton. [3]Excludes the area and population of the town of St. George. [4]Includes the 2.0 sq mi (5.2 sq km) area of the former U.S. military base closed in 1995. [5]Includes 0.4 sq mi (1.1 sq km) of uninhabited islands. [6]Detail does not add to total given because of rounding. [7]Excludes 8,335 short-term visitors, 901 institutionalized persons, and 39 transients. [8]The economy of Bermuda is overwhelmingly based on service industries such as tourism, insurance companies, offshore financial centres, e-commerce companies, and ship repair facilities. [9]Unemployed. [10]Excludes 138 mi (222 km) of paved private roads. [11]1996. [12]Excludes beds in geriatric, rehabilitation, and hospice units.

Internet resources for further information:
- **Bermuda Online: Economy http://bermuda-online.org/economy.htm**

Bhutan

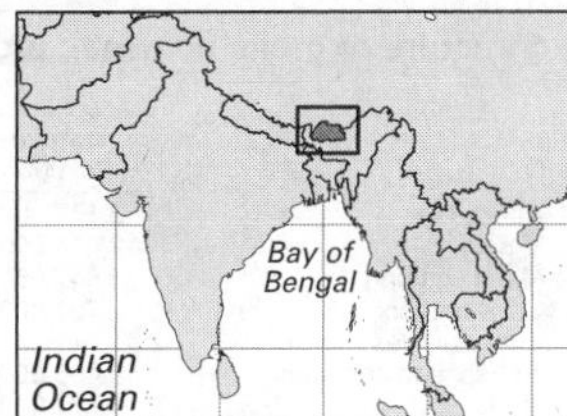

Official name: Druk-Yul (Kingdom of Bhutan).
Form of government: constitutional[1] monarchy with one legislative house (National Assembly [150[2]]).
Chief of state: Monarch[1].
Head of government: Prime Minister[1].
Capital: Thimphu.
Official language: Dzongkha (a Tibetan dialect).
Official religion: Mahāyāna Buddhism.
Monetary unit: 1 ngultrum[3] (Nu) = 100 chetrum; valuation (Sept. 8, 2003) 1 U.S.$ = Nu 45.87; 1 £ = Nu 72.72.

Area and population

		area		population
				2000
Districts	**Capitals**	sq mi	sq km	estimate
Bumthang	Jakar	1,150	2,990	...
Chirang	Damphu	310	800	...
Dagana	Dagana	540	1,400	...
Gaylegphug	Gaylegphug	1,020	2,640	...
Ha	Ha	830	2,140	...
Lhuntshi	Lhuntshi	1,120	2,910	...
Mongar	Mongar	710	1,830	...
Paro	Paro	580	1,500	...
Pema Gatsel	Pema Gatsel	150	380	...
Punakha	Punakha	2,330	6,040	...
Samchi	Samchi	830	2,140	...
Samdrup Jongkhar	Samdrup Jongkhar	900	2,340	...
Shemgang	Shemgang	980	2,540	...
Tashigang	Tashigang	1,640	4,260	...
Thimphu	Thimphu	630	1,620	...
Tongsa	Tongsa	570	1,470	...
Wangdi Phodrang	Wangdi Phodrang	1,160	3,000	...
TOTAL		18,150[4, 5]	47,000[4, 5]	677,932[6]

Demography

Population (2003): 685,000[6].
Density (2003): persons per sq mi 37.7; persons per sq km 14.6.
Urban-rural (2000): urban 21.0%; rural 79.0%.
Sex distribution (2000): male 50.50%; female 49.50%.
Age breakdown (2000): under 15, 42.1%; 15–29, 26.5%; 30–44, 16.6%; 45–59, 9.4%; 60–74, 4.8%; 75 and over, 0.6%.
Population projection: (2010) 793,000; (2020) 965,000.
Doubling time: 27 years.
Ethnic composition (1993): Bhutiā (Ngalops) 50.0%; Nepalese (Gurung) 35.0%; Sharchops 15.0%.
Religious affiliation (2000): Buddhist 74.0%; Hindu 20.5%; other 5.5%.
Major cities (2002): Thimphu 45,000; Phuntsholing (1997) 45,000.

Vital statistics

Birth rate per 1,000 population (2002): 34.9 (world avg. 21.3).
Death rate per 1,000 population (2002): 8.7 (world avg. 9.1).
Natural increase rate per 1,000 population (2002): 26.2 (world avg. 12.2).
Total fertility rate (avg. births per childbearing woman; 2002): 5.1.
Marital status of population 15 years and over (1985): married 71.2%; single 19.7%; widowed 7.5%; divorced 1.6%.
Life expectancy at birth (2002): male 62.0 years; female 64.0 years.
Major causes of death (percentage distribution; 1989): respiratory tract infections 19.5%; diarrhea/dysentery 15.2%; skin infections 12.2%; parasitic worm infestations 10.0%; malaria 9.4%.

National economy

Budget (2001). Revenue: Nu 4,595,500,000 (tax revenue 41.7%, nontax revenue 58.3%). Expenditures: Nu 10,716,500,000 (capital expenditures 58.6%, current expenditures 41.4%).
Public debt (external, outstanding; 2001): U.S.$265,200,000.
Production (metric tons except as noted). Agriculture, forestry, fishing (2002): corn (maize) 48,500, rice 44,300, oranges 30,000, potatoes 22,000, sugarcane 12,800, apples 5,100, wheat 4,350, millet 3,800, green peppers and chilies 2,900, barley 1,700, pulses 1,600; livestock (number of live animals) 355,400 cattle, 41,400 pigs, 31,300 goats, 29,900 horses, 22,880 sheep; roundwood (2001) 4,417,723 cu m; fish catch (2000) 330. Mining and quarrying (1998): limestone 376,700; dolomite 240,300; gypsum 62,300; iron ore 5,000. Manufacturing (value in Nu '000,000; 2000): cement 696.7; chemical products 474.6; alcoholic beverages 255.0; wood board products 228.6; processed fruits 108.5. Construction: n.a. Energy production (consumption): electricity (kW-hr; 2000) 2,131,000,000 (445,600,000); coal (metric tons; 1999) 50,000 (66,000); crude petroleum, none (n.a.); petroleum products (metric tons; 1999) none (44,000); natural gas, none (n.a.).
Household income and expenditure. Average household size (1980) 5.4; income per household: n.a.; sources of income: n.a.; expenditure: n.a.
Population economically active (1999): total 358,950; activity rate of total population 52.9% (participation rates: ages 15–64, 98.6%; female 31.8%; unemployed 1.4%).

Price and earnings indexes (1995 = 100)

	1995	1996	1997	1998	1999	2000	2001
Consumer price index	100.0	108.8	115.9	128.1	136.8	142.3	147.2
Earnings index	...	...	...	...	...	...	...

Gross national product (2001): U.S.$500,000,000 (U.S.$640 per capita).

Structure of gross domestic product and labour force

	2000		1999	
	in value Nu '000,000	% of total value	labour force	% of labour force
Agriculture	7,769.1	36.8	...	...
Mining	341.0	1.6	...	...
Manufacturing	1,734.7	8.2	...	...
Construction	2,717.3	12.9	...	...
Trade	1,465.3	6.9	...	...
Public utilities	2,519.8	11.9	...	...
Transportation and communications	1,863.2	8.8	...	...
Finance	1,324.1	6.3	...	...
Pub. admin., defense; Services	1,920.0	9.1	...	...
Other	–528.0[7]	–2.5[7]	...	...
TOTAL	21,126.5	100.0	358,950	100.0

Tourism (2000): receipts from visitors U.S.$10,000,000; expenditures by nationals abroad, n.a.
Land use (1995): forested 72.5%; meadows and pastures 3.9%; agricultural and under permanent cultivation 7.7%; other 15.9%.

Foreign trade[9]

Balance of trade (current prices)

	1996–97	1997–98	1998–99	1999–2000	2000–01
U.S.$'000,000	–31.9	–24.7	–57.5	–70.7	–103.0
% of total	13.8%	10.0%	21.5%	23.6%	31.4%

Imports (1999): U.S.$182,100,000 (machinery and transport equipment 41.7%, of which computers and related goods 11.0%, road vehicles 10.5%; food 13.9%, of which cereals 7.6%; refined petroleum 7.2%). *Major import sources* (2000–01): India 74.0%; Singapore 12.7%[9]; Thailand 3.1%[9].
Exports (1999): U.S.$116,000,000 (electricity 40.4%, calcium carbide 10.8%, ferro-silicon 10.8%; cement 10.7%). *Major export destinations* (2000–01): India 94.4%; Bangladesh 4.2%[9].

Transport and communications

Transport. Railroads: none. Roads (1999): total length 2,259 mi, 3,636 km (paved 60%). Vehicles (1999): passenger cars 6,468; trucks and buses 3,273. Merchant marine: none. Air transport (1998): passenger-mi 30,000,000, passenger-km 49,000,000; short ton-mi cargo 2,700,000, metric ton-km cargo 4,000,000; airports (2000) with scheduled flights 1.

Communications

Medium	date	unit	number	units per 1,000 persons
Radio	1997	receivers	37,000	19
Television	1999	receivers	13,000	20
Telephones	2002	main lines	19,600	28.0
Personal computers	2002	units	10,000	14.0
Internet	2002	users	17,980	24.5

Education and health

Educational attainment: n.a. *Literacy* (1995 est.): total population age 15 and over literate 42.2%; males literate 56.2%; females literate 28.1%.

Education (2000)

	schools	teachers	students	student/ teacher ratio
Primary (age 7–11)	269	2,867	115,884	40.4
Secondary (age 12–16)	85			
Voc., teacher tr.	9	160	2,060	12.9
Higher	7	159	1,862	11.7

Health: physicians (1999) 103 (1 per 6,384 persons); hospital beds (1994) 970 (1 per 825 persons); infant mortality rate per 1,000 live births (2002) 55.0.
Food (1975–77): daily per capita caloric intake 2,058 (vegetable products 98%, animal products 2%); 89% of FAO recommended minimum requirement.

Military

Total active duty personnel (2001): about 6,000 (army 100%).

[1]There is no formal constitution, but a form of constitutional monarchy is in place; reforms in July 1998 curtailed the powers of the monarchy. [2]Includes 45 nonelective seats occupied by representatives of the King and religious groups. [3]Indian currency is also accepted legal tender; the ngultrum is at par with the Indian rupee. [4]2,700 sq mi (7,000 sq km) are not included in the estimated district area totals. [5]Three districts are not listed: Chhukha, created in 1987 from Samchi, Paro, and Thimphu districts; Gasa, created in 1992 from Punakha; and Tashi Yangtse, created in 1992 from Tashigang. [6]Excludes nearly 100,000 Bhutanese of Nepalese origin declared stateless by the Bhutanese government in 1990. [7]Imputed bank service charges. [8]Imports c.i.f.; exports f.o.b. [9]1999.

Internet resources for further information:
- **Bhutan News Online**
  http://www.bhutannewsonline.com
- **Planning Commission: Royal Government of Bhutan**
  http://www.pcs.gov.bt

Bolivia

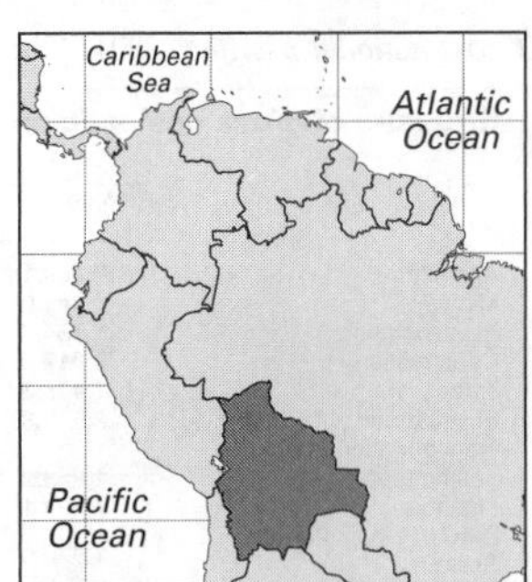

Official name: República de Bolivia (Republic of Bolivia).
Form of government: unitary multiparty republic with two legislative houses (Chamber of Senators [27]; Chamber of Deputies [130]).
Head of state and government: President.
Capitals: La Paz (administrative); Sucre (judicial).
Official languages: Spanish; Aymara; Quechua.
Official religion: Roman Catholicism.
Monetary unit: 1 boliviano (Bs) = 100 centavos; valuation (Sept. 8, 2003) 1 U.S.$ = Bs 7.74; 1 £ = Bs 12.27.

Area and population

Departments	Capitals	area sq mi	area sq km	population 2001 census
Beni	Trinidad	82,458	213,564	362,521
Chuquisaca	Sucre	19,893	51,524	531,522
Cochabamba	Cochabamba	21,479	55,631	1,455,711
La Paz	La Paz	51,732	133,985	2,350,466
Oruro	Oruro	20,690	53,588	391,870
Pando	Cobija	24,644	63,827	52,525
Potosí	Potosí	45,644	118,218	709,013
Santa Cruz	Santa Cruz	143,098	370,621	2,029,471
Tarija	Tarija	14,526	37,623	391,226
TOTAL		424,164	1,098,581	8,274,325

Demography

Population (2003): 8,586,000.
Density (2003): persons per sq mi 20.2, persons per sq km 7.8.
Urban-rural (2001): urban 62.4%; rural 37.6%.
Sex distribution (2001): male 49.84%; female 50.16%.
Age breakdown (2001): under 15, 38.6%; 15–29, 27.4%; 30–44, 17.0%; 45–59, 10.0%; 60–74, 5.2%; 75 and over, 1.8%.
Population projection: (2010) 9,499,000; (2020) 10,747,000.
Doubling time: 38 years.
Ethnic composition (1996): Indian 55.0%; mestizo 30.0%; white 15.0%.
Religious affiliation (1995): Roman Catholic 88.5%; Protestant 9.0%; other 2.5%.
Major cities (2001): Santa Cruz 1,116,059; La Paz 789,585 (urban agglomeration 1,499,000); El Alto 647,350[1]; Cochabamba 516,683; Oruro 201,230; Sucre 193,873.

Vital statistics

Birth rate per 1,000 population (2002): 26.4 (world avg. 21.3).
Death rate per 1,000 population (2002): 8.1 (world avg. 9.1).
Natural increase rate per 1,000 population (2002): 18.3 (world avg. 12.2).
Total fertility rate (avg. births per childbearing woman; 2002): 3.4.
Life expectancy at birth (2002): male 61.9 years; female 67.1 years.
Major causes of death (percentage of total registered deaths; 1980–81): infectious and parasitic diseases 23.9%; diseases of the circulatory system 19.5%; diseases of the respiratory system 14.0%; accidents, homicides, and violence 9.8%; diseases of the digestive system 8.6%.

National economy

Budget (2002). Revenue: Bs 13,558,000,000 (tax revenue 74.3%, of which value-added taxes 25.2%, taxes on hydrocarbons 19.3%, import duties 12.7%; nontax revenue 11.3%; foreign grants 9.4%; other 5.0%). Expenditures: Bs 18,857,000,000 (current expenditure 75.1%; capital expenditure 24.9%).
Production (metric tons except as noted). Agriculture, forestry, fishing (2002): sugarcane 4,320,784, soybeans 1,166,660, potatoes 944,216, corn (maize) 724,613, bananas 714,191, cassava 519,763, rice 248,211, sunflower seeds 193,812, sorghum 165,557, wheat 143,480; livestock (number of live animals) 8,901,631 sheep, 6,576,277 cattle, 2,850,547 pigs, 1,500,500 goats, 632,000 asses, 323,000 horses; roundwood (2001) 2,721,520 cu m; fish catch (2000) 6,511. Mining and quarrying (metric tons of pure metal; 2000): zinc 149,134; tin 12,503; lead 9,523; silver 434; gold 12.0. Manufacturing (value added in U.S.$'000,000; 1998): petroleum products 399; food products 222; beverages 141; nonmetal mineral products 75; textiles 30; printing and publishing 24; nonferrous metals 20. Energy production (consumption): electricity (kW-hr; 2000) 3,498,000,000 (2,904,900,000); coal, none (none); crude petroleum (barrels; 2000) 10,106,000 (8,911,000); petroleum products (metric tons; 1999) 1,347,000 (1,725,000); natural gas (cu m; 2000) 3,597,500,000 (1,544,200,000).
Population economically active (2000): total 3,346,500; activity rate of total population 43.5% (participation rates [1997]: ages 15–64, 72.1%; female [2000] 44.1%; unemployed [2000] 5.0%).

Price and earnings indexes (1995 = 100)

	1997	1998	1999	2000	2001	2002
Consumer price index	117.7	126.8	129.5	135.5	137.6	138.9
Monthly earnings index[2]	117.1	146.3	161.0	173.2	...	...

Tourism (2001): receipts U.S.$156,000,000; expenditures U.S.$118,000,000.
Gross national product (at current market prices; 2001): U.S.$8,100,000,000 (U.S.$950 per capita).

Structure of gross domestic product and labour force

	2000 in value Bs '000[3]	% of total value[3]	labour force[4]	% of labour force[4]
Agriculture	3,172,000	15.5	1,250,500	37.4
Mining	2,414,000	11.8	35,300	1.0
Manufacturing	3,647,000	17.8	320,100	9.6
Construction	731,000	3.6	218,900	6.5
Public utilities	5	5	15,900	0.5
Transp. and commun.	2,456,000	12.0	144,300	4.3
Trade	1,871,000	9.1	660,500	19.7
Finance	2,903,000	14.2	115,800	3.5
Pub. admin., defense	1,996,000	9.8	72,700	2.2
Services	1,269,000[5]	6.2[5]	344,980	10.3
Other	—	—	167,520[6]	5.0[6]
TOTAL	20,459,000	100.0	3,346,500	100.0

Public debt (external, outstanding; 2001): U.S.$3,116,000,000.
Household income and expenditure. Average household size (2000): 4.0; expenditure (1988): food 35.5%, transportation and communications 17.7%, housing 14.8%, household durable goods 7.3%, clothing and footwear 5.1%, beverages and tobacco 4.5%, recreation 2.7%, health 2.1%.
Land use (1994): forested 53.5%; meadows and pastures 24.4%; agricultural and under permanent cultivation 2.2%; other 19.9%.

Foreign trade[7]

Balance of trade (current prices)

	1996	1997	1998	1999	2000	2001
U.S.$'000,000	–313.4	–531.6	–721.0	–487.9	–375.0	–227.3
% of total	12.1%	18.6%	24.6%	18.8%	13.2%	8.1%

Imports (2000): U.S.$1,848,700,000 (machinery and apparatus 23.4%; chemicals and chemical products 14.0%; transportation equipment 13.3%; food 9.7%; iron and steel 5.6%; refined petroleum 4.4%). *Major import sources:* U.S. 22.0%; Brazil 14.4%; Argentina 14.3%; Chile 8.3%; Japan 5.5%.
Exports (2000): U.S.$1,456,700,000 (food 16.9%, of which soybean oilcake 9.7%; zinc ores and concentrates 11.7%; aircraft 9.6%; natural gas 8.7%; gold 6.0%; soybean oil 4.7%; tin 4.5%). *Major export destinations:* U.S. 24.0%; Colombia 13.2%; U.K. 11.5%; Brazil 11.4%; Switzerland 11.2%.

Transport and communications

Transport. Railroads (2000): route length 2,242 mi, 3,608 km; (1997) passenger-mi 139,746,000, passenger-km 224,900,000; short ton-mi cargo 574,600,000, metric ton-km cargo 838,900,000. Roads (1999): total length 32,445 mi, 52,216 km (paved 6%). Vehicles (2001): passenger cars 254,175; trucks and buses 194,510. Air transport (2000): passenger-mi 1,189,653,000, passenger-km 1,914,566,000; short ton-mi cargo 132,083,000, metric ton-km cargo 192,838,000; airports (2000) with scheduled flights 14.

Communications

Medium	date	unit	number	units per 1,000 persons
Daily newspapers	2000	circulation	448,000	65
Radio	2000	receivers	5,510,000	676
Television	2000	receivers	970,000	119
Telephones	2002	main lines	563,900	68
Cellular telephones	2002	subscribers	872,700	105
Personal computers	2002	units	190,000	23
Internet	2002	users	180,000	22

Education and health

Educational attainment (1992). Percentage of population age 25 and over having: no formal schooling 23.3%; some primary 20.3%; primary education 21.7%; some secondary 9.0%; secondary 6.5%; some higher 5.0%; higher 4.8%; not specified 9.4%. *Literacy* (2001): total population age 15 and over literate 87.1%; males literate 93.3%; females literate 81.1%.

Education (2000)

	schools	teachers	students	student/ teacher ratio
Primary (age 6–13)	9,758[8]	64,306	1,531,200	23.8
Secondary (age 14–17)	724[8]	15,110	332,980	22
Higher	12	6,860	175,490	25.6

Health (2000): physicians 2,941 (1 per 2,772 persons); hospital beds 11,410 (1 per 715 persons); infant mortality rate (2002) 57.5.
Food (2001): daily per capita caloric intake 2,267 (vegetable products 84%, animal products 16%); 95% of FAO recommended minimum requirement.

Military

Total active duty personnel (2002): 31,500 (army 79.4%, navy 11.1%, air force 9.5%). *Military expenditure as percentage of GNP* (1998): 1.8% (world 2.4%); per capita expenditure U.S.$18.

[1]Within La Paz urban agglomeration. [2]December. [3]In 1990 prices. [4]Population 10 years of age and over. [5]Services includes Public utilities. [6]Unemployed. [7]Import figures are f.o.b. in balance of trade and c.i.f. for commodities and trading partners. [8]1986–87.

Internet resources for further information:
- **Instituto Nacional de Estadística http://www.ine.gov.bo**

Bosnia and Herzegovina[1]

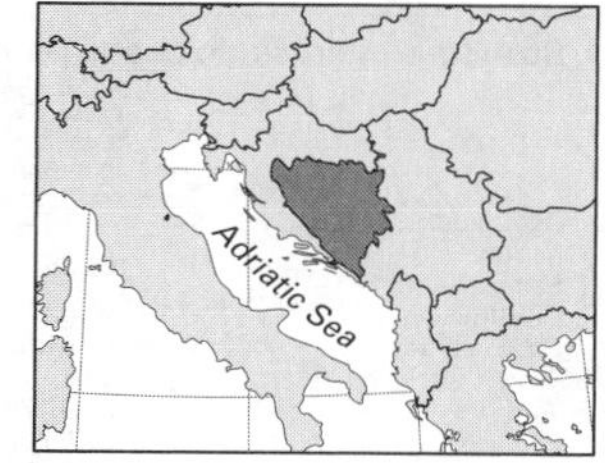

Official name: Bosna i Hercegovina (Bosnia and Herzegovina).
Form of government: federal multiparty republic with bicameral legislature (House of Peoples [15[2]]; House of Representatives [42]).
Chiefs of state: nominally a tripartite presidency.
International authority: High Representative[1].
Head of government: Prime Minister (Chairman of the Council of Ministers).
Capital: Sarajevo.
Official language: Bosnian.
Official religion: none.
Monetary unit: 1 marka[3, 4, 5] (KM) = 100 fenning; valuation (Sept. 8, 2003) 1 U.S.$ = KM 1.81; 1 £ = KM 2.87.

Area and population

Autonomous regions Cantons	Principal cities	area sq mi	area sq km	population 2002 estimate[6]
Federation of Bosnia and Herzegovina	Sarajevo	10,081	26,110	2,312,397
Central Bosnia	Travnik	1,231	3,189	239,728
Goražde	Goražde	195	505	35,258
Neretva	Mostar	1,699	4,401	217,333
Posavina	Orašje	125	325	43,706
Sarajevo	Sarajevo	493	1,277	400,498
Tuzla-Podrinje	Tuzla	1,023	2,649	507,490
Una-Sava	Bihać	1,593	4,125	305,905
Western Bosnia	Livno	1,905	4,934	83,974
Western Herzegovina	Ljubuški	526	1,362	81,304
Zenica-Doboj	Zenica	1,291	3,343	397,201
Republika Srpska	Banja Luka	9,686	25,087	1,392,000[7]
TOTAL		19,767	51,197	3,704,397

Demography

Population (2003)[8]: 3,720,000.
Density (2003)[8]: persons per sq mi 188.1, persons per sq km 72.7.
Urban-rural (2002): urban 43.4%; rural 56.6%.
Sex distribution (2001): male 50.46%; female 49.54%.
Age breakdown (2001): under 15, 20.1%; 15–29, 22.2%; 30–44, 25.8%; 45–59, 17.4%; 60–74, 12.2%; 75 and over, 2.3%.
Population projection: (2010) 3,834,000; (2020) 3,908,000.
Ethnic composition (1999): Bosniac 44.0%; Serb 31.0%; Croat 17.0%; other 8.0%.
Religious affiliation (1999): Sunnī Muslim 43.0%; Serbian Orthodox 30.0%; Roman Catholic 18.0%; other (mostly nonreligious) 9.0%.
Major cities (1991): Sarajevo 360,000[9] (urban agglomeration [2001] 552,000); Banja Luka 160,000[9]; Zenica 96,027; Tuzla 83,770; Mostar 75,865.

Vital statistics

Birth rate per 1,000 population (2001): 9.9 (world avg. 21.3); legitimate 89.4%; illegitimate 10.6%.
Death rate per 1,000 population (2001): 8.0 (world avg. 9.1).
Natural increase rate per 1,000 population (2001): 1.9 (world avg. 12.2).
Total fertility rate (avg. births per childbearing woman; 2001): 1.4.
Marriage rate per 1,000 population (2001): 5.3.
Life expectancy at birth (2001): male 64.6 years; female 70.2 years.
Major causes of death per 100,000 population (2001): circulatory diseases 440.8; malignant neoplasms (cancers) 144.4; accidents, violence, and poisoning 51.8; digestive system diseases 22.7; respiratory diseases 20.1.

National economy

Budget (2001)[10]. Revenue: KM 1,653,100,000 (tax revenue 90.8%, nontax revenue 6.4%, special revenue/grants 2.8%). Expenditures: KM 1,887,600,000 (wages and contributions 24.1%, transfers to households 22.6%, defense 15.4%).
Gross national product (2001): U.S.$5,000,000,000 (U.S.$1,240 per capita).

Structure of gross domestic product and labour force

	2001 in value KM '000,000	2001 % of total value	1990 labour force[11]	1990 % of labour force[11]
Agriculture	1,114	10.6	39,053	3.8
Manufacturing, mining	1,246	11.9	496,190	48.3
Construction	439	4.2	74,861	7.3
Public utilities	691	6.6	22,345	2.2
Transp. and commun.	948	9.0	68,798	6.7
Trade, restaurants	1,199	11.4	130,914	12.8
Finance, real estate	530	5.1	38,686	3.8
Pub. admin., defense	1,265	12.1		
Services	1,170	11.2	155,411	15.1
Other	1,878[12]	17.9[12]		
TOTAL	10,480	100.0	1,026,258	100.0

Production (metric tons except as noted). Agriculture, forestry, fishing (2002): corn (maize) 530,000, potatoes 310,000, wheat 297,000, cabbages 60,000, oats 55,000, plums 27,000, tomatoes 23,500, tobacco 3,444; livestock (number of live animals) 670,000 sheep, 440,000 cattle, 300,000 pigs; roundwood (2001) 3,818,000 cu m; fish catch (2000) 2,500. Mining (2000): iron ore (gross weight) 100,000; bauxite 75,000; kaolin 3,000; barite (concentrate) 2,000. Manufacturing (1996): cement 150,000; crude steel 115,000; pig iron 100,000. Energy production (consumption): electricity (kW-hr; 1999) 2,615,000,000 (2,846,000,000); lignite (metric tons; 1999) 1,848,000 (1,848,000); petroleum products (metric tons; 1999) none (598,000); natural gas (cu m; 1999) none (292,400,000).
Public debt (external, outstanding; 2001): U.S.$2,045,000,000.
Population economically active (2001): total 1,015,169; activity rate of total population 27.4% (participation rates: ages 15–64 [1991] 35.6%; female [1990] 37.7%; unemployed 41.0%).

Price and earnings indexes (1995 = 100)

	1995	1996	1997	1998	1999	2000
Retail price index[13]	100.0	75.5	83.7	87.9	87.6	88.7
Monthly earnings index	...	...	...	...	...	...

Household income and expenditure. Average household size (1991) 3.4; income per household: n.a.; sources of income (1990): wages 53.2%, transfers 18.2%, self-employment 12.0%, other 16.6%; expenditure: n.a.
Tourism (2001): receipts from visitors U.S.$14,000,000; expenditures by nationals abroad, n.a.
Land use (1994): forested 53.1%; meadows and pastures 23.5%; agricultural and under permanent cultivation 15.7%; other 7.7%.

Foreign trade

Balance of trade (current prices)

	1998	1999	2000	2001
KM '000,000	–4,077	–4,673	–4,317	–4,692
% of total	66.2%	63.0%	48.8%	49.7%

Imports (2001): KM 7,062,000,000. *Major import sources:* Croatia 15.2%; Italy 13.2%; Slovenia 13.0%; Germany 10.4%; Yugoslavia 7.4%.
Exports (2001): KM 2,370,000,000. *Major export destinations:* Italy 21.7%; Yugoslavia 19.3%; Germany 13.8%; Croatia 9.9%; Switzerland 9.6%.

Transport and communications

Transport. Railroads (2001)[14]: length 1,031 km; passenger-km 38,740,000; metric ton-km cargo 239,138,000. Roads (2001): total length 21,846 km (paved 64%). Vehicles (1996): passenger cars 96,182; trucks and buses 10,919. Air transport (1998)[15]: passenger-km 40,390,000; metric ton-km 430,000. Airports (2000) with scheduled flights 1.

Communications

Medium	date	unit	number	units per 1,000 persons
Daily newspapers	2000	circulation	563,000	152
Radio	2000	receivers	900,000	243
Television	2000	receivers	411,000	111
Telephones	2002	main lines	490,200	120
Cellular telephones	2002	subscribers	376,100	92
Internet	2002	users	100,000	24

Education and health

Educational attainment: n.a. *Literacy:* n.a.

Education (1990–91)

	schools	teachers	students	student/ teacher ratio
Primary (age 7–14)	2,205	23,369	539,875	23.1
Secondary (age 15–18)	238	9,030	172,063	19.1
Higher	44	2,802	37,541	13.4

Health: physicians (1998) 5,000 (1 per 700 persons); hospital beds (1996) 15,586 (1 per 208 persons); infant mortality rate (2002) 23.5.
Food (2001): daily per capita caloric intake 2,845 (vegetable products 85%, animal products 15%); 112% of FAO recommended minimum requirement.

Military

Total active duty personnel (2002): n.a.; in January 2003 about 13,000 troops of the NATO-commanded Stabilization Force were stationed in Bosnia and Herzegovina to assure implementation of the Dayton accords. *Military expenditure as percentage of GNP* (1999): 4.5% (world 2.4%); per capita expenditure U.S.$75.

[1]Government structure provided for by Dayton accords and constitutions of 1993 and 1994 is being implemented in stages since formal signing of peace accord on Dec. 14, 1995. [2]All seats are nonelective. [3]An interim currency, the marka (or "convertible mark"; KM), was introduced on June 22, 1998, to replace another interim currency, the Bosnian dinar (BD), at a rate of 1 KM to 100 BD. [4]The KM is pegged to the euro from Jan. 1, 2002. [5]The euro also circulates as semiofficial legal tender. [6]January 1. [7]Estimated figure by Republika Srpska government. [8]Excludes refugees in adjacent countries and Western Europe. [9]1997. [10]Combined total for the separately constructed budgets of the Federation of Bosnia and Herzegovina and Republika Srpska. [11]Excludes 28,000 workers in the private sector. [12]Taxes on products and imports less subsidies. [13]Federation of Bosnia and Herzegovina only. [14]1991–95 war destroyed much infrastructure; limited service resumed in 1998. [15]Air Bosna only.

Internet resources for further information:
- **Central Bank of Bosnia and Herzegovina http://www.cbbh.gov.ba**
- **NATO Stabilization Force http://www.nato.int/sfor**

Botswana

Official name: Republic of Botswana.
Form of government: multiparty republic with one legislative body[1] (National Assembly [47[2]]).
Head of state and government: President.
Capital: Gaborone.
Official language: English[3].
Official religion: none.
Monetary unit: 1 pula (P) = 100 thebe; valuation (Sept. 8, 2003) 1 U.S.$ = P 4.90; 1 £ = P 7.77.

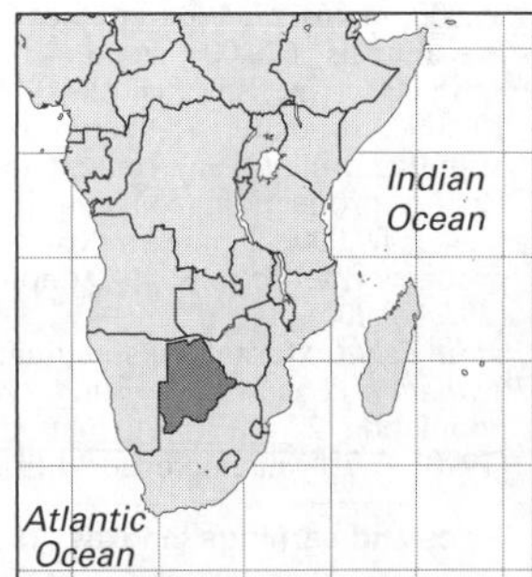

Area and population

Districts	Capitals	area sq mi	area sq km	population 2001 census
Central	Serowe	57,039	147,730	501,381
Ghanzi	Ghanzi	45,525	117,910	33,170
Kgalagadi	Tsabong	41,290	106,940	42,049
Kgatleng	Mochudi	3,073	7,960	73,507
Kweneng	Molepolole	13,857	35,890	230,335
North East	Masunga	1,977	5,120	49,399
North West				
Chobe	Maun	8,031	20,800	18,258
Ngamiland	Maun	33,359	86,400	75,070
Okavango	Maun	8,776	22,730	49,642
South East	Ramotswa	687	1,780	60,623
Southern	Kanye	10,991	28,467	171,652
Towns				
Francistown	—	31	79	83,023
Gaborone	—	65	169	186,007
Jwaneng	—	39	100	15,179
Lobatse	—	16	42	29,689
Orapa	—	7	17	9,151
Selebi-Pikwe	—	23	60	49,849
Sowa	—	61	159	2,879
TOTAL		224,848[4]	582,356[4]	1,680,863

Demography

Population (2003): 1,663,000.
Density (2003): persons per sq mi 7.4, persons per sq km 2.9.
Urban-rural (2002): urban 49.4%; rural 50.6%.
Sex distribution (2000): male 48.58%; female 51.42%.
Age breakdown (2000): under 15, 40.6%; 15–29, 30.8%; 30–44, 15.0%; 45–59, 7.7%; 60–74, 4.3%; 75 and over, 1.6%.
Population projection: (2010) 1,510,000; (2020) 1,225,000.
Doubling time: n.a.; doubling time exceeds 100 years.
Ethnic composition (2000): Tswana 66.8%; Kalanga 14.8%; Ndebele 1.7%; Herero 1.4%; San (Bushman) 1.3%; Afrikaner 1.3%.
Religious affiliation (2000): traditional beliefs 38.8%; African Christian 30.7%; Protestant 10.9%; Roman Catholic 3.7%.
Major cities (2001): Gaborone 186,007; Francistown 83,023; Molepolole 54,561; Selebi-Pikwe 49,849; Maun 43,776.

Vital statistics

Birth rate per 1,000 population (2002): 28.0 (world avg. 21.3).
Death rate per 1,000 population (2002): 26.3 (world avg. 9.1).
Natural increase rate per 1,000 population (2002): 1.7 (world avg. 12.2).
Total fertility rate (avg. births per childbearing woman; 2002): 3.6.
Marriage rate per 1,000 population: n.a.
Life expectancy at birth (2002): male 36.9 years; female 37.6 years.

National economy

Budget (2000–01). Revenue: P 14,115,100,000 (tax revenue 85.6%, of which mineral royalties 59.3%, customs and excise taxes 15.5%; nontax revenue 14.0%, of which property income 8.5%; grants 0.4%). Expenditures: P 11,536,500,000 (education 15.8%, defense 8.9%, health 8.6%, interest 0.9%).
Population economically active (2000): total 574,160; activity rate of total population 35.1% (participation rates: ages 15–64, 58.3%; female 44.3%; unemployed 15.8%).

Price and earnings indexes (1995 = 100)

	1996	1997	1998	1999	2000	2001	2002
Consumer price index	110.1	119.7	127.7	137.5	149.4	159.2	172.1
Annual earnings index	105.1	110.4	142.5	...	...	...	...

Tourism: receipts (2001) U.S.$245,000,000; expenditures (1999) U.S.$143,000,000.
Production (metric tons except as noted). Agriculture, forestry, fishing (2002): cereals 26,600 (of which sorghum 15,000, corn [maize] 10,000), pulses 17,500; livestock (number of live animals) 2,250,000 goats, 1,700,000 cattle, 370,000 sheep; roundwood (2001) 744,809 cu m; fish catch (2000) 166. Mining and quarrying (2000): soda ash 190,000; copper ore (metal content) 38,420; nickel ore (metal content) 34,465; diamonds 24,218,000 carats. Manufacturing (value added in P '000,000; 1994): food products 164.3; wearing apparel 78.9; paper and paper products 28.0; industrial chemicals 18.7; wood products 17.5. Energy production (consumption): electricity (kW-hr; 2000) 500,000,000 (1,450,000,000); coal (metric tons; 2000) 962,000 (971,000); crude petroleum (2001) none (n.a.); natural gas (2000) none (none).
Gross national product (2001): U.S.$5,300,000,000 (U.S.$3,100 per capita).

Structure of gross domestic product and labour force

	2000–01 in value P '000,000	2000–01 % of total value	2000 labour force	2000 % of labour force
Agriculture	716.0	2.4	95,283	16.6
Mining	10,286.5	35.0	11,219	2.0
Manufacturing			42,626	7.4
Construction	1,562.7	5.3	44,940	7.8
Public utilities	691.5	2.4	2,222	0.4
Transp. and commun.	1,089.1	3.7	13,800	2.4
Trade[5]	3,197.7	10.9	73,446	12.8
Finance	3,159.0	10.8	22,068	3.8
Pub. admin., defense	4,654.2	15.9	73,217	12.8
Services	1,090.2	3.7	104,613	18.2
Other	2,905.6[6]	9.9[6]	90,728[7]	15.8[7]
TOTAL	29,352.5	100.0	574,160	100.0

Public debt (external, outstanding; 2001): U.S.$349,200,000.
Household income and expenditure. Average household size (2000) 4.4; average annual income per household (1985–86) P 3,910 (U.S.$2,080); sources of income (1987): wages and salaries 73.3%, self-employment 15.9%, transfers 10.8%; expenditure (1996): food 25.5%, transportation 19.7%, alcohol and tobacco products 13.5%, housing 12.2%, clothing and footwear 5.8%.
Land use (1994): forest 46.8%; pasture 45.2%; agriculture 0.7%; other 7.3%.

Foreign trade[8]

Balance of trade (current prices)

	1996	1997	1998	1999	2000	2001
P '000,000	+2,413	+2,135	–816	+2,063	+3,222	+3,750
% of total	17.4%	11.4%	4.5%	9.2%	13.2%	15.1%

Imports (2001): P 10,557,000,000 (machinery and apparatus 19.7%; food, beverages, and tobacco 14.0%; transport equipment 12.2%; chemical and rubber products 10.3%; wood and paper products 8.8%). *Major import sources:* Customs Union of Southern Africa (CUSA) 77.6%; Europe 12.3%, of which U.K. 4.4%; Zimbabwe 3.9%; U.S. 1.8%.
Exports (2001): P 14,307,000,000 (diamonds 84.5%; copper-nickel matte 4.2%; meat products 2.6%; vehicles and parts 2.1%; textiles 1.3%). *Major export destinations*: U.K. 85.9%; CUSA 6.5%; Zimbabwe 2.6%.

Transport and communications

Transport. Railroads (2000–01): length 705 mi, 1,135 km; passenger-km 106,000,000; metric ton-km cargo 747,000. Roads (2000): total length 6,500 mi, 10,479 km (paved 55%). Vehicles (2001): passenger cars 52,873; trucks and buses 63,945. Air transport (2001)[9]: passenger-km 76,000,000; metric ton-km cargo 283,000; airports (1998) 7.

Communications

Medium	date	unit	number	units per 1,000 persons
Daily newspapers	2000	circulation	44,200	27
Radio	2000	receivers	254,000	155
Television	2000	receivers	40,900	25
Telephones	2001	main lines	142,600	85
Cellular telephones	2002	subscribers	415,000	241
Personal computers	2001	units	65,000	39
Internet	2000	users	25,000	15

Education and health

Educational attainment (1993). Percentage of population age 25 and over having: no formal schooling 34.7%; primary education 44.1%; some secondary 19.8%; postsecondary 1.4%. *Literacy* (2000): total population over age 15 literate 934,200 (77.2%); males literate 449,200 (74.4%); females literate 485,000 (79.8%).

Education (1999)

	schools	teachers	students	student/ teacher ratio
Primary (age 6–13)	736	11,950	323,874	27.1
Secondary (age 14–18)	265	8,470	148,195	17.5
Voc., teacher tr.	53	2,889[10]	12,397	...
Higher	1	697	9,595	13.8

Health (2000): physicians 465 (1 per 4,482 persons); hospital beds 3,716 (1 per 440 persons); infant mortality rate (2002) 64.7.
Food (2001): daily per capita caloric intake 2,292 (vegetable products 83%, animal products 17%); 99% of FAO recommended minimum requirement.

Military

Total active duty personnel (2002): 9,000 (army 94.4%, navy, none [land locked], air force 5.6%). *Military expenditure as percentage of GNP* (1999): 4.7% (world 2.4%); per capita expenditure U.S.$142.

[1]In addition, the House of Chiefs, a 15-member body consisting of chiefs, subchiefs, and associated members, serves in an advisory capacity to the government. [2]Includes four specially elected members, the speaker elected from outside of the National Assembly, and 2 ex officio members. [3]Tswana is the national language. [4]Detail does not add to total given because of rounding. [5]Includes hotels. [6]Imputed bank service charge. [7]Unemployed. [8]Imports c.i.f.; exports f.o.b. [9]Air Botswana only. [10]1997.

Internet resources for further information:
- **Central Statistical Office http://www.cso.gov.bw/cso**
- **Republic of Botswana: The Government of Botswana Web Site http://www.gov.bw/home.html**

Brazil

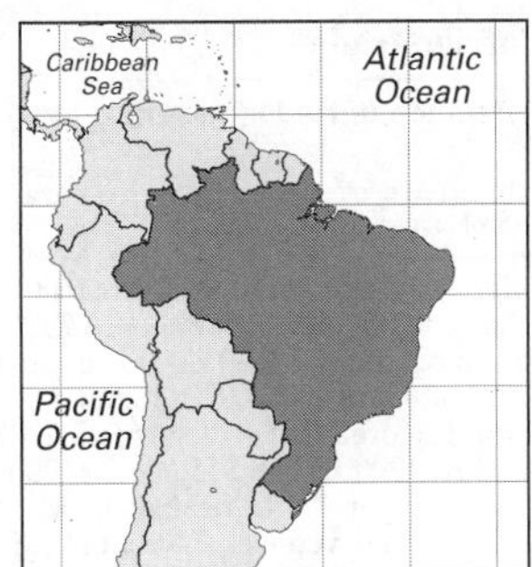

Official name: República Federativa do Brasil (Federative Republic of Brazil).
Form of government: multiparty federal republic with 2 legislative houses (Federal Senate [81]; Chamber of Deputies [513]).
Chief of state and government: President.
Capital: Brasília.
Official language: Portuguese.
Official religion: none.
Monetary unit: 1 real[1] (R$; plural reais) = 100 centavos; valuation (Sept. 8, 2003) 1 U.S.$ = 2.91 reais; 1 £ = 4.62 reais.

Area and population

		area		population
States	**Capitals**	sq mi	sq km	2002[2] estimate
Acre	Rio Branco	58,889	152,522	586,942
Alagoas	Maceió	10,741	27,818	2,887,535
Amapá	Macapá	55,142	142,816	516,511
Amazonas	Manaus	606,546	1,570,947	2,961,801
Bahia	Salvador	217,867	564,273	13,323,212
Ceará	Fortaleza	56,260	145,712	7,654,535
Espírito Santo	Vitória	17,779	46,047	3,201,722
Goiás	Goiânia	131,320	340,118	5,210,335
Maranhão	São Luís	128,154	331,918	5,803,224
Mato Grosso	Cuiabá	348,799	903,386	2,604,742
Mato Grosso do Sul	Campo Grande	137,893	357,140	2,140,624
Minas Gerais	Belo Horizonte	226,469	586,552	18,343,517
Pará	Belém	481,741	1,247,703	6,453,683
Paraíba	João Pessoa	21,753	56,341	3,494,893
Paraná	Curitiba	76,943	199,282	9,798,006
Pernambuco	Recife	38,041	98,527	8,084,667
Piauí	Teresina	97,032	251,312	2,898,223
Rio de Janeiro	Rio de Janeiro	16,911	43,798	14,724,475
Rio Grande do Norte	Natal	20,493	53,077	2,852,784
Rio Grande do Sul	Porto Alegre	108,778	281,734	10,408,540
Rondônia	Porto Velho	91,724	237,564	1,431,777
Roraima	Boa Vista	86,532	224,118	346,871
Santa Catarina	Florianópolis	36,790	95,285	5,527,707
São Paulo	São Paulo	95,822	248,177	38,177,742
Sergipe	Aracaju	8,480	21,962	1,846,039
Tocantins	Palmas	107,065	277,298	1,207,014
Federal District				
Distrito Federal	Brasília	2,240	5,802	2,145,839
Disputed areas[3]		1,088	2,819	—
TOTAL		3,287,292[4]	8,514,047[4, 5]	174,632,960

Demography

Population (2003): 178,470,000.
Density (2003): persons per sq mi 54.3, persons per sq km 21.0.
Urban-rural (2000): urban 81.2%; rural 18.8%.
Sex distribution (2000): male 49.22%; female 50.78%.
Age breakdown (2000)[6]: under 15, 29.0%; 15–29, 28.4%; 30–44, 22.2%; 45–59, 12.5%; 60–74, 6.3%; 75 and over, 1.6%.
Population projection: (2010) 192,879,000; (2020) 209,793,000.
Doubling time: 54 years.
Racial composition (1999)[7]: white 54.0%; mulatto and mestizo 39.9%; black and black/Amerindian 5.4%; Asian 0.5%; Amerindian 0.2%.
Religious affiliation (1995)[8]: Catholic 74.3%[9], of which Roman Catholic 72.3%[9]; Protestant 23.2%, of which Pentecostal 19.1%; other Christian 0.9%; New-Religionist 0.3%; Buddhist 0.3%; Jewish 0.2%; Muslim 0.1%; other 0.7%.
Major cities[10] *and metropolitan areas* (2002)[2]: São Paulo 9,969,100 (18,390,800); Rio de Janeiro 5,937,300 (11,121,300); Salvador 2,519,500 (3,132,000); Belo Horizonte 2,284,500 (5,011,400); Fortaleza 2,219,800 (3,107,300); Brasília 2,052,100 (3,121,100); Curitiba 1,644,600 (2,866,000); Manaus 1,479,200 (1,488,800); Recife 1,449,100 (3,425,400); Porto Alegre 1,342,900 (3,765,500); Belém 1,314,200 (1,878,500); Goiânia 1,121,800 (1,726,300); Guarulhos 1,108,300[11]; Campinas 978,400 (2,437,500).

Other principal cities[10] **(2002)**[2]

	population		population		population
Aracaju	474,000	Maceió	831,200	São Gonçalo	914,500[11]
Campo Grande	684,500	Natal	734,500	São Jose dos Campos	552,900
Contagem	551,800[12]	Nova Iguaçu	780,300[13]	São Luis	872,800
Cuiabá	493,200	Osasco	670,300[11]	Sorocaba	510,500
Duque de Caxias	794,900[13]	Ribeirão Preto	518,300	Teresina	700,800
Jaboatão	587,900[14]	Santo André	656,100[11]	Uberlândia	516,500
João Pessoa	619,000	São Bernardo do Campo	719,100[11]		
Juiz de Fora	467,800				

Families (1999). Average family size 3.7; (1996) 1–2 persons 25.2%, 3 persons 20.3%, 4 persons 22.2%, 5–6 persons 23.3%, 7 or more persons 9.0%.
Domestic migration. Percent of population moving to different *município* between 1991 and 1996: 7.6%.
Number of emigrants/immigrants (1986–96): 2,355,057/169,303. Emigrants' most popular destinations in order of preference are the United States, Japan, and the United Kingdom.

Vital statistics

Birth rate per 1,000 population (2002): 19.7 (world avg. 21.3).
Death rate per 1,000 population (2002): 6.7 (world avg. 9.1).
Natural increase rate per 1,000 population (2002): 13.0 (world avg. 12.2).
Total fertility rate (avg. births per childbearing woman; 2002): 2.2.
Marriage rate per 1,000 population (1995): 4.7.
Divorce rate per 1,000 population (1995): 0.6.
Life expectancy at birth (2000): male 58.5 years; female 67.6 years.
Major causes of death per 100,000 population (1998; based on incomplete registration of deaths): diseases of the circulatory system 153.2; accidents, murder, and violence 70.3; malignant neoplasms (cancers) 66.2; diseases of the respiratory system 55.0; infectious and parasitic diseases 29.1; diseases of the digestive system 24.3; endocrine, metabolic, and nutritional disorders 23.8; ill-defined conditions 82.8.

Social indicators

Educational attainment (1996). Percentage of population age 25 and over having: no formal schooling or less than one year of primary education 17.7%; lower primary only 19.1%; upper primary 30.7%; complete primary to some secondary 11.6%; complete secondary to some higher 13.9%; complete higher 6.2%; unknown 0.8%.

Distribution of income (1995)

percentage of national income by decile/quintile

1	2	3	4	5	6	7	8	9	10 (highest)
0.8	1.7	—5.7—		—9.9—		—17.7—		16.3	47.9

Quality of working life. Proportion of labour force participating in national social insurance system (1990): 50.1%. Proportion of formally employed population receiving minimum wage (1993): 25.0%.
Access to services (1999)[7]. Proportion of households having access to: electricity 94.8%, of which urban households having access 99.2%, rural households having access 75.4%; safe public (piped) water supply 79.8%, of which urban households having access 92.3%, rural households having access 24.9%; public (piped) sewage system 43.6%, of which urban households having access 52.5%, rural households having access 4.5%; no sewage disposal 8.5%, of which urban households having no disposal 2.9%, rural households having no disposal 32.9%.
Social participation. Voting is mandatory for national elections; abstention is punishable by a fine. Trade union membership in total workforce (1991): 16,748,155. Practicing Roman Catholic population in total affiliated Roman Catholic population (2000): large cities 10–15%; towns and rural areas 60–70%.
Social deviance. Annual murder rate per 100,000 population (1996): Brazil 23, Rio de Janeiro only 69, São Paulo only 55.
Leisure. Favourite leisure activities include: playing soccer, dancing, rehearsing all year in neighbourhood samba groups for celebrations of Carnival, and competing in water sports, volleyball, and basketball.
Material well-being (1999)[7]. Households possessing: telephone lines (1997) 27.9%, of which urban 33.2%, rural 4.9%; television receiver 87.7%, of which urban 93.2%, rural 63.8%; refrigerator 82.8%, of which urban 89.7%, rural 52.5%; washing machine 32.8%, of which urban 38.0%, rural 10.0%.

National economy

Gross national product (at current market prices; 2001): U.S.$528,900,000,000 (U.S.$3,070 per capita).

Structure of gross domestic product and labour force

	2000		1999	
	in value R$'000,000[1, 15]	% of total value	labour force[7, 16]	% of labour force
Agriculture	74,426	6.8	17,372,000	21.9
Mining	24,270	2.2	783,000	1.0
Public utilities	34,071	3.2		
Manufacturing	216,388	19.9	8,279,000	10.4
Construction	88,227	8.1	4,743,000	6.0
Transportation and communications	60,084	5.5	2,815,000	3.5
Trade	69,986	6.4	9,618,000[17]	12.1[17]
Finance, real estate	176,888	16.3	1,314,000[18]	1.7[18]
Pub. admin., defense	159,443	14.7	26,721,000[19]	33.7[19]
Services	224,133	20.6		
Other	–41,216[20]	–3.8[20]	7,670,000[21]	9.7[21]
TOTAL	1,086,700	100.0[5]	79,315,000	100.0

Budget (1998). Revenue R$237,187,000,000 (current revenue 95.8%, of which social contributions 32.6%, sales tax 20.3%, tax on income and profit 19.4%, nontax revenue 16.3%; capital revenue 4.2%). Expenditures: R$245,032,-100,000 (social security and welfare 47.3%; interest on debt 14.3%; defense and public order 6.6%; health 6.2%; education 6.1%; economic affairs 4.8%; other 14.7%).
Public debt (external, outstanding; 2001): U.S.$93,467,000,000.
Production ('000 metric tons except as noted). Agriculture, forestry, fishing (2002): sugarcane 360,566, soybeans 41,903, corn (maize) 35,479, cassava 23,108, oranges 18,694, rice 10,489, bananas 6,369, tomatoes 3,518, dry beans 3,017, wheat 2,926, potatoes 2,865, coconuts 2,695, coffee 2,390, seed cotton 2,172, cashew apples 1,600, papayas 1,500, pineapples 1,469, onions 1,132, grapes 1,099, apples 858, sorghum 814, tobacco 654, lemons and limes 580, maté 535, oil palm fruit 450, peanuts (groundnuts) 192, cashews 184, sisal 177, cacao beans 172, garlic 113, natural rubber 96, Brazil nuts 26; livestock (number of live animals) 176,000,000 cattle, 30,000,000 pigs, 15,000,000 sheep, 5,900,000 horses; roundwood (2002) 237,467,063 cu m, of which fuelwood 134,473,063 cu m, sawlogs and veneer logs 49,290,000 cu m, pulpwood 45,860,000 cu m; fish catch (2001) 847, of which freshwater fishes 299. Mining and quarrying (value of export production in U.S.$'000,000; 1998): iron ore 3,066; ferroniobium 242; silicon 135; bauxite 122; kaolin (clay) 106; ferrosilicon 101; granite (1996) 97; copper 89; manganese 52; nickel 52; gold production for both domestic use and export 1,594,000 troy oz; Brazil is also a

world-leading producer of high-quality grade quartz and tantalum. Manufacturing (value added in R$'000,000; 1999): food 28,208; transport equipment 15,588, of which cars 12,513; fabricated and base metals 12,922; electrical machinery 11,670; industrial chemicals 9,871; printing and publishing 8,771; paper and paper products 8,440; plastics and rubber products 7,908; pharmaceuticals 7,642.
Land use (1994): forested 57.7%; meadows and pastures 21.9%; agricultural and under permanent cultivation 6.0%; other 14.4%.

Manufacturing enterprises (1995)

	no. of enter- prises	number of labourers[22]	wages of labourers as a % of avg. of all mfg. wages	value added in producer's prices (in R$'000,000)[1]
Industrial chemicals	1,817	218,756	164.3	21,937
Transport equipment	711	262,712	157.7	20,434
Food products	4,241	527,064	60.6	18,117
Fabricated metals, iron and steel, and nonferrous metals	2,050	325,406	114.2	13,813
Electrical machinery	1,081	191,740	126.6	9,563
Nonelectrical machinery	1,694	227,196	124.7	8,122
Paper and paper products	676	103,339	114.1	5,667
Nonmetallic mineral products	1,508	126,925	88.2	5,125
Pharmaceuticals	359	51,953	178.6	4,958
Textiles	1,192	208,857	66.8	4,907
Publishing and printing	782	105,165	132.1	4,807
Clothing and footwear	1,681	299,193	49.8	4,706
Beverages	451	76,452	87.1	4,027
Plastics	724	101,971	81.0	3,111
Paints, soaps, and perfumes	249	31,143	116.7	2,553
Rubber products	407	49,368	111.5	1,767

Population economically active (1999)[7, 16]: total 79,315,000; activity rate of total population 49.5% (participation rates: ages 15–59 72.4%; female 40.2%; unemployed 9.7%).

Price and earnings indexes (1995 = 100)

	1996	1997	1998	1999	2000	2001	2002
Consumer price index	115.8	123.8	127.7	133.9	143.4	153.2	166.3
Monthly earnings index[23]	118.3	128.5	138.8	146.8	161.8	...	...

Tourism (2001): receipts from visitors U.S.$3,701,000,000; expenditures by nationals abroad U.S.$3,199,000,000.

Retail trade enterprises (1996)

	no. of businesses	total no. of employees	annual wage as a % of all trade wages	annual values of sales in R$'000,000[1]
General merchandise stores (including food products)	10,382	437,452	131.2	35,766
Vehicles, new and used	9,348	202,892	229.9	30,926
Gas stations	20,388	210,250	124.7	23,199
Electronics, kitchen equipment, musical instruments	18,245	158,755	143.7	14,855
Metal products, lumber, glass, and construction materials	81,303	386,285	90.1	14,047
Vehicles, parts	55,534	252,731	110.6	10,881
Pharmaceutical and cosmetic products	50,778	240,633	94.2	9,658
Clothing and apparel	128,908	428,150	76.4	9,023
Food, beverages, and tobacco	135,672	378,102	60.7	6,900

Households. Average household size (2000) 3.8.
Family income and expenditure. Average family size (1999) 3.7[7]; annual income per family (1999) R$10,500 (U.S.$5,900[7, 24]); sources of income (1987–88)[25]: wages and salaries 62.4%, self-employed 14.7%, transfers 10.9%, other 12.0%; expenditure (1995–96)[26]: housing, energy, and household furnishings 28.8%, food and beverages 23.4%, transportation and communications 13.8%, health care 9.2%, education and recreation 8.4%.

Financial aggregates[27]

	1997	1998	1999	2000	2001	2002
Exchange rate, reais[1] per:						
U.S. dollar	1.116	1.209	1.789	1.955	2.320	3.533
£	1.846	2.011	2.892	2.917	3.365	2.355
SDR	1.506	1.702	2.455	2.547	2.916	4.804
International reserves (U.S.$)						
Total (excl. gold; '000,000)	50,827	42,580	34,796	32,488	35,740	37,683
SDRs ('000,000)	1	2	10	—	11	275
Reserve pos. in IMF ('000,000)	—	—	—	—	—	—
Foreign exchange ('000,000)	50,826	42,578	34,786	32,488	35,729	37,409
Gold ('000,000 fine troy oz)	3.03	4.60	3.17	1.89	0.46	0.44
% world reserves	0.34	0.48	0.44	0.20	0.05	0.05
Interest and prices						
Central bank discount (%)	45.09	39.41	21.37	18.52	21.43	18.52
Govt. bond yield (%)	...	...	...	...	...	...
Industrial share prices	...	...	...	...	...	...
Balance of payments (U.S.$'000,000)						
Balance of visible trade	–8,372	–6,603	–1,260	–696	+2,645	+13,143
Imports, f.o.b.	61,358	57,739	49,272	55,783	55,579	47,219
Exports, f.o.b.	52,986	51,136	48,012	55,087	58,224	60,362
Balance of invisibles	–23,839	–27,226	–24,140	–23,936	–25,853	–20,829
Balance of payments current account	–30,491	–33,829	–25,400	–24,632	–23,208	–7,696

Energy production (consumption): electricity (kW-hr; 2000) 348,000,000,000 (331,000,000,000); coal (metric tons; 2000) 6,974,000 ([1999] 19,296,000); crude petroleum (barrels; 2001) 468,873,000 ([1999] 579,500,000); petroleum products (metric tons; 1999) 67,449,000 (73,349,000); natural gas (cu m; 2001) 13,999,000,000 ([1999] 6,053,200,000).

Foreign trade[28]

Balance of trade (current prices)

	1996	1997	1998	1999	2000	2001
U.S.$'000,000	–5,453	–8,372	–6,603	–1,260	–697	+2,645
% of total	5.4%	7.3%	6.1%	1.4%	0.6%	2.3%

Imports (2000): U.S.$55,783,000,000 (machinery and apparatus 32.5%; chemicals and chemical products 16.7%; mineral fuels 13.7%; motor vehicles 8.8%; food products 3.4%). *Major import sources:* United States 23.1%; Argentina 12.3%; Germany 7.9%; Japan 5.3%; Italy 3.9%; France 3.4%; Algeria 2.7%; South Korea 2.5%; Venezuela 2.4%; United Kingdom 2.2%.
Exports (2000): U.S.$55,086,000,000 (food 16.7%, of which meat 3.5%, coffee 2.8%, sugar 2.2%, orange juice 1.9%; transportation equipment 14.4%, of which road vehicles 7.9%, aircraft 6.5%; machinery and apparatus 13.2%; soybeans [all forms] 7.6%; chemicals and chemical products 7.4%; iron and steel 6.7%; iron ore and concentrates 5.5%; paper and cellulose 4.6%). *Major export destinations:* United States 23.9%; Argentina 11.3%; The Netherlands 5.1%; Germany 4.6%; Japan 4.5%; Italy 3.9%; Belgium 3.2%; Mexico 3.1%; France 3.1%; United Kingdom 2.7%.

Transport and communications

Transport. Railroads (1998)[29]: route length 18,458 mi, 29,706 km; passenger-mi 8,676,000,000, passenger-km 12,667,000,000; short ton-mi cargo (2000) 106,077,000,000, metric ton-km cargo 154,870,000,000. Roads (1999): total length 1,071,816 mi, 1,724,924 km (paved 9%). Vehicles (2001): passenger cars 23,241,966; trucks and buses 3,897,140. Air transport (2001)[30]: passenger-mi 26,145,000,000, passenger-km 42,077,000,000; short ton-mi cargo 907,308,000, metric ton-km cargo 1,324,646,000; airports (1995) with scheduled flights 139.

Communications

Medium	date	unit	number	units per 1,000 persons
Daily newspapers	2000	circulation	7,390,000	43
Radio	2000	receivers	74,400,000	433
Television	2000	receivers	58,900,000	343
Telephones	2002	main lines	38,810,000	223
Cellular telephones	2002	subscribers	34,881,000	201
Personal computers	2002	units	13,000,000	75
Internet	2002	users	14,300,000	82

Education and health

Literacy (2000): total population age 15 and over literate 86.7%.

Education (2000)

	schools	teachers	students	student/ teacher ratio
Primary (age 7–14)	181,504	1,538,011	35,717,948	23.2
Secondary (age 15–17)	19,456	430,467	8,192,948	19.0
Higher	1,097	173,836	2,369,945	13.6

Health: physicians (1999) 429,808 (1 per 395 persons); hospital beds (1999) 484,945 (1 per 343 persons); infant mortality rate per 1,000 live births (2002) 31.8.
Food (2001): daily per capita caloric intake 3,002 (vegetable products 80%, animal products 20%); 126% of FAO recommended minimum requirement.

Military

Total active duty personnel (2002): 287,600 (army 65.7%, navy 16.9%, air force 17.4%). *Military expenditure as percentage of GNP* (1999): 1.9% (world 2.4%); per capita expenditure U.S.$59.

[1]The real (R$) replaced the cruzeiro real (CR$) on July 1, 1994, at a rate of 2,750 cruzeiros reais to 1 real (a rate par to the U.S.$ on that date). Previously, the cruzeiro real replaced the cruzeiro (Cr$) at a rate of 1,000 cruzeiros to 1 cruzeiro real on Aug. 2, 1993; the cruzeiro replaced the new cruzado (NCz$) at a rate of 1 to 1 on March 16, 1990; and the new cruzado replaced the (old) cruzado (Cz$) at a rate of 1,000 (old) to 1 new on Jan. 15, 1989. [2]July 1. [3]Area in dispute between Ceará and Piauí. [4]Total area including inland water per survey of late 1990s. [5]Detail does not add to total given because of rounding. [6]Estimated figures. [7]Excludes rural population of Acre, Amapá, Amazonas, Pará, Rondônia, and Roraima. [8]Christian data include nominal Christians. [9]Includes syncretic Afro-Catholic cults having Spiritist beliefs and rituals. [10]Populations are for *municípios,* which may include adjacent urban or rural districts. [11]Within São Paulo metropolitan area. [12]Within Belo Horizonte metropolitan area. [13]Within Rio de Janeiro metropolitan area. [14]Within Recife metropolitan area. [15]Current prices. [16]Excludes members of armed forces in barracks. [17]Excludes restaurants and hotels. [18]Includes activities not adequately defined. [19]Includes restaurants and hotels. [20]Less imputed bank service charges. [21]Unemployed. [22]End of year. [23]Minimum wages. [24]Based on end-of-year exchange rate. [25]Based on 10,408,833 families in Brazil's nine largest metropolitan regions. [26]Based on survey of 11 metropolitan areas only. [27]End-of-period figures. [28]Imports f.o.b. [29]Includes suburban services. [30]TAM Regional, TAM Meridional, VARIG, and VASP airlines only.

Internet resources for further information:

- **IBGE: Instituto Brasileiro de Geografia e Estatística http://www.ibge.gov.br/english/default.php#**
- **Central Bank of Brazil: Economic Data http://www.bcb.gov.br/defaulti.htm**

Brunei

Official name: Negara Brunei Darussalam (State of Brunei, Abode of Peace).
Form of government: monarchy (sultanate)[1].
Head of state and government: Sultan.
Capital: Bandar Seri Begawan.
Official language: Malay[2].
Official religion: Islam.
Monetary unit: 1 Brunei dollar (B$) = 100 cents; valuation (Sept. 8, 2003) 1 U.S.$ = B$1.76; 1 £ = B$2.78.

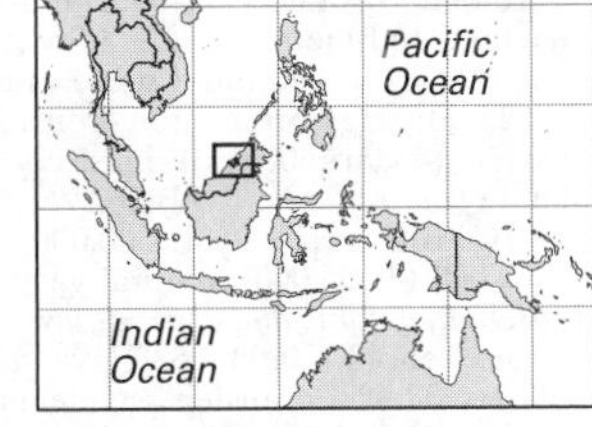

Area and population

Districts	Capitals	area sq mi	area sq km	population 2001 census
Belait	Kuala Belait	1,052	2,724	55,602
Brunei and Muara	Bandar Seri Begawan	220	571	230,030
Temburong	Bangar	504	1,304	8,563
Tutong	Tutong	450	1,166	38,649
TOTAL		2,226	5,765	332,844

Demography

Population (2003): 344,000.
Density (2003): persons per sq mi 154.5, persons per sq km 59.7.
Urban-rural (2002): urban 73.0%; rural 27.0%.
Sex distribution (2002): male 52.35%; female 47.65%.
Age breakdown (2002): under 15, 30.2%; 15–29, 27.0%; 30–44, 25.2%; 45–59, 13.2%; 60–74, 3.6%; 75 and over, 0.8%.
Population projection: (2010) 393,000; (2020) 458,000.
Doubling time: 42 years.
Ethnic composition (2001): Malay 66.8%; Chinese 11.1%; other indigenous 3.5%; other 18.6%.
Religious affiliation (2000): Muslim 64.4%; traditional beliefs 11.2%; Buddhist 9.1%; Christian 7.7%; other religions and nonreligious 7.6%.
Major cities (1991): Bandar Seri Begawan (1999) 85,000[3]; Kuala Belait 21,163; Seria 21,082; Tutong 13,049.

Vital statistics

Birth rate per 1,000 population (2002): 20.1 (world avg. 21.3).
Death rate per 1,000 population (2002): 3.4 (world avg. 9.1).
Natural increase rate per 1,000 population (2002): 16.7 (world avg. 12.2).
Total fertility rate (avg. births per childbearing woman; 2002): 2.4.
Marriage rate per 1,000 population (1998): 5.5.
Divorce rate per 1,000 population (1998): 0.1.
Life expectancy at birth (2002): male 71.7 years; female 76.6 years.
Major causes of death per 100,000 population (1999): cardiovascular disease 70.0; malignant neoplasms (cancers) 50.0; diseases of the respiratory system 28.2; accidents, poisoning, and violence 15.5; congenital anomalies 7.6.

National economy

Budget (1998). Revenue: B$2,775,000,000 (tax revenue 54.6%, of which corporate income tax 47.3%, import duty 7.2%; nontax revenue 45.4%, of which property income 33.8%, commercial receipts 10.9%). Expenditures: B$4,295,000,000 (current expenditure 65.5%; capital expenditure 34.5%).
Public debt (external, outstanding; 1999): U.S.$902,000,000.
Tourism (1998): receipts from visitors U.S.$37,000,000; expenditures by nationals abroad U.S.$1,000,000.
Production (metric tons except as noted). Agriculture, forestry, fishing (2002): vegetables and melons 9,800, fruits (excluding melons) 4,150, cassava 1,800, pineapples 900, bananas 640, rice 360; livestock (number of live animals) 7,000 buffalo, 6,500 pigs, 12,500 chickens; roundwood (2001) 228,550 cu m; fish catch (2000) 2,594. Mining and quarrying: other than petroleum and natural gas, none except sand and gravel for construction. Manufacturing (1998): gasoline 187,600; distillate fuel oils 147,800; kerosene 76,500. Energy production (consumption): electricity (kW-hr; 1999) 2,434,000,000 (2,434,000,000); coal, none (none); crude petroleum (barrels; 2001) 71,000,000 ([1999] 2,300,000); petroleum products (metric tons; 1999) 1,007,000 (1,011,000); natural gas (cu m; 2001) 11,000,000,000 (1,371,000,000).
Gross national product (at current market prices; 2001): U.S.$8,169,000,000 (U.S.$24,630 per capita).

Structure of gross domestic product and labour force

	2001		1995	
	in value B$'000,000	% of total value	labour force	% of labour force
Agriculture	210.0	2.6	1,976	1.7
Mining, Manufacturing	3,140.9	41.2	9,959[4]	8.8[4]
Construction	425.2	5.6	38,128	33.5
Public utilities	65.2	0.9	[4]	[4]
Transportation and communications	434.4	5.7	4,320	3.8
Trade	705.0	9.3	11,821	10.4
Finance	701.0	9.2	5,149	4.5
Services	2,138.7	28.1	42,333[5]	37.3[5]
Other	−201.2[6]	−2.6[6]	...	...
TOTAL	7,619.2	100.0	113,686	100.0

Population economically active (2001): total 145,600; activity rate of total population 43.9% (participation rates: ages 15–64, 65.9%; female 41.4%; unemployed [2002] 4.6%).

Price and earnings indexes (1998 = 100)

	1998	1999	2000	2001
Consumer price index	100.0	99.9	101.2	101.7
Earnings index	...	...	...	...

Household income and expenditure. Average household size (2000) 6.1; income per household: n.a.; sources of income: n.a.; expenditure (1990): food 38.7%, transportation and communications 19.9%, housing 18.6%, clothing 6.4%, other 16.4%.
Land use (1994): forested 85.4%; meadows and pastures 1.1%; agricultural and under permanent cultivation 1.3%; other 12.2%.

Foreign trade[7]

Balance of trade (current prices)

	1996	1997	1998	1999	2000	2001
B$'000,000	+153	+819	+856	+2,074	+4,826	+4,446
% of total	2.1%	11.5%	15.5%	31.5%	55.8%	51.7%

Imports (2001): B$2,076,000,000 (basic manufactures 30.7%, machinery and transport equipment 30.3%, food and live animals 16.4%, chemicals and chemical products 7.6%). *Major import sources:* Singapore 23.4%, Malaysia 22.0%; United States 9.2%; Japan 6.4%; Hong Kong 5.0%.
Exports (2001): B$6,522,000,000 ([1999] crude petroleum and partly refined petroleum 43.4%, natural gas 37.7%, petroleum products 2.2%). *Major export destinations* (2001): Japan 46.0%; South Korea 11.9%; Thailand 11.8%; Singapore 8.4%; United States 7.5%.

Transport and communications

Transport. Railroads[8]: length 12 mi, 19 km. Roads (1998): total length 1,256 mi, 2,021 km (paved 75%). Vehicles (2001): passenger cars 188,720; trucks and buses 17,828. Marine transport (1998): cargo loaded 25,900,000 metric tons, cargo unloaded 1,195,200 metric tons. Air transport (1998): passenger-mi 1,742,000,000, passenger-km 2,803,000,000; short ton-mi cargo 75,020,000, metric ton-km cargo 109,527,000; airports (2001) with scheduled flights 1.

Communications

Medium	date	unit	number	units per 1,000 persons
Daily newspapers	2001	circulation	70,500	213
Radio	2000	receivers	362,712	1,120
Television	2000	receivers	216,223	668
Telephones	2001	main lines	82,600	249
Cellular telephones	2001	subscribers	131,246	395
Personal computers	2001	units	25,000	75
Internet	2001	users	35,000	104

Education and health

Educational attainment (1991). Percentage of population age 25 and over having: no formal schooling 17.0%; primary education 43.3%; secondary 26.3%; postsecondary and higher 12.9%; not stated 0.5%. *Literacy* (2000): percentage of total population age 15 and over literate 91.5%; males literate 95.0%; females literate 88.0%.

Education (2001)

	schools	teachers	students	student/ teacher ratio
Primary (age 5–11)[9]	186	3,806	59,369	15.6
Secondary (age 12–20)	40	2,891	34,809	12.0
Voc., teacher tr.	6	505	2,509	5.0
Higher	3	403	3,885	9.6

Health (2000): physicians 309 (1 per 1,047 persons); hospital beds 926 (1 per 365 persons); infant mortality rate per 1,000 live births (2002) 14.0.
Food (2001): daily per capita caloric intake 2,814 (vegetable products 80%, animal products 20%); 120% of FAO recommended minimum requirement.

Military

Total active duty personnel (2002): 7,000 (army 70.0%, navy 14.3%, air force 15.7%). British troops (a Gurkha batallion): 1,100. *Military expenditure as percentage of GNP* (1999): 4.0% (world 2.4%); per capita expenditure U.S.$897.

[1]A nonelective 21-member body advises the sultan on legislative matters. [2]All official documents that must be published by law in Malay are also required to be issued in an official English version. [3]Urban agglomeration. [4]Mining and Manufacturing includes Public utilities. [5]Includes 38,068 government employees. [6]Less imputed bank service charge. [7]Imports c.i.f.; exports f.o.b. [8]Privately owned. [9]Includes preprimary.

Internet resources for further information:
- **Brunei Darussalam http://www.brunet.bn**
- **The Government of Brunei Darussalam http://www.brunei.gov.bn/index.htm**

Bulgaria

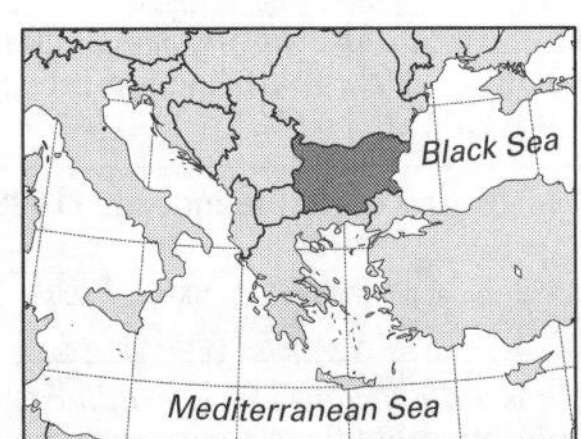

Official name: Republika Bŭlgaria (Republic of Bulgaria).
Form of government: unitary multiparty republic with one legislative body (National Assembly [240]).
Chief of state: President.
Head of government: Prime Minister.
Capital: Sofia.
Official language: Bulgarian.
Official religion: none[1].
Monetary unit: 1 lev (Lw; leva)[2] = 100 stotinki; valuation (Sept. 8, 2003) 1 U.S.$ = 1.76 (new) leva; 1 £ = 2.80 (new) leva.

Area and population

Districts	area sq km	population 2002[3] estimate	Districts	area sq km	population 2002[3] estimate
Blagoevgrad	6,452.3	339,790	Ruse	2,791.3	266,894
Burgas	7,747.9	422,458	Shumen	3,379.8	203,383
Dobrich	4,723.2	213,325	Silistra	2,847.0	140,784
Gabrovo	2,023.0	142,850	Sliven	3,544.1	217,226
Khaskovo	5,539.0	275,183	Smolyan	3,193.9	138,802
Kurdzhali	3,208.8	163,341	Sofiya[4]	7,059.0	270,459
Kyustendil	3,051.5	160,702	Sofiya-Grad[5]	1,344.4	1,178,579
Lovech	4,128.5	167,931	Stara Zagora	5,152.0	368,771
Montana	3,627.6	179,741	Targovishte	2,560.2	140,860
Pazardzhik	4,459.3	308,719	Varna	3,818.9	461,174
Pernik	2,392.8	148,251	Veliko Turnovo	4,662.6	291,121
Pleven	4,338.0	325,531	Vidin	3,033.4	128,050
Plovdiv	5,962.2	714,779	Vratsa	3,937.6	223,358
Razgrad	2,637.6	144,818	Yambol	3,355.5	154,215
			TOTAL	110,971.4	7,891,095

Demography

Population (2003): 7,786,000.
Density (2003): persons per sq mi 181.7, persons per sq km 70.2.
Urban-rural (2001): urban 69.4%; rural 30.6%.
Sex distribution (2002): male 48.68%; female 51.32%.
Age breakdown (2002)[3]: under 15, 15.0%; 15–29, 21.3%; 30–44, 20.4%; 45–59, 20.9%; 60–74, 16.1%; 75 and over, 6.3%.
Population projection: (2010) 7,229,000; (2020) 6,528,000.
Ethnic composition (2000): Bulgarian 79.8%; Turkish 9.6%; Roma (Gypsy) 5.4%; Macedonian 2.5%; Pomak 0.9%; other 1.8%.
Religious affiliation (1995): Bulgarian Orthodox 36.5%; Sunnī Muslim 13.1%; Protestant 1.4%; Roman Catholic 0.8%; other/nonreligious 48.2%.
Major cities (2001): Sofia 1,099,507; Plovdiv 340,122; Varna 313,408.

Vital statistics

Birth rate per 1,000 population (2001): 8.6 (world avg. 21.3).
Death rate per 1,000 population (2001): 14.2 (world avg. 9.1).
Natural increase rate per 1,000 population (2001): –5.6 (world avg. 12.2).
Total fertility rate (avg. births per childbearing woman; 2001): 1.2.
Life expectancy at birth (2001): male 68.5 years; female 75.2 years.
Major causes of death per 100,000 population (2001): diseases of the circulatory system 944.2; malignant neoplasms (cancers) 195.7; accidents, poisoning, and violence 55.1; diseases of the respiratory system 46.6.

National economy

Budget (2001). Revenue: 10,268,300,000 leva (tax revenue 74.8%, of which social insurance 24.3%, value-added tax 23.9%, income and profit tax 12.4%, excises 10.8%, customs and duties 1.9%, other 1.5%; nontax revenue 23.1%; grants 2.1%). Expenditures: 10,212,600,000 leva (social insurance 35.5%; administration and defense 13.4%; capital expenditure 10.7%; interest on debt 10.7%; health 9.6%; wages 7.6%; public safety 5.2%; education 4.5%).
Public debt (external, outstanding; 2001): U.S.$7,378,000,000.
Gross national product (2001): U.S.$13,200,000,000 (U.S.$1,650 per capita).

Structure of gross domestic product and labour force

	2001 in value '000,000 leva	% of total value	labour force	% of labour force
Agriculture, forestry, and fishing	3,578.6	12.1	774,100	21.5
Manufacturing, mining	4,951.5	16.7	627,300	17.5
Construction	1,162.3	3.9	127,000	3.5
Transp. and commun.	3,369.7	11.4	214,200	5.9
Trade	2,204.2	7.4	449,700	12.5
Public utilities, housing	1,323.4	4.5	58,600	1.6
Finance, real estate	789.6	2.7	166,100	4.6
Pub. admin., defense	12,233.8[6]	41.3[6]	96,900	2.7
Services			426,300	11.8
Other			662,300[7]	18.4[7]
TOTAL	29,613.1	100.0	3,602,500	100.0

Production (metric tons except as noted). Agriculture, forestry, fishing (2002): wheat 4,888,648, corn (maize) 1,206,000, barley 1,187,859, sunflower seeds 523,000, grapes 400,000, tomatoes 390,000; livestock (number of live animals) 2,418,490 sheep, 1,013,740 pigs, 898,559 goats, 634,540 cattle; roundwood (2001) 3,991,890 cu m; fish catch (2000) 10,652. Mining and quarrying (2000): iron (metal content) 178,000; copper (metal content) 107,000; gold 2,347 kg. Manufacturing (value of production in '000,000 [old] leva; 1998): refined petroleum products 1,466,259; food, beverages, and tobacco 1,391,751; machine and metalworking 1,368,609; metallurgy 1,074,263; basic chemicals 585,935. Construction (2001): residential 541,324 sq m; nonresidential 140,255. Energy production (consumption): electricity (kW-hr; 2001) 43,968,000,000 (43,968,000,000); hard coal (metric tons; 1999) 122,000 (3,211,000); lignite (metric tons; 1999) 26,176,000 (25,559,000); crude petroleum (barrels; 2000) 301,000 ([1999] 41,500,000); petroleum products (metric tons; 1999) 4,839,000 (3,555,000); natural gas (cu m; 1999) 28,200,000 (3,202,300,000).
Household income and expenditure. Average household size (2001) 3.0; income per household (2001) 4,532 leva (U.S.$2,280); sources of income: wages and salaries 37.8%, transfer payments 24.4%, self-employment in agriculture 14.2%, other 23.6%; expenditure (2001): food 42.7%, housing and energy 11.5%, transportation 5.0%, health 3.7%, clothing 3.4%, education and culture 3.1%, household durable goods 2.7%, other 27.9%.
Population economically active (2001): total 3,602,500; activity rate of total population 45.3% (participation rates: age 16–59 [male], 16–54 [female] 54.2%; female 46.4%; unemployed 18.4%).

Price and earnings indexes (1995 = 100)

	1996	1997	1998	1999	2000	2001	2002
Consumer price index	221.6	2,567.0	3,047.2	3,124.8	3,447.1	3,700.8	3,915.9
Monthly earnings index	174.4	1,864.4	...	...	...	...	...

Tourism (2001): receipts U.S.$1,201,000,000; expenditures U.S.$569,000,000.

Foreign trade[8]

Balance of trade (current prices)

	1997	1998	1999	2000	2001	2002
U.S.$'000,000	+380	–381	–1,081	–1,175	–1,576	–1,619
% of total	4.0%	4.3%	11.9%	10.9%	13.4%	12.7%

Imports (2001): U.S.$7,224,000,000 (crude petroleum and natural gas 17.2%; machinery and apparatus 12.9%; textiles 10.0%; transport equipment 8.2%; plastics and rubber 3.9%). *Major import sources:* Russia 19.9%; Germany 15.3%; Italy 9.6%; France 6.0%; Turkey 3.8%.
Exports (2001): U.S.$5,096,000,000 (clothing and footwear 20.0%; base and fabricated metals 15.2%, of which iron and steel 6.9%; mineral fuels 13.5%, of which petroleum products 8.9%; machinery and apparatus 6.0%). *Major export destinations:* Italy 15.0%; Germany 9.6%; Greece 8.8%; Turkey 8.1%; France 5.6%; Belgium 5.6%; U.S. 5.5%.

Transport and communications

Transport. Railroads (2001): track length 6,402 km; passenger-km 2,990,000,000; metric ton-km cargo 4,904,000,000. Roads (2001): length 37,296 km (paved 92%). Vehicles (2001): cars 2,085,730; trucks and buses 288,832. Merchant marine (2001): vessels (100 gross tons and over) 93; deadweight tonnage 1,701,398. Air transport (2001): passenger-mi 1,115,000,000, passenger-km 1,795,400,000; short ton-mi cargo 1,599,000, metric ton-km cargo 2,335,000; airports (2000) with scheduled flights 3.

Communications

Medium	date	unit	number	units per 1,000 persons
Daily newspapers	2000	circulation	2,060,000	257
Television	2000	receivers	3,600,000	449
Telephones	2002	main lines	2,922,000	375
Cellular telephones	2001	subscribers	1,550,000	191
Personal computers	2002	units	270,000	35
Internet	2001	users	605,000	75

Education and health

Educational attainment (1992). Percentage of population age 25 and over having: no formal schooling 4.7%; incomplete primary education 12.5%; primary 31.9%; secondary 35.7%; higher 15.0%. *Literacy* (1999): total population age 15 and over literate 98.3%; males 98.9%; females 97.7%.

Education (2001–02)

	schools	teachers	students	student/ teacher ratio
Primary (age 6–14) / Secondary (age 15–17)	2,812	63,261	839,518	13.3
Voc., teacher tr.	399	20,462	212,933	10.4
Higher	42	23,891	228,394	9.6

Health (2002): physicians 27,186 (1 per 290 persons); hospital beds 56,984 (1 per 138 persons); infant mortality rate per 1,000 live births (2001) 13.5.
Food (2001): daily per capita caloric intake 2,626 (vegetable products 73%, animal products 27%); 105% of FAO recommended minimum requirement.

Military

Total active duty personnel (2002): 68,450 (army 45.3%, navy 6.4%, air force 26.0%, other 22.3%). *Military expenditure as percentage of GNP* (1999): 3.0% (world 2.4%); per capita expenditure U.S.$158.

[1]Bulgaria has no official religion; the 1991 constitution, however, refers to Eastern Orthodoxy as the "traditional" religion. [2]The lev was re-denominated as of July 5, 1999; as of this date 1,000 (old) leva = 1 (new) lev. [3]January 1. [4]District nearly encircles Sofiya-Grad district on north, east, and south. [5]Sofiya-Grad includes Sofia city and immediately adjacent urban and rural areas. [6]Includes hotels, restaurants (usually included with Trade). [7]Unemployed. [8]Imports f.o.b. in balance of trade and c.i.f. for commodities and trading partners.

Internet resources for further information:

- **National Statistical Institute http://www.nsi.bg**
- **Bulgarian National Bank http://www.bnb.bg**

Burkina Faso

Official name: Burkina Faso (Burkina Faso).
Form of government: multiparty republic with one advisory body (Chamber of Representatives [178[1]]) and one legislative body (National Assembly [111]).
Chief of state: President.
Head of government: Prime Minister.
Capital: Ouagadougou.
Official language: French.
Official religion: none.
Monetary unit: 1 CFA franc (CFAF) = 100 centimes; valuation (Sept. 8, 2003) 1 U.S.$ = CFAF 594.70; 1 £ = CFAF 942.93[2].

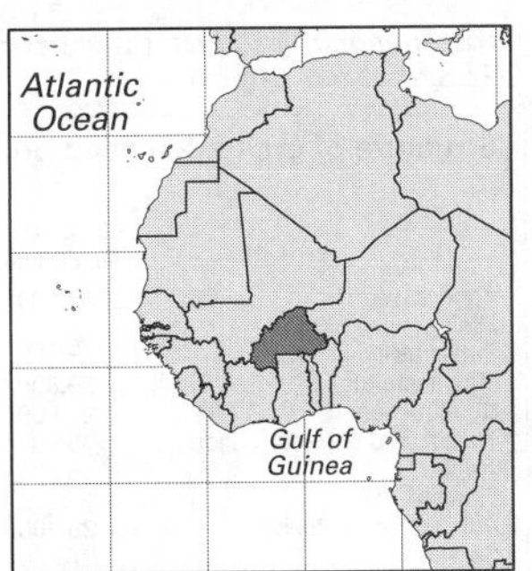

Population[3]

Provinces[4]	population	Provinces[4]	population	Provinces[4]	population
Balé	169,543	Komondjari	49,389	Passoré	271,216
Bam	212,295	Kompienga	73,949	Poni	196,568
Banwa	214,234	Kossi	217,866	Sanguié	249,169
Bazèga	214,450	Koulpélogo	188,760	Sanmatenga	460,684
Bougouriba	76,444	Kouritenga	250,699	Séno	202,972
Boulgou	415,414	Kourwéogo	117,370	Sissili	153,560
Boulkiemdé	421,083	Léraba	93,351	Soum	253,867
Comoé	240,942	Loroum	111,707	Sourou	189,726
Ganzourgou	257,707	Mouhoun	237,048	Tapoa	235,288
Gnagna	307,386	Nahouri	121,314	Tuy	160,249
Gourma	221,956	Namentenga	251,909	Yagha	116,985
Houet	674,916	Nayala	136,273	Yatenga	443,967
Ioba	159,422	Noumbiel	51,449	Ziro	117,774
Kadiogo	976,513	Oubritenga	198,130	Zondoma	127,580
Kénédougou	198,936	Oudalan	136,583	Zoundwéogo	196,698
				TOTAL	10,373,341

Demography

Area: 103,456 sq mi, 267,950 sq km.
Population (2003): 13,228,000.
Density (2003): persons per sq mi 127.9, persons per sq km 49.4.
Urban-rural (2002): urban 16.9%; rural 83.1%.
Sex distribution (2002): male 49.23%; female 50.77%.
Age breakdown (2002): under 15, 46.1%; 15–29, 27.4%; 30–44, 14.5%; 45–59, 7.5%; 60–74, 3.7%; 75 and over, 0.8%.
Population projection: (2010) 15,748,000; (2020) 19,965,000.
Ethnic composition (1995): Mossi 47.9%; Fulani 10.3%; Lobi 6.9%; Bobo 6.9%; Mande 6.7%; Senufo 5.3%; Grosi 5.0%; Gurma 4.8%; Tuareg 3.1%.
Religious affiliation (2000): Muslim 48.6%; traditional beliefs 34.1%; Christian 16.7%, of which Roman Catholic 9.5%.
Major cities (1996): Ouagadougou 709,736; Bobo-Dioulasso 309,771; Koudougou 72,490; Ouahigouya 52,193; Banfora 49,724.

Vital statistics

Birth rate per 1,000 population (2002): 45.1 (world avg. 21.3).
Death rate per 1,000 population (2002): 18.8 (world avg. 9.1).
Natural increase rate per 1,000 population (2002): 26.3 (world avg. 12.2).
Total fertility rate (avg. births per childbearing woman; 2002): 6.4.
Life expectancy at birth (2002): male 43.4 years; female 46.0 years.

National economy

Budget (2001). Revenue: CFAF 376,300,000,000 (tax revenue 56.7%, of which sales tax 29.7%, personal income taxes 14.9%, import duties 10.4%; grants 38.4%; nontax revenue 4.9%). Expenditures: CFAF 457,500,000,000 (investment expenditure 52.6%, wages and salaries 21.5%; transfers 11.3%; debt service 3.8%; other 10.8%).
Household income and expenditure. Average household size (2000) 6.0; average annual income per household (1985) CFAF 303,000 (U.S.$640); sources of income: n.a.; expenditure (1998)[5]: food 33.9%, transportation 15.6%, electricity and fuel 10.5%, clothing 6.4%, health 4.2%, education 3.4%.
Production (metric tons except as noted). Agriculture, forestry, fishing (2002): sorghum 1,373,300, millet 994,700, corn (maize) 653,100, sugarcane 420,000, seed cotton 400,000, peanuts (groundnuts) 323,600, shea nuts 110,500, rice 89,100, sesame 34,400; livestock (number of live animals) 9,450,000 goats, 7,411,000 sheep, 5,092,000 cattle, 23,000,000 chickens; roundwood (2001) 11,835,529 cu m; fish catch (2000) 8,505. Mining and quarrying (2002): gold 624 kg[6]. Manufacturing (2002): sugar 47,743; edible oils 19,636; flour 10,005; soap 9,923; beer 546,000 hectolitres; soft drinks 250,000 hectolitres; bicycles 20,849 units; mopeds 19,702 units; cigarettes 78,000,000 packets. Construction (value added in CFAF; 1995): 62,400,000,000. Energy production (consumption): electricity (kW-hr; 2002) 361,000,000 (361,000,000); crude petroleum (barrels; 1999) none (none); petroleum products (metric tons; 2001) none (294,000).
Population economically active (1996): total 5,075,615; activity rate 49.2% (participation rates: over age 10, 70.0%; female 48.2%; unemployed 1.4%).

Price and earnings indexes (1995 = 100)

	1996	1997	1998	1999	2000	2001	2002
Consumer price index	106.2	108.6	114.2	112.9	112.5	118.0	116.8
Earnings index	...	...	...	...	...	...	...

Gross national product (2001): U.S.$2,500,000,000 (U.S.$220 per capita).

Structure of gross domestic product and labour force

	2002		1996	
	in value CFAF '000,000	% of total value	labour force	% of labour force
Agriculture	692,600	31.8	4,513,868	88.9
Mining	274,600	12.6	3,979	0.1
Manufacturing			71,565	1.4
Construction	96,600	4.4	21,076	0.4
Public utilities	31,700	1.4	2,813	0.1
Transp. and commun.	84,000	3.9	20,580	0.4
Trade	306,800	14.1	224,581	4.4
Finance	...	...	13,131	0.3
Pub. admin., defense Services	671,900	30.8	103,926	2.0
Other	21,000[7]	1.0[7]	100,096[8]	2.0[8]
TOTAL	2,179,200	100.0	5,075,615	100.0

Public debt (external, outstanding; 2001): U.S.$1,310,000,000.
Tourism: receipts (2001) U.S.$34,000,000; expenditures (1994) U.S.$23,000,000.
Land use (1994): forest 50.5%; pasture 21.9%; agriculture 13.0%; other 14.6%.

Foreign trade

Balance of trade (current prices)

	1996	1997	1998	1999	2000	2001
CFAF '000,000,000	–168.9	–164.0	–183.8	–201.2	–222.4	–204.5
% of total	42.9%	38.0%	32.5%	39.2%	43.2%	37.7%

Imports (2001): CFAF 373,300,000,000 (capital equipment 30.9%, petroleum products 18.2%, food products 14.4%, raw materials 9.8%). *Major import sources* (2000): Côte d'Ivoire 22.7%; France 22.4%; other EC 20.0%; Japan 5.6%; China 4.1%.
Exports (2001): CFAF 168,800,000,000 (raw cotton 56.9%, live animals 11.4%, hides and skins 6.9%, shea nuts 2.7%, gold 2.1%). *Major export destinations* (2000): France 21.6%; Côte d'Ivoire 11.5%; Belgium-Luxembourg 8.4%; Italy 7.7%; Singapore 5.6%; Mali 5.0%.

Transport and communications

Transport. Railroads (1995)[9]: route length 386 mi, 622 km; passenger-km 202,000,000; metric ton-km cargo 45,000,000. Roads (1996): total length 7,519 mi, 12,100 km (paved 16%). Vehicles (1996): passenger cars 38,220; trucks and buses 17,980. Air transport (1998)[10]: passenger-km 264,000,000; metric ton-km cargo 39,000,000; airports (2000) 2.

Communications

Medium	date	unit	number	units per 1,000 persons
Daily newspapers	2000	circulation	12,200	1.0
Radio	2000	receivers	428,000	35
Television	2000	receivers	147,000	12
Telephones	2001	main lines	57,600	4.7
Cellular telephones	2001	subscribers	75,000	6.1
Personal computers	2001	units	17,000	1.4
Internet	2001	users	21,000	1.7

Education and health

Educational attainment (1985). Percentage of population age 10 and over having: no formal schooling 86.1%; some primary 7.3%; general secondary 2.2%; specialized secondary and postsecondary 3.8%; other 0.6%. *Literacy* (2000): percentage of total population age 15 and over literate 23.9%; males literate 33.9%; females literate 14.1%.

Education (1995–96)

	schools	teachers	students	student/ teacher ratio
Primary (age 7–12)	3,568	14,037	702,204	50.0
Secondary (age 13–19)	252	4,162	137,257	33.0
Vocational	41	731	9,539	13.0
Higher	9	632	9,531	15.1

Health (1995): physicians 361 (1 per 29,385 persons); hospital beds (1991) 5,041 (1 per 1,837 persons); infant mortality rate (2002) 100.9.
Food (2001): daily per capita caloric intake 2,485 (vegetable products 95%, animal products 5%); 105% of FAO recommended minimum requirement.

Military

Total active duty personnel (2002): 10,200 (army 98.0%, air force 2.0%). *Military expenditure as percentage of GNP* (1999): 1.6% (world 2.4%); per capita expenditure U.S.$4.

[1]All seats are appointed or indirectly elected. [2]Formerly pegged to the French franc and since Jan. 1, 2002, to the euro at the rate of €1 = CFAF 655.96. [3]As of October 1996 census. [4]Includes 15 provinces formally created in January 1997. [5]Weights of consumer price index components; Ouagadougou only. [6]Officially marketed gold only; does not include substantial illegal production. [7]Includes indirect taxes less imputed bank service charges and subsidies. [8]Includes 71,280 unemployed. [9]Passenger-km and metric ton-km cargo figures are based on traffic between Abidjan, Côte d'Ivoire, and Ouagadougou. [10]Air Afrique, an airline jointly owned by 11 African countries (including Burkina Faso), was declared bankrupt in February 2002.

Internet resources for further information:
- **Embassy of Burkina Faso http://www.burkinaembassy-usa.org**

Burundi

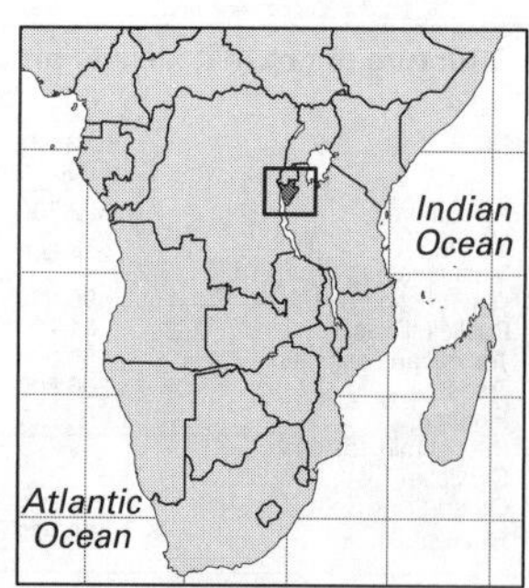

Official name: Republika y'u Burundi (Rundi); République du Burundi (French) (Republic of Burundi).
Form of government: transitional regime[1] with one legislative body (Transitional Assembly[2] [178]).
Head of state and government: President assisted by Vice President.
Capital: Bujumbura.
Official languages: Rundi; French.
Official religion: none.
Monetary unit: 1 Burundi franc (FBu) = 100 centimes; valuation (Sept. 8, 2003) 1 U.S.$ = FBu 1,075; 1 £ = FBu 1,704.

Area and population		area		population
				1990
Provinces	Capitals	sq mi	sq km	census
Bubanza	Bubanza	420	1,089	222,953
Bujumbura	Bujumbura	476[3]	1,232[3]	608,931[4]
Bururi	Bururi	952	2,465	385,490
Cankuzo	Cankuzo	759	1,965	142,707
Cibitoke	Cibitoke	631	1,636	279,843
Gitega	Gitega	764	1,979	565,174
Karuzi	Karuzi	563	1,457	287,905
Kayanza	Kayanza	476	1,233	443,116
Kirundo	Kirundo	658	1,703	401,103
Makamba	Makamba	757	1,960	223,799
Muramvya	Muramvya	269	696	441,653[5]
Muyinga	Muyinga	709	1,836	373,382
Mwaro	Mwaro	324	840	[5]
Ngozi	Ngozi	569	1,474	482,246
Rutana	Rutana	756	1,959	195,834
Ruyigi	Ruyigi	903	2,339	238,567
Urban Province				
Bujumbura	—	34	87	[4]
TOTAL LAND AREA		10,020	25,590	
INLAND WATER		721	1,867	
TOTAL		10,740[6]	27,816[6]	5,292,703

Demography

Population (2003): 6,096,000.
Density (2003)[7]: persons per sq mi 608.4, persons per sq km 238.2.
Urban-rural (2002): urban 9.3%; rural 90.7%.
Sex distribution (2002): male 49.57%; female 50.43%.
Age breakdown (2001): under 15, 46.7%; 15–29, 27.2%; 30–44, 14.5%; 45–59, 7.3%; 60–74, 3.2%; 75 and over, 1.1%.
Population projection: (2010) 7,296,000; (2020) 9,174,000.
Doubling time: 32 years.
Ethnic composition (1995): Rundi 98.0%, of which Hutu 82.5%, Tutsi 14.5%; Twa Pygmy 1.0%; other 1.0%.
Religious affiliation (1990): Roman Catholic 65.1%; Protestant 13.8%; Muslim 1.6%; nonreligious 18.6%; traditional beliefs 0.3%; other 0.6%.
Major cities (1990): Bujumbura (2001) 346,000; Gitega 101,827; Bururi 15,816; Ngozi 14,511; Cibitoke 8,280.

Vital statistics

Birth rate per 1,000 population (2002): 39.7 (world avg. 21.3).
Death rate per 1,000 population (2002): 17.8 (world avg. 9.1).
Natural increase rate per 1,000 population (2002): 21.9 (world avg. 12.2).
Total fertility rate (avg. births per childbearing woman; 2002): 6.0.
Life expectancy at birth (2002): male 42.5 years; female 43.9 years.
Major causes of death: n.a.; however, major health problems include malaria, influenza, diarrheal diseases, measles, and AIDS.

National economy

Budget (2000). Revenue: FBu 114,200,000,000 (tax revenue 82.0%, of which taxes on goods and services 41.0%, taxes on international trade 20.0%, income tax 17.5%; grants 13.9%; nontax revenue 4.1%). Expenditures: FBu 124,100,000,000 (current expenditure 74.9%, of which goods and services 30.1%, wages and salaries 27.3%, public debt 11.9%, subsidies and transfers 8.0%; capital expenditure 25.1%).
Production (metric tons except as noted). Agriculture, forestry, fishing (2002): bananas 1,548,897, sweet potatoes 780,839, cassavas 712,713, dry beans 248,914, sugarcane 200,000, corn (maize) 124,395, yams and taros 94,624, sorghum 70,000, rice 60,920, potatoes 27,319, coffee 13,020, tea 8,840; livestock (number of live animals) 750,000 goats, 315,000 cattle, 230,000 sheep, 4,300,000 chickens; roundwood (2001) 8,284,615 cu m; fish catch (2000) 10,055. Mining and quarrying (2001): gemstones 16,500 kg; gold 415 kg. Manufacturing (2000): beer 723,763 hectolitres; carbonated beverages 119,867 hectolitres; cottonseed oil 104,370 litres; cigarettes 286,240,000 units; blankets 141,854 units. Energy production (consumption): electricity (kW-hr; 2001) 107,774,000 (108,800,000); coal, none (none); crude petroleum, none (none); petroleum products (metric tons; 2001) none (48,093); natural gas, none (none); peat (metric tons; 1998) 12,000 (12,000).
Household income and expenditure. Average household size (2000) 5.1; income per household: n.a.; sources of income: n.a.; expenditure[8]: (1991) food 51.9%, energy and housing 27.0%, transportation 5.3%, clothing 5.3%, furniture 4.9%.
Land use (1994): forested 12.7%; meadows and pastures 38.6%; agricultural and under permanent cultivation 45.9%; other 2.8%.

Gross national product (at current market prices; 2000): U.S.$700,000,000 (U.S.$100 per capita).

Structure of gross domestic product and labour force	2000		1990	
	in value FBu '000,000	% of total value	labour force	% of labour force
Agriculture	184,000	36.0	2,574,443	93.1
Mining }	5,100	1.0	1,419	—
Public utilities }			1,672	0.1
Manufacturing	59,800	11.7	33,867	1.2
Construction	20,600	4.0	19,737	0.7
Transp. and communications	38,700	7.6	8,504	0.3
Trade	36,800	7.2	25,822	0.9
Finance	...	...	2,005	0.1
Pub. admin., defense	83,200	16.3 }	85,191	3.1
Services	27,200	5.3 }		
Other	55,600[9]	10.9[9]	13,270	0.5
TOTAL	511,000	100.0	2,765,945[6]	100.0

Public debt (external, outstanding; 2001): U.S.$974,000,000.
Population economically active (1997): total 3,475,000; activity rate of total population 63.1% (participation rates [1991]: ages 15–64, 91.4%; female 48.9%; unemployed, n.a.).

Price and earnings indexes (1995 = 100)	1996	1997	1998	1999	2000	2001	2002
Consumer price index	126.4	165.8	186.5	192.8	239.7	261.9	256.3
Earnings index	...	...	...	...	...	...	...

Tourism (2001): receipts from visitors U.S.$1,200,000; expenditures by nationals abroad U.S.$20,000,000.

Foreign trade[10]

Balance of trade (current prices)	1997	1998	1999	2000	2001	2002
FBu '000,000	–12,482	–41,639	–35,337	–70,836	–83,271	–92,161
% of total	16.9%	42.1%	36.3%	50.1%	56.6%	61.5%

Imports (2000): FBu 106,059,000,000 (consumption goods 33.6%, of which food and food products 9.0%; capital goods 24.6%; petroleum products 12.6%). *Major import sources* (2001): Belgium 15.5%; Saudi Arabia 10.9%; Tanzania 8.1%; France 7.8%; Kenya 6.7%; Japan 5.0%.
Exports (2000): FBu 35,223,000,000 (coffee 69.1%, tea 24.6%, manufactured products 4.9%). *Major export destinations* (2001): United Kingdom 31.0%; Belgium 10.5%; Germany 7.8%; The Netherlands 7.3%; Kenya 6.9%; Rwanda 5.7%.

Transport and communications

Transport. Railroads: none. Roads (1999): total length 8,997 mi, 14,480 km (paved 7%). Vehicles (1996): passenger cars 19,200; trucks and other vehicles 18,240. Air transport (2000)[11]: passenger arrivals and departures 58,402; cargo loaded and unloaded 3,905 metric tons; airports (2001) 1.

Communications				units
Medium	date	unit	number	per 1,000 persons
Daily newspapers	1996	circulation	20,000	3.2
Radio	2000	receivers	1,260,000	220
Television	2000	receivers	171,000	30
Telephones	2001	main lines	20,000	2.9
Cellular telephones	2001	subscribers	20,000	2.9
Internet	2001	users	6,000	0.9

Education and health

Educational attainment: n.a. *Literacy* (2000): percentage of total population age 15 and over literate 48.0%; males literate 56.2%; females literate 40.4%.

Education (1998)	schools	teachers	students	student/ teacher ratio
Primary (age 6–11)	1,512	12,107	557,344	46.0
Secondary (age 12–18) } Vocational and teacher training }	400	3,548	56,872	16.0
Higher	...	379	5,037	13.3

Health (1999): physicians 357 (1 per 15,695 persons); hospital beds 3,380 (1 per 1,657 persons); infant mortality rate per 1,000 live births (2002) 71.5.
Food (2001): daily per capita caloric intake 1,612 (vegetable products 98%, animal products 2%); 72% of FAO recommended minimum requirement.

Military

Total active duty personnel (2002): 45,000 (army 100%); South African peacekeeping troops (September 2003) 1,600[12]. *Military expenditure as percentage of GNP* (1999): 7.0% (world 2.4%); per capita expenditure U.S.$8.

[1]Transitional government following military coup of July 1996 was modified into a "new" transitional government between November 2001 and November 2004 per implementation of the Tutsi-Hutu agreement (Arusha Accords) on July 23, 2001. [2]"New" transitional body installed January 2002. [3]Unverified figure. [4]Bujumbura (province) includes Bujumbura urban province. [5]Muramvya includes Mwaro. [6]Detail does not add to total given because of rounding. [7]Based on land area. [8]Weights of consumer price index components. [9]Indirect taxes less subsidies. [10]Imports c.i.f.; exports f.o.b. [11]Figures for Bujumbura airport only. [12]Ceasefire of December 2002 was ineffective in September 2003.

Cambodia

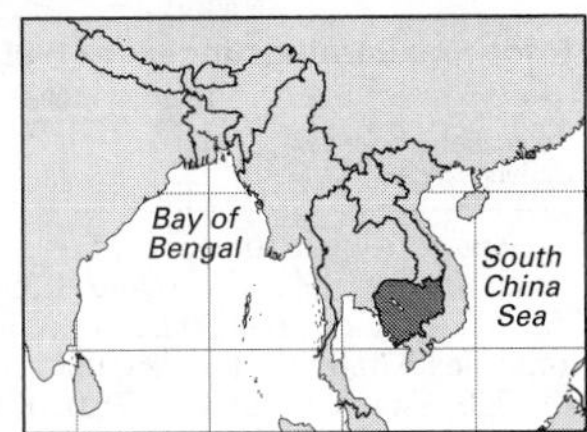

Official name: Preah Reach Ana Pak Kampuchea (Kingdom of Cambodia).
Form of government: constitutional monarchy with two legislative houses (Senate [61[1]]; National Assembly [122]).
Chief of state: King.
Head of government: Prime Minister[2].
Capital: Phnom Penh.
Official language: Khmer.
Official religion: Buddhism.
Monetary unit: 1 riel = 100 sen; valuation (Sept. 8, 2003) 1 U.S.$ = 3,835 riels; 1 £ = 6,081 riels.

Area and population

Provinces	Capitals	area sq mi	area sq km	population 1998 census
Banteay Mean Chey	...	2,579	6,679	577,772
Bat Dambang	Bat Dambang	4,518	11,702	793,129
Kampong Cham	Kampong Cham	3,783	9,799	1,608,914
Kampong Chhnang	Kampong Chhnang	2,132	5,521	417,693
Kampong Spueu	Kampong Spueu	2,709	7,017	598,882
Kampong Thum	Kampong Thum	5,334	13,814	569,060
Kampot	Kampot	1,881	4,873	528,405
Kandal	...	1,378	3,568	1,075,125
Kaoh Kong	Krong Kaoh Kong	4,309	11,160	132,106
Kracheh	Kracheh	4,283	11,094	263,175
Mondol Kiri	Senmonorom	5,517	14,288	32,407
Otdar Mean Cheay	...	2,378	6,158	68,279
Pousat	Pousat	4,900	12,692	360,445
Preah Vihear	Phum Tbeng Mean Cheay	5,324	13,788	119,261
Prey Veaeng	Prey Veaeng	1,885	4,883	946,042
Rotanak Kiri	Lumphat	4,163	10,782	94,243
Siem Reab	Siem Reab	3,976	10,299	696,164
Stueng Traeng	Stueng Traeng	4,283	11,092	81,074
Svay Rieng	Svay Rieng	1,145	2,966	478,252
Takaev	Takaev	1,376	3,563	790,168
Municipalities				
Kaeb	...	130	336	28,660
Pailin	...	310	803	22,906
Phnom Penh	...	112	290	999,804
Preah Sihanouk	...	335	868	155,690
TOTAL LAND AREA		68,740	178,035	
INLAND WATER		1,158	3,000	
TOTAL		69,898	181,035	11,437,656

Demography

Population (2003): 13,125,000.
Density (2003)[3]: persons per sq mi 190.9, persons per sq km 73.7.
Urban-rural (2002): urban 17.0%; rural 83.0%.
Sex distribution (2002): male 48.41%; female 51.59%.
Age breakdown (2002): under 15, 39.3%; 15–29, 28.8%; 30–44, 18.5%; 45–59, 8.8%; 60–74, 3.7%; 75 and over, 0.9%.
Population projection: (2010) 14,902,000; (2020) 17,863,000.
Ethnic composition (1994): Khmer 88.6%; Vietnamese 5.5%; Chinese 3.1%; Cham 2.3%; other (Thai, Lao, and Kola) 0.5%.
Religious affiliation (2000): Buddhist 84.7%; Chinese folk religionist 4.7%; traditional beliefs 4.3%; Muslim 2.3%; Christian 1.1%; other 2.9%.
Major urban areas (1998): Phnom Penh (2001) 1,109,000; Bat Dambang 124,290; Sisophon 85,382; Siem Reab 83,715; Preah Sihanouk 66,723.

Vital statistics

Birth rate per 1,000 population (2002): 35.2 (world avg. 21.3).
Death rate per 1,000 population (2002): 10.6 (world avg. 9.1).
Natural increase rate per 1,000 population (2002): 24.6 (world avg. 12.2).
Total fertility rate (avg. births per childbearing woman; 2002): 4.9.
Life expectancy at birth (2002): male 54.0 years; female 59.0 years.
Major causes of death per 100,000 population: n.a.; however, major health problems include tuberculosis, malaria, and pneumonia. Violence, acts of war, and military ordnance (especially unexploded mines) remain hazards.

National economy

Budget (2001). Revenue: 1,520,000,000,000 riels (indirect taxes 37.6%, of which value-added taxes 26.5%; taxes on international trade 24.7%; nontax revenue 27.9%). Expenditures: 2,329,000,000,000 riels (current expenditure 58.1%, of which civil administration 30.2%, defense and security 16.7%; development expenditure 41.9%).
Public debt (external, outstanding; 2001): U.S.$2,401,000,000.
Production (metric tons except as noted). Agriculture, forestry, fishing (2002): rice 3,740,002, cassava 186,800, corn (maize) 168,700, sugarcane 168,650, bananas 146,000, coconuts 70,000, oranges 63,000, mangoes 35,000, rubber 32,365, soybeans 21,250, tobacco leaves 4,692; livestock (number of live animals) 2,924,457 cattle, 2,105,435 pigs, 625,912 buffalo; roundwood (2001) 10,045,319 cu m; fish catch (2000) 298,798. Mining and quarrying: legal mining is confined to fertilizers, salt, and construction materials. Manufacturing (value added in '000,000 riels; 1995): glass and glass products 42,659; wearing apparel 37,567; rubber products 30,114; processed meat, fish, fruits, and vegetables 24,521; sawmilling and planing of wood 18,099; tobacco products 10,163. Energy production (consumption): electricity (kW-hr; 1999) 222,000,000 (222,000,000); petroleum products (metric tons; 1999) negligible (171,000); crude petroleum (barrels; 1999) none (none).
Household income and expenditure. Average household size (2000) 5.7.

Gross national product (2001): U.S.$3,300,000,000 (U.S.$270 per capita).

Structure of gross domestic product and labour force

	2001 in value '000,000,000 riels	2001 % of total value	2000 labour force[4]	2000 % of labour force[4]
Agriculture	4,930.0	36.9	3,889,048	73.7
Mining	23.8	0.2	3,328	0.1
Manufacturing	2,100.6	15.7	367,286	7.0
Construction	742.9	5.6	69,773	1.3
Public utilities	56.8	0.4	3,799	0.1
Transp. and commun.	940.9	7.0	119,596	2.3
Trade	1,867.0	14.0	455,102	8.6
Finance	990.5	7.4	16,636	0.3
Public admin., defense	369.4	2.8	146,986	2.8
Services	551.1	4.1	203,623	3.9
Other	791.9[5]	5.9[5]	—	—
TOTAL	13,364.9	100.0	5,275,177	100.0[6]

Population economically active (2000)[4]: total 5,275,177; activity rate of total population 45.4% (participation rates: ages 15 and over, 69.9%; female 54.6%; unemployed 5.3%).

Price and earnings indexes (1995 = 100)

	1995	1996	1997	1998	1999	2000	2001
Consumer price index	100.0	110.1	113.6	130.4	135.6	134.5	133.7
Earnings index	...	...	...	...	...	...	...

Tourism (2001): receipts U.S.$304,000,000; expenditures U.S.$35,000,000.
Land use (1994): forested 69.1%; meadows and pastures 8.5%; agricultural and under permanent cultivation 21.7%; other 0.7%.

Foreign trade

Balance of trade (current prices)

	1997	1998	1999	2000	2001
U.S.$'000,000	–264	–264	–292	–452	–476
% of total	14.4%	13.2%	11.7%	14.0%	13.9%

Imports (2001): U.S.$1,951,000,000 (retained imports 91.1%; imports for reexport 8.9%). *Major import sources:* Thailand *c.* 35%; Singapore *c.* 27%; Vietnam *c.* 8%; Hong Kong *c.* 8%; China *c.* 6%.
Exports (2001): U.S.$1,475,000,000 (domestic exports 87.8%, of which garments *c.* 75%, rubber 3.4%[7], sawn timber and logs 2.2%[7]; reexports 12.2%). *Major export destinations:* U.S. *c.* 64%; U.K. *c.* 10%; Germany *c.* 8%.

Transport and communications

Transport. Railroads (1998): length (1999) 403 mi, 649 km; passenger-km 49,894,000; metric ton-km 75,700,000. Roads (1999): total length 22,226 mi, 35,769 km (paved 12%). Vehicles (2001): passenger cars 312,303; trucks and buses 67,954. Air transport (1997): airports with scheduled flights 8.

Communications

Medium	date	unit	number	units per 1,000 persons
Daily newspapers	2000	circulation	24,000	2.0
Radio	2000	receivers	1,480,000	119
Television	2000	receivers	99,500	8.0
Telephones	2001	main lines	33,500	2.5
Cellular telephones	2001	subscribers	223,500	17
Personal computers	2001	units	20,000	1.5
Internet	2001	users	10,000	0.7

Education and health

Educational attainment (1998). Percentage of population age 25 and over having: no formal schooling 2.1%; some primary education 56.6%; primary 24.7%; some secondary 11.8%; secondary and above 4.8%. *Literacy* (2000): percentage of total population age 15 and over literate 68.5%; males literate 79.8%; females literate 57.1%.

Education (2001–02)

	schools	teachers	students	student/ teacher ratio
Primary (age 6–10)	5,471	54,519	2,705,453	49.6
Secondary (age 11–16)	542	24,884	465,039	18.7
Voc., teacher tr.[8]	...	2,315	9,983	4.3
Higher[8]	...	1,001	8,901	8.9

Health: physicians (2001) 2,047 (1 per 5,862 persons); hospital beds 10,900 (1 per 1,100 persons); infant mortality rate (2002) 74.0.
Food (2001): daily per capita caloric intake 1,967 (vegetable products 91%, animal products 9%); 89% of FAO recommended minimum requirement.

Military

Total active duty personnel (2001)[9]: 125,000 (army 60.0%, navy 2.4%, air force 1.6%, provincial 36.0%). *Military expenditure as percentage of GNP* (1999): 4.0% (world 2.4%); per capita expenditure U.S.$28.

[1]All seats appointed in 1999; all seats to be elected in future. [2]A single prime minister was head of government from November 1998 per the king's forced moral persuasion. [3]Based on land area. [4]Employed only. [5]Indirect taxes less imputed bank service charge. [6]Detail does not add to total given because of rounding. [7]Includes estimates for illegal exports. [8]1997–98. [9]Figures include provincial forces and exclude paramilitary forces.

Internet resources for further information:

- **National Institute of Statistics http://www.nis.gov.kh**

Cameroon

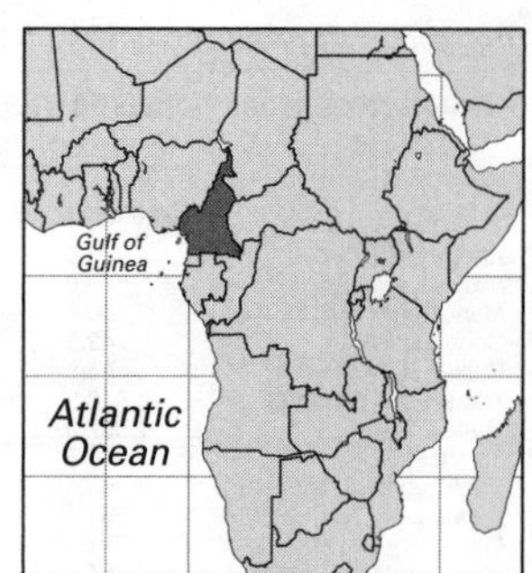

Official name: République du Cameroun (French); Republic of Cameroon (English).
Form of government: unitary multiparty republic with one legislative house (National Assembly [180]).
Chief of state: President.
Head of government: Prime Minister.
Capital: Yaoundé.
Official languages: French; English.
Official religion: none.
Monetary unit: 1 CFA franc (CFAF) = 100 centimes; valuation (Sept. 8, 2003) 1 U.S.$ = CFAF 594.70; 1 £ = CFAF 942.93[1].

Area and population

Regions	Capitals	area sq mi	area sq km	population 1987 census
Adamoua	Ngaoundéré	24,591	63,691	495,200
Centre	Yaoundé	26,613	68,926	1,651,600
Est	Bertoua	42,089	109,011	517,200
Extrême-Nord	Maroua	13,223	34,246	1,855,700
Littoral	Douala	7,814	20,239	1,354,800
Nord	Garoua	25,319	65,576	832,200
Nord-Ouest	Bamenda	6,877	17,810	1,237,400
Ouest	Bafoussam	5,356	13,872	1,339,800
Sud	Ebolowa	18,189	47,110	373,800
Sud-Ouest	Buea	9,448	24,471	838,000
LAND AREA		179,519	464,952	
INLAND WATER		4,051	10,492	
TOTAL		183,569[2]	475,442[2]	10,495,700

Demography

Population (2003): 15,746,000.
Density (2003)[3]: persons per sq mi 87.7, persons per sq km 33.9.
Urban-rural (2002): urban 49.7%; rural 50.3%.
Sex distribution (2002): male 50.27%; female 49.73%.
Age breakdown (2002): under 15, 42.6%; 15–29, 28.8%; 30–44, 15.2%; 45–59, 8.4%; 60–74, 4.0%; 75 and over, 1.0%.
Population projection: (2010) 17,938,000; (2020) 20,946,000.
Doubling time: 34 years.
Ethnic composition (1983): Fang 19.6%; Bamileke and Bamum 18.5%; Duala, Luanda, and Basa 14.7%; Fulani 9.6%; Tikar 7.4%; Mandara 5.7%; Maka 4.9%; Chamba 2.4%; Mbum 1.3%; Hausa 1.2%; French 0.2%; other 14.5%.
Religious affiliation (2000): Roman Catholic 26.4%; traditional beliefs 23.7%; Muslim 21.2%; Protestant 20.7%.
Major cities (1999): Douala 1,448,300; Yaoundé 1,372,800; Garoua (1992) 160,000; Maroua (1992) 140,000; Bafoussam (1992) 120,000.

Vital statistics

Birth rate per 1,000 population (2002): 35.9 (world avg. 21.3).
Death rate per 1,000 population (2002): 15.3 (world avg. 9.1).
Natural increase rate per 1,000 population (2002): 20.6 (world avg. 12.2).
Total fertility rate (avg. births per childbearing woman; 2002): 4.7.
Life expectancy at birth (2002): male 47.2 years; female 49.1 years.
Major causes of death per 100,000 population: n.a.; however, major health problems include measles, malaria, tuberculosis of respiratory system, anemias, meningitis, and intestinal obstruction and hernia.

National economy

Budget (2000–01). Revenue: CFAF 1,326,000,000,000 (oil revenue 33.0%; taxes on goods and services 32.9%; income tax 16.6%; customs duties 11.2%). Expenditures: CFAF 1,175,000,000,000 (current expenditure 80.9%, of which wages and salaries 28.8%, debt service 20.9%, goods and services 20.0%, transfers 11.3%; capital expenditure 19.1%).
Public debt (external, outstanding; 2001): U.S.$6,313,000,000.
Gross national product (2001): U.S.$8,700,000,000 (U.S.$580 per capita).

Structure of gross domestic product and labour force

	2000–01 in value CFAF '000,000,000	2000–01 % of total value	1985 labour force	1985 % of labour force
Agriculture	2,699	42.7	2,900,871	74.0
Mining	246	3.9	1,793	0.1
Manufacturing	669	10.6	174,498	4.5
Construction	229	3.6	66,684	1.7
Public utilities	95	1.5	3,522	0.1
Transp. and commun.			51,688	1.3
Trade			154,014	3.9
Finance	2,205	34.9	8,009	0.2
Services				
Public admin., defense			292,922	7.5
Other	177[4]	2.8[4]	263,634	6.7
TOTAL	6,320	100.0	3,917,635	100.0

Household income and expenditure. Average household size (2000) 5.5; average annual income per household: n.a.; sources of income: n.a.; expenditure (1993)[5]: food 49.1%, housing 18.0%, transportation and communications 13.0%, health 8.6%, clothing 7.6%, recreation 2.4%.
Population economically active (1991): total 4,740,000; activity rate of total population 40.0% (participation rates [1985]: ages 15–69, 66.3%; female 38.5%; unemployed, n.a.).

Price and earnings indexes (1995 = 100)

	1995	1996	1997	1998	1999	2000	2001
Consumer price index	100.0	103.9	108.9	112.4	114.4	115.8	116.8
Earnings index	...	...	...	...	...	...	...

Production (metric tons except as noted). Agriculture, forestry, fishing (2002): cassava 1,900,000, sugarcane 1,350,000, plantains 1,200,000, corn (maize) 750,000, bananas 630,000, sorghum 450,000, vegetables and melons 450,000, tomatoes 370,000, yams 260,000, seed cotton 200,000, peanuts (groundnuts) 200,000, sweet potatoes 175,000, palm oil 150,000, cacao 125,000, coffee 78,000, millet 71,000, rice 62,000, natural rubber 55,000, avocados 52,000; livestock (number of live animals) 5,900,000 cattle, 4,400,000 goats, 3,800,000 sheep, 1,350,000 pigs; roundwood (2001) 10,991,669 cu m; fish catch (2000) 112,159. Mining and quarrying (2002): pozzolana 620,000; aluminum 80,000; gold 1,000 kg. Manufacturing (value added in CFAF '000,000; 1998): wood and wood products 75,261; beverages 71,233; food 61,353; rubber and plastic products 33,467; nonferrous metals 26,987; chemicals 23,966; refined petroleum products 16,394; paper products 14,292; tobacco products 13,064; electrical machinery 7,459; transport equipment 5,471. Energy production (consumption): electricity (kW-hr; 2000) 2,719,000,000 (2,719,000,000); coal (metric tons; 1999) 1,000 (1,000); crude petroleum (barrels; 1999) 49,400,000 (10,700,000); petroleum products (metric tons; 1999) 1,332,000 (1,345,000); natural gas, none (none).
Land use (1994): forested 77.1%; meadows and pastures 4.3%; agricultural and under permanent cultivation 15.1%; other 3.5%.
Tourism (2000): receipts U.S.$39,000,000; expenditures (1995) U.S.$105,-000,000.

Foreign trade

Balance of trade (current prices)

	1996–97	1997–98	1998–99	1999–2000	2000–01	2001–02
CFAF '000,000,000	+380.5	+295.8	+205.8	+460.5	+382.4	+159.5
% of total	21.3%	13.9%	11.0%	20.3%	14.2%	7.1%

Imports (2000–01): CFAF 1,157,800,000,000 (minerals and other raw materials *c.* 21%, semifinished goods *c.* 16%, industrial equipment *c.* 13%, food and beverages *c.* 11%, transport equipment *c.* 10%). *Major import sources:* France *c.* 24%; Nigeria *c.* 20%; Germany *c.* 5%; U.S. *c.* 5%; Japan *c.* 5%; Belgium-Luxembourg *c.* 5%.
Exports (2000–01): CFAF 1,540,200,000,000 (crude petroleum 50.6%, lumber 13.4%, cocoa beans 6.3%, aluminum 4.6%, cotton 4.2%, coffee 3.7%). *Major export destinations:* Italy *c.* 24%; France *c.* 9%; Spain *c.* 9%; The Netherlands *c.* 7%; China *c.* 7%; Taiwan *c.* 7%.

Transport and communications

Transport. Railroads (2001): route length 631 mi, 1,016 km; passenger-mi 147,800,000, passenger-km 237,800,000; short ton-mi cargo 585,000,000, metric ton-km cargo 854,600,000. Roads (1999): total length 30,630 mi, 49,300 km (paved 8%). Vehicles (1997): passenger cars 98,000; trucks and buses 64,350. Merchant marine (1992): vessels (100 gross tons and over) 47; total deadweight tonnage 39,797. Air transport (2001): passenger-mi 494,960,000; passenger-km 796,567,000; short ton-mi cargo 15,928,000, metric ton-km cargo 23,255,000; airports (1998) with scheduled flights 5.

Communications

Medium	date	unit	number	units per 1,000 persons
Daily newspapers	2000	circulation	104,000	7.0
Radio	2000	receivers	2,410,000	163
Television	2000	receivers	503,000	34
Telephones	2001	main lines	101,400	6.7
Cellular telephones	2002	subscribers	563,000	36
Personal computers	2001	units	60,000	3.9
Internet	2001	users	45,000	3.0

Education and health

Educational attainment: n.a. *Literacy* (2000): percentage of total population age 15 and over literate 75.8%; males literate 82.4%; females literate 69.5%.

Education (1998)

	schools	teachers	students	student/ teacher ratio
Primary (age 6–14)	9,459	41,142	2,133,707	51.9
Secondary (age 15–24)	700[6]	19,515	341,439	17.5
Vocational	324[6]	7,245[6]	122,122	...
Higher[7]	6	2,645	66,902	25.3

Health: physicians (1996) 1,031 (1 per 13,510 persons); hospital beds (1988) 29,285 (1 per 371 persons); infant mortality rate (2002) 71.0.
Food (2001): daily per capita caloric intake 2,242 (vegetable products 94%, animal products 6%); 97% of FAO recommended minimum requirement.

Military

Total active duty personnel (2002): 14,100 (army 88.7%, navy 9.2%, air force 2.1%). *Military expenditure as percentage of GNP* (1999): 1.8% (world 2.4%); per capita expenditure U.S.$10.

[1]Formerly pegged to the French franc and since Jan. 1, 2002, to the euro at the rate of 1 € = CFAF 655.96. [2]Detail does not add to total given because of rounding. [3]Based on land area. [4]Indirect taxes. [5]Weights of consumer price index components. [6]1995–96. [7]1990–91.

Internet resources for further information:
- **Investir en Zone Franc http://www.izf.net/izf/Index.htm**

Canada

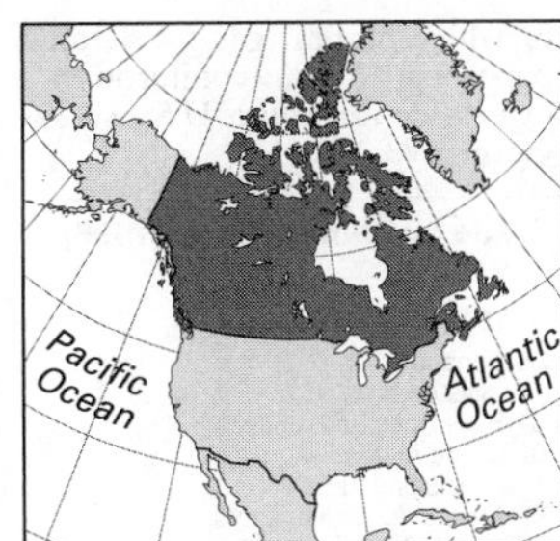

Official name: Canada.
Form of government: federal multiparty parliamentary state with two legislative houses (Senate [105]; House of Commons [301]).
Chief of state: Queen of Canada (British Monarch).
Representative of chief of state: Governor-General.
Head of government: Prime Minister.
Capital: Ottawa.
Official languages: English; French.
Official religion: none.
Monetary unit: 1 Canadian dollar (Can$) = 100 cents; valuation (Sept. 8, 2003) 1 U.S.$ = Can$1.37; 1 £ = Can$2.18

Area and population

Provinces	Capitals	area sq mi	area sq km	population 2002 estimate[1]
Alberta	Edmonton	255,541	661,848	3,113,600
British Columbia	Victoria	364,764	944,735	4,141,300
Manitoba	Winnipeg	250,116	647,797	1,150,800
New Brunswick	Fredericton	28,150	72,908	756,700
Newfoundland and Labrador	St. John's	156,453	405,212	531,600
Nova Scotia	Halifax	21,345	55,284	944,800
Ontario	Toronto	415,599	1,076,395	12,068,300
Prince Edward Island	Charlottetown	2,185	5,660	139,900
Quebec	Quebec	595,391	1,542,056	7,455,200
Saskatchewan	Regina	251,367	651,036	1,011,800
Territories				
Northwest Territories	Yellowknife	519,735	1,346,106	41,400
Nunavut[2]	Iqaluit	808,185	2,093,190	28,700
Yukon Territory	Whitehorse	186,272	482,443	29,900
TOTAL		3,855,103	9,984,670	31,414,000

Demography

Population (2003): 31,590,000.
Density (2003)[3]: persons per sq mi 8.9, persons per sq km 3.5.
Urban-rural (2001): urban 78.9%; rural 21.1%.
Sex distribution (2002): male 49.51%; female 50.49%.
Age breakdown (2002): under 15, 18.5%; 15–29, 20.3%; 30–44, 24.1%; 45–59, 20.2%; 60–74, 11.2%; 75 and over, 5.7%.
Population projection: (2010) 33,174,000; (2020) 35,277,000.
Ethnic origin (2000): Anglo-Canadian 45.5%; French-Canadian 23.5%; Chinese 3.4%; British expatriates 3.3%; Indo-Pakistani 2.6%, of which Punjabi 2.3%; German 2.4%; Italian 2.2%; U.S. white 1.8%; Métis (part-Indian) 1.8%; Indian 1.5%, of which detribalized 0.5%; Jewish 1.4%; Arab 1.3%; Ukrainian 1.2%; Eskimo (Inuit) 0.1%; other 8.0%.
Religious affiliation (2001): Christian 77.1%, of which Roman Catholic 43.2%, Protestant 28.3%, unspecified Christian 2.6%, Orthodox 1.7%, other Christian 1.3%; Muslim 2.0%; Jewish 1.1%; Hindu 1.0%; Buddhist 1.0%; Sikh 0.9%; nonreligious 16.5%; other 0.4%.
Major metropolitan areas (2002): Toronto 5,029,900; Montreal 3,548,800; Vancouver 2,122,700; Ottawa-Hull 1,128,900; Calgary 993,200; Edmonton 967,200; Quebec 697,800; Hamilton 686,900; Winnipeg 685,500; Kitchener 438,000.

Other metropolitan areas (2002)

	population		population		population
Chicoutimi-Jonquière	156,900	Regina	197,000	Sherbrooke	156,500
Halifax	363,200	St. Catharines–Niagara	392,300	Sudbury	155,900
London	427,300	St. John's	177,200	Trois Rivières	141,400
Oshawa	310,000	Saskatoon	231,800	Victoria	318,900
				Windsor	319,900

Place of birth (2001): 81.6% native-born; 18.4% foreign-born, of which U.K. 2.0%, other European 5.7%, Asian countries 5.8%, U.S. 0.8%, other 4.1%.
Mobility (2001). Population living in the same residence as in 1996: 58.1%; different residence, same municipality 22.4%; same province, different municipality 3.3%; different province 12.7%; different country 3.5%.
Households (2001). Total number of households 11,562,975. Average household size 2.6; (1997) 1 person 25.2%, 2 persons 33.0%, 3 persons 16.7%, 4 persons 16.3%, 5 or more persons 8.8%. Family households (2001): 8,371,020 (72.4%), nonfamily 3,191,955 (27.6%, of which 1 person 75.6%).
Immigration (2002): permanent immigrants admitted 222,447; (2000) from Asia 62.1%, of which India 11.6%, Philippines 5.6%, Vietnam 0.7%, Hong Kong 0.3%; United States 2.4%; United Kingdom 2.1%; refugee arrivals (2002) 27,899.

Vital statistics

Birth rate per 1,000 population (2002): 10.4 (world avg. 21.3); (1997) legitimate 72.3%; illegitimate 27.7%.
Death rate per 1,000 population (2002): 7.4 (world avg. 9.1).
Natural increase rate per 1,000 population (2002): 3.0 (world avg. 12.2).
Total fertility rate (avg. births per childbearing woman; 2002): 1.6.
Marriage rate per 1,000 population (2002): 4.9.
Divorce rate per 1,000 population (2002): 2.2.
Life expectancy at birth (2002): male 76.1 years; female 81.5 years.
Major causes of death per 100,000 population (1998): diseases of the circulatory system 214.8; malignant neoplasms (cancers) 183.5; diseases of the respiratory system 55.7; accidents and violence 29.0 (including suicide 12.0).

Social indicators

Educational attainment (2001). Percentage of population age 15 and over having: incomplete primary education 2.2%; complete primary education 7.6%; some secondary and complete secondary 49.5%; postsecondary 25.3%; university degree 15.4%.

Distribution of income (1996)

percentage of household income by quintile

1	2	3	4	5 (highest)
6.1%	11.9%	17.4%	24.0%	40.6%

Quality of working life. Average workweek (2000): 31.6 hours. Annual rate per 100,000 workers for (1997): injury, accident, or industrial illness 1,330; death 2.7. Average days lost to labour stoppages per 1,000 employee-workdays (2001): 0.7. Average duration of journey to work (2001): n.a.; mode of transportation: automobile 80.7%, public transportation 10.5%, walking 6.6%, other 2.2%. Labour force covered by a pension plan (2000): 33.8%.
Access to services. Proportion of households having access to: electricity (2002) 100.0%; public water supply (1996) 99.8%; public sewage collection (1996) 99.3%.
Social participation. Eligible voters participating in last national election (November 2000): 61.2%. Population over 18 years of age participating in voluntary work (2000): 26.7%. Union membership in total workforce (1999): 32.9%. Attendance at religious services on a weekly basis (2001): 20.0%.
Social deviance (2000). Offense rate per 100,000 population for: violent crime 981, of which assault 758.9, sexual assault 78.2, homicide 1.6; property crime 4,067, of which auto theft 521, burglary 954.
Leisure (1998). Favourite leisure activities (hours weekly): television (2001) 21.2; social time 13.3; reading 2.8; sports and entertainment 1.4.
Material well-being (1999). Households possessing: automobile 64.4%; telephone 98.2%; cellular phone 31.9%; colour television 99.9%; refrigerator 99.6%; central air conditioner 34.0%; cable television 73.3%; video recorder 88.6%; microwave oven 89.4%; home computers 49.8%; Internet access 33.1%.

National economy

Gross national product (2001): U.S.$681,600,000,000 (U.S.$21,930 per capita).

Structure of gross domestic product and labour force

	2002 in value Can$'000,000[4]	% of total value	labour force	% of labour force
Agriculture	19,822	2.0	602,000	3.6
Mining	36,517	3.7		
Manufacturing	164,765	16.9	2,326,200	13.9
Construction	51,156	5.2	882,800	5.3
Public utilities	27,851	2.9	131,500	0.7
Transportation	44,674	4.6	756,200	4.5
Trade	113,759	11.6	2,430,000	14.6
Finance	195,246	20.0	895,600	5.4
Pub. admin., defense	55,172	5.6	778,000	4.7
Services[5]	268,263	27.5	6,609,500	39.6
Other	—	—	1,277,600[6]	7.7[6]
TOTAL	977,225[7]	100.0	16,689,400	100.0

Budget (2001). Revenue: Can$227,436,000,000 (tax revenue 91.4%, of which individual income taxes 39.4%, contributions to social security 21.1%, value-added tax 12.5%, corporate income tax 11.0%, import duties 1.3%; nontax revenue 8.6%). Expenditures: Can$212,611,000,000 (social services and welfare 46.4%, public debt interest 13.3%, defense and social protection 9.4%, education 2.2%, health 1.0%).
National debt (2001): Can$629,090,000,000.
Tourism (2001): receipts U.S.$10,774,000,000; expenditures U.S.$11,624,000,000.

Manufacturing, mining, and construction enterprises (2000)

	no. of establishments[8]	no. of employees	weekly wages as a % of avg. of all wages[9]	annual value added (Can$'000,000)[10]
Manufacturing				
Transport equipment	1,224	255,500	148.4	27,656
Food and beverages	3,202	239,500	100.2	21,577[11]
Chemicals and related products	1,396	95,700	147.5	14,884
Electrical and electronic products	1,176	139,700	140.1	13,264
Metal fabricating	3,287	191,500	123.2	11,418
Primary metals	417	87,300	153.9	11,171
Wood products (excl. furniture)	2,201	150,700	111.9	11,163
Paper and related products	651	105,400	154.4	11,132
Nonelectrical machinery	4,000	95,700	145.9	9,756
Rubber and plastic products	1,394	98,700	111.3	9,271
Furniture and fixtures	1,965	67,300	99.7	4,928
Nonmetallic mineral products	1,519	54,300	121.5	4,362
Printing, publishing, and related products	4,655	157,100	109.6	4,184
Wearing apparel	1,923	93,200	72.6	2,799
Textiles	1,057	54,700	101.9	2,048
Petroleum and coal products	170	15,400	186.1	1,815
Tobacco products industries	17	4,400	201.3	[11]
Mining	13,692	140,900	180.5	36,517
Construction	203,253	557,700	115.4	51,117

Production (metric tons except as noted). Agriculture, forestry, fishing (2002): wheat 15,689,000, corn (maize) 9,069,000, barley 7,282,600, potatoes 4,645,000, rapeseed 3,577,100, oats 2,748,000, vegetables 2,435,000 (of which tomatoes

690,000, carrots 280,000, onions 190,000, cabbage 160,000), soybeans 2,334,000, dry peas 1,365,000, linseed 679,400, sugar beets 540,000, apples 460,000; livestock (number of live animals) 14,367,100 pigs, 13,699,500 cattle, 993,600 sheep; roundwood (2001) 176,692,000 cu m; fish catch (2001) 1,116,902. Mining and quarrying (value of production in Can$'000,000; 1999): gold 2,133; potash 1,776; nickel 1,563; zinc 1,533; iron ore 1,420; copper 1,361; sand and gravel 862; stone 732; diamonds 582. Manufacturing (value of shipments in Can$'000,000; 2002): transportation equipment 119,746; food 62,911; chemicals 37,679; paper products 32,726; petroleum and coal 32,250; primary metals 32,216; wood industries 29,498; fabricated metal products 27,510; machinery 24,113; rubber and plastic products 23,002; computers and electronic products 21,255.

Retail trade (2002)

	no. of enter-prises	no. of employees[12]	weekly wages as a % of all wages[9, 12]	annual sales (Can$'000,000)
Motor vehicle dealers	...	326,400[13]	143.5	89,979.0
Food stores	...	496,700	84.2	66,424.8
Clothing and footwear stores	...	144,600	79.4	27,229.0
Home furnishings and electronics	...	173,200	81.7	24,501.5
Automotive stores	...	[13]	143.5	23,078.5
Service stations	...	[13]	143.5	22,679.5
Furniture and appliance stores	...	87,000	119.2	18,275.9
Pharmacies	...	54,200	...	14,356.7
Sporting goods	...	...	...	11,686.9
Hardware stores	...	...	81.7	8,113.0
Electronics, including computers	...	[14]	92.0	8,108.2
Personal care products	...	[14]	79.4	7,620.0
Other	...	235,300[14]	92.0	53,767.7

Energy production (consumption): electricity (kW-hr; 1999) 578,244,000,000 (549,364,000,000); hard coal (metric tons; 2001) 59,042,000 (59,042,000); lignite (metric tons; 1999) 35,959,000 (36,806,000); crude petroleum (barrels; 1999) 615,800,000 (530,500,000); petroleum products (metric tons; 1999) 102,628,000 (88,147,000); natural gas (cu m; 1999) 174,005,700,000 (85,079,600,000).

Population economically active (2002): total 16,689,400; activity rate of total population 53.2% (participation rates: ages 15 and over 66.9%; female 46.4%; unemployed 7.7%).

Price and earnings indexes (1995 = 100)

	1996	1997	1998	1999	2000	2001	2002
Consumer price index	101.6	103.2	104.2	106.0	108.9	111.7	114.2
Hourly earnings index[15]	103.0	103.7	105.8	107.3	110.1	111.9	114.9

Household income and expenditure (2001). Average household size 2.6; average annual income per family (2001) Can$70,814 (U.S.$44,820); sources of income (1995): wages and salaries 57.0%, transfer payments 20.7%, property and entrepreneurial income 13.7%, profits 8.6%; expenditure (2001): housing 26.7%, food, alcohol, and tobacco 18.8%, transportation and communications 18.5%, recreation 8.4%, utilities 6.4%, clothing 5.8%, household durable goods 4.0%, health 3.5%, education 2.2%.

Financial aggregates

	1997	1998	1999	2000	2001	2002
Exchange rate, Can$ per:						
U.S. dollar	1.42	1.53	1.44	1.50	1.59	1.58
£	2.34	2.55	2.33	2.24	2.29	2.37
SDR	1.93	2.16	1.98	1.95	2.00	2.15
International reserves (U.S.$)						
Total (excl. gold; '000,000)	17,823	23,308	28,126	31,924	33,962	36,984
SDRs ('000,000)	1,126	1,098	527	574	614	719
Reserve pos. in IMF ('000,000)	1,575	2,299	3,168	2,509	2,863	3,580
Foreign exchange ('000,000)	15,122	19,991	24,432	28,841	30,484	32,685
Gold ('000,000 fine troy oz)	3.09	2.49	1.81	1.18	1.05	0.60
% world reserves	0.35	0.26	0.18	0.12	0.11	0.06
Interest and prices						
Central bank discount (%)	4.50	5.25	5.00	6.00	2.50	3.00
Govt. bond yield (%)	6.42	5.47	5.69	5.89	5.78	5.66
Industrial share prices (1995 = 100)	145.7	152.4	159.2	216.7	174.4	158.7
Balance of payments (U.S.$'000,000)						
Balance of visible trade, of which:	+18,565	+15,922	+28,291	+45,579	+45,864	+36,838
Imports, f.o.b.	200,498	204,617	220,203	243,899	226,495	227,240
Exports, f.o.b.	219,063	220,539	248,494	289,468	272,359	264,078
Balance of invisibles	–26,798	–23,761	–26,526	–24,974	–28,442	–21,929
Balance of payments, current account	–8,233	–7,839	+1,765	+20,595	+17,442	+14,909

Land use (1994): forested 53.6%; meadows and pastures 3.0%; agricultural and under permanent cultivation 4.9%; built-on, wasteland, and other 38.5%.

Foreign trade

Balance of trade (current prices)

	1997	1998	1999	2000	2001	2002[16]
Can$'000,000,000	+25.5	+19.8	+35.1	+56.3	+58.9	+43.2
% of total	4.5%	3.2%	5.2%	7.3%	7.9%	6.3%

Imports (2000): Can$354,728,000,000 (machinery and apparatus 32.4%; transport equipment 19.5%, of which road vehicles 17.1%; chemicals and chemical products 8.1%; food, beverages, and tobacco 4.8%; crude and refined petroleum 4.6%). *Major import sources:* U.S. 64.4%; Japan 4.7%; U.K. 3.6%; Mexico 3.4%; China 3.2%; Germany 2.2%; South Korea 1.4%.

Exports (2000): Can$410,994,000,000 (transport equipment 23.9%, of which road vehicles 20.9%; machinery and apparatus 16.3%; mineral fuels 13.1%, of which natural gas 5.4%, crude petroleum 4.7%; food 5.4%; paper and paperboard 3.8%; coniferous wood 2.9%; nonferrous metals 2.9%). *Major export destinations:* U.S. 87.2%; Japan 2.2%; U.K. 1.4%; China 0.9%; Germany 0.8%.

Trade by commodities (1998)

	imports		exports	
SITC Group	U.S.$'000,000	%	U.S.$'000,000	%
00 Food and live animals	9,629.6	4.8	12,443.0	5.8
01 Beverages and tobacco	1,065.2	0.5	1,039.0	0.5
02 Crude materials, excluding fuels	5,718.0	2.8	19,337.5	9.0
03 Mineral fuels, lubricants, and related materials	6,847.8	3.5	17,584.3	8.2
04 Animal and vegetable oils, fats, and waxes	...	...	...	...
05 Chemicals and related products, n.e.s.	16,363.1	8.1	11,792.8	5.5
06 Basic manufactures	27,121.9	13.5	34,591.1	16.1
07 Machinery and transport equipment	105,052.9	52.2	88,180.3	41.2
08 Miscellaneous manufactured articles	23,369.9	11.6	13,996.2	6.5
09 Goods not classified by kind	5,568.9	2.8	14,280.2	6.7
TOTAL	201,219.3[17]	100.0[17]	214,187.9[17]	100.0[17]

Direction of trade (1999)

	imports		exports	
	U.S.$'000,000	%	U.S.$'000,000	%
Africa	1,440	0.7	993	0.4
Asia	28,838	13.8	11,587	4.9[17]
China	6,017	2.9	1,673	0.7
Japan	10,104	4.8	5,254	2.2
Taiwan	3,100	1.5	740	0.3
Other	9,617	4.6	3,920	1.6
Americas	153,335	73.2	211,454	89.4
Mexico	6,263	3.0	1,025	0.4
United States	143,498	68.5	208,013	88.0
Other Americas	3,574	1.7	2,416	1.0
Europe	24,904	11.9	11,587	4.9
EU	21,524	10.3	10,427	4.4
Other Europe	3,380	1.6	1,160	0.5
Oceania	1,077	0.5	758	0.3
TOTAL	214,161[17, 18]	100.0[17, 18]	237,337[17]	100.0[17]

Transport and communications

Transport. Railroads (1998): length 65,403 km; (1999) passenger-km 1,592,000,000; (1999) metric ton-km cargo 297,249,000,000. Roads (1999): total length 901,903 km (paved 35%). Vehicles (1998): passenger cars 13,887,270; trucks and buses 3,694,125. Air transport (2001): passenger-km 67,027,355,000; metric ton-km cargo 1,726,120,000; airports (1997) 269.

Communications

Medium	date	unit	number	units per 1,000 persons
Daily newspapers	2000	circulation	4,890,000	159
Radio	2000	receivers	32,200,000	1,047
Television	2000	receivers	21,700,000	716
Telephones	2002	main lines	19,962,100	636
Cellular telephones	2002	subscribers	11,849,000	377
Personal computers	2002	units	15,300,000	487
Internet	2002	users	15,200,000	484

Education and health

Literacy (2002): total population age 15 and over literate virtually 100%.

Education (1998–99)

	schools	teachers	students	student/ teacher ratio
Primary (age 6–14) Secondary (age 14–18)	16,215	296,901	5,496,976	18.5
Postsecondary[19]	199	24,488[20]	397,725	16.2[20]
Higher[21]	76	33,365	578,624	17.3

Health: physicians (2000) 60,559 (1 per 508 persons); hospital beds (1997) 161,867 (1 per 185 persons); infant mortality rate (2001) 5.0.

Food (2001): daily per capita caloric intake 3,176 (vegetable products 70%, animal products 30%); 121% of FAO recommended minimum requirement.

Military

Total active duty personnel (2002): 52,300 (army 36.9%, navy 17.2%, air force 25.8%, not identified by service 20.1%). *Military expenditure as percentage of GNP* (1999): 1.4% (world 2.4%); per capita expenditure U.S.$269.

[1]July 1 estimate based on adjusted 2001 census figure. [2]Nunavut came into existence on April 1, 1999. [3]Based on land area of 3,551,023 sq mi (9,093,507 sq km). [4]At prices of 1997. [5]Services includes communications. [6]Unemployed. [7]GDP at current values in 2002 was Can$1,154,949,000,000. [8]1993. [9]Excludes agriculture, fishing and trapping, private household services, religious organizations, and the military. [10]For 2002 in constant dollars of 1997. [11]Food and beverages includes tobacco. [12]2000. [13]Motor vehicle dealers includes Service stations and Automotive stores. [14]Other includes Electronics and Personal care products. [15]Manufacturing only. [16]Excludes December. [17]Detail does not add to total because of discrepancies in estimates. [18]Total for imports includes U.S.$3,299,000,000 (1.7% of total imports; mostly special transactions) not distributable by region. [19]Community colleges. [20]1997–98. [21]Universities only.

Internet resources for further information:

- **Statistics Canada http://www.statcan.ca**

Cape Verde

Official name: República de Cabo Verde (Republic of Cape Verde).
Form of government: multiparty republic with one legislative house (National Assembly [72]).
Chief of state: President.
Head of government: Prime Minister.
Capital: Praia.
Official language: Portuguese.
Official religion: none.
Monetary unit: 1 escudo (C.V.Esc.)[1] = 100 centavos; valuation (Sept. 8, 2003) 1 U.S.$ = C.V.Esc. 108.95; 1 £ = C.V.Esc. 172.75.

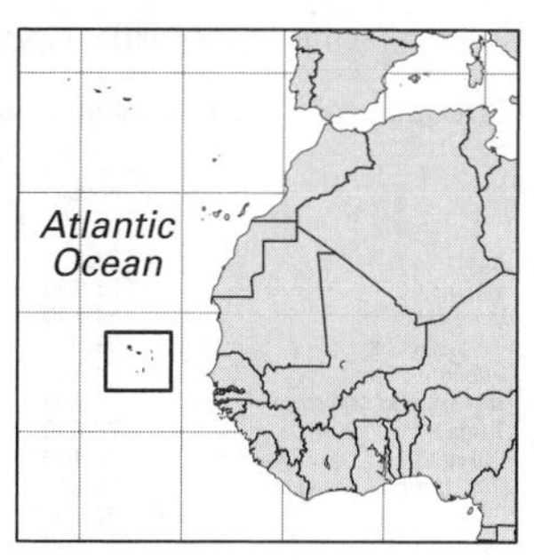

Area and population

Island Groups / Islands/Counties[2] / Counties	Capitals	area sq mi	area sq km	population 2000 census
Leeward Islands		696[3]	1,803	287,323
Brava	Nova Sintra	26	67	6,820
Fogo				
Mosteiros[4]	...	184	476	9,479
São Filipe	São Filipe			27,930
Maio	Porto Inglês	104	269	6,742
Santiago		383	991	236,352
Praia	Praia	153	396	106,052
Santa Catarina	Assomada	94	243	49,970
Santa Cruz	Pedra Badejo	58	149	32,822
São Domingos[4]	...	78	203	13,296
São Miguel[4]	...			16,153
Tarrafal	Tarrafal			18,059
Windward Islands		861[3]	2,230	147,489
Boa Vista	Sal Rei	239	620	4,193
Sal	Santa Maria	83	216	14,792
Santo Antão		300	779	47,124
Paúl	Pombas	21	54	8,325
Porto Novo	Porto Novo	215	558	17,239
Ribeira Grande	Ponta do Sol	64	167	21,560
São Nicolau	Ribeira Brava	150	388	13,536
São Vicente[5]	Mindelo	88	227	67,844
TOTAL		1,557	4,033	434,812

Demography

Population (2003): 438,000.
Density (2003): persons per sq mi 281.3, persons per sq km 108.6.
Urban-rural (2002): urban 63.5%; rural 36.5%.
Sex distribution (2002): male 48.39%; female 51.61%.
Age breakdown (2002): under 15, 41.0%; 15–29, 26.7%; 30–44, 17.0%; 45–59, 6.8%; 60–74, 5.8%; 75 and over, 2.7%.
Population projection: (2010) 458,000; (2020) 476,000.
Doubling time: 35 years.
Ethnic composition (2000): Cape Verdean *mestico* (black-white admixture) 69.6%; Fulani 12.2%; Balanta 10.0%; Mandyako 4.6%; Portuguese white 2.0%; other 1.6%.
Religious affiliation (2000): Roman Catholic 91.4%; Muslim 2.8%; other 5.8%.
Major cities (2000): Praia 94,757; Mindelo 62,970; São Filipe 7,894.

Vital statistics

Birth rate per 1,000 population (2002): 26.9 (world avg. 21.3); (1989) legitimate 28.9%; illegitimate 71.1%.
Death rate per 1,000 population (2002): 6.9 (world avg. 9.1).
Natural increase rate per 1,000 population (2002): 20.0 (world avg. 12.2).
Total fertility rate (avg. births per childbearing woman; 2002): 3.8.
Marriage rate per 1,000 population (1990): 4.5.
Life expectancy at birth (2002): male 65.5 years; female 73.2 years.
Major causes of death per 100,000 population (1987): enteritis and other diarrheal diseases 97.4; heart disease 77.9; malignant neoplasms (cancers) 47.9; pneumonia 46.4; accidents, poisoning, and violence 44.0.

National economy

Budget (2001). Revenue: C.V.Esc. 14,900,000,000 (tax revenue 87.2%, of which taxes on international trade 35.6%, income taxes 32.2%, sales taxes 14.1%; nontax revenue 12.8%). Expenditures: C.V.Esc. 21,200,000,000 (current expenditure 69.8%, of which wages and salaries 31.1%, transfers 26.9%, public debt 6.6%, goods and services 2.9%; capital expenditure 30.2%).
Public debt (external, outstanding; 2001): U.S.$340,200,000.
Production (metric tons except as noted). Agriculture, forestry, fishing (2002): corn (maize) 20,000, sugarcane 14,000, bananas 6,000, coconuts 6,000, vegetables (including melons) 5,000, fruits (except melons) 4,700, sweet potatoes 3,800; livestock (number of live animals) 200,000 pigs, 112,000 goats, 22,000 cattle; roundwood, n.a.; fish catch (2000) 10,821. Mining and quarrying (2000): salt 2,000. Manufacturing (1999): flour 15,901; bread 5,628[6]; soap 833; paint 628[7]; canned tuna 337[6]; cigarettes 41 kg; beer 4,104,546 litres; soft drinks 922,714[7] litres. Energy production (consumption): electricity (kW-hr; 2001) 164,332,000 (127,049,000); coal, none (none); crude petroleum, none (none); petroleum products (metric tons; 2001) none (101,619); natural gas, none (none).
Tourism: receipts from visitors (2000) U.S.$40,800,000; expenditures by nationals abroad (1999) U.S.$41,000,000.
Land use (1994): forest 0.2%; pasture 6.2%; agriculture 11.2%; other 82.4%.
Gross national product (2001): U.S.$600,000,000 (U.S.$1,340 per capita).

Structure of gross domestic product and labour force

	2001 in value C.V.Esc. '000,000	2001 % of total value	1990 labour force	1990 % of labour force
Agriculture	6,888.7	10.3	29,876	24.7
Manufacturing	6,098.3	9.1	5,520	4.6
Public utilities			883	0.7
Mining			410	0.3
Construction	5,196.2	7.8	22,722	18.9
Transp. and commun.	12,197.7	18.3	6,138	5.1
Trade	12,402.2	18.6	12,747	10.6
Finance	7,686.1	11.5	821	0.7
Pub. admin., defense	9,311.9	14.0	17,358	14.4
Services	1,967.8	3.0		
Other	4,946.1[8]	7.4[8]	24,090	20.0
TOTAL	66,695	100.0	120,565	100.0

Population economically active (2000): total 174,644; activity rate of total population 40.2% (participation rates [1990]: ages 15–64, 64.3%; female [2000] 39.0%; unemployed [2000] 17.4%).

Price and earnings indexes (1995 = 100)

	1995	1996	1997	1998	1999	2000	2001
Consumer price index	100.0	106.0	115.0	120.0	126.0	123.0	127.0
Monthly earnings index	...	...	...	...	...	...	...

Household income and expenditure. Average household size (2000) 4.6; income per household: n.a.; sources of income: n.a.; expenditure (1988): food 51.1%, housing, fuel, and power 13.5%, beverages and tobacco 11.8%, transportation and communications 8.8%, household durable goods 6.9%, other 7.9%.

Foreign trade[9]

Balance of trade (current prices)

	1997	1998	1999	2000	2001
C.V.Esc. '000,000	–20,469	–21,582	–25,746	–26,313	–29,317
% of total	88.8%	91.4%	91.7%	91.2%	92.4%

Imports (2000): C.V.Esc. 27,585,000,000 (food 32.8%, machinery and apparatus 16.1%, transport equipment 9.5%, base and fabricated metals 6.5%). *Major import sources* (2001–02): Portugal 54.8%; The Netherlands 13.4%; Spain 4.9%; Belgium 4.1%; Brazil 3.6%.
Exports (2000): C.V.Esc. 1,272,000,000 (shoes and shoe parts 51.8%, clothing 35.1%, fish 4.8%). *Major export destinations* (2001–02): Portugal 91.7%; United States 2.1%; Germany 1.6%.

Transport and communications

Transport. Railroads: none. Roads (1999): total length 684 mi, 1,100 km (paved [1996] 78%). Vehicles (2000): passenger cars 13,473; trucks and buses 3,085. Air transport (2001)[10]: passenger-mi 171,000,000, passenger-km 276,000,000; short ton-mi cargo (1998) 16,200,000, metric ton-km cargo 26,000,000; airports (1997) with scheduled flights 9.

Communications

Medium	date	unit	number	units per 1,000 persons
Radio	1997	receivers	71,000	179
Television	2000	receivers	2,000	4.6
Telephones	2002	main lines	70,200	16
Cellular telephones	2002	subscribers	42,900	98
Internet	2001	users	16,000	36

Education and health

Educational attainment (1990). Percentage of population age 25 and over having: no formal schooling 47.9%; primary 40.9%; incomplete secondary 3.9%; complete secondary 1.4%; higher 1.5%; unknown 4.4%. *Literacy* (2000): total population age 15 and over literate 73.8%; males 84.5%; females 65.7%.

Education (1997–98)

	schools	teachers	students	student/teacher ratio
Primary (age 7–12)	370[11]	3,219	91,636[12]	...
Secondary (age 13–17) / Vocational	...	1,372	40,214[12]	...
Higher	...	...	1,600[13]	...

Health (2000): physicians 102 (1 per 4,274 persons); hospital beds 689 (1 per 631 persons); infant mortality rate per 1,000 live births (2002) 50.5.
Food (2001): daily per capita caloric intake 3,308 (vegetable products 85%, animal products 15%); 141% of FAO recommended minimum requirement.

Military

Total active duty personnel (2001): 1,200 (army 83.3%, air force 8.3%, coast guard 8.4%). *Military expenditure as percentage of GNP* (1999): 0.9% (world 2.4%); per capita expenditure U.S.$13.

[1]Formerly pegged to the Portuguese escudo and since Jan. 1, 2002, to the euro at the rate of €1 = C.V.Esc. 110.27. [2]Island/county areas are coterminous except Fogo, Santiago, and Santo Antão islands. [3]Detail does not add to total given because of rounding. [4]Created after the 1990 census. [5]Includes Santa Luzia Island, which is uninhabited. [6]1995. [7]1996. [8]Taxes and duties on imports. [9]Imports c.i.f., exports f.o.b.; excludes reexports of fuel. [10]TACV airline only. [11]1991. [12]1999–2000. [13]Students abroad in 1996–97.

Internet resources for further information:
- **Instituto Nacional de Estatística de Cabo Verde http://www.ine.cv**
- **Banco de Cabo Verde http://www.bcv.cv**

Central African Republic

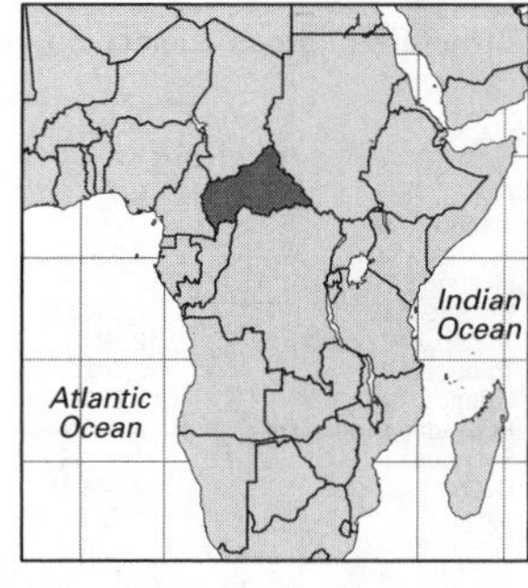

Official name: République Centrafricaine (Central African Republic).
Form of government: military regime with one advisory body (National Transitional Council [63])[1].
Chief of state: President assisted by Prime Minister[1].
Capital: Bangui.
Official languages: French; Sango.
Official religion: none.
Monetary unit: 1 CFA franc (CFAF) = 100 centimes; valuation (Sept. 8, 2003) 1 U.S.$ = CFAF 594.70; 1 £ = CFAF 942.93[2].

Area and population

		area		population
Prefectures	**Capitals**	sq mi	sq km	1988 census
Bamingui-Bangoran	Ndélé	22,471	58,200	28,643
Basse-Kotto	Mobaye	6,797	17,604	194,750
Haut-Mbomou	Obo	21,440	55,530	27,113
Haute-Kotto	Bria	33,456	86,650	58,838
Kemo	Sibut	6,642	17,204	82,884
Lobaye	Mbaïki	7,427	19,235	169,554
Mambéré-Kadéï	Berbérati	11,661	30,203	230,364
Mbomou	Bangassou	23,610	61,150	119,252
Nana-Gribizi	Kaga-Bandoro	7,721	19,996	95,497
Nana-Mambéré	Bouar	10,270	26,600	191,970
Ombella-M'poko	Boali	12,292	31,835	180,857
Ouaka	Bambari	19,266	49,900	208,332
Ouham	Bossangoa	19,402	50,250	262,950
Ouham-Pendé	Bozoum	12,394	32,100	287,653
Sangha-Mbaéré	Nola	7,495	19,412	65,961
Vakaga	Birao	17,954	46,500	32,118
Autonomous commune				
Bangui	Bangui	26	67	451,690
TOTAL		240,324	622,436	2,688,426

Demography

Population (2003): 3,684,000.
Density (2003): persons per sq mi 15.3, persons per sq km 5.9.
Urban-rural (2002): urban 41.7%; rural 58.3%.
Sex distribution (2002): male 49.47%; female 50.53%.
Age breakdown (2002): under 15, 43.4%; 15–29, 28.5%; 30–44, 14.7%; 45–59, 8.3%; 60–74, 4.2%; 75 and over, 0.9%.
Population projection: (2010) 4,073,000; (2020) 4,557,000.
Doubling time: 41 years.
Ethnolinguistic composition (1988): Gbaya (Baya) 23.7%; Banda 23.4%; Mandjia 14.7%; Ngbaka 7.6%; Sara 6.5%; Mbum 6.3%; Kare 2.4%; French 0.1%; other 15.3%.
Religious affiliation (2000): Christian 67.8%, of which Roman Catholic 18.4%, Protestant 14.4%, African Christian 11.6%, other Christian 23.4%; Muslim 15.6%; traditional beliefs 15.4%; other 1.2%.
Major cities (1994): Bangui 524,000; Berbérati 47,000; Bouar 43,000; Bambari 41,000; Carnot 41,000; Bossangoa 33,000.

Vital statistics

Birth rate per 1,000 population (2002): 36.3 (world avg. 21.3).
Death rate per 1,000 population (2002): 19.5 (world avg. 9.1).
Natural increase rate per 1,000 population (2002): 16.8 (world avg. 12.2).
Total fertility rate (avg. births per childbearing woman; 2002): 4.8.
Life expectancy at birth (2002): male 40.7 years; female 43.5 years.

National economy

Budget (2001). Revenue: CFAF 63,200,000,000 (1999; taxes 88.0%, of which international trade tax 38.0%, indirect domestic tax 30.1%, taxes on income and profits 19.9%; nontax receipts 12.0%). Expenditures: CFAF 97,200,000,000 (current expenditure 61.2%, of which wages 30.5%; public investment program 38.8%).
Production (metric tons except as noted). Agriculture, forestry, fishing (2002): cassava 563,000, yams 400,000, peanuts (groundnuts) 127,800, bananas 118,000, corn (maize) 113,000, taro 110,000, sugarcane 90,000, plantains 83,000, sorghum 52,900, sesame seeds 39,400, pulses 32,000, seed cotton 30,000, paddy rice 27,400, coffee 13,000; livestock (number of live animals; 2002) 3,273,000 cattle, 2,921,000 goats, 738,000 pigs, 4,575,000 chickens; roundwood (2001) 3,058,000 cu m; fish catch (2000) 15,120. Mining and quarrying (2000): gold 38.7 kg, diamonds 460,000 carats[3]. Manufacturing (value added in U.S.$'000; 1994): food, beverages, and tobacco 19,000; chemical products 3,000; wood products 2,000; textiles, wearing apparel, and leather products 1,000; transport equipment 1,000. Construction (1992)[4]: residential 10,052 sq m; nonresidential 82,411 sq m. Energy production (consumption): electricity (kW-hr; 1999) 107,000,000 (107,000,000); coal, none (none); crude petroleum, none (none); petroleum products (metric tons; 1999) none (87,000); natural gas, none (none).
Household income and expenditure. Average household size (2000) 5.9; average annual income per household (1988) CFAF 91,985 (U.S.$435); sources of income: n.a.; expenditure (1991)[5]: food 70.5%, clothing 8.5%, other manufactured products 7.6%, energy 7.3%, services (including transportation and communications, recreation, and health) 6.1%.

Gross national product (2001): U.S.$1,000,000,000 (U.S.$260 per capita).

Structure of gross domestic product and labour force

	1999		1988	
	in value CFAF '000,000	% of total value	labour force	% of labour force
Agriculture	326,800	50.1	1,113,900	80.4
Mining	26,200	4.0	15,400	1.1
Manufacturing	54,500	8.4	22,400	1.6
Construction	29,500	4.5	7,000	0.5
Public utilities	4,600	0.7	1,500	0.1
Transp. and commun.	15,400	2.4	1,500	0.1
Trade	78,800	12.1	118,000	8.5
Services	40,100	6.1	15,600	1.1
Pub. admin., defense	35,900	5.5	91,700	6.6
Other	40,700[6]	6.2[6]	—	—
TOTAL	652,500	100.0	1,387,000	100.0

Public debt (external, outstanding; 2001): U.S.$756,900,000.
Population economically active (2000): total 1,752,000; activity rate of total population 50.0% (participation rates [1988] ages 15–64, 78.3%; [1988] female 46.8%; unemployed, n.a.).

Price and earnings indexes (1995 = 100)

	1996	1997	1998	1999	2000	2001	2002
Consumer price index[4]	103.7	105.4	103.4	101.9	105.2	108.8	112.4
Earnings index	...	...	...	...	...	...	...

Land use (1994): forest 75.0%; meadows 4.8%; agriculture 3.2%; other 17.0%.
Tourism (1998): receipts U.S.$6,000,000; expenditures (1997) U.S.$39,000,000.

Foreign trade

Balance of trade (current prices)

	1996	1997	1998	1999	2000	2001
CFAF '000,000,000	–3.1	+9.1	+2.9	+9.4	+31.0	+15.7
% of total	3.1%	5.3%	1.7%	5.5%	15.7%	8.5%

Imports (2001): CFAF 84,800,000,000 (1996; road vehicles 18.3%, machinery and apparatus 15.8%, raw cotton 9.7%, refined petroleum 8.0%, food 7.0%). *Major import sources* (1999): France *c.* 34%; Cameroon *c.* 12%; Belgium *c.* 7%; U.K. *c.* 4%; Japan *c.* 3%.
Exports (2001): CFAF 100,500,000,000 (wood 41.3%, diamonds 41.0%, cotton 7.4%, coffee 1.8%). *Major export destinations* (1999): Belgium *c.* 65%; Spain *c.* 6%; Indonesia *c.* 4%; France *c.* 3%; United Kingdom *c.* 3%.

Transport and communications

Transport. Railroads: none. Roads (1999): total length 14,795 mi, 23,810 km (paved 3%). Vehicles (1996): passenger cars 8,900; trucks and buses 7,000. Air transport (1998)[7]: passenger-km 258,000,000; metric ton-km cargo 38,000,000; airports (2001) 1.

Communications

Medium	date	unit	number	units per 1,000 persons
Daily newspapers	2000	circulation	7,000	2.0
Radio	2000	receivers	280,000	80
Television	2000	receivers	21,000	6.0
Telephones	2001	main lines	10,000	2.6
Cellular telephones	2001	subscribers	11,000	2.9
Personal computers	2001	units	7,000	1.9
Internet	2001	users	2,000	0.5

Education and health

Educational attainment (1988). Percentage of population age 10 and over having: no formal schooling 59.3%; primary education 29.6%; lower secondary 7.5%; upper secondary 2.3%; higher 1.3%. *Literacy* (2000): total population age 15 and over literate 46.7%; males literate 59.7%; females literate 34.9%.

Education (1998)

	schools	teachers	students	student/ teacher ratio
Primary (age 6–11)	...	3,125	284,398	91.0
Secondary (age 12–18)	46[8]	845[8]	42,263[9]	...
Vocational	[10]	[10]	1,477[9]	...
Higher[11]	1	300	6,229	20.8

Health (1995): physicians 112 (1 per 28,600 persons); hospital beds (1991) 4,258 (1 per 672 persons); infant mortality rate (2002) 94.5.
Food (2001): daily per capita caloric intake 1,949 (vegetable products 90%, animal products 10%); 86% of FAO recommended minimum requirement.

Military

Total active duty personnel (2002): 2,550 (army 54.9%; navy, none; air force 5.9%; paramilitary [gendarmerie] 39.2%). *Military expenditure as percentage of GNP* (1999): 2.8% (world 2.4%); per capita expenditure U.S.$8.

[1]From March 15, 2003, coup d'état; expect transitional government until January 2005. [2]Formerly pegged to the French franc and since Jan. 1, 2002, to the euro at the rate of €1 = CFAF 655.96. [3]Export figure; an unknown but substantial amount is believed to be smuggled out of the country annually. [4]Bangui only. [5]Weights of consumer price index components. [6]Indirect taxes and customs duties. [7]Air Afrique, an airline jointly owned by 11 African countries (including the Central African Republic), was declared bankrupt in February 2002. [8]1990–91. [9]1991–92. [10]Included with secondary. [11]University of Bangui only.

Internet resources for further information:
- **Investir en Zone Franc http://www.izf.net/izf/Index.htm**

Chad

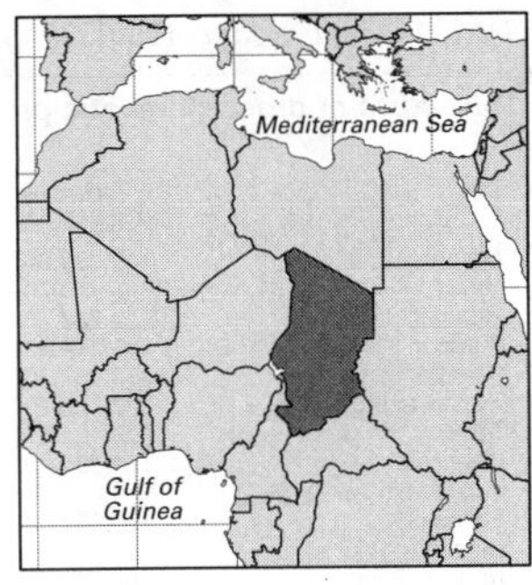

Official name: Jumhūrīyah Tshad (Arabic); République du Tchad (French) (Republic of Chad).
Form of government: unitary republic with one legislative body (National Assembly [155]).
Chief of state: President.
Head of government: Prime Minister.
Capital: N'Djamena.
Official languages: Arabic; French.
Official religion: none.
Monetary unit: 1 CFA franc (CFAF) = 100 centimes; valuation (Sept. 8, 2003) 1 U.S.$ = CFAF 594.70; 1 £ = CFAF 942.93[1].

Area and population

		area		population
Préfectures[2]	**Capitals**	sq mi	sq km	1993 census
Batha	Ati	34,285	88,800	288,458
Biltine	Biltine	18,090	46,850	184,807
Borkou-Ennedi-Tibesti	Faya Largeau	231,795	600,350	73,185
Chari-Baguirmi	N'Djamena	32,010	82,910	1,251,906
Guéra	Mongo	22,760	58,950	306,253
Kanem	Mao	44,215	114,520	279,927
Lac	Bol	8,620	22,320	252,932
Logone Occidental	Moundou	3,357	8,695	455,489
Logone Oriental	Doba	10,825	28,035	441,064
Mayo-Kebbi	Bongor	11,625	30,105	825,158
Moyen-Chari	Sarh	17,445	45,180	738,595
Ouaddaï	Abéché	29,436	76,240	543,900
Salamat	Am Timan	24,325	63,000	184,403
Tandjilé	Laï	6,965	18,045	453,854
TOTAL		495,755[3]	1,284,000	6,279,931

Demography

Population (2003): 9,253,000.
Density (2003): persons per sq mi 18.7, persons per sq km 7.2.
Urban-rural (2002): urban 24.1%; rural 75.9%.
Sex distribution (2002): male 48.62%; female 51.38%.
Age breakdown (2002): under 15, 47.8%; 15–29, 26.2%; 30–44, 14.1%; 45–59, 7.5%; 60–74, 3.6%; 75 and over, 0.8%.
Population projection: (2010) 11,302,000; (2020) 14,671,000.
Doubling time: 23 years.
Ethnolinguistic composition (1993): Sara 27.7%; Sudanic Arab 12.3%; Mayo-Kebbi peoples 11.5%; Kanem-Bornu peoples 9.0%; Ouaddaï peoples 8.7%; Hadjeray (Hadjaraï) 6.7%; Tangale (Tandjilé) peoples 6.5%; Gorane peoples 6.3%; Fitri-Batha peoples 4.7%; Fulani (Peul) 2.4%; other 4.2%.
Religious affiliation (1993): Muslim 53.9%; Christian 34.7%, of which Roman Catholic 20.3%, Protestant 14.4%; traditional beliefs 7.4%; other 4.0%.
Major cities (1993): N'Djamena 530,965; Moundou 282,103; Bongor 196,713; Sarh 193,753; Abéché 187,936; Doba 185,461.

Vital statistics

Birth rate per 1,000 population (2002): 47.6 (world avg. 21.3).
Death rate per 1,000 population (2002): 16.4 (world avg. 9.1).
Natural increase rate per 1,000 population (2002): 31.2 (world avg. 12.2).
Total fertility rate (avg. births per childbearing woman; 2002): 6.5.
Life expectancy at birth (2002): male 47.0 years; female 50.5 years.

National economy

Budget (2000). Revenue: CFAF 128,200,000,000 (tax revenue 53.3%, of which income tax 19.0%, taxes on international trade 17.0%, taxes on goods and services 14.7%, other taxes 2.6%; grants 37.4%; nontax revenue 9.3%). Expenditures: CFAF 203,200,000,000 (current expenditure 49.2%, of which government salaries 19.7%, materials and supply 10.2%, defense 7.5%, transfer payments 5.9%, debt service 5.1%, other 0.8%; capital expenditure 50.8%).
Public debt (external, outstanding; 2001): U.S.$992,000,000.
Tourism (1998): receipts from visitors U.S.$10,000,000; expenditures by nationals abroad (1994) U.S.$26,000,000.
Production (metric tons except as noted). Agriculture, forestry, fishing (2002): peanuts (groundnuts) 448,089, sorghum 428,000, millet 369,000, cassava 310,000, yams 230,000, seed cotton 170,000, corn (maize) 115,000, rice 115,000; livestock (number of live animals) 5,900,000 cattle, 5,500,000 goats, 2,450,000 sheep, 725,000 camels, 5,000,000 chickens; roundwood (2001) 6,761,676 cu m; fish catch (2000) 84,000. Mining and quarrying (1997): aggregate (gravel) 170,000; limited commercial production of natron (10,000) and salt; artisanal gold production. Manufacturing (2000): cotton fibre (1998) 86,260; refined sugar 27,000; gum arabic 3,420; woven cotton fabrics 1,000,000 metres; edible oil 10,000,000 hectolitres; beer 78,000,000 hectolitres; cigarettes 30,000,000 packs; bicycles (1998) 3,444 units. Energy production (consumption): electricity (kW-hr; 2000) 86,400,000 (81,800,000); coal, none (none); crude petroleum, none[4] (none); petroleum products (metric tons; 1999) none (40,000); natural gas, none (none).
Household income and expenditure. Average household size (2000) 4.2; average annual income per household (1993) CFAF 96,806 (U.S.$458); sources of income (1995–96; urban): informal-sector employment and entrepreneurship 36.7%, transfers 24.8%, wages 23.6%, ownership of real estate 8.6%; expenditure (1983)[5]: food 45.3%, health 11.9%, energy 5.8%, clothing 3.3%.
Population economically active (1997): total 3,433,000; activity rate of total population 47.9% (participation rates: over age 15, 72.3%; female 44.5%; unemployed [1993] 0.6%).

Price and earnings indexes (1995 = 100)

	1996	1997	1998	1999	2000	2001	2002
Consumer price index	112.4	118.7	133.1	124.1	128.8	144.8	152.3
Earnings index	...	...	...	...	...	...	...

Gross national product (2001): U.S.$1,600,000,000 (U.S.$200 per capita).

Structure of gross domestic product and labour force

	2000		1993	
	in value CFAF '000,000	% of total value	labour force	% of labour force
Agriculture	349,000	34.8	1,903,492	83.0
Mining	31,200	3.1	...	...
Manufacturing	108,400	10.8	33,670	1.5
Construction	19,700	2.0	10,885	0.5
Public utilities	5,900	0.6	756	—
Transp. and commun. }	244,600	24.4	13,252	0.6
Trade and finance }			179,169	7.8
Pub. admin., defense	114,700	11.4	61,875	2.7
Services	96,400	9.6	79,167	3.4
Other	32,500[6]	3.2[6]	9,311	0.4
TOTAL	1,002,400	100.0[3]	2,293,603	100.0

Land use (1994): forested 25.7%; meadows and pastures 35.7%; agricultural and under permanent cultivation 2.6%; other 36.0%.

Foreign trade

Balance of trade (current prices)

	1996	1997	1998	1999	2000	2001
CFAF '000,000,000	–3.2	+3.2	–11.5	–22.1	–35.5	–199.1
% of total	1.3%	1.2%	3.6%	7.3%	12.0%	43.4%

Imports (2001): CFAF 328,700,000,000 (petroleum sector 61.3%; non-petroleum sector 38.7%). *Major import sources* (1999): France *c.* 37%; Cameroon *c.* 22%; Nigeria *c.* 10%; India *c.* 4%.
Exports (2001): CFAF 129,600,000,000 (cattle, sheep, and goats 39.5%; cotton fibre 37.2%; other 23.3%). *Major export destinations* (1999): Portugal *c.* 29%; Germany *c.* 15%; Taiwan *c.* 8%; U.S. *c.* 7%; France *c.* 5%; Brazil *c.* 5%.

Transport and communications

Transport. Railroads: none. Roads (1999): total length 33,400 km (paved 1%). Vehicles (1996): passenger cars 10,560; trucks and buses 14,550. Air transport (1996)[7]: passenger-km 233,000,000; metric ton-km cargo 37,000,000; airports (2000) with scheduled flights 1.

Communications

Medium	date	unit	number	units per 1,000 persons
Daily newspapers	1997	circulation	2,000	0.2
Radio	2000	receivers	1,990,000	236
Television	2000	receivers	8,420	1.0
Telephones	2001	main lines	11,000	1.4
Cellular telephones	2002	subscribers	34,200	4.3
Personal computers	2001	units	12,000	1.5
Internet	2001	users	4,000	0.5

Education and health

Educational attainment (1993). Percentage of economically active population age 15 and over having: no formal schooling 81.1%; Qur'anic education 4.2%; primary education 11.2%; secondary education 2.7%; higher education 0.3%; professional education 0.5%. *Literacy* (2000): percentage of total population age 15 and over literate 42.6%; males literate 51.6%; females literate 34.0%.

Education (1996–97)

	schools	teachers	students	student/ teacher ratio
Primary (age 6–12)	2,660	10,151	680,909	67.1
Secondary (age 13–19)	153	2,598	97,011	37.3
Voc., teacher tr.	18	194	2,778	14.5
Higher[8]	8	288	3,274	11.4

Health (2000): physicians 1,667 (1 per 4,471 persons); hospital beds (1993) 3,962 (1 per 1,521 persons); infant mortality rate (2002) 96.7.
Food (2001): daily per capita caloric intake 2,245 (vegetable products 94%, animal products 6%); 94% of FAO recommended minimum requirement.

Military

Total active duty personnel (2002): 30,350[9] (army 82.4%; navy, none; air force 1.2%; paramilitary [gendarmerie] 16.4%). *Military expenditure as percentage of GNP* (1999): 2.4% (world 2.4%); per capita expenditure U.S.$5.

[1]Formerly pegged to the French franc and since Jan. 1, 2002, to the euro at the rate of €1 = CFAF 655.96. [2]Chad was administratively reorganized into 28 departments and 1 commune in 1999; area and population details are not available. [3]Detail does not add to total given because of rounding. [4]Significant crude petroleum production began in July 2003. [5]Capital city only. [6]VAT and import taxes. [7]One-eleventh portion of total traffic of Air Afrique; Air Afrique, an airline jointly owned by 11 African countries (including Chad) was declared bankrupt in February 2002. [8]Universities and equivalent institutions only. [9]Excludes 900 French troops.

Internet resources for further information:
- **Embassy of Chad in the U.S. http://www.chadembassy.org**
- **Investir en Zone Franc http://www.izf.net/izf/Index.htm**

Chile

Official name: República de Chile (Republic of Chile).
Form of government: multiparty republic with two legislative houses (Senate [48[1]]; Chamber of Deputies [120]).
Head of state and government: President.
Capital: Santiago[2].
Official language: Spanish.
Official religion: none.
Monetary unit: 1 peso (Ch$) = 100 centavos; valuation (Sept. 8, 2003) 1 U.S.$ = Ch$681.45; 1 £ = Ch$1,080.

Area and population[3]

Regions	Capitals	area sq mi	area sq km	population 2002 census[4]
Aisén del General Carlos Ibáñez del Campo	Coihaique	41,890	108,495	91,492
Antofagasta	Antofagasta	48,668	126,049	493,984
Araucanía	Temuco	12,294	31,842	869,535
Atacama	Copiapó	29,026	75,176	254,336
Bío-Bío	Concepción	14,310	37,063	1,861,562
Coquimbo	La Serena	15,668	40,580	603,210
Libertador General Bernardo O'Higgins	Rancagua	6,327	16,387	780,627
Los Lagos	Puerto Montt	25,874	67,013	1,073,135
Magallanes y la Antártica Chilena	Punta Arenas	51,080	132,297	150,826
Maule	Talca	11,697	30,296	908,097
Santiago, Región Metropolitana de	Santiago	5,947	15,403	6,061,185
Tarapacá	Iquique	22,818	59,099	428,594
Valparaíso	Valparaíso	6,331	16,396	1,539,852
TOTAL		291,930	756,096	15,116,435

Demography

Population (2003): 15,326,000.
Density (2003): persons per sq mi 52.5, persons per sq km 20.3.
Urban-rural (2002): urban 86.6%; rural 13.4%.
Sex distribution (2002): male 49.19%; female 50.81%.
Age breakdown (2001): under 15, 28.1%; 15–29, 24.2%; 30–44, 22.7%; 45–59, 14.6%; 60–74, 7.7%; 75 and over, 2.7%.
Population projection: (2010) 16,607,000; (2020) 18,320,000.
Ethnic composition (2000): mestizo 72.4%; local white 20.8%; Araucanian (Mapuche) 4.7%; European 1.0%; other 1.1%.
Religious affiliation (2000): Roman Catholic *c.* 63%; independent Christian *c.* 20%; Protestant *c.* 2%; other/unaffiliated Christian *c.* 4%; atheist/nonreligious *c.* 9%; other *c.* 1%.
Major cities[5] (2002): Greater Santiago 4,647,444; Puente Alto 501,042; Concepción 376,043; Viña del Mar 298,828; Antofagasta 298,153; Valparaíso 270,242.

Vital statistics

Birth rate per 1,000 population (2001): 16.8 (world avg. 21.3).
Death rate per 1,000 population (2001): 5.6 (world avg. 9.1).
Natural increase rate per 1,000 population (2001): 11.2 (world avg. 12.2).
Total fertility rate (avg. births per childbearing woman; 2000): 2.2.
Life expectancy at birth (2001): male 72.6 years; female 79.4 years.
Major causes of death per 100,000 population (1999): diseases of the circulatory system 155.7; malignant neoplasms (cancers) 122.5; diseases of the respiratory system 78.6; accidents and adverse effects 25.2.

National economy

Budget (2001). Revenue: Ch$9,537,200,000,000 (income from taxes 76.2%, nontax revenue 23.5%, capital 0.3%). Expenditures: Ch$9,932,200,000,000 (pensions 29.5%, wages 19.0%, capital expenditure 15.0%, interest 2.1%).
Population economically active (1999): total 5,822,700; activity rate of total population 38.6% (participation rates [1995]: ages 15–64, 58.6%; female 32.4%; unemployed [2002] 9.0%).

Price and earnings indexes (1995 = 100)

	1996	1997	1998	1999	2000	2001	2002
Consumer price index	107.4	113.9	119.8	123.8	128.5	133.1	136.4
Hourly earnings index	114.8	124.7	134.5	142.4	149.9	157.8	165.0

Production (metric tons except as noted). Agriculture, forestry, fishing (2002): sugar beets 3,540,000, wheat 1,819,000, grapes 1,720,000, potatoes 1,303,000, tomatoes 1,287,000, apples 1,050,000, corn (maize) 924,000, oats 416,000, onions (dry) 287,000, rice 142,000; livestock (number of live animals) 4,100,000 sheep, 3,566,000 cattle, 2,750,000 pigs; roundwood (2001) 37,790,000 cu m; fish catch (2001) 3,717,000. Mining (metal content; 2001): iron ore 5,520,000; copper 4,739,000; molybdenum 33,492; zinc 32,762; silver 1,347,000 kg; gold 42,673 kg. Manufacturing (value added in Ch$'000,000; 1997): food products 3,810,200; metal and metal products 2,631,900; petroleum and petroleum products 1,100,200; paper and paper products 964,900; beverages 807,400; nonmetallic mineral products 593,000. Energy production (consumption): electricity (kW-hr; 2001) 41,292,000,000 ([1999] 31,204,000,000); coal (metric tons; 2001) 480,000 ([1999] 5,939,000); crude petroleum (barrels; 1999) 1,793,000 (72,373,000); petroleum products (metric tons; 1999) 8,748,000 (10,709,000); natural gas (cu m; 1999) 2,069,700,000 (4,477,100,000).

Gross national product (2001): U.S.$70,600,000,000 (U.S.$4,590 per capita).

Structure of gross domestic product and labour force

	2001 in value Ch$'000,000[7]	2001 % of total value	1998[6] labour force	1998[6] % of labour force
Agriculture	2,052,900	5.6	770,000	13.1
Mining	3,050,700	8.3	70,300	1.2
Manufacturing	5,722,100	15.7	754,200	12.9
Public utilities	1,214,800	3.3	28,400	0.5
Construction	2,952,500	8.1	406,100	6.9
Transp. and commun.	2,727,900	7.5	430,200	7.3
Trade	3,904,100	10.7	995,500	17.0
Finance	4,557,200	12.5	425,800	7.3
Pub. admin., defense / Services / Other	10,350,800[8]	28.3[8]	1,494,200	25.5
Other			489,400[9]	8.3[9]
TOTAL	36,583,000[10]	100.0	5,864,100	100.0

Public debt (external, outstanding; 2001): U.S.$5,544,000,000.
Household income and expenditure. Average household size (2002) 3.4; average annual income per household (1994) Ch$5,981,706 at November prices (U.S.$12,552); sources of income (1990): wages and salaries 75.1%, transfer payments 12.0%, other 12.9%; expenditure (1989): food 27.9%, clothing 22.5%, housing 15.2%, transportation 6.4%.
Tourism (2001): receipts U.S.$788,000,000; expenditures U.S.$1,040,000,000.

Foreign trade[11]

Balance of trade (current prices)

	1997	1998	1999	2000	2001	2002[12]
U.S.$'000,000	−1,396	−2,010	+2,459	+2,155	+2,093	+2,238
% of total	3.8%	5.8%	7.7%	5.9%	6.0%	7.1%

Imports (2001): U.S.$17,181,000,000 (machinery and fabricated metals 29.4%; chemical products and mineral fuels 19.7%; copper 12.5%). *Major import sources:* Argentina 17.8%; U.S. 16.8%; Brazil 8.7%; Germany 4.0%; Japan 3.3%.
Exports (2001): U.S.$17,620,000,000 (copper 37.9%; food and food products 24.8%, of which raw fruit 7.8%; paper and paper products 6.4%). *Major export destinations:* U.S. 19.4%; Japan 12.1%; U.K. 7.0%; Brazil 4.8%; France 3.4%.

Transport and communications

Transport. Railroads (2001): route length 5,282 mi, 8,501 km; passenger-km 870,836,000; metric ton-km cargo 3,318,000,000. Roads (1996): total length 49,590 mi, 79,800 km (paved 14%). Vehicles (2001): passenger cars 1,351,900; trucks and buses 693,000. Air transport (1999): passenger-km 10,650,500,000; metric ton-km cargo 2,107,000,000; airports (1998) with scheduled flights 23.

Communications

Medium	date	unit	number	units per 1,000 persons
Daily newspapers	2000	circulation	1,450,000	98
Radio	2000	receivers	5,230,000	354
Television	2000	receivers	3,580,000	242
Telephones	2002	main lines	3,467,200	230
Cellular telephones	2002	subscribers	6,446,000	428
Personal computers	2002	units	1,796,000	119
Internet	2001	users	3,102,200	208

Education and health

Educational attainment (1992). Percentage of population age 25 and over having: no formal schooling 5.7%; primary education 44.2%; secondary 42.2%; higher 7.9%. *Literacy* (1995): total population age 15 and over literate 95.2%; males literate 95.4%; females literate 95.0%.

Education (1995)

	schools	teachers	students	student/teacher ratio
Primary (age 6–13)	8,702	80,155	2,149,501	26.8
Secondary (age 14–17)[13]	...	51,042	679,165	13.3
Higher	...	18,084[14]	367,094	...

Health: physicians (2000) 17,720 (1 per 834 persons); hospital beds (1999) 42,163 (1 per 346 persons); infant mortality rate (2001) 9.4.
Food (2001): daily per capita caloric intake 2,868 (vegetable products 78%, animal products 22%); 118% of FAO recommended minimum requirement.

Military

Total active duty personnel (2002): 80,500 (army 55.9%, navy 28.6%, air force 15.5%). *Military expenditure as percentage of GNP* (1999): 3.0% (world 2.4%); per capita expenditure U.S.$133.

[1]Includes 9 nonelective seats and one former president serving as Senator-for-life. [2]Legislative bodies meet in Valparaíso. [3]Excludes the 480,000-sq mi (1,250,000-sq km) section of Antarctica claimed by Chile (and administered as part of Magallanes y la Antártica Chilena region) and "inland" (actually tidal) water areas. The 2002 census population of Chilean-claimed Antarctica is 130. [4]Final. [5]Preliminary census populations of single communes except Greater Santiago and Concepción, which is a total for 3 communes. [6]Excludes all or some classes or elements of the military. [7]In constant prices of 1996. [8]Less imputed bank service charges, import duties, and value-added tax on imports. [9]Unemployed. [10]Detail does not add to total given because of rounding. [11]Imports f.o.b. in balance of trade and c.i.f. in commodities and trading partners. [12]Excludes December. [13]Includes vocational. [14]Universities only.

Internet resources for further information:

- **Instituto Nacional de Estadísticas http://www.ine.cl**
- **Banco Central de Chile http://www.bcentral.cl/eng**

China

Official name: Chung-hua Jen-min Kung-ho-kuo (People's Republic of China).
Form of government: single-party people's republic with one legislative house (National People's Congress [2,916[1]]).
Chief of state: President.
Head of government: Premier.
Capital: Peking (Beijing).
Official language: Mandarin Chinese.
Official religion: none.
Monetary unit: 1 Renminbi (yuan) (Y) = 10 jiao = 100 fen; valuation (Sept. 8, 2003) 1 U.S.$ = Y 8.28; 1 £ = Y 13.12.

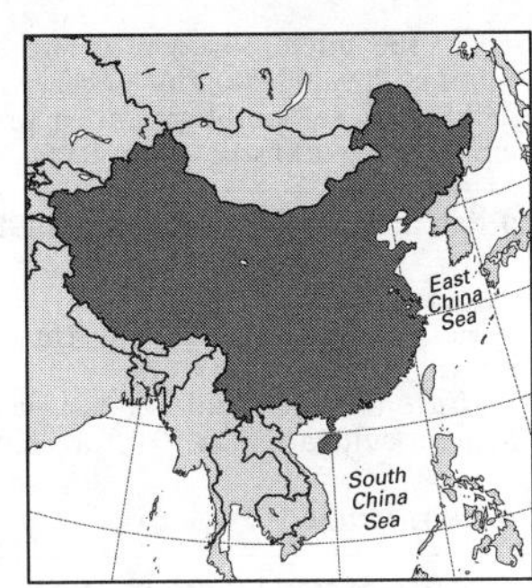

Area and population[2, 3]

Provinces	Capitals	area sq mi	area sq km	population 2000 estimate
Anhwei (Anhui)	Ho-fei (Hefei)	54,000	139,900	59,860,000
Chekiang (Zhejiang)	Hang-chou (Hangzhou)	39,300	101,800	46,770,000
Fukien (Fujian)	Fu-chou (Fuzhou)	47,500	123,100	34,710,000
Hainan (Hainan)	Hai-k'ou (Haikou)	13,200	34,300	7,870,000
Heilungkiang (Heilongjiang)	Harbin	179,000	463,600	36,890,000
Honan (Henan)	Cheng-chou (Zhengzhou)	64,500	167,000	92,560,000
Hopeh (Hebei)	Shih-chia-chuang (Shijiazhuang)	78,200	202,700	67,440,000
Hunan (Hunan)	Ch'ang-sha (Changsha)	81,300	210,500	64,400,000
Hupeh (Hubei)	Wu-han (Wuhan)	72,400	187,500	60,280,000
Kansu (Gansu)	Lan-chou (Lanzhou)	141,500	366,500	25,620,000
Kiangsi (Jiangxi)	Nan-ch'ang (Nanchang)	63,600	164,800	41,400,000
Kiangsu (Jiangsu)	Nanking (Nanjing)	39,600	102,600	74,380,000
Kirin (Jilin)	Ch'ang-ch'un (Changchun)	72,200	187,000	27,280,000
Kwangtung (Guangdong)	Canton (Guangzhou)	76,100	197,100	86,420,000
Kweichow (Guizhou)	Kuei-yang (Guiyang)	67,200	174,000	35,250,000
Liaoning (Liaoning)	Shen-yang (Shenyang)	58,300	151,000	42,380,000
Shansi (Shanxi)	T'ai-yüan (Taiyuan)	60,700	157,100	32,970,000
Shantung (Shandong)	Chi-nan (Jinan)	59,200	153,300	90,790,000
Shensi (Shaanxi)	Sian (Xi'an)	75,600	195,800	36,050,000
Szechwan (Sichuan)	Ch'eng-tu (Chengdu)	210,800	546,000	83,290,000
Tsinghai (Qinghai)	Hsi-ning (Xining)	278,400	721,000	5,180,000
Yunnan (Yunnan)	K'un-ming (Kunming)	168,400	436,200	42,880,000
Autonomous regions				
Inner Mongolia (Nei Monggol)	Hu-ho-hao-t'e (Hohhot)	454,600	1,177,500	23,760,000
Kwangsi Chuang (Guangxi Zhuang)	Nan-ning (Nanning)	85,100	220,400	44,890,000
Ningsia Hui (Ningxia Hui)	Yin-ch'uan (Yinchuan)	25,600	66,400	5,620,000
Sinkiang Uighur (Xinjiang Uygur)	Wu-lu-mu-ch'i (Urumqi)	635,900	1,646,900	19,250,000
Tibet (Xizang)	Lhasa	471,700	1,221,600	2,620,000
Municipalities				
Chungking (Chongqing)	—	8,900	23,000	30,900,000
Peking (Beijing)	—	6,500	16,800	13,820,000
Shanghai (Shanghai)	—	2,400	6,200	16,740,000
Tientsin (Tianjin)	—	4,400	11,300	10,010,000
TOTAL		3,696,100[4]	9,572,900[4]	1,262,280,000[5]

Demography

Population (2003): 1,288,892,000.
Density (2003): persons per sq mi 348.7, persons per sq km 134.6.
Urban-rural (2002): urban 37.7%; rural 62.3%.
Sex distribution (2002): male 51.46%; female 48.54%.
Age breakdown (2000): under 15, 22.9%; 15–29, 25.4%; 30–44, 25.6%; 45–59, 15.7%; 60–74, 8.2%; 75 and over, 2.2%.
Population projection: (2010) 1,344,786,000; (2020) 1,426,184,000.
Doubling time: 99 years.
Ethnic composition (2000): Han (Chinese) 91.53%; Chuang 1.30%; Manchu 0.86%; Hui 0.79%; Miao 0.72%; Uighur 0.68%; Tuchia 0.65%; Yi 0.62%; Mongolian 0.47%; Tibetan 0.44%; Puyi 0.24%; Tung 0.24%; Yao 0.21%; Korean 0.15%; Pai 0.15%; Hani 0.12%; Kazakh 0.10%; Li 0.10%; Tai 0.09%; other 0.54%.
Religious affiliation (2000): nonreligious 42.1%; Chinese folk-religionist 28.5%; Buddhist 8.4%; atheist 8.1%; Christian 7.1%; traditional beliefs 4.3%; Muslim 1.5%.
Major cities (2000[6]): Shanghai 9,231,900; Peking 6,997,000; Tientsin 4,868,800; Wu-han 4,344,600; Shen-yang 3,896,000; Chungking 3,650,100; Canton 3,365,400; Harbin 2,590,000; Nanking 2,471,700; Sian 2,440,400; Ch'eng-tu 2,212,100; Ch'ang-ch'un 2,113,400; Talien (Dalian) 2,031,100; T'ai-yüan 1,794,600; Chi-nan 1,733,500; Ch'ing-tao (Qingdao) 1,730,300; Cheng-chou 1,515,400; K'un-ming 1,460,000; Tzu-po (Zibo) 1,459,300; Lan-chou 1,454,900; Hang-chou 1,392,900; Ch'ang-sha 1,392,900; Shijiazhuang 1,377,000.
Households. Average household size (2000) 3.4; total households 351,233,698, of which family households 340,491,197 (96.9%), collective 10,742,501 (3.1%).

Vital statistics

Birth rate per 1,000 population (2001): 13.4 (world avg. 21.3).
Death rate per 1,000 population (2001): 6.4 (world avg. 9.1).
Natural increase rate per 1,000 population (2001): 7.0 (world avg. 12.2).
Total fertility rate (avg. births per childbearing woman; 2001): 1.8.
Marriage rate per 1,000 population (2001): 6.3.
Divorce rate per 1,000 population (2001): 1.0.
Life expectancy at birth (2002): male 69.0 years; female 73.0 years.
Major causes of death per 100,000 population (1998)[7]: diseases of the circulatory system 244.3; malignant neoplasms (cancers) 139.3; diseases of the respiratory system 86.8; accidents, violence, and intoxication 38.7; digestive diseases 18.7.

Social indicators

Educational attainment (2000). Percentage of population age 15 and over having: no schooling and incomplete primary 15.6%; completed primary 35.7%; some secondary 34.0%; complete secondary 11.1%; some postsecondary through advanced degree 3.6%.

Distribution of urban household income (1996)

avg. per capita income by quintile (avg. Y 4,845 [U.S.$583])

first quintile	second quintile	third quintile	fourth quintile	fifth quintile
Y 2,801	Y 3,780	Y 4,580	Y 5,599	Y 8,039

Quality of working life. Average workweek (1998): 40 hours. Annual rate per 100,000 workers for (1997)[8]: injury or accident 0.7; industrial illness, n.a.; death 1.4. Funds for pensions and social welfare relief (2001): Y 26,668,000,000.
Access to services. Proportion of communes having access to electricity (1979) 87.1%. Percentage of urban population with: safe public water supply (1996) 95.0%; public sewage collection, n.a.; public fire protection, n.a.
Social participation. Eligible voters participating in last national election: n.a. Population participating in voluntary work: n.a. Trade union membership in total labour force (1996): 14.7%. Practicing religious population in total affiliated population: n.a.
Social deviance. Annual reported arrest rate per 100,000 population (1986) for: property violation 20.7; infringing personal rights 7.2; disruption of social administration 3.3; endangering public security 1.0[9].
Material well-being. Urban households possessing (number per household; 2002[6]): bicycles 1.6; colour televisions 1.2; washing machines 0.9; refrigerators 0.8; cameras 0.4. Rural families possessing (number per family; 2002): bicycles 1.2; colour televisions 0.5; washing machines 0.3; refrigerators 0.1; cameras 0.03.

National economy

Gross national product (2001): U.S.$1,131,200,000,000 (U.S.$890 per capita).

Structure of gross domestic product and labour force

	2001 in value Y '000,000	% of total value	labour force ('000)	% of labour force
Agriculture	1,460,990	15.2	329,740	44.3
Mining } Manufacturing }	4,260,710	44.4	5,610	0.8
			80,830	10.9
Construction	646,200	6.7	36,690	4.9
Public utilities	...	...	2,880	0.4
Transp. and commun.	522,210	5.5	20,370	2.7
Trade	782,350	8.2	47,370	6.3
Finance	...	...	4,430	0.6
Pub. admin.	...	...	11,010	1.5
Services	1,920,870	20.0	205,390[10]	27.6[10]
Other	...	...	...	...
TOTAL	9,593,330	100.0	744,320	100.0

Budget (2001). Revenue: Y 1,638,604,000,000 (tax revenue 93.4%, of which VAT 32.7%, corporate income taxes 12.6%, consumption tax 5.6%; nontax revenue 6.6%). Expenditures: Y 1,890,258,000,000 (economic development 34.2%; education, health, and science 27.6%; administration 18.9%; debt payment 10.6%; defense 7.6%; other 1.1%).
Public debt (external, outstanding; 2001): U.S.$91,706,000,000.
Tourism (2001): receipts from visitors U.S.$17,792,000,000; expenditures by nationals abroad U.S.$13,909,000,000.

Retail and catering enterprises (1996)

	no. of enter-prises	no. of employees	annual wage as a % of all wages	annual gross output value (Y '000,000)
Retail trade	13,963,162	31,892,181	...	...
Food, beverage, and tobacco	5,177,416	10,738,924	...	241,350
Articles for daily use	3,242,769	8,614,944	...	88,470
Textile goods, garments, shoes, and hats	2,018,136	4,030,888	...	125,250
Sundry goods for daily use	799,486	1,670,984	...	...
Hardware, electrical appliances, and chemicals	583,466	1,828,788	...	...
Medicines and medical appliances	123,534	405,424	...	57,980
Books and newspapers	140,856	365,424	...	23,110
Other	1,877,499	4,236,805	...	...
Catering trade	2,587,730	7,753,108	...	...
Restaurants	1,181,732	4,321,824	...	...
Fast-food eateries	397,561	1,049,829	...	...
Other	1,008,437	2,381,455	...	...

Production (metric tons except as noted). Agriculture, forestry, fishing (2002): grains—rice 176,553,000, corn (maize) 123,175,000, wheat 91,290,240, sorghum 2,731,000, barley 2,470,000, millet 2,070,779; oilseeds—soybeans 16,900,328, peanuts (groundnuts) 15,006,087, rapeseed 10,530,021, sunflower seeds 1,900,000; fruits and nuts—watermelons 57,530,082, apples 20,434,763, pears 9,090,565, cantaloupes 8,630,911, oranges 3,675,639; other—sweet potatoes 114,289,100, sugarcane 82,278,000, potatoes 65,052,119, cabbage 26,812,396, tomatoes 25,466,211, cucumbers 22,924,218, onions 15,621,572, eggplants 15,430,000, seed cotton 14,760,000, sugar beets 11,562,000, garlic 8,694,066, tobacco leaves 2,394,215, tea 759,837; livestock (number of live animals) 464,695,016 pigs, 161,492,200 goats, 136,972,415 sheep, 106,175,000 cattle, 22,248,850 water buffalo, 8,815,000 asses, 8,262,280 horses, 3,923,600,000 chickens, 661,250,000 ducks; roundwood (2001) 284,910,000 cu m; fish catch (2001) 44,063,000, of which aquaculture 25,680,000. Mining and quarrying (2001): metal content of mine output—zinc 1,700,000, lead 676,000, copper 587,000, antimony 150,000, tin 95,000, tungsten 38,500; metal ores—iron ore 220,000,000, bauxite 9,800,000, manganese ore 2,500,000, vanadium 30,000, silver 1,910, gold 185; nonmetals—salt 34,105,000, soda ash 9,144,000, gypsum 6,800,000, barite 3,600,000, magnesite 3,580,000, talc 3,500,000, fluorspar 2,450,000, asbestos 360,000. Manufacturing (2001): cement 661,040,000; steel products 160,676,000; pig iron 155,554,000; rolled steel 151,634,000; paper and paperboard 37,771,000; chemical fertilizer 33,830,000; sulfuric acid 22,300,000; cotton fabrics 11,716,000; cotton yarn 7,606,000; sugar 6,531,000; colour television sets 40,937,000 units; bicycles 29,023,000 units; household refrigerators 13,513,000 units; household washing machines 13,416,000 units; motor vehicles 2,342,000 units. Distribution of industrial production (percentage of total value of output by sector; 2001): state-operated enterprises 26.8%; urban collectives 16.6%; rural collectives 23.2%; privately operated enterprises 33.4%. Retail sales (percentage of total sales by sector; 2001): state-operated enterprises 25.3%; collectives 29.8%; privately operated enterprises 44.9%.

Manufacturing and mining enterprises (1996)

	no. of enter-prises	no. of employees[11]	annual wages as a % of avg. of all wages	annual gross output value (Y '000,000)
Manufacturing				
Machinery, transport equipment, and metal manufactures,	23,032	21,560	...	880,886
of which,				
Metal products	2,641	1,810,000	...	23,593
Industrial equipment	8,875	7,020,000	...	183,951
Transport equipment	4,303	3,540,000	...	187,581
Electronic goods	1,579	1,630,000	...	70,046
Measuring equipment	1,179	820,000	...	14,738
Textiles	4,031	6,340,000	...	161,949
Garments	1,177	1,680,000	...	11,359
Foodstuffs,	18,191	4,710,000	...	383,264
of which,				
Food processing	14,520	3,170,000	...	196,393
Beverages	3,367	1,210,000	...	70,368
Tobacco manufactures	304	330,000	...	116,503
Chemicals,	10,707	8,140,000	...	537,768
of which,				
Pharmaceuticals	2,044	1,020,000	...	53,749
Plastics	1,667	1,050,000	...	15,167
Secondary forest products (including paper and stationery)	3,664	2,310,000	...	51,238
Primary forest products	877	1,140,000	...	16,750
Mining				
Nonferrous and ferrous metals	1,163	810,000	...	22,711
Crude petroleum	71	1,250,000	...	149,525
Coal	2,011	5,050,000	...	105,946

Energy production (consumption): electricity (kW-hr; 2002) 1,602,156,000,000 ([1999] 1,230,520,000,000); coal (metric tons; 2002) 1,108,000,000 ([1999] 1,305,761,000); crude petroleum (barrels; 2002) 1,247,000,000 ([1999] 1,386,900,000); petroleum products (metric tons; 1999) 140,644,000 (160,622,000); natural gas (cu m; 2002) 32,819,000,000 ([1999] 31,074,900,000).

Financial aggregates[12]

	1996	1997	1998	1999	2000	2001	2002
Exchange rate, Y per:							
U.S. dollar	8.30	8.28	8.28	8.28	8.28	8.28	8.28
£	12.95	13.58	13.74	13.41	12.59	11.92	12.42
SDR	11.93	11.17	11.66	11.36	10.78	10.40	11.25
International reserves (U.S.$)							
Total (excl. gold; '000,000)	107,039	142,762	149,188	157,728	168,278	215,605	291,128
SDRs ('000,000)	614	602	676	741	798	851	998
Reserve pos. in IMF ('000,000)	1,396	2,270	3,553	2,312	1,905	2,590	3,723
Foreign exchange	105,029	139,890	144,959	154,675	165,574	212,165	286,407
Gold ('000,000 fine troy oz)	12.7	12.7	12.7	12.7	12.7	16.1	19.3
% world reserves	1.4	1.4	1.4	1.3	1.3	1.7	2.1
Interest and prices							
Central bank discount (%)	9.00	8.55	4.59	3.24	3.24	3.24	2.70
Govt. bond yield (%)	...	...	...	...	...	...	...
Industrial share prices	...	...	...	...	...	...	...
Balance of payments (U.S.$'000,000)							
Balance of visible trade, of which:	+19,535	+46,222	+46,614	+35,982	+34,474	+34,017	+44,167
Imports, f.o.b.	−131,542	−136,448	−136,915	−158,734	−214,657	−232,058	−281,484
Exports, f.o.b.	151,077	182,670	183,529	194,716	249,131	266,075	325,651
Balance of invisibles	−12,292	−9,259	−15,142	−20,540	−13,956	−16,616	−8,745
Balance of payments, current account	+7,243	+36,963	+31,472	+21,115	+20,518	+17,401	+35,422

Household income and expenditure. Average household size (2001) 3.5; rural households 4.4, urban households 3.1. Average annual per capita income of household (2001): rural households Y 2,366 (U.S.$286), urban households Y 6,907 (U.S.$834). Sources of income (2001): rural households—income from household businesses 77.9%, wages 16.6%, transfers 4.3%, other 1.2%; urban households—wages 73.9%, transfers 19.7%, business income 5.8%, other 0.6%. Expenditure: rural (urban) households—food 47.7% (37.9%), housing 16.0% (10.3%), education and recreation 11.1% (13.0%), transportation and communications 6.3% (8.6%), clothing 5.7% (10.1%), health and personal effects 5.6% (6.5%), household furnishings 4.4% (8.3%).

Population economically active (2001): total 744,320,000; activity rate of total population 58.5% (participation rates: over age 15, 77.7%; female 37.8%; registered unemployed in urban areas 3.6%). Urban employed workforce (2001): 239,400,000; by sector: state enterprises 76,400,000, collectives 28,130,000, self-employment or privately run enterprises 134,870,000. Rural employed workforce 490,850,000.

Price and earnings indexes (1995 = 100)

	1996	1997	1998	1999	2000	2001	2002
Consumer price index	108.3	111.3	110.5	109.0	109.3	109.8	108.9
Annual earnings index[13]	112.1	116.1	114.8	121.8	131.4	145.9	...

Land use (1999): meadows and pastures 42.9%; agricultural and under permanent cultivation 14.5%; forested and other 42.6%.

Foreign trade[14]

Balance of trade (current prices)

	1997	1998	1999	2000	2001	2002
U.S.$'000,000	+46,222	+46,614	+35,982	+34,474	+34,017	+44,167
% of total	14.5%	14.5%	10.2%	7.4%	6.8%	7.3%

Imports (2000): U.S.$225,094,000,000 (machinery and apparatus 38.0%, of which transistors/microcircuits 9.4%, telecommunications equipment 5.5%; crude petroleum 6.6%; artificial resins and plastic materials 5.8%; textile yarn, fabrics, and made-up articles 5.8%; iron and steel 4.4%). *Major import sources:* Japan 18.4%; unspecified Asia (mostly Taiwan) 11.3%; South Korea 10.3%; United States 9.9%; Germany 4.6%; Hong Kong 4.2%; free zones 3.2%; Russia 2.6%; Malaysia 2.4%; Singapore 2.2%.

Exports (2000): U.S.$249,203,000,000 (machinery and apparatus 29.5%, of which computers and related units 7.5%, telecommunications equipment and related parts 5.0%; wearing apparel 14.5%; textile yarn, fabrics, and made-up articles 6.5%; toys, games, and sporting goods 4.1%). *Major export destinations:* United States 20.9%; Hong Kong 17.9%; Japan 16.7%; South Korea 4.5%; Germany 3.7%; The Netherlands 2.7%; United Kingdom 2.5%; Singapore 2.3%.

Transport and communications

Transport. Railroads (2001): route length 43,531 mi, 70,057 km; passenger-mi 296,195,000,000, passenger-km 476,680,000,000; short ton-mi cargo 998,313,000,000, metric ton-km cargo 1,457,510,000,000. Roads (2001): total length 1,055,094 mi, 1,698,012 km (paved, n.a.). Vehicles (2001): passenger cars 9,939,600; trucks and buses 7,652,400. Air transport (2001): passenger-mi 67,816,000,000, passenger-km 109,140,000,000; short ton-mi cargo 2,995,000,000, metric ton-km cargo 4,372,000,000; airports (1996) with scheduled flights 113.

Communications

Medium	date	unit	number	units per 1,000 persons
Daily newspapers	1994	circulation	27,790,000	23
Radio	2000	receivers	428,000,000	339
Television	2000	receivers	370,000,000	293
Telephones	2002	main lines	214,420,000	167
Cellular telephones	2002	subscribers	206,620,000	161
Personal computers	2001	units	25,000,000	19
Internet	2001	users	33,700,000	26

Education and health

Literacy (2000): total population age 15 and over literate 90.9%; males literate 95.1%; females literate 86.5%.

Education (2001)

	schools	teachers	students	student/ teacher ratio
Primary (age 7–13)	491,273	5,798,000	125,435,000	21.6
Secondary (age 13–17)	80,432	4,188,000	78,360,000	18.7
Secondary specialized	2,690	184,000	3,917,000	21.3
Voc., teacher tr.	8,372	352,000	5,326,000	15.1
Higher	1,225	532,000	7,191,000	13.5

Health (2001): physicians 2,100,000 (1 per 592 persons); hospital beds 3,201,000 (1 per 418 persons); infant mortality rate per 1,000 live births (2002) 37.0.

Food (2001): daily per capita caloric intake 2,963 (vegetable products 80%, animal products 20%); 126% of FAO recommended minimum.

Military

Total active duty personnel (2002): 2,270,000 (army 70.5%, navy 11.0%, air force 18.5%). *Military expenditure as percentage of GNP* (1999): 2.3% (world 2.4%); per capita expenditure U.S.$71.

[1]As of March 2003; 36 seats are allotted to Hong Kong and 12 to Macau. [2]Names of the provinces, autonomous regions, and municipalities are stated in conventional form, followed by Pinyin transliteration; names of capitals are stated in conventional form or Wade-Giles transliteration, followed by Pinyin transliteration. [3]Data for Taiwan, Quemoy and Matsu (parts of Fukien province occupied by Taiwan); Hong Kong (which reverted to China from British administration on July 1, 1997) and Macau (which reverted to China from Portuguese administration on Dec. 20, 1999) are excluded. [4]Includes 4,600 sq mi (11,900 sq km) not shown separately. [5]Sum of provincial and autonomous region populations; national total may differ. [6]January 1. [7]Based on urban sample population. [8]Reported cases. [9]Excludes arrests for anti-Communist activities. [10]Includes 6,810,000 registered unemployed. [11]In state-owned and collective-owned industries only. [12]Exchange rates and international reserves are period average figures. [13]Average annual wage in industrial establishments in urban areas. [14]Imports f.o.b. in balance of trade and c.i.f. in commodities and trading partners.

Internet resource for further information:

- **Embassy of The People's Republic of China http://www.china-embassy.org**
- **China Statistical Information Net http://www.stats.gov.cn/english**

Colombia

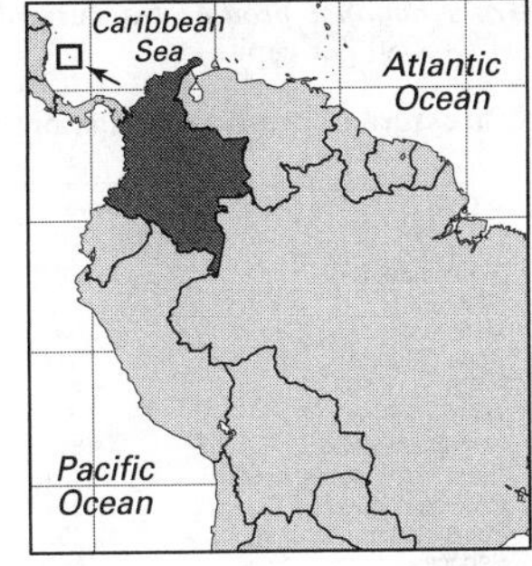

Official name: República de Colombia (Republic of Colombia).
Form of government: unitary, multiparty republic with two legislative houses (Senate [102]; House of Representatives [166[1]]).
Head of state and government: President.
Capital: Bogotá.
Official language: Spanish.
Official religion: none.
Monetary unit: 1 peso (Col$) = 100 centavos; valuation (Sept. 8, 2003) 1 U.S.$ = Col$2,819; 1 £ = Col$4,470.

Area and population

Departments	Capitals	area sq mi	area sq km	population 1999 estimate
Antioquia	Medellín	24,445	63,912	5,300,000
Atlántico	Barranquilla	1,308	3,388	2,081,000
Bolívar	Cartagena	10,030	25,978	1,951,000
Boyacá	Tunja	8,953	23,189	1,355,000
Caldas	Manizales	3,046	7,888	1,094,000
Caquetá	Florencia	34,349	88,965	410,000
Cauca	Popayán	11,316	29,308	1,234,000
Cesar	Valledupar	8,844	22,905	944,000
Chocó	Quibdó	17,965	46,530	406,000
Córdoba	Montería	9,660	25,020	1,308,000
Cundinamarca	Bogotá, D.C.	8,735	22,623	2,099,000
Huila	Neiva	7,680	19,890	911,000
La Guajira	Riohacha	8,049	20,848	475,000
Magdalena	Santa Marta	8,953	23,188	1,260,000
Meta	Villavicencio	33,064	85,635	686,000
Nariño	Pasto	12,845	33,268	1,603,000
Norte de Santander	Cúcuta	8,362	21,658	1,316,000
Orinoquía-Amazonía[2]	...	186,519	483,083	1,162,000
Quindío	Armenia	712	1,845	552,000
Risaralda	Pereira	1,598	4,140	928,000
San Andrés y Providencia	San Andrés	17	44	71,000
Santander	Bucaramanga	11,790	30,537	1,939,000
Sucre	Sincelejo	4,215	10,917	779,000
Tolima	Ibagué	9,097	23,562	1,293,000
Valle	Cali	8,548	22,140	4,104,000
Capital District				
Bogotá		613	1,587	6,276,000
TOTAL		440,762[3]	1,141,568[3]	41,537,000[4]

Demography

Population (2003): 41,662,000[5].
Density (2003): persons per sq mi 94.5, persons per sq km 36.5.
Urban-rural (2002): urban 75.5%; rural 24.5%.
Sex distribution (2002): male 49.10%; female 50.90%.
Age breakdown (2002): under 15, 31.6%; 15–29, 26.0%; 30–44, 24.3%; 45–59, 12.0%; 60–74, 5.7%; 75 and over, 0.4%.
Population projection: (2010) 46,109,000; (2020) 52,199,000.
Ethnic composition (2000): mestizo 47.3%; mulatto 23.0%; white 20.0%; black 6.0%; black-Amerindian 1.0%; Amerindian/other 2.7%.
Religious affiliation (1995): Roman Catholic 91.9%; other 8.1%.
Major cities (1999): Bogotá, D.C., 6,276,428; Cali 2,110,571; Medellín 1,957,928; Barranquilla 1,226,292; Bucaramanga 520,874.

Vital statistics

Birth rate per 1,000 population (2002): 22.0 (world avg. 21.3).
Death rate per 1,000 population (2002): 5.7 (world avg. 9.1).
Natural increase rate per 1,000 population (2002): 16.3 (world avg. 12.2).
Total fertility rate (avg. births per childbearing woman; 2002): 2.6.
Life expectancy at birth (2002): male 67.0 years; female 74.8 years.
Major causes of death per 100,000 population (1994): accidents, violence, and suicides 114.5, of which homicide with firearms 73.1; malignant neoplasms (cancers) 58.3; ischemic heart disease 50.4; infectious and parasitic diseases 13.7.

National economy

Budget (1999)[6]. Revenue: Col$41,457,000,000,000 (tax revenue 61.7%, nontax revenue 38.3%). Expenditures: Col$50,441,000,000,000 (current expenditure 73.6%; capital expenditure 26.4%).
Public debt (external, outstanding; 2001): U.S.$21,777,000,000.
Population economically active (2000): total 15,417,000; activity rate 38.8% (participation rates: ages 15–69, 64.3%; female 38.0%; unemployed 20.2%).

Price and earnings indexes (1995 = 100)

	1996	1997	1998	1999	2000	2001	2002
Consumer price index	120.2	142.4	169.0	187.4	204.7	221.0	235.0
Earnings index	107.4	108.9	109.2	112.3	114.7	...	...

Production (metric tons except as noted). Agriculture, forestry, fishing (2002): sugarcane 38,200,000, plantains 2,827,024, potatoes 2,697,980, rice 2,353,440, cassava 2,214,990, bananas 1,650,000, corn 1,331,160, coffee 660,000; livestock (number of live animals) 27,000,000 cattle, 2,260,000 sheep, 2,150,000 pigs; roundwood (2001) 12,501,000 cu m; fish catch (2000) 191,430. Mining and quarrying (2001): nickel (metal content) 52,962; gold 21,813 kg; emeralds 5,500,000 carats. Manufacturing (value added in Col$'000,000; 1997): processed food 11,133,000; beverages 3,165,400; petroleum products 2,483,600; textiles 2,244,200; transport equipment 2,186,600; chemicals 2,170,300; machinery and electrical apparatus 1,707,300; paper products 1,649,000; fabricated metal products 1,334,500. Energy production (consumption): electricity (kW-hr; 1999) 44,148,000,000 (44,154,000,000); coal (metric tons; 1999) 32,677,000 (3,945,000); crude petroleum (barrels; 2001) 243,208,000 ([1999] 109,400,000); petroleum products (metric tons; 1999) 13,025,000 (9,514,000); natural gas (cu m; 1999) 7,574,400,000 (7,574,400,000).
Gross national product (2001): U.S.$81,600,000,000 (U.S.$1,890 per capita).

Structure of gross domestic product and labour force

	2000			
	in value Col$'000,000	% of total value	labour force	% of labour force
Agriculture	21,745,142	12.8	3,221,000	20.9
Mining	12,998,058	7.7	359,000[7]	2.3[7]
Manufacturing	21,761,444	12.8	1,951,000	12.7
Construction	6,216,386	3.7	700,000	4.5
Public utilities	6,992,144	4.1	[7]	[7]
Transp. and commun.	12,551,115	7.4	842,000	5.5
Trade	18,803,503	11.1	3,469,000	22.5
Finance	24,898,482	14.7	621,000	4.0
Pub. admin., defense; Services	38,204,472	22.5	4,240,000	27.5
Other	5,533,202[8]	3.3[8]	14,000[9]	0.1[9]
TOTAL	169,703,948	100.0[3]	15,417,000	100.0

Household income and expenditure. Average household size (2000) 5.0; expenditure (1992): food 34.2%, transportation 18.5%, housing 7.8%, health care 6.4%.
Tourism (2001): receipts U.S.$1,209,000,000; expenditures U.S.$1,160,000,000.

Foreign trade[10]

Balance of trade (current prices)

	1997	1998	1999	2000	2001	2002
U.S.$'000,000	–3,855	–3,782	+917	+1,502	–577	–790
% of total	14.3%	14.8%	4.1%	6.1%	2.3%	3.2%

Imports (2002): U.S.$12,690,000,000 (capital goods 32.5%, consumer goods 21.3%). *Major import sources:* U.S. 31.7%; Venezuela 6.2%; Mexico 5.3%; Brazil 5.1%; Japan 4.9%.
Exports (2002): U.S.$11,900,000,000 (crude and refined petroleum 27.5%, chemicals and chemical products 12.4%, coal 8.3%, food, beverages, and tobacco 7.9%, machinery and equipment 7.6%, coffee 6.5%). *Major export destinations:* U.S. 43.0%; Venezuela 9.4%; Ecuador 6.8%; Peru 2.9%; Germany 2.8%.

Transport and communications

Transport. Railroads (2000): route length 1,960 mi, 3,154 km; passenger-km (1992) 15,524,000; metric ton-km cargo (1999) 473,000,000. Roads (1999): total length 71,400 mi, 114,912 km (paved 14%). Vehicles (1999): cars 762,000; trucks 672,000. Air transport (2001): passenger-km 5,858,369,000; metric ton-km cargo 33,037,000; airports (1998) 43.

Communications

Medium	date	unit	number	units per 1,000 persons
Daily newspapers	1996	circulation	1,800,000[11]	46[11]
Radio	2000	receivers	21,600,000	544
Television	2000	receivers	11,200,000	282
Telephones	2002	main lines	7,766,000	179
Cellular telephones	2002	subscribers	4,597,000	106
Personal computers	2002	units	2,135,000	50
Internet	2002	users	1,982,000	46

Education and health

Educational attainment (1985). Percentage of population age 25 and over having: no schooling 15.3%; primary education 50.1%; secondary 25.4%; higher 6.8%; not stated 2.4%. *Literacy* (1999): population age 15 and over literate 91.5%; males literate 91.5%; females literate 91.5%.

Education (1999)

	schools	teachers	students	student/ teacher ratio
Primary (age 6–10)	60,183	214,911	5,162,260	24.0
Secondary (age 11–16)	13,421	200,337	3,594,083	17.9
Higher[12]	266	75,568	673,353	8.9

Health (1997): physicians 40,355 (1 per 1,102 persons); hospital beds 40,043 (1 per 1,000 persons); infant mortality rate (2002) 23.2.
Food (2001): daily per capita caloric intake 2,580 (vegetable products 84%, animal products 16%); 111% of FAO recommended minimum requirement.

Military

Total active duty personnel (2002): 158,000 (army 86.1%, navy 9.5%, air force 4.4%). *Military expenditure as percentage of GNP* (1999): 3.2% (world 2.4%); per capita expenditure U.S.$68.

[1]Two seats are occupied by representatives from indigenous communities. [2]Geographic designation for eight political entities in eastern Colombia elevated to departmental status in the early 1990s. [3]Detail does not add to total given because of rounding. [4]De jure estimates. [5]Excludes at least 2,000,000 Colombians who left the country since 1997 because of the violence and high unemployment. [6]Preliminary. [7]Mining includes Public utilities. [8]Import duties and VAT, less imputed bank service charges. [9]Activities not adequately described. [10]Imports c.i.f.; exports f.o.b. [11]Circulation for 26 newspapers only. [12]1996.

Internet resources for further information:
- **National Administration Department of Statistics http://www.dane.gov.co**

Comoros[1]

Official name: L'Union des Comores (French); Udzima wa Komori (Comorian); (Union of the Comoros)[2].
Form of government: republic[3].
Head of state and government: President assisted by Vice Presidents.
Capital: Moroni.
Official languages: Comorian (Shikomor); Arabic; French.
Official religion: Islam.
Monetary unit: 1 Comorian franc[4] (CF) = 100 centimes; valuation (Sept. 8, 2003) 1 U.S.$ = CF 454.33; 1 £ = CF 720.36.

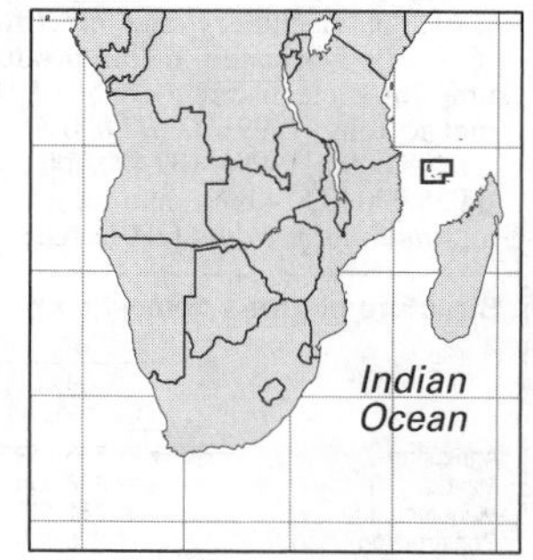

Area and population

		area		population
Autonomous islands	Capitals	sq mi	sq km	2000 estimate
Mwali (Mohéli)	Fomboni	112	290	28,600
Ngazidja (Grande-Comore)	Moroni	443	1,148	261,100
Nzwani (Anjouan)	Mutsamudu	164	424	219,500
TOTAL		719	1,862	509,200[5]

Demography

Population (2003): 584,000[6].
Density (2003): persons per sq mi 812.2, persons per sq km 313.6.
Urban-rural (2002): urban 33.8%; rural 66.2%.
Sex distribution (2002): male 49.62%; female 50.38%.
Age breakdown (2002): under 15, 42.9%; 15–29, 27.8%; 30–44, 16.6%; 45–59, 8.1%; 60–74, 3.9%; 75 and over, 0.7%.
Population projection: (2010) 672,000; (2020) 822,000.
Doubling time: 23 years.
Ethnic composition (2000): Comorian (a mixture of Bantu, Arab, Malay, and Malagasy peoples) 97.1%; Makua 1.6%; French 0.4%; Arab 0.1%; other 0.8%.
Religious affiliation (2000): Sunnī Muslim 98.0%; Christian 1.2%; other 0.8%.
Major cities (1991): Moroni (1995) 34,168 (urban agglomeration [2001] 49,000); Mutsamudu 16,785; Domoni 10,400; Fomboni 5,633.

Vital statistics

Birth rate per 1,000 population (2002): 39.0 (world avg. 21.3).
Death rate per 1,000 population (2002): 9.1 (world avg. 9.1).
Natural increase rate per 1,000 population (2002): 29.9 (world avg. 12.2).
Total fertility rate (avg. births per childbearing woman; 2002): 5.3.
Marriage rate per 1,000 population: n.a.[7]
Divorce rate per 1,000 population: n.a.
Life expectancy at birth (2002): male 58.6 years; female 63.1 years.
Major causes of death per 100,000 population: n.a.; however, major diseases include malaria (afflicts 80–90% of the adult population), tuberculosis, leprosy, and kwashiorkor (a nutritional deficiency disease).

National economy

Budget (2000). Revenue: CF 15,557,000,000 (tax revenue 62.5%, of which taxes on international trade 40.9%, income and profit taxes 12.2%, sales tax 7.7%; grants 29.2%; nontax revenue 8.3%). Expenditures: CF 17,649,000,000 (current expenditures 68.4%, of which wages 34.5%, goods and services 23.3%, interest on debt 5.4%, transfers 4.8%; development expenditures 31.6%).
Production (metric tons except as noted). Agriculture, forestry, fishing (2002): coconuts 76,000, bananas 60,000, cassava 55,000, rice 17,000, taro 9,000, corn (maize) 4,000, cloves 2,700, vanilla 140, ylang-ylang essence 40; other export crops grown in small quantities include coffee, cinnamon, and tuberoses; livestock (number of live animals; 2002) 115,000 goats, 52,000 cattle, 21,000 sheep; roundwood (2001) 8,650; fish catch (2000) 13,200. Mining and quarrying: sand, gravel, and crushed stone from coral mining for local construction. Manufacturing: products of small-scale industries include processed vanilla and ylang-ylang, cement, handicrafts, soaps, soft drinks, woodwork, and clothing. Construction: n.a. Energy production (consumption): electricity (kW-hr; 2001) 36,578,000 (19,780,000); coal, none (none); crude petroleum, none (none); petroleum products (metric tons; 1999) none (26,000); natural gas, none (none).
Population economically active (2000): total 156,000; activity rate of total population 28.4% (participation rates: [1991] ages 10 years and over, 57.8%; female 40.0%; unemployed [2000] 20%).

Price and earnings indexes (1995 = 100)

	1995	1996	1997	1998	1999	2000
Consumer price index	100.0	102.4	104.0	105.9	106.8	111.7
Monthly earnings index	100.0	...	...	...	...	...

Tourism: receipts from visitors (2000) U.S.$15,000,000; expenditures by nationals abroad (1998) U.S.$3,000,000.
Household income and expenditure. Average household size (1995) 6.3[8]; average annual income per household (1995) CF 188,985 (U.S.$505)[8]; sources of income: n.a.; expenditure (1993)[9]: food and beverages 67.3%, clothing and footwear 11.6%, tobacco and cigarettes 4.1%, energy 3.8%, health 3.2%, education 2.5%, transportation 2.2%, other 5.3%.
Land use (1994)[10]: forested 17.9%; meadows and pastures 6.7%; agricultural and under permanent cultivation 44.9%; other 30.5%.

Gross national product (at current market prices; 2001): U.S.$200,000,000 (U.S.$380 per capita).

Structure of gross domestic product and labour force

	2001		1980	
	in value CF '000,000	% of total value	labour force[11]	% of labour force
Agriculture, fishing	49,480	40.9	53,063	53.3
Mining	...	...	62	0.1
Manufacturing	5,037	4.2	3,946	4.0
Construction	7,557	6.2	3,267	3.3
Public utilities	1,857	1.5	129	0.1
Transportation and communications	6,415	5.3	2,118	2.1
Trade, restaurants, hotels	30,481	25.2	1,873	1.9
Finance, insurance	5,217	4.3	237	0.2
Public admin., defense	17,309	14.3	2,435	2.5
Services	668	0.6	4,646	4.7
Other	–3,018[12]	–2.5[12]	27,687[13]	27.8[13]
TOTAL	121,003	100.0	99,463	100.0

Public debt (external, outstanding; 2001): U.S.$220,800,000.

Foreign trade[14]

Balance of trade (current prices)

	1996	1997	1998	1999	2000	2001
CF '000,000,000	–22.2	–23.6	–19.6	–20.7	–16.7	–18.6
% of total	82.0%	81.8%	78.8%	70.9%	57.0%	50.5%

Imports (2001): CF 27,776,000,000 (food products 28.1%, of which rice 11.3%, meat and fish 8.0%; vehicles 15.6%; petroleum products 15.3%; unspecified 30.1%). *Major import sources:* EU *c.* 49%; United Arab Emirates *c.* 11%; South Africa *c.* 10%; Pakistan *c.* 9%.
Exports (2001): CF 9,144,000,000 (vanilla 59.1%, cloves 26.6%, ylang-ylang 10.9%). *Major export destinations:* France *c.* 47%; United States *c.* 30%.

Transport and communications

Transport. Railroads: none. Roads (1996): total length 559 mi, 900 km (paved 76%). Vehicles (1996): passenger cars 9,100; trucks and buses 4,950. Merchant marine (1992): vessels (100 gross tons and over) 6; total deadweight tonnage 3,579. Air transport (1996): passenger-mi 1,900,000, passenger-km 3,000,000; short ton-mi cargo, n.a., metric ton-mi cargo, n.a.; airports (2002) with scheduled flights 4.

Communications

Medium	date	unit	number	units per 1,000 persons
Daily newspapers	1997	circulation	0	0
Radio	1997	receivers	90,000	170
Television	1997	receivers	1,000	1.8
Telephones	2002	main lines	10,300	14
Personal computers	2001	units	4,000	5.5
Internet	2001	users	2,500	3.4

Education and health

Educational attainment (1980). Percentage of population age 25 and over having: no formal schooling 56.7%; Qur'anic school education 8.3%; primary 3.6%; secondary 2.0%; higher 0.2%; not specified 29.2%. *Literacy* (2000): total population age 15 and over literate 55.9%; males literate 63.2%; females literate 48.7%.

Education (1998)

	schools	teachers	students	student/ teacher ratio
Primary (age 7–12)	348	2,381	82,789	34.8
Secondary (age 13–19)	...	591	28,599	48.4
Higher	...	67	649	9.7

Health (1995): physicians 64[15] (1 per 7,800[15] persons); hospital beds 1,450[15] (1 per 342[15] persons); infant mortality rate per 1,000 live births (2002) 81.8.
Food (2001): daily per capita caloric intake 1,735 (vegetable products 94%, animal products 6%); 74% of FAO recommended minimum requirement.

Military

Total active duty personnel (1997): 1,500. *Military expenditure as percentage of GNP:* n.a.

[1]Excludes Mayotte, an overseas possession of France, unless otherwise indicated. [2]New official name effective with the swearing in of the first president of the new union on May 26, 2002. [3]New constitution effective from mid-2002 grants each island greater powers. [4]Formerly pegged to the French franc and since Jan. 1, 2002, to the euro at the rate of €1 = CF 491.97. [5]Projection based on 1991 census. [6]Includes Comorians living abroad in France or Mayotte. [7]In the early 1990s, 20% of adult men had more than one wife. [8]Based on sample survey of 2,004 households on all three islands. [9]Weights of consumer price index components for Moroni. [10]Includes Mayotte. [11]The wage labour force was very small in 1995; total of less than 7,000 including government employees, and less than 2,000 excluding them. [12]Less imputed bank service charge. [13]Not adequately defined. [14]Imports c.i.f.; exports f.o.b. [15]Estimated figure.

Internet resources for further information:
- **Indian Ocean Commission http://www.coi-info.org**
- **UN Development Programme http://www.km.undp.org**

Congo, Democratic Republic of the

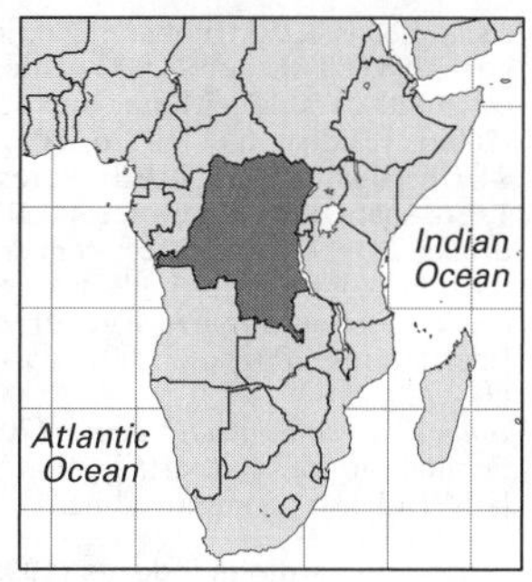

Official name: République Democratique du Congo (Democratic Republic of the Congo).
Form of government: transitional regime[1] with two legislative bodies (Senate [120]; National Assembly [500]).
Head of state and government: President assisted by Vice Presidents[1].
Capital: Kinshasa.
Official languages: French; English.
Official religion: none.
Monetary unit: Congo franc (FC)[2]; valuation (Sept. 8, 2003) 1 U.S.$ = FC 432.00; 1 £ = FC 684.96.

Area and population

		area		population
Provinces	**Capitals**	sq mi	sq km	1998 estimate
Bandundu	Bandundu	114,154	295,658	5,201,000
Bas-Congo	Matadi	20,819	53,920	2,835,000
Equateur	Mbandaka	155,712	403,292	4,820,000
Kasai-Occidental	Kananga	59,746	154,742	3,337,000
Kasai-Oriental	Mbuji-Mayi	65,754	170,302	3,830,000
Katanga	Lubumbashi	191,845	496,877	4,125,000
Maniema	Kindu	51,062	132,250	1,246,787
Nord-Kivu	Goma	22,967	59,483	3,564,434
Orientale	Kisangani	194,302	503,239	5,566,000
Sud-Kivu	Bukavu	25,147	65,130	2,837,779
City				
Kinshasa	—	3,848	9,965	4,787,000
TOTAL		905,354[3]	2,344,858	42,150,000

Demography

Population (2003): 52,771,000[4].
Density (2003): persons per sq mi 58.3, persons per sq km 22.5.
Urban-rural (2002): urban 30.7%; rural 69.3%.
Sex distribution (2002): male 49.38%; female 50.62%.
Age breakdown (2002): under 15, 48.3%; 15–29, 27.2%; 30–44, 13.6%; 45–59, 6.9%; 60–74, 3.2%; 75 and over, 0.8%.
Population projection: (2010) 64,714,000; (2020) 84,418,000.
Ethnic composition (1983): Luba 18.0%; Kongo 16.1%; Mongo 13.5%; Rwanda 10.3%; Azande 6.1%; Bangi and Ngale 5.8%; Rundi 3.8%; Teke 2.7%; Boa 2.3%; Chokwe 1.8%; Lugbara 1.6%; Banda 1.4%; other 16.6%.
Religious affiliation (1995): Roman Catholic 41.0%; Protestant 32.0%; indigenous Christian 13.4%, of which Kimbanguist 13.0%; other Christian 0.8%; Muslim 1.4%; traditional beliefs and other 11.4%.
Major cities (1994): Kinshasa 4,655,313; Lubumbashi 851,381; Mbuji-Mayi 806,475; Kolwezi 417,800; Kisangani 417,517; Kananga 393,030.

Vital statistics

Birth rate per 1,000 population (2002): 45.6 (world avg. 21.3).
Death rate per 1,000 population (2002): 15.1 (world avg. 9.1).
Natural increase rate per 1,000 population (2002): 30.5 (world avg. 12.2).
Total fertility rate (avg. births per childbearing woman; 2002): 6.8.
Life expectancy at birth (2002): male 46.6 years; female 50.9 years.

National economy

Budget (2000). Revenue: FC 15,091,000,000 (tax revenue 83.3%, of which sales tax 24.4%, taxes on international trade 23.8%, corporate tax 23.8%; nontax revenue 16.7%). Expenditures: FC 32,988,000,000 (goods and services 45.4%; wages and salaries 22.2%; interest on debt 18.7%).
Public debt (external, outstanding; 2001): U.S.$7,584,000,000.
Tourism (1998): receipts U.S.$2,000,000; expenditures (1997) U.S.$7,000,000.
Production (metric tons except as noted). Agriculture, forestry, fishing (2002): cassava 14,929,410, sugarcane 1,550,000, plantains 1,200,000, corn (maize) 1,153,990, oil palm fruit 900,000, peanuts (groundnuts) 355,180, rice 314,614, bananas 313,382, sweet potatoes 219,926, papayas 210,000, yams 200,000, pineapples 192,080, coffee 32,077, seed cotton 30,000, natural rubber 7,000; livestock (number of live animals) 4,003,880 goats, 953,066 pigs; roundwood (2001) 69,733,688 cu m; fish catch (2000) 208,862. Mining and quarrying (2001): copper (metal content) 37,800; cobalt (metal content) 4,700; zinc (metal content) 1,300; gold 69 kg; diamonds 18,200,000 carats. Manufacturing (2000): butter 2,052,000; steel 259,000; explosives 246,000; cement 169,000; sugar 80,000; soap 28,000; tires 107,000 units; printed fabrics 14,334,000 sq m; cotton fabrics 2,361,000 sq m; shoes 962,000 pairs; beer 1,710,000 hectolitres; soft drinks 810,000 hectolitres. Energy production (consumption): electricity (kW-hr; 2000) 5,813,000,000 (5,813,000,000); coal (metric tons; 1999) 96,000 (143,000); crude petroleum (barrels; 2000) 8,500,000 ([1999] 571,000); petroleum products (metric tons; 1999) 183,000 (505,000); natural gas, none (none).
Household income and expenditure. Average household size (1998) 2.3; expenditure (1985): food 61.7%, housing and energy 11.5%, clothing and footwear 9.7%, transportation 5.9%, furniture and utensils 4.9%.
Gross national product (at current market prices; 2001): U.S.$4,200,000,000 (U.S.$80 per capita).

Structure of gross domestic product and labour force

	2001		2000	
	in value FC '000,000	% of total value	labour force	% of labour force
Agriculture	824,300	56.3	13,074,000	63.2
Mining	142,000	9.7		
Manufacturing	57,100	3.9		
Construction	64,400	4.4		
Public utilities	11,700	0.8		
Transp. and commun.	39,500	2.7	7,612,000	36.8
Trade	218,200	14.9		
Pub. admin., defense	26,400	1.8		
Finance and services	60,200	4.1		
Other	20,200[5]	1.4[5]		
TOTAL	1,464,000	100.0	20,686,000	100.0

Population economically active (2000): total 20,686,000; activity rate 42.6% (participation rates: over age 10, n.a.; female n.a.).

Price and earnings indexes (1995 = 100)

	1996	1997	1998	1999	2000
Consumer price index	759	2,139	5,027	29,357	179,368
Earnings index	...	...	...	...	...

Land use (1994): forested 76.7%; meadows and pastures 6.6%; agricultural and under permanent cultivation 3.5%; other 13.2%.

Foreign trade

Balance of trade (current prices)

	1996	1997	1998	1999	2000	2001[6]
U.S.$'000,000	+249	+56	−50	−175	−212	+73
% of total	8.2%	2.2%	2.1%	8.6%	13.5%	4.3%

Imports (2000): U.S.$680,000,000 (non-petroleum sector 92.9%, petroleum sector 7.1%). *Major import sources* (2001): Belgium 17.5%; South Africa 15.9%; Nigeria 10.3%; France 5.1%; Kenya 5.0%.
Exports (2000): U.S.$892,000,000 (diamonds 52.5%, crude petroleum 22.8%, cobalt 8.0%, coffee 6.2%, copper 4.8%, gold 2.4%). *Major export destinations* (2001): Belgium 62.1%; U.S. 14.7%; Finland 8.0%; India 4.8%; Italy 2.0%.

Transport and communications

Transport. Railroads (1996)[7]: length 5,138 km; passenger-km 29,000,000[8]; metric ton-km cargo 176,000,000[8]. Roads (1996): total length 154,027 km (paved 2%). Vehicles (1996): passenger cars 787,000; trucks and buses 60,000. Air transport (1996): passenger-km 279,000,000; metric ton-km cargo 42,000,000; airports (1997) with scheduled flights 22.

Communications

Medium	date	unit	number	units per 1,000 persons
Daily newspapers	1996	circulation	124,000	2.7
Radio	2000	receivers	18,700,000	386
Television	1997	receivers	6,478,000	135
Telephones	2001	main lines	20,000	0.4
Cellular telephones	2001	subscribers	150,000	2.9
Internet	2001	users	6,000	0.1

Education and health

Educational attainment: n.a. *Literacy* (2000): percentage of total population age 15 and over literate 61.4%; males literate 73.1%; females literate 50.2%.

Education (1998)

	schools	teachers	students	student/ teacher ratio
Primary (age 6–11)	17,585	154,618	4,022,411	26.0
Secondary (age 12–17) / Voc., teacher tr.	6,007	89,461	1,234,528	13.8
Higher	...	3,788	60,341	15.9

Health: physicians (1996) 3,129 (1 per 14,494 persons); hospital beds (1986) 68,508 (1 per 487 persons); infant mortality rate (2002) 98.5.
Food (2001): daily per capita caloric intake 1,535 (vegetable products 98%, animal products 2%); 68% of FAO recommended minimum requirement.

Military

Total active duty personnel: new national army being created from August 2003; UN peacekeepers (July 2003): 6,800. *Military expenditure as percentage of GNP* (1997): 14.4% (world 2.4%); per capita expenditure U.S.$102.

[1]Per signing of Sun City accord, ending nearly five years of civil war beginning in August 1998; transitional constitution effective from April 5–6, 2003, created a two-year interim administration. [2]The Congo franc (FC) replaced the new zaïre (NZ) at a rate of FC 1 to NZ 100,000 on July 1, 1998; the new zaïre (NZ) had replaced the (old) zaïre (Z) at a rate of 3,000,000 (old) zaïres to 1 NZ on Oct. 22, 1993. [3]Detail does not add to total given because of rounding. [4]2003 population estimate adjusted for about 3 million deaths associated with the civil war and other civil unrest between August 1998 and June 2003. [5]Import duties. [6]Preliminary data. [7]Traffic statistics are for services operated by the Zaire National Railways (SNCZ), which controls more than 90% of the country's total rail facility. [8]1994.

Internet resources for further information:
- **Permanent Mission of the Democratic Republic of the Congo http://www.un.int/drcongo**

Congo, Republic of the

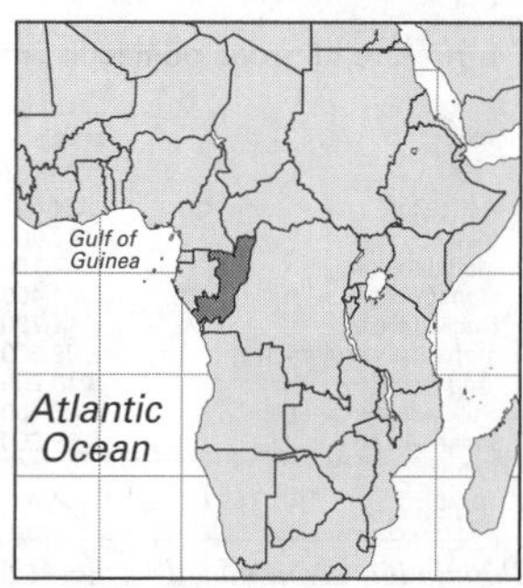

Official name: République du Congo (Republic of the Congo).
Form of government: republic[1] with two legislative houses (Senate[2] [66[3]]; National Assembly [137[4]]).
Chief of state and government: President.
Capital: Brazzaville.
Official language: French[5].
Official religion: none.
Monetary unit: 1 CFA franc (CFAF) = 100 centimes; valuation (Sept. 8, 2003) 1 U.S.$ = CFAF 594.70; 1 £ = CFAF 942.93[6].

Area and population

		area		population
Regions	Capitals	sq mi	sq km	1992 estimate
Bouenza	Madingou	4,733	12,258	177,357
Cuvette Est / Cuvette Ouest	Owando / Ewo	28,900	74,850	151,839
Kouilou	Pointe-Noire	5,270	13,650	89,296
Lékoumou	Sibiti	8,089	20,950	74,420
Likouala	Impfondo	25,500	66,044	70,675
Niari	Loubomo	10,007	25,918	120,077
Plateaux	Djambala	14,826	38,400	119,722
Pool	Kinkala	13,110	33,955	182,671
Sangha	Ouesso	21,542	55,795	35,961
Communes				
Brazzaville	—	39	100	937,579
Loubomo	—	7	18	83,605
Mossendjo	—	2	5	16,405
Nkayi	—	3	8	42,465
Ouesso	—	2	5	16,171
Pointe-Noire	—	17	44	576,206
TOTAL		132,047	342,000	2,694,449

Demography

Population (2003): 3,724,000.
Density (2003): persons per sq mi 28.2, persons per sq km 10.9.
Urban-rural (2002): urban 66.1%; rural 33.9%.
Sex distribution (2002): male 49.36%; female 50.64%.
Age breakdown (2002): under 15, 38.9%; 15–29, 29.6%; 30–44, 17.7%; 45–59, 8.4%; 60–74, 4.4%; 75 and over, 1.0%.
Population projection: (2010) 4,532,000; (2020) 5,960,000.
Doubling time: 44 years.
Ethnic composition (1983): Kongo 51.5%; Teke 17.3%; Mboshi 11.5%; Mbete 4.9%; Punu 3.0%; Sango 2.7%; Maka 1.8%; Pygmy 1.5%; other 5.8%.
Religious affiliation (2000): Roman Catholic 49.3%; Protestant 17.0%; African Christians 12.6%; unaffiliated Christians 11.9%; traditional beliefs 4.8%; other 4.4%.
Major cities (1992): Brazzaville (urban agglomeration; 2001) 1,360,000; Pointe-Noire 576,206; Loubomo 83,605; Nkayi 42,465; Mossendjo 16,405.

Vital statistics

Birth rate per 1,000 population (2002): 30.2 (world avg. 21.3).
Death rate per 1,000 population (2002): 14.0 (world avg. 9.1).
Natural increase rate per 1,000 population (2002): 16.2 (world avg. 12.2).
Total fertility rate (avg. births per childbearing woman; 2002): 3.8.
Life expectancy at birth (2002): male 49.5 years; female 51.5 years.
Major causes of morbidity and mortality in the 1990s included malaria, acute respiratory infections, diarrhea, trauma, helminthiasis, and sexually transmitted diseases.

National economy

Budget (2001). Revenue: CFAF 631,800,000,000 (petroleum revenue 68.2%; nonpetroleum receipts 31.2%; grants 0.6%). Expenditures: CFAF 645,900,000,000 (current expenditure 68.2%, of which debt service 23.5%, salaries 18.3%, transfers and subsidies 11.3%; capital expenditure 31.8%).
Public debt (external, outstanding; 2001): U.S.$3,631,000,000.
Household income and expenditure. Average household size (1984) 5.2.
Gross national product (at current market prices; 2001): U.S.$2,000,000,000 (U.S.$640 per capita).

Structure of gross domestic product and labour force

	2000		1991	
	in value CFAF '000,000	% of total value	labour force	% of labour force
Agriculture, forestry, fishing	121,600	5.3	471,000	59.1
Petroleum	1,502,300	65.5		
Manufacturing, mining	79,700	3.5	101,000	12.7
Construction	56,500	2.5		
Public utilities	15,600	0.7		
Trade	138,500	6.0		
Transp. and commun.	86,000	3.8	225,000	28.2
Pub. admin., defense	125,100	5.5		
Services	113,400	4.9		
Other	53,800[7]	2.3[7]	—	—
TOTAL	2,292,500	100.0	797,000	100.0

Production (metric tons except as noted). Agriculture, forestry, fishing (2002): cassava 861,583, sugarcane 458,649, oil palm fruit 90,000, bananas 84,393, plantains 71,000, mangoes 24,638, peanuts (groundnuts) 23,650, coffee 1,687, cacao beans 1,253, rubber 1,200; livestock (number of live animals) 294,150 goats, 96,000 sheep, 93,000 cattle; roundwood (2001) 2,420,297 cu m; fish catch (2000) 50,180. Mining and quarrying (2000): gold 10 kg. Manufacturing (2000): residual fuel oil 262,000; distillate fuel oils 96,000; refined sugar 74,726; aviation gas 50,000; kerosene 36,000; gasoline 35,000; wheat flour 1,636; soap 1,620; cigarettes 4,000,000 cartons; beer 526,000 hectolitres; soft drinks 290,000 hectolitres; veneer sheets (1998) 52,000 cu m. Energy production (consumption): electricity (kW-hr; 2000) 298,000,000 (560,000,000); crude petroleum (barrels; 1999) 99,400,000 (4,600,000); petroleum products (metric tons; 2001) 383,000 (165,400); natural gas (cu m; 1999) 142,700,000 (142,700,000).
Population economically active (2000): total 1,232,000; activity rate of total population 35.7% (participation rates [1984]: ages 15–64, 54.0%; female [1997] 43.4%; unemployed n.a.).

Price and earnings indexes (1995 = 100)

	1996	1997	1998	1999	2000	2001	2002
Consumer price index	110.0	...	124.1	130.8	129.7	129.8	135.4
Earnings index	...	...	...	...	...	...	...

Land use (1994): forested 58.3%; meadows and pastures 29.3%; agricultural and under permanent cultivation 0.5%; other 11.9%.
Tourism (1999): receipts U.S.$12,000,000; expenditures U.S.$60,000,000.

Foreign trade

Balance of trade (current prices)

	1996	1997	1998	1999	2000	2001
CFAF '000,000,000	+574.2	+502.4	+477.6	+638.7	+1,432.9	+957.0
% of total	48.9%	39.9%	42.0%	49.8%	62.8%	49.6%

Imports (2001): CFAF 486,200,000,000 (non-petroleum sector 84.0%; petroleum sector 16.0%). *Major import sources* (1999): France *c.* 23%; U.S. *c.* 8%; Italy *c.* 8%; Hong Kong *c.* 5%; Belgium *c.* 4%.
Exports (2001): CFAF 1,443,200,000,000 (crude petroleum 89.6%, wood and wood products 5.1%, petroleum products 1.3%, sugar 0.7%). *Major export destinations* (1999): Taiwan *c.* 32%; U.S. *c.* 23%; South Korea *c.* 15%; Germany *c.* 7%; China *c.* 3%.

Transport and communications

Transport. Railroads: (1998) length 894 km; passenger-km 242,000,000; metric ton-km cargo 135,000,000. Roads (2001): total length 17,244 km (paved 7%). Vehicles (1997): passenger cars 37,240; trucks and buses 15,500. Air transport (1998)[8]: passenger-km 258,272,000; metric ton-km cargo 13,524,000; airports (1998) with scheduled flights 10.

Communications

Medium	date	unit	number	units per 1,000 persons
Daily newspapers	2000	circulation	10,300	3.0
Radio	2000	receivers	424,000	123
Television	2000	receivers	114,000	13
Telephones	2002	main lines	22,000	7.1
Cellular telephones	2002	subscribers	221,800	67
Internet	2001	users	1,000	0.3

Education and health

Educational attainment (1984). Percentage of population age 25 and over having: no formal schooling 58.7%; primary education 21.4%; secondary education 16.9%; postsecondary 3.0%. *Literacy* (2000): total population age 15 and over literate 80.7%; males literate 87.5%; females literate 74.4%.

Education (1998)

	schools	teachers	students	student/ teacher ratio
Primary (age 6–13)	1,168	4,515	270,451	59.9
Secondary (age 14–18)	...	5,094	114,450	22.5
Voc., teacher tr.[9]	...	1,746	23,606	13.5
Higher	...	1,341[9]	16,862	12.4

Health: physicians (1995) 632 (1 per 4,083 persons); hospital beds (1989) 4,817 (1 per 446 persons); infant mortality rate per 1,000 live births (2002) 96.8.
Food (2001): daily per capita caloric intake 2,221 (vegetable products 94%, animal products 6%); 100% of FAO recommended minimum requirement.

Military

Total active duty personnel (2002): 10,000 (army 80.0%, navy 8.0%, air force 12.0%). *Military expenditure as percentage of GNP* (1999): 3.5% (world 2.4%); per capita expenditure U.S.$21.

[1]New constitution effective from Aug. 10, 2002. [2]First elections to new Senate held in July 2002. [3]Includes 6 vacant seats in Pool region. [4]Includes 8 vacant seats in Pool region. [5]"Functional" national languages are Lingala and Monokutuba. [6]Formerly pegged to the French franc and since Jan. 1, 2002, to the euro at a rate of €1 = CFAF 655.96. [7]Import duties. [8]Represents 1/11 of the traffic of Air Afrique; Air Afrique, an airline jointly owned by 11 African countries (including Republic of the Congo), was declared bankrupt in February 2002. [9]1996–97.

Internet resources for further information:

- **Investir en Zone Franc http://www.izf.net/izf/Index.htm**

Costa Rica

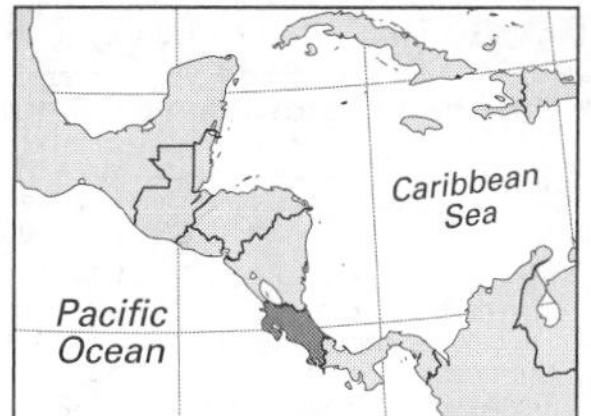

Official name: República de Costa Rica (Republic of Costa Rica).
Form of government: unitary multiparty republic with one legislative house (Legislative Assembly [57]).
Head of state and government: President.
Capital: San José.
Official language: Spanish.
Official religion: Roman Catholicism.
Monetary unit: 1 Costa Rican colón (₡) = 100 céntimos; valuation (Sept. 8, 2003) 1 U.S.$ = ₡406.16; 1 £ = ₡643.99.

Area and population		area		population
				2000
Provinces	Capitals	sq mi	sq km	census
Alajuela	Alajuela	3,766	9,753	716,286
Cartago	Cartago	1,207	3,125	432,395
Guanacaste	Liberia	3,915	10,141	264,238
Heredia	Heredia	1,026	2,657	354,732
Limón	Limón	3,547	9,188	339,295
Puntarenas	Puntarenas	4,354	11,277	357,483
San José	San José	1,915	4,959	1,345,750
TOTAL		19,730	51,100	3,810,179[1]

Demography

Population (2003): 4,171,000.
Density (2003): persons per sq mi 211.4; persons per sq km 81.6.
Urban-rural (2000): urban 59.5%; rural 40.5%.
Sex distribution (2002): male 50.54%; female 49.46%.
Age breakdown (2002): under 15, 30.7%; 15–29, 27.3%; 30–44, 21.7%; 45–59, 12.5%; 60–74, 5.7%; 75 and over, 2.1%.
Population projection: (2010) 4,732,000; (2020) 5,474,000.
Doubling time: 45 years.
Ethnic composition (2000): white 77.0%; mestizo 17.0%; black/mulatto 3.0%; East Asian (mostly Chinese) 2.0%; Amerindian 1.0%.
Religious affiliation (1995): Roman Catholic 86.0%; Protestant 9.3%, of which Pentecostal 4.9%; other Christian 2.4%; other 2.3%.
Major cities (2000): San José 309,672[2] (urban agglomeration 983,000[3]); Limón 60,298[4]; Alajuela 42,889[4]; San Isidro de El General 41,221[4]; Cartago 39,958[5]; Liberia 39,242[4].

Vital statistics

Birth rate per 1,000 population (2002): 19.8 (world avg. 21.3); (1999) legitimate 51.0%; illegitimate 49.0%.
Death rate per 1,000 population (2002): 4.3 (world avg. 9.1).
Natural increase rate per 1,000 population (2002): 15.5 (world avg. 12.2).
Total fertility rate (avg. births per childbearing woman; 1999): 2.6.
Marriage rate per 1,000 population (1999): 7.1.
Divorce rate per 1,000 population (1995): 1.4.
Life expectancy at birth (2002): male 73.7 years; female 78.9 years.
Major causes of death per 100,000 population (1999): diseases of the circulatory system 127.6; malignant neoplasms (cancers) 87.2; accidents and violence 50.1; diseases of the respiratory system 44.5.

National economy

Budget (2000). Revenue: ₡610,138,000,000 (taxes on goods and services 63.8%, income and profit taxes 21.8%, import duties 7.7%, other 6.7%). Expenditures: ₡761,306,000,000 (current expenditures 90.1%, of which transfers 30.5%, wages 29.7%, interest on debt 23.0%; development expenditures 9.9%).
Public debt (external, outstanding; 2001): U.S.$3,424,000,000.
Gross national product (2001): U.S.$15,700,000,000 (U.S.$4,060 per capita).

Structure of gross domestic product and labour force	2000			
	in value ₡'000,000	% of total value	labour force	% of labour force
Agriculture, forestry, fishing	420,369	8.6	269,200	19.4
Mining	6,954	0.1	2,610	0.2
Manufacturing	1,085,501	22.2	190,260	13.7
Construction	176,270	3.6	89,720	6.4
Public utilities	118,136	2.4	10,880	0.8
Transp. and commun.	371,182	7.6	78,830	5.7
Trade, restaurants	882,631	18.0	266,830	19.2
Finance, real estate	225,756	4.6	64,260	4.6
Public administration	173,155	3.5	337,090	24.2
Services	817,425	16.7		
Other	618,071[6]	12.6[6]	80,880[7]	5.8[7]
TOTAL	4,895,450	100.0[8]	1,390,560	100.0

Production (metric tons except as noted). Agriculture, forestry, fishing (2002): sugarcane 3,700,000, bananas 2,140,000, pineapples 1,015,000, oil palm fruit 692,398, oranges 400,000, rice 250,000, coffee 140,220, cassava 105,031, potatoes 82,225, plantains 70,000, other products include other tropical fruits, cut flowers, and ornamental plants grown for export; livestock (number of live animals) 1,219,500 cattle, 475,000 pigs, 17,000,000 chickens; roundwood (2001) 5,161,232 cu m; fish catch (2000) 37,658, of which shrimp 3,684. Mining and quarrying: limestone (1997) 1,500,000; gold (1999) 300 kg. Manufacturing (value added in ₡'000,000; 1997): food products 91,065; beverages 50,898; fertilizers and pesticides 21,713; electrical machinery 18,366, of which radio, television, and communications equipment 15,075; plastic products 14,732; paper and paper products 13,722; apparel 12,556. Energy production (consumption): electricity (kW-hr; 1999) 6,438,000,000 (6,560,000,000); coal, none (none); crude petroleum (barrels; 1999) none (7,000); petroleum products (metric tons; 1999) 2,000 (1,803,000); natural gas, none (none).
Population economically active (2000): total 1,390,560; activity rate of total population 39.9% (participation rates: ages 12–59, 53.4%; female 32.1%; unemployed 5.2%).

Price and earnings indexes (1996 = 100)	1996	1997	1998	1999	2000	2001	2002
Consumer price index	100.0	113.3	126.5	139.1	154.5	171.8	187.5
Monthly earnings index[9]	100.0	115.3	134.6	156.5	183.7	...	...

Tourism (2001): receipts U.S.$1,278,000,000; expenditures U.S.$467,000,000.
Household income and expenditure. Average household size (2000) 4.1; average annual household income (1997) ₡1,468,597 (U.S.$6,314); sources of income (1987–88): wages and salaries 61.0%, self-employment 22.6%, transfers 9.6%; expenditure (1987–88): food and beverages 39.1%, housing and energy 12.1%, transportation 11.6%, household furnishings 10.9%.
Land use (1994): forested 30.8%; meadows and pastures 45.8%; agricultural and under permanent cultivation 10.4%; other 13.0%.

Foreign trade[10]

Balance of trade (current prices)[11]	1997	1998	1999	2000	2001	2002
U.S.$'000,000	–764	–713	+308	–483	–1,548	–1,922
% of total	8.3%	6.1%	2.3%	3.9%	13.4%	15.5%

Imports (2000): U.S.$6,380,000,000 ([12]general merchandise 68%; goods for reassembly 32%). *Major import sources:* U.S. 53.1%; Mexico 6.2%; Venezuela 5.3%; Japan 3.4%; Spain 2.3%.
Exports (2000): U.S.$5,897,000,000 (components for microprocessors 28.0%, bananas 9.0%, processed food and tobacco products 6.5%, coffee 4.7%, tropical fruit 3.4%). *Major export destinations:* U.S. 51.8%; The Netherlands 6.7%; U.K. 5.1%; Guatemala 3.3%; Nicaragua 3.0%.

Transport and communications

Transport. Railroads[13]. Roads (1999): total length 22,292 mi, 35,876 km (paved 17%). Vehicles (1999): passenger cars 326,524; trucks and buses 181,272. Air transport (2001)[14]: passenger-mi 1,332,000,000, passenger-km 2,143,000,000; short-ton mi cargo (1999) 58,013,000, metric ton-km cargo 84,697,000; airports (1996) 14.

Communications				units per 1,000
Medium	date	unit	number	persons
Daily newspapers	1996	circulation	320,000	94
Radio	2000	receivers	3,200,000	816
Television	2000	receivers	907,000	231
Telephones	2002	main lines	1,038,000	251
Cellular telephones	2002	subscribers	528,000	128
Personal computers	2001	units	700,000	170
Internet	2001	users	384,000	93

Education and health

Educational attainment (1996). Percentage of population age 5 and over having: no formal schooling 11.7%; incomplete primary education 28.5%; complete primary 25.8%; incomplete secondary 16.0%; complete secondary 9.0%; higher 8.5%; other/unknown 0.5%. *Literacy* (1999): total population age 15 and over literate 95.5%; males literate 95.4%; females literate 95.5%.

Education (1999)	schools	teachers	students	student/ teacher ratio
Primary (age 7–12)	3,768	20,185	535,057	26.5
Secondary (age 13–17)	468	11,891	235,425	19.8
Higher	52	...	59,947	...

Health (1997): physicians 5,500 (1 per 630 persons); hospital beds 5,953 (1 per 582 persons); infant mortality rate per 1,000 live births (2002) 10.9.
Food (2001): daily per capita caloric intake 2,761 (vegetable products 80%, animal products 20%); 123% of FAO recommended minimum requirement.

Military

Paramilitary expenditure as percentage of GNP (1999): 0.5% (world 2.4%); per capita expenditure U.S.$19. The army was officially abolished in 1948. Paramilitary (police) forces had 8,400 members in 2002.

[1]Adjusted census total for underenumeration equals 3,925,331. [2]Population of San José canton. [3]2001 est. [4]District population. [5]Population of three districts. [6]Taxes less imputed bank service charge. [7]Includes 8,940 not adequately defined and 71,940 unemployed. [8]Detail does not add to total given because of rounding. [9]Data for June only. [10]Imports c.i.f.; exports f.o.b. [11]Includes goods imported for reassembly and reexported. [12]Estimated figures. [13]National rail service was not in regular service from 1995 through 2000. [14]Lacsa (Costa Rican Airlines) only.

Internet resources for further information:
- **Central Bank of Costa Rica: Economic Indicators http://websiec.bccr.fi.cr/indicadores/indice.web**
- **Government of Costa Rica http://www.casapres.go.cr**

Côte d'Ivoire

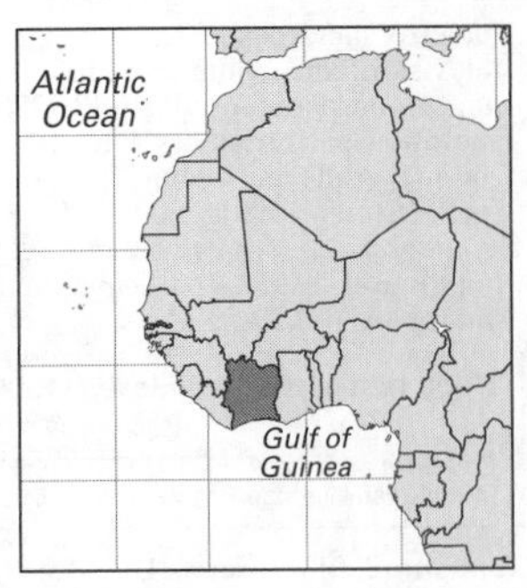

Official name: République de Côte d'Ivoire (Republic of Côte d'Ivoire [Ivory Coast][1]).
Form of government: interim regime[2] with one legislative house (National Assembly [225[3]]).
Chief of state and government: President assisted by Prime Minister.
De facto capital: Abidjan.
Official language: French.
Official religion: none.
Monetary unit: 1 CFA franc (CFAF) = 100 centimes; valuation (Sept. 8, 2003) 1 U.S.$ = CFAF 594.70; 1 £ = CFAF 942.93.[4]

Area and population

Regions	Capitals	area sq mi	area sq km	population 2000 estimate
Agnebi	Agboville	3,510	9,080	641,400
Bafing	Touba	3,370	8,720	158,700
Bas-Sassandra	San-Pédro	9,960	25,800	937,700
Denguélé	Odienné	7,950	20,600	246,400
Dix-huit Montagnes	Man	6,410	16,600	1,051,600
Fromager	Gagnoa	2,660	6,900	604,800
Haut-Sassandra	Daloa	5,870	15,200	1,055,600
Lacs	Yamoussoukro	3,450	8,940	531,600
Lagunes	Abidjan	5,480	14,200	3,894,300
Marahoué	Bouaflé	3,280	8,500	579,800
Moyen-Cavally	Guiglo	5,460	14,150	394,200
Moyen-Comoé	Abengourou	2,660	6,900	434,200
Nzi-Comoé	Dimbokro	7,550	19,560	809,400
Savanes	Korhogo	15,570	40,323	1,081,000
Sud-Bandama	Divo	4,110	10,650	735,100
Sud-Comoé	Aboisso	2,410	6,250	328,500
Vallée du Bandama	Bouaké	11,020	28,530	1,188,000
Worodougou	Séguéla	8,460	21,900	356,000
Zanzan	Bondoukou	14,670	38,000	746,300
TOTAL		123,863[5]	320,803	15,774,600

Demography

Population (2003): 16,631,000.
Density (2003): persons per sq mi 134.3, persons per sq km 51.8.
Urban-rural (2002): urban 44.0%; rural 56.0%.
Sex distribution (2002): male 50.28%; female 49.72%.
Age breakdown (2002): under 15, 45.6%; 15–29, 28.7%; 30–44, 14.4%; 45–59, 7.6%; 60–74, 3.0%; 75 and over, 0.7%.
Population projection: (2010) 18,526,000; (2020) 21,026,000.
Ethnolinguistic composition (1998)[6]: Akan 42.1%; Mande 26.5%; other 31.4%.
Religious affiliation (1998): Muslim 38.6%; Christian 30.4%; nonreligious 16.7%; animist 11.9%; other 2.4%.
Major cities (1995): Abidjan (1999) 3,199,000; Bouaké 330,000; Daloa 123,000; Yamoussoukro 110,000.

Vital statistics

Birth rate per 1,000 population (2002): 40.4 (world avg. 21.3).
Death rate per 1,000 population (2001): 18.4 (world avg. 9.1).
Natural increase rate per 1,000 population (2002): 22.0 (world avg. 12.2).
Total fertility rate (avg. births per childbearing woman; 2002): 5.6.
Life expectancy at birth (2002): male 40.4 years; female 45.3 years.

National economy

Budget (2000). Revenue: CFAF 1,237,100,000,000 (tax revenue 87.1%, of which import taxes and duties 29.2%, export taxes 13.2%, taxes on profits 11.6%, income tax 10.2%; nontax revenue 12.9%). Expenditures: CFAF 1,358,200,000,000 (wages and salaries 33.0%; debt service 22.7%; capital expenditure 15.4%; transfers 13.1%; other 15.8%).
Production (metric tons except as noted). Agriculture, forestry, fishing (2002): yams 3,000,000, cassava 1,700,000, plantains 1,410,000, oil palm fruit 1,400,000, cacao beans 1,000,000, rice 818,000, corn (maize) 625,000, cotton seed 280,000, bananas 270,000, coffee 198,000, rubber 123,000; livestock (number of live animals) 1,522,000 sheep, 1,476,000 cattle, 1,191,000 goats, 32,625,000 chickens; roundwood (2001) 12,083,092 cu m; fish catch (2000) 81,519. Mining and quarrying (2001): gold 3,100 kg; diamonds 320,000 carats. Manufacturing (value added in CFAF '000,000,000; 1997): food 156.6, of which cocoa and chocolate 72.4, vegetable oils 62.7; chemicals 60.2; wood products 55.9; refined petroleum 46.0; textiles 37.9; tobacco 27.6; fabricated metal products 25.9. Energy production (consumption): electricity (kW-hr; 1999) 2,924,000,000 (2,924,000,000); crude petroleum (barrels; 1999) 10,800,000 (34,000,000); petroleum products (metric tons; 1999) 4,045,000 (2,418,000); natural gas (cu m; 1999) 1,510,400,000 (1,510,400,000).
Household income and expenditure. Average household size (2000) 7.8; expenditure (1992–93)[7]: food 48.0%, transportation 12.2%, clothing 10.1%, energy and water 8.5%, housing 7.8%, household equipment 3.4%.
Population economically active (2000): total 6,531,000; activity rate of total population 40.9% (participation rates [1994] over ages 10, 64.3%; female 33.0%; unemployed [1996] 38.8%).

Price and earnings indexes (1995 = 100)

	1996	1997	1998	1999	2000	2001	2002
Consumer price index	102.5	106.6	111.6	112.5	115.2	120.2	123.9
Minimum earnings index	102.7	108.3	…	…	…	…	…

Gross national product (2001): U.S.$10,300,000,000 (U.S.$630 per capita).

Structure of gross domestic product and labour force

	1999 in value CFAF '000,000,000	1999 % of total value	2000 labour force	2000 % of labour force
Agriculture	1,795.2	26.0	3,211,000	49.2
Manufacturing, mining, and public utilities	1,466.4	21.3	3,320,000	50.8
Construction	352.8	5.1		
Transp. and commun.	592.8	8.6		
Trade	1,042.6	15.1		
Public admin., defense	525.8	7.6		
Services	875.5	12.7		
Other (customs receipts)	248.6	3.6		
TOTAL	6,899.7	100.0	6,531,000	100.0

Public debt (external, outstanding; 2001): U.S.$8,590,000,000.
Tourism (2001): receipts U.S.$48,000,000; expenditures U.S.$192,000,000.

Foreign trade[8]

Balance of trade (current prices)

	1996	1997	1998	1999	2000	2001
CFAF '000,000,000	+933	+1,046	+1,015	+1,167	+1,058	+1,123
% of total	25.8%	25.2%	23.0%	25.5%	23.6%	24.1%

Imports (2001): CFAF 1,768,000,000,000 (crude and refined petroleum 28.8%, food products 22.5%, machinery and transport equipment 20.4%). *Major import sources* (2000): Nigeria 26.6%; France 20.3%; Belgium 4.0%; Italy 3.6%; Germany 3.6%.
Exports (2001): CFAF 2,891,000,000,000 (cocoa beans and products 33.2%, crude petroleum and petroleum products 13.7%, wood and wood products 7.1%, coffee beans 3.6%). *Major export destinations* (2000): France 14.9%; The Netherlands 9.7%; United States 8.3%; Mali 5.7%; Italy 4.8%; Senegal 4.0%.

Transport and communications

Transport. Railroads (1999): route length 655 km; passenger-km 93,100,000; metric ton-km cargo 537,600,000. Roads (1999): total length 50,400 km (paved 9.7%). Vehicles (1996): passenger cars 293,000; trucks and buses 163,000. Air transport (1998): passenger-km 318,000,000; metric ton-km cargo 44,000,000; airports (1999) 5.

Communications

Medium	date	unit	number	units per 1,000 persons
Daily newspapers	2000	circulation	1,440,000	91
Radio	2000	receivers	2,170,000	137
Television	2000	receivers	950,000	60
Telephones	2002	main lines	336,100	20
Cellular telephones	2002	subscribers	1,027,100	62
Personal computers	2002	units	118,000	7.2
Internet	2002	users	90,000	5.5

Education and health

Educational attainment (1988). Percentage of population age 6 and over having: no formal schooling 60.0%; Koranic school 3.6%; primary education 24.8%; secondary 10.7%; higher 0.9%. *Literacy* (2000): percentage of population age 15 and over literate 46.8%; males 54.5%; females 38.6%.

Education (1998–99)

	schools	teachers	students	student/ teacher ratio
Primary (age 7–12)	7,599[9]	40,529[9]	1,910,820	…
Secondary (age 13–19)	147[9]	15,959[9]	565,856	…
Vocational[10]	…	1,424	11,037	7.8
Higher	7[10]	1,657[10]	47,187	…

Health: physicians (1996) 1,318 (1 per 11,111 persons); hospital beds (1993) 7,928 (1 per 1,698 persons); infant mortality rate (2001) 99.6.
Food (2001): daily per capita caloric intake 2,594 (vegetable products 97%, animal products 3%); 112% of FAO recommended minimum requirement.

Military

Total active duty personnel: [11]. *Military expenditure as percentage of GNP* (1999): 0.8% (world avg. 2.4%); per capita expenditure U.S.$5.

[1]Since 1986, Côte d'Ivoire has requested that the French form of the country's name be used as the official protocol version in all languages. [2]Referendum approving new constitution took place on July 24, 2000. Constitution was ineffective in September 2003 pending final resolution of September 2002–July 2003 civil war. [3]Includes vacant/unoccupied seats. [4]Formerly pegged to the French franc and since Jan. 1, 2002, to the euro at the rate of €1 = CFAF 655.96. [5]Detail does not add to total given because of rounding. [6]Local population only; foreigners constitute 26% of the population and two-thirds of all foreigners are from Burkina Faso. [7]Weights of consumer price index components for a worker's family living in the capital city. [8]Imports are f.o.b. in balance of trade and commodities and c.i.f. for trading partners. [9]1996–97. [10]1994–95. [11]New national army to be created pending final resolution of 2002–03 civil war. Peacekeeping troops (September 2003): West African regional (ECOWAS) 1,300; French 4,000.

Internet resources for further information:

- **Investir en Zone Franc http://www.izf.net/izf/Index.htm**

Croatia

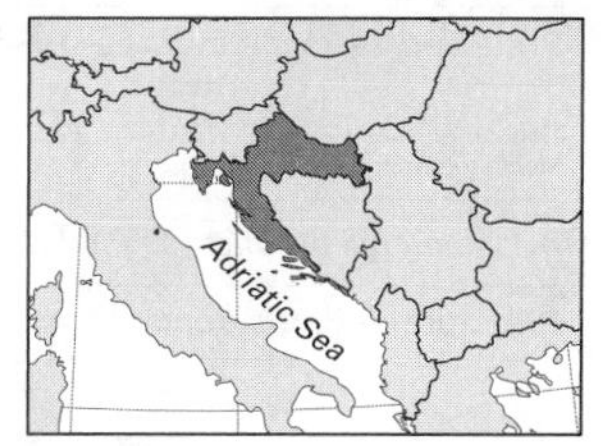

Official name: Republika Hrvatska (Republic of Croatia).
Form of government: multiparty republic with one legislative house (House of Representatives [140[1]])[2].
Head of state: President.
Head of government: Prime Minister.
Capital: Zagreb.
Official language: Croatian (Serbo-Croatian).
Official religion: none.
Monetary unit: 1 kuna (HrK; plural kune) = 100 lipa; valuation (Sept. 8, 2003) 1 U.S.$ = HrK 6.78; 1 £ = HrK 10.74.

Area and population

Counties	area sq km	population 2001 census	Counties	area sq km	population 2001 census
Bjelovar-Bilogora	2,638	133,084	Šibenik-Knin	2,994	112,891
Dubrovnik-Neretva	1,782	122,870	Sisak-Moslavina	4,448	185,387
Istria	2,813	206,344	Slavonski Brod-Posavina	2,027	176,765
Karlovac	3,622	141,787	Split-Dalmatia	4,524	463,676
Koprivnica-Križevci	1,734	124,467	Varaždin	1,260	184,769
Krapina-Zagorje	1,230	142,432	Virovitica-Podravina	2,021	93,389
Lika-Senj	5,350	53,677	Vukovar-Srijem	2,448	204,768
Medimurje	730	118,426	Zadar	3,643	162,045
Osijek-Baranja	4,149	330,506	Zagreb	3,078	309,696
Požega-Slavonia	1,821	85,831	**City**		
Primorje-Gorski kotar	3,590	305,505	Zagreb	640	779,145
			TOTAL	56,542	4,437,460

Demography

Population (2003): 4,428,000.
Density (2003): persons per sq mi 202.8, persons per sq km 78.3.
Urban-rural (2002): urban 58.1%; rural 41.9%.
Sex distribution (2001): male 48.13%; female 51.87%.
Age breakdown (2001): under 15, 17.1%; 15–29, 20.3%; 30–44, 21.4%; 45–59, 19.5%; 60–74, 16.3%; 75 and over, 5.4%.
Population projection: (2010) 4,349,000; (2020) 4,187,000.
Ethnic composition (2001): Croat 89.6%; Serb 4.5%; Bosniac 0.5%; Italian 0.4%; Hungarian 0.4%; other 4.6%.
Religious affiliation (2000): Christian 95.2%, of which Roman Catholic 88.5%, Eastern Orthodox 5.6%, Protestant 0.6%; Sunnī Muslim 2.3%; nonreligious/atheist 2.5%.
Major cities (2001): Zagreb 691,724; Split 175,140; Rijeka 143,800; Osijek 90,411; Zadar 69,556.

Vital statistics

Birth rate per 1,000 population (2001): 10.0 (world avg. 21.3); (1999) legitimate 91.8%; illegitimate 8.2%.
Death rate per 1,000 population (2001): 11.5 (world avg. 9.1).
Natural increase rate per 1,000 population (2001): –1.5 (world avg. 12.2).
Total fertility rate (avg. births per childbearing woman; 2001): 1.4.
Marriage rate per 1,000 population (2000): 4.9.
Divorce rate per 1,000 population (2000): 0.9.
Life expectancy at birth (2001): male 70.8 years; female 77.7 years.
Major causes of death per 100,000 population (2000): diseases of the circulatory system 600.8; cancers 263.8; accidents, violence, and poisoning 65.3; diseases of the digestive system 56.4; diseases of the respiratory system 46.0.

National economy

Budget (2001). Revenue: HrK 55,303,800,000 (tax revenue 84.9%, of which sales tax 40.7%, excise taxes 14.2%, income tax 6.8%; nontax revenue 15.1%). Expenditures: HrK 57,308,100,000 (social security and welfare 43.2%; education 10.7%; public order 8.3%; defense 7.4%).
Population economically active (2001): total 1,728,503; activity rate 39.0% (participation rates: ages 15–64, 57.9%; female 43.0%; unemployed 22.0%).

Price and earnings indexes (1995 = 100)

	1996	1997	1998	1999	2000	2001	2002
Consumer price index	104.3	108.6	115.6	119.6	125.9	131.9	134.5
Annual earnings index	111.8	130.7	147.5	168.1	182.9	...	...

Production (metric tons except as noted). Agriculture, forestry, fishing (2002): corn (maize) 2,501,774, sugar beets 1,183,445, wheat 988,175, potatoes 736,198, grapes 370,930, barley 170,946, soybeans 129,470, cabbage 127,553, tomatoes 71,400, sunflower seed 62,965, apples 59,143, plums 20,543; livestock (number of live animals) 1,286,000 pigs, 580,016 sheep, 417,113 cattle, poultry 11,665,000; roundwood (2001) 3,468,000 cu m; fish catch (2000) 28,062. Mining and quarrying (2000): gypsum 100,000; ferrochromium 16,000. Manufacturing (value added in U.S.$'000,000; 1996): food products 895; transport equipment 425; electrical machinery 362; textiles 285; wearing apparel 260. Energy production (consumption): electricity (kW-hr; 2001) 11,674,000,000 ([1999] 14,599,000,000); hard coal (metric tons; 1999) 15,000 (316,000); lignite (metric tons; 1999) none (31,000); crude petroleum (barrels; 1999) 9,475,000 (41,000,000); petroleum products (metric tons; 1999) 5,103,000 (4,060,000); natural gas (cu m; 2001) 2,009,000,000 ([1999] 2,610,600,000).
Gross national product (2001): U.S.$19,900,000,000 (U.S.$4,550 per capita).

Structure of gross domestic product and labour force

	2001 in value HrK '000,000	% of total value	labour force	% of labour force
Agriculture	13,113	7.8	111,233	6.4
Mining	38,008	22.5	7,733	0.4
Manufacturing			287,030	16.6
Public utilities			27,655	1.6
Construction	8,186	4.8	90,222	5.2
Transp. and commun.	15,105	8.9	96,768	5.6
Trade	24,002	14.2	282,235	16.3
Finance, real estate	20,266	12.0	99,378	5.7
Pub. admin., defense	28,528	16.9	121,332	7.0
Services			224,722	13.0
Other	21,764[3]	12.9[3]	380,195[4]	22.0[4]
TOTAL	168,972	100.0	1,728,503	100.0[5]

Public debt (external, outstanding; 2001): U.S.$6,400,000,000.
Household income and expenditure. Average household size (2001) 3.0; income per household HrK 64,288 (U.S.$8,700); sources: wages 42.8%, self-employment 22.5%, pension 20.6%, other 14.1%; expenditure (2001): food and nonalcoholic beverages 33.7%, housing and energy 13.4%, transportation 11.5%, clothing 9.1%, recreation and culture 5.9%, household furnishings 5.6%, alcoholic beverages and tobacco 4.1%, other 16.7%.
Tourism (2001): receipts from visitors U.S.$3,335,000,000; expenditures by nationals abroad U.S.$606,000,000.
Land use (1994): forest 37.1%; pasture 19.3%; agriculture 21.6%; other 22.0%.

Foreign trade[6]

Balance of trade (current prices)

	1996	1997	1998	1999	2000	2001
U.S.$'000,000	–3,623	–5,196	–4,147	–3,299	–3,204	–4,012
% of total	28.5%	38.2%	31.1%	27.3%	26.0%	29.7%

Imports (2001): U.S.$9,044,000,000 (machinery and transport equipment 33.2%, chemical products 11.5%, base and fabricated metals 10.1%, crude and refined petroleum 9.2%). *Major import sources:* Germany 17.1%; Italy 16.9%; Slovenia 7.9%; Russia and other countries of former U.S.S.R. 7.2%; Austria 7.0%.
Exports (2001): U.S.$4,659,000,000 (machinery and transport equipment 29.4%, chemical and chemical products 10.6%, clothing 10.5%, crude petroleum and petroleum products 7.4%, food 6.9%). *Major export destinations:* Italy 23.7%; Germany 14.8%; Bosnia and Herzegovina 12.0%; Slovenia 9.1%; Austria 5.7%.

Transport and communications

Transport. Railroads (2001): length 2,726 km; passenger-km 1,234,000,000; metric ton-km cargo 2,148,000,000. Roads (2001): total length 28,275 km (paved 82%). Vehicles (2001): passenger cars 1,195,450; trucks and buses 124,669. Air transport (2001): passenger-km 921,053,000; metric ton-km cargo 3,597,000; airports (2001) 4.

Communications

Medium	date	unit	number	units per 1,000 persons
Daily newspapers	1996	circulation	515,000	118
Radio	2000	receivers	1,120,000	252
Television	2000	receivers	1,693,000	380
Telephones	2002	main lines	1,879,000	388
Cellular telephones	2002	subscribers	2,278,000	470
Personal computers	2002	units	760,000	157
Internet	2002	users	789,000	163

Education and health

Educational attainment (1991). Percentage of population age 15 and over having: no schooling or unknown 10.1%; less than full primary education 21.2%; primary 23.4%; secondary 36.0%; postsecondary and higher 9.3%. *Literacy* (1999): population age 15 and over literate 98.2%; males 99.3%; females 97.1%.

Education (2001–02)

	schools	teachers	students	student/ teacher ratio
Primary (age 7–14)	2,134	27,502	400,100	14.5
Secondary (age 15–18)	645	19,718	195,000	9.9
Higher	89	7,622	100,297	13.2

Health (1999): physicians 8,046 (1 per 529 persons); hospital beds 27,000 (1 per 158 persons); infant mortality rate per 1,000 live births (2001) 7.2.
Food (2001): daily per capita caloric intake 2,676 (vegetable products 76%, animal products 24%); 105% of FAO recommended minimum requirement.

Military

Total active duty personnel (2002): 51,000 (army 88.2%, navy 5.9%, air force and air defense 5.9%). *Military expenditure as percentage of GNP* (1999): 6.4% (world 2.4%); per capita expenditure U.S.$491.

[1]Includes six seats representing Croatians abroad. [2]A constitutional amendment in March 2001 abolished the former upper house (House of Counties). [3]Import and turnover taxes less imputed bank service charges. [4]Unemployed. [5]Detail does not add to total given because of rounding. [6]Imports f.o.b. in balance of trade and c.i.f. for commodities and trading partners.

Internet resources for further information:
- **Croatian Bureau of Statistics http://www.dzs.hr/Eng/ouraddress.htm**
- **Ministry of Foreign Affairs http://www.mvp.hr**

Cuba

Official name: República de Cuba (Republic of Cuba).
Form of government: unitary socialist republic with one legislative house (National Assembly of the People's Power [609]).
Head of state and government: President.
Capital: Havana.
Official language: Spanish.
Official religion: none.
Monetary unit: 1 Cuban peso (CUP) = 100 centavos; valuation (Sept. 8, 2003) 1 U.S.$ = 21.00 CUP; 1 £ = 33.30 CUP.

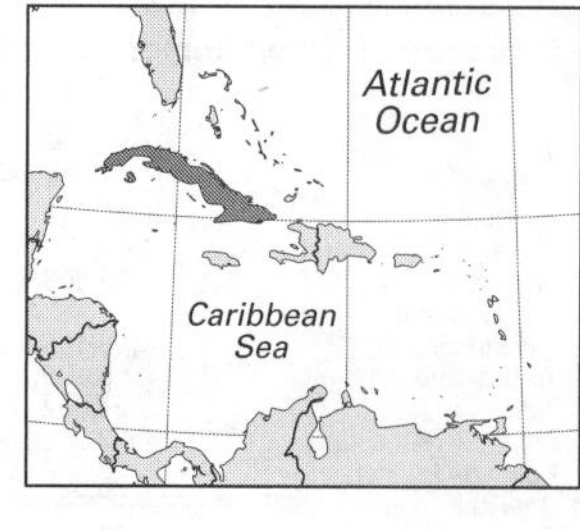

Area and population

Provinces	Capitals	area sq mi	area sq km	population 2002[1] estimate
Camagüey	Camagüey	6,174	15,990	791,800
Ciego de Avila	Ciego de Avila	2,668	6,910	413,500
Cienfuegos	Cienfuegos	1,613	4,178	398,600
Ciudad de la Habana[2]	—	281	727	2,181,500
Granma	Bayamo	3,232	8,372	835,200
Guantánamo	Guantánamo	2,388	6,186	516,300
Holguín	Holguín	3,591	9,301	1,035,800
La Habana[3]	Havana	2,213	5,731	711,600
Las Tunas	Las Tunas	2,544	6,589	532,600
Matanzas	Matanzas	4,625	11,978	665,400
Pinar del Río	Pinar del Río	4,218	10,925	739,400
Sancti Spíritus	Sancti Spíritus	2,604	6,744	463,300
Santiago de Cuba	Santiago de Cuba	2,382	6,170	1,041,400
Villa Clara	Santa Clara	3,345	8,662	836,400
Special municipality				
Isla de la Juventud	Nueva Gerona	926	2,398	80,600
TOTAL		42,804	110,861	11,243,400

Demography

Population (2003): 11,295,000.
Density (2003): persons per sq mi 263.9, persons per sq km 101.9.
Urban-rural (2002): urban 75.5%; rural 24.5%.
Sex distribution (2002): male 49.93%; female 50.07%.
Age breakdown (2002): under 15, 21.0%; 15–29, 21.6%; 30–44, 27.3%; 45–59, 16.3%; 60–74, 9.7%; 75 and over, 4.1%.
Population projection: (2010) 11,450,000; (2020) 11,531,000.
Ethnic composition (1994): mixed 51.0%; white 37.0%; black 11.0%; other 1.0%.
Religious affiliation (1995): Roman Catholic 39.5%; Protestant 2.4%; other Christian 0.2%; other (mostly Santería) 57.9%.
Major cities (1999): Havana (2002)[1] 2,181,500; Santiago de Cuba 441,524; Camagüey 306,049; Holguín 259,300; Santa Clara 210,100; Guantánamo 208,030.

Vital statistics

Birth rate per 1,000 population (2002): 12.6 (world avg. 21.3).
Death rate per 1,000 population (2002): 7.2 (world avg. 9.1).
Natural increase rate per 1,000 population (2002): 5.4 (world avg. 12.2).
Total fertility rate (avg. births per childbearing woman; 2002): 1.7.
Marriage rate per 1,000 population (2001): 4.8.
Divorce rate per 1,000 population (2001): 2.3.
Life expectancy at birth (2002): male 74.4 years; female 79.0 years.
Major causes of death per 100,000 population (1998): heart disease 142.6; malignant neoplasms (cancers) 111.0; cerebrovascular disease 52.9; accidents 39.0; influenza and pneumonia 31.3; diseases of the blood vessels 21.9.

National economy

Budget (2000). Revenue: CUP 14,505,000,000. Expenditures: CUP 15,243,000,000 (capital expenditure 18.0%, education 13.9%, health 11.3%, defense 6.1%, other 50.7%).
Public debt (external, outstanding; 2002): U.S.$12,300,000,000.
Production (metric tons except as noted). Agriculture, forestry, fishing (2002): sugarcane 32,100,000, bananas 678,691, oranges and tangerines 563,293, plantains 380,000, potatoes 345,365, rice 325,539, cassava 300,000, tobacco leaves 31,751; livestock (number of live animals) 4,038,400 cattle, 1,307,300 pigs, 11,215,000 chickens; roundwood (2001) 1,696,000 cu m; fish catch (2000) 108,846. Mining and quarrying (2001): nickel (metal content) 72,619; cobalt (metal content) 3,910. Manufacturing (value added in U.S.$'000,000; 1990): tobacco products 2,629; food products 1,033; beverages 358; chemical products 354; transport equipment 225; nonelectrical machinery 176. Energy production (consumption): electricity (kW-hr; 2001) 15,301,000,000 (15,301,000,000); coal (metric tons; 1999) none (14,000); crude petroleum (barrels; 2000) 17,380,000 ([1999] 18,900,000); petroleum products (metric tons; 1999) 991,000 (5,923,000); natural gas (cu m; 1999) 460,000,000 (460,000,000).
Household income and expenditure. Average household size (2000) 3.6; average annual income per household (1982) CUP 3,680 (U.S.$4,330); sources of income (1982): wages and salaries 57.3%, bonuses and other payments 42.7%; personal consumption (1989): food 26.7%, other retail purchases 60.5%.
Tourism: receipts from visitors (2001) U.S.$1,692,000,000; expenditures by nationals abroad (1990) U.S.$48,000,000.
Population economically active (2002): total 4,300,000; activity rate 38.2% (participation rates: n.a.; female [1998] 37.0%; unemployed [2002] 3.5%).

Price and earnings indexes (1994 = 100)

	1994	1995	1996	1997	1998
Consumer price index	100.0	88.5	84.2	85.8	88.2
Monthly earnings index	...	...	...	...	...

Gross domestic product (2002): U.S.$25,900,000,000 (U.S.$2,300 per capita).

Structure of gross domestic product and labour force

	2001 in value CUP '000,000[4]	2001 % of total value	1989 labour force	1989 % of labour force
Agriculture	1,768.0	6.5	721,100	20.4
Mining	417.7	1.5	} 767,500	} 21.8
Manufacturing	4,751.6	17.4		
Public utilities	576.3	2.1		
Construction	1,779.5	6.5	344,300	9.8
Transp. and commun.	2,874.9	10.5	235,900	6.7
Finance, insurance	2,039.0	7.4	21,700	0.6
Trade	7,608.4	27.8	395,300	11.2
Public administration	—	—	151,700	4.3
Services	5,123.0	18.7	835,700	23.7
Other	435.3[5]	1.6[5]	53,400	1.5
TOTAL	27,373.7	100.0	3,526,600	100.0

Land use (1994): forested 23.7%; meadows and pastures 27.0%; agricultural and under permanent cultivation 30.7%; other 18.6%.

Foreign trade[6]

Balance of trade (current prices)

	1997	1998	1999	2000	2001[7]
U.S.$'000,000	–1,200	–1,300	–1,800	–1,600	–3,000
% of total	25.2%	25.5%	39.1%	30.8%	45.5%

Imports (1996): U.S.$3,481,000,000 (refined petroleum 20.2%; food and live animals 19.8%, of which cereals 11.4%; machinery and transport equipment 16.1%, of which power-generating machinery 7.4%; crude petroleum 7.2%). *Major import sources* (2001): Spain 12.7%; France 6.5%; Canada 5.7%; China 5.3%; Italy 5.0%.
Exports (1996): U.S.$1,849,000,000 (raw sugar 51.5%; nickel [all forms] 22.6%; fresh and frozen fish 6.7%; raw tobacco and tobacco products 5.9%; medicinal and pharmaceutical products 2.8%). *Major export destinations* (2001): The Netherlands 22.4%; Russia 13.3%; Canada 13.3%; Spain 7.3%; China 6.2%.

Transport and communications

Transport. Railroads (2001): length 2,987 mi, 4,807 km; (1997) passenger-km 1,684,000; metric ton-km cargo 821,500,000. Roads (1997): total length 37,815 mi, 60,858 km (paved 49%). Vehicles (1998): passenger cars 172,574; trucks and buses 185,495. Air transport (2000): passenger-km 2,769,162,000; metric ton-km cargo 49,294,000; airports with scheduled flights (1999) 14.

Communications

Medium	date	unit	number	units per 1,000 persons
Daily newspapers	2000	circulation	1,280,000	114
Radio	2000	receivers	5,320,000	354
Television	2000	receivers	3,580,000	242
Telephones	2001	main lines	573,000	51
Cellular telephones	2001	subscribers	8,100	0.7
Personal computers	2001	units	220,000	20
Internet	2001	users	120,000	11

Education and health

Educational attainment (1981). Percentage of population age 25 and over having: no formal schooling or some primary education 39.6%; completed primary 26.6%; secondary 29.6%; higher 4.2%. *Literacy* (2000): total population age 15 and over literate 96.9%; males 96.9%; females 96.8%.

Education (2000–01)

	schools	teachers	students	student/ teacher ratio
Primary (age 6–11)	8,868	75,900	950,400	12.5
Secondary (age 12–17)	1,887	76,000	911,100	12.0
Voc., teacher tr.	...	27,267[8]	244,253[8]	9.0[8]
Higher	48	20,800	116,700	5.6

Health (2001): physicians 66,285 (1 per 169 persons); hospital beds 82,000 (1 per 137 persons); infant mortality rate per 1,000 live births (2001) 6.2.
Food (2001): daily per capita caloric intake 2,564 (vegetable products 86%, animal products 14%); 111% of FAO recommended minimum requirement.

Military

Total active duty personnel (2002): 46,000 (army 76.1%, navy 6.5%, air force 17.4%). *Military expenditure as percentage of GDP* (1999): 1.9% (world 2.4%); per capita expenditure: U.S.$57.

[1]January 1. [2]Province coextensive with the city of Havana. [3]Province bordering the city of Havana on the east, south, and west. [4]At constant 1981 prices. [5]Import duties. [6]Imports are f.o.b. in balance of trade and trading partners and c.i.f. for commodities. [7]Based on balance of estimated imports for 2001 and estimated exports for 2002. [8]1995–96.

Internet resources for further information:

- **Oficina Nacional de Estadísticas**
  http://www.cubagob.cu/otras_info/estadisticas.htm
- **Naciones Unidas en Cuba**
  http://www.onu.org.cu/uunn/homepage/index2.html

Cyprus

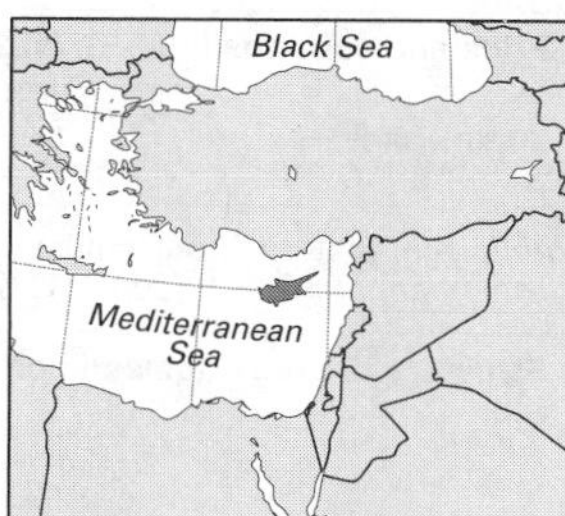

Island of Cyprus

Area: 3,572 sq mi, 9,251 sq km.
Population (2003): 921,000[1].

Two de facto states currently exist on the island of Cyprus: the Republic of Cyprus (ROC), predominantly Greek in character, occupying the southern two-thirds of the island, which is the original and still the internationally recognized de jure government of the whole island; and the Turkish Republic of Northern Cyprus (TRNC), proclaimed unilaterally Nov. 15, 1983, on territory originally secured for the Turkish Cypriot population by the July 20, 1974, intervention of Turkey. Only Turkey recognizes the TRNC, and the two ethnic communities have failed to reestablish a single state. Provision of separate data below does not imply recognition of either state's claims but is necessitated by the lack of unified data.

Republic of Cyprus

Official name: Kipriakí Dhimokratía (Greek); Kıbrıs Cumhuriyeti (Turkish) (Republic of Cyprus).
Form of government: unitary multiparty republic with a unicameral legislature (House of Representatives [80[2]]).
Head of state and government: President.
Capital: Lefkosia (Nicosia).
Official languages: Greek; Turkish.
Monetary unit: 1 Cyprus pound (£C) = 100 cents; valuation (Sept. 8, 2003) 1 £C = U.S.$1.90 = £1.20.

Demography

Area[3]: 2,276 sq mi, 5,896 sq km.
Population (2003): 714,000[4].
Urban-rural (2001): urban 68.8%; rural 31.2%.
Age breakdown (2002)[5]: under 15, 21.5%; 15–29, 22.6%; 30–44, 22.0%; 45–59, 17.8%; 60–74, 11.2%; 75 and over, 4.9%.
Ethnic composition (2000): Greek Cypriot 91.8%; Armenian 3.3%; Arab 2.9%, of which Lebanese 2.5%; British 1.4%; other 0.6%.
Religious affiliation (2001): Greek Orthodox 94.8%; Roman Catholic 2.1%, of which Maronite 0.6%; Anglican 1.0%; Muslim 0.6%; other 1.5%.
Urban areas (2001): Lefkosia 198,697[6]; Limassol 156,458; Larnaca 70,147.

Vital statistics

Birth rate per 1,000 population (2001): 11.7 (world avg. 21.3).
Death rate per 1,000 population (2001): 6.9 (world avg. 9.1).
Natural increase rate per 1,000 population (2001): 4.8 (world avg. 12.2).
Life expectancy at birth (2001): male 76.1 years; female 81.0 years.

National economy

Budget (2001). Revenue: £C 2,073,100,000 (indirect taxes 34.8%, direct taxes 31.8%, social security contributions 19.7%). Expenditures: £C 2,239,700,000 (current expenditures 90.0%, development expenditures 10.0%).
Tourism (2001): receipts U.S.$1,961,000,000; expenditures U.S.$283,000,000.
Household expenditure (2000): housing and energy 21.3%, food and beverages 20.0%, transportation and communications 19.2%.
Gross national product (2001): U.S.$9,400,000,000 (U.S.$12,320 per capita).

Structure of gross domestic product and labour force

	2001			
	in value £C '000,000	% of total value	labour force	% of labour force
Agriculture, fishing	219.4	3.7	24,700	7.6
Mining	15.0	0.3	600	0.2
Manufacturing	562.7	9.6	37,200	11.4
Construction	398.5	6.8	26,900	8.2
Public utilities	115.2	2.0	1,500	0.5
Transportation and communications	557.8	9.5	22,200	6.8
Trade	1,267.7	21.6	88,200	27.0
Finance, insurance	1,194.3	20.3	31,100	9.5
Pub. admin., defense	805.6	13.7	74,700	22.9
Services	467.0	8.0		
Other	264.0[7]	4.5[7]	19,100[8]	5.9[8]
TOTAL	5,867.2	100.0	326,200	100.0

Production. Agriculture (in '000 metric tons; 2002): potatoes 142.0, barley 125.7, grapes 88.0, oranges 36.5, grapefruit 27.8, olives 17.5. Manufacturing (value added in £C '000,000; 1999): food 102.7; cement, bricks, and tiles 47.1; tobacco products 46.3; beverages 45.3; fabricated metal products 35.1. Energy production: electricity (kW-hr; 2001) 3,552,000,000.

Foreign trade[9]

Imports (2001): £C 2,528,700,000 (consumer goods 24.4%; for reexport 13.9%; mineral fuels 10.5%; capital goods 10.2%). *Major import sources:* U.S. 9.4%; Greece 8.9%; U.K. 8.8%; Italy 8.8%; Germany 6.8%; Japan 6.1%.
Exports (2001): £C 628,000,000 (reexports 53.7%[10]; domestic exports 37.2%, of which pharmaceuticals 6.3%, clothing 3.1%; ships' stores 9.1%). *Major export destinations:* U.K. 18.7%; Russia 8.6%; Greece 8.4%; U.A.E. 7.8%; Syria 6.0%.

Transport and communications

Transport. Roads (2001): total length 11,408 km (paved 58%). Vehicles (2001): cars 268,200; trucks and buses 136,200. Air transport (2002)[11]: passenger-km 3,276,000,000; metric ton-km cargo 40,392,000; airports (2000) 2.

Communications

Medium	date	unit	number	units per 1,000 persons
Television	1999	receivers	120,000	180
Telephones	2002	main lines	427,400	616
Cellular telephones	2002	subscribers	417,900	597
Personal computers	2002	units	210,000	300
Internet	2002	users	170,000	247

Education and health

Educational attainment (2001). Percentage of population age 15 and over having: no formal schooling 2.1%; incomplete primary 6.4%; complete primary 20.6%; secondary 48.3%; higher education 22.3%; not stated 0.3%.

Education (1997–98)

	schools	teachers	students	student/ teacher ratio
Primary (age 6–11)	372	3,521	64,592	18.3
Secondary (age 12–17) Vocational	125	5,032	61,703	12.3
Higher	34	835	10,527	12.6

Health (2000): physicians 1,824 (1 per 372 persons); hospital beds 3,147 (1 per 216 persons); infant mortality rate per 1,000 live births (2002) 7.7.

Internet resources for further information:
- **Central Bank of Cyprus http://www.centralbank.gov.cy**
- **Rep. of Cyprus Statistical Service http://www.pio.gov.cy/dsr**

Turkish Republic of Northern Cyprus

Official name: Kuzey Kıbrıs Türk Cumhuriyeti (Turkish) (Turkish Republic of Northern Cyprus).
Capital: Lefkoşa (Nicosia).
Official language: Turkish.
Monetary unit: 1 Turkish lira (TL) = 100 kurush; valuation (Sept. 8, 2003) 1 U.S.$ = TL 1,384,000; 1 £ = TL 2,194,401.
Population (2003): 207,000[1] (Lefkoşa 39,176[12]; Gazimağusa [Famagusta] 27,637[12]; Girne [Kyrenia] 14,205[12]).
Ethnic composition (1996): Turkish Cypriot/Turkish 96.4%; other 3.6%.

Structure of gross domestic product and labour force

	2001			
	in value TL '000,000,000	% of total value	labour force	% of labour force
Agriculture and fishing	78,627.2	7.4	14,931	16.6
Mining and manufacturing	63,210.0	5.9	8,715	9.6
Construction	38,923.3	3.6	14,104	15.6
Public utilities	58,526.4	5.5	1,376	1.5
Transportation and communications	133,453.3	12.5	8,104	9.0
Trade, restaurants	165,151.9	15.4	9,630	10.7
Pub. admin.	199,156.5	18.6	18,084	20.0
Finance, real estate	121,271.8	11.3	14,401	15.9
Services	133,995.8	12.5		
Other	78,108.3[13]	7.3[13]	1,021[14]	1.1[14]
TOTAL	1,070,424.5	100.0	90,366	100.0

Budget (2001). Revenue: U.S.$418,200,000 (foreign aid 46.8%, direct taxes 24.2%, indirect taxes 18.8%, loans 6.4%). Expenditures: U.S.$418,200,000 (wages 32.9%, social transfers 29.8%, defense 8.3%, investments 8.2%).
Imports (2001): U.S.$272,000,000 (machinery and transport equipment 21.7%, food 21.7%). *Major import sources:* Turkey 63.7%; U.K. 10.5%.
Exports (2001): U.S.$34,600,000 (ready-made garments 32.1%, citrus fruits 28.6%). *Major export destinations:* Turkey 37.0%; U.K. 33.2%.

Education (2001–02)

	schools	teachers	students	student/ teacher ratio
Primary (age 7–11)	94	1,177	15,584	13.2
Secondary (age 12–17)	52	1,442	15,631	10.8
Vocational	13	438	2,177	5.0
Higher	6	884[15]	26,321	24.8[15]

Health (2001): physicians 472 (1 per 450 persons); hospital beds 1,002 (1 per 236 persons); infant mortality rate per 1,000 live births (1999) 3.7.

Internet resources for further information:
- **Turkish Republic of Northern Cyprus http://www.cypnet.com/.ncyprus/root.html**

[1]Includes 80,000 "settlers" from Turkey and 40,000 Turkish military in the TRNC; excludes 3,200 British military in the Sovereign Base Areas (SBA) in the ROC and 1,200 UN peacekeeping forces. [2]Twenty-four seats reserved for Turkish Cypriots are not occupied. [3]Area includes 99 sq mi (256 sq km) of British military SBA and *c.* 107 sq mi (*c.* 278 sq km) of the UN Buffer Zone. [4]Excludes British and UN military forces. [5]January 1. [6]ROC only. [7]Import duties less imputed bank service charges. [8]Includes 3,200 unemployed. [9]Imports c.i.f.; exports f.o.b. [10]Mainly cigarettes, vehicles, and consumer electronics. [11]Cyprus Airways. [12]1996 census. [13]Import duties. [14]Unemployed. [15]1998–99.

Czech Republic

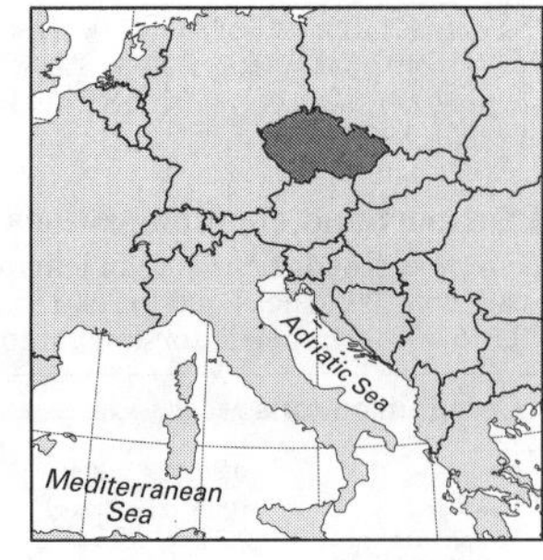

Official name: Česká Republika.
Form of government: unitary multiparty republic with two legislative houses (Senate [81]; Chamber of Deputies [200]).
Chief of state: President.
Head of government: Prime Minister.
Capital: Prague.
Official language: Czech.
Official religion: none.
Monetary unit: 1 koruna (Kč) = 100 halura; valuation (Sept. 8, 2003) 1 U.S.$ = 29.62 Kč
1 £ = 46.97 Kč

Area and population

Regions[1]	area sq km	population 2001 census	Regions[1]	area sq km	population 2001 census
Brno	7,067	1,127,718	Pardubice	4,519	508,281
Budejovice	10,056	625,267	Plzeň	7,560	550,688
Hradec Králové	4,757	550,724	Střed	11,014	1,122,473
Jihlava	6,925	519,211	Ústí	5,335	820,219
Karlovy Vary	3,315	304,343	Zlín	3,965	595,010
Liberec	3,163	428,184			
Olomouc	5,139	639,369	**Capital city**		
Ostrava	5,555	1,269,467	Prague (Praha)	496	1,169,106
			TOTAL	78,866	10,230,060

Demography

Population (2003): 10,202,000.
Density (2003): persons per sq mi 335.0, persons per sq km 129.4.
Urban-rural (2001): urban 74.6%; rural 25.4%.
Sex distribution (2001): male 48.70%; female 51.30%.
Age breakdown (2001): under 15, 16.2%; 15–29, 23.5%; 30–44, 20.2%; 45–59, 21.6%; 60–74, 13.0%; 75 and over, 5.5%.
Population projection: (2010) 10,128,000; (2020) 9,924,000.
Ethnic composition (2001): Czech 90.4%; Moravian 3.7%; Slovak 1.9%; Polish 0.5%; German 0.4%; Silesian 0.1%; Rom (Gypsy) 0.1%; other 2.9%.
Religious affiliation (2000): Catholic 43.8%, of which Roman Catholic 40.4%, Hussite Church of the Czech Republic 2.2%; nonreligious 31.9%; atheist 5.0%; Protestant 3.1%; Orthodox Christian 0.6%; Jewish 0.1%; other (mostly unaffiliated Christian) 15.5%.
Major cities (2001): Prague 1,169,106; Brno 376,172; Ostrava 314,102; Plzeň 163,791; Olomouc 101,624; Liberec 97,677.

Vital statistics

Birth rate per 1,000 population (2001): 8.9 (world avg. 21.3); legitimate 76.5%; illegitimate 23.5%.
Death rate per 1,000 population (2001): 10.5 (world avg. 9.1).
Natural increase rate per 1,000 population (2001): –1.6 (world avg. 12.2).
Total fertility rate (avg. births per childbearing woman; 2001): 1.1.
Marriage rate per 1,000 population (2001): 5.1.
Divorce rate per 1,000 population (2001): 3.1.
Life expectancy at birth (2001): male 72.1 years; female 78.5 years.
Major causes of death per 100,000 population (2001): diseases of the circulatory system 532.7; malignant neoplasms (cancers) 264.1; accidents, poisoning, and violence 64.1; diseases of the respiratory system 43.2.

National economy

Budget (2001). Revenue: Kč 626,216,000,000 (tax revenue 95.6%, of which social security contributions 37.4%, value-added tax 18.6%, personal income tax 13.4%, corporate tax 9.4%, excise tax 9.3%; nontax revenue 4.4%). Expenditures: Kč 693,920,000,000 (social security and welfare 39.3%; education 11.6%; health 6.1%; defense 5.4%; police 3.9%).
Production (metric tons except as noted). Agriculture, forestry, fishing (2002): cereals 6,577,276 (of which wheat 3,866,470, barley 1,792,560, corn [maize] 616,234), sugar beets 3,832,466, potatoes 1,105,967, rapeseed 709,533; livestock (number of live animals) 3,440,925 pigs, 1,520,136 cattle, 96,286 sheep, 16,564,000 chickens; roundwood (2001) 14,374,000 cu m; fish catch (2000) 24,129. Mining and quarrying (2000): kaolin 5,573,000; feldspar 337,000. Manufacturing (value added in Kč '000,000,000; 1998): nonelectrical machinery and apparatus 47.0; food products 37.4; fabricated metals 35.2; motor vehicles 34.2; electrical machinery and apparatus 31.1; iron and steel 25.5. Construction (2001): 196,700,000,000 Kč. Energy production (consumption): electricity (kW-hr; 2001) 74,647,000,000 (65,108,000,000); hard coal (metric tons; 2001) 15,138,000 (15,138,000); lignite (metric tons; 2001) 50,968,000 (50,968,000); crude petroleum (barrels; 2000) 1,176,500 (39,826,000); petroleum products (metric tons; 2000) 6,132,000 (7,998,000); natural gas (cu m; 2000) 219,000,000 (9,428,000,000).
Tourism (2001): receipts from visitors U.S.$3,106,000,000; expenditures by nationals abroad U.S.$1,388,000,000.
Household income and expenditure. Average household size (2001) 2.5; disposable income per household (2000) Kč 286,920 (U.S.$8,900); sources of income (2001): wages and salaries 67.4%, transfer payments 21.5%, self-employment 6.7%, other 4.4%; expenditure (2001): food and beverages 25.3%, housing and utilities 19.8%, transportation and communications 14.4%, recreation 10.5%, household furnishings 6.9%.
Population economically active (2002): total 4,769,727; activity rate of total population 46.6% (participation rates: ages 15–64, 60.9%; female 44.3%; unemployed [2003] 9.9%).

Price and earnings indexes (1995 = 100)

	1997	1998	1999	2000	2001	2002
Consumer price index	118.0	130.7	133.5	138.7	145.2	147.8
Annual earnings index	130.8	143.1	155.1	165.2	179.1	192.3

Public debt (external, outstanding; 2001): U.S.$5,915,000,000.
Gross national product (2001): U.S.$54,300,000,000 (U.S.$5,310 per capita).

Structure of gross domestic product and labour force

	2001		2002	
	in value Kč '000,000	% of total value	labour force	% of labour force
Agriculture, forestry	82,600	3.8	195,264	4.1
Mining	2	2	56,030	1.2
Manufacturing	652,100[2]	30.2[2]	1,389,903	29.1
Construction	141,900	6.6	367,706	7.7
Public utilities	2	2	68,870	1.4
Transportation and communications	162,900	7.6	349,018	7.3
Trade, hotels	337,400	15.6	906,093	19.0
Finance, real estate	311,400	14.4	518,484	10.9
Pub. admin., defense } Services }	296,900	13.8	195,066	4.1
			723,293	15.2
Other	172,600[3]	8.0[3]	—	—
TOTAL	2,157,800	100.0	4,769,727	100.0

Land use (2001): forested 33.5%; meadows and pastures 12.2%; agricultural and under permanent cultivation 42.0%; other 12.3%.

Foreign trade

Balance of trade (current prices)

	1997	1998	1999	2000	2001	2002
Kč '000,000	–139,269	–76,319	–64,413	–120,825	–116,685	–74,455
% of total	8.8%	4.3%	3.4%	5.1%	4.4%	2.9%

Imports (2002): Kč 1,326,339,000,000 (machinery and apparatus 31.2%; base and fabricated metals 10.9%; chemicals and chemical products 10.4%; motor vehicles 9.7%). *Major import sources:* Germany 32.5%; Italy 5.4%; Slovakia 5.2%; France 4.8%; China 4.6%; Russia 4.5%.
Exports (2002): Kč 1,251,884,000,000 (machinery and apparatus 31.9%, of which computers 6.2%; motor vehicles 16.7%; fabricated metals 6.5%; base metals 5.4%; chemicals and chemical products 5.4%). *Major export destinations:* Germany 36.5%; Slovakia 7.7%; United Kingdom 5.8%; Austria 5.5%; Poland 4.7%; France 4.7%.

Transport and communications

Transport. Railroads (2001): length 9,444 km; passenger-km 7,299,000,000; metric ton-km cargo 16,882,000,000. Roads (2001): total length 125,905 km (paved, n.a.). Vehicles (2001): passenger cars 3,529,791; trucks and buses 381,876. Air transport (2001): passenger-km 6,398,920,000; metric ton-km 29,209,000; airports (2001) with scheduled flights 2.

Communications

Medium	date	unit	number	units per 1,000 persons
Daily newspapers	2000	circulation	1,210,000	118
Television	2000	receivers	3,289,000	341
Telephones	2002	main lines	3,860,800	378
Cellular telephones	2002	subscribers	8,610,200	849
Personal computers	2001	units	1,500,000	147
Internet	2001	users	1,500,000	147

Education and health

Educational attainment (2001). Percentage of population age 15 and over having: no formal schooling 0.2%; primary education 21.6%; secondary 68.7%; higher 9.5%. *Literacy* (2001): 99.8%.

Education (2001–02)

	schools	teachers	students	student/ teacher ratio
Primary (age 6–14)	4,263	67,594	1,028,000	15.2
Secondary (age 15–18)	346	11,000	136,729	12.4
Voc., teacher tr.	1,388	10,669	197,229	18.5
Higher[4]	24	13,332	219,514	16.5

Health (2002): physicians 41,293 (1 per 248 persons); hospital beds 119,481 (1 per 86 persons); infant mortality rate per 1,000 live births (2001) 4.0.
Food (2001): daily per capita caloric intake 3,097 (vegetable products 74%, animal products 26%); 125% of FAO recommended minimum requirement.

Military

Total active duty personnel (2002): 49,450 (army 73.5%, air force 22.9%, ministry of defense 3.6%). *Military expenditure as percentage of GNP* (1999): 2.3% (world 2.4%); per capita expenditure: U.S.$292.

[1]New local government structure as of November 2000 elections. [2]Manufacturing includes Mining and Public utilities. [3]Taxes less subsidies and imputed bank charges. [4]Universities only.

Internet resources for further information:
- **Czech Statistical Office http://www.czso.cz**

Denmark

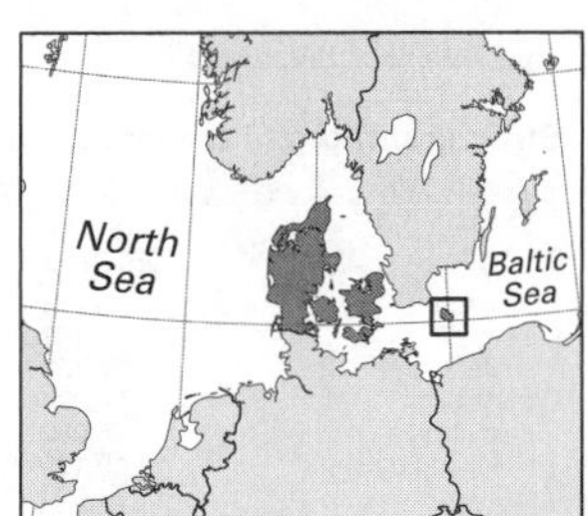

Official name: Kongeriget Danmark (Kingdom of Denmark).
Form of government: parliamentary state and constitutional monarchy with one legislative house (Folketing [179]).
Chief of state: Danish Monarch.
Head of government: Prime Minister.
Capital: Copenhagen.
Official language: Danish.
Official religion: Evangelical Lutheran.
Monetary unit: 1 Danish krone (Dkr; plural kroner) = 100 øre; valuation (Sept. 8, 2003) 1 U.S.$ = Dkr 6.73; 1 £ = Dkr 10.67.

Area and population[1]		area		population
Counties	**Capitals**	sq mi	sq km	2003 estimate[2]
Århus	Århus	1,761	4,561	649,177
Bornholm	Rønne	227	589	44,060
Frederiksborg	Hillerød	520	1,347	372,276
Fyn	Odense	1,346	3,486	473,471
København	—	204	528	618,016
Nordjylland	Ålborg	2,383	6,173	495,625
Ribe	Ribe	1,209	3,132	224,257
Ringkøbing	Ringkøbing	1,874	4,854	275,044
Roskilde	Roskilde	344	891	236,151
Sønderjylland	Åbenrå	1,521	3,939	253,013
Storstrøm	Nykøbing Falster	1,312	3,398	261,188
Vejle	Vejle	1,157	2,997	353,284
Vestsjælland	Sorø	1,152	2,984	300,729
Viborg	Viborg	1,592	4,122	234,496
Municipalities				
Copenhagen (København)	—	34	88	501,285
Frederiksberg	—	3	9	91,435
TOTAL		16,640[3]	43,098	5,383,507

Demography

Population (2003): 5,387,000.
Density (2003): persons per sq mi 323.7, persons per sq km 125.0.
Urban-rural (2003): urban 85.3%; rural 14.7%.
Sex distribution (2003): male 49.46%; female 50.54%.
Age breakdown (2003): under 15, 18.8%; 15–29, 17.7%; 30–44, 22.3%; 45–59, 20.9%; 60–74, 13.3%; 75 and over, 7.0%.
Population projection: (2010) 5,504,000; (2020) 5,640,000.
Ethnic composition (2001)[4]: Danish 95.2%; Asian 1.7%, of which Turkish 0.7%; residents of pre-1992 Yugoslavia 0.7%; African 0.5%; German 0.2%; English 0.2%; other 1.5%.
Religious affiliation (1998): Christian 87.5%, of which Evangelical Lutheran 85.8%; Muslim 2.2%; other/nonreligious 10.3%.
Major urban areas (2003): Greater Copenhagen 1,085,813; Århus 222,559; Odense 145,374; Ålborg 121,100; Esbjerg 72,613.

Vital statistics

Birth rate per 1,000 population (2002): 12.0 (world avg. 21.3).
Death rate per 1,000 population (2002): 10.8 (world avg. 9.1).
Natural increase rate per 1,000 population (2002): 1.2 (world avg. 12.2).
Total fertility rate (avg. births per childbearing woman; 2002): 1.7.
Marriage rate per 1,000 population (2002): 6.9.
Divorce rate per 1,000 population (2002): 2.8.
Life expectancy at birth (2002): male 74.8 years; female 79.4 years.
Major causes of death per 100,000 population (1999): diseases of the circulatory system 400.2; malignant neoplasms (cancers) 300.0.

National economy

Budget (2000). Revenue: Dkr 476,420,000,000 (tax revenue 86.8%, nontax revenue 11.7%, other 1.5%). Expenditures: Dkr 452,939,000,000 (social security and welfare 40.9%, education 12.7%, public service 8.4%, economic affairs 7.5%, defense 4.1%).
National debt (end of year; 2001): Dkr 679,957,000,000.
Tourism (2001): receipts U.S.$3,923,000,000; expenditures U.S.$4,684,000,000.
Population economically active (2002): total 2,892,800; activity rate of total population 53.9% (participation rates: ages 16–66, 77.8%; female 46.9%; unemployed 3.8%).

Price and earnings indexes (1995 = 100)	1996	1997	1998	1999	2000	2001	2002
Consumer price index	102.1	104.4	106.3	108.9	112.1	114.7	117.5
Hourly earnings index	...	...	...	...	...	...	...

Household income and expenditure. Average household size (2001) 2.2; annual disposable income per household (2000) Dkr 259,589 (U.S.$32,115); expenditure (2000): housing 22.3%, transportation and communications 16.1%, food 11.3%, recreation 11.1%, energy 6.8%, household furnishings 6.3%.
Production (in Dkr '000,000 except as noted). Agriculture, forestry, fishing (value added; 2001): meat 24,884 (of which pork 21,069, beef 2,178), milk 11,327, cereals 8,095 (of which wheat 4,012, barley 3,469), furs 2,659, flowers and plants 2,535; livestock (number of live animals) 12,732,035 pigs, 1,796,118 cattle; roundwood (2002) 1,446,000 cu m; fish catch (2000) 1,577,698 metric tons. Mining and quarrying (2001): sand and gravel 23,000,000 cu m; chalk 410,000 metric tons. Manufacturing (value added in U.S.$'000,000; 1998): nonelectrical machinery and apparatus 3,874; food products 3,848; fabricated metals 2,228; printing and publishing 2,177; plastic and rubber products 1,114; furniture 1,089. Energy production (consumption): electricity (kW-hr; 2001) 36,006,000,000 ([1999] 42,363,000,000); coal (metric tons; 2001) none (6,984,000); crude petroleum (barrels; 2001) 129,844,000 ([1999] 57,599,000); petroleum products (metric tons; 2001) 8,860,000 (7,547,000); natural gas (cu m; 2001) 8,153,000,000 (4,366,000,000).
Gross national product (2001): U.S.$164,000,000,000 (U.S.$30,600 per capita).

Structure of gross domestic product and labour force	2002			
	in value Dkr '000,000	% of total value	labour force	% of labour force
Agriculture, fishing	29,998	2.6	102,300	3.5
Mining	29,739	2.6		
Manufacturing	192,338	16.5	453,800	15.7
Construction	57,625	5.0	173,300	6.0
Public utilities	25,888	2.2	14,400	0.5
Transp. and commun.	94,249	8.1	179,000	6.2
Trade, restaurants	165,560	14.2	494,900	17.1
Finance, real estate	293,019	25.2	375,600	13.0
Pub. admin., defense Services	314,829	27.1	974,300	33.7
Other	–40,869[5]	–3.5[5]	125,200[6]	4.3[6]
TOTAL	1,162,377[2]	100.0	2,892,800	100.0

Land use (1994): forested 10.5%; meadows and pastures 7.5%; agricultural and under permanent cultivation 55.9%; other 26.1%.

Foreign trade[7]

Balance of trade (current prices)	1997	1998	1999	2000	2001	2002
Dkr '000,000	+24,353	+13,776	+32,418	+46,201	+53,295	+57,884
% of total	4.0%	2.2%	5.0%	6.1%	6.7%	7.0%

Imports (2001): Dkr 369,582,000,000 (machinery and apparatus [including parts] 22.9%; transport equipment and parts 10.5%; food, beverages, and tobacco 8.5%; clothing and footwear 5.0%; fuels 4.7%). *Major import sources:* Germany 22.0%; Sweden 12.0%; U.K. 7.5%; The Netherlands 7.0%; France 5.7%.
Exports (2001): Dkr 422,877,000,000 (machinery and apparatus 27.5%; agricultural products 19.2%, of which swine 5.7%; mineral fuels and lubricants 6.8%; pharmaceuticals 6.7%; furniture 3.8%). *Major export destinations:* Germany 19.7%; Sweden 11.7%; U.K. 9.4%; U.S. 7.0%; Norway 5.6%; France 5.1%.

Transport and communications

Transport. Railroads (2001): route length 2,743 km; passenger-km 5,318,000,000; metric ton-km cargo 2,025,000,000. Roads (2001): total length 71,663 km (paved 100%). Vehicles (2001): passenger cars 1,854,060; trucks and buses 335,690. Air transport (2001)[8]: passenger-km 8,942,000,000; metric ton-km cargo 183,152,000; airports (1996) with scheduled flights 13.

Communications				units
Medium	date	unit	number	per 1,000 persons
Daily newspapers	2000	circulation	1,510,000	283
Radio	2000	receivers	7,200,000	1,349
Television	2000	receivers	4,310,000	807
Telephones	2002	main lines	3,737,000	696
Cellular telephones	2002	subscribers	4,479,000	833
Personal computers	2002	units	2,500,000	465
Internet	2002	users	3,100,000	577

Education and health

Educational attainment (2000). Percentage of population age 25–69 having: completed lower secondary or not stated 34.6%; completed upper secondary or vocational 42.3%; undergraduate 17.6%; graduate 5.5%. *Literacy:* 100%.

Education (2001)	schools	teachers[9]	students	student/ teacher ratio
Primary/lower secondary (age 7–15)	3,036	58,500	664,224	...
Upper secondary (age 16–18)	154	11,000	64,451	...
Vocational	165	12,000	174,827	...
Higher	154	8,000	174,615	...

Health: physicians (1994) 14,497 (1 per 358 persons); hospital beds (2000) 22,927 (1 per 233 persons); infant mortality rate per 1,000 live births (2002) 4.8.
Food (2001): daily per capita caloric intake 3,454 (vegetable products 60.5%, animal products 39.5%); 128% of FAO recommended minimum requirement.

Military

Total active duty personnel (2002): 22,700 (army 62.6%, navy 17.6%, air force 19.8%). *Military expenditure as percentage of GNP* (1999): 1.6% (world 2.4%); per capita expenditure U.S.$524.

[1]Excludes the Faroe Islands and Greenland. [2]January 1. [3]Detail does not add to total given because of rounding. [4]Based on nationality. [5]Taxes on products less imputed bank service charges. [6]Includes 14,700 not adequately defined and 110,500 unemployed. [7]Imports c.i.f., exports f.o.b. [8]Danish share of Scandinavian Airlines System (scheduled air service only) and Maersk Air. [9]1993–94.

Internet resources for further information:
- **Statistics Denmark http://www.dst.dk/yearbook**

Djibouti

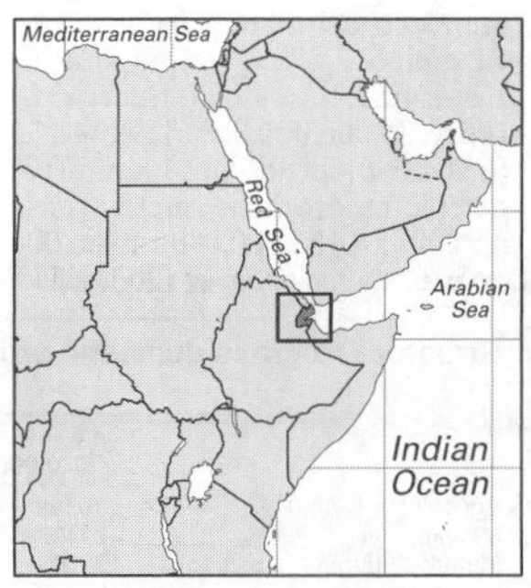

Official name: Jumhūrīyah Jībūtī (Arabic); République de Djibouti (French) (Republic of Djibouti).
Form of government: multiparty republic with one legislative house (National Assembly [65]).
Head of state and government: President.
Capital: Djibouti.
Official languages: Arabic; French.
Official religion: none.
Monetary unit: 1 Djibouti franc (DF) = 100 centimes; valuation (Sept. 8, 2003) 1 U.S.$ = DF 177.72; 1 £ = DF 281.79.

Area and population

		area[1]		population
Districts	**Capitals**	sq mi	sq km	1991 estimate
ʿAlī Sabīḥ (Ali-Sabieh)	ʿAlī Sabīḥ	925	2,400	45,900
Dikhil	Dikhil	2,775	7,200	52,900
Djibouti	Djibouti	225	600	329,300
Obock	Obock	2,200	5,700	20,700
Tadjoura (Tadjourah)	Tadjoura	2,825	7,300	45,100
TOTAL		8,950	23,200	493,900[2]

Demography

Population (2003): 457,000.
Density (2003): persons per sq mi 51.1, persons per sq km 19.7.
Urban-rural (2002): urban 84.2%; rural 15.8%.
Sex distribution (2002): male 51.55%; female 48.45%.
Age breakdown (2002): under 15, 43.0%; 15–29, 28.1%; 30–44, 13.2%; 45–59, 10.5%; 60–74, 4.6%; 75 and over, 0.6%.
Population projection: (2010) 526,000; (2020) 627,000.
Doubling time: 27 years.
Ethnic composition (2000): Somali 46.0%; Afar 35.4%; Arab 11.0%; mixed African and European 3.0%; French 1.6%; other/unspecified 3.0%.
Religious affiliation (1995): Sunnī Muslim 97.2%; Christian 2.8%, of which Roman Catholic 2.2%, Orthodox 0.5%, Protestant 0.1%.
Major city and towns (1991): Djibouti 383,000[3]; ʿAlī Sabīḥ 8,000; Tadjoura 7,500; Dikhil 6,500.

Vital statistics

Birth rate per 1,000 population (2002): 40.3 (world avg. 21.3).
Death rate per 1,000 population (2002): 14.3 (world avg. 9.1).
Natural increase rate per 1,000 population (2002): 26.0 (world avg. 12.2).
Total fertility rate (avg. births per childbearing woman; 2002): 5.6.
Life expectancy at birth (2002): male 49.7 years; female 53.5 years.
Major causes of death (percentage of total deaths [infants and children to age 10, district of Djibouti only]; 1984): diarrhea and acute dehydration 16.0%; malnutrition 16.0%; poisoning 11.0%; tuberculosis 6.0%; acute respiratory disease 6.0%; malaria 6.0%; anemia 6.0%; heart disease 2.0%; kidney disease 1.0%; other ailments 19.0%; no diagnosis 11.0%.

National economy

Budget (2000). Revenue: DF 23,739,000,000 (tax revenue 91.2%, of which indirect taxes 45.3%, direct taxes 38.9%, income and profit tax 6.7%; nontax revenue 8.8%). Expenditures: DF 32,813,000,000 (current expenditures 92.0%, of which general administration 22.7%, defense 13.7%, education 10.0%, health 4.6%; capital expenditures 8.0%).
Tourism (1998): receipts from visitors U.S.$4,000,000; expenditures by nationals abroad U.S.$4,000,000.
Production (metric tons except as noted). Agriculture, forestry, fishing (2002): vegetables and melons 24,210 (of which tomatoes 1,100, onions 110, eggplant 33); lemons and limes 1,800, tropical fruit 1,100; livestock (number of live animals) 512,000 goats, 475,000 sheep, 270,000 cattle, 67,500 camels, 8,700 asses; roundwood, n.a.; fish catch (2000) 350. Mining and quarrying: mineral production limited to locally used construction materials and evaporated salt (2001) 173,000. Manufacturing (2000): structural detail, n.a.; main products include furniture, nonalcoholic beverages, meat and hides, light electromechanical goods, and mineral water. Energy production (consumption): electricity (kW-hr; 2001) 235,262,000 (182,870,000); coal, none (none); crude petroleum, none (none); petroleum products (metric tons; 1999) none (125,000); natural gas, none (none); geothermal, wind, and solar resources are substantial but largely undeveloped.
Population economically active (1991): total 282,000; activity rate of total population 61.5% (participation rates: over age 10, 70.4%; female 40.8%; unemployed [2000] *c.* 50%).

Price and earnings indexes (1995 = 100)

	1995	1996	1997	1998	1999	2000	2001
Inflation rate[4]	100.0	96.1	95.6	95.7	97.9	98.6	100.3
Earnings index	...	...	...	...	...	...	...

Household income and expenditure. Average household size (2000) 5.3; income per household: n.a.; sources of income: n.a.; expenditure (expatriate households; 1984): food 50.3%, energy 13.1%, recreation 10.4%, housing 6.4%, clothing 1.7%, personal effects 1.4%, health care 1.0%, household goods 0.3%, other 15.4%.

Gross national product (2001): U.S.$600,000,000 (U.S.$890 per capita).

Structure of gross domestic product and labour force

	2000		1991	
	in value DF '000,000[5]	% of total value[5]	labour force	% of labour force
Agriculture	3,274	4.0	212,000	75.2
Mining	138	0.2		
Manufacturing	2,750	3.4	31,000	11.0
Construction	4,924	6.1		
Public utilities	5,083	6.3		
Transp. and commun.	19,105	23.6		
Trade	14,530	18.0		
Finance	10,258	12.7	39,000	13.8
Pub. admin., defense	19,392	24.0		
Services	1,354	1.7		
Other	—	—	...	...
TOTAL	80,808	100.0	282,000	100.0

Public debt (external, outstanding; 2001): U.S.$234,900,000.
Land use (1994): forested 0.9%; meadows and pastures 56.1%; agricultural and under permanent cultivation[6]; built-on, wasteland, and other 43.0%.

Foreign trade

Balance of trade (current prices)[7]

	1996	1997	1998	1999	2000	2001
U.S.$'000,000	–161.1	–161.4	–180.5	–182.5	–194.9	–187.4
% of total	67.0%	65.3%	60.4%	56.9%	56.4%	55.3%

Imports (1999): U.S.$152,700,000[8] (food and beverages 25.0%; machinery and electric appliances 12.5%; khat 12.2%; petroleum products 10.9%; transport equipment 10.3%). *Major import sources* (2001): Saudi Arabia 18.5%; France 16.1%; Ethiopia 10.3%; China 8.1%; Italy 3.8%.
Exports (2001): U.S.$10,200,000[8] (aircraft parts 24.5%; hides and skins of cattle, sheep, goats, and camels 20.6%; unspecified special transactions 8.8%; leather 7.8%; live animals 6.9%). *Major export destinations* (2001): Somalia 44.8%; France 23.5%; Yemen 19.2%; Ethiopia 3.5%; United Arab Emirates 3.3%.

Transport and communications

Transport. Railroads (2000): length 62 mi, 100 km; (1999) passenger-mi 50,331,000, passenger-km 81,000,000; short ton-mile cargo 165,347,000, metric ton-km cargo 266,100,000. Roads (1999): total length 1,796 mi, 2,890 km (paved 13%). Vehicles (1996): passenger cars 9,200; trucks and buses 2,040. Merchant marine (2000): vessels (100 gross tons and over) 13; total deadweight tonnage 4,356. Air transport (2001): passengers handled 94,590; metric tons of freight handled 6,652; airports (2000) with scheduled flights 1.

Communications

Medium	date	unit	number	units per 1,000 persons
Daily newspapers	1995	circulation	500	0.8
Radio	1997	receivers	52,000	84
Television	2000	receivers	45,000	104
Telephones	2002	main lines	10,100	15
Cellular telephones	2002	subscribers	15,000	23
Personal computers	2002	units	10,000	15
Internet	2002	users	4,500	6.9

Education and health

Educational attainment: n.a. *Literacy* (2000): percentage of population age 15 and over literate 64.6%; males literate 75.6%; females literate 54.4%.

Education (2000–01)

	schools	teachers	students	student/teacher ratio
Primary (age 6–11)	73	1,127	37,938	33.7
Secondary (age 12–18) / Voc., teacher tr.	26[9]	628[10]	16,121	...
Higher	1[9]	13[9]	478	...

Health (1996): physicians 60 (1 per 7,100 persons); hospital beds[11] (1989) 1,383 (1 per 369 persons); infant mortality rate per 1,000 live births (2002) 99.7.
Food (2001): daily per capita caloric intake 2,218 (vegetable products 88%, animal products 12%); 96% of FAO recommended minimum requirement.

Military

Total active duty personnel (2002): 9,850[12] (army 81.3%, navy 2.0%, air force 2.5%, paramilitary 14.2%). Foreign troops (September 2003): French 2,700; U.S. 1,500; German 800. *Military expenditure as percentage of GNP* (1999): 4.3% (world 2.4%); per capita expenditure U.S.$51.

[1]Original figures are those given in sq km; sq mi equivalent is rounded to appropriate level of generality. [2]Includes refugees. [3]1995 estimate. [4]Estimated figures. [5]At factor cost. [6]In 1988–89 only 1,005 acres (407 hectares) of land were cultivated. [7]Includes trade with Ethiopia (via rail) comprising *c.* 20% of all imports and *c.* 75% of all exports. [8]Excludes Ethiopian trade via rail. [9]1991. [10]1995–96. [11]Public health facilities only. [12]Excluding foreign troops.

Dominica

Official name: Commonwealth of Dominica.
Form of government: multiparty republic with one legislative house (House of Assembly [32[1]]).
Chief of state: President.
Head of government: Prime Minister.
Capital: Roseau.
Official language: English.
Official religion: none.
Monetary unit: 1 East Caribbean dollar (EC$) = 100 cents; valuation (Sept. 8, 2003) 1 U.S.$ = EC$2.70; 1 £ = EC$4.28.

Area and population	area		population
			1991
Parishes	sq mi	sq km	census
St. Andrew	69.3	179.6	11,106
St. David	49.0	126.8	6,977
St. George	20.7	53.5	20,365
St. John	22.5	58.5	4,990
St. Joseph	46.4	120.1	6,183
St. Luke	4.3	11.1	1,552
St. Mark	3.8	9.9	1,943
St. Patrick	32.6	84.4	8,929
St. Paul	26.0	67.4	7,495
St. Peter	10.7	27.7	1,643
TOTAL	285.3[2]	739.0[2]	71,183[3]

Demography

Population (2003): 69,700.
Density (2003)[2]: persons per sq mi 240.3, persons per sq km 92.9.
Urban-rural (2002): urban 71.4%; rural 28.6%.
Sex distribution (2002): male 50.32%; female 49.68%.
Age breakdown (2002): under 15, 28.3%; 15–29, 25.5%; 30–44, 25.5%; 45–59, 11.7%; 60–74, 7.0%; 75 and over, 2.0%.
Population projection: (2010) 70,000; (2020) 75,000.
Doubling time: 68 years.
Ethnic composition (2000): black 88.3%; mulatto 7.3%; black-Amerindian 1.7%; British expatriates 1.0%; Indo-Pakistani 1.0%; other 0.7%.
Religious affiliation (1991): Roman Catholic 70.1%; six largest Protestant groups 17.2%, of which Seventh-day Adventist 4.6%, Pentecostal 4.3%, Methodist 4.2%; other 8.9%; nonreligious 2.9%; unknown 0.9%.
Major towns (1991): Roseau 15,853; Portsmouth 3,621; Marigot 2,919; Atkinson 2,518; Mahaut 2,372.

Vital statistics

Birth rate per 1,000 population (2002): 17.3 (world avg. 21.3); (1991) legitimate 24.1%; illegitimate 75.9%.
Death rate per 1,000 population (2002): 7.1 (world avg. 9.1).
Natural increase rate per 1,000 population (2002): 10.2 (world avg. 12.2).
Total fertility rate (avg. births per childbearing woman; 2002): 2.0.
Marriage rate per 1,000 population (1996): 3.1.
Divorce rate per 1,000 population (1996): 0.7.
Life expectancy at birth (2002): male 71.0 years; female 76.9 years.
Major causes of death per 100,000 population (1994): diseases of the circulatory system 237.8, of which hypertensive disease 93.8, diseases of pulmonary circulation and other forms of heart disease 72.0; malignant neoplasms (cancers) 125.0; endocrine and metabolic disorders 59.8; infectious and parasitic diseases 46.2; diseases of the respiratory system 38.0.

National economy

Budget (2000–01). Revenue: EC$194,900,000 (tax revenue 79.2%, of which consumption taxes on imports 39.1%, income taxes 19.9%; nontax revenue 13.8%; grants 7.0%). Expenditures: EC$270,800,000 (current expenditures 84.2%, of which wages 42.8%, debt payment 13.6%; development expenditures 15.8%).
Public debt (external, outstanding; 2001): U.S.$184,500,000.
Land use (1994): forested 66.0%; meadows and pastures 3.0%; agricultural and under permanent cultivation 23.0%; other 8.0%.
Tourism: receipts from visitors (2000) U.S.$47,000,000; expenditures by nationals abroad U.S.$9,000,000.
Gross national product (2001): U.S.$200,000,000 (U.S.$3,200 per capita).

Structure of gross domestic product and labour force	2000		1997	
	in value EC$'000,000[4]	% of total value[4]	labour force	% of labour force
Agriculture	110.6	18.0	6,100	18.2
Mining	5.2	0.8	...	...
Manufacturing	54.7	8.9	2,250	6.7
Construction	52.2	8.5	2,150	6.4
Public utilities	33.5	5.5	280	0.8
Transportation and communications	104.2	17.0	1,500	4.5
Trade, hotels, restaurants	88.2	14.4	5,030	15.1
Finance, real estate	91.5	14.9	1,390	4.2
Services	9.7	1.6	4,370	13.1
Pub. admin., defense	119.4	19.4	1,530	4.6
Other	–55.3[5]	–9.0[5]	8,820[6]	26.4[6]
TOTAL	613.9	100.0	33,420	100.0

Population economically active (1997): total 33,420; activity rate of total population 45.8% (participation rates: ages 15–64 [1991] 62.4%; female 45.8%; unemployed 23.1%).

Price and earnings indexes (1995 = 100)	1995	1996	1997	1998	1999	2000	2001
Consumer price index	100.0	101.7	104.2	105.2	106.4	107.3	109.3
Earnings index	...	...	...	...	...	...	...

Household income and expenditure. Average household size (1991) 3.6; income per household: n.a.; sources of income: n.a.; expenditure (1984)[7]: food and nonalcoholic beverages 43.1%, housing and utilities 16.1%, transportation 11.6%, clothing and footwear 6.5%, household furnishings 6.0%.
Production (metric tons except as noted). Agriculture, forestry, fishing (2002): bananas 29,018[8], root crops 25,600 (of which dasheens 13,011, yams 8,000, tanias 4,550), grapefruit 17,000, coconuts 11,500, oranges 7,200, plantains 5,700, mangoes 1,900, limes 1,000, pepper 101[9], bay oil 54[9]; livestock (number of live animals: 1999) 13,400 cattle, 9,700 goats, 7,600 sheep; roundwood, n.a.; fish catch (2000) 1,157 metric tons. Mining and quarrying: pumice, limestone, and sand and gravel are quarried primarily for local consumption. Manufacturing (value of production in EC$'000; 2000): toilet and laundry soap 18,815; toothpaste 10,063; crude coconut oil 1,758; other products include fruit juices, beer, garments, bottled spring water, and cardboard boxes. Energy production (consumption): electricity (kW-hr; 2000) 74,000,000 (74,000,000); coal, none (none); crude petroleum, none (none); petroleum products (metric tons; 1999) none (26,000); natural gas, none (none).

Foreign trade[10]

Balance of trade (current prices)	1996	1997	1998	1999	2000	2001
EC$'000,000	–212.4	–193.3	–196.8	–233.6	–251.6	–268.7
% of total	43.4%	40.3%	36.6%	44.4%	46.3%	48.1%

Imports (2000): EC$397,700,000 (food and beverages 19.3%; machinery and apparatus 17.7%; refined petroleum 8.6%; road vehicles 8.3%). *Major import sources:* U.S. 37.5%; Trinidad and Tobago 16.3%; U.K. 7.7%; Japan 6.3%; Canada 4.2%.
Exports (2000): EC$147,300,000 (agricultural exports 37.5%, of which bananas 25.9%; coconut-based soaps 25.0%; perfumery and cosmetics 13.7%). *Major export destinations:* U.K. 24.8%; Jamaica 23.7%; France (significantly Guadeloupe) 8.5%; U.S. 7.4%; Antigua and Barbuda 7.4%.

Transport and communications

Transport. Railroads: none. Roads (1999): total length 485 mi, 780 km (paved 50%). Vehicles (1994): passenger cars 6,581; trucks and buses 2,825. Merchant marine (1992): vessels (100 gross tons and over) 7; total deadweight tonnage 3,153. Air transport: (1991) passenger arrivals 43,312, passenger departures, n.a.; (1997) cargo unloaded 575 metric tons, cargo loaded 363 metric tons; airports (1996) with scheduled flights 2.

Communications				units
Medium	date	unit	number	per 1,000 persons
Radio	1997	receivers	46,000	608
Television	2000	receivers	15,700	220
Telephones	2002	main lines	25,400	326
Cellular telephones	2002	subscribers	9,400	120
Personal computers	2002	units	12,500	160
Internet	2000	users	6,000	77

Education and health

Educational attainment (1991). Percentage of population age 25 and over having: no formal schooling 4.2%; primary education 78.4%; secondary 11.0%; higher vocational 2.3%; university 2.8%; other/unknown 1.3%. *Literacy* (1996): total population age 15 and over literate, 94.0%.

Education (1997–98)	schools	teachers	students	student/ teacher ratio
Primary	63	587	13,636	23.2
Secondary	15	293	5,455	18.6
Higher[11]	2	34	484	14.2

Health (1998): physicians 38 (1 per 2,007 persons); hospital beds 262 (1 per 291 persons); infant mortality rate per 1,000 live births (2002) 15.9.
Food (2001): daily per capita caloric intake 2,995 (vegetable products 77%, animal products 23%); 124% of FAO recommended minimum requirement.

Military

Total active duty personnel (2002): none[12].

[1]Includes 22 seats that are elective (including speaker if elected from outside of the House of Assembly) and 10 seats that are nonelective (including 9 appointees of the president and the attorney general serving ex officio). [2]Total area of Dominica per more recent survey is 290 sq mi (750 sq km). [3]March 2001 preliminary census total equals 71,727. [4]At current factor cost. [5]Less imputed banking service charge. [6]Includes 7,720 unemployed and 1,100 unclassified by economic activity. [7]Weights of consumer price index components. [8]Export production only. [9]1998. [10]Imports c.i.f.; exports f.o.b. [11]1992–93. [12]300-member police force includes a coast guard unit.

Internet resources for further information:
- **Eastern Caribbean Central Bank http://www.eccb-centralbank.org**

Dominican Republic

Official name: República Dominicana (Dominican Republic).
Form of government: multiparty republic with two legislative houses (Senate [32]; Chamber of Deputies [150]).
Head of state and government: President.
Capital: Santo Domingo.
Official language: Spanish.
Official religion: none[1].
Monetary unit: 1 Dominican peso (RD$) = 100 centavos; valuation (Sept. 8, 2003) 1 U.S.$ = RD$27.60; 1 £ = RD$43.76.

Area and population

Provinces	area sq km	population 2002[2] census	Provinces	area sq km	population 2002[2] census
Azua	2,532	202,565	Peravia	998	160,328
Baoruco	1,283	92,111	Puerto Plata	1,857	288,602
Barahona	1,739	174,043	Salcedo	440	91,030
Dajabón	1,021	58,150	Samaná	854	92,102
Duarte	1,605	274,858	San Cristóbal	1,265	499,998
Elías Piña	1,424	59,669	San José de Ocoa	650	59,335
El Seíbo (El Seybo)	1,786	81,326	San Juan	3,571	232,674
Espaillat	838	210,897	San Pedro de Macorís	1,255	284,997
Hato Mayor	1,329	81,074	Sánchez Ramírez	1,196	154,312
Independencia	2,008	46,870	Santiago	2,836	810,462
La Altagracia	3,010	179,041	Santiago Rodríguez	1,112	54,629
La Romana	654	202,320	Santo Domingo	1,296	1,822,028
La Vega	2,286	378,523	Valverde	823	144,297
María Trinidad Sánchez	1,271	126,848			
Monseñor Nouel	992	153,213	**National district**		
Monte Cristi	1,925	104,795	Santo Domingo (city)	104	916,398
Monte Plata	2,633	173,471	TOTAL	48,671[3, 4]	8,230,722
Pedernales	2,077	19,756			

Demography

Population (2003): 8,716,000.
Density (2003): persons per sq mi 463.8, persons per sq km 179.1.
Urban-rural (2000): urban 66.0%; rural 34.0%.
Sex distribution (2002): male 49.85%; female 50.15%.
Age breakdown (2000): under 15, 34.5%; 15–29, 27.3%; 30–44, 20.3%; 45–59, 10.8%; 60–74, 5.7%; 75 and over, 1.4%.
Population projection: (2010) 9,521,000; (2020) 10,625,000.
Doubling time: 40 years.
Ethnic composition (2000): mulatto 69.5%; white 17.0%; local black 9.4%; Haitian black 2.4%; other/unknown 1.7%.
Religious affiliation (1995): Roman Catholic 81.8%; Protestant 6.4%; other Christian 0.6%; other 11.2%.
Major urban centres (2000): Santo Domingo (urban agglomeration; 2001) 2,629,000; Santiago 580,745; San Cristóbal 199,693; San Francisco de Macorís 198,068; La Romana 189,900; San Pedro de Macorís 179,786.

Vital statistics

Birth rate per 1,000 population (2002): 24.3 (world avg. 21.3).
Death rate per 1,000 population (2002): 6.7 (world avg. 9.1).
Natural increase rate per 1,000 population (2002): 17.6 (world avg. 12.2).
Total fertility rate (avg. births per childbearing woman; 2002): 2.9.
Marriage rate per 1,000 population (1994): 2.0.
Life expectancy at birth (2002): male 66.8 years; female 69.8 years.
Major causes of death per 100,000 population (1994)[5]: diseases of the circulatory system 160; accidents and violence 60; malignant neoplasms (cancers) 56; infectious and parasitic diseases 54.

National economy

Budget (2002). Revenue: RD$67,009,000,000 (tax revenue 94.5%, of which taxes on goods and services 45.5%, income taxes 25.0%, import duties 21.2%; nontax revenue 5.5%). Expenditures: RD$75,789,000,000 (current expenditures 63.1%; development expenditures 36.9%).
Public debt (external, outstanding; 2001): U.S.$3,749,000,000.
Gross national product (2001): U.S.$19,000,000,000 (U.S.$2,230 per capita).

Structure of gross domestic product and labour force

	2002		1997	
	in value RD$'000,000	% of total value	labour force	% of labour force
Agriculture	46,931	11.8	529,000	16.7
Mining	5,719	1.4	8,400	0.3
Manufacturing	63,920	16.1	483,300	15.3
Construction	50,743	12.8	153,600	4.9
Public utilities	9,980	2.5	20,300	0.6
Transp. and commun.	55,061	13.9	202,700	6.4
Trade, restaurants	50,928	12.9	647,600	20.5
Finance, real estate	31,287	7.9	34,000	1.1
Pub. admin., defense	30,726	7.8	125,400	4.0
Services, other	50,822	12.9	447,500	14.2
Unemployed	—	—	503,700	16.0
TOTAL	396,117	100.0	3,155,500	100.0

Production (metric tons except as noted). Agriculture, forestry, fishing (2002): sugarcane 4,846,485, rice 730,705, bananas 502,877, plantains 192,000, cacao beans 49,670, coffee 49,022; livestock (number of live animals) 2,159,623 cattle, 577,000 pigs, 46,000,000 chickens; roundwood (2001) 562,300 cu m; fish catch (2000) 13,154. Mining (2000): nickel (metal content) 68,300; gold 40,700 troy oz[6]. Manufacturing (1998)[7]: cement 1,872,000; refined sugar 105,000; beer 2,990,000 hectolitres; rum 420,000 hectolitres. Energy production (consumption): electricity (kW-hr; 2002) 10,449,000,000 (6,808,000,000); coal (metric tons; 1999) none (78,000); crude petroleum (barrels; 2002) none (14,400,000); petroleum products (metric tons; 1999) 1,774,000 (6,667,000); natural gas, none (none).
Tourism (2001): receipts U.S.$2,689,000,000; expenditures U.S.$340,000,000.
Population economically active (1997): total 3,155,500; activity rate of total population 39.5% (participation rates: ages 15–64 [1993] 54.3%; female [1993] 24.9%; unemployed [2002] 16.1%).

Price and earnings indexes (1995 = 100)

	1996	1997	1998	1999	2000	2001	2002
Consumer price index	105.4	114.1	119.7	127.4	137.2	149.4	154.6[8]
Annual earnings index[9]	100.0	120.0	120.0	...	...	...	...

Household income and expenditure. Average household size (2002) 3.5.
Land use (1994): forested 12.4%; meadows and pastures 43.4%; agricultural and under permanent cultivation 30.6%; other 13.6%.

Foreign trade[10]

Balance of trade (current prices)

	1997	1998	1999	2000	2001	2002
U.S.$'000,000	–1,995	–2,616	–2,905	–3,741	–3,503	–3,699
% of total	17.8%	20.8%	22.0%	24.6%	24.9%	26.3%

Imports (2002): U.S.$8,882,000,000 (imports for free zones 29.8%, refined petroleum 14.6%, machinery and apparatus 11.4%, transport equipment 10.5%, food 5.4%). *Major import sources* (1998): U.S. *c.* 65%; Venezuela *c.* 6%; Mexico *c.* 4%; Japan *c.* 3%.
Exports (2002): U.S.$5,183,000,000 (reexports of free zones 83.6%, ferronickel 3.0%, ships' stores 2.2%, raw sugar 1.4%, cacao and cocoa 1.3%). *Major export destinations* (1998): U.S. *c.* 87%; Belgium-Luxembourg *c.* 2%; U.K. *c.* 2%.

Transport and communications

Transport. Railroads (1997)[11]: route length 1,083 mi, 1,743 km. Roads (1999): total length 7,829 mi, 12,600 km (paved 49%). Vehicles (1998): passenger cars 353,177; trucks and buses 200,347. Air transport (1997)[12]: passenger-mi 9,823,000, passenger-km, 15,808,000; short ton-mi cargo 7,962,000, metric ton-km cargo 11,624,000; airports (2002) 6.

Communications

Medium	date	unit	number	units per 1,000 persons
Daily newspapers	1996	circulation	416,000	53
Radio	2000	receivers	1,510,000	181
Television	2000	receivers	810,000	97
Telephones	2002	main lines	955,100	110
Cellular telephones	2002	subscribers	1,270,100	147
Internet	2001	users	186,000	21

Education and health

Educational attainment: n.a. *Literacy* (1995): total population age 15 and over literate, *c.* 4,164,000 (82.1%); males literate, *c.* 2,118,000 (82.0%); females literate, *c.* 2,046,000 (82.2%).

Education (1996–97)

	schools	teachers	students	student/ teacher ratio
Primary (age 6–13)	4,001[13]	39,860	1,360,044	34.1
Secondary (age 14–17)	...	11,033	329,944	29.9
Voc. teacher tr.	...	1,297	22,795	17.6
Higher	...	9,041	176,995	19.6

Health: physicians (1997) 17,460 (1 per 460 persons); hospital beds (1996) 11,921 (1 per 662 persons); infant mortality rate per 1,000 live births (2002) 35.1.
Food (2001): daily per capita caloric intake 2,333 (vegetable products 86%, animal products 14%); 96% of FAO recommended minimum.

Military

Total active duty personnel (2002): 24,500 (army 61.2%, navy 16.3%, air force 22.4%). *Military expenditure as percentage of GNP* (1999): 0.7% (world 2.4%); per capita expenditure U.S.$15.

[1]Roman Catholicism is the state religion per concordat with Vatican City. [2]Preliminary unadjusted results. [3]Detail does not add to total given because of rounding. [4]Mainland total is 48,512 sq km and offshore islands total 159 sq km. [5]Projected rates based on about 50% of total deaths. [6]The mining of gold was temporarily suspended from 1999 through late 2002. [7]Excludes free-zone sector for reexport (significantly ready-made garments but also services, cigars, and footwear) employing (2000) 195,000. [8]Second quarter. [9]Minimum wage for medium-sized businesses in private sector. [10]Includes free zones. [11]Most track is privately owned and serves the sugar industry only. [12]Aerochago and Dominair airlines. [13]1994–95.

Internet resources for further information:
- **Banco Central de la República Dominicana http://www.bancentral.gov.do**
- **Oficina Nacional de Estadística http://www.one.gov.do**

East Timor

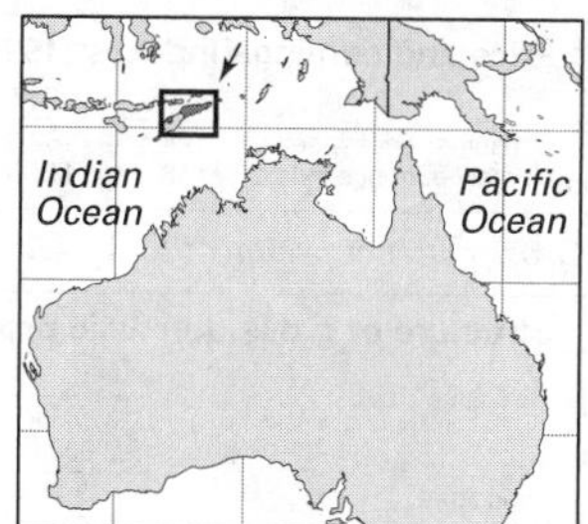

Official name: Repúblika Demokrátika Timor Lorosa'e (Tetum); República Democrática de Timor-Leste (Portuguese) (Democratic Republic of East Timor)[1].
Form of government: republic with one legislative body (National Parliament [88]).
Chief of state: President.
Head of government: Prime Minister.
Capital: Dili.
Official languages: Tetum; Portuguese[2].
Official religion: none.
Monetary unit: 1 United States dollar (U.S.$) = 100 cents; valuation (Sept. 8, 2003) 1 U.S.$ = £0.63.

Area and population

		area		population
Districts	Capitals	sq mi	sq km	1999 census[3]
Aileu	Aileu	281	729	32,500
Ainaro	Ainaro	308	797	44,100
Ambeno (Ocussi) exclave	Pante Macassar	315	815	54,500
Baucau (Baukau)	Baucau	577	1,494	97,600
Bobonaro	Maliana	528	1,368	90,700
Cova Lima	Suai	473	1,226	63,900
Dili	Dili	144	372	179,600
Ermera	Ermera	288	746	89,500
Lautem	Los Palos	657	1,702	52,100
Liquiça	Liquiça	210	543	54,800
Manatuto	Manatuto	659	1,706	34,900
Manufahi	Same	512	1,325	37,200
Viqueque	Viqueque	688	1,781	59,600
TOTAL		5,639[4]	14,604	891,000

Demography

Population (2003): 778,000.
Density (2003): persons per sq mi 138.0, persons per sq km 53.3.
Urban-rural (2001): urban 24.0%; rural 76.0%.
Sex distribution (2000): male 51.70%; female 48.30%.
Age breakdown (2000): under 15, 43.0%; 15–29, 23.9%; 30–44, 17.9%; 45–59, 10.5%; 60–74, 4.1%; 75 and over, 0.6%.
Population projection: (2010) 976,000; (2020) 1,138,000.
Doubling time: 70 years.
Ethnic composition (1999): East Timorese *c.* 80%; other (nearly all Indonesian, and particularly West Timorese) *c.* 20%.
Religious affiliation (2000): Roman Catholic *c.* 87%; Protestant *c.* 5%; Muslim *c.* 3%; traditional beliefs *c.* 3%; other *c.* 2%.
Major cities (2000): Dili 48,200; Dare 17,100; Baucau 14,200; Maliana 12,300; Ermera 12,000.

Vital statistics

Birth rate per 1,000 population (2003): 27.7 (world avg. 21.2).
Death rate per 1,000 population (2003): 6.4 (world avg. 8.9).
Natural increase rate per 1,000 population (2003): 21.3 (world avg. 13.2).
Total fertility rate (avg. births per childbearing woman; 2003): 3.8.
Marriage rate per 1,000 population (1997–98): 0.4.
Divorce rate per 1,000 population (1997–98): 0.1.
Life expectancy at birth (2001): male 56.0 years; female 59.0 years.
Major causes of death per 100,000 population (2002): n.a.[5]

National economy

Budget (2002). Revenue: U.S.$54,000,000 (tax revenue 45.6%; grants 42.0%; nontax revenue 12.4%). Expenditures: U.S.$53,100,000 (current expenditure 78.2%; development expenditure 21.8%).
Public debt (external, outstanding; 2001): n.a.
Production (metric tons except as noted). Agriculture, forestry, fishing (1998): corn (maize) (2001) 69,000, rice (2001) 58,000, cassava (2001) 55,000, sweet potatoes 12,000, coffee (2001) 6,000, mangoes 5,300, peanuts (groundnuts) 4,700, bananas 3,200, candlenut (1997) 1,055; livestock (number of live animals) 378,000 pigs (1996), 187,000 goats (1996), 137,000 cattle (1996), 541,000 chickens; roundwood, n.a.; sandalwood exports were formerly more significant; fish catch (1997) 2,804, of which marine 2,424. Mining and quarrying (2001): commercial quantities of marble are exported. Manufacturing (2001): principally the production of textiles, garments, handicrafts, bottled water, and processed coffee. Energy production (consumption): electricity (kW-hr; 1998) 40,000,000 (n.a.); coal, n.a. (n.a.); crude petroleum, n.a. (n.a.); petroleum products, n.a. (n.a.); natural gas, n.a. (n.a.).
Household income and expenditure. Average household size (1995) 4.9[6]; average annual income per household, n.a.[7]; sources of income, n.a.; expenditure, n.a.
Population economically active (2001): total 232,000[8]; activity rate of total population 28%[8] (participation rates: ages 15–64, 57%[8]; female, n.a.; unofficially unemployed [2000] 80%).

Price and earnings indexes (1995 = 100)

	1996	1997	1998	1999	2000	2001	2002
Consumer price index[8, 9]	105.0	115.5	207.9	499.0	598.8	598.8	623.7
Hourly earnings index	...	...	...	...	...	...	...

Gross national product (2002): U.S.$393,000,000 (U.S.$530 per capita).

Structure of gross domestic product and labour force

	2000		1998	
	in value U.S.$'000,000[10]	% of total value	labour force	% of labour force
Agriculture	83.2	26.0	...	75.0
Mining	11	11	...	...
Manufacturing	11	11	...	...
Public utilities	11	11	...	...
Construction	44.8	14.0	...	...
Transp. and commun.	22.4	7.0	...	...
Trade, hotels	25.6	8.0	...	...
Finance, insurance	11	11	...	...
Services	11	11	...	...
Pub. admin., defense	105.6	33.0	...	13.0
Other	38.4	12.0	...	12.0
TOTAL	320.0	100.0	...	100.0

Tourism: receipts, n.a.; expenditures, n.a.; available beds for tourists (1998) 580.
Land use (2000)[8]: forested 34%; agricultural and under permanent cultivation 15%; meadows and pastures 10%; other 41%.

Foreign trade

Balance of trade (current prices)

	1996	1997	1998	1999	2000	2001
U.S.$'000,000	−88	−90	−80	−36	−84	−229
% of total	50.0%	46.4%	42.1%	28.1%	...	93.5%

Imports (1998): U.S.$135,000,000 (foodstuffs 26%, of which rice 10%; construction materials 15%; petroleum products 10%; unspecified 49%). *Major import sources:* Indonesia nearly 100%.
Exports (1998): U.S.$55,000,000 (agricultural products 93%, of which nonfood crops [nearly all coffee] 51%, livestock 22%, food crops 15%; garments, bottled water, handicrafts, and other manufactured goods 5%). *Major export destinations:* Indonesia 96%.

Transport and communications

Transport. Railroads (2002): none. Roads (December 1999): total length 879 mi (1,414 km)[12]. Vehicles (1998): passenger cars 3,156; trucks and buses 7,140. Air transport: airports (2001) with scheduled flights 1.

Communications

Medium	date	unit	number	units per 1,000 persons
Daily newspaper	2002	circulation	1,500	2.0
Television[13]	2002	receivers	...	...
Telephones	1996	main lines	6,600	8.0

Education and health

Educational attainment: n.a. *Literacy* (2001): total population age 15 and over literate 203,000 (48%); males literate, n.a.; females literate, n.a.

Education (1998–99)[14]

	schools	teachers	students	student/ teacher ratio
Primary (age 7–12)	784	6,641	166,153	25.0
Secondary (age 13–18)	150	2,989	44,739	15.0
Voc., teacher tr.	17	492	4,699	9.6
Higher[15]	1	...	4,500	...

Health: physicians (1996–97) 122 (1 per 6,590 persons); hospital beds (1999) 560 (1 per 1,277 persons); infant mortality rate (2001) 70–90%.

Military

Total active duty personnel (2002): 636[16] (army 94.3%, naval element 5.7%)[17].
Military expenditure as percentage of GNP: n.a.

[1]Admitted to the UN in September 2002 with the official name of the Democratic Republic of Timor-Leste. [2]Indonesian and English are "working" languages. [3]Per Indonesian source. [4]Detail does not add to total given because of rounding. [5]The health sector faces immense difficulties; malaria is endemic and prevalence rates for tuberculosis and leprosy are 2.4% and 1.2%, respectively. [6]Pro-Indonesian militia destroyed about 30% of all housing in 1999. [7]Minimum annual wage (1999) U.S.$276; average public administration wage (1999) U.S.$1,020. [8]Estimated figures. [9]Dili only. [10]Breakdown by sector is estimated. [11]Included with Other. [12]57% of paved roads were in poor or damaged condition in late 1999; gravel roads were not usable for most vehicles. [13]Locally produced television service commenced in May 2002. [14]75–80% of all primary and secondary schools were either partially or completely destroyed in 1999. By mid-2001 373 schools were operational once again. [15]2001. [16]To be expanded to 1,500 troops by the end of 2003. [17]UN presence (August 2003): 3,400 military, 400 police.

Internet resources for further information:
- **Asia Observer**
  http://www.asiaobserver.com
- **Asian Development Bank: Key Indicators**
  http://www.adb.org/Documents/Books/Key_Indicators/2003/default.asp

Ecuador

Official name: República del Ecuador (Republic of Ecuador).
Form of government: unitary multiparty republic with one legislative house (National Congress [125]).
Head of state and government: President.
Capital: Quito.
Official language: Spanish[1].
Official religion: none.
Monetary unit[2]: 1 dollar (U.S.$); valuation (Sept. 8, 2003) 1 U.S.$ = £ 0.63.

Area and population		area		population
				2001
Regions		sq mi	sq km	census
Provinces	**Capitals**			
Amazonica				
Morona-Santiago	Macas	13,100	33,930	115,412
Napo	Tena	9,918	25,690	79,139
Orellana	Francisco de Orellana			86,493
Pastaza	Puyo	11,496	29,774	61,779
Sucumbíos	Nueva Loja	7,076	18,327	128,995
Zamora-Chinchipe	Zamora	8,923	23,111	76,601
Costa				
El Oro	Machala	2,259	5,850	525,763
Esmeraldas	Esmeraldas	5,884	15,239	385,223
Guayas	Guayaquil	7,916	20,503	3,309,034
Los Ríos	Babahoyo	2,770	7,175	650,178
Manabí	Portoviejo	7,289	18,879	1,186,025
Insular				
Galápagos	Puerto Baquerizo Moreno	3,093	8,010	18,640
Sierra				
Azuay	Cuenca	3,137	8,125	599,546
Bolívar	Guaranda	1,521	3,940	169,370
Cañar	Azogues	1,205	3,122	206,981
Carchi	Tulcán	1,392	3,605	152,939
Chimborazo	Riobamba	2,536	6,569	403,632
Cotopaxi	Latacunga	2,344	6,072	349,540
Imbabura	Ibarra	1,760	4,559	344,044
Loja	Loja	4,257	11,026	404,835
Pichincha	Quito	4,987	12,915	2,388,817
Tungurahua	Ambato	1,288	3,335	441,034
TOTAL		105,037[3, 4]	272,045[4]	12,156,608[5]

Demography

Population (2003): 13,003,000.
Density (2003): persons per sq mi 123.8, persons per sq km 47.8.
Urban-rural (2002): urban 63.4%; rural 36.6%.
Sex distribution (2001): male 49.51%; female 50.49%.
Age breakdown (2002): under 15, 35.3%; 15–29, 28.5%; 30–44, 19.2%; 45–59, 10.5%; 60–74, 4.8%; 75 and over, 1.7%.
Population projection: (2010) 14,274,000; (2020) 15,968,000.
Ethnic composition (2000): mestizo 42.0%; Amerindian 40.8%; white 10.6%; black 5.0%; other 1.6%.
Religious affiliation (2000): Roman Catholic 94.1%; Protestant 1.9%; other 4.0%.
Major cities (2001): Guayaquil 1,985,379; Quito 1,399,378; Cuenca 277,374; Machala 204,578; Santo Domingo de los Colorados 200,421; Manta 183,166.

Vital statistics

Birth rate per 1,000 population (2002): 24.9[6] (world avg. 21.3).
Death rate per 1,000 population (2002): 5.3[6] (world avg. 9.1).
Natural increase rate per 1,000 population (2002): 19.6[6] (world avg. 12.2).
Total fertility rate (avg. births per childbearing woman; 2000): 3.2.
Life expectancy at birth (2002): male 69.1 years; female 74.9 years.
Major causes of death per 100,000 population (1995): circulatory diseases 55.1; accidents and violence 29.2; pneumonia 27.2; diabetes mellitus 15.4.

National economy

Budget (2002). Revenue: U.S.$4,526,000,000 (nonpetroleum revenue 72.4%, of which value-added tax 33.8%, income tax 14.8%; petroleum revenue 27.6%). Expenditures: U.S.$4,694,000,000 (current expenditure 73.9%; capital expenditure 26.1%).
Public debt (external, outstanding; 2001): U.S.$11,149,000,000.
Production (metric tons except as noted). Agriculture, forestry, fishing (2002): bananas 6,500,000, sugarcane 5,669,900, rice 1,283,390, corn (maize) 386,320; livestock (live animals) 5,578,396 cattle, 2,805,597 sheep, 2,380,716 pigs; roundwood (2001) 10,919,709 cu m; fish catch (2000) 654,658. Mining and quarrying (2000): limestone 3,147,000; gold 2,823 kg. Manufacturing (value added in S/. '000,000; 1998): refined petroleum 14,320,504; food products 1,943,917; nonmetallic mineral products 785,400; chemical products 744,731; textiles 418,672. Energy production (consumption): electricity (kW-hr; 1999) 10,305,000,000 (10,305,000,000); crude petroleum (barrels; 2001) 146,200,000 ([1999] 52,691,000); petroleum products (metric tons; 1999) 6,611,000 (5,462,000); natural gas (cu m; 1999) 606,000,000 (606,000,000).
Household income and expenditure. Average household size (2001) 4.1; average annual income per household (1995) S/. 9,825,610 (U.S.$3,830); sources of income (1995): self-employment 70.9%, wages 16.0%, transfer payments 6.7%, other 6.4%; expenditure (1995): food and tobacco 37.9%, transportation and communications 15.0%, clothing 9.2%, household furnishings 6.5%.
Population economically active (2001): total 4,124,185; activity rate of total population 49.6% (participation rates: ages 15 and over, 72.8%; female 42.3%; unemployed 13.3%).

Price and earnings indexes (1995 = 100)							
	1996	1997	1998	1999	2000	2001	2002
Consumer price index	124.4	162.5	221.1	336.7	660.2	908.9	1,022.4
Monthly earnings index[7]	136.4	171.8	217.0	292.7	...	...	...

Gross national product (2001): U.S.$14,000,000,000 (U.S.$1,080 per capita).

Structure of gross domestic product and labour force	2000		2001	
	in value S/. '000,000	% of total value	labour force	% of labour force
Agriculture	33,928	10.0	391,300	9.5
Mining	66,767	19.6	18,300	0.4
Manufacturing	57,518	16.9	610,600	14.8
Construction	11,500	3.4	234,900	5.7
Public utilities	848	0.2	27,800	0.7
Transp. and commun.	31,144	9.2	244,600	5.9
Trade	58,046	17.1	1,184,900	28.7
Finance	30,386	8.9	191,700	4.6
Pub. admin., defense	19,746	5.8	159,900	3.9
Services	34,608	10.2	511,700	12.4
Other	–4,469[8]	–1.3[8]	548,300[9]	13.3[9]
TOTAL	340,022	100.0	4,124,200	100.0[3]

Tourism (2001): receipts U.S.$430,000,000; expenditures U.S.$340,000,000.

Foreign trade[10]

Balance of trade (current prices)						
	1997	1998	1999	2000	2001	2002
U.S.$'000,000	+744	–810	+1,714	+1,526	–258	–955
% of total	7.6%	8.8%	23.8%	18.3%	2.7%	8.7%

Imports (2000): U.S.$3,446,000,000 (chemicals and chemical products 23.5%; machinery and apparatus 21.1%; mineral fuels and lubricants 8.2%; food and live animals 7.6%). *Major import sources* (2001): U.S. 29.4%; Colombia 10.3%; Japan 8.2%; Venezuela 4.7%; Chile 4.5%.
Exports (2000): U.S.$4,822,000,000 (mineral fuels and lubricants 50.7%, of which crude petroleum 44.5%; food 35.7%, of which bananas 17.0%, fish and crustaceans 11.8%; cut flowers 3.2%). *Major export destinations* (2001): U.S. 36.2%; Colombia 5.0%; South Korea 4.6%; Germany 4.3%; Japan 4.0%.

Transport and communications

Transport. Railroads (2000): route length 956 km; passenger-km (1998) 44,000,000; metric ton-km cargo (1996) 1,000,000. Roads (1999): total length 43,197 km (paved 19%). Vehicles (1996): passenger cars 464,902; trucks and buses 52,630. Air transport (2001)[11]: passenger-km 901,000,000; metric ton-km cargo 14,344,000.

Communications				units
Medium	date	unit	number	per 1,000 persons
Daily newspapers	1996	circulation	820,000	70
Radio	2000	receivers	5,190,000	418
Television	2000	receivers	2,710,000	213
Telephones	2002	main lines	1,426,200	110
Cellular telephones	2002	subscribers	1,560,900	121
Personal computers	2002	units	403,000	31
Internet	2002	users	503,300	39

Education and health

Educational attainment (1990). Percentage of population age 25 and over having: no formal schooling 2.2%; incomplete primary 54.3%; primary 28.0%; postsecondary 15.5%. *Literacy* (1995): total population age 15 and over literate 90.1%; males 92.0%; females 88.2%.

Education (1996–97)	schools	teachers	students[12]	student/ teacher ratio
Primary (age 4–12)	17,367	74,601	2,147,446	...
Secondary (age 12–18) Vocational	...	62,630[13]	950,834	...
Higher	...	12,856[14]	115,554	...

Health (2000): physicians 18,335 (1 per 456 persons); hospital beds 19,564 (1 per 427 persons); infant mortality rate (2002) 33.0.
Food (2001): daily per capita caloric intake 2,333 (vegetable products 86%, animal products 14%); 103% of FAO recommended minimum requirement.

Military

Total active duty personnel (2002): 59,500 (army 84.0%, navy 9.3%, air force 6.7%). *Military expenditure as percentage of GNP* (1999): 3.7% (world 2.4%); per capita expenditure U.S.$38.

[1]Quechua and Shuar are also official languages for the indigenous peoples. [2]The United States dollar was formally adopted as the national currency on Sept. 9, 2000; the pegged value of the Sucre (S/.), the former national currency, to the U.S. dollar was S/. 25,000 = 1 U.S.$. [3]Detail does not add to total given because of rounding. [4]Includes 884 sq mi (2,289 sq km) in nondelimited areas. [5]Total includes 72,588 persons in nondelimited areas. [6]Excluding nomadic Indian tribes. [7]General minimum wage. [8]Minus imputed bank service charges plus gross import duties. [9]Unemployed. [10]Import figures are f.o.b. in balance of trade and c.i.f. for commodities and trading partners. [11]Ecuatoviana and TAME airlines. [12]2000. [13]1992–93. [14]1990–91.

Internet resources for further information:
- **Instituto Nacional de Estadística y Censos http://www.inec.gov.ec**
- **Banco Central del Ecuador http://www.bce.fin.ec**

Egypt

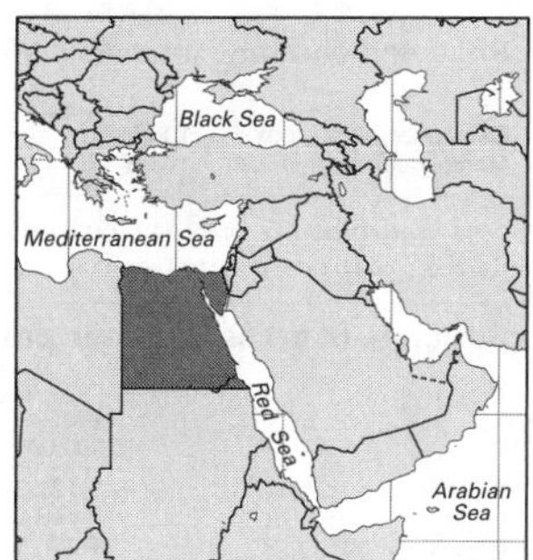

Official name: Jumhūrīah Miṣr al-ʿArabīyah (Arab Republic of Egypt).
Form of government: republic with one legislative house (People's Assembly [454[1]]).
Chief of state: President.
Head of government: Prime Minister.
Capital: Cairo.
Official language: Arabic.
Official religion: Islam.
Monetary unit: 1 Egyptian pound (£E) = 100 piastres; valuation (Sept. 8, 2003) 1 U.S.$ = £E 6.14; 1 £ = £E 9.73.

Area and population

Regions / Governorates	Capitals	area sq mi	area sq km	population 2001 estimate
Frontier				
Al-Baḥr al-Aḥmar	Al-Ghurdaqah	78,643	203,685	172,000
Janūb Sīnāʾ	Aṭ-Ṭūr	12,796	33,140	60,000
Maṭrūḥ	Marsā Maṭrūḥ	81,897	212,112	240,000
Shamāl Sīnāʾ	Al-ʿArish	10,646	27,574	280,000
Al-Wādī al-Jadīd	Al-Kharijah	145,369	376,505	156,000
Lower Egypt				
Al-Buḥayrah	Damanhūr	3,911	10,129	4,339,000
Ad-Daqahlīyah	Al-Manṣūrah	1,340	3,471	4,570,000
Dumyāṭ	Dumyāṭ	227	589	995,000
Al-Gharbīyah	Ṭanṭā	750	1,942	3,661,000
Al-Ismāʿīlīyah (Ismailia)	—	557	1,442	789,000
Kafr ash-Shaykh	Kafr ash-Shaykh	1,327	3,437	2,403,000
Al-Minūfīyah	Shibīn al-Kawm	592	1,532	2,994,000
Al-Qalyūbīyah	Banhā	387	1,001	3,584,000
Ash-Sharqīyah	Az-Zaqāzīq	1,614	4,180	4,691,000
Upper Egypt				
Aswān	Aswān	262	679	1,043,000
Asyūṭ	Asyūṭ	600	1,553	3,122,000
Banī Suwayf	Banī Suwayf	510	1,322	2,062,000
Al-Fayyūm	Al-Fayyūm	705	1,827	2,208,000
Al-Jīzah	Al-Jīzah	32,859	85,105	5,208,000
Al-Minyā	Al-Minyā	873	2,262	3,687,000
Qinā	Qinā	693	1,796	2,697,000
Sawhāj	Sawhāj	597	1,547	3,481,000
Urban				
Būr Saʿīd (Port Said)	—	28	72	506,000
Al-Iskandarīyah (Alexandria)	—	1,034	2,679	3,577,000
Al-Qāhirah (Cairo)	—	83	214	7,283,000
Al-Uqṣur (Luxor)	—	21	55	392,000
As-Suways (Suez)	—	6,888	17,840	452,000
TOTAL		385,210[2]	997,690	64,652,000[3]

Demography

Population (2003): 68,185,000.
Density (2003): persons per sq mi 177.0, persons per sq km 68.3.
Urban-rural (2002): urban 42.7%; rural 57.3%.
Sex distribution (2002): male 50.45%; female 49.55%.
Age breakdown (2002): under 15, 33.9%; 15–29, 28.1%; 30–44, 19.4%; 45–59, 12.0%; 60–74, 5.5%; 75 and over, 1.1%.
Population projection: (2010) 77,085,000; (2020) 88,917,000.
Doubling time: 36 years.
Ethnic composition (2000): Egyptian Arab 84.1%; Sudanese Arab 5.5%; Arabized Berber 2.0%; Bedouin 2.0%; Rom (Gypsy) 1.6%; other 4.8%.
Religious affiliation (1997): Sunnī Muslim 89%; Christian 11%[4].
Major cities ('000; 1996): Cairo 6,789 (10,345[5]); Alexandria 3,328; Al-Jīzah 2,222; Shubrā al-Khaymah 871; Port Said 470; Suez 418.

Vital statistics

Birth rate per 1,000 population (2002): 24.9 (world avg. 21.3).
Death rate per 1,000 population (2002): 5.4 (world avg. 9.1).
Natural increase rate per 1,000 population (2002): 19.5 (world avg. 12.2).
Total fertility rate (avg. births per childbearing woman; 2002): 3.1.
Life expectancy at birth (2002): male 67.6 years; female 72.7 years.

National economy

Budget (2000–01). Revenue: £E 97,938,000,000 (income and profits taxes 28.4%, sales taxes 18.4%, customs duties 13.3%, oil revenue 4.7%, Suez Canal fees 3.6%). Expenditures: £E 111,669,000,000 (current expenditure 76.7%, of which wages and pensions 25.7%, public debt interest 18.3%, defense 3.3%; capital expenditure 23.3%).
Public debt (external, outstanding; 2001): U.S.$25,243,000,000.
Population economically active (1999–2000): total 18,818,000; activity rate 29.7% (participation rates [1998] ages 15–64, 45.9%; female 21.4%; unemployed 8.1%).

Price and earnings indexes (1995 = 100)

	1996	1997	1998	1999	2000	2001	2002
Consumer price index	108.3	112.8	114.4	120.4	123.7	126.5	129.9
Annual earnings index	...	...	...	...	...	...	...

Production ('000; metric tons except as noted). Agriculture, forestry, fishing (2002): sugarcane 15,706, corn (maize) 6,800, tomatoes 6,329, wheat 6,183, rice 5,600, potatoes 1,903, oranges 1,725, dates 1,113; livestock ('000; number of live animals) 4,672 sheep, 3,810 cattle, 3,550 buffalo, 92,000 chickens; roundwood (2001) 16,600,028 cu m; fish catch (2000) 724. Mining and quarrying (1999–2000): gypsum 3,027; iron ore 2,932; salt 1,990; phosphate rock 1,177; kaolin 205. Manufacturing (1999–2000): cement 26,000; nitrate fertilizers 1,550; sugar 1,285; cotton yarn 280; refrigerators 585,000 units; automobiles 48,167 units. Energy production (consumption): electricity ('000,000 kW-hr; 1999) 69,045 (69,045); coal ('000 metric tons; 1999) none (1,310); crude petroleum ('000 barrels; 1999) 278,500 (225,900); petroleum products ('000 metric tons; 1999) 29,503 (21,749); natural gas ('000,000 cu m; 2000) 21,000 ([1999] 16,728).
Gross national product (2001): U.S.$99,600,000,000 (U.S.$1,530 per capita).

Structure of gross domestic product and labour force

	2000–01[6]		1998	
	in value £E '000,000	% of total value	labour force	% of labour force
Agriculture	49,110	16.1	4,807,000	26.4
Mining (petroleum) }	78,871	25.8	47,400	0.3
Manufacturing }			2,207,600	12.1
Construction	18,261	6.0	1,320,100	7.2
Public utilities	5,634	1.8	207,000	1.1
Transp. and commun.	27,616[7]	9.0[7]	1,060,200	5.8
Trade, hotels	72,719[8]	23.8[8]	2,319,800	12.7
Finance	[8]	[8]	458,400	2.5
Pub. admin., defense	23,252	7.6	1,631,700	9.0
Services	30,308	9.9	2,691,500	14.8
Other	—	—	1,480,000[9]	8.1[9]
TOTAL	305,771	100.0	18,230,700	100.0

Household income and expenditure. Average household size (2000) 4.7; household income: n.a.; expenditure: n.a.
Tourism (2001): receipts U.S.$3,800,000,000; expenditures U.S.$1,132,000,000.

Foreign trade[10]

Balance of trade (current prices)

	1999–2000	2000–01	2001–02
U.S.$'000,000	−11,472	−9,363	−8,001
% of total	47.3%	39.8%	37.6%

Imports (1999): U.S.$15,962,000,000 (machinery and apparatus 22.6%; food 18.3%, of which cereals 8.1%; chemicals and chemical products 11.5%; iron and steel 5.6%). *Major import sources* (2001): U.S. 18.6%; Italy 6.6%; Germany 6.5%; France 4.9%; China 4.4%.
Exports (1999): U.S.$3,501,000,000 (crude petroleum 27.4%; refined petroleum 8.4%; food 7.9%; wearing apparel 7.9%; raw cotton 6.8%). *Major export destinations* (2001): Italy 15.0%; U.S. 14.4%; U.K. 9.3%; France 4.7%; Germany 4.1%.

Transport and communications

Transport. Railroads (1999): length 4,810 km; passenger-km (1998) 56,667,000,000; metric ton-km cargo (1996) 4,117,000,000. Roads (1999): length 64,000 km (paved 78%). Vehicles (1998): passenger cars 1,154,753; trucks and buses 510,766. Inland water (2000): Suez Canal, number of transits 14,141; metric ton cargo 438,962,000. Air transport (2001): passenger-km 8,892,000,000; metric ton-km cargo 239,040,000; airports (1998) 11.

Communications

Medium	date	unit	number	units per 1,000 persons
Daily newspapers	2000	circulation	2,780,000	43
Radio	2000	receivers	21,900,000	418
Television	2000	receivers	12,200,000	189
Telephones	2002	main lines	6,688,400	104
Cellular telephones	2002	subscribers	4,412,000	67
Personal computers	2001	units	1,000,000	16
Internet	2001	users	600,000	9.3

Education and health

Literacy (2000): total population age 15 and over literate 55.3%; males 66.6%; females 43.8%.

Education (1999–2000)

	schools	teachers	students	student/ teacher ratio
Primary (age 6–11)[11, 12]	15,533	314,528	7,224,989	23.0
Secondary (age 12–17)[11, 12]	9,149	272,687	5,385,314	19.7
Vocational	1,826	140,050	1,913,022	13.7
Higher	356[13]	...	1,316,491[14]	...

Health: physicians (1996) 129,000 (1 per 472 persons); hospital beds (1994) 113,020 (1 per 515 persons); infant mortality rate (2000) 62.3.
Food (2001): daily per capita caloric intake 3,385 (vegetable products 92%, animal products 8%); 133% of FAO recommended minimum requirement.

Military

Total active duty personnel (2002): 443,000 (army 72.2%, navy 4.3%, air force [including air defense] 23.5%). *Military expenditure as percentage of GNP* (1999): 2.7% (world 2.4%); per capita expenditure U.S.$36.

[1]Includes 10 nonelective seats. [2]Detail does not add to total given because of rounding. [3]January 1. [4]According to the 1986 census, the Christian population of Egypt was 5.9% of the total; this figure is considered by some external authorities to understate significantly the Christian population. [5]1999 urban agglomeration. [6]At 1996–97 factor cost. [7]Transportation includes earnings from traffic on the Suez Canal. [8]Trade, hotels includes Finance. [9]Unemployed. [10]Imports c.i.f.; exports f.o.b. [11]Data exclude 2,631 primary and 1,081 secondary schools, and 707,633 primary and 269,469 secondary students in the Al-Azhar education system. [12]Includes preparatory. [13]1998–99. [14]1996–97.

Internet resources for further information:

- **Egypt State Information Service http://www.sis.gov.eg**
- **Ministry of Economy http://www.economy.gov.eg**

El Salvador

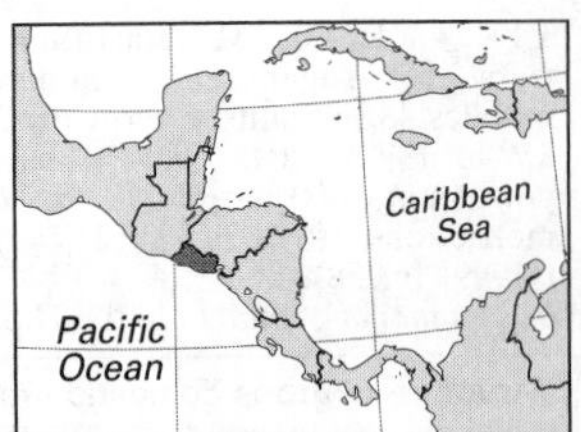

Official name: República de El Salvador (Republic of El Salvador).
Form of government: republic with one legislative house (Legislative Assembly [84]).
Chief of state and government: President.
Capital: San Salvador.
Official language: Spanish.
Official religion: none[1].
Monetary unit[2]: 1 colón (₡) = 100 centavos; valuation (Sept. 8, 2003) 1 U.S.$ = ₡8.75; 1 £ = ₡13.88.

Area and population

		area		population
Departments	Capitals	sq mi	sq km	2000 estimate
Ahuachapán	Ahuachapán	479	1,240	319,781
Cabañas	Sensuntepeque	426	1,104	152,842
Chalatenango	Chalatenango	779	2,017	196,587
Cuscatlán	Cojutepeque	292	756	202,951
La Libertad	Nueva San Salvador	638	1,653	682,093
La Paz	Zacatecoluca	473	1,224	292,887
La Unión	La Unión	801	2,074	289,022
Morazán	San Francisco	559	1,447	173,501
San Miguel	San Miguel	802	2,077	480,276
San Salvador	San Salvador	342	886	1,985,294
San Vicente	San Vicente	457	1,184	161,104
Santa Ana	Santa Ana	781	2,023	550,209
Sonsonate	Sonsonate	473	1,225	450,118
Usulután	Usulután	822	2,130	338,334
TOTAL		8,124	21,041[3]	6,274,999

Demography

Population (2003): 6,515,000.
Density (2003): persons per sq mi 801.9, persons per sq km 309.6.
Urban-rural (2002): urban 61.5%; rural 38.5%.
Sex distribution (2002): male 48.67%; female 51.33%.
Age breakdown (2002): under 15, 37.1%; 15–29, 28.7%; 30–44, 17.2%; 45–59, 9.8%; 60–74, 5.0%; 75 and over 2.2%.
Population projection: (2010) 7,154,000; (2020) 8,005,000.
Doubling time: 32 years.
Ethnic composition (2000): mestizo 88.3%; Amerindian 9.1%, of which Pipil 4.0%; white 1.6%; other/unknown 1.0%.
Religious affiliation (1995): Roman Catholic 78.2%; Protestant 17.1%, of which Pentecostal 13.3%; other Christian 1.9%; other 2.8%.
Major cities[4] (1998): San Salvador 467,004 (urban agglomeration 1,856,788); Soyapango 282,066[5]; Santa Ana 241,266; San Miguel 227,414.

Vital statistics

Birth rate per 1,000 population (2002): 27.9 (world avg. 21.3); (1998) legitimate 27.2%; illegitimate 72.8%.
Death rate per 1,000 population (2002): 6.0 (world avg. 9.1).
Natural increase rate per 1,000 population (2002): 21.9 (world avg. 12.2).
Total fertility rate (avg. births per childbearing woman; 2002): 3.2.
Marriage rate per 1,000 population (1998): 4.4.
Life expectancy at birth (2002): male 67.0 years; female 74.4 years.
Major causes of death per 100,000 population (1998)[6]: accidents and violence 118; diseases of the circulatory system 89; diseases of the respiratory system 60; malignant neoplasms (cancers) 58; ill-defined conditions 116.

National economy

Budget. Revenue (2001): U.S.$1,499,400,000 (sales taxes 57.2%, corporate taxes 13.1%, individual income taxes 11.4%, import duties 9.7%). Expenditures: U.S.$1,968,600,000 (education 23.3%, police 15.7%, economic services 14.7%, social services 12.7%, health 11.1%, defense 6.6%).
Public debt (external, outstanding; 2001): U.S.$3,257,000,000.
Production (metric tons except as noted). Agriculture, forestry, fishing (2002): sugarcane 4,932,516, corn (maize) 637,040, sorghum 139,163, coffee 91,513, dry beans 81,709, bananas 65,000, yautia 52,000, avocados 40,000, tobacco 1,100; livestock (number of live animals) 1,392,114 cattle, 153,463 pigs; roundwood (2001) 5,200,129 cu m; fish catch (2000) 9,851, of which crustaceans 3,730. Mining and quarrying (1997): limestone 3,000,000 metric tons. Manufacturing (value added in U.S.$'000,000; 1998): food products 306; wearing apparel 249; drugs and medicines 128; textiles 120; beverages 112; soaps, cleansers, and cosmetics 92; nonmetallic mineral products 76. Energy production (consumption): electricity (kW-hr; 1999) 3,769,000,000 (4,019,000,000); coal, none (none); crude petroleum (barrels; 1999) none (7,132,000); petroleum products (metric tons; 1999) 932,000 (1,704,000); natural gas, none (none).
Household income and expenditure. Average household size (2000) 4.5; average income per household (1992–93) ₡22,930 (U.S.$2,562); expenditure (1990–91)[7]: food and beverages 37.0%, housing 12.1%, transportation and communications 10.2%, clothing and footwear 6.7%.
Land use (1994): forested 5.0%; meadows and pastures 29.5%; agricultural and under permanent cultivation 35.2%; other 30.3%.
Population economically active (1999): total 2,444,900; activity rate of total population 40.1% (participation rates: ages 15–64 (1995) 62.9%; female 40.7%; unemployed 7.0%).

Price and earnings indexes (1995 = 100)

	1996	1997	1998	1999	2000	2001	2002
Consumer price index	109.8	114.7	117.6	118.2	120.9	125.5	127.8
Monthly earnings index	108.5	116.7	121.9	...	...	...	...

Gross national product (at current market prices; 2001): U.S.$13,000,000,000 (U.S.$2,040 per capita).

Structure of gross domestic product and labour force

	2000		1999	
	in value ₡'000,000	% of total value	labour force	% of labour force
Agriculture	11,121.0	9.6	503,300	20.6
Mining	496.0	0.4	1,800	0.1
Manufacturing	27,234.6	23.6	426,600	17.4
Construction	5,107.7	4.4	130,900	5.4
Public utilities	2,520.1	2.2	8,500	0.3
Transp. and commun.	9,736.9	8.4	100,300	4.1
Trade	21,692.0	18.8	578,500	23.7
Finance, real estate	18,580.4	16.1	84,500	3.5
Public admin., defense	8,710.0	7.5	113,100	4.6
Services	7,642.2	6.6	327,200	13.4
Other	2,769.2[8]	2.4[8]	170,200[9]	7.0[9]
TOTAL	115,610.1	100.0	2,444,900	100.0[3]

Tourism (2001): receipts U.S.$235,000,000; expenditures U.S.$195,000,000.

Foreign trade[10]

Balance of trade (current prices)

	1997	1998	1999	2000	2001	2002
U.S.$'000,000	–1,318	–1,527	–1,585	–2,006	–2,163	–2,198
% of total	21.4%	23.8%	24.0%	25.4%	27.4%	26.9%

Imports (2000): U.S.$4,947,000,000 (imports for reexport 23.3%; machinery and apparatus 15.5%; chemicals and chemical products 11.2%; food 10.4%; petroleum [all forms] 10.3%). *Major import sources* (2002): U.S. 49.6%; Guatemala 8.1%; Honduras 3.0%; Costa Rica 2.9%; unspecified 30.4%.
Exports (2000): U.S.$2,941,000,000 (reexports [mostly clothing] 54.4%; coffee 10.1%; paper and paper products 2.8%; yarn, fabrics, made-up articles 2.7%). *Major export destinations:* U.S. 67.0%; Guatemala 11.5%; Honduras 5.9%; Nicaragua 3.8%; unspecified 6.9%.

Transport and communications

Transport. Railroads (2001): operational route length 283 km; (1997) passenger-km 7,100,000; (1996) metric ton-km cargo 17,300,000. Roads (1999): total length 10,029 km (paved 20%). Vehicles (1997): passenger cars 177,488; trucks and buses 184,859. Air transport (2001)[11]: passenger-km 6,150,000,000; metric ton-km cargo 379,000; airports (2001) with scheduled flights 1.

Communications

Medium	date	unit	number	units per 1,000 persons
Daily newspapers	2000	circulation	217,000	35
Radio	2000	receivers	2,970,000	478
Television	2000	receivers	1,250,000	201
Telephones	2002	main lines	667,700	103
Cellular telephones	2002	subscribers	888,800	138
Personal computers	2001	units	140,000	22
Internet	2002	users	300,000	46

Education and health

Educational attainment (1992). Percentage of population over age 25 having: no formal schooling 34.7%; incomplete primary education 37.6%; complete primary[12] 10.8%; secondary 9.4%; higher technical 2.4%; incomplete undergraduate 1.1%; complete undergraduate 2.9%; other/unknown 1.1%.
Literacy (1999): total population age 15 and over literate 78.3%; males literate 81.3%; females literate 75.6%.

Education (2000)

	schools	teachers	students	student/ teacher ratio
Primary (age 7–15)	5,090	26,209	1,212,622	46.3
Secondary (age 16–18)	...	9,255[13]	147,867	15.5[13]
Higher	...	7,501	114,675	15.3

Health: physicians (1997) 6,177 (1 per 936 persons); hospital beds (1996) 9,571 (1 per 593 persons); infant mortality rate per 1,000 live births (2002) 26.7.
Food (2001): daily per capita caloric intake 2,512 (vegetable products 89%, animal products 11%); 110% of FAO recommended minimum requirement.

Military

Total active duty personnel (2002): 15,000 (army 89.3%, navy 4.2%, air force 6.5%). *Military expenditure as percentage of GNP* (1999): 0.9% (world 2.4%); per capita expenditure U.S.$18.

[1]Roman Catholicism, although not official, enjoys special recognition in the constitution. [2]The U.S. dollar was legal tender in El Salvador from Jan. 1, 2001 (along with the colón) at a pegged rate of 1 U.S.$ = ₡8.75. [3]Detail does not add to total given because of rounding. [4]Populations are for *municipios* (urban centres that may include adjacent rural areas). [5]Within San Salvador urban agglomeration. [6]Projected rates based on about 78% of total deaths. [7]536,628 urban households only. [8]Import duties. [9]Unemployed. [10]Imports c.i.f., exports f.o.b. (including assembled components for reexport). [11]TACA International Airlines only. [12]Education completed through ninth grade. [13]1996.

Internet resources for further information:
- **Banco Central de Reserva de El Salvador http://www.bcr.gob.sv**

Equatorial Guinea

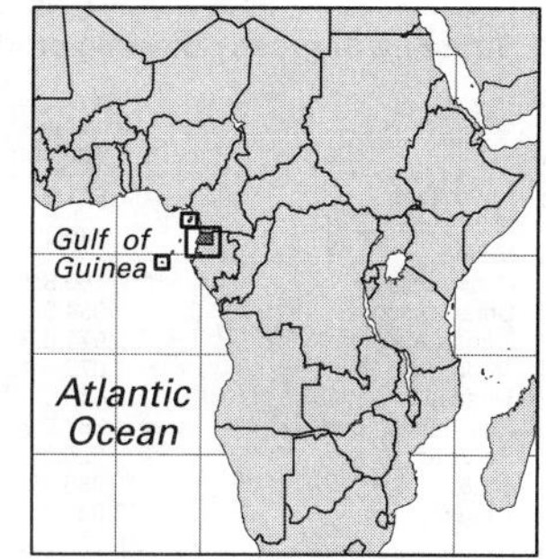

Official name: República de Guinea Ecuatorial (Spanish); République du Guinée Équatoriale (French) (Republic of Equatorial Guinea).
Form of government: republic with one legislative house (House of Representatives of the People [80]).
Chief of state: President.
Head of government: Prime Minister.
Capital: Malabo[1].
Official languages: Spanish; French.
Official religion: none.
Monetary unit: 1 CFA franc (CFAF) = 100 centimes; valuation (Sept. 8, 2003) 1 U.S.$ = CFAF 594.70; 1 £ = CFAF 942.93[2].

Area and population

Regions		area		population
Provinces	Capitals	sq mi	sq km	1994 census
Insular		785[3]	2,034	90,500
Annobón	Palé	7	17	2,800
Bioko Norte	Malabo	300	776	75,100
Bioko Sur	Luba	479	1,241	12,600
Continental		10,045[3]	26,017	315,600
Centro-Sur	Evinayong	3,834	9,931	60,300
Kie-Ntem	Ebebiyin	1,522	3,943	92,800
Litoral[4]	Bata	2,573	6,665	100,000
Wele-Nzas	Mongomo	2,115	5,478	62,500
TOTAL		10,831[3]	28,051	406,200[3]

Demography

Population (2003): 494,000.
Density (2003): persons per sq mi 45.6, persons per sq km 17.6.
Urban-rural (2002): urban 49.3%; rural 50.7%.
Sex distribution (2002): male 48.77%; female 51.23%.
Age breakdown (2002): under 15, 42.4%; 15–29, 27.0%; 30–44, 16.2%; 45–59, 8.3%; 60–74, 4.8%; 75 and over, 1.3%.
Population projection: (2010) 590,000; (2020) 736,000.
Doubling time: 28 years.
Ethnic composition (1995): Fang 82.9%; Bubi 9.6%; other 7.5%.
Religious affiliation (2000): Roman Catholic 80.1%; Muslim 4.0%; African Christian 3.7%; Protestant 3.1%; other 9.1%.
Major cities (2003): Malabo 92,900; Bata 66,800; Mbini 11,600; Ebebiyin 9,100; Luba 6,800.

Vital statistics

Birth rate per 1,000 population (2002): 37.3 (world avg. 21.3); legitimate, n.a.; illegitimate, n.a.
Death rate per 1,000 population (2002): 12.8 (world avg. 9.1).
Natural increase rate per 1,000 population (2002): 24.5 (world avg. 12.2).
Total fertility rate (avg. births per childbearing woman; 2002): 4.8.
Marriage rate per 1,000 population: n.a.
Divorce rate per 1,000 population: n.a.
Life expectancy at birth (2002): male 52.3 years; female 56.5 years.
Major causes of death per 100,000 population: n.a.; however, major diseases include malaria (about 24% of total mortality), respiratory infections (12% of mortality), cholera, leprosy, trypanosomiasis (sleeping sickness), and waterborne (especially gastrointestinal) diseases.

National economy

Budget (1998). Revenue: CFAF 76,974,000,000 (domestic revenue 97.7%, of which oil revenue 69.5%, tax revenue 19.0%, nontax revenue 9.2%; foreign grants 2.3%). Expenditures: CFAF 80,728,000,000 (current expenditure 63.6%, of which goods and services 16.0%, salaries 11.3%, transfers 9.0%, interest on debt 5.5%; capital expenditure 36.4%).
Public debt (external, outstanding; 2001): U.S.$192,100,000.
Gross national product (at current market prices; 2003): U.S.$2,200,000,000[5] (U.S.$4,400[5] per capita).

Structure of gross domestic product and labour force

	1998		1997	
	in value CFAF '000,000	% of total value	labour force	% of labour force
Agriculture, fishing	40,480	15.0	...	...
Forestry	17,719	6.6	...	...
Crude petroleum	164,969	61.3	...	...
Manufacturing	1,007	0.4	...	...
Construction	7,752	2.9	...	...
Public utilities	3,368	1.3	...	...
Transportation and communications	2,100	0.8	...	...
Trade	9,625	3.6	...	...
Finance, real estate	2,135	0.8	...	...
Pub. admin., defense	12,723	4.7	...	...
Services	4,959	1.8	...	...
Other	2,427[6]	0.9[6]	...	...
TOTAL	269,266[3]	100.0[3]	177,000	100.0

Production (metric tons except as noted). Agriculture, forestry, fishing (2002): roots and tubers 105,000 (of which cassava 45,000, sweet potatoes 36,000), palm oil 35,000, bananas 20,000, coconuts 6,000, cacao beans 4,000, coffee 3,500; livestock (number of live animals) 37,600 sheep, 9,000 goats, 6,100 pigs, 5,000 cattle; roundwood (2001) 811,000 cu m; fish catch (2000) 3,634. Mining and quarrying: gold (2002) 500 kg. Manufacturing: methanol (2002) 719,000; sawn timber (1998) 21,500 cu m; processed timber (1998) 3,900 cu m. Energy production (consumption): electricity (kW-hr; 1999) 21,000,000 (21,000,000); coal, none (none); crude petroleum (barrels; 2002) 69,000,000 ([1999] 1,200,000); petroleum products (metric tons; 1999) none (52,000); natural gas (2002) 1,050,000,000 (n.a.).
Population economically active (1997): total 177,000; activity rate of total population 40.0% (participation rates: ages 15–64, 74.7%; female 35.4%; unemployed [1983] 24.2%).

Price and earnings indexes (1995 = 100)

	1992	1993	1994	1995	1996	1997	1998
Consumer price index	61.3	64.1	89.7	100.0	104.5	107.7	116.2
Earnings index	...	...	...	...	...	...	...

Household income and expenditure. Average household size (1980) 4.5; income per household: n.a.; sources of income (1988): wages and salaries 57.0%, business income 42.0%, other 1.0%; expenditure (1988): food and beverages 62.0%, clothing and footwear 10.0%; medical care 6.0%.
Tourism: tourism is a government priority but remains undeveloped.
Land use (1994): forested 65.2%; meadows and pastures 3.7%; agricultural and under permanent cultivation 8.2%; built-on, wasteland, and other 22.9%.

Foreign trade[7]

Balance of trade (current prices)

	1996	1997	1998	1999	2000	2001
CFAF '000,000,000	–16.3	+76.1	–5.5	+167.5	+532.3	+753.3
% of total	6.9%	15.3%	1.1%	23.7%	42.2%	38.8%

Imports (2001): CFAF 593,400,000,000 (for petroleum sector 80.8%; other machinery and apparatus 11.6%; petroleum products 4.8%). *Major import sources* (1999): United States *c.* 60%; France *c.* 12%; Spain *c.* 8%; Italy *c.* 6%; Cameroon *c.* 3%.
Exports (2001): CFAF 1,346,700,000,000 (crude petroleum 91.6%; methanol 4.5%; wood 2.9%; cocoa beans 0.1%). *Major export destinations* (1999): Spain *c.* 46%; China *c.* 24%; Japan *c.* 7%; United States *c.* 7%; Chile *c.* 5%.

Transport and communications

Transport. Railroads: none. Roads (1999): total length 1,790 mi, 2,880 km (paved 13%). Vehicles (1994): passenger cars 6,500; trucks and buses 4,000. Air transport (1998): passenger-mi 2,500,000, passenger-km 4,000,000; (1996) short ton-mi cargo 700,000, metric ton-km cargo 1,000,000; airports (1998) with scheduled flights 1.

Communications

Medium	date	unit	number	units per 1,000 persons
Daily newspapers	1996	circulation	2,000	4.9
Radio	1997	receivers	180,000	428
Television	1997	receivers	4,000	9.8
Telephones	2002	main lines	8,800	18
Cellular telephones	2002	units	27,000	55
Personal computers	2002	units	4,000	7.2
Internet	2002	users	1,700	3.5

Education and health

Educational attainment (1983). Percentage of population age 15 and over having: no schooling 35.4%; some primary education 46.6%; primary 13.0%; secondary 2.3%; postsecondary 1.1%; not specified 1.6%. *Literacy* (2000): percentage of total population age 15 and over literate 83.2%; males literate 92.5%; females literate 74.4%.

Education (1998)

	schools	teachers	students	student/ teacher ratio
Primary (age 6–11)	483	1,322	74,940	56.7
Secondary (age 12–17)	...	763	18,802	24.6
Voc., teacher tr.[8]	...	122	2,105	17.3
Higher[8]	...	58	578	10.0

Health: physicians (1996) 106 (1 per 4,065 persons); hospital beds (1990) 992 (1 per 350 persons); infant mortality rate per 1,000 live births (2002) 90.7.
Food: daily per capita caloric intake, n.a.

Military

Total active duty personnel (2002): 1,320 (army 83.3%, navy 9.1%, air force 7.6%). *Military expenditure as percentage of GNP* (1999): 3.2% (world 2.4%); per capita expenditure U.S.$40.

[1]Construction work on new capital complex in Malabo suburbs underway in late 2003. [2]Formerly pegged to the French franc and since Jan. 1, 2002, to the euro at the rate of CFAF 655.96 = €1. [3]Detail does not add to total given because of rounding. [4]Includes three islets in Corisco Bay. [5]Estimated figure of the Bank of Central African States. [6]Import duties. [7]Imports c.i.f.; exports f.o.b. [8]1993–94.

Internet resources for further information:
- **Investir en Zone Franc http://www.izf.net/izf/Index.htm**

Eritrea

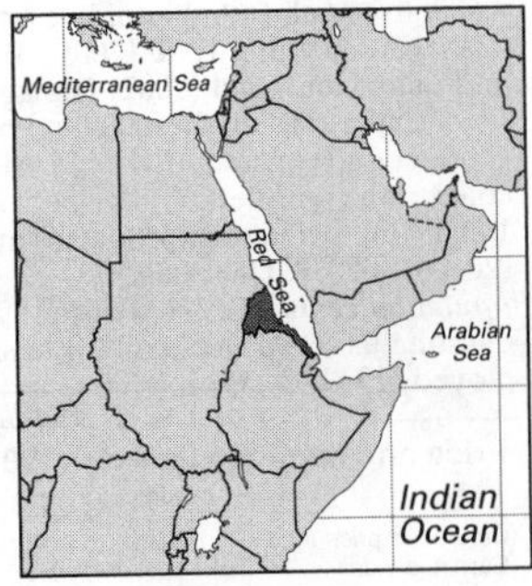

Official name: State of Eritrea.
Form of government: transitional regime with one interim legislative body (Transitional National Assembly [150][1]).
Head of state and government: President.
Capital: Asmara.
Official language: none.
Official religion: none.
Monetary unit: 1 nakfa[2] (Nfa) = 100 cents; valuation (May 15, 2003) 1 U.S.$ = Nfa 13.79; 1 £ = Nfa 22.30.

Area and population

		area[3]		population
Regions	Capitals	sq mi	sq km	2002 estimate[4]
Anseba	Keren	8,960	23,200	580,700
Debub	Mendefera	3,090	8,000	1,018,000
Debub-Keih-Bahri	Asseb (Aseb)	10,660	27,600	274,800
Gash-Barka	Barentu	12,820	33,200	747,200
Maekel	Asmara (Asmera)	500	1,300	727,800
Semien-Keih-Bahri	Massawa (Mitsiwa)	10,730	27,800	569,000
TOTAL		46,760	121,100	3,917,500

Demography

Population (2003): 4,141,000[5].
Density (2003)[6]: persons per sq mi 106.2, persons per sq km 41.0.
Urban-rural (2002): urban 19.1%; rural 80.9%.
Sex distribution (2002): male 49.77%; female 50.23%.
Age breakdown (2002): under 15, 44.5%; 15–29, 27.4%; 30–44, 14.1%; 45–59, 8.8%; 60–74, 4.2%; 75 and over, 1.0%.
Population projection[5]: (2010) 5,256,000; (2020) 6,584,000.
Doubling time: 26 years.
Ethnolinguistic composition (2000): Tigrinya (Tigray) 51.8%; Tigré 17.9%; Afar 8.1%; Saho 4.3%; Kunama 4.1%; other 13.8%.
Religious affiliation (2000): Christian 50.5%, of which Eritrean Orthodox 46.1%; Muslim 44.7%; other 4.8%.
Major cities (2000): Asmara (2001) 503,000; Keren 70,000; Mendefera 65,000; Asseb (2003) 56,300; Massawa 35,000.

Vital statistics

Birth rate per 1,000 population (2002): 40.0 (world avg. 21.3).
Death rate per 1,000 population (2002): 13.1 (world avg. 9.1).
Natural increase rate per 1,000 population (2002): 26.9 (world avg. 12.2).
Total fertility rate (avg. births per childbearing woman; 2002): 5.8.
Marriage rate per 1,000 population (1992): 6.8.
Divorce rate per 1,000 population: n.a.
Life expectancy at birth (2002): male 51.6 years; female 55.6 years.
Major causes of death per 100,000 population: n.a.; morbidity (principal causes of illness) arises mainly in malaria and other infectious diseases, parasitic infections, malnutrition, diarrheal diseases, and dysenteries.

National economy

Budget (2001). Revenue: Nfa 3,361,900,000 (grants 40.9%; tax revenue 38.0%, of which direct taxes 17.0%, import duties 12.2%; nontax revenue 15.9%; extraordinary revenue 5.2%). Expenditures: Nfa 4,545,300,000 (current expenditure 72.3%; capital expenditure 27.7%).
Public debt (external, outstanding; 2001): U.S.$397,600,000.
Production (metric tons except as noted). Agriculture, forestry, fishing (2001): sorghum 86,990, roots and tubers 85,000, barley 44,633, wheat 36,418, pulses 32,000, vegetables 28,000, millet 14,788, corn (maize) 9,257, chickpeas 8,283, sesame seeds 4,000, dry beans 3,000, peanuts (groundnuts) 1,369; livestock (number of live animals; 2002) 2,200,000 cattle, 1,700,000 goats, 1,575,000 sheep, 75,000 camels; roundwood (2001) 2,285,476; fish catch (2000) 12,612, of which artisanal fisheries 1,012. Mining and quarrying (2001): salt 200,000; marble and granite are quarried, as are sand and aggregate (gravel) for construction. Manufacturing (gross value in Nfa '000; 2000): food production 321,000; beverages 288,000; nonmetallic products 151,000; textile products 91,000; leather products and shoes 57,000; chemical products 56,000; metal products 38,000; paper and printing products 32,000. Energy production (consumption): electricity (kW-hr; 2002) 249,117,000 (194,161,000); crude petroleum, none (none); petroleum products (metric tons; 1999) n.a. (182,000); natural gas, none (none).
Land use (1994): forested 7.3%; agricultural and under permanent cultivation 5.1%; meadows and pastures 69.0%; other (predominantly barren land) 18.6%.
Household income and expenditure. Average household size (2000) 5.3; average annual income per household: n.a.; sources of income: n.a.; expenditure: n.a.
Population economically active (1996): 1,649,000; activity rate of total population 41.4%.

Price and earnings indexes (December 1996 = 100)

	1996	1997	1998	1999	2000	2001
Consumer price index[7]	100.0	107.7	117.4	129.8	164.7	177.4
Earnings index	...	...	...	...	...	...

Gross national product (at current market prices; 2001): U.S.$700,000,000 (U.S.$160 per capita).

Structure of gross domestic product

	2002	
	in value Nfa '000,000	% of total value
Agriculture	941.3	10.4
Manufacturing } Mining }	942.4	10.4
Public utilities	100.8	1.1
Construction	954.0	10.6
Transp. and commun.	1,071.3	11.9
Trade	1,672.4	18.5
Finance	448.0	5.0
Pub. admin., defense	1,387.6	15.4
Services	528.0	5.8
Other	985.4[8]	10.9[8]
TOTAL	9,031.2	100.0

Tourism (2001): receipts from visitors U.S.$74,000,000.

Foreign trade[9]

Balance of trade (current prices)

	1996	1997	1998	1999	2000	2001
U.S.$'000,000	–418	–441	–499	–481	...	–440
% of total	68.7%	80.4%	89.9%	90.2%	...	88.0%

Imports (1998): U.S.$527,000,000 (machinery and transport equipment 38.3%, food products 17.1%, chemicals and chemical products 5.7%, animal and vegetable oils 2.6%). *Major import sources* (2001): Italy 18.7%; Saudi Arabia 16.6%; United Arab Emirates 15.3%; United States 4.8%.
Exports (1998): U.S.$28,000,000 (crude materials [including hides and skins] 45.5%, food and live animals 29.6%, manufactured goods 13.2%, machinery and transport equipment 2.4%, chemicals and chemical products 2.1%). *Major export destinations* (2001): The Sudan 48.9%; Italy 8.2%; Germany 3.5%.

Transport and communications

Transport. Railroads (2001): the 190-mi (306-km) rail line that formerly connected Massawa and Agordat is currently under reconstruction; a 51-mi (82-km) section between Massawa and Embatkala was reopened in stages in 2001. Roads (1999): total length 2,491 mi, 4,010 km (paved 22%). Vehicles (1996): automobiles 5,940, trucks and buses, n.a. Merchant marine: vessels (100 gross tons and over) n.a. Air transport (1999)[10]: passenger arrivals and departures 93,007; short ton cargo handled 2,974, metric ton cargo handled 3,279; airports (2000) with scheduled flights 2.

Communications

Medium	date	unit	number	units per 1,000 persons
Daily newspapers	2000	circulation	104,000	28
Radio	2000	receivers	1,650,000	444
Television	2000	receivers	96,500	26
Telephones	2002	main lines	35,900	9.0
Personal computers	2002	units	10,000	2.5
Internet	2002	users	9,000	2.3

Education and health

Literacy (2000): total population age 15 and over literate, 55.7%; males 67.3%; females 44.5%.

Education (1996–97)

	schools	teachers	students	student/ teacher ratio
Primary (age 7–12)	549	5,476	240,737	44.0
Secondary (age 13–18)	86[11]	1,959	88,054	44.9
Voc., teacher tr.	4[11]	112	1,145	10.2
Higher[12]	1	198	3,096	15.6

Health (1993): physicians 69 (1 per 36,000 persons); hospital beds (1986–87): 2,449 (1 per 1,100 persons); infant mortality rate per 1,000 live births (2002) 77.1.
Food (2001): daily per capita caloric intake 1,690 (vegetable 94%, animal products 6%); 76% of FAO recommended minimum requirement.

Military

Total active duty personnel (2002): 172,200 (army 98.7%, navy 0.8%, air force 0.5%). UN peacekeeping force along Eritrean–Ethiopian border (August 2003): 4,100. *Military expenditure as percentage of GNP* (1999): 27.4% (world 2.4%); per capita expenditure U.S.$52.

[1]New constitution adopted in May 1997 was still not implemented in 2003. [2]The nakfa was introduced in July 1997 as the new national currency. [3]Approximate figures. The published total area is 46,774 sq mi (121,144 sq km); water area is 7,776 sq mi (20,140 sq km). [4]Unofficial figures. [5]Estimate of the UN *World Population Prospects* (2002 revision). [6]Based on land area only. [7]Asmara only; year-end. [8]Including indirect taxes less subsidies. [9]Imports c.i.f.; exports f.o.b. [10]Asmara airport only. [11]1992–93. [12]1997–98.

Estonia

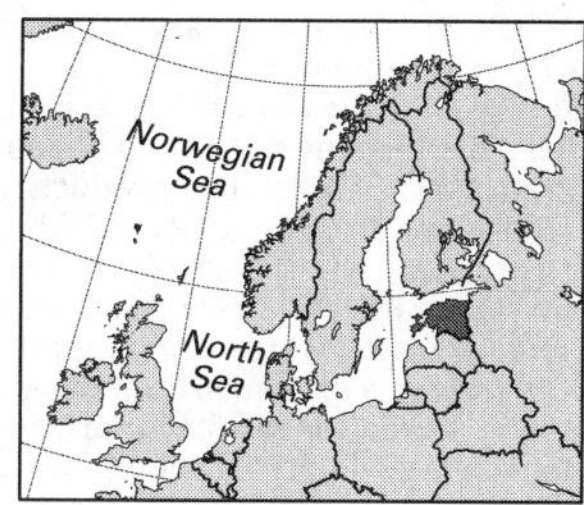

Official name: Eesti Vabariik (Republic of Estonia).
Form of government: unitary multiparty republic with a single legislative body (Riigikogu[1] [101]).
Chief of state: President.
Head of government: Prime Minister.
Capital: Tallinn.
Official language: Estonian.
Official religion: none.
Monetary unit: 1 kroon (EEK) = 100 senti; valuation (Sept. 8, 2003) 1 U.S.$ = EEK 14.19; 1 £ = EEK 22.49.

Area and population

		area		population
Counties	Capitals	sq mi	sq km	2000 census[2]
Harju	Tallinn	1,672	4,332	525,700
Hiiu	Kärdla	395	1,023	10,400
Ida-Viru	Jõhvi	1,299	3,364	179,700
Järva	Paide	1,013	2,623	38,800
Jõgeva	Jõgeva	1,005	2,604	38,300
Lääne	Haapsalu	920	2,383	28,600
Lääne-Viru	Rakvere	1,338	3,465	67,800
Pärnu	Pärnu	1,856	4,806	91,200
Põlva	Põlva	836	2,165	32,700
Rapla	Rapla	1,151	2,980	37,600
Saare	Kuressaare	1,128	2,922	36,000
Tartu	Tartu	1,156	2,993	149,600
Valga	Valga	789	2,044	35,800
Viljandi	Viljandi	1,321	3,422	58,000
Võru	Võru	890	2,305	39,900
TOTAL		16,769[3, 4, 5]	43,431[3, 4, 5]	1,370,100

Demography

Population (2003): 1,353,000.
Density (2003)[3]: persons per sq mi 80.7, persons per sq km 31.2.
Urban-rural (2002): urban 69.4%; rural 30.6%.
Sex distribution (2003[6]): male 46.09%; female 53.91%.
Age breakdown (2002): under 15, 15.8%; 15–29, 22.7%; 30–44, 21.5%; 45–59, 19.1%; 60–74, 14.9%; 75 and over, 6.0%.
Population projection: (2010) 1,316,000; (2020) 1,278,000.
Ethnic composition (2000): Estonian 67.9%; Russian 25.6%; Ukrainian 2.1%; Belarusian 1.3%; Finnish 0.9%; other 2.2%.
Religious affiliation (1995): Christian 38.1%, of which Orthodox 20.4%, Evangelical Lutheran 13.7%; other (mostly nonreligious) 61.9%.
Major cities (2001[6]): Tallinn 399,850; Tartu 101,240; Narva 68,538; Kohtla-Järve 47,484; Pärnu 44,978.

Vital statistics

Birth rate per 1,000 population (2002): 9.6 (world avg. 21.3); legitimate 43.7%; illegitimate 56.3%.
Death rate per 1,000 population (2002): 13.5 (world avg. 9.1).
Natural increase rate per 1,000 population (2002): –3.9 (world avg. 12.2).
Total fertility rate (avg. births per childbearing woman; 2002): 1.4.
Marriage rate per 1,000 population (2002): 4.3.
Divorce rate per 1,000 population (2002): 3.0.
Life expectancy at birth (2002): male 64.4 years; female 76.6 years.
Major causes of death per 100,000 population (2002): diseases of the circulatory system 734.8; malignant neoplasms (cancers) 252.2; accidents, violence, and homicide 147.9; diseases of the digestive system 49.5.

National economy

Budget (2001). Revenue: EEK 36,881,000,000 (social security contributions 31.2%, value-added taxes 23.4%, personal income taxes 19.2%, excise taxes 9.3%). Expenditures: EEK 36,548,000,000 (social security and welfare 31.5%, health 16.3%, education 7.3%, police 7.2%, defense 5.0%).
Public debt (external, outstanding; 2001): U.S.$187,000,000.
Production (metric tons except as noted). Agriculture, forestry, fishing (2002): barley 249,400, potatoes 210,900, wheat 74,400, rapeseed 63,900, oats 61,700, rye 41,500; livestock (number of live animals) 345,000 pigs, 260,500 cattle; roundwood (2001) 10,200,000 cu m; fish catch (2000) 113,371. Mining and quarrying (2002): oil shale 11,800,000; peat 823,800. Manufacturing (value of production in EEK '000,000; 2001): food products 9,282; wood products (excluding furniture) 7,321; fabricated metal products 4,251; furniture 4,143; textiles 3,554; printing and publishing 2,618. Energy production (consumption): electricity (kW-hr; 2002) 8,527,000,000 (5,686,000,000); hard coal (metric tons; 2002) none (60,000); lignite (metric tons; 1999) 10,687,000 (12,685,000); crude petroleum, none (n.a.); petroleum products (metric tons; 1999) none (991,000); natural gas (cu m; 2002) none (743,000,000).
Tourism (2001): receipts U.S.$507,000,000; expenditures U.S.$191,000,000.
Population economically active (2002): total 652,700; activity rate of total population 48.0% (participation rates: ages 15–74, 62.3%; female 48.9%; unemployed 10.3%).

Price and earnings indexes (1995 = 100)

	1996	1997	1998	1999	2000	2001	2002
Consumer price index	123.1	136.1	147.2	152.1	158.2	167.3	173.3
Annual earnings index	118.7	123.0	141.1	152.1	168.2	189.9	...

Household income and expenditure (2002). Average household size (2000) 2.2; average disposable income per household (1998) EEK 53,049 (U.S.$3,769); sources of income: wages and salaries 64.5%, transfers 25.0%, self-employment 5.2%, other 5.3%; expenditure: food and beverages 32.6%, housing 15.7%, transportation and communications 13.1%, clothing and footwear 6.2%.
Gross national product (2001): U.S.$5,300,000,000 (U.S.$3,870 per capita).

Structure of gross domestic product and labour force

	2001		2002	
	in value EEK '000,000	% of total value	labour force	% of labour force
Agriculture, fishing, forestry	4,959.0	5.1	38,800	5.9
Mining	891.8	0.9	5,700	0.9
Manufacturing	16,137.9	16.5	128,200	19.6
Public utilities	2,756.1	2.8	10,500	1.6
Construction	5,406.8	5.5	38,900	6.0
Trade, restaurants	13,569.0	14.0	104,200	16.0
Transp. and commun.	14,410.3	14.7	54,500	8.3
Finance, real estate	13,807.3	14.1	52,200	8.0
Pub. admin., defense	3,864.2	3.9	33,200	5.1
Services	11,947.2	12.2	117,300	18.0
Other	10,144.9[7]	10.4[7]	69,200[8]	10.6[8]
TOTAL	97,894.5	100.0[9]	652,700	100.0

Land use (1994): forest 44.7%; pasture 7.2%; agriculture 32.2%; other 15.9%.

Foreign trade[10]

Balance of trade (current prices)

	1997	1998	1999	2000	2001	2002
EEK '000,000	–20,925	–20,945	–17,070	–18,985	–17,241	–22,609
% of total	20.4%	19.2%	16.5%	15.1%	13.0%	16.6%

Imports (2001): EEK 75,073,000,000 (electrical and nonelectrical machinery 33.5%, textiles and apparel 10.3%, foodstuffs 9.4%, transport equipment 8.9%). *Major import sources:* Finland 29.9%; Germany 11.2%; Sweden 10.0%; Russia 7.8%; Latvia 4.0%.
Exports (2001): EEK 57,832,000,000 (electrical and nonelectrical machinery 33.1%, wood and paper products 15.2%, textiles and apparel 14.0%). *Major export destinations:* Finland 33.9%; Sweden 14.0%; Germany 6.9%; Latvia 6.9%; United Kingdom 4.2%.

Transport and communications

Transport. Railroads (2002): route length 963 km; passenger-km 177,000,000; metric ton-km cargo 9,697,000,000. Roads (2000): total length 16,430 km (paved 51%). Vehicles (2002): passenger cars 400,700; trucks and buses 85,700. Air transport (2002)[11]: passenger-km 355,000,000; metric ton-km cargo 5,000,000; airports (2001) 1.

Communications

Medium	date	unit	number	units per 1,000 persons
Daily newspapers	1996	circulation	255,000	174
Radio	2000	receivers	1,500,000	1,096
Television	2000	receivers	809,000	591
Telephones	2002	main lines	477,600	350
Cellular telephones	2002	subscribers	882,300	650
Personal computers	2002	units	285,000	210
Internet	2002	users	560,000	413

Education and health

Education (2002–03)

	schools	teachers	students	student/ teacher ratio
Primary (age 7–12) } Secondary (age 13–17) }	592	15,762[12]	200,500	13.5[12]
Vocational	79	1,279[12]	28,100	24.1[12]
Higher[13]	14	...	46,801	...

Health (2002): physicians 4,190 (1 per 324 persons); hospital beds 8,088 (1 per 168 persons); infant mortality rate per 1,000 live births (2002) 5.7.
Food (2001): daily per capita caloric intake 3,048 (vegetable products 75%, animal products 25%); 119% of FAO recommended minimum requirement.

Military

Total active duty personnel (2002): 5,510 (army 88.0%, navy 8.0%, air force 4.0%). *Military expenditure as a percentage of GNP* (1999): 1.5% (world 2.4%); per capita expenditure U.S.$120.

[1]Official legislation bans translation of parliament's name. [2]March 2000 final de jure figures. [3]Based on area used by Estonian government to calculate population densities. [4]Total area including the Estonian portion of Lake Peipus (590 sq mi [1,529 sq km]), Lake Võrtsjärv, and Muuga harbour is 17,462 sq mi (45,227 sq km). [5]Total includes 1,596 sq mi (4,133 sq km) of Baltic Sea islands. [6]As of January 1. [7]Includes net taxes (EEK 11,595,300) less imputed bank service charges (EEK 1,450,400,000). [8]Includes 2,000 not adequately defined and 67,200 unemployed. [9]Detail does not add to total given because of rounding. [10]Imports c.i.f.; exports f.o.b. [11]Estonian Air. [12]2000–01. [13]Universities only.

Internet resources for further information:
- **Statistical Office of Estonia http://www.stat.ee**

Ethiopia

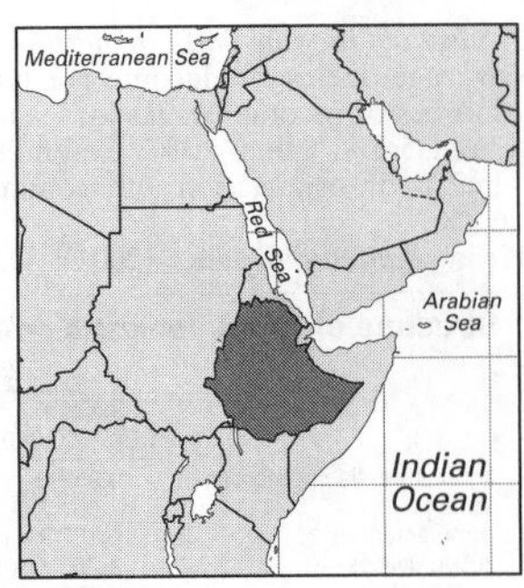

Official name: Federal Democratic Republic of Ethiopia.
Form of government: federal republic[1] with two legislative houses (Federal Council [108]; Council of People's Representatives [546]).
Chief of state: President.
Head of government: Prime Minister.
Capital: Addis Ababa.
Official language: none[2].
Official religion: none.
Monetary unit: 1 birr (Br) = 100 cents; valuation (Sept. 8, 2003) 1 U.S.$ = Br 8.55; 1 £ = Br 13.56.

Area and population

Regional states	Capitals	area sq mi	area sq km	population 1994 census
Afar	Aysaita	...	...	1,106,383
Amhara	Bahir Dar	66,000	170,000	13,834,297
Benishangul/ Gumuz	Asosa	20,000	51,000	460,459
Gambella	Gambella	9,758	25,274	181,862
Harari	Harer (Harar)	131	340	131,139
Oromiya	Addis Ababa	136,560	353,690	18,732,525
Somali	Jijiga	116,000	300,000	3,383,165
Southern Nations, Nationalities and Peoples'	Awasa	44,000	114,000	10,377,028
Tigray	Mekele	31,000	80,000	3,136,267
Cities				
Addis Ababa	...	208	540	2,112,737
Dire Dawa	...	500	1,300	251,864
TOTAL		437,794	1,133,882	53,707,726[3]

Demography

Population (2003): 66,558,000.
Density (2003): persons per sq mi 152.0, persons per sq km 58.7.
Urban-rural (2002): urban 15.9%; rural 84.1%.
Sex distribution (2002): male 49.97%; female 50.03%.
Age breakdown (2002): under 15, 44.9%; 15–29, 28.0%; 30–44, 14.5%; 45–59, 8.2%; 60–74, 3.7%; 75 and over, 0.7%.
Population projection: (2010) 75,066,000; (2020) 85,965,000.
Doubling time: 34 years.
Ethnolinguistic composition (1994): Oromo 31.8%; Amharic 29.3%; Somali 6.2%; Tigrinya 5.9%; Walaita 4.6%; Gurage 4.2%; Sidamo 3.4%; Afar 1.9%; Hadya-Libide 1.7%; other 11.0%.
Religious affiliation (1994): Ethiopian Orthodox 50.3%; Muslim 32.9%; Protestant 10.1%; traditional beliefs 4.8%; Roman Catholic 0.6%; other 1.3%.
Major cities (1994): Addis Ababa 2,112,737; Dire Dawa 164,851; Harer 131,139; Nazret 127,842; Gonder 112,249.

Vital statistics

Birth rate per 1,000 population (2002): 40.4 (world avg. 21.3).
Death rate per 1,000 population (2002): 20.0 (world avg. 9.1).
Natural increase rate per 1,000 population (2002): 20.4 (world avg. 12.2).
Total fertility rate (avg. births per childbearing woman; 2002): 5.7.
Life expectancy at birth (2002): male 40.7 years; female 42.5 years.
Major causes of death: n.a.

National economy

Budget (1999–2000). Revenue: Br 11,222,000,000 (tax revenue 57.8%, of which import duties 22.5%, income and profit tax 19.3%, sales tax 12.8%, export duties 1.3%; nontax revenue 26.9%; grants 15.3%). Expenditures: Br 17,184,000,000 (current expenditure 80.0%, of which defense 39.8%, wages 20.5%, education and health 12.2%, debt payment 6.5%; capital expenditure 20.0%).
Public debt (external, outstanding; 2001): U.S.$5,532,000,000.
Tourism (2001): receipts U.S.$75,000,000; expenditures U.S.$44,000,000.
Gross national product (2001): U.S.$6,737,000,000 (U.S.$100 per capita).

Structure of gross domestic product and labour force

	2000–01 in value Br '000,000[5]	2000–01 % of total value	1995[4] labour force	1995[4] % of labour force
Agriculture	7,831	45.1	21,605,317	87.8
Manufacturing, mining	1,158	6.7	401,535	1.6
Construction	431	2.5	61,232	0.2
Public utilities	243	1.4	17,066	0.1
Transp. and commun.	1,081	6.2	103,154	0.4
Trade	1,469	8.5	935,937	3.8
Finance	1,207	7.0	19,451	0.1
Pub. admin., defense	2,513	14.5	1,252,224	5.1
Services	1,424	8.2		
Other	—	—	210,184[6]	0.9[6]
TOTAL	17,357	100.0[7]	24,606,100	100.0

Production (metric tons except as noted). Agriculture, forestry, fishing (2002): corn (maize) 2,600,000, sugarcane 2,500,000, sorghum 1,820,000, wheat 1,250,000, barley 830,000, potatoes 415,000, millet 378,000, coffee 235,000, seed cotton 45,500, sesame seed 12,000; livestock (number of live animals) 35,500,000 cattle, 11,438,200 sheep, 9,622,088 goats, 5,297,500 horses, mules, and asses, 326,470 camels; roundwood (2001) 91,282,543 cu m; fish catch (2000) 15,681. Mining and quarrying (1999–2000): rock salt 60,900; tantalum 47,000 kg; niobium 7,870 kg; gold 5,200 kg. Manufacturing (value added in Br '000; 1998): food 876,077; beverages 640,263; nonmetallic mineral products 258,151; chemicals and chemical products 219,673; textiles 215,421; cigarettes 177,383; leather products and footwear 167,355. Energy production (consumption): electricity (kW-hr; 1999) 1,650,000,000 (1,650,000,000); coal, none (n.a.); crude petroleum (barrels; 1999) none (4,700,000); petroleum products (metric tons; 1999) 632,000 (1,724,000); natural gas, none (none).
Land use (1994): forest 13.3%; pasture 20.0%; agriculture 11.0%; other 55.7%.
Population economically active (2000): total 27,781,000; activity rate of total population 44.3% (participation rates [1999]: ages over 15, 80.5%; female [1999] 45.5%; unemployed, n.a.).

Price index (1995 = 100)

	1996	1997	1998	1999	2000	2001	2002
Consumer price index	94.9	97.2	99.7	107.6	108.3	99.5	101.0

Household income and expenditure. Average household size (2000) 5.2; income per household: n.a.; sources of income: n.a.; expenditure: n.a.

Foreign trade[8]

Balance of trade (current prices)

	1996	1997	1998	1999	2000	2001
U.S.$'000,000	−586	−414	−800	−920	−645	−1,193
% of total	41.3%	26.0%	41.7%	49.6%	39.9%	57.9%

Imports (2000): U.S.$1,260,000,000 (machinery and apparatus 19.8%, refined petroleum 19.6%, road vehicles 12.0%, chemicals and chemical products 11.3%, iron and steel 5.6%). *Major import sources:* Yemen 19.1%; Italy 8.9%; Japan 8.2%; China 7.7%; India 5.2%; Germany 5.2%.
Exports (2000): U.S.$482,000,000 (coffee 53.0%, leather 8.5%, nonmonetary gold 5.7%, sesame seeds 4.6%). *Major export destinations:* Germany 19.6%; Japan 11.7%; Djibouti 10.7%; Saudi Arabia 8.1%; Italy 6.7%; Somalia 6.1%.

Transport and communications

Transport. Railroads (2001): length 681 km[9]; (1996–97) passenger-km 157,000,000; (1996–97) metric ton-km cargo 106,000,000. Roads (2001): total length 29,799 km (paved 13%). Vehicles (1999): passenger cars 54,240; trucks and buses 34,333. Air transport (2001)[10]: passenger-km 118,366,000; metric ton-km cargo 203,000; airports (1997) 31.

Communications

Medium	date	unit	number	units per 1,000 persons
Daily newspapers	1997	circulation	86,000	1.5
Radio	2000	receivers	11,800,000	189
Television	2000	receivers	376,000	6.0
Telephones	2002	main lines	368,200	5.5
Cellular telephones	2002	subscribers	50,400	0.7
Personal computers	2002	units	100,000	1.5
Internet	2002	users	50,000	0.7

Education and health

Educational attainment: n.a. *Literacy* (2000): total population age 15 and over literate 39.1%; males 47.2%; females 30.9%.

Education (1999–2000)

	schools	teachers	students	student/ teacher ratio
Primary (age 7–12)	11,490	115,777	6,462,503	55.8
Secondary (age 13–18)	410	13,154	571,719	43.5
Voc., teacher tr.	62	1,309	12,551	9.6
Higher	6	1,779	40,894	23.0

Health: physicians: n.a.; hospital beds: n.a.; infant mortality rate (2002) 104.3.
Food (2000): daily per capita caloric intake 2,023 (vegetable products 95%, animal products 5%); 87% of FAO recommended minimum requirement.

Military

Total active duty personnel (2002): 252,500 (army 99.0%, air force 1.0%); UN peacekeeping personnel along Ethiopian-Eritrean border (August 2003): 4,100. *Military expenditure as percentage of GNP* (1999): 8.8% (world 2.4%); per capita expenditure U.S.$9.

[1]Federal republic formally established on Aug. 22, 1995. [2]Amharic is the "working" language. [3]Represents sum of regional state populations; reported census total is 53,477,265. [4]For ages 10 and up. [5]At 1980–81 factor cost. [6]First-time job seekers. [7]Detail does not add to total given because of rounding. [8]Imports f.o.b. in balance of trade and c.i.f. for commodities and trading partners. [9]Length of Ethiopian segment of Addis Ababa–Djibouti railroad. [10]Ethiopian Airlines only.

Internet resources for further information:
- **Ethiopian Embassy (Washington, D.C.) http://www.ethiopianembassy.org**
- **National Bank of Ethiopia http://www.nbe.gov.et**

Faroe Islands[1]

Official name: Føroyar (Faroese); Færøerne (Danish) (Faroe Islands).
Political status: self-governing region of the Danish realm with a single legislative body (Lagting [32]).
Chief of state: Danish Monarch represented by High Commissioner.
Head of home government: Prime Minister.
Capital: Tórshavn (Thorshavn).
Official languages: Faroese; Danish.
Official religion: Evangelical Lutheran.
Monetary unit: 1 Danish krone[2] (Dkr) = 100 øre; valuation (Sept. 8, 2003) 1 U.S.$ = Dkr 6.73; 1£ = Dkr 10.67.

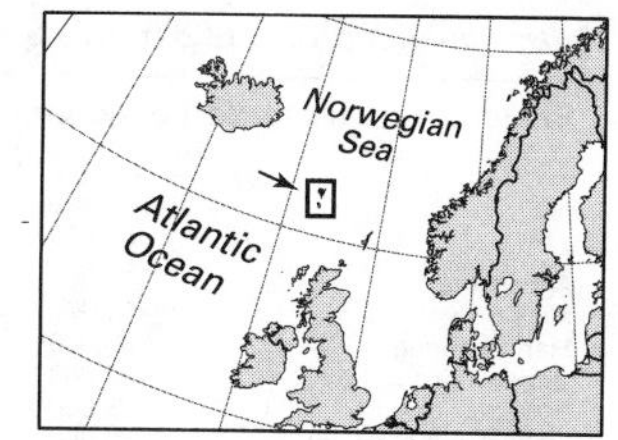

Area and population

Districts	Capitals	area sq mi	area sq km	population 2002[3] estimate
Klaksvík	Klaksvík	4.9	12.7	5,220
Nordhara Eysturoy (Østerø Nordre)	Eidhi	48.4	125.4	1,599
Nordhoy (Norderøernes)	...	88.1	228.1	720
Sandoy (Sandø)	Húsavík	48.1	124.7	1,494
Streymoy (Strømø)	Vestmanna	145.6	377.0	3,285
Sudhuroy (Suderø)	Tvøroyri	64.4	166.8	5,064
Sydhra Eysturoy (Østerø Søndre)	Runavík	62.1	160.9	8,806
Tórshavn (Thorshavn)	Tórshavn	5.9	15.3	18,071
Vágar (Vágø)	Midvágs	72.6	187.9	2,737
TOTAL		540.1	1,398.8	46,996

Demography

Population (2003): 48,000.
Density (2002): persons per sq mi 88.9, persons per sq km 34.3.
Urban-rural (2001): urban[4] 38.5%; rural 61.5%.
Sex distribution (2001): male 51.88%; female 48.12%.
Age breakdown (2001): under 15, 23.7%; 15–29, 19.3%; 30–44, 21.0%; 45–59, 18.4%; 60–74, 11.2%; 75 and over, 6.4%.
Population projection: (2010) 50,000; (2020) 53,000.
Ethnic composition (2000): Faroese 97.0%; Danish 2.5%; other Scandinavian 0.4%; other 0.1%.
Religious affiliation (1995): Evangelical Lutheran Church of Denmark 80.8%; Plymouth Brethren 10.1%; Roman Catholic 0.2%; other (mostly nonreligious) 8.9%.
Major towns (2002[3]): Tórshavn 18,070; Klaksvík 4,773; Runavík 2,516; Tvøroyri 1,837.

Vital statistics

Birth rate per 1,000 population (2002): 13.7 (world avg. 21.3); (1998) legitimate 62.0%; illegitimate 38.0%.
Death rate per 1,000 population (2002): 8.7 (world avg. 9.1).
Natural increase rate per 1,000 population (2002): 5.0 (world avg. 12.2).
Total fertility rate (avg. births per childbearing woman; 2002): 2.3.
Marriage rate per 1,000 population (2001): 5.9.
Divorce rate per 1,000 population (2001): 0.8.
Life expectancy at birth (2002): male 75.3 years; female 82.2 years.
Major causes of death per 100,000 population (1999): diseases of the circulatory system 339.2; malignant neoplasms (cancers) 257.2; diseases of the respiratory system 48.8; accidents 39.9; other 166, of which suicide 2.2.

National economy

Budget (2002). Revenue: Dkr 3,762,060,000 (income taxes 44.5%, customs and excise duties 32.9%, transfers from the Danish government 16.7%). Expenditures: Dkr 3,586,220,000 (health and social welfare 46.6%, education 17.6%, debt service 10.5%, agriculture, fishing, and commerce 4.1%).
Gross national product (at current market prices; 2000): U.S.$1,029,000,000 (U.S.$22,460 per capita).

Structure of gross domestic product and labour force

	2001		2002	
	in value Dkr '000,000	% of total value	labour force	% of labour force
Agriculture	57	0.7	...	...
Fishing[5]	1,865	21.7	...	...
Mining	497	5.8	...	...
Manufacturing[6]	290	3.4	...	...
Construction	471	5.5	...	...
Public utilities	186	2.2	...	...
Transp. and commun.	711	8.3	...	...
Trade, hotels	959	11.2	...	...
Finance and real estate	1,205	14.0	...	...
Pub. admin., defense	1,800	20.9	...	...
Services	305	3.5	...	...
Other	250	2.9	...	...
TOTAL	8,598[7]	100.0[7]	29,540	100.0

Production (metric tons except as noted). Agriculture, forestry, fishing (2002): potatoes 1,500, other vegetables, grass, hay, and silage are produced; livestock (number of live animals) 68,100 sheep, 2,000 cattle; fish catch (2001) 524,837 (of which blue whiting 259,761, saithe 45,792, cod 38,706, herring 35,172, capelin 32,110, mackerel 24,005, prawns, shrimps, and other crustaceans 20,239). Mining and quarrying: negligible[8]. Manufacturing (value added in Dkr '000,000; 1999): processed fish 393; all other manufacturing 351; important products include handicrafts and woolen textiles and clothing. Construction (2001): completed dwellings 164. Energy production (consumption): electricity (kW-hr; 2001) 231,000,000 (223,000,000); coal, none (none); crude petroleum, none (none); petroleum products (metric tons; 2001) none (285,603); natural gas, none (none).
Population economically active (2002): total 29,540; activity rate of total population *c.* 62% (participation rates: ages 14–64, n.a.; female [1997] *c.* 46%; unemployed *c.* 2%).

Price and earnings indexes (1995 = 100)

	1996	1997	1998	1999	2000	2001
Consumer price index	102.6	106.0	109.6	114.6	119.6	128.7
Hourly wage index	100.0	101.5	102.5	104.4	109.3	...

Public debt (to Denmark; end of 2001): none.
Household income and expenditure. Average household size: n.a.; average annual income per household: n.a.; sources of income: n.a.; expenditure (1998)[9]: food and beverages 25.1%, transportation and communications 17.7%, housing 12.5%, recreation 11.9%, energy 7.7%.
Tourism (2002): n.a.
Land use (1994): forested, none; meadows and pastures, none; agricultural and under permanent cultivation 2.1%; other 97.9%.

Foreign trade

Balance of trade (current prices)

	1996	1997	1998	1999	2000	2001
Dkr '000,000	+270	+234	+361	–38	–485	+132
% of total	5.9%	4.7%	6.5%	0.6%	6.0%	1.6%

Imports (2001): Dkr 4,147,000,000 (machinery and transport equipment 25.2%, goods for household consumption 24.4%, petroleum products 11.8%). *Major import sources:* Denmark 29.5%; Norway 23.2%; Germany 8.0%; Iceland 6.4%; Sweden 6.0%.
Exports (2001): Dkr 4,279,000,000 (chilled and frozen fish [excluding salmon] 45.1%, salted fish 16.4%, salmon 15.9%, prawns 7.4%, fish meal and fish oil 5.2%, fishing vessels 1.4%). *Major export destinations:* Denmark 25.6%; United Kingdom 17.8%; Spain 11.8%; France 9.9%; Norway 8.6%; Germany 7.5%.

Transport and communications

Transport. Railroads: none. Roads (2001): total length 288 mi, 464 km (paved, n.a.). Vehicles (2001): passenger cars 15,615; trucks, vans, and buses 3,698. Merchant marine (2001): vessels (20 gross tons and over) 251; total gross tonnage 104,711. Air transport (2001): airports with scheduled flights 1.

Communications

Medium	date	unit	number	units per 1,000 persons
Daily newspapers	1996	circulation	6,000	136
Radio	2000	receivers	102,000	2,222
Television	2000	receivers	46,800	1,022
Telephones	2001	main lines	25,471	542
Cellular telephones	2000	subscribers	16,971	370
Internet	1998	users	5,000	113

Education and health

Education (2001–02)

	schools	teachers	students	student/ teacher ratio
Primary (age 6–14)	38	...	5,579	...
Secondary (age 15–17)	23	...	2,019	...
Voc., teacher tr.	11	...	2,195[10]	...
Higher[11]	1	19	173	9.1

Health (2001): physicians 89 (1 per 532 persons); hospital beds 296 (1 per 160 persons); infant mortality rate per 1,000 live births (2002) 6.7.
Food: n.a.

Military

Defense responsibility lies with Denmark.

[1]English-language alternative spelling is Faeroe Islands. [2]The local currency, the Faroese króna (Fkr), is equivalent to the Danish krone. Banknotes used are Faroese or Danish; coins are Danish. [3]January 1. [4]Tórshavn only. [5]Fishing includes fish processing. [6]Manufacturing excludes fish processing. [7]Detail does not add to total given because of rounding. [8]The maritime boundary demarcation agreement between the Shetland Islands (U.K.) and the Faroes in May 1999 allowed for the exploration of deep-sea petroleum. [9]Weights of consumer price index. [10]1996–97. [11]University of the Faroe Islands.

Internet resources for further information:
- **Statistics Faroe Islands**
  http://www.hagstova.Fo/Welcome_uk.html
- **Danmarks Statistik**
  http://www.dst.dk/665

Fiji

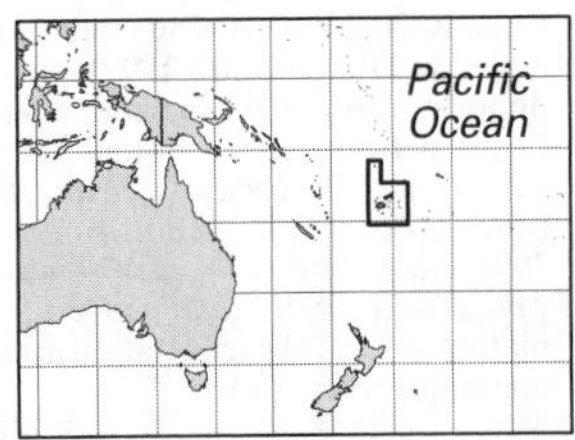

Official name: Republic of the Fiji Islands[1].
Form of government: multiparty republic with two legislative houses (Senate [32[2]]; House of Representatives [72]).
Chief of state: President.
Head of government: Prime Minister.
Capital: Suva.
Official languages: [3].
Official religion: none.
Monetary unit: 1 Fiji dollar (F$) = 100 cents; valuation (Sept. 8, 2003) 1 U.S.$ = F$1.90; 1 £ = F$3.02.

Area and population		area		population
Divisions				1996
Provinces	Capitals	sq mi	sq km	census
Central	Suva			
Naitasiri	—	643	1,666	126,641
Namosi	—	220	570	5,742
Rewa	—	105	272	101,547
Serua	—	320	830	15,461
Tailevu	—	369	955	48,216
Eastern	Levuka			
Kadavu	—	185	478	9,535
Lau	—	188	487	12,211
Lomaiviti	—	159	411	16,214
Rotuma	—	18	46	2,810
Northern	Labasa			
Bua	—	532	1,379	14,988
Cakaudrove	—	1,087	2,816	44,321
Macuata	—	774	2,004	80,207
Western	Lautoka			
Ba	—	1,017	2,634	212,197
Nadroga-Navosa	—	921	2,385	54,083
Ra	—	518	1,341	30,904
TOTAL		7,055[4]	18,272[4]	775,077

Demography

Population (2003): 827,000.
Density (2003): persons per sq mi 117.2, persons per sq km 45.3.
Urban-rural (1996): urban 46.4%; rural 53.6%.
Sex distribution (2000): male 50.88%; female 49.12%.
Age breakdown (2000): under 15, 32.8%; 15–29, 27.9%; 30–44, 20.9%; 45–59, 12.3%; 60–74, 5.0%; 75 and over, 1.1%.
Population projection: (2010) 878,000; (2020) 927,000.
Doubling time: 40 years.
Ethnic composition (2000): Fijian 52.0%; Indian 41.5%[5]; other 6.5%.
Religious affiliation (2000): Christian 56.8%, of which Protestant 37.1%, independent Christian 8.5%, Roman Catholic 8.4%; Hindu 33.3%; Muslim 6.9%; nonreligious 1.3%; Sikh 0.7%; other 1.0%.
Major cities (1996; "urban centres"): Suva 167,421; Lautoka 42,917; Nadi 30,791; Labasa 24,187; Nausori 21,645.

Vital statistics

Birth rate per 1,000 population (2002): 23.2 (world avg. 21.3).
Death rate per 1,000 population (2002): 5.7 (world avg. 9.1).
Natural increase rate per 1,000 population (2002): 17.5 (world avg. 12.2).
Total fertility rate (avg. births per childbearing woman; 2002): 2.8.
Life expectancy at birth (2002): male 66.1 years; female 71.1 years.
Major causes of death per 100,000 population (1987): diseases of the circulatory system 153.4; malignant neoplasms (cancers) 35.5; accidents, poisoning, and violence 32.2; diseases of the respiratory system 31.7.

National economy

Budget (2002). Revenue: F$949,388,000 (customs duties 54.9%, income and estate taxes 29.0%, fees and royalties 5.6%). Expenditures: F$1,345,300,000 (goods and services 42.5%, debt redemption 14.2%, education 12.5%, defense 4.2%).
Production (metric tons except as noted). Agriculture, forestry, fishing (2002): sugarcane 3,300,000, coconuts 170,000, taro 37,880, cassava 33,000, paddy rice 14,700, bananas 6,500, sweet potatoes 6,188, pineapples 3,662; livestock (number of live animals) 340,000 cattle, 247,000 goats, 138,000 pigs; roundwood (2001) 510,000 cu m; fish catch (2000) 39,179. Mining and quarrying (2002): gold 3,725 kg; silver 1,903 kg. Manufacturing (2002): raw sugar 317,000; cement 102,000; flour 59,000; coconut oil 9,000. Energy production (consumption): electricity (kW-hr; 2000) 687,000,000 (687,000,000); coal (metric tons; 1999) none (18,000); petroleum products (metric tons; 1999) none (205,000).
Tourism: receipts from visitors (2001) U.S.$217,000,000; expenditures by nationals abroad (2000) U.S.$78,000,000.
Land use (1994): forested 64.9%; agricultural and under permanent cultivation 14.2%; meadows and pastures 9.5%; other 11.4%.
Population economically active (1996): total 297,770; activity rate of total population 38.4% (participation rates: ages 15–64, 60.6%; female 32.8%; unemployed [2000] 12.2%).

Price and earnings indexes (1995 = 100)	1996	1997	1998	1999	2000	2001	2002
Consumer price index	103.1	106.5	112.6	114.8	116.1	121.0	122.0
Earnings index	...	...	...	...	...	...	...

Gross national product (2001): U.S.$1,800,000,000 (U.S.$2,150 per capita).

Structure of gross domestic product and labour force	2000		1986	
	in value F$'000[6]	% of total value[6]	labour force	% of labour force
Agriculture	342,000	16.8	106,305	44.1
Mining	51,000	2.5	1,345	0.5
Manufacturing	296,000	14.6	18,106	7.5
Construction	88,000	4.3	11,786	4.9
Public utilities	88,000	4.3	2,154	0.9
Transp. and commun.	270,000	13.3	13,151	5.4
Trade	382,000	18.8	26,010	10.8
Finance	248,000	12.2	6,016	2.5
Pub. admin., defense / Services	393,000	19.3	36,619	15.2
Other	–126,000[7]	–6.2[7]	19,668[8]	8.2[8]
TOTAL	2,032,000	100.0[4]	241,160	100.0

Public debt (external, outstanding; 2001): U.S.$159,200,000.
Household income and expenditure. Average household size (2000) 6.1; income per household: n.a.; sources of income: n.a.; expenditure (1991[9]): food, beverages, and tobacco 41.5%, housing and energy 21.4%, transportation and communications 12.9%, household durable goods 6.5%.

Foreign trade[10, 11]

Balance of trade (current prices)	1996	1997	1998	1999	2000	2001
F$'000,000	–335	–496	–418	–578	–513	–584
% of total	13.7%	21.6%	17.5%	19.4%	17.1%	19.3%

Imports (2001): F$1,808,000,000 (machinery and apparatus 16.3%, mineral fuels 15.3%, textiles and wearing apparel 14.5%, live animals and animal products 8.1%, transport equipment 6.4%). *Major import sources:* Australia 39.8%; New Zealand 18.7%; Singapore 5.5%; United States 5.0%; Japan 4.7%.
Exports (2001): F$1,224,000,000 (clothing 25.6%, sugar 18.1%, reexports [mostly petroleum products] 17.7%, fish 8.0%, gold 7.0%). *Major export destinations:* Australia 25.6%; United States 22.5%; United Kingdom 15.1%; other Pacific Islands (excluding New Zealand) 11.2%; Japan 5.0%.

Transport and communications

Transport. Railroads (1999)[12]: length 370 mi, 595 km. Roads (1999): total length 2,140 mi, 3,440 km (paved 49%). Vehicles (2000): passenger cars 50,005; trucks and buses 35,038. Merchant marine (1992): vessels (100 gross tons and over) 64; total deadweight tonnage 60,444. Air transport (2001)[13]: passenger-km 2,537,301,000; metric ton-km cargo 64,881,000; airports (1997) with scheduled flights 13.

Communications				units
Medium	date	unit	number	per 1,000 persons
Daily newspapers	2001	circulation	49,000	60
Radio	1997	receivers	500,000	636
Television	2000	receivers	92,000	114
Telephones	2001	main lines	92,200	111
Cellular telephones	2002	subscribers	89,900	109
Personal computers	2002	units	40,000	49
Internet	2002	users	22,000	27

Education and health

Educational attainment (1986). Percentage of population age 25 and over having: no formal schooling 28.3%; primary only 19.1%; some secondary 44.1%; secondary 4.1%; postsecondary 3.3%; other 1.1%. *Literacy* (2000): total population age 15 and over literate 92.9%; males 94.9%; females 90.8%.

Education (2000)	schools	teachers	students	student/ teacher ratio
Primary (age 5–15)	709[14]	5,082	142,912	28.1
Secondary (age 16–19)	146[14]	3,696	66,905	18.1
Voc., teacher tr.	35[14]	864[15]	9,997[15]	...
Higher[16]	1	355	4,000	11.3

Health (1998): physicians 252 (1 per 3,147 persons); hospital beds 1,797 (1 per 441 persons); infant mortality rate per 1,000 live births (2002) 13.7.
Food (2000): daily per capita caloric intake 2,861 (vegetable products 81%, animal products 19%); 125% of FAO recommended minimum requirement.

Military

Total active duty personnel (2002): 3,500 (army 91.4%, navy 8.6%, air force, none). *Military expenditure as percentage of GNP* (1999): 2.0% (world 2.4%); per capita expenditure U.S.$42.

[1]The long-form name in Fijian is Kai Vakarairai ni Fiji. [2]All seats are nonelected. [3]English, Fijian, and Hindustani (Fijian Hindi) have equal status per 1998 constitution. [4]Detail does not add to total given because of rounding. [5]The emigration of Indian population after the coup in 1987 has resulted in the reemergence of a Fijian majority. [6]Constant 1989 prices. [7]Less imputed bank service charges. [8]Not stated and unemployed. [9]Weights of consumer price index components based on 3,000 urban households. [10]Imports c.i.f.; exports f.o.b. [11]All export data include reexports. [12]Owned by the Fiji Sugar Corporation. [13]Air Pacific only. [14]1995. [15]1998. [16]University of the South Pacific only.

Internet resources for further information:
- **Fiji Islands Statistics Bureau http://www.statsfiji.gov.fj**
- **Fiji Government Online http://www.fiji.gov.fj**

Finland

Official names[1]: Suomen Tasavalta (Finnish); Republiken Finland (Swedish) (Republic of Finland).
Form of government: multiparty republic with one legislative house (Parliament [200]).
Chief of state: President.
Head of government: Prime Minister.
Capital: Helsinki.
Official languages: none[1].
Official religion: none.
Monetary unit: 1 euro (€) = 100 cents; valuation (Sept. 8, 2003) 1 U.S.$ = €0.90; 1 £ = €1.43[2].

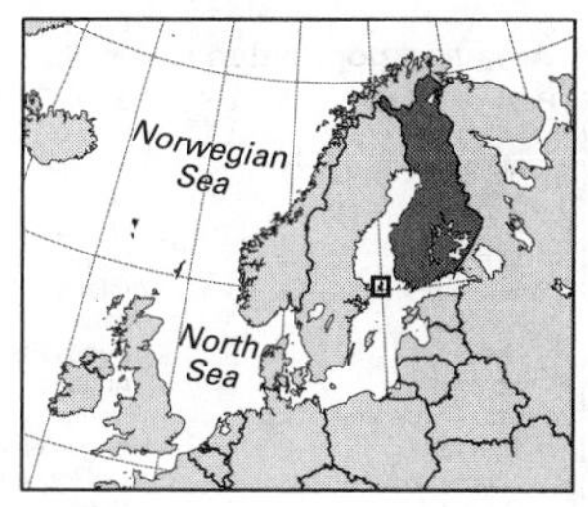

Area and population

Provinces	Capitals	area sq mi	area sq km	population 2002 estimate[3]
Eastern Finland	Mikkeli	23,444	60,720	588,106
Lapland	Rovaniemi	38,203	98,946	189,288
Oulu	Oulu	23,773	61,572	456,502
Southern Finland	Hämeenlinna	13,273	34,378	2,095,416
Western Finland	Turku	31,265	80,976	1,839,581
Autonomous Territory				
Åland (Ahvenamaa)[4]	Mariehamn (Maarianhamina)	599	1,552	26,008
TOTAL		130,559[5, 6]	338,145[5, 6]	5,194,901

Demography

Population (2003): 5,212,000.
Density (2003)[7]: persons per sq mi 44.3, persons per sq km 17.1.
Urban-rural (2002[3]): urban 61.4%; rural 38.6%[8].
Sex distribution (2002[3]): male 48.85%; female 51.15%.
Age breakdown (2002[3]): under 15, 17.9%; 15–29, 18.6%; 30–44, 21.0%; 45–59, 22.1%; 60–74, 13.7%; 75 and over, 6.7%.
Population projection: (2010) 5,267,000; (2020) 5,317,000.
Ethnic composition (2000): Finnish 91.9%; Swedish 5.9%; Karelian 0.8%; Russian 0.2%; other 1.2%.
Religious affiliation (2002[3]): Evangelical Lutheran 84.9%; Finnish (Greek) Orthodox 1.1%; nonreligious 12.9%; other 1.1%.
Major cities (2002[3]): Helsinki 559,718 (metro area 964,953); Espoo 216,836[9]; Tampere 197,774; Vantaa 179,856[9]; Turku 173,686; Oulu 123,274.

Vital statistics

Birth rate per 1,000 population (2002): 10.7 (world avg. 21.3); (2000) legitimate 60.8%; illegitimate 39.2%.
Death rate per 1,000 population (2002): 9.5 (world avg. 9.1).
Natural increase rate per 1,000 population (2002): 1.2 (world avg. 12.2).
Total fertility rate (avg. births per childbearing woman; 2002): 1.7.
Marriage rate per 1,000 population (2000): 5.1.
Divorce rate per 1,000 population (2000): 2.7.
Life expectancy at birth (2002): male 74.6 years; female 81.6 years.
Major causes of death per 100,000 population (1997): ischemic heart diseases 245.4; malignant neoplasms (cancers) 202.7; cerebrovascular diseases 103.2; accidents and violence 83.3; diseases of the respiratory system 77.8.

National economy

Budget (2002). Revenue: €35,326,000,000 (income and property taxes 37.7%, value-added taxes 27.8%, excise duties 13.8%). Expenditures: €35,326,000,000 (social security and health 23.1%, education 15.5%, interest on state debt 10.7%, agriculture and forestry 7.0%, defense 4.9%).
National debt (2001): U.S.$86,666,000,000.
Production (metric tons except as noted). Agriculture, forestry, fishing (2001): silage 6,619,000, barley 1,786,000, oats 1,287,100, sugar beets 1,070,200, potatoes 732,800, sown hay 565,500; livestock (number of live animals; 2001) 1,260,800 pigs, 1,037,400 cattle, 186,000 reindeer; roundwood (2002) 52,210,000 cu m; fish catch (2000) 178,306. Mining and quarrying (2001): chromite (gross weight) 575,000; zinc (metal content) 36,253; gold 5,552 kg. Manufacturing (value added in €'000,000; 2000): radio, television, and communications equipment 6,289; wood pulp, paper, and paper products 5,472; nonelectrical machinery and equipment 3,183; fabricated metals 1,827; food and beverages 1,784; chemicals and chemical products 1,623; printing and publishing 1,616. Energy production (consumption): electricity (kW-hr; 2001) 71,229,000,000 (81,188,000,000); coal (metric tons; 1999) none (5,255,000); crude petroleum (barrels; 1999) none (80,800,000); petroleum products (metric tons; 1999) 12,216,000 (10,112,000); natural gas (cu m; 1999) none (3,979,400,000).
Population economically active (2001): total 2,605,000; activity rate of total population 50.2% (participation rates: ages 15–64, 74.5%; female 47.9%; unemployed 9.1%).

Price and earnings indexes (1995 = 100)

	1997	1998	1999	2000	2001	2002	2003
Consumer price index	101.8	103.2	104.4	108.0	109.8	111.6	111.7[10]
Hourly earnings index	101.4	103.7	104.9	...	...	...	...

Household income and expenditure (2000). Average household size 2.2; disposable income per household €27,608 (U.S.$25,436); sources of gross income: wages and salaries 55.4%, transfer payments 24.3%, other 20.3%; expenditure (1998): housing and energy 27.3%, transportation and communications 18.9%, food, beverages, and tobacco 16.5%.

Gross national product (2001): U.S.$123,400,000 (U.S.$23,780 per capita).

Structure of gross domestic product and labour force

	2001 in value €'000,000	% of total value	labour force	% of labour force
Agriculture, fishing	1,519	1.1	112,000	4.3
Forestry	2,512	1.9	23,000	0.9
Mining	286	0.2	497,000	19.1
Manufacturing	30,358	22.3		
Public utilities	2,219	1.6	...	...
Construction	6,932	5.1	145,000	5.6
Transp. and commun.	11,579	8.5	174,000	6.7
Trade, restaurants	13,165	9.7	357,000	13.7
Finance, real estate	21,044	15.5	301,000	11.6
Pub. admin., defense	20,946	15.4	112,000	4.3
Services	3,497	2.6	638,000	24.5
Other	21,919[11]	16.1[11]	245,000[12]	9.4[12]
TOTAL	135,976	100.0	2,605,000[5]	100.0[5]

Tourism (in U.S.$'000,000; 2001): receipts 1,441; expenditures 1,854.
Land use (1994): forested 76.1%; meadows and pastures 0.4%; agricultural and under permanent cultivation 8.5%; other 15.0%.

Foreign trade[13]

Balance of trade (current prices)

	1997	1998	1999	2000	2001	2002
€'000,000	+8,720	+9,713	+9,554	+12,647	+11,910	+11,140[14]
% of total	13.9%	14.3%	13.9%	14.7%	14.3%	14.8%

Imports (2001): €35,891,000,000 (electrical machinery and apparatus 18.2%; nonelectrical machinery and apparatus 13.8%; mineral fuels 11.6%; automobiles 7.0%). *Major import sources:* Germany 14.5%; Sweden 10.2%; Russia 9.5%; U.S. 6.8%; U.K. 6.4%; France 4.5%.
Exports (2001): €47,800,000,000 (electrical machinery and apparatus 24.3%; paper and paper products 18.8%; nonelectrical machinery and apparatus 11.6%; wood and wood products [excluding furniture] 5.1%). *Major export destinations:* Germany 12.3%; U.S. 9.7%; U.K. 9.6%; Sweden 8.4%; Russia 5.9%; France 4.6%.

Transport and communications

Transport. Railroads: route length (2001) 5,850 km; passenger-km 3,282,000,000; metric ton-km cargo 9,857,000,000. Roads (2001[3, 15]): total length 78,059 km (paved 65%). Vehicles (2001[3]): passenger cars 2,160,603; trucks and buses 312,557. Air transport (2001): passenger-km 13,211,000,000; metric ton-km cargo 179,173,000; airports (2001) 27.

Communications

Medium	date	unit	number	units per 1,000 persons
Daily newspapers	2000	circulation	2,360,000	456
Radio	2000	receivers	8,400,000	1,623
Television	2000	receivers	3,580,000	692
Telephones	2002	main lines	2,850,000	547
Cellular telephones	2002	subscribers	4,400,000	845
Personal computers	2002	units	2,300,000	442
Internet	2002	users	2,650,000	509

Education and health

Educational attainment (end of 2000). Percentage of population age 25 and over having: incomplete upper-secondary education 38.6%; complete upper secondary or vocational 34.5%; higher 26.9%. *Literacy:* virtually 100%.

Education (1999–2000)

	schools	teachers	students	student/ teacher ratio
Primary/lower secondary (age 7–15)	4,101	41,631[16]	591,272	...
Upper secondary (age 16–18)	456	6,693[16]	130,624	...
Voc. (incl. higher)	398	...	258,845	...
Higher[17]	20	7,252[16]	152,466	...

Health (2001): physicians 16,110[18] (1 per 322 persons); hospital beds (2000) 43,250 (1 per 120 persons); infant mortality rate per 1,000 live births (2002) 3.6.
Food (2001): daily per capita caloric intake 3,202 (vegetable products 64.3%, animal products 35.7%); 118% of FAO recommended minimum requirement.

Military

Total active duty personnel (2002): 31,850 (army 77.1%, navy 14.4%, air force 8.5%). *Military expenditure as percentage of GNP* (1999): 1.4% (world 2.4%); per capita expenditure U.S.$344.

[1]Finnish and Swedish were official languages until mid-1995 and national languages thereafter. [2]The Finnish markka (Fmk) was the former monetary unit; on Jan. 1, 2002, Fmk 5.95 = €1. [3]January 1. [4]Has increased autonomy in relationship to Finland from 1993. [5]Detail does not add to total given because of rounding. [6]Total includes land area of 117,558 sq mi (304,473 sq km) and inland water area of 13,001 sq mi (33,672 sq km). [7]Based on land area only. [8]Includes semi-urban. [9]Within Helsinki metro area. [10]July. [11]Taxes less subsidies and imputed bank service charges. [12]Includes 238,000 unemployed persons not previously employed and 7,000 not adequately defined. [13]Imports c.i.f., exports f.o.b. [14]Excludes December. [15]Excludes Åland Islands. [16]1998–99. [17]Universities only. [18]Registered professionals of working age.

Internet resources for further information:
- **Embassy of Finland (Washington, D.C.) http://www.finland.org/facts.html**
- **Statistics Finland http://www.stat.fi/index_en.html**

France

Official name: République Française (French Republic).
Form of government: republic with two legislative houses (Parliament; Senate [321], National Assembly [577]).
Chief of state: President.
Head of government: Prime Minister.
Capital: Paris.
Official language: French.
Official religion: none.
Monetary unit: 1 euro (€) = 100 cents; valuation (Sept. 8, 2003) 1 U.S.$ = €0.90; 1 £ = €1.43[1].

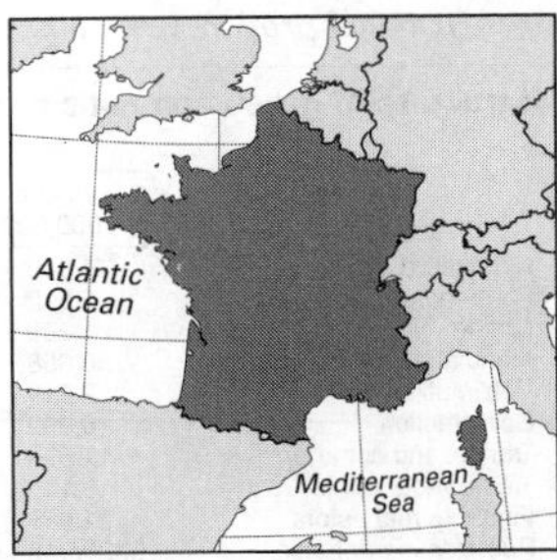

Area and population

Regions / Departments	Capitals	area sq mi	area sq km	population 1999 census
Alsace	Strasbourg			1,734,145
Bas-Rhin	Strasbourg	1,836	4,755	1,026,120
Haut-Rhin	Colmar	1,361	3,525	708,025
Aquitaine	Bordeaux			2,908,359
Dordogne	Périgueux	3,498	9,060	388,293
Gironde	Bordeaux	3,861	10,000	1,287,334
Landes	Mont-de-Marsan	3,569	9,243	327,334
Lot-et-Garonne	Agen	2,070	5,361	305,380
Pyrénées-Atlantiques	Pau	2,952	7,645	600,018
Auvergne	Clermont-Ferrand			1,308,878
Allier	Moulins	2,834	7,340	344,721
Cantal	Aurillac	2,211	5,726	150,778
Haute-Loire	Le Puy-en-Velay	1,922	4,977	209,113
Puy-de-Dôme	Clermont-Ferrand	3,077	7,970	604,266
Basse-Normandie	Caen			1,422,193
Calvados	Caen	2,142	5,548	648,385
Manche	Saint-Lô	2,293	5,938	481,471
Orne	Alençon	2,356	6,103	292,337
Bourgogne (Burgundy)	Dijon			1,610,067
Côte-d'Or	Dijon	3,383	8,763	506,755
Nièvre	Nevers	2,632	6,817	225,198
Saône-et-Loire	Mâcon	3,311	8,575	544,893
Yonne	Auxerre	2,868	7,427	333,221
Bretagne (Brittany)	Rennes			2,906,197
Côtes-d'Armor	Saint-Brieuc	2,656	6,878	542,373
Finistère	Quimper	2,600	6,733	852,418
Ille-et-Vilaine	Rennes	2,616	6,775	867,533
Morbihan	Vannes	2,634	6,823	643,873
Centre	Orléans			2,440,329
Cher	Bourges	2,793	7,235	314,428
Eure-et-Loir	Chartres	2,270	5,880	407,665
Indre	Châteauroux	2,622	6,791	231,139
Indre-et-Loire	Tours	2,366	6,127	554,003
Loir-et-Cher	Blois	2,449	6,343	314,968
Loiret	Orléans	2,616	6,775	618,126
Champagne-Ardenne	Châlons su Marne			1,342,363
Ardemmes	Charleville-Mézières	2,019	5,229	290,130
Aube	Troyes	2,318	6,004	292,131
Haute-Marne	Chaumont	2,398	6,211	194,873
Marne	Châlons-en-Champagne	3,151	8,162	565,229
Corse[2] (Corsica)	Ajaccio			260,196
Corse-du-Sud	Ajaccio	1,550	4,014	118,593
Haute-Corse	Bastia	1,802	4,666	141,603
Franche-Comté	Besançon			1,117,059
Doubs	Besançon	2,021	5,234	499,062
Haute-Saône	Vesoul	2,070	5,360	229,732
Jura	Lons-le-Saunier	1,930	4,999	250,857
Territoire de Belfort	Belfort	235	609	137,408
Haute-Normandie	Rouen			1,780,192
Eure	Évreux	2,332	6,040	541,054
Seine-Maritime	Rouen	2,424	6,278	1,239,138
Île-de-France	Paris			10,952,011
Essonne	Évry	696	1,804	1,134,238
Hauts-de-Seine	Nanterre	68	176	1,428,881
Paris	Paris	40	105	2,125,246
Seine-et-Marne	Melun	2,284	5,915	1,193,767
Seine-Saint-Denis	Bobigny	91	236	1,382,861
Val-de-Marne	Créteil	95	245	1,227,250
Val-d'Oise	Pontoise	481	1,246	1,105,464
Yvelines	Versailles	882	2,284	1,354,304
Languedoc-Roussillon	Montpellier			2,295,648
Aude	Carcassonne	2,370	6,139	309,770
Gard	Nîmes	2,260	5,853	623,125
Hérault	Montpellier	2,356	6,101	896,441
Lozère	Mende	1,995	5,167	73,509
Pyrénées-Orientales	Perpignan	1,589	4,116	392,803
Limousin	Limoges			710,939
Corrèze	Tulle	2,261	5,857	232,576
Creuse	Guéret	2,149	5,565	124,470
Haute-Vienne	Limoges	2,131	5,520	353,893
Lorraine	Metz			2,310,376
Meurthe-et-Moselle	Nancy	2,024	5,241	713,779
Meuse	Bar-le-Duc	2,400	6,216	192,198
Moselle	Metz	2,400	6,216	1,023,447
Vosges	Épinal	2,268	5,874	380,952
Midi-Pyrénées	Toulouse			2,551,687
Ariège	Foix	1,888	4,890	137,205
Aveyron	Rodez	3,373	8,736	263,808
Gers	Auch	2,416	6,257	172,335
Haute-Garonne	Toulouse	2,436	6,309	1,046,338
Haute-Pyrénées	Tarbes	1,724	4,464	222,368
Lot	Cahors	2,014	5,217	160,197
Tarn	Albi	2,223	5,758	343,402
Tarn-et-Garonne	Montauban	1,435	3,718	206,034
Nord-Pas-de-Calais	Lille			3,996,588
Nord	Lille	2,217	5,742	2,555,020
Pas-de-Calais	Arras	2,576	6,671	1,441,568
Area and population (continued)				
Pays de la Loire	Nantes			3,222,061
Loire-Atlantique	Nantes	2,631	6,815	1,134,266
Maine-et Loire	Angers	2,767	7,166	732,942
Mayenne	Laval	1,998	5,175	285,338
Sarthe	Le Mans	2,396	6,206	529,851
Vendée	La Roche-sur-Yon	2,595	6,720	539,664
Picardie (Picardy)	Amiens			1,857,834
Aisne	Laon	2,845	7,369	535,842
Oise	Beauvais	2,263	5,860	766,441
Somme	Amiens	2,382	6,170	555,551
Poitou-Charentes	Poitiers			1,640,068
Charente	Angoulême	2,300	5,956	339,628
Charente-Maritime	La Rochelle	2,650	6,864	557,024
Deux-Sèvres	Niort	2,316	5,999	344,392
Vienne	Poitiers	2,699	6,990	399,024
Provence-Alpes–Côte d'Azur	Marseille			4,506,151
Alpes-de-Haute-Provence	Digne	2,674	6,925	139,561
Alpes-Maritimes	Nice	1,660	4,299	1,011,326
Bouches-du-Rhône	Marseille	1,964	5,087	1,835,719
Hautes-Alpes	Gap	2,142	5,549	121,419
Var	Toulon	2,306	5,973	898,441
Vaucluse	Avignon	1,377	3,567	499,685
Rhône-Alpes	Lyon			5,645,407
Ain	Bourg-en-Bresse	2,225	5,762	515,270
Ardèche	Privas	2,135	5,529	286,023
Drôme	Valence	2,521	6,530	437,778
Haute-Savoie	Annecy	1,694	4,388	631,679
Isère	Grenoble	2,869	7,431	1,094,006
Loire	Saint-Étienne	1,846	4,781	728,524
Rhône	Lyon	1,254	3,249	1,578,869
Savoie	Chambéry	2,327	6,028	373,258
TOTAL		210,026	543,965	58,518,748

Demography

Population (2003): 59,773,000.
Density (2003): persons per sq mi 284.6, persons per sq km 109.9.
Urban-rural (2001): urban 75.5%; rural 24.5%.
Sex distribution (1999): male 48.56%; female 51.44%.
Age breakdown (1999): under 15, 17.9%; 15–29, 20.2%; 30–44, 21.9%; 45–59, 18.7%; 60–74, 13.6%; 75 and over, 7.7%.
Population projection: (2010) 61,507,000; (2020) 63,205,000.
Ethnic composition (2000): French 76.9%; Algerian and Moroccan Berber 2.2%; Italian 1.9%; Portuguese 1.5%; Moroccan Arab 1.5%; Fleming 1.4%; Algerian Arab 1.3%; Basque 1.3%; Jewish 1.2%; German 1.2%; Vietnamese 1.0%; Catalan 0.5%; other 8.1%.
Religious affiliation (2000): Roman Catholic 82.3%; Muslim 7.1%; atheist 4.4%; Protestant 3.7%; Orthodox 1.1%; Jewish 1.0%; other 0.4%.
Major cities (1999): Paris 2,125,246 (metropolitan area 9,644,507); Marseille 798,430 (1,349,772); Lyon 445,452 (1,348,832); Toulouse 390,350 (761,090); Nice 342,738 (888,784); Nantes 270,251 (544,932); Strasbourg 264,115 (427,245); Montpellier 225,392 (287,981); Bordeaux 215,363 (753,931); Rennes 206,229 (272,263); Le Havre 190,905 (248,547); Reims 187,206 (215,581); Lille 184,493 (1,000,900); Saint-Étienne 180,210 (291,960); Toulon 160,639 (519,640).
Mobility (1990). Population living in same residence as in 1982: 51.4%; same region 89.0%; different region 8.8%; different country 2.2%.
Households (1999). Average household size 2.4; 1 person 31.0%, 2 persons 31.1%, 3 persons 16.2%, 4 persons 13.8%, 5 persons or more 7.9%. Family households (1999): 15,942,369 (67.0%); nonfamily 7,865,703 (33.0%).
Immigration (2000): immigrants admitted 53,879 (from Africa 56.0%, of which Algerian 16.9%; from Europe 23.1%; from Asia 12.4%).

Vital statistics

Birth rate per 1,000 population (2001): 13.1 (world avg. 21.3); (2000) legitimate 57.4%; illegitimate 42.6%.
Death rate per 1,000 population (2001): 8.9 (world avg. 9.1).
Natural increase rate per 1,000 population (2001): 4.2 (world avg. 12.2).
Total fertility rate (avg. births per childbearing woman; 2001): 1.9.
Marriage rate per 1,000 population (2001): 5.1.
Divorce rate per 1,000 population (2000): 1.9.
Life expectancy at birth (2002): male 75.5 years; female 83.0 years.
Major causes of death per 100,000 population (1999): heart disease and other circulatory diseases 282.0; malignant neoplasms (cancers) 254.4; respiratory diseases 74.9; accidents and violence 74.4; digestive tract diseases 43.6.

Social indicators

Educational attainment (1990). Percentage of population age 25 and over having: primary 22.1%; lower secondary 7.8%; higher secondary and vocational 29.4%; postsecondary 11.6%; undeclared attainment 29.1%.
Quality of working life. Average workweek (2001): 38.4 hours. Annual rate per 100,000 workers for (1999): injury or accident 4,432 (deaths 0.1%); accidents in transit to work (1994) 708 (deaths 68.3). Average days lost to labour stoppages per 1,000 workers (1994): 21.0. Average length of journey to work (1990): 8.7 mi (14 km).
Access to services (1992). Proportion of dwellings having: central heating 86.0%; piped water 97.0%; indoor plumbing 95.8%.
Social participation. Eligible voters participating in last (June 2002) national election: 64.4%. Population over 15 years of age participating in voluntary associations (1997): 28.0%.
Social deviance. Offense rate per 100,000 population (1998) for: murder 1.6, rape 13.4, other assault 583.8; theft (including burglary and housebreaking) 6,107.6. Incidence per 100,000 in general population of: alcoholism, n.a. (deaths related to alcoholism; 1991) 5.0; suicide (1993) 21.1.
Material well-being (2002). Households possessing: automobile 79%; colour television 94%; VCR (2001) 70%; microcomputer 37%; washing machine 91%; microwave 68%; dishwasher (2001) 39%.

National economy

Gross national product (2001): U.S.$1,380,700,000,000 (U.S.$22,730 per capita).

Structure of gross domestic product and labour force

	2001			
	in value €'000,000	% of total value	labour force[3]	% of labour force[3]
Agriculture	37,781	2.6	348,200	1.6
Mining	...	...	49,500	0.2
Manufacturing	235,769	16.1	3,919,800	17.6
Construction	63,322	4.3	1,256,000	5.6
Public utilities	35,995	2.5	210,100	0.9
Transp. and commun.	56,795	3.9	1,563,100	7.0
Trade, hotels	138,081	9.4	3,659,300	16.4
Finance, real estate	225,463	15.4	3,542,600	15.9
Pub. admin., defense	116,780	8.0	2,353,700	10.6
Services	440,738	30.1	4,955,400	22.2
Other	112,998[4]	7.7[4]	441,700[5]	2.0[5]
TOTAL	1,463,722	100.0	22,302,800[6]	100.0

Budget (2001). Revenue: €244,846,800,000 (value-added taxes 55.7%, personal income tax 21.8%, corporate income tax 20.1%). Expenditures: €268,669,600,000 (current expenditure 89.9%, of which public debt 14.9%, pensions 11.3%, social services 11.3%; development expenditure 10.1%).

Manufacturing enterprises (1995)

	no. of enter-prises[7]	no. of employees	annual salaries as a % of avg. of all salaries[7]	annual value added (F '000,000)
Food products	55,197	545,900	87	208,065
Transport equipment	4,293	508,700	108	167,357
Electrical machinery	15,620	433,600	118	156,221
Iron and steel	27,847	403,800	96	131,376
Mechanical equipment	32,134	390,300	104	127,637
Petroleum refineries	180	46,200	174	117,041
Printing, publishing	30,359	231,900	125	83,083
Textiles and wearing apparel	29,701	281,500	78	63,633
Rubber products	5,875	204,200	94	57,758
Chemical products	1,442	102,100	128	51,146
Paper and paper products	1,916	101,500	102	38,585
Metal products	442	43,700	103	28,115
Glass products	1,536	52,400	104	16,638
Footwear	4,236	55,400	75	12,970

Production (metric tons except as noted). Agriculture, forestry, fishing (2001): wheat 31,572,000, sugar beets 26,841,000, corn (maize) 16,476,000, barley 9,807,000, grapes 7,224,000, potatoes 4,578,000, rapeseed 2,874,000, apples 1,958,000, dry peas 1,665,000, sunflower seeds 1,581,000, triticale 1,488,000, tomatoes 859,000, carrots 650,000, lettuce 491,000, oats 485,000, peaches 460,000, onions 404,000, green peas 243,000; livestock (number of live animals) 20,281,000 cattle, 15,289,000 pigs, 9,327,000 sheep; roundwood 39,831,000 cu m; fish catch 840,000. Mining and quarrying (2001): gypsum 4,500,000; kaolin 375,000; potash 257,000; gold 80,700 troy oz. Manufacturing (value added in F '000,000,000; 1998[8]): transport equipment 157.2, of which motor vehicles 75.7, aircraft 38.8; fabricated metals 83.0; nonelectrical machinery 80.5; electronics, radios, and televisions 58.9; pharmaceuticals 56.6; printing and publishing 55.0, of which publishing 33.9; other electrical machinery 48.6.

Financial aggregates	1997	1998	1999	2000	2001	2002
Exchange rate, F per:[9]						
U.S. dollar	5.99	5.62	1.00	1.07	1.13	0.95
£	9.90	9.35	1.62	1.60	1.65	1.43
SDR	8.08	7.92	1.37	1.40	1.43	1.30
International reserves (U.S.$)						
Total (excl. gold; '000,000)	30,927	44,312	39,701	37,039	31,749	28,365
SDRs ('000,000)	971	1,107	347	402	492	622
Reserve pos. in IMF ('000,000)	2,859	4,452	5,241	4,522	4,894	5,778
Foreign exchange	27,097	38,753	33,933	32,114	26,363	21,965
Gold ('000,000 fine troy oz)	81.89	102.37	97.24	97.25	97.25	97.25
% world reserves	9.2	10.6	10.1	10.2	10.3	10.5
Interest and prices						
Central bank discount (%)	...	...	...	...	...	...
Govt. bond yield (%)	5.63	4.72	4.69	5.45	5.05	4.93
Industrial share prices (1995 = 100)	149.6	201.8	249.7	337.4	270.2	203.7
Balance of payments (U.S.$'000,000)						
Balance of visible trade	+29,280	+27,730	+15,225	+3,695	+2,121	+8,188
Imports, f.o.b.	260,721	277,708	287,481	303,658	293,736	299,755
Exports, f.o.b.	290,001	305,438	302,706	299,963	295,857	307,943
Balance of invisibles	+8,520	+9,970	+19,815	+16,735	+19,239	+17,552
Balance of payments, current account	+37,800	+37,700	+35,040	+20,430	+21,360	+25,740

Public debt (1998): F 5,030,000,000,000 (U.S.$853,000,000,000).

Retail trade enterprises (1995[10])

	no. of enter-prises	no. of employees	weekly wages as a % of all wages	annual turnover (F '000,000)
Large food stores	4,373	385,402	...	617,222
Clothing stores	51,873	195,535	...	126,504
Pharmacies	22,301	126,508	...	121,980
Small food stores	64,565	163,474	...	110,928
butcher shops	21,548	59,962	...	36,732
Furniture stores	7,179	53,080	...	54,390
Electrical and electronics stores	10,990	55,560	...	43,995
Department stores	736	35,074	...	27,741
Publishing and paper	15,083	40,375	...	24,591
Gas, coal, and other energy products	6,042	25,375	...	19,204

Energy production (consumption)[11]: electricity (kW-hr; 2001) 520,000,000,000 ([1999] 467,648,000,000); hard coal (metric tons; 2001) 2,400,000 ([1999] 22,799,000); crude petroleum (barrels; 2001) 11,027,000 ([1999] 608,200,000); petroleum products (metric tons; 1999) 74,800,000 (72,858,000); natural gas (cu m; 2001) 1,982,000,000 ([1999] 41,174,500,000).

Population economically active (2001): total 27,812,600; activity rate of total population 47.0% (participation rates: ages 15–64, 67.6%[12]; female 47.9%; unemployed 12.1%).

Price and earnings indexes (1995 = 100)

	1996	1997	1998	1999	2000	2001	2002
Consumer price index	102.0	103.2	103.9	104.5	106.3	108.0	110.1
Earnings index	101.7	104.5	107.5	109.9	114.9	120.0	124.6

Household income and expenditure. Average household size (1999) 2.5; average annual income per household (1995) F 302,560 (U.S.$60,610); sources of income (1995): wages and salaries 70.0%, self-employment 24.4%, social security 5.6%; expenditure (2001): housing 24.0%, transportation 15.4%, food 14.7%, recreation and education 9.6%, clothing 4.9%.

Tourism (in U.S.$'000,000,000; 2001): receipts U.S.$30.0; expenditures U.S.$17.7.

Land use (1994): forest 27.3%; pasture 19.3%; agriculture 35.4%; other 18.0%.

Foreign trade[13]

Balance of trade (current prices)

	1997[14]	1998	1999	2000	2001	2002[15]
€'000,000,000	+107.3	+11.8	+7.1	−12.6	−4.9	+2.6
% of total	3.3%	4.1%	1.3%	1.9%	0.7%	0.4%

Imports (2000)[16]: U.S.$310,897,000,000 (machinery and apparatus 27.7%; transport equipment 12.6%; chemicals and chemical products 12.3%; petroleum [all forms] 8.1%; food 6.8%). *Major import sources* (2002)[15]: Germany 17.2%; Italy 9.0%; U.S. 8.1%; Spain 7.2%; U.K. 7.2%; Belgium-Luxembourg 7.0%; The Netherlands 4.7%; Japan 3.3%; ASEAN countries 2.5%; Switzerland 2.2%.

Exports (2000)[16]: U.S.$302,248,000,000 (machinery and apparatus 26.0%; transport equipment 18.9%, of which road vehicles 12.5%, aircraft 5.5%; chemicals and chemical products 13.5%; food 7.8%; iron and steel 3.3%; alcoholic beverages 2.4%). *Major export destinations* (2002)[15]: Germany 14.6%; U.K. 10.3%; Spain 9.7%; Italy 9.1%; U.S. 8.2%; Belgium-Luxembourg 7.7%; The Netherlands 4.0%; Switzerland 3.3%; ASEAN 2.5%; CIS 1.9%.

Transport and communications

Transport. Railroads (1999): route length 32,105 km; passenger-km 66,590,000,000; metric ton-km cargo 52,110,000,000. Roads (1999[10]): total length 893,300 km (paved 100%). Vehicles (2000): passenger cars 28,060,000; trucks and buses 5,673,000. Air transport (2000): passenger-km 110,270,500,000; metric ton-km cargo 15,221,900,000; airports (1996) 61.

Communications

Medium	date	unit	number	units per 1,000 persons
Daily newspapers	2000	circulation	11,800,000	201
Radio	2000	receivers	55,900,000	950
Television	2000	receivers	37,000,000	628
Telephones	2002	main lines	33,928,700	569
Cellular telephones	2002	subscribers	38,585,300	647
Personal computers	2002	units	20,700,000	347
Internet	2002	users	18,716,000	314

Education and health

Education (2000–01)

	schools	teachers	students	student/ teacher ratio
Primary (age 6–10)	39,131[17]	211,192	3,839,770	18.2
Secondary (age 11–18) / Voc., teacher tr.	11,052[17]	483,493	5,399,433	11.2
Higher[18]	...	46,196	1,400,393	30.3

Health: physicians (2001) 196,000 (1 per 301 persons); hospital beds (2000) 636,635 (1 per 93 persons); infant mortality rate (2001) 4.5.

Food (2001): daily per capita caloric intake 3,629 (vegetable products 63%, animal products 37%); 129% of FAO recommended minimum requirement.

Military

Total active duty personnel (2002): 260,400 (army 52.6%, navy 17.5%, air force 24.6%, unallocated 5.3%). *Military expenditure as percentage of GNP* (1999): 2.7% (world 2.4%); per capita expenditure U.S.$658.

[1]The French franc was the former monetary unit; on Jan. 1, 2002, F 6.56 = €1. [2]Expect evolving autonomy from central government between 2001 and 2004. [3]Paid employees only; excludes 2,140,300 non-salaried workers and 3,369,500 unemployed. [4]Includes value-added tax and import duties less subsidies and imputed bank service charges. [5]Private households with employed persons. [6]Detail does not add to total given because of rounding. [7]1991. [8]Data unavailable for production of food, beverages, and tobacco products. [9]Beginning in 1999 exchange rates expressed in euros. [10]January 1. [11]Consumption data includes Monaco. [12]1994. [13]Imports c.i.f.; exports f.o.b. [14]In billions of French francs. [15]Excludes December. [16]Includes Monaco. [17]1996–97. [18]Universities only.

Internet resources for further information:

- **INSEE http://www.insee.fr/fr/home/home_page.asp**

French Guiana

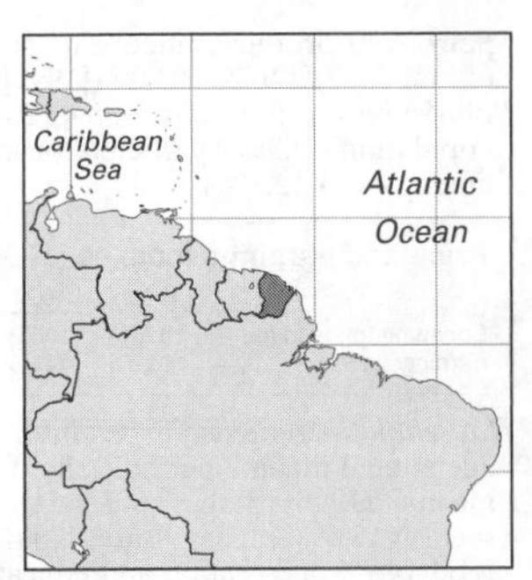

Official name: Département de la Guyane française (Department of French Guiana).
Political status: overseas department of France with two legislative houses (General Council [19]; Regional Council [31]).
Chief of state: President of France.
Heads of government: Prefect (for France); President of the General Council (for French Guiana); President of the Regional Council (for French Guiana).
Capital: Cayenne.
Official language: French.
Official religion: none.
Monetary unit: 1 euro (€) = 100 cents; valuation (Sept. 8, 2003) 1 U.S.$ = €0.90; 1 £ = €1.43[1].

Area and population

		area		population
				1999
Arrondissements	Capitals	sq mi	sq km	census
Cayenne	Cayenne	17,727	45,913	119,660
Saint-Laurent-du-Maroni	Saint-Laurent-du-Maroni	14,526	37,621	37,553
TOTAL		32,253	83,534	157,213

Demography

Population (2003): 178,000.
Density (2003): persons per sq mi 5.5, persons per sq km 2.1.
Urban-rural (2001): urban 75.2%; rural 24.8%.
Sex distribution (1999): male 50.36%; female 49.64%.
Age breakdown (1999): under 15, 34.0%; 15–29, 24.2%; 30–44, 23.3%; 45–59, 12.5%; 60–74, 4.3%; 75 and over, 1.7%.
Population projection: (2010) 208,000; (2020) 252,000.
Doubling time: 41 years.
Ethnic composition (2000): Guianese Mulatto 37.9%; French 8.0%; Haitian 8.0%; Surinamese 6.0%; Antillean 5.0%; Chinese 5.0%; Brazilian 4.9%; East Indian 4.0%; other (other West Indian, Hmong, other South American) 21.2%.
Religious affiliation (2000): Christian 84.6%, of which Roman Catholic 80.0%, Protestant 3.9%; Chinese folk-religionist 3.6%; Spiritist 3.5%; nonreligious/atheist 3.0%; traditional beliefs 1.9%; Hindu 1.6%; Muslim 0.9%; other 0.9%.
Major cities (1999)[2]: Cayenne 50,594 (urban agglomeration 84,181); Saint-Laurent-du-Maroni 19,211; Kourou 19,107; Matoury 18,032[3]; Rémire-Montjoly 15,555[3].

Vital statistics

Birth rate per 1,000 population (2002): 21.7 (world avg. 21.3); (1999) legitimate 18.0%; illegitimate 82.0%.
Death rate per 1,000 population (2002): 4.8 (world avg. 9.1).
Natural increase rate per 1,000 population (2002): 16.9 (world avg. 12.2).
Total fertility rate (avg. births per childbearing woman; 2002): 3.1.
Marriage rate per 1,000 population (1999): 3.5.
Divorce rate per 1,000 population (1998): 1.0.
Life expectancy at birth (2002): male 73.2 years; female 80.0 years.
Major causes of death per 100,000 population (1997): diseases of the circulatory system *c.* 343; malignant neoplasms (cancers) *c.* 196[4]; violence and suicide *c.* 97; infectious and parasitic diseases *c.* 77, of which HIV/AIDS *c.* 43; diseases of the respiratory system *c.* 45; endocrine and metabolic disorders *c.* 43.

National economy

Budget (2000). Revenue: €141,000,000 (direct taxes 32.6%, indirect taxes 29.8%, revenue from French central government 17.7%, development receipts 15.6%). Expenditures: €141,000,000 (current expenditures 83.0%, capital expenditures 17.0%).
Production (metric tons except as noted). Agriculture, forestry, fishing (2002): rice 19,900, cassava 10,375, cabbages 6,350, bananas 4,495, taro 4,095, tomatoes 3,770; livestock (number of live animals) 10,500 pigs, 9,200 cattle; roundwood (2001) 139,200 cu m; fish catch (2000) 5,268. Mining and quarrying: stone, sand, and gravel (2001) 1,500; gold 96,450 troy oz. Manufacturing (2001): pork 1,245; chicken meat 560; finished wood products 3,172 cu m[5]; rum (2000) 3,072 hectolitres; other products include leather goods, clothing, rosewood essence, yogurt, and beer. Number of satellites launched from the Kourou Space Centre (2002): 12[6]. Energy production (consumption): electricity (kW-hr; 2000) 453,000,000 ([1999] 455,000,000); coal, none (none); crude petroleum, none (none); petroleum products (metric tons; 1999) none (292,000); natural gas, none (none).
Household income and expenditure. Average household size (1999) 3.3; income per household (1997) €31,203 (U.S.$33,244); sources of income (1997): wages and salaries and self-employed 72.9%, transfer payments 20.2%; expenditure (1994)[7]: food and beverages 28.7%, housing 11.7%, energy 9.0%, clothing and footwear 6.4%, health 2.7%, other 41.5%.
Land use (1994): forested 90.6%; meadows and pastures 0.1%; agricultural and under permanent cultivation 0.2%; other 9.1%.
Gross national product (1997): U.S.$1,430,000,000 (U.S.$9,410 per capita).

Structure of gross domestic product and labour force

	1997		2002	
	in value €'000,000	% of total value	labour force[8]	% of labour force[8]
Agriculture, forestry, fishing	87	5.7	1,024	2.1
Mining	21	1.4	409	0.8
Manufacturing	127	8.3	1,053	2.1
Construction	156	10.2	2,583	5.2
Public utilities	12	0.8	644	1.3
Finance, real estate[9]	333	21.8	830	1.7
Transp. and commun.	10	0.7	2,134	4.3
Trade, restaurants, hotels	233	15.2	4,815	9.8
Pub. admin., defense	193	12.6	9,758	19.8
Services	360	23.3	14,975	30.4
Other	—	—	11,095	22.5
TOTAL	1,532	100.0	49,320	100.0

Population economically active (1999): total 62,634; activity rate of total population 39.4% (participation rates: age 15 and over 60.5%; female 43.8%; unemployed [March 2003] 22.8%).

Price and earnings indexes (1990 = 100)

	1995	1996	1997	1998	1999	2000	2001
Consumer price index	110.9	111.8	112.9	113.5	113.7	115.3	117.1
Monthly earnings index[10, 11]	112.3	112.3	114.5	127.8	...	...	...

Tourism (2001): receipts U.S.$42,000,000; expenditures, n.a.

Foreign trade

Balance of trade (current prices)

	1997[12]	1998[12]	1999[13]	2000[13]	2001[13]
€'000,000	–2,913	–2,852	–402	–495	–505
% of total	61.4%	70.9%	64%	67%	65%

Imports (2000)[13]: €618,000,000 (food products 19.4%, road vehicles 14.0%, refined petroleum 11.1%, nonelectrical machinery 9.8%). *Major import sources:* France 55.8%; Trinidad and Tobago 10.6%; Italy 2.9%; Japan 2.9%.
Exports (2000)[13]: €123,000,000 (gold 38.2%, shrimp and fish 26.1%, parts for air and space vehicles 14.0%, rice 5.4%). *Major export destinations:* France 63.6%; U.S. 7.4%; Switzerland 5.0%; Guadeloupe 5.0%.

Transport and communications

Transport. Railroads: none. Roads (1996): total length 774 mi, 1,245 km (paved, n.a.). Vehicles (1998): passenger cars 28,200; trucks and buses 9,400. Air transport (2002): passenger arrivals 186,920; passenger departures 192,764; cargo unloaded 4,569 metric tons, cargo loaded 2,119 metric tons; airports (2001) with scheduled flights 1.

Communications

Medium	date	unit	number	units per 1,000 persons
Daily newspapers	1996	circulation	2,000	14
Radio	1997	receivers	104,000	702
Television	1998	receivers	37,000	202
Telephones	1999	main lines	49,000	308
Cellular telephones	2000	subscribers	39,830	220
Personal computers	1999	units	23,000	145
Internet	1999	users	2,000	13

Education and health

Educational attainment (1990). Percentage of population age 25 and over having: incomplete primary education or no declaration 61.7%; completed primary 5.3%; some secondary 15.9%; completed secondary 8.2%; some higher 4.9%; completed higher 4.0%. *Literacy:* n.a.

Education (2000–01)

	schools	teachers	students	student/ teacher ratio
Primary (age 6–11)	86	1,718	20,826	12.1
Secondary (age 12–18)	35	1,385	20,585	14.9
Higher[14]	1	...	666	...

Health: physicians (2000) 219 (1 per 737 persons); hospital beds (2000) 750 (1 per 215 persons); infant mortality rate per 1,000 live births (2002) 13.2.
Food (1992): daily per capita caloric intake 2,900 (vegetable products 70%, animal products 30%); 128% of FAO recommended minimum requirement.

Military

Total active duty personnel (2002): 3,000[15].

[1]The French franc (F) has been replaced by the euro (on Jan. 1, 2002, F 6.56 = €1). [2]Commune population. [3]Within Cayenne urban agglomeration. [4]Excludes breast and lung neoplasms (cancers). [5]1996. [6]In 1991 the European Space Agency accounted for 28.7% of GDP, 28.2% of employed labour force, and 70.9% of imports. [7]Weights of consumer price index components. [8]Employed only. [9]Includes insurance. [10]Index based on end-of-year figures. [11]Based on minimum-level wage in public administration. [12]In F '000,000. [13]Estimated figures. [14]Université des Antilles et de la Guyane, Cayenne campus. [15]Excludes 600 French Foreign Legion troops assigned to guard the Kourou Space Centre.

Internet resources for further information:
- **Chambre de Commerce et l'Industrie: Guyane http://www.guyane.cci.fr**

French Polynesia

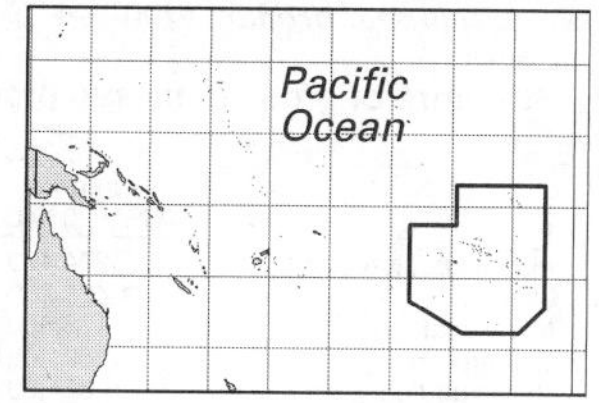

Official name: Territoire de la Polynésie française (French); Polynesia Farani (Tahitian) (Territory of French Polynesia)[1].
Political status: overseas territory[1] (France) with one legislative house (Territorial Assembly [49]).
Chief of state: President of France.
Head of government: High Commissioner (for France); President of the Council of Ministers (for French Polynesia).
Capital: Papeete.
Official languages: French; Tahitian.
Official religion: none.
Monetary unit: 1 Franc de la Comptoirs française du pacifique (CFPF) = 100 centimes; valuation (Sept. 8, 2003)[2] 1 U.S.$ = CFPF 104.80; 1 £ = CFPF 166.17.

Area and population

		area		population
				2002
Circumscriptions	**Capitals**	sq mi	sq km	census
Austral Islands	Mataura	57	148	6,386
Leeward Islands	Uturoa	156	404	30,221
Marquesas Archipelago	Talohae	405	1,049	8,712
Tuamotu–Gambler Islands	Papeete	280	726	15,862
Windward Islands	Papeete	461	1,194	184,224
TOTAL		1,544[3]	4,000[3]	245,405

Demography

Population (2003): 244,000.
Density (2003)[4]: persons per sq mi 180.3, persons per sq km 69.6.
Urban-rural (2002): urban 53.0%; rural 47.0%.
Sex distribution (1996): male 51.92%; female 48.08%.
Age breakdown (1996): under 15, 33.7%; 15–29, 27.3%; 30–44, 21.6%; 45–59, 11.4%; 60–74, 5.0%; 75 and over, 1.0%.
Population projection: (2010) 275,000; (2020) 308,000.
Doubling time: 51 years.
Ethnic composition (1996): Polynesian and part-Polynesian 82.8%; European (mostly French) 11.9%; Asian (mostly Chinese) 4.7%; other 0.6%.
Religious affiliation (1995): Protestant 50.2%, of which Evangelical Church of French Polynesia (Presbyterian) 46.1%; Roman Catholic 39.5%; other Christian 9.9%, of which Mormon 5.9%; other 0.4%.
Major communes (2002): Faaa 28,339[5]; Papeete 26,181 (urban agglomeration [2001] 125,000); Punaauia 23,706[5]; Moorea-Maiao 14,550; Pirae 14,499[5].

Vital statistics

Birth rate per 1,000 population (2002): 18.2 (world avg. 21.3); (1996) legitimate 35.4%; illegitimate 64.6%.
Death rate per 1,000 population (2002): 4.5 (world avg. 9.1).
Natural increase rate per 1,000 population (2002): 13.7 (world avg. 12.2).
Total fertility rate (avg. births per childbearing woman; 2002): 2.2.
Marriage rate per 1,000 population (2000): 4.6.
Life expectancy at birth (2002): male 72.9 years; female 77.7 years.
Major causes of death per 100,000 population (1994–95): diseases of the circulatory system 123; malignant neoplasms (cancers) 104; accidents, suicide, and violence 52; respiratory diseases 47; diseases of the digestive system 17.

National economy

Budget (2001). Revenue: CFPF 108,036,000,000 (indirect taxes 55.1%, direct taxes and nontax revenue 44.9%). Expenditures: CFPF 140,709,000,000 (current expenditure 68.1%, capital expenditure 31.9%).
Production (metric tons except as noted). Agriculture, forestry, fishing (2002): coconuts 88,000, copra (2001) 8,262, cassava 6,000, roots and tubers 5,500, pineapples 3,500, sugarcane 3,200, tomatoes 1,100, watermelon 1,000, cucumbers 1,000, bananas 500; livestock (number of live animals) 34,000 pigs, 16,500 goats, 10,800 cattle; roundwood, n.a.; fish catch (2000) 13,952; export production of black pearls (1998) 6,050 kg. Mining and quarrying: estimated annual production of phosphates ranges from 1,000,000 to 1,200,000 tons. Manufacturing (1999): coconut oil 6,386; other manufactures include *monoï* oil (primarily refined coconut and sandalwood oils), beer, printed cloth, and sandals. Energy production (consumption): electricity (kW-hr; 2001) 495,000,000 ([1999] 365,000,000); coal, none (none); crude petroleum, none (none); petroleum products (metric tons; 1999) none (177,000); natural gas, none (none).
Tourism (1999): receipts from visitors U.S.$394,000,000; expenditures by nationals abroad, n.a.
Household income and expenditure (1986). Average household size (1996) 4.3; average annual income per household CFPF 2,153,112 (U.S.$17,831); sources of income (1993): salaries 61.9%, self-employment 21.5%, transfer payments 16.6%; expenditure: food and beverages 32.1%, household furnishings 12.3%, transportation 12.2%, energy 8.1%, recreation and education 6.9%, clothing 6.3%.
Land use (1998): forested and other 81.4%; meadows and pastures 5.5%; agricultural and under permanent cultivation 13.1%.
Gross national product (at current market prices; 2001): U.S.$4,100,000,000 (U.S.$17,290 per capita).

Structure of gross domestic product and labour force

	1997		1996	
	in value CFPF '000,000	% of total value	labour force	% of labour force
Agriculture, fishing	15,534	4.1	10,888	12.5
Manufacturing[6]	26,360	7.0	6,424	7.4
Construction	20,104	5.3	4,777	5.5
Public utilities[6]	12,221	3.2	459	0.5
Transp. and commun.	27,832	7.4	3,788	4.4
Trade	81,854	21.6	9,357	10.7
Finance, real estate[7]	...	...	1,865	2.1
Pub. admin., defense	97,238	25.7	13,475	15.5
Services[7]	97,360	25.7	23,514	27.0
Other	—	...	12,574[8]	14.4[8]
TOTAL	378,503	100.0	87,121	100.0

Population economically active (1996): total 87,121; activity rate of total population 39.7% (participation rates: ages 14 and over, 68.3%; female 38.7%; unemployed 13.2%).

Price and earnings indexes (1990 = 100)[9]

	1996	1997	1998	1999	2000	2001	2002
Consumer price index	108.0	109.1	110.9	111.8	112.9	113.9	115.0
Monthly earnings index	...	112.7	119.6	124.6	124.6	128.4	...

Public debt (external, outstanding; 1999): U.S.$542,000,000.

Foreign trade[10]

Balance of trade (current prices)

	1997	1998	1999	2000	2001	2002[11]
CFPF '000,000	–82,819	–82,685	–78,463	–97,343	–116,892	–110,297
% of total	71.5%	61.0%	64.8%	67.5%	75.8%	80.7%

Imports (2001): CFPF 135,569,000,000 (machinery and apparatus 19.7%; consumer goods 16.0%; mineral fuels 8.5%). *Major import sources* (2000): France 35.9%; U.S. 13.9%; Australia 9.3%; New Zealand 7.4%; Germany 4.8%.
Exports (2001): CFPF 18,677,000,000 (pearl products 80.0%, of which black cultured pearls 76.1%; fish 7.3%; *nono* fruit 4.6%; coconut oil 1.6%; *monoï* oil 0.8%). *Major export destinations* (2000): Japan 36.9%; Hong Kong 20.9%; France 14.5%; U.S. 12.1%; New Caledonia 5.0%.

Transport and communications

Transport. Railroads: none. Roads (1996): total length 549 mi, 884 km (paved 44%). Motor vehicles: passenger cars (1996) 47,300; trucks and buses (1993) 15,300. Air transport (2001): passengers carried 1,453,513; freight handled 9,834 metric tons; airports (1994) with scheduled flights 17.

Communications

Medium	date	unit	number	units per 1,000 persons
Daily newspapers	1996	circulation	24,000	110
Radio	1997	receivers	128,000	574
Television	2000	receivers	44,500	189
Telephones	2001	main lines	52,500	219
Cellular telephones	2002	subscribers	90,000	375
Personal computers	2001	units	66,000	280
Internet	2002	users	25,000	104

Education and health

Educational attainment (1996). Percentage of population age 15 and over having: no formal schooling 4.9%; primary education 37.4%; secondary 49.0%; higher 8.7%. *Literacy* (2000): total population age 15 and over literate, almost 100%.

Education (1998–99)

	schools	teachers	students	student/ teacher ratio
Primary (age 6–10)[12]	255	2,751	...	...
Secondary (age 11–17) / Vocational	82	2,059	30,473	14.8
Higher[13]	1	54	1,600	29.6

Health: physicians (2001) 433 (1 per 181 persons); hospital beds (1996) 981 (1 per 447 persons); infant mortality rate per 1,000 live births (2002) 9.0.
Food (2001): daily per capita caloric intake 2,889 (vegetable products 72%, animal products 28%); 127% of FAO recommended minimum.

Military

Total active duty personnel (2002): 2,600 French military personnel. *Military expenditure as percentage of GNP:* n.a.

[1]Status change from overseas territory to overseas country is pending per the application of "decentralization" amendments to the French constitution from March 2003. [2]Pegged to the euro on Jan. 1, 2002, at the rate of €1 = CFPF 119.25. [3]Approximate total area including inland water; total land area is 1,359 sq mi (3,521 sq km). [4]Based on land area. [5]Part of Papeete urban agglomeration. [6]The manufacture of energy-generating products is included in Public utilities. [7]Services includes Finance, real estate. [8]Includes not adequately defined and unemployed. [9]All end-of-year. [10]Imports c.i.f.; exports f.o.b. [11]First nine months only. [12]Includes preprimary. [13]University of French Polynesia only; 2000–01.

Internet resources for further information:
- **Institut de la Statistique de la Polynésie Francaise http://www.ispf.pf**

Gabon

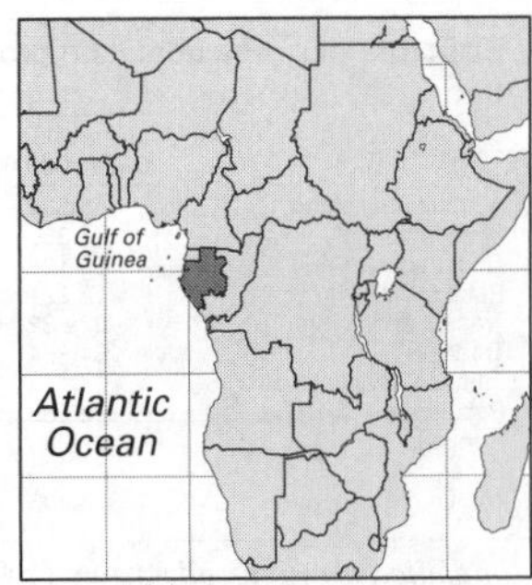

Official name: République Gabonaise (Gabonese Republic).
Form of government: unitary multiparty republic with a Parliament comprising two legislative houses (Senate [91]; National Assembly [120]).
Chief of state: President.
Head of government: Prime Minister.
Capital: Libreville.
Official language: French.
Official religion: none.
Monetary unit: 1 CFA franc (CFAF) = 100 centimes; valuation (Sept. 8, 2003) 1 U.S.$ = CFAF 594.70; 1 £ = CFAF 942.93[1].

Area and population

		area		population
Provinces	Capitals	sq mi	sq km	2002 estimate
Estuaire	Libreville	8,008	20,740	597,200
Haut-Ogooué	Franceville	14,111	36,547	134,500
Moyen-Ogooué	Lambaréné	7,156	18,535	54,600
Ngounié	Mouila	14,575	37,750	100,300
Nyanga	Tchibanga	8,218	21,285	50,800
Ogooué-Ivindo	Makokou	17,790	46,075	63,000
Ogooué-Lolo	Koulamoutou	9,799	25,380	56,600
Ogooué-Maritime	Port-Gentil	8,838	22,890	126,200
Woleu-Ntem	Oyem	14,851	38,465	125,400
TOTAL		103,347[2]	267,667	1,308,600

Demography

Population (2003): 1,329,000.
Density (2003): persons per sq mi 12.9, persons per sq km 5.0.
Urban-rural (1998): urban 46.9%; rural 53.1%.
Sex distribution (2002)[3]: male 49.57%; female 50.43%.
Age breakdown (2002)[3]: under 15, 42.4%; 15–29, 26.1%; 30–44, 16.6%; 45–59, 8.7%; 60–74, 4.8%; 75 and over, 1.4%.
Population projection: (2010) 1,509,000; (2020) 1,781,000.
Doubling time: 28 years.
Ethnic composition (2000): Fang 28.6%; Punu 10.2%; Nzebi 8.9%; French 6.7%; Mpongwe 4.1%.
Religious affiliation (2000): Christian 90.6%, of which Roman Catholic 56.6%, Protestant 17.7%; Muslim 3.1%; traditional beliefs 1.7%.
Major cities (1993): Libreville 362,386; Port-Gentil 80,841; Franceville 30,246; Oyem 22,669; Moanda 21,921.

Vital statistics[3]

Birth rate per 1,000 population (2002): 36.7 (world avg. 21.3).
Death rate per 1,000 population (2002): 10.9 (world avg. 9.1).
Natural increase rate per 1,000 population (2002): 25.8 (world avg. 12.2).
Total fertility rate (avg. births per childbearing woman; 2002): 4.9.
Life expectancy at birth (2001): male 56.0 years; female 59.5 years.
Major causes of death per 100,000 population: n.a.; however, in the 1990s major causes of morbidity and mortality included malaria, shigellosis (infection with dysentery), tetanus, cardiovascular diseases, trypanosomiasis, and tuberculosis.

National economy

Budget (2001). Revenue: CFAF 1,190,100,000,000 (oil revenues 65.7%; taxes on international trade 17.7%; income tax 8.3%; value-added tax 5.1%; other revenues 3.2%). Expenditures: CFAF 976,200,000,000 (current expenditure 81.0%, of which service on public debt 31.0%, wages and salaries 21.9%, transfers 14.3%; capital expenditure 19.0%).
Public debt (external, outstanding; 2000): U.S.$3,512,000,000.
Tourism (2001): receipts from visitors U.S.$7,000,000; expenditures by nationals abroad U.S.$170,000,000.
Production (metric tons except as noted). Agriculture, forestry, fishing (2002): plantains 270,000, sugarcane 235,000, cassava 230,000, yams 155,000, taro 59,000, oil palm fruit 32,000, corn (maize) 26,000, peanuts (groundnuts) 20,000, natural rubber 11,000, cacao beans 600; livestock (number of live animals) 212,000 pigs, 195,000 sheep; roundwood (2001) 3,101,740 cu m; fish catch (2000) 48,028. Mining and quarrying (2001): manganese ore 1,790,000; gold (2000) 70 kg[4]. Manufacturing (1995): fuel oil 295,000; diesel and gas oil 274,000; cement 130,000; kerosene 88,000; wheat flour 27,000; refined sugar 15,000; beer 816,419 hectolitres; soft drinks 415,613 hectolitres; plywood 52,500,000 cu m; textiles are also significant. Energy production (consumption): electricity (kW-hr; 2000) 1,129,000,000 (1,129,000,000); crude petroleum (barrels; 2001) 110,230,000 ([1999] 6,000,000); petroleum products (metric tons; 2000) 593,400 (590,000); natural gas (cu m; 1999) 816,000,000 (816,000,000).
Population economically active (2000): total 555,000; activity rate of total population 44.1% (participation rates [1985] ages 15–64, 68.2%; female 44.5%; unemployed [1996] 20%).

Price and earnings indexes (1995 = 100)

	1996	1997	1998	1999	2000	2001
Consumer price index	100.7	104.7	108.4	107.7	108.3	110.5
Earnings index	103.6	102.5	101.2	…	…	…

Gross national product (2001): U.S.$4,000,000,000 (U.S.$3,160 per capita).

Structure of gross domestic product and labour force

	2001		1993	
	in value CFAF '000,000	% of total value	labour force	% of labour force
Agriculture, forestry, fishing	234,400	6.9	156,000[5]	41.6
Mining	1,481,200	43.7		
Manufacturing	173,500	5.1	43,000[5]	11.5
Construction	62,400	1.8		
Public utilities	35,000	1.0		
Transp. and commun.	157,400	4.6		
Trade	244,900	7.2	115,000[5]	30.7
Finance	19,600	0.6		
Services	384,600	11.4		
Pub. admin., defense	300,300	8.9	61,000[5]	16.2
Other	294,100[6]	8.7[6]	…	…
TOTAL	3,387,400	100.0[2]	376,000[2]	100.0

Household income and expenditure. Average household size (2000) 6.1; income per household: n.a.; sources of income: n.a.; expenditure: n.a.
Land use (1994): forested 77.2%; meadows and pastures 18.2%; agricultural and under permanent cultivation 1.8%; other 2.8%.

Foreign trade

Balance of trade (current prices)

	1996	1997	1998	1999	2000	2001
CFAF '000,000,000	+1,149	+1,196	+439	+978	+1,796	+1,313
% of total	52.3%	51.4%	24.3%	46.6%	61.2%	51.4%

Imports (2001): CFAF 629,000,000,000 (for petroleum sector 34.6%, for mining and forestry sectors 1.7%, other unspecified 63.7%). *Major import sources* (1999): France *c.* 64%; Côte d'Ivoire *c.* 6%; U.S. *c.* 4%; Italy *c.* 3%.
Exports (2001): CFAF 1,942,000,000,000 (crude petroleum and petroleum products 77.8%, wood 12.4%, manganese ore and concentrate 6.2%). *Major export destinations* (1999): U.S. *c.* 46%; France *c.* 19%; China *c.* 8%; Netherlands Antilles *c.* 4%; South Korea *c.* 3%.

Transport and communications

Transport. Railroads (2001): route length 506 mi, 814 km; passenger-km 85,000,000[7]; metric ton-km cargo carried 503,000,000[8]. Roads (1996): total length 4,760 mi, 7,670 km (paved 8%). Vehicles (1997): passenger cars 24,750; trucks and buses 16,490. Air transport (1998): passenger-mi 515,000,000, passenger-km 829,000,000; short ton-mi cargo 76,000,000, metric ton-km cargo 111,000,000; airports (1997) 17.

Communications

Medium	date	unit	number	units per 1,000 persons
Daily newspapers	1997	circulation	33,000	30
Radio	2000	receivers	630,000	501
Television	2000	receivers	410,000	325
Telephones	2001	main lines	37,200	29
Cellular telephones	2001	subscribers	258,100	205
Personal computers	2001	units	15,000	12
Internet	2002	users	25,000	19

Education and health

Educational attainment of economically active population (1993): no formal schooling and incomplete primary education 37.7%; complete primary 32.1%; complete secondary 16.4%; postsecondary certificate or degree 13.8%. *Literacy* (1995): total population age 15 and over literate 63.2%; males literate 73.7%; females literate 53.4%.

Education (1998)

	schools	teachers	students	student/ teacher ratio
Primary	1,175	6,022	265,244	44.0
Secondary	88[9]	3,078	80,282	…
Voc., teacher tr.	11[9]		6,161	…
Higher[10]	2[9]	585	7,473	12.8

Health: physicians (1989) 448 (1 per 2,377 persons); hospital beds (1988) 5,329 (1 per 199 persons); infant mortality rate per 1,000 live births (2002) 55.8.
Food (2001): daily per capita caloric intake 2,602 (vegetable products 87%, animal products 13%); 111% of FAO recommended minimum requirement.

Military

Total active duty personnel (2002): 4,700 (army 68.1%, navy 10.6%, air force 21.3%), excluding 700 French troops. *Military expenditure as percentage of GNP* (1999): 2.4% (world 2.4%); per capita expenditure U.S.$78.

[1]Formerly pegged to the French franc and since Jan. 1, 2002, to the euro at the rate of 1 € = CFAF 655.96. [2]Detail does not add to total given because of rounding. [3]Estimate of the U.S. Bureau of Census International Data Base. [4]Excludes about 400 kg of illegally mined gold smuggled out of Gabon. Uranium mining ceased in 1999. [5]Derived values. [6]Import duties. [7]1996. [8]1995. [9]1995–96. [10]Universities only.

Internet resources for further information:
- **Afristat http://www.afristat.org**
- **Investir en Zone Franc http://www.izf.net/izf/Index.htm**

Gambia, The

Official name: The Republic of The Gambia.
Form of government: multiparty republic with one legislative house (National Assembly [53[1]]).
Head of state and government: President.
Capital: Banjul.
Official language: English.
Official religion: none.
Monetary unit: 1 dalasi (D) = 100 butut; valuation (Sept. 8, 2003) 1 U.S.$ = D 29.50; 1 £ = D 46.77.

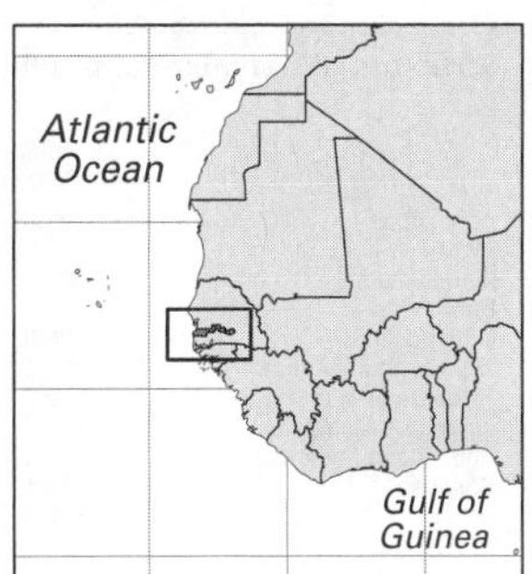

Area and population

		area		population
Divisions	**Capitals**	sq mi	sq km	2002 estimate
Basse	Basse	799	2,069	211,800
Brikama	Brikama	681	1,764	320,700
Janjanbureh	Janjanbureh	493	1,280	120,500
Kanifing[2, 3]	Kanifing	29	76	311,700
Kerewan	Kerewan	871	2,256	213,700
Kuntaur	Kuntaur	623	1,614	92,600
Mansakonko	Mansakonko	625	1,618	89,000
City				
Banjul[3]	—	5	12	57,800
TOTAL		4,127[4, 5]	10,689[5]	1,417,800

Demography

Population (2003): 1,426,000.
Density (2003)[6]: persons per sq mi 428.8, persons per sq km 165.5.
Urban-rural (2002): urban 31.3%; rural 68.7%.
Sex distribution (2002): male 49.95%; female 50.05%.
Age breakdown (2002): under 15, 45.1%; 15–29, 26.3%; 30–44, 15.6%; 45–59, 8.8%; 60–74, 3.5%; 75 and over, 0.7%.
Population projection: (2010) 1,680,000; (2020) 2,015,000.
Doubling time: 24 years.
Ethnic composition (1993): Malinke 34.1%; Fulani 16.2%; Wolof 12.6%; Diola 9.2%; Soninke 7.7%; other 20.2%.
Religious affiliation (1993): Muslim 95.0%; Christian 4.1%; traditional beliefs and other 0.9%.
Major cities/urban areas (1993): Serekunda 151,450[2]; Brikama 42,480; Banjul 42,326 (Greater Banjul 270,540[3]); Bakau 38,062[2]; Farafenni 21,142.

Vital statistics

Birth rate per 1,000 population (2002): 41.3 (world avg. 21.3).
Death rate per 1,000 population (2002): 12.6 (world avg. 9.1).
Natural increase rate per 1,000 population (2002): 28.7 (world avg. 12.2).
Total fertility rate (avg. births per childbearing woman; 2002): 5.6.
Marriage rate per 1,000 population: n.a.
Life expectancy at birth (2002): male 52.0 years; female 56.0 years.
Major causes of death per 100,000 population: n.a.; however, major infectious diseases include malaria, gastroenteritis and dysentery, pneumonia and bronchitis, measles, schistosomiasis, and whooping cough.

National economy

Budget (1999). Revenue: D 944,500,000 (tax revenue 81.9%, of which import duties and excises 29.0%, income taxes 19.4%, sales tax 6.9%; nontax revenue 11.1%; grants 7.0%). Expenditures: D 1,118,200,000 (wages and salaries 26.9%; interest payments 22.2%; goods and services 16.9%; education and culture 13.1%; health 7.9%; defense 3.6%).
Production (metric tons except as noted). Agriculture, forestry, fishing (2002): millet 84,618, peanuts (groundnuts) 71,526, paddy rice 20,452, corn (maize) 18,850, sorghum 15,209, fresh vegetables 9,000, cassava 7,500, pulses (mostly beans) 3,200, palm oil 3,000; livestock (number of live animals) 326,556 cattle, 261,965 goats, 145,593 sheep; roundwood (2001) 723,939 cu m; fish catch (2001) 34,527, of which Atlantic Ocean 32,037, inland water 2,490. Mining and quarrying: sand and gravel are excavated for local use. Manufacturing (value of production in D '000; 1982): processed food, including peanut and palm-kernel oil 62,878; beverages 10,546; textiles 3,253; chemicals and related products 1,031; nonmetals 922; printing and publishing 358; leather 150. Construction: n.a. Energy production (consumption): electricity (kW-hr; 1999) 97,000,000 (97,000,000); coal, none (none); crude petroleum, none (none); petroleum products (metric tons; 1999) none (83,000); natural gas, none (none).
Population economically active (1998): total 575,140; activity rate of total population 47.3% (participation rates: ages 15–64, 86.6%; female 40.0%; unemployed, n.a.).

Price and earnings indexes (1995 = 100)

	1994	1995	1996	1997	1998	1999	2000
Consumer price index	93.5	100.0	101.1	103.9	105.1	109.1	110.0
Earnings index	...	...	...	...	...	...	...

Tourism (1998): receipts from visitors U.S.$49,000,000; expenditures by nationals abroad (1997) U.S.$16,000,000.
Household income and expenditure. Average household size (2000) 7.9; income per household: n.a.; sources of income: n.a.; expenditure (1991)[7]: food and beverages 58.0%, clothing and footwear 17.5%, energy and water 5.4%, housing 5.1%, education, health, transportation and communications, recreation, and other 14.0%.
Public debt (external, outstanding; 2000): U.S.$425,200,000.
Gross national product (at current market prices; 2001): U.S.$400,000,000 (U.S.$320 per capita).

Structure of gross domestic product and labour force

	1999		1993	
	in value D '000,000	% of total value	labour force	% of labour force
Agriculture	1,466.5	29.6	181,752	52.6
Mining	[8]	[8]	398	0.1
Manufacturing	234.6	4.7	21,682	6.3
Construction	236.2[8]	4.8[8]	9,679	2.8
Public utilities	82.0	1.7	1,858	0.5
Transp. and commun.	717.6	14.5	14,203	4.1
Trade	735.0	14.8	54,728	15.8
Finance	299.8	6.0	2,415	0.7
Public administration	421.6	8.5	41,254	11.9
Services	204.4	4.1		
Other	557.9[9]	11.3[9]	17,412[10]	5.0[10]
TOTAL	4,955.6	100.0	345,381	100.0[4]

Land use (1994): forested 10.0%; meadows and pastures 19.0%; agricultural and under permanent cultivation 17.2%; built-on area, wasteland, and other 53.8%.

Foreign trade[11]

Balance of trade (current prices)

	1995	1996	1997	1998	1999
U.S.$'000,000	–195.9	–206.4	–247.4	–231.6	–185.5
% of total	83.9%	88.3%	93.3%	80.1%	91.5%

Imports (1998): U.S.$257,200,000 (food 37.9%, of which rice 15.8%, vegetables 5.1%; machinery and apparatus 10.6%; road vehicles 8.4%; refined petroleum 5.3%). *Major import sources* (1999): Germany 10.4%; U.K. 8.0%; France 5.0%; China 4.8%; Brazil 4.6%; Belgium 4.3%.
Exports (1998): U.S.$25,600,000 (peanuts [groundnuts] 51.6%; fish and crustaceans 9.8%; road vehicles 7.4%; vegetables 7.4%). *Major export destinations* (1999): Belgium 25.6%; U.K. 17.1%; Germany 11.0%; Spain 8.5%; Guinea 7.3%.

Transport and communications

Transport. Railroads: none. Roads (1999): total length 1,678 mi, 2,700 km (paved 35%). Vehicles (1997): passenger cars 7,267; trucks and buses (1996) 9,000. Air transport (1994): passenger-mi 31,100,000, passenger-km 50,000,000; cargo 3,107,000 short ton-mi, metric ton-km 5,000,000; airports (2000) with scheduled flights 1.

Communications

Medium	date	unit	number	units per 1,000 persons
Daily newspapers	2000	circulation	39,400	30
Radio	2000	receivers	520,000	396
Television	2000	receivers	3,940	3.0
Telephones	2001	main lines	35,000	26
Cellular telephones	2001	subscribers	43,000	32
Personal computers	2001	units	17,000	13
Internet	2001	users	18,000	14

Education and health

Educational attainment: n.a. *Literacy* (1998): total population age 15 and over literate 34.6%; males literate 41.9%; females literate 27.5%.

Education (1998–99)

	schools	teachers	students	student/ teacher ratio
Primary (age 8–14)	331	4,572	150,403	32.9
Secondary (age 15–21)[12]	85	1,936	46,769	24.2
Postsecondary	4	155[13]	1,082[13]	7.0[13]

Health (2000): physicians 105 (1 per 12,977 persons); hospital beds 1,140 (1 per 1,199 persons); infant mortality rate per 1,000 live births (2002) 76.4.
Food (2001): daily per capita caloric intake 2,300 (vegetable products 95%, animal products 5%); 97% of FAO recommended minimum requirement.

Military

Total active duty personnel (2002): 800 (army 100%). *Military expenditure as percentage of GNP* (1999): 1.3% (world 2.4%); per capita expenditure U.S.$12.

[1]Includes 5 nonelective seats. [2]Kanifing includes the urban areas of Serekunda and Bakau. [3]Kanifing and Banjul city make up Greater Banjul. [4]Detail does not add to total given because of rounding. [5]Includes inland water area of 802 sq mi (2,077 sq km). [6]Based on land area only. [7]Low-income population in Banjul and Kanifing only; weights of consumer price index components. [8]Construction includes Mining. [9]Indirect taxes. [10]Not adequately defined. [11]Imports c.i.f.; exports f.o.b. (for the most part data exclude the sometimes illegal reexport trade with nearby countries). [12]Includes teacher training and vocational. [13]1994.

Internet resources for further information:

- **Official WWW Site of The Republic of The Gambia http://www.gambia.gm**

Georgia

Official name: Sak'art'velo (Georgia).
Form of government: unitary multiparty republic with a single legislative body (Parliament [235]).
Head of state and government: President, assisted by Minister of State.
Capital: Tbilisi.
Official language: Georgian[1].
Official religion: none[2].
Monetary unit: 1 Georgian lari = 100 tetri; valuation (Sept. 8, 2003) 1 U.S.$ = 2.13 lari; 1 £ = 3.38 lari.

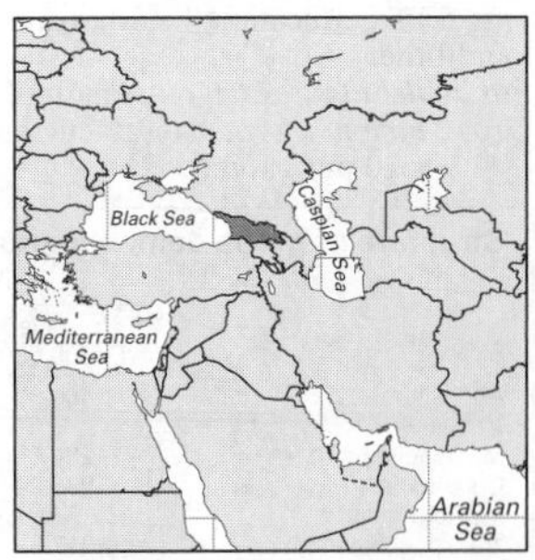

Area and population

Autonomous republics	Capitals	area sq mi	area sq km	population 1993[3] estimate
Abkhazia[4]	Sokhumi (Sukhumi)	3,320	8,600	516,600
Ajaria (Adjara)	Bat'umi	1,158	3,000	386,700
Regions				
Guria	Ozurget'i			160,800
Imereti	K'ut'aisi			788,900
Kakheti	T'elavi			464,000
Kvemo Kartli	Rust'avi			601,500
Mts'khet'a-Mtianeti	Mts'khet'a	21,892	56,700	43,800
Ragha-Lechkhumi & Kvemo Svaneti	Ambrolauri			45,400
Samegrelo & Zemo Svaneti	Zugdidi			418,100
Samtskhe-Javakheti	Akhalts'ikhe			198,800
Shida Kartli[5]	Gori			485,900
City				
Tbilisi (T'bilisi)	...	541	1,400	1,271,800
TOTAL		26,911	69,700	5,405,400[6, 7]

Demography

Population (2003): 4,934,000.
Density (2003): persons per sq mi 183.3, persons per sq km 70.8.
Urban-rural (2001): urban 57.8%; rural 42.2%.
Sex distribution (2001): male 47.81%; female 52.19%.
Age breakdown (2001): under 15, 19.6%; 15–29, 24.0%; 30–44, 22.4%; 45–59, 15.6%; 60–74, 14.4%; 75 and over, 4.0%.
Population projection: (2010) 4,815,000; (2020) 4,785,000.
Ethnic composition (2000): Georgian 57.9%; Mingrelian 9.1%; Armenian 8.1%; Russian 6.3%; Azerbaijani 5.7%; Ossetian 3.0%; Greek 1.9%; Abkhazian 1.8%; other 6.2%.
Religious affiliation (1995): Christian 46.2%, of which Georgian Orthodox 36.7%, Armenian Apostolic 5.6%, Russian Orthodox 2.7%, other Christian 1.2%; Sunni Muslim 11.0%; other (mostly nonreligious) 42.8%.
Major cities (2002): Tbilisi 1,103,500; K'ut'aisi 215,700; Rust'avi 138,200; Bat'umi 124,000; Zugdidi (1997) 105,000.

Vital statistics

Birth rate per 1,000 population (2001): 8.9 (world avg. 21.3).
Death rate per 1,000 population (2001): 9.1 (world avg. 9.1).
Natural increase rate per 1,000 population (2001): –0.2 (world avg. 12.2).
Total fertility rate (avg. births per childbearing woman; 2001): 1.4.
Marriage rate per 1,000 population (2000): 2.8.
Life expectancy at birth (2001): male 61.0 years; female 68.3 years.
Major causes of death per 100,000 population (2000): diseases of the circulatory system 656.2; malignant neoplasms (cancers) 99.7; accidents, poisoning, and violence 27.5; diseases of the respiratory system 24.4.

National economy

Budget (2002). Revenue: 928,600,000 lari (tax revenue 83.1%, of which value-added tax 40.4%, social security tax 17.4%, excise tax 11.3%; nontax revenue 8.5%; grants 8.4%). Expenditures: 920,500,000 lari (current expenditure 99.7%, of which social security and welfare 30.0%, public order 9.1%, health 4.5%, defense 4.4%, education 4.1%; capital expenditure 0.3%).
Public debt (external, outstanding; 2001): U.S.$1,314,000,000.
Population economically active (2000): total 1,748,800[8]; activity rate of total population 35.1% (participation rates [1993]: ages 16–65 [male], 16–60 [female] 55.6%; female 47.8%; unemployed [2000] 12.0%).

Price and earnings indexes (1995 = 100)

	1996	1997	1998	1999	2000	2001	2002
Consumer price index	113.5	122.1	154.4	183.9	191.3	129.8	137.0
Annual earnings index	213.2	319.2	407.2	496.0	382.2	...	...

Production (metric tons except as noted). Agriculture, forestry, fishing (2002): potatoes 414,000, wheat 306,000, corn (maize) 290,000, tomatoes 150,000, grapes 150,000, apples 65,000, tea 20,000; livestock (number of live animals) 1,180,200 cattle, 567,500 sheep; fish catch (2001) 1,910. Mining and quarrying (2001): manganese ore 98,300. Manufacturing (value of production in U.S.$'000,000; 2001)[9]: food products 139.6, basic metals 36.5, transport equipment 27.0, nonmetallic mineral products 25.3. Energy production (consumption): electricity (kW-hr; 2001) 5,700,000,000 (5,700,000,000); coal (metric tons; 2000) 7,300 ([1999] 28,000); crude petroleum (barrels; 2001) 719,000 (719,000); petroleum products (metric tons; 2000) 10,600 ([1999] 1,154,000); natural gas (cu m; 2000) 79,500,000 ([1999] 822,600,000).
Gross national product (2001): U.S.$3,100,000,000 (U.S.$590 per capita).

Structure of net material product and labour force

	2000 in value '000,000 lari	% of total value	labour force[10]	% of labour force[10]
Agriculture	1,191.0	20.0	911,200	52.1
Mining			6,300	0.4
Manufacturing	833.7	14.0	103,900	5.9
Public utilities			29,100	1.7
Construction	226.3	3.8	32,000	1.8
Transp. and commun.	857.5	14.4	71,900	4.1
Trade, restaurants	899.2	15.1	189,800	10.9
Finance, real estate	101.2	1.7	46,700	2.7
Pub. admin., defense	190.6	3.2	105,800	6.0
Services	518.1	8.7	244,700	14.0
Other	1,137.5	19.1	7,400	0.4
TOTAL	5,955.1	100.0	1,748,800	100.0

Household income and expenditure. Average household size (2000) 4.6; income per household: n.a.; sources of income (1993): wages and salaries 34.5%, benefits 21.9%, agricultural income 21.6%, other 22.0%; expenditure (1993): taxes 42.5%, retail goods 32.3%, savings 16.4%, transportation 4.2%.
Tourism (U.S.$'000,000; 2001): receipts 442; expenditures 158.

Foreign trade[11]

Balance of trade (current prices)

	1996	1997	1998	1999	2000	2001
U.S.$'000,000	–488	–704	–608	–364	–321	–364
% of total	55.1%	59.5%	64.1%	43.3%	32.7%	36.3%

Imports (2001): U.S.$684,000,000 (food [all forms] 23.8%; mineral fuels 22.7%; machinery and apparatus 18.3%; transport equipment 7.1%). *Major import sources:* Turkey 15.4%; Russia 13.3%; Azerbaijan 10.7%; Germany 10.1%; Ukraine 7.2%.
Exports (2001): U.S.$320,000,000 (beverages [including wine] 16.7%; iron and steel 15.9%; aircraft and parts 11.3%; food [all forms] 8.8%; mineral fuels 8.6%). *Major export destinations:* Russia 23.0%; Turkey 21.5%; Turkmenistan 9.0%; United Kingdom 7.2%; Switzerland 4.9%.

Transport and communications

Transport. Railroads (2001): 1,546 km; passenger-km 398,000,000; metric ton-km cargo 4,473,000,000. Roads (2001): 20,215 km (paved 93.5%). Vehicles (1999): passenger cars 247,872; trucks and buses 43,421. Air transport (2001): passenger-km 241,000,000; metric ton-km cargo 3,000,000; airports (2001) with scheduled flights 1.

Communications

Medium	date	unit	number	units per 1,000 persons
Radio	2000	receivers	2,790,000	556
Television	2000	receivers	2,380,000	474
Telephones	2002	main lines	648,500	131
Cellular telephones	2002	subscribers	503,600	102
Personal computers	2002	units	156,000	31
Internet	2002	users	73,500	15

Education and health

Education (2000–01)

	schools	teachers	students	student/ teacher ratio
Primary (age 6–9)	1,505	73,000	271,000	9.6
Secondary (age 10–16)	1,652		429,000	
Voc., teacher tr.	140	2,146[12]	32,500	...
Higher	23[12]	25,549[12]	139,000	...

Food (2001): daily per capita caloric intake 2,247 (vegetable products 83%, animal products 17%); 88% of FAO recommended minimum requirement.
Health (2001): physicians 22,000 (1 per 213 persons); hospital beds 24,520 (1 per 208 persons); infant mortality rate per 1,000 live births (2001) 14.9.

Military

Total active duty personnel (2002): 17,500 (army 49.3%, air force 7.1%, navy 10.5%, paramilitary 33.1%).[13] *Military expenditure as percentage of GNP* (1999): 1.2% (world 2.4%); per capita expenditure U.S.$33.

[1]Locally Abkhazian, in Abkhazia. [2]Special recognition is given to the Georgian Orthodox Church. [3]January 1. [4]Abkhazia has had de facto autonomy from Georgia since 1993. Its final status was unresolved in June 2003. [5]The northern 1,505-sq-mi (3,900-sq-km) area of Shida Kartli is the autonomous region of South Ossetia. In March 1997 the separatist region of South Ossetia was given this status by the Georgian government, but its final status was unresolved in June 2003. [6]Excludes population of 23,200 with unknown distribution by autonomous republic or district. [7]January 2002 (rounded, preliminary, and unadjusted) census result (excluding Abkhazia and South Ossetia) is 4.4 million; Abkhazia (2002 est.) 160,000; South Ossetia (2002 est.) 70,000. [8]Excludes informal sector, which was about 750,000 persons in 1998. [9]Excludes Abkhazia and South Ossetia. [10]Employed persons in formal sector only. [11]Imports c.i.f.; exports f.o.b. [12]1996–97. [13]About 3,000 Russian troops acting as a buffer force between Georgians and Abkhazians were in Abkhazia in June 2003.

Internet resources for further information:

- **National Bank of Georgia http://www.nbg.gov.ge**
- **Parliament of Georgia http://www.parliament.ge**

Germany

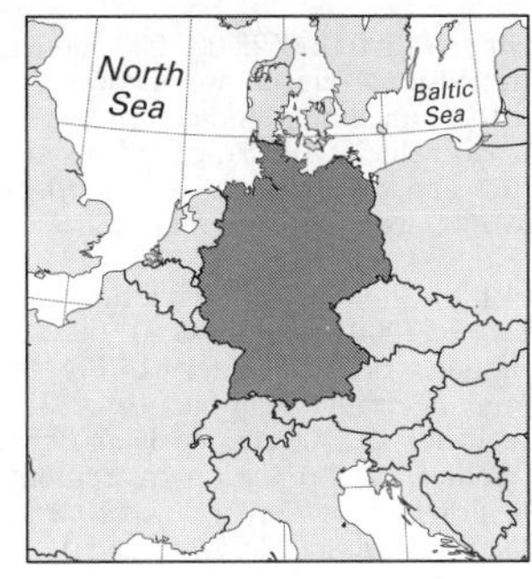

Official name: Bundesrepublik Deutschland (Federal Republic of Germany).
Form of government: federal multiparty republic with two legislative houses (Federal Council [69]; Federal Diet [603]).
Chief of state: President.
Head of government: Chancellor.
Capital: Berlin, some ministries remain in Bonn.
Official language: German.
Official religion: none.
Monetary unit: 1 euro (€) = 100 cents; valuation (Sept. 8, 2003) 1 U.S.$ = €0.90; 1 £ = €1.43[1].

Area and population

States[2] / Administrative districts	Capitals	area sq mi	area sq km	population 2002[3] estimate
Baden-Württemberg	Stuttgart	13,804[4]	35,752	10,600,900[4]
Freiburg	Freiburg im Breisgau	3,613	9,357	2,156,900
Karlsruhe	Karlsruhe	2,671	6,919	2,701,400
Stuttgart	Stuttgart	4,076	10,558	3,964,200
Tübingen	Tübingen	3,443	8,918	1,778,500
Bavaria	Munich	27,240	70,551[4]	12,329,700
Mittelfranken	Ansbach	2,798	7,246	1,698,300
Niederbayern	Landshut	3,988	10,330	1,185,500
Oberbayern	Munich	6,768	17,530	4,138,400
Oberfranken	Bayreuth	2,792	7,230	1,113,800
Oberpfalz	Regensburg	3,741	9,690	1,085,600
Schwaben	Augsburg	3,859	9,994	1,767,200
Unterfranken	Würzburg	3,294	8,532	1,340,900
Berlin	—	344	891	3,388,400
Brandenburg	Potsdam	11,381	29,476	2,593,000
Bremen	Bremen	156	404	659,700
Hamburg	Hamburg	292	755	1,726,400
Hesse	Wiesbaden	8,152	21,114[4]	6,077,800
Darmstadt	Darmstadt	2,874	7,445	3,746,900
Giessen	Giessen	2,078	5,381	1,065,000
Kassel	Kassel	3,200	8,289	1,265,900
Lower Saxony	Hannover	18,383	47,612[4]	7,956,400
Braunschweig	Braunschweig	3,126	8,097	1,666,900
Hannover	Hannover	3,493	9,046	2,163,900
Lüneburg	Lüneburg	5,986	15,505	1,683,400
Weser-Ems	Oldenburg	5,778	14,965	2,442,200
Mecklenburg-West Pomerania	Schwerin	8,946	23,170	1,759,900
North Rhine-Westphalia	Düsseldorf	13,158	34,078[4]	18,052,100[4]
Arnsberg	Arnsberg	3,090	8,002	3,803,300
Cologne (Köln)	Cologne (Köln)	2,844	7,365	4,310,000
Detmold	Detmold	2,517	6,518	2,063,200
Düsseldorf	Düsseldorf	2,042	5,289	5,255,300
Münster	Münster	2,665	6,903	2,620,200
Rhineland-Palatinate	Mainz	7,662[4]	19,846[4]	4,049,100
Saarland	Saarbrücken	992	2,570	1,066,500
Saxony	Dresden	7,109	18,413	4,384,200[4]
Chemnitz	Chemnitz	2,354	6,097	1,602,900
Dresden	Dresden	3,062	7,930	1,695,700
Leipzig	Leipzig	1,693	4,386	1,085,500
Saxony-Anhalt	Magdeburg	7,895[4]	20,447[4]	2,580,600
Dessau	Dessau	1,652	4,280	533,600
Halle	Halle	1,710	4,430	851,500
Magdeburg	Magdeburg	4,532	11,738	1,195,500
Schleswig-Holstein	Kiel	6,089	15,770	2,804,200
Thuringia	Erfurt	6,244	16,171	2,411,400
TOTAL		137,846[4]	357,021[4]	82,440,300

Demography

Population (2003): 82,604,000.
Major cities (2002; *urban agglomerations*[5]): Berlin 3,388,434[6]; Hamburg 1,726,363 (2,664,000); Munich 1,227,958 (2,291,000); Cologne 967,940 (3,050,000); Frankfurt am Main 641,076 (3,681,000); Essen 591,889 (6,531,000[7]); Dortmund 589,240 (6,531,000[7]); Stuttgart 587,152 (2,672,000); Düsseldorf 570,765 (3,233,000); Bremen 540,950 (880,000); Hannover 516,415 (1,283,000); Duisburg 512,030 (6,531,000[7]); Leipzig 493,052; Nuremberg (Nürnberg) 491,307 (1,189,000).

Other principal cities (2002)

	population		population		population
Aachen	245,778	Hamm	183,805	Münster	267,197
Augsburg	257,836	Heidelberg	141,509	Neuss	150,957
Bielefeld	323,373	Herne	174,018	Oberhausen	221,619
Bochum	390,087	Karlsruhe	279,578	Oldenburg	155,908
Bonn	306,016	Kassel	194,748	Osnabrück	164,195
Braunschweig	245,516	Kiel	232,242	Paderborn	140,869
Chemnitz	255,798	Krefeld	239,559	Potsdam	130,435
Darmstadt	138,457	Leverkusen	160,829	Recklingshausen	124,587
Dresden	478,631	Lübeck	213,496	Regensburg	127,198
Erfurt	200,126	Ludwigshafen am Rhein	162,458	Rostock	198,964
Freiburg im Breisgau	208,294	Magdeburg	229,755	Saarbrücken	182,858
Gelsenkirchen	276,740	Mainz	185,293	Solingen	165,032
Göttingen	123,822	Mannheim	308,385	Wiesbaden	271,076
Hagen	202,060	Mönchengladbach	262,963	Wuppertal	364,784
Halle	243,045	Mülheim an der Ruhr	172,332	Würzburg	129,915

Density (2003): persons per sq mi 599.2, persons per sq km 231.4.
Urban-rural (2001): urban 87.7%; rural 12.3%.
Population projection: (2010) 83,065,000; (2020) 82,144,000.
Sex distribution (2000[3]): male 48.79%; female 51.21%.
Age breakdown (2000[3]): under 15, 15.7%; 15–29, 17.6%; 30–44, 24.7%; 45–59, 19.1%; 60–74, 15.9%; 75 and over, 7.0%.
Ethnic composition (by nationality; 2000): German 88.2%; Turkish 3.4%, of which Kurdish 0.7%; Italian 1.0%; Greek 0.7%; Serb 0.6%; Russian 0.6%; Polish 0.4%; other 5.1%.
Religious affiliation (2000): Christian 75.8%, of which Protestant 35.6% (including Lutheran 33.9%), Roman Catholic 33.5%, Orthodox 0.9%, independent Christian 0.9%, other Christian 4.9%; Muslim 4.4%; Jewish 0.1%; nonreligious 17.2%; atheist 2.2%; other 0.3%.
Households (2000). Number of households 38,124,000; average household size 2.2; 1 person 36.0%, 2 persons 33.4%, 3 persons 14.7%, 4 persons 11.5%, 5 or more persons 4.4%.

Vital statistics

Birth rate per 1,000 population (2002): 8.8 (world avg. 21.3); (2001) legitimate 75.0%; illegitimate 25.0%.
Death rate per 1,000 population (2002): 10.3 (world avg. 9.1).
Natural increase rate per 1,000 population (2001): –1.5 (world avg. 12.2).
Total fertility rate (avg. births per childbearing woman; 2002): 1.4.
Marriage rate per 1,000 population (2001): 4.7.
Divorce rate per 1,000 population (2001): 2.4.
Life expectancy at birth (2002): male 75.4 years; female 81.4 years.
Major causes of death per 100,000 population (2001): diseases of the circulatory system 475.6; malignant neoplasms (cancers) 258.6; diseases of the respiratory system 58.9; accidents and other external causes 41.5.

Social indicators

Educational attainment (2000). Percentage of population age 25 and over having: primary and lower secondary 50.6%; intermediate secondary 17.9%; vocational secondary 8.7%; post-secondary and higher (all levels) 22.8%.
Quality of working life. Average workweek (2002): 37.9 hours. Annual rate per 100,000 workers (1993) for: injuries or accidents at work 4,808; deaths, including commuting accidents, 6.7. Proportion of labour force insured for damages of income loss resulting from: injury, virtually 100%; permanent disability, virtually 100%; death, virtually 100%. Average days lost to labour stoppages per 1,000 workers (2000): 0.3.
Access to services. Proportion of dwellings (2002) having: electricity, virtually 100%; piped water supply, virtually 100%; flush sewage disposal (1993) 98.4%; public fire protection, virtually 100%.
Social participation. Eligible voters participating in last (September 2002) national election 79.1%. Trade union membership in total workforce (2002): *c.* 19%. Practicing religious population (1994): 5% of Protestants and 25% of Roman Catholics "regularly" attend religious services.
Social deviance (2000). Offense rate per 100,000 population for: murder and manslaughter 3.8; sexual abuse 37.0, of which rape and forcible sexual assault 11.7, child molestation 10.2; assault and battery 153.2; theft 754.2.
Material well-being (2001[3]; median income). Households possessing: automobile 75.1%; telephone 96.4%; mobile telephone 55.7%; colour television 95.9%; washing machine 95.1%; clothes dryer 33.3%; personal computer 53.4%; dishwasher 51.3%; high-speed internet access 12.0%.

National economy

Budget (2001). Revenue: €922,472,000,000 (taxes 87.9%, loan interest 2.7%, other 9.4%). Expenditures: €972,104,000,000 (current expenditure 66.1%, of which purchase of current goods and services 22.2%, personnel costs 18.6%; capital expenditure 33.9%).
Total national debt (April 2002): €721,620,000,000.
Production (value of production in € except as noted; 2000–01). Agriculture, forestry, fishing: cereal grains 7,573,000,000, flowers and ornamental plants 1,506,000,000, vegetables 1,252,000,000, sugar beets 1,114,000,000, oilseed crops 1,106,000,000, potatoes 1,078,000,000, grapes for wine 980,000,000, tree nurseries 910,000,000, fruits 676,000,000; livestock (number of live animals; 2002) 25,957,000 pigs, 14,226,600 cattle, 2,702,000 sheep, 109,993,000 chickens; roundwood (2001) 39,483,000 cu m; fish catch (metric tons; 2000) 265,580. Mining and quarrying (metric tons; 2001): potash (potassium oxide content) 3,549,000; feldspar 500,000. Manufacturing (value added in U.S.$'000,000; 2000): motor vehicles 72,300; nonelectrical machinery and apparatus 71,800; chemicals (including pharmaceuticals) 62,900; food and beverages 44,700; electrical machinery and apparatus [excluding telecommunications, electronics] 38,600; fabricated metal products 37,000; petroleum products and coal derivatives 28,200; printing and publishing 25,400; rubber products and plastic products 23,700; base metals 22,100. Construction (newly completed buildings, sq m; 2000): residential 34,354,000; nonresidential 44,404,000.

Manufacturing enterprises (2000)

	no. of enterprises	no. of employees	wages as a % of avg. of all wages	annual value added (€'000,000)
Manufacturing	40,052	6,424,000	100.0	600,009
of which				
Machinery (electrical and nonelectrical)	7,996	1,480,000	110.0	119,652
Transport equipment	1,239	967,000	117.8	90,538
Chemical products	1,282	481,000	119.9	68,313
Fabricated metals	7,211	855,000	95.4	63,945
Food and beverages	5,448	599,000	68.2	48,538
Refined petroleum, coke	48	23,000	130.9	30,453
Publishing and printing	2,679	274,000	105.5	27,594
Rubber and plastic products	2,708	359,000	85.5	26,022
Wood and wood products	3,688	329,000	79.7	21,427
Glass and ceramics	2,203	248,000	88.1	20,847
Professional and scientific equipment	1,930	224,000	100.0	17,930
Radio and television	514	161,000	115.4	17,269

Energy production (consumption): electricity (kW-hr; 2001) 565,284,000,000 ([1999] 561,719,000,000); hard coal (metric tons; 2002) 26,364,000 ([1999] 66,268,000); lignite (metric tons; 2002) 181,416,000 ([1999] 162,961,000); crude petroleum (barrels; 2002) 30,177,000 ([1999] 782,000,000); petroleum products (metric tons; 1999) 95,683,000 (106,835,000); natural gas (cu m; 2002) 24,158,000,000 ([1999] 85,267,300,000).

Gross national product (at current market prices; 2001): U.S.$1,939,600,000,000 (U.S.$23,560 per capita).

Structure of gross domestic product and labour force

	2001			
	in value €'000,000	% of total value	labour force	% of labour force
Agriculture	23,250	1.3	942,000	2.3
Public utilities }	41,770	2.3	282,000	0.7
Mining }			139,000	0.3
Manufacturing	442,000	23.8	8,609,000	21.2
Construction	90,960	4.9	2,904,000	7.2
Transp. and commun.	116,990	6.3	2,055,000	5.1
Trade, restaurants	225,720	12.2	6,476,000	16.0
Finance, real estate }	575,370	31.0	4,351,000	10.7
Services }			7,993,000	19.7
Pub. admin., defense	404,540	21.8	3,065,000	7.6
Other	–67,000[8]	–3.6[8]	3,734,000[9]	9.2[9]
TOTAL	1,853,600	100.0	40,550,000	100.0

Household income and expenditure. Average annual income per household (1998) DM 75,144 (U.S.$42,702); sources of take-home income (1997): wages 77.6%, self-employment 12.0%, transfer payments 10.4%; expenditure: rent 24.7%, food and beverages 13.9%, transportation 13.7%, entertainment, education, and leisure 11.8%, household operations, durables, and maintenance 7.0%, clothing and footwear 5.5%.

Financial aggregates[10]

	1996	1997	1998	1999	2000	2001	2002
Exchange rate, DM per[11]:							
U.S. dollar	1.55	1.73	1.76	0.94	1.09	1.12	1.07
£	2.63	2.84	2.91	1.52	1.65	1.61	1.60
SDR	2.24	2.42	2.36	1.37	1.40	1.43	1.30
International reserves (U.S.$)							
Total (excl. gold; '000,000)	83,178	77,587	74,024	61,039	56,890	51,309	51,171
SDRs ('000,000)	1,907	1,788	1,868	1,959	1,763	1,793	1,980
Reserve pos. in IMF ('000,000)	5,468	5,946	8,023	6,419	5,460	5,901	6,695
Foreign exchange	75,083	69,853	64,133	52,661	49,667	43,615	42,495
Gold ('000,000 fine troy oz)	95.18	95.18	118.98	111.52	111.52	111.13	110.79
% world reserves	10.52	10.69	12.31	11.53	11.71	11.79	11.91
Interest and prices							
Central bank discount (%)	2.5	2.5	2.5	...	...	...	...
Govt. bond yield (%)	5.6	5.1	4.4	4.3	5.2	4.7	4.6
Industrial share prices (1995 = 100)[12]	114.1	156.3	200.0	207.3	258.7	197.3	149.0
Balance of payments (U.S.$'000,000,000)							
Balance of visible trade	+69.38	+70.12	+76.91	+70.03	+57.36	+89.20	+122.18
Imports, f.o.b.	453.20	439.90	465.71	472.69	492.42	481.32	492.84
Exports, f.o.b.	522.58	510.02	542.62	542.72	549.78	570.52	615.02
Balance of invisibles	–83.17	–79.26	–89.13	–93.74	–83.20	–88.19	–75.59
Balance of payments, current account	–13.79	–9.14	–12.22	–23.71	–25.84	+1.01	+46.59

Tourism (2001): receipts U.S.$17,225,000,000; expenditures U.S.$46,222,000,000.

Service enterprises (1991)

	no. of enter-prises	no. of employees	weekly wages as a % of all wages	annual turnover (DM '000,000)
Gas	151	37,000	...	42,228
Water	183	40,000	...	3,443
Electrical power	462	296,000	...	147,076
Transport				
air	133	57,390	...	20,270
buses	6,054	192,869	...	12,586
rail	1	416,199	...	14,697
shipping	1,449	9,076	...	...
Communications				
press	2,452	240,075	...	31,096
Postal services	17,616[13]	652,573	...	68,346
Hotels and restaurants	135,141	652,251	...	60,257
Wholesale trade	36,605[13]	1,214,000	...	1,015,984
Retail trade	152,629	2,241,000	...	605,755

Population economically active (2002): total 40,607,000; activity rate of total population 49.3% (participation rates: ages 15–64 [2001], 71.5%; female 44.3%; unemployed 10.0%).

Price and earnings indexes (1995 = 100)

	1997	1998	1999	2000	2001	2002[14]	2003
Consumer price index	103.3	104.3	104.9	107.0	109.6	111.0	112.1[14]
Hourly earnings index[15]	...	108.1	110.8	113.2	115.7	116.9	...

Land use (1994): forest 30.6%; pasture 15.1%; agriculture 19.9%; other 34.4%.

Foreign trade[16]

Balance of trade (current prices)

	1997	1998	1999	2000	2001	2002
€'000,000	+59,549	+64,919	+65,211	+59,129	+95,494	+126,244
% of total	7.0%	7.1%	6.8%	5.2%	8.1%	10.8%

Imports (2002): €522,062,000,000 (machinery and equipment 22.6%, of which televisions, telecommunications equipment, and electronic components 6.0%, office machinery and computers 5.3%; transport equipment 14.3%, of which road vehicles 10.2%; chemicals and chemical products 10.6%; crude petroleum and natural gas 6.0%; food products and beverages 5.0%; base metals 4.8%; wearing apparel 3.1%). *Major import sources:* France 9.5%; The Netherlands 8.3%; U.S. 7.7%; U.K. 6.4%; Italy 6.4%; Belgium 5.2%; Austria 4.1%; China 4.0%; Switzerland 3.7%; Japan 3.6%.

Exports (2002): €648,306,000,000 (machinery and equipment 26.3%, of which nonelectrical machinery 14.1%, televisions, telecommunications equipment, and electronic components 4.8%; transport equipment 23.4%, of which road vehicles 19.1%; chemicals and chemical products 11.8%; base metals 4.5%; medical and precision instruments and watches and clocks 4.0%). *Major export destinations:* France 10.8%; U.S. 10.3%; U.K. 8.4%; Italy 7.3%; The Netherlands 6.1%; Austria 5.1%; Belgium 4.8%; Spain 4.6%; Switzerland 4.1%; Poland 2.5%.

Transport and communications

Transport. Railroads (1998): length 51,209 mi, 82,413 km; (2001) passenger-mi 46,797,000,000, passenger-km 75,314,000,000; (2001) short ton-mi cargo 50,864,000,000, metric ton-km cargo 74,260,000,000. Roads (2002): total length 143,400 mi, 230,800 km (paved 99%). Vehicles (2002[3]): passenger cars 44,383,300; trucks and buses 2,735,600. Air transport (2001): passenger-mi 56,557,000,000, passenger-km 91,020,000,000; short ton-mi cargo 4,791,000,000, metric ton-km cargo 6,995,000,000; airports (1997) 35.

Communications

Medium	date	unit	number	units per 1,000 persons
Daily newspapers	2000	circulation	25,100,000	305
Radio	2000	receivers	77,900,000	948
Television	2000	receivers	48,200,000	586
Telephones	2002	main lines	53,720,000	650
Cellular telephones	2002	subscribers	59,200,000	755
Personal computers	2002	units	35,921,000	435
Internet	2002	users	35,000,000	428

Education and health

Health: physicians (2001) 298,000 (1 per 276 persons); hospital beds (2000) 559,651 (1 per 147 persons); infant mortality rate per 1,000 live births (2002) 4.3.

Education (1999–2000)

	schools	teachers	students	student/ teacher ratio
Primary (age 6–10)	17,503	192,659	3,488,300	17.9
Secondary (age 10–19)	19,897	421,002	5,827,714	13.8
Voc., teacher tr.	9,580	112,577	2,656,450	23.5
Higher[17]	335	152,401	1,838,456	12.1

Food (2001): daily per capita caloric intake 3,567 (vegetable products 71%, animal products 29%); 134% of FAO recommended minimum requirement.

Military

Total active duty personnel (2002): 296,000 (army 68.6%, navy 8.6%, air force 22.8%); German peacekeeping troops abroad (July 2003) 9,000; U.S. troops in Germany (2002) 68,950. *Military expenditure as percentage of GNP* (1999): 1.6% (world 2.4%); per capita expenditure U.S.$395.

[1]The Deutsche Mark (DM) was the former monetary unit; on Jan. 1, 2002, DM 1.96 = €1. [2]State names used in this table are English conventional. [3]January 1. [4]Detail does not add to total given because of rounding. [5]2000 estimate. [6]2002 city population estimate coextensive with urban agglomeration. [7]Part of the Rhine-Ruhr North urban agglomeration. [8]Less imputed bank service charges. [9]Unemployed. [10]End-of-period figures. [11]Beginning in 1999 exchange rates expressed in euros (€). [12]Period averages. [13]1990. [14]Average of first and second quarters. [15]In manufacturing, trade, transportation, and communications. [16]Imports c.i.f.; exports f.o.b. [17]1995–96.

Internet resources for further information:

- **Federal Statistical Office of Germany (in English) http://www.destatis.de/basis/e/bevoe/bev_tab4.htm**

Ghana

Official name: Republic of Ghana.
Form of government: unitary multiparty republic with one legislative house (House of Parliament [200]).
Head of state and government: President.
Capital: Accra.
Official language: English.
Official religion: none.
Monetary unit: 1 cedi (₵) = 100 pesewas; valuation (Sept. 8, 2003) 1 U.S.$ = ₵8,690; 1 £ = ₵13,778.

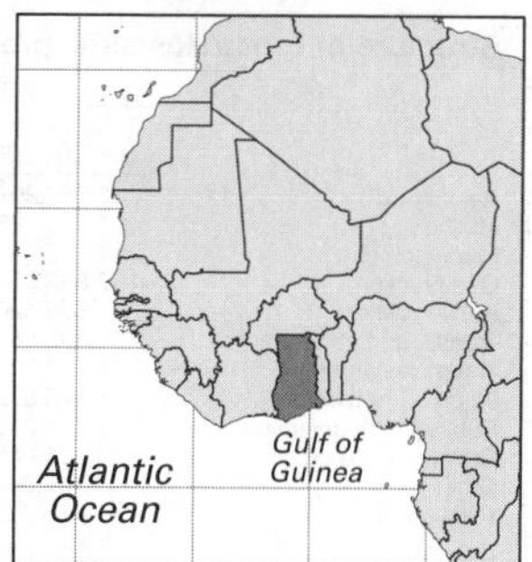

Area and population

Regions	Capitals	area sq mi	area sq km	population 2000 census
Ashanti	Kumasi	9,417	24,389	3,600,358
Brong-Ahafo	Sunyani	15,273	39,557	1,798,058
Central	Cape Coast	3,794	9,826	1,593,888
Eastern	Koforidua	7,461	19,323	2,101,650
Greater Accra	Accra	1,253	3,245	2,903,753
Northern	Tamale	27,175	70,384	1,805,428
Upper East	Bolgatanga	3,414	8,842	919,549
Upper West	Wa	7,134	18,476	575,579
Volta	Ho	7,942	20,570	1,630,254
Western	Sekondi-Takoradi	9,236	23,921	1,916,748
TOTAL		92,098[1]	238,533	18,845,265[2]

Demography

Population (2003): 20,468,000.
Density (2003): persons per sq mi 222.2, persons per sq km 85.8.
Urban-rural (2001): urban 36.4%; rural 63.6%.
Sex distribution (1999): male 49.77%; female 50.23%.
Age breakdown (2000): under 15, 41.9%; 15–29, 27.7%; 30–44, 17.4%; 45–59, 7.8%; 60–74, 4.2%; 75 and over, 1.0%.
Population projection: (2010) 22,230,000; (2020) 24,336,000.
Doubling time: 43 years.
Ethnic composition (2000): Akan 41.6%; Mossi 23.0%; Ewe 10.0%; Ga-Adangme 7.2%; Gurma 3.4%; Nzima 1.8%; Yoruba 1.6%; other 11.4%.
Religious affiliation (2000): Christian 55.4%, of which Protestant 16.6%, African Christian 14.4%, Roman Catholic 9.5%; traditional beliefs 24.4%; Muslim 19.7%; other 0.5%.
Major cities (2001[3]): Accra 1,551,200; Kumasi 610,600; Tamale 259,200; Tema 225,900; Obuasi 118,000.

Vital statistics

Birth rate per 1,000 population (2002): 26.8 (world avg. 21.3).
Death rate per 1,000 population (2002): 10.4 (world avg. 9.1).
Natural increase rate per 1,000 population (2002): 16.4 (world avg. 12.2).
Total fertility rate (avg. births per childbearing woman; 2002): 3.5.
Life expectancy at birth (2002): male 55.9 years; females 57.6 years.
Major causes of death per 100,000 population: n.a.; however, principal infectious diseases as a percentage of outpatients (1989): malaria 43.8%, respiratory infections (including tuberculosis) 8.0%, diarrheal diseases 6.7%, intestinal worms 3.1%.

National economy

Budget (2000). Revenue: ₵5,385,000,000,000 (tax revenue 82.0%, of which indirect taxes 37.5%, direct taxes 26.2%, trade taxes 18.3%; grants 10.7%; nontax revenue 7.3%). Expenditures (2000): ₵7,525,100,000,000 (current expenditure 66.9%, capital expenditure 33.1%).
Public debt (external, outstanding; 2001): U.S.$5,666,000,000.
Household income and expenditure. Average household size (1999) 4.3.
Gross national product (2001): U.S.$5,700,000,000 (U.S.$290 per capita).

Structure of gross domestic product and labour force

	2001		1999	
	in value ₵'000,000,000	% of total value	labour force[4]	% of labour force[5]
Agriculture	13,417	35.2	6,374,500	55.0
Mining	1,796	4.7	81,130	0.7
Manufacturing	3,428	9.0	1,356,030	11.7
Construction	3,347	8.8	162,260	1.4
Public utilities	1,029	2.7	23,180	0.2
Transp. and commun.	1,660	4.4	254,980	2.2
Trade, hotels	2,588	6.8	2,120,970	18.3
Finance	1,630	4.3	92,720	0.8
Pub. admin., defense	3,871	10.2	1,124,230	9.7
Services	1,353	3.5		
Other	3,953[6]	10.4[6]	—	—
TOTAL	38,071[1]	100.0	11,590,000	100.0

Production (metric tons except as noted). Agriculture, forestry, fishing (2002): roots and tubers 15,491,000 (of which cassava 9,731,000, yams 3,900,000, taro 1,860,000), bananas and plantains 2,291,000, cereals 2,162,000 (of which corn [maize] 1,407,000, sorghum 316,000, rice 280,000, millet 159,000), oil palm fruit 1,050,000, cacao 380,000, coconuts 315,000, oranges 300,000, tomatoes 200,000; livestock (number of live animals) 3,410,000 goats, 2,970,000 sheep, 1,430,000 cattle, 22,000,000 chickens; roundwood (2001) 21,979,000 cu m; fish catch (2000) 452,070. Mining and quarrying (2001): manganese (metal content) 260,000; bauxite 715,000; gold 2,137,000 troy oz; gem diamonds 700,000 carats. Manufacturing (value added in ₵; 1993): tobacco 71,474,700,000; footwear 60,350,600,000; chemical products 40,347,600,000; beverages 36,167,000,000; metal products 35,121,700,000; petroleum products 32,143,500,000; textiles 18,278,600,000; machinery and transport equipment 9,525,700,000. Energy production (consumption): electricity (kW-hr; 1999) 5,445,000,000 (5,607,000,000); coal (metric tons; 1999) none (3,000); crude petroleum (barrels; 1999) 66,000 (7,200,000); petroleum products (metric tons; 1999) 911,000 (1,493,000); natural gas, none (none).
Population economically active (1999)[4]: total 11,590,000; activity rate of total population 60.5% (participation rates: over age 15 [1984] 82.5%; female 51.1%; unemployed, n.a.).

Price and earnings indexes (1995 = 100)

	1996	1997	1998	1999	2000	2001	2002
Consumer price index	146.6	187.4	214.8	241.5	302.3	401.8	461.4
Monthly earnings index	...	...	...	...	...	...	...

Tourism (2001): receipts U.S.$448,000,000; expenditures U.S.$100,000,000.
Land use (1994): forest 42.2%; pasture 36.9%; agriculture 19.0%; other 1.9%.

Foreign trade[7]

Balance of trade (current prices)

	1995	1996	1997	1998	1999	2000
U.S.$'000,000	–257	–367	–638	–806	–1,073	–843
% of total	4.6%	10.5%	17.6%	16.2%	23.4%	18.2%

Imports (2000): U.S.$2,933,000,000 (crude and refined petroleum 18.9%, machinery and apparatus 18.8%, road vehicles 11.6%, food 10.9%). *Major import sources:* Nigeria 10.9%; U.K. 9.2%; U.S. 7.5%; Germany 7.1%; The Netherlands 6.3%; Italy 5.0%.
Exports (2000): U.S.$1,671,000,000 (gold 36.7%, cocoa beans 15.5%, aluminum 9.1%, sawn wood 4.9%). *Major export destinations:* Switzerland 23.5%; U.K. 18.9%; The Netherlands 11.2%; U.S. 5.9%; Germany 5.4%.

Transport and communications

Transport. Railroads (2000): route length 592 mi, 953 km; (1993) passenger-km 1,177,000,000; (1994) metric ton-km cargo 125,700,000. Roads (1996): total length 24,000 mi, 38,700 km (paved 40%). Vehicles (1996): passenger cars 90,000; trucks and buses 45,000. Air transport (2001)[8]: passenger-km 1,259,000,000; metric ton-km cargo 32,970,000; airports (1996) with scheduled flights 1.

Communications

Medium	date	unit	number	units per 1,000 persons
Daily newspapers	2000	circulation	273,000	14
Radio	2000	receivers	13,900,000	710
Television	2000	receivers	2,300,000	118
Telephones	2001	main lines	242,100	12
Cellular telephones	2001	subscribers	193,800	9.3
Personal computers	2001	units	70,000	3.3
Internet	2001	users	40,500	1.9

Education and health

Educational attainment (1984). Percentage of population age 25 and over having: no formal schooling 60.4%; primary education 7.1%; middle school 25.4%; secondary 3.5%; vocational and other postsecondary 2.9%; higher 0.6%. *Literacy* (2000): total population age 15 and over literate 8,070,000 (70.2%); males literate 4,520,000 (79.8%); females literate 3,550,000 (61.2%).

Education (1996–97)

	schools	teachers	students	student/ teacher ratio
Primary (age 6–12)	13,014	71,330	2,333,347	32.7
Secondary (age 13–20)	6,384	51,875	932,833	18.0
Voc., teacher tr.[9]	957	422	13,232	31.4
Higher[10]	4	1,432	25,372	17.7

Health: physicians (1994) 735 (1 per 22,970 persons); hospital beds (1994) 26,455 (1 per 638 persons); infant mortality rate per 1,000 live births (2001) 56.5.
Food (2000): daily per capita caloric intake 2,699 (vegetable products 96%, animal products 4%); 118% of FAO recommended minimum requirement.

Military

Total active duty personnel (2002): 7,000 (army 71.4%, navy 14.3%, air force 14.3%). *Military expenditure as percentage of GNP* (1999): 0.8% (world 2.4%); per capita expenditure U.S.$3.

[1]Detail does not add to total given because of rounding. [2]Alternate census total is 18,912,079; unknown if this total is final or unadjusted. [3]January 1. [4]Projected (and estimated total) figures based on Ghana Living Standards Survey (GLSS) of 8,487 labourers. [5]Percentage breakdown of GLSS. [6]Indirect taxes. [7]Imports are f.o.b. in balance of trade and c.i.f. for commodities and trading partners. [8]Ghana Airways only. [9]1989–90. [10]1999–2000; universities only.

Internet resources for further information:
- **UNDP in Ghana http://www.undp-gha.org**
- **Bank of Ghana http://www.bog.gov.gh**

Greece

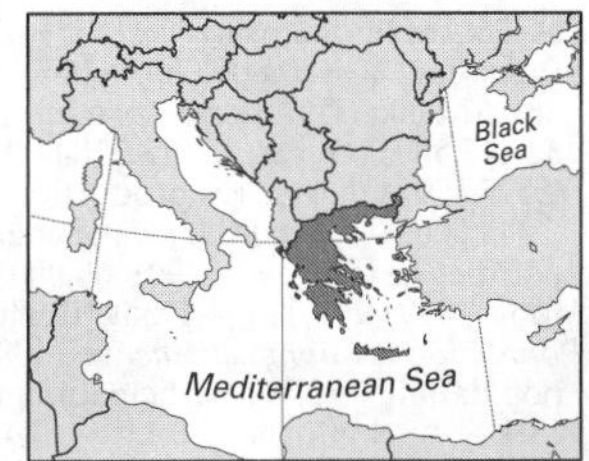

Official name: Ellinikí Dhimokratía (Hellenic Republic).
Form of government: unitary multiparty republic with one legislative house (Greek Chamber of Deputies [300]).
Chief of state: President.
Head of government: Prime Minister.
Capital: Athens.
Official language: Greek.
Official religion: Eastern Orthodox.
Monetary unit: 1 euro (€) = 100 cents; valuation (Sept. 8, 2003) 1 U.S.$ = €0.90; 1 £ = €1.43[1].

Area and population

Regions[2]	Principal cities	area sq mi	area sq km	population 2001 census
Insular				
Aegean Islands	Mitilíni	3,519	9,113	508,807
Crete	Iráklion	3,218	8,336	601,131
Ionian Islands	Kérkira	891	2,307	212,984
Mainland				
Central Greece and Euboea[3]	Lamía	8,147	21,100	829,758
Epirus	Ioánnina	3,553	9,203	353,820
Greater Athens	Athens	1,470	3,808	3,761,810
Macedonia	Thessaloníki	13,195	34,174	2,424,765
Peloponnese	Pátrai	8,278	21,440	1,155,019
Thessaly	Lárisa	5,378	13,930	753,888
Thrace	Alexandroúpolis	3,312	8,578	362,038
TOTAL		50,949[4]	131,957[4]	10,964,020[5]

Demography

Population (2003): 11,001,000.
Density (2003): persons per sq mi 215.9, persons per sq km 83.4.
Urban-rural (2002): urban 60.3%; rural 39.7%.
Sex distribution (2002): male 49.18%; female 50.82%.
Age breakdown (2002): under 15, 14.6%; 15–29, 20.7%; 30–44, 22.3%; 45–59, 18.7%; 60–74, 16.2%; 75 and over, 7.5%.
Population projection: (2010) 11,031,000; (2020) 10,878,000.
Ethnic composition (2000)[6]: Greek 90.4%; Macedonian 1.8%; Albanian 1.5%; Turkish 1.4%; Pomak 0.9%; Roma (Gypsy) 0.8%; other 3.2%.
Religious affiliation (1995): Christian 95.2%, of which Eastern Orthodox 94.0%, Roman Catholic 0.5%; Muslim 1.3%; other 3.5%.
Major cities (2001): Athens 745,514 (urban agglomeration 3,120,000); Thessaloníki 363,987 (urban agglomeration [2000] 789,000); Piraeus (Piraiévs) 175,697[7]; Pátrai 163,446; Peristérion 137,918[7]; Iráklion 137,711.

Vital statistics

Birth rate per 1,000 population (2002): 9.7 (world avg. 21.3); (1998) legitimate 96.2%; illegitimate 3.8%.
Death rate per 1,000 population (2002): 10.0 (world avg. 9.1).
Natural increase rate per 1,000 population (2002): –0.3 (world avg. 12.2).
Total fertility rate (avg. births per childbearing woman; 2002): 1.3.
Marriage rate per 1,000 population (1999): 6.4.
Life expectancy at birth (2002): male 76.2 years; female 81.3 years.
Major causes of death per 100,000 population (1999): diseases of the circulatory system 480.0; malignant neoplasms (cancers) 216.0; ill-defined conditions 66.9; diseases of the respiratory system 66.7.

National economy

Budget (2001). Revenue: Dr 20,596,049,000,000 (indirect taxes 31.9%; direct taxes 22.5%; nontax revenue 28.9%; other 16.7%). Expenditures: Dr 20,596,049,000,000 (current expenditure 86.9%, of which health and social insurance 10.3%, education and culture 6.8%, defense 6.8%; capital expenditure 13.1%).
Public debt (1997): U.S.$18,331,000,000.
Tourism (2001): receipts U.S.$9,121,000,000; expenditures U.S.$4,181,000,000.
Production (metric tons except as noted). Agriculture, forestry, fishing (2002): sugar beets 2,780,000, wheat 2,033,000, corn (maize) 2,014,000, olives 2,000,000, tomatoes 1,700,000, seed cotton 1,180,000, oranges 1,170,000, grapes 1,150,000, peaches and nectarines 930,000, potatoes 875,000, barley 268,000, apples 230,000, tobacco 123,700; livestock (number of live animals) 9,205,000 sheep, 5,023,000 goats, 938,000 pigs; roundwood (2001) 1,915,930 cu m; fish catch (2001) 192,190. Mining and quarrying: bauxite (2001) 1,931,000; crude magnesite 483,000; marble 200,000 cu m. Manufacturing (value added in Dr '000,000,000; 1999): food 573; paints, soaps, varnishes, drugs, and medicines 371; electrical machinery 287; textiles 259; cement, bricks, and tiles 227; beverages 214. Energy production (consumption): electricity (kW-hr; 1999) 49,855,000,000 (50,019,000,000); hard coal (metric tons; 1999) none (1,032,000); lignite (metric tons; 1999) 62,051,000 (60,947,000); crude petroleum (barrels; 1999) 108,000 (117,700,000); petroleum products (metric tons; 1999) 17,271,000 (16,573,000); natural gas (cu m; 1999) 2,900,000 (1,451,900,000).
Household income and expenditure. Average household size (2000) 3.0; income per household (1993–94) Dr 3,900,000 (U.S.$15,660); sources of income (1995): wages and salaries 36.6%, transfer payments 19.0%, other 44.4%; expenditure (1999): food and beverages 24.9%, transportation and communications 14.3%, cafe/hotel expenditures 9.4%, housing 8.1%, household furnishings 7.3%.
Gross national product (2000): U.S.$121,000,000,000 (U.S.$11,430 per capita).

Structure of gross domestic product and labour force

	2000 in value Dr '000,000	2000 % of total value	2001 labour force	2001 % of labour force
Agriculture	2,757,262	6.7	627,000	14.4
Mining	225,183	0.5	17,800	0.4
Manufacturing	4,192,932	10.1	557,400	12.8
Construction	2,583,398	6.2	284,800	6.5
Public utilities	665,420	1.6	34,300	0.8
Transp. and commun.	3,195,964	7.7	250,000	5.7
Trade, restaurants	8,123,638	19.6	928,200	21.3
Finance, real estate	8,446,838	20.4	321,000	7.3
Pub. admin., defense	2,644,010	6.4	897,100	20.6
Services	4,825,045	11.7		
Other	3,747,042[8]	9.1[8]	444,700[9]	10.2[9]
TOTAL	41,406,732	100.0	4,362,300	100.0

Population economically active (2001): total 4,362,300; activity rate of total population 42.1% (participation rates: ages 15–64, 56.9%; female 40.2%; unemployed 10.2%).

Price and earnings indexes (1995 = 100)

	1996	1997	1998	1999	2000	2001	2002
Consumer price index	108.2	114.7	119.6	122.8	126.6	130.9	135.6
Hourly earnings index	108.6	118.3	123.9	...	...	...	...

Land use (1994): forest 20.3%; pasture 40.7%; agriculture 27.2%; other 11.8%.

Foreign trade[10]

Balance of trade (current prices)

	1996	1997	1998	1999	2000	2001
U.S.$'000,000	–17,724	–16,771	–18,656	–18,244	–18,852	–20,444
% of total	42.6%	43.0%	46.5%	46.5%	46.2%	51.9%

Imports (2000): U.S.$29,816,000,000 (machinery and apparatus 18.6%, chemicals and chemical products 11.5%, crude petroleum 10.1%, road vehicles 9.5%, food products 9.1%, ships and boats 5.2%). *Major import sources:* Italy 12.9%; Germany 12.8%; France 7.2%; The Netherlands 5.8%; U.K. 5.0%.
Exports (2000): U.S.$10,964,000,000 (food 14.6%, of which fruits and nuts 6.0%; clothing and apparel 12.8%; refined petroleum 12.5%; machinery and apparatus 9.8%; aluminum 4.2%). *Major export destinations:* Germany 12.3%; Italy 9.2%; U.K. 6.3%; U.S. 5.8%; Turkey 5.0%.

Transport and communications

Transport. Railroads (2000): route length 2,299 km; passenger-km 1,629,000,000; metric ton-km cargo 427,000,000. Roads (1999): total length 117,000 km (paved 92%). Vehicles (2001): passenger cars 3,423,704; trucks and buses 1,112,926. Air transport (2000)[11]: passenger-km 8,856,000,000; metric ton-km cargo 127,488,000; airports (1997) 36.

Communications

Medium	date	unit	number	units per 1,000 persons
Daily newspapers	2000	circulation	1,530,000	140
Radio	2000	receivers	5,220,000	478
Television	2000	receivers	5,330,000	488
Telephones	2001	main lines	5,607,700	529
Cellular telephones	2002	subscribers	9,240,000	839
Personal computers	2001	units	860,000	81
Internet	2002	users	2,000,000	182

Education and health

Educational attainment (1991). Percentage of population age 25 and over having: no formal schooling (illiterate) 6.8%; some primary education 10.6%; completed primary 39.7%; lower secondary 10.8%; higher secondary 20.6%; some postsecondary 4.9%; completed higher 6.6%. *Literacy* (2000): total population age 15 and over literate 97.2%; males 98.6%; females 96.0%.

Education (2001–02)

	schools	teachers	students	student/teacher ratio
Primary (age 6–12)	6,074	49,842	647,041	13.0
Secondary (age 12–18)	3,244	54,123	589,669	10.8
Voc., teacher tr.	591	13,245	154,400	11.7
Higher[12]	18	10,708	163,256	15.2

Health (1999): physicians 46,124 (1 per 235 persons); hospital beds 51,404 (1 per 200 persons); infant mortality rate per 1,000 live births (2002) 5.9.
Food (2001): daily per capita caloric intake 3,754 (vegetable products 78%, animal products 22%); 150% of FAO recommended minimum requirement.

Military

Total active duty personnel (2002): 177,600 (army 70.7%, navy 10.7%, air force 18.6%). *Military expenditure as percentage of GNP* (1999): 4.7% (world 2.4%); per capita expenditure U.S.$573.

[1]The drachma (Dr) was the former monetary unit; on Jan. 1, 2002, Dr 340.75 = €1. [2]Created for planning and economic development; local administration is based on 50 departments, 4 prefectures, and one autonomous self-governing monastic region (Mount Athos). [3]Excluding Greater Athens. [4]Detail does not add to total given because of statistical discrepancy. [5]De facto figure; de jure total equals 10,215,539. [6]Government states there are no ethnic divisions in Greece. [7]Within Athens urban agglomeration. [8]Taxes less imputed bank service charges and subsidies. [9]Unemployed. [10]Imports c.i.f.; exports f.o.b. [11]Olympic Airways. [12]Universities only.

Internet resources for further information:
- **National Statistical Service of Greece http://www.statistics.gr**

Greenland

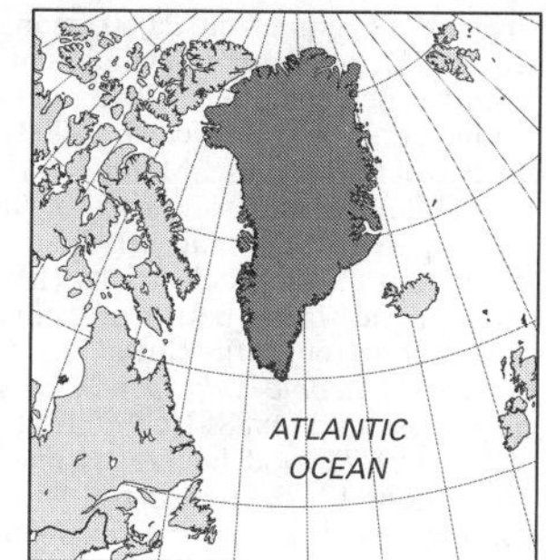

Official name: Kalaallit Nunaat (Greenlandic); Grønland (Danish) (Greenland).
Political status: integral part of the Danish realm with one legislative house (Parliament [31]).
Chief of state: Danish Monarch.
Heads of government: High Commissioner (for Denmark); Prime Minister (for Greenland).
Capital: Nuuk (Godthåb).
Official languages: Greenlandic; Danish.
Official religion: Evangelical Lutheran (Lutheran Church of Greenland).
Monetary unit: 1 Danish krone (Dkr) = 100 øre; valuation (Sept. 8, 2003) 1 U.S.$ = Dkr 6.73; 1 £ = Dkr 10.67.

Area and population

Counties / Communes	area sq mi	area sq km	population 2002[1] estimate
Avanersuaq (Nordgrønland)	...	...	
Qaanaaq (Thule)	...	...	854
Kitaa (Vestgrønland)	...	...	
Aasiaat (Egedesminde)	...	...	3,404
Ilulissat (Jakobshavn)	...	...	4,781
Ivittuut (Ivigtut)	...	...	153
Kangaatsiaq (Kangåtsiaq)	...	...	1,505
Maniitsoq (Sukkertoppen)	...	...	3,703
Nanortalik	...	...	2,516
Narsaq (Narssaq)	...	...	2,051
Nuuk (Godthåb)	...	...	14,272
Paamiut (Frederikshåb)	...	...	2,014
Qaqortoq (Julianehåb)	...	...	3,365
Qasigiannguit (Christianshåb)	...	...	1,462
Qeqertarsuaq (Godhavn)	...	...	1,067
Sisimiut (Holsteinsborg)	...	...	5,960
Upernavik	...	...	2,903
Uummannaq (Umanaq)	...	...	2,738
Tunu (Østgrønland)	...	...	
Illoqqortoormiit (Scoresbysund)	...	...	549
Ammassalik	...	...	2,979
TOTAL (ICE-FREE)	158,475	410,449	
PERMANENT ICE	677,855	1,755,637	
TOTAL	836,330	2,166,086	56,542[2]

Demography

Population (2003): 56,600.
Density[3] (2003): persons per sq mi 0.36, persons per sq km 0.14.
Urban-rural (2001[1]): urban (town) 84.3%; rural (settlement) 15.7%.
Sex distribution (2002[1]): male 53.37%; female 46.63%.
Age breakdown (2002[1]): under 15, 26.4%; 15–29, 19.4%; 30–49, 35.4%; 50–64, 13.5%; 65 and over, 5.3%.
Population projection: (2010) 57,000; (2020) 57,000.
Doubling time: 80 years.
Ethnic composition (2000): Greenland Eskimo 79.1%; Danish 13.6%; other 7.3%.
Religious affiliation (2000): Protestant 69.2%, of which Evangelical Lutheran 64.2%, Pentecostal 2.8%; other Christian 27.4%; other/nonreligious 3.4%.
Major towns (2002[1]): Nuuk (Godthåb) 13,889; Sisimiut (Holsteinsborg) 5,222; Ilulissat (Jakobshavn) 4,285; Aasiaat (Egedesminde) 3,179; Qaqortoq (Julianehåb) 3,086.

Vital statistics

Birth rate per 1,000 population (2002): 16.3 (world avg. 21.3); (1993) legitimate 29.2%; illegitimate 70.8%.
Death rate per 1,000 population (2002): 7.6 (world avg. 9.1).
Natural increase rate per 1,000 population (2002): 8.7 (world avg. 12.2).
Total fertility rate (avg. births per childbearing woman; 2002): 2.4.
Marriage rate per 1,000 population (1993): 7.1.
Divorce rate per 1,000 population (1993): 2.7.
Life expectancy at birth (2002): male 65.1 years; female 72.3 years.
Major causes of death per 100,000 population (1995): diseases of the circulatory system 214.4, of which cerebrovascular disease 68.8, ischemic heart disease 64.9; malignant neoplasms (cancers) 198.7; suicides 90.5; accidents 80.6.

National economy

Budget (2001). Revenue: Dkr 7,648,000,000 (block grant from Danish government 37.9%; income tax 30.5%; import duties 8.8%). Expenditures (2001): Dkr 7,069,000,000 (current expenditure 92.1%, of which social welfare 24.1%, culture and education 21.1%, health 11.9%, defense 3.7%; capital [development] expenditure 7.9%).
Public debt (external, outstanding; 1995): U.S.$243,000,000.
Tourism (2001): number of overnight stays at hotels 189,463, of which visitors from within Greenland 95,007, from Denmark 64,059, from the U.S. 6,622.
Production (metric tons except as noted). Fishing, animal products: fish catch (2000) 259,200 (by local boats 144,400, of which prawn 81,200, halibut 26,300, cod 3,900; by foreign boats 114,800); livestock (number of live animals; 2001) 20,394 sheep, 2,480 reindeer; animal products (value of external sales in Dkr '000; 1998) sealskins 31,044, polar bear skins 579. Mining: [4]. Manufacturing: principally handicrafts and fish processing. Energy production (consumption): electricity (kW-hr; 2001) 284,000,000 ([1999] 260,000,000); coal, none (none); crude petroleum (barrels; 1999) none (1,307,000); petroleum products (metric tons; 1999) none (176,000); natural gas, none (none).
Gross national product (1998): U.S.$1,021,000,000 (U.S.$18,205 per capita).

Structure of gross domestic product and labour force

	1998		1996	
	in value Dkr '000,000	% of total value	labour force	% of labour force
Fishing/fishing industry	...	...	6,380	25.3
Quarrying	...	...	40	0.2
Other manufacturing	...	...	...	...
Construction	...	...	...	...
Transp. and commun.	...	...	...	...
Trade, restaurants	...	...	...	...
Public utilities	...	...	...	...
Public administration, services	...	...	10,080	40.0
Other	...	...	8,670	34.5
TOTAL	7,719	100.0	25,170	100.0

Population economically active (2002): total 31,506; activity rate of total population 55.7% (participation rates: ages 15–62, 82.9%; female [1987] 43.4%; unemployed [2002] 6.5%).

Price and earnings indexes (January 1995 = 100)[5]

	1996	1997	1998	1999	2000	2001
Consumer price index	100.7	101.6	102.1	103.0	104.7	107.9
Monthly earnings index	102.4	103.5	103.0	102.9	...	...

Household income and expenditure. Average household size (1998): 2.6; income per person (1997): Dkr 144,700 (U.S.$17,700); sources of income: n.a.; expenditure (1994): food, beverages, and tobacco 41.6%, housing and energy 22.4%, transportation and communications 10.2%, recreation 6.4%.
Land use (1994): forested 0.03%; meadows and pastures 0.69%; agricultural and under permanent cultivation, none; other (principally ice cap) 99.28%.

Foreign trade

Balance of trade (current prices)

	1996	1997	1998	1999	2000	2001
Dkr '000,000	–578	–688	–1,038	–924	–742	–215
% of total	11.9%	15.1%	23.4%	19.3%	14.4%	4.6%

Imports (2001): Dkr 2,466,000,000 (food, beverages, and tobacco products 17.3%; mineral fuels 16.6%; goods for construction industry 9.2%; machinery 7.0%; transport equipment 3.6%; unspecified 10.7%). *Major import sources* (2000): Denmark 72.8%; Norway 8.9%; Japan 2.6%; Germany 2.4%; Sweden 1.8%.
Exports (2001): Dkr 2,251,000,000 (marine products 87.2%, of which shrimp 54.8%, crab 11.4%). *Major export destinations* (2000): Denmark 86.0%; Japan 6.6%; U.S. 4.7%; Thailand 1.4%.

Transport and communications

Transport. Railroads: none. Roads (1998): total length 93 mi, 150 km (paved 60%). Vehicles (2001): passenger cars 2,485; trucks and buses 1,483. Air transport (1998)[6]: passenger-mi 103,769,000, passenger-km 167,000,000; short ton-mi cargo, n.a.; metric ton-km cargo, n.a.; airports (1998) with scheduled flights 18.

Communications

Medium	date	unit	number	units per 1,000 persons
Daily newspapers	1996	circulation	1,000	18
Radio	1997	receivers	27,000	482
Television	1997	receivers	22,000	393
Telephones	2001	main lines	26,200	467
Cellular telephones	2001	subscribers	16,700	299
Internet	2000	users	20,000	357

Education and health

Educational attainment: n.a. *Literacy* (1999): total population age 15 and over literate: virtually 100%.

Education (2001–02)

	schools	teachers	students	student/ teacher ratio
Primary (age 6–15) / Secondary (age 15–19) / Voc., teacher tr.	87	1,191	11,368	9.5
Higher[7]	1	14	100	7.1

Health (2001): physicians 89 (1 per 632 persons); hospital beds (1993) 465 (1 per 125 persons); infant mortality rate per 1,000 live births (2002) 17.3.

Military

Total active duty personnel. Denmark is responsible for Greenland's defense. Greenlanders are not liable for military service.

[1]January 1. [2]Includes 266 people not distributed by county. [3]Population density calculated with reference to ice-free area only. [4]Production from Greenland's first gold mine was expected to begin in late 2003 or 2004. [5]All figures denote January. [6]Greenlandair only. [7]University of Greenland only.

Internet resources for further information:
- **Greenland Home Rule http://www.gh.gl**
- **Statistics Greenland http://www.statgreen.gl**
- **Danmarks Statistik http://www.dst.dk/yearbook**

Grenada

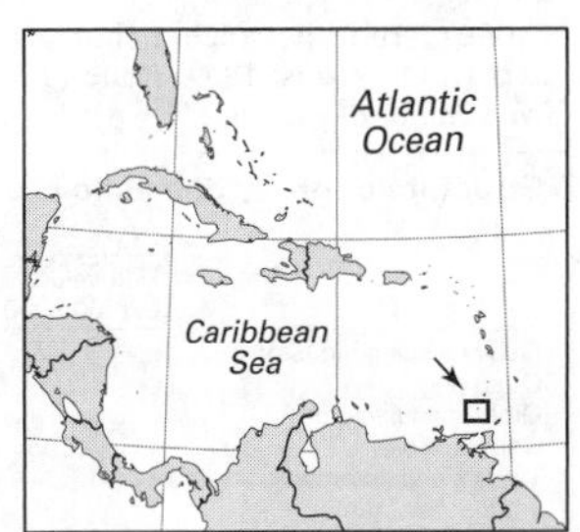

Official name: Grenada.
Form of government: constitutional monarchy with two legislative houses (Senate [13]; House of Representatives [15[1]]).
Chief of state: British Monarch represented by Governor-General.
Head of government: Prime Minister.
Capital: St. George's.
Official language: English.
Official religion: none.
Monetary unit: 1 East Caribbean dollar (EC$) = 100 cents; valuation (Sept. 8, 2003) 1 U.S.$ = EC$2.70; 1 £ = EC$4.28.

Area and population

		area		population
Local Councils	Principal towns	sq mi	sq km	2001[2] census
Carriacou	Hillsborough	10	26	6,063
Petite Martinique	...	3	8	
St. Andrew	Grenville	38	99	24,661
St. David	...	17	44	11,476
St. George	...	25[3]	65[3]	31,651
St. John	Gouyave	14	35	8,557
St. Mark	Victoria	10	25	3,955
St. Patrick	Sauteurs	16	42	10,624
Town				
St. George's	—	[3]	[3]	3,908
TOTAL		133	344	100,895

Demography

Population (2003): 102,000.
Density (2003): persons per sq mi 766.9, persons per sq km 296.5.
Urban-rural (2001)[4]: urban 38.4%; rural 61.6%.
Sex distribution (2000): male 51.70%; female 48.30%.
Age breakdown (2000): under 15, 38.1%; 15–29, 33.3%; 30–44, 17.7%; 45–59, 4.9%; 60–74, 4.7%; 75 and over, 1.3%.
Population projection: (2010) 106,000; (2020) 112,000.
Doubling time: 45 years.
Ethnic composition (2000): black 51.7%; mixed 40.0%; Indo-Pakistani 4.0%; white 0.9%; other 3.4%.
Religious affiliation (1995): Roman Catholic 57.8%; Protestant 37.6%, of which Anglican 14.4%, Pentecostal 8.3%, Seventh-day Adventist 7.0%; other 4.6%, of which Rastafarian *c.* 3.0%.
Major localities (2001): St. George's 3,908 (urban agglomeration 35,559); Gouyave 3,100[5]; Grenville 2,300[5]; Victoria 2,100[5].

Vital statistics

Birth rate per 1,000 population (2002): 23.1 (world avg. 21.3).
Death rate per 1,000 population (2002): 7.6 (world avg. 9.1).
Natural increase rate per 1,000 population (2002): 15.5 (world avg. 12.2).
Total fertility rate (avg. births per childbearing woman; 2002): 2.5.
Marriage rate per 1,000 population (1991): 4.3.
Divorce rate per 1,000 population (1991): 0.8.
Life expectancy at birth (2002): male 62.7 years; female 66.3 years.
Major causes of death per 100,000 population (1995): diseases of the circulatory system 284; malignant neoplasms (cancers) 95; diseases of the genitourinary system 33; endocrine and metabolic diseases 32.

National economy

Budget (2000). Revenue: EC$297,900,000 (tax revenue 89.1%, of which tax on international trade 51.3%, general sales taxes 17.1%, income taxes 17.5%; grants from abroad 10.9%). Expenditures: EC$365,700,000 (current expenditure 63.0%, of which wages 31.3%, transfers 13.2%, debt 11.3%; capital expenditure 37.0%).
Public debt (external, outstanding; 2001): U.S.$160,700,000.
Tourism (2001): receipts from visitors U.S.$63,000,000; expenditures by nationals abroad U.S.$8,000,000.
Gross national product (at current market prices; 2001): U.S.$400,000,000 (U.S.$3,610 per capita).

Structure of gross domestic product and labour force

	2000		1998	
	in value EC$'000,000[6]	% of total value[6]	labour force	% of labour force
Agriculture	70.0	7.7	4,794	11.7
Quarrying	4.4	0.5	58	0.1
Manufacturing	68.9	7.6	2,579	6.3
Construction	93.7	10.3	5,163	12.6
Public utilities	49.6	5.5	505	1.2
Transp. and commun.	211.3	23.4	2,043	5.0
Trade, restaurants	179.7	19.9	8,298	20.2
Finance, real estate	120.4	13.3	1,312	3.2
Pub. admin., defense	148.2	16.4	1,879	4.6
Services	29.4	3.2	6,837	16.7
Other	–70.7[7]	–7.8[7]	7,547[8]	18.4[8]
TOTAL	904.9	100.0	41,015	100.0

Production (metric tons except as noted). Agriculture, forestry, fishing (2002): sugarcane 7,200, coconuts 6,800, bananas 4,100, roots and tubers 3,200, nutmeg 2,747, grapefruit 2,000, mangoes 1,900, avocados 1,750, oranges 900, cacao 737, other crops include cotton, limes, cinnamon, cloves, and pimiento; livestock (number of live animals) 13,100 sheep, 7,100 goats, 5,850 pigs; roundwood, n.a.; fish catch (2000) 1,700. Mining and quarrying: excavation of gravel for local use. Manufacturing (value of production in EC$'000; 1997): wheat flour 13,390; soft drinks 9,798; beer 7,072; animal feed 5,852; rum 5,497; toilet paper 4,237; malt 4,192; stout 3,835; cigarettes 1,053. Energy production (consumption): electricity (kW-hr; 1999) 116,000,000 (116,000,000); coal, none (none); crude petroleum, none (none); petroleum products (metric tons; 1999) none (69,000); natural gas, none (none).
Household income and expenditure. Average household size (1991) 3.7; income per household (1988) EC$7,097 (U.S.$2,629); sources of income: n.a.; expenditure (1987): food, beverages, and tobacco 40.7%, household furnishings and operations 13.7%, housing 11.9%, transportation 9.1%.
Population economically active (1998): total 41,015; activity rate of total population *c.* 46% (participation rate: ages 15–64, *c.* 78%; female 43.5%; unemployed 15.2%).

Price and earnings indexes (1995 = 100)

	1995	1996	1997	1998	1999	2000	2001
Consumer price index	100.0	102.0	103.0	104.7	105.0	108.7	111.4
Annual earnings index	...	...	...	...	...	...	...

Land use (1994): forested 9.0%; meadows and pastures 3.0%; agricultural and under permanent cultivation 35.0%; other 53.0%.

Foreign trade[9]

Balance of trade (current prices)

	1998	1999	2000	2001	2002
U.S.$'000,000	–136.7	–109.8	–135.9	–132.8	–144.7
% of total	59.8%	42.4%	44.6%	51.1%	52.9%

Imports (2002): U.S.$233,200,000 (machinery and transport equipment 27.4%; food 16.6%; chemicals and chemical products 11.1%; mineral fuels 9.8%). *Major import sources:* United States 45.8%; Caricom 25.6%; EU 12.5%, of which United Kingdom 6.0%; Venezuela 4.6%.
Exports (2002): U.S.$59,700,000 (domestic exports 92.1%, of which electronic components 39.2%, nutmeg 21.4%, fish 7.4%, paper products 2.5%, cocoa beans 2.3%; reexports 7.9%). *Major export destinations:* United States 38.9%; EU 34.5%, of which United Kingdom 1.2%; Caricom 22.2%.

Transport and communications

Transport. Railroads: none. Roads (1999): total length 646 mi, 1,040 km (paved 61%). Vehicles (1991)[10]: passenger cars 4,739; trucks and buses 3,068. Air transport (2001)[11]: passengers 331,000; cargo 2,747 metric tons; airports (1998) with scheduled flights 2.

Communications

Medium	date	unit	number	units per 1,000 persons
Radio	1997	receivers	57,000	615
Television	1997	receivers	33,000	353
Telephones	2002	main lines	33,500	317
Cellular telephones	2002	subscribers	7,600	71
Personal computers	2001	units	13,000	130
Internet	2002	users	6,500	61

Education and health

Educational attainment (1991). Percentage of population age 25 and over having: no formal schooling 1.8%; primary education 74.9%; secondary 15.5%; higher 4.7%, of which university 2.8%; other/unknown 3.1%. *Literacy* (1995): total population age 15 and over literate 50,000 (85.0%).

Education (1996–97)

	schools	teachers	students	student/ teacher ratio
Primary (age 5–11)[12]	58	879	23,449	26.7
Secondary (age 12–16)[12]	19[13]	381[13]	7,367	19.3
Vocational	...	...	...	...
Higher[13, 14]	1	66	651	9.9

Health (1997): physicians 80 (1 per 1,236 persons); hospital beds 340 (1 per 290 persons); infant mortality rate per 1,000 live births (2002) 14.6.
Food (2001): daily per capita caloric intake 2,749 (vegetable products 76%, animal products 24%); 114% of FAO recommended minimum requirement.

Military

Total active duty personnel (1997)[15]: *Military expenditure as percentage of GNP:* n.a.; per capita expenditure, n.a.

[1]Excludes the speaker, who may be elected from outside its elected membership. [2]Preliminary noninstitutional figures. [3]St. George local council includes St. George's town. [4]Urban defined as St. George's town and St. George local council. [5]1991. [6]At current prices. [7]Less imputed bank service charges. [8]Includes 1,321 activities not adequately defined and 6,226 unemployed. [9]Imports are f.o.b. in balance of trade and c.i.f. for commodities and trading partners. [10]Registered vehicles only. [11]Point Salines airport. [12]Excludes private schools. [13]1994–95. [14]Excludes Grenada Teachers' College. [15]A 730-member police force includes an 80-member paramilitary unit and a 30-member coast guard unit.

Internet resources for further information:
- **Eastern Caribbean Central Bank http://www.eccb-centralbank.org**
- **Caricom Statistics http://www.caricom.org/CARIStats/index1.html**

Guadeloupe

Official name: Département de la Guadeloupe (Department of Guadeloupe).
Political status: overseas department (France) with two legislative houses (General Council [42]; Regional Council [41]).
Chief of state: President of France.
Heads of government: Commissioner of the Republic (for France); President of the General Council (for Guadeloupe); President of the Regional Council (for Guadeloupe).
Capital: Basse-Terre.
Official language: French.
Official religion: none.
Monetary unit: 1 euro (€) = 100 centimes; valuation (Sept. 8, 2003) 1 U.S.$ = €0.90; 1 £ = €1.43[1].

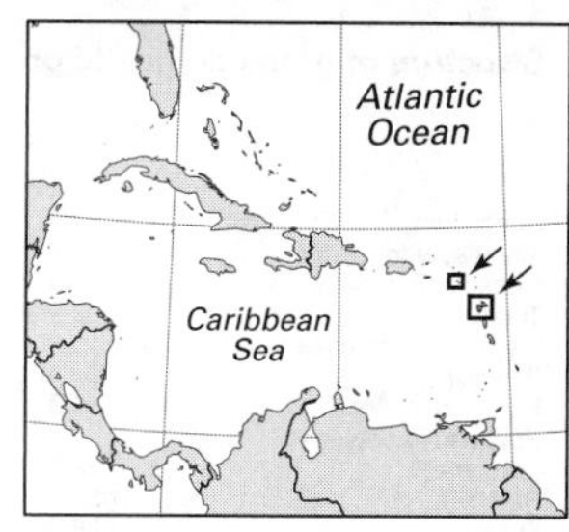

Area and population

		area		population
Arrondissements	**Capitals**	sq mi	sq km	1999 census
Basse-Terre[2]	Basse-Terre	330	855	175,691
Pointe-à-Pitre[3]	Pointe-à-Pitre	299	775	210,875
Saint-Martin–Saint-Barthélemy[4]	Marigot	29	74	35,930
TOTAL		658	1,705	422,496

Demography

Population (2003): 435,000.
Density (2003): persons per sq mi 661.1, persons per sq km 255.1.
Urban-rural (2001): urban 99.6%; rural 0.4%.
Sex distribution (1999): male 48.11%; female 51.89%.
Age breakdown (1999): under 15, 23.6%; 15–29, 22.4%; 30–44, 24.3%; 45–59, 15.7%; 60–74, 9.3%; 75 and over, 4.7%.
Population projection: (2010) 458,000; (2020) 479,000.
Doubling time: 68 years.
Ethnic composition (2000): Creole (mulatto) 76.7%; black 10.0%; Guadeloupe mestizo (French-East Asian) 10.0%; white 2.0%; other 1.3%.
Religious affiliation (1995): Roman Catholic 81.1%; Jehovah's Witness 4.8%; Protestant 4.7%; other 9.4%.
Major communes (1999): Les Abymes 63,054[5]; Saint-Martin (Marigot) 29,078; Le Gosier 25,360[5]; Pointe-à-Pitre 20,948 (urban agglomeration 171,773); Basse-Terre 12,410 (urban agglomeration 54,076).

Vital statistics

Birth rate per 1,000 population (2002): 16.9 (world avg. 21.3); (1997) legitimate 37.0%; illegitimate 63.0%.
Death rate per 1,000 population (2002): 6.6 (world avg. 9.1).
Natural increase rate per 1,000 population (2002): 10.3 (world avg. 12.2).
Total fertility rate (avg. births per childbearing woman; 2002): 2.2.
Marriage rate per 1,000 population (1997): 4.7.
Divorce rate per 1,000 population (1997): 1.3.
Life expectancy at birth (2002): male 74.0 years; female 80.5 years.
Major causes of death per 100,000 population (1996): diseases of the circulatory system 183.7; malignant neoplasms (cancers) 134.8; accidents, violence, and poisoning 68.1; diseases of the respiratory system 32.1; diseases of the digestive system 31.4; endocrine and metabolic diseases 26.2; infectious and parasitic diseases 23.8.

National economy

Budget (1998). Revenue: F 4,227,000,000 (tax revenues 69.0%, of which direct taxes 42.5%, value-added taxes 25.1%; advances, loans, and transfers 26.8%). Expenditures: F 7,874,000,000 (current expenditures 70.6%, capital [development] expenditures 10.6%; advances and loans 18.8%).
Public debt: n.a.
Tourism (2000): receipts from visitors U.S.$418,000,000; expenditures, n.a.
Production (metric tons except as noted). Agriculture, forestry, fishing (2002): sugarcane 798,072, bananas 135,000, yams 10,032, plantains 9,158, pineapples 6,975, sweet potatoes 4,221, melons 4,072, tomatoes 3,071, eggplant 180; livestock (number of live animals) 85,000 cattle, 28,000 goats; roundwood (2001) 15,300 cu m; fish catch (2001) 10,114. Mining and quarrying (2000): pumice 210,000. Manufacturing (2002): cement 284,000; raw sugar 51,726; rum 67,151 hectolitres; other products include clothing, wooden furniture and posts, and metalware. Energy production (consumption): electricity (kW-hr; 1999) 1,218,000,000 (1,218,000,000); coal, none (none); crude petroleum, none (none); petroleum products (metric tons; 1999) none (490,000); natural gas, none (none).
Population economically active (1999): total 191,362; activity rate of total population 45.3% (participation rates: ages 15–64 [1995] 73.2%; female 49.1%; unemployed [2003] 24.1%).

Price and earnings indexes (1998 = 100)

	1998	1999	2000	2001	2002	2003[6]
Consumer price index	100.0	100.4	100.4	103.0	106.6	107.5
Monthly earnings index	...	...	...	...	...	...

Gross domestic product (2000): U.S.$5,153,000,000 (U.S.$12,100 per capita).

Structure of gross domestic product and labour force

	1995		1998	
	in value F '000,000	% of total value	labour force	% of labour force
Agriculture	1,080.7	4.1	8,200	4.5
Mining, manufacturing	1,744.9	6.6	7,900	4.3
Construction	1,880.1	7.2	13,000	7.1
Public utilities	...	...	...	...
Transp. and commun.	2,156.2	8.2	4,200	2.3
Trade, hotels	6,121.6	23.4	20,700	11.4
Finance, real estate	1,043.2	4.0	3,500	1.9
Pub. admin., defense	9,926.7	37.9	43,400	23.8
Services	3,210.2	12.2	24,400	13.4
Other	–957.4[7]	–3.6[7]	56,900[8]	31.2[8]
TOTAL	26,206.2	100.0	182,200	100.0[9]

Household income and expenditure. Average household size (1990) 3.4; income per household (1988) F 105,400 (U.S.$17,700); sources of income (1988): wages and salaries 78.9%, self-employment 12.7%, transfer payments 8.4%; expenditure (1994–95): housing 26.2%, food and beverages 21.4%, transportation and communications 14.1%, household durables 6.0%, culture and leisure 4.2%.
Land use (1994): forest 39.1%; pasture 14.2%; agriculture 16.0%; other 30.7%.

Foreign trade

Balance of trade (current prices)

	1997	1998	1999	2000	2001	2002
€'000,000	–9,274[10]	–9,996[10]	–1,431	–1,666	–1,666	–1,635
% of total	86.3%	88.2%	83.4%	86.2%	83.1%	84.9%

Imports (2001): €1,835,000,000 (food and agriculture products 19.8%, consumer goods 18.6%, machinery and equipment 15.8%). *Major import sources* (1998): France 63.4%; Germany 4.4%; Italy 3.5%; Martinique 3.4%; U.S. 2.9%.
Exports (2001): €169,000,000 (food and agricultural products 58.4% [including bananas, sugar, rum, melons, eggplant, and flowers]). *Major export destinations* (1998): France 68.5%; Martinique 9.4%; Italy 4.8%; Belgium-Luxembourg 3.3%; French Guiana 3.0%.

Transport and communications

Transport. Railroads: none. Roads (1998): total length 1,988 mi, 3,415 km (paved [1986] 80%). Vehicles (1993): passenger cars 101,600; trucks and buses 37,500. Air transport (2002): passenger arrivals and departures 1,807,400; cargo handled 16,179 metric tons, cargo unloaded 5,204 metric tons; airports (1997) with scheduled flights 7.

Communications

Medium	date	unit	number	units per 1,000 persons
Daily newspapers	1995	circulation	35,000	81
Radio	1997	receivers	113,000	258
Television	1999	receivers	118,000	262
Telephones	2001	main lines	210,000	457
Cellular telephones	2002	subscribers	323,500	697
Personal computers	2001	units	100,000	217
Internet	2001	users	20,000	43

Education and health

Educational attainment (1990). Percentage of population age 25 and over having: incomplete primary, or no declaration 59.8%; primary education 14.5%; secondary 19.0%; higher 6.7%. *Literacy* (1992): total population age 15 and over literate 225,400 (90.1%); males literate 108,700 (89.7%); females literate 116,700 (90.5%).

Education (1998–99)

	schools	teachers	students	student/ teacher ratio
Primary (age 6–10)	348	2,936	40,042	13.6
Secondary (age 11–17) Vocational	85	3,392	51,491	15.2
Higher[11]	1	...	10,919	...

Health (1998): physicians 760 (1 per 550 persons); hospital beds 2,796 (1 per 149 persons); infant mortality rate per 1,000 live births (2002) 7.9.
Food (1995): daily per capita caloric intake 2,732 (vegetable products 75%, animal products 25%); 129% of FAO recommended minimum requirement.

Military

Total active duty personnel (2002): French troops in Antilles (Guadeloupe and Martinique) 4,000.

[1]French franc replaced by euro as of Jan. 1, 2002. [2]Comprises Basse-Terre 325 sq mi (842 sq km), pop. 172,693, and Îles des Saintes 5 sq mi (13 sq km), pop. 2,998. [3]Comprises Grande-Terre 230 sq mi (596 sq km), pop. 196,767; Marie-Galante 61 sq mi (158 sq km), pop. 12,488; La Désirade 8 sq mi (21 sq km), pop. 1,620; and the uninhabited Îles de la Petite-Terre. [4]Comprises the French part of Saint-Martin 21 sq mi (53 sq km), pop. 29,078; Saint-Barthélemy 8 sq mi (21 sq km), pop. 6,852; and the small, uninhabited island of Tintamarre. [5]Within Pointe-à-Pitre urban agglomeration. [6]June. [7]Less imputed bank service charges. [8]Includes 55,900 unemployed. [9]Detail does not add to total given because of rounding. [10]In millions of French francs (F). [11]University of Antilles-French Guiana, Guadeloupe campus.

Internet resources for further information:

- **INSEE Guadeloupe**
  http://www.insee.fr/fr/insee_regions/guadeloupe/home/home_page.asp

Guam

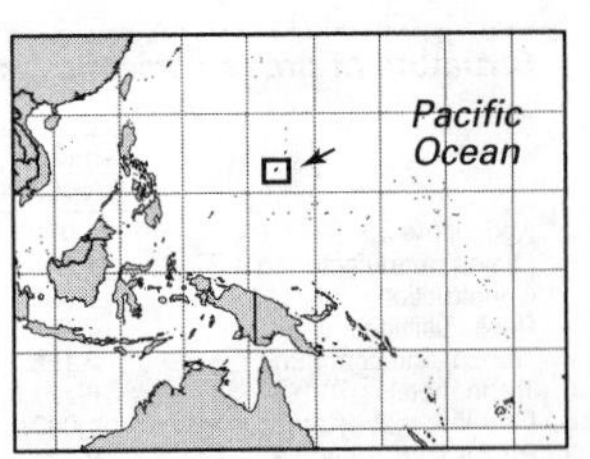

Official name: Teritorion Guam (Chamorro); Territory of Guam (English).
Political status: self-governing, organized, unincorporated territory of the United States with one legislative house (Guam Legislature [15]).
Chief of state: President of the United States.
Head of government: Governor.
Capital: Hagåtña (Agana).
Official languages: Chamorro; English.
Official religion: none.
Monetary unit: 1 United States dollar (U.S.$) = 100 cents; valuation (Sept. 8, 2003) 1 U.S.$ = £0.63.

Area and population	area		population[1]
			2000
Election Districts	sq mi	sq km	census
Agat	11	29	5,656
Asan	6	16	2,090
Barrigada	9	23	8,652
Chalan Pago-Ordot	6	16	5,923
Dededo	30	78	42,980
Hagåtña (Agana)	1	3	1,100
Hagåtña Heights	1	3	3,940
Inarajan	19	49	3,052
Mangilao	10	26	13,313
Merizo	6	16	2,163
Mongmong-Toto-Maite	2	5	5,845
Piti	7	18	1,666
Santa Rita	16	42	7,500
Sinajana	1	3	2,853
Talofofo	17	44	3,215
Tamuning	6	16	18,012
Umatac	6	16	887
Yigo	35	91	19,474
Yona	20	52	6,484
TOTAL	209[2]	541[2, 3]	154,805

Demography

Population (2003): 163,000.
Density (2003)[2]: persons per sq mi 751.2, persons per sq km 290.6.
Urban-rural (2002): urban 40.0%; rural 60.0%.
Sex distribution (2000): male 51.15%; female 48.85%.
Age breakdown (2000): under 15, 30.5%; 15–34, 32.4%; 35–59, 28.9%; 60–74, 6.7%; 75 and over, 1.5%.
Population projection: (2010) 180,000; (2020) 204,000.
Doubling time: 32 years.
Ethnic composition (2000): Pacific Islander 44.6%, of which Chamorro 37.0%; Asian 32.5%, of which Filipino 26.3%, Korean 2.5%; white 6.8%; mixed 13.9%; black 1.0%; other 1.2%.
Religious affiliation (1995): Roman Catholic 74.7%; Protestant 12.8%; other Christian 2.4%; other 10.1%.
Major populated places (2000): Tamuning 10,833; Mangilao 7,794; Yigo 6,391; Astumbo 5,207; Hagåtña 1,122.

Vital statistics

Birth rate per 1,000 population (2002): 26.6 (world avg. 21.3); (2000) legitimate 45.4%; illegitimate 54.6%.
Death rate per 1,000 population (2002): 4.9 (world avg. 9.1).
Natural increase rate per 1,000 population (2002): 21.7 (world avg. 12.2).
Total fertility rate (avg. births per childbearing woman; 2002): 4.0.
Marriage rate per 1,000 population (2000): 9.7.
Divorce rate per 1,000 population (2000): 4.0.
Life expectancy at birth (2002): male 72.0 years; female 77.0 years.
Major causes of death per 100,000 population (2000): ischemic heart diseases 116.9; malignant neoplasms (cancers) 80.7; accidents, poisonings, and violence 49.1, of which suicide 18.7; cerebrovascular disease 37.5; diabetes mellitus 13.6.

National economy

Budget (2001). Revenue: U.S.$662,994,000 (local taxes 63.6%, federal contributions 27.4%, other 9.0%). Expenditures: U.S.$518,433,000 (current expenditures 91.6%, capital expenditures 8.4%).
Production. Agriculture, forestry, fishing (value of production in U.S.$'000; 2000): long beans 234, cucumbers 166, watermelons 106, pineapples 65; livestock (number of live animals [2002]) 200,000 poultry, 5,000 pigs, 680 goats; fish catch (metric tons; 2001) 507, value of aquaculture production (1996) U.S.$1,442,000. Mining and quarrying: sand and gravel. Manufacturing (value of sales in U.S.$'000; 1997): printing and publishing 40,307; food processing 24,333; stone, clay, and glass products 16,914; fabricated metal products 4,367. Construction (gross value of building and construction permits in U.S.$; 2001): residential 59,379,000; nonresidential 57,664,000. Energy production (consumption): electricity (kW-hr; 1999) 830,000,000 (830,000,000); petroleum products (metric tons; 1999) none (1,327,000).
Household income and expenditure. Average household size (2000) 3.9[4]; average annual income per household U.S.$38,983[4]; sources of income: n.a.; expenditure: n.a.
Gross domestic product (2000): U.S.$3,419,920,000 (U.S.$22,120 per capita).

Structure of gross domestic product and labour force	1995		2001	
	in value U.S.$'000,000	% of total value	labour force[5]	% of labour force[5]
Agriculture	[6]	[6]	250	0.4
Manufacturing	[6]	[6]	1,520	2.7
Construction	379.0	12.5	2,810	5.0
Trade	622.9	20.6	13,120	23.4
Transp. and commun.	[6]	[6]	4,670	8.3
Finance	[6]	[6]	2,510	4.5
Pub. admin. (local)	513.3	16.9	12,700	22.6
Pub. admin., defense (federal)	452.7	14.9	3,200	5.7
Services	486.9	16.1	15,360	27.4
Other	575.4[6]	19.0[6]	—	—
TOTAL	3,030.2	100.0	56,140	100.0

Population economically active (2001): total 64,800[7]; activity rate of total population *c.* 42% (participation rates: over age 15, 55.8%; female 45.1%; unemployed [September 2001] 13.5%).

Price and earnings indexes (1996 = 100)	1996	1997	1998	1999	2000	2001
Consumer price index	100.0	101.6	101.2	100.9	104.4	102.6
Hourly earnings index	...	...	...	...	...	...

Tourism (1999): receipts from visitors U.S.$1,908,000,000.
Land use (1998): forested 14.6%; meadows and pastures 14.5%; agricultural and under permanent cultivation 21.8%; other 49.1%.

Foreign trade

Balance of trade (current prices)	1996	1997[8]	1998[8]	1999[8]	2000	2001[8]
U.S.$'000,000	–600	–545	–480	–485	...	–442
% of total	88%	78%	73%	74%	...	78%

Imports (2001): *c.* U.S.$503,000,000[9, 10] (food products and nonalcoholic beverages *c.* 32%; leather products including footwear *c.* 20%; motor vehicles and parts *c.* 12%; clothing *c.* 8%). *Major import sources:* significantly U.S. and Japan.
Exports (2001): U.S.$60,800,000 (food products 52.2%, of which fish 51.4%; petroleum and natural gas products 6.2%; perfumes and colognes 6.0%; tobacco products 5.8%). *Major export destinations:* Japan 50.0%; Palau 9.4%; Federated States of Micronesia 9.1%; Hong Kong 7.4%; Taiwan 4.7%.

Transport and communications

Transport. Railroads: none. Roads (1999): total length 550 mi, 885 km (paved 76%). Vehicles (2001): passenger cars 64,018; trucks and buses 28,322. Air transport (2000): passenger arrivals 1,724,432; passenger departures 1,749,754; cargo loaded and unloaded 35,252 metric tons; airports with scheduled flights 1.

Communications				units per 1,000
Medium	date	unit	number	persons
Daily newspapers	1996	circulation	28,000	178
Radio	1997	receivers	221,000	1,400
Television	1997	receivers	106,000	668
Telephones	2001	main lines	71,784	455
Cellular telephones	2001	subscribers	32,600	207
Internet	2001	users	48,000	305

Education and health

Educational attainment (2000). Percentage of population age 25 and over having: no formal schooling to some secondary education 23.7%; completed secondary 31.9%; some higher 24.5%; undergraduate 15.3%; advanced degree 4.6%. *Literacy:* virtually 100%.

Education (2000–01)	schools	teachers	students	student/ teacher ratio
Primary (age 5–10)	24	1,063	17,001	16.0
Secondary (age 11–18)	11	1,010	18,217	18.0
Higher[11]	1	...	3,462	...

Health (1999): physicians 130[12] (1 per 1,169 persons); hospital beds 192[13] (1 per 792 persons); infant mortality rate per 1,000 live births (2002) 10.0.

Military

Total active duty U.S. personnel (2001): 5,974 (army 3.1%; navy 60.7%; air force 33.2%; coast guard 3.0%).

[1]Includes active-duty military personnel, U.S. Department of Defense employees, their dependents, and Guamanian nationals. [2]Total area per most recent survey including area designated as inland water equals 217 sq mi (561 sq km). [3]Detail does not add to total given because of rounding. [4]Excludes U.S. military and dependents. [5]Per December 2001 survey; employed civilian labour force only, excludes proprietors, self-employed unpaid family workers, domestic servants, and military personnel. [6]Other includes Agriculture, Manufacturing, Transportation and communications, and Finance. [7]Per September survey; excludes nonimmigrant aliens and civilians living on military reservations. [8]Estimated figures. [9]The estimated 1999 import total is based on a projection of summed figures for four months only (January, April, July, and October). [10]Excludes petroleum imports for transshipment. [11]University of Guam only. [12]Members of Guam Medical Society only. [13]Guam Memorial Hospital only.

Internet resources for further information:
- **U.S. Office of Insular Affairs http://www.pacificweb.org**

Guatemala

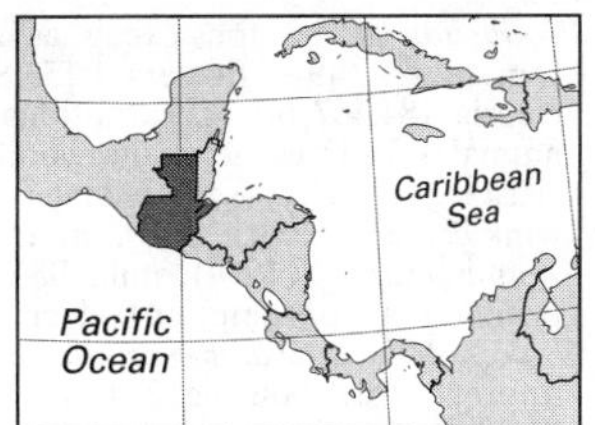

Official name: República de Guatemala (Republic of Guatemala).
Form of government: republic with one legislative house (Congress of the Republic [158]).
Head of state and government: President.
Capital: Guatemala City.
Official language: Spanish.
Official religion: none.
Monetary unit: 1 quetzal (Q) = 100 centavos; valuation (Sept. 8, 2003) 1 U.S.$ = Q 7.96; 1 £ = Q 12.61.

Area and population

Departments	Capitals	area sq mi	area sq km	population 2002 census[1]
Alta Verapaz	Cobán	3,695	9,569	776,246
Baja Verapaz	Salamá	1,198	3,104	215,915
Chimaltenango	Chimaltenango	757	1,960	446,133
Chiquimula	Chiquimula	912	2,361	302,485
El Progreso	Guastatoya (Progreso)	737	1,910	139,490
Escuintla	Escuintla	1,682	4,356	538,746
Guatemala	Guatemala City	856	2,218	2,541,581
Huehuetenango	Huehuetenango	2,813	7,285	846,544
Izabal	Puerto Barrios	3,468	8,981	314,306
Jalapa	Jalapa	792	2,050	242,926
Jutiapa	Jutiapa	1,235	3,199	389,085
Petén	Flores	12,987	33,635	366,735
Quetzaltenango	Quetzaltenango	810	2,098	624,716
Quiché	Santa Cruz del Quiché	3,927	10,172	655,510
Retalhuleu	Retalhuleu	712	1,844	241,411
Sacatepéquez	Antigua Guatemala	178	462	248,019
San Marcos	San Marcos	1,468	3,802	794,951
Santa Rosa	Cuilapa	1,134	2,936	301,370
Sololá	Sololá	405	1,050	307,661
Suchitepéquez	Mazatenango	930	2,409	403,945
Totonicapán	Totonicapán	403	1,043	339,254
Zacapa	Zacapa	1,032	2,673	200,167
TOTAL		42,130[2]	109,117	11,237,196

Demography

Population (2003): 12,347,000.
Density (2003): persons per sq mi 293.1, persons per sq km 113.2.
Urban-rural (2001): urban 39.9%; rural 60.1%.
Sex distribution (2002): male 50.31%; female 49.69%.
Age breakdown (2002): under 15, 41.8%; 15–29, 28.1%; 30–44, 15.9%; 45–59, 8.8%; 60–74, 4.2%; 75 and over, 1.2%.
Population projection: (2010) 14,584,000; (2020) 17,835,000.
Ethnic composition (2000): mestizo 63.7%; Amerindian 33.1%; black 2.0%; white 1.0%; other 0.2%.
Religious affiliation (1995): Roman Catholic 75.9%, of which Catholic/traditional syncretist 25.0%; Protestant 21.8%; other 2.3%.
Major cities (2002)[3]: Guatemala City 942,348 (urban agglomeration [2001] 3,366,000); Mixco 277,400[4]; Villa Nueva 187,700[4]; Quetzaltenango 106,700; Escuintla 65,400.

Vital statistics

Birth rate per 1,000 population (2002): 35.5 (world avg. 21.3).
Death rate per 1,000 population (2002): 6.8 (world avg. 9.1).
Natural increase rate per 1,000 population (2002): 28.7 (world avg. 12.2).
Total fertility rate (avg. births per childbearing woman; 2002): 4.7.
Marriage rate per 1,000 population (1995): 4.6.
Life expectancy at birth (2002): male 65.3 years; female 66.3 years.
Major causes of death per 100,000 population (1988): infectious and parasitic diseases 121.6; diseases of the respiratory system 110.8; perinatal causes 58.7; malnutrition 50.2; dehydration 18.5.

National economy

Budget (2000). Revenue: Q 15,554,320,000 (tax revenue 96.9%, of which VAT 45.2%, income tax 23.7%; grants 2.2%; nontax revenue 0.9%). Expenditures: Q 18,220,750,000 (current expenditures 80.6%; capital expenditures 19.4%).
Public debt (external, outstanding; 2001): U.S.$3,456,000,000.
Tourism (2001): receipts from visitors U.S.$493,000,000; expenditures by nationals abroad U.S.$196,000,000.
Production (metric tons except as noted). Agriculture, forestry, fishing (2002): sugarcane 17,489,900, corn (maize) 1,050,140, bananas 940,388, oil palm fruit 295,000, tomatoes 187,229, coffee 179,836; livestock (number of live animals) 2,540,000 cattle, 778,000 pigs, 26,000,000 chickens; roundwood (2001) 15,336,828 cu m; fish catch (2001) 14,300. Mining and quarrying (2001): gypsum 100,000; gold 4,500 kg; marble 3,800 cu m. Manufacturing (value added in Q '000,000; 1998[5]): food and beverage products 298; clothing and textiles 119; machinery and metal products 55. Energy production (consumption): electricity (kW-hr; 1999) 5,236,000,000 (4,982,000,000); crude petroleum (barrels; 1999) 8,400,000 (7,400,000); petroleum products (metric tons; 1999) 819,000 (2,637,000); natural gas (cu m; 1999) 11,000,000 (11,000,000).
Household income and expenditure. Average household size (2000) 4.5; income per household (1989) Q 4,306 (U.S.$1,529); sources of income: n.a.; expenditure (1981): food 64.4%, housing and energy 16.0%, transportation and communications 7.0%, household furnishings 5.0%, clothing 3.1%.
Gross national product (at current market prices; 2001): U.S.$19,600,000,000 (U.S.$1,680 per capita).

Structure of gross domestic product and labour force

	2000 in value Q '000,000[5]	2000 % of total value	1995 labour force	1995 % of labour force
Agriculture	1,159.1	23.0	1,798,227	58.1
Mining	27.3	0.5	3,095	0.1
Manufacturing	663.2	13.1	420,928	13.6
Construction	210.2	4.2	126,898	4.1
Public utilities	110.3	2.2	9,285	0.3
Transp. and commun.	473.2	9.4	77,377	2.5
Trade	1,239.9	24.6	225,940	7.3
Finance, real estate	499.9	9.9		
Pub. admin., defense	377.2	7.5	371,407	12.0
Services	287.7	5.7		
Other	—	—	61,901	2.0
TOTAL	5,048.0	100.0[2]	3,095,058	100.0

Population economically active (1998–99): total 4,207,946; activity rate of total population 38.9% (participation rates: ages 15–64, 53.4%; female 36.2%; unemployed [1995] 1.4%[6]).

Price and earnings indexes (1995 = 100)

	1996	1997	1998	1999	2000	2001	2002
Consumer price index	111.1	121.3	129.8	136.1	144.2	155.2	167.7
Annual earnings index[7]	121.8	136.7	151.0	...	...	...	...

Land use (1998): forested and nonarable land 58.4%; meadows and pastures 24.0%; agricultural and under permanent cultivation 17.6%.

Foreign trade[8]

Balance of trade (current prices)

	1997	1998	1999	2000	2001	2002[9]
U.S.$'000,000	–1,199	–1,583	–1,613	–1,728	–2,768	–3,086
% of total	20.4%	23.5%	25.2%	24.3%	35.9%	43.2%

Imports (2000): U.S.$4,882,000,000 (machinery and apparatus 22.1%, chemicals and chemical products 16.0%, crude and refined petroleum 11.0%, road vehicles 10.2%). *Major import sources:* United States 39.7%; Mexico 11.7%; El Salvador 6.4%; Venezuela 5.4%; Costa Rica 4.1%.
Exports (2000): U.S.$2,699,000,000 (agricultural products 52.1%, of which coffee 21.3%, sugar 7.1%, bananas 6.6%, spices 3.0%; crude petroleum 5.9%). *Major export destinations:* United States 36.1%; El Salvador 12.6%; Honduras 8.6%; Costa Rica 4.7%; Mexico 4.5%.

Transport and communications

Transport. Railroads (2002): route length 886 km[10]. Roads (1999): total length 14,118 km (paved 35%). Vehicles (1999): passenger cars 578,733; trucks and buses 53,236. Air transport (1998)[11]: passenger-km 480,000,000; metric ton-km cargo 50,000,000; airports (1996) 2.

Communications

Medium	date	unit	number	units per 1,000 persons
Daily newspapers	2000	circulation	377,000	33
Radio	2000	receivers	902,000	79
Television	2000	receivers	697,000	61
Telephones	2001	main lines	756,000	65
Cellular telephones	2001	subscribers	1,134,000	97
Personal computers	2001	units	150,000	13
Internet	2001	users	200,000	17

Education and health

Educational attainment (1994). Percentage of population age 25 and over having: no formal schooling 45.2%; incomplete primary education 20.8%; complete primary 18.0%; some secondary 4.8%; secondary 7.2%; higher 4.0%. *Literacy* (1999): total population age 15 and over literate 68.1%; males literate 75.6%; females literate 60.5%.

Education (1999)

	schools	teachers	students	student/teacher ratio
Primary (age 7–12)	17,905	47,811	1,825,088	38.2
Secondary (age 13–18)	3,118	20,543	305,818	14.9
Higher	1,462	13,105	146,291	11.2

Health (1997): physicians 9,812 (1 per 1,072 persons); hospital beds (1995) 10,974 (1 per 909 persons); infant mortality rate (2002) 39.0.
Food (2001): daily per capita caloric intake 2,203 (vegetable products 91%, animal products 9%); 101% of FAO recommended minimum.

Military

Total active duty personnel (2002): 31,400 (army 93.0%, navy 4.8%, air force 2.2%). *Military expenditure as percentage of GNP* (1999): 0.7% (world 2.4%); per capita expenditure U.S.$10.

[1]Preliminary unadjusted results. [2]Detail does not add to total given because of rounding. [3]Urban populations of municipios. [4]Within Guatemala City urban agglomeration. [5]At prices of 1958. [6]Registered unemployed; majority of economically active population is estimated to be underemployed. [7]Based on employees entitled to social security. [8]Import figures are f.o.b. in balance of trade and c.i.f. for commodities and trading partners. [9]Excludes December. [10]Mostly inoperable in 2001. [11]Aviateca Airlines only.

Internet resources for further information:
- **Banco de Guatemala (Spanish only) http://www.banguat.gob.gt**
- **Instituto Nacional de Estadistica http://www.segeplan.gob.gt/ine/index.htm**

Guernsey[1]

Official name: Bailiwick of Guernsey.
Political status: crown dependency (United Kingdom) with one legislative house (States of Deliberation [57[2, 3, 4]]).
Chief of state: British Monarch represented by Lieutenant Governor.
Head of government: [5].
Capital: St. Peter Port.
Official language: English.
Official religion: n.a.
Monetary unit: 1 Guernsey pound[6] = 100 pence; valuation (Sept. 8, 2003) 1 Guernsey pound = U.S.$1.59.

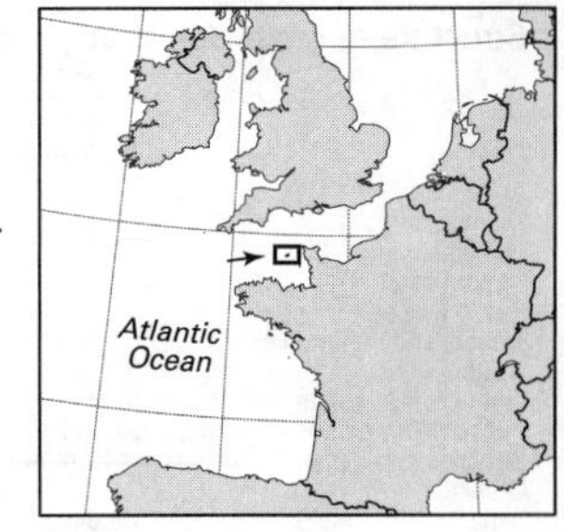

Area and population

	area		population
	sq mi	sq km	2001 census[7]
Parishes of Guernsey			
Castel	3.9	10.1	8,975
Forest	1.6	4.1	1,549
St. Andrew	1.7	4.5	2,409
St. Martin	2.8	7.3	6,267
St. Peter (St. Pierre du Bois)	2.4	6.2	2,188
St. Peter Port	2.6	6.6	16,488
St. Sampson	2.3	6.0	8,592
St. Saviour	2.4	6.3	2,696
Torteval	1.2	3.1	973
Vale	3.4	8.8	9,573
Dependencies of Guernsey			
Alderney	3.1	7.9	2,294
Brechou	0.1	0.3	0
Herm	0.5	1.3	95
Jethou	0.1	0.2	2
Lihou	0.1	0.2	0
Little Sark	0.4	1.0	} 575[8]
Sark (Great Sark)	1.6	4.2	}
TOTAL	30.2	78.1	62,676

Demography

Population (2003)[9]: 63,100.
Density (2002)[9]: persons per sq mi 2,089.4, persons per sq km 807.9.
Sex distribution (2001): male 48.72%; female 51.28%.
Age breakdown (2001): under 15, 17.2%; 15–29, 18.8%; 30–44, 23.2%; 45–59, 20.0%; 60–74, 13.4%; 75 and over, 7.4%.
Population projection[9]: (2010) 64,000; (2020) 65,000.
Population by place of birth (2001): Guernsey 64.3%; United Kingdom 27.4%; Portugal 1.9%; Jersey 0.7%; Ireland 0.7%; Alderney 0.2%; Sark 0.1%; other Europe 3.2%; other 1.5%.
Religious affiliation (*c.* 1990): Anglican 65.2%; other 34.8%.
Major cities (2001)[10]: St. Peter Port 16,488; Vale 9,573; Castel 8,975; St. Sampson 8,592; St. Martin 6,267.

Vital statistics

Birth rate per 1,000 population (2002): 9.7 (world avg. 21.3); (2000) legitimate 65.2%, illegitimate 34.8%.
Death rate per 1,000 population (2002): 9.9 (world avg. 9.1).
Natural increase rate per 1,000 population (2002): –0.2 (world avg. 12.2).
Total fertility rate (avg. births per childbearing woman; 2002): 1.3.
Marriage rate per 1,000 population (2000): 5.7.
Divorce rate per 1,000 population (2000): 2.9.
Life expectancy at birth (2002): male 76.9 years; female 83.0 years.
Major causes of death per 100,000 population (1993): diseases of the circulatory system 423.5; malignant neoplasms (cancers) 288.0; diseases of the respiratory system 133.8; endocrine and metabolic disorders 25.4; accidents, poisoning, and violence 22.0; diseases of the digestive system 11.8.

National economy

Budget (1999). Revenue: £306,991,000 (income tax 79.7%, customs duties and excise taxes 5.7%, document duties 2.7%, corporation taxes 2.1%, automobile taxes 1.9%). Expenditures: £244,418,000 (welfare 31.1%, health 26.2%, education 15.9%, administrative services 6.7%, law and order 4.9%, community services 4.1%).
Public debt: n.a.
Gross national product (at current market prices; 2000): U.S.$1,883,550,000 (U.S.$30,840 per capita).

Structure of gross domestic product and labour force

	2000		2001	
	in value £'000	% of total value	labour force	% of labour force
Horticulture, fishing	24,377	1.9	1,476	4.6
Mining	—	—	—	—
Manufacturing	38,086	3.0	1,798	5.6
Construction	61,727	4.9	2,922	9.0
Public utilities	11	11	454	1.4
Transp. and commun.	11	11	1,228	3.8
Trade, real estate	11	11	5,737	17.8
Finance[12]	500,580	39.9	7,300	22.6
Pub. admin., defense	11	11	1,967	6.1
Services	629,591	50.2	9,411	29.1
TOTAL	1,254,361	100.0[13]	32,293	100.0

Production (metric tons except as noted). Agriculture, forestry, fishing (1999): tomatoes 2,449[14], flowers 1,153,857 boxes, of which roses 287,915 boxes, freesia 184,467 boxes, carnations 161,273 boxes; livestock (number of live animals) 3,262 cattle; roundwood, n.a.; fish catch (2001)[15]: 4,414, of which crustaceans 2,169 (sea spiders and crabs 1,988), mollusks 1,456 (abalones, winkles, and conch 523), marine fish 789. Mining and quarrying: n.a. Manufacturing (1999): milk 98,830 hectolitres. Construction: n.a. Energy production (consumption): electricity (kW-hr; 1999–2000), n.a. (273,013,000).
Household income and expenditure. Average household size (2001) 2.6; expenditure (1996): housing 21.6%, food 12.7%, household goods and services 11.2%, recreation services 9.2%, transportation 8.5%, clothing and footwear 5.6%, personal goods 4.9%, energy 4.1%.
Population economically active (2001): total 32,293; activity rate of total population 51.5% (participation rates: ages 15–64, 80.4%; female 45.3%; unemployed, n.a.).

Retail price and earnings indexes (1994 = 100)

	1995	1996	1997	1998	1999	2000	2001
Consumer price index[16]	103.0	105.5	108.8	113.2	115.7	120.1	124.0
Earnings index	...	...	...	...	...	...	...

Tourism (1996): receipts U.S.$275,000,000.

Foreign trade

Imports (1998): petroleum products are important. *Major import sources* (1998): mostly United Kingdom.
Exports (1998): £93,000,000[17] (manufactured goods *c.* 51%, of which electronic components *c.* 18%, printed products *c.* 10%; agricultural products *c.* 42%, of which flowers *c.* 25%, plants *c.* 10%; fish, crustaceans, and mollusks *c.* 7%). *Major export destinations* (1998): mostly United Kingdom.

Transport and communications

Transport. Railroads: n.a. Vehicles (2000): passenger cars 37,598; trucks and buses 7,338. Air transport: (2000) passenger arrivals 884,284; (1996) freight loaded and unloaded 7,616 metric tons; airports (1999) with scheduled flights 2[18].

Communications

Medium	date	unit	number	units per 1,000 persons
Daily newspapers	1998	circulation	15,784	260
Telephones	2001	main lines	55,000	877
Cellular telephones	2001	subscribers	31,500	502
Internet	2000	users	20,000	320

Education and health

Educational attainment: n.a. *Literacy* (2002): virtually 100%.

Education (2000)

	schools	teachers	students	student/ teacher ratio
Primary (age 5–10)	22[19]	253	4,977	19.9
Secondary (age 11–16)	8[19]	295	3,900	13.2
Higher	1	...	211[20]	...

Health (1999): physicians 93 (1 per 654 persons); hospital beds, n.a.; infant mortality rate per 1,000 live births (2002) 4.9.
Food (2001)[21]: daily per capita caloric intake 3,368 (vegetable products 70%, animal products 30%); 132% of FAO recommended minimum requirement.

Military

Total active duty personnel: n.a.[22].

[1]Data excludes Alderney and Sark unless otherwise noted. [2]Elected only; excludes those serving ex-officio. [3]Headed by the Bailiff. [4]Alderney and Sark have their own parliaments. The States of Alderney has an elected president and 12 people's deputies. The Chief Please of Sark consists of 40 *tenants* or landowners and 12 people's deputies. [5]The government of Guernsey is conducted by committees appointed by the States of Deliberation. [6]Equivalent in value to pound sterling (£). [7]Preliminary. [8]Estimated figure. [9]Includes Alderney, Sark, and other dependencies. [10]Parishes. [11]Services include Trade, real estate, Public utilities, Transportation and communications, and Public administration. [12]Mostly from 79 banks (located offshore) and 581 insurance companies (352 offshore and 217 domestic). [13]Detail does not add to total given because of rounding. [14]1998. [15]Includes Jersey. [16]March. [17]Excluding administrative and financial services. [18]Includes one airport on Alderney. [19]1992. [20]1999. [21]Data for the United Kingdom. [22]The United Kingdom is responsible for defense.

Internet resources for further information:
- **The States of Guernsey**
  http://www.gov.gg

Guinea

Official name: République de Guinée (Republic of Guinea).
Form of government: unitary multiparty republic with one legislative house (National Assembly [114 seats]).
Head of state and government: President assisted by the Prime Minister.
Capital: Conakry.
Official language: French.
Official religion: none.
Monetary unit: 1 Guinean franc (GF) = 100 cauris; valuation (Sept. 8, 2003) 1 U.S.$ = GF 2,000; 1 £ = GF 3,171.

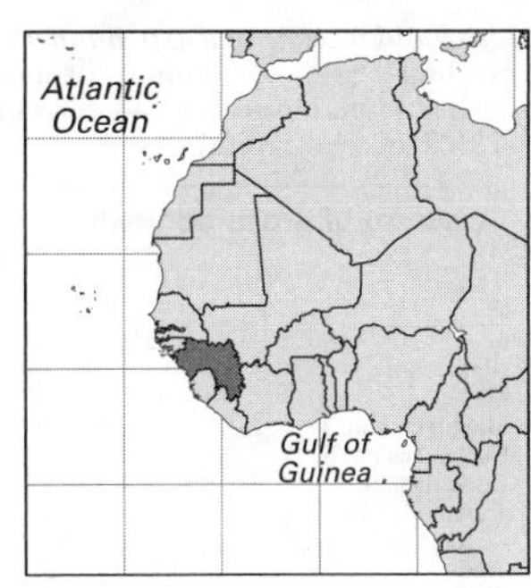

Area and population

Regions[1]	Capitals	area sq mi	area sq km	population 1983 census
Beyla	Beyla	6,738	17,452	161,347
Boffa	Boffa	1,932	5,003	141,719
Boké	Boké	3,881	10,053	225,207
Conakry	Conakry	119	308	705,280
Coyah (Dubréka)	Coyah	2,153	5,576	134,190
Dabola	Dabola	2,317	6,000	97,986
Dalaba	Dalaba	1,313	3,400	132,802
Dinguiraye	Dinguiraye	4,247	11,000	133,502
Faranah	Faranah	4,788	12,400	142,923
Forécariah	Forécariah	1,647	4,265	116,464
Fria	Fria	840	2,175	70,413
Gaoual	Gaoual	4,440	11,500	135,657
Guéckédou	Guéckédou	1,605	4,157	204,757
Kankan	Kankan	7,104	18,400	229,861
Kérouané	Kérouané	3,070	7,950	106,872
Kindia	Kindia	3,409	8,828	216,052
Kissidougou	Kissidougou	3,425	8,872	183,236
Koubia	Koubia	571	1,480	98,053
Koundara	Koundara	2,124	5,500	94,216
Kouroussa	Kouroussa	4,647	12,035	136,926
Labé	Labé	973	2,520	253,214
Lélouma	Lélouma	830	2,150	138,467
Lola	Lola	1,629	4,219	106,654
Macenta	Macenta	3,363	8,710	193,109
Mali	Mali	3,398	8,800	210,889
Mamou	Mamou	2,378	6,160	190,525
Mandiana	Mandiana	5,000	12,950	136,317
Nzérékoré	Nzérékoré	1,460	3,781	216,355
Pita	Pita	1,544	4,000	227,912
Siguiri	Siguiri	7,626	19,750	209,164
Télimélé	Télimélé	3,119	8,080	243,256
Tougué	Tougué	2,394	6,200	113,272
Yomou	Yomou	843	2,183	74,417
TOTAL		94,926[2]	245,857	5,781,014[3]

Demography

Population (2003): 8,480,000.
Density (2003): persons per sq mi 89.3, persons per sq km 34.5.
Urban-rural (2001): urban 27.9%; rural 72.1%.
Sex distribution (2002): male 49.93%; female 50.07%.
Age breakdown (2002): under 15, 44.5%; 15–29, 26.3%; 30–44, 15.5%; 45–59, 8.7%; 60–74, 4.1%; 75 and over, 0.9%.
Population projection: (2010) 9,990,000; (2020) 12,478,000.
Doubling time: 26 years.
Ethnic composition (1996): Fulani 38.6%; Malinke 23.2%; Susu 11.0%; Kissi 6.0%; Kpelle 4.6%; other 16.6%.
Religious affiliation (1996): Muslim 85.0%; Christian 10.0%; other 5.0%.
Major cities (2001): Conakry 1,565,200; Kankan 88,800; Labé 64,500; Kindia 56,000; Nzérékoré 55,000; Kissidougou 40,400.

Vital statistics

Birth rate per 1,000 population (2002): 42.8 (world avg. 21.3).
Death rate per 1,000 population (2002): 15.9 (world avg. 9.1).
Natural increase rate per 1,000 population (2002): 26.9 (world avg. 12.2).
Total fertility rate (avg. births per childbearing woman; 2002): 5.9.
Life expectancy at birth (2002): male 48.1 years; female 50.7 years.

National economy

Budget (2002). Revenue: GF 909,700,000,000 (tax revenue 76.2%, of which value-added tax 20.3%, mining sector 16.0%, tax on trade 15.3%, income tax 10.4%; grants 16.0%; nontax revenue 7.8%). Expenditures: GF 1,281,800,000 (current expenditure 61.5%, of which defense 14.4%, interest 8.2%; capital expenditure 38.5%).
Production (metric tons except as noted). Agriculture, forestry, fishing (2002): cassava 1,137,779, paddy rice 842,521, plantains 430,000, peanuts (groundnuts) 248,316, mangoes 155,812, bananas 150,000, corn (maize) 102,953, pineapples 101,961, coffee 20,500; livestock (number of live animals) 3,128,000 cattle, 1,119,000 goats, 948,500 sheep, 13,300,000 chickens; roundwood (2001) 12,140,757 cu m; fish catch (2001) 90,000. Mining and quarrying (2001): bauxite 17,950,000; alumina 550,000; gold 13,000 kg; diamonds 370,000 carats. Manufacturing (2001): cement 300,000. Energy production (consumption): electricity (kW-hr; 1999) 561,000,000 (561,000,000); petroleum products (metric tons; 1999) none (372,000).
Household income and expenditure. Average household size (2000) 4.0; average annual income per capita, n.a.; expenditure (1985): food 61.5%, health 11.2%, clothing 7.9%, housing 7.3%.
Gross national product (2001): U.S.$3,100,000,000 (U.S.$410 per capita).

Structure of gross domestic product and labour force

	2001 in value GF '000,000,000[4]	2001 % of total value[4]	1983 labour force	1983 % of labour force
Agriculture, forestry, fishing	901.2	18.3	1,423,615	78.2
Mining	801.2	16.3	12,241	0.7
Manufacturing	201.1	4.1	11,215	0.6
Construction	501.2	10.2	9,115	0.5
Public utilities	29.1	0.6	3,205	0.2
Transp. and commun.	281.3	5.7	29,496	1.6
Trade, finance	1,247.8	25.3	40,865	2.0
Pub. admin., defense	257.0	5.2	137,600	7.5
Services	495.2	10.1		
Other	207.3[5]	4.2[5]	155,679	8.5
TOTAL	4,922.4	100.0	1,823,031	100.0

Public debt (external, outstanding; 2001): U.S.$2,844,000,000.
Population economically active (2000): total 4,047,000; activity rate of total population 49.9% (participation rates: n.a.; female, n.a.; unemployed, n.a.).

Price and earnings indexes (1995 = 100)

	1997	1998	1999	2000	2001	2002
Consumer price index	104.9	110.3	116.0	123.9	130.5	134.4
Annual salary index	...	...	...	...	...	...

Tourism (2001): receipts U.S.$14,000,000; expenditures U.S.$15,000,000.
Land use (1994): forest 27.3%; pasture 43.5%; agriculture 3.3%; other 25.9%.

Foreign trade[6]

Balance of trade (current prices)

	1997	1998	1999	2000	2001	2002
U.S.$'000,000	+117.6	+121.0	+53.9	+79.3	+169.2	+50.8
% of total	10.3%	9.6%	4.4%	6.3%	13.1%	3.8%

Imports (2000): U.S.$612,400,000 (refined petroleum 24.8%, food 18.0%, machinery and apparatus 10.0%, road vehicles 8.7%). *Major import sources* (2000): Côte d'Ivoire 21.4%; France 19.8%; U.S. 7.9%; Belgium 7.7%; Japan 5.6%.
Exports (2002): U.S.$700,400,000 (bauxite 43.6%, gold 20.5%, alumina 18.3%, diamonds 4.9%, fish 4.0%, coffee 2.5%). *Major export destinations* (2000): France 33.0%; U.S. 12.8%; Spain 9.6%; Ireland 9.1%; Germany 6.1%.

Transport and communications

Transport. Railroads (2000): route length of operational lines for cargo (mostly bauxite) transport 170 mi, 274 km; passenger-km, n.a.[7]; metric ton-km cargo (1993) 710,000,000. Roads (1999): total length 30,500 km (paved 16.5%). Vehicles (1996): passenger cars 14,100; trucks and buses 21,000. Air transport (1998): passenger-km 50,000,000; metric ton-km cargo 5,000,000; airports (2000) 1.

Communications

Medium	date	unit	number	units per 1,000 persons
Daily newspapers	1988	circulation	13,000	2.0
Radio	2000	receivers	422,000	52
Television	2000	receivers	357,000	44
Telephones	2001	main lines	25,500	3.2
Cellular telephones	2001	subscribers	55,700	6.9
Personal computers	2001	units	32,000	4.0
Internet	2001	users	15,000	1.9

Education and health

Educational attainment of those age 6 and over having attended school (1983): primary 55.2%; secondary 32.7%; vocational 3.4%; higher 8.7%. *Literacy* (1995): percentage of total population age 15 and over literate 35.9%; males literate 49.9%; females literate 21.9%.

Education (1997–98)

	schools	teachers	students	student/ teacher ratio
Primary (age 7–12)	3,723	13,883	674,732	48.6
Secondary (age 13–18)	239	4,958	143,245	28.9
Voc., teacher tr.[8]	55	1,268	8,569	6.8
Higher[9, 10]	2	947	8,151	8.6

Health: physicians (1991) 920 (1 per 6,840 persons); hospital beds (1988) 3,382 (1 per 1,652 persons); infant mortality rate (2002) 94.8.
Food (2001): daily per capita caloric intake 2,362 (vegetable products 96%, animal products 4%); 102% of FAO recommended minimum requirement.

Military

Total active duty personnel (2002): 9,700 (army 87.6%, navy 4.1%, air force 8.2%). *Military expenditure as percentage of GNP* (1999): 1.6% (world 2.4%); per capita expenditure U.S.$7.

[1]Regions represent second-level administration; Guinea is divided into 7 provinces and 1 city (Conakry) at the first level of administration. [2]Detail does not add to total given because of rounding. [3]1996 rounded census total equals 7,156,000. [4]1996 prices. [5]Indirect taxes. [6]Imports f.o.b. in balance of trade and c.i.f. for commodities and trading partners. [7]Passenger service has been limited and irregular since the late 1980s. [8]1995–96. [9]1996–97. [10]Universities only.

Internet resources for further information:

- **Official site of Guinea http://www.guinee.gov.gn**

Guinea-Bissau

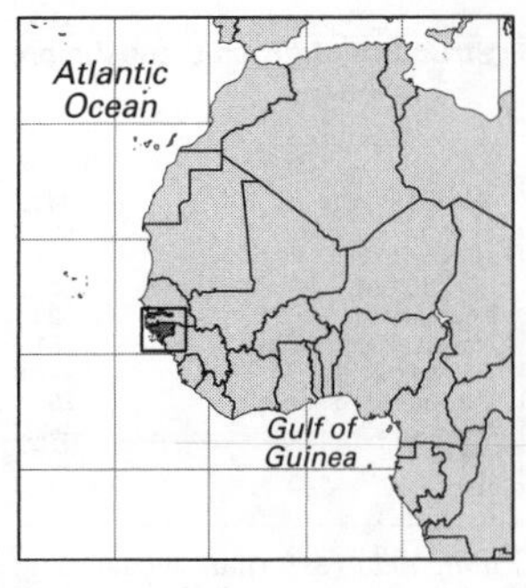

Official name: Républica da Guiné-Bissau (Republic of Guinea-Bissau).
Form of government: military regime[1] with one advisory body (National Transition Council [56]).
Head of state and government: President assisted by the Prime Minister.
Capital: Bissau.
Official language: Portuguese.
Official religion: none.
Monetary unit: 1 CFA franc[2] (CFAF) = 100 centimes; valuation (Sept. 8, 2003) 1 U.S.$ = CFAF 594.70; 1 £ = CFAF 942.93.

Area and population

		area		population
Regions	Chief towns	sq mi	sq km	1991 census
Bafatá	Bafatá	2,309	5,981	143,377
Biombo	Quinhámel	324	840	60,420
Bolama	Bolama	1,013	2,624	26,691
Cacheu	Cacheu	1,998	5,175	146,980
Gabú	Gabú	3,533	9,150	134,971
Oio	Bissorã	2,086	5,403	156,084
Quinara	Fulacunda	1,212	3,138	44,793
Tombali	Catió	1,443	3,736	72,441
Autonomous Sector				
Bissau	—	30	78	197,610
TOTAL		13,948[3]	36,125[3]	983,367

Demography

Population (2003): 1,361,000.
Density (2002)[4]: persons per sq mi 125.3, persons per sq km 48.4.
Urban-rural (2001): urban 32.4%; rural 67.6%.
Sex distribution (1997): male 48.52%; female 51.48%.
Age breakdown (1997): under 15, 42.7%; 15–29, 28.1%; 30–44, 15.4%; 45–59, 9.2%; 60–74, 3.8%; 75 and over, 0.8%.
Population projection: (2010) 1,566,000; (2020) 1,882,000.
Doubling time: 32 years.
Ethnic composition (1995): Balante 30%; Fulani 20%; Mandyako 14%; Malinke 13%; Pepel 7%; nonindigenous Cape Verdean mulatto 2%; other 14%.
Religious affiliation (2000): traditional beliefs 45.2%; Muslim 39.9%; Christian 13.2%, of which Roman Catholic 9.9%; other 1.7%.
Major cities (1997): Bissau 200,000 (urban agglomeration [2001] 292,000); Bafatá 15,000; Cacheu 14,000; Gabú 10,000.

Vital statistics

Birth rate per 1,000 population (2002): 38.8 (world avg. 21.3).
Death rate per 1,000 population (2002): 16.7 (world avg. 9.1).
Natural increase rate per 1,000 population (2002): 22.1 (world avg. 12.2).
Total fertility rate (avg. births per childbearing woman; 2002): 5.1.
Marriage rate per 1,000 population: n.a.
Divorce rate per 1,000 population: n.a.
Life expectancy at birth (2002): male 45.1 years; female 48.9 years.
Major causes of death per 100,000 population: n.a.; however, major diseases include tuberculosis of the respiratory system, whooping cough, typhoid fever, cholera, bacillary dysentery and amebiasis, malaria, pneumonia, and meningococcal infections; malnutrition is widespread.

National economy

Budget (2001). Revenue: CFAF 47,530,000,000 (foreign grants 40.0%; tax revenue 31.0%, of which taxes on international trade 13.6%, general sales tax 7.3%; nontax revenue 29.0%, of which fishing licenses 15.6%). Expenditures: CFAF 63,162,000,000 (current expenditures 65.7%, of which scheduled external interest payments 19.4%; capital expenditures 34.3%).
Public debt (external, outstanding; 2001): U.S.$627,200,000.
Production (metric tons except as noted). Agriculture, forestry, fishing (2002): cashew nuts 80,000, oil palm fruit 80,000, rice 79,900, roots and tubers 65,000, coconuts 46,000, plantains 38,000, millet 26,100, peanuts (groundnuts) 19,000, seed cotton 4,000; livestock (number of live animals) 515,000 cattle, 350,000 pigs, 325,000 goats, 285,000 sheep; roundwood (1999) 592,000 cu m; fish catch (2001) 5,000. Mining and quarrying: extraction of construction materials only. Manufacturing (2000): processed wood 11,200; wood products 4,400; dried and smoked fish 3,500; soap 2,500; vegetable oils 34,000 hectolitres; distilled liquor 11,000 hectolitres. Energy production (consumption): electricity (kW-hr; 1999) 54,000,000 (54,000,000); coal, none (none); crude petroleum, none (none); petroleum products (metric tons; 1999) none (85,000); natural gas, none (none).
Population economically active (1992): total 471,000; activity rate of total population 46.9% (participation rates [1991]: over age 10, 67.1%; female 40.5%; unemployed, n.a.).

Price and earnings indexes (1995 = 100)

	1996	1997	1998	1999	2000	2001	2002
Consumer price index	150.7	224.7	239.4	234.5	254.7	262.8	265.2
Monthly earnings index	...	...	...	...	...	...	...

Household income and expenditure. Average household size (1996) 6.9; income per household: n.a; sources of income: n.a.; expenditure: n.a.
Gross national product (at current market prices; 2001): U.S.$200,000,000 (U.S.$160 per capita).

Structure of gross domestic product and labour force

	2000		1994	
	in value CFAF '000,000	% of total value	labour force	% of labour force
Agriculture	88,015	57.4	365,000	77.2
Mining, Manufacturing, Public utilities	14,979	9.8	21,000 (Mining through Construction)	4.4
Construction	3,427	2.2		
Transportation and communications	5,545	3.6	87,000 (Transportation through Pub. admin.)	18.4
Trade	23,332	15.2		
Finance, services	579	0.4		
Pub. admin., defense	13,835	9.0		
Other	3,702[5]	2.4[5]	...	...
TOTAL	153,413[6]	100.0	473,000	100.0

Tourism: n.a.
Land use (1994): forested 38.1%; meadows and pastures 38.4%; agricultural and under permanent cultivation 12.1%; other 11.4%.

Foreign trade[7]

Balance of trade (current prices)

	1997	1998	1999	2000	2001
U.S.$'000,000	–40.1	–38.9	–30.8	–41.7	–49.5
% of total	29.2%	42.9%	23.1%	25.1%	34.4%

Imports (2001): U.S.$96,700,000 (foodstuffs 18.7%, of which rice 6.6%; transport equipment 13.2%; equipment and machinery 7.7%; fuel and lubricants 6.2%; unspecified 39.3%). *Major import sources:* Portugal 30.9%; Senegal 28.3%; China 11.3%; The Netherlands 6.8%; Japan 5.8%.
Exports (2001): U.S.$47,200,000 (cashews 95.6%; cotton 2.3%; logs 1.5%). *Major export destinations:* India 85.6%; Portugal 3.8%; Senegal 2.5%; France 1.7%.

Transport and communications

Transport. Railroads: none. Roads (1999): total length 2,734 mi, 4,400 km (paved 10%). Vehicles (1996): passenger cars 7,120; trucks and buses 5,640. Air transport (1998): passenger-mi 6,200,000, passenger-km 10,000,000; short ton-mi cargo, n.a., metric ton-km cargo, n.a.; airports (1997) with scheduled flights 2.

Communications

Medium	date	unit	number	units per 1,000 persons
Daily newspapers	2000	circulation	6,390	5.0
Radio	2000	receivers	56,200	44
Television	1997	receivers	0	0
Telephones	2001	main lines	12,000	9.8
Internet	2001	users	4,000	3.3

Education and health

Educational attainment: n.a. *Literacy* (1995): total population age 15 and over literate 54.9%; males literate 68.0%; females literate 42.5%.

Education (1999)

	schools	teachers	students	student/ teacher ratio
Primary (age 7–13)	759	4,306	149,530	...
Secondary (age 13–18)	...	1,913	25,034[8]	...

Health: physicians (1994) 184 (1 per 5,546 persons); hospital beds (1993) 1,300 (1 per 834 persons); infant mortality rate per 1,000 live births (2002) 111.9.
Food (2001): daily per capita caloric intake 2,481 (vegetable products 93%, animal products 7%); 107% of FAO recommended minimum requirement.

Military

Total active duty personnel (2002): 9,250 (army 73.5%, navy 3.8%, air force 1.1%, paramilitary [gendarmerie] 21.6%). *Military expenditure as percentage of GNP* (1999): 2.7% (world 2.4%); per capita expenditure U.S.$4.

[1]From September 2003. [2]Formerly pegged to the French franc and since Jan. 1, 2002, to the euro at the rate of €1 = CFAF 655.96. [3]Includes water area of about 3,089 sq mi (8,000 sq km). [4]Based on land area of 10,859 sq mi (28,125 sq km). [5]Indirect taxes. [6]Detail does not add to total given because of rounding. [7]Imports c.i.f.; exports f.o.b. [8]UNESCO estimate.

Internet resources for further information:
- **Afristat http://www.afristat.org**
- **Investir en Zone Franc http://www.izf.net/izf/Index.htm**

Guyana

Official name: Co-operative Republic of Guyana.
Form of government: unitary multiparty republic with one legislative house (National Assembly [65[1]]).
Head of state and government: President.
Capital: Georgetown.
Official language: English.
Official religion: none.
Monetary unit: 1 Guyana dollar (G$) = 100 cents; valuation (Sept. 8, 2003) 1 U.S.$ = G$179.00; 1 £ = G$283.81.

Area and population

Administrative regions		Capitals	area sq mi	area sq km	population 1986 estimate
Region 1	(Barima–Waini)	Mabaruma	7,853	20,339	18,516
Region 2	(Pomeroon–Supenaam)	Anna Regina	2,392	6,195	41,966
Region 3	(Essequibo Islands–West Demerara)	Vreed en Hoop	1,450	3,755	102,760
Region 4	(Demerara–Mahaica)	Paradise	862	2,233	310,758
Region 5	(Mahaica–Berbice)	Fort Wellington	1,610	4,170	55,556
Region 6	(East Berbice–Corentyne)	New Amsterdam	13,998	36,255	148,967
Region 7	(Cuyuni–Mazaruni)	Bartica	18,229	47,213	17,941
Region 8	(Potaro–Siparuni)	Mahdia	7,742	20,052	5,672
Region 9	(Upper Takutu–Upper Essequibo)	Lethem	22,313	57,790	15,338
Region 10	(Upper Demerara–Berbice)	Linden	6,595	17,081	38,598
TOTAL			83,044[2]	215,083[2]	756,072

Demography

Population (2003): 778,000.
Density (2003)[3]: persons per sq mi 10.2, persons per sq km 3.9.
Urban-rural (2001): urban 36.7%; rural 63.3%.
Sex distribution (2002): male 50.26%; female 49.74%.
Age breakdown (2002): under 15, 27.6%; 15–29, 31.0%; 30–44, 21.3%; 45–59, 12.8%; 60–74, 5.4%; 75 and over, 1.9%.
Population projection: (2010) 782,000; (2020) 759,000.
Doubling time: 77 years.
Ethnic composition (1992–93): East Indian 49.4%; black (African Negro and Bush Negro) 35.6%; mixed 7.1%; Amerindian 6.8%; Portuguese 0.7%; Chinese 0.4%.
Religious affiliation (1995): Christian 40.9%, of which Protestant 27.5% (including Anglican 8.6%), Roman Catholic 11.5%, Ethiopian Orthodox 1.1%; Hindu 34.0%; Muslim 9.0%; other 16.1%.
Major cities (1997): Georgetown 230,000 (urban agglomeration [2001] 280,000); Linden 35,000; New Amsterdam 25,000; Corriverton 24,000.

Vital statistics

Birth rate per 1,000 population (2002): 17.9 (world avg. 21.3).
Death rate per 1,000 population (2002): 8.9 (world avg. 9.1).
Natural increase rate per 1,000 population (2002): 9.0 (world avg. 12.2).
Total fertility rate (avg. births per childbearing woman; 2002): 2.1.
Life expectancy at birth (2002): male 60.9 years; female 66.6 years.
Major causes of death per 100,000 population (1994)[4]: diseases of the circulatory system 274.3, of which cerebrovascular disease 99.2, ischemic heart diseases 75.2, diseases of pulmonary circulation and other forms of heart disease 57.9; accidents and violence 76.1; endocrine and metabolic disorders 58.9; diseases of the respiratory system 50.1.

National economy

Budget (1999): Revenue: G$36,544,000,000 (tax revenue 91.6%, of which consumption taxes 32.0%, income taxes on companies 22.2%, personal income taxes 15.5%, import duties 11.4%; nontax revenue 8.2%). Expenditures: G$41,983,000,000 (current expenditure 71.2%, of which debt charges 13.8%; development expenditure 28.8%).
Production (metric tons except as noted). Agriculture, forestry, fishing (2002): rice 450,000, raw sugar (2001) 284,100, coconuts 45,000, cassava (manioc) 29,000, plantains 17,000, bananas 17,000, mangoes 12,000, oranges 5,000, pineapples 4,500; livestock (number of live animals) 130,000 sheep, 100,000 cattle, 12,500,000 chickens; roundwood (2001) 1,188,420 cu m; fish catch (2001) 54,013, of which shrimps and prawns 27,013. Mining and quarrying (2001): bauxite 2,011,901; gold (2002) 436,668 troy oz; diamonds 184,309 carats. Manufacturing (2002): flour 36,570; rum 145,900 hectolitres; beer and stout 108,500 hectolitres; soft drinks 4,251,000 cases; pharmaceuticals 9,042,000 tablets; garments 4,900,000 units. Construction: n.a. Energy production (consumption): electricity (kW-hr; 1999) 896,000,000 (896,000,000); coal, none (none); crude petroleum, none (none); petroleum products (metric tons; 1999) none (549,000); natural gas, none (none).
Population economically active (1997): total 263,807; activity rate of total population 33.9% (participation rates: ages 15–64 [1992] 59.5%; female 35.2%; unemployed 9.1%).

Price and earnings indexes (1995 = 100)

	1996	1997	1998	1999	2000	2001	2002
Consumer price index[5]	107.1	110.9	116.0	124.7	132.4	135.9	143.1
Earnings index	...	...	...	...	...	...	...

Gross national product (2001): U.S.$600,000,000 (U.S.$840 per capita).

Structure of gross domestic product and labour force

	1999 in value G$'000,000	1999 % of total value	1997 labour force	1997 % of labour force
Sugar	16,142[6]	13.4[6]		
Other agriculture	17,543[7]	14.5[7]	66,789	25.3
Fishing, forestry	8,851	7.3		
Mining	13,923	11.5	7,299	2.8
Manufacturing	3,681[8, 9]	3.1[8, 9]	27,869	10.6
Construction	4,771	4.0	16,545	6.3
Public utilities	[9]	[9]	2,547	0.9
Transp. and commun.	7,138	5.9	20,154	7.6
Trade	4,268	3.5	44,653	16.9
Finance, real estate	7,235	6.0	12,219	4.6
Pub. admin., defense	16,976	14.1	15,219	5.8
Services	1,570	1.3	26,553	10.1
Other	18,570[10]	15.4[10]	23,960[11]	9.1[11]
TOTAL	120,668	100.0	263,807	100.0

Public debt (external, outstanding; 2001): U.S.$1,176,000,000.
Household income and expenditure. Average household size (2000) 4.5.
Tourism: receipts from visitors (1999) U.S.$59,000,000; expenditures by nationals abroad (1997) U.S.$22,000,000.
Land use (1994): forested 83.8%; meadows and pastures 6.3%; agricultural and under permanent cultivation 2.5%; other 7.4%.

Foreign trade[12]

Balance of trade (current prices)

	1997	1998	1999	2000	2001	2002
U.S.$'000,000	–48.2	–54.2	–25.2	–80.2	–93.8	–68.2
% of total	3.9%	4.7%	2.3%	7.4%	8.7%	6.4%

Imports (2002): U.S.$563,100,000 (consumer goods 28.0%, fuels and lubricants 22.3%, capital goods 20.1%). *Major import sources* (2001)[13]: U.S. 24%; Netherlands Antilles 17%; Chile 16%; Trinidad and Tobago 13%; U.K. 6%.
Exports (2002): U.S.$494,900,000 (gold 27.5%, sugar 24.1%, shrimp 10.6%, rice 9.2%, timber 7.2%, bauxite 7.1%). *Major export destinations* (2001)[13]: U.S. 22%; Canada 20%; U.K. 12%; Netherlands Antilles 12%; Belgium 5%.

Transport and communications

Transport. Railroads: [14]. Roads (1999): total length 4,952 mi, 7,970 km (paved 7%). Vehicles (1995): passenger cars 24,000; trucks and buses 9,000. Air transport (1999)[15]: passenger-mi 172,000,000, passenger-km 276,600,000; short ton-mi cargo 1,507,000, metric ton-km cargo 2,200,000; airports (2000) with scheduled flights 1[16].

Communications

Medium	date	unit	number	units per 1,000 persons
Daily newspapers	1996	circulation	42,000	54
Radio	1997	receivers	420,000	539
Television	1999	receivers	60,000	77
Telephones	2002	main lines	80,400	92
Cellular telephones	2002	subscribers	87,300	99
Personal computers	2001	units	23,000	26
Internet	2001	users	95,000	109

Education and health

Educational attainment (1980). Percentage of population age 25 and over having: no formal schooling 8.1%; primary education 72.8%; secondary 17.3%; higher 1.8%. *Literacy* (1999): total population age 15 and over literate 98.4%; males literate 98.8%; females literate 97.9%.

Education (1999–2000)

	schools	teachers	students	student/ teacher ratio
Primary (age 6–11)	428	3,951	105,800	26.8
Secondary (age 12–17)	109	2,764	50,459	18.3
Voc., teacher tr.	7	512	6,266	12.2
Higher	1	371	7,496	20.2

Health: physicians (1998) 334 (1 per 2,326 persons); hospital beds 3,293 (1 per 236 persons); infant mortality rate per 1,000 live births (2002) 37.9.
Food (2001): daily per capita caloric intake 2,515 (vegetable products 85%, animal products 15%); 111% of FAO recommended minimum requirement.

Military

Total active duty personnel (2002): 1,600 (army 87.5%, navy 6.3%, air force 6.2%). *Military expenditure as percentage of GNP* (1999): 0.8% (world 2.4%); per capita expenditure U.S.$7.

[1]Includes 12 indirectly elected seats. [2]Includes inland water area equaling *c.* 7,000 sq mi (*c.* 18,000 sq km). [3]Based on land area only. [4]Projected rates based on about 78% of total deaths. [5]Weights of consumer price index components for Georgetown only. [6]Includes sugar manufacturing. [7]Includes rice manufacturing. [8]Excludes sugar and rice manufacturing. [9]Manufacturing includes Public utilities. [10]Indirect taxes less subsidies. [11]Unemployed. [12]Imports are f.o.b. in balance of trade and commodities and c.i.f. for trading partners. [13]Estimated figures. [14]No public railways. [15]Scheduled traffic only. [16]International only; domestic air service is provided on a charter basis.

Internet resources for further information:

- **Bank of Guyana**
  http://www.bankofguyana.org.gy
- **UNDP Common Country Assessment**
  http://www.undp.org.gy/ccassess.pdf

Haiti

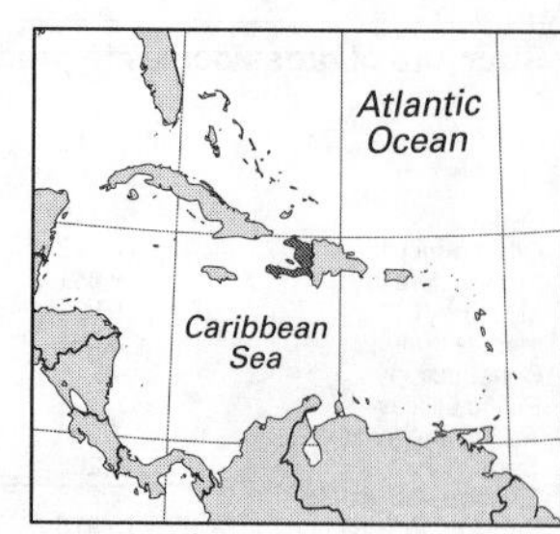

Official name: Repiblik Dayti (Haitian Creole); République d'Haïti (French) (Republic of Haiti).
Form of government: multiparty republic with two legislative houses (Senate [27]; Chamber of Deputies [83]).
Chief of state: President.
Head of government: Prime Minister.
Capital: Port-au-Prince.
Official languages: Haitian Creole; French.
Official religions: [1, 2].
Monetary unit: 1 gourde (G) = 100 centimes; valuation (Sept. 8, 2003) 1 U.S.$ = G 38.00; 1 £ = G 60.25.

Area and population

		area		population
Departements	**Capitals**	sq mi	sq km	1997 estimate
Artibonite	Gonaïves	1,924	4,984	1,052,834
Centre	Hinche	1,419	3,675	508,199
Grand'Anse	Jérémie	1,278	3,310	660,420
Nord	Cap-Haïtien	813	2,106	785,687
Nord-Est	Fort-Liberté	697	1,805	255,601
Nord-Ouest	Port-de-Paix	840	2,176	439,984
Ouest	Port-au-Prince	1,864	4,827	2,651,115
Sud	Les Cayes	1,079	2,794	671,112
Sud-Est	Jacmel	781	2,023	466,810
TOTAL		10,695	27,700	7,491,762[3]

Demography

Population (2003): 7,528,000[4].
Density (2003): persons per sq mi 703.9, persons per sq km 271.8.
Urban-rural (2001): urban 36.3%; rural 63.7%.
Sex distribution (2002): male 49.56%; female 50.44%.
Age breakdown (2002): under 15, 43.2%; 15–29, 28.6%; 30–44, 14.3%; 45–59, 8.2%; 60–74, 4.6%; 75 and over, 1.1%.
Population projection[4]: (2010) 8,555,000; (2020) 10,262,000.
Ethnic composition (2000): black 94.2%; mulatto 5.4%; other 0.4%.
Religious affiliation (1995): Roman Catholic 68.5%[5]; Protestant 24.1%, of which Baptist 5.9%, Pentecostal 5.3%, Seventh-day Adventist 4.6%; other 7.4%.
Major cities (1999): Port-au-Prince 990,558 (metropolitan area [1997] 1,556,588); Carrefour 336,222[6]; Delmas 284,079[6]; Cap-Haïtien 113,555; Pétion-Ville (1997) 76,155[6].

Vital statistics

Birth rate per 1,000 population (2002): 34.4 (world avg. 21.3).
Death rate per 1,000 population (2002): 13.5 (world avg. 9.1).
Natural increase rate per 1,000 population (2002): 20.9 (world avg. 12.2).
Total fertility rate (avg. births per childbearing woman; 2002): 5.0.
Life expectancy at birth (2002): male 50.2 years; female 52.7 years.
Major causes of death per 100,000 population (1999)[7]: infectious and parasitic diseases *c.* 530, of which HIV/AIDS *c.* 74, diarrhea and infectious gastroenteritis *c.* 71; diseases of the circulatory system, n.a.; accidents and violence *c.* 61; neoplasms (cancers) *c.* 38.

National economy

Budget (2002)[8]. Revenue: G 7,721,700,000 (general sales tax 31.3%; customs duties 26.8%; individual taxes on income and profits 20.5%). Expenditures: G 10,376,700,000 (current expenditure 81.6%, of which wages 33.6%, transfers 4.8%, interest on public debt 1.2%; capital expenditure 18.4%).
Production (metric tons except as noted). Agriculture, forestry, fishing (2002): sugarcane 1,010,100, cassava (manioc) 335,000, bananas 295,000, plantains 285,000, mangoes 260,000, yams 198,000, corn (maize) 185,000, sweet potatoes 175,000, rice 104,000, coffee 30,000, sisal 5,700, cacao 4,500; livestock (number of live animals) 1,943,000 goats, 1,450,000 cattle, 1,001,100 pigs, 500,500 horses; roundwood (2001) 2,209,701 cu m; fish catch (2001) 5,000. Mining and quarrying (2001): sand 2,000,000 cu m. Manufacturing (value added in G '000,000; 2001[9]): food and beverages 467.1; textiles, wearing apparel, and footwear 202.4; chemical and rubber products 62.8; tobacco products 37.7. Energy production (consumption): electricity (kW-hr; 1999) 640,000,000 (640,000,000); petroleum products (metric tons; 1999) none (461,000).
Land use (1994): forested 5.1%; meadows and pastures 18.0%; agricultural and under permanent cultivation 33.0%; other 43.9%.
Population economically active (2002): total *c.* 4,100,000; activity rate of total population *c.* 55% (participation rates: ages 15–64 [1990] 64.8%; female [1996] 43.0%; unemployed unofficially [1996] *c.* 60%).

Price and earnings indexes (1995 = 100)

	1996	1997	1998	1999	2000	2001	2002
Consumer price index	120.6	145.4	160.8	174.8	198.7	226.9	249.3
Daily earnings index[10]	100.0	100.0	100.0	100.0	100.0	100.0	...

Household income and expenditure. Average household size (1982) 4.4; average annual income of urban wage earners (1984): G 1,545 (U.S.$309); expenditure (1996)[11]: food, beverages, and tobacco 49.4%, housing and energy 9.1%, transportation 8.7%, clothing and footwear 8.5%.

Public debt (external, outstanding; 2001): U.S.$1,028,000,000.
Gross national product (2001): U.S.$3,900,000,000 (U.S.$480 per capita).

Structure of gross domestic product and labour force

	2001		1990	
	in value G '000,000[9]	% of total value	labour force[12]	% of labour force
Agriculture, forestry	3,445.6	26.5	1,535,444	57.3
Mining	13.7	0.1	24,012	0.9
Manufacturing	983.3	7.6	151,387	5.6
Construction	947.9	7.3	28,001	1.0
Public utilities	59.8	0.5	2,577	0.1
Transp. and commun.	764.6	5.9	20,691	0.8
Trade, restaurants	3,409.8	26.2	352,970	13.2
Finance, real estate	852.1	6.6	5,057	0.2
Services; Pub. admin., defense	2,089.0	16.1	155,347	5.8
Other	425.2[13]	3.2[13]	403,654[14]	15.1[14]
TOTAL	12,991.0	100.0	2,679,140	100.0

Tourism (2001): receipts from visitors U.S.$54,000,000; expenditures by nationals abroad (1998) U.S.$37,000,000.

Foreign trade[15, 16]

Balance of trade (current prices)

	1997	1998	1999	2000	2001	2002
U.S.$'000,000	–497.8	–522.7	–600.4	–698.0	–693.9	–705.8
% of total	54.8%	46.6%	46.9%	52.5%	54.2%	56.3%

Imports (2002): U.S.$1,054,200,000 (food and live animals 22.4%, basic manufactures 19.9%, machinery and transport equipment 15.2%, petroleum and derivatives 14.9%). *Major import sources* (1999)[17]: United States 60%; Dominican Republic 4%; Japan 3%; France 3%; Canada 3%.
Exports (2002): U.S.$274,400,000 (reexports to U.S. 80.8%, of which clothing and apparel 79.1%; mangoes 2.6%; cacao 2.0%; essential oils 1.5%; leather goods 1.1%). *Major export destinations* (1999)[17]: United States 90%; Canada 3%; Belgium 2%, France 2%.

Transport and communications

Transport. Railroad: none. Roads (1999): total length 2,585 mi, 4,160 km (paved 24%). Vehicles (1996): passenger cars 32,000; trucks and buses 21,000. Air transport (2000)[18]: passenger arrivals and departures 924,000; cargo unloaded and loaded 15,300 metric tons; airports (1997) with scheduled flights 2.

Communications

Medium	date	unit	number	units per 1,000 persons
Daily newspapers	2000	circulation	21,500	3.0
Radio	2000	receivers	395,000	55
Television	2000	receivers	35,900	5.0
Telephones	2002	main lines	130,000	16
Cellular telephones	2002	subscribers	140,000	17
Internet	2002	users	80,000	9.6

Education and health

Educational attainment (1986–87). Percentage of population age 25 and over having: no formal schooling 59.5%; primary education 30.5%; secondary 8.6%; vocational and teacher training 0.7%; higher 0.7%. *Literacy* (1995): total population age 15 and over literate 1,930,000 (45.0%); males literate 992,000 (48.0%); females literate 938,000 (42.2%).

Education (1994–95)

	schools	teachers	students	student/ teacher ratio
Primary (age 6–12)	10,071	30,205	1,110,398	36.8
Secondary (age 13–18); Voc., teacher tr.	1,038	...	195,418	...
Higher[19, 20]	2	899	12,348	13.7

Health: physicians (1998) 1,688 (1 per 4,167 persons); hospital beds (1996) 5,241 (1 per 1,242 persons); infant mortality rate (2002) 77.7.
Food (2001): daily per capita caloric intake 2,045 (vegetable products 93%, animal products 7%); 90% of FAO recommended minimum requirement.

Military

Total active duty personnel: [21].

[1]Roman Catholicism has special recognition per concordat with the Vatican. [2]Voodoo became officially sanctioned per governmental decree of April 2003. [3]Official population projection based on 1982 census. [4]De facto estimate(s). [5]About 80% of all Roman Catholics also practice voodoo. [6]Within Port-au-Prince metropolitan area. [7]Projected rates based on about 8% of all deaths. [8]Does not include projects financed with loans and grants. [9]At prices of 1986–87. [10]Standard minimum wage rate. [11]Weights of consumer price index components. [12]The 2002 labour force equaled *c.* 4,100,000, of which formal sector equaled *c.* 110,000 (including 35,000 government employees). [13]Import duties less imputed bank service charges. [14]Includes 63,975 not adequately defined and 339,679 officially unemployed. [15]Includes reexports. [16]Import figures are f.o.b. in balance of trade and c.i.f. in commodities and trading partners. [17]Estimated percentages. [18]Port-au-Prince Airport only. [19]Port-au-Prince universities only. [20]2000–01. [21]The Haitian army was disbanded in 1995. The national police force had 5,300 personnel in 2002.

Internet resources for further information:
- **Embassy of Haiti (Washington, D.C.) http://www.haiti.org**
- **Banque de la République d'Haïti http://www.brh.net**

Honduras

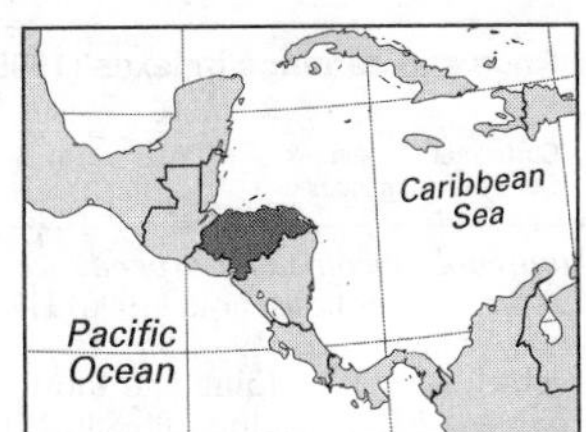

Official name: República de Honduras (Republic of Honduras).
Form of government: multiparty republic with one legislative house (National Assembly [128]).
Head of state and government: President.
Capital: Tegucigalpa.
Official language: Spanish.
Official religion: none.
Monetary unit: 1 Honduran lempira (L) = 100 centavos; valuation (Sept. 8, 2003) 1 U.S.$ = L 17.50; 1 £ = L 27.75.

Area and population

Departments	Administrative centres	area sq mi	area sq km	population 2001 census
Atlántida	La Ceiba	1,641	4,251	344,099
Choluteca	Choluteca	1,626	4,211	390,805
Colón	Trujillo	3,427	8,875	246,708
Comayagua	Comayagua	2,006	5,196	352,881
Copán	Santa Rosa de Copán	1,237	3,203	288,766
Cortés	San Pedro Sula	1,527	3,954	1,202,510
El Paraíso	Yuscarán	2,787	7,218	350,054
Francisco Morazán	Tegucigalpa	3,068	7,946	1,180,676
Gracias a Dios	Puerto Lempira	6,421	16,630	67,384
Intibucá	La Esperanza	1,186	3,072	179,862
Islas de la Bahía	Roatán	100	261	38,073
La Paz	La Paz	900	2,331	156,560
Lempira	Gracias	1,656	4,290	250,067
Ocotepeque	Nueva Ocotepeque	649	1,680	108,029
Olancho	Juticalpa	9,402	24,351	419,561
Santa Bárbara	Santa Bárbara	1,975	5,115	342,054
Valle	Nacaome	604	1,565	151,841
Yoro	Yoro	3,065	7,939	465,414
TOTAL		43,277[1]	112,088[1]	6,535,344[2]

Demography

Population (2003): 6,803,000.
Density (2003)[3]: persons per sq mi 156.6, persons per sq km 60.5.
Urban-rural (2001): urban 53.7%; rural 46.3%.
Sex distribution (2002): male 50.09%; female 49.91%.
Age breakdown (2002): under 15, 41.9%; 15–29, 29.1%; 30–44, 15.3%; 45–59, 8.3%; 60–74, 4.1%; 75 and over, 1.3%.
Population projection: (2010) 7,884,000; (2020) 9,155,000.
Doubling time: 27 years.
Ethnic composition (2000): mestizo 86.6%; Amerindian 5.5%; black (including Black Carib) 4.3%; white 2.3%; other 1.3%.
Religious affiliation (1995): Roman Catholic 86.7%; Protestant 10.4%, of which Pentecostal 5.7%; other 2.9%.
Major cities (2001): Tegucigalpa 769,061; San Pedro Sula 439,086; La Ceiba 114,584; El Progreso 90,475; Choluteca 75,600.

Vital statistics

Birth rate per 1,000 population (2002): 32.3 (world avg. 21.3).
Death rate per 1,000 population (2002): 6.3 (world avg. 9.1).
Natural increase rate per 1,000 population (2002): 26.0 (world avg. 12.2).
Total fertility rate (avg. births per childbearing woman; 2002): 4.2.
Life expectancy at birth (2002): male 65.2 years; female 68.7 years.
Major causes of death (1990): diseases of the circulatory system 19.0% of total; accidents and violence 13.0%; diseases of the respiratory system 9.5%; infectious and parasitic diseases 9.0%; malignant neoplasms (cancers) 8.2%.

National economy

Budget (1999). Revenue: L 14,621,500,000 (tax revenue 92.6%, of which indirect taxes 72.8%, direct taxes 19.8%; nontax revenue 5.1%; transfers 2.3%). Expenditures: L 18,197,700,000 (current expenditure 67.9%; capital expenditure 32.1%).
Public debt (external, outstanding; 2001): U.S.$3,995,000,000.
Production (metric tons except as noted). Agriculture, forestry, fishing (2002): sugarcane 4,300,000, bananas 965,066, oil palm fruit 735,802, corn (maize) 392,214, plantains 260,000, coffee 190,000, oranges 167,226, cantaloupes 131,298, pineapples 61,814; livestock (number of live animals) 1,859,737 cattle, 538,033 pigs, 18,648,000 chickens; roundwood (2001) 9,531,959 cu m; fish catch (2001) 16,451. Mining and quarrying (2001): gypsum 59,500; zinc (metal content) 48,485; silver 35,000 kg; gold 880 kg. Manufacturing (value added in L '000,000; 1996): food products 1,937; wearing apparel 1,266[4]; beverages 700; nonmetallic mineral products 504; wood products 326. Energy production (consumption): electricity (kW-hr; 2001) 4,191,600,000 (4,191,600,000); crude petroleum (barrels; 1999) none (n.a.); petroleum products (metric tons; 1999) none (1,444,000); natural gas (cu m; 1999) none (n.a.).
Population economically active (2001): total 2,438,000; activity rate of total population 38.5% (participation rates: ages 15–64, 64.5%; female 35.7%; unemployed 4.2%).

Price and earnings indexes (1995 = 100)

	1996	1997	1998	1999	2000	2001	2002
Consumer price index	123.8	148.8	169.2	188.9	209.8	230.1	247.8
Daily earnings index[5]	119.3	158.0	184.9	...	...	...	...

Gross national product (at current market prices; 2001): U.S.$5,900,000,000 (U.S.$900 per capita).

Structure of gross domestic product and labour force

	2001 in value L '000,000[6]	% of total value[6]	labour force	% of labour force
Agriculture	12,213	14.1	766,800	31.5
Mining	1,587	1.8	2,900	0.1
Manufacturing	17,540	20.3	356,000	14.6
Construction	4,261	4.9	121,000	5.0
Public utilities	3,728	4.3	8,400	0.3
Transp. and commun.	5,061	5.9	74,300	3.0
Trade	10,916	12.6	559,200	22.9
Finance, real estate	14,605	16.9	65,800	2.7
Public admin., defense	5,667	6.6	380,300	15.6
Services	10,806	12.5		
Other	—	—	103,300[7]	4.2[7]
TOTAL	86,386[8]	100.0[8]	2,438,000	100.0[8]

Household income and expenditure. Average household size (2000) 5.1; sources of income (1985): wages and salaries 58.8%, transfer payments 1.8%, other 39.4%; expenditure (1986): food 44.4%, utilities and housing 22.4%, clothing and footwear 9.0%, household furnishings 8.3%.
Tourism (2001): receipts U.S.$275,000,000; expenditures U.S.$157,000,000.
Land use (1998): forested and other 67.9%; meadows and pastures 13.8%; agricultural and under permanent cultivation 18.3%.

Foreign trade[9]

Balance of trade (current prices)

	1997	1998	1999	2000	2001	2002
U.S.$'000,000	−703	−1,002	−1,512	−1,485	−1,655	−1,585
% of total	19.6%	24.6%	39.4%	35.1%	38.4%	34.4%

Imports (2001): U.S.$2,984,000,000 (food products and live animals 18.3%, machinery and electrical equipment 15.1%, chemicals and chemical products 14.1%, mineral fuels and lubricants 13.2%). *Major import sources:* U.S. 46.2%; Guatemala 9.9%; El Salvador 6.2%; Mexico 4.7%; Costa Rica 3.5%.
Exports (2001): U.S.$1,329,000,000 (bananas 15.4%, shrimp 13.3%, coffee 12.1%, nontraditional exports [including African palm oil, decorative plants, and mangoes] 42.2%). *Major export destinations:* U.S. 45.7%; El Salvador 10.2%; Guatemala 9.7%; Belgium 4.7%; Germany 4.3%.

Transport and communications

Transport. Railroads (2000): serviceable lines *c.* 127 mi (*c.* 205 km); most tracks are out of use but not dismantled. Roads (2001): total length 8,452 mi, 13,603 km (paved 20%). Vehicles (1999): passenger cars 326,541; trucks and buses 59,322. Air transport (1995): passenger-km 341,000,000; metric ton-km cargo 33,000,000; airports (1996) with scheduled flights 8.

Communications

Medium	date	unit	number	units per 1,000 persons
Daily newspapers	2000	circulation	349,000	55
Radio	2000	receivers	2,620,000	412
Television	2000	receivers	610,000	96
Telephones	2002	main lines	322,500	48
Cellular telephones	2002	subscribers	326,500	49
Personal computers	2001	units	80,000	12
Internet	2002	users	200,000	30

Education and health

Educational attainment (1988). Percentage of population age 10 and over having: no formal schooling 33.4%; primary education 50.1%; secondary education 13.4%; higher 3.1%. *Literacy* (2000): total population age 15 and over literate 74.6%; males literate 74.7%; females literate 74.5%.

Education (2001)

	schools	teachers	students	student/ teacher ratio
Primary (age 7–13)	9,746	32,568	1,109,242	34.0
Secondary (age 14–19) Voc., teacher tr.	1,000	15,647	195,072	12.5
Higher	10	3,704	64,142	17.3

Health: physicians (2000) 5,287 (1 per 1,201 persons); hospital beds (2001) 5,069 (1 per 1,287 persons); infant mortality rate (2002) 30.9.
Food (2001): daily per capita caloric intake 2,405 (vegetable products 85%, animal products 15%); 106% of FAO recommended minimum.

Military

Total active duty personnel (2002): 8,300 (army 66.3%, navy 12.0%, air force 21.7%); U.S. troops (August 2003) 500. *Military expenditure as percentage of GNP* (1999): 0.7% (world 2.4%); per capita expenditure U.S.$6.

[1]Area as of 1992 judgment of the International Court of Justice is 43,433 sq mi (112,492 sq km); breakdown by department is not available. [2]Census population adjusted for underenumeration; unadjusted census figure is 6,071,200. [3]Based on the revised area. [4]Important product of the maquiladora sector; garment assembly employed 110,000 in 2001. [5]Official minimum wages in all sectors. [6]At factor cost. [7]Unemployed. [8]Detail does not add to total given because of rounding. [9]Imports c.i.f.; exports f.o.b.

Internet resources for further information:
- **Banco Central de Honduras http://www.bch.hn**
- **Instituto Nacional de Estadística http://www.ine.online.hn**

Hong Kong

Official name: Xianggang Tebie Xingzhengqu (Chinese); Hong Kong Special Administrative Region (English).
Political status: special administrative region[1] (People's Republic of China) with one legislative house (Legislative Council [60[2]]).
Chief of state: President of China.
Head of government: Chief Executive.
Government offices: Central & Western District (formerly Victoria), Hong Kong Island.
Official languages: Chinese; English.
Official religion: none.
Monetary unit: 1 Hong Kong dollar (HK$) = 100 cents; valuation (Sept. 8, 2003) 1 U.S.$ = HK$7.80; 1 £ = HK$12.37.

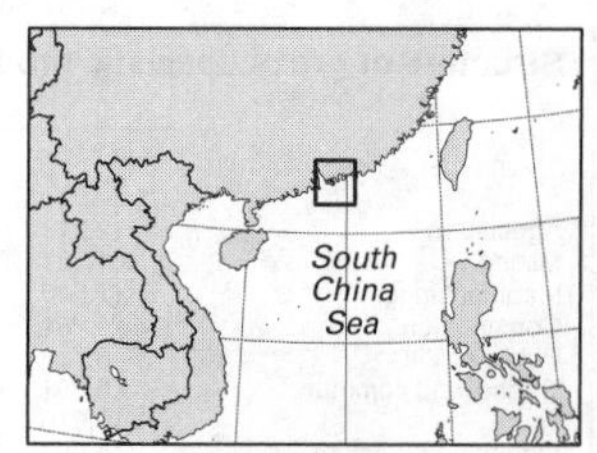

Area and population

Area	area sq mi	area sq km	population 2001 census
Hong Kong Island	31.0	80.4	1,335,469
Kowloon and New Kowloon	18.1	46.9	2,023,979
New Territories	376.0	973.7	3,343,046
Marine	—	—	5,895
TOTAL	425.1	1,101.0	6,708,389

Demography

Population (2003): 6,838,000.
Density (2003): persons per sq mi 16,086, persons per sq km 6,211.
Urban-rural (2002): urban 100.0%.
Sex distribution (2002): male 48.63%; female 51.37%.
Age breakdown (2002): under 15, 16.1%; 15–29, 20.6%; 30–44, 28.9%; 45–59, 19.4%; 60–74, 10.4%; 75 and over, 4.6%.
Population projection: (2010) 7,313,000; (2020) 7,944,000.
Ethnic composition (2003): Chinese 95%; other 5%.
Religious affiliation (1994): Buddhist and Taoist 73.8%; Christian 8.4%, of which Protestant 4.3%, Roman Catholic 4.1%; New Religionist 3.2%; Muslim 0.8%; Hindu 0.2%; nonreligious/atheist 13.5%; other 0.1%.

Vital statistics

Birth rate per 1,000 population (2002): 7.1 (world avg. 21.3).
Death rate per 1,000 population (2002): 5.0 (world avg. 9.1).
Natural increase rate per 1,000 population (2002): 2.1 (world avg. 12.2).
Total fertility rate (avg. births per childbearing woman; 2002): 1.3.
Marriage rate per 1,000 population (2002): 4.7.
Life expectancy at birth (2002): male 78.7 years; female 84.7 years.
Major causes of death per 100,000 population (2002): malignant neoplasms (cancers) 167.8; diseases of the circulatory system 121.3; diseases of the respiratory system 81.1; accidents and poisoning 31.4[3].

National economy

Budget (2001–02). Revenue: HK$174,047,000,000 (earnings and profits taxes 44.8%; indirect taxes 25.9%, of which property taxes 7.2%; capital revenue 12.5%). Expenditures: HK$273,151,000,000 (education 19.3%; health 12.5%; housing 12.1%; social welfare 11.3%; police 8.0%; economic services 5.2%).
Gross domestic product (2000): U.S.$162,397,000,000 (U.S.$24,360 per capita).

Structure of gross domestic product and labour force

	2000			
	in value HK$'000,000	% of total value	labour force	% of labour force
Agriculture	920	0.1	9,300	0.3
Mining	241	—	338,500	10.0
Manufacturing	71,655	5.6		
Construction	64,026	5.0	303,200	9.0
Public utilities	38,853	3.0	16,600	0.5
Transp. and commun.	125,724	9.8	358,700	10.6
Trade	324,622	25.2	985,200	29.1
Finance, insurance, and real estate	291,062	22.6	448,700	13.3
Pub. admin., defense, and services	252,435	19.6	754,200	22.3
Other	117,266[4]	9.1[4]	168,300[5]	5.0[5]
TOTAL	1,286,804	100.0	3,382,700	100.0[6]

Production (metric tons except as noted). Agriculture, forestry, fishing (2000): vegetables 42,500, fruits and nuts 2,022, field crops 508, eggs 3,710,000 units; livestock (number of live animals) 446,000 pigs[7]; roundwood (2001) n.a.; fish catch (2000) 157,012. Manufacturing (value added in HK$'000,000; 1999): publishing and printed materials 10,748; electrical and electronic products 8,279; textiles 7,276; wearing apparel 7,240; food 5,213; machinery and equipment 4,849; transport equipment 3,031; basic metals and fabricated metal products 2,667. Construction (2002)[8]: residential 1,411,000 sq m; nonresidential 549,000 sq m. Energy production (consumption): electricity (kW-hr; 1999) 29,496,000,000 (38,564,000,000); coal (metric tons; 1999) none (6,393,000); petroleum products (metric tons; 1999) none (7,319,000).
Population economically active (2002): total 3,519,000; activity rate of total population 52.0% (participation rates: over age 15, 62.0%; female 44.2%; unemployed 7.2%).

Price and earnings indexes (1995 = 100)

	1996	1997	1998	1999	2000	2001	2002
Consumer price index	106.3	112.5	115.7	111.1	106.9	105.2	102.0
Daily earnings index	...	...	...	...	...	...	...

Household income and expenditure. Average household size (2002) 3.1; annual income per household (1996) HK$210,000 (U.S.$27,600); sources of income: n.a.; expenditure (1994–95): food 29.5%, housing 28.8%, transportation and vehicles 7.8%, clothing and footwear 6.7%, durable goods 5.5%.
Tourism (2001): receipts U.S.$8,241,000,000; expenditures U.S.$12,494,000,000.
Land use (1995): forested 20.1%; agricultural and under permanent cultivation 5.8%; fishponds 1.5%; built-on, scrublands, and other 72.6%.

Foreign trade[9]

Balance of trade (current prices)

	1997	1998	1999	2000	2001	2002
HK$'000,000	–159,141	–81,443	–43,718	–85,273	–87,208	–58,902
% of total	5.8%	2.9%	1.6%	2.6%	2.9%	1.9%

Imports (2002): HK$1,619,419,000,000 (consumer goods 33.5%, capital goods 26.4%, foodstuffs 3.7%, mineral fuels and lubricants 1.9%). *Major import sources:* China 44.3%; Japan 11.3%; Taiwan 7.2%; U.S. 5.6%; Singapore 4.7%; South Korea 4.7%.
Exports (2002): HK$1,560,517,000,000 (reexports 91.6%, of which consumer goods 37.2%, capital goods 24.5%; domestic exports 8.4%, of which clothing accessories and apparel 4.2%). *Major export destinations*[10]: China 39.3%; U.S. 21.3%; Japan 5.4%; U.K. 3.5%; Germany 3.1%.

Transport and communications

Transport. Railroads (2003): route length *c.* 93 mi, *c.* 150 km; passenger-km, n.a.; metric ton-km cargo, n.a. Roads (2002): total length 1,187 mi, 1,911 km (paved 100%). Vehicles (2002): passenger cars 381,757; trucks and buses 145,293. Air transport (2002): passenger arrivals 11,841,000, passenger departures 11,722,000; airports (2002) with scheduled flights 1.

Communications

Medium	date	unit	number	units per 1,000 persons
Daily newspapers	2000	circulation	5,280,000	792
Radio	2000	receivers	4,560,000	684
Television	2000	receivers	3,290,000	493
Telephones	2002	main lines	3,842,900	533
Cellular telephones	2002	subscribers	6,297,500	930
Personal computers	2001	units	2,600,000	387
Internet	2002	users	2,918,800	431

Education and health

Educational attainment (2002). Percentage of population age 15 and over having: no formal schooling 7.0%; primary education 21.0%; secondary 46.8%; matriculation 4.7%; nondegree higher 7.6%; higher degree 12.9%.
Literacy (2000): total population age 15 and over literate 93.5%; males literate 96.5%; females literate 90.2%.

Education (2001–02)

	schools	teachers	students	student/ teacher ratio
Primary (age 6–11)	815	22,845	493,075	21.6
Secondary (age 12–18)	537	25,093	465,503	18.6
Vocational	1[11]	1,033	54,825	53.1
Higher	8	5,620	83,657	14.9

Health (2002): physicians 10,837[12] (1 per 625 persons); hospital beds 35,220 (1 per 192 persons); infant mortality rate per 1,000 live births (2002) 2.4.
Food (2001): daily per capita caloric intake 3,104 (vegetable products 68%, animal products 32%); 136% of FAO recommended minimum requirement.

Military

Total active duty personnel (2003): 4,000 troops of Chinese army to intervene in local matters only at the request of the Hong Kong government; Chinese navy and air force, n.a.

[1]On July 1, 1997, Hong Kong reverted to China as a special administrative region in which the existing socioeconomic system would remain unchanged for a period of 50 years. [2]24 seats are directly elected by ordinary voters; the remaining 36 seats are elected/appointed by special interest groups and a committee. [3]As of 2000. [4]Indirect taxes less subsidies. [5]Unemployed. [6]Detail does not add to total given because of rounding. [7]Excludes local pigs not slaughtered in abattoirs. [8]Usable floor area only. [9]Imports are c.i.f., exports f.o.b. [10]Includes reexports and domestic exports. [11]The Hong Kong Institute of Vocational Education was formed in 1999. It is composed of the two former technical colleges and the seven former technical institutes. [12]Registered personnel; all may not be present and working in the country.

Internet resources for further information:
- **Census and Statistics Department http://www.info.gov.hk/censtatd**

Hungary

Official name: Magyar Köztársaság (Republic of Hungary).
Form of government: unitary multi-party republic with one legislative house (National Assembly [386]).
Chief of state: President.
Head of government: Prime Minister.
Capital: Budapest.
Official language: Hungarian.
Official religion: none.
Monetary unit: 1 forint (Ft) = 100 filler; valuation (Sept. 8, 2003) 1 U.S.$ = Ft 232.32; 1 £ = Ft 368.36.

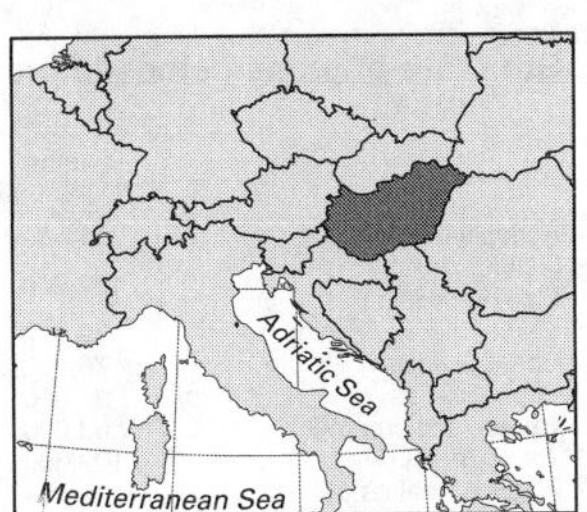

Area and population

Counties	Capitals	area sq mi	area sq km	population 2001 census
Bács-Kiskun	Kecskemét	3,261	8,445	546,753
Baranya	Pécs	1,710	4,430	408,019
Békés	Békéscsaba	2,174	5,631	397,074
Borsod-Abaúj-Zemplén	Miskolc	2,798	7,247	745,154
Csongrád	Szeged	1,646	4,263	433,388
Fejér	Székesfehérvár	1,683	4,359	434,547
Györ-Moson-Sopron	Györ	1,579	4,089	434,956
Hajdú-Bihar	Debrecen	2,398	6,211	553,043
Heves	Eger	1,404	3,637	325,673
Jász-Nagykun-Szolnok	Szolnok	2,155	5,582	415,819
Komárom-Esztergom	Tatabánya	875	2,265	316,780
Nógrád	Salgótarján	982	2,544	220,576
Pest	Budapest[1]	2,468	6,393	1,080,759
Somogy	Kaposvár	2,331	6,036	335,463
Szabolcs-Szatmár-Bereg	Nyíregyháza	2,292	5,937	582,795
Tolna	Szekszárd	1,430	3,703	250,062
Vas	Szombathely	1,288	3,336	268,653
Veszprém	Veszprém	1,781	4,613	374,346
Zala	Zalaegerszeg	1,461	3,784	298,056
Capital city				
Budapest[1]		203	525	1,775,203
TOTAL		35,919	93,030	10,197,119

Demography

Population (2003): 10,136,000.
Density (2003): persons per sq mi 282.2, persons per sq km 109.0.
Urban-rural (2003): urban 65.0%; rural 35.0%.
Sex distribution (2003): male 47.52%; female 52.48%.
Age breakdown (2003): under 15, 16.1%; 15–29, 22.1%; 30–44, 19.7%; 45–59, 21.4%; 60–74, 14.2%; 75 and over, 6.5%.
Population projection: (2010) 9,920,000; (2020) 9,570,000.
Ethnic composition (2000): Hungarian 84.4%; Roma (Gypsy) 5.3%; Ruthenian 2.9%; German 2.4%; Romanian 1.0%; Slovak 0.9%; Jewish 0.6%; other 2.5%.
Religious affiliation (1998): Roman Catholic 57.8%; Reformed 17.7%; Lutheran 3.9%; Jewish 0.2%; nonreligious 18.5%; other/unknown 1.9%.
Major cities (2003): Budapest 1,725,000; Debrecen 206,000; Miskolc 180,000; Szeged 163,000; Pécs 159,000; Györ 130,000.

Vital statistics

Birth rate per 1,000 population (2002): 9.5 (world avg. 21.3); (2002) legitimate 68.7%; illegitimate 31.3%.
Death rate per 1,000 population (2002): 13.1 (world avg. 9.1).
Natural increase rate per 1,000 population (2002): –3.6 (world avg. 12.2).
Total fertility rate (avg. births per childbearing woman; 2002): 1.3.
Marriage rate per 1,000 population (2002): 4.5.
Life expectancy at birth (2001): male 68.2 years; female 76.5 years.
Major causes of death per 100,000 population (2000): diseases of the circulatory system 674.5; malignant neoplasms (cancers) 325.9.

National economy

Budget (2001). Revenue: Ft 6,325,700,000,000 (social security contributions 30.3%, value-added taxes 20.0%, personal income taxes 17.9%). Expenditures: Ft 6,769,100,000,000 (social security and welfare 32.2%, public safety 16.3%, education 10.9%, health 9.2%).
Production (metric tons except as noted). Agriculture, forestry, fishing (2002): corn (maize) 6,087,000, wheat 3,896,000, sugar beets 2,249,000, barley 1,053,000, sunflower seeds 779,000, apples 605,000, grapes 560,000; livestock (number of live animals) 5,082,000 pigs, 770,000 cattle; roundwood (2001) 5,811,000 cu m; fish catch (2001) 19,694. Mining and quarrying (2002): bauxite 720,000. Manufacturing (gross output of production in Ft '000,000,000; 2002): electrical machinery and apparatus 3,091; food, beverages, and tobacco 1,890; transportation equipment 1,659; basic metals 859; chemicals 790; refined petroleum products 502. Energy production (consumption): electricity (kW-hr; 2002) 36,083,000,000 (43,718,000,000); hard coal (metric tons; 2002) 726,000 ([1999] 1,251,000); lignite (metric tons; 2002) 11,582,000 ([1999] 15,451,000); crude petroleum (barrels; 2002) 7,025,000 ([1999] 51,633,000); petroleum products (metric tons; 1999) 6,529,000 (6,269,000); natural gas (cu m; 2002) 3,353,000,000 ([1999] 11,442,100,000).
Land use (1994): forested 19.1%; meadows and pastures 12.4%; agricultural and under permanent cultivation 53.9%; other 14.6%.
Public debt (external, outstanding; 2001): U.S.$12,681,000,000.
Population economically active (2002): total 4,109,400; activity rate of total population 40.4% (participation rates: ages 15–64, 60.0%; female 44.5%; unemployed 5.8%).

Price and earnings indexes (1995 = 100)

	1996	1997	1998	1999	2000	2001	2002
Consumer price index	123.4	146.0	166.7	183.5	201.4	220.3	231.9
Annual earnings index	117.8	145.7	170.7	191.6	215.8	244.1	280.9

Tourism (U.S.$'000,000; 2001): receipts 3,933; expenditures 1,309.
Gross national product (2001): U.S.$49,200,000,000 (U.S.$4,830 per capita).

Structure of gross domestic product and labour force

	2001 in value Ft '000,000	% of total value	labour force	% of labour force
Agriculture, forestry	562,000	3.8	239,400	5.8
Mining	34,300	0.2	13,000	0.3
Manufacturing	3,060,500	20.6	955,800	23.4
Construction	635,800	4.3	272,700	6.7
Public utilities	441,200	3.0	79,500	1.9
Transp. and commun.	1,192,500	8.1	310,900	7.6
Trade, restaurants	1,679,600	11.3	691,400	16.9
Finance, real estate	2,827,400	19.1	298,500	7.3
Public administration, defense	981,400	6.6	289,600	7.1
Services	1,210,000	8.2	708,700	17.3
Other	2,199,000[2]	14.8[2]	234,900[3]	5.7[3]
TOTAL	14,823,900[4]	100.0[4]	4,094,400	100.0

Household income and expenditure. Average household size (2000) 2.7; income per household[5] (2001) Ft 2,898,000 (U.S.$10,300); sources of income (2001): wages 48.3%, transfers 25.7%, self-employment 16.3%, other 9.7%; expenditure (2001): food and beverages 35.1%, transportation and communications 23.2%, housing and energy 17.4%, clothing 6.1%, health 5.4%.

Foreign trade[6]

Balance of trade (current prices)

	1997	1998	1999	2000	2001	2002
Ft '000,000,000	–394	–577	–707	–1,121	–917	–830
% of total	5.2%	5.5%	5.6%	6.6%	5.0%	4.5%

Imports (2001): Ft 9,665,000,000,000 (electrical machinery 17.5%, nonelectrical machinery 14.6%, road vehicles 7.3%, computers and office machines 5.9%, telecommunications equipment 5.9%). *Major import sources:* Germany 24.9%; Italy 7.9%; Austria 7.4%; Russia 7.0%; France 4.7%.
Exports (2001): Ft 8,748,000,000,000 (telecommunications equipment 12.6%, electrical machinery 11.9%, power-generating machinery 10.7%, road vehicles 8.9%, office machines and computers 8.4%). *Major export destinations:* Germany 35.6%; Austria 7.9%; Italy 6.3%; France 6.0%; U.S. 5.0%.

Transport and communications

Transport. Railroads (2001): route length 7,897 km; passenger-km 9,902,000,000; metric ton-km cargo 7,426,000,000. Roads (1999): total length 188,203 km (paved 43%). Vehicles (2002): passenger cars 2,630,000; trucks and buses 387,000. Air transport (2001): passenger-km 3,146,000,000; (2002) metric ton-km cargo 64,400,000; airports (2002) with scheduled flights 1.

Communications

Medium	date	unit	number	units per 1,000 persons
Daily newspapers	1996	circulation	1,895,000	186
Radio	2000	receivers	7,050,000	690
Television	2000	receivers	4,460,000	437
Telephones	2002	main lines	3,666,400	361
Cellular telephones	2002	subscribers	6,562,000	646
Personal computers	2002	units	1,100,000	108
Internet	2002	users	1,600,000	158

Education and health

Educational attainment (1990). Population age 25 and over having: no formal schooling 1.3%; primary education 57.9%; secondary 30.7%; higher 10.1%.

Education (2002–03)

	schools	teachers	students	student/ teacher ratio
Primary (age 6–13)	3,792	89,029	933,100	10.5
Secondary (age 14–17)	1,399	37,083	426,400	11.5
Vocational	627	9,305	130,541	14.0
Higher	66	23,151	381,560	16.5

Health (2001): physicians 33,088[7] (1 per 305 persons); hospital beds 80,383 (1 per 127 persons); infant mortality rate per 1,000 live births (2002) 7.2.
Food (2001): daily per capita caloric intake 3,520 (vegetable products 69%, animal products 31%); 134% of FAO recommended minimum requirement.

Military

Total active duty personnel (2002): 33,400 (army 70.7%, air force 23.1%, headquarters staff 6.2%). *Military expenditure as percentage of GNP* (1999): 1.7% (world 2.4%); per capita expenditures U.S.$185.

[1]Budapest acts as the capital of Pest county even though it is administratively not part of Pest county. [2]Represents net taxes on commodities less imputed bank service charge. [3]Unemployed. [4]Detail does not add to total given because of rounding. [5]Adjusted disposable income including government transfers. [6]Imports c.i.f.; exports f.o.b. [7]In active service.

Internet resources for further information:
- **Hungarian Central Statistical Office**
http://www.ksh.hu/pls/ksh/docs/index_eng.html

Iceland

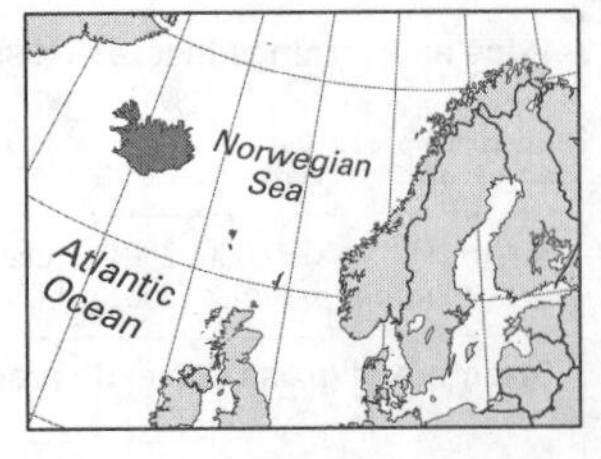

Official name: Lýdhveldidh Ísland (Republic of Iceland).
Form of government: unitary multiparty republic with one legislative house (Althingi [63]).
Chief of state: President.
Head of government: Prime Minister.
Capital: Reykjavík.
Official language: Icelandic.
Official religion: Evangelical Lutheran.
Monetary unit: 1 króna (ISK) = 100 aurar; valuation (Sept. 8, 2003) 1 U.S.$ = ISK 80.73; 1 £ = ISK 128.00.

Area and population

Constituencies[1]	Principal centres	area sq mi	area sq km	population 2002[2] estimate
Austurland	Egilsstadhir	8,773	22,721	11,755
Höfudhborgarsvaedi[3]	Reykjavík	410	1,062	179,781
Nordhurland eystra	Akureyri	8,482	21,968	26,761
Nordhurland vestra	Saudhárkrókur	4,918	12,737	9,213
Sudhurland	Selfoss	9,469	24,526	21,473
Sudhurnes	Keflavík	320	829	16,793
Vestfirdhir	Ísafjördhur	3,633	9,409	7,930
Vesturland	Borgarnes	3,689	9,554	14,495
Unallocated area	—	47	122	0
TOTAL		39,741	102,928	288,201

Demography

Population (2003): 290,000.
Density (2003)[4]: persons per sq mi 31.6, persons per sq km 12.2.
Urban-rural (2001): urban 93.7%; rural 6.3%.
Sex distribution (2002): male 50.06%; female 49.94%.
Age breakdown (2002): under 15, 23.1%; 15–29, 22.4%; 30–44, 22.0%; 45–59, 17.4%; 60–74, 9.8%; 75 and over, 5.3%.
Population projection: (2010) 307,000; (2020) 330,000.
Doubling time: 79 years.
Ethnic composition (2002)[5]: Icelandic 93.6%; European 4.5%, of which Nordic 1.9%; Asian 1.0%; other 0.9%.
Religious affiliation (2001): Protestant 92.2%, of which Evangelical Lutheran 87.1%, other Lutheran 4.1%; Roman Catholic 1.7%; other and not specified 6.1%.
Major cities (2002): Reykjavík 111,748 (urban area 179,781); Kópavogur 24,950[6]; Hafnarfjördhur 20,675[6]; Akureyri 15,840; Gardabær 8,687[6].

Vital statistics

Birth rate per 1,000 population (2001): 14.6 (world avg. 21.3); legitimate 36.7%; illegitimate 63.3%.
Death rate per 1,000 population (2001): 6.1 (world avg. 9.1).
Natural increase rate per 1,000 population (2001): 8.5 (world avg. 12.2).
Total fertility rate (avg. births per childbearing woman; 2001): 1.9.
Marriage rate per 1,000 population (2001): 5.2.
Divorce rate per 1,000 population (2001): 1.9.
Life expectancy at birth (2000–01): male 78.1 years; female 82.2 years.
Major causes of death per 100,000 population (1998): diseases of the circulatory system 270.3, of which ischemic heart diseases 142.1, cerebrovascular disease 68.3; malignant neoplasms (cancers) 184.8; diseases of the respiratory system 54.8; injury and poisoning 42.4.

National economy

Budget (2001). Revenue: ISK 288,848,000,000 (current revenue 94.5%, of which direct taxes 44.6%, indirect taxes 44.3%; development revenue 5.5%). Expenditures: ISK 272,588,000,000 (current expenditure 87.4%; development expenditure 12.6%).
Public debt (2000): U.S.$2,242,600,000.
Production (metric tons except as noted). Agriculture, forestry, fishing (2001): potatoes 11,366, cereals 4,337, cucumbers 1,049, hay 2,391,067 cu m; livestock (number of live animals) 473,535 sheep, 73,809 horses, 70,168 cattle; fish catch (value in ISK '000,000; 2001) 70,885, of which cod 30,045, redfish 4,075, halibut 3,821, herring 3,756, shrimp 3,522. Mining and quarrying (2002): diatomite 31,000. Manufacturing (value added in ISK '000,000; 1996): preserved and processed fish 18,114; other food products 10,848; printing and publishing 6,914; fabricated metal products 6,640; nonferrous metals 2,932; wood furniture 2,379. Energy production (consumption): electricity (kW-hr; 2001) 8,028,000,000 (8,028,000,000); coal (metric tons; 1999) none (60,000); crude petroleum, none (none); petroleum products (metric tons; 1999) none (581,000).
Land use (1994): forested 1.2%; meadows and pastures 22.7%; agricultural and under permanent cultivation 0.1%; other 76.0%.
Population economically active (2001): total 162,700; activity rate of total population 57.1% (participation rates: ages 16–74, 83.6%; female 46.7%; unemployed 2.3%).

Price and earnings indexes (1995 = 100)

	1996	1997	1998	1999	2000	2001	2002
Consumer price index	102.3	104.1	105.9	109.3	114.9	122.3	128.6
Hourly earnings index	...	...	...	...	...	...	...

Tourism (2001): receipts U.S.$335,000,000; expenditures U.S.$416,000,000.
Gross national product (2001): U.S.$8,200,000,000 (U.S.$28,910 per capita).

Structure of gross domestic product and labour force

	2001 in value ISK '000,000[7]	% of total value[7]	labour force	% of labour force
Agriculture	11,400	1.5	6,400	3.9
Fishing	102,200	13.2	6,000	3.7
Fish processing			6,800	4.2
Manufacturing, mining	89,900	11.6	16,400	10.1
Construction	76,000	9.8	11,400	7.0
Public utilities	27,000	3.5	1,500	0.9
Transp. and commun.	63,000	8.1	10,100	6.2
Trade, restaurants	109,600	14.2	29,500	18.1
Finance, real estate	[8]	[8]	20,000	12.3
Public administration	159,400	20.6	6,200	3.8
Services	179,000[8]	23.1[8]	44,700	27.5
Other	–43,300[9]	–5.6[9]	3,700	2.3
TOTAL	774,200	100.0	162,700	100.0

Household income and expenditure. Average household size (2000) 2.8; annual income per household (2001) ISK 2,322,000 (U.S.$22,600); sources of income (2001): wages and salaries 78.6%, pension 10.3%, self-employment 2.0%, other 9.1%; expenditure (2002): food and beverages 20.6%, transportation and communications 18.8%, housing and energy 18.3%, recreation and culture 14.2%, household goods 6.8%.

Foreign trade[10]

Balance of trade (current prices)

	1997	1998	1999	2000	2001	2002
ISK '000,000	–10,127	–31,513	–36,189	–53,949	–24,292	–4,215
% of total	3.7%	9.8%	11.1%	15.3%	5.8%	1.0%

Imports (2002): ISK 207,609,000,000 (machinery and apparatus 20.4%; transport equipment 11.9%; food products 9.5%; crude petroleum and petroleum products 7.9%; clothing and footwear 4.4%). *Major import sources:* U.S. 11.1%; Germany 10.7%; Denmark 8.5%; Norway 8.0%; U.K. 7.4%; The Netherlands 6.0%.
Exports (2002): ISK 203,394,000,000 (marine products 62.8%, of which cod 23.9%, shrimp 6.3%, redfish 5.3%, haddock 4.0%; aluminum 18.9%; medicinal products 3.0%). *Major export destinations:* Germany 18.5%; U.K. 17.6%; U.S. 10.8%; The Netherlands 10.8%; Spain 5.3%.

Transport and communications

Transport. Railroads: none. Roads (2002): total length 8,050 mi, 12,955 km (paved 33%). Vehicles (2002): passenger cars 159,865; trucks and buses 21,701. Air transport (2001)[11]: passenger-mi 2,312,000,000, passenger-km 3,720,000,000; short ton-mi cargo 69,000,000, metric ton-km cargo 101,000,000; airports (1996) with scheduled flights 24.

Communications

Medium	date	unit	number	units per 1,000 persons
Daily newspapers	2000	circulation	100,000	347
Radio	2000	receivers	270,000	960
Television	2000	receivers	143,000	509
Telephones	2001	main lines	190,600	664
Cellular telephones	2002	subscribers	260,000	903
Personal computers	2002	units	130,000	451
Internet	2002	users	175,000	607

Education and health

Educational attainment (2001): Percentage of population ages 25–64 having primary and some secondary education 36.6%; secondary 44.8%; higher 18.6%. *Literacy:* virtually 100%.

Education (2000–01)

	schools	teachers	students	student/teacher ratio
Primary/lower secondary (age 7–15)	193	4,490	44,137	9.8
Upper secondary (age 16–19)	36	2,198	20,740	9.4
Higher	11	1,489	11,964	8.0

Health: physicians (2002) 990 (1 per 289 persons); hospital beds 2,432 (1 per 118 persons); infant mortality rate (2001) 3.0.
Food (2001): daily per capita caloric intake 3,313 (vegetable products 59%, animal products 41%); 121% of FAO recommended minimum requirement.

Military

Total active duty personnel (2002): 120 coast guard personnel; NATO-sponsored U.S.-manned Iceland Defense Force (2003): 1,700. *Military expenditure as percentage of GNP* (1999): none (world average 2.4%).

[1]Constituencies are electoral districts. Actual local administration is based on towns or rural districts. [2]December 1st. [3]In English, Capital Region. [4]Population density calculated with reference to 9,191 sq mi (23,805 sq km) area free of glaciers (comprising 4,603 sq mi [11,922 sq km]), lava fields or wasteland (comprising 24,918 sq mi [64,538 sq km]), and lakes (comprising 1,064 sq mi [2,757 sq km]). [5]By country of birth. [6]Within Reykjavík urban area. [7]Breakdown by sector is estimated. [8]Services include Finance, real estate. [9]Indirect taxes and production of private nonprofit institution less imputed bank service charges and subsidies. [10]Imports c.i.f.; exports f.o.b. [11]Icelandair only.

Internet resources for further information:
- **Statistics Iceland http://www.statice.is**
- **Central Bank of Iceland http://www.sedlabanki.is**

India

Official name: Bharat (Hindi); Republic of India (English).
Form of government: multiparty federal republic with two legislative houses (Council of States [245[1]], House of the People [545[2]]).
Chief of state: President.
Head of government: Prime Minister.
Capital: New Delhi.
Official languages: Hindi; English.
Official religion: none.
Monetary unit: 1 Indian rupee (Re, plural Rs) = 100 paise; valuation (Sept. 8, 2003) 1 U.S.$ = Rs 45.87; 1 £ = Rs 72.72.

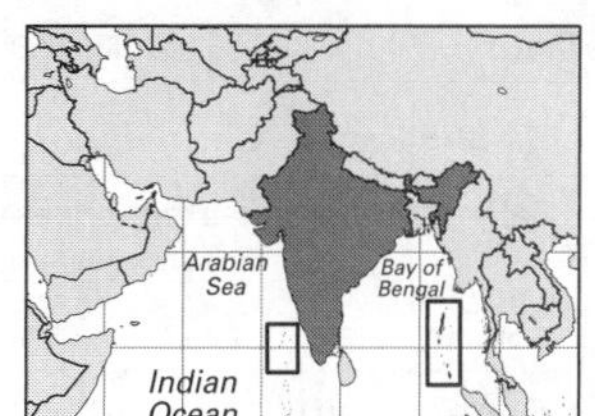

Area and population

		area		population
States	**Capitals**	sq mi	sq km	2001 preliminary census
Andhra Pradesh	Hyderabad	106,204	275,068	75,727,541
Arunachal Pradesh	Itanagar	32,333	83,743	1,091,117
Assam	Dispur	30,285	78,438	26,638,407
Bihar	Patna	38,301	99,200	82,878,796
Chhattisgarh	Raipur	52,199	135,194	20,795,956
Goa	Panaji	1,429	3,702	1,343,998
Gujarat	Gandhinagar	75,685	196,024	50,596,992
Haryana	Chandigarh	17,070	44,212	21,082,989
Himachal Pradesh	Shimla	21,495	55,673	6,077,248
Jammu and Kashmir	Srinagar	39,146	101,387	10,069,917
Jharkhand	Ranchi	28,833	74,677	26,909,428
Karnataka	Bangalore	74,051	191,791	52,733,958
Kerala	Thiruvananthapuram (Trivandrum)	15,005	38,863	31,838,619
Madhya Pradesh	Bhopal	119,016	308,252	60,385,118
Maharashtra	Mumbai (Bombay)	118,800	307,690	96,752,247
Manipur	Imphal	8,621	22,327	2,388,634
Meghalaya	Shillong	8,660	22,429	2,306,069
Mizoram	Aizawl	8,139	21,081	891,058
Nagaland	Kohima	6,401	16,579	1,988,636
Orissa	Bhubaneshwar	60,119	155,707	36,706,920
Punjab	Chandigarh	19,445	50,362	24,289,296
Rajasthan	Jaipur	132,139	342,239	56,473,122
Sikkim	Gangtok	2,740	7,096	540,493
Tamil Nadu	Chennai (Madras)	50,216	130,058	62,110,839
Tripura	Agartala	4,049	10,486	3,191,168
Uttar Pradesh	Lucknow	93,933	243,286	166,052,859
Uttaranchal	Dehra Dun	19,739	51,125	8,479,562
West Bengal	Kolkata (Calcutta)	34,267	88,752	80,221,171
Union Territories				
Andaman and Nicobar Islands	Port Blair	3,185	8,249	356,265
Chandigarh	Chandigarh	44	114	900,914
Dadra and Nagar Haveli	Silvassa	190	491	220,451
Daman and Diu	Daman	43	112	158,059
Lakshadweep	Kavaratti	12	32	60,595
Pondicherry	Pondicherry	190	492	973,829
National Capital Territory				
Delhi[3]	Delhi	573	1,483	13,782,976
TOTAL		1,222,559[4, 5]	3,166,414[4]	1,027,015,247

Demography

Population (2003): 1,065,462,000.
Density (2003)[4]: persons per sq mi 871.5, persons per sq km 336.5.
Urban-rural (2001): urban 27.8%; rural 72.2%.
Sex distribution (2001): male 51.73%; female 48.27%.
Age breakdown (2000): under 15, 33.6%; 15–29, 27.7%; 30–44, 19.8%; 45–59, 11.9%; 60–74, 5.6%; 75 and over, 1.4%.
Population projection: (2010) 1,173,806,000; (2020) 1,312,212,000.
Doubling time: 46 years.
Major cities (2001; *urban agglomerations,* 2001): Greater Mumbai (Greater Bombay) 11,914,398 (16,368,084); Delhi 9,817,439 (12,791,458); Kolkata (Calcutta) 4,580,544 (13,216,546); Bangalore 4,292,223 (5,686,844); Chennai (Madras) 4,216,268 (6,424,624); Ahmadabad 3,515,361 (4,519,278); Hyderabad 3,449,878 (5,533,640); Pune (Poona) 2,540,069 (3,755,525); Kanpur 2,532,138 (2,690,486); Surat 2,433,787 (2,811,466); Jaipur 2,324,319 (2,324,-319); New Delhi[6] 294,783.

Other principal cities (2001)[7]

	population		population		population
Agra	1,259,979	Jodhpur	846,408	Shambajinagar (Aurangabad)	873,037
Allahabad (Prayag Raj)	990,298	Kalyan[9]	1,193,266	Sholapur (Solapur)	873,037
Amritsar	975,695	Kota	537,371	Srinagar	894,940
Bhopal	1,433,875	Lucknow	2,207,340	Thane (Thana)[9]	1,261,517
Chandigarh	808,796	Ludhiana	1,395,053	Thiruvananthapuram (Trivandrum)	744,739
Coimbatore	923,085	Madurai	922,913	Tiruchirappalli	746,062
Faridabad	1,054,981	Meerut	1,074,229	Vadodara (Baroda)	1,306,035
Ghaziabad	968,521	Mysore	742,261	Varanasi (Benares)	1,100,748
Guwahati	808,021	Nagpur	2,051,320	Vijayawada	825,436
Gwalior	826,919	Nashik (Nasik)	1,076,967	Vishakhapatnam	969,608
Howrah (Haora)[8]	1,008,704	Patna	1,376,950		
Hubli-Dharwad	786,018	Pimpri-Chinchwad[10]	1,006,417		
Indore	1,597,441	Rajkot	966,642		
Jabalpur	951,469	Ranchi	846,454		

Linguistic composition (1991)[11]: Hindi 27.58% (including associated languages and dialects, 39.85%); Bengali 8.22%; Telugu 7.80%; Marathi 7.38%; Tamil 6.26%; Urdu 5.13%; Gujarati 4.81%; Kannada 3.87%; Malayalam 3.59%; Oriya 3.32%; Punjabi 2.76%; Assamese 1.55%; Bhili/Bhilodi 0.66%; Santhali 0.62%; Kashmiri 0.47%[12]; Gondi 0.25%; Sindhi 0.25%; Nepali 0.25%; Konkani 0.21%; Tulu 0.18%; Kurukh 0.17%; Manipuri 0.15%; Bodo 0.14%; Khandeshi 0.12%; other 3.26%. Hindi (66.00%) and English (19.00%) are also spoken as lingua francas (second languages).
Religious affiliation (2000): Hindu 73.72%; Muslim 11.96%, of which Sunnī 8.97%, Shīʿī 2.99%; Christian 6.08%, of which Independent 2.99%, Protestant 1.47%, Roman Catholic 1.35%, Orthodox 0.27%; traditional beliefs 3.39%; Sikh 2.16%; Buddhist 0.71%; Jain 0.40%; Bahāʾī 0.12%; Zoroastrian (Parsi) 0.02%; other 1.44%.
Households (2001). Total number of households 191,963,935. Average household size 5.4. Type of household: permanent 51.8%; semipermanent 30.0%; temporary 18.2%. Average number of rooms per household 2.2; 1 room 38.4%, 2 rooms 30.0%, 3 rooms 14.3%, 4 rooms 7.5%, 5 rooms 2.9%, 6 or more rooms 3.7%, unspecified number of rooms 3.2%.

Vital statistics

Birth rate per 1,000 population (2002): 23.8 (world avg. 21.3).
Death rate per 1,000 population (2002): 8.6 (world avg. 9.1).
Natural increase rate per 1,000 population (2002): 15.2 (world avg. 12.2).
Total fertility rate (avg. births per childbearing woman; 2002): 2.9.
Life expectancy at birth (2002): male 62.9 years; female 64.4 years.
Major causes of death per 100,000 population (1987)[13]: diseases of the circulatory system 227; infectious and parasitic diseases 215; diseases of the respiratory system 108; certain conditions originating in the perinatal period 108; accidents, homicide, and other violence 102; diseases of the digestive system 48; diseases of the nervous system 43; malignant neoplasms (cancers) 41; endocrine, metabolic, and nutritional disorders 30; diseases of the blood and blood-forming organs 25; ill-defined conditions 129.

Social indicators

Educational attainment (1991)[14, 15]. Percentage of population age 25 and over having: no formal schooling 57.5%; incomplete primary education 28.0%; complete primary or some secondary 7.2%; complete secondary or higher 7.3%.

Distribution of expenditure (1994)

percentage of household expenditure by decile/quintile

1	2	3	4	5	6	7	8	9	10 (highest)
4.1	5.1	—13.0—		—16.8—		—21.7—		14.3	25.0

Quality of working life. Average workweek (1989): 42 hours[16]. Rate of fatal (nonfatal) injuries per 100,000 industrial workers (1989) 17 (3,625)[16]. Agricultural workers in servitude to creditors (early 1990s) 10–20%.
Access to services (2001). Percentage of total (urban, rural) households having access to: electricity for lighting purposes 55.8% (87.6%, 43.5%); kerosene for lighting purposes 43.3% (11.6%, 55.6%), water closets 18.0% (46.1%, 7.1%), pit latrines 11.5% (14.6%, 10.3%), no latrines 63.6% (26.3%, 78.1%), closed drainage for waste water 12.5% (34.5%, 3.9%), open drainage for waste water 33.9% (43.4%, 30.3%), no drainage for waste water 53.6% (22.1%, 65.8%). Type of fuel used for cooking in households: firewood 52.5% (22.7%, 64.1%), LPG (liquefied petroleum gas) 17.5% (48.0%, 5.7%), kerosene 6.5% (19.2%, 1.6%), crop residue 10.0% (2.1%, 13.1%), cow dung 9.8% (2.0%, 12.8%), electricity 0.2% (0.3%, 0.1%). Source of drinking water: hand pump or tube well 41.3% (21.3%, 48.9%), piped water 36.7% (68.7%, 24.3%), well 18.2% (7.7%, 22.2%), river, canal, spring, public tank, pond, or lake 2.7% (0.7%, 3.5%).
Social participation. Eligible voters participating in September/October 1999 national election: 59.6%. Trade union membership (1998): *c.* 16,000,000 (primarily in the public sector).
Social deviance (1990)[17]. Offense rate per 100,000 population for: murder 4.1; dacoity (gang robbery) 1.3; theft and housebreaking 56.6; riots 12.0. Rate of suicide per 100,000 population (1991): 9.0.
Material well-being (2001). Total (urban, rural) households possessing: television receivers 31.6% (64.3%, 18.9%), telephones 9.1% (23.0%, 3.8%), scooters, motorcycles, or mopeds 11.7% (24.7%, 6.7%), cars, jeeps, or vans 2.5% (5.6%, 1.3%). Households availing banking services 35.5% (49.5%, 30.1%).

National economy

Gross national product (2001): U.S.$477,400,000,000 (U.S.$460 per capita).

Structure of gross domestic product and labour force

	2000–01[18]		1993–94	
	in value Rs '000,000,000[19]	% of total value	labour force	% of labour force
Agriculture, forestry	4,719.8	24.9	240,700,000	64.7
Mining	446.5	2.4	2,600,000	0.7
Manufacturing	2,997.5	15.8	39,100,000	10.5
Construction	1,164.3	6.1	11,900,000	3.2
Public utilities	495.3	2.6	1,500,000	0.4
Transp. and commun.	1,383.3	7.3	10,400,000	2.8
Trade, restaurants	2,612.9	13.8	27,500,000	7.4
Finance, real estate	2,366.5	12.5	38,300,000	10.3
Pub. admin., defense; Services	2,772.4	14.6		
TOTAL	18,958.4[5]	100.0	372,000,000	100.0

Budget (2001–02). Revenue[20]: Rs 2,143,000,000,000 (tax revenue 62.7%, nontax revenue 36.5%, grants 0.8%). Expenditures: Rs 3,589,000,000,000 (current expenditure 87.6%, capital expenditure 12.4%).
Public debt (external, outstanding; 2001): U.S.$82,695,000,000.
Production (in '000 metric tons except as noted). Agriculture, forestry, fishing (2002): cereals 491,174 (of which rice 116,580, wheat 71,814, corn [maize]

10,570, sorghum 7,060, millet 6,150), sugarcane 279,000, fruits 34,720 (of which bananas 16,450, mangoes 11,400, oranges 2,980, apples 1,420, lemons and limes 1,370, pineapples 1,100), oilseeds 16,750 (of which peanuts [groundnuts] 5,400, rapeseed 5,040, soybeans 4,270, sunflower seeds 870, castor beans 590, sesame 580), pulses 10,760 (of which chickpeas 5,320, dry beans 3,000, pigeon peas 2,440), coconuts 9,300, eggplants 8,800, seed cotton 5,580, jute 1,789, tea 826, natural rubber 650, tobacco 575, garlic 497, cashews 460, betel 330, coffee 317, ginger 275, pepper 51; livestock (number of live animals; 2002) 221,900,000 cattle, 124,000,000 goats, 95,100,000 water buffalo, 58,800,000 sheep, 18,000,000 pigs, 900,000 camels; roundwood 319,418,047 cu m, of which fuelwood 300,564,000 cu m, industrial roundwood 18,854,000; fish catch (metric tons; 2001) 5,965,230, of which freshwater fish 2,950,003, marine fish 2,301,609, crustaceans 498,827. Mining and quarrying (2001–02): limestone 129,771; iron ore 52,521[21]; bauxite 8,585; manganese 621[21]; chromium 543[21]; zinc 239[21]; copper 42[21]; gold 88,703 troy oz; gem diamonds 81,448 carats. Manufacturing (value added in Rs '000,000,000; 1999): iron and steel 188.1; industrial chemicals 167.7; paints, soaps, varnishes, drugs, and medicines 164.2; transport equipment 159.7; food products 139.0; textiles 136.8; electrical machinery 118.6; nonelectrical machinery 116.3; refined petroleum 79.2; cements, bricks, and tiles 67.2; fabricated metal products 39.5; nonferrous base metals 37.5.

Manufacturing enterprises (1995–96)[22]

	no. of factories	no. of persons engaged	avg. wages as a % of avg. of all wages	annual value added (Rs '000,000)[23]
Chemicals and chemical products,	9,206	758,500	140.3	237,093
of which synthetic fibres	395	97,100	183.8	68,420
fertilizers/pesticides	753	104,500	217.4	59,521
drugs and medicine	2,542	204,600	129.3	40,050
paints, soaps, and cosmetics	1,958	104,300	129.0	23,459
Transport equipment,	6,120	838,600	142.7	120,207
of which motor vehicles	3,758	392,400	162.4	77,240
motorcycles and bicycles	1,243	124,900	123.6	21,957
Textiles	16,228	1,579,400	80.2	99,855
Iron and steel	3,519	507,700	152.9	97,274
Nonelectrical machinery/apparatus	9,075	548,400	137.2	92,762
Food products,	22,878	1,285,900	60.4	92,163
of which refined sugar	1,285	341,000	92.0	28,125
Electrical machinery/apparatus,	5,472	443,700	149.4	84,320
of which industrial machinery	2,048	165,600	190.8	35,717
Refined petroleum	161	31,100	349.3	52,778
Bricks, cement, plaster products	10,067	394,500	70.3	49,413
Nonferrous basic metals	3,301	228,700	124.3	42,252
Fabricated metal products	7,984	277,700	98.6	32,565
Paper and paper products	2,742	175,200	99.5	26,380
Wearing apparel	3,463	263,700	55.0	23,485

Energy production (consumption): electricity (kW-hr; 2002) 529,692,000,000 ([1999] 533,910,000,000); hard coal (metric tons; 2002) 335,256,000 ([1999] 328,266,000); lignite (metric tons; 2002) 22,824,000 ([1999] 22,522,000); crude petroleum (barrels; 2002) 248,520,000 ([1999] 572,100,000); petroleum products (metric tons; 1999) 60,700,000 (68,164,000); natural gas (cu m; 2002) 29,495,000,000 ([1999] 23,243,500,000).

Financial aggregates[24]

	1997	1998	1999	2000	2001	2002	2003
Exchange rate, Rs per:							
U.S. dollar	39.28	42.48	43.49	46.75	48.18	48.03	46.47[25]
£	64.96	70.67	70.30	69.76	69.88	77.41	76.68[25]
SDR	53.00	59.81	59.69	60.91	60.55	65.30	65.10[25]
International reserves (U.S.$)							
Total (excl. gold; '000,000)	24,688	27,341	32,667	37,902	45,870	67,665	79,519[25]
SDRs ('000,000)	77	83	4	2	5	7	1[25]
Reserve pos. in IMF ('000,000)	287	300	671	637	614	665	972[25]
Foreign exchange ('000,000)	24,324	26,958	31,992	37,264	45,251	66,994	78,546[25]
Gold ('000,000 fine troy oz)	12.740	11.487	11.502	11.502	11.502	11.502	11.502[25]
% world reserves	1.4	1.2	1.2	1.2	1.2	1.2	1.2[25]
Interest and prices							
Central bank discount (%)	9.00	9.00	8.00	8.00	6.50	6.25	6.00[25]
Advance (prime) rate (%)	13.8	13.5	12.5	12.3	12.1	11.9	11.5[25]
Industrial share prices (1995 = 100)[26]	113.2	99.5	123.5	137.3	103.6	97.0	…
Balance of payments (U.S.$'000,000)							
Balance of visible trade	–10,028	–10,752	–8,679	–12,193	…	…	…
Imports, f.o.b.	45,730	44,828	45,556	55,325	…	…	…
Exports, f.o.b.	35,702	34,076	36,877	43,132	…	…	…
Balance of invisibles	+7,063	+3,849	+5,451	+7,995	…	…	…
Balance of payments, current account	–2,965	–6,903	–3,228	–4,198	…	…	…

Land use (1994): forested 23.0%; meadows and pastures 3.8%; agricultural and under permanent cultivation 57.1%; other 16.1%.

Population economically active (1993–94): total 372,000,000; activity rate of total population *c.* 41% (participation rates: n.a.; female 32.5%; unemployed[27]).

Price and earnings indexes (1995 = 100)

	1996	1997	1998	1999	2000	2001	2002
Consumer price index	109.0	116.8	132.2	138.4	144.0	149.3	155.8
Monthly earnings index	98.2	93.9	…	…	…	…	…

Household income and expenditure. Average household size (2001) 5.4; sources of income (1984–85): salaries and wages 42.2%, self-employed 39.7%, interest 8.6%, profits and dividends 6.0%, rent 3.5%; expenditure (1998–99): food, beverages, and tobacco 52.1%, transportation and communications 13.7%, housing and energy 10.2%, clothing and footwear 5.2%, health 4.4%.

Service enterprises (net value added in Rs '000,000,000; 1998–99): wholesale and retail trade 1,562; finance, real estate, and insurance 1,310; transport and storage 804; community, social, and personal services 763; construction 545; electricity, gas, and steam 287.

Tourism (2001): U.S.$3,042,000,000; expenditures (2000) U.S.$2,567,000,000.

Foreign trade[28, 29]

Balance of trade (current prices)

	1996–97	1997–98	1998–99	1999–2000	2000–01	2001–02
U.S.$'000,000	–5,663	–6,478	–9,170	–12,848	–5,976	–7,527
% of total	7.8%	8.5%	12.1%	14.9%	6.3%	8.0%

Imports (2001–02): U.S.$51,087,000,000 (crude petroleum and refined petroleum 27.4%; precious and semiprecious stones 9.0%; gold and silver 8.9%; electronic goods 7.4%; nonelectrical machinery and apparatus 5.8%; organic and inorganic chemicals 5.4%). *Major import sources:* U.S. 6.1%; Switzerland 5.6%; Belgium 5.4%; U.K. 5.0%; Japan 4.0%; Germany 4.0%; China 4.0%; South Africa 2.8%; Singapore 2.5%; Malaysia 2.2%.

Exports (2001–02): U.S.$43,560,000,000 (cut and polished diamonds and jewelry 16.8%; cotton ready-made garments 11.4%; food and agricultural products 10.6%; chemicals and chemical products 8.4%; cotton yarn, fabrics, and thread 7.0%; petroleum products 4.9%; footwear and leather manufactures 4.4%; machinery and apparatus 4.2%; fabricated metals 3.6%). *Major export destinations:* U.S. 19.5%; United Arab Emirates 5.7%; Hong Kong 5.4%; U.K. 4.9%; Germany 4.1%; Japan 3.4%; Belgium 3.2%; Italy 2.8%; France 2.2%; Bangladesh 2.2%; Singapore 2.2%.

Transport and communications

Transport. Railroads (1998–99): route length 39,028 mi, 62,809 km; (2001–02) passenger-mi 309,225,000,000, passenger-km 497,651,000,000; (2001–02) short ton-mi cargo 227,264,000,000, metric ton-km cargo 331,800,000,000. Roads (1999): total length 2,062,727 mi, 3,319,644 km (paved 46%). Vehicles (1997): passenger cars 4,662,000; trucks and buses 2,748,000. Air transport (2001)[30]: passenger-mi 11,969,000,000, passenger-km 19,263,000,000; short ton-mi cargo 308,451,000, metric ton-km cargo 450,331,000; airports (1996) with scheduled flights 66.

Communications

Medium	date	unit	number	units per 1,000 persons
Daily newspapers	2000	circulation	61,000,000	60
Radio	2000	receivers	123,000,000	121
Television	2000	receivers	79,000,000	78
Telephones	2002	main lines	41,420,000	40
Cellular telephones	2002	subscribers	12,688,000	12
Personal computers	2001	units	6,000,000	5.8
Internet	2002	users	16,580,000	16

Education and health

Literacy (2000): percentage of total population age 15 and over literate 57.2%; males literate 68.4%; females literate 45.4%.

Education (2000–01)

	schools	teachers	students	student/ teacher ratio
Primary (age 6–10)	638,738	1,896,791	113,826,978	60.0
Secondary (age 11–17)	293,944	2,332,497	61,802,703	26.5
Higher	38,372	755,798	9,851,291	13.0

Health: physicians (1992) 410,875 (1 per 2,173 persons); hospital beds (1993) 659,000 (1 per 1,364 persons); infant mortality rate (2002) 59.6.

Food (2001): daily per capita caloric intake 2,487 (vegetable products 92%, animal products 8%); 113% of FAO recommended minimum requirement.

Military

Total active duty personnel (2003): 1,326,000 (army 83.0%, navy 4.2%, air force 12.8%); personnel in paramilitary forces 1,089,700. *Military expenditure as percentage of GNP* (1999): 2.5% (world 2.4%); per capita expenditure U.S.$11.

[1]Council of States can have a maximum of 250 members; a maximum of 12 of these members may be nominated by the President. [2]Includes 2 nonelective seats. [3]Bill changing the status of Delhi to full statehood introduced in the House of the People in August 2003. [4]Excludes 46,660 sq mi (120,849 sq km) of territory claimed by India as part of Jammu and Kashmir but occupied by Pakistan or China; inland water constitutes 9.6% of total area of India (including all of Indian-claimed Jammu and Kashmir). [5]Detail does not add to total given because of rounding. [6]Within Delhi urban agglomeration. [7]Preliminary figures. [8]Within Kolkata urban agglomeration. [9]Within Greater Mumbai urban agglomeration. [10]Within Pune urban agglomeration. [11]Mother tongue unless otherwise noted. [12]1981. [13]Projected rates based on about 3.5% of total deaths (317,392 registered deaths out of an estimated total of nearly 9,000,000 deaths). [14]Excludes Jammu and Kashmir. [15]No formal schooling (1991): males 43.3%, females 72.8%; complete secondary or higher education (1991): males 10.6%, females 3.7%. [16]Data apply to the workers employed in the "organized sector" only (28.2 million in 1997–98, of which 19.4 million were employed in the public sector and 8.8 million were employed in the private sector); few legal protections exist for the more than 350 million workers in the "unorganized sector." [17]Crimes reported to National Crime Records Bureau by police authorities of state governments. [18]Provisional. [19]At factor cost. [20]Central government only. [21]Approximate metal content of ore. [22]Establishments using power with at least 10 workers on any workday and all establishments employing 20 or more workers. [23]In factor values. [24]End-of-period unless otherwise noted. [25]June. [26]Period average. [27]Average number of registered unemployed in February 2000 was 40,395,000. [28]Imports c.i.f.; exports f.o.b. [29]Fiscal year beginning April 1. [30]Air India and Indian Airlines.

Internet resources for further information:

- **India Image: Directory of Government Web Sites http://www.nic.in**
- **Census of India http://www.censusindia.net**
- **Reserve Bank of India http://www.rbi.org.in**
- **India Infoline.com http://www.indiainfoline.com**

Indonesia

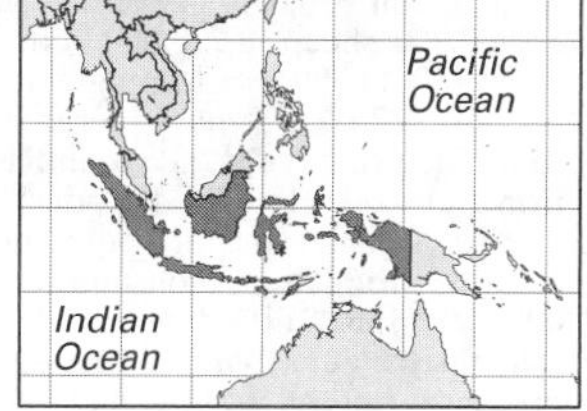

Official name: Republik Indonesia (Republic of Indonesia).
Form of government: unitary multiparty republic with two legislative houses (People's Consultative Assembly [700[1]]; House of People's Representatives [500[2]]).
Head of state and government: President.
Capital: Jakarta.
Official language: Indonesian.
Official religion: monotheism.
Monetary unit: 1 Indonesian rupiah (Rp) = 100 sen; valuation (Sept. 8, 2003) 1 U.S.$ = Rp 8,485; 1 £ = Rp 13,453.

Area and population

Island(s) Provinces	area sq km	population 2000 census[3]
Bali and the Lesser Sunda Islands[4]	73,135	11,112,702
Bali	5,633	3,151,162
East Nusa Tenggara	47,349	3,952,279
West Nusa Tenggara	20,153	4,009,261
Celebes (Sulawesi)[5]	191,800	14,946,488
Central Sulawesi	63,689	2,218,435
Gorontalo[6]	12,151	835,044
North Sulawesi	15,337	2,012,098
Southeast Sulawesi	38,140	1,821,284
South Sulawesi	62,483	8,059,627
Java[5]	127,499	121,352,608
Banten[7]	8,232	8,098,780
Central Java	32,549	31,228,940
East Java	47,923	34,783,640
Jakarta[8]	664	8,389,443
West Java	34,945	35,729,537
Yogyakarta[9]	3,186	3,122,268
Kalimantan[5, 10]	547,891	11,331,558
Central Kalimantan	153,564	1,857,000
East Kalimantan	210,985	2,455,120
South Kalimantan	36,535	2,985,240
West Kalimantan	146,807	4,034,198
Maluku (Moluccas)	77,871	1,990,598
Maluku	...	1,205,539
North Maluku	...	785,059
Papua (Irian Jaya)[5, 11]	421,981	2,220,934
Sumatra[5]	482,393	43,309,707
Aceh[9]	55,390	3,930,905
Bangka-Belitung[6]	[12]	900,197
Bengkulu	19,789	1,567,432
Jambi	53,436	2,413,846
Lampung	35,385	6,741,439
North Sumatra	71,680	11,649,655
Riau[11]	94,561	4,957,627
South Sumatra	109,254[12]	6,899,675
West Sumatra	42,898	4,248,931
TOTAL	1,922,570[4]	206,264,595[4]

Demography

Population (2003): 219,883,000.
Density (2003)[4]: persons per sq mi 296.2, persons per sq km 114.4.
Urban-rural (2002): urban 43.0%; rural 57.0%.
Sex distribution (2000): male 50.14%; female 49.86%.
Age breakdown (2000): under 15, 30.4%; 15–29, 29.3%; 30–44, 21.8%; 45–59, 11.3%; 60–74, 5.8%; 75 and over, 1.4%.
Population projection: (2010) 238,374,000; (2020) 261,053,000.
Ethnolinguistic composition (1990): Javanese 39.4%; Sundanese 15.8%; Indonesian (Malay) 12.1%; Madurese 4.3%; Minang 2.4%; other 26.0%.
Religious affiliation (2000): Muslim 76.5%; Christian 13.1%, of which Protestant 5.7%, independent Christian 4.0%, Roman Catholic 2.7%; Hindu 3.4%; traditional beliefs 2.5%; nonreligious 1.9%; other 2.6%.
Major cities (2000): Jakarta 8,347,083 (urban agglomeration [2001] 11,429,000); Surabaya 2,599,796; Bandung 2,136,260; Medan 1,904,273; Bekasi 1,663,802; Palembang 1,451,419; Semarang 1,348,803; Tangerang 1,325,854.

Vital statistics

Birth rate per 1,000 population (2002): 20.3 (world avg. 21.3).
Death rate per 1,000 population (2002): 7.1 (world avg. 9.1).
Total fertility rate (avg. births per childbearing woman; 2002): 2.3.
Marriage rate per 1,000 population (1999–2000): 9.8[13].
Life expectancy at birth (2002): male 65.0 years; female 69.0 years.

National economy

Budget (2002). Revenue: RP 300,190,000,000,000 (tax revenue 70.3%, of which income tax 33.9%, VAT 21.9%; nontax revenue 29.7%, of which revenue from petroleum 15.9%). Expenditures: RP 327,860,000,000,000 (current expenditure 57.7%; development expenditure 12.3%; expenditure 30.0%).
Public debt (external, outstanding; 2001): U.S.$68,378,000,000.
Population economically active (2001): total 98,812,448; activity rate 46.1% (participation rates: over age 15 [2000] 67.8%; unemployed 8.1%).

Price and earnings indexes (1995 = 100)

	1996	1997	1998	1999	2000	2001	2002
Consumer price index	108.0	115.2	181.7	218.9	227.0	255.9	285.2
Earnings index[14]	105.4	116.1	133.9	155.4	...	...	...

Household income and expenditure. Average household size (2000) 3.9.
Production (metric tons except as noted). Agriculture, forestry, fishing (2002): rice 51,603,748, palm fruit oil 40,000,000, sugarcane 23,400,000, cassava 16,723,257, corn (maize) 9,277,258, natural rubber 1,600,000; livestock (number of live animals) 12,400,000 goats, 11,200,000 cattle, 7,350,000 sheep; roundwood (2001) 119,208,572 cu m; fish catch (2001) 5,068,106. Mining and quarrying (2001): bauxite 1,276,000; copper (metal content) 1,081,000; nickel (metal content) 102,000; silver 348,332 kg; gold 166,091 kg. Manufacturing (value added in RP '000,000,000; 2000)[15]: machinery and transport equipment 57,296; food products 44,736; chemicals and plastics 39,168; textiles 38,471; wood products (including furniture) 14,976; paper and paper products 14,456. Energy production (consumption): electricity (kW-hr; 2000) 90,732,000,000 (90,732,000,000); coal (metric tons; 2001) 90,648,000 ([1999] 15,988,000); crude petroleum (barrels; 2002) 507,807,000 ([1999] 312,200,000); petroleum products (metric tons; 1999) 44,500,000 (44,681,000); natural gas (cu m; 2001) 79,379,000,000 ([1999] 29,919,600,000).
Gross national product (2001): U.S.$144,700,000,000 (U.S.$690 per capita).

Structure of gross domestic product and labour force

	2001			
	in value Rp '000,000,000	% of total value	labour force	% of labour force
Agriculture	244,381	16.4	39,743,908	40.2
Mining	202,680	13.6		
Manufacturing	389,321	26.1	13,177,242	13.3
Public utilities	17,286	1.2		
Construction	84,045	5.6	3,837,554	3.9
Transp. and commun.	79,825	5.3	4,448,279	4.5
Trade	239,959	16.1	17,469,129	17.7
Finance, real estate	92,459	6.2	1,127,823	1.2
Pub. admin., defense	81,851	5.5		
Services	59,167	4.0	11,003,482	11.1
Other	—	—	8,005,031[16]	8.1[16]
TOTAL	1,490,974	100.0	98,812,448	100.0

Tourism (2001): receipts U.S.$5,411,000,000; expenditures U.S.$3,406,000,000.

Foreign trade[17]

Balance of trade (current prices)

	1997	1998	1999	2000	2001	2002
U.S.$'000,000	+11,821	+21,510	+24,661	+28,609	+21,105	+25,702
% of total	12.3%	28.2%	33.9%	29.9%	42.4%	29.1%

Imports (2000): U.S.$33,515,000,000 (machinery and apparatus 18.8%, refined petroleum 10.6%, food and live animals 8.3%, crude petroleum 7.8%, organic chemicals 7.3%). *Major import sources:* Japan 16.0%; Singapore 11.3%; U.S. 10.1%; South Korea 6.2%; China 6.0%.
Exports (2000): U.S.$62,124,000,000 (natural gas 10.7%, crude petroleum 9.8%, garments 7.7%, telecommunications equipment 5.6%, wood products 5.2%, computers and parts 4.9%). *Major export destinations:* Japan 23.2%; U.S. 13.7%; Singapore 10.6%; South Korea 7.0%; China 4.5%.

Transport and communications

Transport. Railroads (2000): route length 6,458 km; passenger-km 19,228,000,000; metric ton-km cargo 4,997,000,000. Roads (1999): length 355,951 km (paved 57%). Vehicles (2000): passenger cars 3,038,913; trucks and buses 2,373,414. Air transport (1999): passenger-km 12,389,000,000; metric ton-km cargo 340,932,000; airports (1996) 81.

Communications

Medium	date	unit	number	units per 1,000 persons
Daily newspapers	2000	circulation	4,870,000	23
Radio	2000	receivers	33,200,000	157
Television	2000	receivers	31,500,000	149
Telephones	2002	main lines	7,632,600	36
Cellular telephones	2002	subscribers	11,700,000	55
Personal computers	2001	units	2,300,000	11
Internet	2001	users	4,000,000	19

Education and health

Educational attainment (2000). Percentage of population age 15 and over having: no schooling or incomplete primary 23.9%; primary and some secondary 53.8%; complete secondary 17.9%; some higher 2.2%; complete higher 2.2%. *Literacy* (2000): total population age 15 and over literate 86.9%; males literate 91.8%; females literate 82.0%.

Education (1999–2000)

	schools	teachers	students	student/ teacher ratio
Primary (age 7–12)	150,612	1,141,168	25,614,836	22.4
Secondary (age 13–18)	28,766	656,850	10,496,957	16.0
Voc., teacher tr.	4,169	131,107	1,882,061	14.4
Higher	1,633	194,828	2,919,846	15.0

Health (1999): physicians 31,603 (1 per 6,605 persons); hospital beds 123,398 (1 per 1,692 persons); infant mortality rate (2002) 40.0.
Food (2001): daily per capita caloric intake 2,931 (vegetable products 96%, animal products 4%); 134% of FAO recommended minimum.

Military

Total active duty personnel (2002): 297,000 (army 77.4%, navy 13.5%, air force 9.1%). *Military expenditure as percentage of GNP* (1999): 1.1% (world 2.4%); per capita expenditure U.S.$7.

[1]Includes the 500 members of the House of People's Representatives plus 200 other appointees. [2]Includes 38 nonelective seats reserved for the military. [3]Adjusted figure. [4]Excludes area and population of East Timor. [5]Includes area and population of nearby islands. [6]Formally established February 2001. [7]Formally established November 2000. [8]Formally a metropolitan district. [9]Formally a special autonomous district. [10]Kalimantan is the name of the Indonesian part of the island of Borneo. [11]Effective government is pending in September 2003 in the new provinces created within Papua and Riau. [12]South Sumatra includes Bangka-Belitung. [13]Muslim population only. [14]Based on minimum monthly wages. [15]Medium and large establishments only. [16]Unemployed. [17]Imports c.i.f.; exports f.o.b.

Internet resources for further information:

- **Central Bureau of Statistics http://www.bps.go.id**

Iran

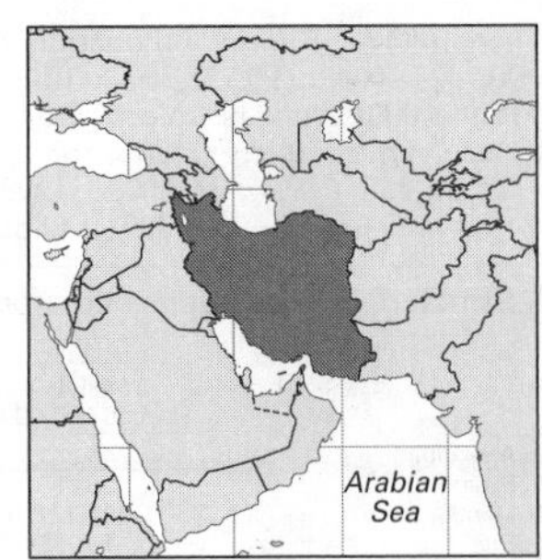

Official name: Jomhūrī-ye Eslamī-ye Irān (Islamic Republic of Iran).
Form of government: unitary Islamic republic with one legislative house (Islamic Consultative Assembly [290]).
Supreme political/religious authority: Leader[1].
Head of state and government: President.
Capital: Tehrān.
Official language: Farsī (Persian).
Official religion: Islam.
Monetary unit: 1 rial (Rls); valuation (Sept. 8, 2003) 1 U.S.$ = Rls 8,315; 1 £ = Rls 13,184.

Area and population

	area	population		area	population
Provinces	sq km	2002 estimate	Provinces	sq km	2002 estimate
Ardabīl	17,881	1,204,410	Khūzestān	63,213	4,506,816
Āzārbāyjān-e Gharbī	37,463	2,774,804	Kohgīlūyeh va		
Āzārbāyjān-e Sharqī	45,481	3,378,242	Būyer Aḥmad	15,563	627,517
Būshehr	23,168	796,639	Kordestān	28,817	1,492,007
Chahār Maḥāll va			Lorestān	28,392	1,671,706
Bakhtīārī	16,201	794,077	Markazi	29,406	1,300,778
Eṣfahān	107,027	4,316,767	Māzandarān	23,833	2,742,885
Fārs	121,825	4,135,251	Qazvīn	15,502	1,066,317
Gilan	13,952	2,310,033	Qom	11,237	971,280
Golestān	20,893	1,555,058	Semnān	96,816	563,959
Hamadān	19,547	1,718,627	Sīstān va		
Hormozgān	71,193	1,235,816	Balūchestān	178,431	2,086,170
Ilām	20,150	550,971	Tehrān	19,196	11,689,301
Kermān	181,814	2,215,376	Yazd	73,467	841,370
Kermānshāh	24,641	1,962,176	Zanjān	21,841	936,985
Khorāsān	302,966	6,094,888	TOTAL	1,629,918[2]	65,540,226

Demography

Population: 66,255,000[3].
Density (2003): persons per sq mi 105.3, persons per sq km 40.6.
Urban-rural (2001): urban 64.7%; rural 35.3%.
Sex distribution (2002): male 51.01%; female 48.99%.
Age breakdown (2002): under 15, 30.8%; 15–29, 34.1%; 30–44, 18.9%; 45–59, 9.6%; 60–74, 5.0%; 75 and over, 1.6%.
Population projection: (2010) 71,482,000; (2020) 79,721,000.
Ethnic composition (1995): Persian 51%; Azerbaijani 24%; Gīlaki/Mazāndarānī 8%; Kurd 7%; Arab 3%; Lurī 2%; Balochi 2%; other 3%.
Religious affiliation (2000): Muslim 95.6% (Shīʿī 90.1%, Sunnī 5.5%); Zoroastrian 2.8%; Christian 0.5%; other 1.1%.
Major cities (1996): Tehrān 6,758,845; Mashhad 1,887,405; Eṣfahān 1,266,072; Tabriz 1,191,043; Shīrāz 1,053,025; Karaj 940,968; Ahvāz 804,980.

Vital statistics

Birth rate per 1,000 population (2002): 18.3 (world avg. 21.3).
Death rate per 1,000 population (2002): 6.3 (world avg. 9.1).
Natural increase rate per 1,000 population (2002): 12.0 (world avg. 12.2).
Total fertility rate (avg. births per childbearing woman; 2002): 2.1.
Life expectancy at birth (2002): male 67.8 years; female 70.4 years.
Major causes of death per 100,000 population (1990)[4]: diseases of the circulatory system 304; accidents and violence 108; malignant neoplasms (cancers) 61; diseases of the respiratory system 48; infectious diseases 34.

National economy

Budget (2001–02). Revenue: Rls 180,975,000,000,000 (petroleum and natural gas revenue 57.0%; taxes 23.0%, of which corporate 6.8%, import duties 6.5%; other 20.0%). Expenditures: Rls 168,992,000,000,000 (current expenditure 66.6%; development expenditures 15.1%; other 18.3%).
Public debt (external, outstanding; 2001): U.S.$5,295,000,000.
Tourism (2001): receipts U.S.$920,000,000; expenditures (1999) U.S.$918,000,000.
Gross national product (2001): U.S.$108,700,000,000 (U.S.$1,680 per capita).

Structure of gross domestic product and labour force

	2002–03		1996	
	in value Rls '000,000,000	% of total value	labour force	% of labour force
Agriculture, forestry	105,027.6	12.2	3,357,263	21.0
Petroleum, natural gas	169,264.2	19.7	119,884	0.7
Other mining	4,554.5	0.5		
Manufacturing	120,533.9	14.0	2,551,962	15.9
Construction	35,259.4	4.1	1,650,481	10.3
Public utilities	12,709.4	1.5	150,631	0.9
Transp. and commun.	74,971.0	8.7	972,792	6.1
Trade, restaurants	116,256.1	13.5	1,927,067	12.0
Finance, real estate	130,179.7	15.1	301,962	1.9
Pub. admin., defense	123,556.5	14.4	1,618,100	10.1
Services	22,282.4	2.6	1,664,402	10.4
Other	–54,061.9[5]	–6.3[5]	1,712,028[6]	10.7[6]
TOTAL	860,532.8	100.0	16,026,572	100.0

Production (metric tons except as noted). Agriculture, forestry, fishing (2002): wheat 12,000,000, sugar beets 5,250,000, potatoes 3,500,000, tomatoes 3,000,000, grapes 2,516,695, apples 2,353,359, rice 2,115,000, barley 2,000,000, oranges 1,878,548, corn (maize) 1,200,000, lemons 1,038,833, dates 874,986, seed cotton 320,000, pistachios 300,000; livestock (number of live animals) 53,900,000 sheep, 8,738,000 cattle; roundwood (2001) 1,323,923 cu m; fish catch (2001) 399,000. Mining and quarrying (2001): iron ore 5,400,000[7]; copper ore 120,000[7]; manganese 105,000[7]; zinc 85,000[7]; chromium 10,000[7]. Manufacturing (value added in Rls '000,000,000; 1996): basic chemicals 4,433; iron and steel 4,105; food products 2,877; nonmetallic mineral products 2,526; textiles 2,363; transport equipment 1,843; nonelectrical machinery 1,282. Energy production (consumption): electricity (kW-hr; 2002–03) 136,231,000,000 (136,231,000,000); coal (metric tons; 1999) 1,337,000 (1,644,000); crude petroleum (barrels; 1999–2000) 1,255,000,000 (496,000,000); petroleum products (metric tons; 1999) 60,509,000 (44,296,000); natural gas (cu m; 2001–02) 86,300,000,000 (66,600,000,000).
Population economically active (2002–03): total 19,819,000; activity rate 30.0% (participation rates: over age 15 [1996] 44.0%; female [1996] 12.7%; unemployed [2002–03] 15.7%).

Price and earnings indexes (1997–98 = 100)

	1997–98	1998–99	1999–2000	2000–01	2001–02	2002–03
Consumer price index	100.0	118.1	141.8	159.7	177.9	206.0
Daily earnings index[8]	100.0	113.3	128.5	142.3	156.1	184.0

Household income and expenditure. Average household size (2000) 4.6; annual average income per urban household (1998–99) Rls 15,151,894 (U.S.$8,644); sources of urban income (1998–99): wages 32.8%, self-employment 29.6%, other 37.6%; expenditure (1997–98): food, beverages, and tobacco 32.5%, housing and energy 27.0%, transportation 11.4%.
Land use (1994): forest 7.0%; pasture 26.9%; agriculture 11.1%; other 55.0%.

Foreign trade

Balance of trade (current prices)

	1996–97	1997–98	1998–99	1999–2000	2000–01	2001–02
U.S.$'000,000	+7,910	+4,258	–1,168	+7,597	+13,375	+5,775
% of total	21.5%	13.1%	4.3%	22.0%	30.7%	13.7%

Imports (2000–01): U.S.$15,086,000,000 (nonelectrical machinery 19.7%, chemicals and chemical products 13.4%, iron and steel 12.1%, cereals and cereal products 9.2%, transportation equipment 7.4%). *Major import sources:* Germany *c.* 10%; U.A.E. *c.* 8%; Italy *c.* 6%; Russia *c.* 6%; South Korea *c.* 5%; Japan *c.* 5%.
Exports (2000–01): U.S.$28,461,000,000 (crude petroleum 75.5%, refined petroleum 8.8%, carpets 2.2%, fruit 1.8%, iron and steel 1.1%). *Major export destinations* (1999–2000): Japan 16.5%; U.K. 15.4%; U.A.E. 7.5%; Italy 7.1%; South Korea 6.4%.

Transport and communications

Transport. Railroads (2002): route length 4,391 mi, 7,066 km; (1999) passenger-km 6,451,000,000; (1999) metric ton-km cargo 14,082,000,000. Roads (1997): length 102,976 mi, 165,724 km (paved 50%). Vehicles (1996): passenger cars 1,793,000; trucks and buses 692,000. Air transport (2001)[9]: passenger-km 6,674,097; metric ton-km cargo 74,989,000; airports (1996) 19.

Communications

Medium	date	unit	number	units per 1,000 persons
Daily newspapers	2000	circulation	1,780,000	28
Radio	2000	receivers	17,900,000	281
Television	2000	receivers	10,400,000	163
Telephones	2002	main lines	13,075,000	200
Cellular telephones	2002	subscribers	2,087,400	32
Personal computers	2001	units	4,500,000	70
Internet	2002	users	1,005,000	16

Education and health

Educational attainment (1986). Percentage of population age 25 and over having: no formal schooling 12.8%; secondary education 38.0%; higher 7.8%.
Literacy (2000): total population age 15 and over literate 76.3%; males literate 83.2%; females literate 69.3%.

Education (2000–01)

	schools	teachers	students	student/ teacher ratio
Primary (age 7–11)	69,149	314,654	7,968,437	25.3
Secondary (age 12–18)[13]	42,079	337,912	9,090,938	26.9
Higher	...	...	1,573,322	...

Health (1998–99): physicians 60,000 (1 per 1,033 persons); hospital beds 98,669 (1 per 628 persons); infant mortality rate (2000) 30.0.
Food (2001): daily per capita caloric intake 2,931 (vegetable products 90%, animal products 10%); 122% of FAO recommended minimum requirement.

Military

Total active duty personnel (2002): 520,000 (revolutionary guard corps 24.0%, army 62.5%, navy 3.5%, air force 10.0%). *Military expenditure as percentage of GNP* (1999): 2.9% (world 2.4%); per capita expenditure U.S.$106.

[1]Not required to be a supreme theological authority. [2]Detail does not add to total given because of rounding. [3]Excludes roughly 1.0 million Afghan refugees in January 2003. [4]Projected rates based on about 20% of total deaths. [5]Less imputed bank service charge. [6]Includes 1,455,000 unemployed. [7]Metal content. [8]Construction sector only. [9]Iran Air.

Internet resources for further information:
- **Statistical Centre of Iran http://www.sci.or.ir**
- **Central Bank of Iran http://cbi.ir**

Iraq

Official name: Al-Jumhūrīyah al-ʿIrāqīyah (Republic of Iraq).
Form of government: coalition provisional authority[1].
Head of state and government: Civil Administrator[1] assisted by the Iraqi Governing Council[2].
Capital: Baghdad.
Official languages: Arabic; Kurdish (locally).
Official religion: Islam.
Monetary unit[3]: 1 (new) Iraqi dinar (ID); valuation (Oct. 15, 2003) 1 U.S.$ = 1,250 (new) ID; 1 £ = 2,088 (new) ID.

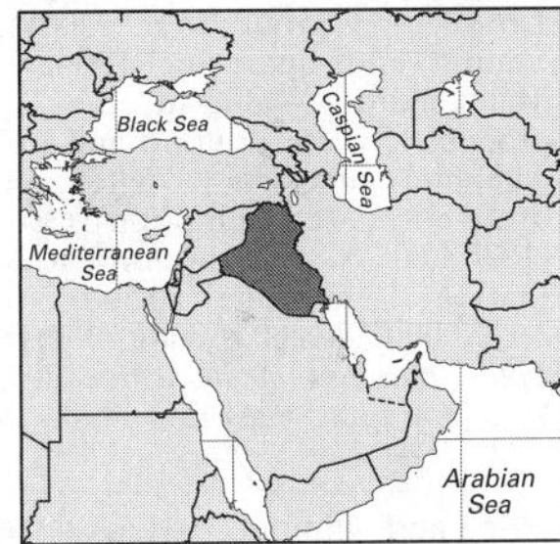

Area and population

Governorates[4]	Capitals	area sq mi	area sq km	population 1991 estimate
Al-Anbār	Ar-Ramādī	53,208	137,808	865,500
Bābil	Al-Ḥillah	2,163	5,603	1,221,100
Baghdād	Baghdad	1,572	4,071	3,910,900
Al-Baṣrah	Al-Baṣrah	7,363	19,070	1,168,800
Dhī Qār	An-Nāṣirīyah	4,981	12,900	1,030,900
Diyālā	Baʿqūbah	6,828	17,685	1,037,600
Karbalāʾ	Karbalāʾ	1,944	5,034	567,600
Maysān	Al-ʿAmārah	6,205	16,072	524,200
Al-Muthannā	As-Samāwah	19,977	51,740	350,000
An-Najaf	An-Najaf	11,129	28,824	666,400
Nīnawā	Mosul	14,410	37,323	1,618,700
Al-Qādisiyah	Ad-Dīwānīyah	3,148	8,153	595,600
Ṣalāḥ ad-Dīn	Tikrīt	9,407	24,363	772,200
At-Taʾmīm	Karkūk (Kirkūk)	3,737	9,679	605,900
Wāsiṭ	Al-kūt	6,623	17,153	605,700
Kurdish Autonomous Region[5]				
Dahūk	Dahūk	2,530	6,553	309,300
Irbīl	Irbīl	5,820	15,074	928,400
As-Sulaymānīyah	As-Sulaymānīyah	6,573	17,023	1,124,200
TOTAL		167,618	434,128	17,903,000

Demography

Population (2003): 24,683,000.
Density (2003): persons per sq mi 147.3, persons per sq km 56.9.
Urban-rural (2000): urban 67.5%; rural 32.5%.
Sex distribution (2001): male 50.57%; female 49.43%.
Age breakdown (2000): under 15, 42.1%; 15–29, 30.4%; 30–44, 15.6%; 45–59, 7.4%; 60–74, 3.5%; 75 and over, 1.0%.
Population projection: (2010) 29,672,000; (2020) 36,908,000.
Doubling time: 25 years.
Ethnic composition (2000): Arab 64.7%; Kurd 23.0%; Azerbaijani 5.6%; Turkmen 1.2%; Persian 1.1%; other 4.4%.
Religious affiliation (2000): Shīʿī Muslim 62.0%; Sunnī Muslim 34.0%; Christian (primarily Chaldean rite and Syrian rite Catholic and Nestorian) 3.2%; other (primarily Yazīdī syncretist) 0.8%.
Major cities (2003)[6]: Baghdad 5,750,000; Mosul 1,800,000; Al-Baṣrah 1,400,000; Irbīl 850,000; Karkūk 750,000.

Vital statistics

Birth rate per 1,000 population (2001): 34.6 (world avg. 21.3).
Death rate per 1,000 population (2001): 6.2 (world avg. 9.1).
Natural increase rate per 1,000 population (2001): 28.4 (world avg. 12.2).
Total fertility rate (avg. births per childbearing woman; 2001): 4.8.
Marriage rate per 1,000 population (1997): 6.3.
Divorce rate per 1,000 population (1997): 1.3.
Life expectancy at birth (2001): male 65.9 years; female 68.0 years.
Major causes of death per 100,000 population (1995): infectious and parasitic diseases 311.6, diseases of the circulatory system 130.2, malignant neoplasms (cancers) 111.5, diseases of the respiratory system 99.5, accidents and violence 65.3.

National economy

Budget (1992). Revenue: ID 13,935,000,000. Expenditures: ID 13,935,000,000. Details of more recent budgets are not available.
Production (metric tons except as noted). Agriculture, forestry, fishing (2002): wheat 800,000, dates 650,000, potatoes 625,000, tomatoes 500,000, barley 500,000, watermelons 380,000, oranges 270,000, grapes 265,000, cucumbers 215,000, cantaloupes 195,000, rice 90,000; livestock (number of live animals) 6,200,000 sheep, 1,400,000 cattle; roundwood (2001) 111,294 cu m; fish catch (2000) 22,511. Mining and quarrying (2002): phosphate rock 100,000. Manufacturing (value added in U.S.$'000,000; 1994): refined petroleum 127; bricks, tiles, and cement 100; industrial chemicals 79; food products 59; metal products 28. Energy production (consumption): electricity (kW-hr; 1999) 30,491,000,000 (30,491,000,000); coal, none (none); crude petroleum (barrels; 2002) 738,400,000 ([1999] 174,900,000); petroleum products (metric tons; 1999) 20,227,000 (18,721,000); natural gas (cu m; 2002) 2,900,000,000 ([1999] 3,180,000,000).
Household income and expenditure (1988). Average household size 8.9; sources of income: self-employment 33.9%, wages and salaries 23.9%, transfers 23.0%, rent 18.6%; expenditure: food and beverages 50.2%, housing and energy 19.9%, clothing and footwear 10.6%.
Gross domestic product (2000): U.S.$20,000,000,000 (U.S.$900 per capita).

Structure of gross domestic product

	2001 in value ID '000,000[7]	2001 % of total value	2000 labour force	2000 % of labour force
Agriculture	1,962,510	24.6	...	...
Mining			...	...
Manufacturing	786,249	9.8	...	...
Public utilities			...	...
Construction	253,375	3.2	...	...
Transp. and commun.	1,241,586	15.5	...	...
Trade	2,083,053	26.1	...	...
Finance, real estate	914,625	11.5	...	...
Pub. admin., defense	921,570	11.5	...	...
Services			...	...
Other	–177,923[8]	–2.2[8]	...	...
TOTAL	7,985,045	100.0	6,339,000	100.0

Public debt (external, outstanding; 1999): U.S.$23,000,000,000.
Population economically active (1996): total 5,573,000; activity rate of total population 27.6% (participation rates: ages 15–64, 45.7%; female 25.0%).

Price index (1995 = 100)

	1990	1991	1992	1993	1994	1995	1996
Consumer price index	0.2	0.6	1.7[9]	5.2[9]	20[9]	100[9]	550[9]

Tourism (1997): receipts U.S.$13,000,000; expenditures, n.a.
Land use (1994): forest 0.4%; pasture 9.1%; agriculture 13.1%; other 77.4%.

Foreign trade[10]

Balance of trade (current prices)

	2001[9]	2002[9]
U.S.$'000,000	+4,900	+5,200
% of total	18.2%	25.0%

Imports (2002): U.S.$7,800,000,000[9] (primarily food, medicine, and consumer goods regulated by the UN). *Major import sources* (2001): France 19.4%; Australia 14.4%; Italy 10.7%; Germany 9.9%; China 6.4%.
Exports (2002): U.S.$13,000,000,000[9] (crude petroleum and petroleum products *c.* 95%). *Major export destinations* (2001): United States 60.6%; France 8.5%; The Netherlands 7.4%; Italy 5.8%; Canada 5.5%.

Transport and communications

Transport. Railroads (1999): route length 2,603 km; passenger-km 499,600,000; metric ton-km cargo 830,200,000. Roads (1999): total length 45,550 km (paved 84%). Vehicles (1998): passenger cars 735,521; trucks and buses 349,202. Air transport: [11].

Communications

Medium	date	unit	number	units per 1,000 persons
Daily newspapers	2000	circulation	431,000	19
Radio	2000	receivers	5,030,000	222
Television	2000	receivers	1,880,000	83
Telephones	1999	main lines	675,000	30

Education and health

Educational attainment (1987). Percentage of population age 10 and over having: no formal schooling 52.8%; primary education 21.5%; secondary 11.6%; higher 4.1%; unknown 10.0%. *Literacy* (1995): total population age 15 and over literate 58.0%; males 70.7%; females 45.0%.

Education (1997–98)

	schools	teachers	students	student/ teacher ratio
Primary (age 6–11)	8,333	141,935	3,029,386	21.3
Secondary (age 12–17)	2,822	54,846	1,020,823	18.6
Voc., teacher tr.	303	8,838	102,004	11.5
Higher	11	12,101	266,505	22.0

Health (1998): physicians 11,046 (1 per 1,937 persons); hospital beds 30,022 (1 per 713 persons); infant mortality rate per 1,000 live births (2001) 60.0.
Food (2000): daily per capita caloric intake 2,197 (vegetable products 96%, animal products 4%); 91% of FAO recommended minimum requirement.

Military

Total active duty personnel: n.a. U.S./allied coalition forces (August 2003): 146,000/30,000. *Military expenditure as percentage of GDP* (1999): 5.5% (world 2.4%); per capita expenditure U.S.$57.

[1]From April 2003. [2]From July 2003. [3]The (new) Iraqi dinar (ID) introduced on Oct. 15, 2003, replaced the (old) Iraqi dinar at a rate of 1 to 1. (Old) Iraqi dinars are to be out of circulation by Jan. 15, 2004. [4]Pre-April 2003 local government structure. [5]De facto self-government from 1992 through March 2003. [6]Unofficial estimate(s). [7]ESCWA estimate; in purchaser's value. [8]Imputed bank service charge. [9]Estimated figure(s). [10]UN-imposed trade sanctions in place from August 1990 to May 2003. [11]Scheduled domestic and limited international air service resumed in 2000 and 2001, respectively.

Internet resources for further information:
- **Council on Foreign Relations http://www.cfr.org**
- **Coalition Provisional Authority http://www.cpa-iraq.org**

Ireland

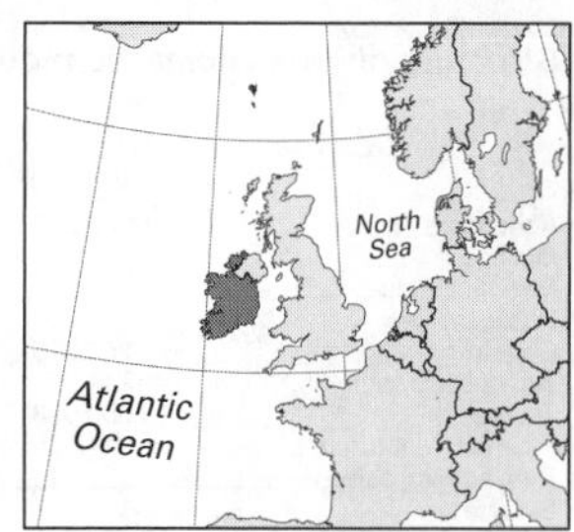

Official name: Éire (Irish); Ireland[1] (English).
Form of government: unitary multi-party republic with two legislative houses (Senate [60[2]]; House of Representatives [166]).
Chief of state: President.
Head of government: Prime Minister.
Capital: Dublin.
Official languages: Irish; English.
Official religion: none.
Monetary unit: 1 euro (€) = 100 cents; valuation (Sept. 8, 2003) 1 U.S.$ = €0.90; 1 £ = €1.43[3].

Area and population

Provinces Counties/County Boroughs (C.B.)	area sq km	population 2002 census	Provinces Counties/County Boroughs (C.B.)	area sq km	population 2002 census
Connacht	17,711	464,296	Westmeath	1,840	71,858
Galway	6,098	143,245	Wexford	2,367	116,596
Galway C.B.	51	65,832	Wicklow	2,027	114,676
Leitrim	1,590	25,799	Munster	24,674	1,100,614
Mayo	5,586	117,446	Clare	3,450	103,277
Roscommon	2,548	53,774	Cork	7,460	324,767
Sligo	1,838	58,200	Cork C.B.	40	123,062
Leinster	19,801[4]	2,105,579	Kerry	4,807	132,527
Carlow	897	46,014	Limerick	2,735	121,281
Dublin C.B.	118	495,781	Limerick C.B.	21	54,023
Dun Laoghaire-Rathdown	126	191,792	Tipperary North Riding	2,046	61,010
Fingal	455	196,413	Tipperary South Riding	2,258	79,121
Kildare	1,695	163,944	Waterford	1,816	56,952
Kilkenny	2,073	80,339	Waterford C.B.	41	44,594
Laoighis	1,720	58,774	Ulster (part of)	8,088	246,714
Longford	1,091	31,068	Cavan	1,932	56,546
Louth	826	101,821	Donegal	4,861	137,575
Meath	2,342	134,005	Monaghan	1,295	52,593
Offaly	2,001	63,663	TOTAL	70,273[4, 5]	3,917,203
South Dublin	224	238,835			

Demography

Population (2003): 3,969,000.
Density (2002): persons per sq mi 146.3, persons per sq km 56.5.
Urban-rural (2002): urban 59.6%; rural 40.4%.
Sex distribution (2002): male 49.68%; female 50.32%.
Age breakdown (2002): under 15, 21.1%; 15–29, 24.4%; 30–44, 22.1%; 45–59, 17.3%; 60–74, 10.2%; 75 and over, 4.9%.
Population projection: (2010) 4,237,000; (2020) 4,566,000.
Ethnic composition (2000): Irish 95.0%; British 1.7%, of which English 1.4%; Ulster Irish 1.0%; U.S. white 0.8%; other 1.5%.
Religious affiliation (2002): Roman Catholic 88.4%; Church of Ireland (Anglican) 3.0%; other Christian 1.6%; nonreligious 3.5%; other 3.5%.
Major cities (2002): Dublin 495,781 (urban agglomeration 1,004,600); Cork 123,062; Galway 65,832; Limerick 54,023; Waterford 44,594.

Vital statistics

Birth rate per 1,000 population (2002): 15.4 (world avg. 21.3).
Death rate per 1,000 population (2002): 7.5 (world avg. 9.1).
Natural increase rate per 1,000 population (2002): 7.9 (world avg. 12.2).
Marriage rate per 1,000 population (2001): 5.0.
Total fertility rate (avg. births per childbearing woman; 2001): 2.0.
Life expectancy at birth (2000–02): male 73.8 years; female 79.5 years.
Major causes of death per 100,000 population (2002): diseases of the circulatory system 295.3; malignant neoplasms (cancers) 191.0; diseases of the respiratory system 110.3; accidents and violence 35.1.

National economy

Budget (2000). Revenue: £Ir 21,741,000,000 (income taxes 33.0%, value-added tax 27.0%, excise taxes 15.4%). Expenditures: £Ir 19,297,000,000 (social welfare 27.9%, health 20.9%, education 14.9%, debt service 10.5%).
Public debt (1996): U.S.$47,876,000,000.
Gross national product (2001): U.S.$87,700,000,000 (U.S.$22,850 per capita).

Structure of gross domestic product and labour force

	2001		2002	
	in value €'000,000[6]	% of total value[6]	labour force	% of labour force
Agriculture	3,969	3.9	120,700	6.6
Mining				
Manufacturing	42,734	41.7	302,900	16.6
Public utilities				
Construction			181,100	9.9
Transp. and commun.	16,224	15.8	110,200	6.0
Trade, hotels			350,700	19.2
Pub. admin., defense	3,563	3.5	89,200	4.9
Services	40,162	39.2	366,000	20.0
Finance			229,100	12.5
Other	–4,257[7]	–4.2[7]	77,200[8]	4.3[8]
TOTAL	102,393[4]	100.0[4]	1,827,100	100.0[4]

Tourism (2001): receipts U.S.$3,547,000,000; expenditures U.S.$2,767,000,000.
Production (metric tons except as noted). Agriculture, forestry, fishing (2002): sugar beets 1,313,000, barley 963,000, wheat 867,000, potatoes 519,000, oats 134,000; livestock (number of live animals) 6,408,000 cattle, 4,807,000 sheep, 1,763,000 pigs; roundwood (2001) 2,455,000 cu m; fish catch (2000) 324,478. Mining and quarrying (2002): zinc ore 252,700[9]; lead ore 32,500[9]. Manufacturing (value added in U.S.$'000,000; 1999): chemicals and chemical products 16,075; printing and publishing 6,925; food and beverages 6,850; computers and parts 4,575; telecommunications and electronics 3,025. Energy production (consumption): electricity (kW-hr; 1999) 23,633,000,000 (18,974,000,000); coal (metric tons; 1999) none (2,514,000); crude petroleum (barrels; 1999) none (20,500,000); petroleum products (metric tons; 1999) 2,717,000 (7,208,000); natural gas (cu m; 1999) 1,341,100,000 (3,624,700,000).
Population economically active (2002): total 1,827,100; activity rate 46.6% (participation rates: ages 15–64 [2000] *c.* 68%; female [2000] 40.3%; unemployed 4.3%).

Price and earnings indexes (1995 = 100)

	1996	1997	1998	1999	2000	2001	2002
Consumer price index	101.7	103.2	105.7	107.4	113.4	118.9	124.5
Weekly earnings index	102.5	107.5	111.9	118.4	126.4	137.9	145.5

Household income and expenditure. Average household size (2002) 2.9; income per household (1994–95): £Ir 16,224 (U.S.$25,100); expenditure (1996)[10]: food and beverages 35.4%, transportation 13.9%, rent/household goods 11.6%.

Foreign trade[11]

Balance of trade (current prices)

	1997	1998	1999	2000	2001	2002
€'000,000	+12,004	+17,607	+22,629	+27,704	+35,306	+38,421
% of total	15.4%	18.1%	20.3%	20.2%	23.5%	25.8%

Imports (2000): €54,858,000,000 (machinery and apparatus 43.4%, of which computers and parts 20.5%, electronic microcircuits 5.1%; chemicals and chemical products 10.8%; road vehicles 7.3%; food 5.1%). *Major import sources:* U.K. 31.3%; U.S. 16.6%; Germany 5.8%; Japan 4.8%; France 4.7%.
Exports (2000): €82,562,000,000 (computers and parts 23.5%; organic chemicals 20.2%; food 7.1%; electronic microcircuits 5.3%; sound-recording devices 5.0%; telecommunications equipment 4.2%). *Major export destinations:* U.K. 21.8%; U.S. 17.2%; Germany 11.3%; France 7.6%; The Netherlands 5.6%.

Transport and communications

Transport. Railroads (2001): route length 1,947 km; passenger-km 1,515,303,000; metric ton-km cargo 515,754,000. Roads (1999): length 92,500 km (paved 94%). Vehicles (2000): passenger cars 1,269,245; trucks and buses 188,814. Air transport (2001)[12]: passenger-km 8,901,000,000; metric ton-km cargo 146,530,000; airports (1996) 9.

Communications

Medium	date	unit	number	units per 1,000 persons
Daily newspapers	2000	circulation	574,000	150
Radio	2000	receivers	2,660,000	695
Television	1999	receivers	2,144,000	578
Telephones	2001	main lines	1,860,000	480
Cellular telephones	2002	subscribers	2,969,000	758
Personal computers	2001	units	1,500,000	387
Internet	2002	users	1,065,000	272

Education and health

Educational attainment (1999). Percentage of population ages 25–64 and over having: no formal schooling through lower secondary 49%; upper secondary 30%; higher 21%, of which university 11%.

Education (1999–2000)

	schools	teachers	students	student/ teacher ratio
Primary (age 6–11)[13]	3,340	21,850	428,339	19.6
Secondary (age 12–18)	782	12,418	203,418	16.4
Voc., teacher tr.		8,683	150,442	17.3
Higher	56	5,644[14]	126,300	19.0[14]

Health: physicians (1998) 8,114 (1 per 457 persons); hospital beds (1997) 13,620 (1 per 270 persons); infant mortality rate (2000) 5.6.
Food (2001): daily per capita caloric intake 3,666 (vegetable products 69%, animal products 31%); 146% of FAO recommended minimum requirement.

Military

Total active duty personnel (2002): 10,460 (army 81.3%, navy 10.5%, air force 8.2%). *Military expenditure as percentage of GNP* (1999): 1.0% (world 2.4%); per capita expenditure U.S.$208.

[1]As provided by the constitution; the 1948 Republic of Ireland Act provides precedent for this longer formulation of the official name but, per official sources, "has not changed the usage *Ireland* as the name of the state in the English language." [2]Includes 11 nonelective seats. [3]The Irish pound was the former monetary unit; on Jan. 1, 2002, 1 £Ir = € 1.27. [4]Detail does not add to total given because of rounding. [5]27,133 sq mi. [6]At factor cost. [7]Less imputed bank service charges and statistical discrepancy. [8]Unemployed. [9]Metal content. [10]November. [11]Imports c.i.f.; exports f.o.b. [12]Aer Lingus only. [13]National schools only. [14]1998–99.

Internet resources for further information:
- **Central Statistics Office (Ireland) http://www.cso.ie**
- **Central Bank of Ireland http://www.centralbank.ie**

Isle of Man

Official name: Isle of Man[1].
Political status: crown dependency (United Kingdom) with two legislative bodies[2] (Legislative Council [11[3]]; House of Keys [24]).
Chief of state: British Monarch represented by Lieutenant-Governor.
Head of government: Chief Minister assisted by the Council of Ministers.
Capital: Douglas.
Official language: English.
Official religion: none.
Monetary unit: 1 Manx pound (£M)[4] = 100 new pence; valuation (Sept. 8, 2003) 1 £M = U.S.$1.59.

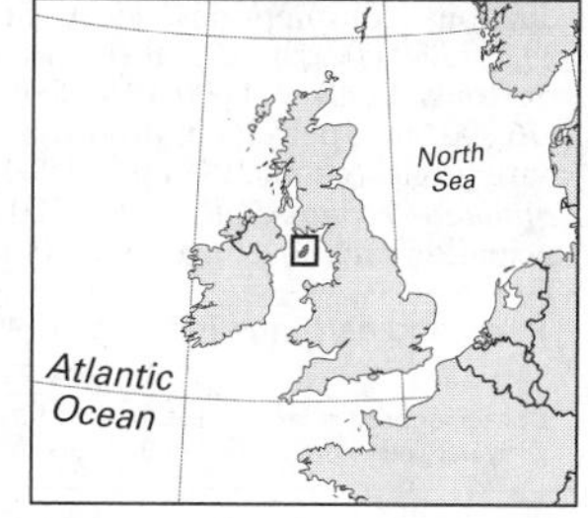

Area and population

	area	population		area	population
	sq km	2001 census		sq km	2001 census
Towns			**Parishes** (cont.)		
Castletown	2.3	3,100	Ballaugh	23.6	868
Douglas	10.1	25,347	Braddan	42.6	2,665
Peel	1.7	3,785	Bride	21.7	408
Ramsey	3.7	7,322	German	45.3	1,010
			Jurby	17.7	677
Villages			Lezayre	62.3	1,134
Laxey	2.4	1,725	Lonan	35.2	1,393
Onchan	24.7	8,803	Malew	47.1	2,262
Port Erin	2.6	3,369	Marown	26.7	1,879
Port St. Mary	1.4	1,941	Maughold	34.5	941
			Michael	33.9	1,431
Parishes			Patrick	42.2	1,305
Andreas	31.1	1,152	Rushen	24.6	1,504
Arbory	17.7	1,714	Santon	16.9	580
			TOTAL	572.0[5]	76,315

Demography

Population (2003): 77,300.
Density (2002): persons per sq mi 349.8, persons per sq km 135.1.
Urban-rural (1999): urban 76.3%; rural 23.7%.
Sex distribution (2001): male 48.97%; female 51.03%.
Age breakdown (2001): under 15, 17.9%; 15–29, 17.5%; 30–44, 22.6%; 45–59, 20.1%; 60–74, 13.6%; 75 and over, 8.3%.
Population projection: (2010) 80,000; (2020) 84,000.
Population by place of birth (2001): Isle of Man 48.0%; United Kingdom 45.2%, of which England 38.2%, Scotland 3.5%, Northern Ireland 2.3%, Wales 1.2%; Ireland 2.3%; other Europe 1.0%; South Africa 0.5%.
Religious affiliation (2000): Christian 63.7%, of which Anglican 40.5%, Methodist 9.9%, Roman Catholic 8.2%; other (mostly nonreligious) 36.3%.
Major towns (2001): Douglas 25,347; Onchan 8,803; Ramsey 7,322; Peel 3,785; Port Erin 3,369.

Vital statistics

Birth rate per 1,000 population (2002): 11.3 (world avg. 21.3); legitimate 64.6%; illegitimate 35.4%.
Death rate per 1,000 population (2002): 10.6 (world avg. 9.1).
Natural increase rate per 1,000 population (2002): 0.7 (world avg. 12.2).
Total fertility rate (avg. births per childbearing woman; 1999): 1.6.
Marriage rate per 1,000 population (2002): 5.6.
Divorce rate per 1,000 population (1996): 4.0.
Life expectancy at birth (1999): male 73.9 years; female 80.8 years.
Major causes of death per 100,000 population (2002): diseases of the circulatory system 563.2, of which ischemic heart diseases 264.1, cerebrovascular disease 132.7; neoplasms (cancers) 278.3; diseases of the respiratory system 106.7.

National economy

Budget (2001–02). Revenue: £466,177,000 (customs duties and excise taxes 64.3%; income taxes 34.8%, of which resident 30.5%, nonresident 4.3%; nontax revenue 0.9%). Expenditures: £360,499,000 (health and social security 39.8%; education 19.1%; transportation 6.8%; home affairs 6.0%; tourism and recreation 5.8%).
Public debt: n.a.
Production. Agriculture, forestry, fishing: main crops include hay, oats, barley, wheat, and orchard crops; livestock (number of live animals; 2001) 167,000 sheep, 33,000 cattle; fish catch (value of principal catch in £; 2001): 2,200,000, of which scallops 1,600,000, queen scallops 600,000. Mining and quarrying: sand and gravel. Manufacturing (value added in U.S.$; 1996–97): electrical and nonelectrical machinery/apparatus, textiles, other 103,700,000; food and beverages 18,600,000. Energy production (consumption): electricity (kW-hr; 2001–02), n.a. (345,000,000); crude petroleum, none (n.a.); petroleum products, n.a. (n.a.); natural gas, none (n.a.).
Household income and expenditure. Average household size (2001) 2.4; income per household (1981–82)[6, 7] £7,479 (U.S.$13,721); sources of income (1981–82)[6, 7]: wages and salaries 64.1%, transfer payments 16.9%, interest and dividends 11.2%, self-employment 6.6%; expenditure (1981–82)[6, 7]: food and beverages 31.0%, transportation 14.9%, energy 11.0%, housing 7.9%, clothing and footwear 7.0%.
Gross national product (at current market prices; 2000–01): U.S.$1,610,000,000 (U.S.$21,300 per capita).

Structure of gross domestic product and labour force

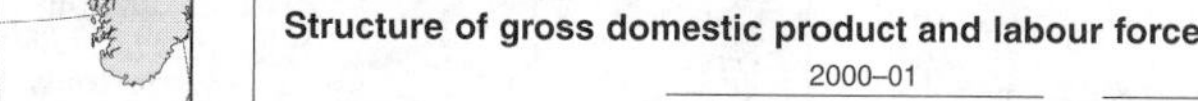

	2000–01		2001	
	in value £'000[8]	% of total value[8]	labour force	% of labour force
Agriculture, fishing	15,824	1.5	543	1.4
Mining, Manufacturing	76,664	7.2	3,185	8.0
Construction	89,600	8.5	2,512	6.3
Public utilities	17,799	1.7	515	1.3
Transp. and commun.	72,256	6.8	2,970	7.5
Trade, hotels	83,452	7.9	7,171	18.1
Finance, real estate, insurance	505,382[9]	47.8[9]	8,959	22.6
Pub. admin., defense	53,566	5.1	3,105	7.8
Services	304,129[9]	28.7[9]	10,090	25.4
Other	–160,538[10]	–15.2[10]	635[11]	1.6[11]
TOTAL	1,058,134	100.0	39,685	100.0

Population economically active (2001): total 39,685; activity rate of total population 52.0% (participation rates: ages 16 and over 64.2%; female 45.4%; unemployed 1.6%).

Price and earnings indexes (1995 = 100)

	1997	1998	1999	2000	2001	2002
Retail price index[12]	105.2	108.3	110.4	113.4	129.3	138.0
Weekly earnings index[12]	110.0	115.0	120.3	123.3	129.3	134.8

Tourism: receipts from visitors (1999) U.S.$90,600,000; expenditures by nationals abroad, n.a.; number of tourists (2001) 201,300.
Land use (2000): meadows and pasture 72%; other 28%.

Foreign trade[13]

Imports: n.a. *Major import sources:* mostly the United Kingdom.
Exports: traditional exports include scallops, herring, beef, lambs, and tweeds. *Major export destinations:* mostly the United Kingdom.

Transport and communications

Transport. Railroads (2001): route length 38 mi, 61 km[14]. Roads (2001): total length, more than 500 mi, more than 805 km (paved, n.a.). Vehicles (2001): passenger cars 45,195; trucks and buses 4,635. Merchant marine (2002): vessels (100 gross tons and over) 246; gross registered tonnage 5,835,174. Air transport (1998)[15]: passenger-mi 526,161,000, passenger-km 846,775,000; short ton-mi cargo 115,000, metric ton-km cargo 168,000; airports (2001) with scheduled flights 1.

Communications

Medium	date	unit	number	units per 1,000 persons
Daily newspapers	2001	circulation	—[16]	—
Television	2000	receivers	28,600	355
Telephones	2001	main lines	56,000	741
Cellular telephones	2001	subscribers	32,000	424

Education and health

Educational attainment: n.a. *Literacy:* n.a.

Education (2001)

	schools	teachers	students	student/ teacher ratio
Primary (age 5–10)	32	...	6,611	...
Secondary (age 11–16)	5	...	5,374	...
Higher	1	...	1,128[17]	...

Health: physicians (2000) 138 (1 per 547 persons); hospital beds (1998) 505 (1 per 143 persons); infant mortality rate per 1,000 live births (2002) 3.0.
Food (2001)[18]: daily per capita caloric intake 3,368 (vegetable products 70%, animal products 30%); 134% of FAO recommended minimum requirement.

Military

Total active duty personnel: [19].

[1]Ellan Vannin in Manx Gaelic. [2]Collective name is Tynwald. [3]Includes 3 nonelected seats. [4]Equivalent in value to pound sterling (£). [5]220.9 sq mi. [6]Fiscal year ending March 31st. [7]Based on survey of 259 households; "high income" and "pensioner" households are excluded. [8]At factor cost. [9]Most GDP in 2000–01 was derived from 60 banks (most of which are "offshore"), 80 investment businesses, and 183 insurance companies. [10]Ownership of dwellings less adjustments. [11]Unemployed. [12]June. [13]Because of the customs union between the Isle of Man and the U.K. since 1980, there are no customs controls on the movement of goods between the Isle of Man and the U.K. [14]Length of three tourist (novel) railways operating in summer. [15]Manx Airlines. [16]Isle of Man has 2 weekly newspapers and 1 biweekly newspaper. [17]Includes enrollees at Isle of Man College and students abroad in 1998–99. [18]Data for United Kingdom. [19]The United Kingdom is responsible for defense.

Internet resources for further information:

- **Isle of Man Government http://www.gov.im**

Israel

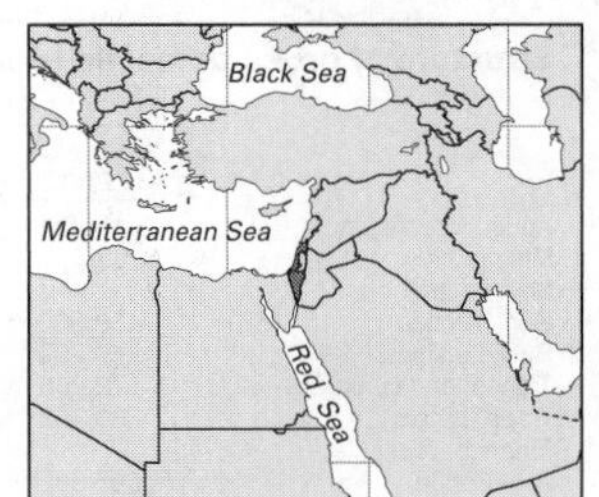

Official name: Medinat Yisra'el (Hebrew); Isrā'īl (Arabic) (State of Israel).
Form of government: multiparty republic with one legislative house (Knesset [120]).
Chief of state: President.
Head of government: Prime Minister.
Capital: Jerusalem is the proclaimed capital of Israel and the actual seat of government, but recognition of its status as capital by the international community has largely been withheld.
Official languages: Hebrew; Arabic.
Official religion: none.
Monetary unit: 1 New (Israeli) sheqel (NIS) = 100 agorot; valuation (Sept. 8, 2003) 1 U.S.$ = NIS 4.45; 1 £ = NIS 7.05.

Area and population

		area[1]		population
				2003[2]
Districts	Capitals	sq mi	sq km	estimate
Central (Ha Merkaz)	Ramla	493	1,276	1,541,100
Haifa (Ḥefa)	Haifa	333	863	838,900
Jerusalem (Yerushalayim)	Jerusalem	225	582	794,100
Northern (Ha Ẓafon)	Tiberias	1,275	3,302	1,127,200
Southern (Ha Darom)	Beersheba	5,494	14,231	948,500
Tel Aviv	Tel Aviv–Yafo	66	171	1,161,100
TOTAL		7,886	20,425	6,410,900[3]

Demography

Population (2003): 6,473,000.
Density (2003)[3]: persons per sq mi 820.8, persons per sq km 316.9.
Urban-rural (2002[2]): urban 91.6%; rural 8.4%.
Sex distribution (2000): male 49.33%; female 50.67%.
Age breakdown (2000): under 15, 28.6%; 15–29, 25.1%; 30–44, 18.7%; 45–59, 14.5%; 60–74, 8.8%; 75 and over, 4.3%.
Population projection: (2010) 7,305,000; (2020) 8,443,000.
Ethnic composition (2000): Jewish 78.1%; Arab and other 21.9%.
Religious affiliation (2000): Jewish 78.1%; Muslim (mostly Sunnī) 15.1%; Christian 2.1%; Druze 1.6%; other 3.1%.
Major cities (2001[2]): Jerusalem 657,500; Tel Aviv–Yafo 354,400; Haifa 270,500; Rishon LeẒiyyon 202,200; Petah Tiqwa 167,500; Ḥolon 165,700.

Vital statistics

Birth rate per 1,000 population (2001): 21.2 (world avg. 21.3); (2000)[4] legitimate 97.2%; illegitimate 2.8%.
Death rate per 1,000 population (2001): 5.8 (world avg. 9.1).
Natural increase rate per 1,000 population (2001): 15.4 (world avg. 12.2).
Total fertility rate (avg. births per childbearing woman; 2001): 2.9.
Marriage rate per 1,000 population (1999): 6.6.
Divorce rate per 1,000 population (1999): 1.7.
Life expectancy at birth (2002): male 76.8 years; female 81.0 years.
Major causes of death per 100,000 population (1997): diseases of the circulatory system 210; malignant neoplasms (cancers) 140; diabetes mellitus 42; accidents and violence 20; diseases of the respiratory system 19.

National economy

Budget (2001). Revenue: NIS 195,376,000,000 (tax revenue 87.8%, of which income tax 39.7%, value-added tax 24.9%, nontax revenue 12.2%). Expenditures: NIS 224,287,000,000 (social security and welfare 28.0%; defense 17.1%; education 13.9%; health 13.5%; interest on loans 11.2%).
Public debt (external, outstanding; 1999): U.S.$27,323,000,000.
Gross national product (2001): U.S.$106,800,000,000 (U.S.$16,750 per capita).

Structure of net domestic product and labour force

	2000		2001	
	in value NIS '000,000	% of total value	labour force	% of labour force
Agriculture	7,502	1.6	43,000	1.7
Manufacturing, mining	74,486	15.5	394,200	15.7
Construction	20,383	4.2	116,700	4.7
Public utilities	8,093	1.7	19,500	0.8
Transp. and commun.	34,181	7.1	149,200	6.0
Trade, hotels	42,832	8.9	396,600	15.8
Finance, real estate	131,422	27.3	351,900	14.1
Public admin., defense	35,872	7.5	126,600	5.1
Services	75,718	15.7	656,400	26.2
Other	49,933[5]	10.4[5]	249,400[6]	10.0[6]
TOTAL	480,780[7]	100.0[7]	2,503,300[7]	100.0[7]

Production (metric tons except as noted). Agriculture, forestry, fishing (2002): potatoes 375,000, tomatoes 352,000, grapefruit and pomelos 255,000, oranges 198,000, wheat 175,000, grapes 114,000, apples 95,000, olives 60,000; livestock (number of live animals) 392,000 sheep, 390,000 cattle; roundwood (2001) 27,000 cu m; fish catch (2000) 25,916. Mining and quarrying (2001): phosphate rock 3,511,000, potash 1,774,000. Manufacturing (value added in U.S.$'000,000; 1998): electronics and telecommunications 2,225; chemicals, chemical products, and refined petroleum 1,950; professional and scientific equipment 1,725; fabricated metals 1,650; food products 1,600. Energy production (consumption): electricity (kW-hr; 2001) 43,838,000,000 ([2000] 39,317,000,000); hard coal (metric tons; 1999) none (9,187,000); lignite (metric tons; 1999) 944,000 (944,000); crude petroleum (barrels; 1999) 29,000 (76,800,000); petroleum products (metric tons; 1999) 9,356,000 (10,730,000); natural gas (cu m; 1999) 9,900,000 (9,900,000).
Population economically active (2001): total 2,503,300; activity rate 40.2% (participation rates: over age 15[8] [2000] 54.3%; female 45.8%; unemployed 9.3%).

Price and earnings indexes (1995 = 100)

	1996	1997	1998	1999	2000	2001	2002
Consumer price index	111.3	121.3	127.9	134.5	136.0	137.6	145.3
Daily earnings index	113.9	130.8	143.9	155.4	165.2	179.3	181.2

Household income and expenditure (2001). Average household size 3.4; net annual income per household (2000) NIS 101,952 (U.S.$25,004); sources of income (2000)[8]: salaries and wages 67.5%, self-employment 11.5%; expenditure (2000): housing 22.0%, transport and communications 19.3%, food and beverages 16.7%.
Tourism (2001): receipts U.S.$2,166,000,000; expenditures U.S.$2,896,000,000.

Foreign trade[9]

Balance of trade (current prices)

	1996	1997	1998	1999	2000	2001
U.S.$'000,000	–9,824	–7,064	–4,736	–6,073	–4,346	–4,242
% of total	19.6%	13.8%	9.4%	10.8%	6.5%	6.8%

Imports (2001): U.S.$33,303,000,000 (machinery and apparatus 29.3%; diamonds 16.8%; chemicals and chemical products 9.5%; crude petroleum and refined petroleum 8.1%; road vehicles 6.5%). *Major import sources:* U.S. 20.1%; Belgium-Luxembourg 8.0%; Germany 7.9%; U.K. 6.6%; Italy 5.0%.
Exports (2001): U.S.$29,061,000,000 (worked diamonds 25.8%; chemicals and chemical products 12.6%; high-tech communications equipment 11.5%; electronic components 8.1%; precision and scientific equipment 6.6%). *Major export destinations:* U.S. 38.2%; Belgium-Luxembourg 5.4%; Germany 4.4%; Hong Kong 4.3%; U.K. 4.2%.

Transport and communications

Transport. Railroads (2001): route length 684 km; passenger-km 961,000,000, metric ton-km cargo 1,098,000,000. Roads (2001): total length 16,563 km (paved 100%). Vehicles (2001): passenger cars 1,460,851; trucks and buses 338,325. Air transport (2000)[10]: passenger-km 14,125,067,000; metric ton-km cargo 1,288,345,000; airports (1999) with scheduled flights 7.

Communications

Medium	date	unit	number	units per 1,000 persons
Daily newspapers	2000	circulation	1,770,000	290
Radio	2000	receivers	3,210,000	526
Television	2000	receivers	2,040,000	335
Telephones	2002	main lines	3,100,000	467
Cellular telephones	2002	subscribers	6,334,000	954
Personal computers	2002	units	1,600,000	246
Internet	2002	users	2,000,000	301

Education and health

Educational attainment (2000). Percentage of population age 15 and over having: no formal schooling 3.3%; primary 1.9%; secondary 57.4%; postsecondary, vocational, and higher 37.4%. *Literacy* (2000): 96.7%.

Education (2000–01)

	schools	teachers	students	student/ teacher ratio
Primary (age 6–13)	2,137	58,785	559,541	9.5
Secondary (age 14–17)[11]	707	76,915	473,092	6.2
Vocational, teacher tr.	113	...	118,605	...
Higher	7	10,171	219,763	21.6

Health (2000): physicians 21,500 (1 per 284 persons); hospital beds 38,577 (1 per 158 persons); infant mortality rate (2001) 5.4.
Food (2001): daily per capita caloric intake 3,512 (vegetable products 81.1%, animal products 18.9%); 137% of FAO recommended minimum.

Military

Total active duty personnel (2002): 161,500 (army 74.3%, navy 4.0%, air force 21.7%). *Military expenditure as percentage of GNP* (1999): 8.8% (world 2.4%); per capita expenditure U.S.$1,510.

[1]Excluding West Bank (2,278 sq mi [5,900 sq km]), Gaza Strip (140 sq mi [363 sq km]), Golan Heights (454 sq mi [1,176 sq km]), East Jerusalem (27 sq mi [70 sq km]), Sea of Galilee (63 sq mi [164 sq km]), and the Dead Sea (120 sq mi [310 sq km]). [2]January 1. [3]Includes 2003 population of Golan Heights (36,000) and East Jerusalem and excludes 2003 Jewish population of the West Bank and Gaza Strip (230,000). [4]Jewish population only. [5]Taxes on products less imputed bank service charges, subsidies, and statistical discrepancy. [6]Includes 16,300 not adequately classified and 233,100 unemployed. [7]Detail does not add to total given because of rounding. [8]Money income only. [9]Excludes trade with Gaza Strip and the West Bank. [10]El Al only. [11]Includes intermediate schools.

Internet resources for further information:
- **Central Bureau of Statistics (Israel) http://www.cbs.gov.il/engindex.htm**

Italy

Official name: Repubblica Italiana (Italian Republic).
Form of government: republic with two legislative houses (Senate [321[1]]; Chamber of Deputies [630]).
Chief of state: President.
Head of government: Prime Minister.
Capital: Rome.
Official language: Italian.
Official religion: none.
Monetary unit: 1 euro (€) = 100 cents; valuation (Sept. 8, 2003) 1 U.S.$ = €0.90; 1 £ = €1.43[2].

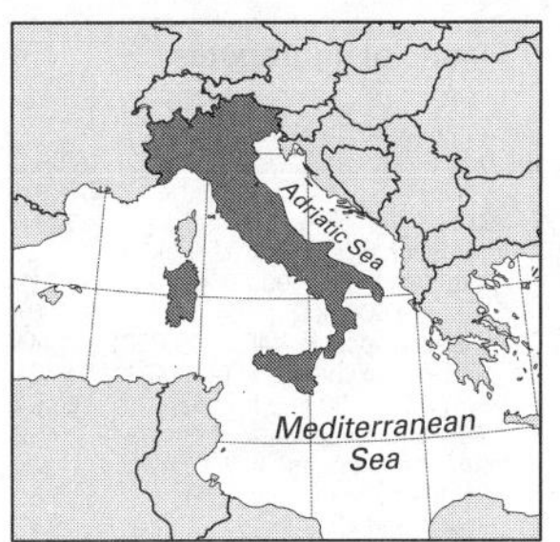

Area and population

Regions / Provinces	Capitals	area sq mi	area sq km	population 2001 census
Abruzzo	L'Aquila	4,168	10,794	1,244,226
Chieti	Chieti	999	2,587	379,471
L'Aquila	L'Aquila	1,944	5,034	289,853
Pescara	Pescara	473	1,225	292,355
Teramo	Teramo	752	1,948	282,547
Basilicata	Potenza	3,858	9,992	595,727
Matera	Matera	1,331	3,447	203,063
Potenza	Potenza	2,527	6,545	392,664
Calabria	Catanzaro	5,823	15,080	1,993,274
Catanzaro	Catanzaro	924	2,392	367,592
Cosenza	Cosenza	2,568	6,650	727,267
Crotone	Crotone	662	1,716	163,058
Reggio di Calabria	Reggio di Calabria	1,229	3,183	563,405
Vibo Valentia	Vibo Valentia	440	1,139	171,952
Campania	Naples	5,249	13,595	5,652,492
Avellino	Avellino	1,078	2,792	428,314
Benevento	Benevento	800	2,071	286,040
Caserta	Caserta	1,019	2,639	853,009
Napoli	Naples	452	1,171	3,009,678
Salerno	Salerno	1,900	4,922	1,075,451
Emilia-Romagna	Bologna	8,542	22,123	3,960,549
Bologna	Bologna	1,429	3,702	910,592
Ferrara	Ferrara	1,016	2,632	342,704
Forlì-Cesena	Forlì	969	2,510	356,327
Modena	Modena	1,039	2,690	628,180
Parma	Parma	1,332	3,449	384,989
Piacenza	Piacenza	1,000	2,589	263,309
Ravenna	Ravenna	718	1,859	350,879
Reggio nell'Emilia	Reggio nell'Emilia	885	2,292	453,039
Rimini	Rimini	154	400	270,530
Friuli-Venezia Giulia	Trieste	3,029	7,845	1,180,375
Gorizia	Gorizia	180	467	136,183
Pordenone	Pordenone	878	2,273	285,409
Trieste	Trieste	82	212	240,549
Udine	Udine	1,889	4,893	518,234
Lazio	Rome	6,642	17,203	4,976,184
Frosinone	Frosinone	1,251	3,239	447,950
Latina	Latina	869	2,251	489,599
Rieti	Rieti	1,061	2,749	144,597
Roma	Rome	2,066	5,352	3,608,784
Viterbo	Viterbo	1,395	3,612	285,254
Liguria	Genoa	2,092	5,418	1,560,748
Genova	Genoa	709	1,836	870,553
Imperia	Imperia	446	1,155	204,233
La Spezia	La Spezia	341	882	215,137
Savona	Savona	596	1,545	270,825
Lombardy	Milan	9,211	23,857	8,922,463
Bergamo	Bergamo	1,051	2,722	968,723
Brescia	Brescia	1,846	4,782	1,106,373
Como	Como	497	1,288	537,046
Cremona	Cremona	684	1,771	334,087
Lecco	Lecco	315	816	311,122
Lodi	Lodi	302	783	195,474
Mantova	Mantova	903	2,339	375,159
Milano	Milan	765	1,980	3,614,108
Pavia	Pavia	1,145	2,965	489,751
Sondrio	Sondrio	1,240	3,212	176,565
Varese	Varese	463	1,199	814,055
Marche	Ancona	3,743	9,693	1,463,868
Ancona	Ancona	749	1,940	447,613
Ascoli Piceno	Ascoli Piceno	806	2,087	365,216
Macerata	Macerata	1,071	2,774	301,302
Pesaro e Urbino	Pesaro	1,117	2,892	349,737
Molise	Campobasso	1,713	4,438	316,548
Campobasso	Campobasso	1,123	2,909	227,090
Isernia	Isernia	590	1,529	89,458
Piedmont	Turin	9,807[3]	25,399	4,166,442
Alessandria	Alessandria	1,375	3,560	414,384
Asti	Asti	583	1,511	207,671
Biella	Biella	352	913	187,041
Cuneo	Cuneo	2,665	6,903	554,992
Novara	Novara	530	1,373	344,010
Torino	Turin	2,637	6,830	2,122,704
Verbano-Cusio-Ossola	Verbania	858	2,221	158,999
Vercelli	Vercelli	806	2,088	176,641
Puglia	Bari	7,470	19,348	3,983,487
Bari	Bari	1,980	5,129	1,541,314
Brindisi	Brindisi	710	1,838	403,923
Foggia	Foggia	2,774	7,185	677,515
Lecce	Lecce	1,065	2,759	785,969
Taranto	Taranto	941	2,437	574,766
Sardinia	Cagliari	9,301	24,090	1,599,511
Cagliari	Cagliari	2,662	6,895	749,393
Nuoro	Nuoro	2,720	7,044	260,345
Oristano	Oristano	1,016	2,631	149,620
Sassari	Sassari	2,903	7,520	440,153
Sicily	Palermo	9,926	25,709	4,866,202
Agrigento	Agrigento	1,175	3,042	441,669
Caltanissetta	Caltanissetta	822	2,128	272,402
Catania	Catania	1,371	3,552	1,040,547
Enna	Enna	989	2,562	177,291
Messina	Messina	1,254	3,248	641,753
Palermo	Palermo	1,927	4,992	1,198,644
Ragusa	Ragusa	623	1,614	292,000
Siracusa	Siracusa	814	2,109	391,515
Trapani	Trapani	951	2,462	410,381
Trentino-Alto Adige	Bolzano	5,258	13,618	937,107
Bolzano-Bozen	Bolzano	2,857	7,400	460,665
Trento	Trento	2,401	6,218	476,442
Tuscany	Florence	8,877	22,992[3]	3,460,835
Arezzo	Arezzo	1,248	3,232	323,011
Firenze	Florence	1,365	3,536	927,835
Grosseto	Grosseto	1,739	4,504	209,295
Livorno	Livorno	468	1,213	316,757
Lucca	Lucca	684	1,773	364,113
Massa-Carrara	Massa-Carrara	447	1,157	197,411
Pisa	Pisa	945	2,448	381,119
Pistoia	Pistoia	373	965	268,180
Prato	Prato	133	344	225,672
Siena	Siena	1,475	3,821	247,442
Umbria	Perugia	3,265	8,456	815,588
Perugia	Perugia	2,446	6,334	597,470
Terni	Terni	819	2,122	218,118
Valle d'Aosta	Aosta	1,259	3,262	119,356
Veneto	Venice	7,090	18,364	4,490,586
Belluno	Belluno	1,420	3,678	209,033
Padova	Padova	827	2,142	845,203
Rovigo	Rovigo	691	1,789	240,102
Treviso	Treviso	956	2,477	793,209
Venezia	Venice	950	2,460	800,370
Verona	Verona	1,195	3,096	814,295
Vicenza	Vicenza	1,051	2,722	788,374
TOTAL		116,324[3, 4]	301,277[3, 4]	56,305,568[5]

Demography

Population (2003): 57,033,000.
Density (2003): persons per sq mi 490.2, persons per sq km 189.3.
Urban-rural (2001): urban 67.1%; rural 32.9%.
Sex distribution (2000): male 48.55%; female 51.45%.
Age breakdown (2000): under 15, 14.4%; 15–29, 19.5%; 30–44, 23.1%; 45–59, 19.1%; 60–74, 16.1%; 75 and over, 7.8%.
Population projection: (2010) 57,124,000; (2020) 56,079,000.
Ethnolinguistic composition (2000): Italian 96.0%; North African Arab 0.9%; Italo-Albanian 0.8%; Albanian 0.5%; German 0.4%; Austrian 0.4%; other 1.0%.
Religious affiliation (2000): Roman Catholic 79.6%; nonreligious 13.2%; Muslim 1.2%; other 6.0%.
Major cities and urban agglomerations (2001/2000[6]): Rome 2,459,776 (2,649,000); Milan 1,182,693 (4,251,000); Naples 993,386 (3,012,000); Turin 857,433 (1,294,000); Palermo 652,640; Genoa 603,560 (890,000); Bologna 369,955; Florence 352,227 (778,000); Bari 312,452; Catania 306,464; Venice 266,181; Verona 243,474; Messina 236,621; Trieste 209,520.
National origin (1991): Italian 99.3%; foreign-born 0.7%, of which European 0.3%, African 0.2%, Asian 0.1%, other 0.1%.
Households. Average household size (2000) 2.6; composition of households: 1 person 23.3%, 2 persons 26.1%, 3 persons 23.0%, 4 persons 20.2%, 5 or more persons 7.4%. Family households (1991): 15,538,335 (73.8%); nonfamily 5,527,105 (26.2%), of which one-person 19.5%.
Immigration (1997): immigrants 162,857, from Europe 41.1%, of which EU countries 14.2%; Africa 25.5%; Asia 19.0%; Western Hemisphere 14.0%.

Vital statistics

Birth rate per 1,000 population (2002): 9.3 (world avg. 21.3); (1998) legitimate 91.0%; illegitimate 8.0%.
Death rate per 1,000 population (2002): 10.3 (world avg. 9.1).
Natural increase rate per 1,000 population (2002): –1.0 (world avg. 12.2).
Total fertility rate (avg. births per childbearing woman; 2002): 1.3.
Marriage rate per 1,000 population (2001): 4.7.
Divorce rate per 1,000 population (1994): 0.5.
Life expectancy at birth (2002): male 76.5 years; female 82.5 years.
Major causes of death per 100,000 population (1998): diseases of the circulatory system 432.5; malignant neoplasms 266.7; diseases of the respiratory system 68.6; diseases of the digestive system 45.1; accidents and violence 37.5.

Social indicators

Educational attainment (1995). Percentage of labour force age 15 and over having: basic literacy or primary education 40.4%; secondary 30.5%; post-secondary technical training 5.1%; some college 19.2%; college degree 4.3%.
Quality of working life. Average workweek (2001): 39.3 hours. Annual rate per 100,000 workers (2000) for: injury or accident 4,030; death 7. Percentage of labour force insured for damages or income loss (1992) resulting from: injury 100%; permanent disability 100%; death 100%. Number of working days lost to labour stoppages per 1,000 workers (1996): 97. Average duration of journey to work: n.a. Rate per 1,000 workers of discouraged (unemployed no longer seeking work; 1990): 1.1.
Material well-being. Rate per 1,000 of population possessing (1995): telephone 434; automobile 550; television 436.
Social participation. Eligible voters participating in last national election (May 13, 2001): 81.2%. Trade union membership in total workforce (1990): *c.* 28%.
Social deviance (2000). Offense rate per 100,000 population for: murder 1.3; rape 4.1; assault 210.4[7]; theft, including burglary and housebreaking 2,466; drug trafficking 61.1; suicide 6.3[8].
Access to services (2002). Nearly 100% of dwellings have access to electricity, a safe water supply, and toilet facilities.
Leisure (1998). Favourite leisure activities (as percentage of household spending on culture): cinema 21.8%; sporting events 14.6%; theatre 13.8%.

National economy

Gross national product (2001): U.S.$1,123,800,000,000 (U.S.$19,390 per capita).

Structure of gross domestic product and labour force

	2001			
	in value €'000,000	% of total value	labour force	% of labour force
Agriculture	30,754	2.5	1,126,000	4.7
Mining	9	9	64,000	0.3
Manufacturing	228,533[9]	18.8[9]	4,907,000	20.5
Construction	55,584	4.6	1,707,000	7.1
Public utilities	30,783	2.5	162,000	0.7
Transportation and communications	81,089	6.7	1,180,000	4.9
Trade	191,246	15.7	4,296,000	18.0
Finance	298,950	24.6	2,209,000	9.2
Pub. admin., defense	60,896	5.0	1,987,000	8.3
Services	156,989	12.9	3,973,000	16.6
Other	81,868[10]	6.7[10]	2,287,000[11]	9.6[11]
TOTAL	1,216,694[3]	100.0	23,901,000[3]	100.0[3]

Budget (1999). Revenue: Lit 620,534,000,000,000 (income taxes 46.9%, of which individual 37.5%, corporate 9.4%; value-added and excise taxes 30.6%). Expenditures: Lit 668,251,000,000,000 (1995; debt service 27.5%; social security 18.4%; education 9.1%; transportation 4.7%; defense 2.8%).
Public debt (1999): U.S.$766,000,000,000.
Tourism (2001): receipts U.S.$25,787,000,000; expenditures U.S.$14,215,000,000.

Manufacturing, mining, and construction enterprises (1995)

	no. of enterprises	no. of employees[12]	hourly wages as a % of avg. of all wages	annual value added (Lit '000,000,000)
Manufacturing				
Metal products	5,780	360,979	...	36,249
Machinery (nonelectrical)	4,503	379,027	...	35,221
Industrial chemicals	1,206	180,836	...	27,505
Electrical machinery	2,962	303,439	...	26,306
Food products	2,549	224,025	...	22,878
Transport equipment	1,122	275,077	...	22,642
Printing, publishing[13]	2,086	148,757	...	16,150
Pottery, ceramics, and glass	2,128	149,586	...	14,361
Textiles[14]	3,514	215,387	...	14,335
Rubber and plastic products	1,836	123,119	...	12,711
Wearing apparel	2,436	114,059	...	7,279
Paper and paper products[13]	...	...	...	...
Petroleum and gas	108	22,566	...	4,221
Mining and quarrying	340	20,013	...	5,991
Construction	6,228	1,564,100	...	94,887

Production (metric tons except as noted). Agriculture, forestry, fishing (2002): sugar beets 11,500,000, corn (maize) 10,937,000, grapes 7,872,000, wheat 7,765,000, tomatoes 6,054,689, olives 2,732,000, apples 2,222,000, potatoes 2,075,000, oranges 1,917,000, peaches and nectarines 1,632,000, rice 1,371,000, barley 1,217,000, soybeans 549,000; livestock (number of live animals) 10,952,000 sheep, 8,410,000 pigs, 7,068,000 cattle, 100,000,000 chickens; roundwood (2003) 8,099,000 cu m; fish catch (2000) 513,474. Mining and quarrying (2001): loam rock 13,973,000; rock salt 3,281,300; feldspar 3,092,400; barite 10,800; lead 4,000. Manufacturing (2001): cement 38,964,900; crude steel 26,526,200; pig iron 10,562,000; glass containers 2,899,000; sulfuric acid 1,581,200; cotton and wool 981,153[15]; wine 58,072,000 hectolitres[15]; beer 11,123,000 hectolitres[15]; olive oil (2000) 493,000 hectolitres; 8,333,500 washing machines; 6,844,300 refrigerators; 2,209,500 motorized road vehicles, of which 1,271,800 automobiles, 633,100 motorcycles, 304,600 trucks and buses; (2000) 1,350,115 colour televisions. Construction (1998): residential 56,268,471 cu m; commercial 67,443,808 cu m.

Service enterprises (1999)

	no. of enterprises[16]	no. of employees	hourly wage as a % of all wages	annual value added €'000,000
Public utilities	...	146,593	...	18,083
Transportation and communications	...	1,142,666	...	51,835
Real estate, research	...	1,828,536	...	66,887
Wholesale and retail trade	...	3,115,825	...	85,832
Health and social services	...	456,997	...	14,469
Hotels, restaurants	...	796,081	...	15,903

Energy production (consumption): electricity (kW-hr; 2001) 278,904,000,000 ([1999] 316,631,000,000); hard coal (metric tons; 1999) negligible (17,069,000); lignite (metric tons; 1999) 115,000 (150,000); crude petroleum (barrels; 2001) 27,714,000 ([1999] 632,600,000); petroleum products (metric tons; 1999) 84,086,000 (83,603,000); natural gas (cu m; 2001) 15,298,000,000 ([1999] 66,568,000,000).
Population economically active (2001): total 23,901,000; activity rate of total population 42.4% (participation rates: ages 15–64, 63.0%; female 38.7%; unemployed 9.6%).

Price and earnings indexes (1995 = 100)

	1997	1998	1999	2000	2001	2002
Consumer price index	106.1	108.2	110.0	112.8	115.9	118.3
Earnings index	106.9	109.9	112.4	114.7	116.6	119.6

Household income and expenditure (2000). Average household size 2.6; average annual income per household: n.a.; sources of income (1996): salaries and wages 38.8%, property income and self-employment 38.5%, transfer payments 22.0%; expenditure (2001): housing 34.9%, food and beverages 18.9%, transportation and communications 16.7%, leisure 6.3%, other 16.2%.

Financial aggregates

	1997	1998	1999	2000	2001	2002
Exchange rate, Lit per[17]:						
U.S. dollar	1,759.2	1,653.1	0.9954	1.0747	1.1347	0.9536
£	2,909.4	2,749.9	1.6090	1.6037	1.6458	1.5370
SDR	2,373.6	2,327.6	1.3662	1.4002	1.4260	1.2964
International reserves (U.S.$)						
Total (excl. gold; '000,000)	55,739	29,888	22,422	25,567	24,419	28,603
SDRs ('000,000)	67	111	168	238	297	108
Reserve pos. in IMF ('000,000)	2,241	4,330	3,546	2,906	3,217	3,907
Foreign exchange ('000,000)	54,431	25,447	18,623	22,423	20,905	24,588
Gold ('000,000 fine troy oz)	66.67	83.36	78.83	78.83	78.83	78.83
% world reserves	7.5	8.6	8.2	8.3	8.4	8.5
Interest and prices						
Central bank discount (%)	5.50	3.00	...	...	...	...
Govt. bond yield (%)	6.47	4.55	4.04	5.29	4.64	4.48
Industrial share prices (1995 = 100)	137.7	220.5	245.5	319.0	258.8	205.2
Balance of payments (U.S.$'000,000)						
Balance of visible trade	39,877	35,361	23,436	9,548	15,539	16,533
Imports, f.o.b.	−200,527	−206,941	−212,420	−230,925	−229,392	−237,147
Exports, f.o.b.	240,404	242,572	235,856	240,473	244,931	253,680
Balance of invisibles	−7,474	−15,363	−15,326	−16,477	−16,191	−23,274
Balance of payments, current account	32,403	19,998	8,110	−5,781	−652	−6,741

Land use (1994): forest 23.0%; pasture 15.4%; agriculture 37.9%; other 23.7%.

Foreign trade[18]

Balance of trade (current prices)

	1996	1997	1998	1999	2000	2001
U.S.$'000,000	+43,983	+29,949	+26,512	+14,907	+1,781	+8,262
% of total	9.6%	6.7%	5.8%	3.3%	0.4%	1.7%

Imports (2000): U.S.$235,859,000,000 (machinery 20.5%, chemicals 12.0%, road vehicles 11.0%, crude petroleum 7.2%, food 6.9%, iron and steel 3.6%). *Major import sources:* Germany 17.5%; France 11.2%; The Netherlands 5.7%; U.K. 5.4%; U.S. 5.3%; Spain 4.1%; Belgium 4.0%; Switzerland 3.0%.
Exports (2000): U.S.$237,640,000,000 (machinery and apparatus 27.7%, chemicals and chemical products 9.1%, road vehicles 8.1%, apparel and clothing accessories 5.6%, textile yarn and fabrics 5.1%, food 4.3%). *Major export destinations:* Germany 15.0%; France 12.5%; U.S. 10.3%; U.K. 6.8%; Spain 6.2%; Switzerland 3.3%; Belgium 2.7%; The Netherlands 2.6%.

Transport and communications

Transport. Railroads: (2002) length 19,786 km; (2001) passenger-km 46,675,000,000; (2001) metric ton-km cargo 24,995,000,000. Roads (1997): total length 654,676 km (paved 100%). Vehicles (1999): passenger cars 31,953,247; trucks and buses 3,302,569. Air transport (2001)[19]: passenger-km 36,524,000,000; metric ton-km cargo 1,530,000,000; airports (1997) 34.

Communications

Medium	date	unit	number	units per 1,000 persons
Daily newspapers	2000	circulation	5,920,000	104
Radio	2000	receivers	50,000,000	878
Television	2000	receivers	28,100,000	494
Telephones	2002	main lines	27,452,000	486
Cellular telephones	2002	subscribers	52,316,000	843
Personal computers	2001	units	11,300,000	195
Internet	2002	users	17,000,000	301

Education and health

Literacy (2000): total population age 15 and over literate 48,100,000 (98.4%); males literate 23,800,000 (98.9%); females literate 24,300,000 (98.0%).

Education (2000–01)

	schools	teachers	students	student/ teacher ratio
Primary (age 6–10)	18,854	287,344	1,576,456	5.5
Secondary (age 11–18)	7,906	209,829	1,776,950	8.5
Voc., teacher tr.	6,637	307,279	2,565,029	8.3
Higher[20]	74	54,856	1,702,575	31.0

Health: physicians (1998) 356,821 (1 per 160 persons); hospital beds (1999) 270,773 (1 per 213 persons); infant mortality rate (2002) 6.2.
Food (2001): daily per capita caloric intake 3,680 (vegetable products 75%, animal products 25%); 146% of FAO recommended minimum requirement.

Military

Total active duty personnel (2002): 216,800 (army 59.0%, navy 17.5%, air force 23.4%). *Military expenditure as percentage of GNP* (1999): 2.0% (world 2.4%); per capita expenditure U.S.$412.

[1]Includes 6 nonelective seats in late 2003 (4 presidential appointees and 2 former presidents serving ex officio). [2]The Italian lira (Lit) was the former monetary unit; on Jan. 1, 2002, Lit 1,936 = €1. [3]Detail does not add to total given because of rounding. [4]The total area for Italy, per 2000 survey, is 116,345 sq mi (301,333 sq km). [5]Preliminary de jure figure; final de jure figure equals 56,995,744. [6]Major city populations are 2001 preliminary census figures; urban agglomeration populations are 2000 estimates by the UN. [7]1995. [8]1996. [9]Manufacturing includes Mining. [10]Other includes indirect import charges and building rental less imputed bank service charges. [11]Unemployed. [12]Total number of persons engaged. [13]Printing, publishing includes Paper and paper products. [14]1993. [15]1999. [16]Enterprises with 20 or more persons engaged. [17]Beginning in 1999 exchange rates in euros. [18]Imports c.i.f.; exports f.o.b. [19]Alitalia only. [20]2001–02.

Internet resources for further information:
- **National Statistical Institute http://www.istat.it/English**

Jamaica

Official name: Jamaica.
Form of government: constitutional monarchy[1] with two legislative houses (Senate [21]; House of Representatives [60]).
Chief of state: British Monarch represented by Governor-General.
Head of government: Prime Minister.
Capital: Kingston.
Official language: English.
Official religion: none.
Monetary unit: 1 Jamaica dollar (J$) = 100 cents; valuation (Sept. 8, 2003) 1 U.S.$ = J$58.70; 1 £ = J$93.07.

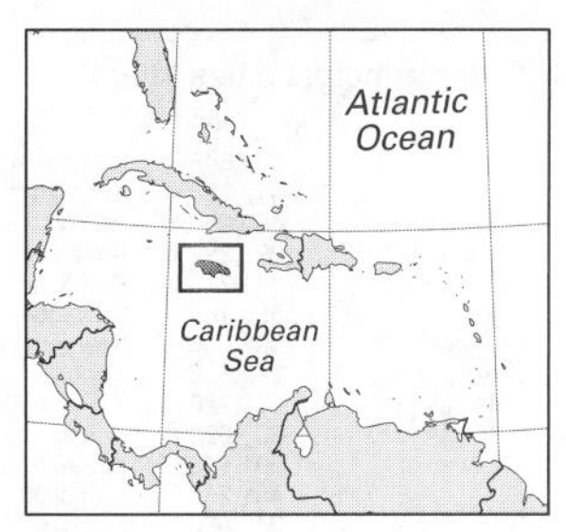

Area and population

Parishes	Capitals	area sq mi	area sq km	population 2001 census[2]
Clarendon	May Pen	462	1,196	237,000
Hanover	Lucea	174	450	67,000
Kingston	[3]	8	22	96,100
Manchester	Mandeville	321	830	185,800
Portland	Port Antonio	314	814	80,200
Saint Andrew	[3]	166	431	555,800
Saint Ann	Saint Ann's Bay	468	1,213	166,800
Saint Catherine	Spanish Town	460	1,192	482,300
Saint Elizabeth	Black River	468	1,212	146,400
Saint James	Montego Bay	230	595	175,100
Saint Mary	Port Maria	236	611	111,500
Saint Thomas	Morant Bay	287	743	91,600
Trelawny	Falmouth	338	875	73,100
Westmoreland	Savanna-la-Mar	312	807	138,900
TOTAL		4,244	10,991	2,607,600

Demography

Population (2003): 2,644,000.
Density (2003): persons per sq mi 623.0, persons per sq km 240.6.
Urban-rural (2001): urban 52.1%; rural 47.9%.
Sex distribution (2002[4]): male 49.95%; female 50.05%.
Age breakdown (2002[4]): under 15, 30.5%; 15–29, 26.9%; 30–44, 21.9%; 45–59, 11.1%; 60–74, 6.5%; 75 and over, 3.1%.
Population projection: (2010) 2,825,000; (2020) 3,118,000.
Doubling time: 52 years.
Ethnic composition (2000): local black 77.0%; local mulatto 14.6%; Haitian 2.0%; East Indian 1.7%; black-East Indian 1.6%; other 3.1%.
Religious affiliation (1995): Protestant 39.0%, of which Pentecostal 10.5%, Seventh-day Adventist 6.1%, Baptist 5.3%, Anglican 3.7%; Roman Catholic 10.4%; other (including nonreligious) 46.9%[5].
Major cities (1991): Kingston 103,771[6] (metro area 587,798); Spanish Town (2001) 131,056; Portmore 90,138; Montego Bay 83,446; May Pen 46,785.

Vital statistics

Birth rate per 1,000 population (2002): 20.0 (world avg. 21.3).
Death rate per 1,000 population (2002): 6.5 (world avg. 9.1).
Natural increase rate per 1,000 population (2002): 13.5 (world avg. 12.2).
Total fertility rate (avg. births per childbearing woman; 2001): 2.1.
Marriage rate per 1,000 population (1996): 7.4.
Life expectancy at birth (2001): male 73.5 years; female 77.5 years.
Major causes of death per 100,000 population (1991): diseases of the circulatory system 189.4; malignant neoplasms (cancers) 84.1; endocrine and metabolic disorders 51.3; diseases of the respiratory system 30.1.

National economy

Budget (2000–01). Revenue J$101,018,000,000 (tax revenue 86.2%, of which income taxes 35.1%, consumption taxes 26.4%, custom duties 8.4%; nontax revenue 7.7%; bauxite levy 2.7%; capital revenue 1.7%; grants 1.7%). Expenditures: J$104,171,000,000 (current expenditure 91.0%, of which debt interest 41.2%, wages 33.8%; capital expenditure 9.0%).
Production (metric tons except as noted). Agriculture, forestry, fishing (2002): sugarcane 2,400,000, citrus fruits 221,000, vegetables and melons 197,000, coconuts 170,000, yams 158,000, bananas 130,000, plantains 29,000, tomatoes 24,000, cabbages 22,000, coffee 2,700; livestock (number of live animals) 440,000 goats, 400,000 cattle, 180,000 pigs; roundwood (2002) 866,628 cu m; fish catch (1999) 12,658. Mining and quarrying (2002): bauxite 13,139,000; alumina 3,630,000; gypsum (2001) 317,000. Manufacturing (2001): cement 595,064; animal feeds 384,569; sugar 205,128; flour 129,836; molasses 86,983; beer 622,000 hectolitres; rum [and other distilled spirits] 223,000 hectolitres; cigarettes 1,024,933,000 units. Energy production (consumption): electricity (kW-hr; 1999) 6,609,000,000 (6,609,000,000); coal (metric tons; 1999) none (72,000); crude petroleum (barrels; 1999) none (3,200,000); petroleum products (metric tons; 1999) 520,000 (3,286,000).
Population economically active (April 2001): total 1,105,800; activity rate of total population 42.4% (participation rates: ages 14 and over 63.0%; female 43.9%; unemployed 14.8%).

Price and earnings indexes (1995 = 100)

	1996	1997	1998	1999	2000	2001	2002
Consumer price index	126.4	138.6	150.6	159.5	172.6	184.6	197.7
Earnings index	...	...	...	...	...	...	...

Gross national product (2001): U.S.$7,300,000,000 (U.S.$2,800 per capita).

Structure of gross domestic product and labour force

	2001 in value J$'000,000	2001 % of total value	2000 labour force	2000 % of labour force
Agriculture	22,888	6.8	195,700	17.7
Mining	14,820	4.4	4,600	0.4
Manufacturing	46,554	13.9	69,600	6.3
Construction	34,763	10.4	81,500	7.4
Public utilities	14,125	4.2	6,300	0.6
Transp. and commun.	37,809	11.3	59,400	5.4
Trade	87,879	26.3	206,300	18.7
Pub. admin., defense	40,296	12.0	254,800	23.0
Finance, real estate	43,141	12.9	53,100	4.8
Services	9,673	2.9	2,300	0.2
Other	–17,249[7]	–5.1[7]	171,800[8]	15.5[8]
TOTAL	334,699	100.0	1,105,400	100.0

Public debt (external, outstanding; 2001): U.S.$3,947,000,000.
Household income and expenditure. Average household size (1991) 4.2; average annual income per household (1988) J$8,356 (U.S.$1,525); sources of income (1989): wages and salaries 66.1%, self-employment 19.3%, transfers 14.6%; expenditure (1988)[9]: food and beverages 55.6%, housing 7.9%, fuel and other household supplies 7.4%, health care 7.0%, transportation 6.4%.
Tourism: receipts (2001) U.S.$1,233,000,000; expenditures U.S.$206,000,000.

Foreign trade[10]

Balance of trade (current prices)

	1996	1997	1998	1999	2000	2001
U.S.$'000,000	–1,567	–1,838	–1,714	–1,656	–1,907	–2,140
% of total	36.1%	41.6%	40.7%	39.9%	42.4%	46.6%

Imports (2001): U.S.$3,365,000,000 (consumer goods 29.4%, capital goods 16.8%, refined petroleum and other fuels and lubricants 12.4%, crude petroleum 5.0%). *Major import sources* (2001): U.S. 44.8%; Caricom 12.7%; Latin American countries 10.5%; EU 9.3%, of which U.K. 3.0%.
Exports (2001): U.S.$1,225,000,000 (alumina 52.5%, bauxite 7.7%, wearing apparel 7.2%, refined sugar 5.8%, coffee 2.5%, rum 2.4%). *Major export destinations:* U.S. 31.1%; EU 29.4%, of which U.K. 12.8%; Canada 15.6%; Norway 7.5%; Caricom 4.1%.

Transport and communications

Transport. Railroads (2000): route length 211 mi; 339 km; passenger-mi 12,127,000, passenger-km 19,516,000; short ton-mi cargo 1,700,000, metric ton-km cargo 2,482,000. Roads (1999): total length 11,620 mi, 18,700 km (paved 70%). Vehicles (2000–01): passenger cars 168,179, trucks and buses 62,634. Air transport (2001)[11]: passenger-km 4,411,851,000; metric ton-km cargo 50,743,000; airports (2000) with scheduled flights 4.

Communications

Medium	date	unit	number	units per 1,000 persons
Daily newspapers	2000	circulation	161,000	62
Radio	2000	receivers	2,030,000	784
Television	2000	receivers	502,000	194
Telephones	2001	main lines	512,600	197
Cellular telephones	2001	subscribers	700,000	269
Personal computers	2001	units	130,000	50
Internet	2001	users	100,000	38

Education and health

Educational attainment (1982). Percentage of population age 25 and over having: no formal schooling 3.2%; some primary education 79.8%; some secondary 15.0%; complete secondary and higher 2.0%. *Literacy* (2000): total population age 15 and over literate 88%; males 83%; females 91%.

Education (2000–01)

	schools	teachers	students	student/ teacher ratio
Primary (age 6–11)[12]	788[13]	10,215	334,735	32.8
Secondary (age 12–16)	135	9,077	174,094	19.2
Voc., teacher tr.	17	1,083	17,768	16.4
Higher[14]	1	418	8,191	19.6

Health (2000)[15]: physicians 435 (1 per 5,988 persons); hospital beds 3,511 (1 per 742 persons); infant mortality rate (2001) 14.2.
Food (2001): daily per capita caloric intake 2,705 (vegetable products 85%, animal products 15%); 121% of FAO recommended minimum requirement.

Military

Total active duty personnel (2002): 2,830 (army 88.3%, coast guard 6.7%, air force 5.0%). *Military expenditure as percentage of GNP* (1999): 0.8% (world 2.4%); per capita expenditure U.S.$19.

[1]Jamaica is to become a republic by 2007 per announcement of prime minister in September 2003. [2]Final adjusted (rounded) figure. [3]The parishes of Kingston and Saint Andrew are jointly administered from the Half Way Tree section of Saint Andrew. [4]January 1. [5]Includes *c.* 0.7% Rastafarian. [6]City of Kingston is coextensive with Kingston parish. [7]Less imputed service charges. [8]Unemployed. [9]Weights of consumer price index components. [10]Imports c.i.f.; exports f.o.b. [11]Air Jamaica only. [12]Includes lower-secondary students at all-age schools. [13]1991–92. [14]1996–97. [15]Public health only.

Internet resources for further information:
- **Statistics Institute of Jamaica http://www.statinja.com**

Japan

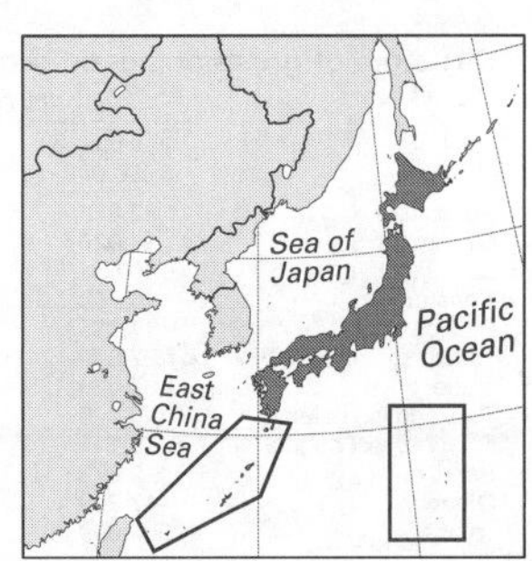

Official name: Nihon (Japan).
Form of government: constitutional monarchy with a national Diet consisting of two legislative houses (House of Councillors [247]; House of Representatives [480]).
Symbol of state: Emperor.
Head of government: Prime Minister.
Capital: Tokyo.
Official language: Japanese.
Official religion: none.
Monetary unit: 1 yen (¥) = 100 sen; valuation (Sept. 8, 2003) 1 U.S.$ = ¥116.74; 1 £ = ¥185.10.

Area and population

Regions / Prefectures	Capitals	area sq mi	area sq km	population 2002 estimate
Chūbu		25,786	66,786	21,718,000
Aichi	Nagoya	1,991	5,156	7,123,000
Fukui	Fukui	1,617	4,189	828,000
Gifu	Gifu	4,092	10,598	2,111,000
Ishikawa	Kanazawa	1,616	4,185	1,180,000
Nagano	Nagano	5,245	13,585	2,217,000
Niigata	Niigata	4,858	12,582	2,465,000
Shizuoka	Shizuoka	3,003	7,779	3,786,000
Toyama	Toyama	1,640	4,247	1,119,000
Yamanashi	Kōfu	1,724	4,465	889,000
Chūgoku		12,322	31,913	7,718,000
Hiroshima	Hiroshima	3,273	8,477	2,878,000
Okayama	Okayama	2,746	7,112	1,953,000
Shimane	Matsue	2,590	6,707	757,000
Tottori	Tottori	1,354	3,507	612,000
Yamaguchi	Yamaguchi	2,359	6,110	1,518,000
Hokkaidō		32,221	83,453	5,670,000
Hokkaidō	Sapporo	32,221	83,453	5,670,000
Kantō		12,518	32,422	40,871,000
Chiba	Chiba	1,991	5,156	5,994,000
Gumma	Maebashi	2,457	6,363	2,032,000
Ibaraki	Mito	2,354	6,096	2,990,000
Kanagawa	Yokohama	932	2,415	8,625,000
Saitama	Saitama	1,466	3,797	7,001,000
Tochigi	Utsunomiya	2,474	6,408	2,010,000
Tokyo-to	Tokyo	844	2,187	12,219,000
Kinki		12,783	33,108	22,754,000
Hyōgo	Kōbe	3,240	8,392	5,578,000
Kyōto-fu	Kyōto	1,781	4,613	2,642,000
Mie	Tsu	2,230	5,776	1,861,000
Nara	Nara	1,425	3,691	1,438,000
Ōsaka-fu	Ōsaka	731	1893	8,815,000
Shiga	Ōtsu	1,551	4,017	1,359,000
Wakayama	Wakayama	1,825	4,726	1,061,000
Kyūshū		17,157	44,436	14,786,000
Fukuoka	Fukuoka	1,919	4,971	5,043,000
Kagoshima	Kagoshima	3,547	9,187	1,779,000
Kumamoto	Kumamoto	2,859	7,404	1,858,000
Miyazaki	Miyazaki	2,986	7,734	1,167,000
Nagasaki	Nagasaki	1,580	4,092	1,507,000
Ōita-ken	Ōita	2,447	6,338	1,219,000
Okinawa	Naha	877	2,271	1,339,000
Saga	Saga	942	2,439	874,000
Shikoku		7,259	18,802	4,137,000
Ehime	Matsuyama	2,192	5,676	1,486,000
Kagawa	Takamatsu	724	1,876	1,021,000
Kōchi	Kōchi	2,743	7,105	810,000
Tokushima	Tokushima	1,600	4,145	820,000
Tohoku		25,825	66,886	9,778,000
Akita	Akita	4,483	11,612	1,176,000
Aomori	Aomori	3,709	9,606	1,469,000
Fukushima	Fukushima	5,321	13,782	2,120,000
Iwate	Morioka	5,899	15,278	1,407,000
Miyagi	Sendai	2,813	7,285	2,371,000
Yamagata	Yamagata	3,600	9,323	1,235,000
TOTAL		145,898[1]	377,873[1]	127,435,000[2]

Demography

Population (2003): 127,546,000.
Density (2003): persons per sq mi 874.2, persons per sq km 337.5.
Urban-rural (2001): urban 78.9%; rural 21.1%.
Sex distribution (2002): male 48.9%; female 51.1%.
Age breakdown (2002): under 15, 14.2%; 15–29, 19.3%; 30–44, 20.0%; 45–59, 21.5%; 60–74, 17.1%; 75 and over, 7.9%.
Population projection: (2010) 127,920,000; (2020) 125,541,000.
Doubling time: not applicable; doubling time exceeds 100 years.
Composition by nationality (2002): Japanese 98.7%; Korean 0.5%; Chinese 0.3%; other 0.5%.
Immigration (2000): permanent immigrants/registered aliens admitted 1,686,444, from North and South Korea 37.7%, Taiwan, Hong Kong, and China 19.9%, Brazil 15.1%, Philippines 8.6%, Peru 2.7%, United States 2.6%, Thailand 1.7%, Indonesia 1.1%, United Kingdom 1.0%, Vietnam 0.6%, Canada 0.6%, India 0.6%, Pakistan 0.4%, other 7.4%.
Major cities (2002): Tokyo 8,025,538; Yokohama 3,433,612; Ōsaka 2,484,326; Nagoya 2,109,681; Sapporo 1,822,992; Kōbe 1,478,380; Kyōto 1,387,264; Fukuoka 1,302,454; Kawasaki 1,245,780; Hiroshima 1,113,786; Saitama[3] 1,029,327; Kita-Kyūshū 999,806; Sendai 986,713.

Other principal cities (2002)

	population		population		population
Akashi	291,649	Kagoshima	544,840	Nishinomiya	436,877
Akita	319,926	Kakogawa	265,393	Ōita	437,699
Amagasaki	463,256	Kanazawa	439,892	Okayama	621,809
Aomori	297,292	Kashiwa	326,097	Okazaki	336,169
Asahikawa	361,372	Kasugai	288,208	Ōtsu	291,322
Chiba	880,164	Kawagoe	325,373	Sagamihara	600,386
Fujisawa	382,038	Kawaguchi	463,879	Sakai	787,833
Fukui	249,656	Kōchi	326,490	Shimonoseki	246,924
Fukushima	288,926	Koriyama	330,776	Shizuoka	468,775
Fukuyama	381,098	Koshigaya	308,413	Suita	342,112
Funabashi	551,918	Kumamoto	653,835	Takamatsu	333,387
Gifu	401,269	Kurashiki	432,938	Takasaki	241,672
Hachinohe	243,880	Machida	384,572	Takatsuki	353,362
Hachiōji	521,359	Maebashi	283,005	Tokorozawa	330,020
Hakodate	284,690	Matsudo	464,224	Tokushima	262,286
Hamamatsu	573,504	Matsuyama	473,039	Toyama	321,049
Higashi-Ōsaka	496,747	Mito	246,095	Toyohashi	356,794
Himeji	475,892	Miyazaki	305,270	Toyonaka	387,869
Hirakata	401,753	Morioka	281,182	Toyota	342,835
Hiratsuka	252,982	Nagano	359,045	Utsunomiya	443,404
Ibaraki	257,577	Nagasaki	419,901	Wakayama	391,008
Ichihara	280,313	Naha	303,146	Yamagata	250,316
Ichikawa	447,686	Nara	364,411	Yao	268,012
Ichinomiya	277,473	Neyagawa	248,464	Yokkaichi	288,319
Iwaki	363,526	Niigata	514,678	Yokosuka	434,613

Religious affiliation (1995): Shintō and related religions 93.1%[4]; Buddhism 69.6%; Christian 1.2%; other 8.1%.
Households (2000). Total households 46,782,000; average household size 2.7; composition of households 1 person 27.6%, 2 persons 25.1%, 3 persons 18.8%, 4 persons 16.9%, 5 persons 6.8%, 6 or more persons 4.8%. Family households 33,769,000 (72.2%); nonfamily 13,013,000 (27.8%).

Type of household (1998)

Total number of occupied dwelling units: 43,922,000

	number of dwellings	percentage of total
by kind of dwelling		
exclusively for living	41,744,000	95.0
mixed use	124,000	0.3
combined with nondwelling	2,054,000	4.7
detached house	23,469,000	56.2
apartment building	16,420,000	39.3
tenement (substandard or overcrowded building)	1,735,000	4.2
other	120,000	0.3
by legal tenure of householder		
owned	26,468,000	60.3
rented	16,730,000	38.1
other	724,000	1.6
by kind of amenities		
flush toilet	36,461	83.0
bathroom	41,919	95.4
by year of construction		
prior to 1945	1,647,000	3.8
1945–70	8,077,000	18.9
1971–80	11,492,000	26.8
1981–90	11,973,000	28.0
1991–98 (Sept.)	9,650,000	22.5

Mobility (2002). Percentage of total population moving: within a prefecture 2.5%; between prefectures 2.1%.

Vital statistics

Birth rate per 1,000 population (2001): 9.3 (world avg. 21.3).
Death rate per 1,000 population (2001): 7.7 (world avg. 9.1).
Natural increase rate per 1,000 population (2001): 1.6 (world avg. 12.2).
Total fertility rate (avg. births per childbearing woman; 2001): 1.3.
Marriage rate per 1,000 population (2001): 6.4; average age at first marriage (1996) men 28.5 years, women 26.4 years.
Divorce rate per 1,000 population (2001): 2.3.
Life expectancy at birth (2001): male 78.1 years; female 84.9 years.
Major causes of death per 100,000 population (2001): circulatory diseases 329.2, of which cerebrovascular disease 103.6; malignant neoplasms (cancers) 236.2; pneumonia and bronchitis 78.8; accidents and adverse effects 63.8, of which suicide 23.1; nephritis, nephrotic syndrome, and nephrosis 13.9; cirrhosis of the liver 12.5; diabetes mellitus 9.5.

Social indicators

Educational attainment (1998). Percentage of population ages 25–64 having: no formal schooling through complete primary education 2.4%; incomplete through complete secondary 79.9%; postsecondary 17.7%.

Distribution of income (2000)

percentage of average household income by quintile

1	2	3	4	5 (highest)
11.2	15.3	18.7	23.0	31.7

Quality of working life. Average hours worked per month (2002): 153.1. Annual rate of industrial deaths per 100,000 workers (2001): 2.7. Proportion of labour force insured for damages or income loss resulting from injury, permanent disability, and death (2001): 65.4%. Average man-days lost to labour stoppages per 1,000,000 workdays (1998): 6.8. Average duration of journey to work (1996): 19.0 minutes. Rate per 1,000 workers of discouraged workers (unemployed no longer seeking work: 1997): 89.4.

Access to services (1989). Proportion of households having access to: gas supply 64.6%; safe public water supply 94.0%; public sewage collection 89.4%.
Social participation. Eligible voters participating in last national election (June 2000): 62.5%. Population 15 years and over participating in social-service activities on a voluntary basis (1991): 26.3%. Trade union membership in total workforce (2002): 20.2%.
Social deviance (2001). Offense rate per 100,000 population for: homicide 0.6; robbery 1.2; larceny and theft 14.2. Incidence in general population of: alcoholism per 100,000 population, n.a.; drug and substance abuse 0.1. Rate of suicide per 100,000 population: 23.1.

Leisure/use of personal time

Discretionary daily activities (1996)
(Population age 10 years and over)

	weekly average hrs./min.
Total discretionary daily time	6:12
of which	
Hobbies and amusements	0:36
Sports	0:13
Learning (except schoolwork)	0:12
Social activities	0:04
Associations	0:27
Radio, television, newspapers, and magazines	2:59
Rest and relaxation	1:15
Other activities	0:20

Major leisure activities (1996)
(Population age 15 years and over)

	percentage of participation		
	male	female	total
Sports	81.7	70.5	76.1
Light gymnastics	25.9	30.6	28.3
Swimming	24.6	20.9	22.8
Bowling	33.7	24.6	29.2
Learning (except schoolwork)	30.7	30.6	30.6
Travel (1991)			
Domestic	72.7	68.3	70.4
Foreign	10.4	7.6	9.0

Material well-being (2001). Households possessing: automobile 84.4%; telephone, virtually 100%; colour television receiver 99.3%; refrigerator 98.4%; air conditioner 87.2%; washing machine 99.3%; vacuum cleaner 98.2%; videocassette recorder 79.6%; camera 86.8%; microwave oven 96.2%; compact disc player 60.5%; personal computer 57.2%; cellular phone 78.6%.

National economy

Gross national product (at current market prices; 2001): U.S.$4,523,300,000,000 (U.S.$35,610 per capita).

Structure of gross domestic product and labour force

	2001		2002	
	in value ¥'000,000,000	% of total value	labour force	% of labour force
Agriculture, fishing	6,973.0	1.4	2,960,000	4.4
Mining	662.6	0.1	50,000	0.1
Manufacturing	104,230.8	20.5	12,220,000	18.3
Construction	35,762.3	7.0	6,180,000	9.2
Public utilities	14,494.8	2.9	340,000	0.5
Transportation and communications	32,161.5	6.3	4,010,000	6.0
Trade	70,524.6	13.9	14,380,000	21.5
Finance	101,020.7	19.9	2,410,000	3.6
Pub. admin., defense	47,122.2	9.3	20,750,000	31.0
Services	110,702.5	21.8		
Other	−16,199.6[5]	−3.2[5]	3,590,000[6]	5.4[6]
TOTAL	507,455.4	100.0[2]	66,890,000	100.0

Budget (2002–03). Revenue: ¥81,230,000,000,000 (government bonds 36.9%; income tax 19.5%; corporation tax 13.8%; value-added tax 12.1%; stamp and customs duties 3.9%). Expenditures: ¥81,230,000,000,000 (social security 22.5%; debt service 20.5%; public works 10.3%; national defense 6.1%).
Public debt (1998): U.S.$2,412,200,000,000 (¥278,847,900,000,000).

Financial aggregates

	1996	1997	1998	1999	2000	2001	2002
Exchange rate[7], ¥ per:							
U.S. dollar	116.00	129.95	115.60	102.20	114.90	131.80	119.90
£	196.97	214.11	192.30	165.20	171.45	191.16	193.25
SDR	166.80	175.34	162.77	140.27	149.70	165.64	163.01
International reserves (U.S.$)							
Total (excl. gold; '000,000)	216,648	219,648	215,471	286,916	354,902	395,155	461,186
SDRs ('000,000)	2,648	2,638	2,663	2,656	2,437	2,377	2,524
Reserve pos. in IMF ('000,000)	6,671	9,144	9,593	6,552	5,253	5,051	7,203
Foreign exchange ('000,000)	207,335	207,866	203,215	277,708	347,212	387,727	451,458
Gold ('000,000 fine troy oz)	24.23	24.23	24.23	24.23	24.55	24.60	24.60
% world reserves	2.7	2.7	2.5	2.6	2.6	2.6	2.6
Interest and prices							
Central bank discount (%)[7]	0.50	0.50	0.50	0.50	0.50	0.10	0.10
Govt. bond yield (%)	2.23	1.69	1.10	1.77	1.75	1.33	1.25
Industrial share prices (1995 = 100)	116.3	101.1	85.4	100.4	112.0	86.5	70.3
Balance of payments (U.S.$'000,000,000)							
Balance of visible trade	83.56	101.60	122.39	123.32	116.72	70.21	93.83
Imports, f.o.b.	316.72	307.64	251.66	280.37	342.80	313.38	301.75
Exports, f.o.b.	400.28	409.24	374.04	403.69	459.51	383.59	395.58
Balance of invisibles	−17.68	−7.25	−1.69	−16.45	0.16	19.07	18.62
Balance of payments, current account	65.88	94.35	120.70	106.87	116.88	89.28	112.45

Manufacturing and mining enterprises (2002)

	no. of establishments	avg. no. of persons engaged	annual wages as a % of avg. of all mfg. wages	annual value added (¥'000,000,000)
Electrical machinery	42,164	1,829,000	112.1	13,293
Food, beverages, and tobacco	66,507	1,488,000	70.1	7,888
Transport equipment	25,756	1,026,000	125.3	9,174
Chemical products	9,099	495,000	136.6	8,479
Nonelectrical machinery	73,782	1,168,000	112.9	7,176
Fabricated metal products	81,544	856,000	93.3	5,920
Printing and publishing	57,364	697,000	120.9	5,598
Ceramic, stone, and clay	28,148	413,000	104.6	2,702
Plastic products	28,120	472,000	90.7	4,265
Iron and steel	7,662	264,000	117.0	2,297
Paper and paper products	15,271	286,000	103.9	1,930
Apparel products	51,078	487,000	51.5	1,612
Precision instruments	11,793	250,000	103.4	2,426
Nonferrous metal products	5,830	181,000	111.6	1,380
Rubber products	7,798	161,000	85.1	1,560
Textiles	35,611	246,000	85.3	1,303
Furniture and fixtures	33,349	220,000	76.8	1,395
Lumber and wood products	22,055	192,000	82.7	900
Petroleum and coal products	1,379	38,000	161.9	883
Leather products	9,871	65,000	65.2	312
Mining and quarrying	3,764	47,000	101.3	839

Energy production (consumption): electricity (kW-hr; 1999) 1,066,130,000,000 (1,066,130,000,000); coal (metric tons; 1999) 3,922,000 (137,492,000); crude petroleum (barrels; 1999) 2,800,000 (1,546,700,000); petroleum products (metric tons; 1999) 183,706,000, of which (by volume [1998]) diesel 32.8%, heavy fuel oil 21.7%, gasoline 21.7%, kerosene and jet fuel 12.0% (193,294,000); natural gas (cu m; 1999) 2,279,600,000 (74,066,700,000). Composition of energy supply by source (1998): crude oil and petroleum products 50.9%, coal 17.0%, nuclear power 14.2%, natural gas 12.8%, hydroelectric power 4.1%, other 1.0%. Domestic energy demand by end use (1998): mining and manufacturing 46.3%, residential and commercial 26.3%, transportation 25.2%, other 2.2%.
Population economically active (2002): total 66,890,000; activity rate of total population 52.5% (participation rates: age 15 and over, 63.9%; female 40.9%; unemployed 5.4%).

Price and earnings indexes (1995 = 100)

	1996	1997	1998	1999	2000	2001	2002
Consumer price index	100.1	101.9	102.5	102.2	101.5	100.8	99.8
Monthly earnings index	101.9	103.4	103.1	103.6	104.6	104.7	99.0

Household income and expenditure (2002). Average household size 2.7; average annual income per household ¥6,338,000 (U.S.$51,400); sources of income (1994): wages and salaries 59.0%, transfer payments 20.5%, self-employment 12.8%, other 7.3%; expenditure (2002): food 23.3%, transportation and communications 12.0%, recreation 10.1%, fuel, light, and water charges 6.9%, housing 6.5%, clothing and footwear 4.7%, education 4.2%, medical care 3.8%, furniture and household utensils 3.4%.
Tourism (2001): receipts from visitors U.S.$3,301,000,000; expenditures by nationals abroad U.S.$26,530,000,000.

Retail and wholesale trade and services (2002)

	no. of establishments	avg. no. of employees	annual sales (¥'000,000,000)
Retail trade	1,300,043	7,974,000	135,125
Food and beverages	466,590	3,162,000	41,238
Grocery	36,469	755,000	15,080
Liquors	65,098	194,000	3,785
General merchandise	4,995	542,000	17,318
Department stores	2,029	523,000	16,938
Motor vehicles and bicycles	89,091	556,000	16,217
Furniture and home furnishings	120,743	535,000	11,884
Apparel and accessories	185,939	720,000	10,980
Gasoline service stations	65,261	425,000	11,137
Books and stationery	59,327	703,000	4,839
Wholesale trade	379,547	4,004,000	413,547
Machinery and equipment	97,730	1,167,000	146,500
Motor vehicles and parts	18,218	189,000	16,487
General machinery except electrical	34,970	334,000	24,277
General merchandise	1,156	40,000	48,129
Farm, livestock, and fishery products	38,300	413,000	40,267
Food and beverages	83,597	919,000	43,983
Minerals and metals	17,106	202,000	43,859
Building materials	86,803	767,000	91,132
Textiles, apparel, and accessories	31,281	328,000	20,889
Chemicals	16,006	168,000	21,266
Drugs and toilet goods	18,730	247,000	21,575

Production (metric tons except as noted). Agriculture, forestry, fishing (2002): rice 11,111,000, sugar beets 4,098,000, potatoes 2,980,000, cabbages 2,500,000, sugarcane 1,400,000, onions 1,270,000, sweet potatoes 1,030,000, apples 911,000, wheat 827,800, tomatoes 800,000, cucumbers 740,000, carrots 700,000, watermelons 570,000, lettuce 560,000, eggplant 450,000, pears 375,500, spinach 320,000, cantaloupes 305,000, soybeans 270,200, persimmons 269,300, grapes 231,700, pumpkins 220,000, taro 218,000, barley 217,000, strawberries 210,000, yams 200,000, peaches 175,100, peppers 171,000, cauliflower 115,000, plums 112,700; livestock (number of live animals) 9,612,000 pigs, 4,564,000 cattle, 283,102,000 chickens; roundwood (2001) 16,236,538 cu m; fish catch (2000) 5,752,178, of which squid 671,100, scallops 515,000, cod 398,900, crabs 42,000. Mining and quarrying (2001):

limestone 182,255,000; silica stone 14,213,000; dolomite 3,389,000; pyrophyllite 403,000; zinc 44,519; lead 4,997; copper 744; silver 80,397 kg; gold 7,815 kg. Manufacturing (2001): crude steel 102,866,000; steel products 78,927,000; cement 76,550,000; pig iron 78,836,000; sulfuric acid 6,727,000; plastic products 6,300,000; fertilizers 4,200,000; newsprint 3,210,000; cotton fabrics 710,000,000 sq m; synthetic fabrics 1,920,000 sq m; finished products (in number of units) 420,000,000 watches and clocks, 51,062,000 industrial robots, 46,072,000 cellular phones, 12,421,000 air conditioners, 11,350,000 computers, 9,777,000 passenger cars, 9,112,000 cameras, 8,993,000 video cameras, 5,446,000 vacuum cleaners, 4,184,000 bicycles, 4,059,000 automatic washing machines, 3,875,000 electric refrigerators, 3,130,000 colour television receivers, 2,675,000 microwave ovens, 2,398,000 photocopy machines, 2,328,000 motorcycles, 1,916,000 facsimile machines, 1,185,000 videocassette recorders. Construction (value in ¥'000,000; 2001): residential 42,700,000; nonresidential 28,271,000.

Land use (1999): forested 66.4%; meadows and grassland 0.9%; agricultural and under permanent cultivation 12.9%; other 19.8%.

Foreign trade[8]

Balance of trade (current prices)

	1997	1998	1999	2000	2001	2002
¥'000,000,000	+9,982	+13,991	+12,279	+10,716	+6,564	+9,931
% of total	10.9%	16.0%	14.8%	11.6%	7.2%	10.5%

Imports (2001): ¥42,415,500,000,000 (machinery and apparatus 28.5%, of which computers and office machinery 6.5%; crude and refined petroleum 13.3%; food products 12.4%, chemicals and chemical products 7.3%, apparel and clothing accessories 5.5%). *Major import sources:* U.S. 18.1%; China 16.6%; South Korea 4.9%; Indonesia 4.3%; Australia 4.1%; Taiwan 4.1%; Malaysia 3.7%; U.A.E. 3.7%; Germany 3.6%; Saudi Arabia 3.5%.

Exports (2001): ¥48,979,200,000,000 (machinery and apparatus 44.4%, of which electronic microcircuits 7.4%, computers and office machinery 5.8%; road vehicles and parts 18.6%; base and fabricated metals 5.9%; precision instruments 5.4%). *Major export destinations:* U.S. 30.0%; China 7.7%; South Korea 6.3%; Taiwan 6.0%; Hong Kong 5.8%; Germany 3.9%; Singapore 3.6%; U.K. 3.0%; Thailand 2.9%; The Netherlands 2.8%.

Trade by commodity group (2001)

	imports		exports	
SITC group	U.S.$'000,000	%	U.S.$'000,000	%
00 Food and live animals	38,583	11.0	2,608	0.6
01 Beverages and tobacco	4,479	1.3		
02 Crude materials, excluding fuels	22,485[9]	6.4[9]	3,349[9]	0.8[9]
03 Mineral fuels, lubricants, and related materials	70,424	20.2	…	…
04 Animal and vegetable oils, fats, and waxes	[9]	[9]	[9]	[9]
05 Chemicals and related products, n.e.s.	24,961	7.2	29,662	7.4
06 Basic manufactures	25,872	7.4	44,825	11.1
07 Machinery and transport equipment	95,143	27.2	269,888	66.9
08 Miscellaneous manufactured articles	54,905	15.7	36,226	9.0
09 Goods not classified by kind	12,448	3.6	16,806	4.2
TOTAL	349,300	100.0	403,364	100.0

Direction of trade (2001)

	imports		exports	
	U.S.$'000,000	%	U.S.$'000,000	%
Africa	4,931	1.4	4,311	1.1
Asia	192,798	55.2	174,136	43.2
South America	9,119	2.6	4,891	1.2
North America and Central America	71,584	20.5	140,641	34.9
United States	63,758	18.3	122,549	30.4
other North and Central America	7,826	2.2	18,092	4.5
Europe	53,659	15.4	69,037	17.1
EU	44,594	12.8	64,469	16.0
Russia	4,062	1.2	1,439	0.4
other Europe	5,003	1.4	3,129	0.7
Oceania	17,209	4.9	10,348	2.6
TOTAL	349,300	100.0	403,364	100.0[2]

Transport and communications

Transport. Railroads (2001): length 14,698 mi, 23,654 km; rolling stock—(1995) locomotives 1,787, (1995) passenger cars 25,973, (1995) freight cars 12,688; passengers carried 21,700,000,000; passenger-mi 239,489,000,000, passenger-km 385,421,000,000; short ton-mi cargo 15,200,000,000, metric ton-km cargo 22,193,000,000. Roads (2002): total length 765,600 mi, 1,232,000 km (paved 82%). Vehicles (2002): passenger cars 42,655,000; trucks and buses 18,200,000. Merchant marine (2001): vessels (100 gross tons and over) 7,924; total deadweight tonnage 16,653,000. Air transport (2000): passengers carried 205,106,000; passenger-mi 159,337,000,000, passenger-km 256,428,000,000; short ton-mi cargo 6,712,000,000, metric ton-km cargo 9,800,000,000; airports (1996) with scheduled flights 73.

Urban transport (2000)[10]: passengers carried 57,719,000, of which by rail 34,020,000, by road 19,466,000, by subway 4,233,000.

Distribution of traffic (2001)

	cargo carried ('000,000 tons)	% of national total	passengers carried ('000,000)	% of national total
Road	5,578	90.6	64,590	74.7
Rail (intercity)	59	1.0	21,720	25.1
Inland water	520	8.4	112	0.1
Air	1	0.0	95	0.1
TOTAL	6,158	100.0	86,517	100.0

Communications

Medium	date	unit	number	units per 1,000 persons
Daily newspapers	2000	circulation	73,300,000	578
Radio	2000	receivers	121,000,000	956
Television	2000	receivers	92,000,000	725
Telephones	2001	main lines	76,000,000	597
Cellular telephones	2002	subscribers	79,083,000	621
Personal computers	2002	units	48,700,000	383
Internet	2002	users	57,200,000	449

Radio and television broadcasting (2001): total radio stations 1,586, of which commercial 707; total television stations 15,088, of which commercial 8,299. Commercial broadcasting hours (by percentage of programs; 2001): reports—radio 12.6%, television 21.4%; education—radio 2.4%, television 12.1%; culture—radio 13.5%, television 24.8%; entertainment—radio 69.0%, television 39.2%. Advertisements (daily average; 2001): radio 158, television 431.

Other communications media (2001)

	titles		titles
Print		**Cinema**	
Books (new)	71,073	Feature films	640
of which		Domestic	293
Social sciences	14,648	Foreign	347
Fiction	12,119		
Arts	10,199		traffic ('000)
Engineering	7,709		
Natural sciences	5,385	**Post**	
History	5,148	Postal offices	24,773
Philosophy	2,967	Mail	26,216,000
Magazines/journals	4,447	Domestic	25,578,000
Weekly	145	International	638,000
Monthly	2,793	Parcels	411,000,000
		Domestic	387,000,000
		International	24,000,000

Education and health

Literacy: total population age 15 and over literate, virtually 100%.

Education (2002)

	schools	teachers	students	student/teacher ratio
Primary (age 6–11)	23,316	410,505	7,239,000	17.6
Secondary (age 12–17)	16,427	516,325	7,792,000	15.1
Higher	1,289	174,006	3,110,349	17.9

Health (2000): physicians 243,201 (1 per 522 persons); dentists 90,857 (1 per 1,396 persons); nurses 1,042,468 (1 per 122 persons); pharmacists 217,477 (1 per 583 persons); midwives 24,511 (1 per 5,176 persons); hospital beds 1,646,797 (1 per 77 persons), of which general 76.5%, mental 21.7%, other 1.8%; infant mortality rate per 1,000 live births (2001) 3.1.

Food (2001): daily per capita caloric intake 2,768 (vegetable products 79%, animal products 21%); 118% of FAO recommended minimum requirement.

Military

Total active duty personnel (2002): 239,900 (army 61.8%, navy 18.5%, air force 19.0%); U.S. troops (2002) 38,500. *Military expenditure as percentage of GNP* (1999): 1.0% (world 2.4%); per capita expenditure U.S.$342.

[1]Regional prefecture areas do not sum to total given because of particular excluded inland water areas. [2]Detail does not add to total given because of rounding. [3]Saitama was created in 2001 with the merger of the cities of Urawa, Omiya, and Yono. [4]Many Japanese practice both Shintōism and Buddhism. [5]Import duties and statistical discrepancy less imputed bank service charge. [6]Unemployed. [7]End of period. [8]Imports c.i.f.; exports f.o.b. [9]Crude materials includes Animal and vegetable oils, fats, and waxes. [10]Tokyo, Nagoya, and Ōsaka metropolis traffic range only.

Internet resources for further information:

- **Bank of Japan http://www.boj.or.jp/en/index.htm**
- **Statistics Bureau and Statistics Center (Japan) http://www.stat.go.jp/english/index.htm**

Jersey

Official name: Bailiwick of Jersey.
Political status: crown dependency (United Kingdom) with one legislative house (States of Jersey [57][1]).
Chief of state: British Monarch represented by Lieutenant Governor.
Head of government: [2].
Capital: Saint Helier.
Official language: English[3].
Official religion: none.
Monetary unit: 1 Jersey pound (£J) = 100 pence; valuation (Sept. 8, 2003) 1 Jersey pound = U.S.$1.59; at par with the British pound.

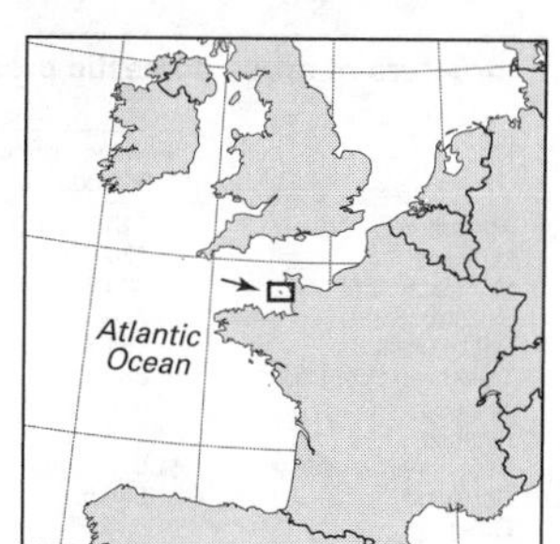

Area and population

Parishes	area sq mi	area sq km	population 2001 census
Grouville	3.0	7.8	4,702
St. Brelade	4.9	12.8	10,134
St. Clement	1.6	4.2	8,196
St. Helier	4.1	10.6	28,310
St. John	3.4	8.7	2,618
St. Lawrence	3.7	9.5	4,702
St. Martin	3.8	9.9	3,628
St. Mary	2.5	6.5	1,591
St. Ouen	5.8	15.0	3,803
St. Peter	4.5	11.6	4,293
St. Saviour	3.6	9.3	12,491
Trinity	4.7	12.3	2,718
TOTAL	45.6	118.2	87,186

Demography

Population (2003): 87,700.
Density (2003): persons per sq mi 1,906.5, persons per sq km 743.2.
Sex distribution (2001): male 48.73%; female 51.27%.
Age breakdown (2001): under 15, 16.9%; 15–29, 18.4%; 30–44, 25.9%; 45–59, 19.7%; 60–74, 12.6%; 75 and over, 6.5%.
Population projection: (2010) 89,000; (2020) 89,000.
Population by place of birth (2001): Jersey 52.6%; United Kingdom, Guernsey, or Isle of Man 35.8%; Portugal 5.9%; France 1.2%; other 4.5%.
Religious affiliation (2000)[4]: Christian 86.0%, of which Anglican 44.1%, Roman Catholic 14.6%, other Protestant 6.9%, unaffiliated Christian 20.1%; nonreligious/atheist 13.4%; other 0.6%.
Major cities (2001)[5]: St. Helier 28,310; St. Saviour 12,491; St. Brelade 10,134.

Vital statistics

Birth rate per 1,000 population (2002): 10.9 (world avg. 21.3).
Death rate per 1,000 population (2002): 9.2 (world avg. 9.1).
Natural increase rate per 1,000 population (2002): 1.7 (world avg. 12.2).
Total fertility rate (avg. births per childbearing woman; 2000): 1.6.
Marriage rate per 1,000 population (2001): 7.6.
Divorce rate per 1,000 population (2001): 3.2.
Life expectancy at birth (2002): male 76.3 years; female 81.4 years.
Major causes of death per 100,000 population (2000): diseases of the circulatory system *c.* 328, malignant neoplasms (cancers) *c.* 255, diseases of the respiratory system *c.* 136, accidents and violence *c.* 35, diseases of the digestive system *c.* 35.

National economy

Budget (2001). Revenue: £400,085,000 (income tax 86.8%, import duties 8.7%, interest payment 1.5%, other 3.0%). Expenditures: £369,138,000 (current expenditure 79.3%, of which health 25.7%, education 19.0%, social security 18.2%, public services 5.1%; capital expenditure 20.7%).
Production. Agriculture, forestry, fishing: fruits and vegetables, mostly potatoes and greenhouse tomatoes; greenhouse flowers are important export crops; livestock (number of live animals; 2001) 4,552 mature dairy cattle; roundwood, none; fish catch (metric tons; 2001)[4]: 3,927, of which crustaceans (including lobsters and crabs) 2,169, mollusks (including abalones, winkles, and conch) 969, marine fish 789. Mining and quarrying: n.a. Manufacturing: light industry, mainly electrical goods, textiles and clothing. Energy production (consumption): electricity (kW-hr; 2001) 153,000,000 (567,000,000); crude petroleum, none (n.a.); petroleum products, n.a. (n.a.); natural gas, none (n.a.).
Gross national product (at current market prices; 2000): U.S.$2,880,000,000 (U.S.$33,220 per capita).

Structure of gross domestic product and labour force

	1996		2001	
	in value[6] £J '000,000	% of total value	labour force	% of labour force
Agriculture, fishing	74	5.0	1,750	3.8
Mining / Construction	...	...	4,320	9.3
Manufacturing	30	2.0	1,400	3.0
Public utilities	...	...	560	1.2
Transp. and commun.	...	...	2,590	5.6
Trade, hotels, restaurants	354[7]	24.0[7]	9,780	21.0
Finance, real estate[8]	811	55.0	11,340	24.3
Pub. admin., defense	...	...	13,840	29.7
Services	...	...		
Other	206[9]	14.0[9]	1,022[10]	2.1[10]
TOTAL	1,475	100.0	46,602	100.0

Household income and expenditure. Average household size (2001) 2.4; average annual income of workers (2001) £22,700 (U.S.$35,200); sources of income: n.a.; expenditure (1998–99)[11]: housing 20.1%, recreation 16.5%, transportation 12.8%, household furnishings 11.6%, food 11.5%, alcoholic beverages 6.0%, clothing and footwear 5.5%.
Population economically active (2001): total 46,602; activity rate of total population 53.4% (participation rates: ages 15–64, 81.7%; female 45.5%; unemployed 2.1%).

Price index (1995 = 100)[12]

	1996	1997	1998	1999	2000	2001	2002
Consumer price index	103.6	107.2	111.7	115.6	120.2	124.9	130.2

Public debt: none.
Tourism (1996): receipts U.S.$429,000,000; expenditures by nationals abroad, n.a.; number of visitors for at least one night (2001) 470,000.
Land use (1997): land under cultivation 56.8%; other 43.2%.

Foreign trade

Imports: [13]. *Major import sources* (2001): mostly the United Kingdom.
Exports: [13]; agricultural and marine exports (2001): £40,626,000 (potatoes 67.4%, greenhouse tomatoes 19.1%, flowers 3.3%, zucchini 3.0%, crustaceans 2.0%, mollusks 2.0%). *Major export destinations:* mostly the United Kingdom.

Transport and communications

Transport. Railroads: none. Roads (1995): total length 346 mi, 557 km (paved 100%). Vehicles (2001): passenger cars 71,059; trucks and buses 10,576. Air transport (1999)[14]: passenger-mi 553,291,000, passenger-km 890,438,000; short ton-mi cargo 632,000, metric ton-km cargo 923,000; airports (1999) with scheduled flights 1.

Communications

Medium	date	unit	number	units per 1,000 persons
Daily newspapers	2002	circulation	22,897	262
Telephones	2001	main lines	73,900	848
Cellular telephones	2001	subscribers	61,400	704
Internet	2001	users	8,000	92

Education and health

Educational attainment (2001). Percentage of male population (16–64), female population (16–59) having: no formal degree 34.1%; primary education, n.a.; secondary, n.a.; undergraduate 7.1%; graduate (advanced degree) 4.1%.
Literacy (2002): 100.0%.

Education (2002)

	schools	teachers	students	student/ teacher ratio
Primary (age 5–10)	21	...	7,386	...
Secondary (age 11–16)	10	...	5,715	...
Voc., teacher tr.	...	...	...	...
Higher[15]	1	...	582	...

Health: physicians (2001) 174 (1 per 500 persons); hospital beds (1995) 651 (1 per 130 persons); infant mortality rate per 1,000 live births (2002) 5.2.
Food: daily per capita caloric intake, n.a.

Military

Total active duty personnel (2002): none; defense is the responsibility of the United Kingdom.

[1]53 elected members include 12 senators popularly elected for six-year terms, 12 constables popularly elected triennially, and 29 deputies also popularly elected triennially; 4 nonelected members include the bailiff, the dean of Jersey, the attorney general, and the solicitor general. [2]Executive committees appointed by the States of Jersey (alternately called States Assembly). [3]Until the 1960s French was an official language of Jersey and is still used by the court and legal professions; Jerriais, a Norman-French dialect, is spoken by a small number of residents. [4]Includes Guernsey. [5]Population of parishes. [6]Calculation based on percentage distribution. [7]Represents tourism-related businesses. [8]Jersey is an international finance centre with 79 banks in 1998 and over 33,000 registered companies; of more than U.S.$160,000,000,000 deposited in the island, 62 percent is in foreign (not £J or £) currency. [9]Represents investment income from abroad received by residents. [10]Unemployed seeking work. [11]Weights of retail price index components. [12]June. [13]Customs ceased recording imports and exports as of 1980. [14]Jersey European Airways. [15]2001; Highlands College.

Internet resources for further information:

- **States of Jersey**
  http://www.gov.je

Jordan

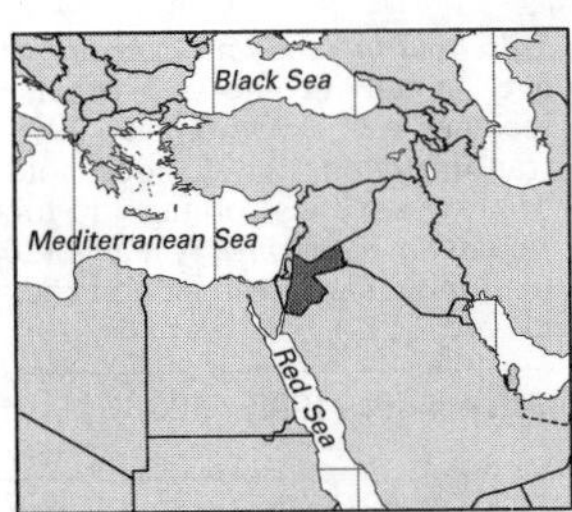

Official name: Al-Mamlakah al-Urdunnīyah al-Hāshimīyah (Al-Urdun) (Hashemite Kingdom of Jordan).
Form of government: constitutional monarchy with two legislative houses (Senate [40[1]]; House of Representatives [110]).
Head of state and government: King assisted by Prime Minister.
Capital: Amman.
Official language: Arabic.
Official religion: Islam.
Monetary unit: 1 Jordan dinar (JD) = 1,000 fils; valuation (Sept. 8, 2003) JD 1.00 = U.S.$1.41 = £0.89.

Area and population

		area		population
				2002
Governorates	Capitals	sq mi	sq km	estimate[2]
ʿAjlūn	ʿAjlun	159	412	115,000
ʿAmman	Amman	3,178	8,231	1,971,800
Al-ʿAqabah	Al-ʿAqabah	2,542	6,583	104,200
Al-Balqāʾ	Aṣ-Ṣalt	415	1,076	339,900
Irbid	Irbid	626	1,621	924,500
Jarash	Jarash	155	402	152,400
Al-Karak	Al-Karak	1,242	3,217	208,300
Maʿān	Maʿān	12,804	33,163	101,000
Mādabā	Mādabā	775	2,008	132,100
Al-Mafraq	Al-Mafraq	10,207	26,435	238,900
Aṭ-Ṭafīlah	Aṭ-Ṭafīlah	816	2,114	78,800
Az-Zarqāʾ	Az-Zarqāʾ	1,575	4,080	815,100
TOTAL		34,495[3]	89,342	5,182,000

Demography

Population (2003): 5,395,000.
Density (2003): persons per sq mi 156.4, persons per sq km 60.4.
Urban-rural (2000): urban 74.2%; rural 25.8%.
Sex distribution (2002): male 52.38%; female 47.62%.
Age breakdown (2002): under 15, 36.6%; 15–29, 30.4%; 30–44, 19.8%; 45–59, 8.0%; 60–74, 4.3%; 75 and over, 0.9%.
Population projection: (2010) 6,302,000; (2020) 7,462,000.
Doubling time: 32 years.
Ethnic composition (2000): Arab 97.8%, of which Jordanian 32.4%, Palestinian 32.2%, Iraqi 14.0%, Bedouin 12.8%; Circassian 1.2%; other 1.0%.
Religious affiliation (2000): Sunnī Muslim 93.5%; Christian 4.1%; other 2.4%.
Major cities (1994): Amman 969,598; Az-Zarqāʾ 350,849; Irbid 208,329; Ar-Ruṣayfah 137,247; Wādi Essier 89,104; Al-ʿAqabah 62,773.

Vital statistics

Birth rate per 1,000 population (2002): 24.6 (world avg. 21.3).
Death rate per 1,000 population (2002): 2.6 (world avg. 9.1).
Natural increase rate per 1,000 population (2002): 22.0 (world avg. 12.2).
Total fertility rate (avg. births per childbearing woman; 2002): 3.1.
Life expectancy at birth (2002): male 75.3 years; female 80.3 years.
Major causes of death per 100,000 population: n.a.

National economy

Budget (2002 est.). Revenue: JD 2,029,500,000 (taxes 52.8%, of which sales tax 25.2%, custom duties 10.6%, income and profits taxes 9.7%; nontax revenue 33.5%, of which licenses and fees 12.7%; foreign grants 13.7%). Expenditures: JD 2,289,100,000 (current expenditure 78.5%, of which defense 24.1%, social security and other transfers 22.1%, wages 17.8%, interest expense 12.4%; capital expenditure 21.5%).
Public debt (external, outstanding; 2001): U.S.$6,600,000,000.
Production (metric tons except as noted). Agriculture, forestry, fishing (2002): tomatoes 359,830, olives 180,900, cucumbers 150,000, citrus fruits 121,900, potatoes 105,330, watermelons 71,780, zucchini (2001) 57,500, barley 56,700, bananas 47,400, apples 39,230, grapes 34,770; livestock (number of live animals) 1,457,910 sheep, 557,260 goats; roundwood (2001) 233,544 cu m; fish catch (2001) 1,060. Mining and quarrying (2002): phosphate ore 7,107,200; potash 1,956,200. Manufacturing (value added in JD '000; 1997): chemicals 130,276; nonmetallic mineral products, pottery, and china 114,897; tobacco 96,380; food products 80,994; refined petroleum 60,028; plastic products 25,627. Energy production (consumption): electricity (kW-hr; 2002) 7,864,900,000 (7,864,900,000); crude petroleum (barrels; 2001) 14,600 ([1999] 25,600,000); petroleum products (metric tons; 2002) 3,627,000 ([1999] 4,192,000); natural gas (cu m; 2001) 290,000,000 ([2000] 283,000,000).
Land use (1994): forest 0.8%; pasture 8.9%; agriculture 4.6%; other 85.7%.
Tourism (2001): receipts U.S.$700,000,000; expenditures U.S.$420,000,000.
Population economically active (1993): total 859,300; activity rate of total population 22.2% (participation rates: over age 15, 43.6%; female 14.0%; unemployed [2001] 16.0%).

Price and earnings indexes (1995 = 100)

	1996	1997	1998	1999	2000	2001	2002
Consumer price index	106.5	109.7	113.1	113.8	114.6	116.6	118.7
Daily earnings index	...	...	...	...	...	...	...

Gross national product (2001): U.S.$8,800,000,000 (U.S.$3,750 per capita).

Structure of gross domestic product and labour force

	2001		1993	
	in value JD '000,000	% of total value	labour force	% of labour force
Agriculture	115.6	1.8	54,995	6.4
Mining	176.7	2.8	91,086	10.6
Manufacturing	833.8	13.3		
Construction	226.6	3.6	60,151	7.0
Public utilities	134.8	2.2	6,015	0.7
Transp. and commun.	880.1	14.1	57,573	6.7
Trade[4]	650.3	10.4	129,754	15.1
Finance	1,134.3	18.1	24,920	2.9
Pub. admin., defense	1,077.4	17.2		
Services[5]	334.5	5.3	434,806	50.6
Other	695.9[6]	11.1[6]		
TOTAL	6,260.0	100.0[3]	859,300	100.0

Household income and expenditure. Average household size (2000) 7.5; income per household (1997) JD 5,464 (U.S.$7,700); sources of income (1997): wages and salaries 52.4%, rent and property income 24.5%, transfer payments 12.8%, self-employment 10.3%; expenditure (1997): food and beverages 44.3%, housing and energy 23.5%, transportation 8.2%, clothing and footwear 6.2%, education 4.5%, health care 2.5%.

Foreign trade[7]

Balance of trade (current prices)

	1997	1998	1999	2000	2001	2002
JD '000,000	–1,608	–1,436	–1,336	–1,913	–1,827	–1,586
% of total	38.2%	36.0%	34.0%	41.5%	36.0%	29.0%

Imports (2002[8]): JD 3,213,000,000 (food products 14.1%; machinery and apparatus 13.9%; crude petroleum 11.6%; transport equipment 11.2%; chemicals and chemical products 11.1%). *Major import sources:* Iraq 15.4%; Germany 9.3%; United States 7.2%; China 6.5%; France 4.1%.
Exports (2002[8]): JD 1,776,000,000 (domestic goods 78.5%, of which chemicals and chemical products 19.7% [including medicines and pharmaceuticals 7.4%], clothing 17.4%, potash 6.6%, vegetables 5.3%, phosphates 5.0%; reexports 21.5%). *Major export destinations*[9]: Iraq 20.2%; United States 18.5%; India 10.3%; Saudi Arabia 6.9%; Israel 5.8%.

Transport and communications

Transport. Railroads (2000): route length 677 km; passenger-km 2,100,000; metric ton-km cargo 348,000,000. Roads (1998): total length 7,133 km (paved 100%). Vehicles (2001): passenger cars 245,357; trucks and buses 110,920. Air transport (2001)[10]: passenger-km 3,848,000,000; metric ton-km cargo 181,408,000; airports (1999) 3.

Communications

Medium	date	unit	number	units per 1,000 persons
Daily newspapers	2000	circulation	383,000	77
Radio	2000	receivers	1,850,000	372
Television	2000	receivers	417,000	84
Telephones	2002	main lines	680,000	127
Cellular telephones	2002	subscribers	866,000	167
Personal computers	2001	units	170,000	33
Internet	2002	users	234,000	45

Education and health

Educational attainment (2000). Percentage of population age 25 and over having: no formal schooling 16.7%; primary education 49.2%; secondary 16.7%; postsecondary and vocational 9.5%; higher 8.2%. *Literacy* (2003): percentage of population age 15 and over literate 91.3%; males literate 95.9%; females literate 86.3%.

Education (2001)

	schools	teachers	students	student/ teacher ratio
Primary (age 6–14)	2,708	50,562	1,173,314	23.2
Secondary (age 15–17)	912	11,254	129,984	11.6
Voc., teacher tr.	214	3,026	43,861	14.5
Higher	22	6,036	153,965	25.5

Health: physicians (2000) 9,493 (1 per 523 persons); hospital beds (1999) 8,726 (1 per 553 persons); infant mortality rate per 1,000 live births (2002) 19.6.
Food (2001): daily per capita caloric intake 2,769 (vegetable products 89%, animal products 11%); 113% of FAO recommended minimum requirement.

Military

Total active duty personnel (2002): 100,240 (army 84.5%, navy 0.5%, air force 15.0%). *Military expenditure as percentage of GDP* (1999): 9.2% (world 2.4%); per capita expenditure U.S.$150.

[1]Appointed by king. [2]January 1. [3]Detail does not add to total given because of rounding. [4]Includes hotels. [5]Includes domestic help employed in households. [6]Net taxes on products less imputed bank service charges. [7]Imports c.i.f.; exports f.o.b. [8]Excludes December. [9]Domestic exports only. [10]Royal Jordanian airlines only.

Internet resources for further information:
- **Dept. of Statistics http://www.dos.gov.jo**
- **Central Bank of Jordan http://www.cbj.gov.jo**

Kazakhstan

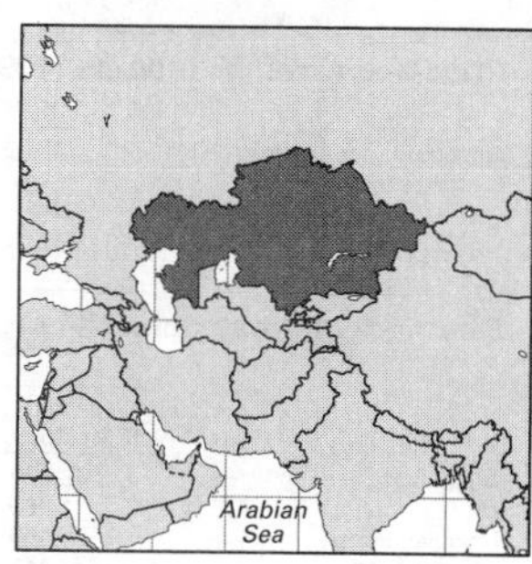

Official name: Qazaqstan Respūblīkasy (Republic of Kazakhstan).
Form of government: unitary republic with a Parliament consisting of two chambers (Senate [39[1]] and Assembly [77]).
Head of state and government: President assisted by Prime Minister.
Capital: Astana[2].
Official language: Kazakh[3].
Official religion: none.
Monetary unit: 1 tenge (T) = 100 tiyn; valuation (Sept. 8, 2003) 1 U.S.$ = 148.42 tenge; 1 £ = 235.33 tenge.

Area and population

Provinces	Capitals	area sq mi	area sq km	population 2001[4] estimate
Almaty	Taldykorgan	86,450	223,900	1,561,800
Aqmola	Kokshetau	56,450	146,200	810,300
Aqtöbe	Aqtöbe	116,050	300,600	672,600
Atyraū	Atyraū	45,800	118,600	447,100
Batys Qazaqstan	Oral	58,400	151,300	604,400
Mangghystaū	Aqtaū	63,950	165,600	323,700
Ongtüstik Qazaqstan	Shymkent	45,300	117,300	2,025,400
Pavlodar	Pavlodar	48,200	124,800	776,800
Qaraghandy	Qaraghandy	165,250	428,000	1,381,600
Qostanay	Qostanay	75,700	196,000	972,300
Qyzylorda[5]	Qyzylorda	87,250	226,000	605,500
Shyghys Qazaqstan	Öskemen	109,400	283,300	1,504,300
Soltüstik Qazaqstan	Petropavl	37,850	98,000	706,400
Zhambyl	Taraz	55,700	144,300	985,700
Cities				
Almaty[6]	—	100	300	1,139,900
Astana[2]	—	250	700	324,100
TOTAL		1,052,100	2,724,900	14,841,900

Demography

Population (2003): 14,790,000.
Density (2003): persons per sq mi 14.1, persons per sq km 5.4.
Urban-rural (2001): urban 56.3%; rural 43.7%.
Sex distribution (2001): male 48.07%; female 51.93%.
Age breakdown (2001): under 15, 26.7%; 15–29, 27.1%; 30–44, 21.5%; 45–59, 13.2%; 60–74, 9.2%; 75 and over, 2.3%.
Population projection: (2010) 14,499,000; (2020) 14,779,000.
Ethnic composition (1999): Kazakh 53.4%; Russian 30.0%; Ukrainian 3.7%; Uzbek 2.5%; German 2.4%; Tatar 1.7%; other 6.3%.
Religious affiliation (1995): Muslim (mostly Sunnī) 47.0%; Russian Orthodox 8.2%; Protestant 2.1%; other (mostly nonreligious) 42.7%.
Major cities (1999): Almaty[5] 1,130,068; Qaraghandy (Karaganda) 436,900; Shymkent (Chimkent) 360,100; Taraz 330,100; Astana 319,318[2].

Vital statistics

Birth rate per 1,000 population (2001): 14.9 (world avg. 21.3); (2000) legitimate 76.1%, illegitimate 23.9%.
Death rate per 1,000 population (2001): 10.0 (world avg. 9.1).
Natural increase rate per 1,000 population (2001): 4.9 (world avg. 12.2).
Total fertility rate (avg. births per childbearing woman; 2001): 2.0.
Life expectancy at birth (2002): male 58.3 years; female 71.1 years.
Major causes of death per 100,000 population (2000): diseases of the circulatory system 500.5; accidents, poisoning, and violence 140.7; malignant neoplasms (cancers) 129.1; diseases of the respiratory system 71.1.

National economy

Budget (2001). Revenue: 743,550,000,000 tenge (tax revenue 91.1%, of which income and profits taxes 34.8%, sales tax 29.3%, social security 17.5%; nontax revenue 8.9%). Expenditures: 749,092,000,000 tenge (social security 24.9%, education 14.0%, health 8.3%, debt 6.7%, defense 4.3%).
Population economically active (2001): total 7,479,100; activity rate of total population 50.4% (participation rates: ages 16–59 [male], 16–54 [female] 73.6%; female 46.0%; unemployed 12.8%).

Price and earnings indexes (1995 = 100)

	1996	1997	1998	1999	2000	2001	2002
Consumer price index	139.3	163.4	175.0	189.6	214.6	232.6	246.3
Monthly earnings index	142.9	178.5	202.3	247.9	300.3	362.5	425.5

Production (metric tons except as noted). Agriculture, forestry, fishing (2002): wheat 12,699,975, potatoes 2,257,000, barley 2,208,925, tomatoes 448,855, corn (maize) 435,208, sugar beets 372,205, oats 183,225; livestock (number of live animals) 9,207,500 sheep and goats, 4,281,700 cattle; roundwood (1998) 315,000 cu m; fish catch (2000) 31,071. Mining and quarrying (2000): iron ore 13,828,000; bauxite 3,730,000; chromite 2,607,000; copper (metal content) 430,200; zinc (metal content) 322,100; gold 28,171 kg. Manufacturing (value of production in '000,000 tenge; 2002): metallurgy 396,000; food 307,000; oil and nuclear energy 149,000; machinery 69,000; textiles 44,000. Energy production (consumption): electricity (kW-hr; 2002) 58,464,000,000 ([1999] 50,490,000,000); hard coal (metric tons; 2002) 70,608,000 ([1999] 43,364,000); lignite (metric tons; 2002) 2,616,000 ([1999] 1,744,000); crude petroleum (barrels; 2002) 348,224,000 ([1999] 30,000,000); petroleum products (metric tons; 1999) 5,648,000 (5,481,000); natural gas (cu m; 2002) 9,112,000,000 ([1999] 8,196,700,000).

Gross national product (2001): U.S.$20,100,000,000 (U.S.$1,350 per capita).

Structure of gross domestic product and labour force

	2002 in value '000,000 tenge	% of total value	labour force[7]	% of labour force[7]
Agriculture	298,000	8.0	2,381,000	35.5
Manufacturing, mining, public utilities	1,099,000	29.3	824,000	12.3
Construction	230,000	6.1	268,000	4.0
Transp. and commun.	430,000	11.5	504,000	7.5
Trade	450,000	12.0	1,064,000	15.8
Finance	496,000	13.2	253,000	3.8
Pub. admin., defense } Services }	744,000	19.9	281,000	4.2
			1,134,000	16.9
Other	—	—	...	...
TOTAL	3,747,000	100.0	6,709,000	100.0

Public debt (external, outstanding; 2001): U.S.$3,446,000,000.
Household income and expenditure. Average household size (1999) 3.6; sources of income (2001): salaries and wages 72.1%, social benefits 9.2%; expenditure (2001): food and beverages 56.0%, housing 11.7%.
Tourism (2001): receipts U.S.$395,000,000; expenditures U.S.$474,000,000.

Foreign trade[8]

Balance of trade (current prices)

	1997	1998	1999	2000	2001	2002[9]
U.S.$'000,000	+2,196	+1,086	+1,912	+4,087	+2,284	+2,855
% of total	20.3%	11.1%	20.6%	28.8%	15.2%	19.8%

Imports (2000): U.S.$5,052,000,000 (machinery and apparatus 27.4%; mineral fuels and lubricants 11.5%; chemicals and chemical products 11.4%; transport equipment 11.1%). *Major import sources:* Russia 48.7%; Germany 6.6%; U.S. 5.5%; U.K. 4.3%; Italy 3.1%.
Exports (2000): U.S.$9,139,000,000 (crude petroleum 49.4%; nonferrous metals 13.7%, of which copper 7.5%; iron and steel 12.0%; cereals 6.0%). *Major export destinations:* Russia 19.5%; Bermuda 14.9%; British Virgin Islands 11.6%; Italy 9.8%; China 7.3%.

Transport and communications

Transport. Railroads (2001): route length 13,500 km; passenger-km 10,384,000,000; metric ton-km cargo 135,653,000,000. Roads (1999): total length 109,445 km (paved 90%). Vehicles (2001): passenger cars 1,000,298; trucks and buses 278,711. Air transport (2001): passenger-km 1,901,100,000; metric ton-km cargo 44,000,000; airports (1999) with scheduled flights 20.

Communications

Medium	date	unit	number	units per 1,000 persons
Radio	2000	receivers	6,270,000	422
Television	2000	receivers	3,580,000	241
Telephones	2001	main lines	1,939,600	121
Cellular telephones	2001	subscribers	582,000	36
Internet	2001	users	150,000	9.3

Education and health

Educational attainment (1999). Population age 25 and over having: no formal schooling or some primary education 9.1%; primary education 23.1%; secondary and some postsecondary 57.8%; higher 10.0%. *Literacy* (1999): 99.0%.

Education (1999–2000)

	schools	teachers	students	student/ teacher ratio
Primary (age 7–13)	1,447	62,700	1,208,300	19.3
Secondary (age 14–17)	8,309	176,900	1,913,100	10.8
Voc., teacher tr.	293	...	89,900	...
Higher	170	39,187[10]	440,700	...

Health (2001): physicians 51,300 (1 per 289 persons); hospital beds 110,200 (1 per 134 persons); infant mortality rate per 1,000 live births (2001) 19.4.
Food (2001): daily per capita caloric intake 2,477 (vegetable products 73%, animal products 27%); 97% of FAO minimum requirement.

Military

Total active duty personnel (2002): 60,000 (army 68.3%, air force 31.7%). *Military expenditure as percentage of GNP* (1999): 0.9% (world avg. 2.4%); per capita expenditure U.S.$40.

[1]Includes 7 nonelective seats. [2]City of Akmola (Kazakh: Aqmola; capital replacing Almaty) was renamed Astana on May 6, 1998. [3]Russian has equal status with Kazakh at state-owned organizations and bodies of local government per a law effective July 16, 1997. [4]January 1. [5]Includes an area of 6,000 sq km enclosing the Bayqongyr (Baykonur) space launch facilities and the city of Bayqongyr (formerly Leninsk) leased to Russia in 1995 for a period of 20 years. [6]Formerly known as Alma-Ata. [7]Employed only. [8]Imports c.i.f.; exports f.o.b. [9]Excludes December. [10]1995–96.

Internet resources for further information:
- **National Bank of Kazakhstan http://www.nationalbank.kz**
- **Agency on Statistics of Kazakhstan http://www.stat.kz/en/releases**

Kenya

Official name: Jamhuri ya Kenya (Swahili); Republic of Kenya (English).
Form of government: unitary multiparty republic with one legislative house (National Assembly [224[1]]).
Head of state and government: President.
Capital: Nairobi.
Official languages: Swahili; English.
Official religion: none.
Monetary unit: 1 Kenya shilling[2] (K Sh) = 100 cents; valuation (Sept. 8, 2003) 1 U.S.$ = K Sh 77.00; 1 £ = K Sh 122.09.

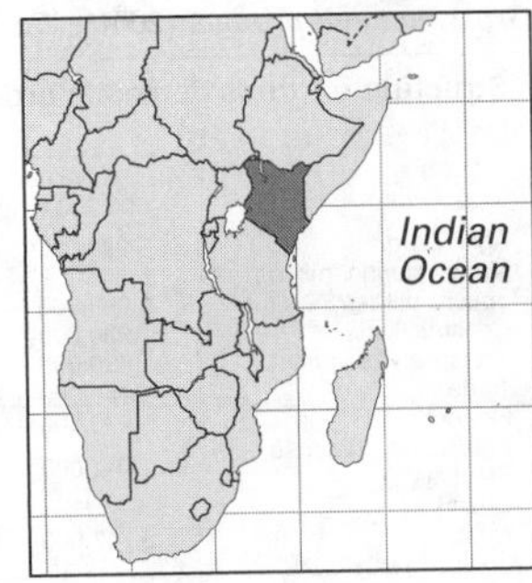

Area and population

Provinces	Provincial headquarters	area sq mi	area sq km	population 1999 census[3]
Central	Nyeri	5,087	13,176	3,724,159
Coast	Mombasa	32,279	83,603	2,487,264
Eastern	Embu	61,734	159,891	4,631,779
North Eastern	Garissa	48,997	126,902	962,143
Nyanza	Kisumu	6,240	16,162	4,392,196
Rift Valley	Nakuru	67,131	173,868	6,987,036
Western	Kakamega	3,228	8,360	3,358,776
Special area				
Nairobi	—	264	684	2,143,254
TOTAL		224,961[4, 5]	582,646[5]	28,686,607

Demography

Population (2003): 31,639,000.
Density (2003): persons per sq mi 140.6, persons per sq km 54.3.
Urban-rural (2002): urban 34.4%; rural 65.6%.
Sex distribution (2001): male 50.16%; female 49.84%.
Age breakdown (2001): under 15, 41.9%; 15–29, 32.1%; 30–44, 14.6%; 45–59, 7.0%; 60–74, 3.4%; 75 and over, 1.0%.
Population projection: (2010) 33,654,000; (2020) 34,848,000.
Doubling time: 54 years.
Ethnic composition (1989): Kikuyu 17.7%; Luhya 12.4%; Luo 10.6%; Kalenjin 9.8%; Kamba 9.8%; other 39.7%.
Religious affiliation (2000): Christian 79.3%, of which Roman Catholic 22.0%, African Christian 20.8%, Protestant 20.1%; Muslim 7.3%; other 13.4%.
Major cities (1999)[6]: Nairobi 2,143,254; Mombasa 665,018; Nakuru 219,366; Kisumu 194,390; Eldoret 167,016; Thika 82,665.

Vital statistics

Birth rate per 1,000 population (2002): 29.8 (world avg. 21.3).
Death rate per 1,000 population (2002): 15.7 (world avg. 9.1).
Natural increase rate per 1,000 population (2002): 14.1 (world avg. 12.2).
Total fertility rate (avg. births per childbearing woman; 2000): 3.7.
Life expectancy at birth (2002): male 45.3 years; female 45.8 years.
Major causes of death per 100,000 population: n.a.; however, major infectious diseases include AIDS, malaria, gastroenteritis, venereal diseases, diarrhea and dysentery, trachoma, amebiasis, and schistosomiasis.

National economy

Budget (2001–02). Revenue: K Sh 206,665,600,000 (tax revenue 86.6%, of which income and profit taxes 29.0%, value-added tax 27.2%, import duties 15.3%; nontax revenue 13.4%). Expenditures: K Sh 235,832,000,000 (recurrent expenditure 80.4%, of which administration 29.7%, education 22.2%, defense 6.1%, health 6.0%; development expenditure 19.6%).
Public debt (external, outstanding; 2001): U.S.$4,930,000,000.
Production (metric tons except as noted). Agriculture, forestry, fishing (2002): sugarcane 5,150,000, corn (maize) 2,800,000, potatoes 1,000,000, plantains 870,000, cassava 610,000, pineapples 600,000, sweet potatoes 550,000, tea 287,000, wheat 280,000, tomatoes 270,000, pulses 230,000, bananas 210,000, sorghum 130,000, coffee 59,300, sisal 20,000, seed cotton 20,000, tobacco 18,000, cashew nuts 12,500, sunflower seeds 12,200; livestock (number of live animals) 13,500,000 cattle, 9,000,000 goats, 8,000,000 sheep; roundwood (2001) 21,803,900 cu m; fish catch (2001) 164,151, of which freshwater fish 95.5%. Mining and quarrying (2000): soda ash 238,200; fluorite 100,100; salt 16,400. Manufacturing (value added in K£'000[2]; 1995): food products 847,000; beverages and tobacco 249,000; machinery and transport equipment 226,000; chemical products 181,000; metal products 131,000; textiles 94,000; paper and paper products 86,000; plastic products 75,000; clothing and footwear 58,000. Energy production (consumption): electricity (kW-hr; 2001) 4,338,400,000 (3,654,800,000); coal (metric tons; 1999) none (98,000); crude petroleum (barrels; 1999) none (15,700,000); petroleum products (metric tons; 2001) 1,695,600 (2,385,200); natural gas, none (none).
Household income and expenditure. Average household size (1998) 3.4; average annual income per household: n.a.; sources of income: n.a.; expenditure (1993–94): food 42.4%, housing and energy 24.1%, clothing and footwear 9.1%, transportation 6.4%, other 18.0%.
Tourism (2001): receipts from visitors U.S.$308,000,000; expenditures by nationals abroad U.S.$143,000,000.
Population economically active (2001): total 12,952,000; activity rate of total population 42.1% (participation rates [1985]: ages 15–64, 76.2%; female [1997] 46.1%; unemployed, n.a.).

Price and earnings indexes (1995 = 100)

	1996	1997	1998	1999	2000	2001	2002
Consumer price index	108.9	121.2	129.4	136.8	150.5	159.1	162.2
Earnings index	...	...	...	...	...	...	...

Gross national product (2001): U.S.$10,700,000,000 (U.S.$350 per capita).

Structure of gross domestic product and labour force

	2001 in value K Sh '000,000	% of total value	labour force	% of labour force
Agriculture	146,639	19.0	312,500[7]	2.4[7]
Mining	1,260	0.2	5,200[7]	—[7]
Manufacturing	96,969	12.5	216,600[7]	1.7[7]
Construction	33,161	4.3	76,800[7]	0.6[7]
Public utilities	8,937	1.2	21,400[7]	0.2[7]
Transp. and commun.	53,107	6.9	84,300[7]	0.7[7]
Trade	194,611	25.2	156,900[7]	1.2[7]
Finance	115,046	14.9	83,800[7]	0.6[7]
Pub. admin., defense / Services	123,163	15.8	719,600[7]	5.6[7]
Other	—	—	11,274,900[8]	87.0[8]
TOTAL	772,893	100.0	12,952,000	100.0

Land use (1994): forest 29.5%; pasture 37.4%; agriculture 8.0%; other 25.1%.

Foreign trade[9]

Balance of trade (current prices)

	1997	1998	1999	2000	2001	2002
K Sh '000,000	–70,714	–71,780	–76,246	–104,430	–98,070	–118,675
% of total	22.8%	22.8%	23.8%	28.3%	24.3%	27.2%

Imports (2002): K Sh 277,275,000,000 (crude petroleum and petroleum products 22.8%, machinery and transport equipment 19.3%, chemicals and chemical products 14.1%). *Major import sources* (2001): U.S. 16.4%; U.A.E. 10.7%; Saudi Arabia 7.8%; South Africa 7.1%; U.K. 7.1%.
Exports (2002): K Sh 158,600,000,000 (tea 21.4%, horticultural products [mostly cut flowers] 13.8%, petroleum products 7.6%, coffee 4.1%, other [including nontraditional fruits and vegetables, iron and steel, and fish] 53.1%). *Major export destinations* (2001): Uganda 17.4%; U.K. 12.5%; The Netherlands 6.5%; Pakistan 6.1%; U.S. 5.6%.

Transport and communications

Transport. Railroads (2000): route length 1,678 mi, 2,700 km; passenger-mi 187,600,000; passenger-km 302,000,000; short ton-mi cargo 967,000,000, metric ton-km cargo 1,557,000,000. Roads (1999): total length 39,600 mi, 63,800 km (paved 14%). Vehicles (2000): passenger cars 244,836; trucks and buses 96,726. Air transport (1998): passenger-mi 1,299,000,000, passenger-km 2,091,000,000; short ton-mi cargo 151,000,000, metric ton-km cargo 243,000,000; airports (1997) with scheduled flights 11.

Communications

Medium	date	unit	number	units per 1,000 persons
Daily newspapers	2000	circulation	303,000	10
Radio	2000	receivers	6,760,000	223
Television	2000	receivers	758,000	25
Telephones	2002	main lines	328,100	16
Cellular telephones	2002	subscribers	1,325,200	42
Personal computers	2001	units	175,000	5.6
Internet	2001	users	500,000	16

Education and health

Educational attainment: n.a. *Literacy* (1999): total population over age 15 literate 81.5%; males literate 88.3%; females literate 74.8%.

Education (2001)

	schools[10]	teachers	students	student/ teacher ratio
Primary (age 5–11)	15,906	185,720	6,314,500	34.0
Secondary (age 12–17)	2,878	48,129	818,200	17.0
Voc., teacher tr.	62	...	44,700	...
Higher[11]	14	4,392[10]	62,100	...

Health (2001): physicians 4,630 (1 per 6,645 persons); hospital beds 57,540 (1 per 535 persons); infant mortality rate per 1,000 live births (2002): 64.1.
Food (2001): daily per capita caloric intake 2,058 (vegetable products 88%, animal products 12%); 89% of FAO recommended minimum requirement.

Military

Total active duty personnel (2001): 24,400 (army 82.0%, navy 5.7%, air force 12.3%). *Military expenditure as percentage of GNP* (1999): 1.9% (world 2.4%); per capita expenditure U.S.$7.

[1]Includes 14 nonelective seats. [2]Kenya pound (K£) as a unit of account equals 20 K Sh. [3]Preliminary. [4]Detail does not add to total given because of rounding. [5]Includes water area of 4,336 sq mi (11,230 sq km). [6]Population of urban core(s). [7]Formally employed only. [8]Includes informally employed, small-scale farmers and pastoralists, unemployed, self-employed, and unpaid family workers. [9]Import figures are c.i.f. [10]1993. [11]Universities only.

Internet resources for further information:
- **Central Bank of Kenya http://www.centralbank.go.ke**
- **Central Bureau of Statistics http://www.cbs.go.ke**

Kiribati

Official name: Republic of Kiribati.
Form of government: unitary republic with a unicameral legislature (House of Assembly [42[1]]).
Head of state and government: President.
Capital: Bairiki, on Tarawa Atoll.
Official language: English.
Official religion: none.
Monetary unit: 1 Australian dollar ($A) = 100 cents; valuation (Sept. 8, 2003) 1 U.S.$ = $A 1.55; 1 £ = $A 2.46.

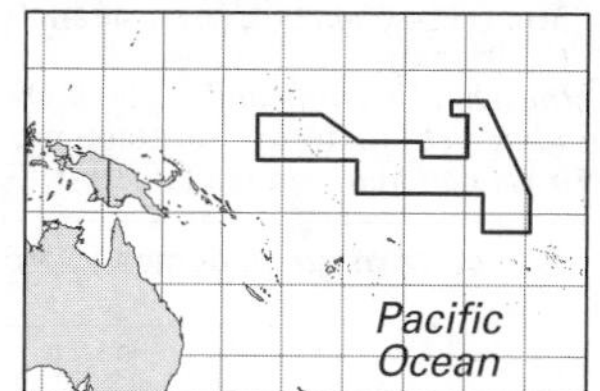

Area and population

Island Groups / Islands	Capitals	area[2] sq mi	area[2] sq km	population 2000 census
Gilberts Group		110.2[3]	285.5[3]	78,158
Abaiang	Tuarabu	6.8	17.5	5,794
Abemama	Kariatebike	10.6	27.4	3,142
Aranuka	Takaeang	4.5	11.6	966
Arorae	Roreti	3.7	9.5	1,225
Banaba	Anteeren	2.4	6.3	276
Beru	Taubukinberu	6.8	17.7	2,732
Butaritari	Butaritari	5.2	13.5	3,464
Kuria	Tabontebike	6.0	15.5	961
Maiana	Tebangetua	6.4	16.7	2,048
Makin	Makin	3.1	7.9	1,691
Marakei	Rawannawi	5.4	14.1	2,544
Nikunau	Rungata	7.4	19.1	1,733
Nonouti	Teuabu	7.7	19.9	3,176
Onotoa	Buariki	6.0	15.6	1,668
Tabiteuea, North	Utiroa	10.0	25.8	3,365
Tabiteuea, South	Buariki	4.6	11.9	1,217
Tamana	Bakaka	1.8	4.7	962
Tarawa, North	Abaokoro	5.9	15.3	4,477
Tarawa, South	Bairiki	6.1	15.8	36,717
Line and Phoenix Group		202.7[3]	525.0[3]	6,336
Northern Line		166.7	431.7	6,275
Kiritimati (Christmas)	London	150.0	388.4	3,431
Tabuaeran (Fanning)	Paelau	13.0	33.7	1,757
Teraina (Washington)	Washington	3.7	9.6	1,087
Southern Line and Phoenix Group		36.1	93.4	61
Kanton (Canton) in Phoenix Group	Kanton	3.6	9.2	61
TOTAL		312.9	810.5	84,494

Demography

Population (2003): 87,900.
Density (2003)[4]: persons per sq mi 314.0, persons per sq km 121.1.
Urban-rural (2002): urban 40.0%; rural 60.0%.
Sex distribution (2000): male 49.29%; female 50.71%.
Age breakdown (1995): under 15, 41.2%; 15–29, 25.8%; 30–44, 18.3%; 45–59, 9.3%; 60–74, 4.4%; 75 and over, 1.0%.
Population projection: (2010) 95,300; (2020) 106,900.
Doubling time: 30 years.
Ethnic composition (2000): Micronesian 98.8%; Polynesian 0.7%; European 0.2%; other 0.3%.
Religious affiliation (2000): Roman Catholic 54.6%; Kiribati Protestant (Congregational) 37.0%; Mormon 2.7%; Bahā'ī 2.4%; other Protestant 2.3%; other/nonreligious 1.0%.
Major city (1999): Tarawa (urban area) 32,000.

Vital statistics

Birth rate per 1,000 population (2002): 31.6 (world avg. 21.3).
Death rate per 1,000 population (2002): 8.8 (world avg. 9.1).
Total fertility rate (avg. births per childbearing woman; 2002): 4.3.
Natural increase rate per 1,000 population (2002): 22.8 (world avg. 12.2).
Marriage rate per 1,000 population (1988): 5.2.
Life expectancy at birth (2002): male 57.6 years; female 63.6 years.
Major causes of death per 100,000 population (1993): senility without mention of psychosis 61.2; stroke 39.1; diarrhea 37.8; hepatitis 32.5; diabetes mellitus 28.6; malnutrition 23.4; meningitis 18.2.

National economy

Budget (2000). Revenue: $A 107,800,000 (nontax revenue 59.5%, tax revenue 22.9%, grants 17.6%). Expenditures: $A 90,000,000 (current expenditures 87.2%, capital expenditures 12.8%).
Public debt (external, outstanding; 1999): U.S.$9,500,000.
Tourism: receipts from visitors (2001) U.S.$3,200,000; expenditures by nationals abroad (1999) U.S.$2,000,000.
Land use (1994): forest 2.7%; agricultural and under permanent cultivation 50.7%; other 46.6%.
Production (metric tons except as noted). Agriculture, forestry, fishing (2002): coconuts 96,000, roots and tubers 7,200 (of which taro 1,700), vegetables and melons 5,600, bananas 4,600, tropical fruit 1,250; livestock (number of live animals) 12,000 pigs, 450,000 chickens; fish catch 32,375. Mining and quarrying: none. Manufacturing (1996): processed copra 9,321; other important products are processed fish, baked goods, clothing, and handicrafts. Energy production (consumption): electricity (kW-hr; 1999) 7,000,000 (7,000,000); petroleum products (metric tons; 1999) none (8,000).
Gross national product (2001): U.S.$100,000,000 (U.S.$830 per capita).

Structure of gross domestic product and labour force

	2001 in value $A '000	2001 % of total value	2000 labour force	2000 % of labour force
Agriculture, fishing	4,592	7.1	30,966[5]	71.7[5]
Mining	—	—	—	—
Manufacturing	717	1.1	150	0.4
Construction	3,714	5.7	346	0.8
Public utilities	988	1.5	187	0.4
Transp. and commun.	7,734	11.9	944	2.2
Trade	11,167	17.2	1,181	2.7
Finance	4,795	7.4	317	0.7
Pub. admin., defense	30,213	46.6	5,821	13.5
Services	904[6]	1.5[6]	2,649	6.1
Other			644[7]	1.5[7]
TOTAL	64,824	100.0	43,205	100.0

Population economically active (1995): total 38,407; activity rate of total population 49.5% (participation rates: over age 15, 84.0%; female 47.8%; unemployed [2000] 1.5%).

Price and earnings indexes (1998 = 100)

	1998	1999	2000	2001	2002
Consumer price index[8]	100.0	101.8	102.2	108.2	111.7
Earnings index	...	...	...	...	...

Household income and expenditure. Average household size (1995) 6.5; expenditure (1996)[9]: food 45.0%, nonalcoholic beverages 10.0%, transportation 8.0%, energy 8.0%, education 8.0%.

Foreign trade

Balance of trade (current prices)

	1995	1996	1997	1998	1999	2000
$A '000,000	–37.5	–41.8	–44.1	–42.6	–49.7	–57.2
% of total	65.2%	75.4%	72.3%	69.6%	63.8%	72.8%

Imports (1999): $A 63,700,000 (food and live animals 28.3%; machinery and transport equipment 22.6%; mineral fuels 10.3%; beverages and tobacco products 7.7%). *Major import sources* (2001): Australia 26.5%; Poland 15.7%; Fiji 14.8%; United States 9.5%; Japan 8.0%.
Exports (1999): $A 14,000,000 (domestic exports 92.6%, of which copra 63.9%, seaweed 5.1%, other [including fish for food and pet fish] 23.6%; reexports 7.4%). *Major export destinations* (2001): Japan 45.8%; Thailand 24.8%; South Korea 10.7%; Bangladesh 5.5%; Brazil 3.0%.

Transport and communications

Transport. Roads (1996): total length 416 mi, 670 km (paved 5%). Vehicles (2000)[10]: passenger cars 477; trucks and buses 277. Air transport (1996): passenger-mi 4,350,000, passenger-km 7,000,000; short ton-mi cargo 621,000, metric ton-km cargo 1,000,000; airports 9.

Communications

Medium	date	unit	number	units per 1,000 persons
Radio	2000	receivers	32,600	386
Television	2000	receivers	3,030	36
Telephones	2001	main lines	3,600	42
Cellular telephones	2001	subscribers	500	5.8
Personal computers	2001	units	2,000	25
Internet	2001	users	2,000	25

Education and health

Educational attainment (1995). Percentage of population age 25 and over having: no schooling 7.8%; primary education 68.5%; secondary or higher 23.7%.
Literacy (1995): population age 15 and over literate 90%.

Education (2001)

	schools	teachers	students	student/ teacher ratio
Primary (age 6–13)	88	627	16,096	25.7
Secondary (age 14–18)	19	324	5,743	17.7
Voc., teacher tr.	2	39	1,501	38.5
Higher[11]	—	—	—	—

Health: physicians (1998) 26 (1 per 3,378 persons); hospital beds (1990) 283 (1 per 253 persons); infant mortality rate per 1,000 live births (2002) 52.6.
Food (2001): daily per capita caloric intake 2,922 (vegetable products 88%, animal products 12%); 128% of FAO recommended minimum requirement.

[1]Includes two nonelective members. [2]Includes uninhabited islands. [3]Detail does not add to total given because of rounding. [4]Based on inhabited island areas (280 sq mi [726 sq km]) only. [5]Includes 30,712 persons engaged in "village work" (subsistence agriculture or fishing). [6]Indirect taxes less subsidies and imputed bank service charge and unknown. [7]Unemployed. [8]Urban Tarawa only. [9]Weights of consumer price index components. [10]Registered vehicles in South Tarawa only. [11]129 students overseas in 2001.

Internet resources for further information:
- **United Nations Development Programme, Common Country Assessments http://www.undp.org.fj/CCAs.htm**
- **Key Indicators of Developing Asian and Pacific Countries http://www.adb.org/Documents/Books/Key_Indicators/2003**

Korea, North

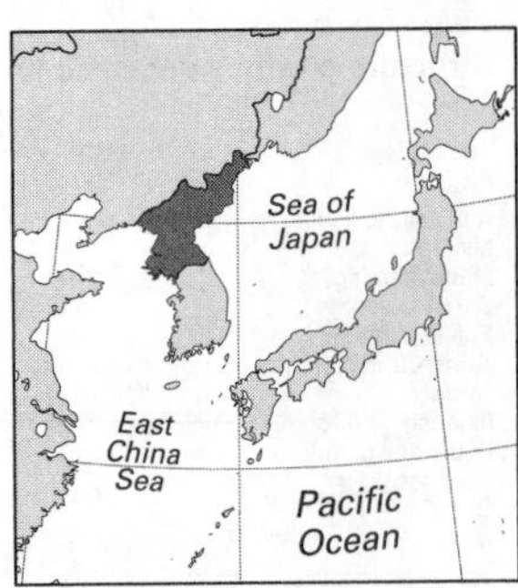

Official name: Chosŏn Minjujuŭi In'min Konghwaguk (Democratic People's Republic of Korea).
Form of government: unitary single-party republic with one legislative house (Supreme People's Assembly [687]).
Head of state and government: Chairman of the National Defense Commission[1].
Capital: P'yŏngyang.
Official language: Korean.
Official religion: none.
Monetary unit: 1 won = 100 chŏn; valuation (April 15, 2003) 1 U.S.$ = 142 won[2]; 1 £ = 223 won[2].

Area and population

Provinces	Capitals	area sq mi	area sq km	population 1987 estimate
Chagang-do	Kanggye	6,551	16,968	1,156,000
Kangwŏn-do	Wŏnsan	4,306	11,152	1,227,000
North Hamgyŏng (Hamgyŏng-pukto)	Ch'ŏngjin	6,784[3]	17,570[3]	2,003,000[3]
North Hwanghae (Hwanghae-pukto)	Sariwŏn	3,091	8,007	1,409,000
North P'yŏngan (P'yŏngan-pukto)	Sinŭiju	4,656[4]	12,059[4]	2,380,000[5]
South Hamgyŏng (Hamgyŏng-namdo)	Hamhŭng	7,324	18,970	2,547,000
South Hwanghae (Hwanghae-namdo)	Haeju	3,090	8,002	1,914,000
South P'yŏngan (P'yŏngan-namdo)	P'yŏngsan	4,470	11,577	2,653,000
Yanggang-do	Hyesan	5,528	14,317	628,000
Special administrative region[6]				
Sinŭiju	—	51	132	[5]
Special cities				
Kaesŏng	—	485	1,255	331,000
Najin Sŏnbong	—	[3]	[3]	[3]
Namp'o	—	291	753	715,000
P'yŏngyang	—	772	2,000	2,355,000
Special district				
Hyangsan-chigu	—	[4]	[4]	28,000
TOTAL		47,399	122,762	19,346,000

Demography

Population (2003): 22,466,000.
Density (2003): persons per sq mi 474.0, persons per sq km 183.0.
Urban-rural (2001): urban 60.5%; rural 39.5%.
Sex distribution (2000): male 48.48%; female 51.52%.
Age breakdown (2000): under 15, 25.6%; 15–29, 24.5%; 30–44, 24.7%; 45–59, 14.4%; 60–74, 9.0%; 75 and over, 1.8%.
Population projection: (2010) 23,802,000; (2020) 25,210,000.
Ethnic composition (1999): Korean 99.8%; Chinese 0.2%.
Religious affiliation (2000): nonreligious 55.6%; atheist 15.6%; Ch'ŏndogyo 12.9%; traditional beliefs 12.3%; Christian 2.1%; Buddhist 1.5%.
Major cities (1993): P'yŏngyang (2001) 3,164,000[7]; Namp'o (2000) 1,022,000[7]; Hamhŭng 709,000; Ch'ŏngjin 582,480; Kaesŏng 334,433; Sinŭiju 326,011.

Vital statistics

Birth rate per 1,000 population (2002): 18.7 (world avg. 21.3).
Death rate per 1,000 population (2002): 6.9 (world avg. 9.1).
Natural increase rate per 1,000 population (2002): 11.8 (world avg. 12.2).
Total fertility rate (avg. births per childbearing woman; 2002): 2.3.
Marriage rate per 1,000 population (1987): 9.3.
Divorce rate per 1,000 population (1987): 0.2.
Life expectancy at birth (2002): male 67.8 years; female 73.3 years.
Major causes of death per 100,000 population (1986); diseases of the circulatory system 224.9; malignant neoplasms (cancers) 69.0; diseases of the digestive system 51.6; diseases of the respiratory system 46.7.

National economy

Budget (1999). Revenue: 19,801,000,000 won (turnover tax and profits from state enterprises). Expenditures: 20,018,200,000 won (1994; national economy 67.8%, social and cultural affairs 19.0%, defense 11.6%).
Population economically active (1997)[8]: total 11,898,000; activity rate of total population 55.8% (participation rates [1988–93]: ages 15–64, 49.5%; female 46.0%; unemployed, n.a.).
Production (metric tons except as noted). Agriculture, forestry, fishing (2002): rice 2,190,000, potatoes 1,884,000, corn (maize) 1,651,000, cabbages 680,000, apples 660,000, soybeans 360,000, sweet potatoes 340,000, wheat 130,000, pears 130,000, peaches and nectarines 115,000, watermelons 105,000, tomatoes 70,000, barley 69,000, cucumbers and gherkins 65,000, tobacco leaves 63,000, millet 45,000, oats 11,000; livestock (number of live animals) 3,152,000 pigs, 2,693,000 goats, 575,000 cattle, 170,000 sheep; roundwood (2000) 4,900,000 cu m; fish catch (2000): 267,550. Mining and quarrying (2001): iron ore (metal content) 300,000; magnesite 1,000,000; phosphate rock 350,000; sulfur 240,000; zinc (metal content) 100,000; lead (metal content) 60,000; copper (metal content) 13,000; silver 40; gold 2,000 kg. Manufacturing (1999): cement 16,000,000; crude steel 8,100,000; pig iron 6,600,000; coke 3,400,000; steel semimanufactures 2,700,000[9]; chemical fertilizers 2,500,000[9]; meat 259,200[9]; gasoline 8,600,000[10] barrels; textile fabrics 350,000,000 sq m[9]. Energy production (consumption): electricity (kW-hr; 1999) 31,450,000,000 (31,450,000,000); hard coal (metric tons; 1999) 4,197,000 (59,129,000); lignite (metric tons; 1999) 20,800,000 (20,800,000); crude petroleum (barrels; 1999) none (14,000,000); petroleum products (metric tons; 1999) 2,480,000 (3,795,000).
Household income and expenditure. Average household size (1999) 4.6.
Public debt (external, outstanding; 1999): U.S.$12,000,000,000.
Gross national product (1999): U.S.$9,912,000,000 (U.S.$457 per capita).

Structure of gross domestic product and labour force

	1999 in value U.S.$'000,000	1999 % of total value	1997 labour force	1997 % of labour force
Agriculture	...	25.0	3,853,000	32.4
Mining and manufacturing				
Construction				
Public utilities	...	60.0		
Transp. and commun.			8,045,000	67.6
Trade				
Finance	...	...		
Pub. admin., defense				
Services	...	15.0		
Other				
TOTAL	22,600	100.0	11,898,000	100.0

Land use (1994): forested 61.2%; meadows and pastures 0.4%; agricultural and under permanent cultivation 16.6%; other 21.8%.

Foreign trade

Balance of trade (current prices)

	1996	1997	1998	1999	2000	2001
U.S.$'000,000	–1,050	–390	–320	–540	–961	–1,021
% of total	36.3%	18.1%	22.2%	29.8%	40.1%	38.2%

Imports (2001): U.S.$1,847,000,000 ([11]food, beverages, and other agricultural products 23.7%, machinery and apparatus 15.0%, mineral fuels and lubricants 14.3%, textiles and clothing 12.6%). *Major import sources:* China 31.0%; Japan 13.5%; South Korea 12.3%; India 8.4%; Singapore 6.1%.
Exports (2001): U.S.$826,000,000 ([11]live animals and agricultural products 30.2%, textiles and wearing apparel 21.6%, machinery and apparatus 15.1%, base and fabricated metals 9.3%). *Major export destinations:* Japan 27.3%; South Korea 21.3%; China 20.2%; Hong Kong 4.6%; Thailand 3.0%.

Transport and communications

Transport. Railroads (1999): length 8,533 km. Roads (1998): total length 14,544 mi, 23,407 km (paved 8%). Vehicles (1990): passenger cars 248,000. Air transport (1997): passenger-mi 177,712,000, passenger-km 286,000,000; short ton-mi cargo 18,600,000; metric ton-km cargo 30,000,000; airports (2001) with scheduled flights 1.

Communications

Medium	date	unit	number	units per 1,000 persons
Daily newspapers	2000	circulation	4,500,000	208
Radio	2000	receivers	3,330,000	154
Television	2000	receivers	1,170,000	54
Telephones	1999	main lines	1,100,000	46

Education and health

Educational attainment (1987–88). Percentage of population age 16 and over having attended or graduated from postsecondary-level school: 13.7%.
Literacy (1997): 95%.

Education (1988)

	schools	teachers	students	student/ teacher ratio
Primary (age 6–9)	4,810	59,000	1,543,000	26.2
Secondary (age 10–15)	4,840	111,000	2,468,000	22.2
Voc., teacher tr.	...	...	...	...
Higher	46	23,000	325,000	14.1

Health (1993): physicians 61,200 (1 per 370 persons); hospital beds (1989) 290,590 (1 per 74 persons); infant mortality rate (2002) 26.5.
Food (2001): daily per capita caloric intake 2,201 (vegetable products 94.2%, animal products 5.8%); 94% of FAO recommended minimum requirement.

Military

Total active duty personnel (2002): 1,082,000 (army 87.8%, navy 4.2%, air force 8.0%). *Military expenditure as percentage of GNP* (1999): 18.8% (world 2.4%); per capita expenditure U.S.$199.

[1]Position in effect from Sept. 5, 1998, is the declared "highest office of state." It is defined as an enhanced military post with revised constitutional powers. [2]Exchange rate per government announcement in August 2002. Black market rate in April 2003: 1 U.S.$ equals as much as 700 won. [3]North Hamgyŏng includes Najin Sŏnbong special city created in 2001. [4]North P'yŏngan includes special district of Hyangsan-chigu. [5]North P'yŏngan includes Sinŭiju. [6]Economic trade zone formally established September 2002. [7]Urban agglomeration. [8]The Democratic People's Republic of Korea categorizes economically active as including students in higher education, retirees, and heads of households, as well as those in the civilian labour force. [9]1994. [10]1996. [11]Data for commodities exclude trade with South Korea.

Internet resources for further information:
- **Digital KOTRA: North Korean Economy**
  http://crm.kotra.or.kr/main
- **United States Department of Energy**
  http://www.eia.doe.gov/emeu/cabs/nkorea.html

Korea, South

Official name: Taehan Min'guk (Republic of Korea).
Form of government: unitary multiparty republic with one legislative house (National Assembly [273]).
Head of state and government: President, assisted by Prime Minister.
Capital: Seoul.
Official language: Korean.
Official religion: none.
Monetary unit: 1 won (W) = 100 chon; valuation (Sept. 8, 2003) 1 U.S.$ = W 1,172; 1 £ = W 1,857.

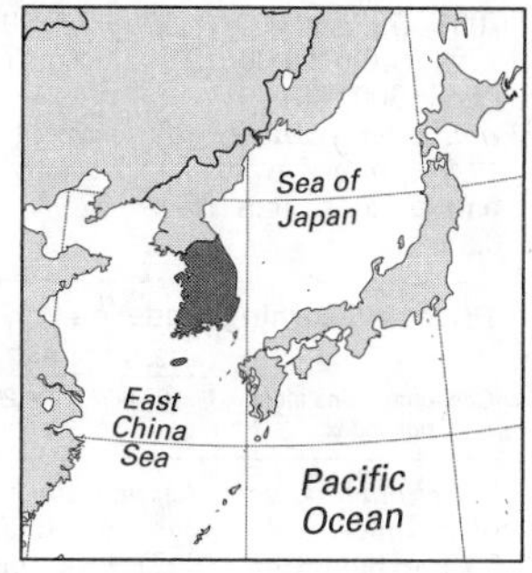

Area and population

Provinces	Capitals	area sq mi	area sq km	population 2000 census
Cheju	Cheju	713	1,847	513,260
Kangwŏn	Ch'unch'ŏn'	6,414	16,612	1,487,011
Kyŏnggi	Suwŏn	3,914	10,137	8,984,134
North Chŏlla	Chŏnju	3,109	8,051	1,890,669
North Ch'ungch'ŏng	Ch'ŏngju	2,870	7,432	1,466,567
North Kyŏngsang	Taegu	7,345	19,024	2,724,931
South Chŏlla	Kwangju	4,629	11,990	1,996,456
South Ch'ungch'ŏng	Taejŏn	3,319	8,597	1,845,321
South Kyŏngsang	Ch'angwŏn	4,061	10,517	2,978,502
Metropolitan cities				
Inch'ŏn	Inch'ŏn	378	980	2,475,139
Kwangju	Kwangju	193	501	1,352,797
Pusan	Pusan	294	762	3,662,884
Sŏul (Seoul)	Seoul	234	606	9,895,217
Taegu	Taegu	342	886	2,480,578
Taejŏn	Taejŏn	209	540	1,368,207
Ulsan	Ulsan	408	1,056	1,014,428
TOTAL		38,432	99,538	46,136,101

Demography

Population (2003): 47,925,000.
Density (2002): persons per sq mi 1,247.0, persons per sq km 481.5.
Urban-rural (2002): urban 83.0%; rural 17.0%.
Sex distribution (2002): male 50.34%; female 49.66%.
Age breakdown (2002): under 15, 20.6%; 15–29, 24.1%; 30–44, 26.9%; 45–59, 16.5%; 60–74, 9.4%; 75 and over, 2.5%.
Population projection: (2010) 49,594,000; (2020) 50,650,000.
Ethnic composition (2000): Korean 97.7%; Japanese 2.0%; U.S. white 0.1%; Han Chinese 0.1%; other 0.1%.
Religious affiliation (1995): religious 50.7%, of which Buddhist 23.2%, Protestant 19.7%, Roman Catholic 6.6%, Confucian 0.5%, Wonbulgyo 0.2%, Ch'ŏndogyo 0.1%, other 0.4%; nonreligious 49.3%.
Major cities (2000): Seoul 9,853,972; Pusan 3,655,437; Taegu 2,473,990; Inch'ŏn 2,466,338; Taejŏn 1,365,961.

Vital statistics

Birth rate per 1,000 population (2002): 12.9 (world avg. 21.3).
Death rate per 1,000 population (2002): 5.9 (world avg. 9.1).
Natural increase rate per 1,000 population (2002): 7.0 (world avg. 12.2).
Total fertility rate (avg. births per childbearing woman; 2002): 1.5.
Marriage rate per 1,000 population (2000): 7.0.
Divorce rate per 1,000 population (2000): 2.5.
Life expectancy at birth (2002): male 71.5 years; female 79.1 years.
Major causes of death per 100,000 population (2000): malignant neoplasms (cancers) 125.6; diseases of the circulatory system 124.6; accidents, poisoning, and violence 61.4; diseases of the respiratory system 34.3.

National economy

Budget (2002). Revenue: W 105,876,700,000,000 (tax revenue 88.6%, of which income and profits taxes 34.3%, value-added tax 30.2%; nontax revenue 11.4%). Expenditures: W 105,876,700,000,000 (economic services 25.9%, education 17.4%, defense 16.2%, social services 13.1%).
Public debt (external, outstanding; 2001): U.S.$33,742,000,000.
Production (metric tons except as noted). Agriculture, forestry, fishing (2002): rice 6,650,000, cabbages 3,420,000, dry onions 1,074,000, tangerines, mandarins, etc. 780,000, potatoes 750,000, pears 417,000, garlic 407,000; livestock (number of live animals) 8,811,000 pigs, 1,951,000 cattle, 107,000,000 chickens; roundwood (2001) 3,986,806 cu m; fish catch (2000) 2,146,393. Mining and quarrying (2001): iron ore 195,000. Manufacturing (units; 2001): transistors 21,126,000,000; mobile phones 89,834,000; colour television receivers 15,914,000; room air conditioners 5,955,659; computer mainframes 3,920,832; rice cookers 2,998,000; passenger cars 2,155,000; cement 53,062,000 metric tons. Energy production (consumption): electricity (kW-hr; 1999) 266,818,000,000 (266,818,000,000); coal (metric tons; 1999) 57,000,000 (58,682,000); crude petroleum (barrels; 1999) none (873,900,000); petroleum products (metric tons; 1999) 96,499,000 (62,047,000); natural gas (cu m; 1999) none (17,828,200,000).
Household income and expenditure (2001). Average household size 3.5; annual income per household W 31,501,200 (U.S.$24,400); sources of income: wages 84.2%, other 15.8%; expenditure: food and beverages 26.3%, transportation and communications 16.3%, education 11.3%.
Gross national product (2001): U.S.$447,600,000,000 (U.S.$9,460 per capita).

Structure of gross domestic product and labour force

	2000 in value W '000,000,000[1]	2000 % of total value[1]	2000 labour force	2000 % of labour force
Agriculture	24,859.8	6.0	2,288,000	10.4
Mining	1,439.4	0.3	18,000	0.1
Manufacturing	163,014.5	39.6	4,244,000	19.3
Construction	36,881.8	9.0	1,583,000	7.2
Public utilities	12,265.2	3.0	63,000	0.3
Transp. and commun.	41,276.1	10.0	1,260,000	5.7
Trade	58,469.5	14.2	5,943,000	27.1
Finance	83,860.0	20.4	2,089,000	9.5
Pub. admin., defense	29,171.7	7.1	753,000	3.4
Services	30,396.9	7.4	2,798,000	12.8
Other	–69,946.4[2]	–17.0[2]	911,000[3]	4.2[3]
TOTAL	411,688.5	100.0	21,950,000	100.0

Population economically active (2001): total 22,181,000; activity rate 46.9% (participation rates: ages 15–64, 64.6%; female 41.3%; unemployed [2002] 3.1%).

Price and earnings indexes (1995 = 100)

	1996	1997	1998	1999	2000	2001	2002
Consumer price index	104.9	109.6	117.8	118.8	121.5	126.4	129.9
Monthly earnings index	112.2	118.0	114.3	131.3	142.5	151.5	169.7

Tourism (2001): receipts U.S.$6,373,000,000; expenditures U.S.$6,547,000,000.

Foreign trade[4]

Balance of trade (current prices)

	1997	1998	1999	2000	2001	2002
U.S.$'000,000	–8,452	+39,031	+23,934	+11,787	+9,341	+10,812
% of total	3.0%	17.3%	9.1%	3.5%	3.2%	3.4%

Imports (2001): U.S.$141,098,000,000 (electric and electronic products 19.4%, crude petroleum 15.1%, nonelectrical machinery and transport equipment 14.5%, chemicals and chemical products 9.2%, food and live animals 4.8%). *Major import sources:* Japan 18.9%; U.S. 15.9%; China 9.4%; Saudi Arabia 5.7%; Australia 3.9%.
Exports (2001): U.S.$150,439,000,000 (electric and electronic products 25.0%, transport equipment 17.0%, nonelectrical machinery and apparatus 15.6%, chemicals and chemical products 8.3%). *Major export destinations:* U.S. 20.7%; China 12.1%; Japan 11.0%; Hong Kong 6.3%; Taiwan 3.9%.

Transport and communications

Transport. Railroads (2001): length 6,819 km; passenger-km 29,172,000,000; metric ton-km cargo 10,492,000,000. Roads (2001): total length 91,396 km (paved 77%). Vehicles (2001): passenger cars 8,889,000; trucks and buses 3,768,000. Air transport (2002)[5]: passenger-km 48,325,000,000; metric ton-km cargo 4,590,000,000; airports (1996) with scheduled flights 14.

Communications

Medium	date	unit	number	units per 1,000 persons
Daily newspapers	2000	circulation	18,500,000	393
Radio	2000	receivers	48,600,000	1,033
Television	2000	receivers	17,100,000	364
Telephones	2002	main lines	23,257,000	489
Cellular telephones	2002	subscribers	32,342,000	680
Personal computers	2002	units	26,458,000	556
Internet	2002	users	26,270,000	552

Education and health

Educational attainment (1995). Percentage of population age 25 and over having: no formal schooling 8.5%; primary education or less 17.7%; some secondary and secondary 53.1%; postsecondary 20.6%. *Literacy* (1995): total population age 15 and over literate 98.0%; males 99.3%; females 96.7%.

Education (2001)

	schools	teachers	students	student/ teacher ratio
Primary (age 6–13)	13,739	171,690	4,634,571	27.0
Secondary (age 14–19)	4,739	197,699	3,742,325	18.9
Voc., teacher tr.	169	12,607	974,067	77.3
Higher[6]	162	43,309	1,729,638	39.9

Health (2001): physicians 75,295 (1 per 629 persons); hospital beds 288,952 (1 per 164 persons); infant mortality rate (2002) 7.4.
Food (2001): daily per capita caloric intake 3,055 (vegetable products 85%, animal products 15%); 130% of FAO recommended minimum.

Military

Total active duty personnel (2002): 686,000 (army 81.6%, navy 9.2%, air force 9.2%); U.S. military forces (2002): 37,000. *Military expenditure as percentage of GNP* (1999): 2.9% (world 2.4%); per capita expenditure U.S.$246.

[1]At 1995 constant prices. [2]Import duties less imputed bank service charges. [3]Includes 22,000 inadequately defined and 889,000 unemployed. [4]Imports c.i.f.; exports f.o.b. [5]Scheduled flights of Asiana and Korean Air only. [6]Excludes graduate schools.

Internet resources for further information:
- **National Statistical Office http://www.nso.go.kr/eng**

Kuwait

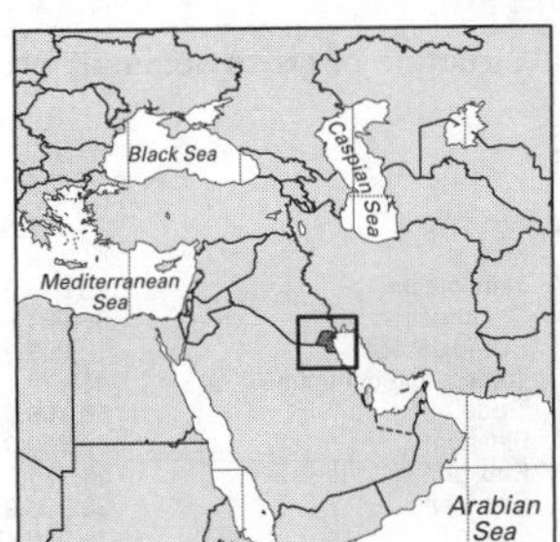

Official name: Dawlat al-Kuwayt (State of Kuwait).
Form of government: constitutional monarchy with one legislative body (National Assembly [50[1]]).
Head of state and government: Emir assisted by the Prime Minister[2].
Capital: Kuwait (city)[3].
Official language: Arabic.
Official religion: Islam.
Monetary unit: 1 Kuwaiti dinar (KD) = 1,000 fils; valuation (Sept. 8, 2003) 1 KD = U.S.$3.34 = £2.11.

Area and population

Governorates	Capitals	area sq mi	area sq km	population 2001 estimate
Al-Aḥmadī	Al-Aḥmadī	1,977	5,120	364,484
Al-ʿAṣimah	Kuwait (city)	77	200	388,532
Al-Farwānīyah	Al-Farwānīyah	73	190	572,252
Al-Jahrāʾ	Al-Jahrāʾ	4,336	11,230	282,353
Ḥawallī	Ḥawallī }	69	178	488,294
Mubārak al-Kabīr	… }			144,981
Islands[4]	—	347	900	…
TOTAL		6,880[5]	17,818	2,240,896[6]

Demography

Population (2003): 2,439,000.
Density (2003): persons per sq mi 354.5, persons per sq km 136.9.
Urban-rural (2001): urban 96.1%; rural 3.9%.
Sex distribution (2002): male 60.26%; female 39.74%.
Age breakdown (2002): under 15, 28.3%; 15–29, 30.6%; 30–44, 24.5%; 45–59, 12.4%; 60–74, 3.7%; 75 and over, 0.5%.
Population projection: (2010) 2,944,000; (2020) 3,529,000.
Doubling time: 36 years.
Ethnic composition (2000): Arab 74%, of which Kuwaiti 30%, Palestinian 17%, Jordanian 10%, Bedouin 9%; Kurd 10%; Indo-Pakistani 8%; Persian 4%; other 4%.
Religious affiliation (1995): Muslim 85%, of which Sunnī 45%, Shīʿī 30%, other Muslim 10%; other (mostly Christian and Hindu) 15%.
Major cities (1995): As-Sālimīyah 130,215; Qalīb ash-Shuyūkh 102,178; Ḥawallī 82,238; Kuwait (city) 28,859 (urban agglomeration [2001] 888,000).

Vital statistics

Birth rate per 1,000 population (2002): 21.8 (world avg. 21.3).
Death rate per 1,000 population (2002): 2.5 (world avg. 9.1).
Natural increase rate per 1,000 population (2002): 19.3 (world avg. 12.2).
Total fertility rate (avg. births per childbearing woman; 2002): 3.1.
Marriage rate per 1,000 population (2000): 4.9.
Divorce rate per 1,000 population (1999): 3.9.
Life expectancy at birth (2002): male 75.6 years; female 77.4 years.
Major causes of death per 100,000 population (2000): circulatory diseases 75.5; accidents and violence 24.6; cancers 22.3; congenital anomalies 13.2; endocrine and metabolic diseases 10.9; respiratory diseases 9.1.

National economy

Budget[7] (2002–03). Revenue: KD 3,521,700,000 (oil revenue 84.1%). Expenditures: KD 5,428,000,000 (wages 29.5%, transfers 29.1%, economic development 11.7%, other 29.7%).
Tourism (2001): receipts from visitors U.S.$104,000,000; expenditures by nationals abroad U.S.$2,843,000,000.
Gross national product (2001): U.S.$37,400,000,000 (U.S.$18,270 per capita).

Structure of gross domestic product and labour force

	2002 in value KD '000,000	% of total value	labour force[8]	% of labour force
Agriculture	48.1	0.4	21,800	1.6
Mining (petroleum sector)	4,406.2[9]	41.0[9]	8,300	0.6
Manufacturing	736.6[9]	6.9[9]	83,200	6.1
Construction	258.7	2.4	107,900	7.9
Public utilities	276.0	2.6	8,300	0.6
Transp. and commun.	563.9	5.3	43,700	3.2
Trade, hotels	764.2	7.1	219,700	16.1
Finance and business services	1,456.0	13.6	58,700	4.3
Pub. admin., defense	1,108.3	10.3 }	721,300	52.9
Services	1,555.1	14.5 }		
Other	–435.6[10]	–4.1[10]	91,400[11]	6.7[11]
TOTAL	10,737.5	100.0	1,364,300	100.0

Production (metric tons except as noted). Agriculture, forestry, fishing (2002): tomatoes 35,127, cucumbers and gherkins 33,004, eggplants 12,002, onions 3,327, garlic 448; livestock (number of live animals) 800,000 sheep, 130,000 goats, 18,000 cattle, 9,000 camels; fish catch (2001) 6,041. Mining and quarrying (2001): sulfur 524,000; lime 40,000. Manufacturing (value added in KD '000,000; 1997): refined petroleum products 3,632; industrial chemicals 962; fabricated metal products 68; food products 55; clothing and apparel 37. Construction (floor area of new construction; 1998): residential 2,983,000 sq m; nonresidential 220,000 sq m. Energy production (consumption): electricity (kW-hr; 1999) 32,106,000,000 (32,106,000,000); crude petroleum (barrels; 2001) 733,500,000 ([1999] 329,900,000); petroleum products (metric tons; 1999) 40,619,000 (9,902,000); natural gas (cu m; 1999) 8,686,300,000 (8,686,300,000).
Population economically active (2002): total 1,364,290, of which Kuwaiti 19.5%, non-Kuwaiti 80.5%; activity rate of total population 56.4% (participation rates: ages 15–59, 72.9%; female [1995] 26.1%; [2000] unemployed 0.8%).

Price and earnings indexes (1995 = 100)

	1996	1997	1998	1999	2000	2001	2002
Consumer price index	103.6	104.2	104.4	100.9	101.3	111.3	112.8
Earnings index	…	…	…	…	…	…	…

Household income and expenditure. Average household size (1995) 3.9; sources of income (1986): wages and salaries 53.8%, self-employment 20.8%, other 25.4; expenditure (1992): food, beverages, and tobacco 37.0%, housing and energy 18.7%, transportation 15.3%, household appliances and services 11.1%, clothing and footwear 10.0%, education and health 2.5%.
Land use (1994): forest 0.1%; pasture 7.7%; agriculture 0.3%; other 91.9%.

Foreign trade[12]

Balance of trade (current prices)

	1997	1998	1999	2000	2001	2002
KD '000,000	+1,813	+285	+1,384	+3,767	+2,577	+1,979
% of total	26.6%	5.2%	23.0%	46.2%	35.2%	25.2%

Imports (2001): KD 2,371,000,000 (machinery and apparatus 20.0%, transport equipment 17.2%, base and fabricated metals 8.5%, chemicals and chemical products 7.5%, textiles and wearing apparel 7.0%). *Major import sources:* U.S. 19.1%; Germany 14.1%; Japan 12.3%; U.K. 10.8%; Italy 8.1%.
Exports (2001): KD 4,948,000,000 (crude petroleum and petroleum products 92.8%, plastics 4.0%). *Major export destinations:* Japan 28.7%; South Korea 17.1%; U.S. 16.8%; Singapore 10.3%; Taiwan 9.4%.

Transport and communications

Transport. Railroads: none. Roads (1997): total length 2,765 mi, 4,450 km (paved 81%). Vehicles (1998): passenger cars 747,042; trucks and buses 140,480. Air transport (2002): passenger-mi 3,933,000,000, passenger-km 6,330,000,000; short ton-mi cargo 174,183,000, metric ton-km cargo 254,302,000; airports (2001) with scheduled flights 1.

Communications

Medium	date	unit	number	units per 1,000 persons
Daily newspapers	2000	circulation	836,000	374
Radio	2000	receivers	1,400,000	624
Television	2000	receivers	1,090,000	486
Telephones	2001	main lines	472,400	207
Cellular telephones	2002	subscribers	877,900	386
Personal computers	2001	units	272,000	120
Internet	2001	users	200,000	88

Education and health

Educational attainment (1988). Percentage of population age 25 and over having: no formal schooling 44.8%; primary education 8.6%; some secondary 15.1%; complete secondary 15.1%; higher 16.4%. *Literacy* (2000): total population age 15 and over literate 82.0%; males literate 84.0%; females literate 79.7%.

Education (2000–01)

	schools	teachers	students	student/teacher ratio
Primary (age 6–9)[13, 14]	349	17,385	193,582	11.1
Secondary (age 10–17)[13]	117	9,234	76,221	8.3
Voc., teacher tr.[13]	40	1,107	2,997	2.7
Higher[15]	1	918	17,447	19.0

Health (2002): physicians 3,780 (1 per 625 persons); hospital beds 5,200 (1 per 455 persons); infant mortality rate per 1,000 live births 10.9.
Food (2001): daily per capita caloric intake 3,170 (vegetable products 78%, animal products 22%); 131% of FAO recommended minimum requirement.

Military

Total active duty personnel (2002): 15,500 (army [including central staff] 71.0%, navy 12.9%, air force 16.1%); U.S. troops (October 2003) 34,000. *Military expenditure as percentage of GNP* (1999): 7.7% (world 2.4%); per capita expenditure U.S.$1,410.

[1]Excludes cabinet ministers not elected to National Assembly serving ex officio. [2]As of July 13, 2003, the office of prime minister became separated from the role of emir for the first time since independence in 1961. [3]Officially Al-Kuwayt; Kuwait is variant. [4]Būbiyān Island 333 sq mi (863 sq km) and Warbah Island 14 sq mi (37 sq km). [5]Detail does not add to total given because of rounding. [6]Sum of governorate populations. Actual mid-year est. pop. is 2,243,080. [7]Approved budget. [8]Rounded figures are derived from percentages. [9]Manufacturing includes petroleum products; Mining (petroleum sector) excludes petroleum products. [10]Includes import duties less imputed bank service charges. [11]Not stated. [12]Imports c.i.f.; exports f.o.b. [13]Government schools only. [14]Includes intermediate. [15]University only.

Internet resources for further information:
- **Central Bank of Kuwait http://www.cbk.gov.kw**
- **Ministry of Planning http://www.mop.gov.kw/MopWebSite/english/default.asp**

Kyrgyzstan

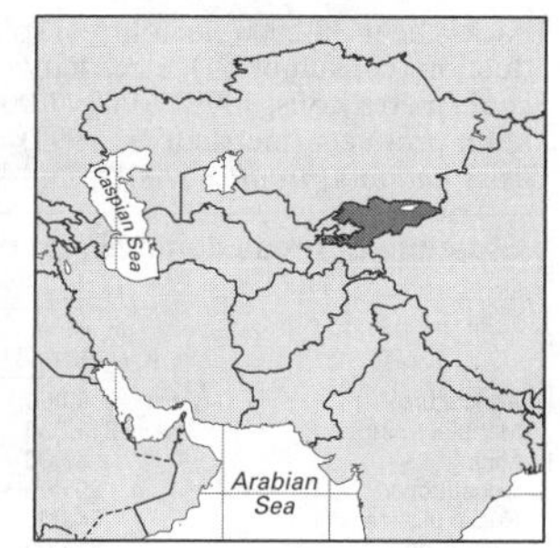

Official name: Respublika Kirgizstan (Kyrgyz); Kyrgyz Respublikasy (Russian) (Kyrgyz Republic).
Form of government: unitary multiparty republic with two legislative houses (Assembly of People's Representatives [45]; Legislative Assembly [60]).
Head of state and government: President assisted by Prime Minister.
Capital: Bishkek.
Official languages: Kyrgyz; Russian.
Official religion: none.
Monetary unit: 1 som (K.S.) = 100 tyiyn; valuation (Sept. 8, 2003) 1 U.S.$ = K.S. 42.75; 1 £ = K.S. 67.78.

Area and population

Provinces	Capitals	area sq mi	area sq km	population 1999 census
Batken	Batken	6,573	17,024	382,426
Chüy (Chu)	Tokmok[1]	7,214	18,684	770,811
Jalal-Abad (Dzhalal-Abad)	Jalal-Abad (Dzhalal-Abad)	12,992	33,648	869,259
Naryn	Naryn	18,035	46,710	249,115
Osh	Osh	11,261	29,165	1,175,998
Talas	Talas	4,419	11,446	199,872
Ysyk-Köl (Issyk-Kul)	Ysyk-Köl (Issyk-Kul)	16,646	43,114	413,149
City				
Bishkek (Frunze)	—	49	127	762,308
TOTAL		77,199[2, 3]	199,945[2, 3]	4,822,938

Demography

Population (2003): 5,059,000.
Density (2003): persons per sq mi 65.5, persons per sq km 25.3.
Urban-rural (1999): urban 34.3%; rural 65.7%.
Sex distribution (2001): male 48.84%; female 51.16%.
Age breakdown (2001): under 15, 35.0%; 15–29, 28.1%; 30–44, 18.6%; 45–59, 9.2%; 60–74, 7.0%; 75 and over, 2.1%.
Population projection: (2010) 5,539,000; (2020) 6,144,000.
Doubling time: 53 years.
Ethnic composition (1999): Kyrgyz 64.9%; Uzbek 13.8%; Russian 12.5%; Hui 1.1%; Ukrainian 1.0%; Uighur 1.0%; other 5.7%.
Religious affiliation (1997): Muslim (mostly Sunnī) 75.0%; Christian 6.7%, of which Russian Orthodox 5.6%; other (mostly nonreligious) 18.3%.
Major cities (1999): Bishkek (Frunze) 750,327; Osh 208,520; Jalal-Abad 70,401; Tokmok 59,409; Kara-Köl 47,159.

Vital statistics

Birth rate per 1,000 population (2001): 20.6 (world avg. 21.3); (1994) legitimate 83.2%; illegitimate 16.8%.
Death rate per 1,000 population (2001): 7.3 (world avg. 9.1).
Natural increase rate per 1,000 population (2001): 13.3 (world avg. 12.2).
Total fertility rate (avg. births per childbearing woman; 2001): 2.5.
Marriage rate per 1,000 population (1999): 5.6.
Divorce rate per 1,000 population (1999): 4.6.
Life expectancy at birth (2001): male 64.0 years; female 72.0 years.
Major causes of death per 100,000 population (1999): diseases of the circulatory system 285.6; diseases of the respiratory system 84.2; malignant neoplasms (cancers) 59.9; accidents, poisoning, and violence 45.4.

National economy

Budget (2001). Revenue: K.S. 12,544,000,000 (tax revenue 73.2%, of which VAT 33.6%, taxes on income 16.0%, excise taxes 8.8%, other taxes 14.8%; nontax revenue 21.3%; grants 5.5%). Expenditures: K.S. 13,133,000,000 (education 21.7%; general public services 16.0%; social security 10.8%; health 10.5%; defense 7.5%).
Public debt (external, outstanding; 2001): U.S.$1,256,000,000.
Land use (1994): forest 3.7%; pasture 45.4%; agriculture 7.2%; other 43.7%.
Population economically active (2001): total 1,939,000; activity rate of total population 39.2% (participation rates [2000]: ages 16–59 [male], 16–54 [female] 62.0%; female (1999) 44.9%; unemployed [2001] 7.8%).

Price and earnings indexes (1995 = 100)

	1996	1997	1998	1999	2000	2001	2002
Consumer price index	131.9	162.9	179.9	244.5	290.2	310.3	316.9
Monthly earnings index	133.3	184.7	228.3	285.1	328.6	...	...

Production (metric tons except as noted). Agriculture, forestry, fishing (2002): mixed grasses and legumes 2,900,000, wheat 1,306,000, potatoes 1,244,000, sugarbeets 525,000, corn (maize) 428,000, seed cotton 98,000, tobacco leaves 8,183; livestock (number of live animals) 3,104,000 sheep, 988,000 cattle, 350,000 horses; roundwood (2001) 26,000 cu m; fish catch (2001) 201. Mining and quarrying (2002): mercury 300; antimony 200; gold (2001) 24,600 kg. Manufacturing (value of production in '000,000 som; 2001): ferrous metals 21,268; nonferrous metals 21,243; flour 3,914; nonelectrical machinery 2,518; textiles 2,216; tobacco products 1,375. Energy production (consumption): electricity (kW-hr; 2001) 13,667,000,000 (11,503,000,000); hard coal (metric tons; 1999) 97,000 (878,000); lignite (metric tons; 1999) 320,000 (346,000); crude petroleum (barrels; 2001) 553,000 (553,000); petroleum products (metric tons; 2001) 131,000 (387,000); natural gas (cu m; 2001) 32,800,000 (655,700,000).
Household income and expenditure. Average household size (1999) 4.3; income per household (1994) 4,359 som (U.S.$325); sources of income (1999): wages and salaries 29.2%, self-employment 25.6%, other 45.2%; expenditure (1990): food and clothing 48.0%, health care 13.1%, housing 5.9%.
Gross national product (2001): U.S.$1,400,000,000 (U.S.$280 per capita).

Structure of gross domestic product and labour force

	2001 in value K.S. '000,000	2001 % of total value	1999 labour force	1999 % of labour force
Agriculture	25,554.6	34.6	924,300	48.6
Mining			9,500	0.5
Manufacturing	16,596.4	22.5	127,000	6.7
Public utilities			22,100	1.2
Construction	2,793.8	3.8	45,200	2.4
Transp. and commun.	3,230.5	4.4	65,800	3.4
Trade	9,343.9	12.6	195,200	10.3
Finance	866.7	1.2	35,800	1.9
Public admin., defense	3,729.1	5.0	65,700	3.4
Services	6,412.0	8.7	273,700	14.4
Other	5,356.3[4]	7.2[4]	136,800[5]	7.2[5]
TOTAL	73,883.3	100.0	1,901,100	100.0

Tourism (2001): receipts from visitors, U.S.$24,000,000; expenditures by nationals abroad, U.S.$12,000,000.

Foreign trade[6]

Balance of trade (current prices)

	1996	1997	1998	1999	2000	2001
U.S.$'000,000	–251.7	–15.2	–220.7	–88.6	+4.0	+39.9
% of total	19.2%	1.2%	17.1%	8.7%	0.4%	4.3%

Imports (2001): U.S.$467,200,000 (petroleum and natural gas 22.6%, machinery and apparatus 21.0%, food products 11.7%, chemicals and chemical products 9.5%). *Major import sources:* Russia 18.2%; Kazakhstan 17.5%; Uzbekistan 14.3%; China 10.4%; United States 5.7%.
Exports (2001): U.S.$476,200,000 (nonferrous metals [significantly gold] 51.7%, machinery and apparatus 12.0%, electricity 9.8%, agricultural products [significantly tobacco] 9.5%). *Major export destinations:* Switzerland 26.1%; Germany 19.8%; Russia 13.5%; Uzbekistan 10.1%; Kazakhstan 8.2%.

Transport and communications

Transport. Railroads (2000): length 424 km; passenger-km 44,000,000; metric ton-km cargo 348,000,000. Roads (1999): total length 18,500 km (paved 91%). Vehicles (2000): passenger cars 187,322; trucks and buses, n.a. Air transport (1999): passenger-km 532,000,000; metric ton-km cargo 56,000,000; airports with scheduled flights 2.

Communications

Medium	date	unit	number	units per 1,000 persons
Daily newspapers	2000	circulation	73,000	15
Radio	2000	receivers	542,000	111
Television	2000	receivers	239,000	49
Telephones	2002	main lines	394,800	79
Cellular phones	2002	subscribers	53,100	10
Personal computers	2002	units	65,000	13
Internet	2002	users	152,000	30

Education and health

Educational attainment (1999). Percentage of population age 15 and over having: primary education 6.3%; some secondary 18.3%; completed secondary 50.0%; some postsecondary 14.9%; higher 10.5%. *Literacy* (1999): total population age 15 and over literate 97.5%; males 98.5%; females 96.5%.

Education (1999–2000)

	schools	teachers	students	student/ teacher ratio
Primary (age 6–13)	1,985	19,200	466,200	24.3
Secondary (age 14–17)	1,474[7]	36,600	633,900	17.3
Voc., teacher tr.	53[7]	5,100	52,200	10.2
Higher	23	8,400	159,200	19.0

Health (1997): physicians 15,100 (1 per 307 persons); hospital beds 40,700 (1 per 114 persons); infant mortality rate per 1,000 live births (2001) 39.0.
Food (2001): daily per capita caloric intake 2,882 (vegetable products 81%, animal products 19%); 111% of FAO recommended minimum.

Military

Total active duty personnel (2002): 10,900 (army 78.0%, air force 22.0%)[8]. *Military expenditure as percentage of GNP* (1999): 2.4% (world 2.4%); per capita expenditure U.S.$62.

[1]As of March 2003. [2]Includes *c.* 480 sq mi (*c.* 1,250 sq km) ceded to China in May 2002. [3]Detail does not add to total given because of statistical discrepancy. [4]Taxes on products less imputed bank service charge. [5]Unemployed. [6]Imports are f.o.b. in balance of trade and c.i.f. for commodities and trading partners. [7]1993–94. [8]U.S. and coalition troops (May 2003) 1,500. Russian air base (not affiliated with coalition forces) opened in Kyrgyzstan in October 2003.

Internet resources for further information:
- **National Statistical Committee of the Kyrgyz Republic http://nsc.bishkek.su/English/index.html**
- **Embassy of the Kyrgyz Republic http://www.kyrgyzstan.org**

Laos

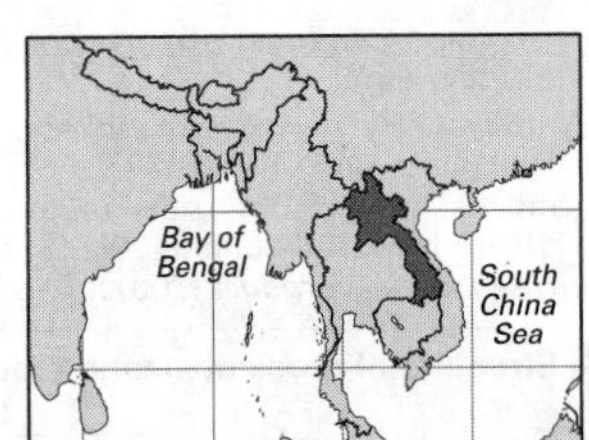

Official name: Sathalanalat Paxathipatai Paxaxôn Lao (Lao People's Democratic Republic).
Form of government: unitary single-party people's republic with one legislative house (National Assembly [109]).
Chief of state: President.
Head of government: Prime Minister.
Capital: Vientiane (Viangchan).
Official language: Lao.
Official religion: none.
Monetary unit: 1 kip (KN) = 100 at; valuation (Sept. 8, 2003) 1 U.S.$ = KN 7,600; 1 £ = KN 12,050.

Area and population

Provinces	Capitals	area sq mi	area sq km	population 1996 estimate
Attapu	Attapu	3,985	10,320	87,700
Bokèo	Houayxay	2,392	6,196	114,900
Bolikhamxai	Pakxan	5,739	14,863	164,900
Champasak	Pakxé	5,952	15,415	503,300
Houaphan	Xam Nua	6,371	16,500	247,300
Khammouan	Thakhek	6,299	16,315	275,400
Louangnamtha	Louangnamtha	3,600	9,325	115,200
Louangphrabang	Louangphrabang	6,515	16,875	367,200
Oudomxay	Xay	5,934	15,370	211,300
Phôngsali	Phôngsali	6,282	16,270	153,400
Salavan	Salavan	4,128	10,691	258,300
Savannakhét	Savannakhét	8,407	21,774	674,900
Special Region	...	2,743	7,105	54,200
Viangchan	Muang Phôn-Hông	6,149	15,927	286,800
Xaignabouli	Xaignabouli	6,328	16,389	293,300
Xékong	Thong	2,959	7,665	64,200
Xiangkhoang	Phônsavan	6,131	15,880	201,200
Municipalities				
Viangchan	Vientiane (Viangchan)	1,514	3,920	531,800
TOTAL		91,429[1]	236,800	4,605,300

Demography

Population (2003): 5,657,000.
Density (2003): persons per sq mi 61.9, persons per sq km 23.9.
Urban-rural (2002): urban 25.0%; rural 75.0%.
Sex distribution (2002): male 49.97%; female 50.03%.
Age breakdown (2000): under 15, 42.8%; 15–29, 27.0%; 30–44, 16.3%; 45–59, 8.3%; 60–74, 4.6%; 75 and over, 1.0%.
Population projection: (2010) 6,592,000; (2020) 7,967,000.
Doubling time: 28 years.
Ethnic composition (2000): Lao-Lum (Lao) 53.0%; Lao-Theung (Mon-Khmer) 23.0%; Lao-Tai (Tai) 13.0%; Lao-Soung (Miao [Hmong] and Man [Yao]) 10.0%; other (ethnic Chinese or Vietnamese) 1.0%.
Religious affiliation (2000): Buddhist 48.8%; traditional beliefs 41.7%; nonreligious 4.3%; Christian 2.1%; other 3.1%.
Major cities (2003): Vientiane 194,200 (urban agglomeration [2001] 663,000); Savannakhét 58,200; Pakxé 50,100; Xam Nua 40,700; Muang Khammouan 27,300; Louangphrabang 26,400.

Vital statistics

Birth rate per 1,000 population (2002): 36.0 (world avg. 21.3).
Death rate per 1,000 population (2002): 12.8 (world avg. 9.1).
Natural increase rate per 1,000 population (2002): 23.2 (world avg. 12.2).
Total fertility rate (avg. births per childbearing woman; 2002): 5.0.
Life expectancy at birth (2002): male 52.0 years; female 55.9 years.
Major causes of death per 100,000 population (incomplete, 1990): malaria 7.6; pneumonia 3.0; meningitis 1.5; diarrhea 1.2; tuberculosis 0.8.

National economy

Budget (2001–02). Revenue: KN 2,481,000,000,000 (tax revenue 82.3%; nontax revenue 17.7%). Expenditures: KN 3,614,000,000,000 (capital expenditure 59.9%, of which foreign-financed 34.8%; current expenditure 40.1%).
Public debt (external, outstanding; 2001): U.S.$2,456,000,000.
Tourism (2001): receipts from visitors U.S.$104,000,000; expenditures by nationals abroad U.S.$8,000,000.
Population economically active (2000): total 2,625,000; activity rate of total population *c.* 50% (participation rates: ages 15–64, n.a.; female *c.* 47%; unemployed [1994] 2.6%).

Price and earnings indexes (1995 = 100)

	1996	1997	1998	1999	2000	2001	2002
Consumer price index	113.0	144.1	275.2	628.7	786.4	847.8	937.9
Earnings index	...	...	...	...	...	...	...

Production (metric tons except as noted). Agriculture, forestry, fishing (2002): rice 2,410,000, sugarcane 210,000, corn (maize) 113,000, sweet potatoes 102,000, cassava 70,000, pineapples 35,000, potatoes 35,000, oranges 28,000, bananas 23,500, coffee 18,000, seed cotton 10,145; livestock (number of live animals) 1,425,900 pigs, 1,150,000 cattle, 1,060,000 water buffalo, 15,000,000 chickens; roundwood (2001) 6,455,000 cu m; fish catch (2000) 71,300. Mining and quarrying (2002): gypsum 130,000; tin (metal content) 350; gold (2003) 115,000 troy oz[2]. Manufacturing (1998): plastic products 3,225; tobacco 1,000; detergent 912; nails 624; clothing 23,000,000 pieces; cigarettes 55,000,000 packs; beer 332,000 hectolitres; soft drinks 125,000 hectolitres. Energy production (consumption): electricity (kW-hr; 1999) 1,225,000,000 (497,000,000); coal (metric tons; 1999) 1,000 (1,000); crude petroleum, none (none); petroleum products (metric tons; 1999) none (119,000); natural gas, none (none).
Gross national product (2001): U.S.$1,600,000,000 (U.S.$300 per capita).

Structure of gross domestic product and labour force

	2001 in value KN '000,000[3]	2001 % of total value	2000 labour force	2000 % of labour force
Agriculture	606,000	50.9	2,007,000	76.5
Manufacturing	211,000	17.7		
Mining	6,000	0.5		
Construction	29,000	2.4		
Public utilities	34,000	2.8		
Transp. and commun.	71,000	6.0	618,000	23.5
Trade	114,000	9.6		
Finance	44,000	3.7		
Pub. admin., defense	34,000	2.8		
Services	33,000	2.8		
Other	9,000	0.8		
TOTAL	1,191,000	100.0	2,625,000	100.0

Household income and expenditure. Average household size (1995) 6.1; average annual income per household KN 3,710 (U.S.$371); sources of income: n.a.; expenditure: n.a.
Land use (1994): forested 54.4%; meadows and pastures 3.5%; agricultural and under permanent cultivation 3.9%; other 38.2%.

Foreign trade[4]

Balance of trade (current prices)

	1997	1998	1999	2000	2001	2002
U.S.$'000,000	–347	–183	–214	–218	–197	–133
% of total	32.6%	19.9%	25.6%	23.7%	22.9%	18.3%

Imports (2000): U.S.$569,000,000 (consumption goods 50.6%, mineral fuels 13.9%, materials for garment assembly 10.6%, construction and electrical equipment 7.6%). *Major import sources* (2001): Thailand 52.0%; Vietnam 26.5%; China 5.7%; Singapore 3.3%; Japan 1.5%.
Exports (2000): U.S.$351,000,000 (electricity 32.0%, garments 26.1%, wood products [mostly logs and timber] 24.8%, motorcycles 6.3%). *Major export destinations* (2001): Vietnam 41.5%; Thailand 14.8%; France 6.1%; Germany 4.6%; Belgium 2.2%.

Transport and communications

Transport. Railroads: none. Roads (1999): total length 13,494 mi, 21,716 km (paved [1995] 45%). Vehicles (1996): passenger cars 16,320; trucks and buses 4,200. Air transport (1997): passenger-mi 29,000,000, passenger-km 48,000,000; short ton-mi cargo 3,000,000, metric ton-km cargo 5,000,000; airports (1996) with scheduled flights 11.

Communications

Medium	date	unit	number	units per 1,000 persons
Daily newspapers	2000	circulation	21,100	4.0
Radio	2000	receivers	781,000	148
Television	2000	receivers	52,800	10
Telephones	2002	main lines	61,900	11
Cellular telephones	2002	subscribers	55,200	10
Personal computers	2002	units	15,000	2.7
Internet	2002	users	18,000	3.3

Education and health

Educational attainment (1985). Percentage of population age 6 and over having: no schooling 49.3%; primary 41.2%; secondary 9.1%; higher 0.4%. *Literacy* (1995): total population age 15 and over literate 56.6%; males literate 69.4%; females literate 44.4%.

Education (1996–97)

	schools	teachers	students	student/ teacher ratio
Primary (age 6–10)	7,896	25,831	786,335	30.4
Secondary (age 11–16)	...	10,717	180,160	16.8
Voc., teacher tr.	...	1,600[5]	9,400[5]	5.9[5]
Higher	...	1,369	12,732	9.3

Health: physicians (1996) 1,167 (1 per 4,115 persons); hospital beds (1990) 10,364 (1 per 402 persons); infant mortality rate (2002) 90.8.
Food (2001): daily per capita caloric intake 2,309 (vegetable products 93%, animal products 7%); (2001) 108% of FAO recommended minimum requirement.

Military

Total active duty personnel (2002): 29,100 (army 88.0%, air force 12.0%). *Military expenditure as percentage of GNP* (1999): 2.0% (world 2.4%); per capita expenditure U.S.$5.

[1]Detail does not add to total given because of rounding. [2]Gold production began February 2003; production figure is through mid-September 2003 only. [3]At constant 1990 prices. [4]Imports c.i.f.; exports f.o.b. [5]1995–96.

Internet resources for further information:
- **Asian Development Bank: Key Indicators 2002 http://www.adb.org**

Latvia

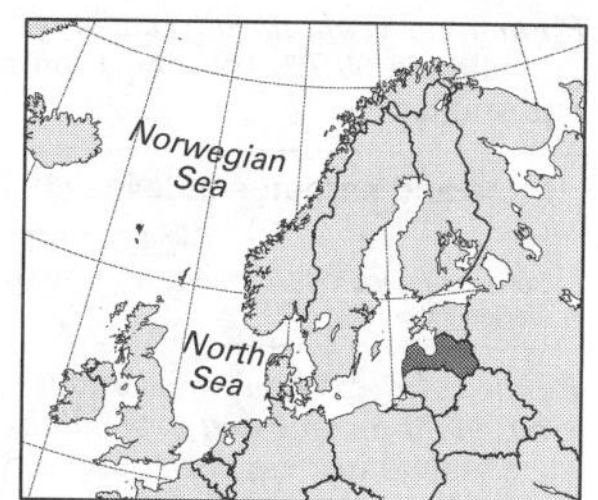

Official name: Latvijas Republika (Republic of Latvia).
Form of government: unitary multiparty republic with a single legislative body (Parliament, or Saeima [100]).
Chief of state: President.
Head of government: Prime Minister.
Capital: Riga.
Official language: Latvian.
Official religion: none.
Monetary unit: 1 lats (Ls; plural lati) = 100 santimi; valuation (Sept. 8, 2003) 1 U.S.$ = 0.57 lats; 1 £ = 0.91 lats.

Area and population

Cities	area sq km	population 2002[1] estimate	Districts	area sq km	population 2002[1] estimate
Daugavpils	72	113,409	Jelgava	1,604	37,086
Jelgava	60	65,927	Krāslava	2,285	36,203
Jūrmala	100	55,328	Kuldīga	2,502	37,584
Liepāja	60	87,505	Liepāja	3,594	46,170
Rēzekne	17	38,054	Limbaži	2,602	39,920
Riga	307	747,157	Ludza	2,569	34,380
Ventspils	46	44,004	Madona	3,346	45,517
			Ogre	1,840	63,028
Districts			Preiļi	2,041	41,041
Aizkraukle	2,565	41,546	Rēzekne	2,655	43,012
Alūksne	2,243	26,020	Rīga (Riga)	3,059	145,261
Balvi	2,386	29,843	Saldus	2,182	38,311
Bauska	1,882	52,517	Talsi	2,751	48,959
Cēsis	3,067	59,914	Tukums	2,447	55,050
Daugavpils	2,525	42,193	Valka	2,437	33,597
Dobele	1,633	39,791	Valmiera	2,365	59,593
Gulbene	1,877	27,937	Ventspils	2,472	14,529
Jēkabpils	2,998	55,182	TOTAL	64,589	2,345,768

Demography

Population (2003): 2,324,000.
Density (2003): persons per sq mi 93.2, persons per sq km 36.0.
Urban-rural (2002): urban 67.8%; rural 32.2%.
Sex distribution (2002): male 46.03%; female 53.97%.
Age breakdown (2000): under 15, 18.1%; 15–29, 21.2%; 30–44, 21.4%; 45–59, 18.3%; 60–74, 15.7%; 75 and over, 5.3%.
Population projection: (2010) 2,213,000; (2020) 2,065,000.
Ethnic composition (2002): Latvian 58.2%; Russian 29.2%; Belarusian 4.0%; Ukrainian 2.6%; Polish 2.5%; Lithuanian 1.4%; other 2.1%.
Religious affiliation (1995): Christian 39.6%, of which Protestant 16.7% (of which Lutheran 14.6%), Roman Catholic 14.9%, Orthodox 8.0%; Jewish 0.6%; other (mostly nonreligious) 59.8%.
Major cities (2002[1]): Riga 747,157; Daugavpils 113,409; Liepāja 87,505; Jelgava 65,927; Jūrmala 55,328.

Vital statistics

Birth rate per 1,000 population (2002): 8.6 (world avg. 21.3); (1998) legitimate 62.9%; illegitimate 37.1%.
Death rate per 1,000 population (2001): 13.9 (world avg. 9.1).
Natural increase rate per 1,000 population (2002): –5.3 (world avg. 12.2).
Total fertility rate (avg. births per childbearing woman; 2000): 1.1.
Marriage rate per 1,000 population (2002): 4.2.
Divorce rate per 1,000 population (2002): 2.6.
Life expectancy at birth (2002): male 65.2 years; female 76.6 years.
Major causes of death per 100,000 population (2000): diseases of the circulatory system 755.8; malignant neoplasms (cancers) 235.6; accidents, poisoning, and violence 209.8, of which suicide 32.6; diseases of the digestive system 42.3.

National economy

Budget (2001). Revenue: Ls 1,244,100,000 (social security contributions 35.3%, value-added taxes 28.2%, income taxes 14.3%, excises 13.0%, nontax revenue 9.2%). Expenditures: Ls 1,399,800,000 (social security and welfare 40.7%, health 11.0%, police 7.0%, education 6.3%, defense 3.1%).
Public debt (external, outstanding; 2001): U.S.$978,000,000.
Production (metric tons except as noted). Agriculture, forestry, fishing (2002): grasses for forage and silage 14,000,000, potatoes 768,400, sugar beets 622,300, wheat 519,500, barley 262,400, rye 101,500; livestock (number of live animals) 453,000 pigs, 388,000 cattle; roundwood (2001) 14,037,000 cu m; fish catch 105,000. Mining and quarrying (2001): peat 555,003. Manufacturing (value added in Ls '000,000; 1998): alcoholic beverages 79.4; sawn wood 64.4; veneer/plywood 37.6; dairy products 30.5; wearing apparel 30.4; bakery products 29.8; fish processing 24.2. Energy production (consumption): electricity (kW-hr; 2001) 4,236,000,000 ([2002] 6,323,000,000); coal (2002) none (102,000); crude petroleum[2], none (none); petroleum products[2] (2002) none (1,084,000); natural gas (cu m; 2002) none (1,610,000,000).
Household income and expenditure. Average household size (2000) 2.7; annual disposable income per household (2002) Ls 2,076 (U.S.$3,460); sources of income (1998): wages and salaries 55.8%, pensions and transfers 25.7%; expenditure (2001–02): food, beverages, and tobacco 40.0%, transportation and communications 15.0%, housing and energy 14.0%.
Tourism (in U.S.$'000,000; 2001): receipts 120; expenditures 224.
Gross national product (2001): U.S.$7,600,000,000 (U.S.$3,230 per capita).

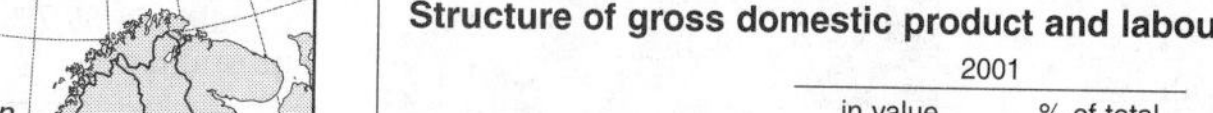

Structure of gross domestic product and labour force

	2001 in value Ls '000,000	2001 % of total value	2002 labour force	2002 % of labour force
Agriculture, forestry	174.3	3.7	153,000	13.6
Mining and quarrying	5.6	0.1	} 193,000	} 17.2
Manufacturing	624.9	13.2		
Public utilities	158.7	3.3		
Construction	259.7	5.5	60,000	5.3
Transp. and commun.	645.4	13.6	86,000	7.7
Trade, restaurants	845.2	17.8	172,000	15.3
Finance, real estate	674.5	14.2	52,000	4.6
Pub. admin., defense	271.1	5.7	68,000	6.1
Services	544.8	11.5	204,000	18.2
Other	536.6[3]	11.3[3]	135,000[4]	12.0[4]
TOTAL	4,740.8	100.0[5]	1,123,000	100.0

Population economically active (2002): total 1,123,000; activity rate of total population 48.1% (participation rates: ages 15–64 [2000] 67.5%; female [2000] 48.5%; unemployed 12.0%).

Price and earnings indexes (1995 = 100)

	1996	1997	1998	1999	2000	2001	2002
Consumer price index	117.6	127.5	133.5	136.6	140.3	143.7	146.5
Annual earnings index	114.9	139.7	148.8	154.7	159.7	167.5	178.0

Land use (1994): forested 44.4%; meadows and pastures 12.4; agricultural and under permanent cultivation 27.0%; other 16.2%.

Foreign trade[6]

Balance of trade (current prices)

	1997	1998	1999	2000	2001	2002
Ls '000,000	–610	–812	–716	–803	–945	–1,088
% of total	23.9%	27.5%	26.2%	26.2%	27.4%	27.9%

Imports (2002): Ls 2,497,000,000 (machinery and apparatus 21.3%, chemicals and chemical products 10.5%, transport vehicles 9.8%, mineral fuels 9.7%). *Major import sources:* Germany 17.2%; Lithuania 9.8%; Russia 8.8%; Finland 8.0%; Sweden 6.4%.
Exports (2002): Ls 1,409,000,000 (wood and wood products [mostly sawn wood] 33.6%, base and fabricated metals [mostly iron and steel] 13.2%, textiles and clothing 12.8%). *Major export destinations:* Germany 15.5%; U.K. 14.6%; Sweden 10.5%; Lithuania 8.4%; Estonia 6.0%.

Transport and communications

Transport. Railroads (2002): length 2,270 km; passenger-km (2000) 715,000,000; metric-km cargo 15,020,000,000. Roads (1999): total length 73,227 km (paved 39%). Vehicles (2002): passenger cars 552,200; trucks and buses 113,900. Air transport (1999): passenger-km 238,000,000; metric ton-km cargo 10,000,000; airports with scheduled flights (2001) 2.

Communications

Medium	date	unit	number	units per 1,000 persons
Daily newspapers	2000	circulation	586,000	247
Radio	2000	receivers	1,650,000	695
Television	2000	receivers	1,870,000	789
Telephones	2002	main lines	701,200	279
Cellular telephones	2002	subscribers	917,200	394
Personal computers	2002	units	400,000	171
Internet	2002	users	310,000	133

Education and health

Educational attainment (2000). Percentage of population age 15 and over having: some and complete primary education 8.5%; lower secondary 26.5%; upper secondary 51.1%; higher 13.9%. *Literacy* (2000): 99.8%.

Education (2000–01)

	schools	teachers	students	student/ teacher ratio
Primary } Secondary }	1,074	25,795	359,818	13.9
Vocational	...	5,439	48,625	8.9
Higher	33	4,486[7]	101,270	...

Health (2002): physicians 7,900 (1 per 295 persons); hospital beds 18,200 (1 per 128 persons); infant mortality rate per 1,000 live births (2002) 9.9.
Food (2001): daily per capita caloric intake 2,809 (vegetable products 72%, animal products 28%); 110% of FAO recommended minimum requirement.

Military

Total active duty personnel (2002): 5,500[8] (army 78.2%, navy 16.9%, air force 4.9%). *Military expenditure as percentage of GNP* (1999): 0.9% (world 2.4%); per capita expenditure U.S.$59.

[1]January 1. [2]Large volumes of Russian crude and refined petroleum are exported through Latvia. [3]Indirect taxes less subsidies. [4]Unemployed. [5]Detail does not add to total given because of rounding. [6]Imports c.i.f.; exports f.o.b. [7]1996–97. [8]Excludes 3,200 border guards classified as paramilitary.

Internet resources for further information:
- **Bank of Latvia http://www.bank.lv**
- **Central Statistical Bureau of Latvia http://www.csb.lv**

Lebanon

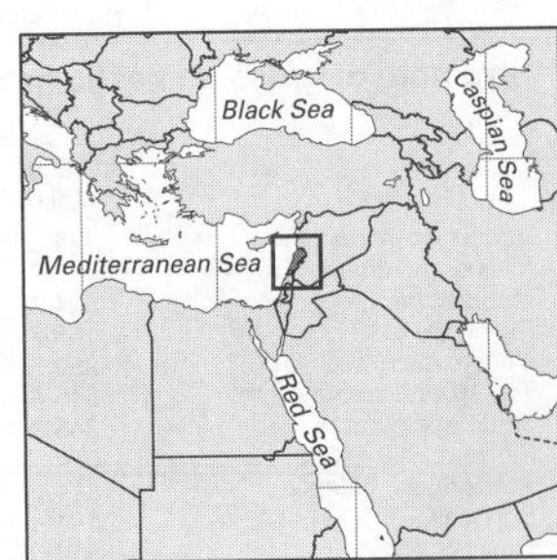

Official name: Al-Jumhūrīyah al-Lubnānīyah (Lebanese Republic).
Form of government: unitary multiparty republic with one legislative house (National Assembly [128])[1].
Chief of state: President.
Head of government: Prime Minister.
Capital: Beirut.
Official language: Arabic.
Official religion: none.
Monetary unit: 1 Lebanese pound (£L) = 100 piastres; valuation (Sept. 8, 2003) 1 U.S.$ = £L 1,514; 1 £ = £L 2,401.

Area and population

		area		population
Governorates	Capitals	sq mi	sq km	1996 estimate
Bayrūt	Beirut (Bayrūt)	7	18	407,403
Al-Biqāʿ	Zaḥlah	1,653	4,280	399,890
Jabal Lubnān	Bʿabdā	753	1,950	1,145,458
Al-Janūb	Sidon (Ṣaydā)	364	943	283,056
An-Nabaṭīyah	An-Nabaṭīyah	408	1,058	205,412
Ash-Shamāl	Tripoli (Ṭarābulus)	765	1,981	670,609
TOTAL		4,016[2]	10,400[2]	3,111,828

Demography

Population (2003): 3,728,000[3].
Density (2003): persons per sq mi 928.3, persons per sq km 358.5.
Urban-rural (2001): urban 90.1%; rural 9.9%.
Sex distribution (2002): male 48.48%; female 51.52%.
Age breakdown (2002): under 15, 27.4%; 15–29, 32.2%; 30–44, 21.0%; 45–59, 10.1%; 60–74, 7.1%; 75 and over, 2.2%.
Population projection: (2010) 4,056,000; (2020) 4,417,000.
Doubling time: 50 years.
Ethnic composition (2000): Arab 84.5%, of which Lebanese 71.2%, Palestinian 12.1%; Armenian 6.8%; Kurd 6.1%; other 2.6%.
Religious affiliation (1995): Muslim 55.3%, of which Shiʿi 34.0%, Sunnī 21.3%; Christian 37.6%, of which Catholic 25.1% (Maronite 19.0%, Greek Catholic or Melchite 4.6%), Orthodox 11.7% (Greek Orthodox 6.0%, Armenian Apostolic 5.2%), Protestant 0.5%; Druze 7.1%.
Major cities (1998): Beirut 1,100,000 (urban agglomeration 2,115,000[4]); Tripoli 200,000; Sidon 140,000; Tyre (Ṣūr) 110,000; An-Nabaṭīyah 84,000; Jūniyah 75,000.

Vital statistics

Birth rate per 1,000 population (2002): 20.0 (world avg. 21.3).
Death rate per 1,000 population (2002): 6.4 (world avg. 9.1).
Natural increase rate per 1,000 population (2002): 13.6 (world avg. 12.2).
Total fertility rate (avg. births per childbearing woman; 2002): 2.0.
Life expectancy at birth (2002): male 69.4 years; female 74.3 years.
Major causes of death: n.a.

National economy

Budget (2000). Revenue: £L 4,091,435,000,000 (1998; tax revenue 74.6%, of which customs revenues 44.1%, income tax 9.0%, taxes on goods and services 8.4%, property tax 8.4%, miscellaneous taxes and fees 2.1%; nontax revenue 25.4%). Expenditures: £L 8,190,034,000,000 (current expenditures 81.1%, of which debt service 40.0%, public services 13.3%, defense 9.7%, education 8.3%, social security 6.4%, health 2.6%; capital expenditures 18.9%).
Production (metric tons except as noted). Agriculture, forestry, fishing (2002): potatoes 257,000, tomatoes 247,000, cucumbers and gherkins 161,000, oranges 155,800, onions 144,200, wheat 139,500, grapes 116,200, apples 112,000, lemons and limes 103,100, olives 85,800; livestock (number of live animals) 385,000 goats, 350,000 sheep, 79,000 cattle, 33,000,000 chickens; roundwood (2001) 89,426 cu m; fish catch (2001) 3,970. Mining and quarrying (1996): lime 16,000; salt 4,000; gypsum 2,000. Manufacturing (2001): cement 2,727,000; flour 420,000; olive oil 7,000. Construction (2001): 6,923,000 sq m[5]. Energy production (consumption): electricity (kW-hr; 2001) 10,452,000,000 ([1999] 9,880,000,000); coal, n.a. (115,000); crude petroleum (barrels; 1998) none (1,358,000); petroleum products (metric tons; 2001) none (4,784,000).
Gross national product (2001): U.S.$17,600,000,000 (U.S.$4,010 per capita).

Structure of gross domestic product and labour force

	1995			
	in value U.S.$'000,000	% of total value	labour force	% of labour force
Agriculture	380	4.0	143,900	14.0
Mining	—	—		
Manufacturing	1,235	13.0	277,600	27.0
Construction	950	10.0		
Public utilities Transp. and commun.	2,375[6]	25.0[6]		
Trade	2,660	28.0	606,500	59.0
Finance Real estate and business services Services	1,900	20.0		
Pub. admin., defense	6	6		
TOTAL	9,500	100.0	1,028,000	100.0

Population economically active (1997): total 1,362,000; activity rate of total population 39.7% (participation rates: over age 15, n.a.; female, n.a.; unemployed 8.5%).

Price and earnings indexes (1995 = 100)

	1995	1996	1997	1998	1999
Consumer price index[7]	100.0	108.0	110.8	113.4	116.1
Wages index	...	...	...	...	...

Public debt (external, outstanding; 2001): U.S.$8,957,000,000.
Household income and expenditure. Average household size (2000) 4.5; average annual income per household (1994)[7] £L 2,400,000 (U.S.$1,430); sources of income: n.a.; expenditure: n.a.
Tourism (2001): receipts from visitors U.S.$837,000,000.
Land use (1994): forested 7.8%; meadows and pastures 1.0%; agricultural and under permanent cultivation 29.9%; wasteland and other areas 61.3%.

Foreign trade[8]

Balance of trade (current prices)

	1997	1998	1999	2000	2001	2002
U.S.$'000,000	–6,824	–6,408	–5,530	–5,514	–6,423	–5,399
% of total	84.1%	82.9%	80.3%	79.4%	78.7%	72.1%

Imports (2002): U.S.$6,445,000,000 (mineral products 15.1%, machinery and apparatus 13.4%, food and live animals 13.3%, chemicals and chemical products 9.8%). *Major import sources:* Italy 10.8%; Germany 9.0%; France 8.0%; U.S. 7.2%; China 6.7%.
Exports (2002): U.S.$1,046,000,000 (precious metal [significantly gold] jewelry 20.5%, machinery and apparatus 11.4%, chemicals and chemical products 10.3%, food and beverages 9.8%, paper and paper products 9.4%). *Major export destinations:* Switzerland 12.6%; Saudi Arabia 9.2%; U.A.E. 9.1%; Syria 7.2%; Iraq 6.8%.

Transport and communications

Transport. Railroads: [9]. Roads (1996): total length 6,350 km (paved 95%). Vehicles (1997): passenger cars 1,299,398; trucks and buses 85,242. Merchant marine (1992): vessels (100 gross tons and over) 163; total deadweight tonnage 438,165. Air transport (2001)[10]: passenger-km 1,661,000,000; metric ton-km cargo 216,700,000; airports (1999) 1.

Communications

Medium	date	unit	number	units per 1,000 persons
Daily newspapers	2000	circulation	383,000	107
Radio	2000	receivers	2,460,000	687
Television	2000	receivers	1,200,000	335
Telephones	2002	main lines	678,800	198
Cellular telephones	2002	subscribers	775,100	227
Personal computers	2002	units	275,000	81
Internet	2002	users	400,000	117

Education and health

Educational attainment: n.a. *Literacy* (2000): total population age 15 and over literate 87.4%; males literate 93.1%; females literate 82.2%.

Education (1996–97)

	schools	teachers	students	student/teacher ratio
Primary (age 5–9)	2,160	...	382,309	...
Secondary (age 10–16)	...	...	292,002	...
Voc., teacher tr.	275[11]	7,745	55,848	7.2
Higher	20	10,444[12]	81,588[12]	7.8[12]

Health (1997): physicians 7,203 (1 per 476 persons); hospital beds (1995) 11,596 (1 per 319 persons); infant mortality rate per 1,000 live births (2002) 27.4.
Food (2001): daily per capita caloric intake 3,184 (vegetable products 85%, animal products 15%); 128% of FAO recommended minimum.

Military

Total active duty personnel (2002): Lebanese national armed forces 71,830 (army 97.5%, navy 1.1%, air force 1.4%). External regular military forces include: UN peacekeeping force in Lebanon (July 2002) 3,400; Syrian army 18,000. *Military expenditure as percentage of GNP* (1999): 4.0% (world 2.4%); per capita expenditure: U.S.$185.

[1]The current legislature was elected between August and September 2000; one-half of its membership is Christian and one-half Muslim/Druze. [2]Includes water area of 66 sq mi (170 sq km) not distributed by governorate. [3]Excludes about 400,000 Palestinian refugees. [4]2001. [5]Permits authorized. [6]Public utilities and Transportation and communications includes Public administration, defense. [7]ESCWA estimate for Beirut only. [8]Imports are c.i.f. [9]Apart from a 14-mi (23-km) section delivering oil from the Zahrani refinery to a thermal power station serving Beirut, no passenger or general cargo track was in use in 2001. [10]For Middle East Airlines and Trans-Mediterranean Airways. [11]1994–95. [12]1995–96.

Internet resources for further information:
- **Central Administration for Statistics http://www.cas.gov.lb**
- **Central Bank of Lebanon http://www.bdl.gov.lb**

Lesotho

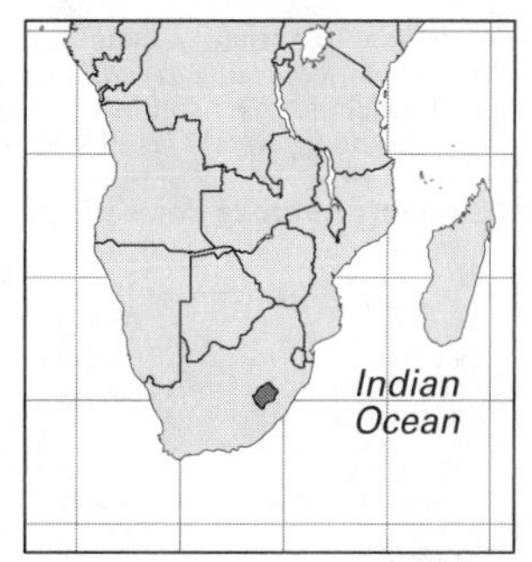

Official name: Lesotho (Sotho); Kingdom of Lesotho (English).
Form of government: constitutional monarchy with 2 legislative houses (Senate [33[1]]; National Assembly [120]).
Chief of state: King.
Head of government: Prime Minister.
Capital: Maseru.
Official languages: Sotho; English.
Official religion: Christianity.
Monetary unit: 1 loti (plural maloti [M]) = 100 lisente; valuation (Sept. 8, 2003) 1 U.S.$ = M 7.42; 1 £ = M 11.77.

Area and population

Districts	Capitals	area sq mi	area sq km	population 2002 census[2]
Berea	Teyateyaneng	858	2,222	300,557
Butha-Buthe	Butha-Buthe	682	1,767	126,907
Leribe	Hlotse	1,092	2,828	362,339
Mafeteng	Mafeteng	818	2,119	238,946
Maseru	Maseru	1,652	4,279	477,599
Mohale's Hoek	Mohale's Hoek	1,363	3,530	206,842
Mokhotlong	Mokhotlong	1,573	4,075	89,705
Qacha's Nek	Qacha's Nek	907	2,349	80,323
Quthing	Quthing	1,126	2,916	140,641
Thaba-Tseka	Thaba-Tseka	1,649	4,270	133,680
TOTAL		11,720	30,355	2,157,539

Demography

Population (2003): 1,802,000[3].
Density (2002): persons per sq mi 153.8, persons per sq km 59.4.
Urban-rural (2001)[2]: urban 13.4%; rural 86.6%.
Sex distribution (2001)[2]: male 50.62%; female 49.38%.
Age breakdown (2001)[2]: under 15, 35.3%; 15–29, 31.4%; 30–44, 14.8%; 45–59, 10.0%; 60–74, 5.9%; 75 and over, 2.6%.
Population projection[3]: (2010) 1,757,000; (2020) 1,663,000.
Doubling time: 50 years.
Ethnic composition (2000): Sotho 80.3%; Zulu 14.4%; other 5.3%.
Religious affiliation (2000): Christian 91.0%, of which Roman Catholic 37.5%, Protestant (mostly Presbyterian) 13.0%, African Christian 11.8%; other (mostly traditional beliefs) 9.0%.
Major urban centres (1996): Maseru 137,837 (urban agglomeration [2001] 271,000); Teyateyaneng 48,869; Maputsoe 27,951; Hlotse 23,122; Mafeteng 20,804.

Vital statistics

Birth rate per 1,000 population (2002): 30.7 (world avg. 21.3).
Death rate per 1,000 population (2002): 16.8 (world avg. 9.1).
Natural increase rate per 1,000 population (2002): 13.9 (world avg. 12.2).
Total fertility rate (avg. births per childbearing woman; 2002): 4.0.
Life expectancy at birth (2002): male 46.3 years; female 47.8 years.
Major causes of death per 100,000 population: n.a.; 31% of total population was HIV positive in 2002.

National economy

Budget (2000–01). Revenue: M 2,752,200,000 (customs receipts 40.9%, grants and nontax revenue 29.4%, income tax 11.4%, sales tax 10.2%). Expenditures: M 2,897,900,000 (personal emoluments 31.8%, capital expenditure 17.8%, subsidies and transfers 9.6%, interest payments 9.0%).
Public debt (external, outstanding; 2001): U.S.$573,300,000.
Production (metric tons except as noted). Agriculture, forestry, fishing (2002): corn (maize) 300,000, potatoes 90,000, wheat 51,000, sorghum 46,000, vegetables 18,000, fruit 13,000, dry beans 8,000; livestock (number of live animals) 850,000 sheep, 650,000 goats, 540,000 cattle, 154,000 asses, 100,000 horses; roundwood (2001) 2,028,134 cu m; fish catch (2001) 32. Mining and quarrying (2001): diamonds 1,140 carats. Manufacturing (value added in U.S.$'000,000; 1995): food products 58; beverages 38; textiles 14; chemical products 9; metal products 4; wearing apparel 4. Energy production (consumption): electricity, data for Lesotho included with South Africa; coal, none (none); petroleum, none (n.a.); natural gas, none (none).
Tourism (2001): receipts from visitors U.S.$23,000,000; expenditures by nationals abroad U.S.$9,000,000.
Population economically active (1993): total 617,871; activity rate of total population 45.1% (participation rates: ages 15–64 [1986] 79.8%; female 23.7%; unemployed [2001] *c.* 40%).

Price and earnings indexes (July 1996 = 100)

	1996	1997	1998	1999	2000	2001	2002
Consumer price index[4]	100	110	119	133	143	155	174
Annual earnings index	...	...	...	...	...	...	...

Household income and expenditure. Average household size (2000) 5.0; average annual income per household: n.a.; sources of income: n.a.; expenditure (1989): food 48.0%, clothing 16.4%, household durable goods 11.9%, housing and energy 10.1%, transportation 4.7%.
Gross national product (at current market prices; 2001): U.S.$1,100,000,000 (U.S.$530 per capita).

Structure of gross domestic product and labour force

	2002 in value M '000,000	2002 % of total value	2001 labour force	2001 % of labour force
Agriculture	1,178.1	15.7	329,000	37.6
Mining	10.0	0.1	545,000[5]	62.4
Manufacturing	1,353.0	18.0		
Construction	1,220.4	16.2		
Public utilities	348.9	4.6		
Transp. and commun.	256.8	3.4		
Trade	738.8	9.8		
Finance	1,033.8	13.7		
Pub. admin., defense	511.7	6.8		
Services	772.7	10.3		
Other	106.4[6]	1.4[6]		
TOTAL	7,530.6	100.0	874,000	100.0

Land use (1998): meadows and pastures 65.9%; agricultural and under permanent cultivation 10.7%; other 23.4%.

Foreign trade[7]

Balance of trade (current prices)

	1996	1997	1998	1999	2000	2001
M '000,000	–3,491	–3,818	–3,590	–3,707	–3,582	–3,398
% of total	68.3%	67.9%	61.8%	63.7%	55.0%	41.2%

Imports (2001): M 5,824,000,000 (1999; food products 15.3%, unspecified commodities 84.7%). *Major import sources* (2001): Customs Union of Southern Africa (mostly South Africa) 82.8%; Asian countries 14.9%.
Exports (2001): M 2,426,000,000 (manufactured goods [mostly clothing] 74.7%, machinery and transport equipment 10.5%, beverages 3.6%, wool 2.5%). *Major export destinations:* North America (mostly the United States) 62.8%; Customs Union of Southern Africa (mostly South Africa) 37.0%.

Transport and communications

Transport. Railroads (2001): length 1.6 mi, 2.6 km. Roads (1999): total length 3,691 mi, 5,940 km (paved 18%). Vehicles (1996): passenger cars 12,610; trucks and buses 25,000. Air transport (1999): passenger-km, negligible (less than 500,000); metric ton-km cargo, negligible; airports (1997) with scheduled flights 1.

Communications

Medium	date	unit	number	units per 1,000 persons
Daily newspapers	2000	circulation	14,300	8
Radio	2000	receivers	94,600	53
Television	2000	receivers	28,600	16
Telephones	2002	main lines	34,000	16
Cellular telephones	2002	subscribers	92,000	43
Personal computers	...	units	...	...
Internet	2001	users	5,000	2.3

Education and health

Educational attainment (1986–87). Percentage of population age 10 and over having: no formal education 22.9%; primary 52.8%; secondary 23.2%; higher 0.6%. *Literacy* (1995): total population age 15 and over literate 849,700 (71.3%); males literate 468,000 (81.1%); females literate 381,700 (62.3%).

Education (2002)

	schools	teachers	students	student/ teacher ratio
Primary (age 6–12)	1,333	8,908	418,668	47.0
Secondary (age 13–17)	224	3,384	81,130	24.0
Vocational	8	172	1,859	10.8
Higher	1	436[8]	6,273	8.0

Health: physicians (1995) 105 (1 per 18,527 persons); hospital beds (1992) 2,400 (1 per 765 persons); infant mortality rate per 1,000 live births (2002) 82.6.
Food (2001): daily per capita caloric intake 2,320 (vegetable products 97%, animal products 3%); 102% of FAO recommended minimum requirement.

Military

Total active duty personnel (2002): 2,000[9]. *Military expenditure as percentage of GNP* (1999): 2.6% (world 2.4%); per capita expenditure U.S.$14.

[1]All seats are nonelective. [2]De jure figure including absentee miners working in South Africa. [3]De facto figure(s). [4]As of June. [5]Includes 61,400 mine workers in South Africa. [6]Indirect taxes less imputed bank service charges. [7]Import figures are f.o.b. in balance of trade and c.i.f. in commodities and trading partners. [8]1998. [9]Royal Lesotho Defence Force.

Internet resources for further information:
- **Central Bank of Lesotho http://www.centralbank.org.ls**
- **Bureau of Statistics http://www.bos.gov.ls**

Liberia

Official name: Republic of Liberia.
Form of government: transitional regime[1].
Head of state and government: Chairman[1].
Capital: Monrovia.
Official language: English.
Official religion: none.
Monetary unit: 1 Liberian dollar (L$) = 100 cents; valuation (Sept. 30, 2003) 1 U.S.$ = L$49.00; 1 £ = L$81.69.

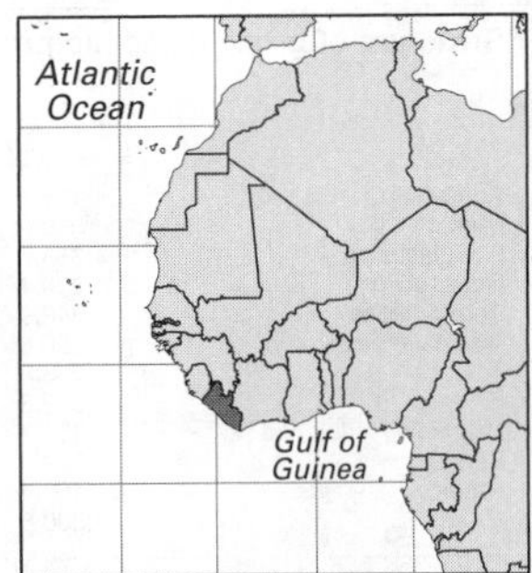

Area and population

Counties	Capitals	area sq mi	area sq km	population 1999 estimate
Bomi	Tubmanburg	755	1,955	114,316
Bong	Gbarnga	3,127	8,099	299,825
Gbarpolu	Bopulu	2,982	7,723	[2]
Grand Bassa	Buchanan	3,382	8,759	215,338
Grand Cape Mount	Robertsport	2,250	5,827	120,141
Grand Gedeh	Zwedru	6,575[3]	17,029[3]	94,497[3]
Grand Kru	Barclayville	[4]	[4]	39,062
Lofa	Voinjama	4,493	11,367	351,492[2]
Margibi	Kakata	1,260	3,263	219,417
Maryland	Harper	2,066[4]	5,351[4]	71,977
Montserrado	Bensonville	1,058	2,740	843,783
Nimba	Sanniquellie	4,650	12,043	338,887
River Gee	Fish Town	[3]	[3]	[3]
Rivercess	Rivercess City	1,693	4,385	38,167
Sinoe	Greenville	3,959	10,254	79,241
TOTAL		38,250[5]	99,067[5, 6]	2,826,143

Demography

Population (2003): 3,317,000.
Density (2003)[5]: persons per sq mi 87.9, persons per sq km 33.9.
Urban-rural (2001): urban 45.5%; rural 54.5%.
Sex distribution (2002): male 49.47%; female 50.53%.
Age breakdown (2001): under 15, 43.2%; 15–29, 27.0%; 30–44, 15.1%; 45–59, 9.4%; 60–74, 4.2%; 75 and over, 1.1%.
Population projection: (2010) 3,935,000; (2020) 4,900,000.
Doubling time: 25 years.
Ethnic composition (2000): Kpelle 18.9%; Bassa 13.1%; Grebo 10.3%; Gio (Dan) 7.4%; Kru 6.9%; Mano 6.1%; Loma 5.3%; Kissi 3.8%; Krahn 3.7%; Americo-Liberians 2.4%[7]; other 22.1%.
Religious affiliation (1995): traditional beliefs 63.0%; Christian 21.0%, of which Protestant 13.5%, African Christian 5.1%, Roman Catholic 2.4%; Muslim 16.0%.
Major cities (2002): Monrovia 543,000; Zwedru 33,800; Buchanan 27,000; Yekepa 22,500; Harper 19,600.

Vital statistics

Birth rate per 1,000 population (2002): 45.8 (world avg. 21.3).
Death rate per 1,000 population (2002): 17.9 (world avg. 9.1).
Natural increase rate per 1,000 population (2002): 27.9 (world avg. 12.2).
Total fertility rate (avg. births per childbearing woman; 2002): 6.3.
Marriage rate per 1,000 population: n.a.
Divorce rate per 1,000 population: n.a.
Life expectancy at birth (2002): male 47.2 years; female 49.6 years.
Major causes of death per 100,000 population: n.a.; however, violence and acts of war were major causes of both morbidity and mortality from 1990 onward.

National economy

Budget (2002). Revenue: U.S.$72,700,000 (tax revenue 96.7%, of which import duties 23.1%, income and profit taxes 19.8%, maritime revenue 18.4%, stamps and land rental 17.9%, petroleum sales tax 8.3%; nontax revenue 3.3%). Expenditures: U.S.$80,100,000 (development expenditures [including national security] 67.5%; current expenditures 32.5%, of which wages 16.7%, interest on debt 7.9%, goods and services 7.4%).
Population economically active (1997): total 1,183,000; activity rate 51.4% (participation rates: ages 10–64 [1994] 64.0%; female 39.5%; unemployed [1996] 95%).

Price and earnings indexes (1998 = 100)

	1998	1999	2000	2001	2002
Consumer price index	100.0	105.6	111.1	124.6	142.3
Earnings index	...	...	...	...	...

Production (metric tons except as noted). Agriculture, forestry, fishing (2002): cassava 445,100, natural rubber 219,800, rice 187,000, oil palm fruit 174,000, bananas 110,000, plantains 39,500, yams 20,000, cacao beans 626, coffee 439; livestock (number of live animals) 220,000 goats, 210,000 sheep, 130,000 pigs, 5,000,000 chickens; roundwood (2001) 5,261,930 cu m; fish catch (2001) 11,300. Mining and quarrying (2001): diamonds 170,000 carats; gold 1,000 kg. Manufacturing (2000): palm oil 42,000; cement 15,000; cigarettes 22,000,000 units[8]. International maritime licensing (fees earned; 2002): more than U.S.$13,000,000. Energy production (consumption): electricity (kW-hr; 1999) 519,000,000 (519,000,000); coal, none (none); crude petroleum, none (none); petroleum products (metric tons; 1999) none (128,000); natural gas, none (none).

Public debt (external, outstanding; 2001): U.S.$1,012,000,000.
Household income and expenditure. Average household size (1983) 4.3; income per household: n.a.; sources of income: n.a.; expenditure: n.a.
Gross national product (2001): U.S.$500,000,000 (U.S.$140 per capita).

Structure of gross domestic product and labour force

	2002		2000	
	in value U.S.$'000,000[9]	% of total value	labour force	% of labour force
Agriculture	420.4	78.5	829,000	67.0
Mining / Manufacturing	23.5	4.4	408,000	33.0
Construction	7.6	1.4		
Public utilities	2.6	0.5		
Transp. and commun.	26.0	4.9		
Trade	18.7	3.5		
Finance	12.8	2.3		
Pub. admin., defense	11.3	2.1		
Services	12.6	2.4		
Other	...	...	...	...
TOTAL	535.5	100.0	1,237,000	100.0

Land use (1994): forested 47.8%; meadows and pastures 20.8%; agricultural and under permanent cultivation 3.8%; other 27.6%.

Foreign trade

Balance of trade (current prices)

	1997	1998	1999	2000	2001
U.S.$'000,000	–217.9	–118.5	–150.7	–64.9	–69.0
% of total	81.1%	58.1%	56.1%	21.2%	21.2%

Imports (2001): U.S.$196,900,000 (food and live animals 31.1%, of which rice 14.0%; petroleum and petroleum products 20.7%; machinery and transport equipment 18.0%). *Major import sources* (1999): South Korea *c.* 27%; Japan *c.* 25%; Germany *c.* 14%; Singapore *c.* 7%; Croatia *c.* 5%.
Exports (2001): U.S.$127,900,000 (logs and timber 54.1%, rubber 42.2%). *Major export destinations* (2001): Norway *c.* 24%; Germany *c.* 11%; United States *c.* 9%; France *c.* 8%; Singapore *c.* 7%.

Transport and communications

Transport. Railroads (2001): route length 304 mi, 490 km; (1998) short ton-mi cargo 534,000,000, metric ton-km cargo 860,000,000. Roads (1999): total length 6,600 mi, 10,600 km (paved 6%). Vehicles (1996): passenger cars 9,400; trucks and buses 25,000. Air transport (1992): passenger-mi 4,300,000, passenger-km 7,000,000; short ton-mi cargo 621,000, metric ton-km cargo 1,000,000; airports (2000) with scheduled flights 2.

Communications

Medium	date	unit	number	units per 1,000 persons
Daily newspapers	2000	circulation	37,800	12
Radio	2000	receivers	863,000	274
Television	2000	receivers	78,700	25
Telephones	1999	main lines	6,600	2.2

Education and health

Educational attainment, n.a. *Literacy* (2000): total population age 15 and over literate 54.0%.

Education (1998)

	schools	teachers	students	student/ teacher ratio
Primary (age 6–12)	...	10,047	395,611	39.4
Secondary (age 13–18)	...	6,621	113,878	17.2
Higher	...	633	20,804	32.9

Health: physicians (1992) 257 (1 per 8,333 persons); hospital beds, n.a.; infant mortality rate (2002) 133.8.
Food (2001): daily per capita caloric intake 1,946 (vegetable products 97%, animal products 3%); 84% of FAO recommended minimum requirement.

Military

Total active duty personnel: UN peacekeeping troops (November 2003) 4,000 (authorized number is 15,000); the disarming of 60,000 marauding bands of fighters to begin in earnest in early 2004. *Military expenditure as percentage of GNP* (1999): 1.2% (world 2.4%); per capita expenditure U.S.$2.

[1]Transitional government established in October 2003 was expected to be in place for two years. [2]Gbarpolu (created late 2000) included with Lofa. [3]River Gee (created mid-2000) included with Grand Gedeh. [4]Grand Kru included with Maryland. [5]Total area per more recent survey is 37,743 sq mi (97,754 sq km). [6]Detail does not add to total given because of rounding. [7]Descendants of freed U.S. slaves. [8]1992. [9]At constant prices of 1992.

Libya

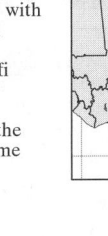

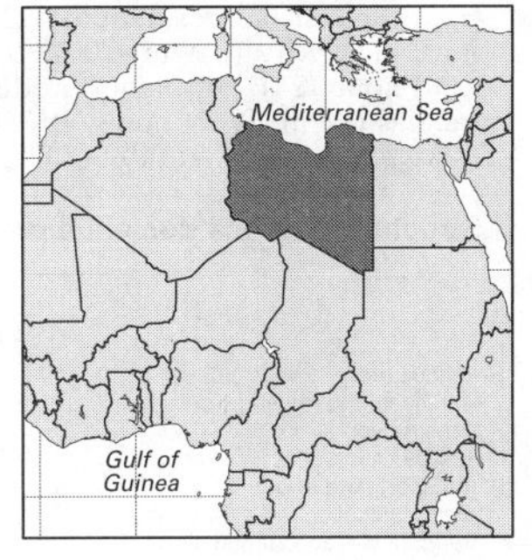

Official name: Al-Jamāhīrīyah al-ʿArabīyah al-Lībīyah ash-Shaʿbīyah al-Ishtirākīyah al-ʿUẓmā (Socialist People's Libyan Arab Jamahiriya).
Form of government: socialist state with one policy-making body (General People's Congress [760]).
Chief of state: Muammar al-Qaddafi (de facto)[1]; Secretary of General People's Congress (de jure).
Head of government: Secretary of the General People's Committee (prime minister).
Capital: Tripoli[2].
Official language: Arabic.
Official religion: Islam.
Monetary unit: 1 Libyan dinar (LD) = 1,000 dirhams; valuation (Sept. 8, 2003) 1 U.S.$ = LD 1.41; 1 £ = LD 2.23.

Area and population

Administrative regions[3]	Capitals	area sq mi	area sq km	population 1995 census[4]
Banghāzī	Banghāzī	...	...	665,615
Al-Bāṭin	...	...	...	151,240
Fazzān	...	...	...	314,029
Al-Jabal al-Akhḍar	Al-Bayḍā'	...	...	381,165
Al-Jabal al-Gharbī	Gharyān	...	...	316,970
Al-Jufrah	...	...	...	39,335
Miṣrātah (Misurata)	...	...	...	488,573
Najghaza	...	...	...	244,553
Sofuljin	...	...	...	76,401
Ṭarābulus	Tripoli (Ṭarābulus)	...	...	1,313,996
Al-Wāḥah	...	...	...	62,056
Al-Wasṭa	...	...	...	240,574
Az-Zāwiyah	Az-Zāwiyah	...	...	517,395
TOTAL		679,362	1,759,540	4,811,902

Demography

Population (2003): 5,551,000.
Density (2003): persons per sq mi 8.2, persons per sq km 3.2.
Urban-rural (2001): urban 88.0%; rural 12.0%.
Sex distribution (2001): male 51.41%; female 48.59%.
Age breakdown (2001): under 15, 35.4%; 15–29, 31.7%; 30–44, 19.1%; 45–59, 8.0%; 60–74, 4.5%; 75 and over, 1.3%.
Population projection: (2010) 6,332,000; (2020) 7,378,000.
Doubling time: 29 years.
Ethnic composition (2000): Arab 87.1%, of which Libyan 57.2%, Bedouin 13.8%, Egyptian 7.7%, Sudanese 3.5%, Tunisian 2.9%; Berber 6.8%, of which Arabized 4.2%; other 6.1%.
Religious affiliation (1995): Sunnī Muslim 96.1%; other 3.9%.
Major cities (1995): Tripoli 1,140,000 (urban agglomeration [2001] 1,776,000); Banghāzī 650,000 (urban agglomeration [2000] 829,000); Miṣrātah 280,000; Surt 150,000.

Vital statistics

Birth rate per 1,000 population (2002): 27.6 (world avg. 21.3).
Death rate per 1,000 population (2002): 3.5 (world avg. 9.1).
Natural increase rate per 1,000 population (2002): 24.1 (world avg. 12.2).
Total fertility rate (avg. births per childbearing woman; 2002): 3.6.
Marriage rate per 1,000 population: n.a.
Divorce rate per 1,000 population: n.a.
Life expectancy at birth (2002): male 73.7 years; female 78.1 years.
Major causes of death per 100,000 population: n.a.; however, the main causes of hospital mortality in 1987 were injuries and poisoning 15.5%, diseases of the circulatory system 11.6%, conditions originating in the perinatal period 11.4%, diseases of the respiratory system 7.0%, neoplasms (cancers) 4.4%.

National economy

Budget (2001). Revenue: LD 5,998,800,000 (oil revenues 60.1%, other 39.9%). Expenditures: LD 5,625,600,000 (current expenditures 63.9%, development expenditures 27.3%, extraordinary expenditures 8.8%).
Production (metric tons except as noted). Agriculture, forestry, fishing (2002): watermelons 218,000, potatoes 195,000, dry onions 182,000, olives 170,000, tomatoes 160,000, dates 133,500, wheat 130,000, barley 80,000; livestock (number of live animals; 2001) 4,130,000 sheep, 1,265,000 goats, 220,000 cattle, 72,000 camels, 25,000,000 chickens; roundwood (2001) 652,000 cu m; fish catch (2000) 33,487. Mining and quarrying (2001): lime 250,000; gypsum 150,000; salt 40,000. Manufacturing (value of production in LD '000,000; 1996): base metals 212, electrical equipment 208, petrochemicals 175, food products 79, cement and other building materials 68. Energy production (consumption): electricity (kW-hr; 2001) 20,180,000,000 (18,770,000,000); coal (metric tons; 1999) none (5,000); crude petroleum (barrels; 2002) 482,000,000 ([1999] 120,500,000); petroleum products (metric tons; 2001) 15,070,700 (6,629,200); natural gas (cu m; 2001) 6,174,000,000 (4,265,100,000).
Land use (1994): forested 0.5%; meadows and pastures 7.6%; agricultural and under permanent cultivation 1.2%; desert and built-up areas 90.7%.
Population economically active (1996): total 1,224,000; activity rate of total population 26.1% (participation rates [1993]: ages 10 and over, 35.2%; female 9.8%; unemployed [2000] 30.0%).

Price index (1995 = 100)

	1991	1992	1993	1994	1995	1996	1997
Cost of living index[5]	64.7	70.7	78.5	90.1	100.0	113.2	129.1

Public debt (2001): U.S.$2,359,000,000.
Gross domestic product (2000): U.S.$38,000,000,000 (U.S.$6,200 per capita).

Structure of gross domestic product and labour force

	2001 in value LD '000,000[6]	2001 % of total value	1996 labour force	1996 % of labour force
Agriculture	1,512.5	8.6	219,500	17.9
Oil and natural gas	6,009.0	34.1	31,000	2.5
Other mining	340.0	1.9		
Manufacturing	1,040.0	5.9	128,500	10.5
Construction	1,185.0	6.7	171,000	14.0
Public utilities	309.5	1.8	35,500	2.9
Transp. and commun.	1,315.5	7.5	104,000	8.5
Trade	1,803.5	10.3	73,000	6.0
Finance, insurance	881.0	5.0	22,000	1.8
Pub. admin., defense Services	3,208.5	18.2	439,500	35.9
TOTAL	17,604.5	100.0	1,224,000	100.0

Household income and expenditure. Average household size (2000) 6.3; income per household: n.a.; sources of income: n.a.; expenditure: n.a.
Tourism (2000): receipts U.S.$114,000,000; expenditures U.S.$17,000,000.

Foreign trade

Balance of trade (current prices)

	1997	1998	1999	2000	2001[7]	2002[7]
U.S.$'000,000	+2,716	+471	+2,974	...	+2,950	+3,100
% of total	15.9%	3.9%	25.7%	...	14%	24%

Imports (2001): U.S.$8,700,000,000 (1997; machinery 25.9%, food products 20.0%, road vehicles 10.1%, chemical products 7.5%). *Major import sources* (2001): Italy 28.5%; Germany 12.1%; U.K. 6.6%; Tunisia 6.0%; France 5.9%.
Exports (2001): U.S.$7,500,000,000 (crude petroleum *c.* 85%, refined petroleum *c.* 11%, natural gas *c.* 2%). *Major export destinations:* Italy 39.8%; Germany 15.6%; Spain 14.1%; Turkey 6.4%; France 5.5%.

Transport and communications

Transport. Railroads: none. Roads (1999): total length 83,200 km (paved 57%). Vehicles (1996): passenger cars 809,514; trucks and buses 357,528. Air transport (2001): passenger-km 410,000,000; metric ton-km cargo 259,000; airports with scheduled flights: n.a.

Communications

Medium	date	unit	number	units per 1,000 persons
Daily newspapers	2000	circulation	78,600	14
Radio	2000	receivers	1,430,000	259
Television	2000	receivers	717,000	133
Telephones	2001	main lines	610,000	115
Cellular telephones	2001	subscribers	50,000	9.0
Internet	2001	users	20,000	3.6

Education and health

Educational attainment (1984). Percentage of population age 25 and over having: no formal schooling (illiterate) 59.7%; incomplete primary education 15.4%; complete primary 8.5%; some secondary 5.2%; secondary 8.5%; higher 2.7%. *Literacy* (1998): percentage of total population age 15 and over literate 78.1%; males literate 89.6%; females literate 65.4%.

Education (1995–96)

	schools	teachers	students	student/ teacher ratio
Primary (age 6–12)	2,733[8]	122,020	1,333,679	10.9
Secondary (age 13–18)	...	17,668	189,202[9]	...
Voc., teacher tr.	480	...	147,689[10]	...
Higher	13	...	126,348	...

Health: physicians (1997) 6,092 (1 per 781 persons); hospital beds (1998) 18,100[11] (1 per 312 persons); infant mortality rate (2002) 27.9.
Food (2001): daily per capita caloric intake 3,333 (vegetable products 89%, animal products 11%); 141% of FAO recommended minimum requirement.

Military

Total active duty personnel (2002): 76,000 (army 59.2%, navy 10.5%, air force 30.3%). *Military expenditure as percentage of GNP* (1995): 6.1% (world 2.4%); per capita expenditure U.S.$342.

[1]No formal titled office exists. [2]Policy-making body (General People's Congress) may meet in Surt or Tripoli. [3]Libya is divided into 25 administrative entities as of 1998. [4]Preliminary. [5]Tripoli only. [6]At factor cost. [7]Estimated figures. [8]1994–95. [9]1992–93. [10]1993–94. [11]Includes beds in clinics.

Internet resources for further information:
- **Central Bank of Libya**
  http://www.cbl-ly.com/eng/about.html

Liechtenstein

Official name: Fürstentum Liechtenstein (Principality of Liechtenstein).
Form of government: constitutional monarchy with one legislative house (Diet [25]).
Chief of state: Prince[1].
Head of government: Prime Minister.
Capital: Vaduz.
Official language: German.
Official religion: none.
Monetary unit: 1 Swiss franc (Sw F) = 100 centimes; valuation (Sept. 8, 2003) 1 U.S.$ = Sw F 1.39; 1 £ = Sw F 2.21.

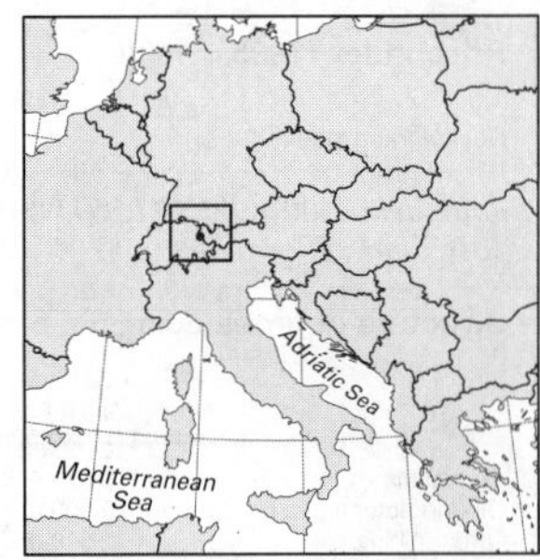

Area and population

Regions / Communes	area sq mi	area sq km	population 2002[2] estimate
Oberland (Upland)	48.3	125.2	22,266
Balzers	7.6	19.6	4,299
Planken	2.0	5.3	357
Schaan	10.3	26.8	5,556
Triesen	10.2	26.4	4,509
Triesenberg	11.5	29.8	2,596
Vaduz	6.7	17.3	4,949
Unterland (Lowland)	13.4[3]	34.8	11,259
Eschen	4.0	10.3	3,863
Gamprin	2.4	6.1	1,207
Mauren	2.9	7.5	3,457
Ruggell	2.9	7.4	1,754
Schellenberg	1.4	3.5	978
TOTAL	61.8[3]	160.0	33,525

Demography

Population (2003): 34,100.
Density (2003): persons per sq mi 550.0, persons per sq km 213.1.
Urban-rural (2001): urban 21.2%; rural 78.8%.
Sex distribution (2001): male 48.72%; female 51.28%.
Age breakdown (2001): under 15, 18.5%; 15–29, 22.4%; 30–44, 25.4%; 45–59, 19.4%; 60–74, 9.8%; 75 and over, 4.5%.
Population projection: (2010) 36,000; (2020) 38,000.
Ethnic composition (2001): Liechtensteiner 65.7%; Swiss 11.2%; Austrian 6.0%; German 3.4%; Italian 3.3%; other 10.4%.
Religious affiliation (1998): Roman Catholic 80.0%; Protestant 7.5%; Muslim 3.3%; Eastern Orthodox 0.7%; atheist 0.6%; other 7.9%.
Major cities (2002): Schaan 5,556; Vaduz 4,949.

Vital statistics

Birth rate per 1,000 population (2002): 11.2 (world avg. 21.3); (1997) legitimate 86.0%; illegitimate 14.0%.
Death rate per 1,000 population (2002): 6.8 (world avg. 9.1).
Natural increase rate per 1,000 population (2002): 4.4 (world avg. 12.2).
Total fertility rate (avg. births per childbearing woman; 2002): 1.5.
Marriage rate per 1,000 population (1998): 13.2.
Divorce rate per 1,000 population (1994): 1.4.
Life expectancy at birth (2002): male 75.4 years; female 82.7 years.
Major causes of death per 100,000 population (1998): diseases of the circulatory system 284.2; malignant neoplasms (cancers) 128.0; old age 49.9; diseases of the respiratory system 31.2; accidents, poisonings, and acts of violence 28.1; diseases of the digestive tract 24.9.

National economy

Budget (2001). Revenue: Sw F 804,100,000 (taxes and duties 85.8%, investment income 5.5%, charges and fees 5.0%, real estate capital-gains taxes and death and estate taxes 3.7%). Expenditures: Sw F 751,400,000 (financial affairs 34.8%, social welfare 19.5%, education 14.1%, general administration 10.2%, public safety 5.5%, transportation 4.8%).
Public debt: none.
Tourism (2001): 123,273 tourist overnight stays; receipts from visitors, n.a.; expenditures by nationals abroad, n.a.
Population economically active (2002[2]): total 17,011; activity rate of total population 50.7% (participation rates: ages 15–64, 71.4%; female 40.4%; unemployed 2.1%).

Price and earnings indexes (1995 = 100)

	1995	1996	1997	1998	1999	2000	2001
Consumer price index	100.0	100.8	101.3	101.3	102.2	103.8	105.0
Earnings index	...	...	...	...	...	...	...

Household income and expenditure. Average household size (1990) 2.7; income per household: n.a.; sources of income: n.a.; expenditure: n.a.
Production (metric tons except as noted). Agriculture, forestry, fishing (2002): significantly market gardening, other crops include cereals and apples; livestock (number of live animals) 6,000 cattle, 3,000 pigs, 2,900 sheep; commercial timber (1999) 22,000 cu m; fish catch, n.a. Mining and quarrying: n.a. Manufacturing (2000): small-scale precision manufacturing includes optical lenses, electron microscopes, electronic equipment, and high-vacuum pumps; metal manufacturing, construction machinery, and ceramics are important; dairy products and wine are also produced. Construction (2000): residential 273,935 cu m; nonresidential 592,737 cu m. Energy production (consumption): electricity (kW-hr; 2001) 93,282,000 (313,450,000); coal (metric tons; 2000) none (24); petroleum products (metric tons; 2000) none (47,100); natural gas (cu m; 1994) none (19,350,000).
Gross national product (1999): U.S.$2,664,000,000 (U.S.$63,550 per capita[4]).

Structure of gross domestic product and labour force

	1999 in value Sw F '000,000	1999 % of total value	2002[2] labour force	2002[2] % of labour force
Agriculture	...	...	322	1.9
Manufacturing, mining	1,600[5]	40.0[5]	4,386	25.8
Construction	...	...	1,648	9.7
Public utilities	...	...	154	0.9
Transportation and communications	...	...	585	3.4
Trade, public accommodation	...	...	2,291	13.5
Finance, insurance, real estate	1,200	30.0	1,280	7.5
Pub. admin., defense }	960	24.0	1,269	7.5
Services }			4,722	27.8
Other	240	6.0	354[6]	2.1[6]
TOTAL	4,000	100.0	17,011[7]	100.0[3]

Land use (2001): forested 34.8%; meadows and pastures 15.7%; agricultural and under permanent cultivation 24.3%; other 25.2%.

Foreign trade[8, 9]

Balance of trade (current prices)

	1995	1996	1997	1998	1999	2000
Sw F '000,000	+1,078	+1,165	+1,515	+2,394	+1,632	+1,576
% of total	33.5%	34.0%	39.1%	49.1%	39.5%	35.1%

Imports (2000): Sw F 1,456,000,000 (machinery and apparatus 30.4%, glass [all forms] and ceramics 11.0%, fabricated metals 10.0%, iron and steel 5.7%, transport equipment 5.7%). *Major import sources:* Germany 34.6%; Austria 31.8%; Italy 7.9%; U.S. 6.1%; France 3.5%.
Exports (2000): Sw F 3,032,000,000 (machinery and apparatus [mostly electronic products and precision tools] 35.1%, fabricated metals 15.2%, glass and ceramic products [including lead crystal and specialized dental products] 9.9%, food products 5.3%). *Major export destinations:* Germany 25.8%; U.S. 20.0%; Austria 8.4%; France 7.8%; Italy 6.5%.

Transport and communications

Transport. Railroads (1998): length 11.5 mi, 18.5 km; passenger and cargo traffic, n.a. Roads (1999): total length 201 mi, 323 km. Vehicles (2002): passenger cars 23,265; trucks and buses 2,824. Merchant marine: none. Air transport: the nearest scheduled airport service is through Zürich, Switzerland.

Communications

Medium	date	unit	number	units per 1,000 persons
Daily newspapers	1998	circulation	17,900	565
Radio	1997	receivers	21,000	658
Television	1997	receivers	12,000	364
Telephones	2000	main lines	20,072	615

Education and health

Educational attainment (1990). Percentage of population not of preschool age or in compulsory education having: no formal schooling 0.3%; primary and lower secondary education 39.3%; higher secondary and vocational 47.6%; some postsecondary 7.4%; university 4.2%; other and unknown 1.1%.
Literacy: virtually 100%.

Education (1998–99)

	schools	teachers	students	student/ teacher ratio
Primary (age 7–12)	14	151	2,048	13.6
Secondary (age 13–19)	9	162	1,859	11.5
Vocational[10]	2	309	2,307	7.5

Health: physicians (2000) 46 (1 per 714 persons); hospital beds (1997) 108 (1 per 288 persons); infant mortality rate per 1,000 live births (2002) 4.9.
Food (1999)[11]: daily per capita caloric intake 3,600 (vegetable products 65%, animal products 35%); 134% of FAO recommended minimum requirement.

Military

Total active duty personnel: none; Liechtenstein has had no standing army since 1868. *Military expenditure as percentage of GNP:* none.

[1]Increased power as of March 2003 referendum. [2]January 1. [3]Detail does not add to total given because of rounding. [4]Includes 9,700 foreign workers domiciled abroad. [5]Includes other undefined economic sectors. [6]Unemployed. [7]Excludes 11,772 foreign employees. [8]Excludes trade with Switzerland and transshipments through Switzerland. [9]Liechtenstein has formed a customs union with Switzerland since 1923. [10]1997–98. [11]Figures are derived from statistics for Switzerland and Austria.

Internet resources for further information:
- **Liechtenstein News**
http://www.news.li/index.htm

Lithuania

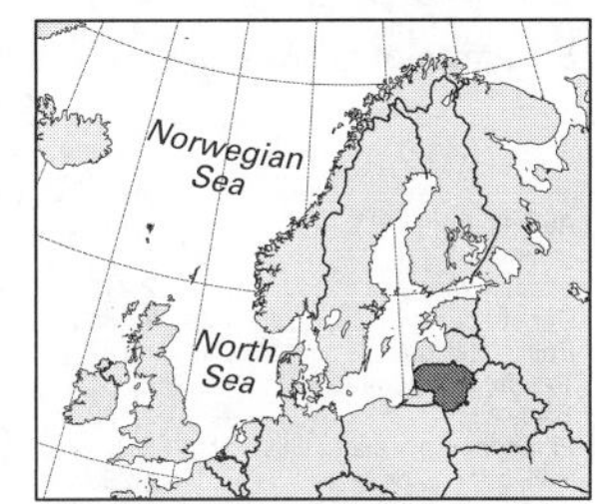

Official name: Lietuvos Respublika (Republic of Lithuania).
Form of government: unitary multiparty republic with a single legislative body, the Seimas (141).
Head of state: President.
Head of government: Prime Minister.
Capital: Vilnius.
Official language: Lithuanian.
Official religion: none.
Monetary unit: 1 litas (LTL) = 100 centai; valuation (Sept. 8, 2003) 1 U.S.$ = LTL 3.13; 1 £ = LTL 4.96[1].

Area and population

Provinces	Capitals	area sq mi	area sq km	population 2003[2] estimate
Alytus	Alytus	2,095	5,425	186,337
Kaunas	Kaunas	3,112	8,060	696,123
Klaipėda	Klaipėda	2,011	5,209	383,951
Marijampolė	Marijampolė	1,723	4,463	187,577
Panevėžys	Panevėžys	3,043	7,881	297,514
Šiauliai	Šiauliai	3,297	8,540	367,175
Tauragė	Tauragė	1,703	4,411	133,469
Telšiai	Telšiai	1,680	4,350	179,148
Utena	Utena	2,780	7,201	183,143
Vilnius	Vilnius	3,768	9,760	848,164
TOTAL		25,212	65,300	3,462,601

Demography

Population (2003): 3,454,000.
Density (2003): persons per sq mi 137.0, persons per sq km 52.9.
Urban-rural (2002): urban 66.9%; rural 33.1%.
Sex distribution (2002): male 46.74%; female 53.26%.
Age breakdown (2001): under 15, 19.5%; 15–29, 21.2%; 30–44, 22.8%; 45–59, 17.2%; 60–74, 14.2%; 75 and over, 5.1%.
Population projection: (2010) 3,321,000; (2020) 3,140,000.
Ethnic composition (2001): Lithuanian 83.5%; Polish 6.7%; Russian 6.3%; Belarusian 1.2%; Ukrainian 0.7%; other 1.6%.
Religious affiliation (2001): Roman Catholic 79.0%; nonreligious 9.5%; Orthodox 4.8%, of which Old Believers 0.8%; Protestant 1.0%; unknown 5.4%; other 0.3%.
Major cities (2003[2]): Vilnius 553,283; Kaunas 373,669; Klaipėda 192,066; Šiauliai 132,714; Panevėžys 118,824; Alytus 71,745.

Vital statistics

Birth rate per 1,000 population (2001): 9.1 (world avg. 21.3); (2001) legitimate 74.6%; illegitimate 25.4%.
Death rate per 1,000 population (2001): 11.6 (world avg. 9.1).
Natural increase rate per 1,000 population (2001): –2.5 (world avg. 12.2).
Total fertility rate (avg. births per childbearing woman; 2001): 1.3.
Marriage rate per 1,000 population (2001): 4.5.
Divorce rate per 1,000 population (2001): 3.2.
Life expectancy at birth (2001): male 65.9 years; female 77.4 years.
Major causes of death per 100,000 population (2001): diseases of the circulatory system 628.2; malignant neoplasms (cancers) 223.9; accidents, injury, homicide 145.8, of which suicide 46.6.

National economy

Budget (2002). Revenue: LTL 15,112,000,000 (tax revenue 92.5%, of which value-added tax 25.2%, individual income tax 23.6%, social security tax 22.7%, excise tax 10.6%; nontax revenue 7.5%). Expenditures: LTL 15,907,000,000 (current expenditure 90.0%, of which social security and welfare 28.0%, wages 23.2%; capital expenditure 10.0%).
Gross national product (2001): U.S.$11,700,000,000 (U.S.$3,350 per capita).

Structure of gross national product and labour force

	2002		2001	
	in value LTL '000,000	% of total value	labour force	% of labour force
Agriculture, forestry	3,219	6.4	271,700	15.6
Mining	288	0.6	3,300	0.2
Manufacturing	8,867	17.5	272,500	15.6
Construction	2,964	5.8	94,400	5.4
Public utilities	1,911	3.8	34,500	2.0
Transp. and commun.	6,241	12.3	92,000	5.3
Trade, restaurants	8,972	17.7	261,800	15.0
Finance, real estate	4,776	9.4	70,400	4.0
Pub. admin., defense	2,497	4.9	77,100	4.4
Services	5,241	10.3	346,100	19.8
Other	5,703[3]	11.3[3]	221,500[4]	12.7[4]
TOTAL	50,679	100.0	1,745,300	100.0

Production (metric tons except as noted). Agriculture, forestry, fishing (2002): hay 2,500,000, potatoes 1,531,300, wheat 1,165,100, sugar beets 1,052,000, barley 800,000, rye 360,000, apples 145,000, cabbages 112,000, rapeseed 105,600, oats 104,000; livestock (number of live animals) 1,010,800 pigs, 751,500 cattle; roundwood (2001) 5,700,000 cu m; fish catch (2001) 153,932. Mining and quarrying (2002): limestone 857,500; peat 262,700. Manufacturing (value of production in LTL '000,000; 2000): food and beverages 4,952; refined petroleum products 4,303; wearing apparel 2,034; textiles 1,248; chemicals and chemical products 1,231; wood and wood products (excluding furniture) 1,164. Energy production (consumption): electricity (kW-hr; 2000) 11,388,000,000 ([1999] 10,853,000,000); coal (metric tons; 1999) none (174,000); crude petroleum (barrels; 1999) 1,700,000 (31,900,000); petroleum products (metric tons; 2002) 6,543,500 (2,756,000); natural gas (cu m; 1999) none (2,176,900,000).
Public debt (external outstanding; 2000): U.S.$2,188,300,000.
Population economically active (2001): total 1,745,300; activity rate of total population 50.2% (participation rates: ages 15–64, 69.3%; female 49.8%; registered unemployed 12.7%).

Price and earnings indexes (1995 = 100)

	1996	1997	1998	1999	2000	2001	2002
Consumer price index	124.6	135.7	142.5	143.6	145.1	147.0	147.4
Annual earnings index	135.1	166.7	187.7	198.6	197.2	199.0	206.8

Household income and expenditure. Average household size (2000) 2.7; average annual household disposable income (1997): LTL 12,914 (U.S.$3,228); sources of income (2001): wages and salaries 53.6%, transfers 24.2%, self-employment 11.3%; expenditure (2001): food and beverages 42.4%, housing and energy 13.6%, transportation and communications 11.8%, clothing and footwear 6.5%.
Land use (1994): forested 30.4%; meadows and pastures 7.6%; agricultural and under permanent cultivation 53.9%; other 8.1%.
Tourism (2001): receipts from visitors U.S.$383,000,000; expenditures by nationals abroad U.S.$218,000,000.

Foreign trade[5]

Balance of trade (current prices)

	1997	1998	1999	2000	2001	2002
LTL '000,000	–7,136	–8,332	–7,323	–6,588	–7,081	–7,940
% of total	18.8%	21.9%	23.4%	17.8%	16.2%	16.4%

Imports (2002): LTL 28,220,000,000 (mineral fuels [mostly crude petroleum] 17.8%, machinery and apparatus 17.5%, transport equipment 16.4%, chemicals and chemical products 8.7%, textiles and clothing 7.9%). *Major import sources:* Russia 21.4%; Germany 17.2%; Italy 4.9%; Poland 4.8%; France 3.9%.
Exports (2002): LTL 20,280,000,000 (mineral fuels [mostly refined petroleum] 19.0%, transport equipment [mostly auto components] 15.9%, textiles and clothing 15.0%, agricultural and food products 10.8%, machinery and apparatus 9.9%). *Major export destinations:* United Kingdom 13.5%; Russia 12.1%; Germany 10.3%; Latvia 9.6%; Denmark 5.0%.

Transport and communications

Transport. Railroads (2001): route length 1,054 mi, 1,696 km; passenger-mi 331,000,000, passenger-km 533,000,000; short ton-mi cargo 5,302,000,000, metric ton-km cargo 7,741,000,000. Roads (2002): total length 47,580 mi, 76,573 km (paved 91%). Vehicles (2002): passenger cars 1,133,477; trucks and buses 104,544. Air transport (2001): passenger-mi 301,000,000; passenger-km 484,000,000; short ton-mi cargo 2,055,000, metric ton-km cargo 3,000,000; airports with scheduled flights (2001) 3.

Communications

Medium	date	unit	number	units per 1,000 persons
Daily newspapers	1996	circulation	344,000	93
Radio	2000	receivers	1,750,000	500
Television	2000	receivers	1,450,000	422
Telephones	2002	main lines	935,900	271
Cellular telephones	2002	subscribers	1,631,600	472
Personal computers	2001	units	260,000	71
Internet	2001	users	250,000	68

Education and health

Educational attainment (2001). Percentage of population age 10 and over having: no schooling and incomplete primary education 5.1%; complete primary 20.8%; incomplete and complete secondary 42.2%; postsecondary 31.9%, of which university 12.6%. *Literacy* (2000): total population age 15 and over literate 99.6%.

Education (2002–03)

	schools	teachers	students	student/ teacher ratio
Primary (age 7–10)[6] / Secondary (age 11–18)	2,172	50,200	594,300	11.8
Voc., teacher tr.	82	4,700	44,400	9.4
Higher	70	14,200	168,200	11.8

Health (2002[2]): physicians 14,031 (1 per 248 persons); hospital beds 32,104 (1 per 108 persons); infant mortality rate per 1,000 live births (2001) 7.7.
Food (2001): daily per capita caloric intake 3,384 (vegetable products 76%, animal products 24%); 132% of FAO recommended minimum requirement.

Military

Total active duty personnel (2002): 13,500[7] (army 60.0%, navy 4.8%, air force 7.4%, centrally controlled staff 13.3%, volunteer national defense force 14.5%). *Military expenditure as percentage of GNP* (1999): 1.3% (world 2.4%); per capita expenditure U.S.$87.

[1]Pegged to the euro from Feb. 2, 2002, at the rate of 1€ = LTL 3.45. [2]January 1. [3]Taxes less imputed bank service charges and subsidies. [4]Unemployed. [5]Imports c.i.f.; exports f.o.b. [6]Excludes special education. [7]Excludes 13,850 in paramilitary.

Internet resources for further information:

- **Lithuanian Department of Statistics http://www.std.lt**
- **Bank of Lithuania http://www.lbank.lt/eng/default.htm**

Luxembourg

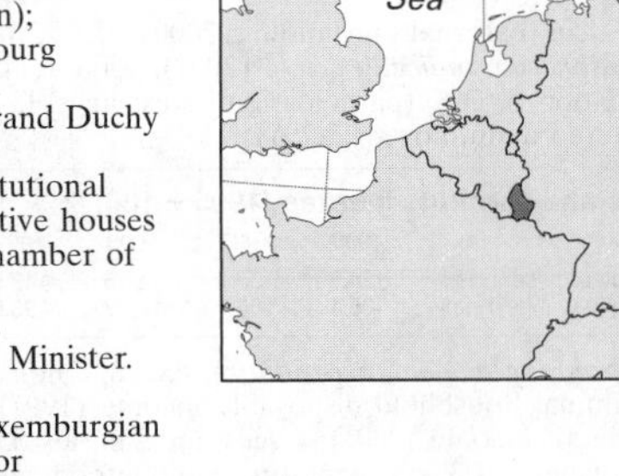

Official name: Groussherzogtum Lëtzebuerg (Luxemburgian); Grand-Duché de Luxembourg (French); Grossherzogtum Luxemburg (German) (Grand Duchy of Luxembourg).
Form of government: constitutional monarchy with two legislative houses (Council of State [21][1]; Chamber of Deputies [60]).
Chief of state: Grand Duke.
Head of government: Prime Minister.
Capital: Luxembourg.
Official language: none; Luxemburgian (national); French (used for most official purposes); German (lingua franca).
Official religion: none.
Monetary unit: 1 € (euro) = 100 cents; valuation (Sept. 8, 2003) 1 U.S.$ = €0.90; 1 £ = €1.43[2].

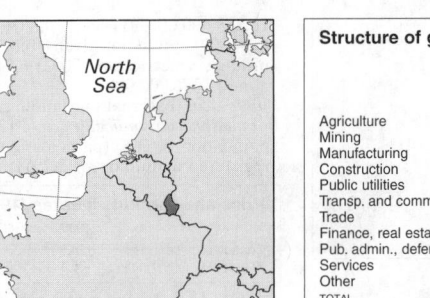

Area and population

Districts / Cantons	area sq mi	area sq km	population 2001 census
Diekirch	447	1,157	67,487
Clervaux	128	332	12,411
Diekirch	92	239	26,748
Redange	103	267	13,689
Vianden	21	54	2,920
Wiltz	102	265	11,719
Grevenmacher	203	525	51,960
Echternach	72	186	14,141
Grevenmacher	82	211	21,664
Remich	49	128	16,155
Luxembourg	349	904	320,317
Capellen	77	199	30,523
Esch	94	243	134,846
Luxembourg (Ville et Campagne)	92	238	131,652
Mersch	86	224	23,296
TOTAL	999	2,586	439,764

Demography

Population (2003): 453,000.
Density (2003): persons per sq mi 453.5, persons per sq km 175.2.
Urban-rural (2002): urban 91.9%; rural 8.1%.
Sex distribution (2003): male 49.30%; female 50.70%.
Age breakdown (2001): under 15, 18.9%; 15–29, 18.2%; 30–44, 25.4%; 45–59, 18.7%; 60–74, 13.1%; 75 and over, 5.7%.
Population projection: (2010) 494,000; (2020) 550,000.
Ethnic composition (nationality; 2003): Luxemburger 61.9%; Portuguese 13.5%; French 4.8%; Italian 4.2%; Belgian 3.5%; German 2.3%; English 1.0%; other 8.8%.
Religious affiliation (1996): Roman Catholic 95.1%; other 4.9%.
Major cities (2001)[3]: Luxembourg 76,687; Esch-sur-Alzette 27,186; Dudelange 17,348; Schifflange 7,854; Bettembourg 7,162.

Vital statistics

Birth rate per 1,000 population (2002): 12.0 (world avg. 21.3); (1998) legitimate 82.5%; illegitimate 17.5%.
Death rate per 1,000 population (2002): 8.4 (world avg. 9.1).
Natural increase rate per 1,000 population (2002): 3.6 (world avg. 12.2).
Total fertility rate (avg. births per childbearing woman; 2002): 1.6.
Marriage rate per 1,000 population (2002): 4.5.
Divorce rate per 1,000 population (2002): 2.4.
Life expectancy at birth (2002): male 74.9 years; female 81.0 years.
Major causes of death per 100,000 population (2002): diseases of the circulatory system 321.5; malignant neoplasms (cancers) 205.4.

National economy

Budget (2002). Revenue: €5,977,200,000 (direct taxes 47.4%, indirect taxes 38.5%, other 14.1%). Expenditures: €5,976,100,000 (current expenditure 85.7%, development expenditure 14.3%).
National debt (2002): U.S.$578,000,000.
Production (metric tons except as noted). Agriculture, forestry, fishing (2002): corn (maize) 138,721, wheat 67,126, barley 65,000, potatoes 20,105, apples 13,000, grapes (2001) 1,298 ha (3,208 acres); livestock (number of live animals; 2000) 205,072 cattle, 80,141 pigs; roundwood (2001) 142,150 cu m. Mining and quarrying (2002): limited quantities of limestone and slate. Manufacturing (2002): rolled steel 4,467,000; crude steel 2,736,000; cement 800,000; wine 153,900 hectolitres. Energy production (consumption): electricity (kW-hr; 2000) 1,124,000,000 (6,445,000,000); coal (metric tons; 1999) none (153,000); crude petroleum, none (none); petroleum products (metric tons; 1999) none (1,754,000); natural gas (cu m; 1999) none (781,900,000).
Land use (1992): forested 34.2%; meadows and pastures 25.6%; agricultural and under permanent cultivation 23.2%; other 17.0%.
Tourism (2001): receipts from visitors U.S.$1,782,000,000; expenditures U.S.$1,467,000,000.
Gross national product (2001): U.S.$17,600,000,000 (U.S.$39,840 per capita).

Structure of gross domestic product and labour force

	2001 in value €'000,000	2001 % of total value	2002 labour force	2002 % of labour force
Agriculture	144.9	0.7	3,600	1.3
Mining	30.5	0.1	34,300	12.0
Manufacturing	2,415.9	11.4		
Construction	1,332.2	6.3	28,100	9.8
Public utilities	227.1	1.1	1,600	0.6
Transp. and commun.	2,331.1	11.0	23,100	8.1
Trade	2,572.5	12.1	53,400	18.7
Finance, real estate	8,299.3	39.1	79,300	27.7
Pub. admin., defense	1,230.2	5.8	14,900	5.2
Services	2,248.8	10.6	47,400	16.6
Other	391.0[4]	1.8[4]	—	—
TOTAL	21,223.5	100.0	285,700	100.0

Population economically active (2002): total 285,700; activity rate of total population 63.9% (participation rates: ages 15–64 [2001] 64.4%; female [2001] 40.2%; unemployed [2002] 3.0%).

Price and earnings indexes (1995 = 100)

	1996	1997	1998	1999	2000	2001	2002
Consumer price index	101.4	102.8	103.8	104.8	108.2	111.1	113.4
Hourly earnings index	...	...	...	...	...	...	...

Household income and expenditure. Average household size (2000) 2.5; income per household (2002) €61,800 (U.S.$55,600); sources of income (1992): wages and salaries 67.1%, transfer payments 28.1%, self-employment 4.8%; expenditure (2002): food, beverages, and tobacco 21.0%, housing 20.7%, transportation and communications 19.3%, entertainment and education 8.6%, household goods and furniture 8.3%, clothing and footwear 5.3%, health 1.4%.

Foreign trade[5]

Balance of trade (current prices)

	1997	1998	1999	2000	2001	2002
€'000,000	−2,283	−2,513	−2,967	−3,032	−3,253	−3,170
% of total	15.4%	14.8%	16.7%	15.0%	15.2%	15.0%

Imports (2001): €12,335,000,000 (machinery and apparatus 21.5%, transport equipment 15.2%, base and fabricated metals 11.3%, chemicals and chemical products 10.1%). *Major import sources:* Belgium 34.3%; Germany 25.1%; France 12.8%; The Netherlands 5.8%; U.S. 5.1%.
Exports (2001): €9,082,000,000 (base and fabricated metals [mostly iron and steel] 28.1%, machinery and apparatus 24.0%, chemicals and chemical products 6.3%, transport equipment 4.3%, food products 4.2%). *Major export destinations:* Germany 24.6%; France 19.6%; Belgium 12.3%; U.K. 8.2%; Italy 6.2%.

Transport and communications

Transport. Railroads (2002): route length 170 mi, 274 km; passenger-mi 166,500,000, passenger-km 268,000,000; short ton-mi cargo 420,000,000, metric ton-km cargo 613,000,000. Roads (1999): total length 3,209 mi, 5,166 km (paved 100%). Vehicles (2003): passenger cars 287,245; trucks and buses 22,691. Air transport (2002): passengers carried 1,517,000; cargo 578,944 metric tons; airports (2002) with scheduled flights 1.

Communications

Medium	date	unit	number	units per 1,000 persons
Daily newspapers	1996	circulation	135,000	325
Radio	2000	receivers	300,000	685
Television	2000	receivers	170,000	391
Telephones	2001	main lines	350,000	783
Cellular telephones	2002	subscribers	455,000	1,018
Personal computers	2001	units	230,000	515
Internet	2001	users	100,000	227

Education and health

Educational attainment: n.a. *Literacy* (2001): virtually 100% literate.

Education (2000–01)

	schools	teachers	students	student/teacher ratio
Primary (age 6–11)[6]	...	2,135	31,278	14.7
Secondary (age 12–18)	...	3,125	9,859	...
Voc., teacher tr.	...		21,359	...
Higher	5	...	2,533	...

Health (2002): physicians 1,137 (1 per 393 persons); hospital beds 3,035 (1 per 147 persons); infant mortality rate per 1,000 live births (2002) 5.0.
Food (1995): daily per capita caloric intake 3,530 (vegetable products 68%, animal products 32%); 134% of FAO recommended minimum.

Military

Total active duty personnel (2002): 900 (army 100.0%). *Military expenditure as percentage of GNP* (1999): 0.8% (world 2.4%); per capita expenditure U.S.$326.

[1]Has limited legislative authority. [2]The Luxembourg franc was the former monetary unit; on Jan. 1, 2002, Lux F 40.34 = €1. [3]Populations of localities (comparable to cities proper or towns proper). [4]Imputed bank service charges. [5]Imports c.i.f.; exports f.o.b. [6]Public schools only.

Internet resources for further information:
- **STATEC: Luxembourg in Figures http://statec.gouvernement.lu/html_en**

Macau

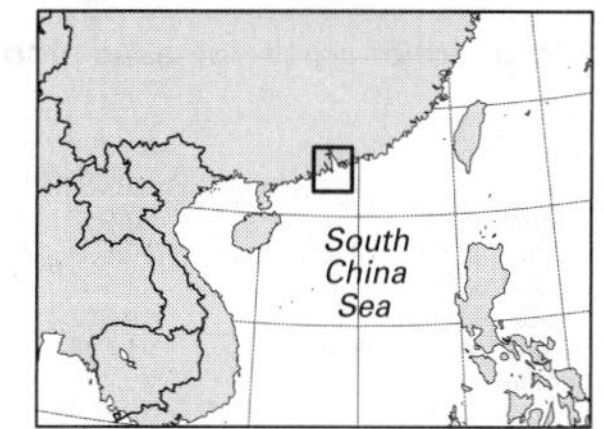

Official name: Aomen Tebie Xingzhengqu (Chinese); Região Administrativa Especial de Macau (Portuguese) (Macau Special Administrative Region).
Political status: special administrative region (China[1]) with one legislative house (Legislative Council [27[2]]).
Chief of state: President of China.
Head of government: Chief Executive.
Capital: Macau.
Official languages: Chinese; Portuguese.
Official religion: none.
Monetary unit: 1 pataca (MOP) = 100 avos; valuation (Sept. 8, 2003) 1 U.S.$ = MOP 8.03; 1 £ = MOP 12.74.

Area and population

	area		population
Geographic areas	sq mi	sq km	2001 census
Macau peninsula	3.3	8.5	388,647
Islands	5.3	13.8	44,690
Coloane	2.9	7.6	2,904
Taipa	2.4	6.2	41,786
Marine	—	—	1,898
Embankment[3]	1.7	4.5	—
TOTAL	10.3	26.8	435,235

Demography

Population (2003): 443,000.
Density (2003): persons per sq mi 43,000, persons per sq km 16,530.
Urban-rural (2003): urban, virtually 100%[4].
Sex distribution (2002): male 47.95%; female 52.05%.
Age breakdown (2001): under 15, 21.7%; 15–29, 22.2%; 30–44, 29.1%; 45–59, 17.5%; 60–74, 6.6%; 75 and over, 2.9%.
Population projection: (2010) 468,000; (2020) 507,000.
Doubling time: over 100 years.
Nationality (2001)[5]: Chinese 95.2%; Portuguese 2.0%; Filipino 1.2%; other 1.6%.
Religious affiliation (1998): nonreligious 60.8%; Buddhist 16.7%; other 22.5%.
Major city (2000 est.): Macau 437,900.

Vital statistics

Birth rate per 1,000 population (2002): 7.2 (world avg. 21.3).
Death rate per 1,000 population (2002): 3.2 (world avg. 9.1).
Natural increase rate per 1,000 population (2002): 4.0 (world avg. 12.2).
Total fertility rate (avg. births per childbearing woman; 2002): 1.1.
Marriage rate per 1,000 population (2002): 2.8.
Divorce rate per 1,000 population (2002): 0.9.
Life expectancy at birth (2002): male 77.0 years; female 82.0 years.
Major causes of death per 100,000 population (1999): diseases of the circulatory system 107.9; malignant neoplasms (cancers) 83.7; diseases of the respiratory system 38.4; accidents, poisoning, and violence 26.3; diseases of the digestive system 12.1; diseases of the genitourinary system 9.4; infectious and parasitic diseases 7.5; endocrine and metabolic disorders 6.4; diseases of the nervous system 2.9.

National economy

Budget (1998). Revenue: MOP 14,831,099,000 (recurrent receipts 69.1%, autonomous agency receipts 21.4%, capital receipts 2.2%). Expenditures: MOP 14,831,099,000 (recurrent payments 61.1%, autonomous agency expenditures 21.4%, capital payments 17.5%).
Tourism: receipts from visitors (2001) U.S.$3,745,000,000; expenditures by nationals abroad (1999) U.S.$131,000,000.
Land use (1992): built-on area, wasteland, and other 100.0%.
Gross domestic product (at current market prices; 2002): U.S.$6,731,246,000 (U.S.$15,320 per capita).

Structure of gross domestic product and labour force

	2001		2002	
	in value MOP '000,000	% of total value	labour force	% of labour force
Agriculture and mining	6	6	6	6
Manufacturing	4,238.3	8.5	40,900	19.2
Construction	997.2	2.0	15,000	7.0
Public utilities	1,545.7	3.1	...	...
Transportation and communications	3,340.8	6.7	12,800	6.0
Trade	5,883.7	11.8	54,000	25.3
Finance	10,919.8	21.9	17,100	8.0
Public administration / Services[7]	25,778.8	51.7	59,000	27.7
Other	–2,842.1[8]	–5.7[8]	14,400[9]	6.8[9]
TOTAL	49,862.2	100.0	213,200	100.0

Production (metric tons except as noted). Agriculture, forestry, fishing (1999): eggs 650; livestock (number of live animals) 500,000 chickens; fish catch (2000) 1,500. Quarrying (value added in MOP '000,000; 1997): 13. Manufacturing (value added in MOP '000,000; 2001): wearing apparel 2,090; textiles 522; printing and publishing 95; food products 93; chemicals 73; footwear 70. Construction (2002): residential 36,387 sq m; nonresidential 66,162 sq m. Energy production (consumption): electricity (kW-hr; 1999) 1,531,000,000 (1,726,000,000); petroleum products (metric tons; 1999) none (494,000).
Public debt (long-term, external; 1999): U.S.$706,000,000.
Population economically active (2001): total 231,266; activity rate of total population 53.1% (participation rates: over age 14, 66.1%; female 46.5%; unemployed 7.0%).

Price and earnings indexes (1995 = 100)

	1997	1998	1999	2000	2001	2002
Consumer price index[10]	102.8	103.0	99.7	98.1	96.2	93.7
Earnings index	...	...	...	...	...	...

Household income and expenditure. Average household size (2001) 3.1; annual income per household MOP 181,884 (U.S.$22,764); sources of income: n.a.; expenditure (1987–88): food 38.3%, housing 19.7%, education, health, and other services 12.1%, transportation 7.4%, clothing and footwear 6.8%, energy 4.0%, household durable goods 3.7%, other goods 8.0%.

Foreign trade[11]

Balance of trade (current prices)

	1997	1998	1999	2000	2001	2002
MOP '000,000	+526	+1,487	+1,280	+2,283	–697	–1,398
% of total	1.6%	4.6%	3.8%	5.9%	1.9%	3.6%

Imports (2002): MOP 20,323,000,000 (textile materials 32.3%; capital goods 13.8%; clothing and footwear 13.3%; food, beverages, and tobacco 11.4%). *Major import sources:* China 41.7%; Hong Kong 14.5%; Taiwan 6.7%; Japan 6.7%; France 4.3%.
Exports (2002): MOP 18,925,000,000 (domestic exports 78.1%, of which machine-knitted clothing 42.1%, machine-woven clothing 27.4%, footwear 3.6%; reexports 21.9%). *Major export destinations:* United States 48.4%; China 15.6%; Germany 7.5%; Hong Kong 5.8%; United Kingdom 5.4%.

Transport and communications

Transport. Railroads: none. Roads (1999): total length 167 mi, 269 km (paved 100%). Vehicles (1999): passenger cars 47,776; trucks and buses 5,812. Air transport (2001)[12]: passenger-mi 1,185,567,000, passenger-km 1,907,988,000; short ton-mi cargo 15,491,000, metric ton-km cargo 22,616,000.

Communications

Medium	date	unit	number	units per 1,000 persons
Daily newspapers	2000	circulation	210,100	488
Radio	2000	receivers	215,300	500
Television	2000	receivers	123,100	286
Telephones	2002	main lines	176,100	399
Cellular telephones	2002	subscribers	276,100	625
Personal computers	2001	units	80,000	179
Internet	2001	users	101,000	225

Education and health

Educational attainment (2001). Population age 25 and over having: no formal schooling 7.6%; incomplete primary education 13.6%; completed primary 26.6%; some secondary 23.9%; completed secondary and post-secondary 28.3%. *Literacy* (2001): percentage of population age 15 and over literate 91.3%; males literate 95.3%; females literate 87.8%.

Education (2001–02)

	schools	teachers[13]	students	student/ teacher ratio[13]
Primary (age 6–11)	80	1,744	43,709	27.1
Secondary (age 12–18)	54	1,577	38,751	17.9
Voc., teacher tr.	4	47	2,381	14.9
Higher	11	818	8,520	9.4

Health (2002): physicians 915 (1 per 480 persons); hospital beds 990 (1 per 444 persons); infant mortality rate per 1,000 live births 8.0.
Food (1998): daily per capita caloric intake 2,471 (vegetable products 76%, animal products 24%); 108% of FAO recommended minimum requirement.

Military

Total active duty personnel: Chinese troops (2001) 500.

[1]Macau reverted to Chinese sovereignty on Dec. 20, 1999. [2]Includes 10 directly elected seats, 7 seats appointed by the chief executive, and 10 seats appointed by special-interest groups. [3]Landfill linking Coloane and Taipa. [4]About 0.5% of Macau's population live on sampans and other vessels. [5]Resident population. [6]Negligible. [7]Includes gambling. [8]Imputed bank service charge. [9]Includes 1,800 in activities undefined and 12,600 unemployed. [10]Excluding rent; base year is July 1995–June 1996. [11]Includes reexports. [12]Air Macau only. [13]1997–98.

Internet resources for further information:
- **Government of Macau Special Administrative Region, P.R.C. http://www.macau.gov.mo/index_en.html**
- **Macau Census and Statistics Service http://www.dsec.gov.mo/e_index.html**

Macedonia

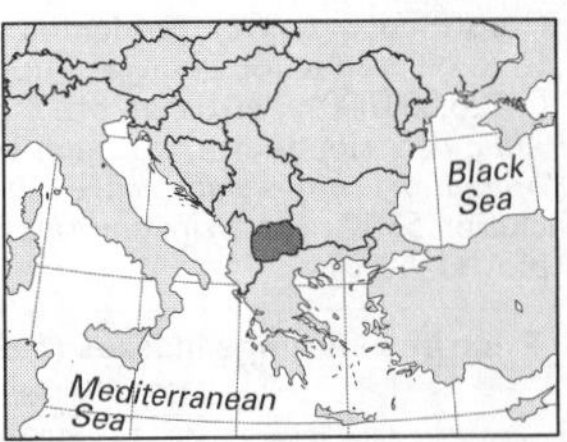

Official name[1]: Republika Makedonija (Republic of Macedonia).
Form of government: unitary multiparty republic with a unicameral legislative (Assembly [120]).
Head of state: President.
Head of government: Prime Minister.
Capital: Skopje.
Official languages[2]: Macedonian; Albanian.
Official religion: none.
Monetary unit: denar; valuation (Sept. 8, 2003) 1 U.S.$ = 56.57 denar; 1 £ = 89.70 denar.

Area and population

Former administrative districts[3]	area sq km	population 1994 census
Berovo	806	19,737
Bitola	1,798	106,012
Brod	924	10,912
Debar	274	26,449
Delčevo	589	25,052
Demir Hisar	443	10,321
Gevgelija	757	34,767
Gostivar	1,341	108,189
Kavadarci	1,132	41,801
Kičevo	854	53,044
Kočani	570	48,105
Kratovo	376	10,855
Kriva Palanka	720	25,112
Kruševo	239	11,981
Kumanovo	1,212	126,543
Negotino	734	23,094
Ohrid	1,069	60,841
Prilep	1,675	93,248
Probištip	326	16,373
Radoviš	735	30,378
Resen	739	17,467
Skopje	1,818	541,280
Štip	815	50,531
Struga	507	62,305
Strumica	952	89,759
Sveti Nikole	649	21,391
Tetovo	1,080	174,748
Titov Veles	1,536	65,523
Valandovo	331	12,049
Vinica	432	19,010
TOTAL	25,713[4]	1,936,877

Demography

Population (2003): 2,056,000.
Density (2003): persons per sq mi 207.1, persons per sq km 80.0.
Urban-rural (2000): urban 62.0%; rural 38.0%.
Sex distribution (2001): male 50.06%; female 49.94%.
Age breakdown (2001): under 15, 22.9%; 15–29, 24.4%; 30–44, 21.5%; 45–59, 16.8%; 60–64, 11.2%; 65 and over, 3.2%.
Population projection: (2010) 2,122,000; (2020) 2,185,000.
Ethnic composition (2000): Macedonian 53.9%; Albanian 18.0%; Turkish 7.7%; Roma (Gypsy) 5.3%; Aromanian 5.0%; Serbian 2.1%; Croat 2.0%; other 6.0%.
Religious affiliation (1995): Serbian (Macedonian) Orthodox 54.2%; Sunnī Muslim 30.0%; other 15.8%.
Major cities (1994): Skopje 440,577; Bitola 75,386; Prilep 67,371; Kumanovo 66,237; Tetovo 50,376.

Vital statistics

Birth rate per 1,000 population (2001): 13.5 (world avg. 21.3); (2000) legitimate 90.2%; illegitimate 9.8%.
Death rate per 1,000 population (2001): 7.7 (world avg. 9.1).
Natural increase rate per 1,000 population (2001): 5.8 (world avg. 12.2).
Total fertility rate (avg. births per childbearing woman; 2001): 1.6.
Marriage rate per 1,000 population (2000): 7.0.
Life expectancy at birth (2001): male 71.8 years; female 76.4 years.
Major causes of death per 100,000 population (1997): diseases of the circulatory system 462.8; malignant neoplasms 138.3; diseases of the respiratory system 39.5; accidents, violence, and poisoning 32.4.

National economy

Budget (2002). Revenue: 53,089,000,000 denar (tax revenue 94.2%, of which value-added tax 33.7%, excise taxes 20.6%, income and profit tax 19.6%, import duties 10.0%; nontax revenue 5.8%). Expenditure: 59,979,000,000 denar (wages and salaries 29.5%, pensions 26.1%, goods and services 20.0%, interest 6.1%).
External debt (2001): U.S.$1,136,000,000.
Production (metric tons except as noted). Agriculture, forestry, fishing (2002): wheat 267,100, potatoes 183,000, corn (maize) 140,200, grapes 119,000, tomatoes 109,500, tobacco leaves 22,044; livestock (number of live animals) 1,233,800 sheep, 259,000 cattle; roundwood (2001) 740,000 cu m; fish catch (2000) 1,834 (all freshwater). Mining and quarrying (2000)[5]: zinc (electrolytic only) 62,800; lead 25,000; copper 19,000; silver 20,000 kg. Manufacturing (1998): cement 461,195; steel sheets 276,464; detergents 21,990; wool yarn 3,252; refrigerators 4,007 units; freezers 3,488 units; leather footwear 1,382,000 pairs; cotton fabric 13,700,000 sq m; cigarettes 7,009,000 units. Energy production (consumption): electricity (kW-hr; 1999) 6,862,000,000 (6,759,000,000); hard coal (metric tons; 1999) none (181,000); lignite (metric tons; 1999) 7,375,000 (7,529,000); crude petroleum (barrels; 1999) none (4,400,000); petroleum products (metric tons; 1999) 589,000 (823,000); natural gas (cu m; 1999) none (39,200,000).
Household income and expenditure. Average household size (1994) 3.8; income per household (2000) U.S.$3,798; sources of income (2000): wages and salaries 54.2%, transfer payments 22.6%, savings 3.2%, other 20.0%; expenditure: food 38.4%, transportation and communications 9.7%, fuel and lighting 8.2%, beverages and tobacco 7.6%.
Gross national product (2001): U.S.$3,500,000,000 (U.S.$1,690 per capita).

Structure of gross domestic product and labour force

	2001 in value '000,000 denar	2001 % of total value	2000 labour force	2000 % of labour force
Agriculture	22,957	9.8	123,038	15.2
Mining and manufacturing	40,899	17.5	148,633	18.3
Construction	11,801	5.0	35,712	4.4
Public utilities	10,041	4.3	10,627	1.3
Transp. and commun.	21,694	9.3	27,486	3.4
Trade	29,486	12.7	68,732	8.5
Finance	15,724	6.8	15,667	1.9
Pub. admin., defense	14,445	6.2	32,508	4.0
Services	22,286	9.5	118,419	14.6
Other	44,508	18.9	230,178[6]	28.4[6]
TOTAL	233,841	100.0	811,000	100.0

Population economically active (2000): total 811,000; activity rate 39.9% (participation rates: ages 15–64, 52.9%; female 38.5%; unemployed [2002] 31.9%).

Price and earnings indexes (1997 = 100)

	1997	1998	1999	2000	2001	2002
Consumer price index	100.0	100.6	99.2	99.9	99.2	99.2
Annual earnings index	100.0	103.7	106.6	112.5	115.9[7]	...

Tourism (2000): receipts from visitors U.S.$37,000,000; expenditures by nationals abroad U.S.$34,000,000.

Foreign trade[8]

Balance of trade (current prices)

	1997	1998	1999	2000	2001	2002
U.S.$'000,000	−542	−604	−604	−766	−533	−809
% of total	18.0%	18.7%	20.2%	22.5%	18.7%	26.7%

Imports (2001): U.S.$1,688,000,000 (mineral fuels 13.9%, machinery and apparatus 13.0%, food and live animals 11.5%, chemicals and chemical products 10.2%). *Major import sources* (2002): Germany 14.3%; Greece 12.1%; Yugoslavia 9.4%; Slovenia 6.6%; Bulgaria 6.5%; Italy 6.0%.
Exports (2001): U.S.$1,155,000,000 (clothing 27.7%, iron and steel 16.9%, tobacco [all forms] 6.5%, nonferrous base metals 6.4%, beverages 4.0%). *Major export destinations* (2002): Yugoslavia 22.1%; Germany 21.0%; Greece 10.4%; Italy 7.1%; United States 7.0%.

Transport and communications

Transport. Railroads (1999): length 575 mi, 925 km; passenger-km 150,000,000; metric ton-km cargo 380,000,000. Roads (2000): length 7,782 mi, 12,522 km (paved 58%). Vehicles (2000): passenger cars 299,588; trucks and buses 23,261. Air transport (2001)[9]: passenger-km 168,000,000; metric ton-km cargo 130,000; airports (2002) with scheduled flights 2.

Communications

Medium	date	unit	number	units per 1,000 persons
Daily newspapers	2000	circulation	89,400	44
Radio	2000	receivers	415,000	205
Television	2000	receivers	571,000	282
Telephones	2001	main lines	538,000	264
Cellular telephones	2001	subscribers	223,300	109
Personal computers	2001	units	...	...
Internet	2001	users	70,000	34

Education and health

Educational attainment (1994). Percentage of population age 15 and over having: less than full primary education 25.0%; primary 33.4%; secondary 32.3%; postsecondary and higher 8.7%; unknown 0.6%. *Literacy* (1998): 94.6%.

Education (1999–2000)

	schools	teachers	students	student/ teacher ratio
Primary (age 7–14)	1,036	13,782	252,212	18.3
Secondary (age 15–18)	96	5,557	89,775	16.2
Higher[10]	31	1,495	40,246	26.9

Health (2000): physicians 4,455 (1 per 454 persons); hospital beds 10,248 (1 per 198 persons); infant mortality rate per 1,000 live births (2001) 13.0.
Food (2001): daily per capita caloric intake 2,552 (vegetable products 80%, animal products 20%); 100% of FAO recommended minimum requirement.

Military

Total active duty personnel (2002): 12,300 (army 91.9%, headquarters staff 8.1%). *Military expenditure as percentage of GNP* (1999): 2.5% (world 2.4%); per capita expenditure U.S.$112.

[1]Member of the United Nations under the name The Former Yugoslav Republic of Macedonia (FYROM). [2]Albanian was made an official language in June 2002. [3]Local government was reorganized into 123 municipalities in 1996. [4]Total includes 280 sq km of inland water not distributed by district. [5]Contained metal. [6]Unemployed. [7]Does not include last quarter. [8]Imports c.i.f.; exports f.o.b. [9]Macedonian Airline. [10]2000–01.

Internet resources for further information:
- **National Bank of the Republic of Macedonia http://www.nbrm.gov.mk**
- **State Statistical Office http://www.stat.gov.mk/english/index_eng.htm**

Madagascar

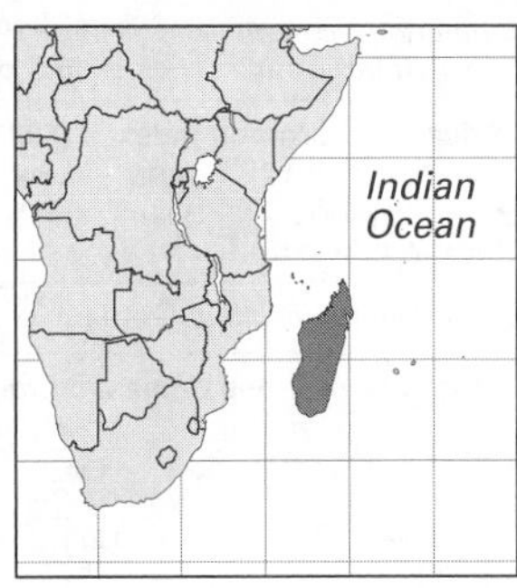

Official name: Repoblikan'i Madagasikara (Malagasy); République de Madagascar (French) (Republic of Madagascar).
Form of government: federal[1] multiparty republic with two legislative houses (Senate [90]; National Assembly [160]).
Heads of state and government: President assisted by Prime Minister.
Capital: Antananarivo.
Official languages: [2].
Official religion: none.
Monetary unit: 1 ariary[3] (MGA) = 5 iraimbilanja; valuation (Sept. 8, 2003) 1 U.S.$ = MGA 1,190; 1 £ = MGA 1,887.

Area and population

Autonomous provinces[1]	Capitals	area sq mi	area sq km	population 2001 estimate
Antananarivo	Antananarivo	22,503	58,283	4,580,788
Antsirañana	Antsirañana	16,620	43,046	1,188,425
Fianarantsoa	Fianarantsoa	39,526	102,373	3,366,291
Mahajanga	Mahajanga	57,924	150,023	1,733,917
Toamasina	Toamasina	27,765	71,911	2,593,063
Toliary	Toliary	62,319	161,405	2,229,550
TOTAL		226,658	587,041	15,692,034

Demography

Population (2003): 16,606,000.
Density (2003): persons per sq mi 73.3, persons per sq km 28.3.
Urban-rural (2001): urban 30.1%; rural 69.9%.
Sex distribution (2000): male 49.70%; female 50.30%.
Age breakdown (2000): under 15, 45.0%; 15–29, 26.5%; 30–44, 15.8%; 45–59, 7.9%; 60–74, 3.8%; 75 and over, 1.0%.
Population projection: (2010) 20,134,000; (2020) 25,847,000.
Doubling time: 23 years.
Ethnic composition (2000): Malagasy 95.9%, of which Merina 24.0%, Betsimisaraka 13.4%, Betsileo 11.3%, Tsimihety 7.0%, Sakalava 5.9%; Makua 1.1%; French 0.6%; Comorian 0.5%; Reunionese 0.4%; other 1.5%.
Religious affiliation (2000): Christian 49.5%, of which Protestant 22.7%, Roman Catholic 20.3%; traditional beliefs 48.0%; Muslim 1.9%; other 0.6%.
Major cities (2001): Antananarivo 1,403,449; Toamasina 179,045; Antsirabe 160,356; Fianarantsoa 144,225; Mahajanga 135,660.

Vital statistics

Birth rate per 1,000 population (2002): 42.4 (world avg. 21.3).
Death rate per 1,000 population (2002): 12.2 (world avg. 9.1).
Natural increase rate per 1,000 population (2002): 30.2 (world avg. 12.2).
Total fertility rate (avg. births per childbearing woman; 2002): 5.8.
Life expectancy at birth (2000): male 52.7 years; female 57.3 years.
Major causes of death per 100,000 population: n.a.; however, major causes of death in the 1990s included maternal and perinatal diseases, malaria, infectious and parasitic diseases, malnutrition, diarrhea, and respiratory diseases.

National economy

Budget (2000). Revenue: FMG 3,068,000,000,000 (taxes 96.9%, of which duties on trade 51.9%, value-added tax 16.7%, income tax 15.2%; nontax receipts 3.1%). Expenditures: FMG 4,168,600,000,000 (current expenditure 57.6%, of which general administration 21.1%, debt service 14.7%, education 13.3%, defense 7.7%, health 4.4%, agriculture 2.0%; capital expenditure 42.4%).
Public debt (external, outstanding; 2001): U.S.$3,793,000,000.
Production (metric tons except as noted). Agriculture, forestry, fishing (2002): paddy rice 2,670,600, cassava 2,510,000, sugarcane 2,223,400, sweet potatoes 525,700, potatoes 296,000, bananas 290,000, mangoes 210,000, taro 200,000, corn (maize) 180,600, dry beans 84,000, oranges 83,000, coffee 64,600, pineapples 51,000, seed cotton 28,000, cloves (whole and stem) 15,500, vanilla 1,518; livestock (number of live animals) 11,000,000 cattle, 1,600,000 pigs, 1,350,000 goats; roundwood (2001) 10,012,542 cu m; fish catch (2000) 139,373, of which crustaceans (1999) 15,199. Mining and quarrying (2001): chromite ore 42,500; graphite 2,013; mica 90; gold 5 kg (illegally smuggled, *c.* 3,500 kg); sapphires (value of exports in U.S.$'000,000; 1999) 12.5. Manufacturing (2000): refined sugar 62,487; cement 50,938; soap 15,385; cigarettes 3,633[4]; beer 645,300 hectolitres; fuel oil 225,700 cu m; gas oil 150,400 cu m; gasoline 122,600 cu m; kerosene 65,200 cu m; shoes 873,000 pairs. Energy production (consumption): electricity (kW-hr; 1999) 794,000,000 (794,000,000); coal (metric tons; 1999) none (8,000); crude petroleum (barrels; 1999) none (2,900,000); petroleum products (metric tons; 1999) 301,000 (522,000); natural gas, none (n.a.).
Population economically active (1993): total 5,914,000; activity rate of total population 48.9% (participation rates [1995]: over age 10, 59.4%; female 38.4%; unemployed, n.a.).

Price and earnings indexes (1995 = 100)

	1996	1997	1998	1999	2000	2001	2002
Consumer price index[5]	119.8	125.1	132.9	146.1	163.7	175.0	202.9
Annual earnings index	...	...	...	...	...	...	...

Gross national product (2001): U.S.$4,200,000,000 (U.S.$270 per capita).

Structure of gross domestic product and labour force

	2000 in value FMG '000,000[6]	2000 % of total value[6]	1993 labour force	1993 % of labour force
Agriculture	6,858	29.1	5,100,000	86.2
Manufacturing, Mining	3,412	14.4	86,000	1.5
Public utilities, Construction	396	1.7	46,000	0.8
Transp. and commun.	4,501	19.1	42,000	0.7
Trade	2,927	12.4	149,000 (Trade and Finance)	2.5 (Trade and Finance)
Finance	[7]	[7]		
Services	4,404[7]	18.7[7]	243,000	4.1
Pub. admin., defense	1,412	6.0	208,000	3.5
Other	–327[8]	–1.4[8]	40,000	0.7
TOTAL	23,583	100.0	5,914,000	100.0

Household income and expenditure. Average household size (1993) 4.6[9]; expenditure (1983)[5, 10]: food 60.4%, fuel and light 9.1%, clothing and footwear 8.6%, household goods and utensils 2.4%.
Land use (1994): forest 39.9%; pasture 41.3%; agriculture 5.3%; other 13.5%.
Tourism (2001): receipts from visitors U.S.$115,000,000; expenditures by nationals abroad U.S.$115,000,000.

Foreign trade[11]

Balance of trade

	1997	1998	1999	2000	2001
FMG '000,000,000	–892	–815	–995	–702	+97
% of total	14.7%	12.5%	11.9%	5.9%	0.8%

Imports (2001): FMG 7,363,000,000,000 (petroleum [all forms] 15.0%, machinery and apparatus 14.7%, consumer goods 11.8%, other [mostly imports for EPZ[12]] 39.3%). *Major import sources:* France 21.5%; China 9.1%; South Africa 5.5%; Japan 4.4%; U.S. 4.2%.
Exports (2001): FMG 6,356,000,000,000 (EPZ[12] exports [mostly textiles and clothing] 35.3%, vanilla 17.0%, cloves 9.9%, shellfish 9.6%). *Major export destinations:* France 29.7%; U.S. 13.9%; Mauritius 2.6%; unspecified countries 34.7%.

Transport and communications

Transport. Railroads: route length (2003) 560 mi, 901 km[13]; (2000) passenger-mi 15,209,000, passenger-km 24,471,000; (2000) short ton-mi cargo 18,630,000, metric ton-km cargo 27,200,000. Roads (1999): total length 30,968 mi, 49,827 km (paved 12%). Vehicles (1996): passenger cars 62,000; trucks and buses 16,460. Air transport (2001): passenger-km 1,223,000,000; metric ton-km cargo 47,855,000; airports (1994) with scheduled flights 44.

Communications

Medium	date	unit	number	units per 1,000 persons
Daily newspapers	2000	circulation	77,500	5.0
Radio	2000	receivers	3,350,000	216
Television	2000	receivers	375,000	24
Telephones	2001	main lines	58,400	3.7
Cellular telephones	2001	subscribers	147,500	9.0
Personal computers	2001	users	40,000	2.4
Internet	2001	users	35,000	2.1

Education and health

Educational attainment: n.a. *Literacy* (2000): percentage of total population age 15 and over literate 66.5%; males literate 73.6%; females literate 59.7%.

Education (1998–99)

	schools	teachers	students	student/ teacher ratio
Primary (age 6–13)	14,438	42,678	2,012,416	47.2
Secondary (age 14–18)	...	18,987	334,250	17.6
Voc., teacher tr.[14]	...	1,150	8,479	7.3
Higher	6	1,471	31,013	21.1

Health: physicians (1996) 1,470 (1 per 9,351 persons); hospital beds (1990) 10,800 (1 per 1,064 persons); infant mortality rate (2002) 81.9.
Food (2001): daily per capita caloric intake 2,072 (vegetable products 91%, animal products 9%); 91% of FAO recommended minimum requirement.

Military

Total active duty personnel (2002): 13,500 (army 92.6%, navy 3.7%, air force 3.7%). *Military expenditure as percentage of GNP* (1999): 1.2% (world 2.4%); per capita expenditure U.S.$3.

[1]Each of the six autonomous provinces is adopting its own statutory laws per article 2 of the 1998 constitution. [2]The 1998 constitution identifies Malagasy as the "national" language, although neither Malagasy nor French, the languages of the two official texts of the constitution, is itself "official." [3]The ariary (MGA), the precolonial currency of Madagascar, replaced the Malagasy franc (FMG) in July 2003 at a rate of 1 MGA = FMG 5. [4]1999. [5]Antananarivo only. [6]At factor cost. [7]Services includes Finance. [8]Less imputed bank charges. [9]Malagasy households only. [10]Weights of consumer price index components; excludes housing. [11]Imports are f.o.b. in balance of trade and c.i.f. for commodities and trading partners. [12]Export-processing zones. [13]Railroad infrastructure was either inoperable or in poor condition in June 2003. [14]1995–96.

Internet resources for further information:

- **Institut National de la Statistique**
  http://www.cite.mg/instat/Prod/Annuaire/tab_jas.htm

Malawi

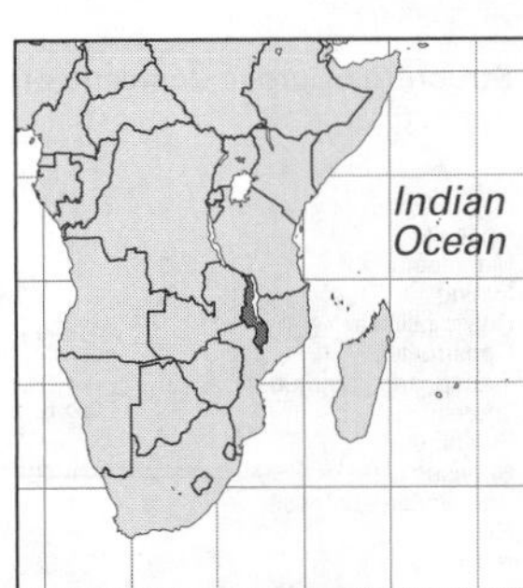

Official name: Republic of Malawi.
Form of government: multiparty republic with one legislative house (National Assembly [192]).
Head of state and government: President.
Capital: Lilongwe[1].
Official language: none.
Official religion: none.
Monetary unit: 1 Malawi kwacha (MK) = 100 tambala; valuation (Sept. 8, 2003) 1 U.S.$ = MK 107.75; 1 £ = MK 170.84.

Area and population		area		population
Regions				1998
Districts	**Capitals**	sq mi	sq km	census
Central	Lilongwe	13,742	35,592	4,066,340
Dedza	Dedza	1,399	3,624	486,682
Dowa	Dowa	1,174	3,041	411,387
Kasungu	Kasungu	3,042	7,878	480,659
Lilongwe	Lilongwe	2,378	6,159	1,346,360
Mchinji	Mchinji	1,296	3,356	324,941
Nkhotakota	Nkhotakota	1,644	4,259	229,460
Ntcheu	Ntcheu	1,322	3,424	370,757
Ntchisi	Ntchisi	639	1,655	167,880
Salima	Salima	848	2,196	248,214
Northern	Mzuzu	10,398	26,931	1,233,560
Chitipa	Chitipa	1,656	4,288	126,799
Karonga	Karonga	1,295	3,355	194,572
Likoma	Likoma	7	18	8,074
Mzimba	Mzimba	4,027	10,430	610,994
Nkhata Bay	Nkhata Bay	1,572	4,071	164,761
Rumphi	Rumphi	1,841	4,769	128,360
Southern	Blantyre	12,260	31,753	4,633,968
Balaka	Balaka	847	2,193	253,098
Blantyre	Blantyre	777	2,012	809,397
Chikwawa	Chikwawa	1,836	4,755	356,682
Chiradzulu	Chiradzulu	296	767	236,050
Machinga	Machinga	1,456	3,771	369,614
Mangochi	Mangochi	2,422	6,273	610,239
Mulanje	Mulanje	794	2,056	428,322
Mwanza	Mwanza	886	2,295	138,015
Nsanje	Nsanje	750	1,942	194,924
Phalombe	Phalombe	538	1,394	231,990
Thyolo	Thyolo	662	1,715	458,976
Zomba	Zomba	996	2,580	546,661
TOTAL LAND AREA		36,400	94,276	
INLAND WATER		9,347	24,208	
TOTAL		45,747	118,484	9,933,868

Demography

Population (2003): 11,651,000.
Density (2003)[2]: persons per sq mi 320.1, persons per sq km 123.6.
Urban-rural (2002): urban 15.1%; rural 84.9%.
Sex distribution (2001): male 49.39%; female 50.61%.
Age breakdown (2001): under 15, 44.4%; 15–29, 30.4%; 30–44, 13.5%; 45–59, 7.2%; 60–74, 3.7%; 75 and over, 0.8%.
Population projection: (2010) 13,416,000; (2020) 16,150,000.
Ethnic composition (2000): Chewa 34.7%; Maravi 12.2%; Ngoni 9.0%; Yao 7.9%; Tumbuka 7.9%; Lomwe 7.7%; Ngonde 3.5%; other 17.1%.
Religious affiliation (1995): Christian 50.3%, of which Protestant 20.5%, Roman Catholic 18.0%; Muslim 20.0%; traditional beliefs 10.0%; other 19.7%.
Major cities (1998): Blantyre 502,053; Lilongwe 440,471; Mzuzu 86,980; Zomba 65,915; Karonga 27,811.

Vital statistics

Birth rate per 1,000 population (2001): 37.8 (world avg. 21.3).
Death rate per 1,000 population (2001): 22.8 (world avg. 9.1).
Natural increase rate per 1,000 population (2001): 15.0 (world avg. 12.2).
Total fertility rate (avg. births per childbearing woman; 2001): 5.2.
Life expectancy at birth (2001): male 36.6 years; female 37.6 years.
Major causes of death per 100,000 population (1986)[3]: infectious and parasitic diseases 711; malnutrition 267; diseases of the respiratory system 265.

National economy

Budget (2001–02). Revenue: MK 22,853,200,000 (tax revenue 72.5%, of which surtax 21.5%, income and profit tax 17.1%, import tax 8.4%; grants 19.8%; nontax revenue 7.7%). Expenditures: MK 30,476,300,000 (current expenditure 86.7%; capital expenditure 9.9%; other 3.4%).
Public debt (external, outstanding; 2001): U.S.$2,483,000,000.
Production (metric tons except as noted). Agriculture (2002): sugarcane 1,900,000, corn (maize) 1,603,000, cassava 1,540,000, potatoes 1,082,000, plantains 200,000, peanuts (groundnuts) 158,000, tobacco leaves 69,401, tea 38,000, coffee 3,600; livestock (number of live animals) 1,700,000 goats, 750,000 cattle, 456,000 pigs; roundwood (2001) 5,515,659 cu m; fish catch (2000) 45,530. Mining and quarrying (1999): limestone 171,900; gemstones 649 kg. Manufacturing (value added in MK '000,000; 1998): beverages 793; food products 571; chemicals 505, of which industrial 245; fabricated metal products 278. Energy production (consumption): electricity (kW-hr; 1999) 883,000,000 (881,000,000); coal (metric tons; 1999) none (17,000); petroleum products (metric tons; 1999) none (206,000).
Land use (1994): forested 39.3%; meadows and pastures 19.6%; agricultural and under permanent cultivation 18.1%; other 23.0%.

Population economically active (1998): total 4,509,290; activity rate 45.4% (participation rates: ages 10 and over 66.9%; female 50.2%).

Price and earnings indexes (1995 = 100)	1995	1996	1997	1998	1999	2000	2001
Consumer price index	100.0	137.6	150.2	194.9	282.4	365.6	465.2
Earnings index	...	...	...	...	...	...	...

Gross national product (2001): U.S.$1,700,000,000 (U.S.$160 per capita).

Structure of gross domestic product and labour force	2000		1998	
	in value MK '000,000[4]	% of total value[4]	labour force	% of labour force
Agriculture	5,210	39.2	3,765,827	83.6
Mining	188	1.4	2,499	0.1
Manufacturing	1,705	12.8	118,483	2.6
Construction	288	2.2	73,402	1.6
Public utilities	189	1.4	7,319	0.2
Transp. and commun.	552	4.2	32,623	0.7
Trade	2,760	20.8	257,389	5.7
Finance	1,242	9.3	13,957	0.3
Public administration	1,282	9.6	101,433	2.2
Services	271	2.0	85,996	1.9
Other	–387[5]	–2.9[5]	50,362[6]	1.1[6]
TOTAL	13,300	100.0	4,509,290	100.0

Household income and expenditure. Average household size (1998) 4.3; income per household: n.a.; sources of income: n.a.; expenditure (2001)[7]: food 55.5%, clothing and footwear 11.7%, housing 9.6%, household goods 8.4%.
Tourism: receipts (2001) U.S.$28,000,000; expenditures (1994) U.S.$15,000,000.

Foreign trade[8]

Balance of trade (current prices)	1997	1998	1999	2000	2001	2002[9]
MK '000,000	–4,168	–3,361	–9,788	–8,658	–7,664	–15,605
% of total	19.0%	9.3%	19.7%	15.5%	10.7%	20.6%

Imports (2001): MK 39,480,000,000 (1998; food 16.4%, of which cereals 13.1%; machinery and apparatus 15.3%; chemicals and chemical products 13.2%; road vehicles 11.6%; mineral fuels 9.6%). *Major import sources* (2001): South Africa 39.7%; Zimbabwe 16.0%; Zambia 10.9%; India 3.2%; Germany 2.7%.
Exports (2001): MK 31,816,000,000 (tobacco 57.7%; sugar 12.5%; tea 7.7%; apparel 1.7%; coffee 1.4%). *Major export destinations:* South Africa 19.1%; U.S. 15.4%; Germany 11.2%; Japan 7.6%; The Netherlands 5.4%.

Transport and communications

Transport. Railroads (1995–96): route length 495 mi, 797 km; passenger-km 18,048,000; metric ton-km cargo 43,431,000. Roads (1998): total length 10,222 mi, 16,451 km (paved 19%). Vehicles (1996): passenger cars 27,000; trucks and buses 29,700. Air transport (2001)[10]: passenger-km 241,000,000; metric ton-km cargo 798,000; airports (1998) 5.

Communications				units per 1,000
Medium	date	unit	number	persons
Daily newspapers	1996	circulation	22,000[11]	2.3[11]
Radio	2000	receivers	5,426,000	499
Television	2000	receivers	32,600	3.0
Telephones	2001	main lines	54,100	4.7
Cellular telephones	2001	subscribers	55,700	4.8
Personal computers	2001	units	13,000	1.1
Internet	2001	users	20,000	1.7

Education and health

Educational attainment (1987). Percentage of population age 25 and over having: no formal education 55.0%; primary education 39.8%; secondary and higher 5.2%. *Literacy* (2000): total population age 15 and over literate 60.1%; males literate 74.5%; females literate 46.5%.

Education (1995–96)	schools	teachers	students	student/ teacher ratio
Primary (age 6–13)	3,706	49,138	2,887,107	58.8
Secondary (age 14–18)	...	2,948	139,386	47.3
Voc., teacher tr.	...	224	2,525	11.3
Higher	6[12]	329	3,872	11.8

Health: physicians (1989) 186 (1 per 47,634 persons); hospital beds (1998) 14,200 (1 per 746 persons); infant mortality rate (2001) 121.0.
Food (2001): daily per capita caloric intake 2,168 (vegetable products 97%, animal products 3%); 93% of FAO recommended minimum requirement.

Military

Total active duty personnel (2002): 5,300 (army 100%; navy, none; air force, none). *Military expenditure as percentage of GNP* (1999): 0.6% (world 2.4%); per capita expenditure U.S.$1.

[1]Judiciary meets in Blantyre. [2]Based on land area. [3]Estimates based on reported inpatient deaths in hospitals, constituting an estimated 8% of total deaths. [4]At constant prices of 1994. [5]Less imputed bank service charges. [6]Unemployed. [7]Weights of consumer price index components. [8]Imports c.i.f.; exports f.o.b. [9]Excludes December. [10]Air Malawi only. [11]Circulation for one newspaper only. [12]Universities only.

Internet resources for further information:
- **National Statistical Office of Malawi http://www.nso.malawi.net**

Malaysia

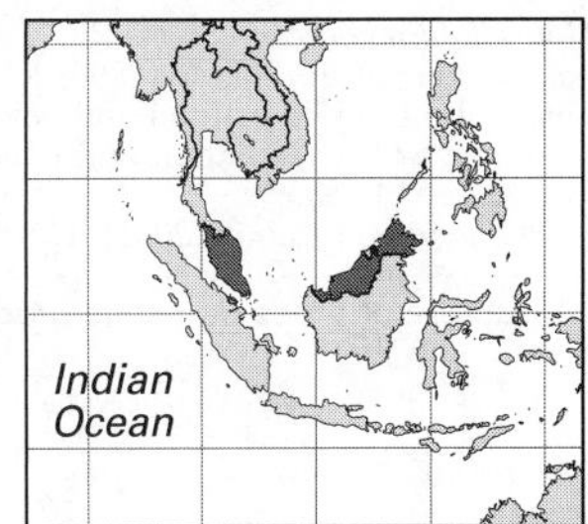

Official name: Malaysia.
Form of government: federal constitutional monarchy with two legislative houses (Senate [70[1]]; House of Representatives [193]).
Chief of state: Yang di-Pertuan Agong (Paramount Ruler).
Head of government: Prime Minister.
Capital: Kuala Lumpur[2].
Official language: Malay.
Official religion: Islam.
Monetary unit: 1 ringgit, or Malaysian dollar (RM) = 100 cents; valuation[3] (Sept. 8, 2003) 1 U.S.$ = RM 3.80; 1 £ = RM 6.03.

Area and population		area		population
Regions				2000
States	**Capitals**	sq mi	sq km	census
East Malaysia				
Sabah	Kota Kinabalu	28,424	73,619	2,603,485
Sarawak	Kuching	48,050	124,450	2,071,506
West Malaysia (Peninsular Malaysia)				
Johor	Johor Bahru	7,331	18,987	2,740,625
Kedah	Alor Setar	3,639	9,425	1,649,756
Kelantan	Kota Baharu	5,801	15,024	1,313,014
Melaka	Melaka	638	1,652	635,791
Negeri Sembilan	Seremban	2,565	6,644	859,924
Pahang	Kuantan	13,886	35,965	1,288,376
Perak	Ipoh	8,110	21,005	2,051,236
Perlis	Kangar	307	795	204,450
Pulau Pinang	George Town	398	1,031	1,313,449
Selangor	Shah Alam	3,054	7,910	4,188,876[4]
Terengganu	Kuala Terengganu	5,002	12,955	898,825
Federal Territories				
Kuala Lumpur	—	94	243	1,379,310
Labuan	—	36	92	76,067
Putrajaya	—	19	50	[4]
TOTAL		127,355	329,847	23,274,690

Demography

Population (2003): 25,225,000.
Density (2003): persons per sq mi 198.1, persons per sq km 76.5.
Urban-rural (2002): urban 59.0%; rural 41.0%.
Sex distribution (2000): male 50.50%; female 49.50%.
Age breakdown (2000): under 15, 33.0%; 15–29, 28.3%; 30–44, 21.0%; 45–59, 11.6%; 60–74, 4.9%; 75 and over, 1.2%.
Population projection: (2010) 28,414,000; (2020) 32,614,000.
Ethnic composition (2000): Malay and other indigenous 61.3%; Chinese 24.5%; Indian 7.2%; other nonindigenous 1.1%; noncitizen 5.9%.
Religious affiliation (2000): Muslim 60.4%; Buddhist 19.2%; Christian 9.1%; Hindu 6.3%; Chinese folk religionist 2.6%; other 2.4%.
Major cities (2000[5]): Kuala Lumpur 1,297,526; Ipoh 566,211; Kelang 563,173; Petaling Jaya 438,084; Johor Bahru 384,613.

Vital statistics

Birth rate per 1,000 population (2003): 21.4 (world avg. 21.3).
Death rate per 1,000 population (2003): 4.4 (world avg. 9.1).
Natural increase rate per 1,000 population (2003): 17.0 (world avg. 12.2).
Total fertility rate (avg. births per childbearing woman; 2000): 3.1.
Life expectancy at birth (2003): male 70.6 years; female 75.5 years.
Major causes of death per 100,000 population (1998): diseases of the circulatory system 37.7; malignant neoplasms (cancers) 20.7; infectious and parasitic diseases 16.1; accidents and violence 12.8; respiratory diseases 10.5.

National economy

Budget (2001). Revenue: RM 79,567,000,000 (income tax 52.9%, nontax revenue 25.1%, taxes on goods and services 16.9%, taxes on international trade 5.1%). Expenditures: RM 63,757,000,000 (education 22.6%, interest payments 15.1%, defense and internal security 13.0%, social security 8.7%, health 7.3%, transport 2.1%, agriculture 2.1%).
Tourism (2001): receipts from visitors U.S.$6,374,000,000; expenditures by nationals abroad (2000) U.S.$2,052,000,000.
Population economically active (1999): total 9,010,000; activity rate 39.7% (participation rates: ages 15–64, 60.6%; female [2000] 34.7%; unemployed 3.0%).

Price index (1995 = 100)	1996	1997	1998	1999	2000	2001	2002
Consumer price index	103.5	106.2	111.8	114.9	116.7	118.3	120.5

Production (metric tons except as noted). Agriculture, forestry, fishing (2002): palm fruit oil 67,400,000, rice 2,091,000, coconuts 700,000, rubber 589,400, bananas 500,000, pepper 28,600; livestock (number of live animals) 1,824,200 pigs, 747,600 cattle; roundwood (2001) 16,346,500 cu m; fish catch (2000) 1,441,018. Mining and quarrying (2001): iron ore 376,000; struverite 9,657; tin (metal content) 4,973; gold 3,965 kg. Manufacturing (2001): cement 13,820,000; iron and steel bars and rods 2,712,200; refined sugar 1,210,400; plywood 3,940,200 cu m; radio receivers 29,184,000 units; automotive tires 26,507,000 units. Energy production (consumption): electricity (kW-hr; 1999) 65,189,000,000 (65,189,000,000); coal (metric tons; 2001) 540,000 ([1999] 2,180,000); crude petroleum (barrels; 2001) 247,000,000[6] ([1999] 125,100,000); petroleum products (metric tons; 1999) 16,566,000 (19,704,000); natural gas (cu m; 2001) 46,378,000,000 ([1999] 24,771,800,000).
Gross national product (2001): U.S.$79,300,000,000 (U.S.$3,330 per capita).

Structure of gross domestic product and labour force	2000			
	in value RM '000,000	% of total value	labour force	% of labour force
Agriculture	17,687	8.4	1,408,000	14.7
Mining	14,416	6.9	41,000	0.4
Manufacturing	69,867	33.4	2,559,000	26.7
Construction	6,996	3.3	755,000	7.9
Public utilities	7,886	3.8	75,000	0.8
Transp. and commun.	16,694	8.0	462,000	4.8
Trade	30,949	14.8	1,584,000	16.5
Finance	26,161	12.5	509,000	5.3
Pub. admin., defense	30,057	14.4	981,000	10.3
Services			899,000	9.4
Other	–11,348[7]	–5.5[7]	302,000	3.2
TOTAL	209,365	100.0	9,575,000	100.0

Public debt (external, outstanding; 2001): U.S.$24,068,000,000.
Household income and expenditure. Average household size (2000) 4.5; annual income per household (1997) RM 31,280 (U.S.$11,120); sources of income: n.a.; expenditure (1983): food 28.7%, transportation 20.9%, recreation and education 11.0%, housing 10.2%, household durable goods 7.7%.

Foreign trade[8]

Balance of trade (current prices)	1997	1998	1999	2000	2001	2002
RM '000,000	–50	+58,440	+73,080	+61,810	+54,050	+50,970
% of total	0.0%	11.4%	12.8%	9.0%	8.8%	7.7%

Imports (2002): RM 303,510,000,000 (microcircuits, transistors, and valves 29.2%; computers, office machines, and parts 6.9%; telecommunications equipment 4.3%; other electrical machinery 6.6%). *Major import sources:* Japan 17.8%; U.S. 16.4%; Singapore 12.0%; China 7.8%; Taiwan 5.6%; South Korea 5.3%.
Exports (2002): RM 354,480,000,000 (microcircuits, transistors, and valves 20.5%; computers, office machines, and parts 18.4%; telecommunications equipment 5.4%; fixed vegetable oils 3.9%; crude petroleum 3.3%). *Major export destinations:* U.S. 20.2%; Singapore 17.1%; Japan 11.2%; Hong Kong 5.7%; China 5.6%.

Transport and communications

Transport. Railroads (2000): route length 2,227 km; passenger-km 1,241,000,000[9]; metric ton-km cargo 918,000,000[9]. Roads (2000): total length 66,445 km (paved 76%). Vehicles (2000): passenger cars 4,212,567; trucks and buses 713,946. Air transport (2001): passenger-km 35,658,000,000; metric ton-km cargo 3,456,000,000; airports (1997) 39.

Communications				units
Medium	date	unit	number	per 1,000 persons
Daily newspapers	2000	circulation	3,672,000	158
Radio	2000	receivers	9,762,000	420
Television	2000	receivers	3,900,000	168
Telephones	2001	main lines	4,738,000	199
Cellular telephones	2001	subscribers	7,128,000	300
Personal computers	2001	units	3,000,000	126
Internet	2001	users	5,700,000	239

Education and health

Educational attainment (1996). Percentage of population age 25 and over having: no formal schooling 16.7%; primary education 33.7%; secondary 42.8%; higher 6.8%. *Literacy* (2000): total population age 15 and over literate 87.5%; males literate 91.4%; females literate 83.4%.

Education (2000)	schools	teachers	students	student/ teacher ratio
Primary (age 7–12)	7,231	154,509	2,934,000	19.0
Secondary (age 13–19)	1,561	107,598	1,938,000	18.0
Voc., teacher tr.[10]	80	5,111	51,000	10.0
Higher	55	19,702	344,000	17.5

Health (2000): physicians 15,619 (1 per 1,488 persons); hospital beds 44,126 (1 per 527 persons); infant mortality rate per 1,000 live births (2002) 7.9.
Food (2001): daily per capita caloric intake 2,927 (vegetable products 82%, animal products 18%); 131% of FAO recommended minimum.

Military

Total active duty personnel (2002): 100,000 (army 80.0%, navy 12.0%, air force 8.0%). *Military expenditure as percentage of GDP* (1999): 2.3% (world 2.4%); per capita expenditure U.S.$78.

[1]Includes 40 appointees of the Paramount Ruler; the remaining 30 are indirectly elected at different times. [2]The transfer to the new federal administrative centre at Putrajaya is occurring between 1999 and 2012. [3]Pegged to the U.S. dollar at RM 3.80 = 1 U.S.$ on Oct. 6, 2000. [4]Selangor includes population data for Putrajaya. [5]Preliminary. [6]Production for Sabah and Sarawak only. [7]Net bank service charges. [8]Imports c.i.f.; exports f.o.b. [9]Peninsular Malaysia and Singapore. [10]1999.

Internet resources for further information:
- **Department of Statistics http://www.statistics.gov.my**
- **Malaysian Information Services (English) http://penerangan.gov.my**

Maldives

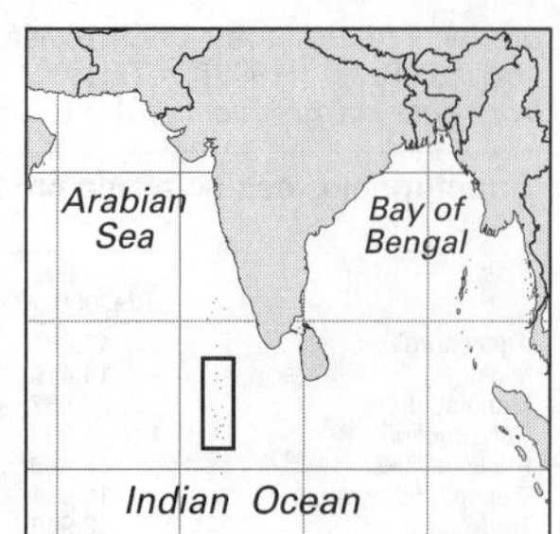

Official name: Divehi Jumhuriyya (Republic of Maldives).
Form of government: republic with one legislative house (Majlis[1] [42[2]]).
Head of state and government: President.
Capital: Male.
Official language: Divehi.
Official religion: Islam.
Monetary unit: 1 Maldivian rufiyaa (Rf) = 100 laari; valuation (Sept. 8, 2003) 1 U.S.$ = Rf 12.80; 1 £ = Rf 20.30.

Area and population[3]

Administrative atolls	Capitals	area sq mi	area sq km	population 2000 census
North Thiladhunmathi (Haa-Alifu)	Dhidhdhoo	...	...	14,161
South Thiladhunmathi (Haa-Dhaalu)	Nolhivaranfaru	...	...	16,956
North Miladhunmadulu (Shaviyani)	Farukolhu-funadhoo	...	...	11,406
South Miladhunmadulu (Noonu)	Manadhoo	...	...	10,429
North Maalhosmadulu (Raa)	Ugoofaaru	...	...	14,486
South Maalhosmadulu (Baa)	Eydhafushi	...	...	9,612
Faadhippolhu (Lhaviyani)	Naifaru	...	...	9,385
Male (Kaafu)	Thulusdhoo	...	...	13,474
Ari Atoll Uthuru Gofi (Alifu)	Rasdhoo	...	...	5,518
Ari Atoll Dhekunu Gofi (Alifu)	Mahibadhoo	...	...	7,803
Felidhu Atoll (Vaavu)	Felidhoo	...	...	1,753
Mulakatholhu (Meemu)	Muli	...	...	5,084
North Nilandhe Atoll (Faafu)	Magoodhoo	...	...	3,827
South Nilandhe Atoll (Dhaalu)	Kudahuvadhoo	...	...	5,067
Kolhumadulu (Thaa)	Veymandoo	...	...	9,305
Hadhdhunmathi (Laamu)	Hithadhoo	...	...	11,588
North Huvadhu Atoll (Gaafu-Alifu)	Viligili	...	...	8,249
South Huvadhu Atoll (Gaafu-Dhaalu)	Thinadhoo	...	...	11,886
Foammulah (Gnyaviyani)	Foahmulah	...	...	7,528
Addu Atoll (Seenu)	Hithadhoo	...	...	18,515
Capital island				
Male (Maale)		...	...	74,069
TOTAL		115	298	270,101

Demography

Population (2003): 285,000.
Density (2003): persons per sq mi 2,478, persons per sq km 956.4.
Urban-rural (2002): urban 27.0%; rural 73.0%.
Sex distribution (2003): male 50.73%; female 49.27%.
Age breakdown (2003): under 15, 36.1%; 15–29, 31.7%; 30–44, 18.0%; 45–59, 7.9%; 60–74, 5.2%; 75 and over, 1.1%.
Population projection: (2010) 318,000; (2020) 372,000.
Doubling time: 23 years.
Ethnic composition (2000): Maldivian 98.5%; Sinhalese 0.7%; other 0.8%.
Religious affiliation: virtually 100% Sunnī Muslim.
Major city (2000): Male 74,069.

Vital statistics

Birth rate per 1,000 population (2002): 36.1 (world avg. 21.3).
Death rate per 1,000 population (2002): 6.1 (world avg. 9.1).
Natural increase rate per 1,000 population (2002): 30.0 (world avg. 12.2).
Total fertility rate (avg. births per childbearing woman; 2002): 5.4.
Marriage rate per 1,000 population (2001): 11.6.
Divorce rate per 1,000 population (2001): 5.5.
Life expectancy at birth (2002): male 68.0 years; female 67.0 years.
Major causes of death per 100,000 population (1988): rheumatic fever 106.0; ischemic heart diseases 65.0; bronchitis, emphysema, and asthma 61.0; tetanus 23.5; tuberculosis 13.0; accidents and suicide 10.0.

National economy

Budget (2001). Revenue: Rf 2,513,200,000 (nontax revenue 50.8%, taxation 41.4%, foreign aid 7.3%). Expenditures: Rf 2,886,200,000 (general public services 42.1%, of which defense 15.2%; education 18.5%; health 10.4%; transportation and communications 8.9%; transfer payments 2.3%).
Public debt (external, outstanding; 2001): U.S.$180,700,000.
Production (metric tons except as noted). Agriculture, forestry, fishing (2001): vegetables and melons 28,000, coconuts 15,000, fruits (excluding melons) 9,000, roots and tubers (including cassava, sweet potatoes, and yams) 8,000; fish catch 127,184. Mining and quarrying: coral for construction materials. Manufacturing: details, n.a.; however, major industries include boat building and repairing, coir yarn and mat weaving, coconut and fish processing, lacquerwork, garment manufacturing, and handicrafts. Energy production (consumption): electricity (kW-hr; 1999) 93,000,000 (93,000,000); petroleum products (metric tons; 1999) none (152,000).
Tourism (2001): receipts from visitors U.S.$331,000,000; expenditures by nationals abroad U.S.$45,000,000.
Population economically active (2000): total 87,987; activity rate of total population 32.6% (participation rates: ages 15–64, 58.5%; female 33.8%; unemployed 2.0%).

Price index (1995 = 100)

	1996	1997	1998	1999	2000	2001	2002
Consumer price index	106.3	114.3	112.7	116.0	114.7	115.4	116.5

Household income and expenditure. Average household size (2000) 6.8; annual income per household (1990) Rf 2,616 (U.S.$274); sources of income: n.a.; expenditure (1981)[4]: food and beverages 61.8%, housing equipment 17.0%, clothing 8.0%, recreation and education 5.9%, transportation 2.6%, health 2.5%, rent 1.6%.
Gross national product (2001): U.S.$600,000,000 (U.S.$2,170 per capita).

Structure of gross domestic product and labour force

	2000 in value Rf '000[5]	% of total value	labour force	% of labour force
Agriculture[6]	549,200	8.7	11,789	13.4
Mining	35,600	0.6	473	0.5
Manufacturing } Public utilities }	738,900	11.8	11,081	12.6
			1,132	1.3
Construction	166,800	2.6	3,691	4.2
Transp. and commun.	986,100	15.7	7,873	9.0
Trade	2,377,900	37.9	15,606	17.7
Finance	882,900	14.1	1,690	1.9
Pub. admin., defense	773,900	12.3 }	18,089	20.6
Services	136,400	2.2 }		
Other	−369,400	−5.9	16,563	18.8
TOTAL	6,278,300	100.0	87,987	100.0

Land use (1994): forested 3.3%; meadows and pastures 3.3%; agricultural and under permanent cultivation 10.0%; built-on, wasteland, and other 83.4%.

Foreign trade[7, 8]

Balance of trade (current prices)

	1996	1997	1998	1999	2000	2001
U.S.$'000,000	−221.8	−255.8	−258.4	−310.7	−279.9	−285.2
% of total	58.1%	57.9%	57.5%	62.9%	56.3%	56.4%

Imports (2001): U.S.$395,400,000 (food products 36.9%; petroleum products 12.1%; transport equipment 10.5%; construction-related goods 10.2%). *Major import sources:* Asian countries 69%, of which Singapore 25%, Sri Lanka 13%, India 10%, Malaysia 9%; European countries 14%.
Exports (2001): U.S.$110,200,000 (domestic exports 69.1%, of which fish 32.5%, garments 29.3%, live tropical fish 2.8%; reexports 30.9%, of which jet fuel 25.6%). *Major export destinations:* United States 39%; Sri Lanka 21%; European countries 15%.

Transport and communications

Transport. Railroads: none. Roads: total length, n.a. Vehicles (1999): passenger cars 3,037; trucks and buses 1,003. Merchant marine (1992): vessels (100 gross tons and over) 44; total deadweight tonnage 78,994. Air transport (1997): passengers carried 189,000; passenger-km 292,000,000; airports (1997) with scheduled flights 5.

Communications

Medium	date	unit	number	units per 1,000 persons
Daily newspapers	1996	circulation	5,000	19
Radio	1997	receivers	34,000	129
Television	2000	receivers	10,900	40
Telephones	2001	main lines	27,200	101
Cellular telephones	2001	subscribers	18,400	68
Personal computers	2001	units	6,000	22
Internet	2001	users	10,000	37

Education and health

Educational attainment (1990). Percentage of population age 15 and over having: no standard passed 25.6%; primary standard 37.2%; middle standard 25.9%; secondary standard 6.3%; preuniversity 3.4%; higher 0.4%; not stated 1.2%. *Literacy* (1995): total population age 15 and over literate 93.2%; males literate 93.0%; females literate 93.3%.

Education (1998)

	schools	teachers	students	student/ teacher ratio
Primary (age 6–11)	228	1,992	48,895	24.5
Secondary (age 11–18)	...	...	15,933[9]	...
Voc., teacher tr.	...	...	452[9]	...
Higher	—	—	—	—

Health (2001): physicians 263 (1 per 1,049 persons); hospital beds (2000) 470 (1 per 577 persons); infant mortality rate per 1,000 live births (2002) 38.0.
Food (2001): daily per capita caloric intake 2,587 (vegetable products 75%, animal products 25%); 117% of FAO recommended minimum requirement.

Military

Total active duty personnel: Maldives maintains a single security force numbering about 700–1,000; it performs both army and police functions.

[1]Also known or translated as People's Majlis, Citizens' Council, or Citizens' Assembly. [2]Excludes eight nonelective seats. [3]Maldives is divided into 20 administrative districts corresponding to atoll groups; arrangement shown here is from north to south. Total area excludes 34,634 sq mi (89,702 sq km) of tidal waters. [4]Weights of consumer price index components. [5]At 1995 prices. [6]Primarily fishing. [7]Imports c.i.f.; exports f.o.b. [8]Exports include reexports. [9]1992.

Internet resources for further information:
- **Ministry of Planning and National Development http://www.planning.gov.mv/index2.htm**

Mali

Official name: République du Mali (Republic of Mali).
Form of government: multiparty republic with one legislative house (National Assembly [147]).
Chief of state: President.
Head of government: Prime Minister.
Capital: Bamako.
Official language: French.
Official religion: none.
Monetary unit: 1 CFA franc (CFAF) = 100 centimes; valuation (Sept. 8, 2003) 1 U.S.$ = CFAF 594.70; 1 £ = CFAF 942.93[1].

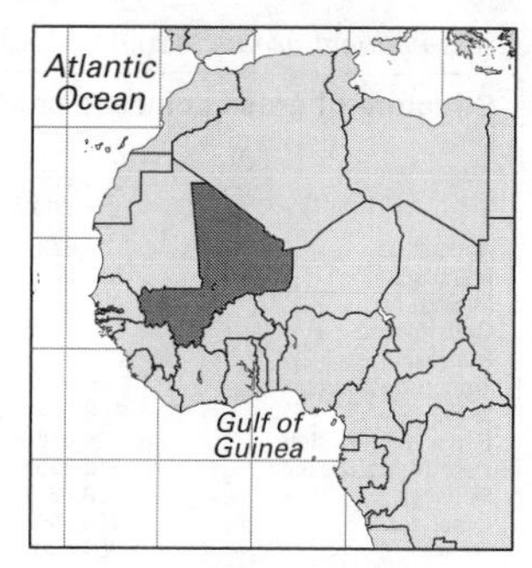

Area and population

Regions	Capitals	area sq mi	area sq km	population 1998 census
Gao	Gao	65,858	170,572	495,178
Kayes	Kayes	46,233	119,743	1,424,657
Kidal	Kidal	58,467	151,430	65,524
Koulikoro	Koulikoro	37,007	95,848	1,620,811
Mopti	Mopti	30,509	79,017	1,405,370
Ségou	Ségou	25,028	64,821	1,652,594
Sikasso	Sikasso	27,135	70,280	1,839,747
Tombouctou	Tombouctou (Timbuktu)	191,743	496,611	496,312
District				
Bamako	Bamako	97	252	1,178,977
TOTAL		482,077	1,248,574	10,179,170[2]

Demography

Population (2003): 11,626,000.
Density (2003): persons per sq mi 24.1, persons per sq km 9.3.
Urban-rural (1998): urban 28.7%; rural 71.3%.
Sex distribution (2001): male 48.9%; female 51.1%.
Age breakdown (2001): under 15, 47.2%; 15–29, 26.8%; 30–44, 13.3%; 45–59, 7.9%; 60–74, 4.0%; 75 and over, 0.8%.
Population projection: (2010) 14,012,000; (2020) 17,847,000.
Doubling time: 23 years.
Ethnic composition (2000): Bambara 30.6%; Senufo 10.5%; Fula Macina (Niafunke) 9.6%; Soninke 7.4%; Tuareg 7.0%; Maninka 6.6%; Songhai 6.3%; Dogon 4.3%; Bobo 3.5%; other 14.2%.
Religious affiliation (2000): Muslim 82%; traditional beliefs 16%; Christian 2%.
Major cities (1998): Bamako 1,016,167; Sikasso 113,803; Ségou 90,898; Mopti 79,840; Gao 54,903.

Vital statistics

Birth rate per 1,000 population (2001): 48.8 (world avg. 21.3).
Death rate per 1,000 population (2001): 18.7 (world avg. 9.1).
Natural increase rate per 1,000 population (2001): 30.1 (world avg. 12.2).
Total fertility rate (avg. births per childbearing woman; 2001): 6.8.
Life expectancy at birth (2001): male 45.8 years; female 48.2 years.
Major causes of death per 100,000 population: n.a.; morbidity ([notified cases of illness] by cause as a percentage of all reported infectious disease; 1985): malaria 62.1%; measles 10.3%; amebiasis 10.3%; syphilis and gonococcal infections 6.0%; influenza 4.9%.

National economy

Budget (2002). Revenue: CFAF 379,400,000,000 (tax revenue 82.7%, nontax revenue 17.3%). Expenditures: CFAF 601,500,000,000 (current expenditure 46.7%, of which wages and salaries 14.9%, education 4.9%, interest on public debt 3.5%; capital expenditure 53.3%).
Public debt (external, outstanding; 2001): U.S.$2,616,000,000.
Tourism (2000): receipts from visitors U.S.$71,000,000; expenditures by nationals abroad U.S.$41,000,000.
Population economically active (2001): total 5,895,000; activity rate of total population 53.7% (participation rates: ages 15–64, n.a.; female, n.a.; unemployed, n.a.).

Price and earnings indexes (1995 = 100)

	1996	1997	1998	1999	2000	2001	2002
Consumer price index	106.8	106.4	110.7	109.4	108.6	114.3	120.0
Hourly earnings index[3]	103.2	106.0	109.0[4]	...	...	...	...

Production (metric tons except as noted). Agriculture, forestry, fishing (2002): millet 1,034,211, sorghum 951,417, rice 926,497, seed cotton 611,938, corn (maize) 320,502, sugarcane 300,000, peanuts (groundnuts) 257,108, sweet potatoes 74,483; livestock (number of live animals) 15,000,000 goats and sheep, 6,818,000 cattle, 700,000 asses, 470,000 camels, 170,000 horses, 85,000 pigs; roundwood (2001) 5,200,428 cu m; fish catch (2001) 109,900. Mining and quarrying (2002): limestone 20,000[5]; phosphate 3,000[5]; iron oxide 708[5]; gypsum 500; gold 63,000 kg; silver 1,000 kg. Manufacturing (2000): cement 40,000; sugar 28,000; soap 10,097[6]; soft drinks 68,609 hectolitres[6]; beer 41,690 hectolitres[6]; shoes 111,000 pairs[6]; cigarettes 51,400 cartons. Construction: n.a. Energy production (consumption): electricity (kW-hr; 1999) 404,000,000 (404,000,000); coal, none (n.a.); crude petroleum, none (n.a.); petroleum products (metric tons; 1999) none (161,000); natural gas, none (n.a.).
Gross national product (2001): U.S.$2,500,000,000 (U.S.$230 per capita).

Structure of gross domestic product and labour force

	2001 in value CFAF '000,000	% of total value	labour force	% of labour force
Agriculture	986,800	47.6	4,580,000	77.7
Mining	169,900	8.2		
Manufacturing	88,900	4.2		
Construction	114,100	5.5		
Public utilities	29,800	1.4	1,315,000	22.3
Transp. and commun.	85,700	4.1		
Trade, Finance	268,900	13.0		
Pub. admin., defense	129,500	6.3		
Services	71,600	3.5	...	...
Other	128,400[7]	6.2[7]	...	...
TOTAL	2,073,600	100.0	5,895,000	100.0

Household income and expenditure. Average household size (2000) 5.6; average annual income per household: n.a.; sources of income: n.a.; expenditure: n.a.
Land use (1994): forested 5.7%; meadows and pastures 24.6%; forest 9.7%; agricultural and under permanent cultivation 2.1%; other 63.6%.

Foreign trade

Balance of trade (current prices)

	1996	1997	1998	1999	2000	2001
CFAF '000,000,000	−60.7	+9.2	−1.2	−21.2	−33.4	−2.4
% of total	12.1%	1.4%	0.2%	2.9%	4.1%	0.2%

Imports (2001): CFAF 532,900,000,000 (machinery and apparatus 46.0%, petroleum products 25.9%, food products 13.0%). *Major import sources* (1999)[8]: African countries *c.* 51%, of which Côte d'Ivoire *c.* 20%; France *c.* 18%; Germany *c.* 3%; Hong Kong *c.* 3%.
Exports (2001): CFAF 530,500,000,000 (gold 66.7%, raw cotton and cotton products 15.7%, live animals 8.5%). *Major export destinations* (1999)[8]: Italy *c.* 12%; Taiwan *c.* 10%; Thailand *c.* 10%; South Korea *c.* 9%; Canada *c.* 8%; Portugal *c.* 5%.

Transport and communications

Transport. Railroads (1999): route length 453 mi, 729 km; passenger-mi 130,000,000, passenger-km 210,000,000; short ton-mi cargo 165,000,000, metric ton-km cargo 241,000,000. Roads (1996): total length 9,383 mi, 15,100 km (paved 12%). Vehicles (1996): passenger cars 26,190; trucks and buses 18,240. Merchant marine: vessels (100 gross tons and over) none. Air transport (1999)[9]: passenger-mi 146,000,000, passenger-km 235,000,000; short ton-mi cargo 25,000,000, metric ton-km cargo 36,000,000; airports (1999) 9.

Communications

Medium	date	unit	number	units per 1,000 persons
Daily newspapers	1997	circulation	45,000	4.6
Radio	2000	receivers	597,000	56
Television	2000	receivers	149,000	14
Telephones	2001	main lines	49,900	4.3
Cellular phones	2001	subscribers	45,300	3.9
Personal computers	2001	units	14,000	1.2
Internet	2001	users	30,000	2.6

Education and health

Educational attainment: n.a. *Literacy* (2000): percentage of total population age 15 and over literate 41.5%; males literate 48.9%; females literate 34.4%.

Education (2000–01)

	schools	teachers	students	student/ teacher ratio
Primary (age 6–14)	2,871	14,962	1,115,563	74.5
Secondary (age 15–17)	...	...	257,574	...
Vocational	...	...	47,883	...
Higher	...	1,312	28,000	21.3

Health: physicians (1993) 483 (1 per 18,376 persons); hospital beds (1998) 2,412 (1 per 4,168 persons); infant mortality rate per 1,000 live births (2001) 121.4.
Food (2001): daily per capita caloric intake 2,376 (vegetable products 91%, animal products 9%); 101% of FAO recommended minimum requirement.

Military

Total active duty personnel (2002): 7,350 (army 100.0%). *Military expenditure as percentage of GNP* (1999): 2.3% (world 2.4%); per capita expenditure U.S.$6.

[1]Formerly pegged to the French franc, and since Jan. 1, 2002, to the euro at the rate of €1 = CFAF 655.96. [2]Excludes 772,006 Malians living abroad. [3]Minimum wage for nonagricultural workers. [4]As of November 1. [5]1997. [6]1995. [7]Import taxes. [8]Estimated figures. [9]Represents 1/11 of the traffic of Air Afrique, which was operated by 11 West African states and was declared bankrupt in February 2002.

Internet resources for further information:
- **Embassy of Mali (Washington, D.C.) http://www.maliembassy-usa.org**
- **Investir en Zone Franc http://www.izf.net/izf/Index.htm**

Malta

Official name: Repubblikka ta' Malta (Maltese); Republic of Malta (English).
Form of government: unitary multiparty republic with one legislative house (House of Representatives [65]).
Chief of state: President.
Head of government: Prime Minister.
Capital: Valletta.
Official languages: Maltese; English.
Official religion: Roman Catholicism.
Monetary unit: 1 Maltese lira (Lm) = 100 cents = 1,000 mils; valuation (Sept. 8, 2003) 1 U.S.$ = Lm 0.39; 1 £ = Lm 0.61.

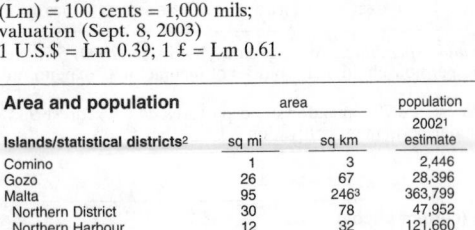

Area and population

Islands/statistical districts[2]	area sq mi	area sq km	population 2002[1] estimate
Comino	1	3	2,446
Gozo	26	67	28,396
Malta	95	246[3]	363,799
Northern District	30	78	47,952
Northern Harbour	12	32	121,660
South Eastern District	20	53	54,149
Southern Harbour	6	15	85,495
Western District	27	69	54,543
TOTAL	122	316	394,641[4]

Demography

Population (2003): 399,000.
Density (2003): persons per sq mi 3,270, persons per sq km 1,263.
Urban-rural (2000): urban 90.5%; rural 9.5%.
Sex distribution (2002): male 49.54%; female 50.46%.
Age breakdown (2002): under 15, 18.7%; 15–29, 22.1%; 30–44, 20.1%; 45–59, 22.0%; 60–74, 11.8%; 75 and over, 5.3%.
Population projection: (2010) 419,000; (2020) 440,000.
Ethnic composition (2000): Maltese 93.8%; British 2.1%; Arab 2.0%; Italian 1.5%; other 0.6%.
Religious affiliation (2000): Roman Catholic 94.5%; other 5.5%.
Major localities (2002[1]): Birkirkara 22,208; Qormi 18,501; Mosta 17,847; Zabbar 15,003; Valletta 7,199 (urban agglomeration [2001] 82,000).

Vital statistics

Birth rate per 1,000 population (2002): 9.9 (world avg. 21.3); legitimate 85.4%; illegitimate 14.6%.
Death rate per 1,000 population (2002): 7.9 (world avg. 9.1).
Natural increase rate per 1,000 population (2002): 2.0 (world avg. 12.2).
Total fertility rate (avg. births per childbearing woman; 2000): 1.9.
Marriage rate per 1,000 population (2000): 6.5.
Life expectancy at birth (2002): male 75.8 years; female 80.5 years.
Major causes of death per 100,000 population (2002): diseases of the circulatory system 335.4; malignant neoplasms 185.6; diseases of the respiratory system 88.0; accidents, poisonings, and violence 31.4; endocrine and metabolic diseases 26.3; diseases of the digestive system 26.3.

National economy

Budget (2001). Revenue: Lm 797,400,000 (social security 22.5%; income tax 20.9%; value-added tax 14.4%; grants and loans 13.6%). Expenditures: Lm 766,700,000 (recurrent expenditures 80.2%, of which social security 24.1%, education 6.1%; capital expenditure 10.5%; public debt service 9.3%).
Public debt (2001): U.S.$616,000,000.
Production (metric tons except where noted). Agriculture, forestry, fishing (2002): vegetables 49,200 (of which melons 12,800, tomatoes 7,400, onions 4,392, cabbage 3,900, garlic 551), potatoes 27,500, wheat 9,600, barley 2,200; livestock (number of live animals; 2002) 79,300 pigs, 18,000 cattle, 6,600 sheep; fish catch (2000) 987,294. Quarrying (2002): small quantities of limestone and salt. Manufacturing (value added in U.S.$'000,000; 1998): telecommunications equipment and electronics 149; food products 69; wearing apparel 63; beverages 55; printing and publishing 52. Energy production (consumption): electricity (kW-hr; 1999) 1,840,000,000 (1,840,000,000); coal (metric tons; 1999) none (322,000); crude petroleum, none (none); petroleum products (metric tons; 1999) none (878,000).
Population economically active (1998): total 144,824; activity rate of total population 38.4% (participation rates: ages 15–64 [1985] 45.9%; female 27.6%; unemployed [2001] 6.1%).

Price and earnings indexes (1995 = 100)

	1996	1997	1998	1999	2000	2001	2002
Consumer price index	102.1	105.2	107.7	110.0	112.6	115.9	118.5
Average weekly earnings	104.3	...	...	...	...	...	...

Household income and expenditure. Average household size (2001) 3.1; average annual income per household (1982) Lm 4,736 (U.S.$11,399); sources of income (1993): wages and salaries 63.8%, professional and unincorporated enterprises 19.3%, rents, dividends, and interest 16.9%; expenditure (2000): food and beverages 36.6%, transportation and communications 23.4%, recreation, entertainment, and education 9.4%, household furnishings and operations 7.6%.
Tourism (2001): receipts from visitors U.S.$579,000,000; expenditures by nationals abroad U.S.$160,000,000.

Gross national product (2001): U.S.$3,600,000,000 (U.S.$9,210 per capita).

Structure of gross domestic product and labour force

	2001 in value Lm '000	% of total value	labour force	% of labour force
Agriculture	32,678	2.3	2,956	1.9
Manufacturing	318,677	23.0	32,532	21.0
Mining }	41,303	3.0	1,015	0.7
Construction }			10,075	6.5
Public utilities	5	5	3,352	2.2
Transp. and commun.	95,413	6.9	10,485	6.8
Trade	153,504	11.1	32,881	21.3
Finance, real estate	126,278	9.1	12,377	8.0
Pub. admin., defense	312,595[5]	22.6[5]	12,804	8.3
Services	160,763	11.6	26,499	17.1
Other	143,695	10.4	9,638[6]	6.2[6]
TOTAL	1,384,906	100.0	154,614	100.0

Land use (1994): agricultural and under permanent cultivation 40.6%; other (infertile clay soil with underlying limestone) 59.4%.

Foreign trade[7]

Balance of trade (current prices)

	1996	1997	1998	1999	2000	2001
Lm '000,000	–383.7	–355.3	–322.9	–345.1	–420.0	–345.7
% of total	23.5%	22.0%	18.5%	17.9%	16.4%	16.4%

Imports (2000): Lm 1,492,400,000 (electronic microcircuits 37.3%, refined petroleum 7.0%, chemicals and chemical products 6.9%, food 6.0%). *Major import sources* (2001): Italy 17.3%; France 10.3%; Singapore 8.3%; Japan 7.6%; U.K. 7.5%.
Exports (2000): Lm 1,072,400,000 (electronic microcircuits 62.1%, apparel and clothing accessories 5.9%, refined petroleum 4.4%, children's toys and games 4.3%). *Major export destinations* (2001): U.S. 15.2%; Germany 13.4%; Singapore 11.6%; France 8.9%; U.K. 8.7%.

Transport and communications

Transport. Railroads: none. Roads (1997): total length 1,219 mi, 1,961 km (paved 94%). Vehicles (2000): passenger cars 202,883; trucks and buses 52,604. Air transport (2001): passenger-mi 1,469,000,000, passenger-km 2,364,000,000; (2000) short ton-mi cargo 9,789,000; metric ton-km cargo 14,292,000; airports (1999) with scheduled flights 1.

Communications

Medium	date	unit	number	units per 1,000 persons
Daily newspapers	1996	circulation	54,000	145
Radio	1997	receivers	255,000	680
Television	2000	receivers	217,000	556
Telephones	2002	main lines	207,300	523
Cellular telephones	2002	subscribers	276,900	699
Personal computers	2001	units	90,000	230
Internet	2001	users	99,000	253

Education and health

Educational attainment (2001). Percentage of population age 15 and over having: no formal schooling 4.3%; primary education 34.4%; general secondary 37.6%; vocational secondary 5.7%; some postsecondary 11.8%; undergraduate 5.4%; graduate 0.8%. *Literacy* (2000): total population age 15 and over literate 279,000 (92.1%).

Education (1995–96)

	schools	teachers	students	student/ teacher ratio
Primary (age 5–10)	111	1,990	33,530[8]	17.8
Secondary (age 11–17)	59	2,679	27,647[8]	20.9
Voc., teacher tr.	22	541	4,539	8.4
Higher[9]	1	522	6,420	12.3

Health (1996): physicians 925 (1 per 403 persons); hospital beds 2,140 (1 per 174 persons); infant mortality rate per 1,000 live births (2001) 4.3.
Food (2001): daily per capita caloric intake 3,495 (vegetable products 73%, animal products 27%); 141% of FAO recommended minimum requirement.

Military

Total active duty personnel (2002): 2,140 (army 100%). *Military expenditure as percentage of GNP* (1999): 0.8% (world 2.4%); per capita expenditure U.S.$73.

[1]January 1. [2]Actual local administration in 2002 was based on 3 regions divided into 68 local councils. [3]Detail does not add to total given because of rounding. [4]Includes foreign workers and foreign residents (9,564 persons as of Jan. 1, 2002). [5]Pub. admin., defense includes Public utilities. [6]Includes 9,432 unemployed. [7]Imports c.i.f.; exports f.o.b. [8]2000–01. [9]University of Malta only; full-time faculty and students in 2000–01.

Internet resources for further information:
- **National Statistics Office http://www.nso.gov.mt**
- **Central Bank of Malta http://www.centralbankmalta.com**

Marshall Islands

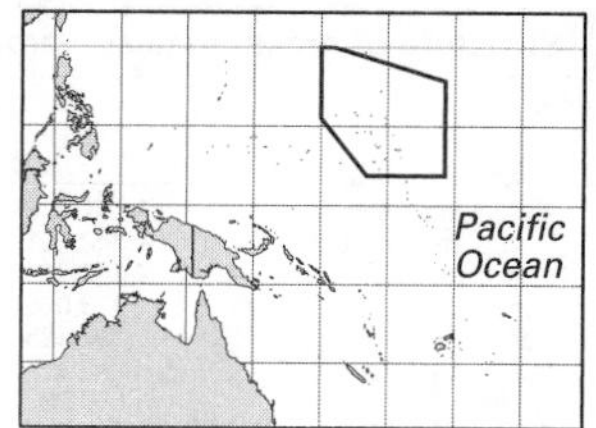

Official name: Majōl (Marshallese); Republic of the Marshall Islands (English).
Form of government: unitary republic with two legislative houses (Council of Iroij [12][1]; Nitijela [33]).
Head of state and government: President.
Capital: Majuro[2].
Official languages: Marshallese (Kajin-Majōl); English.
Official religion: none.
Monetary unit: 1 U.S. dollar (U.S.$) = 100 cents; valuation (Sept. 8, 2003) 1 U.S.$ = £0.63.

Area and population

Atolls/Islands	area sq mi	area sq km	population 1999 census
Ailinglaplap	5.67	14.69	1,959
Ailuk	2.07	5.36	514
Arno	5.00	12.95	2,069
Aur	2.17	5.62	537
Bikini	2.32	6.01	13
Ebon	2.22	5.75	902
Enewetak	2.26	5.85	853
Jabat	0.22	0.57	95
Jaluit	4.38	11.34	1,669
Kili	0.36	0.93	774
Kwajalein	6.33	16.39	10,903
Lae	0.56	1.45	322
Lib	0.36	0.93	147
Likiep	3.96	10.26	527
Majuro[2]	3.75	9.71	23,682
Maloelap	3.79	9.82	856
Mejit	0.72	1.86	416
Mili	6.15	15.93	1,032
Namorik	1.07	2.77	772
Namu	2.42	6.27	903
Rongelap	3.07	7.95	19
Ujae	0.72	1.86	440
Ujelang	0.67	1.74	0
Utirik	0.94	2.43	433
Wotho	1.67	4.33	145
Wotje	3.16	8.18	866
Other atolls	4.04	10.46	0
TOTAL	70.05[3, 4]	181.43[3, 4]	50,848

Demography

Population (2003): 56,400.
Density (2003): persons per sq mi 805.1, persons per sq km 310.9.
Urban-rural (2001): urban 65.4%; rural 34.6%.
Sex distribution (1999): male 51.20%; female 48.80%.
Age breakdown (1999): under 15, 42.9%; 15–29, 28.7%; 30–44, 16.7%; 45–59, 8.2%; 60–74, 2.6%; 75 and over, 0.9%.
Population projection: (2010) 66,000; (2020) 78,000.
Doubling time: 24 years.
Ethnic composition (nationality; 2000): Marshallese 88.5%; U.S. white 6.5%; other Pacific islanders and East Asians 5.0%.
Religious affiliation (1995): Protestant 62.8%; Roman Catholic 7.1%; Mormon 3.1%; Jehovah's Witness 1.0%; other 26.0%.
Major towns (1999): Majuro[2] 19,300; Ebeye 9,300; Laura 2,300; Ajeltake 1,200; Enewetak 820.

Vital statistics

Birth rate per 1,000 population (2002): 34.5 (world avg. 21.3).
Death rate per 1,000 population (2002): 5.1 (world avg. 9.1).
Natural increase rate per 1,000 population (2000): 29.4 (world avg. 12.2).
Total fertility rate (avg. births per childbearing woman; 2002): 4.2.
Life expectancy at birth (2002): male 67.2 years; female 71.1 years.
Major causes of death per 100,000 population (1990–93)[5]: infectious and parasitic diseases 169.9; circulatory diseases 155.1; respiratory diseases 105.1; malignant neoplasms (cancers) 68.4; digestive diseases 63.3.

National economy

Budget (1997–98). Revenue: U.S.$61,400,000 (U.S. government grants 59.7%, income tax 12.7%, import tax 10.7%, value-added and excise taxes 4.4%, fishing rights 2.9%, fees and charges 2.1%). Expenditures: U.S.$50,900,000 (wages and salaries 33.4%, goods and services 32.4%, capital expenditures 14.3%, interest payments 10.8%, subsidies 7.1%).
Public debt (external, outstanding; 1996–97): U.S.$124,900,000.
Production (metric tons except as noted). Agriculture, forestry, fishing (value of production for household consumption in U.S.$'000; 1999): fish 3,920; pork 1,496; breadfruit 646; chickens 591; coconuts 434; taro 166; bananas 108; foreign fish catch (1999) 12,993, of which Japanese 6,762. Mining and quarrying: for local construction only. Manufacturing (2000): copra 2,706; coconut oil and processed (chilled or frozen) fish are important products; the manufacture of handicrafts and personal items (clothing, mats, boats, etc.) by individuals is also significant. Energy production (consumption): electricity (kW-hr; 2000) 63,049,000 (63,049,000); coal, none (none); petroleum products, n.a. (n.a.).
Tourism (2000): receipts U.S.$4,000,000; expenditures, n.a.
Gross national product (at current market prices; 2001): U.S.$100,000,000 (U.S.$2,190 per capita).

Structure of gross domestic product and labour force

	2000 in value U.S.$'000	2000 % of total value	1999 labour force	1999 % of labour force
Agriculture	13,208	13.5	2,355	16.0
Mining	284	0.3	—	—
Manufacturing	1,721	1.8	1,447	9.9
Public utilities	2,189	2.2	274	1.9
Construction	10,375	10.6	863	5.9
Transp. and commun.	5,215	5.4	867	5.9
Trade, restaurants, hotels	17,082	17.5	1,210	8.2
Finance, insurance, real estate	15,688	16.1	814	5.5
Public administration } Services }	30,902	31.7	5,119	34.9
Other	879[6]	0.9[6]	1,728[7]	11.8[7]
TOTAL	97,543	100.0	14,677	100.0

Household income and expenditure. Average household size (1999) 7.8; annual median income per household (1999) U.S.$6,840; sources of income: n.a.; expenditure (1982): food 57.7%, housing 15.6%, clothing 12.0%, personal effects and other 14.7%.
Population economically active (1999): total 14,677; activity rate of total population 28.9% (participation rates: over age 15, 53.1%; female [1988] 30.1%; unemployed 9.5%).

Price and earnings indexes (1995 = 100)

	1994	1995	1996	1997	1998	1999	2000
Consumer price index[8]	92.4	100.0	109.6	114.9	117.4	119.4	117.1
Earnings index	...	...	...	...	...	...	...

Land use (1989)[9]: forested 22.5%; meadows and pastures 13.5%; agricultural and under permanent cultivation 33.1%; other 30.9%.

Foreign trade[10]

Balance of trade (current prices)

	1995	1996	1997	1998	1999	2000
U.S.$'000,000	−52.0	−53.6	−45.2	−61.5	−61.2	−60.9
% of total	53.0%	58.6%	58.9%	84.1%	79.9%	80.8%

Imports (2000): U.S.$68,200,000 (mineral fuels and lubricants 43.6%; machinery and transport equipment 16.9%; food, beverages, and tobacco 10.9%). *Major import sources:* U.S. 61.4%; Japan 5.1%; Australia 2.0%; Hong Kong 1.9%; Taiwan 1.3%.
Exports (2000): U.S.$7,300,000 (chilled and frozen fish, n.a.; copra cake 16.2%; crude coconut oil 14.7%; aquarium fish 6.2%). *Major export destinations:* U.S. *c.* 71%; other *c.* 29%.

Transport and communications

Transport. Roads: only Majuro and Kwajalein have paved roads. Vehicles (1999): passenger cars 1,404; trucks and buses 139. Air transport (2001)[11]: passenger-km 24,972,000; metric ton-km cargo 183,000; airports (1997) 25.

Communications

Medium	date	unit	number	units per 1,000 persons
Telephones	2001	main lines	4,200	60
Cellular telephones	2001	subscribers	500	7.0
Internet	2001	users	900	13
Personal computers	2001	units	4,000	50

Education and health

Educational attainment (1999). Percentage of population age 25 and over having: no formal schooling 3.1%; elementary education 35.5%; secondary 46.5%; some higher 12.3%; undergraduate degree 1.7%; advanced degree 0.9%. *Literacy* (latest): total population age 15 and over literate 19,377 (91.2%); males literate 9,993 (92.4%); females literate 9,384 (90.0%).

Education (1998)

	schools	teachers	students	student/ teacher ratio
Primary (age 6–14)	103	548	12,421	22.7
Secondary (age 15–18)	16	162	2,667	16.5
Voc., teacher tr.	...	...	...	...
Higher[12]	1	25	1,149	46.0

Health (1997): physicians 34 (1 per 1,785 persons); hospital beds 129 (1 per 470 persons); infant mortality rate per 1,000 live births (2002) 32.7.

Military

The United States provides for the defense of the Republic of the Marshall Islands under the 1984 and 2003 compacts of free association.

[1]Council of Iroij is an advisory body only. [2]Local name is Rita. [3]Land area only; excludes lagoon area of 4,507 sq mi (11,673 sq km). [4]Detail does not add to total given because of rounding. [5]Registered deaths only. [6]Import duties less imputed bank service charges. [7]Represents sum of not stated and unemployed. [8]Majuro only. [9]Data are for the former Trust Territory of the Pacific Islands. [10]Imports c.i.f.; exports f.o.b. [11]Air Marshall Islands only. [12]1994.

Internet resources for further information:
- **RMI Online, Internet Guide to the Republic of the Marshall Islands http://www.rmiembassyus.org**
- **U.S. Office of Insular Affairs http://www.pacificweb.org**

Martinique

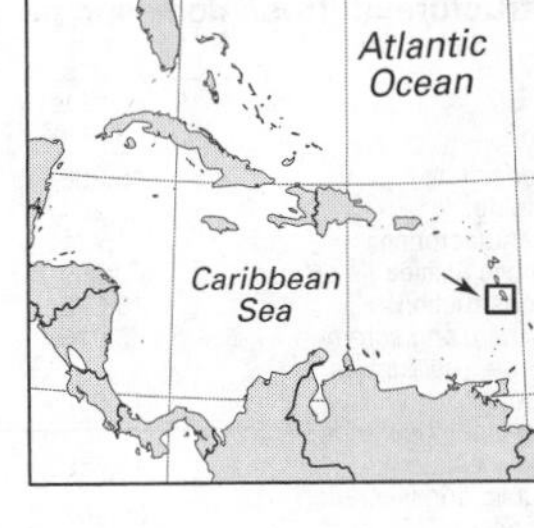

Official name: Département de la Martinique (Department of Martinique).
Political status: overseas department (France) with two legislative houses (General Council [45]; Regional Council [41]).
Chief of state: President of France.
Heads of government: Prefect (for France); President of the General Council (for Martinique); President of the Regional Council (for Martinique).
Capital: Fort-de-France.
Official language: French.
Official religion: none.
Monetary unit: 1 euro (€) = 100 cents; valuation (Sept. 8, 2003) 1 U.S.$ = €0.90; 1 £ = €1.43[1].

Area and population

		area		population
				1999
Arrondissements	**Capitals**	sq mi	sq km	census
Fort-de-France	Fort-de-France	66	171	166,139
Le Marin	Le Marin	158	409	106,818
La Trinité	La Trinité	131	338	85,006
Saint-Pierre	Saint-Pierre	81	210	23,464
TOTAL		436	1,128	381,427

Demography

Population (2003): 393,000.
Density (2003): persons per sq mi 901.4, persons per sq km 348.4.
Urban-rural (2001): urban 95.2%; rural 4.8%.
Sex distribution (2001): male 49.47%; female 50.53%.
Age breakdown (2001): under 15, 23.1%; 15–29, 23.3%; 30–44, 26.3%; 45–59, 13.8%; 60–74, 9.1%; 75 and over, 4.4%.
Population projection: (2010) 404,000; (2020) 419,000.
Doubling time: 77 years.
Ethnic composition (2000): mixed race (black/white/Asian) 93.4%; French (metropolitan and Martinique white) 3.0%; East Indian 1.9%; other 1.7%.
Religious affiliation (1995): Roman Catholic 86.5%; Protestant 8.0% (mostly Seventh-day Adventist); Jehovah's Witness 1.6%; other 3.9%, including Hindu, syncretist, and nonreligious.
Major communes (1999): Fort-de-France 94,049; Le Lamentin 35,460; Le Robert 21,201; Schoelcher 20,845; Sainte-Marie 20,058.

Vital statistics

Birth rate per 1,000 population (2002): 15.4 (world avg. 21.3); (1997) legitimate 31.8%; illegitimate 68.2%.
Death rate per 1,000 population (2002): 6.4 (world avg. 9.1).
Natural increase rate per 1,000 population (2002): 9.0 (world avg. 12.2).
Total fertility rate (avg. births per childbearing woman; 2001): 1.4.
Marriage rate per 1,000 population (1999): 4.2.
Divorce rate per 1,000 population (1999): 0.9.
Life expectancy at birth (2002): male 79.2 years; female 77.9 years.
Major causes of death per 100,000 population (1996): diseases of the circulatory system 206.8; malignant neoplasms (cancers) 150.3; accidents, poisoning, and violence 47.2; diseases of the respiratory system 36.3; endocrine and metabolic disorders 27.8; diseases of the digestive system 27.2.

National economy

Budget (1999). Revenue: F 1,298,000,000 (general receipts from French central government and local administrative bodies 45.0%; tax receipts 34.0%, of which indirect taxes 19.5%, direct taxes 14.5%). Expenditures: F 1,298,000,000 (health and social assistance 42.0%; wages and salaries 16.7%; other administrative services 7.2%; debt amortization 5.0%).
Public debt (1994): U.S.$186,700,000.
Production (metric tons except as noted). Agriculture, forestry, fishing (2002): bananas 303,800, sugarcane 207,000, pineapples 18,000, plantains 16,000, roots and tubers 13,250, lettuce 7,800, yams 7,500, tomatoes 6,100, cucumbers and gherkins 4,000, melons 2,240, sweet potatoes 1,170, coconuts 1,150; livestock (number of live animals) 35,000 pigs, 34,000 sheep, 25,000 cattle, 17,000 goats; roundwood (2001) 12,000 cu m; fish catch (2000) 6,365. Mining and quarrying (2001): salt 200,000, pumice 130,000. Manufacturing (2002): cement (2001) 220,000; sugar 5,340; rum 91,629 hectolitres; other products include clothing, fabricated metals, and yawls and sails. Energy production (consumption): electricity (kW-hr; 1999) 1,082,000,000 (1,082,000,000); coal, none (none); crude petroleum (barrels; 1999) none (5,900,000); petroleum products (metric tons; 1999) 751,000 (575,000); natural gas, none (none).
Household income and expenditure. Average household size (1999) 3.0; annual net income per household (1997) €29,516 (U.S.$33,174); sources of income (1997): wages and salaries 49.0%, inheritance or endowment 16.4%, self-employment 14.7%, other 19.9%; expenditure (1993): food and beverages 32.1%, transportation and communications 20.7%, housing and energy 10.6%, household durable goods 9.4%, clothing and footwear 8.0%.
Tourism (2001): receipts from visitors U.S.$245,000,000; expenditures by nationals abroad, n.a.; number of visitors (2000) 816,000.
Gross domestic product (2000): U.S.$5,064,000,000 (U.S.$13,160 per capita).

Structure of gross domestic product and labour force

	1995		1998	
	in value F '000,000	% of total value	labour force	% of labour force
Agriculture, fishing	1,151,952	4.1	7,650	4.6
Mining, manufacturing	1,502,161	5.3	7,103	4.3
Construction	2,249,756	7.9	10,405	6.3
Public utilities	973,068	3.4		
Transp. and commun.	1,797,425	6.3	4,383	2.6
Trade, restaurants, hotels	5,660,282	20.0	16,196	9.8
Finance, real estate, insurance	1,180,409	4.2	25,909	15.6
Pub. admin., defense	13,159,431	46.4	18,742	11.3
Services			25,667	15.5
Other	693,355[2]	2.4[2]	49,845[3]	30.0[3]
TOTAL	28,367,839	100.0	165,900	100.0

Population economically active (1998): total 165,900; activity rate of total population 43.7% (participation rates: ages 15–64, 70.7%; female 45.9%; unemployed [March 2003] 22.2%).

Price and earnings indexes (1995 = 100)

	1995	1996	1997	1998	1999	2000	2001
Consumer price index[4]	100.0	106.6	113.8	121.6	130.0	135.4	142.7
Monthly earnings index[5]	100.0	100.9	104.9	106.3	106.3	106.8	...

Land use (1998): forested 43.2%; meadows and pastures 12.5%; agricultural and under permanent cultivation 18.1%; other 26.2%.

Foreign trade[6]

Balance of trade (current prices)

	1998	1999	2000	2001
€'000,000	–1,266	–1,355	–1,438	–1,604
% of total	71.0%	72.2%	71.0%	74.5%

Imports (2001): €1,878,000,000 (consumer goods *c.* 20%, processed foods, beverages, and tobacco *c.* 18%, automobiles *c.* 12%). *Major import sources* (2000): France 63.5%; Venezuela 5.8%; Germany 3.9%; Italy 3.1%; Netherlands Antilles 2.3%.
Exports (2001): €274,000,000 (bananas *c.* 35%, processed foods and beverages [significantly rum] *c.* 21%, machinery and apparatus *c.* 15%, refined petroleum *c.* 9%). *Major export destinations* (2000): France 57.8%; Guadeloupe 21.4%; French Guiana 3.7%; U.K. 3.4%; Belgium 2.7%.

Transport and communications

Transport. Railroads: none. Roads (1994): total length 1,291 mi, 2,077 km (paved [1988] 75%). Vehicles (1998): passenger cars 147,589; trucks and buses 35,615. Air transport (2001): passenger arrivals 706,929, passenger departures 701,597; cargo loaded 5,656 metric tons; cargo unloaded 9,303 metric tons; airports (2000) 1.

Communications

Medium	date	unit	number	units per 1,000 persons
Daily newspapers	1996	circulation	32,000	83
Radio	1997	receivers	82,000	213
Television	1999	receivers	66,000	168
Telephones	2001	main lines	172,192	417
Cellular telephones	2002	subscribers	319,900	790
Personal computers	2001	units	52,000	130
Internet	2001	users	40,000	100

Education and health

Educational attainment (1990). Percentage of population age 25 and over having: incomplete primary, or no declaration 54.3%; primary education 18.0%; secondary 20.0%; higher 7.7%. *Literacy:* n.a.

Education (2001–02)

	schools	teachers	students	student/ teacher ratio
Primary (age 6–11)	273	3,260	53,347	16.4
Secondary (age 12–18)	78	4,257	51,057	12.0
Vocational[7]	15	896[8]	7,661	...
Higher	1	...	11,755[9]	...

Health (2000): physicians 762 (1 per 507 persons); hospital beds 2,674 (1 per 144 persons); infant mortality rate per 1,000 live births (2002) 7.6.
Food (1998): daily per capita caloric intake 2,865 (vegetable products 75%, animal products 25%); 118% of FAO recommended minimum requirement.

Military

Total active duty personnel (2003): 4,100 French troops.

[1]The French franc was the former monetary unit; on Jan. 1, 2002, F 6.56 = €1. [2]Statistical discrepancy. [3]Unemployed. [4]Figures are end-of-year. [5]Based on minimum-level wage of public employees. [6]Imports c.i.f.; exports f.o.b. [7]1998–99. [8]1995–96. [9]Total enrollment of the University of the Antilles and French Guiana at 7 sites.

Internet resources for further information:
- **INSEE: Martinique http://www.insee.fr/fr/insee_regions/Martinique**
- **Martinique Chamber of Commerce and Industry http://www.martinique.cci.fr**

Mauritania

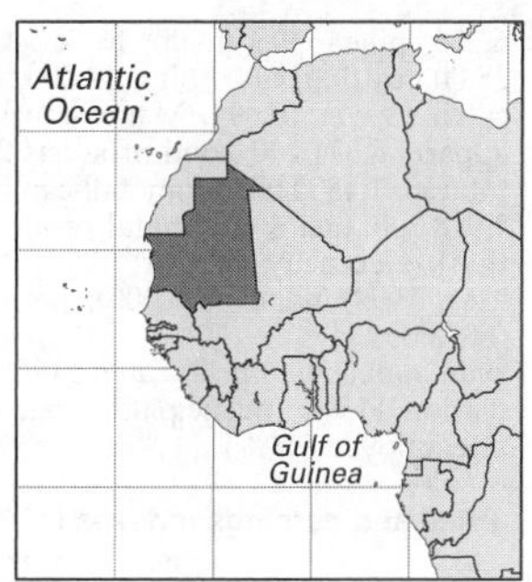

Official name: Al-Jumhūrīyah al-Islāmīyah al-Mūrītānīyah (Arabic) (Islamic Republic of Mauritania).
Form of government: unitary multiparty republic with two legislative houses (Senate [56]; National Assembly [81]).
Head of state and government: President assisted by the Prime Minister.
Capital: Nouakchott.
Official language: Arabic[1].
Official religion: Islam.
Monetary unit: 1 ouguiya (UM) = 5 khoums; valuation (Sept. 8, 2003) 1 U.S.$ = UM 265.00; 1 £ = UM 420.17.

Area and population

Regions	Capitals	area sq mi	area sq km	population 2000 census[2]
El-ʾAçâba	Kiffa	14,100	36,600	242,265
Adrar	Atar	83,100	215,300	69,542
Brakna	Aleg	13,000	33,800	247,006
Dakhlet Nouadhibou	Nouadhibou	8,600	22,300	79,516
Gorgol	Kaédi	5,300	13,600	242,711
Guidimaka	Sélibaby	4,000	10,300	177,707
Hodh ech-Chargui	Néma	70,600	182,700	281,600
Hodh el-Gharbi	ʿAyoûn el-ʾAtroûs	20,600	53,400	212,156
Inchiri	Akjoujt	18,100	46,800	11,500
Tagant	Tidjikdja	36,800	95,200	76,620
Tiris Zemmour	Zouérate	97,600	252,900	41,121
Trarza	Rosso	25,800	66,800	268,220
Capital District				
Nouakchott	Nouakchott	400	1,000	558,195
TOTAL		398,000[3]	1,030,700	2,508,159

Demography

Population (2003): 2,696,000.
Density (2003): persons per sq mi 6.8, persons per sq km 2.6.
Urban-rural (1999): urban 56.5%; rural 43.5%.
Sex distribution (2000): male 48.68%; female 51.32%.
Age breakdown (2000): under 15, 46.2%; 15–29, 26.6%; 30–44, 15.6%; 45–59, 7.8%; 60–74, 3.3%; 75 and over, 0.5%.
Population projection: (2010) 3,290,000; (2020) 4,181,000.
Doubling time: 24 years.
Ethnic composition (1993)[4]: Moor 70% (of which about 40% "black" Moor [Ḥarāṭīn, or African Sudanic] and about 30% "white" Moor [Bidan, or Arab-Berber]); other black African 30% (mostly Wolof, Tukulor, Soninke, and Fulani).
Religious affiliation (2000): Sunnī Muslim 99.1%; traditional beliefs 0.5%; Christian 0.3%; other 0.1%.
Major cities (2000): Nouakchott 558,195[5]; Nouadhibou 72,337; Rosso 48,922; Boghé 37,531; Adel Bagrou 36,007.

Vital statistics

Birth rate per 1,000 population (2001): 42.5 (world avg. 21.3).
Death rate per 1,000 population (2001): 13.3 (world avg. 9.1).
Natural increase rate per 1,000 population (2001): 29.2 (world avg. 12.2).
Total fertility rate (avg. births per childbearing woman; 2001): 6.1.
Life expectancy at birth (2001): male 49.2 years; female 53.7 years.

National economy

Budget (2001). Revenue: UM 51,800,000,000 (tax revenue 70.3%, of which taxes on goods and services 35.1%, income taxes 21.8%, import taxes 11.8%; nontax revenue 29.7%, of which fishing royalties and penalties 10.2%). Expenditures: UM 54,400,000,000 (current expenditure 78.2%, of which wages and salaries 22.5%, interest on public debt 13.3%, defense 8.1%; capital expenditure 21.8%).
Land use (1994): forested 4.3%; meadows and pastures 38.3%; agricultural and under permanent cultivation 0.2%; desert 57.2%.
Production (metric tons except as noted). Agriculture, forestry, fishing (2002): rice 67,900, millet 51,500, sorghum 25,405, cow peas 24,000, dates 20,000, pulses 16,000; livestock (number of live animals) 7,600,000 sheep, 5,100,000 goats, 1,500,000 cattle, 1,230,000 camels; roundwood (2001) 1,470,448 cu m; fish catch (metric tons; 2001) 83,596, of which octopuses 20,308[6]. Mining and quarrying (gross weight; 2001): iron ore 12,000,000; gypsum 100,000. Manufacturing (1996): cow's milk 91,000[7]; goat's milk 77,000[7]; meat 58,200, of which fresh mutton and lamb 24,600, fresh beef and veal 10,200; hides and skins 4,600; cement, tiles, and bricks 5.9[8]; fabricated metal products 5.4[8]; paper and paper products 2.1[8]. Energy production (consumption): electricity (kW-hr; 2001) 246,284,000 (189,516,000); coal (metric tons; 1999) none (6,000); crude petroleum (barrels; 1999) none (7,100,000); petroleum products (metric tons; 1999) 858,000 (958,000); natural gas, none (none).
Population economically active (1994): total 687,000; activity rate of total population 31.3% (participation rates: over age 10 [1991] 45.5%; female 22.9%).

Price and earnings indexes (1995 = 100)

	1996	1997	1998	1999	2000	2001	2002
Consumer price index[9]	104.7	109.5	118.3	123.1	127.1	133.1	138.2
Hourly earnings index[10]	100.0	100.0	100.0	100.0	...	...	...

Household income and expenditure. Average household size (2000): 5.3; expenditure (1990): food and beverages 73.1%, clothing and footwear 8.1%, energy and water 7.7%, transportation and communications 2.0%.
Gross national product (2001): U.S.$1,000,000,000 (U.S.$360 per capita).

Structure of gross domestic product and labour force

	2001		1988	
	in value UM '000,000	% of total value	labour force	% of labour force
Agriculture, livestock	46,492	18.9	225,238	38.5
Mining	31,524	12.8	6,322	1.1
Manufacturing	20,530	8.4	5,630	1.0
Public utilities }	15,137	6.2	1,326	0.2
Construction }			12,291	2.1
Transp. and commun.	24,298	9.9	8,378	1.4
Trade and finance	43,519	17.7	73,451	12.5
Services	13,255	5.4 }	86,807	14.8
Pub. admin., defense	26,389	10.7 }		
Other	24,452[11]	10.0[11]	166,366[12]	28.4[12]
TOTAL	245,596	100.0	585,809	100.0

Public debt (external, outstanding; 2001): U.S.$1,865,000,000.
Tourism (1999): receipts U.S.$28,000,000; expenditures U.S.$55,000,000.

Foreign trade

Balance of trade (current prices)

	1997	1998	1999	2000	2001
SDR '000,000[13]	+38	+1	+21	+12	−9
% of total	7.0%	0.2%	4.5%	2.2%	1.6%

Imports (2001): SDR 280,000,000[13] (imports for National Industrial and Mining Company 29.6%; petroleum products 26.5%; public investment including food aid 7.0%). *Major import sources:* France *c.* 23%; Belgium-Luxembourg *c.* 9%; Spain *c.* 6%; Germany *c.* 5%; Italy *c.* 5%.
Exports (2001): SDR 271,000,000[13] (iron ore 54.6%; fish 45.4%, of which cephalopods 26.7%). *Major export destinations:* Italy *c.* 15%; France *c.* 15%; Spain *c.* 12%; Japan *c.* 9%; Belgium-Luxembourg *c.* 8%.

Transport and communications

Transport. Railroads (1998): route length 437 mi, 704 km; passenger-km, negligible; (1997) metric ton-km cargo 2,340,000,000. Roads (1996): total length 4,760 mi, 7,660 km (paved 11%). Vehicles (1996): passenger cars 18,810; trucks and buses 10,450. Air transport (1998)[14]: passenger-km 258,263,000; metric ton-km cargo 13,524,000; airports (1997) with scheduled flights 9.

Communications

Medium	date	unit	number	units per 1,000 persons
Daily newspapers	1996	circulation	1,000	0.4
Radio	1997	receivers	360,000	147
Television	1999	receivers	247,000	100
Telephones	2002	main lines	32,000	12
Cellular telephones	2002	subscribers	245,700	92
Personal computers	2001	units	27,000	9.8
Internet	2001	users	10,000	3.7

Education and health

Educational attainment (1988). Percentage of population age 25 and over having: no formal schooling 60.8%; primary and incomplete secondary 34.1%; secondary 3.8%; higher 1.3%. *Literacy* (1995): percentage of total population age 15 and over literate 37.7%; males literate 49.6%; females literate 26.3%.

Education (1998–99)

	schools	teachers	students	student/ teacher ratio
Primary (age 6–11)	2,676	7,366	346,222	47.0
Secondary (age 12–17)	... }	2,185	60,029	...
Voc., teacher tr.[15]	... }		2,812	...
Higher	...	270[16]	12,912	...

Health: physicians (1994) *c.* 200 (1 per 11,085 persons); hospital beds (1988) 1,556 (1 per 1,217 persons); infant mortality rate per 1,000 live births (2001) 75.2.
Food (2001): daily per capita caloric intake 2,764 (vegetable products 84%, animal products 16%); 120% of FAO recommended minimum requirement.

Military

Total active duty personnel (2002): 15,000 (army 95.2%, navy 3.2%, air force 1.6%). *Military expenditure as percentage of GNP* (1999): 4.0% (world 2.4%); per capita expenditure U.S.$14.

[1]The 1991 constitution names Arabic as the official language and the following as national languages: Arabic, Fulani, Soninke, and Wolof. [2]Final figures. [3]Detail does not add to total given because of rounding. [4]Estimated figures. [5]Limits are coextensive with the capital district. [6]Fish catch (2000) including foreign fishing vessels equals 544,925 metric tons. [7]1994. [8]1993 value added of production in U.S.$'000,000. [9]Nouakchott only. [10]Minimum wage. [11]Indirect taxes. [12]Mostly unemployed. [13]Special Drawing Rights of IMF; conversion rate to UM or U.S.$ is unknown. [14]Data represent 1/11 of the total scheduled traffic of Air Afrique; Air Afrique was declared bankrupt in February 2002. [15]1995–96. [16]Excludes health-related programs.

Internet resources for further information:

- **Office National de la Statistique**
  http://www.ons.mr

Mauritius

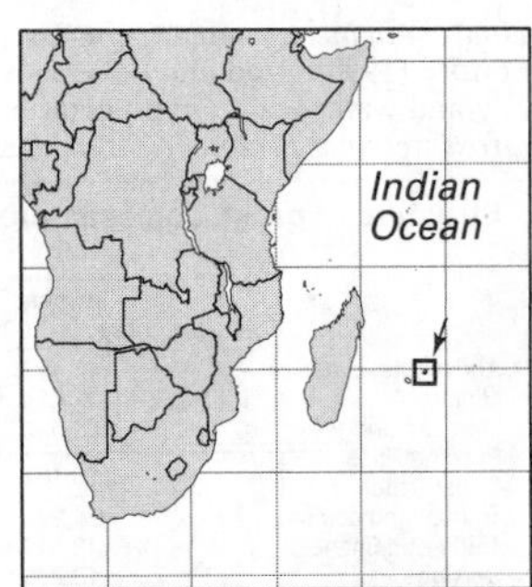

Official name: Republic of Mauritius.
Form of government: republic with one legislative house (National Assembly [70[1]]).
Chief of state: President.
Head of government: Prime Minister.
Capital: Port Louis.
Official language: English.
Official religion: none.
Monetary unit: 1 Mauritian rupee (Mau Re; plural Mau Rs) = 100 cents; valuation (Sept. 8, 2003) 1 U.S.$ = Mau Rs 28.95; 1 £ = Mau Rs 45.90.

Area and population

Islands Districts/Dependencies	Administrative Centres	area sq mi	area sq km	population 2002 estimate
Mauritius		720	1,865[2]	1,174,021
Black River	Tamarin	100	259	64,040
Flacq	Centre de Flacq	115	298	130,846
Grand Port	Mahébourg	100	260	109,513
Moka	Moka	89	231	77,224
Pamplemousses	Pamplemousses	69	179	126,402
Plaines Wilhems	Rose Hill	78	203	366,691
Port Louis	Port Louis	17	43	129,681
Rivière du Rempart	Poudre d'Or	57	148	101,848
Savanne	Souillac	95	245	67,776
Mauritian dependencies				
Agalega[3]	...	27	70	289
Cargados Carajos Shoals (Saint Brandon)[3]	—	0.4	1	0
Rodrigues[4]	Port Mathurin	40	104	36,175
TOTAL		788[2]	2,040	1,210,485

Demography

Population (2003): 1,221,000.
Density (2003): persons per sq mi 1,549.6, persons per sq km 598.6.
Urban-rural (2002): urban 42.5%; rural 57.5%.
Sex distribution (2003): male 49.49%; female 50.51%.
Age breakdown (2000): under 15, 25.7%; 15–29, 25.6%; 30–44, 24.7%; 45–59, 15.1%; 60–74, 6.8%; 75 and over, 2.1%.
Population projection: (2010) 1,295,000; (2020) 1,390,000.
Doubling time: 73 years.
Ethnic composition (2000): Indo-Pakistani 67.0%; Creole (mixed Caucasian, Indo-Pakistani, and African) 27.4%; Chinese 3.0%; other 2.6%.
Religious affiliation (2000)[5]: Hindu 49.6%; Christian 32.2%, of which Roman Catholic 23.6%; Muslim 16.6%; Buddhist 0.4%; other 1.2%.
Major urban areas (2000)[5]: Port Louis 144,303; Beau Bassin-Rose Hill 103,872; Vacoas-Phoenix 100,066; Curepipe 78,920; Quatre Bornes 75,884.

Vital statistics

Birth rate per 1,000 population (2002): 16.5[6] (world avg. 21.3).
Death rate per 1,000 population (2002): 6.9[6] (world avg. 9.1).
Natural increase rate per 1,000 population (2002): 9.6[6] (world avg. 12.2).
Total fertility rate (avg. births per childbearing woman; 2002): 2.0[6].
Marriage rate per 1,000 population (2002): 8.6[6].
Divorce rate per 1,000 population (2002): 1.1[6].
Life expectancy at birth (2001): male 67.3 years; female 75.3 years.
Major causes of death per 100,000 population (2002)[6]: diseases of the circulatory system 351.3; malignant neoplasms (cancers) 72.7; diseases of the respiratory system 57.1; homicide, suicide, and accidents 44.1.

National economy

Budget (2001–02). Revenue: Mau Rs 28,319,500,000 (tax revenue 82.2%, of which taxes on goods and services 39.2%, import duties 20.8%, income tax 12.6%; nontax revenue 16.2%; grants 1.1%). Expenditures: Mau Rs 33,385,800,000 (social security 21.8%; government services 18.1%; education 15.4%; economic services 12.3%; interest on debt 10.6%; health 8.7%).
Tourism (2001): receipts from visitors U.S.$525,000,000; expenditures by nationals abroad (2000) U.S.$182,000,000.
Public debt (external, outstanding; 2001): U.S.$765,000,000.
Gross national product (2001): U.S.$4,600,000,000 (U.S.$3,830 per capita).

Structure of gross domestic product and labour force

	2002 in value Mau Rs '000,000	% of total value	labour force[7]	% of labour force[7]
Agriculture	8,810	5.6	25,258	8.5
Mining	80	0.1	170	0.1
Manufacturing	30,330	19.3	111,017	37.5
Construction	8,035	5.1	13,027	4.4
Public utilities	3,150	2.0	3,041	1.0
Transp. and commun.	19,350	12.3	17,521	5.9
Trade	23,510	14.9	34,051	11.5
Finance	25,965	16.5	15,745	5.3
Pub. admin., defense	19,215	12.2	67,670	22.9
Services	5,790	3.7	7,103	2.4
Other	13,070[8]	8.3[8]	1,597	0.5
TOTAL	157,305	100.0	296,200[9]	100.0[9]

Production (metric tons except as noted). Agriculture, forestry, fishing (2002): sugarcane 4,874,000, vegetables 21,000, roots and tubers 15,000, potatoes 14,000, tomatoes 12,000, carrots 8,700, cabbages 8,300, onions 7,200, bananas 6,700, pineapples 1,900; livestock (number of live animals) 93,000 goats, 28,000 cattle, 14,000 pigs, 12,000 sheep; roundwood (2001) 17,000 cu m; fish catch (2001) 10,694. Manufacturing (value added in Mau Rs '000; 1999): apparel 8,871,200; food products 2,094,800; textiles 1,707,200; beverages and tobacco 1,480,800; nonmetallic mineral products 1,080,100; chemical products 1,018,800; metal and metal products 774,100. Energy production (consumption): electricity (kW-hr; 1999) 1,441,000,000 (1,441,000,000); coal (metric tons; 1999) none (136,000); petroleum products (metric tons; 1999) none (687,000).
Population economically active (2002): total 541,100; activity rate of total population 44.7% (participation rates: ages 15 and over, 59.8%; female 34.6%; unemployed 9.7%).

Price and earnings indexes (1995 = 100)

	1996	1997	1998	1999	2000	2001	2002
Consumer price index	106.6	113.8	121.6	130.0	135.4	142.7	152.3
Earnings index	...	...	...	...	...	...	...

Household income and expenditure. Average household size (2000) 4.2; annual income per household (1996–97) Mau Rs 122,148 (U.S.$6,263); sources of income (1990): salaries and wages 48.4%, entrepreneurial income 41.2%, transfer payments 10.4%; expenditure (1996–97): food, beverages, and tobacco 45.2%, transportation and communications 14.2%, housing and household furnishings 13.2%, clothing and footwear 7.9%.
Land use (1994): forested 21.7%; meadows and pastures 3.4%; agricultural and under permanent cultivation 52.2%; other 22.7%.

Foreign trade[10]

Balance of trade (current prices)

	1997	1998	1999	2000	2001	2002[11]
Mau Rs '000,000	–12,399	–9,691	–16,604	–14,046	–10,429	–6,519
% of total	16.5%	11.7%	17.2%	14.7%	9.9%	7.6%

Imports (2001): Mau Rs 57,940,000,000 (fabrics and yarn 18.3%; food and live animals 14.3%; machinery and apparatus 14.3%; refined petroleum 9.5%; transport equipment 8.1%). *Major import sources:* South Africa 13.9%; France 9.3%; India 7.9%; China 7.1%; Germany 5.4%.
Exports (2001): Mau Rs 47,511,000,000 (domestic exports 91.8%, of which clothing 54.4%, sugar 18.0%, fabric, yarn, and made-up articles 4.7%; reexports 4.1%; ships' stores and bunkers 4.1%). *Major export destinations:* U.K. 31.3%; U.S. 20.3%; France 18.7%; Madagascar 6.1%; Italy 3.8%.

Transport and communications

Transport. Railroads: none. Roads (1998): total length 1,184 mi, 1,905 km (paved 93%). Vehicles (2002): passenger cars 61,885; trucks and buses 13,892. Air transport (1998)[12]: passenger-km 3,858,695; metric ton-km cargo 819,432,000; airports (1998) with scheduled flights 1.

Communications

Medium	date	unit	number	units per 1,000 persons
Daily newspapers	2000	circulation	84,300	71
Radio	2000	receivers	450,000	379
Television	2000	receivers	318,000	268
Telephones	2002	main lines	325,774	269
Cellular telephones	2002	subscribers	350,000	289
Personal computers	2001	units	130,000	108
Internet	2002	users	180,000	149

Education and health

Educational attainment (1990). Percentage of population age 25 and over having: no formal education 18.3%; incomplete primary 42.6%; primary 6.1%; incomplete secondary 18.0%; secondary 13.1%; higher 1.9%. *Literacy* (1995): percentage of total population age 15 and over literate 82.9%; males literate 87.1%; females literate 78.8%.

Education (2002)

	schools	teachers	students	student/ teacher ratio
Primary (age 5–12)	290	5,256	132,432	25.2
Secondary (age 12–20)	143	5,553	99,687	18.0
Voc., teacher tr.	13	380	5,966	15.7
Higher[13]	3	461	6,429	13.9

Health (2002): physicians 1,186 (1 per 1,123 persons); hospital beds (2001) 3,709[14] (1 per 303 persons); infant mortality rate per 1,000 live births 14.9[6].
Food (2001): daily per capita caloric intake 2,995 (vegetable products 86%, animal products 14%); 132% of FAO recommended minimum requirement.

Military

Total active duty personnel: none; however, a special 2,000-person paramilitary force ensures internal security. *Military expenditure as percentage of GNP* (1999): 0.2% (world 2.4%); per capita expenditure U.S.$7.

[1]Includes 8 "bonus" seats allocated to minor parties. [2]Detail does not add to total given because of rounding. [3]Administered directly from Port Louis. [4]Local autonomy status granted by Mauritius in November 2001. [5]Based on census. [6]Excludes Agalega and Cargados Carajos Shoals. [7]Employed persons in large establishments only. [8]Indirect taxes less imputed bank service charges. [9]Total labour force equals 541,100 and includes 193,800 employees of small businesses or self-employed and 51,100 unemployed. [10]Imports c.i.f.; exports f.o.b. [11]Excludes fourth quarter. [12]Air Mauritius only. [13]1998. [14]Island of Mauritius only; the island of Rodrigues in 2002 had 183 hospital beds.

Internet resources for further information:
- **Central Statistical Office http://statsmauritius.gov.mu**

Mayotte

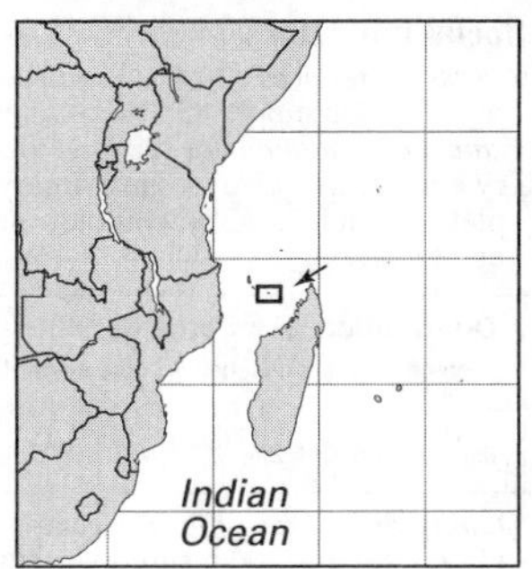

Official name: Collectivité Départementale de Mayotte[1] (Departmental Collectivity of Mayotte).
Political status: overseas dependency of France[2] with one legislative house (General Council [19]).
Chief of state: President of France.
Head of government: Prefect (for France); President of the General Council (for Mayotte).
Capitals: Dzaoudzi (French administrative); Mamoudzou (local administrative)[3].
Official language: French.
Official religion: none.
Monetary unit: 1 euro (€) = 100 cents; valuation (Sept. 28, 2003) 1 U.S.$ = €0.90; 1 £ = €1.43[4].

Area and population

Islands / Communes	Capitals	area sq mi	area sq km	population 2002 census
Grande Terre				
Acoua	Acoua	4.9	12.6	4,605
Bandraboua	Bandraboua	12.5	32.4	7,501
Bandrele	Bandrele	14.1	36.5	5,537
Boueni	Boueni	5.4	14.1	5,151
Chiconi	Chiconi	3.2	8.3	6,167
Chirongui	Chirongui	10.9	28.3	5,696
Dembeni	Dembeni	15.0	38.8	7,825
Kani-Keli	Kani-Keli	7.9	20.5	4,336
Koungou	Koungou	11.0	28.4	15,383
Mamoudzou	Mamoudzou	16.2	41.9	45,485
M'tsangamouji	M'tsangamouji	8.4	21.8	5,382
M'tzamboro	M'tzamboro	5.3	13.7	7,068
Ouangani	Ouangani	7.3	19.0	5,569
Sada	Sada	4.3	11.2	6,963
Tsingoni	Tsingoni	13.4	34.8	7,779
Petite Terre				
Dzaoudzi-Labattoir	Dzaoudzi	2.6	6.7	12,308
Pamandzi	Pamandzi	1.7	4.3	7,510
TOTAL		144.1[5]	373.3[5]	160,265

Demography

Population (2003): 166,000.
Density (2003): persons per sq mi 1,152, persons per sq km 443.9.
Urban-rural (1985): urban 59.7%; rural 40.3%.
Sex distribution (2001): male 52.44%; female 47.56%.
Age breakdown (2001): under 15, 46.6%; 15–29, 24.9%; 30–44, 18.3%; 45–59, 7.4%; 60–74, 2.4%; 75 and over, 0.4%.
Population projection: (2010) 216,000; (2020) 292,000.
Doubling time: 70 years.
Place of birth (1997): Mayotte 73.6%[6]; nearby islands of the Comoros 19.9%[6]; metropolitan France 2.8%; other 3.7%.
Ethnic composition (2000): Comorian (Mauri, Mahorais) 92.3%; Swahili 3.2%; white (French) 1.8%; Makua 1.0%; other 1.7%.
Religious affiliation (2000): Sunnī Muslim 96.5%; Christian, principally Roman Catholic, 2.2%; other 1.3%.
Major towns (2002[7]): Mamoudzou 45,485; Koungou 15,383; Dzaoudzi 12,308.

Vital statistics

Birth rate per 1,000 population (2002): 43.6 (world avg. 21.3).
Death rate per 1,000 population (2002): 8.6 (world avg. 9.1).
Natural increase rate per 1,000 population (2002): 35.0 (world avg. 12.2).
Total fertility rate (avg. births per childbearing woman; 2002): 6.2.
Marriage rate per 1,000 population: n.a.; *marital status of adult population* (1997): monogamous marriage 48.5%, polygamous marriage 6.9%, other 44.6%.
Divorce rate per 1,000 population (1997): 16.2.
Life expectancy at birth (2002): male 58.1; female 62.4.
Major causes of death per 100,000 population: n.a.

National economy

Budget (1997). Revenue: F 1,022,400,000 (1993; current revenue 68.8%, of which subsidies 40.0%, indirect taxes 16.8%, direct taxes 4.9%; development revenue 31.2%, of which loans 11.6%, subsidies 7.9%). Expenditures: F 964,200,000 (current expenditure 75.2%; development expenditure 24.8%).
Public debt: n.a.
Production (metric tons except as noted). Agriculture, forestry, fishing (1997): bananas 30,200, cassava 10,000, cinnamon 27,533 kg, ylang-ylang 14,300 kg, vanilla 4,417 kg; livestock (number of live animals; 1997) 25,000 goats, 17,000 cattle, 2,000 sheep; roundwood, n.a.; fish catch (1999) 1,502. Mining and quarrying: negligible. Manufacturing: mostly processing of agricultural products and materials used in housing construction (including siding and roofing materials, joinery, and latticework). Construction (public works authorized in F '000; 1999): residential 128,991; nonresidential 119,294. Energy production (consumption): electricity (kW-hr; 1999) 68,387,000 (68,387,000); coal, none (none); crude petroleum, none (none); petroleum products, none (n.a.); natural gas, none (none).
Tourism (number of visitors; 1999): 21,000; receipts U.S.$10,000,000.
Gross national product (1998): U.S.$486,409,000 (U.S.$3,704 per capita).

Structure of gross domestic product and labour force

	1997 in value U.S.$'000	% of total value	labour force	% of labour force
Agriculture, forestry, and fishing	...	...	4,824	11.2
Mining	...	...	80	0.2
Manufacturing	...	...	1,083	2.5
Construction	...	...	3,840	9.0
Public utilities	...	...	399	0.9
Transp. and commun.	...	...	1,563	3.6
Trade	...	...	3,057	7.1
Finance, insurance, real estate	...	...	647	1.5
Pub. admin., defense	...	...	4,526	10.6
Services	...	...	5,074	11.8
Other	...	...	17,803[8]	41.6[8]
TOTAL	154,900	100.0	42,896	100.0

Household income and expenditure. Average household size (1997) 4.6; expenditure (1991)[9]: food 42.2%, clothing and footwear 31.5%, household furnishings 8.8%, energy and water 6.8%, transportation 5.1%.
Population economically active (1997): total 42,896; activity rate of total population 32.7% (participation rates: ages 15–64, 58.6%; female 43.4%; unemployed 41.5%).

Price and earnings indexes (1995 = 100)

	1995	1996	1997	1998	1999
Consumer price index	100.0	105.3	108.9	111.1	112.2
Monthly earnings index[10]	100.0	106.3	109.5	112.2	113.4

Land use (1987): meadows 35.0%; agricultural 29.0%; other 36.0%.

Foreign trade

Balance of trade (current prices)

	1998	1999	2000	2001
€'000,000	−136.5	−126.7	−147.8	−171.5
% of total	95.9%	96.2%	96.2%	95.7%

Imports (2001): €175,388,000 (food products 24.3%; machinery and apparatus 21.4%; transport equipment 13.0%; metals and metal products 9.4%). *Major import sources* (1997): France 66.0%; South Africa 14.0%; Asia 11.0%.
Exports (2001): €3,863,000 (traditional exports 18.3%, of which ylang-ylang 17.4%, vanilla 0.9%; unspecified commodities 81.7%). *Major export destinations* (1997): France 80.0%; Comoros 15.0%.

Transport and communications

Transport. Railroads: none. Roads (1998): total length 145 mi, 233 km (paved 77%). Vehicles (1998): 8,213. Merchant marine: n.a. Air transport (1998): passenger arrivals and departures 88,034; cargo unloaded and loaded 1,012 metric tons; airports (2000) with scheduled flights 1.

Communications

Medium	date	unit	number	units per 1,000 persons
Daily newspapers[11]	1998	circulation	...	...
Radio	1996	receivers	50,000	427
Television	1999	receivers	3,500	30
Telephones	2001	main lines	10,000	70

Education and health

Educational attainment (1991). Percentage of population age 25 and over having: no formal education 72.8%; primary 14.2%; lower secondary 7.5%; higher secondary 3.2%; higher 2.3%. *Literacy* (1997): total population age 15 and over literate 63,053 (86.1%).

Education (2001–02)

	schools	teachers	students	student/teacher ratio
Primary (age 6–11)	112	555[12]	28,591	38.9[12]
Secondary (age 12–18)	14	246[12]	15,626	16.2[12]
Voc., teacher tr.	2[13]	...	1,733	...
Higher	—	—	—	—

Health: physicians (1997) 57 (1 per 2,304 persons); hospital beds 186 (1 per 706 persons); infant mortality rate per 1,000 live births (2002) 67.8.

Military

Total active duty personnel (2001): 4,200 French troops are assigned to Mayotte and Réunion.

[1]Mahoré in Shimaoré, the local Swahili-based language. [2]Final status of Mayotte has not yet been determined; it is claimed by Comoros as an integral part of that country. [3]Representatives of the French government in Mayotte continue to occupy offices in the original capital of Dzaoudzi. Local administrative (General Council) offices are in Mamoudzou. [4]The French franc was the former monetary unit; on Jan. 1, 2002, F 6.56 = €1. [5]Revised area as of 2002 census equals 144.5 sq mi (374.2 sq km). [6]Nearly all ethnic Comorian (a mixture of Bantu, Arab, and Malagasy peoples). [7]Population of communes. [8]Unemployed. [9]Weights of consumer price index components. [10]Based on minimum-level wage of public employees. [11]One weekly newspaper has a total circulation of 15,000. [12]1992–93. [13]1997.

Internet resources for further information:
- **Ministère de l'Outre-Mer http://www.outre-mer.gouv.fr**
- **Le Portail de l'ile au Lagon http://www.mayotte-online.com**

Mexico

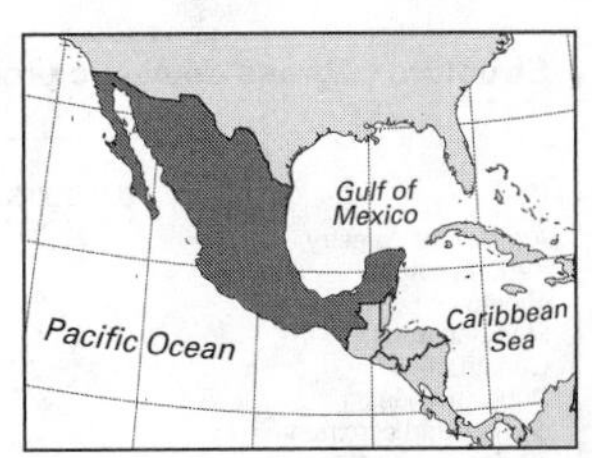

Official name: Estados Unidos Mexicanos (United Mexican States).
Form of government: federal republic with two legislative houses (Senate [128]; Chamber of Deputies [500]).
Head of state and government: President.
Capital: Mexico City.
Official language: Spanish.
Official religion: none.
Monetary unit: 1 Mexican peso (Mex$) = 100 centavos; valuation (Sept. 8, 2003) 1 U.S.$ = Mex$10.85; 1 £ = Mex$17.21.

Area and population

		area		population
States	Capitals	sq mi	sq km	2000 census
Aguascalientes	Aguascalientes	2,112	5,471	944,285
Baja California	Mexicali	26,997	69,921	2,487,367
Baja California Sur	La Paz	28,369	73,475	424,041
Campeche	Campeche	19,619	50,812	690,689
Chiapas	Tuxtla Gutiérrez	28,653	74,211	3,920,892
Chihuahua	Chihuahua	94,571	244,938	3,052,907
Coahuila de Zaragoza	Saltillo	57,908	149,982	2,298,070
Colima	Colima	2,004	5,191	542,627
Durango	Durango	47,560	123,181	1,448,661
Guanajuato	Guanajuato	11,773	30,491	4,663,032
Guerrero	Chilpancingo	24,819	64,281	3,079,649
Hidalgo	Pachuca	8,036	20,813	2,235,591
Jalisco	Guadalajara	31,211	80,836	6,322,002
México	Toluca	8,245	21,355	13,096,686
Michoacán de Ocampo	Morelia	23,138	59,928	3,985,667
Morelos	Cuernavaca	1,911	4,950	1,555,296
Nayarit	Tepic	10,417	26,979	920,185
Nuevo León	Monterrey	25,067	64,924	3,834,141
Oaxaca	Oaxaca	36,275	93,952	3,438,765
Puebla	Puebla	13,090	33,902	5,076,686
Querétaro de Arteaga	Querétaro	4,420	11,449	1,404,306
Quintana Roo	Chetumal	19,387	50,212	874,963
San Luis Potosí	San Luis Potosí	24,351	63,068	2,299,360
Sinaloa	Culiacán	22,521	58,328	2,536,844
Sonora	Hermosillo	70,291	182,052	2,216,969
Tabasco	Villahermosa	9,756	25,267	1,891,829
Tamaulipas	Ciudad Victoria	30,650	79,384	2,753,222
Tlaxcala	Tlaxcala	1,551	4,016	962,646
Veracruz–Llare	Xalapa (Jalapa)	27,683	71,699	6,908,975
Yucatán	Mérida	14,827	38,402	1,658,210
Zacatecas	Zacatecas	28,283	73,252	1,353,610
Federal District				
Distrito Federal	—	571	1,479	8,605,239
CONTINENTAL AREA		756,066[1]	1,958,201[1]	
LAND		736,949	1,908,690	
WATER		19,117	49,511	
INSULAR AREA[2]		1,979	5,127	
TOTAL		758,449[3]	1,964,375[3]	97,483,412

Demography

Population (2003): 100,588,000.
Density (2003): persons per sq mi 132.6, persons per sq km 51.2.
Urban-rural (2000): urban 74.6%; rural 25.4%.
Sex distribution (2000): male 48.82%; female 51.18%.
Age breakdown (2000): under 15, 33.8%; 15–29, 29.8%; 30–44, 19.1%; 45–59, 10.7%; 60–74, 5.2%; 75 and over, 1.4%.
Population projection: (2010) 109,166,000; (2020) 120,937,000.
Doubling time: 39 years.
Ethnic composition (2000): mestizo 64.3%; Amerindian 18.0%, of which detribalized 10.5%; Mexican white 15.0%; Arab 1.0%; Mexican black 0.5%; Spaniard 0.3%; U.S. white 0.2%; other 0.7%.
Religious affiliation (2000): Roman Catholic 90.4%; Protestant (including Evangelical) 3.8%; other 5.8%.
Major cities (2000): Mexico City 8,591,309 (urban agglomeration [2001] 18,268,000); Guadalajara 1,647,000 (urban agglomeration 3,697,000); Puebla 1,270,989 (urban agglomeration 1,888,000); Ciudad Netzahualcóyotl 1,224,500; Juárez 1,190,000; Tijuana 1,150,000; Monterrey 1,108,400 (urban agglomeration 3,267,000); León 1,019,510; Mérida 660,848; Chihuahua 650,000.
Place of birth (1990): 93.1% native-born; 6.9% foreign-born and unknown.
Households. Total households (2000) 21,954,733; distribution by size (2000): 1 person 6.0%, 2 persons 12.3%, 3 persons 17.2%, 4 persons 21.8%, 5 persons 17.7%, 6 persons 10.9%, 7 or more persons 14.1%.
Emigration (2000): legal immigrants into the United States 173,900.

Vital statistics

Birth rate per 1,000 population (2000): 23.2 (world avg. 21.3).
Death rate per 1,000 population (2000): 5.0 (world avg. 9.1).
Natural increase rate per 1,000 population (2000): 18.2 (world avg. 12.2).
Total fertility rate (avg. births per childbearing woman; 2001): 2.3.
Marriage rate per 1,000 population (2001): 6.8.
Divorce rate per 1,000 population (2001): 0.6.
Life expectancy at birth (2001): male 68.6 years; female 74.8 years.
Major causes of death per 100,000 population (2001): diseases of the circulatory system 101.3; diabetes mellitus 64.0; malignant neoplasms 59.9; accidents and violence 52.8; diseases of the digestive system 43.5; diseases of the respiratory system 38.0.

Social indicators

Access to services (2000). Proportion of dwellings having: electricity 94.8%; piped water supply 83.3%; drained sewage 76.2%.
Educational attainment (2000). Population age 15 and over having: no primary education 10.3%; some primary 18.1%; completed primary 19.4%; incomplete secondary 5.3%; complete secondary 19.1%; some higher 16.8%; higher 11.0%.

Distribution of income (2000)

percentage of household income by decile

1	2	3	4	5	6	7	8	9	10 (highest)
0.4	1.5	2.4	3.4	4.7	6.2	8.1	11.0	16.7	45.6

Quality of working life. Average workweek (1999): 44.4 hours[4]. Annual rate (1992) per 100,000 insured workers for: temporary disability 6,426; indemnification for permanent injury 239; death 18. Labour stoppages (2001): 35, involving 23,234 workers.
Social participation. Eligible voters participating in last national election (2000): 64%. Trade union membership in total workforce: n.a. Practicing religious population in total affiliated population: national average of weekly attendance (1993) 11%.
Social deviance (1991). Criminal cases tried by local authorities per 100,000 population for: murder 60.3; rape 22.4; other assault 301.0; theft 703.8. Incidence per 100,000 in general population of: alcoholism (2000) 7.6; drug and substance abuse 26.6; suicide (2001) 3.1.

National economy

Gross national product (2001): U.S.$550,200,000,000 (U.S.$5,530 per capita).

Structure of gross domestic product and labour force

	2001			
	in value Mex$'000,000[5]	% of total value	labour force	% of labour force
Agriculture	218,770	3.8	7,074,400	17.8
Mining	72,144	1.2	127,200	0.3
Manufacturing	1,037,134	17.8	7,373,000	18.6
Construction	262,631	4.5	2,396,900	6.0
Public utilities	62,526	1.1	194,900	0.5
Transp. and commun.	595,607	10.2	1,776,700	4.5
Trade	1,105,047	19.0	10,821,400	27.3
Finance	642,115	11.0	1,504,600	3.8
Pub. admin., defense	1,380,406	23.7	1,682,100	4.2
Services			6,054,000	15.3
Other	452,211[6]	7.7[6]	677,600[7]	1.7[7]
TOTAL	5,828,591	100.0	39,682,800	100.0

Budget (2001). Revenue: Mex$939,114,500,000 (income tax 30.4%, VAT 22.2%, royalties 21.7%, excise tax 11.8%, import duties 3.1%, other 10.8%). Expenditures: Mex$996,950,600,000 (current expenditure 63.4%, of which social security and welfare 41.8%, interest on public debt 16.7%; capital expenditure 36.6%).
Public debt (external, outstanding; 2001): U.S.$86,199,000,000.
Tourism (2001): receipts from visitors U.S.$8,401,000,000; expenditures by nationals abroad U.S.$5,502,000,000.

Manufacturing (2000)

	no. of enter-prises[8]	no. of employees ('000)	yearly wages as a % of avg. of all wages	value added (U.S.$'000,000)
Manufacturing	266,033	1,476,309	100.0	60,760
Transport equipment	...	105,429	105.4	9,439
Food	91,894	247,869	91.5	8,883
Chemicals	7,321	131,530	165.7	8,726
Beverages	...	110,074	92.9	5,422
Nonmetallic mineral products	24,397	46,520	99.4	3,580
Electrical machinery	...	132,335	93.0	3,484
Iron and steel	401	34,591	135.3	2,891
Nonelectrical machinery	...	49,374	105.1	2,254
Paper and paper products	15,022	51,860	91.9	2,243
Rubber and plastic	...	85,470	103.8	2,031
Metal products	...	60,180	83.2	1,691
Automobile parts	...	49,737	102.4	1,585
Tobacco	...	4,337	169.3	1,104
Nonferrous metals	...	19,627	95.1	1,093

Production (metric tons except as noted). Agriculture, forestry, fishing (2002): sugarcane 46,000,000, corn (maize) 17,500,000, sorghum 5,800,000, oranges 3,843,960, wheat 3,272,660, tomatoes 2,083,558, bananas 2,076,729, chilies and green peppers 1,755,758, lemons and limes 1,680,323, dry beans 1,647,670, mangoes 1,412,980, watermelons 1,225,713, coconuts 959,000, avocados 897,231, barley 838,583, papayas 688,642, pineapples 584,590, grapes 446,470, carrots 378,517, coffee (green) 319,835, cauliflower 200,000; livestock (number of live animals) 30,600,000 cattle, 17,000,000 pigs, 9,400,000 goats, 8,100,000 ducks, 6,700,000 sheep, 6,255,000 horses, 5,850,000 turkeys, 3,280,000 mules, 3,260,000 asses, 520,800,000 chickens; roundwood (2001) 45,156,319 cu m; fish catch (2001) 1,519,009. Mining and quarrying (2001): salt 8,501,000, gypsum 6,237,056, iron 5,539,944, silica 1,696,695, phosphate 878,177, dolomite 670,797, fluorite 619,000, sulfur 572,000, zinc 402,330, copper 343,445, lead 146,830, barite 145,789, manganese 99,751, silver 2,759,985 kg, gold 25,749 kg. Manufacturing (gross value of production in Mex$'000; 1998): machinery and equipment 423,579,725; food, beverages, and tobacco products 279,104,375; chemical products 212,479,904; metal products 108,951,844; paper and paper products 56,522,215; mineral products 55,612,499; textiles 54,458,821.
Household income and expenditure. Average household size (2000) 4.4; income per household (2000) Mex$15,762 (U.S.$1,667); sources of income (2000): wages and salaries 63.4%, property and entrepreneurship 23.6%, transfer

payments 10.0%, other 2.9%; expenditure (2000): food, beverages, and tobacco 29.9%, transportation and communications 17.8%, education 17.3%, housing (includes household furnishings) 16.5%, clothing and footwear 5.8%, health and medical services 3.6%.

Trade and service enterprises (1998)

	no. of establish-ments	no. of employees	yearly wage as a % of avg. of all wages	annual income (Mex$'000,000)[8]
Trade	1,497,828	3,790,764	...	565,728,373
Wholesale	110,180	864,569	...	249,597,035
Retail	1,387,648	2,926,195	...	316,131,338
Boutiques (excluding food products)	536,900	1,192,597	...	108,507,889
Food and tobacco speciality stores	768,799	1,234,656	...	65,305,180
Automobile, tire, and auto parts dealers	41,236	164,493	...	47,888,576
Supermarkets and grocery stores	24,697	254,497	...	48,769,283
Gasoline stations	4,345	53,610	...	32,517,091
Other	11,671	26,342	...	13,143,319
Services[8]	711,843	2,766,750	...	200,001,682
Professional services	130,475	652,148	...	53,533,318
Food and beverage services	677	11,258	...	1,012,369
Transp. and travel agencies	9,967	62,767	...	11,858,406
Lodging	9,913	151,445	...	8,960,922
Automotive repair	112,293	252,950	...	7,263,560
Educational services (private)	20,622	247,086	...	10,815,238
Medical and social assistance	79,748	203,348	...	7,497,794
Amusement services (cinemas and theatres)	4,855	65,608	...	9,845,129
Recreation[8]	20,973	65,936	...	3,065,672
Other repair[8]	72,129	104,478	...	2,625,370
Commercial and professional organizations[8]	1,946	11,946	...	264,770
Other[8]	248,245	937,780	...	83,259,134

Energy production (consumption): electricity (kW-hr; 2001) 187,812,000,000 ([1999] 230,431,000,000); hard coal (metric tons; 1999) 2,304,000 (2,754,000); lignite (metric tons; 1999) 8,845,000 (9,473,000); crude petroleum (barrels; 2001) 1,132,300,000 ([1999] 498,800,000); petroleum products (metric tons; 1999) 75,898,000 (85,258,000); natural gas (cu m; 2001) 46,620,000,000 ([1999] 30,853,200,000).

Population economically active (2001): total 39,682,800; activity rate of total population 39.9% (participation rates: ages 15–64 [1999] 63.4%; female 29.9%; unemployed [2002] 4.4%).

Price and earnings indexes (1995 = 100)

	1996	1997	1998	1999	2000	2001	2002
Consumer price index	134.4	162.1	187.9	219.1	239.9	255.1	268.0
Monthly earnings index	90.1	89.6	92.1	93.5	99.1	105.8	107.4

Financial aggregates[9]

	1996	1997	1998	1999	2000	2001	2002
Exchange rate, Mex$ per:							
U.S. dollar	7.599	7.919	9.136	9.560	9.572	9.142	10.313
£	11.867	12.969	15.133	15.470	14.283	13.260	16.686
SDR	11.289	10.906	13.890	13.059	12.472	11.489	14.020
International reserves (U.S.$)							
Total (excl. gold; '000,000)	19,433	28,797	31,799	31,782	35,509	44,741	50,594
SDRs ('000,000)	257	661	337	790	366	356	392
Reserve pos. in IMF ('000,000)	—	—	—	—	—	—	308
Foreign exchange	19,176	28,136	31,461	30,992	35,142	44,384	49,895
Gold ('000,000 fine troy oz)	0.26	0.19	0.22	0.16	0.25	0.23	0.23
% world reserves	0.03	0.02	0.03	0.02	0.02	0.02	0.02
Interest and prices							
Treasury bill rate	31.39	19.80	24.76	21.41	15.24	11.31	7.09
Balance of payments (U.S.$'000,000)							
Balance of visible trade,	+6,531	+623	–7,743	–5,581	–8,003	–9,729	–7,997
of which:							
Imports, f.o.b.	–89,469	–109,808	–125,243	–141,973	–174,458	–168,276	–168,679
Exports, f.o.b.	96,000	110,431	117,500	136,392	166,455	158,547	160,682
Balance of invisibles	–8,454	–8,077	–8,044	–8,473	–10,134	–8,362	–6,023
Balance of payments, current account	–2,328	–7,454	–15,724	–14,324	–18,137	–18,091	–14,020

Land use (1994): forest 25.5%; pasture 39.0%; agriculture 13.0%; other 22.5%.

Foreign trade

Balance of trade (current prices)

	1997	1998	1999	2000	2001	2002
U.S.$'000,000	+623	–7,913	–5,584	–8,133	–9,729	–7,997
% of total	0.3%	3.3%	2.0%	2.4%	3.0%	2.4%

Imports (2002): U.S.$168,679,000,000 (non-maquiladora sector 64.8%, of which machinery and apparatus 18.9%, transport and communications equipment 13.0%, chemicals and chemical products 7.4%, processed food, beverages, and tobacco 3.7%; maquiladora sector 35.2%, of which electrical machinery, apparatus, and electronics 15.9%, nonelectrical machinery and apparatus 5.4%, textiles and clothing 3.3%, rubber and plastic products 3.0%). *Major import sources:* U.S. 63.2%; Japan 5.5%; China 3.7%; Germany 3.6%; Canada 2.7%; Taiwan 2.5%; South Korea 2.3%.

Exports (2002): U.S.$160,682,000,000 (non-maquiladora sector 51.4%, of which road vehicles and parts 16.0%, machinery and apparatus 8.9%, crude petroleum 8.2%; maquiladora sector 48.6%, of which electrical machinery, apparatus, and electronics 24.2%, nonelectrical machinery and apparatus 10.2%, textiles and clothing 4.3%). *Major export destinations:* U.S. 89.0%; Canada 1.7%; South America 1.5%; Caribbean countries 1.4%; Central America 1.1%; Germany 0.9%; Spain 0.8%.

Trade by commodity group (1998)

	imports		exports	
SITC group	U.S.$'000,000	%	U.S.$'000,000	%
00 Food and live animals	5,285	4.2	6,135	5.2
01 Beverages and tobacco	...	...	1,035	0.9
02 Crude materials, excluding fuels	4,263	3.4	1,696	1.4
03 Mineral fuels, lubricants, and related materials	2,747	2.2	6,980	5.9
04 Animal and vegetable oils, fats, and waxes	590	0.5	—	—
05 Chemicals and related products, n.e.s.	10,718	8.6	4,231	3.6
06 Basic manufactures	21,537	17.2	11,976	10.2
07 Machinery and transport equipment	59,850	47.8	68,011	58.0
08 Miscellaneous manufactured articles	15,773	12.6	16,976	14.5
09 Goods not classified by kind	4,210	3.4	285	0.3
TOTAL[10]	125,193[11]	100.0[11]	117,325	100.0

Direction of trade (1999)

	imports		exports	
	U.S.$'000,000	%	U.S.$'000,000	%
Western Hemisphere	112,011	78.8	127,982	93.6
United States	105,267	74.1	120,393	88.1
Latin America and the Caribbean	3,795	2.7	5,198	3.8
Canada	2,949	2.0	2,391	1.7
Europe	15,208	10.7	5,889	4.3
EU	14,006	9.9	5,197	3.8
EFTA	776	0.5	455	0.3
Russia	—	—	—	—
Other Europe	426	0.3	237	0.2
Asia	13,354	9.4	2,353	1.7
Japan	5,083	3.6	776	0.6
Other Asia	8,271	5.8	1,577	1.1
Africa	398	0.3	159	0.1
Other	1,093	0.8	320	0.2
TOTAL	142,064	100.0	136,703	100.0[11]

Transport and communications

Transport. Railroads (2000): route length 16,563 mi, 26,656 km; (1998) passenger-mi 677,000,000, passenger-km 1,089,000,000; (2001) short ton-mi cargo 32,433,000, metric ton-km cargo 47,336,000,000. Roads (2000): total length 207,438 mi, 333,840 km (paved 32%). Vehicles (1999): passenger cars 9,842,006; trucks and buses 4,749,789. Air transport (2002): passenger-mi 16,120,000,000, passenger-km 25,944,000,000; short ton-mi cargo 40,990,000,-000, metric ton-km cargo 244,632,000,000; airports (2001) 85.

Communications

Medium	date	unit	number	units per 1,000 persons
Daily newspapers	2000	circulation	9,580,000	98
Radio	2000	receivers	32,300,000	330
Television	2000	receivers	27,700,000	283
Telephones	2002	main lines	14,941,600	147
Cellular telephones	2002	subscribers	25,928,000	254
Personal computers	2001	units	6,900,000	69
Internet	2002	users	4,663,000	46

Education and health

Literacy (2000): total population age 15 and over literate 91.4%; males literate 93.4%; females literate 89.5%.

Education (2001–02)

	schools	teachers	students	student/ teacher ratio
Primary (age 6–12)	99,230	609,654	14,843,400	24.3
Secondary (age 12–18)	39,691	536,579	8,600,700	16.0
Voc., teacher tr.[12]	6,610	63,674	883,000	13.9
Higher	4,183	216,804	2,147,100	9.9

Health (2000): physicians 140,629 (1 per 695 persons); hospital beds 77,144 (1 per 1,267 persons); infant mortality rate per 1,000 live births (2001) 26.0.

Food (2001): daily per capita caloric intake 3,160 (vegetable products 82%, animal products 18%); 136% of FAO recommended minimum requirement.

Military

Total active duty personnel (2002): 192,770 (army 74.7%, navy 19.2%, air force 6.1%). *Military expenditure as percentage of GNP* (1999): 0.6% (world 2.4%); per capita expenditure U.S.$27.

[1]Continental area per more recent survey equals 756,470 sq mi (1,959,248 sq km). [2]Uninhabited (nearly all Pacific) islands directly administered by federal government. [3]Total area based on most recent survey figure for continental area. [4]Manufacturing only. [5]At factor cost. [6]Imputed bank service charge. [7]Unemployed. [8]1993. [9]Exchange rates and treasury bill rates are expressed in period averages; international reserves are expressed in end-of-period rates. [10]Totals include adjustments of unspecified nature. [11]Detail does not add to total given because of rounding. [12]1996–97.

Internet resources for further information:

- **National Institute of Statistics, Geography, and Informatics http://www.inegi.gob.mx/difusion/ingles/portadai.html**
- **Banco de México http://www.banxico.org.mx**

Micronesia

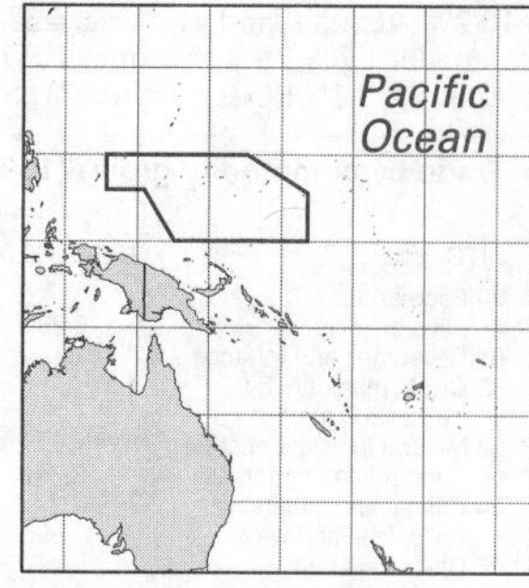

Official name: Federated States of Micronesia.
Form of government: federal nonparty republic in free association with the United States with one legislative house (Congress [14])[1].
Head of state and government: President.
Capital: Palikir, on Pohnpei.
Official language: none.
Official religion: none.
Monetary unit: 1 U.S. dollar (U.S.$) = 100 cents; valuation (Sept. 8, 2003) 1 U.S.$ = £0.63.

Area and population

States / Major Islands	Capitals	area sq mi	area sq km	population 2000 census
Chuuk (Truk)	Weno (Moen)	49.1	127.2	53,595
Chuuk Islands		...	...	40,465
Kosrae	Lelu	42.3	109.6	7,686
Kosrae Island		42.3	109.6	7,686
Pohnpei (Ponape)	Kolonia	133.3	345.2	34,486
Pohnpei Island		129.0	334.1	32,178
Yap	Colonia	45.9	118.9	11,241
Yap Island		38.7	100.2	7,391
TOTAL		270.8[2]	701.4[2]	107,008

Demography

Population (2003): 112,000.
Density (2003): persons per sq mi 413.3, persons per sq km 159.8.
Urban-rural (2000): urban 28.5%; rural 71.5%.
Sex distribution (2000): male 50.64%; female 49.36%.
Age breakdown (2000): under 15, 40.3%; 15–29, 28.4%; 30–44, 16.9%; 45–59, 9.1%; 60–74, 3.9%; 75 and over, 1.4%.
Population projection: (2010) 118,000; (2020) 124,000.
Doubling time: 32 years.
Ethnic composition (2000): Chuukese/Mortlockese 33.6%; Pohnpeian 24.9%; Yapese 10.6%; Kosraean 5.2%; U.S. white 4.5%; Asian 1.3%; other 19.9%.
Religious affiliation (2000): Roman Catholic 52.7%; Protestant 41.7%, of which Congregational 40.1%; Mormon 1.0%; other/unknown 4.6%.
Major towns (2000): Weno, in Chuuk state 13,900; Tol, in Chuuk state 9,500; Palikir, on Pohnpei 6,227; Kolonia, on Pohnpei 5,681; Colonia, on Yap 3,350.

Vital statistics

Birth rate per 1,000 population (2002): 27.2 (world avg. 21.3); legitimate, n.a.; illegitimate, n.a.
Death rate per 1,000 population (2002): 5.3 (world avg. 9.1).
Natural increase rate per 1,000 population (2002): 21.9 (world avg. 12.2).
Total fertility rate (avg. births per childbearing woman; 2002): 3.6.
Marriage rate per 1,000 population: n.a.
Divorce rate per 1,000 population: n.a.
Life expectancy at birth (2002): male 67.1 years; female 70.6 years.
Major causes of death per 100,000 population (1998)[3]: diseases of the circulatory system 89.7; malignant neoplasms (cancers) 50.5; homicide, suicide, and accidents 48.6; diseases of the respiratory system 47.7; infectious and parasitic diseases 38.3; endocrine and metabolic diseases 33.6.

National economy

Budget (2001–02). Revenue: U.S.$160,400,000 (external grants 71.2%, tax revenue 17.7%, nontax revenue [including fishing rights fees] 11.1%). Expenditures: U.S.$154,800,000 (current expenditures 83.4%, capital expenditure 16.6%).
Public debt (external, outstanding; 2000): U.S.$85,700,000.
Population economically active (2000): total 37,414; activity rate of total population 35.0% (participation rates: ages 15–64, 61.7%; female 42.9%; unemployed 22.0%).

Price and earnings indexes (1995 = 100)

	1996	1997	1998	1999	2000	2001
Price index	103.1	105.2	106.8	109.6	111.8	114.0
Annual wage index	97.5	94.2	...	...	...	...

Production (metric tons except as noted). Agriculture, forestry, fishing (2002): coconuts 140,000, cassava 11,800, sweet potatoes 3,000, bananas 2,000; livestock (number of live animals) 32,000 pigs, 13,900 cattle, 4,000 goats; fish catch (2001) 18,100, of which skipjack tuna 10,300, yellowfin tuna 5,300. Mining and quarrying: quarrying of sand and aggregate for local construction only. Manufacturing: n.a.; however, copra and coconut oil, traditionally important products, are being displaced by garment production; the manufacture of handicrafts and personal items (clothing, mats, boats, etc.) by individuals is also important. Energy production (consumption): electricity (kW-hr; 1997) 100,333,000 (100,333,000); coal, none (none); crude petroleum, none (none); petroleum products (metric tons; 1992) none (77,000); natural gas, none (none).
Household income and expenditure. Average household size (2000) 6.7; annual income per household U.S.$8,944 (median income: U.S.$4,618); sources of income (1994): wages and salaries 51.8%, operating surplus 23.0%, social security 2.1%; expenditure (1985): food and beverages 73.5%.

Land use: n.a.
Gross national product (2001): U.S.$300,000,000 (U.S.$2,150 per capita).

Structure of gross domestic product and labour force

	1996 in value U.S.$'000,000	1996 % of total value	2000 labour force	2000 % of labour force
Agriculture and fishing[4]	34.7	19.1	15,216	40.7
Mining	0.7	0.4	1,164	3.1
Manufacturing	2.6	1.4		
Construction	1.9	1.0	781	2.1
Public utilities	2.0	1.1	360	1.0
Transp. and commun.	8.5	4.7	806	2.2
Finance	4.2	2.3	726	1.9
Services	3.1	1.7	1,445	3.9
Trade, hotels	43.6	24.0	2,540	6.8
Public administration	80.4	44.3	6,137	16.4
Other	...	...	8,239[5]	22.0[5]
TOTAL	181.6[2]	100.0	37,414	100.0[2]

Tourism (1998): receipts from visitors U.S.$2,513,000; expenditures by nationals abroad, n.a.

Foreign trade

Balance of trade (current prices)

	1994	1995	1996	1997	1998	1999
U.S.$'000,000	–50.5	–60.3	–73.4	–67.2	–46.1	–10.2
% of total	24.4%	43.4%	77.4%	80.7%	87.4%	70.6%

Imports (1999): U.S.$12,328,000 (food and live animals 24.8%, mineral fuels 20.3%, machinery and transport equipment 19.5%, beverages and tobacco products 6.0%). *Major import sources* (2000): United States 43.9%; Australia 19.8%; Japan 12.5%.
Exports (1999): U.S.$2,128,000 (fish 92.0%, bananas 1.2%). *Major export destinations* (1996): Japan 79.0%; United States 18.3%.

Transport and communications

Transport. Railroads: none. Roads (1990): total length 140 mi, 226 km (paved 17%). Vehicles (1998): passenger cars 2,044; trucks and buses 354. Air transport: n.a.; airports (1997) with scheduled flights 4.

Communications

Medium	date	unit	number	units per 1,000 persons
Radio	1996	receivers	70,000	667
Television	1999	receivers	2,400	21
Telephones	2001	main lines	10,000	93
Cellular telephones	2001	subscribers	49,900	466
Internet	2000	users	4,000	37

Education and health

Educational attainment (2000). Percentage of population age 25 and over having: no formal schooling 12.3%; primary education 37.0%; some secondary 18.3%; secondary 12.9%; some college 18.4%. *Literacy* (2000): total population age 10 and over literate 72,140 (92.4%); males literate 36,528 (92.9%); females literate 35,612 (91.9%).

Education (1997–98)

	schools	teachers	students	student/teacher ratio
Elementary (age 6–12)	171	1,486	25,915	18.6
Secondary (age 13–18)	24	418	6,809	16.2
College	1	71	1,884	26.5

Health (1998): physicians 68 (1 per 1,677 persons); hospital beds (1997) 260 (1 per 447 persons); infant mortality rate per 1,000 live births (2003) 33.5.
Food: daily per capita caloric intake, n.a.

Military

External security is provided by the United States.

[1]The compact of free association (from 1986) between the United States and the Federated States of Micronesia (FSM) was renewed in 2003 for another 20 years. Terms of the new compact included a cut in U.S. grants after 2004. [2]Detail does not add to total given because of rounding. [3]Based on registered deaths only. [4]Includes subsistence farming and fishing. [5]Unemployed.

Internet resources for further information:
- **General Information on The FSM**
  http://www.boh.com/econ/pacific
- **U.S. Office on Insular Affairs**
  http://www.pacificweb.org

Moldova

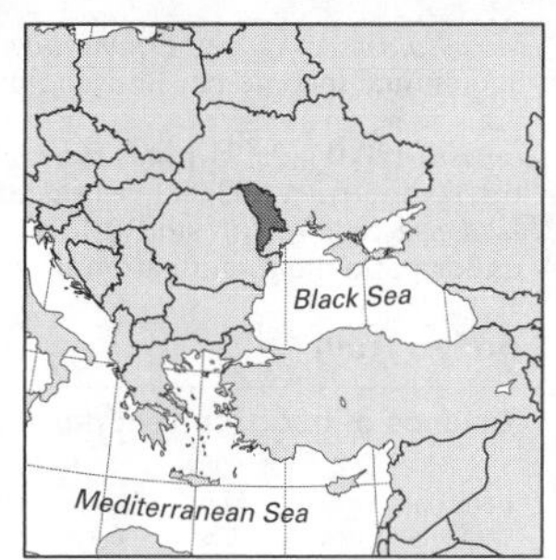

Official name: Republica Moldova (Republic of Moldova).
Form of government: unitary parliamentary republic with a single legislative body (Parliament [101]).
Head of state: President.
Head of government: Prime Minister.
Capital: Chişinău.
Official language: Romanian[1].
Official religion: none.
Monetary unit: 1 Moldovan leu (plural lei) = 100 bani; valuation (Sept. 8, 2003) free rate, 1 U.S.$ = 13.74 Moldovan lei; 1 £ = 21.79 Moldovan lei.

Area and population

Counties	Capitals	area: sq mi	area: sq km	population: 2003[2] estimate
Bălţi	Bălţi	1,576	4,081	500,900
Cahul	Cahul	941	2,438	190,800
Chişinău	Chişinău	1,073	2,780	382,400
Edinet	Edinet	1,231	3,187	279,100
Lăpuşna	Lăpuşna	1,327	3,436	276,300
Orhei	Orhei	1,100	2,850	300,400
Soroca	Soroca	1,221	3,162	274,600
Taraclia	Taraclia	395	1,022	45,600
Tighina	Tighina	1,119	2,899	169,000
Ungheni	Ungheni	971	2,516	260,300
City District				
Chişinău	—	189	490	779,400
Autonomous Region				
Găgăuzia	Comrat	580	1,503	158,900
Disputed Territory[3]				
Stonga Nistruli (Transdniester)[4]	Tiraspol	1,343	3,479	630,000
TOTAL		13,066	33,843	4,248,000[5, 6]

Demography

Population (2003): 4,267,000[5, 7].
Density (2003): persons per sq mi 326.6, persons per sq km 126.1.
Urban-rural (2002): urban 45.3%; rural 54.7%.
Sex distribution (2002): male 47.84%; female 52.16%.
Age breakdown (2001): under 15, 22.4%; 15–29, 25.5%; 30–44, 21.1%; 45–59, 16.6%; 60–74, 11.0%; 75 and over, 3.4%.
Population projection: (2010) 4,230,000; (2020) 4,163,000.
Ethnic composition (2000): Moldovan 48.2%; Ukrainian 13.8%; Russian 12.9%; Bulgarian 8.2%; Roma (Gypsy) 6.2%; Gagauz 4.2%; other 6.5%.
Religious affiliation (1995): Orthodox 46.0%, of which Romanian Orthodox 35.0%, Russian Orthodox 9.5%; Muslim 5.5%; Catholic 1.8%, of which Roman Catholic 0.6%; Protestant 1.7%; Jewish 0.9%; other (mostly nonreligious) 44.1%.
Major cities (2003)[5]: Chişinău 662,400; Tiraspol 185,000; Bălţi 145,900; Tighina 125,000; Râbniţa 62,000.

Vital statistics

Birth rate per 1,000 population (2002): 9.9 (world avg. 21.3); (1995) legitimate 87.7%; illegitimate 12.3%.
Death rate per 1,000 population (2002): 11.5 (world avg. 9.1).
Natural increase rate per 1,000 population (2002): –1.6 (world avg. 12.2).
Total fertility rate (avg. births per childbearing woman; 2002): 1.7.
Marriage rate per 1,000 population (2001): 6.8.
Life expectancy at birth (2001): male 60.2 years; female 69.3 years.
Major causes of death per 100,000 population (1994): circulatory diseases 500.7; cancers 136.1; accidents and violence 113.3; digestive system diseases 110.4.

National economy

Budget (2001). Revenue: 5,393,000,000 lei (value-added tax 27.8%; social fund contributions 24.2%; excise taxes 12.6%; profits tax 6.5%; duties and customs taxes 4.3%). Expenditures: 5,661,000,000 lei (current expenditures 75.4%, of which social fund expenditures 24.3%, education 16.3%, interest payments 14.1%, health care 9.6%; capital expenditure 24.6%).
Public debt (external, outstanding; 2001): U.S.$779,000,000.
Production (metric tons except as noted). Agriculture, forestry, fishing (2002): corn (maize) 1,192,770, wheat 1,122,270, sugar beets 1,116,034, grapes 660,218, potatoes 324,938, sunflower seeds 320,101, apples 271,000, tobacco leaves 11,567; livestock (number of live animals) 834,870 sheep, 448,898 pigs, 404,845 cattle; roundwood (2001) 56,800 cu m; fish catch (2000) 1,319. Mining and quarrying (2000): sand and gravel 277,000; gypsum 32,100. Manufacturing ('000,000 lei; 1995): food 1,446,824; machinery 383,153; construction materials 164,198; textiles 57,283. Energy production (consumption): electricity (kW-hr; 1999) 3,814,000,000 (5,378,000,000); coal (metric tons; 1999) none (229,000); crude petroleum (barrels; 1999) none (none); petroleum products (metric tons; 1999) none (450,000); natural gas (cu m; 1999) none (2,418,200,000).
Population economically active (2001): total 1,616,700; activity rate of total population 37.8% (participation rates: ages 15–64, n.a.; female 50.1%; unemployed 7.3%).

Price and earnings indexes (1995 = 100)

	1996	1997	1998	1999	2000	2001	2002
Consumer price index	120.9	130.6	139.2	203.2	266.8	292.9	307.9
Earnings index	...	...	...	...	...	...	...

Gross national product (at current market prices; 2001): U.S.$1,500,000,000 (U.S.$400 per capita).

Structure of gross domestic product and labour force

	2000: in value '000,000 lei[8]	2000: % of total value	2001: labour force	2001: % of labour force
Agriculture	3,919	24.7	764,800	47.3
Manufacturing, mining	2,446	15.4	138,800	8.6
Public utilities	358	2.3	26,400	1.6
Construction	423	2.7	43,200	2.7
Transp. and commun.	1,434	9.0	64,300	4.0
Trade[9]	2,135	13.4	163,800	10.1
Finance			28,700	1.8
Pub. admin., defense }	4,248	26.7	65,800	4.1
Services			203,200	12.6
Other	927[10]	5.8[10]	117,700[11]	7.3[11]
TOTAL	15,890	100.0	1,616,700	100.0[6]

Tourism (2001): receipts from visitors U.S.$46,000,000; expenditures by nationals abroad U.S.$88,000,000.
Household income and expenditure. Average household size (1989) 3.4; annual average income per household (2002) U.S.$1,200; sources of income (1994): wages and salaries 41.2%, social benefits 15.3%, agricultural income 10.4%, other 33.1%; expenditure (2001): food and drink 60.4%, housing 13.5%, utilities 10.5%, transportation 8.9%, clothing 7.6%, health 3.9%.
Land use (1994): forest 10.6%; pasture 10.9%; agriculture 75.9%; other 2.6%.

Foreign trade

Balance of trade (current prices)

	1997	1998	1999	2000	2001	2002
U.S.$'000,000	–297	–392	–122	–306	–327	–393
% of total	14.5%	23.7%	11.7%	24.5%	22.3%	21.6%

Imports (2002): U.S.$1,103,000,000 (mineral products 21.7%; machinery and apparatus 14.0%; chemicals and chemical products 10.7%; textiles 10.0%). *Major import sources:* Ukraine 20.4%; Russia 15.3%; Romania 11.4%; Germany 9.2%; Italy 7.5%.
Exports (2002): U.S.$710,000,000 (processed food, beverages [significantly wine], and tobacco products 37.8%; textiles and wearing apparel 16.7%; vegetables, fruits, seeds, and nuts 15.0%). *Major export destinations:* Russia 35.4%; Ukraine 9.1%; Italy 9.1%; Romania 8.4%; Germany 7.4%.

Transport and communications

Transport. Railroads (2000): length 2,710 km; passenger-km 315,000,000; metric ton-km cargo 1,513,000,000. Roads (1999): total length 12,657 km (paved 87%). Vehicles (1999): passenger cars 232,278; trucks and buses 66,012. Air transport (2000): passenger-km 253,000,000; metric ton-km cargo 4,100,000; airports (2001) 1.

Communications

Medium	date	unit	number	units per 1,000 persons
Daily newspapers	2000	circulation	660,000	154
Radio	2000	receivers	3,250,000	758
Television	2000	receivers	1,270,000	297
Telephones	2001	main lines	676,100	154
Cellular telephones	2001	subscribers	210,000	48
Personal computers	2001	units	70,000	16
Internet	2001	users	60,000	14

Education and health

Educational attainment: n.a. *Literacy* (2000): total population age 15 and over literate 98.9%; males 99.5%; females 98.3%.

Education (2002–03)

	schools	teachers	students	student/ teacher ratio
Primary (age 7–13) } Secondary (age 14–17)	1,580	42,300	542,600	12.8
Voc., teacher tr.	83	2,300	22,600	9.8
Higher[12]	45	5,300	95,039	17.9

Health (2001): physicians 12,800 (1 per 334 persons); hospital beds 25,000 (1 per 171 persons); infant mortality rate per 1,000 live births (2001) 42.7.
Food (2001): daily per capita caloric intake 2,766 (vegetable products 86%, animal products 14%); 108% of FAO recommended minimum requirement.

Military

Total active duty personnel (2003): 6,910 (army 84.1%, air force 15.9%). Opposition forces in Transdniester (excluding militia; 2003) *c.* 9,500. *Military expenditure as percentage of GNP* (1999): 1.6% (world 2.4%); per capita expenditure U.S.$10.

[1]Officially designated Moldovan per constitution. [2]January 1. [3]Breakaway area from 1991. [4]Also known as Transnistria. [5]De jure figure including Moldovans working abroad (particularly in Western Europe). [6]Detail does not add to total given because of rounding. [7]Estimate of UN *World Population Prospects (2002 revision).* [8]Excludes Stonga Nistruli (Transdniester). [9]Includes hotels. [10]Import and production taxes less subsidies. [11]Includes unemployed. [12]Universities only.

Internet resources for further information:
- **Department for Statistics and Sociology http://www.statistica.md/statistics**
- **Moldovan Economic Trends http://www.met.dnt.md**

Monaco

Official name: Principauté de Monaco (Principality of Monaco).
Form of government: constitutional monarchy with one legislative body (National Council [24]).
Chief of state: Prince.
Head of government[1]: Minister of State assisted by the Council of Government.
Capital: [2].
Official language: French.
Official religion: Roman Catholicism.
Monetary unit: 1 euro[3] (€) = 100 centimes; valuation (Sept. 8, 2003) 1 U.S.$ = €0.90; 1 £ = €1.43.

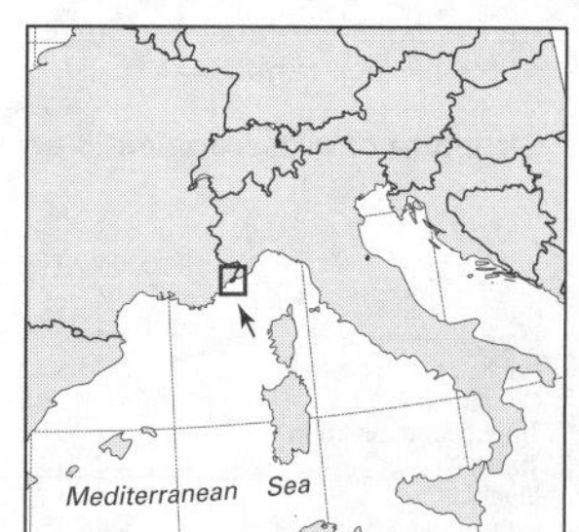

Area and population		area		population
				2000
Quarters	**Capitals**[2]	sq mi	sq km	census
Fontvieille	—	0.13	0.33	3,292
La Condamine	—	0.23	0.61	12,187
Monaco-Ville	—	0.07	0.19	1,034
Monte-Carlo	—	0.32	0.82	15,507
TOTAL		0.75	1.95	32,020

Demography

Population (2003): 32,400.
Density (2003): persons per sq mi 43,200, persons per sq km 16,615.
Urban-rural (2000): urban 100%; rural 0%.
Sex distribution (2000): male 47.58%; female 52.42%.
Age breakdown (2000): under 15, 15.1%; 15–29, 14.0%; 30–44, 21.2%; 45–59, 21.3%; 60–74, 17.2%; 75 and over, 11.2%.
Population projection: (2010) 33,000; (2020) 35,000.
Doubling time: not applicable.
Ethnic composition (2000): French 45.8%; Ligurian (Genoan) 17.2%; Monegasque 16.9%; British 4.5%; Jewish 1.7%; other 13.9%.
Religious affiliation (2000): Christian 93.2%, of which Roman Catholic 89.3%; Jewish 1.7%; nonreligious and other 5.1%.

Vital statistics

Birth rate per 1,000 population (2002): 23.0 (world avg. 21.3).
Death rate per 1,000 population (2002): 16.2 (world avg. 9.1).
Natural increase rate per 1,000 population (2002): 6.8 (world avg. 12.2).
Total fertility rate (avg. births per childbearing woman; 2002): 1.8.
Marriage rate per 1,000 population (2002): 5.4.
Divorce rate per 1,000 population (2002): 2.1.
Life expectancy at birth (2002): male 74.9 years; female 83.0 years.
Major causes of death per 100,000 population: n.a.; however, principal causes are those of a developed country with an older population.

National economy

Budget (2001). Revenue: €624,254,804 (value-added taxes *c.* 50%[4], state-run monopolies *c.* 20%). Expenditures: €621,041,725 (current expenditure 65.5%, capital expenditure 34.5%).
Public debt: n.a.
Production. Agriculture, forestry, fishing: some horticulture and greenhouse cultivation; no agriculture as such. Mining and quarrying: none. Manufacturing (value of export sales in €'000,000; 2001): chemicals, cosmetics, perfumery, and pharmaceuticals 347; plastic products 179; light electronics and precision instruments 81; paper and card manufactures 45; textiles 26. Energy production (consumption): electricity (kW-hr; 2001), n.a. (475,000,000 [imported from France]); coal, none (n.a.); crude petroleum, none (n.a.); natural gas, none (n.a.).
Gross national product (2002): U.S.$849,000,000 (U.S.$26,300 per capita).

Distribution of value of sales and labour force	1992		2001	
	in value F '000,000	% of total value	labour force	% of labour force
Agriculture	...	...		
Manufacturing	3,650	11.3		
Construction } Public utilities }	5	5	6,920	17.5
Hotels, restaurants	1,140	3.5		
Transp. and commun.	...	...		
Finance, real estate	3,780[5]	11.6[5]		
Services	23,870	73.6	32,623	82.5
Pub. admin., defense	...	...		
Other	—	—		
TOTAL	32,440	100.0	39,543[6]	100.0[6]

Population economically active (2001): total 39,543, of which Monegasque 3,471, foreign workers 36,072; female participation in labour force 42.4%; unemployed, n.a.

Price and earnings indexes (1995 = 100)	1996	1997	1998	1999	2000	2001	2002
Consumer price index[7]	102.0	103.2	103.9	104.5	106.3	108.1	110.1
Earnings index[7]	101.9	104.7	107.6	110.0	115.0	120.2	124.6

Household income and expenditure. Average household size (1998) 2.2; average annual income per household: n.a.; sources of income: n.a.; expenditure: n.a.
Tourism (2001): 2,174 hotel rooms; 798,000 overnight stays; 3 casinos run by the state attract 400,000 visitors annually.
Land use (2000): forested 0%; meadows and pastures 0%; agricultural and under permanent cultivation 0%; built-up and other 100%.

Foreign trade[8]

Balance of trade (current prices)	1998	1999	2000	2001
€'000,000	–69	–54	+20	+9
% of total	9.6%	6.4%	2.1%	1.1%

Imports (2001): €394,000,000 (consumer goods and parts for industrial production [including pharmaceuticals, perfumes, clothing, publishing] 23.8%, food products 22.6%, transport equipment and parts 20.0%). *Major import sources:* EEC 64.0%; U.S., Japan, Switzerland, and Norway 11.6%; African countries 8.8%.
Exports (2001): €403,000,000 (rubber and plastic products, glass, construction materials, organic chemicals, and paper and paper products 31.4%, products of automobile industry 21.4%, consumer goods 17.0%). *Major export destinations:* EEC 63.5%; U.S., Japan, Switzerland, and Norway 10.6%; African countries 8.6%.

Transport and communications

Transport. Railroads (2001): length 1.1 mi, 1.7 km; passengers 2,171,100; cargo 3,357 tons. Roads (2001): total length 31 mi, 50 km (paved 100%). Vehicles (1997): passenger cars 21,120; trucks and buses 2,770. Air transport: airports with scheduled flights, none[9].

Communications				units
Medium	date	unit	number	per 1,000 persons
Daily newspapers	1999	circulation	10,000	300
Radio	1997	receivers	34,000	1,030
Television	1997	receivers	25,000	758
Telephones	1999	main lines	33,000	990
Cellular telephones	1999	subscribers	12,000	360

Education and health

Education (2002–03)	schools	teachers	students	student/ teacher ratio
Primary (age 6–10)	7	...	1,899	...
Secondary (age 11–17)	4	...	3,140	...
Higher	1	53	650	12.3

Literacy: virtually 100%.
Health (2002): physicians 156 (1 per 207 persons); hospital beds 521 (1 per 62 persons); infant mortality rate per 1,000 live births (2000) 5.9.
Food: daily per capita caloric intake, n.a.; assuming consumption patterns similar to France (2000) 3,591 (vegetable products 62%, animal products 38%); 143% of FAO recommended minimum requirement.

Military

Defense responsibility lies with France according to the terms of the Versailles Treaty of 1919.

[1]Under the authority of the prince. [2]The principality is a single administrative unit, and no separate area within it is distinguished as capital. [3]French franc (F) replaced by euro on Jan. 1, 2002. [4]On hotels, banks, and the industrial sector. [5]Finance, real estate includes Construction and Public utilities. [6]Includes 36,072 foreigners. [7]The index is for France. [8]Excludes trade with France; Monaco has participated in a customs union with France since 1963. [9]Fixed-wing service is provided at Nice, France; helicopter service is available at Fontvieille.

Internet resources for further information:
- **La Principauté de Monaco**
  http://www.monaco.gouv.mc
- **Monaco—Monte-Carlo**
  http://www.monte-carlo.mc

Mongolia

Official name: Mongol Uls (Mongolia).
Form of government: unitary multiparty republic with one legislative house (State Great Hural [76]).
Chief of state: President.
Head of government: Prime Minister.
Capital: Ulaanbaatar (Ulan Bator).
Official language: Khalkha Mongolian.
Official religion: none.
Monetary unit: 1 tugrik (Tug) = 100 möngö; valuation (Sept. 8, 2003) 1 U.S.$ = Tug 1,126; 1 £ = Tug 1,785.

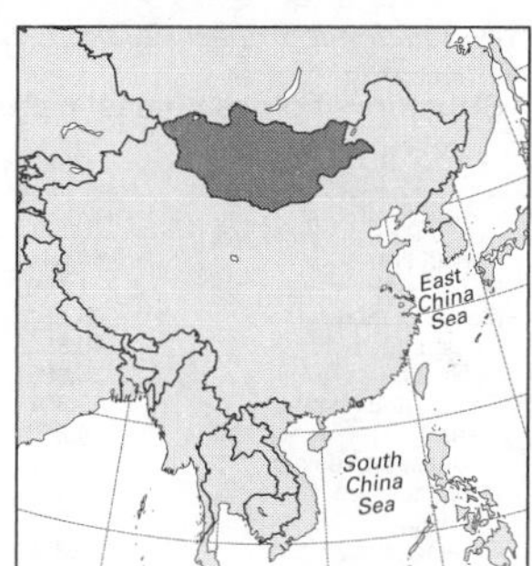

Area and population

Provinces	Capitals	area[1] sq mi	area[1] sq km	population 2002[2] estimate
Arhangay	Tsetserleg	21,400	55,300	98,300
Bayan-Ölgiy	Ölgiy	17,600	45,700	96,900
Bayanhongor	Bayanhongor	44,800	116,000	85,700
Bulgan	Bulgan	18,800	48,700	63,300
Darhan-Uul	Darhan	1,270	3,280	86,000
Dornod	Choybalsan	47,700	123,600	74,500
Dornogovĭ	Saynshand	42,300	109,500	51,500
Dundgovĭ	Manalgovi	28,800	74,700	51,300
Dzavhan	Uliastay	31,900	82,500	86,800
Govĭ-Altay	Altay	54,600	141,400	64,200
Govĭ-Sümber	Choyr	2,140	5,540	12,400
Hentiy	Öndörhaan	31,000	80,300	71,900
Hovd	Hovd	29,400	76,100	88,700
Hövsgöl	Mörön	38,800	100,600	120,900
Ömnögovĭ	Dalandzadgad	63,900	165,400	47,300
Orhon	Erdenet	320	840	76,500
Övörhangay	Arvayheer	24,300	62,900	114,000
Selenge	Sühbaatar	15,900	41,200	101,700
Sühbaatar	Baruun-Urt	31,800	82,300	56,000
Töv	Dzüünmod	28,600	74,000	96,300
Uvs	Ulaangom	26,900	69,600	85,800
Autonomous municipality				
Ulaanbaatar	—	1,800	4,700	812,500
TOTAL	…	603,930[3]	1,564,160	2,442,500

Demography

Population (2003): 2,493,000.
Density (2003): persons per sq mi 4.1, persons per sq km 1.6.
Urban-rural (2002): urban 56.4%; rural 43.6%.
Sex distribution (2002): male 49.53%; female 50.47%.
Age breakdown (2002): under 15, 32.7%; 15–29, 31.4%; 30–44, 21.2%; 45–59, 9.2%; 60–69, 3.4%; 70 and over, 2.1%.
Population projection: (2010) 2,748,000; (2020) 3,097,000.
Doubling time: 50 years.
Ethnic composition (2000): Khalkha Mongol 81.5%; Kazakh 4.3%; Dörbed Mongol 2.8%; Bayad 2.1%; Buryat Mongol 1.7%; Dariganga Mongol 1.3%; Zakhchin 1.3%; Tuvan (Uriankhai) 1.1%; other 3.9%.
Religious affiliation (1995): Tantric Buddhist (Lamaism) 96.0%; Muslim 4.0%.
Major cities (2000): Ulaanbaatar (Ulan Bator) 760,077; Erdenet 68,310; Darhan 65,791; Choybalsan 41,714; Ulaangom 26,319.

Vital statistics

Birth rate per 1,000 population (2001): 20.5 (world avg. 21.3); legitimate 82.2%; illegitimate 17.8%.
Death rate per 1,000 population (2001): 6.6 (world avg. 9.1).
Natural increase rate per 1,000 population (2001): 13.9 (world avg. 12.2).
Total fertility rate (avg. births per childbearing woman; 2001): 2.2.
Marriage rate per 1,000 population (2001): 5.1.
Divorce rate per 1,000 population (2001): 1.5.
Life expectancy at birth (2001): male 62.1 years; female 66.5 years.
Major causes of death per 100,000 population (2001): diseases of the circulatory system 103.7; malignant neoplasms (cancers) 56.2; diseases of the digestive system 22.0; diseases of the respiratory system 21.0; accidents 15.8.

National economy

Budget (2002). Revenue: Tug 466,527,000,000 (taxes 76.4%, of which VAT 25.2%, income tax 15.2%, social security contributions 11.4%, customs duties 11.2%; nontax revenue 23.6%). Expenditures: Tug 536,549,300,000 (education, health, social services 52.3%; wages 19.6%; capital investment 11.9%; interest 3.3%; other 12.9%).
Public debt (external; 2001): U.S.$823,800,000.
Tourism (2001): receipts U.S.$55,000,000; expenditures U.S.$39,000,000.
Population economically active (2002[2]): total 872,600; activity rate of total population 35.7% (participation rates: ages 15 and over 62.2%; female 49.8%; unemployed 4.6%).

Price and earnings indexes (1995 = 100)

	1995	1996	1997	1998	1999	2000	2001
Consumer price index	100.0	149.3	203.9	223.0	239.9	267.7	284.4
Monthly earnings index	100.0	146.4	185.4	234.4	…	…	…

Production (metric tons except as noted). Agriculture, forestry, fishing (2002): wheat 149,336, potatoes 65,560, vegetables and melons 45,000; livestock (number of live animals) 11,937,300 sheep, 8,858,000 goats, 3,100,000 horses, 2,053,700 cattle, 352,000 camels, 15,000 pigs; roundwood (2001) 631,000 cu m; fish catch (2001) 425. Mining and quarrying (2002): copper 376,300; fluorspar concentrate 159,800; molybdenum 3,384; gold 12,097 kg. Manufacturing (value added by manufacturing in Tug '000,000; 2001): textiles 82,486; food and beverages 81,319; clothing and apparel 23,007; printing 6,380; nonmetallic mineral products 6,088; chemicals 4,849; wood products 2,694; leather and footwear 1,573. Construction (Tug '000,000; 2001): residential 69; nonresidential 238. Energy production (consumption): electricity (kW-hr; 2001) 3,017,000,000 (3,213,000,000); hard coal (metric tons; 1999) 892,000 (977,000); lignite (metric tons; 1999) 4,061,000 (4,061,000); petroleum products (metric tons; 1999) none (391,000).
Gross national product (2001): U.S.$1,000,000,000 (U.S.$400 per capita).

Structure of gross domestic product and labour force

	2001 in value Tug '000,000	2001 % of total value	2002[2] labour force	2002[2] % of labour force
Agriculture	300,644.7	26.0	402,400	46.1
Mining	135,418.1	11.7	19,900	2.3
Manufacturing	83,484.7	7.2	55,600	6.4
Construction	23,702.3	2.0	20,400	2.3
Public utilities	27,386.1	2.4	17,800	2.0
Transp. and commun.	135,759.8	11.7	35,100	4.0
Trade	284,465.7	24.6	106,800	12.2
Finance, real estate	40,459.3	3.5	14,200	1.6
Public admin., defense	52,244.2	4.5	41,000	4.7
Services	107,627.5	9.3	119,200	13.7
Other	–32,984.3[4]	–2.8[4]	40,200[5]	4.6[5]
TOTAL	1,158,208.1	100.0[3]	872,600	100.0[3]

Household income and expenditure (2001): Average household size 4.4; annual income per household (2001) Tug 1,226,000 (U.S.$1,100); sources of income (2001): wages 29.2%, self-employment 28.6%, transfer payments 8.0%, other 34.2%; expenditure (2001): food 42.5%, clothing 16.2%, transportation and communications 7.8%, education 7.1%, housing 6.8%, health care 1.7%.
Land use (1998): forest and other 24.4%; pasture 74.8%; agriculture 0.8%.

Foreign trade

Balance of trade (current prices)

	1998	1999	2000	2001	2002
U.S.$'000,000	–41.0	–58.6	–78.7	–116.2	–158.1
% of total	4.2%	6.1%	6.8%	10.0%	13.6%

Imports (2002): U.S.$659,000,000 (machinery and apparatus 19.5%, food and agricultural products 19.0%, mineral fuels 18.6%, textiles and clothing 12.7%). *Major import sources:* Russia 34.1%; China 24.4%; South Korea 12.2%; Japan 6.2%; Germany 4.5%.
Exports (2002): U.S.$500,900,000 (2001; copper concentrate 28.1%, gold 14.3%, cashmere [all forms] 13.4%, fluorspar 3.8%). *Major export destinations* (2002): China 42.4%; United States 31.6%; Russia 8.6%; South Korea 4.4%; Australia 3.5%.

Transport and communications

Transport. Railroads (2001): length 1,815 km; passenger-km (2001): 1,062,200,000; metric ton-km cargo 5,287,900,000. Roads (2001): total length 49,250 km (paved 4%). Vehicles (2001): passenger cars 53,200; trucks and buses 36,600. Air transport (2001): passenger-km 538,900,000; metric ton-km cargo 9,500,000; airports (2001) with scheduled flights 1.

Communications

Medium	date	unit	number	units per 1,000 persons
Daily newspapers	1996	circulation	68,000	27
Radio	2000	receivers	368,000	154
Television	2000	receivers	169,100	58
Telephones	2001	main lines	124,300	52
Cellular telephones	2001	subscribers	195,000	76
Personal computers	2001	units	35,000	14
Internet	2001	users	40,000	16

Education and health

Educational attainment (2000). Percentage of population age 10 and over having: no formal education 11.6%; primary education 23.5%; secondary 46.1%; vocational secondary 11.2%; higher 7.6%. *Literacy* (2000): percentage of total population age 15 and over literate 98.9%; males 99.1%; females 98.8%.

Education (2001–02)

	schools	teachers	students	student/ teacher ratio
Primary (age 6–12) / Secondary (age 13–16)	700	20,076	510,300	25.4
Vocational (age 16–18)	32	985	15,000	15.2
Higher	178	5,400	92,300	17.1

Health (2001): physicians 6,639 (1 per 365 persons); hospital beds 18,100 (1 per 135 persons); infant mortality rate per 1,000 live births (2001) 29.5.
Food (2001): daily per capita caloric intake 1,974 (vegetable products 60%, animal products 40%); 81% of FAO recommended minimum.

Military

Total active duty personnel (2002): 9,100 (army 82.4%, air force 17.6%). *Military expenditure as percentage of GNP* (1999): 2.1% (world 2.4%); per capita expenditure U.S.$5.

[1]Rounded figures. [2]January 1. [3]Detail does not add to total given because of rounding. [4]Imputed bank service charges. [5]Unemployed.

Internet resources for further information:
- **National Statistical Office of Mongolia http://www.nso.mn/eng/index.htm**

Morocco

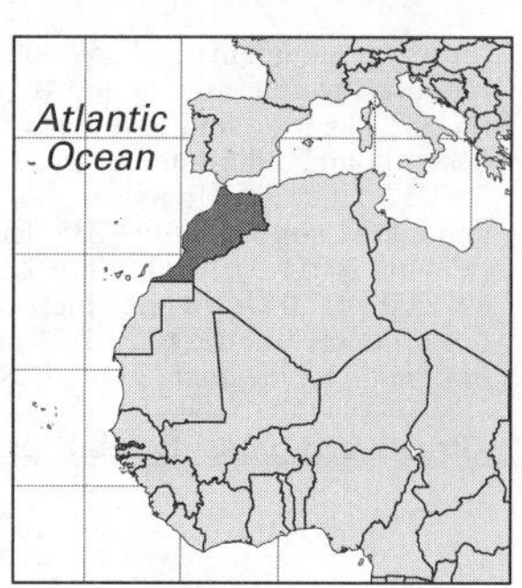

Official name: Al-Mamlakah al-Maghribīyah (Kingdom of Morocco).
Form of government: constitutional monarchy with two legislative houses (House of Councillors [270[1]]; House of Representatives [325]).
Chief of state and head of government: King assisted by Prime Minister.
Capital: Rabat.
Official language: Arabic.
Official religion: Islam.
Monetary unit: 1 Moroccan dirham (DH) = 100 Moroccan francs; valuation (Sept. 8, 2003) 1 U.S.$ = DH 9.77; 1 £ = DH 15.49.

Population (2002 estimate)[2]

Provinces	Administrative centres	Population
Chaouia-Ouardigha	Settat	1,663,000
Doukkala-Abda	Safi	1,984,000
Fès-Boulemane	Fès	1,586,000
Gharb-Chrarda-Béni Hsen	Kénitra	1,868,000
Grand Casablanca	Casablanca	3,546,000
Guelmim-Es Semara	Guelmim	436,000
Laâyoune-Bojador-Sakia El-Hamra	Laâyoune	217,000
Marrakech-Tensift-El Haouz	Marrakech	3,027,000
Meknès-Tafilalt	Meknès	2,119,000
Oriental	Oujda	1,914,000
Oued Eddahab-Lagouira[3]	Dakhla	52,000
Rabat-Salé-Zemmour-Zaër	Rabat	2,389,000
Sous-Massa-Draâ	Agadir	3,081,000
Tadla-Azilal	Béni Mellal	1,474,000
Tangier-Tetouan	Tangier	2,430,000
Taza-Al Hoceïma-Taounate	Al-Hoceïma	1,845,000
TOTAL		29,631,000

Demography

Area[2]: 274,461 sq mi, 710,850 sq km.
Population (2003)[2]: 30,097,000.
Density (2003)[2]: persons per sq mi 109.7, persons per sq km 42.4.
Urban-rural (1999): urban 52.7%; rural 47.3%.
Sex distribution (1999): male 49.89%; female 50.11%.
Age breakdown (1999): under 15, 35.7%; 15–29, 28.9%; 30–44, 18.9%; 45–59, 9.2%; 60–74, 5.3%; 75 and over, 2.0%.
Population projection[2]: (2010) 33,562,000; (2020) 38,281,000.
Doubling time: 40 years.
Ethnolinguistic composition (1995): Arab 65%; Berber 33%; other 2%.
Religious affiliation (2000): Muslim (mostly Sunnī) 98.3%; Christian 0.6%; other 1.1%.
Major urban areas (2000): Casablanca 3,357,000; Rabat-Salé 1,616,000; Fès 907,000; Marrakech 822,000; Agadir (1994) 524,564; Tangier (1994) 497,147.

Vital statistics

Birth rate per 1,000 population (2002): 23.6 (world avg. 21.3).
Death rate per 1,000 population (2002): 5.9 (world avg. 9.1).
Natural increase rate per 1,000 population (2002): 17.7 (world avg. 12.2).
Total fertility rate (avg. birth per childbearing woman; 2002): 3.0.
Life expectancy at birth (2002): male 67.5 years; female 72.1 years.
Major causes of death (1989)[4]: childhood diseases 22.9%; circulatory diseases 15.4%; accidents 7.3%; infectious and parasitic diseases 6.3%; malignant neoplasms (cancers) 5.6%.

National economy

Budget. Revenue (2002): DH 98,261,000,000 (value-added tax 24.4%; taxes on income and profits 16.6%; excise taxes 16.4%; international trade 14.5%; stamp tax 5.1%). Expenditures (2002): DH 118,999,000,000 (current expenditure 76.2%, of which wages 40.8%, debt payment 14.8%; capital expenditure 17.8%; transfers 6.0%).
Public debt (external, outstanding; 2001): U.S.$14,325,000,000.
Production (metric tons except as noted). Agriculture, forestry, fishing (2002): wheat 3,356,000, sugar beets 2,985,900, barley 1,669,000, potatoes 1,334,000, tomatoes 991,000, oranges 723,100, olives 420,000; livestock (number of live animals) 16,335,000 sheep, 5,090,000 goats, 2,669,000 cattle, 1,000,000 asses; roundwood (2001) 971,000 cu m; fish catch (2001) 1,083,000, of which sardines 763,000, octopuses 113,000. Mining and quarrying (2001): phosphate rock 21,983,000[5]; barite 471,000; zinc (metal content) 89,300; lead (metal content) 76,700; silver 280,000 kg[6]. Manufacturing (value added in DH '000,000; 2001): food 55,815; textiles 26,017; electronic products 7,010. Energy production (consumption): electricity (kW-hr; 2001) 13,339,000,000 ([1999] 15,004,000,000); coal (metric tons; 2001) 135,000 ([1999] 3,568,000); crude petroleum (barrels; 1999) 84,000 (53,600,000); petroleum products (metric tons; 1999) 6,080,000 (6,941,000); natural gas (cu m; 2001) 44,000,000 ([1999] 44,000,000).
Population economically active (2001): total 10,230,000; activity rate 35.4% (participation rates: ages 15–64, n.a.; female, n.a.; unemployed 12.5%).

Price and earnings indexes (1995 = 100)

	1996	1997	1998	1999	2000	2001	2002
Consumer price index	103.0	103.9	106.9	107.6	109.7	110.4	113.5
Earnings index	...	...	...	...	...	...	...

Gross national product (2001): U.S.$34,700,000,000 (U.S.$1,190 per capita).

Structure of gross domestic product and labour force

	2001			
	in value DH '000,000	% of total value	labour force	% of labour force
Agriculture	60,546	15.8	3,900,000	38.1
Mining	7,446	1.9	1,169,000	11.4
Manufacturing	64,851	16.9		
Construction	19,352	5.1	598,000	5.9
Public utilities	26,589	7.0		
Transp. and commun.	26,367	6.9	317,000	3.1
Trade	44,533	11.6	1,155,000	11.3
Finance, real estate	...	...	835,000	8.2
Pub. admin., defense	58,138	15.2	976,000	9.5
Services	46,713	12.2		
Other	28,362	7.4	1,280,000[7]	12.5[7]
TOTAL	382,897	100.0	10,230,000	100.0

Tourism (2001): receipts U.S.$2,526,000; expenditures U.S.$360,000,000.
Household income and expenditure. Average household size (1998) 5.7; expenditure (1994)[8]: food 45.2%, housing 12.5%, transportation 7.6%.

Foreign trade[9]

Balance of trade (current prices)

	1997	1998	1999	2000	2001	2002
DH '000,000	–30,467	–30,068	–32,314	–43,700	–43,641	–43,693
% of total	25.5%	18.0%	18.0%	21.7%	21.3%	20.3%

Imports (2002): DH 129,346,000,000 (machinery and apparatus 19.3%; mineral fuels 15.6%, of which crude petroleum 10.0%; food, beverages, and tobacco 11.8%, of which wheat 4.5%; cotton fabric and fibres 6.4%). *Major import sources* (2001): France 24.1%; Spain 10.3%; U.K. 6.2%; Italy 5.0%; Germany 5.0%.
Exports (2002)[10]: DH 85,653,000,000 (garments 21.4%; food, beverages, and tobacco 20.5%, of which crustaceans and mollusks 6.6%; knitwear 10.4%; phosphoric acid 6.8%; machinery and apparatus 6.6%; phosphates 5.2%). *Major export destinations* (2001): France 32.8%; Spain 15.3%; U.K. 8.6%; Italy 5.7%; Germany 4.2%.

Transport and communications

Transport. Railroads (2002): route length 1,907 km; passenger-km 2,145,000,000; metric ton-km cargo 4,974,000,000. Roads (2001): total length 57,226 km (paved 56%). Vehicles (1998): passenger cars 1,111,846; trucks and buses 392,602. Air transport (2001)[11]: passenger-km 7,362,000,000; metric ton-km cargo 76,005,000; airports (2002) 15.

Communications

Medium	date	unit	number	units per 1,000 persons
Daily newspapers	2000	circulation	740,000	26
Radio	2000	receivers	6,920,000	243
Television	2000	receivers	4,720,000	166
Telephones	2002	main lines	1,127,400	38
Cellular telephones	2002	subscribers	6,198,000	209
Personal computers	2002	units	500,000	17
Internet	2002	users	400,000	13

Education and health

Educational attainment (1982). Percentage of population age 25 and over having: no formal education 47.8%; some primary education 47.8%; some secondary 3.8%; higher 0.6%. *Literacy* (2000): total population over age 15 literate 48.9%; males literate 61.1%; females literate 35.1%.

Education (1999–2000)

	schools	teachers	students	student/ teacher ratio
Primary (age 7–12)	6,565	127,582	3,669,605	28.7
Secondary (age 13–17)	1,664	88,301	1,438,988	16.3
Vocational[12]	69	...	22,791	...
Higher	68	9,667	266,507	27.6

Health (2002): physicians 13,955 (1 per 2,123 persons); hospital beds (1994) 26,407 (1 per 978 persons); infant mortality rate (2002) 46.9.
Food (2001): daily per capita caloric intake 3,046 (vegetable products 93%, animal products 7%); 126% of FAO recommended minimum requirement.

Military

Total active duty personnel (2002): 196,300 (army 89.1%, navy 4.0%, air force 6.9%). *Military expenditure as percentage of GNP* (1999): 4.3% (world 2.4%); per capita expenditure U.S.$49.

[1]All seats indirectly elected: 162 by regional councils; 108 by industry, agriculture, and trade unions. [2]Includes Western Sahara, annexure of Morocco whose unresolved political status (from 1991) is to be eventually decided by an internationally sponsored referendum; Western Sahara area: 97,344 sq mi, 252,120 sq km; Western Sahara population (2002 est.) 256,000. [3]Includes Aousserd province created in late 1990s. [4]Registered deaths of urban population only. [5]Includes Western Sahara production of 1,500,000. [6]Includes smelter bullion. [7]Includes 1,275,000 unemployed. [8]Weights of consumer price index components. [9]Imports c.i.f.; exports f.o.b. [10]Cannabis is an important illegal export. [11]Royal Air Maroc only. [12]Excludes teacher training.

Internet resources for further information:
- **Moroccan Central Statistical Office http://www.statistic.gov.ma**
- **Bank al-Maghrib http://www.bkam.ma**

Mozambique

Official name: República de Moçambique (Republic of Mozambique).
Form of government: multiparty republic with a single legislative house (Assembly of the Republic [250]).
Head of state and government: President.
Capital: Maputo.
Official language: Portuguese.
Official religion: none.
Monetary unit: 1 metical (Mt; plural meticais) = 100 centavos; valuation (Sept. 8, 2003) 1 U.S.$ = Mt 23,326; 1 £ = Mt 36,984.

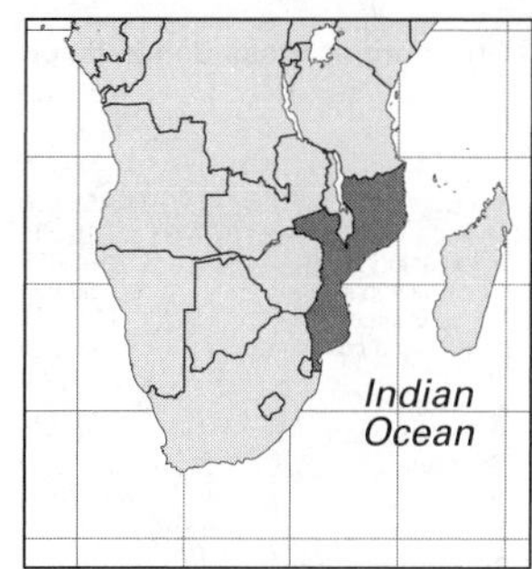

Area and population

Provinces	Capitals	area sq mi	area sq km	population 2002 estimate
Cabo Delgado	Pemba	31,902	82,625	1,525,634
Gaza	Xai-Xai	29,231	75,709	1,266,431
Inhambane	Inhambane	26,492	68,615	1,326,848
Manica	Chimoio	23,807	61,661	1,207,332
Maputo	Maputo	9,944	25,756	1,003,992
Nampula	Nampula	31,508	81,606	3,410,141
Niassa	Lichinga	49,828	129,055	916,672
Sofala	Beira	26,262	68,018	1,516,166
Tete	Tete	38,890	100,724	1,388,205
Zambézia	Quelimane	40,544	105,008	3,476,484
City				
Maputo	—	232	602	1,044,618
TOTAL LAND AREA		308,642[1]	799,379	
INLAND WATER		5,019	13,000	
TOTAL		313,661	812,379	18,082,523

Demography

Population (2003): 18,568,000.
Density (2003): persons per sq mi 59.2, persons per sq km 22.9.
Urban-rural (2001): urban 33.3%; rural 66.7%.
Sex distribution (2002): male 48.12%; female 51.88%.
Age breakdown (2001): under 15, 42.7%; 15–29, 29.2%; 30–44, 15.2%; 45–59, 8.4%; 60–74, 3.8%; 75 and over, 0.7%.
Population projection: (2010) 19,721,000; (2020) 20,547,000.
Doubling time: 44 years.
Ethnic composition (2000): Makuana 15.3%; Makua 14.5%; Tsonga 8.6%; Sena 8.0%; Lomwe 7.1%; Tswa 5.7%; Chwabo 5.5%; other 35.3%.
Linguistic composition (1997): Makua 26.3%; Tsonga 11.4%; Lomwe 7.6%; Sena 7.0%; Portuguese 6.5%; Chuaba 6.3%; other Bantu languages 33.0%; other 1.9%.
Religious affiliation (2000): traditional beliefs 50.4%; Christian 38.4%, of which Roman Catholic 15.8%, Protestant 8.9%; Muslim 10.5%.
Major cities (1997): Maputo 989,386; Matola 440,927; Beira 412,588; Nampula 314,965; Chimoio 177,608.

Vital statistics

Birth rate per 1,000 population (2002): 37.8 (world avg. 21.3).
Death rate per 1,000 population (2002): 22.2 (world avg. 9.1).
Natural increase rate per 1,000 population (2002): 15.6 (world avg. 12.2).
Total fertility rate (avg. births per childbearing woman; 2002): 5.0.
Life expectancy at birth (2002): male 40.0 years; female 38.4 years.

National economy

Budget (2001). Revenue: Mt 19,253,000,000 (grants 50.1%; tax revenue 44.6%, of which sales tax 27.9%, customs taxes 7.7%, individual income tax 7.7%; nontax revenue 5.3%). Expenditures: Mt 23,221,000,000 (current expenditures 45.2%, of which administrative salaries 21.1%, goods and services 10.3%, transfers 9.6%; capital expenditures 44.9%; net lending 9.9%).
Public debt (external, outstanding; 2000): U.S.$4,599,000,000.
Production (metric tons except as noted). Agriculture, forestry, fishing (2001): cassava 5,361,974, corn (maize) 1,143,263, sugarcane 397,276, sorghum 313,787, coconuts 300,000, rice 166,945, peanuts (groundnuts) 109,175, bananas 59,000, cashews 57,894; livestock (number of live animals) 1,320,000 cattle, 392,000 goats, 180,000 pigs, 125,000 sheep, 28,000,000 chickens; roundwood (2001) 18,043,000 cu m; fish catch (2000) 39,065. Mining and quarrying (2000): gold 23 kg[2]; semiprecious gemstones 3,400 carats. Manufacturing (gross production value in Mt '000,000; 1998): beverages and tobacco 1,753,706; food 1,238,569; chemicals 497,406; nonmetallic mineral products 485,289; machinery and transport equipment 226,169; textiles 209,169; iron and steel 76,042. Energy production (consumption): electricity (kW-hr; 1999) 7,355,000,000 (2,028,000,000); coal (metric tons; 2001) 17,700 ([1999] 37,000); crude petroleum, none (none); petroleum products (metric tons; 1999) none (359,000); natural gas (cu m; 2001) 60,000,000 (n.a.).
Household income and expenditure. Average family size (1997) 4.1; income per household: n.a.; source of income (1992–93)[3]: wages and salaries 51.6%, self-employment 12.5%, barter 11.5%, private farming 7.7%; expenditure (1992–93)[3]: food, beverages, and tobacco 74.6%, housing and energy 11.7%, transportation and communications 4.7%, clothing and footwear 3.7%, education and recreation 1.4%, health 0.8%.
Population economically active (1999): total 9,985,000; activity rate 59.3% (participation rates: over age 15, n.a.; female, n.a.; unemployed, n.a.).

Price and earnings indexes (1995 = 100)

	1996	1997	1998	1999	2000	2001	2002
Consumer price index	148.5	159.4	161.8	166.4	187.6	204.6	238.9
Monthly earnings index	...	...	...	...	...	...	...

Gross national product (2001): U.S.$3,800,000,000 (U.S.$210 per capita).

Structure of gross domestic product and labour force

	2001 in value Mt '000,000	2001 % of total value	1991 labour force	1991 % of labour force
Agriculture	15,510,000	20.8	6,870,000	81.4
Mining, Manufacturing	8,206,000	11.0	766,000	9.1
Construction	8,761,000	11.7		
Public utilities	1,573,000	2.1		
Transp. and commun.	11,982,000	16.0		
Finance	4,437,000	5.9	798,000	9.5
Trade	13,643,000	18.3		
Pub. admin., defense	5,320,000	7.1		
Services	5,243,000	7.0		
Other	...	...	...	...
TOTAL	74,675,000	100.0[1]	8,434,000	100.0

Land use (1994): forested 22.1%; meadows and pastures 56.1%; agricultural and under permanent cultivation 4.0%; other 17.8%.

Foreign trade[4]

Balance of trade (current prices)

	1997	1998	1999	2000	2001	2002
U.S.$'000,000	–454	–491	–806	–682	–725	–1,276
% of total	49.7%	50.1%	58.7%	48.4%	17.5%	27.8%

Imports (2000): U.S.$1,162,300,000 (1999; road vehicles 24.6%; machinery and apparatus 17.4%; food and live animals 16.7%, of which cereals 11.1%; refined petroleum 9.8%). *Major import sources:* South Africa 49.8%; European Union 28.6%, of which Portugal 7.6%; Japan 4.6%; U.S. 3.5%.
Exports (2000): U.S.$364,000,000 (prawns 25.1%; electricity 18.4%; aluminum 16.5%; cotton 7.0%; cashews 5.6%). *Major export destinations:* Zimbabwe 17.7%; South Africa 14.6%; Portugal 11.6%; Spain 10.7%; U.S. 4.7%.

Transport and communications

Transport. Railroads (1999): route length 1,940 mi, 3,123 km; (2001) passenger-mi 88,234,540, passenger-km 142,000,000; (2001) short ton-mi cargo 530,489,128, metric ton-km cargo 774,500,000. Roads (1996): total length 18,890 mi, 30,400 km (paved 19%). Vehicles (1995): passenger cars 84,000; trucks and buses 26,800. Air transport: (2001) passenger-mi 169,261,188, passenger-km 272,400,000; (1999) short ton-mi cargo 3,790,000, metric ton-km cargo 6,100,000; airports (1997) with scheduled flights 7.

Communications

Medium	date	unit	number	units per 1,000 persons
Daily newspapers	2000	circulation	53,000	3.0
Radio	2000	receivers	778,000	44
Television	2000	receivers	88,400	5.0
Telephones	2001	main lines	89,400	4.4
Cellular telephones	2001	subscribers	169,900	8.4
Personal computers	2001	units	70,000	3.5
Internet	2001	users	15,000	0.7

Education and health

Literacy (2000): percentage of total population age 15 and over literate 43.8%; males literate 59.9%; females literate 28.4%.

Education (1997)

	schools	teachers	students	student/ teacher ratio
Primary (age 7–12)	6,025	32,670	1,899,531	58.1
Secondary (age 13–18)	75	1,555	51,554	33.2
Voc., teacher tr.	25	565	12,001	21.2
Higher	3	954	7,156	7.5

Health: physicians (1996) 120[5] (1 per 124,697 persons); hospital beds (1997) 12,630 (1 per 1,210 persons); infant mortality rate per 1,000 live births (2002) 138.5.
Food (2001): daily per capita caloric intake 1,980 (vegetable products 98%, animal products 2%); 85% of FAO recommended minimum requirement.

Military

Total active duty personnel (2002): *c.* 11,100 (army 86%, navy 5%, air force 9%). *Military expenditure as percentage of GNP* (1999): 2.5% (world 2.4%); per capita expenditure U.S.$5.

[1]Detail does not add to total given because of rounding. [2]Official figures; unofficial artisanal production is 4,000–5,000 kg. [3]City of Maputo only. [4]Imports are f.o.b. in balance of trade and c.i.f. for commodities and trading partners. [5]Government personnel only.

Internet resources for further information:
- **Instituto Nacional de Estatística http://www.ine.gov.mz**
- **Banco de Moçambique http://www.bancomoc.mz**

Myanmar (Burma)

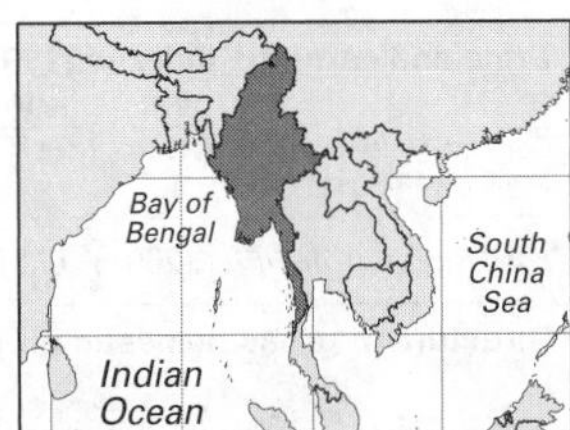

Official name: Pyidaungzu Myanma Naingngandaw (Union of Myanmar).
Form of government: military regime.
Head of state and government: Chairman of the State Peace and Development Council, assisted by Prime Minister.
Capital: Yangôn (Rangoon).
Official language: Burmese.
Official religion: none.
Monetary unit: 1 Myanmar kyat (K) = 100 pyas; valuation[1] (Sept. 8, 2003) 1 U.S.$ = K 6.20; 1 £ = K 9.83.

Area and population

Divisions	Capitals	area sq mi	area sq km	population 1994 estimate
Irrawaddy (Ayeyarwady)	Bassein (Pathein)	13,567	35,138	6,107,000
Magwe (Magway)	Magwe (Magway)	17,305	44,820	4,067,000
Mandalay	Mandalay	14,295	37,024	5,823,000
Pegu (Bago)	Pegu (Bago)	15,214	39,404	4,607,000
Sagaing	Sagaing	36,535	94,625	4,889,000
Tenasserim (Tanintharyi)	Tavoy (Dawei)	16,735	43,343	1,187,000
Yangôn	Yangôn (Rangoon)	3,927	10,171	5,037,000
States				
Chin	Hakha	13,907	36,019	438,000
Kachin	Myitkyinā	34,379	89,041	1,135,000
Karen	Pa-an (Hpa-an)	11,731	30,383	1,323,000
Kayah	Loi-kaw	4,530	11,733	228,000
Mon	Moulmein (Mawlamyine)	4,748	12,297	2,183,000
Rakhine (Arakan)	Sittwe (Akyab)	14,200	36,778	2,482,000
Shan	Taunggyi	60,155	155,801	4,416,000
TOTAL		261,228	676,577	43,922,000

Demography

Population (2003): 42,511,000.
Density (2003): persons per sq mi 162.7, persons per sq km 62.8.
Urban-rural (2002): urban 29.0%; rural 71.0%.
Sex distribution (2002): male 49.81%; female 50.19%.
Age breakdown (2002): under 15, 28.5%; 15–29, 30.8%; 30–44, 22.0%; 45–59, 11.4%; 60 and over, 5.7%.
Population projection: (2010) 43,721,000; (2020) 44,825,000.
Doubling time: 58 years.
Ethnic composition (2000): Burman 55.9%; Karen 9.5%; Shan 6.5%; Han Chinese 2.5%; Mon 2.3%; Yangbye 2.2%; Kachin 1.5%; other 19.6%.
Religious affiliation (2000): Buddhist 72.7%; Christian 8.3%; Muslim 2.4%; Hindu 2.0%; traditional beliefs 12.6%; other 2.0%.
Major cities (1993 est.): Yangôn (Rangoon) 3,361,700; Mandalay 885,300; Moulmein (Mawlamyine) 307,600; Pegu (Bago) 190,900; Bassein (Pathein) 183,900.

Vital statistics

Birth rate per 1,000 population (2002): 23.5 (world avg. 21.3).
Death rate per 1,000 population (2002): 11.6 (world avg. 9.1).
Natural increase rate per 1,000 population (2002): 11.9 (world avg. 12.2).
Total fertility rate (avg. births per childbearing woman; 2002): 2.9.
Life expectancy at birth (2002): male 54.0 years; female 59.0 years.
Major causes of death per 100,000 population (1994): infectious and parasitic diseases 27.7; circulatory diseases 17.4; respiratory diseases 15.1; malignant neoplasms (cancers) 7.6; malnutrition 3.2.

National economy

Budget (2000–01). Revenue: K 134,550,000,000 (revenue from taxes 56.4%, of which taxes on goods and services 32.8%, taxes on income 19.4%; nontax revenue 43.4%; foreign grants 0.2%). Expenditures: K 221,255,000,000 (defense 28.7%; agriculture and forestry 17.4%; education 14.2%; public works and housing 9.2%).
Public debt (external, outstanding; 2001): U.S.$5,007,000,000.
Tourism (2001): receipts from visitors U.S.$45,000,000; expenditures by nationals abroad U.S.$27,000,000.
Production (metric tons except as noted). Agriculture, forestry, fishing (2002): rice 21,900,000, sugarcane 6,333,000, dry beans 1,467,330, peanuts (groundnuts) 700,000, corn (maize) 660,000, plantains 400,000, sesame seeds 225,000, seed cotton 152,694, natural rubber 35,662, opium poppy (2000) 1,085; livestock (number of live animals) 11,551,000 cattle, 4,498,680 pigs, 2,252,020 buffalo; roundwood (2001) 39,365,000 cu m; fish catch (2001) 1,288,134. Mining and quarrying (2001): copper (metal content) 26,300; jade 1,700,000 kg; rubies, sapphires, and spinel 8,630,000 carats. Manufacturing (2001): cement 384,000; refined sugar 101,000; fertilizers 60,100; paper 20,600; cotton yarn 5,500; plywood 28,000 cu m; cigarettes 1,991,000,000 units[2]; clay bricks 68,000,000 units[2]. Energy production (consumption): electricity (kW-hr; 1999) 4,558,000,000 (4,558,000,000); hard coal (metric tons; 1999) 42,000 (38,000); lignite (metric tons; 1999) 106,000 (106,000); crude petroleum (barrels; 2001) 3,300,000 ([1999] 7,600,000); petroleum products (metric tons; 1999) 847,000 (1,755,000); natural gas (cu m; 2001) 6,800,300,000 ([1999] 1,551,700,000).
Household income and expenditure. Average household size (2000) 4.8; average annual income per household: n.a.; sources of income: n.a.; expenditure (1994)[3]: food and beverages 67.1%, fuel and lighting 6.6%, transportation 4.0%, charitable contributions 3.1%, medical care 3.1%.
Gross national product (1996): U.S.$119,334,000,000 (U.S.$2,610 per capita).

Structure of gross domestic product and labour force

	2000–01 in value K '000,000	2000–01 % of total value	1997–98 labour force[4]	1997–98 % of labour force[4]
Agriculture	1,458,270	57.1	12,093,000	65.9
Mining	15,234	0.5	121,000	0.7
Manufacturing	195,876	7.7	1,666,000	9.1
Construction	50,263	2.0	400,000	2.2
Public utilities	3,445	0.1	26,000	0.1
Transp. and commun.	149,669	5.9	495,000	2.7
Trade	601,690	23.6	1,781,000	9.7
Finance	2,587	0.1	1,485,000	8.1
Public administration	40,260	1.6		
Services	35,429	1.4	270,000	1.5
TOTAL	2,552,723	100.0	18,337,000	100.0

Population economically active (1999): total 23,700,000; activity rate of total population 57.1% (participation rates: ages 15–64, n.a.; female, n.a.; unemployed 4.1%).

Price index (1995 = 100)

	1996	1997	1998	1999	2000	2001	2002
Consumer price index	116.3	150.8	228.5	270.5	270.2	327.2	514.0

Land use (1994): forested 49.3%; meadows and pastures 0.5%; agricultural and under permanent cultivation 15.3%; other 34.9%.

Foreign trade[5]

Balance of trade (current prices)[6]

	1996–97	1997–98	1998–99	1999–2000	2000–01	2001–02
K '000,000	–6,291	–7,919	–10,116	–7,318	–2,638	–1,346
% of total	36.4%	38.0%	42.8%	29.0%	9.7%	3.5%

Imports (2000–01[6]): K 14,900,000,000 (machinery and transport equipment 25.2%, chemicals and chemical products 12.9%, mineral fuels 7.7%, food and live animals 3.9%). *Major import sources* (2001): China 21.8%; Singapore 16.6%; Thailand 13.9%; South Korea 9.1%; Malaysia 8.0%; Japan 7.1%.
Exports (2000–01[6]): K 12,262,000,000 (domestic exports 68.6%, of which food 26.1% [including pulses 13.5%], mineral fuels [significantly natural gas] 9.6%, teak and other hardwood 6.5%; reexports [significantly garments] 31.4%). *Major export destinations* (2001): Thailand 26.0%; United States 16.2%; India 10.2%; China 5.0%; Singapore 3.6%.

Transport and communications

Transport. Railroads (2000): route length 3,955 km; passenger-km 4,451,000,000; metric ton-km cargo 1,222,000,000. Roads (1996): total length 28,200 km (paved 12%). Vehicles (1999): passenger cars 171,300; trucks and buses 83,400. Air transport (1999): passenger-km 355,000,000; metric ton-km cargo 40,000,000; airports (1996) 19.

Communications

Medium	date	unit	number	units per 1,000 persons
Daily newspapers	2000	circulation	376,000	9.0
Radio	2000	receivers	2,760,000	66
Television	2000	receivers	292,000	7.0
Telephones	2001	main lines	281,200	5.8
Cellular telephones	2001	subscribers	13,800	0.3
Personal computers	2001	units	55,000	1.1
Internet	2001	users	10,000	0.2

Education and health

Educational attainment: n.a. *Literacy* (2000): total population age 15 and over literate 84.7%; males literate 89.0%; females literate 80.5%.

Education (1997–98)

	schools	teachers	students	student/ teacher ratio
Primary (age 5–9)	35,877	167,134	5,145,400	30.8
Secondary (age 10–15)	2,091	56,955	1,545,600	27.1
Voc., teacher tr.[7]	103	2,462	25,374	10.3
Higher	923	17,089	385,300	22.5

Health (1999): physicians 14,622 (1 per 2,838 persons); hospital beds (1997) 28,943 (1 per 1,433 persons); infant mortality rate per 1,000 live births (2002) 88.0.
Food (2001): daily per capita caloric intake 2,822 (vegetable products 96%, animal products 4%); 132% of FAO recommended minimum requirement.

Military

Total active duty personnel (2002): 444,000 (army 95.7%, navy 2.3%, air force 2.0%). *Military expenditure as percentage of GNP* (1999): 7.8% (world 2.4%); per capita expenditure U.S.$112.

[1]Pegged rate to the Special Drawing Right of the International Monetary Fund; the illegal black market rate in April 2003 was about 1 U.S.$ = K 1,000. [2]1999. [3]Yangôn only. [4]Employed only. [5]Imports c.i.f.; exports f.o.b. [6]Fiscal year beginning April 1. [7]1994–95.

Internet resources for further information:

- **Key Indicators of Developing Asian and Pacific Countries http://www.adb.org/Documents/Books/Key_Indicators/default.asp**

Namibia

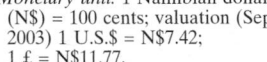

Official name: Republic of Namibia.
Form of government: republic with two legislative houses (National Council [26]; National Assembly [72[1]]).
Head of state and government: President.
Capital: Windhoek.
Official language: English.
Official religion: none.
Monetary unit: 1 Namibian dollar (N$) = 100 cents; valuation (Sept. 8, 2003) 1 U.S.$ = N$7.42; 1 £ = N$11.77.

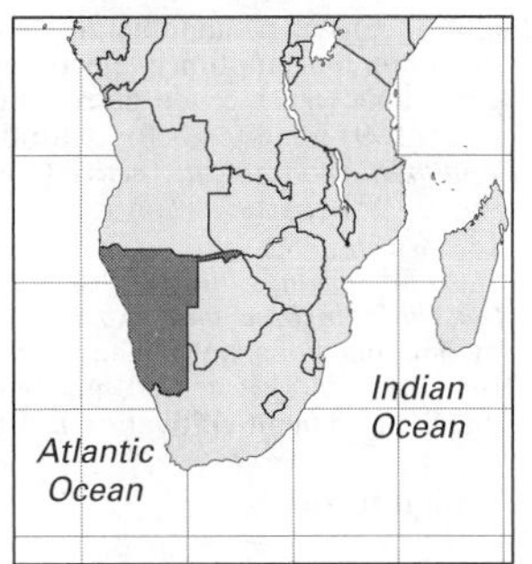

Area and population

Regions	Largest towns	area sq mi	area sq km	population 2001 census
Erongo	Walvis Bay	24,602	63,719	107,629
Hardap	Rehoboth	42,428	109,888	67,998
Karas	Keetmanshoop	62,288	161,324	69,677
Khomas	Windhoek	14,210	36,804	250,305
Kunene	Khorixas	55,697	144,254	68,224
Liambezi (Caprivi)	Katima Mulilo	7,541	19,532	79,852
Ohangwena	Oshikango	4,086	10,582	227,728
Okavango	Rundu	16,763	43,417	201,093
Omaheke	Gobabis	32,715	84,731	67,496
Omusati	Ongandjera	5,265	13,637	228,364
Oshana	Oshakati	2,042	5,290	161,977
Oshikoto	Tsumeb	10,273	26,607	160,788
Otjozondjupa	Otjiwarongo	40,667	105,327	135,723
TOTAL		318,580[2]	825,118[2]	1,826,854

Demography

Population (2003): 1,927,000.
Density (2003): persons per sq mi 6.0, persons per sq km 2.3.
Urban-rural (2001): urban 31.4%; rural 68.6%.
Sex distribution (2001): male 48.73%; female 51.27%.
Age breakdown (1999): under 15, 43.2%; 15–29, 28.6%; 30–44, 15.1%; 45–59, 7.7%; 60–74, 4.0%; 75 and over, 1.4%.
Population projection: (2010) 2,036,000; (2020) 2,081,000.
Doubling time: 41 years.
Ethnic composition (2000): Ovambo 34.4%; mixed race (black/white) 14.5%; Kavango 9.1%; Afrikaner 8.1%; San (Bushmen) and Bergdama 7.0%; Herero 5.5%; Nama 4.4%; Kwambi 3.7%; German 2.8%; other 10.5%.
Religious affiliation (2000): Protestant (mostly Lutheran) 47.5%; Roman Catholic 17.7%; African Christian 10.8%; traditional beliefs 6.0%; other 18.0%.
Major cities (2001): Windhoek 216,000[3]; Walvis Bay 40,849; Swakopmund 25,442[4]; Rehoboth 21,782; Rundu 19,597.

Vital statistics

Birth rate per 1,000 population (2002): 34.7 (world avg. 21.3).
Death rate per 1,000 population (2002): 17.6 (world avg. 9.1).
Natural increase rate per 1,000 population (2002): 17.1 (world avg. 12.2).
Total fertility rate (avg. births per childbearing woman; 2002): 4.8.
Life expectancy at birth (2002): male 46.1 years; female 43.8 years.
Major causes of death per 100,000 population (1999)[5]: infectious and parasitic diseases *c.* 58%, of which AIDS-related *c.* 22%, tuberculosis *c.* 10%, malaria *c.* 5%; diseases of the circulatory system *c.* 8%; malignant neoplasms (cancers) *c.* 4%.

National economy

Budget (2002–03). Revenue: N$10,256,000,000 (taxes on income and profits 38.5%; taxes on international trade 25.3%; taxes on goods and services 23.6%; nontax revenue 9.7%). Expenditures: N$12,257,000,000 (current expenditure 84.3%; development expenditure 15.7%).
Public debt (external, outstanding 1998): U.S.$747,700,000.
Production (metric tons except as noted). Agriculture, forestry, fishing (2002): roots and tubers 270,000, millet 65,000, corn (maize) 27,700, fruits 11,000, vegetables 11,000, pulses 8,500, sorghum 8,100, wheat 6,100; livestock (number of live animals) 2,509,000 cattle, 2,370,000 sheep, 1,769,000 goats; fish catch (2000) 283,015. Mining and quarrying (2001): gem diamonds (2002) 1,550,000 carats; fluorite 81,200; zinc (metal content) 31,803; marble 20,000; copper (metal content) 12,392; uranium oxide 2,640; silver 407,639 troy oz; gold 91,662 troy oz. Manufacturing: n.a.; products include cut gems (primarily diamonds), fur products (from Karakul sheep), processed foods (fish, meats, and dairy products), textiles, carved wood products, refined metals (copper and lead). Energy production (consumption): electricity (kW-hr; 2001) 27,000,000 (603,000,000); coal (metric tons; 2000) none (3,000); petroleum products (metric tons; 2001) none (n.a.).
Population economically active: total (1991) 493,580; activity rate of total population, 34.9% (participation rates: ages 15–64, 61.3%; female 43.5%; unemployed 20.1%).

Price and earnings indexes (1995 = 100)

	1997	1998	1999	2000	2001	2002
Consumer price index	117.5	124.8	135.5	147.7	161.8	180.2
Earnings index	...	...	...	...	...	...

Gross national product (2001): U.S.$3,500,000,000 (U.S.$1,960 per capita).

Structure of gross domestic product and labour force

	2001 in value N$'000,000	2001 % of total value	1991 labour force[6]	1991 % of labour force[6]
Agriculture	2,431	8.9	189,929	38.5
Mining	3,489	12.8	14,686	3.0
Manufacturing	2,638	9.7	22,884	4.6
Construction	773	2.8	18,638	3.8
Public utilities	652	2.4	2,974	0.6
Transp. and commun.	1,435	5.3	9,322	1.9
Trade, hotels	3,481	12.8	37,820	7.7
Finance, real estate			8,547	1.7
Services				
Public administration and defense	12,332	45.3	89,541	18.1
Other			99,239[7]	20.1[7]
TOTAL	27,231	100.0	493,580	100.0

Household income and expenditure. Average household size (2001) 5.1; average annual income per household, n.a.; sources of income (1992): wages and salaries 69.0%, income from property 25.6%, transfer payments 5.4%; expenditure: n.a.
Tourism (2001): receipts U.S.$404,000,000; expenditures (1998) U.S.$88,000,000.
Land use (1994): forested 15.2%; meadows and pastures 46.2%; agricultural and under permanent cultivation 0.8%; other 37.8%.

Foreign trade[8]

Balance of trade (current prices)

	1996	1997	1998	1999	2000	2001
N$'000,000	−396	−1,232	−1,562	−1,453	−1,099	−1,572
% of total	3.9%	9.1%	10.3%	8.8%	6.5%	8.1%

Imports (1997): N$7,718,000,000 (food, beverages, and tobacco 24.1%; machinery and apparatus 15.0%; transport equipment 14.7%; base and fabricated metals 7.5%). *Major import sources* (2000): South Africa 86.4%; Germany 2.0%; U.K. 2.0%; U.S. 1.3%.
Exports (2001): N$8,901,000,000 (diamonds 45.4%; metals 18.6%, of which gold 2.3%, zinc 1.5%, other [mostly uranium and copper] 14.8%; fish 10.4%; meat [mostly beef] 7.0%). *Major export destinations* (1998): U.K. *c.* 43%; South Africa *c.* 26%; Spain *c.* 14%; France *c.* 8%.

Transport and communications

Transport. Railroads: route length (1999) 1,480 mi, 2,382 km; (1995–96) passenger-km 48,300,000; (1995–96) metric ton-km 1,082,000,000. Roads (2000): total length 41,301 mi, 66,467 km (paved 7%). Vehicles (1996): passenger cars 74,875; trucks and buses 66,500[9]. Air transport (2001)[10]: passenger-km 624,000,000; metric ton-km cargo 72,575,000; airports (1997) 11.

Communications

Medium	date	unit	number	units per 1,000 persons
Daily newspapers	2000	circulation	34,700	19
Radio	2000	receivers	258,000	141
Television	2000	receivers	69,400	38
Telephones	2001	main lines	117,400	66
Cellular telephones	2001	subscribers	100,000	56
Personal computers	2001	units	65,000	36
Internet	2001	users	45,000	25

Education and health

Educational attainment (1991). Percentage of population age 25 and over having: no formal schooling 35.1%; primary education 31.9%; secondary 28.5%; higher 4.5%. *Literacy* (2000): total population age 15 and over literate 830,200 (82.1%); males literate 416,000 (82.9%); females literate 414,200 (81.2%).

Education (1998)

	schools	teachers	students	student/ teacher ratio
Primary (age 6–12)	1,362	11,992	386,647	32.2
Secondary (age 13–19)	114[11]	5,093	110,076	21.6
Higher	24[11]	619	12,787	20.7

Health: physicians (2000) 244[12] (1 per 7,500 persons); hospital beds (2000) 6,739[12] (1 per 271 persons); infant mortality rate per 1,000 live births (2002) 67.3.
Food (2001): daily per capita caloric intake 2,745 (vegetable products 85%, animal products 15%); 120% of FAO recommended minimum requirement.

Military

Total active duty personnel (2002): 9,000 (army 100.0%). *Military expenditure as percentage of GNP* (1999): 2.9% (world 2.4%); per capita expenditure U.S.$53.

[1]72 elected and up to 6 appointed members. [2]Detail does not add to total given because of rounding. [3]Urban agglomeration. [4]Population of constituency (second-order administrative subdivision). [5]Percentage of total number of deaths at public hospitals. [6]Includes more than 140,000 nonwage (informal) workers. [7]Unemployed. [8]Imports are f.o.b. in balance of trade and c.i.f. for commodities and trading partners. [9]1995. [10]Air Namibia only. [11]1994. [12]Public sector only.

Internet resources for further information:
- **Bank of Namibia http://www.bon.com.na**

Nauru

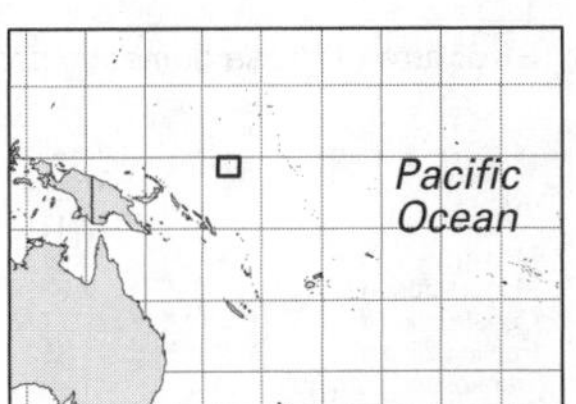

Official name: Naoero (Nauruan[1]); (Republic of Nauru).
Form of government: republic with one legislative house (Parliament [18]).
Head of state and government: President.
Capital: [2].
Official language: none[1].
Official religion: none.
Monetary unit: 1 Australian dollar ($A) = 100 cents; valuation (Sept. 8, 2003) 1 U.S.$ = $A 1.55; 1 £ = $A 2.46.

Area and population

	area		population
Districts	sq mi	sq km	1992 census[3]
Aiwo	0.4	1.1	1,072
Anabar	0.6	1.5	320
Anetan	0.4	1.0	427
Anibare	1.2	3.1	165
Baitsi	0.5	1.2	450
Boe	0.2	0.5	750
Buada	1.0	2.6	661
Denigomodu	0.3	0.9	2,548
Ewa	0.5	1.2	355
Ijuw	0.4	1.1	206
Meneng	1.2	3.1	1,269
Nibok	0.6	1.6	577
Uaboe	0.3	0.8	447
Yaren	0.6	1.5	672
TOTAL	8.2	21.2	9,919

Demography

Population (2003): 12,600.
Density (2003): persons per sq mi 1,536.6, persons per sq km 594.3.
Urban-rural (2001): urban 100%.
Sex distribution (2001): male 50.50%; female 49.50%.
Age breakdown (2001): under 15, 40.3%; 15–29, 26.8%; 30–44, 19.0%; 45–59, 10.7%; 60–74, 3.0%; 75 and over, 0.2%.
Population projection: (2010) 14,000; (2020) 17,000.
Doubling time: 35 years.
Ethnic composition (1992): Nauruan 68.9%; other Pacific Islander 23.7%, of which Kiribati 12.8%, Tuvaluan 8.7%; Asian 5.9%, of which Filipino 2.5%, Chinese 2.3%; other 1.5%.
Religious affiliation (1995): Protestant 53.5%, of which Congregational 35.3%, Pentecostal 4.8%; Roman Catholic 27.5%; other 19.0%.
Major cities: none; population of Yaren district (1996) 700.

Vital statistics

Birth rate per 1,000 population (2001): 27.2 (world avg. 21.3); legitimate, n.a.; illegitimate, n.a.
Death rate per 1,000 population (2001): 7.2 (world avg. 9.1).
Natural increase rate per 1,000 population (2001): 20.0 (world avg. 12.2).
Total fertility rate (avg. births per childbearing woman; 2001): 3.6.
Marriage rate per 1,000 population (1995): 5.3.
Divorce rate per 1,000 population: n.a.
Life expectancy at birth (2001): male 57.7 years; female 64.9 years.
Major causes of death per 100,000 population: n.a.[4]

National economy

Budget (1999). Revenue: $A 38,700,000[5]. Expenditures: $A 37,200,000.
Public debt (external, outstanding; beginning of 1996): *c.* U.S.$150,000,000.
Tourism: receipts from visitors, virtually none; expenditures by nationals abroad, n.a.
Gross national product (at current market prices; 1997): U.S.$128,000,000 (U.S.$11,538 per capita).

Distribution of gross domestic product and labour force

	1997			
	in value U.S.$'000,000	% of total value	labour force[6, 7, 8]	% of labour force
Agriculture	...	...	...	...
Mining (phosphate)	...	...	528	24.7
Manufacturing	...	...	...	...
Construction	...	...	...	...
Public utilities	...	...	...	...
Transportation and communications	...	...	...	...
Hotels	...	...	137	6.4
Finance[9]	...	...	33	1.6
Services	...	...	...	...
Pub. admin.	...	...	1,238	58.0
Other	...	...	198	9.3
TOTAL	540	100.0	2,134	100.0

Production (metric tons except as noted). Agriculture, forestry, fishing (2002): coconuts 1,600, vegetables 450, tropical fruit (including mangoes) 275; almonds, figs, and pandanus are also cultivated, but most foodstuffs and beverages (including water) are imported; livestock (number of live animals) 2,800 pigs; roundwood, none; fish catch (2001) 250. Mining and quarrying (2001): phosphate rock (gross weight) 400,000. Manufacturing: none; virtually all consumer manufactures are imported. Construction: n.a. Energy production (consumption): electricity (kW-hr; 1999) 33,000,000 (33,000,000); coal, none (n.a.); crude petroleum, none (n.a.); petroleum products (metric tons; 1999) none (44,000); natural gas, none (n.a.).
Population economically active (1992): 2,453[7, 10]; activity rate of total population 35.9% (participation rates: over age 15, n.a.; female, n.a.; unemployed, 18.2%).
Price and earnings indexes: [11].
Household income and expenditure. Average household size (1992) 10.0[6]; income per household: n.a.; sources of income: n.a.; expenditure: n.a.
Land use (1995): forested, nil; meadows and pastures, nil; agricultural and under permanent cultivation *c.* 10%[12]; other *c.* 90%[13].

Foreign trade

Balance of trade (current prices)

	1994	1995	1996	1997	1998	1999
U.S.$'000,000	+20.0	+0.2	+3.3	+10.1	+20.0	+20.0
% of total	33.3%	0.4%	4.6%	24.9%	33.3%	33.3%

Imports (1999): U.S.$20,000,000 (agricultural products 65.0%, of which food 45.0%; remainder 35.0%). *Major import sources* (2001): Australia 49.4%; United States 16.9%; Indonesia 7.9%; India 4.8%; United Kingdom 4.6%.
Exports (1999): U.S.$40,000,000 (phosphate, virtually 100%). *Major export destinations* (2001): New Zealand 28.6%; Australia 23.6%; Thailand 14.7%; South Korea 11.5%; Japan 9.6%.

Transport and communications

Transport. Railroads (2001): length 3 mi, 5 km; passenger traffic, n.a.; metric ton-km cargo, n.a. Roads (2001): total length 19 mi, 30 km (paved 79%). Vehicles (1989): passenger cars, trucks, and buses 1,448. Merchant marine (1992): vessels 2, total deadweight tonnage 5,791. Air transport (1996): passenger-mi 151,000,000, passenger-km 243,000,000; short ton-mi cargo 15,000,000, metric ton-km cargo 24,000,000; airports (2001) with scheduled flights 1.

Communications

Medium	date	unit	number	units per 1,000 persons
Daily newspapers	—	circulation	—	—
Radio	1997	receivers	7,000	609
Television	1997	receivers	500	48
Telephones	1998	main lines	1,700	149
Cellular telephones	1998	subscribers	850	75
Personal computers	1998	units	...	...
Internet	1998	users	...	...

Education and health

Educational attainment (1992)[7]. Percentage of population age 5 and over having: primary education or less 77.4%; secondary education 12.9%; higher 4.1%; not stated 5.6%. *Literacy* (1999): total population age 15 and over literate 99%.

Education (2002)[7]

	schools	teachers	students	student/ teacher ratio
Primary (age 6–13)	5	64[14]	1,566	...
Secondary (age 14–17)	4	53[14]	609	...

Health: physicians (1995) 17 (1 per 637 persons); hospital beds (1990) 207 (1 per 46 persons); infant mortality rate per 1,000 live births (2001) 10.7.
Food (2000)[15]: daily per capita caloric intake 2,991 (vegetable products 70%, animal products 30%); 131% of FAO recommended minimum requirement.

Military

Total active duty personnel (2002): Nauru does not have any military establishment. The defense is assured by Australia, but no formal agreement exists.

[1]Nauruan is the national language; English is the language of business and government. [2]Government offices are located in Yaren district. [3]Preliminary. [4]Morbidity is often associated with dietary and social problems (particularly obesity and alcoholism). [5]Largely from phosphate exports. [6]Employed only. [7]Nauruan only. [8]Most non-Nauruans are phosphate industry contract workers. [9]400 offshore banks were registered in Nauru in mid-2001. [10]Excludes activity not stated. [11]Minimum wage remained constant between November 1992 and the end of 1997. [12]Cultivatable coastal strip. [13]Phosphate-extracted interior wasteland. [14]1997. [15]Data for Oceania.

Nepal

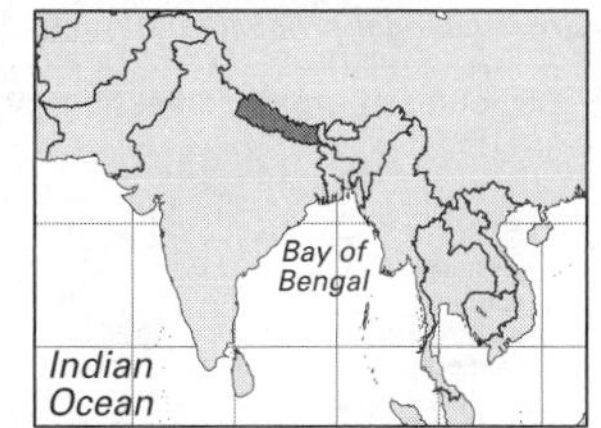

Official name: Nepal Adhirajya (Kingdom of Nepal).
Form of government: constitutional monarchy[1].
Chief of state: King.
Head of government: Prime Minister.
Capital: Kathmandu.
Official language: Nepali.
Official religion: Hinduism.
Monetary unit: 1 Nepalese rupee (NRs) = 100 paisa (pice); valuation (Sept. 8, 2003) 1 U.S.$ = NRs 74.60; 1 £ = NRs 118.28.

Area and population

Development regions	Capitals	area sq mi	area sq km	population 2001 census[2]
Eastern	Dhankuta	10,987	28,456	5,344,476
Central	Kathmandu	10,583	27,410	8,031,629
Western	Pokhara	11,351	29,398	4,571,013
Mid-western	Surkhet	16,362	42,378	3,012,975
Far-western	Dipayal	7,544	19,539	2,191,330
TOTAL		56,827	147,181	23,151,423

Demography

Population (2003): 24,172,000.
Density (2002): persons per sq mi 425.4, persons per sq km 164.2.
Urban-rural (2002): urban 13.0%; rural 87.0%.
Sex distribution (2001): male 49.96%; female 50.04%.
Age breakdown (2001): under 15, 39.3%; 15–29, 27.0%; 30–44, 17.1%; 45–59, 10.1%; 60–74, 5.2%; 75 and over, 1.3%.
Population projection: (2010) 28,061,000; (2020) 33,600,000.
Doubling time: 29 years.
Ethnic composition (2000): Nepalese 55.8%; Maithili 10.8%; Bhojpuri 7.9%; Tharu 4.4%; Tamang 3.6%; Newar 3.0%; Awadhi 2.7%; Magar 2.5%; Gurkha 1.7%; other 7.6%.
Religious affiliation (2001): Hindu 80.6%; Buddhist 10.7%; Muslim 4.2%; Kirat (local traditional belief) 3.6%; Christian 0.5%; other 0.4%.
Major cities (2001): Kathmandu 696,852; Biratnagar 166,902; Lalitpur 161,617; Pokhara 159,104; Birganj 112,031.

Vital statistics

Birth rate per 1,000 population (2002): 34.2 (world avg. 21.3).
Death rate per 1,000 population (2002): 10.0 (world avg. 9.1).
Natural increase rate per 1,000 population (2002): 24.2 (world avg. 12.2).
Total fertility rate (avg. births per childbearing woman; 2002): 4.5.
Life expectancy at birth (2002): male 60.0 years; female 59.0 years.
Major causes of death per 100,000 population: n.a.; however, the leading causes of mortality are infectious and parasitic diseases, diseases of the respiratory system, and diseases of the nervous system.

National economy

Budget (2001). Revenue: NRs 48,596,000,000 (taxes on goods and services 34.1%, taxes on international trade 28.1%, income taxes 19.0%, state property revenues 1.9%, other 16.9%). Expenditures: NRs 74,289,000,000 (current expenditure 59.3%, of which education 14.0%, defense 7.8%, health 2.8%; development expenditure 40.7%, of which economic services 25.7%).
Public debt (external, outstanding; 2002): U.S.$2,933,000,000.
Production (metric tons except as noted). Agriculture, forestry, fishing (2002): rice 4,130,000, sugarcane 2,248,000, corn (maize) 1,511,000, potatoes 1,473,000, wheat 1,258,000, millet 282,000; livestock (number of live animals) 6,979,000 cattle, 6,607,000 goats, 3,701,000 buffalo, 934,000 pigs, 840,000 sheep; roundwood (2002) 13,988,000 cu m; fish catch (2000) 31,723. Mining and quarrying (2001): limestone 280,000; talc 6,000; salt 2,000. Manufacturing (value added in U.S.$'000,000; 1996): textiles 99; tobacco products 46; beverages 35; food products 30; wearing apparel 24. Energy production (consumption): electricity (kW-hr; 1999) 1,398,000,000 (1,535,000,000); coal (metric tons; 1999) 18,000 (419,000); petroleum products (metric tons; 1999) none (673,000).
Tourism (2001): receipts from visitors U.S.$140,000,000; expenditures by nationals abroad U.S.$80,000,000.
Population economically active (2001): total 11,138,000; activity rate of total population *c.* 48% (participation rates: ages 10 years and over, 58.2%[3]; female [1991] 45.5%; unemployed 5.1%).

Price and earnings indexes (1995 = 100)

	1996	1997	1998	1999	2000	2001	2002
Consumer price index	109.2	113.6	125.0	134.4	137.9	141.7	145.6
Monthly earnings index[4]	100.0	100.0	124.1	124.1	145.9	…	…

Household income and expenditure (1984–85). Average household size (2001) 5.4; income per household NRs 14,796 (U.S.$853); sources of income: self-employment 63.4%, wages and salaries 25.1%, rent 7.5%, other 4.0%; expenditure: food and beverages 61.2%, housing 17.3%, clothing 11.7%, health care 3.7%, education and recreation 2.9%, transp. and commun. 1.2%.
Gross national product (at current market prices; 2001): U.S.$5,800,000,000 (U.S.$250 per capita).

Structure of gross domestic product and labour force

	2000–01 in value NRs '000,000	2000–01 % of total value	1999 labour force[5]	1999 % of labour force[5]
Agriculture	149,040	36.3	7,203,000	76.1
Mining	1,981	0.5	8,000	0.1
Manufacturing	35,566	8.7	552,000	5.8
Construction	39,571	9.6	344,000	3.7
Public utilities	6,989	1.7	26,000	0.3
Transp. and commun.	33,050	8.1	135,000	1.4
Trade	45,381	11.0	522,000	5.5
Finance	41,835	10.2	51,000	0.5
Services	40,060	9.8	614,000	6.5
Other	16,721[6]	4.1[6]	8,000	0.1
TOTAL	410,194	100.0	9,463,000	100.0

Land use (1994): forested 42.0%; meadows and pastures 14.6%; agricultural and under permanent cultivation 17.2%; other 26.2%.

Foreign trade[7]

Balance of trade (current prices)

	1997	1998	1999	2000	2001	2002
NRs '000,000	–74,419	–50,613	–55,969	–54,569	–55,141	–66,368
% of total	61.2%	44.7%	40.5%	32.3%	33.3%	42.9%

Imports (2000–01): NRs 115,687,000,000 (basic manufactures [including fabrics, yarns, and made-up articles] 35.6%, machinery and transport equipment 19.9%, chemicals and chemical products 11.2%, mineral fuels [mostly refined petroleum] 9.7%). *Major import sources* (2001): India 36.7%; Argentina 15.5%; China 15.3%; U.A.E. 5.8%; Singapore 5.1%.
Exports (2000–01): NRs 55,654,000,000 (ready-made garments 23.6%, carpets 15.4%, pashminas[8] 12.4%, vegetable ghee 6.4%). *Major export destinations* (2001): U.S. 30.7%; India 30.2%; Germany 11.6%; Argentina 7.4%; Japan 2.3%.

Transport and communications

Transport. Railroads (2002): route length 59 km; passengers carried 1,600,000; freight handled 22,000 metric tons. Roads (1997): total length 7,700 km (paved 42%). Vehicles (2000): passenger cars 53,073; trucks and buses 32,065. Air transport (2000): passenger-km 1,023,000,000; metric ton-km cargo 108,000,000; airports (1996) with scheduled flights 24.

Communications

Medium	date	unit	number	units per 1,000 persons
Daily newspapers	1996	circulation	250,000	11
Radio	2000	receivers	883,000	39
Television	2000	receivers	159,000	7.0
Telephones	2002	main lines	327,700	14
Cellular telephones	2002	subscribers	21,900	0.9
Personal computers	2002	units	80,000	3.5
Internet	2002	users	60,000	2.6

Education and health

Educational attainment (1981). Percentage of population age 25 and over having: no formal schooling 41.2%; primary education 29.4%; secondary 22.7%; higher 6.8%. *Literacy* (2001): total population age 15 and over literate *c.* 53%; males literate *c.* 60%; females literate *c.* 43%.

Education (2000)

	schools	teachers	students	student/ teacher ratio
Primary (age 6–10)	25,927	97,879	3,623,150	37.0
Secondary (age 11–15) / Vocational	11,639	44,873	1,330,360	29.6
Higher	2	6,313	149,060	23.6

Health (1999): physicians 1,259 (1 per 17,589 persons); hospital beds 5,190 (1 per 4,267 persons); infant mortality rate per 1,000 live births (2002) 72.0.
Food (2001): daily per capita caloric intake 2,459 (vegetable products 94%, animal products 6%); 112% of FAO recommended minimum.

Military

Total active duty personnel (2002): 51,000 (army 100.0%). *Military expenditure as percentage of GNP* (1999): 0.8% (world 2.4%); per capita expenditure U.S.$2.

[1]Bicameral parliament dissolved by the monarch from May 2002 through mid-November 2003. [2]Final figures adjusted for undercount. [3]Usually economically active. [4]Minimum monthly wage rates for unskilled industrial workers; 1994–95 = 100. [5]Employed only. [6]Includes indirect taxes less imputed bank service charges. [7]Imports c.i.f.; exports f.o.b. [8]Fine shawls made of cashmere or cashmere-silk blend.

Internet resources for further information:
- **Central Bank of Nepal http://www.nrb.org.np**
- **National Planning Commission http://npc.gov.np:8080**

Netherlands, The

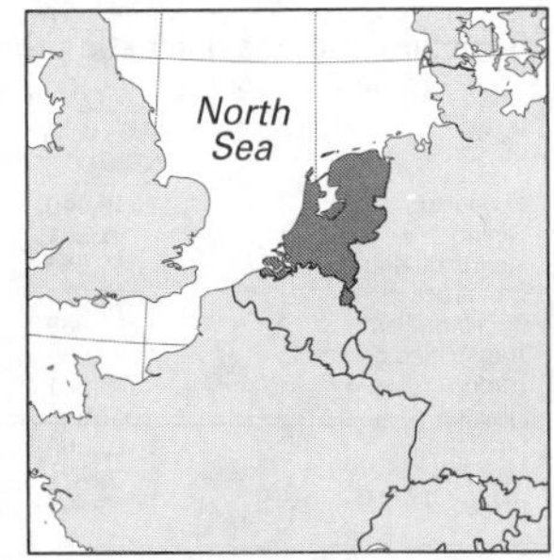

Official name: Koninkrijk der Nederlanden (Kingdom of The Netherlands).
Form of government: constitutional monarchy with a parliament (States General) comprising two legislative houses (First Chamber [75]; Second Chamber [150]).
Chief of state: Monarch.
Head of government: Prime Minister.
Seat of government: The Hague.
Capital: Amsterdam.
Official language: Dutch.
Official religion: none.
Monetary unit: 1 euro (€) = 100 cents; valuation (Sept. 8, 2003) 1 U.S.$ = €0.90; 1 £ = €1.43[1].

Area and population

		area		population
Provinces	**Capitals**	sq mi	sq km	2002[2] estimate
Drenthe	Assen	1,035	2,680	479,000
Flevoland	Lelystad	931	2,412	342,000
Friesland	Leeuwarden	2,217	5,741	636,000
Gelderland	Arnhem	1,983	5,137	1,949,000
Groningen	Groningen	1,146	2,968	570,000
Limburg	Maastricht	853	2,209	1,143,000
Noord-Brabant	's-Hertogenbosch	1,962	5,082	2,391,000
Noord-Holland	Haarlem	1,567	4,059	2,559,000
Overijssel	Zwolle	1,321	3,421	1,094,000
Utrecht	Utrecht	556	1,439	1,140,000
Zeeland	Middelburg	1,133	2,934	377,000
Zuid-Holland	The Hague	1,331	3,446	3,424,000
TOTAL		16,034[3, 4]	41,528[4]	16,105,000[3]

Demography

Population (2003): 16,238,000.
Density (2003)[5]: persons per sq mi 1,241.5, persons per sq km 479.4.
Urban-rural (2001): urban 89.6%; rural 10.4%.
Sex distribution (2002[2]): male 49.50%; female 50.50%.
Age breakdown (2000[2]): under 15, 18.6%; 15–29, 19.3%; 30–44, 24.2%; 45–59, 19.8%; 60–74, 12.1%; 75 and over, 6.0%.
Population projection: (2010) 16,913,000; (2020) 17,524,000.
Ethnic composition (by place of origin [including 2nd generation]; 2002[2]): Netherlander 81.6%; Indonesian 2.5%; German 2.5%; Turkish 2.1%; Surinamese 2.0%; Moroccan 1.8%; Netherlands Antillean/Aruban 0.8%; other 6.7%[6].
Religious affiliation (1999[2]): Roman Catholic 31.0%; Reformed (NHK) 14.0%; other Reformed 7.0%; Muslim 4.5%; Hindu 0.5%; nonreligious and other 43.0%.
Major urban agglomerations (2000[2]): Amsterdam 1,002,868; Rotterdam 989,956; The Hague 610,245; Utrecht 366,186; Eindhoven 302,274.

Vital statistics

Birth rate per 1,000 population (2001): 12.6 (world avg. 21.3); legitimate 72.8%; illegitimate 27.2%.
Death rate per 1,000 population (2001): 8.8 (world avg. 9.1).
Natural increase rate per 1,000 population (2001): 3.8 (world avg. 12.2).
Total fertility rate (avg. births per childbearing woman; 2001): 1.7.
Marriage rate per 1,000 population (2000): 5.3.
Life expectancy at birth (2001): male 75.8 years; female 80.7 years.
Major causes of death per 100,000 population (2000): diseases of the circulatory system 310.1; malignant neoplasms (cancers) 237.9; diseases of the respiratory system 92.5; accidents and violence 32.6.

National economy

Budget (1997). Revenue: f. 324,360,000,000 (social security taxes 41.1%, income and corporate taxes 24.8%, value-added and excise taxes 22.7%, property taxes 3.0%). Expenditures: f. 337,620,000,000 (social security and welfare 37.4%, health 14.8%, education 10.0%, interest payments 9.1%, defense 3.9%, transportation 3.5%).
Public debt (2002): U.S.$240,951,000,000.
Production (metric tons except as noted). Agriculture, forestry, fishing (2002): potatoes 7,363,000, sugar beets 6,250,000, wheat 1,057,000, onions 882,000, tomatoes 580,000, carrots 375,000, apples 333,000, barley 315,000, flowering bulbs and tubers 59,800 acres (24,200 hectares), of which tulips 26,200 acres (10,600 hectares), cut flowers/plants under glass 14,392 acres (5,823 hectares); livestock (number of live animals; 2002) 11,648,000 pigs, 3,858,000 cattle, 1,186,000 sheep; roundwood (2002) 839,000 cu m; fish catch (2000) 495,804. Manufacturing (value added in €'000,000; 2000): food, beverages, and tobacco 11,625; chemicals and chemical products 8,314; electric/electronic machinery 6,429; printing and publishing 5,699. Energy production (consumption): electricity (kW-hr; 2000) 89,580,000,000 ([1999] 93,505,000,000); coal (metric tons; 1999) negligible (12,090,000); crude petroleum (barrels; 2000) 9,389,000 ([1999] 377,100,000); petroleum products (metric tons; 1999) 61,688,000 (29,802,000); natural gas (cu m; 2000) 67,864,000,000 ([1999] 50,699,000,000).
Household income and expenditure. Average household size (2003) 2.3; disposable income per household (2000) €26,653 (U.S.$24,521); sources of income (1996): wages 48.4%, transfers 28.5%, self-employment 11.3%; expenditure (2000): housing and energy 23.2%, food and beverages 14.2%, transportation and communications 11.7%, textiles and clothing 6.4%.

Gross national product (2001): U.S.$390,300,000,000 (U.S.$24,330 per capita).

Structure of gross domestic product and labour force

	1999		2001	
	in value f. '000,000	% of total value	labour force	% of labour force
Agriculture	20,554	2.5	224,000	2.8
Mining	14,503	1.8	9,000	0.1
Manufacturing	125,570	15.2	1,115,000	13.8
Construction	43,091	5.2	508,000	6.3
Public utilities	13,046	1.6	34,000	0.4
Transp. and commun.	55,723	6.8	486,000	6.0
Trade	112,907	13.7	1,545,000	19.1
Finance, real estate	199,652	24.2	1,251,000	15.5
Pub. admin., defense	87,044	10.6	541,000	6.7
Services	84,717	10.3	1,613,000	19.9
Other	67,176[7]	8.1[7]	756,000[8]	9.4[8]
TOTAL	823,983	100.0	8,086,000[3]	100.0

Population economically active (1998): total 7,735,000; activity rate of total population 49.3% (participation rates: ages 15–64, 72.9%; female 42.5%; unemployed [February 2001–January 2002] 2.0%).

Price and earnings indexes (1995 = 100)

	1997	1998	1999	2000	2001	2002	2003[9]
Consumer price index	104.2	106.3	108.6	111.4	116.4	120.5	123.4
Hourly earnings index	104.8	108.1	111.3	115.4	120.2	124.8	127.5

Tourism (2001): receipts U.S.$6,723,000,000; expenditures U.S.$12,016,000,000.
Land use (1994): forested 10.3%; meadows and pastures 31.0%; agricultural and under permanent cultivation 28.0%; other 30.7%.

Foreign trade[10]

Balance of trade (current prices)

	1997	1998	1999	2000	2001	2002
€'000,000	+32,732[11]	+26,926[11]	+9,325	+12,367	+23,682	+31,053
% of total	4.4%	4.5%	2.5%	2.8%	5.2%	7.1%

Imports (2001): €217,151,000,000 (computers and related equipment 11.9%, chemicals and chemical products 11.4%, mineral fuels 10.1%, food 8.2%, road vehicles 7.0%). *Major import sources:* Germany 18.5%; U.S. 9.8%; Belgium-Luxembourg 9.3%; U.K. 8.9%; France 5.7%.
Exports (2001): €240,833,000,000 (chemicals and chemical products 15.4%, food 12.3%, computers and related equipment 11.7%, mineral fuels 9.2%). *Major export destinations:* Germany 25.6%; Belgium-Luxembourg 11.9%; U.K. 11.2%; France 10.3%; Italy 6.2%.

Transport and communications

Transport. Railroads (2001): length 2,809 km; passenger-km 14,392,000,000; metric ton-km cargo 4,293,000,000. Roads (1999): total length 116,500 km (paved 90%). Vehicles (2002): passenger cars 6,711,000; trucks and buses 997,000. Air transport (2001)[12]: passenger-km 57,848,000,000; metric ton-km cargo 4,464,000,000; airports (1996) 6.

Communications

Medium	date	unit	number	units per 1,000 persons
Daily newspapers	2000	circulation	4,870,000	306
Radio	2000	receivers	15,600,000	980
Television	2000	receivers	8,570,000	538
Telephones	2001	main lines	10,003,000	625
Cellular telephones	2002	subscribers	11,700,000	720
Personal computers	2001	units	6,900,000	429
Internet	2002	users	8,590,000	529

Education and health

Educational attainment (2001). Percentage of population ages 15–64 having: primary education 14.1%; lower secondary 9.3%; upper secondary/vocational 54.3%; tertiary vocational 15.1%; university 6.9%; unknown 0.3%.

Education (2001–02)[13]

	schools	teachers	students	student/ teacher ratio
Primary (age 6–12)	7,397	...	1,604,000	...
Secondary (age 12–18)	795	...	904,000	...
Vocational[14]	64	...	258,000	...
Higher[15]	13	...	159,000	...

Health (2000): physicians 27,161 (1 per 586 persons); hospital beds 90,747 (1 per 175 persons); infant mortality rate per 1,000 live births (2001) 5.4.
Food (2001): daily per capita caloric intake 3,282 (vegetable products 64%, animal products 36%); 117% of FAO recommended minimum requirement.

Military

Total active duty personnel (2002): 47,430 (army 48.8%, navy 25.6%, air force 18.5%, paramilitary 7.0%). *Military expenditure as percentage of GNP* (1999): 1.8% (world 2.4%); per capita expenditure U.S.$445.

[1]The Netherlands guilder (f.) was the former monetary unit; on Jan. 1, 2002, f. 2.20 = €1. [2]January 1. [3]Detail does not add to total given because of rounding. [4]Includes inland water area totaling 1,343 sq mi (3,479 sq km) and coastal water totaling 1,612 sq mi (4,176 sq km). [5]Based on land area only (13,079 sq mi [33,873 sq km]). [6]Includes Netherlander-EU country 4.7%. [7]Imputed value-added tax less subsidies and bank service charges. [8]Includes 220,000 registered unemployed. [9]April. [10]Imports c.i.f.; exports f.o.b. [11]In guilders. [12]KLM only. [13]Public schools only. [14]Colleges only. [15]Universities.

Internet resources for further information:
- **Statistics Netherlands http://www.cbs.nl/en**

Netherlands Antilles

Official name: Nederlandse Antillen (Netherlands Antilles).
Political status: nonmetropolitan territory of The Netherlands with one legislative house (States of the Netherlands Antilles [22]).
Chief of state: Dutch Monarch represented by Governor.
Head of government: Prime Minister.
Capital: Willemstad.
Official language: Dutch.
Official religion: none.
Monetary unit: 1 Netherlands Antillean guilder (NA f.) = 100 cents; valuation (Sept. 8, 2003) 1 U.S.$ = NA f. 1.79; 1 £ = NA f. 2.84.

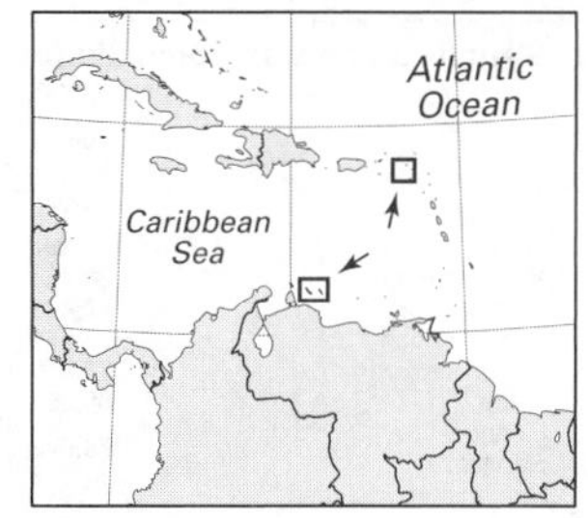

Area and population

Island councils	Capitals	area sq mi	area sq km	population 2001 census
Leeward Islands				
Bonaire	Kralendijk	111	288	10,791
Curaçao	Willemstad	171	444	130,627
Windward Islands				
Saba	The Bottom	5	13	1,349
Sint Eustatius, or Statia	Oranjestad	8	21	2,292
Sint Maarten (Dutch part only)	Philipsburg	13	34	30,594
TOTAL		308	800	175,653

Demography

Population (2003): 169,000.
Density (2003): persons per sq mi 548.7, persons per sq km 211.3.
Urban-rural (2001): urban 69.6%; rural 30.4%.
Sex distribution (2001): male 46.98%; female 53.02%.
Age breakdown (2001): under 15, 24.2%; 15–29, 18.2%; 30–44, 25.5%; 45–59, 19.0%; 60–74, 9.4%; 75 and over, 3.7%.
Population projection: (2010) 169,000; (2020) 169,000.
Ethnic composition (2000): local black-other (Antillean Creole) 81.1%; Dutch 5.3%; Surinamese 2.9%; other (significantly West Indian black) 10.7%.
Religious affiliation (2001): Roman Catholic 72.0%; Protestant 16.0%; Spiritist 0.9%; Buddhist 0.5%; Jewish 0.4%; Bahā'ī 0.3%; Hindu 0.2%; Muslim 0.2%; other/unknown 9.5%.
Major cities (2001): Willemstad (urban agglomeration) 125,000; Kralendijk 7,900; Philipsburg 6,300.

Vital statistics

Birth rate per 1,000 population (2001): 13.6 (world avg. 21.3); (1988)[1] legitimate 51.6%; illegitimate 48.4%.
Death rate per 1,000 population (2001): 6.4 (world avg. 9.1).
Natural increase rate per 1,000 population (2001): 7.2 (world avg. 12.2).
Total fertility rate (avg. births per childbearing woman; 2001): 2.1.
Marriage rate per 1,000 population (1999): 4.7.
Divorce rate per 1,000 population (1999): 2.6.
Life expectancy at birth (2001): male 72.8 years; female 77.2 years.
Major causes of death per 100,000 population (1993): infectious and parasitic diseases/diseases of the respiratory system 209.0; diseases of the circulatory system 180.2; malignant neoplasms (cancers) 117.7.

National economy

Budget (2002). Revenue: NA f. 616,500,000 (tax revenue 86.5%, of which sales tax 40.6%, import duties 20.6%, excise on gasoline 12.7%; nontax revenue 11.7%; grants 1.8%). Expenditures: NA f. 669,000,000 (current expenditures 94.7%, of which transfers 32.0%, wages 31.1%, interest payments 16.1%, goods and services 12.9%; development expenditures 5.3%).
Production (metric tons except as noted). Agriculture, forestry, fishing: [2]; livestock (number of live animals; 2002) 13,000 goats, 7,300 sheep, 2,600 asses, 135,000 chickens; roundwood, n.a.; fish catch (2001) 950. Mining and quarrying (2001): salt 500,000, sulfur by-product 30,000. Manufacturing (1996): residual fuel oil 5,013,000; gas-diesel oils 2,218,000; other manufactures include electronic parts, cigarettes, textiles, rum, and Curaçao liqueur. Energy production (consumption): electricity (kW-hr; 2000) 1,120,500,000 ([1999] 1,114,000,000); coal, none (none); crude petroleum (barrels; 1999) none (105,900,000); petroleum products (metric tons; 1999) 10,286,000 (591,000); natural gas, none (none).
Land use (1998): forested, negligible; meadows and pastures, negligible; agricultural and under permanent cultivation 10.0%; other (dry savanna) 90.0%.
Tourism (2000): receipts from visitors U.S.$765,000,000; expenditures by nationals abroad U.S.$339,000,000.
Household income and expenditure. Average household size (2001) 2.9; income per household: n.a.; sources of income: n.a.; expenditure (1996)[3, 4]: housing 26.5%, transportation and communications 19.9%, food 14.7%, household furnishings 8.8%, recreation and education 8.2%, clothing and footwear 7.5%.
Gross national product (at current market prices; 1997): U.S.$2,609,000,000 (U.S.$12,490 per capita).

Structure of gross domestic product and labour force

	1997 in value NA f. '000,000	1997 % of total value	2001 labour force	2001 % of labour force
Agriculture, forestry	28.7	0.6	441	0.5
Mining			131	0.2
Manufacturing	271.0	6.0	4,619	5.7
Construction	330.6	7.3	5,335	6.5
Public utilities	194.4	4.3	1,131	1.4
Transp. and commun.	500.1	11.0	5,410	6.6
Trade, hotels, restaurants	1,089.6	24.0	19,002	23.3
Finance, real estate, insurance	1,173.1	25.9	10,103	12.4
Pub. admin., defense	748.1	16.5	5,997	7.3
Services	423.2	9.3	15,961	19.6
Other	–221.7[5]	–4.9[5]	13,428[6]	16.5[6]
TOTAL	4,537.1	100.0	81,558	100.0

Population economically active (2001): total 81,558; activity rate of total population 46.4% (participation rates: ages 15–64, 68.7%; female 49.0%; unemployed [2002] 14.2%).

Price and earnings indexes (1996 = 100)

	1995	1996	1997	1998	1999	2000	2001
Consumer price index	96.5	100.0	103.3	104.4	104.8	110.9	117.0
Monthly earnings index[7]	...	100.0	100.0	100.0	...	...	...

Public debt (external, outstanding; 1999): U.S.$294,600,000.

Foreign trade

Balance of trade (current prices)

	1997	1998	1999	2000	2001	2002[8]
NA f. '000,000	–1,723	–1,616	–1,709	–1,764	–1,866	–1,309
% of total	52.6%	50.4%	53.3%	46.3%	48.7%	49.2%

Imports (2001): NA f. 2,850,000,000 (nonpetroleum domestic imports 67.8%, crude petroleum and petroleum products 17.6%, imports of Curaçao free zone 14.6%). *Major import sources* (2000): United States 25.8%; Mexico 20.7%; Gabon 6.6%; Italy 5.8%; The Netherlands 5.5%.
Exports (2001): NA f. 984,000,000 (goods procured in ports for ships' bunkers 37.7%, reexports of Curaçao free zone 30.9%, nonpetroleum domestic exports 18.3%). *Major export destinations* (2000): United States 35.9%; Guatemala 9.4%; Venezuela 8.7%; France 5.4%; Singapore 2.8%.

Transport and communications

Transport. Railroads: none. Roads (1992): total length 367 mi, 590 km (paved 51%). Vehicles (1999): passenger cars 74,840; trucks and buses 17,415. Air transport (2000)[9]: passenger arrivals and departures 911,000; freight loaded and unloaded 14,500 metric tons; airports (2000) with scheduled flights 5.

Communications

Medium	date	unit	number	units per 1,000 persons
Daily newspapers	1996	circulation	70,000	341
Radio	1997	receivers	217,000	1,039
Television	1997	receivers	69,000	330
Telephones	1999	main lines	79,000	386
Cellular telephones	1998	subscribers	16,000	77

Education and health

Educational attainment (2001). Percentage of population 25 and over having: no formal schooling 0.8%; primary education 24.2%; lower secondary 42.8%; upper secondary 16.8%; higher 11.4%; unknown 4.0%. *Literacy* (1995): total population age 15 and over literate 194,900 (96.6%); males literate 93,300 (96.6%); females literate 101,600 (96.6%).

Education (1999–2000)

	schools	teachers	students	student/ teacher ratio
Primary (age 6–12)	90	1,139[10]	23,205	21.1[10]
Secondary (age 12–17)	22	461[10]	8,112	18.2[10]
Voc., teacher tr.	32	853[10]	7,576	9.7[10]
Higher	2	123	825	6.7

Health (2001): physicians 333 (1 per 520 persons); hospital beds 1,343 (1 per 129 persons); infant mortality rate per 1,000 live births (2001) 11.4.
Food (2001): daily per capita caloric intake 2,565 (vegetable products 72%, animal products 28%); 106% of FAO recommended minimum requirement.

Military

Total active duty personnel (2002): a 20-member Dutch naval/air force contingent is stationed in the Netherlands Antilles and Aruba.

[1]Excludes Sint Eustatius. [2]Mostly tomatoes, beans, cucumbers, gherkins, melons, and lettuce grown on hydroponic farms; aloes grown for export, divi-divi pods, and sour orange fruit are nonhydroponic crops. [3]Curaçao only. [4]Weights of consumer price index components. [5]Less imputed bank service charges. [6]Includes 11,876 unemployed. [7]Minimum wages only. [8]Excludes fourth quarter. [9]Curaçao airport only. [10]1996–97.

Internet resources for further information:
- **Central Bank of the Netherlands Antilles http://www.centralbank.an**
- **Central Bureau of Statistics http://central-bureau-of-statistics.an/default.asp**

New Caledonia

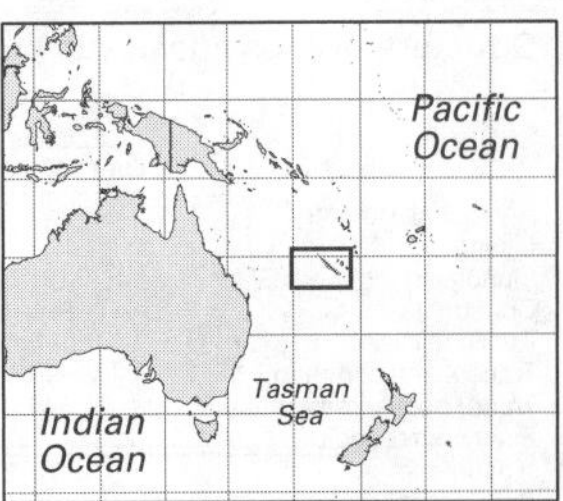

Official name: Nouvelle-Calédonie (New Caledonia).
Political status[1]: overseas collectivity (France) with one legislative house (Congress[2] [54]).
Chief of state: President of France represented by High Commissioner.
Head of government: President.
Capital: Nouméa.
Official language: none[3].
Official religion: none.
Monetary unit: 1 franc of the Comptoirs français du Pacifique (CFPF) = 100 centimes; valuation (Sept. 8, 2003)[4] 1 U.S.$ = CFPF 104.80; 1 £ = CFPF 166.17.

Area and population

Provinces Island(s)	Capitals	area sq mi	area sq km	population 1996 census
Loyauté (Loyalty)	Wé	765	1,981	20,877
Lifou		466	1,207	10,007
Maré		248	642	6,896
Ouvéa		51	132	3,974
Nord (Northern)	Koné	3,305	8,561	41,413
Belep		27	70	923
New Caledonia (part)		3,278	8,491	40,490
Sud (Southern)	Nouméa	3,102	8,033	134,546
New Caledonia (part)		3,043	7,881	132,875
Pins		59	152	1,671
TOTAL		7,172	18,575	196,836

Demography

Population (2003): 220,000.
Density (2003): persons per sq mi 30.7, persons per sq km 11.8.
Urban-rural (2002): urban 79.0%; rural 21.0%.
Sex distribution (1996): male 51.23%; female 48.77%.
Age breakdown (1996): under 15, 30.7%; 15–29, 27.2%; 30–44, 21.3%; 45–59, 13.3%; 60–74, 5.9%; 75 and over, 1.6%.
Population projection: (2010) 240,000; (2020) 265,000.
Doubling time: 48 years.
Ethnic composition (1996): Melanesian 45.3%, of which local (Kanak) 44.1%, Vanuatuan 1.2%; European 34.1%; Wallisian or Futunan 9.0%; Indonesian 2.6%; Tahitian 2.6%; Vietnamese 1.4%; other 5.0%.
Religious affiliation (2000): Roman Catholic 54.2%; Protestant 14.0%; Muslim 2.7%; other Christian 2.1%; other 27.0%.
Major cities (1996): Nouméa 76,293 (urban agglomeration 118,823); Mont-Dore 20,780[5]; Dumbéa 13,888[5].

Vital statistics

Birth rate per 1,000 population (2002): 19.9 (world avg. 21.3); (1996) legitimate 36.4%; illegitimate 63.6%.
Death rate per 1,000 population (2002): 5.6 (world avg. 9.1).
Natural increase rate per 1,000 population (2002): 14.3 (world avg. 12.2).
Total fertility rate (avg. births per childbearing woman; 2002): 2.4.
Marriage rate per 1,000 population (2001): 4.3.
Divorce rate per 1,000 population (1999): 0.8.
Life expectancy at birth (2002): male 70.3 years; female 76.4 years.
Major causes of death per 100,000 population (1999): diseases of the circulatory system 143.5; malignant neoplasms (cancers) 119.9; accidents, poisonings, and violence 95.4; diseases of the respiratory system 52.0.

National economy

Budget (1999). Revenue: CFPF 77,477,000,000 (indirect taxes 49.7%, direct taxes 30.9%, French government subsidies 8.6%, tobacco excises 6.3%). Expenditures: CFPF 74,218,000,000 (current expenditure 93.4%, development expenditure 6.6%).
Production (metric tons except as noted). Agriculture, forestry, fishing (2002): coconuts 16,000, yams 11,000, vegetables 3,900, fruit 3,000, sweet potatoes 3,000, corn (maize) 2,500; livestock (number of live animals; 2000) 122,000 cattle, 40,000 pigs, 500,000 poultry; roundwood (1998) 4,800 cu m; fish catch (1999) 5,088, of which shrimp 1,906, tuna 1,616, sea cucumbers 493. Mining and quarrying (metric tons; 1999): nickel ore 6,562,000, of which nickel content (1997) 110,000; cobalt (1997) 800. Manufacturing (metric tons; 2000): cement (1999) 92,714; ferronickel (metal content) 43,914; nickel matte (metal content) 13,549; other manufactures include beer, copra cake, and soap. Energy production (consumption): electricity (kW-hr; 1999) 1,614,000,000 (1,614,000,000); coal (metric tons; 1999) none (160,000); crude petroleum, none (none); petroleum products (metric tons; 1999) none (405,000); natural gas, none (none).
Population economically active (1996): total 80,589; activity rate of total population 40.9% (participation rates: over age 14, 57.3%; female 39.7%; unemployed 18.6%).

Price and earnings indexes (1995 = 100)[6]

	1995	1996	1997	1998	1999	2000	2001
Consumer price index	100.0	101.7	103.7	104.0	104.1	106.5	108.9
Earnings index[7]	100.0	101.2	103.1	104.4	105.0	106.1	135.3

Public debt (external, outstanding; 1999): U.S.$746,000,000.
Gross national product (2001): U.S.$3,200,000,000 (U.S.$15,060 per capita).

Structure of gross domestic product and labour force

	1997 in value CFPF '000,000	1997 % of total value	1996 labour force	1996 % of labour force
Agriculture	6,439	1.9	4,663	5.8
Mining	13,307	3.8	4,408[8]	5.5[8]
Manufacturing	38,766	11.1	3,072[9]	3.8[9]
Construction	17,447	5.0	6,890	8.5
Public utilities	5,370	1.5	697	0.8
Transp. and commun.	23,415	6.7	2,968	3.7
Trade	80,054	22.9	8,375	10.4
Finance }	76,543	21.9	5,550	6.9
Services }			17,218	21.4
Pub. admin., defense	87,919	25.2	10,536	13.1
Other	—	—	16,212[10]	20.1[10]
TOTAL	349,260	100.0	80,589	100.0

Household income and expenditure (1991). Average household size (1996) 3.8; average annual income per household CFPF 3,361,233 (U.S.$32,879)[11]; sources of income: wages and salaries 68.2%, transfer payments 13.7%, other 18.1%; expenditure: food and beverages 25.9%, housing 20.4%, transportation and communications 16.1%, recreation 4.8%.
Tourism: receipts from visitors (2000) U.S.$110,000,000.
Land use (1994): forested 38.7%; meadows and pastures 11.8%; agricultural and under permanent cultivation 0.7%; other 48.8%.

Foreign trade[12]

Balance of trade (current prices)

	1997	1998	1999	2000	2001	2002
CFPF '000,000	–40,949	–58,910	–60,521	–41,312	–63,824	–68,022
% of total	26.2%	42.0%	36.6%	20.8%	34.6%	36.5%

Imports (2002): CFPF 127,123,000,000 (machinery and apparatus 18.2%, food 15.6%, transportation equipment 15.2%, mineral products [mostly coal and refined petroleum] 13.4%, chemicals and chemical products 8.4%). *Major import sources:* France 39.6%; other EU 13.3%; Australia 12.9%; Singapore 10.0%.
Exports (2002): CFPF 59,101,000,000 (ferronickel 64.2%, nickel matte 13.0%, nickel ore 12.3%, shrimp 2.3%). *Major export destinations* (2001): France 24.9%; Japan 24.1%; Taiwan 16.8%; Spain 7.7%; Australia 5.6%.

Transport and communications

Transport. Railroads: none. Roads (2000): total length 3,375 mi, 5,432 km (paved [1993] 52%). Vehicles: passenger cars (1996) 56,700; trucks and buses (1993) 21,200. Air transport (2001)[13]: passenger arrivals 173,913, passenger departures 172,854; freight unloaded 3,661 metric tons, freight loaded 1,401 metric tons; airports (1999) with scheduled flights 11.

Communications

Medium	date	unit	number	units per 1,000 persons
Daily newspapers	1996	circulation	24,000	121
Radio	1997	receivers	107,000	533
Television	1999	receivers	101,000	480
Telephones	2000	main lines	51,000	237
Cellular telephones	2000	subscribers	49,900	232
Internet	2000	users	24,000	111

Education and health

Educational attainment (1996). Percentage of population age 14 and over having: no formal schooling 5.7%; primary education 28.9%; lower secondary 30.2%; upper secondary 24.6%; higher 10.5%. *Literacy:* n.a.

Education (2000)

	schools	teachers	students	student/ teacher ratio
Primary (age 6–10)	204	1,809	23,748	13.1
Secondary (age 11–17) } Vocational }	72	2,283	28,198	12.4
Higher	4[14]	55	2,069	37.6

Health (1999): physicians 418 (1 per 497 persons); hospital beds 838 (1 per 248 persons); infant mortality rate per 1,000 live births (2002) 8.2.
Food (2001): daily per capita caloric intake 2,770 (vegetable products 76%, animal products 24%); 120% of FAO recommended minimum requirement.

Military

Total active duty personnel (2001): 3,100 French troops. *Military expenditure as percentage of GNP:* n.a.

[1]The Nouméa Accord granting New Caledonia limited autonomy (with likely independence by 2013) was formally signed on May 5, 1998. New Caledonia became an overseas collectivity per March 2003 amendments to the French constitution. [2]Operates in association with 3 provincial assemblies. [3]Kanak languages and French have special recognition per Nouméa Accord. [4]Pegged to the euro on January 1, 2002, at €1 = CFPF 119.25. [5]Within Nouméa urban agglomeration. [6]All figures are end-of-year. [7]Based on minimum hourly wage. [8]Includes metallurgy. [9]Excludes metallurgy. [10]Includes 1,194 military conscripts and 15,018 unemployed. [11]Includes both monetary (92%) and nonmonetary income (8%). [12]Imports c.i.f.; exports f.o.b. [13]La Tontouta international airport only. [14]1996.

Internet resources for further information:

- **Ministère de l'Outre-Mer http://www.outre-mer.gouv.fr**
- **New Caledonia Economic Development Agency http://www.adecal.nc**

New Zealand

Official name: New Zealand (English); Aotearoa (Māori).
Form of government: constitutional monarchy with one legislative house (House of Representatives [120[1]]).
Chief of state: British Monarch, represented by Governor-General.
Head of government: Prime Minister.
Capital: Wellington.
Official languages: English; Māori.
Official religion: none.
Monetary unit: 1 New Zealand dollar ($NZ) = 100 cents; valuation (Sept. 8, 2003) 1 U.S.$ = $NZ 1.74; 1 £ = $NZ 2.76.

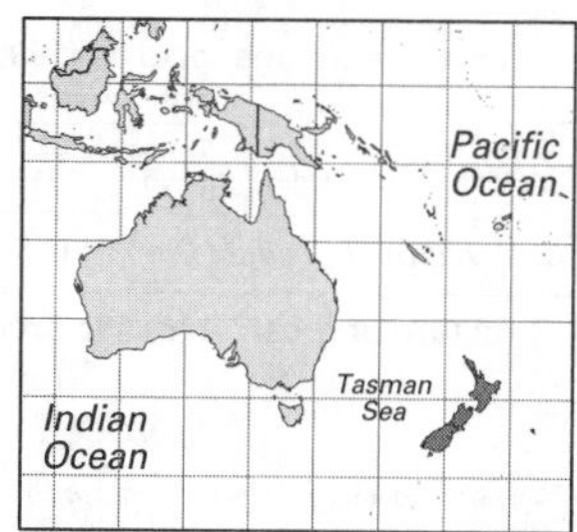

Area and population

Islands / Regional Councils	area sq mi	area sq km	population 2001 census
North Island	44,702	115,777	2,870,688
Auckland	...	...	1,173,639
Bay of Plenty	...	...	245,100
Gisborne[2]	...	...	44,142
Hawkes Bay	...	...	146,109
Manawatu-Wanganui	...	...	222,123
Northland	...	...	144,363
Taranaki	...	...	102,684
Waikato	...	...	364,986
Wellington	...	...	427,542
South Island	58,384	151,215	949,242
Canterbury	...	...	494,952
Marlborough[2]	...	...	42,528
Nelson[2]	...	...	43,560
Otago	...	...	194,487
Southland	...	...	94,371
Tasman[2]	...	...	44,880
West Coast	...	...	34,464
Offshore islands	1,368	3,542	819
TOTAL	104,454	270,534	3,820,749

Demography

Population (2003): 4,001,000[3].
Density (2003): persons per sq mi 38.3, persons per sq km 14.8.
Urban-rural (2002): urban 86.0%; rural 14.0%.
Sex distribution (2001): male 48.73%; female 51.27%.
Age breakdown (2001): under 15, 22.9%; 15–29, 20.1%; 30–44, 23.0%; 45–59, 17.9%; 60–74, 10.7%; 75 and over, 5.4%.
Population projection: (2010) 4,216,000; (2020) 4,480,000.
Ethnic composition (2001): European 73.8%; Māori (local Polynesian) 13.5%; Asian 6.1%; other Pacific Peoples (mostly other Polynesian) 6.0%; other 0.6%.
Religious affiliation (2001): Christian 55.2%, of which Anglican 15.3%, Roman Catholic 12.7%, Presbyterian 11.3%; nonreligious 26.9%; Buddhist 1.1%; Hindu 1.0%; other religions/not specified 15.8%.
Major urban areas (2001): Auckland 1,074,513; Wellington 339,750; Christchurch 334,107; Hamilton 166,128; Dunedin 107,088.

Vital statistics

Birth rate per 1,000 population (2002): 14.2 (world avg. 21.3); (1996) legitimate 58.0%; illegitimate 42.0%.
Death rate per 1,000 population (2002): 7.6 (world avg. 9.1).
Natural increase rate per 1,000 population (2002): 6.6 (world avg. 12.2).
Total fertility rate (avg. births per childbearing woman; 2002): 1.8.
Life expectancy at birth (2002): male 75.1 years; female 81.2 years.
Major causes of death per 100,000 population (1998): diseases of the circulatory system 298.2; malignant neoplasms (cancers) 209.5; diseases of the respiratory system 59.4; accidents, suicide, homicide, and other violence 46.1.

National economy

Budget (2000–01). Revenue: $NZ 37,156,000,000 (income taxes 59.4%, taxes on goods and services 34.4%, nontax revenue 6.2%). Expenditures: $NZ 37,019,000,000 (social welfare 37.0%, health 19.0%, education 17.6%).
Production (metric tons except as noted). Agriculture, forestry, fishing (2002): apples 537,000, barley 406,000, wheat 355,000, corn (maize) 157,000; livestock (number of live animals) 43,142,000 sheep, 9,633,000 cattle, 358,000 pigs; roundwood (2000) 20,523,000 cu m; fish catch (2000) 647,000. Mining and quarrying (2001): limestone 4,746,000; iron ore and sand concentrate 1,636,000; gold 9,850 kg. Manufacturing (1999): wood pulp 1,572,277; chemical fertilizers 1,365,000; wool yarn 23,500; wine 602,000 hectolitres; carpets 9,980,000 sq m[4]. Energy production (consumption): electricity (kW-hr; 1999) 38,102,000,000 (38,102,000,000); hard coal (metric tons; 1999) 3,456,000 (1,882,000); lignite (metric tons; 1999) 255,000 (259,000); crude petroleum (barrels; 1999) 14,700,000 (35,200,000); petroleum products (metric tons; 1999) 4,830,000 (4,996,000); natural gas (cu m; 1999) 5,174,600,000 (5,174,100,000).
Household income and expenditure. Average household size (1998) 2.8; annual income per household[5] (2000–01) $NZ 53,076 (U.S.$24,403); sources of income (1998): wages and salaries 65.8%, transfer payments 15.2%, self-employment 9.8%, other 9.2%; expenditure (2000–01): housing 23.9%, food 16.5%, transportation 15.9%, household goods 12.8%, clothing 3.2%.
Tourism (2001): receipts U.S.$2,250,000,000; expenditures U.S.$1,340,000,000.
Gross national product (2001): U.S.$51,000,000,000 (U.S.$13,250 per capita).

Structure of gross domestic product and labour force

	2001–02 in value $NZ '000,000[6]	2001–02 % of total value	2001 labour force	2001 % of labour force
Agriculture } Mining }	8,991	8.3	166,100	8.6
			3,700	0.2
Manufacturing	16,886	15.6	288,900	15.0
Construction	3,872	3.6	112,200	5.8
Public utilities	2,041	1.9	10,100	0.5
Transp. and commun.	11,164	10.3	112,400	5.8
Trade	16,699	15.4	393,600	20.5
Finance	26,878	24.8	232,000	12.1
Pub. admin., defense	4,349	4.0 }	499,600	25.9
Services	13,328	12.3 }		
Other	4,152	3.8	107,100[7]	5.6[7]
TOTAL	108,360	100.0	1,925,700	100.0

Population economically active (2000): total 1,923,700; activity rate 50.1% (participation rates: over age 15, 66.2%; female 45.3%; unemployed 5.7%).

Price and earnings indexes (1995 = 100)

	1996	1997	1998	1999	2000	2001	2002
Consumer price index	102.3	103.5	104.8	104.7	107.4	110.3	113.2
Hourly earnings index[8]	103.7	107.2	...	...	...	...	...

Land use (1999): pasture 49.6%; agriculture 12.2%; forest and other 38.2%.

Foreign trade[9]

Balance of trade (current prices)

	1997	1998	1999	2000	2001	2002[10]
$NZ '000,000	+1,007	+812.0	–1,896	+347	+2,987	+760
% of total	2.4%	1.8%	3.9%	0.6%	4.8%	1.3%

Imports (2001–02[11]): $NZ 32,165,000,000 (machinery and apparatus 21.4%, crude and refined petroleum 13.7%, vehicles 13.4%, plastics 3.7%). *Major import sources:* Australia 21.4%; U.S. 13.7%; Japan 10.8%; China 7.2%; Germany 4.7%.
Exports (2001–02[11]): $NZ 31,676,000,000 (domestic exports 96.2%, of which dairy products 20.6%, beef and sheep meat 12.7%, wood and paper products 10.8%, machinery and apparatus 6.1%, fruits and nuts 3.7%; reexports 3.8%). *Major export destinations:* Australia 19.9%; U.S. 15.3%; Japan 11.5%; U.K. 4.9%; South Korea 4.5%; China 4.5%.

Transport and communications

Transport. Railroads (1999): route length 3,912 km; passengers carried (2001–02) 14,330,000; metric ton-km cargo (1998) 3,960,000,000. Roads (1999): total length 92,075 km (paved 62%). Vehicles (2002): passenger cars 1,960,503; trucks and buses 374,005. Air transport[12] (1999): passenger-km 19,879,000,000; metric ton-km cargo 851,744,000; airports (1997) 36.

Communications

Medium	date	unit	number	units per 1,000 persons
Daily newspapers	2000	circulation	799,000	207
Radio	2000	receivers	3,850,000	997
Television	2000	receivers	2,010,000	522
Telephones	2002	main lines	1,765,000	448
Cellular telephones	2002	subscribers	2,436,000	618
Personal computers	2002	units	1,765,000	448
Internet	2002	users	1,908,000	484

Education and health

Educational attainment (1991). Percentage of population age 25 and over having: primary and some secondary education 54.9%; secondary 31.1%; higher 6.9%; not specified 7.1%. *Literacy:* virtually 100.0%.

Education (1999)

	schools	teachers	students	student/ teacher ratio
Primary (age 5–12)[13]	2,366	25,832	478,065	18.5
Secondary (age 13–17)	335	15,401	226,164	14.7
Voc., teacher tr.	29	5,428	111,855	20.6
Higher[14]	7	5,008	105,996	21.2

Health (2001): physicians 12,505 (1 per 306 persons); hospital beds 23,741 (1 per 161 persons); infant mortality rate per 1,000 live births (2002) 6.2.
Food (2001): daily per capita caloric intake 3,235 (vegetable products 67%, animal products 33%); 123% of FAO recommended minimum requirement.

Military

Total active duty personnel (2002): 8,710 (army 52.0%, air force 22.7%, navy 25.3%). *Military expenditure as percentage of GNP* (1999): 1.2% (world 2.4%); per capita expenditure U.S.$156.

[1]Includes seven elected seats allocated to Māoris. [2]Reorganized as a unitary authority that is administered by a district council with regional powers. [3]Adjusted for undercount of the 2001 census including New Zealand residents temporarily overseas. [4]1996–97. [5]Gross income. [6]Constant 1995–96 prices. [7]Mostly unemployed. [8]In manufacturing. [9]Import figures are f.o.b. in balance of trade and c.i.f. in commodities and trading partners. [10]Excludes December. [11]Beginning October 1. [12]Air New Zealand only. [13]Includes composite schools that provide both primary and secondary education. [14]Universities only.

Internet resources for further information:
- **Statistics New Zealand/Te Tari Tatau http://www.stats.govt.nz/statsweb.nsf**
- **The Press On-Line New Zealand News http://www.press.co.nz**

Nicaragua

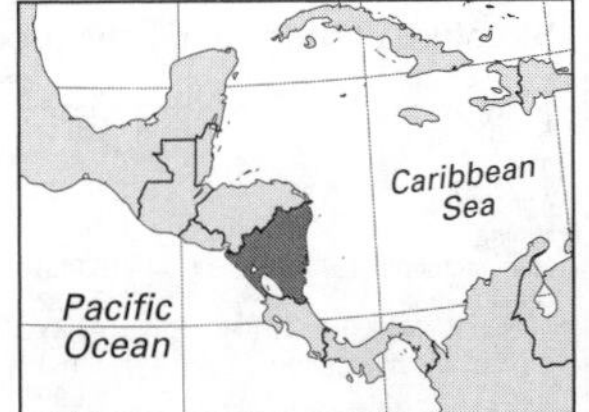

Official name: República de Nicaragua (Republic of Nicaragua).
Form of government: unitary multiparty republic with one legislative house (National Assembly [92[1]]).
Head of state and government: President.
Capital: Managua.
Official language: Spanish.
Official religion: none.
Monetary unit: 1 córdoba oro (C$) = 100 centavos; valuation (Sept. 8, 2003) 1 U.S.$ = C$15.19; 1 £ = C$24.08.

Area and population

Departments	Capitals	area[2] sq mi	area[2] sq km	population 2003 estimate[3]
Boaco	Boaco	1,613	4,177	169,443
Carazo	Jinotepe	417	1,081	178,818
Chinandega	Chinandega	1,862	4,822	439,986
Chontales	Juigalpa	2,502	6,481	181,793
Estelí	Estelí	861	2,230	214,399
Granada	Granada	402	1,040	191,927
Jinotega	Jinotega	3,714	9,620	298,754
León	León	2,107	5,457	395,251
Madriz	Somoto	659	1,708	133,974
Managua	Managua	1,338	3,465	1,374,025
Masaya	Masaya	236	611	315,630
Matagalpa	Matagalpa	2,627	6,804	485,537
Nueva Segovia	Ocotal	1,194	3,093	212,557
Río San Juan	San Carlos	2,912	7,541	95,110
Rivas	Rivas	835	2,162	168,517
Autonomous regions				
North Atlantic	Puerto Cabezas	12,549	32,501	250,071
South Atlantic	Bluefields	10,636	27,546	376,548
TOTAL LAND AREA		46,464	120,340[4]	
INLAND WATER		3,874	10,034	
TOTAL		50,337[4]	130,373[4]	5,482,340

Demography

Population (2003): 5,482,000.
Density (2003)[5]: persons per sq mi 108.9, persons per sq km 42.1.
Urban-rural (2001): urban 56.5%; rural 43.5%.
Sex distribution (2000): male 49.96%; female 50.04%.
Age breakdown (2000): under 15, 39.7%; 15–29, 30.6%; 30–44, 17.0%; 45–59, 8.2%; 60–74, 3.7%; 75 and over, 0.8%.
Population projection: (2010) 6,378,000; (2020) 7,679,000.
Doubling time: 30 years.
Ethnic composition (2000): mestizo (Spanish/Indian) 63.1%; white 14.0%; black 8.0%; multiple ethnicities 5.0%; other 9.9%.
Religious affiliation (1995): Roman Catholic 85.1%; Protestant 11.6%, of which Evangelical 8.8%; nonreligious 1.3%; other 2.0%.
Major cities (1995): Managua (2001) 1,039,000[6]; León 123,865; Chinandega 97,387; Masaya 88,971; Granada 71,783; Estelí 71,550.

Vital statistics

Birth rate per 1,000 population (2002): 27.0 (world avg. 21.3).
Death rate per 1,000 population (2002): 4.8 (world avg. 9.1).
Natural increase rate per 1,000 population (2002): 22.2 (world avg. 12.2).
Total fertility rate (avg. births per childbearing woman; 2002): 3.1.
Life expectancy at birth (2002): male 67.4 years; female 71.4 years.
Major causes of death per 100,000 population (2000)[7]: diseases of the circulatory system 63; malignant neoplasms 30; accidents, injuries, and violence 20; diseases of the respiratory system 18; infectious and parasitic diseases 15.

National economy

Budget (2001). Revenue: C$7,654,000,000 (tax revenue 96.1%, of which tax on goods and services 67.1%, tax on income and profits 17.0%, import duties 7.7%; nontax revenue 3.9%). Expenditures: C$14,282,100,000 (current expenditure 64.6%, development expenditure 35.4%).
Public debt (external, outstanding; 2001): U.S.$5,437,000,000.
Production (metric tons except as noted). Agriculture, forestry, fishing (2002): sugarcane 3,389,000, corn (maize) 483,330, rice 264,000, dry beans 183,000, sorghum 90,000, oranges 73,000, bananas 54,000, cassava 52,000, coffee 48,000, soybeans 3,400; livestock (number of live animals) 3,350,000 cattle, 420,000 pigs; roundwood 5,920,000 cu m; fish catch (2000) 33,437, of which crustaceans 11,379. Mining and quarrying (2001): gold 117,350 troy oz. Manufacturing (value added in C$'000,000; 2000[8]): food 1,936; beverages 1,261; cement, bricks, tiles 538; refined petroleum 212; chemical products 191. Energy production (consumption): electricity (kW-hr; 1999) 2,148,000,000 (2,208,000,000); coal, none (none); crude petroleum (barrels; 1999) none (5,900,000); petroleum products (metric tons; 1999) 810,000 (1,155,000); natural gas, none (none).
Tourism (2001): receipts from visitors U.S.$109,000,000; expenditures by nationals abroad U.S.$76,000,000.
Land use (1994): forested 26.3%; meadows and pastures 45.3%; agricultural and under permanent cultivation 10.5%; other 17.9%.
Population economically active (2000): total 1,815,300; activity rate of total population 35.8% (participation rates: ages 15–64, 64.1%; female 29.5%; unemployed 9.8%).

Price and earnings indexes (1995 = 100)

	1996	1997	1998	1999	2000	2001	2002
Consumer price index	111.6	121.9	137.8	153.3	171	183.5	190.9
Monthly earnings index	106	119	138	167	...	...	...

Gross national product (2000): U.S.$2,053,000,000 (U.S.$410 per capita).

Structure of gross domestic product and labour force

	2001 in value C$'000	% of total value	labour force	% of labour force
Agriculture, forestry	11,024,400	32.4	728,000	38.3
Mining	242,700	0.7	10,800	0.6
Manufacturing	4,833,800	14.2	132,300	7.0
Construction	2,169,100	6.4	105,200	5.5
Public utilities	372,700	1.1	6,100	0.3
Transp. and commun.	1,137,800	3.4	52,600	2.8
Trade, restaurants	7,624,800	22.4	278,000	14.6
Finance, real estate	1,735,500	5.1	22,500	1.2
Pub. admin., defense	3,021,300	8.9	65,000	3.4
Services	1,843,400	5.4	303,300	16.0
Other	—	—	202,800[9]	10.7[9]
TOTAL	34,005,500	100.0	1,900,400[4]	100.0[4]

Household income and expenditure. Average household size (1995) 5.8.

Foreign trade[10]

Balance of trade (current prices)

	1997	1998	1999	2000	2001	2002
U.S.$'000,000	−794	−824	−1,154	−1,008	−1,028	−1,040
% of total	40.8%	41.8%	51.4%	43.9%	46.5%	46.6%

Imports (2001): U.S.$1,788,000,000 (nondurable consumer goods 26.5%, capital goods for industry 12.8%, crude petroleum 9.6%, transport equipment 8.0%). *Major import sources:* U.S. 27.4%; Venezuela 10.8%; Costa Rica 10.7%; Guatemala 8.2%; Mexico 6.9%; El Salvador 6.3%.
Exports (2001): U.S.$592,000,000 (manufactured products 24.7%, coffee 17.7%, beef 11.1%, sugar 8.3%, shrimp 6.4%, lobster 6.4%, gold 5.0%). *Major export destinations:* U.S. 28.2%; El Salvador 12.7%; Honduras 8.0%; Germany 6.4%; Costa Rica 5.5%.

Transport and communications

Transport. Railroads: [11]. Roads (1999): total length 16,382 km (paved 11%). Vehicles (2000): passenger cars 61,357; trucks and buses 91,014. Air transport (1999): passenger-km 67,000,000; metric ton-km cargo 7,000,000; airports (1997) with scheduled flights 10.

Communications

Medium	date	unit	number	units per 1,000 persons
Daily newspapers	2000	circulation	152,000	30
Radio	2000	receivers	1,370,000	270
Television	2000	receivers	350,000	69
Telephones	2002	main lines	171,600	32
Cellular telephones	2002	subscribers	239,900	45
Personal computers	2002	units	90,000	17
Internet	2002	users	150,000	28

Education and health

Educational attainment (1995). Percentage of population age 25 and over having: no formal schooling 30.6%; no formal schooling (literate) 3.9%; primary education 39.2%; secondary 17.0%; technical 3.1%; incomplete undergraduate 2.2%; complete undergraduate 4.0%. *Literacy* (2000): total population age 15 and over literate 66.5%; males literate 66.3%; females literate 66.8%.

Education (2000)

	schools	teachers	students	student/ teacher ratio
Primary (age 7–12)	7,224[12]	21,020	838,437	39.9
Secondary (age 13–18)	451[13]	5,970	315,354	52.8
Higher	10[13]	3,840	56,160	14.6

Health: physicians (1997) 3,725 (1 per 1,255 persons); hospital beds (1996) 6,666 (1 per 674 persons); infant mortality rate (2002) 32.5.
Food (2001): daily per capita caloric intake 2,256 (vegetable products 92%, animal products 8%); 99% of FAO recommended minimum requirement.

Military

Total active duty personnel (2002): 14,000 (army 85.7%, navy 5.7%, air force 8.6%). *Military expenditure as percentage of GNP* (1999): 1.2% (world 2.4%); per capita expenditure U.S.$5.

[1]Includes 2 unsuccessful 2001 presidential candidates meeting special conditions. [2]Lakes and lagoons are excluded from the areas of departments and autonomous regions. [3]Official projection based on 1995 census. [4]Detail does not add to total given because of rounding. [5]Based on land area. [6]Population of urban agglomeration. [7]Estimates. [8]At prices of 1980. [9]Represents unemployed. [10]Imports f.o.b. in balance of trade and c.i.f. in commodities and trading partners. [11]Public railroad service ended in January 1994; private rail service (2000) 4 mi (6 km). [12]1998. [13]1994.

Internet resources for further information:
- **Central Bank of Nicaragua http://www.bcn.gob.ni/english**
- **Instituto Nacional de Estadísticas y Censos http://www.inec.gob.ni**

Niger

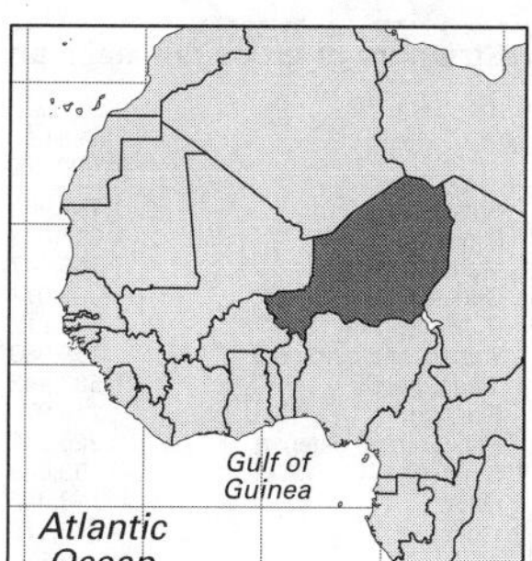

Official name: République du Niger (Republic of Niger).
Form of government: multiparty republic with one legislative house (National Assembly [83]).
Head of state and government: President, assisted by Prime Minister.
Capital: Niamey.
Official language: French.
Official religion: none.
Monetary unit: 1 CFA franc (CFAF) = 100 centimes; valuation (Sept. 8, 2003) 1 U.S.$ = CFAF 594.70; 1 £ = CFAF 942.93[1].

Area and population		area[2]		population
Departments	**Capitals**	sq mi	sq km	1990 estimate
Agadez	Agadez	244,869	634,209	189,000
Diffa	Diffa	54,138	140,216	227,000
Dosso	Dosso	11,970	31,002	982,000
Maradi	Maradi	14,896	38,581	1,415,000
Tahoua	Tahoua	41,188	106,677	1,373,000
Tillabéri	Tillabéri	34,604	89,623	1,818,000[3]
Zinder	Zinder	56,151	145,430	1,467,000
City				
Niamey	Niamey	259	670	[3]
TOTAL		458,075	1,186,408	7,471,000[4]

Demography

Population (2003): 11,380,000.
Density (2003)[2]: persons per sq mi 23.3, persons per sq km 9.0.
Urban-rural (2000): urban 20.1%; rural 79.9%.
Sex distribution (2001): male 49.93%; female 50.07%.
Age breakdown (2001): under 15, 48.0%; 15–29, 26.3%; 30–44, 14.1%; 45–59, 7.8%; 60–74, 3.2%; 75 and over, 0.6%.
Population projection: (2010) 13,647,000; (2020) 13,647,000.
Doubling time: 26 years.
Ethnolinguistic composition (2000): Zerma- (Djerma-) Songhai 25.7%; Tazarawa 14.9%; Fulani (Peul) 11.1%; Hausa 6.6%; other 41.7%.
Religious affiliation (2000): Sunnī Muslim 90.7%; traditional beliefs 8.7%; Christian 0.5%; other 0.1%.
Major cities (1988): Niamey 391,876 (urban agglomeration [2001] 821,000); Zinder 119,827; Maradi 110,005; Tahoua 49,948; Agadez 32,272.

Vital statistics

Birth rate per 1,000 population (2002): 50.2 (world avg. 21.3).
Death rate per 1,000 population (2002): 21.9 (world avg. 9.1).
Natural increase rate per 1,000 population (2002): 28.3 (world avg. 12.2).
Total fertility rate (avg. births per childbearing woman; 2002): 7.0.
Marriage rate per 1,000 population: n.a.
Divorce rate per 1,000 population: n.a.
Life expectancy at birth (2002): male 42.2 years; female 42.2 years.
Major causes of death: n.a.; however, among selected major causes of infectious disease registered at medical facilities were malaria, measles, diarrhea, meningitis, pneumonia, diphtheria, tetanus, viral hepatitis, and poliomyelitis; malnutrition and shortages of trained medical personnel are widespread.

National economy

Budget (2000). Revenue: CFAF 162,166,000,000 (taxes 63.4%, external aid and gifts 32.1%, nontax revenue 4.5%). Expenditures: CFAF 204,800,000,000 (current expenditures 67.6%, of which education 13.7%, defense 6.8%, economic services 4.5%, health 3.9%; development expenditures 32.4%).
Public debt (external, outstanding; 2001): U.S.$1,371,000,000.
Tourism (2000): receipts from visitors U.S.$24,000,000; expenditures by nationals abroad U.S.$28,000,000.
Gross national product (2001): U.S.$2,000,000,000 (U.S.$180 per capita).

Structure of gross domestic product and labour force	2000		1988	
	in value CFAF '000,000	% of total value	labour force[5]	% of labour force[5]
Agriculture	484,400	37.8	1,764,049	76.2
Mining	87,500	6.8	5,295	0.2
Manufacturing	87,000	6.8	65,793	2.8
Construction	24,100	1.9	13,742	0.6
Public utilities	28,800	2.2	1,778	0.1
Transp. and commun.	60,900	4.8	14,764	0.6
Trade and finance	237,100	18.5	210,354	9.1
Pub. admin., defense	109,600	8.6	59,271	2.6
Services	131,400	10.3	63,991	2.8
Other	29,600[6]	2.3[6]	116,657	5.0
TOTAL	1,280,400	100.0	2,315,694	100.0

Production (metric tons except as noted). Agriculture, forestry, fishing (2002): millet 2,000,000, sorghum 655,729, cowpeas 350,000, onions 271,218, sugarcane 211,354, peanuts (groundnuts) 129,336, cassava 105,494, tomatoes 99,266, rice 76,400, tobacco leaf 164; livestock (number of live animals) 6,900,000 goats, 4,500,000 sheep, 2,260,000 cattle, 580,000 asses, 415,000 camels, 105,000 horses; roundwood 8,601,400 cu m; fish catch (2000) 16,265. Mining and quarrying: salt (1997) 3,000; uranium (2000) 2,898. Manufacturing (value added in CFAF '000,000; 1998): paper and products 3,171; food 1,697; soaps and other chemical products 1,547; textiles 784. Construction (value added in CFAF; 1994): 16,100,000,000. Energy production (consumption): electricity (kW-hr; 2000) 199,200,000 (326,600,000); coal (metric tons; 1999) 175,000 (175,000); crude petroleum, none (none); petroleum products (metric tons; 2000) none (165,700); natural gas, none (none).
Population economically active (1988)[5]: total 2,315,694; activity rate of total population 31.9% (participation rates: ages 15–64, 55.2%; female 20.4%).

Price and earnings indexes (1995 = 100)	1996	1997	1998	1999	2000	2001	2002
Consumer price index	105.3	108.4	113.3	110.7	113.9	118.5	121.6
Annual earnings index	...	...	...	...	...	...	...

Household income and expenditure. Average household size (1998) 6.3; income per household: n.a.; expenditure (1987): food and beverages 43.1%, housing 22.8%, clothing 10.0%.
Land use (1994): forested 2.0%; meadows and pastures 8.2%; agricultural and under permanent cultivation 2.9%; other (largely desert) 86.9%.

Foreign trade

Balance of trade (current prices)	1996	1997	1998	1999	2000	2001
CFAF '000,000	+90,200	+72,500	–41,300	–29,900	–28,900	–37,500
% of total	20.1%	17.2%	9.5%	7.8%	6.7%	8.7%

Imports (2000): CFAF 230,400,000,000 (food products 27.5%, petroleum products 20.7%, capital goods 19.4%, intermediate goods 7.5%). *Major import sources:* France 20.1%; Côte d'Ivoire 13.2%; Nigeria 10.3%; Japan 6.2%; Germany 2.2%.
Exports (2000): CFAF 201,200,000,000 (2001; uranium 31.9%, livestock [mostly live cattle, sheep, and goats] 20.6%, cowpeas 9.6%). *Major export destinations:* France 48.1%; Nigeria 40.6%; Côte d'Ivoire 1.6%.

Transport and communications

Transport. Railroads: none. Roads (1999): total length 6,276 mi, 10,100 km (paved 8%). Vehicles (1996): passenger cars 38,220, trucks and buses 15,200. Air transport (1998)[7]: passenger-mi 160,477,000, passenger-km 258,263,000; short ton-mi cargo 9,263,000, metric ton-km cargo 13,524,000; airports (1999) with scheduled flights 6.

Communications				units
Medium	date	unit	number	per 1,000 persons
Daily newspapers	1996	circulation	2,000	0.2
Radio	2000	receivers	1,270,000	121
Television	2000	receivers	388,000	37
Telephones	2001	main lines	21,700	1.9
Cellular telephones	2001	subscribers	1,800	0.1
Personal computers	2001	units	6,000	0.5
Internet	2001	users	12,000	1.1

Education and health

Educational attainment (1988). Percentage of population age 25 and over having: no formal schooling 85.0%; Koranic education 11.2%; primary education 2.5%; secondary 1.1%; higher 0.2%. *Literacy* (1995): total population age 15 and over literate 641,000 (13.6%); males literate 482,000 (20.9%); females literate 159,000 (6.6%).

Education (1997–98)	schools	teachers	students	student/ teacher ratio
Primary (age 7–12)	3,175	11,545	482,065	41.8
Secondary (age 13–19)[8]	...	3,579	97,675	27.3
Voc., teacher tr.[8]	...	215	2,145	10.0
Higher[9]	2	355	5,569	15.7

Health: physicians (1997) 324 (1 per 28,171 persons); hospital beds, n.a.; infant mortality rate per 1,000 live births (2002) 124.6.
Food (2001): daily per capita caloric intake 2,118 (vegetable products 94%, animal products 6%); 90% of FAO recommended minimum requirement.

Military

Total active duty personnel (2002): 5,300 (army 98.1%, air force 1.9%). *Military expenditure as percentage of GNP* (1999): 1.2% (world 2.4%); per capita expenditure U.S.$2.

[1]Formerly pegged to the French franc and since Jan. 1, 2002, to the euro at the rate of 1€ = CFAF 655.96. [2]The departmental areas and total shown are based on old survey. The total area, according to a more recent survey, is 489,000 sq mi (1,267,000 sq km). [3]Tillabéri includes Niamey. [4]June 2001 preliminary census total equals 10,790,352. [5]Excluding nomadic population. [6]Import taxes and duties. [7]Represents 1/11 of the traffic of Air Afrique, which is operated by 11 West African states. [8]1996–97. [9]Université de Niamey and École Nationale d'Administration du Niger only.

Internet resources for further information:
- **Niger Profile**
  http://www.nigerembassyusa.org/profile.html
- **Investir en zone franc**
  http://www.izf.net/izf/Index.htm

Nigeria

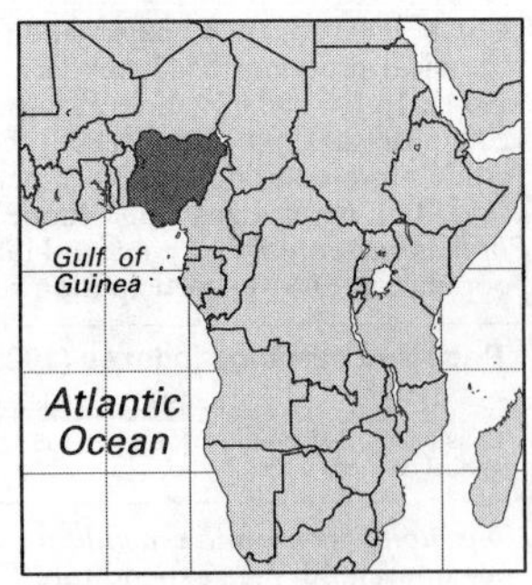

Official name: Federal Republic of Nigeria.
Form of government: federal republic with two legislative bodies (Senate [109]; House of Representatives [360]).
Head of state and government: President.
Capital: Abuja.
Official language: English.
Official religion: none.
Monetary unit: 1 Nigerian naira (₦) = 100 kobo; valuation (Sept. 8, 2003) 1 U.S.$ = ₦131.15; 1 £ = ₦207.95.

Area and population

States[1]	area sq km	population 1995 estimate	States[1]	area sq km	population 1995 estimate
Abia	6,320	2,569,362[2]	Kebbi	36,800	2,305,768
Adamawa	36,917	2,374,892	Kogi	29,833	2,346,936
Akwa Ibom	7,081	2,638,413	Kwara	36,825	1,751,464
Anambra	4,844	3,094,783	Lagos	3,345	6,357,253
Bauchi	45,837	4,801,569[3]	Nassarawa	27,117	[6]
Bayelsa	10,773	[4]	Niger	76,363	2,775,526
Benue	34,059	3,108,754	Ogun	16,762	2,614,747
Borno	70,898	2,903,238	Ondo	14,606	4,343,230[5]
Cross River	20,156	2,085,926	Osun	9,251	2,463,185
Delta	17,698	2,873,711	Oyo	28,454	3,900,803
Ebonyi	5,670	[2]	Plateau	30,913	3,671,498[6]
Edo	17,802	2,414,919	Rivers	11,077	4,454,337[4]
Ekiti	6,353	[5]	Sokoto	25,973	4,911,118[7]
Enugu	7,161	3,534,633[2]	Taraba	54,473	1,655,443
Gombe	18,768	[3]	Yobe	45,502	1,578,172
Imo	5,530	2,779,028	Zamfara	39,762	[7]
Jigawa	23,154	3,164,134			
Kaduna	46,053	4,438,007	**Federal Capital**		
Kano	20,131	6,297,165	**Territory**		
Katsina	24,192	4,336,363	Abuja	7,315	423,391
			TOTAL	923,768	98,967,768

Demography

Population (2003): 125,275,000.
Density (2003): persons per sq mi 351.2, persons per sq km 135.6.
Urban-rural (2002): urban 44.9%; rural 55.1%.
Sex distribution (2001): male 50.60%; female 49.40%.
Age breakdown (2001): under 15, 43.7%; 15–29, 27.8%; 30–44, 15.3%; 45–59, 8.6%; 60–74, 3.9%; 75 and over, 0.7%.
Population projection: (2010) 147,677,000; (2020) 179,288,000.
Ethnic composition (2000): Yoruba 17.5%; Hausa 17.2%; Igbo (Ibo) 13.3%; Fulani 10.7%; Ibibio 4.1%; Kanuri 3.6%; Egba 2.9%; Tiv 2.6%; Bura 1.1%; Nupe 1.0%; Edo 1.0%; other 25.0%.
Religious affiliation (2000): Christian 45.9%, of which independent Christian 15.0%, Anglican 13.0%, other Protestant 9.0%, Roman Catholic 8.0%; Muslim 43.9%; African indigenous 9.8%; other 0.4%.
Major cities (1991): Lagos 5,197,247 (urban agglomeration [2000] 13,427,000); Kano 2,166,554; Ibadan (2000) 1,731,000; Kaduna 993,642; Benin City 762,719; Port Harcourt 703,421; Maiduguri 618,278; Zaria 612,257; Ilorin 532,089.

Vital statistics

Birth rate per 1,000 population (2002): 39.2 (world avg. 21.3).
Death rate per 1,000 population (2002): 13.6 (world avg. 9.1).
Natural increase rate per 1,000 population (2002): 25.7 (world avg. 12.2).
Total fertility rate (avg. births per childbearing woman; 2002): 5.5.
Life expectancy at birth (2002): male 51.4 years; female 51.6 years.

National economy

Budget (2000). Revenue: ₦1,927,087,000,000 (tax revenue 33.1%, of which petroleum profit tax 17.3%, import duties, excise taxes, and fees 6.0%; non-tax revenue 66.9%, of which oil export proceeds 49.1%). Expenditures: ₦1,834,305,000,000 (1999; recurrent expenditure 75.6%, of which debt service 18.8%, education 5.2%, defense 4.6%; capital expenditure 24.4%).
Production (metric tons except as noted). Agriculture, forestry, fishing (2002): cassava 34,476,000, yams 26,849,000, sorghum 7,704,000, millet 6,100,000, corn (maize) 4,934,000, taro 3,929,000, rice 3,192,000, peanuts (groundnuts) 2,699,000, sweet potatoes 2,503,000, cow peas 2,389,000, plantains 1,999,000, tomatoes 879,000; livestock 27,000,000 goats, 22,000,000 sheep, 20,000,000 cattle, 5,500,000 pigs; roundwood 69,482,328 cu m; fish catch (2000) 467,095. Mining and quarrying (2000): limestone 2,000,000; marble 30,000. Manufacturing (value added in ₦'000,000; 1995): food and beverages 25,415; textiles 16,193; chemical products 11,181; machinery and transport equipment 5,639; paper products 2,828. Energy production (consumption): electricity (kW-hr; 1999) 16,138,000,000 (16,138,000,000); coal (metric tons; 1999) 60,000 (60,000); crude petroleum (barrels; 2001) 757,498,000 (106,580,000); petroleum products (metric tons; 1999) 8,458,000 (8,079,000); natural gas (cu m; 2001) 757,498,000 (106,580,000).
Household income and expenditure. Avg. household size (1995) 4.7; annual income per household (1992–93) ₦15,000 (U.S.$760); sources of income: n.a.; expenditures: n.a.
Gross national product (at current market prices; 2001): U.S.$37,100,000,000 (U.S.$290 per capita).

Structure of gross domestic product and labour force

	2000		1986	
	in value ₦'000,000	% of total value	labour force	% of labour force
Agriculture	1,191,989	28.5	13,259,000	43.1
Mining[8]	1,657,876	39.7	6,800	0.1
Manufacturing	166,247	4.0	1,263,700	4.1
Construction	31,017	0.7	545,600	1.8
Public utilities	2,212	0.1	130,400	0.4
Transp. and commun.	108,080	2.6	1,111,900	3.6
Trade, hotels	533,442	12.8	7,417,400	24.1
Finance	216,270	5.1	120,100	0.4
Pub. admin., defense	226,306	5.4	4,902,100	15.9
Services	53,688	1.3		
Other	–8,948[9]	–0.2[9]	2,008,500[10]	6.5[10]
TOTAL	4,178,179	100.0	30,765,500	100.0

Public debt (external, outstanding; 2001): U.S.$29,215,000,000.
Population economically active (1993–94): total 29,000,000; activity rate 31.0% (participation rates: ages 15–59, 64.4%; female 44.0%).

Price and earnings indexes (1995 = 100)

	1996	1997	1998	1999	2000	2001	2002
Consumer price index	129.3	139.9	154.3	161.7	185.2	209.2	236.1
Earnings index	...	...	...	...	...	...	...

Tourism (2001): receipts U.S.$158,000,000; expenditures U.S.$700,000,000.
Land use (1994): forest 15.7%; pasture 43.9%; agriculture 35.9%; other 4.5%.

Foreign trade[11]

Balance of trade (current prices)

	1997	1998	1999	2000	2001	2002
U.S.$'000,000	+5,706	+644	+5,268	+12,254	+5,675	+7,560
% of total	23.1%	3.4%	23.5%	41.3%	19.7%	33.4%

Imports (2002): U.S.$7,547,000,000 ([2000] machinery and apparatus 21.1%; chemicals and chemical products 20.1%; food 18.9%, of which cereals 7.1%; road vehicles 10.4%; iron and steel 6.2%). *Major import sources* (2001): U.K. 9.4%; U.S. 9.2%; China 8.8%; Germany 8.5%; France 7.2%; The Netherlands 5.3%.
Exports (2002): U.S.$15,107,000,000 (crude petroleum 98.3%, remainder 1.7%). *Major export destinations* (2001): U.S. 40.5%; Spain 8.5%; Brazil 6.7%; India 6.5%; France 5.2%.

Transport and communications

Transport. Railroads (2000): length 3,505 km; passenger-km 179,000,000[12]; metric ton-km cargo 120,000,000[12]. Roads (1999): total length 62,598 km (paved 19%). Vehicles (1996): passenger cars 773,000; trucks and buses 68,300[13]. Air transport[14] (2000): passenger-km 111,566,000; metric ton-km cargo 2,068,000; airports (1998) 12.

Communications

Medium	date	unit	number	units per 1,000 persons
Daily newspapers	2000	circulation	2,770,000	24
Radio	2000	receivers	23,000,000	200
Television	2000	receivers	7,840,000	68
Telephones	2002	main lines	702,000	5.8
Cellular telephones	2002	subscribers	1,633,100	14.6
Personal computers	2002	units	800,000	6.8
Internet	2002	users	200,000	1.8

Education and health

Literacy (2002): total population age 15 and over literate 40,700,000 (64.1%); males literate 22,600,000 (62.3%); females literate 18,100,000 (56.2%).

Education (2002)

	schools	teachers	students	student/ teacher ratio
Primary (age 6–12)	49,343	537,741	29,575,790	55.0
Secondary (age 12–17)	10,000	187,126	7,485,072	40.0
Higher	158	...	1,249,776	...

Health (2002): physicians 25,914 (1 per 4,722 persons); hospital beds 54,872 (1 per 2,230 persons); infant mortality rate (2002) 72.2.
Food (2001): daily per capita caloric intake 2,747 (vegetable products 97%, animal products 3%); 116% of FAO recommended minimum requirement.

Military

Total active duty personnel (2002): 78,500 (army 79.0%, navy 8.9%, air force 12.1%). *Military expenditure as percentage of GNP* (1999): 1.7% (world 2.4%); per capita expenditure U.S.$13.

[1]In October 1996 six new states were created: Bayelsa, Ebonyi, Ekiti, Gombe, Nassarawa, and Zamfara. [2]Ebonyi is included partly in Abia and partly in Enugu. [3]Bauchi includes Gombe. [4]Rivers includes Bayelsa. [5]Ondo includes Ekiti. [6]Plateau includes Nassarawa. [7]Sokoto includes Zamfara. [8]Includes ₦1,653,212,000,000 (39.5%) from petroleum and natural gas. [9]Less subsidies. [10]Includes 1,263,000 unemployed. [11]Imports c.i.f.; exports f.o.b. [12]1997. [13]1995. [14]Nigeria Airways only.

Internet resources for further information:
- **Information on corporate Nigeria http://www.nigeriabusinessinfo.com**
- **Central Bank of Nigeria http://www.cenbank.org/welcome.htm**

Northern Mariana Islands

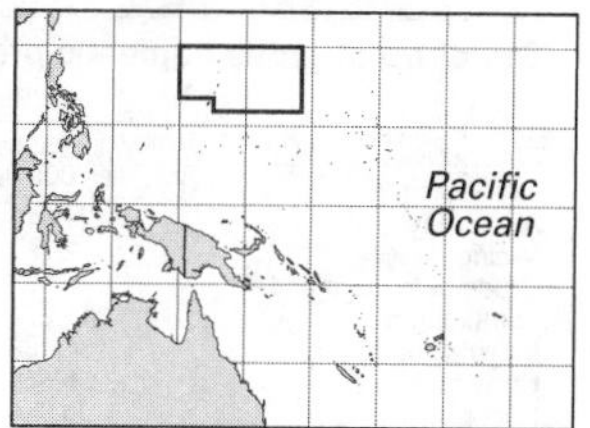

Official name: Commonwealth of the Northern Mariana Islands.
Political status: self-governing commonwealth in association with the United States, having two legislative houses (Senate [9]; House of Representatives [18])[1].
Chief of state: President of the United States.
Head of government: Governor.
Capital: Capital Hill, Saipan.
Official languages: Chamorro, Carolinian, and English.
Official religion: none.
Monetary unit: 1 dollar (U.S.$) = 100 cents; valuation (Sept. 8, 2003) 1 U.S.$ = £0.63.

Area and population

		area		population
Municipal councils	Major villages	sq mi	sq km	2000 census
Northern Islands[2]	...	55.3	143.2	6
Rota (island)	Songsong	32.8	85.0	3,283
Saipan (island)	San Antonio	46.5	120.4	62,392
Tinian[3]	San Jose	41.9	108.5	3,540
TOTAL		176.5[4]	457.1[4]	69,221[5]

Demography

Population (2003): 73,300.
Density (2003): persons per sq mi 398.4, persons per sq km 153.7.
Urban-rural (2002)[6]: urban 90.0%; rural 10.0%.
Sex distribution (2000): male 46.21%; female 53.79%.
Age breakdown (2000): under 15, 22.5%; 15–34, 45.8%; 35–59, 29.0%; 60–74, 2.3%; 75 and over, 0.4%.
Population projection: (2010) 73,000; (2020) 73,000.
Doubling time: 39 years.
Ethnic composition (2000)[7]: Filipino 26.2%; Chinese 22.1%; Chamorro 21.3%; Carolinian 3.8%; other Asian 7.5%; other Pacific Islander 6.6%; white 1.8%; multiethnic and other 10.7%.
Religious affiliation (1995)[8]: Roman Catholic 59.6%; Protestant 18.7%; other Christian 1.4%; other 20.3%.
Major villages (2000)[6, 9]: San Antonio 4,741; Garapan 3,588; Capital Hill 1,498; Songsong (on Rota) 1,411; San Jose (on Tinian) 1,361.

Vital statistics

Birth rate per 1,000 population (2002): 20.0 (world avg. 21.3).
Death rate per 1,000 population (2002): 2.4 (world avg. 9.1).
Natural increase rate per 1,000 population (2002): 17.6 (world avg. 12.2).
Total fertility rate (avg. births per childbearing woman; 2002): 1.4.
Marriages per 1,000 population ages 15 and older (2000): 526.3.
Divorce rate per 1,000 population (2000): 16.9.
Life expectancy at birth (2002): male 72.9 years; female 79.2 years.
Major causes of death per 100,000 population (1994–96 avg.): diseases of the circulatory system 53.3, of which cerebrovascular disease 25.8, ischemic heart diseases 21.8; malignant neoplasms (cancers) 33.3; accidents 29.8; diabetes mellitus 10.9.

National economy

Budget (2001). Revenue: U.S.$255,391,000 (tax revenue 70.6%, of which local revenue 83.3%, income tax 22.8%, corporate tax 21.3%, excise tax 8.5%; non-tax revenue 29.4%). Expenditures: U.S.$245,200,000 (health 20.4%, education 20.1%, general government 15.0%, social services 12.0%, public safety 9.3%).
Tourism (1998): receipts from visitors U.S.$394,000,000; expenditures by nationals abroad, n.a.
Land use (1990): forested, n.a.; meadows and pastures 3.7%; agricultural and under permanent cultivation 4.0%; other 92.3%.
Gross national product (1999): U.S.$664,600,000 (U.S.$9,600 per capita).

Structure of labour force

	2000	
	labour force	% of labour force
Agriculture, forestry, and fishing	623	1.4
Mining and quarrying	—	—
Manufacturing	17,398	39.1
Public utilities	2,117	4.8
Construction	2,785	6.2
Transp. and commun.	1,449	3.3
Trade	3,736	8.4
Finance, insurance, and real estate	1,013	2.3
Pub. admin., defense	2,583	5.8
Services	10,446	23.5
Other	2,321	5.2
TOTAL	44,471	100.0

Production (metric tons except as noted). Agriculture, forestry, fishing (1989): melons 165, cucumbers 83, bananas 46, betelnuts 38, Chinese cabbage 33, coconuts 30, eggplant 23; livestock (number of live animals; 1997) 1,789 cattle, 831 pigs, 249 goats, 29,409 chickens; roundwood, n.a.; fish catch (2000) 189. Mining and quarrying: negligible amount of quarrying for building material. Manufacturing (value of sales in U.S.$'000,000; 1997): garments 700; stone, glass, or ceramic products 21; food products 6. Construction (new permits in U.S.$'000,000; 1998): 63.3. Energy production (consumption): electricity (kW-hr) n.a.[10]; coal, none (none); crude petroleum, none (none); petroleum products, none (none); natural gas, none (none).
Population economically active (2000): total 44,471; activity rate of total population 64.2% (participation rates: ages 16 and over, 84.1%; female 49.9%; unemployed 3.9%).

Price index (1990 = 100)

	1992	1993	1994	1995	1996	1997	1998
Consumer price index	116.9	122.0	125.4	127.7	131.5	132.9	132.5

Public debt (external, outstanding; 1999): U.S.$146,000,000.
Household income and expenditure. Average household size (2000) 3.7; average income per household (2000) U.S.$37,015; sources of income (1994): wages 83.9%, interest and rental 7.2%, self-employment 7.2%, transfer payments 1.7%.

Foreign trade

Balance of trade (current prices)

	1989	1990	1991
U.S.$'000,000	−162	−138	−129
% of total	34.7%	25.3%	19.7%

Imports (1997): U.S.$836,200,000 (clothing and accessories 37.0%, foodstuffs 9.6%, petroleum and petroleum products 8.2%, transport equipment and parts 5.0%, construction materials 4.2%). *Major import sources:* Guam 35.6%, Hong Kong 24.0%, Japan 14.1%, South Korea 9.6%, United States 7.6%.
Exports (2002): U.S.$817,000,000[11] (garments and accessories 99.8%, of which cotton garments 69.8%; remainder 0.2%). *Major export destinations:* nearly all to the United States.

Transport and communications

Transport. Railroads: none. Roads (1998): total length *c.* 225 mi, *c.* 360 km (paved, nearly 100%). Vehicles (2001): passenger cars 11,019; trucks and buses 4,928. Merchant marine (1992): vessels (100 gross tons and over) 2; total deadweight tonnage 856. Air transport (1999)[12]: aircraft landings 23,853; boarding passengers 562,364; airports (1999) with scheduled flights 2[13].

Communications

Medium	date	unit	number	units per 1,000 persons
Radio	1999	receivers	10,500	152
Television	1999	receivers	4,100	59
Telephones	2000	main lines	26,800	506
Cellular telephones	2000	subscribers	3,000	57
Personal computers	...	units	...	...
Internet	...	users	...	...

Education and health

Educational attainment (2000). Percentage of population age 25 and over having: no formal schooling 0.0%; primary education 13.7%; some secondary 17.0%; completed secondary 35.6%; some postsecondary 12.6%; completed undergraduate or higher 21.1%. *Literacy* (1990): total population age 10 and over literate 35,490 (98.8%); males literate 18,790 (99.0%); females literate 16,700 (98.6%).

Education (2000–01)

	schools	teachers	students	student/ teacher ratio
Primary (age 6–11)	12[14]	392[15]	7,446	19
Secondary (age 12–17)	6[14]	266[15]	4,927	18.5
Vocational	—	—	—	—
Higher[16]	1	504	2,383	4.7

Health: hospital beds (1998): 74 (1 per 899 persons); infant mortality rate per 1,000 live births (2002): 7.5.
Food: n.a.

Military

The United States is responsible for military defense; headquarters of the U.S. Pacific Command are in Hawaii.

[1]Residents elect a nonvoting representative to U.S. Congress. [2]Comprises the islands of Agrihan, Pagan, and Alamagan, as well as seven other uninhabited islands: Farallon de Pajaros (Uracas), Maug (East, West, and North islands), Asuncion, Guguan, Serigan, Anatahan, and Farallon de Medinilla. [3]Comprises Tinian island and Aguijan island. [4]Area measured at high tide; at low tide, total dry land area is 184.0 square miles (476.6 square km). [5]The 1995 census totaling 58,846 included 27,478 U.S. citizens and 31,368 aliens working primarily in the garment industry. [6]All of Saipan was designated an urban area in 2002. [7]Includes aliens. [8]Unofficial estimate. [9]All villages are unincorporated census designated places. [10]The installed electrical capacity in 1992 was 114,020 kilowatts. [11]To U.S. only. [12]Saipan International Airport only. [13]International flights are regularly scheduled at Saipan and at Rota; Tinian has nonscheduled domestic service. Additional domestic airports mainly handle charter flights. [14]Excludes 18 private schools. [15]Estimate. [16]Northern Marianas College; 1995–96.

Internet resources for further information:
- **Bank of Hawaii: Economics Research Center http://www.boh.com/econ/pacific**
- **CNMI: Central Statistics Division http://www.commerce.gov.mp/csdhome.htm**

Norway

Official name: Kongeriket Norge (Kingdom of Norway).
Form of government: constitutional monarchy with one legislative house (Parliament [165]).
Chief of state: King.
Head of government: Prime Minister.
Capital: Oslo.
Official language: Norwegian.
Official religion: Evangelical Lutheran.
Monetary unit: 1 Norwegian krone (NKr) = 100 øre; valuation (Sept. 8, 2003) 1 U.S.$ = NKr 7.47; 1 £ = NKr 11.84.

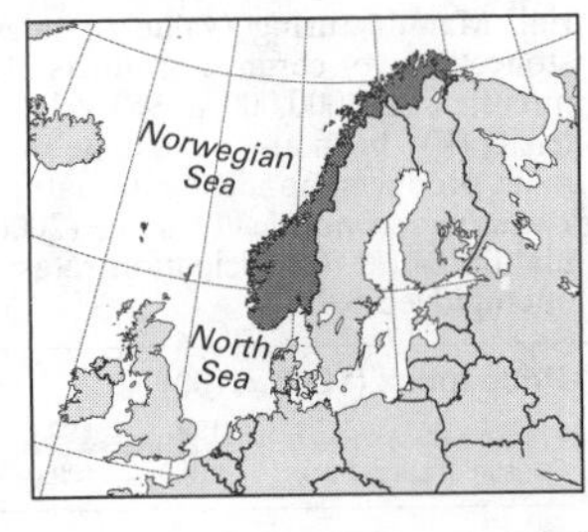

Area and population

Counties	Capitals	area[1] sq mi	area[1] sq km	population 2003[2] estimate
Akershus	Oslo	1,898	4,917	483,283
Aust-Agder	Arendal	3,557	9,212	103,195
Buskerud	Drammen	5,763	14,927	241,371
Finnmark	Vadsø	18,779	48,637	73,514
Hedmark	Hamar	10,575	27,388	188,281
Hordaland	Bergen	6,036	15,634	441,660
Møre og Romsdal	Molde	5,832	15,104	244,309
Nordland	Bodø	14,798	38,327	236,950
Nord-Trøndelag	Steinkjer	8,647	22,396	127,610
Oppland	Lillehammer	9,726	25,191	183,582
Oslo	Oslo	175	454	517,401
Østfold	Moss	1,615	4,183	255,122
Rogaland	Stavanger	3,529	9,141	385,020
Sogn og Fjordane	Leikanger	7,189	18,620	107,274
Sør-Trøndelag	Trondheim	7,271	18,838	268,188
Telemark	Skien	5,913	15,315	165,855
Troms	Tromsø	10,032	25,984	152,247
Vest-Agder	Kristiansand	2,811	7,281	159,219
Vestfold	Tønsberg	856	2,216	218,171
TOTAL		125,004[3]	323,758[3]	4,552,252[4]

Demography

Population (2003): 4,569,000.
Density (2003): persons per sq mi 36.6, persons per sq km 14.1.
Urban-rural (1990): urban 75.0%; rural 25.0%.
Sex distribution (2003[2]): male 49.56%; female 50.44%.
Age breakdown (2003[2]): under 15, 20.0%; 15–29, 18.7%; 30–44, 22.4%; 45–59, 19.7%; 60–74, 11.4%; 75 and over, 7.8%.
Population projection: (2010) 4,736,000; (2020) 4,989,000.
Ethnic composition (2000): Norwegian 93.8%; Vietnamese 2.4%; Swedish 0.5%; Punjabi 0.4%; Urdu 0.3%; U.S. white 0.3%; Lapp 0.3%; Danish 0.3%; other 1.7%.
Major cities (2003)[2, 5]: Oslo 517,401 (urban agglomeration [2001] 787,000); Bergen 235,423; Trondheim 152,699; Stavanger 111,007; Bærum 102,529.

Vital statistics

Birth rate per 1,000 population (2001): 12.6 (world avg. 21.3); (1999) legitimate 49.1%; illegitimate 50.9%.
Death rate per 1,000 population (2001): 9.8 (world avg. 9.1).
Natural increase rate per 1,000 population (2001): 2.8 (world avg. 12.2).
Total fertility rate (avg. births per childbearing woman; 2001): 1.8.
Marriage rate per 1,000 population (2000): 5.0.
Divorce rate per 1,000 population (2000): 2.2.
Life expectancy at birth (2000): male 76.0 years; female 81.4 years.
Major causes of death per 100,000 population (1999): malignant neoplasms (cancers) 239.4; ischemic heart disease 196.0; cerebrovascular disease 106.1.

National economy

Budget (2001). Revenue: NKr 829,345,000,000 (value-added taxes 30.7%, tax on income 28.6%, social security taxes 20.2%). Expenditures: NKr 617,372,000,000 (social security and welfare 37.8%, health 15.9%, education 13.6%, debt service 4.6%).
Land use (1994): forested 27.2%; meadows and pastures 0.4%; agricultural and under permanent cultivation 2.9%; built-up and other 69.5%.
Production (metric tons except as noted). Agriculture, forestry, fishing (2002): barley 601,000, potatoes 389,000, oats 312,000, wheat 268,000; livestock (number of live animals) 2,396,000 sheep, 967,200 cattle; roundwood (2002) 8,649,000 cu m; fish catch (2001) 2,682,516, of which herring 581,161, capelin 482,834, cod 208,839[6], mackerel 180,602. Mining and quarrying (2001): ilmenite concentrate 600,000, iron ore (metal content) 340,000, cobalt 3,134. Manufacturing (value added in NKr '000,000; 1999): machinery and transport equipment 30,514; food products 29,361; paper and paper products 19,125; chemical and refined petroleum products 12,411; wood products 4,804; primary aluminum 1,068,000 metric tons. Energy production (consumption): electricity (kW-hr; 1999) 123,977,000,000 (122,167,000,000); coal (metric tons; 1999) 489,000 (1,045,000); crude petroleum (barrels; 2001) 1,275,000,000 ([1999] 112,000,000); petroleum products (metric tons; 1999) 17,766,000 (11,232,000); natural gas (cu m; 2001) 57,848,000,000 ([1999] 5,607,000,000).
Household income and expenditure. Average household size (2001) 2.3; consumption expenditure per household (1998) NKr 357,458 (U.S.$47,376); expenditure (1996–98): transportation 24.1%, housing 16.6%, food 12.9%, recreation and education 11.3%, household furniture and equipment 8.7%.
Gross national product (2001): U.S.$160,800,000,000 (U.S.$35,630 per capita).

Structure of gross domestic product and labour force

	2001 in value NKr '000,000	2001 % of total value	2001 labour force	2001 % of labour force
Agriculture	25,010	1.7	89,000	3.8
Mining	2,769	0.2	7	7
Crude petroleum and natural gas	311,274	20.6	32,000	1.4
Manufacturing	131,432	8.7	290,000[7]	12.3[7]
Construction	56,654	3.7	152,000	6.4
Public utilities	30,844	2.0	18,000	0.8
Transp. and commun.	119,351	7.9	169,000	7.1
Trade	141,378[8]	9.4[8]	398,000	16.9
Finance	247,619	16.4	273,000	11.6
Pub. admin., defense	233,950	15.5	855,000	36.2
Services	68,652	4.5		
Other	141,935	9.4	84,000[9]	3.5[9]
TOTAL	1,510,866[3]	100.0	2,362,000[3]	100.0

Population economically active (1999): total 2,333,000; activity rate of total population 52.4% (participation rates: ages 16–64 [1996] 79.1%; female 46.0%; unemployed 4.9%).

Price and earnings indexes (1995 = 100)

	1996	1997	1998	1999	2000	2001	2002
Consumer price index	101.3	103.9	106.2	108.7	112.0	115.4	116.9
Hourly earnings index	...	...	...	...	...	...	...

National debt (2002): U.S.$53,125,000,000.
Tourism (2001): receipts U.S.$2,037,000,000; expenditures U.S.$4,305,000,000.

Foreign trade[10]

Balance of trade (current prices)

	1997	1998	1999	2000	2001	2002
NKr '000,000	+90,189	+25,998	+84,886	+219,605	+233,805	+208,365
% of total	15.1%	4.5%	13.8%	27.6%	28.3%	27.4%

Imports (2001): NKr 296,161,000,000 (machinery and transport equipment 42.1%, of which road vehicles 8.7%; ships 3.4%; chemicals and chemical products 9.5%; metals and metal products 7.7%; food products 6.7%; petroleum products 3.0%). *Major import sources:* Sweden 15.2%; Germany 12.6%; U.K. 7.9%; Denmark 7.1%; U.S. 7.1%.
Exports (2001): NKr 529,966,000,000 (crude petroleum 44.3%; natural gas 11.5%; machinery and transport equipment 11.4%; metals and metal products 7.9%; fish 5.6%). *Major export destinations:* U.K. 19.6%; Germany 12.2%; The Netherlands 10.4%; France 9.4%; Sweden 8.0%.

Transport and communications

Transport. Railroads (2001): route length 4,178 km; passenger-km 2,536,000,000; metric ton-km cargo 2,451,000,000. Roads (2002): total length 91,545 km (paved 74%[11]). Vehicles (2001): passenger cars 1,872,862; trucks and buses 444,626. Air transport (2001): passenger-km 4,120,000,000; metric ton-km cargo (2000) 1,254,364,000; airports (1996) 50.

Communications

Medium	date	unit	number	units per 1,000 persons
Daily newspapers	2000	circulation	2,620,000	585
Radio	2000	receivers	4,110,000	915
Television	2000	receivers	3,000,000	669
Telephones	2002	main lines	3,325,000	732
Cellular telephones	2002	subscribers	3,842,000	846
Personal computers	2002	units	2,300,000	507
Internet	2001	users	2,300,000	510

Education and health

Educational attainment (2000). Percentage of population age 16 and over having: primary and lower secondary education 21.5%; higher secondary 55.0%; higher 21.3%; unknown 2.2%. *Literacy* (2000): virtually 100% literate.

Education (2000–01)

	schools	teachers	students	student/ teacher ratio
Primary (age 7–12)	3,260	45,247	590,471	13.0
Secondary (age 13–18) and vocational	696	20,567	220,328	10.7
Higher	70	12,071	191,454	15.9

Health: physicians (1996) 15,368 (1 per 285 persons); hospital beds (2000) 22,486 (1 per 199 persons); infant mortality rate (1999) 3.9.
Food (2001): daily per capita caloric intake 3,382 (vegetable products 67%, animal products 33%); 126% of FAO recommended minimum requirement.

Military

Total active duty personnel (2002): 25,800 (army 57.0%, navy 23.6%, air force 19.4%). *Military expenditure as percentage of GNP* (1999): 2.2% (world avg. 2.4%); per capita expenditure U.S.$742.

[1]Excludes Svalbard (23,560 sq mi [61,020 sq km]) and Jan Mayen (146 sq mi [377 sq km]). [2]January 1. [3]Detail does not add to total given because of rounding. [4]Includes Norwegian population of Svalbard and Jan Mayen, registered as residents on the mainland. [5]Population of municipalities. [6]Norwegian catches on quotas bought from other countries are included. [7]Manufacturing includes mining. [8]Includes hotels. [9]Unemployed. [10]Imports c.i.f.; exports f.o.b. [11]1998.

Internet resources for further information:
- **Statistics Norway http://www.ssb.no/www-open/english**

Oman

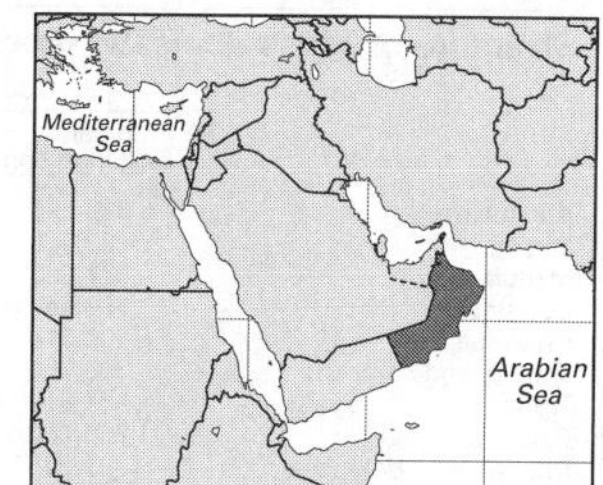

Official name: Salṭanat ʻUmān (Sultanate of Oman).
Form of government: monarchy with two advisory bodies (Council of State [41[1]]; Consultative Council [83]).
Head of state and government: Sultan.
Capital: Muscat.
Official language: Arabic.
Official religion: Islam.
Monetary unit: 1 rial Omani (RO) = 1,000 baizas; valuation (Sept. 8, 2003) 1 RO = U.S.$2.60 = £1.64.

Area and population

		area[2]		population
Regions	Capitals	sq mi	sq km	2000 estimate
Al-Bāṭinah	Ar-Rustāq; Ṣuḥār	4,850	12,500	667,053
Ad-Dākhilīyah	Nizwā; Samā'il	12,300	31,900	272,141
Ash-Sharqīyah	Ibrā; Ṣūr	14,200	36,800	307,000
Al-Wusṭa	Haymā'	30,750	79,700	20,000
Aẓ-Ẓāhirah	Al-Buraymī; ʻIbrī	17,000	44,000	214,997
Governorates				
Masqaṭ	Muscat (Masqaṭ)	1,350	3,500	661,145
Musandam	Khaṣab	700	1,800	34,007
Ẓufār (Dhofar)	Ṣalālah	38,350	99,300	224,993
TOTAL		119,500	309,500	2,401,336

Demography

Population (2003): 2,621,000.
Density (2003): persons per sq mi 21.9, persons per sq km 8.5.
Urban-rural (2001): urban 76.5%; rural 23.5%.
Sex distribution (2000): male 56.8%; female 43.2%.
Age breakdown (2000): under 15, 36.8%; 15–29, 29.7%; 30–44, 22.1%; 45–59, 7.9%; 60 and over, 3.5%.
Population projection: (2010) 3,189,000; (2020) 4,009,000.
Doubling time: 21 years.
Ethnic composition (2000): Omani Arab 48.1%; Indo-Pakistani 31.7%, of which Balochi 15.0%, Bengali 4.4%, Tamil 2.5%; other Arab 7.2%; Persian 2.8%; Zanzibari (blacks originally from Zanzibar) 2.5%; other 7.7%.
Religious affiliation (2000): Muslim 87.4%, of which Ibāḍiyah Muslim *c.* 75% (principal minorities are Sunnī Muslim and Shīʻī Muslim); Hindu 5.7%; Christian 4.9%; Buddhist 0.8%; other 1.2%.
Major cities (1993): As-Sīb 155,000[3]; Ṣalālah 116,000; Bawshar 107,500[3]; Ṣuḥār 84,300; ʻIbrī 76,000; Muscat 40,900 (urban agglomeration [2001] 540,000).

Vital statistics

Birth rate per 1,000 population (2002): 37.8 (world avg. 21.3).
Death rate per 1,000 population (2002): 4.0 (world avg. 9.1).
Natural increase rate per 1,000 population (2002): 33.7 (world avg. 12.2).
Total fertility rate (avg. births per childbearing woman; 2002): 6.0.
Life expectancy at birth (2002): male 70.2 years; female 74.6 years.
Major causes of death per 100,000 population: n.a.; however, the main causes of hospital deaths in 1995 were diseases of the circulatory system 34.1%, infectious diseases 11.1%, malignant neoplasms (cancers) 9.4%, perinatal problems 7.2%, diseases of the respiratory system 6.3%.

National economy

Budget (2002). Revenue: RO 3,007,000,000 (oil revenue 75.7%; other 24.3%). Expenditures: RO 2,937,300,000 (current expenditure 77.3%, of which civil ministries 39.0%, defense 32.6%, interest paid on loans 2.4%; capital expenditure 20.0%; other 2.7%).
Public debt (external, outstanding; 2001): U.S.$2,691,000,000.
Gross national product (2001): U.S.$14,900,000,000 (U.S.$6,180 per capita).

Structure of gross national product and labour force

	2002			
	in value RO '000,000	% of total value	labour force[4]	% of labour force[4]
Agriculture, fishing	161.8	2.1	65,900	9.9
Oil and natural gas	3,267.7[5]	41.9[5]		
Other mining	15.9	0.2	5,975	0.9
Manufacturing	602.9[5]	7.7[5]	70,627	10.6
Construction	197.4	2.5	134,179	20.1
Public utilities	81.7	1.1	1,365	0.2
Transp. and commun.	534.4	6.9	4,660	0.7
Trade, restaurants, hotels	984.9	12.6	171,060	25.7
Finance, real estate	634.3	8.1	6,283	1.0
Pub. admin., defense	775.2	9.9	118,632	17.8
Services	726.2	9.3	86,516	13.0
Other	–178.9[6]	–2.3[6]	912	0.1
TOTAL	7,803.5	100.0	666,109	100.0

Tourism (2001): receipts U.S.$118,000,000; expenditures U.S.$367,000,000.
Household income and expenditure. Average household size (1999) 6.9; expenditure (1990): housing and utilities 27.8%, food, beverage, and tobacco 26.4%, transportation 19.8%, clothing and shoes 7.8%, household goods and furniture 6.1%, education, health services, entertainment, and other 12.1%.
Production (metric tons except as noted). Agriculture, forestry, fishing (2002): dates 248,458, bananas 33,680, watermelons 29,914, dry onions 17,360, potatoes 12,688, mangoes 10,945, papayas 2,360, tobacco leaves 1,270; livestock (number of live animals) 998,000 goats, 354,000 sheep, 314,000 cattle, 122,700 camels; fish catch (2000) 123,706. Mining and quarrying (2001): marble 156,000; chromite (gross weight) 30,100; gold 1,000 kg. Manufacturing (value added in U.S.$'000,000; 1998): bricks, tiles, and cement 119; food products 116; petroleum products 116; fabricated metals 45; garments 42; furniture 31. Energy production (consumption): electricity (kW-hr; 1999) 11,236,000,000 (11,236,000,000); crude petroleum (barrels; 2002) 327,300,000 ([2001] 20,100,000); petroleum products (metric tons; 1999) 4,056,000 (2,989,000); natural gas (cu m; 2001) 9,100,000,000 (6,300,000,000).
Population economically active (1993)[7]: total 704,798; activity rate of total population 34.9% (participation rates: over age 15, 60.9%; female 9.7%; unemployed [1996] *c.* 20%).

Price and earnings indexes (1995 = 100)

	1996	1997	1998	1999	2000	2001	2002
Consumer price index	100.3	100.0	99.5	99.8	98.7	97.7	97.0
Earnings index	...	...	...	...	...	...	...

Land use (1994): meadows and pastures 4.7%; agricultural and under permanent cultivation 0.3%; other (mostly desert and developed area) 95.0%.

Foreign trade[8]

Balance of trade (current prices)

	1996	1997	1998	1999	2000	2001
RO '000,000	+1,208	+1,158	+118	+1,130	+2,586	+2,216
% of total	27.1%	24.5%	2.9%	25.5%	42.3%	35.2%

Imports (2001): RO 2,229,000,000 (machinery and apparatus 26.4%; motor vehicles and parts 13.2%; food and live animals 12.1%; beverages and tobacco 8.9%; chemicals and chemical products 7.2%). *Major import sources:* United Arab Emirates 28.4%; Japan 15.4%; United States 6.8%; United Kingdom 6.0%; Germany 4.2%.
Exports (2001): RO 4,258,000,000 (domestic exports 86.4%, of which crude and refined petroleum 69.6%, natural gas 10.6%, base and fabricated [mostly copper] metals 1.0%, live animals and animal products 1.0%; reexports 13.6%, of which motor vehicles and parts 4.5%, beverages and tobacco products 3.5%). *Major export destinations*[9]: United Arab Emirates 35.6%; Iran 20.7%; Saudi Arabia 8.6%; United States 4.5%; Tanzania 2.7%.

Transport and communications

Transport. Railroads: none. Roads (1999): total length 20,518 mi, 33,020 km (paved 24%). Vehicles (2000): passenger cars 280,977; trucks and buses 124,582. Air transport (2001)[10]: passenger-mi 589,680,000, passenger-km 949,000,000; short ton-mi cargo 5,537,000, metric ton-km cargo 8,084,000; airports (1999) with scheduled flights 6.

Communications

Medium	date	unit	number	units per 1,000 persons
Daily newspapers	1996	circulation	63,000	28
Radio	2000	receivers	1,490,000	621
Television	2000	receivers	1,350,000	563
Telephones	2001	main lines	235,300	90
Cellular telephones	2001	subscribers	324,500	124
Personal computers	2001	units	85,000	34
Internet	2001	users	120,000	46

Education and health

Educational attainment (1993). Percentage of population age 15 and over having: no formal schooling (illiterate) 41.2%; no formal schooling (literate) 14.9%; primary 18.9%; secondary 21.1%; higher technical 2.0%; higher undergraduate 1.5%; higher graduate 0.1%; other 0.3%. *Literacy* (2000): percentage of total population age 15 and over literate 71.7%; males literate 80.1%; females literate 61.6%.

Education (2000–01)

	schools	teachers	students	student/ teacher ratio
Primary (age 6–14)	294	9,238	253,430	27.4
Secondary (age 15–17)[11, 12]	674	12,646	227,026	18.0
Voc., teacher tr.[12]	10	954	9,936	10.4
Higher[13]	1	833	9,075	10.9

Health (1998): physicians 3,061 (1 per 747 persons); hospital beds 5,075 (1 per 444 persons); infant mortality rate per 1,000 live births (2002) 21.8.

Military

Total active duty personnel (2002): 41,700 (army 60.0%, navy 10.1%, air force 9.8%, royal household 20.1%); U.S. troops in Oman (May 2003) 2,700. *Military expenditure as percentage of GNP* (1999): 15.3% (world 2.4%); per capita expenditure U.S.$726.

[1]All seats are nonelected. [2]Approximate; no comprehensive survey of surface area has ever been carried out in Oman. [3]Within Muscat urban agglomeration. [4]Employed only; includes 547,477 expatriate workers in private sector and 118,632 government employees, of which 78.6% are Omani. [5]Manufacturing includes petroleum products; Oil and natural gas excludes petroleum products. [6]Includes import taxes less bank service charges. [7]Non-Omani workers constituted 61.3% of the labour force in 1993. [8]Imports are f.o.b. in balance of trade and c.i.f. for commodities and trading partners. [9]Excludes petroleum and natural gas; includes reexports. [10]Oman Air only. [11]Includes preparatory. [12]1998–99. [13]University only.

Internet resources for further information:
- **Ministry of Information http://www.omanet.com**
- **Central Bank of Oman http://www.cbo-oman.org/pub_annual.htm**

Pakistan

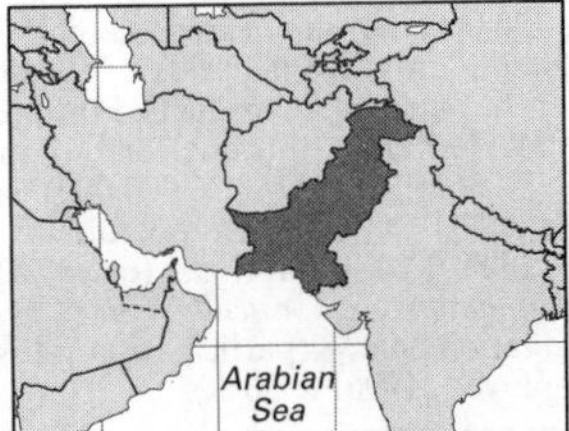

Official name: Islam-i Jamhuriya-e Pakistan (Islamic Republic of Pakistan).
Form of government: military-backed constitutional regime with two legislative houses (Senate [100]; National Assembly [342]).
Chiefs of state and government: President[1] assisted by Prime Minister.
Capital: Islamabad.
Official language: Urdu.
Official religion: Islam.
Monetary unit: 1 Pakistan rupee (PRs) = 100 paisa; valuation (Sept. 8, 2003) 1 U.S.$ = PRs 57.78; 1 £ = PRs 91.61.

Area and population

		area[2]		population
Provinces	Capitals	sq mi	sq km	2003 estimate[3]
Balochistan	Quetta	134,051	347,190	7,450,000
North-West Frontier	Peshawar	28,773	74,521	20,170,000
Punjab	Lahore	79,284	205,345	82,710,000
Sindh	Karachi	54,407	140,914	34,240,000
Federally Administered Tribal Areas	...	10,509	27,220	3,420,000
Federal Capital Area				
Islamabad	...	350	906	1,040,000
TOTAL		307,374	796,096	149,030,000

Demography

Population (2003)[3]: 149,030,000.
Density (2003)[2, 3]: persons per sq mi 484.8, persons per sq km 187.2.
Urban-rural (2002)[3, 4]: urban 38.0%; rural 62.0%.
Sex distribution (2002)[3, 4]: male 51.92%; female 48.08%.
Age breakdown (1998)[3, 4]: under 15, 43.2%; 15–29, 26.9%; 30–44, 15.6%; 45–59, 8.8%; 60–74, 4.3%; 75 and over, 1.2%.
Population projection[3]: (2010) 169,480,000; (2020) 197,538,000.
Doubling time: 32 years.
Ethnic composition (2000): Punjabi 52.6%; Pashtun 13.2%; Sindhi 11.7%; Urdu-speaking muhajirs 7.5%; Balochi 4.3%; other 10.7%.
Religious affiliation (2000): Muslim 96.1%[5]; Christian 2.5%; Hindu 1.2%; others (including Ahmadiyah) 0.2%.
Major cities (1998): Karachi 9,269,000; Lahore 5,063,000; Faisalabad 1,977,000; Rawalpindi 1,406,000; Multan 1,182,000; Islamabad 525,000.

Vital statistics

Birth rate per 1,000 population (2002): 30.4 (world avg. 21.3).
Death rate per 1,000 population (2002): 9.0 (world avg. 9.1).
Natural increase rate per 1,000 population (2002): 21.4 (world avg. 12.2).
Total fertility rate (avg. births per childbearing woman; 2002): 4.3.
Life expectancy at birth (2002): male 61.0 years; female 62.7 years.
Major cause of death (percentage of total deaths; 1987): malaria 18.2%; childhood diseases 12.1%; diseases of digestive system 9.8%; diseases of respiratory system 9.2%; infection of intestinal tract 7.7%.

National economy

Budget (2001–02). Revenue: PRs 632,799,000,000 (sales tax 26.9%, nontax receipts 26.0%, income taxes 22.4%, customs duties 8.0%, excise taxes 7.4%). Expenditures: PRs 773,289,000,000 (public-debt service 41.4%, defense 19.6%, development 16.1%, general administration 6.6%, grants and subsidies 3.3%).
Public debt (external, outstanding; 2001): U.S.$26,801,000,000.
Production (metric tons except as noted). Agriculture, forestry, fishing (2002): sugarcane 48,041,600, wheat 18,226,100, rice 6,343,000, seed cotton 5,040,000, potatoes 1,721,600, corn (maize) 1,689,000, chickpeas 362,100, rapeseed 230,000; livestock (number of live animals) 50,900,000 goats, 24,398,000 sheep, 24,000,000 buffalo, 22,857,000 cattle, 153,000,000 chickens; roundwood (2002) 27,691,679 cu m; fish catch (2000) 627,314. Mining and quarrying (2001–02): limestone 9,805,000; rock salt 1,359,000; gypsum 328,000; silica sand 157,000; chromite 15,984. Manufacturing (2001–02): cement 9,935,000; urea 4,216,200; refined sugar 3,246,600; cotton yarn 1,808,600; vegetable ghee 774,000; jute textiles 82,000; cotton textiles 568,400,000 sq m; cigarettes 55,320,000,000 units; motor-vehicle tires 1,463,000 units; bicycles 553,400 units; (2000–01) sewing machines 26,900 units. Energy production (consumption): electricity (kW-hr; 2001) 67,704,000,000 ([1999] 65,402,000,000); coal (metric tons; 1999) 3,461,000 (4,371,000); crude petroleum (barrels; 2000–01) 21,100,000 ([1999] 49,300,000); petroleum products (metric tons; 1999) 5,985,000 (16,701,000); natural gas (cu m; 2000–01) 24,800,000,000 ([1999] 19,413,800,000).
Population economically active (2002): total 41,540,000; activity rate of total population 28.5% (participation rates: ages 15–64 [1999] 43.1%; female [1996–97] 14.4%; unemployed 7.8%).

Price index (1995 = 100)

	1996	1997	1998	1999	2000	2001	2002
Consumer price index	110.4	122.9	130.6	136.0	141.9	146.4	151.2

Gross national product (2001): U.S.$60,000,000,000 (U.S.$420 per capita).

Structure of gross domestic product and labour force

	2001–02		2001	
	in value PRs '000,000	% of total value	labour force	% of labour force
Agriculture	829,398	22.3	18,160,000	44.6
Mining	22,803	0.6	4,330,000	10.7
Manufacturing	537,035	14.4		
Construction	103,157	2.8	2,170,000	5.3
Public utilities	106,614	2.9	260,000	0.6
Transp. and commun.	393,799	10.6	1,890,000	4.7
Trade	511,819	13.7	5,060,000	12.4
Finance	265,760	7.1		
Pub. admin., defense	321,090	8.6	5,630,000	13.8
Services	336,843	9.0		
Other	298,293	8.0	3,190,000[6]	7.9[6]
TOTAL	3,726,611	100.0	40,690,000	100.0

Household income and expenditure (1988). Average household size 6.3; income per household PRs 25,572 (U.S.$1,420); sources of income: self-employment 56.0%, wages and salaries 22.0%, other 22.0%; expenditure: food 47.0%, housing 12.0%, clothing and footwear 8.0%, other 33.0%.
Tourism (2001): receipts U.S.$92,000,000; expenditures U.S.$255,000,000.
Land use (1999): pasture 6.5%; agriculture 28.4%; forest and other 65.1%.

Foreign trade[7]

Balance of trade (current prices)

	1996–97	1997–98	1998–99	1999–2000	2000–01	2001–02
U.S.$'000,000	–3,145	–1,868	–2,085	–1,412	–1,269	–360
% of total	16.3%	10.0%	12.2%	7.9%	6.6%	1.9%

Imports (2001–02): U.S.$10,339,000,000 (machinery and apparatus 15.6%; refined petroleum 15.2%; chemicals and chemical products 14.4%; crude petroleum 11.9%; food 8.0%; transport equipment 4.8%). *Major import sources* (2000–01): U.A.E. 12.5%; Saudi Arabia 11.7%; Kuwait 8.9%; Japan 5.4%; U.S. 5.2%; China 4.9%.
Exports (2001–02): U.S.$9,135,000,000 (textiles 63.6%, of which cotton yarn and fabric 22.6%, bedding 10.1%, ready-made garments 9.6%, knitwear 9.3%; leather and leather products 7.4%; rice 4.9%; sporting goods 3.3%; carpets 2.7%). *Major export destinations:* EU 27.4%, of which U.K. 7.2%, Germany 4.9%; U.S. 24.7%; U.A.E. 7.9%; Hong Kong 4.8%.

Transport and communications

Transport. Railroads (2000–01): route length 7,791 km; passenger-km 19,590,000,000; metric ton-km cargo 4,520,000,000. Roads (2001–02): total length 156,375 mi, 251,661 km (paved 59%). Vehicles (2001): passenger cars 758,600; trucks and buses 253,100. Air transport (2000–01): passenger-km 9,739,000,000; (1999) metric ton-km cargo 329,832,000; airports (1997) 35.

Communications

Medium	date	unit	number	units per 1,000 persons
Daily newspapers	2000	circulation	4,190,000	30
Radio	2000	receivers	14,700,000	121
Television	2000	receivers	18,300,000	131
Telephones	2001	main lines	3,400,000	24
Cellular telephones	2001	subscribers	800,000	5.5
Personal computers	2001	units	600,000	4.1
Internet	2001	users	500,000	3.4

Education and health

Educational attainment (1990). Percentage of population age 25 and over having: no formal schooling 73.8%; some primary education 9.7%; secondary 14.0%; postsecondary 2.5%. *Literacy* (2000): total population age 15 and over literate 43.2%; males literate 57.5%; females literate 27.9%.

Education (2000–01)

	schools	teachers	students	student/ teacher ratio
Primary (age 5–9)	165,700	373,900	20,999,000	56.2
Secondary (age 10–14)	31,600	320,100	6,576,000	20.5
Voc., teacher tr.	580	7,062	75,000	10.6
Higher	1,187	41,673	1,067,999	25.6

Health (2001): physicians 96,248 (1 per 1,516 persons); hospital beds 97,945 (1 per 1,490 persons); infant mortality rate per 1,000 live births (2002) 78.5.
Food (2001): daily per capita caloric intake 2,457 (vegetable products 81%, animal products 19%); 106% of FAO recommended minimum.

Military

Total active duty personnel (2002): 620,000 (army 88.7%, navy 4.0%, air force 7.3%). *Military expenditure as percentage of GNP* (1999): 5.9% (world 2.4%); per capita expenditure U.S.$25.

[1]Military leader (from October 1999) who was sworn in as president in June 2001. [2]Excludes 32,494-sq-mi (84,159-sq-km) area of Pakistani-administered Jammu and Kashmir (comprising both Azad Kashmir [AK] and the Northern Areas [NA]). [3]Excludes Afghan refugees (2003; 1,500,000) and the 2003 populations of AK (3,100,000) and NA (1,050,000). [4]Excludes Federally Administered Tribal Areas. [5]Mostly Sunnī, with Shīʿī comprising about 17% of total population. [6]Unemployed. [7]Import figures are f.o.b. in balance of trade and c.i.f. for commodities and trading partners.

Internet resources for further information:
- **Economic Survey, Ministry of Finance http://www.finance.gov.pk**
- **Statistics Division: Government of Pakistan http://www.statpak.gov.pk**

Palau

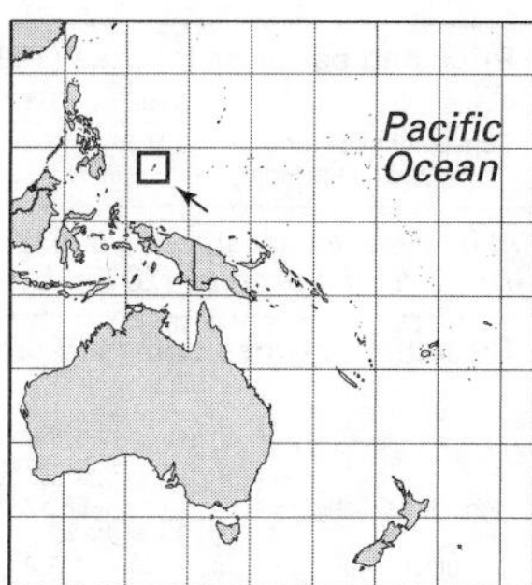

Official name: Belu'u er a Belau (Palauan); Republic of Palau (English).
Form of government: unitary republic with a national congress composed of two legislative houses (Senate [14]; House of Delegates [16]).
Head of state and government: President.
Capital: Koror (acting)[1].
Official languages[2]: Palauan; English.
Official religion: none.
Monetary unit: 1 U.S. dollar (U.S.$) = 100 cents; valuation (Sept. 8, 2003) 1 U.S.$ = £0.63.

Area and population

States	area sq mi	area sq km	population 2000 census
Aimeliik	20	52	272
Airai	17	44	2,104
Angaur	3	8	188
Hatobohel	1	3	23
Kayangel	1	3	138
Koror	7	18	13,303
Melekeok	11	28	239
Ngaraard	14	36	638
Ngarchelong	4	10	267
Ngardmau	18	47	286
Ngatpang	18	47	367
Ngchesar	16	41	280
Ngeremlengui	25	65	221
Ngiwal	10	26	193
Peleliu	5	13	571
Sonsorol	1	3	39
Other			
Rock Islands	18	47	—
TOTAL	188[3]	488[3]	19,129

Demography

Population (2003): 20,200.
Density (2003): persons per sq mi 107.4, persons per sq km 41.4.
Urban-rural (2002): urban 73.0%; rural 27.0%.
Sex distribution (2000): male 54.63%; female 45.37%.
Age breakdown (2000): under 15, 23.9%; 15–29, 24.2%; 30–44, 29.9%; 45–59, 14.2%; 60–74, 5.5%; 75 and over 2.3%.
Population projection: (2010) 22,200; (2020) 24,200.
Doubling time: 58 years.
Ethnic composition (1997): Palauan 74.5%; Filipino 16.0%; Chinese 3.2%; other Micronesian and other 6.3%.
Religious affiliation (1995): Roman Catholic 38.4%; Protestant 24.7%; Modekngei (marginal Christian sect) 26.5%; other 10.4%.
Major city (2000): Koror 13,303.

Vital statistics

Birth rate per 1,000 population (2002): 19.3 (world avg. 21.3).
Death rate per 1,000 population (2002): 7.1 (world avg. 9.1).
Natural increase rate per 1,000 population (2002): 12.2 (world avg. 12.2).
Total fertility rate (avg. births per childbearing woman; 2002): 2.5.
Marriage rate per 1,000 population: n.a.
Divorce rate per 1,000 population: n.a.
Life expectancy at birth (2002): male 66.1 years; female 72.5 years.
Major causes of death per 100,000 population (1999): diseases of the circulatory system 227.4; malignant and benign neoplasms (cancers) 119.1; accidents, poisoning, and violence 92.1; endocrine, nutritional, metabolic, and immunity disorders 59.6; diseases of the respiratory system 43.3; diseases of the digestive system 21.7; diseases of the genitourinary system 21.7; infectious and parasitic diseases 16.2.

National economy

Budget (2002). Revenue: U.S.$70,058,000 (grants from the U.S. 49.4%; tax revenue 36.0%; nontax revenue 14.6%). Expenditures: U.S.$79,691,000 (current expenditure 74.6%, of which wages and salaries 38.1%; capital expenditure 25.4%).
Public debt (external, outstanding; 2000): U.S.$20,000,000.
Production (metric tons except as noted). Agriculture, forestry, fishing (value of sales in U.S.$; 1998): eggs (1999) 609,626, fruit and vegetables 97,225, root crops (taro, cassava, sweet potatoes) 6,566, betel nuts 4,291; livestock (number of live animals; 2001) 702 pigs, 21,189 poultry; roundwood, n.a.; fish catch (2001; pounds) 593,473, of which sturgeon and unicorn fish 101,613, parrot fish 57,516, rabbit fish 25,613, groupers 23,835, emperor fish 20,586, crabs 17,347, wrasses 14,315, tuna and mackerel 13,366. Mining and quarrying: n.a. Manufacturing: includes handicrafts and small items. Construction: n.a. Energy production (consumption): electricity (kW-hr; 1999) 210,000,000 (210,000,000); coal, none (n.a.); crude petroleum, none (n.a.); petroleum products (metric tons; 1999), none (79,000); natural gas, none (n.a.).
Tourism (2002): receipts from visitors U.S.$66,100,000.
Population economically active (2000): total 9,845; activity rate of total population 51.5% (participation rates: over age 15, 67.6%; female [1995] 39.6%; unemployed 2.3%).

Gross national product (at current market prices; 2001): U.S.$100,000,000 (U.S.$6,780 per capita).

Structure of gross domestic product and labour force

	2001 in value U.S.$'000	2001 % of total value	2000 labour force	2000 % of labour force
Agriculture, fisheries	4,771	4.0	215 (with Mining)	2.2 (with Mining)
Mining	240	0.2		
Manufacturing	1,774	1.5	345	3.5
Public utilities	3,741	3.1	[4]	[4]
Construction	9,181	7.6	1,112	11.3
Transportation and communications	10,855	9.0	765[4]	7.8[4]
Trade	36,756	30.4	2,619	26.6
Finance	9,683	8.0	116	1.2
Public administration, defense	30,860	25.5	3,203	32.5
Services	10,381	8.6	1,246	12.6
Other	2,592[5]	2.1[5]	224[6]	2.3[6]
TOTAL	120,834	100.0	9,845	100.0

Household income and expenditure. Average household size (2000) 5.7; income per household (1989) U.S.$8,882; sources of income (1989): wages 63.7%, social security 12.0%, self-employment 7.4%, retirement 5.5%, interest, dividend, or net rental 4.3%, remittance 4.1%, public assistance 1.0%, other 2.0%; expenditure (1997): food 42.2%, beverages and tobacco 14.8%, entertainment 13.1%, transportation 6.4%, clothing 5.7%, household goods 2.7%, other 15.1%.
Land use: n.a.

Foreign trade

Balance of trade (current prices)

	1997	1998	1999	2000	2001	2002
U.S.$'000	–57,500	–54,800	–92,400	–111,500	–86,700	–77,200
% of total	70.9%	71.2%	79.8%	82.0%	82.8%	81.1%

Imports (2001): U.S.$95,700,000 (machinery and transport equipment 24.2%; food and live animals 15.2%; mineral fuels and lubricants 10.4%; beverages and tobacco products 8.3%; chemicals and chemical products 7.4%). *Major import sources:* United States 39.3%; Guam 14.0%; Japan 10.2%; Singapore 7.7%; South Korea 6.4%; Taiwan 5.3.
Exports (2001): U.S.$9,000,000 (mostly high-grade tuna and garments). *Major export destinations:* mostly U.S., Japan, and Taiwan.

Transport and communications

Transport. Railroads: none. Roads (1993): total length 40 mi, 64 km (paved 59%). Vehicles (2001): passenger cars and trucks 4,452. Merchant marine (1991): vessels (100 gross tons and over) 4; total deadweight tonnage, n.a. Air transport (2001): passenger arrivals 64,143, passenger departures 61,472; airports (1997) with scheduled flights 1.

Communications

Medium	date	unit	number	units per 1,000 persons
Radio	1997	receivers	12,000	663.0
Television	1997	receivers	11,000	606.0
Telephones	1994	main lines	2,615	160.0

Education and health

Educational attainment (1997). Percentage of population age 25 and over having: no formal schooling 0.1%; some primary education 4.4%; completed primary 5.7%; some secondary 16.3%; completed secondary 41.0%; some postsecondary 13.0%; higher 19.5%. *Literacy* (1997): total population age 15 and over literate 99.9%.

Education (2001–02)

	schools	teachers	students	student/teacher ratio
Primary (age 6–13)	23	235	3,033	12.9
Secondary (age 14–18)	6	132	1,168	8.8
Higher[7]	1	25	598	23.9

Health: physicians (1998) 20 (1 per 906 persons); hospital beds (1990) 70 (1 per 200 persons); infant mortality rate per 1,000 live births (1999) 17.7.
Food: daily per capita caloric intake, n.a.

Military

The United States is responsible for the external security of Palau, as specified in the Compact of Free Association of Oct. 1, 1994.

[1]New capital buildings at Melekeok on Babelthuap were not completed as of November 2003. [2]Sonsorolese-Tobian is also, according to official sources, considered an official language. [3]Detail does not add to total given because of rounding. [4]Transportation and communications includes Public utilities. [5]Includes import duties and imputed bank service charge. [6]Unemployed. [7]Palau Community College.

Internet resources for further information:

- **Republic of Palau Economic Report (Bank of Hawaii)** **http://www.boh.com/econ/pacific**
- **Department of the Interior: Office of Insular Affairs** **http://www.pacificweb.org**

Panama

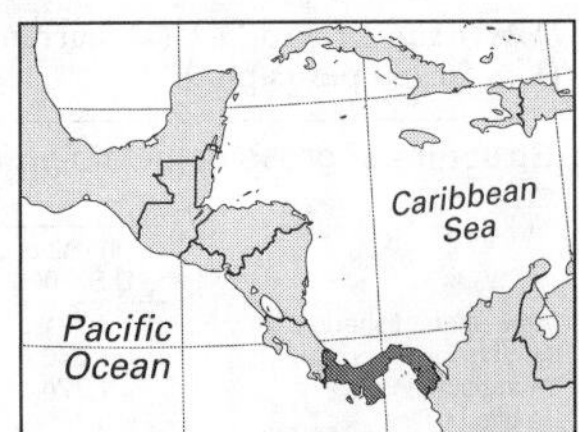

Official name: República de Panamá (Republic of Panama).
Form of government: multiparty republic with one legislative house (Legislative Assembly [71]).
Head of state and government: President assisted by Vice Presidents.
Capital: Panama City.
Official language: Spanish.
Official religion: none.
Monetary unit: 1 balboa (B) = 100 cents; valuation (Sept. 8, 2003) 1 U.S.$ = B 1.00; 1 £ = B 1.59.

Area and population

		area		population
Provinces	**Capitals**	sq mi	sq km	2000 census
Bocas del Toro	Bocas del Toro	1,788	4,631	89,269
Chiriquí	David	2,498	6,471	368,790
Coclé	Penonomé	1,902	4,927	202,461
Colón	Colón	1,888	4,890	204,208
Darién[1]	La Palma	4,282	11,091	39,151
Herrera	Chitré	904	2,341	102,465
Los Santos	Las Tablas	1,469	3,805	83,495
Panamá	Panama City	3,719	9,633	1,385,052
Veraguas	Santiago	4,119	10,668	209,076
Indigenous districts				
Emberá	Unión Chocó	1,698	4,398	8,246
Kuna de Madungandí	...	895	2,319	3,305
Kuna de Wargandí[1]	...	299	775	1,133
Kuna Yala (San Blas)	El Porvenir	910	2,357	32,446
Ngöbe Buglé	Quebrada Guabo	2,576	6,673	110,080
TOTAL		28,950[2]	74,979	2,839,177[3]

Demography

Population (2003): 3,116,000.
Density (2003): persons per sq mi 107.6, persons per sq km 41.6.
Urban-rural (1999): urban 56.0%; rural 44.0%.
Sex distribution (2000): male 50.46%; female 49.54%.
Age breakdown (1999): under 15, 31.7%; 15–29, 27.4%; 30–44, 20.9%; 45–59, 12.0%; 60–74, 5.9%; 75 and over, 2.1%.
Population projection: (2010) 3,504,000; (2020) 4,011,000.
Doubling time: 46 years.
Ethnic composition (2000): mestizo 58.1%; black and mulatto 14.0%; white 8.6%; Amerindian 6.7%; Asian 5.5%; other 7.1%.
Religious affiliation (1995): Roman Catholic 82.2%; unaffiliated Christian 12.9%; other (mostly ethnoreligionist) 4.9%.
Major cities (2000): Panama City 415,964 (urban agglomeration [2001] 1,202,000); San Miguelito 293,745[4]; David 77,734[5]; Arraiján 63,753[5]; La Chorrera 55,871; Colón 42,133.

Vital statistics

Birth rate per 1,000 population (2002): 21.2 (world avg. 21.3).
Death rate per 1,000 population (2002): 6.1 (world avg. 9.1).
Natural increase rate per 1,000 population (2002): 15.1 (world avg. 12.2).
Total fertility rate (avg. births per childbearing woman; 2002): 2.6.
Marriage rate per 1,000 population (1997): 4.1[6].
Divorce rate per 1,000 population (1997): 0.7[6].
Life expectancy at birth (2002): male 70.1 years; female 75.0 years.
Major causes of death per 100,000 population (2000): diseases of the circulatory system 101.7; malignant neoplasms (cancers) 62.7; accidents 28.7; diseases of the respiratory system 27.5; infectious and parasitic diseases 30.9.

National economy

Budget (2000). Revenue: B 2,688,400,000 (tax revenue 62.6%, of which income taxes 12.6%, social security contributions 18.5%, corporate tax 5.8%; nontax revenue 37.4%, of which entrepreneurial and property income 21.1%). Expenditures: B 2,803,900,000 (social security and welfare 20.9%; health 17.2%; education 16.6%; defense 7.1%; economic affairs 7.0%).
Production (metric tons except as noted). Agriculture, forestry, fishing (2002): sugarcane 1,440,612, bananas 600,000, rice 320,226, plantains 105,000, corn (maize) 94,500, oranges 46,600, yams 16,720, coffee 13,900, tobacco 2,130; livestock (number of live animals) 1,533,461 cattle, 280,000 pigs, 170,000 horses; roundwood 1,321,388 cu m; fish catch (value of production in B '000,000; 1998): fish 63, shrimps 40. Mining and quarrying (2001): limestone 270,000; gold 48,600 troy oz. Manufacturing (value of production in B '000,000; 1998): food products 1,203, of which meat 341, dairy products 144; refined petroleum 299; beverages 176; cement, bricks, and tiles 154. Energy production (consumption): electricity (kW-hr; 2001) 4,858,000,000 ([1999] 4,870,000,000); coal (metric tons; 1999) none (70,000); crude petroleum (barrels; 1999) none (18,400,000); petroleum products (metric tons; 1999) 2,281,000 (2,228,000); natural gas (cu m; 1999) none (61,500,000).
Tourism (2001): receipts from visitors U.S.$626,000,000; expenditures by nationals abroad U.S.$176,000,000.
Household income and expenditure. Average household size (2000) 4.2; average annual income per household (1990) B 5,450 (U.S.$5,450); expenditure, n.a.
Population economically active (1998)[6]: total 1,083,580; activity rate of total population 42.2%[7] (participation rates: ages 15–69 [1997] 64.3%, female [1997] 35.6%, unemployed 13.6%).

Price and earnings indexes (1995 = 100)

	1996	1997	1998	1999	2000	2001	2002
Consumer price index	101.3	102.5	103.2	104.5	106.0	106.3	107.4
Monthly earnings index	...	...	...	...	...	...	...

Public debt (external, outstanding; 2001): U.S.$6,332,000,000.
Gross national product (2001): U.S.$9,500,000,000 (U.S.$3,260 per capita).

Structure of gross domestic product and labour force

	2000		2001	
	in value B '000,000	% of total value	labour force[6]	% of labour force[6]
Agriculture, fishing	682.7	6.8	220,700	18.7
Mining	42.8	0.4	2,200	0.2
Manufacturing	712.9	7.1	91,300	7.7
Construction	492.8	4.9	67,800	5.8
Public utilities	399.0	4.0	9,900	0.8
Transp. and commun.	1,727.5	17.2	77,700	6.6
Trade, restaurants	1,758.8	17.6	220,000	18.7
Finance, real estate	2,659.6	26.6	55,500	4.7
Pub. admin. }	1,716.2	17.1	66,600	5.7
Services }			204,100	17.3
Other	–173.3[8]	–1.7[8]	163,100[9]	13.8[9]
TOTAL	10,019.0	100.0	1,177,900	100.0

Land use (1994): forested 43.8%; meadows and pastures 19.8%; agricultural and under permanent cultivation 8.9%; other 27.5%.

Foreign trade[10, 11]

Balance of trade (current prices)

	1996	1997	1998	1999	2000	2001
B '000,000	–2,215	–2,358	–2,714	–2,781	–2,626	–2,155
% of total	66.2%	64.5%	65.8%	66.2%	62.8%	57.1%

Imports (2001): B 2,964,000,000 (mineral fuels 21.0%, of which crude petroleum 14.4%; machinery and apparatus 19.1%; chemicals and chemical products 11.2%; transport equipment 8.7%). *Major import sources:* U.S. 32.5%; Colón Free Zone 11.9%; Ecuador 8.0%; Colombia 5.7%; Venezuela 5.2%.
Exports (2001): B 809,000,000 (bananas 15.1%; fish 11.9%; shrimps 8.7%; petroleum products 7.1%; unspecified 38.6%). *Major export destinations:* U.S. 48.1%; Nicaragua 5.1%; Costa Rica 4.8%; Belgium 4.5%; Sweden 3.7%.

Transport and communications

Transport. Railroads (2000): route length 220 mi, 354 km. Roads (1997): total length 7,022 mi, 11,301 km (paved 33%). Vehicles: passenger cars (1998) 228,722; trucks and buses 84,020. Panama Canal traffic (2000–01): oceangoing transits 12,197; cargo 196,242,000 metric tons. Air transport (2001)[12]: passenger-km 3,004,000,000; metric ton-km cargo 25,235,000; airports (1996) 10.

Communications

Medium	date	unit	number	units per 1,000 persons
Daily newspapers	2000	circulation	183,000	62
Radio	2000	receivers	884,000	300
Television	2000	receivers	572,000	194
Telephones	2001	main lines	430,000	148
Cellular telephones	2001	subscribers	600,000	207
Personal computers	2001	units	110,000	38
Internet	2000	users	90,000	32

Education and health

Educational attainment (1990). Percentage of population age 25 and over having: no formal schooling 11.6%; primary 41.6%; secondary 28.7%; undergraduate 12.4%; graduate 0.7%; other/unknown 5.0%. *Literacy* (2000): total population age 15 and over literate 91.3%; males 92.5%; females 91.3%.

Education (1997)

	schools	teachers	students	student/ teacher ratio
Primary (age 6–11)	2,866	15,058	377,898	25.1
Secondary (age 12–17) } Voc., teacher tr. }	417	12,450	223,155	17.9
Higher	14	6,409	95,341	14.9

Health (1998): physicians 3,518 (1 per 772 persons); hospital beds 7,287 (1 per 373 persons); infant mortality rate per 1,000 live births (2002) 21.9.
Food (2001): daily per capita caloric intake 2,386 (vegetable products 76%, animal products 24%); 103% of FAO recommended minimum requirement.

Military

Total active duty personnel (2002): none; Panama has an 11,800-member national police force. *Military expenditure as percentage of GNP* (1999): 1.4% (world avg. 2.4%); per capita expenditure U.S.$45.

[1]Kuna de Wargandí indigenous district (*comarca*) was created in 2000 from part of Darién province. [2]Detail does not add to total given because of rounding. [3]Census adjusted for undercount equals 2,938,548. [4]District adjacent to Panama City within Panama City urban agglomeration. [5]Population of *cabecera*. [6]Excludes indigenous population. [7]Estimated figure. [8]Imputed finance service charges less import duties. [9]Includes 161,400 unemployed. [10]Imports c.i.f.; exports f.o.b. [11]Excludes Colón Free Zone (2001 imports c.i.f. B 4,760,000,000; 2001 reexports f.o.b. B 5,406,000,000, of which textiles and clothing 25.9%, machinery and apparatus 23.7%). [12]COPA only.

Internet resources for further information:

- **Contraloría General de la República Panamá http://www.contraloria.gob.pa/index.htm**

Papua New Guinea

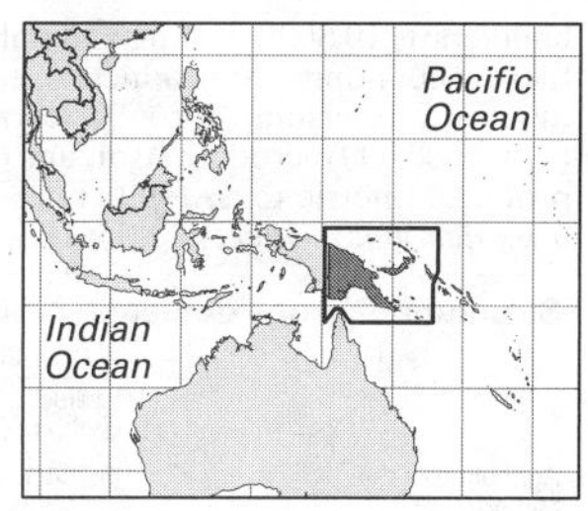

Official name: Independent State of Papua New Guinea.
Form of government: constitutional monarchy with one legislative house (National Parliament [109]).
Chief of state: British Monarch represented by Governor-General.
Head of government: Prime Minister.
Capital: Port Moresby.
Official language: English[1].
Official religion: none.
Monetary unit: 1 Papua New Guinea kina (K) = 100 toea; valuation (Sept. 8, 2003) 1 U.S.$ = K 3.38; 1 £ = K 5.36.

Area and population

		area		population
Provinces	Administrative centres	sq mi	sq km	2000 census
Central	Port Moresby	11,400	29,500	183,983
East New Britain	Rabaul	6,000	15,500	220,133
East Sepik	Wewak	16,550	42,800	343,181
Eastern Highlands	Goroka	4,300	11,200	432,972
Enga	Wabag	4,950	12,800	295,031
Gulf	Kerema	13,300	34,500	106,898
Madang	Madang	11,200	29,000	365,106
Manus	Lorengau	800	2,100	43,387
Milne Bay	Alotau	5,400	14,000	210,412
Morobe	Lae	13,300	34,500	539,404
National Capital District	Port Moresby	100	240	254,158
New Ireland	Kavieng	3,700	9,600	118,350
Oro (Northern)	Popondetta	8,800	22,800	133,065
Sandaun (West Sepik)	Vanimo	14,000	36,300	185,741
Simbu (Chimbu)	Kundiawa	2,350	6,100	259,703
Southern Highlands	Mendi	9,200	23,800	546,265
West New Britain	Kimbe	8,100	21,000	184,508
Western	Daru	38,350	99,300	153,304
Western Highlands	Mount Hagen	3,300	8,500	440,025
Autonomous region (pending)				
Bougainville[2]	Arawa	3,600	9,300	175,160
TOTAL		178,704[3]	462,840	5,190,786

Demography

Population (2003): 5,583,000.
Density (2003): persons per sq mi 31.2, persons per sq km 12.1.
Urban-rural (2001): urban 17.6%; rural 82.4%.
Sex distribution (2000): male 51.30%; female 48.70%.
Age breakdown (2000): under 15, 38.8%; 15–29, 28.7%; 30–44, 17.1%; 45–59, 9.7%; 60–74, 4.7%; 75 and over, 1.0%.
Population projection: (2010) 6,430,000; (2020) 7,637,000.
Ethnic composition (1983)[4]: New Guinea Papuan 84.0%; New Guinea Melanesian 15.0%; other 1.0%.
Religious affiliation (2000): Christian 95.1%, of which non-Anglican Protestant 56.6%, Roman Catholic 30.0%, Anglican 6.7%; traditional beliefs 3.6%; Bahā'ī 0.8%; other 0.5%.
Major cities (2000): Port Moresby 254,158; Lae 78,038; Madang 27,394; Wewak 19,724; Goroka 18,618.

Vital statistics

Birth rate per 1,000 population (2002): 31.6 (world avg. 21.3).
Death rate per 1,000 population (2002): 7.8 (world avg. 9.1).
Natural increase rate per 1,000 population (2002): 23.8 (world avg. 12.2).
Total fertility rate (avg. births per childbearing woman; 2002): 4.2.
Life expectancy at birth (2002): male 61.7 years; female 66.0 years.
Major causes of death per 100,000 population (1993): acute respiratory infections 34.6; pneumonia 27.8; meningitis 7.6; conditions originating from perinatal period 6.2; malaria 3.8.

National economy

Budget (2001). Revenue: K 2,859,000,000 (tax revenue 86.6%, of which value-added tax 27.0%, corporate tax 24.2%, income tax 22.7%, excise tax 6.5%; nontax revenue 13.4%). Expenditures (2000): K 3,081,800,000 (current expenditure 70.8%, of which transfer to provincial governments 16.8%, interest payments 12.4%; development expenditure 29.2%).
Public debt (external, outstanding; 2001): U.S.$1,413,000,000.
Production (metric tons except as noted). Agriculture, forestry, fishing (2002): oil palm fruit 1,250,000, bananas 725,000, coconuts 513,000, sweet potatoes 490,000, sugarcane 425,000, yams 232,000, taro 174,000, cassava 125,000, coffee 62,500, cacao 45,000, tea 9,000, natural rubber 7,300; livestock (number of live animals) 1,650,000 pigs, 3,800,000 chickens; roundwood (2002) 8,597,000 cu m; fish catch (2000) 50,556. Mining and quarrying (2000): copper (metal content) 200,900; gold 74,300 kg; silver 73,200 kg. Manufacturing (1998): palm oil 241,485; copra 124,349; wood products (excluding furniture) 3,054,000 cu m. Energy production (consumption): electricity (kW-hr; 1999) 1,784,000,000 (1,784,000,000); coal (metric tons; 1999) none (1,000); crude petroleum (barrels; 2000) 33,000,000 ([1999] 513,000); natural gas (cu m; 1999) 83,500,000 (83,500,000); petroleum products (metric tons; 1999) 49,000 (717,000).
Land use (1997): forested 92.3%; agricultural and under permanent cultivation 1.5%; meadows and pastures 0.2%; other 6.0%.
Gross national product (2001): U.S.$3,000,000,000 (U.S.$580 per capita).

Structure of gross domestic product and labour force

	2001		1980	
	in value K '000,000	% of total value	labour force[5]	% of labour force[5]
Agriculture	2,848	28.3	564,500	77.0
Mining	2,745	27.2	4,300	0.6
Manufacturing	859	8.5	14,000	1.9
Construction	349	3.5	21,600	2.9
Public utilities	132	1.3	2,800	0.4
Transp. and commun.	431	4.3	17,400	2.4
Trade	866	8.6	25,100	3.4
Finance	358	3.5	4,500	0.6
Pub. admin., defense Services	1,253	12.4	77,100	10.5
Other	238[6]	2.4[6]	1,500	0.2
TOTAL	10,079	100.0	732,800	100.0[3]

Population economically active (1990)[5]: total 1,715,330; activity rate 36.9% (participation rates: over age 10, n.a.; female 41.5%; unemployed 7.7%).

Price and earnings indexes (1995 = 100)

	1996	1997	1998	1999	2000	2001	2002
Consumer price index	111.6	116.0	131.8	151.5	175.1	191.4	214.0
Weekly earnings index	...	...	...	...	...	...	...

Tourism (2001): receipts U.S.$101,000,000; expenditures U.S.$38,000,000.

Foreign trade[7]

Balance of trade (current prices)

	1997	1998	1999	2000	2001
U.S.$'000,000	+213	+424	+494	...	+609
% of total	5.2%	12.9%	13.9%	...	19.3%

Imports (2000): U.S.$1,035,000,000 (petroleum products *c.* 22%; food *c.* 16%; transport equipment *c.* 14%; nonelectrical machinery *c.* 12%; chemicals and chemical products *c.* 7%). *Major import sources* (2000): Australia 55.8%; Japan 11.3%; U.S. 6.5%; Singapore 5.4%; New Zealand 3.5%.
Exports (2002): U.S.$1,638,000,000 (gold 36.0%; crude petroleum 22.5%; copper 16.0%; logs 5.7%; palm oil 5.1%). *Major export destinations* (2002): Australia 49.3%; Singapore 18.8%; New Zealand 4.4%; Japan 4.2%; Malaysia 2.8%.

Transport and communications

Transport. Railroads: none. Roads (1996): total length 19,600 km (paved 4%). Vehicles (1998): passenger cars 21,700; trucks and buses 89,700. Air transport (1999): passenger-km 641,000,000; metric ton-km cargo 80,000,000; airports (1999) with scheduled flights 42.

Communications

Medium	date	unit	number	units per 1,000 persons
Daily newspapers	2000	circulation	72,600	14
Radio	2000	receivers	446,000	86
Television	2000	receivers	88,200	17
Telephones	2001	main lines	62,000	12
Cellular telephones	2001	units	10,700	2.0
Internet	2001	users	300,000	61

Education and health

Educational attainment (1990). Percentage of population age 25 and over having: no formal schooling 82.6%; some primary education 8.2%; completed primary 5.0%; some secondary 4.2%. *Literacy* (2000): total population age 15 and over literate 63.9%; males literate 70.6%; females literate 56.8%.

Education (1997)

	schools	teachers	students	student/ teacher ratio
Primary (age 7–12)	3,518	13,457[8]	587,788	...
Secondary (age 13–16)	159	2,415[9]	74,873	...
Voc., teacher tr.	128	878[9]	15,422	...
Higher	3	957[8]	9,220	...

Health: physicians (1998) 342 (1 per 13,708 persons); hospital beds (1993) 14,119 (1 per 294 persons); infant mortality rate (2002) 56.5.
Food (2001): daily per capita caloric intake 2,193 (vegetable products 91%, animal products 9%); 96% of FAO recommended minimum.

Military

Total active duty personnel (2002): 3,100 (army 80.6%, navy 12.9%, air force 6.5%). *Military expenditure as percentage of GNP* (1999): 1.1% (world 2.4%); per capita expenditure U.S.$7.

[1]The national languages are English, Tok Pisin (English Creole), and Motu. [2]Formal peace agreement signed on Aug. 30, 2001, ended nine years of civil war and promised Bougainville autonomy; internationally supported autonomy process under way through October 2003. [3]Detail does not add to total given because of rounding. [4]Papua New Guinea has several thousand separate communities, most with only a few hundred people. [5]Citizens of Papua New Guinea over age 10 involved in "money-raising activities" only. [6]Import duties. [7]Imports c.i.f.; exports f.o.b. [8]1995. [9]1992.

Internet resources for further information:
- **National Statistical Office of Papua New Guinea http://www.nso.gov.pg**
- **Bank of Papua New Guinea http://www.bankpng.gov.pg**

Paraguay

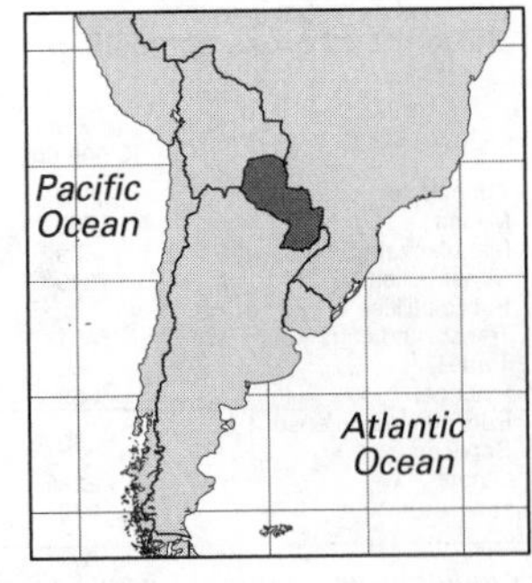

Official name: República del Paraguay (Spanish); Tetã Paraguáype (Guaraní) (Republic of Paraguay).
Form of government: multiparty republic with two legislative houses (Senate [46[1]]; Chamber of Deputies [80]).
Head of state and government: President.
Capital: Asunción.
Official languages: Spanish; Guaraní.
Official religion: none[2].
Monetary unit: 1 Paraguayan Guaraní (₲) = 100 céntimos; valuation (Sept. 8, 2003) 1 U.S.$ = ₲6,295; 1 £ = ₲9,981.

Area and population

Regions Departments	Capitals	area sq mi	 sq km	population 2002 census
Occidental		95,338	246,925	142,501
Alto Paraguay	Fuerte Olimpo	31,795	82,349	15,008
Boquerón	Filadelfia	35,393	91,669	45,617
Presidente Hayes	Pozo Colorado	28,150	72,907	81,876
Oriental		61,710	159,827	5,063,600
Alto Paraná	Ciudad del Este	5,751	14,895	563,042
Amambay	Pedro Juan Caballero	4,994	12,933	113,888
Asunción[3]	—	45	117	513,399
Caaguazú	Coronel Oviedo	4,430	11,474	448,983
Caazapá	Caazapá	3,666	9,496	139,241
Canindeyú	Salto del Guairá	5,663	14,667	140,551
Central	Asunción	952	2,465	1,363,399
Concepción	Concepción	6,970	18,051	180,277
Cordillera	Caacupé	1,910	4,948	234,805
Guairá	Villarrica	1,485	3,846	176,933
Itapúa	Encarnación	6,380	16,525	463,410
Misiones	San Juan Bautista	3,690	9,556	103,633
Ñeembucú	Pilar	4,690	12,147	76,738
Paraguarí	Paraguarí	3,361	8,705	226,514
San Pedro	San Pedro	7,723	20,002	318,787
TOTAL		157,048	406,752	5,206,101[4]

Demography

Population (2003): 5,642,000.
Density (2003): persons per sq mi 35.9, persons per sq km 13.9.
Urban-rural (2000): urban 54.5%; rural 45.5%.
Sex distribution (2000): male 50.43%; female 49.57%.
Age breakdown (1999): under 15, 39.3%; 15–29, 26.2%; 30–44, 17.9%; 45–59, 9.9%; 60–74, 5.1%; 75 and over, 1.6%.
Population projection: (2010) 6,622,000; (2020) 8,082,000.
Ethnic composition (2000): mixed (white/Amerindian) 85.6%; white 9.3%, of which German 4.4%, Latin American 3.4%; Amerindian 1.8%; black 1.0%; other 2.3%.
Religious affiliation (1995): Roman Catholic 88.5%; Protestant 5.0%; other 6.5%.
Major urban areas (2002): Asunción 513,399 (urban agglomeration [2001] 1,302,000); Ciudad del Este 223,350; Encarnación 69,769; Pedro Juan Caballero 64,153; Caaguazú 50,329.

Vital statistics

Birth rate per 1,000 population (2001): 30.9 (world avg. 21.3).
Death rate per 1,000 population (2001): 4.8 (world avg. 9.1).
Natural increase rate per 1,000 population (2001): 26.1 (world avg. 12.2).
Total fertility rate (avg. births per childbearing woman; 2001): 4.1.
Marriage rate per 1,000 population (1999): 3.6[5].
Life expectancy at birth (2001): male 71.4 years; female 76.5 years.
Major causes of death per 100,000 population (1998)[6]: diseases of the circulatory system 129; malignant neoplasms (cancers) 63; accidents 54; diseases of the respiratory system 40; infectious and parasitic diseases 29.

National economy

Budget (1999): Revenue: ₲4,011,200,000,000 (tax revenue 69.4%, of which taxes on goods and services 39.0%, income tax 13.4%, customs duties 10.3%, social security 6.7%; nontax revenue including grants 30.6%). Expenditures: ₲4,605,800,000,000 (current expenditure 75.6%; capital expenditure 24.4%).
Public debt (external, outstanding; 2001): U.S.$2,119,000,000.
Population economically active (1996): total 1,747,488; activity rate 35.3% (participation rates [1992]: ages 12 and over, 51.0%; female 23.8%; unemployed [1998] 7.2%).

Price index (1995 = 100)

	1996	1997	1998	1999	2000	2001	2002
Consumer price index	109.8	117.5	131.0	139.9	152.4	163.5	180.7

Production (metric tons except as noted). Agriculture, forestry, fishing (2002): cassava 4,142,000, soybeans 3,276,000, sugarcane 3,210,000, corn (maize) 783,000, wheat 355,000, oranges 210,000, seed cotton 153,000, sweet potatoes 132,000, bananas 65,000; livestock (number of live animals) 9,900,000 cattle, 2,750,000 pigs, 15,500,000 chickens; roundwood 9,787,000 cu m; fish catch (2001) 25,000. Mining and quarrying (2002): hydraulic cement 650,000; kaolin 66,700; gypsum 4,300. Manufacturing (value added in constant prices of 1982, ₲'000,000; 1998): food products 59,100; wood products and furniture 23,500; handicrafts 10,300; printing and publishing 9,200; leather and hides 7,000; textiles 6,600; nonmetal products 6,600; petroleum products 3,800. Energy production (consumption): electricity (kW-hr; 2000) 51,500,000,000 (2,000,000,000); crude petroleum (barrels; 1999) none (872,000); petroleum products (metric tons; 1999) 116,000 (1,369,000).
Gross national product (2001): U.S.$7,600,000,000 (U.S.$1,350 per capita).

Structure of gross domestic product and labour force

	2000 in value ₲'000,000,000	 % of total value	1996 labour force	 % of labour force
Agriculture	6,764.1	25.1	559,042	32.0
Mining	97.2	0.4	2,568	0.1
Manufacturing	3,689.2	13.7	181,983	10.4
Construction	1,615.1	6.0	142,678	8.2
Public utilities	1,635.7	6.1	13,150	0.8
Transp. and commun.	1,303.2	4.8	55,972	3.2
Trade Finance	6,250.4	23.2	224,210	12.8
Pub. admin., defense Services	2,147.9	8.0	330,697	18.9
Other	3,418.3	12.7	237,188[7]	13.6[7]
TOTAL	26,921.1	100.0	1,747,488	100.0

Household income and expenditure. Average household size (2000) 4.4; sources of income (1989): wages and salaries 33.9%, transfer payments 2.5%.
Tourism (2001): receipts U.S.$77,000,000; expenditures U.S.$91,000,000.

Foreign trade

Balance of trade (current prices)

	1996	1997	1998	1999	2000	2001
U.S.$'000,000	−1,807	−1,956	−1,457	−984	−1,181	−999
% of total	46.4%	46.1%	41.8%	39.9%	40.4%	33.5%

Imports (2001): U.S.$1,989,000,000 (machinery and apparatus 18.0%, fuels and lubricants 15.2%, chemicals and pharmaceuticals 10.3%, transport equipment 9.5%, food products 6.3%, tobacco products 5.2%). *Major import sources:* Brazil 28.3%; Argentina 24.1%; U.S. 6.0%; Japan 4.3%; Uruguay 3.5%.
Exports (2001): U.S.$990,000,000[8] (soybeans 36.0%, cotton 9.1%, processed meats 7.7%, leather and leather products 5.8%, soybean flour 5.8%, wood manufactures 4.8%). *Major export destinations:* Brazil 28.1%; Uruguay 18.2%; Chile 6.2%; Argentina 6.1%; Italy 4.3%.

Transport and communications

Transport. Railroads (1998): route length 441 km; passenger-km 3,000,000; metric ton-km cargo 5,500,000. Roads (1999): total length 29,500 km (paved 51%). Vehicles (2002): passenger cars 274,186; trucks 189,115. Air transport (2000): passenger-km 270,503,000; metric ton-km cargo 24,346,000; airports (1998) 5.

Communications

Medium	date	unit	number	units per 1,000 persons
Daily newspapers	2000	circulation	227,000	43
Radio	2000	receivers	961,000	182
Television	2000	receivers	1,150,000	218
Telephones	2002	main lines	273,200	47
Cellular telephones	2002	subscribers	1,667,000	288
Personal computers	2001	units	60,000	11
Internet	2002	users	100,000	17

Education and health

Educational attainment (1999). Percentage of population age 15 and over having: no formal schooling 5.5%; primary education 52.8%; secondary 34.0%; higher 7.6%; not stated 0.1%. *Literacy* (1999): percentage of total population age 15 and over literate 92.3%; males literate 94.1%; female literate 90.6%.

Education (1998)

	schools	teachers	students	student/ teacher ratio
Primary (age 7–12)	6,143	59,423	933,289	15.7
Secondary (age 13–18)[9]	1,846	17,668[10]	332,703	16.6[10]
Higher	2	742[11]	42,302	…

Health (1995): physicians 3,730 (1 per 1,294 persons); hospital beds 6,759 (1 per 714 persons); infant mortality rate per 1,000 live births (2001) 29.8.
Food (2001): daily per capita caloric intake 2,576 (vegetable products 78%, animal products 22%); 112% of FAO recommended minimum requirement.

Military

Total active duty personnel (2002): 18,600 (army 80.1%, navy 10.8%, air force 9.1%). *Military expenditure as percentage of GNP* (1999): 1.1% (world 2.4%); per capita expenditure U.S.$15.

[1]Includes one nonelective seat. Former president Juan Carlos Wasmosy became senator-for-life in August 1998. [2]Roman Catholicism, although not official, enjoys special recognition in the 1992 constitution. [3]Asunción is the capital city, not a department. [4]Preliminary figure; adjusted preliminary total equals 5,534,378. [5]Civil Registry records only. [6]Reporting areas only (constituting about 67 percent of the total population). [7]Includes 171,312 unemployed. [8]Excludes value of hydroelectricity exports to Brazil and Argentina. [9]Includes vocational and teacher training. [10]1996. [11]1993–94.

Internet resources for further information:
- **Banco Central del Paraguay http://www.bcp.gov.py**
- **Dirección General Estadística, Encuestas y Censos http://www.dgeec.gov.py/index.htm**

Peru

Official name: República del Perú (Spanish) (Republic of Peru).
Form of government: unitary multiparty republic with one legislative house (Congress [120]).
Head of state and government: President, assisted by Prime Minister.
Capital: Lima.
Official languages: Spanish; Quechua; Aymara.
Official religion: Roman Catholicism.
Monetary unit: 1 nuevo sol (S/.) = 100 céntimos; valuation (Sept. 8, 2003) 1 U.S.$ = S/. 3.48; 1 £ = S/. 5.52.

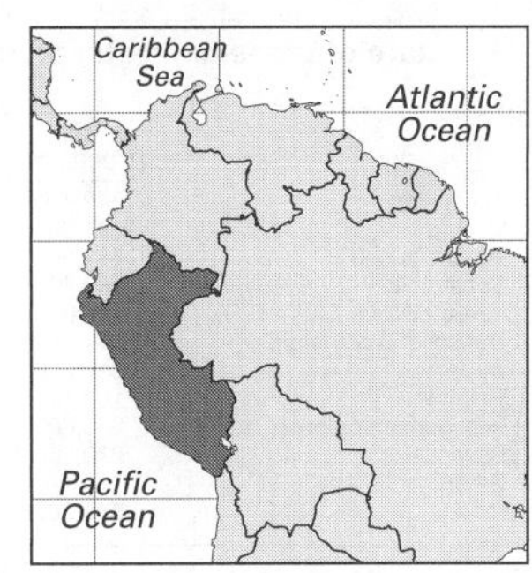

Area and population

Regions[1]	area sq km	population 2002 estimate	Regions[1]	area sq km	population 2002 estimate
Amazonas	39,249	428,095	Lambayeque	14,231	1,121,358
Ancash	35,877	1,107,828	Lima	34,802	7,748,528
Apurímac	20,896	463,131	Loreto	368,852	907,341
Arequipa	63,345	1,101,005	Madre de Dios	85,183	99,452
Ayacucho	43,815	550,751	Moquegua	15,734	156,750
Cajamarca	33,318	1,498,567	Pasco	25,320	264,702
Callao	147	787,154	Piura	35,892	1,636,047
Cusco	72,104	1,208,689	Puno	71,999[2]	1,263,995
Huancavelica	22,131	443,213	San Martin	51,253	757,740
Huánuco	36,887	811,865	Tacna	16,076	294,214
Ica	21,328	687,334	Tumbes	4,669	202,088
Junín	44,197	1,246,663	Ucayali	102,411	456,340
La Libertad	25,500	1,506,122	TOTAL	1,285,216[2]	26,748,972

Demography

Population (2002): 27,148,000.
Density (2002): persons per sq mi 54.7, persons per sq km 21.1.
Urban-rural (2000): urban 73.1%; rural 26.9%.
Sex distribution (2000): male 49.59%; female 50.41%.
Age breakdown (2000): under 15, 33.4%; 15–29, 29.1%; 30–44, 19.3%; 45–59, 10.9%; 60–74, 5.7%; 75 and over, 1.6%.
Population projection: (2010) 29,952,000; (2020) 33,923,000.
Doubling time: 40 years.
Ethnic composition (2000): Quechua 47.0%; mestizo 31.9%; white 12.0%; Aymara 5.4%; Japanese 0.5%; other 3.2%.
Religious affiliation (2000): Roman Catholic 95.7%; other (of which mostly Protestant) 4.3%.
Major cities (1998 est.): metropolitan Lima 7,060,600; Arequipa 710,103; Trujillo 603,657; Chiclayo 469,200; Iquitos 334,013.

Vital statistics

Birth rate per 1,000 population (2002): 23.4 (world avg. 21.3).
Death rate per 1,000 population (2002): 5.7 (world avg. 9.1).
Natural increase rate per 1,000 population (2002): 17.7 (world avg. 12.2).
Total fertility rate (avg. births per childbearing woman; 2002): 2.9.
Life expectancy at birth (2002): male 68.2 years; female 73.1 years.
Major causes of death per 100,000 population (2000): diseases of the circulatory system 536.0; malignant neoplasms (cancers) 522.6; respiratory diseases 453.5; accidents, poisoning, and violence 274.0; infectious diseases 243.2.

National economy

Budget (2001). Revenue: S/. 27,039,000,000 (taxes on goods and services 56.7%, income taxes 20.8%, nontax revenue 15.1%, import duties 10.1%, payroll tax 3.1%). Expenditures: S/. 32,378,000,000 (current expenditure 73.7%, capital expenditure 13.8%, interest payments 12.5%).
Public debt (external, outstanding; 2001): U.S.$18,831,000,000.
Tourism (2001): receipts U.S.$817,000,000; expenditures U.S.$566,000,000.
Production (metric tons except as noted). Agriculture, forestry, fishing (2002): sugarcane 8,422,000, potatoes 3,299,000, rice 2,124,000, corn (maize) 2,099,000, plantains 1,560,000, cassava 887,000; livestock (number of live animals) 14,300,000 sheep, 4,950,000 cattle, 2,800,000 pigs, 2,010,000 goats, 90,000,000 chickens; roundwood 9,928,385 cu m; fish catch (2000) 10,665,420. Mining and quarrying (2001): iron ore 3,892,000; zinc (metal) 201,498; copper (metal) 471,875; lead (metal) 121,181; silver (metal) 1,184; gold 4,438,000 troy oz. Manufacturing (value in S/. '000,000[3]; 1996): processed foods 275.1; base metal products 188.6; textiles and leather products 129.5; industrial chemicals 112.3; wood products 80.0. Construction (value in S/. '000,000[3]; 1996): residential 32.1; nonresidential 26.8. Energy production (consumption): electricity (kW-hr; 1999) 19,051,000,000 (19,051,000,000); coal (metric tons; 1999) 16,000 (339,000); crude petroleum (barrels; 1999) 44,100,000 (62,100,000); petroleum products (metric tons; 1999) 7,484,000 (8,167,000); natural gas (cu m; 1999) 869,900,000 (869,900,000).
Population economically active (1998): total 7,407,280; activity rate of total population 45.7% (participation rates: over age 15, 66.9%; female 43.8%; unemployed 7.7%).

Price and earnings indexes (1995 = 100)

	1996	1997	1998	1999	2000	2001	2002
Consumer price index	111.5	121.1	129.9	134.4	139.4	142.2	142.4
Monthly earnings index[4]	106.8	114.8	120.5	122.1	...	...	...

Gross national product (at current market prices; 2000): U.S.$52,200,000,000 (U.S.$1,980 per capita).

Structure of gross domestic product and labour force

	2001 in value S/.'000[3]	% of total value	labour force	% of labour force
Agriculture	14,536,300	7.8	667,800	8.1
Mining	10,021,500	5.4	45,900	0.6
Manufacturing	27,230,200	14.5	956,400	11.6
Construction	9,389,600	5.0	341,300	4.1
Public utilities	4,447,700	2.4	20,400	0.2
Transp. and commun.	15,386,000	8.2	641,000	7.7
Trade	33,222,400	17.7	2,718,300	32.9
Finance	43,208,100	23.1	390,500	4.7
Pub. admin., defense	13,908,100	7.4	298,100	3.6
Other	15,901,100[4]	8.5[4]	2,191,700[5]	26.5[5]
TOTAL	187,251,000	100.0	8,271,400	100.0

Household income and expenditure. Average household size (1993) 5.1; income per household (1988) U.S.$2,173; sources of income (1991): self-employment 67.1%, wages 23.3%, transfers 7.6%; expenditure (1990): food 29.4%, recreation and education 13.2%, household durables 10.1%.
Land use (1998): forest and other 75.7%; pasture 21.1%; agricultural 3.2%.

Foreign trade[6]

Balance of trade (current prices)

	1997	1998	1999	2000	2001	2002
U.S.$'000,000	–1,712	–2,466	–616	–303	–65	+265
% of total	11.1%	17.6%	4.8%	2.1%	0.5%	1.8%

Imports (2001): U.S.$7,316,000,000 (machinery and apparatus 25.0%, chemicals and chemical products 16.1%, crude and refined petroleum 11.9%, food 11.0%). *Major import sources:* U.S. 23.1%; Argentina 6.2%; Japan 5.9%; Chile 5.9%; Colombia 5.2%.
Exports (2001): U.S.$6,826,000,000 (gold 17.1%, fish foodstuffs for animals 12.3%, refined copper and copper products 11.7%, apparel and clothing accessories 7.4%, crude and refined petroleum 6.1%, zinc ores and concentrates 5.2%). *Major export destinations:* U.S. 24.8%; U.K. 13.5%; China 6.2%; Japan 5.6%; Switzerland 4.5%.

Transport and communications

Transport. Railroads (2000): route length 1,608 km; (1996) passenger-km 171,091,000; (1996) metric ton-km cargo 850,329,000. Roads (1999): total length 78,128 km (paved 13%). Vehicles (1999): passenger cars 684,533; trucks and buses 403,652. Air transport (1998): passenger-km 3,014,000,000; metric ton-km cargo 286,000,000; airports (1996) 27.

Communications

Medium	date	unit	number	units per 1,000 persons
Daily newspapers	1996	circulation	2,000,000	84
Radio	1997	receivers	7,080,000	273
Television	1999	receivers	3,840,000	148
Telephones	2001	main lines	2,022,300	78
Cellular telephones	2001	subscribers	1,545,000	59
Personal computers	2001	units	1,250,000	48
Internet	2001	users	3,000,000	115

Education and health

Educational attainment (1993). Percentage of population age 15 and over having: no formal schooling 12.3%; less than primary education 0.3%; primary 31.5%; secondary 35.5%; higher 20.4%. *Literacy* (2000): total population age 15 and over literate 89.9%; males 94.7%; females 85.3%.

Education (2000)

	schools	teachers	students	student/ teacher ratio
Primary (age 6–11)	33,709	173,877	4,254,384	24.5
Secondary (age 12–16)	8,879	137,431	2,257,400	16.4
Higher	2,161	57,874	1,495,957	25.8

Health: physicians (1997) 22,930 (1 per 1,075 persons); hospital beds (1996) 35,638 (1 per 680 persons); infant mortality rate per 1,000 live births (2002) 38.2.
Food (2001): daily per capita caloric intake 2,610 (vegetable products 87%, animal products 13%); 111% of FAO recommended minimum requirement.

Military

Total active duty personnel (2002): 110,000 (army 63.6%, navy 22.7%, air force 13.6%). *Military expenditure as percentage of GNP* (1999): 2.4% (world 2.4%); per capita expenditure U.S.$45.

[1]Elections to newly decentralized regions held in November 2002. [2]Includes the 4,996 sq km area of the Peruvian part of Lake Titicaca. [3]At market prices. [4]Includes services, import duties, and other taxes on products. [5]Includes services and 651,500 unemployed. [6]Imports are f.o.b. in balance of trade and c.i.f. in commodities and trading partners.

Internet resources for further information:
- **Instituto Nacional de Estadística e Informática (Spanish) http://www.inei.gob.pe**
- **Banco Central de Reserva del Peru http://www.bcrp.gob.pe/English/Index_eng.htm**

Philippines

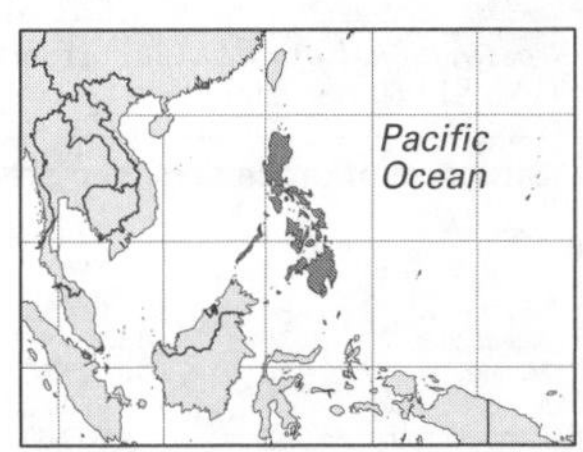

Official name: Republika ng Pilipinas (Pilipino); Republic of the Philippines (English).
Form of government: unitary republic with two legislative houses (Senate [24]; House of Representatives [214]).
Chief of state and head of government: President.
Capital: Quezon City/Manila[1].
Official languages: Pilipino; English.
Official religion: none.
Monetary unit: 1 Philippine peso (₱) = 100 centavos; valuation (Sept. 8, 2003) 1 U.S.$ = ₱ 54.93; 1 £ = ₱ 87.09.

Area and population

Regions	Capitals	area sq mi	area sq km	population 2000 census
Bicol	Legaspi	6,808	17,633	4,674,855
Cagayan Valley	Tuguegarao	10,362	26,838	2,813,159
Caraga	Butuan	7,277	18,847	2,095,367
Central Luzon	San Fernando	7,039	18,231	8,030,945
Central Mindanao	Cotabato	5,549	14,373	2,598,210
Central Visayas	Cebu	5,773	14,951	5,701,064
Cordillera Administrative	...	7,063	18,294	1,365,220
Eastern Visayas	Tacloban	8,275	21,432	3,610,355
Ilocos	San Fernando	4,958	12,840	4,200,478
National Capital	Manila	246	636	9,932,560
Northern Mindanao	Cagayan de Oro	5,418	14,033	2,747,585
Southern Mindanao	Davao	10,479	27,141	5,189,335
Southern Tagalog[2]	...	18,117	46,924	11,793,655
Western Mindanao	Zamboanga	6,194	16,042	3,091,208
Western Visayas	Iloilo	7,808	20,223	6,208,733
Autonomous region				
Muslim Mindanao	Sultan Kudarat	4,493	11,638	2,412,159
TOTAL		115,860[3]	300,076	76,498,735[4]

Demography

Population (2003): 81,161,000.
Density (2002): persons per sq mi 700.5, persons per sq km 270.5.
Urban-rural (2002): urban 60.0%; rural 40.0%.
Sex distribution (2002): male 50.37%; female 49.63%.
Age breakdown (2002): under 15, 35.1%; 15–29, 28.1%; 30–44, 19.3%; 45–59, 11.2%; 60–74, 5.0%; 75 and over, 1.3%.
Population projection: (2010) 92,330,000; (2020) 107,235,000.
Doubling time: 33 years.
Ethnolinguistic composition (by mother tongue of households; 1995): Pilipino (Tagalog) 29.3%; Cebuano 23.3%; Ilocano 9.3%; Hiligaynon Ilongo 9.1%; Bicol 5.7%; Waray 3.8%; Pampango 3.0%; Pangasinan 1.8%; other 14.7%.
Religious affiliation (1996): Roman Catholic 82.9%; Protestant 5.4%; Muslim 4.6%; Aglipayan (Philippine Independent Church) 2.6%; other 4.5%.
Major cities (2000): Quezon City 2,173,831; Manila 1,581,082 (Metro Manila, 9,932,560); Caloocan 1,177,604; Davao 1,147,116; Cebu 718,821.

Vital statistics

Birth rate per 1,000 population (2002): 26.2 (world avg. 21.3).
Death rate per 1,000 population (2002): 5.2 (world avg. 9.1).
Natural increase rate per 1,000 population (2002): 21.0 (world avg. 12.2).
Total fertility rate (avg. births per childbearing woman; 2002); 3.2.
Life expectancy at birth (2002): male 68.0 years; female 72.0 years.
Major causes of death per 100,000 population (1998): circulatory diseases 132.6; respiratory diseases 75.9; malignant neoplasms (cancers) 43.9; accidents 40.8; tuberculosis 38.3; diabetes mellitus 12.1.

National economy

Budget (2001). Revenue: ₱ 563,732,000,000 (income taxes 39.6%, international duties 17.1%, sales tax 15.4%, nontax revenues 12.8%). Expenditures: ₱ 706,327,000,000 (debt service 24.6%, education 17.2%, economic affairs 12.9%, public order 6.8%, defense 4.6%).
Production (metric tons except as noted). Agriculture, forestry, fishing (2002): sugarcane 25,835,000, coconuts 13,682,560, rice 13,270,653, bananas 5,264,470, corn (maize) 4,319,262, pineapples 1,635,930; livestock (number of live animals) 11,652,700 pigs, 6,250,000 goats, 3,122,026 buffalo, 125,730,000 chickens; roundwood (2001) 16,013,084 cu m; fish catch (2001) 2,280,512. Mining and quarrying (2001): nickel (metal content) 27,359; copper (metal content) 20,322; chrome (metal content) 2,569; gold 33,840 kg; silver 33,600 kg. Manufacturing (gross value added in ₱ '000,000; 2001): food products 361,217; electrical machinery 95,592; petroleum and coal products 73,280; chemicals 58,487; beverages and tobacco 49,933. Energy production (consumption): electricity (kW-hr; 2001) 47,049,000,000 (47,049,000,000); hard coal (metric tons; 2001) 1,235,000 ([1999] 6,375,000); crude petroleum (barrels; 1999) 342,000 (120,700,000); petroleum products (metric tons; 1999) 14,700,000 (15,532,000); natural gas, none (none).
Household income and expenditure (2000). Average household size 5.0; income per family ₱ 144,506 (U.S.$3,150); sources of income: wages 52.1%, entrepreneurial income 25.1%, receipts from abroad 11.1%, rent 3.6%, other 8.1%; expenditure: food, beverage, and tobacco 45.4%, housing 14.2%, transportation 6.8%, fuel and power 6.3%, education 4.2%, personal care 3.6%.
Gross national product (at current market prices; 2001): U.S.$80,800,000,000 (U.S.$1,030 per capita).

Structure of gross domestic product and labour force

	2001 in value ₱ '000,000	% of total value	labour force	% of labour force
Agriculture	549,400	15.1	11,253,000	33.7
Mining	21,200	0.6	103,000	0.3
Manufacturing	831,600	22.8	2,892,000	8.7
Construction	182,400	5.0	1,571,000	4.7
Public utilities	116,300	3.2	116,000	0.3
Transp. and commun.	247,600	6.8	2,171,000	6.5
Trade	517,500	14.2	6,226,000	18.7
Finances	160,100	4.4	848,000	2.5
Pub. admin., defense	343,600	9.4	1,385,000	4.2
Services	670,300	18.4	3,521,000	10.6
Others	—	—	3,268,000[5]	9.8[5]
TOTAL	3,640,000	100.0[3]	33,354,000	100.0

Public debt (external, outstanding; 2001): U.S.$34,190,000,000.
Population economically active (2001): total 33,354,000; activity rate 42.6% (participation rates: ages 15 and over 69.9%; female 38.6%; unemployed [July 2002] 11.2%).

Price index (1995 = 100)

	1996	1997	1998	1999	2000	2001	2002
Consumer price index	109.0	115.4	126.6	135.1	141.0	149.6	154.2

Tourism (2001): receipts U.S.$1,723,000,000; expenditures U.S.$1,224,000,000.

Foreign trade[6]

Balance of trade (current prices)

	1996	1997	1998	1999	2000	2001
U.S.$'000,000	–11,884	–10,706	–164	+4,294	+6,691	+2,599
% of total	22.4%	17.5%	0.3%	6.5%	9.6%	4.2%

Imports (2001): U.S.$29,551,000,000 (electronic components 16.0%, computer parts 9.3%, crude petroleum 9.0%, chemicals and chemical products 8.5%, food 7.4%, telecommunications equipment 5.8%). *Major import sources:* Japan 20.6%; United States 16.9%; South Korea 6.6%; Singapore 6.1%; Taiwan 5.4%; Hong Kong 4.3%.
Exports (2001): U.S.$32,150,000,000 (electronic microcircuits 34.4%, computers and computer parts 21.9%, apparel and clothing accessories 7.5%, food 4.0%). *Major export destinations:* United States 27.5%; Japan 15.7%; The Netherlands 9.3%; Singapore 7.2%; Taiwan 6.6%; Hong Kong 4.9%.

Transport and communications

Transport. Railroads (2000): route length 897 km; passenger-km 12,000,000; metric ton-km cargo 660,000,000. Roads (2000): total length 201,994 km (paved 39%). Vehicles (2001): passenger cars 729,350; trucks and buses 285,282. Air transport (2001)[7]: passenger-km 13,448,457,000; metric ton-km cargo 263,545,000; airports (1996) with scheduled flights 21.

Communications

Medium	date	unit	number	units per 1,000 persons
Daily newspapers	2000	circulation	6,300,000	82
Radio	2000	receivers	12,400,000	161
Television	2000	receivers	11,100,000	144
Telephones	2001	main lines	3,100,000	40
Cellular telephones	2001	subscribers	10,568,000	137
Personal computers	2001	units	1,700,000	22
Internet	2001	users	2,000,000	26

Education and health

Education attainment (1995). Percentage of population age 15 and over having: no schooling 3.7%; elementary education 35.8%; secondary 38.4%; post-secondary 21.9%; not stated 0.2%. *Literacy* (2000): total population age 15 and over literate 95.3%; males literate 95.1%; females literate 95.5%.

Education (2001–02)

	schools	teachers	students	student/teacher ratio
Primary (age 7–12)	40,761	331,448	12,826,218	38.7
Secondary (age 13–16)	7,683	112,210	5,813,879	51.8
Higher	1,603	66,876[8]	2,373,486	30.2[8]

Health: physicians (1996) 86,000 (1 per 813 persons); hospital beds (2001) 79,444 (1 per 985 persons); infant mortality rate per 1,000 live births (2002) 30.0.
Food (2001): daily per capita caloric intake 2,372 (vegetable products 85%, animal products 15%); 105% of FAO recommended minimum.

Military

Total active duty personnel (2002): 106,000 (army 62.3%, navy 22.6%, air force 15.1%). *Military expenditure as percentage of GNP* (1999): 1.4% (world 2.4%); per capita expenditure U.S.$14.

[1]And other Manila suburbs of the National Capital Region (Greater Manila). [2]The two new regions of Calabarzon and Mimaropa were created from Southern Tagalog in 2002. [3]Detail does not add to total given because of rounding. [4]Includes foreign-service employees stationed abroad. [5]Unemployed. [6]Import figures are f.o.b. in balance of trade and trading partners and c.i.f. for commodities. [7]Philippines Airlines only. [8]1995–96.

Internet resources for further information:
- **National Statistics Office http://www.census.gov.ph**
- **Government Website http://www.neda.gov.ph**

Poland

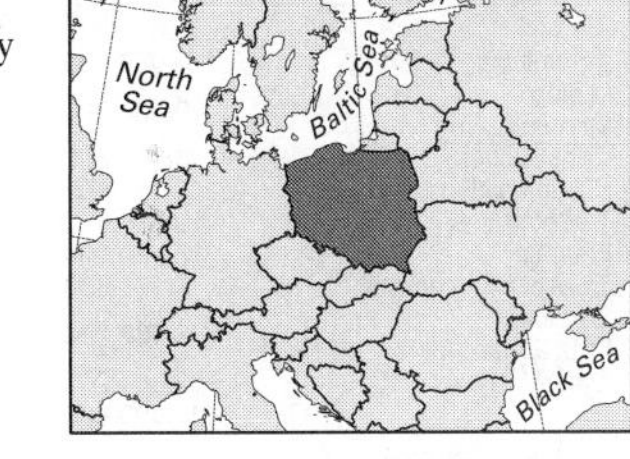

Official name: Rzeczpospolita Polska (Republic of Poland).
Form of government: unitary multiparty republic with two legislative houses (Senate [100]; Diet [460]).
Chief of state: President.
Head of government: Prime Minister.
Capital: Warsaw.
Official language: Polish.
Official religion: none[1].
Monetary unit: 1 zloty (Zł) = 100 groszy; valuation (Sept. 8, 2003) 1 U.S.$ = Zł 4.02; 1 £ = Zł 6.37.

Area and population

Provinces[3]	Capitals	area sq mi	area sq km	population 2002[2] estimate
Dolnośląskie	Wrocław	7,702	19,948	2,970,100
Kujawsko-pomorskie	Bydgoszcz/Toruń	6,938	17,970	2,101,700
Lubelskie	Lublin	9,697	25,114	2,227,600
Lubuskie	Gorzów Wielkopolski/ Zielona Góra	5,399	13,984	1,024,500
Łódzkie	Łódź	7,034	18,219	2,632,900
Małopolskie	Kraków	5,847	15,144	3,240,900
Mazowieckie	Warsaw (Warszawa)	13,744	35,598	5,079,000
Opolskie	Opole	3,634	9,412	1,080,500
Podkarpackie	Rzeszów	6,921	17,926	2,131,400
Podlaskie	Białystok	7,792	20,180	1,219,900
Pomorskie	Gdańsk	7,063	18,293	2,204,400
Śląskie	Katowice	4,747	12,294	4,830,400
Świętokrzyskie	Kielce	4,507	11,672	1,319,600
Warmińsko-Mazurskie	Olsztyn	9,345	24,203	1,469,300
Wielkopolskie	Poznań	11,516	29,826	3,366,000
Zachodniopomorskie	Szczecin	8,843	22,902	1,734,500
TOTAL		120,728[4]	312,685	38,632,500[4]

Demography

Population (2003): 38,623,000.
Density (2003): persons per sq mi 319.9, persons per sq km 123.5.
Urban-rural (2001): urban 61.7%; rural 38.3%.
Sex distribution (2002): male 48.43%; female 51.57%.
Age breakdown (2000): under 15, 19.1%; 15–29, 24.3%; 30–44, 21.3%; 45–59, 18.7%; 60–74, 12.2%; 75 and over, 4.4%.
Population projection: (2010) 38,691,000; (2020) 38,455,000.
Ethnolinguistic composition (1997): Polish 94.2%; Ukrainian 3.9%; German 1.3%; Belarusian 0.6%.
Religious affiliation (1995): Roman Catholic 90.7%; Ukrainian Catholic 1.4%; Polish Orthodox 1.4%; Protestant 0.5%; Jehovah's Witness 0.5%; other (mostly nonreligious) 5.5%.
Major cities (2002): Warsaw 1,671,670 (urban agglomeration; 2001) 2,282,000; Łódź 789,318; Kraków 758,544; Wrocław 640,367; Poznań 578,886; Gdańsk 461,334.

Vital statistics

Birth rate per 1,000 population (2002): 9.3 (world avg. 21.3); (2000) legitimate 87.9%; illegitimate 12.1%.
Death rate per 1,000 population (2002): 9.4 (world avg. 9.1).
Natural increase rate per 1,000 population (2002): –0.1 (world avg. 12.2).
Total fertility rate (avg. births per childbearing woman; 2001): 1.3.
Marriage rate per 1,000 population (2002): 5.0.
Divorce rate per 1,000 population (2002): 1.2.
Life expectancy at birth (2001): male 69.9 years; female 78.1 years.
Major causes of death per 100,000 population (2001): diseases of the circulatory system 449.8; malignant neoplasms (cancers) 228.3; accidents, poisoning, and violence 64.8; diseases of the respiratory system 40.8.

National economy

Budget (2002). Revenue: Zł 143,022,000,000 (value-added tax 40.0%, income tax 27.3%, excise tax 21.9%, nontax revenue 10.8%). Expenditures: Zł 182,922,000,000 (social security and welfare 25.2%, public debt 13.1%, education 12.2%, defense 5.1%).
Gross national product (2001): U.S.$163,600,000,000 (U.S.$4,230 per capita).

Structure of gross domestic product and labour force

	2001 in value Zł '000,000	2001 % of total value	2002[3] labour force	2002[3] % of labour force
Agriculture	24,731.9	3.2	4,296,800	24.2
Mining	15,283.4	2.0	216,500	1.2
Manufacturing	118,590.1	15.6	2,501,500	14.1
Public utilities	24,213.6	3.2	245,600	1.4
Construction	48,194.5	6.3	737,100	4.1
Transp. and commun.	48,191.9	6.3	714,400	4.0
Trade, restaurants	142,645.0	18.7	2,186,400	12.3
Finance, real estate	100,687.2	13.2	1,128,700	6.3
Pub. admin., defense	45,155.9	5.9	525,700	3.0
Services	88,401.2	11.6	2,117,900	11.9
Other	105,261.5[5]	13.8[5]	3,115,100[6]	17.5[6]
TOTAL	761,356.2	100.0[4]	17,785,700	100.0

Production (metric tons except as noted). Agriculture, forestry, fishing (1999): (gross value of production in Zł '000,000) potatoes 4,066, wheat 3,747, fruit 3,578, vegetables 3,484, rye 1,420, sugar beets 1,254; livestock (number of live animals) 18,538,000 pigs, 6,555,000 cattle; roundwood (2001) 21,170,000 cu m; fish catch (2001) 254,149. Mining and quarrying (2000): sulfur 1,369,000; copper ore (metal content) 390,700; silver (recoverable metal content) 1,144. Manufacturing (value added in Zł '000,000; 1999): food products 13,764; beverages 13,582; transport equipment 10,596; nonelectrical machinery 7,542; electrical machinery 7,506. Energy production (consumption): electricity ('000,000 kW-hr; 2002) 140,880 ([1999] 139,197); hard coal ('000 metric tons; 2002) 104,112 ([1999] 89,040); lignite ('000 metric tons; 2002) 58,212 ([1999] 60,826); crude petroleum (barrels; 1999) 3,200,000 (122,600,000); petroleum products (metric tons; 1999) 15,784,000 (17,787,000); natural gas (cu m; 2002) 5,255,000,000 ([1999] 10,657,300,000).
Public debt (external, outstanding; 2001): U.S.$24,828,000,000.
Population economically active (2002[3]): total 17,785,700; activity rate of total population 46.0% (participation rates: 15 and over, 55.0%; female 45.7%; unemployed 17.5%).

Price and earnings indexes (1995 = 100)

	1996	1997	1998	1999	2000	2001	2002
Consumer price index	119.8	137.9	154.1	165.3	182.1	192.1	195.7
Annual earnings index	126.3	151.6	174.2	189.9	209.6	224.1	232.7

Household income and expenditure. Average household size (2002) 2.9; average annual income (2002) Zł 25,600 (U.S.$6,400); sources of income (2001): wages 46.7%, transfers 33.8%, self-employment 13.9%; expenditure (2001): food, beverages, and tobacco 28.0%, housing and energy 25.6%, transportation and communications 14.6%, recreation 6.6%.
Tourism (2001): receipts U.S.$4,815,000,000; expenditures U.S.$3,500,000,000.
Land use (1994): forest 28.8%; meadow 13.3%; agricultural and under permanent cultivation 47.0%; other 10.9%.

Foreign trade[7]

Balance of trade (current prices)

	1997	1998	1999	2000	2001	2002
Zł '000,000	–54,418	–67,443	–73,656	–75,163	–58,138	–57,478
% of total	24.4%	26.2%	25.3%	21.4%	16.4%	14.7%

Imports (2001): Zł 206,253,000,000 (machinery and apparatus 26.1%, chemicals and chemical products 13.9%, road vehicles 7.8%, crude petroleum 5.7%, food 5.3%, textile yarn and fabrics 5.2%). *Major import sources:* Germany 24.0%; Russia 8.8%; Italy 8.3%; France 6.8%; U.K. 4.2%.
Exports (2001): Zł 148,115,000,000 (machinery and apparatus 20.4%, road vehicles 8.9%, food 7.1%, furniture and furniture parts 6.9%, chemicals and chemical products 5.9%, apparel and clothing accessories 5.4%, ships and boats 5.2%). *Major export destinations:* Germany 34.4%; Italy 5.4%; France 5.4%; U.K. 5.0%; The Netherlands 4.7%.

Transport and communications

Transport. Railroads (2002): length 22,981 km; passenger-km 20,809,000,000; metric ton-km cargo 47,756,000. Roads (1999): total length 381,046 km (paved 66%). Vehicles (2001[3]): passenger cars 9,991,260; trucks and buses 1,783,008. Air transport (2002)[8]: passenger-km 6,672,000,000; metric ton-km cargo 80,000,000; airports (1997) 8.

Communications

Medium	date	unit	number	units per 1,000 persons
Daily newspapers	2000	circulation	4,170,000	108
Radio	2000	receivers	20,200,000	523
Television	2000	receivers	15,500,000	400
Telephones	2001	main lines	11,400,000	295
Cellular telephones	2002	subscribers	14,000,000	363
Personal computers	2001	units	3,300,000	85
Internet	2001	users	3,800,000	98

Education and health

Educational attainment (1995). Percentage of population age 15 and over having: no formal schooling/incomplete primary education 6.3%; primary 33.7%; secondary/vocational 53.2%; higher 6.8%. *Literacy* (2000): 99.8%.

Education (2000–01)

	schools	teachers	students	student/ teacher ratio
Primary (age 7–12)	16,766	226,400	3,220,600	14.2
Secondary (age 13–18)	8,587	115,700	2,114,100	18.3
Voc., teacher tr.	8,251	89,700	1,527,900	17.0
Higher	310	79,900	1,584,800	19.8

Health (2002[3]): physicians 86,608 (1 per 446 persons); hospital beds 188,038 (1 per 205 persons); infant mortality rate per 1,000 live births (2002) 7.5.
Food (2001): daily per capita caloric intake 3,397 (vegetable products 75%, animal products 25%); 130% of FAO recommended minimum requirement.

Military

Total active duty personnel (2003): 163,000 (army 63.8%, navy 8.8%, air force 22.4%, other 5.0%). *Military expenditure as percentage of GNP* (1999): 2.1% (world 2.4%); per capita expenditure U.S.$173.

[1]Roman Catholicism has special recognition per 1997 concordat with Vatican City. [2]January 1. [3]Administrative organization effective from Jan. 1, 1999. [4]Detail does not add to total given because of rounding. [5]Taxes less subsidies. [6]Unemployed. [7]Imports c.i.f.; exports f.o.b. [8]LOT only.

Internet resources for further information:
- **Polish Official Statistics**
  http://www.stat.gov.pl/english/index.htm

Portugal

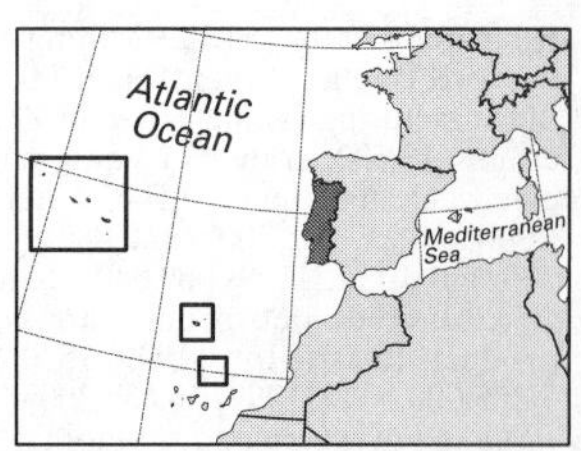

Official name: República Portuguesa (Portuguese Republic).
Form of government: republic with one legislative house (Assembly of the Republic [230]).
Chief of state: President.
Head of government: Prime Minister.
Capital: Lisbon.
Official language: Portuguese.
Official religion: none.
Monetary unit: 1 euro (€) = 100 cents; valuation (Sept. 8, 2003) 1 U.S.$ = €0.90; 1 £ = €1.43[1].

Area and population

		area[2, 3]		population
Continental Portugal		sq mi	sq km	2001 census
Regions	**Principal cities**			9,656,471
Alentejo	Évora	12,080	31,280	760,896
Algarve	Faro	1,920	4,970	420,166
Centre (Centro)	Coimbra	11,030	28,570	2,303,579
Lisbon and Tagus Valley (Lisboa e Vale do Tejo)	Lisbon	1,140	2,950	2,576,823
North (Norte)	Porto	8,220	21,280	3,595,007
Insular Portugal				
Autonomous Regions				491,788
Azores (Açores)	Ponta Delgado	897	2,322	240,565
Madeira	Funchal	303	785	251,223
TOTAL		35,580[4]	92,152[4]	10,148,259[5]

Demography

Population (2003): 10,181,000.
Density (2003): persons per sq mi 286.1, persons per sq km 110.5.
Urban-rural (2001): urban 65.8%; rural 34.2%.
Sex distribution (2001): male 48.34%; female 51.66%.
Age breakdown (2000): under 15, 17.1%; 15–29, 23.0%; 30–44, 21.5%; 45–59, 17.8%; 60–74, 14.5%; 75 and over, 6.1%.
Population projection: (2010) 10,273,000; (2020) 10,190,000.
Ethnic composition (2000): Portuguese 91.9%; mixed race people from Angola, Mozambique, and Cape Verde 1.6%; Brazilian 1.4%; Marrano 1.2%; other European 1.2%; Han Chinese 0.9%; other 1.8%.
Religious affiliation (2000): Christian 92.4%, of which Roman Catholic 87.4%, independent Christian 2.7%, Protestant 1.3%, other Christian 1.0%; nonreligious/atheist 6.5%; Buddhist 0.6%; other 0.5%.
Major cities (2001)[6]: Lisbon 564,657 (urban agglomeration 3,447,173); Porto 263,131; Amadora 175,872; Braga 164,193; Coimbra 148,474; Funchal 103,962.

Vital statistics

Birth rate per 1,000 population (2002): 11.5 (world avg. 21.3).
Death rate per 1,000 population (2002): 10.2 (world avg. 9.1).
Natural increase rate per 1,000 population (2002): 1.3 (world avg. 12.2).
Total fertility rate (avg. births per childbearing woman; 2002): 1.5.
Life expectancy at birth (2002): male 72.7 years; females 79.9 years.
Major causes of death per 100,000 population (1998): circulatory diseases 426.5; malignant neoplasms (cancers) 213.9; respiratory diseases 94.9.

National economy

Budget (2001). Revenue: Esc 5,793,400,000,000 (taxes on goods and services 52.0%, income taxes 39.5%). Expenditures: Esc 6,616,800,000,000 (current expenditure 89.2%, development expenditure 10.8%).
Public debt (1996): U.S.$40,504,000,000.
Production (metric tons except as noted). Agriculture, forestry, fishing (2002): potatoes 1,200,000, tomatoes 994,300, grapes 900,000, corn (maize) 851,000, sugar beets 600,000, wheat 387,000, olives 320,000, apples 240,000, oranges 220,000, cork (1998) 163,000; livestock (number of live animals) 5,478,000 sheep, 2,389,000 pigs, 1,399,000 cattle; roundwood (2002) 8,742,000 cu m; fish catch (2000) 194,691. Mining and quarrying (2001): marble 1,000,000; copper (metal content) 83,000; tin (metal content) 1,200; silver 23,100 kg. Manufacturing (value added in Esc '000,000; 1998): machinery and transport equipment 605,966, of which transport equipment 231,893; petroleum refining 517,170; wearing apparel and footwear 307,275; food and beverages 290,051; textiles 283,268; tobacco 187,220; printing and publishing 165,341. Energy production (consumption): electricity (kW-hr; 1999) 43,383,000,000 (42,523,000,000); coal (metric tons; 1999) negligible (6,126,000); crude petroleum (barrels; 1999) none (94,800,000); petroleum products (metric tons; 1999) 11,410,000 (12,434,000); natural gas (cu m; 1999) none (2,312,400,000).
Tourism (2001): receipts U.S.$5,479,000,000; expenditures U.S.$2,105,000,000.
Population economically active (2001): total 5,211,300; activity rate of total population 51.3% (participation rates: ages 15–64 [1997], 68.5%; female 45.6%; unemployed 4.1%).

Price and earnings indexes (1995 = 100)

	1996	1997	1998	1999	2000	2001	2002
Consumer price index	103.1	105.3	108.3	110.8	114.0	118.9	123.1
Annual earnings index	...	...	...	...	...	...	...

Gross national product (at current market prices; 2001): U.S.$109,300,000,000 (U.S.$10,900 per capita).

Structure of gross domestic product and labour force

	2002		2001	
	in value €'000	% of total value	labour force	% of labour force
Agriculture	4,083,800	3.2	628,700	12.1
Mining	20,958,200	16.2	16,200	0.3
Manufacturing			1,081,900	20.8
Construction	8,450,800	6.5	581,200	11.1
Public utilities	3,151,400	2.4	36,200	0.7
Trade, hotels	19,816,900	15.3	752,200	14.4
Finance	13,920,600	10.8	566,200	10.9
Transp. and commun.	7,171,900	5.5	194,200	3.7
Services	38,982,000	30.1	678,300	13.0
Pub. admin., defense			321,500	6.2
Other	12,864,200[7]	9.9[7]	354,500[8]	6.8[8]
TOTAL	129,399,800	100.0[4]	5,211,300	100.0

Household income and expenditure. Average household size (1999) 3.1; sources of income (1995): wages and salaries 44.4%, self-employment 23.4%, transfers 22.2%; expenditure (1994–95): food 23.9%, housing 20.6%, transportation and communications 18.9%.
Land use (1994): forest 35.9%; pasture 10.9%; agriculture 31.5%; other 21.7%.

Foreign trade[9]

Balance of trade (current prices)

	1997	1998	1999	2000	2001	2002
€'000,000	−1,945[10]	−2,454[10]	−13,790	−16,912	−15,667	−13,568
% of total	18.8%	21.6%	22.5%	24.2%	22.7%	20.0%

Imports (2000): €43,358,000,000 (road vehicles 14.1%; nonelectrical machinery and apparatus 11.4%; mineral fuels and lubricants 10.3%; electrical machinery and telecommunications equipment 9.9%; food products 9.3%; chemicals and chemical products 9.1%). *Major import sources* (2001): Spain 26.5%; Germany 13.9%; France 10.3%; Italy 6.7%; U.K. 5.0%.
Exports (2000): €26,446,000,000 (machinery and apparatus 19.7%, of which telecommunications equipment 4.2%; road vehicles 13.5%; apparel and clothing accessories 11.6%; footwear 5.7%; chemicals and chemical products 5.5%; fabrics 4.7%). *Major export destinations* (2001): Germany 19.2%; Spain 18.6%; France 12.6%; U.K. 10.3%; U.S. 5.8%.

Transport and communications

Transport. Railroads (1999): route length 3,579 km; passenger-km 4,380,000,000; metric ton-km cargo 2,560,000,000. Roads (1999): total length 68,732 km (paved 86%). Vehicles (1998): passenger cars 3,200,000; trucks and buses 1,097,000. Air transport (2001): passenger-km 10,457,000,000; metric ton-km cargo 53,865,000; airports (2000) 16.

Communications

Medium	date	unit	number	units per 1,000 persons
Daily newspapers	2000	circulation	324,000	32
Radio	2000	receivers	3,080,000	304
Television	2000	receivers	6,380,000	630
Telephones	2002	main lines	4,361,000	419
Cellular telephones	2002	subscribers	8,528,900	819
Personal computers	2002	units	1,394,000	134
Internet	2002	users	3,700,000	355

Education and health

Educational attainment (1991). Percentage of population age 25 and over having: no formal schooling 16.1%; some primary education 61.5%; some secondary 10.6%; postsecondary 3.5%. *Literacy* (2000): total population age 15 and over literate 92.2%; males literate 94.8%; females literate 90.0%.

Education (1998–99)

	schools	teachers	students	student/ teacher ratio
Primary (age 5–11)	12,635	145,513	1,563,700	10.7
Secondary (age 12–19)				
Vocational	215	6,895	80,130[11]	...
Higher	282	16,192[11]	346,034	...

Health (1998): physicians 31,087 (1 per 321 persons); hospital beds 39,870 (1 per 250 persons); infant mortality rate per 1,000 live births (2002) 5.8.
Food (2001): daily per capita caloric intake 3,751 (vegetable products 71%, animal products 29%); 153% of FAO recommended minimum requirement.

Military

Total active duty personnel (2003): 44,900 (army 59.5%, navy 24.4%, air force 16.1%). *Military expenditure as percentage of GNP* (1999): 2.1% (world 2.4%); per capita expenditure U.S.$240.

[1]The escudo was the former monetary unit; on Jan. 1, 2002, Esc 200.48 = €1. [2]Includes new areas based on regional boundaries changed in *c.* 2001. [3]Regional figures are rounded. [4]Detail does not add to total given because of rounding. [5]Final de facto figure; final de jure figure equals 10,356,117. [6]De jure figures. [7]Includes imputed bank service charges. [8]Includes 143,200 inadequately defined and 211,500 unemployed. [9]Imports c.i.f.; exports f.o.b. [10]In billions of escudos. [11]1996–97.

Internet resources for further information:
- **Instituto Nacional de Estatística http://www.ine.pt**
- **Banco de Portugal http://www.bportugal.pt**

Puerto Rico

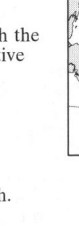

Official name: Estado Libre Asociado de Puerto Rico; Commonwealth of Puerto Rico.
Political status: self-governing commonwealth in association with the United States, having two legislative houses (Senate [27[1]]; House of Representatives [51[1]]).
Chief of state: President of the United States.
Head of government: Governor.
Capital: San Juan.
Official languages: Spanish; English.
Monetary unit: 1 U.S. dollar (U.S.$) = 100 cents; valuation (Sept. 8, 2003) 1 £ = U.S.$1.59.

Population (2000 census)

Municipios	population	Municipios	population	Municipios	population
Adjuntas	19,143	Fajardo	40,712	Naguabo	23,753
Aguada	42,042	Florida	12,367	Naranjito	29,709
Aguadilla	64,685	Guánica	21,888	Orocovis	23,844
Agunas Buenas	29,032	Guayama	44,301	Patillas	20,152
Aibonito	26,493	Guayanilla	23,072	Peñuelas	26,719
Añasco	28,348	Guaynabo	100,053	Ponce	186,475
Arecibo	100,131	Gurabo	36,743	Quebradillas	25,450
Arroyo	19,117	Hatillo	38,925	Rincón	14,767
Barceloneta	22,322	Hormigueros	16,614	Río Grande	52,362
Barranquitas	28,909	Humacao	59,035	Sabana Grande	25,935
Bayamón	224,044	Isabela	44,444	Salinas	31,113
Cabo Rojo	46,911	Jayuya	17,318	San Germán	37,105
Caguas	140,502	Juana Díaz	50,531	San Juan	434,374
Camuy	35,244	Juncos	36,452	San Lorenzo	40,997
Canóvanas	43,335	Lajas	26,261	San Sebastián	44,204
Carolina	186,076	Lares	34,415	Santa Isabel	21,665
Cataño	30,071	Las Marías	11,061	Toa Alta	63,929
Cayey	47,370	Las Piedras	34,485	Toa Baja	94,085
Ceiba	18,004	Loíza	32,537	Trujillo Alto	75,728
Ciales	19,811	Luquillo	19,817	Utuado	35,336
Cidra	42,753	Manatí	45,409	Vega Alta	37,910
Coamo	37,597	Maricao	6,449	Vega Baja	61,929
Comerío	20,002	Maunabo	12,741	Vieques	9,106
Corozal	36,867	Mayagüez	98,434	Villalba	27,913
Culebra	1,868	Moca	39,697	Yabucoa	39,246
Dorado	34,017	Morovis	29,965	Yauco	46,384
				TOTAL	3,808,610

Demography

Area: 3,515 sq mi, 9,104 sq km.
Population (2003): 3,879,000.
Density (2003): persons per sq mi 1,103.6, persons per sq km 426.1.
Urban-rural (2001): urban 75.6%; rural 24.4%.
Sex distribution (2000): male 48.14%; female 51.86%.
Age breakdown (2000): under 15, 23.8%; 15–34, 30.1%; 35–54, 25.7%; 55–64, 9.2%; 65 and over, 11.2%.
Population projection: (2010) 4,001,000; (2020) 4,109,000.
Doubling time: 99 years.
Ethnic composition (2000): local white 72.1%; black 15.0%; mulatto 10.0%; U.S. white 2.2%; other 0.7%.
Religious affiliation (2000): Roman Catholic 75.0%; Protestant 13.1%; independent Christian 6.4%; other 5.6%.
Major urban agglomerations (1998): San Juan 2,004,054; Ponce 366,273; Caguas 315,921; Mayagüez 258,283; Arecibo 176,814.

Vital statistics

Birth rate per 1,000 population (2002): 14.4 (world avg. 21.3).
Death rate per 1,000 population (2002): 7.6 (world avg. 9.1).
Natural increase rate per 1,000 population (2002): 6.8 (world avg. 12.2).
Total fertility rate (avg. births per childbearing woman; 2002): 1.9.
Marriage rate per 1,000 population (1996): 8.7.
Life expectancy at birth (2002): male 73.1 years; female 81.5 years.
Major causes of death per 100,000 population (1993): heart disease 142.6; cancers 95.4; diabetes 55.1; cerebrovascular disease 38.0; pneumonia and influenza 29.2.

National economy

Budget. Revenue (2000–01): U.S.$11,208,442,000 (tax revenue 57.3%, of which income taxes 40.5%, excise taxes 16.0%, intergovernment transfers 34.0%). Expenditures: U.S.$10,336,782,000 (welfare 22.3%; education 22.3%; public safety and protection 15.7%; debt service 9.8%; health 9.2%).
Public debt (outstanding; 1999): U.S.$22,678,200,000.
Tourism (2001): receipts U.S.$2,728,000,000; expenditures U.S.$1,004,000,000.
Production (in metric tons except as noted). Agriculture, forestry, fishing (2002): sugarcane 320,000, plantains 82,000, bananas 50,000, oranges 25,712, mangoes 17,375, pineapples 15,000, coffee 12,800, pumpkins, squash, and gourds 11,000; livestock (number of live animals) 390,000 cattle, 118,000 pigs; roundwood, n.a.; fish catch (2000) 4,308 metric tons. Mining (value of production in U.S.$'000; 1999): crushed stone 57. Manufacturing (value added in U.S.$'000,000; 1997): chemicals, pharmaceuticals, and allied products 21,393; food 3,532; machinery and metal products 2,940; petroleum products 849; clothing 679. Energy production (consumption): electricity (kW-hr; 1999) 20,370,000,000 ([2001] 20,500,000,000); coal (metric tons; 2001) none (172,000); crude petroleum (barrels; 2001) none (58,400,000); petroleum products (metric tons; 1999) 2,432,000 (4,688,000); natural gas, none (none).

Gross national product (2001): U.S.$45,300,000,000 (U.S.$11,783 per capita).

Structure of gross domestic product and labour force

	1999–2000		2001	
	in value U.S.$'000,000	% of total value	labour force	% of labour force
Agriculture	449,700	0.7	23,000	1.8
Manufacturing	27,441,900	43.5	147,000	11.3
Mining	1,862,700	2.9	2,000	0.2
Construction			85,000	6.6
Public utilities	4,057,400	6.4	15,000	1.2
Transp. and commun.			41,000	3.2
Trade	8,437,300	13.4	238,000	18.4
Finance, real estate	8,920,200	14.1	45,000	3.5
Pub. admin., defense	5,477,800	8.7	555,000	42.8
Services	6,678,900	10.6		
Other	–176,200[2]	–0.3[2]	147,000[3]	11.3[3]
TOTAL	63,149,700	100.0	1,297,000[4]	100.0[4]

Population economically active (1997): total 1,298,000; activity rate 34.1% (participation rates: ages 16 and over, 48.0%; female 39.5%; unemployed 13.1%).

Price and earnings indexes (1995 = 100)

	1993	1994	1995	1996	1997	1998	1999
Consumer price index	93.5	96.2	100.0	105.1	110.8	117.0	123.2
Hourly earnings index[5]	...	...	...	...	...	...	...

Household income and expenditure (1999). Average family size (2000) 3.0; income per family U.S.$32,892; sources of income: wages and salaries 60.6%, transfers 31.3%, rent 6.5%, self-employment 6.1%; expenditure: food and beverages 18.8%, health care 17.8%, transportation 12.8%, housing 12.1%, household furnishings 11.6%, clothing 7.9%, recreation 7.7%.

Foreign trade

Balance of trade (current prices)

	1996	1997	1998	1999	2000	2001
U.S.$'000,000	+3,800	+2,500	+8,500	+9,600	+11,500	+17,800
% of total	9.0%	5.5%	16.3%	15.9%	17.6%	23.4%

Imports (2001): U.S.$29,100,000,000 (incomplete breakdown; compounds used in the manufacture of medicines and pharmaceuticals 19.6%, refined petroleum 6.6%, passenger motor vehicles 5.5%). *Major import sources:* U.S. 53.4%; Ireland 16.3%; Japan 4.5%; U.S. Virgin Islands 2.7%.
Exports (2001): U.S.$46,900,000,000 (antibiotics 13.1%, antidepressants and tranquilizers 11.1%, analgesics and antipyretics 7.4%, other medicines and pharmaceuticals 19.5%). *Major export destinations:* U.S. 88.2%; U.K. 1.5%; Dominican Republic 1.4%.

Transport and communications

Transport. Railroads (1988)[6]: length 59 mi, 96 km. Roads (1996): total length 8,948 mi, 14,400 km (paved 100%). Vehicles (1996): passenger cars 878,000; trucks and buses 190,000. Air transport (1998): passenger arrivals and departures 9,285,000; cargo loaded and unloaded 275,500 metric tons[7]; airports (1998) with scheduled flights 7.

Communications

Medium	date	unit	number	units per 1,000 persons
Daily newspapers	2000	circulation	481,000	126
Radio	2000	receivers	2,830,000	742
Television	2000	receivers	1,260,000	330
Telephones	2001	main lines	1,330,000	336
Cellular telephones	2001	subscribers	1,211,000	307
Internet	2001	users	600,000	152

Education and health

Educational attainment (2000). Percentage of population age 25 and over having: no formal schooling to secondary education 25.4%; some upper secondary to some higher 60.0%; undergraduate or graduate degree 18.3%.
Literacy (2000): total population age 15 and over literate 93.8%; males literate 93.7%; females literate 94.0%.

Education (1985–86)

	schools	teachers	students	student/ teacher ratio
Primary (age 5–12)	1,542	18,359	427,582	23.3
Secondary (age 13–18)	395	13,612	334,661	24.6
Voc., teacher tr.	52	...	149,191	...
Higher	45	9,045	156,818	17.3

Health: physicians (1999) 6,650 (1 per 571 persons); hospital beds (1993–94) 9,598 (1 per 381 persons); infant mortality rate (2002) 8.6.

Military

Total active duty personnel (2001): 2,840 U.S. personnel[8].

[1]Number of members per constitution. Excludes additional seats allotted to either the Senate or House of Representatives to meet 1/3 total representation requirements for minority parties per constitution. [2]Statistical discrepancy. [3]Unemployed. [4]Detail does not add to total given because of rounding. [5]Manufacturing sector only. [6]Privately owned railway for sugarcane transport only. [7]Handled by the Luis Muñoz Marín International Airport only. [8]The U.S. naval base at Ceiba is scheduled to close in 2004.

Internet resources for further information:

- **Junta de Plantificacion http://www.jp.gobierno.pr**
- **Global Development Bank http://www.gdb-pur.com**

Qatar

Official name: Dawlat Qaṭar (State of Qatar).
Form of government: constitutional emirate[1].
Heads of state and government: Emir assisted by Prime Minister.
Capital: Doha.
Official language: Arabic.
Official religion: Islam.
Monetary unit: 1 riyal (QR) = 100 dirhams; valuation (Sept. 8, 2003) 1 U.S.$ = QR 3.64; 1 £ = QR 5.77.

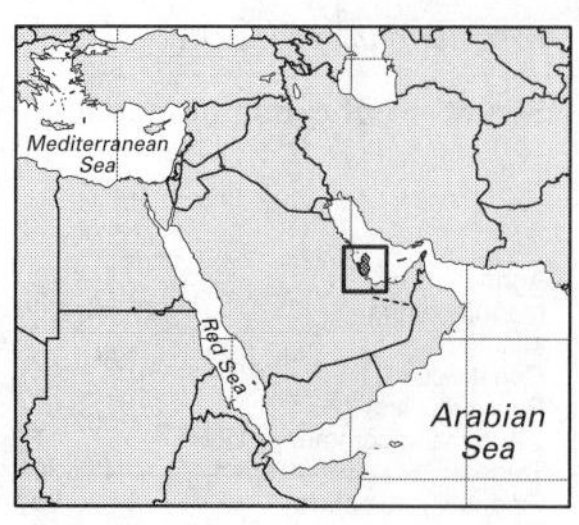

Area and population

Municipalities	Capitals	area sq mi	area sq km	population 1997 census
Ad-Dawḥah (Doha)	—	51	132	264,009
Al-Ghuwayrīyah	Al-Ghuwayrīyah	240	622	1,716
Jarayān al-Bāṭinah	Jarayān al-Bāṭinah	1,434	3,715	4,742
Al-Jumaylīyah	Al-Jumaylīyah	991[2]	2,565[2]	9,836
Al-Khawr	Al-Khawr	385	996	17,793
Ar-Rayyān	Ar-Rayyān	343	889	169,774
Ash-Shamāl	Madinat ash-Shamāl	348	901	4,059
Umm Ṣalāl	Umm Ṣalāl Muḥammad	190	493	18,392
Al-Wakrah	Al-Wakrah	430	1,114	31,702
TOTAL		4,412[3]	11,427[3]	522,023

Demography

Population (2003): 626,000.
Density (2003): persons per sq mi 141.9, persons per sq km 54.8.
Urban-rural (2001): urban 92.9%; rural 7.1%.
Sex distribution (2002): male 65.6%; female 34.4%.
Age breakdown (2002): under 15, 25.2%; 15–29, 23.2%; 30–44, 25.2%; 45–59, 21.0%; 60–74, 4.8%; 75 and over, 0.6%.
Population projection: (2010) 689,000; (2020) 773,000.
Doubling time: 59 years.
Ethnic composition (2000): Arab 52.5%, of which Palestinian 13.4%, Qatari 13.3%, Lebanese 10.4%, Syrian 9.4%; Persian 16.5%; Indo-Pakistani 15.2%; black African 9.5%; other 6.3%.
Religious affiliation (2000): Muslim (mostly Sunnī) 82.7%; Christian 10.4%; Hindu 2.5%; other 4.4%.
Major cities (1997): Ad-Dawḥah (Doha) 264,009 (urban agglomeration [1999] 391,000); Ar-Rayyān 161,453; Al-Wakrah 20,205; Umm Ṣalāl 15,935.

Vital statistics

Birth rate per 1,000 population (2002): 15.8 (world avg. 21.3).
Death rate per 1,000 population (2002): 4.3 (world avg. 9.1).
Natural increase rate per 1,000 population (2002): 11.5 (world avg. 12.2).
Total fertility rate (avg. births per childbearing woman; 2002): 3.1.
Marriage rate per 1,000 population (1994): 2.8.
Divorce rate per 1,000 population (1994): 1.0.
Life expectancy at birth (2002): male 70.4 years; female 75.5 years.
Major causes of death per 100,000 population (1992): diseases of the circulatory system 56.9; injuries and poisoning 36.0; neoplasms (including benign neoplasms) 21.4; certain conditions originating in the perinatal period 11.1; diseases of the respiratory system 7.5; endocrine, metabolic, and nutritional diseases and immunity disorders 7.3; diseases of the digestive system 3.4; signs, symptoms, and ill-defined conditions 10.9.

National economy

Budget (2002–03). Revenue: QR 26,636,000,000 (crude oil about 90%). Expenditures: QR 22,516,000,000 (current expenditure 80.8%, of which wages and salaries 25.5%; capital expenditure 19.2%).
Production (metric tons except as noted). Agriculture, forestry, fishing (2002): dates 16,500, tomatoes 11,000, pumpkin and squash 8,500, barley 4,650, dry onions 4,000, melons 3,450, watermelons 1,400; livestock (number of live animals; 2002) 200,000 sheep, 179,000 goats, 50,000 camels, 15,000 cattle; fish catch (2001) 7,142. Mining and quarrying (2001): limestone 900,000; sulfur 220,824; gypsum, sand and gravel, and clay are also produced. Manufacturing (value added in QR '000,000; 1998): industrial chemicals 516; fertilizers and pesticides 474; iron and steel 459; wearing apparel 235; pottery, china, and earthenware 194; cement and plaster 157; refined petroleum 112. Construction (1992): residential 12,420 units; nonresidential 1,416 units. Energy production (consumption): electricity (kW-hr; 1999) 8,164,000,000 (8,164,000,000); coal, none (n.a.); crude petroleum (barrels; 2001) 243,788,000 ([1999] 28,100,000); petroleum products (metric tons; 1999) 5,489,000 (1,482,000); natural gas (cu m; 1999) 29,819,900,000 (21,994,200,000).
Tourism (1997): receipts and expenditures, n.a.; total number of tourists staying in hotels 435,000.
Population economically active (2001): total 317,000; activity rate of total population 53.1% (participation rates [1997]: ages 15–64, 59.7%; female [1997] 21.0%; unemployed, n.a.).

Price and earnings indexes (1995 = 100)

	1996	1997	1998	1999	2000	2001	2002
Consumer price index	107.4	110.4	113.3	115.7	117.7	119.3	120.5
Earnings index	...	...	...	...	...	...	...

Gross national product (2001): U.S.$7,200,000,000 (U.S.$12,000 per capita).

Structure of gross domestic product and labour force

	2002 in value QR '000,000	2002 % of total value	2001 labour force	2001 % of labour force
Agriculture	255	0.4	4,000	1.3
Oil sector	37,500	58.9	313,000	98.7
Manufacturing	3,600	5.7		
Construction	2,390	3.8		
Public utilities	795	1.3		
Transportation	2,120	3.3		
Trade	3,795	6.0		
Finance	4,793	7.5		
Pub. admin., defense; Services; Other	8,330	13.1		
TOTAL	63,578	100.0	317,000	100.0

Household income and expenditure. Average household size (2000) 7.0; income per household: n.a., sources of income, n.a.; expenditure (1993): food 28.7%, transportation 19.3%, housing 12.4%, clothing 10.6%, education 7.6%, health 1.2%.
Land use (1994): meadows and pastures 4.5%; agricultural and under permanent cultivation 0.7%; built-up, desert, and other 94.7%.

Foreign trade[4]

Balance of trade (current prices)

	1997	1998	1999	2000	2001	2002
QR '000,000	+3,143	+7,134	+18,062	+31,538	+27,243	+24,412
% of total	12.6%	24.2%	52.4%	59.7%	52.5%	43.7%

Imports (2001): QR 13,678,000,000 (machinery and apparatus 35.6%, of which general industrial machinery 11.8%, specialized machinery 6.4%; road vehicles 11.6%; food and live animals 9.7%; chemicals and chemical products 6.9%). *Major import sources:* U.S. 13.8%; Italy 9.8%; Japan 9.5%; Germany 9.2%; U.K. 9.1%; Saudi Arabia 5.4%.
Exports (2001): QR 38,969,000,000 (crude petroleum 52.4%; liquefied natural gas 35.5%; chemicals and chemical products 4.3%). *Major export destinations:* Japan 51.8%; South Korea 20.0%; Singapore 6.9%; U.S. 3.5%.

Transport and communications

Transport. Railroads: none. Roads (1996): total length 764 mi, 1,230 km (paved 90%). Vehicles (2000): passenger cars 199,600; trucks and buses 92,900. Merchant marine (2001): vessels (100 gross tons and over) 68; total deadweight tonnage 690,812. Air transport (2001)[5]: passenger-mi 2,133,650,000, passenger-km 3,433,790,000; short ton-mi cargo 83,432,000, metric ton-km cargo 121,809,000; airports (2001) with scheduled flights 1.

Communications

Medium	date	unit	number	units per 1,000 persons
Daily newspapers	1995	circulation	90,000	161
Radio	1997	receivers	250,000	432
Television	1998	receivers	490,000	846
Telephones	2002	main lines	176,500	289
Cellular telephones	2001	subscribers	266,700	437
Personal computers	2001	units	110,000	180
Internet	2001	users	70,000	156

Education and health

Educational attainment (1986). Percentage of population age 25 and over having: no formal education 53.3%, of which illiterate 24.3%; primary 9.8%; preparatory (lower secondary) 10.1%; secondary 13.3%; postsecondary 13.3%; other 0.2%. *Literacy* (2000): total population age 15 and over literate 81.2%; males literate 80.4%; females literate 83.1%.

Education (1995–96)[6]

	schools	teachers	students	student/teacher ratio
Primary (age 6–11)	174	5,864	53,631	9.1
Secondary (age 12–17)	123	3,738	37,924	10.1
Vocational[7]	3	120	670	5.6
Higher[8]	1	643	8,475	13.2

Health: physicians (1996) 703 (1 per 793 persons); hospital beds (1995) 892 (1 per 555 persons); infant mortality rate per 1,000 live births (2002) 20.3.

Military

Total active duty personnel (2002): 12,400 (army 68.5%, navy 14.5%, air force 16.9%); U.S. troops (2002) 3,300. *Military expenditure as percentage of GNP* (1999): 10.0% (world 2.4%); per capita expenditure U.S.$1,470.

[1]Referendum on new draft constitution approved April 29, 2003. Expect new legislative assembly in 2004. [2]Includes the area of the unpopulated and formerly disputed (with Bahrain) Hawar Islands. The International Court of Justice awarded Hawar to Bahrain in early 2001. Qatar was awarded jurisdiction over some nearby islets. [3]Includes approximately 4 sq mi (10 sq km) of area not distributed by municipalities. [4]Imports f.o.b. in balance of trade and c.i.f. in commodities and trading partners. [5]Qatar Airways. [6]Public schools only; available detail for private schools (1991–92) included 17,728 primary students, 1,695 secondary students, and 1,465 teachers. [7]1994–95. [8]1996–97.

Internet resources for further information:
- **Qatar Central Bank http://www.qcb.gov.qa**
- **Qatar Embassy, Washington, D.C. http://www.qatarembassy.org**

Réunion

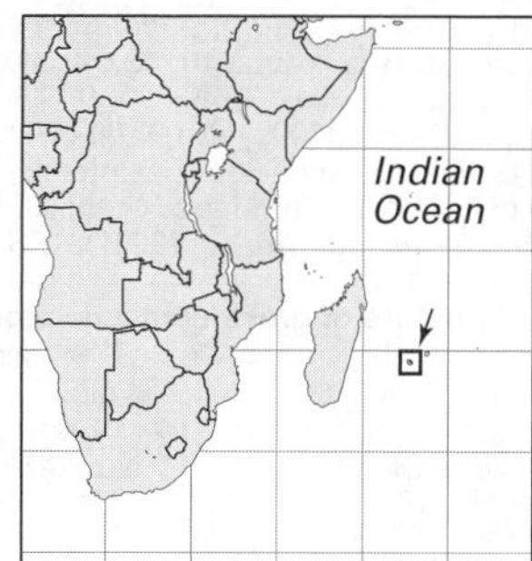

Official name: Département de la Réunion (Department of Réunion).
Political status: overseas department (France) with two legislative houses (General Council [47]; Regional Council [45]).
Chief of state: President of France.
Heads of government: Prefect (for France); President of General Council (for Réunion); President of Regional Council (for Réunion).
Capital: Saint-Denis.
Official language: French.
Official religion: none.
Monetary unit: 1 euro (€) = 100 cents; valuation (Sept. 8, 2003) 1 U.S.$ = €0.90; 1 £ = €1.43[1].

Area and population

		area		population
Arrondissements	Capitals	sq mi	sq km	1999 census
Saint-Benoît	Saint-Benoît	285	737	101,804
Saint-Denis	Saint-Denis	163	421	236,599
Saint-Paul	Saint-Paul	180	467	138,551
Saint-Pierre	Saint-Pierre	341	883	229,346
TOTAL		968[2, 3]	2,507[2, 3]	706,300

Demography

Population (2003): 760,000.
Density (2002): persons per sq mi 767.6, persons per sq km 296.4.
Urban-rural (1999): urban 71.6%; rural 28.4%[4].
Sex distribution (1999): male 49.15%; female 50.85%.
Age breakdown (1999): under 15, 27.0%; 15–29, 24.8%; 30–44, 24.4%; 45–59, 13.8%; 60–74, 7.2%; 75 and over, 2.8%.
Population projection: (2010) 826,000; (2020) 905,000.
Doubling time: 49 years.
Ethnic composition (2000): mixed race (black-white-South Asian) 42.6%; local white 25.6%; South Asian 23.0%, of which Tamil 20.0%; Chinese 3.4%; East African 3.4%; Malagasy 1.4%; other 0.6%.
Religious affiliation (1995): Roman Catholic 89.4%; Pentecostal 2.7%; other Christian 1.8%; other (mostly Muslim) 6.1%.
Major cities (1999): Saint-Denis 131,557[5] (agglomeration 158,139); Saint-Paul 87,712[5]; Saint-Pierre 68,915[5] (agglomeration 129,238); Le Tampon 60,323[5, 6]; Saint-Louis 43,519[5].

Vital statistics

Birth rate per 1,000 population (2002): 20.7 (world avg. 21.3); (1997) legitimate 41.5%; illegitimate 58.5%.
Death rate per 1,000 population (2002): 5.5 (world avg. 9.1).
Natural increase rate per 1,000 population (2002): 15.2 (world avg. 12.2).
Total fertility rate (avg. births per childbearing woman; 2002): 2.6.
Marriage rate per 1,000 population (1998): 4.8.
Divorce rate per 1,000 population (1997): 1.3.
Life expectancy at birth (2001): male 71.0 years; female 76.4 years.
Major causes of death per 100,000 population (1996): diseases of the circulatory system 170.7; malignant neoplasms (cancers) 98.0; accidents, suicide, and violence 53.0; diseases of the respiratory system 48.5.

National economy

Budget (1998). Revenue: F 4,624,000,000 (receipts from the French central government and local administrative bodies 52.7%, tax receipts 20.2%, loans 8.9%). Expenditures: F 4,300,000,000 (current expenditures 68.7%, development expenditures 31.3%).
Public debt (external, outstanding): n.a.
Tourism (2001): receipts U.S.$244,000,000; expenditures U.S.$309,000,000.
Gross national product (1998): U.S.$5,070,000,000 (U.S.$7,270 per capita).

Structure of gross domestic product and labour force

	1996		1999	
	in value €'000,000	% of total value	labour force	% of labour force
Agriculture, fishing	219	3.2	9,562	3.2
Manufacturing, mining / Public utilities	451	6.7	13,424	4.5
Construction	396	5.9	11,003	3.7
Transp. and commun.	339	5.0	5,494	1.8
Trade, restaurants	832	12.3	24,658	8.2
Finance, real estate, business services	1,114	16.5	16,076	5.4
Pub. admin., defense	3,063	45.4	40,019	13.4
Services			54,408	18.2
Other	339[7]	5.0[7]	124,203[8]	41.6[8]
TOTAL	6,753	100.0	298,847	100.0

Production (metric tons except as noted). Agriculture, forestry, fishing (2001): sugarcane 1,850,000, corn (maize) 17,000, bananas 10,200, pineapples 10,000, cabbages 8,500, tomatoes 5,400, lettuce 4,500, potatoes 4,000, carrots 3,800, eggplants 3,200, pimento 800, ginger 200, vanilla 35, tobacco 20, geranium essence (1998) 6.3; livestock (number of live animals) 78,000 pigs, 37,000 goats, 30,000 cattle; roundwood (2002) 36,100 cu m; fish catch (2002) 3,635. Mining and quarrying: gravel and sand for local use. Manufacturing (value added in F '000,000; 1997): food and beverages 1,019, of which meat and milk products 268; construction materials (mostly cement) 394; fabricated metals 258; printing and publishing 192. Energy production (consumption): electricity (kW-hr; 2000) 1,757,000,000 ([1999] 1,570,000,000); petroleum products (metric tons; 1999) none (708,000).
Population economically active (1998): total 288,760; activity rate of total population 41.2% (participation rates: ages 15–64, 57.5%; female 44.3%; unemployed [2000] 36.5%).

Price and earnings indexes (December 1997 = 100)[9]

	1996	1997	1998	1999	2000	2001	2002
Consumer price index	98.6	100.0	100.9	101.9	104.1	106.2	108.8[10]
Monthly earnings index[11]	98.9	100.0	101.4	102.8	103.4	108.5	109.1[10]

Household income and expenditure. Average household size (1999) 3.3; average annual income per household (1997) F 136,800 (U.S.$23,438); sources of income (1997): wages and salaries and self-employment 41.8%, transfer payments 41.3%, other 16.9%; expenditure (1994–95): food and beverages 22.0%, transportation and communications 19.0%, housing and energy 10.0%, household furnishings 8.0%, recreation 6.0%.
Land use (1994): forested 35.2%; meadows and pastures 4.8%; agricultural and under permanent cultivation 19.6%; other 40.4%.

Foreign trade

Balance of trade (current prices)

	1997[12]	1998	1999	2000	2001	2002
€'000,000	–13,011	–2,155	–2,226	–2,503	–2,556	–2,746
% of total	83.9%	85.3%	84.6%	84.7%	84.8%	86.2%

Imports (2002): €2,966,000,000 (food and agricultural products 18.2%, automobiles 12.9%, electrical machinery and electronics 9.0%, pharmaceuticals and medicines 8.4%, clothing and footwear 7.9%). *Major import sources* (1998): France 66.0%; EC 14.0%.
Exports (1998): €185,700,000 (sugar 58.9%, machinery, apparatus, and transport equipment 17.5%, rum 2.5%, lobster 1.7%). *Major export destinations* (1998): France 70.0%; EC 9.0%; Madagascar 4.5%; Mauritius 2.3%.

Transport and communications

Transport. Railroads: [13]. Roads (1994): total length 1,711 mi, 2,754 km (paved [1991] 79%). Vehicles (1999): passenger cars 190,300; trucks and buses 44,300. Air transport (2001)[14]: passenger arrivals 747,044, passenger departures 744,788; cargo unloaded 17,945 metric tons, cargo loaded 8,881 metric tons; airports (2001) with scheduled flights 2.

Communications

Medium	date	unit	number	units per 1,000 persons
Daily newspapers	1996	circulation	83,000	123
Radio	1997	receivers	173,000	252
Television	1998	receivers	130,000	186
Telephones	1999	main lines	268,496	378
Cellular telephones	2000	subscribers	276,100	382
Personal computers	1999	units	32,000	45
Internet	2000	users	130,000	180

Education and health

Educational attainment (1986–87). Percentage of population age 25 and over having: no formal schooling 18.8%; primary education 44.3%; lower secondary 21.6%; upper secondary 11.0%; higher 4.3%. *Literacy* (1996): total population age 16–66 literate 373,487 (91.3%); males literate 179,154 (89.9%); females literate 194,333 (92.7%).

Education (2001–02)

	schools	teachers	students	student/ teacher ratio
Primary (age 6–10)	354[15]	...	77,792	...
Secondary (age 11–17)	118	7,868	98,848	12.6
Higher[16]	1	343	10,637	31.0

Health (2002): physicians 1,137 (1 per 449 persons); hospital beds (2000) 2,124 (1 per 337 persons); infant mortality rate per 1,000 live births (2002) 8.3.
Food (2001): daily per capita caloric intake, n.a.

Military

Total active duty personnel (2003): 3,600 French troops[17].

[1]The French franc was the former monetary unit; on Jan. 1, 2002, F 6.56 = €1. [2]Detail does not add to total given because of rounding. [3]Indian Ocean islets administered by France from Réunion are excluded from total. Islets between Africa and Réunion, which have no permanent population, are: Îles Glorieuses 1.9 sq mi (5.0 sq km), Île Juan de Nova 1.7 sq mi (4.4 sq km), Île Tromelin 0.4 sq mi (1.0 sq km), Bassas da India 0.1 sq mi (0.2 sq km), Île Europa 7.8 sq mi (20.2 sq km). The French overseas territory of French Southern and Antarctic Territories has been administered from Réunion since April 2000. It comprises 2 archipelagos and 2 islands in the South Indian Ocean as well as the French-claimed part of Antarctica. Non-Antarctic scientific population in summer (2000) 172; non-Antarctic area 4,844 sq mi (7,796 sq km). [4]Includes semi-urban. [5]Population of commune. [6]Within Saint-Pierre agglomeration. [7]Less imputed bank service charges. [8]Unemployed. [9]Indexes refer to December. [10]September. [11]Minimum salary in public administration. [12]In F '000,000. [13]No public railways; railways in use are for sugar industry. [14]Saint-Denis airport only. [15]2000–01. [16]University only. [17]Includes troops stationed on Mayotte.

Internet resources for further information:
- **INSEE: Réunion http://www.insee.fr/fr/insee_regions/reunion/home/home_page.asp**
- **Ministère de l'Outre-mer (Paris) http://www.outre-mer.gouv.fr**

Romania

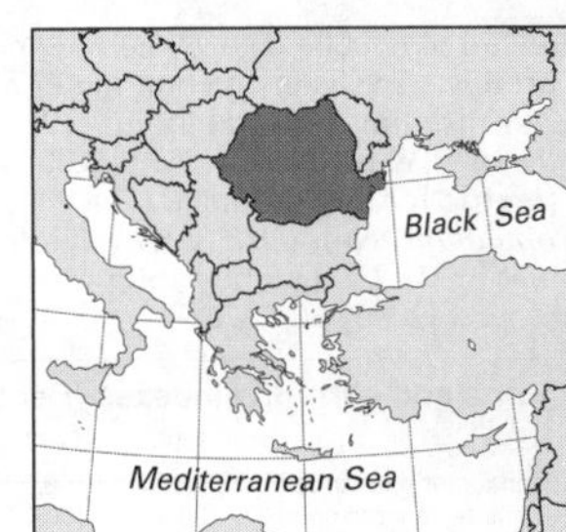

Official name: România (Romania).
Form of government: unitary republic with two legislative houses (Senate [143]; Assembly of Deputies [345[1]]).
Chief of state: President.
Head of government: Prime Minister.
Capital: Bucharest.
Official language: Romanian.
Official religion: none.
Monetary unit: 1 Romanian leu (plural lei) = 100 bani; valuation (Sept. 8, 2003) 1 U.S.$ = 34,039 lei; 1 £ = 53,971 lei.

Area and population

Counties	area sq km	population 2002 census[2]	Counties	area sq km	population 2002 census[2]
Alba	6,231	382,999	Iași	5,469	819,044
Arad	7,652	461,730	Ilfov	1,593	300,109
Argeș	6,801	653,903	Maramureș	6,215	510,688
Bacău	6,606	708,751	Mehedinți	4,900	306,118
Bihor	7,535	600,223	Mureș	6,696	579,862
Bistrița-Năsăud	5,305	312,325	Neamț	5,890	557,084
Botoșani	4,965	454,023	Olt	5,507	490,276
Brăila	4,724	588,366	Prahova	4,694	829,224
Brașov	5,351	373,897	Sălaj	3,850	248,407
Buzău	6,072	494,982	Satu Mare	4,405	369,096
Călărași	5,074	324,629	Sibiu	5,422	422,224
Caraș-Severin	8,503	333,396	Suceava	8,555	690,941
Cluj	6,650	703,269	Teleorman	5,760	436,926
Constanța	7,055	715,172	Timiș	8,692	677,744
Covasna	3,705	222,274	Tulcea	8,430	258,639
Dâmbovița	4,036	541,326	Vâlcea	5,705	413,570
Dolj	7,413	734,823	Vaslui	5,297	455,550
Galați	4,425	619,522	Vrancea	4,863	390,268
Giurgiu	3,511	298,022	**Municipality**		
Gorj	5,641	387,407	Bucharest	227	1,921,751
Harghita	6,610	326,020	TOTAL	237,500	21,698,181
Hunedoara	7,016	487,115			
Ialomița	4,449	296,486			

Demography

Population (2003): 21,616,000.
Density (2003): persons per sq mi 235.7, persons per sq km 91.0.
Urban-rural (2002): urban 52.7%; rural 47.3%.
Sex distribution (2002): male 48.77%; female 51.23%.
Age breakdown (2002): under 15, 18.4%; 15–29, 24.1%; 30–44, 21.0%; 45–59, 17.7%; 60–74, 14.3%; 75 and over, 4.5%.
Population projection: (2010) 21,265,000; (2020) 20,571,000.
Ethnic composition (2002): Romanian 89.5%; Hungarian 6.6%; Roma (Gypsy) 2.5%; other 1.4%.
Religious affiliation (2002): Romanian Orthodox 86.7%; Protestant 6.4%; Roman Catholic 4.7%; Greek Orthodox 0.9%; Muslim 0.3%; other 1.0%.
Major cities (2000): Bucharest 2,009,200; Iași 345,795; Constanța 337,216; Timișoara 329,554; Cluj-Napoca 329,310; Galați 326,956.

Vital statistics

Birth rate per 1,000 population (2000): 10.8 (world avg. 21.3).
Death rate per 1,000 population (2000): 12.3 (world avg. 9.1).
Natural increase rate per 1,000 population (2000): –1.7 (world avg. 12.2).
Total fertility rate (avg. births per childbearing woman; 2001): 1.4.
Marriage rate per 1,000 population (1995): 6.8.
Life expectancy at birth (2001): male 67.8 years; female 74.5 years.
Major causes of death per 100,000 population (2000): circulatory disease 1,439.9; malignant neoplasms (cancers) 187.2; respiratory disease 67.7; diseases of the digestive system 65.6.

National economy

Budget ('000,000 lei; 2000). Revenue: 119,763,500 (value-added tax 42.1%, excise tax 17.2%, personal income tax 16.6%, nontax revenue 4.5%). Expenditures: 105,923,100 (economic affairs 23.0%, education 19.0%, defense 13.3%, public order 13.2%).
Public debt (external, outstanding; 2001): U.S.$6,682,000,000.
Population economically active (2001): total 11,446,900; activity rate 52.6% (participation rates: ages 15–64, 74.5%; female 46.2%; unemployed 6.6%).

Price and earnings indexes (1995 = 100)

	1996	1997	1998	1999	2000	2001	2002
Consumer price index	138.8	353.7	562.7	820.4	1,195.1	1,607.0	1,969.2
Annual earnings index	149.0	295.0	502.9	719.6	1,006.0	1,413.3	1,796.3

Household income and expenditure. Average household size (2000) 3.1; income per household, n.a.; sources of income, n.a.
Production (metric tons). Agriculture (2002): corn (maize) 8,500,000, wheat 4,380,000, potatoes 4,000,000, grapes 895,000, sugar beets 870,000, plums 530,000; livestock (number of live animals) 7,251,000 sheep, 4,446,800 pigs, 2,799,800 cattle; roundwood (2002) 15,154,000 cu m; fish catch (2000) 17,099. Mining (2000): iron (metal content) 55,000; bauxite 135,000; zinc (metal content of concentrate) 27,455; lead (metal content of concentrate) 18,744; copper (metal content of concentrate) 16,079. Manufacturing (value-added in '000,000,000,000 lei; 1996): food products 5.8; beverages 3.0; iron and steel 1.6; glass products 1.5; textiles 1.4; motor vehicles 1.3; electrical machinery 0.9. Construction (1995): 9,300 dwelling units. Energy production (consumption): electricity (kW-hr; 2001) 53,640,000,000 ([1999] 49,883,000,000); hard coal (metric tons; 2000) 3,240,000 ([1999] 3,651,000); lignite (metric tons; 2001) 29,431,000 ([1999] 24,092,000); crude petroleum (barrels; 2001) 45,164,000 ([1999] 78,100,000); petroleum products (metric tons; 1999) 8,533,000 (8,235,000); natural gas (cu m; 2001) 12,172,000,000 ([1999] 14,425,700,000).
Gross national product (2001): U.S.$38,600,000,000 (U.S.$1,720 per capita).

Structure of gross domestic product and labour force

	2000		2001	
	in value '000,000,000 lei	% of total value	labour force	% of labour force
Agriculture	90,929.3	11.4	4,526,800	39.5
Industry[3]	219,861.1	27.6	2,373,700	20.7
Construction	38,127.3	4.8	430,000	3.8
Transp. and commun.	370,916.4	46.5	519,400	4.5
Trade			1,082,800	9.5
Finance			200,000	1.7
Pub. admin.			581,400	5.1
Services			982,800	8.6
Other	78,699.6[4]	9.9[4]	750,000[5]	6.6[5]
TOTAL	796,533.7	100.0[6]	11,446,900	100.0

Tourism (2001): receipts U.S.$362,000,000; expenditures U.S.$449,000,000.

Foreign trade[7]

Balance of trade (current prices)

	1997	1998	1999	2000	2001	2002
U.S.$'000,000	–1,980	–2,611	–1,087	–1,683	–2,973	–2,611
% of total	10.5%	13.6%	6.0%	7.5%	11.5%	8.6%

Imports (2001): U.S.$15,552,000,000 (nonelectrical machinery and apparatus 11.9%, fabrics 11.6%, electrical machinery and telecommunications equipment 10.9%, chemicals and chemical products 9.3%, crude and refined petroleum 8.7%). *Major import sources:* Italy 20.0%; Germany 15.2%; Russia 7.6%; France 6.3%; Hungary 3.9%.
Exports (2001): U.S.$11,385,000,000 (apparel and clothing accessories 24.4%, electrical machinery and telecommunications equipment 8.0%, iron and steel 7.2%, nonelectrical machinery and apparatus 6.7%, footwear 5.6%, refined petroleum 5.3%). *Major export destinations:* Italy 25.1%; Germany 15.6%; France 8.1%; U.K. 5.2%; Turkey 4.0%.

Transport and communications

Transport. Railroads (2000): length 11,385 km; passenger-km 11,632,000,000; metric ton-km cargo 17,982,000,000. Roads (2001): length 198,603 km (paved 64%). Vehicles (2000): cars 3,128,782; trucks and buses 461,635. Air transport (2002): passenger-km 1,908,000,000; metric ton-km cargo 8,664,000; airports (2001) 8.

Communications

Medium	date	unit	number	units per 1,000 persons
Daily newspapers	2000	circulation	6,560,000	300
Radio	2000	receivers	7,310,000	334
Television	2000	receivers	8,340,000	381
Telephones	2001	main lines	4,094,000	183
Cellular telephones	2001	subscribers	3,860,000	172
Personal computers	2002	units	898,000	40
Internet	2002	users	1,800,000	81

Education and health

Educational attainment (1992). Percentage of population age 25 and over having: no schooling 5.4%; some primary education 24.4%; some secondary 63.2%; postsecondary 6.9%. *Literacy* (2000): total population age 15 and over literate 98.1%; males 99.0%; females 97.3%.

Education (2000–01)

	schools	teachers	students	student/ teacher ratio
Primary (age 6–9)	12,709	162,606	2,411,505	14.8
Secondary (age 10–17)	1,367	64,018	687,919	10.7
Voc., teacher tr.	201	6,387	330,655	51.8
Higher	126	27,959	533,152	19.1

Health: physicians (1998) 40,658 (1 per 543 persons); hospital beds (1992) 174,900 (1 per 130 persons); infant mortality rate (2002) 18.9.
Food (2001): daily per capita caloric intake 3,407 (vegetable products 80%, animal products 20%); 125% of FAO recommended minimum requirement.

Military

Total active duty personnel (2002): 99,200 (army 66.5%, navy 6.3%, air force 17.1%, other 10.1%). *Military expenditure as percentage of GNP* (2001): 1.6% (world 2.4%); per capita expenditure U.S.$97.

[1]Includes 18 elective seats for minority parties. [2]Preliminary. [3]Mining, manufacturing, and public utilities. [4]Taxes less imputed bank charges. [5]Unemployed. [6]Detail does not add to total given because of rounding. [7]Imports f.o.b. in balance of trade and c.i.f. in commodities and trading partners.

Internet resources for further information:
- **Embassy of Romania (Washington, D.C.) http://www.roembus.org**
- **National Institute of Statistics http://www.insse.ro/NIS.htm**
- **National Bank of Romania http://www.bnro.ro/def_en.htm**

Russia

Official name: Rossiyskaya Federatsiya (Russian Federation).
Form of government: federal multiparty republic with a bicameral legislative body (Federal Assembly comprising a Federation Council [178] and a State Duma [450]).
Head of state: President.
Head of government: Prime Minister.
Capital: Moscow.
Official language: Russian.
Official religion: none.
Monetary unit: 1 ruble (Rub) = 100 kopecks; valuation (Sept. 8, 2003) market rate, 1 U.S.$ = Rub 30.68; 1 £ = Rub 48.65.

Area and population

		area		population
Federal districts[1]	**Capitals**	sq mi	sq km	2002 census
Central	Moscow (Moskva)	251,200	650,700	37,991,000
Belgorod (region)	Belgorod	10,500	27,100	1,512,400
Bryansk (region)	Bryansk	13,500	34,900	1,378,900
Ivanovo (region)	Ivanovo	8,400	21,800	1,148,900
Kaluga (region)	Kaluga	11,500	29,900	1,040,900
Kostroma (region)	Kostroma	23,200	60,100	737,500
Kursk (region)	Kursk	11,500	29,800	1,235,600
Lipetsk (region)	Lipetsk	9,300	24,100	1,213,400
Moscow (city)		[2]	[2]	10,101,500
Moskva (Moscow; region)	Moscow (Moskva)	18,200[2]	47,000[2]	6,627,000
Oryol (region)	Oryol	9,500	24,700	860,600
Ryazan (region)	Ryazan	15,300	39,600	1,228,000
Smolensk (region)	Smolensk	19,200	49,800	1,050,500
Tambov (region)	Tambov	13,200	34,300	1,179,600
Tula (region)	Tula	9,900	25,700	1,675,700
Tver (region)	Tver	32,500	84,100	1,472,600
Vladimir (region)	Vladimir	11,200	29,000	1,524,900
Voronezh (region)	Voronezh	20,200	52,400	2,379,000
Yaroslavl (region)	Yaroslavl	14,100	36,400	1,367,700
Far Eastern	Khabarovsk	2,400,000	6,215,900	6,686,700
Amur (region)	Blagoveshchensk	140,400	363,700	902,500
Chukot (autonomous district)	Anadyr	284,800	737,700	53,600
Kamchatka (region)	Petropavlovsk-Kamchatsky	66,000	170,800	333,800
Khabarovsk (territory)	Khabarovsk	304,500	788,600	1,435,400
Koryak (autonomous district)	Palana	116,400	301,500	25,000
Magadan (region)	Magadan	178,100	461,400	182,700
Primorye (territory)	Vladivostok	64,100	165,900	2,068,200
Sakha (republic)	Yakutsk	1,198,200	3,103,200	948,100
Sakhalin (region)	Yuzhno-Sakhalinsk	33,600	87,100	546,500
Yevreyskaya (autonomous region)	Birobidzhan	13,900	36,000	190,900
Northwest	St. Petersburg	648,000	1,677,900	13,986,000
Arkhangelsk (region)	Arkhangelsk	158,700	411,000	1,294,200
Kaliningrad (region)	Kaliningrad	5,800	15,100	955,200
Kareliya (republic)	Petrozavodsk	66,600	172,400	716,700
Komi (republic)	Kudymkar	160,600	415,900	1,019,000
Leningrad (region)	St. Petersburg	33,200[3]	85,900[3]	1,671,100
Murmansk (region)	Murmansk	55,900	144,900	893,300
Nenets (autonomous district)	Naryan-Mar	68,100	176,400	41,500
Novgorod (region)	Novgorod	21,400	55,300	694,700
Pskov (region)	Pskov	21,400	55,300	760,900
St. Petersburg (city)		[3]	[3]	4,669,400
Vologda (region)	Vologda	56,300	145,700	1,270,000
Siberia	Novosibirsk	1,974,800	5,114,800	20,064,300
Agin Buryat (autonomous district)	Aginskoye	7,300	19,000	72,200
Altay (republic)	Gorno-Altaysk	35,700	92,600	202,900
Altay (territory)	Barnaul	65,300	169,100	2,607,200
Buryatiya (republic)	Ulan-Ude	135,600	351,300	981,000
Chita (region)	Chita	159,300	412,500	1,084,000
Evenk (autonomous district)	Tyra	296,400	767,600	17,700
Irkutsk (region)	Irkutsk	287,900	745,500	2,446,300
Kemerovo (region)	Kemerovo	36,900	95,500	2,900,200
Khakassia (republic)	Abakan	23,900	61,900	546,100
Krasnoyarsk (territory)	Krasnoyarsk	274,100	710,000	2,908,700
Novosibirsk (region)	Novosibirsk	68,800	178,200	2,692,200
Omsk (region)	Omsk	53,900	139,700	2,079,200
Taymyr (Dolgano-Nenets) (autonomous district)	Dudinka	332,900	862,100	39,800
Tomsk (region)	Tomsk	122,400	316,900	1,046,000
Tuva (republic)	Kyzyl-Orda	65,800	170,500	305,500
Ust-Ordyn Buryat	Ust-Ordinsky	8,600	22,400	135,300
Southern	Rostov-na-Donu	227,300	589,200	22,914,200
Adygeya (republic)	Maykop	2,900	7,600	447,000
Astrakhan (region)	Astrakhan	17,000	44,100	1,007,200
Chechnia (republic)	Grozny	6,010	15,700	1,100,300
Dagestan (republic)	Makhachkala	19,400	50,300	2,584,200
Ingushetiya (republic)	Magas	1,390	3,600	468,900
Kabardino-Balkariya (republic)	Nalchik	4,800	12,500	900,500
Kalmykiya (republic)	Elista	29,400	76,100	292,400
Karachayevo-Cherkessia (republic)	Cherkessk	5,400	14,100	439,700
Krasnodar (territory)	Krasnodar	29,300	76,000	5,124,400
Rostov (region)	Rostov-na-Donu	38,900	100,800	4,406,700
Severnaya Osetiya–Alania (republic)	Vladikavkaz	3,100	8,000	709,900
Stavropol (territory)	Stavropol	25,700	66,500	2,730,500
Volgograd (region)	Volgograd	44,000	113,900	2,702,500
Urals	Yekaterinburg	690,600	1,788,900	12,381,500
Chelyabinsk (region)	Chelyabinsk	33,900	87,900	3,606,100
Khanty-Mansi (autonomous district)	Khanty-Mansiysk	202,000	523,100	1,433,100
Kurgan (region)	Kurgan	27,400	71,000	1,019,900
Sverdlovsk (region)	Sverdlovsk	75,200	194,800	4,489,800
Tyumen (region)	Tyumen	62,400	161,800	1,325,200
Yamalo-Nenets (autonomous district)	Salekhard	289,700	750,300	507,400
Area and population (continued)				
Volga	Nizhny Novgorod	400,900	1,038,300[4]	31,158,200
Bashkortostan (republic)	Ufa	55,400	143,600	4,012,900
Chuvashiya (republic)	Cheboksary	7,100	18,300	1,313,900
Kirov (region)	Kirov	46,600	120,800	1,503,600
Komi-Permyak (autonomous district)	Syktyvkar	12,700	32,900	135,900
Mari-El (republic)	Toshkar-Ola	9,000	23,200	728,000
Mordoviya (republic)	Saransk	10,100	26,200	888,700
Nizhny Novgorod (region)	Nizhny Novgorod	29,700	76,900	3,524,000
Orenburg (region)	Orenburg	47,900	124,000	2,177,500
Penza (region)	Penza	16,700	43,200	1,453,400
Perm (region)	Perm	49,300	127,700	2,688,500
Samara (region)	Samara	20,700	53,600	3,239,800
Saratov (region)	Saratov	38,700	100,200	2,669,300
Tatarstan (republic)	Kazan	26,300	68,000	3,779,800
Udmurtia (republic)	Izhevsk	16,300	42,100	1,570,500
Ulyanovsk (Simbirsk; region)	Simbirsk	14,400	37,300	1,382,300
TOTAL		6,592,800	17,075,400[4]	145,181,900

Demography

Population (2003): 144,893,000.
Density (2003): persons per sq mi 22.0, persons per sq km 8.5.
Urban-rural (2003): urban 73.3%; rural 26.7%.
Sex distribution (2002): male 46.74%; female 53.26%.
Age breakdown (2002): under 15, 16.8%; 15–29, 23.3%; 30–44, 22.7%; 45–59, 18.3%; 60 and over, 18.9%.
Population projection: (2010) 142,689,000; (2020) 139,331,000.
Ethnic composition (2000): Russian 80.2%; Tatar 3.8%; Ukrainian 2.3%; Chuvash 1.2%; Jewish 1.1%; Bashkir 0.9%; Mordvin 0.7%; Chechen 0.6%; Belorussian 0.6%; German 0.5%; Armenian 0.5%; Mari 0.5%; Udmurt 0.5%; Avar (Dagestani) 0.4%; other 6.2%.
Religious affiliation (1997): Russian Orthodox 16.3%; Muslim 7.6%; other Orthodox 1.6%; Protestant 0.9%; Jewish 0.4%; Roman Catholic 0.3%; other Catholic 0.3%; other (mostly nonreligious) 72.6%.
Major cities (2002): Moscow 10,101,500; St. Petersburg 4,669,400; Novosibirsk 1,425,600; Nizhny Novgorod 1,311,200; Yekaterinburg 1,293,000; Samara 1,158,100; Omsk 1,133,900; Kazan 1,105,300; Chelyabinsk 1,078,300; Rostov-na-Donu 1,070,200; Ufa 1,042,400; Volgograd 1,012,800.

Other principal cities (2002)

	population		population		population
Astrakhan	506,400	Lipetsk	506,000	Simbirsk (Ulyanovsk)	632,600
Barnaul	603,500	Naberezhnye Chelny	510,000	Tolyatti	701,900
Irkutsk	593,400	Novokuznetsk	550,100	Tomsk	487,700
Izhevsk	632,100	Orenburg	548,800	Tula	472,300
Kemerovo	485,000	Penza	518,200	Tyumen	510,700
Khabarovsk	582,700	Perm	1,000,100	Vladivostok	591,800
Krasnodar	644,800	Ryazan	521,700	Voronezh	848,700
Krasnoyarsk	911,700	Saratov	873,500	Yaroslavl	613,200

Migration (2002): immigrants 184,612; emigrants 106,685.
Refugees (2002): 828,784, of which from Kazakhstan 301,137, Uzbekistan 106,299, Tajikistan 86,041, Georgia 62,868.
Households (1999). Total households 52,116,000; average household size 2.8; distribution by size (1995): 1 person 19.2%; 2 persons 26.2%; 3 persons 22.6%; 4 persons 20.5%; 5 persons or more 11.5%.

Vital statistics

Birth rate per 1,000 population (2002): 9.6 (world avg. 21.3); (2001) legitimate 70.5%; illegitimate 29.5%.
Death rate per 1,000 population (2002): 16.3 (world avg. 9.1).
Natural increase rate per 1,000 population (2002): –6.5 (world avg. 12.2).
Total fertility rate (avg. births per childbearing woman; 2002): 1.3.
Marriage rate per 1,000 population (2002): 7.1.
Divorce rate per 1,000 population (2002): 6.0.
Life expectancy at birth (2002): male 58.5 years; female 71.9 years.
Major causes of death per 100,000 population (2002): circulatory diseases 909; accidents, poisoning, and violence 230, of which suicide 39, murder 31, alcohol poisoning 28; malignant neoplasms (cancers) 204; respiratory diseases 70; digestive diseases 52; infectious and parasitic diseases 25.0.

Social indicators

Educational attainment (1998). Percentage of population age 16 and over having: primary or no formal education 11.2%; some secondary 25.3%; secondary and some postsecondary 40.9%; higher and postgraduate 22.6%.
Quality of working life (2002). Average workweek: 40 hours. Annual rate per 100,000 workers of: injury or accident 460; industrial illness 22.2; death 13.8. Average days lost to labour strikes per 1,000 employees (1999): 35.7.
Access to services (1990). Proportion of dwellings having access to: electricity, virtually 100%; safe public water supply 94%; public sewage collection 92%; central heating 92%; bathroom 87%; gas 72%; hot water 79%.
Social participation. Eligible voters participating in last national election (2000): 64.2%. Trade union membership in total workforce (2000[5]): 100%.
Social deviance. Offense rate per 100,000 population (2002) for: murder 22.5; rape 5.6; serious injury 40.7; larceny-theft 761.5. Incidence per 100,000 population (2000) of: alcoholism (1992) 1,727.5; substance abuse 25.6; suicide 39.2.
Material well-being (2002). Durable goods possessed per 100 households: automobiles 27; personal computers 7; television receivers 126; refrigerators and freezers 113; washing machines 93; VCRs 50; motorcycles 26; bicycles 71.

National economy

Public debt (external, outstanding: 2001): U.S.$101,918,000,000.
Budget (2001). Revenue: Rub 2,438,105,000,000 (tax revenue 83.3%, of which value-added tax 26.2%, social security tax 25.4%, individual income tax 9.0%, excise tax 8.5%; nontax revenue 16.7%). Expenditures: Rub 2,202,868,000,000 (current expenditure 91.3%, of which social security

33.7%, defense 12.6%, public services 8.2%, law enforcement 5.9%; capital expenditure 8.7%).
Gross national product (2001): U.S.$253,400,000,000 (U.S.$1,750 per capita).

Structure of gross domestic product and labour force

	2002			
	in value Rub '000,000	% of total value	labour force	% of labour force
Agriculture	666,000	6.1	7,933,000	11.0
Mining Manufacturing	2,882,000	26.5	14,768,000	20.5
Public utilities			3,295,000	4.6
Construction	797,000	7.3	5,140,000	7.1
Transp. and commun.	1,089,000	10.0	5,141,000	7.1
Trade	2,480,000	22.8	10,463,000	14.5
Finance	1,577,000	14.5	818,000	1.1
Services	881,000	8.1	15,272,500	21.2
Pub. admin., defense	491,000	4.5	2,935,000	4.1
Other	—	—	6,153,500[6]	8.6[6]
TOTAL	10,863,000	100.0[7]	71,919,000	100.0[7]

Production (metric tons except as noted). Agriculture, forestry, fishing (2002): wheat 50,557,000, potatoes 31,900,000, barley 18,688,000, sugar beets 15,500,000, vegetables (other than potatoes) 13,800,000, rye 7,139,000, oats 5,700,000, sunflower seeds 3,600,000, apples 1,800,000, peas 1,578,000, corn (maize) 1,541,000, rice 483,000, buckwheat 304,000; livestock (number of live animals) 27,106,000 cattle, 16,047,500 pigs, 13,035,000 sheep; roundwood (2002) 176,900,000 cu m; fish catch (2000) 4,047,659. Mining and quarrying (2000): iron ore 84,200,000; copper (metal content) 570,000; nickel (metal content) 270,000; zinc (metal content) 130,000; chrome ore (marketable) 100,000; platinum 30,000; vanadium 9,000; silver 370,000 kg; gold 143,000 kg. Manufacturing (2002): crude steel 59,800,000; rolled steel 46,300,000; pig iron 44,700,000; cement 37,700,000; mineral fertilizers 13,600,000; sulfuric acid 8,600,000; cellulose 5,568,000; paper 3,524,000; synthetic resins and plastics 2,875,000; cardboard 2,397,000; detergents 528,000; synthetic fibres 158,000; cotton fabrics 2,326,000,000 sq m; silk fabrics 148,000,000 sq m; linen fabrics 138,000,000 sq m; wool fabrics 50,400,000 sq m; cigarettes 310,000,000,000 units; watches 6,100,000 units; refrigerators 1,933,000 units; television receivers 1,822,000 units; washing machines 1,357,000 units; passenger cars 961,000 units; vacuum cleaners 777,000 units; bicycles 509,000 units; motorcycles 20,900 units; footwear 41,200,000 pairs; beer 70,200,000 hectolitres; vodka and liquors 13,900,000 hectolitres; champagne 8,100,000 hectolitres; grape wine 3,250,000 hectolitres.

Manufacturing, mining, and construction enterprises (1995)

	no. of enter-prises	no. of employees	monthly wages as a % of avg. of all wages	value added (Rub '000,000,000)
Manufacturing				
Machinery and metal products	48,905	4,842,000	80.1	27,234
Fuel and energy	1,758	1,554,000	228.9	44,211
Metallurgy	2,158	1,248,000	121.9	26,437
Chemicals	23,027	2,432,000	95.9	17,934
Light industry	23,007	1,368,000	60.1	2,931
Food	14,713	1,514,000	105.3	12,886
Other industries	19,073	2,085,000	...	4,685
Building materials	8,359	994,000	110.4	3,761

Energy production (consumption): electricity (kW-hr; 2002) 889,000,000,000 ([2000] 863,700,000,000); hard coal (metric tons; 2002) 253,000,000 ([1999] 169,622,000); lignite (metric tons; 2000) 86,300,000 ([1999] 83,500,000); crude petroleum (barrels; 2002) 2,785,400,000 ([1999] 1,249,700,000); petroleum products (metric tons; 1999) 149,996,000 (102,297,000); natural gas (cu m; 2002) 595,000,000,000 ([1999] 313,407,700,000); peat (metric tons; 2002) 2,200,000 (2,200,000).
Population economically active (2002): total 71,919,000; activity rate of total population 50.0% (participation rates: ages over 15, 82.6%; female 48.6%; unemployed 8.6%).

Price and earnings indexes (1995 = 100)

	1996	1997	1998	1999	2000	2001	2002
Consumer price index	147.7	169.5	216.4	401.8	485.2	589.5	682.6
Monthly earnings index	164.8	203.9	235.0	363.6	554.5	845.6	1,211

Household income and expenditure. Average household size (2002) 2.8; income per household: Rub 52,400 (U.S.$1,692); sources of income (2002): wages 66.2%, pensions and stipends 14.9%, income from entrepreneurial activities 12.0%, property income 4.9%, other 2.0%; expenditure (2002): food 41.7%, clothing 13.3%, housing 6.2%, furniture and household appliances 5.7%, alcohol and tobacco 3.2%, transportation 2.7%.
Tourism (2001): receipts U.S.$3,750,000,000; expenditures U.S.$10,360,000,000.

Foreign trade[8]

Balance of trade (current prices)

	1997	1998	1999	2000	2001	2002
U.S.$'000,000	+9,932	+11,067	+32,077	+55,440	+57,670	+40,867
% of total	5.9%	8.0%	26.9%	36.5%	41.0%	23.6%

Imports (2001): U.S.$41,528,000,000 (machinery and apparatus 21.8%, of which general industrial machinery 5.9%; food and live animals 16.1%; chemicals and chemical products 12.1%; road vehicles 4.5%; iron and steel 3.5%). *Major import sources* (2002): Germany 14.3%; Belarus 8.8%; Ukraine 7.0%; U.S. 6.4%; China 5.2%; Italy 4.8%; Kazakhstan 4.2%; France 4.1%; Finland 3.3%; Poland 2.8%.

Exports (2001): U.S.$99,198,000,000 (fuels and lubricants 53.9%, of which crude petroleum 24.8%, natural gas 18.0%, refined petroleum 9.5%; nonferrous metals 6.8%; iron and steel 5.6%; chemicals and chemical products 4.8%; machinery and apparatus 4.6%; special transactions 11.6%). *Major export destinations* (2002): Germany 7.6%; Italy 7.0%; The Netherlands 6.8%; China 6.4%; Belarus 5.5%; Ukraine 5.5%; Switzerland 5.1%; U.S. 3.8%; U.K. 3.6%; Poland 3.5%.

Trade by commodity group (2001)[9]

	imports		exports	
SITC group	U.S.$'000,000	%	U.S.$'000,000	%
0 Food and live animals	6,705	16.1	1,212	1.2
3 Mineral fuels, lubricants	1,013	2.4	53,478	53.9
5 Chemicals, related products	5,023	12.1	4,802	4.8
67 Iron and steel	1,471	3.5	5,582	5.6
68 Nonferrous metals	372	0.9	6,765	6.8
74 General industrial machinery	2,467	5.9	1,283	1.3
76 Telecommunications, incl. parts	1,433	3.5	—	—
78 Road vehicles	1,869	4.5	826	0.8
TOTAL (all groups)	41,528		99,197	

Direction of trade (2001)

	imports		exports	
	U.S.$'000,000	%	U.S.$'000,000	%
Africa	405	1.0	942	0.9
Americas	5,433	13.1	6,875	6.9
United States	3,208	7.7	2,876	2.9
Asia (excl. former U.S.S.R.)	5,401	13.0	15,772	15.9
China	1,617	3.9	3,878	3.9
Asia (former U.S.S.R. only)	2,833	6.8	47,449	4.8
Europe	23,058	55.5	58,598	59.1
EU	15,282	36.8	33,295	33.6
Eastern Europe	2,218	5.3	11,279	11.4
Europe (former U.S.S.R. only)	4,552	11.0	11,150	11.2
Oceania	177	0.4	20	—
TOTAL	41,528[10]		99,198[10]	

Transport and communications

Transport. Railroads (2002): length 139,000 km; passenger-km 152,900,000,000; metric ton-km cargo 1,510,000,000. Roads (2002): total length 593,000 km (paved 91%). Vehicles (2000): passenger cars 20,247,800; trucks and buses (1999) 5,021,000. Air transport (2002): passenger-km 64,700,000,000; metric ton-km cargo 2,700,000,000; airports (1998) 75.

Distribution of traffic (2000)

	cargo carried ('000,000 tons)	% of national total	passengers carried ('000,000)	% of national total
Intercity transport			23,502	54.5
Road	550	21.5	22,033	51.1
Rail	1,046	40.9	1,419	3.3
Sea and river	134	5.2	27	0.1
Air	0.8	...	23	...
Pipeline	829	32.4	—	—
Urban transport	—	—	19,628	45.5
TOTAL	2,559.8	100.0	43,130	100.0

Communications

Medium	date	unit	number	units per 1,000 persons
Daily newspapers	2000	circulation	15,300,000	105
Radio	2000	receivers	61,100,000	418
Television	2000	receivers	61,500,000	421
Telephones	2002	main lines	35,500,000	242
Cellular telephones	2002	subscribers	17,668,100	121
Personal computers	2002	units	13,000,000	89
Internet	2002	users	6,000,000	41

Education and health

Education (2002–03)

	schools	teachers	students	student/ teacher ratio
Primary (age 6–13) Secondary (age 14–17)	67,431	1,719,000	18,918,000	11.0
Voc., teacher tr.	2,626	134,200	2,489,000	18.5
Higher	1,039	291,800	5,948,000	20.4

Health (2002): physicians 678,000 (1 per 212 persons); hospital beds 1,653,000 (1 per 87 persons); infant mortality rate per 1,000 live births (2002) 13.3.
Food (2001): daily per capita caloric intake 3,014 (vegetable products 78%; animal products 22%); 115% of FAO recommended minimum requirement.

Military

Total active duty personnel (2002): 988,100 (army 32.5%, navy 17.4%, air force 18.7%, strategic deterrent forces 10.1%, other 21.3%[11]). *Military expenditure as percentage of GNP* (1999): 5.6% (world 2.4%); per capita expenditure U.S.$239.

[1]Federal districts were formally established in May 2000. [2]Moskva (Moscow; region) includes Moscow (city). [3]Leningrad region includes the city of St. Petersburg. [4]Detail does not add to total given because of statistical discrepancy. [5]State enterprises only. [6]Unemployed. [7]Detail does not add to total given because of rounding. [8]Imports c.i.f.; exports f.o.b. [9]Selected commodities only. [10]Includes unspecified. [11]Represents about 210,000 military personnel not included elsewhere (including Ministry of Defense staff and centrally controlled units for electronic warfare).

Internet resources for further information:
- **Russian Statistical Agency http://www.gks.ru/eng/default.asp**

Rwanda

Official name: Repubulika y'u Rwanda (Rwanda); République Rwandaise (French); Republic of Rwanda (English).
Form of government: multiparty republic with two legislative bodies (Senate [26]; Chamber of Deputies [80])[1].
Head of state and government: President assisted by Prime Minister.
Capital: Kigali.
Official languages: Rwanda; French; English.
Official religion: none.
Monetary unit: 1 Rwanda franc (RF); valuation (Sept. 8, 2003) 1 U.S.$ = RF 535.80; 1 £ = RF 849.54.

Area and population

Provinces	Capitals	area sq mi	area sq km	population 2002 preliminary census
Butare	Butare	709	1,837	722,616
Byumba[2]	Byumba	1,838	4,761	712,372
Cyangugu	Cyangugu	713	1,847	609,504
Gikongoro	Gikongoro	794	2,057	492,607
Gisenyi	Gisenyi	791	2,050	867,225
Gitarama	Gitarama	845	2,189	864,594
Kibungo[2]	Kibungo	1,562	4,046	707,548
Kibuye	Kibuye	658	1,705	467,745
Kigali (city)	—	1,204	3,118	608,141
Kigali Ngali	Kigali (city)			792,542
Ruhengeri	Ruhengeri	642	1,663	894,179
Umutara[2]	Nyagatare	...	...	423,642
TOTAL LAND AREA		9,758[3]	25,273	
LAKE KIVU (Rwandan part)		411	1,065	
TOTAL		10,169	26,338	8,162,715

Demography

Population (2003): 8,387,000.
Density (2002)[4]: persons per sq mi 758.2, persons per sq km 292.7.
Urban-rural (2001): urban 6.3%; rural 93.7%.
Sex distribution (2001): male 49.60%; female 50.40%.
Age breakdown (2001): under 15, 43.0%; 15–29, 30.4%; 30–44, 15.0%; 45–59, 7.3%; 60–74, 3.5%; 75 and over, 0.8%.
Population projection: (2010) 9,559,000; (2020) 11,557,000.
Doubling time: 47 years.
Ethnic composition (1996): Hutu 80.0%; Tutsi 19.0%; Twa 1.0%.
Religious affiliation (2000): Roman Catholic 51.0%; Protestant 28.8%; traditional beliefs 9.0%; Muslim 7.9%; independent Christian 2.1%; other 1.2%.
Major cities (1991): Kigali (1999) 369,000; Ruhengeri 29,578; Butare 28,645; Gisenyi 21,918.

Vital statistics

Birth rate per 1,000 population (2001): 34.0 (world avg. 21.3).
Death rate per 1,000 population (2001): 21.1 (world avg. 9.1).
Natural increase rate per 1,000 population (2001): 12.9 (world avg. 12.2).
Total fertility rate (avg. births per childbearing woman; 2001): 4.9.
Marriage rate per 1,000 population: n.a.
Life expectancy at birth (2001): male 38.4 years; female 39.7 years.
Major causes of death per 100,000 population: n.a.; however, principal causes are malaria, bronchopneumonia, diarrhea, AIDS, pulmonary diseases, cerebrospinal meningitis, kwashiorkor, and road accidents.

National economy

Budget (2001). Revenue: RF 149,500,000,000 (grants 42.3%; taxes on goods and services 27.4%; income tax 16.0%; import and export duties 7.4%; nontax revenue 6.9%). Expenditures: RF 189,200,000,000 (current expenditures 56.8%, of which wages 28.4%, education 15.8%, defense 15.1%, health 2.7%, debt payment 1.5%; capital expenditure 43.2%).
Production (metric tons except as noted). Agriculture, forestry, fishing (2002): plantains 2,784,870, sweet potatoes 1,292,361, potatoes 1,038,931, cassava 1,031,077, sorghum 194,351, corn (maize) 91,686, coffee 19,400, tea 14,900; livestock (number of live animals) 815,000 cattle, 760,000 goats, 260,000 sheep, 180,000 pigs; roundwood (2002) 7,836,000 cu m; fish catch (2000) 6,996. Mining and quarrying (2001): cassiterite (tin content) 171; niobium 76; tantalum 50; gold 10 kg. Manufacturing (value added in RF '000,000; 2000): food and nonalcoholic beverages 37,981; nonmetallic products 3,109; metal products 1,087; chemicals 965; textiles 791; paper 615. Energy production (consumption): electricity (kW-hr; 2000) 110,800,000 (210,770,000); petroleum products (metric tons; 1999) none (173,000); natural gas (cu m; 2000) 1,373,000,000 ([1999] 205,000).
Population economically active (1996): total 3,021,000; activity rate of total population 50.8% (participation rates: ages 14 and over, 86.0%; female 49.0%; unemployed, n.a.).

Price index (1995 = 100)

	1997	1998	1999	2000	2001	2002
Consumer price index	120.3	127.8	124.7	130.1	133.9	137.2

Land use (1994): forested 10.1%; meadows and pastures 28.4%; agricultural and under permanent cultivation 47.4%; other 14.1%.

Gross national product (2001): U.S.$1,900,000,000 (U.S.$220 per capita).

Structure of gross domestic product and labour force

	2000 in value RF '000,000	2000 % of total value	2001 labour force	2001 % of labour force
Agriculture	292,300	41.4	3,897,000	90.2
Mining	11,500	1.6		
Manufacturing	68,600	9.7		
Construction	60,500	8.6		
Public utilities	3,700	0.5		
Transp. and commun.	49,700	7.0	424,000	9.8
Trade	71,000	10.1		
Pub. admin., defense	52,800	7.5		
Services	95,600	13.5		
Other	—	—		
TOTAL	705,700	100.0[3]	4,321,000	100.0

Public debt (external, outstanding; 2001): U.S.$1,163,000,000.
Household income and expenditure. Average household size (1991) 4.7; average annual income per household, n.a.; sources of income: n.a.; expenditure: n.a.
Tourism: receipts (1993) U.S.$2,000,000; expenditures (1992) U.S.$17,000,000.

Foreign trade

Balance of trade (current prices)

	1996	1997	1998	1999	2000	2001
U.S.$'000,000	–156.9	–184.5	–168.5	–186.7	–168.6	–147.4
% of total	56.0%	52.5%	56.8%	60.0%	55.0%	44.9%

Imports (2000): U.S.$239,800,000 (capital goods 22.1%, food 19.4%, energy products 18.7%, intermediate goods 18.1%). *Major import sources* (2002): Kenya 21.9%; Germany 8.4%; Belgium 7.9%; Israel 4.3%; U.S. 3.5%.
Exports (2001): U.S.$90,400,000 (niobium and tantalum 45.2%, tea 25.6%, coffee 20.1%). *Major export destinations* (2002): Indonesia 30.8%; Germany 14.6%; Hong Kong 8.9%; South Africa 5.5%.

Transport and communications

Transport. Railroads: none. Roads (1999): total length 7,460 mi, 12,000 km (paved 8%). Vehicles (1996): passenger cars 13,000; trucks 17,100. Air transport (2000)[5]: passengers embarked and disembarked 101,000; cargo loaded and unloaded 4,300 metric tons; airports (2002) with scheduled flights 2.

Communications

Medium	date	unit	number	units per 1,000 persons
Daily newspapers	1995	circulation	500	0.1
Radio	1997	receivers	601,000	101
Telephones	2001	main lines	21,500	2.7
Cellular telephones	2001	subscribers	65,000	8.2
Internet	2001	users	20,000	2.5

Education and health

Educational attainment: n.a. *Literacy* (2000): percentage of total population age 15 and over literate 66.8%; males literate 73.7%; females literate 60.2%.

Education (1998)

	schools	teachers	students	student/ teacher ratio
Primary (age 7–15)	1,710[6]	23,730	1,288,669	54.3
Secondary (age 16–19)[7]	...	3,413[6]	91,219	...
Higher	...	646[6]	5,678	...

Health: physicians (1992) 150 (1 per 50,000 persons); hospital beds (1990) 12,152 (1 per 588 persons); infant mortality rate (2001) 107.0.
Food (2001): daily per capita caloric intake 2,086 (vegetable products 97%, animal products 3%); 90% of FAO recommended minimum requirement.

Military

Total active duty personnel (2002): 60,000–75,000 (army 100%). *Military expenditure as percentage of GNP* (1999): 4.5% (world 2.4%); per capita expenditure U.S.$12.

[1]Referendum on new draft constitution approved May 26, 2003. Executive and legislative elections in August/September 2003 ended 9 years of transitional rule. [2]Umutara prefecture created in 1996 from parts of Byumba and Kibungo prefectures. [3]Detail does not add to total given because of rounding. [4]Based on land area. [5]Kigali airport only. [6]1991–92. [7]Includes vocational and teacher training.

Internet resources for further information:

- **Republic of Rwanda (official website)**
  http://www.rwanda1.com/government/rwandalaunch.html
- **Banque Nationale du Rwanda**
  http://www.bnr.rw/bnrnet

Saint Kitts and Nevis

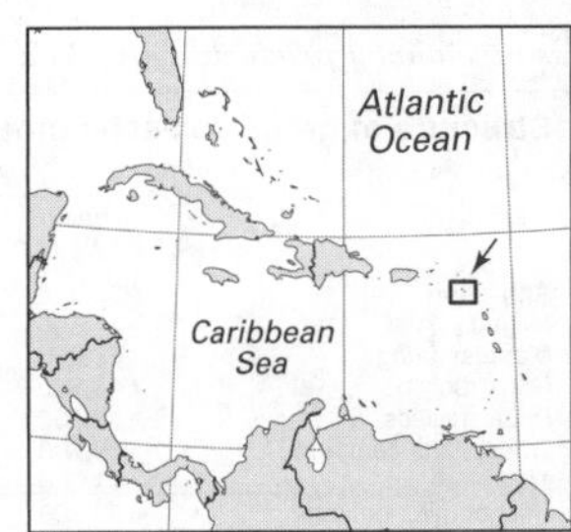

Official name: Federation of Saint Kitts and Nevis[1].
Form of government: constitutional monarchy with one legislative house (National Assembly [15[2]]).
Chief of state: British Monarch represented by Governor-General.
Head of government: Prime Minister.
Capital: Basseterre.
Official language: English.
Official religion: none.
Monetary unit: 1 Eastern Caribbean dollar (EC$) = 100 cents; valuation (Sept. 8, 2003) 1 U.S.$ = EC$2.70; 1 £ = EC$4.28.

Area and population

		area		population
				2001
Islands	Capitals	sq mi	sq km	census[3]
Nevis[4]	Charlestown	36.0	93.2	11,181
St. Kitts	Basseterre	68.0	176.2	34,703
TOTAL		104.0	269.4	45,884

Demography

Population (2003): 46,400.
Density (2003): persons per sq mi 446.2, persons per sq km 172.5.
Urban-rural (2000): urban 34.2%; rural 65.8%.
Sex distribution (2001): male 49.70%; female 50.30%.
Age breakdown (2000): under 15, 30.3%; 15–29, 24.9%; 30–44, 22.2%; 45–59, 11.2%; 60–74, 7.1%; 75 and over, 4.3%.
Population projection: (2010) 48,000; (2020) 53,000.
Doubling time: 72 years.
Ethnic composition (2000): black 90.4%; mulatto 5.0%; Indo-Pakistani 3.0%; white 1.0%; other/unspecified 0.6%.
Religious affiliation (1995): Protestant 84.6%, of which Anglican 25.2%, Methodist 25.2%, Pentecostal 8.4%, Moravian 7.6%; Roman Catholic 6.7%; Hindu 1.5%; other 7.2%.
Major towns (2001): Basseterre 13,033; Charlestown (1994) 1,411.

Vital statistics

Birth rate per 1,000 population (2001): 17.4 (world avg. 21.3); (1983) legitimate 19.2%; illegitimate 80.8%.
Death rate per 1,000 population (2002): 7.6 (world avg. 9.1).
Natural increase rate per 1,000 population (2001): 9.8 (world avg. 12.2).
Total fertility rate (avg. births per childbearing woman; 2000): 2.5.
Marriage rate per 1,000 population (2001): 7.1.
Divorce rate per 1,000 population (2002): 0.5.
Life expectancy at birth (2000): male 68.0 years; female 71.8 years.
Major causes of death per 100,000 population (1985): diseases of the circulatory system 443.2, of which cerebrovascular disease 220.5, diseases of pulmonary circulation and other heart disease 122.7; malignant neoplasms (cancers) 95.5.

National economy

Budget (2001). Revenue: EC$270,100,000 (tax revenue 72.8%, of which import duties 34.0%, taxes on income and profits 21.4%, taxes on domestic goods and services 14.1%; nontax revenue 28.1%). Expenditures: EC$406,000,000 (current expenditure 75.6%; development expenditure 24.4%).
Production (metric tons except as noted). Agriculture, forestry, fishing (2002): sugarcane 191,400, tropical fruit 1,300, coconuts 1,000, roots and tubers 700, pulses 210, potatoes 160, sweet potatoes 150, tomatoes 100, cabbages 60, onions 60; sea island cotton is grown on Nevis; livestock (number of live animals) 14,400 goats, 14,000 sheep, 4,300 cattle, 4,000 pigs; roundwood, n.a.; fish catch (2001) 291. Mining and quarrying: excavation of sand for local use. Manufacturing (2001): raw sugar 20,193; carbonated beverages 45,000 hectolitres[5]; beer 20,000 hectolitres[5]; other manufactures include electronic components, garments, footwear, and batik. Construction (value added; 1994): EC$57,000,000. Energy production (consumption): electricity (kW-hr; 1999) 98,000,000 (98,000,000); coal, none (none); crude petroleum, none (none); petroleum products (metric tons; 1999) none (33,000); natural gas, none (none).
Gross national product (2001): U.S.$300,000,000 (U.S.$6,630 per capita).

Structure of gross domestic product and labour force

	2000		1994	
	in value EC$'000,000	% of total value	labour force[6]	% of labour force[6]
Sugarcane	6.1	0.8	1,525[7]	9.2[7]
Other agriculture, forestry, fisheries	17.2	2.2	914	5.5
Mining	2.5	0.3	29	0.2
Manufacturing	72.1	9.1	1,290[8]	7.8[8]
Construction	140.3	17.6	1,745	10.5
Public utilities	17.7	2.2	416	2.5
Transp. and commun.	106.4	13.4	534	3.2
Trade, restaurants	155.1	19.5	3,367	20.3
Finance, real estate	139.3	17.5	3,708[9]	22.3[9]
Pub. admin., defense	152.2	19.1	2,738	16.5
Services	34.6	4.3	[9]	[9]
Other	–47.1[10]	–5.9[10]	342	2.1
TOTAL	796.3[11]	100.0[11]	16,608	100.0[11]

Household income and expenditure. Average household size (2001) 2.9; average annual income per wage earner (1994) EC$9,940 (U.S.$3,681); sources of income: n.a.; expenditure (1978)[12]: food, beverages, and tobacco 55.6%, household furnishings 9.4%, housing 7.6%, clothing and footwear 7.5%, fuel and light 6.6%, transportation 4.3%, other 9.0%.
Public debt (external, outstanding; 2001): U.S.$186,000,000.
Population economically active (1980): total 17,125; activity rate of total population 39.5% (participation rates: ages 15–64, 69.5%; female 41.0%; unemployed [1997] 4.5%).

Price and earnings indexes (1995 = 100)

	1996	1997	1998	1999	2000	2001
Consumer price index	102.1	111.2	115.0	119.5	122.1	125.9
Earnings index	...	...	...	...	...	...

Land use (1994): forested 17%; meadows and pastures 3%; agricultural and under permanent cultivation 39%; other 41%.
Tourism: receipts from visitors (2001) U.S.$62,000,000; expenditures by nationals abroad (2000) U.S.$9,000,000.

Foreign trade[13]

Balance of trade (current prices)

	1997	1998	1999	2000	2001
U.S.$'000,000	–106.1	...	–124.9	–163.1	–158.2
% of total	56.3%	...	69.1%	71.4%	71.9%

Imports (2001): U.S.$189,200,000 (machinery and apparatus 22.4%; food 14.4%; fabricated metals 7.9%; chemicals and chemical products 6.9%; refined petroleum 6.4%). *Major import sources* (2002): United States 41.5%; Trinidad and Tobago 16.2%; Canada 9.8%; United Kingdom 6.9%; Japan 4.0%.
Exports (2001): U.S.$31,000,000 (electrical switches, relays, and fuses 56.1%; raw sugar 21.0%; telecommunications equipment [parts] 3.2%). *Major export destinations* (2002): United States 66.6%; United Kingdom 7.6%; Canada 6.8%; Portugal 6.0%; Germany 2.9%.

Transport and communications

Transport. Railroads (2000)[14]: length 36 mi, 58 km. Roads (2001): total length 197 mi, 318 km (paved 44%). Vehicles (2001): passenger cars 5,826; trucks and buses 2,989. Merchant marine (1992): vessels (100 gross tons and over) 1; total deadweight tonnage 550. Air transport (2001)[15]: passenger arrivals 135,237; passenger departures 134,937; cargo handled 1,802; airports (1998) with scheduled flights 2.

Communications

Medium	date	unit	number	units per 1,000 persons
Radio	1997	receivers	28,000	701
Television	1997	receivers	10,000	264
Telephones	2002	main lines	23,500	500
Cellular telephones	2000	units	5,000	106
Personal computers	1999	units	5,000	106
Internet	1999	users	9,000	120

Education and health

Educational attainment (1991). Percentage of population age 25 and over having: no formal schooling 1.6%; primary education 45.8%; secondary 38.4%; higher 5.2%. *Literacy* (1990): total population age 15 and over literate 25,500 (90.0%); males literate 13,100 (90.0%); females literate 12,400 (90.0%).

Education (2001–02)

	schools	teachers	students	student/ teacher ratio
Primary (age 5–12)[16]	24	301	5,608	18.6
Secondary (age 13–17)[16]	7	389	4,445	11.4
Higher[17]	1	51	394	7.7

Health (2001): physicians 49 (1 per 936 persons); hospital beds 178 (1 per 258 persons); infant mortality rate per 1,000 live births (2001): 12.5.
Food (2001): daily per capita caloric intake 2,997 (vegetable products 74%, animal products 26%); 124% of FAO recommended minimum requirement.

Military

Total active duty personnel: in July 1997 the National Assembly approved a bill creating a 50-member army. *Military expenditure as percentage of GNP* (1998): 3.5%[18] (world, n.a.); per capita expenditure U.S.$226[18].

[1]Both Saint Christopher and Nevis and the Federation of Saint Christopher and Nevis are officially acceptable, variant, short- and long-form names of the country. [2]Includes 4 nonelective seats. [3]Preliminary figures. [4]Nevis has full internal self-government. The Nevis legislature is subordinate to the National Assembly only with regard to external affairs and defense. [5]1995. [6]Employed persons only. [7]Includes sugar manufacturing. [8]Excludes sugar manufacturing. [9]Finance, real estate includes Services. [10]Imputed service charge. [11]Detail does not add to total given because of rounding. [12]Weights of consumer price index components. [13]Imports c.i.f.; exports f.o.b. [14]Light railway serving the sugar industry on Saint Kitts. [15]Saint Kitts airport only. [16]Public schools only. [17]1992–93. [18]Includes expenditure for police.

Internet resources for further information:

- **Official Web site of the Government of St. Kitts & Nevis**
  http://www.stkittsnevis.net
- **Eastern Caribbean Central Bank**
  http://www.eccb-centralbank.org

Saint Lucia

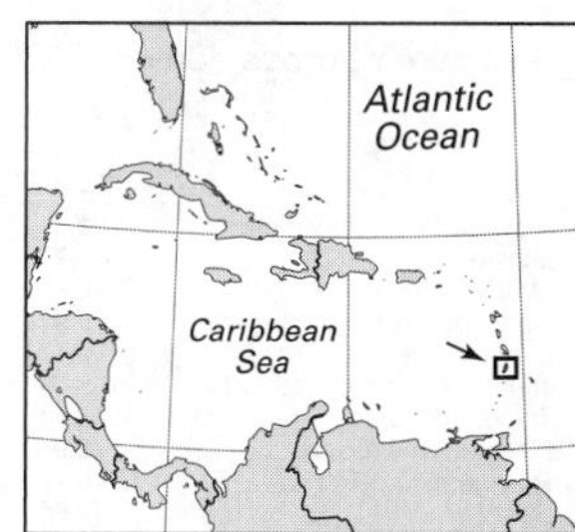

Official name: Saint Lucia.
Form of government: constitutional monarchy with a Parliament consisting of two legislative chambers (Senate [11]; House of Assembly [17[1]]).
Chief of state: British Monarch represented by Governor-General.
Head of government: Prime Minister.
Capital: Castries.
Official language: English.
Official religion: none.
Monetary unit: 1 Eastern Caribbean dollar (EC$) = 100 cents; valuation (Sept. 8, 2003) 1 U.S.$ = EC$2.70; 1 £ = EC$4.28.

Area and population

		area		population
Districts	Capitals	sq mi	sq km	2001 census
Anse-la-Raye	Anse-la-Raye	18	47	5,954
Canaries	Canaries			1,741
Castries	Castries	31	79	60,390
Choiseul	Choiseul	12	31	5,993
Dennery	Dennery	27	70	12,537
Gros Islet	Gros Islet	39	101	19,409
Laborie	Laborie	15	38	7,329
Micoud	Micoud	30	78	15,892
Soufrière	Soufrière	19	51	7,337
Vieux Fort	Vieux Fort	17	44	14,561
TOTAL		238[2]	617[2]	151,143[3]

Demography

Population (2003): 162,000.
Density (2003): persons per sq mi 680.7, persons per sq km 262.6.
Urban-rural (2001): urban 38.0%; rural 62.0%.
Sex distribution (2000): male 49.04%; female 50.96%.
Age breakdown (2000): under 15, 31.8%; 15–29, 29.6%; 30–44, 20.5%; 45–59, 10.2%; 60–74, 5.3%; 75 and over, 2.6%.
Population projection: (2010) 177,000; (2020) 199,000.
Doubling time: 43 years.
Ethnic composition (2000): black 50%; mulatto 44%; East Indian 3%; white 1%; other 2%.
Religious affiliation (2001): Roman Catholic 67.5%; Protestant 22.0%, of which Seventh-day Adventist 8.4%, Pentecostal 5.6%; Rastafarian 2.1%; nonreligious 4.5%; other/unknown 3.9%.
Major urban area (2001): Castries 35,070.

Vital statistics

Birth rate per 1,000 population (2002): 21.4 (world avg. 21.3); legitimate 14.3%; illegitimate 85.7%.
Death rate per 1,000 population (2002): 5.3 (world avg. 9.1).
Natural increase rate per 1,000 population (2002): 16.1 (world avg. 12.2).
Total fertility rate (avg. births per childbearing woman; 2002): 2.3.
Marriage rate per 1,000 population (2000): 4.1.
Divorce rate per 1,000 population (2000): 0.3.
Life expectancy at birth (2002): male 69.3 years; female 76.7 years.
Major causes of death per 100,000 population (1996): diseases of the circulatory system 282.9; malignant neoplasms (cancers) 74.1; diseases of the respiratory system 41.5; infectious and parasitic diseases 37.4; endocrine and metabolic disorders 19.0; ill-defined conditions 63.2.

National economy

Budget (2001). Revenue: EC$460,900,000 (tax revenue 86.2%, of which consumption duties on imported goods 41.5%; taxes on income and profits 29.0%; goods and services 15.4%; nontax revenue 9.7%; grants 3.8%). Expenditures: EC$528,800,000 (current expenditures 76.8%; development expenditures and net lending 23.2%).
Public debt (external, outstanding; 2001): U.S.$168,200,000.
Production (metric tons except as noted). Agriculture, forestry, fishing (2002): bananas 92,000, mangoes 28,000, coconuts 14,000, yams 4,500, grapefruit 2,973, tropical fruit 2,800, plantains 1,300, cassava 1,000, vegetables 1,000, oranges 602; livestock (number of live animals) 14,950 pigs, 12,500 sheep, 12,400 cattle, 9,800 goats; roundwood, n.a.; fish catch (2000) 1,759. Mining and quarrying: excavation of sand for local construction and pumice. Manufacturing (value of production in EC$'000; 1998): alcoholic beverages and tobacco 31,120; paper products and cardboard boxes 28,747; electrical and electronic components 16,245; food 9,535; garments 6,563; textiles 3,999; refined coconut oil 2,330; copra 1,330. Energy production (consumption): electricity (kW-hr; 1999) 254,000,000 (254,000,000); coal, none (none); crude petroleum, none (none); petroleum products (metric tons; 1999) none (105,000); natural gas, none (none).
Population economically active (1998): total 73,660; activity rate of total population 49.2% (participation rates: ages 15–64, 79.1%; female 44.4%; unemployed [2001] 18.9%).

Price and earnings indexes (1995 = 100)

	1996	1997	1998	1999	2000	2001	2002
Consumer price index	100.9	100.9	104.2	107.7	111.8	111.9	113.7
Earnings index	...	...	...	...	...	...	...

Gross national product (at current market prices; 2001): U.S.$600,000,000 (U.S.$3,950 per capita).

Structure of gross domestic product and labour force

	2001		2000	
	in value EC$'000,000[4]	% of total value[4]	labour force	% of labour force
Agriculture	94.04	6.3	12,560	16.1
Mining	6.08	0.4	—	—
Manufacturing	73.14	4.9	6,610	8.4
Construction	125.08	8.4	6,460	8.3
Public utilities	76.16	5.1	530	0.7
Transportation and communications	311.71	20.9	4,540	5.8
Trade, restaurants	376.03	25.3	17,230	22.1
Finance, real estate	249.35	16.7	2,320	3.0
Pub. admin., defense	222.82	15.0	8,180	10.5
Services	78.54	5.3	4,360	5.6
Other	–124.10[5]	–8.3[5]	15,210[6]	19.5[6]
TOTAL	1,488.85	100.0	78,000	100.0

Household income and expenditure. Average household size (2001) 3.3; income per household: n.a.; sources of income: n.a.; expenditure.
Land use (1994): forested 13%; meadows and pastures 5%; agricultural and under permanent cultivation 30%; other 52%.
Tourism: receipts from visitors (2001) U.S.$232,000,000; expenditures by nationals abroad (2000) U.S.$33,000,000.

Foreign trade[7]

Balance of trade (current prices)

	1996	1997	1998	1999	2000	2001
U.S.$'000,000	–233.9	–271.1	–273.0	–298.9	–311.7	–231.0
% of total	59.5%	68.9%	68.7%	72.8%	78.2%	72.1%

Imports (2001): U.S.$275,800,000 (food products 23.0%; machinery and apparatus 14.9%; refined petroleum 9.8%; chemicals and chemical products 7.9%). *Major import sources:* United States 41.8%; Trinidad and Tobago 15.8%; United Kingdom 9.0%; Japan 4.2%; Canada 3.4%.
Exports (2001): U.S.$44,800,000 (bananas 46.9%; beer and ale 18.1%; clothing 7.1%; electrical and electronic components 6.5%). *Major export destinations:* United Kingdom 47.3%; United States 17.6%; Barbados 13.4%; Antigua and Barbuda 3.1%.

Transport and communications

Transport. Railroads: none. Roads (1999): total length 750 mi, 1,210 km (paved 5%). Vehicles (2001): passenger cars 22,453; trucks and buses 8,972. Air transport (2000)[8]: passenger arrivals and departures 726,000; cargo unloaded and loaded 4,200 metric tons; airports (2000) with scheduled flights 2.

Communications

Medium	date	unit	number	units per 1,000 persons
Radio	1997	receivers	100,000	668
Television	1997	receivers	40,000	267
Telephones	1999	main lines	44,465	289
Cellular telephones	1998	subscribers	1,900	12.5

Education and health

Educational attainment (2000). Percentage of population age 15 and over having: no formal schooling 6.5%; primary education 56.2%; secondary 27.5%; higher vocational 4.5%; university 2.7%; other/unknown 2.6%. *Literacy* (2000): 90.2%.

Education (2000–01)

	schools	teachers	students	student/ teacher ratio
Primary (age 5–11)	82	1,052	28,618	27.2
Secondary (age 12–16)	18	678	12,865	19.0
Higher	...	127	1,403	11.0

Health (1998): physicians 60 (1 per 2,533 persons); hospital beds 521 (1 per 292 persons); infant mortality rate per 1,000 live births (2002) 14.8.
Food (2001): daily per capita caloric intake 2,849 (vegetable products 72%, animal products 28%); 118% of FAO recommended minimum requirement.

Military

Total active duty personnel (2000): [9].

[1]Represents elected seats only. Attorney general and speaker serve ex officio. [2]Total includes the uninhabited 30 sq mi (78 sq km) Central Forest Reserve. [3]Preliminary enumerated household population; preliminary household pop. adjusted for under-enumeration equals 157,775; total adjusted pop. (including institutionalized individuals but excluding visitors) equals 158,361. [4]At factor cost in current prices. [5]Less imputed bank service charges. [6]Includes 13,630 unemployed. [7]Imports c.i.f.; exports f.o.b. [8]Combined data for both Castries and Vieux Fort airports. [9]The 300-member police force includes a specially trained paramilitary unit and a coast guard unit.

Internet resources for further information:

- **Saint Lucian Government Statistics Department http://www.stats.gov.lc**
- **Eastern Caribbean Central Bank http://www.eccb-centralbank.org**

Saint Vincent and the Grenadines

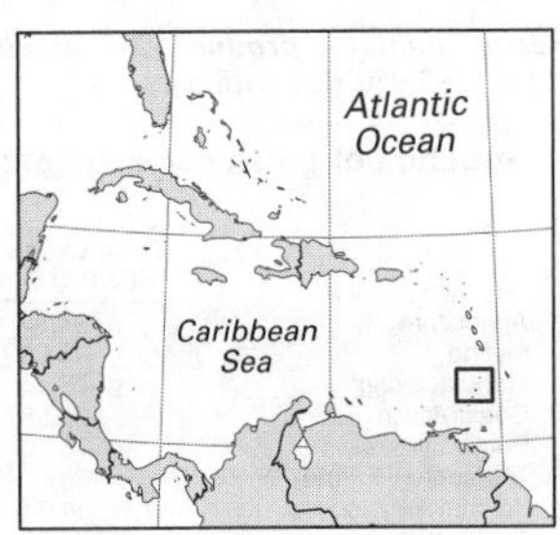

Official name: Saint Vincent and the Grenadines.
Form of government: constitutional monarchy with one legislative house (House of Assembly [21[1]]).
Chief of state: British Monarch represented by Governor-General.
Head of government: Prime Minister.
Capital: Kingstown.
Official language: English.
Official religion: none.
Monetary unit: 1 Eastern Caribbean dollar (EC$) = 100 cents; valuation (Sept. 8, 2003) 1 U.S.$ = EC$2.70; 1 £ = EC$4.28.

Area and population

Census Divisions[3]	area sq mi	area sq km	population 2001[2] estimate
Island of Saint Vincent			
Barrouallie	14.2	36.8	5,459
Bridgetown	7.2	18.6	7,908
Calliaqua	11.8	30.6	21,305
Chateaubelair	30.9	80.0	6,346
Colonarie	13.4	34.7	8,284
Georgetown	22.2	57.5	7,668
Kingstown (city)	1.9	4.9	16,239
Kingstown (suburbs)	6.4	16.6	11,295
Layou	11.1	28.7	6,294
Marriaqua	9.4	24.3	9,307
Sandy Bay	5.3	13.7	2,932
Saint Vincent Grenadines			
Northern Grenadines	9.0	23.3	5,789
Southern Grenadines	7.5	19.4	2,995
TOTAL	150.3	389.3[4]	111,821

Demography

Population (2003): 113,000.
Density (2002): persons per sq mi 753.3, persons per sq km 290.5.
Urban-rural (2000): urban 54.4%; rural 45.6%.
Sex distribution (2000): male 49.90%; female 50.10%.
Age breakdown (1999): under 15, 31.3%; 15–29, 31.2%; 30–44, 19.6%; 45–59, 9.4%; 60–74, 5.9%; 75 and over, 2.6%.
Population projection: (2010) 115,000; (2020) 115,000.
Doubling time: 61 years.
Ethnic composition (1999): black 65.5%; mulatto 23.5%; Indo-Pakistani 5.5%; white 3.5%; black-Amerindian 2.0%.
Religious affiliation (1995): Protestant 57.6%; unaffiliated Christian 20.6%; Roman Catholic 10.7%; Hindu 3.3%; Muslim 1.5%; other/nonreligious 6.3%.
Major city (2000[2]): Kingstown 16,209.

Vital statistics

Birth rate per 1,000 population (2001): 18.0 (world avg. 21.3); (1999) legitimate 17.9%; illegitimate 82.1%.
Death rate per 1,000 population (2001): 6.6 (world avg. 9.1).
Natural increase rate per 1,000 population (2001): 11.4 (world avg. 12.2).
Total fertility rate (avg. births per childbearing woman; 2000): 2.1.
Marriage rate per 1,000 population (2000): 6.0.
Divorce rate per 1,000 population (2000): 0.5.
Life expectancy at birth (2001): male 70.8 years; female 74.3 years.
Major causes of death per 100,000 population (1999): diseases of the circulatory system 242.8; malignant neoplasms (cancers) 138.0; endocrine and metabolic disorders 86.9; infectious and parasitic diseases 75.3; diseases of the respiratory system 66.2.

National economy

Budget (2002). Revenue: EC$312,000,000 (current revenue 80.8%, of which taxes on international trade and transactions 38.8%, income tax 25.6%, taxes on goods and services 15.7%; grants 5.1%; nontax revenue 13.8%; capital revenue 0.3%). Expenditures: EC$348,000,000 (current expenditure 81.3%, development expenditure 18.7%).
Public debt (external, outstanding; 2001): U.S.$163,000,000.
Production (metric tons except as noted). Agriculture, forestry, fishing (2000): bananas 45,951, coconuts 23,700, eddoes and dasheens[5] 4,400, plantains 2,048, corn (maize) 2,000, sweet potatoes 1,850, oranges 960, ginger 528, arrowroot starch 209, nutmegs 195; soursops, guavas, mangoes, and papayas are also grown; livestock (number of live animals) 13,000 sheep, 9,500 pigs, 6,200 cattle; roundwood, n.a.; fish catch 7,294. Mining and quarrying: sand and gravel for local use. Manufacturing (value added in EC$'000,000; 2000): beverages and tobacco products 17.4; food 15.6; paper products and publishing 3.6; textiles, clothing, and footwear 3.3. Energy production (consumption): electricity (kW-hr; 1999) 85,000,000 (85,000,000); coal, none (none); crude petroleum, none (none); petroleum products (metric tons; 1999) none (53,000); natural gas, none (none).
Tourism: receipts from visitors (2000) U.S.$80,000,000; expenditures by nationals abroad (2000) U.S.$9,000,000.
Land use (1994): forested 36%; meadows and pastures 5%; agricultural and under permanent cultivation 28%; other 31%.
Gross national product (2001): U.S.$300,000,000 (U.S.$2,740 per capita).

Structure of gross domestic product and labour force

	2000 in value EC$'000,000	2000 % of total value	1991 labour force	1991 % of labour force
Agriculture, forestry, fishing	82.4	10.8	8,377	20.1
Mining	1.7	0.2	98	0.2
Manufacturing	46.0	6.0	2,822	6.8
Construction	85.9	11.3	3,535	8.5
Public utilities	50.1	6.6	586	1.4
Transp. and commun.	155.1	20.3	2,279	5.5
Trade, restaurants	156.4	20.5	6,544	15.7
Finance, real estate	78.9	10.3	1,418	3.4
Pub. admin., defense	140.9	18.5	7,696	18.5
Services	14.8	1.9		
Other	–49.3[6]	–6.4[6]	8,327[7]	20.0[7]
TOTAL	762.9	100.0	41,682	100.0[4]

Population economically active (1991): total 41,682; activity rate of total population 39.1% (participation rates: ages 15–64, 67.5%; female 35.9%; unemployed [1996] more than 30%).

Price and earnings indexes (1995 = 100)

	1996	1997	1998	1999	2000	2001	2002
Consumer price index	104.4	104.9	107.1	108.2	108.4	109.3	110.2
Daily earnings index	...	...	...	...	...	...	...

Household income and expenditure. Average household size (1991) 3.9; income per household (1988) EC$4,579 (U.S.$1,696); sources of income: n.a.; expenditure: n.a.

Foreign trade[8]

Balance of trade (current prices)

	1997	1998	1999	2000	2001	2002
U.S.$'000,000	–127.2	–151.2	–161.1	–111.5	–140.8	–136.3
% of total	58.2%	60.1%	61.9%	51.8%	60.6%	64.1%

Imports (2001): U.S.$186,500,000 (food products 20.4%; machinery and transport equipment 19.0%; chemicals and chemical products 9.8%; fuels 9.0%). *Major import sources:* U.S. 34.5%; Caricom countries 31.2%, of which Trinidad and Tobago 19.9%; U.K. 9.8%; Japan 3.5%.
Exports (2001): U.S.$45,700,000 (domestic exports 86.9%, of which bananas 28.4%, packaged flour 13.2%, packaged rice 9.2%, eddoes and dasheens[5] 3.4%; reexports 13.1%). *Major export destinations:* Caricom countries 53.7%, of which Trinidad and Tobago 17.0%, Barbados 9.8%, St. Lucia 7.9%; U.K. 36.8%.

Transport and communications

Transport. Railroads: none. Roads (1999): total length 646 mi, 1,040 km (paved 31%). Vehicles (1999): passenger cars 7,989; trucks and buses 3,920. Merchant marine (1997): vessels (100 gross tons and over) 946; total deadweight tonnage 1,253,000. Air transport (2000): passenger arrivals 132,445; passenger departures 134,012; airports (1998) with scheduled flights 5.

Communications

Medium	date	unit	number	units per 1,000 persons
Radio	1995	receivers	65,000	591
Television	1995	receivers	17,700	161
Telephones	2001	main lines	26,100	233
Cellular telephones	2002	subscribers	10,000	85
Internet	2002	users	7,000	60
Personal computers	2002	units	14,000	192

Education and health

Educational attainment (1980). Percentage of population age 25 and over having: no formal schooling 2.4%; primary education 88.0%; secondary 8.2%; higher 1.4%. *Literacy* (1991): total population age 15 and over literate 64,000 (96.0%).

Education (2000)

	schools	teachers	students	student/ teacher ratio
Primary (age 5–11)	60	987	20,530	20.8
Secondary (age 12–18)	21	406	7,939	19.6
Voc., teacher tr.	4	48	904	18.8

Health (1998): physicians 59 (1 per 1,883 persons); hospital beds (2000) 209 (1 per 535 persons); infant mortality rate per 1,000 live births (2001) 16.6.
Food (2001): daily per capita caloric intake 2,609 (vegetable products 83%, animal products 17%); 108% of FAO recommended minimum requirement.

Military

Total active duty personnel (1992): 634-member police force includes a coast guard and paramilitary unit.

[1]Includes 6 nonelective seats; excludes speaker who may be elected from within or from outside of the House of Assembly membership. [2]January 1. [3]For statistical purposes and the election of legislative representatives only. [4]Detail does not add to total given because of rounding. [5]Varieties of taro roots. [6]Net of indirect taxes less imputed bank service charges. [7]Unemployed. [8]Imports c.i.f.; exports f.o.b.

Internet resources for further information:
- **Eastern Caribbean Central Bank http://www.eccb-centralbank.org**

Samoa[1]

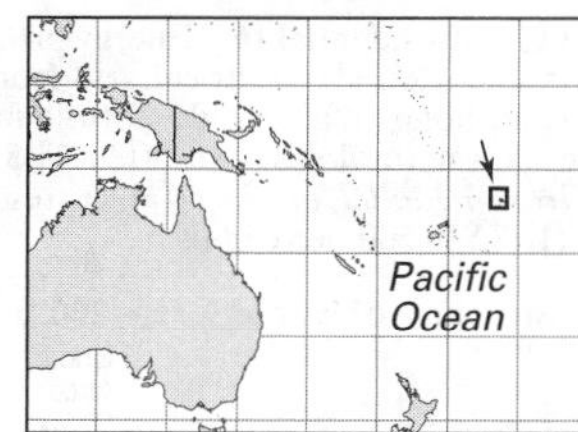

Official name: Malo Sa'oloto Tuto'atasi o Samoa (Samoan); Independent State of Samoa (English).
Form of government: constitutional monarchy[2] with one legislative house (Legislative Assembly [49]).
Chief of state: Head of State.
Head of government: Prime Minister.
Capital: Apia.
Official languages: Samoan; English.
Official religion: none.
Monetary unit: 1 tala (SA$[3], plural tala) = 100 sene; valuation (Sept. 8, 2003) 1 U.S.$ = SA$3.05; 1 £ = SA$4.83.

Area and population

Islands / Political Districts	area sq mi	area sq km	population 2001 census
Savai'i	659	1,707	42,400[4]
Fa'aseleleaga			...
Gaga'emauga			...
Gaga'ifomauga			...
Palauli			...
Satupa'itea			...
Vaisigano			...
Upolu	432	1,119	134,400[4]
A'ana			...
Aiga-i-le-Tai			...
Atua			...
Tuamasaga			...
Vaa-o-Fonoti			...
TOTAL	1,093[5]	2,831[5]	176,848[6]

Demography

Population (2003): 179,000.
Density (2003): persons per sq mi 163.8, persons per sq km 63.2.
Urban-rural (2002): urban 22.0%; rural 78.0%.
Sex distribution (2001): male 52.0%[4]; female 48.0%[4].
Age breakdown (1991): under 15, 40.6%; 15–29, 29.9%; 30–44, 14.6%; 45–59, 8.8%; 60–74, 5.0%; 75 and over, 1.1%.
Population projection: (2010) 193,000; (2020) 215,000.
Doubling time: 31 years.
Ethnic composition (1997): Samoan (Polynesian) 92.6%; Euronesian (European and Polynesian) 7.0%; European 0.4%.
Religious affiliation (1995): Mormon 25.8%; Congregational 24.6%; Roman Catholic 21.3%; Methodist 12.2%; Pentecostal 8.0%; Seventh-day Adventist 3.9%; other Christian 1.7%; other 2.5%.
Major towns: Apia (2001) 38,836; Safotulafai (2003) 1,800; Falelatai (2003) 1,800.

Vital statistics

Birth rate per 1,000 population (2002): 28.0 (world avg. 21.3).
Death rate per 1,000 population (2002): 5.6 (world avg. 9.1).
Natural increase rate per 1,000 population (2002): 22.4 (world avg. 12.2).
Total fertility rate (avg. births per childbearing woman; 2002): 4.2.
Marriage rate per 1,000 population: n.a.
Divorce rate per 1,000 population: n.a.
Life expectancy at birth (2002): male 67.0 years; female 73.0 years.
Major causes of death (percent distribution; 1992): congestive heart failure 14.0%; malignant neoplasms (cancers) 11.0%; cerebrovascular diseases 8.0%; injury and poisoning 8.0%; pneumonia 6.0%; septicemia 6.0%; diabetes mellitus 4.0%; intestinal infectious diseases 2.0%.

National economy

Budget (2000–01). Revenue: SA$262,400,000 (tax revenue 66.6%, grants 24.8%, nontax revenue 8.6%). Expenditures: SA$281,700,000 (current expenditure 58.4%, development expenditure 36.6%, net lending 5.0%).
Production (metric tons except as noted). Agriculture, forestry, fishing (2002): coconuts 140,000, bananas 21,500, taro 17,000, pineapples 4,600, papayas 3,600, mangoes 2,500, avocados 1,000, cacao beans 500; livestock (number of live animals) 201,000 pigs, 28,000 cattle, 450,000 chickens; roundwood (2001) 131,000 cu m; fish catch (2000) 13,004. Mining and quarrying: n.a. Manufacturing (in WS$'000; 1990): beer 8,708; cigarettes 6,551; coconut cream 5,576; sawn wood 3,662; coconut oil 3,442; corned meat 2,905; soap 1,487; paints 1,457. Construction (permits issued in WS$; 1995): residential 7,749,000; commercial, industrial, and other 30,867,000. Energy production (consumption): electricity (kW-hr; 1999) 66,000,000 (66,000,000); coal, none (n.a.); crude petroleum, none (n.a.); petroleum products (metric tons; 1999) none (45,000).
Household income and expenditure. Average household size (1999) 5.4; income per household: n.a.; sources of income: n.a.; expenditure: n.a.
Population economically active (2001): total 50,000; activity rate of total population 28.3% (participation rates: ages 15–64, n.a.; female [1991] 32.0%).

Price and earnings indexes (1995 = 100)

	1996	1997	1998	1999	2000	2001	2002
Consumer price index	105.4	112.6	115.1	115.4	116.5	121.2	130.8
Earnings index	...	...	...	...	...	...	...

Gross national product (at current market prices; 2001): U.S.$300,000,000 (U.S.$1,490 per capita).

Structure of gross domestic product and labour force

2001	in value SA$'000	% of total value	labour force	% of labour force
Agriculture	121,500	14.3	20,600	41.2
Mining	...	...		
Manufacturing	137,000	16.1		
Construction	59,500	7.0		
Public utilities	25,500	3.0		
Transp. and commun.	116,800	13.7		
Trade	175,800	20.6	29,400	58.8
Finance	59,300	7.0		
Pub. admin., defense	69,500	8.2		
Services	92,400	10.9		
Other	–5,800[7]	–0.7[7]		
TOTAL	851,500	100.0[6]	50,000	100.0

Public debt (external, outstanding; 2001): U.S.$143,300,000.
Tourism: receipts from visitors (2001) U.S.$39,000,000; expenditures by nationals abroad (1999) U.S.$4,000,000.
Land use (1994): forested 47.3%; meadows and pastures 0.4%; agricultural and under permanent cultivation 43.1%; other 9.2%.

Foreign trade[8]

Balance of trade (current prices)

	1997	1998	1999	2000	2001	2002
SA$'000,000	–218.8	–230.1	–293.6	–303.9	–396.2	–407.9
% of total	74.5%	67.5%	72.9%	77.2%	79.0%	81.5%

Imports (2001–02): SA$465,000,000 (petroleum products 10.2%, imports for government 5.2%, unspecified 84.6%). *Major import sources:* New Zealand 34.4%; Australia 26.6%; United States 11.8%; Fiji 8.7%; Japan 6.6%.
Exports (2001–02): SA$49,500,000 (fresh fish 66.9%, garments 11.5%, beer 6.7%, coconut cream 6.6%). *Major export destinations:* American Samoa 52.3%; United States 32.2%; New Zealand 6.8%; Germany 3.4%; Australia 2.7%.

Transport and communications

Transport. Railroads: none. Roads (1996): total length 491 mi, 790 km (paved 42%). Vehicles (1995): passenger cars 1,068; trucks and buses 1,169. Merchant marine (2001): vessels (100 gross tons and over) 7; total deadweight tonnage (1992) 6,501. Air transport (1999): passenger-km 244,000,000; metric ton-km cargo 23,000,000; airports (1997) with scheduled flights 3.

Communications

Medium	date	unit	number	units per 1,000 persons
Radio	1997	receivers	178,000	1,035
Television	1998	receivers	9,000	52
Telephones	2002	main lines	10,300	57
Cellular telephones	2002	subscribers	2,700	15
Personal computers	2002	units	1,000	6.7
Internet	2002	users	4,000	22

Education and health

Educational attainment: n.a. *Literacy* (2000): total population over age 15 literate 80.2%; males 81.2%; females 79.0%.

Education (1998)

	schools	teachers	students	student/ teacher ratio
Primary (age 5–11)	155[9]	1,233[10]	35,749[10]	23.9[10]
Secondary (age 12–18)	...	665[9]	12,672[9]	19.1[9]
Higher[11]	1	28	328	11.7

Health: physicians (1996) 62 (1 per 2,919 persons); hospital beds (1991) 863 (1 per 255 persons); infant mortality rate per 1,000 live births (2002) 26.0.
Food (1992): daily per capita caloric intake 2,828 (vegetable products 74%, animal products 26%); 124% of FAO recommended minimum requirement.

Military

No military forces are maintained; New Zealand is responsible for defense.

[1]In July 1997 the short-form name of the country was officially changed from Western Samoa to Samoa. [2]According to the constitution, the current Head of State, paramount chief HH Malietoa Tanumafili II, will hold office for life. Upon his death, the monarchy will functionally cease, and future Heads of State will be elected by the Legislative Assembly. [3]Symbol of the monetary unit changed from WS$ to SA$ as of July 1997. [4]Rounded census figure. [5]Total includes 2 sq mi (5 sq km) of uninhabited islands. [6]Detail does not add to total given because of rounding. [7]Less imputed bank service charges. [8]Imports c.i.f.; exports f.o.b. [9]1996. [10]1999. [11]National University of Samoa only.

Internet resources for further information:
- **Central Bank of Samoa http://www.cbs.gov.ws**

San Marino

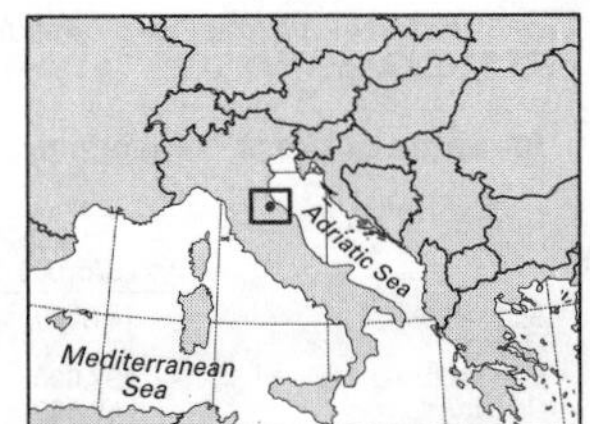

Official name: Serenissima Repubblica di San Marino (Most Serene Republic of San Marino).
Form of government: unitary multiparty republic with one legislative house (Great and General Council [60]).
Head of state and government: Captains-Regent (2).
Capital: San Marino.
Official language: Italian.
Official religion: none.
Monetary unit: 1 euro (€) = 100 cents; valuation (Sept. 8, 2003) 1 U.S.$ = €0.90; 1 £ = €1.43[1].

Area and population

Castles	Capitals	area sq mi	area sq km	population 2003[2] estimate
Acquaviva	Acquaviva	1.88	4.86	1,602
Borgo Maggiore	Borgo Maggiore	3.48	9.01	5,916
Chiesanuova	Chiesanuova	2.11	5.46	969
Città	San Marino	2.74	7.09	4,483
Domagnano	Domagnano	2.56	6.62	2,651
Faetano	Faetano	2.99	7.75	1,050
Fiorentino	Fiorentino	2.53	6.57	2,031
Montegiardino	Montegiardino	1.28	3.31	786
Serravalle/Dogano	Serravalle	4.07	10.53	9,265
TOTAL		23.63[3]	61.20	28,753

Demography

Population (2003): 29,200.
Density (2003): persons per sq mi 1,235.7, persons per sq km 477.1.
Urban-rural (1999): urban 96.2%; rural 3.8%.
Sex distribution (2003[2]): male 48.94%; female 51.06%.
Age breakdown (2003[2]): under 15, 14.1%; 15–29, 16.6%; 30–44, 27.3%; 45–59, 19.7%; 60–74, 14.2%; 75 and over, 8.1%.
Population projection: (2010) 32,000; (2020) 35,000.
Ethnic composition (2003[2]): Sammarinesi 85.7%; Italian 13.0%; other 1.3%.
Religious affiliation (2000): Roman Catholic 88.7%; Pentecostal 1.8%; other 9.5%.
Major cities (2000): Serravalle/Dogano 8,547; San Marino 4,439; Borgo Maggiore 2,394[4]; Murata 1,549[4]; Domagnano 1,048[4].

Vital statistics

Birth rate per 1,000 population (2002): 10.4 (world avg. 21.3); (1985) legitimate 95.2%; illegitimate 4.8%.
Death rate per 1,000 population (2002): 7.1 (world avg. 9.1).
Natural increase rate per 1,000 population (2002): 3.3 (world avg. 12.2).
Total fertility rate (avg. births per childbearing woman; 2002): 1.3.
Marriage rate per 1,000 population (2002): 7.3.
Divorce rate per 1,000 population (1991–95): 1.0.
Life expectancy at birth (2000): male 77.6 years; female 85.0 years.
Major causes of death per 100,000 population (1994–98): disease of the circulatory system 338.3; malignant neoplasms (cancers) 224.5; accidents, violence, and suicide 60.9; diseases of the respiratory system 9.5.

National economy

Budget (2003). Revenue: €505,341,000 (1997; taxes on goods and services 37.2%, taxes on income and profits 31.6%, social security 19.7%). Expenditures: €505,341,000 (1997; current expenditures 90.4%, of which social security and subsidies 48.2%, wages and salaries 31.2%; capital expenditures 6.9%; other 2.7%).
Public debt (external outstanding; 2000): U.S.$3,873,000.
Tourism: number of tourist arrivals (2002) 3,102,453; receipts from visitors (1994) U.S.$252,500,000; expenditures by nationals abroad, n.a.
Population economically active (2002): total 20,205; activity rate of total population 70.3% (participation rates: ages 15–64, 72.1%; female 40.3%; unemployed 3.9%).

Price and earnings indexes (1995 = 100)

	1993	1994	1995	1996	1997	1998	1999
Consumer price index	91.6	95.3	100.0	104.1	106.2	108.6	112.1
Annual earnings index	87.9	93.9	100.0	110.9	118.4	...	...

Household income and expenditure. Total number of households (2003[2]) 11,723; average household size (2003[2]) 2.5; income per household: n.a.; sources of income: n.a.; expenditure (1991)[5]: food, beverages, and tobacco 22.1%, housing, fuel, and electrical energy 20.9%, transportation and communications 17.6%, clothing and footwear 8.0%, furniture, appliances, and goods and services for the home 7.2%, education 7.1%, health and sanitary services 2.6%, other goods and services 14.5%.
Production (metric tons except as noted). Agriculture, forestry, fishing[6]: wheat *c.* 4,400, grapes *c.* 700, barley *c.* 500; livestock (number of live animals; 1998) 831 cattle, 748 pigs. Manufacturing (1998): processed meats 324,073 kg, of which beef 226,570 kg, pork 87,764 kg, veal 7,803 kg; cheese 61,563 kg; butter 12,658 kg; milk 1,167,620 litres; yogurt 5,131 litres; other major products include electrical appliances, musical instruments, printing ink, paint, cosmetics, furniture, floor tiles, gold and silver jewelry, clothing, and postage stamps. Construction (new units completed; 1998): residential 69; nonresidential 165. Energy production (consumption): all electrical power is imported via electrical grid from Italy (consumption [2001] 193,371,696); coal, none (n.a.); crude petroleum, none (n.a.); petroleum products, none (n.a.); natural gas, none ([2001] 50,641,790).
Gross national product (at current market prices; 1999): U.S.$715,300,000 (U.S.$26,600 per capita).

Structure of labour force (2002)

	labour force[7]	% of labour force[7]
Agriculture	24	0.1
Manufacturing	6,022	34.7
Construction and public utilities	1,351	7.8
Transportation and communications	371	2.1
Trade	2,701	15.6
Finance and insurance	636	3.7
Services	1,950	11.2
Public administration and defense	4,303	24.8
Other	11[8]	—
TOTAL	17,369	100.0

Land use (1985): agricultural and under permanent cultivation 74%; meadows and pastures 22%; forested, built-on, wasteland, and other 4%.

Foreign trade[9]

Balance of trade (current prices)

	1994	1995	1996	1997	1998	1999
U.S.$'000,000	–41.2	–3.3	+22.6	–34.0	–17.9	–28.0
% of total	1.3%	0.1%	0.7%	1.0%	0.5%	0.8%

Imports (1999): U.S.$1,707,000,000 (manufactured goods of all kinds, petroleum products, electricity, and gold). *Major import source:* Italy[9].
Exports (1999): U.S.$1,679,000,000 (goods include electronics, postage stamps, leather products, ceramics, wine, wood products, and building stone). *Major export destination:* Italy[10].

Transport and communications

Transport. Railroads: none (nearest rail terminal is at Rimini, Italy, 17 mi [27 km] northeast). Roads (2001): total length 156 mi, 252 km. Vehicles (2002): passenger cars 28,470; trucks and buses 2,748. Merchant marine: vessels (100 gross tons and over) none. Air transport: airports with scheduled flights, none; there is, however, a heliport that provides passenger and cargo service between San Marino and Rimini, Italy, during the summer months.

Communications

Medium	date	unit	number	units per 1,000 persons
Daily newspapers	1996	circulation	2,000	72
Radio	1998	receivers	16,000	610
Television	1998	receivers	9,055	358
Telephones	2002	main lines	20,601	716
Cellular telephones	2002	subscribers	16,759	583
Internet	2002	users	5,800	202

Education and health

Educational attainment (2003[2]). Percentage of population age 14 and over having: basic literacy or primary education 41.0%; some secondary 25.0%; secondary 27.0%; higher degree 7.0%. *Literacy* (1997[2]): total population age 15 and over literate 21,885 (99.1%); males literate 10,546 (99.4%); females literate 11,339 (98.8%).

Education (2002–03)

	schools	teachers	students	student/ teacher ratio
Primary (age 6–10)	14	242	1,343	5.4
Secondary (age 11–18)[11]	7	227	2,162	8.7
Higher	1	27	950	35.6

Health (2002): physicians 117 (1 per 230 persons); hospital beds 134 (1 per 191 persons); infant mortality rate per 1,000 live births (2002) 6.8.
Food (2000)[12]: daily per capita caloric intake 3,661 (vegetable products 74%, animal products 26%); 146% of FAO recommended minimum requirement.

Military

Total active duty personnel (2000): none[13]. *Military expenditure as percentage of national budget* (1992): 1.0% (world 3.6%); per capita expenditure (1987) U.S.$155.

[1]Italian lira replaced by euro (€) from Jan. 1, 2002. [2]January 1. [3]Detail does not add to total given because of rounding. [4]1997. [5]Weighting coefficients for component expenditures are those of the 1991 official Italian consumer price index for the North-Central region of Italy. [6]Early 1980s. [7]Employed only. [8]Unspecified workers. [9]A customs union with Italy has existed since 1862. [10]In the late 1990s Italy accounted for 87% of all foreign trade. [11]Includes vocational schools. [12]Figures are for Italy. [13]Defense is provided by a public security force of about 50.

Internet resources for further information:
- **San Marino http://www.esteri.sm/eindex.htm**

São Tomé and Príncipe

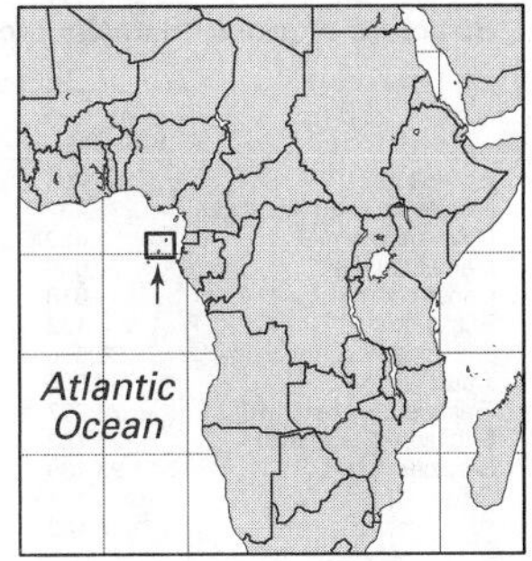

Official name: República democrática de São Tomé e Príncipe (Democratic Republic of São Tomé and Príncipe).
Form of government: multiparty republic with one legislative house (National Assembly [55]).
Chief of state: President.
Head of government: Prime Minister.
Capital: São Tomé.
Official language: Portuguese.
Official religion: none.
Monetary unit: 1 dobra (Db) = 100 cêntimos; valuation (Sept. 8, 2003) 1 U.S.$ = Db 8,700; 1 £ = Db 13,794.

Area and population

Islands / Districts	Capitals	area sq mi	area sq km	population 2001 census
São Tomé		332	859	131,633
Aqua Grande	São Tomé	7	17	51,886
Cantagalo	Santana	46	119	13,258
Caué	São João Angolares	103	267	5,501
Lemba	Neves	88	229	10,696
Lobata	Guadalupe	41	105	15,187
Mé-Zóchi	Trindade	47	122	35,105
Autonomous Island		55	142	5,966
Príncipe (Pagué)	Santo António	55	142	5,966
TOTAL		386[1]	1,001	137,599

Demography

Population (2003): 142,000.
Density (2003): persons per sq mi 367.9, persons per sq km 141.9.
Urban-rural (1999): urban 46.0%; rural 54.0%.
Sex distribution (2001): male 49.28%, female 50.72%.
Age breakdown (2001): under 15, 47.7%; 15–29, 27.5%; 30–44, 12.6%; 45–59, 6.3%; 60–74, 4.5%; 75 and over, 1.4%.
Population projection: (2010) 158,200; (2020) 185,000.
Doubling time: 20 years.
Ethnic composition (2000): black-white admixture 79.5%; Fang 10.0%; angolares (descendants of former Angolan slaves) 7.6%; Portuguese 1.9%; other 1.0%.
Religious affiliation (1995): Roman Catholic, about 89.5%; remainder mostly Protestant, predominantly Seventh-day Adventist and an indigenous Evangelical Church.
Major cities (2001): São Tomé 51,886; Trindade 14,700[2]; Santo Amaro 7,400[2]; Santana 7,000[2]; Neves 7,000[2].

Vital statistics

Birth rate per 1,000 population (2002): 42.3 (world avg. 21.3).
Death rate per 1,000 population (2002): 7.3 (world avg. 9.1).
Natural increase rate per 1,000 population (2002): 35.0 (world avg. 12.2).
Total fertility rate (avg. births per childbearing woman; 2002): 6.1.
Marriage rate per 1,000 population: n.a.
Divorce rate per 1,000 population: n.a.
Life expectancy at birth (2002): male 64.5 years; female 65.9 years.
Major causes of death per 100,000 population (1987): malaria 160.6; direct obstetric causes 76.7; pneumonia 74.0; influenza 61.5; anemias 47.3; hypertensive disease 32.1.

National economy

Budget (2000). Revenue: Db 183,400,000,000 (grants 56.4%; taxes 32.4%, of which sales taxes 10.9%, import taxes 9.8%, income and profit taxes 9.1%; nontax revenue 11.2%). Expenditures: Db 244,400,000,000 (capital expenditure 63.3%; recurrent expenditure 36.7%, of which personnel costs 11.8%, debt service 10.0%, goods and services 6.2%, transfers 3.0%, defense 0.5%).
Public debt (external, outstanding; 2000): U.S.$294,400,000.
Production (metric tons except as noted). Agriculture, forestry, fishing (2002): oil palm fruit 40,000, bananas 35,000, coconuts 26,600, taro 25,000, vegetables 6,200, cassava 5,500, cacao 4,000, fruits (other than melon) 2,500, corn (maize) 2,500, cinnamon 30, coffee 20; livestock (number of live animals) 4,800 goats, 4,100 cattle, 2,600 sheep, 2,100 pigs; roundwood (2001) 9,000 cu m; fish catch (2001) 3,500, principally marine fish and shellfish. Mining and quarrying: some quarrying to support local construction industry. Manufacturing (value in Db; 1995): beer 880,000; clothing 679,000; lumber 369,000; bakery products 350,000; palm oil 228,000; soap 133,000; ceramics 87,000. Energy production (consumption): electricity (kW-hr; 2000) 26,050,000 (16,574,000); coal, none (n.a.); crude petroleum, none (n.a.); petroleum products (metric tons; 1999) none (29,000); natural gas, none (n.a.).
Household income and expenditure. Average household size (1981) 4.0; income per household: n.a.; sources of income: n.a.; expenditure (1995)[3]: food 71.9%, housing and energy 10.2%, transportation and communications 6.4%, clothing and other items 5.3%, household durable goods 2.8%, education and health 1.7%.
Tourism (1997): receipts from visitors U.S.$2,000,000; expenditures by nationals abroad U.S.$1,000,000.
Population economically active (1994): total 51,789; activity rate of total population 40.8% (participation rates: ages 15–64 [1981] 61.1%; female [1991] 32.4%; unemployed [1994] 29.0%).

Price and earnings indexes (1995 = 100)

	1995	1996	1997	1998	1999	2000
Consumer price index	100.0	137.6	175.8	209.7	233.6	233.9
Earnings index	...	...	...	...	...	...

Gross national product (2000): U.S.$43,000,000 (U.S.$290 per capita).

Structure of gross domestic product and labour force

	2000		1998	
	in value Db '000,000	% of total value	labour force[4]	% of labour force[4]
Agriculture	74,300	20.1	16,004	41.5
Mining	...	...	...	...
Manufacturing / Public utilities	20,300	5.5	2,420	6.2
Construction	43,700	11.8	3,515	9.1
Transp. and commun.	85,700	23.2	2,819	7.3
Trade			5,350	13.9
Finance	32,100	8.7	215	0.6
Pub. admin., defense	84,800	22.9	3,338	8.7
Services	28,800	7.8	...	...
Other	...	...	4,921	12.8
TOTAL	369,700	100.0	38,582	100.0[1]

Land use (1994): meadows and pastures 1.3%; agricultural and under permanent cultivation 54.0%; forest, built-on, wasteland, and other 44.7%.

Foreign trade

Balance of trade (current prices)

	1997	1998	1999	2000	2001	2002
U.S.$'000,000	–13.9	–12.1	–18.0	–19.1	–21.2	–19.3
% of total	56.7%	56.3%	69.8%	74.9%	76.3%	63.7%

Imports (2002): U.S.$24,800,000 ([5]investment goods 52.9%, food and other agricultural products 20.2%, petroleum products 17.9%). *Major import sources:* Portugal 38.9%; U.S. 22.2%; U.K. 9.3%.
Exports (2002): U.S.$5,500,000 (cocoa beans 80.0%; other exports include copra, coffee, and palm oil). *Major export destinations:* The Netherlands 27.3%; Portugal 18.2%; Canada 9.1%.

Transport and communications

Transport. Railroads: none. Roads (1999): total length 199 mi, 320 km (paved 68%). Vehicles (1996): passenger cars 4,040; trucks and buses 1,540. Merchant marine (2000): vessels (100 gross tons and over) 39; total deadweight tonnage 149,048. Air transport (1998): passenger-mi 6,000,000, passenger-km 9,000,000; short ton-mi cargo 700,000, short ton-km cargo 1,000,000; airports (2000) 2.

Communications

Medium	date	unit	number	units per 1,000 persons
Radio	1997	receivers	38,000	272
Television	1997	receivers	23,000	163
Telephones	2002	main lines	6,200	41
Cellular telephones	2002	subscribers	500	3.2
Internet	2001	users	11,000	73

Education and health

Educational attainment: n.a. *Literacy* (1991): total population age 15 and over literate 73.0%; males literate 85.0%; females literate 62.0%.

Education (1998)

	schools	teachers[6]	students	student/ teacher ratio
Primary (age 6–13)	71	638	20,287	34.1[6]
Secondary (age 14–18)[7]	11	415	11,814	29.6[6]
Voc., teacher tr.	...	...	...	...
Higher	...	...	...	...

Health: physicians (1996) 61 (1 per 2,147 persons); hospital beds (1983) 640 (1 per 158 persons); infant mortality rate per 1,000 live births (2002) 47.5.
Food (2001): daily per capita caloric intake 2,567 (vegetable products 96%, animal products 4%); 109% of FAO recommended minimum requirement.

Military

Total active duty personnel (1995): 600[8]. *Military expenditure as percentage of GNP* (1999): 1.0% (world 2.4%); per capita expenditure U.S.$3.

[1]Detail does not add to total given because of rounding. [2]2004. [3]Weights based on CPI components. [4]Employed only. [5]Based on imports for 2000 equaling U.S.$22,300,000. [6]1997. [7]Includes vocational. [8]A 5-member crew of the Portuguese air force is stationed in São Tomé and Príncipe to provide humanitarian assistance.

Internet resources for further information:
- **UN Development Programme: Human Development Indicators (2003) http://www.undp.org/hdr2003/indicator/cty_f_STP.html**

Saudi Arabia

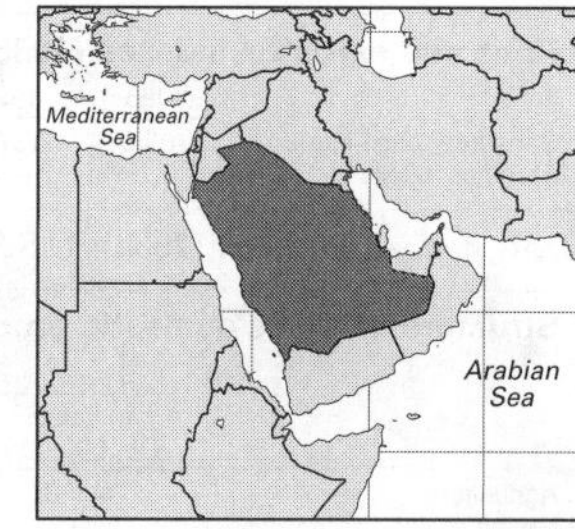

Official name: Al-Mamlakah al-ʿArabīyah as-Saʿūdīyah (Kingdom of Saudi Arabia).
Form of government: monarchy[1].
Heads of state and government: King assisted by Crown Prince.
Capital: Riyadh.
Official language: Arabic.
Official religion: Islam.
Monetary unit: 1 Saudi riyal (SRls) = 100 halalah; valuation (Sept. 8, 2003) 1 U.S.$ = SRls 3.75; 1 £ = SRls 5.94.

Area and population

Geographic Regions / Administrative Regions	Capitals	area sq mi	area sq km	population 2000 estimate
Al-Gharbīyah (Western)		121,637	315,039	7,304,025
Al-Bāḥah	Al-Bāḥah	3,830	9,921	476,382
Al-Madīnah al-Munawwarah	Medina (Al-Madīnah)	58,684	151,990	1,378,870
Makkah al-Mukarramah	Mecca (Makkah)	59,123	153,128	5,448,773
Al-Janūbīyah (Southern)		91,844	237,875	3,106,074
ʿAsīr	Abha	29,611	76,693	1,637,464
Jīzān	Jīzān	4,506	11,671	1,083,022
Najrān	Najrān	57,727	149,511	385,588
Ash-Shamālīyah (Northern)		138,256	358,081	1,197,700
Al-Ḥudūd ash-Shamālīyah (Northern Borders)	ʿArʿar	43,165	111,797	249,544
Al-Jawf	Sakākah	38,692	100,212	354,450
Tabūk	Tabūk	56,399	146,072	593,706
Ash-Sharqīyah (Eastern)		259,662	672,522	3,008,913[2]
Ash-Sharqīyah (Eastern)	Ad-Dammām	259,662	672,522	3,008,913[2]
Al-Wūsṭā (Central)		218,601	566,173	6,230,172
Ḥāʾil	Ḥāʾil	40,111	103,887	519,984
Al-Qaṣīm	Buraydah	22,412	58,046	979,858
Ar-Riyāḍ	Riyadh (Ar-Riyāḍ)	156,078	404,240	4,730,330
TOTAL		830,000	2,149,690	20,846,884

Demography

Population (2003): 24,008,000[3].
Density (2002): persons per sq mi 28.9, persons per sq km 11.2.
Urban-rural (2001): urban 86.7%; rural 13.3%.
Sex distribution (2002): male 55.04%; female 44.96%.
Age breakdown (2002): under 15, 42.6%; 15–29, 23.5%; 30–44, 16.8%; 45–59, 12.5%; 60–74, 3.9%; 75 and over, 0.7%.
Population projection: (2010) 28,990,000; (2020) 36,022,000.
Doubling time: 22 years.
Ethnic composition (2000): Arab 88.1%, of which Saudi Arab 74.2%, Bedouin 3.9%, Gulf Arab 3.0%; Indo-Pakistani 5.5%; African black 1.5%; Filipino 1.0%; other 3.9%.
Religious affiliation (1992): Sunnī Muslim 93.3%; Shīʿī Muslim 3.3%; Christian 3.0%; other 0.4%.
Major urban agglomerations (2000): Riyadh 4,549,000; Jiddah 3,192,000; Mecca 1,335,000; Medina 891,000; Ad-Dammām 764,000.

Vital statistics

Birth rate per 1,000 population (2002): 37.3 (world avg. 21.3).
Death rate per 1,000 population (2002): 5.9 (world avg. 9.1).
Natural increase rate per 1,000 population (2002): 31.4 (world avg. 12.2).
Total fertility rate (avg. births per childbearing woman; 2002): 6.2.
Life expectancy at birth (2002): male 66.7 years; female 70.2 years.
Major causes of death per 100,000 population: n.a.

National economy

Budget (2001). Revenue: SRls 215,000,000,000 (oil revenues 78.6%). Expenditures: SRls 215,000,000,000 (defense and security 36.7%, human resource development 24.7%, public administration, municipal transfers, and subsidies 17.4%, health and social development 8.4%).
Production (metric tons except as noted). Agriculture, forestry, fishing (2002): alfalfa 2,000,000, wheat 1,800,000, dates 783,000, potatoes 400,000, tomatoes 310,000, watermelons 275,000, sorghum 200,000, grapes 117,000, cantaloupes 105,000, barley 100,000, dry onions 97,000; livestock (number of live animals) 8,000,000 sheep, 4,650,000 goats, 415,000 camels, 330,000 cattle; fish catch (2000) 55,654. Mining and quarrying (2001): gypsum 450,000; silver 15,000 kg; gold 5,000 kg. Manufacturing (value added in U.S.$'000,000; 1995): industrial chemicals 3,014; cement, glass, and other nonmetal mineral products 943; refined petroleum 830; metal products 589; iron and steel 561; food, beverages, and tobacco 493; plastic products 221. Energy production (consumption): electricity (kW-hr; 1999) 121,616,000,000 (121,616,000,000); coal, none (none); crude petroleum (barrels; 2001) 2,862,000,000 ([1999] 515,500,000); petroleum products (metric tons; 1999) 92,255,000 (43,454,000); natural gas (cu m; 1999) 46,198,400,000 (46,198,400,000).
Population economically active (2001): total 7,305,000, of which 3,808,800 foreign workers and 3,496,200 Saudi nationals; activity rate of total population 31.3% (participation rates, n.a.; female, n.a.; unemployed [2002] 11.0%).

Price and earnings indexes (1995 = 100)

	1996	1997	1998	1999	2000	2001	2002
Consumer price index	101.2	101.3	100.7	99.3	98.5	98.1	97.6
Earnings index	...	...	...	...	...	...	...

Gross national product (2000): U.S.$149,932,000,000 (U.S.$7,230 per capita).

Structure of gross domestic product and labour force

2001	in value SRls '000,000	% of total value	labour force	% of labour force
Agriculture	35,708	5.1	567,500	7.8
Petroleum and natural gas	238,492	34.1	113,300	1.6
Other mining	2,650	0.4		
Manufacturing[4]	70,096	10.0	616,800	8.4
Construction	43,018	6.2	1,051,500	14.4
Public utilities	3,152	0.5	96,600	1.3
Transp. and commun.	30,500	4.4	303,500	4.2
Trade	49,506	7.1	1,050,300	14.4
Finance, real estate[5]	78,297	11.2	350,500	4.8
Pub. admin., defense	123,753	17.7	922,600	12.6
Services	23,130	3.3	2,232,400	30.6
Other	101[6]	—		
TOTAL	698,403	100.0	7,305,000[7, 8]	100.0[7, 8]

Household income and expenditure. Average household size (2000) 6.8; income per household: n.a.; sources of income: n.a.; expenditure (1994)[9]: food and tobacco 38.5%, transportation and communications 16.4%, housing 15.2%.
Tourism (in U.S.$'000,000): receipts (1997) 1,420; expenditures, n.a.
Land use (1994): forested 0.8%; meadows and pastures 55.8%; agricultural and under permanent cultivation 1.8%; built-on, waste, and other 41.6%.

Foreign trade[10]

Balance of trade (current prices)

	1996	1997	1998	1999	2000	2001
SRls '000,000,000	+123.5	+119.8	+33.0	+85.1	+177.1	+157.2
% of total	37.3%	35.8%	12.8%	28.9%	43.8%	40.2%

Imports (2001): SRls 116,930,000,000 (transport equipment 21.3%, of which road vehicles 16.5%; machinery and apparatus 20.6%, of which general industrial machinery 5.7%; food and live animals 13.5%; chemicals and chemical products 9.6%; iron and steel 4.0%). *Major import sources* (2001): U.S. 17.8%; Japan 11.2%; Germany 8.0%; U.K. 6.9%; China 4.6%.
Exports (2001): SRls 274,085,000,000 (crude petroleum 72.8%; refined petroleum 16.0%; organic chemicals 3.6%; polyethylene 1.6%). *Major export destinations* (2002): U.S. 18.7%; Japan 15.7%; South Korea 10.2%; Singapore 5.1%; China 4.6%.

Transport and communications

Transport. Railroads (2001): route length 1,390 km; passenger-km 222,000,000; metric ton-km cargo 856,000,000. Roads (2002): total length 157,000 km (paved 29%). Vehicles (1996): passenger cars 1,744,000; trucks and buses 1,192,000. Air transport (2001): passenger-km 20,216,000,000[11]; metric ton-km cargo 798,968,000[11]; airports (1998) with scheduled flights 28.

Communications

Medium	date	unit	number	units per 1,000 persons
Daily newspapers	1996	circulation	1,105,000	59
Radio	2000	receivers	7,180,000	326
Television	2000	receivers	5,810,000	264
Telephones	2002	main lines	3,318,000	144
Cellular telephones	2002	subscribers	5,008,000	217
Personal computers	2002	units	3,000,000	130
Internet	2002	users	1,419,000	62

Education and health

Educational attainment (2000). Percentage of Saudi (non-Saudi) population age 10 and over who: are illiterate 19.9% (12.1%), are literate/have primary education 39.5% (40.6%), have some/completed secondary education 34.2% (36.0%), have at least begun university education 6.4% (11.3%).

Education (2000–01)

	schools	teachers	students	student/teacher ratio
Primary (age 6–12)	12,585	195,201	2,308,460	11.8
Secondary (age 13–18)	9,774	151,851	1,878,114	12.4
Voc., teacher tr.	95	7,028	81,177	11.6
Higher[12]	75	10,554	190,478	18.0

Health (2001): physicians 31,983 (1 per 709 persons); hospital beds 46,855 (1 per 484 persons); infant mortality rate per 1,000 live births (2002) 49.6.
Food (2001): daily per capita caloric intake 2,841 (vegetable products 85%, animal products 15%); 119% of FAO recommended minimum requirement.

Military

Total active duty personnel (2002): 124,500 (army 60.2%, navy 12.4%, air force 27.4%); U.S. military withdrew in 2003. *Military expenditure as percentage of GNP* (1999): 14.9% (world 2.4%); per capita expenditure U.S.$996.

[1]Assisted by the Consultative Council consisting of 120 appointed members. [2]Geographic and administrative regions are coextensive. [3]Expatriates comprise 25% of total population. [4]Includes refined petroleum. [5]Includes business services. [6]Other equals import duties less imputed bank services charge. [7]Includes 3,808,800 (52.1%) foreign workers in the private sector. [8]Detail does not add to total given because of rounding. [9]Urban middle-income households only. [10]Imports c.i.f., exports f.o.b. [11]Saudi Arabian Airlines only. [12]1999–2000.

Internet resources for further information:
- **Ministry of Information http://www.saudinf.com**

Senegal

Official name: République du Sénégal (Republic of Senegal).
Form of government: multiparty republic with one legislative house (National Assembly [120]).
Head of state and government: President assisted by Prime Minister.
Capital: Dakar.
Official language: French.
Official religion: none.
Monetary unit: 1 CFA franc (CFAF) = 100 centimes; valuation (Sept. 8, 2003) 1 U.S.$ = CFAF 594.70; 1 £ = CFAF 942.91[1].

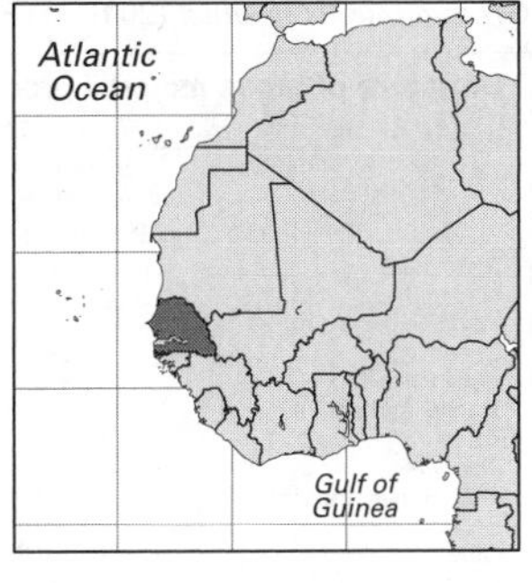

Area and population

Regions	Capitals	area sq mi	area sq km	population 2001 estimate
Dakar	Dakar	212	550	2,411,528
Diourbel	Diourbel	1,683	4,359	930,008
Fatick	Fatick	3,064	7,935	639,075
Kaolack	Kaolack	6,181	16,010	1,128,128
Kolda	Kolda	8,112	21,011	834,753
Louga	Louga	11,270	29,188	559,268
Matam	Matam	9,685	25,083	291,555
Saint-Louis	Saint-Louis	7,353	19,044	571,885
Tambacounda	Tambacounda	23,012	59,602	530,332
Thiès	Thiès	2,549	6,601	1,348,637
Ziguinchor	Ziguinchor	2,834	7,339	557,606
TOTAL		75,955	196,722	9,802,775

Demography

Population (2003): 10,095,000.
Density (2003): persons per sq mi 132.9, persons per sq km 51.3.
Urban-rural (2000): urban 47.4%; rural 52.6%.
Sex distribution (2002): male 49.07%; female 50.93%.
Age breakdown (2002): under 15, 44.1%; 15–29, 27.8%; 30–44, 15.6%; 45–59, 7.9%; 60–74, 3.6%; 75 and over, 1.0%.
Population projection: (2010) 11,869,000; (2020) 14,422,000.
Doubling time: 27 years.
Ethnic composition (2000): Wolof 34.6%; Peul (Fulani) and Tukulor 27.1%; Serer 12.0%; Malinke (Mandingo) 9.7%; other 16.6%.
Religious affiliation (2000): Muslim 87.6%; traditional beliefs 6.2%; Christian 5.5%, of which Roman Catholic 4.7%; other 0.7%.
Major cities (2001): Dakar 2,411,528[2]; Thiès 273,599; Kaolack 243,209; Ziguinchor 216,971; Saint-Louis 154,496.

Vital statistics

Birth rate per 1,000 population (2002): 36.8 (world avg. 21.3).
Death rate per 1,000 population (2002): 11.0 (world avg. 9.1).
Natural increase rate per 1,000 population (2002): 25.8 (world avg. 12.2).
Total fertility rate (avg. births per childbearing woman; 2002): 5.0.
Marriage rate per 1,000 population: n.a.[3].
Life expectancy at birth (2002): male 54.7 years; female 57.7 years.
Major causes of death: n.a.; major diseases are malaria, tetanus, meningitis, and tuberculosis.

National economy

Budget (2001). Revenue: CFAF 664,400,000,000 (tax revenue 77.5%, of which oil revenue 12.7%; nontax revenue 13.2%; grants 9.3%). Expenditures: CFAF 733,800,000,000 (current expenditures 70.4%, of which wages 24.2%, education 21.0%, health 5.6%, interest payment 4.1%; development expenditure 29.6%).
Public debt (external, outstanding; 2001): U.S.$2,961,000,000.
Production (metric tons except as noted). Agriculture, forestry, fishing (2002): sugarcane 890,000, peanuts (groundnuts) 501,298, millet 414,687, watermelons 224,064, paddy rice 177,756, sorghum 143,892, cassava 110,617, corn (maize) 97,858, oil palm fruit 65,000; livestock (number of live animals) 4,900,000 sheep, 4,000,000 goats, 3,230,000 cattle, 492,000 horses; roundwood (2001) 5,971,559 cu m; fish catch (2001) 405,409, of which crustaceans and mollusks 22,288. Mining and quarrying (2001): phosphate 1,890,000; salt 130,000. Manufacturing (CFAF '000,000; 1997): food 72,853; industrial chemicals 39,421; cement 12,782; textiles 10,274; fabricated metal products 8,264; tobacco products 6,231. Energy production (consumption): electricity (kW-hr; 2001) 1,651,200,000 (1,651,200,000); coal, none (none); crude petroleum (barrels; 1999) none (6,200,000); petroleum products (metric tons; 1999) 864,000 (1,082,000); natural gas, none (none).
Population economically active (2001): total 4,294,000; activity rate of total population 44.6% (participation rates: n.a.; female, n.a.; unemployed, n.a.).

Price and earnings indexes (1995 = 100)

	1996	1997	1998	1999	2000	2001	2002
Consumer price index	102.8	104.4	105.6	106.5	107.2	110.5	113.0
Hourly earnings index	...	...	...	...	...	...	...

Household income and expenditure. Average household size (2000) 8.7.
Tourism (2000): receipts U.S.$140,000,000; expenditures (1999) U.S.$54,000,-000.
Gross national product (at current market prices; 2001): U.S.$4,000,000,000 (U.S.$490 per capita).

Structure of gross domestic product and labour force

	2001 in value CFAF '000,000,000[4]	2001 % of total value[4]	1991 labour force	1991 % of labour force
Agriculture	412.3	18.8	1,789,467	65.3
Mining	304.8	13.9	1,998	0.1
Manufacturing			161,124	5.9
Public utilities	42.5	1.9	...	...
Construction	105.0	4.8	60,935	2.2
Transp. and commun.	272.7	12.5	58,081	2.1
Trade, hotels	464.0	21.2	378,241	13.8
Finance	...	...	4,623	0.2
Services	404.8	18.5	...	...
Pub. admin., defense	183.8	8.4	268,721	9.8
Other	—	—	16,286	0.6
TOTAL	2,189.9	100.0	2,739,476	100.0

Land use (1994): forested 39.5%; meadows and pastures 29.6%; agricultural and under permanent cultivation 12.2%; other 18.7%.

Foreign trade[5]

Balance of trade (current prices)

	1996	1997	1998	1999	2000	2001
U.S.$'000,000	–276	–271	–293	–326	–417	–425
% of total	12.3%	13.0%	12.9%	13.5%	18.5%	17.5%

Imports (2001): U.S.$1,730,000,000 (food and live animals 22.3%, of which cereals 13.2%, rice 8.2%; mineral fuels and lubricants 16.8%, of which crude petroleum 9.8%; machinery and apparatus 15.1%; chemicals and chemical products 11.1%). *Major import sources:* France 27.8%; Nigeria 9.8%; Thailand 7.7%; Germany 4.8%; United States 4.2%.
Exports (2001): U.S.$785,000,000 (fresh fish 16.1%; refined petroleum 15.5%; fresh crustaceans and mollusks 12.0%; bunkers and ships' stores 12.0%; phosphorous pentoxide and phosphoric acids 9.5%; peanut [groundnut] oil 9.1%). *Major export destinations:* France 16.7%; India 12.4%; Greece 7.3%; Mali 6.9%.

Transport and communications

Transport. Railroads: (2001) route length 563 mi, 906 km; (1998) passenger-km 63,400,000; metric ton-km cargo 435,200,000. Roads (1996): total length 9,060 mi, 14,700 km (paved 29%). Vehicles (1999): passenger cars 98,260; trucks and buses 35,753. Air transport (1999)[6]: passenger-km 241,000,000; metric ton-km cargo 37,000,000; airports (1996) with scheduled flights 7.

Communications

Medium	date	unit	number	units per 1,000 persons
Daily newspapers	2000	circulation	47,000	5.0
Radio	2000	receivers	1,320,000	141
Television	2000	receivers	376,000	40
Telephones	2002	main lines	224,600	30
Cellular telephones	2002	subscribers	553,400	57
Personal computers	2002	units	200,000	20
Internet	2002	users	105,000	11

Education and health

Educational attainment: n.a. *Literacy* (2000): percentage of total population age 15 and over literate 37.3%; males literate 47.3%; females literate 27.6%.

Education (1999–2000)

	schools	teachers	students	student/ teacher ratio
Primary (age 6–12)	4,751	23,198	1,107,712	47.8
Secondary (age 13–18)	566	10,040	245,121	24.4
Vocational	12	384	4,425	11.5
Higher[7]	2	963	22,157	23.0

Health: physicians (1996) 649 (1 per 13,162 persons); hospital beds (1998) 3,582 (1 per 2,500 persons); infant mortality rate per 1,000 live births (2002): 58.6.
Food (2001): daily per capita caloric intake 2,277 (vegetable products 91%, animal products 9%); 95% of FAO recommended minimum requirement.

Military

Total active duty personnel (2003): 13,620[8] (army 87.4%, navy 7.0%, air force 5.6%). *Military expenditure as percentage of GNP* (1999): 1.7% (world 2.4%); per capita expenditure U.S.$8.

[1]Formerly pegged to the French franc and since Jan. 1, 2002, to the euro at the rate of 1€ = CFAF 656.96. [2]Population of Dakar region. Populations for departments (second-order administrative subdivisions) within Dakar region are: Dakar 919,683; Pikine 754,372; Guédiawaye 452,168; Rufisque 285,305. [3]In 1996 about half of all women lived in polygamous unions. [4]At constant prices of 1987. [5]Imports f.o.b. in balance of trade and c.i.f. in commodities and trading partners. [6]Air Afrique, an airline jointly owned by 11 African countries (including Senegal), was declared bankrupt in February 2002. [7]Universities only; 2000–01. [8]Excludes 950 French troops.

Internet resources for further information:
- **République du Sénégal (French language only)**
http://www.primature.sn
- **Investir en Zone Franc**
http://www.izf.net/izf/Index.htm

Serbia and Montenegro

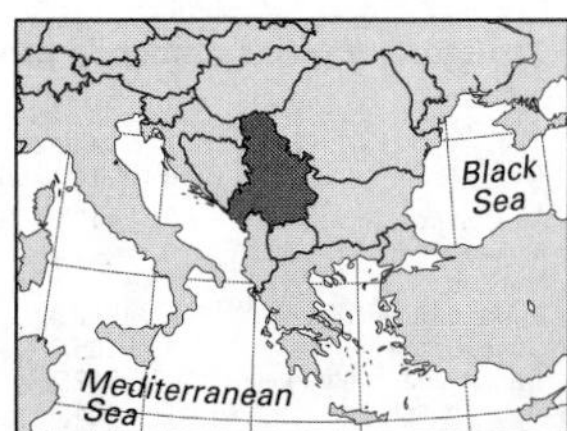

Official name: Srbija i Crna Gora (Serbia and Montenegro[1]).
Form of government: state union ("loose confederation") with one legislative house (Parliament [126]).
Head of state and government: President assisted by Council of Ministers.
Administrative centres: [2].
Official language: none.
Official religion: none.
Monetary unit: 1 Serbian dinar[3] = 100 paras; valuation (Sept. 8, 2003) 1 U.S.$ = 59.91 Serbian dinars; 1 £ = 94.99 Serbian dinars.

Area and population

		area		population
Republics	Capitals	sq mi	sq km	2001 estimate
Montenegro (Crna Gora)	Podgorica	5,333	13,812	658,000
Serbia (Srbija)	Belgrade	21,609	55,968	5,731,000
Autonomous province[4]				
Vojvodina	Novi Sad	8,304	21,506	1,937,000
Geographic region				
Kosovo (Kosova)[5]	Priština	4,203	10,887	2,325,000
TOTAL		39,449	102,173	10,651,000

Demography

Population (2003): 10,527,000.
Density (2003): persons per sq mi 266.9, persons per sq km 103.0.
Urban-rural (2002): urban 51.7%; rural 48.3%.
Sex distribution (2001): male 48.64%; female 51.36%.
Age breakdown (2001): under 15, 19.5%; 15–29, 22.5%; 30–44, 19.4%; 45–59, 18.4%; 60–74, 14.6%; 75 and over, 5.6%.
Population projection: (2010) 10,498,000; (2020) 10,357,000.
Ethnic composition (2000): Serb 62.1%; Albanian 17.1%; Montenegrin 4.3%; Hungarian 4.3%; Croat 3.1%; Bosniak Muslim 1.8%; Romany (Gypsy) 1.4%; Slovak 0.9%; Romanian 0.8%; other 4.2%.
Religious affiliation (1995): Serbian Orthodox 62.6%; Muslim 19.0%; Roman Catholic 5.8%; other, mostly nonreligious 12.6%.
Major cities (2000[6]): Belgrade 1,194,878; Priština 186,611; Novi Sad 182,778; Niš 182,583; Kragujevac 154,489; Podgorica 130,875.

Vital statistics

Birth rate per 1,000 population (2002): 12.4 (world avg. 21.3).
Death rate per 1,000 population (2002): 11.2 (world avg. 9.1).
Natural increase rate per 1,000 population (2002): 1.2 (world avg. 12.2).
Total fertility rate (avg. births per childbearing woman; 2002): 2.0.
Life expectancy at birth (2002): male 69.7 years; female 74.8 years.
Major causes of death per 100,000 population (1997): diseases of the circulatory system 585.0; malignant neoplasms (cancers) 169.0; accidents, violence, and poisoning 45.0; diseases of the respiratory system 39.0.

National economy

Budget (2001)[7]. Revenue: 421,000,000,000 Yugoslav new dinars (tax revenue 91.5%, of which social security tax 26.8%, VAT 26.2%, income tax 12.5%, excise tax 11.9%; nontax revenue 8.5%). Expenditure: 477,000,000,000 Yugoslav new dinars (transfers 50.1%, wages 20.7%, other 29.2%).
Public debt (external, outstanding; 2001): U.S.$6,002,000,000.
Production[8] (metric tons except as noted). Agriculture, forestry, fishing (2002): corn (maize) 5,597,207, wheat 2,245,030, sugar beets 2,098,080, potatoes 1,030,622, grapes 429,765, cabbages 354,686, plums 205,371, raspberries 94,400; livestock (number of live animals) 3,608,000 pigs, 1,691,000 sheep, 1,355,000 cattle; roundwood (2001) 2,936,000 cu m; fish catch (2000) 9,940. Mining and quarrying (2000): bauxite 630,000; copper (metal content) 52,000; lead (metal content) 12,000. Manufacturing (2000): cement 2,117,000; wheat flour 840,000; crude steel 682,000; pig iron 563,000; sulfuric acid 211,000[9]; nitric acid 185,000[9]; electrolytic copper 94,000[9]; welded pipes 43,000[9]; rolled copper 27,055[9]; refined lead 22,900; medicines 22,871[9]. Energy production (consumption): electricity (kW-hr; 2001) 34,594,000,000 (34,594,000,000); hard coal (metric tons; 2000) 88,000 ([1999] 162,000); lignite (metric tons; 2000) 33,638,000 ([1999] 33,261,000); crude petroleum (barrels; 2001) 5,534,000,000 (5,534,000,000); petroleum products (metric tons; 1999) 1,041,000 (2,244,000); natural gas (cu m; 1999) 773,500,000 (1,730,700,000).
Population economically active (2001)[8]: total 3,092,000; activity rate 37.1% (participation rates: over age 15 [1998] 58.3%; female [1995] 43.7%; [2002] unemployed 29.6%[8]).

Price and earnings indexes (1997 = 100)

	1997	1998	1999	2000	2001	2002
Consumer price index	100.0	129.9	188.2	349.3	660.0	770.0
Annual earnings index	100.0	132.4	163.0	318.6	690.5	...

Household income and expenditure[8]. Average household size (2000) 4.2; income per household (2000) 93,185 Yugoslav new dinars (U.S.$7,280); sources of income (2000): wages and salaries 50.6%, pensions 21.2%, self-employment 9.5%, other 18.7%; expenditure (2000): food 47.0%, fuel and light 9.9%, beverages and tobacco 7.3%, clothing and footwear 6.6%, transportation and communications 6.2%, health 5.6%, education 2.1%, housing 1.3%, other 14.0%.

Gross domestic product (2001): U.S.$9,900,000,000 (U.S.$930 per capita).

Structure of gross material product and labour force

	1999[8]		2002[8]	
	in value '000,000 Yugoslav new dinars	% of total value	labour force	% of labour force
Agriculture	37,227	18.9	87,000	2.8
Mining	50,102	25.5	40,000	1.3
Manufacturing			591,000	18.9
Construction	8,220	4.2	97,000	3.1
Public utilities	7,879	4.0	58,000	1.9
Transp. and commun.	16,439	8.4	138,000	4.4
Trade	17,669	9.0	267,000	8.5
Finance	16,912	8.6	87,000	2.8
Pub. admin., defense	10,274	5.2	72,000	2.3
Services	17,133	8.7	764,000	24.4
Other	14,661[10]	7.5[10]	924,000[11]	29.6[11]
TOTAL	196,516	100.0	3,125,000	100.0

Tourism (2001): receipts from visitors U.S.$40,000,000; expenditures, n.a.

Foreign trade

Balance of trade (current prices)

	1997	1998	1999	2000	2001	2002
U.S.$'000,000	–2,431	–1,991	–1,798	–1,988	–2,934	–4,045
% of total	33.9%	25.8%	37.5%	36.6%	43.5%	47.1%

Imports (2002): U.S.$6,320,000,000 (machinery and transport equipment 25.8%; mineral fuels 16.9%, of which crude petroleum 7.6%; chemical products 11.0%; food 7.0%). *Major import sources:* Germany 13.1%; Russia 12.5%; Italy 10.3%; Hungary 4.4%; Slovenia 3.8%.
Exports (2002): U.S.$2,275,000,000 (food 21.2%, of which refined sugar 4.0%, frozen raspberries 3.9%; machinery and transport equipment 11.2%; chemical products 7.4%; aluminum 6.9%). *Major export destinations:* Bosnia and Herzegovina 14.6%; Italy 14.5%; Germany 10.7%; Macedonia 9.1%; Switzerland 7.5%.

Transport and communications

Transport. Railroads (2001): length 4,058 km; passenger-km 1,292,000,000; metric ton-km cargo 2,027,000,000. Roads (2000): total length 44,777 km (paved 63%). Vehicles (1998): passenger cars 1,863,315; trucks and buses 158,667. Air transport (2001): passenger-km 997,000,000; metric ton-km cargo 7,838,000,000; airports (2000) 5.

Communications

Medium	date	unit	number	units per 1,000 persons
Daily newspapers	2000	circulation	1,130,000	107
Radio	2000	receivers	3,130,000	297
Television	2000	receivers	2,980,000	282
Telephones	2002	main lines	2,493,000	233
Cellular telephones	2002	subscribers	2,750,400	257
Personal computers	2002	units	290,000	27
Internet	2002	users	640,000	60

Education and health

Educational attainment (1991). Percentage of population age 15 and over having: less than full primary education 33.5%; primary 25.0%; secondary 32.2%; postsecondary and higher 9.3%. *Literacy* (1991): total population age 10 and over literate 93.0%; males literate 97.2%; females literate 88.9%.

Education (2000–01)

	schools	teachers	students	student/teacher ratio
Primary (age 7–14)	4,087	48,868	787,423	16.1
Secondary (age 15–18)	518	26,740	355,424	13.3
Higher	51	1,612	50,901	31.6

Health (2000): physicians 27,010 (1 per 394 persons); hospital beds 56,928 (1 per 187 persons); infant mortality rate per 1,000 live births (2000) 13.0.
Food (2001): daily per capita caloric intake 2,778 (vegetable products 65%, animal products 35%); 109% of FAO recommended minimum.

Military

Total active duty personnel (2003)[12]: 74,200 (army 84.1%, air force 10.8%, navy 5.1%). *Military expenditure as percentage of government expenditure* (1991): 3.9% (world 4.0%); per capita expenditure U.S.$176.

[1]Replaced Yugoslavia per effective date of new constitution (Feb. 4, 2003). [2]No capital per 2003 constitution; principal executive and legislative bodies meet in Belgrade; the principal judicial body meets in Podgorica. [3]Replaced Yugoslav new dinar on Feb. 4, 2003, at rate of 1 to 1. Montenegro and Kosovo (Kosova) use the euro adopted on Jan. 1, 2002. [4]Vojvodina is administratively part of the Republic of Serbia. [5]Region under interim UN administration from June 1999. [6]January 1. [7]Consolidated general government. [8]Excludes Kosovo. [9]1998. [10]Taxes on products less subsidies. [11]Unemployed. [12]About 18,000 troops from many NATO and non-NATO countries were deployed in Kosovo in August 2003.

Internet resources for further information:

- **Serbia and Montenegro Statistical Office http://www.szs.sv.gov.yu/homee.htm**
- **National Bank of Serbia http://www.nbs.yu/english/index.htm**

Seychelles

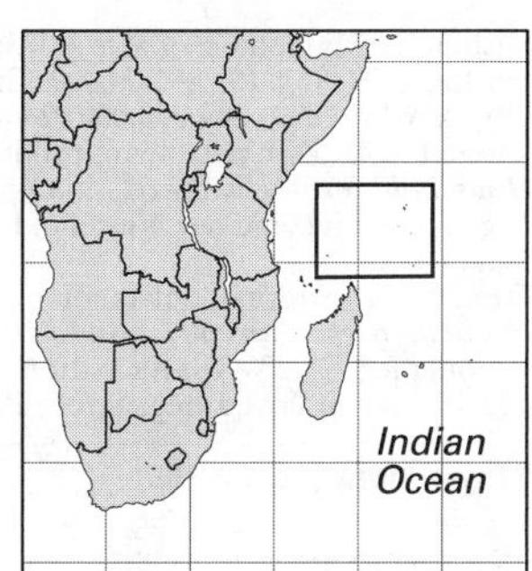

Official name: Repiblik Sesel (Creole); Republic of Seychelles (English); République des Seychelles (French).
Form of government: multiparty republic with one legislative house (National Assembly [34]).
Head of state and government: President.
Capital: Victoria.
Official languages: none[1].
Official religion: none.
Monetary unit: 1 Seychelles rupee (SR) = 100 cents; valuation (Sept. 8, 2003) 1 U.S.$ = SR 5.62; 1 £ = SR 8.91.

Area and population

Island Groups	Capital	area sq mi	area sq km	population 1997 census
Central (Granitic) group				
La Digue and satellites	—	6	15	1,998
Mahé and satellites	Victoria	59	153	67,338
Praslin and satellites	—	15	40	6,091
Silhouette	—	8	20	449
Other islands	—	2	4	0
Outer (Coralline) islands	—	86	223	0
TOTAL		176	455	75,876[2]

Demography

Population (2003): 81,500.
Density (2003): persons per sq mi 463.1, persons per sq km 179.1.
Urban-rural (2002): urban 64.6%; rural 35.4%.
Sex distribution (2000): male 49.57%; female 50.43%.
Age breakdown (2000): under 15, 28.8%; 15–29, 29.6%; 30–44, 24.6%; 45–59, 8.6%; 60–74, 5.8%; 75 and over, 2.6%.
Population projection: (2010) 84,000; (2020) 88,000.
Doubling time: 65 years.
Ethnic composition (2000): Seychellois Creole (mixture of Asian, African, and European) 93.2%; British 3.0%; French 1.8%; Chinese 0.5%; Indian 0.3%; other unspecified 1.2%.
Religious affiliation (2000): Roman Catholic 90.4%; Anglican 6.7%; Hindu 0.6%; other (mostly nonreligious) 2.3%.
Major city (1999): Victoria 28,000.

Vital statistics

Birth rate per 1,000 population (2002): 17.3 (world avg. 21.3); (1998) legitimate 24.7%; illegitimate 75.3%.
Death rate per 1,000 population (2002): 6.6 (world avg. 9.1).
Natural increase rate per 1,000 population (2002): 10.7 (world avg. 12.2).
Total fertility rate (avg. births per childbearing woman; 2002): 1.8.
Marriage rate per 1,000 population (2000): 6.0.
Divorce rate per 1,000 population (2000): 1.1.
Life expectancy at birth (2002): male 65.5 years; female 76.6 years.
Major causes of death per 100,000 population (2000): diseases of the circulatory system 190.0; malignant neoplasms (cancers) 89.0; accidents 61.0; diseases of the respiratory system 60.0; infectious and parasitic diseases 35.9; diseases of the digestive system 23.0.

National economy

Budget (2000). Revenue: SR 1,332,700,000 (tax revenue 71.0%, of which customs taxes and duties 23.7%, sales tax 19.7%, tax on income and profit 18.3%; nontax revenue 25.3%; grants 3.7%). Expenditures: SR 1,674,800,000 (current expenditure 76.1%, of which debt service 15.7%, wages and salaries 13.0%, education 8.1%, health 7.9%; capital expenditure 23.9%).
Tourism (2001): receipts from visitors U.S.$113,000,000; expenditures by nationals abroad U.S.$30,000,000.
Land use (1994): forested 11.1%; agricultural and under permanent cultivation 15.6%; built-on, wasteland, and other 73.3%.
Gross national product (2001): U.S.$500,000,000 (U.S.$6,530 per capita).

Structure of gross domestic product and labour force

2000	in value SR '000,000	% of total value	labour force[3]	% of labour force[3]
Agriculture	83.3	2.4	2,290	7.2
Manufacturing	498.8	14.5	3,835	12.0
Construction, mining	341.1	9.9	2,502	7.8
Public utilities	86.7	2.5	934	2.9
Trade	804.2	23.3	7,033	22.0
Transportation and communications	614.7	17.8	3,343	10.5
Pub. admin., defense	440.3	12.8	11,998 (Pub. admin., defense; Finance; Services)	37.6
Finance; Services	449.4	13.0		
Other	131.9[4]	3.8[4]	...	...
TOTAL	3,450.4	100.0	31,935	100.0

Production (metric tons except as noted). Agriculture, forestry, fishing (2002): coconuts 3,200, bananas 1,970, tea 231, cinnamon 230; livestock (number of live animals) 18,500 pigs, 5,150 goats, 1,400 cattle, 540,000 chickens; fish catch (2000) 40,608, of which (1998) jack 30.2%, snapper 18.3%, capitaine 8.3%, mackerel 4.8%. Mining and quarrying (1998): guano 5,000. Manufacturing (2000): canned tuna 28,781; copra 377; tea 246; soft drinks 88,060 hectolitres; beer and stout 70,460 hectolitres; fruit juices 30,540 hectolitres; cigarettes 40,000,000 units. Energy production (consumption): electricity (kW-hr; 2002) 170,000,000 ([2000] 166,500,000); coal, none (n.a.); crude petroleum, none (n.a.); petroleum products (metric tons; 1999) none (70,000); natural gas, none (n.a.).
Population economically active (2000): total 31,935; activity rate of total population 39.4% (participation rates: ages 15–64, 81.5%; female 43.0%; unemployed [1999] 11.5%).

Price and earnings indexes (1995 = 100)

	1996	1997	1998	1999	2000	2001	2002
Consumer price index	98.9	99.5	102.1	108.6	115.4	122.2	122.5
Monthly earnings index	...	...	...	...	...	...	...

Public debt (external, outstanding; 2001): U.S.$117,100,000.
Household income and expenditure. Average household size (1997) 4.2; average annual income per household (1978) SR 18,480 (U.S.$2,658); sources of income: wages and salaries 77.2%, self-employment 3.8%, transfer payments 3.2%; expenditure (1991–92): food and beverages 47.6%, housing 15.1%, clothing and footwear 8.6%, transportation 8.0%, energy and water 7.4%, recreation 6.7%, household and personal goods 6.6%.

Foreign trade[5]

Balance of trade (current prices)

	1997	1998	1999	2000	2001	2002
SR '000,000	–1,142	–1,372	–1,542	–841	–1,513	–1,046
% of total	50.1%	51.6%	49.9%	27.5%	37.5%	29.5%

Imports (2002): SR 2,295,000,000 (food and beverages 30.4%, of which fish, crustaceans, and mollusks 16.8%; mineral fuels 14.3%; base and fabricated metals 8.9%; ships and boats 7.6%). *Major import sources:* Saudi Arabia 14.0%; France 11.8%; South Africa 10.8%; Spain 8.6%; Italy 8.4%; Germany 8.1%.
Exports (2002): SR 1,249,000,000 (domestic exports 76.7%, of which canned tuna 67.5%, other processed fish 3.8%, fresh and frozen fish 1.5%; reexports 23.3%, of which petroleum products 20.3%). *Major export destinations*[6]: United Kingdom 41.9%; France 29.9%; Italy 9.3%; Germany 8.3%.

Transport and communications

Transport. Railroads: none. Roads (2000): total length 275 mi, 443 km (paved 88%). Vehicles (2000): passenger cars 6,970; trucks and buses 2,483. Merchant marine (1992): vessels (100 gross tons and over) 9; total deadweight tonnage 3,337. Air transport (2000): passenger arrivals 157,000, passenger departures 158,000; metric ton cargo unloaded 4,592; metric ton cargo loaded 1,801; airports (2000) with scheduled flights 2.

Communications

Medium	date	unit	number	units per 1,000 persons
Daily newspapers	1996	circulation	3,000	46
Radio	1997	receivers	42,000	560
Television	2000	receivers	16,000	203
Telephones	2001	main lines	21,400	267
Cellular telephones	2001	subscribers	44,100	552
Personal computers	2002	units	13,000	157
Internet	2001	users	9,000	112

Education and health

Educational attainment (1994). Percentage of population age 12 and over having: primary education 37.0%; some secondary 16.8%; complete secondary 19.0%; vocational 15.2%; postsecondary 3.0%; not stated 9.0%. *Literacy* (2000): total population age 12 and over literate 91.0%; males literate 92.0%; females literate 91.0%.

Education (2001)

	schools	teachers	students	student/ teacher ratio
Primary (age 6–15)	26	712	9,782	14.1
Secondary (age 16–18)	14	525	7,514	14.1
Voc., teacher tr.	11	216	1,740	8.1

Health (2000): physicians 105 (1 per 854 persons); hospital beds 420 (1 per 193 persons); infant mortality rate per 1,000 live births (2002) 16.7.
Food (2001): daily per capita caloric intake 2,461 (vegetable products 81%, animal products 19%); 105% of FAO recommended minimum requirement.

Military

Total active duty personnel (2002): 450[7]. *Military expenditure as percentage of GNP* (1997): 3.8% (world 2.6%); per capita expenditure U.S.$194.

[1]Creole, English, and French are all national languages per 1993 constitution. [2]2002 preliminary census total equals 81,177. [3]Excludes unemployed, self-employed, and domestic workers. [4]Import duties less bank service charges. [5]Imports c.i.f.; exports f.o.b. [6]Domestic exports only. [7]All services form part of the army.

Internet resources for further information:
- **Seychelles in Figures http://www.seychelles.net/misdstat**
- **Central Bank of Seychelles http://www.cbs.sc**

Sierra Leone

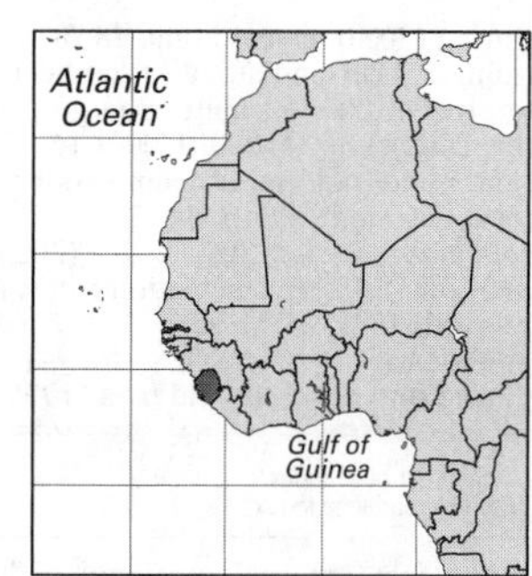

Official name: Republic of Sierra Leone.
Form of government: republic with one legislative body (Parliament [124[1]]).
Head of state and government: President.
Capital: Freetown.
Official language: English.
Official religion: none.
Monetary unit: 1 leone (Le) = 100 cents; valuation (Sept. 8, 2003) 1 U.S.$ = Le 2,353; 1 £ = Le 3,730.

Area and population

Provinces Districts	Capitals	area sq mi	area sq km	population 1985 census[2]
Eastern Province	Kenema	6,005	15,553	960,551
Kailahun	Kailahun	1,490	3,859	233,839
Kenema	Kenema	2,337	6,053	337,055
Kono	Sefadu	2,178	5,641	389,657
Northern Province	Makeni	13,875	35,936	1,259,641
Bombali	Makeni	3,083	7,985	317,729
Kambia	Kambia	1,200	3,108	186,231
Koinaduga	Kabala	4,680	12,121	183,286
Port Loko	Port Loko	2,208	5,719	329,344
Tonkolili	Magburaka	2,704	7,003	243,051
Southern Province	Bo	7,604	19,694	741,377
Bo	Bo	2,015	5,219	268,671
Bonthe (incl. Sherbro)	Bonthe	1,339	3,468	105,007
Moyamba	Moyamba	2,665	6,902	250,514
Pujehun	Pujehun	1,585	4,105	117,185
Western Area[3]	Freetown	215	557	554,243
TOTAL		27,699	71,740	3,515,812

Demography

Population (2003): 4,971,000.
Density (2003): persons per sq mi 179.5, persons per sq km 64.3.
Urban-rural (2000): urban 36.6%; rural 63.4%.
Sex distribution (2000): male 48.44%; female 51.56%.
Age breakdown (2000): under 15, 44.7%; 15–29, 26.1%; 30–44, 14.9%; 45–59, 9.2%; 60–74, 4.3%; 75 and over, 0.8%.
Population projection: (2010) 5,859,000; (2020) 6,979,000.
Doubling time: 27 years.
Ethnic composition (2000): Mende 26.0%; Temne 24.6%; Limba 7.1%; Kuranko 5.5%; Kono 4.2%; Fulani 3.8%; Bullom-Sherbro 3.5%; other 25.3%.
Religious affiliation (2000): Sunnī Muslim 45.9%; traditional beliefs 40.4%; Christian 11.4%; other 2.3%.
Major cities (2003): Freetown (urban agglomeration; 2001) 837,000; Koidu 113,700; Makeni 110,700; Bo 82,400; Kenema 72,400.

Vital statistics

Birth rate per 1,000 population (2000): 45.6 (world avg. 21.3).
Death rate per 1,000 population (2000): 19.6 (world avg. 9.1).
Natural increase rate per 1,000 population (2000): 26.0 (world avg. 12.2).
Total fertility rate (avg. births per childbearing woman; 2000): 6.1.
Life expectancy at birth (2000): male 42.4 years; female 48.2 years.
Major causes of death per 100,000 population: n.a.; however, the major diseases are malaria, tuberculosis, leprosy, measles, tetanus, and diarrhea.

National economy

Budget (2002). Revenue: Le 239,425,000,000 (customs duties and excise taxes 64.0%, income tax 25.1%, other 10.9%). Expenditures: Le 701,834,000,000 (recurrent expenditures 65.1%, of which wages and salaries 18.8%, goods and services 12.9%, defense and security 12.9%, debt service 9.4%; capital expenditures 34.9%).
Gross national product (2001): U.S.$700,000,000 (U.S.$140 per capita).

Structure of gross domestic product and labour force

	1994–95 in value Le '000,000	1994–95 % of total value	2001 labour force	2001 % of labour force
Agriculture	275,327.5	38.8	1,046,000	61.6
Mining	119,229.2	16.8		
Manufacturing	61,475.3	8.7		
Construction	15,788.2	2.2		
Public utilities	2,816.8	0.4		
Transp. and commun.	61,267.5	8.6		
Trade[4]	98,270.1	13.8	651,000	38.4
Finance	14,732.2	2.1		
Pub. admin., defense	19,844.9	2.8		
Services	12,308.9	1.7		
Other	29,329.7[5]	4.1[5]		
TOTAL	710,389.3[6]	100.0	1,697,000	100.0

Production (metric tons except as noted). Agriculture, forestry, fishing (2002): cassava 260,000, rice 250,000, oil palm fruit 180,000, pulses 53,000, sweet potatoes 30,000, plantains 30,000, sugarcane 24,000, coffee 17,000, peanuts (groundnuts) 16,000, tomatoes 13,500, cacao beans 10,920, sorghum 9,000, mangoes 6,500, millet 4,500; livestock (number of live animals) 400,000 cattle, 370,000 sheep, 220,000 goats, 55,000 pigs; roundwood (2002) 5,497,220 cu m; fish catch (2001) 74,660. Mining and quarrying (2001): rutile, none[7]; diamonds 600,000 carats; gold 30 kg. Manufacturing (value added in Le '000,000; 1993): food 36,117; chemicals 10,560; earthenware 1,844; printing and publishing 1,171; metal products 1,073; furniture 647. Construction (value added in Le; 1994–95): 15,788,200,000. Energy production (consumption): electricity (kW-hr; 1999) 244,000,000 (244,000,000); crude petroleum (barrels; 1999) none (1,745,000); petroleum products (metric tons; 1999) 182,000 (143,000).
Household income and expenditure. Average household size (2000) 6.5; average annual income per household, n.a.; sources of income, n.a.; expenditure, n.a.
Public debt (external, outstanding; 2001): U.S.$1,014,000,000.
Population economically active (2001): total 1,697,000; activity rate of total population 35.2% (participation rates [1991]: ages 10–64, 53.3%; female 32.4%; unemployed [registered; 1992] 10.6%).

Price index (1995 = 100)

	1996	1997	1998	1999	2000	2001	2002
Consumer price index	123.1	141.5	191.8	257.2	255.1	260.4	251.8

Tourism (1999): receipts U.S.$8,000,000; expenditures U.S.$4,000,000.
Land use (1994): forest 28.5%; pasture 30.7%; agriculture 7.5%; other 33.3%.

Foreign trade[8]

Balance of trade (current prices)

	1997	1998	1999	2000	2001	2002
Le '000,000	–64,598	–137,744	–142,509	–287,868	–313,608	–452,828
% of total	67.7%	86.8%	86.3%	84.3%	73.0%	68.9%

Imports (2001): Le 371,506,000,000 (food and live animals 28.2%; fuels 23.4%; machinery and transport equipment 20.3%; chemicals and chemical products 4.8%). *Major import sources:* U.K. 25.3%; The Netherlands 10.1%; U.S. 7.9%; Germany 6.3%; Italy 5.6%.
Exports (2001): Le 57,898,000,000 (diamonds 89.9%; cacao 1.0%; rutile, none[7]; reexports 2.7%). *Major export destinations:* Belgium 40.6%; U.S. 9.1%; U.K. 8.5%; Germany 7.8%; Japan 5.6%.

Transport and communications

Transport. Railroads (1995): length 52 mi, 84 km. Roads (1996): total length 7,270 mi, 11,700 km (paved 11%). Vehicles (1996): passenger cars 17,640; trucks and buses 10,890. Air transport (1996): passenger-mi 15,000,000, passenger-km 24,000,000; short ton-mi cargo 1,400,000, metric ton-km cargo 2,000,000; airports (2001) with scheduled flights 1.

Communications

Medium	date	unit	number	units per 1,000 persons
Daily newspapers	2000	circulation	17,700	4.0
Radio	2000	receivers	1,140,000	259
Television	2000	receivers	57,400	13
Telephones	2001	main lines	22,700	4.7
Cellular telephones	2002	subscribers	66,300	13
Personal computers	1999	units	100	—
Internet	2002	users	8,000	1.6

Education and health

Educational attainment (1985). Percentage of population age 5 and over having: no formal schooling 64.1%; primary education 18.7%; secondary 9.7%; higher 1.5%. *Literacy* (1995): total population age 15 and over literate 791,000 (31.4%); males literate 555,000 (45.4%); females 236,000 (18.2%).

Education (1992–93)

	schools	teachers	students	student/ teacher ratio
Primary (age 5–11)	1,643	10,595	267,425	25.2
Secondary (age 12–18)	167	4,313	70,900	16.4
Voc., teacher tr.	44	709	7,756	10.9
Higher[9]	2	257	2,571	10.0

Health: physicians (1996) 339 (1 per 13,696 persons); hospital beds (1988) 4,025 (1 per 980 persons); infant mortality rate per 1,000 live births (2000) 148.7.
Food (2000): daily per capita caloric intake 1,863 (vegetable products 97%, animal products 3%); 81% of FAO recommended minimum requirement.

Military

Total active duty personnel (2002): 13,000 (army 96.7%, navy 3.3%, air force, none); UN peacekeeping troops (August 2003) 11,900. *Military expenditure as percentage of GNP* (1999): 3.0% (world 2.4%); per capita expenditure U.S.$4.

[1]Includes 12 paramount chiefs elected to represent each of the provincial districts. [2]Preliminary figures exclude adjustment for underenumeration; adjusted total is 3,760,000. [3]Not officially a province; the administration of the Western Area is split among Greater Freetown (the city and its suburbs) and other administrative bodies. [4]Includes hotels. [5]Import duties less imputed bank service charges. [6]Detail does not add to total given because of rounding. [7]Production at world's richest deposit was halted between 1995 and September 2003 because of the civil war and its lasting effects. [8]Imports c.i.f.; exports f.o.b. [9]1990–91.

Internet resources for further information:
- **Sierra Leone Annual Statistical Digest, 2001 http://www.sierra-leone.org/cso2001-index.html**

Singapore

Official name: Hsin-chia-p'o Kung-ho-kuo (Mandarin Chinese); Republik Singapura (Malay); Singapore Kudiyarasu (Tamil); Republic of Singapore (English).
Form of government: unitary multiparty republic with one legislative house (Parliament [90[1]]).
Chief of state: President[2].
Head of state government: Prime Minister[3].
Capital: Singapore.
Official languages: Chinese; Malay; Tamil; English.
Official religion: none.
Monetary unit: 1 Singapore dollar (S$) = 100 cents; valuation (Sept. 8, 2003) 1 U.S.$ = S$1.76; 1 £ = S$2.78.

Population (2002 estimate)	
De facto population	4,171,300[4]
De jure population	3,378,300[5]

Demography

Area: 264.6 sq mi, 685.4 sq km.
Population (2003): 4,233,000.
Density (2003): persons per sq mi 15,974, persons per sq km 6,180.
Urban-rural: urban 100.0%.
Sex distribution (2000)[6]: male 49.96%; female 50.04%.
Age breakdown (2000)[6]: under 15, 21.5%; 15–34, 30.1%; 35–54, 33.9%; 55–74, 12.1%; 75 and over, 2.4%.
Population projection: (2010) 4,561,000; (2020) 4,799,000.
Ethnic composition (2000)[6]: Chinese 76.7%; Malay 13.9%; Indian 7.9%; other 1.5%.
Religious affiliation (2000)[7]: Buddhist 42.5%; Muslim 14.9%; Christian 14.6%; Taoist 8.5%; Hindu 4.0%; traditional beliefs 0.6%; nonreligious 14.9%.

Vital statistics

Birth rate per 1,000 population (2002)[6]: 11.4 (world avg. 21.3).
Death rate per 1,000 population (2002)[6]: 4.4 (world avg. 9.1).
Natural increase rate per 1,000 population (2002)[6]: 7.0 (world avg. 12.2).
Total fertility rate (avg. births per childbearing woman; 2002)[6]: 1.4.
Marriage rate per 1,000 population (2002)[6]: 4.8.
Life expectancy at birth (2002)[6]: male 76.8 years; female 80.6 years.
Major causes of death per 100,000 population (2001)[6]: diseases of the circulatory system 164.4; malignant neoplasms (cancers) 130.5; diseases of the respiratory system 50.0; accidents and violence 31.0.

National economy

Budget (2002). Revenue: S$25,401,200,000 (income tax 45.5%, nontax revenue 15.4%, goods and services tax 8.3%, motor vehicle taxes 6.1%, customs and excise duties 6.7%). Expenditures: S$27,121,000,000 (security 34.5%, development expenditure 29.0%, education 17.6%, health 5.9%, trade and industry 2.0%).
Production (metric tons except as noted). Agriculture, forestry, fishing (2002): vegetables and fruits 4,800; livestock (number of live animals) 190,000 pigs, 2,000,000 chickens; fish catch (2001) 10,483. Mining and quarrying (value of output in S$; 1994): granite 75,800,000. Manufacturing (value added in S$'000,000; 1998): electronic products 17,241.5; chemical products 5,268.0; machinery and equipment 5,026.4; transport equipment 4,082.3; fabricated metal products 2,821.7; petroleum products 1,909.5. Energy production (consumption): electricity (kW-hr; 1999) 29,520,000,000 (29,520,000,000); crude petroleum (barrels; 1999) none (325,700,000); petroleum products (metric tons; 1999) 35,415,000 (15,305,000).
Population economically active (2002): total 2,128,500[6]; activity rate of total population 63.0% (participation rates: ages 15 and over, 64.7%; female 43.8%; unemployed 4.3%).

Price and earnings indexes (1995 = 100)

	1996	1997	1998	1999	2000	2001	2002
Consumer price index	101.4	103.4	103.1	103.2	104.6	105.6	105.2
Monthly earnings index	105.8	111.8	114.9	118.0	128.4	131.4	...

Gross national product (2001): U.S.$88,800,000,000 (U.S.$21,500 per capita).

Structure of gross domestic product and labour force

	2002		2001	
	in value S$'000,000	% of total value	labour force	% of labour force
Agriculture, Quarrying	166.1	0.1	6,300	0.3
Manufacturing	41,204.3	26.5	384,600	18.1
Construction	8,375.6	5.4	124,900	5.9
Public utilities	2,763.0	1.7	10,400	0.5
Transp. and commun.	17,943.8	11.5	228,200	10.8
Trade	23,355.7	15.0	431,900	20.4
Finance	43,780.0	28.1	351,800	16.6
Services	18,654.4	12.0	508,700	24.0
Other	–316.3[7]	–0.2[7]	72,900[8]	3.4[8]
TOTAL	155,726.6	100.0[9]	2,119,700	100.0

Household income and expenditure. Average household size (2000) 3.7; income per household (2000) S$59,316 (U.S.$34,406); sources of income: n.a.; expenditure (1998): food 23.7%, transportation and communications 22.8%, housing costs and furnishings 21.6%, education 6.9%, clothing and footwear 4.1%, health 3.3%, other 17.6%.
Tourism (2001): receipts from visitors U.S.$5,081,000,000; expenditures by nationals abroad U.S.$4,647,000,000.

Foreign trade[10]

Balance of trade (current prices)

	1997	1998	1999	2000	2001	2002
S$'000,000	–10,993	+8,896	+6,147	+5,651	+10,335	+15,590
% of total	2.4%	2.5%	1.6%	1.2%	2.4%	5.8%

Imports (2002): S$208,311,000,000 (electronic valves [including integrated circuits and semiconductors] 20.7%; crude and refined petroleum 13.0%; computers and related parts 11.6%; chemicals and chemical products 6.2%; telecommunications equipment 4.3%). *Major import sources:* Malaysia 18.2%; U.S. 14.2%; Japan 12.5%; China 7.6%; Thailand 4.6%; Taiwan 4.6%.
Exports (2002): S$223,901,000,000 (electronic valves 23.5%; computers and related parts 20.3%; crude and refined petroleum 10.2%, chemicals and chemical products 9.3%, of which organic chemicals 3.9%; telecommunications equipment 4.7%). *Major export destinations:* Malaysia 17.4%; U.S. 14.7%; Hong Kong 9.2%; Japan 7.1%; China 5.5%; Taiwan 5.0%.

Transport and communications

Transport. Railroads (2003): length 131 km. Roads (2000): total length 3,122 km (paved 99%). Vehicles (2002): passenger cars 423,380; trucks and buses 138,638. Air transport (2002): passenger-km 94,572,000,000; metric ton-km cargo 10,527,000,000; airports (2003) 1.

Communications

Medium	date	unit	number	units per 1,000 persons
Daily newspapers	2000	circulation	1,197,301	298
Radio	2000	receivers	2,700,000	672
Television	2000	receivers	1,220,000	304
Telephones	2002	main lines	1,927,200	463
Cellular telephones	2002	subscribers	3,312,600	795
Personal computers	2001	units	2,100,000	508
Internet	2002	users	2,247,000	540

Education and health

Educational attainment (2000)[6]. Percentage of population age 15 and over having: no schooling 19.6%; primary education 23.1%; secondary 39.5%; post-secondary 17.8%. *Literacy* (2000)[6]: total population age 15 and over literate 93.0%.

Education (2000)

	schools	teachers	students	student/ teacher ratio
Primary (age 6–11)	201	12,287	305,992	24.5
Secondary (age 12–18)	180	11,340	201,107	17.7
Voc., teacher tr.	10	1,257	15,974	12.7
Higher	8	7,318	111,538	15.2

Health (2001): physicians 5,577 (1 per 585[6] persons); hospital beds 11,897 (1 per 277[6] persons); infant mortality rate per 1,000 live births (2002) 2.5.
Food (1988–90): daily per capita caloric intake 3,121 (vegetable products 76%, animal products 24%); 136% of FAO recommended minimum requirement.

Military

Total active duty personnel (2002): 60,500 (army 82.7%, navy 7.4%, air force 9.9%). *Military expenditure as percentage of GNP* (1999): 4.8% (world 2.4%); per capita expenditure U.S.$1,100.

[1]Includes 6 nonelective seats. [2]Title per constitution is Head of State. [3]Has principal executive authority per constitution. [4]The de facto population figure (as of the 2000 census) includes citizens (2,973,091), noncitizens with permanent residency status (290,118), and temporary residents (754,524). [5]The de jure population figure excludes temporary residents. [6]Based on de jure population. [7]Imputed bank service charges. [8]Unemployed. [9]Detail does not add to total given because of rounding. [10]Imports c.i.f., exports f.o.b.

Internet resources for further information:
- **Statistics Singapore http://www.singstat.gov.sg**

Slovakia

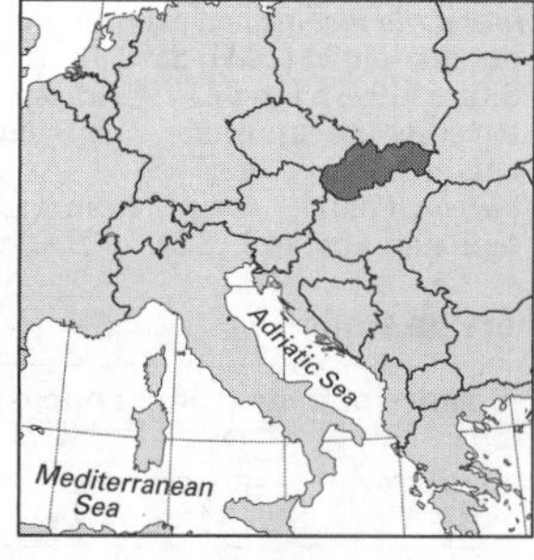

Official name: Slovenská Republika (Slovak Republic).
Form of government: unitary multiparty republic with one legislative house (National Council [150]).
Chief of state: President.
Head of government: Prime Minister.
Capital: Bratislava.
Official language: Slovak.
Official religion: none.
Monetary unit: 1 Slovak koruna (Sk) = 100 halura; valuation (Sept. 8, 2003) 1 U.S.$ = Sk 37.88; 1 £ = Sk 60.06.

Area and population

		area		population
Regions[1]	**Capitals**	sq mi	sq km	2001 census
Banská Bystrica	Banská Bystrica	3,651	9,455	662,121
Bratislava	Bratislava	793	2,053	599,015
Košice	Košice	2,607	6,753	766,012
Nitra	Nitra	2,449	6,343	713,422
Prešov	Prešov	3,472	8,993	789,968
Trenčín	Trenčín	1,738	4,501	605,582
Trnava	Trnava	1,602	4,148	551,003
Žilina	Žilina	2,621	6,788	692,332
TOTAL		18,933	49,035[2]	5,379,455[3]

Demography

Population (2003): 5,402,000.
Density (2002): persons per sq mi 285.3, persons per sq km 110.2.
Urban-rural (2002): urban 57.6%; rural 42.4%.
Sex distribution (2001): male 48.56%; female 51.44%.
Age breakdown (2001): under 15, 18.9%; 15–29, 25.1%; 30–44, 21.5%; 45–59, 18.9%; 60–74, 11.0%; 75 and over, 4.6%.
Population projection: (2010) 5,434,000; (2020) 5,428,000.
Ethnic composition (2001): Slovak 85.8%; Hungarian 9.7%; Rom (Gypsy) 1.7%; Czech 0.8%; Ruthenian and Ukrainian 0.7%; other 1.3%.
Religious affiliation (2001): Roman Catholic 68.9%; Protestant 9.2%, of which Slovak Evangelical 6.9%, Reformed Christian 2.0%; Greek Catholic 4.1%; Eastern Orthodox 0.9%; nonreligious and other 16.9%.
Major cities (2001): Bratislava 428,672; Košice 236,093; Prešov 92,786; Nitra 87,285; Žilina 85,400; Banská Bystrica 83,056.

Vital statistics

Birth rate per 1,000 population (2002): 10.4 (world avg. 21.3); (1999) legitimate 83.1%; illegitimate 16.9%.
Death rate per 1,000 population (2002): 9.6 (world avg. 9.1).
Natural increase rate per 1,000 population (2002): 0.8 (world avg. 12.2).
Total fertility rate (avg. births per childbearing woman; 2002): 1.3.
Marriage rate per 1,000 population (2002): 4.4.
Divorce rate per 1,000 population (2002): 1.8.
Life expectancy at birth (2002): male 69.6 years; female 77.7 years.
Major causes of death per 100,000 population (1999): diseases of the circulatory system 531; malignant neoplasms (cancers) 221; diseases of the digestive system 49; diseases of the respiratory system 48.

National economy

Budget (2000). Revenue: Sk 347,600,000,000 (tax revenue 87.4%, of which social security contribution 33.3%, value-added tax 20.3%, income tax 11.9%; nontax revenue 12.6%). Expenditures: Sk 378,800,000,000 (current expenditures 89.4%, of which social welfare 32.5%, wages 15.8%, health 12.8%, debt service 6.3%; investment 10.6%).
Production (metric tons except as noted). Agriculture, forestry, fishing (2002): wheat 1,554,000, sugar beets 1,340,000, corn [maize] 754,000, barley 695,000, potatoes 484,000, rapeseed 257,000, sunflower seeds 117,000, rye 96,000; livestock (number of live animals) 1,554,000 pigs, 608,000 cattle, 316,000 sheep; roundwood (2002) 5,765,400 cu m; fish catch (2001) 3,142. Mining and quarrying (2000): iron ore (metal content) 300,000; gold 306 kg. Manufacturing (value added in Sk '000,000; 1998): food 10,203; nonelectrical machinery 10,116; transport equipment 9,422; crude steel and pig iron 8,204; electrical machinery 6,738; paper 6,346; refined petroleum 6,303; chemicals 6,286. Energy production (consumption): electricity (kW-hr; 2002) 32,436,000,000 ([2000] 22,957,000,000); hard coal (metric tons; 1999) none (5,525,000); lignite 3,748,000 (5,134,000); crude petroleum (barrels; 1999) 484,000 (39,800,000); petroleum products (metric tons; 1999) 4,218,000 (2,045,000); natural gas (cu m; 2000) 358,800,000 ([1999] 6,910,000,000).
Population economically active (2001): total 2,665,837; activity rate of total population 49.6% (participation rates: ages 15–64, 79.6%; female 47.7%; unemployed 18.0%).

Price and earnings indexes (1995 = 100)

	1996	1997	1998	1999	2000	2001	2002
Consumer price index	105.8	112.3	119.8	132.5	148.4	159.3	164.6
Annual earnings index	114.6	127.2	136.1	148.3	162.0	177.6	...

Household income and expenditure. Average household size (1999) 3.3; gross income per household (2001) Sk 89,352 (U.S.$1,848); sources of income (2001): wages and salaries 67.1%, transfer payments 15.8%, other 17.1%; expenditure (2001): food, beverages, and tobacco 27.4%, housing and energy 17.2%, transportation and communications 13.7%, clothing and footwear 8.6%.
Public debt (external, outstanding; 2001): U.S.$5,498,000,000.
Gross national product (2001): U.S.$20,300,000,000 (U.S.$3,760 per capita).

Structure of gross domestic product and labour force

	2000		2002	
	in value Sk '000,000	% of total value	labour force[4]	% of labour force[4]
Agriculture	36,000	4.1	131,400	6.2
Mining and manufacturing	200,200	22.6	640,900[5]	30.1[5]
Construction	42,300	4.8	176,000	8.3
Public utilities	32,900	3.7	[5]	[5]
Transp. and commun.	90,100	10.1	154,400	7.3
Trade	134,200	15.1	340,000	16.0
Finance	[6]	[6]	143,100	6.7
Pub. admin., defense	106,100	12.0	149,700	7.0
Services	163,900[6]	18.5[6]	391,300	18.4
Other	81,500[7]	9.2[7]	600	—
TOTAL	887,200	100.0[2]	2,127,000[2, 8]	100.0[8]

Tourism: receipts from visitors (2001) U.S.$639,000,000; expenditure by nationals abroad U.S.$287,000,000.
Land use (1994): forested 40.6%; meadows and pastures 17.0%; agricultural and under permanent cultivation 32.9%; other 9.5%.

Foreign trade

Balance of trade (current prices)

	1997	1998	1999	2000	2001	2002
U.S.$'000,000	−2,081	−2,353	−1,093	−904	−2,135	−2,117
% of total	9.7%	9.9%	5.1%	3.7%	7.8%	6.9%

Imports (2002): U.S.$16,502,000,000 (machinery and apparatus 25.6%, mineral fuels 14.6%, transport equipment 12.8%, base and fabricated metals 8.9%). *Major import sources:* Germany 22.6%; Czech Republic 15.2%; Russia 12.5%; Italy 6.9%; France 4.4%.
Exports (2002): U.S.$14,385,000,000 (transport equipment [mostly road vehicles] 21.2%, machinery and apparatus 18.8%, base and fabricated metals [mostly iron and steel] 14.3%, mineral fuels 7.2%). *Major export destinations:* Germany 26.0%; Czech Republic 15.2%; Italy 10.7%; Austria 7.7%; Hungary 5.5%; Poland 5.3%.

Transport and communications

Transport. Railroads (2001): length 3,665 km; (1998) passenger-km 3,092,000,000; metric ton-km cargo 11,754,000,000. Roads (2001): total length 17,735 km (paved, n.a.). Vehicles (2001): passenger cars 1,293,000; trucks and buses 120,000. Merchant marine: n.a. Air transport (2000): passenger-km 250,900,000; metric ton-km cargo 220,000; airports (2000) with scheduled flights 2.

Communications

Medium	date	unit	number	units per 1,000 persons
Daily newspapers	2000	circulation	938,000	174
Radio	2000	receivers	5,200,000	965
Television	2000	receivers	2,190,000	407
Telephones	2002	main lines	1,402,700	261
Cellular telephones	2002	subscribers	2,923,400	544
Personal computers	2002	units	970,000	180
Internet	2002	users	863,000	160

Education and health

Educational attainment (1991). Percentage of adult population having: incomplete primary education 0.7%; primary and incomplete secondary 37.9%; complete secondary 50.9%; higher 9.5%; unknown 1.0%. *Literacy* (2001): total population age 15 and over literate 100%.

Education (2000–01)

	schools	teachers	students	student/teacher ratio
Primary (age 6–14)	2,447	39,745	650,966	16.4
Secondary (age 15–18)	212	6,259	82,147	13.1
Voc., teacher tr.	368	11,255	111,128	9.9
Higher	20	9,047	125,896	13.9

Health (2001): physicians 20,430 (1 per 263 persons); hospital beds 54,759 (1 per 98 persons); infant mortality rate per 1,000 live births (2002) 8.1.
Food (2000): daily per capita caloric intake 3,133 (vegetable products 75%, animal products 25%); 127% of FAO recommended minimum requirement.

Military

Total active duty personnel (2002): 26,200 (army 49.6%, air force 38.9%, headquarters staff 11.5%). *Military expenditure as percentage of GNP* (1999): 1.8% (world 2.4%); per capita expenditure U.S.$187.

[1]Based on administrative reorganization effective from July 1996. [2]Detail does not add to total given because of rounding. [3]De jure figure; 2001 de facto census total equals 5,193,376. [4]Employed only. [5]Mining and manufacturing includes Public utilities. [6]Services includes Finance. [7]Bank service charges and indirect taxes. [8]Excluding unemployed and women on regular and additional maternity leave and armed forces.

Internet resources for further information:

- **National Bank of Slovakia**
  http://www.nbs.sk

Slovenia

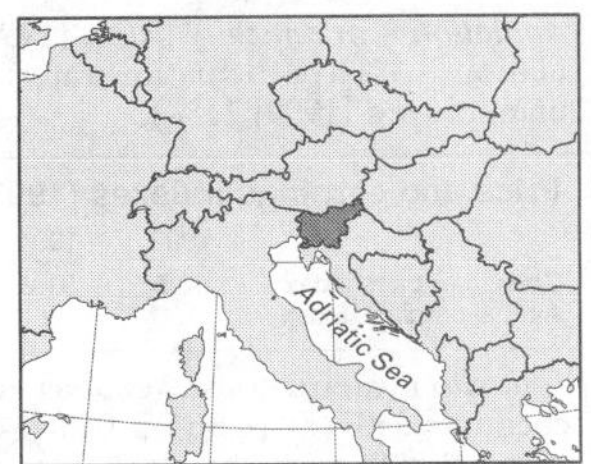

Official name: Republika Slovenija (Republic of Slovenia).
Form of government: unitary multiparty republic with two legislative houses (National Council [40]; National Assembly [90]).
Head of state: President.
Head of government: Prime Minister.
Capital: Ljubljana.
Official language: Slovene.
Official religion: none.
Monetary unit: 1 Slovene tolar (SIT; plural tolarjev) = 100 stotin; valuation (Sept. 8, 2003) 1 U.S.$ = SIT 213.07; 1 £ = SIT 337.83.

Area and population

		area		population
				2002
Statistical regions[1]	**Principal cities**	sq mi	sq km	census
Gorenjska	Kranj	825	2,137	195,885
Goriška	Nova Gorica	898	2,325	118,511
Jugovzhodna Slovenija	Novo Mesto	653	1,690	136,474
Koroška	Ravne na Koroškem	401	1,041	73,296
Notranjsko-kraška	Postojna	562	1,456	50,243
Obalno Kraško	Koper	403	1,044	102,070
Osrednjeslovenska	Ljubljana	1,367	3,540	488,364
Podravska	Maribor	838	2,170	310,743
Pomurska	Murska Sobota	516	1,337	120,875
Savinjska	Celje	920	2,384	253,574
Spodnjeposavska	Krško	342	885	68,565
Zasavska	Trbovlje	102	264	45,436
TOTAL		7,827	20,273	1,964,036

Demography

Population (2003): 1,971,000.
Density (2003): persons per sq mi 251.8, persons per sq km 97.2.
Urban-rural (2002): urban 50.8%; rural 49.2%.
Sex distribution (2002): male 48.81%; female 51.19%.
Age breakdown (2002): under 15, 15.3%; 15–29, 21.6%; 30–44, 22.7%; 45–59, 20.5%; 60–74, 14.3%; 75 and over, 5.6%.
Population projection: (2010) 2,004,000; (2020) 2,019,000.
Ethnic composition (2002)[2]: Slovene 91.2%; Serb 2.2%; Croat 2.0%; Bosniac (ethnic Muslim) 1.8%; other 2.8%.
Religious affiliation (2000): Christian 92.1%, of which Roman Catholic 83.5%, unaffiliated Christian 4.7%, Protestant 1.6%, Orthodox 0.6%; nonreligious/atheist 7.8%; other 0.1%.
Major cities (2002)[3]: Ljubljana 265,881; Maribor 110,668; Kranj 51,225; Celje 48,081; Koper 47,539.

Vital statistics

Birth rate per 1,000 population (2001): 9.3 (world avg. 21.3); legitimate 60.6%; illegitimate 39.4%.
Death rate per 1,000 population (2001): 10.0 (world avg. 9.1).
Natural increase rate per 1,000 population (2001): –0.7 (world avg. 12.2).
Total fertility rate (avg. births per childbearing woman; 2001): 1.3.
Marriage rate per 1,000 population (2001): 3.5.
Divorce rate per 1,000 population (2001): 1.1.
Life expectancy at birth (2001): male 71.2 years; female 79.2 years.
Major causes of death per 100,000 population (2000): diseases of the circulatory system 377.5; malignant neoplasms (cancers) 242.7; accidents and violence 77.6; diseases of the respiratory system 74.4.

National economy

Budget (2001). Revenue: SIT 1,968,000,000,000 (taxes on goods and services 34.2%, social security contributions 31.6%, personal income tax 18.2%, nontax revenue 7.1%). Expenditures: SIT 2,031,000,000,000 (current expenditures 90.2%, development expenditures 9.8%).
Public debt (external, outstanding; 2001): U.S.$2,700,000,000.
Production (metric tons except as noted). Agriculture, forestry, fishing (2002): silage 1,085,000, corn (maize) 255,000, sugar beets 190,000, wheat 175,000, potatoes 150,000, grapes 126,800, apples 75,000; livestock (number of live animals) 599,895 pigs, 477,075 cattle; roundwood (2001) 2,283,000 cu m; fish catch (2001) 3,040. Mining and quarrying (2000): dimension stone 105,000. Manufacturing (value added in SIT '000,000; 1998): base and fabricated metals 111,182; food, beverages, and tobacco products 96,223; electrical machinery 92,709; chemicals and chemical products 91,311; textiles 71,477. Energy production (consumption): electricity (kW-hr; 2001) 14,466,000,000 (11,091,000,000); hard coal (metric tons; 1999) 6,000 (476,000); lignite (metric tons; 1999) 3,974,000 (3,884,000); crude petroleum (barrels; 1999) 7,000 (1,900,000); petroleum products (metric tons; 1999) 206,000 (2,334,000); natural gas (cu m; 1999) 5,800,000 (1,017,800,000).
Land use (1994): forest 53.2%; pasture 24.8%; agricultural 11.6%; other 10.4%.
Household income and expenditure (2001). Average household size (2002) 2.8; income per household SIT 3,090,000 (U.S.$12,800); sources of income: wages 60.0%, transfers 26.6%; expenditure: transportation and communications 25.8%, food and beverages 17.8%, housing 10.4%, recreation 9.3%.
Gross national product (at current market prices; 2001): U.S.$19,400,000,000 (U.S.$9,760 per capita).

Structure of gross domestic product and labour force

	2001			
	in value SIT '000,000	% of total value	labour force[4]	% of labour force[4]
Agriculture, forestry	124,621	2.7	90,000	9.3
Mining	36,393	0.8	6,000	0.6
Manufacturing	1,082,244	23.7	277,000	28.5
Construction	236,420	5.2	55,000	5.6
Public utilities	134,556	2.9	11,000	1.1
Transp. and commun.	313,330	6.9	57,000	5.9
Trade, restaurants	591,345	13.0	147,000	15.1
Finance, real estate	666,531	14.6	69,000	7.1
Pub. admin., defense	236,766	5.2	48,000	4.9
Services	620,943	13.6	143,000	14.7
Other	523,042[5]	11.5[5]	69,000[6]	7.1[6]
TOTAL	4,566,191	100.0[7]	972,000	100.0[7]

Population economically active (2002): total 949,078; activity rate 48.3% (participation rates: ages 15 and over 57.0%; female 45.4%; unemployed 13.8%).

Price and earnings indexes (1995 = 100)

	1996	1997	1998	1999	2000	2001	2002
Consumer price index	109.9	119.1	128.5	136.4	148.4	161.0	173.0
Annual earnings index	114.8	127.9	140.1	153.2	169.2	187.5	207.5

Tourism (2001): receipts U.S.$996,000,000; expenditures U.S.$519,000,000.

Foreign trade[8]

Balance of trade (current prices)

	1997	1998	1999	2000	2001	2002
U.S.$'000,000	–985	–1,062	–1,537	–1,384	–893	–575
% of total	5.6%	5.5%	8.3%	7.3%	4.6%	2.7%

Imports (2002): U.S.$10,928,000,000 (machinery and transport equipment 34.0%, of which road vehicles 10.7%; chemicals and chemical products 13.4%; mineral fuels 7.0%; food products 5.2%). *Major import sources:* Germany 19.2%; Italy 17.9%; France 10.3%; Austria 8.3%; Croatia 3.6%.
Exports (2002): U.S.$10,353,000,000 (machinery and transport equipment 37.1%, of which road vehicles 12.5%, electrical machinery and apparatus 11.5%; chemicals and chemical products 12.4%, of which medicines and pharmaceuticals 5.8%; furniture and parts 7.0%). *Major export destinations:* Germany 24.8%; Italy 12.1%; Croatia 8.7%; Austria 7.1%; France 6.7%.

Transport and communications

Transport. Railroads (2001): length 764 mi, 1,229 km; passenger-km 715,000,000; metric ton-km cargo 2,837,000,000. Roads (1999): total length 12,507 mi, 20,128 km (paved 81%). Vehicles: passenger cars (2001) 862,648; trucks and buses (1999) 67,111. Air transport (2001): passenger-km 790,000,000; metric ton-km cargo 4,108,000; airports (2001) with scheduled flights 3.

Communications

Medium	date	unit	number	units per 1,000 persons
Daily newspapers	2000	circulation	334,000	171
Radio	2000	receivers	792,000	405
Television	2000	receivers	720,000	368
Telephones	2002	main lines	811,400	407
Cellular telephones	2002	subscribers	1,667,000	835
Internet	2002	users	800,000	401
Personal computers	2002	units	600,000	301

Education and health

Educational attainment (2002). Percentage of population age 15 and over having: no formal schooling 0.7%; incomplete and complete primary education 32.2%; secondary 54.1%; some higher 5.1%; undergraduate 6.9%; advanced degree 1.0%. *Literacy* (2000): 99.7%.

Education (1999–2000)

	schools	teachers	students	student/ teacher ratio
Primary (age 7–14)	443	15,287	185,034	12.1
Secondary (age 15–18)	149	9,351	102,969	11.0
Higher[9]	...	4,666	88,100	18.9

Health (2000): physicians 4,483 (1 per 436 persons); hospital beds 10,745 (1 per 182 persons); infant mortality rate per 1,000 live births (2001) 4.4.

Military

Total active duty personnel (2002): 9,000 (army 100%). *Military expenditure as percentage of GNP* (1999): 1.4% (world 2.4%); per capita expenditure U.S.$227.

[1]Actual first-order administration is based on 192 municipalities. [2]Prorating 8.9% of population not responding to census questionnaire. [3]Populations of municipalities, which may include nearby small towns and rural areas. [4]May. [5]Import taxes less imputed bank service charges. [6]Includes 57,000 unemployed and 12,000 not distributed. [7]Detail does not add to total given because of rounding. [8]Imports c.i.f.; exports f.o.b. [9]2001–02.

Internet resources for further information:
- **Statistical Office of the Republic of Slovenia http://www.sigov.si/zrs/eng/index.html**
- **Bank of Slovenia http://www.bsi.si**

Solomon Islands

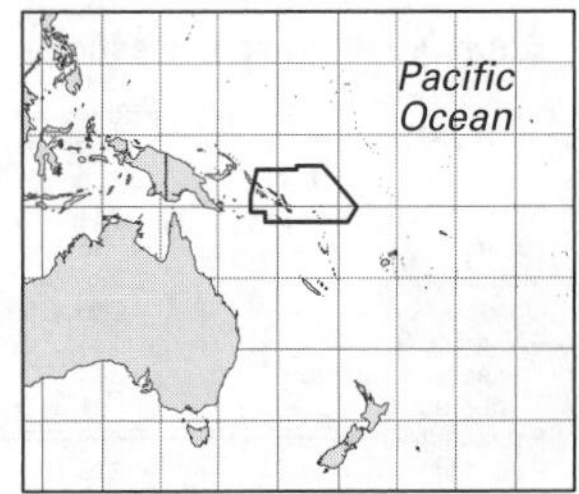

Official name: Solomon Islands.
Form of government: constitutional monarchy[1] with one legislative house (National Parliament [50]).
Chief of state: British Monarch represented by Governor-General.
Head of government: Prime Minister.
Capital: Honiara.
Official language: English.
Official religion: none.
Monetary unit: 1 Solomon Islands dollar (SI$) = 100 cents; valuation (Sept. 8, 2003) 1 U.S.$ = SI$7.53; 1 £ = SI$11.94.

Area and population

Provinces	Capitals	area sq mi	area sq km	population 1999 census
Central Islands	Tulagi	237	615	21,577
Choiseul	Taro	1,481	3,837	20,008
Guadalcanal	Honiara	2,060	5,336	60,275
Isabel	Buala	1,597	4,136	20,421
Makira-Ulawa	Kira Kira	1,231	3,188	31,006
Malaita	Auki	1,631	4,225	122,620
Rennell and Bellona	Tigoa	259	671	2,377
Temotu	Santa Cruz	334	865	18,912
Western	Gizo	2,114	5,475	62,739
Capital Territory				
Honiara	—	8	22	49,107
TOTAL		10,954[2]	28,370	409,042

Demography

Population (2003): 450,000.
Density (2003): persons per sq mi 41.1, persons per sq km 15.9.
Urban-rural (2002): urban 21.0%; rural 79.0%.
Sex distribution (1999): male 51.68%; female 48.32%.
Age breakdown (1996): under 15, 43.7%; 15–29, 28.7%; 30–44, 15.2%; 45–59, 8.1%; 60–74, 3.6%; 75 and over, 0.7%.
Population projection: (2010) 542,000; (2020) 673,000.
Doubling time: 21 years.
Ethnic composition (2002): Melanesian 93.0%; Polynesian 4.0%; Micronesian 1.5%; other 1.5%.
Religious affiliation (2000): Christian 90.8%, of which Protestant 74.0% (including Church of Melanesia [Anglican] 38.2%), Roman Catholic 10.8%; traditional beliefs 3.1%; other 6.1%.
Major cities (1999): Honiara 49,107 (urban agglomeration [2001] 78,000); Noro 3,482; Gizo 2,960; Auki 1,606; Tulagi 1,333.

Vital statistics

Birth rate per 1,000 population (2002): 33.3 (world avg. 21.3).
Death rate per 1,000 population (2002): 4.2 (world avg. 9.1).
Natural increase rate per 1,000 population (2002): 29.1 (world avg. 12.2).
Total fertility rate (avg. births per childbearing woman; 2002): 4.5.
Marriage rate per 1,000 population: n.a.
Life expectancy at birth (2002): male 69.4 years; female 74.4 years.
Major causes of death per 100,000 population (1990): respiratory diseases 22.4; diarrheal diseases 13.6; malaria 10.0.

National economy

Budget (2002). Revenue: SI$288,350,000 (current revenue 91.1%, of which tax 84.4%, nontax 6.7%; grants 8.9%). Expenditures: SI$401,900,000 (current expenditure 75.3%; capital expenditure 24.7%).
Tourism: receipts from visitors (1999) U.S.$6,000,000; expenditures by nationals abroad U.S.$7,000,000.
Land use (1994): forested 87.5%; meadows and pastures 1.4%; agricultural and under permanent cultivation 2.0%; other 9.1%.
Gross national product (at current market prices; 2001): U.S.$300,000,000 (U.S.$590 per capita).

Structure of gross domestic product and labour force

	2000		1993	
	in value SI$'000[3]	% of total value	labour force[4]	% of labour force[4]
Agriculture	116,000	42.1	8,106	27.4
Mining	8,600	3.1	2,844	9.6
Manufacturing	13,400	4.9		
Construction	7,600	2.8	977	3.3
Public utilities	3,600	1.3	245	0.8
Transportation and communications	15,500	5.6	1,723	5.8
Trade	29,700	10.8	3,390	11.5
Finance	12,900	4.7	1,144	3.9
Pub. admin., defense	68,000	24.7	4,303	14.6
Services			6,845	23.1
Other	...	...	...	...
TOTAL	275,300	100.0	29,577	100.0

Household income and expenditure. Average household size (1999) 6.3; average annual income per household[5] (1991) U.S.$2,387; sources of income (1983): wages and salaries 74.1%, other 25.9%; expenditure (1992)[6]: food 46.8%, housing 11.0%, household operations 10.9%, transportation 9.9%, recreation and health 7.9%.

Population economically active (1993): total 29,577[4]; activity rate of total population 8.3% (participation rates: ages 15–60 [1986] 98.6%; female 22.6%; unemployed [1999] 11%).

Price and earnings indexes (1995 = 100)

	1993	1994	1995	1996	1997	1998	1999
Consumer price index	80.5	91.2	100.0	111.8	120.8	135.7	146.9
Annual earnings index	...	...	...	...	...	...	...

Production (metric tons except as noted). Agriculture, forestry, fishing (2002): coconuts 330,000, palm oil fruit 140,000, sweet potatoes 84,000, taro 36,000, yams 31,500, vegetables 5,700, cacao beans 3,000; livestock (number of live animals) 68,000 pigs, 13,000 cattle, 220,000 chickens; roundwood (2002) 692,000 cu m; fish catch (2000) 23,458. Mining and quarrying (1999): gold 3,456 kg[7]. Manufacturing (2002): vegetable oils and fats 50,000, palm oil 35,000, coconut oil 15,000, dried coconut 8,100. Energy production (consumption): electricity (kW-hr; 1999) 33,000,000 (33,000,000); coal none (n.a.); petroleum products (metric tons; 1999) none (54,000); natural gas, none (n.a.).
Public debt (external, outstanding; 2001): U.S.$130,900,000.

Foreign trade[8]

Balance of trade (current prices)

	1998	1999	2000	2001	2002
SI$'000,000	−7.1	+69.0	−167.7	−183.3	−46.3
% of total	0.6%	6.0%	19.3%	26.9%	5.6%

Imports (2002): SI$436,300,000 (food and live animals 24.9%, mineral fuels and lubricants 17.3%, machinery and transport equipment 13.2%, unspecified 33.9%). *Major import sources:* Australia 31.5%; Singapore 19.8%; New Zealand 5.2%; Fiji 4.6%; Papua New Guinea 4.5%.
Exports (2002): SI$390,000,000 (timber 65.2%, fish products 18.1%, cacao beans 7.1%, gold, none[7]). *Major export destinations:* Japan 17.1%; South Korea 16.7%; Philippines 6.8%; Thailand 6.7%; China 6.5%.

Transport and communications

Transport. Railroads: none. Roads (1996): total length 1,360 km (paved 2.5%). Vehicles (1993): passenger cars 2,052; trucks and buses 2,574. Air transport (1999): passenger-km 47,278,000; metric ton-km cargo 1,250,000; airports (1997) with scheduled flights 21.

Communications

Medium	date	unit	number	units per 1,000 persons
Radio	1997	receivers	57,000	141
Television	2000	receivers	9,570	23
Telephones	2002	main lines	6,600	15
Cellular telephones	2002	subscribers	1,000	2.2
Personal computers	2002	units	18,000	41
Internet	2002	users	2,200	5.0

Education and health

Educational attainment (1986)[9]. Percentage of population age 25 and over having: no schooling 44.4%; primary education 46.2%; secondary 6.8%; higher 2.6%. *Literacy* (1999): total population age 15 and over literate 181,000 (76%); males 102,500 (83%); females 78,500 (68%).

Education (1994)

	schools	teachers	students	student/teacher ratio
Primary (age 7–12)	520	2,510	73,120	29.1
Secondary (age 13–18)	23	618	7,981	12.9
Voc., teacher tr.[10]	1	...	...	...
Higher[10]	1	...	...	...

Health: physicians (1999) 53 (1 per 7,692 persons); hospital beds (1997) 210 (1 per 1,957 persons); infant mortality rate per 1,000 live births (2002) 23.7.
Food (2001): daily per capita caloric intake 2,272 (vegetable products 92%, animal products 8%); 100% of FAO recommended minimum requirement.

Military

Total active duty personnel (2003): none; multinational regional intervention force (primarily Australian) for combating violence and lawlessness (from July 2003): 1,800; number of troops declining from October 2003.

[1]New constitution implementing a federal structure was being drafted in November 2003. [2]Detail does not add to total given because of rounding. [3]At 1985 factor cost. [4]Persons employed in the monetary sector only; 1990 = 100. [5]Public-service earnings. [6]Retail price index components. [7]Production at the country's only gold mine was suspended from 2000 through September 2003 because of civil unrest. [8]Imports c.i.f.; exports f.o.b. [9]Honiara only; a 1993 survey of rural households returned an average household income of U.S.$330. [10]Vocational and teacher training are carried out at the College of Higher Education.

Internet resources for further information:

- **Solomon Islands Government Ministries http://www.commerce.gov.sb**

Somalia[1]

Official name: Soomaaliya (Somali) (Somalia).
Form of government: transitional regime[2] with one legislative body (Transitional National Assembly [245[3]]).
Head of state and government: President assisted by Prime Minister.
Capital: Mogadishu.
Official languages: Somali; Arabic.
Official religion: Islam.
Monetary unit: 1 Somali shilling (So.Sh.) = 100 cents; valuation (Sept. 8, 2003) 1 U.S.$ = So.Sh. 2,620[4]; 1 £ = So.Sh. 4,154.

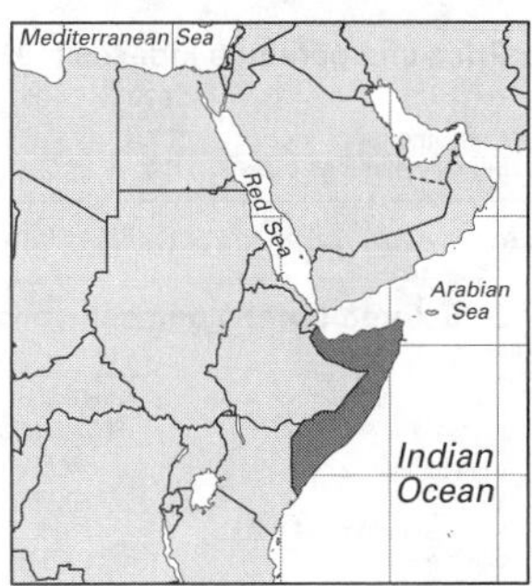

Area and population

		area		population
				1980
Regions	Principal cities	sq mi	sq km	estimate
Bakool[5]	Xuddur	10,000	27,000	148,700
Banaadir	Mogadishu (Muqdisho)	400	1,000	520,100
Bari[6]	Boosaaso	27,000	70,000	222,300
Bay[5]	Baydhabo	15,000	39,000	451,000
Galguduud	Dhuusamarreeb	17,000	43,000	255,900
Gedo[5]	Garbahaarrey	12,000	32,000	235,000
Hiiraan	Beledweyne	13,000	34,000	219,300
Jubbada Dhexe[5]	Bu'aale	9,000	23,000	147,800
Jubbada Hoose[5]	Kismaayo	24,000	61,000	272,400
Mudug[6]	Gaalkacyo	27,000	70,000	311,200
Nugaal[6]	Garoowe	19,000	50,000	112,200
Sanaag[7]	Ceerigaabo	21,000	54,000	216,500
Shabeellaha Dhexe	Jawhar	8,000	22,000	352,000
Shabeellaha Hoose[5]	Marka	10,000	25,000	570,700
Togdheer[7]	Burao	16,000	41,000	383,900
Woqooyi Galbeed[7]	Hargeysa	17,000	45,000	655,000
TOTAL		246,000[8]	637,000	5,074,000

Demography

Population (2003): 8,025,000.
Density (2003): persons per sq mi 31.5, persons per sq km 12.2.
Urban-rural (2001): urban 27.9%; rural 72.1%.
Sex distribution (2000): male 50.18%; female 49.82%.
Age breakdown (2000): under 15, 44.4%; 15–29, 26.8%; 30–44, 17.9%; 45–59, 6.6%; 60–74, 3.5%; 75 and over, 0.8%.
Population projection: (2010) 9,922,000; (2020) 13,023,000.
Doubling time: 24 years.
Ethnic composition (2000): Somali 92.4%[9]; Arab 2.2%; Afar 1.3%; other 4.1%.
Religious affiliation (1995): Sunnī Muslim 99.9%; other 0.1%.
Major cities (1990): Mogadishu 1,212,000[10]; Hargeysa 90,000; Kismaayo 90,000; Berbera 70,000; Marka 62,000.

Vital statistics

Birth rate per 1,000 population (2001): 47.2 (world avg. 21.3).
Death rate per 1,000 population (2001): 18.4 (world avg. 9.1).
Natural increase rate per 1,000 population (2001): 28.8 (world avg. 12.2).
Total fertility rate (avg. births per childbearing woman; 2000): 7.1.
Life expectancy at birth (2001): male 45.0 years; female 48.3 years.

National economy

Budget (1991). Revenue: So.Sh. 151,453,000,000 (domestic revenue sources, principally indirect taxes and import duties 60.4%; external grants and transfers 39.6%). Expenditures: So.Sh. 141,141,000,000 (general services 46.9%; economic and social services 31.2%; debt service 7.0%).
Public debt (external, outstanding; 2001): U.S.$1,795,000,000.
Production (metric tons except as noted). Agriculture, forestry, fishing (2002): fruits (excluding melons) 220,000, sugarcane 210,000, corn (maize) 210,000, sorghum 90,000, cassava 85,000, bananas 60,000, sesame seed 25,000, beans 16,500, dates 11,000, seed cotton 6,000, other forest products include khat, frankincense, and myrrh; livestock (number of live animals) 13,100,000 sheep, 12,700,000 goats, 6,200,000 camels, 5,300,000 cattle; roundwood (2001) 9,936,520 cu m; fish catch (2000) 20,200. Mining and quarrying (2001): gypsum 1,500; salt 1,000. Manufacturing (value added in So.Sh. '000,000; 1988): food 794; cigarettes and matches 562; hides and skins 420; paper and printing 328; plastics 320; chemicals 202; beverages 144. Energy production (consumption): electricity (kW-hr; 1999) 280,000,000 (280,000,000); coal, none (none); crude petroleum (barrels; 1991) none (806,000); petroleum products (metric tons; 1991) none (59,000); natural gas, none (none).
Household income and expenditure. Average household size (1980) 4.9; income per household: n.a.; sources of income: n.a.; expenditure (1983)[11]: food and tobacco 62.3%, housing 15.3%, clothing 5.6%, energy 4.3%, other 12.5%.
Population economically active (2001): total 3,906,000; activity rate of total population 52.2% (participation rates: n.a.; female, n.a.; unemployed, n.a.).

Price and earnings indexes (1990 = 100)

	1989	1990	1991	1992	1993	1994	1995
Consumer price index[12]	100.0	240.0	372.2	507.4	630.7	749.8	872.1
Earnings index	...	...	...	...	...	...	...

Gross national product (1996): U.S.$706,000,000 (U.S.$110 per capita).

Structure of gross domestic product and labour force

	1991		2001	
	in value So.Sh. '000,000	% of total value	labour force	% of labour force
Agriculture	867,500	64.5	2,762,000	70.7
Mining	2,700	0.2		
Manufacturing	59,200	4.4		
Construction	51,100	3.8		
Public utilities	9,400	0.7		
Transp. and commun.	80,700	6.0		
Trade	125,000	9.3	1,144,000	29.3
Finance	45,700	3.4		
Pub. admin., defense	80,700	6.0		
Services	30,900	2.3		
Other	–8,100	–0.6		
TOTAL	1,344,900[8]	100.0	3,906,000	100.0

Tourism: n.a.
Land use (1994): forest 25.5%; pasture 68.6%; agriculture 1.6%; other 4.3%.

Foreign trade[13]

Balance of trade (current prices)

	1996	1997	1998	1999	2000	2001
U.S.$'000,000	–128	–132	–118	–166	–184	–184
% of total	29.9%	29.6%	31.6%	41.1%	39.7%	39.7%

Imports (2001): U.S.$324,000,000 (agricultural products 17.1%, of which cereals 5.7%, refined sugar 4.4%; unspecified 82.9%). *Major import sources* (2002): Djibouti 30%; Kenya 14%; Brazil 11%; Thailand 5%; United Kingdom 5%.
Exports (2001): U.S.$140,000,000 (agricultural products 46.9%, of which goats 20.4%, sheep 15.5%, camels 10.0%; wood charcoal 4.5%). *Major export destinations:* United Arab Emirates 47%; Yemen 23%; Oman 10%; Kuwait 4%; India 3%.

Transport and communications

Transport. Railroads: none. Roads (1996): total length 13,700 mi, 22,100 km (paved 12%). Vehicles (1996): passenger cars 1,020; trucks and buses 6,440. Merchant marine (1992): vessels (100 gross tons and over) 28; total deadweight tonnage 18,496. Air transport (1991): passenger-mi 81,000,000, passenger-km 131,000,000; short ton-mi cargo 3,000,000, metric ton-km cargo 5,000,000; airports (2002) with scheduled flights 1.

Communications

Medium	date	unit	number	units per 1,000 persons
Daily newspapers	1996	circulation	10,000	1.2
Radio	1997	receivers	470,000	53
Television	1997	receivers	135,000	15
Telephones	1999	main lines	15,000	2.1

Education and health

Educational attainment: n.a. *Literacy* (1995): percentage of total population age 15 and over literate 24%; males literate 36%; females literate 14%.

Education (1989–90)

	schools	teachers	students	student/ teacher ratio
Primary (age 6–14)	1,125	8,208	377,000	20.9
Secondary (age 15–18)	82	2,109	44,000	20.3
Voc., teacher tr.	21	498	10,400	9.7
Higher	1	549	4,640	...

Health: physicians (1997) 265 (1 per 25,034 persons); hospital beds (1985) 5,536 (1 per 1,130 persons); infant mortality rate (2001) 124.0.
Food (2000): daily per capita caloric intake 1,628 (vegetable products 62%, animal products 38%); 70% of FAO recommended minimum requirement.

Military

Total active duty personnel: clan warfare between 1991 and late 2003. *Military expenditure as percentage of GNP* (1990): 0.9% (world 4.3%); per capita expenditure U.S.$1.

[1]Proclamation of the "Republic of Somaliland" in May 1991 on territory corresponding to the former British Somaliland (which unified with the former Italian Trust Territory of Somalia to form Somalia in 1960) had not received international recognition as of October 2003. This entity represented about a quarter of Somalia's territory. [2]From August 2000; effective control in Mogadishu vicinity only in 2003. [3]Includes 44 seats allotted to each of 4 major clans, 24 seats allotted to minor clans and tribes, 25 seats allotted to women, and 20 nominees of president. [4]Official rate ineffective; in September 2003 about 18,000 So.Sh. equaled 1 U.S.$ on the black market. [5]Part of "autonomous region" of Southwestern Somalia from April 2002. [6]Part of "autonomous region" of Puntland from 1998. [7]Part of "Republic of Somaliland" from 1991. [8]Detail does not add to total given because of rounding. [9]The Somali are divided into six major clans, of which four are predominantly pastoral (representing *c.* 70% of the population) and two are predominantly agricultural (representing *c.* 20% of the population); the remainder are urban dwellers with less clan identification. [10]2001. [11]Mogadishu only. [12]Reported inflation rate. [13]Imports c.i.f.; exports f.o.b.

Internet resources for further information:
- **The ACG Somalia Page http://www.abyssiniacybergateway.net/somalia**
- **UN Development Programme in Somalia http://www.so.undp.org**

South Africa

Official name: Republic of South Africa (English).
Form of government: multiparty republic with two legislative houses (National Council of Provinces [90]; National Assembly [400]).
Head of state and government: President.
Capitals (de facto): Pretoria/Tshwane[1] (executive); Bloemfontein/Mangaung[1] (judicial); Cape Town (legislative).
Official languages: [2].
Official religion: none.
Monetary unit: 1 rand (R) = 100 cents; valuation (Sept. 8, 2003) 1 U.S.$ = R 7.42; 1 £ = R 11.77.

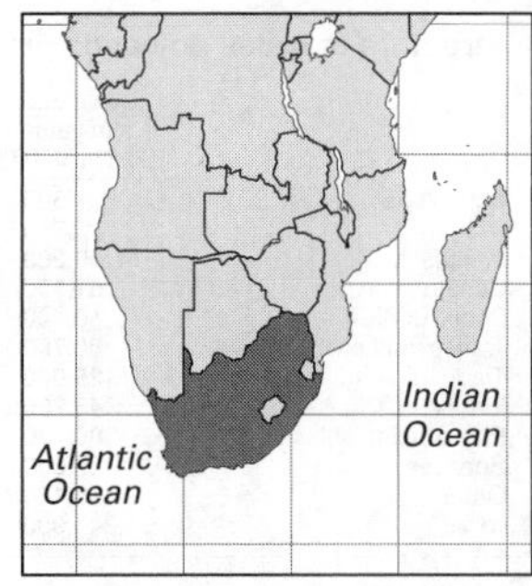

Area and population

Provinces	Capitals	area sq mi	area sq km	population 2001 census
Eastern Cape	Bisho	65,475	169,580	6,436,763
Free State	Bloemfontein	49,993	129,480	2,706,775
Gauteng	Johannesburg	6,568	17,010	8,837,178
KwaZulu–Natal	Pietermaritzburg	35,560	92,100	9,426,017
Limpopo	Polokwane	47,842	123,910	5,273,642
Mpumalanga	Nelspruit	30,691	79,490	3,122,990
Northern Cape	Kimberley	139,703	361,830	822,727
North West	Mafikeng/Mmabatho	44,911	116,320	3,669,349
Western Cape	Cape Town	49,950	129,370	4,524,335
TOTAL		470,693	1,219,090	44,819,778

Demography

Population (2003): 45,349,000.
Density (2003): persons per sq mi 96.3, persons per sq km 37.2.
Urban-rural (2002): urban 57.7%; rural 42.3%.
Sex distribution (2001): male 47.82%; female 52.18%.
Age breakdown (2001): under 15, 32.0%; 15–29, 29.5%; 30–44, 20.2%; 45–59, 11.0%; 60–74, 5.5%; 75 and over, 1.8%.
Population projection: (2010) 45,261,000; (2020) 43,996,000.
Ethnic composition (2001): black 78.4%, of which Zulu 23.8%, Xhosa 17.6%, Pedi 9.4%, Tswana 8.2%, Sotho 7.9%, Tsonga 4.4%, Swazi 2.7%, other black 4.4%; white 9.6%; Coloured 8.9%; Asian 2.5%; other 0.6%.
Religious affiliation (2000): Christian 83.1%, of which black independent churches 39.1%, Protestant 31.8%, Roman Catholic 7.1%; traditional beliefs 8.4%; Hindu 2.4%; Muslim 2.4%; nonreligious 2.4%; other 1.3%.
Major cities (2003): Cape Town 2,733,000; Durban 2,396,100[3]; Johannesburg 1,675,200[3]; Pretoria 1,249,700; Port Elizabeth 848,400.

Vital statistics

Birth rate per 1,000 population (2001): 19.8 (world avg. 21.3).
Death rate per 1,000 population (2001): 15.0 (world avg. 9.1).
Natural increase rate per 1,000 population (2001): 4.8 (world avg. 12.2).
Marriage rate per 1,000 population (1998): 3.4.
Total fertility rate (avg. births per childbearing woman; 2001): 2.4.
Life expectancy at birth (2001): male 50.7 years; female 51.4 years.
Major causes of death per 100,000 population (1996): diseases of the circulatory system 507.6; accidents and violence 444.8; diseases of the respiratory system 226.9; malignant neoplasms (cancers) 220.8; endocrine and metabolic diseases 76.7; infectious and parasitic diseases 41.5.

National economy

Budget (2001–02). Revenue: R 248,447,200,000 (personal income taxes 36.6%, value-added taxes 23.6%, company income taxes 17.7%, other 22.1%). Expenditures: R 262,589,800,000 (transfer to provinces 46.2%, interest on public debt 18.1%, police and prisons 9.2%, defense 6.1%).
Public debt (external, outstanding; 2001): U.S.$7,941,000,000.
Production (in R '000,000 except as noted). Agriculture, forestry, fishing (in value of production; 2000): poultry 8,270, corn (maize) 5,654, beef 3,904, temperate fruits 2,975, sugarcane 2,530, vegetables 2,516, milk 2,229, wheat 2,100, citrus fruits 1,835, potatoes 1,599, sheep and goat meat 1,322; roundwood (2001) 30,616,000 cu m; fish catch (2001) 647,763 metric tons. Mining and quarrying (in value of sales; 2000): platinum-group metals 27,111; gold 25,272; rough diamonds 10,015,000 carats; coal 19,520; iron ore (1998) 2,492; copper (1998) 1,612; nickel (1997) 1,004. Manufacturing (value added in U.S.$'000,000; 1999): food products 2,225; iron and steel 2,225; transport equipment 2,100; fabricated metals 1,400; electrical machinery 1,325; refined petroleum 1,325; nonferrous base metals 1,200. Energy production (consumption): electricity (kW-hr; 2002) 217,704,000,000 ([2001] 182,565,000,000); coal (metric tons; 2002) 222,456,000 ([2000] 159,937,000); crude petroleum (barrels; 2000) 5,456,000 ([1999] 186,800,000[4]); petroleum products (metric tons; 1999) 23,292,000[4] (16,806,000[4]); natural gas (cu m; 2000): 1,400,000,000 (1,400,000,000).
Household income and expenditure. Average household size (2001) 3.8; average annual disposable income per household (1996)[5] R 47,600 (U.S.$11,070); expenditure (1998): food, beverages, and tobacco 31.3%; transportation 14.3%; housing 9.3%; household furnishings and operation 8.9%.
Population economically active (2001): total 15,358,000; activity rate of total population 34.5% (participation rates: over age 15, 50.7%; female 46.7%; unemployed [2001] 29.5%).

Price and earnings indexes (1995 = 100)

	1996	1997	1998	1999	2000	2001	2002
Consumer price index	107.4	116.5	124.6	131.1	138.1	145.9	159.3
Monthly earnings index	...	...	...	...	...	...	...

Gross national product (2001): U.S.$121,900,000,000 (U.S.$2,820 per capita).

Structure of gross domestic product and labour force

	2002		2001	
	in value R '000,000	% of total value	labour force	% of labour force
Agriculture	37,674	3.4	1,051,000	6.8
Mining	80,586	7.3	487,000	3.2
Manufacturing	188,182	17.1	1,605,000	10.5
Construction	27,545	2.5	594,000	3.9
Public utilities	23,965	2.2	95,000	0.6
Transp. and commun.	96,086	8.7	543,000	3.5
Trade	132,691	12.1	2,397,000	15.6
Finance, real estate	194,591	17.7	975,000	6.3
Pub. admin., defense	157,936	14.4	3,043,000	19.8
Services	59,659	5.4		
Other	99,799[6]	9.1[6]	4,568,000[7]	29.7[7]
TOTAL	1,098,714	100.0[8]	15,358,000	100.0[8]

Tourism (2000): receipts U.S.$2,501,000,000; expenditures U.S.$1,917,000,000.
Land use (1994): forest 6.7%; pasture 66.7%; agriculture 10.8%; other 15.8%.

Foreign trade

Balance of trade (current prices)

	1997	1998	1999	2000	2001	2002
U.S.$'000,000	+2,324	+2,056	+4,073	+4,316	+4,860	+4,372
% of total	3.9%	3.6%	7.7%	7.3%	8.6%	7.6%

Imports (2001): U.S.$24,188,000,000 (nonelectrical machinery 18.0%, crude petroleum 12.9%, chemicals and chemical products 11.9%, electrical machinery 11.5%). *Major import sources* (2001): U.S. 11.0%; Germany 10.5%; U.K. 7.4%; Japan 5.5%; China 4.4%; unspecified 17.1%.
Exports (2001): U.S.$27,928,000,000 (diamonds 18.6%, gold 12.6%, iron and steel 7.8%, food 6.5%, nonelectrical machinery 6.3%, industrial chemicals 6.2%, road vehicles 5.6%, coal 5.2%). *Major export destinations* (2002): U.K. 12.9%; U.S. 12.8%; Germany 9.1%; Japan 8.9%; Italy 5.8%.

Transport and communications

Transport. Railroads: route length (2001) 20,384 km; passenger-km 3,930,000,000; metric ton-km cargo 106,786,000,000. Roads (1999): length 331,265 km (paved 41%). Vehicles (2002): passenger cars 4,135,037; trucks and buses 2,202,032. Air transport (2000)[9]: passenger-km 19,320,000,000; metric ton-km cargo 677,048,000; airport (1996) 24.

Communications

Medium	date	unit	number	units per 1,000 persons
Daily newspapers	2000	circulation	1,590,000	32
Radio	2000	receivers	16,800,000	338
Television	2000	receivers	6,310,000	127
Telephones	2002	main lines	4,895,000	108
Cellular telephones	2002	subscribers	12,081,000	266
Personal computers	2002	units	3,300,000	73
Internet	2002	users	3,100,000	68

Education and health

Educational attainment (2000). Percentage of population age 20 and over having: no formal schooling 17.9%; some primary education 16.0%; complete primary/some secondary 37.2%; complete secondary 20.4%; higher 8.5%. *Literacy* (2000): total population age 15 and over literate: 85.3%; males 86.0%; females 84.6%.

Education (2000)

	schools	teachers	students	student/ teacher ratio
Primary (age 6–12)	17,213	183,639	6,266,223	34.1
Secondary (age 13–17)[10]	10,547	177,084	5,588,866	31.6
Higher[11]	21	...	169,604	...

Health: physicians (2000) 29,788 (1 per 1,453 persons); hospital beds (1998) 144,363 (1 per 290 persons); infant mortality rate (2001) 58.1.
Food (2001): daily per capita caloric intake 2,889 (vegetable products 87%, animal products 13%); 114% of FAO recommended minimum.

Military

Total active duty personnel (2002): 60,000 (army 67.1%, navy 8.3%, air force 15.4%, intraservice medical service 9.2%). *Military expenditure as percentage of GNP* (1999): 1.5% (world 2.4%); per capita expenditure U.S.$45.

[1]Renamed within larger municipality in December 2000. [2]Afrikaans; English; Ndebele; Pedi (North Sotho); Sotho (South Sotho); Swazi; Tsonga; Tswana (West Sotho); Venda; Xhosa; Zulu. [3]Name change pending. [4]Includes Botswana, Lesotho, Namibia, and Swaziland. [5]Estimated figures. [6]Taxes on products less subsidies on products. [7]Includes 43,000 not adequately defined and 4,525,000 unemployed. [8]Detail does not add to total given because of rounding. [9]SAA only. [10]Includes combined and intermediate. [11]Universities only.

Internet resources for further information:
- **South African Reserve Bank http://www.reservebank.co.za**
- **Statistics South Africa http://www.statssa.gov.za**

Spain

Official name: Reino de España (Kingdom of Spain).
Form of government: constitutional monarchy with two legislative houses (Senate [259[1]]; Congress of Deputies [350]).
Chief of state: King.
Head of government: Prime Minister.
Capital: Madrid.
Official languages: Castilian Spanish[2].
Official religion: none.
Monetary unit: 1 euro (€) = 100 céntimos; valuation (Sept. 8, 2003) 1 U.S.$ = €0.90; 1 £ = €1.43[3].

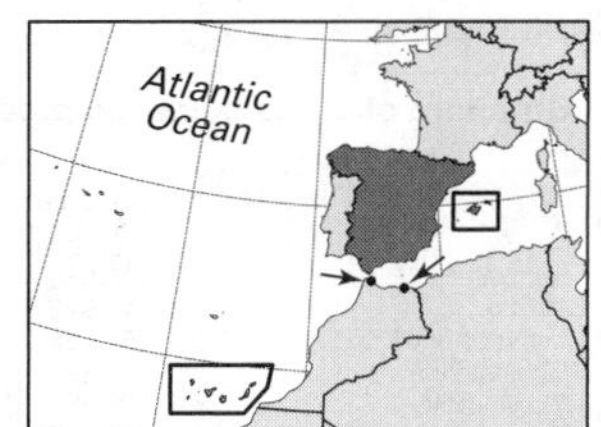

Area and population		area		population
				2001
Autonomous communities	**Capitals**	sq mi	sq km	census
Andalucía	Seville	33,820	87,595	7,357,558
Aragón	Zaragoza	18,425	47,720	1,204,215
Asturias	Oviedo	4,094	10,604	1,062,998
Baleares (Balearic Islands)	Palma de Mallorca	1,927	4,992	841,669
Canarias (Canary Islands)	Santa Cruz de Tenerife	2,893	7,492	1,694,477
Cantabria	Santander	2,054	5,321	535,131
Castilla-La Mancha	Toledo	30,680	79,461	1,760,516
Castilla y León	Valladolid	36,380	94,224	2,456,474
Cataluña	Barcelona	12,399	32,113	6,343,110
Extremadura	Mérida	16,075	41,634	1,058,503
Galicia	Santiago	11,419	29,575	2,695,880
La Rioja	Logroño	1,948	5,045	276,702
Madrid	Madrid	3,100	8,028	5,423,384
Murcia	Murcia	4,368	11,314	1,197,646
Navarra	Pamplona	4,012	10,391	555,829
País Vasco (Basque Country)	Vitoria (Gasteiz)	2,793	7,234	2,082,587
Valenciana	Valencia	8,979	23,255	4,162,776
Autonomous cities				
Ceuta	—	8	20	71,505
Melilla	—	5	12	66,411
TOTAL		195,379	506,030	40,847,371

Demography

Population (2003): 42,600,000.
Density (2003): persons per sq mi 218.0, persons per sq km 84.2.
Urban-rural (2002): urban 77.8%; rural 22.2%.
Sex distribution (2002): male 48.95%; female 51.05%.
Age breakdown (2002): under 15, 14.6%; 15–29, 21.7%; 30–44, 24.0%; 45–59, 18.0%; 60–74, 14.2%; 75 and over, 7.5%.
Population projection: (2010) 42,600,000; (2020) 42,600,000.
Ethnic composition (2000): Spaniard 44.9%; Catalonian 28.0%; Galician 8.2%; Basque 5.5%; Aragonese 5.0%; Extremaduran 2.8%; Rom (Gypsy) 2.0%; other 3.6%.
Religious affiliation (2000): Roman Catholic 92.0%; Muslim 0.5%; Protestant 0.3%; other 7.2%.
Major cities (2001): Madrid 2,938,723; Barcelona 1,503,884; Valencia 738,441; Seville 684,633; Zaragoza 614,905.

Vital statistics

Birth rate per 1,000 population (2001): 10.0 (world avg. 21.3).
Death rate per 1,000 population (2001): 8.9 (world avg. 9.1).
Total fertility rate (avg. births per childbearing woman; 2001): 1.2.
Life expectancy at birth (2001): male 75.6 years; female 82.5 years.
Major causes of death per 100,000 population (1999): circulatory diseases 332.5; malignant neoplasms (cancers) 238.7; respiratory diseases 114.1; digestive diseases 47.9; accidents, poisonings, violence 41.4.

National economy

Budget (2002). Revenue: €108,824,300,000 (direct taxes 46.6%, of which income tax 27.2%; indirect taxes 41.8%, of which value-added tax on products 27.8%; other taxes 11.6%). Expenditures: €112,586,900,000 (public debt 15.7%; health 9.8%; pensions 5.7%; defense 5.6%; public works 4.4%).
Tourism (2001): receipts U.S.$32,873,000,000; expenditures U.S.$5,974,000,000.
Gross national product (2001): U.S.$588,000,000,000 (U.S.$14,300 per capita).

Structure of gross domestic product and labour force				
	2001			
	in value €'000,000	% of total value	labour force	% of labour force
Agriculture	21,001	3.2	1,019,200	5.7
Mining	103,511	15.9	63,300	0.4
Manufacturing			3,005,600	16.9
Public utilities	19,221	2.9	98,800	0.6
Construction	53,673	8.2	1,850,200	10.4
Transp. and commun.	...	...	965,200	5.4
Trade and hotels	418,235	64.2	3,526,200	19.8
Finance			1,630,400	9.2
Services			2,778,600	15.6
Pub. admin., defense			1,008,100	5.6
Other	35,999[4]	5.5[4]	1,869,000[5]	10.5[5]
TOTAL	651,641[6]	100.0[6]	17,814,600	100.0[6]

Production (metric tons except as noted). Agriculture, forestry, fishing (2002): barley 8,332,900, sugar beets 7,877,000, wheat 6,782,000, grapes 5,609,300, corn (maize) 4,394,500, olives 4,303,700, tomatoes 3,878,400, potatoes 3,103,000, oranges 2,865,800; livestock (number of live animals) 24,300,624 sheep, 23,857,776 pigs, 6,411,000 cattle; roundwood (2001) 15,839,000 cu m; fish catch (2001) 1,289,081. Mining and quarrying (metal content in metric tons; 2001): zinc 164,900; lead 49,500. Manufacturing (value added in €'000,000; 2001): transport equipment 35,774; petroleum products 26,242; food products 14,771; chemical products 14,137; plastics 11,893; pharmaceutical products 10,050; furniture 9,653; alcoholic beverages 9,195. Energy production (consumption): electricity (kW-hr; 2000) 212,244,000,000 ([1999] 218,290,000,000); hard coal (metric tons; 2001) 10,491,000 ([1999] 31,466,000); lignite (metric tons; 1999) 12,527,000 (12,156,000); crude petroleum (barrels; 2001) 2,505,000 ([1999] 431,100,000); petroleum products (metric tons; 1999) 51,542,000 (50,645,000); natural gas (cu m; 2001) 180,000,000 ([1999] 16,107,600,000).
Public debt (2001): €307,434,000,000.
Population economically active (2001): total 17,814,600; activity rate of total population 43.7% (participation rates: ages [1995] 16–64, 60.7%; female 39.2%; unemployed 10.5%).

Price and earnings indexes (1995 = 100)							
	1996	1997	1998	1999	2000	2001	2002
Consumer price index	103.6	105.6	107.5	110.0	113.8	116.8	121.5
Monthly earnings index	105.3	109.6	112.7	115.5	118.2	122.8	127.8

Household income and expenditure. Average household size (2000) 3.2; income per household (2000) Ptas 3,205,693 (U.S.$18,470); expenditure (1995): housing 26.0%, food 24.0%, transportation 12.8%, clothing/footwear 7.4%.

Foreign trade[7]

Balance of trade (current prices)						
	1997	1998	1999	2000	2001	2002
U.S.$'000,000	–13,407	–20,758	–30,339	–34,820	–32,539	–33,098
% of total	5.9%	8.5%	11.9%	13.0%	12.1%	11.6%

Imports (2001): U.S.$154,993,000,000 (road vehicles 15.6%, nonelectrical machinery 13.3%, chemicals and chemical products 11.2%, electrical machinery 8.7%, crude and refined petroleum 8.6%). *Major import sources* (2002): France 16.9%; Germany 16.5%; Italy 8.6%; U.K. 6.4%; The Netherlands 4.8%.
Exports (2001): U.S.$116,149,000,000 (road vehicles 23.0%; machinery 16.0%; food 12.0%, of which fruits and vegetables 6.3%; chemicals and chemical products 9.7%). *Major export destinations* (2002): France 18.9%; Germany 11.4%; Portugal 9.5%; U.K. 9.5%; Italy 9.3%.

Transport and communications

Transport. Railroads (2001): route length 13,832 km; passenger-km 19,190,000,000; metric ton-km cargo 12,216,000,000. Roads (1999): length 346,548 km (paved 99%). Vehicles (2001): cars 18,151,000; trucks and buses 4,005,000. Air transport (1999): passenger-km 60,696,083,000; metric ton-km cargo 6,406,562,000; airports (1997) with scheduled flights 25.

Communications				units per 1,000
Medium	date	unit	number	persons
Daily newspapers	2000	circulation	4,060,000	100
Radio	2000	receivers	13,500,000	333
Television	2000	receivers	24,000,000	591
Telephones	2001	main lines	18,705,600	460
Cellular telephones	2001	subscribers	33,475,000	823
Personal computers	2002	units	7,972,000	196
Internet	2002	users	7,856,000	193

Education and health

Educational attainment (1997). Percentage of economically active population age 16 and over having: no formal schooling 6.4%[8]; primary 26.6%; secondary 58.9%; higher 8.1%. *Literacy* (2000): 97.6%.

Education (2001–02)	schools	teachers	students	student/ teacher ratio
Primary (age 6–11)	8,547	170,691	2,475,027	14.5
Secondary (age 12–18)[9]	4,319	264,464	3,116,895	11.8
Higher	1,774	98,567	1,508,116	15.3

Health: physicians (2000) 179,033 (1 per 227 persons); hospital beds (1999) 164,097 (1 per 246 persons); infant mortality rate (2001) 4.7.
Food (2000): daily per capita caloric intake 3,352 (vegetable products 73%, animal products 27%); 136% of FAO recommended minimum requirement.

Military

Total active duty personnel (2003): 150,700 (army 63.4%, navy 15.2%, air force 15.1%, other 6.3%). *Military expenditure as percentage of GNP* (1999): 1.3% (world 2.4%); per capita expenditure U.S.$192.

[1]Includes 51 indirectly elected seats. [2]The constitution states that "Castilian is the Spanish official language of the State," but that "all other Spanish languages (including Euskera [Basque], Catalan, and Galician) will also be official in the corresponding Autonomous Communities." [3]The peseta (Pta) was the former monetary unit; on Jan. 1, 2002, Ptas 166.33 = €1. [4]Import taxes and value-added tax on products. [5]Unemployed. [6]Detail does not add to total given because of rounding. [7]Imports are f.o.b. in balance of trade. [8]Includes illiterate. [9]Includes vocational.

Internet resources for further information:
- **Banco de España http://www.bde.es**
- **National Institute of Statistics http://www.ine.es**

Sri Lanka

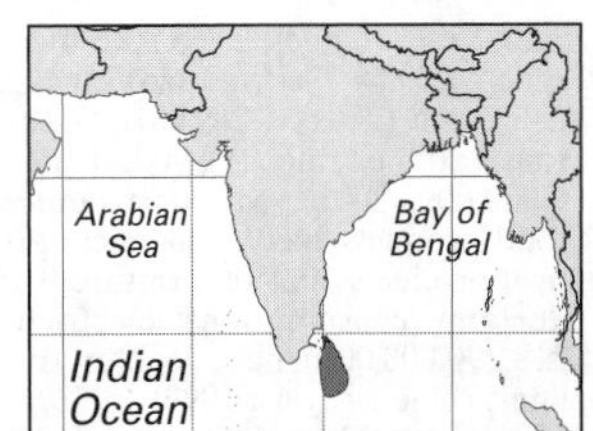

Official name: Śri Lanka Prajatantrika Samajavadi Janarajaya (Sinhala); Ilangai Jananayaka Socialisa Kudiarasu (Tamil) (Democratic Socialist Republic of Sri Lanka).
Form of government: unitary multiparty republic with one legislative house (Parliament [225]).
Head of state and government: President assisted by Prime Minister.
Capitals: Colombo (executive); Sri Jayewardenepura Kotte (Colombo suburb; legislative and judicial).
Official languages: Sinhala; Tamil.
Official religion: none.
Monetary unit: 1 Sri Lanka rupee (SL Rs) = 100 cents; valuation (Sept. 8, 2003) 1 U.S.$ = SL Rs 96.15; 1 £ = SL Rs 152.45.

Area and population

Districts	Capitals	area sq mi	area sq km	population 2001 census[1]
Amparai	Amparai	1,705	4,415	589,344
Anuradhapura	Anuradhapura	2,772	7,179	746,466
Badulla	Badulla	1,104	2,861	774,555
Batticaloa	Batticaloa	1,102	2,854	486,447[2]
Colombo	Colombo	270	699	2,234,289
Galle	Galle	638	1,652	990,539
Gampaha	Gampaha	536	1,387	2,066,096
Hambantota	Hambantota	1,007	2,609	525,370
Jaffna	Jaffna	396	1,025	490,621[2]
Kalutara	Kalutara	617	1,598	1,060,800
Kandy	Kandy	749	1,940	1,272,463
Kegalle	Kegalle	654	1,693	779,774
Kilinochchi	Kilinochchi	494	1,279	127,263[2]
Kurunegala	Kurunegala	1,859	4,816	1,452,369
Mannar	Mannar	771	1,996	151,577[2]
Matale	Matale	770	1,993	442,427
Matara	Matara	495	1,283	761,236
Monaragala	Monaragala	2,177	5,639	396,173
Mullaitivu	Mullaitivu	1,010	2,617	121,667[2]
Nuwara Eliya	Nuwara Eliya	672	1,741	700,083
Polonnaruwa	Polonnaruwa	1,271	3,293	359,197
Puttalam	Puttalam	1,186	3,072	705,342
Ratnapura	Ratnapura	1,264	3,275	1,008,164
Trincomalee	Trincomalee	1,053	2,727	340,158[2]
Vavuniya	Vavuniya	759	1,967	149,835[2]
TOTAL		25,332	65,610	18,732,255

Demography

Population (2003): 19,065,000.
Density (2003): persons per sq mi 752.6, persons per sq km 290.6.
Urban-rural (2002): urban 25.0%; rural 75.0%.
Sex distribution (2001): male 49.47%; female 50.53%.
Age breakdown (2001): under 15, 27.9%; 15–29, 27.1%; 30–44, 22.7%; 45–59, 13.6%; 60–74, 7.0%; 75 and over, 1.7%.
Population projection: (2010) 20,046,000; (2020) 21,121,000.
Ethnic composition (2000): Sinhalese 72.4%; Tamil 17.8%; Sri Lankan Moor 7.4%; other 2.4%.
Religious affiliation (2000): Buddhist 68.4%; Hindu 11.3%; Christian 9.4%; Muslim 9.0%; other 1.9%.
Major cities (2001)[1]: Colombo 642,163; Dehiwala–Mount Lavinia 209,787; Moratuwa 177,190; Negombo 121,933; Sri Jayewardenepura Kotte 115,826.

Vital statistics

Birth rate per 1,000 population (2002): 17.3 (world avg. 21.3).
Death rate per 1,000 population (2002): 6.3 (world avg. 9.1).
Natural increase rate per 1,000 population (2002): 11.0 (world avg. 12.2).
Total fertility rate (avg. births per childbearing woman; 2002): 2.1.
Marriage rate per 1,000 population (1997): 8.9.
Life expectancy at birth (2002): male 70.0 years; female 76.0 years.
Major causes of death per 100,000 population (1996): violence and poisoning 127.5; diseases of the circulatory system 123.8; diseases of the respiratory system 35.1; diseases of the nervous system 32.4; malignant neoplasms (cancers) 17.2.

National economy

Budget (2001). Revenue: SL Rs 231,463,000,000 (sales tax 19.7%, excise taxes 19.4%, income taxes 15.0%, nontax revenue 11.6%). Expenditures: SL Rs 383,686,000,000 (interest payments 24.6%, defense 17.8%, social welfare 13.4%).
Public debt (external, outstanding; 2001): U.S.$7,472,000,000.
Production (metric tons except as noted). Agriculture, forestry, fishing (2002): rice 2,794,000, coconuts 1,900,000, sugarcane 1,050,000, plantains 610,000, tea 310,000, natural rubber 87,000; livestock (number of live animals) 1,565,000 cattle, 661,200 buffalo; roundwood (2001) 6,468,369 cu m; fish catch (2001) 312,676. Mining and quarrying (2001); graphite 6,585; sapphires 453,800 carats; diamonds, n.a. Manufacturing (value added, in U.S.$'000,000; 1995): food, beverages, and tobacco 601; textiles and apparel 391; petrochemicals 116. Energy production (consumption): electricity (kW-hr; 2001) 6,520,000,000 (6,520,000,000); coal (metric tons; 1999) none (negligible); crude petroleum (barrels; 1999) none (13,600,000); petroleum products (metric tons; 1999) 1,694,000 (2,677,000).

Gross national product (2001): U.S.$16,630,000,000 (U.S.$880 per capita).

Structure of gross domestic product and labour force

	2001 in value SL Rs '000,000	2001 % of total value	2000 labour force[3]	2000 % of labour force[3]
Agriculture	215,929	15.5	2,290,000	33.5
Mining	17,922	1.3	77,800	1.1
Manufacturing	261,428	18.7	1,013,200	14.8
Construction	91,720	6.5	320,600	4.7
Public utilities	32,685	2.3	25,000	0.4
Transp. and commun.	153,149	11.0	278,100	4.1
Trade	325,249	23.3	767,700	11.2
Finance	118,492	8.5	122,600	1.8
Pub. admin., defense	120,550	8.6	1,153,700	16.9
Services	33,962	2.4		
Other	26,346[4]	1.9[4]	778,600[5]	11.5[5]
TOTAL	1,397,452	100.0	6,827,300	100.0

Population economically active: total (2001) 6,729,700[3]; activity rate *c.* 40% (participation rates: ages 10 and over, 48.3%; female 33.3%; unemployed 7.8%).

Price and earnings indexes (1995 = 100)

	1996	1997	1998	1999	2000	2001	2002
Consumer price index	115.9	127.0	138.9	145.4	154.4	176.3	193.1
Average wage index[6]	109.3	117.0	132.1	134.3	237.3	141.7	152.8

Household income and expenditure (1992). Average household size (2000) 4.6[3]; income per household SL Rs 116,100 (U.S.$2,600); sources of income: wages 48.5%, property income and self-employment 41.8%, transfers 9.7%; expenditure: food 58.6%, transportation 16.0%, clothing 8.4%.
Tourism (2001): receipts U.S.$211,000,000; expenditures U.S.$245,000,000.

Foreign trade[7]

Balance of trade (current prices)

	1997	1998	1999	2000	2001	2002
SL Rs '000,000	–71,833	–69,740	–96,717	–134,176	–102,591	–134,641
% of total	11.6%	10.1%	12.9%	13.8%	10.6%	13.0%

Imports (2002): SL Rs 584,491,000,000 (textiles [mostly yarns and fabrics] 21.6%; petroleum and natural gas 12.9%; foods 11.4%; machinery and equipment 10.5%). *Major import sources:* India 13.9%; Hong Kong 8.2%; Singapore 7.2%; Japan 5.9%; South Korea 5.0%; Taiwan 4.8%.
Exports (2002): SL Rs 449,850,000,000 (clothing and accessories 51.6%; tea 13.5%; precious and semiprecious stones 5.9%; rubber products 3.9%). *Major export destinations:* U.S. 38.9%; U.K. 13.0%; Belgium-Luxembourg 5.7%; Germany 4.4%; India 3.8%.

Transport and communications

Transport. Railroads (2001): route length 1,449 km; (1998) passenger-km 3,264,000,000; (1998) metric ton-km cargo 132,000,000. Roads (1996): total length 99,200 km (paved 40%). Vehicles (2001): passenger cars 353,701; trucks and buses 244,166. Air transport (2001): passenger-km 4,126,000,000; metric ton-km cargo 224,000,000; airports (2001) 1.

Communications

Medium	date	unit	number	units per 1,000 persons
Daily newspapers	2000	circulation	539,000	29
Radio	2000	receivers	3,870,000	208
Television	2000	receivers	2,060,000	111
Telephones	2002	main lines	883,100	47
Cellular telephones	2002	subscribers	931,600	49
Personal computers	2002	units	250,000	13
Internet	2002	users	200,000	11

Education and health

Educational attainment: n.a. *Literacy* (2000): percentage of population age 15 and over literate 91.6%; males literate 94.4%; females literate 89.0%.

Education (2000–01)

	schools	teachers	students	student/teacher ratio
Primary (age 5–10) Secondary (age 11–17)	10,977	199,948	4,337,161	21.7
Voc., teacher tr.	36	574	11,270	19.6
Higher	12	2,999	48,899	16.3

Health (1999): physicians 6,938 (1 per 2,740 persons); hospital beds (1997) 52,298 (1 per 355 persons); infant mortality rate (2001) 12.2.
Food (2001): daily per capita caloric intake 2,274 (vegetable products 93%, animal products 7%); 102% of FAO recommended minimum.

Military

Total active duty personnel (2002): 157,900 (army 74.7%, navy 13.0%, air force 12.2%). *Military expenditure as percentage of GNP* (1999): 4.7% (world 2.4%); per capita expenditure U.S.$38.

[1]Provisional figures (except for 7 districts experiencing civil war). [2]Registrar-general estimates. [3]Excludes 7 districts experiencing civil war. [4]Import duties. [5]Mainly unemployed. [6]Agricultural minimum rates. [7]Imports c.i.f.; exports f.o.b.

Internet resources for further information:
- **Central Bank of Sri Lanka http://www.centralbanklanka.org**
- **Department of Census and Statistics http://www.statistics.gov.lk**

Sudan, The

Official name: Jumhūrīyat as-Sūdān (Republic of the Sudan).
Form of government: military regime[1] with one legislative body (National Assembly [360[2]]).
Head of state and government: President.
Capitals: Khartoum (executive); Omdurman (legislative).
Official language: Arabic[3].
Official religion: [4].
Monetary unit: 1 Sudanese dinar (Sd)[5]; valuation (Sept. 8, 2003) 1 U.S.$ = Sd 261.00; 1 £ = Sd 413.83.

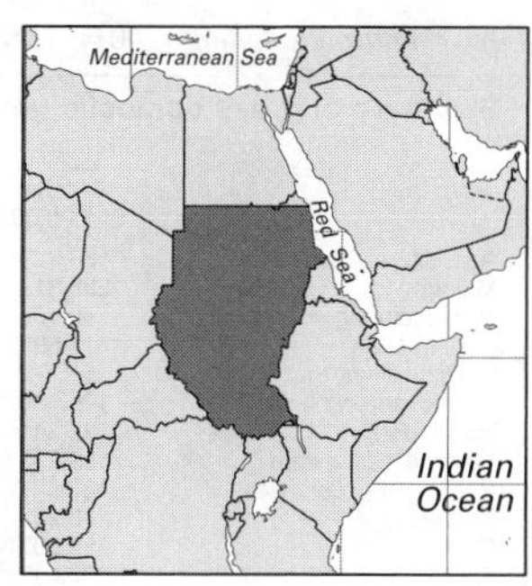

Area and population	area	population		**States**[6]	area	population
		2000				2000
States[6]	sq km	estimate			sq km	estimate
Bahr el-Ghazal[7]	...	2,256,942		Red Sea	...	709,637
Blue Nile	...	633,129		River Nile	...	895,893
Equatoria	...	1,234,486		Sinnar	...	1,132,758
Gedaref	...	1,414,531		Southern Darfur	...	2,708,007
Gezira	...	3,310,928		Southern Kordofan	...	1,066,117
Kassalā	...	1,433,730		Upper Nile	...	1,342,943
Khartoum	...	4,740,290		Western Darfur	...	1,531,682
Northern	...	578,376		Western Kordofan	...	1,078,330
Northern Darfur	...	1,409,894		White Nile	...	1,431,701
Northern Kordofan	...	1,439,930		TOTAL	2,503,890[8]	30,349,304[9, 10]

Demography

Population (2003): 38,114,000.
Density (2003): persons per sq mi 39.4, persons per sq km 15.2.
Urban-rural (2002): urban 37.1%; rural 62.9%.
Sex distribution (2001): male 50.64%; female 49.36%.
Age breakdown (2001): under 15, 44.6%; 15–29, 27.6%; 30–44, 15.6%; 45–59, 8.4%; 60–74, 3.3%; 75 and over, 0.5%.
Population projection: (2010) 45,485,000; (2020) 56,162,000.
Doubling time: 25 years.
Ethnic composition (1983): Sudanese Arab 49.1%; Dinka 11.5%; Nuba 8.1%; Beja 6.4%, Nuer 4.9%; Zande 2.7%; Bari 2.5%; Fur 2.1%; other 12.7%.
Religious affiliation (2000): Sunnī Muslim 70.3%; Christian 16.7%, of which Roman Catholic *c.* 8%, Anglican *c.* 6%; traditional beliefs 11.9%; other 1.1%.
Major cities (1993): Omdurman 1,267,077; Khartoum 924,505; Khartoum North 879,105; Port Sudan 305,385; Kassalā 234,270; Nyala 228,778.

Vital statistics

Birth rate per 1,000 population (2001): 37.9 (world avg. 21.3).
Death rate per 1,000 population (2001): 10.0 (world avg. 9.1).
Natural increase rate per 1,000 population (2001): 27.9 (world avg. 12.2).
Total fertility rate (avg. births per childbearing woman; 2001): 5.3.
Life expectancy at birth (2001): male 55.9 years; female 58.1 years.
Major causes of death per 100,000 population: n.a.

National economy

Budget (2001). Revenue: Sd 365,200,000,000[5] (tax revenue 51.5%, of which custom duties 21.3%, VAT 10.3%; nontax revenue 48.5%). Expenditures: Sd 418,800,000,000[5] (current expenditure 81.9%, of which wages 31.4%; development expenditure 18.1%).
Public debt (external, outstanding; 2001): U.S.$8,489,000,000.
Production (metric tons except as noted). Agriculture, forestry, fishing (2002): sugarcane 5,000,000, sorghum 2,800,000, peanuts (groundnuts) 945,000, millet 618,000, sesame seeds 274,000, wheat 247,000, seed cotton 193,000, dates 177,000, tea 173,000, gum arabic 15,700; livestock (number of live animals) 47,043,000 sheep, 40,000,000 goats, 38,325,000 cattle, 3,203,000 camels; roundwood (2002) 19,241,332 cu m; fish catch (2001) 51,000. Mining and quarrying (2001): salt 120,000; gold 6,800 kg. Manufacturing (2000): raw sugar 689,000[11]; flour 600,000; cement 189,600[11]; vegetable oils 120,000; cattle hides and horsehides 8,500,000 units; shoes 50,000,000 pairs. Energy production (consumption): electricity (kW-hr; 2000) 2,569,200,000 (1,337,000,000); coal, none (none); crude petroleum (barrels; 2001) 145,100,000 ([1999] 4,400,000); petroleum products (metric tons; 2001) 2,674,700 ([2000] 1,753,000); natural gas, none (none).
Gross national product (2001): U.S.$10,700,000,000 (U.S.$340 per capita).

Structure of gross domestic product and labour force

	2001		2000	
	in value Sd '000,000,000	% of total value	labour force[12]	% of labour force[12]
Agriculture	1,543.0	45.6	7,454,000	61.1
Mining	293.2	8.7	}	
Manufacturing	265.8	7.9		
Construction	153.4	4.5		
Public utilities	57.5	1.7		
Transportation and communications }				
Trade, hotels }	864.9	25.6	4,753,000	38.9
Finance }				
Services }				
Pub. admin., defense	202.8	6.0		
Other	—	—	}	
TOTAL	3,380.6	100.0	12,207,000	100.0

Population economically active (2000): total 12,207,000; activity rate of total population 37.8% (participation rates: n.a.; female 29.9%; unemployed, n.a.).

Price and earnings indexes (1995 = 100)							
	1995	1996	1997	1998	1999	2000	2001
Consumer price index	100.0	232.8	341.5	399.9	463.8	488.3	525.5
Earnings index	...	...	...	...	...	...	...

Household income and expenditure. Average household size (2000): 6.1; income per household: n.a.; expenditure: n.a.
Tourism (2001): receipts from visitors U.S.$56,000,000; expenditures by nationals abroad U.S.$74,000,000.
Land use (1994): forested 18.1%; meadows and pastures 46.3%; agricultural and under permanent cultivation 5.5%; desert and other 30.1%.

Foreign trade[13]

Balance of trade (current prices)						
	1996	1997	1998	1999	2000	2001
U.S.$'000,000	–884	–985	–1,329	–635	+254	+113
% of total	41.6%	45.2%	52.7%	28.8%	7.6%	3.4%

Imports (2001): U.S.$1,586,000,000 (machinery and equipment 27.9%; foodstuffs 16.4%, of which wheat and wheat flour 8.7%; transport equipment 12.8%; chemicals and chemical products 7.8%). *Major import sources* (2002): China 19.8%; Saudi Arabia 6.9%; India 5.5%; Germany 5.5%; U.K. 5.4%.
Exports (2001): U.S.$1,699,000,000 (crude petroleum 74.7%; refined petroleum 6.3%; sesame seeds 6.2%; gold 2.6%; cotton 2.6%). *Major export destinations* (2002): China 55.3%; Japan 13.9%; Saudi Arabia 5.4%; South Korea 3.8%; Egypt 3.3%.

Transport and communications

Transport. Railroads: route length (2000) 5,901 km; (2001) passenger-km 78,000,000; metric ton-km cargo 1,250,000,000. Roads (1999): total length 11,900 km (paved 36%). Vehicles (1996): passenger cars 285,000; trucks and buses 53,000. Air transport (2001): passenger-km 803,000,000; metric ton-km cargo 54,542,000; airports (1997) with scheduled flights 3.

Communications				units
Medium	date	unit	number	per 1,000 persons
Daily newspapers	2000	circulation	912,000	26
Radio	2000	receivers	16,300,000	464
Television	2000	receivers	9,580,000	273
Telephones	2002	main lines	671,800	21
Cellular telephones	2002	subscribers	190,800	5.9
Personal computers	2002	units	200,000	6.1
Internet	2002	users	84,000	2.6

Education and health

Educational attainment: n.a. *Literacy* (2000): total population age 15 and over literate 55.8%; males 69.5%; females 46.3%.

Education (1999–2000)	schools	teachers	students	student/ teacher ratio
Primary (age 7–12)	11,923	117,151	3,137,494	26.8
Secondary (age 13–18)	1,694	21,114	401,424	19.0
Vocational[14]	...	761	26,421	34.7
Higher[15]	19	1,417[14]	200,538	...

Health: physicians (1997) 3,423 (1 per 9,395 persons); hospital beds (1997) 22,656 (1 per 1,420 persons); infant mortality rate (2001) 68.7.
Food (2001): daily per capita caloric intake 2,288 (vegetable products 80%, animal products 20%); 97% of FAO recommended minimum.

Military

Total active duty personnel (2003): 104,500 (army 95.7%, navy 1.4%, air force 2.9%); main opposition force (Sudanese People's Liberation Army) roughly 25,000. *Military expenditure as percentage of GNP* (1999): 4.8% (world 2.4%); per capita expenditure U.S.$33.

[1]A state of emergency introduced Dec. 12, 1999, was still in effect in November 2003. [2]Includes 90 indirectly elected or appointed seats. [3]English has been designated the "principal" language in southern Sudan. [4]Islamic law and custom are sources of national law per 1998 constitution. [5]The Sudanese dinar (Sd), introduced May 1992 at a value equal to 10 Sudanese pounds (LSd), officially replaced the Sudanese pound on March 1, 1999. [6]Local administrative reorganization into 26 new states was announced in February 1994 and confirmed in June 1998. Names listed below are English-language variants; six southern states are excluded. [7]Includes Western Bahr el-Ghazal and Northern Bahr el-Ghazal. [8]Including *c.* 130,000 sq km of inland water area. [9]Summary total; actual total per official source is 31,081,000. [10]Population estimates are unavailable for six states in southern Sudan experiencing civil war since 1983. [11]2001. [12]FAO estimate. [13]Imports c.i.f.; exports f.o.b. [14]1996–97. [15]Universities only.

Internet resources for further information:
- **Bank of Sudan**
  http://www.bankofsudan.org

Suriname

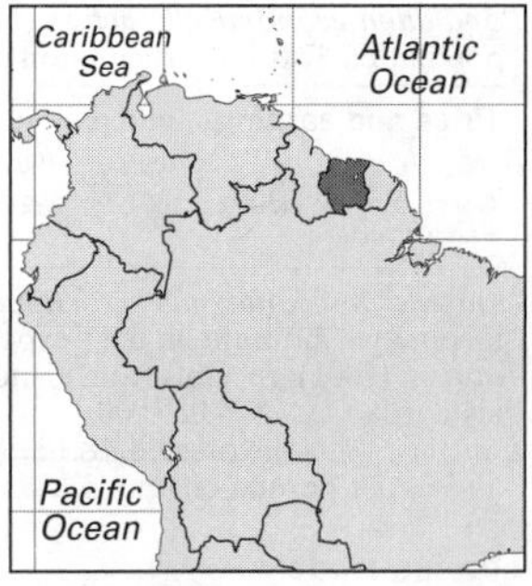

Official name: Republiek Suriname (Republic of Suriname).
Form of government: multiparty republic with one legislative house (National Assembly [51]).
Head of state and government: President.
Capital: Paramaribo.
Official language: Dutch.
Official religion: none.
Monetary unit: 1 Suriname guilder (Sf) = 100 cents; valuation (Sept. 8, 2003) 1 U.S.$ = Sf 2,515; 1 £ = Sf 3,988[1].

Area and population

Districts	Capitals	area sq mi	area sq km	population 1996 estimate
Brokopondo	Brokopondo	2,843	7,364	7,200
Commewijne	Nieuw Amsterdam	908	2,353	20,900
Coronie	Totness	1,507	3,902	2,900
Marowijne	Albina	1,786	4,627	12,600
Nickerie	Nieuw Nickerie	2,067	5,353	33,600
Para	Onverwacht	2,082	5,393	14,400
Saramacca	Groningen	1,404	3,636	13,000
Sipaliwini	2	50,412	130,566	23,500
Wanica	Lelydorp	171	443	72,400
Town district				
Paramaribo	Paramaribo	71	183	222,800
TOTAL		63,251[3]	163,820[3]	423,400[4]

Demography

Population (2003): 435,000.
Density (2003): persons per sq mi 6.9, persons per sq km 2.7.
Urban-rural (2001): urban 74.8%; rural 25.2%.
Sex distribution (2000): male 50.77%; female 49.23%.
Age breakdown (2000): under 15, 32.1%; 15–29, 27.2%; 30–44, 22.7%; 45–59, 9.9%; 60–74, 6.4%; 75 and over, 1.7%.
Population projection: (2010) 441,000; (2020) 439,000.
Doubling time: 52 years.
Ethnic composition (1999): Indo-Pakistani 37.0%; Suriname Creole 31.0%; Javanese 15.0%; Bush Negro 10.0%; Amerindian 2.5%; Chinese 2.0%; white 1.0%; other 1.5%.
Religious affiliation (2000): Christian 50.4%, of which Roman Catholic 22.3%, Protestant (mostly Moravian) 17.1%, unaffiliated/other Christian 11.0%; Hindu 17.8%; Muslim 13.9%; nonreligious 4.8%; Spiritists (including followers of Voodoo) 3.5%; traditional beliefs 1.9%; other 7.7%.
Major cities (1996/1997): Paramaribo 222,800 (urban agglomeration 289,000); Lelydorp 15,600; Nieuw Nickerie 11,100; Mungo (Moengo) 6,800; Meerzorg 6,600.

Vital statistics

Birth rate per 1,000 population (2002): 20.0 (world avg. 21.3).
Death rate per 1,000 population (2002): 6.7 (world avg. 9.1).
Natural increase rate per 1,000 population (2002): 13.3 (world avg. 12.2).
Total fertility rate (avg. births per childbearing woman; 2002): 2.4.
Marriage rate per 1,000 population (1991): 4.9.
Divorce rate per 1,000 population (1991): 2.5.
Life expectancy at birth (2002): male 66.8 years; female 72.0 years.
Major causes of death per 100,000 population (1992): noncommunicable diseases 769.0; external and other causes 608.1; communicable and perinatal diseases 232.8; ill-defined diseases 279.0.

National economy

Budget (1998). Revenue: Sf 137,200,000,000 (indirect taxes 40.4%; direct taxes 36.2%; bauxite levy 10.9%; grants 12.5%). Expenditures: Sf 188,000,000,000 (current expenditures 90.2%, of which wages and salaries 39.1%, transfers 11.7%, debt service 1.3%; capital expenditures 9.8%).
Production (metric tons except as noted). Agriculture, forestry, fishing (2002): rice 192,000, sugarcane 120,000, bananas 43,000, plantains 11,000, oranges 10,300, coconuts 8,000, cassava 5,235; livestock (number of live animals) 136,000 cattle, 24,000 pigs, 2,200,000 chickens; roundwood (2002) 199,545 cu m; fish catch (2001) 18,915, of which shrimp 7,390. Mining and quarrying (2001): bauxite 4,512,000; alumina 1,900,000; gold 300 kg[5]. Manufacturing (value of production at factor cost in Sf; 1993): food products 992,000,000; beverages 558,000,000; tobacco 369,000,000; chemical products 291,000,000; pottery and earthenware 258,000,000; wood products 180,000,000. Energy production (consumption): electricity (kW-hr; 1999) 1,640,000,000 (1,640,000,000); hard coal (metric tons) none (none); crude petroleum (barrels; 2001) 5,000,000 ([1999] 1,200,000); petroleum products (metric tons; 1999) none[6] (490,000); natural gas, none (none).
Population economically active (1999): total 84,646[7]; activity rate of total population 19.8%[7] (participation rates[8]: [1992] ages 15–64, 56.0%; female 34.4%; unemployed 14.0%).

Price and earnings indexes (1995 = 100)

	1996	1997	1998	1999	2000	2001	2002
Consumer price index	99.3	106.4	126.6	251.8	401.2	556.3	616.6[9]
Earnings index	…	…	…	…	…	…	…

Gross national product (2001): U.S.$800,000,000 (U.S.$1,810 per capita).

Structure of gross domestic product and labour force

	2001 in value Sf '000,000	2001 % of total value	1999 labour force[7]	1999 % of labour force[7]
Agriculture, forestry	165,227	10.3	4,456	5.3
Mining	298,318	18.7	1,127	2.0
Manufacturing	89,102	5.6	2,863	3.4
Construction	51,598	3.2	4,953	5.9
Public utilities	54,273	3.4	1,000	1.2
Transp. and commun.	124,630	7.8	5,817	6.9
Trade, hotels	192,341	12.0	17,262	20.4
Finance, real estate	199,232	12.5	4,544	5.4
Pub. admin., defense	123,529	7.7	27,305	32.3
Services	116,202	7.3		
Other	182,897[10]	11.5[10]	14,720[11]	17.4[11]
TOTAL	1,597,347[4]	100.0	84,646[4]	100.0[4]

Household income and expenditure. Average household size (1998) 4.8; income per household: n.a.; sources of income: n.a.; expenditure: n.a.
Public debt (external, outstanding; 1996): U.S.$216,500,000.
Tourism (2001): receipts from visitors U.S.$14,000,000; expenditures by nationals abroad U.S.$29,000,000.
Land use (1994): forested 96.2%; meadows and pastures 0.1%; agricultural and under permanent cultivation 0.4%; other 3.3%.

Foreign trade[12]

Balance of trade (current prices)

	1996	1997	1998	1999	2000
U.S.$'000,000	–29.2	–83.8	–60.3	…	–12.5
% of total	3.3%	7.4%	5.9%	…	1.2%

Imports (2000): U.S.$526,500,000 (nonelectrical machinery 22.5%, food products 13.4%, road vehicles 13.2%, chemicals and chemical products 10.2%, refined petroleum 5.8%). *Major import sources* (2001): U.S. *c.* 34%; The Netherlands *c.* 17%; Trinidad and Tobago *c.* 13%; Netherlands Antilles *c.* 8%; Japan *c.* 5%.
Exports (2000): U.S.$514,000,000 (alumina 62.1%, gold 11.4%, crustaceans and mollusks 7.0%, crude petroleum 4.3%, refined petroleum 2.3%, rice 2.2%). *Major export destinations* (2001): U.S. *c.* 26%; Norway *c.* 16%; France *c.* 10%; The Netherlands *c.* 9%; Canada *c.* 7%.

Transport and communications

Transport. Railroads (1997)[13]: length 187 mi, 301 km; passengers, not applicable; cargo, n.a. Roads (1996): total length 2,815 mi, 4,530 km (paved 26%). Vehicles (2000): passenger cars 61,365; trucks and buses 23,220. Air transport (1998): passenger-mi 666,109,000, passenger-km 1,072,000,000; short ton-mi cargo 86,988,000, metric ton-km cargo 127,000,000; airports with scheduled flights 1.

Communications

Medium	date	unit	number	units per 1,000 persons
Daily newspapers	1996	circulation	50,000	122
Radio	1997	receivers	300,000	728
Television	2000	receivers	109,000	253
Telephones	2001	main lines	77,400	176
Cellular telephones	2001	subscribers	87,000	197
Personal computers	2001	units	20,000	45
Internet	2001	users	14,500	33

Education and health

Educational attainment: n.a. *Literacy* (2001): total population age 15 and over literate 92.2%; males literate 93.6%; females literate 90.7%.

Education (1995–96)

	schools	teachers	students	student/ teacher ratio
Primary (age 6–11)	304	3,611	75,585	20.9
Secondary (age 12–18)	104	2,286	31,918	13.9
Teacher training	1	…	1,462	…
Higher[14]	1	286	3,081	10.8

Health: physicians (1998) 166 (1 per 2,518 persons); hospital beds (1998) 1,449 (1 per 288 persons); infant mortality rate per 1,000 live births (2002) 25.4.
Food (2001): daily per capita caloric intake 2,643 (vegetable products 86%, animal products 14%); 117% of FAO recommended minimum requirement.

Military

Total active duty personnel (2002): 1,840[15] (army 76.1%, navy 13.0%, air force 10.9%). *Military expenditure as percentage of GNP* (1999): 1.8% (world 2.4%); per capita expenditure U.S.$33.

[1]Suriname guilder (Sf) to be replaced by Suriname dollar (S$) in January 2004; Sf 1,000 will equal 1 S$. [2]No capital; administered from Paramaribo. [3]Area excludes 6,809 sq mi (17,635 sq km) of territory disputed with Guyana. [4]Detail does not add to total given because of rounding. [5]Recorded production; unrecorded production may be as high as 30,000 kg. [6]Production of petroleum products began in 2000; data not available. [7]Based on sample survey. [8]Districts of Wanica and Paramaribo only. [9]July. [10]Taxes on products less imputed bank service charges. [11]Includes 11,812 unemployed. [12]Imports c.i.f.; exports f.o.b. [13]There are no public railways operating in Suriname. [14]Anton de Kom University of Suriname; 2001–02. [15]All services are part of the army.

Internet resources for further information:
- **Suriname http://www.sesrtcic.org/statistics/coustats.shtml**
- **Caricom Statistics http://www.caricom.org/CARIStats/handbookpub.html**

Swaziland

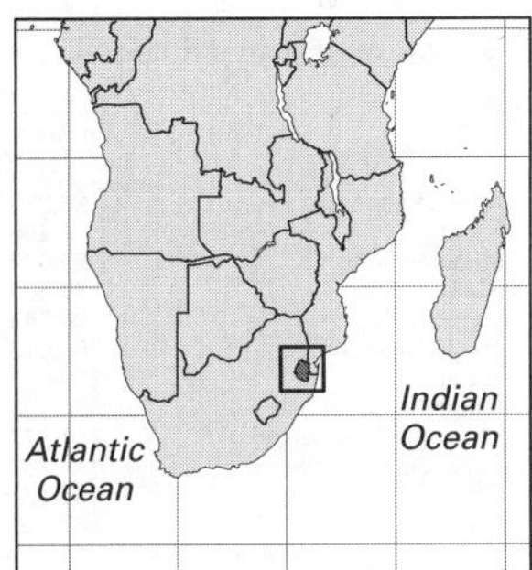

Official name: Umbuso weSwatini (Swazi); Kingdom of Swaziland (English).
Form of government: monarchy[1] with two legislative houses (Senate [30[2]]; House of Assembly [65[3]]).
Head of state and government: King, assisted by Prime Minister.
Capitals: Mbabane (administrative and judicial); Lozitha and Ludzidzini (royal); Lobamba (legislative).
Official languages: Swati (Swazi); English.
Official religion: none.
Monetary unit: 1 lilangeni[4] (plural emalangeni [E]) = 100 cents; valuation (Sept. 8, 2003) 1 U.S.$ = E 7.42; 1 £ = E 11.77.

Area and population

		area		population
				1997
Districts	**Capitals**	sq mi	sq km	census
Hhohho	Mbabane	1,378	3,569	269,826
Lubombo	Siteki	2,296	5,947	201,696
Manzini	Manzini	1,571	4,068	292,100
Shiselweni	Nhlangano	1,459	3,780	217,100
TOTAL		6,704	17,364	980,722[5]

Demography

Population (2003): 1,077,000.
Density (2002): persons per sq mi 160.7; persons per sq km 62.0.
Urban-rural (2001): urban 26.7%; rural 73.3%.
Sex distribution (1997): male 48.28%; female 51.72%.
Age breakdown (1997): under 15, 42.5%; 15–29, 29.2%; 30–44, 15.5%; 45–59, 7.8%; 60–74, 3.3%; 75 and over, 1.2%; unknown 0.5%.
Population projection: (2010) 1,084,000; (2020) 1,062,000.
Doubling time: 64 years.
Ethnic composition (2000): Swazi 82.3%; Zulu 9.6%; Tsonga 2.3%; Afrikaner 1.4%; mixed (black-white) 1.0%; other 3.4%.
Religious affiliation (2000): Christian 67.5%, of which African indigenous 45.6%, Protestant 15.2%, Roman Catholic 5.4%; traditional beliefs 12.2%; other (mostly unaffiliated Christian) 20.3%.
Major cities (1997): Mbabane 57,992; Manzini 25,571 (urban agglomeration 78,734); Big Bend 9,374; Mhlume 7,661; Malkerns 7,400.

Vital statistics

Birth rate per 1,000 population (2002): 30.2 (world avg. 21.3).
Death rate per 1,000 population (2002): 19.3 (world avg. 9.1).
Natural increase rate per 1,000 population (2002): 10.9 (world avg. 12.2).
Total fertility rate (avg. births per childbearing woman; 2002): 4.0.
Life expectancy at birth (2002): male 42.9 years; female 39.9 years.
Major causes of death (1992)[6]: accidents and injuries 15.8%; infectious intestinal diseases 13.3%; tuberculosis 10.3%; malnutrition 6.2%; respiratory diseases 5.3%; circulatory diseases 5.0%; digestive diseases 4.6%.

National economy

Budget (2001–02). Revenue: E 3,094,000,000 (receipts from Customs Union of Southern Africa 48.6%; tax on income and profits 23.4%; sales tax 13.2%; foreign-aid grants 3.9%). Expenditures: E 3,409,000,000 (current expenditure 74.4%; development expenditure 25.4%; net lending 0.2%).
Gross national product (2001): U.S.$1,400,000,000 (U.S.$1,300 per capita).

Structure of gross domestic product and labour force

	2001			
	in value E '000	% of total value	labour force[7]	% of labour force[7]
Agriculture	1,055,100	9.6	195,098[8]	49.8[8]
Mining	24,900	0.2	620	0.1
Manufacturing	2,757,100	25.1	19,898	5.1
Construction	452,000	4.1	5,779	1.5
Public utilities	111,700	1.0	1,409	0.3
Transp. and commun.	391,300	3.6	12,509	3.2
Trade	689,200	6.3		
Finance	326,200	3.0	7,492	1.9
Pub. admin., defense	1,367,900	12.5	25,323	6.5
Services	82,600	0.8		
Other	3,713,000[9]	33.8[9]	123,872[10]	31.6[10]
TOTAL	10,971,000	100.0	392,000	100.0

Population economically active (2001): total 392,000; activity rate of total population 39.3% (participation rates: ages 15 and over, n.a.; female n.a.; unemployed 31.6%).

Price and earnings indexes (1995 = 100)

	1996	1997	1998	1999	2000	2001	2002
Consumer price index	106.4	114.0	123.3	130.8	146.7	155.4	174.1
Weekly earnings index[11]	100.0	95.7	95.7	98.3	...	...	...

Public debt (external, outstanding; 2001): U.S.$235,500,000.
Production (metric tons except as noted). Agriculture, forestry, fishing (2002): sugarcane 4,000,000, corn (maize) 85,000, grapefruit and pomelo 37,000, oranges 36,000, seed cotton 22,500, pineapples 19,700; livestock (number of live animals) 615,000 cattle, 422,000 goats; roundwood (2002) 890,000 cu m; fish catch (2000) 139. Mining and quarrying (2001): stone 350,000 cu m. Manufacturing (value added in U.S.$'000; 1994): food and beverages 244,000, of which beverage processing 153,000; paper and paper products 35,000; textiles 19,000; printing and publishing products 18,000; clothing 7,000; metal and metal products 7,000. Energy production (consumption): electricity (kW-hr; 2000) 265,000,000 (702,000,000); coal (metric tons; 2001) 380,000 (n.a.); crude petroleum, n.a. (n.a.).
Household income and expenditure. Average household size (1986) 5.7; annual income per household (1985) E 332 (U.S.$151); sources of income (1985): wages and salaries 44.4%, self-employment 22.2%, transfers 12.2%, other 21.2%; expenditure (1985): food and beverages 33.5%, rent and fuel 13.4%, household durable goods 12.8%, transportation and communications 8.8%, clothing and footwear 6.0%, recreation 3.3%.
Tourism (2001): receipts U.S.$28,000,000; expenditures U.S.$44,000,000.

Foreign trade[12]

Balance of trade (current prices)

	1996	1997	1998	1999	2000	2001
U.S.$'000,000	–204	–104	–106	–131	–136	–73
% of total	10.7%	5.1%	5.2%	6.5%	7.0%	4.3%

Imports (2001): U.S.$832,000,000 (food and live animals 15.6%; machinery and apparatus 13.6%; chemicals and chemical products 13.2%; road vehicles 9.5%; refined petroleum 9.2%). *Major import sources:* South Africa 94.5%; Hong Kong 1.0%; Japan 0.9%.
Exports (2001): U.S.$678,000,000 (soft drink [including sugar and fruit juice] concentrates *c.* 38%; sugar *c.* 14%; apparel and clothing accessories *c.* 12%; wood pulp *c.* 9%). *Major export destinations:* South Africa 78.0%; Mozambique 4.6%; U.S. 4.0%.

Transport and communications

Transport. Railroads (2001): route length 187 mi, 301 km; passenger-km, n.a.[13]; metric ton-km cargo 700,000,000. Roads (1996): total length 2,367 mi, 3,810 km (paved 29%). Vehicles (1998): passenger cars 34,064; trucks and buses 35,030. Air transport: (1998) passenger-mi 26,718,910, passenger-km 43,000,000; (1995) short ton-mi cargo 87,000, metric ton-km cargo 127,000; airports (1997) with scheduled flights 1.

Communications

Medium	date	unit	number	units per 1,000 persons
Daily newspapers	2000	circulation	27,100	26
Radio	2000	receivers	169,000	162
Television	2000	receivers	124,000	110
Telephones	2002	main lines	35,100	34
Cellular telephones	2002	subscribers	63,000	61
Personal computers	2002	units	25,000	24
Internet	2002	users	20,000	19

Education and health

Educational attainment (1986). Percentage of population age 25 and over having: no formal schooling 42.1%; some primary education 23.9%; complete primary 10.5%; some secondary 19.2%; complete secondary and higher 4.3%.
Literacy (2000): total population age 15 and over literate 79.6%; males literate 80.8%; females literate 78.6%.

Education (2001)

	schools	teachers	students	student/ teacher ratio
Primary (age 6–13)	541	6,594	212,064	32.2
Secondary (age 14–18)	182	3,647	61,335	16.8
Voc., teacher tr.	5	...	1,822	...
Higher	1	...	3,692	...

Health: physicians (1996) 148 (1 per 6,663 persons); hospital beds (2000) 1,570[14] (1 per 665 persons); infant mortality rate per 1,000 live births (2002) 66.5.
Food (2001): daily per capita caloric intake 2,593 (vegetable products 85%, animal products 15%); 112% of FAO recommended minimum requirement.

Military

Total active duty personnel: n.a. *Military expenditure as percentage of GNP* (1999): 1.5% (world 2.4%); per capita expenditure U.S.$20.

[1]Effectiveness of constitution accepted by the King in November 2003 was unclear in December 2003. [2]Includes 20 nonelective seats. [3]Includes 10 nonelective seats. [4]The lilangeni is at par with the South African rand. [5]Final results, includes 51,005 residents abroad. [6]Percentage of deaths of known cause at government, mission, and private hospitals. [7]Formally employed only (except for Agriculture and Other). [8]Includes informally employed (mostly in Agriculture). [9]Includes indirect taxes less imputed bank service charges and subsidies. [10]Unemployed. [11]Manufacturing sector only. [12]Imports f.o.b. in balance of trade and c.i.f. in commodities and trading partners. [13]Scheduled passenger train service was terminated in January 2001. [14]Excludes National Psychiatric Hospital.

Internet resources for further information:

- **Central Bank of Swaziland**
  http://www.centralbank.sz
- **Swaziland Government**
  http://www.gov.sz

Sweden

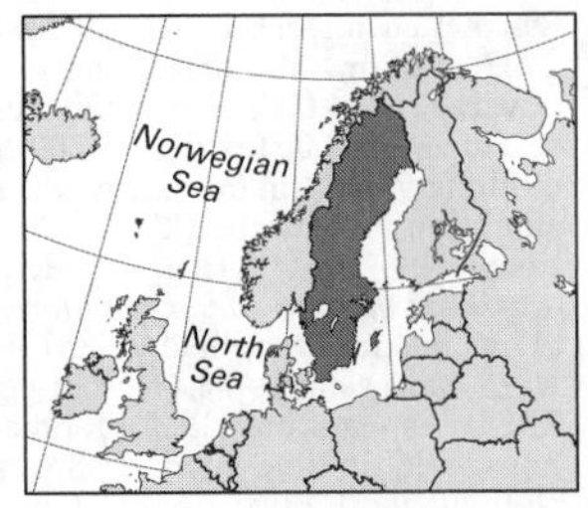

Official name: Konungariket Sverige (Kingdom of Sweden).
Form of government: constitutional monarchy and parliamentary state with one legislative house (Parliament [349]).
Chief of state: King.
Head of government: Prime Minister.
Capital: Stockholm.
Official language: Swedish.
Official religion: none[1].
Monetary unit: 1 Swedish krona (SKr) = 100 ore; valuation (Sept. 8, 2003) 1 U.S.$ = SKr 8.26; 1 £ = SKr 13.10.

Area and population

	area	population		area	population
		2002[2]			2002[2]
Counties	sq km	estimate	Counties	sq km	estimate
Blekinge	2,941	150,036	Skåne	11,027	1,143,513
Dalarna	28,193	276,765	Södermanland	6,062	258,389
Gävleborg	18,192	277,171	Stockholm	6,490	1,849,206
Gotland	3,140	57,458	Uppsala	6,989	298,556
Halland	5,454	278,236	Värmland	17,586	273,716
Jämtland	49,443	127,953	Västerbotten	55,401	254,936
Jönköping	10,475	327,917	Västernorrland	21,678	244,734
Kalmar	11,171	234,776	Västmanland	6,302	258,855
Kronoberg	8,458	176,955	Västra Götaland	23,942	1,507,182
Norrbotten	98,911	253,945	TOTAL LAND AREA	410,934	
Örebro	8,517	273,419	INLAND WATER	39,030	
Östergötland	10,562	413,401	TOTAL	449,964	8,937,119

Demography

Population (2003): 8,958,000.
Density (2003)[3]: persons per sq mi 56.5, persons per sq km 21.8.
Urban-rural (2001[4]): urban 81.2%; rural 18.8%.
Sex distribution (2002[4]): male 49.48%; female 50.52%.
Age breakdown (2002[4]): under 15, 18.2%; 15–29, 18.1%; 30–44, 20.8%; 45–59, 20.6%; 60–74, 13.4%; 75 and over, 8.9%.
Population projection: (2010) 9,245,000; (2020) 9,696,000.
Ethnic composition (2002[4])[5]: Swedish 88.5%; other European 6.9%, of which Finnish 2.2%, Serb/Montenegrin 0.8%, Bosniac 0.6%; Asian 3.0%, of which Iranian 0.6%; African 0.6%; other 1.0%.
Religious affiliation (1999): Church of Sweden 86.5% (about 30% nonpracticing); Muslim 2.3%; Roman Catholic 1.8%; Pentecostal 1.1%; other 8.3%.
Major cities (2002[4]): Stockholm 754,948; Göteborg 471,267; Malmö 262,397; Uppsala 191,110; Linköping 134,039; Västerås 127,799.

Vital statistics

Birth rate per 1,000 population (2001): 10.3 (world avg. 21.3); legitimate 44.5%; illegitimate 55.5%.
Death rate per 1,000 population (2001): 10.3 (world avg. 9.1).
Natural increase rate per 1,000 population (2001): 0.0 (world avg. 12.2).
Total fertility rate (avg. births per childbearing woman; 2001): 1.6.
Marriage rate per 1,000 population (2001): 4.0.
Divorce rate per 1,000 population (2001): 2.4.
Life expectancy at birth (2001): male 77.1 years; female 81.9 years.
Major causes of death per 100,000 population (1999): heart disease 503.0; malignant neoplasms (cancers) 238.3; cerebrovascular disease 116.4.

National economy

Budget (2001). Revenue: SKr 755,126,000,000 (value-added and excise taxes 36.0%, social security 31.6%, income and capital gains taxes 17.9%, property taxes 5.3%). Expenditures: SKr 716,379,000,000 (health and social affairs 30.6%, debt service 11.3%, defense 6.3%, education 5.7%).
Public debt (2000): U.S.$61,046,000,000.
Production (metric tons except as noted). Agriculture, forestry, fishing (2002): sugar beets 2,800,000, wheat 2,117,000, barley 1,778,500, oats 1,186,000, potatoes 907,000, rapeseed 159,900; livestock (number of live animals) 1,882,000 pigs, 1,637,000 cattle, 427,000 sheep; roundwood (2002) 67,500,000 cu m; fish catch (2001) 305,700. Mining and quarrying (2001): iron ore 19,486,000; zinc (metal content) 156,300; copper (metal content) 74,300; silver (metal content) 306,000 kg. Manufacturing (value added, in U.S.$'000,000; 1999): telecommunications equipment, electronics 9,200; nonelectrical machinery and apparatus 6,100; road vehicles 6,000; paper and paper products 5,950; fabricated metals 4,050; printing and publishing 3,500; food products 3,450. Energy production (consumption): electricity (kW-hr; 2002) 143,136,000,000 ([2000] 160,203,000,000); coal (metric tons; 1999) none (3,011,000); crude petroleum (barrels; 1999) none (143,400,000); petroleum products (metric tons; 1999) 17,768,000 (12,921,000); natural gas (cu m; 1999) none (850,900,000).
Household income and expenditure. Average household size (2000) 2.2; average annual disposable income per household (2000) SKr 239,000 (U.S.$26,091); sources of income (1996): wages and salaries 59.2%, transfer payments 26.1%, other 14.7%; expenditure (1996): housing 27.6%, transportation and communications 17.1%, food and beverages 16.5%, recreation 9.1%, energy 5.8%.
Tourism (2001): receipts U.S.$4,162,000,000; expenditures U.S.$6,803,000,000.
Gross national product (at current market prices; 2001): U.S.$225,900,000,000 (U.S.$25,400 per capita).

Structure of gross domestic product and labour force

	2001			
	in value SKr '000,000	% of total value	labour force	% of labour force
Agriculture	33,236	1.5	96,000	2.1
Mining	5,266	0.2		
Manufacturing	395,099	18.2	777,000	17.6
Public utilities	44,580	2.1		
Construction	84,349	3.9	232,000	5.3
Transp. and commun.	160,013	7.4	804,000	18.2
Trade	239,003	11.0		
Finance, real estate	494,130	22.8	601,000	13.6
Pub. admin., defense	411,577	19.0	232,000	5.3
Services	114,769	5.3	1,491,000	33.8
Other	185,174[6]	8.5[6]	181,000[7]	4.1[7]
TOTAL	2,167,196	100.0[8]	4,414,000	100.0

Population economically active (2001): total 4,414,000; activity rate of total population 49.5% (participation rates: ages 16–64 [2000] 77.9%; female 47.8%; unemployed 4.0%).

Price and earnings indexes (1995 = 100)

	1996	1997	1998	1999	2000	2001	2002
Consumer price index	100.5	101.0	100.9	101.3	102.3	104.8	107.1
Hourly earnings index	106.6	111.3	115.3	117.4	121.4	125.0	129.2

Land use (1994): forest 68.0%; pasture 1.4%; agriculture 6.8%; other 23.8%.

Foreign trade[9]

Balance of trade (current prices)

	1997	1998	1999	2000	2001	2002
SKr '000,000	+131,400	+130,200	+133,000	+129,700	+127,300	+146,600
% of total	11.6%	10.7%	10.5%	16.3%	9.8%	10.3%

Imports (2001): SKr 656,200,000,000 (nonelectrical machinery and apparatus 16.6%; electrical machinery and apparatus 14.0%; chemicals and chemical products 10.8%; road vehicles 9.3%; crude and refined petroleum 7.8%). *Major import sources* (2002): Germany 18.5%; Denmark 8.8%; U.K. 8.6%; Norway 8.2%; The Netherlands 6.7%.
Exports (2001): SKr 783,500,000,000 (nonelectrical machinery and apparatus 16.9%; electrical machinery and apparatus 15.2%, of which telecommunications equipment, electronics 9.3%; road vehicles 12.1%; paper and paper products 8.5%; medicines and pharmaceuticals 5.5%; iron and steel 5.0%). *Major export destinations* (2002): U.S. 11.6%; Germany 10.1%; Norway 9.0%; U.K. 8.2%; Denmark 5.9%.

Transport and communications

Transport. Railroads (2001): length 6,994 mi, 11,255 km; (2000) passenger-km 8,251,000,000; metric ton-km cargo 20,088,000,000. Roads (2002[4]): total length 262,200 mi, 422,000 km (public 50.2%). Vehicles (2001[4]): passenger cars 4,019,000; trucks and buses 410,000. Air transport (2002)[10]: passenger-km 10,896,000; metric ton-km cargo 266,676,000; airports (2001) 49.

Communications

Medium	date	unit	number	units per 1,000 persons
Daily newspapers	2000	circulation	3,830,000	432
Radio	2000	receivers	8,270,000	932
Television	2000	receivers	5,090,000	574
Telephones	2002	main lines	6,441,000	720
Cellular telephones	2002	subscribers	7,915,000	885
Personal computers	2001	units	4,600,000	517
Internet	2002	users	5,125,000	573

Education and health

Educational attainment (2002[4]). Percentage of population age 16–74 having: lower secondary education 27%; incomplete or complete upper secondary education 45%; up to 3 years postsecondary 12%; 3 years or more postsecondary 14%; unknown 2%. *Literacy* (2002): virtually 100%.

Education (1999–2000)

	schools	teachers	students	student/ teacher ratio
Primary (age 7–12)	5,048	100,827	1,034,881	10.3
Secondary (age 13–18)		30,295	312,936	10.3
Higher	64	...	372,108	...

Health (2001): physicians 25,200 (1 per 354 persons); hospital beds 29,122 (1 per 306 persons); infant mortality rate per 1,000 live births (2001) 3.7.
Food (2001): daily per capita caloric intake 3,164 (vegetable 70%, animal 30%); 118% of FAO recommended minimum requirement.

Military

Total active duty personnel (2002): 33,900 (army 56.3%, navy 20.9%, air force 22.7%). *Military expenditure as percentage of GNP* (1999): 2.3% (world 2.4%); per capita expenditure U.S.$601.

[1]As of Jan. 1, 2000, the Church of Sweden (Lutheran Church) ceased being the official religion. [2]September 30. [3]Density based on land area only. [4]January 1. [5]By place of birth. [6]Taxes less subsidies and imputed bank service charges. [7]Includes 175,000 unemployed. [8]Detail does not add to total given because of rounding. [9]Imports c.i.f.; exports f.o.b. [10]Includes SAS international and domestic traffic applicable to Sweden.

Internet resources for further information:
- **Statistics Sweden http://www.scb.se/indexeng.asp**

Switzerland

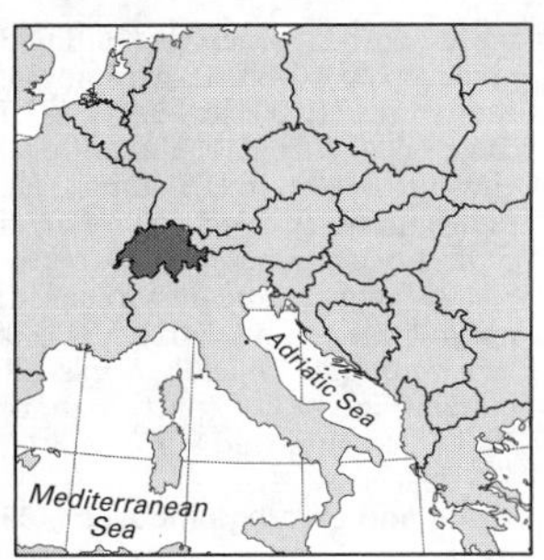

Official name: Confédération Suisse (French); Schweizerische Eidgenossenschaft (German); Confederazione Svizzera (Italian) (Swiss Confederation)[1].
Form of government: federal state with two legislative houses (Council of States [46]; National Council [200]).
Head of state and government: President of the Federal Council.
Capitals: Bern (administrative); Lausanne (judicial).
Official languages: French; German; Italian; Romansh (locally).
Official religion: none.
Monetary unit: 1 Swiss Franc (Sw F) = 100 centimes; valuation (Sept. 8, 2003) 1 U.S.$ = Sw F 1.39; 1 £ = Sw F 2.21.

Area and population

Cantons	Capitals	area sq mi	area sq km	population 2000 census
Aargau	Aarau	542	1,404	547,493
Appenzell Ausser-Rhoden[2]	Herisau	94	243	53,504
Appenzell Inner-Rhoden[2]	Appenzell	66	172	14,618
Basel-Landschaft[2]	Liestal	200	518	259,374
Basel-Stadt[2]	Basel	14	37	188,079
Bern	Bern	2,301	5,959	957,197
Fribourg	Fribourg	645	1,671	241,706
Genève	Geneva	109	282	413,673
Glarus	Glarus	264	685	38,183
Graubünden	Chur	2,743	7,105	187,058
Jura	Delémont	324	838	68,224
Luzern	Luzern	576	1,493	350,504
Neuchâtel	Neuchâtel	310	803	167,949
Nidwalden[2]	Stans	107	276	37,235
Obwalden[2]	Sarnen	190	491	32,427
Sankt Gallen	Sankt Gallen	782	2,026	452,837
Schaffhausen	Schaffhausen	115	298	73,392
Schwyz	Schwyz	351	908	128,704
Solothurn	Solothurn	305	791	244,341
Thurgau	Frauenfeld	383	991	228,875
Ticino	Bellinzona	1,086	2,812	306,846
Uri	Altdorf	416	1,077	34,777
Valais	Sion	2,017	5,224	272,399
Vaud	Lausanne	1,240	3,212	640,657
Zug	Zug	92	239	100,052
Zürich	Zürich	668	1,729	1,247,906
TOTAL		15,940	41,284	7,288,010[3]

Demography

Population (2003): 7,336,000.
Density (2003): persons per sq mi 460.2, persons per sq km 177.7.
Urban-rural (2001): urban 67.3%; rural 32.7%.
Sex distribution (2001[4]): male 48.86%; female 51.14%.
Age breakdown (2001[4]): under 15, 17.4%; 15–29, 18.3%; 30–44, 24.4%; 45–59, 19.8%; 60–74, 13.0%; 75 and over, 7.1%.
Population projection: (2010) 7,549,000; (2020) 7,675,000.
National composition (2001[4]): Swiss 80.2%; Yugoslav 4.8%; Italian 4.5%; Portuguese 1.9%; German 1.5%; Spanish 1.2%; other 5.9%.
Religious affiliation (2000): Roman Catholic 41.8%; Protestant 35.2%; Muslim 4.3%; Orthodox 1.8%; Jewish 0.2%; nonreligious 11.1%; other 5.6%.
Major urban agglomerations (2002[4]): Zürich 967,600; Geneva 470,400; Basel 402,000; Bern 320,700; Lausanne 292,300; Luzern 184,600.

Vital statistics

Birth rate per 1,000 population (2002): 10.0 (world avg. 21.3); legitimate 90.0%; illegitimate 10.0%.
Death rate per 1,000 population (2002): 8.4 (world avg. 9.1).
Natural increase rate per 1,000 population (2002): 1.6 (world avg. 12.2).
Total fertility rate (avg. births per childbearing woman; 2002): 1.4.
Marriage rate per 1,000 population (2001): 4.9.
Divorce rate per 1,000 population (2001): 2.1.
Life expectancy at birth (2002): male 77.4 years; female 83.1 years.
Major causes of death per 100,000 population (1998): diseases of the circulatory system 357.2; malignant neoplasms (cancers) 212.2; diseases of the respiratory system 63.8; accidents, suicide, violence 50.0.

National economy

Budget (2002)[5]. Revenue: Sw F 130,595,000,000 (1997; social security contributions 46.7%, taxes on goods and services 20.2%, income taxes 11.6%). Expenditures: Sw F 132,989,000,000 (1997; social security and welfare 50.5%, health 19.7%, economic affairs 10.4%, defense 5.2%, education 2.3%).
National debt (end of year; 2001): Sw F 106,810,000,000.
Tourism (2001): receipts from visitors U.S.$7,309,000,000; expenditures by nationals abroad U.S.$6,180,000,000.
Production (metric tons except as noted). Agriculture, forestry, fishing (2002): sugar beets 1,100,000, cow's milk (2001) 626,000, wheat 584,000, potatoes 515,000, barley 265,800, apples 170,000, grapes 153,000; livestock (number of live animals) 1,593,000 cattle, 1,536,000 pigs; roundwood (2002) 4,344,000 cu m; fish catch (2000) 2,759. Mining (1999): salt 300,000.[6] Manufacturing (value added in Sw F '000,000; 1998): nonelectrical machinery and transport equipment 20,757; chemicals and chemical products 13,026; fabricated metal products 8,143; food 5,667; electrical machinery 4,883. Energy production (consumption): electricity (kW-hr; 2000) 63,374,000,000 (56,304,000,000); coal (metric tons; 1999) none (111,000); crude petroleum (barrels; 1999) none (37,200,000); petroleum products (metric tons; 2000) 4,861,000 ([1999] 10,759,000); natural gas (cu m; 1999) negligible (2,917,000,000).
Gross national product (2001): U.S.$277,200,000,000 (U.S.$38,330 per capita).

Structure of gross domestic product and labour force

	1999[7]		2000	
	in value Sw F '000,000	% of total value	labour force	% of labour force
Agriculture	7,474	2.2	177,000	4.4
Manufacturing	69,261	20.6	705,000	17.7
Mining	665	0.2	5,000	0.1
Public utilities	8,593	2.6	24,000	0.6
Construction	20,436	6.1	299,000	7.5
Transp. and commun.	22,236	6.6	255,000	6.4
Trade, restaurants	49,438	14.7	875,000	22.0
Finance, insurance	85,086	25.4	592,000	14.9
Pub. admin., defense	42,686	12.7	152,000	3.8
Services	24,651	7.4	824,000	20.7
Other	5,012[8]	1.5[8]	77,000[9]	1.9[9]
TOTAL	335,538[10]	100.0	3,985,000[11]	100.0

Population economically active (2000): total 3,985,000[11]; activity rate of total population 55.6% (participation rates: ages 15 and over, 67.4%; female 44.2%; unemployed [2001] 1.9%).

Price and earnings indexes (1995 = 100)

	1996	1997	1998	1999	2000	2001	2002
Consumer price index	100.8	101.3	101.4	102.2	103.8	104.8	105.5
Annual earnings index	101.2	101.7	102.4	102.7	102.3	104.8	...

Household income and expenditure (2000). Average household size 2.4; average gross income per household Sw F 104,352 (U.S.$64,400); sources of income (2000): work 72.4%, transfers 22.3%; expenditure (2000): housing 17.6%, taxes 13.6%, recreation, entertainment, restaurants 13.2%, social security contribution 9.5%, health 8.8%, food 8.3%, transportation 7.5%.

Foreign trade[12]

Balance of trade (current prices)

	1997	1998	1999	2000	2001	2002
Sw F '000,000	+330	+2,247	+1,030	–2,066	+1,665	+7,255
% of total	0.1%	1.0%	0.5%	0.8%	0.6%	2.9%

Imports (2002): Sw F 123,125,000,000 (chemical products 22.1%, machinery 21.1%, vehicles 10.4%, food products 8.0%). *Major import sources:* Germany 32.3%; Italy 10.8%; France 10.4%; The Netherlands 5.4%; U.S. 5.3%.
Exports (2002): Sw F 130,380,000,000 (chemicals and chemical products 34.4%, machinery 24.3%, precision instruments, watches, jewelry 17.3%, fabricated metals 7.5%). *Major export destinations:* Germany 20.8%; U.S. 11.0%; France 9.2%; Italy 8.3%; U.K. 4.9%.

Transport and communications

Transport. Railroads: length (1999) 3,129 mi, 5,035 km; passenger-km 14,104,000,000; metric ton-km cargo 8,688,000,000. Roads (1998): total length 44,248 mi, 71,211 km. Vehicles (2001): passenger cars 3,629,713; trucks and buses 289,897. Air transport (2001)[13]: passenger-km 32,981,000,000; metric ton-km cargo 1,793,704,000; airports (1996) with scheduled flights 5.

Communications

Medium	date	unit	number	units per 1,000 persons
Daily newspapers	2000	circulation	2,650,000	369
Radio	2000	receivers	7,200,000	1,002
Television	2000	receivers	3,940,000	548
Telephones	2002	main lines	5,335,000	733
Cellular telephones	2002	subscribers	5,734,000	787
Personal computers	2002	units	4,225,000	580
Internet	2001	users	2,917,000	404

Education and health

Educational attainment (2000). Percentage of resident Swiss and resident alien population age 25–64 having: compulsory education 19.0%; secondary 56.8%; higher 24.2%.
Health (1999): physicians 27,863 (1 per 256 persons); hospital beds (1998) 45,959 (1 per 155 persons); infant mortality rate per 1,000 live births (2002) 4.5.
Food (2001): daily per capita caloric intake 3,440 (vegetable products 66%, animal products 34%); 129% of FAO recommended minimum.

Military

Total active duty personnel (2002): 3,500[14]. *Military expenditure as percentage of GNP* (1999): 1.2% (world 2.4%); per capita expenditure U.S.$469.

[1]Long-form name in Romansh is Confederaziun Svizra. [2]Demicanton; functions as a full canton. [3]Population estimate (Jan. 1, 2002): 7,261,000, of which 1,458,000 resident aliens excluding refugees. [4]January 1. [5]Consolidated central government. [6]Cut and polished diamond exports (1998): U.S.$1,340,000,000. [7]1990 prices. [8]Import duties less imputed bank charges. [9]Unemployed. [10]GDP in 2002 was Sw F 416,840,000,000. [11]Labour force includes about 956,000 foreign workers. [12]Imports c.i.f.; exports f.o.b. [13]Swissair only. [14]Excludes 351,000 reservists.

Internet resources for further information:
- **Embassy of Switzerland (Washington, D.C.) http://www.swissemb.org**
- **Swiss Federal Statistical Office http://www.statistik.admin.ch**

Syria

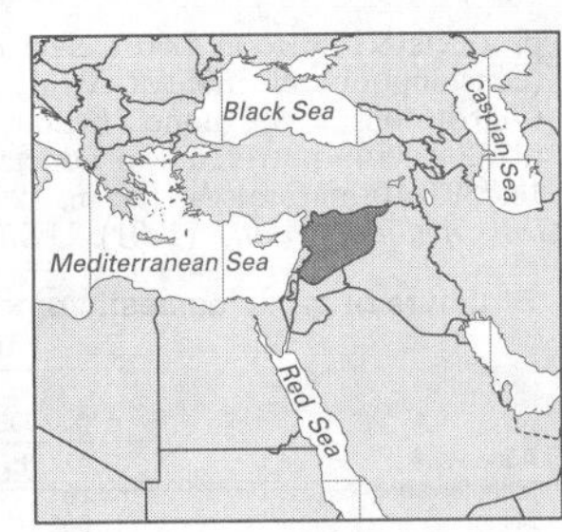

Official name: Al-Jumhūrīyah al-ʿArabīyah as-Sūrīyah (Syrian Arab Republic).
Form of government: unitary multiparty republic with one legislative house (People's Council [250[1]]).
Head of state and government: President.
Capital: Damascus.
Official language: Arabic.
Official religion: none[2].
Monetary unit: 1 Syrian pound (LS) = 100 piastres; valuation[3] (Sept. 8, 2003) 1 U.S.$ = LS 46.00; 1 £ = LS 72.94.

Area and population

Governorates	Capitals	area sq mi	area sq km	population 2001 estimate
Darʿā	Darʿā	1,440	3,730	758,000
Dayr az-Zawr	Dayr az-Zawr	12,765	33,060	891,000
Dimashq	Damascus	6,962	18,032	2,162,000
Ḥalab	Aleppo	7,143	18,500	3,622,000
Ḥamāh	Ḥamāh	3,430	8,883	1,305,000
Al-Ḥasakah	Al-Ḥasakah	9,009	23,334	1,235,000
Ḥimṣ	Homs (Ḥimṣ)	16,302	42,223	1,457,000
Idlib	Idlib	2,354	6,097	1,093,000
Al-Lādhiqīyah	Latakia	887	2,297	861,000
Al-Qunayṭirah	Al-Qunayṭirah (abandoned)	719[4]	1,861[4]	64,000
Ar-Raqqah	Ar-Raqqah	7,574	19,616	674,000
As-Suwaydāʾ	As-Suwaydāʾ	2,143	5,550	302,000
Ṭarṭūs	Ṭarṭūs	730	1,892	664,000
Municipality				
Damascus	—	41	105	1,632,000
TOTAL		71,498[4, 5]	185,180[4]	16,720,000

Demography

Population (2003): 17,586,000.
Density (2003): persons per sq mi 246.0, persons per sq km 95.0.
Urban-rural (2001): urban 51.8%; rural 48.2%.
Sex distribution (2001): male 51.15%; female 48.85%.
Age breakdown (2001): under 15, 40.4%; 15–29, 30.1%; 30–44, 15.6%; 45–59, 8.8%; 60 and over, 5.1%.
Population projection: (2010) 20,606,000; (2020) 24,676,000.
Doubling time: 28 years.
Ethnic composition (2000): Syrian Arab 74.9%; Bedouin Arab 7.4%; Kurd 7.3%; Palestinian Arab 3.9%; Armenian 2.7%; other 3.8%.
Religious affiliation (1992): Muslim 86.0%, of which Sunnī 74.0%, ʿAlawite (Shīʿī) 12.0%; Christian 5.5%; Druze 3.0%; other 5.5%.
Major cities: Aleppo (2000) 2,229,000[6]; Damascus (2001) 2,195,000[6]; Homs (Ḥimṣ) (2000) 811,000[6]; Latakia (1994) 306,535; Ḥamāh (1994) 229,000.

Vital statistics

Birth rate per 1,000 population (2002): 30.1 (world avg. 21.3).
Death rate per 1,000 population (2002): 5.1 (world avg. 9.1).
Natural increase rate per 1,000 population (2002): 25.0 (world avg. 12.2).
Total fertility rate (avg. births per childbearing woman; 2002): 3.8.
Marriage rate per 1,000 population (2000)[7]: 8.0.
Life expectancy at birth (2001): male 67.6 years; female 70.0 years.
Major causes of death per 100,000 population (1989): n.a.; however, the leading causes of mortality among the total population were diseases of the circulatory system 39.6%, injuries and poisoning 9.1%, diseases of the nervous system 7.4%, diseases of the respiratory system 7.4%.

National economy

Budget (2000). Revenue: LS 275,400,000,000 (taxes 31.2%, revenue from loans 13.4%, transit duties 8.0%, other 47.4%). Expenditures: LS 275,400,000,000 (current expenditures 52.1%, capital [development] expenditures 47.9%).
Public debt (external, outstanding; 2001): U.S.$15,811,000,000.
Gross national product (2001): U.S.$17,300,000,000 (U.S.$1,040 per capita).

Structure of gross domestic product and labour force

	2000 in value LS '000,000	% of total value	labour force	% of labour force
Agriculture	229,452	25.6	1,430,000	29.0
Mining Manufacturing Public utilities	267,568	29.8	585,000	11.8
Construction	28,795	3.2	554,000	11.2
Transp. and commun.	113,615	12.7	237,000	4.8
Trade	134,239	15.0	648,000	13.1
Finance	32,402	3.6		
Pub. admin.	68,982	7.7	1,014,000	20.5
Services	21,581	2.4		
Other	...	...	469,000[8]	9.5[8]
TOTAL	896,634	100.0	4,937,000	100.0[5]

Production (metric tons except as noted). Agriculture, forestry, fishing (2002): wheat 4,755,440, sugar beets 1,480,500, olives 998,988, seed cotton 802,178, tomatoes 545,962, potatoes 515,153, watermelons 480,087, oranges 427,148, grapes 368,893, apples 215,762, eggplants 120,000; livestock (number of live animals) 13,497,481 sheep, 931,886 goats, 866,675 cattle; roundwood (2001) 50,400 cu m; fish catch (2001) 13,369. Mining and quarrying (2001): phosphate rock 2,043,000; gypsum 345,000; salt 106,000. Manufacturing (2000): cement 4,631,000; fertilizers 452,766; cottonseed cake 288,000; soap 88,863; olive oil 80,000; glass and pottery products 59,862; vegetable oil 45,087; television receivers 169,291 units; refrigerators 130,159 units. Energy production (consumption): electricity (kW-hr; 2000) 23,946,000,000 (23,946,000,000); coal, none (none); crude petroleum (barrels; 2002) 191,900,000 ([1999] 87,800,000); petroleum products (metric tons; 1999) 11,789,000 (11,400,000); natural gas (cu m; 2001) 5,833,000,000 (5,833,000,000).
Population economically active (2000): total 4,937,000; activity rate of total population 30.3% (participation rates: ages 15 and over, 50.9%; female 19.8%; unemployed 9.5%).

Price and earnings indexes (1995 = 100)

	1995	1996	1997	1998	1999	2000	2001
Consumer price index	100.0	108.2	110.8	110.2	107.3	106.8	107.3
Earnings index	...	...	...	...	...	...	...

Average household size (2000): 6.0; income per household: n.a.; sources of income: n.a.; expenditure: n.a.
Tourism (2000): receipts U.S.$1,082,000,000; expenditures (2001) U.S.$610,000,000.
Land use (1994): steppe and pasture 45.2%; agricultural and under permanent cultivation 30.1%; forested 2.6%; other 22.1%.

Foreign trade[9]

Balance of trade (current prices)

	1996	1997	1998	1999	2000	2001
U.S.$'000,000	+82	+129	–890	–222	+819	+492
% of total	1.0%	1.7%	13.7%	3.2%	9.7%	5.0%

Imports (2000): U.S.$3,815,000,000 (food 14.6%, of which cereals 4.9%; chemicals and chemical products 12.9%; nonelectrical machinery and equipment 10.9%; iron and steel 10.7%; textile yarn 7.5%). *Major import sources:* Germany 6.8%; U.S. 6.8%; Italy 6.2%; Ukraine 6.2%; China 5.3%; Turkey 5.0%; South Korea 5.0%.
Exports (2000): U.S.$4,634,000,000 (crude petroleum 69.1%; refined petroleum 7.0%; raw cotton 4.1%; vegetables 2.9%; apparel and clothing accessories 2.8%). *Major export destinations:* Italy 32.0%; France 22.5%; Turkey 10.4%; Saudi Arabia 5.9%; Lebanon 4.1%.

Transport and communications

Transport. Railroads (2001)[10]: route length 2,676 km; passenger-km 304,000,000; metric ton-km cargo 1,491,000,000. Roads (2000): total length 44,575 km (paved 21%). Vehicles (2000): passenger cars 138,823; trucks and buses (1998) 282,664. Air transport (2001): passenger-km 1,626,950; metric ton-km cargo 15,357,000; airports with scheduled flights 5.

Communications

Medium	date	unit	number	units per 1,000 persons
Daily newspapers	2000	circulation	326,000	20
Radio	2000	receivers	4,500,000	276
Television	2000	receivers	1,090,000	67
Telephones	2002	main lines	2,099,300	123
Cellular telephones	2002	units	400,000	24
Personal computers	2002	units	330,000	19
Internet	2002	users	220,000	13

Education and health

Educational attainment: n.a. *Literacy* (2000): percentage of population age 15 and over literate 74.4%; males literate 88.3%; females literate 60.5%.

Education (2000)

	schools	teachers	students	student/ teacher ratio
Primary (age 6–11)	11,482	121,880	2,774,922	22.8
Secondary (age 12–18)	2,911	63,889	955,290	15.0
Voc., teacher tr.	587	15,103	134,473	8.9
Higher[11]	4	5,664	155,137	27.4

Health (2000): physicians 22,408 (1 per 746 persons); hospital beds 18,370 (1 per 910 persons); infant mortality rate (2001) 33.8.
Food (2001): daily per capita caloric intake 3,038 (vegetable products 88%, animal products 12%); 123% of FAO recommended minimum.

Military

Total active duty personnel (2002): 319,000 (army 67.4%, navy 1.3%, air force 12.5%, air defense 18.8%); troops stationed in Lebanon (October 2003) 20,000. *Military expenditure as percentage of GNP* (1999): 7.0% (world 2.4%); per capita expenditure U.S.$280.

[1]Elections held March 2003. [2]Islam is required to be the religion of the head of state and is the basis of the legal system. [3]Exchange rate most commonly used for commerce; Syria had two different exchange rates in September 2003. [4]Includes territory in the Golan Heights recognized internationally as part of Syria. [5]Detail does not add to total given because of rounding. [6]Population of urban agglomeration. [7]Syrian Arabs only. [8]Unemployed. [9]Imports c.i.f.; exports f.o.b. [10]Excludes length of Syrian part of railway opened in August 2000 linking Aleppo, Syria, and Mosul, Iraq. [11]University-level institutions only.

Internet resources for further information:
- **Ministry of Economy and Foreign Trade http://www.syrecon.org/right_frame1.html**

Taiwan

Official name: Chung-hua Min-kuo (Republic of China).
Form of government: multiparty republic with a Legislature (Legislative Yuan [225])[1].
Chief of state: President.
Head of government: Premier.
Capital: Taipei.
Official language: Mandarin Chinese.
Official religion: none.
Monetary unit: 1 New Taiwan dollar (NT$) = 100 cents; valuation (Sept. 8, 2003) 1 U.S.$ = NT$34.12; 1 £ = NT$54.09.

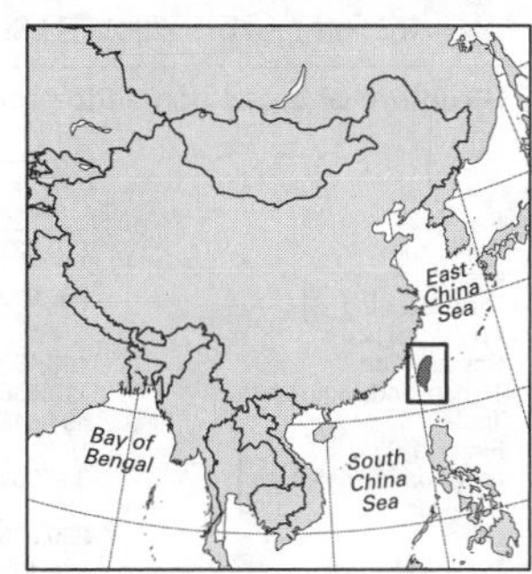

Area and population

Taiwan area Counties	area sq km	population 2003 estimate	Municipalities	area sq km	population 2003 estimate
Chang-hua	1,074	1,316,256	Chia-i	60	268,263
Chia-i	1,902	561,747	Chi-lung	133	391,657
Hsin-chu	1,428	453,906	Hsin-chu	104	379,938
Hua-lien	4,629	351,631	Kao-hsiung	154	1,508,917
I-lan	2,137	463,954	T'ai-chung	163	999,476
Kao-hsiung	2,793	1,235,203	T'ai-nan	176	746,287
Miao-li	1,820	560,581	Taipei	272	2,638,065
Nan-t'ou	4,106	541,222			
P'eng-hu	127	92,366	**non-Taiwan area Counties**		
P'ing-tung	2,776	905,660			
T'ai-chung	2,051	1,513,537	Kinmen (Quemoy) }		
T'ai-nan	2,016	1,106,919	Lienchiang (Matsu) }	179	68,274
T'ai-pei	2,052	3,651,248			
T'ai-tung	3,515	243,581			
T'ao-yüan	1,221	1,799,061	TOTAL	36,179[2]	22,540,155
Yün-lin	1,291	742,406			

Demography

Population (2003)[3]: 22,569,000.
Density (2003)[2, 3]: persons per sq mi 1,615.3, persons per sq km 623.7.
Urban-rural (1991)[4]: urban 74.7%; rural 25.3%.
Sex distribution (2003)[3]: male 50.98%; female 49.02%.
Age breakdown (2002)[3]: under 15, 20.8%; 15–29, 24.9%; 30–44, 25.3%; 45–59, 16.7%; 60–74, 9.1%; 75 and over, 3.2%.
Population projection: (2010) 23,395,000; (2020) 24,218,000.
Ethnic composition (1997): Han Chinese, Chinese mainland minorities, and others 98.2%; indigenous tribal peoples 1.8%, of which Ami 0.6%.
Religious affiliation (1997)[5, 6]: Buddhism 22.4%; Taoism 20.7%; I-kuan Tao 4.3%; Protestant 1.6%; Roman Catholic 1.4%; other Christian 0.3%; Muslim 0.2%; Bahā'ī 0.1%; other (mostly Christian folk-religionists) 49.0%.
Major cities (2003): Taipei 2,638,065; Kao-hsiung 1,508,917; T'ai-chung 999,476; T'ai-nan 746,287; Chi-lung 391,657; Chung-ho (1998) 388,174.

Vital statistics

Birth rate per 1,000 population (2002): 10.2 (world avg. 21.3).
Death rate per 1,000 population (2002): 5.2 (world avg. 9.1).
Natural increase rate per 1,000 population (2002): 5.0 (world avg. 12.2).
Total fertility rate (avg. births per childbearing woman; 2002): 1.3.
Life expectancy at birth (2000): male 73.6 years; female 79.3 years.
Major causes of death per 100,000 population (2001)[4]: malignant neoplasms 147.6; cerebrovascular diseases 58.8; heart disease 49.2; accidents and suicide 42.6; diabetes 40.8; liver diseases 23.5; kidney diseases 18.2; pneumonia 16.8.

National economy

Budget (1999[7]). Revenue: NT$3,391,948,000,000 (income taxes 18.0%, business tax 9.1%, commodity tax 6.5%, land tax 6.4%, customs duties 4.6%). Expenditures: NT$3,371,702,000,000 (administration and defense 24.5%, education 19.4%).
Population economically active (May 2003): total 10,022,000; activity rate of total population 44.4% (participation rates: [December 2002] over age 15, *c.* 57%; female [May 2003] 40.4%; unemployed [May 2003] 5.0%).

Price and earnings indexes (1995 = 100)

	1996	1997	1998	1999	2000	2001	2002
Consumer price index	103.1	104.0	105.7	105.9	107.2	107.2	106.9
Monthly earnings index[8]	104.2	108.9	112.0	115.8	119.2	...	...

Production (metric tons except as noted). Agriculture, forestry, fishing (2000): sugarcane 2,894,000, rice 1,559,000, citrus fruits 440,382, pineapples 357,535, bananas 198,454, sweet potatoes 198,000; livestock (number of live animals) 7,494,954 pigs, 202,491 goats, 161,700 cattle; timber 21,134 cu m; fish catch 1,356,275. Mining and quarrying (2000): marble 17,800,000. Manufacturing (2002): cement 19,228,026; steel ingots 18,240,256; paperboard 3,274,932; fertilizers (2000) 1,706,861; polyester filament 1,603,096; polyvinyl chloride plastics 1,483,947; telephones 4,722,353 units; televisions 1,014,755 units. Energy production (consumption): electricity (kW-hr; 2002) 165,901,000,000 (151,193,000,000); coal (metric tons; 2001)[9] (48,000,000); crude petroleum (barrels; 2002) 349,000 (360,000,000); natural gas (cu m; 2001) 918,000,000 (8,264,000,000).
Tourism (2001): receipts from visitors U.S.$3,991,000,000; expenditures by nationals abroad U.S.$6,379,000,000.
Gross national product (2002): U.S.$283,375,000,000 (U.S.$12,570 per capita).

Structure of gross domestic product and labour force[4]

	2002			
	in value NT$'000,000	% of total value	labour force[10]	% of labour force[10]
Agriculture	180,857	1.8	709,000	7.1
Mining	42,024	0.4	9,000	0.1
Manufacturing	2,505,856	25.7	2,563,000	25.7
Construction	252,950	2.6	725,000	7.3
Public utilities	219,975	2.3	35,000	0.3
Transp. and commun.	677,728	7.0	477,000	4.8
Trade	1,883,665	19.4	1,693,000	17.0
Finance	2,294,642	23.6	953,000	9.5
Pub. admin., defense	1,023,175	10.5 }	2,290,000	23.0
Services	1,005,747	10.3 }		
Other	–352,268[11]	–3.6[11]	515,000[12]	5.2[12]
TOTAL	9,734,351	100.0	9,969,000	100.0

Household income and expenditure (1999). Average household size (2003) 3.2; income per household NT$1,181,082 (U.S.$37,153); expenditure: food, beverages, and tobacco 25.1%, rent, fuel, and power 24.9%, education and recreation 13.0%, transportation 11.1%, health care 11.0%, clothing 4.1%.

Foreign trade[13]

Balance of trade (current prices)

	1997	1998	1999	2000	2001	2002
U.S.$'000,000	+7,656	+5,917	+10,901	+8,310	+15,629	+18,050
% of total	3.2%	2.7%	4.7%	2.8%	6.8%	7.4%

Imports (2002): U.S.$112,591,000,000 (electronic machinery 28.5%, nonelectrical machinery 16.0%, minerals 11.2%, chemicals 10.1%, metals and metal products 8.2%, precision instruments, clocks, watches, and musical instruments 5.8%). *Major import sources:* Japan 24.2%; U.S. 16.1%; South Korea 6.8%; Germany 3.9%; Malaysia 3.7%.
Exports (2002): U.S.$130,641,000,000 (nonelectrical machinery, electrical machinery, and electronics 57.4%, textile products 10.0%, plastic articles 5.9%, transportation equipment 3.7%). *Major export destinations:* Hong Kong 23.6%; U.S. 20.5%; Japan 9.2%; Singapore 3.2%; Germany 2.9%.

Transport and communications

Transport. Railroads (2002)[14]: route length 1,119 km; passenger-km 9,666,000,000, metric ton-km cargo 919,000,000. Roads (2002): total length 20,816 km[15] (paved, n.a.). Vehicles (2002): passenger cars 4,989,000; trucks and buses 882,000. Air transport (1998): passenger-km 39,218,000,000; metric ton-km cargo 4,129,300,000; airports (1996) 13.

Communications

Medium	date	unit	number	units per 1,000 persons
Radio	1996	receivers	8,620,000	402
Television	1999	receivers	9,200,000	418
Telephones	2002	main lines	13,234,000	589
Cellular telephones	2002	subscribers	23,905,000	1,064
Personal computers	2002	units	8,887,000	396
Internet	2002	users	7,454,000	332

Education and health

Educational attainment (1999). Percentage of population age 25 and over having: no formal schooling 7.0%; less than complete primary education 6.3%; primary 21.3%; incomplete secondary 25.7%; secondary 21.8%; some college 10.4%; higher 7.5%. *Literacy* (1999): population age 15 and over literate 16,414,896 (94.6%); males 8,641,549 (97.6%); females 7,773,347 (91.4%).

Education (2002–03)

	schools	teachers	students	student/ teacher ratio
Primary (age 6–12)	2,627	104,300	1,918,034	18.4
Secondary (age 13–18) } Vocational }	1,188	97,710	1,679,959	17.2
Higher	154	46,042	1,240,330	26.9

Health (2001): physicians 30,562 (1 per 731 persons); hospital beds 127,676 (1 per 175 persons); infant mortality rate per 1,000 live births (2000) 7.1.

Military

Total active duty personnel (2002): 370,000 (army 64.8%, navy 16.8%, air force 18.4%). *Military expenditure as percentage of GNP* (1999): 5.2% (world 2.4%); per capita expenditure U.S.$690.

[1]The National Assembly became a nonstanding body with limited specialized authority per April 2000 amendment; the Legislature is the formal lawmaking body. [2]Total area per more recent survey is 36,188 sq km (13,972 sq mi). [3]Includes Quemoy and Matsu groups. [4]For Taiwan area only, excluding Quemoy and Matsu groups. [5]Formal subscribers to religious beliefs. [6]Almost all Taiwanese adults engage in religious practices stemming from one or a combination of traditional folk religions. [7]General government. [8]In manufacturing. [9]Coal production ceased in 2000. [10]Civilian persons only. [11]Import duties less imputed bank service charge. [12]Unemployed. [13]Imports c.i.f.; exports f.o.b. [14]Taiwan Railway Administration only. [15]Excludes urban.

Internet resources for further information:
- **Taiwan Yearbook 2003**
  http://www.gio.gov.tw/taiwan-website/5-gp/yearbook
- **Directorate-General of Budget, Accounting and Statistics (Taiwan)**
  http://www.dgbasey.gov.tw/english/dgbas_e0.htm

Tajikistan

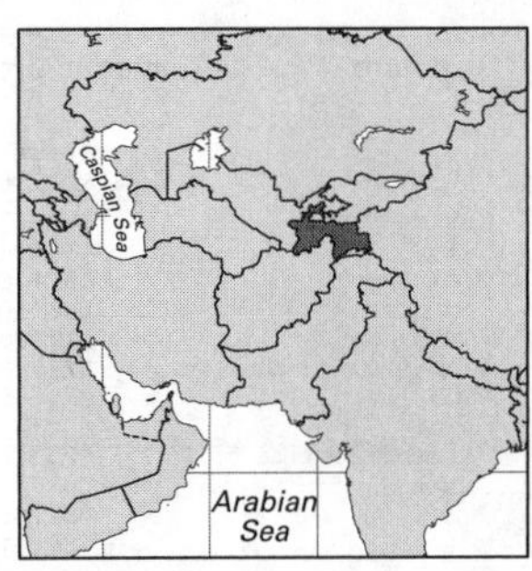

Official name: Jumhurii Tojikiston (Republic of Tajikistan).
Form of government: parliamentary republic with two legislative houses (National Assembly [33[1]]; Assembly of Representatives [63]).
Chief of state: President.
Head of government: Prime Minister.
Capital: Dushanbe.
Official language: Tajik (Tojik).
Official religion: none.
Monetary unit: 1 somoni[2] = 100 dinars; valuation (Sept. 1, 2003) 1 U.S.$ = 3.16 somoni; 1 £ = 4.99 somoni.

Area and population		area		population
				2000
Oblasts	**Capitals**	sq mi	sq km	census
Khatlon (Qŭrghonteppa)	Qŭrghonteppa	9,500	24,600	2,151,000
Sughd	Khujand	10,100	26,100	1,870,000
Autonomous oblast				
Kŭhistoni Badakhshon (Gorno-Badakhshan)	Khorugh	24,600	63,700	206,000
City				
Dushanbe	—	100	300	562,000
Other[3]	—	11,000	28,400	1,338,000
TOTAL		55,300[4]	143,100[4]	6,127,000

Demography

Population (2003): 6,535,000.
Density (2003): persons per sq mi 118.2, persons per sq km 45.7.
Urban-rural (2000): urban 26.6%; rural 73.4%.
Sex distribution (2000): male 50.30%; female 49.70%.
Age breakdown (2000): under 15, 39.4%; 15–29, 27.7%; 30–44, 18.4%; 45–59, 7.6%; 60–74, 5.4%; 75 and over, 1.5%.
Population projection: (2010) 7,047,000; (2020) 8,105,000.
Doubling time: 32 years.
Ethnic composition (2000): Tajik 80.0%; Uzbek 15.3%; Russian 1.1%; Tatar 0.3%; other 3.3%.
Religious affiliation (1995): Sunnī Muslim 80.0%; Shīʿī Muslim 5.0%; Russian Orthodox 1.5%; Jewish 0.1%; other (mostly nonreligious) 13.4%.
Major cities (2002): Dushanbe 575,900; Khujand 147,400; Kulyab 79,500; Kurgan-Tyube 61,200; Ura-Tyube 51,700.

Vital statistics

Birth rate per 1,000 population (2001): 27.2 (world avg. 21.3); (1994) legitimate 90.8%; illegitimate 9.2%.
Death rate per 1,000 population (2001): 5.1 (world avg. 9.1).
Natural increase rate per 1,000 population (2001): 22.1 (world avg. 12.2).
Total fertility rate (avg. births per childbearing woman; 2001): 4.4.
Marriage rate per 1,000 population (2001): 4.6.
Divorce rate per 1,000 population (1994): 0.8.
Life expectancy at birth (2001): male 59.9 years; female 66.9 years.
Major causes of death per 100,000 population (1999): diseases of the circulatory system 211.5; diseases of the respiratory system 56.3; infectious and parasitic diseases 31.6; violence, poisoning, and accidents 28.3; malignant neoplasms (cancers) 27.9; diseases of the digestive system 19.0.

National economy

Budget (2001). Revenue: 342,316,000 somoni (tax revenue 91.6%, of which value-added tax 25.1%, taxes on aluminum and cotton 18.3%, customs duties 15.1%, income and profit taxes 13.8%, excise taxes 4.5%; nontax revenue 8.4%). Expenditures: 338,418,000 somoni (current expenditures 77.5%, of which state authorities 19.7%, education 18.9%, state bodies and administration 11.7%, defense 8.7%, health 7.3%, law enforcement 4.1%, debt payment 4.1%; capital expenditures 22.5%).
Production (metric tons except as noted). Agriculture, forestry, fishing (2002): raw seed cotton 515,000, potatoes 400,000, wheat 361,000, tomatoes 170,000, grapes 100,000; livestock (number of live animals) 1,490,000 sheep, 1,091,000 cattle, 779,000 goats; roundwood, n.a.; fish catch (2001) 145. Mining and quarrying (2000): antimony (metal content) 2,000; gold 2,700 kg. Manufacturing (value of production in '000,000 somoni[5]; 2001): nonferrous metals 442,000[6]; food 138,000; textiles 104,000; grain mill products 51,000; basic chemicals 10,000. Energy production (consumption): electricity (kW-hr; 2001) 14,400,000,000 (13,500,000,000); coal (metric tons; 2001) 24,900 (122,000); crude petroleum (barrels; 1999) 139,000 (95,000); petroleum products (metric tons; 1999) none (1,116,000); natural gas (cu m; 1999) 34,100,000 (763,500,000).
Public debt (external, outstanding; 2001): U.S.$789,000,000.
Population economically active (2002): total 1,829,000; activity rate of total population 29.6% (participation rates: ages 15–59 [male], 15–54 [female] 55.1%; female [1996] 46.5%; unemployed 2.3%).

Price and earnings indexes (1995 = 100)	1995	1996	1997	1998	1999	2000	2001
Consumer price index	100.0	298.0	511.0	524.8	682.8	1,097	1,234
Monthly earnings index	100.0	383.7	680.6	1,175	1,488	2,049	...

Gross national product (2001): U.S.$1,000,000,000 (U.S.$180 per capita).

Structure of gross domestic product and labour force	2001			
	in value '000 somoni	% of total value	labour force	% of labour force
Agriculture	670,027	26.7	1,167,000	62.3
Mining; Manufacturing	566,822	22.6	131,000	7.0
Public utilities	...	...	...	...
Construction	103,682	4.1	31,000	1.7
Transp. and commun.	112,588	4.5	43,000	2.3
Trade	494,642	19.7	140,000	7.5
Finance			...	...
Pub. admin., defense	334,034 (Finance, Pub. admin., defense, Services)	13.3	26,000	1.4
Services			291,000	15.5
Other	230,305[7]	9.2[7]	43,000[8]	2.3[8]
TOTAL	2,512,100	100.0[9]	1,872,000	100.0

Tourism (2001): receipts from visitors U.S.$100,000; expenditures by nationals abroad U.S.$3,000,000.
Land use (1994): forest 3.8%; pasture 24.8%; agriculture 6.0%; other 65.4%.
Household income and expenditure. Average household size (2000) 5.9; (1995) income per household 18,744 Tajik rubles[2] (U.S.$114); sources of income (1995): wages and salaries 34.5%, self-employment 34.0%, borrowing 2.4%, pension 2.0%, other 27.1%; expenditure: food 81.5%, clothing 10.2%, transport 2.5%, fuel 2.1%, other 3.7%.

Foreign trade

Balance of trade (current prices)	1997	1998	1999	2000	2001	2002
U.S.$'000,000	–61	–139	–27	–46	–121	–124
% of total	3.9%	10.6%	2.0%	2.8%	12.4%	8.1%

Imports (2001): U.S.$773,000,000 (alumina 23.9%, petroleum products and natural gas 12.9%, electricity 12.7%, grain and flour 8.0%). *Major import sources* (2000): Uzbekistan 28.8%; Russia 16.1%; Ukraine 13.1%; Kazakhstan 12.8%; Azerbaijan 9.8%.
Exports (2001): U.S.$652,000,000 (aluminum 61.0%, electricity 12.1%, cotton fibre 10.9%). *Major export destinations* (2000): Russia 37.4%; The Netherlands 25.7%; Uzbekistan 14.1%; Switzerland 10.4%; Italy 2.8%.

Transport and communications

Transport. Railroads (2001): length 299 mi, 482 km; passenger-mi 20,000,000, passenger-km 32,000,000; short ton-mi cargo 855,000,000, metric ton-km cargo 1,248,000,000. Roads (1996): total length 8,500 mi, 13,747 km (paved 83%). Vehicles (1996): passenger cars 680,000; trucks and buses 8,190. Air transport (2001)[10]: passenger-mi 376,000,000, passenger-km 605,000,000; short ton-mi cargo 3,316,000, metric ton-km cargo 4,841,000; airports (2002) 2.

Communications				units
Medium	date	unit	number	per 1,000 persons
Daily newspapers	2000	circulation	123,000	20
Radio	2000	receivers	870,000	141
Television	2000	receivers	2,010,000	326
Telephones	2002	main lines	232,700	37
Cellular phones	2002	subscribers	13,200	2.1
Personal computers	...	units	...	...
Internet	2002	users	3,500	0.5

Education and health

Educational attainment (1989). Percentage of population age 25 and over having: primary education or no formal schooling 16.3%; some secondary 21.1%; completed secondary and some postsecondary 55.1%; higher 7.5%. *Literacy* (2000): percentage of total population age 15 and over literate 99.2%; males literate 99.6%; females literate 98.8%.

Education (2001–02)	schools	teachers	students	student/ teacher ratio
Primary (age 6–13)	660	100,200 (Primary and Secondary)	1,520,000 (Primary and Secondary)	15.2 (Primary and Secondary)
Secondary (age 14–17)[11]	2,861			
Voc., teacher tr.	55	...	29,842[12]	...
Higher	31	6,100	84,400	13.8

Health (1998): physicians 14,292 (1 per 416 persons); hospital beds 36,920 (1 per 161 persons); infant mortality rate per 1,000 live births (2001) 54.0.
Food (2001): daily per capita caloric intake 1,662 (vegetable products 92%, animal products 8%); 65% of FAO recommended minimum requirement.

Military

Total active duty personnel (2002): 6,000 (army 100%); Russian troops (2003) more than 20,000 troops including 11,000 along the Tajik-Afghan border. *Military expenditure as percentage of GNP* (1999): 1.3% (world 2.4%); per capita expenditure U.S.$13.

[1]Eight members are appointed by the President. [2]The somoni (equal to 1,000 Tajik rubles) was introduced on Oct. 30, 2000. [3]No oblast-level administration. [4]Includes *c.* 400 sq mi (*c.* 1,035 sq km) ceded to China in May 2002. [5]At 1998 constant prices. [6]Aluminum production by weight in 2001 equaled 289,100 metric tons. [7]Indirect taxes. [8]Unemployed. [9]Detail does not add to total given because of rounding. [10]Tajikistan Airlines only. [11]Excludes special education. [12]1994–95.

Internet resources for further information:

- **Key Indicators of Developing Asian and Pacific Countries http://www.adb.org/Documents/Books/Key_Indicators/default.asp**

Tanzania

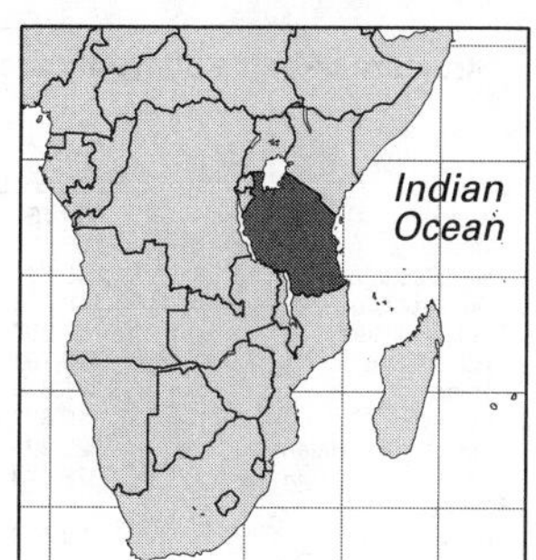

Official name: Jamhuri ya Muungano wa Tanzania (Swahili); United Republic of Tanzania (English).
Form of government: unitary multiparty republic with one legislative house (National Assembly [274]).
Head of state and government: President.
Seat of government: Dar es Salaam (pending capital, Dodoma)[1].
Official languages: Swahili; English.
Official religion: none.
Monetary unit: 1 Tanzania shilling (T Sh) = 100 cents; valuation (Sept. 8, 2003) 1 U.S.$ = T Sh 1,046; 1 £ = T Sh 1,659.

Area and population

Administrative regions	area sq km	population 2002 census	Administrative regions	area sq km	population 2002 census
Mainland Tanzania (Tanganyika)			Rukwa	68,635	1,141,743
Arusha	36,486	1,292,973	Ruvuma	63,498	1,117,166
Dar es Salaam	1,393	2,497,940	Shinyanga	50,781	2,805,580
Dodoma	41,311	1,698,996	Singida	49,341	1,090,758
Iringa	56,864	1,495,333	Tabora	76,151	1,717,908
Kagera	28,388	2,033,888	Tanga	26,808	1,642,015
Kigoma	37,037	1,679,109	**Autonomous territory**		
Kilimanjaro	13,309	1,381,149	Zanzibar and Pemba[2]		
Lindi	66,046	791,306	Pemba	906	362,166
Manyara	45,820	1,040,461	Zanzibar	1,554	622,459
Mara	19,566	1,368,602	TOTAL LAND AREA	883,749	
Mbeya	60,350	2,070,046	INLAND WATER	59,050	
Morogoro	70,799	1,759,809	TOTAL	942,799[3]	34,569,232
Mtwara	16,707	1,128,523			
Mwanza	19,592	2,942,148			
Pwani (Coast)	32,407	889,154			

Demography

Population (2003): 35,078,000.
Density (2003)[4]: persons per sq mi 102.7, persons per sq km 39.7.
Urban-rural (2002): urban 33.3%; rural 66.7%.
Sex distribution (2001): male 49.72%; female 50.28%.
Age breakdown (2001): under 15, 44.8%; 15–29, 28.9%; 30–44, 14.2%; 45–59, 7.6%; 60–74, 3.6%; 75 and over, 0.9%.
Population projection: (2010) 40,216,000; (2020) 47,729,000.
Doubling time: 31 years.
Ethnolinguistic composition (2000): Sukuma 9.5%; Hehet and Bena 4.5%; Gogo 4.4%; Haya 4.2%; Nyamwezi 3.6%; Makonde 3.3%; Chagga 3.0%; Ha 2.9%; other 64.6%.
Religious affiliation (2000): Christian 46.9%; Muslim 31.8%; ethnoreligionist 16.1%.
Major urban districts (2002): Dar es Salaam 2,497,940[5]; Zanzibar 391,002[6]; Dodoma 324,347; Arusha 282,712; Mbeya 266,422.

Vital statistics

Birth rate per 1,000 population (2002): 40.0 (world avg. 21.3).
Death rate per 1,000 population (2002): 17.3 (world avg. 9.1).
Natural increase rate per 1,000 population (2002): 22.7 (world avg. 12.2).
Total fertility rate (avg. births per childbearing woman; 2002): 5.3.
Life expectancy at birth (2002): male 43.5 years; female 46.0 years.
Major causes of death per 100,000 population: n.a.; however, the major diseases include HIV/AIDS, malaria, schistosomiasis, tuberculosis, and sleeping sickness.

National economy

Budget (2001–02). Revenue: T Sh 1,422,802,000,000 (import duties 28.3%, grants 26.7%, income tax 15.5%, sales and value-added tax 15.2%). Expenditures: T Sh 1,466,138,000,000 (current payments 68.3%, interest payments on debt 8.2%, capital expenditure 23.5%).
Tourism (2001): receipts from visitors U.S.$725,000,000; expenditures by nationals abroad U.S.$330,000,000.
Land use (1995): forested 37.0%; meadows and pastures 39.6%; agricultural and under permanent cultivation 4.2%; other 19.2%.
Gross national product (2000)[7]: U.S.$9,400,000,000 (U.S.$270 per capita).

Structure of gross domestic product and labour force

	2000			
	in value T Sh '000,000[7]	% of total value	labour force	% of labour force
Agriculture	3,003,903	45.1	14,551,000	80.4
Mining	99,519	1.5		
Manufacturing	499,726	7.4		
Construction	343,354	5.2		
Public utilities	112,753	1.7		
Transp. and commun.	328,259	4.9		
Trade	823,025	12.4	3,537,000	19.6
Finance	377,996	5.7		
Pub. admin., defense	516,865	7.8		
Services	709,617	10.6		
Other	−151,359[8]	−2.3[8]		
TOTAL	6,663,658	100.0	18,088,000	100.0

Public debt (external, outstanding; 2001): U.S.$5,758,000,000.
Production (metric tons except as noted). Agriculture (2002): cassava 6,880,000, corn (maize) 2,700,500, sweet potatoes 950,100, sorghum 650,000, rice 514,000, seed cotton 243,000, bananas 150,400, cashew nuts 121,900, coffee 58,100, tea 25,500, tobacco leaves 24,470; livestock (number of live animals) 17,700,000 cattle, 11,650,000 goats, 3,550,000 sheep, 29,000,000 chickens; roundwood 23,438,758 cu m; fish catch (2001) 336,200. Mining and quarrying (2001): gold 30,088 kg; garnets 19,508 kg; tanzanites 5,473 kg; sapphires 3,576 kg; diamonds 254,300 carats. Manufacturing (2001): cement 900,000; sugar 161,600; iron sheets 25,900; rolled steel 16,100; beer 1,757,000 hectolitres; cigarettes 3,500,000,000 units; textiles 84,300,000 sq m. Energy production (consumption): electricity (kW-hr; 1999) 2,552,000,000 (2,552,-000,000); coal (metric tons; 1999) 5,000 (5,000); crude petroleum (barrels; 1999) none (4,500,000); petroleum products (metric tons; 1999) 613,000 (692,000); natural gas, none (none).
Population economically active (2001): total 18,556,000; activity rate 55.5% (participation rates [1991]: over age 10, 87.8%; female 40.0%).

Price index (1995 = 100)

	1996	1997	1998	1999	2000	2001	2002
Consumer price index	121.0	140.4	158.4	170.9	181.0	190.3	199.0

Household income and expenditure. Average household size (1998) 5.4; income per household: n.a.; sources of income: n.a.; expenditure (1994): food 64.2%, clothing 9.9%, housing 8.3%, energy 7.6%, transportation 4.1%.

Foreign trade[9]

Balance of trade (current prices)

	1997	1998	1999	2000	2001	2002
T Sh '000,000,000	−244	−516	−649	−537	−626	−547
% of total	20.9%	39.7%	44.1%	33.6%	31.5%	24.4%

Imports (2002): T Sh 1,601,000,000,000 (consumer goods 31.0%, of which food products 8.8%; machinery and apparatus 22.2%; transport equipment 13.2%; crude and refined petroleum 11.8%). *Major import sources:* South Africa 11.4%; Japan 8.4%; India 6.5%; Russia 6.1%; U.A.E. 5.9%; U.K. 5.7%; Kenya 5.7%.
Exports (2002): T Sh 846,000,000,000 (minerals [mostly gold, significantly diamonds and other gemstones] 42.4%; cashews 5.8%; tobacco 5.6%; coffee 4.0%; tea 3.4%; other [significantly fish products] 38.8%). *Major export destinations:* U.K. 18.5%; France 17.4%; Japan 11.0%; India 7.3%; The Netherlands 6.2%.

Transport and communications

Transport. Railroads (1997): length 3,569 km; passenger-journeys 694,000,-000[10]; metric ton-km cargo 1,354,000,000[10]. Roads (1999): length 88,200 km (paved 4.2%). Vehicles (1996): passenger cars 23,760; trucks and buses 115,700. Air transport (2001)[11]: passenger-km 155,000,000; metric ton-km 2,772,000; airports (1999) with scheduled flights 11.

Communications

Medium	date	unit	number	units per 1,000 persons
Daily newspapers	2000	circulation	130,000	4.0
Radio	2000	receivers	9,130,000	281
Television	2000	receivers	650,000	20
Telephones	2002	main lines	161,600	4.7
Cellular telephones	2002	subscribers	670,000	19
Personal computers	2002	units	144,000	4.2
Internet	2002	users	80,000	2.3

Education and health

Educational attainment: n.a. *Literacy* (2000): percentage of population age 15 and over literate 75.1%; males 83.9%; females 66.5%.

Education (1998)[7]

	schools	teachers	students	student/ teacher ratio
Primary (age 7–13)	11,339	106,329	4,042,568	38.0
Secondary (age 14–19)	491[12]	11,691	226,903	19.4
Teacher training	40[12]	1,062	9,136	8.6
Higher	...	2,064	18,867	9.1

Health (1993): physicians 1,365 (1 per 20,511 persons); hospital beds 26,820 (1 per 1,000 persons); infant mortality rate (2002) 105.3.
Food (2001): daily per capita caloric intake 1,997 (vegetable products 94%, animal products 6%); 86% of FAO recommended minimum requirement.

Military

Total active duty personnel (2002): 27,000 (army 85.2%, navy 3.7%, air force 11.1%). *Military expenditure as percentage of GNP* (1999): 1.4% (world 2.4%); per capita expenditure U.S.$4.

[1]As of 2002 only the prime minister's office and legislature were located in Dodoma; the scheduled completion date for the move of all government offices to Dodoma is 2005. [2]Has local internal government structure; Zanzibar has 3 administrative regions, Pemba has 2. [3]A recent survey indicates a total area of 945,090 sq km (364,901 sq mi). [4]Based on land area only. [5]Combined population of 3 urban districts. [6]Combined population of 2 urban districts. [7]Mainland Tanzania only. [8]Bank service charge. [9]Imports f.o.b. in balance of trade and c.i.f. in commodities and trading partners. [10]Tanzanian Railways only; 1995. [11]Air Tanzania only. [12]1994.

Internet resources for further information:

- **National Bureau of Statistics http://www.tanzania.go.tz/statistics.html#top**
- **Bank of Tanzania http://www.bot-tz.org**

Thailand

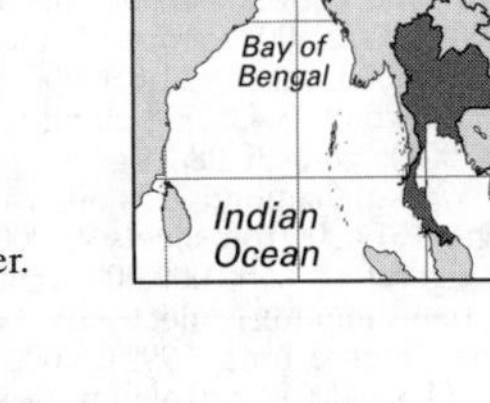

Official name: Muang Thai, or Prathet Thai (Kingdom of Thailand).
Form of government: constitutional monarchy with two legislative houses (Senate [200]; House of Representatives [500]).
Chief of state: King.
Head of government: Prime Minister.
Capital: Bangkok.
Official language: Thai.
Official religion: Buddhism.
Monetary unit: 1 Thai baht (B) = 100 stangs; valuation (Sept. 8, 2003) 1 U.S.$ = B 40.67; 1 £ = B 64.48.

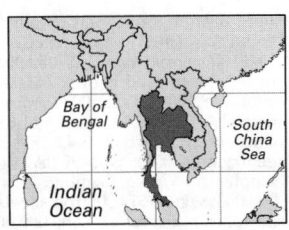

Area and population

Regions[1]	area sq mi	area sq km	population 2000 final census
Bangkok Metropolis	606	1,569	6,320,200
Central	39,512	102,336	14,101,500
Northeastern	65,195	168,855	20,759,900
Northern	65,500	169,644	11,367,800
Southern	27,303	70,715	8,067,800
TOTAL	198,116	513,119	60,617,200

Demography

Population (2003): 64,022,000.
Density (2003): persons per sq mi 323.2, persons per sq km 124.8.
Urban-rural (2001): urban 28.6%; rural 71.4%.
Sex distribution (2000): male 49.24%; female 50.76%.
Age breakdown (2000): under 15, 24.1%; 15–29, 25.6%; 30–44, 25.9%; 45–59, 15.0%; 60–74, 7.5%; 75 and over, 1.9%.
Population projection: (2010) 67,828,000; (2020) 71,650,000.
Doubling time: 87 years.
Ethnic composition (2000): Tai peoples 81.4%, of which Thai (Siamese) 34.9%, Lao 26.5%; Han Chinese 10.6%; Malay 3.7%; Khmer 1.9%; other 2.4%.
Religious affiliation (2000): Buddhist 94.2%; Muslim 4.6%; Christian and other 1.2%.
Major cities (2000)[2]: Bangkok 6,320,174; Samut Prakan 378,694; Nonthaburi 291,307; Udon Thani 220,493; Nakhon Ratchasima 204,391.

Vital statistics

Birth rate per 1,000 population (2002): 14.0 (world avg. 21.3).
Death rate per 1,000 population (2002): 6.0 (world avg. 9.1).
Natural increase rate per 1,000 population (2002): 8.0 (world avg. 12.2).
Total fertility rate (avg. births per childbearing woman; 2002): 1.8.
Marriage rate per 1,000 population (2000): 5.4.
Divorce rate per 1,000 population (2000): 1.1.
Life expectancy at birth (2002): male 70.0 years; female 75.0 years.
Major causes of death per 100,000 population (1998): diseases of the circulatory system 75.9; accidents, homicide, and poisonings 51.0; malignant neoplasms (cancers) 49.2.

National economy

Budget (2001–02). Revenue: B 903,550,000,000 (tax revenue 90.3%, of which income taxes 28.7%, VAT 26.1%, taxes on international trade 11.5%, consumption tax 10.8%; nontax revenue 9.7%). Expenditures: B 1,023,000,000,000 (education 21.8%; defense 7.5%; agriculture 7.4%; health 7.1%; social security 6.9%; public order 5.5%).
Public debt (external, outstanding; 2001): U.S.$26,411,000,000.
Production (metric tons except as noted). Agriculture, forestry, fishing (2002): sugarcane 62,350,000, rice 25,945,000, cassava 16,870,000, corn (maize) 4,170,000, natural rubber 2,460,000, pineapples 1,978,822, bananas 1,750,000, mangoes 1,700,000, coconuts 1,396,000, tobacco 73,000; livestock (number of live animals) 6,688,904 pigs, 4,640,355 cattle, 1,800,000 buffalo, 121,000,000 chickens; roundwood (2001) 27,351,000 cu m; fish catch (2001) 2,881,316, of which mollusks 249,867. Mining and quarrying (2001): gypsum 6,191,000; dolomite 871,300; feldspar 710,500; zinc [metal content] 24,000; gemstones (significantly rubies and sapphires) 1,071,000 carats. Manufacturing (2001): cement 27,913,000; refined sugar 4,865,000; crude steel 2,127,000; paper products 917,000; tin plate (2002) 233,000; beer 12,380,000 hectolitres. Energy production (consumption): electricity (kW-hr; 2002) 108,418,000,000 (105,182,000,000); hard coal (metric tons; 1999) negligible (3,145,000); lignite (metric tons; 2001) 19,619,000 ([1999] 18,844,000); crude petroleum (barrels; 2001) 22,600,000 ([1999] 273,400,000); petroleum products (metric tons; 1999) 35,286,000 (31,406,000); natural gas (cu m; 2001) 20,633,000,000 ([1999] 16,875,200,000).
Tourism (2001): receipts from visitors U.S.$6,371,000,000; expenditures by nationals abroad U.S.$2,179,000,000.
Population economically active (2001): total 33,920,000; activity rate of total population 53.9% (participation rates: over age 14, 72.1%; female [2000] 45.0%; unemployed 3.2%).

Price and earnings indexes (1995 = 100)

	1996	1997	1998	1999	2000	2001	2002
Consumer price index	105.8	111.8	120.8	121.1	123.0	125.1	125.9
Monthly earnings index	108.5	117.0	...	...	...	...	...

Gross national product (2001): U.S.$118,500,000,000 (U.S.$1,940 per capita).

Structure of gross domestic product and labour force

	2001 in value B '000,000	% of total value	labour force	% of labour force
Agriculture	436,160	8.5	13,590,000	40.1
Mining	125,869	2.5	470,000	1.4
Manufacturing	1,706,695	33.5	5,680,000	16.7
Construction	148,996	2.9	1,580,000	4.7
Public utilities	167,850	3.3	170,000	0.5
Transp. and commun.	410,701	8.0	1,020,000	3.0
Trade	875,850	17.2	4,490,000	13.2
Finance	319,623	6.3		
Pub. admin., defense	229,425	4.5	5,600,000	16.5
Services	678,473	13.3		
Other	—	—	1,320,000[3]	3.9[3]
TOTAL	5,099,642	100.0	33,920,000	100.0

Household income and expenditure (1998). Average household size (2000) 3.9; average annual income per household B 149,904 (U.S.$3,624); sources of income: wages and salaries 40.1%, self-employment 29.8%, transfer payments 7.9%, other 22.2%; expenditure: food, tobacco, and beverages 37.7%, housing 21.4%, transportation and communications 13.3%, medical and personal care 5.1%, clothing 3.5%, education 2.3%.
Land use (1998): meadows and pastures 1.6%; agricultural and under permanent cultivation 39.8%; forested and other 58.6%.

Foreign trade[4]

Balance of trade (current prices)

	1997	1998	1999	2000	2001	2002
U.S.$'000,000	+1,572	+16,238	+14,013	+11,700	+8,582	+9,775
% of total	1.4%	18.2%	14.1%	9.4%	7.3%	7.9%

Imports (2001): U.S.$62,057,000,000 (electrical machinery 22.1%, of which electronic components and parts 10.9%; nonelectrical machinery 17.4%, of which computers and parts 6.3%; chemicals and chemical products 10.3%; crude petroleum 9.3%). *Major import sources* (2002): Japan 23.0%; U.S. 9.6%; China 7.6%; Malaysia 5.6%; Singapore 4.5%.
Exports (2001): U.S.$65,113,000,000 (food products 14.9%, of which fish, crustaceans, and mollusks 6.2%; computers and parts 12.3%; microcircuits and other electronics 7.2%; chemicals and chemical products 5.7%; garments and clothing accessories 5.6%). *Major export destinations* (2002): U.S. 19.6%; Japan 14.5%; Singapore 8.1%; Hong Kong 5.4%; China 5.2%.

Transport and communications

Transport. Railroads (2000): route length 4,041 km; passenger-km 10,040,000,000; metric ton-km cargo 3,347,000,000. Roads (2001): total length 53,436 km (paved 98%). Vehicles (2002): passenger cars 2,281,000; trucks and buses 4,145,000. Air transport (1999): passenger-km 38,345,195,000; metric ton-km cargo 1,670,717,000; airports (1996) 25.

Communications

Medium	date	unit	number	units per 1,000 persons
Daily newspapers	2000	circulation	3,990,000	64
Radio	2000	receivers	14,700,000	235
Television	2000	receivers	17,700,000	284
Telephones	2002	main lines	6,499,800	105
Cellular telephones	2002	subscribers	16,117,000	260
Personal computers	2002	units	2,461,000	40
Internet	2002	users	4,800,000	78

Education and health

Educational attainment (2000). Percentage of population age 6 and over having: no formal schooling 8.5%; primary education 59.0%; lower secondary 12.5%; upper secondary 11.2%; some higher 2.2%; undergraduate 5.2%; advanced degree 0.4%; other/unknown 1.0%. *Literacy* (2000): 95.5%.

Education (1997–98)

	schools	teachers	students	student/ teacher ratio
Primary (age 7–12)	34,001[5]	445,542[6]	5,927,902	19.3[6]
Secondary (age 13–18)	2,318[6]	107,025[6]	3,358,470	19.8[6]
Voc., teacher tr.	679[6]	40,116[6]	738,861	19.8[6]
Higher	102[6]	38,423[5]	1,522,142	31.8[5]

Health (2001): physicians 18,531 (1 per 3,395 persons); hospital beds 141,380 (1 per 445 persons); infant mortality rate (2002) 21.0.
Food (2001): daily per capita caloric intake 2,486 (vegetable products 88%, animal products 12%); 112% of FAO recommended minimum requirement.

Military

Total active duty personnel (2002): 306,000 (army 62.1%, navy 22.2%, air force 15.7%). *Military expenditure as percentage of GNP* (1999): 1.7% (world 2.4%); per capita expenditure U.S.$34.

[1]Actual local administration is based on 76 provinces. [2]Preliminary census figures. [3]Unemployed. [4]Import figures are f.o.b. in balance of trade and c.i.f. for commodities and trading partners. [5]1995–96. [6]1993.

Internet resources for further information:
- **National Statistical Office Thailand**
  http://www.nso.go.th
- **Bank of Thailand**
  http://www.bot.or.th

Togo

Official name: République Togolaise (Togolese Republic).
Form of government: multiparty republic[1] with one legislative body (National Assembly [81]).
Chief of state: President[1].
Head of government: Prime Minister.
Capital: Lomé.
Official language: French.
Official religion: none.
Monetary unit: 1 CFA franc (CFAF) = 100 centimes; valuation (Sept. 8, 2003) 1 U.S.$ = CFAF 594.70; 1 £ = CFAF 942.93[2].

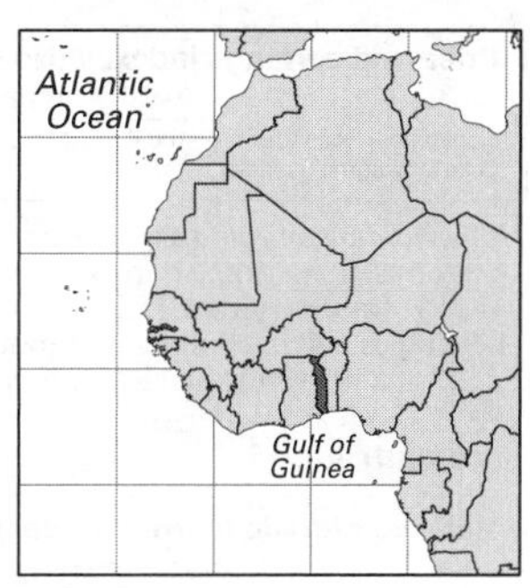

Area and population		area		population
Regions				1989
Prefectures	Capitals	sq mi	sq km	estimate
Centrale	Sokodé			339,000
Sotouboua	Sotouboua	2,892	7,491	162,500
Tchamba	Tchamba	1,214	3,143	54,500
Tchaoudjo	Sokodé	984	2,549	122,000
De la Kara	Kara			531,500
Assoli	Bafilo	362	938	41,000
Bassar	Bassar	2,444	6,330	152,000
Binah	Pagouda	180	465	61,000
Doufelgou	Niamtougou	432	1,120	75,000
Kéran	Kandé	419	1,085	49,500
Kozah	Kara	653	1,692	153,000
Des Plateaux	Atakpamé			810,500
Amou	Amlamé	773	2,003	98,500
Haho	Notsé	1,406	3,641	139,000
Kloto	Kpalimé	1,072	2,777	233,500
Ogou	Atakpamé	2,349	6,083	204,000
Wawa	Badou	954	2,471	135,500
Des Savanes	Dapaong			410,500
Oti	Sansanné-Mango	1,453	3,762	98,500
Tône	Dapaong	1,869	4,840	312,000
Maritime	Lomé			1,299,500
Golfe	Lomé	133	345	560,000
Lacs	Aného	275	713	172,500
Vo	Vogan	290	750	125,000
Yoto	Tabligbo	483	1,250	187,000
Zio	Tsévié	1,288	3,337	255,000
TOTAL		21,925	56,785	3,391,000

Demography

Population (2003): 5,429,000.
Density (2003): persons per sq mi 247.6, persons per sq km 95.6.
Urban-rural (2002): urban 33.9%; rural 66.1%.
Sex distribution (2001): male 49.22%; female 50.78%.
Age breakdown (2001): under 15, 45.6%; 15–29, 28.1%; 30–44, 14.8%; 45–59, 7.5%; 60–74, 3.3%; 75 and over, 0.7%.
Population projection: (2010) 6,256,000; (2020) 7,195,000.
Ethnic composition (2000): Ewe 22.2%; Kabre 13.4%; Wachi 10.0%; Mina 5.6%; Kotokoli 5.6%; Bimoba 5.2%; Losso 4.0%; Gurma 3.4%; Lamba 3.2%; Adja 3.0%; other 24.4%.
Religious affiliation (2000): Christian 37.8%, of which Roman Catholic 24.3%; traditional beliefs 37.7%; Muslim 18.9%; other 5.6%.
Major cities (2003): Lomé 676,400 (urban agglomeration 749,700); Sokodé 84,200; Kpalimé 75,200; Atakpamé 64,300; Kara 49,800.

Vital statistics

Birth rate per 1,000 population (2002): 36.1 (world avg. 21.3).
Death rate per 1,000 population (2002): 11.4 (world avg. 9.1).
Natural increase rate per 1,000 population (2002): 24.7 (world avg. 12.2).
Total fertility rate (avg. births per childbearing woman; 2002): 5.1.
Life expectancy at birth (2002): male 51.9 years; female 55.8 years.

National economy

Budget (2002). Revenue: CFAF 128,300,000,000 (tax revenue 92.5%, nontax revenue 4.8%, grants 2.7%). Expenditures: CFAF 135,300,000,000 (current expenditure 89.4%, capital expenditure 10.6%).
Public debt (external, outstanding; 2001): U.S.$1,203,000,000.
Production (metric tons except as noted). Agriculture, forestry, fishing (2002): cassava 651,530, yams 549,070, corn (maize) 463,930, seed cotton 175,000, sorghum 141,723, vegetables 130,000, oil palm fruit 130,000, rice 63,693, coffee 17,000, cacao beans 8,000; livestock (number of live animals) 1,700,000 sheep, 1,460,000 goats, 300,000 pigs, 278,500 cattle; roundwood 5,835,447 cu m; fish catch (2000) 22,379. Mining and quarrying: limestone (2001) 2,400,000; phosphate rock (2002) 1,380,000. Manufacturing (value added in CFAF '000,000; 1998): food products, beverages, and tobacco manufactures 41,400; metallic goods 12,000; nonmetallic manufactures 8,500; textiles, clothing, and leather 4,900; wood products 4,700; paper, printing, and publishing 4,600; chemicals 3,600. Energy production (consumption): electricity (kW-hr; 1999) 94,000,000 (529,000,000); petroleum products (metric tons; 1999) 366,000 (342,000).
Household income and expenditure. Average household size (1999) 6.0; expenditure (1987): food and beverages 45.9%, services 20.5%, household durable goods 13.9%, clothing 11.4%, housing 5.9%.
Gross national product (at current market prices; 2001): U.S.$1,300,000,000 (U.S.$270 per capita).

Structure of gross domestic product and labour force	1999		2000	
	in value CFAF '000,000,000	% of total value	labour force	% of labour force
Agriculture	366.3	41.8	1,142,000	59.7
Mining	44.9	5.1		
Manufacturing	80.6	9.2		
Construction	32.3	3.7		
Public utilities	27.8	3.2		
Transp. and commun.	47.5	5.4	771,000	40.3
Trade and finance	150.7	17.2		
Pub. admin., defense	60.9	6.9		
Services	66.1	7.5		
TOTAL	877.1	100.0	1,913,000	100.0

Population economically active (2000): total 1,913,000; activity rate of total population 38.1% (participation rates: over age 15, 70.7%; female 39.9%; unemployed [1994] 16–18%).

Price and earnings indexes (1995 = 100)	1996	1997	1998	1999	2000	2001	2002
Consumer price index	104.7	113.3	114.4	114.3	116.5	121.1	124.8
Hourly earnings index	...	...	...	...	...	...	...

Tourism (2001): receipts U.S.$11,000,000; expenditures U.S.$5,000,000.

Foreign trade[3]

Balance of trade (current prices)	1997	1998	1999	2000	2001	2002
U.S.$'000,000	–283.5	–293.5	–307.9	–131.9	–134.8	–172.7
% of total	28.9%	27.2%	29.9%	25.6%	23.4%	17.0%

Imports (2001): U.S.$355,000,000 (food 18.2%, of which cereals 9.4%; refined petroleum 15.7%; chemicals and chemical products 10.4%; machinery and apparatus 9.8%; cement 8.8%; iron and steel 8.8%). *Major import sources:* France 19.1%; Canada 6.5%; Italy 6.1%; Côte d'Ivoire 5.7%; Germany 4.5%.
Exports (2001): U.S.$220,200,000 (cement 29.4%, phosphates 20.3%, cotton 10.1%, iron and steel 8.6%). *Major export destinations:* Ghana 22.4%; Benin 16.9%; Burkina Faso 10.4%; Philippines 6.3%; Niger 4.5%.

Transport and communications

Transport. Railroads (1999): route length 395 km; (1998) passenger-km 35,200,000; metric ton-km cargo 758,700,000. Roads (1999): total length 7,520 km (paved 32%). Vehicles (1996): passenger cars 79,200; trucks and buses 34,240. Air transport[4]: airports (1998) 2.

Communications Medium	date	unit	number	units per 1,000 persons
Daily newspapers	2000	circulation	20,100	4.0
Radio	2000	receivers	1,330,000	265
Television	2000	receivers	161,000	32
Telephones	2002	main lines	51,200	10
Cellular telephones	2002	subscribers	170,000	34
Personal computers	2002	units	150,000	30
Internet	2002	users	200,000	40

Education and health

Educational attainment (1981). Percentage of population age 25 and over having: no formal schooling 76.5%; primary education 13.5%; secondary 8.7%; higher 1.3%. *Literacy* (2000): total population age 15 and over literate 57.1%; males 72.4%; females 42.5%.

Education (1996–97)	schools	teachers	students	student/ teacher ratio
Primary (age 6–11)	3,283[5]	18,535	859,574	46.4
Secondary (age 12–18)	314[6]	4,736[6]	169,178	...
Vocational	...	653	9,076	13.9
Higher[7]	1	443	11,639	26.3

Health: physicians (1995) 320 (1 per 13,158 persons); hospital beds (1990) 5,307 (1 per 694 persons); infant mortality rate (2002) 69.8.
Food (2001): daily per capita caloric intake 2,287 (vegetable products 97%, animal products 3%); 99% of FAO recommended minimum requirement.

Military

Total active duty personnel (2003): 8,550 (army 94.7%, navy 2.3%, air force 3.0%). *Military expenditure as percentage of GNP* (1999): 1.8% (world 2.4%); per capita expenditure U.S.$5.

[1]Personal military-supported rule from 1967 continues under constitution approved by referendum in September 1992. [2]Formerly pegged to the French franc and since Jan. 1, 2002, to the euro at the rate of €1 = CFAF 655.96. [3]Import figures are c.i.f. (except in 2002 balance of trade). [4]Air Afrique, an airline jointly owned by 11 African countries (including Togo), was declared bankrupt in February 2002. [5]1995–96. [6]1990. [7]University only.

Internet resources for further information:

- **AFRISTAT http://www.afristat.org**
- **Investir en Zone Franc http://www.izf.net/izf/index.htm**

Tonga

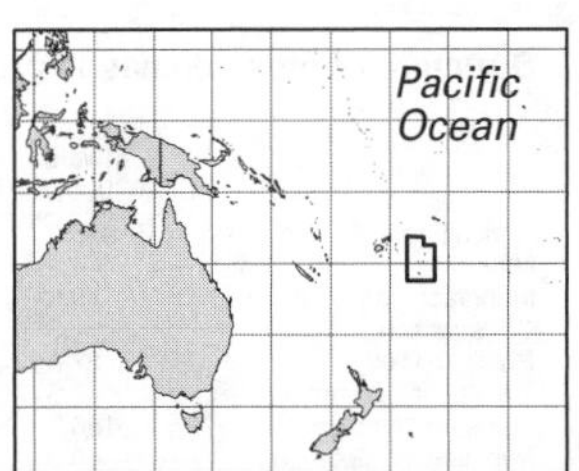

Official name: Pule'anga Fakatu'i 'o Tonga (Tongan); Kingdom of Tonga (English).
Form of government: constitutional monarchy with one legislative house (Legislative Assembly [30[1]]).
Head of state and government: King assisted by Privy Council.
Capital: Nuku'alofa.
Official languages: Tongan; English.
Official religion: none.
Monetary unit: 1 pa'anga (T$) = 100 seniti; valuation (Sept. 8, 2003) 1 U.S.$ = T$2.17; 1 £ = T$3.44.

Area and population		area		population
				1996
Divisions	Capitals	sq mi	sq km	census[2]
'Eua[3]	'Ohonua	33.7	87.4	4,934
Ha'apai[4]	Pangai	42.5	110.0	8,138
Niuas[5]	Hihifo	27.7	71.7	2,018
Tongatapu[3]	Nuku'alofa	100.6	260.5	66,979
Vava'u[4]	Neiafu	46.0	119.2	15,715
TOTAL LAND AREA		278.1[6]	720.3[6]	
INLAND WATER		11.4	29.6	
TOTAL		289.5	749.9	97,784

Demography

Population (2003): 102,000.
Density (2003)[7]: persons per sq mi 366.8, persons per sq km 141.6.
Urban-rural (2002): urban 39.0%; rural 61.0%.
Sex distribution (2002): male 50.93%; female 49.07%.
Age breakdown (1996): under 15, 39.1%; 15–29, 28.0%; 30–44, 15.1%; 45–59, 10.0%; 60–74, 6.0%; 75 and over, 1.8%.
Population projection: (2010) 106,000; (2020) 113,000.
Doubling time: 38 years.
Ethnic composition (1996): Tongan and part Tongan 98.2%; other 1.8%.
Religious affiliation (1998): Free Wesleyan 41.2%; Roman Catholic 15.8%; Mormon 13.6%; other (mostly other Protestant) 29.4%.
Major cities (1986): Nuku'alofa (1996) 22,400[8]; Neiafu 3,879; Haveluloto 3,070.

Vital statistics

Birth rate per 1,000 population (2002): 24.1 (world avg. 21.3).
Death rate per 1,000 population (2002): 5.6 (world avg. 9.1).
Natural increase rate per 1,000 population (2002): 18.5 (world avg. 12.2).
Total fertility rate (avg. births per childbearing woman; 2002): 3.0.
Marriage rate per 1,000 population (1994): 7.7.
Divorce rate per 1,000 population (1994): 0.8.
Life expectancy at birth (2002): male 66.1 years; female 71.1 years.
Major causes of death per 100,000 population (1993)[9]: circulatory diseases 58.1; nervous system diseases 51.0; senility 27.6; diabetes mellitus 17.3.

National economy

Budget (2002). Revenue: T$93,200,000 (foreign-trade taxes 52.0%, government services revenue 13.7%, income tax 16.7%, sales taxes 8.2%). Expenditures: T$99,400,000 (2001; general administration 20.9%, education 14.0%, health 10.2%, social security 6.7%, agriculture 6.5%, law and order 5.7%, defense 4.6%).
Public debt (external, outstanding; 2001): U.S.$62,700,000.
Production (metric tons except as noted). Agriculture, forestry, fishing (2002): coconuts 57,700, pumpkins, squash, and gourds 17,000, cassava 9,000, vegetables 5,500, sweet potatoes 5,500, yams 4,400, vanilla 14; livestock (number of live animals) 80,853 pigs, 12,500 goats, 11,400 horses, 11,250 cattle, 300,000 chickens; roundwood 2,100 cu m; fish catch (2000) 3,531. Mining and quarrying: coral and sand for local use. Manufacturing (output in T$'000,000; 1996): food products and beverages 8,203; paper products 1,055; chemical products 964; metal products 889; textile and wearing apparel 742; nonmetallic products 715. Energy production (consumption): electricity (kW-hr; 2002) 36,176,000 (36,176,000); crude petroleum, none (none); petroleum products (metric tons; 1999) n.a. (39,000).
Tourism: receipts (2001) U.S.$7,000,000; expenditures (1997) U.S.$3,000,000.
Gross national product (2001): U.S.$200,000,000 (U.S.$1,530 per capita).

Structure of gross domestic product and labour force	2001–02		1996	
	in value T$'000,000	% of total value	labour force	% of labour force
Agriculture	70.2	23.7	9,953	29.3
Mining	1.1	0.4	43	0.1
Manufacturing	13.7	4.6	6,710	19.8
Construction	16.9	5.7	500	1.5
Public utilities	5.5	1.9	504	1.5
Transp. and commun.	19.7	6.6	1,209	3.6
Trade	33.8	11.4	2,506	7.4
Finance	35.9	12.1	657	1.9
Pub. admin., defense	47.8	16.1	3,701	10.9
Services	14.6	4.9	3,623	10.7
Other	37.3	12.6	4,502	13.3
TOTAL	296.5	100.0	33,908	100.0

Population economically active (1996): total 33,908; activity rate 34.7% (participation rates: ages 15 and over 57.0%; female 36.0%; unemployed 13.3%).

Price and earnings indexes (November 1995 = 100)	1998	1999	2000	2001	2002
Consumer price index	106.4	110.5	116.4	124.3	137.3
Quarterly earnings index	...	...	...	...	...

Household income and expenditure. Average household size (1996) 6.0; income per household: n.a.; sources of income: n.a.; expenditure (1991–92)[10]: food 43.2%, transportation 15.5%, household 14.2%, housing 6.4%, tobacco and beverages 5.4%, clothing and footwear 4.2%.
Land use (1994): forest 11.1%; pasture 5.6%; agriculture 66.7%; other 16.6%.

Foreign trade[11]

Balance of trade (current prices)	1996–97	1997–98	1998–99	1999–2000	2000–01	2001–02
U.S.$'000,000	–47.0	–66.2	–43.5	–43.0	–49.9	–44.0
% of total	64.0%	73.6%	64.3%	65.5%	67.6%	55.1%

Imports (2000–01): U.S.$70,100,000 (food and live animals 32.3%, mineral fuels and chemical products 25.6%, machinery and transport equipment 11.2%). *Major import sources* (2002): New Zealand 30.8%; Fiji 20.7%; U.S. 14.3%; Australia 13.2%; China 6.2%.
Exports (2000–01): U.S.$6,700,000 (squash 40.8%, fish 27.7%, root crops 15.4%, kava 2.3%, vanilla beans 2.3%). *Major export destinations* (2002): Japan 43.3%; U.S. 41.0%; Greece 3.8%; New Zealand 3.6%; Taiwan 2.7%.

Transport and communications

Transport. Railroads: none. Roads (1996): total length 680 km (paved 27%). Vehicles (1998): passenger cars 6,419, commercial vehicles 9,189. Air transport (1999): passenger-km 19,000,000; metric ton-km cargo 2,000,000; airports (1996) with scheduled flights 6.

Communications				units per 1,000
Medium	date	unit	number	persons
Daily newspapers	2000	circulation	12,300	123
Radio	1997	receivers	61,000	619
Television	1997	receivers	2,000	21
Telephones	2002	main lines	11,200	113
Cellular telephones	2002	subscribers	3,400	34
Personal computers	2002	units	2,000	20
Internet	2002	users	2,900	29

Education and health

Educational attainment (1996). Percentage of population age 25 and over having: primary education 26%; lower secondary 58%; upper secondary 8%; higher 6%; not stated 2%. *Literacy* (1996): 98.5%.

Education (1999)	schools	teachers	students	student/ teacher ratio
Primary (age 6–11)	117	745	16,206	21.8
Secondary (age 12–18)	39	961	13,987	14.6
Voc., teacher tr.	5	67	755	11.3
Higher[12]	1	19	226	11.9

Health: physicians (1997) 43 (1 per 2,279 persons); hospital beds (1992) 307 (1 per 320 persons); infant mortality rate per 1,000 live births (2002) 13.7.
Food (1992): daily per capita caloric intake 2,946 (vegetable products 82%, animal products 18%); 129% of FAO recommended minimum requirement.

Military

Total active duty personnel (1999): 125-member naval force; an air force was created in 1996. *Military expenditure as percentage of GNP:* n.a.

[1]Includes 12 nonelective seats and 9 nobles elected by the 33 hereditary nobles of Tonga. [2]Final figures. [3]'Eua and Tongatapu together comprise Tongatapu island group. [4]Also the name of an island group. [5]Also known as Niuatoputapu island group. [6]Total includes 27.6 sq mi (71.5 sq km) of uninhabited islands. [7]Based on land area. [8]Population of urban agglomeration (2001) is 33,000. [9]Reported inpatient deaths at all hospitals. [10]Current weight of consumer price index components. [11]Imports f.o.b. in balance of trade and c.i.f. in commodities and trading partners. [12]1992.

Internet resources for further information:
- **Secretariat of the Pacific Community http://www.spc.org.nc**

Trinidad and Tobago

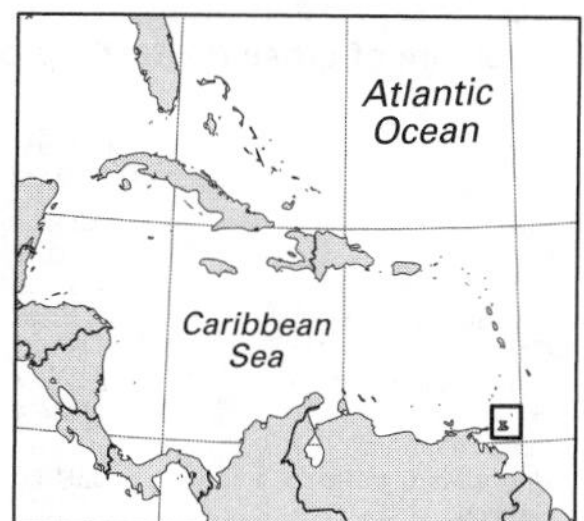

Official name: Republic of Trinidad and Tobago.
Form of government: multiparty republic with two legislative houses (Senate [31]; House of Representatives [36[1]]).
Chief of state: President.
Head of government: Prime Minister.
Capital: Port of Spain.
Official language: English.
Official religion: none.
Monetary unit: 1 Trinidad and Tobago dollar (TT$) = 100 cents; valuation (Sept. 8, 2003) 1 U.S.$ = TT$6.15; 1 £ = TT$9.75.

Area and population

	area[2] sq km	population 2000 census[3]		area[2] sq km	population 2000 census[3]
Trinidad			**Cities**		
Counties	4,828	1,208,282	Port of Spain	10	49,031
Couva/Tabaquite/Talparo	701	162,779	San Fernando	8	55,419
Diego Martin	122	105,720	**Boroughs**		
Mayaro/Rio Claro	907	33,480	Arima	10	32,278
Penal/Debe	259	83,609	Chaguanas	60	67,433
Princes Town	551	91,947	Point Fortin	23	19,056
Sangre Grande	881	64,343	**Tobago (Unitary State)**	300	54,084
San Juan/Laventille	200	157,295	TOTAL	5,128	1,262,366
Siparia	570	81,917			
Tunapuna/Piarco	526	203,975			

Demography

Population (2003): 1,279,000.
Density (2003): persons per sq mi 646.0, persons per sq km 249.1.
Urban-rural (2002): urban 74.5%; rural 25.5%.
Sex distribution (2001): male 51.22%; female 48.78%.
Age breakdown (2001): under 15, 24.3%; 15–29, 27.1%; 30–44, 22.5%; 45–59, 15.5%; 60–74, 7.7%; 75 and over, 2.9%.
Population projection: (2010) 1,304,000; (2020) 1,339,000.
Ethnic composition (2000): black 39.2%; East Indian 38.6%; mixed 16.3%; Chinese 1.6%; white 1.0%; other/not stated 3.3%.
Religious affiliation (1990): six largest Protestant bodies 29.7%; Roman Catholic 29.4%; Hindu 23.7%; Muslim 5.9%; other 11.3%.
Major cities (2000)[3]: Chaguanas 67,433; San Fernando 55,149; Port of Spain 49,031; Arima 32,278; Point Fortin 19,056; Scarborough 15,830.

Vital statistics

Birth rate per 1,000 population (2001): 12.8 (world avg. 21.3).
Death rate per 1,000 population (2001): 8.2 (world avg. 9.1).
Natural increase rate per 1,000 population (2001): 4.6 (world avg. 12.2).
Total fertility rate (avg. births per childbearing woman; 2001): 1.8.
Marriage rate per 1,000 population (1996): 5.6.
Divorce rate per 1,000 population (1996): 1.2.
Life expectancy at birth (2001): male 67.4 years; female 72.8 years.
Major causes of death per 100,000 population (1994): diseases of the circulatory system 286.4; malignant neoplasms (cancers) 94.3; endocrine and metabolic disorders 90.0; accidents, violence, and homicide 52.8.

National economy

Budget (2001–02). Revenue: TT$14,672,000,000 (income taxes 31.5%; petroleum sector 29.0%; sales tax 23.7%; taxes on international trade 5.7%; other 10.1%). Expenditures: TT$13,861,000,000 (current expenditures 90.4%, of which transfers and subsidies 33.9%, wages 30.9%, interest payment 16.8%, other 8.8%; development expenditures 9.6%).
Production (metric tons except as noted). Agriculture, forestry, fishing (2002): sugarcane 1,050,000, coconuts 24,000, oranges 4,987, rice 3,882, pigeon peas 2,780, cocoa 1,218, coffee 243, nutmeg 140; livestock (number of live animals) 60,500 goats, 31,600 cattle, 25,000,000 chickens; roundwood (2000) 116,500 cu m; fish catch (2001) 9,683. Mining and quarrying (2000): natural asphalt 9,900. Manufacturing (2000): anhydrous ammonia and urea 3,718,700; methanol 2,480,200; steel billets 743,800; cement 742,700; steel wire rods 630,800; refined sugar 51,500; beer and stout 523,800 hectolitres; rum 146,000 hectolitres. Energy production (consumption): electricity (kW-hr; 1999) 5,247,000,000 (5,247,000,000); crude petroleum (barrels; 2000) 39,337,000 ([1999] 55,500,000); petroleum products (metric tons; 1999) 7,521,000 (742,000); natural gas (cu m; 2000) 15,483,000,000 ([1999] 10,382,400,000).
Household income and expenditure. Average household size (2000) 3.7; average income per household, n.a.; expenditure (1993): food, beverages, and tobacco 25.5%, housing 21.6%, transportation 15.2%, household furnishings 14.3%, clothing and footwear 10.4%.
Tourism (2001): receipts from visitors U.S.$201,000,000; expenditures by nationals abroad (1998) U.S.$67,000,000.
Land use (1994): forested 45.8%; meadows and pastures 2.1%; agricultural and under permanent cultivation 23.8%; other 28.3%.
Gross national product (at current market prices; 2001): U.S.$7,800,000,000 (U.S.$5,960 per capita).

Structure of gross domestic product and labour force

	2002		2001	
	in value TT$'000,000	% of total value	labour force	% of labour force
Agriculture	800	0.9	40,300	7.0
Petroleum	11,693	13.7	16,600	2.9
Manufacturing[4]	15,812	18.5	52,700	9.1
Construction	5,952	7.0	71,200	12.3
Public utilities }	12,377	14.5	7,500	1.3
Transp. and commun. }			38,900	6.7
Trade	19,248	22.5	89,900	15.6
Finance, real estate	14,437	16.9	41,000	7.1
Pub. admin., defense } Services }	7,187	8.4	156,100	27.1
Other	–2,001[5]	–2.3[5]	62,700[6]	10.9[6]
TOTAL	85,503	100.0[7]	576,900	100.0

Population economically active (2001): total 576,900; activity rate of total population 45.5% (participation rates: ages 15 and over 60.7%; female 36.6%; unemployed 10.9%).

Price and earnings indexes (1995 = 100)

	1996	1997	1998	1999	2000	2001	2002
Consumer price index	103.4	107.2	113.2	117.1	121.2	126.0	133.2
Weekly earnings index[8]	102.5	109.5	114.9	...	...	...	...

Public debt (external, outstanding; 2001): U.S.$1,452,000,000.

Foreign trade[9]

Balance of trade (current prices)

	1997	1998	1999	2000	2001	2002
TT$'000,000	–2,818	–4,666	+398	+6,082	+7,363	+1,470
% of total	8.1%	14.1%	1.1%	12.7%	13.1%	3.1%

Imports (2001): TT$24,510,000,000 (crude petroleum 19.3%, general industrial machinery 16.1%, floating docks 9.3%, food products 7.5%, refined petroleum 4.1%). *Major import sources:* United States 34.4%; Venezuela 11.1%; Brazil 5.1%; United Kingdom 4.9%; Panama 4.6%.
Exports (2001): TT$31,873,000,000 (refined petroleum 29.4%, floating docks 12.6%, crude petroleum 9.3%, anhydrous ammonia 8.5%, iron and steel 5.7%, methanol 5.0%). *Major export destinations:* United States 42.3%; Mexico 7.4%; Jamaica 7.0%; Barbados 5.5%; France 3.9%.

Transport and communications

Transport. Railroads: none. Roads (1999): total length 7,900 km (paved 51%). Vehicles (1996): passenger cars 122,000; trucks and buses 24,000. Air transport (2001)[10]: passenger-km 2,496,000,000; metric ton-km cargo 56,236,000; airports (2000) with scheduled flights 2.

Communications

Medium	date	unit	number	units per 1,000 persons
Daily newspapers	2000	circulation	155,000	123
Radio	2000	receivers	672,000	532
Television	2000	receivers	429,000	340
Telephones	2000	main lines	325,100	250
Cellular telephones	2002	subscribers	361,900	278
Personal computers	2002	units	104,000	80
Internet	2002	users	138,000	106

Education and health

Educational attainment (1990). Percentage of population age 25 and over having: no formal schooling 4.5%; primary education 56.4%; secondary 32.1%; higher 3.4%; other/not stated 3.6%. *Literacy* (2000): total population age 15 and over literate 93.8%; males 95.5%, females 92.1%.

Education (1999–2000)

	schools	teachers	students	student/teacher ratio
Primary (age 5–11)	481	7,311[11]	162,736	24.8[11]
Secondary (age 12–16)	...	5,070[11]	105,500	20.6[11]
Higher[12]	1	477	7,585	15.9

Health: physicians (1999) 1,171 (1 per 1,076 persons); hospital beds 4,384 (1 per 287 persons); infant mortality rate (2001) 25.6.
Food (2001): daily per capita caloric intake 2,756 (vegetable products 84%, animal products 16%); 114% of FAO recommended minimum requirement.

Military

Total active duty personnel (2002): 2,700 (army 74.1%, coast guard 25.9%). *Military expenditure as percentage of GNP* (1999): 1.4% (world 2.4%); per capita expenditure U.S.$78.

[1]Excludes speaker, who may be elected from outside the House of Representatives. [2]Area figures for counties are estimated. [3]Preliminary figures. [4]Includes petroleum refining and petrochemicals. [5]Net of value-added taxes less imputed bank service charges. [6]Unemployed. [7]Detail does not add to total given because of rounding. [8]Manufacturing only. [9]Imports c.i.f.; exports f.o.b. [10]BWIA only. [11]1996–97. [12]University of the West Indies.

Internet resources for further information:
- **Central Bank of Trinidad and Tobago http://www.central-bank.org.tt**
- **Central Statistical Office http://www.cso.gov.tt**

Tunisia

Official name: Al-Jumhūrīyah at-Tūnisīyah (Republic of Tunisia).
Form of government: multiparty republic[1] with one legislative house (Chamber of Deputies [182]).
Chief of state: President.
Head of government: Prime Minister.
Capital: Tunis.
Official language: Arabic.
Official religion: Islam.
Monetary unit: 1 dinar (D) = 1,000 millimes; valuation (Sept. 8, 2003) 1 U.S.$ = D 1.31; 1 £ = D 2.08.

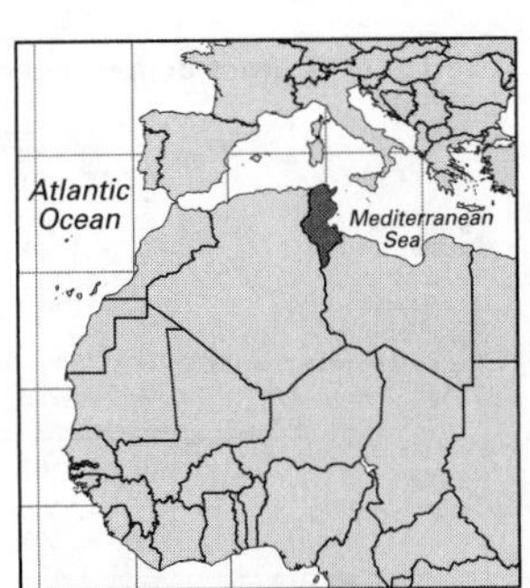

Area and population

Governorates	Capitals	area sq mi	area sq km	population 2002 estimate
Al-Ariānah	Al-Ariānah	192	498	382,600
Bājah	Bājah	1,374	3,558	320,200
Banzart	Bizerte (Banzart)	1,423	3,685	527,600
Bin ʿArūs	Bin ʿArūs	294	761	467,200
Jundūbah	Jundūbah	1,198	3,102	430,100
Al-Kāf	Al-Kāf	1,917	4,965	281,900
Madanīn	Madanīn	3,316	8,588	432,000
Al-Mahdīyah	Al-Mahdīyah	1,145	2,966	376,400
Manūbah	Manūbah	410	1,060	327,000
Al-Munastīr	Al-Munastīr	393	1,019	429,100
Nābul	Nābul	1,076	2,788	649,900
Qābis	Qābis	2,770	7,175	337,000
Qafṣah	Qafṣah	3,471	8,990	333,400
Al-Qaṣrayn	Al-Qaṣrayn	3,114	8,066	424,800
Al-Qayrawān	Al-Qayrawān	2,591	6,712	571,000
Qibilī	Qibilī	8,527	22,084	144,200
Ṣafāqis	Ṣafāqis	2,913	7,545	832,500
Sīdī Bū Zayd	Sīdī Bū Zayd	2,700	6,994	404,100
Siliānah	Siliānah	1,788	4,631	258,100
Sūsah	Sūsah	1,012	2,621	510,000
Tatāuīn	Tatāuīn	15,015	38,889	150,500
Tawzar	Tawzar	1,822	4,719	98,500
Tūnis	Tunis (Tūnis)	134	346	933,700
Zaghwān	Zaghwān	1,069	2,768	157,300
TOTAL		63,170[2]	163,610[2]	9,779,100

Demography

Population (2003): 9,888,000.
Density (2003): persons per sq mi 156.5, persons per sq km 60.4.
Urban-rural (2002): urban 63.4%; rural 36.6%.
Sex distribution (2002): male 50.30%; female 49.70%.
Age breakdown (2002): under 15, 27.9%; 15–29, 30.6%; 30–44, 21.6%; 45–59, 10.8%; 60–74, 7.8%; 75 and over, 1.3%.
Population projection: (2010) 10,624,000; (2020) 11,601,000.
Doubling time: 58 years.
Ethnic composition (2000): Tunisian Arab 67.2%; Bedouin Arab 26.6%; Algerian Arab 2.4%; Berber 1.4%; other 2.4%.
Religious affiliation (2000): Sunnī Muslim 98.9%; Christian 0.5%; other 0.6%.
Major cities (2003): Tunis 699,700 (urban agglomeration [2001] 1,927,000); Ṣafāqis 270,700; Al-Ariānah 217,100[3]; Ettadhamen 188,700[3]; Sūsah 155,900; Al-Qayrawān 117,700.

Vital statistics

Birth rate per 1,000 population (2002): 16.7 (world avg. 21.3).
Death rate per 1,000 population (2002): 5.8 (world avg. 9.1).
Natural increase rate per 1,000 population (2002): 10.9 (world avg. 12.2).
Total fertility rate (avg. births per childbearing woman; 2002): 2.1.
Marriage rate per 1,000 population (1995): 6.0.
Life expectancy at birth (2002): male 71.0 years; female 75.1 years.
Major causes of death: n.a.

National economy

Budget (2002). Revenue: D 11,533,000,000 (tax revenue 91.5%, of which goods and services 34.4%, income tax 22.1%, social security 18.9%, import duties 9.9%; nontax revenue 8.5%). Expenditures: D 11,533,000,000 (current expenditure 79.8%, of which interest on public debt 8.5%; development expenditure 20.2%).
Public debt (external, outstanding; 2001): U.S.$9,085,000,000.
Production (metric tons except as noted). Agriculture, forestry, fishing (2002): olives 1,500,000, tomatoes 810,000, cereals 538,300, watermelons 400,000, potatoes 300,000, dates 110,000, oranges 106,000, apples 100,000; livestock (live animals) 6,850,000 sheep, 1,450,000 goats, 760,000 cattle; roundwood (2002) 2,329,317 cu m; fish catch (2001) 97,103. Mining and quarrying (2002): phosphate rock 8,144,000; iron ore 198,000; zinc (metal content) 35,692. Manufacturing (2002): cement 6,022,000; phosphoric acid 1,219,000; lime 471,000; crude steel 220,000; pig iron 152,000. Energy production (consumption): electricity (kW-hr; 2001) 9,787,000,000 ([2000] 8,150,400,000); coal (metric tons; 1999) none (1,000); crude petroleum (barrels; 2001) 25,712,000 ([1999] 12,800,000); petroleum products (metric tons; 1999) 1,731,000 (3,593,000); natural gas (cu m; 2001) 2,143,100,000 ([1999] 1,810,100,000).
Household income and expenditure. Average household size (2000) 4.7; income per household D 6,450 (U.S.$4,640); expenditure (2000): food and beverages 38.0%, housing and energy 21.5%, household durables 11.1%, health and personal care 10.0%, transportation 9.7%, recreation 8.7%, other 1.0%.
Gross national product (2001): U.S.$20,000,000,000 (U.S.$2,070 per capita).

Structure of gross domestic product and labour force

	2001 in value D '000,000	2001 % of total value	2002 labour force	2002 % of labour force
Agriculture	3,347.0	11.6	709,000	21.0
Mining	220.1	0.8		
Public utilities	1,351.9	4.7	1,144,400	33.9
Manufacturing	5,325.6	18.5		
Construction	1,391.2	4.8		
Transp. and commun.	2,390.7	8.3		
Trade	7,784.4	27.0		
Finance			1,522,300	45.1
Pub. admin., defense	3,913.5	13.6		
Services				
Other	3,068.7[4]	10.7[4]	...	...
TOTAL	28,793.1	100.0	3,375,700	100.0

Population economically active (2002): total 3,375,700; activity rate of total population 34.5% (participation rates: age 15 and over 48.0%; female 24.3%; unemployed 14.9%).

Price and earnings indexes (1995 = 100)

	1996	1997	1998	1999	2000	2001	2002
Consumer price index	103.7	107.5	110.9	113.9	117.2	119.5	122.8
Hourly earnings index	...	...	...	...	...	...	...

Tourism (2001): receipts U.S.$1,605,000,000; expenditures U.S.$273,000,000.
Land use (1994): forested 4.3%; meadows and pastures 20.0%; agricultural and under permanent cultivation 31.9%; other 43.8%.

Foreign trade[5]

Balance of trade (current prices)

	1997	1998	1999	2000	2001	2002
D '000,000	–2,645	–2,971	–3,103	–3,733	–4,193	–3,762
% of total	17.7%	18.6%	18.2%	18.9%	18.1%	16.2%

Imports (2002): D 13,511,000,000 (nonelectrical machinery and equipment 19.6%, fabric 12.7%, food products 10.5%, electrical machinery and equipment 10.0%, crude and refined petroleum 8.3%). *Major import sources:* France 25.6%; Italy 19.5%; Germany 8.9%; Spain 5.0%; U.S. 3.2%.
Exports (2002): D 9,749,000,000 (clothing 30.4%, knitwear 8.4%, crude petroleum 7.3%, phosphates and phosphate derivatives 6.8%, electrical cable and wire 4.7%). *Major export destinations:* France 31.3%; Italy 21.6%; Germany 11.5%; Spain 4.8%; Libya 4.6%.

Transport and communications

Transport. Railroads (2001): route length 2,169 km; passenger-km 1,283,500,000; metric ton-km cargo 2,286,100,000. Roads (1997): total length 23,100 km (paved 79%). Vehicles (2000): passenger cars 482,700; trucks and buses 250,300. Air transport (2001)[6]: passenger-km 2,696,313,000; metric ton-km cargo 20,104,000; airports (1998) 5.

Communications

Medium	date	unit	number	units per 1,000 persons
Daily newspapers	1996	circulation	280,000	31
Radio	1997	receivers	2,060,000	224
Television	1999	receivers	1,800,000	190
Telephones	2002	main lines	1,148,000	117
Cellular telephones	2002	subscribers	503,900	51
Personal computers	2002	units	300,000	31
Internet	2002	users	505,500	52

Education and health

Educational attainment: n.a. *Literacy* (2000): total population age 10 and over literate 74.4%; males literate 83.5%; females literate 65.3%.

Education (2001–02)

	schools	teachers	students	student/teacher ratio
Primary (age 6–11)	4,518	60,566	1,325,707	21.9
Secondary (age 12–18)	1,356	57,821	1,074,391	18.6
Higher	128	11,412	226,102	19.8

Health (2002): physicians 8,463 (1 per 1,156 persons); hospital beds 16,682 (1 per 586 persons); infant mortality rate (2002) 22.1.
Food (2001): daily per capita caloric intake 3,293 (vegetable products 89%, animal products 11%); 138% of FAO recommended minimum requirement.

Military

Total active duty personnel (2002): 35,000 (army 77.1%, navy 12.9%, air force 10.0%). *Military expenditure as percentage of GNP* (1999): 1.8% (world 2.4%); per capita expenditure U.S.$38.

[1]A single party dominates the political system in practice. [2]Total includes 3,506 sq mi- (9,080 sq km-) area of saline lakes that are not distributed by governorate. [3]Within Tunis urban agglomeration. [4]Indirect taxes less subsidies. [5]Imports c.i.f.; exports f.o.b. [6]Tunis Air only.

Internet resources for further information:
- **Central Bank of Tunisia http://www.bct.gov.tn/english**
- **National Statistics Institute (French only) http://www.ins.nat.tn**

Turkey

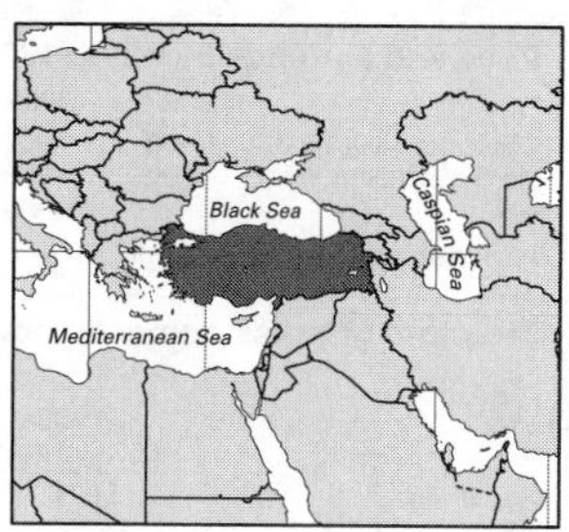

Official name: Türkiye Cumhuriyeti (Republic of Turkey).
Form of government: multiparty republic with one legislative house (Turkish Grand National Assembly [550]).
Chief of state: President.
Head of government: Prime Minister.
Capital: Ankara.
Official language: Turkish.
Official religion: none.
Monetary unit: 1 Turkish lira (TL) = 100 kurush; valuation (Sept. 8, 2003) 1 U.S.$ = TL 1,384,000; 1 £ = TL 2,194,401.

Area and population

Geographic regions[2]	Largest cities	area[1] sq mi	area[1] sq km	population 2000 census
Aegean	İzmir	34,920	90,442	8,938,781
Black Sea	Samsun	32,080	83,088	7,120,747
Central Anatolia	Ankara	97,218	251,793	16,073,370
East Anatolia	Diyarbakir	67,916	175,901	8,004,382
Marmara	Istanbul	24,539	63,556	16,414,533
Mediterranean	Adana	28,485	73,775	7,703,621
South Eastern Anatolia	Gaziantep	13,521	35,020	3,548,493
TOTAL		299,158[3]	774,815[3]	67,803,927

Demography

Population (2003): 70,597,000.
Density (2003): persons per sq mi 236.0, persons per sq km 91.1.
Urban-rural (2001): urban 66.2%; rural 33.8%.
Sex distribution (2000): male 50.57%; female 49.43%.
Age breakdown (2000): under 15, 29.1%; 15–29, 28.8%; 30–44, 21.5%; 45–59, 11.8%; 60–74, 6.8%; 75 and over, 2.0%.
Population projection: (2010) 77,300,000; (2020) 84,864,000.
Doubling time: 58 years.
Ethnic composition (2000)[4]: Turk 65.1%; Kurd 18.9%; Crimean Tatar 7.2%; Arab 1.8%; Azerbaijani 1.0%; Yoruk 1.0%; other 5.0%.
Religious affiliation (2000): Muslim 97.2%, of which Sunnī *c.* 67%, Shīʿī *c.* 30% (including nonorthodox Alevi *c.* 26%); Christian (mostly Eastern Orthodox) 0.6%; other 2.2%.
Major urban agglomerations (2001): Istanbul 10,243,000; Ankara 4,611,000; İzmir 3,437,000; Bursa (2000) 1,166,000; Adana (2000) 1,091,000.

Vital statistics

Birth rate per 1,000 population (2002): 18.0 (world avg. 21.3).
Death rate per 1,000 population (2002): 6.0 (world avg. 9.1).
Natural increase rate per 1,000 population (2002): 12.0 (world avg. 12.2).
Total fertility rate (avg. births per childbearing woman; 2002): 2.1.
Marriage rate per 1,000 population (1998): 7.6.
Divorce rate per 1,000 population (1997): 0.5.
Life expectancy at birth (2002): male 69.2 years; female 74.0 years.
Major causes of death per 100,000 population (1995)[5]: diseases of the circulatory system 322; malignant neoplasms (cancers) 71; accidents and violence 32; infectious and parasitic diseases 20; ill-defined conditions 129.

National economy

Budget (2002). Revenue: TL 71,218,000,000,000,000 (tax revenue 81.3%, of which tax on income 26.7%; nontax revenue 9.8%; special funds 8.4%). Expenditures: TL 98,131,000,000,000,000 (interest payments 43.6%, personnel 22.3%, investments 5.8%).
Public debt (external, outstanding; 2001): U.S.$56,004,000,000.
Production (in '000 metric tons except as noted). Agriculture, forestry, fishing (2002): wheat 21,000, sugar beets 13,000, tomatoes 9,000, barley 7,500, potatoes 5,000, grapes 3,600, corn (maize) 2,500, apples 2,500, seed cotton 2,400, olives 1,500, oranges 1,200, sunflower seeds 800, hazelnuts 625, lentils 480, peaches 450, raisins 250[6], tobacco 154, tea 120[6], garlic 110, attar of roses 800 kg[7]; livestock (number of live animals) 26,972,000 sheep, 10,548,000 cattle, 615,000[8] angora goats; roundwood 18,465,000 cu m; fish catch (2000) 582,376. Mining (2001): boron minerals 4,000,000; chromite 390,000; copper ore (metal content) 52,000. Manufacturing (1995)[9]: refined petroleum 4,583; food products 3,944; textiles 3,907; transport equipment 3,048; iron and steel 2,453; paints, soaps, and pharmaceuticals 2,301. Energy production (consumption): electricity (kW-hr; 2001) 123,096,000,000 ([1999] 118,485,000,000); hard coal (metric tons; 2001) 3,719,000 ([1999] 10,854,000); lignite (metric tons; 2001) 57,157,000 ([1999] 64,078,000); crude petroleum (barrels; 2001) 18,218,000 ([1999] 188,500,000); petroleum products (metric tons; 1999) 21,850,000 (24,801,000); natural gas (cu m; 2000) 611,800,000 ([1999] 12,598,600,000).
Tourism (2001): receipts from visitors U.S.$8,932,000,000; expenditures by nationals abroad U.S.$1,738,000,000.
Population economically active (1997)[10]: total 22,359,000; activity rate of total population 35.8% (participation rates: ages 15–64, 53.1%; female 26.8%; unemployed [2000] 6.6%).

Price and earnings indexes (1995 = 100)

	1995	1996	1997	1998	1999	2000	2001
Consumer price index	100.0	180.3	335.0	618.5	1,019.7	1,579.6	2,439.0
Annual earnings index[11]	100.0	190.4	376.8	650.3	...	...	...

Gross national product (2001): U.S.$167,300,000,000 (U.S.$2,530 per capita).

Structure of gross domestic product and labour force

	2001 in value TL '000,000,000	2001 % of total value	1998 labour force[9]	1998 % of labour force[9]
Agriculture	23,427,659	12.9	8,918,000	39.6
Mining	2,128,387	1.2	154,000	0.7
Manufacturing	36,730,882	20.2	3,267,000	14.5
Construction	9,202,185	5.1	1,277,000	5.7
Public utilities	7,015,153	3.9	115,000	0.5
Transp. and commun.	28,462,322	15.7	957,000	4.3
Trade	37,867,860	20.9	2,860,000	12.7
Finance, real estate	15,130,893	8.3	511,000	2.3
Pub. admin., defense	18,781,015	10.3	3,026,000	13.4
Services	7,622,726	4.2		
Other	–4,960,521[12]	–2.7[12]	1,428,000[13]	6.3[13]
TOTAL	181,408,561	100.0	22,513,000	100.0

Household income and expenditure (1994). Average household size (1999) 4.6; income per household TL 165,089,000 (U.S.$5,576); expenditure: food, tobacco, and café expenditures 38.5%, housing 22.8%, clothing 9.0%.
Land use (1994): forested 26.2%; meadows and pastures 16.1%; agricultural and under permanent cultivation 36.1%; other 21.6%.

Foreign trade[14]

Balance of trade (current prices)

	1997	1998	1999	2000	2001	2002
U.S.$'000,000	–22,298	–18,947	–14,084	–26,782	–10,065	–15,450
% of total	29.8%	26.0%	20.9%	32.5%	13.8%	17.8%

Imports (2002): U.S.$51,203,000,000 (mineral fuels 17.6%, of which crude petroleum 8.0%; nonelectrical machinery 15.9%; electrical machinery 8.5%; iron and steel 5.7%; plastics and plastic products 4.7%). *Major import sources:* Germany 13.7%; Italy 8.1%; Russia 7.6%; U.S. 6.0%; France 5.9%; U.K. 4.8%.
Exports (2002): U.S.$35,753,000,000 (textiles, apparel, and clothing accessories 25.4%; vehicles 9.0%; electrical and electronic machinery 8.1%; nonelectrical machinery 6.1%; iron and steel 6.0%; raw and prepared fruits and vegetables 5.7%). *Major export destinations:* Germany 16.6%; U.S. 9.2%; U.K. 8.5%; Italy 6.4%; France 6.0%.

Transport and communications

Transport. Railroads (2000): length 5,388 mi, 8,671 km; passenger-km 6,122,000,000; metric ton-km cargo 10,032,000,000. Roads (2000): total length 238,379 mi, 383,636 km (paved [1997] 25%). Vehicles (2000): passenger cars 4,283,080; trucks and buses 1,488,016. Air transport (2000)[15]: passenger-km 16,492,416; metric ton-km cargo 379,630,000; airports (1996) 26.

Communications

Medium	date	unit	number	units per 1,000 persons
Daily newspapers	2000	circulation	7,480,000	111
Radio	2000	receivers	38,600,000	573
Television	2000	receivers	30,300,000	449
Telephones	2002	main lines	18,914,900	281
Cellular telephones	2002	subscribers	23,374,400	348
Personal computers	2002	units	3,000,000	45
Internet	2002	users	4,900,000	73

Education and health

Educational attainment (1993). Percentage of population age 25 and over having: no formal schooling 30.5%; incomplete primary education 6.6%; complete primary 40.4%; incomplete secondary 3.1%; complete secondary or higher 19.1%; unknown 0.3%. *Literacy* (2000): total population age 15 and over literate 85.1%; males literate 93.5%; females literate 76.5%.

Education (1998)

	schools	teachers	students	student/ teacher ratio
Primary (age 6–10)	45,112	317,795	9,625,400	30.3
Secondary (age 11–16)	2,598	71,344	1,282,600	18.0
Voc., teacher tr.	3,367	74,559	998,000	13.4
Higher	1,222	60,129	1,465,000	24.4

Health: physicians (2001) 82,920 (1 per 826 persons); hospital beds (1999) 172,112 (1 per 385 persons); infant mortality rate (2002) 45.8.
Food (2000): daily per capita caloric intake 3,343 (vegetable products 90%, animal products 10%); 133% of FAO recommended minimum requirement.

Military

Total active duty personnel (2002): 514,850 (army 78.1%, navy 10.2%, air force 11.7%). *Military expenditure as percentage of GNP* (1999): 5.3% (world 2.4%); per capita expenditure U.S.$154.

[1]Estimated figures. [2]Administratively divided into 81 provinces as of 2000. [3]Detail does not add to total given because of rounding. [4]Per unofficial source. [5]Projected rates based on about 42% of total deaths. [6]1998. [7]1993. [8]1997. [9]Value added in U.S.$'000,000. [10]Civilian population only. [11]Istanbul wage earners only. [12]Import duties less imputed bank charges. [13]Unemployed. [14]Imports c.i.f.; exports f.o.b. [15]Turkish Airlines only.

Internet resources for further information:
- **Ministry of Foreign Affairs http://www.mfa.gov.tr**
- **Central Bank of Turkey http://www.tcmb.gov.tr**
- **State Institute of Statistics http://www.die.gov.tr**

Turkmenistan

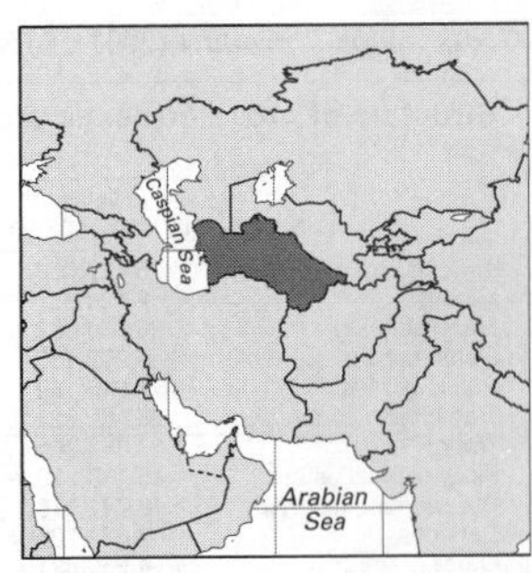

Official name: Türkmenistan (Turkmenistan).
Form of government: unitary republic with one legislative body (Majlis [Parliament; 50]).
Head of state and government: President assisted by the People's Council.
Capital: Ashgabat (formerly Ashkhabad).
Official language: Turkmen.
Official religion: none.
Monetary unit: manat; valuation (Sept. 17, 2003) 1 U.S.$ = 5,148 manat; 1 £ = 8,285 manat.

Area and population

Provinces	Capitals	area sq mi	area sq km	population 2001 estimate
Ahal	Ashgabat	37,500[1]	97,100[1]	767,700
Balkan	Balkanabat	53,500	138,600	468,900
Dashhowuz	Dashhowuz	28,100	72,700	1,165,000
Lebap	Turkmenabad (Chärjew)	36,000	93,200	1,130,700
Mary	Mary	33,400	86,400	1,251,300
City				
Ashgabat	—	[1]	[1]	695,300
TOTAL		188,500	488,100[2]	5,478,900

Demography

Population (2003): 4,867,000[3].
Density (2003): persons per sq mi 25.7, persons per sq km 10.0.
Urban-rural (2002): urban 44.9%; rural 55.1%.
Sex distribution (2001): male 49.44%; female 50.56%.
Age breakdown (2001): under 15, 37.9%; 15–29, 27.9%; 30–44, 23.7%; 45–59, 6.5%; 60–74, 3.5%; 75 and over, 0.5%.
Population projection[3]: (2010) 5,412,000; (2020) 6,211,000.
Doubling time: 39 years.
Ethnic composition (1997): Turkmen 77.0%; Uzbek 9.2%; Russian 6.7%; Kazakh 2.0%; Tatar 0.8%; other 4.3%.
Religious affiliation (1995): Muslim (mostly Sunnī) 87.0%; Russian Orthodox 2.4%; other (mostly nonreligious) 10.6%.
Major cities (1999): Ashgabat (2002) 743,000; Turkmenabad 203,000; Dashhowuz 165,000; Mary 123,000; Balkanabat 108,000.

Vital statistics

Birth rate per 1,000 population (2001): 28.6 (world avg. 21.3); (1998) legitimate 96.2%; illegitimate 3.8%.
Death rate per 1,000 population (2001): 8.0 (world avg. 9.1).
Natural increase rate per 1,000 population (2001): 20.6 (world avg. 12.2).
Total fertility rate (avg. births per childbearing woman; 2001): 3.5.
Marriage rate per 1,000 population (1998): 5.4.
Divorce rate per 1,000 population (1994): 1.5.
Life expectancy at birth (2001): male 57.5 years; female 64.8 years.
Major causes of death per 100,000 population (1998): diseases of the circulatory system 314.6; diseases of the respiratory system 101.1; infectious and parasitic diseases 99.1; accidents, poisoning, and violence 59.3; malignant neoplasms (cancers) 43.9; diseases of the digestive system 30.2.

National economy

Budget (1999). Revenue: 3,693,100,000,000 manat (value-added tax 25.6%, pension and social security fund 22.5%, repayments of scheduled gas 13.0%, excise tax 10.2%, personal income tax 6.1%). Expenditures: 3,894,300,000,000 manat (education 26.9%, pension and social security 15.6%, defense and security 14.9%, health 14.1%, agriculture 5.7%).
Public debt (external, outstanding; 2000): U.S.$1,731,000,000.
Production (metric tons except as noted). Agriculture, forestry, fishing (2002): wheat 2,033,000, seed cotton 600,000, vegetables and melons 327,000, watermelons 230,000, fruit excluding watermelons 185,000; livestock (number of live animals) 6,375,000 sheep and goats, 860,000 cattle, 4,800,000 poultry; roundwood (2000) 2,000,000 cu m; fish catch (2000) 12,775. Mining and quarrying (2000): gypsum 100,000, sodium sulfate 60,000, sulfur 9,000, iodine 355. Manufacturing (value of production in '000,000 manat; 1994): ferrous and nonferrous metals 278; machinery and metalworks 223; food products 129; chemical products 90; construction materials 52; wood products 31. Construction (1994): 1,700,000 sq m. Energy production (consumption): electricity (kW-hr; 1999) 8,860,000,000 (7,460,000,000); crude petroleum (barrels; 2001) 58,000,000 (19,000,000); petroleum products (metric tons; 1999) 6,092,000 (2,333,000); natural gas (cu m; 2001) 46,439,000,000 (7,362,000,000).
Household income and expenditure. Average household size (2000) 4.7; income per household: n.a.; sources of income (1998): wages and salaries 70.6%, pensions and grants 20.9%, self-employment (mainly agricultural income) 2.3%, nonwage income of workers 1.1%; expenditure (1998): food 45.2%, clothing and footwear 16.8%, furniture 13.3%, transportation 7.6%, health 7.0%.
Population economically active (2000): total 1,950,000; activity rate of total population 42.0% (participation rates [1996]: ages 16–59 [male], 16–54 [female] 73.0%; female 42.7%; unemployed, n.a.).

Price and earnings indexes (1994 = 100)[4]

	1994	1995	1996	1997	1998
Consumer price index	100	1,362	7,431	27,502	32,122
Monthly earnings index	100	739	6,334	11,282	16,163

Gross national product (2001): U.S.$5,100,000,000 (U.S.$950 per capita).

Structure of gross domestic product and labour force

	2000 in value '000,000 manat	2000 % of total value	1998 labour force	1998 % of labour force
Agriculture	5,903,300	25.8	892,400	48.5
Mining } Manufacturing }	8,644,500	37.8	226,800	12.3
Public utilities }			48,300	2.6
Construction	2,244,000	9.8	108,200	5.9
Transp. and commun.	1,043,700	4.6	90,700	4.9
Trade	1,008,100	4.4	115,800	6.4
Finance }			12,600	0.7
Public administration, defense }	4,051,000	17.7	28,800	1.6
Services }			284,900	15.5
Other }			30,200	1.6
TOTAL	22,894,600	100.0[2]	1,838,700	100.0

Tourism: receipts from visitors (1998) U.S.$192,000,000; expenditures (1997) U.S.$125,000,000.
Land use (1994): forested 8.2%; meadows and pastures 61.6%; agricultural and under permanent cultivation 3.0%; other 27.2%.

Foreign trade[5]

Balance of trade (current prices)

	1994	1995	1996	1997	1998	1999	2000
U.S.$'000,000	+485	+536	+329	−231	−523	+707	+721
% of total	12.5%	15.4%	10.8%	13.0%	30.0%	26.5%	16.8%

Imports (2000): U.S.$1,785,000,000 (machinery and equipment 43.8%, basic manufactures 21.4%, food products 10.1%, chemicals 8.9%, mineral fuels 1.2%). *Major import sources* (2001): Turkey 14.2%; U.S. 13.9%; Ukraine 12.6%; U.A.E. 8.1%; Russia 7.8%; Germany 6.2%; Iran 5.0%; Uzbekistan 1.8%.
Exports (2000): U.S.$2,506,000,000 (natural gas and oil products 81.0%, crude materials except fuels 10.3%). *Major export destinations* (2001): Iran 17.7%; Turkey 15.1%; Ukraine 12.1%; Germany 10.9%; Switzerland 7.0%; Tajikistan 3.4%; Afghanistan 3.1%.

Transport and communications

Transport. Railroads (1999): length 1,437 mi, 2,313 km; passenger-km 701,000,000; metric ton-km cargo 7,337,000,000. Roads (1999): total length 24,000 km (paved 81%). Vehicles (1995): passenger cars 220,000; trucks and buses 58,200. Air transport (2001)[6]: passenger-km 1,631,000,000; metric ton-km cargo 35,000,000; airports (2002) with scheduled flights 1.

Communications

Medium	date	unit	number	units per 1,000 persons
Radio	2000	receivers	1,190,000	256
Television	2000	receivers	911,000	196
Telephones	2001	main lines	387,600	80
Cellular phones	2001	subscribers	9,500	2.1
Internet	2001	users	8,000	1.6

Education and health

Educational attainment: n.a. *Literacy* (1999): total population age 15 and over literate 98.0%.

Education (1994–95)

	schools	teachers	students	student/ teacher ratio
Primary (age 6–13) } Secondary (age 14–17) }	1,900	72,900	940,600	12.9
Voc., teacher tr.	78	...	26,000	...
Higher	15	...	29,435[7]	...

Health (1995): physicians 13,500 (1 per 330 persons); hospital beds 46,000 (1 per 97 persons); infant mortality rate per 1,000 live births (2001) 73.2.
Food (2001): daily per capita caloric intake 2,738 (vegetable products 97%, animal products 3%); 107% of FAO recommended minimum requirement.

Military

Total active duty personnel (2002): 17,500 (army 82.9%, air force 17.1%). *Military expenditure as percentage of GNP* (1999): 3.4% (world 2.4%); per capita expenditure U.S.$122.

[1]Ahal includes Ashgabat. [2]Detail does not add to total given because of rounding. [3]UN estimate; official Turkmen estimates are significantly higher. [4]December. [5]Import data in balance of trade is c.i.f. [6]Turkmenavia only. [7]1995–96.

Internet resources for further information:
- **United Nations in Turkmenistan http://www.untuk.org**
- **Interstate Statistical Committee of the Commonwealth of Independent States http://www.cisstat.com/eng/macro0.htm**

Tuvalu

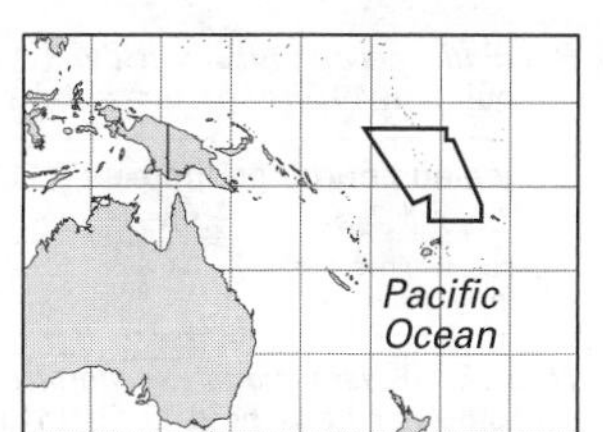

Official name: Tuvalu.
Form of government: constitutional monarchy with one legislative house (Parliament [12]).
Chief of state: British Monarch, represented by Governor-General.
Head of government: Prime Minister.
Capital: government offices are at Vaiaku, Fongafale islet, of Funafuti atoll.
Official language: none.
Official religion: none.
Monetary units[1]: 1 Tuvalu dollar = 1 Australian dollar ($T = $A) = 100 Tuvalu and Australian cents; valuation (Sept. 8, 2003) 1 U.S.$ = $A 1.55; 1 £ = $A 2.46.

Area and population

	area		population
Islands[2]	sq mi	sq km	2000 estimate
Funafuti	1.08	2.79	4,590
Nanumaga	1.07	2.78	770
Nanumea	1.49	3.87	1,010
Niulakita	0.16	0.42	3
Niutao	0.98	2.53	1,120[3]
Nui	1.09	2.83	690
Nukufetau	1.15	2.99	800
Nukulaelae	0.70	1.82	360
Vaitupu	2.16	5.60	1,410
TOTAL	9.90[4, 5]	25.63[4]	10,750

Demography

Population (2003): 10,200.
Density (2003): persons per sq mi 1,030, persons per sq km 398.
Urban-rural (2002): urban 54.0%; rural 46.0%.
Sex distribution (2000): male 48.65%; female 51.35%.
Age breakdown (2000): under 15, 33.7%; 15–29, 22.1%; 30–44, 21.9%; 45–59, 12.8%; 60–74, 7.3%; 75 and over, 2.2%.
Population projection: (2010) 11,000; (2020) 13,000.
Doubling time: 50 years.
Ethnic composition (2000): Tuvaluan (Polynesian) 96.3%; mixed (Pacific Islander/European/Asian) 1.0%; Micronesian 1.0%; European 0.5%; other 1.2%.
Religious affiliation (1995): Church of Tuvalu (Congregational) 85.4%; Seventh-day Adventist 3.6%; Roman Catholic 1.4%; Jehovah's Witness 1.1%; Bahā'ī 1.0%; other 7.5%.
Major locality (2001): Fongafale, on Funafuti atoll, 5,000.

Vital statistics

Birth rate per 1,000 population (2002): 21.4 (world avg. 21.3).
Death rate per 1,000 population (2002): 7.5 (world avg. 9.1).
Natural increase rate per 1,000 population (2002): 13.9 (world avg. 12.2).
Total fertility rate (avg. births per childbearing woman; 2002): 3.1.
Marriage rate per 1,000 population: n.a.
Divorce rate per 1,000 population: n.a.
Life expectancy at birth (2002): male 64.8 years; female 69.2 years.
Major causes of death per 100,000 population (1985): diseases of the digestive system 170.0; diseases of the circulatory system 150.0; diseases of the respiratory system 120.0; diseases of the nervous system 120.0; malignant neoplasms (cancers) 70.0; infectious and parasitic diseases 40.0; endocrine and metabolic disorders 20.0; ill-defined conditions 430.0.

National economy

Budget (2001). Revenue: $A 33,519,000. Expenditures: $A 24,091,000.
Public debt (external; 1993): U.S.$6,000,000.
Gross national product (1998): U.S.$14,700,000 (U.S.$1,400 per capita).

Structure of gross domestic product and labour force

	1998		1991	
	in value $A '000[6]	% of total value[6]	labour force	% of labour force
Agriculture, fishing, forestry	3,484	15.8	4,020	68.0
Mining	638	2.9	—	—
Manufacturing[7]	881	4.0	60	1.0
Construction	2,951	13.4	240	4.0
Public utilities	574	2.6	—	—
Transp. and commun.	1,380	6.2	60	1.0
Trade, hotels, and restaurants	2,972	13.5	240	4.0
Finance	2,376	10.8	—	—
Pub. admin., defense Services	4,806	21.8	1,290	22.0
Other	1,983	9.0	...	...
TOTAL	22,045	100.0	5,910	100.0

Production (metric tons except as noted). Agriculture[8], forestry, fishing (2002): coconuts 1,000, tropical fruit 400, vegetables 380, bananas 250, roots and tubers 120, other agricultural products include breadfruit, pulaka (taro), pandanus fruit, sweet potatoes, and pawpaws; livestock (number of live animals) 13,200 pigs, 10,000 ducks, 40,000 chickens; forestry, n.a.; fish catch (2001) 400. Mining and quarrying[9]: n.a. Manufacturing: tiny amounts of copra, handicrafts, and garments. Overseas employment (2000) of Tuvaluan seafarers contributes about U.S.$5,000,000 annually to the Tuvalu economy. Energy production (consumption): electricity (kW-hr; 1992) 1,300,000 (1,300,000); coal, none (none); crude petroleum, none (n.a.); petroleum products, none (n.a.); natural gas, none (none).
Tourism (1998): receipts from visitors U.S.$200,000; expenditures by nationals abroad, n.a.
Population economically active (1991): total 5,910; activity rate of total population 65.3% (participation rates: ages 15–64, 85.5%; female [1979] 51.3%; unemployed [1979] 4.0%).

Price and earnings indexes (1990 = 100)

	1994	1995	1996	1997	1998	1999	2000
Consumer price index	103.7	109.0	109.8	111.5	112.4	113.5	119.5
Earnings index	...	...	...	...	...	...	...

Household income and expenditure. Average household size (1994): Funafuti 7.0, other islands 5.8; average annual gross income per household (1994): Funafuti $A 12,012 (U.S.$8,789), other islands $A 3,536 (U.S.$2,587); sources of income (1987): agriculture and other 45.0%, cash economy only 38.0%, overseas remittances 17.0%; expenditure (1992)[10]: food 45.5%, housing and household operations 11.5%, transportation 10.5%, alcohol and tobacco 10.5%, clothing 7.5%, other 14.5%.
Land use (1987): agricultural and under permanent cultivation 73.6%[11]; scrub 16.1%; other 10.3%.

Foreign trade

Balance of trade (current prices)

	1995	1996	1997	1998	1999	2000
$A '000	–6,373	–5,638	–7,771	–11,341	–14,353	–22,250
% of total	94.4%	88.6%	91.2%	98.8%	77.3%	89.1%

Imports (1999): $A 16,461,000 (food 26%, machinery and transport equipment 25%, refined petroleum 9%, chemicals and chemical products 5%, beverages and tobacco 5%). *Major import sources:* Australia 38%; Fiji 32%; New Zealand 11%; Japan 6%; China 2%.
Exports (1999): $A 2,108,000 (primarily copra, stamps, and handicrafts). *Major export destinations* (1995): South Africa 64%; Colombia 9%; Belgium-Luxembourg 9%.

Transport and communications

Transport. Railroads: none. Roads (2000): total length 28 km (paved, none). Vehicles[12]: n.a. Merchant marine (1992): vessels (100 gross tons and over) 6; total deadweight tonnage 16,005. Air transport: n.a.; airports (2001) 1.

Communications

Medium	date	unit	number	units per 1,000 persons
Radio	1997	receivers	4,000	384
Television	1996	receivers	100	13
Telephones	1999	main lines	630	55

Education and health

Educational attainment (mid-1990s). Percentage of population age 15 and over (on Funafuti) having: no formal schooling through completed primary education 31.9%; some secondary 46.6%; completed secondary to some higher 18.6%; completed higher 2.9%. *Literacy* (1990): total population literate in Tuvaluan 8,593 (95.0%); literacy in English estimated at 45.0%.

Education (1998)

	schools	teachers[13]	students	student/ teacher ratio
Primary (age 5–11)	12	91[13]	1,811[13]	19.9[13]
Secondary (age 12–18)[14]	1	31	345	11.1
Vocational[15]	1	10	58	...
Higher	—	—	—	—

Health (1999): physicians 8 (1 per 1,375 persons); hospital beds (1990) 30 (1 per 302 persons); infant mortality rate per 1,000 live births (2002): 22.0.

Military

Total active duty personnel: none; Tuvalu relies on Australian-trained volunteers from Fiji and Papua New Guinea.

[1]The value of the Tuvalu dollar is pegged to the value of the Australian dollar, which is also legal currency in Tuvalu. [2]Local government councils have been established on all islands except Niulakita. [3]Niutao includes Niulakita. [4]Another survey puts the area at 9.4 sq mi (24.4 sq km). [5]Detail does not add to total given because of rounding. [6]In purchasers' values. [7]Including cottage industry. [8]Because of poor soil quality, only limited subsistence agriculture is possible on the islands. [9]Research into the mineral potential of Tuvalu's maritime exclusive economic zone (289,500 sq mi [750,000 sq km] of the Pacific Ocean) is currently being conducted by the South Pacific Geo-Science Commission. [10]Weights of consumer price index components. [11]Capable of supporting coconut palms, pandanus, and breadfruit. [12]There are several cars, tractors, trailers, and light trucks on Funafuti; a few motorcycles are in use on most islands. [13]1994. [14]2000. [15]1991.

Internet resources for further information:
- **United Nations Development Programme, Common Country Assessments http://www.undp.org.fj/CCAs.htm**
- **Secretariat of Pacific Communities http://www.spc.org**

Uganda

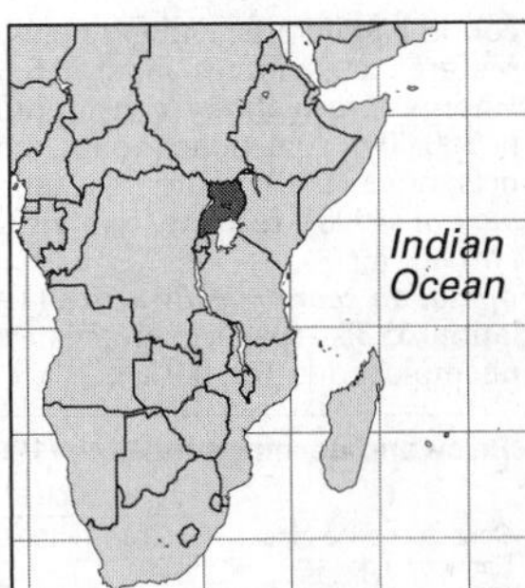

Official name: Republic of Uganda.
Form of government: nonparty republic with one legislative house (Parliament [305[1]]).
Head of state and government: President.
Capital: Kampala.
Official language: English[2].
Official religion: none.
Monetary unit: 1 Uganda shilling (U Sh) = 100 cents; valuation (Sept. 8, 2003) 1 U.S.$ = U Sh 2,001; 1 £ = U Sh 3,173.

Area and population

		area		population
				2002
Geographic regions[3]	Principal cities	sq mi	sq km	census[4]
Central	Kampala	23,749	61,510	6,683,887
Eastern	Jinja	15,426	39,953	6,301,677
Northern	Gulu	32,687	84,658	5,345,964
Western	Mbarara	21,204	54,917	6,417,449
TOTAL		93,065[5, 6]	241,038[5]	24,748,977

Demography

Population (2003): 25,437,000.
Density (2002)[7]: persons per sq mi 334.3, persons per sq km 129.1.
Urban-rural (1999–2000): urban 13.0%; rural 87.0%.
Sex distribution (2002): male 48.99%; female 51.01%.
Age breakdown (2000): under 15, 51.1%; 15–29, 26.2%; 30–44, 13.6%; 45–59, 5.7%; 60–74, 2.9%; 75 and over, 0.5%.
Population projection: (2010) 32,424,000; (2020) 45,826,000.
Doubling time: 27 years.
Ethnolinguistic composition (1991): Ganda 18.1%; Nkole 10.7%; Kiga 8.4%; Soga 8.2%; Lango 5.9%; Lugbara 4.7%; Gisu 4.5%; Acholi 4.4%.
Religious affiliation (1995): Christian 66%, of which Roman Catholic 33%, Protestant 33% (of which mostly Anglican); traditional beliefs 18%; Muslim 16%.
Major cities (2002): Kampala 1,208,544[8]; Gulu 113,144; Lira 89,871; Jinja 86,520; Mbale 70,437.

Vital statistics

Birth rate per 1,000 population (2000): 48.0 (world avg. 21.3).
Death rate per 1,000 population (2000): 22.4 (world avg. 9.1).
Natural increase rate per 1,000 population (2000): 25.6 (world avg. 12.2).
Total fertility rate (avg. births per childbearing woman; 2000): 7.0.
Life expectancy at birth (2000): male 42.2 years; female 43.7 years.

National economy

Budget (2001–02). Revenue: U Sh 1,977,500,000,000 (taxes 58.4%, of which VAT 19.9%, excise taxes 18.3%, income taxes 14.4%, tax on international trade 5.9%; grants 36.6%; nontax revenue 5.0%). Expenditures: U Sh 2,565,000,000,000 (current expenditures 55.8%, of which public administration 14.3%, education 14.1%, defense 8.2%, health 6.4%, public order 4.5%; capital expenditures 44.2%).
Public debt (external, outstanding; 2001): U.S.$3,306,000,000.
Production (metric tons except as noted). Agriculture, forestry, fishing (2002): plantains 9,600,000, cassava 5,300,000, sweet potatoes 2,515,000, sugarcane 1,600,000, corn (maize) 1,174,000, millet 590,000, potatoes 510,000, sorghum 430,000, coffee 198,000, peanuts (groundnuts) 148,000, rice 114,000; livestock (number of live animals) 5,900,000 cattle, 5,600,000 goats, 1,550,000 pigs, 1,200,000 sheep, 25,500,000 chickens; roundwood 38,316,824 cu m; fish catch (2001) 356,032. Mining and quarrying (2001): cobalt 634; gold (metal content) 56 kg. Manufacturing (2001): cement 431,084; sugar 130,326; soap 90,807; metal products 77,049; footwear 1,979,000 pairs; beer 1,079,000 hectolitres; soft drinks 816,860 hectolitres. Energy production (consumption): electricity (kW-hr; 2001) 1,534,700,000 (1,534,700,000); coal (metric tons) none (none); crude petroleum (barrels) none (none); petroleum products (metric tons; 1999) none (396,000); natural gas (cu m) none (none).
Tourism (2001): receipts from visitors U.S.$158,000,000; expenditures by nationals abroad (1999) U.S.$141,000,000.
Gross national product (2001): U.S.$5,900,000,000 (U.S.$260 per capita).

Structure of gross domestic product and labour force

	2000–01		2001	
	in value U Sh '000,000	% of total value	labour force	% of labour force
Agriculture	3,673,126	39.7	9,326,000	79.6
Mining	63,566	0.7		
Manufacturing	799,777	8.6		
Construction	786,881	8.5		
Public utilities	128,730	1.4		
Transp. and commun.	541,119	5.9	2,388,000	20.4
Trade	1,299,629	14.0		
Finance; Pub. admin., defense; Services	895,121	9.7		
Other	1,067,979	11.5		
TOTAL	9,255,928	100.0	11,714,000	100.0

Population economically active (2001): total 11,714,000; activity rate of total population 49.3% (participation rates: ages 15–64, 78.9%[9]; female 35.2%).

Price and earnings indexes (1995 = 100)

	1995	1996	1997	1998	1999	2000	2001
Consumer price index	100.0	107.2	114.6	114.6	121.9	125.4	127.9
Earnings index	...	...	...	...	...	...	...

Household income and expenditure (1999–2000)[9]. Average household size 5.2; income per household U Sh 141,000 (U.S.$91[10]); sources of income: wages and self-employment 78.0%, transfers 13.0%, rent 9.0%; expenditure: food and beverages 51.0%, rent, energy, and services 17.0%, education 7.0%, household durable goods 6.0%, transportation 5.0%, health 4.0%.
Land use (1994): forest 31.5%; pasture 9.1%; agriculture 34.0%; other 25.4%.

Foreign trade[11]

Balance of trade (current prices)

	1996	1997	1998	1999	2000	2001
U Sh '000,000,000	–633.8	–831.1	–952.7	–1,207.0	–1,727.0	–1,995.9
% of total	34.1%	41.1%	50.1%	44.6%	53.2%	55.4%

Imports (2001–02): U.S.$1,084,900,000 (machinery and apparatus 28.3%, refined petroleum 16.1%, food and live animals 15.9%, road vehicles 15.8%, pharmaceuticals 4.9%). *Major import sources* (2001): Kenya 28.0%; Japan 7.5%; U.K. 7.2%; India 6.6%; United Arab Emirates 5.6%; U.S. 2.8%.
Exports (2001–02): U.S.$475,500,000 (unroasted coffee 21.6%, fish products 17.0%, tea 5.7%, cereal 2.8%, cotton 2.8%). *Major export destinations* (2001): Switzerland 15.5%; Kenya 13.1%; The Netherlands 11.7%; Hong Kong 5.9%; South Africa 5.6%; Belgium 3.6%.

Transport and communications

Transport. Railroads (2000): route length 1,241 km; passenger-km (1996) 28,000,000; metric ton-km cargo 199,494,000. Roads (1996): total length 26,800 km (paved 7.7%). Vehicles (2000): passenger cars 49,016; trucks and buses 55,683. Merchant marine (1992): vessels (100 gross tons and over) 2. Air transport (1999): passenger-km 356,000,000; metric ton-km cargo 54,000,000; airports (2002) 1.

Communications

Medium	date	unit	number	units per 1,000 persons
Daily newspapers	2000	circulation	45,900	2.0
Radio	2000	receivers	2,920,000	127
Television	2000	receivers	620,000	27
Telephones	2002	main lines	55,000	2.2
Cellular telephones	2002	subscribers	393,300	16
Personal computers	2002	units	82,000	3.3
Internet	2002	users	70,000	2.8

Education and health

Educational attainment (1991). Percentage of population age 25 and over having: no formal schooling or less than one full year 46.9%; primary education 42.1%; secondary 10.5%; higher 0.5%. *Literacy* (1999–2000): population age 10 and over literate 65.0%; males literate 74.0%; females literate 57.0%.

Education (1999)

	schools	teachers	students	student/ teacher ratio
Primary (age 5–11)[12]	8,531	109,733	6,591,429	60.1
Secondary (age 12–15)[12]	...	22,599	427,492	18.9
Voc., teacher tr.[12, 13]	...	2,094	38,500	18.4
Higher[14]	1	1,134	14,279	12.6

Health: physicians (1993) 840 (1 per 22,399 persons); hospital beds (1989) 20,136 (1 per 817 persons); infant mortality rate (2000) 93.3.
Food (2001): daily per capita caloric intake 2,398 (vegetable products 94%, animal products 6%); 103% of FAO recommended minimum requirement.

Military

Total active duty personnel (2002): 50,000–60,000[15]. *Military expenditure as percentage of GNP* (1999): 2.3% (world 2.4%); per capita expenditure U.S.$6.

[1]Includes 10 ex officio members (ministers who are not elected to Parliament). [2]The constitution was translated into six local languages in 1999 including Ganda (Luganda), Acholi, Teso (Ateso), Lugbara, and two others. [3]The 39 administrative districts in Uganda as of 1994 were increased to 45 administrative districts in 1997. Eight additional administrative districts were announced in November 2000 and 3 more in July 2001, for a total of 56 administrative districts. [4]Revised preliminary. [5]Includes water area of 16,984 sq mi (43,989 sq km); Uganda's portion of Lake Victoria comprises 11,954 sq mi (30,960 sq km). [6]Detail does not add to total given because of rounding. [7]Based on land area only. [8]Urban agglomeration. [9]Based on nationally representative household survey. [10]The household income for urban areas is U Sh 302,900 (U.S.$195). [11]Imports c.i.f.; exports f.o.b. [12]Public sector only. [13]1998. [14]University only. [15]Breakdown by branch of service is unavailable.

Internet resources for further information:
- **Uganda Bureau of Statistics http://www.ubos.org**
- **Bank of Uganda http://www.bou.or.ug**

Ukraine

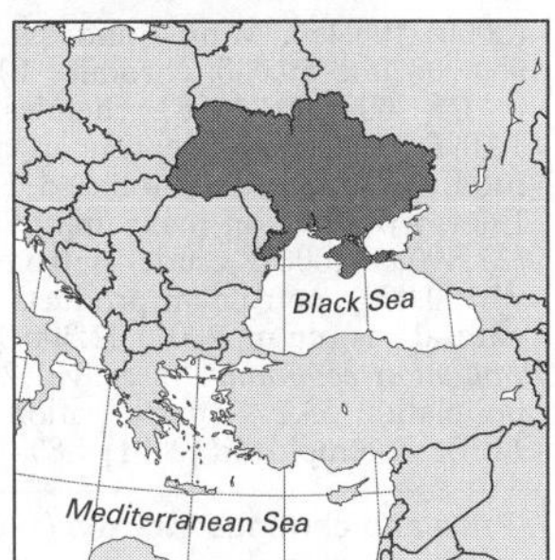

Official name: Ukrayina (Ukraine).
Form of government: unitary multiparty republic with a single legislative body (Supreme Council [450]).
Head of state: President.
Head of government: Prime Minister.
Capital: Kiev (Kyyiv).
Official language: Ukrainian.
Official religion: none.
Monetary unit: hryvnya (pl. hryvnyas)[1]; (Sept. 8, 2003) free rate, 1 U.S.$ = 5.33 hryvnyas; 1 £ = 8.46 hryvnyas.

Area and population

Autonomous republic	area sq km	population 2003[2] estimate	Provinces	area sq km	population 2003[2] estimate
Crimea (Krym)	26,100	2,018,400	Kyyiv (Kiev)	28,100	1,808,300
Cities			Luhansk	26,700	2,507,300
Kiev	800	2,621,700	Lviv	21,800	2,611,000
Sevastopol	900	378,500	Mykolayiv	24,600	1,251,500
			Odessa	33,300	2,448,200
Provinces			Poltava	28,800	1,609,400
Cherkasy	20,900	1,386,600	Rivne	20,100	1,168,300
Chernihiv	31,900	1,225,200	Sumy	23,800	1,279,900
Chernivtsi	8,100	918,500	Ternopil	13,800	1,134,200
Dnipropetrovsk	31,900	3,532,800	Vinnytsya	26,500	1,753,900
Donetsk	26,500	4,774,400	Volyn	20,200	1,054,700
Ivano-Frankivsk	13,900	1,403,700	Zakarpatska	12,800	1,253,900
Kharkiv	31,400	2,887,900	Zaporizhzhya	27,200	1,909,300
Kherson	28,500	1,161,400	Zhytomyr	29,900	1,373,900
Khmelnytsky	20,600	1,414,900	TOTAL	603,700	48,003,500
Kirovohrad	24,600	1,115,700			

Demography

Population (2003): 47,856,000.
Density (2003): persons per sq mi 205.3, persons per sq km 79.3.
Urban-rural (2001): urban 67.2%; rural 32.8%.
Sex distribution (2001): male 46.42%; female 53.58%.
Age breakdown (2001): under 15, 17.3%; 15–29, 22.3%; 30–44, 21.7%; 45–59, 17.8%; 60–74, 15.7%; 75 and over, 5.2%.
Population projection: (2010) 45,970,000; (2020) 44,148,000.
Ethnic composition (2001): Ukrainian 77.8%; Russian 17.3%; Belarusian 0.6%; Moldovan 0.5%; Crimean Tatar 0.5%; other 3.3%.
Religious affiliation (1995): Ukrainian Orthodox (Russian patriarchy) 19.5%; Ukrainian Orthodox (Kiev patriarchy) 9.7%; Ukrainian Catholic (Uniate) 7.0%; Protestant 3.6%; other Orthodox 1.6%; Roman Catholic 1.2%; Jewish 0.9%; other (mostly nonreligious) 56.5%.
Major cities (2001): Kiev 2,621,700[3]; Kharkiv 1,470,000; Dnipropetrovsk 1,064,000; Odessa 1,029,000; Donetsk 1,016,000; Zaporizhzhya 814,000.

Vital statistics

Birth rate per 1,000 population (2002): 9.6 (world avg. 21.3); (1993) legitimate 87.0%; illegitimate 13.0%.
Death rate per 1,000 population (2002): 16.4 (world avg. 9.1).
Natural increase rate per 1,000 population (2002): –6.8 (world avg. 12.2).
Total fertility rate (avg. births per childbearing woman; 2002): 1.3.
Life expectancy at birth (2002): male 60.9 years; female 72.1 years.
Major causes of death per 100,000 population (2000): circulatory diseases 942.2; neoplasms (cancers) 197.3; accidents 149.4; respiratory diseases 77.0.

National economy

Budget (2001). Revenue: 54,569,300,000 hryvnyas (tax revenue 81.1%, of which social security contribution 36.0%, taxes on goods and services 29.1%, income tax 11.6%, other 4.4%; nontax revenue 9.1%; other 9.8%). Expenditures: 58,973,600,000 hryvnyas (social security 43.2%; economy 8.2%; debt payment 6.7%; education 6.2%; public order 6.1%; defense 5.8%; health 1.9%).
Production (metric tons except as noted). Agriculture, forestry, fishing (2002): wheat 20,550,000, potatoes 16,100,000, sugar beets 14,400,000, barley 10,358,000, corn (maize) 4,171,000, rye 1,500,000, oats 942,000; livestock (number of live animals) 9,421,000 cattle, 8,370,000 pigs, 1,875,000 sheep and goats; roundwood (2002) 9,859,300 cu m; fish catch (2000) 423,693. Mining and quarrying (2000): iron ore 55,883,000; manganese (metal content) 930,000; uranium 600,000. Manufacturing (value of production in '000,000 hryvnyas; 1998): iron and steel 14,525; food and beverages 12,974; nonelectrical machinery 3,838; fabricated metal products 2,919; industrial chemicals 2,741. Energy production (consumption): electricity (kW-hr; 2002) 172,800,000,000 ([1999] 168,679,000,000); hard coal (2002) 59,400,000,000 ([1999] 87,745,000); lignite (2001) 1,035,000 ([1999] 1,532,000); crude petroleum (barrels; 2001) 27,150,000 ([2000] 126,290,000); petroleum products (barrels; 1999) 12,359,000 (15,557,000); natural gas (cu m; 2002) 17,700,000,000 (76,089,500,000).
Population economically active (2002): total 22,701,700; activity rate of total population 47.2% (participation rates: ages 16–59 [male], 15–64 [female] 56.6%; female 48.8%; unemployed 10.1% [registered 5.8%]).

Price and earnings indexes (1997 = 100)

	1997	1998	1999	2000	2001	2002
Consumer price index	100.0	110.6	135.7	174.0	196.8	198.4
Monthly earnings index	100.0	107.3	124.0	160.8	...	...

Public debt (external; 2001): U.S.$8,197,000,000.
Gross national product (2001): U.S.$35,200,000,000 (U.S.$720 per capita).

Structure of gross domestic product and labour force

	2002 in value '000,000 hryvnyas	2002 % of total value	2000 labour force	2000 % of labour force
Agriculture	29,632	13.4	4,977,000	27.6
Mining, Manufacturing, Public utilities	67,238	30.5	3,532,000	19.6
Construction	7,504	3.4	895,000	4.9
Transp. and commun.	25,291	11.5	1,228,000	6.8
Trade	21,773	9.9	1,406,000	7.8
Finance, Pub. admin., defense, Services	40,392	18.3	3,318,000	18.4
Other	28,726[4]	13.0[4]	2,707,600[5]	15.0[5]
TOTAL	220,556	100.0	18,063,600[6]	100.0[7]

Tourism (2001): receipts U.S.$2,725,000,000; expenditures U.S.$2,179,000,000.
Household income and expenditure (1996). Average household size (2002): 2.7; income per household (2002) 7,900 hryvnyas (U.S.$1,500); sources of income (2002): wages and salaries 42.8%, subsidies and pensions 20.4%, remuneration from abroad 8.6%, sales of agricultural products 5.0%, other 23.2%; expenditures (2002): food and beverages 62.8%, consumer goods 30.0%, housing 7.2%.

Foreign trade

Balance of trade (current prices)

	1997	1998	1999	2000	2001	2002
U.S.$'000,000	–4,205	–2,584	+244	+829	+198	+710
% of total	12.0%	8.6%	0.9%	2.7%	0.6%	1.9%

Imports (2002): U.S.$17,959,000,000 (fuel and energy products 41.0%, machinery 22.4%, chemicals and chemical products 13.1%, food and raw materials 6.6%). *Major import sources:* Russia 37.4%; Germany 9.8%; Turkmenistan 3.4%; U.S. 2.8%; Belarus 1.6%.
Exports (2002): U.S.$18,669,000,000 (ferrous and nonferrous metals 39.3%, wood and wood products 14.5%, food and raw materials 13.2%, machinery 11.5%, chemicals and chemical products 10.0%). *Major export destinations:* Russia 17.6%; Turkey 6.8%; Germany 4.2%; China 3.9%; U.S. 2.9%.

Transport and communications

Transport. Railroads (2001): length 22,218 km; (1999) passenger-km 47,600,000,000; metric ton-km cargo 156,336,000,000. Roads (2002): total length 169,679 km (paved 97%). Vehicles (2000): passenger cars 5,250,100. Air transport (1999): passenger-km 1,312,000,000; metric ton-km cargo 138,000,000; airports (1999) with scheduled flights 12.

Communications

Medium	date	unit	number	units per 1,000 persons
Daily newspapers	2000	circulation	4,970,000	101
Radio	2000	receivers	43,800,000	889
Television	2000	receivers	22,500,000	456
Telephones	2001	main lines	10,669,600	212
Cellular telephones	2001	subscribers	2,224,600	44
Personal computers	2002	units	951,000	19
Internet	2002	users	1,000,000	20

Education and health

Educational attainment: n.a. *Literacy* (1999): percentage of total population age 15 and over literate 99.6%; males literate 99.7%; females literate 99.5%.

Education (2001–02)

	schools	teachers	students	student/ teacher ratio
Primary (age 6–13), Secondary (age 14–17)	22,200	568,000	6,601,000	11.6
Voc., teacher tr.	1,003	...	533,600	...
Higher	979	...	2,109,300	...

Health (2002): physicians 224,000 (1 per 215 persons); hospital beds 465,000 (1 per 104 persons); infant mortality rate per 1,000 live births (2002) 21.1.
Food (2001): daily per capita caloric intake 3,008 (vegetable products 80%, animal products 20%); 118% of FAO recommended minimum requirement.

Military

Total active duty personnel (2002): 302,300 (army 49.9%, air force 16.2%, navy 4.5%, headquarters 14.9%, paramilitary 14.5%). *Military expenditure as percentage of GNP* (1999): 3.0% (world 2.4%); per capita expenditure U.S.$103.

[1]On Sept. 2, 1996, the karbovanets, a transitional currency, was replaced by the hryvnya at a 100,000-to-1 ratio. [2]January 1. [3]2003. [4]Less imputed bank service charges, net indirect taxes, and taxes on production. [5]Unemployed. [6]Excludes about 4,500,000 self-employed, including employment in personal farms. [7]Detail does not add to total given because of rounding.

Internet resources for further information:
- **National Bank of Ukraine http://www.bank.gov.ua/ENGL/DEFAULT.htm**

United Arab Emirates

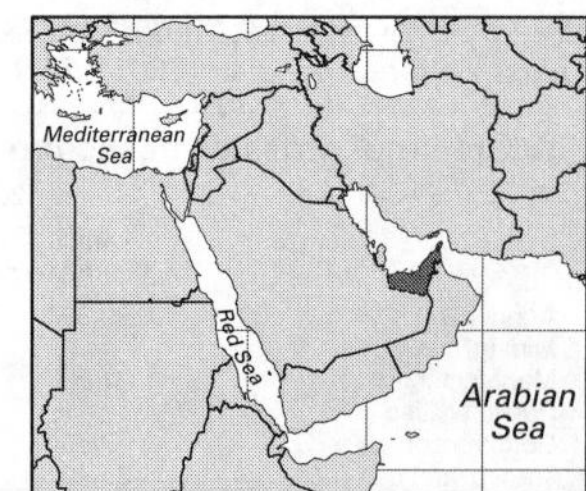

Official name: Al-Imārāt al-ʿArabīyah al-Muttaḥidah (United Arab Emirates).
Form of government: federation of seven emirates with one appointive advisory body (Federal National Council [40[1]]).
Chief of state: President.
Head of government: Prime Minister.
Capital: Abu Dhabi.
Official language: Arabic.
Official religion: Islam.
Monetary unit: 1 U.A.E. dirham (Dh) = 100 fils; valuation (Sept. 8, 2003) 1 U.S.$ = Dh 3.67; 1 £ = Dh 5.82.

Area and population

		area[2]		population
Emirates	Capitals	sq mi	sq km	2001 estimate
Abū Ẓaby (Abu Dhabi)	Abu Dhabi	28,210	73,060	1,362,000
ʿAjmān (Ajman)	ʿAjmān	100	260	196,000
Dubayy (Dubai)	Dubai	1,510	3,900	1,029,000
Al-Fujayrah (Fujairah)	Al-Fujayrah	500	1,300	106,000
Raʾs al-Khaymah (Ras al-Khaimah)	Raʾs al-Khaymah	660	1,700	181,000
Ash-Shāriqah (Sharjah)	Sharjah	1,000	2,600	562,000
Umm al-Qaywayn (Umm al-Qaiwain)	Umm al-Qaywayn	300	780	52,000
TOTAL		32,280	83,600	3,488,000

Demography

Population (2003): 3,818,000.
Density (2003): persons per sq mi 118.3, persons per sq km 45.7.
Urban-rural (2001): urban 87.2%; rural 12.8%.
Sex distribution (2001): male 67.63%; female 32.37%.
Age breakdown (2001): under 15, 26.2%; 15–29, 29.2%; 30–44, 33.4%; 45–59, 9.6%; 60–74, 1.4%; 75 and over, 0.2%.
Population projection: (2010) 4,299,000; (2020) 4,889,000.
Doubling time: 50 years.
Ethnic composition (2000): Arab 48.1%, of which U.A.E. Arab 12.2%, U.A.E Bedouin 9.4%, Egyptian Arab 6.2%, Omani Arab 4.1%, Saudi Arab 4.0%; South Asian 35.7%, of which Pashtun 7.1%, Balochi 7.1%, Malayali 7.1%; Persian 5.0%; Filipino 3.4%; white 2.4%; other 5.4%.
Religious affiliation (1995): Muslim 96.0% (Sunnī 80.0%, Shīʿī 16.0%); other (mostly Christian and Hindu) 4.0%.
Major cities (1995): Dubai (2000) 886,000; Abu Dhabi (2001) 471,000; Sharjah 320,095; Al-ʿAyn 225,970; ʿAjmān 114,395; Raʾs al-Khaymah 77,550.

Vital statistics

Birth rate per 1,000 population (2001): 18.1 (world avg. 21.3).
Death rate per 1,000 population (2001): 3.8 (world avg. 9.1).
Natural increase rate per 1,000 population (2001): 14.3 (world avg. 12.2).
Total fertility rate (avg. births per childbearing woman; 2001): 1.6.
Marriage rate per 1,000 population (1999): 3.5.
Divorce rate per 1,000 population (1999): 0.9.
Life expectancy at birth (2001): male 71.8 years; female 76.9 years.
Major causes of death per 100,000 population (1998): cardiovascular diseases 44.1; accidents and poisoning 31.1; malignant neoplasms (cancers) 15.3; congenital anomalies 9.4.

National economy

Budget (2001). Revenue: Dh 82,480,000,000 (oil revenue 58.5%, non-oil revenue 41.5%). Expenditures: Dh 96,083,000,000 (current expenditures 80.5%, capital [development] expenditure 19.5%).
Gross national product (2001): U.S.$69,568,000,000 (U.S.$19,945 per capita).

Structure of gross domestic product and labour force

	2002		2001	
	in value Dh '000,000[3]	% of total value[3]	labour force	% of labour force
Agriculture	9,499	3.6	128,000	6.9
Crude petroleum production, Mining and quarrying	72,146	27.7	26,000	1.4
Manufacturing	37,398	14.3	246,000	13.3
Construction	17,988	6.9	302,000	16.3
Public utilities	5,125	2.0	31,000	1.7
Transp. and commun.	20,177	7.7	109,000	5.9
Trade	30,095	11.5	448,000	24.2
Finance, real estate	38,323	14.7	71,000	3.8
Pub. admin., defense	28,756	11.0	214,000	11.5
Services	6,573	2.5	278,000	15.0
Other	–5,432[4]	–2.0[4]	—	—
TOTAL	260,648	100.0[5]	1,853,000[6]	100.0

Public debt: n.a.
Tourism (2001): receipts U.S.$1,064,000,000.
Production (metric tons except as noted). Agriculture, forestry, fishing (2002): dates 760,000, spinach 620,000, tomatoes 400,000, cabbages 290,000, cantaloupes and watermelons 175,631, eggplants 140,000, onions 84,000, pumpkins and squash 41,500, cucumbers and gherkins 37,000, lemons and limes 16,195, mangoes 9,137; livestock (number of live animals) 1,300,000 goats, 510,000 sheep, 220,000 camels, 100,000 cattle, 17,000,000 chickens; fish catch (2000) 105,456. Mining and quarrying (2001): aluminum 500,000; gypsum 90,000; lime 50,000; chromite 10,000. Manufacturing (value of production in Dh '000,000; 1998): chemical products (including refined petroleum) 10,096; textiles and wearing apparel 2,397; fabricated metal products 1,999; food, beverages, and tobacco 1,510; cement, bricks, and ceramics 1,409. Energy production (consumption): electricity (kW-hr; 1999) 31,890,000,000 (31,890,000,000); crude petroleum (barrels; 2001) 740,000,000 ([1999] 93,100,000); petroleum products (metric tons; 1999) 20,359,000 (7,026,000); natural gas (cu m; 2001) 41,300,000,000 ([1999] 29,969,200,000).
Population economically active (2001): total 1,853,000; activity rate of total population 53.1% (participation rates [1995]: over age 15, 55.4%; female 11.7%; unemployed [2001] 1.8%).

Price and earnings indexes (1995 = 100)

	1995	1996	1997	1998	1999	2000	2001
Consumer price index	100.0	102.6	104.7	106.8	108.9	110.7	113.1
Annual earnings index	100.0	103.0	102.7	...	...	...	...

Household income and expenditure. Average household size (2000) 5.0; income per household: n.a.; sources of income: n.a.; expenditure (1996): rent, fuel, and light 36.1%, transportation and communications 14.9%, food 14.4%, education, recreation, and entertainment 10.3%, durable household goods 7.4%, clothing 6.7%.
Land use (1994): forested, virtually none; meadows and pastures 2.4%; agricultural and under permanent cultivation 0.5%; built-on, wasteland, and other 97.1%.

Foreign trade

Balance of trade (current prices)

	1996	1997	1998	1999	2000	2001
Dh '000,000,000	+27.2	+39.6	+17.2	+31.6	+69.0	+56.3
% of total	12.5%	15.3%	7.6%	13.4%	23.4%	23.1%

Imports (2001): Dh 120,600,000,000[7] (machinery and transport equipment 37.6%, food 23.2%, textiles 13.9%, basic manufactures 8.4%, chemicals 6.3%, optical and medical equipment 2.8%). *Major import sources:* Japan 10.2%; United States 9.6%; United Kingdom 8.8%; China 8.6%; Germany 6.7%; India 6.7%; Italy 6.2%; South Korea 5.3%.
Exports (2001): Dh 176,900,000,000 (domestic exports 71.1%, of which crude petroleum 36.7%, natural gas 7.1%, refined petroleum products 4.6%, nonmonetary gold 4.4%; reexports 28.9%). *Major export destinations:* Japan 36.4%; India 7.5%; South Korea 7.1%; Singapore 6.3%; Iran 3.8%; Oman 3.4%.

Transport and communications

Transport. Railroads: none. Roads (1999): total length 2,355 mi, 3,791 km (paved 100%). Vehicles (1996): passenger cars 201,000; trucks and buses 56,950. Air transport (2002)[8]: passenger-mi 18,747,000,000, passenger-km 30,170,000,000; short ton-mi cargo 1,343,000,000, metric ton-km cargo 1,960,764,000; airports (2001) with scheduled flights 6.

Communications

Medium	date	unit	number	units per 1,000 persons
Daily newspapers	2000	circulation	507,000	156
Radio	2000	receivers	1,030,000	318
Television	2000	receivers	948,000	292
Telephones	2002	main lines	1,093,700	342
Cellular telephones	2002	subscribers	2,428,100	759
Personal computers	2002	units	450,000	141
Internet	2002	users	1,175,600	367

Education and health

Educational attainment (1995). Percentage of population age 10 and over having: no formal schooling 47.6%; primary education 27.8%; secondary 16.0%; higher 8.6%. *Literacy* (2000): total population age 15 and over literate 76.3%; males literate 75.0%; females literate 79.3%.

Education (1998–99)

	schools	teachers	students	student/ teacher ratio
Primary (age 6–11)	...	16,148[9]	270,486	16.1[9]
Secondary (age 12–18)	...	12,388[10]	198,439	12.0[10]
Vocational	...	249[9]	3,113	7.7[9]
Higher	4[9]	510[10]	17,950[9]	19.2[10]

Health (1999): physicians 6,059 (1 per 485 persons); hospital beds 7,448 (1 per 394 persons); infant mortality rate per 1,000 live births (2001) 16.7.
Food (2001): daily per capita caloric intake 3,192 (vegetable products 75%, animal products 25%); 132% of FAO recommended minimum requirement.

Military

Total active duty personnel (2002): 41,500 (army 84.3%, navy 6.0%, air force 9.7%). *Military expenditure as percentage of GDP* (1999): 4.1% (world 2.4%); per capita expenditure U.S.$935.

[1]All appointed seats. [2]Approximate figures. [3]At factor cost. [4]Imputed bank service charges. [5]Detail does not add to total given because of rounding. [6]Excludes defense personnel. [7]Breakdown is given for imports for the Emirates of Abu Dhabi, Dubai, and Sharjah only, which is 90% of total imports. [8]Emirates Air only. [9]1996–97. [10]1994–95.

Internet resources for further information:
- **Government of United Arab Emirates http://www.uae.gov.ae**
- **Central Bank of the United Arab Emirates http://www.cbuae.gov.ae**

United Kingdom

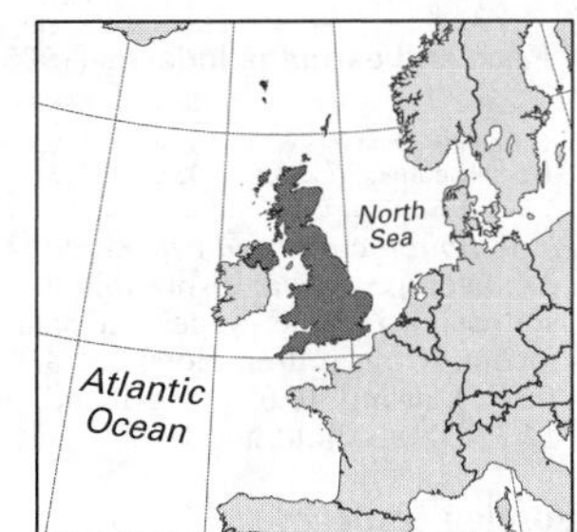

Official name: United Kingdom of Great Britain and Northern Ireland.
Form of government: constitutional monarchy with two legislative houses (House of Lords [688]; House of Commons [659]).
Chief of state: Sovereign.
Head of government: Prime Minister.
Capital: London.
Official language: English.
Official religion: Churches of England and Scotland "established" (protected by the state, but not "official") in their respective countries; no established church in Northern Ireland or Wales.
Monetary unit: 1 pound sterling (£) = 100 new pence; valuation (Sept. 8, 2003) 1 £ = U.S.$1.59; 1 U.S.$ = £0.63.

Population (2001 census[1])

Countries[2]	population		population		population
England	49,138,831	Peterborough	156,060	Scotland	5,062,011
Counties		Plymouth	240,718	**Unitary Districts**	
Bedfordshire	381,571	Poole	138,299	Aberdeen City	212,125
Buckinghamshire	479,028	Portsmouth	186,704	Aberdeenshire	226,871
Cambridgeshire	552,655	Reading	143,124	Angus	108,400
Cheshire	673,777	Redcar and		Argyll and Bute	91,306
Cornwall	501,267	Cleveland	139,141	City of Edinburgh	448,624
Cumbria	487,607	Rutland	34,560	Clackmannanshire	48,077
Derbyshire	734,581	Slough	119,070	Dumfries and	
Devon	704,499	South		Galloway	147,765
Dorset	390,986	Gloucestershire	217,478	Dundee City	145,663
Durham	493,470	Southampton	245,644	East Ayrshire	120,235
East Sussex	492,324	Southend-on-Sea	160,256	East Dumbarton-	
Essex	1,310,922	Stockton-on-		shire	108,243
Gloucestershire	564,559	Tees	178,405	East Lothian	90,088
Hampshire	1,240,032	Stoke-on-Trent	240,643	East Renfrewshire	89,311
Hertfordshire	1,033,977	Swindon	180,061	Eilean Siar[5]	26,502
Isle of Wight[3]	132,719	Telford and		Falkirk	145,191
Kent	1,329,653	Wrenkin	158,285	Fife	349,429
Lancashire	1,134,976	Thurrock	143,042	Glasgow City	577,869
Leicestershire	609,579	Torbay	129,702	Highland	208,914
Lincolnshire	646,646	Warrington	191,084	Inverclyde	84,203
Norfolk	796,733	West Berkshire	144,445	Midlothian	80,941
North Yorkshire	569,660	Windsor and		Moray	86,940
Northamptonshire	629,676	Maidenhead	133,606	North Ayrshire	135,817
Northumberland	307,186	Wokingham	150,257	North Lanarkshire	321,067
Nottinghamshire	748,503	York	181,131	Orkney Islands	19,245
Oxfordshire	605,492	**Metropolitan**		Perth and Kinross	134,949
Shropshire	283,240	**Counties/Greater**		Renfrewshire	172,867
Somerset	498,093	**London**		Scottish Borders	106,764
Staffordshire	806,737	Greater London[4]	7,172,036	Shetland Islands	21,988
Suffolk	668,548	Greater		South Ayrshire	112,097
Surrey	1,059,015	Manchester	2,482,352	South Lanarkshire	302,216
Warwickshire	505,885	Merseyside	1,362,034	Stirling	86,212
West Sussex	753,612	South Yorkshire	1,266,337	West Dumbarton-	
Wiltshire	432,973	Tyne and Wear	1,075,979	shire	93,378
Worcestershire	542,107	West Midlands	2,555,596	West Lothian	158,714
Unitary Districts		West Yorkshire	2,079,217		
Bath and				Northern Ireland	1,685,267
NE Somerset	169,045	Wales	2,903,085	**Districts**	
Blackburn with		**Unitary Districts**		Antrim	48,366
Darwen	137,471	Blaenau Gwent	70,058	Ards	73,244
Blackpool	142,284	Bridgend	128,650	Armagh	54,263
Bournemouth	163,441	Caerphilly	169,521	Ballymena	58,610
Bracknell Forest	109,606	Cardiff	305,340	Ballymoney	26,894
Brighton and		Carmarthenshire	173,635	Banbridge	41,392
Hove	247,820	Ceredigion	75,384	Belfast	277,391
Bristol	380,615	Conway	109,597	Carrickfergus	37,659
Darlington	174,844	Denbighshire	93,092	Castlereagh	66,488
Derby	97,822	Flintshire	148,565	Coleraine	56,315
East Riding of		Gwynedd	116,838	Cookstown	32,581
Yorkshire	221,716	Isle of Anglesey	66,828	Craigavon	80,671
Halton	314,076	Merthyr Tydfil	55,983	Derry	105,066
Hartlepool	118,215	Monmouthshire	84,879	Down	63,828
Herefordshire	88,629	Neath and		Dungannon	47,735
Kingston upon		Port Talbot	134,471	Fermanagh	57,527
Hull	243,595	Newport	137,017	Larne	30,832
Leicester	279,923	Pembrokeshire	112,901	Limvady	32,422
Luton	184,390	Powys	126,344	Lisburn	108,694
Medway	249,502	Rhondda, Cynon,		Magherafelt	39,780
Middlesborough	134,847	Taff	231,952	Moyle	15,933
Milton Keynes	207,063	Swansea	223,293	Newry and Mourne	87,058
NE Lincolnshire	157,983	Torfaen	90,967	Newtownabbey	79,995
North Lincolnshire	152,839	The Vale of		North Down	76,323
North Somerset	188,556	Glamorgan	119,293	Omagh	47,952
Nottingham	266,995	Wrexham	128,477	Strabane	38,248
				TOTAL	58,789,194

Demography

Population (2003): 59,164,000.
Area: 94,248 sq mi, 244,101 sq km, of which England 50,351 sq mi, 130,410 sq km; Wales 8,015 sq mi, 20,758 sq km; Scotland 30,421 sq mi, 78,789 sq km; Northern Ireland (figures represent remainder) 5,461 sq mi, 14,144 sq km.
Density (2003): persons per sq mi 627.7, persons per sq km 242.4.
Urban-rural (2001): urban 89.5%; rural 10.5%.
Age breakdown (2001): under 15, 18.9%; 15–29, 18.8%; 30–44, 22.5%; 45–59, 18.9%; 60–74, 13.3%; 75 and over, 7.6%.
Ethnic composition (2001): white 92.1%; black 2.0%, of which Caribbean origin 1.0%, African origin 0.8%; Asian Indian 1.8%; Pakistani 1.3%; Bangladeshi 0.5%; Chinese 0.4%; other and not stated 1.9%.
Population projection: (2010) 60,350,000; (2020) 62,197,000.
Sex distribution (2001): male 48.62%; female 51.38%.
Religious affiliation (2001): Christian 71.6%, of which Anglican 29.0%, Roman Catholic 11.0%; Muslim 2.7%; Hindu 1.0%; Sikh 0.6%; Jewish 0.5%; nonreligious 15.5%; other 8.1%.
Major cities (2001; urban agglomeration [2000]): Greater London 7,188,000; Birmingham 976,000 (2,272,000); Manchester 439,000 (2,252,000); Leeds 716,000 (1,433,000); Newcastle 260,000 (1,026,000); Liverpool 439,000 (951,000); Glasgow 579,000; Edinburgh 449,000; Bristol 405,000; Cardiff 305,000; Belfast 277,000.
Mobility (1991)[6]. Population living in the same residence as 1990: 90.1%; different residence, same country (of Great Britain) 8.1%; different residence, different country of Great Britain 1.2%; from outside Great Britain 0.6%.
Households (2002)[6]. Average household size 2.4; 1 person 29%, couple 29%, couple with 1–2 children 19%, couple with 3 or more children 10%, single parent with children 9%, other 4%.
Immigration (2001): permanent residents 372,000, from Australia 13.4%, Bangladesh, India, and Sri Lanka 6.2%, South Africa 4.8%, New Zealand 4.3%, Pakistan 3.5%, United States 3.2%, Canada 1.6%, other 63.0%, of which EU 22.3%.

Vital statistics

Birth rate per 1,000 population (2001): 11.4 (world avg. 21.3); legitimate 60.0%; illegitimate 40.0%.
Death rate per 1,000 population (2001): 10.0 (world avg. 9.1).
Natural increase rate per 1,000 population (2001): 1.4 (world avg. 12.2).
Total fertility rate (avg. births per childbearing woman; 2001): 1.5.
Marriage rate per 1,000 population (2001): 10.4.
Divorce rate per 1,000 population (2001): 2.7.
Life expectancy at birth (2002): male 75.7 years; female 80.4 years.
Major causes of death per 100,000 population (2000): diseases of the circulatory system 396.0, of which ischemic heart disease 207.6, cerebrovascular disease 100.2; malignant neoplasms (cancers) 257.2; diseases of the respiratory system 170.6, of which pneumonia 101.5; diseases of the digestive system 42.8; diseases of the genitourinary system 14.1; diseases of the endocrine system 13.7, of which diabetes mellitus 10.8; suicide 7.2.

Social indicators

Educational attainment (1999). Percentage of population age 25–64 having: up to lower secondary education only 38%; completed secondary 37%; higher 25%, of which at least some university 17%.

Distribution of disposable income (2000–01)

percentage of household income by quintile				
1	2	3	4	5 (highest)
8.8	12.0	17.4	26.1	35.7

Quality of working life (2002). Average full-time workweek (hours): male 39.6, female 34.4. Annual rate per 100,000 workers for (2000–01)[6]: injury or accident 2,778.6; death 5.0. Proportion of labour force (employed persons) insured for damages or income loss resulting from: injury 100%; permanent disability 100%; death 100%. Average days lost to labour stoppages per 1,000 employee workdays (2001): 20.
Access to services (2000). Proportion of households having access to: bath or shower 100%; toilet 100%.
Social participation. Eligible voters participating in last national election (June 2001): 59.4%. Population age 16 and over participating in voluntary work (2001)[6]: 39%. Trade union membership in total workforce (2001) 29.1%.
Social deviance (2001–02)[7]. Offense rate per 100,000 population for: theft and handling stolen goods 3,856.2; vandalism 1,809.9; burglary 1,296.2; violence against the person 1,105.6; fraud and forgery 539.2; robbery 205.8; sexual offense 69.7.
Leisure (1994). Favourite leisure activities (hours weekly): watching television 17.1; listening to radio 10.3; reading 8.8, of which books 3.8, newspapers 3.3; gardening 2.1.
Material well-being (2001). Households possessing: automobile 74.0%, telephone 94.0%, television receiver (2000) 98.3%, refrigerator/freezer 95.0%, washing machine 93.0%, central heating 92.0%, video recorder 90.0%.

National economy

Budget (2001–02). Revenue: £388,357,000,000 (production and import taxes 35.5%, income tax 28.1%, social security contributions 16.3%). Expenditures: £380,867,000,000 (social protection 41.8%, health 16.1%, education 12.3%, defense 7.3%).
Gross national product (2001): U.S.$1,476,800,000,000 (U.S.$25,120 per capita).

Structure of gross domestic product and labour force

	2001		2002	
	in value £'000,000	% of total value	labour force	% of labour force
Agriculture	8,241	0.8	255,000	0.9
Mining[8]	25,665	2.6	75,000	0.3
Manufacturing	153,132	15.5	3,668,000	12.6
Construction	47,327	4.8	1,186,000	4.1
Public utilities	15,713	1.6	177,000	0.6
Transp. and commun.	70,252	7.1	1,524,000	5.2
Trade[9]	136,125	13.7	6,162,000	21.1
Finance	255,871	25.9	4,969,000	17.0
Pub. admin., defense	42,096	4.3	1,382,000	4.7
Services	159,170	16.1	6,277,000	21.5
Other	75,422[10]	7.6[10]	3,508,000[11]	12.0[11]
TOTAL	989,014	100.0	29,183,000	100.0

Total national debt (March 31, 2000): £426,239,200,000 (U.S.$679,894,200,000).
Land use (1994): forested 10.4%; meadows and pastures 45.9%; agricultural and under permanent cultivation 24.8%; other 18.9%.
Tourism (2001): receipts from visitors U.S.$16,283,000,000; expenditures by nationals abroad U.S.$36,483,000,000.
Production (value of production in £'000,000). Agriculture, forestry, fishing (2001): wheat 1,322, vegetables 970, barley 726, potatoes 600, rapeseed 275, sugar beets 255, fruit 243, oats 64; livestock (number of live animals) 36,716,000 sheep, 10,602,000 cattle, 5,845,000 pigs; roundwood (2002) 7,577,000 cu m; fish catch (2001) 530,000 tons. Mining and quarrying (2000): limestone and dolomite 662; sand and gravel 619; china clay (kaolin) 234. Manufacturing (value added in £'000,000; 2000): electrical and optical equipment 21,137; food and beverages 20,628; paper, printing, and publishing 19,575; metal manufacturing 16,275; transport equipment 15,968; chemicals and chemical products 14,918; machinery and equipment 12,319; textiles and leather products 7,159. Construction (value in £; 2001)[6]: residential 8,796,000,000; nonresidential 1,437,000,000.

Financial aggregates

	1996	1997	1998	1999	2000	2001	2002
Exchange rate							
U.S. dollar per £	1.56	1.64	1.66	1.62	1.52	1.44	1.50
SDRs per £	1.18	1.22	1.18	1.18	1.14	1.15	1.18
International reserves (U.S.$)							
Total (excl. gold; '000,000,000)	39.90	32.32	32.21	35.87	43.89	37.28	39.36
SDRs ('000,000,000)	0.34	0.47	0.47	0.51	0.33	0.29	0.36
Reserve pos. in IMF ('000,000)	2.43	2.97	4.38	5.28	4.28	5.05	6.21
Foreign exchange	37.12	28.88	27.36	30.08	39.28	31.94	32.79
Gold ('000,000 fine troy oz)	18.43	18.42	23.00	20.55	15.67	11.42	10.09
% world reserves	2.0	2.1	2.4	2.1	1.6	1.2	1.1
Interest and prices							
Central bank discount (%)	…	…	…	…	…	…	…
Govt. bond yield (%) long term	8.10	7.09	5.45	4.70	4.68	4.78	4.83
Industrial share prices (1995 = 100)	113.3	128.3	150.5	…	…	…	…
Balance of payments (U.S.$'000,000,000,000)							
Balance of visible trade	–21.23	–20.2	–36.13	–44.3	–45.89	–48.21	–53.05
Imports, f.o.b.	–282.48	–301.74	–307.85	–313.18	–330.27	–321.86	–332.38
Exports, f.o.b.	261.25	281.54	271.72	268.88	284.38	273.65	279.33
Balance of invisibles	7.79	17.35	28.17	12.47	17.21	30.32	38.64
Balance of payments, current account	–13.44	–2.85	–7.96	–31.83	–28.68	–17.89	–14.41

Manufacturing, mining, and construction enterprises (2001)

	no. of enterprises	no. of employees	annual costs as a % of avg. of employment costs[12]	annual value added (£'000,000)
Manufacturing				
Food, beverages, and tobacco	7,706	515,000	86.6	20,370
Paper and paper products; printing and publishing	32,493	475,000	101.5	19,444
Chemical products	3,864	251,000	138.8	14,850
Metal manufacturing	31,629	487,000	92.3	15,269
Machinery and equipment	13,650	355,000	104.3	11,696
Mineral products (nonmetallic)	5,439	134,000	93.7	4,852
Electrical and optical equipment	16,141	475,000	118.3	16,070
Transport equipment	5,665	390,000	120.0	17,411
Rubber and plastics	7,021	233,000	92.3	7,632
Textiles	11,310	210,000	66.5	5,147
Wood and wood products	8,444	89,000	68.2	2,345
Other manufacturing	20,155	229,000	76.8	6,452
Mining				
Extraction of coal, mineral oil, and natural gas	444	39,000	…	20,629
Extraction of minerals other than fuels	1,224	33,000	…	1,798
Construction	192,000	1,367,000	…	47,969

Retail trade and service enterprises (2001)

	no. of-enterprises	no. of employees	weekly wage as a % of all wages	annual turnover (£'000,000)
Food, beverages, and tobacco	27,074	993,000	…	85,534
of which				
meats	8,485	46,000	…	2,216
Household goods,	23,553	319,000	…	29,151
of which				
electronics, appliances	7,157	101,000	…	10,821
furniture	10,592	119,000	…	8,784
Clothing and footwear	17,869	446,000	…	25,963
Pharmaceuticals and cosmetics	6,915	110,000	…	9,543
Business services,	534,956	4,273,000	…	265,631
of which				
real estate	30,779	79,000	…	32,779
Transp. and commun.	81,154	1,621,000	…	181,669
Hotels, restaurants	118,988	1,792,000	…	49,902
Social services,	35,622	1,026	…	16,233
of which				
health	9,683	453,000	…	7,575

Energy production (consumption): electricity (kW-hr; 2001) 352,985,000,000 ([1999] 384,816,000,000); hard coal (metric tons; 2000) 31,200,000 ([1999] 58,800,000); crude petroleum (barrels; 2000) 884,273,000 (620,500,000); petroleum products (metric tons; 1999) 83,344,000 (73,223,000); natural gas (cu m; 2000) 128,425,000,000 ([1999] 105,612,300,000).
Population economically active (2002): total 29,183,000, activity rate of total population 59.6% (participation rates: ages 16–64, 74.4%; female 45.9%; unemployed 5.2%).

Price and earnings indexes (1995 = 100)

	1996	1997	1998	1999	2000	2001	2002
Consumer price index	102.4	105.7	109.3	111.0	114.2	116.3	118.2
Monthly earnings index	103.5	108.0	113.5	119.0	124.5	129.9	134.6

Household income and expenditure (2000–01). Average household size (2002) 2.4; average annual disposable income per household £21,242 (U.S.$31,395); sources of income: wages and salaries 67.0%, social security benefits 12.0%, income from self-employment 8.9%, dividends and interest 4.0%; expenditure: housing 16.6%, food and beverages 16.0%, transport and vehicles 14.3%, household goods 8.5%, clothing 5.7%.

Foreign trade[13]

Balance of trade (current prices)

	1997	1998	1999	2000	2001	2002
£'000,000	–15,540	–25,466	–29,765	–34,856	–37,271	–39,272
% of total	4.3%	7.2%	8.2%	8.6%	9.1%	9.6%

Imports (2001): £222,944,000,000 (machinery and transport equipment 43.9%, of which electrical equipment 19.7%, road vehicles 11.7%; chemicals 10.2%, of which organic chemicals 2.1%, plastics 1.1%; food 6.4%; clothing and footwear 5.1%; petroleum and petroleum products 4.2%; textiles 2.8%; paper and paperboard 1.8%). *Major import sources:* U.S. 13.2%; Germany 12.7%; France 8.6%; The Netherlands 6.7%; Belgium-Luxembourg 5.7%; Italy 4.4%; Ireland 4.2%; Japan 4.1%; Spain 3.1%; Hong Kong 2.6%.
Exports (2001): £185,673,000,000 (machinery and transport equipment 46.1%, of which electrical equipment 22.2%, road vehicles 7.3%; chemicals 14.7%, of which medicinal products 4.9%, organic chemicals 3.1%; petroleum and petroleum products 7.8%; professional and scientific 4.1%; food 2.9%; iron and steel products 2.3%). *Major export destinations:* U.S. 15.4%; Germany 12.5%; France 10.2%; The Netherlands 7.7%; Ireland 7.3%; Belgium-Luxembourg 5.2%; Italy 4.4%; Spain 4.4%; Sweden 2.1%; Japan 2.0%; Switzerland 1.9%.

Transport and communications

Transport. Railroads (2001–02)[6]: length 19,883 mi[14], 32,000 km[14]; passenger-mi 24,298,000,000, passenger-km 39,104,000,000; ton-mi cargo 13,493,000,000, metric ton-km cargo 19,700,000,000. Roads (2001): total length 243,831 mi, 392,408 km (paved 100%). Vehicles (2001): passenger cars 23,899,000, trucks and buses 2,544,000. Merchant marine (2001): vessels (over 100 gross tons) 594; total deadweight tonnage 12,100,000. Air transport (2001): passenger-mi 154,700,000,000, passenger-km 249,000,000,000; short ton-mi cargo 3,559,000,000, metric ton-km cargo 5,196,000,000; airports (2001) 150[14].

Communications

Medium	date	unit	number	units per 1,000 persons
Daily newspapers	2000	circulation	19,300,000	329
Radio	2000	receivers	84,500,000	1,432
Television	1999	receivers	38,800,000	652
Telephones	2002	main lines	35,145,000	595
Cellular telephones	2002	subscribers	49,921,000	845
Personal computers	2002	units	23,972,000	406
Internet	2002	users	24,000,000	406

Education and health

Literacy (2002): total population literate, virtually 100%.

Education (2002)[15]

	schools	teachers	students	student/ teacher ratio
Primary (age 5–10)	22,800	231,400	5,083,400	25.9
Secondary (age 11–19)	4,306	241,000	3,948,000	16.4
Voc., teacher tr.	…	…	586,000[16]	…
Higher[17]	89	*c.* 48,000[18]	*c.* 810,000[18]	*c.* 17.0[18]

Health: physicians (2001) 71,107[6] (1 per 826 persons); hospital beds (2000) 242,671 (1 per 246 persons); infant mortality rate (2002) 4.7.
Food (2001): daily per capita caloric intake 3,368 (vegetable products 70%, animal products 30%); 134% of FAO recommended minimum requirement.

Military

Total active duty personnel (2002): 210,450 (army 54.5%, navy 20.1%, air force 25.4%); U.S. troops (2002) 9,500. *Military expenditure as percentage of GNP* (1999): 2.5% (world 2.4%); per capita expenditure U.S.$615.

[1]Preliminary. [2]The reorganization of first-order administrative units was completed in 1999: England's former 46 counties (including 7 metropolitan counties) reorganized into 35 counties, 45 unitary districts, 6 metropolitan counties, and Greater London; Wales's former 8 counties reorganized into 22 unitary districts; Scotland's former 9 regions and 3 island councils reorganized into 32 unitary districts; Northern Ireland did not change. [3]Only unitary district with county status. [4]Has administrative authority from July 2000. [5]Formerly Western Isles. [6]Great Britain only. [7]England and Wales only. [8]Includes petroleum extraction. [9]Includes hotels and restaurants. [10]Plus rent and value-added taxes; less imputed bank service charges. [11]Includes 1,524,000 unemployed. [12]Wages in manufacturing account for *c.* 90% of employment costs. [13]Imports c.i.f. [14]Estimate. [15]Public sector only. [16]1992–93. [17]Universities only. [18]1994–95.

Internet resources for further information:
- **Office for National Statistics http://www.statistics.gov.uk**

United States

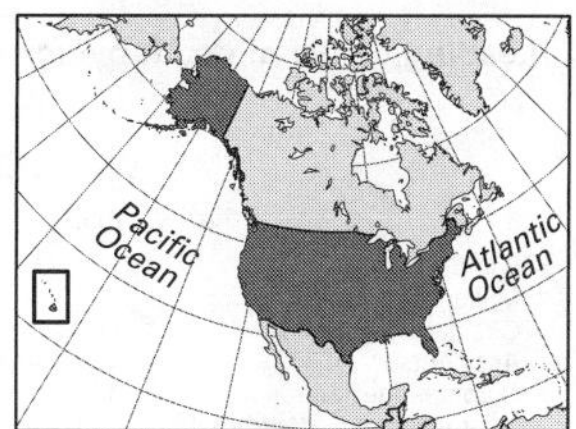

Official name: United States of America.
Form of government: federal republic with two legislative houses (Senate [100]; House of Representatives [435[1]]).
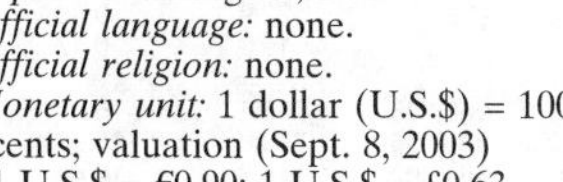
Head of state and government: President.
Capital: Washington, D.C.
Official language: none.
Official religion: none.
Monetary unit: 1 dollar (U.S.$) = 100 cents; valuation (Sept. 8, 2003) 1 U.S.$ = €0.90; 1 U.S.$ = £0.63.

Area and population

States	Capitals	area sq mi	area sq km	population 2002 estimate
Alabama	Montgomery	51,718	133,950	4,486,508
Alaska	Juneau	587,875	1,522,595	643,786
Arizona	Phoenix	114,006	295,275	5,456,453
Arkansas	Little Rock	53,182	137,741	2,710,079
California	Sacramento	158,647	410,895	35,116,033
Colorado	Denver	104,100	269,619	4,506,542
Connecticut	Hartford	5,006	12,966	3,460,503
Delaware	Dover	2,026	5,247	807,385
Florida	Tallahassee	58,680	151,981	16,713,149
Georgia	Atlanta	58,930	152,629	8,560,310
Hawaii	Honolulu	6,459	16,729	1,244,898
Idaho	Boise	83,574	216,456	1,341,131
Illinois	Springfield	57,918	150,008	12,600,620
Indiana	Indianapolis	36,420	94,328	6,159,068
Iowa	Des Moines	56,276	145,755	2,936,760
Kansas	Topeka	82,282	213,110	2,715,884
Kentucky	Frankfort	40,411	104,664	4,092,891
Louisiana	Baton Rouge	47,719	123,592	4,482,646
Maine	Augusta	33,128	85,801	1,294,464
Maryland	Annapolis	10,455	27,078	5,458,137
Massachusetts	Boston	8,262	21,399	6,427,801
Michigan	Lansing	96,705	250,466	10,050,446
Minnesota	St. Paul	86,943	225,182	5,019,720
Mississippi	Jackson	47,695	123,530	2,871,782
Missouri	Jefferson City	69,709	180,546	5,672,579
Montana	Helena	147,046	380,849	909,453
Nebraska	Lincoln	77,359	200,360	1,729,180
Nevada	Carson City	110,567	286,368	2,173,491
New Hampshire	Concord	9,283	24,043	1,275,056
New Jersey	Trenton	7,790	20,176	8,590,300
New Mexico	Santa Fe	121,598	314,939	1,855,059
New York	Albany	53,013	137,304	19,157,532
North Carolina	Raleigh	52,672	136,420	8,320,146
North Dakota	Bismarck	70,704	183,123	634,110
Ohio	Columbus	44,828	116,104	11,421,267
Oklahoma	Oklahoma City	69,903	181,049	3,493,714
Oregon	Salem	97,052	251,364	3,521,515
Pennsylvania	Harrisburg	45,759	118,516	12,335,091
Rhode Island	Providence	1,213	3,142	1,069,725
South Carolina	Columbia	31,117	80,593	4,107,183
South Dakota	Pierre	77,121	199,743	761,063
Tennessee	Nashville	42,145	109,155	5,797,289
Texas	Austin	266,873	691,201	21,779,893
Utah	Salt Lake City	84,904	219,901	2,316,256
Vermont	Montpelier	9,615	24,903	616,592
Virginia	Richmond	40,598	105,149	7,293,542
Washington	Olympia	68,126	176,446	6,068,996
West Virginia	Charleston	24,232	62,761	1,801,873
Wisconsin	Madison	65,500	169,645	5,441,196
Wyoming	Cheyenne	97,819	253,351	498,703
District				
District of Columbia	—	68	176	570,898
TOTAL		3,675,031[2]	9,518,323[2]	288,368,698[3]

Demography

Population (2003): 291,587,000[4].
Density (2003): persons per sq mi 80.7, persons per sq km 31.1.
Urban-rural (2000): urban 79.0%; rural 21.0%.
Sex distribution (2002): male 49.12%; female 50.88%.
Age breakdown (2000): under 15, 21.4%; 15–29, 20.8%; 30–44, 23.3%; 45–59, 18.2%; 60–74, 10.4%; 75 and over, 5.9%.
Population projection: (2010) 310,489,000; (2020) 337,474,000.
Doubling time: not applicable; doubling time exceeds 100 years.
Population by race and Hispanic[5] origin (2000): non-Hispanic white 70.5%; Hispanic 12.5%; non-Hispanic black 12.3%; Asian and Pacific Islander 3.8%; American Indian and Eskimo 0.9%.
Religious affiliation (1995): Christian 85.3%, of which Protestant 57.9%, Roman Catholic 21.0%, other Christian 6.4%; Jewish 2.1%; Muslim 1.9%; nonreligious 8.7%; other 2.0%.
Mobility (2000). Population living in the same residence as in 1999: 84.0%; different residence, same county 9.0%; different county, same state 3.0%; different state 3.0%; moved from abroad 1.0%.
Households (2000). Total households 105,480,000 (married-couple families 54,493,000 [51.7%]). Average household size (2000) 2.7; 1 person 25.9%, 2 persons 32.1%, 3 persons 16.9%, 4 persons 14.9%, 5 or more persons 10.2%. Family households: 71,787,000 (68.1%); nonfamily 33,693,000 (31.9%), of which 1-person 80.8%.
Place of birth (2000): native-born 245,708,000 (89.6%); foreign-born 28,379,000 (10.4%), of which Mexico 7,841,000, the Philippines 1,222,000, China and Hong Kong 1,067,000, India 1,007,000, Cuba 952,000, Vietnam 863,000, El Salvador 765,000, South Korea 701,000.

Components of population change (1990–99)

States	Net change in population	Annual percentage change	Births	Deaths	Net migration
Alabama	329,473	0.8	568,961	387,158	147,670
Alaska	69,457	1.3	98,976	22,291	–7,228
Arizona	1,112,993	2.9	670,677	317,200	759,516
Arkansas	200,749	0.9	330,123	244,180	114,806
California	3,333,694	1.2	5,227,258	2,039,044	145,480
Colorado	761,660	2.3	513,908	225,699	473,451
Connecticut	–5,085	–0.1	423,922	268,782	–160,225
Delaware	87,370	1.3	97,768	58,165	47,767
Florida	2,173,173	1.7	1,781,648	1,370,234	1,761,759
Georgia	1,310,091	2.0	1,053,424	525,580	782,247
Hawaii	77,268	0.7	173,388	67,676	–28,444
Idaho	244,966	2.4	166,298	77,951	156,619
Illinois	697,768	0.6	1,735,493	971,944	–65,781
Indiana	398,745	0.8	779,368	482,740	102,117
Iowa	92,582	0.4	349,191	256,794	185
Kansas	176,464	0.7	348,226	215,686	43,924
Kentucky	273,933	0.8	494,758	340,897	120,072
Louisiana	150,209	0.4	629,286	362,228	–116,849
Maine	25,112	0.2	137,791	107,664	–5,015
Maryland	390,881	0.9	687,293	375,178	78,766
Massachusetts	158,744	0.3	778,803	506,880	–113,179
Michigan	568,488	0.6	1,287,572	763,166	44,082
Minnesota	399,843	0.9	603,264	338,093	134,672
Mississippi	193,144	0.8	389,349	246,225	50,020
Missouri	351,437	0.7	697,038	492,127	146,526
Montana	83,714	1.1	103,358	69,332	49,688
Nebraska	87,611	0.6	217,510	139,754	9,855
Nevada	607,578	4.5	227,622	110,437	490,393
New Hampshire	91,882	0.9	142,027	83,680	33,535
New Jersey	395,662	0.5	1,079,022	667,367	–15,993
New Mexico	224,775	1.5	254,934	111,862	81,703
New York	205,823	0.1	2,539,280	1,519,562	–813,895
North Carolina	1,018,341	1.6	967,386	586,354	637,309
North Dakota	–5,134	–0.1	78,833	54,150	–29,817
Ohio	409,539	0.4	1,454,713	957,171	–88,003
Oklahoma	212,468	0.7	437,373	298,499	73,594
Oregon	473,817	1.7	399,411	255,204	329,610
Pennsylvania	111,174	0.1	1,438,566	1,163,384	–164,008
Rhode Island	–12,645	–0.1	125,103	89,187	–48,561
South Carolina	399,426	1.2	498,067	301,259	202,618
South Dakota	37,129	0.6	98,048	62,765	1,846
Tennessee	606,332	1.3	687,916	463,719	382,135
Texas	3,057,806	1.8	3,025,567	1,254,005	1,286,244
Utah	406,986	2.3	369,419	98,393	135,960
Vermont	30,982	0.6	67,101	44,797	8,678
Virginia	683,715	1.1	872,681	477,233	288,267
Washington	889,692	1.8	729,025	372,964	533,631
West Virginia	13,451	0.1	198,388	184,750	–187
Wisconsin	358,492	0.8	637,733	412,353	133,112
Wyoming	26,013	0.6	60,099	32,704	–1,382
District					
District of Columbia	–87,900	–1.7	87,167	59,836	–115,231
TOTAL/RATE	23,899,888	1.0	36,820,132	20,934,303	8,014,059

Major cities (2002): New York 8,084,316; Los Angeles 3,798,981; Chicago 2,886,251; Houston 2,009,834; Philadelphia 1,492,231; Phoenix 1,371,960; San Diego 1,259,532; Dallas 1,211,467; San Antonio 1,194,222; Detroit 925,051.

Other principal cities (2002)

	population		population		population
Akron	214,349	Fresno	445,227	Omaha	399,357
Albuquerque	463,874	Honolulu	378,155	Pittsburgh	327,898
Anaheim	332,642	Indianapolis	783,612	Portland (Ore.)	539,438
Anchorage	268,983	Jacksonville	762,461	Raleigh	306,944
Arlington (Tex.)	349,944	Jersey City	240,100	Riverside	274,226
Atlanta	424,868	Kansas City (Mo.)	443,471	Rochester	217,158
Austin	671,873	Las Vegas	508,604	Sacramento	435,245
Bakersfield	260,969	Lexington (Ky.)	263,618	St. Louis	338,353
Baltimore	638,614	Lincoln	232,362	St. Paul	284,037
Baton Rouge	225,702	Long Beach	472,412	St. Petersburg	248,546
Birmingham	239,416	Louisville	237,498	San Francisco	764,049
Boston	589,281	Madison	215,211	San Jose	900,443
Buffalo	287,698	Memphis	648,882	Santa Ana	343,413
Charlotte	580,597	Mesa (Ariz.)	426,841	Seattle	570,426
Cincinnati	323,885	Miami	374,791	Shreveport	199,033
Cleveland	467,851	Milwaukee	590,895	Stockton	262,835
Colorado Springs	371,182	Minneapolis	375,635	Tampa	315,140
Columbus	725,228	Nashville	545,915	Toledo	309,106
Corpus Christi	278,520	New Orleans	473,681	Tucson	503,151
Denver	560,415	Newark	277,000	Tulsa	391,908
El Paso	577,415	Norfolk	239,036	Virginia Beach	433,934
Fort Wayne	210,070	Oakland	402,777	Washington, D.C.	570,898
Fort Worth	567,516	Oklahoma City	519,034	Wichita	355,126

Immigration (2001): permanent immigrants admitted 1,064,318, from Mexico 19.2%, India 6.2%, former U.S.S.R. 5.2%, China 4.8%, the Philippines 4.8%, Africa 4.7%, Vietnam 3.3%, El Salvador 2.9%, Canada 2.8%, Cuba 2.4%, Haiti 2.1%, Dominican Republic 2.0%, South Korea 1.9%, Jamaica 1.4%, other 36.3%. Refugees (end of 2000) 508,222[6]. Asylum seekers (end of 2000): 386,330[6].

Vital statistics

Birth rate per 1,000 population (2000): 14.7 (world avg. 21.3); legitimate 66.8%; illegitimate 33.2%.
Death rate per 1,000 population (2000): 8.7 (world avg. 9.1).
Natural increase rate per 1,000 population (2000): 6.0 (world avg. 12.2).
Total fertility rate (avg. births per childbearing woman; 2000): 2.0.
Marriage rate per 1,000 population (2001): 8.4; median age at first marriage (1991): men 26.3 years, women 24.1 years.
Divorce rate per 1,000 population (2001): 4.0.

Life expectancy at birth (2000): white male 74.8 years, black and other male (1996) 68.9 years; white female 80.4 years, black and other female 76.1 (1996) years.

Vital statistics (2000)

States	Live births	Birth rate per 1,000 population	Death rate per 1,000 population	Infant mortality rate per 1,000 live births[7]	Abortion rate per 1,000 live births[8]	Life expectancy[9]
Alabama	63,299	14.4	10.3	9.8	248.8	73.6
Alaska	9,974	16.0	4.7	5.7	196.1	...
Arizona	85,273	17.5	8.3	6.8	248.3	76.1
Arkansas	37,783	14.7	11.0	8.0	170.5	74.3
California	531,959	15.8	6.8	5.4	434.8	75.9
Colorado	65,438	15.8	6.6	6.7	294.7	77.0
Connecticut	43,026	13.0	9.2	6.1	383.7	76.9
Delaware	11,051	14.5	9.0	7.4	582.5	74.8
Florida	204,125	13.3	10.7	7.4	466.3	75.8
Georgia	132,644	16.7	8.1	8.2	329.5	73.6
Hawaii	17,551	14.9	7.0	7.0	430.1	78.2
Idaho	20,366	16.0	7.5	6.7	111.1	76.9
Illinois	185,036	15.2	8.8	8.5	366.0	74.9
Indiana	87,699	14.7	9.3	8.0	169.1	75.4
Iowa	38,266	13.3	9.8	5.7	163.0	77.3
Kansas	39,666	14.9	9.3	7.3	268.8	76.8
Kentucky	56,029	14.1	9.9	7.6	152.7	74.4
Louisiana	67,898	15.5	9.4	9.2	228.7	73.0
Maine	13,603	10.8	9.8	4.8	215.8	73.1
Maryland	74,316	14.2	8.4	8.4	428.2	76.4
Massachusetts	81,614	13.2	9.1	5.2	502.5	74.8
Michigan	136,171	13.7	8.8	8.1	364.0	75.0
Minnesota	67,604	14.0	7.8	6.2	237.0	77.8
Mississippi	44,075	15.8	10.3	10.1	72.6	73.0
Missouri	76,463	13.9	10.0	7.8	150.7	75.3
Montana	10,957	12.3	9.1	6.7	270.3	76.2
Nebraska	24,646	14.8	9.0	6.8	172.4	76.9
Nevada	30,829	16.4	8.1	6.6	640.0	74.2
New Hampshire	14,609	12.0	8.0	5.8	204.1	76.7
New Jersey	115,632	14.1	9.2	6.7	531.4	75.4
New Mexico	27,223	14.2	7.7	6.9	185.9	75.7
New York	258,737	14.2	8.7	6.4	648.5	74.7
North Carolina	120,311	15.5	9.3	9.1	344.5	74.5
North Dakota	7,676	12.2	9.3	6.8	117.6	77.6
Ohio	155,472	13.8	9.6	8.2	266.1	75.3
Oklahoma	49,782	14.7	10.4	8.5	196.9	75.1
Oregon	45,804	13.7	8.8	5.8	373.8	76.4
Pennsylvania	146,281	12.2	10.9	7.3	270.1	75.4
Rhode Island	12,505	12.6	10.1	5.7	468.8	76.5
South Carolina	56,114	14.3	9.4	10.2	216.1	73.5
South Dakota	10,345	14.0	9.5	8.9	95.2	76.9
Tennessee	79,611	14.4	10.0	7.7	245.9	74.3
Texas	363,414	17.8	7.3	6.2	275.7	75.1
Utah	47,353	21.9	5.7	4.8	101.0	77.7
Vermont	6,500	10.9	8.6	5.8	294.1	76.5
Virginia	98,938	14.2	8.1	5.8	334.8	75.2
Washington	81,036	13.9	7.6	5.0	323.8	76.8
West Virginia	20,865	11.6	11.7	7.4	141.5	74.3
Wisconsin	69,326	13.1	8.8	6.7	192.6	76.9
Wyoming	6,253	13.0	8.1	6.9	...	76.2
District						
District of Columbia	7,666	14.8	11.5	15.0	2,333.3	68.0
TOTAL/RATE	4,058,814	14.7	8.7	7.1	349.8	75.8

Major causes of death per 100,000 population (2000): cardiovascular diseases 339.3, of which ischemic heart disease 186.6, cerebrovascular diseases 60.3, atherosclerosis 5.2; malignant neoplasms (cancers) 200.5; diseases of the respiratory system 69.2, of which pneumonia 24.5; accidents and adverse effects 34.0, of which motor-vehicle accidents 15.2; diabetes mellitus 24.9; suicide 10.3; chronic liver disease and cirrhosis 9.5; AIDS 5.2.

Morbidity rates of infectious diseases per 100,000 population (1998): chlamydia 223.4; gonorrhea 131.7; chicken pox 30.5; AIDS 17.2; salmonellosis 16.2; syphilis 14.0; shigellosis 8.7; hepatitis A (infectious) 8.6; tuberculosis 6.8; lyme disease 6.2; hepatitis B (serum) 3.8; pertussis 2.7.

Leading cause of death by age group (1998)

	Number of deaths			Total death rate per 100,000 population	Percentage of all deaths
	Total	Male	Female		
All ages[10]	2,337,256	1,157,260	1,179,996	864.7	100.0
1 to 4 years	5,251	2,920	2,331	34.6	0.22
Accidents	1,935	1,155	780	12.7	0.08
Congenital anomalies	564	287	277	3.7	0.02
Malignant neoplasms	365	189	176	2.4	0.02
Homicide	399	223	175	2.6	0.02
Circulatory diseases	214	114	100	1.4	0.01
5 to 14 years	7,791	4,686	3,105	19.9	0.33
Accidents	3,254	2,086	1,158	8.3	0.14
Malignant neoplasms	1,013	582	431	2.6	0.04
Homicide	460	257	203	1.2	0.02
Circulatory diseases	326	191	135	0.9	0.01
Suicide	324	241	83	0.8	0.01
15 to 24 years	30,627	22,717	7,910	82.3	1.31
Accidents	13,349	9,887	3,462	35.9	0.57
Homicide	5,506	4,720	785	14.8	0.24
Suicide	4,135	3,532	603	11.1	0.18
Malignant neoplasms	1,699	1,029	670	4.6	0.07
Circulatory diseases	1,057	672	385	2.8	0.04
25 to 44 years	131,382	86,354	45,028	157.7	5.62
Accidents	27,172	20,232	6,940	32.6	1.16
Malignant neoplasms	21,407	9,684	11,723	25.7	0.92
Circulatory diseases	16,800	11,796	5,004	20.2	0.72
Suicide	12,202	9,700	2,502	14.6	0.52
HIV infection	8,658	6,509	2,149	10.4	0.37
45 to 64 years	380,203	231,861	146,342	664.0	16.27
Malignant neoplasms	132,771	70,736	62,035	231.9	5.68
Circulatory diseases	100,124	70,138	29,986	174.9	4.28
Accidents	18,286	12,971	5,315	31.9	0.78
Diabetes mellitus	13,091	7,139	5,952	22.9	0.56
Liver disease and cirrhosis	11,023	8,031	2,992	19.3	0.47
65 and over	1,753,220	792,612	960,608	5,096.4	75.01
Circulatory diseases	605,673	270,637	335,036	1,760.6	25.91
Malignant neoplasms	384,186	199,794	184,392	1,116.8	16.44
Pneumonia and influenza	82,989	35,790	47,199	241.2	3.55
Diabetes mellitus	48,974	20,862	28,112	142.4	2.10
Accidents	32,975	16,176	16,799	95.9	1.41

Incidence of chronic health conditions per 1,000 population (1996): arthritis 126.8; chronic sinusitis 125.0; deformities or orthopedic impairments 111.2; hypertension 106.8; hay fever 89.4; hearing impairment 83.1; heart conditions 77.9; asthma 55.0; chronic bronchitis 53.4; migraine 43.5.

Social indicators

Educational attainment (2000). Percentage of population age 25 and over having: primary and incomplete secondary 15.9%; secondary 33.1%; some post-secondary 25.4%; 4-year higher degree 17.0%; advanced degree 8.6%. Number of earned degrees (2000): bachelor's degree 1,237,875; master's degree 457,056; doctor's degree 44,808; first-professional degrees (in fields such as medicine, theology, and law) 80,057.

Distribution of income (1999)

percentage of disposable family income by quintile

1	2	3	4	5 (highest)
4.3	9.9	15.6	23.0	47.2

Quality of working life (2001). Average workweek: 39.2 hours. Annual death rate per 100,000 workers for (2000): 4.5; leading causes of occupational deaths (1999): transportation incidents 43.4%, contact with objects/equipment 17.1%, assaults/violent acts 14.8%. Average days per 1,000 workdays lost to labour stoppages (2000): 1.8. Average duration of journey to work (2000): 20.7 minutes (private automobile 87.9%, of which drive alone 75.7%, car-pool 12.2%; take public transportation 4.7%; walk 2.9%; work at home 3.3%; other 1.2%). Rate per 1,000 employed workers of discouraged workers (unemployed no longer seeking work; 2000): 1.8.

Access to services (1995). Proportion of occupied dwellings having access to: electricity, virtually 100.0%; safe public water supply 99.4% (12.6% from wells); public sewage collection 77.0%, septic tanks 22.8%.

Social participation. Eligible voters participating in last presidential election (2000): 51.2%. Population age 18 and over participating in voluntary work (1999): 66.0%. Trade-union membership in total workforce (2000): 14.9%.

Social deviance (2002). Offense rate per 100,000 population for: murder 6.0; rape 33.9; robbery 158.6; aggravated assault 326.4; motor-vehicle theft 464.3; burglary and housebreaking 774.7; larceny-theft 2,540.1; drug-abuse violation 587.1; drunkenness 149.1. Estimated drug and substance users (population age 12 and over; 1999)[11]: cigarettes 57,296,000; binge alcohol[12] 44,486,000; marijuana 11,476,000; other illicit drugs 6,645,000. Rate per 100,000 population of suicide (1999): 10.7.

Leisure (1997). Favourite leisure activities (percentage of total population age 18 and over that undertook activity at least once in the previous year): exercise program 76.0%, movie 66.0%, home improvement 66.0%, amusement park 57.0%, playing sports 45.0%, charity work 43.0%, sports event 41.0%.

Material well-being (1995). Occupied dwellings with householder possessing: automobile 95.6%; telephone 93.9%; radio receiver 99.0%; television receiver 98.3%; videocassette recorder 81.0%; washing machine 78.3%; air conditioner 69.7%; cable television 63.4%.

Recreational expenditures (2000): U.S.$574,200,000,000 (television and radio receivers, computers, and video equipment 18.6%; golfing, bowling, and other participatory activities 11.0%; nondurable toys and sports equipment 10.5%; sports supplies 10.1%; magazines and newspapers 5.7%; books and maps 5.3%; spectator amusements 4.8%, of which theatre and opera 1.7%, spectator sports 1.6%, movies 1.4%; flowers, seeds, and potted plants 3.0%; other 31.0%).

National economy

Budget (2001). Revenue: U.S.$2,136,900,000,000 (individual income tax 48.8%, social-insurance taxes and contributions 36.4%, corporation income tax 10.4%, excise taxes 3.4%, customs duties 1.0%). Expenditures: U.S.$1,856,200,000,000 (social security and medicare 37.5%, defense 16.1%, interest on debt 11.1%, other 35.3%).

Total national debt (2002): U.S.$6,137,100,000,000.

Manufacturing, mining, and construction enterprises (2000)

	no. of enterprises	no. of employees	hourly wages as a % of all wages	value added (U.S.$'000,000)
Manufacturing				
Chemical and related products	13,426	886,000	131.0	191,100
Transportation equipment	12,766	1,873,000	137.2	182,900
Electric and electronic machinery, and computers	24,189	2,146,000	100.9	181,200
Machinery, except electrical	29,442	1,378,000	113.2	167,600
Food and related products	26,401	1,468,000	90.1	137,000

Manufacturing, mining, and construction enterprises (2000) (continued)

	no. of enter-prises	no. of employees	hourly wages as a % of all wages	value added (U.S.$'000,000)
Manufacturing (continued)				
Fabricated metal products	61,144	1,791,000	100.4	108,700
Printing and publishing	39,035	813,000	104.0	105,500
Rubber and plastic products	16,292	1,057,000	92.2	60,200
Paper and related products	5,790	554,000	118.0	59,900
Primary metals	6,300	602,000	119.9	52,900
Lumber and wood	17,328	598,000	85.4	44,400
Stone, clay, and glass products	16,537	524,000	102.9	43,900
Petroleum and coal products	2,210	109,000	162.1	36,500
Furniture and fixtures	19,848	640,000	84.6	26,700
Textile-mill products	6,881	216,000	79.8	24,700
Apparel and related products	16,505	510,000	66.3	23,600
Beverages and tobacco products	2,869	169,000	127.4	22,300
Leather and leather products	1,783	69,000	72.6	4,000
Miscellaneous manufacturing industries	31,303	732,000	85.1	29,100
Mining[13]				
Oil and gas extraction	8,312	110,881	124.1	82,350
Coal mining	1,511	87,965	142.7	15,567
Nonmetallic, except fuels	5,344	95,887	112.0	12,253
Metal mining	493	45,467	126.2	7,387
Construction[13]				
Special trade contractors	414,602	3,441	130.4	307,743
General contractors and operative builders	199,289	1,342,953	124.3	198,827
Heavy construction contractors	42,557	880,400	121.5	105,639

Gross national product (2001): U.S.$9,780,800,000,000 (U.S.$34,280 per capita).

Structure of gross domestic product and labour force

	2001		2000	
	in value U.S.$'000,000,000	% of total value	labour force[14]	% of labour force[14]
Agriculture	140.6	1.4	3,457,000	2.5
Mining	139.0	1.4	521,000	0.4
Manufacturing	1,423.0	14.1	19,940,000	14.2
Construction	480.0	4.8	9,433,000	6.7
Public utilities	221.9	2.2	1,447,000	1.0
Transp. and commun.	597.6	5.9	9,433,000	6.7
Trade, hotels	1,700.9	16.9	27,832,000	19.8
Finance, real estate	2,076.9	20.6	8,294,000	5.9
Public administration, defense	1,281.3	12.7	7,082,000	5.0
Services	2,138.2	21.2	47,770,000	33.9
Other	–117.2[15]	–1.2[15]	5,654,000[16]	4.0[16]
TOTAL	10,082.2	100.0	140,863,000	100.0[17]

Gross domestic product and national income

(in U.S.$'000,000,000)

	1996	1997	1998	1999	2000
Gross domestic product	7,576.1	8,110.9	8,511.0	9,299.2	9,963.1
By type of expenditure					
Personal consumption expenditures	5,151.4	5,493.7	5,807.9	6,268.7	6,757.3
Durable goods	632.1	673.0	724.7	761.3	820.3
Nondurable goods	1,545.1	1,600.6	1,662.4	1,845.5	2,010.0
Services	2,974.3	3,220.1	3,420.8	3,661.9	3,927.0
Gross private domestic investment	1,117.0	1,256.0	1,367.1	1,650.1	1,832.7
Fixed investment	1,101.5	1,188.6	1,307.8	1,606.8	1,778.2
Changes in business inventories	15.4	67.4	59.3	43.3	54.5
Net exports of goods and services	–98.7	–93.4	–151.2	–254.0	–370.7
Exports	855.2	965.4	959.0	990.2	1,097.3
Imports	953.9	1,058.8	1,110.2	1,224.2	1,468.0
Government purchases of goods and services	1,406.4	1,454.6	1,487.1	1,634.4	1,743.7
Federal	523.1	520.2	520.6	568.6	595.2
State and local	886.8	934.4	966.5	1,003.8	1,148.6
By major type of product					
Goods output	2,799.8	2,978.5	3,104.0	3,510.2	3,793.4
Durable goods	1,232.3	1,343.8	1,416.2	1,687.3	1,843.9
Nondurable goods	1,567.5	1,634.8	1,687.8	1,831.9	1,949.5
Services	4,105.2	4,414.1	4,641.0	4,934.6	5,254.0
Structures	671.1	718.3	765.9	854.3	915.6
National income (incl. capital consumption adjustment)	6,164.2	6,646.5	6,994.7	7,469.7	8,002.0
By type of income					
Compensation of employees	4,448.5	4,687.2	4,981.0	5,299.8	5,638.2
Proprietors' income	527.7	551.2	577.2	663.5	710.4
Rental income of persons	150.2	158.2	162.6	143.4	140.0
Corporate profits	670.2	817.9	824.6	856.0	946.2
Net interest	403.3	432.0	449.3	507.1	567.2
By industry division (excl. capital consumption adjustment)					
Agriculture, forestry, fishing	114.1	106.0	104.2	109.2	…
Mining and construction	325.9	357.6	381.1	433.1	…
Manufacturing	1,069.1	1,150.0	1,168.7	1,193.3	…
Durable	628.6	659.4	684.2	704.6	…
Nondurable	440.5	491.6	484.4	488.7	…
Transportation	196.5	208.0	216.2	236.9	…
Communications	148.5	139.3	149.3	161.9	…
Public utilities	126.5	133.6	135.3	135.9	…
Wholesale and retail trade	857.8	927.4	989.2	1,077.0	…
Finance, insurance, real estate	1,037.0	1,192.0	1,273.5	1,366.9	…
Services	1,441.1	1,513.6	1,624.9	1,782.9	…
Government and government enterprise	843.1	877.5	906.3	953.2	…
Other	–8.9	–8.0	–20.4	–11.0	…

Business activity (1997): number of businesses 23,645,000 (sole proprietorships 72.6%, active corporations 19.9%, active partnerships 7.5%), of which services 10,114,000, wholesaling and retailing 4,455,000; business receipts U.S.$18,057,000,000,000 (active corporations 88.0%, sole proprietorships 4.8%, active partnerships 7.2%), of which wholesaling and retailing U.S.$5,136,000,000,000, services U.S.$2,130,000,000,000; net profit U.S.$1,270,000,000,000 (active corporations 72.0%, sole proprietorships 14.7%, partnerships 13.3%), of which services U.S.$203,000,000,000, wholesaling and retailing U.S.$10,000,000,000. New business starts and business failures (1995): total number of new business starts 168,158; total failures 71,194, of which commercial service 21,850, retail trade 12,952; failure rate per 10,000 concerns 90.0; current liabilities of failed concerns U.S.$37,507,000,000; average liability U.S.$526,830. Business expenditures for new plant and equipment (1995): total U.S.$594,465,000,000, of which trade, services, and communications U.S.$244,829,000,000, manufacturing businesses U.S.$172,308,000,000 (durable goods 53.0%, nondurable goods 47.0%), public utilities U.S.$42,816,000,000, transportation U.S.$37,021,000,000, mining and construction U.S.$35,985,000.

Components of gross domestic product (2001)

States	Gross state product (U.S.$'000,000,000)	Personal income (U.S.$'000,000,000)	Disposable personal income (U.S.$'000,000,000)	Per capita disposable personal income (U.S.$)
Alabama	119.9	109.0	95.9	21,481
Alaska	27.7	19.7	17.2	27,131
Arizona	156.3	135.2	116.5	21,942
Arkansas	67.7	61.7	54.2	20,151
California	1,344.6	1,127.4	929.7	26,947
Colorado	167.9	145.6	122.3	27,683
Connecticut	159.3	143.6	115.6	33,765
Delaware	36.3	25.6	21.7	27,237
Florida	472.1	467.2	402.6	24,554
Georgia	296.1	238.4	203.7	24,296
Hawaii	42.4	35.0	30.4	24,810
Idaho	37.0	32.0	27.7	20,967
Illinois	457.3	408.9	345.9	27,711
Indiana	192.2	168.3	145.5	23,801
Iowa	89.6	79.7	69.4	23,754
Kansas	85.1	76.8	66.0	24,506
Kentucky	118.5	101.9	87.9	21,631
Louisiana	137.7	107.5	95.1	21,286
Maine	36.0	33.9	29.2	22,663
Maryland	186.1	187.9	156.9	29,197
Massachusetts	284.9	247.8	202.2	31,694
Michigan	325.4	295.1	251.3	25,158
Minnesota	184.8	163.0	137.3	27,622
Mississippi	67.3	61.9	55.4	19,401
Missouri	178.8	157.8	136.3	24,217
Montana	21.7	21.3	18.6	20,544
Nebraska	56.1	48.9	42.3	24,707
Nevada	42.4	62.9	54.0	25,637
New Hampshire	47.7	42.7	36.8	29,259
New Jersey	363.1	323.7	268.9	31,693
New Mexico	54.4	42.4	37.2	20,340
New York	799.2	682.2	559.0	29,402
North Carolina	281.7	224.4	192.9	23,567
North Dakota	18.3	16.2	14.4	22,691
Ohio	372.6	325.5	277.7	24,420
Oklahoma	91.8	85.8	74.8	21,613
Oregon	118.6	97.2	82.1	23,650
Pennsylvania	404.0	376.2	322.0	26,203
Rhode Island	36.5	31.8	27.3	25,769
South Carolina	113.4	99.9	87.0	21,423
South Dakota	23.2	19.9	17.7	23,454
Tennessee	178.4	153.6	136.7	23,819
Texas	742.3	607.5	533.4	25,015
Utah	68.5	54.9	47.2	20,803
Vermont	18.4	17.2	14.8	24,064
Virginia	261.4	232.1	193.9	26,972
Washington	219.9	189.1	160.3	26,773
West Virginia	42.3	40.9	36.2	20,068
Wisconsin	173.5	156.2	133.5	24,710
Wyoming	19.3	14.2	12.2	24,575
District				
District of Columbia	59.4	23.2	18.9	33,031
TOTAL/AVERAGE	9,899.1	8,620.8	7,315.7	25,688

Retail and wholesale trade and services (2000)

	no. of establish-ments	no. of employees	hourly wage as a % of all wages	annual sales or receipts (U.S.$'000,000)
Retail trade	1,113,600	14,841,000	68.7	3,105,585
Automotive dealers	124,500	1,866,000	93.5	927,141
Food stores	154,500	3,004,000	68.8	464,288
General merchandise group stores	39,600	2,526,000	74.7	417,852
Eating and drinking places	483,000	8,113,000	50.0[7, 18]	303,905
Building materials, hardware, garden supply, and mobile home dealers	91,900	1,235,000	74.2	298,604
Gasoline service stations	119,600	937,000	93.5	199,420
Apparel and accessory stores	150,900	1,369,000	67.8	169,815
Drugstores and proprietary stores	81,200	914,000	79.8	152,780
Furniture, home furnishings, equipment stores	64,800	549,000	92.2	90,503
Electronics and appliances	45,600	407,000	75.1	88,678
Sporting goods, book and music stores	65,000	616,000	92.1	74,080
Liquor stores	28,500	134,000	…	23,400
Wholesale trade	446,200	6,112,000	110.1	2,755,500
Durable goods	288,600	3,627,000	114.9	1,435,100
Professional and commercial equipment	44,400	763,000	136.6	279,300
Machinery, equipment, and supplies	73,700	796,000	115.9	257,900
Electrical goods	38,300	535,000	117.5	239,500
Motor vehicles, automotive equipment	28,400	402,000	101.8	195,700
Computers and software	…	…	…	164,700

Retail and wholesale trade and services (2000) (continued)

	no. of establish-ments	no. of employees	hourly wage as a % of all wages	annual sales or receipts (U.S.$'000,000)
Metals and minerals, except petroleum	12,100	173,000	109.1	103,300
Lumber and other construction materials	15,100	184,000	101.8	71,500
Hardware, plumbing, heating equipment and supplies	21,400	249,000	106.4	65,500
Furniture and home furnishings	14,900	167,000	100.8	46,500
Miscellaneous durable goods	40,200	355,000	89.6	175,900
Nondurable goods	157,700	2,487,000	97.3	1,320,500
Groceries and related products	39,700	875,000	101.5	387,900
Petroleum and products	10,700	132,000	93.8	171,900
Drugs, drug proprietaries, and druggists' sundries	7,400	210,000	142.6	166,300
Farm-products raw materials	9,500	92,000	79.2	106,200
Apparel and accessories	20,000	214,000	97.6	94,200
Paper and paper products	14,900	232,000	104.9	79,000
Beer, wine, and distilled alcoholic beverages	4,600	153,000	115.0	71,700
Chemicals and allied products	15,300	166,000	119.7	60,000
Miscellaneous nondurable goods	35,400	409,000	84.0	184,300
Services	3,842,000	61,662,000	101.6	1,843,800[13]
Health	659,000	14,109,000	107.1	398,500[13]
Business, except computer services	623,000	5,645,000	100.9	304,400[13]
Computer and data-processing services	100,000	1,171,000	168.4	224,100[13]
Legal services	177,000	1,089,000	145.3	122,600[13]
Automotive repair, services, garages	164,000	856,000	86.7	99,600[13]
Management and public relations	47,000	2,874,000	139.6	101,300[13]
Hotels and motels	60,000	1,768,000	70.1	97,900[13]
Amusement and recreation	64,000	1,279,000	76.4	67,900[13]
Engineering services	102,000	1,213,000	139.5	108,600[13]
Personal services	199,000	1,293,000	72.2	53,100[13]
Motion pictures	23,000	304,000	111.4	67,900[13]

Production. Agriculture, forestry, fishing (value of production/catch in U.S.$'000,000 except as noted; 2000): corn (maize) 18,621, soybeans 13,073, wheat 5,970, cotton lint 4,781, grapes 3,063, potatoes 2,539, tobacco 2,056, oranges 1,752, apples 1,554, head lettuce 1,259, tomatoes 1,160, rice 1,073, strawberries 1,013, almonds 852, peanuts (groundnuts) 844, sorghum 822, onions 732, cottonseed 677, barley 632, bell peppers 614, broccoli 597, peaches 495, sweet corn 474, carrots 436, dry beans 423, grapefruit 423, cantaloupes 359, cabbage 332, lemons 318, avocados 318, sweet cherries 286, cauliflower 259, pears 255, sunflower seeds 241, watermelons 236, pecans 234; livestock (number of live animals) 98,048,000 cattle, 59,337,000 pigs, 7,215,000 sheep, 5,320,000 horses, 1,720,000,000 chickens; roundwood 500,434,000 cu m; fish and shellfish catch 3,467, of which fish 1,558 (including salmon 359, Alaska pollack 163), shellfish 1,909 (including shrimp 560, crabs 521). Mining (metal content in metric tons except as noted; 2001): iron 37,800,000; copper 1,340,000; zinc 830,000; lead 420,000; molybdenum 38,300; vanadium 2,700; mercury 550; silver 1,800,000 kg; gold 350,000 kg; helium 101,000,000 cu m. Quarrying (metric tons; 2000): crushed stone 1,300,000,000; sand and gravel 1,139,000,000; cement 75,000,000; common salt 45,000,000; clay 40,700,000; phosphate rock 34,200,000; lime 20,000,000; gypsum 18,800,000. Manufacturing (value added in U.S.$'000,000; 1999): transportation equipment 268,511, of which motor vehicle parts 86,310, motor vehicles 80,134, aerospace products and parts 73,897; computers and electronic products 265,442, of which semiconductors and related components 102,003; chemicals and chemical products 229,284, of which pharmaceuticals and medicine 74,108; food 177,659; fabricated metal products 142,451; nonelectrical machinery 138,798; paper and paper products 74,602; plastics 72,183; base metals 66,733; printing 62,428; electrical machinery 60,458. Construction (completed; 2000): private U.S.$640,654,000,000, of which residential U.S.$374,274,000,000, nonresidential U.S.$210,140,000,000; public U.S.$174,860,000,000.

Energy production (consumption): electricity (kW-hr; 2001) 3,778,500,000,000 ([1999] 4,005,256,000,000); hard coal (metric tons; 1999) 915,998,000 (884,033,000); lignite (metric tons; 1999) 78,361,000 (81,484,000); crude petroleum (barrels; 2001) 2,163,000,000 ([1999] 5,524,300,000); petroleum products (metric tons; 1999) 750,886,000 (753,174,000); natural gas (cu m; 2001) 549,557,000,000 ([1999] 653,144,900,000). Domestic production of energy by source (1998): coal 32.5%, natural gas 26.3%, crude petroleum 18.0%, nuclear power 9.8%, renewable energy 9.1%, other 4.3%.

Energy consumption by source (1999): petroleum and petroleum products 39.7%, natural gas 23.3%, coal 21.4%, nuclear electric power 8.1%, hydroelectric and thermal 7.5%; by end use: industrial 37.8%, residential and commercial 35.4%, transportation 26.8%.

Energy consumption by source and by state (1999)

('000,000,000,000 Btu)

States	Petroleum	Natural gas	Coal	Hydroelectric power	Nuclear electric power
Alabama	551	345	855	80	328
Alaska	253	420	11	9	0.0
Arizona	497	163	404	104	323
Arkansas	384	266	267	28	137
California	3,383	2,182	64	425	355
Colorado	426	318	355	17	0.0
Connecticut	440	135	0.0	14	135
Delaware	141	58	36	0.0	0.0
Florida	1,912	542	672	2	335
Georgia	1,044	341	790	28	334
Hawaii	214	3	3	1	0.0
Idaho	170	72	8	140	0.0
Illinois	1,340	1,058	837	2	868

Energy consumption by source and by state (1999) (continued)

('000,000,000,000 Btu)

States	Petroleum	Natural gas	Coal	Hydroelectric power	Nuclear electric power
Indiana	899	577	1,451	4	0.0
Iowa	419	236	416	10	39
Kansas	437	302	329	0.0	97
Kentucky	726	220	885	27	0.0
Louisiana	1,452	1,558	228	8	139
Maine	250	6	3	81	0.0
Maryland	584	201	304	15	141
Massachusetts	639	356	13	15	48
Michigan	1,098	930	823	11	155
Minnesota	661	346	336	59	142
Mississippi	483	346	138	0.0	90
Missouri	781	270	686	18	91
Montana	174	64	174	143	0.0
Nebraska	246	121	196	18	107
Nevada	221	157	180	29	0.0
New Hampshire	188	21	35	25	92
New Jersey	1,236	641	68	0.0	308
New Mexico	257	225	298	3	0.0
New York	1,653	1,251	188	265	393
North Carolina	937	229	708	40	399
North Dakota	123	59	412	28	0.0
Ohio	1,340	878	1,379	4	175
Oklahoma	500	543	334	32	0.0
Oregon	392	219	39	475	0.0
Pennsylvania	1,385	696	1,143	16	756
Rhode Island	99	86	0.1	10	0.0
South Carolina	467	163	403	7	540
South Dakota	115	36	46	71	0.0
Tennessee	713	286	626	74	289
Texas	5,565	3,982	1,535	13	391
Utah	262	169	382	13	0.0
Vermont	85	8	2	61	43
Virginia	864	275	402	6	301
Washington	878	277	96	988	65
West Virginia	220	147	977	10	0.0
Wisconsin	668	379	472	23	122
Wyoming	156	102	495	12	0.0
District					
District of Columbia	34	33	0.6	0.0	0.0
TOTAL	37,962	22,298	20,504.7	3,464	7,738

Household income[19] level by selected characteristics (2000)

Characteristics	Number of households ('000)	Number ('000): Under $15,000	$15,000–$34,999	$35,000–$74,999	$75,000 and over	Median income ($)
Total/Average	106,418	16,952	27,584	36,570	25,313	42,151
Age of householder						
15 to 24 years	6,393	1,506	2,445	1,922	520	27,711
25 to 34 years	18,554	2,098	4,881	7,722	3,853	44,477
35 to 44 years	23,904	2,163	4,921	9,561	7,259	53,243
45 to 54 years	21,797	2,082	3,918	7,823	7,975	58,217
55 to 64 years	13,944	2,220	3,221	4,773	3,728	44,993
65 years and over	21,826	6,883	8,198	4,769	1,978	23,047
Size of household						
One person	27,820	10,112	9,524	6,362	1,820	21,468
Two persons	35,388	3,716	9,987	13,028	8,657	44,530
Three persons	17,259	1,530	3,425	6,922	5,382	54,196
Four persons	15,430	904	2,614	6,073	5,840	61,847
Five persons	6,686	425	1,239	2,597	2,424	60,295
Six persons	2,396	154	502	1,000	740	54,841
Seven or more persons	1,439	108	293	589	449	54,663
Educational attainment of householder						
Total[20]	100,025	15,446	25,139	34,646	24,795	43,556
Less than 9th grade	6,753	2,898	2,302	1,244	308	17,557
Some high school	9,111	3,023	3,224	2,276	587	22,753
High school graduate	30,785	5,248	9,363	11,410	4,765	36,722
Some college, no degree	18,165	2,155	4,834	7,087	4,089	44,449
Associate degree	8,214	730	1,888	3,351	2,246	50,356
Bachelor's degree	17,521	1,006	2,607	6,462	7,446	65,922
Master's degree	6,435	265	685	2,076	3,410	77,935
Professional degree	1,641	70	145	342	1,085	100,000
Doctorate degree	1,400	51	91	398	859	93,361

Household income and expenditure. Average household size (2000) 2.7; median annual income per household (2001) U.S.$42,228, of which median Asian and Pacific Islander household U.S.$53,635, median non-Hispanic household U.S.$46,305, median Hispanic[5] household U.S.$33,565, median black (including Hispanic) household U.S.$29,470; sources of personal income (2000): wages and salaries 57.6%, self-employment 8.6%, transfer payments 8.5%, other 25.3%; expenditure (1999): transportation 18.9%, housing 18.9%, food at home 7.9%, household furnishings 7.2%, fuel and utilities 6.4%, food away from home 5.7%, recreation 5.5%, health 5.3%, wearing apparel 4.7%, education 1.7%, other 17.8%.

Financial aggregates

	1997	1998	1999	2000	2001	2002	2003[21]
Exchange rate, U.S.$ per:							
£[22]	1.65	1.66	1.62	1.49	1.44	1.50	1.63
SDR[22]	1.38	1.36	1.37	1.32	1.27	1.29	1.40
International reserves (U.S.$)[23]							
Total (excl. gold; '000,000,000)	58.91	70.71	60.50	56.60	57.63	67.96	69.57
SDRs ('000,000,000)	10.03	10.60	10.35	10.54	10.78	12.17	11.65
Reserve pos. in IMF ('000,000,000)	18.07	24.11	17.97	14.82	17.87	21.98	22.74
Foreign exchange ('000,000,000)	30.81	36.00	32.18	31.24	29.98	33.82	35.19

Financial aggregates (continued)

	1997	1998	1999	2000	2001	2002	2003[21]
Gold ('000,000 fine troy oz)	261.61	261.78	261.67	261.61	262.00	262.00	261.55
% world reserves	29.52	27.09	27.13	27.52	27.83	28.16	28.40
Interest and prices							
Central bank discount (%)[23]	5.00	4.50	5.00	6.00	1.25	0.75	2.00
Govt. bond yield (%)[22]	6.35	5.26	5.64	6.03	5.02	4.61	3.98
Industrial share prices[22] (1995 = 100)	159.3	198.7	251.3	272.8	215.2	178.4	176.1
Balance of payments (U.S.$'000,000,000)							
Balance of visible trade	–196.18	–244.74	–343.72	–449.79	–424.11	–479.38	...
Imports, f.o.b.	–876.51	–917.12	–1,029.99	–1,224.43	–1,145.95	–1,164.76	...
Exports, f.o.b.	680.33	672.38	686.27	774.63	721.84	685.38	...
Balance of invisibles	68.50	40.07	52.85	38.33	30.37	–1.48	...
Balance of payments, current account	–127.68	–204.67	–290.87	–411.46	–393.74	–480.86	...

Average employee earnings

	average hourly earnings in U.S.$		average weekly earnings in U.S.$	
	Feb. 1999	Feb. 2000	Feb. 1999	Feb. 2000
Manufacturing				
Durable goods	13.66	14.19	564.16	588.89
Lumber and wood products	11.26	11.61	453.78	469.04
Furniture and fixtures	11.06	11.50	440.17	457.70
Stone, clay, and glass products	13.64	13.99	576.96	593.18
Primary metal industries	15.41	16.29	673.42	723.28
Fabricated metal products	13.29	13.65	555.52	576.03
Machinery, except electrical	14.72	15.39	619.71	652.54
Electrical and electronic equipment	13.25	13.71	544.58	567.59
Transportation equipment	17.50	18.65	768.25	818.74
Instruments and related products	13.94	14.41	578.51	595.13
Miscellaneous manufacturing	11.17	11.56	442.33	455.46
Nondurable goods	12.97	13.38	525.29	543.23
Food and kindred products	11.91	12.25	489.50	501.03
Tobacco manufactures	17.80	17.32	662.16	680.68
Textile mill products	10.60	10.84	426.12	447.69
Apparel and other textile products	8.65	9.01	322.65	338.78
Paper and allied products	15.70	16.03	675.10	689.29
Printing and publishing	13.67	14.13	515.36	536.53
Chemicals and allied products	17.20	17.80	734.44	756.50
Petroleum and coal products	21.43	22.03	927.92	962.71
Rubber and miscellaneous plastics products	12.16	12.53	503.42	518.74
Leather and leather products	9.56	9.87	355.63	370.13
Nonmanufacturing				
Metal mining	18.16	18.63	793.59	815.99
Coal mining	19.11	19.40	865.68	873.00
Oil and gas extraction	16.98	16.68	696.18	738.47
Nonmetallic minerals, except fuels	14.81	15.22	662.00	672.02
Construction	16.66	17.37	633.08	672.09
Transportation and public utilities	15.56	16.06	606.84	613.49
Wholesale trade	14.38	14.96	550.75	571.47
Retail trade	8.98	9.34	256.83	266.19
Finance, insurance, and real estate	14.55	14.91	528.17	536.76
Hotels, motels, and tourist courts	9.20	9.53	280.60	289.71
Health services	14.06	14.55	462.57	480.15
Legal services	18.74	19.75	652.15	693.23
Miscellaneous services	18.38	18.67	637.79	681.46

Median household income[19]

(in constant 1999 U.S.$)

States	1995	1996	1997	1998	1999
Alabama	28,413	32,175	33,153	37,067	36,213
Alaska	52,422	56,042	49,818	51,812	51,509
Arizona	33,739	33,593	33,984	37,909	37,119
Arkansas	28,219	28,800	27,156	28,276	29,762
California	40,457	41,211	41,203	41,838	43,744
Colorado	44,499	43,482	44,876	47,628	48,346
Connecticut	43,993	44,723	45,657	47,535	50,798
Delaware	38,182	41,739	44,669	42,374	46,839
Florida	32,517	32,535	33,688	35,680	35,876
Georgia	37,276	34,505	38,056	39,519	39,433
Hawaii	46,844	44,354	42,490	41,729	44,373
Idaho	35,721	36,855	34,674	37,490	35,906
Illinois	41,618	41,999	42,852	44,132	46,392
Indiana	36,496	37,320	40,367	40,608	40,929
Iowa	38,829	35,262	35,067	37,837	41,238
Kansas	33,168	34,600	37,857	37,522	37,476
Kentucky	32,588	34,417	34,723	37,053	33,901
Louisiana	30,553	32,133	34,524	32,436	32,695
Maine	37,013	36,841	34,018	36,427	38,932
Maryland	44,865	46,713	48,459	51,121	52,310
Massachusetts	42,168	41,936	43,620	43,280	44,192
Michigan	39,820	41,650	40,214	42,745	46,238
Minnesota	41,467	43,525	44,182	48,984	47,240
Mississippi	29,011	28,326	29,582	29,763	32,540
Missouri	38,070	36,383	37,942	41,089	41,466
Montana	30,343	30,457	30,322	32,274	31,244
Nebraska	35,997	36,117	36,011	37,217	38,787
Nevada	39,446	40,923	40,331	40,634	41,680
New Hampshire	42,821	41,843	42,556	45,951	46,167
New Jersey	48,017	50,403	49,846	50,926	49,930
New Mexico	28,413	26,637	31,229	32,240	32,475
New York	36,105	37,599	37,159	38,220	40,058
North Carolina	34,959	37,802	37,202	36,630	37,340
North Dakota	31,799	33,416	32,864	30,973	32,877

Median household income[19] (continued)

(in constant 1999 U.S.$)

States	1995	1996	1997	1998	1999
Ohio	38,197	36,176	37,507	39,785	39,617
Oklahoma	28,763	29,133	32,543	34,472	32,919
Oregon	39,763	37,686	38,663	39,930	40,713
Pennsylvania	37,741	37,057	38,943	39,877	37,995
Rhode Island	38,654	39,273	36,119	41,585	42,936
South Carolina	31,780	36,808	35,564	34,002	36,563
South Dakota	32,334	31,351	30,823	33,510	35,982
Tennessee	31,719	32,694	31,800	34,844	36,536
Texas	35,024	35,117	36,408	36,573	38,978
Utah	39,879	39,328	44,401	45,277	46,094
Vermont	36,976	34,358	36,385	40,242	41,630
Virginia	39,597	41,635	44,590	44,312	45,750
Washington	38,882	38,943	46,256	48,468	45,639
West Virginia	27,198	26,808	28,533	27,294	29,433
Wisconsin	44,771	42,474	41,100	42,240	45,825
Wyoming	34,467	32,867	34,693	36,029	37,395
District					
District of Columbia	33,613	33,942	33,071	34,171	38,686
U.S. AVERAGE	37,251	37,686	38,411	39,744	40,816

Average annual expenditure of "consumer units" (households, plus individuals sharing households or budgets; 2000): total U.S.$38,045, of which housing U.S.$12,319, transportation U.S.$7,417, food U.S.$5,158, pensions and social security U.S.$2,966, health care U.S.$2,066, clothing U.S.$1,856, other U.S.$6,263.

Selected household characteristics (2000). Total number of households 104,705,000, of which (family households by race) white 84.8%, black 12.2%, other 3.0%; in central cities 31.4%[24], in suburbs 46.3%[24], outside metropolitan areas 22.3%[24]; (by tenure[24]) owned 64,045,000 (64.7%), rented 34,946,000 (35.3%); family households 72,025,000, of which married couple 76.8%, female head with own children[25] under age 18, 10.5%, female head without own children[25] under 18, 7.1%; nonfamily households 32,680,000, of which female living alone 47.6%, male living alone 34.2%, other 18.2%.

Population economically active (2001): total 141,815,000[14]; activity rate of total population 49.8% (participation rates: age 16 and over 66.9%; female 46.7%; unemployed [November 2003] 5.9%).

Price and earnings indexes (1995 = 100)

	1996	1997	1998	1999	2000	2001	2002
Consumer price index	102.9	105.3	107.0	109.3	113.0	116.2	118.0
Hourly earnings index	103.3	106.4	109.1	112.4	116.2	120.0	123.7

Tourism (1999): receipts from visitors U.S.$94,657,000,000; expenditures by nationals abroad U.S.$80,756,000,000; number of foreign visitors (2000) 50,891,000,000 (14,594,000 from Canada, 10,322,000 from Mexico, 11,597,000 from Europe); number of nationals traveling abroad 60,816,000 (18,849,000 to Mexico, 15,114,000 to Canada).

Land use (1997): forested 20.9%; meadows and pastures 27.1%; agricultural and under permanent cultivation 21.1%; other 30.9%.

Foreign trade

Balance of trade (current prices)

	1996	1997	1998	1999	2000	2001
U.S.$'000,000,000	–189.2	–181.9	–231.1	–343.3	–434.3	–410.2
% of total	13.4%	11.7%	14.5%	20.0%	21.7%	21.9%

Imports (2000): U.S.$1,216,743,000,000 (manufactured goods 84.8%, of which motor vehicles and parts 13.3%, electrical machinery 8.9%, computers and office equipment 7.5%, petroleum and petroleum products 7.4%, chemicals and chemical products 6.0%, wearing apparel 5.3%; food and live animals 3.1%). *Major import sources:* Canada 19.0%; Japan 12.0%; Mexico 11.2%; China 8.2%; Germany 4.8%; United Kingdom 3.6%; Taiwan 3.3%; South Korea 3.3%; France 2.4%; Italy 2.1%; Malaysia 2.1%; Singapore 1.6%; Thailand 1.3%; Philippines 1.1%; Brazil 1.1%.

Exports (2000): U.S.$782,429,000,000 (manufactured goods 79.7%, of which electrical machinery 11.4%, chemicals and related products 10.2%, motor vehicles 7.3%, scientific and precision equipment 3.9%; food and live animals 6.4%). *Major export destinations:* Canada 22.9%; Mexico 14.2%; Japan 8.3%; United Kingdom 5.3%; Germany 3.7%; South Korea 3.6%; Taiwan 3.1%; The Netherlands 2.8%; France 2.6%; Singapore 2.3%; Brazil 2.0%.

Trade by commodity group (2000)

	imports		exports	
SITC Group	U.S.$'000,000	%	U.S.$'000,000	%
00 Food and live animals	39,547[26]	3.1[26]	40,242[26]	5.4[26]
01 Beverages and tobacco	9,736	0.8	6,821	0.9
02 Crude materials, excluding fuels	24,086	1.9	29,014	3.9
03 Mineral fuels, lubricants, and related materials	139,706	11.1	13,813	1.9
04 Animal and vegetable oils, fat, and waxes	[26]	[26]	[26]	[26]
05 Chemicals and related products, n.e.s.	74,562	5.9	80,021	10.8
06 Basic manufactures	142,245	11.3	73,265	9.8
07 Machinery and transport equipment	563,304	44.8	382,362	51.4
08 Miscellaneous manufactured articles	210,503	16.7	86,191	11.6
09 Goods not classified by kind	52,899	4.2	30,295	4.1
TOTAL	1,258,080[27]	100.0[27]	743,404[27]	100.0[27]

Direction of trade (2000)

	imports		exports	
	U.S.$'000,000	%	U.S.$'000,000	%
Africa	26,983	2.2	7,565	1.0
South Africa	4,317	0.4	3,100	0.4
Other Africa	22,666	1.8	4,465	0.6
Americas	439,960	35.5	342,144	44.3
Canada	229,191	18.5	174,616	22.6
Caribbean countries and Central America	20,969	1.7	21,867	2.9
Mexico	135,080	10.9	107,751	13.9
South America	54,720	4.4	37,803	4.9
Asia	501,526	40.5	220,872	28.6
China	106,215	8.6	15,964	2.1
Japan	149,520	12.1	64,538	8.4
Other Asia	245,791	19.8	140,370	18.1
Europe	260,752	21.1	186,787	24.2
EU	223,295	18.0	164,593	21.3
Russia	7,830	0.6	2,301	0.3
Other Europe	29,627	2.5	19,893	2.6
Oceania	8,879	0.7	14,316	1.9
Australia	6,693	0.5	12,332	1.6
Other Oceania	2,186	0.2	1,984	0.3
TOTAL	1,238,200[27]	100.0	771,991[27]	100.0

Transport and communications

Transport. Railroads (1998): length 132,000 mi, 212,433 km; (1999) passenger-mi 13,402,000,000, passenger-km 21,568,000,000; short ton-mi cargo (1997) 1,421,000,000,000, metric ton-km cargo (1997) 2,075,000,000. Roads (2000): total length 3,936,229 mi, 6,334,747 km (paved 91%). Vehicles (2000): passenger cars 133,621,000; trucks and buses 87,107,000. Merchant marine (1999): vessels (1,000 gross tons and over) 579; total deadweight tonnage 16,747,000. Air transport (2002): passenger-mi 992,849,000,000, passenger-km 1,598,000,000,000; short ton-mi cargo 54,302,000,000, metric ton-km cargo 87,390,000,000; localities (1996) with scheduled flights 834[28]. Certified route passenger/cargo air carriers (1992) 77; operating revenue (U.S.$'000,000; 1991) 74,942, of which domestic 56,119, international 18,823; operating expenses 76,669, of which domestic 56,596, international 20,073.

Intercity passenger and freight traffic by mode of transportation (1999)

	cargo traffic ('000,000,000 ton-mi)	% of nat'l total	passenger traffic ('000,000,000 passenger-mi)	% of nat'l total
Rail	1,499	40.3	14	0.6
Road	1,093	29.4	1,885	78.5
Inland water	486	13.1	—	—
Air	14	0.4	501	20.9
Petroleum pipeline	623	16.8	—	—
TOTAL	3,715	100.0	2,400	100.0

Communications

Medium	date	unit	number	units per 1,000 persons
Daily newspapers	2000	circulation	55,773,000	198
Radio	2000	receivers	598,000,000	2,118
Television	2000	receivers	241,000,000	854
Telephones	2002	main lines	190,000,000	659
Cellular telephones	2002	subscribers	140,767,000	488
Personal computers	2001	units	178,000,000	623
Internet	2002	users	155,000,000	538

Other communications media (2000)

	titles		titles
Print		Engineering	265
Books (new)	122,108	Fine and applied arts	145
of which		General interest	181
Agriculture	1,073	History	151
Art	5,980	Home economics	90
Biography	3,899	Industrial arts	106
Business	4,068	Journalism and commun.	90
Education	3,378	Labour and industrial relations	70
Fiction	14,617	Law	273
General works	1,318	Library and information sciences	118
History	7,931	Literature and language	158
Home economics	2,513	Mathematics and science	238
Juvenile	8,690	Medicine	182
Language	2,536	Philosophy and religion	130
Law	3,070	Physical education and recreation	151
Literature	3,371	Political science	136
Medicine	6,234	Psychology	138
Music	1,582	Sociology and anthropology	149
Philosophy, psychology	5,556	Zoology	94
Poetry, drama	2,479		
Religion	6,206	**Cinema**	
Science	8,464	Feature films	478
Sociology, economics	14,908		
Sports, recreation	3,483		(pieces of mail)
Technology	8,582	**Post**	
Travel	3,170	Mail	207,483,000,000
Periodicals[7]	3,731	Domestic	206,381,000,000
of which		International	1,102,000,000
Agriculture	153		
Business and economics	262		
Chemistry and physics	170		
Children's periodicals	78		
Education	203		

Education and health

Literacy: n.a.

Education (2001–02)

	schools	teachers	students	student/ teacher ratio
Primary (age 5–13)[29]	...	2,206,000	38,163,000	17.3
Secondary and vocational (age 14–17)	...	1,341,000	14,902,000	11.1
Higher, including teacher-training colleges	4,064[7]	1,012,000	15,300,000	15.1

Food (2001): daily per capita caloric intake 3,776 (vegetable products 73%, animal products 27%); 143% of FAO recommended minimum requirement. Per capita consumption of major food groups (kilograms annually; 2001): milk 256.6; fresh vegetables 124.5; cereal products 116.9; fresh fruits 113.4; red meat 72.5; potatoes 64.4; poultry products 47.8; sugar 32.6; fats and oils 32.5; fish and shellfish 21.2.

Health (2000): doctors of medicine 813,800[30] (1 per 346 persons), of which office-based practice 490,400 (including specialties in internal medicine 18.1%, general and family practice 13.8%, pediatrics 8.6%, obstetrics and gynecology 6.5%, anesthesiology 5.6%, psychiatry 5.1%, general surgery 5.0%, orthopedics 3.5%, ophthalmology 3.2%); doctors of osteopathy 44,900; nurses 2,201,810 (1 per 128 persons); dentists 170,000 (1 per 1,696 persons); hospital beds 984,000 (1 per 293 persons), of which nonfederal 94.6% (community hospitals 83.7%, psychiatric 8.8%, long-term general and special 1.8%), federal 5.4%; infant mortality rate per 1,000 live births (2000) 7.1.

Military

Total active duty personnel (2003): 1,427,000 (army 34.0%, navy 28.0%, air force 25.8%, marines 12.2%). *Military expenditure as percentage of GNP* (1999): 3.0% (world 2.4%); per capita expenditure U.S.$1,030. *Security assistance to the world* (2002): U.S.$7,209,000,000, for underwriting the purchase of U.S. weapons 50.6%, of which Israel 28.3%, Egypt 18.0%, Jordan 1.0%; for economic support 30.5%, of which Israel 10.0%, Egypt 9.1%, Jordan 2.1%; for the Andean Counterdrug Initiative 9.2%; for nonproliferation, antiterrorism, and de-mining 4.3%; for international narcotics and law enforcement 3.0%; for peacekeeping operations 1.9%.

[1]Excludes 4 nonvoting delegates from the District of Columbia, the U.S. Virgin Islands, American Samoa, and Guam; a nonvoting resident commissioner from Puerto Rico; and a nonvoting resident representative from the Northern Mariana Islands. [2]Total area per most recent official survey equals 3,675,267 sq mi (9,518,898 sq km), of which land area equals 3,536,278 sq mi (9,158,918 sq km), inland water area equals 78,937 sq mi (204,446 sq km), and Great Lakes water area equals 60,052 sq mi (155,534 sq km). [3]Excludes 231,000 military personnel overseas; adjusted census total announced December 2002 equaled 284,683,782. [4]Includes military personnel residing overseas. [5]Persons of Hispanic origin may be of any race. [6]Estimate of the UN High Commissioner of Refugees. [7]1999. [8]1995. [9]1989–91. [10]Includes deaths with age not known. [11]Individuals who used drugs at least once within month prior to survey. [12]Drinking 5 or more drinks on the same occasion on at least one day in the past 30 days per survey. [13]1997. [14]Excludes military personnel overseas. [15]Statistical discrepancy. [16]Unemployed. [17]Detail does not add to total given because of rounding. [18]Excludes tips. [19]Gross income from all sources, including transfer payments to individuals. [20]Householder 25 years old or older. [21]July. [22]Period average. [23]End-of-period. [24]1994. [25]"Own children" includes adopted children and stepchildren. [26]Animal and vegetable oils included in Food and live animals. [27]Detail does not add to total given because of statistical discrepancies in the data. [28]Includes 292 localities in Alaska. [29]Primary includes kindergarten. [30]737,500 professionally active.

Internet resources for further information:

- **U.S. Census Bureau**
  http://www.census.gov
- **Statistical Abstract of the United States**
  http://www.census.gov/prod/www/statistical-abstract-us.html

Uruguay

Official name: República Oriental del Uruguay (Oriental Republic of Uruguay).
Form of government: republic with two legislative houses (Senate [31][1]; Chamber of Representatives [99]).
Head of state and government: President.
Capital: Montevideo.
Official language: Spanish.
Official religion: none.
Monetary unit: 1 peso uruguayo[2] ($U) = 100 centesimos; valuation (Sept. 8, 2003) 1 U.S.$ = $U 27.73; 1 £ = $U 43.96.

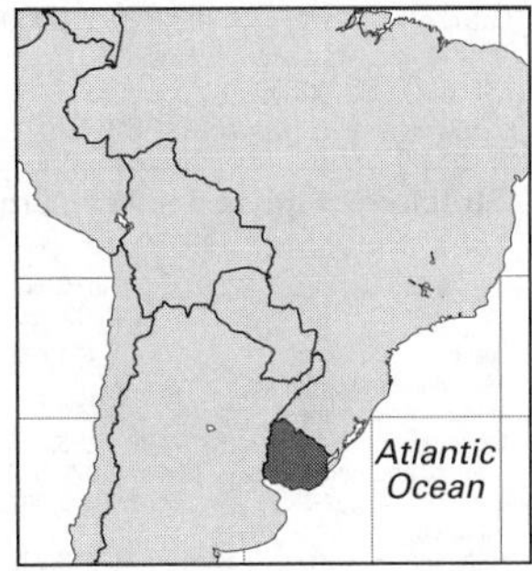

Area and population		area		population
Departments	Capitals	sq mi	sq km	2002 estimate
Artigas	Artigas	4,605	11,928	78,220
Canelones	Canelones	1,751	4,536	513,279
Cerro Largo	Melo	5,270	13,648	86,075
Colonia	Colonia del Sacramento	2,358	6,106	126,472
Durazno	Durazno	4,495	11,643	57,609
Flores	Trinidad	1,986	5,144	25,414
Florida	Florida	4,022	10,417	68,627
Lavalleja	Minas	3,867	10,016	62,493
Maldonado	Maldonado	1,851	4,793	151,953
Montevideo	Montevideo	205	530	1,382,149
Paysandú	Paysandú	5,375	13,922	118,183
Río Negro	Fray Bentos	3,584	9,282	54,867
Rivera	Rivera	3,618	9,370	105,544
Rocha	Rocha	4,074	10,551	72,492
Salto	Salto	5,468	14,163	127,863
San José	San José de Mayo	1,927	4,992	105,786
Soriano	Mercedes	3,478	9,008	84,165
Tacuarembó	Tacuarembó	5,961	15,438	87,693
Treinta y Tres	Treinta y Tres	3,679	9,529	51,984
TOTAL LAND AREA		67,574	175,016	
INLAND WATER		463	1,199	
TOTAL		68,037	176,215	3,360,868

Demography

Population (2003): 3,380,000.
Density (2003): persons per sq mi 49.7, persons per sq km 19.2.
Urban-rural (2001): urban 92.1%; rural 7.9%.
Sex distribution (2001): male 48.43%; female 51.57%.
Age breakdown (2001): under 15, 24.6%; 15–29, 22.8%; 30–44, 19.7%; 45–59, 15.5%; 60–74, 11.8%; 75 and over, 5.6%.
Population projection: (2010) 3,517,000; (2020) 3,719,000.
Ethnic composition (2000): white (mostly Spanish, Italian, or mixed Spanish-Italian) 94.5%; mestizo 3.1%; mulatto 2.0%; other 0.4%.
Religious affiliation (2000): Roman Catholic 78.2%[3]; Protestant 3.3%; other Christian 5.3%; Jewish 1.2%; atheist 6.3%; other 5.7%.
Major cities (1996): Montevideo 1,378,707; Salto 93,113; Paysandú 74,568; Las Piedras 66,584; Rivera 62,859.

Vital statistics

Birth rate per 1,000 population (2002): 17.3 (world avg. 21.3).
Death rate per 1,000 population (2002): 9.0 (world avg. 9.1).
Total fertility rate (avg. births per childbearing woman; 2002): 2.4.
Marriage rate per 1,000 population (2001): 4.2.
Divorce rate per 1,000 population (2001): 2.0.
Life expectancy at birth (2002): male 72.3 years; female 79.2 years.
Major causes of death per 100,000 population (1999): diseases of the circulatory system 330.4; malignant neoplasms 221.7; suicides, accidents, and injury 56.9.

National economy

Budget (2001). Revenue: $U 62,708,000,000 (taxes on goods and services 38.7%, social security contributions 23.4%, income taxes 15.2%, import tax 2.9%, nontax revenue 7.2%). Expenditures: $U 77,487,000,000 (social security and welfare 56.5%, general public services 4.6%, education 7.6%, health 6.6%, capital expenditure 3.9%).
Public debt (external, outstanding; 2001): U.S.$6,110,000,000.
Production (metric tons except as noted). Agriculture, forestry, fishing (2002): rice 939,489, wheat 270,000, sugarcane 170,000, corn (maize) 163,400, oranges 155,000, sunflower seeds 150,300; livestock (number of live animals) 11,667,000 cattle, 11,250,000 sheep; roundwood 5,674,646 cu m. Mining and quarrying (2002): limestone 1,300,000; gypsum 183,000; gold 66,841 troy oz. Manufacturing (value added in $U '000,000; 1998): food products 6,955; refined petroleum 4,966; beverages 3,175; paints, soaps, and varnishes 2,337; textiles (excluding wearing apparel) 2,156. Energy production (consumption): electricity (kW-hr; 1999) 7,193,000,000 (7,716,000,000); coal (metric tons; 1999) none (1,000); crude petroleum (barrels; 1999) none (11,500,000); petroleum products (metric tons; 1997) 1,317,000 (1,665,000).
Land use (1998): forested and other 15.2%; meadows and pastures 77.3%; agricultural and under permanent cultivation 7.5%.
Household income and expenditure. Avg. household size (1999) 3.3; avg. annual income per household, n.a.; expenditure: n.a.
Gross national product (2001): U.S.$19,200,000,000 (U.S.$5,710 per capita).

Structure of gross domestic product and labour force

	2001		2000	
	in value $U '000,000	% of total value	labour force	% of labour force
Agriculture	15,864.3	6.4	42,400	3.4
Mining	730.0	0.3	1,700	0.1
Manufacturing	40,988.1	16.5	158,200	12.8
Construction	13,418.3	5.4	88,700	7.2
Public utilities	10,514.4	4.2	13,100	1.1
Transp. and commun.	23,143.7	9.3	61,500	5.0
Trade	31,977.8	12.9	214,100	17.3
Finance	73,102.9	29.4	72,000	5.8
Pub. admin., defense	24,580.5	9.9	415,500	33.7
Services	28,714.1	11.5		
Other	–14,414.7[4]	–5.8[4]	168,100[5]	13.6[5]
TOTAL	248,619.4	100.0	1,235,300	100.0

Population economically active (2001): total 1,239,500[6]; activity rate 46.9% (participation rates: ages 14 and over, 56.1%; female 45.0%).

Price and earnings indexes (1995 = 100)

	1996	1997	1998	1999	2000	2001	2002
Consumer price index	128.3	153.8	170.4	180.0	188.6	196.8	224.3
Monthly earnings index[7]	126.0	146.4	161.6	169.9	175.2	...	...

Tourism (2001): receipts U.S.$561,000,000; expenditures U.S.$252,000,000.

Foreign trade[8]

Balance of trade (current prices)

	1996	1997	1998	1999	2000	2001
U.S.$'000,000	–925.6	–1,001.1	–1,039.8	–1,119.7	–1,171.1	–1,000.4
% of total	16.2%	15.5%	15.8%	20.0%	20.3%	19.5%

Imports (2000): U.S.$3,465,809,000 (machinery and appliances 19.3%; mineral products 15.8%; chemical products 13.3%; transport equipment 8.8%; synthetic plastics, resins, and rubber 7.2%; processed foods 7.1%; textiles 4.6%). *Major import sources:* Argentina 24.1%; Brazil 19.2%; United States 9.7%; Spain 4.6%; Italy 3.3%; France 3.2%.
Exports (2000): U.S.$2,294,557,000 (live animals and live-animal products 29.2%; textiles and textile products 11.8%; hides and skins 11.5%; vegetable products 11.1%; processed foods 5.0%). *Major export destinations:* Brazil 23.1%; Argentina 17.9%; United States 7.8%; Germany 3.9%.

Transport and communications

Transport. Railroads (1998): track length 3,002 km; passenger-km 14,000,000; metric ton-km cargo 244,000,000. Roads (1997): length 8,683 km[9] (paved 30%). Vehicles (1997): passenger cars 516,889; trucks and buses 50,264. Air transport (1998): passenger-km 642,000,000; metric ton-km cargo 70,000,000; airports (1997) 1.

Communications

Medium	date	unit	number	units per 1,000 persons
Daily newspapers	2000	circulation	973,000	293
Radio	2000	receivers	2,000,000	603
Television	2000	receivers	1,760,000	536
Telephones	2002	main lines	946,500	280
Cellular telephones	2002	subscribers	652,000	193
Personal computers	2001	units	370,000	110
Internet	2001	users	400,000	119

Education and health

Educational attainment (1996). Percentage of population age 25 and over having: no formal schooling 3.4%; primary education 53.6%; secondary 31.7%; higher 10.1%; unknown 1.2%. *Literacy* (2000 est.): population age 15 and over literate 97.7%; males 97.3%; females 98.1%.

Education (2000)

	schools	teachers	students	student/ teacher ratio
Primary (age 6–11)	2,409	17,311	351,525	20.3
Secondary (age 12–17)	400	20,476	210,208	10.3
Vocational	106	...	59,716	...
Higher	6	6,887	69,827	10.1

Health (1999): physicians 12,357 (1 per 263 persons); hospital beds 6,651 (1 per 488 persons); infant mortality rate (2002) 14.3.
Food (2001): daily per capita caloric intake 2,848 (vegetable products 65%, animal products 35%); 107% of FAO recommended minimum.

Military

Total active duty personnel (2002): 23,900 (army 63.6%, navy 23.8%, air force 12.6%). *Military expenditure as percentage of GNP* (1999): 1.3% (world 2.4%); per capita expenditure U.S.$83.

[1]Includes the vice president, who serves as ex officio presiding officer. [2]The peso uruguayo (Uruguayan peso [$U]) replaced the new Uruguayan peso (NUr$) on March 1, 1993. [3]About 30–40% of Roman Catholics are estimated to be nonreligious. [4]Includes indirect taxes less imputed bank service charges. [5]Includes unemployed not previously employed. [6]From urban areas only. [7]December 1995 = 100. [8]Import figures are c.i.f. [9]Excludes streets under local control.

Internet resources for further information:
- **Instituto Nacional de Estadística—Uruguay http://www.ine.gub.uy**

Uzbekistan

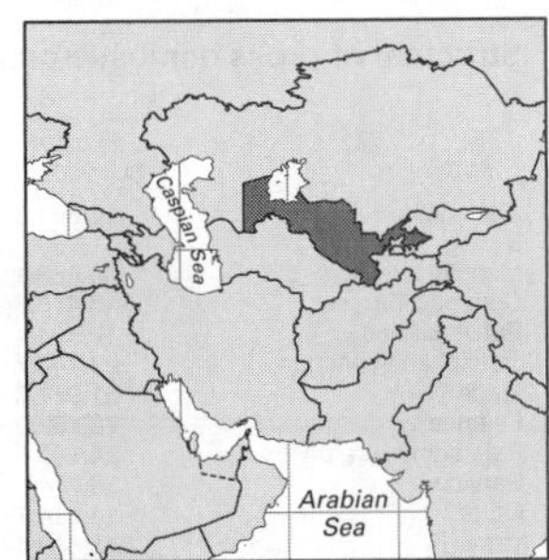

Official name: Ŭzbekiston Respublikasi (Republic of Uzbekistan).
Form of government: multiparty republic with a single legislative body (Supreme Assembly [250])[1].
Heads of state and government: President assisted by Prime Minister.
Capital: Tashkent (Toshkent).
Official language: Uzbek.
Official religion: none.
Monetary unit: sum (plural sumy); valuation (Sept. 8, 2003) 1 U.S.$ = 973.83 sumy; 1 £ = 1,544 sumy.

Area and population

Autonomous republic	Administrative centres	area sq mi	area sq km	population 2002 estimate[2]
Qoraqalpoghiston	Nuqus	63,700	164,900	1,633,900
Provinces				
Andijon	Andijon	1,600	4,200	2,286,000
Buxoro	Bukhara (Buxoro)	15,200	39,400	1,534,900
Farghona	Fergana (Farghona)	2,700	7,100	2,761,300
Jizzakh	Jizzakh	7,900	20,500	1,026,000
Khorazm	Urganch	2,400	6,300	1,402,600
Namangan	Namangan	3,100	7,900	2,049,900
Nawoiy	Nawoiy	42,800	110,800	877,100
Qashqadaryo	Qarshi	11,000	28,400	2,302,000
Samarqand	Samarkand (Samarqand)	6,300	16,400	2,749,100
Sirdaryo	Guliston	2,000	5,100	670,800
Surkhondaryo	Termiz	8,000	20,800	1,846,400
Tashkent (Toshkent)	Tashkent (Toshkent)	6,000[3]	15,600[3]	4,986,800
City				
Tashkent (Toshkent)	—	[3]	[3]	2,120,000
TOTAL		172,700	447,400	26,127,400

Demography

Population (2003): 25,640,000.
Density (2003): persons per sq mi 148.5, persons per sq km 57.3.
Urban-rural (2002): urban 36.6%; rural 63.4%.
Sex distribution (2001): male 49.55%; female 50.45%.
Age breakdown (2001): under 15, 36.4%; 15–29, 28.6%; 30–44, 19.6%; 45–59, 8.5%; 60–74, 5.4%; 75 and over, 1.5%.
Population projection: (2010) 28,354,000; (2020) 31,793,000.
Doubling time: 44 years.
Ethnic composition (1998): Uzbek 75.8%; Russian 6.0%; Tajik 4.8%; Kazakh 4.1%; Tatar 1.6%; other 7.7%.
Religious affiliation (2000): Muslim (mostly Sunnī) 76.2%; nonreligious 18.1%; Russian Orthodox 0.8%; Jewish 0.2%; other 4.7%.
Major cities (1999): Tashkent 2,142,700; Namangan 376,600; Samarkand 362,300; Andijon 323,900; Bukhara 237,900.

Vital statistics

Birth rate per 1,000 population (2001): 21.7 (world avg. 21.3); (1994) legitimate 96.5%; illegitimate 3.5%.
Death rate per 1,000 population (2001): 5.9 (world avg. 9.1).
Natural increase rate per 1,000 population (2001): 15.8 (world avg. 12.2).
Total fertility rate (avg. births per childbearing woman; 2001): 3.1.
Marriage rate per 1,000 population (1999): 7.1.
Divorce rate per 1,000 population (1994): 1.1.
Life expectancy at birth (2001): male 66.0 years; female 72.0 years.
Major causes of death per 100,000 population (1998): diseases of the circulatory system 291.8; diseases of the respiratory system 85.9; accidents, poisoning, and violence 45.1; infectious and parasitic diseases 45.0; cancers 39.5; diseases of the digestive system 30.7; diseases of the nervous system 12.9.

National economy

Budget (1999). Revenue: 611,897,000,000 sumy (taxes on income and profits 30.5%, value-added tax 27.3%, excise taxes 22.8%, property and land taxes 12.1%, other 7.3%). Expenditures: 654,259,000,000 sumy (social and cultural affairs 36.7%, investments 18.7%, national economy 10.4%, transfers 10.4%, administration 2.2%, interest on debt 1.9%, other 19.2%).
Household income and expenditure (1995). Average household size (2000) 5.5; income per household 35,165 sumy (U.S.$1,040); sources of income: wages and salaries 63.0%, subsidies, grants, and nonwage income 34.9%, other 2.1%; expenditure: food and beverages 71%, clothing and footwear 14%, recreation 6%, household durables 4%, housing 3%.
Public debt (external, outstanding; 2001): U.S.$3,759,000,000.
Production (metric tons except as noted). Agriculture, forestry, fishing (2002): wheat 4,956,000, seed cotton 3,200,000, vegetables 2,300,000, fruit (except grapes) and berries 1,100,000, potatoes 730,000, grapes 570,000, rice 143,100, barley 129,000; livestock (number of live animals) 8,220,000 sheep, 5,400,000 cattle, 830,000 goats, 14,500,000 chickens; roundwood (2001) 24,980 cu m; fish catch (2000) 8,529. Mining and quarrying (2000): copper (metal content) 91,800; gold 62,276 kg. Manufacturing (metric tons except as noted; 1998): cement 3,358,000; cotton fibre 1,138,000; mineral fertilizer 897,000; steel 360,000; ferrous metal products 322,000; television sets 192,468 units; passenger cars 54,456 units; video recorders 50,096 units; refrigerators 16,000 units; tractors 3,000 units. Energy production (consumption): electricity (kW-hr; 2001) 47,961,000,000 (48,455,000,000); hard coal (metric tons; 1999) 69,000 (69,000); lignite (metric tons; 1999) 2,901,000 (2,829,000); crude petroleum (barrels; 1999) 33,800,000 (32,000,000); petroleum products (metric tons; 1999) 6,298,000 (5,961,000); natural gas (cu m; 2002) 58,429,000,000 (50,630,000,000).
Gross national product (2001): U.S.$13,800,000,000 (U.S.$550 per capita).

Structure of gross domestic product and labour force

	2001 in value '000,000 sumy	2001 % of total value	2000 labour force	2000 % of labour force
Agriculture	1,471,675	30.2	3,083,000	34.3
Manufacturing, mining, and public utilities	590,014	12.1	1,145,000	12.7
Construction	286,646	5.9	676,000	7.5
Transp. and commun.	379,542	7.8	382,000	4.3
Trade	492,001	10.1	754,000	8.4
Finance, Pub. admin., defense, Services	945,928	19.4	2,042,000	22.7
Other	702,607[4]	14.4[4]	901,000[5]	10.0[5]
TOTAL	4,868,413	100.0[6]	8,983,000	100.0[6]

Population economically active (2001): total 9,136,000; activity rate of total population 36.5% (participation rates: ages 16–59 [male], 16–54 [female] 70.4%; female [1994] 43.0%; unemployed [official rate] 0.4%).

Price and earnings indexes (1995 = 100)

	1994	1995	1996	1997	1998	1999
Consumer price index	44.4	100.0	...	...	...	...
Monthly earnings index	25.7	100.0	204.5	345.0	508.3	826.9

Tourism (2001): receipts U.S.$72,000,000.
Land use (1994): forested 2.9%; meadows and pastures 46.5%; agricultural and under permanent cultivation 10.1%; other 40.5%.

Foreign trade[7]

Balance of trade (current prices)

	1998	1999	2000	2001	2002
U.S.$'000,000	+239.5	+125.1	+317.3	+33.5	+276.4
% of total	3.5%	2.0%	5.1%	0.5%	4.8%

Imports (2002): U.S.$2,712,000,000 (machinery and metalworking products 48.9%, food products 21.3%, other 29.8%). *Major import sources:* Russia 20.5%; South Korea 17.4%; Germany 8.9%; Kazakhstan 7.5%; U.S. 6.4%; Ukraine 6.3%.
Exports (2002): U.S.$2,988,400,000 (cotton fibre 41.5%, energy 22.7%, gold 6.0%, other 29.8%). *Major export destinations* (2002): Russia 17.3%; Ukraine 10.2%; Italy 8.3%; Tajikistan 7.8%; South Korea 7.1%; Poland 4.7%; Kazakhstan 4.2%.

Transport and communications

Transport. Railroads (2000): length 3,950 km; (1999) passenger-km 1,900,000,000; (1999) metric ton-km cargo 13,900,000,000. Roads (1997): total length 84,400 km (paved 87%). Vehicles (1994): passenger cars 865,300; buses 14,500. Air transport (2000)[8]: passenger-km 3,732,000,000; metric ton-km cargo 76,600,000; airports (1998) with scheduled flights 9.

Communications

Medium	date	unit	number	units per 1,000 persons
Daily newspapers	2000	circulation	74,200	3.0
Television	2000	receivers	6,830,000	276
Telephones	2002	main lines	1,670,000	66
Cellular telephones	2002	subscribers	186,900	7.4
Internet	2002	users	275,000	11

Education and health

Educational attainment: n.a. *Literacy* (2000): percentage of total population age 15 and over literate 99.2% (male 99.6%, female 98.8%).

Education (1995–96)

	schools	teachers	students	student/ teacher ratio
Primary (age 6–13), Secondary (age 14–17)	9,300	413,000	5,090,000	12.3
Voc., teacher tr.[9]	248	22,164[10]	240,100	...
Higher[10]	55	...	272,300	...

Health (1995): physicians 76,200 (1 per 302 persons); hospital beds 192,000 (1 per 120 persons); infant mortality rate per 1,000 live births (2001) 38.0.
Food (2001): daily per capita caloric intake 2,379 (vegetable products 82%, animal products 18%); 93% of FAO recommended minimum requirement.

Military

Total active duty personnel (2002): 50,000–55,000 (army *c.* 75%, air force *c.* 25%). *Military expenditure as percentage of GNP* (1999): 1.7% (world 2.4%); per capita expenditure U.S.$38.

[1]Official approval of future bicameral legislature announced in August 2003. [2]Unofficial figures; 2003 estimate for country is not based on these estimates. [3]Tashkent province includes Tashkent city. [4]Includes value-added taxes: excise taxes plus net import taxes minus subsidies. [5]Includes 863,000 persons on forced leave and 38,000 unemployed. [6]Detail does not add to total given because of rounding. [7]Imports c.i.f., exports f.o.b. [8]Uzbekistan Airways. [9]1998. [10]1992–93.

Internet resources for further information:
- **UNDP in Uzbekistan http://www.undp.uz**

Vanuatu

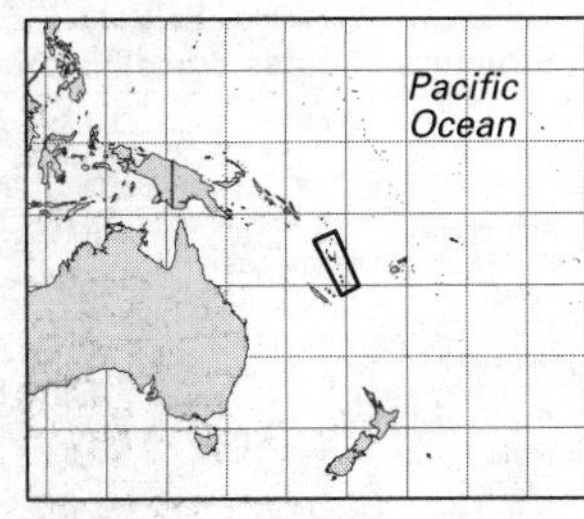

Official name: Ripablik blong Vanuatu (Bislama); République de Vanuatu (French); Republic of Vanuatu (English).
Form of government: republic with a single legislative house (Parliament [52]).
Chief of state: President.
Head of government: Prime Minister.
Capital: Vila.
Official languages: Bislama; French; English.
Official religion: none.
Monetary unit: vatu (VT); valuation (Sept. 8, 2003) 1 U.S.$ = VT 123.15; 1 £ = VT 195.26.

Area and population

		area		population
				1999
Provinces	Capitals	sq mi	sq km	census
Malampa	Lakatoro	1,073	2,779	32,705
Penama	Longana	463	1,198	26,646
Sanma	Luganville	1,640	4,248	36,084
Shefa	Vila	562	1,455	54,439
Tafea	Isangel	628	1,627	29,047
Torba	Sola	341	882	7,757
TOTAL		4,707	12,190[1]	186,678[2]

Demography

Population (2003): 204,000.
Density (2003): persons per sq mi 43.3, persons per sq km 16.7.
Urban-rural (2002): urban 21.0%; rural 79.0%.
Sex distribution (1999): male 51.46%; female 48.54%.
Age breakdown (1999): under 15, 37.8%; 15–29, 29.4%; 30–44, 18.2%; 45–59, 9.7%; 60–74, 4.0%; 75 and over, 0.9%.
Population projection: (2010) 240,000; (2020) 290,000.
Doubling time: 42 years.
Ethnic composition (1999): Ni-Vanuatu 98.7%; European and other Pacific Islanders 1.3%.
Religious affiliation (2000): Christian 89.3%, of which Protestant 53.7%, Anglican 18.2%, Roman Catholic 15.5%; Custom (traditional beliefs) 3.5%; Bahā'ī 2.9%; other 4.3%.
Major towns (1999): Vila (Port-Vila) 30,139; Luganville 11,360.

Vital statistics

Birth rate per 1,000 population (2002): 24.8 (world avg. 21.3).
Death rate per 1,000 population (2002): 8.3 (world avg. 9.1).
Natural increase rate per 1,000 population (2002): 16.5 (world avg. 12.2).
Total fertility rate (avg. births per childbearing woman; 2002): 3.1.
Marriage rate per 1,000 population: n.a.
Divorce rate per 1,000 population: n.a.
Life expectancy at birth (2002): male 59.9 years; female 62.8 years.
Major causes of death per 100,000 population (1994)[3]: diseases of the circulatory system 39.0; diseases of the respiratory system 30.4; malignant neoplasms (cancers) 29.2; infectious and parasitic diseases 25.0; diseases of the digestive system 9.7.

National economy

Budget (2001). Revenue: VT 6,887,000,000 (tax revenue 84.0%, of which taxes on goods and services 48.4%, tax on import duties 33.2%; foreign grants 6.4%; nontax revenue 9.4%). Expenditures: VT 7,885,000,000 (wages and salary 47.4%; goods and services 23.3%; transfers 10.1%; interest payments 3.1%; other [including technical assistance] 16.0%).
Public debt (external, outstanding; 2001): U.S.$64,500,000.
Production (metric tons except as noted). Agriculture, forestry, fishing (2002): coconuts 200,000, roots and tubers 45,000, bananas 13,000, vegetables and melons 10,000, peanuts (groundnuts) 2,500, cacao beans 794, corn (maize) 700; livestock (number of live animals) 151,000 cattle, 62,000 pigs, 12,000 goats, 340,000 chickens; roundwood 119,000 cu m; fish catch (2000) 73,490, of which tuna 71,120. Mining and quarrying: small quantities of coral-reef limestone, crushed stone, sand, and gravel. Manufacturing (value added in VT '000,000; 1995): food, beverages, and tobacco 645; wood products 423; fabricated metal products 377; paper products 125; chemical, rubber, plastic, and nonmetallic products 84; textiles, clothing, and leather 54. Energy production (consumption): electricity (kW-hr; 1999) 38,000,000 (38,000,000); coal, none (none); crude petroleum, none (none); petroleum products (metric tons; 1999) none (26,000); natural gas, none (none).
Land use (1994): forested 75.0%; meadows and pastures 2.0%; agricultural 11.8%; other 11.2%.
Population economically active (1999): total 76,370; activity rate of total population 40.9% (participation rates: ages 15–64, 78.2%; female 49.6%; unemployed, n.a.).

Price and earnings indexes (1995 = 100)

	1995	1996	1997	1998	1999	2000	2001
Consumer price index	100.0	100.9	103.8	107.2	109.3	112.0	116.1
Earnings index	...	...	...	...	...	...	...

Gross national product (2001): U.S.$200,000,000 (U.S.$1,050 per capita).

Structure of gross domestic product and labour force

	2001		1989	
	in value VT '000,000	% of total value	labour force	% of labour force
Agriculture	5,097	15.0	49,811	74.4
Mining	...	...	1	—
Manufacturing	1,363	4.0	891	1.3
Construction	1,071	3.2	1,302	1.9
Public utilities	685	2.0	109	0.2
Transportation and communications	4,508	13.2	1,031	1.5
Trade	13,507	39.7	2,713	4.1
Finance	4,058	11.9	646	1.0
Pub. admin., defense	4,663	13.7	7,892	11.8
Services	760	2.2		
Other	–1,671[6]	–4.9[6]	2,561	3.8
TOTAL	34,041	100.0	66,957	100.0

Household income and expenditure (1985)[4]. Average household size (1989) 5.1; income per household U.S.$11,299; sources of income: wages and salaries 59.0%, self-employment 33.7%; expenditure (1990)[4, 5]: food and nonalcoholic beverages 30.5%, housing 20.7%, transportation 13.2%, health and recreation 12.3%, tobacco and alcohol 10.4%.
Tourism (2001): receipts from visitors U.S.$46,000,000; expenditures by nationals abroad U.S.$8,000,000.

Foreign trade[7]

Balance of trade (current prices)

	1996	1997	1998	1999	2000	2001
VT '000,000	–7,520	–6,801	–6,943	–9,120	–8,673	–10,340.0
% of total	52.7%	45.4%	44.5%	57.8%	54.3%	–61.8%

Imports (2001): VT 13,532,000,000 (machinery and transport equipment 23.8%, food and live animals 16.6%, basic manufactures 12.6%, mineral fuels 13.7%, chemical products 10.7%, other manufactured articles 8.2%). *Major import sources:* Japan 26.1%; Australia 16.9%; Singapore 14.5%; Germany 11.0%.
Exports (2001): VT 3,192,000,000 (timber 10.5%, copra 10.1%, beef 7.5%). *Major export destinations*[8]: Indonesia 34.8%; Greece 15.5%; Japan 14.2%; South Korea 1.1%.

Transport and communications

Transport. Railroads: none. Roads (1996): total length 665 mi, 1,070 km (paved 24%). Vehicles (1996): passenger cars 4,000; trucks and buses 2,600. Merchant marine (1992): vessels (100 gross tons and over) 280; total deadweight tonnage 3,259,594. Air transport (2001)[9]: passenger-mi 131,755,000, passenger-km 212,039,000; short ton-mi cargo 1,301,000, metric ton-km 1,899,000; airports (1996) with scheduled flights 29.

Communications

Medium	date	unit	number	units per 1,000 persons
Radio	1997	receivers	62,000	350
Television	2000	receivers	2,280	12
Telephones	2002	main lines	6,600	32
Cellular telephones	2002	subscribers	490	2.4
Personal computers	2002	units	3,000	15
Internet	2002	users	7,000	34

Education and health

Educational attainment (1999). Percentage of population age 15 and over having: no formal schooling 18.0%; incomplete primary education 20.6%; completed primary 35.5%; some secondary 12.2%; completed secondary 8.5%; higher 5.2%, of which university 1.3%. *Literacy* (1998): total population age 15 and over literate 64%.

Education (1992)

	schools	teachers	students	student/ teacher ratio
Primary (age 6–11)[10]	272	852	26,267	30.8
Secondary (age 11–18)	27	220	4,269	19.4
Voc., teacher tr.	...	...	444	...
Higher	1[11]	13[12]	124[13]	...

Health (1997): physicians 21 (1 per 8,524 persons); hospital beds 573 (1 per 312 persons); infant mortality rate per 1,000 live births (2002) 59.6.
Food (2001): daily per capita caloric intake 2,565 (vegetable products 87%, animal products 13%); 113% of FAO recommended minimum.

Military

Total active duty personnel: Vanuatu has a paramilitary force of about 300.

[1]Detail does not add to total given because of rounding. [2]De jure figure. [3]Deaths reported to the Ministry of Health only. [4]Vila and Luganville only. [5]Weights of consumer price index components. [6]Imputed bank service charges. [7]Imports c.i.f.; exports f.o.b. [8]Destination of domestic exports only. [9]Air Vanuatu only. [10]Excludes independent private schools. [11]1989. [12]1983. [13]1991.

Internet resources for further information:
- **Vanuatu Statistics Office http://www.vanuatustatistics.gov.vu**
- **United Nations Development Programme, Common Country Assessments http://www.undp.org.fj/CCAs.htm**
- **Secretariat of the Pacific Community http://www.spc.int/stats/Vanuatu**

Venezuela

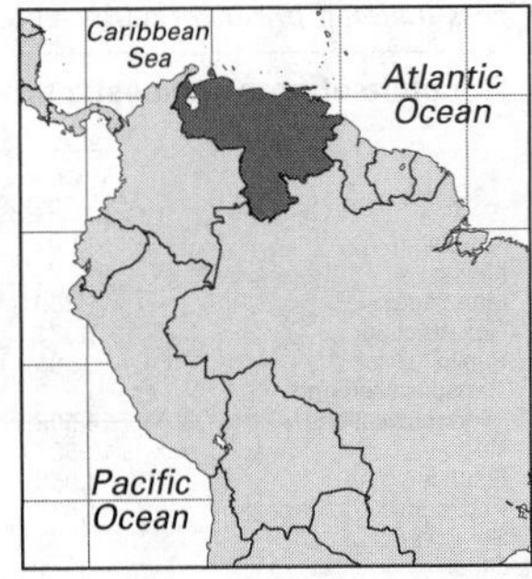

Official name: República Bolivariana de Venezuela (Bolivarian Republic of Venezuela).
Form of government: federal multiparty republic with a unicameral legislature (National Assembly [165]).
Head of state and government: President.
Capital: Caracas.
Official languages: Spanish and Indian languages[1].
Official religion: none.
Monetary unit: 1 bolívar (B, plural Bs) = 100 céntimos; valuation (Sept. 8, 2003) 1 U.S.$ = Bs 1,598; 1 £ = Bs 2,534.

Area and population

		area		population
States	**Capitals**	sq mi	sq km	2001 census[2]
Amazonas	Puerto Ayacucho	69,554	180,145	70,464
Anzoátegui	Barcelona	16,700	43,300	1,222,225
Apure	San Fernando de Apure	29,500	76,500	377,756
Aragua	Maracay	2,708	7,014	1,449,616
Barinas	Barinas	13,600	35,200	624,508
Bolívar	Ciudad Bolívar	91,900	238,000	1,214,846
Carabobo	Valencia	1,795	4,650	1,932,168
Cojedes	San Carlos	5,700	14,800	253,105
Delta Amacuro	Tucupita	15,500	40,200	97,987
Falcón	Coro	9,600	24,800	763,188
Guárico	San Juan de Los Morros	25,091	64,986	627,086
Lara	Barquisimeto	7,600	19,800	1,556,415
Mérida	Mérida	4,400	11,300	715,268
Miranda	Los Teques	3,070	7,950	2,330,872
Monagas	Maturín	11,200	28,900	712,626
Nueva Esparta	La Asunción	440	1,150	373,851
Portuguesa	Guanare	5,900	15,200	725,740
Sucre	Cumaná	4,600	11,800	786,483
Táchira	San Cristóbal	4,300	11,100	992,669
Trujillo	Trujillo	2,900	7,400	608,563
Vargas	La Guaira	578	1,497	298,109
Yaracuy	San Felipe	2,700	7,100	499,049
Zulia	Maracaibo	24,400	63,100	2,983,679
Other federal entities				
Dependencias Federales[3]	—	50	120	1,651
Distrito Federal	Caracas	167	433	1,836,286
TOTAL		353,841[4]	916,445	23,054,210

Demography

Population (2003): 25,699,000.
Density (2002): persons per sq mi 72.6, persons per sq km 28.0.
Urban-rural (2000): urban 87.1%; rural 12.9%.
Sex distribution (2000): male 50.31%; female 49.69%.
Age breakdown (2000): under 15, 34.0%; 15–29, 27.5%; 30–44, 20.2%; 45–59, 11.7%; 60–74, 5.2%; 75 and over, 1.4%.
Population projection: (2010) 28,955,000; (2020) 33,300,000.
Ethnic composition (1993): mestizo 67%; white 21%; black 10%; Indian 2%.
Religious affiliation (2000): Roman Catholic 89.5%; Protestant 2.0%; other Christian 1.4%; Spiritist 1.1%; nonreligious/atheist 2.2%; other 3.8%.
Major cities (2001): Caracas 1,836,000[2] (urban agglomeration 3,177,000); Maracaibo 1,609,000[2]; Valencia 1,196,000[2]; Barquisimeto 811,000[2]; Ciudad Guayana 629,000[2].

Vital statistics

Birth rate per 1,000 population (2002): 20.2 (world avg. 21.3).
Death rate per 1,000 population (2002): 4.9 (world avg. 9.1).
Natural increase rate per 1,000 population (2002): 15.3 (world avg. 12.2).
Total fertility rate (avg. births per childbearing woman; 2002): 2.4.
Marriage rate per 1,000 population (2000): 3.8.
Divorce rate per 1,000 population (2000): 0.8.
Life expectancy at birth (2002): male 70.5 years; female 76.8 years.
Major causes of death per 100,000 population (1996): heart diseases 102.9; cancers 59.0; accidents 35.8; cardiovascular diseases 33.0.

National economy

Budget (2000). Revenue: Bs 14,664,587,000,000 (oil revenues 59.2%, value-added tax 17.3%, income tax 9.0%, import duties 7.3%). Expenditures: Bs 17,238,854,000,000 (subsidies 50.5%, wages and salaries 19.1%, debt service 11.6%, goods and services 2.7%, capital expenditure 14.5%).
Production (metric tons except as noted). Agriculture, forestry, fishing (2002): sugarcane 6,909,000, corn (maize) 1,805,000, rice 790,000, plantains 760,000, bananas 750,000, cassava 625,000, sorghum 553,000, potatoes 330,000; livestock (number of live animals) 14,500,000 cattle, 5,655,000 pigs, 4,000,000 goats, 115,000,000 chickens; roundwood (2002) 4,667,000 cu m; fish catch (2001) 418,000. Mining and quarrying (2001): iron ore 16,902,000; bauxite 4,526,000; gold 9,076 kg; diamonds 52,804 carats. Manufacturing (value added in 1984 Bs '000,000; 1997): ferrous and nonferrous metals 16,355; food products 13,277; chemicals 10,004; beverages 9,480; clothing, textiles, leather, and shoes 8,311; metal products 6,413. Energy production (consumption): electricity (kW-hr; 1999) 83,570,000,000 (83,570,000,000); coal (metric tons; 1999) 6,979,000 (50,000); crude petroleum (barrels; 2001) 972,000,000 ([1999] 391,100,000); petroleum products (metric tons; 1999) 55,263,000 (20,116,000); natural gas (cu m; 1999) 21,334,100,000 (21,334,100,000).
Gross national product (2001): U.S.$117,200,000,000 (U.S.$4,760 per capita).

Structure of gross domestic product and labour force

	2001		2000	
	in value Bs '000,000[5]	% of total value[5]	labour force	% of labour force
Agriculture	29,166	4.9	950,000	9.2
Petroleum and natural gas } Mining	135,609	22.6	53,000	0.5
Manufacturing	113,618	18.9	1,191,000	11.5
Construction	33,467	5.6	741,000	7.2
Public utilities	11,276	1.9	58,000	0.6
Transp. and commun.	39,103	6.5	608,000	5.9
Trade	63,835	10.6 }	2,752,000	26.6
Finance	55,262	9.2 }		
Pub. admin., defense	46,208	7.7 }	2,598,000	25.2
Services	59,803	10.0 }		
Other	12,434	2.1	1,376,000[6]	13.3[6]
TOTAL	599,781	100.0	10,327,000	100.0

Public debt (external, outstanding; 2001): U.S.$24,916,000,000.
Population economically active (1997): total 9,507,125; activity rate 41.7% (participation rates: over age 15, 64.6%; female 35.9%; unemployed 10.6%).

Price index (1995 = 100)

	1996	1997	1998	1999	2000	2001	2002
Consumer price index	199.9	299.9	407.2	503.2	584.7	658.0	805.6

Household income and expenditure. Average household size (1990) 5.1; average annual income per household (1981) Bs 42,492 (U.S.$9,899); expenditure (1995): food 40.6%, housing 13.8%, transportation and communications 8.6%, clothing 5.3%, health 3.1%, education and recreation 2.9%.
Tourism (2001): receipts U.S.$643,000,000; expenditures U.S.$1,801,000,000.
Land use (1998): forest and other 75.3%; pasture 20.7%; agriculture 4.0%.

Foreign trade[7]

Balance of trade (current prices)

	1996	1997	1998	1999	2000	2001
Bs '000,000	+5,996.8	+3,858.3	+1,642.2	+5,201.4	+11,694.7	+5,658.0
% of total	44.3%	23.1%	9.6%	25.6%	37.1%	19.2%

Imports (2000): U.S.$9,907,500,000 (nonelectrical machinery 18.8%, chemicals and chemical products 13.8%, transport equipment 11.6%, electrical machinery 11.1%). *Major import sources:* U.S. 37.8%; Colombia 7.4%; Brazil 5.0%; Italy 4.4%; Mexico 4.3%.
Exports (2000): U.S.$21,602,200,000 (crude petroleum 58.9%, refined petroleum 26.6%, iron and steel 2.7%, aluminum 2.5%). *Major export destinations:* U.S. 59.6%; Netherlands Antilles 5.6%; Brazil 3.6%; Colombia 2.8%.

Transport and communications

Transport. Railroads (1996): length (1994) 627 km; passenger-km 149,905; metric ton-km cargo 54,474,000. Roads (1999): total length 96,155 km (paved 34%). Vehicles (1997): passenger cars 1,505,000; trucks and buses 542,000. Merchant marine (1992): vessels (over 100 gross tons) 271; total deadweight tonnage 1,355,419. Air transport (1998): passenger-km 3,133,000,000; metric ton-km cargo 332,000,000; airports (1997) with scheduled flights 20.

Communications

Medium	date	unit	number	units per 1,000 persons
Daily newspapers	2000	circulation	5,000,000	206
Radio	2000	receivers	7,140,000	294
Television	2000	receivers	4,490,000	185
Telephones	2002	main lines	2,841,800	112
Cellular telephones	2002	subscribers	6,463,600	256
Personal computers	2002	units	1,536,000	61
Internet	2002	users	1,274,400	51

Education and health

Educational attainment (1993). Percentage of population age 25 and over having: no formal schooling 8.0%; primary education or less 43.7%; some secondary and secondary 38.3%; postsecondary 10.0%. *Literacy* (1995 est.): total population age 15 and over literate 91.1%; males 91.8%; females 90.3%.

Education (1998–99)

	schools	teachers[8]	students	student/ teacher ratio
Primary (age 7–12)	17,372	186,658	4,299,671	...
Secondary (age 13–17)[9]	2,524	61,761	400,794	...
Higher	99[10]	43,833[10]	717,192	12.6[11]

Health (1997): physicians 28,341 (1 per 804 persons); hospital beds 38,924 (1 per 585 persons); infant mortality rate (2002) 24.6.
Food (2001): daily per capita caloric intake 2,376 (vegetable products 83%, animal products 17%); 96% of FAO recommended minimum.

Military

Total active duty personnel (2002): 82,300 (army 69.3%, navy 22.2%, air force 8.5%). *Military expenditure as percentage of GNP* (1999): 1.4% (world 2.4%); per capita expenditure U.S.$61.

[1]31 indigenous Indian languages were made official in May 2002. [2]Preliminary unadjusted census results. [3]A new federal entity (the Caribbean Federal Territory) was under consideration in 2003. [4]Detail does not add to total given because of rounding. [5]At constant 1984 prices. [6]Mostly unemployed. [7]Imports and exports are f.o.b. in balance of trade. [8]1997–98. [9]Includes vocational and teacher training. [10]1990–91. [11]1991–92.

Internet resources for further information:
- **Banco Central de Venezuela http://www.bcv.org.ve**

Vietnam

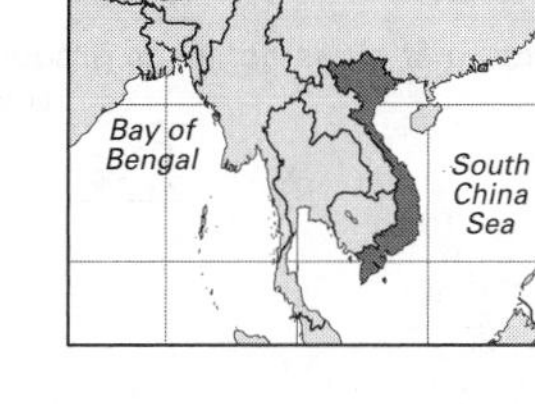

Official name: Cong Hoa Xa Hoi Chu Nghia Viet Nam (Socialist Republic of Vietnam).
Form of government: socialist republic with one legislative house (National Assembly [498]).
Head of state: President.
Head of government: Prime Minister.
Capital: Hanoi.
Official language: Vietnamese.
Official religion: none.
Monetary unit: 1 dong (D) = 10 hao = 100 xu; valuation (Sept. 8, 2003) 1 U.S.$ = D 15,524; 1 £ = D 24,613.

Area and population

Economic regions[1]	Principal cities	area sq mi	area sq km	population 1999 census
Central Highlands	Buon Ma Thuot	17,740	45,946	3,062,293
Mekong River Delta	Long Xuyen	15,274	39,559	16,131,984
North Central Coast	Hue	19,758	51,174	10,007,215
North East	Thai Nguyen	25,871	67,005	10,860,417
North West	Hoa Binh	15,426	39,955	2,227,686
Northeastern South Region	Ho Chi Minh City	16,437	42,572	12,708,882
Red River Delta	Hanoi	4,833	12,517	14,800,066
South Central Coast	Da Nang	13,040	33,773	6,525,841
TOTAL		128,379[2]	332,501[2]	76,324,384[2]

Demography

Population (2003): 81,377,000.
Density (2003): persons per sq mi 633.9, persons per sq km 244.7.
Urban-rural (1999): urban 23.5%; rural 76.5%.
Sex distribution (1999): male 49.15%; female 50.85%.
Age breakdown (2001): under 15, 32.1%; 15–29, 29.4%; 30–44, 21.1%; 45–59, 9.7%; 60–74, 5.8%; 75 and over, 1.9%.
Population projection: (2010) 84,128,000; (2020) 100,079,000.
Doubling time: 46 years.
Ethnic composition (2000): Vietnamese 85.0%; Han Chinese 3.5%; Montagnards 1.9%; Tho (Tay) 1.6%; Tai 1.5%; Muong 1.4%; Khmer 1.2%; Nung 1.0%; other 2.9%.
Religious affiliation (1995): Buddhist 66.7%; Christian 8.7%, of which Roman Catholic 7.7%, Protestant 1.0%; Cao Dai (a New-Religionist group) 3.5%; Hoa Hao (a New-Religionist group) 2.1%; other 19.0%.
Major cities (1992): Ho Chi Minh City 4,549,000[3]; Hanoi 2,154,900[4]; Haiphong 783,133; Da Nang 382,674; Buon Ma Thuot 282,095; Nha Trang 221,331; Hue 219,149; Can Tho 215,587.

Vital statistics

Birth rate per 1,000 population (2002): 19.6 (world avg. 21.3).
Death rate per 1,000 population (2002): 6.2 (world avg. 9.1).
Natural increase rate per 1,000 population (2002): 13.4 (world avg. 12.2).
Total fertility rate (avg. births per childbearing woman; 2002): 2.3.
Life expectancy at birth (2002): male 67.3 years; female 72.4 years.

National economy

Budget (2002). Revenue: D 106,900,000,000,000 (tax revenue 81.9%, of which corporate income taxes 24.4%, turnover taxes 21.5%, taxes on trade 18.7%; nontax revenues 14.0%; grants 1.9%). Expenditures: D 120,484,000,000,000 (current expenditures 65.4%, of which social services 31.9%; capital expenditures 29.1%; other 5.5%).
Public debt (external, outstanding; 2001): U.S.$11,427,000,000.
Gross national product (2001): U.S.$32,800,000,000 (U.S.$410 per capita).

Structure of gross domestic product and labour force

	2001 in value D '000,000,000	2001 % of total value	1997 labour force	1997 % of labour force
Agriculture, forestry, fishing	114,412	23.6	25,400,000	68.5
Public utilities	16,197	3.3	200,000	0.5
Mining	44,544	9.2	200,000	0.5
Manufacturing	95,129	19.6	3,300,000	8.9
Construction	27,421	5.7	1,000,000	2.7
Transp. and commun.	19,431	4.0	900,000	2.4
Trade and restaurants	83,701	17.3	3,200,000	8.6
Finance, insurance	33,092	6.8	700,000	1.9
Pub. admin., defense, services, other	50,566	10.5	2,200,000	5.9
TOTAL	484,493	100.0	37,000,000[5]	100.0[5]

Tourism (1997): receipts from visitors U.S.$88,000,000; expenditures by nationals abroad, n.a.
Production (metric tons except as noted). Agriculture, forestry, fishing (2002): rice 34,064,000, sugarcane 16,824,000, cassava 4,158,000, corn (maize) 2,315,000, sweet potatoes 1,725,000, bananas 1,044,000, coconuts 838,000, coffee 689,000, oranges 442,000, groundnuts (peanuts) 397,000, pineapples 348,000, natural rubber 331,400, tea 90,000, pimento 77,000; livestock (number of live animals) 60,000,000 ducks, 23,170,000 pigs, 4,063,000 cattle, 2,814,000 buffalo; roundwood (2002) 30,730,000 cu m, of which fuelwood 26,547,000 cu m, industrial roundwood 4,183,000 cu m; fish catch (2001) 1,491,000, of which marine fish 1,321,000. Mining and quarrying (2001): phosphate rock (gross weight) 750,000; tin (metal content) 3,500. Manufacturing (gross value of production in D '000,000,000; 1998[6]): food and beverages 36.5; cement, bricks, pottery, and glass 13.7; textiles 8.4; chemicals and chemical products 8.1; footwear and leather tanning 7.1; electric and electronic products 6.2. Energy production (consumption): electricity (kW-hr; 1999) 23,559,000,000 (23,559,000,000); coal (metric tons; 1999) 9,629,000 (6,298,000); crude petroleum (barrels; 1999) 107,800,000 ([1997] 293,200); petroleum products (metric tons; 1999) 157,000 (7,518,000); natural gas (cu m; 1999) 1,096,500,000 (1,096,500,000).
Population economically active (2000): total 38,400,000; activity rate 49.5% (participation rates [1989]: ages 15–64, 79.9%; female 51.7%; unemployed [2000] 4.4%).

Price and earnings indexes (1995 = 100)

	1996	1997	1998	1999	2000	2001	2002
Consumer price index	105.7	109.1	117.0	121.8	119.7	119.2	123.8
Earnings index	...	...	...	...	...	...	...

Household income and expenditure. Average household size (1989) 4.8; income per household (1990)[7] D 577,008 (U.S.$93); sources of income: n.a.; expenditure (1990): food 62.4%, clothing 5.0%, household goods 4.6%, education 2.9%, housing 2.5%.
Land use (1994): forested 29.6%; meadows and pastures 1.0%; agricultural and under permanent cultivation 21.5%; other 47.9%.

Foreign trade[8]

Balance of trade (current prices)

	1996	1997	1998	1999	2000
U.S.$'000,000	–2,775	–1,247	–989	+972	+375
% of total	32.1%	6.4%	5.0%	4.4%	1.3%

Imports (2000): U.S.$15,637,000,000 (machinery equipment [including aircraft] 16.4%; petroleum products 13.2%; textiles, clothing, and leather 8.5%; iron and steel 5.2%; motorcycles 5.0%; fertilizers 3.3%; unspecified 48.4%). *Major import sources:* Singapore 15.1%; Japan 14.0%; South Korea 11.9%; China 10.9%; Thailand 5.9%.
Exports (2000): U.S.$14,448,000,000 (crude petroleum 24.2%; garments 13.1%; fish, crustaceans, and mollusks 10.2%; footwear 10.1%; electronic products 5.4%; rice 4.6%; coffee 3.5%). *Major export destinations:* Japan 18.6%; Australia 9.7%; Germany 7.7%; China 6.6%; U.S. 6.1%; Singapore 5.8%; France 3.6%.

Transport and communications

Transport. Railroads (1999): route length 1,952 mi, 3,142 km; passenger-mi 1,694,000,000, passenger-km 2,727,000,000; short ton-mile cargo 958,000,000, metric ton-km cargo 1,398,000,000. Roads (1996): total length 58,000 mi, 93,300 km (paved 25%). Vehicles (1994): passenger cars, trucks, and buses 200,000. Air transport (1999)[9]: passenger-mi 2,380,000,000, passenger-km 3,831,000,000; short ton-mile cargo 67,436,000, metric ton-km cargo 98,455,000; airports (1997) with scheduled flights 12.

Communications

Medium	date	unit	number	units per 1,000 persons
Daily newspapers	2000	circulation	313,000	4.0
Radio	2000	receivers	8,520,000	109
Television	2000	receivers	14,500,000	185
Telephones	2002	main lines	3,929,100	48
Cellular telephones	2002	subscribers	1,638,000	20
Personal computers	2002	units	800,000	10
Internet	2002	users	1,500,000	18

Education and health

Educational attainment (1989). Percentage of population age 25 and over having: no formal education (illiterate) 16.6%; incomplete and complete primary 69.8%; incomplete and complete secondary 10.6%; higher 2.6%; unknown 0.4%. *Literacy* (2000): percentage of population age 15 and over literate 93.3%; males 95.7%; females 91.0%.

Education (1999–2000)

	schools	teachers	students	student/ teacher ratio
Primary (age 7–12)	...	340,900	10,063,000	29.5
Secondary (age 13–18)	...	273,900	7,743,600	28.3
Vocational[10]	...	9,336	172,400	18.5
Higher	109[11]	26,100[12]	682,300[12]	26.1[12]

Health (1999): physicians 37,100 (1 per 2,092 persons); hospital beds (1997) 197,900 (1 per 380 persons); infant mortality rate (2002) 31.8.
Food (2001): daily per capita caloric intake 2,533 (vegetable products 89%, animal products 11%); 117% of FAO recommended minimum requirement.

Military

Total active duty personnel (2002): 484,000 (army 85.1%, navy 8.7%, air force 6.2%). *Military expenditure as percentage of GNP* (1997): 2.4% (world 2.5%); per capita expenditure U.S.$44.

[1]Eight economic regions are divided into 57 provinces and 4 municipalities as of the administrative reorganization of 1997. [2]Total represents sum of parts; actual reported total figure may differ. [3]1999. [4]1993. [5]Detail does not add to total given because of rounding. [6]Estimated figures at prices of 1994. [7]Wage workers and government officials only. [8]Imports are f.o.b. in balance of trade and c.i.f. in commodities and trading partners. [9]Vietnam Airlines only. [10]1996–97. [11]1995–96. [12]1998–99.

Internet resources for further information:
- **Ministry of Foreign Affairs http://www.mofa.gov.vn**

Virgin Islands (U.S.)

Official name: Virgin Islands of the United States.
Political status: organized unincorporated territory of the United States with one legislative house (Senate [15]).
Chief of state: President of the United States.
Head of government: Governor.
Capital: Charlotte Amalie.
Official language: English.
Official religion: none.
Monetary unit: 1 U.S. dollar (U.S.$) = 100 cents; valuation (Sept. 8, 2003) 1 £ = U.S.$1.59.

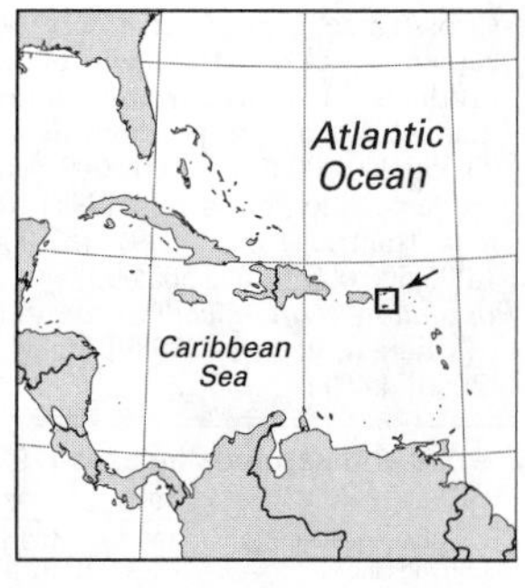

Area and population

		area		population
Islands[1]	Principal towns	sq mi	sq km	2000 census
St. Croix	Christiansted	84	218	53,234
St. John	Cruz Bay[2]	20	52	4,197
St. Thomas	Charlotte Amalie	32	83	51,181
TOTAL		136	353	108,612[3]

Demography

Population (2003): 111,000.
Density (2003): persons per sq mi 816.7, persons per sq km 315.3.
Urban-rural (1998): urban 45.7%; rural 54.3%.
Sex distribution (2000): male 46.91%; female 53.09%.
Age breakdown (2000): under 15, 27.8%; 15–29, 22.4%; 30–44, 17.9%; 45–59, 19.1%; 60–74, 9.7%; 75 and over, 3.1%.
Population projection: (2010) 118,000; (2020) 126,000.
Doubling time: 75 years.
Ethnic composition (2000): black 61.1%; white 15.0%; Puerto Rican 12.0%; French Creole 9.0%; British 1.0%; other 1.9%.
Religious affiliation (2000): Christian 96.3%, of which Protestant 51.0% (including Anglican 13.0%), Roman Catholic 27.5%, independent Christian 12.2%; nonreligious 2.2%; other 1.5%.
Major towns (2000): Charlotte Amalie 11,004 (urban agglomeration 18,914); Christiansted 2,637; Frederiksted 732.

Vital statistics

Birth rate per 1,000 population (2002): 15.1 (world avg. 21.3); (1998) legitimate 30.2%[4]; illegitimate 69.8%.
Death rate per 1,000 population (2002): 5.8 (world avg. 9.1).
Natural increase rate per 1,000 population (2002): 9.3 (world avg. 12.2).
Total fertility rate (avg. births per childbearing woman; 2002): 2.2.
Marriage rate per 1,000 population (1993): 35.1.
Divorce rate per 1,000 population (1993): 4.5.
Life expectancy at birth (2002): male 74.6 years; female 82.5 years.
Major causes of death per 100,000 population (1997): diseases of the heart 111.3; malignant neoplasms (cancers) 103.9; cerebrovascular diseases 44.5; diabetes mellitus 32.3; accidents 31.4; homicide 27.1.

National economy

Budget. Revenue (1998): U.S.$459,485,000 (personal income tax 45.7%, gross receipts tax 18.5%, property tax 9.9%, corporate income tax 5.4%, excise tax 3.7%). Expenditures (1998): U.S.$398,394,000 (education 30.4%, health 17.8%, executive branch 7.8%, public safety 7.6%, public works 6.3%, College of the Virgin Islands 5.7%).
Production. Agriculture, forestry, fishing (value of sales in U.S.$'000; 1998): milk 1,263, livestock and livestock products 655 (of which cattle and calves 439, hogs and pigs 46), ornamental plants and other nursery products 364, vegetables 329 (notably tomatoes and cucumbers), fruits and nuts 185 (notably mangoes, bananas, and avocados), poultry 21; livestock (number of live animals: 2002) 8,000 cattle, 4,000 goats, 3,200 sheep, 2,600 hogs and pigs, 3,500 chickens; roundwood, n.a.; fish catch (2001) 300 metric tons. Mining and quarrying: sand and crushed stone for local use. Manufacturing (U.S.$'000[5]; 1997): food and food products 31,949; stone, clay, and glass products 21,897; print and publishing 21,127; transportation equipment 4,920; fabricated metal products 3,352. Construction: n.a. Energy production (consumption): electricity (kW-hr; 1999) 1,086,000,000 (1,086,000,000); coal (metric tons; 1999) none (255,000); crude petroleum (barrels; 1999) none (124,200,000); petroleum products (metric tons; 1999) 15,309,000 (2,421,000); natural gas, none (none).
Tourism (2001): receipts from visitors U.S.$1,196,000,000; number of hotel rooms 5,049; occupancy percentage 56.6%; expenditures by nationals abroad, n.a.
Household income and expenditure. Average household size (2000) 2.6; average annual income per household (2000) U.S.$34,991; sources of income (1984): wages and salaries 65.7%, transfer payments 13.0%, interest, dividends, and rent 12.7%, self-employment 2.6%; expenditure, n.a.
Population economically active (2000)[6]: total 50,933; activity rate of total population 46.9% (participation rates: ages 16–64, 72.5%[7]; female 47.8%[7]; unemployed 8.6%).

Price and earnings indexes (1995 = 100)

	1994	1995	1996	1997
Consumer price index	...	...	...	...
Hourly earnings index[8]	93.0	100.0	115.6	109.9

Gross national product (at current market prices; 1997): U.S.$2,666,000,000 (U.S.$18,287 per capita).

Structure of gross domestic product and labour force

	2001		1995	
	in value U.S.$'000,000	% of total value	labour force[9]	% of labour force[9]
Agriculture, fishing	...	...	3,110	6.5
Mining	...	...	10	10
Manufacturing	...	...	2,370[11]	5.0[11]
Construction	...	...	1,140[10]	2.4[10]
Public utilities	...	...	11	11
Transp. and commun.	...	...	2,560	5.4
Trade, hotels, restaurants	...	...	9,740	20.4
Finance, insurance, real estate	...	...	1,830	3.8
Pub. admin., defense	...	...	13,770	28.8
Services	...	...	10,490	21.9
Other	...	...	2,800[12]	5.8[12]
TOTAL	2,069[13]	100.0	47,810	100.0

Public debt (1999): U.S.$1,200,000,000.
Land use (1994): forested 5.9%; meadows and pastures 26.5%; agricultural and under permanent cultivation 20.6%; other 47.0%.

Foreign trade[14]

Balance of trade (current prices)

	1996	1997	1998	1999	2000	2001
U.S.$'000,000	+56.6	−372.3	−120.3	−99.4	−149.5	−374.5
% of total	0.8%	5.1%	2.2%	1.5%	1.4%	4.2%

Imports (2001): U.S.$4,608,700,000[15]. *Major import sources:* United States 15.8%; other countries 84.2%.
Exports (2001): U.S.$4,234,200,000[16]. *Major export destinations* (1995): United States 92.7%; other countries 7.3%.

Transport and communications

Transport. Railroads: none. Roads (1996): total length 532 mi, 856 km (paved, n.a.). Vehicles (1993): passenger cars 51,000; trucks and buses 13,300. Merchant marine (1992): vessels (100 gross tons and over) 1. Shipping (1988): cruise ship arrivals 1,228; passenger arrivals 1,062,010. Air transport (1989)[17]: passenger arrivals and departures 1,897,000; cargo loaded and unloaded 4,600 metric tons; airports (1999) with scheduled flights 2.

Communications

Medium	date	unit	number	units per 1,000 persons
Daily newspapers	2000	circulation	43,000	364
Radio	1996	receivers	107,000	927
Television	2000	receivers	64,700	594
Telephones	2001	main lines	69,400	635
Cellular telephones	2001	subscribers	41,000	375
Internet	2002	users	30,000	273

Education and health

Educational attainment (1997). Percentage of population age 25 and over having: incomplete primary education 4.4%; completed lower secondary 18.5%; incomplete upper secondary 27.3%; completed upper secondary 24.0%; incomplete undergraduate 14.0%; completed undergraduate 11.8%. *Literacy:* n.a.

Education (1997–98)[18]

	schools	teachers	students	student/ teacher ratio
Primary (age 5–12)	62[19]	777	11,926	15.3
Secondary (age 12–18)	...	782	9,982	12.8
Higher	1	266[19]	3,103	11.0[19]

Health (1999): physicians 178 (1 per 607 persons); hospital beds, n.a.; infant mortality rate per 1,000 live births (2002) 8.6.
Food: daily per capita caloric intake, n.a.

Military

Total active duty personnel: no domestic military force is maintained; the United States is responsible for defense and external security.

[1]May be administered by officials assigned by the governor. [2]Census designated place. [3]De jure figure. [4]Percentage of legitimate births may be an underestimation due to the common practice of consensual marriage. [5]Figures are for value of sales. [6]Excludes armed forces. [7]1990. [8]Service workers only. [9]Employed labour force as of September 30; excludes armed forces. [10]Construction includes Mining. [11]Manufacturing includes Public utilities. [12]Includes 2,740 unemployed. [13]Tourism accounts for more than 70% of gross domestic product. [14]Imports c.i.f. [15]Breakdown of 1992 imports from U.S. only, totaling U.S.$1,768,000,000: crude petroleum 60.7%, food and beverages 4.5%, iron and steel (all forms) 4.5%, fuel oils 3.2%. [16]Breakdown of 1999 exports to U.S. only, totaling U.S.$2,971,899,000: petroleum products 90.4%, chemicals and chemical products 2.4%, antibiotics 0.4%, alcoholic beverages 0.3%. [17]St. Croix and St. Thomas airports. [18]Public schools only. [19]1992–93.

Internet resources for further information:
- **Office of Insular Affairs**
  http://www.pacificweb.org
- **U.S. Census Bureau: Economic Census of Outlying Areas**
  http://www.census.gov/csd/oat

Yemen

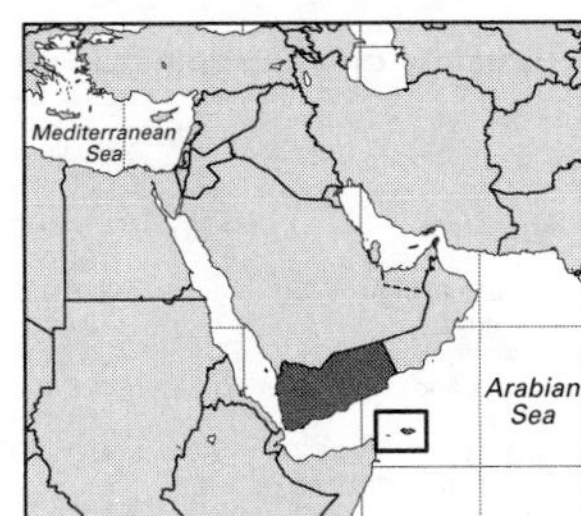

Official name: Al-Jumhūrīyah al-Yamanīyah (Republic of Yemen).
Form of government: multiparty republic with two legislative houses (Consultative Council [111 nonelected seats]; House of Representatives [301]).
Head of state: President.
Head of government: Prime Minister.
Capital: Sanaa.
Official language: Arabic.
Official religion: Islam.
Monetary unit: 1 Yemeni Rial (YRls) = 100 fils; valuation (Sept. 8, 2003) 1 U.S.$ = YRls 178.01; 1 £ = YRls 282.24.

Area and population

		area[1]		population
Governorates	Capitals	sq mi	sq km	2001 estimate
Abyān	Zinjibār	8,297	21,489	432,529
ʿAdan	Aden	2,695	6,980	519,822
ʿAmrān[2]	ʿAmrān	...	...	993,722
Al-Bayḍāʾ	Al-Bayḍāʾ	4,310	11,170	579,955
Al-Ḍāliʿ[2]	Al-Ḍāliʿ	...	...	415,066
Dhamār	Dhamār	3,430	8,870	1,234,424
Ḥaḍramawt	Al-Mukallā	59,991	155,376	890,247
Ḥajjah	Ḥajjah	3,700	9,590	1,404,554
Al-Ḥudaydah	Al-Ḥudaydah	5,240	13,580	2,004,049
Ibb	Ibb	2,480	6,430	2,074,139
Al-Jawf	Al-Jawf	...	...	447,020
Laḥij	Laḥij	4,928	12,766	664,070
Al-Mahrah	Al-Ghayḍah	25,618	66,350	72,555
Al-Maḥwīt	Al-Maḥwīt	830	2,160	464,158
Maʾrib	Maʾrib	15,400	39,890	233,695
Ṣaʿdah	Ṣaʿdah	4,950	12,810	614,682
Ṣanʿāʾ	Sanaa	7,745	20,063	1,394,947
Shabwah	ʿAtāq	28,536	73,908	469,256
Taʿizz	Taʿizz	4,020	10,420	2,363,486
City				
Sanaa	—	95	247	1,590,624
TOTAL		[3]	[3]	18,862,999

Demography

Population (2003): 20,010,000.
Density (2002)[4]: persons per sq mi 93.4, persons per sq km 36.1.
Urban-rural (2001): urban 25.0%; rural 75.0%.
Sex distribution (2000): male 50.98%; female 49.02%.
Age breakdown (2000): under 15, 47.5%; 15–29, 27.8%; 30–44, 13.2%; 45–59, 7.1%; 60–74, 3.3%; 75 and over, 1.1%.
Population projection: (2010) 25,602,000; (2020) 36,537,000.
Doubling time: 20 years.
Ethnic composition (2000): Arab 92.8%; Somali 3.7%; black 1.1%; Indo-Pakistani 1.0%; other 1.4%.
Religious affiliation (2000): Muslim 98.9%, of which Sunnī *c.* 60%, Shīʿī *c.* 40%; Hindu 0.7%; Christian 0.2%; other 0.2%.
Major cities (2001): Sanaa 1,590,624; Aden 509,886; Taʿizz 450,000; Al-Ḥudaydah 425,000; Al-Mukallā 165,000.

Vital statistics

Birth rate per 1,000 population (2002): 43.3 (world avg. 21.3).
Death rate per 1,000 population (2002): 9.3 (world avg. 9.1).
Natural increase rate per 1,000 population (2002): 34.0 (world avg. 12.2).
Total fertility rate (avg. births per childbearing woman; 2002): 6.9.
Life expectancy at birth (2002): male 58.8 years; female 62.5 years.
Major causes of death per 100,000 population: n.a.; however, infant, child, and maternal mortality were very high in the late 1990s.

National economy

Budget (2000). Revenue: YRls 388,950,000,000 (1999; tax revenue 90.1%, of which oil revenue 64.1%, taxes on income and profits 9.4%, customs duties 7.8%; nontax revenue 9.9%). Expenditures: YRls 422,250,000,000 (1999; wages and salaries 23.0%; defense 18.1%; economic development 17.5%; interest on debt 13.8%; subsidies 7.7%).
Population economically active (1999): total 4,118,000; activity rate of total population 24.3% (participation rates [1994]: age 15 and over, 45.8%; female 18.2%; unemployed [1995] 30%).

Price index (1995 = 100)

	1993	1994	1995	1996	1997	1998	1999
Consumer price index	44.0	64.0	100.0	130.0	137.0	148.0	167.9

Production (metric tons except as noted). Agriculture, forestry, fishing (2002): sorghum 360,000, tomatoes 261,692, potatoes 208,597, grapes 162,726, oranges 158,940, wheat 150,000, bananas 95,860, onions 79,147, papayas 70,740, millet 68,554; livestock (number of live animals) 5,028,968 sheep, 4,452,540 goats, 1,400,584 cattle, 500,000 asses, 198,434 camels, 34,800,000 chickens; roundwood (2002) 326,262 cu m; fish catch (2000) 114,751. Mining and quarrying (2001): salt 150,000; gypsum 100,000. Manufacturing (value of production in YRls '000,000; 1996): food, beverages, and tobacco 43,927; chemicals and chemical products 42,369; nonmetallic mineral products 8,571; paper products 8,562; basic metal industries 3,040; clothing, textiles, and leather 1,693; wood products 392. Construction: n.a. Energy production (consumption): electricity (kW-hr; 1999) 2,960,000,000 (2,960,000,000); coal, none (none); crude petroleum (barrels; 2001) 165,200,000 ([1999] 50,600,000); petroleum products (metric tons; 1999) 5,275,000 (4,000,000); natural gas (cu m; 2000) none (none).
Gross national product (2001): U.S.$8,200,000,000 (U.S.$450 per capita).

Structure of gross domestic product and labour force

	2001		1999	
	in value YRls '000,000[5]	% of total value[5]	labour force	% of labour force
Agriculture	243,044	15.5	1,996,000	48.5
Mining	492,753	31.5	13,000	0.3
Manufacturing	106,175	6.8	206,000	5.0
Public utilities	11,656	0.8	382,000	9.3
Construction	61,681	3.9	21,000	0.5
Transp. and commun.	169,381	10.8	210,000	5.1
Trade	181,958	11.6	440,000	10.7
Finance, real estate	119,590	7.7	49,000	1.2
Pub. admin., defense	166,129	10.6	389,000	9.4
Services	12,565	0.8	412,000	10.0
Other	–242[6]	—[6]	...	...
TOTAL	1,564,690	100.0	4,118,000	100.0

Household income and expenditure. Average household size (1998) 7.1; income per household YRls 29,035 (U.S.$217).
Tourism (2001): receipts U.S.$38,000,000; expenditures U.S.$70,000,000.
Public debt (external, outstanding; 2001): U.S.$4,062,000,000.
Land use (1994): forest 3.8%; pasture 30.4%; agriculture 2.9%; other 62.9%.

Foreign trade[7]

Balance of trade

	1996	1997	1998	1999	2000	2001
U.S.$'000,000	+636.9	+490.2	–669.9	+431.9	+1,755.1	+905.5
% of total	13.5%	10.9%	18.3%	9.7%	27.4%	16.4%

Imports (2000): U.S.$2,323,700,000 (food and live animals 29.6%, of which cereals and related products 13.5%; machinery 20.8%; mineral fuels 12.0%; chemicals and chemical products 9.7%). *Major import sources:* U.A.E. 12.5%; Saudi Arabia 12.4%; India 5.5%; Kuwait 5.2%; U.S. 4.9%.
Exports (2000): U.S.$4,078,800,000 (crude petroleum 96.5%; raw materials 0.5%). *Major export destinations:* India 18.3%; Thailand 18.0%; South Korea 13.2%; China 9.6%.

Transport and communications

Transport. Railroads: none. Roads (1996): total length 64,725 km (paved 8.1%). Vehicles (1996): passenger cars 240,567; trucks and buses 291,149. Air transport (2000): passenger-km 1,574,000,000; metric ton-km cargo 32,000,000; airports (1998) with scheduled flights 12.

Communications

Medium	date	unit	number	units per 1,000 persons
Daily newspapers	2000	circulation	270,000	15
Radio	2000	receivers	1,170,000	65
Television	2000	receivers	5,100,000	283
Telephones	2002	main lines	542,200	28
Cellular telephones	2002	subscribers	411,100	21
Internet	2002	users	100,000	5.1
Personal computers	2002	units	145,000	7.4

Education and health

Educational attainment (1998). Percentage of population age 10 and over having: no formal schooling 49.5%; reading and writing ability 32.2%; primary education 11.0%; secondary education 4.6%; higher 2.7%. *Literacy* (2000): percentage of total population age 15 and over literate 46.3%; males literate 67.5%; females literate 25.2%.

Education (2001–02)

	schools	teachers	students	student/ teacher ratio
Primary (age 7–12)	11,013[8]	113,812	3,401,508	29.9
Secondary (age 13–18)[9]	1,224[10]	14,063	484,573	34.6
Voc., teacher tr.[9, 10]	125	369	15,074	40.9
Higher[9]	7[11]	3,429	184,072	53.7

Health (1998): physicians 3,883 (1 per 4,211 persons); hospital beds 9,143 (1 per 1,788 persons); infant mortality rate per 1,000 live births (2002) 66.8.
Food (2001): daily per capita caloric intake 2,050 (vegetable products 94%, animal products 6%); 85% of FAO recommended minimum requirement.

Military

Total active duty personnel (2002): 66,500 (army 90.2%, navy 2.3%, air force 7.5%). *Military expenditure as percentage of GNP* (1999): 6.1% (world 2.4%); per capita expenditure U.S.$22.

[1]Governorate area figures are based on a pre-1998 survey and are sometimes rounded. [2]Created in 1998 from parts of three other governorates. [3]An agreement to resolve the long-undemarcated northeastern boundary with Saudi Arabia (which increased Yemen's total area to roughly 214,300 sq mi [555,000 sq km]) was signed in June 2000. [4]Based on the total area estimate of 214,300 sq mi (555,000 sq km). [5]In purchasers' value at current prices. [6]Includes import duties of 28.4 million Yemeni Rials less imputed bank service charges. [7]Imports c.i.f. in balance of trade and f.o.b. in commodities and trading partners. [8]1993–94. [9]Public schools only, which comprise the vast majority of schools in Yemen. [10]1994–95. [11]1999–2000.

Internet resources for further information:
- **Central Bank of Yemen http://www.centralbank.gov.ye**

Zambia

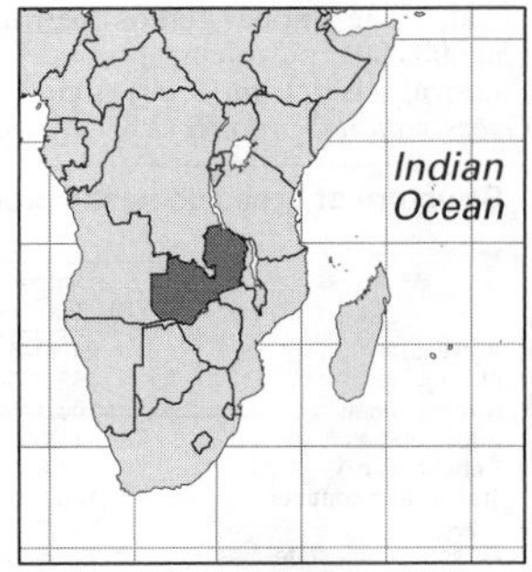

Official name: Republic of Zambia.
Form of government: multiparty republic with one legislative house (National Assembly [158[1]]).
Head of state and government: President.
Capital: Lusaka.
Official language: English.
Official religion: none[2].
Monetary unit: 1 Zambian kwacha (K) = 100 ngwee; valuation (Sept. 8, 2003) 1 U.S.$ = K 4,790; 1 £ = K 7,595.

Area and population

		area		population
Provinces	Capitals	sq mi	sq km	2000 census[3]
Central	Kabwe	36,446	94,394	1,006,766
Copperbelt	Ndola	12,096	31,328	1,657,646
Eastern	Chipata	26,682	69,106	1,300,973
Luapula	Mansa	19,524	50,567	784,613
Lusaka	Lusaka	8,454	21,896	1,432,401
North-Western	Solwezi	48,582	125,827	610,975
Northern	Kasama	57,076	147,826	1,407,088
Southern	Livingstone	32,928	85,283	1,302,660
Western	Mongu	48,798	126,386	782,509
TOTAL		290,585[4]	752,612[4]	10,285,631

Demography

Population (2003): 10,812,000.
Density (2003): persons per sq mi 37.2, persons per sq km 14.4.
Urban-rural (2001): urban 43.9%; rural 56.1%.
Sex distribution (2000): male 49.30%; female 50.70%.
Age breakdown (2000): under 15, 47.6%; 15–29, 30.6%; 30–44, 12.4%; 45–59, 5.5%; 60–74, 3.1%; 75 and over, 0.8%.
Population projection: (2010) 11,768,000; (2020) 13,558,000.
Doubling time: 44 years.
Ethnolinguistic composition (1990): Bemba peoples 39.7%; Maravi (Nyanja) peoples 20.1%; Tonga peoples 14.8%; North-Western peoples 8.8%; Barotze peoples 7.5%; Tumbuka peoples 3.7%; Mambwe peoples 3.4%; other 2.0%.
Religious affiliation (1995): Christian 47.8%, of which Protestant 22.9%, Roman Catholic 16.9%, African Christian 5.6%; traditional beliefs 27.0%; Muslim 1.0%; other 24.2%.
Major cities (1999): Lusaka 1,269,848 (urban agglomeration [2001] 1,718,000); Kitwe 467,084; Ndola 441,624; Kabwe 233,197; Chingola 211,755.

Vital statistics

Birth rate per 1,000 population (2002): 40.1 (world avg. 21.3).
Death rate per 1,000 population (2002): 24.3 (world avg. 9.1).
Natural increase rate per 1,000 population (2002): 15.8 (world avg. 12.2).
Total fertility rate (avg. births per childbearing woman; 2002): 5.4.
Life expectancy at birth (2002): male 35.3 years; female 35.3 years.
Major causes of death per 100,000 population: n.a.

National economy

Budget (2001). Revenue: K 2,509,000,000,000 (tax revenue 97.6%, of which income tax 38.0%, value-added tax 32.7%, excise taxes 14.6%; nontax revenue 2.4%). Expenditures: K 4,212,000,000,000 (current expenditures 61.2%, of which wages 21.0%, transfers 8.4%; capital expenditures 38.8%).
Public debt (external, outstanding; 2001): U.S.$4,394,000,000.
Production (metric tons except as noted). Agriculture, forestry, fishing (2002): sugarcane 1,800,000, cassava 950,000, corn (maize) 900,000, fruits and vegetables 380,000, wheat 75,000, seed cotton 62,000, sweet potatoes 53,000, peanuts (groundnuts) 42,000, millet 38,000, sunflower seeds 10,000, tobacco 4,800; livestock (number of live animals) 2,600,000 cattle, 1,270,000 goats, 340,000 pigs, 30,000,000 chickens; roundwood (2001) 8,053,000 cu m; fish catch (2001) 70,911. Mining and quarrying (2001): copper (metal content) 233,000; cobalt (metal content) 8,000; emeralds 7,000 kg[5]. Manufacturing (value added in K '000,000; 1994): food products 39,765.1; beverages 36,596.5; chemicals and pharmaceuticals 32,141.5; textiles 15,358.5; tobacco 14,060.2; iron and steel, nonferrous metals, and fabricated metal products 13,874.6. Energy production (consumption): electricity (kW-hr; 1999) 8,065,000,000 (6,529,000,000); coal (metric tons; 1999) 184,000 (177,000); crude petroleum (barrels; 1999) none (1,800,000); petroleum products (metric tons; 1999) 207,000 (391,000); natural gas, none (none).
Household income and expenditure. Average household size (2000) 3.9; average annual income per household: n.a.; sources of income: n.a.; expenditure: n.a.
Tourism (2001): receipts U.S.$117,000,000; expenditures 44,000,000.
Population economically active (1996): total 3,454,000; activity rate of total population 38.2% (participation rates [1991]: over age 10, 52.6%; female 29.6%; unemployed, n.a.).

Price and earnings indexes (1996 = 100)

	1996	1997	1998	1999	2000	2001	2002
Consumer price index	100.0	123.3	153.5	214.1	266.1	300.3	367.1
Earnings index	...	...	...	...	...	...	...

Gross national product (2001): U.S.$3,300,000,000 (U.S.$320 per capita).

Structure of gross domestic product and labour force

	2001		1990	
	in value K '000,000[6]	% of total value	labour force	% of labour force
Agriculture	418,900	15.9	1,872,000	68.9
Mining	182,900	7.0	56,800	2.1
Manufacturing	278,600	10.6	50,900	1.9
Construction	137,800	5.2	29,100	1.1
Public utilities	82,100	3.1	8,900	0.3
Transp. and commun.	162,100	6.2	25,600	0.9
Trade	544,100	20.7	30,700	1.1
Finance	452,200	17.2	24,200	0.9
Pub. admin., defense Services	204,000	7.8	111,600	4.1
Other	166,500[7]	6.3[7]	506,100	18.6
TOTAL	2,629,200	100.0	2,716,000[4]	100.0[4]

Land use (1994): forest 43.0%; pasture 40.4%; agriculture 7.1%; other 9.5%.

Foreign trade[8]

Balance of trade (current prices)

	1997	1998	1999	2000	2001	2002
U.S.$'000,000	+54	–155	–115	–232	–108	–233
% of total	2.5%	8.7%	7.1%	13.5%	4.5%	10.7%

Imports (2001): U.S.$1,307,000,000 (nonelectrical machinery and equipment 18.5%, chemicals and chemical products 15.4%, transport equipment 10.3%, printed matter 9.6%, refined petroleum 7.7%). *Major import sources:* South Africa 53.7%; U.K. 15.5%; Zimbabwe 8.0%; China 2.9%.
Exports (2001): U.S.$985,000,000 (copper 54.6%, other base metals [including cobalt] 10.0%, manufactures of base metals 6.9%, raw sugar 3.7%, cotton yarn 3.1%). *Major export destinations:* U.K. 52.9%; South Africa 22.9%; Switzerland 6.1%; Republic of the Congo 3.4%.

Transport and communications

Transport. Railroads (2002)[9]: length 787 mi, 1,266 km; (1997) passenger-mi 166,000,000, passenger-km 267,000,000; short ton-mi cargo 316,000,000, metric ton-km cargo 462,000,000. Roads (1999): total length 24,170 mi, 38,898 km (paved 18%). Vehicles (1996): passenger cars 157,000; trucks and buses 81,000. Air transport (1999): passenger-mi 21,100,000, passenger-km 34,000,000; short ton-mi cargo 2,000,000, metric ton-km cargo 3,000,000; airports (1998) 4.

Communications

Medium	date	unit	number	units per 1,000 persons
Daily newspapers	2000	circulation	125,000	12
Radio	2000	receivers	1,510,000	145
Television	2000	receivers	1,400,000	134
Telephones	2002	main lines	87,700	8.2
Cellular telephones	2002	subscribers	139,100	13
Internet	2002	users	52,400	4.9
Personal computers	2002	units	80,000	7.5

Education and health

Educational attainment (1993)[10]. Percentage of population age 14 and over having: no formal schooling 18.6%; some primary education 54.8%; some secondary 25.1%; higher 1.5%. *Literacy* (2000): population age 15 and over literate 78.1%; males literate 85.2%; females literate 71.5%.

Education (1998)

	schools	teachers	students	student/ teacher ratio
Primary (age 7–13)	4,221	34,810	1,557,257	44.7
Secondary (age 14–18)	246[11]	10,000	290,085	29.0
Voc., teacher tr.	4[11]	...	...	...
Higher	2[11]	640[11]	22,701	...

Health: physicians (1995) 647 (1 per 14,492 persons); hospital beds (1989) 22,461 (1 per 349 persons); infant mortality rate per 1,000 live births (2002) 100.2.
Food (2001): daily per capita caloric intake 1,885 (vegetable products 95%, animal products 5%); 82% of FAO recommended minimum requirement.

Military

Total active duty personnel (2002): 21,600 (army 92.6%; navy, none; air force 7.4%). *Military expenditure as percentage of GNP* (1999): 1.0% (world 2.4%); per capita expenditure U.S.$3.

[1]Includes 8 nonelective seats. [2]In 1996 Zambia was declared a Christian nation per the preamble of a constitutional amendment. [3]Preliminary and unadjusted for undercount/overcount. [4]Detail does not add to total given because of rounding. [5]In 1999 legal and illegal exports of emeralds were estimated to equal U.S.$20,000,000 (about 20% of world total). [6]At constant prices of 1994. [7]Less imputed bank service charge. [8]Imports f.o.b. in balance of trade and c.i.f. in commodities and trading partners. [9]Excludes Tanzania-Zambia Railway Authority (TAZARA) data. [10]Based on a sample survey of 35,502 persons. [11]1996.

Internet resources for further information:
- **Zambian Department of Census and Statistics http://www.zamstats.gov.zm**
- **Bank of Zambia http://www.boz.zm**

Zimbabwe

Official name: Republic of Zimbabwe.
Form of government: multiparty republic with one legislative house (House of Assembly [150[1]]).
Head of state and government: President.
Capital: Harare.
Official language: English.
Official religion: none.
Monetary unit: 1 Zimbabwe dollar (Z$) = 100 cents; valuation (Sept. 8, 2003) 1 U.S.$ = Z$824.00; 1 £ = Z$1,307.[2]

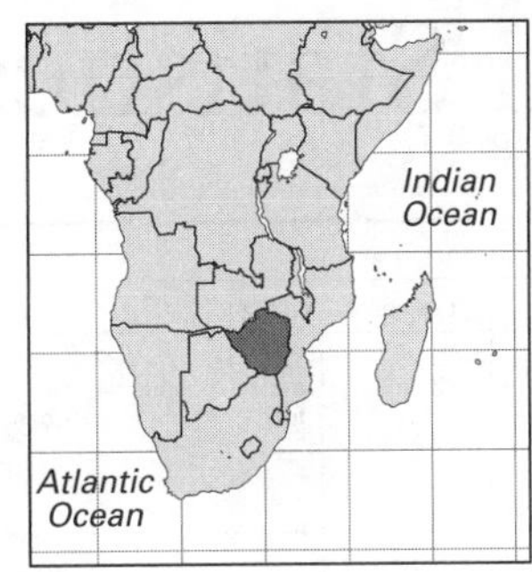

Area and population

Provinces	Capitals	area sq mi	area sq km	population 2002 preliminary census
Bulawayo[3]	—	185	479	676,787
Harare[3]	—	337	872	1,903,510
Manicaland	Mutare	14,077	36,459	1,566,889
Mashonaland Central	Bindura	10,945	28,347	998,265
Mashonaland East	Marondera	12,444	32,230	1,125,355
Mashonaland West	Chinhoyi	22,178	57,441	1,222,583
Masvingo	Masvingo	21,840	56,566	1,318,705
Matabeleland North	Lupane	28,967	75,025	701,359
Matabeleland South	Gwanda	20,916	54,172	654,879
Midlands	Gweru	18,983	49,166	1,466,331
TOTAL		150,872	390,757	11,643,663

Demography

Population (2003): 11,719,000.
Density (2003): persons per sq mi 77.7, persons per sq km 30.0.
Urban-rural (2001): urban 36.0%; rural 64.0%.
Sex distribution (2002): male 48.40%; female 51.60%.
Age breakdown (2000): under 15, 39.6%; 15–29, 33.1%; 30–44, 14.8%; 45–59, 7.2%; 60–74, 4.1%; 75 and over, 1.2%.
Population projection: (2010) 12,044,000; (2020) 11,957,000.
Doubling time: 87 years.
Ethnic composition (2000): Shona 67.1%; Ndebele 13.0%; Chewa 4.9%; British 3.5%; other 11.5%.
Religious affiliation (1995): Christian 45.4%, of which Protestant (including Anglican) 23.5%, African indigenous 13.5%, Roman Catholic 7.0%; animist 40.5%; other 14.1%.
Major cities (2002): Harare 1,444,534; Bulawayo 676,787; Chitungwiza (1992) 274,035; Mutare (1992) 131,808; Gweru (1992) 124,735.

Vital statistics

Birth rate per 1,000 population (2002): 30.7 (world avg. 21.3).
Death rate per 1,000 population (2002): 22.8 (world avg. 9.1).
Natural increase rate per 1,000 population (2002): 7.9 (world avg. 12.2).
Total fertility rate (avg. births per childbearing woman; 2002): 3.7.
Life expectancy at birth (2002): male 41.6 years; female 38.8 years.
Major causes of death per 100,000 population (1990): infectious and parasitic diseases 64.7; accidents and poisoning 44.4; diseases of the circulatory system 40.9; diseases of the respiratory system 39.5; malignant neoplasms (cancers) 28.4; diseases of the digestive system 12.1.

National economy

Budget (2002). Revenue: Z$300,385,000,000 (tax revenue 93.5%, of which income tax 53.0%, sales tax 24.1%, customs duties 9.0%, excise tax 6.2%; nontax revenue 6.5%). Expenditures: Z$351,321,000,000 (current expenditures 91.3%, of which goods and services 61.5%, transfer payments 15.7%, interest payments 14.1%; development expenditure 7.2%; net lending 1.5%).
Population economically active (1992): total 3,600,000; activity rate of total population 34.6% (participation rates: over age 15, 63.4%; female 39.8%; unemployed, n.a.).

Price and earnings indexes (1995 = 100)

	1996	1997	1998	1999	2000	2001	2002
Consumer price index	121	154	226	355	550	1,167	3,490
Earnings index	…	…	…	…	…	…	…

Production (metric tons except as noted). Agriculture, forestry, fishing (2002): sugarcane 4,700,000, corn (maize) 499,000, seed cotton 200,400, cassava 175,000, tobacco leaves 174,000, peanuts (groundnuts) 165,000, wheat 150,000, oranges 90,000, bananas 85,000, soybeans 83,000, sorghum 80,000, tea 22,400; livestock (number of live animals) 5,753,000 cattle, 2,970,000 goats, 605,000 pigs, 600,000 sheep; roundwood 9,107,600 cu m; fish catch (2000) 13,300. Mining and quarrying (value of production in Z$'000,000; 2000): gold 8,521; asbestos 2,776; coal 2,690; nickel 2,178; chrome 778; granite 552. Manufacturing (value added in U.S.$'000,000; 1998): beverages 171; foodstuffs 148; textiles 99; iron and steel 86; fabricated metal products 64; cement, bricks, and tiles 63; tobacco products 51. Energy production (consumption): electricity (kW-hr; 2000) 7,016,000,000 ([1999] 12,362,000,000); coal (metric tons; 2000) 3,986,000 ([1999] 4,977,000); crude petroleum, none (none); petroleum products (metric tons; 1999) none (1,421,000); natural gas, none (none).
Public debt (external, outstanding; 2001): U.S.$2,847,000,000.
Household income and expenditure. Average household size (1992) 4.8; income per household Z$1,689 (U.S.$332); expenditure (1990[4]): food, beverages, and tobacco 39.1%, housing 18.7%, clothing and footwear 9.8%, transportation 8.4%, education 7.6%, household durable goods 7.2%.
Gross national product (2001): U.S.$6,200,000,000 (U.S.$480 per capita).

Structure of gross domestic product and labour force

	1999 in value Z$'000,000[5]	1999 % of total value[5]	2000 labour force[6]	2000 % of labour force[6]
Agriculture	35,812	19.4	325,000	26.3
Mining	3,380	1.8	45,000	3.6
Manufacturing	30,538	16.5	181,000	14.6
Construction	5,132	2.8	54,000	4.4
Public utilities	5,171	2.8	11,000	0.9
Transp. and commun.	11,373	6.2	44,000	3.6
Trade	36,261	19.7	103,000	8.3
Finance	26,917	14.6	35,000	2.8
Pub. admin., defense	22,913	12.4	440,000	35.5
Services	8,273	4.5		
Other	−1,357[7]	−0.7[7]	—	—
TOTAL	184,413	100.0	1,238,000	100.0

Tourism: receipts (2001) U.S.$81,000,000; expenditures (1998) U.S.$131,-000,000.

Foreign trade

Balance of trade (current prices)

	1996	1997	1998	1999	2000	2001
U.S.$'000,000	+249	−230	−95	+258	+346	−170
% of total	5.2%	4.5%	2.4%	7.1%	8.5%	5.0%

Imports (2001): U.S.$1,779,000,000 (machinery and transport equipment 28.1%, chemicals and chemical products 22.9%, petroleum products 15.7%, food 3.8%, electricity 3.1%). *Major import sources* (2002): South Africa 47.7%; Democratic Republic of the Congo 5.7%; Mozambique 5.3%; Germany 3.1%; U.K. 3.1%.
Exports (2001): U.S.$1,609,000,000 (tobacco 36.9%, gold 14.0%, horticultural products [including cut flowers] 7.4%, ferroalloys 5.1%, cotton lint 5.1%, sugar 4.4%). *Major export destinations* (2001): South Africa 17.7%; U.K. 12.6%; Germany 8.3%; China 7.1%; Japan 6.6%.

Transport and communications

Transport. Railroads (2001): route length 3,077 km; (1998) passenger-km 408,223,000; (1998) metric ton-km cargo 4,603,000. Roads (1996): total length 18,338 km (paved 47%). Vehicles (2000): passenger cars 573,000; trucks and buses 39,000. Air transport (2001)[8]: passenger-km 723,000,000; metric ton-km cargo 28,829,000; airports (1997) with scheduled flights 7.

Communications

Medium	date	unit	number	units per 1,000 persons
Daily newspapers	2000	circulation	205,000	18
Radio	2000	receivers	4,110,000	362
Television	1999	receivers	2,074,000	183
Telephones	2002	main lines	287,900	24
Cellular telephones	2002	subscribers	353,000	30
Personal computers	2002	units	600,000	52
Internet	2002	users	500,000	43

Education and health

Educational attainment (1992). Percentage of population age 25 and over having: no formal schooling 22.3%; primary 54.3%; secondary 13.1%; higher 3.4%. *Literacy* (1995): percentage of total population age 15 and over literate 85.1%; males literate 90.4%; females literate 79.9%.

Education (1998)

	schools	teachers	students	student/ teacher ratio
Primary (age 7–13)	4,706	64,538	2,507,098	38.8
Secondary (age 14–19)	1,530	30,482	847,296	27.8
Voc., teacher tr.[9]	25	1,479	27,431	18.5
Higher[10]	28[9]	3,581	46,492	13.0

Health: physicians (1996) 1,603 (1 per 6,904 persons); hospital beds (1996) 22,975 (1 per 501 persons); infant mortality rate (2002) 65.9.
Food (2001): daily per capita caloric intake 2,133 (vegetable products 92%, animal products 8%); 89% of FAO recommended minimum requirement.

Military

Total active duty personnel (2002): 36,000 (army 88.9%, air force 11.1%). *Military expenditure as percentage of GNP* (1999): 5.0% (world 2.4%); per capita expenditure U.S.$23.

[1]Includes 30 nonelective seats. [2]Black market rate in August 2003 was 1 U.S.$ = Z$4,000. [3]City with provincial status. [4]Based on consumer price index. [5]At factor cost. [6]Wage-earning workers only. [7]Less imputed bank service charges. [8]Air Zimbabwe only. [9]1992. [10]Includes postsecondary vocational and teacher training at the higher level.

Internet resources for further information:
- **Reserve Bank of Zimbabwe http://www.rbz.co.zw**

Comparative National Statistics

World and regional summaries

region/bloc	area and population, 2003						gross national product, 2000						labour force, 1990		
	area		population			population projection, 2020	total ('000,000 U.S.$)	% agricul-ture	% industry	% ser-vices	growth rate, 1990–99	GNP per capita (U.S.$)	total ('000)	% male	% female
	square miles	square kilometres	total	per sq mi	per sq km										
World	52,424,911	135,780,131	6,258,041,000	119.4	46.1	7,428,533,500	31,252,121	4	28	68	2.5	5,330	2,353,806	63.8	36.2
Africa	11,714,700	30,341,175	835,479,000	71.3	27.5	1,132,265,000	550,247	16	30	53	2.5	730	242,784	65.6	34.4
Central Africa	2,552,967	6,612,155	97,909,000	38.4	14.8	147,774,000	25,549	17	36	21	1.3	540	26,428	64.7	35.3
East Africa	2,473,674	6,406,668	257,986,000	104.3	40.3	346,889,000	66,770	28	17	54	2.9	270	85,082	58.8	41.2
North Africa	3,287,612	8,514,830	183,897,000	55.9	21.6	242,818,000	244,873	16	33	51	3.3	1,450	40,016	84.6	15.4
Southern Africa	1,032,304	2,673,657	51,818,000	50.2	19.4	50,027,000	140,652	3	28	68	1.3	2,850	14,532	64.3	35.7
West Africa	2,368,143	6,133,865	243,869,000	103.0	39.8	344,757,000	72,403	31	30	38	3.0	310	76,726	63.8	36.2
Americas	16,244,419	42,072,851	857,602,000	52.8	20.4	1,021,535,500	12,126,348	2	23	75	3.0	14,870	293,723	66.5	33.5
Anglo-America[2]	8,301,333	21,500,356	323,304,000	38.9	15.0	373,384,000	10,252,979	1	22	76	3.0	32,830	135,438	58.7	41.3
Canada	3,849,674	9,970,610	31,590,000	8.2	3.2	35,277,000	647,829	3	27	70	2.8	21,130	13,360	60.2	39.8
United States	3,615,215	9,363,364	291,587,000	80.7	31.1	337,974,000	9,601,505	1	22	77	3.0	34,100	122,005	58.6	41.4
Latin America	7,943,086	20,572,495	534,298,000	67.3	26.0	648,151,500	1,873,369	7	29	64	3.4	3,720	158,285	73.1	26.9
Caribbean	90,706	234,924	37,802,000	416.7	160.9	43,683,500	124,590	5	33	56	2.8	3,330	13,813	66.9	33.1
Central America	202,246	523,816	38,753,000	191.6	74.0	52,542,000	63,867	17	21	63	4.4	1,770	9,520	78.5	21.5
Mexico	756,066	1,958,201	100,588,000	133.0	51.4	120,937,000	497,025	4	27	69	2.8	5,070	30,487	72.9	27.1
South America	6,894,068	17,855,554	357,155,000	51.8	20.0	430,989,000	1,187,887	8	30	63	3.6	3,580	104,465	73.6	26.4
Andean Group	2,112,164	5,470,481	131,424,000	62.2	24.0	164,457,000	270,788	9	32	59	3.8	2,380	34,715	75.6	24.4
Brazil	3,300,171	8,547,404	178,470,000	54.1	20.9	209,793,000	610,058	8	31	60	3.0	3,580	55,026	72.6	27.4
Other South America	1,481,733	3,837,669	47,261,000	31.9	12.3	56,739,000	307,041	5	24	70	4.8	6,500	14,724	72.4	27.6
Asia	12,309,306	31,880,824	3,804,957,000	309.1	119.3	4,515,504,000	8,491,380	8	35	57	3.7	2,400	1,464,452	64.5	35.5
Eastern Asia	4,546,130	11,774,466	1,519,172,000	334.2	129.0	1,663,351,000	6,470,963	4	36	59	3.1	4,340	775,590	57.4	42.6
China	3,696,100	9,572,900	1,288,892,000	348.7	134.6	1,426,184,000	1,062,919	18	49	33	10.8	840	669,693	56.7	43.3
Japan	145,884	377,837	127,546,000	874.3	337.6	125,541,000	4,519,067	2	33	66	1.4	35,620	62,202	62.1	37.9
South Korea	38,432	99,538	47,925,000	1,247.0	481.5	50,650,000	421,069	6	49	45	5.7	8,910	18,664	66.2	33.8
Other Eastern Asia	665,714	1,724,191	54,809,000	82.3	31.8	60,976,000	467,908	1	22	73	5.5	8,940	25,031	58.8	41.2
South Asia	1,936,365	5,015,158	1,420,523,000	733.6	283.2	1,777,681,000	563,681	28	23	48	5.5	460	411,136	77.4	22.6
India	1,222,243	3,165,596	1,065,462,000	871.7	336.6	1,312,212,000	454,800	28	24	48	5.9	450	322,944	74.8	25.2
Pakistan	307,374	796,096	149,030,000	484.8	187.2	197,538,000	61,022	24	18	58	3.5	440	33,698	87.5	12.5
Other South Asia	406,748	1,053,466	206,031,000	506.5	195.6	267,931,000	47,859	35	28	36	4.9	590	54,494	86.2	13.8
Southeast Asia	1,742,098	4,512,012	538,536,000	309.1	119.4	649,928,000	661,194	21	30	49	5.3	1,290	189,297	63.0	37.0
Southwest Asia	4,084,713	10,579,188	326,726,000	80.0	30.9	424,544,000	795,542	10	36	52	2.8	2,620	88,429	69.4	30.6
Central Asia	1,545,789	4,003,445	56,891,000	36.8	14.2	67,032,000	33,915	16	25	58	–4.3	610	20,728	54.8	45.2
Gulf Cooperation Council	1,031,352	2,671,071	34,186,000	33.1	12.8	50,010,000	261,751	4	51	45	2.2	8,880	6,511	91.7	8.3
Iran	630,830	1,633,841	66,255,000	105.0	40.6	79,721,000	106,707	21	30	50	3.4	1,680	15,253	82.0	18.0
Other Southwest Asia	876,742	2,270,831	169,394,000	193.2	74.6	227,781,000	393,169	11	28	57	4.0	2,530	45,936	68.7	31.3
Europe	8,868,823	22,970,277	727,671,000	82.0	31.7	720,965,000	9,627,957	3	27	70	1.3	13,260	340,666	57.1	42.9
Eastern Europe	7,437,283	19,262,609	333,661,000	44.9	17.3	319,999,000	719,022	7	32	61	–3.2	2,140	171,080	50.6	49.4
Russia	6,592,800	17,075,400	144,893,000	22.0	8.5	139,331,000	241,027	7	35	59	–6.0	1,660	72,286	47.6	52.4
Ukraine	233,100	603,700	47,856,000	205.3	79.3	44,148,000	34,595	11	30	59	–10.8	700	25,401	48.0	52.0
Other Eastern Europe	611,383	1,583,509	140,912,000	230.5	89.0	136,520,000	443,400	7	30	62	1.3	3,140	73,393	54.4	45.6
Western Europe	1,431,540	3,707,668	394,010,000	275.2	106.3	400,966,000	8,908,935	2	27	71	1.8	22,850	169,586	63.6	36.4
European Union (EU)	1,249,629	3,236,522	380,951,000	304.9	117.7	387,021,000	8,457,121	2	27	71	1.8	19,950	163,771	63.6	36.4
France	210,026	543,965	59,773,000	284.6	109.9	63,205,000	1,438,293	3	22	75	1.5	24,090	25,404	60.1	39.9
Germany	137,847	357,021	82,604,000	599.2	231.4	82,144,000	2,063,734	1	31	68	1.4	25,120	38,981	60.7	39.3
Italy	116,345	301,333	57,033,000	490.2	189.3	56,079,000	1,163,211	3	31	67	1.4	20,160	23,339	68.1	31.9
Spain	195,364	505,990	42,600,000	218.1	84.2	40,566,000	595,255	3	24	73	2.3	15,080	14,456	75.5	24.5
United Kingdom	94,251	244,110	59,164,000	627.7	242.4	62,197,000	1,459,500	1	26	73	2.5	24,430	27,766	61.4	38.6
Other EU	495,796	1,284,103	79,777,000	160.9	62.1	82,830,000	1,737,128	3	25	72	2.4	22,140	33,825	63.4	36.6
Non-EU	181,911	471,146	13,059,000	71.8	27.7	13,945,000	451,814	2	29	67	1.7	35,640	5,815	61.9	38.1
Oceania	3,287,663	8,515,005	32,332,000	9.8	3.8	38,264,000	456,189	4	21	74	3.9	14,780	12,181	63.0	37.0
Australia	2,969,978	7,692,208	19,880,000	6.7	2.6	22,577,000	388,252	3	22	76	4.1	20,240	20,240	61.9	38.1
Pacific Ocean Islands	317,685	822,797	12,452,000	39.2	15.1	15,687,000	67,937	9	21	64	2.9	5,810	4,218	65.0	35.0

[1]Refers only to the outstanding long-term external public and publicly guaranteed debt of the 137 countries that report under the World Bank's Debtor Reporting System (DRS). [2]Anglo-America includes

Africa

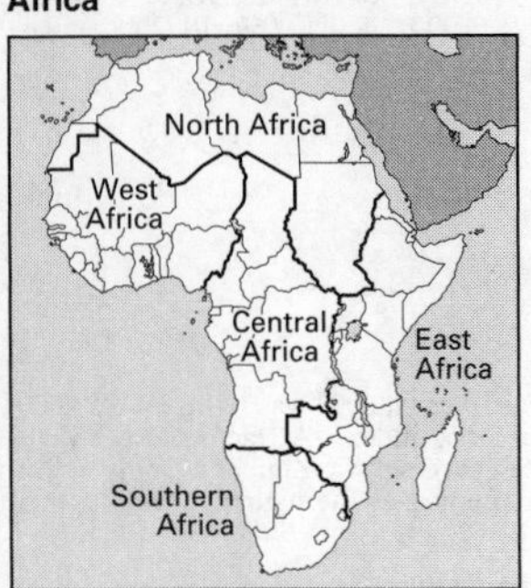

Americas

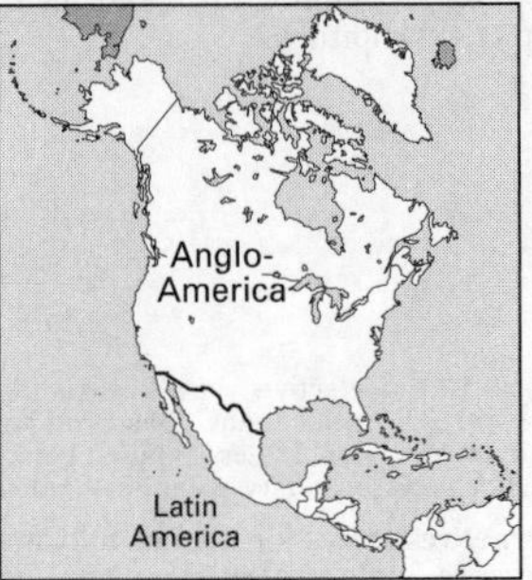

Asia

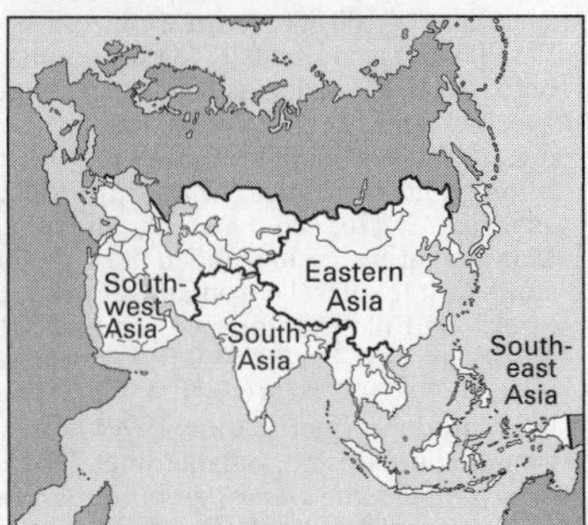

economic indicators							social indicators									region/bloc
pop. per 1,000 ha of arable land, 2002	electricity consump-tion (kW-hr per capita), 1998	trade ('000,000 U.S.$), 1999			debt ('000,000 U.S.$), 1999[1]		life expec-tancy (years), 2000		health			food (% FAO recom-mended minimum), 1998	literacy (%) (latest)		
		imports (c.i.f.)	exports (f.o.b.)	balance	total	% of GNP	male	female	pop. per doctor (latest)	infant mor-tality per 1,000 births, 2001	pop. having safe water (%); (1989–98)		male	female	
4,570	2,428	5,785,724	5,667,433	−118,291	1,464,107	24.0	64.3	68.3	730	55.2	76	118	83.7	71.0	World
4,600	521	124,113	119,194	−4,919	236,331	48.0	51.1	53.1	2,560	86.7	57	104	65.9	45.5	Africa
4,450	114	6,281	11,402	+5,122	34,588	134.3	47.3	50.4	12,890	107.3	44	83	77.7	56.4	Central Africa
5,760	139	18,145	9,269	−8,876	45,902	77.9	44.9	46.3	13,620	94.8	44	84	65.4	44.1	East Africa
4,460	749	48,990	36,052	−12,938	87,534	44.0	63.2	66.7	890	59.0	82	125	64.8	40.1	North Africa
3,160	4,221	32,634	32,131	−503	10,458	7.7	50.2	52.4	1,610	63.1	70	116	81.6	80.0	Southern Africa
4,280	140	18,064	30,341	+12,277	57,849	79.6	50.3	51.5	6,260	85.6	52	113	58.4	37.5	West Africa
2,370	6,511	1,640,288	1,264,753	−375,535	398,042	20.6	68.6	74.8	520	25.1	83	128	91.3	89.9	Americas
1,430	14,427	1,275,874	931,894	−343,979	—	—	74.3	80.0	370	6.8	91	140	96.1	95.7	Anglo-America[2]
690	17,486	215,555	238,778	+23,223	—	—	76.0	83.0	540	5.1	100	119	96.6	96.6	Canada
1,630	14,089	1,059,220	692,784	−366,436	—	—	74.1	79.7	360	6.9	90	142	95.7	95.3	United States
3,940	1,805	364,414	332,859	−31,555	398,042	20.6	65.2	71.6	690	32.4	78	119	87.8	85.6	Latin America
6,600	1,702	54,781	47,226	−7,555	10,091	26.6	67.3	72.0	380	43.8	77	102	83.8	83.0	Caribbean
5,940	712	21,925	12,058	−9,868	24,967	41.2	67.1	72.5	950	34.3	76	105	73.6	68.1	Central America
4,070	1,933	145,556	136,263	−9,293	87,531	18.6	68.5	74.7	810	26.2	85	135	91.8	87.4	Mexico
3,630	1,890	142,151	137,312	−4,839	275,453	20.2	63.8	70.6	710	32.9	76	117	88.4	87.0	South America
8,950	1,580	48,780	59,046	+10,266	87,634	26.6	68.0	71.7	830	31.0	79	106	92.6	88.7	Andean Group
3,280	2,177	60,793	51,120	−9,673	95,233	13.0	58.5	67.6	770	38.0	76	122	83.3	83.2	Brazil
1,610	1,726	32,578	27,146	−5,432	92,586	30.4	71.8	78.4	410	20.9	71	129	96.0	95.7	Other South America
7,890	1,183	1,475,600	1,676,841	+201,241	595,398	20.9	65.9	68.9	970	53.5	75	117	81.2	63.7	Asia
11,360	1,788	919,675	1,082,099	+162,425	166,210	12.1	69.9	74.3	610	34.2	71	125	91.4	77.0	Eastern Asia
10,350	926	165,699	194,931	+29,232	108,163	11.1	69.0	73.0	620	37.0	67	126	89.9	72.7	China
28,460	8,285	309,995	417,610	+107,616	—	—	77.5	84.0	530	3.4	97	123	100.0	100.0	Japan
27,710	5,218	119,751	143,685	+23,934	57,231	14.2	72.0	79.0	740	7.0	93	131	99.3	96.7	South Korea
18,910	3,686	324,230	325,873	+1,643	816	94.7	71.3	77.2	500	31.0	96	107	95.9	91.4	Other Eastern Asia
6,890	439	67,099	51,878	−15,221	139,322	24.4	61.4	62.3	2,100	70.4	80	108	62.4	35.5	South Asia
6,480	505	42,425	33,207	−9,218	82,380	18.5	61.9	63.1	1,920	64.9	81	112	65.5	37.7	India
6,850	419	10,159	8,383	−1,776	28,514	48.5	61.0	60.0	1,840	85.0	79	106	50.0	24.4	Pakistan
10,250	116	14,515	10,287	−4,228	28,428	41.3	59.2	60.0	5,080	80.6	78	89	53.5	30.9	Other South Asia
9,940	686	301,916	349,480	+47,564	186,531	37.6	65.9	69.8	3,120	40.0	70	120	91.8	83.3	Southeast Asia
3,690	2,301	186,911	193,385	+6,473	103,335	25.5	66.4	71.0	610	45.2	79	116	86.7	72.4	Southwest Asia
1,900	2,399	9,215	10,877	+1,662	9,819	25.1	63.1	71.0	330	45.4	85	98	98.8	96.1	Central Asia
8,910	7,140	65,737	91,749	+26,013	1,768	12.8	67.8	71.3	620	45.7	95	122	73.8	55.8	Gulf Cooperation Council
4,570	1,573	12,622	19,726	+7,104	6,184	5.6	68.3	71.5	1,200	30.0	95	117	78.4	65.8	Iran
4,220	1,688	99,338	71,032	−28,306	85,563	35.5	66.4	70.6	690	49.3	65	122	87.8	68.1	Other Southwest Asia
2,510	5,738	2,459,253	2,531,996	+72,742	232,295	28.0	66.2	74.2	300	9.4	99	125	99.0	97.5	Europe
1,550	4,355	227,417	220,533	−6,884	232,295	28.0	63.5	73.9	290	15.4	95	116	99.1	96.6	Eastern Europe
1,150	5,488	40,429	74,663	+34,234	120,375	32.1	59.9	72.4	240	15.3	...	111	99.5	96.8	Russia
1,480	3,385	11,846	11,582	−265	10,027	26.7	60.6	72.0	330	21.7	97	112	99.5	97.4	Ukraine
2,450	3,534	175,142	134,288	−40,854	101,893	24.4	68.2	76.1	370	13.7	94	122	98.7	96.1	Other Eastern Europe
5,260	6,960	2,231,837	2,311,463	+79,627	—	—	68.6	74.3	300	5.0	100	134	98.9	98.2	Western Europe
5,180	6,696	2,109,241	2,152,830	+43,589	—	—	68.3	74.1	290	5.1	100	134	98.8	98.1	European Union (EU)
3,220	7,613	286,593	296,025	+9,432	—	—	74.8	82.9	330	4.5	100	141	98.9	98.7	France
6,970	6,785	464,318	535,530	+71,212	—	—	74.4	80.6	290	4.3	100	128	100.0	100.0	Germany
7,260	5,244	216,451	230,094	+13,643	—	—	75.9	82.5	180	5.8	100	143	97.8	96.4	Italy
3,080	5,014	147,866	111,493	−36,373	—	—	75.6	82.5	240	5.0	99	136	98.1	95.1	Spain
10,240	6,329	327,576	273,492	−54,084	—	—	75.4	80.2	720	5.8	100	129	100.0	100.0	United Kingdom
4,960	8,113	666,438	706,196	+39,758	—	—	42.5	45.8	320	5.2	100	132	97.9	97.2	Other EU
9,170	14,899	122,595	158,633	+36,038	—	—	76.4	81.9	480	3.7	100	123	99.9	99.9	Non-EU
96,340	8,140	86,469	74,649	−11,821	2,042	33.7	0.5	0.5	480	26.2	86	117	96.3	94.0	Oceania
390	10,520	65,515	58,016	−7,499	—	—	76.6	82.0	400	6.0	95	120	99.5	99.5	Australia
5,620	4,029	20,955	16,633	−4,322	2,042	33.7	67.1	71.6	770	42.8	68	111	89.8	82.7	Pacific Ocean Islands

Canada, the United States, Greenland, Bermuda, and St. Pierre and Miquelon.

Europe

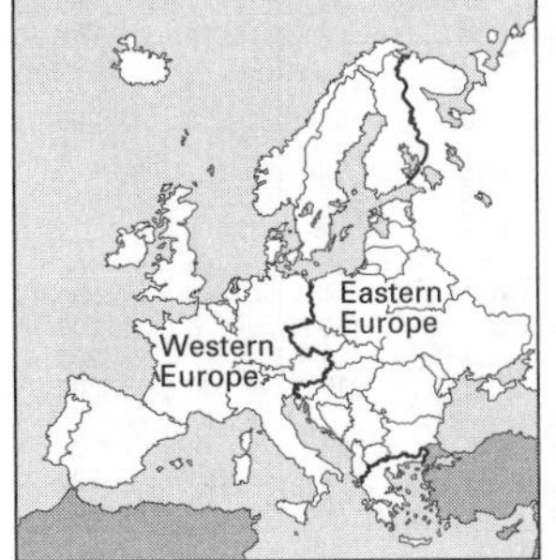

Eastern Europe

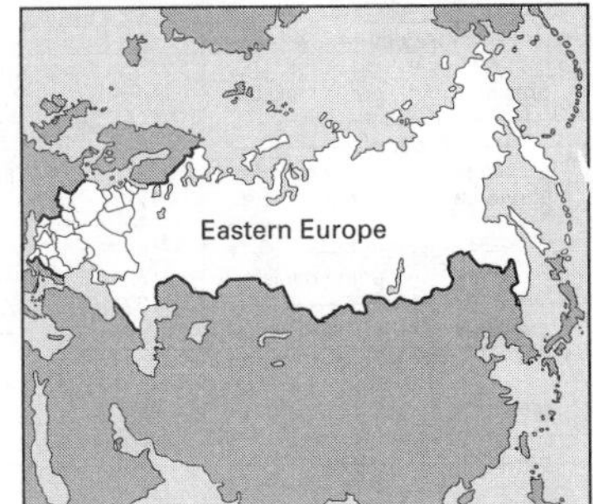

Oceania

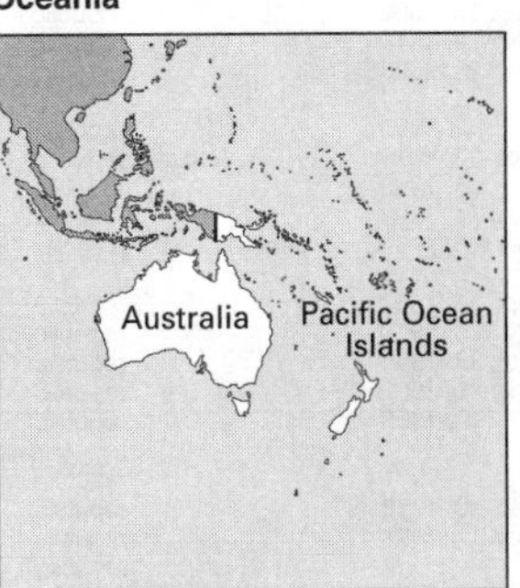

Government and international organizations

This table summarizes principal facts about the governments of the countries of the world, their branches and organs, the topmost layers of local government constituting each country's chief administrative subdivisions, and the participation of their central governments in the principal intergovernmental organizations of the world.

In this table "date of independence" may refer to a variety of circumstances. In the case of the newest countries, those that attained full independence after World War II, the date given is usually just what is implied by the heading—the date when the country, within its present borders, attained full sovereignty over both its internal and external affairs. In the case of longer established countries, the choice of a single date may be somewhat more complicated, and grounds for the use of several different dates often exist. The reader should refer to appropriate Britannica articles on national histories and relevant historical acts.

The date of the current, or last, constitution is in some ways a less complicated question, but governments sometimes do not, upon taking power, either adhere to existing constitutional forms or trouble to terminate the previous document and legitimize themselves by the installation of new constitutional forms. Often, however, the desire to legitimize extraconstitutional political activity by associating it with existing forms of long precedent leads to partial or incomplete modification, suspension, or abrogation of a constitution, so that the actual day-to-day conduct of government may be largely unrelated to the provisions of a constitution still theoretically in force. When a date in this column is given in italics, it refers to a document that has been suspended, abolished by extraconstitutional action, or modified extensively.

The characterizations adopted under "type of government" represent a compromise between the forms provided for by the national constitution and the more pragmatic language that a political scientist might adopt to describe these same systems. For an explanation of the application of these terms in the Britannica World Data, *see* the Glossary at page 501.

The positions denoted by the terms "chief of state" and "head of government" are usually those identified with those functions by the constitution. The duties of the chief of state may range from largely ceremonial responsibilities, with little or no authority over the day-to-day conduct of government, to complete executive authority as the effective head of government. In certain countries, an official of a political party or a revolutionary figure outside the constitutional structure may exercise the powers of both positions.

Membership in the legislative house(s) of each country as given here includes all elected or appointed members, as well as ex officio members (those who by virtue of some other office or title are members of the body), whether voting or nonvoting. The legislature of a country with a unicameral system is shown as the upper house in this table.

The number of administrative subdivisions for each country is listed down to the second level. In some instances, planning or statistical sub-

Government and international organizations

country	date of independence[a]	date of current or last constitution[b]	type of government	executive branch[c]		legislative branch[d]		admin. subdivisions		seaward claims	
				chief of state	head of government	upper house (members)	lower house (members)	first-order (number)	second-order (number)	territorial (nautical miles)	fishing/economic (nautical miles)
Afghanistan	Aug. 19, 1919	[1]	[2]	——president——		—	—	...	...	—	—
Albania	Nov. 28, 1912	Nov. 28, 1998	republic	president	prime minister	140	—	12	36	12	[3]
Algeria	July 5, 1962	Dec. 7, 1996[4]	republic	president	prime minister	144	389	48	553	12	[5]
American Samoa	—	July 1, 1967	territory (U.S.)	U.S. president	governor	18	20	4	14	12	200
Andorra	Dec. 6, 1288	May 4, 1993	parl. coprincipality	[7]	head of govt.	28	—	7	...	—	—
Angola	Nov. 11, 1975	Aug. 27, 1992	republic	——president[8]——		220	—	18	163	12	200
Antigua and Barbuda	Nov. 1, 1981	Nov. 1, 1981	constitutional monarchy	British monarch	prime minister	17	17[9]	30	—	12[10]	200[10]
Argentina	July 9, 1816	Aug. 24, 1994[11]	federal republic	——president[12]——		72	257	24	503	12	200
Armenia	Sept. 23, 1991	July 5, 1995	republic	president	prime minister	131	—	11	930	—	—
Aruba	—	Jan. 1, 1986	overseas territory (Neth.)	Dutch monarch	[13]	21	—	...	...	12	200
Australia	Jan. 1, 1901	July 9, 1900	federal parl. state[15]	British monarch	prime minister	76	150	8	*c.* 900	12	200
Austria	Oct. 30, 1918	Oct. 1, 1920[16]	federal state	president	chancellor	64	183	9	99	—	—
Azerbaijan	Aug. 30, 1991	Aug. 24, 2002[17]	republic	——president[8]——		125[18]	—	...	...	...	...
Bahamas, The	July 10, 1973	July 10, 1973	constitutional monarchy	British monarch	prime minister	16	40	32	80	12	200
Bahrain	Aug. 15, 1971	Feb. 14, 2002	constitutional monarchy	monarch	prime minister	40	40	...	—	12	[19]
Bangladesh	March 26, 1971	Dec. 16, 1972	republic	president	prime minister	330	—	7	64	12	200
Barbados	Nov. 30, 1966	Nov. 30, 1966	constitutional monarchy	British monarch	prime minister	21	30	—	—	12	200
Belarus	Aug. 25, 1991	Nov. 27, 1996[20]	republic	——president[8]——		62[18]	110[18]	7	118	—	—
Belgium	Oct. 4, 1830	Feb. 17, 1994	fed. const. monarchy	monarch	prime minister	71[21]	150	[22]	589	12	[23]
Belize	Sept. 21, 1981	Sept. 21, 1981	constitutional monarchy	British monarch	prime minister	8	29	[24]	...	12[25]	200
Benin	Aug. 1, 1960	Dec. 2, 1990	republic	——president——		83	—	12	77	200	200
Bermuda	—	June 8, 1968	dependent territory (U.K.)	British monarch	[26]	11	36	11	—	12	200
Bhutan	March 24, 1910	—	[27]	monarch	chairman CM	150	—	20	196	—	—
Bolivia	Aug. 6, 1825	Feb. 2, 1967	republic	——president——		27	130	9	112	—	—
Bosnia and Herzegovina	March 3, 1992	Dec. 14, 1995[28]	federal republic	[29]	chairman CM	15	42	2	10[30]	...	...
Botswana	Sept. 30, 1966	Sept. 30, 1966	republic	——president——		15[31]	47	16	...	—	—
Brazil	Sept. 7, 1822	Oct. 5, 1988[16]	federal republic	——president——		81	513	27	5,561	12	200
Brunei	Jan. 1, 1984	*Sept. 29, 1959*[32]	monarchy (sultanate)	——sultan——		21[31]	—	4	38	12	200
Bulgaria	Oct. 5, 1908	July 12, 1991	republic	president	prime minister	240	—	28	259	12	200
Burkina Faso	Aug. 5, 1960	June 11, 1991	republic	president	prime minister	178[31]	111	45	382	—	—
Burundi	July 1, 1962	July 23, 2001[33]	republic[2]	——president[34]——		178	—	17	116	—	—
Cambodia	Nov. 9, 1953	March 4, 1999[35]	constitutional monarchy	king	prime minister	61	123	24	183	12	200
Cameroon	Jan. 1, 1960	Jan. 18, 1996	republic	president	prime minister	180	—	10	58	...	...
Canada	July 1, 1867	April 17, 1982	federal parl. state[15]	Canadian GG[36]	prime minister	105	301	13	...	12	200
Cape Verde	July 5, 1975	Sept. 25, 1992	republic	president	prime minister	72	—	17	...	12[10]	200[10]
Central African Republic	Aug. 13, 1960	*Jan. 14, 1995*	military regime	——president[8]——		63	—	17	69	—	—
Chad	Aug. 11, 1960	April 14, 1996	republic	president	prime minister	155	—	29	...	—	—
Chile	Sept. 18, 1810	March 11, 1981	republic	——president——		48	120	13	51	12	200
China	1523 BC	Dec. 4, 1982	people's republic	president	premier SC	2,916	—	31	332	12	200
Colombia	July 20, 1810	July 5, 1991	republic	——president——		102	166	33	1,097	12	200
Comoros	July 6, 1975	June 5, 2002[37]	federal republic[38]	——president[39]——		...	...	3	...	12[10]	200[10]
Congo, Dem. Rep. of the	June 30, 1960	April 15, 2003[40]	republic[2]	——president[39]——		120	500	11	...	12	...
Congo, Rep. of the	Aug. 15, 1960	Aug. 10, 2002	republic	——president——		66[18]	137[18]	16	47	200	[3]
Costa Rica	Sept. 15, 1821	Nov. 9, 1949	republic	——president——		57	—	7	81	12	200
Côte d'Ivoire	Aug. 7, 1960	July 23, 2000	republic	——president[8]——		225	—	19	...	12	200
Croatia	June 25, 1991	Dec. 22, 1990	republic	president	prime minister	140[41]	—	21	123	12	...
Cuba	May 20, 1902	Feb. 24, 1976	socialist republic	——president——		609	—	15	169	12	200
Cyprus[43]	Aug. 16, 1960	Aug. 16, 1960	republic	——president——		56[44]	—	...	647	12	...
Czech Republic	Jan. 1, 1993	Jan. 1, 1993	republic	president	prime minister	81	200	14	76	—	—
Denmark	*c.* 800	June 5, 1953	constitutional monarchy	monarch	prime minister	179	—	16	275	12	200
Djibouti	June 27, 1977	Sept. 15, 1992	republic	——president——		65	—	5	...	12	200
Dominica	Nov. 3, 1978	Nov. 3, 1978	republic	president	prime minister	32	—	37	—	12	200
Dominican Republic	Feb. 27, 1844	Nov. 28, 1966	republic	——president——		32	150	32	160	6	200
East Timor	May 20, 2002	May 20, 2002	republic	president	prime minister	88	—	4	13	12	200
Ecuador	May 24, 1822	Aug. 10, 1998	republic	——president——		125	—	22	216	200	200
Egypt	Feb. 28, 1922	Sept. 11, 1971	republic	president	prime minister	454	—	27	186	12[46]	...
El Salvador	Jan. 30, 1841	Dec. 20, 1983	republic	——president——		84	—	14	262	200	200
Equatorial Guinea	Oct. 12, 1968	Nov. 17, 1991	republic	president	prime minister	80	—	7	18	12	200
Eritrea	May 24, 1993	[47]	republic[2]	——president——		150	—	6	...	12	[48]
Estonia	Feb. 24, 1918	July 3, 1992	republic	president	prime minister	101	—	15	46	12[49]	[49]

divisions may be substituted when administrative subdivisions do not exist.

Finally, in the second half of the table are listed the memberships each country maintains in the principal international intergovernmental organizations of the world. This part of the table may also be utilized to provide a complete membership list for each of these organizations as of Dec. 1, 2003.

Notes for the column headings

a. The date may also be either that of the organization of the present form of government or the inception of the present administrative structure (federation, confederation, union, etc.).
b. Constitutions whose dates are in italic type had been wholly or substantially suspended or abolished as of late 2003.
c. For abbreviations used in this column see the list on the facing page.
d. When a legislative body has been adjourned or otherwise suspended, figures in parentheses indicate the number of members in the legislative body as provided for in constitution or law.
e. States contributing funds to or receiving aid from UNICEF in 1997.
f. 15 nations with judicial representation in ICJ in 2003.

International organizations, conventions

ACP	African, Caribbean, and Pacific (Cotonou Agreement) states
ADB	Asian Development Bank
APEC	Asia-Pacific Economic Co-operation
AU	African Union
CARICOM	Caribbean Community and Common Market
ECOWAS	Economic Community of West African States
EU	The European Union
FAO	Food and Agriculture Org.
FZ	The Franc Zone
GCC	Gulf Cooperation Council
I-ADB	Inter-American Development Bank
IAEA	International Atomic Energy Agency
IBRD	International Bank for Reconstruction and Development
ICAO	International Civil Aviation Org.
ICJ	International Court of Justice
IDA	International Development Association
IDB	Islamic Development Bank
IFC	International Finance Corporation
ILO	International Labour Org.
IMF	International Monetary Fund
IMO	International Maritime Org.
ITU	International Telecommunication Union
LAS	League of Arab States (Arab League)
OAS	Organization of American States
OPEC	Organization of the Petroleum Exporting Countries
PC	Pacific Community
UNCTAD	United Nations Conference on Trade and Development
UNESCO	United Nations Educational Scientific and Cultural Org.
UNICEF	United Nations Children's Fund
UNIDO	United Nations Industrial Development Org.
UPU	Universal Postal Union
WHO	World Health Org.
WIPO	World Intellectual Property Org.
WMO	World Meteorological Org.
WTO	World Trade Org.

Abbreviations used in the executive-branch column

CM	Council of Ministers
FC	Federal Council
GG	Governor-General
GPC	General People's Committee
NDC	National Defense Commission
NTG	National Transitional Government
PC	People's Council
PNA	Palestine National Authority
SC	State Council
SPDC	State Peace and Development Council

membership in international organizations																																					country
United Nations (date of admission)	UN organs★ and affiliated intergovernmental organizations																				The Commonwealth	regional multipurpose						economic									
	UNCTAD★	UNICEF★e	ICJ★f	FAO	IAEA	IBRD	ICAO	IDA	IFC	ILO	IMF	IMO	ITU	UNESCO	UNIDO	UPU	WHO	WIPO	WMO	WTO		AU	EU	GCC	LAS	OAS	PC	ACP	ADB	APEC	CARICOM	ECOWAS	FZ	I-ADB	IDB	OPEC	
1946	●	●		●	●	●	●	●	●	●	●		●	●	●	●	●		●										●						●		Afghanistan
1955	●	●		●	●	●	●	●	●	●	●	●	●	●	●	●	●	●	●	●															●		Albania
1962	●	●		●	●	●	●	●	●	●	●	●	●	●	●	●	●	●	●	6		●			●										●	●	Algeria
—													●			●											●										American Samoa
1993	●						●						●	●			●	●	●	6																	Andorra
1976	●	●		●	●	●	●	●	●	●	●	●	●	●	●	●	●	●	●	●		●						●									Angola
1981	●	●		●		●	●		●	●	●	●	●	●		●	●	●	●	●	●					●		●			●						Antigua and Barbuda
1945	●	●		●	●	●	●	●	●	●	●	●	●	●	●	●	●	●	●	●						●								●			Argentina
1992	●	●		●	●	●	●	●	●	●	●		●	●	●	●	●	●	●	●																	Armenia
—											●			14		●			●																		Aruba
1945	●	●		●	●	●	●	●	●	●	●	●	●	●		●	●	●	●	●	●						●		●	●							Australia
1955	●	●		●	●	●	●	●	●	●	●	●	●	●	●	●	●	●	●	●			●						●					●			Austria
1992	●	●		●	●	●	●	●	●	●	●	●	●	●	●	●	●	●	●	6									●						●		Azerbaijan
1973	●	●		●		●	●		●	●	●	●	●	●	●	●	●	●	●	6	●					●		●			●			●			Bahamas, The
1971	●	●		●		●	●		●	●	●	●	●	●	●	●	●	●	●	●				●	●										●		Bahrain
1974	●	●		●	●	●	●	●	●	●	●	●	●	●	●	●	●	●	●	●	●								●						●		Bangladesh
1966	●	●		●		●	●	●	●	●	●	●	●	●	●	●	●	●	●	●	●					●		●			●			●			Barbados
1945	●	●			●	●	●		●	●	●		●	●	●	●	●	●	●	6																	Belarus
1945	●	●		●	●	●	●	●	●	●	●	●	●	●	●	●	●	●	●	●			●						●					●			Belgium
1981	●	●		●		●	●	●	●	●	●	●	●	●	●	●	●	●	●	●	●					●		●			●			●			Belize
1960	●	●		●	●	●	●	●	●	●	●	●	●	●	●	●	●	●	●	●		●						●				●	●		●		Benin
—													●			●			●												14						Bermuda
1971	●	●		●		●	●	●			●		●	●	●	●	●	●		6									●								Bhutan
1945	●	●		●	●	●	●	●	●	●	●	●	●	●	●	●	●	●	●	●						●								●			Bolivia
1992	●	●		●	●	●	●	●	●	●	●	●	●	●	●	●	●	●	●	6																	Bosnia and Herzegovina
1966	●	●		●	●	●	●	●	●	●	●		●	●	●	●	●	●	●	●	●	●						●									Botswana
1945	●	●	●	●	●	●	●	●	●	●	●	●	●	●	●	●	●	●	●	●						●								●			Brazil
1984	●					●	●				●	●	●			●	●	●	●	●	●									●					●		Brunei
1955	●	●		●	●	●	●		●	●	●	●	●	●	●	●	●	●	●	●																	Bulgaria
1960	●	●		●	●	●	●	●	●	●	●		●	●	●	●	●	●	●	●		●						●				●	●		●		Burkina Faso
1962	●	●		●		●	●	●	●	●	●		●	●	●	●	●	●	●	●		●						●									Burundi
1955	●	●		●		●	●	●	●	●	●	●	●	●	●	●	●	●	●	●									●								Cambodia
1960	●	●		●	●	●	●	●	●	●	●	●	●	●	●	●	●	●	●	●	●	●						●					●		●		Cameroon
1945	●	●		●	●	●	●	●	●	●	●	●	●	●		●	●	●	●	●	●					●			●	●				●			Canada
1975	●	●		●		●	●	●	●	●	●	●	●	●	●	●	●	●	●	6		●						●				●					Cape Verde
1960	●	●		●	●	●	●	●	●	●	●		●	●	●	●	●	●	●	●		●						●					●				Central African Republic
1960	●	●		●		●	●	●	●	●	●		●	●	●	●	●	●	●	●		●						●					●		●		Chad
1945	●	●		●	●	●	●	●	●	●	●	●	●	●	●	●	●	●	●	●						●				●				●			Chile
1945	●	●	●	●	●	●	●	●	●	●	●	●	●	●	●	●	●	●	●	●									●	●							China
1945	●	●		●	●	●	●	●	●	●	●	●	●	●	●	●	●	●	●	●						●								●			Colombia
1975	●	●		●		●	●	●	●	●	●	●	●	●	●	●	●		●			●			●			●					●		●		Comoros
1960	●	●		●	●	●	●	●	●	●	●	●	●	●	●	●	●	●	●	●		●						●									Congo, Dem. Rep. of the
1960	●	●		●		●	●	●	●	●	●	●	●	●	●	●	●	●	●	●		●						●					●				Congo, Rep. of the
1945	●	●		●	●	●	●	●	●	●	●	●	●	●	●	●	●	●	●	●						●								●			Costa Rica
1960	●	●		●	●	●	●	●	●	●	●	●	●	●	●	●	●	●	●	●		●						●				●	●				Côte d'Ivoire
1992	●	●		●	●	●	●	●	●	●	●	●	●	●	●	●	●	●	●	●														●			Croatia
1945	●	●		●	●		●			●		●	●	●	●	●	●	●	●	●						42											Cuba
1960	●	●		●	●	●	●	●	●	●	●	●	●	●	●	●	●	●	●	●	●		45														Cyprus[43]
1993	●	●		●	●	●	●	●	●	●	●	●	●	●	●	●	●	●	●	●			45														Czech Republic
1945	●	●		●	●	●	●	●	●	●	●	●	●	●	●	●	●	●	●	●			●						●					●			Denmark
1977	●	●				●	●	●	●	●	●	●	●	●	●	●	●	●	●	●		●			●			●							●		Djibouti
1978	●	●		●		●		●	●	●	●	●	●	●	●	●	●	●	●	●	●					●		●			●						Dominica
1945	●	●		●	●	●	●	●	●	●	●	●	●	●	●	●	●	●	●	●						●		●						●			Dominican Republic
2002						●		●		●	●			●	●		●											●	●								East Timor
1945	●	●		●	●	●	●	●	●	●	●	●	●	●	●	●	●	●	●	●						●								●			Ecuador
1945	●	●	●	●	●	●	●	●	●	●	●	●	●	●	●	●	●	●	●	●		●			●										●		Egypt
1945	●	●		●	●	●	●	●	●	●	●	●	●	●	●	●	●	●	●	●						●								●			El Salvador
1968	●	●		●		●	●	●	●	●	●	●	●	●	●	●	●	●				●						●					●				Equatorial Guinea
1993	●	●		●	●	●	●	●	●	●	●	●	●	●	●	●	●	●	●			●						●									Eritrea
1991	●	●		●	●	●	●		●	●	●	●	●	●	●	●	●	●	●	●			45														Estonia

Government and international organizations (continued)

country	date of independence[a]	date of current or last constitution[b]	type of government	executive branch[c]		legislative branch[d]		admin. subdivisions		seaward claims	
				chief of state	head of government	upper house (members)	lower house (members)	first-order (number)	second-order (number)	territorial (nautical miles)	fishing/economic (nautical miles)
Ethiopia	*c.* 1000 BC	Aug. 22, 1995	federal republic	president	prime minister	108	546	11	57	—	—
Faroe Islands	—	April 1, 1948	part of Danish realm	Danish monarch	[50]	32	—	9	48	...	200[51]
Fiji	Oct. 10, 1970	July 27, 1998	republic	president	prime minister	32	72	4	15	12[10]	200[10]
Finland	Dec. 6, 1917	March 1, 2000	republic	president	prime minister	200	—	6	19	12[52]	[49]
France	August 843	Oct. 4, 1958[16]	republic	president	prime minister	321	577	22	96	12	200
French Guiana	—	Feb. 28, 1983	overseas dept. (Fr.)	French president	[53]	19	31	2	22	12	200
French Polynesia	—	Sept. 6, 1984	overseas territory (Fr.)[54]	French president	[55]	49	—	5	48	12	200
Gabon	Aug. 17, 1960	March 26, 1991	republic	president	prime minister	91	120	9	37	12	200
Gambia, The	Feb. 18, 1965	Jan. 16, 1997	republic	president		53	—	8	45	12	200
Gaza Strip	—	May 4, 1994[56]	interim authority	chairman PNA[8]		89	—	5	...	...	...
Georgia	April 9, 1991	Oct. 17, 1995	republic	president[58]		235	—	12	74	...	...
Germany	May 5, 1955	May 23, 1949	federal republic	president	chancellor	69	603	16	32	12[51]	...
Ghana	March 6, 1957	Jan. 7, 1993	republic	president		200	—	10	110	12	200
Greece	Feb. 3, 1830	April 6, 2001[59]	republic	president	prime minister	300	—	55	1,033	6/10	[3]
Greenland	—	May 1, 1979	part of Danish realm	Danish monarch	[50]	31	—	18	...	3	200
Grenada	Feb. 7, 1974	Feb. 7, 1974	constitutional monarchy	British monarch	prime minister	13	15	9	...	12	200
Guadeloupe	—	Feb. 28, 1983	overseas dept. (Fr.)	French president	[53]	42	41	3	34	12	200
Guam	—	Aug. 1, 1950	territory (U.S.)	U.S. president	governor	15	—	...	—	12	200
Guatemala	Sept. 15, 1821	Jan. 14, 1986	republic	president		158	—	22	313	12	200
Guernsey	—	Jan. 1, 1949[16]	crown dependency (U.K.)	British monarch[60]	[61]	59	—	2	10	3	12
Guinea	Oct. 2, 1958	Dec. 23, 1990[40]	republic	president[8]		114	—	8	34	12	200
Guinea-Bissau	Sept. 10, 1974	*May 11, 1991*	military regime[2]	president[8]		56	—	9	37	12	200
Guyana	May 26, 1966	Oct. 6, 1980	cooperative republic	president		65	—	10	71	12	200
Haiti	Jan. 1, 1804	March 29, 1987	republic	president	prime minister	27	83	9	41	12	200
Honduras	Nov. 5, 1838	Jan. 20, 1982	republic	president		128	—	18	298	12	200
Hong Kong	—	July 1, 1997	[62]	Chinese president	chief executive	60	—	18	298	12	[3]
Hungary	Nov. 16, 1918	Aug. 20, 1949[63]	republic	president	prime minister	386	—	20	195	—	—
Iceland	June 17, 1944	June 17, 1944	republic	president	prime minister	63	—	8	122	12	200
India	Aug. 15, 1947	Jan. 26, 1950	federal republic	president	prime minister	245	545	35	593	12	200
Indonesia	Aug. 17, 1945	Aug. 17, 1945	republic	president		700	500	31	...	12[10]	200[10]
Iran	Oct. 7, 1906	Dec. 2–3, 1979	Islamic republic	president[64]		290	—	28	299	12	50[65]
Iraq	Oct. 3, 1932	Oct. 16, 2003[66]	[67]	civil administrator[68]		—	—	...	...	12	[3]
Ireland	Dec. 6, 1921	Dec. 29, 1937	republic	president	prime minister	60	166	34	86	12	200
Isle of Man	—	1961[16]	crown dependency (U.K.)	British monarch[60]	chief minister	11	24	24	—	12[69]	...
Israel	May 14, 1948	June 1950[16]	republic	president	prime minister	120	—	6	15	12	[3]
Italy	March 17, 1861	Jan. 1, 1948	republic	president	prime minister	321	630	20	103	12	[3]
Jamaica	Aug. 6, 1962	Aug. 6, 1962	constitutional monarchy	British monarch	prime minister	21	60	13	—	12	200
Japan	*c.* 660 BC	May 3, 1947	constitutional monarchy	[70]	prime minister	247	480	47	3,230	12[71]	200
Jersey	—	Jan. 1, 1949[16]	crown dependency (U.K.)	British monarch[60]	[72]	57	—	12	—	12	...
Jordan	May 25, 1946	Jan. 8, 1952	constitutional monarchy	king[8]		40	110	12	18	3	[3]
Kazakhstan	Dec. 16, 1991	Sept. 6, 1995	republic	president[8]		39	77	16	160	—	—
Kenya	Dec. 12, 1963	Dec. 12, 1963	republic	president		224	—	8	...	12	200
Kiribati	July 12, 1979	July 12, 1979	republic	president		42	—	...	...	12[10]	200[10]
Korea, North	Sept. 9, 1948	Sept. 5, 1998[73]	socialist republic	chairman NDC		687	—	14	172	12	200
Korea, South	Aug. 15, 1948	Feb. 25, 1988	republic	president[8]		273	—	16	195	12	200
Kuwait	June 19, 1961	Nov. 16, 1962	const. mon. (emirate)	emir[8]		50[74]	—	6	...	12	[3]
Kyrgyzstan	Aug. 31, 1991	May 5, 1993	republic	president[8]		45	60	8	42	—	—
Laos	Oct. 23, 1953	Aug. 15, 1991	republic	president	prime minister	109	—	18	133	—	—
Latvia	Nov. 18, 1918	Nov. 7, 1922	republic	president	prime minister	100	—	33	70	12	[75]
Lebanon	Nov. 26, 1941	Sept. 21, 1990	republic	president	prime minister	128	—	6	...	12	[3]
Lesotho	Oct. 4, 1966	April 2, 1993	constitutional monarchy	king	prime minister	33[31]	120	10	...	—	—
Liberia	July 26, 1847	Aug. 18, 2003[76]	republic	chairman NTG		...	...	15	...	200	[3]
Libya	Dec. 24, 1951	March 2, 1977	socialist state[77]	leader[78]	sec. GPC	760	—	25	...	12	[3]
Liechtenstein	July 12, 1806	Oct. 5, 1921[79]	constitutional monarchy	prince	head of govt.	25	—	11	—	—	—
Lithuania	Feb. 16, 1918	Nov. 6, 1992	republic	president	prime minister	141	—	10	60	12	...
Luxembourg	May 10, 1867	Oct. 17, 1868	constitutional monarchy	grand duke	prime minister	21[31]	60	3	12	—	—
Macau	—	Dec. 20, 1999	[62]	Chinese president	chief executive	27	—	8	...	...	...
Macedonia	Nov. 17, 1991	Nov. 16, 2001[80]	republic	president	prime minister	120	—	123	...	—	—
Madagascar	June 26, 1960	April 8, 1998	federal republic	president[8]		90	160	6	28	12	200
Malawi	July 6, 1964	May 18, 1994	republic	president		192	—	3	27	—	—
Malaysia	Aug. 31, 1957	Aug. 31, 1957	fed. const. monarchy	paramount ruler	prime minister	70	193	16	137	12	200
Maldives	July 26, 1965	Jan. 1, 1998	republic	president		42[74]	—	21	201	12[10]	200
Mali	Sept. 22, 1960	Feb. 25, 1992	republic	president	prime minister	147	—	9	49	—	—
Malta	Sept. 21, 1964	Dec. 13, 1974	republic	president	prime minister	65	—	1	68	12	25
Marshall Islands	Dec. 22, 1990	May 1, 1979	republic	president		12[31]	33	...	—	12[10]	200
Martinique	—	Feb. 28, 1983	overseas dept. (Fr.)	French president	[53]	45	41	4	34	12	200
Mauritania	Nov. 28, 1960	July 21, 1991	republic	president[8]		56	81	13	53	12	200
Mauritius	March 12, 1968	March 12, 1992	republic	president	prime minister	70	—	11	130	12	200
Mayotte	—	July 11, 2001	dept. collectivity (Fr.)	French president	[81]	19	—	17	—	12	200
Mexico	Sept. 16, 1810	Feb. 5, 1917	federal republic	president		128	500	32	2,445	12	200
Micronesia	Dec. 22, 1990	Jan. 1, 1981	federal republic	president		14	—	4	74	12	200
Moldova	Aug. 27, 1991	Aug. 27, 1994	parliamentary republic	president	prime minister	101	—	13	...	—	—
Monaco	Feb. 2, 1861	Dec. 17, 1962	constitutional monarchy	prince	min. of state[82]	24	—	—	—	12	[3]
Mongolia	March 13, 1921	Feb. 12, 1992	republic	president	prime minister	76	—	22	340	—	—
Morocco	March 2, 1956	Oct. 7, 1996	constitutional monarchy	king[8]		270	325	17[83]	71[83]	12	200
Mozambique	June 25, 1975	Nov. 30, 1990	republic	president		250	—	11	112	12	200
Myanmar (Burma)	Jan. 4, 1948	*Jan. 4, 1974*	republic	chairman SPDC[8]		(492)	—	14	58	12	200
Namibia	March 21, 1990	March 21, 1990	republic	president		26	72[74]	13	—	12	200
Nauru	Jan. 31, 1968	Jan. 31, 1968	republic	president		18	—	1	—	12	200
Nepal	Nov. 13, 1769	Nov. 9, 1990	constitutional monarchy	king	prime minister	(60)	(205)	5[85]	75	—	—
Netherlands, The	March 30, 1814	Feb. 17, 1983	constitutional monarchy	monarch	prime minister	75	150	12	489	12	[23]
Netherlands Antilles	—	Dec. 29, 1954	overseas territory (Neth.)	Dutch monarch	[13]	22	—	5	—	12	200
New Caledonia	—	March 19, 2003	overseas collectivity (Fr.)	French president[86]	president	54	—	3	33	12	200
New Zealand	Sept. 26, 1907	June 30, 1852[16]	constitutional monarchy	British monarch	prime minister	120	—	12	74	12	200
Nicaragua	April 30, 1838	Jan. 9, 1987	republic	president		92	—	17	151	12	200

membership in international organizations

United Nations (date of admission)	UN organs★ and affiliated intergovernmental organizations																				The Commonwealth	regional multipurpose						economic									country
	UNCTAD★	UNICEF★[e]	ICJ★[f]	FAO	IAEA	IBRD	ICAO	IDA	IFC	ILO	IMF	IMO	ITU	UNESCO	UNIDO	UPU	WHO	WIPO	WMO	WTO		AU	EU	GCC	LAS	OAS	PC	ACP	ADB	APEC	CARICOM	ECOWAS	FZ	I-ADB	IDB	OPEC	
1945	●	●		●	●	●	●	●	●	●	●	●	●	●	●	●	●	●	●			●						●									Ethiopia
—												14				●																					Faroe Islands
1970	●	●		●		●	●	●	●	●	●	●	●	●	●	●	●	●	●	●	●						●	●	●								Fiji
1955	●	●		●	●	●	●	●	●	●	●	●	●	●	●	●	●	●	●	●			●						●					●			Finland
1945	●	●	●	●	●	●	●	●	●	●	●	●	●	●	●	●	●	●	●	●			●				●		●				●	●			France
—													●			●																	●				French Guiana
—													●			●			●								●						●				French Polynesia
1960	●	●		●	●	●	●	●	●	●	●	●	●	●	●	●	●	●	●	●		●						●					●				Gabon
1965	●	●		●		●	●	●	●	●	●	●	●	●	●	●	●	●	●	●	●	●						●				●			●		Gambia, The
—		●														●									●[57]										●[57]		Gaza Strip
1992	●	●		●	●	●	●	●	●	●	●	●	●	●	●	●	●	●	●	●																	Georgia
1973	●	●	●	●	●	●	●	●	●	●	●	●	●	●	●	●	●	●	●	●			●						●					●			Germany
1957	●	●		●	●	●	●	●	●	●	●	●	●	●	●	●	●	●	●	●	●	●						●				●					Ghana
1945	●	●		●	●	●	●	●	●	●	●	●	●	●	●	●	●	●	●	●			●														Greece
—																●																					Greenland
1974	●	●		●		●	●	●	●	●	●	●	●	●	●	●	●	●		●	●					●		●			●						Grenada
—													●			●																	●				Guadeloupe
—													●			●											●										Guam
1945	●	●		●	●	●	●	●	●	●	●	●	●	●	●	●	●	●	●	●						●								●			Guatemala
—													●			●																					Guernsey
1958	●	●		●		●	●	●	●	●	●	●	●	●	●	●	●	●	●	●		●						●				●			●		Guinea
1974	●	●		●		●	●	●	●	●	●	●	●	●	●	●	●	●	●	●		●						●				●	●		●		Guinea-Bissau
1966	●	●		●		●	●	●	●	●	●	●	●	●	●	●	●	●	●	●	●					●		●			●			●			Guyana
1945	●	●		●	●	●	●	●	●	●	●	●	●	●	●	●	●	●	●	●						●		●			●			●			Haiti
1945	●	●		●	●	●	●	●	●	●	●	●	●	●	●	●	●	●	●	●						●								●			Honduras
—		●									●	14		●		●			●	●									●	●							Hong Kong
1955	●	●		●	●	●	●	●	●	●	●	●	●	●	●	●	●	●	●	●			45														Hungary
1946	●	●		●	●	●	●	●	●	●	●	●	●	●		●	●	●	●	●																	Iceland
1945	●	●		●	●	●	●	●	●	●	●	●	●	●	●	●	●	●	●	●	●								●								India
1950	●	●		●	●	●	●	●	●	●	●	●	●	●	●	●	●	●	●	●									●	●					●	●	Indonesia
1945	●	●		●	●	●	●	●	●	●	●	●	●	●	●	●	●	●	●																●	●	Iran
1945	●	●		●	●	●	●	●	●	●	●	●	●	●	●	●	●	●	●						●										●	●	Iraq
1955	●	●		●	●	●	●	●	●	●	●	●	●	●	●	●	●	●	●	●			●														Ireland
—													●			●																					Isle of Man
1949	●	●		●	●	●	●	●	●	●	●	●	●	●	●	●	●	●	●	●														●			Israel
1955	●	●		●	●	●	●	●	●	●	●	●	●	●	●	●	●	●	●	●			●						●					●			Italy
1962	●	●		●	●	●	●		●	●	●	●	●	●	●	●	●	●	●	●	●					●		●			●			●			Jamaica
1956	●	●	●	●	●	●	●	●	●	●	●	●	●	●	●	●	●	●	●	●									●	●				●			Japan
—													●			●																					Jersey
1955	●	●	●	●	●	●	●	●	●	●	●	●	●	●	●	●	●	●	●	●					●										●		Jordan
1992	●	●		●	●	●	●	●	●	●	●	●	●	●	●	●	●	●	●	6									●						●		Kazakhstan
1963	●	●		●	●	●	●	●	●	●	●	●	●	●	●	●	●	●	●	●	●	●						●									Kenya
1999	●	●		●		●	●	●	●		●	●	●	●		●	●				●						●	●	●								Kiribati
1991	●	●		●			●					●	●	●	●	●	●	●	●																		Korea, North
1991	●	●		●	●	●	●	●	●	●	●	●	●	●	●	●	●	●	●	●									●	●							Korea, South
1963	●	●		●	●	●	●	●	●	●	●	●	●	●	●	●	●	●	●	●				●	●										●	●	Kuwait
1992	●	●		●	●	●	●	●	●	●	●		●	●	●	●	●	●	●	●									●						●		Kyrgyzstan
1955	●	●		●		●	●	●	●	●	●		●	●	●	●	●	●	●	6									●								Laos
1991	●	●		●	●	●	●	●	●	●	●	●	●	●		●	●	●	●	●			45														Latvia
1945	●	●		●	●	●	●	●	●	●	●	●	●	●	●	●	●	●	●	6					●										●		Lebanon
1966	●	●		●		●	●	●	●	●	●		●	●	●	●	●	●	●	●	●	●						●									Lesotho
1945	●	●		●	●	●	●	●	●	●	●	●	●	●	●	●	●	●	●			●						●				●					Liberia
1955	●	●		●	●	●	●	●	●	●	●	●	●	●	●	●	●	●	●						●										●	●	Libya
1990	●				●								●			●	●	●		●																	Liechtenstein
1991	●	●		●	●	●	●		●	●	●	●	●	●	●	●	●	●	●	●			45														Lithuania
1945	●	●		●	●	●	●	●	●	●	●	●	●	●	●	●	●	●	●	●			●														Luxembourg
—				●							●	14		14		●			●	●																	Macau
1993	●	●		●	●	●	●	●	●	●	●	●	●	●	●	●	●	●	●	●																	Macedonia
1960	●	●	●	●	●	●	●	●	●	●	●	●	●	●	●	●	●	●	●	●		●						●									Madagascar
1964	●	●		●		●	●	●	●	●	●	●	●	●	●	●	●	●	●	●	●	●						●									Malawi
1957	●	●		●	●	●	●	●	●	●	●	●	●	●	●	●	●	●	●	●	●								●	●					●		Malaysia
1965	●	●		●		●	●	●	●		●	●	●	●	●	●	●		●	●	●								●						●		Maldives
1960	●	●		●	●	●	●	●	●	●	●		●	●	●	●	●	●	●	●		●						●				●	●		●		Mali
1964	●	●		●	●	●	●			●	●	●	●	●	●	●	●	●	●	●	●		45														Malta
1991	●	●		●	●	●	●	●	●		●	●	●	●			●										●	●	●								Marshall Islands
—													●			●																	●				Martinique
1961	●	●		●		●	●	●	●	●	●	●	●	●	●	●	●	●	●	●		●			●			●							●		Mauritania
1968	●	●		●	●	●	●	●	●	●	●	●	●	●	●	●	●	●	●	●	●	●						●									Mauritius
—													●			●																	●				Mayotte
1945	●	●		●	●	●	●	●	●	●	●	●	●	●	●	●	●	●	●	●						●				●				●			Mexico
1991	●	●				●	●	●	●		●		●	●			●		●								●	●	●								Micronesia
1992	●	●		●	●	●	●	●	●	●	●	●	●	●	●	●	●	●	●	●																	Moldova
1993	●	●			●		●					●	●	●	●	●	●	●																			Monaco
1961	●	●		●	●	●	●	●	●	●	●	●	●	●	●	●	●	●	●	●									●								Mongolia
1956	●	●		●	●	●	●	●	●	●	●	●	●	●	●	●	●	●	●	●					●										●		Morocco
1975	●	●		●		●	●	●	●	●	●	●	●	●	●	●	●	●	●	●	●	●						●							●		Mozambique
1948	●	●		●	●	●	●	●	●	84	●	●	●	●	●	●	●	●	●	●									●								Myanmar (Burma)
1990	●	●		●	●	●	●		●	●	●	●	●	●	●	●	●	●	●	●	●	●						●									Namibia
1999				●			●						●	●		●	●				●						●	●	●								Nauru
1955	●	●		●		●	●	●	●	●	●	●	●	●	●	●	●	●	●	●									●								Nepal
1945	●	●	●	●	●	●	●	●	●	●	●	●	●	●	●	●	●	●	●	●			●						●					●			Netherlands, The
—											●			14		●			●																		Netherlands Antilles
—													●			●			●								●						●				New Caledonia
1945	●	●		●	●	●	●	●	●	●	●	●	●	●	●	●	●	●	●	●	●						●		●	●							New Zealand
1945	●	●		●	●	●	●	●	●	●	●	●	●	●	●	●	●	●	●	●						●								●			Nicaragua

Government and international organizations (continued)

country	date of independence[a]	date of current or last constitution[b]	type of government	executive branch[c]		legislative branch[d]		admin. subdivisions		seaward claims	
				chief of state	head of government	upper house (members)	lower house (members)	first-order (number)	second-order (number)	territorial (nautical miles)	fishing/economic (nautical miles)
Niger	Aug. 3, 1960	Aug. 9, 1999	republic	—president[8]—		83	—	8	35	—	—
Nigeria	Oct. 1, 1960	May 5, 1999	federal republic	—president—		109	360	37	768	12	200
Northern Mariana Is.	—	Jan. 9, 1978	commonwealth (U.S.)	U.S. president	governor	9	18	4	—	12	200
Norway	June 7, 1905	May 17, 1814	constitutional monarchy	king	prime minister	165	—	19	439	4	200
Oman	Dec. 20, 1951	Nov. 6, 1996[87]	monarchy (sultanate)	—sultan—		—[88]—		8	60	12	200
Pakistan	Aug. 14, 1947	Aug. 14, 1973	republic	—president[8]—		100	342	5	28	12	200
Palau	Oct. 1, 1994	Jan. 1, 1981	republic	—president—		14	16	16	—	3	200
Panama	Nov. 3, 1903	May 20, 1983[35]	republic	—president[39]—		71	—	14	75	12	200
Papua New Guinea	Sept. 16, 1975	Sept. 16, 1975	constitutional monarchy	British monarch	prime minister	109	—	20	267	3/12	200[10]
Paraguay	May 14, 1811	June 22, 1992	republic	—president—		46	80	18	235	—	—
Peru	July 28, 1821	Dec. 29, 1993	republic	—president[8]—		120	—	25	194	200	200
Philippines	July 4, 1946	Feb. 11, 1987	republic	—president—		24	214	18	79	[89]	200[10]
Poland	Nov. 10, 1918	Oct. 17, 1997	republic	president	prime minister	100	460	16	373	12	...
Portugal	*c.* 1140	April 25, 1976	republic	president	prime minister	230	—	7	308	12	200
Puerto Rico	—	July 25, 1952	commonwealth (U.S.)	U.S. president	governor	27[90]	51[90]	78	—	12	200
Qatar	Sept. 3, 1971	April 29, 2003[91]	constitutional emirate[92]	—emir[8]—		...	...	9	—	12	...
Réunion	—	Feb. 28, 1983	overseas dept. (Fr.)	French president	[53]	47	45	4	24	12	200
Romania	May 21, 1877	Dec. 13, 1991	republic	president	prime minister	143	345	42	2,687	12[46]	200[46]
Russia	Dec. 8, 1991	Dec. 24, 1993	federal republic	president	prime minister	178	450	7	89	12	200
Rwanda	July 1, 1962	June 4, 2003	republic	—president[8]—		26	80	12	105	—	—
St. Kitts and Nevis	Sept. 19, 1983	Sept. 19, 1983	constitutional monarchy	British monarch	prime minister	15	—	1	—	12	200
St. Lucia	Feb. 22, 1979	Feb. 22, 1979	constitutional monarchy	British monarch	prime minister	11	17[9]	10	—	12	200
St. Vincent	Oct. 27, 1979	Oct. 27, 1979	constitutional monarchy	British monarch	prime minister	21	—	...	—	12	200
Samoa	Jan. 1, 1962	Oct. 28, 1960	[93]	head of state	prime minister	49	—	11	—	12	200
San Marino	855	Oct. 8, 1600	republic	—captains-regent (2)—		60	—	9	—	—	—
São Tomé and Príncipe	July 12, 1975	Sept. 10, 1990	republic	president	prime minister	55	—	1	6	12[10]	200[10]
Saudi Arabia	Sept. 23, 1932	[94]	monarchy	—king[95]—		120[31]	—	13	103	12	[3]
Senegal	Aug. 20, 1960	Jan. 7, 2001	republic	—president[8]—		120	—	11	34	12[46]	200[46]
Serbia and Montenegro	Dec. 1, 1918	Feb. 4, 2003	state union[96]	—president[97]—		126	—	2	...	12	...
Seychelles	June 29, 1976	June 21, 1993	republic	—president—		34	—	...	...	12	200
Sierra Leone	April 27, 1961	Oct. 1, 1991	republic	—president—		124	—	13	150	12	200
Singapore	Aug. 9, 1965	June 3, 1959[16]	republic	president	prime minister	90	—	—	—	3	...
Slovakia	Jan. 1, 1993	Jan. 1, 1993	republic	president	prime minister	150	—	8	79	—	—
Slovenia	June 25, 1991	Dec. 23, 1991	republic	president	prime minister	40	90	192	—	...	...
Solomon Islands	July 7, 1978	July 7, 1978	constitutional monarchy	British monarch	prime minister	50	—	10	183	12[10]	200[10]
Somalia	July 1, 1960	July–August 2000[98]	republic[2, 99]	—president[8]—		245[18]	—	5	...	200	200
South Africa	May 31, 1910	June 30, 1997	republic	—president—		90	400	9	360	12	200
Spain	1492	Dec. 29, 1978	constitutional monarchy	king	prime minister	259	350	19	50	12	200[100]
Sri Lanka	Feb. 4, 1948	Sept. 7, 1978	republic	—president[8]—		225	—	25	319	12	200
Sudan, The	Jan. 1, 1956	June 30, 1998	military regime	—president—		360	—	26	...	12	[3]
Suriname	Nov. 25, 1975	Nov. 25, 1987	republic	—president—		51	—	10	...	12	200
Swaziland	Sept. 6, 1968	Nov. 14, 2003[101]	monarchy[101]	—king[8]—		30[31]	65[31]	4	55	—	—
Sweden	before 836	Jan. 1, 1975	constitutional monarchy	king	prime minister	349	—	21	289	12	[19]
Switzerland	Sept. 22, 1499	Jan. 1, 2000	federal state	—president FC—		46	200	26	187	—	—
Syria	April 17, 1946	March 14, 1973	republic	—president—		250	—	14	60	35	[3]
Taiwan	Oct. 25, 1945	Dec. 25, 1947[16]	republic	president	premier	225	—	2	25	24	200
Tajikistan	Sept. 9, 1991	Nov. 6, 1994	republic	president	prime minister	33	63	4	...	—	—
Tanzania	Dec. 9, 1961	April 25, 1977	republic	—president—		274	—	1	26	12	200
Thailand	1350	Oct. 11, 1997	constitutional monarchy	king	prime minister	200	500	76	795	12	200
Togo	April 27, 1960	Sept. 27, 1992	republic	president	prime minister	81	—	5	21	30	200
Tonga	June 4, 1970	Nov. 4, 1875	hereditary monarchy	—monarch—		30	—	...	...	12	200
Trinidad and Tobago	Aug. 31, 1962	July 27, 1976	republic	president	prime minister	31	36	16	...	12[10]	200[10]
Tunisia	March 20, 1956	June 1, 2002[35]	republic	president	prime minister	182	—	24	257	12	...
Turkey	Oct. 29, 1923	Nov. 7, 1982	republic	president	prime minister	550	—	81	849	12[102]	200[103]
Turkmenistan	Oct. 27, 1991	May 18, 1992	republic	—president PC—		50	—	6	...	—	—
Tuvalu	Oct. 1, 1978	Oct. 1, 1986	constitutional monarchy	British monarch	prime minister	12	—	8	—	12[10]	200[10]
Uganda	Oct. 9, 1962	Oct. 8, 1995	republic	—president—		305	—	56	165	—	—
Ukraine	Aug. 24, 1991	June 28, 1996	republic	president	prime minister	450	—	27	485	12	200
United Arab Emirates	Dec. 2, 1971	Dec. 2, 1971	federation of emirates	president	prime minister	40[31]	—	7	—	12	200
United Kingdom	Dec. 6, 1921	[104]	constitutional monarchy	monarch	prime minister	688	659	3	...	12[69]	200
United States	July 4, 1776	March 4, 1789	federal republic	—president—		100	435	51	3,043	12	200
Uruguay	Aug. 25, 1828	Feb. 15, 1967	republic	—president—		31	99	19	...	12	200
Uzbekistan	Aug. 31, 1991	Dec. 8, 1992	republic	—president[8]—		250	—	14	162	—	—
Vanuatu	July 30, 1980	July 30, 1980	republic	president	prime minister	52	—	6	...	12[10]	200[10]
Venezuela	July 5, 1811	Dec. 20, 1999	federal republic	—president—		165	—	25	332	12	200
Vietnam	Sept. 2, 1945	April 15, 1992	socialist republic	president	prime minister	498	—	8	61	12	200
Virgin Islands (U.S.)	—	July 22, 1954	territory (U.S.)	U.S. president	governor	15	—	...	...	12	200
West Bank	—	May 4, 1994[56]	interim authority	—chairman PNA—		89	—	11	...	—	—
Western Sahara	—	—	annexure of Morocco	—	—	—	—	...	...	12	200
Yemen	December 1918	Sept. 29, 1994	republic	president	prime minister	111[31]	301	20	...	12	200
Zambia	Oct. 24, 1964	May 28, 1996[4]	republic	—president—		158	—	9	72	—	—
Zimbabwe	April 18, 1980	April 18, 1980	republic	—president—		150	—	10	80	—	—

[1]Draft constitution unveiled November 2003. [2]Transitional government. [3]Territorial sea claim. [4]Date president signed new constitution. [5]Varies between 32 and 52 nautical miles. [6]Observer. [7]President of France and Bishop of Urgell, Spain. [8]Assisted by the prime minister. [9]Excludes possible ex officio members. [10]Measured from claimed archipelagic baselines. [11]Promulgation date of significant amendments to July 9, 1853, constitution. [12]Assisted by the ministerial coordinator. [13]Executive responsibilities divided between (for The Netherlands) the governor and (locally) the prime minister. [14]Associate member. [15]Formally a constitutional monarchy. [16]Evolving body of constitutional law. [17]Date of referendum approving significant constitutional amendments. [18]Statutory number of seats. [19]Defined by equidistant line. [20]Legal status is controversial. [21]Excludes children of the monarch serving ex officio from age 18. [22]10 provincial councils; 5 region/community councils. [23]Defined by coordinates of points. [24]6 districts; 8 town boards. [25]3 nautical miles from the mouth of the Sarstoon River (southern boundary with Guatemala) to Ranguana Caye. [26]Executive responsibilities divided between (for the U.K.) the governor and (locally) the premier. [27]Resembles a constitutional monarchy without a formal constitution. [28]Date of international treaty confirming the existence of a single state under the final international authority of the high representative. [29]Tripartite presidency. [30]Cantons only; Republika Srpska has no cantons. [31]Body with limited or no legislative authority. [32]Sections of the constitution have been suspended since 1962. [33]Implementation date of Arusha Accords. [34]Assisted by the vice president. [35]Date significant amendments adopted. [36]Governor-general can exercise all the powers of the reigning monarch of the Commonwealth. [37]Effective date of new government. [38]In actuality, a loose union of semiautonomous islands. [39]Assisted by vice presidents. [40]Transitional constitution. [41]Elected seats for resident Croatians only. [42]Suspended membership. [43]Republic of Cyprus only. [44]24 seats reserved for Turkish Cypriots are not occupied. [45]New member as of May 2004. [46]Zone defined by geographic coordinates. [47]Constitution adopted in May 1997 had not been promulgated as of November 2003. [48]Partially delimited by Eritrea–Yemeni arbitration. [49]Defined by coordinates in some parts of the Gulf of Finland. [50]Executive responsibilities divided between (for Denmark) the high commissioner and (locally) the prime minister. [51]Or agreed boundaries or median line. [52]3 nautical miles in the Gulf of Finland. [53]Executive responsibilities divided among (for France) the prefect and (locally) the president of the General Council and the president of the Regional Council. [54]Status change pending as of November 2003. [55]Executive responsibilities divided between (for France) the high commissioner and (locally)

United Nations (date of admission)	UNCTAD★	UNICEF★e	ICJ★f	FAO	IAEA	IBRD	ICAO	IDA	IFC	ILO	IMF	IMO	ITU	UNESCO	UNIDO	UPU	WHO	WIPO	WMO	WTO	The Commonwealth	AU	EU	GCC	LAS	OAS	PC	ACP	ADB	APEC	CARICOM	ECOWAS	FZ	I-ADB	IDB	OPEC	country
membership in international organizations:	UN organs★ and affiliated intergovernmental organizations																				The Commonwealth	regional multipurpose						economic									
1960	●	●		●	●	●	●	●	●	●	●		●	●	●	●	●	●	●	●		●						●				●	●		●		Niger
1960	●	●		●	●	●	●	●	●	●	●	●	●	●	●	●	●	●	●	●	●	●						●				●				●	Nigeria
—																●											●										Northern Mariana Is.
1945	●	●		●	●	●	●	●	●	●	●	●	●	●	●	●	●	●	●	●									●					●			Norway
1971	●	●		●		●	●	●	●	●	●	●	●	●	●	●	●	●	●	●				●	●										●		Oman
1947	●	●		●	●	●	●	●	●	●	●	●	●	●	●	●	●	●	●	●	42								●						●		Pakistan
1994	●	●		●		●	●	●	●		●			●			●										●	●									Palau
1945	●	●		●	●	●	●	●	●	●	●	●	●	●	●	●	●	●	●	●						●								●			Panama
1975	●	●		●		●	●	●	●	●	●	●	●	●	●	●	●	●	●	●	●						●	●	●	●							Papua New Guinea
1945	●	●		●	●	●	●	●	●	●	●	●	●	●	●	●	●	●	●	●						●								●			Paraguay
1945	●	●		●	●	●	●	●	●	●	●	●	●	●	●	●	●	●	●	●						●				●				●			Peru
1945	●	●		●	●	●	●	●	●	●	●	●	●	●	●	●	●	●	●	●									●	●							Philippines
1945	●	●		●	●	●	●	●	●	●	●	●	●	●	●	●	●	●	●	●			45														Poland
1955	●	●		●	●	●	●	●	●	●	●	●	●	●	●	●	●	●	●	●			●											●			Portugal
—				14									●			●	14																				Puerto Rico
1971	●	●		●	●	●	●			●	●	●	●	●	●	●	●	●	●	●				●	●										●	●	Qatar
—													●			●																	●				Réunion
1955	●	●		●	●	●	●		●	●	●	●	●	●	●	●	●	●	●	●																	Romania
1991	●	●	●		●	●	●	●	●	●	●	●	●	●	●	●	●	●	●	6										●							Russia
1962	●	●		●		●	●	●	●	●	●		●	●	●	●	●	●	●	●		●						●									Rwanda
1983	●	●		●		●	●	●	●	●	●	●		●	●	●	●	●		●	●					●		●			●						St. Kitts and Nevis
1979	●	●		●		●	●	●	●	●	●	●	●	●	●	●	●	●	●	●	●					●		●			●						St. Lucia
1980	●	●		●		●	●	●		●	●	●	●	●	●	●	●	●		●	●					●		●			●						St. Vincent
1976	●	●		●		●	●	●	●		●	●	●	●		●	●	●	●	6	●						●	●	●								Samoa
1992	●	●		●		●	●			●	●	●	●	●		●	●	●	●																		San Marino
1975	●	●		●		●	●	●		●	●	●	●	●	●	●	●	●	●			●						●									São Tomé and Príncipe
1945	●	●		●	●	●	●	●	●	●	●	●	●	●	●	●	●	●	●	6				●	●										●	●	Saudi Arabia
1960	●	●		●	●	●	●	●	●	●	●	●	●	●	●	●	●	●	●	●		●						●				●	●		●		Senegal
1945	●	●		●	●	●	●	●	●	●	●	●	●	●	●	●	●	●	●	6																	Serbia and Montenegro
1976	●	●		●	●	●	●	●	●	●	●	●	●	●	●	●	●	●	●	6	●	●						●									Seychelles
1961	●	●	●	●	●	●	●	●	●	●	●	●	●	●	●	●	●	●	●	●	●	●						●				●			●		Sierra Leone
1965	●	●			●	●	●	●	●	●	●	●	●			●	●	●	●	●	●								●	●							Singapore
1993	●	●	●	●	●	●	●	●	●	●	●	●	●	●	●	●	●	●	●	●			45														Slovakia
1992	●	●		●	●	●	●	●	●	●	●	●	●	●	●	●	●	●	●	●			45											●			Slovenia
1978	●	●		●		●	●	●	●	●	●	●	●	●		●	●	●	●	●	●						●	●	●								Solomon Islands
1960	●	●		●		●	●	●	●	●	●	●	●	●	●	●	●	●	●			●			●			●							●		Somalia
1945	●	●		●	●	●	●	●	●	●	●	●	●	●	●	●	●	●	●	●	●	●						●									South Africa
1955	●	●		●	●	●	●	●	●	●	●	●	●	●	●	●	●	●	●	●			●						●					●			Spain
1955	●	●		●	●	●	●	●	●	●	●	●	●	●	●	●	●	●	●	●	●								●								Sri Lanka
1956	●	●		●	●	●	●	●	●	●	●	●	●	●	●	●	●	●	●	6		●			●			●							●		Sudan, The
1975	●	●		●		●	●		●	●	●	●	●	●	●	●	●	●	●	●						●		●			●			●	●		Suriname
1968	●	●		●		●	●	●	●	●	●	●	●	●	●	●	●	●	●	●	●	●						●									Swaziland
1946	●	●		●	●	●	●	●	●	●	●	●	●	●	●	●	●	●	●	●			●						●					●			Sweden
2002	●	●		●	●	●	●	●	●	●	●	●	●	●	●	●	●	●	●	●									●					●			Switzerland
1945	●	●		●	●	●	●	●	●	●	●	●	●	●	●	●	●	●	●						●										●		Syria
—																				●									●	●							Taiwan
1992	●	●		●	●	●	●	●	●	●	●		●	●	●	●	●	●	●	6									●						●		Tajikistan
1961	●	●		●	●	●	●	●	●	●	●	●	●	●	●	●	●	●	●	●	●	●						●									Tanzania
1946	●	●		●	●	●	●	●	●	●	●	●	●	●	●	●	●	●	●	●									●	●							Thailand
1960	●	●		●		●	●	●	●	●	●	●	●	●	●	●	●	●	●	●		●						●				●	●		●		Togo
1999	●	●		●		●	●	●	●		●	●	●	●	●	●	●	●		6	●						●	●	●								Tonga
1962	●	●		●		●	●	●	●	●	●	●	●	●	●	●	●	●	●	●	●					●		●			●			●			Trinidad and Tobago
1956	●	●		●	●	●	●	●	●	●	●	●	●	●	●	●	●	●	●	●		●			●										●		Tunisia
1945	●	●		●	●	●	●	●	●	●	●	●	●	●	●	●	●	●	●	●									●						●		Turkey
1992	●	●		●		●	●		●	●	●	●	●	●	●	●	●	●	●										●						●		Turkmenistan
2000	●	●											●	●		●	●				●						●	●	●								Tuvalu
1962	●	●		●	●	●	●	●	●	●	●		●	●	●	●	●	●	●	●	●	●						●							●		Uganda
1945	●	●			●	●	●		●	●	●	●	●	●	●	●	●	●	●	6																	Ukraine
1971	●	●		●	●	●	●	●	●	●	●	●	●	●	●	●	●	●	●	●				●	●										●	●	United Arab Emirates
1945	●	●	●	●	●	●	●	●	●	●	●	●	●	●	●	●	●	●	●	●	●		●				●		●					●			United Kingdom
1945	●	●	●	●	●	●	●	●	●	●	●	●	●	●		●	●	●	●	●						●	●		●	●				●			United States
1945	●	●		●	●	●	●		●	●	●	●	●	●	●	●	●	●	●	●						●								●			Uruguay
1992	●	●		●	●	●	●	●	●	●	●		●	●	●	●	●	●	●	6									●								Uzbekistan
1981	●	●		●		●	●	●	●	●	●	●	●	●	●	●	●		●	●	●						●	●	●								Vanuatu
1945	●	●	●	●	●	●	●		●	●	●	●	●	●	●	●	●	●	●	●						●								●		●	Venezuela
1977	●	●		●	●	●	●	●	●	●	●	●	●	●	●	●	●	●	●	6									●	●							Vietnam
—													●			●															●						Virgin Islands (U.S.)
—		●																							● [57]										● [57]		West Bank
—																						105															Western Sahara
1947	●	●		●	●	●	●	●	●	●	●	●	●	●	●	●	●	●	●	6					●										●		Yemen
1964	●	●		●	●	●	●	●	●	●	●		●	●	●	●	●	●	●	●	●	●						●									Zambia
1980	●	●		●	●	●	●	●	●	42	●		●	●	●	●	●	●	●	●	42	●						●									Zimbabwe

the president of the territorial government. [56]Date of agreement providing for Palestinian self-rule. [57]As Palestine. [58]Assisted by the minister of state. [59]Date parliament approved constitutional amendments for 78 articles. [60]Represented by the lieutenant governor. [61]Executive committees appointed by the States of Deliberation. [62]Special administrative region (China). [63]Has been significantly amended. [64]Shares coexecutive authority with spiritual leader. [65]Sea of Oman only; median line boundaries in Persian Gulf. [66]UN approval date of U.S. resolution on Iraqi economic and political reconstruction. [67]Coalition provisional authority. [68]Assisted by the Iraqi Governing Council. [69]Median line boundary between the Isle of Man and the United Kingdom. [70]The emperor is the symbol of state. [71]3 nautical miles in 5 straits. [72]Executive committees appointed by the States Assembly. [73]Essentially 1992 constitution with new preamble. [74]Elected seats only. [75]Limits established by international agreements with Estonia, Lithuania, and Sweden. [76]Date of peace accord. [77]Formally a *jamahiriya,* translated as "the masses of people"; in fact, a military dictatorship. [78]De facto chief of state. [79]Prince granted extensive new authority per March 2003 constitutional amendment. [80]Date parliament adopted significant constitutional amendments. [81]Executive responsibilities divided between (for France) the prefect and (locally) the president of the General Council. [82]Under prince's authority. [83]Includes Western Sahara annexure. [84]Expelled. [85]Development regions. [86]Represented by high commissioner. [87]Basic law promulgated by sultan. [88]Has 2 consultative bodies with advisory authority only. [89]Rectangle defined by coordinates; claim extends beyond 12 mi. [90]Excludes additional seats for both houses of the legislature to meet 1/3 total representation requirements for minority parties per constitution. [91]Date of referendum approving draft constitution. [92]Per effective implementation of constitution. [93]Mixed political system approximating a constitutional monarchy. [94]Royal decrees from March 1, 1992, created first written rules of governance. [95]Assisted by crown prince; crown prince has assumed some powers of king because of king's illness. [96]"Loose confederation." [97]Assisted by Council of Ministers. [98]Transitional national charter. [99]Effective control in Mogadishu vicinity only. [100]Atlantic Ocean only. [101]Effectiveness of new constitution unclear in December 2003. [102]Black Sea and Mediterranean Sea; 6 nautical miles in Aegean Sea. [103]In the Black Sea only. [104]Based on evolving body of statutes and common law. [105]Membership held by the Sahrawi Arab Democratic Republic.

Area and population

This table provides the area and population for each of the countries of the world and for all but the smallest political dependencies having a permanent civilian population. The data represent the latest published and unpublished data for both the surveyed area of the countries and their populations, the latter both as of a single year (2003) to provide the best comparability and as of a recent census to provide the fullest comparison of certain demographic measures that are not always available between successive national censuses. The 2003 midyear estimates represent a combination of national, United Nations (UN) or other international organizations, and *Encyclopædia Britannica* estimates so as to give the best fit to available published series, to take account of unpublished information received via Internet, facsimile, or correspondence, and to incorporate the results of very recent censuses for which published analyses are not yet available.

One principal point to bear in mind when studying these statistics is that all of them, whatever degree of precision may be implied by the exactness of the numbers, are estimates—all of varying, and some of suspect, accuracy—even when they *contain* a very full enumeration. The United States—which has a long tradition both of census taking and of the use of the most sophisticated analytical tools in processing the data—is unable to determine within 1.2% (the estimated 2000 undercount) its total population nationally. And that is an *average* underenumeration. In states and larger cities, where enumeration of particular populations, including illegal, is more difficult, the accuracy of the enumerated count may be off as much as 3.1% at a state level (in New Mexico, for instance) and by a greater percent for a single city. The high accuracy attained by census operations in China may approach 0.25% of rigorously maintained civil population registers. Other national census operations not so based, however, are inherently less accurate. For example, Ethiopia's first-ever census in 1984 resulted in figures that were 30% or more above prevailing estimates; Nigeria's 1991 census corrected decades of miscounts and was well below prevailing estimates. An undercount of 2–8% is more typical, but even census operations offering results of 30% or more above or below prevailing estimates can still represent well-founded benchmarks from which future planning may proceed. The editors have tried to take account of the range of variation and accuracy in published data, but it is difficult to establish a value for many sources of inaccuracy unless some country or agency has made a conscientious effort to establish both the relative accuracy (precision) of its estimate and the absolute magnitude of the quantity it is trying to measure—for example, the number of people in Cambodia who died at the hands of the Khmer Rouge. If a figure of 2,000,000 is adopted, what is its accuracy: ± 1%, 10%, 50%? Are the original data documentary or evidentiary, complete or incomplete, analytically biased or unbiased, in good agreement with other published data?

Many similar problems exist and in endless variations: What is the extent of eastern European immigration to western Europe in search of jobs? How many registered and unregistered refugees from Afghanistan, Sierra Leone, or Burundi are there in surrounding countries? How many undocumented aliens are there in the United Kingdom, Japan, or the United States? How many Tamils have left Sri Lanka as a result of civil unrest in their homeland? How many Amerindians exist (remain, preserving their original language and a mode of life unassimilated by the larger national culture) in the countries of South America?

Still, much information is accurate, well founded, and updated regularly.

Area and population

country	area			population (latest estimate)					population (recent census)				
	square miles	square kilo-metres	rank	total midyear 2003	rank	density per sq mi	density per sq km	% annual growth rate 1998–2003	census year	total	male (%)	female (%)	urban (%)
Afghanistan	249,347	645,807	41	28,717,000	38	115.2	44.5	3.6	1979	13,051,358[1]	51.4	48.6	15.1
Albania	11,082	28,703	142	3,166,000	132	285.7	110.3	0.3	1989	3,182,417	51.5	48.5	35.7
Algeria	919,595	2,381,741	11	31,800,000	34	34.6	13.4	1.6	1998	29,272,343	50.6	49.4	80.8
American Samoa	77	200	206	61,200	207	794.8	306.0	2.0	2000	57,291	51.4[2]	48.6[2]	33.4[2]
Andorra	179	464	194	66,900	204	373.7	144.2	0.4	2000[3]	65,971	52.2	47.8	93.0[4]
Angola	481,354	1,246,700	24	10,766,000	73	22.4	8.6	2.0	1970	5,673,046	52.1	47.9	14.2
Antigua and Barbuda	171	442	196	76,800	201	449.1	173.8	1.9	1991	63,896	48.2	51.8	36.2
Argentina	1,073,400	2,780,092	8	36,846,000	32	34.3	13.3	1.0	1991	32,615,528	48.9	51.1	88.4
Armenia	11,484	29,743	141	3,061,000	134	266.5	102.9	–0.8	1989	3,287,677	49.3	50.7	67.8
Aruba	75	193	207	92,700	196	1,236.0	480.3	0.9	1991	66,687	49.2	50.8	...
Australia	2,969,978	7,692,208	6	19,880,000	52	6.7	2.6	1.2	1996	17,892,423	49.5	50.5	89.3
Austria	32,383	83,871	114	8,054,000	89	248.7	96.0	0.0	1991	7,795,786	48.2	51.8	64.5
Azerbaijan	33,400	86,600	113	8,235,000	88	246.6	95.1	0.8	1999	7,953,000	48.8	51.2	56.9[4]
Bahamas, The	5,382	13,939	159	314,000	175	58.3	22.5	1.3	1990	255,095	49.0	51.0	64.3
Bahrain	276	716	186	674,000	161	2,442.0	941.3	2.2	1991	508,037	57.9	42.1	88.4
Bangladesh	56,977	147,570	93	133,107,000	8	2,336.2	902.0	1.0	1991	111,455,185	51.4	48.6	20.2
Barbados	166	430	197	272,000	178	1,638.6	632.6	0.4	1990[6]	257,083	47.7	52.3	37.9[7]
Belarus	80,153	207,595	85	9,881,000	81	123.3	47.6	–0.4	1999	10,045,237[6]	47.0[6]	53.0[6]	69.3[6]
Belgium	11,787	30,528	139	10,341,000	75	877.3	338.7	0.3	1991	9,978,681	48.9	51.1	96.6[8]
Belize	8,867	22,965	150	269,000	179	30.3	11.7	2.5	2000	240,204	50.5	49.5	47.7
Benin	43,484	112,622	101	7,041,000	94	161.9	62.5	3.1	1992	4,915,555	48.6	51.4	35.7
Bermuda	21	54	213	64,000	205	3,047.6	1,185.2	0.6	1991[6]	58,460	48.5	51.5	100.0
Bhutan	18,150	47,000	131	685,000	160	37.7	14.6	1.9	...	...	51.6[10]	48.4[10]	7.0[10]
Bolivia	424,164	1,098,581	28	8,586,000	85	20.2	7.8	1.8	1992	6,420,792	49.4	50.6	57.5
Bosnia and Herzegovina	19,767	51,197	127	3,720,000	127	188.1	72.7	2.6	1991	4,377,033	49.9	50.1	39.6
Botswana	224,848	582,356	47	1,663,000	146	7.4	2.9	1.3	1991	1,326,796	47.8	52.2	23.9
Brazil	3,287,292	8,514,047	5	178,470,000	5	54.3	21.0	1.3	1991	146,825,475	49.4	50.6	75.6
Brunei	2,226	5,765	168	344,000	174	154.5	59.7	2.2	1991	260,482	52.8	47.2	66.6
Bulgaria	42,846	110,971	103	7,786,000	91	181.7	70.2	–0.9	2001	7,977,646	48.7	51.3	67.2[11]
Burkina Faso	103,456	267,950	75	13,228,000	62	127.9	49.4	2.7	1996	10,312,609	48.2	51.8	15.0[10]
Burundi	10,740	27,816	145	6,096,000	100	567.6	219.2	2.1	1990[6]	5,292,793	48.6	51.4	6.3
Cambodia	69,898	181,035	89	13,125,000	63	187.8	72.5	1.8	1998	11,437,656	48.2	51.8	20.9
Cameroon	183,569	475,442	53	15,746,000	59	85.8	33.1	2.1	1987	10,516,232	49.0	51.0	38.3
Canada	3,855,103	9,984,670	2	31,590,000	36	8.2	3.2	0.9	1996	28,846,761	49.1	50.9	77.9
Cape Verde	1,557	4,033	170	438,000	169	281.3	108.6	0.7	2000	434,812	48.4	51.6	53.3
Central African Republic	240,324	622,436	43	3,684,000	128	15.3	5.9	1.7	1988	2,688,426	49.1	50.9	36.5
Chad	495,755	1,284,000	21	9,253,000	82	18.7	7.2	3.3	1993	6,279,931	47.9	52.1	21.4
Chile	291,930	756,096	38	15,326,000	60	52.5	20.3	1.1	1992	13,348,401	49.1	50.9	83.5
China	3,696,100	9,572,900	3	1,288,892,000	1	348.7	134.6	0.9	2000	1,265,830,000	51.6	48.4	36.1
Colombia	440,762	1,141,568	26	41,662,000	29	94.5	36.5	1.7	1993	33,109,840	49.2	50.8	70.3[7]
Comoros	719	1,862	176	584,000	163	812.2	313.6	2.0	1991	446,817	49.5	50.5	28.5
Congo, Dem. Rep. of the	905,354	2,344,858	12	52,771,000	23	58.3	22.5	2.4	1984	29,671,407	49.2	50.8	29.1[12]
Congo, Rep. of the	132,047	342,000	63	3,724,000	126	28.2	10.9	2.8	1984[6]	1,909,248	48.7	51.3	52.0
Costa Rica	19,730	51,100	128	4,171,000	119	211.4	81.6	2.2	2000	3,824,593	50.0	50.0	51.9[10]
Côte d'Ivoire	123,863	320,803	68	16,631,000	56	134.3	51.8	1.7	1988	10,815,694	51.1	48.9	39.0
Croatia	21,831	56,542	126	4,428,000	116	202.8	78.3	0.0	1991	4,784,265	48.5	51.5	54.3
Cuba	42,804	110,861	104	11,295,000	70	263.9	101.9	0.3	1993	10,904,466	50.3	49.7	74.4
Cyprus[13]	3,572	9,251	165	921,000	155	257.8	99.6	0.8	1992[6, 14]	615,013	49.8	50.2	67.7
Czech Republic	30,450	78,866	117	10,202,000	76	335.0	129.4	–0.2	1991	10,302,215	48.5	51.5	75.2
Denmark	16,640	43,098	133	5,387,000	109	323.7	125.0	0.4	1999[3]	5,313,577	49.4	50.6	85.0
Djibouti	8,950	23,200	149	457,000	165	51.1	19.7	1.6	1983	273,974	51.9	48.1	82.8[12]
Dominica	290	750	184	69,700	203	240.3	92.9	–0.9	1991	71,183	49.8	50.2	...
Dominican Republic	18,792	48,671	130	8,716,000	84	463.8	179.1	1.5	1993	7,293,390	48.7	51.3	56.1
East Timor	5,639	14,604	158	778,000	157	138.0	53.3	0.8	1990	747,750	51.7	48.3	7.8
Ecuador	105,037	272,045	73	13,003,000	64	123.8	47.8	1.6	1990	9,648,189	49.7	50.3	55.4

The sources of these data are censuses; national population registers (cumulated periodically); registration of migration, births, deaths, and so on; sample surveys to establish demographic conditions; and the like.

The statistics provided for area and population by country are ranked, and the population densities based on those values are also provided. The population densities, for purposes of comparison within this table, are calculated on the bases of the 2003 midyear population estimate as shown and of total area of the country. Elsewhere in individual country presentations the reader may find densities calculated on more specific population figures and more specialized area bases: land area for Finland (because of its many lakes) or ice-free area for Greenland (most of which is ice cap). The data in this section conclude with the estimated average annual growth rate for the country (including both natural growth and net migration) during the five-year period 1998–2003.

In the section containing census data, information supplied includes the census total (usually de facto, the population actually present, rather than de jure, the population legally resident, who might be anywhere); the male-female breakdown; the proportion that is urban (usually according to the country's own definition); and finally an analysis of the age structure of the population by 15-year age groups. This last analysis may be particularly useful in distinguishing the type of population being recorded—young, fast-growing nations show a high proportion of people under 30 (many countries in sub-Saharan Africa and the Middle East have about 40% of their population under 15 years), while other nations (for example, Sweden, which suffered no age-group losses in World War II) exhibit quite uniform proportions.

Finally, a section is provided giving the population of each country at 10-year intervals from 1950 to 2020. The data for years past represent the best available analysis of the published data by the country itself, by the demographers of the UN, demographers of the U.S. Bureau of the Census, International Data Base, or by the editors of Britannica. The projections for 2010 and 2020 similarly represent the best fit of available data through the autumn of 2003. The evidence of the last 30 years with respect to similar estimates published about 1970, however, shows how cloudy is the glass through which these numbers are read. In 1970 no respectable Western analyst would have imagined proposing that mainland China could achieve the degree of birth control that it apparently has since then; on the other hand, even the Chinese admit that their methods have been somewhat Draconian and that they have already seen some backlash in terms of higher birth rates among those who have so far postponed larger families. How much is "some" by 2010? Compound that problem with all the social, economic, political, and biological factors (including the impact of AIDS) that can affect 217 countries' populations, and the difficulty facing the prospective compiler of such projections may be appreciated.

Specific data about the vital rates affecting the data in this table may be found in great detail in both the country statistical boxes in "The Nations of the World" section and in the *Vital statistics, marriage, family* table, beginning at page 770.

Percentages in this table for male and female population will always total 100.0, but percentages by age group may not, for reasons such as non-response on census forms, "don't know" responses (which are common in countries with poor birth registration systems), and the like.

age distribution (%)						population (by decade, '000s)								country
0–14	15–29	30–44	45–59	60–74	75 and over	1950	1960	1970	1980	1990	2000	2010 projection	2020 projection	
44.5	26.9	15.8	8.6	3.6	0.6	8,150	9,829	12,431	14,985	14,750	25,889	33,864	41,735	Afghanistan
33.0	28.9	18.5	11.7	5.9	1.9	1,227	1,623	2,157	2,671	3,289	3,113	3,335	3,548	Albania
36.2	30.6	17.7	8.9	5.1	1.5	8,753	10,800	13,746	18,740	25,017	30,245	35,549	40,479	Algeria
38.1[2]	29.0[2]	18.1[2]	9.4[2]	4.3[2]	1.1[2]	19	20	27	32	47	58	71	86	American Samoa
15.4	20.9	29.3	18.6	10.5	5.3	6	8	19	33	53	66	70	74	Andorra
41.7	23.2	17.0	7.4	3.8	1.0	4,118	4,797	5,606	6,736	8,049	10,132	12,250	14,473	Angola
30.4	27.8	20.5	10.2	7.7	3.4	45	55	66	69	64	74	80	84	Antigua and Barbuda
30.6	23.3	19.3	13.9	9.6	3.3	17,150	20,616	23,962	28,094	32,527	35,726	39,769	43,486	Argentina
30.3	25.7	20.8	13.6	6.4	3.2	1,354	1,867	2,518	3,096	3,545	3,112	2,991	2,926	Armenia
24.4	22.0	27.0	16.1	7.2	3.0	51	57	61	60	64	91	96	98	Aruba
21.5[5]	22.3[5]	23.1[5]	17.1[5]	11.0[5]	5.0[5]	8,219	10,315	12,552	14,741	17,065	19,222	21,082	22,577	Australia
17.4	23.7	21.6	17.2	13.4	6.7	6,935	7,048	7,447	7,549	7,729	8,038	8,130	8,225	Austria
31.8	25.6	24.1	9.5	7.6	1.4	2,896	3,895	5,172	6,165	7,166	8,048	8,839	9,717	Azerbaijan
32.2	30.8	19.7	10.6	5.0	1.8	79	110	170	210	256	304	336	363	Bahamas, The
31.7	28.4	28.2	8.0	3.1	0.6	110	149	210	334	503	638	748	838	Bahrain
41.5	25.2	16.2	8.1	4.3	1.1	45,646	54,622	67,403	88,077	109,897	129,800	147,253	170,108	Bangladesh
24.1	27.1	22.1	11.4	9.9	5.4	209	232	235	249	261	268	278	283	Barbados
19.5	21.8	23.4	16.4	—18.9—		7,745	8,190	9,040	9,650	10,186	10,005	9,598	9,195	Belarus
18.2	21.8	22.5	16.9	14.1	6.6	8,639	9,153	9,690	9,859	9,967	10,251	10,458	10,529	Belgium
43.9[9]	27.9[9]	14.9[9]	7.2[9]	4.4[9]	1.6[9]	68	90	120	146	189	250	316	383	Belize
48.6	24.2	14.5	6.6	4.1	1.9	1,673	2,055	2,620	3,444	4,662	6,428	8,504	10,647	Benin
19.5	24.0	26.8	16.4	—13.3—		37	43	53	55	59	63	67	69	Bermuda
40.2[10]	26.0[10]	17.4[10]	10.1[10]	5.2[10]	1.1[10]	...	...	...	...	519	638	793	965	Bhutan
41.2	26.2	16.8	8.9	—6.5—		2,766	3,434	4,346	5,441	6,574	8,153	9,499	10,747	Bolivia
23.5[8]	26.3[8]	22.6[8]	16.9[8]	8.9[8]	2.7[8]	2,662	3,240	3,703	4,092	4,424	3,704	3,834	3,908	Bosnia and Herzegovina
42.8	27.3	14.3	7.3	4.1	2.2	430	497	584	914	1,312	1,636	1,510	1,225	Botswana
34.7	28.1	19.3	10.6	5.7	1.6	53,975	72,742	95,988	121,614	148,809	171,796	192,879	209,793	Brazil
34.5	29.3	24.2	7.9	—4.1—		45	83	128	185	258	324	393	458	Brunei
20.5[11]	19.2[11]	—39.8[11]—		—20.5[11]—		7,251	7,867	8,490	8,862	8,718	8,012	7,229	6,528	Bulgaria
47.9[5]	26.8[5]	12.9[5]	7.6[5]	3.9[5]	0.9[5]	4,376	4,866	5,626	6,942	9,090	12,217	15,748	19,965	Burkina Faso
46.4	25.3	15.4	7.0	4.0	1.7	2,363	2,812	3,513	4,138	5,285	5,713	7,296	9,174	Burundi
42.8	26.1	17.2	8.5	4.3	1.1	4,163	5,364	6,984	6,586	9,271	12,433	14,902	17,863	Cambodia
46.4	24.5	14.6	8.7	4.1	1.6	4,888	5,609	6,727	8,748	11,685	14,792	17,938	20,946	Cameroon
19.9	20.9	25.7	17.2	11.1	5.2	13,737	17,909	21,324	24,516	27,701	30,777	33,174	35,277	Canada
43.6[10]	24.8[10]	17.1[10]	5.8[10]	6.3[10]	2.4[10]	146	197	269	296	349	423	458	476	Cape Verde
43.2	27.5	15.0	9.2	4.1	0.8	1,260	1,467	1,827	2,244	2,803	3,501	4,073	4,557	Central African Republic
48.1	24.6	14.7	7.2	4.2	1.3	2,608	3,042	3,731	4,542	6,030	8,419	11,302	14,671	Chad
29.4	27.3	21.2	12.2	7.2	2.5	6,082	7,608	9,496	11,147	13,100	14,779	16,607	18,320	Chile
27.7[2]	31.0[2]	20.7[2]	12.1[2]	6.9[2]	1.7[2]	556,613	667,070	818,316	981,242	1,133,683	1,261,379	1,344,786	1,426,184	China
34.5	28.5	20.1	10.0	5.3	1.6	11,592	15,953	21,430	26,583	32,859	39,686	46,109	52,199	Colombia
47.6[8]	27.0[8]	13.1[8]	7.7[8]	3.5[8]	1.0[8]	148	183	236	334	429	549	672	822	Comoros
47.3[12]	25.9[12]	14.1[12]	8.1[12]	3.8[12]	0.8[12]	12,184	15,438	20,603	27,909	37,370	48,571	64,714	84,418	Congo, Dem. Rep. of the
44.7	27.2	13.3	9.1	4.6	0.7	808	1,004	1,323	1,804	2,494	3,447	4,532	5,960	Congo, Rep. of the
32.1[10]	27.1[10]	21.6[10]	11.7[10]	5.6[10]	1.9[10]	862	1,236	1,758	2,302	3,051	3,925	4,732	5,474	Costa Rica
46.8	27.3	15.0	7.5	2.8	0.6	2,775	3,803	5,521	8,427	12,505	15,827	18,526	21,026	Côte d'Ivoire
19.4	20.7	22.7	18.3	12.9	4.5	3,850	4,045	4,169	4,377	4,842	4,446	4,349	4,187	Croatia
22.3	29.4	21.3	14.8	8.4	3.9	5,850	7,028	8,572	9,780	10,603	11,199	11,450	11,531	Cuba
25.4	22.0	22.3	15.4	10.2	4.7	494	573	615	658	751	900	954	990	Cyprus[13]
21.0	21.8	22.6	16.8	12.7	5.1	8,925	9,539	9,805	10,326	10,363	10,243	10,128	9,924	Czech Republic
18.2	19.2	22.4	20.5	12.6	7.1	4,271	4,581	4,929	5,123	5,140	5,337	5,504	5,640	Denmark
39.4	32.9	16.9	7.4	2.8	0.6	60	78	158	279	366	431	526	627	Djibouti
33.3	28.3	16.3	9.7	—11.8—		51	60	70	75	73	72	70	75	Dominica
36.5[15]	29.5[15]	18.4[15]	9.6[15]	4.8[15]	1.2[15]	2,353	3,231	4,423	5,697	7,076	8,354	9,521	10,625	Dominican Republic
...	...	...	...	...	...	433	501	604	581	740	702	976	1,138	East Timor
38.8	28.5	17.3	9.0	4.7	1.7	3,387	4,439	5,970	7,961	10,264	12,420	14,274	15,968	Ecuador

Area and population (continued)

country	area			population (latest estimate)					population (recent census)				
	square miles	square kilometres	rank	total midyear 2003	rank	density per sq mi	density per sq km	% annual growth rate 1998–2003	census year	total	male (%)	female (%)	urban (%)
Egypt	385,210	997,690	30	68,185,000	16	177.0	68.3	1.9	1996	59,312,914	51.2	48.8	42.6
El Salvador	8,124	21,041	151	6,515,000	98	801.9	309.6	1.7	1992	5,118,599	48.6	51.4	50.4
Equatorial Guinea	10,831	28,051	144	494,000	164	45.6	17.6	2.7	1983	300,060	48.8	51.2	28.2
Eritrea	46,774	121,144	99	4,141,000	120	88.5	34.2	3.6	1984	2,703,998	49.9	50.1	15.1
Estonia	17,462	45,227	132	1,353,000	149	77.5	29.9	–0.5	2000	1,376,700[6]	46.1	53.9	74.3[10]
Ethiopia	437,794	1,133,882	27	66,558,000	17	152.0	58.7	2.1	1994	53,477,265	50.3	49.7	14.4[12]
Faroe Islands	540	1,399	178	48,000	210	88.9	34.3	1.5	1999[3]	45,409	51.8	48.2	...
Fiji	7,055	18,272	155	827,000	156	117.2	45.3	0.7	1996	775,077	50.8	49.2	46.4
Finland	130,559	338,145	64	5,212,000	110	39.9	15.4	0.2	1990	4,998,478	48.5	51.5	79.7
France	210,026	543,965	49	59,773,000	20	284.6	109.9	0.5	1999	58,518,748	48.6	51.4	75.5
French Guiana	32,253	83,534	116	178,000	185	5.5	2.1	3.0	1999	157,274	50.4	49.6	77.8[4]
French Polynesia	1,544	4,000	171	244,000	181	158.0	61.0	1.8	1996	219,521	51.9	48.1	40.1[4]
Gabon	103,347	267,667	76	1,329,000	150	12.9	5.0	2.0	1993	1,011,710	49.3	50.7	73.2
Gambia, The	4,127	10,689	163	1,426,000	147	345.5	133.4	3.0	1993	1,038,145	50.1	49.9	36.7
Gaza Strip	140	363	200	1,304,000	151	9,314.3	3,592.3	4.5	1995[3, 17]	1,054,000	50.9	49.1	...
Georgia	26,911	69,700	121	4,934,000	113	183.3	70.8	–0.7	1989	5,443,359	47.2	52.8	55.7
Germany	137,847	357,021	62	82,604,000	12	599.2	231.4	0.1	1998[3]	82,037,000	48.8	51.2	87.5[10]
Ghana	92,098	238,533	81	20,468,000	50	222.2	85.8	1.7	1984	12,296,081	49.3	50.7	32.0
Greece	50,949	131,957	96	11,001,000	71	215.9	83.4	0.4	1991	10,264,156	49.3	50.7	58.9
Greenland	836,330	2,166,086	13	56,600	208	0.07	0.03	0.2	2000[3]	56,124	53.4	46.6	81.5
Grenada	133	344	202	102,000	194	766.9	296.5	0.5	1991	95,597	48.8	51.2	33.5
Guadeloupe	658	1,705	177	435,000	170	661.1	255.1	0.7	1999	422,496	48.1	51.9	99.7[4]
Guam	217	561	191	163,000	188	751.2	290.6	1.6	1990	133,152	53.3	46.7	38.2
Guatemala	42,130	109,117	105	12,347,000	65	293.1	113.2	2.7	1994	8,331,874	49.3	50.7	35.0
Guernsey	30	78	211	63,100	206	2,103.3	809.0	0.4	1996[18]	58,681	48.1	51.9	...
Guinea	94,926	245,857	78	8,480,000	86	89.3	34.5	1.6	1996	7,165,750	48.8	51.2	26.0
Guinea-Bissau	13,948	36,125	137	1,361,000	148	97.6	37.7	2.2	1991	983,367	48.4	51.6	20.3[8]
Guyana	83,044	215,083	84	778,000	157	9.4	3.6	0.0	1991	701,704	49.2	50.8	35.4[12]
Haiti	10,695	27,700	146	7,528,000	92	703.9	271.8	1.6	1982	5,053,792	48.5	51.5	20.6
Honduras	43,433	112,492	102	6,803,000	96	156.6	60.5	2.5	1988	4,376,839	49.6	50.4	39.4
Hong Kong	425	1,101	180	6,838,000	95	16,089.4	6,210.7	0.9	2001	6,715,000	49.0	51.0	100.0
Hungary	35,919	93,030	110	10,136,000	78	282.2	109.0	–0.3	1990	10,375,323	48.1	51.9	61.8
Iceland	39,741	102,928	106	290,000	176	7.3	2.8	1.1	1999[3]	278,717	50.1	49.9	93.5
India	1,222,559	3,166,414	7	1,065,462,000	2	871.5	336.5	1.6	2001	1,027,015,247	51.7	48.3	27.8
Indonesia	742,308	1,922,570	16	219,883,000	4	296.2	114.4	1.3	1990	178,631,196	49.9	50.1	30.9
Iran	629,315	1,629,918	18	66,255,000	18	105.3	40.6	1.4	1996	60,055,488	50.8	49.2	61.3
Iraq	167,618	434,128	58	24,683,000	44	147.3	56.9	2.9	1997	22,017,983	49.7	50.3	74.5[12]
Ireland	27,133	70,273	122	3,969,000	121	146.3	56.5	1.3	1996	3,626,087	49.6	50.4	57.0
Isle of Man	221	572	190	77,300	200	349.8	135.1	1.0	1996[6]	71,714	48.5	51.5	74.7
Israel[21, 22]	7,886	20,425	152	6,473,000	99	820.8	316.9	2.2	1995[6, 23]	5,548,523	49.3	50.7	92.9[12]
Italy	116,345	301,333	71	57,033,000	22	490.2	189.3	0.0	1991	57,103,833	48.6	51.4	67.1[24]
Jamaica	4,244	10,991	162	2,644,000	136	623.0	240.6	0.7	1991	2,374,193	49.0	51.0	50.4
Japan	145,898	377,873	61	127,546,000	9	874.2	337.5	0.2	1995	125,570,246	49.0	51.0	78.1
Jersey	46	118	210	87,700	198	1,906.5	743.2	0.4	1996	85,150	48.6	51.4	...
Jordan[25]	34,495	89,342	112	5,395,000	108	156.4	60.4	2.9	1994	4,139,458	52.2	47.8	78.3
Kazakhstan	1,052,090	2,724,900	9	14,790,000	61	14.1	5.4	–0.4	1999	15,049,100	48.5[26]	51.5[26]	57.2[26]
Kenya	224,961	582,646	46	31,639,000	35	140.6	54.3	1.6	1999	28,686,607	49.5	50.5	32.2[4]
Kiribati	313	811	182	87,900	197	280.8	108.4	1.3	1995	77,658	49.5	50.5	36.5
Korea, North	47,399	122,762	98	22,466,000	48	474.0	183.0	0.9	1993	21,213,378	48.7	51.3	58.9
Korea, South	38,432	99,538	108	47,925,000	24	1,247.0	481.5	0.7	1995[6]	44,608,726	50.2	49.8	81.0[12]
Kuwait	6,880	17,818	156	2,439,000	140	354.5	136.9	1.7	1995	1,575,983	58.0	42.0	97.0[12]
Kyrgyzstan	77,199	199,945	86	5,059,000	111	65.5	25.3	1.4	1999	4,822,938	49.4	50.6	34.8
Laos	91,429	236,800	83	5,657,000	101	61.9	23.9	2.4	1995	4,581,258	49.5	50.5	20.7[12]
Latvia	24,938	64,589	124	2,324,000	141	93.2	36.0	–0.7	2000	2,375,339	46.0	54.0	69.2
Lebanon	4,016	10,400	164	3,728,000	125	928.3	358.5	1.4	1970	2,126,325	50.8	49.2	60.1
Lesotho	11,720	30,355	140	1,802,000	145	153.8	59.4	0.6	1996[6]	1,960,069	49.2	50.8	16.9
Liberia	37,743	97,754	109	3,317,000	131	87.9	33.9	4.6	1984	2,101,628	50.6	49.4	38.8
Libya	679,362	1,759,540	17	5,551,000	104	8.2	3.2	2.0	1995[6]	4,404,986	50.8	49.2	85.3[12]
Liechtenstein	62	160	209	34,100	212	550.0	213.1	1.5	1999[3]	32,426	48.7	51.3	22.2[4]
Lithuania	25,212	65,300	123	3,454,000	129	137.0	52.9	–0.5	1989	3,689,779	47.4	52.6	68.0
Luxembourg	999	2,586	173	453,000	166	453.5	175.2	1.3	1991	384,634	49.0	51.0	85.9[8]
Macau	10.3	26.8	214	443,000	168	43,009.7	16,529.9	0.8	1991	339,464	48.5	51.5	97.0
Macedonia	9,928	25,713	148	2,056,000	142	207.1	80.0	0.6	1994	1,945,932	50.4	49.6	58.7
Madagascar	226,658	587,041	45	16,606,000	57	73.3	28.3	2.6	1993[6]	12,092,157	49.5	50.5	26.4[12]
Malawi	45,747	118,484	100	11,651,000	67	254.7	98.3	2.4	1998	9,933,868	49.0	51.0	14.0
Malaysia	127,355	329,847	66	25,225,000	43	198.1	76.5	2.9	2000	22,202,614	50.4	49.6	50.6[9]
Maldives	115	298	204	285,000	177	2,478.3	956.4	1.8	2000	269,010	51.2	48.8	25.5[29]
Mali	482,077	1,248,574	23	11,626,000	68	24.1	9.3	2.9	1987	7,696,348	48.9	51.1	22.0
Malta	122	316	203	399,000	172	3,270.5	1,262.7	0.7	1995	378,132	49.4	50.6	90.3[4]
Marshall Islands	70	181	208	56,400	209	805.7	311.6	1.8	1999	50,865	51.2	48.8	64.5[30]
Martinique	436	1,128	179	393,000	173	901.4	348.4	0.6	1999	381,427	47.4	52.6	94.6[4]
Mauritania	398,000	1,030,700	29	2,696,000	135	6.8	2.6	2.6	2000	2,548,157	48.7	51.3	57.7[10]
Mauritius	788	2,040	175	1,221,000	153	1,549.5	598.5	1.0	1990	1,056,827	49.9	50.1	39.3
Mayotte	144	374	199	166,000	187	1,152.8	443.9	4.0	1997	131,320	50.7	49.3	...
Mexico	758,449	1,964,375	15	100,588,000	11	132.6	51.2	1.2	2000	97,361,711	48.6	51.4	71.3
Micronesia	271	701	187	112,000	192	413.3	159.8	0.8	1994	105,506	51.1	48.9	28.0[12]
Moldova	13,066	33,843	138	4,267,000	117	326.6	126.1	–0.2	1989	4,337,592	47.5	52.5	46.9
Monaco	0.75	1.95	217	32,400	213	43,200.0	16,615.4	0.5	1990	29,972	47.5	52.5	100.0
Mongolia	603,909	1,564,116	19	2,493,000	138	4.1	1.6	1.4	2000	2,382,500	49.6	50.4	58.6
Morocco[32]	177,117	458,730	55	29,835,000	37	168.4	65.0	1.6	1994	25,821,571[33]	49.7[33]	50.3[33]	51.7[33]
Mozambique	313,661	812,379	35	18,568,000	54	59.2	22.9	1.8	1997	16,099,246	47.9	52.1	28.6
Myanmar (Burma)	261,228	676,577	40	42,511,000	28	162.7	62.8	0.6	1983	35,307,913	49.6	50.4	24.0
Namibia	318,580	825,118	34	1,927,000	144	6.0	2.3	2.0	1991	1,401,711	48.6	51.4	32.8
Nauru	8.2	21.2	216	12,600	216	1,536.6	594.3	2.0	1992	9,919	51.2	48.8	100.0
Nepal	56,827	147,181	94	24,172,000	45	425.4	164.2	2.2	1991	18,491,097	49.9	50.1	9.6

age distribution (%)						population (by decade, '000s)								country
0–14	15–29	30–44	45–59	60–74	75 and over	1950	1960	1970	1980	1990	2000	2010 projection	2020 projection	
37.7	27.6	18.6	10.4	5.0	0.7	20,461	26,085	33,329	40,546	51,959	63,978	77,085	88,917	Egypt
38.7	28.7	16.0	9.2	5.4	1.9	1,951	2,578	3,598	4,586	5,110	6,209	7,154	8,005	El Salvador
41.7	25.1	15.7	11.2	5.3	1.0	226	254	294	219	354	456	590	736	Equatorial Guinea
46.1	23.0	15.9	8.9	4.4	1.6	1,140	1,420	1,831	2,381	3,103	3,712	5,256	6,584	Eritrea
17.7[10]	22.1[10]	21.4[10]	18.4[10]	15.0[10]	5.4[10]	1,101	1,216	1,360	1,477	1,569	1,370	1,316	1,278	Estonia
46.1[16]	26.0[16]	15.1[16]	8.3[16]	3.8[16]	0.7[16]	20,175	24,252	29,673	36,413	47,958	62,651	75,066	85,965	Ethiopia
23.8	19.4	21.0	18.2	11.3	1.8	31	35	39	43	48	46	50	53	Faroe Islands
35.4	27.4	20.7	11.4	4.2	0.9	289	394	520	634	737	810	878	927	Fiji
19.3	20.5	24.6	17.1	12.9	5.7	4,009	4,430	4,606	4,800	4,986	5,176	5,267	5,317	Finland
17.9	20.2	21.9	18.7	13.6	7.7	41,736	45,684	50,770	53,880	56,710	58,893	61,507	63,205	France
34.0	24.2	23.3	12.5	4.3	1.7	27	33	49	68	116	164	208	252	French Guiana
33.7	27.3	21.6	11.4	5.0	1.0	62	84	117	151	197	235	275	308	French Polynesia
33.8[15]	23.7[15]	17.0[15]	17.4[15]	6.9[15]	1.2[15]	469	486	529	695	953	1,258	1,509	1,781	Gabon
43.8	27.7	15.1	6.8	3.5	1.4	294	355	469	652	936	1,312	1,680	2,015	Gambia, The
50.3	25.8	13.1	6.2	3.7	0.9	245	308	370	456	630	1,145	1,693	2,325	Gaza Strip
24.8	24.1	19.2	17.5	10.8	3.6	3,516	4,147	4,694	5,048	5,457	5,020	4,815	4,785	Georgia
15.8	17.9	24.6	19.3	15.5	6.9	68,377	72,674	77,709	78,275	79,365	82,188	83,065	82,144	Germany
45.0	26.4	14.6	8.1	4.1	1.8	5,297	6,958	8,789	11,016	15,400	19,509	22,230	24,336	Ghana
19.3	22.2	20.3	18.3	14.1	5.9	7,566	8,327	8,793	9,643	10,161	10,913	11,031	10,878	Greece
27.1	19.2	29.3	16.4	—8.0—		23	32	46	50	56	56	57	57	Greenland
42.5[8]	30.4[8]	12.9[8]	6.6[8]	5.5[8]	2.1[8]	76	90	95	89	95	100	106	112	Grenada
23.6	22.4	24.3	15.7	9.3	4.7	206	265	320	327	388	426	458	479	Guadeloupe
30.0	30.0	22.6	10.8	5.5	1.1	60	67	86	107	134	155	180	204	Guam
44.0	26.1	15.8	8.3	—5.8—		2,969	3,963	5,243	6,820	8,749	11,423	14,584	17,835	Guatemala
17.6	20.6	22.3	19.0	13.2	7.3	44	45	51	53	61	62	64	65	Guernsey
44.1[5]	26.5[5]	15.9[5]	9.0[5]	3.9[5]	0.6[5]	2,550	3,136	3,897	4,688	6,122	8,117	9,990	12,478	Guinea
43.9[8]	26.5[8]	16.1[8]	8.8[8]	3.7[8]	1.0[8]	573	617	620	789	996	1,278	1,566	1,882	Guinea-Bissau
35.4[8]	31.5[8]	17.8[8]	9.0[8]	4.8[8]	1.5[8]	428	560	714	759	759	772	782	759	Guyana
39.2	26.9	15.6	10.0	5.4	2.9	3,097	3,723	4,605	5,056	6,075	7,177	8,555	10,262	Haiti
46.8	25.8	14.4	7.9	3.8	1.4	1,431	1,952	2,683	3,635	4,876	6,352	7,884	9,155	Honduras
16.5	21.6	29.0	18.0	10.6	4.3	1,974	3,074	3,942	5,063	5,705	6,665	7,313	7,944	Hong Kong
21.3	19.4	22.5	17.9	13.4	5.6	9,338	9,984	10,337	10,707	10,374	10,211	9,920	9,570	Hungary
23.3	22.7	22.4	16.5	10.0	5.1	143	176	204	228	255	281	307	330	Iceland
33.1[19]	27.8[19]	19.9[19]	12.1[19]	5.6[19]	1.5[19]	357,561	442,344	554,911	688,856	846,418	1,016,938	1,173,806	1,312,212	India
36.6	28.3	18.1	10.6	5.2	1.1	79,538	95,931	119,998	150,128	182,117	211,559	238,374	261,053	Indonesia
44.3	26.6	15.1	8.2	4.8	0.8	16,913	21,554	28,359	38,783	54,134	63,664	71,482	79,721	Iran
43.8[20]	30.2[20]	14.5[20]	6.9[20]	3.6[20]	1.0[20]	5,163	6,822	9,413	13,233	18,135	22,676	29,672	36,908	Iraq
26.7	24.1	20.2	13.8	10.6	4.6	2,969	2,834	2,954	3,421	3,506	3,826	4,237	4,566	Ireland
17.6	19.0	20.6	19.5	14.4	8.9	55	49	52	64	69	76	80	84	Isle of Man
29.2	25.0	19.6	13.1	9.1	4.0	1,258	2,114	2,958	3,862	4,613	6,098	7,305	8,443	Israel[21, 22]
15.9	23.7	20.9	18.4	14.4	6.7	47,104	50,200	53,822	56,434	56,749	56,967	57,124	56,079	Italy
34.4	30.6	16.6	9.0	—9.4—		1,403	1,629	1,891	2,133	2,369	2,590	2,825	3,118	Jamaica
15.9	21.5	19.7	22.0	15.0	5.9	83,625	94,096	104,331	116,807	123,537	126,867	127,920	125,541	Japan
15.5[9]	24.9[9]	23.5[9]	17.0[9]	11.9[9]	6.8[9]	57	63	71	76	84	87	89	89	Jersey
41.3	31.8	14.6	8.1	3.4	0.8	1,095	1,384	1,795	2,183	3,306	4,970	6,302	7,462	Jordan[25]
31.9[26]	26.3[26]	19.4[26]	13.2[26]	6.9[26]	2.3[26]	6,693	9,982	13,106	14,994	16,708	14,869	14,499	14,779	Kazakhstan
47.8[26]	27.6[26]	13.1[26]	6.6[26]	3.4[26]	1.5[26]	6,121	8,157	11,272	16,698	23,934	30,310	33,654	34,848	Kenya
41.2	25.8	18.3	9.3	4.4	1.0	33	41	49	58	71	84	95	107	Kiribati
29.5[15]	31.9[15]	21.3[15]	11.0[15]	5.0[15]	1.2[15]	9,471	10,392	13,912	17,114	20,019	21,648	23,802	25,210	Korea, North
23.0	27.6	25.7	14.5	7.4	1.9	21,147	25,012	32,241	38,124	42,869	47,008	49,594	50,650	Korea, South
25.4[27]	26.4[27]	34.4[27]	11.1[27]	—2.7[27]—		145	292	748	1,358	2,141	2,236	2,944	3,529	Kuwait
37.5[26]	27.0[26]	16.3[26]	10.9[26]	6.2[26]	2.1[26]	1,740	2,173	2,965	3,631	4,395	4,884	5,539	6,144	Kyrgyzstan
45.4[12]	26.5[12]	14.9[12]	8.1[12]	4.2[12]	1.0[12]	1,755	2,177	2,713	3,205	4,132	5,279	6,592	7,967	Laos
21.4[26]	21.7[26]	20.3[26]	19.2[26]	12.0[26]	5.3[26]	1,949	2,121	2,359	2,512	2,713	2,373	2,213	2,064	Latvia
42.6	23.8	16.7	9.1	—7.7—		1,364	1,786	2,383	3,086	3,147	3,578	4,056	4,417	Lebanon
43.1	27.6	15.0	8.6	4.8	0.9	734	853	1,028	1,277	1,570	1,785	1,757	1,663	Lesotho
43.2	28.2	14.7	7.7	4.4	1.8	824	1,055	1,397	1,892	2,189	3,149	3,935	4,900	Liberia
45.4[12]	26.4[12]	14.7[12]	9.1[12]	3.7[12]	0.6[12]	1,029	1,349	1,986	3,043	4,306	5,237	6,332	7,378	Libya
18.7	20.6	25.8	20.5	9.7	4.7	14	16	21	26	29	33	36	38	Liechtenstein
22.6	23.8	20.0	17.9	10.9	4.8	2,553	2,765	3,138	3,436	3,698	3,500	3,321	3,140	Lithuania
17.3	21.5	23.8	17.5	12.8	7.1	296	314	339	364	382	436	494	550	Luxembourg
24.1	27.2	29.4	9.6	7.3	2.3	188	169	221	243	332	431	468	507	Macau
24.8	24.1	22.3	15.8	10.6	2.4	1,230	1,392	1,568	1,795	1,909	2,024	2,122	2,185	Macedonia
45.1[15]	26.8[15]	15.1[15]	7.7[15]	4.3[15]	1.0[15]	4,620	5,482	6,766	8,677	11,522	15,506	20,134	25,847	Madagascar
45.7[28]	29.2[28]	13.2[28]	7.5[28]	3.7[28]	0.7[28]	2,817	3,450	4,489	6,129	9,215	10,874	13,416	16,150	Malawi
36.7[9]	27.6[9]	20.0[9]	9.9[9]	4.6[9]	1.2[9]	6,187	7,908	10,466	13,764	17,857	23,242	28,414	32,614	Malaysia
46.4[29]	26.2[29]	14.3[29]	7.7[29]	4.3[29]	0.9[29]	79	92	115	155	215	271	318	372	Maldives
46.1	23.9	15.0	8.9	4.9	1.2	3,688	4,486	5,525	6,731	8,228	10,665	14,012	17,847	Mali
21.9	20.9	22.5	18.8	11.6	4.3	312	329	326	364	360	390	419	440	Malta
51.0[30]	24.5[30]	14.6[30]	5.5[30]	3.6[30]	0.8[30]	11	15	22	31	46	53	66	78	Marshall Islands
22.0	21.0	24.4	16.0	11.1	5.5	222	282	325	326	360	386	404	419	Martinique
46.2[10]	26.6[10]	15.6[10]	7.8[10]	3.3[10]	0.5[10]	960	1,057	1,227	1,550	1,963	2,487	3,291	4,181	Mauritania
29.7	28.9	22.3	10.9	6.6	1.6	479	662	829	966	1,059	1,187	1,295	1,390	Mauritius
43.5	29.9	15.6	6.6	2.7	1.7	17	25	35	52	89	147	216	292	Mayotte
38.3	29.4	16.6	8.9	4.5	1.7	27,737	36,945	50,596	67,570	81,700	97,743	109,116	120,937	Mexico
46.4[31]	26.8[31]	12.6[31]	8.5[31]	4.5[31]	1.1[31]	32	45	61	73	96	107	118	124	Micronesia
27.9	22.9	21.0	15.6	9.7	2.9	2,341	3,004	3,595	4,010	4,364	4,283	4,230	4,163	Moldova
12.3	16.7	21.2	20.4	17.9	10.8	18	21	24	27	30	32	33	35	Monaco
41.9[26]	29.2[26]	14.6[26]	8.5[26]	—5.8[26]—		747	931	1,248	1,663	2,086	2,390	2,748	3,097	Mongolia
37.0[16]	29.6[16]	17.3[16]	9.2[16]	5.4[16]	1.5[16]	8,953	11,640	15,126	19,206	23,986	28,460	33,261	37,924	Morocco[32]
43.5[20]	28.6[20]	15.1[20]	8.5[20]	3.6[20]	0.7[20]	6,250	7,472	9,304	12,103	12,649	17,673	19,721	20,547	Mozambique
38.6	28.7	15.5	10.9	5.2	1.1	19,488	22,836	27,386	33,283	38,526	41,772	43,721	44,825	Myanmar (Burma)
41.7	28.8	14.7	7.8	—6.9—		464	591	765	975	1,409	1,826	2,036	2,081	Namibia
41.8	25.0	20.7	8.2	—2.8—		3	4	7	8	10	12	14	17	Nauru
42.3	25.7	16.7	9.7	4.7	0.9	8,502	9,839	11,880	14,559	18,142	22,648	28,061	33,600	Nepal

Area and population (continued)

country	area			population (latest estimate)					population (recent census)				
	square miles	square kilo-metres	rank	total midyear 2003	rank	density		% annual growth rate 1998–2003	census year	total	male (%)	female (%)	urban (%)
						per sq mi	per sq km						
Netherlands, The	16,034	41,528	134	16,238,000	58	1,012.7	391.0	0.7	2000	15,864,000	49.5	50.5	89.4[10]
Netherlands Antilles	308	800	183	169,000	186	548.7	211.3	–1.2	1992	189,474	47.9	52.1	...
New Caledonia	7,172	18,575	154	220,000	182	30.7	11.8	1.5	1996	196,836	51.2	48.8	60.4
New Zealand	104,454	270,534	74	4,001,000	121	38.3	14.8	1.0	1996	3,681,546	49.1	50.9	85.0
Nicaragua	50,337	130,373	97	5,482,000	105	108.9	42.0	2.6	1995	4,357,099	49.3	50.7	54.4
Niger	489,000	1,267,000	22	11,380,000	69	23.3	9.0	2.9	1988	7,228,552	49.5	50.5	15.3
Nigeria	356,669	923,768	32	125,275,000	10	351.2	135.6	2.9	1991	88,514,501	50.3	49.7	35.0[7]
Northern Mariana Islands	184	477	193	73,300	202	398.4	153.7	2.5	1995	58,846	49.8	50.2	28.0[2]
Norway	125,004	323,758	67	4,569,000	115	36.6	14.1	0.6	1990	4,247,546	49.4	50.6	72.0
Oman	119,500	309,500	70	2,621,000	137	21.9	8.5	2.8	1993	2,018,074	58.4	41.6	71.7
Pakistan[34]	307,374	796,096	36	149,030,000	6	484.8	187.2	2.2	1998	130,579,571	52.0	48.0	33.3
Palau	188	488	192	20,200	215	107.4	41.4	1.9	2000	19,129	54.6	45.4	71.4[29]
Panama	28,950	74,979	118	3,116,000	133	107.6	41.6	1.9	2000	2,839,177	50.5	49.5	56.3
Papua New Guinea	178,704	462,840	54	5,583,000	103	31.2	12.1	2.8	2000	5,130,000	51.9	48.1	15.2[2]
Paraguay	157,048	406,752	59	5,642,000	102	35.9	13.9	2.2	1992	4,123,550	50.2	49.8	50.5
Peru	496,225	1,285,216	20	27,148,000	39	54.7	21.1	1.6	1993	22,639,443	49.7	50.3	70.1
Philippines	115,860	300,076	72	81,161,000	14	700.5	270.5	2.1	1995	68,613,706	50.4	49.6	54.0[12]
Poland	120,728	312,685	69	38,623,000	30	319.9	123.5	0.0	1988	37,878,641	48.7	51.3	61.2
Portugal	35,580	92,152	111	10,181,000	77	286.1	110.5	0.2	2001	10,318,084[6]	48.3[6]	51.7[6]	48.2[9]
Puerto Rico	3,515	9,104	166	3,879,000	123	1,103.6	426.1	0.5	2000	3,808,610	48.1	51.9	71.2[2]
Qatar	4,412	11,427	161	626,000	162	141.9	54.8	2.9	1997	522,023	65.6	34.4	91.4[12]
Réunion	968	2,507	174	760,000	159	785.1	303.2	1.7	1999	706,180	49.1	50.9	70.3[4]
Romania	91,699	237,500	82	21,616,000	49	235.7	91.0	–0.4	1992	22,760,449	49.1	50.9	54.4
Russia	6,592,800	17,075,400	1	144,893,000	7	22.0	8.5	–0.3	1989	147,400,537	46.9	53.1	73.6
Rwanda	10,169	26,338	147	8,387,000	87	824.8	318.4	5.0	1991	7,164,994	48.7	51.3	5.4
St. Kitts and Nevis	104	269	205	46,400	211	446.2	172.5	0.9	1991	40,618	49.1	50.9	48.9[7]
St. Lucia	238	617	189	162,000	189	680.7	262.6	1.3	1991	133,308	48.5	51.5	44.1[7]
St. Vincent and the Grenadines	150	389	198	113,000	191	753.3	290.5	0.2	1991	106,499	49.9	50.1	24.6
Samoa	1,093	2,831	172	179,000	184	163.8	63.2	0.8	1991	161,298	52.5	47.5	21.2
San Marino	24	61	212	29,200	214	1,216.7	478.7	1.5	1997	25,872[3]	49.3	50.7	96.0[12]
São Tomé and Príncipe	386	1,001	181	142,000	190	367.9	141.9	1.6	1991	117,504	49.4	50.6	44.1[24]
Saudi Arabia	830,000	2,149,690	14	24,008,000	46	28.9	11.2	3.0	1992	16,948,388	55.9	44.1	77.3[7]
Senegal	75,955	196,722	87	10,095,000	79	132.9	51.3	2.4	1988	6,928,405	48.7	51.3	38.6
Serbia and Montenegro	39,449	102,173	107	10,527,000	74	266.9	103.0	–0.1	1991	10,394,026	49.6	50.4	53.2[7]
Seychelles	176	455	195	81,500	199	463.1	179.1	1.2	1997	75,876	49.5	50.5	54.8[12]
Sierra Leone	27,699	71,740	119	4,971,000	112	179.5	69.3	3.4	1985	3,517,530	49.6	50.4	31.8
Singapore	265	685	188	4,233,000	118	15,973.6	6,179.6	1.5	2000[6]	3,263,209	50.0	50.0	100.0
Slovakia	18,933	49,035	129	5,402,000	107	285.3	110.2	0.1	1991	5,268,935	48.9	51.1	56.8
Slovenia	7,827	20,273	153	1,971,000	143	251.8	97.2	0.2	1991	1,974,839	48.5	51.5	48.9
Solomon Islands	10,954	28,370	143	450,000	167	41.1	15.9	2.7	1986	285,176	51.9	48.1	15.7
Somalia	246,000	637,000	42	8,025,000	90	32.6	12.6	3.2	1975	4,089,203	50.1	49.9	25.4
South Africa	470,693	1,219,090	25	45,349,000	26	96.3	37.2	1.5	1996	40,583,573	48.1	51.9	53.7
Spain	195,379	506,030	51	42,600,000	27	218.0	84.2	0.4	1991	38,999,181	49.1	50.9	75.3
Sri Lanka	25,332	65,610	122	19,065,000	53	752.6	290.6	0.8	1981	14,848,364	50.8	49.2	21.5
Sudan, The	966,757	2,503,890	10	38,114,000	31	39.4	15.2	2.9	1993	24,940,683	50.2	49.8	31.3[12]
Suriname	63,251	163,820	91	435,000	170	6.9	2.7	0.5	1980	354,860	49.5	50.5	49.1[12]
Swaziland	6,704	17,364	157	1,077,000	154	160.7	62.0	1.4	1997	929,718	47.3	52.7	23.1
Sweden	173,732	449,964	56	8,958,000	83	51.6	19.9	0.2	1999[3]	8,861,426	49.4	50.6	83.3[4]
Switzerland	15,940	41,284	135	7,336,000	93	460.2	177.7	0.6	1990[36]	6,873,687	49.3	50.7	68.9
Syria	71,498	185,180	88	17,586,000	55	246.0	95.0	2.6	1994	13,812,284	50.7	49.3	52.2[12]
Taiwan	13,972	36,188	136	22,569,000	47	1,615.3	623.7	0.7	1990[6]	20,393,628	52.1	47.9	74.5
Tajikistan	55,300	143,100	95	6,535,000	97	118.2	45.7	1.9	1989	5,108,576	49.7	50.3	32.6
Tanzania	364,901	945,090	31	35,078,000	33	96.1	37.1	2.7	1988	23,174,336	48.9	51.1	18.5
Thailand	198,116	513,119	50	64,022,000	19	323.2	124.8	0.9	2000	60,606,947	49.2	50.8	31.1
Togo	21,925	56,785	125	5,429,000	106	247.6	95.6	2.7	1981	2,719,567	48.7	51.3	15.2
Tonga	290	750	185	102,000	194	351.7	136.0	0.6	1996[6]	97,784	50.7	49.3	32.1
Trinidad and Tobago	1,980	5,128	169	1,279,000	152	646.0	249.4	0.4	1990	1,234,388	50.1	49.9	64.8
Tunisia	63,170	163,610	92	9,888,000	80	156.5	60.4	1.2	1994	8,785,711	50.6	49.4	61.0
Turkey	299,158	774,815	37	70,597,000	15	236.0	91.1	1.7	1997	62,865,574	50.7[2]	49.3[2]	65.0
Turkmenistan	188,500	488,100	52	4,867,000	114	25.8	10.0	1.7	1995	4,483,251	49.6	50.4	46.0
Tuvalu	9.9	25.6	215	10,200	217	1,030.3	398.4	0.2	1991	9,043	48.4	51.6	42.5
Uganda	93,065	241,038	80	25,437,000	42	273.3	105.5	3.5	1991	16,671,705	49.1	50.9	11.3
Ukraine	233,100	603,700	44	47,856,000	25	205.3	79.3	–1.0	1989	51,706,746	46.3	53.7	66.9
United Arab Emirates	32,280	83,600	115	3,818,000	124	118.3	45.7	6.1	1995	2,411,041	66.6	33.4	77.3
United Kingdom	94,248	244,101	79	59,164,000	21	627.7	242.4	0.3	1991[6]	56,467,000	48.4	51.6	89.1[7]
United States	3,615,215[37]	9,363,364[37]	4	291,587,000	3	80.7	31.1	1.1	2000	281,421,906	49.1	50.9	75.2[2]
Uruguay	68,037	176,215	90	3,380,000	130	49.7	19.2	0.7	1996	3,151,662	48.4	51.6	89.3
Uzbekistan	172,700	447,400	57	25,640,000	41	148.5	57.3	1.3	1989	19,905,158	49.3	50.7	40.7
Vanuatu	4,707	12,190	160	204,000	183	43.3	16.7	2.5	1999	193,219	51.5	48.5	21.5
Venezuela	353,841	916,445	33	25,699,000	40	72.6	28.0	2.0	1990	19,405,429	49.7	50.3	84.0
Vietnam	128,379	332,501	65	81,377,000	13	633.9	244.7	1.4	1999	76,324,753	49.2	50.8	23.5
Virgin Islands (U.S.)	136	352	201	111,000	193	816.2	315.3	0.7	1990	101,809	48.3	51.7	37.2
West Bank[38]	2,270	5,900	167	2,467,000	139	1,086.8	418.1	3.7	1995[3, 17]	1,707,000	51.2	48.8	...
Western Sahara	97,344	252,120	77	262,000	180	2.7	1.0	2.3	1994	252,146	...	...	90.7
Yemen	214,300	555,000	48	20,010,000	51	93.4	36.1	3.5	1994	14,587,807	51.2	48.8	23.5
Zambia	290,585	752,612	39	10,812,000	72	37.2	14.4	1.5	1990	7,818,447	49.2	50.8	42.0
Zimbabwe	150,872	390,757	60	11,719,000	66	77.7	30.0	1.1	1992	10,412,548	48.8	51.2	30.6

[1]Settled population only. [2]1990 census. [3]Civil register; not a census. [4]1999 estimate. [5]1996 estimate. [6]Data are for de jure population. [7]1990 estimate. [8]1991 estimate. [9]1991 census. [10]2000 estimate. [11]1992 census. [12]1995 estimate. [13]Data are for the island of Cyprus (excepting census information). [14]Republic of Cyprus only. [15]1993 estimate. [16]1994 estimate. [17]Projections from 1995 demographic survey. [18]Data exclude Alderney (population 2,297) and Sark (population 604). [19]2001 estimate. [20]1997 estimate. [21]Area figures exclude the West Bank, East Jerusalem, Gaza Strip, and Golan Heights. [22]Population figures include Golan Heights and East Jerusalem and exclude Israelis in the West Bank and Gaza Strip. [23]Includes East

age distribution (%)						population (by decade, '000s)								country
0–14	15–29	30–44	45–59	60–74	75 and over	1950	1960	1970	1980	1990	2000	2010 projection	2020 projection	
18.6	19.3	24.2	19.8	12.1	6.0	10,090	11,494	13,020	14,127	14,951	15,917	16,694	17,231	Netherlands, The
26.0	23.9	25.5	14.3	7.3	3.0	112	136	163	174	188	177	169	169	Netherlands Antilles
30.7	27.2	21.3	13.3	5.9	1.6	59	79	110	140	171	211	240	265	New Caledonia
23.0	22.3	23.0	16.2	10.6	4.9	1,909	2,377	2,820	3,144	3,452	3,859	4,216	4,480	New Zealand
45.1	27.5	15.0	7.2	3.7	1.4	1,134	1,542	2,123	2,919	3,824	5,073	6,378	7,679	Nicaragua
48.7	24.8	14.6	6.8	3.6	1.5	2,482	3,168	4,182	5,629	7,729	10,480	13,647	17,112	Niger
45.5[8]	26.0[8]	15.3[8]	8.8[8]	3.8[8]	0.6[8]	29,790	37,446	47,980	64,325	86,018	115,224	147,677	179,288	Nigeria
24.6	31.9	31.6	9.6	1.8	0.5	6	9	10	17	44	70	73	73	Northern Mariana Islands
18.8	22.9	22.1	15.1	13.9	7.2	3,265	3,581	3,877	4,086	4,241	4,487	4,736	4,989	Norway
41.0	25.5	21.9	7.8	2.9	0.9	489	499	779	1,060	1,625	2,401	3,189	4,009	Oman
43.2	26.9	15.6	8.8	4.3	1.2	39,448	50,387	65,706	85,219	109,710	139,760	169,480	197,538	Pakistan[34]
23.9	24.2	29.9	14.2	5.5	2.3	7	9	12	13	15	19	22	24	Palau
32.0	26.8	20.6	12.0	6.1	2.5	860	1,126	1,506	1,949	2,411	2,948	3,504	4,011	Panama
41.9[2]	28.5[2]	16.6[2]	8.7[2]	— 3.2[2] —		1,412	1,747	2,288	2,991	3,758	5,187	6,430	7,637	Papua New Guinea
40.1	27.6	18.7	8.3	4.2	1.1	1,488	1,842	2,350	3,114	4,219	5,282	6,622	8,082	Paraguay
37.0	28.6	17.7	9.8	— 7.0 —		7,632	9,931	13,193	17,324	21,753	25,939	29,958	33,923	Peru
38.3	28.4	18.3	9.5	4.3	1.2	20,988	27,561	36,850	48,286	60,937	76,797	92,330	107,235	Philippines
25.4	21.2	23.3	15.5	10.4	4.2	24,824	29,561	32,526	35,578	38,057	38,649	38,691	38,455	Poland
20.0[9]	23.7[9]	20.2[9]	17.1[9]	13.7[9]	5.3[9]	8,443	9,037	9,044	9,778	9,923	10,133	10,273	10,190	Portugal
23.8	23.2	20.6	17.1	10.5	4.8	2,218	2,360	2,722	3,210	3,537	3,816	4,001	4,109	Puerto Rico
29.7[20]	30.7[20]	31.0[20]	7.0[20]	1.4[20]	0.2[20]	47	59	151	229	423	579	689	773	Qatar
27.0	24.8	24.4	13.8	7.2	2.8	244	338	447	507	601	722	826	905	Réunion
22.4	22.9	20.8	17.1	— 16.8 —		16,311	18,403	20,253	22,201	23,207	21,881	21,265	20,571	Romania
23.1	22.0	21.9	17.6	11.2	4.2	101,937	119,632	130,245	139,045	148,082	146,093	142,689	139,331	Russia
45.6	28.6	12.4	8.4	3.9	0.9	2,162	2,887	3,776	5,157	6,775	7,724	9,559	11,557	Rwanda
36.9[8]	31.8[8]	14.5[8]	6.0[8]	6.9[8]	3.8[8]	49	51	46	44	41	45	48	53	St. Kitts and Nevis
36.8	29.4	16.3	8.7	6.3	2.5	79	86	101	115	134	156	177	199	St. Lucia
37.2	29.5	16.1	8.3	6.4	2.5	67	80	86	99	105	112	115	115	St. Vincent and the Grenadines
40.5	30.0	14.6	8.7	— 6.0 —		82	111	143	155	160	175	193	215	Samoa
14.6	20.5	25.9	18.5	13.8	6.7	13	15	19	21	23	27	32	35	San Marino
46.9	26.2	12.2	8.0	— 6.7 —		60	64	74	94	116	135	158	185	São Tomé and Príncipe
41.8	26.8	20.4	7.0	3.0	1.0	3,201	4,075	5,745	9,604	16,554	22,010	28,990	36,022	Saudi Arabia
47.5	26.1	13.6	7.8	— 5.0 —		2,500	3,187	4,158	5,538	7,345	9,393	11,869	14,422	Senegal
22.8	21.6	21.7	17.1	12.2	3.5	7,131	8,050	8,691	9,522	10,156	10,555	10,498	10,357	Serbia and Montenegro
28.8	27.4	22.6	10.6	7.5	3.1	34	42	54	63	70	79	84	88	Seychelles
43.9[35]	25.6[35]	15.7[35]	9.6[35]	4.5[35]	0.7[35]	1,944	2,242	2,657	3,239	4,054	4,415	5,859	6,979	Sierra Leone
21.5	21.2	28.4	18.2	8.2	2.5	1,022	1,639	2,075	2,414	3,047	4,018	4,561	4,799	Singapore
25.0	22.7	22.8	14.6	10.7	4.2	3,463	3,994	4,528	4,984	5,256	5,391	5,434	5,428	Slovakia
20.0	22.4	23.7	17.4	11.9	4.6	1,467	1,558	1,676	1,833	1,896	1,956	2,004	2,019	Slovenia
47.3	25.7	13.9	8.1	— 4.9 —		107	126	163	232	315	416	542	673	Solomon Islands
45.6	24.9	15.5	7.4	— 5.4 —		2,438	2,956	3,667	5,791	6,675	7,253	9,922	13,023	Somalia
33.9	28.6	19.4	9.8	5.3	1.8	13,683	17,396	22,657	29,140	36,848	43,698	45,261	43,996	South Africa
19.4	24.9	20.0	16.5	13.6	5.6	27,868	30,303	33,779	37,636	38,798	40,599	42,600	42,600	Spain
35.3	29.6	17.9	10.6	5.2	1.4	7,483	9,701	12,295	14,543	16,830	18,595	20,046	21,121	Sri Lanka
43.0	27.0	16.4	9.3	3.7	0.6	8,051	10,589	13,788	19,064	26,627	35,080	45,485	56,162	Sudan, The
39.3	29.5	13.8	10.0	4.5	2.8	208	285	373	355	395	429	441	439	Suriname
44.3	28.6	14.4	7.7	3.4	1.6	273	351	443	596	847	1,044	1,084	1,062	Swaziland
18.5	18.3	20.7	20.3	13.3	8.9	7,014	7,480	8,042	8,310	8,559	8,872	9,245	9,696	Sweden
16.8	22.8	23.2	18.0	12.5	6.7	4,715	5,429	6,270	6,362	6,712	7,184	7,549	7,675	Switzerland
44.7	28.2	14.8	7.3	— 5.0 —		3,495	4,533	6,258	8,774	12,436	16,306	20,606	24,676	Syria
27.1	27.8	23.1	12.3	7.9	1.8	7,619	10,668	14,583	17,642	20,279	22,185	23,395	24,218	Taiwan
42.9	28.1	13.8	9.0	4.6	1.6	1,532	2,083	2,942	3,968	5,213	6,169	7,047	8,105	Tajikistan
45.8	26.7	13.5	7.8	4.5	1.7	7,935	10,260	13,842	18,939	24,354	32,497	40,216	47,729	Tanzania
28.8[2]	30.4[2]	21.2[2]	12.3[2]	5.7[2]	1.6[2]	20,010	26,392	35,037	46,538	56,096	62,408	67,828	71,650	Thailand
49.8	24.8	13.1	6.8	3.3	2.0	1,172	1,456	1,964	2,596	3,705	5,033	6,256	7,195	Togo
39.1	28.0	15.1	10.0	6.0	1.8	50	65	80	92	96	100	106	113	Tonga
33.5	27.2	19.9	10.7	6.4	2.3	668	828	941	1,082	1,235	1,263	1,304	1,339	Trinidad and Tobago
34.8	28.5	18.8	9.6	6.4	1.9	3,517	4,149	5,099	6,443	8,207	9,563	10,624	11,601	Tunisia
35.0[2]	28.6[2]	18.4[2]	10.9[2]	5.6[2]	1.6[2]	21,122	28,217	35,758	44,439	56,098	67,418	77,200	84,864	Turkey
40.5[26]	28.8[26]	15.5[26]	9.1[26]	4.7[26]	1.4[26]	1,211	1,594	2,189	2,861	3,668	4,643	5,412	6,211	Turkmenistan
34.6	24.0	20.7	11.3	— 9.2 —		5	5	6	8	9	10	11	13	Tuvalu
47.3	27.7	13.1	6.9	3.7	1.3	5,522	7,262	9,728	12,298	16,447	22,962	32,424	45,826	Uganda
21.5	21.0	20.6	18.5	10.7	7.7	36,906	42,783	47,317	50,034	51,892	49,235	45,970	44,148	Ukraine
26.3	29.2	33.2	9.6	1.4	0.3	70	90	223	1,042	1,844	3,247	4,299	4,839	United Arab Emirates
19.1	21.9	21.2	16.7	14.1	7.0	50,290	52,372	55,632	56,330	57,436	58,654	60,350	62,197	United Kingdom
21.4	20.8	23.3	18.2	10.4	5.9	152,271	180,671	204,879	227,726	249,806	282,434	310,489	337,474	United States
25.1	22.9	19.6	15.1	12.2	5.1	2,194	2,531	2,824	2,914	3,041	3,322	3,517	3,719	Uruguay
40.8	28.4	15.0	9.3	4.7	1.8	6,314	8,559	11,973	15,977	20,515	24,741	28,354	31,793	Uzbekistan
45.5[26]	26.6[26]	15.2[26]	8.4[26]	3.7[26]	0.6[26]	52	66	85	117	147	190	240	290	Vanuatu
38.3	28.1	18.6	9.3	4.5	1.2	5,094	7,579	10,721	15,091	19,502	24,277	28,955	33,300	Venezuela
39.0[26]	28.7[26]	16.0[26]	9.1[26]	5.6[26]	1.6[26]	27,367	33,648	42,898	53,005	66,074	78,137	89,128	100,079	Vietnam
28.9	23.7	22.0	16.0	7.3	2.2	27	32	64	97	101	109	118	126	Virgin Islands (U.S.)
44.6	28.4	14.0	7.4	4.4	1.2	...	...	608	733	1,011	2,211	2,995	3,731	West Bank[38]
...	...	...	...	...	...	14	32	76	126	191	245	301	357	Western Sahara
47.6[16]	28.7[16]	11.9[16]	7.4[16]	3.6[16]	0.7[16]	4,316	5,211	6,290	8,140	11,944	18,017	25,662	36,537	Yemen
47.3	28.2	12.9	7.3	3.5	0.7	2,440	3,141	4,228	5,977	8,200	10,419	11,768	13,558	Zambia
45.1	28.3	14.0	7.2	3.9	1.2	2,853	4,011	5,515	7,170	10,154	11,367	12,044	11,957	Zimbabwe

Jerusalem and Israelis in the West Bank, Gaza Strip, and Golan Heights. [24]1992 estimate. [25]Excludes the West Bank. [26]1989 census. [27]1998 official country estimate including nonresidents. [28]1998 estimate. [29]1995 census. [30]1988 census. [31]1980 census. [32]Excludes Western Sahara, an annexure of Morocco. [33]Includes Western Sahara. [34]Excludes Afghan refugees (2003; *c.* 1.5 million) and the area (32,494 sq mi [84,159 sq km]) and population (2003; *c.* 4.15 million) of Pakistani-occupied Jammu and Kashmir. [35]1985 estimate. [36]Includes resident aliens; excludes seasonal workers. [37]Includes inland water area of 78,937 sq mi (204,446 sq km); excludes Great Lakes water area of 60,052 sq mi (155,534 sq km). [38]Excludes East Jerusalem.

Major cities and national capitals

The following table lists the principal cities or municipalities (those exceeding 100,000 in population [75,000 for Anglo-America, Australia, and the United Kingdom]) of the countries of the world, together with figures for each national capital (indicated by a ★), regardless of size.

Most of the populations given refer to a so-called city proper, that is, a legally defined, incorporated, or chartered area defined by administrative boundaries and by national or state law. Some data, however, refer to the municipality, or commune, similar to the medieval city-state in that the city is governed together with its immediately adjoining, economically dependent areas, whether urban or rural in nature. Some countries define no other demographic or legal entities within such communes or municipalities, but many identify a centre, seat, head (*cabecera*), or locality that corresponds to the most densely populated, compact, contiguous core of the municipality. Because the amount of work involved in carefully defining these "centres" may be considerable, the necessary resources usually exist only at the time of a national census (generally 5 or 10 years apart). Between censuses, therefore, it may be possible only to track the growth of the municipality as a whole. Thus, in order to provide the most up-to-date data for cities in this table, figures referring to municipalities or communes may be given (identified by the abbreviation "MU"), even though the country itself may define a smaller, more closely knit city proper. Specific identification of municipalities is provided in this table *only* when the country also publishes data for a more narrowly defined city proper; it is *not* provided when the sole published figure is the municipality, whether or not this is the proper local administrative term for the entity.

Populations for urban agglomerations as defined by the United Nations are occasionally inset beneath the populations of cities proper. Specifically that is when the urban agglomeration populations are at least three times the size of cities proper.

For certain countries, more than one form of the name of the city is given, usually to permit recognition of recent place-name changes or of *forms* of the place-name likely to be encountered in press stories if the title of the city's entry in the *Encyclopædia Britannica* is spelled according to a different romanization or spelling policy.

Chinese names for China are usually given in their Pinyin spelling, the official Chinese system encountered in official documents and maps. For Taiwan, the Wade-Giles spelling of place-names is used.

Sources for this data were often national censuses and statistical abstracts of the countries concerned, supplemented by Internet sources.

Internet sources for further information

- City Population: http://www.citypopulation.de/cities.html
- The World Gazetteer: http://www.gazetteer.de/st/stata.htm

Major cities and national capitals

country city	population
Afghanistan (early 1990s est.)	
Herāt	186,800
★ Kābul	700,000[1]
agglomeration	2,454,000[2]
Kandahār (Qandahār)	237,500
Mazār-e Sharīf	127,800
Albania (1999 est.)	
★ Tiranë	279,000
Algeria (1998)	
★ Algiers	1,519,570
Annaba	348,554
Batna	242,514
Béchar	131,010
Bejaïa	147,076
Biskra (Beskra)	170,956
Blida (el-Boulaida)	226,512
Bordj Bou Arreridj	128,535
Constantine (Qacentina)	462,187
Djelfa	154,265
Ech-Cheliff (el-Asnam)	179,768
El-Eulma	105,130
El-Wad	104,801
Ghardaïa	110,724
Ghilizane	104,285
Guelma	108,734
Jijel	106,003
Khenchela	106,082
Médéa	123,535
Mostaganem	124,399
Oran (Wahran)	692,516
Saïda	110,865
Sétif (Stif)	211,859
Sidi bel Abbès	180,260
Skikda	152,335
Souq Ahras	115,882
Tébessa (Tbessa)	153,246
Tihert	145,332
Tlemcen (Tilimsen)	155,162
Touggourt	113,625
Wargla (Ouargla)	129,402
American Samoa (1990)	
★ Fagatogo (legislative and judicial)	2,323[3]
★ Utulei (executive)	930[3]
Andorra (1999 est.)	
★ Andorra la Vella	21,513
Angola (1999 est.)	
Huambo	400,000[4]
★ Luanda	2,555,000
Antigua and Barbuda (1991)	
★ Saint John's	22,342
Argentina (1999 est.)	
Almirante Brown	550,000
Avellaneda	342,193
Bahía Blanca	281,161
Belén de Escobar	192,992
Berazategui	296,759
★ Buenos Aires	2,904,192
agglomeration	12,423,000
Caseros	341,398
Catamarca	140,000
Comodoro Rivadavia	144,074
Concordia	131,716
Córdoba	1,275,585
Corrientes	325,628
Esteban Echeverría	234,188
Florencio Valera	331,358
Formosa	197,057
General San Martín	409,879
General Sarmiento	209,450
Godoy Cruz	205,955
Hurlingham	165,986
Ituzaingo	154,437
José Carlos Paz	219,624
La Matanza (San Justo)	1,241,264
La Plata	556,308
La Rioja	138,074
Lanús	470,000
Las Heras	183,511
Lomas de Zamora	609,621
Mar del Plata	579,483
Mendoza	119,681
Mercedes	100,876
Merlo	430,213
Moreno	398,023
Morón	340,645
Neuquén	327,374
Paraná	256,602
Pilar	166,587
Posadas	250,000
Quilmes	550,069
Resistencia	280,000
Río Cuarto	150,000
Rosario	1,000,000
Salta	457,223
San Carlos de Bariloche	105,093
San Fernando	146,896
San Isidro	296,935
San Juan	120,000
San Luis	146,855
San Miguel	246,503
San Miguel de Tucumán	519,252
San Nicolás de los Arroyos	132,909
San Rafael	111,066
San Salvador de Jujuy	226,961
Santa Fe	400,000
Santiago del Estero	202,876
Tigre	299,376
Trelew	101,425
Vicente López	279,464
Villa Krause	100,000
Villa Nueva	224,116
Armenia (1995 est.)	
Gyumri (Kumayri; Leninakan)	120,000[5]
★ Yerevan	1,248,700
Aruba (1998 est.)	
★ Oranjestad	28,000
Australia (1998 est.)	
Adelaide UC[6]	978,100[7]
Adelaide	12,922
Charles Sturt	103,012
Marion	77,547
Onkaparinga	146,367
Port Adelaide Enfield	101,225
Salisbury	112,344
Tea Tree Gully	96,972
Brisbane UC[6]	1,291,117[7]
Brisbane	848,741
Ipswich	132,232
Logan	165,924
Canberra-Queanbeyan UC[6]	322,723[7]
★ Canberra	306,000
Melbourne UC[6]	2,865,329[7]
Banyule	119,486
Bayside	88,449
Boroondara	157,208
Brimbank	158,032
Casey	160,845
Dandenong	132,091
Darebin	129,005
Frankston	111,081
Glen Eira	122,535
Hobsons Bay	80,825
Hume	126,350
Kingston	132,895
Knox	141,016
Manningham	112,503
Maroondah	97,321
Melbourne	44,619
Monash	161,996
Moonee Valley	111,898
Moreland	137,258
Port Philip	78,680
Stonnington	90,546
Whitehorse	145,611
Whittlesea	111,040
Wyndham	80,931
Perth UC[6]	1,096,829[7]
Gosnells	79,372
Melville	95,854
Perth	5,957
Stirling	175,569
Wanneroo	154,641
Sydney UC[6]	3,276,207[7]
Bankstown	167,839
Blacktown	248,525
Blue Mountains	75,855
Campbelltown	149,489
Canterbury	140,435
Fairfield	190,920
Gosford	155,144
Holroyd	86,280
Liverpool	137,066
Parramatta	144,366
Penrith	171,420
Randwick	125,359
Rockdale	90,372
Ryde	97,598
South Sydney	83,752
Sydney	24,883
Other cities	
Ballarat	80,330
Bendigo	86,451
Cairns	118,834
Geelong	186,307
Gold Coast	380,270
Lake Macquarie	180,826
Newcastle	139,171
Shoalhaven	81,253
Toowoomba	86,968
Townsville	87,235
Wollongong	185,397
Austria (2001)	
Graz	226,424
Innsbruck	113,826
Linz	186,298
Salzburg	144,816
★ Vienna	1,562,676
Azerbaijan (1997 est.)	
★ Baku (Baky)	1,727,200
Gäncä (Gyandzha)	291,900
Sumqayit (Sumgait)	248,500
Bahamas, The (1999 est.)	
★ Nassau	214,000[8]
Bahrain (1999 est.)	
★ Al-Manāmah	162,000
Bangladesh (1991)	
Barisal	170,232
Bogra	120,170
Brahmanbaria	109,032
Chittagong	1,392,860
Comilla	135,313
★ Dhaka (Dacca)	3,612,850
agglomeration	11,726,000[2]
Dinajpur	127,815
Jamalpur	103,556
Jessore	139,710
Khulna	663,340
Mymensingh	188,713
Naogaon	101,266
Narayanganj	276,549
Nawabganj (Nowabgonj)	130,577
Pabna	103,277
Rajshahi	294,056
Rangpur	191,398
Sylhet	117,396
Tangail	106,004
Tongi	168,702
Barbados (1990)	
★ Bridgetown	6,070
agglomeration	133,000[2]
Belarus (1998 est.)	
Baranovichi (Baranavichy)	173,000
Bobruysk (Babrujsk)	227,000
Borisov (Barysau)	153,000
Brest (Bierascie)	297,000
Gomel (Homiel)	513,000
Grodno (Horadnia)	306,000
Lida	100,000
★ Minsk	1,717,000
Mogilyov (Mahilou)	369,000
Mozyr (Mazyr)	109,000
Orsha (Vorsha)	138,000
Pinsk	132,000
Soligorsk	102,000
Vitebsk (Viciebsk)	364,000
Belgium (2000 est.)	
Antwerp	446,525
Brugge (Bruges)	116,246
★ Brussels	133,859
agglomeration	1,121,000[2]
Charleroi	200,827
Ghent	224,180
Liège (Luik)	185,639
Namur	105,419
Schaerbeek	105,692
Belize (2000)	
★ Belmopan	8,130
Benin (1992)	
★ Cotonou (official)	533,212
Djougou	132,192
Parakou	106,708
★ Porto-Novo (de facto)	177,660
Bermuda (1995 est.)	
★ Hamilton	1,100
Bhutan (1999 est.)	
★ Thimphu	28,000
Bolivia (2000 est.)	
Cochabamba	607,129
El Alto	568,919
★ La Paz (administrative)	1,000,899
Oruro	232,311
Potosí	147,351
Quillacollo	132,579
Santa Cruz	1,016,137
★ Sucre (judicial)	192,238
Tarija	135,679
Bosnia and Herzegovina (1997 est.)	
Banja Luka	160,000
★ Sarajevo	360,000
Botswana (1997 est.)	
★ Gaborone	183,487
Brazil (2000)[9]	
Águas Lindas de Goiás	105,216
Alagoinhas	112,339
Alvorada	182,864
Americana	181,650
Ananindeua	391,994
Anápolis	279,752
Angra dos Reis	114,237

country / city	population
Aparecida de Golânia	334,994
Apucarana	100,241
Aracaju	460,898
Araçatuba	164,440
Araguaina	105,701
Arapiraca	152,281
Araraquara	173,086
Barbacena	103,522
Barra Mansa	164,963
Barreiras	115,331
Barueri	208,028
Bauru	310,208
Belém	1,271,615
Belford Roxo	433,120
Belo Horizonte	2,229,697
Betim	295,480
Blumenau	241,987
Boa Vista	196,942
Botucatu	103,793
Bragança Paulista	110,982
★ Brasília	1,954,442
Cabo (de Santo Agostinho)	134,356
Cabo Frio	106,326
Cachoeirinha	107,472
Cachoeiro de Itapemirim	154,771
Camaçari	153,829
Camaragibe	128,627
Campina Grande	336,218
Campinas	951,824
Campo Grande	654,832
Campos	363,489
Canoas	305,711
Carapicuíba	343,668
Cariacica	312,542
Caruaru	217,084
Cascavel	228,340
Castanhal	121,174
Catanduva	104,195
Caucaia	225,854
Caxias	103,276
Caxias do Sul	333,201
Chapecó	134,210
Colombo	174,971
Contagem	531,715
Cotia	148,082
Criciúma	152,903
Cubatão	107,260
Cuiabá	475,632
Curitiba	1,586,898
Diadema	356,389
Divinópolis	177,729
Dourados	149,679
Duque de Caxias	767,724
Embu	206,781
Feira de Santana	431,458
Ferraz	140,777
Florianópolis	321,778
Fortaleza	2,138,234
Foz do Iguaçu	256,349
Franca	281,869
Francisco Morato	133,085
Franco de Rocha	100,241
Garanhuns	103,283
Goiânia	1,083,396
Governador Valadares	235,881
Gravataí	211,969
Guarapuava	141,575
Guarujá	265,076
Guarulhos	1,048,280
Hortolândia	151,669
Ibirité	132,131
Ilhéus	161,898
Imperatriz	218,555
Indaiatuba	144,528
Ipatinga	210,777
Itaboraí	176,767
Itabuna	190,888
Itajaí	141,932
Itapecerica da Serra	127,783
Itapetininga	111,774
Itapevi	162,421
Itaquaquecetuba	272,416
Itu	123,881
Jaboatão	567,319
Jacareí	183,444
Jaú	106,954
Jequié	130,207
João Pessoa	594,922
Joinville	414,350
Juàzeiro	132,796
Juàzeiro do Norte	201,950
Juiz de Fora	443,359
Jundiaí	299,669
Lages	152,320
Lauro de Freitas	108,111
Limeira	237,959
Londrina	433,264
Luziânia	129,905
Macaé	125,118
Macapá	270,077
Maceió	794,894
Magé	193,784
Manaus	1,394,724
Marabá	134,258
Maracanaú	174,037
Marília	189,533
Maringá	283,792
Mauá	363,112
Mogi Guaçu	116,117
Moji das Cruzes	301,551
Montes Claros	288,534
Mossoró	197,067
Natal	709,422
Nilópolis	153,572
Niterói	458,465
Nossa Senhora de Socorro	130,255
Nova Friburgo	151,820
Nova Iguaçu	915,364
Novo Hamburgo	231,833
Olinda	361,300
Osasco	650,993
Palmas	133,471
Paranaguá	122,179
Parnaíba	124,942
Parnamirim	107,927
Passo Fundo	163,748
Patos de Minas	111,159
Paulista	262,072
Pelotas	300,952
Petrolina	166,113
Petrópolis	270,489
Pindamonhangaba	118,793
Pinhais	100,601
Piracicaba	316,518
Poços de Caldas	130,594
Ponta Grossa	266,552
Porto Alegre	1,320,069
Porto Velho	273,496
Praia Grande	191,811
Presidente Prudente	185,150
Queimados	121,681
Recife	1,421,947
Ribeirão das Neves	245,143
Ribeirão Pires	104,336
Ribeirão Preto	502,333
Rio Branco	226,054
Rio Claro	163,341
Rio de Janeiro	5,850,544
Rio Grande	179,422
Rio Verde	106,109
Rondonópolis	141,660
Sabará	111,897
Salvador	2,439,881
Santa Bárbara d'Oeste	167,574
Santa Luzia	184,026
Santa Maria	230,464
Santa Rita	100,259
Santarém	186,518
Santo André	648,443
Santos	415,543
São Bernardo do Campo	688,161
São Caetano do Sul	140,144
São Carlos	183,369
São Gonçalo	889,828
São João de Meriti	449,562
São José	167,268
São José do Rio Prêto	336,998
São José dos Campos	532,403
São José dos Pinhais	183,259
São Leopoldo	192,756
São Luís	834,968
São Paulo	9,785,640
São Vicente	302,541
Sapucaia do Sul	121,739
Serra	320,965
Sete Lagoas	180,211
Sobral	134,371
Sorocaba	487,907
Sumaré	193,266
Susano (Suzano)	221,192
Taboão da Serra	197,460
Taubaté	229,810
Teófilo Otoni	102,500
Teresina	676,596
Teresopolis	114,688
Timon	111,967
Uberaba	243,406
Uberlândia	487,887
Uruguaiana	118,181
Varginha	103,499
Várzea Grande	210,849
Viamão	210,873
Vila Velha	343,567
Vitória	291,889
Vitória da Conquista	225,430
Volta Redonda	242,773
Brunei (1991)	
★ Bandar Seri Begawan	21,484
agglomeration	85,000[2]
Bulgaria (1999 est.)	
Burgas	195,255
Dobrich	100,399
Pleven	121,952
Plovdiv	342,584
Ruse	166,467
Sliven	105,530
★ Sofia	1,122,302
Stara Zagora	147,939
Varna	299,801
Burkina Faso (1993 est.)	
Bobo Dioulasso	300,000
Koudougou	105,000
★ Ouagadougou	690,000
Burundi (1994 est.)	
★ Bujumbura	300,000
Gitega	101,827[10]
Cambodia (1999 est.)	
★ Phnom Penh	938,000
Cameroon (1992 est.)	
Bafoussam	120,000
Bamenda	110,000[5]
Douala	1,200,000
Garoua	160,000
Maroua	140,000
Nkongsamba	112,000[5]
★ Yaoundé	800,000
Canada (1996)	
Abbotsford	105,403
Barrie	79,191
Brampton	268,251
Brantford	84,764
Burlington	136,976
Burnaby	179,209
Calgary	768,082
Cambridge	101,429
Cape Breton	114,733
Coquitlam	101,820
Delta	95,411
East York	107,822
Edmonton	616,306
Etobicoke	328,718
Gatineau	100,702
Gloucester	104,022
Guelph	95,821
Halifax	113,910
Hamilton	322,352
Kamloops	76,394
Kelowna	89,442
Kitchener	178,420
Laval	330,343
London	325,646
Longueuil	127,977
Markham	173,383
Mississauga	544,382
Montreal	1,016,376
Montréal-Nord	81,581
Nepean	115,100
Niagara Falls	76,917
North York	589,653
Oakville	128,405
Oshawa	134,364
★ Ottawa	323,340
Pickering	78,989
Prince George	75,150
Quebec	167,264
Regina	180,400
Richmond	148,867
Richmond Hill	101,725
Saanich	101,388
Saint Catharines	130,926
Saint-Hubert	77,042
Saint John's	101,936
Saskatoon	193,647
Sault Sainte Marie	80,054
Scarborough	558,960
Sherbrooke	76,786
Sudbury	92,059
Surrey	304,477
Thunder Bay	113,662
Toronto	653,734
Vancouver	514,008
Vaughan	132,549
Waterloo	77,949
Windsor	197,694
Winnipeg	618,477
York	146,534
Cape Verde (2000)	
★ Praia	94,757
Central African Republic (1995 est.)	
★ Bangui	553,000
Chad (1993; MU)	
Abéché	187,936
Bongor	196,713
Doba	185,461
Moundou	282,103
★ N'Djamena	530,965
Sarh	193,753
Chile (1999 est.)	
Antofagasta	243,038
Arica	178,547
Calama	121,326
Chillán	162,969
Concepción	362,589
Copiapó	114,615
Coquimbo	126,886
Iquique	159,815
La Serena	123,166
Los Angeles	109,606
Osorno	126,645
Puente Alto	363,012
Puerto Montt	128,945
Punta Arenas	120,148
Quilpué	114,617
Rancagua	202,067
San Bernardo	223,055
★ Santiago	202,010[11]
(administrative) agglomeration	4,640,635
Talca	174,858
Talcahuano	269,265
Temuco	253,451
Valdívia	122,166
★ Valparaíso (legislative)	283,489
Viña del Mar	330,736
China (1999 est.)[12]	
Acheng	234,057
Aksu	220,415
Altay	106,665
Anda	180,795
Ankang	173,450
Anlu	112,529
Anning	128,275
Anqing	356,920
Anqiu	193,258
Anshan	1,285,849
Anshun	217,215
Anyang	527,982
Baicheng	269,732
Baise	119,150
Baishan	253,631
Baiyin	258,885
Baoding	570,167
Baoji	447,105
Baoshan	100,797
Baotou	1,092,819
Bazhong	137,627
Bei'an	217,980
Beihai	196,256
★ Beijing (Peking)	6,633,929
Beiliu	140,015
Beining	101,273
Beipiao	202,807
Bengbu	506,239
Benxi	827,203
Bijie	101,171
Binzhou	230,174
Botou	103,337
Bozhou	253,544
Cangzhou	304,010
Cenxi	113,589
Changchun	2,072,324
Changde	384,433
Changge	117,166
Changji	192,000
Changning	134,592
Changsha	1,334,036
Changshu	264,472
Changyi	133,754
Changzhi	387,002
Changzhou	772,700
Chaohu	280,409
Chaoyang (*Fujian*)	389,558
Chaoyang (*Liaoning*)	295,302
Chaozhou	257,521
Chengde	298,895
Chengdu	2,146,126
Chenghai	166,621
Chenzhou	274,338
Chibi	158,125
Chifeng	453,946
Chongqing (Chungking)	3,193,889
Chuxiong	115,887
Chuzhou	187,985
Cixi	132,588
Conghua	128,328
Da'an	153,718
Dachuan	200,785
Dafeng	153,147
Dali	175,847
Dalian	2,000,944
Dandong	578,723
Dangyang	114,885
Danjiangkou	152,396
Danyang	211,875
Danzhou	212,572
Daqing	811,154
Dashiqiao	186,201
Datong	928,293
Daye	128,561
Dehui	149,275
Dengzhou	119,036
Dexing	104,945
Deyang	246,221
Dezhou	310,538
Dingzhou	131,992
Donggang	104,971
Dongguan	378,354
Dongsheng	113,436
Dongtai	231,444
Dongying	479,941
Dujiangyan	154,867
Dunhua	257,190
Duyun	150,950
Emeishan	124,471
Enping	164,929
Enshi	125,937
Ezhou	301,248
Fangchenggang	119,444
Fanyu	345,275
Feicheng	301,981
Fengcheng (*Guangdong*)	173,112
Fengcheng (*Jiangxi*)	221,652
Fengnan	121,767
Foshan	411,107
Fu'an	100,793
Fujin	123,280
Fuqing	139,426
Fushun	1,271,113
Fuxin	682,966
Fuyang (*Anhui*)	319,816
Fuzhou	1,057,372
Gaizhou	175,467
Ganzhou	271,952
Gao'an	130,520
Gaomi	224,162
Gaoming	121,732
Gaoyao	142,335
Gaoyou	135,728
Gaozhou	204,028
Gejiu	218,921
Genhe	173,188
Gongyi	118,985
Gongzhuling	352,978
Guanghan	121,228
Guangshui	137,189
Guangyuan	257,411
Guangzhou (Canton)	3,306,277
Guichi	103,860
Guigang	290,829
Guilin	458,333
Guiping	151,341
Guixi	102,536
Guiyang	1,320,566
Gujiao	104,560
Haicheng	259,725
Haikou	438,262
Hailar	209,294
Hailin	242,389
Hailun	154,148
Haimen	355,232
Haining	122,973
Hami	205,310
Hancheng	108,702
Hanchuan	171,827
Handan	1,005,834
Hangzhou	1,346,148
Hanzhong	215,284
Harbin	2,586,978
Hebi	276,808
Hechi	108,942
Hechuan	202,218
Hefei	1,000,655
Hegang	591,254
Heihe	112,961
Helong	135,328
Hengshui	212,516
Hengyang	584,346
Heshan	117,049

Major cities and national capitals (continued)

country city	population
Heyuan	164,986
Heze	307,445
Hezhou	113,031
Hohhot	754,749
Honghu	201,421
Hongjiang	130,713
Hongta	110,048
Houma	103,578
Huadian	197,759
Huadu	195,921
Huai'an	155,657
Huaibei	574,904
Huaihua	225,414
Huainan	823,395
Huaiyin	320,841
Huanggang	241,268
Huangshan	130,623
Huangshi	569,394
Huazhou	183,394
Huichun	134,379
Huiyang	192,713
Huizhou	287,178
Hulin	152,353
Huludao	447,986
Huzhou	296,962
Jiamusi	579,093
Ji'an (*Jiangxi*)	178,957
Jiangdu	182,208
Jiangjin	222,571
Jiangmen	333,154
Jiangyan	149,706
Jiangyin	339,420
Jiangyou	221,960
Jianyang (*Sichuan*)	161,496
Jiaohe	170,881
Jiaonan	186,424
Jiaozhou	188,192
Jiaozuo	536,021
Jiaxing	261,465
Jiayuguan	114,510
Jieyang	204,134
Jilin	1,165,418
Jimo	149,083
Jinan	1,713,036
Jinchang	141,578
Jincheng	200,659
Jingdezhen	315,036
Jingjiang	136,204
Jingmen	388,780
Jingzhou	596,860
Jinhua	199,649
Jining (*Inner Mongolia*)	206,514
Jining (*Shandong*)	427,256
Jinjiang	126,102
Jinzhou	658,589
Jishou	114,650
Jiujiang	361,645
Jiutai	198,316
Jixi	752,840
Jiyuan	241,406
Jurong	108,555
Kaifeng	569,300
Kaili	149,939
Kaiping	188,795
Kaiyuan (*Liaoning*)	132,481
Kaiyuan (*Yunnan*)	104,329
Karamay	225,251
Kashgar (Kashi)	205,056
Korla	200,374
Kuitun	144,048
Kunming	1,350,640
Kunshan	177,003
Laiwu	382,785
Laixi	118,709
Laiyang	166,824
Laizhou	206,786
Langfang	241,984
Langzhong	112,118
Lanxi	103,792
Lanzhou	1,429,673
Laohekou	162,343
Lechang	177,572
Leiyang	163,278
Leizhou	226,310
Lengshuijiang	176,182
Leping	129,376
Leqing	103,118
Leshan	410,423
Lhasa	121,568
Lianjiang	246,638
Lianyuan	133,059
Lianyungang	447,918
Liaocheng	275,271
Liaoyang	570,483
Liaoyuan	391,841
Liling	135,453
Linchuan	232,592
Linfen	257,684
Lingbao	114,053
Lingyuan	141,481
Linhai	127,378
Linhe	186,234
Linjiang	114,072
Linqing	143,203
Linyi	569,419
Linzhou	110,526
Liu'an	282,880
Liupanshui	502,327
Liuyang	133,723
Liuzhou	775,823
Liyang	292,482
Longhai	101,884
Longjing	144,940
Longkou	221,823
Longyan	237,385
Loudi	222,375
Lufeng	260,804
Luoding	338,722
Luohe	306,565
Luoyang	1,002,178
Luzhou	371,843
Ma'anshan	393,174
Macheng	175,322
Manzhouli	143,711
Maoming	302,022
Meihekou	255,514
Meizhou	230,419
Mianyang	396,055
Mingguang	112,715
Mishan	153,717
Mudanjiang	641,347
Muling	134,632
Nan'an	108,684
Nanchang	1,264,739
Nanchong	390,603
Nanhai	381,322
Nanjing (Nanking)	2,388,915
Nankang	102,222
Nanning	984,061
Nanping	230,931
Nantong	468,215
Nanyang	477,128
Nehe	128,191
Neijiang	320,777
Ning'an	143,722
Ningbo	704,819
Ningguo	108,767
Panjin	471,729
Panshi	165,101
Panzhihua	488,911
Penglai	114,440
Pengzhou	122,074
Pingdingshan	619,694
Pingdu	198,558
Pingliang	124,447
Pingxiang	392,286
Pizhou	159,194
Pulandian	166,331
Puning	312,498
Putian	145,051
Puyang	289,232
Qianjiang	313,500
Qidong	231,611
Qilin	210,230
Qingdao	1,702,108
Qingyuan	193,284
Qingzhou	193,996
Qinhuangdao	485,143
Qinzhou	172,379
Qiongshan	144,979
Qiqihar (Tsitsihar)	1,115,766
Qitaihe	289,111
Qixia	115,089
Quanzhou	281,906
Qufu	157,201
Quzhou	151,122
Renqiu	158,242
Rizhao	322,190
Rongcheng	203,263
Rugao	276,028
Rui'an	164,563
Rushan	116,166
Ruzhou	102,691
Sanhe	108,252
Sanmenxia	189,084
Sanming	199,201
Sanshui	145,279
Sanya	161,869
Shanghai	8,937,175
Shangqiu	317,948
Shangrao	168,263
Shangyu	116,279
Shangzhi	228,273
Shantou	831,949
Shanwei	171,380
Shaoguan	431,053
Shaoxing	233,954
Shaoyang	311,261
Shenyang	3,876,289
Shenzhen	899,111
Shihezi	330,535
Shijiazhuang	1,338,796
Shishou	140,634
Shiyan	377,232
Shizuishan	313,842
Shouguang	202,067
Shuangcheng	172,936
Shuangliao	135,663
Shuangyashan	431,170
Shulan	208,723
Shunde	339,392
Shuozhou	134,645
Sihui	125,065
Siping	382,652
Songyuan	303,821
Songzi	148,183
Suihua	262,117
Suining	229,229
Suizhou	333,766
Suqian	115,368
Suzhou (*Anhui*)	325,724
Suzhou (*Jiangsu*)	845,687
Tai'an	518,117
Taicang	119,862
Taishan	355,017
Taixing	185,270
Taiyuan	1,768,530
Taizhou (*Jiangsu*)	219,968
Taizhou (*Zhejiang*)	239,271
Tangshan	1,210,842
Taonan	156,464
Tengzhou	452,009
Tianchang	167,508
Tianjin (Tientsin)	4,835,327
Tianmen	367,036
Tianshui	301,570
Tiefa	165,956
Tieli	272,841
Tieling	313,991
Tongchuan	304,809
Tonghua	362,577
Tongliao	305,885
Tongling	292,721
Tongxiang	109,976
Tongzhou	365,003
Tumen	102,191
Ulanhot	182,128
Ürümqi	1,258,457
Wafangdian	305,249
Weifang	621,125
Weihai	287,872
Weinan	210,079
Wendeng	183,952
Wenling	134,074
Wenzhou	512,523
Wuchang	227,856
Wuchuan	184,812
Wudalianchi	157,547
Wuhai	316,718
Wuhan	3,911,824
Wuhu	495,765
Wujiang	176,514
Wujin	141,495
Wuwei	181,328
Wuxi	940,858
Wuxian	176,694
Wuxue	142,136
Wuzhou	253,159
Xiamen (Amoy)	593,401
Xi'an (Sian)	2,294,790
Xiangcheng	103,692
Xiangfan	597,604
Xiangtan	518,783
Xiangxiang	103,871
Xianning	249,234
Xiantao	412,434
Xianyang	460,976
Xiaogan	224,026
Xiaoshan	220,815
Xiaoyi	117,133
Xichang	174,781
Xingcheng	120,431
Xinghua	199,023
Xingning	206,712
Xingping	108,491
Xingtai	387,081
Xinhui	269,528
Xining	604,812
Xinmin	123,655
Xintai	381,637
Xinxiang	583,408
Xinyang	366,304
Xinyi (*Guangdong*)	170,368
Xinyi (*Jiangsu*)	127,496
Xinyu	250,666
Xinzheng	136,980
Xinzhou	143,840
Xishan	171,316
Xuanwei	120,046
Xuanzhou	136,914
Xuchang	275,743
Xuzhou	1,044,729
Ya'an	119,320
Yakeshi	391,627
Yan'an	133,226
Yancheng	332,125
Yangchun	206,440
Yangjiang	295,672
Yangquan	447,229
Yangzhou	395,048
Yanji	329,112
Yantai	818,646
Yanzhou	199,491
Yibin	288,039
Yichang	481,277
Yicheng	116,586
Yichun (*Heilongjiang*)	802,931
Yichun (*Jiangxi*)	198,799
Yima	116,760
Yinchuan	469,180
Yingcheng	120,499
Yingde	205,782
Yingkou	498,300
Yingtan	110,671
Yining	230,429
Yixing	258,808
Yiyang	297,000
Yizheng	166,358
Yong'an	130,688
Yongcheng	118,659
Yongchuan	186,482
Yongzhou	276,669
Yuanjiang	140,406
Yuanping	101,689
Yuci	243,948
Yueyang	448,249
Yuhang	152,429
Yulin (*Guangxi*)	190,418
Yulin (*Shaanxi*)	106,391
Yumen	116,194
Yuncheng	172,620
Yunfu	168,371
Yushu	171,692
Yuyao	136,464
Yuzhou	133,619
Zalantun	143,273
Zaoyang	211,295
Zaozhuang	741,421
Zengcheng	197,023
Zhangjiagang	168,546
Zhangjiajie	115,896
Zhangjiakou	660,504
Zhangqiu	207,212
Zhangshu	112,600
Zhangye	114,592
Zhangzhou	231,333
Zhanjiang	588,583
Zhaodong	227,218
Zhaoqing	311,571
Zhaotong	104,382
Zhaoyuan	172,646
Zhengzhou	1,465,069
Zhenjiang	469,977
Zhijiang	126,808
Zhongshan	390,060
Zhongxiang	224,442
Zhoukou	189,377
Zhoushan	196,368
Zhuanghe	161,223
Zhucheng	145,952
Zhuhai	371,116
Zhuji	116,116
Zhumadian	204,020
Zhuozhou	109,390
Zhuzhou	528,958
Zibo	1,458,060
Zigong	464,497
Zixing	123,747
Ziyang	145,665
Zoucheng	302,856
Zunyi	464,945
Colombia (1999 est.)	
Armenia	281,422
Barrancabermeja	178,020
Barranquilla	1,223,260
Bello	333,470
Bucaramanga	515,555
Buenaventura	224,336
Buga	110,699
Cali	2,077,386
Cartagena	805,757
Cartago	125,884
Cúcuta	606,932
Dos Quebradas	159,363
Envigado	135,848
Florencia	108,574
Floridablanca	221,913
Girardot	110,963
Ibagué	393,664
Itagüí	228,985
Maicao	108,053
Manizales	337,580
Medellín	1,861,265
Montería	248,245
Neiva	300,052
Palmira	226,509
Pasto	332,396
Pereira	381,725
Popayán	200,719
Santa Marta	359,147
★ Santafé de Bogotá, D.C.	6,260,862
Sincelejo	220,704
Soacha	272,058
Sogamoso	107,728
Soledad	295,058
Tuluá	152,488
Tunja	109,740
Valledupar	263,247
Villavicencio	273,140
Comoros (1995 est.)	
★ Moroni	34,168
Congo, Dem. Rep. of the (1994 est.)	
Boma	135,284
Bukavu	201,569
Butembo	109,406
Goma	109,094
Kalemi	101,309
Kananga	393,030
Kikwit	182,142
★ Kinshasa	4,655,313
Kisangani	417,517
Kolwezi	417,810
Likasi	299,118
Lubumbashi	851,381
Matadi	172,730
Mbanadaka	169,841
Mbuji-Mayi	806,475
Mwene-Ditu	137,459
Tshikapa	180,860
Uvira	115,590
Congo, Rep. of the (1992 est.)	
★ Brazzaville	937,579
Pointe-Noire	576,206
Costa Rica (2000 est.)	
★ San José	344,349[13]
Côte d'Ivoire (1995 est.)	
★ Abidjan (de facto; legislative)	3,199,000[2]
Bouaké	330,000
Daloa	123,000
Korhogo	109,445[14]
★ Yamoussoukro (de jure; administrative)	110,000
Croatia (2001)	
Rijeka	147,709
Split	173,692
★ Zagreb	682,598[15]
Cuba (1994 est.)	
Bayamo	137,663
Camagüey	293,961
Ciego de Avila	104,060[5]
Cienfuegos	132,038
Guantánamo	207,796
★ Havana	2,198,392[16]
Holguín	242,085
Las Tunas	126,930
Manzanillo	109,471[5]
Matanzas	123,843
Pinar del Río	128,570
Santa Clara	205,400
Santiago de Cuba	440,084
Cyprus (1998 est.)	
Limassol	152,900
★ Lefkosia (Nicosia)	194,100[17]
Czech Republic (2000 est.)	
Brno	383,569
Olomouc	103,015
Ostrava	321,263
Plzeň	167,534
★ Prague	1,186,855
Denmark (2000 est.; MU)	
Ålborg	161,161
Århus	284,846
★ Copenhagen	495,699
Odense	183,912

country city	population
Djibouti (1995 est.)	
★ Djibouti	383,000
Dominica (1991)	
★ Roseau	15,853
Dominican Republic (1993)	
La Romana	140,204
San Francisco de Macorís	108,485
San Pedro de Macorís	124,735
Santiago	365,463
★ Santo Domingo	1,609,966[18]
East Timor (1999 est.)	
★ Dili	65,000
Ecuador (1997 est.)	
Ambato	160,302
Cuenca	255,028
Duran	135,675
Eloy Alfaro	120,364[4]
Esmeraldas	117,722
Guayaquil	1,973,880
Ibarra	119,243
Loja	117,365
Machala	197,350
Manta	156,981
Milagro	119,371
Portoviejo	167,956
Quevedo	120,640
★ Quito	1,487,513
Riobamba	117,270
Santo Domingo	183,219
Egypt (1996)	
Alexandria	3,328,196
Al-ʿArīsh	100,447
Aswān	219,017
Asyūṭ	343,498
Banhā	145,792
Banī Suwayf	172,032
Bilbays	113,608
Būr Saʿīd (Port Said)	469,533
★ Cairo	6,789,479
Damanhūr	212,203
Al-Fayyūm	260,964
Al-Ismāʿīlīyah	254,477
Al-Jīzah (Giza)	2,221,868
Kafr ad-Dawwar	231,978
Kafr ash-Shaykh	124,819
Al-Maḥallah al-Kubrā	395,402
Mallawī	119,283
Al-Manṣūrah	369,621
Al-Minyā	201,360
Mīt Ghamr	101,801
Qinā	171,275
Sawhāj	170,125
Shibīn al-Kawm	159,909
Shubrā al-Khaymah	870,716
As-Suways (Suez)	417,610
Ṭanṭā	371,010
Al-Uqṣur (Luxor)	360,503
Az-Zaqāzīq	267,351
El Salvador (1992)	
Mejicanos	131,972[19]
San Miguel	127,696
★ San Salvador	415,346
Santa Ana	139,389
Soyapango	261,122[19]
Equatorial Guinea (1995 est.)	
★ Malabo	47,500
Eritrea (1995 est.)	
★ Asmara	431,000
Estonia (2000 est.)	
★ Tallinn	404,000
Tartu	101,000
Ethiopia (1994)	
★ Addis Ababa	2,112,737
Dire Dawa	164,851
Gonder	112,249
Harer (Harar)	131,139
Jima	106,842
Nazret	127,842
Faroe Islands (2000 est.)	
★ Tórshavn	16,474
Fiji (1996)	
★ Suva	77,366
Finland (2000 est.)	
Espoo	209,667
★ Helsinki	551,123
Oulu	117,670
Tampere	193,174
Turku	172,107
Vantaa	176,386
France (1999)	
Aix-en-Provence	134,222
Amiens	135,501
Angers	151,279
Besançon	117,304
Bordeaux	215,118
Boulogne-Billancourt	106,367
Brest	149,634
Caen	113,987
Clermont-Ferrand	137,140
Dijon	149,867
Grenoble	153,317
Le Havre	190,651
Le Mans	146,105
Lille	182,228
Limoges	133,960
Lyon	445,257
Marseille	797,486
Metz	123,776
Montpellier	225,392
Mulhouse	110,359
Nancy	103,605
Nantes	268,695
Nice	342,738
Nîmes	133,424
Orléans	112,833
★ Paris	2,123,261
agglomeration	9,608,000[2]
Perpignan	105,115
Reims	187,206
Rennes	206,229
Rouen	106,035
Saint-Étienne	179,755
Strasbourg	263,940
Toulon	159,389
Toulouse	390,413
Tours	132,820
Villeurbanne	124,215
French Guiana (1999)	
★ Cayenne	50,594
French Polynesia (1996)	
★ Papeete	25,353
agglomeration	121,000[2]
Gabon (1993)	
★ Libreville	362,386
Gambia, The (1993)	
★ Banjul	42,407
agglomeration	270,540
Gaza Strip (1999 est.)	
★ Gaza (Ghazzah; acting administrative centre)	388,031
Jabālyah	113,901[20]
Khān Yūnus	123,175[20]
Georgia (1997 est.)	
Bat'umi (Batumi)	137,100
K'ut'aisi (Kutaisi)	240,000
Rust'avi (Rustavi)	158,000
★ T'bilisi (Tbilisi)	1,398,968[16]
Zugdidi	105,000[21]
Germany (1999 est.)	
Aachen	243,600
Augsburg	254,500
Bergisch Gladbach	105,963[16]
★ Berlin	3,392,900
Bielefeld	321,600
Bochum	392,900
Bonn	304,100
Bottrop	121,500
Braunschweig	246,800
Bremen	542,300
Bremerhaven	123,800
Chemnitz	266,000
Cologne (Köln)	963,200
Cottbus	112,200
Darmstadt	137,600
Dortmund	590,300
Dresden	477,700
Duisburg	521,300
Düsseldorf	568,500
Erfurt	202,100
Erlangen	100,600
Essen	600,700
Frankfurt am Main	644,700
Freiburg im Breisgau	201,000
Fürth	109,700
Gelsenkirchen	283,300
Gera	115,800
Göttingen	127,366[16]
Hagen	206,400
Halle	258,500
Hamburg	1,701,800
Hamm	181,500
Hannover	515,200
Heidelberg	139,400
Heilbronn	119,900
Herne	176,200
Hildesheim	105,405[16]
Ingolstadt	114,500
Kaiserslautern	100,300
Karlsruhe	276,700
Kassel	196,700
Kiel	235,500
Koblenz	108,700
Krefeld	242,800
Leipzig	490,000
Leverkusen	161,100
Lübeck	213,800
Ludwigshafen	164,200
Magdeburg	238,000
Mainz	185,600
Mannheim	308,400
Moers	106,704[16]
Mönchengladbach	264,100
Mülheim an der Ruhr	174,300
Munich (München)	1,193,600
Münster	264,700
Neuss	149,206[16]
Nürnberg	486,400
Oberhausen	222,300
Offenbach am Main	116,400
Oldenburg	154,100
Osnabrück	164,900
Paderborn	131,851[16]
Pforzheim	117,500
Potsdam	129,500
Recklinghausen	126,241[16]
Regensburg	125,200
Remscheid	119,500
Reutlingen	109,882[16]
Rostock	205,900
Saarbrücken	186,402[16]
Salzgitter	113,700
Schwerin	104,200
Siegen	110,847[16]
Solingen	165,400
Stuttgart	581,200
Ulm	116,000
Wiesbaden	268,200
Witten	103,872[16]
Wolfsburg	122,200
Wuppertal	370,700
Würzburg	126,000
Zwickau	104,900
Ghana (1998 est.)	
★ Accra	1,446,000
Kumasi	578,000
Tamale	229,000
Tema	300,000
Greece (1991)	
★ Athens	772,072
Iráklion	116,178
Kallithéa	114,233
Larissa	112,777
Pátrai (Patras)	153,344
Peristérion	137,288
Piraiévs (Piraeus)	182,671
Thessaloníki	383,967
Greenland (2000 est.)	
★ Nuuk (Godthåb)	13,838
Grenada (1991)	
★ Saint George's	4,621
agglomeration	35,000[2]
Guadeloupe (1999)	
★ Basse-Terre	12,549
Guam (1995 est.)	
★ Hagåtña (Agana)	2,000
Guatemala (1994)	
★ Guatemala City	823,301
agglomeration	3,119,000[2]
Mixco	209,791[22]
Villa Nueva	101,295[22]
Guernsey (1996)	
★ St. Peter Port	16,194
Guinea (1999 est.)	
★ Conakry	1,764,000
Guinea-Bissau (1999 est.)	
★ Bissau	274,000
Guyana (1999 est.)	
★ Georgetown	275,000
Haiti (1997 est.)	
Cap-Haïtien	107,026
Carrefour	306,074
Delmas	257,247
★ Port-au-Prince	917,112
Honduras (1999 est.)	
El Progreso	104,100
La Ceiba	103,400
San Pedro Sula	452,100
★ Tegucigalpa	988,400[23]
Hong Kong (2001 est.)	
★ Hong Kong	6,732,100[24]
Hungary (2000 est.)	
★ Budapest	1,811,552
Debrecen	203,648
Győr	127,119
Kecskemét	105,606
Miskolc	172,357
Nyíregyháza	112,419
Pécs	157,332
Szeged	158,158
Székesfehérvár	105,119
Iceland (1999 est.)	
★ Reykjavík	109,184
India (1991)	
Abohar	107,163
Adoni	136,182
Agartala	157,358
Agra	891,790
Ahmadabad	2,876,710
Ahmadnagar	181,339
Aizawl	155,240
Ajmer	402,700
Akola	328,034
Alandur	125,244
Alappuzha (Alleppey)	174,666
Alibag	328,640
Aligarh	480,520
Allahabad (Prayag Raj)	792,858
Alwar	205,086
Ambala	119,338
Ambattur	215,424
Amravati	421,576
Amritsar	708,835
Amroha	137,061
Anand	110,266
Anantapur	174,924
Ara (Arrah)	157,082
Asansol	262,188
Avadi	183,215
Baharampur	115,144
Bahraich	135,400
Bally	184,474
Balurghat	119,796
Bangalore	2,660,088
Bankura	114,876
Baranagar (Barahanagar)	224,821
Barasat	102,660
Barddhaman (Burdwan)	245,079
Bareilly	587,211
Barrackpore	133,265
Basirhat	101,409
Bathinda (Bhatinda)	159,042
Beawar	105,363
Belgaum	326,399
Bellary	245,391
Bhagalpur	253,225
Bharatpur	148,519
Bharuch (Broach)	133,102
Bhatpara	304,952
Bhavnagar	402,338
Bhilainagar	395,360
Bhilwara	183,965
Bhimavaram	121,314
Bhind	109,755
Bhiwandi	379,070
Bhiwani	121,629
Bhopal	1,062,771
Bhubaneshwar	411,542
Bhuj	102,176
Bhusawal	145,143
Bid (Bhir)	112,434
Bidar	108,016
Bidhan Nagar	100,048
Bihar Sharif	201,323
Bijapur	186,939
Bikaner	416,289
Bilaspur	179,833
Bokaro (Bokaro Steel City)	333,683
Brahmapur	210,418
Budaun	116,695
Bulandshahr	127,201
Burhanpur	172,710
Burnpur	174,933
Champdani	101,067
Chandannagar	120,378
Chandigarh	504,094
Chandrapur	226,105
Chennai (Madras)	3,841,396
Chhapra	136,877
Chittoor	133,462
Coimbatore	816,321
Cuddalore	144,561
Cuddapah	121,463
Cuttack	403,418
Dabgram	147,217
Darbhanga	218,391
Davanagere	266,082
Dehra Dun	270,159
Delhi	7,206,704
Dewas	164,364
Dhanbad	151,789
Dhule (Dhulia)	278,317
Dibrugarh	120,127
Dindigul	182,447
Durg	150,645
Durgapur	425,836
Eluru	212,866
Erode	159,232
Etawah	124,072
Faizabad	124,437
Faridabad	617,717
Farrukhabad-cum-Fatehgarh	194,567
Fatehpur	117,675
Fīrozabad	215,128
Gadag-Betigeri	134,051
Gandhidham	104,585
Gandhinagar	123,359
Ganganagar	161,482
Gaya	219,675
Ghaziabad	454,156
Gondia	109,470
Gorakhpur	505,566
Gudivada	101,656
Gulbarga	304,099
Guna	100,490
Guntakal	107,592
Guntur	471,051
Gurgaon	121,486
Guwahati (Gauhati)	584,342
Gwalior	690,765
Habra	100,223
Haldia	100,347
Haldwani-cum-Kathgodam	104,195
Halisahar	114,028
Haora (Howrah)	950,435
Hapur	146,262
Haridwar (Hardwar)	147,305
Hathras	113,285
Hindupur	104,651
Hisar (Hissar)	172,677
Hoshiarpur	122,705
Hubli-Dharwad	648,298
Hugli-Chunchura	151,806
Hyderabad	3,145,939
Ichalkaranji	214,950
Imphal	198,535
Indore	1,091,674
Ingraj Bazar (English Bazar)	139,204
Jabalpur	741,927
Jaipur	1,458,183
Jalandhar (Jullundur)	509,510
Jalgaon	242,193
Jalna	174,985
Jammu	225,000[5, 25]
Jamnagar	341,637
Jamshedpur	478,950
Jaunpur	136,062
Jhansi	300,850
Jodhpur	666,279
Junagadh	130,484
Kakinada	279,980
Kalyan	1,014,557
Kamarhati	266,889
Kanchipuram	144,955
Kanchrapara	100,194
Kanpur	1,874,409

Major cities and national capitals (continued)

country city	population
Karimnagar	148,583
Karnal	173,751
Katihar	135,436
Khammam	127,992
Khandwa	143,133
Kharagpur	177,989
Kochi (Cochin)	564,589
Kolhapur	406,370
Kolkata (Calcutta)	4,399,819
Kollam (Quilon)	139,852
Korba	124,501
Kota	537,371
Kozhikode (Calicut)	419,831
Krishnanagar	121,110
Kukatpalle	186,963
Kulti-Barakar	108,518
Kumbakonam	139,483
Kurnool	236,800
Lalbahadur Nagar	155,514
Latur	197,408
Lucknow	1,619,115
Ludhiana	1,042,740
Machilipatnam (Masulipatam)	159,110
Madurai	940,989
Mahbubnagar	116,833
Malegaon	342,595
Malkajgiri	127,178
Mandya	120,265
Mangalore	273,304
Mango	108,100
Mathura	226,691
Maunath Bhanjan	136,697
Medinipur (Midnapore)	125,498
Meerut	753,778
Mira-Bhayandar	175,605
Miraj	121,593
Mizapur-cum-Vindhyachal	169,336
Modinagar	101,660
Moga	108,304
Moradabad	429,214
Morena	147,124
Mumbai (Bombay)	9,925,891
Munger (Monghyr)	150,112
Murwara (Katni)	163,431
Muzaffarnagar	240,609
Muzaffarpur	241,107
Mysore	480,692
Nadiad	167,051
Nagercoil	190,084
Nagpur	1,624,752
Naihati	132,701
Nanded (Nander)	275,083
Nandyal	119,813
Nashik (Nasik)	656,925
Navadwip	125,037
Navsari	126,089
Nellore	316,606
New Bombay	307,724
★ New Delhi	301,297
Neyveli	118,080
Nizamabad	241,034
Noida	146,514
North Barrackpore	100,606
North Dum Dum	149,965
Ongole	100,836
Palghat (Palakkad)	123,289
Pali	136,842
Pallavaram	111,866
Panihati	275,990
Panipat	191,212
Parbhani	190,255
Pathankot	123,930
Patiala	238,368
Patna	917,243
Pilibhit	106,605
Pimpri-Chinchwad	517,083
Pondicherry	203,065
Porbandar	116,671
Proddatur	133,914
Pune	1,566,651
Puri	125,199
Purnia (Purnea)	114,912
Qutubullapur	106,591
Rae Bareli	129,904
Raichur	157,551
Raiganj	151,045
Raipur	438,639
Raj Nandgaon	125,371
Rajahmundry	324,851
Rajapalaiyam	114,202
Rajkot	559,407
Ramagundam	214,384
Rampur	243,742
Ranchi	599,306
Ratlam	183,375
Raurkela Civil Township	140,408

country city	population
Raurkela Steel Township	215,509
Rewa	128,981
Rishra	102,815
Rohtak	216,096
Sagar	195,346
Saharanpur	374,945
Salem	366,712
Sambalpur	131,138
Sambhal	150,869
Sangli	193,197
Satna	156,630
Shahjahanpur	237,713
Shambajinagar (Aurangābād)	573,272
Shantipur	109,956
Shiliguri (Siliguri)	216,950
Shillong	131,719
Shimoga	179,258
Shivpuri	108,277
Sholapur (Solapur)	604,215
Shrirampur	137,028
Sikandarabad (Secundarabad) Cantonment	171,148
Sikar	148,272
Silchar	115,483
Sirsa	112,841
Sitapur	121,842
Sonipat (Sonepat)	143,922
South Dum Dum	232,811
Srinagar	700,000[5, 25]
Surat	1,498,817
Surendranagar	106,110
Tambaram	107,187
Tenali	143,726
Thalassery (Tellicherry)	103,579
Thane (Thana)	803,389
Thanjavur	202,013
Thiruvananthapuram (Trivandrum)	524,006
Tiruchchirappalli	387,223
Tirunelueli	135,825
Tirupati	174,369
Tirupper (Tiruppur)	235,661
Tiruvannamalai	109,196
Tiruvottiyur	168,642
Titagarh	114,085
Tonk	100,079
Tumkur	138,903
Tuticorin	199,854
Udaipur	308,571
Ujjain	362,266
Ulhasnagar	369,077
Uluberia	155,172
Unnao	107,425
Uttarpara-Kotrung	101,268
Vadodara (Baroda)	1,031,346
Valparai	106,523
Varanasi (Benares)	929,270
Vellore	175,061
Vijayawada	701,827
Vishakhapatnam	752,037
Vizianagaram	160,359
Warangal	447,657
Wardha	102,985
Yamunanagar	144,346
Yavatmal (Yeotmal)	108,578
Indonesia (1995 est.)[26]	
Ambon	249,312
Balikpapan	338,752
Banda Aceh	143,360[10]
Bandar Lampung	457,927[10]
Bandung	2,356,120
Banjarmasin	482,931
Bekasi	644,284[10]
Bengkulu	146,395[10]
Binjai	127,184[10]
Blitar	112,986[10]
Bogor	285,114
Cianjur	114,335[10]
Cibinong	101,317[10]
Cilacap	206,928[10]
Cilegon-Merak	116,981[10]
Cimahi	344,607[10]
Ciomas	187,379[10]
Ciparay	111,467[10]
Ciputat	270,815[10]
Cirebon	254,406
Citeurup	105,079[10]
Denpasar	345,150[10]
Depok (*West Java*)	106,825[10]
Depok (*Yogyakarta*)	661,495[10]
★ Jakarta	9,112,652
Jambi	385,201
Jember	218,529[10]
Karawang (Krawang)	145,041[10]
Kediri	253,760

country city	population
Klaten	103,327[10]
Kupang	129,259[10]
Lhokseumawe	109,569[10]
Madiun	171,532
Magelang	123,800
Malang	716,862
Manado	332,288
Mataram	275,089[10]
Medan	1,843,919
Padang	534,474
Palembang	1,222,764
Palu	142,767[10]
Pangkalpinang	108,377[10]
Pasuruan	133,685[9]
Pekalongan	301,504
Pekanbaru	438,638
Pemalang	103,540[10]
Pematang Siantar	203,056
Percut	129,036[10]
Pondokgede	263,152[10]
Pontianak	409,632
Probolinggo	120,770
Purwokerto	202,452[10]
Salatiga	103,000
Samarinda	399,175
Semarang	1,104,405
Serang	122,429[10]
Sukabumi	125,766
Surabaya	2,663,820
Surakarta	516,594
Taman	106,975[10]
Tangerang	887,952[10]
Tanjung Balai	101,644[10]
Tanjung Karang	680,332
Tasikmalaya	179,766[10]
Tebingtinggi	129,300
Tegal	289,744
Ujung Pandang	1,060,257
Waru	124,282[10]
Yogyakarta	418,944
Iran (1996)	
Ābādān	206,073
Ahvāz	804,980
Āmol	159,092
Andīmeshk	106,923
Arāk	380,755
Ardabīl	340,386
Bābol	158,346
Bandar 'Abbās	273,578
Bandar-e Būshehr (Būshehr)	143,641
Bīrjand	127,608
Bojnūrd	134,835
Borūjerd	217,804
Būkān	120,020
Dezfūl	202,639
Emāmshahr (Shāhrūd)	104,765
Eṣfahān (Isfahan)	1,266,072
Gonbad-e Kavus	111,253
Gorgān	188,710
Hamadān	401,281
Īlām	126,346
Islāmshahr (Eslāmshahr)	265,450
Karaj	940,968[27]
Kāshān	201,372
Kermān	384,991
Kermānshāh (Bākhtarān)	692,986
Khomeynīshahr	165,888
Khorramābād	272,815
Khorramshahr	105,636
Khvoy (Khoy)	148,944
Mahābād	107,799
Malāyer	144,373
Marāgheh	132,318
Marv Dasht	103,579
Mashhad (Meshed)	1,887,405
Masjed-e Soleymān	116,882
Najafābād	178,498
Neyshābūr	158,847
Orūmīyeh	435,200
Qā'emshahr	143,286
Qarchak	142,690
Qazvīn	291,117
Qods	138,278
Qom	777,677
Rasht	417,748
Sabzevār	170,738
Sanandaj	277,808
Saqqez	115,394
Sārī	195,882
Sāveh	111,245
Shahr-e Kord	100,477
Shīrāz	1,053,025
Sīrjān	135,024
Tabrīz	1,191,043

country city	population
★ Tehrān	6,758,845
Varāmīn	107,233
Yazd	326,776
Zābol	100,888
Zāhedān	419,518
Zanjān	286,295
Iraq (1987)	
Al-'Amārah	208,797
★ Baghdad	4,689,000[2, 28]
Ba'qūbah	114,516[29]
Al-Baṣrah	406,296
Al-Ḥillah	268,834
Dīwanīyah	196,519
Irbīl	485,968
Karbalā'	296,705
Karkūk	418,624
Al-Kūt	183,183
Mosul	664,221
An-Najaf	309,010
An-Nāṣirīyah	265,937
Ar-Ramādī	192,556
As-Sulaymānīyah	364,096
Ireland (1996)	
Cork	127,092[30]
★ Dublin	480,996[30]
Isle of Man (1996)	
★ Douglas	23,487
Israel (1999 est.)	
Ashdod	155,800
Bat Yam	137,000
Beersheba (Be'er Sheva')	163,700
Bene Beraq	133,900
Haifa (Ḥefa)	265,700
Ḥolon	163,100
★ Jerusalem (Yerushalayim, Al-Quds)	633,700
Netanya	154,900
Petah Tiqwa	159,400
Ramat Gan	126,900
Rishon LeẒiyyon	188,200
Tel Aviv–Yafo	348,100
Italy (2000 est.)[31]	
Bari	331,848
Bergamo	117,837
Bologna	381,161
Brescia	191,317
Cagliari	165,926
Catania	337,862
Ferrara	132,127
Florence (Firenze)	376,682
Foggia	154,891
Forlì	107,475
Genoa (Genova)	636,104
Latina	114,099
Livorno	161,673
Messina	259,156
Milan (Milano)	1,300,977
Modena	176,022
Monza	119,516
Naples (Napoli)	1,002,619
Novara	102,037
Padua (Padova)	211,391
Palermo	683,794
Parma	168,717
Perugia	156,673
Pescara	115,698
Prato	172,473
Ravenna	138,418
Reggio di Calabria	179,617
Reggio nell'Emilia	143,664
Rimini	131,062
★ Rome (Roma)	2,643,581
Salerno	142,055
Sassari	120,803
Siracusa (Syracuse)	126,282
Taranto	208,214
Terni	107,770
Trento	104,906
Trieste	216,459
Turin (Torino)	903,703
Venice (Venezia)	277,305
Verona	255,268
Vicenza	109,738
Jamaica (1991)	
★ Kingston	103,771
agglomeration	655,000[2]
Japan (1995)	
Abiko	124,257
Ageo	206,090
Aizuwakamatsu	119,640
Akashi	287,606

country city	population
Akishima	107,292
Akita	311,948
Amagasaki	488,586
Anjō	149,464
Aomori	294,167
Asahikawa	360,568
Asaka	110,789
Ashikaga	165,828
Atsugi	208,627
Beppu	128,255
Chiba	856,878
Chigasaki	212,874
Chōfu	198,574
Daitō	128,838
Ebetsu	115,495
Ebina	113,430
Fuchu	216,211
Fuji	229,187
Fujieda	124,822
Fujinomiya	119,536
Fujisawa	368,651
Fukaya	100,285
Fukui	255,604
Fukuoka	1,284,795
Fukushima	285,754
Fukuyama	374,517
Funabashi	540,817
Gifu	407,134
Habikino	117,735
Hachinohe	242,654
Hachiōji	503,363
Hadano	164,722
Hakodate	298,881
Hamamatsu	561,606
Handa	106,452
Higashi-Hiroshima	113,939
Higashi-Kurume	111,097
Higashi-Murayama	135,112
Higashi-Ōsaka	517,232
Hikone	103,508
Himeji	470,986
Hino	166,537
Hirakata	400,144
Hiratsuka	253,822
Hirosaki	177,972
Hiroshima	1,108,888
Hitachi	199,244
Hitachinaka	146,750
Hōfu	118,803
Hoya	100,260
Ibaraki	258,233
Ichihara	277,061
Ichikawa	440,555
Ichinomiya	267,362
Iida	106,772
Ikeda	104,293
Ikoma	106,726
Imabari	120,214
Iruma	144,402
Ise	102,632
Isesaki	120,236
Ishinomaki	121,208
Itami	188,431
Iwaki	360,598
Iwakuni	107,386
Iwatsuki	109,546
Izumi	157,300
Joetsu	132,205
Kadoma	140,506
Kagamigahara	131,955
Kagoshima	546,282
Kakogawa	260,567
Kamakura	170,329
Kanazawa	453,975
Kariya	125,305
Kashihara	121,988
Kashiwa	317,750
Kasugai	277,589
Kasukabe	200,121
Kawachi-Nagano	117,082
Kawagoe	323,353
Kawaguchi	448,854
Kawanishi	144,539
Kawasaki	1,202,820
Kiryū	120,377
Kisarazu	123,499
Kishiwada	194,818
Kita-Kyūshū	1,019,598
Kitami	110,452
Kobe	1,423,792
Kochi	321,999
Kodaira	172,946
Kofu	201,124
Koganei	109,279
Kokubunji	105,786
Komaki	137,165
Komatsu	107,965
Koriyama	326,833
Koshigaya	298,253

country city	population
Kumagaya	156,429
Kumamoto	650,341
Kurashiki	422,836
Kure	209,485
Kurume	234,433
Kusatsu	101,828
Kushiro	199,323
Kuwana	103,044
Kyōto	1,463,822
Machida	360,525
Maebashi	284,788
Matsubara	134,457
Matsudo	461,503
Matsue	147,416
Matsumoto	205,523
Matsuyama	460,968
Matsuzaka	122,449
Minō	127,542
Misato	133,600
Mishima	107,890
Mitaka	165,721
Mito	246,347
Miyakonojō	132,714
Miyazaki	300,068
Moriguchi	157,306
Morioka	286,478
Muroran	109,766
Musashino	135,051
Nagano	358,516
Nagaoka	190,470
Nagareyama	146,245
Nagasaki	438,635
Nagoya	2,152,184
Naha	301,890
Nara	359,218
Narashino	152,887
Neyagawa	258,443
Niigata	494,769
Niihama	127,917
Niiza	144,726
Nishinomiya	390,389
Nobeoka	126,629
Noda	119,790
Numazu	212,241
Obihiro	171,715
Odawara	200,103
Ōgaki	149,759
Ōita	426,979
Okayama	615,757
Okazaki	322,621
Okinawa	115,336
Ōme	137,234
Ōmiya	433,755
Ōmuta	145,085
Ōsaka	2,602,421
Ōta	143,057
Ōtaru	157,022
Ōtsu	276,332
Oyama	150,115
Saga	171,231
Sagamihara	570,597
Sakai	802,993
Sakata	101,230
Sakura	162,624
Sapporo	1,757,025
Sasebo	244,909
Sayama	162,240
Sendai	971,297
Seto	129,393
Shimizu	240,174
Shimonoseki	259,795
Shizuoka	474,092
Sōka	217,930
Suita	342,760
Suzuka	179,800
Tachikawa	157,884
Tajimi	101,270
Takamatsu	331,004
Takaoka	173,607
Takarazuka	202,544
Takasaki	238,133
Takatsuki	362,270
Tama	148,113
Tokorozawa	320,406
Tokushima	268,706
Tokuyama	108,671
★ Tokyo	7,967,614
Tomakomai	169,328
Tondabayashi	121,690
Tottori	146,330
Toyama	325,375
Toyohashi	352,982
Toyokawa	114,380
Toyonaka	398,908
Toyota	341,079
Tsu	163,156
Tsuchiura	132,243
Tsukuba	156,012
Tsuruoka	100,538
Ube	175,116
Ueda	123,284
Uji	184,830
Urawa	453,300
Urayasu	123,654
Utsunomiya	435,357
Wakayama	393,885
Yachiyo	154,509
Yaizu	115,931
Yamagata	254,488
Yamaguchi	135,579
Yamato	203,933
Yao	276,664
Yatsushiro	107,709
Yokkaichi	285,779
Yokohama	3,307,136
Yokosuka	432,193
Yonago	134,762
Zama	118,159
Jersey (1996)	
★ St. Helier	27,523
Jordan (1994)	
★ Amman	969,598
Irbid	208,329
Ar-Ruṣayfah	137,247
Az-Zarqā'	350,849
Kazakhstan (1999)	
Almaty (Alma-Ata)	1,129,400
Aqtaū (Aktau; Shevchenko)	143,400
Aqtöbe (Aktyubinsk)	253,100
★ Astana (Aqmola; Tselinograd)	313,000
Atyraū (Guryev)	142,500
Ekibastuz	127,200
Kökshetaū (Kokchetav)	123,400
Oral (Uralsk)	195,500
Ōskemen (Ust-Kamenogorsk)	311,000
Pavlodar	300,500
Petropavl (Petropavlovsk)	203,500
Qaraghandy (Karaganda)	436,900
Qostanay (Kustanay)	221,400
Qyzylord (Kzyl-Orda)	157,400
Rūdny	109,500
Semey (Semipalatinsk)	269,600
Shymkent (Shimkent; Chimkent)	360,100
Taraz (Auliye-Ata; (Dzhambul)	330,100
Temirtaū	170,500
Kenya (1999)	
Eldoret	111,882[32]
Kisumu	192,733[32]
Machakos	143,274
Meru	126,427
Mombasa	461,753[32]
★ Nairobi	2,143,254
Nakuru	231,262
Nyeri	101,238
Kiribati (1990)	
★ Bairiki	2,226
agglomeration	32,000[2]
Korea, North (1987 est.)	
Anju	186,000
Ch'ŏngjin	582,480[1]
Haeju	195,000
Hamhŭng-Hungnam	709,000[1]
Hŭich'ŏn	163,000
Kaesŏng	334,433[1]
Kanggye	211,000
Kimch'aek (Songjin)	179,000
Kusŏng	177,000
Namp'o	731,448[1]
★ P'yŏngyang	3,136,000[2, 28]
Sinp'o	158,000
Sinŭiju	326,011[1]
Sunch'ŏn	356,000
Tanch'ŏn	284,000
Tŏkch'ŏn	217,000
Wŏnsan	274,000
Korea, South (1995)	
Andong	188,443
Ansan	510,314
Anyang	591,106
Asan	154,663
Ch'angwŏn	481,694
Chech'ŏn	137,070
Cheju (Jeju)	258,511
Chinhae	125,997
Chinju	329,886
Ch'ŏnan	330,259
Ch'ŏngju	531,376
Chŏng-ŭp	139,011
Chŏnju	563,153
Ch'unch'ŏn	234,528
Ch'ungju	205,206
Hanam	115,812
Iksan (Iri)	322,685
Inch'ŏn (Incheon)	2,308,188
Kangnŭng	220,403
Kimch'ŏn	147,027
Kimhae	256,370
Kimje	115,427
Kŏje	147,562
Kongju	131,229
Koyang	518,282
Kumi	311,431
Kunp'o	235,233
Kunsan	266,569
Kuri	142,173
Kwangju	1,257,636
Kwangmyŏng	350,914
Kwangyang	122,052
Kyŏngju	273,968
Kyŏngsan	173,746
Masan	441,242
Miryang	121,501
Mokp'o	247,452
Naju	107,831
Namwon	103,544
Namyangju	229,060
P'ohang	508,899
Poryŏng	122,604
Puch'ŏn	779,412
Pusan (Busan)	3,814,325
P'yŏngt'aek	312,927
Sach'ŏn	113,494
Sangju	124,116
★ Seoul (Sŏul)	10,231,217
Shihŭng	133,443
Sŏngnam	869,094
Sŏsan	134,746
Sunch'ŏn	249,263
Suwŏn	755,550
Taegu	2,449,420
Taejŏn	1,272,121
Tongyŏng	131,717
Ŭijŏngbu	276,111
Ŭiwang	108,788
Ulsan	967,429
Wŏnju	237,460
Yŏngch'ŏn	113,511
Yŏngju	131,097
Yŏsu	183,596
Kuwait (1995)	
As-Sālimīyah	130,215
★ Kuwait (Al-Kuwayt)	28,859
agglomeration	1,165,000[2]
Qalīb ash-Shuyūkh	102,178
Kyrgyzstan (1999 est.)	
★ Bishkek (Frunze)	619,000[28]
Osh	220,500[33]
Laos (1999 est.)	
★ Vientiane (Viangchan)	534,000
Latvia (2000 est.)	
Daugavpils	114,510
★ Rīga	788,283
Lebanon (1998 est.)	
Baalbek (Ba'labakk)	150,000
★ Beirut (Bayrūt)	1,500,000
Jūniyah	100,000
Tripoli (Ṭarābulus)	160,000
Lesotho (1996 est.)	
★ Maseru	160,100
agglomeration	373,000[2]
Liberia (1999 est.)	
★ Monrovia	479,000[28]
Libya (1995 est.)	
Banghāzī	650,000
Miṣrātah	280,000
Surt (Sirte)	150,000
★ Tripoli (Ṭarābulus)	1,140,000
Liechtenstein (2000 est.)	
★ Vaduz	5,043
Lithuania (2000 est.)	
Kaunas	412,614
Klaipėda	202,484
Panevėžys	133,696
Šiauliai	146,570
★ Vilnius	577,969
Luxembourg (1999 est.)	
★ Luxembourg	79,800
Macau (2000 est.)	
★ Macau	440,000
Macedonia (1994)	
★ Skopje (Skopije)	444,299
Madagascar (1993)	
★ Antananarivo	1,103,304
Antsirabe	126,062
Fianarantsoa	109,248
Mahajanga	106,780
Toamasina	137,782
Malawi (1998 est.)	
★ Blantyre (executive; judicial)	478,155
★ Lilongwe (ministerial; financial; legislative)	435,964
Malaysia (1991)	
Alor Setar	125,026
George Town (Pinang)	219,376
Ipoh	382,633
Johor Baharu	328,646
Kelang (Port Kelang)	243,698
Kota Baharu	219,713
★ Kuala Lumpur	1,145,075
Kuala Terengganu	228,659
Kuantan	198,356
Kuching	147,729
Petaling Jaya	254,849
Sandakan	126,092
Selayang Baru	124,606
Seremban	182,584
Shah Alam	101,773
Sibu	126,384
Sungai Petani	115,719
Taiping	183,165
Maldives (1995)	
★ Male	62,973
Mali (1996 est.)	
★ Bamako	809,552
Ségou	106,799
Malta (1999 est.)	
★ Valletta	7,100
agglomeration	102,000
Marshall Is. (1999)	
★ Majuro	23,676
Martinique (1999)	
★ Fort-de-France	94,049
Mauritania (1999 est.)	
★ Nouakchott	881,000
Mauritius (1999 est.)	
★ Port Louis	147,648
Beau Bassin/Rose Hill	101,273
Mayotte (1997; MU)	
★ Dzaoudzi (French administrative)	10,796
★ Mamoudzou (local administrative)	32,774
Mexico (2000 est.)	
Acapulco	619,253[34]
Aguascalientes	594,056[34]
Atizapán de Zaragoza (Ciudad López Mateos)	467,000
Boca del Río	124,000
Campeche	195,000
Cancún	400,000
Celaya	270,000
Chalco	123,000
Chetumal	118,000
Chihuahua	650,000
Chilpancingo	140,000
Chimalhuacán	488,000
Ciudad Acuña (Acuña)	108,000
Ciudad Apodaca (Apodaca)	273,000
Ciudad del Carmen	115,000
Ciudad Madero	182,012[34]
Ciudad Obregón	250,000
Ciudad Santa Catarina (Santa Catarina)	226,500
Ciudad Valles	105,000
Ciudad Victoria (Victoria)	248,000
Coacalco	250,000
Coatzacoalcos	229,000
Colima	119,186[34]
Córdoba	138,000
Cuautitlán Izcalli	435,000
Cuautla Morelos	137,000
Cuernavaca	330,000
Culiacán	536,942[34]
Durango	430,000
Ecatepec (de Morelos)	1,619,000
Ensenada	222,687[34]
General Escobedo	230,000
Gómez Palacio	210,000
Guadalajara	1,647,000
Guadalupe	668,500
Hermosillo	544,889[34]
Heroica Nogales (Nogales)	157,000
Huixquilucan	110,000
Iguala	105,000
Irapuato	320,000
Ixtapaluca	240,000
Jiutepec	140,000
Juárez (Ciudad Juárez)	1,190,000
La Paz	162,795[34]
León	1,019,510[34]
Los Mochis	200,000
Los Reyes la Paz	213,040[34]
Matamoros	370,000
Mazatlán	325,000
Mérida	660,848[34]
Metepec	160,000
Mexicali	550,000
★ Mexico City	8,591,309[34]
Minatitlán	150,000
Monclova	192,000
Monterrey	1,108,400
Morelia	549,404[34]
Naucalpan	840,000
Nezahualcóyotl	1,224,500
Nicolás Romero	218,000
Nuevo Laredo	309,000
Oaxaca	252,586[34]
Orizaba	118,400
Pachuca	231,089[34]
Piedras Negras	125,000
Poza Rica de Hidalgo	151,500
Puebla	1,270,989[34]
Puerta Vallarta	150,000
Querétaro	535,468[34]
Reynosa	398,000
Salamanca	140,000
Saltillo	560,000
San Cristóbal de las Casas	112,000
San Luis Potosí	628,134[34]
San Luis Río Colorado	125,000
San Nicolás de los Garzas	495,540[34]
San Pablo de las Salinas	150,000
San Pedro Garza García	126,000
Soledad de Graciano Sanchez	170,000
Tampico	294,789[34]
Tapachula	180,000
Tehuacán	204,358[34]
Tepic	265,681[34]
Texcoco (de Mora)	105,000
Tijuana	1,150,000
Tlalnepantla	715,000
Tlaquepaque	460,000
Toluca	435,000
Tonala	310,000
Torreón	505,000
Tultilan (Buenavista)	192,000
Tuxtla Gutiérrez	425,000
Uruapan	227,000
Valle de Chalco (Xico)	323,000
Veracruz	410,000
Villahermosa	330,605[34]
Xalapa (Jalapa Enríquez)	375,000
Zacatecas	113,780[34]
Zamora de Hidalgo	121,000
Zapopan	912,000
Micronesia	
★ Palikir	—
Moldova (1999 est.)	
Bălţi (Beltsy)	156,600
★ Chişinău (Kishinyov)	655,000
Tighina (Bendery)	128,000[33]
Tiraspol	200,700
Monaco (2000 est.)	
★ Monaco	31,700
Mongolia (2000 est.)	
★ Ulaanbaatar (Ulan Bator)	691,000

Major cities and national capitals (continued)

country city	population
Morocco (1994)	
Agadir	155,240
Beni-Mellal	140,212
Casablanca	2,940,623
El-Jadida	119,083
Fès	541,162
Kenitra	292,627
Khouribga	152,090
Ksar el-Kebir	107,065
Marrakech	621,914
Meknès	459,958
Mohammedia	170,083
Nador	112,450
Oujda	365,582
★ Rabat	623,457
Safi	262,276
Salé	504,420
Tanger	521,735
Temera	126,303
Tétouan	277,516
Mozambique (1997)	
Beira	412,588
Chimoio	177,608
★ Maputo (Lourenço Marques)	989,386
Matola	440,927
Mocuba	124,650
Nacala	164,309
Nampula	314,965
Quelimane	153,187
Tete	104,832
Xai-Xai	103,251
Myanmar (Burma) (1993 est.)	
Bassein (Pathein)	183,900
Henzada	104,700
Lashio	107,600
Mandalay	885,300
Meiktila	129,700
Mergui	122,700
Monywa	138,600
Moulmein (Mawlamyine)	307,600
Myingyan	103,600
Pegu (Bago)	190,900
Pyay (Prome, Pye)	105,700
Sittwe (Akyab)	137,600
Taunggyi	131,500
★ Yangôn (Rangoon)	3,361,700
Namibia (1997 est.)	
★ Windhoek	169,000
Nauru (1992)	
★ Yaren	672
Nepal (2000 est.; MU)	
Biratnagar	168,544
Birganj	103,880
★ Kathmandu	701,499
Lalitpur (Patan)	157,475
Pokhara	168,806
Netherlands, The (1999 est.)	
Almere	136,157
Amersfoort	123,367
★ Amsterdam (capital)	727,053
Apeldoorn	152,860
Arnhem	137,222
Breda	159,042
Dordrecht	119,462
Ede	101,542
Eindhoven	199,877
Emmen	105,497
Enschede	148,814
Groningen	171,193
Haarlem	148,262
Haarlemmermeer	109,377
Leiden	117,389
Maastricht	121,479
Nijmegen	151,864
Rotterdam	592,665
's-Hertogenbosch	128,009
★ The Hague (seat of government)	440,743
Tilburg	190,559
Utrecht	232,718
Zaanstad	135,126
Zoetermeer	108,899
Zwolle	104,431
Netherlands Antilles (1999 est.)	
★ Willemstad	123,000
New Caledonia (1996)	
★ Nouméa	76,293
New Zealand (1999 est.)	
Auckland	381,800
Christchurch	324,200
Dunedin	119,600
Hamilton	117,100
Manukau	281,800
North Shore	187,700
Waitakere	170,600
★ Wellington	166,700
Nicaragua (1995)	
León	123,865
★ Managua	864,201
Niger (1994 est.)	
★ Niamey	420,000
Zinder	100,000
Nigeria (1991)	
Aba	500,183
Abeokuta	352,735
★ Abuja	107,069
Ado-Ekiti	156,122
Akure	239,124
Awka	104,682
Bauchi	206,537
Benin City	762,719
Bida	111,245
Calabar	310,839
Damaturu	141,897
Ede	142,363
Effon-Alaiye	158,977
Enugu	407,756
Gboko	101,281
Gombe	163,604
Gusau	132,393
Ibadan	1,835,300
Ife	186,856
Ijebu-Ode	124,313
Ikare	103,843
Ikire	111,435
Ikorodu	184,674
Ikot Ekpene	119,402
Ilawe-Ekiti	104,049
Ilesha	139,445
Ilorin	532,089
Ise	108,136
Iseyin	170,936
Iwo	125,645
Jimeta	141,724
Jos	510,300
Kaduna	993,642
Kano	2,166,554
Katsina	259,315
★ Lagos	5,195,247
agglomeration	12,763,000[2]
Maiduguri	618,278
Makurdi	151,515
Minna	189,191
Mubi	128,900
Nnewi	121,065
Ogbomosho	433,030
Okene	312,775
Okpogho	105,127
Ondo	146,051
Onitsha	350,280
Oshogbo	250,951
Owerri	119,711
Owo	157,181
Oyo	369,894
Port Harcourt	703,421
Sagamu	127,513
Sango Otta	103,332
Sapele	109,576
Sokoto	329,639
Suleja	105,075
Ugep	134,773
Umuahia	147,167
Warri	363,382
Zaria	612,257
Northern Mariana Is. (1995 est.)	
★ Capital Hill[35]	2,698
Norway (2000 est.; MU)	
Bærum	101,494
Bergen	229,496
★ Oslo	507,467
Stavanger	108,818
Trondheim	148,859
Oman (1993)	
As-Sib	155,000
Bawshar	107,500
★ Muscat	40,900
agglomeration	887,000[2]
Salālah	116,000
Pakistan (1998)	
Abbottabad	105,999[36]
Bahawalnagar	109,642
Bahawalpur	403,408[36]
Burewala	149,857
Chiniot	169,282
Chishtian Mandi	101,659
Daska	101,500
Dera Ghazi Khan	188,149
Faisalabad (Lyallpur)	1,977,246
Gojra	114,967
Gujranwala	1,124,799
Gujrat	250,121
Hafizabad	130,216
Hyderabad	1,151,274[36]
★ Islamabad	524,500
Jacobabad	137,773
Jaranwala	103,308
Jhang Sadar	292,214
Jhelum	145,847
Kamoke	150,984
Karachi	9,269,265[36]
Kasur	241,649
Khairpur	102,188
Khanewal	132,962
Khanpur	117,764
Kohat	125,271[36]
Lahore	5,063,499[36]
Larkana	270,366
Mardan	244,511[36]
Mingaora	174,469
Mirpur Khas	184,465
Multan	1,182,441[36]
Muridike	108,578
Muzaffargarh	121,641
Nawabshah	183,110
Okara	200,901
Pakpattan	107,791
Peshawar	988,055[36]
Quetta	560,307
Rahimyar Khan	228,479
Rawalpindi	1,406,214[36]
Sadiqabad	141,509
Sahiwal	207,388
Sargodha	455,360[36]
Shekhupura	271,875
Shikarpur	133,259
Sialkot	417,597[36]
Sukkur	329,176
Tando Adam	103,363
Wah	198,431[36]
Palau (2000)	
★ Koror	13,303
Panama (2000)	
★ Panama City	415,964
San Miguelito	293,745[37]
Papua New Guinea (1999 est.)	
Lae	113,118[38]
★ Port Moresby (National Capital District)	298,145
Paraguay (1992)	
★ Asunción	500,938
Ciudad del Este	133,881
San Lorenzo	133,395
Peru (1998 est.)	
Arequipa	710,103
Ayacucho	118,960
Cajamarca	108,009
Chiclayo	469,200
Chimbote	298,800
Chincha Alta	130,000
Cusco	278,590
Huancayo	305,039
Huánuco	129,688
Ica	194,820
Iquitos	334,013
Juliaca	180,000
Lima agglomeration	7,060,600
Ate	324,799[33]
Callao	407,904[33]
Carabayllo	115,000[33]
Chorrillos	238,739[33]
Comas	434,690[33]
El Agustino	159,707[33]
Independencia	191,151[33]
La Victoria	213,239[33]
★ Lima	316,322[33]
Los Olivos	281,115[33]
Lurigancho	110,347[33]
Puente Piedra	131,000[33]
Rímac	190,836[33]
San Borja	109,233[33]
San Juan de Lurigancho	652,681[33]
San Juan de Miraflores	329,023[33]
San Martin de Porras	411,000[33]
San Miguel	126,825[33]
Santa Anita	131,519[33]
Santiago de Surco	224,866[33]
Ventanilla	105,824[33]
Villa el Salvador	296,000[33]
Villa Maria del Triunfo	301,505[33]
Piura	308,155
Pucallpa	220,866
Puno	101,578
Sullana	170,000
Tacna	215,683
Trujillo	603,657
Philippines (2000)	
Angeles	263,971
Antipolo	200,000[39]
Bacolod	429,076
Bacoor	305,699
Baguio	252,386
Baliuag	119,675
Biñan	201,186
Binangonan	187,691
Butuan	120,000[39]
Cagayan de Oro	345,000[39]
Cainta	242,511
Calamba	160,000[39]
Cebu	718,821
Cotabato	163,849
Dagupan	130,328
Dasmariñas	250,000[39]
Davao	700,000[39]
Dumaguete	102,265
General Mariano Alvarez	112,446
General Santos	250,000[39]
Iloilo	365,820
Kalookan (Caloocan)	1,177,604
Lapu-Lapu	217,019
Las Piñas	472,780
Lucena	196,075
Makati	444,867
Malabon	338,855
Malolos	175,291
Mandaluyong	278,474
Mandaue	259,728
★ Manila	1,581,082
Metro Manila	9,932,560
Marawi	131,090
Marikina	391,170
Meycauayan	163,037
Muntinglupa	379,310
Naga	137,810
Navotas	230,403
Olongapo	194,260
Parañaque	449,811
Pasay	354,908
Pasig	505,058
★ Quezon City	2,173,831
San Fernando	221,857
San Juan del Monte	117,680
San Pablo	105,000[39]
San Pedro	231,403
Santa Rosa	185,633
Tacloban	178,639
Tagig	467,375
Taytay	198,183
Valenzuela	485,433
Zamboanga	135,000[39]
Poland (1999 est.)	
Białystok	283,937
Bielsko-Biała	180,307
Bydgoszcz	386,855
Bytom	205,560
Chorzów	121,708
Częstochowa	257,812
Dąbrowa Górnicza	131,037
Elbląg	129,782
Gdańsk	458,988
Gdynia	253,521
Gliwice	212,164
Gorzów Wielkopolski	126,019
Grudziadz	102,434
Jastrzębie-Zdrój	102,294
Kalisz	106,641
Katowice	345,934
Kielce	212,383
Koszalin	112,375
Kraków	740,666
Legnica	109,335
Łódź	806,728
Lublin	356,251
Olsztyn	170,904
Opole	129,553
Płock	131,011
Poznań	578,235
Radom	232,262
Ruda Śląska	159,665
Rybnik	144,582
Rzeszów	162,049
Słupsk	102,370
Sosnowiec	244,102
Szczecin	416,988
Tarnów	121,494
Toruń	206,158
Tychy	133,178
Wałbrzych	136,923
★ Warsaw (Warszawa)	1,618,468
Włocławek	123,373
Wrocław	637,877
Zabrze	200,177
Zielona Góra	118,182
Portugal (2001)	
Amadora	174,788
Braga	105,000
Coimbra	103,000
Funchal	102,521
★ Lisbon	556,797
agglomeration	3,754,000[2]
Porto	262,928
Puerto Rico (2000)	
Bayamón	203,499[40]
Carolina	168,164[40]
Ponce	155,038[40]
★ San Juan	421,958[40]
agglomeration	1,366,000[2]
Qatar (1997)	
★ Doha	264,009
Ar-Rayyān	161,453
Réunion (1999)	
★ Saint-Denis	131,557
Romania (1997 est.)	
Arad	184,619
Bacău	209,689
Baia Mare	149,496
Botoșani	129,285
Brăila	234,648
Brașov	317,772
★ Bucharest	2,027,512
Buzău	149,080
Cluj-Napoca	332,792
Constanța	344,876
Craiova	312,891
Drobeta-Turnu Severin	117,882
Galați	331,360
Iași	348,399
Oradea	223,288
Piatra Neamț	125,121
Pitești	187,181
Ploiești	253,414
Râmnicu Vâlcea	119,340
Satu Mare	129,886
Sibiu	168,949
Suceava	118,162
Timișoara	334,098
Târgu Mureș	165,534
Russia (1999 est.)	
Abakan	169,000
Achinsk	122,400
Almetyevsk	141,000
Angarsk	266,600
Arkhangelsk	366,200
Armavir	166,600
Arzamas	111,300
Astrakhan	488,000
Balakovo	206,300
Balashikha	134,200
Barnaul	586,200
Belgorod	339,100
Berezniki	182,200
Biysk	225,700
Blagoveshchensk	220,900
Bratsk	252,500
Bryansk	461,100
Cheboksary	458,000
Chelyabinsk	1,086,300
Cherepovets	324,500
Cherkessk	122,200
Chita	314,300
Dimitrovgrad	137,200
Dzerzhinsk	278,900
Elektrostal	147,600
Elista	101,700
Engels	189,100
Glazov	106,000
Grozny (Dzhokhar)	186,000
Irkutsk	596,400
Ivanovo	463,400

country city	population
Izhevsk	655,300
Kaliningrad	427,200
Kaliningrad (*Moscow oblast*)	134,000[38]
Kaluga	342,400
Kamensk-Uralsky	192,000
Kamyshin	126,000
Kansk	107,500
Kazan	1,100,800
Kemerovo	496,300
Khabarovsk	614,000
Khimki	133,500
Kineshma	100,000
Kirov	466,100
Kiselyovsk	111,100
Kislovodsk	120,800
Kolomna	151,500
Kolpino	141,200
Komsomolsk-na-Amure	295,100
Kostroma	289,300
Kovrov	161,200
Krasnodar	643,400
Krasnoyarsk	877,800
Kurgan	367,200
Kursk	445,400
Leninsk-Kuznetsky	115,600
Lipetsk	521,600
Lyubertsy	165,100
Magadan	121,800
Magnitogorsk	428,100
Makhachkala	334,900
Maykop	167,000
Mezhdurechensk	104,500
Miass	166,900
Michurinsk	121,800
★ Moscow	8,389,700
Murmansk	382,700
Murom	143,200
Mytishchi	155,700
Naberezhnye Chelny (Brezhnev)	518,300
Nakhodka	159,800
Nalchik	234,700
Nevinnomyssk	132,700
Nikolo-Beryozovka (Neftekamsk)	116,500
Nizhnekamsk	222,000
Nizhnevartovsk	235,600
Nizhny Novgorod (Gorky)	1,364,900
Nizhny Tagil	395,800
Noginsk	117,800
Norilsk	146,500
Novgorod	231,700
Novocheboksarsk	123,600
Novocherkassk	186,500
Novokuybyshevsk	116,400
Novokuznetsk	562,800
Novomoskovsk	139,600
Novorossiysk	204,300
Novoshakhtinsk	103,100
Novosibirsk	1,402,400
Novotroitsk	109,700
Obninsk	108,500
Odintsovo	127,600
Oktyabrsky	111,700
Omsk	1,157,600
Orekhovo-Zuyevo	125,500
Orenburg	526,800
Orsk	274,400
Oryol	346,500
Penza	533,300
Perm	1,017,100
Pervouralsk	136,400
Petropavlovsk-Kamchatsky	196,700
Petrozavodsk	282,500
Podolsk	195,900
Prokopyevsk	240,500
Pskov	202,900
Pyatigorsk	133,100
Rostov-na-Donu	1,017,300
Rubtsovsk	163,900
Ryazan	531,300
Rybinsk (Andropov)	241,800
Saint Petersburg (Leningrad)	4,169,400
Salavat	156,400
Samara (Kuybyshev)	1,168,000
Saransk	316,600
Sarapul	106,800
Saratov	881,000
Sergiev Posad (Zagorsk)	111,800
Serov	100,400
Serpukhov	134,600
Severodvinsk	231,800
Seversk	118,600[39]
Shakhty	224,400
Shchyolkovo	104,900[39]
Simbirsk (Ulyanovsk)	671,700
Smolensk	355,700
Sochi	359,300
Solikamsk	106,400
Stary Oskol	211,800
Stavropol	345,100
Sterlitamak	263,600
Surgut	276,100
Syktyvkar	230,900
Syzran	188,100
Taganrog	287,600
Tambov	315,100
Tobolsk	100,000[39]
Tolyatti	720,300
Tomsk	481,400
Tula	513,100
Tver (Kalinin)	457,100
Tyumen	503,800
Ufa	1,088,900
Ulan-Ude	371,400
Usolye-Sibirskoye	104,100
Ussuriysk	158,400
Ust-Ilimsk	105,500
Velikiye Luki	117,100
Vladikavkaz (Ordzhonikidze)	310,600
Vladimir	339,200
Vladivostok	613,100
Volgodonsk	179,200
Volgograd	1,000,000
Vologda	304,300
Volzhsky	289,500
Voronezh	908,000
Votkinsk	102,000
Yakutsk	195,500
Yaroslavl	620,600
Yekaterinburg (Sverdlovsk)	1,272,900
Yelets	120,300
Yoshkar-Ola	249,800
Yuzhno-Sakhalinsk	179,900
Zelenodolysk	100,600
Zelenograd	206,800
Zheleznodorozhny	100,400
Zlatoust	198,400
Rwanda (1996 est.)	
★ Kigali	356,000
St. Kitts and Nevis (1994 est.)	
★ Basseterre	12,605
St. Lucia (1997 est.)	
★ Castries	16,187
agglomeration	57,000[2]
St. Vincent and the Grenadines (1999 est.)	
★ Kingstown	16,175
Samoa (1999 est.)	
★ Apia	38,000
San Marino (1997 est.)	
★ San Marino	2,294
São Tomé and Príncipe (1991)	
★ São Tomé	43,420
Saudi Arabia (1992)	
Abhā	112,316
'Ar'ar	108,055
Buraydah	248,636
Ad-Dammām	482,321
Ḥafar al-Bāṭin	137,793
Ḥā'il	176,757
Al-Hufūf	225,847
Jiddah	2,046,251
Al-Jubayl	140,828
Khamīs Mushayṭ	217,870
Al-Kharj	152,071
Al-Khubar	141,683
Mecca (Makkah)	965,697
Medina (Al-Madīnah)	608,295
Al-Mubarraz	219,123
★ Riyadh (Ar-Riyāḍ)	2,776,096
Tabūk	292,555
Aṭ-Ṭā'if	416,121
Ath-Thuqbah	125,650
Yanbu' al-Baḥr	119,819
Senegal (1998 est.)	
★ Dakar	1,999,000[2, 28]
Kaolack	200,000
Mbour	109,317[33]
Rufisque	185,142[33]
Saint-Louis	180,000[33]
Thiès	320,000
Ziguinchor	180,555[33]
Serbia and Montenegro (2000 est.)[41]	
★ Belgrade (Beograd)	1,194,878
Kragujevac	154,489
Niš	182,583
Novi Sad	182,778
Podgorica (Titograd)	130,875
Priština	186,611
Prizren	115,711
Seychelles (1997)	
★ Victoria	24,701[28]
Sierra Leone (1999 est.)	
★ Freetown	822,000[28]
Singapore (2000 est.)[42]	
★ Singapore	3,278,000
Slovakia (2000 est.)	
★ Bratislava	448,292
Košice	241,874
Slovenia (2000 est.)	
★ Ljubljana	270,986
Solomon Islands (2000 est.)	
★ Honiara	50,100
Somalia (1999 est.)	
★ Mogadishu	1,162,000[28]
South Africa (1996)[28]	
Alberton	147,948
Benoni	365,467
★ Bloemfontein[43] (de facto judicial)	333,769
Boksburg	260,905
Botshabelo	177,971
Brakpan	171,359
★ Cape Town (de facto legislative)	2,415,408
Carletonville	164,367
Durban	2,117,650
East London	212,323
Johannesburg	1,480,530
Kimberley	170,432
Klerksdorp	137,318
Krugersdorp	203,168
Mdantsane	182,998
Midrand	126,400
Newcastle	219,682
Paarl	140,376
Pietermaritzburg	378,126
Port Elizabeth	749,921
Potchefstroom	101,682
★ Pretoria[44] (de facto executive)	1,104,479
Rustenburg	104,537
Somerset West	112,489
Soweto	1,098,094
Springs	160,795
Tembisa	282,272
Uitenhage	192,120
Vanderbijlpark	253,335
Vereeniging	346,780
Verwoerdburg	114,575
Welkom	203,296
Westonaria	113,932
Witbank	167,183
Spain (1998 est.)	
Albacete	145,454
Alcalá de Henares	163,831
Alcorcón	143,970
Algeciras	101,972
Alicante (Alacant)	272,432
Almería	168,025
Badajoz	134,710
Badalona	209,606
Barakaldo	98,649
Barcelona	1,505,581
Bilbao	358,467
Burgos	161,984
Cádiz	143,129
Cartagena	175,628
Castellón de la Plana (Castelló de la Plana)	137,741
Córdoba	309,961
Coruña, A (Coruña, La)	243,134
Donostia–San Sebastián	178,229
Elche (Elx)	191,713
Fuenlabrada	167,458
Getafe	143,629
Gijón	265,491
Granada	241,471
Hospitalet de Llobregat	248,521
Huelva	139,991
Jaén	107,184
Jerez de la Frontera	181,602
Laguna, La	127,945
Leganés	173,163
León	139,809
Lleida (Lérida)	112,207
Logroño	125,617
★ Madrid	2,881,506
Málaga	528,079
Mataró	103,265
Móstoles	195,311
Murcia	349,040
Ourense (Orense)	107,965
Oviedo	199,549
Palma (de Mallorca)	319,181
Palmas de Gran Canaria, Las	352,641
Pamplona (Iruña)	171,150
Sabadell	184,859
Salamanca	158,457
Santa Coloma de Gramanet	120,958
Santa Cruz de Tenerife	211,930
Santander	184,165
Sevilla (Seville)	701,927
Tarragona	112,795
Terrassa (Tarrasa)	165,654
Valencia (València)	739,412
Valladolid	319,946
Vigo	283,110
Vitoria–Gasteiz	216,527
Zaragoza (Saragossa)	603,367
Sri Lanka (1997 est.; MU)	
★ Colombo (administrative)	800,982
Dehiwala-Mount Lavinia	220,780
Galle	123,616
Jaffna	145,600
Kandy	150,532
Moratuwa	213,000
Negombo	136,850
★ Sri Jayawardenepura Kotte (legislative and judicial)	118,000[45, 46]
Sudan, The (1993)	
Al-Fāshir	141,884
Juba	114,980
Kassalā	234,270
★ Khartoum (executive)	924,505
Khartoum North	879,105
Kūstī	173,599
Nyala	228,778
★ Omdurman (legislative)	1,267,077
Port Sudan	305,385
Al-Qaḍārif	189,384
Al-Ubayyiḍ	228,096
Wad Madanī	218,714
Suriname (1999 est.)	
★ Paramaribo	233,000[28]
Swaziland (1998 est.)	
★ Lobamba (legislative)	...
★ Lozitha (royal)	...
★ Ludzidzini (royal)	...
★ Mbabane (administrative)	60,000
Sweden (2000 est.; MU)	
Göteborg	462,470
Helsingborg	116,870
Jönköping	116,344
Linköping	132,500
Malmö	257,574
Norrköping	122,212
Örebro	123,503
★ Stockholm	743,703
Umeå	103,970
Uppsala	188,478
Västerås	125,433
Switzerland (1999 est.)	
Basel (Bâle)	168,735
★ Bern (Berne)	123,254
Geneva (Genève)	172,809
Lausanne	114,161
Zürich	336,821
Syria (1994)	
Aleppo (Ḥalab)	1,582,930
★ Damascus (Dimashq)	1,394,322
Dar'ā	180,093[45]
Dayr az-Zawr	140,459
Dūmā	131,158[45]
Ḥamāh	264,348
Āl-Ḥasakah	106,000[47]
Homs (Ḥims)	540,133
Jaramānah	138,469[45]
Latakia (al-Ladhiqiyah)	311,784
Al-Qāmishlī	144,286
Ar-Raqqah	165,195
Ṭarṭūs	136,812[45]
Taiwan (2000 est.)	
Chang-hua	227,715
Chi-lung (Keelung)	385,201
Chia-i	265,109
Chung-ho	392,176
Chung-li	318,649
Feng-shan	318,562
Fêng-yüan	161,032
Hsi-chih	154,976
Hsin-chu	361,958
Hsin-chuang	365,048
Hsin-tien	263,603
Hua-lien	108,407
Kao-hsiung	1,475,505
Lu-chou	160,516
Nan-t'ou	104,723
Pa-te	161,700
Pan-ch-'iao (T'ai-pei-hsien)	523,850
P'ing-chen	188,344
P'ing-tung	214,727
San-chu'ung	380,084
Shu-lin	151,260
T'ai-chung	940,589
T'ai-nan	728,060
T'ai-p'ing	165,524
T'ai-tung	111,039
★ Taipei (T'ai-pei)	2,641,312
Ta-li	171,940
T'ao-yuan	316,438
T'u-ch'eng	224,897
Yung-ho	227,700
Yung-k'ang	193,005
Tajikistan (1998 est.)	
★ Dushanbe	513,000
Khujand (Khudzhand; Leninabad)	163,000[1]
Tanzania (1988)	
Arusha	102,544
★ Dar es Salaam	1,747,000[4]
★ Dodoma (legislative)	189,000[4]
Mbeya	130,798
Morogoro	117,760
Mwanza	172,287
Tanga	137,364
Zanzibar	157,634
Thailand (1999 est.)	
★ Bangkok (Krung Thep)	6,320,174[34]
Chiang Mai	171,594
Hat Yai	156,812
Khon Kaen	126,500[39]
Nakhon Ratchasima	181,400[39]
Nakhon Si Thammarat	105,176
Nonthaburi	292,100[39]
Pak Kret	140,725[38]
Surat Thani	112,504
Ubon Ratchathani	116,300[39]
Udon Thani	156,038
Togo (1999 est.)	
★ Lomé	790,000[28]
Tonga (1999 est.)	
★ Nuku'alofa	37,000
Trinidad and Tobago (1996 est.)	
★ Port-of-Spain	43,396
Tunisia (1994)	
Aryānah	152,700
Ettadhamen	149,200
Kairouan	102,600
Ṣafāqis (Sfax)	230,900
Sūsah	125,000
★ Tunis	674,100
Turkey (1997)	
Adana	1,041,509
Adıyaman	212,475

Major cities and national capitals (continued)

country / city	population
Afyon	113,510
Aksaray	101,187
Alanya	117,311
★ Ankara	2,984,099
Antakya (Hatay)	139,046
Antalya	512,086
Aydın	133,757
Balıkesir	189,987
Batman	212,726
Bismil	101,409
Bursa	1,066,559
Çorlu	123,266
Çorum	147,112
Denizli	233,651
Diyarbakır	511,640
Edirne	115,083
Elazığ	250,534
Erzincan	102,304
Erzurum	298,735
Eskişehir	454,536
Gaziantep	712,800
Gebze	235,211
Hatay	139,046
İçel (Mersin)	501,398
İskenderun	161,728
Isparta	134,271
Istanbul	8,260,438
İzmir	2,081,556
Kahramanmaraş (Maras)	303,594
Karabük	103,806
Karaman	104,154
Kayseri	498,233
Kırıkkale	203,496
Kızıltepe	112,015
Kocaeli (İzmit)	198,200
Konya	623,333
Kütahya	162,319
Malatya	400,248
Manisa	201,340
Ordu	117,699
Osmaniye	160,854
Sakarya (Adapazarı)	183,265
Samsun	338,387
Siirt	107,067
Sivas	232,352
Sultanbeyli	144,932
Tarsus	190,184
Tekirdağ	100,557
Trabzon	182,552
Urfa (Şanlıurfa)	410,762
Uşak	124,356
Van	226,965
Viranşehir	106,363
Zonguldak	106,176
Turkmenistan (1999 est.)	
★ Ashkhabad (Ashgabat)	605,000
Chärjew (Chardzhev; Chardzhou)	203,000
Dashhowuz (Dashkhovuz; Tashauz)	165,000
Mary	123,000
Nebitdag	119,000
Tuvalu (1999 est.)	
★ Funafuti	6,000
Uganda (1999 est.)	
★ Kampala	1,154,000[28]
Ukraine (1998 est.)	
Alchevsk	120,900
Berdyansk	132,300
Bila Tserkva (Belaya Tserkov)	215,200
Cherkasy (Cherkassy)	310,600
Chernihiv (Chernigov)	310,800
Chernivtsi (Chernovtsy)	259,000
Dniprodzerzhynsk (Dneprodzerzhinsk)	275,000
Dnipropetrovsk (Dnepropetrovsk)	1,122,400
Donetsk	1,065,400
Horlivka (Gorlovka)	309,300
Ivano-Frankivsk (Ivano-Frankovsk)	237,400
Kam'yanets-Podilskyy (Kamenets-Podolsky)	108,000
Kerch	167,400
Kharkiv (Kharkov)	1,521,400
Kherson	358,700
Khmelnytskyy (Khmelnitsky)	260,100
★ Kiev (Kyyiv)	2,620,900
Kirovohrad	270,200
Kostyantynivka (Konstantinovka)	100,100
Kramatorsk	190,800
Krasnyy Luch	104,500
Kremenchuk (Kremenchug)	240,700
Kryvyy Rih (Krivoy Rog)	715,400
Luhansk (Voroshilovgrad)	475,300
Lutsk	217,900
Lviv (Lvov)	793,700
Lysychansk (Lisichansk)	119,000
Makiyivka (Makeyevka)	394,800
Mariupol (Zhdanov)	504,400
Melitopol	171,000
Mykolayiv (Nikolayev)	517,900
Nikopol	152,000
Odesa (Odessa)	1,027,400
Oleksandriya (Aleksandriya)	101,000
Pavlohrad	130,000
Poltava	317,300
Rivne (Rovno)	244,900
Sevastopol	356,000
Simferopol	341,000
Slov'yansk (Slavyansk)	129,600
Stakhanov	104,500
Sumy	299,800
Syeverodonetsk	129,200
Ternopil (Ternopol)	235,100
Uzhhorod	125,500
Vinnytsya (Vinnitsa)	389,100
Yenakiyeve (Yenakiyevo)	108,700
Yevpatoriya	113,500
Zaporizhzhya (Zaporozhye)	863,100
Zhytomyr (Zhitomir)	297,700
United Arab Emirates (1995)	
★ Abu Dhabi (Abū Ẓaby)	398,695
'Ajmān	114,395
Al-'Ayn	225,970
Dubai (Dubayy)	669,181
Sharjah (Ash-Shāriqah)	320,095
United Kingdom (1999 est.)	
England[48]	
Barnsley	220,937
Birmingham	961,041
Blackburn with Darwen	136,612
Blackpool	151,200
Bolton	258,584
Bournemouth	160,700
Bracknell Forest	110,000
Bradford	457,344
Brighton and Hove	245,000
Bristol	399,600
Bury	176,760
Calderdale	191,585
Cambridge	91,933
Canterbury	123,947
Carlisle	100,562
Chester	115,971
Coventry	294,387
Darlington	101,000
Derby	235,238
Doncaster	288,854
Dudley	304,615
Durham	80,669
Exeter	98,125
Gateshead	199,588
Gloucester	101,608
Halton	123,038
Kingston upon Hull	266,900
Kirklees	373,127
Knowsley	152,091
Lancaster	123,856
Leeds	680,722
Leicester	270,493
Lincoln	81,987
Liverpool	452,450
★ London (Greater London)	7,187,300[16, 49]
Luton	181,500
Manchester	404,861
Milton Keynes	204,415
Newcastle upon Tyne	259,541
North Tyneside	192,286
Norwich	120,895
Nottingham	284,000
Oldham	216,531
Oxford	134,800
Peterborough	159,900
Plymouth	255,800
Poole	139,200
Portsmouth	190,400
Reading	142,851
Rochdale	202,164
Rotherham	251,637
St. Albans	128,700
St. Helens	178,764
Salford	220,463
Sandwell	290,091
Sefton	289,542
Sheffield	501,202
Slough	108,000
Solihull	199,859
South Tyneside	154,697
Southampton	214,859
Southend	172,300
Stockport	284,395
Stockton-on-Tees	179,000
Stoke-on-Trent	254,300
Sunderland	289,040
Swindon	177,118
Tameside	216,431
Thurrock	132,283
Torbay	119,674
Trafford	212,731
Wakefield	310,915
Walsall	259,488
Warrington	187,000
Wigan	306,521
Winchester	96,386
Windsor and Maidenhead	132,465
Wirral	330,795
Wolverhampton	242,190
Worcester	89,481
York	175,925
Northern Ireland[50]	
Belfast	297,200
Craigavon	79,100
Derry (Londonderry)	104,700
Lisburn	106,600
Newtonabbey	79,600
Scotland[51]	
Aberdeen	213,070
Dundee	146,690
Edinburgh	450,180
Glasgow	619,680
Wales[52]	
Cardiff	315,040
Conwy	110,600
Neath Port Talbot	139,459
Newport	136,800
Rhondda, Cynon, Taff	240,117
Swansea	230,200
Torfaen	90,527
Wrexham	125,200
United States (2000)	
Abilene (*Texas*)	115,930
Akron (*Ohio*)	217,074
Albany (*Ga.*)	76,939
Albany (*N.Y.*)	95,658
Albuquerque (*N.M.*)	448,607
Alexandria (*Va.*)	128,283
Alhambra (*Calif.*)	85,804
Allentown (*Pa.*)	106,632
Amarillo (*Texas*)	173,627
Anaheim (*Calif.*)	328,014
Anchorage (*Alaska*)	260,283
Ann Arbor (*Mich.*)	114,024
Antioch (*Calif.*)	90,532
Arden-Arcade (*Calif.*)[53]	96,025
Arlington (*Texas*)	332,969
Arlington (*Va.*)[53]	189,453
Arlington Heights (*Ill.*)	76,031
Arvada (*Colo.*)	102,153
Athens (*Ga.*)	100,266
Atlanta (*Ga.*)	416,474
Augusta (*Ga.*)	195,182
Aurora (*Colo.*)	276,393
Aurora (*Ill.*)	142,990
Austin (*Texas*)	656,562
Bakersfield (*Calif.*)	247,057
Baldwin Park (*Calif.*)	75,837
Baltimore (*Md.*)	651,154
Baton Rouge (*La.*)	227,818
Beaumont (*Texas*)	113,866
Beaverton (*Ore.*)	76,129
Bellevue (*Wash.*)	109,569
Berkeley (*Calif.*)	102,743
Billings (*Mont.*)	89,847
Birmingham (*Ala.*)	242,820
Bloomington (*Minn.*)	85,172
Boise (*Idaho*)	185,787
Boston (*Mass.*)	589,141
Boulder (*Colo.*)	94,673
Brandon (*Fla.*)[52]	77,895
Brick Township (*N.J.*)[53]	76,119
Bridgeport (*Conn.*)	139,529
Brockton (*Mass.*)	94,304
Brownsville (*Texas*)	139,722
Buena Park (*Calif.*)	78,282
Buffalo (*N.Y.*)	292,648
Burbank (*Calif.*)	100,316
Cambridge (*Mass.*)	101,355
Camden (*N.J.*)	79,904
Canton (*Mich.*)[53]	76,366
Canton (*Ohio*)	80,806
Cape Coral (*Fla.*)	102,286
Carlsbad (*Calif.*)	78,247
Carrollton (*Texas*)	109,576
Carson (*Calif.*)	89,730
Cary (*N.C.*)	94,536
Cedar Rapids (*Iowa*)	120,758
Chandler (*Ariz.*)	176,581
Charleston (*S.C.*)	96,650
Charlotte (*N.C.*)	540,828
Chattanooga (*Tenn.*)	155,554
Cheektowaga (*N.Y.*)[53]	79,988
Chesapeake (*Va.*)	199,184
Chicago (*Ill.*)	2,896,016
Chula Vista (*Calif.*)	173,556
Cicero (*Ill.*)	85,616
Cincinnati (*Ohio*)	331,285
Citrus Heights (*Calif.*)	85,071
Clarksville (*Tenn.*)	103,455
Clearwater (*Fla.*)	108,787
Cleveland (*Ohio*)	478,403
Clifton (*N.J.*)	78,672
Clinton Township (*Mich.*)[53]	95,648
Colorado Springs (*Colo.*)	360,890
Columbia (*Md.*)[53]	88,254
Columbia (*Mo.*)	84,531
Columbia (*S.C.*)	116,278
Columbus (*Ga.*)	185,781
Columbus (*Ohio*)	711,470
Compton (*Calif.*)	93,493
Concord (*Calif.*)	121,780
Coral Springs (*Fla.*)	117,549
Corona (*Calif.*)	124,966
Corpus Christi (*Texas*)	277,454
Costa Mesa (*Calif.*)	108,724
Cranston (*R.I.*)	79,269
Dallas (*Texas*)	1,188,580
Daly City (*Calif.*)	103,621
Davenport (*Iowa*)	98,359
Davie (*Fla.*)	75,720
Dayton (*Ohio*)	166,179
Dearborn (*Mich.*)	97,775
Decatur (*Ill.*)	81,860
Denton (*Texas*)	80,537
Denver (*Colo.*)	554,636
Des Moines (*Iowa*)	198,682
Detroit (*Mich.*)	951,270
Dover Township (*N.J.*)[52]	86,327
Downey (*Calif.*)	107,323
Duluth (*Minn.*)	86,918
Durham (*N.C.*)	187,035
East Los Angeles (*Calif.*)[53]	124,283
Edison (*N.J.*)[53]	97,687
El Cajon (*Calif.*)	94,869
El Monte (*Calif.*)	115,965
El Paso (*Texas*)	563,662
Elgin (*Ill.*)	94,487
Elizabeth (*N.J.*)	120,568
Erie (*Pa.*)	103,717
Escondido (*Calif.*)	133,559
Eugene (*Ore.*)	137,893
Evansville (*Ind.*)	121,582
Everett (*Wash.*)	91,488
Fairfield (*Calif.*)	96,178
Fall River (*Mass.*)	91,938
Fargo (*N.D.*)	90,599
Farmington Hills (*Mich.*)	82,111
Fayetteville (*N.C.*)	121,015
Federal Way (*Wash.*)	83,259
Flint (*Mich.*)	124,943
Fontana (*Calif.*)	128,929
Fort Collins (*Colo.*)	118,652
Fort Lauderdale (*Fla.*)	152,397
Fort Smith (*Ark.*)	80,268
Fort Wayne (*Ind.*)	205,727
Fort Worth (*Texas*)	534,694
Fremont (*Calif.*)	203,413
Fresno (*Calif.*)	427,652
Fullerton (*Calif.*)	126,003
Gainesville (*Fla.*)	95,447
Garden Grove (*Calif.*)	165,196
Garland (*Texas*)	215,768
Gary (*Ind.*)	102,746
Gilbert (*Ariz.*)	109,697
Glendale (*Ariz.*)	218,812
Glendale (*Calif.*)	194,973
Grand Prairie (*Texas*)	127,427
Grand Rapids (*Mich.*)	197,800
Greeley (*Colo.*)	76,930
Green Bay (*Wis.*)	102,313
Greensboro (*N.C.*)	223,891
Gresham (*Ore.*)	90,205
Hammond (*Ind.*)	83,048
Hampton (*Va.*)	146,437
Hartford (*Conn.*)	121,578
Hawthorne (*Calif.*)	84,112
Hayward (*Calif.*)	140,030
Henderson (*Nev.*)	175,381
Hialeah (*Fla.*)	226,419
High Point (*N.C.*)	85,839
Hollywood (*Fla.*)	139,357
Honolulu (*Hawaii*)[53]	371,657
Houston (*Texas*)	1,953,631
Huntington Beach (*Calif.*)	189,594
Huntsville (*Ala.*)	158,216
Independence (*Mo.*)	113,288
Indianapolis (*Ind.*)	791,926
Inglewood (*Calif.*)	112,580
Irvine (*Calif.*)	143,072
Irving (*Texas*)	191,615
Jackson (*Miss.*)	184,256
Jacksonville (*Fla.*)	735,617
Jersey City (*N.J.*)	240,055
Joliet (*Ill.*)	106,221
Kalamazoo (*Mich.*)	77,145
Kansas City (*Kan.*)	146,866
Kansas City (*Mo.*)	441,545
Kendall (*Fla.*)[53]	75,226
Kenosha (*Wis.*)	90,352
Killeen (*Texas*)	86,911
Knoxville (*Tenn.*)	173,890
Lafayette (*La.*)	110,257
Lakeland (*Fla.*)	78,452
Lakewood (*Calif.*)	79,345
Lakewood (*Colo.*)	144,126
Lancaster (*Calif.*)	118,718
Lansing (*Mich.*)	119,128
Laredo (*Texas*)	176,576
Las Vegas (*Nev.*)	478,434
Lawrence (*Kan.*)	80,098
Lawton (*Okla.*)	92,757
Lewisville (*Texas*)	77,737
Lexington (*Ky.*)	260,512
Lincoln (*Neb.*)	225,581
Little Rock (*Ark.*)	183,133
Livonia (*Mich.*)	100,545
Long Beach (*Calif.*)	461,522
Los Angeles (*Calif.*)	3,694,820
Louisville (*Ky.*)	256,231
Lowell (*Mass.*)	105,167
Lubbock (*Texas*)	199,564
Lynn (*Mass.*)	89,050
McAllen (*Texas*)	106,414
Macon (*Ga.*)	97,255
Madison (*Wis.*)	208,054
Manchester (*N.H.*)	107,006
Memphis (*Tenn.*)	650,100
Mesa (*Ariz.*)	396,375
Mesquite (*Texas*)	124,523
Metairie (*La.*)[53]	146,136
Miami (*Fla.*)	362,470
Miami Beach (*Fla.*)	87,933
Midland (*Texas*)	94,996
Milwaukee (*Wis.*)	596,974
Minneapolis (*Minn.*)	382,618
Mission Viejo (*Calif.*)	93,102
Mobile (*Ala.*)	198,915
Modesto (*Calif.*)	188,856
Montgomery (*Ala.*)	201,568
Moreno Valley (*Calif.*)	142,381

[1]1993 estimate. [2]1999 estimate. [3]Eight villages, including Fagatogo, Utulei, and Pago Pago, are collectively known as Pago Pago (1999 agglomeration pop. 14,000). [4]1995 estimate. [5]1991 estimate. [6]Urban Centre ("urban agglomeration") as defined by 1996 census. [7]1996 census. [8]Estimated population of New Providence and adjacent islands. [9]Preliminary census populations for urban areas of *municípios*. [10]1990 census. [11]1992 census. [12]Excludes agricultural population within city limits. [13]San Jose canton. [14]1988 census. [15]As of 1998 administrative reorganization. [16]1998 estimate. [17]Excludes Lefkoşa (Turkish Nicosia), whose population per 1996 census was 36,834. [18]Population of the urban area of the National District. [19]Within San Salvador metropolitan area. [20]1997 census. [21]Includes internally displaced persons from Abkhazia. [22]Within Guatemala City metropolitan area. [23]Population includes Comayagüela. [24]Urban population; Hong Kong is 100% urban. [25]Census not taken because of civil unrest. [26]Urban population (may or may not be city proper; not urban agglomeration). [27]Population of Greater Karaj. [28]Urban agglomeration(s). [29]1985 estimate. [30]County borough population. [31]Commune population. [32]1989 census. [33]1996 estimate. [34]2000 census. [35]Census designated place on the island of Saipan. [36]Includes

country city	population
Naperville (*Ill.*)	128,358
Nashua (*N.H.*)	86,605
Nashville (*Tenn.*)	545,524
New Bedford (*Mass.*)	93,768
New Haven (*Conn.*)	123,626
New Orleans (*La.*)	484,674
New York City (*N.Y.*)	8,008,278
Newark (*N.J.*)	273,546
Newport News (*Va.*)	180,150
Newton (*Mass.*)	83,829
Norfolk (*Va.*)	234,403
Norman (*Okla.*)	95,694
North Charleston (*S.C.*)	79,641
North Las Vegas (*Nev.*)	115,488
Norwalk (*Calif.*)	103,298
Norwalk (*Conn.*)	82,951
Oakland (*Calif.*)	399,484
Oceanside (*Calif.*)	161,029
Odessa (*Texas*)	90,943
Ogden (*Utah*)	77,226
Oklahoma City (*Okla.*)	506,132
Olathe (*Kan.*)	92,962
Omaha (*Neb.*)	390,007
Ontario (*Calif.*)	158,007
Orange (*Calif.*)	128,821
Orem (*Utah*)	84,324
Orlando (*Fla.*)	185,951
Overland Park (*Kan.*)	149,080
Oxnard (*Calif.*)	170,358
Palm Bay (*Fla.*)	79,413
Palmdale (*Calif.*)	116,670
Paradise (*Nev.*)[52]	186,070
Parma (*Ohio*)	85,655
Pasadena (*Calif.*)	133,936
Pasadena (*Texas*)	141,674
Paterson (*N.J.*)	149,222
Pembroke Pines (*Fla.*)	137,427
Peoria (*Ariz.*)	108,364
Peoria (*Ill.*)	112,936
Philadelphia (*Pa.*)	1,517,550
Phoenix (*Ariz.*)	1,321,045
Pittsburgh (*Pa.*)	334,563
Plano (*Texas*)	222,030
Plantation (*Fla.*)	82,934
Pomona (*Calif.*)	149,473
Pompano Beach (*Fla.*)	78,191
Port St. Lucie (*Fla.*)	88,769
Portland (*Ore.*)	529,121
Portsmouth (*Va.*)	100,565
Providence (*R.I.*)	173,618
Provo (*Utah*)	105,166
Pueblo (*Colo.*)	102,121
Quincy (*Mass.*)	88,025
Racine (*Wis.*)	81,855
Raleigh (*N.C.*)	276,093
Rancho Cucamonga (*Calif.*)	127,743
Reading (*Pa.*)	81,207
Redding (*Calif.*)	80,865
Redwood City (*Calif.*)	75,402
Reno (*Nev.*)	180,480
Rialto (*Calif.*)	91,873
Richardson (*Texas*)	91,802
Richmond (*Calif.*)	99,216
Richmond (*Va.*)	197,790
Riverside (*Calif.*)	255,166
Roanoke (*Va.*)	94,911
Rochester (*Minn.*)	85,806
Rochester (*N.Y.*)	219,773
Rockford (*Ill.*)	150,115
Roseville (*Calif.*)	79,921
Roswell (*Ga.*)	79,334
Sacramento (*Calif.*)	407,018
St. Louis (*Mo.*)	348,189
St. Paul (*Minn.*)	287,151
St. Petersburg (*Fla.*)	248,232
Salem (*Ore.*)	136,924
Salinas (*Calif.*)	151,060
Salt Lake City (*Utah*)	181,743
San Angelo (*Texas*)	88,439
San Antonio (*Texas*)	1,144,646
San Bernardino (*Calif.*)	185,401
San Buenaventura (Ventura) (*Calif.*)	100,916
San Diego (*Calif.*)	1,223,400
San Francisco (*Calif.*)	776,733
San Jose (*Calif.*)	894,943
San Leandro (*Calif.*)	79,452
San Mateo (*Calif.*)	92,482
Sandy (*Utah*)	88,418
Sandy Springs (*Ga.*)[53]	85,781
Santa Ana (*Calif.*)	337,977
Santa Barbara (*Calif.*)	92,325
Santa Clara (*Calif.*)	102,361
Santa Clarita (*Calif.*)	151,088
Santa Maria (*Calif.*)	77,423
Santa Monica (*Calif.*)	84,084
Santa Rosa (*Calif.*)	147,595
Savannah (*Ga.*)	131,510
Schaumburg (*Ill.*)	75,386
Scottsdale (*Ariz.*)	202,705
Scranton (*Pa.*)	76,415
Seattle (*Wash.*)	563,374
Shreveport (*La.*)	200,145
Silver Spring (*Md.*)[53]	76,540
Simi Valley (*Calif.*)	111,351
Sioux City (*Iowa*)	85,013
Sioux Falls (*S.D.*)	123,975
Somerville (*Mass.*)	77,478
South Bend (*Ind.*)	107,789
South Gate (*Calif.*)	96,375
Southfield (*Mich.*)	78,296
Spokane (*Wash.*)	195,629
Spring Valley (*Nev.*)[53]	117,390
Springfield (*Ill.*)	111,454
Springfield (*Mass.*)	152,082
Springfield (*Mo.*)	151,580
Stamford (*Conn.*)	117,083
Sterling Heights (*Mich.*)	124,471
Stockton (*Calif.*)	243,771
Sunnyvale (*Calif.*)	131,760
Sunrise (*Fla.*)	85,779
Sunrise Manor (*Nev.*)[53]	156,120
Syracuse (*N.Y.*)	147,306
Tacoma (*Wash.*)	193,556
Tallahassee (*Fla.*)	150,624
Tampa (*Fla.*)	303,447
Tempe (*Ariz.*)	158,625
Thornton (*Colo.*)	82,384
Thousand Oaks (*Calif.*)	117,005
Toledo (*Ohio*)	313,619
Topeka (*Kan.*)	122,377
Torrance (*Calif.*)	137,946
Trenton (*N.J.*)	85,403
Troy (*Mich.*)	80,959
Tucson (*Ariz.*)	486,699
Tulsa (*Okla.*)	393,049
Tuscaloosa (*Ala.*)	77,906
Tyler (*Texas*)	83,650
Vacaville (*Calif.*)	88,625
Vallejo (*Calif.*)	116,760
Virginia Beach (*Va.*)	425,257
Visalia (*Calif.*)	91,565
Vista (*Calif.*)	89,857
Waco (*Texas*)	113,726
Warren (*Mich.*)	138,247
Warwick (*R.I.*)	85,808
★ Washington, D.C.	572,059
Waukegan (*Ill.*)	87,901
Waterbury (*Conn.*)	107,271
West Covina (*Calif.*)	105,080
West Palm Beach (*Fla.*)	82,103
West Valley City (*Utah*)	108,896
Westland (*Mich.*)	86,602
Westminster (*Calif.*)	88,207
Westminster (*Colo.*)	100,940
Whittier (*Calif.*)	83,680
Wichita (*Kan.*)	344,284
Wichita Falls (*Texas*)	104,197
Wilmington (*N.C.*)	75,838
Winston-Salem (*N.C.*)	185,776
Worcester (*Mass.*)	172,648
Yonkers (*N.Y.*)	196,086
Youngstown (*Ohio*)	82,026
Yuma (*Ariz.*)	77,515
Uruguay (1996)	
★ Montevideo	1,378,707
Uzbekistan (1998 est.)	
Andijon (Andizhan)	288,000
Angren	132,000[1]
Bukhoro (Bukhara)	220,000
Chirchiq (Chirchik)	156,000[1]
Farghona (Fergana)	203,000
Jizzakh (Dzhizak)	116,000[1]
Marghilon (Margilan)	129,000[1]
Namangan	291,000
Nawoiy (Navoi)	115,000[1]
Nukus	185,000[1]
Olmaliq (Almalyk)	116,000[1]
Qarshi (Karshi)	177,000[1]
Qŭqon (Kokand)	184,000[1]
Samarqand (Samarkand)	388,000
★ Tashkent (Toshkent)	2,124,000
Urganch (Urgench)	135,000[1]
Vanuatu (1999 est.)	
★ Vila	30,139
Venezuela (2000 est.)[54]	
Acarigua	166,720
Barcelona	311,475
Barinas	228,598
Barquisimeto	875,790
Baruta	213,373
Cabimas	214,000
Calabozo	102,000
★ Caracas	1,975,787
Carúpano	121,892
Catia la Mar	118,466
Ciudad Bolívar	312,691
Ciudad Guayana (San Felix de Guayana)	704,168
Ciudad Ojeda	103,835
Coro	158,763
Cúa	101,868
Cumaná	269,428
El Límon	119,602
El Tigre	119,609
Guacara	137,816
Guanare	112,000
Guarenas	170,204
Guatire	115,264
Los Teques	183,142
Maracaibo	1,764,038
Maracay	459,007
Mariara	101,115
Maturín	283,318
Mérida	230,101
Ocumare del Tuy	101,707
Petare	520,982
Puerto Cabello	169,959
Puerto La Cruz	205,635
Punto Fijo	109,362
San Cristóbal	307,184
Santa Teresa	126,930
Turmero	226,084
Valencia	1,338,833
Valera	116,036
Vietnam (1992 est.)	
Bien Hoa	273,879[32]
Cam Pha	109,086
Cam Ranh	114,041[32]
Can Tho	215,587
Da Lat	106,409
Da Nang	382,674
Haiphong	783,133
★ Hanoi	1,073,760
Ho Chi Minh City (Saigon)	3,015,743
Hong Gai	127,484
Hue	219,149
Long Xuyen	132,681
My Tho	108,404
Nam Dinh	171,699
Nha Trang	221,331
Phan Thiet	114,236[32]
Qui Nhon	163,385
Rach Gia	141,132
Thai Nguyen	127,643
Vinh	112,455
Vung Tau	145,145
Virgin Islands (U.S.) (1990)	
★ Charlotte Amalie	12,331
West Bank (1997)	
Hebron (Al-Khalīl)	119,401
Nābulus	100,231
★ Rām Allāh (Ramallah) (acting administrative centre)	18,017
Western Sahara (1998 est.)	
Laayoune (El Aaiún)	164,000[55]
Yemen (1994)	
Aden	398,300
Al-Ḥudaydah	298,500
Ibb	103,300
Al-Mukallā	122,400
★ Ṣan'ā'	954,400
Ta'izz	317,600
Zambia (1990)	
Chingola	167,954
Kabwe	166,519
Kitwe	338,207
Luanshya	146,275
★ Lusaka	1,577,000[2, 28]
Mufulira	152,944
Ndola	376,311
Zimbabwe (1998 est.)	
Bulawayo	790,000
Chitungwiza	600,000
Gweru	170,000
★ Harare	1,686,000[2, 28]
Kwekwe	100,000
Mutare	165,000

cantonment(s). [37]Urban district adjacent to Panama City. [38]1997 estimate. [39]2000 estimate. [40]Urban population. [41]Unofficial estimate. [42]Urban population; Singapore is 100% urban. [43]Bloemfontein was absorbed into the larger municipality of Manguang in December 2000. [44]Pretoria was absorbed into the larger municipality of Tshwane in December 2000. [45]1994 estimate. [46]Population refers to Kotte only. [47]1992 estimate. [48]All cities and borough councils of England after the local government reorganization of 1995–98. [49]32 borough councils, not listed separately, constitute London (Greater London). [50]Cities and borough councils of Northern Ireland with more than 75,000 population. [51]Cities of Scotland after the local government reorganization of 1994–96. Borough councils do not exist in Scotland. [52]Cities and boroughs in Wales with more than 75,000 population after the local government reorganization of 1994–96. [53]Unincorporated place. [54]Projections based on 1990 census. [55]Urban population of Laayoune and northern Western Sahara.

Language

This table presents estimated data on the principal language communities of the countries of the world. The countries, and the principal languages (occasionally, language families) represented in each, are listed alphabetically. A bullet (●) indicates those languages that are official in each country. The sum of the estimates equals the 2003 population of the country given in the "Area and population" table.

The estimates represent, so far as national data collection systems permit, the distribution of mother tongues (a mother tongue being the language spoken first and, usually, most fluently by an individual). Many countries do not collect any official data whatever on language use, and published estimates not based on census or survey data usually span a substantial range of uncertainty. The editors have adopted the best-founded distribution in the published literature (indicating uncertainty by the degree of rounding shown) but have also adjusted or interpolated using data not part of the base estimate(s). Such adjustments have not been made to account for large-scale refugee movements, as these are of a temporary nature.

A variety of approaches have been used to approximate mother-tongue distribution when census data were unavailable. Some countries collect data on ethnic or "national" groups only; for such countries ethnic distribution often had to be assumed to conform roughly to the distribution of language communities. This approach, however, should be viewed with caution, because a minority population is not always free to educate its children in its own language and because better economic opportunities often draw minority group members into the majority-language community. For some countries, a given individual may be visible in national statistics only as a passport-holder of a foreign country, however long he may remain resident. Such persons, often guest workers, have sometimes had to be assumed to be speakers of the principal language of their home country. For other countries, the language mosaic may be so complex, the language communities so minute in size, scholarly study so inadequate, or the census base so obsolete that it was possible only to assign percentages to entire groups, or families, of related languages, despite their mutual unintelligibility (Papuan and Melanesian languages in Papua New Guinea, for instance). For some countries in the Americas, so few speakers of any single indigenous language remain that it was necessary to combine these groups as *Amerindian* so as to give a fair impression of their aggregate size within their respective countries.

No systematic attempt has been made to account for populations that may legitimately be described as bilingual, unless the country itself collects data on that basis, as does Bolivia or the Comoros, for example. Where a nonindigenous official or excolonial language constitutes a lingua franca of the country, however, speakers of the language as a second tongue are shown in italics, even though very few may speak it as a mother tongue. Lingua franca figures that are both italicized and indented are not included in population totals. No comprehensive effort has been made to distinguish between dialect communities *usually* classified as belonging to the same language, though such distinctions were possible for some countries—*e.g.*, between French and Occitan (the dialect of southern France) or among the various dialects of Chinese.

In giving the names of Bantu languages, grammatical particles specific to a language's autonym (name for itself) have been omitted (the form *Rwanda* is used here, for example, rather than *kinyaRwanda* and *Tswana* instead of *seTswana*). Parenthetical alternatives are given for a number of languages that differ markedly from the name of the people speaking them (such as Kurukh, spoken by the Oraon tribes of India) or that may be combined with other groups sometimes distinguishable in national data but appearing here under the name of the largest member—*e.g.*, "Tamil (and other Indian languages)" combining data on South Asian Indian populations in Singapore. The term *creole* as used here refers to distinguishable dialectal communities related to a national, official, or former colonial language (such as the French creole that survives in Mauritius from the end of French rule in 1810).

Internet resources for further information:

- *Ethnologue* (14th ed.; Summer Institute of Linguistics) http://www.ethnologue.com
- Joshua Project 2000—People's List (Christian interfaith missionary database identifying some 2,000 ethnolinguistic groups) http://www.ad2000.org/peoples/index.htm
- U.S. Census Bureau: http://www.census.gov/ftp/pub/ipc/www/idbconf.html (especially tables 57 and 59)

Language

Major languages by country	Number of speakers
Afghanistan[1]	
Indo-Aryan languages	
Pashai	178,000
Iranian languages	
Balochi	266,000
● Dari (Persian)	
Chahar Aimak	810,000
Hazara	2,530,000
Tajik	5,859,000
Nuristani group	222,000
Pamir group	178,000
● Pashto	15,046,000
Turkic languages	
Turkmen	555,000
Uzbek	2,530,000
Other	544,000
Albania[1]	
● Albanian	3,102,000
Greek	59,000
Macedonian	4,600
Other	900
Algeria	
● Arabic	27,346,000
Berber	4,454,000
English	...
French	*6,243,000*
American Samoa	
● English	1,900
English (lingua franca)	*60,000*
● Samoan	56,000
Tongan	1,900
Other	1,900
Andorra[2]	
● Catalan (Andorran)	22,000
French	5,000
Portuguese	7,000
Spanish	29,000
Other	4,000
Angola[1]	
Ambo (Ovambo)	255,000
Chokwe	457,000
Herero	74,000
Kongo	1,423,000
Luchazi	255,000
Luimbe-Nkangala	584,000
Lunda	127,000
Luvale (Lwena)	382,000
Mbunda	127,000
Mbundu	2,325,000
Nyaneka-Nkhumbi	584,000
Ovimbundu (Umbundu)	4,003,000
● Portuguese	*3,822,000*
Other	170,000
Antigua and Barbuda	
● English	*76,800*
English/English Creole	72,000
Other	4,200
Argentina	
Amerindian languages	109,000
Italian	647,000
● Spanish	35,682,000
Other	408,000
Armenia	
● Armenian	2,853,000
Azerbaijani (Azeri)	80,000
Other	128,000
Aruba	
● Dutch	4,800
English	8,700
Papiamento	71,500
Spanish	6,800
Other	1,000
Australia	
Aboriginal languages	53,000
Arabic	194,000
Cantonese	227,000
Dutch	48,000
● English	16,141,000
English (lingua franca)	*19,189,000*
French	47,000
German	115,000
Greek	310,000
Hungarian	31,000
Indonesian Malay	31,000
Italian	439,000
Macedonian	82,000
Maltese	53,000
Mandarin	105,000
Pilipino (Filipino)	81,000
Polish	73,000
Portuguese	28,000
Russian	36,000
Serbo-Croatian	122,000
Spanish	104,000
Turkish	51,000
Vietnamese	160,000
Other/not stated	1,352,000
Austria	
Czech	19,000
● German	7,409,000
Hungarian	34,000
Polish	19,000
Romanian	17,000
Serbo-Croatian	175,000
Slovene	30,000
Turkish	122,000
Other	229,000
Azerbaijan	
Armenian	163,000
● Azerbaijani (Azeri)	7,326,000
Lezgi (Lezgian)	184,000
Russian	249,000
Other	317,000
Bahamas, The	
● English	...
English/English Creole	282,000
French (Haitian) Creole	32,000
Bahrain[2]	
● Arabic	459,000
English	...
Other	215,000
Bangladesh[1]	
● Bengali	130,078,000
Chakma	496,000
English	*3,503,000*
Garo	124,000
Khasi	103,000
Marma (Magh)	258,000
Mro	41,000
Santhali	93,000
Tripuri	93,000
Other	1,824,000
Barbados	
Bajan (English Creole)	259,000
● English	...
Other	13,000
Belarus	
● Belarusian	6,488,000
Polish	49,000
● Russian	3,155,000
Ukrainian	129,000
Other	59,000
Belgium[2, 3]	
Arabic	161,000
● Dutch (Flemish; Netherlandic)	6,128,000
● French (Walloon)	3,376,000
● German	101,000
Italian	252,000
Spanish	50,000
Turkish	91,000
Other	181,000
Belize	
● English	136,000
English Creole (lingua franca)	*202,000*
Garifuna (Black Carib)	18,000
German	4,300
Mayan languages	26,000
Spanish	85,000
Spanish (lingua franca)	*149,000*
Benin[1]	
Adja	782,000
Aizo (Ouidah)	606,000
Bariba	606,000
Dendi	154,000
Djougou	209,000
Fon	2,799,000
● French	*661,000*
Fula (Fulani)	397,000
Somba (Ditamari)	463,000
Yoruba (Nago)	859,000
Other	165,000
Bermuda	
● English	64,000
Portuguese	*6,100*
Bhutan[1]	
Assamese	104,000
● Dzongkha (Bhutia)	343,000
Nepali (Hindi)	239,000
Bolivia	
● Aymara	278,000
Guaraní	10,000
● Quechua	700,000
● Spanish	3,583,000
Spanish-Amerindian (multilingual), of which	3,943,000
Spanish-Aymara	*1,699,000*
Spanish-Guaraní	*31,000*
Spanish-Quechua	*2,224,000*
Other	72,000
Bosnia and Herzegovina[1]	
● Bosnian	1,637,000
● Croatian	630,000
● Serbian	1,153,000
Other	300,000
Botswana[1]	
● English (lingua franca)	*665,000*
Khoekhoe (Hottentot)	41,000
Ndebele	21,000
San (Bushman)	58,000
Shona	207,000
Tswana	1,255,000
Tswana (lingua franca)	*1,330,000*
Other	81,000
Brazil[1]	
Amerindian languages	183,000
German	978,000
Italian	752,000
Japanese	677,000
● Portuguese	174,226,000
Other	1,655,000
Brunei	
Chinese	32,000
English	10,400
English-Chinese	7,300
● Malay	159,000
Malay-Chinese	3,100
Malay-Chinese-English	13,500
Malay-English	101,000
Other	18,700
Bulgaria[1]	
● Bulgarian	6,480,000
Macedonian	191,000
Romany	286,000
Turkish	734,000
Other	95,000
Burkina Faso[4]	
Dogon	44,000
French	44,000
● French (lingua franca)	*5,419,000*
Fula (Fulani)	1,272,000
Gur (Voltaic) languages	
Bwamu	288,000
Gouin (Cerma)	77,000
Grusi (Gurunsi) group	
Ko	22,000
Lyele	321,000
Nuni	155,000
Sissala	11,000
Lobi	254,000
Moore (Mossi) group	
Dagara	409,100
Gurma	752,000
Kusaal	22,000
Moore (Mossi)	6,636,000
Senufo group	
Minianka	—
Senufo	188,000
Kru languages	
Seme (Siamou)	22,000
Mande languages	
Bobo	299,000
Busansi (Bisa)	476,000
Dyula (Jula)	343,000
Marka	221,000
Samo	310,000
Tamashek (Tuareg)	122,000
Other	940,000
Burundi[1]	
● French	*285,000*
● Rundi	3,015,000
Hutu	2,542,000

Major languages by country	Number of speakers
Tutsi	447,000
Twa	31,000
Other[5]	61,000
Cambodia[1]	
Cham	308,000
Chinese	403,000
● Khmer	11,629,000
Vietnamese	722,000
Other[6]	64,000
Cameroon[1]	
Chadic languages	
Buwal	307,000
Hausa	194,000
Kotoko	174,000
Mandara (Wandala)	889,000
Masana (Masa)	623,000
● English	*7,868,000*
● French	*4,700,000*
Niger-Congo languages	
Adamawa-Ubangi languages	
Chamba	378,000
Gbaya (Baya)	194,000
Mbum	204,000
Atlantic languages	
Fula (Fulani)	1,512,000
Benue-Congo languages	
Bamileke (Medumba)-Widikum (Mogha-mo)-Bamum (Mum)	2,922,000
Basa (Bassa)	174,000
Duala	1,717,000
Fang (Pangwe)-Beti-Bulu	3,096,000
Ibibio (Efik)	20,000
Igbo	82,000
Jukun	102,000
Lundu	429,000
Maka	777,000
Tikar	1,165,000
Tiv	409,000
Wute	51,000
Saharan languages	
Kanuri	51,000
Semitic languages	
Arabic	153,000
Other	123,000
Canada	
● English	18,703,000
● French	7,349,000
English-French	119,000
English-other	276,000
French-other	40,000
English-French-other	10,000
Arabic	164,000
Chinese	793,000
Cree	85,000
Dutch	148,000
Eskimo (Inuktitut) languages	30,000
German	499,000
Greek	135,000
Italian	537,000
Pilipino (Filipino)	149,000
Polish	236,000
Portuguese	234,000
Punjābī	224,000
Spanish	236,000
Ukrainian	180,000
Vietnamese	118,000
Other	1,327,000
Cape Verde	
Crioulo (Portuguese Creole)	438,000
● Portuguese	...
Central African Republic	
Banda	858,000
● French	*942,000*
Gbaya (Baya)	869,000
Mandjia	544,000
Mbum	230,000
Ngbaka	283,000
Nzakara	63,000
● Sango (lingua franca)	*3,244,000*
Sara	241,000
Zande (Azande)	73,000
Other	523,000
Chad[1]	
● Arabic	1,140,000
Bagirmi	143,000
Fitri-Batha	428,000
● French	*2,774,000*
Fula (Fulani)	230,000
Gorane	581,000
Hadjarai	614,000
Kanem-Bornu	833,000
Lac-Iro	55,000
Mayo-Kebbi	1,063,000
Ouaddai	811,000
Sara	2,554,000
Tandjile	603,000
Other	197,000
Chile[1]	
Araucanian (Mapuche)	1,421,000
Aymara	81,000
Rapa Nui	35,000
● Spanish	13,740,000
China[1]	
Achang	31,000
Bulang (Blang)	92,000
Ch'iang (Qiang)	225,000
Chinese (Han)	1,185,204,000
Cantonese (Yüeh [Yue])	*51,093,000*
Hakka	*28,612,000*
Hsiang (Xiang)	*39,853,000*
Kan (Gan)	*22,481,000*
● Mandarin	*918,652,000*
Min	*39,853,000*
Wu	*84,814,000*
Ching-p'o (Jingpo)	133,000
Chuang (Zhuang)	17,607,000
Daghur (Daur)	133,000
Evenk (Ewenki)	31,000
Gelo	501,000
Hani (Woni)	1,431,000
Hui	9,772,000
Kazak	1,267,000
Korean	2,187,000
Kyrgyz	164,000
Lahu	470,000
Li	1,267,000
Lisu	654,000
Manchu	11,169,000
Maonan	82,000
Miao	8,410,000
Mongol	5,467,000
Mulam	184,000
Na-hsi (Naxi)	317,000
Nu	31,000
Pai (Bai)	1,809,000
Pumi	31,000
Puyi (Chung-chia)	2,892,000
Salar	102,000
She	715,000
Shui	388,000
Sibo (Xibe)	194,000
Tai (Dai)	1,165,000
Tajik	41,000
Tibetan	5,222,000
Tu (Monguor)	215,000
T'u-chia (Tujia)	6,489,000
Tung (Dong)	2,861,000
Tung-hsiang (Dongxiang)	429,000
Uighur	8,206,000
Wa (Va)	399,000
Yao	2,422,000
Yi	7,470,000
Other	1,012,000
Colombia[1]	
Amerindian languages	352,000
Arawakan	39,000
Cariban	29,000
Chibchan	176,000
Other	107,000
English Creole	49,000
● Spanish	40,910,000
Comoros	
● Arabic	...
● Comorian	374,000
Comorian-French	65,000
Comorian-Malagasy	28,000
Comorian-Arabic	8,600
Comorian-Swahili	2,600
Comorian-French-other	20,000
● French	*104,000*
Other	2,600
Congo, Dem. Rep. of the[1]	
Boa	1,239,000
Chokwe	965,000
● English	...
● French	*4,062,000*
Kongo	8,470,000
Kongo (lingua franca)	*16,250,000*
Lingala (lingua franca)	*36,562,000*
Luba	9,486,000
Lugbara	853,000
Mongo	7,109,000
Ngala and Bangi	3,047,000
Rundi	2,031,000
Rwanda	5,423,000
Swahili (lingua franca)	*25,390,000*
Teke	1,442,000
Zande (Azande)	3,219,000
Other	9,486,000
Congo, Rep. of the[1]	
Bobangi	39,000
● French	*1,960,000*
Kongo	1,908,000
Kota	39,000
Lingala (lingua franca)	...
Maka	65,000
Mbete	183,000
Mboshi	431,000
Monokutuba (lingua franca)	*2,221,000*
Punu	118,000
Sango	105,000
Teke	640,000
Other	196,000
Costa Rica	
Chibchan languages	12,500
Bribrí	8,000
Cabécar	4,600
Chinese	8,000
English Creole	83,000
● Spanish	4,044,000
Other	11,000
Côte d'Ivoire[1]	
Akan (including Baule and Anyi)	4,996,000
● French	*8,326,000*
Gur ([Voltaic] including Senufo and Lobi)	1,946,000
Kru (including Bete)	1,748,000
Malinke (including Dyula and Bambara)	1,905,000
Southern Mande (including Dan and Guro)	1,280,000
Other (non-Ivoirian population)	4,756,000
Croatia	
● Serbo-Croatian (Croatian)	4,252,000
Other	176,000
Cuba	
● Spanish	11,295,000
Cyprus (island)[1]	
● Greek	685,000
● Turkish	203,000
Other	32,000
Czech Republic[1]	
Bulgarian	3,000
● Czech	8,282,000
German	48,000
Greek	3,000
Hungarian	20,000
Moravian	1,313,000
Polish	60,000
Romanian	1,000
Romany	33,000
Russian	5,000
Ruthenian	2,000
Silesian	44,000
Slovak	312,000
Ukrainian	8,000
Other	70,000
Denmark[2]	
Arabic	39,000
● Danish	5,102,000
English	20,000
German	26,000
South Slavic languages	39,000
Turkish	47,000
Other	120,000
Djibouti[1]	
Afar	162,000
● Arabic	51,000
● French	*71,000*
Somali	203,000
Gadabourski	...
Issa	...
Issaq	...
Other	41,000
Dominica	
● English	...
English Creole	69,700
French Creole	*63,000*
Dominican Republic	
French (Haitian) Creole	176,000
● Spanish	8,540,000
East Timor	
Portuguese	80,000
Tetum (Tetun)	608,000
Other	310,000
Ecuador	
Quechuan (and other Amerindian languages)	915,000
● Spanish	12,088,000
Egypt[1]	
● Arabic	67,367,000
Other	818,000
El Salvador	
● Spanish	6,515,000
Equatorial Guinea[1]	
Bubi	51,000
Fang	401,000
● French	...
Krio (English Creole)	...
● Spanish	...
Other	41,000
Eritrea	
Cushitic languages	
Afar	180,000
Bilin	130,000
Hadareb (Beja)	160,000
Saho	120,000
Nilotic languages	
Kunama	110,000
Nara	90,000
Semitic languages	
Arabic (Rashaida)	10,000
Tigré	1,310,000
Tigrinya	2,031,000
Estonia[1]	
Belarusian	20,000
● Estonian	883,000
Finnish	12,000
Russian	380,000
Ukrainian	34,000
Other	25,000
Ethiopia[1]	
Afar	1,205,000
Agew (Awngi)	607,000
Amharic	18,668,000
Berta	149,000
Gedeo	548,000
Gumuz	129,000
Gurage	2,708,000
Hadya–Libida	1,085,000
Kaffa	717,000
Kambata	797,000
Kimant	199,000
Oromo (Oromifa)	20,291,000
Sidamo	2,161,000
Somali	3,973,000
Tigrinya	3,764,000
Walaita	3,883,000
Other	5,705,000
Faroe Islands	
● Danish	...
● Faroese	48,000
Fiji[1]	
● English	*172,000*
Fijian	420,000
Hindi	361,000
Other	45,000
Finland	
Finnish	4,820,000
Russian	26,000
Sami (Lapp)	2,000
Swedish	295,000
Other	68,000
France	
Arabic[7]	1,514,000
English[7]	81,000
● French[7, 8, 9]	55,974,000
Basque	*102,000*
Breton	*813,000*
Catalan (Rousillonais)	*264,000*
Corsican	*81,000*
Dutch (Flemish)	*91,000*
German (Alsatian)	*1,016,000*
Occitan	*711,000*
Italian[7]	264,000
Polish[7]	51,000
Portuguese[7]	691,000
Spanish[7]	224,000
Turkish[7]	213,000
Other[7]	762,000
French Guiana	
Amerindian languages	3,200
● French	...
French/French Creoles	167,000
Other	7,600
French Polynesia[10]	
Chinese	13,600
● French	197,000
Polynesian languages	271,000
● Tahitian	...
Other	48,000
Gabon[1]	
Fang	476,000
● French	*1,108,000*
Kota	44,000
Mbete	188,000
Mpongwe (Myene)	199,000
Punu, Sira, Nzebi	222,000
Teke	22,000
Other	177,000
Gambia, The[1]	
● English	...
Gambians	
Aku (Krio)	8,300
Atlantic languages	
Diola (Jola)	131,000
Fula (Fulani)	230,000
Manjak	23,000
Serer	34,000
Wolof	179,000
Mande languages	
Bambara	10,000
Malinke	486,000
Soninke	109,000
Other	18,000
non-Gambians	196,000
Gaza Strip	
Arabic	1,297,000
Hebrew	6,800
Georgia	
Abkhaz	88,000
Armenian	343,000
Azerbaijani (Azeri)	274,000
● Georgian (Kartuli)	3,514,000
Ossetian	118,000
Russian	441,000
Other	157,000
Germany[2]	
● German	75,429,000
Greek	362,000
Italian	613,000
Kurdish	*402,000*
Polish	281,000
South Slavic languages	1,196,000
Turkish	2,120,000
Other	2,603,000
Ghana[1]	
Akan	10,732,000
● English	*1,436,000*
Ewe	2,431,000
Ga-Adangme	1,593,000
Gurma	681,000
Hausa (lingua franca)	*12,262,000*
Mole-Dagbani (Moore)	3,238,000
Yoruba	272,000
Other	1,520,000
Greece	
● Greek	10,834,000
Turkish	104,000
Other	63,000
Greenland[2]	
● Danish	7,100
● Greenlandic	50,000
Grenada	
● English	...
English/English Creole	102,000
Guadeloupe	
● French	...
French/French Creole	414,000
Other	21,000
Guam	
Asian languages	10,800
● Chamorro	34,000
● English	59,000
English (lingua franca)	*153,000*
Philippine languages	34,000
Other Pacific Island languages	10,500
Guatemala	
Garífuna (Black Carib)	26,000
Mayan languages	3,416,000
Cakchiquel	873,000
Kekchí	471,000
Mam	265,000
Quiché	985,000
● Spanish	6,311,000
Guernsey	
● English	63,000
Norman French	...
Guinea[1]	
Atlantic languages	
Basari-Konyagi	102,000
Fula (Fulani)	3,269,000
Kissi	511,000
Other	261,000
● French	*795,000*
Mande languages	
Kpelle	397,000
Loma	193,000
Malinke	1,964,000
Susu	931,000
Yalunka	250,000
Other	590,000
Other	11,400
Guinea-Bissau[1]	
Balante	411,000
Crioulo (Portuguese Creole)	*601,000*
Ejamat	32,000
French	*137,000*
Fula (Fulani)	295,000
Malinke	179,000
Mandyako	148,000
Mankanya	53,000
Pepel	137,000
● Portuguese	*148,000*
Other	106,000
Guyana	
Amerindian languages	
Arawakan	11,000
Cariban	17,000
● English	...
English/English Creoles	750,000

Language (continued)

Major languages by country	Number of speakers
Haiti	
● French	*1,535,000*
● Haitian (French) Creole	7,528,000
Honduras	
English Creole	13,000
Garifuna (Black Carib)	86,000
Miskito	12,000
● Spanish	6,611,000
Other	82,000
Hong Kong	
Chinese	
● Cantonese	6,059,000
Cantonese (lingua franca)	*6,549,000*
Chiu Chau	98,000
Fukien (Min)	130,000
Hakka	114,000
Putonghua (Mandarin)	76,000
Putonghua (lingua franca)	*1,239,000*
Sze Yap	27,000
● English	151,000
English (lingua franca)	*2,156,000*
Japanese	14,000
Pilipino (Filipino)	7,000
Other	164,000
Hungary	
German	40,000
● Hungarian	9,984,000
Romanian	10,000
Romany	51,000
Serbo-Croatian	20,000
Slovak	10,000
Other	20,000
Iceland[2]	
● Icelandic	278,000
Other	12,000
India	
Afro-Asiatic languages	
Arabic	32,000
Austroasiatic languages	
Ho	1,198,000
Kharia	284,000
Khasi	1,146,000
Korku	589,000
Munda	526,000
Mundari	1,083,000
Santhali	6,568,000
Savara (Sora)	347,000
Other Austroasiatic	200,000
Dravidian languages	
Gondi	2,680,000
Kannada	41,239,000
Khond	273,000
Koya	336,000
Kui	809,000
Kurukh (Oraon)	1,797,000
Malayalam	38,254,000
Tamil	66,745,000
Telugu	83,129,000
Tulu	1,955,000
Other Dravidian	694,000
English	221,000
● English (lingua franca)	*202,831,000*
Indo-Iranian (Indo-Aryan) languages	
Assamese	16,468,000
Bengali	87,638,000
Bhili (Bhilodi)	7,020,000
Barel	*586,000*
Bhilali	*586,000*
Gujarati	51,212,000
Halabi	673,000
● Hindi	424,684,000
Awadhi	*610,000*
Baghelkhandi	*1,745,000*
Bagri	*746,000*
Banjari	*1,114,000*
Bhojpuri	*29,090,000*
Bundelkhandi	*2,091,000*
Chhattisgarhi	*13,336,000*
Dhundhari	*1,219,000*
Garhwali	*2,354,000*
Harauti	*1,555,000*
Haryanvi	*452,000*
Hindi	*293,936,000*
Kangri	*620,000*
Khortha (Khotta)	*1,324,000*
Kumauni	*2,165,000*
Lamani (Banjari)	*2,585,000*
Magahi (Magadhi)	*13,305,000*
Maithili	*9,784,000*
Malvi	*3,741,000*
Mandeali	*557,000*
Marwari	*5,885,000*
Mewari	*2,659,000*
Nagpuri	*977,000*
Nimadi	*1,787,000*
Pahari	*2,743,000*
Rajasthani	*16,784,000*
Sadani (Sadri)	*1,976,000*
Surgujia	*1,314,000*
Surjapuri	*462,000*
Other Hindi dialects	*7,766,000*
Hindi (lingua franca)	*703,078,000*
Kashmiri	4,960,000
Khandeshi	1,230,000
Konkani	2,218,000
Lahnda	32,000
Marathi	78,673,000
Nepali (Gorkhali)	2,617,000
Oriya	35,333,000
Punjabi	29,437,000
Sanskrit	63,000
Sindhi	2,669,000
Kachchhi	*715,000*
Urdu	54,659,000
Sino-Tibetan languages	
Adi	200,000
Angami	126,000
Ao	221,000
Bodo/Boro	1,534,000
Dimasa	116,000
Garo	851,000
Karbi/Makir	462,000
Konyak	179,000
Lotha	105,000
Lushai (Mizo)	683,000
Manipuri (Meithei)	1,597,000
Miri/Mishing	494,000
Nissi/Dafla	221,000
Rabha	179,000
Sema	210,000
Tangkhul	126,000
Thado	137,000
Tripuri	872,000
Kokbarak	*652,000*
Other Sino-Tibetan languages	1,902,000
Other	5,560,000
Indonesia	
Balinese	3,655,000
Banjarese	3,844,000
Batak	4,884,000
Buginese	4,842,000
● Indonesian (Malay)	26,627,000
Javanese	86,697,000
Madurese	9,516,000
Minangkabau	5,189,000
Sundanese	34,673,000
Other	39,956,000
Iran[1]	
Armenian	317,000
Iranian languages	
Bakhtyari (Luri)	1,110,000
Balochi	1,511,000
● Farsi (Persian)	30,232,000
Farsi (lingua franca)	*54,843,000*
Gilaki	3,498,000
Kurdish	6,044,000
Luri	2,864,000
Mazandarani	2,388,000
Other	1,437,000
Semitic languages	
Arabic	1,427,000
Other	159,000
Turkic languages	
Afshari	750,000
Azerbaijani (Azeri)	11,138,000
Qashqa'i	845,000
Shahsavani	402,000
Turkish (mostly Pishagchi, Bayat, and Qajar)	476,000
Turkmen	1,036,000
Other	137,000
Other	486,000
Iraq[1]	
● Arabic	19,026,000
Assyrian	207,000
Azerbaijani (Azeri)	424,000
Kurdish	4,678,000
Persian	207,000
Other	141,000
Ireland	
● English	3,751,000
● Irish[11]	62,000
Irish	*1,571,000*
Isle of Man	
● English	77,000
Israel[12]	
● Arabic	1,165,000
● Hebrew	4,079,000
Russian	583,000
Other	646,000
Italy[1]	
Albanian	117,000
Catalan	29,000
French	302,000
German	302,000
Greek	39,000
● Italian	52,956,000
Rhaetian	722,000
Friulian	702,000
Ladin	20,000
Romany	107,000
Sardinian	1,492,000
Slovene	117,000
Other	127,000
Jamaica	
● English	...
English/English Creoles	2,492,000
Hindī and other Indian languages	51,000
Other	101,000
Japan[2]	
Ainu[1]	15,000
Chinese	241,000
English	80,000
● Japanese	126,406,000
Korean	663,000
Philippine languages	90,000
Other	50,000
Jersey	
● English	82,200
French	...
Norman French	*5,500*
Jordan[1]	
● Arabic	5,287,000
Armenian	54,000
Kabardian (Circassian)	54,000
Kazakhstan[1]	
Azerbaijani (Azeri)	89,000
Belarusian	149,000
German	456,000
● Kazakh	6,800,000
Korean	89,000
Russian	5,135,000
Tatar	288,000
Uighur	169,000
Ukrainian	734,000
Uzbek	337,000
Other	545,000
Kenya[1]	
Arabic	83,000
Bantu languages	
Bajun (Rajun)	73,000
Basuba	125,000
Embu	375,000
Gusii (Kisii)	1,949,000
Kamba	3,565,000
Kikuyu	6,609,000
Kuria	188,000
Luhya	4,378,000
Mbere	125,000
Meru	1,731,000
Nyika (Mijikenda)	1,512,000
Pokomo	83,000
Swahili	10,000
● Swahili (lingua franca)	*20,849,000*
Taita	313,000
Cushitic languages	
Oromo languages	
Boran	146,000
Gabbra	63,000
Gurreh	167,000
Orma	63,000
Somali languages	
Degodia	198,000
Ogaden	52,000
Somali	323,000
● English (lingua franca)	*2,815,000*
Nilotic languages	
Kalenjin	3,409,000
Luo	4,034,000
Masai	500,000
Sambur	156,000
Teso	271,000
Turkana	427,000
Other	709,000
Kiribati[1]	
● English	*22,000*
Kiribati (Gilbertese)	87,000
Tuvaluan (Ellice)	500
Other	600
Korea, North[1]	
Chinese	31,000
● Korean	22,435,000
Korea, South[1]	
Chinese	51,000
● Korean	47,874,000
Kuwait	
● Arabic	1,900,000
Other	539,000
Kyrgyzstan[1]	
Azerbaijani (Azeri)	21,000
German	31,000
Kazakh	52,000
● Kyrgyz	3,021,000
● Russian	817,000
Tajik	41,000
Tatar	62,000
Ukrainian	83,000
Uzbek	714,000
Other	217,000
Laos[1]	
● Lao-Lum (Lao)	3,004,000
Lao-Soung (Miao [Hmong] and Man [Yao])	569,000
Lao-Tai (Tai)	733,000
Lao-Theung (Mon-Khmer)	1,301,000
Other[13]	52,000
Latvia[1]	
Belarusian	87,000
● Latvian	1,298,000
Lithuanian	29,000
Polish	48,000
Russian	755,000
Ukrainian	69,000
Other	39,000
Lebanon[1]	
● Arabic	3,468,000
Armenian	219,000
French	*896,000*
Other	42,000
Lesotho[1]	
● English	*429,000*
● Sotho	1,533,000
Zulu	270,000
Liberia[1]	
Atlantic (Mel) languages	
Gola	137,000
Kissi	137,000
● English	*661,000*
Krio (English Creole)	*2,939,000*
Kru languages	
Bassa	462,000
Belle	21,000
De (Dewoin, Dey)	11,000
Grebo	294,000
Krahn	126,000
Kru (Krumen)	241,000
Mande (Northern) languages	
Gbandi	95,000
Kpelle	640,000
Loma	189,000
Malinke (Mandingo)	168,000
Mende	21,000
Vai	116,000
Mande (Southern) languages	
Gio (Dan)	262,000
Mano	231,000
Other	168,000
Libya	
● Arabic	5,334,000
Berber	54,000
Other[14]	163,000
Liechtenstein[2]	
● German	30,000
Italian	1,100
Other	3,200
Lithuania[1]	
Belarusian	43,000
● Lithuanian	2,907,000
Polish	235,000
Russian	220,000
Ukrainian	23,000
Other	24,000
Luxembourg[2]	
Belgian	11,000
Dutch	2,800
English	3,500
French	13,500
German	7,800
Italian	14,200
Luxemburgian	197,000
Portuguese	182,200
Other	21,300
Macau	
Chinese	
● Cantonese (Yüeh [Yue])	381,000
Mandarin	5,000
Other Chinese languages	40,000
English	2,000
● Portuguese	10,000
Other	5,000
Macedonia[1]	
Albanian	470,000
● Macedonian	1,368,000
Romany	46,000
Serbo-Croatian	41,000
Turkish	82,000
Vlach	9,000
Other	39,000
Madagascar[1]	
French	*2,464,000*
Malagasy	16,435,000
Other	171,000
Malawi[1]	
Chewa (Maravi)	6,802,000
● English	*606,000*
Lomwe	2,144,000
Ngoni	746,000
Yao	1,538,000
Other	393,000
Malaysia	
Bajau	163,000
Chinese	1,464,000
Chinese-others	824,000
Dusun	260,000
English	130,000
English-others	282,000
English (lingua franca)	*7,700,000*
Iban	597,000
Iban-others	98,000
● Malay	10,877,000
Malay-others	3,861,000
Tamil	976,000
Tamil-others	11,000
Other	5,683,000
Maldives	
● Divehi (Maldivian)	285,000
Mali[1]	
Afro-Asiatic languages	
Berber languages	
Tamashek (Tuareg)	848,000
Semitic languages	
Arabic (Mauri)	185,000
● French	*1,195,000*
Niger-Congo languages	
Atlantic languages	
Dogon	467,000
Fula (Fulani) and Tukulor	1,619,000
Gur (Voltaic) languages	
Bwa (Bobo)	283,000
Moore (Mossi)	44,000
Senufo and Minianka	1,391,000
Mande languages	
Bambara	3,705,000
Bambara (lingua franca)	*9,236,000*
Bobo Fing	11,000
Dyula (Jula)	337,000
Malinke, Khasonke, and Wasulunka	771,000
Samo (Duun)	76,000
Soninke	1,021,000
Nilo-Saharan languages	
Songhai	837,000
Other	33,000
Malta[1]	
● English	14,000
English (lingua franca)	*99,000*
● Maltese	380,000
Other	5,200
Marshall Islands[2]	
● English	*56,000*
● Marshallese	55,000
Other	1,700
Martinique	
● French	...
French/French Creole	380,000
Other	13,300
Mauritania[1]	
● Arabic	...
French	*274,000*
Fula (Fulani)	30,000
Hassānīyah Arabic	2,199,000
Soninke	71,000
Tukulor	142,000
Wolof	182,000
Zenaga	30,000
Other	41,000
Mauritius	
Bhojpuri	233,000
Bhojpuri-other	26,000
Chinese	4,000
● English	2,000
French	42,000
French Creole	754,000
French Creole-other	108,000
Hindi	16,000
Marathi	8,000
Tamil	9,000
Telugu	7,000
Urdu	8,000
Other	3,000
Mayotte[15]	
● Arabic	...
● French	68,000
Mahorais (local dialect of Comorian Swahili)	140,000
Other Comorian Swahili dialects	62,000
Malagasy	54,000
Other	10,000
Mexico	
Amerindian languages	7,278,000
Amuzgo	50,000
Aztec (Nahuatl)	1,744,000
Chatino	49,000
Chinantec	159,000

Major languages by country	Number of speakers
Chocho	1,200
Chol	194,000
Chontal	53,000
Cora	20,000
Cuicatec	16,000
Huastec	180,000
Huave	17,000
Huichol	38,000
Kanjobal	11,000
Mame	11,000
Mayo	44,000
Mazahua	172,000
Mazatec	254,000
Mixe	139,000
Mixtec	538,000
Otomí	360,000
Popoluca	66,000
Purépecha (Tarasco)	143,000
Tarahumara	92,000
Tepehua	11,000
Tepehuan	31,000
Tlapanec	123,000
Tojolabal	46,000
Totonac	287,000
Trique	25,000
Tzeltal	344,000
Tzotzil	362,000
Yaqui	16,000
Yucatec (Mayan)	948,000
Zapotec	533,000
Zoque	64,000
Other	496,000
● Spanish	85,871,000
Spanish-Amerindian languages	*5,987,000*
Micronesia	
Chuukese (Trukese)/Mortlockese	56,000
English	1,500
Kosraean	7,700
Pohnpeian	28,000
Polynesian languages	1,600
Woleaian	4,700
Yapese	6,000
Other	1,400
Moldova	
Bulgarian	70,000
Gagauz	139,000
● Romanian (Moldovan)	2,646,000
Russian	985,000
Ukrainian	368,000
Other	60,000
Monaco[2]	
English	2,100
● French	13,600
Italian	5,200
Monegasque	5,200
Other	6,300
Mongolia[1]	
Bayad	49,000
Buryat	43,000
Darhat	18,000
Dariganga	35,000
Dörbet	68,000
Dzakhchin	27,000
Kazakh	147,000
● Khalkha (Mongolian)	1,962,000
Khalkha (lingua franca)	*2,232,000*
Ould	10,000
Torgut	13,000
Tuvan (Uryankhai)	25,000
Other	98,000
Morocco	
● Arabic	19,390,000
Berber	9,845,000
French	*11,905,000*
Other	600,000
Mozambique	
Bantu languages	
Chuabo	1,167,000
Lomwe	1,410,000
Makua	4,883,000
Sena	1,303,000
Tsonga (Changana)	2,120,000
Other Bantu languages	6,128,000
● Portuguese	1,206,000
Portuguese (lingua franca)	*7,363,000*
Other	350,000
Myanmar (Burma)[1]	
● Burmese	29,312,000
Burmese (lingua franca)	*34,017,000*
Chin	927,000
Kachin (Ching-p'o)	581,000
Karen	2,648,000
Kayah	173,000
Mon	1,029,000
Rakhine (Arakanese)	1,915,000
Shan	3,595,000
Other	2,332,000
Namibia	
Afrikaans	183,000
Caprivi	90,000
● English	15,000
English (lingua franca)	*370,000*
German	17,000
Herero	154,000
Kavango (Okavango)	187,000
Nama	240,000
Ovambo (Ambo [Kwanyama])	976,000
San (Bushman)	37,000
Tswana	8,700
Other	18,500
Nauru	
Chinese	1,100
English	1,000
English (lingua franca)	*11,000*
Kiribati (Gilbertese)	2,200
Nauruan	7,300
Tuvaluan (Ellice)	1,100
Nepal	
Austroasiatic (Munda) languages	
Santhali	39,000
English	*7,147,000*
Indo-Aryan languages	
Bengali	39,000
Bhojpuri	1,801,000
Dhanwar	29,000
Hindi	225,000
Hindi (Awadhi dialect)	490,000
Maithili	2,869,000
● Nepali (Eastern Pahari)	12,169,000
Rajbansi	108,000
Tharu	1,302,000
Urdu	264,000
Tibeto-Burman languages	
Bhutia (Sherpa)	157,000
Chepang	29,000
Gurung	294,000
Limbu	333,000
Magar	558,000
Newari	901,000
Rai and Kiranti	578,000
Tamang	1,185,000
Thakali	9,800
Thami	20,000
Other	773,000
Netherlands, The[2]	
Arabic	133,000
● Dutch	15,556,000
Dutch and Frisian	*613,000*
Turkish	105,000
Other	444,000
Netherlands Antilles	
● Dutch	...
English	14,000
Papiamento	145,000
Other	10,000
New Caledonia[1]	
● French	75,000
Indonesian	5,000
Melanesian languages	99,000
Polynesian languages	26,000
Vietnamese	3,100
Other	12,000
New Zealand	
● English	3,483,000
English-Māori	155,000
● Māori	15,000
Other	349,000
Nicaragua	
English Creole	31,000
Misumalpan languages	
Miskito	90,000
Sumo	9,000
● Spanish	5,350,000
Other	2,300
Niger[1]	
Atlantic languages	
Fula (Fulani)	1,106,000
Berber languages	
Tamashek (Tuareg)	1,185,000
Chadic languages	
Hausa	6,029,000
Hausa (lingua franca)	*8,016,000*
● French	*1,694,000*
Gur (Voltaic) languages	
Gurma	34,000
Saharan languages	
Kanuri	508,000
Teda (Tubu)	45,000
Semitic languages	
Arabic	34,000
Songhai and Zerma	2,416,000
Other	23,000
Nigeria[1]	
Arabic	305,000
Bura	1,932,000
Edo	4,271,000
● English/English Creole (lingua franca)	*56,943,000*
Fula (Fulani)	14,134,000
Hausa	26,743,000
Hausa (lingua franca)	*63,044,000*
Ibibio	7,016,000
Igbo (Ibo)	22,574,000
Ijo (Ijaw)	2,237,000
Kanuri	5,186,000
Nupe	1,525,000
Tiv	2,847,000
Yoruba	26,743,000
Other	9,762,000
Northern Mariana Islands	
● Carolinian	3,100
● Chamorro	16,000
Chinese	16,900
● English	8,000
English (lingua franca)	*66,000*
Philippine languages	17,600
Other Pacific Island languages	3,900
Other	6,700
Norway[2]	
Danish	18,000
English	24,000
● Norwegian	4,411,000
Swedish	13,000
Other	102,000
Oman	
● Arabic (Omani)	2,012,000
Other	609,000
Pakistan	
Balochi	4,484,000
Brahui	1,821,000
English (lingua franca)	*16,842,000*
Pashto	19,579,000
Punjabi	
Hindko	3,621,000
Punjabi	71,778,000
Sindhi	
Saraiki	14,642,000
Sindhi	17,537,000
● Urdu	11,326,000
Other	4,242,000
Palau	
Chinese	300
● English	600
English (lingua franca)	*20,000*
● Palauan	17,000
Philippine languages	2,000
Other	700
Panama	
Amerindian languages	
Bokotá	5,500
Chibchan	
Guaymí (Ngõbe Buglé)	166,000
Kuna	63,000
Teribe	3,000
Chocó	
Emberá	20,000
Wounaan	3,000
Arabic	18,000
Chinese	9,000
English	...
English Creoles	436,000
● Spanish	2,393,000
Papua New Guinea[1]	
● English	*159,000*
Melanesian languages	1,121,000
Motu	*181,000*
Papuan languages	4,349,000
Tok Pisin (English Creole)	*3,624,000*
Other	113,000
Paraguay	
German	51,000
● Guaraní	2,267,000
Guaraní-Spanish	2,739,000
Portuguese	174,000
● Spanish	369,000
Other	41,000
Peru	
Amerindian languages	
● Aymara	624,000
● Quechua	4,465,000
Other	190,000
● Spanish	21,657,000
Other	212,000
Philippines	
Aklanon	595,000
Bantoanon	74,000
Bicol	4,614,000
Bilaan	43,000
Bontoc	64,000
Butuanon	85,000
Cebuano	18,882,000
Chavacano	500,000
Chinese	74,000
Davaweno (Mansaka)	553,000
● English (lingua franca)	*42,207,000*
Hiligaynon	7,389,000
Ibaloi (Nabaloi)	138,000
Ibanag	298,000
Ifugao	223,000
Ilocano	7,559,000
Ilongot	117,000
Kalinga	138,000
Kankanai	308,000
Kinaray-a (Hamtikanon)	510,000
Maguindanao	1,180,000
Manobo	542,000
Maranao	1,031,000
Masbateño	564,000
Palawano	85,000
Pampango	2,424,000
Pangasinan	1,467,000
● Pilipino (Filipino; Tagalog)	23,761,000
Romblon	255,000
Samal	510,000
Sambal	213,000
Subanon	330,000
Surigaonon	595,000
Tau Sug	936,000
Tboli	106,000
Tinggian	74,000
Tiruray	74,000
Waray-Waray	3,094,000
Yakan	160,000
Other	1,595,000
Poland	
Belarusian	190,000
German	500,000
● Polish	37,704,000
Ukrainian	230,000
Portugal[2]	
● Portuguese	10,079,000
Other	102,000
Puerto Rico	
● English	543,000
● Spanish	3,297,000
Other	39,000
Qatar[2]	
● Arabic	250,000
Other[16]	376,000
Réunion	
Chinese	21,000
Comorian	21,000
● French	*232,000*
French Creole	697,000
Malagasy	11,000
Tamil	*148,000*
Other	11,000
Romania[1]	
Bulgarian	8,000
Czech	4,000
German	64,000
Hungarian	1,427,000
Polish	4,000
● Romanian	19,346,000
Romany (Tigani)	540,000
Russian	43,000
Serbo-Croatian	26,000
Slovak	22,000
Tatar	22,000
Turkish	43,000
Ukrainian	64,000
Other	43,000
Russia[1]	
Adyghian	119,000
Armenian	713,000
Avar	604,000
Azerbaijani (Azeri)	336,000
Bashkir	1,375,000
Belarusian	972,000
Buryat	453,000
Chechen	898,000
Chuvash	1,722,000
Dargin	353,000
Georgian (Kartuli)	132,000
German	788,000
Ingush	253,000
Kabardian	367,000
Kalmyk	166,000
Karachay	150,000
Kazakh	569,000
Komi-Permyak	147,000
Komi-Zyryan	354,000
Kumyk	286,000
Lak	117,000
Lezgi (Lezgian)	295,000
Mari	66,000
Mordvin	723,000
Ossetian	463,000
Romanian	95,000
Romany	130,000
● Russian	118,000,000
Tabasaran	97,000
Tatar	5,519,000
Tuvan	198,000
Udmurt	713,000
Ukrainian	3,446,000
Uzbek	127,000
Yakut	441,000
Other	3,836,000
Rwanda	
● English	...
● French	*576,000*
● Rwanda	8,387,000
St. Kitts and Nevis	
● English	...
English/English Creole	46,400
St. Lucia	
● English	32,000
English/French Creole	130,000
St. Vincent and the Grenadines	
● English	...
English/English Creole	112,000
Other	1,000
Samoa	
● English	1,000
● Samoan	85,000
Samoan-English	93,000
San Marino[1]	
● Italian (Romagnolo)	29,000
São Tomé and Príncipe	
Crioulo (Portuguese Creole)	124,000
English	...
French	1,000
● Portuguese	...
Other	17,000
Saudi Arabia[1]	
● Arabic	22,809,000
Other	1,199,000
Senegal	
● French	*3,547,000*
Senegalese	
Bambara	91,000
Diola	497,000
Fula (Fulani)-Tukulor	2,199,000
Malinke (Mandingo)	375,000
Serer	1,267,000
Soninke	132,000
Wolof	4,865,000
Wolof (lingua franca)	*8,108,000*
Other	446,000
non-Senegalese	223,000
Serbia and Montenegro[1]	
Albanian	1,738,000
Hungarian	346,000
Macedonian	49,000
Romanian	40,000
Romany	148,000
● Serbo-Croatian (Serbian)	7,920,000
Serbo-Croatian (lingua franca)	*9,974,000*
Slovak	69,000
Vlach	20,000
Other	198,000
Seychelles	
English	3,000
English (lingua franca)	*29,000*
French	1,000
French (lingua franca)	*78,000*
Seselwa (French Creole)	75,000
Other	3,000
Sierra Leone[1]	
Atlantic languages	
Bullom-Sherbro	190,000
Fula (Fulani)	190,000
Kissi	114,000
Limba	418,000
Temne	1,578,000
● English	*475,000*
Krio (English Creole [lingua franca])	*4,182,000*
Mande languages	
Kono-Vai	257,000
Kuranko	171,000
Mende	1,720,000
Susu	76,000
Yalunka	171,000
Other	86,000
Singapore[1]	
Chinese	3,253,000
● English	*1,585,000*
● Malay	589,000
● Mandarin Chinese	*1,837,000*
● Tamil (and other Indian languages)	335,000
Other	56,000
Slovakia[1]	
Czech, Moravian, and Silesian	59,000
German	5,000
Hungarian	569,000

Language (continued)

Major languages by country	Number of speakers
Polish	3,000
Romany	90,000
Ruthenian, Ukrainian, and Russian	35,000
● Slovak	4,626,000
Other	15,000
Slovenia	
Hungarian	9,000
Serbo-Croatian	156,000
● Slovene	1,732,000
Other	74,000
Solomon Islands[1]	
● English	*9,000*
Melanesian languages	385,000
Papuan languages	39,000
Polynesian languages	16,000
Solomon Island Pidgin (English Creole)	*157,000*
Other	10,000
Somalia[1]	
● Arabic	...
English	...
● Somali	7,892,000
Other	133,000
South Africa	
● Afrikaans	5,961,000
● English	3,675,000
Nguni	
● Ndebele	717,000
● Swazi	1,210,000
● Xhosa	7,888,000
● Zulu	10,667,000
Sotho	
● North Sotho (Pedi)	4,213,000
● South Sotho	3,540,000
● Tswana (Western Sotho)	3,675,000
● Tsonga	1,972,000
● Venda	1,031,000
Other	224,000
Spain	
Basque (Euskera)	641,000
● Castilian Spanish	30,373,000
Catalan (Català)	6,886,000
Galician (Gallego)	2,604,000
Other	305,000
Sri Lanka	
English	10,000
English-Sinhala	1,051,000
English-Sinhala-Tamil	684,000
English-Tamil	218,000
● Sinhala	11,510,000
Sinhala-Tamil	1,785,000
● Tamil	3,748,000
Other	60,000
Sudan, The[1]	
● Arabic	18,818,000
Arabic (lingua franca)	*22,816,000*
Bari	934,000
Beja	2,434,000
Dinka	4,400,000
Fur	782,000
Lotuko	565,000
Nubian languages	3,086,000
Nuer	1,869,000
Shilluk	652,000
Zande (Azande)	1,032,000
Other	3,542,000
Suriname	
● Dutch	*111,000*
English/English Creole	*415,000*
Sranantonga	172,000
Sranantonga-other	172,000
Other (mostly Hindi, Javanese, and Saramacca)	91,000
Swaziland[1]	
● English	*50,000*
● Swazi	976,000
Zulu	20,000
Other	81,000
Sweden[2]	
Arabic	69,000
Danish	41,000
English	32,000
Finnish	211,000
German	46,000
Iranian languages[1]	50,000
Norwegian	47,000
Polish	39,000
South Slavic languages[1]	117,000
Spanish	57,000
● Swedish	8,021,000
Turkish	29,000
Other	199,000
Switzerland	
● French	1,410,000
● German	4,669,000
● Italian	562,000
Romansch	41,000
Other	654,000
Syria[1]	
● Arabic	15,829,000
Kurdish	1,585,000
Other	173,000
Taiwan	
Austronesian languages	
Ami	140,000
Atayal	91,000
Bunun	43,000
Paiwan	69,000
Puyuma	10,000
Rukai	11,000
Saisiyat	6,000
Tsou	7,000
Yami	4,000
Chinese languages	
Hakka	2,481,000
● Mandarin	4,535,000
Min (South Fukien)	15,049,000
Other	122,000
Tajikistan	
Russian	633,000
● Tajik (Tojik)	4,066,000
Uzbek	1,515,000
Other	322,000
Tanzania[1]	
Chaga (Chagga), Pare	1,719,000
● English	*3,775,000*
Gogo	1,381,000
Ha	1,202,000
Haya	2,066,000
Hehet	2,414,000
Iramba	1,003,000
Luguru	1,719,000
Luo	288,000
Makonde	2,066,000
Masai	348,000
Ngoni	467,000
Nyakusa	1,898,000
Nyamwesi (Sukuma)	7,401,000
Shambala	1,500,000
● Swahili	3,100,000
Swahili (lingua franca)	*31,790,000*
Tatoga	258,000
Yao	854,000
Other	5,394,000
Thailand[1]	
Chinese	7,764,000
Karen	226,000
Malay	2,328,000
Mon-Khmer languages	
Khmer	810,000
Kuy	687,000
Other	226,000
Tai languages	
Lao	17,221,000
● Thai (Siamese)	33,662,000
Other	441,000
Other	656,000
Togo[1]	
Atlantic (Mel) languages	
Fula (Fulani)	74,000
Benue-Congo languages	
Ana (Ana-Ife)	136,000
Nago	14,000
Yoruba	11,000
Chadic languages	
Hausa	15,000
● French	*2,704,000*
Gur (Voltaic) languages	
Basari	95,000
Chakossi (Akan)	64,000
Chamba	53,000
Dye (Gangam)	51,000
Gurma	184,000
Kabre	748,000
Konkomba	77,000
Kotokoli (Tem)	313,000
Moba	292,000
Moore (Mossi)	14,000
Namba (Lamba)	166,000
Naudemba (Losso)	223,000
Tamberma	30,000
Yanga	16,000
Kwa languages	
Adele	11,000
Adja (Aja)	170,000
Ahlo	10,000
Akposo	145,000
Ane (Basila)	307,000
Anlo	4,300
Anyaga	11,000
Ewe	1,259,000
Fon	54,000
Hwe	6,500
Kebu	63,000
Kpessi	4,300
Peda-Hula (Pla)	22,000
Watyi (Ouatchi)	559,000
Other	229,000
Tonga	
● English	*31,000*
● Tongan	100,000
Other	2,000
Trinidad and Tobago	
● English	...
English Creole[17]	37,000
Hindi	45,000
Trinidad English	1,195,000
● Other	3,000
Tunisia	
● Arabic	6,911,000
Arabic-French	2,596,000
Arabic-French-English	309,000
Arabic-other	10,000
Other-no Arabic	31,000
Other	31,000
Turkey[1]	
Arabic	967,000
Kurdish[18]	7,482,000
● Turkish	61,825,000
Other	323,000
Turkmenistan[1]	
Armenian	37,000
Azerbaijani (Azeri)	40,000
Balochi	40,000
Kazakh	96,000
Russian	328,000
Tatar	40,000
● Turkmen	3,731,000
Ukrainian	25,000
Uzbek	446,000
Other	85,000
Tuvalu	
English	...
Kiribati (Gilbertese)	800
Tuvaluan (Ellice)	9,400
Uganda[1]	
Bantu languages	
Amba	98,000
Ganda (Luganda)	4,603,000
Gisu (Masaba)	1,145,000
Gwere	415,000
Kiga (Chiga)	2,127,000
Konjo	556,000
Nkole (Nyankole and Hororo)	2,727,000
Nyole	349,000
Nyoro	753,000
Ruli	109,000
Rundi	153,000
Rwanda	818,000
Samia	338,000
Soga	2,094,000
Swahili (lingua franca)	*8,944,000*
Toro	742,000
Central Sudanic languages	
Lugbara	1,200,000
Madi	196,000
Ndo	251,000
● English	*2,727,000*
Nilotic languages	
Acholi	1,124,000
Alur	600,000
Kakwa	131,000
Karamojong	535,000
Kumam	175,000
Lango	1,494,000
Padhola	382,000
Sebei (Kupsabiny)	164,000
Teso	1,527,000
Other (mostly Gujarati and Hindi)	633,000
Ukraine	
Belarusian	145,000
Bulgarian	154,000
Hungarian	145,000
Polish	29,000
Romanian	318,000
Russian	15,714,000
● Ukrainian	30,937,000
Other	414,000
United Arab Emirates[2]	
● Arabic	1,606,000
Other[16]	2,212,000
United Kingdom	
● English	57,559,000
Scots-Gaelic	79,000
Welsh	565,000
Other	961,000
United States	
Amharic	42,000
Arabic	683,000
Armenian	225,000
Bengali	53,000
Cajun	42,000
Chinese (including Formosan)	2,247,000
Czech	117,000
Danish	42,000
Dutch	180,000
English	239,407,000
English (lingua franca)	*282,724,000*
Finnish	64,000
French	2,150,000
French Creole (mostly Haitian)	233,000
German	1,537,000
Greek	406,000
Gujarati	262,000
Hebrew	217,000
Hindi (including Urdu)	645,000
Hungarian	131,000
Ilocano	53,000
Italian	1,121,000
Japanese	531,000
Korean	994,000
Kru (Gullah)	85,000
Lithuanian	74,000
Malayalam	42,000
Miao (Hmong)	187,000
Mon-Khmer (mostly Cambodian)	202,000
Navajo	198,000
Norwegian	106,000
Pennsylvania Dutch	106,000
Persian	347,000
Polish	742,000
Portuguese	627,000
Punjābī	64,000
Romanian	85,000
Russian	785,000
Samoan	42,000
Serbo-Croatian	260,000
Slovak	106,000
Spanish	31,230,000
Swedish	95,000
Syriac	42,000
Tagalog	1,361,000
Tai (including Laotian)	300,000
Turkish	53,000
Ukrainian	127,000
Vietnamese	1,122,000
Yiddish	199,000
Other	858,000
Uruguay	
● Spanish	3,235,700
Other	114,000
Uzbekistan[1]	
Kazakh	1,046,000
Russian	1,542,000
Tajik	1,232,000
Tatar	414,000
● Uzbek	19,429,000
Other	1,977,000
Vanuatu[19]	
● Bislama (English Creole)	116,000
● English	58,000
● French	29,000
Other	1,900
Venezuela	
Amerindian languages	
Goajiro	170,000
Warrau (Warao)	21,000
Other	160,000
● Spanish	24,795,000
Other	553,000
Vietnam[1]	
Bahnar	177,000
Cham	125,000
Chinese (Hoa)	1,142,000
French	*395,000*
Hre	125,000
Jarai	312,000
Khmer	1,132,000
Koho	114,000
Man (Mien, or Yao)	602,000
Miao (Meo, or Hmong)	716,000
Mnong	83,000
Muong	1,162,000
Nung	903,000
Rade (Rhadé)	249,000
Roglai	96,000
San Chay (Cao Lan)	146,000
San Diu	125,000
Sedang	125,000
Stieng	62,000
Tai	1,329,000
Tho (Tay)	1,515,000
● Vietnamese	70,972,000
Other	168,000
Virgin Islands (U.S.)	
● English	91,000
French	2,800
Spanish	15,000
Other	2,800
West Bank[20]	
Arabic	2,275,000
Hebrew	192,000
Western Sahara	
Arabic	262,000
Yemen[1]	
● Arabic	19,930,000
Other	80,000
Zambia[21]	
Bemba group	
Bemba	3,217,000
Bemba (lingua franca)	*5,643,000*
Bisa	124,000
Lala	260,000
Lamba	237,000
Other	451,000
● English	124,000
English (lingua franca)	*2,032,000*
Lozi (Barotse) group	
Lozi (Barotse)	688,000
Other	124,000
Mambwe group	
Lungu	79,000
Mambwe	124,000
Mwanga (Winawanga)	148,000
Other	11,000
North-Western group	
Kaonde	248,000
Lunda	214,000
Luvale (Luena)	192,000
Other	293,000
Nyanja (Maravi) group	
Chewa	621,000
Ngoni	181,000
Nsenga	463,000
Nyanja (Maravi)	847,000
Nyanja (lingua franca)	*2,822,000*
Other	68,000
Tonga (Ila-Tonga) group	
Ila	102,000
Lenje	169,000
Tonga	1,185,000
Other	135,000
Tumbuka group	
Senga	79,000
Tumbuka	316,000
Other	11,000
Other	102,000
Zimbabwe	
● English	258,000
English (lingua franca)	*5,477,000*
Ndebele (Nguni)	1,902,000
Nyanja	269,000
Shona	8,453,000
Other	837,000

[1]Figures given represent ethnolinguistic groups. [2]Data refer to nationality (usually resident aliens holding foreign passports). [3]Data are partly based on place of residence. [4]Majority of population speak Moore (language of the Mossi); Dyula is language of commerce. [5]Swahili also spoken. [6]English and French also spoken. [7]Based on "nationality" at 1982 census. [8]Includes naturalized citizens. [9]French is the universal language throughout France; traditional dialects and minority languages are retained regionally in the approximate numbers shown, however. [10]Data reflect multi-lingualism; 2000 population estimate is 233,000. [11]Refers to Irish speakers in Gaeltacht areas. [12]Includes the population of the Golan Heights and East Jerusalem; excludes the Israeli population in the West Bank and Gaza Strip. [13]English and French also spoken. [14]English and Italian also spoken. [15]Data reflect ability to speak the language, not mother tongue; 2003 population estimate is 160,000. [16]Mostly Pakistanis, Indians, and Iranians. [17]Spoken on Tobago only. [18]Other estimates of the Kurdish population range from 6 percent to 20–25 percent. [19]Data reflect multilingualism; 2000 population is 190,000. [20]Excludes East Jerusalem. [21]Groups are officially defined geographic divisions; elements comprising them are named by language.

Religion

The following table presents statistics on religious affiliation for each of the countries of the world. An assessment was made for each country of the available data on distribution of religious communities within the total population; the best available figures, whether originating as census data, membership figures of the churches concerned, or estimates by external analysts in the absence of reliable local data, were applied as percentages to the estimated 2001 midyear population of the country to obtain the data shown below.

Several concepts govern the nature of the available data, each useful separately but none the basis of any standard of international practice in the collection of such data. The word "affiliation" was used above to describe the nature of the relationship joining the religious bodies named and the populations shown. This term implies some sort of formal, usually documentary, connection between the religion and the individual (a baptismal certificate, a child being assigned the religion of its parents on a census form, maintenance of one's name on the tax rolls of a state religion, etc.) but says nothing about the nature of the individual's personal religious practice, in that the individual may have lapsed, never been confirmed as an adult, joined another religion, or may have joined an organization that is formally atheist.

The user of these statistics should be careful to note that not only does the nature of the affiliation (with an organized religion) differ greatly from country to country, but the social context of religious practice does also. A country in which a single religion has long been predominant will often show more than 90% of its population to be *affiliated*, while in actual fact, no more than 10% may actually *practice* that religion on a regular basis. Such a situation often leads to undercounting of minority religions (where someone [head of household, communicant, child] is counted at all), blurring of distinctions seen to be significant elsewhere (a Hindu country may not distinguish Protestant [or even Christian] denominations; a Christian country may not distinguish among its Muslim or Buddhist citizens), or double-counting in countries where an individual may conscientiously practice more than one "religion" at a time.

Until 1989 communist countries had for long consciously attempted to ignore, suppress, or render invisible religious practice within their borders. Countries with large numbers of adherents of traditional, often animist, religions and belief systems usually have little or no formal methodology for defining the nature of local religious practice. On the other hand, countries with strong missionary traditions, or good census organizations, or few religious sensitivities may have very good, detailed, and meaningful data.

The most comprehensive works available are DAVID B. BARRETT (ed.), *World Christian Encyclopedia* (2001); and PETER BRIERLEY, *World Churches Handbook* (1997).

Religion

Religious affiliation	2001 population
Afghanistan	
Sunnī Muslim	23,090,000
Shīʿī Muslim	2,310,000
other	490,000
Albania	
Muslim	1,200,000
Roman Catholic	520,000
Albanian Orthodox	320,000
other	1,050,000
Algeria	
Sunnī Muslim	30,550,000
Ibāḍīyah Muslim	180,000
other	90,000
American Samoa	
Congregational	23,800
Roman Catholic	11,300
other	23,400
Andorra	
Roman Catholic	60,000
other	7,000
Angola	
Roman Catholic	6,440,000
Protestant	1,550,000
African Christian	710,000
other	1,660,000
Antigua and Barbuda	
Protestant	30,000
Anglican	23,000
Roman Catholic	8,000
other	10,000
Argentina	
Roman Catholic	29,920,000
Protestant	2,040,000
Muslim	730,000
Jewish	500,000
nonreligious	880,000
other	3,430,000
Armenia	
Armenian Apostolic (Orthodox)	2,454,000
other	1,353,000
Aruba	
Roman Catholic	80,000
other	18,000
Australia	
Roman Catholic	5,230,000
Anglican	4,260,000
Uniting Church	1,460,000
Presbyterian	740,000
other Protestant	1,400,000
Orthodox	540,000
nonreligious	3,220,000
other	2,510,000
Austria	
Roman Catholic	6,060,000
Protestant (mostly Lutheran)	430,000
atheist and nonreligious	690,000
other	890,000
Azerbaijan	
Shīʿī Muslim	5,299,000
Sunnī Muslim	2,271,000
other	535,000
Bahamas, The	
Protestant	135,000
Roman Catholic	50,000
Anglican	32,000
other	77,000
Bahrain	
Shīʿī Muslim	420,000
Sunnī Muslim	140,000
other	140,000
Bangladesh	
Muslim	112,660,000
Hindu	16,260,000
other	2,360,000
Barbados	
Anglican	89,000
Protestant	80,000
Roman Catholic	12,000
other	88,000
Belarus	
Belarusian Orthodox	3,151,000
Roman Catholic	1,772,000
other	5,062,000
Belgium	
Roman Catholic	8,310,000
nonreligious	600,000
other	1,360,000
Belize	
Roman Catholic	143,000
Protestant	67,000
Anglican	17,000
other	20,000
Benin	
Voodoo (traditional beliefs)	3,390,000
Roman Catholic	1,370,000
Muslim	1,320,000
other	500,000
Bermuda	
Anglican	23,700
Methodist	10,400
Roman Catholic	8,800
other	20,900
Bhutan	
Lamaistic Buddhist	510,000
Hindu	140,000
other	40,000
Bolivia	
Roman Catholic	7,540,000
Protestant	770,000
other	210,000
Bosnia and Herzegovina	
Sunnī Muslim	1,690,000
Serbian Orthodox	1,180,000
Roman Catholic	710,000
other	350,000
Botswana	
African Christian	490,000
Protestant	170,000
Roman Catholic	60,000
other (mostly traditional beliefs)	870,000
Brazil	
Roman Catholic (including syncretic Afro-Catholic cults having Spiritist beliefs and rituals)	124,470,000
Evangelical Protestant	39,850,000
other	7,800,000
Brunei	
Muslim	222,000
other	121,000
Bulgaria	
Bulgarian Orthodox	5,690,000
Muslim (mostly Sunnī)	940,000
other	1,320,000
Burkina Faso	
Muslim	5,960,000
traditional beliefs	4,180,000
Christian	2,040,000
other	80,000
Burundi	
Roman Catholic	4,050,000
nonreligious	1,160,000
other (mostly Protestant)	1,020,000
Cambodia	
Buddhist	10,780,000
Chinese folk-religionist	600,000
traditional beliefs	550,000
Muslim	290,000
other	500,000
Cameroon	
Roman Catholic	4,180,000
traditional beliefs	3,750,000
Muslim	3,350,000
Protestant	3,270,000
other	1,250,000
Canada	
Roman Catholic	14,010,000
Protestant	8,620,000
Anglican	2,490,000
Eastern Orthodox	440,000
Jewish	360,000
Muslim	290,000
Buddhist	190,000
Hindu	180,000
Sikh	170,000
nonreligious	3,880,000
other	380,000
Cape Verde	
Roman Catholic	370,000
other	35,000
Central African Republic	
Roman Catholic	660,000
Muslim	560,000
traditional beliefs	550,000
Protestant	520,000
other	1,290,000
Chad	
Muslim	4,690,000
Roman Catholic	1,770,000
Protestant	1,250,000
traditional beliefs	640,000
other	350,000
Chile	
Roman Catholic	11,810,000
Evangelical Protestant	1,910,000
other	1,690,000
China	
nonreligious	661,390,000
Chinese folk-religionist	256,260,000
atheist	152,990,000
Buddhist	108,110,000
Christian	76,540,000
Muslim	18,360,000
traditional beliefs	1,280,000
Colombia	
Roman Catholic	39,590,000
other	3,480,000
Comoros	
Sunnī Muslim	555,000
other	11,000
Congo, Dem. Rep. of the	
Roman Catholic	21,990,000
Protestant	16,950,000
African Christian	7,170,000
traditional beliefs	5,740,000
Muslim	750,000
other	1,040,000
Congo, Rep. of the	
Roman Catholic	1,430,000
Protestant	490,000
African Christian	360,000
other	610,000
Costa Rica	
Roman Catholic	3,380,000
Protestant	360,000
other	190,000
Côte d'Ivoire	
Muslim	6,340,000
Roman Catholic	3,400,000
traditional beliefs	2,790,000
nonreligious	2,220,000
Protestant	870,000
other	770,000
Croatia	
Roman Catholic	3,890,000
Serbian Orthodox	250,000
Sunnī Muslim	100,000
Protestant	30,000
other	130,000
Cuba	
Roman Catholic	4,420,000
Protestant	270,000
other (mostly Santeria)	6,500,000
Cyprus	
Greek Orthodox	630,000
Muslim (mostly Sunnī)	200,000
other (mostly Christian)	40,000
Czech Republic	
Roman Catholic	4,010,000
Evangelical Church of Czech Brethren	200,000
Czechoslovak Hussite	180,000
Silesian Evangelical	30,000
Eastern Orthodox	20,000
atheist and nonreligious	4,100,000
other	1,730,000
Denmark	
Evangelical Lutheran	4,600,000
Muslim	120,000
other	640,000
Djibouti	
Sunnī Muslim	434,000
other	27,000
Dominica	
Roman Catholic	50,000
Protestant	12,000
other	10,000
Dominican Republic	
Roman Catholic	7,110,000
Protestant	560,000
other	1,020,000
East Timor	
Roman Catholic	780,000
Protestant	50,000
Muslim	30,000
other	40,000
Ecuador	
Roman Catholic	11,910,000
Protestant	440,000
other	530,000
Egypt	
Sunnī Muslim	58,060,000
Coptic Orthodox[1]	6,520,000
other	660,000
El Salvador	
Roman Catholic	4,880,000
Protestant	1,070,000
other	290,000
Equatorial Guinea	
Roman Catholic	390,000
other	110,000
Eritrea	
Eritrean Orthodox	1,980,000
Muslim	1,920,000
other	400,000

Religion (continued)

Religious affiliation	2001 population
Estonia	
Estonian Orthodox	277,000
Evangelical Lutheran	187,000
other	899,000
Ethiopia	
Ethiopian Orthodox	33,110,000
other Christian	7,090,000
Muslim (mostly Sunnī)	21,710,000
traditional beliefs	3,180,000
other	820,000
Faroe Islands	
Evangelical Lutheran	38,000
other	9,000
Fiji	
Christian (mostly Methodist and Roman Catholic)	437,000
Hindu	316,000
Muslim	65,000
other	9,000
Finland	
Evangelical Lutheran	4,420,000
other	770,000
France	
Roman Catholic	38,690,000
nonreligious	9,230,000
Muslim	4,180,000
atheist	2,380,000
Protestant	720,000
Jewish	590,000
other	3,290,000
French Guiana	
Roman Catholic	91,000
other	77,000
French Polynesia	
Protestant	119,000
Roman Catholic	94,000
other	25,000
Gabon	
Roman Catholic	690,000
Protestant	220,000
African Christian	170,000
other	160,000
Gambia, The	
Muslim (mostly Sunnī)	1,340,000
other	70,000
Gaza Strip	
Muslim (mostly Sunnī)	1,190,000
other	20,000
Georgia	
Georgian Orthodox	1,828,000
Sunnī Muslim	549,000
Armenian Apostolic (Orthodox)	279,000
Russian Orthodox	133,000
other (mostly nonreligious)	2,200,000
Germany	
Protestant (mostly Evangelical Lutheran)	29,330,000
Roman Catholic	27,590,000
Muslim	3,660,000
atheist	1,800,000
other (mostly nonreligious)	20,020,000
Ghana	
traditional beliefs	4,860,000
Muslim	3,910,000
Protestant	3,310,000
African Christian	2,870,000
Roman Catholic	1,890,000
other	3,050,000
Greece	
Greek Orthodox	10,010,000
Muslim	360,000
other	500,000
Greenland	
Evangelical Lutheran	36,500
other	19,800
Grenada	
Roman Catholic	54,000
Anglican	14,000
other	34,000
Guadeloupe	
Roman Catholic	350,000
other	82,000
Guam	
Roman Catholic	118,000
Protestant	19,000
other	21,000
Guatemala	
Roman Catholic	8,880,000
Evangelical Protestant	2,540,000
other	270,000
Guernsey	
Anglican	42,000
other	22,000
Guinea	
Muslim	6,470,000
Christian	760,000
other	380,000
Guinea-Bissau	
traditional beliefs	590,000
Muslim	530,000
Christian	170,000
other	20,000
Guyana	
Hindu	264,000
Protestant	145,000
Roman Catholic	89,000
Muslim	70,000
Anglican	67,000
other	142,000
Haiti	
Roman Catholic	4,770,000
Protestant	1,590,000
other	610,000
Honduras	
Roman Catholic	5,740,000
Evangelical Protestant	690,000
other	200,000
Hong Kong	
Buddhist and Taoist	4,970,000
Protestant	290,000
Roman Catholic	280,000
other	1,200,000
Hungary	
Roman Catholic	6,120,000
Protestant	2,470,000
nonreligious	750,000
other	850,000
Iceland	
Evangelical Lutheran	260,000
other	20,000
India	
Hindu	759,350,000
Sunnī Muslim	92,380,000
traditional beliefs	34,930,000
Shīʿī Muslim	30,790,000
independent	30,750,000
Sikh	22,290,000
Protestant	15,130,000
Roman Catholic	13,940,000
Buddhist	7,290,000
Jain	4,160,000
atheist	1,670,000
Bahāʾī	1,190,000
Zoroastrian (Parsi)	210,000
nonreligious	12,910,000
other	3,000,000
Indonesia	
Muslim	185,060,000
Protestant	12,820,000
Roman Catholic	7,600,000
Hindu	3,880,000
Buddhist	2,190,000
other	660,000
Iran	
Shīʿī Muslim	57,180,000
Sunnī Muslim	3,460,000
Zoroastrian	1,780,000
Bahāʾī	430,000
Christian	340,000
other	250,000
Iraq	
Shīʿī Muslim	13,890,000
Sunnī Muslim	8,510,000
Christian	750,000
other	180,000
Ireland	
Roman Catholic	3,500,000
other	320,000
Isle of Man	
Anglican	30,000
Methodist	7,000
Roman Catholic	6,000
other	31,000
Israel	
Jewish[2]	4,960,000
Muslim (mostly Sunnī)	930,000
other	360,000
Italy	
Roman Catholic	46,260,000
nonreligious and atheist	9,600,000
Muslim	680,000
other	1,350,000
Jamaica	
Protestant	1,020,000
Roman Catholic	270,000
Anglican	100,000
other	1,230,000
Japan	
Shintoist[3]	118,270,000
Buddhist[3]	88,490,000
Christian	1,470,000
other	10,250,000
Jersey	
Anglican	55,000
Roman Catholic	21,000
other	14,000
Jordan	
Sunnī Muslim	4,800,000
Christian	210,000
other	120,000
Kazakhstan	
Muslim (mostly Sunnī)	6,988,000
Russian Orthodox	1,216,000
Protestant	318,000
other (mostly nonreligious)	6,345,000
Kenya	
Roman Catholic	6,780,000
African Christian	6,400,000
Protestant	6,170,000
traditional beliefs	3,540,000
Anglican	2,900,000
Muslim	2,240,000
Orthodox	720,000
other	2,030,000
Kiribati	
Roman Catholic	50,000
Congregational	36,000
other	9,000
Korea, North	
atheist and nonreligious	15,000,000
traditional beliefs	3,430,000
Ch'ŏndogyo	3,050,000
other	480,000
Korea, South	
nonreligious	23,490,000
Buddhist	11,040,000
Protestant	9,370,000
Roman Catholic	3,160,000
Confucian	230,000
Wonbulgyo	90,000
other	290,000
Kuwait	
Sunnī Muslim	1,020,000
Shīʿī Muslim	680,000
other Muslim	230,000
other (mostly Christian and Hindu)	340,000
Kyrgyzstan	
Muslim (mostly Sunnī)	3,701,000
Russian Orthodox	276,000
other (mostly nonreligious)	958,000
Laos	
Buddhist	2,750,000
traditional beliefs	2,350,000
other	540,000
Latvia	
Roman Catholic	350,000
Evangelical Lutheran	345,000
Russian Orthodox	181,000
other (mostly nonreligious)	1,482,000
Lebanon	
Shīʿī Muslim	1,230,000
Sunnī Muslim	770,000
Maronite Catholic	690,000
Druze	260,000
Greek Orthodox	220,000
Armenian Apostolic (Orthodox)	190,000
Greek Catholic (Melchite)	170,000
other	110,000
Lesotho	
Roman Catholic	820,000
Protestant	280,000
African Christian	260,000
traditional beliefs	170,000
Anglican	100,000
other	550,000
Liberia	
traditional beliefs	1,390,000
Christian	1,270,000
Muslim	520,000
other	60,000
Libya	
Sunnī Muslim	5,040,000
other	200,000
Liechtenstein	
Roman Catholic	26,000
other	7,000
Lithuania	
Roman Catholic	2,660,000
Russian Orthodox	90,000
other (mostly nonreligious)	940,000
Luxembourg	
Roman Catholic	400,000
other	40,000
Macau	
nonreligious	271,000
Buddhist	75,000
other	100,000
Macedonia	
Serbian (Macedonian) Orthodox	1,210,000
Sunnī Muslim	580,000
other	260,000
Madagascar	
traditional beliefs	7,670,000
Roman Catholic	3,250,000
Protestant	3,630,000
other	1,420,000
Malawi	
Roman Catholic	2,600,000
Protestant	2,070,000
African Christian	1,770,000
Muslim	1,560,000
traditional beliefs	820,000
other	1,730,000
Malaysia	
Muslim	10,770,000
Chinese folk-religionist	5,450,000
Christian	1,880,000
Hindu	1,660,000
Buddhist	1,500,000
other	1,350,000
Maldives	
Sunnī Muslim	273,000
other	2,000
Mali	
Muslim	9,010,000
traditional beliefs	1,760,000
Christian	220,000
other	10,000
Malta	
Roman Catholic	363,000
other	21,000
Marshall Islands	
Protestant	32,800
Roman Catholic	3,700
other	15,700
Martinique	
Roman Catholic	336,000
other	52,000
Mauritania	
Sunnī Muslim	2,720,000
other	20,000
Mauritius	
Hindu	610,000
Roman Catholic	330,000
Muslim	190,000
other	70,000
Mayotte	
Sunnī Muslim	153,000
Christian	5,000
Mexico	
Roman Catholic	90,370,000
Protestant	3,820,000
other Christian	1,820,000
other (mostly nonreligious)	3,970,000
Micronesia	
Roman Catholic	63,600
Protestant	40,100
other	14,200
Moldova	
Romanian Orthodox	1,263,000
Russian (Moldovan) Orthodox	342,000
other (mostly nonreligious)	2,007,000
Monaco	
Roman Catholic	28,000
other	4,000
Mongolia	
Tantric Buddhist (Lamaist)	2,340,000
Muslim	100,000
Morocco	
Muslim (mostly Sunnī)	28,730,000
other	500,000
Mozambique	
traditional beliefs	9,750,000
Roman Catholic	3,060,000
Muslim	2,040,000
Protestant	1,720,000
African Christian	1,400,000
other	1,400,000
Myanmar (Burma)	
Buddhist	37,560,000
Christian	2,060,000
Muslim	1,610,000
traditional beliefs	480,000
Hindu	210,000
other	70,000
Namibia	
Protestant (mostly Lutheran)	850,000
Roman Catholic	320,000
African Christian	200,000
other	430,000
Nauru	
Protestant	6,100
Roman Catholic	3,300
other	2,700
Nepal	
Hindu	19,180,000
traditional beliefs	2,350,000
Buddhist	2,050,000
Muslim	970,000
Christian	600,000
other	140,000
Netherlands, The	
Roman Catholic	4,950,000
Dutch Reformed Church (NHK)	2,240,000
Reformed Churches	1,120,000
Muslim	720,000
nonreligious	6,550,000
other	400,000
Netherlands Antilles	
Roman Catholic	152,000
other	54,000
New Caledonia	
Roman Catholic	132,000
Protestant	31,300
other	52,200

Religious affiliation	2001 population
New Zealand	
Anglican	674,000
Roman Catholic	505,000
Presbyterian	489,000
Methodist	130,000
Baptist	57,000
Mormon	44,000
Ratana	39,000
nonreligious	954,000
other	969,000
Nicaragua	
Roman Catholic	3,590,000
Protestant	810,000
other (mostly nonreligious)	520,000
Niger	
Sunnī Muslim	9,390,000
traditional beliefs	900,000
other	70,000
Nigeria	
Muslim	55,600,000
traditional beliefs	12,500,000
Christian	58,100,000
other	500,000
Northern Mariana Islands	
Roman Catholic	53,600
other	19,700
Norway	
Evangelical Lutheran (Church of Norway)	3,990,000
other	530,000
Oman	
Ibāḍīyāh Muslim	1,840,000
Sunnī Muslim	350,000
Hindu	190,000
Christian	100,000
other	20,000
Pakistan	
Sunnī Muslim	113,950,000
Shīʿī Muslim	25,010,000
Christian	3,560,000
Hindu	1,730,000
other	370,000
Palau	
Roman Catholic	7,600
Modekne	5,200
Protestant	4,900
other	2,100
Panama	
Roman Catholic	2,330,000
Protestant	420,000
other	150,000
Papua New Guinea	
Protestant	3,180,000
Roman Catholic	1,500,000
Anglican	210,000
other	420,000
Paraguay	
Roman Catholic	4,990,000
Protestant	280,000
other	370,000
Peru	
Roman Catholic	23,170,000
Protestant	1,730,000
other (mostly nonreligious)	1,190,000
Philippines	
Roman Catholic	63,530,000
Protestant	4,160,000
Muslim	3,500,000
Aglipayan	2,010,000
Church of Christ (Iglesia ni Cristo)	1,790,000
other	1,620,000
Poland	
Roman Catholic	35,050,000
Polish Orthodox	550,000
other (mostly nonreligious)	3,050,000
Portugal	
Roman Catholic	9,520,000
other	810,000
Puerto Rico	
Roman Catholic	2,480,000
Protestant	1,080,000
other	270,000
Qatar	
Muslim (mostly Sunnī)	490,000
Christian	60,000
other	40,000
Réunion	
Roman Catholic	599,000
Hindu	33,000
other	102,000
Romania	
Romanian Orthodox	19,460,000
Roman Catholic	1,140,000
other	1,810,000
Russia	
Russian Orthodox	23,580,000
Muslim	10,980,000
Protestant	1,320,000
Jewish	590,000
other (mostly nonreligious)	107,960,000
Rwanda	
Roman Catholic	3,730,000
Protestant	1,530,000
traditional beliefs	660,000
Muslim	580,000
Anglican	570,000
other	260,000
St. Kitts and Nevis	
Anglican	10,000
Methodist	10,000
other	15,000
Pentecostal	7,000
other	12,000
St. Lucia	
Roman Catholic	125,000
Protestant	20,000
other	13,000
St. Vincent and the Grenadines	
Anglican	20,000
Pentecostal	17,000
Methodist	12,000
Roman Catholic	12,000
other	52,000
Samoa	
Mormon	46,200
Congregational	44,000
Roman Catholic	38,100
Methodist	21,800
other	29,100
San Marino	
Roman Catholic	24,000
other	3,000
São Tomé and Príncipe	
Roman Catholic	111,000
African Christian	16,000
other	20,000
Saudi Arabia	
Sunnī Muslim	20,490,000
Shīʿī Muslim	840,000
Christian	840,000
Hindu	250,000
other	330,000
Senegal	
Sunnī Muslim	9,010,000
traditional beliefs	640,000
Roman Catholic	480,000
other	160,000
Serbia and Montenegro	
Serbian Orthodox	6,680,000
Sunnī Muslim	2,030,000
Roman Catholic	620,000
other (mostly nonreligious)	1,350,000
Seychelles	
Roman Catholic	69,800
other	10,800
Sierra Leone	
Sunnī Muslim	2,490,000
traditional beliefs	2,190,000
Christian	620,000
other	130,000
Singapore	
Buddhist and Taoist	1,695,000
Muslim	495,000
Christian	485,000
Hindu	133,000
nonreligious	493,000
other	21,000
Slovakia	
Roman Catholic	3,270,000
Slovak Evangelical	340,000
other (mostly nonreligious)	1,800,000
Slovenia	
Roman Catholic	1,650,000
other	340,000
Solomon Islands	
Protestant	173,000
Anglican	149,000
Roman Catholic	83,000
other	75,000
Somalia	
Sunnī Muslim	7,364,000
other	125,000
South Africa	
Christian	36,220,000
independents	17,040,000
Protestant	13,860,000
Roman Catholic	3,090,000
traditional beliefs	3,660,000
Hindu	1,050,000
Muslim	1,050,000
Bahāʾī	260,000
Jewish	170,000
nonreligious	1,050,000
other	130,000
Spain	
Roman Catholic	36,920,000
Muslim	200,000
other (mostly nonreligious)	3,010,000
Sri Lanka	
Buddhist	13,270,000
Hindu	2,190,000
Muslim	1,750,000
Roman Catholic	1,300,000
other	900,000
Sudan, The	
Sunnī Muslim	25,360,000
Christian	6,020,000
traditional beliefs	4,300,000
other	390,000
Suriname	
Hindu	119,000
Roman Catholic	91,000
Muslim	85,000
Protestant	71,000
other	68,000
Swaziland	
African Christian	480,000
Protestant	160,000
traditional beliefs	120,000
other	340,000
Sweden	
Church of Sweden (Lutheran)	7,690,000
other	1,200,000
Switzerland	
Roman Catholic	3,330,000
Protestant	2,890,000
other	1,000,000
Syria	
Sunnī Muslim	12,380,000
Shīʿī Muslim	2,010,000
Christian	920,000
Druze	500,000
other	920,000
Taiwan	
nonreligious	10,670,000
Buddhist	5,100,000
Taoist	4,040,000
I Kuan Tao	990,000
Protestant	440,000
Roman Catholic	320,000
Tien Te Chiao	210,000
Tien Ti Chiao	190,000
Confucianism (Li)	150,000
Hsuan Yuan Chiao	140,000
Muslim	50,000
Shinto (Tenrikyo)	20,000
Bahāʾī	20,000
Tajikistan	
Sunnī Muslim	4,920,000
Shīʿī Muslim	310,000
Russian Orthodox	90,000
atheist	120,000
other (mostly nonreligious)	820,000
Tanzania	
Christian	18,260,000
Muslim	11,520,000
traditional beliefs	5,830,000
other	620,000
Thailand	
Buddhist	57,920,000
Muslim	2,850,000
Christian	440,000
other	40,000
Togo	
traditional beliefs	1,940,000
Roman Catholic	1,250,000
Sunnī Muslim	970,000
Protestant	530,000
other	450,000
Tonga	
Free Wesleyan	44,000
Roman Catholic	16,000
other	41,000
Trinidad and Tobago	
Roman Catholic	380,000
Hindu	308,000
Protestant	244,000
Anglican	142,000
Muslim	76,000
other	149,000
Tunisia	
Sunnī Muslim	9,720,000
other	104,000
Turkey	
Muslim (mostly Sunnī)	64,360,000
nonreligious	1,340,000
other	530,000
Turkmenistan	
Muslim (mostly Sunnī)	4,752,000
Russian Orthodox	129,000
other (mostly nonreligious)	581,000
Tuvalu	
Congregational	9,400
other	1,600
Uganda	
Roman Catholic	10,050,000
Anglican	9,450,000
Muslim (mostly Sunnī)	1,250,000
traditional beliefs	1,050,000
other	2,190,000
Ukraine	
Ukrainian Orthodox (Russian patriarchy)	9,491,000
Ukrainian Orthodox (Kiev patriarchy)	4,746,000
Ukrainian Autocephalous Orthodox	332,000
Ukrainian Catholic (Uniate)	3,417,000
Protestant	1,736,000
Roman Catholic	576,000
Jewish	423,000
other (mostly nonreligious)	28,044,000
United Arab Emirates	
Sunnī Muslim	2,490,000
Shīʿī Muslim	500,000
other	120,000
United Kingdom	
Christian	49,510,000
Anglican	26,140,000
Roman Catholic	5,590,000
Protestant	5,020,000
Eastern Orthodox	370,000
other Christian	12,390,000
Muslim	1,220,000
Hindu	440,000
Jewish	310,000
Sikh	240,000
other (mostly nonreligious and atheist)	8,240,000
United States	
Christian (professing)	242,011,000
Christian (affiliated)	196,929,000
independent	80,639,000
Protestant	66,287,000
Roman Catholic	59,542,000
Eastern Orthodox	5,915,000
Anglican	2,464,000
other Christian	10,348,000
multi-affiliated Christians	−28,266,000
Christian (unaffiliated)	45,082,000
non-Christian	44,056,000
nonreligious	25,745,000
Jewish	5,771,000
Muslim	4,242,000
Buddhist	2,515,000
atheist	1,181,000
Hindu	1,059,000
New-Religionist	832,000
Bahāʾī	773,000
Ethnic religionist	447,000
Sikh	240,000
Chinese folk-religionist	80,000
other	1,171,000
Uruguay	
Roman Catholic	2,590,000
Protestant	150,000
Mormon	50,000
Jewish	30,000
other	480,000
Uzbekistan	
Muslim (mostly Sunnī)	19,156,000
Russian Orthodox	195,000
other (mostly nonreligious)	5,804,000
Vanuatu	
Presbyterian	70,000
Roman Catholic	28,000
Anglican	27,000
other	69,000
Venezuela	
Roman Catholic	22,050,000
other	2,590,000
Vietnam	
Buddhist	53,290,000
Roman Catholic	6,180,000
New-Religionist	
Cao Dai	2,810,000
Hoa Hao	1,690,000
other	16,500,000
Virgin Islands (U.S.)	
Protestant	56,000
Roman Catholic	41,000
other	24,000
West Bank	
Muslim (mostly Sunnī)	1,860,000
Jewish[4]	230,000
Christian and other	180,000
Western Sahara	
Sunnī Muslim	250,000
other	1,000
Yemen	
Muslim (mostly Sunnī)	18,050,000
other	20,000
Zambia	
traditional beliefs	2,640,000
Protestant	2,240,000
Roman Catholic	1,650,000
other	3,240,000
Zimbabwe	
African Christian	4,580,000
traditional beliefs	3,430,000
Protestant	1,400,000
Roman Catholic	1,090,000
other	870,000

[1]Official 1986 census figure is 5.9 percent. [2]Includes the Golan Heights and East Jerusalem; excludes the West Bank and Gaza Strip. [3]Many Japanese practice both Shintoism and Buddhism. [4]Excludes East Jerusalem.

Vital statistics, marriage, family

This table provides some of the basic measures of the factors that influence the size, direction, and rates of population change within a country. The accuracy of these data depends on the effectiveness of each respective national system for registering vital and civil events (birth, death, marriage, etc.) and on the sophistication of the analysis that can be brought to bear upon the data so compiled.

Data on birth rates, for example, depend not only on the completeness of registration of births in a particular country but also on the conditions under which those data are collected: Do all births take place in a hospital? Are the births reported comparably in all parts of the country? Are the records of the births tabulated at a central location in a timely way with an effort to eliminate inconsistent reporting of birth events, perinatal mortality, etc.? Similar difficulties attach to death rates but with the added need to identify "cause of death." Even in a developed country such identifications are often left to nonmedical personnel, and in a developing country with, say, only one physician for every 10,000 population, there will be too few physicians to perform autopsies to assess accurately the cause of death after the fact and also too few to provide ongoing care at a level where records would permit inference about cause of death based on prior condition or diagnosis.

Calculating natural increase, which at its most basic is simply the difference between the birth and death rates, may be affected by the differing degrees of completeness of birth and death registration for a given country. The total fertility rate may be understood as the average number of children that would be borne per woman if all childbearing women lived to the end of their childbearing years and bore children at each age at the average rate for that age. Calculating a meaningful fertility rate requires analysis of changing age structure of the female population over time, changing mortality rates among mothers and their infants, and changing medical practice at births, each improvement of natural survivorship or medical support leading to greater numbers of live-born children and greater numbers of children who survive their first year (the basis for measurement of infant mortality, another basic indicator of demographic conditions and trends within a population).

As indicated above, data for causes of death are not only particularly difficult to obtain, since many countries are not well equipped to collect the data, but also difficult to assess, as their accuracy may be suspect and their meaning may be subject to varying interpretation. Take the case of a citizen of a less developed country who dies of what is clearly a lung infection: Was the death complicated by chronic malnutrition, itself complicated by a parasitic infestation, these last two together so weakening the subject that he died of an infection that he might have survived had his general health been better? Similarly, in a developed country: Someone may die from what is identified in an autopsy as a cerebrovascular accident, but if that accident occurred in a vascular system that was weakened by diabetes, what was the actual cause of death? Statistics on causes of death seek to identify the "underlying" cause (that which sets the final train of events leading to death in motion) but often must settle for the most proximate cause or symptom. Even this kind of analysis may be misleading for those charged with interpreting the data with a view to ordering health-care priorities for a particular country. The eight groups of causes of death utilized here include most, but not all, of the detailed causes classified by the World Health Organization and would not, thus, aggregate to the country's crude death rate for the same year. Among the lesser causes excluded by the present classification are: benign neoplasms; nutritional disorders; anemias; mental disorders; kidney and genito-urinary

Vital statistics, marriage, family

country	vital rates						causes of death (rate per 100,000 population)								
	year	birth rate per 1,000 population	death rate per 1,000 population	infant mortality rate per 1,000 live births	rate of natural increase per 1,000 population	total fertility rate	year	infectious and parasitic diseases	malignant neoplasms (cancers)	endocrine and metabolic disorders	diseases of the nervous system	diseases of the circulatory system	diseases of the respiratory system	diseases of the digestive system	accidents, poisoning, and violence
Afghanistan	2000	41.8	18.0	149.3	23.8	5.9	...	...	...	...	...	...	...	...	...
Albania	2000	19.5	6.0	41.3	13.5	2.4	1993	10.8	53.8	5.1	24.1	187.0	84.5	16.5	41.7
Algeria	2000	19.8	5.5	51.1	14.3	2.8	...	...	...	...	...	...	...	...	...
American Samoa	2000	25.8	4.3	10.6	21.5	3.6	1990	16.4[4]	46.8	16.4[5]	...	131.1[6]	65.6[7]	...	58.5
Andorra	1999	12.6[8]	3.1[8]	4.1[9]	9.5[8]	1.2[10]	...	...	...	...	...	...	...	...	...
Angola	2000	46.9	25.0	195.8	21.9	6.5	...	...	...	...	...	...	...	...	...
Antigua and Barbuda	2000	20.2	6.0	23.0	14.2	2.3	1995	10.4	96.2	57.7	13.3	242.6	42.9	19.2	37.0
Argentina	2000	18.6	7.6	18.3	11.0	2.5	1996	28.1	145.7	19.1[5]	9.7	297.3	64.8	32.5	52.2
Armenia	2000	11.0	9.5	41.5	1.5	1.5	1997	9.2	96.5	32.6	4.4	336.6	38.9	23.9	37.9
Aruba	2000	13.1	6.1	6.5	7.0	1.8	1998	26.1	118.0	29.3[5]	4.3	184.0	35.9	14.1	52.2
Australia	2000	13.0	7.6	6.0	5.4	1.8	1995	6.0	190.0	23.0	17.0	296.0	52.0	21.0	41.0
Austria	1999	9.5	9.4	4.4	0.1	1.3	1997	2.5	233.5	19.9	0.5[14]	532.6	29.9	28.4	54.9
Azerbaijan	2001	13.7	6.2	83.4[10]	7.5	1.6	1995	29.7	61.9	11.8	11.3	335.3	84.9	34.3	45.9
Bahamas, The	2000	19.5	6.8	17.0	12.7	2.3	1995	13.3	85.6	36.3	0.7	160.1	26.6	14.4	40.0
Bahrain	2000	20.6	3.9	20.5	16.7	2.8	1998	5.4	37.8	22.7	4.6	85.9	22.7	13.3	14.5
Bangladesh	2000	27.0	9.1	73.0	17.9	3.0	...	...	...	...	...	...	...	...	...
Barbados	2000	13.6	8.7	12.4	4.9	1.6	1995	27.3	162.5	149.2	22.7	365.5	55.7	34.1	36.0
Belarus	1999	9.3	14.2	11.5	–4.9	1.3[19]	1997	8.8	191.9	8.7[20]	11.5	673.9	68.7	27.5	154.5
Belgium	2000	10.9	10.1	4.8	0.8	1.5	1994	13.4	275.0	21.7	29.2	383.4	92.5	42.6	68.5
Belize	2000	32.3	4.8	26.0	27.5	4.1	1995	23.5	37.7	22.1	6.9	118.9	47.5	16.1	67.3
Benin	2000	44.8	14.5	90.8	30.3	6.3	...	...	...	...	...	...	...	...	...
Bermuda	1999	13.2	7.1	3.2[21]	6.1	1.8	1990	...	181.5	...	...	344.4	25.2	...	38.6
Bhutan	2001	35.2	9.0	56.0	26.2	5.2	...	...	...	...	...	...	...	...	...
Bolivia	2000	31.9	23.3	62.0[23]	23.3	3.7	...	...	...	...	...	...	...	...	...
Bosnia and Herzegovina	2000	12.9	7.9	25.2	5.0	1.7	1989	9.9	122.6[24]	12.6	11.9	344.1	29.0	29.2	47.1
Botswana	2001	28.8	24.8	63.2	4.0	3.7	...	...	...	...	...	...	...	...	...
Brazil	2000	18.8	9.4	38.0	9.4	2.1	1996	33.5	65.9	23.3[20]	9[13]	159.1	56.4	25.9	75.9
Brunei	1999	22.3	2.8	6.0	19.5	2.7	...	...	...	...	...	...	...	...	...
Bulgaria	1999	8.8	13.6	14.6	–4.8	1.2	1998	9.4	192.9	25.4	9.7	954.4	67.6	38.8	60.7
Burkina Faso	2000	45.3	17.0	108.5	28.3	6.4	...	...	...	...	...	...	...	...	...
Burundi	2000	40.5	16.4	71.5	24.1	6.3	...	...	...	...	...	...	...	...	...
Cambodia	2001	35.9	10.7	76.0	25.2	5.0	...	...	...	...	...	...	...	...	...
Cameroon	2000	36.6	11.9	70.9	24.7	4.9	...	...	...	...	...	...	...	...	...
Canada	2000	11.3	7.4	5.1	3.9	1.6	1997	8.3	195.6	23.7	21.9	264.8	66.8	25.4	43.5
Cape Verde	2000	29.7	7.4	54.6	22.3	4.2	...	...	...	...	...	...	...	...	...
Central African Republic	2000	37.5	18.4	106.7	19.1	5.0	...	...	...	...	...	...	...	...	...
Chad	2000	48.8	15.7	96.7	33.1	5.7	...	...	...	...	...	...	...	...	...
Chile	2000	17.2	5.5	9.6	11.7	2.2	1994	14.2	111.9	16.5	8.6	149.5	61.2	37.2	63.6
China	2001	14.9	7.0	38.0	7.9	1.8	1994[26]	15.2	117.7	17.2[20]	4.4	206.4	125.3	25.3	56.6
Colombia	2000	22.9	5.7	24.7	17.2	2.7	1994	13.7	58.3	15.2	4.6	125.3	34.3	15.7	119.5
Comoros	2000	40.0	9.6	86.3	30.4	5.4	...	...	...	...	...	...	...	...	...
Congo, Dem. Rep. of the	2000	46.4	15.4	101.6	31.0	6.9	...	...	...	...	...	...	...	...	...
Congo, Rep. of the	2000	38.6	16.4	101.6	22.2	5.1	...	...	...	...	...	...	...	...	...
Costa Rica	1999	21.7	4.2	11.8	17.5	2.6	1994	9.7	80.0	12.6	8.5	126.6	40.6	24.6	49.7
Côte d'Ivoire	2000	40.8	16.6	95.1	24.2	5.8	...	...	...	...	...	...	...	...	...
Croatia	1999	9.9	11.4	7.4	–1.5	1.9[10]	1996	8.8	227.2	25.4[20]	8.0	547.4	41.4	52.1	70.7
Cuba	2000	12.7	7.3	7.5	5.4	1.6	1995	12.8	133	25.9	11.1	305.5	64.1	24.9	84.6
Cyprus	1999	12.8	7.6	8.1[10]	5.2	2.0	...	...	...	...	...	...	...	...	...
Czech Republic	1999	8.7	10.7	4.6	–2.0	1.1	1998	2.6	272.1	15.0	11.6	586.7	39.9	40.4	68.1
Denmark	2000	12.6	10.9	5.0	1.7	1.7	1996	10.1	289.2	16.5	15.3	428.4	108.1	46.1	64.1

diseases not classifiable under the main groups; maternal deaths (for which data *are* provided, however, in the "Health services" table); diseases of the skin and musculoskeletal systems; congenital and perinatal conditions; and general senility and other ill-defined (ill-diagnosed) conditions, a kind of "other" category.

Expectation of life is probably the most accurate single measure of the quality of life in a given society. It summarizes in a single number all of the natural and social stresses that operate upon individuals in that society. The number may range from as few as 40 years of life in the least developed countries to as much as 80 years for women in the most developed nations. The lost potential in the years separating those two numbers is prodigious, regardless of how the loss arises—wars and civil violence, poor public health services, or poor individual health practice in matters of nutrition, exercise, stress management, and so on.

Data on marriages and marriage rates probably are less meaningful in terms of international comparisons than some of the measures mentioned above because the number, timing, and kinds of social relationships that substitute for marriage depend on many kinds of social variables—income, degree of social control, heterogeneity of the society (race, class, language communities), or level of development of civil administration (if one must travel for a day or more to obtain a legal civil ceremony, one may forgo it). Nevertheless, the data for a single country say specific things about local practice in terms of the age at which a man or woman typically marries, and the overall rate will at least define the number of legal civil marriages, though it cannot say anything about other, less formal arrangements (here the figure for the legitimacy rate for children in the next section may identify some of the societies in which economics or social constraints may operate to limit the number of marriages that are actually confirmed on civil registers). The available data usually include both first marriages and remarriages after annulment, divorce, widowhood, or the like.

The data for families provide information about the average size of a family unit (individuals related by blood or civil register) and the average number of children under a specified age (set here at 15 to provide a consistent measure of social minority internationally, though legal minority depends on the laws of each country). When well-defined family data are not collected as part of a country's national census or vital statistics surveys, data for households have been substituted on the assumption that most households worldwide represent families in some conventional sense. But increasing numbers of households worldwide are composed of unrelated individuals (unmarried heterosexual couples, aged [or younger] groups sharing limited [often fixed] incomes for reasons of economy, or homosexual couples). Such arrangements do not yet represent great numbers overall. Increasing numbers of census programs, however, even in developing countries, are making more adequate provision for distinguishing these nontraditional, often nonfamily households.

Internet resources for further information:

- World Health Organization (World) http://www.who.ch
- Pan American Health Organization (the Americas) http://www.paho.org
- National Center for Health Statistics (U.S.) http://www.cdc.gov/nchs
- U.S. Census Bureau: International Data Base (World) http://www.census.gov/ipc/www/idbprint.html

expectation of life at birth (latest year)		nuptiality, family, and family planning																country
		marriages			age at marriage (latest)						families (F), households (H) (latest)							
		year	total number	rate per 1,000 population	groom (percent)			bride (percent)			families (households)		children		induced abortions		
male	female				19 and under	20–29	30 and over	19 and under	20–29	30 and over	total ('000)	size	number under age 15	percent legitimate	number	ratio per 100 live births	
46.6	45.1	...	...	...	...	...	...	...	...	...	H 2,110	H 6.2	H 2.8[1]	...	...	...	Afghanistan
68.8	74.9	1997	25,260	6.8	1.5[2]	80.4[2]	18.1[2]	24.0[2]	71.4[2]	4.6[2]	F 675	F 3.9	F 1.6	...	...	...	Albania
68.3	71.0	1996	156,870	5.6	0.7[3]	67.1[3]	32.2[3]	29.8[3]	61.4[3]	8.8[3]	H 4,102	H 7.1	H 3.0	...	...	...	Algeria
70.7	79.8	1993	325	6.1	...	...	...	...	...	...	H 7	H 7.0	H 2.7	72.0	...	...	American Samoa
80.6	86.6	1998	208	3.2	...	...	...	...	...	...	...	...	...	...	...	...	Andorra
37.1	39.6	...	...	...	...	...	...	...	...	...	...	H 5.0	...	...	...	...	Angola
68.2	72.8	1998	1,418	22.1	1.0[11]	37.4[12]	61.6	3.7[11]	52.4[12]	43.9	H 18	H 3.2	H 1.2	23.4	...	...	Antigua and Barbuda
71.7	78.6	1996	148,721	4.2	5.6	71.5	22.9	26.0	58.6	15.4	H 10,097	H 3.2	H 1.0	67.5	...	...	Argentina
62.0	71.0	1995	14,200	4.2	5.0[13]	73.8[13]	21.2[13]	39.3[13]	49.9[13]	10.8[13]	H 559	H 4.5	H 1.8	86.0	30,571	59.8	Armenia
75.0	81.9	1998	564	6.1	...	...	...	...	...	...	H 19	H 3.6	...	57.5	...	...	Aruba
76.0	81.0	1996	109,386	6.0	0.7	54.5	44.8	3.6	63.6	32.8	H 6,636	H 2.6	H 0.6	75.0	...	...	Australia
75.1	80.9	1998	39,143	4.8	1.1[15]	49.9[15]	49.0[15]	4.2[15]	62.0[15]	33.8[15]	H 3,058	H 2.6	H 0.5	69.5	...	...	Austria
68.0	75.0	1994	47,147	6.3	1.2[16]	80.4[16]	18.4[16]	24.8[16]	63.9[16]	11.3[16]	H 1,381	H 5.2	H 1.7	94.8	42,134	23.2	Azerbaijan
68.3	73.9	1996	2,628	9.3	...	14.0	86.0	—	26.1	73.9	H 74	H 3.9	...	45.7	...	...	Bahamas, The
70.6	75.5	1998	3,677	5.7	2.6[17]	65.4[17]	32.0[17]	28.0[17]	54.6[17]	17.4[17]	H 67	H 6.5	H 2.2	100.0	...	...	Bahrain
59.0	60.0	1997	1,181,000	9.7	...	...	...	...	...	...	H 19,980	H 5.6	...	...	...	...	Bangladesh
70.4	75.6	1995	3,564	13.5	0.1[18]	40.2[18]	59.7[18]	1.4[18]	53.6[18]	44.9[18]	H 67	H 3.5	H 1.5	26.9	723	19.6	Barbados
62.2	73.9	1997	69,735	6.8	5.4[15]	69.8[15]	24.8[15]	27.1[15]	53.1[15]	19.8[15]	H 2,796	H 3.6	H 0.8	82.2	174,098	181.7	Belarus
74.5	81.3	1996	50,601	5.0	0.6[17]	59.5[17]	39.9[17]	4.0[17]	66.3[17]	29.7[17]	F 3,613	F 2.7	F 0.5	88.7	...	...	Belgium
68.7	73.3	1997	1,543	6.6	6.3[17]	58.4[17]	35.3[17]	23.4[17]	51.0[17]	25.6[17]	H 42	H 5.3	H 2.2	40.3	990	15.1	Belize
49.2	51.2	...	...	...	...	...	...	...	...	...	...	H 5.9	...	...	...	...	Benin
74.9	78.9	1994	944	15.4	0.2[22]	37.4[22]	62.4[22]	1.5[22]	49.4[22]	49.1[22]	H 24	H 2.5	H 0.5	61.7	92	11.0	Bermuda
61.0	64.0	...	...	...	...	...	...	...	...	...	...	H 5.4	...	...	...	...	Bhutan
66.3	61.2	...	...	...	...	...	...	...	...	...	H 1,655	H 3.8	H 1.6	80.9	...	...	Bolivia
68.8	74.4	1991	27,923	6.0	2.3	74.2	23.5	28.6	58.9	12.5	H 1,203	H 3.4	H 1.1	92.6	...	...	Bosnia and Herzegovina
36.8	37.5	1986	1,638	1.5	—	33.0	67.0	5.0	69.2	25.8	H 125	H 5.7	H 2.0	28.8	17	0.1	Botswana
58.5	67.6	1995	...	4.7	7.0[13]	68.7[13]	24.3[13]	31.2[13]	54.3[13]	14.5[13]	F 39,768	F 3.9	1.2	...	...	...	Brazil
74.0	76.0	1995	1,793	6.1	10.6[25]	50.1[25]	39.3[25]	11.4[25]	54.7[25]	33.9[25]	H 45	H 5.8	H 2.0	99.6	...	...	Brunei
67.5	74.6	1996	...	4.3	3.4[17]	73.1[17]	23.5[17]	26.9[17]	60.4[17]	12.7[17]	H 2,795	H 3.0	...	74.3	97,023	134.8	Bulgaria
46.3	47.2	...	...	...	...	...	...	...	...	...	...	H 6.2	...	...	...	...	Burkina Faso
45.2	47.2	...	...	...	...	...	...	...	...	...	...	H 5.0	...	...	...	...	Burundi
54.0	59.0	...	...	...	...	...	...	...	...	...	...	H 5.6	...	...	...	...	Cambodia
54.0	55.6	...	...	...	...	...	...	...	...	...	...	H 5.7	...	...	...	...	Cameroon
76.0	83.0	1995	160,256	5.4	0.9	49.3	49.8	3.6	57.9	38.5	H 11,580	H 2.5	H 0.6	83.8	70,549	18.7	Canada
65.6	72.3	1994	1,200	3.2	...	...	...	...	...	...	F 59	F 5.1	...	28.9	...	...	Cape Verde
42.3	45.8	...	...	...	...	...	...	...	...	...	...	H 5.9	...	...	...	...	Central African Republic
48.5	52.6	...	...	...	...	...	...	...	...	...	...	H 5.0	...	...	...	...	Chad
72.4	79.2	1996	83,547	5.8	4.7	67.5	27.8	18.6	62.2	19.2	H 3,537	H 3.8	...	61.9	67	—	Chile
69.0	73.0	1994	9,290,027	7.8	...	...	...	...	...	...	H 278.6[27]	H 4.1	H 1.1	...	10,500,000	47.7	China
66.4	74.3	...	...	...	...	...	...	...	...	...	F 4,772	F 5.3	F 2.5	75.2	...	...	Colombia
57.8	62.2	...	...	...	...	...	...	...	...	...	...	H 5.6	...	...	...	...	Comoros
47.6	50.8	...	...	...	...	...	...	...	...	...	...	H 2.3	...	...	...	...	Congo, Dem. Rep. of the
44.5	50.5	...	...	...	...	...	...	...	...	...	H 326	H 4.7	H 2.0	...	...	...	Congo, Rep. of the
74.2	79.9	1997	22,422	6.5	7.1[17]	60.9[17]	32.0[17]	26.3[17]	52.0[17]	94.7[17]	H 772	H 4.1	...	50.3	...	...	Costa Rica
43.7	46.6	...	...	...	...	...	...	...	...	...	...	H 8.0	...	...	...	...	Côte d'Ivoire
70.0	77.5	1997	24,517	5.3	1.2[15]	65.2[15]	33.6[15]	13.9[15]	66.8[15]	19.3[15]	H 1,544	H 3.1	H 0.6	92.7	12,339	22.9	Croatia
73.8	78.5	1997	60,220	5.4	5.2[17]	51.8[17]	43.0[17]	18.0[17]	49.4[17]	32.6[17]	F 2,860	F 3.7	H 1.6	...	83,963	57.1	Cuba
75.3	80.1	1996	5,761	7.8	0.8	54.6	44.6	8.1	64.2	27.7	H 160	H 3.5	H 1.1	99.6	...	...	Cyprus
71.1	78.2	1997	57,086	5.6	3.7[15]	66.5[15]	29.8[15]	15.0[15]	65.8[15]	19.2[15]	H 3,557	H 2.9	...	79.4	48,086	53.2	Czech Republic
74.3	79.1	1997	34,108	6.5	0.4[17]	36.2[17]	63.4[17]	1.4[17]	47.9[17]	50.7[17]	H 2,027	H 2.2	...	53.5	17,720	53.2	Denmark

Vital statistics, marriage, family (continued)

country	vital rates						causes of death (rate per 100,000 population)								
	year	birth rate per 1,000 population	death rate per 1,000 population	infant mortality rate per 1,000 live births	rate of natural increase per 1,000 population	total fertility rate	year	infectious and parasitic diseases	malignant neoplasms (cancers)	endocrine and metabolic disorders	diseases of the nervous system	diseases of the circulatory system	diseases of the respiratory system	diseases of the digestive system	accidents, poisoning, and violence
Djibouti	2000	41.0	14.9	103.3	26.1	5.8	…	…	…	…	…	…	…	…	…
Dominica	2000	18.3	7.3	17.1	11.0	2.0	1994	23.1	125.0	59.8	9.5	237.8	38.0	21.7	28.5
Dominican Republic	2000	25.2	4.7	35.9	20.5	3.0	1985[28]	85	45	15[5]	7[14]	165	41	25	*56*
East Timor[29]	…	…	…	…	…	…	…	…	…	…	…	…	…	…	…
Ecuador	2000[1]	26.5	5.5	35.1	21.0	3.2	1995	29.7	50.8	17.5	7.2	80.8	46.0	23.1	65.1
Egypt	2000	25.4	7.8	62.3	17.6	3.2	1992	49.0	22.4	17.3	9.5	313.5	83.4	33.5	28.8
El Salvador	2000	29.0	6.3	29.2	22.7	3.4	1994[30]	42	52	9[5]	2[14]	124	36	14	135
Equatorial Guinea	2000	38.1	13.4	94.8	24.7	4.9	…	…	…	…	…	…	…	…	…
Eritrea	2000	42.7	12.3	76.7	30.4	5.9	…	…	…	…	…	…	…	…	…
Estonia	2000	9.6	13.5	8.4	–3.9	1.2	1995	13.7	221.1	8.2	13.0	771.9	42.5	36.0	198.8
Ethiopia	2000	45.1	17.6	101.3	27.5	7.1	…	…	…	…	…	…	…	…	…
Faroe Islands	2000	13.6	8.7	6.9	22.3	2.3	1992	4.3	191.3	14.9[5]	—	352.8	59.5	14.9	57.4
Fiji	2000	23.5	5.8	14.5	17.7	2.9	…	…	…	…	…	…	…	…	…
Finland	1999	11.2	9.5	4.2	1.7	1.7	1995	7.7	196.6	12.5	20.1	459.7	73.6	38.0	85.8
France	2000	12.3	9.1	4.8	3.2	1.7	1994	12.8	207.7	27.8	20.7	288.2	63.9	43.9	76.1
French Guiana	2000	22.4	4.8	14.0	17.6	3.2	1989	61.7	58.1	16.3	10.9	114.3	20.9	13.6	98.0
French Polynesia	2001	20.7	4.8	9.0	15.9	2.5	1994–95	14.0	104.0	14.0	10.0	123.0	47.0	17.0	52.0
Gabon	2001	27.4	17.2	94.9	10.2	3.7	…	…	…	…	…	…	…	…	…
Gambia, The	2000	42.3	13.2	79.3	29.1	5.8	…	…	…	…	…	…	…	…	…
Gaza Strip	2000	43.1	4.3	26.0	38.8	6.6	…	…	…	…	…	…	…	…	…
Georgia	2000	10.9	14.5	52.9	–3.6	1.4	1990	12.7	100.8	14.6	4.3	548.4	43.3	8.5	56.1
Germany	2000	9.4	10.5	4.8	–1.1	1.4	1995	7.4	260.7	34.5	18.0	525.7	66.0	51.2	48.2
Ghana	2001	29.0	10.3	56.5	18.7	3.8	…	…	…	…	…	…	…	…	…
Greece	2000	11.7	10.5	6.7[23]	1.2	1.3	1998	6.7	213.4	8.3	9.4	492.4	54.9	22.1	42.8
Greenland	2000	16.9	7.6	18.3	9.3	2.4	1995	29.5	198.7	3.9	1.8	214.4	9.6	5.7	206.5
Grenada	2000	23.2	8.0	14.6	15.2	3.2	1987	9.6	82.8	57.3	7.4	264.3	45.6	38.2	…
Guadeloupe	2000	17.3	6.0	9.8	11.3	1.9	1996	23.8	134.8	26.2	…	183.7	32.1	31.4	68.1
Guam	2001	27.0	4.8	10.0	22.2	4.0	1994	1.4	60.0	26.5[5]	6.8	141.8	27.9	1.4	64.1
Guatemala	2000	35.1	6.9	47.0	28.2	4.7	…	…	…	…	…	…	…	…	…
Guernsey	2000	10.5	9.3	5.1	1.2	1.3	1996	5.3	282.3	15.9	15.9	441.1	150.0	49.4	24.7
Guinea	2001	39.8	17.5	120.0	22.3	5.4	…	…	…	…	…	…	…	…	…
Guinea-Bissau	2000	39.6	15.6	112.3	24.0	5.3	…	…	…	…	…	…	…	…	…
Guyana	2000	17.9	8.4	39.1	9.5	2.1	1994	38.9	33.5	45.7	10.6	212.8	44.5	27.6	59.0
Haiti	2000	32.0	15.1	97.1	16.9	4.5	…	…	…	…	…	…	…	…	…
Honduras	2000	32.7	5.3	31.3	27.4	4.3	…	…	…	…	…	…	…	…	…
Hong Kong	2000	8.1	5.1	2.9	3.0	1.3	1998	14.4	160.5	7.4	3.9	126.7	99.6	21.0	21.2
Hungary	1999	9.4	14.2	8.4	–4.8	1.3	1995	7.9	322.0	20.1	11.5	721.4	63.0	115.6	111.5
Iceland	1999	14.8	6.9	2.4	7.9	2.0	1995	6.7	176.4	3.7	19.5	308.6	82.0	3.0	56.6
India	2000	24.8	8.9	64.9	15.9	3.1	…	…	…	…	…	…	…	…	…
Indonesia[29]	2001	20.8	7.2	42.0	13.6	2.4	…	…	…	…	…	…	…	…	…
Iran	2000	18.3	5.5	30.0	12.8	2.2	1990[34]	*34*	*61*	*12*[20]	*26*	*304*	*48*	*24*	*108*
Iraq	2000	35.0	6.4	62.5	28.6	4.9	…	…	…	…	…	…	…	…	…
Ireland	2000	14.5	8.1	5.6	6.4	1.9	1997	4.8	205.6	10.8[5]	0.2[14]	369.9	153.4	9.4	38.4
Isle of Man	1999	12.3	13.5	3.7[35]	–1.2	1.6	1998	2.8	298.4	11.1	31.8	504.3	225.2	38.7	52.5
Israel	2000	21.7	6.0	5.1	15.7	3.0	1995	10.4	148.9	23.4	11.5	278.4	26.5	23.1	35.8
Italy	2000	9.1	10.0	5.9	–0.9	1.2	1995	13.3	258.2	34.7	20.3	424.3	59.1	47.0	49.0
Jamaica	2000	20.0	5.1	14.6	14.9	2.8[36]	1991	8.1	84.1	51.3	7.5	189.5	30.2	14.1	8.4
Japan	1999	9.3	7.8	3.4	1.5	1.4	1997	14.6	220.4	12.4	7.0	237.7	98.0	30.0	52.4
Jersey	2000	11.7	9.3	5.7	2.4	1.6	…	…	…	…	…	…	…	…	…
Jordan	2000	26.2	2.6	21.1	23.6	3.4	…	…	…	…	…	…	…	…	…
Kazakhstan	2001	16.5	10.1	43.0	6.4	2.0	1996	45.7	133.0	10.9	1.4	436.2	71.0	32.9	101.1
Kenya	2000	29.4	14.1	68.7	15.3	3.7	…	…	…	…	…	…	…	…	…
Kiribati	2000	33.1	8.4	56.8[23]	24.7	4.4[23]	…	…	…	…	…	…	…	…	…
Korea, North	2000	20.4	6.9	24.3	13.5	2.3	…	…	…	…	…	…	…	…	…
Korea, South	1999	15.3	5.8	10.0	9.5	1.7	1997	10.8	115.4	20.2	5.1	121.5	24.4	34.4	70.6
Kuwait	2000	22.0	2.4	11.5	19.6	3.3	1997	5.4	22.7	10.6	3.1	84.6	11.0	4.7	34.8
Kyrgyzstan	2001	20.6	7.3	39.0	13.3	2.5	1996	12.6	25.7	8.3	1.5	278.5	75.0	9.8	21.4
Laos	2001	36.5	13.1	91.0	23.4	5.0	…	…	…	…	…	…	…	…	…
Latvia	1999	8.0	13.5	11.4	–5.5	1.2	1998	19.5	231.8	12.2[20]	12.7	775.6	34.6	42.2	161.8
Lebanon	2000	20.3	6.4	29.3	13.9	2.1	…	…	…	…	…	…	…	…	…
Lesotho	2000	31.7	14.6	83.0	17.1	4.2	…	…	…	…	…	…	…	…	…
Liberia	2000	47.2	16.6	134.6	30.6	6.4	…	…	…	…	…	…	…	…	…
Libya	2000	27.7	3.5	30.1	24.2	3.7	…	…	…	…	…	…	…	…	…
Liechtenstein	2000	11.8	6.7	5.7	5.1	1.5	1997	23.0[13]	199.7	…	6.6[13]	613.9	29.0	22.6	146.9
Lithuania	2000	9.2	10.5	8.5	–1.3	1.4	1995	16.4	203.2	8.0	10.3	654.2	40.5	32.1	176.0
Luxembourg	2000	12.5	8.9	4.8	3.6	1.7	1995	4.6	248.5	21.7	14.9	375.1	61.5	40.2	59.0
Macau	2001	9.4	4.5	8.0	4.9	1.1	1998	10.0	77.8	3.9	1.7	117.1	39.3	11.1	23.9
Macedonia	2000	13.7	7.7	13.4	6.0	1.8	1997	17.6	138.3	24.1[5]	28.0	462.8	39.5	15.9	32.4
Madagascar	2000	42.9	12.7	87.0	30.2	5.8	…	…	…	…	…	…	…	…	…
Malawi	2000	38.5	22.4	122.3	16.1	6.3	…	…	…	…	…	…	…	…	…
Malaysia	2001	23.5	4.4	7.9	19.1	3.1[23]	1997	15.2	19.8	3.8	1.1	37.2	8.7	2.1	13.2
Maldives	2001	36.3	6.3	40.0	30.0	5.5	…	…	…	…	…	…	…	—	…
Mali	2000	49.2	19.1	123.3	30.1	6.9	…	…	…	…	…	…	…	…	…
Malta	2000	12.8	7.7	5.9	5.1	1.9	1997	5.1	281.9	25.1	12.8	354.1	70.9	26.1	28.5
Marshall Islands	2000	41.8	4.9	41.0	36.9	6.6	1993[37]	169.9	68.4	…	—	155.1	105.1	63.3	36.7
Martinique	2000	16.1	6.4	8.0	9.7	1.8	1996	21.9	150.1	27.7	…	206.6	36.3	27.2	47.2
Mauritania	2000	43.4	14.0	78.1	29.4	6.3	…	…	…	…	…	…	…	…	…
Mauritius	2000	16.7	6.8	17.7	9.9	2.0	1996	12.1	56.8	24.9	0.8	291.2	34.9	21.7	46.2
Mayotte	2000	45.3	9.1	71.3	36.2	6.3	…	…	…	…	…	…	…	…	…
Mexico	2000	23.2	5.1	26.2	18.1	2.7	1995	22.0	52.9	46.9	6.7	106.8	47.1	42.1	62.4
Micronesia	2000	27.1	6.0	33.5	21.1	3.8	…	…	…	…	…	…	…	…	…
Moldova	2000	12.9	12.6	43.3	0.3	1.6	1995	14.6	133.3	10.7	11.8	559.4	76.3	114.7	113.7
Monaco	2000	9.9	13.1	5.9	–3.2	1.8	…	…	…	…	…	…	…	…	…
Mongolia	2001	22.4	7.5	61.0	14.9	2.4	1994[38]	33	118	3	14	200	110	55	64
Morocco	2001	24.2	5.9	48.1	18.3	3.0	1992	10.2	14.0	12.2	4.9	35.5	9.5	7.9	19.2

expectation of life at birth (latest year)		nuptiality, family, and family planning															country
		marriages			age at marriage (latest)						families (F), households (H) (latest)						
		year	total number	rate per 1,000 population	groom (percent)			bride (percent)			families (households)		children		induced abortions		
male	female				19 and under	20–29	30 and over	19 and under	20–29	30 and over	total ('000)	size	number under age 15	percent legitimate	number	ratio per 100 live births	
49.0	52.7	...	...	...	...	...	...	...	...	...	...	H 5.6	...	96.8	...	...	Djibouti
70.5	76.3	1996	230	3.1	—	37.0	63.0	2.7	56.2	41.1	H 19	H 3.6	H 2.2	24.1	...	...	Dominica
71.1	75.4	1994	14,883	2.0	...	...	...	...	...	...	H 1,804	H 3.9	...	32.8	562	0.5	Dominican Republic
...	...	...	...	...	...	...	...	...	...	...	... ...	...	... ...	...	...	...	East Timor[29]
68.3	74.0	1996	72,094	6.2	12.6	61.7	25.7	32.6	51.4	16.0	...	H 4.1	...	67.9	...	...	Ecuador
61.3	65.5	1994	451,817	3.2	3.4	58.7	37.9	11.2	77.1	11.7	H 9,733	H 4.9	H 2.1	100.0	...	...	Egypt
66.1	73.5	1994	27,761	5.1	6.6[25]	54.8[25]	38.6[25]	21.5[25]	51.4[25]	27.1[25]	H 1,092	H 4.8	...	29.4	...	...	El Salvador
51.5	55.7	...	...	...	...	...	...	...	...	...	...	H 4.5	...	...	...	...	Equatorial Guinea
53.4	58.3	1992	68	...	...	...	...	...	...	...	...	[31, 32]	...	...	...	...	Eritrea
65.4	76.1	1998	5,430	3.7	3.2[15]	56.4[15]	40.4[15]	13.9[15]	53.9[15]	32.2[15]	H 427	H 3.1	H 0.8	47.8	16,887	127.1	Estonia
44.4	45.9	...	...	...	...	...	...	...	...	...	...	H 4.5[31, 32]	...	...	...	...	Ethiopia
75.0	81.9	1990	203	4.3	...	...	...	...	...	...	F 14	F 3.0	F 0.9	57.5	26	3.3	Faroe Islands
65.5	70.5	1995	7,903	9.9	...	...	...	...	...	...	F 97	F 6.0	F 2.5	82.7	...	...	Fiji
73.7	81.0	1998	24,023	4.7	1.0[15]	47.1[15]	51.9[15]	3.5[15]	55.9[15]	40.6[15]	H 2,270	H 2.2	...	61.3	10,437	17.2	Finland
74.9	82.9	1997	283,984	4.8	0.2[17]	51.9[17]	47.9[17]	1.4[17]	63.2[17]	35.4[17]	H 20,899	H 2.6	H 1.0	63.9	157,886	22.2	France
72.8	79.6	1992	716	5.3	...	...	...	...	...	...	H 33	H 3.4	H 1.2	20.3	388	16.8	French Guiana
70.0	75.0	1996	1,200	5.7	...	...	...	...	...	...	H 40	H 4.3	H 1.7	40.5	...	...	French Polynesia
48.5	50.8	...	...	...	...	...	...	...	...	...	H 136	H 4.0	...	...	...	...	Gabon
50.9	54.7	...	...	...	...	...	...	...	...	...	...	H 8.3	...	...	...	...	Gambia, The
69.6	72.1	...	...	...	...	...	...	...	...	...	...	...	...	...	...	...	Gaza Strip
60.9	68.2	1996	19,253	3.7	9.1	59.4	31.5	32.7	51.2	16.1	H 1,244	H 4.1	H 1.1	82.3	43,549	77.3	Georgia
74.3	80.8	1997	422,319	5.1	0.7[15]	44.6[15]	54.7[15]	3.7[15]	56.3[15]	40.0[15]	H 37,457	H 2.2	H 0.3	82.0	97,937	12.8	Germany
55.9	58.7	...	...	...	...	...	...	...	...	...	H 2,355	H 4.9	H 2.2	...	...	...	Ghana
75.9	81.2	1998	55,489	5.3	0.9[17]	53.6[17]	45.5[17]	9.6[17]	68.9[17]	21.5[17]	H 2,990	H 3.3	H 0.7	96.7	12,289	12.1	Greece
64.5	71.7	1996	208	3.7	1.1[2]	44.6[2]	54.3[2]	2.7[2]	59.6[2]	37.7[2]	F 31	F 1.8	F 0.5	29.2	962	80.7	Greenland
62.7	66.3	1991	...	4.3	...	...	...	...	...	...	H 24	H 3.7	H 2.2	18.1	...	...	Grenada
73.8	80.3	1997	1,936	4.7	0.5[2]	51.4[2]	48.0[2]	7.2[2]	61.4[2]	31.4[2]	H 112	H 3.4	H 0.9	37.0	561	8.7	Guadeloupe
72.0	77.0	1995	1,507	10.1	3.0[25]	55.5[25]	41.5[25]	9.2[25]	59.3[25]	31.5[25]	H 31	H 4.0	H 1.3	50.1	...	...	Guam
63.5	69.0	1997	51,526	4.9	18.3	56.1	25.6	41.1	40.8	18.1	H 1,806	H 5.2	...	34.8	...	...	Guatemala
76.7	82.8	1996	340	5.8	...	...	...	...	...	...	H 21	H 2.6	H 0.5	73.2	...	...	Guernsey
43.5	48.4	...	...	...	...	...	...	...	...	...	H 1,064	H 4.1	...	...	...	...	Guinea
46.8	51.4	...	...	...	...	...	...	...	...	...	H 124	H 6.9	H 2.8	11.3	...	...	Guinea-Bissau
61.1	67.2	...	...	...	...	...	...	...	...	...	H 150	H 5.1	H 2.1	...	...	...	Guyana
47.5	51.1	...	...	...	...	...	...	...	...	...	H 1,147	H 4.4	H 1.8	...	...	...	Haiti
67.9	72.1	...	...	...	...	...	...	...	...	...	H 463	H 5.7	H 2.8	...	...	...	Honduras
77.0	82.2	1999	31,300	4.6	0.9[15]	42.7[15]	56.4[15]	3.0[15]	63.5[15]	33.5[15]	H 1,840	H 3.3	...	94.5	17,600	25.2	Hong Kong
66.3	75.1	1998	45,500	4.5	3.7[15]	69.1[15]	27.2[15]	17.5[15]	64.8[15]	17.7[15]	F 3,058	F 2.9	F 0.8	72.0	76,600	72.8	Hungary
77.5	81.4	1998	1,238	5.6	0.1[15]	40.7[15]	59.2[15]	1.2[15]	55.6[15]	43.2[15]	H 85	H 2.9	H 1.3	37.4	858	19.8	Iceland
61.9	63.1	...	...	...	...	...	...	...	...	...	H 151,033	H 5.6	H 2.4	...	581,215	...	India
65.0	69.0	1992–93[33]	1,423,774	7.6	...	...	...	...	...	...	H 39,695	H 4.5	H 1.8	...	...	...	Indonesia[29]
68.3	71.5	1996	479,263	7.8	...	...	...	...	...	...	H 9,759	H 4.8	H 2.2	...	...	...	Iran
65.5	67.6	1992	144,055	7.8	...	...	...	...	...	...	H 1,873	H 8.9	H 4.1	...	...	...	Iraq
74.1	79.7	1999	18,526	4.9	0.7[13]	62.2[13]	37.1[13]	1.6[13]	74.7[13]	23.7[13]	H 541	H 3.3	H 1.3	65.5	...	...	Ireland
73.9	80.8	1998	435	6.0	0.2	39.5	60.3	1.6	45.1	53.3	H 29,377	H 2.4	...	68.1	...	...	Isle of Man
76.6	80.5	1997	32,510	5.6	3.5[13]	74.0[13]	22.5[13]	21.2[13]	68.3[13]	10.5[13]	H 1,355	H 3.7	H 1.1	98.5	16,903	14.7	Israel
75.9	82.4	1997	275,381	4.8	0.6[17]	56.2[17]	43.2[17]	4.8[17]	71.5[17]	23.7[17]	F 19,766	F 2.6	F 0.5	90.2	134,137	25.5	Italy
73.3	77.3	1996	18,708	7.4	...	...	...	...	...	...	H 554	H 4.2	H 1.4	14.9	...	...	Jamaica
77.5	84.0	1996	795,000	6.3	1.2	61.6	37.2	2.6	77.0	20.4	H 43,447	H 2.8	...	99.0	338,867	28.1	Japan
76.1	81.1	1994	542	6.4	...	...	...	...	...	...	H 29	H 2.6	H 0.4	88.1	296	28.0	Jersey
74.9	79.9	1996	102,558	6.4	4.4[17]	70.0[17]	25.6[17]	37.3[17]	54.7[17]	8.0[17]	H 11,891	H 6.1	H 3.4	...	...	...	Jordan
59.0	71.0	1996	102,558	6.4	6.0	71.5	22.5	27.9	56.5	15.6	H 3,824	H 4.0	H 1.4	86.6	193,462	76.4	Kazakhstan
47.0	49.0	...	...	...	...	...	...	...	...	...	H 1,938	H 3.4	H 2.7	...	...	...	Kenya
56.5	62.4	...	...	...	...	...	...	...	...	...	H 11	H 6.6	H 2.5	...	...	...	Kiribati
67.8	73.9	...	...	...	...	...	...	...	...	...	H 4,054	H 4.8	H 1.7	...	...	...	Korea, North
70.5	78.4	1995	320,395	7.1	0.3	67.7	32.0	1.7	86.1	12.2	H 12,961	H 3.7	H 1.0	99.5	...	...	Korea, South
75.3	76.9	1997	9,612	5.3	6.1[25]	72.2[25]	21.7[25]	35.9[25]	53.3[25]	10.8[25]	H 246	H 3.9	H 1.6	100.0	...	...	Kuwait
64.0	72.0	1995	26,866	6.0	5.4	79.0	15.6	38.1	52.0	9.9	H 856	H 4.2	H 1.9	83.2	27,111	23.1	Kyrgyzstan
53.0	55.0	...	...	...	...	...	...	...	...	...	...	H 6.0	...	...	...	...	Laos
64.9	76.2	1998	9,641	3.9	—	61.7	38.3	—	69.0	31.0	H 732	H 2.7	H 0.8	62.9	24,227	122.5	Latvia
68.9	73.7	...	...	...	...	...	...	...	...	...	H 405	H 5.3	H 2.2	...	...	...	Lebanon
49.8	51.8	...	...	...	...	...	...	...	...	...	H 330	H 4.8	H 2.0	...	...	...	Lesotho
49.6	52.5	...	...	...	...	...	...	...	...	...	H 474	H 5.0	...	...	...	...	Liberia
73.3	77.7	...	...	...	...	...	...	...	...	...	F 383	F 5.4	F 2.9	...	...	...	Libya
75.2	82.5	1998	423	13.2	—	54.5	44.5	0.0	66.3	29.2	H 8	H 3.0	H 0.7	86.0	...	...	Liechtenstein
67.6	77.9	1997	18,769	5.0	7.1[15]	68.5[15]	24.4[15]	23.0[15]	57.8[15]	19.2[15]	H 1,000	H 2.9	H 0.8	82.0	27,829	71.0	Lithuania
73.8	80.6	1997	2,007	4.8	0.9[15]	49.1[15]	50.0[15]	4.0[15]	61.6[15]	34.4[15]	H 145	H 2.6	H 0.5	82.5	...	...	Luxembourg
77.0	81.0	1998	1,451	3.4	0.6[15]	38.6[15]	60.8[15]	2.8[15]	58.0[15]	39.2[15]	H 99	H 3.5	H 0.9	99.3	...	...	Macau
71.6	76.2	1998	13,993	7.0	5.0	75.1	19.9	26.5	63.8	9.7	H 468	H 3.8	H 1.3	90.5	18,754	57.9	Macedonia
52.7	57.3	...	...	...	...	...	...	...	...	...	H 1,709	H 4.7	H 2.0	...	...	...	Madagascar
37.2	38.0	...	...	...	...	...	...	...	...	...	...	H 4.3	...	...	...	...	Malawi
70.3	75.2	...	...	...	...	...	...	...	...	...	H 3,580	H 4.9	...	...	...	...	Malaysia
68.0	66.0	1995	4,998	19.7	13.7[18]	58.2[18]	29.1[18]	...	...	...	...	H 7.2	...	...	...	...	Maldives
45.5	47.8	...	...	...	...	...	...	...	...	...	H 1,364	H 5.0	...	...	...	...	Mali
75.5	80.6	1998	2,376	6.3	2.0[15]	74.0[15]	24.0[15]	9.5[15]	76.0[15]	14.5[15]	H 76	H 3.3	H 1.2	91.8	...	...	Malta
63.7	67.4	...	...	...	...	...	...	...	...	...	H 5	H 8.7	...	...	...	...	Marshall Islands
75.5	80.6	1993	1,555	4.2	0.1[25]	46.8[25]	53.1[25]	3.3[25]	61.5[25]	35.2[25]	H 107	H 3.3	H 0.8	34.1	1,753	30.6	Martinique
48.7	52.9	...	...	...	...	...	...	...	...	...	H 246	H 5.0	... ...	...	...	...	Mauritania
67.0	75.0	1997	10,887	9.5	1.8[15]	56.2[15]	42.0[15]	25.8[15]	54.0[15]	20.2[15]	F 155	F 5.3	F 2.0	72.8	...	...	Mauritius
57.4	61.6	...	...	...	...	...	...	...	...	...	H 19	H 4.9	H 2.3	89.2	...	...	Mayotte
68.5	74.7	1996	670,523	6.9	14.0	65.1	20.9	32.5	54.7	12.8	H 17,152	H 5.1	H 2.0	72.5	28,734	1.0	Mexico
66.7	70.6	...	...	...	...	...	...	...	...	...	H 11	H 6.8	...	...	...	...	Micronesia
59.9	69.2	1996	26,089	6.0	8.2[17]	70.0[17]	21.8[17]	38.2[17]	45.0[17]	16.8[17]	H 1,144	H 3.4	H 1.1	89.6	44,252	78.4	Moldova
74.9	83.0	...	...	...	...	...	...	...	...	...	H 14	H 2.2	H 0.3	96.8	...	...	Monaco
61.0	65.0	1996	14,200	6.0	...	...	...	...	...	...	F 428	F 4.8	...	...	...	...	Mongolia
67.2	71.7	...	...	...	...	...	...	...	...	...	H 2,819	H 5.8	H 2.5	...	...	...	Morocco

Vital statistics, marriage, family (continued)

country	vital rates						causes of death (rate per 100,000 population)								
	year	birth rate per 1,000 population	death rate per 1,000 population	infant mortality rate per 1,000 live births	rate of natural increase per 1,000 population	total fertility rate	year	infectious and parasitic diseases	malignant neoplasms (cancers)	endocrine and metabolic disorders	diseases of the nervous system	diseases of the circulatory system	diseases of the respiratory system	diseases of the digestive system	accidents, poisoning, and violence
Mozambique	2000	38.0	23.3	139.9	14.5	4.9	...	...	...	...	...	...	...	...	...
Myanmar (Burma)	2000	24.2	11.7	89.0	12.5	3.0	...	...	...	...	...	...	...	...	...
Namibia	2001	34.7	20.9	71.7	13.8	4.8	...	...	...	...	...	...	...	...	...
Nauru	2000	22.9	5.1	11.1[23]	17.8	3.8[23]	...	...	...	...	...	...	...	...	...
Nepal	2001	34.7	10.3	74.0	24.4	4.6	...	...	...	...	...	...	...	...	...
Netherlands, The	1999	12.7	8.9	5.2	3.8	1.6[10]	1995	7.6	236.1	28.1	13.3	335.1	81.8	32.6	33.5
Netherlands Antilles	1999	13.7	6.5	11.7[10]	7.2	2.1[10]	1995[39]	16.7	149.0	61.7	9.9	71.6	40.8	21.4	47.6
New Caledonia	2001	20.1	4.9	7.0	15.2	2.5	1996	17.6	110.6	8.1[16]	14.6	124.2	60.3	19.6	63.7
New Zealand	2001	14.7	6.9	5.9	7.8	2.0	1996	5.6	200.7	22.1	12.3	317.2	86.4	20.9	46.7
Nicaragua	2000	28.3	4.9	34.8	23.4	3.3	1994[38]	*68*	*62*	*25*	*12*	*156*	*64*	*29*	*120*
Niger	2000	51.5	23.2	124.9	28.3	7.2	...	...	...	...	...	...	...	...	...
Nigeria	2000	40.2	13.7	74.2	26.5	5.7	...	...	...	...	...	...	...	...	...
Northern Mariana Islands	2000	20.7	2.2	5.9[23]	18.5	1.8[23]	1994–96	[40]	33.3	10.9[5]	—	53.3	12.6[40]	—	47.0
Norway	2000	13.2	9.8	3.9	3.4	1.9[23]	1994	8.3	238.3	16.4	16.4	450.1	102.2	29.8	51.8
Oman	2000	38.1	4.2	23.3	33.9	6.1	...	...	...	...	...	...	...	...	...
Pakistan	2001	36.8	10.0	89.0	26.8	5.2	...	...	...	...	...	...	...	...	...
Palau	2000	21.1	7.2	17.7[23]	13.9	2.5[23]	1993	43.6	136.9	...	...	192.9	43.6	...	112.0
Panama	2000	19.5	5.0	20.8	14.5	2.3	1997	21.2	64.4	18.2[5]	1.3[14]	122.1	25.4	9.6	37.1
Papua New Guinea	2000	32.7	8.0	59.9	24.7	4.4	...	...	...	...	...	...	...	...	...
Paraguay	2000	31.3	4.8	30.8	26.5	4.2	1994[41]	*29*	*53*	*18*	*6*	*162*	*31*	*18*	*48*
Peru	2000	24.5	5.8	40.6	18.7	3.0	...	...	...	...	...	...	...	...	...
Philippines	2001	26.7	5.3	31.0	21.4	3.3	1996	66.7	42.9	11.0[5]	7.1	136.3	76.9	22.4	43.4
Poland	1999	9.9	9.9	8.9	0.0	1.4[10]	1995	6.4	202.3	14.0	8.1	504.5	34.3	33.0	74.5
Portugal	2000	11.5	10.2	6.1	1.3	1.5	1995	10.2	201.7	43.9	10.0	438.9	80.2	45.7	59.8
Puerto Rico	2000	15.5	7.7	9.7	7.8	1.9	1993	59.4	122.2	66.7	19.2	242.3	80.5	43.9	34.1
Qatar	2000	16.1	4.2	22.1	11.9	3.3	1992	3.4	21.4[24]	7.3[22]	2.6	59.9	7.5	3.4	36.0
Réunion	2000	21.8	5.6	8.7	16.2	1.3	1993	14.9	99.7	22.5	16.0	170.1	41.5	59.5[42]	65.3
Romania	2000	10.8	12.3	19.8	–1.5	1.4	1995	14.1	164.1	10.4	8.8	736.1	75.8	68.2	78.7
Russia	2000	8.3	14.7	16.9	–6.4	1.3	1998	19.0	203.0	11.0[13]	10.9[13]	749.0	57.0	38.0	185.0
Rwanda	2000	35.8	21.0	120.1	14.8	5.1	...	...	...	...	...	...	...	...	...
St. Kitts and Nevis	2000	19.1	9.4	16.7	9.7	2.4	1995	57.8	108.0	55.3	20.1	482.4	65.3	50.3	45.2
St. Lucia	2000	22.2	5.4	16.8	16.8	2.4	1995	20.7	98.6	79.3	13.8	226.9	29.7	21.4	50.3
St. Vincent and the Grenadines	2000	18.3	6.2	17.7[23]	12.1	2.1	1997	36.8	90.0	56.6	14.4	228.4	42.2	28.8	—
Samoa	2001	28.2	5.7	27.0	22.5	4.3	1992[37]	3.1	11.2	9.9	3.1	24.2	9.9	6.8	2.5
San Marino	2000	10.9	7.7	6.3	3.2	1.3	1991–95	...	229.4	2.4[5]	...	324.8	10.7	...	45.2
São Tomé and Príncipe	2000	43.0	7.8	50.4	35.2	6.1	...	...	...	...	...	...	...	...	...
Saudi Arabia	2000	37.5	6.0	52.9	31.5	6.3	...	...	...	...	...	...	...	...	...
Senegal	2000	37.9	8.6	58.1	29.3	5.2	...	...	...	...	...	...	...	...	...
Serbia and Montenegro	1997	12.4	10.6	14.3	1.8	1.7	1995	9.0	167.7[24]	23.8	10.1	573.7	40.9	28.3	42.2
Seychelles	2000	18.0	6.7	17.7	11.3	1.9	1994	43.3	128.6	16.2	16.2	288.4	98.8	39.3	43.3
Sierra Leone	2000	45.6	19.6	148.7	26.0	6.1	...	...	...	...	...	...	...	...	...
Singapore	2000	13.6	4.5	2.5	9.1	1.6	1995	12.4	130.5	10.9	3.0	186.1	97.5	13.7	37.3
Slovakia	2000	10.2	9.8	8.3	0.4	1.3	1997	4.0	209.0	12.0	5.0	529.0	70.0	41.0	69.0
Slovenia	1999	8.8	9.5	4.5	–0.7	1.2	1997	4.4	243.9	36.4	9.0	381.1	81.0	55.2	88.6
Solomon Islands	2001	38.3	4.8	22.0	33.5	5.4	...	...	...	...	...	...	...	...	...
Somalia	2000	47.7	18.7	125.8	29.0	7.2	...	...	...	...	...	...	...	...	...
South Africa	2000	21.6	14.7	58.9	6.9	2.5	1995	71.3	55.8	20.5	10.2	98.5	51.9	15.1	112.0
Spain	2000	9.8	9.1	5.0	0.7	1.2[23]	1995	5.9	219.8	23.1	0.4	333.6	28.0	20.4	41.3
Sri Lanka	2000	17.5	5.8	17.0	11.7	2.1	...	...	...	...	...	...	...	...	...
Sudan, The	2000	38.6	10.3	70.2	28.3	5.5	...	...	...	...	...	...	...	...	...
Suriname	2000	21.1	5.7	25.1	15.4	2.5	1992[43]	*40*	*68*	*40*	*11*	*193*	*37*	*32*	*71*
Swaziland	2000	40.6	20.4	109.0	20.2	5.9	...	...	...	...	...	...	...	...	...
Sweden	2000	10.0	10.6	3.5	–0.6	1.5	1995	8.6	234.6	23.2	14.3	525.5	85.8	33.8	48.9
Switzerland	1999	11.0	8.7	3.4	2.3	1.5	1994	16.3	238.7	23.3[20]	18.1	381.5	64.2	27.1	69.3
Syria	2000	31.1	5.3	34.8	25.8	4.1	...	...	...	...	...	...	...	...	...
Taiwan	2000	13.8	5.7	7.1	8.1	1.8	1992	...	101.5	23.7[5]	...	140.1[18]	24.3[44]	18.2[44]	63.7[44]
Tajikistan	2001	24.7	6.4	54.0	18.3	4.4	1993	128.3	40.7	8.8[2, 20]	7.9[2]	222.8	158.7	20.7	181.3
Tanzania	2000	40.2	12.9	81.0	27.3	5.5	...	...	...	...	...	...	...	...	...
Thailand	2001	16.1	6.0	18.0	10.1	1.8	1994	27.6	49.0	7.5	11.0	89.8	91.4	18.4	73.8
Togo	2000	38.0	11.2	71.6	26.8	5.5	...	...	...	...	...	...	...	...	...
Tonga	2000	27.2	6.1	37.9[23]	21.1	3.6[23]	1992	16.3	54.9	15.2	6.1	158.5	31.5	18.3	4.1
Trinidad and Tobago	1997	14.5	7.2	17.1	7.3	1.8[10]	1994	11.6	94.4	119.3	14.7	286.5	49.0	28.6	52.8
Tunisia	2000	17.1	5.6	25.8	11.5	2.1	...	...	...	...	...	...	...	...	...
Turkey	2000	18.7	6.0	48.9	12.7	2.2	1993[44]	24	80	9[5]	2[13]	369	19	10	33
Turkmenistan	2000	28.9	9.0	73.3	19.9	1.8	1994	75.7	55.4	11.2	7.6	337.2	150.3	7.6	60.1
Tuvalu	2000	21.4	7.8	26.2[19]	13.6	3.1[19]	...	...	...	...	...	...	...	...	...
Uganda	2000	48.0	18.4	93.3	29.6	7.0	...	...	...	...	...	...	...	...	...
Ukraine	2000	7.9[45]	13.9[45]	21.7	–6.0[45]	1.3	1996	17.7	192.5	8.3[20]	1.2	784.5	75.3	4.9	157.2
United Arab Emirates	2000	18.0	3.7	8.8[23]	14.3	3.3	...	...	...	...	...	...	...	...	...
United Kingdom	2000	11.7	10.4	5.6	1.3	1.7	1997	6.8	261.2	13.8	18.5	442.1	165.8	39.5	32.7
United States	1999	14.3	8.7	6.9	5.6	2.0	1997	19.6[46]	201.6	30.3	21.0	354.4	85.2	29.5	55.9
Uruguay	2000	17.4	9.1	15.1	8.3	2.4	1990	16.0	222.8	25.5	16.2	378.4	76.3	39.1	61.7
Uzbekistan	2001	21.7	5.9	38.0	15.8	3.1	1993	38.0	48.2	9.4[25]	8.9[25]	300.3	113.8	31.4	49.5
Vanuatu	2001	32.1	5.6	30.0	26.5	4.4	1994[37]	25.0	29.2	9.1	5.5	39.0	30.4	9.7	9.1
Venezuela	2000	21.1	4.9	26.2	16.2	2.5	1994	33.0	60.5	24.1	7.4	144.7	31.9	19.3	74.1
Vietnam	2000	21.6	6.3	31.1	15.3	2.5	...	...	...	...	...	...	...	...	...
Virgin Islands (U.S.)	2000	16.0	5.4	9.6	10.6	2.3	...	...	...	...	...	...	...	...	...
West Bank	2000	36.7	4.5	22.3	32.2	5.0	...	...	...	...	...	...	...	...	...
Western Sahara	2000	45.1	16.1	133.6	29.0	6.6	...	...	...	...	...	...	...	...	...
Yemen	2000	43.4	9.9	70.3	33.5	7.1	...	...	...	...	...	...	...	...	...
Zambia	2000	41.9	22.1	92.4	19.8	5.6	...	...	...	...	...	...	...	...	...
Zimbabwe	2000	25.0	22.4	62.3	2.6	3.3	1990	64.7	28.4	4.9	9.4	40.8	39.5	12.1	44.9

[1]Excludes nomadic tribes. [2]1991. [3]1986. [4]Septicemia only. [5]Diabetes mellitus only. [6]Cerebrovascular disease and heart disease only. [7]Chronic obstructive pulmonary diseases, pneumonia, and influenza only. [8]Official government figures. [9]1998–2000 average. [10]2000. [11]Under 21 years of age. [12]21–29 years of age. [13]1994. [14]Meningitis only. [15]1996. [16]1989. [17]1995. [18]1993. [19]1998. [20]Includes nutritional disorders. [21]1996–98 average. [22]1990. [23]1999. [24]Includes benign neoplasms (cancers). [25]1992. [26]Results based on a sample population of about 100,000. [27]Millions of households. [28]Projected rates based on about 60 percent of the total deaths. [29]Indonesia includes East Timor. [30]Projected rates based on about 75 percent of the total deaths.

expectation of life at birth (latest year)		nuptiality, family, and family planning																country
		marriages			age at marriage (latest)						families (F), households (H) (latest)							
					groom (percent)			bride (percent)			families (households)		children		induced abortions			
male	female	year	total number	rate per 1,000 popu-lation	19 and under	20–29	30 and over	19 and under	20–29	30 and over	total ('000)	size	number under age 15	percent legiti-mate	number	ratio per 100 live births		
38.3	36.7	...	...	...	...	...	...	...	...	...	F 1,860	F 4.4	F 2.0	73.1	...	...		Mozambique
59.0	63.0	...	...	...	...	...	...	...	...	...	...	H 5.6	...	...	...	...		Myanmar (Burma)
42.5	38.7	...	...	...	...	...	...	...	...	...	...	H 5.2	...	...	...	...		Namibia
57.0	64.1	1995	57	5.3	...	...	...	...	...	...	H 1	H 8.0	H 2.6	...	...	...		Nauru
59.0	59.0	...	...	...	...	...	...	...	...	...	H 3,345	H 5.6	H 2.3	...	...	...		Nepal
75.2	80.7	1998	87,000	5.5	0.5[15]	47.4[15]	52.1[15]	3.2[15]	60.9[15]	35.9[15]	H 6,185	H 2.3	H 0.4	77.3	22,441	11.8		Netherlands, The
72.6	77.0	1998	1,276	6.1	...	...	...	...	...	...	H 41	H 3.7	H 2.1	51.6	...	...		Netherlands Antilles
72.0	77.0	1999	934	4.5	0.1[12]	46.5[12]	53.4[12]	5.0[12]	61.2[12]	33.8[12]	H 51	H 3.8	...	36.4	...	...		New Caledonia
75.7	80.8	1996	21,506	6.0	0.8[12]	50.6[12]	48.6[12]	3.2[12]	60.8[12]	36.0[12]	H 1,178	H 2.8	H 0.7	58.0	11,460	19.3		New Zealand
66.8	70.8	1991	13,122	3.3	...	...	...	...	...	...	H 752	H 5.8	...	...	...	...		Nicaragua
41.4	41.1	...	...	...	...	...	...	...	...	...	H 1,130	H 6.3	...	...	...	...		Niger
51.6	51.6	...	...	...	...	...	...	...	...	...	H 21,283	H 4.7	...	...	...	...		Nigeria
72.0	78.4	...	...	...	...	...	...	...	...	...	H 7	H 4.6	H 1.5	51.2	...	...		Northern Mariana Islands
75.6	81.1	1996	23,172	5.3	0.4	43.5	56.1	2.1	59.1	38.8	H 1,864	H 2.3	...	51.0	13,672	22.6		Norway
69.7	74.0	...	...	...	...	...	...	...	...	...	...	H 8.0	...	...	...	...		Oman
61.0	60.0	...	...	...	...	...	...	...	...	...	...	H 6.3	...	...	...	...		Pakistan
65.2	71.5	...	...	...	...	...	...	...	...	...	...	H 4.9	...	...	...	...		Palau
72.7	78.3	1995	8,841	3.4	2.4	52.3	45.3	10.4	57.2	32.4	H 524	H 4.4	H 1.5	25.5	...	...		Panama
61.1	65.3	...	...	...	...	...	...	...	...	...	H 674	H 4.6	...	...	...	...		Papua New Guinea
71.2	76.3	1994	23,649	5.0	4.2[25]	64.8[25]	31.0[25]	30.4[25]	50.2[25]	19.4[25]	H 868	H 4.7	1.9	68.7	...	...		Paraguay
67.6	72.5	1993	90,000	4.1	...	...	...	...	...	...	H 3,099	H 5.1	...	57.8	...	...		Peru
68.0	72.0	1993	474,407	7.1	4.9	66.3	28.8	18.0	63.8	18.2	F 9,566	F 5.7	F 2.4	93.9	2,315	...		Philippines
69.0	77.6	1996	203,641	5.3	2.8	77.2	20.0	16.6	70.5	12.9	F 9,435	F 3.6	F 0.9	95.0	491	0.1		Poland
72.2	79.5	1997	63,542	6.5	3.1[15]	70.0[15]	26.9[15]	13.9[15]	68.1[15]	18.0[15]	H 3,150	H 3.1	H 0.8	85.5	...	...		Portugal
71.1	80.3	1996	32,572	8.7	8.5	53.8	37.7	19.4	49.3	31.4	H 1,005	H 3.6	H 1.0	59.6	...	...		Puerto Rico
69.9	74.9	1996	1,641	2.9	4.9	67.5	27.6	29.6	59.7	10.7	H 61	H 6.4	...	...	...	...		Qatar
69.3	76.2	1996	3,313	4.9	1.2[22]	65.2[22]	33.6[22]	12.5[22]	66.8[22]	20.7[22]	H 185	H 3.5	...	44.1	4,302	31.7		Réunion
66.1	74.0	1997	147,105	6.5	2.6[15]	76.0[15]	21.4[15]	25.4[15]	62.1[15]	12.5[15]	H 7,115	H 3.1	...	...	456,221	197.2		Romania
59.9	72.4	1995	1,074,900	7.3	6.5	64.5	29.0	28.5	47.7	23.8	H 40,426	H 3.2	H 0.8	70.5	2,766,362	202.8		Russia
38.6	40.1	...	...	...	...	...	...	...	...	...	H 1,509	H 4.7	2.3	94.9	...	...		Rwanda
67.9	73.7	...	...	...	...	...	...	...	...	...	H 12	H 3.7	H 1.4	19.2	...	...		St. Kitts and Nevis
68.7	76.1	1997	467	3.1	0.8[16]	34.4[16]	64.8[16]	3.5[16]	45.1[16]	51.4[16]	H 33	H 4.0	H 2.0	14.2	...	...		St. Lucia
70.6	74.1	1997	508	4.6	1.0[25]	37.0[25]	62.0[25]	4.8[25]	46.3[25]	48.9[25]	H 27	H 3.9	H 2.0	...	...	...		St. Vincent and the Grenadines
67.0	73.0	1997	...	4.6	0.5[18]	51.0[18]	48.5[18]	8.0[18]	65.0[18]	27.0[18]	F 20	F 7.8	F 3.8	43.5	...	...		Samoa
77.6	85.0	1996	191	7.5	0.6[16]	75.1[16]	24.3[16]	5.3[16]	85.3[16]	9.5[16]	H 9	H 2.6	H 0.4	95.2	...	...		San Marino
63.8	66.7	...	...	...	...	...	...	...	...	...	...	H 4.0	...	...	...	...		São Tomé and Príncipe
66.1	69.5	...	...	...	...	...	...	...	...	...	H 1,513	H 6.1	...	...	...	...		Saudi Arabia
60.6	63.8	...	...	...	...	...	...	...	...	...	...	H 8.7	...	...	...	...		Senegal
69.9	74.7	1997	56,004	5.3	2.3[17]	64.5[17]	33.2[17]	18.7[17]	63.5[17]	17.8[17]	H 2,870	H 3.6	H 0.9	...	91,474	65.1		Serbia and Montenegro
64.9	76.1	1996	875	11.4	2.0[13]	45.8[13]	42.2[13]	11.2[13]	51.5[13]	29.6[13]	H 13	H 4.8	H 1.9	27.2	387	22.8		Seychelles
42.4	48.2	...	...	...	...	...	...	...	...	...	...	H 6.6	...	...	...	...		Sierra Leone
76.0	80.0	1997	25,667	6.9	0.5	57.3	42.2	3.1	74.5	22.4	H 662	H 4.2	H 1.3	...	14,362	29.6		Singapore
69.7	78.0	1996	27,484	5.1	6.0[17]	76.2[17]	17.8[17]	27.4[17]	62.4[17]	10.2[17]	...	H 3.2	...	83.1	35,879	58.4		Slovakia
71.0	79.0	1996	7,555	3.8	0.5	63.2	36.3	5.8	72.7	21.5	H 637	H 3.1	...	64.4	10,218	54.4		Slovenia
68.0	70.0	...	...	...	...	...	...	...	...	...	...	H 5.8	...	...	...	...		Solomon Islands
44.7	47.9	...	...	...	...	...	...	...	...	...	...	H 4.9	...	...	...	...		Somalia
50.4	51.8	1995	148,148	3.6	0.3	39.7	60.0	2.8	54.9	42.3	H 8,688	H 4.6	...	75.9	...	...		South Africa
74.4	81.6	1996	194,635	5.0	1.2[17]	62.5[17]	36.3[17]	5.0[17]	72.8[17]	22.2[17]	F 10,665	F 3.5	...	89.5	47,832	13.1		Spain
71.0	76.0	1996	170,444	9.3	1.3	64.3	34.4	16.7	67.1	16.2	H 3,282	H 4.6	...	96.3	...	...		Sri Lanka
55.5	57.7	...	...	...	...	...	...	...	...	...	H 3,471	H 5.3	...	...	...	...		Sudan, The
68.7	74.1	1995	2,249	5.5	...	...	...	...	...	...	...	H 4.8	...	...	...	...		Suriname
39.5	41.4	...	...	...	...	...	...	...	...	...	H 122	H 5.7	...	...	1,145	...		Swaziland
77.0	82.4	1996	33,484	3.4	0.3	40.5	59.2	1.5	54.0	44.5	H 3,670	H 2.1	H 0.5	46.1	32,117	33.7		Sweden
76.7	82.6	1997	37,575	5.3	0.4[15]	43.6[15]	56.0[15]	2.8[15]	58.8[15]	38.4[15]	H 3,250	H 2.0	0.4	91.2	...	...		Switzerland
67.4	69.6	1994	115,994	8.4	...	...	...	...	...	...	F 1,151	H 6.2	F 2.4	...	...	...		Syria
73.6	79.3	1998	145,678	6.7	1.5[22]	62.3[22]	36.2[22]	6.0[22]	77.7[22]	16.3[22]	H 5,964	H 3.6	H 1.0	97.2	...	...		Taiwan
65.0	71.0	1994	38,820	6.8	10.7	80.6	8.7	49.6	45.7	4.7	H 799	H 6.1	H 2.7	93.0	35,709	22.0		Tajikistan
51.3	53.2	...	...	...	...	...	...	...	...	...	H 3,435	H 5.2	H 2.3	...	...	...		Tanzania
71.0	76.0	1995	470,751	7.9	...	...	...	...	...	...	H 15,551	H 3.8	...	...	...	...		Thailand
52.8	56.7	...	...	...	...	...	...	...	...	...	H 479	H 6.0	...	...	...	...		Togo
67.7	72.2	1994	748	7.7	16.3	63.0	20.7	5.1	65.0	29.9	F 15	F 6.3	F 2.7	80.6	...	...		Tonga
65.4	70.6	1996	7,118	5.6	4.3	54.9	40.8	20.0	52.8	27.2	H 301	H 3.8	H 1.3	...	9	—		Trinidad and Tobago
72.1	75.4	1997	57,100	6.2	...	60.5[25]	39.5[25]	24.7[25]	62.7[25]	20.2[25]	H 1,703	H 5.1	H 1.9	99.8	23,300	10.9		Tunisia
68.6	73.4	1996	486,734	7.8	5.9[17]	74.5[17]	19.6[17]	31.4[17]	58.5[17]	10.1[17]	...	H 4.5	...	...	...	...		Turkey
57.3	64.7	1993	42,106	10.7	3.0[16]	87.4[16]	9.6[16]	16.1[16]	77.1[16]	6.8[16]	H 598	H 5.6	H 2.4	96.5	39,068	31.3		Turkmenistan
62.7	65.1	...	...	...	...	...	...	...	...	...	H 1	H 6.4	H 2.2	82.2	...	...		Tuvalu
42.2	43.7	...	...	...	...	...	...	...	...	...	H 2,766	H 4.8	...	...	...	...		Uganda
60.6	72.0	1997	345,000	6.5	7.5	68.4	24.1	35.2	45.9	18.9	H 14,507	H 3.2	H 0.8	89.2	957,022	159.5		Ukraine
71.6	76.6	1995	...	2.7	...	...	...	...	...	...	H 247	H 5.3	...	...	...	...		United Arab Emirates
75.0	80.5	1995	282,900	5.5	0.8	49.1	50.1	3.6	57.4	39.0	H 29,533	H 2.4	H 1.7	63.2	167,297	22.8		United Kingdom
74.1	79.7	1996	2,324,000	8.8	4.3[22]	51.8[22]	43.9[22]	10.9[22]	55.8[22]	35.3[22]	H 96,391	H 2.6	F 1.0	67.2	1,359,145	32.0		United States
71.9	78.8	1996	17,596	5.5	6.9[25]	57.2[25]	35.9[25]	23.5[25]	51.4[25]	25.1[25]	H 863	H 3.3	H 0.9	73.8	...	...		Uruguay
66.0	72.0	1994	176,300	7.8	11.2	80.7	8.1	49.3	45.3	5.4	H 3,415	H 5.5	H 2.4	95.8	120,434	18.3		Uzbekistan
67.0	70.0	...	...	...	...	...	...	...	...	...	H 28	H 5.1	H 2.2	...	113	2.4		Vanuatu
70.1	76.3	1996	81,951	3.7	9.5	58.7	31.8	27.9	51.7	20.4	H 2,707	H 5.3	H 2.2	47.0	...	...		Venezuela
66.8	71.9	...	...	...	...	...	...	...	...	...	H 12,958[47]	H 4.8[47]	H 1.9[47]	...	...	...		Vietnam
74.2	82.5	1993	3,646	35.1	0.4	33.6	66.0	1.9	45.9	52.2	H 32	H 3.1	H 1.0	30.2	...	...		Virgin Islands (U.S.)
70.4	73.9	...	...	...	...	...	...	...	...	...	...	...	...	...	...	...		West Bank
48.7	51.3	...	...	...	...	...	...	...	...	...	...	...	...	...	...	...		Western Sahara
58.1	61.6	...	...	...	...	...	...	...	...	...	H 1,848	H 5.6	...	...	...	...		Yemen
37.1	37.4	...	...	...	...	...	...	...	...	...	H 1,370	H 4.4	H 2.1	...	...	...		Zambia
39.2	36.4	...	...	...	...	...	...	...	...	...	H 2,166	H 4.8	1.1	95.8	...	...		Zimbabwe

[31]Ethiopia includes Eritrea. [32]Based on a sample registration scheme. [33]Muslims only. [34]Projected rates based on about 20 percent of the total deaths. [35]1997–99 average. [36]1997. [37]Registered deaths only. [38]Projected rates based on about 45 percent of the total deaths. [39]Includes Aruba. [40]Diseases of the respiratory system included in infectious and parasitic diseases. [41]Reporting areas only (constituting about 75 percent of the total population). [42]Includes all deaths associated with alcoholism. [43]Projected rates based on about 70 percent of the total deaths. [44]Projected rates based on about 35 percent of the total deaths. [45]Average of April to September only. [46]Of which AIDS, 6.2. [47]Private households only.

National product and accounts

This table furnishes, for most of the countries of the world, breakdowns of (1) gross national product (GNP)—its global and per capita values, and purchasing power parity (PPP), (2) growth rates (1990–99) and principal industrial and accounting components of gross domestic product (GDP), and (3) principal elements of each country's balance of payments, including international goods trade, invisibles, external public debt outstanding, and tourism payments.

Measures of national output. The two most commonly used measures of national output are GDP and GNP. Each of these measures represents an aggregate value of goods and services produced by a specific country. The GDP, the more basic of these, is a measure of the total value of goods and services produced entirely within a given country. The GNP, the more comprehensive value, is composed of both domestic production (GDP) and the net income from current (short-term) transactions with other countries. When the income received from other countries is greater than payments to them, a country's GNP is greater than its GDP. In theory, if all national accounts could be equilibrated, the global summation of GDP would equal GNP.

In the first section of the table, data are provided for the nominal and real GNP. ("Nominal" refers to value in current prices for the year indicated and is distinguished from a "real" valuation, which is one adjusted to eliminate the effect of recent inflation [most often] or, occasionally, of deflation between two given dates.) Both the total and per capita values of this product are denominated in U.S. dollars for ease of comparison, as is a new value for GNP per capita adjusted for purchasing power parity. The latter is a concept that provides a better approximation of the ability of equivalent values of two (or more) national currencies to purchase comparable quantities of goods and services in their respective domestic markets and may differ substantially from two otherwise equal GNP per capita values based solely on currency exchange rates. Beside these are given figures for average annual growth of total and per capita real GNP. GNP per capita provides a rough measure of annual national income per person, but values should be compared cautiously, as they are subject to a number of distortions, notably of exchange rate, but also of purchasing power parity and in the existence of elements of national production that do not enter the monetary economy in such a way as to be visible to fiscal authorities (*e.g.*, food, clothing, or housing produced and consumed within families or communal groups or services exchanged). For reasons of comparability, the majority of the data in this section are taken from the World Bank's *The World Bank Atlas* (annual).

The internal structure of the national product. GDP/GNP values allow comparison of the relative size of national economies, but further information is provided when these aggregates are analyzed according to their industrial sectors of origin, component kinds of expenditure, and cost components.

The distribution of GDP for ten industrial sectors, usually compiled from national sources, is aggregated into three major industrial groups:

1. The primary sector, composed of agriculture (including forestry and fishing) and mineral production (including fossil fuels).

National product and accounts

country	gross national product (GNP), 1999			gross domestic product (GDP), 1990–99			origin of gross domestic product (GDP) by economic sector, 1998 (%)										
	nominal ('000,000 U.S.$)	per capita		average annual growth rates, 1990–99			primary		secondary			tertiary					other
		nominal (U.S.$)	purchasing power parity (PPP; U.S.$)	real GDP (%)	population (%)	real GDP per capita (%)	agriculture	mining	manufacturing	construction	public utilities	transp., communications	trade	financial svcs.	other svcs.	government	
Afghanistan	5,666[1]	250[1]	...	...	...	...	...	...	...	...	...	...	...	...	...	...	...
Albania	3,146	930	3,240	3.4	0.6	2.8	54	[2]	12[2]	13	[2]	3		—18—			—
Algeria	46,548	1,550	4,840	1.7	2.2	–0.5	11	23	10	11	—		—24—			13	8
American Samoa	253[1]	4,300[1]	...	...	...	...	...	...	...	...	...	...	...	...	...	...	...
Andorra	850[3]	13,100[3]	...	...	...	...	...	...	...	...	...	...	...	...	...	...	...
Angola	3,276	270	1,100	–0.5	2.3	–2.8	13	45	6	6	—	—18—			—11—		1
Antigua and Barbuda	606	8,990	9,870	3.8	1.1	2.7	3	1	2	10	3	17	19	14	6	15	10
Argentina	296,097	7,550	11,940	4.9	1.3	3.6	5[3]	2[3]	20[3]	6[3]	2[3]	6[3]	14[3]	18[3]	—24[3]—		3[3]
Armenia	1,878	490	2,360	–3.1	0.8	–3.9	31	[2]	22[2]	9	[2]	5	9		—25—		–1
Aruba	1,728[4, 5]	18,700[4, 5]	...	...	...	...	...	...	...	...	...	...	...	...	...	...	...
Australia	397,345	20,950	23,850	4.1	1.2	2.9	3	4	13	6	2	8	10	16	33	4	1
Austria	205,743	25,430	24,600	1.9	0.5	1.4	3	1	24	7	3	8	19	18	6	10	1
Azerbaijan	3,705	460	2,450	–9.5	1.2	–10.7	20[3]	[2]	25[2, 3]	14[3]	[2]	10[3]		—31[3]—			—
Bahamas, The	3,288[3]	11,830[3]	...	...	...	...	1[6]	15[6]	17[6]	6[6]	2[6]	11[6]	11[6]	19[6]	5[6]	19[6]	–6[6]
Bahrain	4,909[4]	7,640[4]	...	...	...	...	1[7]	17[7]	22[7]	6[7]	2[7]	9[7]	11[7]	18[7]	5[7]	19[7]	–10[7]
Bangladesh	41,071	370	1,530	4.7	1.6	3.1	23	1	18	7	1	10	15	11	11	2	1
Barbados	2,294	8,600	14,010	1.8	0.3	1.5	6	1	10	8	4	8	35	—17—		12	–1
Belarus	26,299	2,620	6,880	–3.1	–0.2	–2.9	13	[8]	36[8]	7	4	12	12		—16—		—
Belgium	252,051	24,650	25,710	1.7	0.3	1.4	1[3]	—	21[3]	5[3]	2[3]	8[3]	12[3]	14[3]	7[3]	24[3]	6[3]
Belize	673	2,730	4,750	3.2	2.5	0.7	18	1	13	5	2	12	15	8	6	6	14
Benin	2,320	380	920	5.0	3.2	1.8	38[3]	[8]	9[3, 8]	4[3]	1[3]	7[3]	18[3]	9[3]	—7[3]—		7[3]
Bermuda	2,128[3]	34,950[3]	...	...	...	...	...	...	...	...	...	...	...	...	...	...	...
Bhutan	399	510	1,260	6.1	2.7	3.4	38	2	12	11	11	8	7	5	—9—		–3
Bolivia	8,092	990	2,300	4.2	2.4	1.8	15	11	18	5	1	12	9	13	6	10	—
Bosnia and Herzegovina	4,706	1,210	...	...	...	...	12	...	24	6	3	9	19	4	14	8	—
Botswana	5,139	3,240	6,540	3.8	2.0	1.8	3	36	5	6	2	4	18	8	4	14	—
Brazil	730,424	4,350	6,840	3.0	1.5	1.5	7[3]	1[3]	19[3]	9[3]	3[3]	5[3]	7[3]	20[3]	11[3]	13[3]	5[3]
Brunei	7,209[4]	22,280[4]	...	...	...	...	3	[8]	37[8]	7	1	4	10	9	—33—		–4
Bulgaria	11,572	1,410	5,070	–2.8	–0.7	–2.1	19	1	17	3	4	7	7	2	—29—		11
Burkina Faso	2,602	240	960	4.2	2.8	1.4	30	[8]	20[8]	5	1	4	12		—22—		6
Burundi	823	120	570	–3.9	1.1	–5.0	46	1[9]	9	5	[9]	4	4	—2—		18	11
Cambodia	3,023	260	1,350	5.2	3.3	1.9	51	—	6	7	1	4	15	5	7	3	1
Cameroon	8,798	600	1,490	1.3	2.8	–1.5	41	5	10	4	1			—35—			4
Canada	614,003	20,140	25,440	2.8	1.1	1.7	2	4	18	6	3	8	12	16	24	6	1
Cape Verde	569	1,330	4,450	4.6	1.4	3.2	12	—	10	9	—	18	19	12	7	14	–1
Central African Republic	1,035	290	1,150	2.0	2.3	–0.3	49	4	8	4	1	2	12	—6—		6	8
Chad	1,555	210	840	2.5	3.4	–0.9	37	1	12	2	1	—24—		—9—		11	3
Chile	69,602	4,630	8,410	7.1	1.5	5.6	7	9	15	5	2	9	18	17	6	2	10
China	979,894	780	3,550	10.8	1.3	9.5	18	[2]	42[2]	7	[2]	6	8		—18—		1
Colombia	90,007	2,170	5,580	3.3	1.9	1.4	14	4	14	5	...	8	12	—34—		9	—
Comoros	189	350	1,430	–0.1	3.0	–3.1	40	...	4	6	1	5	25	3	1	13	2
Congo, Dem. Rep. of the	5,433[4]	110[4]	...	...	...	...	58[7]	4[7]	6[7]	2[7]	2[7]	3[7]	17[7]	—6[7]—		1[7]	1[7]
Congo, Rep. of the	1,571	550	540	–0.8	2.5	–3.3	11[7]	33[7]	8[7]	2[7]	1[7]	12[7]	9[7]	—8[7]—		13[7]	3[7]
Costa Rica	12,828	3,570	7,880	5.0	2.0	3.0	15	[8]	19[8]	2	3	6	21	12	8	14	—
Côte d'Ivoire	10,387	670	1,540	3.6	3.0	0.6	28	[2]	20[2]	5	[2]	8	15	—12—		8	4
Croatia	20,222	4,530	7,260	0.4	–0.6	1.0	7	[8]	24[8]	6	3	8	12	13	—14—		13
Cuba	18,600[5]	1,700[5]	...	...	...	...	7[3]	2[3]	37[3]	5[3]	2[3]	4[3]	21[3]	2[3]	—19[3]—		2[3]
Cyprus[10]	9,086	11,950	19,080	4.2	1.4	2.8	4	—	11	8	2	9	20	19	10	14	3
Czech Republic	51,623	5,020	12,840	0.9	–0.0	0.9	4	[2]	32[2]	7	[2]	9	12	17	—13—		6
Denmark	170,685	32,050	25,600	2.4	0.4	2.0	4[3]	1[3]	20[3]	6[3]	2[3]	10[3]	13[3]	19[3]	6[3]	22[3]	–3[3]
Djibouti	511	790	...	–3.0	2.1	–5.1	3	—	5	8	5	17	16	10	5	20	11
Dominica	238	3,260	5,040	2.4	0.6	1.8	20	1	9	8	5	17	14	14	1	19	–8
Dominican Republic	16,130	1,920	5,210	5.7	1.8	3.9	12	2	17	12	2	12	20	9	8	8	–2
East Timor	113[4, 5]	130[4, 5]	...	...	...	...	...	...	...	...	...	...	...	...	...	...	...
Ecuador	16,841	1,360	2,820	2.1	2.1	0.0	17[3]	15[3]	15[3]	2[3]	1[3]	9[3]	15[3]	12[3]	6[3]	7[3]	1[3]

2. The secondary sector, composed of manufacturing, construction, and public utilities.
3. The tertiary sector, which includes transportation and communications, trade (wholesale and retail), restaurants and hotels, financial services (including banking, real estate, insurance, and business services), other services (community, social, and personal), and government services.

The category "other" contains adjustments such as import duties and bank service charges that are not distributed by sector.

There are three major domestic components of GDP expenditure: private consumption (analyzed in greater detail in the "Household budgets and consumption" table), government spending, and gross domestic investment. The fourth, nondomestic, component of GDP expenditure is net foreign trade; values are given for both exports (a positive value) and imports (a negative value, representing obligations to other countries). The sum of these five percentages, excluding statistical discrepancies and rounding, should be 100% of the GDP.

Balance of payments (external account transactions). The external account records the sum (net) of all economic transactions of a current nature between one country and the rest of the world. The account shows a country's net of overseas receipts and obligations, including not only the trade of goods and merchandise but also such invisible items as services, interest and dividends, short- and long-term investments, tourism, transfers to or from overseas residents, etc. Each transaction gives rise either to a foreign claim for payment, recorded as a deficit (*e.g.*, from imports, capital outflows), or a foreign obligation to pay, recorded as a surplus (*e.g.*, from exports, capital inflows) or a domestic claim on another country. Any international transaction automatically creates a deficit in the balance of payments of one country and a surplus in that of another. Values are given in U.S. dollars for comparability.

External public debt. Because the majority of the world's countries are in the less developed bloc, and because their principal financial concern is often external debt and its service, data are given for outstanding external public and publicly guaranteed long-term debt rather than for total public debt, which is the major concern in the developed countries. For comparability, the data are given in U.S. dollars. The data presented in the table come from the World Bank's *Global Development Finance* (formerly *World Debt Tables*).

Tourist trade. Net income or expenditure from tourism (in U.S. dollars for comparability) is often a significant element in a country's balance of payments. Receipts from foreign nationals reflect payments for goods and services from foreign currency resources by tourists in the given country. Expenditures by nationals abroad are also payments for goods and services, but in this case made by the residents of the given country as tourists abroad. The majority of the data in this section are compiled by the World Tourism Organization.

gross domestic product (GDP) by type of expenditure, 1998 (%)					external public debt outstanding (long-term, disbursed only), 1999						balance of payments, 1999 (current external transactions; '000,000 U.S.$)			tourist trade, 1997 ('000,000 U.S.$)		country
consumption		gross domestic investment	foreign trade		total ('000,000 U.S.$)	creditors (%)		debt service			net transfers		current balance of payments	receipts from foreign nationals	expenditures by nationals abroad	
private	government		exports	imports		official	private	total ('000,000 U.S.$)	repayment (%) principal	repayment (%) interest	goods, merchandise	invisibles				
…	…	…	…	…	…	…	…	…	…	…	…	…	…	1	1	Afghanistan
…	…	…	…	…	849.1	70.7	29.3	27.1	28.4	71.6	−663.0	507.6	−155.4	27	5	Albania
51	17	27	28	−23	25,913	71.3	28.7	4,885	64.7	35.3	3,360	−3,340	20	20	64	Algeria
…	…	…	…	…	…	…	…	…	…	…	…	…	…	10	…	American Samoa
…	…	…	…	…	…	…	…	…	…	…	…	…	…	…	…	Andorra
…	…	…	…	…	9,248	39.6	60.4	1,099	89.6	10.4	1,463.5[4]	−3,323.1[4]	−1,857.6[4]	9	73	Angola
58	22	32	73	−84	…	…	…	…	…	…	−321.3[4]	232.7[4]	−88.6[4]	260	26	Antigua and Barbuda
—71—		20	10	−13	84,568	24.8	75.2	12,170	48.1	51.9	−770	−11,676	−12,446	5,069	2,680	Argentina
103	11	19	19	−53	681.9	100.0	—	39.8	64.6	35.4	−474.0	167.0	−307.1	7	41	Armenia
73	13	11	—2—		…	…	…	…	…	…	−591.7	258.5	−333.2	666	130	Aruba
59	18	24	20	−22	…	…	…	…	…	…	−9,730	−13,340	−23,070	9,026	6,129	Australia
55	20	26	44	−45	…	…	…	…	…	…	−3,649	−2,098	−5,747	12,393	10,992	Austria
78[3]	12[3]	38[3]	28[3]	−55[3]	493.3	91.1	8.9	49.8	81.5	18.5	−408.2	−191.5	−599.7	159	72	Azerbaijan
66[7]	15[7]	23[7]	54[7]	−58[7]	…	…	…	…	…	…	−1,428.2	756.3	−671.9	1,416	250	Bahamas, The
51	21	18	78	−68	…	…	…	…	…	…	672.1	−1,012.5	−340.4	260	129	Bahrain
78	14	13	19	−23	16,962	99.4	0.6	675	72.3	27.7	−1,962.1	1,670.6	−291.5	59	170	Bangladesh
59	21	20	58	−57	359.1	75.4	24.6	84.2	64.4	35.6	−691.7	565.9	−125.8	717	74	Barbados
58	20	27	60	−65	851	52.8	47.2	141	64.5	35.5	−570.0	376.3	−193.7	25	114	Belarus
54	21	21	76	−72	…	…	…	…	…	…	6,642	6,732	13,374	5,275	8,275	Belgium
65	17	27	52	−61	294.6	73.6	26.4	40.2	59.6	40.4	−128.8	51.4	−77.4	87	30	Belize
81	9	18	27	−35	1,472	99.8	0.2	56	64.3	35.7	−158.3[4]	6.8[4]	−151.5[4]	31	7	Benin
…	…	…	…	…	…	…	…	…	…	…	…	…	…	474	148	Bermuda
36[1]	29[1]	44[1]	34[1]	−44[1]	181.8	100.0	—	6.9	71.0	29.0	−24.8[4]	−21.7[4]	−46.5[4]	6	…	Bhutan
75	14	23	20	−32	3,864	99.4	0.6	257	57.0	43.0	−488.0	−67.8	−555.8	170	172	Bolivia
—100—		38	35	−73	1,826	92.6	7.4	388	64.3	35.7	−2,072.0	1,284.6	−787.4	15	…	Bosnia and Herzegovina
28	29	28	56	−41	442.3	95.2	4.8	82.5	74.7	25.3	674.5	−157.7	516.8	184	140	Botswana
64	18	21	7	−10	95,233	33.8	66.2	24,374	72.1	27.9	−1,261	−24,139	−25,400	2,595	6,583	Brazil
…	…	…	…	…	…	…	…	…	…	…	175[4]	1,910[4]	2,085[4]	39	…	Brunei
72	15	14	44	−45	7,602	32.8	67.2	632	49.5	50.5	−1,081.0	396.3	−684.7	368	222	Bulgaria
81	10	24	15	−30	1,295	99.7	0.3	53	69.8	30.2	−184.5	−38.6	−223.1	39	32	Burkina Faso
96	12	3	8	−19	1,050	99.9	0.1	20	70.0	30.0	−42.3	15.3	−27.0	1	10	Burundi
96[1]	7[1]	16[1]	28[1]	−46[1]	2,136	100.0	—	28	51.8	48.2	−209.5	143.5	−66.0	143	12	Cambodia
71	9	18	26	−27	7,614	95.2	4.8	346	47.8	52.2	112.4	−343.7	−231.3	39	107	Cameroon
59	20	20	41	−40	…	…	…	…	…	…	22,756	−25,029	−2,273	8,770	11,304	Canada
68	23	40	25	−57	265.1	95.7	4.3	21.6	84.7	15.3	−185.6[4]	127.6[4]	−58.0[4]	15	17	Cape Verde
84	12	14	16	−25	830.1	96.1	3.9	11.9	60.9	39.1	−8.3[4]	−79.1[4]	−87.4[4]	5	39	Central African Republic
90	10	15	18	−33	1,045	98.5	1.5	27	61.1	38.9	−50.3[4]	−155.8[4]	−206.1[4]	9	24	Chad
67	11	26	25	−29	5,655	37.1	62.9	780	60.1	39.9	1,664	−1,744	−80	1,021	946	Chile
46	12	38	—4—		108,163	46.6	53.4	15,668	68.2	31.8	36,207	−20,540	15,667	12,074	10,166	China
68	19	20	15	−22	19,434	39.6	60.4	4,775	65.5	34.5	1,776	−1,837	−61	955	958	Colombia
91[1]	15[1]	19[1]	20[1]	−45[1]	179.9	100.0	—	7.1	87.3	12.7	−35.6[4]	40.8[4]	5.2[4]	26	8	Comoros
81[7]	5[7]	9[7]	28[7]	−23[7]	8,188	93.8	6.2	—	—	—	830[1]	−1,375[1]	−515[1]	2	7	Congo, Dem. Rep. of the
46	16	26	67	−55	3,932	80.1	19.9	—	—	—	644.1	−885.7	−241.6	3	36	Congo, Rep. of the
56	16	28	50	−50	3,186	64.0	36.0	475	70.3	29.7	659.6	−1,309.1	−649.5	719	358	Costa Rica
64	11	19	44	−37	9,699	74.8	28.2	992	53.8	46.2	1,832.3[4]	−2,144.9[4]	−312.6[4]	88	282	Côte d'Ivoire
59[1]	29[1]	22[1]	42[1]	−52[1]	5,433	26.3	73.7	667	47.1	52.9	−3,298.7	1,776.5	−1,522.2	2,529	521	Croatia
71[1]	24[1]	7[1]	16[1]	−18[1]	…	…	…	…	…	…	…	…	…	1,338	…	Cuba
64	19	25	44	−52	…	…	…	…	…	…	−2,309.2	2,075.5	−233.7	1,639	278	Cyprus[10]
52	19	30	60	−61	13,440	8.6	91.4	2,470	62.5	37.5	−1,902	870	−1,032	3,647	2,380	Czech Republic
51	26	21	35	−33	…	…	…	…	…	…	6,689	−3,725	2,964	3,156	4,128	Denmark
79	24	15	45	−64	252.7	100.0	—	3.0	68.3	31.7	−179.7[4]	165.3[4]	−14.4[4]	4	5	Djibouti
58[3]	21[3]	34[3]	51[3]	−63[3]	89.0	100.0	—	9.3	75.3	23.7	−58.4	29.0	−29.4	37	7	Dominica
75	8	26	47	−56	3,665	80.5	19.5	331	52.3	47.7	−2,904.4	2,475.2	−429.2	2,107	242	Dominican Republic
…	…	…	…	…	…	…	…	…	…	…	…	…	…	…	…	East Timor
70	12	25	25	−32	12,756	42.7	57.3	1,382	45.2	54.8	1,655	−700	955	290	227	Ecuador

National product and accounts (continued)

country	gross national product (GNP), 1999			gross domestic product (GDP), 1990–99			origin of gross domestic product (GDP) by economic sector, 1998 (%)										
	nominal ('000,000 U.S.$)	per capita		average annual growth rates, 1990–99			primary		secondary			tertiary					other
		nominal (U.S.$)	purchasing power parity (PPP; U.S.$)	real GDP (%)	popu-lation (%)	real GDP per capita (%)	agri-culture	mining	manu-facturing	con-struction	public util-ities	transp., commu-nications	trade	finan-cial svcs.	other svcs.	govern-ment	
Egypt	86,544	1,380	3,460	4.6	2.2	2.4	16[3]	[8]	27[3, 8]	5[3]	2[3]	11[3]	19[3]	6[3]	—7[3]—		7[3]
El Salvador	11,806	1,920	4,260	4.6	1.8	2.8	12	—	22	4	2	8	19	12	7	14	—
Equatorial Guinea	516	1,170	3,910	18.9	2.6	16.3	22	61	—	3	1	1	4	1	2	5	—
Eritrea	779	200	1,040	5.6	3.4	2.2	15	—	13	11	1	9	20	4	1	17	9
Estonia	4,906	3,400	8,190	–1.2	–0.9	–0.3	6	1	14	5	3	12	18	13	14	4	10
Ethiopia	6,524	100	620	5.3	2.9	2.4	46	[8]	7[8]	3	2	6	9	7	8	13	–1
Faroe Islands	976[4]	24,620[4]	...	...	...	...	...	...	...	...	...	...	...	...	...	...	...
Fiji	1,848	2,310	4,780	2.2	1.0	1.2	16	3	15	5	5	14	16	14	—20—		–8
Finland	127,764	27,730	22,600	2.4	0.4	2.0	4	—	22	4	2	8	11	11	9	16	13
France	1,453,211	24,170	23,020	1.5	0.4	1.1	3[3]	1[3]	22[3]	5[3]	3[3]	6[3]	14[3, 11]	5[3]	18[3, 11]	19[3]	6[3]
French Guiana	1,543[7]	10,580[7]	...	...	...	...	...	...	...	...	...	...	...	...	...	...	...
French Polynesia	3,908	16,930	22,200	1.6	1.7	–0.1	...	...	...	...	...	...	...	...	...	...	...
Gabon	3,987	3,300	5,280	1.8	1.2	0.6	7[3]	43[3]	6[3]	4[3]	1[3]	5[3]	8[3]	—11[3]—		9[3]	6[3]
Gambia, The	415	330	1,550	3.0	3.6	–0.6	24	—	5	5	2	14	17	7	5	9	12
Gaza Strip	1,368[4, 5]	1,320[4, 5]	...	...	...	...	13	—	10	8	2	5	15	23	8	16	—
Georgia	3,362	620	2,540	...	...	...	32	[2]	13[2]	4	[2]	11	11	11	—13—		5
Germany	2,103,804	26,620	23,510	1.4	0.4	1.0	1	[2]	25[2]	5	[2]	—17—		30	—21—		1
Ghana	7,451	400	1,850	4.1	2.5	1.6	36	5	9	9	3	4	7	4	3	10	10
Greece	127,648	12,110	15,800	2.5	0.7	1.8	14[3]	1[3]	14[3]	6[3]	2[3]	7[3]	14[3]	3[3]	11[3]	19[3]	9[3]
Greenland	1,142[3]	20,380[3]	...	...	...	...	...	...	...	...	...	...	...	...	...	...	...
Grenada	334	3,440	6,300	2.9	0.7	2.2	9[3]	1[3]	7[3]	7[3]	5[3]	24[3]	20[3]	14[3]	3[3]	16[3]	–6[3]
Guadeloupe	3,706[5, 7]	9,200[5, 7]	...	...	...	...	...	...	...	...	...	...	...	...	...	...	...
Guam	3,301[4, 5]	20,660[4, 5]	...	...	...	...	...	...	...	...	...	...	...	...	...	...	...
Guatemala	18,625	1,680	3,630	4.2	2.7	1.5	23	1	14	2	3	9	25	10	6	8	–1
Guernsey[12]	1,902	29,810	...	...	...	...	...	...	...	...	...	...	...	...	...	...	...
Guinea	3,556	490	1,870	3.9	2.4	1.5	21	16	4	9	1	6	—28—		9	4	2
Guinea-Bissau	194	160	630	0.7	2.6	–1.9	62	[2]	9[2]	3	[2]	2	19	—1—		3	1
Guyana	651	760	3,330	5.6	0.4	5.2	29	14	9[13]	5	[13]	6	4	6	1	11	15
Haiti	3,584	460	1,470	–2.1	1.3	–3.4	30	—	7	12	1	2	13	8	5	18	4
Honduras	4,829	760	2,270	3.6	3.3	0.3	19	2	19	5	5	5	12	17	11	6	–1
Hong Kong	165,122	24,570	22,570	3.7	1.8	1.9	—	—	6	6	3	9	23	24	—19—		10
Hungary	46,751	4,640	11,050	1.1	–0.3	1.4	6[3]	[8]	20[3, 8]	4[3]	3[3]	9[3]	10[3]	16[3]	13[3]	6[3]	13[3]
Iceland	8,197	29,540	27,210	2.7	0.9	1.8	9[3]	—	13[3]	6[3]	3[3]	6[3]	10[3]	15[3]	5[3]	14[3]	18[3]
India	441,834	440	2,230	5.9	1.8	4.1	25	2	15	4	2	7	14	10	6	5	10
Indonesia	125,043	600	2,660	4.6	1.6	3.0	19	13	26	5	1	5	15	8	3	4	1
Iran	113,729	1,810	5,520	3.4	1.5	1.9	20	12	16	4	2	8	17	10	2	10	–1
Iraq	11,500[1, 5]	600[1, 5]	...	...	...	...	...	...	...	...	...	...	...	...	...	...	...
Ireland	80,559	21,470	22,460	6.8	0.7	6.1	8[1]	[14]	38[1, 14]	[14]	[14]	—18[1]—		—31[1]—		5[1]	—
Isle of Man	1,319[4, 5]	18,270[4, 5]	...	...	...	...	2[3]	—	12[3]	7[3]	3[3]	10[3]	12[3]	59[3]	4[3]	6[3]	–15[3]
Israel	99,574	16,310	18,070	5.2	2.9	2.3	2[3]	[2]	19[2, 3]	9	[2]	6[3]	12[3]	30[3]	—28[3]—		–6[3]
Italy	1,162,910	20,170	22,000	1.4	0.2	1.2	3[1]	4[1]	16[1]	5[1]	6[1]	6[1]	19[1]	5[1]	13[1]	22[1]	1[1]
Jamaica	6,311	2,430	3,390	0.4	1.0	–0.6	7	5	14	10	2	11	23	12	3	12	1
Japan	4,054,545	32,030	25,170	1.4	0.3	1.1	2[3]	—	24[3]	10[3]	3[3]	7[3]	12[3]	19[3]	20[3]	8[3]	–5[3]
Jersey	2,670[1, 5]	30,940[1, 5]	...	...	...	...	...	...	...	...	...	...	...	...	...	...	...
Jordan	7,717	1,630	3,880	5.4	4.3	1.1	3	3	12	4	2	14	11	16	5	18	12
Kazakhstan	18,732	1,250	4,790	–6.1	–1.2	–4.9	8	[2]	22[2]	4	[2]	11	17	—37—			1
Kenya	10,696	360	1,010	2.3	2.6	–0.3	30[1]	—	10[1]	5[1]	1[1]	8[1]	19[1]	18[1]	—8[1]—		—
Kiribati	81	910	...	3.6	2.6	1.0	12[1]	—	1[1]	3[1]	2[1]	12[1]	19[1]	6[1]	3[1]	33[1]	9[1]
Korea, North	17,700[3]	740[3]	...	...	...	...	...	...	...	...	...	...	...	...	...	...	...
Korea, South	397,910	8,490	15,530	5.7	1.0	4.7	5	—	31	10	2	7	11	20	8	8	–2
Kuwait	35,152[3]	22,110[3]	...	...	...	...	—	31	12	3	—	6	10	14	—26—		–2
Kyrgyzstan	1,465	300	2,420	–5.4	1.0	–6.4	41	[2]	17[2]	3	[2]	2	12	—14—		3	8
Laos	1,476	290	1,430	6.5	2.7	3.8	52	—	17	3	2	6	12	3	1	3	1
Latvia	5,913	2,430	6,220	–4.7	–1.0	–3.7	8[1]	[8]	19[1, 8]	4[1]	5[1]	—51[1]—					13[1]
Lebanon	15,796	3,700	...	7.0	1.3	5.7	...	...	...	...	...	...	...	...	...	...	...
Lesotho	1,158	550	2,350	4.3	2.2	2.1	12[1]	—	14[1]	18[1]	3[1]	3[1]	10[1]	8[1]	1[1]	18[1]	13[1]
Liberia	1,174[1]	490[1]	...	...	...	...	78	2	5	2	—	5	3	3	2	2	–2
Libya	32,663[4, 5]	6,700[4, 5]	...	...	...	...	...	...	...	...	...	...	...	...	...	...	—
Liechtenstein	714[1, 5]	23,000[1, 5]	...	...	...	...	...	...	...	...	...	...	...	...	...	...	...
Lithuania	9,751	2,640	6,490	–4.0	–0.1	–3.9	9	[8]	17[8]	8	4	9	16	9	11	6	11
Luxembourg	18,545	42,930	41,230	5.2	1.4	3.8	1	—	17	7	1	—24—		45	—19—		–14
Macau	6,161	14,200	16,940	3.7	3.0	0.7	...	...	...	...	...	...	...	...	...	...	...
Macedonia	3,348	1,660	4,590	–0.7	0.8	–1.5	10	[8]	22[8]	6	3	6	13	6	—19—		15
Madagascar	3,712	250	790	1.8	3.0	–1.2	33	[8]	—12[8]—			—42—				5	8
Malawi	1,961	180	570	2.0	1.1	0.9	36	1	13	2	1	4	25	9	2	10	–3
Malaysia	76,944	3,390	7,640	7.4	2.7	4.7	9	8	28	4	3	8	16	13	—16—		–5
Maldives	322	1,200	...	6.3	2.4	3.9	16	2	7[13]	11	[13]	7	20	—29—		8	—
Mali	2,577	240	740	3.7	2.6	1.1	44	6	9	5	—	5	—16—		7	4	4
Malta	3,492	9,210	...	5.0	0.8	4.2	2	[15]	19	3[15]	7	6	10	17	9	14	13
Marshall Islands	99	1,950	...	...	...	...	15[3]	—	2[3]	7[3]	2[3]	7[3]	18[3]	15[3]	—30[3]—		4[3]
Martinique	4,271[3, 5]	11,320[3, 5]	...	...	...	...	...	...	...	...	...	...	...	...	...	...	...
Mauritania	1,001	390	1,550	4.3	3.0	1.3	22[3]	10[3]	10[3]	—9[3]—		8[3]	15[3]	—7[3]—		10[3]	9[3]
Mauritius	4,157	3,540	8,950	5.1	1.2	3.9	7	—	21	5	2	10	15	14	5	9	12
Mayotte	486[4]	3,700[4]	...	...	...	...	...	...	...	...	...	...	...	...	...	...	...
Mexico	428,877	4,440	8,070	2.8	1.8	1.0	5	1	21	5	1	11	20	14	—23—		–1
Micronesia	212	1,830	...	–0.2	1.6	–1.8	19[1]	—	1[1]	1[1]	1[1]	5[1]	24[1]	3[1]	3[1]	42[1]	1[1]
Moldova	1,481	410	2,100	–11.0	–0.2	–10.8	21	[8]	17[8]	4	2	4	7	6	—12—		27
Monaco	793[1, 5]	25,000[1, 5]	...	...	...	...	...	...	...	...	...	...	...	...	...	...	...
Mongolia	927	390	1,610	0.8	1.4	–0.6	33	[8]	24[8]	3	—	7	19	—14—			—
Morocco	33,715	1,190	3,320	2.1	1.7	0.4	15[3]	2[3]	18[3]	5[3]	9[3]	6[3]	19[3]	—13[3]—			13[3]
Mozambique	3,804	220	810	6.9	3.1	3.8	32	—	8	8	1	11	23	—	12	3	2
Myanmar (Burma)	55,700[3, 5]	1,190[3, 5]	...	...	...	...	53	—	6	2	—	5	30	2	—2—		—
Namibia	3,211	4,890	5,580	3.2	2.4	0.8	9[3]	12[3]	12[3]	3[3]	3[3]	4[3]	9[3]	8[3]	3[3]	23[3]	14[3]
Nauru	128[4]	11,540[4]	...	...	...	...	...	...	...	...	...	...	...	...	...	...	...
Nepal	5,173	220	1,280	4.8	2.5	2.3	38	1	9	10	2	8	11	10	—9—		2

gross domestic product (GDP) by type of expenditure, 1998 (%)					external public debt outstanding (long-term, disbursed only), 1999						balance of payments, 1999 (current external transactions; '000,000 U.S.$)			tourist trade, 1997 ('000,000 U.S.$)		country
consumption		gross domestic invest-ment	foreign trade		total ('000,000 U.S.$)	creditors (%)		debt service			net transfers		current balance of payments	receipts from foreign nationals	expendi-tures by nationals abroad	
private	govern-ment		exports	imports		offi-cial	private	total ('000,000 U.S.$)	repayment (%)		goods, merchan-dise	invisibles				
									princi-pal	inter-est						
74	10	22	17	–23	25,998	97.9	2.1	1,478	56.8	43.2	–9,928	8,293	–1,635	3,727	1,347	Egypt
86	10	17	23	–36	2,649	91.8	8.2	254	54.3	45.7	–1,358.9	1,117.0	–241	75	75	El Salvador
…	…	…	102	–173	207.9	93.7	6.3	1.7	58.8	41.2	26.5[4]	–400.1[4]	–373.6[4]	2	8	Equatorial Guinea
…	…	…	…	…	253.8	100.0	—	3.9	16.7	83.3	–498.9[4]	323.5[4]	–175.4[4]	75	…	Eritrea
59	22	29	78	–88	205.5	81.8	18.2	61.2	80.5	19.5	–877.5	582.9	–294.6	465	118	Estonia
79	14	18	16	–26	5,360	97.6	2.4	147	62.6	37.4	–797.1	480.9	–316.2	36	40	Ethiopia
…	…	…	…	…	…	…	…	…	…	…	51.6[4]	102.4[4]	154.0[4]	…	…	Faroe Islands
72	18	12	67	–69	120.7	100.0	—	29.2	75.3	24.7	–115.6	128.3	12.7	297	53	Fiji
39	21	19	50	–30	…	…	…	…	…	…	11,655	–4,067	7,588	1,963	2,270	Finland
54	24	19	26	–23	…	…	…	…	…	…	19,390	17,190	36,580	28,009	16,576	France
…	…	…	…	…	…	…	…	…	…	…	…	…	…	…	…	French Guiana
…	…	…	…	…	…	…	…	…	…	…	…	…	…	359	…	French Polynesia
40[3]	11[3]	26[3]	64[3]	–42[3]	3,290	96.1	3.9	487	52.6	47.4	202.5[3]	34.6[3]	237.1[3]	7	178	Gabon
76	17	18	51	–62	425.4	100.0	—	16.6	67.2	32.8	–69.0[4]	52.7[4]	–16.3[4]	32	16	Gambia, The
…	…	…	…	…	…	…	…	…	…	…	…	…	…	…	…	Gaza Strip
…	…	…	…	…	1,308	99.8	0.2	80	48.1	51.9	–533.9	335.5	–198.4	416	228	Georgia
57	19	22	29	–27	…	…	…	…	…	…	72,000	–91,310	–19,310	16,509	46,200	Germany
77	10	25	34	–47	5,647	91.2	8.8	391	68.3	31.7	–1,111.5	345.5	–766.0	266	22	Ghana
71	15	21	18	–25	…	…	…	…	…	…	–17,947	12,845	–5,102	3,771	1,325	Greece
…	…	…	…	…	…	…	…	…	…	…	…	…	…	…	…	Greenland
61	18	44	53	–76	122.2	93.9	6.1	6.4	73.4	26.6	–133.4[4]	43.9[4]	–89.5[4]	61	5	Grenada
…	…	…	…	…	…	…	…	…	…	…	…	…	…	499	…	Guadeloupe
…	…	…	…	…	…	…	…	…	…	…	…	…	…	…	…	Guam
87	6	16	19	–27	3,129	80.0	20.0	313	58.5	41.5	1,445.1	–2,471.0	–1,025.9	325	119	Guatemala
…	…	…	…	…	…	…	…	…	…	…	…	…	…	…	…	Guernsey[12]
77	7	17	22	–23	3,057	99.1	0.9	114	61.4	38.6	94.5	–246.1	–151.6	5	23	Guinea
100	9	11	15	–35	837.1	99.9	0.1	8.6	44.2	55.8	–14.4	–12.6	–27.0	…	…	Guinea-Bissau
43[3]	20[3]	43[3]	78[3]	–84[3]	1,238	96.6	3.4	74	52.7	47.3	–25	–50	–75	39	22	Guyana
—103—		13	13	–29	1,049	100.0	—	43	65.1	34.9	–469.7	410.1	–59.6	97	37	Haiti
67	10	30	44	–51	4,231	96.7	3.3	296	59.3	40.7	–709.1	172.3	–536.8	146	62	Honduras
61	9	30	127	–127	…	…	…	…	…	…	–3,159	14,635	11,476	9,242	…	Hong Kong
62	11	29	51	–53	16,064	14.0	86.0	3,282	69.5	30.5	–2,189	83	–2,106	2,582	1,153	Hungary
62	21	22	35	–39	…	…	…	…	…	…	–308	–292	–600	173	324	Iceland
66	13	23	12	–13	82,380	71.1	28.9	8,221	62.7	37.3	–8,029	5,245	–2,784	3,152	1,342	India
53	4	35	40	–33	72,554	75.5	24.5	9,192	59.5	40.5	20,644	–14,859	5,785	5,437	2,436	Indonesia
65	13	22	8	–8	6,184	59.4	40.6	2,971	86.6	13.4	6,215	–1,488	4,727	327	253	Iran
…	…	…	…	…	…	…	…	…	…	…	…	…	…	13	…	Iraq
51	13	24	84	–72	…	…	…	…	…	…	24,178	–23,583	595	3,189	2,223	Ireland
…	…	…	…	…	…	…	…	…	…	…	…	…	…	…	…	Isle of Man
61	30	20	32	–43	…	…	…	…	…	…	–4,408	2,527	–1,881	2,741	3,570	Israel
60	18	20	24	–22	…	…	…	…	…	…	20,383	–14,079	6,304	29,714	16,631	Italy
67	18	29	43	–56	2,905	77.5	22.5	648	52.3	47.7	–1,137.7	882.0	–255.7	1,131	181	Jamaica
61	10	26	11	–9	…	…	…	…	…	…	123,320	–16,450	106,870	4,326	33,041	Japan
…	…	…	…	…	…	…	…	…	…	…	…	…	…	…	…	Jersey
70	27	25	49	–70	7,546	83.2	16.8	559	52.6	47.4	–1,460.1	1,865.0	404.9	774	398	Jordan
75	11	18	32	–37	2,995	77.0	23.0	629	71.7	28.3	343.7	–514.7	–171.0	289	445	Kazakhstan
74	16	17	25	–32	5,385	90.2	9.8	533	78.9	21.1	–829.2	840.2	11.0	377	194	Kenya
…	…	…	…	…	…	…	…	…	…	…	–31.6[1]	29.3[1]	–2.3[1]	2	4	Kiribati
…	…	…	…	…	…	…	…	…	…	…	…	…	…	…	…	Korea, North
55	11	21	48	–35	57,231	27.1	72.9	23,000	81.4	18.6	28,371	–3,894	24,477	5,116	6,262	Korea, South
56	31	14	45	–47	…	…	…	…	…	…	5,571	–509	5,062	188	2,558	Kuwait
88	18	16	36	–58	1,130.4	97.2	2.8	16.5	8.2	91.8	–84.4	–168.9	–253.3	7	4	Kyrgyzstan
…	…	…	…	…	2,471	100.0	—	29	69.0	31.0	–189.5	68.4	–121.1	73	21	Laos
64	26	23	48	–61	864.8	70.2	29.8	41.4	50.7	49.3	–1,027	380	–647	192	326	Latvia
…	…	…	…	…	5,568	16.4	83.6	653	45.6	54.4	…	…	…	1,000	…	Lebanon
116	20	46	27	–109	661.8	91.6	8.4	44.6	55.8	44.2	–606.7	385.9	–220.8	20	8	Lesotho
…	…	…	…	…	1,062	80.7	19.3	—	—	—	–118.5[4]	76.6[4]	–41.9[4]	…	…	Liberia
55[3]	27[3]	12[3]	29[3]	–23[3]	…	…	…	…	…	…	2,974	–838	2,136	6	215	Libya
…	…	…	…	…	…	…	…	…	…	…	…	…	…	…	…	Liechtenstein
63	25	24	47	–59	1,891.5	34.2	65.8	166.7	54.3	45.7	–1,404.6	210.6	–1,194.0	399	290	Lithuania
46	17	21	116	–99	…	…	…	…	…	…	–2,449	3,761	1,312	297	…	Luxembourg
40	11	18	76	–46	…	…	…	…	…	…	…	…	…	2,947	153	Macau
74	18	23	43	–58	1,135	75.4	24.6	377	85.0	15.0	–420.3	108.6	–311.7	14	27	Macedonia
89	7	12	21	–30	4,023	99.1	0.9	147	46.9	53.1	–154[4]	–147[4]	–301[4]	73	48	Madagascar
85	14	14	30	–42	2,596	99.3	0.7	44	62.5	37.5	–93.0[1]	–0.3[1]	–92.7[1]	7	17	Malawi
42	10	27	114	–93	18,929	24.2	75.8	2,278	52.3	47.7	22,648	–10,042	12,606	2,703	2,478	Malaysia
…	…	…	…	…	192.5	84.9	15.1	16.7	73.7	26.3	–262.6	192.6	–70.0	286	38	Maldives
70	14	24	24	–33	2,798	100.0	—	85	75.3	24.7	9.7[3]	–187.7[3]	–178.0[3]	26	42	Mali
62	20	23	88	–94	…	…	…	…	…	…	–571.4	449.0	–112.4	664	191	Malta
…	…	…	…	…	…	…	…	…	…	…	–35.8[3]	52.2[3]	16.4[3]	3	…	Marshall Islands
…	…	…	…	…	…	…	…	…	…	…	…	…	…	400	…	Martinique
69[3]	20[3]	17[3]	42[3]	–49[3]	2,138	99.1	0.9	88	68.2	31.8	40.0[4]	37.2[4]	77.2[4]	11	24	Mauritania
63	12	25	67	–67	1,155	45.8	54.2	161	62.4	37.6	–547.2	494.9	52.4	475	177	Mauritius
…	…	…	…	…	…	…	…	…	…	…	…	…	…	…	…	Mayotte
68	9	24	31	–33	87,531	24.9	75.1	16,015	61.4	38.6	–5,581	–8,585	–14,166	7,594	3,892	Mexico
…	…	…	…	…	…	…	…	…	…	…	–52.0[3]	115.8[3]	63.8[3]	…	…	Micronesia
71	24	30	—–25—		722	82.5	17.5	98	55.1	44.9	–128.0	83.3	–44.7	4	…	Moldova
…	…	…	…	…	…	…	…	…	…	…	…	…	…	…	…	Monaco
65[3]	16[3]	23[3]	1[3]	–5[3]	816.3	97.4	2.6	20.9	57.2	42.8	–56.4	–55.8	–112.2	22	21	Mongolia
65	18	22	22	–26	17,284	75.9	24.1	2,985	64.6	35.4	–2,448	2,277	–171	1,443	315	Morocco
88	9	23	12	–32	4,625	99.7	0.3	68	47.8	52.2	–491.0[4]	61.7[4]	–429.3[4]	…	…	Mozambique
—89—		12	0	–1	5,333	90.1	9.9	88	72.7	27.3	–1,035.2	669.5	–365.7	34	25	Myanmar (Burma)
55[3]	31[3]	20[3]	53[3]	–58[3]	…	…	…	…	…	…	–172.6[4]	334.4[4]	161.8[4]	336	99	Namibia
…	…	…	…	…	…	…	…	…	…	…	…	…	…	…	…	Nauru
81	9	21	24	–35	2,910	99.3	0.7	99	69.7	30.3	–880.7	891.3	10.6	119	103	Nepal

National product and accounts (continued)

country	gross national product (GNP), 1999			gross domestic product (GDP), 1990–99			origin of gross domestic product (GDP) by economic sector, 1998 (%)										
	nominal ('000,000 U.S.$)	per capita		average annual growth rates, 1990–99			primary		secondary			tertiary					other
		nominal (U.S.$)	purchasing power parity (PPP; U.S.$)	real GDP (%)	popu-lation (%)	real GDP per capita (%)	agri-culture	mining	manu-factur-ing	con-struc-tion	public util-ities	transp., commu-nications	trade	finan-cial svcs.	other svcs.	govern-ment	
Netherlands, The	397,384	25,140	24,410	2.7	0.6	2.1	3	2	17	5	2	7	15	26	11	12	—
Netherlands Antilles	2,400[3, 5]	11,500[3, 5]	…	…	…	…	1[7]	—	7[7]	7[7]	4[7]	13[7]	25[7]	17[7]	9[7]	18[7]	–1[7]
New Caledonia	3,169	15,160	21,130	1.4	2.2	–0.8	2[3]	4[3]	11[3]	5[3]	2[3]	7[3]	23[3]	—20[3]—		25[3]	–1[3]
New Zealand	53,299	13,990	17,630	3.0	1.2	1.8	7	1	17	3	3	11	15	22	—22—		1
Nicaragua	2,012	410	2,060	3.3	2.9	0.4	28	2	21	5	3	5	18	7	4	8	–1
Niger	1,974	190	740	1.8	2.8	–1.0	37[3]	4[3]	7[3]	2[3]	2[3]	6[3]	17[3]	—21[3]—			4[3]
Nigeria	31,600	260	770	2.4	2.9	–0.5	37	26	5	1	—	3	16	5	1	1	5
Northern Mariana Is.	665	9,600	…	…	…	…	…	…	…	…	…	…	…	…	…	…	…
Norway	149,280	33,470	28,140	3.8	0.6	3.2	2	11	12	4	2	9	10	17	5	16	12
Oman	13,135[4]	5,950[4]	…	…	…	…	2[1]	43[1]	4[1]	2[1]	1[1]	6[1]	13[1]	8[1]	8[1]	12[1]	1[1]
Pakistan	62,915	470	1,860	3.5	2.5	1.0	24	—	15	3	4	9	15	8	7	7	8
Palau	129[4, 5]	7,140[4, 5]	…	…	…	…	5	—	1	8	—	16	27	12	7	22	2
Panama	8,657	3,080	5,450	4.3	1.9	2.4	8	—	10	4	4	13	21	25	6	10	–1
Papua New Guinea	3,834	810	2,260	4.9	2.6	2.3	24	26	9	6	1	5	9	1	—13—		6
Paraguay	8,374	1,560	4,380	2.5	2.7	–0.2	28	—	14	5	6	5	23	3	10	6	—
Peru	53,705	2,130	4,480	5.0	1.8	3.2	6[3]	2[3]	19[3]	11[3]	1[3]	4[3]	16[3]	14[3]	13[3]	7[3]	7[3]
Philippines	77,967	1,050	3,990	3.2	2.3	0.9	17	1	22	6	3	5	14	12	11	10	–1
Poland	157,429	4,070	8,390	4.6	0.2	4.4	5	3	22	8	3	6	21	15	3	13	1
Portugal	110,175	11,030	15,860	2.4	0.1	2.3	…	…	…	…	…	…	…	…	…	…	…
Puerto Rico	25,380[3]	7,010[3]	…	…	…	…	1[1]	[15]	41[1]	2[1, 15]	[16]	8[1, 16]	14[1]	13[1]	11[1]	11[1]	–1[1]
Qatar	6,473[4]	11,600[4]	…	…	…	…	1[3]	38[3]	7[3]	7[3]	1[3]	4[3]	8[3]	10[3]	—24[3]—		…
Réunion	5,680[3]	8,260[3]	…	…	…	…	…	…	…	…	…	…	…	…	…	…	…
Romania	33,034	1,470	5,970	–0.9	–0.4	–0.5	19[1]	[2]	34[1, 2]	7[1]	[2]	9[1]	10[1]	—17[1]—			4[1]
Russia	328,995	2,250	6,990	–6.0	–0.1	–5.9	7	[2]	33[2]	8	[2]	—23—		14	9	6	—
Rwanda	2,041	250	880	–2.7	0.3	–3.0	44	—	13	7	—	4	11	—15—		7	–1
St. Kitts	259	6,330	10,400	4.2	–0.7	4.9	6[1]	—	11[1]	12[1]	2[1]	16[1]	23[1]	16[1]	4[1]	18[1]	–8[1]
St. Lucia	590	3,820	5,200	2.4	1.5	0.9	7	—	5	6	4	15	23	15	3	13	9
St. Vincent	301	2,640	4,990	3.3	0.7	2.6	9	—	6	12	5	17	15	8	2	15	11
Samoa	181	1,070	4,070	2.0	0.6	1.4	17[3]	…	19[3]	5[3]	2[3]	11[3]	17[3]	11[3]	7[3]	9[3]	2[3]
San Marino	883[3, 5]	34,330[3, 5]	…	…	…	…	…	…	…	…	…	…	…	…	…	…	…
São Tomé and Príncipe	40	270	…	1.1	2.0	–0.9	23[3]	—	4[3]	15[3]	—	—19[3]—		8[3]	9[3]	22[3]	—
Saudi Arabia	139,365	6,900	11,050	2.2	3.3	–1.1	6[1]	36[1]	9[1]	9[1]	—	6[1]	7[1]	5[1]	3[1]	17[1]	2[1]
Senegal	4,685	500	1,400	3.7	3.1	0.6	18	[5]	13[5]	5	2	12	—21—		20	9	—
Serbia and Montenegro	13,742[4]	1,290[4]	…	…	…	…	20	[8]	36[8]	6	3	12	19	—5—			–1
Seychelles	520	6,500	…	2.9	1.6	1.3	3	…	14	9	3	15	24	10	2	13	7
Sierra Leone	653	130	440	–4.9	2.1	–7.0	39[7]	17[7]	9[7]	2[7]	—	9[7]	14[7]	2[7]	2[7]	3[7]	4[7]
Singapore	95,429	24,150	22,310	6.6	1.9	4.7	—	—	24	9	2	14	19	28	—11—		–7
Slovakia	20,318	3,770	10,430	1.8	0.2	1.6	4	1	23	5	3	8	—22—		—29—		5
Slovenia	19,862	10,000	16,050	2.4	–0.1	2.5	4[3]	1[3]	25[3]	5[3]	3[3]	7[3]	13[3]	14[3]	12[3]	5[3]	11[3]
Solomon Islands	320	750	2,050	3.7	3.4	0.3	48[1]	—	3[1]	7[1]	2[1]	6[1]	9[1]	4[1]	—21[1]—		—
Somalia	706[1]	110[1]	…	…	…	…	…	…	…	…	…	…	…	…	…	…	…
South Africa	133,569	3,170	8,710	1.2	1.4	–0.2	4	7	19	3	3	10	13	18	—23—		—
Spain	583,082	14,800	17,850	2.3	0.3	2.0	4[1]	[2]	24[1, 2]	8[1]	[2]	—59[1]—					5[1]
Sri Lanka	15,578	820	3,230	5.3	1.3	4.0	19	2	15	7	1	10	19	9	—13—		5
Sudan, The	9,435	330	…	…	…	…	41	—	9	6	1	6	20	—14—			3
Suriname	684[4]	1,660[4]	…	…	…	…	12[1]	11[1]	13[1]	3[1]	9[1]	15[1]	12[1]	14[1]	—13[1]—		–2[1]
Swaziland	1,379	1,350	4,380	2.3	2.5	–0.2	12	1	27	4	2	4	7	4	1	15	23
Sweden	236,940	26,750	22,510	1.6	0.4	1.2	2[1]	—	20[1]	5[1]	3[1]	6[1]	11[1]	23[1]	4[1]	19[1]	7[1]
Switzerland	273,856	38,380	28,760	0.6	0.7	–0.1	…	…	…	…	…	…	…	…	…	…	…
Syria	15,172	970	3,450	5.5	2.8	2.7	28[1]	7[1]	4[1]	4[1]	1[1]	11[1]	26[1]	5[1]	2[1]	10[1]	—
Taiwan	297,953[4]	13,900[4]	…	…	…	…	3	—	27	4	2	7	17	23	10	10	–3
Tajikistan	1,749	280	…	…	…	…	20	[2]	28[2]	2	[2]	—18—		—22—			10
Tanzania	8,515	260	500	3.0	3.1	–0.1	43[3]	1[3]	6[3]	4[3]	2[3]	5[3]	12[3]	12[3]	2[3]	7[3]	6[3]
Thailand	121,051	2,010	5,950	4.9	1.1	3.8	14	2	28	5	3	8	14	—26—			—
Togo	1,398	310	1,380	2.7	3.2	–0.5	42	6	9	3	3	5	17	—8—		7	—
Tonga	172	1,732	…	1.1	0.4	0.7	32	—	3	5	2	7	11	10	—18—		12
Trinidad and Tobago	6,142	4,750	7,690	2.5	0.5	2.0	2	21	8	10	—	—18—		12	17	9	3
Tunisia	19,757	2,090	5,700	4.5	1.6	2.9	12	1	18	5	5	8	—24—			14	13
Turkey	186,490	2,900	6,440	3.7	1.5	2.2	17	1	19	6	2	14	20	—13—		9	–1
Turkmenistan	3,205	670	3,340	–6.6	3.0	–9.6	25	[2]	30[2]	12	[2]	10	5	—13—			5
Tuvalu	7[1]	650[1]	…	…	…	…	22[7]	2[7]	3[7]	14[7]	2[7]	4[7]	14[7]	10[7]	—28[7]—		—
Uganda	6,794	320	1,160	7.1	3.1	4.0	41[1]	—	7[1]	7[1]	1[1]	4[1]	12[1]	7[1]	5[1]	4[1]	12[1]
Ukraine	41,991	840	3,360	–10.8	–0.5	–10.3	11	[2]	25[2]	5	[2]	13	8	—25—			13
United Arab Emirates	48,673[4]	17,870[4]	…	…	…	…	2[1]	35[1]	9[1]	9[1]	1[1]	6[1]	13[1]	13[1]	2[1]	11[1]	–1[1]
United Kingdom	1,403,843	23,500	22,220	2.5	0.4	2.1	1	2	18	5	2	7	13	23	4	15	10
United States	8,879,500	31,910	31,910	3.0	1.0	2.0	2[3]	1[3]	17[3]	4[3]	3[3]	6[3]	17[3]	19[3]	20[3]	13[3]	—
Uruguay	20,604	6,220	8,750	3.7	0.7	3.0	11	—	20	4	4	10	14	21	—15—		1
Uzbekistan	17,613	720	2,230	–1.2	1.9	–3.1	26	[2]	15[2]	8	[2]	6	8	—21—			16
Vanuatu	227	1,180	2,880	2.3	3.1	–0.8	23	—	5	5	2	7	34	7	—17—		—
Venezuela	87,313	3,680	5,420	1.7	2.2	–0.5	5	12	16	7	2	10	18	16	9	6	–1
Vietnam	28,733	370	1,860	8.0	1.8	6.2	26	[8]	—33[8]—			4	19	7	—12—		–1
Virgin Islands (U.S.)	2,666[3]	18,290[3]	…	…	…	…	…	…	…	…	…	…	…	…	…	…	…
West Bank	2,758[4, 5]	1,680[4, 5]	…	…	…	…	7	[2]	17[2]	11	[2]	[17]	14	11	19[17]	10	13
Western Sahara	60[5, 18]	300[5, 18]	…	…	…	…	…	…	…	…	…	…	…	…	…	…	…
Yemen	6,080	360	730	3.5	3.9	–0.4	24	17	10	4	2	7	14	6	2	14	—
Zambia	3,222	330	720	–0.4	2.0	–2.4	17	6	11	5	4	6	19	16	—9—		7
Zimbabwe	6,302	530	2,690	1.9	1.3	0.6	14[7]	5[7]	18[7]	2[7]	3[7]	5[7]	18[7]	9[7]	11[7]	4[7]	11[7]

gross domestic product (GDP) by type of expenditure, 1998 (%)					external public debt outstanding (long-term, disbursed only), 1999						balance of payments, 1999 (current external transactions; '000,000 U.S.$)			tourist trade, 1997 ('000,000 U.S.$)		country
consumption		gross domestic investment	foreign trade		total ('000,000 U.S.$)	creditors (%)		debt service			net transfers		current balance of payments	receipts from foreign nationals	expenditures by nationals abroad	
private	government		exports	imports		official	private	total ('000,000 U.S.$)	repayment (%) principal	repayment (%) interest	goods, merchandise	invisibles				
59	14	20	55	–49	…	…	…	…	…	…	17,940	–704	17,236	6,219	10,232	Netherlands, The
67[7]	28[7]	19[7]	72[7]	–85[7]	…	…	…	…	…	…	–1,064[4]	1,008[4]	–56[4]	576	243	Netherlands Antilles
…	…	…	…	…	…	…	…	…	…	…	…	…	…	110	…	New Caledonia
65	15	19	31	–30	…	…	…	…	…	…	–435	–3,161	3,596	2,093	1,451	New Zealand
94	14	34	36	–78	5,799	93.3	6.7	137	43.1	56.9	–1,133.2	481.0	–652.2	74	65	Nicaragua
82[3]	16[3]	12[3]	19[3]	–29[3]	1,424	100.0	—	19	52.6	47.7	–17.6[5]	–134.1[5]	–151.7[5]	18	24	Niger
64	14	29	32	–38	22,423	74.3	25.7	835	67.2	32.8	4,288	–3,782	506	118	1,816	Nigeria
…	…	…	…	…	…	…	…	…	…	…	…	…	…	672	…	Northern Mariana Is.
50	22	28	37	–37	…	…	…	…	…	…	10,119	–4,105	6,014	2,226	4,496	Norway
55	24	23	37	–39	1,768	37.4	62.6	711	82.3	17.7	2,918	–3,110	–192	108	47	Oman
72	12	17	16	–17	28,514	92.5	7.5	1,597	63.1	36.9	–1,874[4]	—[4]	–1,874[4]	117	364	Pakistan
…	…	…	…	…	…	…	…	…	…	…	…	…	…	22[7]	…	Palau
58	16	33	90	–97	5,678	23.6	76.4	619	45.7	54.3	–1,415.0	39.0	–1,376.0	374	164	Panama
55[7]	16[7]	18[7]	49[7]	–37[7]	1,517	95.6	4.4	160	66.9	33.1	856.0	–761.3	94.7	72	81	Papua New Guinea
86	8	23	28	–45	1,672	96.7	3.3	183	62.3	37.7	–334.4	270.8	–63.6	753	195	Paraguay
72	9	24	12	–17	20,709	79.7	20.3	1,957	41.3	58.7	–616	–1,206	–1,822	805	485	Peru
73	13	20	51	–58	33,568	63.8	36.2	5,097	68.1	31.9	4,958	2,952	7,910	2,831	1,936	Philippines
63	16	27	25	–32	33,151	75.6	24.4	2,162	39.1	60.9	–15,072	2,585	–12,487	8,679	6,900	Poland
66	20	26	28	–40	…	…	…	…	…	…	–13,766	4,137	–9,629	4,277	2,164	Portugal
…	…	…	…	…	…	…	…	…	…	…	…	…	…	2,046	869	Puerto Rico
…	…	…	…	…	…	…	…	…	…	…	…	…	…	…	…	Qatar
…	…	…	…	…	…	…	…	…	…	…	…	…	…	249	…	Réunion
76	15	18	26	–34	5,985	64.4	35.6	2,754	85.7	14.3	–1,092	–205	–1,297	526	783	Romania
58	19	15	31	–23	120,375	59.1	40.9	4,470	42.9	57.1	36,130	–11,482	24,648	6,900	10,113	Russia
94	9	16	6	–24	1,162	99.9	0.1	20	60.0	40.0	–140.6	138.1	–2.5	…	…	Rwanda
76[1]	18[1]	24[1]	44[1]	–63[1]	131.7	73.4	26.6	16.9	54.4	45.6	…	…	…	72	6	St. Kitts
69	15	19	65	–68	125.6	88.5	11.5	16.4	63.4	36.8	–201.2[4]	160.2[4]	–41.0[4]	282	29	St. Lucia
74	19	32	47	–72	159.8	63.2	36.8	12.6	49.2	50.8	–119.4[4]	75.1[4]	–44.3[4]	70	7	St. Vincent
…	…	…	…	…	156.5	100.0	—	4.8	70.8	29.2	–97.5	78.7	18.8	41	5	Samoa
66[1]	12[1]	17[1]	234[1]	–229[1]	…	…	…	…	…	…	22.6[1]	–11.9[1]	10.7[1]	…	…	San Marino
…	…	…	…	…	232.2	100.0	—	3.9	64.1	35.9	–12.1[4]	3.6[4]	–8.5[4]	2	1	São Tomé and Príncipe
41	32	21	36	–31	…	…	…	…	…	…	25,039	–24,627	412	1,420	…	Saudi Arabia
76	10	20	32	–38	3,111	99.7	0.3	179	68.2	31.8	–284.3[4]	174.6[4]	–109.7[4]	160	77	Senegal
…	…	…	…	…	7,416	44.4	55.6	—	—	—	…	…	…	41	…	Serbia and Montenegro
51	27	37	65	–81	132.2	81.6	18.4	23.4	76.3	23.7	–232.4	118.4	–114.0	122	30	Seychelles
81	11	4	14	–10	938	99.4	0.6	7	57.1	42.9	–126.7[7]	0.2[7]	–126.5[7]	57	2	Sierra Leone
39	10	33	—— 18 ——		…	…	…	…	…	…	11,303	9,951	21,254	6,843	3,224	Singapore
50	22	39	64	–75	4,457	29.6	70.4	639	67.9	32.1	–1,109	–46	–1,155	546	439	Slovakia
56	21	25	57	–58	…	…	…	…	…	…	–1,245.2	462.8	–782.4	1,188	544	Slovenia
…	…	…	…	…	120.4	97.2	2.8	5.5	72.7	27.3	54.5	–33.1	21.5	7	9	Solomon Islands
…	…	…	…	…	1,859	98.2	1.8	—	—	—	…	…	…	…	…	Somalia
63	20	16	26	–25	9,148	—	100.0	3,162	78.5	21.5	4,150	–4,683	–533	2,297	1,947	South Africa
62	16	22	29	–28	…	…	…	…	…	…	–30,339	16,623	–13,716	26,651	4,467	Spain
71	10	25	36	–42	8,182	92.6	7.4	401	64.1	35.9	–707.4	214.4	–493.0	212	180	Sri Lanka
91	4	18	6	–19	8,852	84.8	15.2	12	45.8	54.2	–475.9	11.1	–464.8	4	34	Sudan, The
…	…	…	…	…	…	…	…	…	…	…	–27.2[4]	–127.7[4]	–154.9[4]	17	4	Suriname
63	25	34	76	–99	205.5	100.0	—	29.0	64.3	35.7	–110.8	128.0	17.2	40	37	Swaziland
50	27	17	44	–38	…	…	…	…	…	…	15,714	–9,732	5,982	3,572	6,579	Sweden
60	15	21	40	–36	…	…	…	…	…	…	723	28,476	29,199	7,902	6,904	Switzerland
69	11	20	30	–31	16,142	93.3	6.7	206	61.7	38.3	216	–15	201	1,035	545	Syria
61	14	22	49	–47	…	…	…	…	…	…	10,531[4]	–6,803[4]	3,728[4]	3,402	6,500	Taiwan
…	…	…	…	…	594.9	90.7	9.3	22.6	88.7	11.3	–38[3]	–36[3]	–74[3]	…	…	Tajikistan
85	8	15	19	–28	6,595	96.7	3.3	150	59.3	40.7	–876.0	69.1	–806.9	392	407	Tanzania
50	10	24	56	–40	31,011	71.3	28.7	4,255	60.0	40.0	14,013	1,585	12,428	7,048	1,888	Thailand
81	11	14	34	–40	1,263	100.0	—	26	65.4	34.6	–98.0	–29.1	–127.1	13	19	Togo
…	…	…	…	…	63.5	98.0	2.0	4.3	81.4	18.6	–67.1[4]	47.8[4]	–19.3[4]	14	3	Tonga
62	16	26	48	–54	1,485	46.3	53.7	401	74.1	25.9	–740.8[4]	97.3[4]	–643.5[4]	108	75	Trinidad and Tobago
60	16	28	42	–46	9,487	67.5	32.5	1,359	63.8	36.2	–2,141	1,698	–443	1,423	160	Tunisia
67	12	24	24	–27	50,095	25.8	74.2	8,559	64.0	36.0	–10,443	9,083	–1,360	8,088	1,716	Turkey
…	…	…	…	…	1,678	23.7	76.3	449	86.2	13.8	–523.0[4]	–411.5[4]	–934.5[4]	74	125	Turkmenistan
…	…	…	…	…	…	…	…	…	…	…	…	…	…	0.3	…	Tuvalu
83[3]	10[3]	15[3]	12[3]	–21[3]	3,564	98.0	2.0	126	65.1	34.9	–596.4	45.6	–550.8	135	137	Uganda
59	23	21	40	–43	10,027	61.5	38.5	1,277	62.4	37.6	244	1,414	1,658	270	305	Ukraine
45[1]	16[1]	26[1]	77[1]	–65[1]	…	…	…	…	…	…	8,254[3]	–1,553[3]	6,701[3]	535	…	United Arab Emirates
65	18	18	27	–28	…	…	…	…	…	…	–42,350	26,370	–15,980	20,039	27,710	United Kingdom
67	15	20	11	–13	…	…	…	…	…	…	–343,260	11,780	–331,480	73,268	51,220	United States
71	14	16	22	–22	5,108	42.1	57.9	917	61.6	38.4	–868.4	263.4	–605.0	759	264	Uruguay
…	…	…	…	…	3,421	54.8	45.2	461	65.7	34.3	171[4]	–210[4]	–39[4]	19	…	Uzbekistan
49[5]	27[5]	34[5]	47[5]	–57[5]	63.4	100.0	—	1.6	53.1	46.9	–51.5	48.4	–3.1	51	5	Vanuatu
73	8	20	20	–20	25,216	18.9	81.1	4,148	54.6	45.4	7,606	–3,917	3,689	1,086	2,381	Venezuela
71	7	29	42	–49	20,529	82.2	17.8	1,347	75.8	24.2	–981[4]	–86[4]	–1,067[4]	88	…	Vietnam
…	…	…	…	…	…	…	…	…	…	…	…	…	…	601	…	Virgin Islands (U.S.)
…	…	…	…	…	…	…	…	…	…	…	…	…	…	…	…	West Bank
…	…	…	…	…	…	…	…	…	…	…	…	…	…	…	…	Western Sahara
61[3]	16[3]	28[3]	43[3]	–48[3]	3,729	95.3	4.7	100	46.0	54.0	357.9	219.2	577.1	69	81	Yemen
79	16	14	29	–38	4,498	99.3	0.7	416	69.5	30.5	–148[4]	–121[4]	–269[4]	75	59	Zambia
70[3]	17[3]	20[3]	38[3]	–46[3]	3,211	88.7	11.3	480	71.6	28.4	79[4]	–423[4]	–344[4]	230	118	Zimbabwe

[1]1996. [2]Manufacturing includes mining and public utilities. [3]1997. [4]1998. [5]Gross domestic product (GDP). [6]1994. [7]1995. [8]Manufacturing includes mining. [9]Mining includes public utilities. [10]Republic of Cyprus only. [11]Services includes hotels. [12]Excludes Alderney and Sark. [13]Manufacturing includes public utilities. [14]Manufacturing includes mining, construction, and public utilities. [15]Construction includes mining. [16]Transportation, communications includes public utilities. [17]Services includes transportation, communications. [18]1991.

Employment and labour

This table provides international comparisons of the world's national labour forces—giving their size; composition by demographic component and employment status; and structure by industry.

The table focuses on the concept of "economically active population," which the International Labour Organisation (ILO) defines as persons of all ages who are either employed or looking for work. In general, the economically active population does not include students, persons occupied solely in domestic duties, retired persons, persons living entirely on their own means, and persons wholly dependent on others. Persons engaged in illegal economic activities—smugglers, prostitutes, drug dealers, bootleggers, black marketeers, and others—also fall outside the purview of the ILO definition. Countries differ markedly in their treatment, as part of the labour force, of such groups as members of the armed forces, inmates of institutions, the unemployed (both persons seeking their first job and those previously employed), seasonal and international migrant workers, and persons engaged in informal, subsistence, or part-time economic activities. Some countries include all or most of these groups among the economically active, while others may treat the same groups as inactive.

Three principal structural comparisons of the economically active total are given in the first part of the table: (1) participation rate, or the proportion of the economically active who possess some particular characteristic, is given for women and for those of working age (usually ages 15 to 64), (2) activity rate, the proportion of the total population who *are* economically active, is given for both sexes and as a total, and (3) employment status, usually (and here) grouped as employers, self-employed, employees, family workers (usually unpaid), and others.

Each of these measures indicates certain characteristics in a given national labour market; none should be interpreted in isolation, however, as the meaning of each is influenced by a variety of factors—demographic structure and change, social or religious customs, educational opportunity, sexual differentiation in employment patterns, degree of technological development, and the like. Participation and activity rates, for example, may be high in a particular country because it possesses an older population with few children, hence a higher proportion of working age, or because, despite a young population with many below working age, the economy attracts eligible immigrant workers, themselves almost exclusively of working age. At the same time, low activity and participation rates might be characteristic of a country having a young population with poor employment possibilities or of a country with a good job market distorted by the presence of large numbers of "guest" or contract workers who are not part of the domestic labour force. An illiterate woman in a strongly sex-differentiated labour force is likely to begin and end as a family or

Employment and labour

country	year	economically active population										distribution by economic sector			
		total ('000)	participation rate (%)		activity rate (%)			employment status (%)				agriculture, forestry, fishing		manufacturing; mining, quarrying; public utilities	
			female	ages 15–64	total	male	female	employers, self-employed	employees	unpaid family workers	other	number ('000)	% of econ. active	number ('000)	% of econ. active
Afghanistan	1979	3,941	7.9	49.1	30.3	54.2	4.9	52.2	33.8	14.0	—	2,369	60.1	494	12.5
Albania	1994	1,340	47.0[3]	92.0[3, 4]	57.4[3]	60.8[3]	54.0[3]	…	…	…	…	534	39.9	84[5]	6.3[5]
Algeria	1987	5,341	9.2	44.3	23.6	42.4	4.4	16.8	61.7	2.6	18.9	725	13.6	622	11.6
American Samoa	1990	14.2	41.1	52.6[8]	30.4	34.8	25.7	2.1	92.6	0.2	5.1	0.3	2.3	4.8	33.7
Andorra	1989	25	45.6	74.3	55.1	…	…	…	…	…	…	0.3	1.2	2.7	11.0
Angola	1996	4,581	37.3	65.1[10]	40.0	50.8	29.5	…	…	…	…	3,170	69.2	528	11.5[11]
Antigua and Barbuda	1991	26.8	45.6	69.7	45.1	50.9	39.6	12.1	82.8	0.7	4.4	1.0	3.9	1.9	7.3
Argentina	1995	14,345	36.7	64.5	41.5	53.5	29.9	28.0[13]	60.4[13]	5.0[13]	6.6[13]	1,201[14]	12.0[14]	2,136[14]	21.3[14]
Armenia	1996	1,584	…	75.1[16]	42.1	…	…	…	…	…	…	587	37.1	255	16.1
Aruba	1991	31.1	42.5	67.1	46.7	54.5	39.0	7.0	86.4	0.3	6.3	0.2	0.5	2.3	7.3
Australia	1998[18]	9,343	43.3	73.3[19]	49.8	56.6	43.0	12.7	78.2	0.7	8.4	442	4.7	1,311	14.0
Austria	1998[18]	3,888	43.1	70.7	48.1	56.5	40.3	9.7[20]	87.4[20]	3.0[20]	—	246	6.3	842	21.6
Azerbaijan	1998	3,744	47.8	64.4[16, 20]	47.1	50.1	44.2	…	…	…	…	1,085	29.0	367	9.8
Bahamas, The	1994	139	47.5	77.8	50.7	54.8	46.8	11.6[22]	85.1[22]	0.3[22]	3.0[22]	6.9	5.0	7.3	5.3
Bahrain	1991	226	17.5	66.8	44.6	63.5	18.5	5.1	88.5	0.1	6.3	5	2.3	33	14.6
Bangladesh	1995–96[18]	56,014	38.1	73.7	46.0	55.8	35.7	28.8	12.1	39.1	20.0	34,530	61.6	4,211	7.5
Barbados	1995[18]	137	49.5	79.9	51.8	54.6	49.1	8.8[24]	76.4[24]	0.2[24]	14.6[24]	6.3	4.6	15.6	11.4
Belarus	1999	4,542	52.4	78.2[16]	45.3	46.0	44.7	…	…	…	…	672	14.8	1,258	27.7
Belgium	1992	4,237	42.3	51.5[25]	42.2	49.8	34.9	12.7	72.4	3.4	11.5	95	2.2	788	18.6
Belize	1996	75.5	30.8	58.5[26]	34.1	47.2	21.0	26.2[20]	59.2[20]	4.9[20]	9.8[20]	18.3[13]	31.4[13]	7.0[13]	12.0[13]
Benin	1992	2,085	42.6	73.4	43.0	50.6	35.7	58.4	5.3	30.5	5.8	1,148	55.0	162	7.8
Bermuda	1995	34.1	50.0	63.5[13]	55.8	57.4	54.4	9.7[13]	84.0[13]	0.1[13]	6.2[13]	0.5	1.5	1.4	4.2
Bhutan	…	…	…	…	…	…	…	…	…	…	…	…	…	…	…
Bolivia	1992	2,530	38.2	64.0	39.4	48.7	30.4	41.2	31.5	7.1	20.2	984	38.9	281	11.1
Bosnia and Herzegovina	1990[5]	1,026	36.9	…	22.7	…	…	…	…	…	…	39	3.8	519	50.5
Botswana	1995	440	46.6	65.4	29.9	33.1	27.0	7.9	62.7	7.9	21.5	54	12.2	47	10.8
Brazil	1997	75,213	40.4	66.9	48.2	58.7	38.1	26.3[22]	62.3[22]	7.7[22]	3.7[22]	16,771	22.3	9,281	12.3
Brunei	1991	112	32.9	67.6	43.0	54.6	30.0	3.5	91.4	0.4	4.7	2.2	1.9	11.6	10.4
Bulgaria	1995	3,738	48.4[28]	68.8[28]	46.3[28]	48.7[28]	44.1[28]	8.4	75.9	0.9	14.8	783	20.9	1,003	26.8
Burkina Faso	1995	5,250	45.5	75.8[10]	50.9	56.0	45.9	…	…	…	…	4,397	83.8	298	5.7[11]
Burundi	1990	2,780	52.6	91.4	52.5	51.2	53.8	62.8	5.1	30.3	1.8	2,574	92.6	37	1.3
Cambodia	1993	4,010	55.8	86.2	43.1	39.5	46.4	…	…	…	…	2,454[14]	74.4[14]	220[11, 14]	6.7[11, 14]
Cameroon	1991	4,740	33.2	58.9[10]	40.0	53.9	26.3	60.2[22]	14.6[22]	18.0[22]	7.1[22]	2,856	60.3	628[11]	13.2[11]
Canada	1998[18]	15,631	45.3	75.4	51.0	56.3	45.9	15.8	75.5	0.4	8.3	586	3.7	2,601	16.6
Cape Verde	1990	121	37.1	64.3	35.3	46.9	24.9	24.7	53.7	2.0	19.6	29.9	24.8	6.8	5.7
Central African Republic	1988	1,187	46.8	78.3	48.2	52.2	44.3	75.3	8.0	8.1	8.6	881	74.2	31	2.6
Chad	1991	2,016	18.2	51.6[10]	35.3	56.5	14.7	…	…	…	…	1,489	73.9	149[11]	7.4[11]
Chile	1998[18]	5,852	33.4	59.9	39.3	52.8	26.0	26.4[19]	64.6[19]	3.2[19]	5.8[19]	809	13.8	1,015	17.3
China	1990	657,290	44.9	85.0	57.9	61.8	53.7	…	…	…	…	467,926	71.2	87,275	13.3
Colombia	1985	9,558	32.8	49.4[29]	34.3	46.6	22.3	…	…	…	…	2,412[14]	28.5[14]	1,231[14]	14.5[14]
Comoros	1996	252	38.9	59.2	37.2	44.8	29.3	47.6[14]	25.6[14]	— 26.8[14] —		189	74.7	18[11]	7.1[11]
Congo, Dem. Rep. of the	1996	14,082	35.0	47.9[10]	31.1	40.9	21.6	…	…	…	…	9,124	64.8	2,267[11]	16.1[11]
Congo, Rep. of the	1984	563	45.6	54.0	29.5	33.0	26.2	64.3	31.4	1.2	3.1	294	52.2	50	8.8
Costa Rica	1998	1,377	32.6	59.7[25]	41.2	55.8	26.7	24.0[19]	72.2[19]	3.3[19]	0.6[19]	271	19.7	231	16.8
Côte d'Ivoire	1988	4,263	32.3	66.6	39.4	52.2	26.0	…	…	…	…	2,628	61.6	100	2.3
Croatia	1991	2,040	42.9	65.2	45.3	53.9	37.4	12.7	73.7	2.0	11.6	341	16.7	571	28.0
Cuba	1988	4,570	36.1	56.9[25]	44.2	56.2	32.1	5.7[30]	94.1[30]	0.2[30]	—	791[30]	22.3[30]	668[30]	18.9[30]
Cyprus[31, 32]	1995	303	38.6	71.5	47.0	57.8	36.2	18.7[28]	73.1[28]	6.1[28]	2.1[28]	31	10.1	48	15.9
Czech Republic	1997	5,215	44.1	72.5	50.6	58.2	43.5	12.8	81.6	0.4	5.2	296	5.7	1,617	31.0
Denmark	1998	2,848	46.3	80.3	53.7	58.3	49.2	8.7	85.8	—	5.5	103	3.6	572	20.1
Djibouti	1996	396	41.4	96.3[10]	67.2	79.7	55.0	…	…	…	…	288	72.7	56[11]	14.1[11]
Dominica	1991	26.4	34.5	62.4	38.0	50.0	26.1	29.2[33]	50.6[33]	1.9[33]	18.3[33]	7.3	27.9	2.3	8.8
Dominican Republic	1981	1,915	28.9	53.6	33.9	48.1	19.7	36.5	51.3	3.3	8.9	420	22.0	243	12.7
East Timor	…	…	…	…	…	…	…	…	…	…	…	…	…	…	…
Ecuador	1990	3,360	26.4	55.7	34.8	51.5	18.3	45.7	42.5	4.4	7.4	1,036	30.8	404	12.0
Egypt	1995[18]	17,725	22.0	49.8	29.9	45.9	13.4	24.7[28]	50.0[28]	16.4[28]	9.0[28]	5,221	30.2	2,405	13.9
El Salvador	1997	2,256	36.7	61.4	38.2	50.2	27.0	31.7	48.5	7.4	12.4	607	26.9	373	16.5
Equatorial Guinea	1983	103	35.7	66.7	39.2	52.5	26.9	29.0	16.0	29.9	25.1	59.4	57.9	1.8	1.8
Eritrea	…	…	…	…	…	…	…	…	…	…	…	…	…	…	…
Estonia	1998	711	47.7	71.8[34]	48.9	54.9	43.6	4.8[19]	85.2[19]	0.8[19]	9.2[19]	61	8.6	165	23.2

traditional agricultural worker. Loss of working-age men to war, civil violence, or emigration for job opportunities may also affect the structure of a particular labour market.

The distribution of the economically active population by employment status reveals that a large percentage of economically active persons in some less developed countries falls under the heading "employers, self-employed." This occurs because the countries involved have poor, largely agrarian economies in which the average worker is a farmer who tills his own small plot of land. In countries with well-developed economies, "employees" will usually constitute the largest portion of the economically active.

Caution should be exercised when using the economically active data to make intercountry comparisons, as countries often differ in their choices of classification schemes, definitions, and coverage of groups and in their methods of collection and tabulation of data. The population base containing the economically active population, for example, may range, in developing countries, from age 9 or 10 with no upper limit to, in developed countries, age 18 or 19 upward to a usual retirement age of from 55 to 65, with sometimes a different range for each sex. Data on female labour-force participation, in particular, often lack comparability. In many less developed countries, particularly those dominated by the Islamic faith, a cultural bias favouring traditional roles for women results in the undercounting of economically active women. In other less developed countries, particularly those in which subsistence workers are deemed economically active, the role of women may be overstated.

The second major section of the table provides data on the distribution by economic (also conventionally called industrial) sector of the economically active population. The data usually include such groups as unpaid family workers, members of the armed forces, and the unemployed, the last distributed by industry as far as possible.

The categorization of industrial sectors is based on the divisions listed in the *International Standard Industrial Classification of All Economic Activities*. The "other" category includes persons whose activities were not adequately defined and the unemployed who were not distributable by industrial sector.

A substantial part of the data presented in this table is summarized from various issues of the ILO's *Year Book of Labour Statistics*, which compiles its statistics both from official publications and from information submitted directly by national census and labour authorities. The editors have supplemented and updated ILO statistical data with information from Britannica's holdings of relevant official publications and from direct correspondence with national authorities.

construction		transportation, communications		trade, hotels, restaurants		finance, real estate		public administration, defense		services		other		country
number ('000)	% of econ. active	number ('000)	% of econ. active	number ('000)	% of econ. active	number ('000)	% of econ. active	number ('000)	% of econ. active	number ('000)	% of econ. active	number ('000)	% of econ. active	
51	1.3	66	1.6	138	3.5	[1]	[1]	[1]	[1]	749[1]	19.0[1]	78[2]	2.0[2]	Afghanistan
33[5]	2.5[5]	19[5]	1.4[5]	3[5]	0.2[5]	3[5]	0.2[5]	16[5]	1.2[5]	145[5]	10.8[5]	505[6]	37.7[6]	Albania
690	12.9	216	4.1	391	7.3	143	2.7	[7]	[7]	1,180[7]	22.1[7]	1,374	25.7	Algeria
1.2	8.3	0.8	5.5	1.8	13.0	0.3	2.1	1.4	10.0	2.8	19.8	0.7[9]	5.1[9]	American Samoa
2.9	11.8	...	...	6.0	24.2	1.3	5.4	2.6	10.3	4.1	16.7	0.1	0.5	Andorra
[11]	[11]	[12]	[12]	[12]	[12]	[12]	[12]	[12]	[12]	883[12]	19.3[12]	—	—	Angola
3.1	11.6	2.4	9.0	8.5	31.9	1.5	5.4	[7]	[7]	6.4[7]	23.9[7]	1.9	7.0	Antigua and Barbuda
1,003[14]	10.0[14]	460[14]	4.6[14]	1,702[14]	17.0[14]	396[14]	3.9[14]	[7]	[7]	2,399[7, 14]	23.9[7, 14]	736[14, 15]	7.3[14, 15]	Argentina
68	4.3	24	1.5	110	6.9	[1]	[1]	[1]	[1]	350[1]	22.1[1]	190[17]	12.0[17]	Armenia
3.2	10.4	2.3	7.5	11.0	35.4	2.4	7.8	[7]	[7]	8.6[7]	27.7[7]	1.1[17]	3.5[17]	Aruba
654	7.0	567	6.1	2,279	24.4	1,310	14.0	444	4.7	1,884	20.2	454[17]	4.9[17]	Australia
341	8.8	250	6.4	844	21.7	387	9.9	256	6.6	712	18.3	12[2]	0.3[2]	Austria
150	4.0	167	4.5	772	20.6	10	0.3	[7]	[7]	618[7]	16.5[7]	574[21]	15.3[21]	Azerbaijan
11.6	8.3	11.2	8.1	44.2	31.8	12.9	9.3	10.7	7.7	29.7	21.4	4.5[23]	3.2[23]	Bahamas, The
27	11.8	14	6.1	30	13.2	17	7.6	41	18.1	43	19.0	16[17]	7.3[17]	Bahrain
1,015	1.8	2,308	4.1	6,068	10.8	213	0.4	[7]	[7]	5,092[7]	9.1[7]	2,585[17]	4.6[17]	Bangladesh
12.2	8.9	5.9	4.3	35.3	25.8	8.4	6.1	[7]	[7]	48.8[7]	35.7[7]	4.3[2]	3.1[2]	Barbados
336	7.4	332	7.3	504	11.1	[1]	[1]	[1]	[1]	1,345[1]	29.6[1]	95[9]	2.1[9]	Belarus
245	5.8	257	6.1	634	15.0	342	8.1	7	7	1,393[7]	32.9[7]	484[17]	11.4[17]	Belgium
4.1[13]	7.0[13]	2.9[13]	5.0[13]	10.0[13]	17.2[13]	1.8[13]	3.1[13]	5.4[13]	9.2[13]	6.0[13]	10.3[13]	2.8[13]	4.8[13]	Belize
52	2.5	53	2.5	433	20.7	3	0.1	[7]	[7]	165[7]	7.9[7]	71[21]	3.4[21]	Benin
1.7	5.0	2.2	6.4	10.8	31.6	5.2	15.3	[7]	[7]	12.3[7]	35.9[7]	—	—	Bermuda
...	...	...	...	...	...	...	...	...	...	...	...	...	...	Bhutan
129	5.1	117	4.6	232	9.2	54	2.1	59	2.3	350	13.8	323[15]	12.7[15]	Bolivia
75	7.3	69	6.7	131	12.8	39	3.8	[7]	[7]	155[7]	15.1[7]	—	—	Bosnia and Herzegovina
41	9.3	8	1.8	54	12.3	12	2.7	60	13.6	69	15.7	95[17]	21.6[17]	Botswana
4,583	6.1	2,759	3.7	9,223[27]	12.3[27]	1,287	1.7	[7]	[7]	25,436[7, 27]	33.8[7, 27]	5,882[9]	7.8[9]	Brazil
14.1	12.6	5.4	4.8	15.4	13.8	5.8	5.2	[7]	[7]	52.1[7]	46.6[7]	5.3[17]	4.7[17]	Brunei
188	5.0	251	6.7	357	9.5	51	1.4	76	2.0	532	14.2	497[17]	13.3[17]	Bulgaria
[11]	[11]	[12]	[12]	[12]	[12]	[12]	[12]	[12]	[12]	558[12]	10.6[12]	—	—	Burkina Faso
20	0.7	9	0.3	26	0.9	2.0	0.1	[7]	[7]	85[7]	3.1[7]	27[17]	1.0[17]	Burundi
[11]	[11]	[12]	[12]	[12]	[12]	[12]	[12]	[12]	[12]	625[12, 14]	18.9[12, 14]	—	—	Cambodia
[11]	[11]	[12]	[12]	[12]	[12]	[12]	[12]	[12]	[12]	1,256[12]	26.5[12]	—	—	Cameroon
857	5.5	1,128	7.2	3,585	22.9	2,336	14.9	820	5.2	3,252	20.8	468[2]	3.0[2]	Canada
22.7	18.8	6.1	5.1	12.7	10.6	0.8	0.7	[7]	[7]	17.4[7]	14.4[7]	24.1	20.0	Cape Verde
6	0.5	7	0.6	92	7.8	0.7	0.1	[7]	[7]	70[7]	5.9[7]	100[17]	8.5[17]	Central African Republic
[11]	[11]	[12]	[12]	[12]	[12]	[12]	[12]	[12]	[12]	377[12]	18.7[12]	—	—	Chad
533	9.1	456	7.8	1,075	18.4	437	7.5	[7]	[7]	1,478[7]	25.3[7]	47[15]	0.8[15]	Chile
11,890	1.8	11,814	1.8	25,631	3.9	8,268	1.3	[7]	[7]	34,053[7]	5.2[7]	10,434	1.6	China
242[14]	2.9[14]	353[14]	4.2[14]	1,262[14]	14.9[14]	278[14]	3.3[14]	[7]	[7]	1,998[7, 14]	23.6[7, 14]	691[14, 15]	8.2[14, 15]	Colombia
[11]	[11]	[12]	[12]	[12]	[12]	[12]	[12]	[12]	[12]	46[12]	18.2[12]	—	—	Comoros
[11]	[11]	[12]	[12]	[12]	[12]	[12]	[12]	[12]	[12]	2,691[12]	19.1[12]	—	—	Congo, Dem. Rep. of the
25	4.5	29	5.1	67	11.8	3	0.5	[7]	[7]	85[7]	15.1[7]	10	2.0	Congo, Rep. of the
89	6.5	75	5.5	267	19.4	35	2.6	[7]	[7]	385[7]	27.9[7]	23[23]	1.7[23]	Costa Rica
85	2.0	118	2.8	530	12.4	[1]	[1]	[1]	[1]	591[1]	13.9[1]	210[2]	4.9[2]	Côte d'Ivoire
93	4.5	112	5.5	223	10.9	58	2.8	104	5.1	204	10.0	329[17]	16.1[17]	Croatia
313[30]	8.8[30]	249[30]	7.0[30]	306[30]	8.6[30]	[1]	[1]	[1]	[1]	1,086[1, 30]	30.7[1, 30]	128[30]	3.6[30]	Cuba
26	8.7	19	6.2	77	25.4	23	7.6	[7]	[7]	65[7]	21.6[7]	13	4.4	Cyprus[31, 32]
501	9.6	392	7.5	871	16.7	358	6.9	328	6.3	762	14.6	90[17]	1.7[17]	Czech Republic
185	6.5	191	6.7	467	16.4	321	11.3	175	6.1	821	28.8	18[23]	0.6[23]	Denmark
[11]	[11]	[12]	[12]	[12]	[12]	[12]	[12]	[12]	[12]	52[12]	13.2[12]	—	—	Djibouti
2.8	10.7	1.2	4.6	3.7	13.9	0.8	3.1	1.5	5.8	3.4	13.1	3.2[17]	12.3[17]	Dominica
81	4.3	40	2.1	192	10.0	22	1.2	[7]	[7]	363[7]	18.9[7]	553[15]	28.9[15]	Dominican Republic
...	...	...	...	...	...	...	...	...	...	...	...	...	...	East Timor
197	5.9	131	3.9	477	14.2	81	2.4	[7]	[7]	838[7]	24.9[7]	196[15]	5.8[15]	Ecuador
984	5.7	912	5.3	1,609	9.3	286	1.7	[7]	[7]	4,000[7]	23.2[7]	1,858[23]	10.8[23]	Egypt
159	7.1	103	4.6	462	20.5	32	1.4	[7]	[7]	485[7]	21.5[7]	36[2]	1.6[2]	El Salvador
1.9	1.9	1.8	1.7	3.1	3.0	0.4	0.4	[7]	[7]	8.4[7]	8.2[7]	25.8[17]	25.2[17]	Equatorial Guinea
...	...	...	...	...	...	...	...	...	...	...	...	...	...	Eritrea
48	6.8	60	8.4	105	14.8	44	6.2	37	5.2	122	17.2	68[9]	9.6[9]	Estonia

Employment and labour (continued)

country	year	economically active population										distribution by economic sector			
		total ('000)	participation rate (%)		activity rate (%)			employment status (%)				agriculture, forestry, fishing		manufacturing; mining, quarrying; public utilities	
			female	ages 15–64	total	male	female	employers, self-employed	employees	unpaid family workers	other	number ('000)	% of econ. active	number ('000)	% of econ. active
Ethiopia	1995	24,606	41.1	72.2	43.3	50.3	36.5	58.5[35]	6.5[35]	34.0[35]	1.0[35]	21,605	87.8	419	1.7
Faroe Islands	1977	17.6	27.2	64.0	41.9	58.2	23.9	11.9	86.1	…	2.0	3.3	18.8	3.9	21.9
Fiji	1986	241	21.2	56.0	33.7	52.4	14.5	33.6	42.2	16.3	7.9	106	44.1	22	9.0
Finland	1998	2,532	47.0	73.1	49.1	53.4	45.1	11.9	75.2	0.6	12.3	154	6.1	508	20.1
France	1994[18]	25,871	44.9	67.7	44.8	50.6	39.2	10.2	77.4	—	12.4	1,048	4.1	4,432	17.4
French Guiana	1990	48.8	38.2	67.3	42.5	50.5	33.9	10.6	62.7	2.5	24.2	4.2	8.6	3.1	6.4
French Polynesia	1988	75	37.1	64.8	39.9	48.2	30.9	13.0	55.0	4.0	28.0	7.6	10.0	5.4	7.2
Gabon	1991	504	36.9	56.0[10]	43.9	53.9	30.7	…	…	…	…	338	67.1	71[11]	14.1[11]
Gambia, The	1983	326	46.3	78.2	47.3	51.1	43.6	0.5	78.0	14.3	7.1	240	73.7	9	2.9
Gaza Strip	1996	173	9.0	36.3[25]	18.0	32.0	3.2	15.7	46.8	6.7	30.8	9.0	5.2	17.0[36]	9.8[36]
Georgia	1993	1,920	…	58.1[16, 28]	35.7	…	…	…	…	…	…	562	29.3	303	15.8
Germany	1998	39,709	43.1	70.7	48.4	56.5	40.7	9.1	80.3	1.0	9.6	1,200	3.0	10,019	25.2
Ghana	1984	5,580	51.2	82.5[25]	45.4	44.9	45.8	67.7	15.7	12.2	4.4	3,311	59.3	631	11.3
Greece	1997[18]	4,294	39.2	61.3	40.9	53.0	31.5	29.9	49.2	10.7	10.2	773	18.0	680	15.8
Greenland	1976	21.4	33.4	63.5[25]	43.1	53.0	31.4	12.6	82.5	0.4	4.5	3.2	15.1	3.3	15.3
Grenada	1988	38.9	48.6	72.7[35]	39.9	42.9	37.2	16.0[30]	64.2[30]	0.8[30]	19.0[30]	5.6	14.3	3.3	8.6
Guadeloupe	1990	172	45.5	66.4	44.5	49.6	39.7	13.2	53.7	2.0	31.1	8.4	4.9	9.6	5.6
Guam	1990	66.1	37.4	75.7[8]	49.7	58.4	39.7	2.4	94.4	0.1	3.1	0.5	0.8	3.5	5.3
Guatemala	1999	3,489	22.0	55.0	31.5	48.6	14.0	32.7[33]	47.6[33]	16.2[33]	3.5[33]	1,416[33]	48.9[33]	405[33]	14.0[33]
Guernsey[38]	1996	30.7	44.7	76.4	52.3	60.1	45.1	13.0	87.0	—	—	1.9	6.2	2.5	8.2
Guinea	1983	1,823	39.4	63.5	39.1	48.7	30.1	36.2	15.6	37.6	10.6	1,424	78.1	27	1.5
Guinea-Bissau	1995	491	39.9	65.5[10]	45.8	55.9	36.0	…	…	…	…	373	76.0	20[11]	4.1[11]
Guyana	1992–93	278	34.1	61.8	38.8	51.9	26.0	14.3[14]	63.8[14]	1.9[14]	20.0[14]	50[14]	20.4[14]	41[14]	16.8[14]
Haiti	1990	2,679	40.0	64.8	41.1	50.3	32.3	59.1	16.5	10.4	14.0	1,535	57.3	178	6.6
Honduras	1998[18]	2,135	36.9	61.2[25]	36.9	49.2	25.0	40.6	48.0	11.4	—	738	34.6	380	17.8
Hong Kong	1998[18]	3,359	39.3	70.0	51.1	61.9	40.3	9.9[19]	87.4[19]	0.7[19]	1.9[19]	10	0.3	434	12.9
Hungary	1998[18]	4,011	44.4	58.4	39.3	45.8	33.4	10.6	80.3	0.7	8.4	301	7.5	1,115	27.8
Iceland	1998	152.1	47.1	86.6[8]	55.4	59.2	52.2	17.3	80.3	0.3	2.1	12.8	8.4	27.1	17.8
India	1991	314,131	28.6	60.7[25, 30]	37.5	51.6	22.3	8.8[30]	16.3[30]	3.6[30]	71.3[30]	191,341	60.9	30,423	9.7
Indonesia	1998	92,735	38.8	65.3[25]	45.4	55.8	35.0	42.7[34]	33.0[34]	17.1[34]	7.2[34]	39,415	42.5	10,756	11.6
Iran	1996–97	16,027	12.7	46.8[13]	26.7	45.8	6.9	39.7[13]	45.4[13]	2.3[13]	12.6[13]	3,205[13]	21.8[13]	2,243[13]	15.2[13]
Iraq	1988	4,127	12.0	45.3	24.7	42.3	6.1	25.4[39]	59.5[39]	11.4[39]	3.7[39]	477	11.6	439	10.6
Ireland	1997	1,539	39.1	62.7	42.0	51.6	32.6	17.4	71.1	1.1	10.4	145	9.4	314	20.4
Isle of Man	1991	33.2	42.3	73.2	47.6	56.9	38.9	15.8	80.1	—	4.1	1.2	3.7	3.9	11.6
Israel	1998[18]	2,272	44.3	53.5[25]	40.3	45.2	35.5	13.2	77.7	0.5	8.6	50	2.3	434	19.1
Italy	1994[18]	22,680	36.9	57.4	40.1	52.1	28.8	21.4	62.8	4.0	11.8	1,573	6.9	4,837	21.3
Jamaica	1998	1,129	45.6	69.3[40]	43.9	48.7	39.2	32.3	49.9	1.9	15.9	218[19]	20.0[19]	107[19]	9.8[19]
Japan	1998	67,930	40.7	72.6	53.7	65.1	42.9	11.2	79.0	5.4	4.4	3,440	5.1	14,620	21.5
Jersey	1991	47.5	43.2	66.9[25]	56.5	66.1	47.5	12.6	84.0	…	3.4	2.2	4.7	3.8	8.0
Jordan	1993	859	11.4[42]	43.2[42]	22.2	…	…	22.8[43]	67.2[43]	0.8[43]	9.2[43]	55	6.4	97	11.3
Kazakhstan	1995	6,976	…	71.8[16, 20]	40.8	…	…	…	…	…	…	1,442	20.7	1,372	19.7
Kenya	1996	12,269	38.5	63.6[10]	43.9	53.9	33.8	…	…	…	…	9,100	74.2	1,062[11]	8.7[11]
Kiribati	1990	32.6	46.4	75.6[25]	45.1	48.9	41.4	71.9	25.3	…	2.8	23.1	71.0	0.9	2.8
Korea, North	1985	9,084	46.0	75.3	44.6	48.6	40.6	…	…	…	…	3,726[24]	44.1[24]	2,790[11, 24]	33.0[11, 24]
Korea, South	1998[18]	21,390	39.8	60.7[25]	45.9	54.9	36.8	26.8	57.0	9.3	6.8	2,450	11.5	4,246	19.9
Kuwait	1997	1,217	23.5	61.5[42]	55.1	69.0	33.2	3.9[42]	94.1[42]	0.1[42]	1.9[42]	9[42]	1.3[42]	69[42]	9.4[42]
Kyrgyzstan	1998	1,705	46.1	…	37.2	41.1	33.5	…	…	…	…	831	48.7	104	6.1
Laos	1995	2,166	56.4	83.3	47.3	46.2	52.8	…	…	…	…	1,393[14]	75.7[14]	130[11, 14]	7.1[11, 14]
Latvia	1997	1,186	48.1	70.2	48.0	54.0	42.9	11.1	69.3	5.0	14.6	203	17.1	233	19.6
Lebanon	1997	1,362	21.6	49.3	34.0	55.2	14.2	…	…	…	…	132[44]	19.1[44]	131[44]	18.9[44]
Lesotho	1986	504	27.0	44.0	31.6	47.3	16.7	16.8	55.7	20.5	7.0	131	25.9	142	28.2
Liberia	1984	704	41.0	56.3	33.5	39.1	27.8	59.1	21.6	14.4	5.0	481	68.3	31	4.4
Libya	1991	1,169	9.3	37.1[10]	24.8	42.9	4.9	…	…	…	…	129	11.0	372[11]	31.8[11]
Liechtenstein	1996	16.2	40.3	71.3	52.0	63.7	40.8	6.4	90.8	0.1	2.7	0.3	2.0	4.9	30.2
Lithuania	1998	1,835	47.9	71.7[26]	49.5	54.8	44.9	14.1	69.1	0.2	16.6	317	17.2	411	22.4
Luxembourg	1991[45]	168	36.5	62.5	43.5	56.4	31.2	9.2	85.3	1.1	4.4	5	3.2	26	15.8
Macau	1998[18]	210.7	35.3	70.7[40]	50.2	58.2	43.0	8.0	85.9	1.6	4.5	0.4	0.2	44.5	21.1
Macedonia	1996	789	39.1	60.6	39.6	48.1	31.1	…	…	…	…	103	13.0	165	20.9
Madagascar	1996	5,984	38.2	58.7	39.2	48.9	29.8	…	…	…	…	4,381	73.2	926[11]	15.5[11]
Malawi	1987	3,458	51.0	89.4	43.3	43.9	42.8	4.9	16.2	77.6	1.3	2,968	85.8	114	3.3
Malaysia	1998[18]	8,884	33.5	64.4	40.1	52.0	27.5	21.1[20]	71.4[20]	7.5[20]	—	1,617	18.2	1,986	22.4
Maldives	1990	56.4	19.9	50.2	26.5	41.3	10.8	39.7	49.3	4.5	6.5	14.1	25.0	9.4	16.6
Mali	1987	3,438	37.4	67.4	44.7	57.2	32.7	35.4	5.2	57.6	1.8	2,803	81.5	191	5.6
Malta	1990	132	25.4	47.4[13]	37.2	56.1	18.7	14.1[48]	77.4[48]	…	8.5[48]	3	2.5	38	28.8
Marshall Islands	1988	11.5	30.1	54.1[28]	26.5	37.7	14.8	21.6	58.9	7.1	12.5	2.2	18.7	1.0	9.0
Martinique	1990	165	47.5	68.1	45.9	49.8	42.2	9.5	56.9	1.5	32.1	8.4	5.1	9.7	5.9
Mauritania	1995	704	23.0	44.3[10]	31.0	48.1	14.1	…	…	…	…	437	62.1	84[11]	11.9[11]
Mauritius[49]	1995	484	32.9	63.5	42.9	58.1	28.0	15.1	72.9	2.1	9.9	65	13.5	142	29.4
Mayotte	1991	27.3	29.4	56.4	28.9	39.2	17.7	12.0	42.9	7.3	37.8	3.1	11.4	1.3	4.7
Mexico	1998	39,507	33.7	65.4	41.3	56.1	27.2	30.1[20]	53.8[20]	13.6[20]	2.6[20]	7,842	19.8	7,473	18.9
Micronesia	1990	30.5	29.8[14]	60.6	30.3	…	…	2.7[14]	74.4[14]	0.1[14]	22.7[14]	12.7	41.5	1.6	5.2
Moldova	1996	1,686	…	68.7[16, 19]	39.1	…	…	…	…	…	…	711	42.2	195	11.6
Monaco	1990	12.6	39.7	…	42.0	53.2	31.8	17.4	75.1	0.3	7.2	—	0.3	2.7	21.8
Mongolia	1998	841	48.0	64.3[51]	36.7	38.8	34.6	…	…	…	…	300[20]	35.5[20]	124[20]	14.7[20]
Morocco	1982	5,999	19.7	48.9	29.3	47.1	11.6	27.1	40.5	17.6	14.8	2,352	39.2	1,016	16.9
Mozambique	1996	9,318	46.3	83.2[10]	56.3	61.1	51.5	…	…	…	…	7,360	79.0	987[11]	10.6[11]
Myanmar (Burma)	1997–98[18]	18,337	35.3[48]	64.2[48]	40.2[48]	52.4[48]	28.2[48]	41.4[48]	27.4[48]	30.2[48]	1.0[48]	12,093	65.9	1,831	9.9
Namibia	1991	494	43.6	61.3	35.2	39.9	30.5	17.8	49.1	17.9	15.2	190	38.5	41	8.2
Nauru	1977	2.2	…	…	30.5	…	…	…	…	…	…	…	…	…	…
Nepal	1991	7,340	40.4	57.0[10]	40.0	47.8	32.2	75.8	21.4	2.3	0.4	5,962	81.2	164	2.2
Netherlands, The	1998	7,735	42.5	72.9	49.3	57.2	41.5	10.0	84.8	0.8	4.4	236	3.1	1,162	15.0
Netherlands Antilles	1992	87.8	45.1	68.6	46.3	53.1	40.1	…	…	…	…	0.5	0.6	8.4	9.6
New Caledonia	1989	66	37.5	70.7[53]	40.2	49.1	30.8	16.3	64.3	1.6	17.8	7.8	11.8	6.2	9.3
New Zealand	1998[18]	1,864	45.0	74.0	49.2	54.9	43.6	18.1[20]	73.6[20]	0.8[20]	7.5[20]	161	8.6	326	17.5
Nicaragua	1998	1,630	29.5	61.2	34.1	48.9	19.8	…	…	…	…	457[28]	31.4[28]	183[28]	12.5[28]

construction		transportation, communications		trade, hotels, restaurants		finance, real estate		public administration, defense		services		other		country
number ('000)	% of econ. active	number ('000)	% of econ. active	number ('000)	% of econ. active	number ('000)	% of econ. active	number ('000)	% of econ. active	number ('000)	% of econ. active	number ('000)	% of econ. active	
61	0.2	103	0.4	936	3.8	19	0.1	[7]	[7]	1,252[7]	5.1[7]	210[2]	0.9[2]	Ethiopia
2.0	11.1	1.9	11.1	2.1	11.9	0.3	1.9	[7]	[7]	3.5[7]	20.1[7]	0.6	3.2	Faroe Islands
12	4.9	13	5.5	26	10.8	6	2.5	[7]	[7]	37[7]	15.2[7]	20[17]	8.2[17]	Fiji
163	6.4	178	7.0	366	14.5	269	10.6	148	5.8	653	25.8	95[23]	3.8[23]	Finland
1,443	5.7	1,397	5.5	3,716	14.6	2,340	9.2	[7]	[7]	7,733[7]	30.3[7]	3,376[17]	13.2[17]	France
4.4	9.1	1.9	3.8	4.2	8.5	1.7	3.5	[7]	[7]	17.5[7]	35.9[7]	11.8[9]	24.2[9]	French Guiana
5.5	7.4	2.8	3.7	10.3	13.7	1.2	1.5	[7]	[7]	21.5[7]	28.6[7]	21.1[17]	28.0[17]	French Polynesia
[11]	[11]	[12]	[12]	[12]	[12]	[12]	[12]	[12]	[12]	95[12]	18.8[12]	—	—	Gabon
4	1.3	8	2.5	17	5.1	5	1.4	8	2.5	9	2.9	25	7.7	Gambia, The
17.8	10.3	5.7	3.3	20.8	12.0	[1]	[1]	[1]	[1]	49.3[1, 36]	28.5[1, 36]	53.3[9]	30.8[9]	Gaza Strip
125	6.5	107	5.6	117	6.1	20	1.0	49	2.6	479	24.9	158[17]	8.2[17]	Georgia
3,760	9.5	2,090	5.3	6,924	17.4	4,098	10.3	3,174	8.0	8,182	20.6	262[2]	0.7[2]	Germany
65	1.2	123	2.2	792	14.2	27	0.5	98	1.7	376	6.7	158[9]	2.8[9]	Ghana
262	6.1	264	6.1	933	21.7	268	6.2	285	6.6	593	13.8	235[23]	5.5[23]	Greece
3.1	14.6	1.8	8.6	2.7	12.6	0.3	1.6	[7]	[7]	6.3[7]	29.5[7]	0.6	2.8	Greenland
3.5	9.1	1.7	4.4	5.4	13.9	0.8	2.0	[7]	[7]	5.9[7]	15.3[7]	12.7[17]	32.5[17]	Grenada
14.0	8.1	7.0	4.0	15.0	8.7	2.8	1.6	[7]	[7]	60.8[7]	35.2[7]	54.9[17]	31.8[17]	Guadeloupe
8.0	12.1	4.5	6.8	11.5	17.5	3.9	6.0	17.7	26.7	14.5	21.9	2.0[9]	3.1[9]	Guam
114[33]	3.9[33]	72[33]	2.5[33]	375[33]	12.9[33]	38[33]	1.3[33]	[7]	[7]	417[7]	14.4[7]	60[17]	2.1[17]	Guatemala
2.7	8.7	1.3	4.1	7.0	22.9	8.2	26.6	1.9	6.2	5.0	16.2	0.2	0.8	Guernsey[38]
9	0.5	29	1.6	37	2.0	4	0.2	[7]	[7]	138[7]	7.5[7]	156	8.5	Guinea
[11]	[11]	[12]	[12]	[12]	[12]	[12]	[12]	[12]	[12]	98[12]	20.0[12]	—	—	Guinea-Bissau
7[14]	2.8[14]	9[14]	3.8[14]	15[14]	6.2[14]	3[14]	1.2[14]	30[14]	12.1[14]	29[14]	11.9[14]	61[14, 17]	24.7[14, 17]	Guyana
28	1.0	21	0.8	353	13.2	5	0.2	[7]	[7]	155[7]	5.8[7]	404[17]	15.1[17]	Haiti
111	5.2	55	2.6	440	20.6	52	2.5	[7]	[7]	359[7]	16.8[7]	—	—	Honduras
349	10.4	377	11.2	1,024	30.5	431	12.8	[7]	[7]	718[7]	21.4[7]	16[2]	0.5[2]	Hong Kong
257	6.4	315	7.9	640	16.0	258	6.4	313	7.8	747	18.6	67[23]	1.7[23]	Hungary
11.0	7.2	11.0	7.2	25.7	16.9	14.4	9.5	7.1	4.7	41.4	27.2	1.3[2]	1.1[2]	Iceland
5,543	1.8	8,108	2.6	21,296	6.8	[1]	[1]	[1]	[1]	29,312[1]	9.3[1]	28,199	9.0	India
3,522	3.8	4,154	4.5	16,814	18.1	618	0.7	[7]	[7]	12,394[7]	13.4[7]	5,063[9]	5.5[9]	Indonesia
1,372[13]	9.3[13]	762[13]	5.2[13]	1,238[13]	8.4[13]	195[13]	1.3[13]	[7]	[7]	3,518[7, 13]	23.9[7, 13]	2,203[13, 17]	14.9[13, 17]	Iran
461	11.2	266	6.4	282	6.8	42	1.0	[7]	[7]	2,160[7]	52.3[7]	—	—	Iraq
128	8.3	69	4.5	295	19.2	140	9.1	75	4.8	312	20.3	61[17]	4.0[17]	Ireland
3.4	10.3	2.4	7.3	6.1	18.4	4.4	13.1	[7]	[7]	10.4[7]	31.4[7]	1.4[9]	4.1[9]	Isle of Man
144	6.3	130	5.7	377	16.6	304	13.4	115	5.1	606	26.7	111[17]	4.9[17]	Israel
1,641	7.2	1,080	4.8	4,221	18.6	1,514	6.7	[7]	[7]	5,134[7]	22.6[7]	2,676[9]	11.8[9]	Italy
66[19]	6.1[19]	40[19]	3.7[19]	196[19]	17.9[19]	47[19]	4.3[19]	[7]	[7]	237[7, 19]	21.7[7, 19]	180[17, 19]	16.5[17, 19]	Jamaica
6,670	10.0	4,170	6.1	15,150[41]	22.3[41]	5,930	8.7	[7]	[7]	16,010[7, 41]	23.6[7, 41]	1,810[17]	2.7[17]	Japan
4.4	9.3	2.4	5.0	6.8	14.4	7.4	15.6	3.1	6.5	15.7	33.1	1.6[17]	3.4[17]	Jersey
60	7.0	58	6.7	130	15.1	25	2.9	[7]	[7]	435[7]	50.6[7]	—	—	Jordan
364	5.2	507	7.3	1,035	14.8	334	4.8	[7]	[7]	1,664[7]	23.9[7]	258[17]	3.7[17]	Kazakhstan
[11]	[11]	[12]	[12]	[12]	[12]	[12]	[12]	[12]	[12]	2,107[12]	17.2[12]	—	—	Kenya
0.3	1.0	0.9	2.8	1.3	4.1	0.4	1.4	2.1	6.5	2.3	7.0	1.1[17]	3.4[17]	Kiribati
[11]	[11]	[12]	[12]	[12]	[12]	[12]	[12]	[12]	[12]	1,939[12, 24]	22.9[12, 24]	—	—	Korea, North
1,876	8.8	1,218	5.7	5,911	27.6	1,962	9.2	752	3.5	2,713	12.7	270[15]	1.3[15]	Korea, South
115[42]	15.7[42]	38[42]	5.2[42]	83[42]	11.4[42]	22[42]	3.0[42]	[7]	[7]	384[7, 42]	52.6[7, 42]	11[2, 42]	1.5[2, 42]	Kuwait
51	3.0	75	4.4	178	10.4	15	0.9	61	3.6	258	15.2	132	7.7	Kyrgyzstan
[11]	[11]	[12]	[12]	[12]	[12]	[12]	[12]	[12]	[12]	316[12, 14]	17.2[12, 14]	—	—	Laos
69	5.8	96	8.1	198	16.7	57	4.8	67	5.6	209	17.6	55	4.6	Latvia
43[44]	6.2[44]	48[44]	7.0[44]	115[44]	16.5[44]	24[44]	3.5[44]	[7]	[7]	200[7, 44]	28.8[7, 44]	—	—	Lebanon
28	5.5	8	1.6	24	4.7	2	0.5	[7]	[7]	157[7]	31.1[7]	13	2.6	Lesotho
4	0.6	14	2.0	47	6.7	[1]	[1]	[1]	[1]	63[1]	9.0[1]	64[17]	9.1[17]	Liberia
[11]	[11]	[12]	[12]	[12]	[12]	[12]	[12]	[12]	[12]	668[12]	57.1[12]	—	—	Libya
1.1	7.0	0.5	3.2	2.4	14.8	1.3	7.8	1.0	6.4	4.1	25.4	0.6[17]	3.4[17]	Liechtenstein
128	7.0	119	6.5	302	16.4	70	3.8	82	4.4	347	18.9	61[2]	3.3[2]	Lithuania
14	8.4	11	6.3	29	17.5	15	9.2	21	12.8	31	18.7	14[21]	8.1[21]	Luxembourg
23.0	10.9	14.3	6.8	60.0	28.5	14.4	6.8	16.5	7.8	36.6	17.4	1.0	0.5	Macau
36	4.5	27	3.4	77	9.8	15	1.9	28	3.5	88	11.1	251[46]	31.9[46]	Macedonia
[11]	[11]	[12]	[12]	[12]	[12]	[12]	[12]	[12]	[12]	677[12]	11.3[12]	—	—	Madagascar
46	1.4	25	0.7	94	2.7	6	0.2	[7]	[7]	147[7]	4.3[7]	57	1.7	Malawi
746	8.4	422	4.7	1,616	18.2	426	4.8	[7]	[7]	1,788[7]	20.1[7]	284	3.2	Malaysia
3.2	5.6	5.3	9.4	8.9	15.7	1.1	1.9	[7]	[7]	11.8[7]	21.0[7]	2.7[47]	4.7[47]	Maldives
13	0.4	6	0.2	159	4.6	0.3	—	75	2.2	84	2.4	107	3.1	Mali
6	4.4	9	6.9	13	9.8	5	3.7	[7]	[7]	53[7]	40.0[7]	5[9]	3.8[9]	Malta
1.1	9.4	0.5	4.7	1.4	12.1	0.8	7.3	[7]	[7]	3.1[7]	26.4[7]	1.4[17]	12.5[17]	Marshall Islands
9.3	5.6	6.7	4.0	14.0	8.5	3.0	1.8	[7]	[7]	59.1[7]	35.8[7]	54.8[17]	33.2[17]	Martinique
[11]	[11]	[12]	[12]	[12]	[12]	[12]	[12]	[12]	[12]	183[12]	26.0[12]	—	—	Mauritania
46	9.6	29	5.9	76	15.6	14	2.8	27	5.5	62	12.8	23[2]	4.8[2]	Mauritius[49]
3.1	11.4	1.5	5.4	2.0	7.2	0.1	0.4	[7]	[7]	5.7[7]	21.0[7]	10.5[17]	38.4[17]	Mayotte
2,189	5.5	1,730	4.4	8,777	22.2	1,518	3.8	1,630	4.1	8,051	20.4	298[17]	0.8[17]	Mexico
1.8	6.1	[50]	[50]	[50]	[50]	[50]	[50]	6.3	20.8	3.7[50]	12.1[50]	4.1[9]	13.5[9]	Micronesia
55	3.3	66	3.9	271	16.1	47	2.8	30	1.8	285	16.9	26	1.5	Moldova
0.7	5.3	...	...	2.5	20.2	1.0	8.0	2.8	22.4	1.9	14.9	0.9[21]	7.1[21]	Monaco
33	3.9	38	4.4	62	7.3	[1]	[1]	[1]	[1]	123[1, 20]	14.5[1, 20]	166[20, 21]	19.7[20, 21]	Mongolia
437	7.3	141	2.3	498	8.3	[52]	[52]	533	8.9	474[52]	7.9[52]	548[2]	9.1[2]	Morocco
[11]	[11]	[12]	[12]	[12]	[12]	[12]	[12]	[12]	[12]	971[12]	10.4[12]	—	—	Mozambique
400	2.2	495	2.7	1,781	9.7	...	...	[7]	[7]	1,485[7]	8.1[7]	270	1.5	Myanmar (Burma)
19	3.8	9	1.9	38	7.7	9	1.7	[7]	[7]	6[7]	1.2[7]	183[17]	37.1[17]	Namibia
...	...	...	...	...	...	...	...	...	...	...	...	...	...	Nauru
36	0.5	51	0.7	256	3.5	20	0.3	[7]	[7]	752[7]	10.3[7]	98	1.3	Nepal
451	5.8	442	5.7	1,487	19.2	1,097	14.2	525	6.8	1,833	23.7	498[17]	6.4[17]	Netherlands, The
6.5	7.4	5.0	5.7	20.9	23.8	8.2	9.3	[7]	[7]	24.8[7]	28.2[7]	13.4[9]	15.3[9]	Netherlands Antilles
4.5	6.8	3.1	4.7	9.5	14.3	2.5	3.8	[7]	[7]	22.0[7]	33.4[7]	13.5[9]	16.0[9]	New Caledonia
120	6.5	109	5.8	398	21.3	224	12.0	[7]	[7]	493[7]	26.4[7]	33[17]	1.8[17]	New Zealand
32[28]	2.2[28]	32[28]	2.2[28]	201[28]	13.8[28]	16[28]	1.1[28]	79[28]	5.4[28]	195[28]	13.4[28]	265[9, 28]	18.2[9, 28]	Nicaragua

Employment and labour (continued)

country	year	economically active population										distribution by economic sector			
		total ('000)	participation rate (%)		activity rate (%)			employment status (%)				agriculture, forestry, fishing		manufacturing; mining, quarrying; public utilities	
			female	ages 15–64	total	male	female	employers, self-employed	employees	unpaid family workers	other	number ('000)	% of econ. active	number ('000)	% of econ. active
Niger	1988[54]	2,316	20.4	55.2	31.9	51.1	13.0	51.4	5.0	40.3	3.3	1,764	76.2	73	3.1
Nigeria	1986[18]	30,766	33.3	58.8	31.1	41.1	20.9	64.6	18.8	10.7	5.9	13,259	43.1	1,401	4.6
Northern Mariana Islands	1990	26.6	43.2	83.6[8]	61.3	66.2	55.9	1.4	96.1	0.2	2.3	0.6	2.3	6.0	22.5
Norway	1998	2,317	46.2	80.8	52.3	56.9	47.8	7.4	88.7	0.6	3.2	104	4.5	375	16.2
Oman	1993	705	9.7	60.9	34.9	54.0	8.1	5.2	91.0	0.1	3.7	64	9.1	79	11.3
Pakistan	1996–97[18]	36,407	15.2	51.0	28.7	47.0	9.0	40.6[55]	34.2[55]	19.1[55]	6.1[55]	15,148	41.6	4,222	11.6
Palau	1990	6.1	36.9	64.1[8]	40.2	47.1	32.1	2.5	89.5	0.2	7.8	0.4	7.1	0.2	3.0
Panama	1998	1,049	35.5	66.4	38.4	49.0	27.6	23.9	59.5	2.7	13.9	180	17.2	118	11.3
Papua New Guinea	1980[56]	733	39.8	35.2[10]	24.6	28.3	20.5	72.7	26.4	—	0.9	564	77.0	21	2.9
Paraguay	1982	1,039	19.7	57.5	34.3	54.8	13.6	43.1	37.7	9.2	9.9	446	42.9	129	12.4
Peru	1995	8,906	34.7	60.9	37.8	49.8	26.1	39.8[30]	41.8[30]	8.4[30]	10.0[30]	2,693[20]	32.5[20]	1,091[20]	13.2[20]
Philippines	1998[18]	31,278	37.6	67.9	41.1	51.4	30.8	36.2[19]	41.7[19]	13.7[19]	8.4[19]	11,272	36.0	2,931	9.4
Poland	1998[18]	16,197	45.7	66.1	44.4	49.5	39.5	21.3	69.0	4.5	5.2	3,045	17.7	4,272	24.9
Portugal	1998[18]	5,000	45.0	70.3	50.2	57.3	43.6	24.2	68.0	0.8	7.0	651	13.0	1,243	24.9
Puerto Rico	1998[18]	1,320	42.2	54.5	34.2	41.0	27.9	13.6[34]	85.2[34]	0.7[34]	0.6[34]	35	2.7	203	15.4
Qatar	1988	293	11.2	80.8	53.7	77.3	22.2	1.8[44]	97.7[44]	—	0.5[44]	4.5	1.6	22.0	7.5
Réunion	1990[18]	234	41.1	60.3	39.1	46.8	31.6	8.4	53.1	1.1	37.4	11	4.8	11	4.8
Romania	1998	11,577	45.6	69.0	51.4	57.1	45.9	21.1	55.9	16.7	6.3	4,411	38.1	2,950	25.5
Russia	1996	68,264	46.6	71.9[51]	46.2	52.7	40.5	...	...	...	...	10,079	14.8	15,950	23.4
Rwanda	1996	3,719	47.5	67.5[10]	45.6	48.4	42.8	...	...	...	...	3,375	90.7	133[11]	3.6[11]
St. Kitts and Nevis	1980	17.1	41.0	69.5	39.5	48.4	31.2	9.7	78.5	0.4	11.4	4.5	26.1	3.8	22.3
St. Lucia	1991	53.1	40.3	67.6	39.9	49.1	31.2	21.0[14]	55.8[14]	1.6[14]	21.6[14]	11.6	21.8	7.5	14.0
St. Vincent	1991	41.7	35.9	67.5	39.1	50.3	28.0	18.2	59.6	2.1	20.1	8.4	20.1	3.5	8.4
Samoa	1986	45.6	18.8	48.6[30]	29.0	44.5	11.6	21.1[30]	43.5[30]	35.0[30]	0.4[30]	29.0	63.6	2.4	5.4
San Marino	1998	18.5	39.6	77.9	58.4	66.6	49.2	13.9	79.3	0.2	6.6	0.2	1.4	5.8	31.2
São Tomé and Príncipe	1991	35	33.6	59.1	30.1	40.5	20.0	25.8	68.6	0.7	4.9	13.6	38.4	1.8	5.0
Saudi Arabia	1988	5,369	3.6	59.1	36.3	54.9	3.6	...	...	...	...	192	3.6	595	11.1
Senegal	1995	3,508	38.3	62.1[10]	42.2	52.0	32	...	...	...	...	2,719	77.5	259[11]	7.4[11]
Serbia and Montenegro	1996	3,182	43.4[19]	58.7[25, 34]	30.1	...	...	...	...	...	...	104	3.3	903	28.4
Seychelles	1993[58]	28.1	...	...	38.9	...	...	...	...	...	...	2.2	7.7	4.6[11]	16.4[11]
Sierra Leone	1995	1,648	31.7	54.1[10]	36.5	50.9	22.7	...	...	...	...	964	58.5	319[11]	19.4[11]
Singapore	1998[18]	1,932	41.8	69.0	51.6	60.8	42.6	12.2	83.6	1.0	3.2	4	0.2	429	22.2
Slovakia	1998[18]	2,464	45.6	67.0	45.7	51.1	40.6	6.0	81.9	—	12.1	185	7.5	710	28.8
Slovenia	1998	982	46.3	69.1	49.6	54.5	44.7	11.5	74.7	6.1	7.6	110	11.2	332	33.8
Solomon Islands	1993[59]	29.6	25.6[44]	24.9[44, 60]	13.7[44]	19.7[44]	7.3[44]	29.6[44]	68.6[44]	—	1.8[44]	8.1	27.4	3.1	10.4
Somalia	1996	3,667	39.3	59.9[10]	38.8	47.1	29.9	...	...	...	...	2,446	66.7	417[11]	11.4[11]
South Africa[61]	1991	11,624	39.4	69.3[53]	37.5	45.5	29.5	7.0	74.8	...	18.2	1,224	10.5	2,361	20.3
Spain	1998[18]	16,265	39.2	62.6	41.6	51.9	31.8	11.9	62.4	0.9	24.7	1,286	7.9	2,965	18.2
Sri Lanka	1998	6,693	35.8	58.8[25]	43.4	55.9	30.9	24.9[34]	54.2[34]	7.8[34]	13.1[34]	2,472	36.9	1,028	15.4
Sudan, The	1983[54]	6,343	29.1	57.4	35.1	50.0	20.4	...	...	...	...	4,029	63.5	317	5.0
Suriname	1994[62]	89.8	35.1	52.3	45.2	59.4	31.4	...	...	...	...	4.8	5.3	10.7	11.9
Swaziland	1996	371	37.7	60.5[10]	42.3	55.0	30.6	...	...	...	...	231	62.3	44[11]	11.9[11]
Sweden	1998	4,255	47.5	76.5[8]	48.0	50.9	45.1	9.5	83.6	0.4	6.5	109	2.6	849	20.0
Switzerland	1998[18, 45]	3,975	44.2	67.9[25]	55.9	63.9	48.4	12.8[19]	84.3[19]	2.9[19]	—	179	4.5	715	18.0
Syria	1998[18]	4,411	17.5	51.2	28.3	46.9	9.8	31.0[13]	49.3[13]	13.0[13]	6.7[13]	917[13]	26.3[13]	471[13]	13.5[13]
Taiwan	1996[18]	9,310	39.2	58.4[25]	43.4	51.3	35.0	21.7	67.5	8.1	2.6	918	9.9	2,471	26.5
Tajikistan	1996	1,778	46.5	63.5[16, 20]	30.3	32.5	28.2	...	...	...	...	1,026	57.7	202	11.4
Tanzania	1996	15,170	46.6	74.1[10]	49.7	53.6	45.9	...	...	...	...	11,738	77.4	725[11]	4.8[11]
Thailand	1998[18, 63]	33,352	45.1	73.6[25]	54.5	60.0	49.0	31.2[64]	40.3[64]	19.5[64]	9.1[64]	16,472	49.4	4,449	13.3
Togo	1995	1,575	35.4	57.1[10]	38.1	49.7	26.7	70.3[30]	10.4[30]	11.3[30]	8.0[30]	1,059	67.2	183[11]	11.6[11]
Tonga	1990	32.0	33.0	57.0	33.6	45.2	22.0	33.7	45.4	16.8	4.1	11.7	36.5	5.1	15.8
Trinidad and Tobago	1998	559	38.3	65.4[34]	47.1	57.2	36.6	17.2	69.1	1.6	12.1	41	7.4	88	15.8
Tunisia	1989	2,361	20.9	50.6	29.8	46.5	12.7	20.9	54.9	7.4	16.8	510	21.6	418	17.7
Turkey	1998[18]	23,415	29.0	54.8	36.6	51.4	21.5	27.6[20]	41.5[20]	27.7[20]	3.2[20]	9,601	41.0	3,852	16.5
Turkmenistan	1996	1,680	40.0	71.9[16]	36.1	43.9	28.5	...	...	...	...	746	44.4	165	9.8
Tuvalu	1991	5.9	51.3[43]	85.5	65.3	...	...	0.3[43]	22.2[43]	— 77.5[43] —		4.2	68.0	0.1	2.0
Uganda	1996	9,636	39.9	68.9[10]	44.0	53.2	34.8	...	...	...	...	7,440	77.2	637[11]	6.6[11]
Ukraine	1998	25,936	50.9	74.9	51.6	54.6	49.0	...	...	...	...	5,074	19.6	4,227	16.3
United Arab Emirates	1990	690	10.4[42]	69.0[42]	47.0[42]	67.6[42]	12.9[42]	6.8[14]	92.7[14]	0.1[14]	0.5[14]	43	6.3	94	13.6
United Kingdom	1998	28,713	44.3	76.2[20]	49.2	55.7	43.0	11.2[20]	76.7[20]	0.5[20]	11.6[20]	479	1.7	5,592	19.5
United States	1998[18]	137,674	46.3	79.4[53]	50.9	55.9	46.1	7.5	87.9	0.1	4.5	3,724	2.7	23,723	17.2
Uruguay	1998[65]	1,239	44.0	71.3	47.0	55.8	39.1	22.9[28]	72.3[28]	2.3[28]	2.5[28]	47	3.8	215	17.3
Uzbekistan	1998	8,800	...	72.3	36.7	...	...	...	...	...	...	3,467	39.4	1,114	12.7
Vanuatu	1989	67.0	46.3	85.0	47.0	49.0	44.9	...	...	...	...	49.8	74.4	1.0	1.5
Venezuela	1997[18]	9,507	35.9	67.2	41.7	53.2	30.1	30.2[20]	61.8[20]	1.7[20]	6.3[20]	940	9.9	1,430	15.0
Vietnam	1989	30,521	51.7	79.9	47.4	47.0	47.7	...	...	...	...	20,471	67.1	3,390	11.1
Virgin Islands (U.S.)	1990[18]	47.4	47.8	70.3	46.6	50.3	43.1	7.6	85.5	0.2	6.7	0.6	1.2	3.7	7.8
West Bank	1996	356.9	16.1	42.2[25]	22.7	37.7	7.4	24.5	49.0	8.1	18.5	41.3	11.6	51.8[36]	14.5[36]
Western Sahara	...	...	...	...	...	...	...	...	...	...	...	...	...	...	...
Yemen	1988	3,029	31.6	52.6	26.4	36.8	16.4	...	...	...	...	2,152	71.1	129	4.3
Zambia	1996	3,507	30.3	54.5	36.1	50.9	21.7	22.9[14]	42.5[14]	3.6[14]	31.0[14]	2,322	66.2	428[11]	12.2[11]
Zimbabwe	1992	3,601	39.6	63.4	34.6	42.8	26.7	24.1	43.9	9.2	22.8	2,110[66]	64.7[66]	179[66]	5.5[66]

[1]Services includes finance, real estate and public administration, defense. [2]Unemployed, not previously employed only. [3]Includes emigrant workers (352,000). [4]Ages 15–59 (male) and 15–54 (female). [5]State sector only. [6]Includes nonagricultural private sector (241,000) and unemployed (261,000). [7]Services includes public administration, defense. [8]Ages 16–64. [9]Unemployed only. [10]Over age 10. [11]Manufacturing; mining, quarrying; public utilities includes construction. [12]Services includes transportation, communications; trade, hotels, restaurants; finance, real estate; and public administration, defense. [13]1991. [14]1980. [15]Includes unemployed, not previously employed. [16]Ages 16–59 (male) and 16–54 (female). [17]Mostly unemployed. [18]Excludes all or some classes or elements of the military. [19]1994. [20]1993. [21]Includes unemployed. [22]1990. [23]Mostly unemployed, not previously employed. [24]1982. [25]Over age 15. [26]Ages 14–64. [27]Services includes restaurants and hotels. [28]1992. [29]Over age 12. [30]1981. [31]Republic of Cyprus only. [32]1993 population economically active for Turkish Republic of Northern Cyprus is 75,947. [33]1989. [34]1995.

construction		transportation, communications		trade, hotels, restaurants		finance, real estate		public administration, defense		services		other		country
number ('000)	% of econ. active	number ('000)	% of econ. active	number ('000)	% of econ. active	number ('000)	% of econ. active	number ('000)	% of econ. active	number ('000)	% of econ. active	number ('000)	% of econ. active	
14	0.6	15	0.6	209	9.0	2	0.1	[7]	[7]	123[7]	5.3[7]	117[21]	5.0[21]	Niger
546	1.8	1,112	3.6	7,417	24.1	120	0.4	[7]	[7]	4,902[7]	15.9[7]	2,009[17]	6.5[17]	Nigeria
5.8	21.7	1.4	5.3	5.3	19.8	1.0	3.8	1.4	5.3	4.5	16.9	0.6[9]	2.3[9]	Northern Mariana Islands
145	6.3	170	7.3	411	17.7	229	9.9	152	6.6	655	28.3	75	3.2	Norway
108	15.3	25	3.5	104	14.8	17	2.5	166	23.5	111	15.8	30[23]	4.3[23]	Oman
2,330	6.4	1,971	5.4	5,021	13.8	338	0.9	[7]	[7]	5,395[7]	14.8[7]	1,982[23]	5.4[23]	Pakistan
0.9	14.2	0.4	6.6	1.1	18.7	0.2	2.9	0.8	13.7	1.6	26.1	0.5[9]	7.8[9]	Palau
72	6.9	66	6.3	232	22.1	59	5.6	74	7.0	205	19.5	43[23]	4.1[23]	Panama
22	2.9	1.7	2.4	25	3.4	4	0.6	[7]	[7]	77[7]	10.5[7]	2	0.2	Papua New Guinea
70	6.7	31	2.9	86	8.3	18	1.7	[7]	[7]	174[7]	16.8[7]	86[15]	8.3[15]	Paraguay
308[20]	3.7[20]	364[20]	4.4[20]	1,352[20]	16.3[20]	197[20]	2.4[20]	[7]	[7]	2,287[7, 20]	27.6[7, 20]	—	—	Peru
1,511	4.8	1,885	6.0	4,328[27]	13.8[27]	695	2.2	[7]	[7]	5,631[7, 27]	18.0[7, 27]	3,024[17]	9.7[17]	Philippines
1,248	7.3	1,015	5.9	2,641	15.4	866	5.0	844	4.9	2,754	16.0	511[23]	3.0[23]	Poland
539	10.8	184	3.7	953	19.1	277	5.5	309	6.2	798	16.0	45[2]	0.9[2]	Portugal
103	7.8	50	3.8	266[41]	20.2[41]	44	3.3	[7]	[7]	602[7, 41]	45.6[7, 41]	17[23]	1.3[23]	Puerto Rico
64.2	22.0	11.9	4.1	34.2	11.7	6.2	2.1	[7]	[7]	149.6[7]	51.1[7]	—	—	Qatar
17	7.1	7	3.1	18	7.7	3	1.3	[7]	[7]	79[7]	33.9[7]	87[17]	37.4[17]	Réunion
471	4.1	545	4.7	1,134	9.8	245	2.1	522	4.5	1,006	8.7	291[23]	2.5[23]	Romania
5,516	8.1	5,219	7.6	7,165	10.5	5,077	7.4	2,726	4.0	14,229	20.8	2,314	3.4	Russia
[11]	[11]	[12]	[12]	[12]	[12]	[12]	[12]	[12]	[12]	212[12]	5.7[12]	—	—	Rwanda
0.4	2.5	0.3	1.6	1.3	7.3	0.8	4.7	1.0	5.7	2.9	17.0	2.2[17]	12.8[17]	St. Kitts and Nevis
5.0	9.3	2.7	5.0	11.1	20.8	1.9	3.6	[7]	[7]	9.2[7]	17.2[7]	4.3	8.2	St. Lucia
3.5	8.5	2.3	5.5	6.5	15.7	1.4	3.4	[7]	[7]	7.7[7]	18.5[7]	8.3[9]	20.0[9]	St. Vincent
0.1	0.1	1.5	3.3	1.7	3.7	0.8	1.8	[7]	[7]	9.4[7]	20.7[7]	0.6	1.4	Samoa
1.5	8.2	0.4	1.9	2.8	15.2	1.4	7.8	2.3	12.4	2.8	15.2	1.3[21]	6.8[21]	San Marino
2.9	8.1	2.2	6.2	4.5	12.6	0.2	0.5	[7]	[7]	8.0[7]	22.5[7]	2.4	6.7	São Tomé and Príncipe
1,181	22.0	321	6.0	964	18.0	151	2.8	[7]	[7]	1,965[7]	36.6[7]	—	—	Saudi Arabia
[11]	[11]	[12]	[12]	[12]	[12]	[12]	[12]	[12]	[12]	530[12]	15.1[12]	—	—	Senegal
130	4.1	142	4.5	557[57]	17.5[57]	77	2.4	92	2.9	356	11.2	819[9]	25.7[9]	Serbia and Montenegro
[11]	[11]	3.4	12.2	5.2	18.6	1.0	3.4	2.6	9.1	5.6	20.0	3.6[17]	12.6[17]	Seychelles
[11]	[11]	[12]	[12]	[12]	[12]	[12]	[12]	[12]	[12]	365[12]	22.1[12]	—	—	Sierra Leone
136	7.0	212	11.0	415	21.5	300	15.5	119	6.2	307	15.9	9[2]	0.5[2]	Singapore
222	9.0	176	7.2	368	14.9	127	5.2	162	6.6	400	16.2	113[23]	4.6[23]	Slovakia
56	5.7	53	5.4	163	16.6	68	6.9	42	4.3	134	13.6	2.3[23]	2.4[23]	Slovenia
1.0	3.3	1.7	5.8	3.4	11.5	1.1	3.9	4.3	14.6	6.8	23.1	—	—	Solomon Islands
[11]	[11]	[12]	[12]	[12]	[12]	[12]	[12]	[12]	[12]	804[12]	21.9[12]	—	—	Somalia
526	4.5	497	4.3	1,358	11.7	504	4.3	[7]	[7]	2,641[7]	22.7[7]	2,513[17]	21.6[17]	South Africa[61]
1,546	9.5	828	5.1	3,387	20.8	1,331	8.2	905	5.6	2,634	16.2	1,382[23]	8.5[23]	Spain
309	4.6	268	4.0	594	8.9	117	1.8	[7]	[7]	1,007[7]	15.0[7]	897[17]	13.4[17]	Sri Lanka
139	2.2	215	3.4	294	4.6	21	0.3	[7]	[7]	550[7]	8.7[7]	777[23]	12.3[23]	Sudan, The
4.2	4.6	5.1	5.6	11.4	12.7	3.5	3.9	[7]	[7]	35.7[7]	39.7[7]	14.6[17]	16.3[17]	Suriname
[11]	[11]	[12]	[12]	[12]	[12]	[12]	[12]	[12]	[12]	96[12]	25.9[12]	—	—	Swaziland
244	5.7	285	6.7	663	15.6	519	12.2	218	5.1	1,328	31.2	39[23]	0.9[23]	Sweden
297	7.5	244	6.1	899	22.6	572	14.4	153	3.8	791	19.9	125	3.1	Switzerland
341[13]	9.8[13]	167[13]	4.8[13]	378[13]	10.9[13]	25[13]	0.7[13]	[7]	[7]	951[7, 13]	27.3[7, 13]	235[9, 13]	6.8[9, 13]	Syria
928	10.0	472	5.1	1,976	21.2	567	6.1	324	3.5	1,412	15.2	242[9]	2.6[9]	Taiwan
68	3.8	58	3.3	69	3.9	[1]	[1]	[1]	[1]	309[1]	17.3[1]	46[9]	2.6[9]	Tajikistan
[11]	[11]	[12]	[12]	[12]	[12]	[12]	[12]	[12]	[12]	2,708[12]	17.8[12]	—	—	Tanzania
1,280	3.8	923	2.8	4,464	13.4	[1]	[1]	[1]	[1]	4,584[1]	13.7[1]	1,222[17]	3.7[17]	Thailand
[11]	[11]	[12]	[12]	[12]	[12]	[12]	[12]	[12]	[12]	331[12]	21.0[12]	—	—	Togo
1.3	3.9	1.8	5.7	2.6	8.1	1.2	3.7	[7]	[7]	7.1[7]	22.0[7]	1.3[9]	4.2[9]	Tonga
84	14.9	38	6.8	99	17.6	43	7.7	[7]	[7]	165[7]	29.6[7]	1	0.1	Trinidad and Tobago
248	10.5	96	4.1	217	9.2	15	0.7	[7]	[7]	444[7]	18.8[7]	412[17]	17.5[17]	Tunisia
1,464	6.3	996	4.3	3,075	13.1	536	2.3	[7]	[7]	3,260[7]	13.9[7]	631[2]	2.7[2]	Turkey
155	9.2	83	4.9	107	6.4	55	3.3	25	1.5	300	17.9	44	2.6	Turkmenistan
0.2	4.0	0.1	1.0	0.2	4.0	—	—	[7]	[7]	1.3[7]	22.0[7]	—	—	Tuvalu
[11]	[11]	[12]	[12]	[12]	[12]	[12]	[12]	[12]	[12]	1,559[12]	16.2[12]	—	—	Uganda
1,092	4.2	1,400	5.4	1,514	5.8	213	0.8	[7]	[7]	5,886	22.7	6,509	25.1	Ukraine
119	17.3	72	10.4	101	14.7	19	2.7	[7]	[7]	241[7]	35.0[7]	—	—	United Arab Emirates
2,037	7.1	1,846	6.4	5,695	19.8	4,085	14.2	1,612	5.6	6,857	23.9	509[23]	1.8[23]	United Kingdom
9,094	6.6	8,075	5.9	28,740[41]	20.9[41]	16,151	11.7	[7]	[7]	47,623[7, 41]	34.6[7, 41]	543[23]	0.4[23]	United States
93	7.5	71	5.7	249	20.1	77	6.2	[7]	[7]	465[7]	37.5[7]	23[2]	1.9[2]	Uruguay
841	9.6	362	4.1	715	8.1	284	3.2	[7]	[7]	1,691[7]	19.2[7]	326	3.7	Uzbekistan
1.3	1.9	1.0	1.5	2.7	4.1	0.6	1.0	[7]	[7]	7.9[7]	11.8[7]	2.6	3.8	Vanuatu
841	8.8	578	6.1	2,169	22.8	523	5.5	[7]	[7]	2,616[7]	27.5[7]	410[23]	4.3[23]	Venezuela
581	1.9	576	1.9	1,880	6.2	90	0.3	305	1.0	1,374	4.5	1,854[17]	6.1[17]	Vietnam
5.7	12.0	3.7	7.8	10.3	21.8	3.6	7.7	5.1	10.8	7.8	16.4	6.9	14.6	Virgin Islands (U.S.)
60.8	17.0	15.7	4.4	52.6	14.8	[1]	[1]	[1]	[1]	68.6[1, 36]	19.2[1, 36]	66.0[9]	18.5[9]	West Bank
...	...	...	...	...	...	...	...	...	...	...	...	...	...	Western Sahara
178	5.9	90	3.0	84	2.8	4	0.1	[7]	[7]	391[7]	12.9[7]	—	—	Yemen
[11]	[11]	[12]	[12]	[12]	[12]	[12]	[12]	[12]	[12]	757[12]	21.6[12]	—	—	Zambia
51[66]	1.6[66]	76[66]	2.3[66]	128[66]	3.9[66]	24[66]	0.7[66]	[7]	[7]	397[7, 66]	12.2[7, 66]	277[17, 66]	8.5[17, 66]	Zimbabwe

[35]1984. [36]Services includes public utilities. [37]Ages 15–65. [38]Excludes Alderney and Sark. [39]1977. [40]Ages 14–64. [41]Services includes hotels. [42]1988. [43]1979. [44]1986. [45]Excludes foreign border workers. [46]Includes unemployed, emigrant workers, and employees in private nonagricultural sector. [47]Includes unemployed, previously employed. [48]1983. [49]Island of Mauritius only. [50]Services includes transportation, communications; trade, hotels, restaurants; and finance, real estate. [51]Ages 15–59. [52]Services includes finance, real estate. [53]Ages 20–64. [54]Excludes nomadic population. [55]1996–97. [56]Citizens over age 10 involved in money-raising activities only. [57]Includes arts and crafts and owners and employees of private shops. [58]Excludes domestic workers (private households), self-employed, and family workers. [59]Wage earners only. [60]Over age 14. [61]Excludes the former black independent states of Bophuthatswana, Ciskei, Transkei, and Venda. [62]Districts of Wanica and Paramaribo only. [63]August survey. [64]1994; February survey. [65]Urban areas only. [66]1986–87.

Crops and livestock

This table provides comparative data for selected categories of agricultural production for the countries of the world. The data are taken mainly from the United Nations Food and Agriculture Organization's (FAO's) annual *Production Yearbook* and the online FAOSTAT statistics database (http://apps.fao.org/default.htm).

The FAO depends largely on questionnaires supplied to each country for its statistics, but, where no official or semiofficial responses are returned, the FAO makes estimates, using incomplete, unofficial, or other similarly limited data. And, although the FAO provides standardized guidelines upon which many nations have organized their data collection systems and methods, persistent, often traditional, variations in standards of coverage, methodology, and reporting periods reduce the comparability of statistics that *can* be supplied on such forms. FAO data are based on calendar-year periods; that is, data for any particular crop refer to the calendar year in which the harvest (or the bulk of the harvest) occurred.

In spite of the often tragic food shortages in a number of countries in recent years, worldwide agricultural production is probably more often underreported than overreported. Many countries do not report complete domestic production. Some countries, for example, report only crops that are sold commercially and ignore subsistence crops produced for family or communal consumption, or barter; others may limit reporting to production for export only, to holdings above a certain size, or represent a sampling only.

Methodological problems attach to much smaller elements of the agricultural whole, however. The FAO's cereals statistics relate, ideally, to weight or volume of crops harvested for dry grain (excluding cereal crops used for grazing, harvested for hay, or harvested green for food, feed, or silage). Some countries, however, collect the basic data they report to the FAO on sown or cultivated areas instead and calculate production statistics from estimates of yield. Millet and sorghum, which in many European and North American countries are used primarily as livestock or poultry feed, may be reportable by such countries as animal fodder only, while elsewhere many nations use the same grains for human consumption and report them as cereals. Statistics for tropical fruits are frequently not compiled by producing countries, and coverage is not uniform, with some countries reporting only commercial fruits and others including those consumed for

Crops and livestock

country	crops															
	grains				roots and tubers[a]				pulses[b]				fruits[c]		vegetables[d]	
	production ('000 metric tons)		yield (kg/hectare)		production ('000 metric tons)		yield (kg/hectare)		production ('000 metric tons)		yield (kg/hectare)		production ('000 metric tons)		production ('000 metric tons)	
	1989–91 average	2000	1989–91 average	2000	1989–91 average	2000	1989–91 average	2000	1989–91 average	2000	1989–91 average	2000	1989–91 average	2000	1989–91 average	2000
Afghanistan	2,754	1,913	1,200	795	217	235	16,291	16,786	32	50	913	1,351	615	615	466	652
Albania	792	580	2,609	2,610	88	180	8,409	14,400	20	32	729	926	153	133	377	652
Algeria	2,481	1,226	823	622	962	950	8,862	14,615	49	38	477	435	1,026	1,491	1,087	2,588
American Samoa	…	…	…	…	2	2	3,721	3,361	…	…	…	…	1	1	—	—
Andorra	…	…	…	…	…	…	…	…	…	…	…	…	…	…	…	…
Angola	298	550	350	619	1,815	3,331	4,220	6,071	35	68	273	356	414	423	250	240
Antigua and Barbuda	—	—	—	—	—	—	5,171	4,811	…	…	…	…	9	8	2	2
Argentina	19,916	38,110	2,342	3,522	2,279	3,990	18,183	25,659	249	358	1,105	1,155	5,915	6,531	2,802	3,480
Armenia	282[1]	216	1,500[1]	1,155	365[1]	320	12,080[1]	9,143	3[1]	1	1,714[1]	509	237[1]	227	444[1]	395
Aruba	…	…	…	…	…	…	…	…	…	…	…	…	…	…	…	…
Australia	21,390	30,589	1,665	1,710	1,127	1,333	28,301	32,001	1,530	1,764	1,025	864	2,345	3,016	1,504	1,799
Austria	5,115	4,457	5,443	5,383	810	496	24,907	20,908	119	70	3,555	2,397	946	1,036	455	613
Azerbaijan	1,130[1]	1,530	1,733[1]	2,372	153[1]	450	8,179[1]	11,250	…	21	…	3,443	803[1]	481	771[1]	917
Bahamas, The	1	—	1,522	2,168	1	1	6,900	5,330	1	—	1,199	718	12	22	27	21
Bahrain	…	…	…	…	—	—	14,112	16,000	—	—	836	1,091	14	22	10	12
Bangladesh	28,032	37,785	2,530	3,246	1,643	2,085	9,744	10,959	512	500	699	757	1,329	1,340	1,332	1,785
Barbados	2	2	2,656	2,500	7	7	9,271	9,024	1	1	1,261	1,254	3	3	7	12
Belarus	6,749[1]	4,820	2,610[1]	1,970	9,623[1]	8,500	12,975[1]	12,143	235[1]	380	1,335[1]	1,689	561[1]	262	917[1]	1,247
Belgium[2]	2,236	2,511	6,094	7,168	1,838	3,000	37,421	46,154	18	16	4,062	4,600	372	735	1,438	1,784
Belize	28	49	1,640	2,112	4	4	21,838	21,765	3	5	763	962	134	311	5	5
Benin	566	872	860	1,043	2,102	3,853	9,354	10,825	60	92	552	673	180	221	211	234
Bermuda	…	…	…	…	1	1	20,985	20,735	…	…	…	…	—	—	3	3
Bhutan	102	159	1,089	1,456	52	56	9,910	10,750	2	2	800	800	64	64	9	10
Bolivia	881	1,257	1,426	1,619	1,160	1,562	6,058	7,471	30	32	1,079	1,010	853	1,358	384	587
Bosnia and Herzegovina	1,176[1]	1,311	3,230[1]	2,771	230[1]	365	4,672[1]	8,795	19[1]	19	1,086[1]	1,270	130[1]	146	533[1]	689
Botswana	60	22	308	217	7	13	5,385	7,059	18	17	562	515	11	2	17	17
Brazil	37,702	46,597	1,868	2,690	27,229	26,272	12,567	13,598	2,471	3,063	473	690	30,895	39,910	5,605	7,138
Brunei	1	—	1,793	…	2	2	3,344	4,286	…	…	…	…	5	6	8	9
Bulgaria	8,872	4,545	4,121	2,574	495	566	11,987	10,885	89	41	1,021	819	1,576	743	1,792	1,766
Burkina Faso	1,975	2,453	717	827	70	61	6,032	6,080	56	72	746	935	71	73	229	229
Burundi	296	245	1,299	1,249	1,420	1,462	6,800	6,856	262	219	1,020	842	1,638	1,598	210	200
Cambodia	2,591	3,857	1,431	1,965	105	111	5,366	7,351	9	11	500	438	239	320	472	470
Cameroon	907	1,489	1,182	1,731	2,371	3,356	7,704	8,048	72	176	534	725	1,876	2,456	499	1,676
Canada	52,915	51,315	2,470	2,801	2,903	4,569	24,683	28,887	633	4,439	1,564	1,675	752	785	2,036	2,156
Cape Verde	10	11	287	333	18	9	9,099	7,965	9	3	184	94	15	15	7	17
Central African Republic	103	176	845	1,163	816	961	3,551	3,356	16	31	941	1,069	202	255	60	83
Chad	677	1,248	565	524	628	593	4,692	4,415	35	56	682	691	74	95	109	113
Chile	2,997	2,593	3,862	4,507	858	999	14,315	17,435	131	58	1,156	1,046	2,596	3,781	1,943	2,596
China	390,173	408,431	4,192	4,736	141,074	188,320	14,980	18,224	4,575	4,279	1,354	1,477	21,900	70,432	128,265	278,592
Colombia	4,090	3,362	2,471	3,048	4,342	4,931	11,973	12,206	167	141	691	1,007	5,024	6,732	1,433	1,325
Comoros	19	21	1,289	1,338	58	69	4,884	5,274	7	12	833	1,034	54	62	5	6
Congo, Dem. Rep. of the	1,471	1,621	803	778	19,477	16,748	7,913	13,280	204	168	602	534	3,321	3,013	513	426
Congo, Rep. of the	11	2	885	687	725	864	6,712	7,159	7	8	704	772	156	195	42	42
Costa Rica	262	287	2,775	3,556	152	111	20,865	16,908	34	16	524	544	2,119	3,267	116	334
Côte d'Ivoire	1,241	1,827	884	1,241	4,291	4,996	5,618	5,665	8	8	667	667	1,627	1,956	450	534
Croatia	2,562[1]	2,070	4,128[1]	4,046	517[1]	500	8,085[1]	9,091	22[1]	26	1,914[1]	2,209	539[1]	565	259[1]	504
Cuba	547	555	2,346	2,694	666	775	4,398	5,808	13	17	260	377	1,424	1,343	509	378
Cyprus	107	47	1,901	1,038	187	123	22,328	24,127	2	1	967	1,229	369	381	125	143
Czech Republic	6,622[3]	6,455	4,101[3]	3,910	1,652[3]	1,476	19,261[3]	21,330	175[3]	86	2,371[3]	2,107	496[3]	557	541[3]	492
Denmark	9,211	9,598	5,887	6,224	1,394	1,502	36,010	39,528	481	195	4,303	2,912	88	84	304	309
Djibouti	—	—	…	…	…	…	…	…	…	…	…	…	…	…	22	24
Dominica	—	—	…	…	29	27	9,292	9,251	—	—	450	400	97	72	6	6
Dominican Republic	531	556	3,951	3,690	243	246	7,085	6,890	98	46	937	866	1,560	1,299	245	458
East Timor[4]	…	…	…	…	…	…	…	…	…	…	…	…	…	…	…	…
Ecuador	1,422	2,341	1,718	2,588	500	979	6,596	11,661	40	59	489	723	4,446	8,368	389	418
Egypt	12,672	20,046	5,526	7,494	1,904	2,074	21,762	21,998	542	418	2,951	2,311	4,456	6,576	8,923	13,563
El Salvador	785	793	1,840	2,181	38	89	15,090	14,674	55	72	802	855	290	227	146	145
Equatorial Guinea	…	…	…	…	77	81	2,484	2,531	…	…	…	…	16	20	…	…
Eritrea	175[3]	270	740[3]	531	109[3]	120	2,804[3]	3,093	36[3]	41	545[3]	573	4[3]	4	30[3]	25
Estonia	638[1]	647	1,665[1]	1,781	590[1]	457	13,743[1]	12,026	1[1]	4	1,452[1]	948	33[1]	20	75[1]	55

subsistence as well. Figures on wild fruits and berries are seldom included in national reports at all. FAO vegetable statistics include vegetables and melons grown for human consumption only. Some countries do not make this distinction in their reports, and some exclude the production of kitchen gardens and small family plots, although in certain countries, such small-scale production may account for 20 to 40 percent of total output.

Livestock statistics may be distorted by the timing of country reports. Ireland, for example, takes a livestock enumeration in December that is reported the following year and that appears low against data for otherwise comparable countries because of the slaughter and export of animals at the close of the grazing season. It balances this, however, with a June enumeration, when numbers tend to be high. Milk production as defined by the FAO includes whole fresh milk, excluding milk sucked by young animals but including amounts fed by farmers or ranchers to livestock, but national practices vary. Certain countries do not distinguish between milk cows and other cattle, so that yield per dairy cow must be estimated. Some countries do not report egg production statistics (here given of metric tons), and external estimates must be based on the numbers of chickens and reported or assumed egg-laying rates. Other countries report egg production by number, and this must be converted to weight, using conversion factors specific to the makeup by species of national poultry flocks.

Metric system units used in the table may be converted to English system units as follow:

metric tons × 1.1023 = short tons
kilograms × 2.2046 = pounds
kilograms per hectare × 0.8922 = pounds per acre.

The notes that follow, keyed by references in the table headings, provide further definitional information.

a. Includes such crops as potatoes and cassava.
b. Includes beans and peas harvested for dry grain only. Does not include green beans and green peas.
c. Excludes melons.
d. Includes melons, green beans, and green peas.
e. From cows only.
f. From chickens only.

livestock														country
cattle		sheep		hogs		chickens		milk[e]				eggs[f]		
stock ('000 head)		stock ('000 head)		stock ('000 head)		stock ('000 head)		production ('000 metric tons)		yield (kg/animal)		production (metric tons)		
1989–91 average	2000	1989–91 average	2000	1989–91 average	2000	1989–91 average	2000	1989–91 average	2000	1989–91 average	2000	1989–91 average	2000	
1,600	3,478	14,173	18,000	…	…	7,073	7,000	507	2,100	633	1,207	14,300	18,000	Afghanistan
657	720	1,645	1,941	183	81	4,864	4,000	403	815	1,384	1,701	15,033	21,000	Albania
1,366	1,650	17,302	18,200	5	6	73,000	110,000	595	1,000	940	1,250	122,000	120,000	Algeria
—	—	—	—	11	11	34	37	—	—	…	…	30	30	American Samoa
…	…	…	…	…	…	…	…	…	…	…	…	…	…	Andorra
3,117	4,042	240	350	802	800	6,117	6,000	151	191	483	473	4,000	4,000	Angola
16	16	13	12	2	2	87	90	6	6	936	968	173	150	Antigua and Barbuda
52,633	55,000	28,139	14,500	2,633	4,200	42,333	65,000	6,375	9,800	2,621	4,000	298,453	286,000	Argentina
522[1]	479	858[1]	510	130[1]	71	3,209[1]	2,850	394[1]	470	…	1,793	11,242[1]	18,000	Armenia
…	…	1	—	1	—	50	—	…	…	…	…	…	…	Aruba
23,086	26,716	165,046	115,693	2,617	2,433	56,000	96,000	6,514	11,183	3,945	5,153	179,000	200,000	Australia
2,546	2,150	284	361	3,762	3,790	14,000	14,000	3,344	3,350	3,805	4,716	94,284	92,000	Austria
1,726[1]	1,945	4,714[1]	5,390	84[1]	20	21,267[1]	14,000	798[1]	1,011	…	1,108	37,333[1]	29,000	Azerbaijan
4	1	39	6	12	6	1,733	5,000	1	1	1,000	1,000	1,000	1,000	Bahamas, The
14	11	20	18	…	…	1,000	…	19	14	2,602	1,970	2,800	3,000	Bahrain
23,173	23,652	871	1,121	…	…	90,253	139,000	741	755	206	206	57,000	132,000	Bangladesh
28	23	40	41	29	33	3,437	4,000	14	8	1,784	1,688	2,000	1,000	Barbados
6,216[1]	4,326	332[1]	92	4,397[1]	3,566	47,573[1]	30,000	5,660[1]	4,320	…	2,335	193,200[1]	187,000	Belarus
3,264	3,085	174	152	6,439	7,322	33,000	45,000	3,875	3,600	4,313	5,538	168,171	220,000	Belgium[2]
51	59	4	3	26	24	987	1,000	7	7	1,159	1,059	1,000	2,000	Belize
1,037	1,438	869	645	479	470	23,333	23,000	16	21	130	130	17,000	17,000	Benin
1	1	…	…	1	…	75	…	1	…	2,901	…	472	…	Bermuda
402	…	49	…	69	…	250	…	29	…	257	257	317	…	Bhutan
5,542	6,725	7,573	8,752	2,160	2,793	23,697	74,000	113	213	1,399	1,689	47,333	37,000	Bolivia
438[1]	462	518[1]	662	404[1]	150	5,167[1]	3,000	303[1]	270	…	892	17,833[1]	3,000	Bosnia and Herzegovina
2,694	2,350	317	350	16	6	2,080	4,000	113	102	350	350	2,000	3,000	Botswana
147,797	167,471	20,061	15,000	33,643	27,425	557,282	1,006,000	15,004	22,134	780	1,380	1,244,227	1,400,000	Brazil
2	2	…	…	17	6	2,254	6,000	…	…	…	…	3,083	4,000	Brunei
1,548	682	8,226	2,549	4,219	1,512	34,167	14,000	1,999	1,200	3,370	2,799	129,127	90,000	Bulgaria
3,937	4,704	5,049	6,585	510	610	17,028	22,000	101	163	156	172	15,000	18,000	Burkina Faso
431	320	352	120	92	50	4,000	4,000	33	19	350	285	3,040	3,000	Burundi
2,178	3,000	…	…	1,601	2,600	9,000	13,000	17	20	170	170	9,000	12,000	Cambodia
4,660	5,900	3,407	3,880	1,344	1,430	17,333	30,000	116	125	500	500	11,867	14,000	Cameroon
11,165	12,786	595	695	10,505	12,242	110,000	158,000	7,915	8,090	5,800	7,324	319,000	357,000	Canada
18	22	6	8	115	640	1,000	…	2	5	447	638	1,000	2,000	Cape Verde
2,589	2,950	134	210	430	650	3,000	4,000	46	62	224	264	1,000	1,000	Central African Republic
4,298	5,595	1,926	2,500	14	21	3,950	5,000	116	151	270	270	4,000	4,000	Chad
3,402	4,134	4,803	4,144	1,144	2,465	32,000	70,000	1,353	2,160	1,862	1,350	96,000	95,000	Chile
79,282	104,582	112,299	131,095	360,247	437,551	2,127,000	3,625,000	4,410	7,838	1,562	1,639	6,701,000	19,235,000	China
24,383	26,000	2,547	2,200	2,627	2,800	58,000	100,000	3,897	5,740	963	990	237,000	350,000	Colombia
47	52	13	20	…	…	392	440	4	4	500	500	1,000	1,000	Comoros
1,535	822	934	925	1,050	1,049	25,000	22,000	8	5	851	825	8,143	7,000	Congo, Dem. Rep. of the
65	77	104	116	49	46	2,000	2,000	1	1	500	500	1,170	1,000	Congo, Rep. of the
2,181	1,715	3	3	270	390	14,000	17,000	431	707	1,308	1,537	19,000	27,150	Costa Rica
1,101	1,350	1,137	1,393	361	280	24,333	30,000	18	24	150	168	13,000	18,000	Côte d'Ivoire
566[1]	427	502[1]	528	1,264[1]	1,233	11,665[1]	11,000	643[1]	641	…	2,424	51,167[1]	49,000	Croatia
4,922	4,700	385	310	2,184	2,800	27,876	15,000	1,100	618	1,866	1,200	120,000	74,000	Cuba
50	56	300	240	281	455	3,000	4,000	98	133	4,746	5,583	8,000	11,000	Cyprus
2,234[3]	1,574	205[3]	84	4,179[3]	3,688	25,574[3]	30,000	3,207[3]	2,708	…	4,946	154,226[3]	176,000	Czech Republic
2,227	1,850	164	143	9,390	11,551	16,000	20,000	4,710	4,465	6,227	7,271	83,000	78,000	Denmark
188	269	433	465	…	…	…	…	7	8	350	350	…	…	Djibouti
9	13	7	8	4	5	129	…	5	6	902	910	155	225	Dominica
2,283	1,904	115	105	543	539	31,227	46,000	345	398	1,701	1,657	35,000	61,000	Dominican Republic
…	…	…	…	…	…	…	…	…	…	…	…	…	…	East Timor[4]
4,351	5,110	1,417	2,870	2,213	2,130	52,000	130,000	1,529	1,996	2,092	2,009	51,000	57,000	Ecuador
2,771	3,180	3,310	4,450	24	30	38,000	88,000	974	1,645	689	1,089	144,000	170,000	Egypt
1,213	1,121	5	5	305	300	5,200	8,000	268	401	999	1,148	46,000	53,000	El Salvador
5	5	35	36	5	5	228	245	…	…	…	…	175	190	Equatorial Guinea
1,290[3]	1,800	1,520[3]	1,540	…	…	4,300[3]	4,600	30[3]	41	…	190	5,934[3]	1,000	Eritrea
595[1]	286	116[1]	29	588[1]	281	3,965[1]	2,000	834[1]	600	…	3,750	22,487[1]	17,000	Estonia

Crops and livestock (continued)

country	crops															
	grains				roots and tubers[a]				pulses[b]				fruits[c]		vegetables[d]	
	production ('000 metric tons)		yield (kg/hectare)		production ('000 metric tons)		yield (kg/hectare)		production ('000 metric tons)		yield (kg/hectare)		production ('000 metric tons)		production ('000 metric tons)	
	1989–91 average	2000	1989–91 average	2000	1989–91 average	2000	1989–91 average	2000	1989–91 average	2000	1989–91 average	2000	1989–91 average	2000	1989–91 average	2000
Ethiopia	7,197	7,845	1,409[3]	1,151	2,000[3]	4,140	3,659[3]	7,289	978[3]	747	890[3]	777	228[3]	221	568[3]	575
Faroe Islands	…	…	…	…	1	2	13,663	13,636	…	…	…	…	…	…	…	…
Fiji	30	19	2,289	2,143	36	72	3,739	9,508	—	—	773	1,000	13	13	9	18
Finland	3,845	4,006	3,360	3,380	845	816	20,656	20,400	14	14	2,549	2,222	22	23	205	239
France	57,683	66,542	6,240	7,261	5,213	6,652	29,853	3,985	3,310	2,078	4,735	4,444	10,561	11,137	7,628	7,938
French Guiana	22	20	4,199	2,536	32	14	10,178	5,906	…	…	…	…	7	13	9	20
French Polynesia	…	…	…	…	11	12	12,752	12,778	…	…	…	…	8	7	7	1
Gabon	23	32	1,599	1,728	376	436	5,424	5,888	—	—	639	667	268	304	30	35
Gambia, The	99	144	1,076	1,112	6	6	3,000	3,000	4	4	267	267	4	4	8	8
Gaza Strip	1	1	510	529	23	35	22,624	21,875	…	…	…	…	168	137	140	158
Georgia	457[1]	327	1,823[1]	1,003	223[1]	480	10,300[1]	13,333	…	9	…	928	745[1]	564	1,205[1]	634
Germany	37,910	45,304	5,534	6,369	14,057	12,639	27,747	41,831	337	561	2,770	2,826	4,752	4,793	2,867	2,499
Ghana	1,155	1,686	1,076	1,292	6,608	12,892	8,143	10,725	18	15	102	100	1,147	2,449	414	698
Greece	5,491	4,171	3,727	3,289	1,052	892	19,880	18,938	41	41	1,512	1,598	4,005	4,010	4,070	4,124
Greenland	…	…	…	…	…	…	…	…	…	…	…	…	…	…	…	…
Grenada	—	—	1,000	1,000	4	4	5,214	5,336	1	1	1,080	1,132	26	18	2	3
Guadeloupe	…	…	…	…	20	17	9,649	10,826	—	—	577	3,833	129	159	24	23
Guam	—	—	2,000	2,000	2	2	14,904	14,904	…	…	…	…	2	2	4	5
Guatemala	1,413	1,199	1,950	1,750	61	92	4,861	7,077	135	130	916	816	811	1,263	511	523
Guernsey	…	…	…	…	…	…	…	…	…	…	…	…	…	…	…	…
Guinea	632	973	1,052	1,307	578	1,122	7,320	5,972	60	60	857	857	840	994	432	840
Guinea-Bissau	200	212	1,556	1,398	69	82	6,911	7,087	2	2	960	622	62	74	21	25
Guyana	218	603	3,197	4,086	35	42	10,027	10,000	1	2	612	593	49	40	10	9
Haiti	405	431	996	932	770	769	3,785	3,891	100	75	655	658	1,005	1,037	277	226
Honduras	664	607	1,403	1,370	30	34	8,836	7,223	71	85	746	704	1,399	945	197	269
Hong Kong	—	—	—	—	—	—	—	—	…	…	…	…	4	4	116	59
Hungary	14,592	9,956	5,160	3,623	1,230	768	16,713	17,067	347	118	2,249	1,990	2,184	1,309	1,937	1,279
Iceland	…	…	…	…	11	10	9,159	14,286	…	…	…	…	—	—	2	4
India	195,478	239,914	1,911	2,372	21,280	30,550	15,906	18,024	13,604	13,480	568	564	27,138	49,199	48,971	61,698
Indonesia[4]	51,258	60,169	3,814	4,031	19,270	19,248	11,522	11,555	666	901	1,393	1,603	5,497	7,478	4,336	6,397
Iran	12,973	12,513	1,363	1,627	2,387	3,450	17,394	20,783	398	475	584	571	7,088	11,550	7,743	12,863
Iraq	2,541	795	927	284	196	150	15,980	6,250	19	29	995	1,061	1,457	1,215	2,855	1,908
Ireland	1,950	1,963	6,374	7,134	577	500	25,060	29,412	8	19	4,798	4,524	24	19	235	216
Isle of Man	…	…	…	…	…	…	…	…	…	…	…	…	…	…	…	…
Israel	234	134	2,968	2,354	209	357	32,359	38,551	9	12	1,334	1,906	1,715	1,343	1,143	1,705
Italy	17,921	20,744	4,005	4,989	2,340	2,089	19,637	24,762	221	123	1,430	1,777	17,569	19,413	14,436	15,338
Jamaica	3	2	1,232	1,221	225	291	12,534	16,907	6	5	898	1,114	383	416	108	190
Japan	13,946	12,769	5,645	6,260	5,539	4,554	25,459	26,009	145	105	1,670	1,831	4,838	4,306	14,471	12,851
Jersey	…	…	…	…	…	…	…	…	…	…	…	…	…	…	…	…
Jordan	105	52	1,040	901	59	93	25,459	26,009	6	5	690	837	247	225	709	781
Kazakhstan	22,521[1]	11,583	1,040[1]	945	2,303[1]	1,694	9,742[1]	10,615	96[1]	20	782[1]	764	160[1]	106	1,096[1]	2,192
Kenya	2,893	2,197	1,567	1,329	1,536	1,855	8,200	7,275	219	230	312	329	888	981	629	649
Kiribati	…	…	…	…	7	9	7,449	8,148	…	…	…	…	5	6	4	5
Korea, North	8,244	3,118	3,152	2,443	1,051	1,870	13,414	8,348	325	280	922	848	1,304	1,350	4,344	3,810
Korea, South	8,412	7,498	5,891	6,362	939	1,106	21,133	23,163	45	30	1,134	1,102	2,019	2,468	9,729	10,980
Kuwait	1	3	4,143	2,815	1	29	19,530	25,961	…	…	…	…	2	10	92	130
Kyrgyzstan	1,339[1]	1,550	2,271[1]	2,670	321[1]	1,033	12,190[1]	15,892	…	…	…	…	97[1]	130	291[1]	732
Laos	1,443	2,232	2,688	3,189	246	158	8,150	8,535	12	15	780	954	130	173	89	288
Latvia	1,072[1]	928	1,739[1]	2,194	1,161[1]	747	13,147[1]	14,600	6[1]	3	1,480[1]	1,497	73[1]	52	256[1]	121
Lebanon	80	96	1,955	2,424	249	271	18,708	20,008	28	43	1,631	2,095	1,223	1,313	798	1,324
Lesotho	170	149	805	934	47	90	15,553	16,667	9	11	481	764	18	13	24	18
Liberia	191	200	1,035	1,290	422	440	7,253	6,801	3	3	517	500	111	149	73	76
Libya	284	238	680	728	141	210	7,891	7,000	12	19	1,126	1,379	307	381	708	905
Liechtenstein	…	…	…	…	…	…	…	…	…	…	…	…	…	—	…	…
Lithuania	2,319[1]	2,658	1,974[1]	2,713	1,316[1]	1,792	11,213[1]	16,392	30[1]	145	1,239[1]	2,185	145[1]	79	306[1]	321
Luxembourg[2]	…	…	…	…	…	…	…	…	…	…	…	…	…	…	…	…
Macau	…	…	…	…	7	…	13,394	…	1	…	…	…	—	…	1	…
Macedonia	583[1]	621	2,453[1]	2,867	127[1]	165	9,534[1]	12,445	29[1]	28	1,348[1]	2,555	342[1]	357	462[1]	523
Madagascar	2,541	2,460	1,943	1,761	3,160	3,152	6,359	6,489	67	99	883	909	790	854	328	344
Malawi	1,560	2,463	1,104	1,620	506	2,600	4,294	8,229	253	234	560	562	485	511	252	256
Malaysia	1,886	2,094	2,710	2,910	497	469	9,683	9,306	…	…	…	…	1,126	1,066	334	488
Maldives	—	—	1,125	4,400	7	7	4,537	4,355	—	—	633	750	9	10	20	28
Mali	2,114	2,952	907	1,171	23	34	4,721	4,250	40	98	172	349	15	41	307	320
Malta	8	12	3,422	4,008	17	35	13,181	19,612	1	1	2,336	2,556	14	8	52	64
Marshall Islands	…	…	…	…	…	…	…	…	…	…	…	…	…	…	…	…
Martinique	…	…	…	…	23	18	10,917	10,456	…	1	…	…	273	356	24	28
Mauritania	131	263	831	1,011	6	6	1,933	2,115	28	34	385	330	16	25	11	12
Mauritius	2	—	3,885	5,200	19	18	18,659	19,604	1	2	708	…	8	9	43	85
Mayotte	…	…	…	…	…	…	…	…	…	…	…	…	…	…	…	…
Mexico	23,553	29,550	2,350	2,451	1,302	1,722	11,790	21,553	1,412	1,460	704	595	9,430	12,363	6,604	9,621
Micronesia	…	…	…	…	…	…	…	…	…	…	…	…	…	…	…	…
Moldova	2,274[1]	2,021	3,019[1]	2,348	504[1]	342	7,989[1]	4,866	107[1]	49	1,537[1]	1,092	1,562[1]	749	689[1]	583
Monaco	…	…	…	…	…	…	…	…	…	…	…	…	…	…	…	…
Mongolia	719	190	1,104	956	128	70	10,613	10,747	3	1	708	833	—	—	42	47
Morocco	7,457	2,006	1,346	368	975	1,103	16,319	18,003	386	186	790	743	2,310	2,578	2,941	2,231
Mozambique	629	1,476	404	949	4,122	4,741	4,322	5,826	87	130	301	342	368	260	197	126
Myanmar (Burma)	14,111	20,643	2,738	3,138	212	356	8,579	9,836	434	1,655	674	648	957	1,284	2,027	3,369
Namibia	103	140	482	437	212	255	8,610	8,500	8	9	1,097	1,096	10	11	9	11
Nauru	…	…	…	…	…	…	…	…	…	…	…	…	—	—	—	—
Nepal	5,680	6,986	1,885	2,087	826	1,238	7,398	8,850	168	218	597	729	415	457	962	1,252
Netherlands, The	1,327	1,649	6,909	7,472	6,947	8,200	40,168	44,809	85	19	4,109	4,203	507	756	3,470	3,711
Netherlands Antilles	…	…	…	…	…	…	…	…	…	…	…	…	…	…	…	…
New Caledonia	1	2	1,837	3,736	21	21	6,023	5,778	—	—	393	600	4	3	5	4
New Zealand	783	870	4,886	6,648	277	518	30,899	39,808	62	52	2,941	2,984	806	925	576	995
Nicaragua	453	751	1,483	1,842	77	85	11,790	10,366	69	114	621	652	303	260	35	31

livestock														country
cattle		sheep		hogs		chickens		milk[e]				eggs[f]		
stock ('000 head)		stock ('000 head)		stock ('000 head)		stock ('000 head)		production ('000 metric tons)		yield (kg/animal)		production (metric tons)		
1989–91 average	2000	1989–91 average	2000	1989–91 average	2000	1989–91 average	2000	1989–91 average	2000	1989–91 average	2000	1989–91 average	2000	
29,575[3]	35,000	21,700[3]	21,000	20[3]	24	54,200[3]	56,000	738[3]	930	...	204	73,370[3]	75,000	Ethiopia
2	2	67	68	...	...	...	...	...	...	...	...	...	...	Faroe Islands
274	350	—	7	88	115	3,000	4,000	58	58	1,705	1,800	2,000	4,000	Fiji
1,352	1,087	59	107	1,322	1,351	6,000	6,000	2,712	2,500	5,666	6,452	73,000	59,000	Finland
21,407	20,527	11,196	10,004	11,999	14,635	198,306	233,000	26,334	24,890	4,797	5,630	903,413	1,050,000	France
15	9	4	3	9	11	202	190	—	—	...	581	250	450	French Guiana
8	10	—	—	33	37	100	150	2	1	2,207	2,000	1,000	2,000	French Polynesia
30	36	161	198	160	213	2,217	3,000	1	2	250	250	1,500	1,980	Gabon
333	370	127	195	11	14	1,000	1,000	7	7	175	175	1,000	1,000	Gambia, The
3	3	24	24	...	...	3,000	4,000	7	8	4,000	4,000	5,000	8,000	Gaza Strip
1,051[1]	1,122	1,160[1]	560	525[1]	411	15,113[1]	8,000	450[1]	721	...	1,243	12,717[1]	24,000	Georgia
20,048	14,658	3,824	2,100	33,350	27,049	116,263	108,000	30,976	28,420	4,931	5,880	989,000	880,000	Germany
1,159	1,285	2,199	2,565	495	350	9,682	18,000	23	33	130	130	10,000	19,000	Ghana
651	590	8,684	9,041	1,002	906	27,213	28,000	646	770	2,523	4,400	123,000	110,000	Greece
...	...	21	22	...	...	...	...	...	...	...	...	...	...	Greenland
4	4	11	13	3	5	260	...	1	1	...	800	1,000	1,000	Grenada
70	80	4	4	28	15	311	200	1	...	506	...	1,000	2,000	Guadeloupe
—	—	...	...	4	4	170	...	...	...	...	...	367	1,000	Guam
2,052	2,300	432	551	602	825	14,633	24,000	312	320	680	711	68,000	109,000	Guatemala
...	...	...	...	...	...	...	...	...	...	...	...	...	...	Guernsey
1,491	2,368	429	687	24	54	5,800	9,000	42	62	185	185	6,000	9,000	Guinea
412	530	239	285	290	345	1,000	1,000	12	13	170	170	1,000	1,000	Guinea-Bissau
138	220	129	130	42	20	2,000	13,000	19	13	840	828	1,000	7,000	Guyana
1,067	1,430	120	152	330	1,000	5,167	6,000	25	41	250	250	4,000	4,000	Haiti
2,412	1,950	10	14	589	800	9,436	18,000	346	729	911	1,157	28,000	41,000	Honduras
2	—	—	—	296	110	5,678	3,000	2	—	...	2,236	1,497	10	Hong Kong
1,619	873	2,050	934	7,996	5,335	50,950	26,000	2,733	2,091	4,977	5,532	254,000	177,000	Hungary
75	72	540	465	18	43	450	180	112	107	3,509	3,972	3,000	2,000	Iceland
191,897	218,800	43,706	57,900	11,193	16,500	294,000	402,000	22,259	30,900	880	917	1,161,000	1,782,000	India
10,390	12,102	6,008	9,353	6,008	7,502	577,000	800,000	335	384	1,094	1,151	366,000	406,000	Indonesia[4]
7,382	8,100	44,754	55,000	—	—	162,000	250,000	2,480	4,403	1,014	1,243	310,000	538,000	Iran
1,416	1,350	7,804	6,780	...	...	63,000	23,000	297	319	730	750	64,450	14,000	Iraq
5,923	6,708	5,523	5,393	1,125	1,763	9,000	12,000	5,376	5,448	3,849	4,320	33,000	32,000	Ireland
...	...	...	...	...	...	...	...	...	...	...	...	...	...	Isle of Man
340	388	383	350	122	163	23,000	28,000	964	1,194	8,783	9,787	105,000	92,000	Israel
8,541	7,184	11,088	10,970	9,150	8,403	138,000	100,000	10,893	11,741	3,724	5,499	687,000	768,000	Italy
382	400	2	1	192	180	7,167	11,000	51	53	1,000	1,000	26,000	28,000	Jamaica
4,772	4,658	30	11	11,673	9,980	338,000	298,000	8,169	8,500	5,825	6,641	2,446,228	2,508,000	Japan
...	...	...	...	...	...	...	...	...	...	...	...	...	...	Jersey
35	57	1,660	1,600	...	...	14,000	25,000	60	145	2,485	3,085	32,420	50,000	Jordan
9,336[1]	3,998	33,688[1]	9,776	2,610[1]	1,034	50,400[1]	18,000	5,327[1]	3,600	...	1,829	176,667[1]	86,000	Kazakhstan
13,583	13,794	9,241	7,000	125	170	24,667	27,000	2,297	2,250	499	480	41,440	50,000	Kenya
...	...	...	...	9	12	259	300	...	...	...	...	124	140	Kiribati
1,293	600	385	190	3,215	2,970	21,000	10,000	88	90	2,379	2,308	146,000	95,000	Korea, North
2,149	2,486	3	1	4,792	7,864	70,336	97,000	1,752	2,244	5,944	7,357	399,000	465,000	Korea, South
14	20	197	450	...	...	17,000	33,000	21	42	3,226	606	6,390	20,000	Kuwait
1,124[1]	932	8,261[1]	3,264	257[1]	105	9,867[1]	2,200	918[1]	1,090	...	2,225	22,000[1]	12,000	Kyrgyzstan
853	987	...	...	1,397	1,101	8,165	12,000	9	6	200	200	4,000	8,000	Laos
1,068[1]	378	154[1]	27	865[1]	405	5,397[1]	3,000	1,212[1]	823	...	4,003	25,033[1]	26,000	Latvia
65	77	222	380	46	64	23,000	32,000	94	205	2,826	3,254	35,000	42,000	Lebanon
550	520	1,450	750	62	65	967	2,000	24	24	290	250	826	2,000	Lesotho
38	36	222	210	123	120	3,800	4,000	1	1	130	130	3,904	4,000	Liberia
238	143	5,100	5,100	...	...	15,867	25,000	99	135	1,202	1,205	33,917	59,000	Libya
6	6	3	3	3	3	...	...	13	12	4,645	4,444	...	...	Liechtenstein
1,761[1]	898	52[1]	14	1,579[1]	936	10,860[1]	6,000	2,128[1]	1,560	...	3,156	41,167[1]	37,000	Lithuania
...	...	...	...	...	...	...	...	...	...	...	...	...	...	Luxembourg[2]
...	...	...	...	...	...	450	500	...	...	...	...	638	...	Macau
282[1]	290	2,425[1]	1,600	176[1]	197	4,458[1]	3,000	127[1]	180	...	1,837	25,653[1]	22,000	Macedonia
10,254	10,364	737	800	1,431	900	13,062	20,000	476	535	273	282	15,050	15,000	Madagascar
862	760	151	115	236	240	11,500	15,000	37	35	460	461	11,203	20,000	Malawi
677	723	212	175	2,577	1,829	62,377	120,000	29	42	486	477	287,000	413,000	Malaysia
...	...	...	...	...	...	...	...	...	...	...	...	...	...	Maldives
5,007	6,200	6,072	6,000	59	65	22,000	25,000	123	152	245	245	11,880	12,000	Mali
21	19	6	16	101	80	1,000	1,000	24	48	3,851	5,535	7,000	8,000	Malta
...	...	...	...	...	...	...	...	...	...	...	...	...	...	Marshall Islands
37	30	46	42	39	33	347	250	2	2	756	763	1,000	2,000	Martinique
1,350	1,435	5,067	6,200	...	...	3,800	4,000	97	102	350	350	4,250	5,000	Mauritania
34	29	7	7	12	20	2,200	4,000	25	60	2,500	1,714	4,200	5,000	Mauritius
...	...	...	...	...	...	...	...	...	...	...	...	...	...	Mayotte
32,194	30,293	5,862	5,900	15,715	13,690	240,218	476,000	6,336	9,474	992	1,393	1,066,065	1,666,000	Mexico
...	14	...	...	...	32	...	185	...	...	...	...	...	175	Micronesia
962[1]	416	1,300[1]	974	1,468[1]	705	17,767[1]	14,000	998[1]	550	...	2,321	35,833[1]	32,000	Moldova
...	...	...	...	...	...	...	...	...	...	...	...	...	...	Monaco
2,694	3,500	14,266	14,000	166	19	351	72	320	285	348	320	2,000	340	Mongolia
3,284	2,675	13,528	17,300	9	8	71,200	100,000	929	1,150	521	879	171,000	180,000	Morocco
1,373	1,320	120	125	167	180	21,833	28,000	63	60	170	170	11,333	14,000	Mozambique
9,269	10,964	275	390	2,355	3,914	23,989	44,000	422	612	392	415	35,208	83,000	Myanmar (Burma)
2,104	2,063	3,289	2,100	18	17	1,717	2,200	76	75	401	403	1,000	2,000	Namibia
...	...	...	...	3	3	5	5	...	...	...	...	16	16	Nauru
6,274	7,031	903	900	571	870	12,000	18,000	252	337	366	407	16,133	22,000	Nepal
4,918	4,200	1,663	1,401	13,747	13,140	92,050	106,000	11,198	10,800	6,040	7,200	644,480	660,000	Netherlands, The
1	1	6	7	3	2	125	135	—	—	1,278	1,250	432	1,000	Netherlands Antilles
122	123	3	1	37	40	317	1,000	4	4	600	600	1,367	2,000	New Caledonia
7,987	9,457	57,861	45,800	404	344	9,067	13,000	7,572	12,014	2,835	3,600	46,000	51,000	New Zealand
1,693	1,660	4	4	565	400	4,000	10,000	162	231	797	981	25,500	30,000	Nicaragua

Crops and livestock (continued)

country	crops															
	grains				roots and tubers[a]				pulses[b]				fruits[c]		vegetables[d]	
	production ('000 metric tons)		yield (kg/hectare)		production ('000 metric tons)		yield (kg/hectare)		production ('000 metric tons)		yield (kg/hectare)		production ('000 metric tons)		production ('000 metric tons)	
	1989–91 average	2000	1989–91 average	2000	1989–91 average	2000	1989–91 average	2000	1989–91 average	2000	1989–91 average	2000	1989–91 average	2000	1989–91 average	2000
Niger	2,120	2,738	341	368	180	158	5,570	5,167	312	658	127	172	44	48	274	286
Nigeria	18,100	22,405	1,165	1,212	35,155	64,236	10,370	9,507	1,383	2,158	719	417	6,644	8,900	4,272	7,783
Northern Mariana Islands	...	...	...	...	...	...	...	...	...	...	...	...	...	...	...	...
Norway	1,410	1,322	3,943	3,894	452	446	24,246	24,800	—	—	...	...	100	28	182	144
Oman	5	6	2,124	2,173	5	6	25,208	21,923	...	...	...	...	184	210	155	173
Pakistan	21,038	29,923	1,784	2,401	1,052	2,298	11,467	16,859	1,044	924	553	597	3,871	5,409	3,193	5,042
Palau	...	...	...	...	...	...	...	...	...	...	...	...	...	...	...	...
Panama	336	401	1,884	2,704	66	79	5,901	11,888	9	10	526	442	1,225	1,062	65	162
Papua New Guinea	4	11	2,330	3,981	1,253	1,251	7,270	7,219	2	3	500	526	1,076	1,213	357	387
Paraguay	818	1,266	1,838	2,257	3,479	3,582	15,109	14,312	55	55	959	786	523	533	268	302
Peru	1,983	3,313	2,473	3,116	2,293	4,750	8,066	10,640	107	208	896	1,125	1,922	3,431	918	1,947
Philippines	14,350	16,901	2,018	2,583	2,761	2,704	6,851	6,700	60	58	908	773	8,341	9,804	4,211	4,726
Poland	27,594	22,341	3,231	2,535	33,247	24,232	18,350	19,376	635	305	1,857	2,064	1,792	2,131	5,797	5,700
Portugal	1,673	1,686	2,019	2,737	1,403	1,274	11,596	14,457	51	30	590	574	2,176	1,713	2,063	2,369
Puerto Rico	—	—	7,462	4,000	28	9	6,499	11,246	2	—	569	609	255	179	43	31
Qatar	3	6	2,910	3,418	—	—	9,611	10,375	...	...	...	...	8	18	30	55
Réunion	12	17	5,559	6,724	15	9	11,006	13,043	1	1	1,429	741	44	49	45	68
Romania	18,286	9,594	3,084	1,844	3,159	3,650	10,517	13,129	149	64	889	1,159	2,295	1,947	3,215	4,105
Russia	92,890[1]	64,088	1,612[1]	1,610	36,603[1]	32,597	10,673[1]	10,030	2,880[1]	913	1,383[1]	962	2,989[1]	2,608	10,411[1]	14,809
Rwanda	289	240	1,161	993	1,641	2,124	4,553	4,339	216	231	726	795	3,020	2,272	131	261
St. Kitts and Nevis	...	...	...	...	1	1	3,611	2,861	—	—	1,000	1,000	1	1	—	1
St. Lucia	—	—	699	...	11	11	4,350	3,928	—	—	2,133	2,000	176	128	1	1
St. Vincent and the Grenadines	2	2	3,348	3,333	19	12	4,539	4,525	—	—	1,000	1,000	78	49	3	4
Samoa	...	...	...	...	41	41	5,002	6,164	...	...	...	...	51	43	1	1
San Marino	...	...	...	...	...	...	...	...	...	...	...	...	...	...	...	...
São Tomé and Príncipe	3	2	2,015	2,230	6	33	7,346	9,054	...	...	...	...	10	21	3	6
Saudi Arabia	4,214	2,452	4,177	4,214	59	394	19,121	25,088	7	8	1,832	1,841	832	1,192	1,987	1,821
Senegal	996	963	823	746	67	48	3,990	2,897	19	35	337	314	105	131	197	396
Serbia and Montenegro	7,613[1]	5,238	3,102[1]	2,566	766[1]	690	6,928[1]	6,610	100[1]	107	1,438[1]	1,259	1,391[1]	1,116	1,045[1]	1,106
Seychelles	...	...	...	...	...	...	5,000	5,000	...	...	...	...	2	2	2	2
Sierra Leone	566	222	1,224	1,078	139	271	5,220	4,671	38	52	652	673	163	163	189	182
Singapore	...	...	...	...	—	—	13,933	10,000	...	...	...	...	1	—	8	5
Slovakia	3,494[3]	2,201	4,068[3]	2,705	566[3]	419	13,232[3]	15,474	161[3]	58	2,313[3]	2,055	285[3]	254	528[3]	411
Slovenia	486[1]	502	4,131[1]	5,230	379[1]	194	13,756[1]	19,736	7[1]	5	777[1]	1,594	255[1]	206	77[1]	104
Solomon Islands	1	5	...	...	107	134	17,595	16,947	2	4	1,175	1,296	15	16	6	7
Somalia	497	313	715	565	50	76	10,421	10,000	13	15	263	250	271	216	65	73
South Africa	12,734	13,245	2,053	2,630	1,336	1,737	16,611	22,269	146	96	1,178	955	3,744	4,760	2,021	2,270
Spain	19,306	24,602	2,489	3,600	5,334	3,156	19,439	25,370	238	389	755	840	13,503	14,971	11,026	11,822
Sri Lanka	2,370	2,804	2,924	2,370	547	329	8,845	8,213	50	26	780	618	743	834	578	650
Sudan, The	2,771	3,292	497	501	137	169	2,670	2,595	103	253	1,064	1,593	773	973	922	1,134
Suriname	229	175	3,770	3,499	3	5	11,900	12,000	—	—	690	727	75	81	26	21
Swaziland	127	73	1,401	1,299	9	7	1,665	1,872	5	7	569	957	141	99	13	11
Sweden	5,677	6,200	4,594	5,055	1,132	1,310	32,977	37,222	91	140	2,494	2,669	171	94	261	310
Switzerland	1,331	1,138	6,352	6,387	731	584	37,867	42,628	8	11	4,264	3,516	634	727	308	292
Syria	2,601	3,503	668	1,249	407	450	17,543	20,000	131	198	577	684	1,370	1,880	1,690	1,686
Taiwan	...	...	...	...	...	...	...	...	...	...	...	...	...	...	...	...
Tajikistan	256[1]	455	944[1]	1,198	151[1]	250	12,215[1]	12,500	7[1]	9	742[1]	1,948	248[1]	299	623[1]	490
Tanzania	4,138	3,556	1,389	822	8,167	6,498	8,824	5,637	437	433	501	565	2,093	1,874	1,185	1,166
Thailand	23,624	28,262	2,149	2,463	21,775	18,773	14,245	16,268	377	285	751	806	6,371	7,610	2,514	2,782
Togo	505	759	809	955	913	1,376	7,992	7,247	22	52	202	293	49	49	152	131
Tonga	...	...	...	...	99	92	6,551	10,008	...	...	...	...	15	13	20	7
Trinidad and Tobago	17	12	2,816	2,927	10	12	9,757	10,315	3	4	1,460	2,566	62	80	17	25
Tunisia	1,611	1,095	1,115	923	205	290	12,592	10,741	73	93	663	819	670	933	1,477	2,154
Turkey	28,283	26,657	2,065	2,018	4,321	5,476	22,388	25,935	1,946	1,349	885	974	9,117	10,610	17,963	22,099
Turkmenistan	1,038[1]	1,768	2,870[1]	2,619	32[1]	28	4,750[1]	5,620	...	8	...	2,000	158[1]	206	539[1]	363
Tuvalu	...	...	...	...	...	—	...	...	...	...	...	...	1	1	—	—
Uganda	1,597	2,111	1,483	1,539	5,360	7,842	6,335	7,803	493	585	774	568	8,384	10,195	421	549
Ukraine	37,208[1]	23,760	2,957[1]	1,949	19,129[1]	13,037	12,040[1]	8,357	2,840[1]	680	2,300[1]	1,789	2,597[1]	2,561	5,750[1]	6,040
United Arab Emirates	2	1	1,912	...	4	5	19,300	19,464	...	...	...	...	205	378	270	1,129
United Kingdom	22,644	23,983	6,168	7,165	6,333	6,640	35,916	40,151	745	686	3,401	3,757	515	307	3,580	2,996
United States	292,217	343,866	4,580	5,865	18,530	24,025	32,089	41,047	1,623	1,535	1,839	1,879	25,256	32,570	31,092	37,698
Uruguay	1,230	1,817	2,411	3,326	215	172	7,514	11,701	6	6	979	982	394	541	117	147
Uzbekistan	2,281[1]	3,048	1,714[1]	2,281	468[1]	656	10,083[1]	12,148	...	4	...	667	985[1]	1,422	3,760[1]	3,095
Vanuatu	1	1	515	538	49	65	10,139	13,000	...	...	...	...	18	20	8	10
Venezuela	2,037	1,958	2,484	2,938	682	951	8,676	11,314	57	35	585	730	2,579	2,508	514	1,223
Vietnam	20,008	34,484	3,081	4,120	4,758	4,010	7,432	7,700	187	244	639	736	3,096	4,098	3,625	4,849
Virgin Islands (U.S.)	...	...	...	...	...	...	...	...	...	...	...	...	—	—	...	...
West Bank	...	30	...	...	...	17	...	...	...	2	...	...	...	153	...	228
Western Sahara	...	3	...	794	...	...	...	...	...	...	...	...	...	...	...	...
Yemen	693	695	871	693	153	214	12,223	12,661	64	70	1,424	1,207	314	613	536	553
Zambia	1,467	1,435	1,569	1,570	704	1,084	6,517	6,384	15	15	629	516	105	101	274	270
Zimbabwe	2,391	2,513	1,488	1,406	127	208	4,792	4,856	50	50	694	760	170	200	153	147

livestock														country
cattle		sheep		hogs		chickens		milk[e]				eggs[f]		
stock ('000 head)		stock ('000 head)		stock ('000 head)		stock ('000 head)		production ('000 metric tons)		yield (kg/animal)		production (metric tons)		
1989–91 average	2000	1989–91 average	2000	1989–91 average	2000	1989–91 average	2000	1989–91 average	2000	1989–91 average	2000	1989–91 average	2000	
1,712	2,217	3,100	4,300	37	39	17,833	20,000	140	168	393	400	9,000	9,000	Niger
14,650	19,830	12,477	20,500	3,319	4,855	122,120	126,000	350	386	239	243	313,000	435,000	Nigeria
...	...	...	...	...	...	...	...	...	...	...	...	...	...	Northern Mariana Islands
959	1,042	2,202	2,400	696	690	4,000	23,000	1,944	1,759	5,854	5,429	51,046	49,000	Norway
137	149	141	180	...	...	3,000	3,000	18	19	420	420	6,000	6,000	Oman
17,677	22,000	25,703	24,100	...	...	78,000	148,000	3,525	8,039	842	1,179	211,000	331,000	Pakistan
...	...	...	...	...	...	...	...	...	...	...	...	...	...	Palau
1,401	1,360	...	...	228	280	8,000	12,000	129	157	1,162	1,309	11,117	14,000	Panama
103	87	4	6	997	1,550	3,000	4,000	—	—	...	100	3,000	4,000	Papua New Guinea
7,985	9,910	422	413	2,443	2,700	15,065	25,000	224	330	1,904	2,399	35,000	68,000	Paraguay
4,126	4,903	12,484	14,400	2,417	2,788	62,406	81,000	788	1,048	1,323	2,015	104,000	163,000	Peru
1,644	2,553	30	30	7,968	10,398	77,000	142,000	15	10	1,036	1,037	297,000	539,000	Philippines
9,875	6,083	3,934	362	20,056	17,122	58,196	50,000	15,560	11,731	3,260	3,890	410,255	425,000	Poland
1,355	1,245	5,531	5,850	2,531	2,330	19,667	28,000	1,500	1,850	3,734	5,256	85,400	110,000	Portugal
595	388	7	8	204	175	11,241	12,000	396	357	4,233	3,933	16,690	15,143	Puerto Rico
10	14	126	215	...	...	2,932	4,000	10	11	1,592	1,600	3,000	4,000	Qatar
20	27	2	2	88	89	6,916	11,000	7	14	627	964	4,117	5,000	Réunion
6,029	3,155	12,675	5,951	12,675	7,972	121,000	72,000	3,450	4,500	1,867	2,727	354,367	300,000	Romania
51,939[1]	27,500	46,998[1]	14,000	31,820[1]	18,300	582,667[1]	340,000	45,088[1]	31,560	...	2,447	2,233,333[1]	1,867,000	Russia
592	725	387	320	117	160	1,292	1,000	85	85	579	739	2,000	2,000	Rwanda
4	4	14	7	2	3	56	70	...	...	...	...	347	300	St. Kitts and Nevis
12	12	16	13	12	15	223	260	1	1	1,396	1,389	528	1,000	St. Lucia
6	6	13	13	10	10	205	200	1	1	1,351	1,370	1,000	1,000	St. Vincent and the Grenadines
24	26	...	...	186	179	356	350	1	1	1,000	1,000	192	200	Samoa
...	...	...	...	...	...	...	...	...	...	...	...	...	...	San Marino
4	4	2	3	3	2	124	290	—	—	...	170	175	315	São Tomé and Príncipe
195	297	6,370	7,576	...	...	76,000	130,000	274	601	6,254	8,035	113,005	136,000	Saudi Arabia
2,616	2,960	3,500	4,300	295	330	19,667	45,000	98	105	360	360	15,000	33,000	Senegal
1,925[1]	1,452	2,701[1]	1,917	3,876[1]	4,087	21,920[1]	21,000	1,841[1]	1,825	...	2,100	96,833[1]	76,000	Serbia and Montenegro
2	1	...	...	18	18	293	1,000	—	—	...	6	1,000	2,000	Seychelles
333	420	271	365	50	52	5,900	6,000	17	21	250	250	7,000	8,000	Sierra Leone
—	—	—	—	300	190	3,000	2,000	...	...	...	...	17,000	16,000	Singapore
1,030[3]	665	412[3]	340	2,162[3]	1,593	13,321[3]	12,000	1,206[3]	1,099	...	4,467	79,549[3]	65,000	Slovakia
488[1]	471	23[1]	73	574[1]	558	10,420[1]	7,000	569[1]	634	...	3,132	19,712[1]	23,000	Slovenia
11	12	...	...	53	59	144	185	1	1	650	650	288	372	Solomon Islands
3,967	5,100	12,117	13,100	9	4	2,833	3,000	425	530	398	400	2,000	3,000	Somalia
12,920	13,700	32,060	28,700	1,480	1,535	46,000	61,000	2,426	2,667	2,637	2,667	213,000	339,000	South Africa
5,125	6,203	23,800	23,700	16,720	23,682	75,000	128,000	6,100	5,900	3,728	4,820	649,413	522,000	Spain
1,690	1,617	25	12	88	74	9,000	10,000	172	220	271	319	46,033	51,000	Sri Lanka
20,593	37,093	20,179	42,800	...	...	32,371	42,000	2,252	3,072	480	480	33,212	45,000	Sudan, The
91	106	9	12	29	32	8,000	2,000	17	13	1,832	1,857	3,033	5,000	Suriname
712	610	24	30	23	33	1,133	3,000	42	35	274	302	...	1,000	Swaziland
1,704	1,713	408	437	2,243	1,918	11,433	8,000	3,401	3,300	6,097	7,717	116,333	107,000	Sweden
1,845	1,600	392	450	1,793	1,450	5,912	7,000	3,892	3,910	4,954	5,356	38,000	38,000	Switzerland
786	905	14,571	14,500	1	1	14,405	22,000	782	1,150	2,314	2,556	75,133	120,000	Syria
157	...	...	...	8,813	10,509[5]	80,119	101,838[5]	204	318[5]	4,349	4,802[5]	...	...	Taiwan
1,238[1]	1,042	2,110[1]	1,593	49[1]	1	4,029[1]	1,000	472[1]	306	...	593	14,667[1]	1,000	Tajikistan
13,047	14,380	3,551	4,200	320	350	20,567	28,000	516	685	169	207	41,000	58,000	Tanzania
5,513	6,100	161	41	4,766	7,200	109,000	172,000	137	469	1,886	2,231	430,033	515,000	Thailand
247	215	1,164	740	617	850	6,070	8,000	8	7	225	225	6,000	6,000	Togo
11	9	...	...	94	81	221	266	—	—	...	2	287	28	Tonga
55	35	14	12	53	41	10,000	10,000	11	10	1,593	1,552	9,000	9,000	Trinidad and Tobago
626	790	5,935	6,600	6	6	39,367	37,000	393	890	1,420	1,618	52,250	80,000	Tunisia
12,037	11,031	43,195	29,435	10	5	73,181	237,000	8,183	8,800	1,352	1,600	369,080	660,000	Turkey
962[1]	850	5,793[1]	5,600	203[1]	46	6,900[1]	4,000	565[1]	900	...	1,765	14,933[1]	16,000	Turkmenistan
...	...	...	...	12	13	29	27	...	...	...	...	12	12	Tuvalu
4,777	5,966	1,350	1,980	797	970	18,667	25,000	418	511	350	350	15,000	20,000	Uganda
22,597[1]	10,627	6,658[1]	1,060	16,437[1]	10,073	180,352[1]	105,000	18,363[1]	12,400	...	2,283	664,865[1]	477,000	Ukraine
49	110	255	467	...	...	7,000	15,000	5	9	210	157	10,000	13,000	United Arab Emirates
11,980	11,133	29,241	42,261	7,519	6,482	124,076	157,000	14,976	14,461	5,206	6,190	616,000	588,000	United Kingdom
96,316	98,048	11,384	7,215	54,557	59,337	1,333,000	1,720,000	66,423	76,294	6,673	8,388	4,048,000	5,011,000	United States
9,019	10,800	25,359	13,032	217	380	8,000	13,000	980	1,422	1,562	1,755	26,000	37,000	Uruguay
5,273[1]	5,268	8,681[1]	8,917	524[1]	80	26,867[1]	14,000	3,622[1]	3,692	...	1,605	96,833[1]	69,000	Uzbekistan
124	152	...	...	59	62	306	320	2	3	202	203	312	280	Vanuatu
13,311	15,800	551	781	2,801	4,900	60,000	110,000	1,564	1,311	1,285	1,278	119,000	168,000	Venezuela
3,153	4,137	...	...	12,224	20,194	77,228	196,000	36	42	800	800	97,000	165,000	Vietnam
8	8	3	3	3	3	30	35	2	2	2,725	2,703	120	160	Virgin Islands (U.S.)
...	12	...	352	...	...	...	...	...	27	...	35	...	15,000	West Bank
...	...	...	29	...	...	...	...	...	...	...	...	...	...	Western Sahara
1,154	1,283	3,682	4,760	...	...	16,385	28,000	152	172	600	600	18,000	31,000	Yemen
2,845	2,373	59	140	296	330	16,033	29,000	77	64	300	300	26,000	46,000	Zambia
6,147	5,550	584	530	300	275	12,000	16,000	440	310	417	310	16,000	21,000	Zimbabwe

[1]1992–94 average. [2]Belgium includes Luxembourg. [3]1993–95 average. [4]Indonesia includes East Timor. [5]1995.

Extractive industries

Extractive industries are generally defined as those exploiting in situ natural resources and include such activities as mining, forestry, fisheries, and agriculture; the definition is often confined, however, to nonrenewable resources only. For the purposes of this table, agriculture is excluded; it is covered in the preceding table.

Extractive industries are divided here into three parts: mining, forestry, and fisheries. These major headings are each divided into two main subheadings, one that treats production and one that treats foreign trade. The production sections are presented in terms of volume except for mining, and the trade sections are presented in terms of U.S. dollars. Volume of production data usually imply output of primary (unprocessed) raw materials only, but, because of the way national statistical information is reported, the data may occasionally include some processed and manufactured materials as well, since these are often indistinguishably associated with the extractive process (sulfur from petroleum extraction, cured or treated lumber, or "processed" fish). This is also the case in the trade sections, where individual national trade nomenclatures may not distinguish some processed and manufactured goods from unprocessed raw materials.

Mining. In the absence of a single international source publication or standard of practice for reporting volume or value of mineral production, single-country sources predominantly have been used to compile mining production figures, supplemented by U.S. Bureau of Mines data, by the United Nations' *National Accounts Statistics* (annual; 2 parts), and by industry sources, especially *Mining Journal's Mining Annual Review*. Each country has its own methods of classifying mining data, which do not always accord with the principal mineral production categories adopted in this table—namely, "metals," "nonmetals," and "energy." The available data have therefore been adjusted to accord better with the definition of each group. Included in the "metal" category are all ferrous and nonferrous metallic ores, concentrates, and scrap; the "nonmetal" group includes all nonmetallic minerals (stone, clay, precious gems, etc.) except the mineral fuels; the last group, "energy," is composed predominantly of the natural hydrocarbon fuels, though it may also include manufactured gas.

The contribution (value) of each national mineral sector to its country's gross domestic product is given, as is the distribution by group of that contribution (to gross domestic product and to foreign trade), although statistics regarding the value of mineral production are less readily available in country sources than those regarding trade or volume of minerals produced. Figures for value added by mineral output, though not always available, were sought first, as they provide the most consistent standard to compare the importance of minerals both within a particular national economy and among national mineral sectors worldwide. Where value added to the gross domestic product was not available, gross value of production or sales was substituted and the exception footnoted. Figures for value of production are reported here in millions of U.S. dollars to permit comparisons to be made from country to country. Comparisons can also be made as to the relative importance of each mineral group within a given country.

Extractive industries

country	mining														
	% of GDP, 1998	mineral production (value added)					trade (value)								
		year	total ('000,000 U.S.$)	by kind (%)			year	exports				imports			
				metals[a]	non-metals[b]	energy[c]		total ('000,000 U.S.$)	by kind (%)			total ('000,000 U.S.$)	by kind (%)		
									metals[a]	non-metals[b]	energy[c]		metals[a]	non-metals[b]	energy[c]
Afghanistan	...	...	...	...	...	...	1997	0.1	—	100.0	—	...	...	...	...
Albania	...	1994[1]	81.4	46.1	0.8	53.1	1997	16.5	93.9	6.1	—	12.9	—	34.9	65.1
Algeria	23.0	1998	10,895.7	—	—	100.0	1996	8,931.6	—	0.2	99.8	22.4	—	—	100.0
American Samoa	...	1998	...	—	100.0	—	...	...	...	...	...	...	...	...	...
Andorra	...	...	...	...	...	...	...	...	...	...	...	...	...	...	...
Angola	60.9[2]	1997	3,935.1	—	7.7	92.3	1997	212.6	—	90.4	9.6	...	...	...	...
Antigua and Barbuda	1.5	1998	9.0[12]	—	100.0	—	...	...	...	...	...	...	...	...	...
Argentina	2.4[2]	1997	7,821.8[3]	...	...	...	1997	2,429.7[4]	—	—	100.0[4]	419.5	65.2	1.6	33.2
Armenia	...	1998	...	—100.0—		—	1997	106.9	—	100.0	—	187.2	50.5	49.5	—
Aruba	...	1998	...	—	100.0	—	1997	1.4	—	100.0	—	...	...	...	...
Australia	4.4	1998	15,105.6	...	...	...	1997	17,083.6	40.1	3.6	56.3	3,181.5	3.4	9.0	87.6
Austria	0.5	1995	819.3	2.5	53.5	44.0	1997	484.0[4]	38.5[4]	61.2[4]	0.3[4]	3,055.2	16.7	10.2	73.1
Azerbaijan	...	...	...	...	...	...	1994	...	...	...	...	224.1	—	—	100.0
Bahamas, The	...	1998	...	—	100.0	—	1997	1.2	100.0	—	—	...	...	...	...
Bahrain	13.6	1998	841.2	—	1.5	98.5	1996	2,471.1[6]	0.6[6]	—	99.3[6]	2,002.2	15.8	0.6	83.7
Bangladesh	1.0	1997–98	417.6	—	47.4	52.6	1996	...	...	...	...	80.0	—	77.5	22.5
Barbados	1.0	1998	4.6[3]	—	—100.0[3]—		1997	0.1	100.0	—	—	8.3	—	43.4	56.6
Belarus	...	1998	...	—	—100.0—		1997	175.2	—	92.5	7.5	39.6	—	100.0	—
Belgium	0.3[2]	1997	617.8	—	—100.0—		1997	13,490.0	8.2	88.6	3.3	21,328.3	12.4	54.9	32.7
Belize	0.5	1998	2.5	—	100.0	—	1997	...	...	...	...	3.4	—	14.7	85.3
Benin	0.7[5]	1995	14.4[8]	—	—100.0[8]—		...	...	...	...	...	...	...	...	...
Bermuda	...	...	...	...	...	...	1997	...	...	...	...	14.0	—	100.0	—
Bhutan	2.3[2]	1997	8.5	—	—100.0—		1994	2.9	—	82.8	17.2	1.7	—	29.4	70.6
Bolivia	11.1	1998	686.1	—49.5—		50.5	1997	377.7	72.9	1.1	26.0	17.7	85.9	14.1	—
Bosnia and Herzegovina	...	...	...	...	...	...	1997	2.9	—	—	100.0	...	...	...	...
Botswana	37.6	1997–98	1,950.6	11.4[9]	88.0[9]	0.7[9]	[10]	...	...	...	...	...	...	...	...
Brazil	0.8[2]	1997	6,760.5	...	...	...	1997	3,454.5	92.4	7.6	—	5,433.9	8.2	4.4	87.4
Brunei	36.7	1998	1,777.6	—8.5—		91.5	1997	1,970.2[6]	—	—	100.0[6]	9.3	—	100.0	—
Bulgaria	1.4	1998	167.4	...	...	...	1997	120.4	37.7	62.3	—	1,166.2	13.4	3.4	83.2
Burkina Faso	...	1998	...	—100.0—		—	...	...	...	...	...	...	...	...	...
Burundi	0.6[2]	1995	6.2	...	...	...	...	...	...	...	...	...	...	...	...
Cambodia	0.3	1998	8.8	—	100.0	—	...	...	...	...	...	...	...	...	...
Cameroon	5.5	1997–98	491.5	—	—	100.0	1996	628.8	—	—	100.0	187.6	16.4	4.0	79.6
Canada	3.7	1998	21,998.8	19.4	12.0	68.6	1997	22,630.2	16.3	3.7	79.9	10,037.9	24.5	6.4	69.1
Cape Verde	0.3[9]	1994	0.9	—	100.0	—	...	...	...	...	...	...	...	...	...
Central African Republic	3.8	1998	39.8[11]	—100.0[11]—		—	1997	104.1	—	100.0	—	0.8[4]	—	100.0[4]	—
Chad	...	...	...	...	...	...	...	...	...	...	...	...	...	...	...
Chile	8.5	1998	3,555.7	—100.0—		—	1997	2,553.3	96.9	3.1	—	1,505.5	4.1	—	95.9
China	...	...	...	...	...	...	1997	5,786.1	2.5	24.5	73.0	10,446.5	32.9	5.6	61.5
Colombia	5.5[4]	1996	4,735.4	...	...	...	1997	3,363.5	0.1	4.2	95.7	86.1	20.0	80.0	—
Comoros	—	1998	...	—	100.0	—	...	...	...	...	...	...	...	...	...
Congo, Dem. Rep. of the	22.8[6]	1995	288.6	—100.0—		—	1995	302.7	—	84.5	15.5	3.4	—	100.0	—
Congo, Rep. of the	40.6[13]	1996[13]	978.8[13]	...	...	...	1995	939.5	—	0.3	99.7	5.2	—	48.1	51.9
Costa Rica	...	...	...	...	...	...	1997	5.1	100.0	—	—	123.1[4]	—	7.0[4]	93.0[4]
Côte d'Ivoire	0.2[13]	1998[13]	28.1[13]	...	...	...	1997	132.0	—	100.0	—	489.9[4]	—	3.2[4]	96.8[4]
Croatia	0.4	1998	96.9	...	...	...	1997	135.0	23.1	14.1	62.8	772.7	—	7.3	92.7
Cuba	...	...	...	...	...	...	1997	...	...	...	...	13.3	—	100.0	—
Cyprus	0.3[14]	1998[14]	25.1	—	100.0	—	1997[14]	20.6	46.6	53.4	—	167.9	—	12.9	87.1
Czech Republic	...	...	...	...	...	...	1997	651.0	23.9	11.0	65.1	2,175.5	13.0	4.1	82.9
Denmark	1.4[2]	1997	2,023.8	—	—100.0—		1997	1,193.7	15.2	6.9	77.8	1,004.3	7.7	18.6	73.7
Djibouti	—	1998	...	—	100.0	—	...	...	...	...	...	...	...	...	...
Dominica	0.9	1998	2.0	—	100.0	—	1996	0.9	—	100.0	—	1.1	—	—	100.0
Dominican Republic	2.0	1998	309.3	—100.0—		—	1994	2.7	—	100.0	—	...	...	...	...
East Timor	...	...	...	...	...	...	...	...	...	...	...	...	...	...	...
Ecuador	7.8	1997	1,560.0	—6.8[15]—		93.2[15]	1997	1,404.8	—	—	100.0	95.0	—	9.4	90.6

Since the data for value of mineral production are obtained mostly from country sources, there is some variation (from a standard calendar year) in the time periods to which the data refer. In addition, the time period for which production data are available does not always correspond with the year for which mineral trade data are available.

The Standard International Trade Classification (SITC), Revision 3, was used to determine the commodity groupings for foreign trade statistics. The actual trade data for these groups is taken largely from the United Nations' *International Trade Statistics Yearbook* (2 vol.) and national sources.

Forestry. Data for the production and trade sections of forestry are based on the Food and Agriculture Organization (FAO) of the United Nations' *Yearbook of Forest Products.* Production of roundwood (all wood obtained in removals from forests) is the principal indicator of the volume of each country's forestry sector; this total is broken down further (as percentages of the roundwood total) into its principal components: fuelwood and charcoal, and industrial roundwood. The latter group was further divided to show its principal component, sawlogs and veneer; lesser categories of industrial roundwood could not be shown for reasons of space. These included pitprops (used in mining, a principal consumer of wood) and pulpwood (used in papermaking and plastics). Value of trade in forest products is given for both imports and exports, although exports alone tend to be the significant indicator for producing countries, while imports of wood are rarely a significant fraction of the trade of most importing countries.

Fisheries. Data for nominal (live weight) catches of fish, crustaceans, mollusks, etc., in all fishing areas (marine areas and inland waters) are taken from the FAO *Yearbook of Fishery Statistics* (*Catches and Landings*). Total catch figures are given in metric tons; the catches in inland waters and marine areas are given as percentages of the total catch, as are the main kinds of catch—fish, crustaceans, and mollusks. The total catch figures exclude marine mammals, such as whales and seals; and such aquatic animal products as corals, sponges, and pearls; but include frogs, turtles, and jellyfish. The subtotals by kind of catch, however, exclude the last group, which do not belong taxonomically to the fish, crustaceans, or mollusks.

Figures for trade in fishery products (including processed products and preparations like oils, meals, and animal feeding stuffs) are taken from the FAO's *Yearbook of Fishery Statistics* (*Commodities*). Value figures for trade in fish products are given for both imports and exports.

The following notes further define the column headings:

a. Includes ferrous and nonferrous metallic ores, concentrates, and scraps, such as iron ore, bauxite and alumina, copper, zinc, gold (except unwrought or semimanufactured), lead, or uranium.

b. Includes natural fertilizers; stone, sand, and aggregate; and pearls, precious and semiprecious stones, worked and unworked.

c. Includes hydrocarbon solids, liquids, and gases.

1 cubic metre = 35.3147 cubic feet

1 metric ton = 1.1023 short tons

forestry						fisheries, 1999								country
production of roundwood, 2000				trade (value, '000 U.S.$), 1999		catch (nominal)						trade (value, '000 U.S.$)		
total ('000 cubic metres)	fuelwood, charcoal (%)	industrial roundwood (%)		exports	imports	total ('000 metric tons)	by source (%)		by kind of catch (%)			exports	imports	
		total	sawlogs, veneer				marine	inland	fish	crusta-ceans	mollusks			
8,283	78.8	21.2	10.3	...	1,090	1.2	—	100.0	100.0	—	—	...	...	Afghanistan
409	84.5	15.5	15.5	7,063	17,158	2.7	70.3	29.7	90.8	0.7	8.5	4,804	3,965	Albania
2,795	83.9	16.1	2.4	...	375,546	105.7	100.0	—	96.3	3.6	0.1	2,374	13,268	Algeria
...	...	...	...	...	302[2]	0.5	100.0	—	99.6	0.2	0.2	...	...	American Samoa
...	...	...	...	...	6,383	—	—	100.0	100.0	—	—	...	...	Andorra
6,676	83.3	16.7	1.0	1,635	5,124	177.5	96.6	3.4	98.3	1.4	0.3	10,043	14,523	Angola
...	...	...	...	...	4,604	3.2	100.0	—	69.3	29.2	1.4	644	2,373	Antigua and Barbuda
5,741	19.2	80.8	—	224,651	755,695	1,024.8	98.8	1.2	63.1	2.9	34.1	807,042	88,368	Argentina
36[5]	100.0[5]	—	—	...	386	0.4	—	100.0	100.0	—	—	494	3,136	Armenia
...	...	...	...	6	7,321	0.2	100.0	—	100.0	—	—	...	17,753	Aruba
22,938	11.8	88.2	43.5	709,553	1,523,192	216.3	98.6	1.4	61.5	25.8	12.7	899,040	485,072	Australia
13,276	21.5	78.5	60.5	4,085,669	2,318,823	0.4	—	100.0	100.0	—	—	10,689	204,997	Austria
...	...	...	...	206	28,116	4.7	—	100.0	100.0	—	—	3,850	846	Azerbaijan
17	—	100.0	100.0	...	30,414	10.5	100.0	—	16.9	78.5	4.5	69,591	4,400	Bahamas, The
—	—	—	—	...	25,821	10.3	100.0	—	65.5	34.1	0.4	6,925	3,203	Bahrain
33,629	98.1	1.9	0.5	14,405	92,529	924.1	37.0	63.0	96.6	3.4	—	297,585	2,050	Bangladesh
5	—	100.0	100.0	...	35,503	0.3	100.0	—	100.0	—	—	951	11,044	Barbados
6,136	15.1	84.9	51.6	73,918	63,254	0.5	—	100.0	88.9	—	11.1	14,028	54,905	Belarus
4,400	12.5	87.5	58.0	3,734,032[7]	4,136,516[7]	29.9	98.2	1.8	92.9	5.0	2.1	447,598[7]	1,063,195[7]	Belgium
188	67.2	32.8	32.8	3,763	4,003	39.9	100.0	—	64.3	5.4	30.3	21,163	1,724	Belize
6,140	94.6	5.4	0.6	931	12,324	38.5	22.2	77.8	80.1	19.9	—	1,928	3,457	Benin
...	...	...	...	...	...	0.5	100.0	—	91.1	8.9	—	...	7,569	Bermuda
1,751	97.4	2.6	1.0	156	2,159	0.3	—	100.0	100.0	—	—	...	...	Bhutan
1,906	72.7	27.3	26.3	25,409	40,384	6.1	—	100.0	100.0	—	—	4	2,938	Bolivia
40	...	100.0	100.0	72,219	23,986	2.5	—	100.0	100.0	—	—	...	9,781	Bosnia and Herzegovina
1,702	93.8	6.2	—	...	15,410	2.0	—	100.0	100.0	—	—	54	5,218	Botswana
197,897	57.6	42.4	23.6	2,579,776	811,923	655.0	73.3	26.7	90.6	8.7	0.6	138,232	289,808	Brazil
296	26.7	73.3	69.6	...	8,426	3.2	99.2	0.8	96.7	2.2	1.1	184	8,881	Brunei
4,766	44.2	55.8	34.1	75,289	77,741	10.6	76.6	23.4	64.0	—	36.0	5,774	13,307	Bulgaria
11,095	95.4	4.6	—	...	14,780	7.6	—	100.0	100.0	—	—	5	1,674	Burkina Faso
1,799	83.9	16.1	12.3	...	1,700	9.2	—	100.0	100.0	—	—	334	8	Burundi
8,157	87.3	12.7	5.0	35,010	8,910	269.1	14.2	85.8	98.0	1.3	0.7	30,525	2,796	Cambodia
15,279	82.0	18.0	11.6	386,415	18,650	95.0	63.2	36.8	99.6	0.4	—	6,152	19,783	Cameroon
185,659	2.6	97.4	78.9	25,469,746	3,777,382	1,021.9	96.0	4.0	62.5	26.2	11.4	2,617,759	1,338,973	Canada
...	...	...	...	2,519	3,760	10.4	100.0	—	99.6	0.4	—	1,852	1,013	Cape Verde
3,548	75.7	24.3	15.6	46,659	...	15.0	—	100.0	100.0	—	—	61	448	Central African Republic
1,969	61.4	38.6	0.7	116	1,650	84.0	—	100.0	100.0	—	—	...	28	Chad
27,972	38.6	61.4	42.1	1,530,190	185,022	5,050.5	100.0	—	97.1	0.8	2.1	1,696,819	54,569	Chile
291,330[12]	65.6[12]	34.4[12]	19.1[12]	6,778,898[12]	25,536,650[12]	17,240.0	98.3	1.7	69.9	17.6	12.5	2,959,530	1,127,412	China
17,845	95.4	4.6	4.5	78,486	316,615	117.9	75.6	24.4	94.8	5.0	0.2	183,668	71,028	Colombia
9	—	100.0	100.0	...	185	12.2	100.0	—	100.0	—	—	1	774	Comoros
50,754	92.7	7.3	0.5	20,754	3,968	208.4	1.9	98.1	99.8	0.2	—	431	41,905	Congo, Dem. Rep. of the
3,243	80.1	19.9	8.5	75,946	1,769	43.7	41.7	58.3	86.0	5.3	8.7	1,720	18,631	Congo, Rep. of the
5,397	69.0	31.0	25.9	20,837	240,616	25.7	90.4	9.6	96.1	3.6	0.3	148,321	25,359	Costa Rica
13,396	76.9	23.1	16.3	225,923	45,038	76.0	82.9	17.1	98.7	1.2	0.1	132,249	162,354	Côte d'Ivoire
3,486	31.4	68.6	54.9	229,147	290,892	19.3	97.9	2.1	93.0	1.5	5.5	34,845	34,825	Croatia
1,593	74.5	25.5	8.0	60	24,509	67.3	93.1	6.9	61.4	22.7	15.9	93,296	22,484	Cuba
25	26.4	73.6	579.7	2,127	37,192	5.3	98.7	1.3	93.8	2.8	3.4	4,343	31,891	Cyprus
14,441	6.5	93.5	55.5	868,057	667,290	4.2	—	100.0	100.0	—	—	25,922	73,795	Czech Republic
3,086	32.4	67.6	42.8	398,653	1,329,135	1,405.0	100.0	—	92.4	0.8	6.9	2,884,334	1,771,500	Denmark
—	—	—	—	...	4,475	0.4	100.0	—	100.0	—	—	130	1,253	Djibouti
...	...	...	...	...	8,358	1.2	100.0	—	100.0	—	—	...	1,595	Dominica
562	98.9	1.1	0.6	578	211,782	8.5	91.6	8.4	74.2	10.4	15.4	700	53,102	Dominican Republic
...	...	...	...	...	...	0.5	100.0	—	98.4	1.4	0.2	...	...	East Timor
11,340	47.8	0.1	45.6	72,103	224,328	497.9	99.9	0.1	99.6	0.4	—	954,471	5,060	Ecuador

Extractive industries (continued)

country	mining						trade (value)								
	% of GDP, 1998	mineral production (value added)					year	exports				imports			
		year	total ('000,000 U.S.$)	by kind (%)				total ('000,000 U.S.$)	by kind (%)			total ('000,000 U.S.$)	by kind (%)		
				metals[a]	non-metals[b]	energy[c]			metals[a]	non-metals[b]	energy[c]		metals[a]	non-metals[b]	energy[c]
Egypt	9.8[9]	1994	5,151.3	——1.0——		99.0	1997	704.6	—	5.2	94.8	381.9	40.7	19.2	40.1
El Salvador	0.4	1998	47.6	100.0	—	—	1997	...	...	...	...	151.9	—	5.4	94.6
Equatorial Guinea	61.3	1998	279.6	—	—	100.0	...	...	...	...	...	...	...	...	...
Eritrea	0.1	1998	0.5	——100.0——		—	...	...	...	...	...	...	...	...	...
Estonia	1.0	1998	54.2	—	——100.0——		1997	76.5	79.0	—	21.0	113.1	27.9	20.2	52.0
Ethiopia	0.5	1997–98	33.3	——100.0——		—	1995	...	...	...	...	68.4	—	—	100.0
Faroe Islands	0.2[4]	1996	1.7	...	...	...	...	...	...	...	...	...	...	...	...
Fiji	3.4[4]	1996	42.5	——100.0——		—	1994	0.8	100.0	—	—	5.8	—	41.4	58.6
Finland	0.2	1998	307.4	——100.0——		—	1997	295.9	64.2	33.1	2.8	3,383.4	28.5	8.5	63.1
France	0.8[6]	1995	11,521.0	4.8	14.3	81.0	1997	2,335.7	46.6	32.5	20.9	20,162.7	9.2	5.2	85.5
French Guiana	...	1998	...	——100.0——		—	...	...	...	...	...	...	...	...	...
French Polynesia	...	...	...	...	...	...	1997	191.4	—	100.0	—	...	...	...	...
Gabon	41.8[4]	1996	2,382.8	4.0	—	96.0	1996	2,621.1	2.4	—	97.6	6.7	—	50.7	49.3
Gambia, The	—	1998	...	—	100.0	—	1995	...	...	...	...	1.4	—	—	100.0
Gaza Strip	...	...	...	...	...	...	...	...	...	...	...	...	...	...	...
Georgia	...	...	...	...	...	...	...	...	...	...	...	...	...	...	...
Germany	...	...	...	...	...	...	1997	5,631.4	43.6	21.0	35.3	30,568.8	16.3	5.6	78.1
Ghana	5.2	1998	388.6	——100.0——		—	1997	225.2	—	100.0	—	56.5	100.0	—	—
Greece	0.6[2]	1997	707.9	...	...	...	1997	310.3	40.9	35.9	23.2	1,393.2	6.9	7.2	85.9
Greenland	...	...	...	...	...	...	1997	...	...	...	...	1.6	—	100.0	—
Grenada	1.4	1998	1.3	—	100.0	—	1996	...	...	...	...	2.4	—	25.0	75.0
Guadeloupe	...	1998	...	—	100.0	—	...	...	...	...	...	...	...	...	...
Guam	...	1998	...	—	100.0	—	...	...	...	...	...	...	...	...	...
Guatemala	0.6	1998	30.0	...	...	...	1997	102.9	—	6.2	93.8	172.1	—	—	100.0
Guernsey	...	...	...	...	...	...	...	...	...	...	...	...	...	...	...
Guinea	15.7	1998	645.4[17]	——100.0[17]——		—	1997	396.7	80.3	19.7	—	...	...	...	...
Guinea-Bissau	...	1998	...	—	100.0	—	...	...	...	...	...	...	...	...	...
Guyana	13.6	1998	98.0	——100.0——		—	1997	94.3	100.0	—	—	...	...	...	...
Haiti	0.2	1998	1.8	—	100.0	—	...	...	...	...	...	...	...	...	...
Honduras	1.8	1998	82.3	——100.0——		—	1997	30.6	100.0	—	—	10.1	—	—	100.0
Hong Kong	0.02	1998	39.1	—	100.0	—	1997	2,264.8	27.2	72.8	—	4,639.9	12.9	75.8	11.2
Hungary	0.4[2]	1997	181.5	15.6	26.5	57.9	1997	136.5	99.6	—	0.4	1,747.1	1.9	3.5	94.6
Iceland	...	1998	...	—	100.0	—	1997	19.7	34.0	66.0	—	50.7	68.6	21.5	9.9
India	1.0	1996–97	3,268.9	...	...	...	1997	5,168.2	13.3	86.2	0.5	10,499.3[4]	7.8[4]	31.2[4]	61.0[4]
Indonesia	12.9	1998	12,704.4	——34.7——		65.3	1997	13,660.2	12.7	0.9	86.4	2,138.5	16.9	14.5	68.6
Iran	7.2	1998–99	13,441.8	——9.1——		90.9	1995	18,525.9	1.0	0.4	98.6	1,271.4	17.5	7.5	75.0
Iraq	...	...	...	...	...	...	...	...	...	...	...	...	...	...	...
Ireland	...	...	...	...	...	...	1997	538.5	75.1	16.5	8.4	825.7	14.4	12.9	72.7
Isle of Man	...	1998	...	—	100.0	—	...	...	...	...	...	...	...	...	...
Israel	...	...	...	...	...	...	1997	6,948.8	0.5	99.5	—	7,117.3	0.2	73.3	26.5
Italy	...	...	...	...	...	...	1997	851.4	34.6	57.2	8.2	16,573.7	15.0	9.3	75.7
Jamaica	4.5	1998	310.3	97.2	2.8	—	1997	682.4	100.0	—	—	105.8	—	—	100.0
Japan	0.2[4]	1996	9,863.9	...	...	...	1997	1,315.4	44.0	56.0	—	67,595.7	12.8	5.8	81.4
Jersey	...	...	...	...	...	...	...	...	...	...	...	...	...	...	...
Jordan	3.3	1998	239.3	—	100.0	—	1997	353.6	5.0	95.0	—	416.7[6]	0.6[6]	8.8[6]	90.6[6]
Kazakhstan	...	...	...	...	...	...	1996	837.9	18.9	12.8	68.4	170.9	29.9	25.8	44.3
Kenya	0.2[6]	1995	14.1	——100.0——		—	1997	40.4	—	100.0	—	227.3[4]	—	2.6[4]	97.4[4]
Kiribati	...	...	...	...	...	...	1995	...	...	...	...	0.1	—	100.0	—
Korea, North	...	...	...	...	...	...	1997	90.6	30.8	36.9	32.3	52.7[6]	—	36.1[6]	63.9[6]
Korea, South	0.4	1998	1,141.7	...	...	...	1997	238.6	13.9	53.9	32.2	23,311.9[4]	12.8[4]	3.0[4]	84.2[4]
Kuwait	39.5[6]	1995	10,513.4	—	—	100.0	1997	14,130.4[4]	0.2[4]	—	99.8[4]	60.7	—	100.0	—
Kyrgyzstan	...	...	...	...	...	...	1996	15.8	75.9	—	24.1	118.2	2.5	4.8	92.7
Laos	0.4	1998	5.8	——100.0——		—	...	...	...	...	...	...	...	...	...
Latvia	0.5	1998	116.4	—	——100.0——		1997	32.3	85.1	—	14.9	148.9	13.7	8.1	78.2
Lebanon	...	...	...	...	...	...	1997	130.5	31.0	69.0	—	132.8	—	100.0	—
Lesotho	0.01[4]	1996	0.1	—	100.0	—	[10]	...	...	...	...	...	...	...	...
Liberia	2.4	1998	8.6	—	100.0	—	1997	15.7	100.0	—	—	14.8	—	100.0	—
Libya	25.8[4]	1996	8,441.7	—	7.1	92.9	1997	9,451.2[6]	—	—	100.0[6]	51.2	100.0	—	—
Liechtenstein	...	...	...	...	...	...	...	...	...	...	...	...	...	...	...
Lithuania	0.5	1998	49.3	—	33.9[2]	66.1[2]	1997	130.7	48.7	—	51.3	850.6	2.4	7.0	90.6
Luxembourg	0.2	1998	24.8	—	100.0	—	[7]	...	...	...	...	...	...	...	...
Macau	...	...	...	...	...	...	1997	...	...	...	...	17.3	—	20.8	79.2
Macedonia	...	...	...	...	...	...	1995	29.5	68.1	31.9	—	41.8	6.7	39.5	53.8
Madagascar	0.3[9]	1994	5.2	——100.0——		—	1997	26.6	40.6	59.4	—	79.5	—	—	100.0
Malawi	1.0[9]	1994	12.8	...	...	...	1995	...	...	...	...	5.1	—	62.7	37.3
Malaysia	7.9	1998	3,675.2[3]	...	...	...	1996	5,509.7	2.4	2.3	95.3	1,175.0	43.1	32.2	24.7
Maldives	1.6	1998	2.2	—	100.0	—	...	...	...	...	...	...	...	...	...
Mali	5.5	1998	81.7	——100.0——		—	1997	7.0	—	100.0	—	...	...	...	...
Malta	...	1998	...	—	100.0	—	1996	3.5[6]	97.9[6]	2.1[6]	—	10.2	—	100.0	—
Marshall Islands	0.3[6]	1995	0.3	—	100.0	—	...	...	...	...	...	...	...	...	...
Martinique	...	1998	...	—	100.0	—	1995	4.1	19.4	38.3	42.3	102.5	—	—	100.0
Mauritania	9.6[2]	1997	105.9	——100.0——		—	1997	301.6	100.0	—	—	...	...	...	...
Mauritius	0.1	1998	5.6	—	100.0	—	1996	56.2	—	73.8	26.2	56.2	—	73.8	26.2
Mayotte	...	...	...	...	...	...	...	...	...	...	...	...	...	...	...
Mexico	1.2	1998	5,128.4	...	...	...	1997	11,181.6	4.8	2.3	93.0	1,715.3	39.7	25.2	35.1
Micronesia	...	...	...	...	...	...	...	...	...	...	...	...	...	...	...
Moldova	...	1998	...	—	100.0	—	1997	18.7[6]	100.0[6]	—	—	147.5	—	—	100.0
Monaco	...	...	...	...	...	...	...	...	...	...	...	...	...	...	...
Mongolia	...	...	...	...	...	...	1996	254.1	90.9	9.1	—	...	...	...	...
Morocco	2.2[2]	1997	746.5	...	...	...	1997	751.1	23.6	76.4	—	1,449.6	—	11.3	88.7
Mozambique	...	...	...	...	...	...	1996	8.4	72.6	27.4	—	3.3	—	100.0	—
Myanmar (Burma)	0.4	1998–99	1,107.3	...	...	...	1997	39.0	—	100.0	—	...	...	...	...
Namibia	11.7[2]	1997	382.8	——100.0——		—	[10]	...	...	...	...	...	...	...	...
Nauru	...	1998	...	—	100.0	—	1997	151.6	—	100.0	—	...	...	...	...
Nepal	0.5	1998–99	26.8	——100.0——		—	1995	...	...	...	...	9.1	51.6	—	48.4

forestry						fisheries, 1999								country
production of roundwood, 2000				trade (value, '000 U.S.$), 1999		catch (nominal)						trade (value, '000 U.S.$)		
total ('000 cubic metres)	fuelwood, charcoal (%)	industrial roundwood (%)		exports	imports	total ('000 metric tons)	by source (%)		by kind of catch (%)			exports	imports	
		total	sawlogs, veneer				marine	inland	fish	crusta-ceans	mollusks			
2,883	95.4	4.6	—	11,855	794,951	380.5	40.8	59.2	94.5	4.1	1.4	1,442	153,061	Egypt
5,170	87.4	12.6	12.6	14,360	124,786	15.2	83.9	16.1	24.8	71.1	4.1	33,596	6,640	El Salvador
811	55.1	44.9	44.9	89,885	...	7.0	84.3	15.7	90.8	7.2	2.0	2,565	2,508	Equatorial Guinea
2,285	99.9	0.1	0.1	...	6,833	7.0	100.0	—	98.7	1.1	0.2	973	54	Eritrea
8,910	18.4	81.6	32.0	391,529	112,763	111.8	97.2	2.8	88.9	11.1	—	77,582	30,951	Estonia
89,925	97.3	2.7	—	...	8,894	15.9	—	100.0	100.0	—	—	...	42	Ethiopia
...	...	...	...	221	4,162	358.0	100.0	—	94.1	4.2	1.7	436,000	15,372	Faroe Islands
483	7.7	92.3	40.6	18,189	8,189	36.7	84.7	15.3	56.2	3.4	40.3	22,266	17,294	Fiji
54,263	7.6	92.4	47.9	10,925,450	887,491	160.6	77.1	22.9	99.9	0.1	—	21,493	118,244	Finland
50,170	22.0	78.0	52.8	5,683,978	7,492,308	578.1	99.2	0.8	86.4	3.5	10.1	1,107,169	3,280,940	France
120	49.8	50.2	42.6	2,481	2,424	7.7	100.0	—	45.5	54.5	—	40,495[2]	5,136[2]	French Guiana
...	...	...	...	...	22,201	12.4	99.6	0.4	99.5	0.4	0.1	2,263	6,891	French Polynesia
5,397	48.6	51.4	51.4	380,793	4,799	52.9	84.9	15.1	94.2	5.4	0.4	13,148	6,876	Gabon
618	81.8	18.2	17.2	...	1,416	30.0	91.7	8.3	97.9	1.8	0.3	4,643	848	Gambia, The
...	...	...	...	...	...	3.6	100.0	—	88.1	6.3	5.7	...	...	Gaza Strip
...	...	...	...	11,952	5,749	1.5	93.3	6.7	100.0	—	—	208	2,471	Georgia
37,634	6.8	93.2	62.2	9,923,976	10,776,915	238.9	90.4	9.6	92.0	8.0	—	966,300	2,288,523	Germany
21,907	94.4	5.6	5.2	187,175	24,016	492.8	84.9	15.1	99.1	0.9	—	95,813	20,321	Ghana
2,171	63.3	36.7	31.5	77,993	737,282	136.7	84.5	15.5	78.8	2.5	18.7	278,208	308,553	Greece
—	—	—	—	77	7,179	160.3	100.0	—	48.8	51.2	—	261,255	1,412	Greenland
...	...	...	...	—	5,167	1.6	100.0	—	95.2	4.4	0.4	3,530	2,534	Grenada
15	98.0	2.0	2.0	...	30,639	9.2	100.0	—	92.9	1.6	5.5	266[2]	30,393[2]	Guadeloupe
...	...	...	...	...	...	0.2	100.0	—	98.7	0.4	0.9	...	...	Guam
13,300	96.2	3.8	3.8	17,449	137,727	11.0	36.7	63.3	71.8	28.0	0.2	28,148	6,794	Guatemala
...	...	...	...	...	...	[16]	[16]	[16]	[16]	[16]	[16]	...	...	Guernsey
8,651	92.5	7.5	1.6	6,024	4,542	87.1	95.4	4.6	98.1	0.5	1.5	22,131	14,490	Guinea
592	71.3	28.7	6.8	610	...	5.0	96.0	4.0	81.3	2.4	16.3	6,318	487	Guinea-Bissau
467	2.4	97.6	93.1	36,047	3,239	53.8	98.9	1.1	77.7	22.3	—	34,461	475	Guyana
6,501	96.3	3.7	3.4	...	13,221	5.0	90.0	10.0	86.0	5.0	9.0	9,264	7,990	Haiti
7,413	88.5	11.5	11.5	43,309	59,836	7.2	98.6	1.4	53.7	21.8	24.4	97,207	14,805	Honduras
21[5]	100.0[5]	—	—	2,508,240[5]	3,101,116[5]	127.8	100.0	—	90.4	3.8	5.9	383,398	1,593,661	Hong Kong
5,902	44.0	56.0	23.4	353,145	618,345	7.5	—	100.0	97.6	—	2.4	6,948	39,552	Hungary
—	—	—	—	648	65,695	1,736.3	100.0	—	96.7	2.6	0.7	1,379,379	80,693	Iceland
302,794	92.1	7.9	6.1	54,971	789,321	3,316.8	79.2	20.8	89.3	7.9	2.8	1,019,579	20,188	India
190,601	83.5	16.5	13.0	4,757,769	947,593	4,149.4	92.9	7.1	90.9	6.6	2.6	1,527,092	86,555	Indonesia
1,151	16.5	83.5	26.9	...	201,165	387.2	63.0	37.0	97.3	1.2	1.5	23,945	58,002	Iran
177	66.7	33.3	14.1	...	4,341	24.6	53.2	46.8	100.0	—	—	...	1,277	Iraq
2,673	2.7	97.3	59.4	237,008	730,167	285.9	98.9	1.1	90.0	7.4	2.6	343,826	115,853	Ireland
...	...	...	...	...	...	2.6	100.0	—	3.6	9.0	87.3	...	...	Isle of Man
113	11.5	88.5	31.9	34,467	695,578	5.9	63.5	36.5	94.8	3.2	2.0	8,496	129,891	Israel
9,329	60.9	39.1	22.1	2,581,755	7,096,128	294.2	98.2	1.8	59.0	6.0	35.1	356,976	2,728,568	Italy
706	60.0	40.0	18.7	...	71,424	8.5	94.7	5.3	79.1	4.8	16.1	13,905	32,487	Jamaica
19,031	1.4	98.6	70.4	1,729,858	12,348,306	5,176.5	98.6	1.4	77.0	3.7	19.3	719,839	14,748,712	Japan
...	...	...	...	...	...	3.6[16]	100.0[16]	—[16]	25.7[16]	67.3[16]	7.0[16]	...	...	Jersey
11	63.6	36.4	—	5,420	104,204	0.5	31.4	68.6	100.0	—	—	1,231	21,020	Jordan
315[5]	100.0	—	—	598	48,398	25.8	—	100.0	100.0	—	—	12,257	11,903	Kazakhstan
29,908	93.4	6.6	1.5	2,064	38,124	205.3	3.2	96.8	99.5	0.4	0.2	32,415	5,339	Kenya
...	...	...	...	...	769[5]	48.2	100.0	—	97.0	—	3.0	5,611	299	Kiribati
7,000	78.6	21.4	14.3	15,192	8,781	210.0	90.5	9.5	95.2	—	4.8	71,535	2,579	Korea, North
1,722	1.6	98.4	36.1	1,515,287	2,967,578	2,119.7	99.7	0.3	64.0	4.4	31.5	1,393,428	1,140,022	Korea, South
...	...	...	...	13	97,708	6.3	100.0	—	88.5	11.5	—	4,721	22,111	Kuwait
42[5]	74.5[5]	25.5[5]	21.9[5]	225	9,892	—	100.0	100.0	100.0	—	—	...	2,287	Kyrgyzstan
4,869	82.2	17.8	15.1	26,657	1,704	30.0	—	100.0	100.0	—	—	99	1,157	Laos
14,488	11.6	88.4	58.7	600,131	47,946	125.4	99.5	0.5	97.5	2.5	—	51,849	36,097	Latvia
412	98.3	1.7	1.7	4,885	166,234	3.6	99.4	0.6	94.4	3.5	2.1	...	19,863	Lebanon
1,594	100.0	—	—	...	...	0.03	—	100.0	100.0	—	—	[18]	[18]	Lesotho
3,037	88.9	11.1	5.2	24,492	1,635	15.5	74.1	25.9	97.6	0.2	2.2	64	1,412	Liberia
652	82.2	17.8	9.7	...	33,260	32.5	100.0	—	100.0	—	—	32,654	12,561	Libya
13[5]	30.8[5]	69.2[5]	69.2[5]	...	...	—	...	...	...	...	...	...	...	Liechtenstein
5,346	22.4	77.6	52.4	171,231	113,279	33.6	94.9	5.1	87.6	12.4	—	33,560	52,499	Lithuania
259	6.9	93.1	43.6	[7]	[7]	—	...	...	...	...	...	[7]	[7]	Luxembourg
...	...	...	...	1,841	14,022	1.5	100.0	—	68.0	29.3	2.7	2,852	13,236	Macau
1,047	83.6	16.4	15.7	9,093	150,166	0.1	—	100.0	100.0	—	—	129	9,994	Macedonia
10,359	98.9	1.1	0.8	23,784	5,061	131.6	77.2	22.8	89.5	0.9	9.5	101,061	5,661	Madagascar
9,964	94.8	5.2	1.3	688	5,265	45.4	—	100.0	100.0	—	—	302	236	Malawi
29,461	26.2	73.8	68.6	3,114,963	1,000,476	1,251.8	99.7	0.3	78.3	8.5	13.2	299,437	258,747	Malaysia
...	...	...	...	14	4,220	133.5	100.0	—	99.6	—	0.4	38,907	...	Maldives
6,597	93.7	6.3	0.1	1,648	8,731	98.5	—	100.0	100.0	—	—	378	1,211	Mali
...	...	...	...	—	62,831	1.0	100.0	—	95.7	2.3	1.9	6,751	19,442	Malta
...	...	...	...	...	1,923	0.4	100.0	—	100.0	—	—	1,482	120	Marshall Islands
12	83.3	16.7	16.7	110	22,864	5.0	100.0	—	98.0	2.0	—	168[2]	38,658[2]	Martinique
16	62.5	37.5	6.3	...	6,000	47.8	89.5	10.5	64.7	—	35.2	99,348	524	Mauritania
25	48.0	52.0	28.0	3,741	67,773	12.0	100.0	—	97.2	0.3	2.5	38,558	32,642	Mauritius
...	...	...	...	...	...	1.5	100.0	—	100.0	—	—	3[2]	161[2]	Mayotte
24,122	67.1	32.9	27.0	281,218	2,106,097	1,202.2	92.4	7.6	80.6	7.7	11.7	649,787	125,723	Mexico
...	...	...	...	...	2,110	11.9	100.0	—	99.6	0.2	0.2	459	3,280	Micronesia
58	50.6	49.4	7.7	3,303	23,350	0.5	—	100.0	100.0	—	—	1,381	2,763	Moldova
...	...	...	...	...	...	0.004	100.0	—	100.0	—	—	...	...	Monaco
631	29.5	70.5	70.5	6,289	2,944	0.5	—	100.0	100.0	—	—	232	33	Mongolia
1,123	49.2	50.8	15.7	74,985	336,920	745.4	99.7	0.3	83.2	0.1	16.7	750,764	10,509	Morocco
18,043	92.7	7.3	0.7	14,072	10,075	35.6	69.8	30.2	100.0	—	—	76,861	10,341	Mozambique
22,574	85.2	14.8	10.4	239,712	18,874	851.6	84.8	15.2	98.7	1.3	0.1	158,560	559	Myanmar (Burma)
[19]	[19]	[19]	[19]	...	36,449	299.2	99.5	0.5	91.3	8.4	0.3	344,017	...	Namibia
...	...	...	...	23[5]	205[5]	0.3	100.0	—	100.0	—	—	...	...	Nauru
21,962	97.2	2.8	2.8	1,199	2,572	12.8	—	100.0	100.0	—	—	269	261	Nepal

Extractive industries (continued)

country	mining														
	% of GDP, 1998	mineral production (value added)					trade (value)								
		year	total ('000,000 U.S.$)	by kind (%)			year	exports				imports			
				metals[a]	non-metals[b]	energy[c]		total ('000,000 U.S.$)	by kind (%) metals[a]	non-metals[b]	energy[c]	total ('000,000 U.S.$)	by kind (%) metals[a]	non-metals[b]	energy[c]
Netherlands, The	2.7[6]	1995[3]	9,620.1[3]	...	...	...	1997	6,275.9	19.2	8.5	72.3	12,803.2	12.5	5.9	81.6
Netherlands Antilles	...	1998	...	—	100.0	—	1995	901.5	—	0.1	99.9	900.5	—	—	100.0
New Caledonia	10.7[2]	1997	352.1	100.0	—	—	1997	208.9	100.0	—	—	12.9	—	—	100.0
New Zealand	...	...	...	...	...	...	1996	110.9	31.3	0.4	68.3	854.0	21.1	13.5	65.5
Nicaragua	1.6	1998	34.0	—— 100.0 ——		—	1997	4.0	100.0	—	—	130.0	—	4.6	95.4
Niger	3.5[9]	1994	62.5	—— 100.0 ——		—	...	...	...	...	...	...	...	...	...
Nigeria	26.0	1998	33,716.8	—	0.5	99.5	1995	11,131.5	—	—	100.0	19.9	1.5	98.5	—
Northern Mariana Islands	...	...	...	...	...	...	...	...	...	...	...	...	...	...	...
Norway	10.9	1998	16,068.2	—— 1.8 ——		98.2	1997	24,255.2	0.4	1.0	98.6	1,820.3	73.2	11.3	15.5
Oman	40.6[2]	1997	6,361.2	—	0.7	99.3	1996	5,768.3	—	0.1	99.9	70.7	78.8	21.2	—
Pakistan	0.5	1997–98	301.4	...	...	...	1997	57.3	—	1.4	98.6	338.9	50.5	7.5	42.0
Palau	0.1	1998	0.1	—	100.0	—	...	...	...	...	...	...	...	...	...
Panama	0.2	1998	10.5	—— 100.0 ——		—	1996	6.7	100.0	—	—	324.5	—	—	100.0
Papua New Guinea	26.0	1998	975.2	—— 64.0 ——		36.0	1995	1,123.1	48.0	—	52.0	...	...	...	...
Paraguay	0.3	1998	29.2	—	100.0	—	1996	...	...	...	...	124.9	—	66.9	33.1
Peru	10.9	1998	2,378.8	—— 67.9[6, 20] ——		32.1[6]	1997	1,150.6	79.1	0.1	20.8	564.2	0.4	—	99.6
Philippines	0.7	1998	489.1	57.7[6]	41.3[6]	1.0[6]	1997	567.7	55.4	25.5	19.1	4,078.1	14.2	4.1	81.7
Poland	2.9	1998	4,613.0	...	...	...	1997	1,400.6[4]	7.0[4]	11.6[4]	81.4[4]	3,751.2	11.7	6.5	81.8
Portugal	0.5[6]	1995	529.3	40.2	59.6	0.2	1997	391.8	57.0	35.6	7.5	2,369.2	0.7	7.7	91.6
Puerto Rico	...	...	...	...	...	...	...	...	...	...	...	...	...	...	...
Qatar	38.1[2]	1997	3,502.7[3]	...	...	...	1995	3,000.3	—	0.1	99.9	51.3[9]	75.3[9]	24.7[9]	—
Réunion	...	1998	...	—	100.0	—	1995	0.9	100.0	—	—	15.0	—	—	100.0
Romania	3.3[9]	1994	990.9	—	16.1	83.9	1997	75.6	62.6	37.4	—	1,723.1[9]	9.7[9]	3.7[9]	86.6[9]
Russia	...	...	...	...	...	...	1997	32,522.7	5.6	1.0	93.4	560.0[6]	60.2[6]	16.9[6]	23.0[6]
Rwanda	0.06	1998	1.2	...	...	...	...	...	...	...	...	...	...	...	...
St. Kitts and Nevis	0.3[6]	1995	0.6	—	100.0	—	1997	...	...	...	...	2.1	—	33.3	66.7
St. Lucia	0.5	1998	2.6	—	100.0	—	1996	...	...	...	...	5.1	—	49.0	51.0
St. Vincent	0.3	1998	0.9	—	100.0	—	1997	1.6	—	18.8	81.3	1.6[6]	—	18.8[6]	81.3[6]
Samoa	...	...	...	...	...	...	...	...	...	...	...	...	...	...	...
San Marino	...	...	...	...	...	...	...	...	...	...	...	...	...	...	...
São Tomé and Príncipe	...	1998	—	—	100.0	—	...	...	...	...	...	...	...	...	...
Saudi Arabia	37.2[2]	1997	54,352.5	—— 1.1 ——		98.9	1997	50,116.9[2]	0.1[2]	—	99.9[2]	136.7	88.6	11.4	—
Senegal	0.2	1998	6.3	—	100.0	—	1995	55.8	7.3	92.7	—	102.6	—	13.5	86.5
Serbia and Montenegro	9.5[9]	1994	981.7	12.0	3.1	84.9	1997	16.8	32.1	—	67.9	708.7	23.6	5.9	70.6
Seychelles	...	1998	—	—	100.0	—	1996	...	...	...	...	0.5	—	100.0	—
Sierra Leone	16.8[22]	1994–95	117.7	—— 100.0 ——		—	1995	16.7	25.4	74.6	—	0.6	—	100.0	—
Singapore	0.02	1998	14.3	—	100.0	—	1997	787.1	31.0	41.7	27.3	8,895.9	0.7	9.0	90.3
Slovakia	0.9	1998	178.8	...	...	...	1997	68.5	28.0	72.0	—	1,106.3	8.9	4.1	87.0
Slovenia	1.0[2]	1997	182.6	...	...	...	1997	28.6	100.0	—	—	386.4	23.4	17.1	59.4
Solomon Islands	...	1998	...	—— 100.0[23] ——		—	1996	...	...	...	...	2.0	—	—	100.0
Somalia	...	...	...	...	...	...	...	...	...	...	...	...	...	...	...
South Africa	6.5	1998	8,003.2	...	...	...	1997[10]	7,936.4	23.4	51.1	25.4	3,452.8	9.7	14.3	76.0
Spain	...	...	...	...	...	...	1997	771.2	39.7	55.0	5.3	12,200.5[4]	16.5[4]	4.2[4]	79.3[4]
Sri Lanka	1.9	1998	269.4[24]	—— 100.0[24] ——		—	1995	216.5	—	100.0	—	271.1	—	40.0	60.0
Sudan, The	0.3	1998	27.4	...	...	...	1995	...	...	...	...	34.1	—	—	100.0
Suriname	10.9[4]	1996	58.9[25]	...	...	...	1997	594.7	100.0	—	—	15.9[6]	—	31.4[6]	68.6[6]
Swaziland	0.7	1998	8.9	...	...	...	[10]	...	...	...	...	...	...	...	...
Sweden	0.3[6]	1995	634.3	59.2[9]	40.8[9]	—	1997	1,127.6	83.8	11.2	5.0	4,369.9	13.4	6.2	80.4
Switzerland	...	1998	...	—	100.0	—	1997	1,931.1	15.0	85.0	—	4,056.5	3.0	69.0	28.0
Syria	6.6[9]	1994	2,594.1[8]	—	—— 100.0[8] ——		1995	2,675.5	—	1.4	98.6	21.6	—	—	100.0
Taiwan	0.3[6]	1995	791.6	—	79.6	20.4	1995	843.7	...	...	...	8,035.8	—— 35.8 ——		64.2
Tajikistan	...	...	...	...	...	...	1997	1.0	—	100.0	—	228.0[4]	—	100.0[4]	—
Tanzania	1.3	1998	111.9	...	...	...	...	...	...	...	...	...	...	...	...
Thailand	1.8[2]	1997	2,756.6	...	...	...	1997	1,334.0	9.3	74.9	15.7	5,929.7	4.7	14.2	81.1
Togo	5.8	1998	88.3	—	100.0	—	1997	145.3	—	100.0	—	...	...	...	...
Tonga	0.3[6]	1995	0.4	—	100.0	—	1995	0.1	—	100.0	—	1.3	—	46.2	53.6
Trinidad and Tobago	12.2	1998	708.6	—	—	100.0	1996	492.4	—	—	100.0	476.9	12.7	2.1	85.1
Tunisia	5.6	1998	1,456.4	—— 17.1 ——		82.9	1997	438.9	2.7	11.6	85.7	367.1	—	32.4	67.6
Turkey	1.1	1998	2,160.5	...	...	...	1997	325.8	61.7	38.3	—	5,709.8	21.0	3.3	75.7
Turkmenistan	9.7[2]	1997	204.0	—	—	100.0	1997	489.9	—	0.2	99.8	...	...	...	...
Tuvalu	0.9[6]	1995	0.1	—	100.0	—	...	...	...	...	...	...	...	...	...
Uganda	0.3[26]	1995–96	15.8	—— 100.0 ——		—	1996	...	...	...	...	11.2	—	100.0	—
Ukraine	...	...	...	...	...	...	1997	1,421.6	60.4	19.7	19.8	6,790.7	3.4	3.1	93.5
United Arab Emirates	33.4[9]	1994[3]	12,269.1[3]	...	...	...	1996	23,700.1	0.5	0.5	99.0	233.3	17.1	82.9	—
United Kingdom	1.7	1998	21,115.8	—— 8.5 ——		91.5	1997	18,681.6	5.5	32.6	61.8	16,302.2	16.2	38.7	45.1
United States	1.5[2]	1997	120,500.0	4.8	9.5	85.7	1997	13,394.6	35.4	33.2	31.4	80,065.7	5.6	12.8	81.6
Uruguay	0.2	1997	47.6	—	100.0	—	1997	...	...	...	...	229.7	—	6.4	93.6
Uzbekistan	...	...	...	...	...	...	1997	114.5	—	—	100.0	13.9	100.0	—	—
Vanuatu	...	1998	...	—	100.0	—	1994	...	...	...	...	0.5	—	—	100.0
Venezuela	12.1	1998	10,676.5	—— 6.4 ——		93.6	1997	12,510.3	1.8	—	98.2	132.3	41.5	58.5	—
Vietnam	6.2	1998	1,091.3	—— 9.4 ——		90.6	1997	103.2	1.8	—	98.8	32.1	—	100.0	—
Virgin Islands (U.S.)	...	1998	...	—	100.0	—	...	...	...	...	...	...	...	...	...
West Bank	...	...	...	...	...	...	...	...	...	...	...	...	...	...	...
Western Sahara	...	...	...	...	...	...	...	...	...	...	...	...	...	...	...
Yemen	9.8[9]	1994	1,788.2[8]	—	—— 100.0[8] ——		1995	1,424.0	—	—	100.0	208.4	—	—	100.0
Zambia	6.1	1998	203.0	...	...	...	1995	12.9	—	100.0	—	1.7	100.0	—	—
Zimbabwe	6.9[9]	1994	336.1	...	...	...	1997	95.9	4.9	94.3	0.8	35.3[4]	17.8[4]	37.1[4]	45.0[4]

[1]Gross value of production (output). [2]1997. [3]Mostly crude petroleum and natural gas. [4]1996. [5]1998. [6]1995. [7]Belgium includes Luxembourg. [8]Mostly crude petroleum. [9]1994. [10]South Africa includes Botswana, Lesotho, Namibia, and Swaziland. [11]Mostly diamonds, some gold. [12]China includes Taiwan. [13]Petroleum sector only. [14]Republic of Cyprus only. [15]1993. [16]Jersey includes

country	forestry						fisheries, 1999							
	production of roundwood, 2000				trade (value, '000 U.S.$), 1999		catch (nominal)						trade (value '000 U.S.$)	
	total ('000 cubic metres)	fuelwood, charcoal (%)	industrial roundwood (%)		exports	imports	total ('000 metric tons)	by source (%)		by kind of catch (%)			exports	imports
			total	sawlogs, veneer				marine	inland	fish	crusta-ceans	mollusks		
Netherlands, The	1,039	15.4	84.6	55.1	2,706,468	5,705,731	514.6	99.6	0.4	87.2	2.8	9.9	1,744,665	1,304,585
Netherlands Antilles	...	...	...	...	1,535	19,459	0.9	100.0	—	99.4	—	0.6	1,198	6,380
New Caledonia	5	—	100.0	58.3	...	11,595	3.2	100.0	—	96.1	2.8	1.1	18,766	5,677
New Zealand	17,953	—	100.0	40.4	1,303,550	310,844	594.1	99.8	0.2	93.4	0.7	5.9	712,256	52,445
Nicaragua	4,306	94.7	5.3	5.3	11,725	16,267	20.6	94.6	5.4	46.7	52.3	1.0	78,596	7,843
Niger	6,666	93.8	6.2	—	...	6,334	11.0	—	100.0	100.0	—	—	154	458
Nigeria	100,637	90.6	9.4	7.1	33,457	172,331	455.6	69.4	30.6	92.0	7.2	0.8	19,662	209,959
Northern Mariana Islands	...	...	...	...	...	51[5]	0.2	100.0	—	99.5	0.5	—	...	...
Norway	8,173	8.1	91.9	50.1	1,831,746	1,009,845	2,620.1	100.0	—	97.5	2.5	—	3,764,790	612,469
Oman	...	...	...	...	...	17,179	108.8	100.0	—	92.6	0.5	6.9	38,243	5,077
Pakistan	33,075	92.7	7.3	5.4	...	137,040	654.5	72.5	27.5	93.6	4.9	1.6	141,476	816
Palau	...	...	...	...	...	1,123	1.8	100.0	—	98.0	2.0	—	290	87
Panama	1,052	96.7	3.3	3.3	5,440	67,462	120.5	100.0	—	90.8	7.7	1.5	194,898	15,125
Papua New Guinea	8,597	64.4	35.6	35.6	168,807	12,439	53.7	74.9	25.1	96.9	3.1	—	25,173	7,819
Paraguay	8,097	52.1	47.9	42.2	88,064	31,132	25.0	—	100.0	100.0	—	—	36	1,592
Peru	9,157	80.0	20.0	17.7	71,644	166,328	8,429.3	99.5	0.5	98.4	0.2	1.3	788,411	16,833
Philippines	43,399	91.8	8.2	1.1	52,996	606,710	1,870.5	92.3	7.7	88.1	4.2	7.7	372,274	121,492
Poland	25,652	6.0	94.0	44.1	862,220	1,251,300	235.1	94.1	5.9	89.6	8.3	2.1	282,354	260,653
Portugal	9,878	6.1	84.8	32.7	1,185,978	913,640	207.7	100.0	—	90.3	2.3	7.4	278,586	1,017,066
Puerto Rico	...	...	...	...	...	...	2.1	100.0	—	59.2	7.7	33.1	[21]	[21]
Qatar	...	...	...	...	...	15,654	4.2	100.0	—	98.8	1.2	—	28	2,053
Réunion	36	85.9	14.1	11.6	342	69,029	5.8	100.0	—	95.5	4.5	—	19,662	33,053
Romania	13,148	23.1	76.9	46.7	355,924	172,019	7.8	32.0	68.0	100.0	—	—	7,109	31,911
Russia	158,100	33.1	66.9	30.3	3,190,431	358,552	4,141.2	92.6	7.4	95.9	2.1	2.0	1,247,518	199,065
Rwanda	7,836	95.7	4.3	1.1	...	2,407	6.4	—	100.0	100.0	—	—	...	61
St. Kitts and Nevis	...	...	...	...	33	1,797	0.4	100.0	—	81.5	5.7	12.8	...	729
St. Lucia	...	...	...	...	—	11,692	1.7	100.0	—	96.8	1.7	1.5	6,172	5,186
St. Vincent	...	...	...	...	8	18,545	15.6	100.0	—	100.0	—	—	927	1,537
Samoa	131	53.4	46.6	44.3	1,357	2,542	9.8	100.0	—	99.5	0.3	0.2	11,700	5,984
San Marino	...	...	...	...	...	...	—	100.0	—	100.0	—	—	...	...
São Tomé and Príncipe	9	—	100.0	100.0	504[5]	196[5]	3.8	100.0	—	99.0	—	1.0	3,836	137
Saudi Arabia	...	...	...	...	19,256	778,185	46.9	100.0	—	87.9	10.4	1.7	10,134	99,412
Senegal	5,037	84.2	15.8	0.8	...	45,293	418.1	90.4	9.6	87.8	1.5	10.7	301,498	3,784
Serbia and Montenegro	1,140	4.4	95.6	95.6	44,990	166,400	1.3	33.9	66.1	96.6	0.8	2.6	225	43,088
Seychelles	...	...	...	...	99	1,416	37.8	100.0	—	99.7	—	0.2	12,318	12,904
Sierra Leone	3,419	96.4	3.6	0.1	1,264	2,053	59.4	75.6	24.4	94.9	3.9	1.2	15,654	3,267
Singapore	120[5]	—	—	—	502,202	889,039	5.1	100.0	—	75.4	14.3	10.3	390,062	475,224
Slovakia	5,783	5.9	94.1	42.2	431,828	237,213	1.4	—	100.0	100.0	—	—	1,895	32,269
Slovenia	2,253	23.6	76.4	49.7	399,531	296,900	2.0	88.8	11.2	98.6	—	1.4	6,597	29,280
Solomon Islands	872	15.8	84.2	84.2	51,070	...	82.3	100.0	—	99.9	—	0.1	64,170	75
Somalia	8,329	98.7	1.3	0.3	132[5]	257[5]	20.3	98.8	1.2	95.6	2.0	2.5	4,058	170
South Africa	30,616[19]	39.2[19]	60.8[19]	19.6[19]	827,673	487,114	588.0	99.8	0.2	98.2	0.5	1.3	260,056[18]	55,691[18]
Spain	14,810	11.1	88.9	38.4	1,626,053	3,813,488	1,167.2	99.3	0.7	86.8	3.1	10.1	1,604,237	3,286,831
Sri Lanka	10,344	93.9	6.1	0.6	2,862	81,534	271.6	90.1	9.9	98.7	1.1	0.2	74,120	59,775
Sudan, The	9,682	77.6	22.4	1.3	1,040	16,928	49.5	11.1	88.9	99.7	—	0.3	88	280
Suriname	93	1.1	98.9	96.8	3,249	1,353	13.0	98.5	1.5	98.0	2.0	—	11,640	3,600
Swaziland	890	62.9	37.1	29.2	62,000	—	0.1	—	100.0	100.0	—	—	2,242	9,738
Sweden	61,800	9.5	90.5	49.7	9,720,885	1,615,641	351.3	99.6	0.4	98.9	1.1	—	477,992	715,463
Switzerland	10,428	20.1	79.9	73.9	1,937,022	2,393,070	1.8	—	100.0	100.0	—	—	3,031	375,700
Syria	50	31.5	68.5	31.7	1,040	141,790	7.9	32.7	67.3	99.1	0.9	—	183	49,546
Taiwan	...	...	...	...	...	...	1,099.7	99.9	0.1	70.2	2.6	27.2	1,763,572	556,873
Tajikistan	...	...	...	...	80	4,131	...	—	100.0	100.0	—	—	54	143
Tanzania	39,846	94.2	5.8	0.8	5,939	22,531	310.0	16.1	83.9	99.1	—	0.9	60,202	1,975
Thailand	36,631	92.2	7.9	0.1	758,925	1,006,210	3,004.9	92.5	7.5	86.7	4.3	9.0	4,109,860	840,679
Togo	1,232	74.5	25.5	5.4	974	4,355	22.9	78.2	21.8	100.0	—	—	1,498	12,222
Tonga	2	—	100.0	100.0	...	2,065	3.7	100.0	—	94.3	5.5	0.2	2,625	872
Trinidad and Tobago	44	22.7	77.3	77.3	2,032	65,952	15.0	100.0	—	95.0	5.0	—	12,315	8,009
Tunisia	2,842	92.5	7.5	0.7	14,709	151,980	92.1	99.1	0.9	81.6	7.8	10.6	82,118	13,276
Turkey	17,767	41.3	58.7	29.1	82,545	969,948	575.1	91.3	8.7	97.1	0.4	2.5	98,196	59,207
Turkmenistan	...	...	...	...	501	3,880	8.8	—	100.0	100.0	—	—	316	99
Tuvalu	...	...	...	...	—	323[5]	0.4	100.0	—	100.0	—	—	326	...
Uganda	16,998	81.3	18.7	6.2	...	17,781	226.1	—	100.0	100.0	—	—	24,221	78
Ukraine	10,008	17.6	82.4	62.0	132,755	235,646	407.9	98.9	1.1	98.1	1.4	0.6	75,079	96,776
United Arab Emirates	...	...	...	...	7,290	297,934	117.6	100.0	—	99.9	0.1	—	29,436	28,872
United Kingdom	7,451	3.1	96.9	57.1	2,192,065	8,983,465	837.8	99.8	0.2	85.3	7.5	7.2	1,427,853	2,276,998
United States	500,434	14.4	85.6	49.6	14,783,367	23,721,067	4,749.6	99.2	0.8	79.0	8.3	12.7	2,945,014[21]	9,407,307[21]
Uruguay	6,163	70.3	29.7	22.3	77,918	97,102	103.0	97.6	2.4	79.7	3.3	17.0	98,981	13,418
Uzbekistan	...	...	...	...	240	37,231	2.9	—	100.0	100.0	—	—	44	2,688
Vanuatu	63	38.0	62.0	62.0	3,074	...	94.6	100.0	—	99.1	0.3	0.6	738	681
Venezuela	2,713	33.6	66.4	59.7	65,999	297,987	411.9	91.4	8.6	86.2	2.2	11.6	134,120	40,409
Vietnam	36,730	87.6	12.4	6.6	47,277	132,913	1,200.0	93.8	6.3	70.8	22.3	6.9	940,473	13,801
Virgin Islands (U.S.)	...	...	...	...	...	...	0.8	100.0	—	100.0	—	—	...	...
West Bank	...	...	...	...	...	...	...	...	...	...	...	...	...	...
Western Sahara	...	...	...	...	...	...	—	—	—	—	—	—	...	...
Yemen	—	—	—	—	...	44,915	123.3	100.0	—	96.2	0.4	3.4	19,789	4,636
Zambia	8,053	89.6	10.4	4.0	...	8,809	67.3	—	100.0	100.0	—	—	205	1,404
Zimbabwe	9,253	87.7	12.3	10.1	31,415	33,293	12.4	—	100.0	100.0	—	—	1,462	9,925

Guernsey. [17]Mostly bauxite and diamonds. [18]South Africa includes Lesotho. [19]South Africa includes Namibia. [20]Includes coal mining. [21]United States includes Puerto Rico. [22]1994–95. [23]Mostly gold. [24]Mostly precious and semiprecious stones. [25]Mostly bauxite. [26]1995–96.

Manufacturing industries

This table provides a summary of manufacturing activity by industrial sector for the countries of the world, providing figures for total manufacturing value added, as well as the percentage contribution of 29 major branches of manufacturing activity to the gross domestic product. U.S. dollar figures for total value added by manufacturing are given but should be used with caution because of uncertainties with respect to national accounting methods; purchasing power parities; preferential price structures and exchange rates; labour costs; and costs for material inputs influenced by "most favoured" international trade agreements, barter, and the like.

Manufacturing activity is classified here according to a modification of the International Standard Industrial Classification (ISIC), revision 2, published by the United Nations. A summary of the 2-, 3-, and 4-digit ISIC codes (groups) defining these 29 sectors follows, providing definitional detail beyond that possible in the column headings. Recently available revision 3 data have also been modified to fit into this 29-sector breakdown.

The collection and publication of national manufacturing data is usually carried out by one of three methods: a full census of manufacturing (usually done every 5 to 10 years for a given country), a periodic survey of manufacturing (usually taken at annual or other regular intervals between censuses), and the onetime sample survey (often limited in geographic, sectoral, or size-of-enterprise coverage). The full census is, naturally, the most complete, but, since up to 10 years may elapse between such censuses, it has sometimes been necessary to substitute a survey of more recent date but less complete coverage. In addition to national sources, data published by the United Nations Industrial Development Organization (UNIDO), especially its *International Yearbook of Industrial Statistics* and Geographical Reference Information Guide online; occasional publications of the International Monetary Fund (IMF); and other sources have been used.

ISIC code(s)		Products manufactured
31		Food, beverages, and tobacco
	311 + 312	food including prepared animal feeds
	313	alcoholic and nonalcoholic beverages
	314	tobacco manufactures
32		Textiles, wearing apparel, and leather goods
	321	spinning of textile fibres, weaving and finishing of textiles, knitted articles, carpets, rope, etc.
	322	wearing apparel (including leather clothing; excluding knitted articles and footwear)
	323 + 324	leather products (including footwear; excluding wearing apparel), leather substitutes, and fur products

Manufacturing industries

country	year	total manufacturing value added ('000,000 U.S.$)	(31) food	beverages	tobacco manufactures	(32) textiles (exc. wearing apparel)	wearing apparel	leather and fur products	(33) wood products (exc. furniture)	wood furniture	(34) paper, paper products	printing and publishing	(35) industrial chemicals	paints, soaps, etc.	drugs and medicines
			(311 + 312)	(313)	(314)	(321)	(322)	(323 + 324)	(331)	(332)	(341)	(342)	(351)	(352 exc. 3522)	(3522)
Afghanistan	1988–89[1]	435	18.3	1.9	—	8.0	0.4	16.7	—0.5—		0.9	4.9	4.8	0.2	2.7
Albania	1998[2, 3, 4]	257	14.3	7.5	3.0	—9.6—		11.3	—7.8—		—5.9—		2.8[5]	[5]	[5]
Algeria	1997[3, 4, 7]	1,838	25.2	4.0	6.2	—3.5—		0.8	2.8	1.2	1.6	1.2	4.0	5.7	2.4
American Samoa	1999[8]	345	98.4	—	—	—	1.3	—	—	—	—	—	—	—	—
Andorra	1999[9]	41	—10.4—			7.6	—2.4—		—1.0—		—11.0—		—8.3—		—
Angola	1989	319	20.0	—12.2—		—11.6—			—3.7—		—0.3—		9.1[5]	[5]	[5]
Antigua and Barbuda	2000	13		...	...	...	...	...	...	...	...	...	...	...	...
Argentina	1996[3, 7]	33,015	16.5	6.5	6.2	3.6	1.4	2.1	0.7	0.7[11]	2.6	4.1	4.3	—10.6—	
Armenia	2001[2]	358	—55.0—		4.4	0.7	1.2	0.2	0.7	...	0.2	2.3	—4.4—		
Aruba	1994	89[12]	...	...	...	...	...	...	...	...	...	...	...	...	...
Australia	2000–01	59,557	18.5	0.9	0.6	2.3	1.2	0.5	3.5	2.7[11]	3.2	9.5	3.1	2.4	2.3
Austria	1998[13, 14]	38,375	7.8	1.8	...	2.7	1.1	0.6	4.5	3.5[11]	3.9	...	2.0	1.2	2.4
Azerbaijan	2001[2]	1,325	—34.0—		4.2	1.8	0.6	0.2	0.2	...	0.1	0.7	—9.4—		
Bahamas, The	1992[14]	95	7.4	38.9	—	0.3	3.6	—	—	3.5	...	10.0	...	22.0	...
Bahrain	1992	761	5.0	1.1	—	—	6.5	0.1	0.1	8.4	0.4	4.4	5.6	—	—
Bangladesh	1991–92[3, 7]	1,899	12.7	0.6	12.2	23.5	10.2	3.9	0.7	0.1	2.9	1.2	5.6	4.5	5.8
Barbados	1995	289	18.0	16.9	2.4	0.7	2.1	—	—	1.4	1.0	8.3	5.9	—4.1—	
Belarus	1994[2, 14, 15]	3,006	16.2	...	...	7.0	2.1	2.6	—5.4[16]—		—[16]—		16.3[5]	[5]	[5]
Belgium	1995	53,712	15.4	2.0	0.7	4.3	2.3	0.1	0.6	3.6	2.2	4.6	11.5	—3.8—	
Belize	1992[3]	59	45.9	7.5	3.9	—3.8—			5.5	2.7	1.1	1.5	—14.1—		
Benin	1990	59	20.6	13.1	—	3.2	5.5	6.9	3.6	5.2	—	2.5	—	—9.5—	
Bermuda	1995	170	...	...	...	...	...	...	...	...	...	...	...	...	...
Bhutan	1989[3]	21	6.0	10.1	—	—5.6—			18.1	2.7	0.4	1.0	21.5	—1.7—	
Bolivia	1998[3, 19]	1,086	20.4	13.0	0.5	2.8	1.0	1.1	1.5	0.8[11]	1.7	1.9	0.5	2.6	2.0
Bosnia and Herzegovina	1991	4,021	9.1	2.6	1.7	5.9	4.5	3.3	6.3	4.2	3.9	1.4	5.5	—4.1—	
Botswana	1995	212	32.5	12.7	—	8.0	5.2	2.8	2.4	1.4	2.8	2.8	1.4	—1.4—	
Brazil	1996[13]	153,540	14.4	5.3	1.1	3.5	2.4	2.4	1.2	1.4[11]	4.0	4.7	—12.5—		
Brunei	1998[20]	151	...	...	...	...	...	...	...	...	...	...	...	...	...
Bulgaria	1998[2]	7,669	14.8	5.8	4.8	3.5	3.5	1.3	1.4	1.1[11]	2.0	2.0	—10.3—		
Burkina Faso	1995	162	47.2	15.5	1.2	13.7	1.2	4.4	—	1.2	—	1.2	0.6	—	—
Burundi	1995	117	54.7	21.4	5.1	9.4	—	—	0.9	—	—	0.9	—	—1.7—	
Cambodia	1995[3, 7]	71	—14.2—		5.9	0.7	—21.7—		—10.4[21]—		[21]	0.5	—0.3—		
Cameroon	1997–98[3]	708	14.8	17.2	3.1	8.8	—	0.4	18.1	—	3.4	1.2	—5.8—		
Canada	1999[22]	112,037	10.0	2.5	0.8	2.0	2.2	0.2	4.7	2.6[11]	5.1	5.1	—8.0—		
Cape Verde	1997[2]	78	26.7	20.4	1.9	—	4.9	6.1	5.5	5.7	...	3.0	0.6	7.7	1.7
Central African Republic	1995	36	27.0	13.5	21.6	—	—	—	13.5	2.7	...	5.4	2.7	—5.4—	
Chad	2000	152	...	...	...	...	—	—	—	—	—	—	—	...	—
Chile	1997[3, 23]	18,472	21.9	7.0	3.6	2.1	2.1	1.3	3.6	0.8	6.1	3.3	5.2	5.2	2.0
China	1998[24]	182,196	6.7	3.6	5.9	6.7	—5.0—		0.8	0.5	2.1	1.2	—11.4—		
Colombia	1997[3, 7]	16,696	19.2	10.7	0.5	5.9	3.3	1.3	0.7	0.5	3.4	3.9	4.7	6.6	4.5
Comoros	2000	8.4	...	...	—	...	...	...	...	...	—	—	—	—	—
Congo, Dem. Rep. of the	1990	808	86.7	5.4	1.9	0.6	0.2	0.6	0.1	0.2	—	0.1	0.9	—0.1—	
Congo, Rep. of the	1995	86	26.7	24.4	7.0	2.3	1.2	2.3	3.5	2.3	1.2	1.2	3.5	—4.7—	
Costa Rica	1997[3, 14]	1,412	27.7	15.5	2.8	1.7	3.8	0.6	1.5	0.9	4.2	3.8	6.8	4.4	1.7
Côte d'Ivoire	1997[14, 25]	857	31.3	5.2	5.5	7.6	1.7	0.8	11.2	0.1	2.7	2.3	6.1	6.0	—
Croatia	1999	3,363	—18.7—		1.5	2.1	5.0	1.5	3.2	[26]	1.8	7.3	—10.8—		
Cuba	1995	4,077[27]	15.7	5.4	39.9	3.6	1.9	1.2	1.0	0.8	0.2	1.2	1.9	—7.8—	
Cyprus[28]	1999	971	19.5	8.6	8.8	2.0	6.0	1.9	6.3	5.2[11]	2.0	5.1	0.6	2.6	2.3
Czech Republic	1998[14]	12,920	9.0	2.9	...	3.8	1.7	0.9	2.8	2.0[11]	1.9	3.4	4.2	1.2	1.1
Denmark	1998	25,318	15.2	1.7	1.1	1.8	1.2	0.2	2.7	4.3[11]	2.5	8.6	2.4	2.2	4.1
Djibouti	1992[8]	13	—5.0—			—3.0—			—	—	—0.3—		—1.0—		
Dominica	2000[13]	20	...	...	—	—	...	—	...	...	—	—	—	...	—
Dominican Republic	1990	1,298	31.9	13.8	5.2	3.5	1.2	3.0	0.2	1.5	2.9	1.7	1.6	—3.4—	
East Timor	1996	12	...	...	...	...	...	...	...	...	...	...	...	...	...
Ecuador	1998[3, 7]	4,680	13.7	8.2	0.1	2.2	0.4	0.5	0.9	0.5[11]	1.5	1.1	0.4	2.2	0.3
Egypt	1997–98[13]	6,768	17.1	0.8	0.6	8.7	4.2	0.4	—	0.5[11]	0.9	2.1	5.9	7.2	5.0
El Salvador	1998[3, 19, 29]	1,438	21.3	7.8	—	8.4	17.3	2.5	—	1.0	3.9	3.2	0.7	6.4	8.9
Equatorial Guinea	1990[2]	1.9	27.6	4.1	...	...	2.6	...	...	49.3	...	1.2	...	—13.8—	
Eritrea	1998[3, 7]	58	17.2	34.1	6.1	4.8	1.2	6.3	—	3.2[11]	0.3	1.6	0.4	6.1	—
Estonia	1998[2]	2,675	24.1	4.6	—	7.4	4.1	1.4	10.7	6.7[11]	2.0	5.3	1.7	4.1	0.3

ISIC code(s)		Products manufactured
33		Wood and wood products
	331	sawlogs, wood products (excluding furniture), cane products, and cork products
	332	wood furniture
34		Paper and paper products, printing and publishing
	341	wood pulp, paper, and paper products
	342	printing, publishing, and bookbinding
35		Chemicals and chemical, petroleum, coal, rubber, and plastic products
	351	basic industrial chemicals (including fertilizers, pesticides, and synthetic fibres)
	352 minus 3522	chemical products not elsewhere specified (including paints, varnishes, and soaps and other toiletries)
	3522	drugs and medicines
	353 + 354	refined petroleum and derivatives of petroleum and coal
	355	rubber products
	356	plastic products (excluding synthetic fibres)
36		Glass, ceramic, and nonmetallic mineral products
	361 + 362	pottery, china, glass, and glass products
	369	bricks, tiles, cement, cement products, plaster products, etc.

ISIC code(s)		Products manufactured
37		Basic metals
	371	iron and steel
	372	nonferrous basic metals and processed nickel and cobalt
38		Fabricated metal products, machinery and equipment
	381	fabricated metal products (including cutlery, hand tools, fixtures, and structural metal products)
	382 minus 3825	nonelectrical machinery and apparatus not elsewhere specified
	3825	office, computing, and accounting machinery
	383 minus 3832	electrical machinery and apparatus not elsewhere specified
	3832	radio, television, and communications equipment (including electronic parts)
	384 minus 3843	transport equipment not elsewhere specified
	3843	motor vehicles (excluding motorcycles)
	385	professional and scientific equipment; photographic and optical goods; watches and clocks
39		Other manufactured goods
	390	jewelry, musical instruments, sporting goods, artists' equipment, toys, etc.

			(36)		(37)		(38)								(39)	country
refined petroleum and products	rubber products	plastic products	pottery, china, and glass	bricks, tiles, cement, etc.	iron and steel	non-ferrous metals	fabricated metal products	nonelectrical machinery	office equip., computers	electrical equip.	radio, television	transport equip. exc. motor vehicles	motor vehicles	professional equip.	jewelry, musical instruments	
(353 + 354)	(355)	(356)	(361 + 362)	(369)	(371)	(372)	(381)	(382 exc. 3825)	(3825)	(383 exc. 3832)	(3832)	(384 exc. 3843)	(3843)	(385)	(390)	
—	—	2.1	1.1		0.4	—	—	—	—	—	—	—	0.1	—	37.1	Afghanistan
15.9	[5]	[5]	8.0		11.2[6]		[6]	…	2.3		…	…	…	…	0.4	Albania
…	0.1	1.1	0.5	21.4	6.4	1.3	0.5	1.7		4.3		0.1	2.3	1.2	0.3	Algeria
—	—	—	—	—	—	—	0.3	—	—	—	—	—	—	—	—	American Samoa
—	5.0		0.5		2.5[6]		[6]	14.6				19.6		7.2	9.8	Andorra
20.0	[5]	[5]	11.3		1.9		5.0					4.7		[10]	0.3[10]	Angola
…	…	…	…	…	…	…	…	…	…	…	…	…	…	…	…	Antigua and Barbuda
11.6	1.0	2.5	4.2		4.1	0.6	2.9	3.9	0.1	1.9	1.2	0.5	5.6	0.3	0.4	Argentina
—	0.3		4.1		11.3		1.0	3.2	—	1.3	0.3	0.1		1.0	8.4	Armenia
…	…	…	…	…	…	…	…	…	…	…	…	…	…	…	…	Aruba
1.7	0.8	3.3	1.0	3.4	3.6	6.4	8.0	4.5	0.4	2.7	2.1	2.2	6.8	1.5	0.9	Australia
…	0.7	3.3	1.7	4.3	6.1		8.6	10.4	0.1	4.4	6.3	0.9	5.1	2.0	1.7	Austria
38.1	0.4		2.5		0.8		0.7	2.5	0.1	0.5	0.1	2.7	—	0.2	0.3	Azerbaijan
…	…	…	…	7.0	2.6	—	—	—	—	…	…	—	—	…	…	Bahamas, The
13.7	0.8	—	—	4.5	4.4	33.4	0.3	0.4		3.4	—	3.4	—	—	4.1	Bahrain
0.4	0.5	0.4	1.0	1.7	3.6	0.1	1.2	0.4	—	1.2	0.5	0.8	3.7	—	0.6	Bangladesh
—	6.6	14.9	0.7	2.8	—	—	6.9	3.8		2.4		1.0		—	0.3	Barbados
7.6	[5]	[5]	5.5		3.0		26.8								…	Belarus
1.0	0.6	5.4	2.5	2.1	4.7	1.8	7.1	7.1		7.8		7.0		0.5	1.3	Belgium
—	0.3[17]		[17]	6.2	—	—	2.0	—	—	0.1		4.2		—	1.1	Belize
—	—	—	0.5	24.6	—	—	4.8	—	—	—	—	—	—	—	—	Benin
…	…	…	…	…	…	…	…	…	…	…	…	…	…	…	…	Bermuda
…	0.7	2.2	29.0		…	…	1.0[18]								[18]	Bhutan
36.7	0.1	1.8	1.0	6.8	0.2	0.2	1.2	0.1	—	0.4	—	—	0.2	—	1.5	Bolivia
2.3	0.3	1.3	0.5	3.2	5.5	3.4	10.8	5.0		3.3		8.6		2.6	0.7	Bosnia and Herzegovina
—	0.5	0.5	—	—	—	—	2.4	0.9		0.9		1.4		—	19.8	Botswana
4.6	1.4	2.8	3.5		5.7		4.1	7.1	0.6	2.8	3.7	0.9	8.0	0.9	1.0	Brazil
…	…	…	…	…	…	…	…	…	…	…	…	…	…	…	…	Brunei
10.9	0.9	1.7	4.9		12.5		2.9	8.0	0.6	2.7	0.5	2.4	0.5	0.6	0.4	Bulgaria
—	1.2	0.6	—	—	1.2	—	0.6	—	—	0.6		1.2		—	8.1	Burkina Faso
—	—	0.9	—	1.7	—	—	2.6	—	—	—	—	—	—	—	0.9	Burundi
…	17.4		24.6		3.8		0.5	—	—	—	—	—	—	—	0.1	Cambodia
4.0	7.2	0.9	—	2.8	—	6.5	1.1	—	—	1.8		1.3		—	1.6	Cameroon
0.8	1.9	3.0	2.8		4.7		7.3	4.6		9.8		19.0		[10]	3.0[10]	Canada
…	0.3	…	0.6	1.5	0.1		5.6	0.1	…	—	…	4.1	—	3.5	—	Cape Verde
—	—	—	—	—	—	—	2.7	…	…	—	—	2.7		—	2.7	Central African Republic
—	—	—	—	—	—	—	—	…	—	—	—	…	—	—	…	Chad
3.4	0.9	2.4	0.9	3.6	2.3	12.3	3.9	2.0	—	1.1	0.2	0.8	1.6	0.2	0.2	Chile
3.5	1.4	2.4	1.5	4.5	6.5	2.2	3.3	7.8		13.3		7.2		1.1	1.4	China
5.8	1.1	4.1	2.4	5.7	2.0	0.4	3.4	1.9	—	2.0	0.4	0.7	3.4	0.7	0.8	Colombia
—	—	—	—	—	—	—	—	—	—	—	—	—	—	—	—	Comoros
0.1	—	—	—	0.2	…	…	0.4	0.3		0.2		0.5		—	1.5	Congo, Dem. Rep. of the
—	2.3	—	—	1.2	—	—	7.0	2.3		3.5		3.5		—	—	Congo, Rep. of the
2.9	1.8	4.4	1.3	2.9	…	0.1	2.5	1.8	…	1.0	4.6	1.0	0.1	…	0.2	Costa Rica
9.2	0.1	…	…	2.1	…	…	5.2	0.1		1.1		1.4	0.3	…	0.1	Côte d'Ivoire
11.2	2.5		6.0		2.1		6.7	3.8	0.7	4.0	1.9	5.0	0.6	0.8	2.8[26]	Croatia
…	2.4	2.1	0.5	1.9	0.7	0.9	1.7	1.7		0.9		3.5		0.3	3.0	Cuba
1.3	0.2	3.3	0.4	8.5	1.1		6.7	2.6	—	1.5	—	0.3	0.7	0.4	2.1	Cyprus[28]
…	1.5	2.9	8.3		7.9		9.6	11.3	0.1	5.8	1.6	1.3	8.2	2.2	1.6	Czech Republic
0.3	4.4		1.0	3.2	2.2		8.8	15.3	1.2	3.7	2.6	2.6	1.4	3.7	1.6	Denmark
			0.1		0.1		13.0								77.5	Djibouti
—	—	—	—	…	—	—	…	—	—	…	—	—	—	—	…	Dominica
16.2	0.8	1.6	0.7	3.5	1.8	0.2	3.7	0.5		0.8		0.1		0.2	0.2	Dominican Republic
…	…	…	…	…	…	…	…	…	…	…	…	…	…	…	…	East Timor
56.2	0.3	2.4	0.5	2.9	0.8	0.3	1.4	0.6	—	0.5	—	0.1	1.7	—	0.2	Ecuador
13.7	0.7	1.2	1.7	8.7	4.4	1.3	2.1	3.9	0.4	3.1	0.8	1.0	2.9	0.4	0.2	Egypt
1.2	0.3	4.0	0.1	5.3	1.2	—	2.2	0.7	—	0.8	0.5	1.2	—	—	1.1	El Salvador
…	…	…	…	0.8	…	…	0.6	…	…	…	…	…	…	…	…	Equatorial Guinea
—	—	0.6	0.1	13.4	0.3	—	3.1	0.1	—	0.1	—	—	0.6	0.4	—	Eritrea
0.3	0.2	2.1	1.6	3.8	0.1	0.1	6.7	2.5	1.0	1.6	1.3	1.9	1.6	1.9	0.9	Estonia

Manufacturing industries (continued)

country	year	total manufacturing value added ('000,000 U.S.$)	(31) food (311 + 312)	beverages (313)	tobacco manufactures (314)	(32) textiles (exc. wearing apparel) (321)	wearing apparel (322)	leather and fur products (323 + 324)	(33) wood products (exc. furniture) (331)	wood furniture (332)	(34) paper, paper products (341)	printing and publishing (342)	(35) industrial chemicals (351)	paints, soaps, etc. (352 exc. 3522)	drugs and medicines (3522)
Ethiopia	1997–98[3, 30]	449	28.2	20.6	5.7	6.9	0.6	5.4	0.8	2.0[11]	1.5	3.0	0.6	3.1	3.4
Faroe Islands	1999[8, 31]	117	80.7	...	...	...	0.1	...	...	...	...	...	...	...	...
Fiji	1994	160	42.6	6.1	—	—13.8—		1.3	9.7	1.9	3.8	5.1	—	3.1	—
Finland	2000	28,355	4.8	0.9	0.1	0.9	0.6	0.3	4.4	2.4[11, 34]	17.8	5.2	—5.3—		
France	1998[13, 35]	166,238[36]	...	...	...	2.8	1.8	0.9	1.1	1.7[11]	3.1	5.7	5.7	5.7	4.4
French Guiana	1996[14, 37]	101	—8.5—			—[38]—			...	...	...	3.3[38]	...	...	...
French Polynesia	1993[14]	214	—27.2—		—	...	...	—	...	...	—	—	—	...	—
Gabon	1995	243	9.1	7.0	6.2	0.8	1.7	—	18.1	2.5	0.8	1.2	4.1	—1.7—	
Gambia, The	1995[3, 19]	9.2	—65.0—		—	—8.3—			—6.2[39]—		—	4.2	8.8[5]	[5]	[5]
Gaza Strip[40]	...	...	...	...	...	...	...	...	...	...	...	...	...	...	...
Georgia	2001[2]	292	—47.8—		3.8	0.2	0.5	0.7	0.9	0.5[11, 34]	0.4	3.0	—5.6—		
Germany	2000[35]	552,121	—8.1—		2.2	1.2	0.7	0.2	1.2	[41]	2.4	4.6	—11.4—		
Ghana	1993[3, 35]	610	8.4	9.1	18.1	4.6	—0.5—		15.2	0.8	1.8	1.3	0.9	—8.9—	
Greece	1996[7, 13]	10,948	18.3	6.6	2.0	6.6	5.0	1.4	1.5	1.5[11]	3.1	4.2	3.0	—8.9—	
Greenland	2000[14, 43]	0.5	...	...	...	...	...	...	...	...	...	...	...	...	...
Grenada	1996[44, 45]	21	31.5	51.2	2.0	—	...	—	...	...	6.5	—	—	8.8	...
Guadeloupe	1995[14]	290	—28.8—			...	...	...	...	...	...	...	...	...	...
Guam	1997[1, 14]	165	—14.8—			—[46]—			—[46]—		—	24.4	—[46]—		
Guatemala	1995	1,468	28.7	6.2	3.1	5.7	2.5	1.2	0.8	0.5	1.5	4.5	3.5	—16.4—	
Guernsey	2000[8, 14]	68	...	[47]	...	[47]	...	...	...	7.2[47]	...	21.1	...	...	...
Guinea	1998	158	...	...	...	...	...	...	...	...	...	...	...	...	...
Guinea-Bissau	2001[48]	20	...	...	...	...	...	...	...	...	...	...	...	...	...
Guyana	2001[14, 48]	58	46.4[49]	...	...	...	...	...	...	...	...	...	—	...	...
Haiti	1999[14]	197	—48.6—		3.8	—20.9—			...	...	...	...	—6.3—		
Honduras	1996[13, 19]	575	28.8	10.4	2.9	2.5	18.8	1.0	4.8	1.5	2.9	2.2	0.4	3.7	1.0
Hong Kong	1999[14]	8,477	7.9	[46]	[46]	11.1	11.0	0.1	0.1	0.1	1.3	16.3	—3.3—		
Hungary	1999	8,878	15.1	3.2	0.6	2.3	4.7	1.1	1.5	1.3	1.4	4.0	—7.0—		
Iceland	1996	998	43.6	2.1	...	2.4	1.6	1.2	0.2	3.6	1.1	10.4	1.2	2.0	—
India	1997–98[13, 50]	34,090	9.1	1.3	1.7	9.6	1.8	0.8	0.2	0.1	1.4	1.4	9.2	4.1	4.9
Indonesia	1998[13, 14, 35]	14,799	12.1	0.4	8.8	10.5	3.4	3.7	6.8	2.8[11]	3.5	2.7	10.0	2.2	1.3
Iran	1996–97[7]	16,068	10.2	1.7	1.0	8.6	0.5	1.0	0.6	0.4[11]	1.7	0.9	11.8	3.5	1.6
Iraq	1995	567	9.9	3.4	1.2	3.5	1.2	3.5	—	0.2	3.5	1.4	9.2	—1.1—	
Ireland	1999	45,302	—15.1—		0.5	0.5	0.5	0.1	—0.6—		0.8	15.3	—35.5—		
Isle of Man	1998–99[13, 14]	135	—19.9—		...	...	...	...	...	...	...	...	...	...	...
Israel	1998[19]	15,537	10.3	—1.7—		3.8	1.7	0.4	0.7	1.7[11]	2.3	4.8	—12.5—		
Italy	1998	161,544	7.2	1.4	0.4	6.3	4.0	2.8	1.1	2.5	2.6	3.3	3.6	—6.7—	
Jamaica	2001[3]	566	22.5	14.3	6.8	—2.5—		0.6	—2.7—		—2.9—		8.5[5]	[5]	[5]
Japan	1998	888,152	8.3	2.1	0.7	2.2	1.0	0.4	1.3	0.9[11]	2.6	6.1	3.6	2.9	3.2
Jersey	1996	46	...	...	...	...	...	...	...	...	...	...	...	...	...
Jordan	1998	1,262	10.2	5.7	13.3	2.2	2.0	0.9	1.0	2.6	2.7	2.8	6.9	2.7	5.1
Kazakhstan	1998[2, 14]	5,660	12.9[14]	4.2	3.2	1.1[14]	0.4	0.2	0.4	0.2[11]	—[14]	2.2[14]	2.0	0.3[14]	0.2
Kenya	1998[4, 13]	1,029	36.0	11.2	1.9	4.6	2.0	1.4	1.8	0.9	4.7	2.5	2.4	—6.4—	
Kiribati	1998	0.76	...	...	—	—	—	—	...	—	—	—	—	...	—
Korea, North	...	...	...	...	...	...	...	...	...	...	...	...	...	...	...
Korea, South	1999	168,813	—7.8—		1.1	5.5	1.9	1.0	0.6	[41]	2.3	2.5	—9.5—		
Kuwait	1997[7]	4,310	3.7	1.1	—	0.5	2.7	0.1	0.3	1.0	0.6	0.5	2.4	0.5	—
Kyrgyzstan	1998[2]	494	15.3	2.7	6.1	10.9	0.6	0.4	0.3	0.2[11]	—	0.7	—	—	0.1
Laos	1990[2]	66	4.5	7.4	16.3	—	5.1	0.3	40.1	5.0	—	1.2	—4.0—		
Latvia	1998[13, 14]	1,125	23.3	12.2	...	5.9	4.6	0.5	16.1	2.2[11]	1.1	5.8	0.2	1.0	1.4
Lebanon	1994	1,679	—25.2—		1.9	3.3	9.6	3.0	—3.4—		2.4	2.4	2.4	—	—
Lesotho	1995	134	43.3	28.4	...	10.4	3.0	2.2	...	0.7	...	1.5	...	—6.7—	
Liberia	1999	21	...	...	...	...	...	...	...	...	...	...	...	...	...
Libya	1995	857	4.3	2.2	9.4	3.7	3.3	8.5	0.3	0.2	0.3	1.0	7.0	—5.2—	
Liechtenstein	2000[8, 14, 53]	1,269	—6.1—			—1.7—			...	...	...	...	—10.0—		
Lithuania	1999[2]	4,552	—27.6—		[46]	6.6	10.9	1.2	5.7	[41]	1.4	3.8	—6.5—		
Luxembourg	1999	2,332	—11.0—			—10.0—			1.8	[41]	—7.5—		—6.4—		
Macau	2001	395	2.9	0.8	1.2	16.4	65.9	2.3	—	[41]	0.2	3.0	—2.3—		
Macedonia	1996	603	19.7	4.8	7.5	5.9	8.0	3.9	0.2	2.1	0.9	4.6	5.5	—5.1—	
Madagascar	1995	127	15.0	11.8	0.8	35.4	3.1	2.4	0.8	0.8	3.9	1.6	—	—6.3—	
Malawi	1998	105[13]	17.6	24.4	1.7	5.7	1.4	0.7	—2.0—		—6.5—		7.6[55]	—8.0—	
Malaysia	1997[13]	28,143	6.4	0.8	1.2	3.1	1.6	0.1	5.1	1.4	1.4	2.7	6.6	1.7	0.3
Maldives	2000	63[48]	...	...	—	—	...	—	—	...	—	...	—	...	—
Mali	1990	96	18.4	1.2	13.1	36.5	10.3	0.1	0.1	—	0.4	0.8	0.8	—0.7—	
Malta	1998	739	9.3	7.5	1.2	0.5	8.5	2.0	0.4	4.7[11]	1.4	7.0	1.4	1.6	1.9
Marshall Islands	1997	2.2	...	...	...	...	...	...	...	...	...	...	...	...	...
Martinique	1997	322	...	...	...	...	...	...	...	...	...	...	...	...	...
Mauritania	1997	13	—39.8—			—0.4—			...	...	—3.9—		—14.5—		
Mauritius	1998[7, 57]	785	15.3	—6.8—		7.9	42.2	0.8	0.4	1.0[11]	1.5	3.3[57]	—4.6—		
Mayotte	1992	...	...	...	—	—	—	—	—	—	—	—	—	—	—
Mexico	1999[3, 27]	41,861	8.4	8.9	3.8	1.9	0.5	0.3	0.1	0.2	2.3	0.5	8.8	—8.7—	
Micronesia	1996	2.6[6]	...	...	...	...	...	...	...	...	...	...	...	...	...
Moldova	1998[2, 3, 59]	752	39.8	25.8	5.8	1.6	1.4	2.0	0.5	1.1	1.5	1.6	—	0.4	0.9
Monaco	1992	689[1]	...	...	...	...	...	...	...	...	...	...	...	...	...
Mongolia	1998[3]	44	28.3	10.6	—	34.2	7.4	0.7	2.1	0.1[11]	—	2.6	—	0.2	2.9
Morocco	1998	5,484	16.9	4.7	12.2	8.3	8.8	1.3	1.5	0.3	2.6	1.2	9.8	3.4	2.0
Mozambique	2000[2]	490	15.7	22.4	1.9	4.4	2.6	...	4.5	0.1	—5.9—		—3.8—		
Myanmar (Burma)	1998	2,409[4]	4.0	19.9[4]	28.5	22.9	...	0.4	4.3	...	1.1[4]	...	...	5.4	6.9
Namibia	2001[14]	306	—70.8—		...	...	...	...	...	...	...	...	...	...	...
Nauru	1989	—	—	—	—	—	—	—	—	—	—	—	—	—	—
Nepal	1996–97[3, 7, 14]	381	13.6	9.1	12.0	25.9	6.3	1.3	1.4	0.9[11]	1.7	1.3	...	3.4	2.4
Netherlands, The	1999[3]	48,443	15.0	3.9	5.3	1.8	0.3	0.2	1.0	0.8	3.4	8.6	7.9	—5.5—	
Netherlands Antilles	1997	151	...	...	...	...	...	...	...	...	...	...	...	...	...
New Caledonia	1997[14]	375	—16.5—			...	...	...	...	...	...	...	...	...	
New Zealand	1995	9,878	25.1	3.0	0.6	2.9	2.3	1.1	4.6	1.8	7.7	7.8	3.6	—3.1—	
Nicaragua	2000[14]	331	40.5	25.3	2.2	1.2	0.1	1.2	2.5	0.5	1.0	1.8	—3.9—		

			(36)		(37)		(38)								(39)	country
refined petroleum and products	rubber products	plastic products	pottery, china, and glass	bricks, tiles, cement, etc.	iron and steel	non-ferrous metals	fabricated metal products	nonelectrical machinery	office equip., computers	electrical equip.	radio, television	transport equip. exc. motor vehicles	motor vehicles	professional equip.	jewelry, musical instruments	
(353 + 354)	(355)	(356)	(361 + 362)	(369)	(371)	(372)	(381)	(382 exc. 3825)	(3825)	(383 exc. 3832)	(3832)	(384 exc. 3843)	(3843)	(385)	(390)	
—	2.1	2.0	0.8	8.3	2.6	—	1.2	0.1	—	—	—	—	1.1	—	—	Ethiopia
...	...	...	...	...	...	...	...	...	...	...	...	14.3	...	...	4.9[32]	Faroe Islands
—	0.5	2.0	—	3.0[33]	[33]	—	3.2	1.2	—	—	—	0.4	1.0	—	1.2	Fiji
1.6	0.6	2.6	0.9	2.1	4.5		5.9	10.3	—	3.1	20.4	1.8	1.1	2.3	[34]	Finland
2.6	2.2	3.8	1.9	2.7	3.2	1.3	8.5	8.2	2.5	4.9	6.0	5.0	11.0	2.5	1.0	France
...	...	...	...	...	...	...	...	...	...	...	...	...	...	...	...	French Guiana
—	...	...	...	...	—	—	35.4								...	French Polynesia
10.3	—	—	0.8	5.8	2.1	2.1	8.7	0.8		5.4		7.0		0.4	3.3	Gabon
—	[5]	[5]	—	—	1.8		4.8	0.8						—	[39]	Gambia, The
...	...	...	...	...	...	...	...	...	...	...	...	...	...	...	...	Gaza Strip[40]
0.9	1.9		8.7		12.5		0.9	0.8	—	1.5	0.1	8.8	0.5	0.1	[34]	Georgia
5.1	4.3		3.5		4.0		6.7	13.0	1.1	7.0	2.9	2.0	13.1	3.0	2.3[41]	Germany
8.1	0.6	2.6	4.4		0.7	8.2	3.4	0.3		1.5		0.6[42]		—	[42]	Ghana
4.3	0.5	3.2	7.3		2.3	3.3	3.8	3.6	0.1	2.1	1.7	4.3	0.6	0.4	0.5	Greece
...	...	...	...	...	...	...	...	...	...	...	...	...	...	...	...	Greenland
—	...	—	—	—	—	—	—	—	—	...	...	—	—	—	...	Grenada
...	...	...	...	...	...	...	...	...	...	...	...	...	...	...	...	Guadeloupe
—	—	—	10.3		—	—	2.6	[46]							0.6	Guam
1.1	2.5	4.0	2.5	4.8	2.7	0.1	2.5	0.8		3.4		0.3		0.2	0.4	Guatemala
...	...	...	...	...	...	...	...	9.3		...	21.8	5.6	...	...	...	Guernsey
...	...	...	...	...	...	...	...	...	...	...	...	...	...	...	...	Guinea
...	...	...	...	...	...	...	...	...	...	...	...	...	...	...	...	Guinea-Bissau
—	—	—	—	—	—	—	—	...	—	...	—	—	—	—	...	Guyana
—			1.1		...	...	2.0	...	...	...	...	...	...	...	...	Haiti
0.2	1.1	3.3	0.1	7.5	0.5	0.2	3.6	0.7	—	0.9	0.1	—	0.2	0.1	0.7	Honduras
[46]	[46]	2.0	4.2		1.0		3.1	7.4	3.6	0.4	13.3	4.6		2.5	3.6	Hong Kong
15.0	0.3	3.5	1.7	2.2	1.3	1.2	3.8	4.6		11.6		10.2		2.1	0.4	Hungary
—	—	3.0	0.4	3.7	2.4	4.4	9.9	—	—	—	—	2.4	—	—	4.5	Iceland
2.2	2.2	1.7	0.7	3.7	13.1	2.6	2.4	6.3	0.7	5.1	2.3	3.3	6.2	0.6	1.3	India
1.7	2.0	1.9	...	...	2.5	1.5	2.6	1.3	—	1.4	4.8	6.9	1.4	0.4	1.3	Indonesia
1.9	1.8	1.3	1.4	8.4	15.3	3.1	5.1	6.2	0.1	2.6	1.2	0.8	6.5	0.6	0.2	Iran
25.2	0.5	1.4	0.7	18.2	4.1	—	4.8	2.3		4.4		0.4		—	—	Iraq
[51]	1.2		1.7		0.4		1.4	1.8	10.1	2.0	6.7	0.6	0.4	3.4	1.4[51]	Ireland
...	...	...	...	...	...	...	...	...	...	...	...	...	...	...	...	Isle of Man
—	5.1		3.6		1.8		10.6	4.3		2.4	14.4	5.4		11.2	1.3	Israel
2.1	1.7	3.0	1.6	4.3	3.5	1.2	7.4	13.8		7.4		8.5		2.6	1.1	Italy
14.1	[5]	[5]	7.7		[52]		16.9[52]								0.6	Jamaica
0.8	1.2	3.6	1.0	2.8	3.5	1.1	7.3	11.1	4.8	4.6	8.0	1.4	9.6	2.1	1.7	Japan
...	...	...	...	...	...	...	...	...	...	...	...	...	...	...	...	Jersey
6.5	0.2	3.0	1.1	13.5	2.2	0.7	9.1	1.9		1.8		—	1.2	0.1	0.6	Jordan
7.0[14]	0.3	0.3	0.1	2.6	9.3	20.7	1.6	1.9[14]	0.1	0.5	0.5	0.1[14]	0.1[14]	0.2	0.2[14]	Kazakhstan
0.8	3.1	3.8	0.5	3.8	...	...	6.8	0.6		...	...	2.5		0.1	2.2	Kenya
—	—	—	—	—	—	—	...	—	—	—	—	...	—	—	...	Kiribati
...	...	...	...	...	...	...	...	...	...	...	...	...	...	...	...	Korea, North
3.9	4.2		3.9		6.6		4.0	7.1	2.8	3.7	16.2	4.1	8.7	1.0	1.6[41]	Korea, South
75.2	0.1	1.3	0.3	3.4	0.3	—	2.8	1.3	—	1.0	—	0.4	0.1	—	0.5	Kuwait
0.6	—	—	1.2	9.3	—	40.8	0.4	3.2	0.2	4.3	0.1	—	0.8	1.4	0.4	Kyrgyzstan
—	0.5		0.1	3.8	—	—	10.8	0.5		0.2		—	—	—	0.1	Laos
0.1	0.1	1.0	1.2	2.1	...	0.1	4.0	3.7	0.1	2.3	0.8	3.2	0.5[14]	0.7	0.6	Latvia
1.6	—	3.2	12.0		4.9		8.9	2.2		2.1		1.0		—	10.5	Lebanon
...	...	...	...	0.7	...	...	3.0	...	...	...	...	...	...	...	...	Lesotho
...	...	...	...	...	...	...	...	...	...	...	...	...	...	...	...	Liberia
27.2	0.1	0.8	0.2	21.7	—	—	0.5	—	—	—	—	—	—	—	4.0	Libya
—			11.4		0.6	1.5	17.6	40.6				10.5		...[54]	...	Liechtenstein
13.1	3.0		3.5		0.6		2.0	2.4	0.2	2.3	3.0	2.0	0.1	1.1	3.0[41]	Lithuania
—	12.1		8.6		17.3		12.1	7.6		4.0		0.5		...	0.9[41]	Luxembourg
—	—	0.2	1.3		—	—	0.6	0.3	–0.1	0.2		0.9			1.5[41]	Macau
0.4	0.1	1.2	0.8	0.6	6.2	—	5.4	1.1		9.5		4.7		0.3	1.7	Macedonia
7.9	0.8	0.8	—	2.4	—	—	3.1	—	—	2.4		0.8		—	—	Madagascar
—	0.6	3.2	—	7.5	—	—	8.6	4.5[56]		[55]		[56]		—	...	Malawi
3.4	4.2	3.5	1.6	3.9	2.3	1.0	4.1	3.4	2.6	3.5	26.5	1.4	4.4	1.0	0.7	Malaysia
—	—	...	—	...	—	—	...	—	—	—	—	...	—	—	...	Maldives
0.7	0.3	0.4	—	1.3	—	—	6.2	0.5		1.7		6.5		—	—	Mali
—	3.9	2.1	0.6	2.0	0.1		3.4	2.0	0.2	6.0	20.1	2.8	0.2	4.2	5.1	Malta
...	...	...	...	...	...	...	...	...	...	...	...	...	...	...	...	Marshall Islands
...	...	...	...	...	...	...	...	...	...	...	...	...	...	...	...	Martinique
—			12.2		...	...	29.2								...	Mauritania
—			5.3		1.5		2.3	0.6		1.4		0.4		1.1	3.6	Mauritius
—	—	—	—	...	—	—	—	—	—	—	—	—	—	—	—	Mayotte
0.6[27, 58]	1.3	1.5	2.7	3.7	7.6	3.1	4.1	3.9		6.1		20.5		0.4	0.3	Mexico
...	...	...	...	...	...	...	...	...	...	...	...	...	...	...	...	Micronesia
—	—	0.5	3.8	3.9	0.1	0.1	1.1	5.2	0.2	0.4	0.4	0.1	0.6	0.9	0.3	Moldova
...	...	...	...	...	...	...	...	...	...	...	...	...	...	...	...	Monaco
—	—	—	—	4.4	0.3	—	0.2	0.2	—	0.1	—	0.2	—	1.6	3.6	Mongolia
...	0.9	1.9	1.4	9.3	1.0	0.3	4.3	0.7	0.2	2.2	0.8	0.5	3.0	0.2	0.1	Morocco
0.4	1.1	1.8	10.8		0.1	0.1	23.9	0.1		0.4		0.1		...	0.1	Mozambique
...	1.7	1.0	...	...	1.3	...	0.1	...	...	0.6	...	...	0.9	...	0.9	Myanmar (Burma)
...	...	...	...	...	...	...	...	...	...	...	...	...	...	...	...	Namibia
—	—	—	—	—	—	—	—	—	—	—	—	—	—	—	—	Nauru
0.2	1.3	1.7	0.1	7.2	1.6	0.1	4.8	0.1	—	2.2	0.3	—	—	—	0.5	Nepal
1.8	0.6	3.2	1.6	2.3	3.7		6.2	9.6		10.9		5.1		0.9	0.3	Netherlands, The
...	...	...	...	...	...	...	...	...	...	...	...	...	...	...	...	Netherlands Antilles
...	...	...	...	...	...	47.9	14.4								...	New Caledonia
1.5	0.7	3.6	1.3	2.1	1.8	2.3	7.7	4.8		4.4		4.4		0.4	1.3	New Zealand
4.4	0.1		10.9		...	...	0.7	0.3				0.2		...	3.3	Nicaragua

Manufacturing industries (continued)

country	year	total manufacturing value added ('000,000 U.S.$)	(31) food (311 + 312)	beverages (313)	tobacco manufactures (314)	(32) textiles (exc. wearing apparel) (321)	wearing apparel (322)	leather and fur products (323 + 324)	(33) wood products (exc. furniture) (331)	wood furniture (332)	(34) paper, paper products (341)	printing and publishing (342)	(35) industrial chemicals (351)	paints, soaps, etc. (352 exc. 3522)	drugs and medicines (3522)
Niger	1998[3]	15		19.8			9.1		0.5		37.0				18.0
Nigeria	1995	7,884	17.6	15.3	1.9	10.4	0.1	3.1	0.5	0.9	3.8	3.4	0.3	11.7	
Northern Mariana Islands	1997[1, 14]	762		0.7		[46]	91.8	—	[46]	[46]	[46]	0.7		0.3	
Norway	1998[14]	17,647	12.4	3.9[14]	…	1.2	0.4	0.1	3.8	2.6[11]	4.3	9.9	4.9	1.2	1.6
Oman	1998	689	16.8	2.3	—	1.0	6.1	0.3	3.1	4.5[11]	1.4	3.1	1.0	4.3	0.8
Pakistan	1995–96[3, 19]	6,307	15.2	1.6	6.2	23.5	1.4	1.3	0.2	—	1.6	2.0	8.5	3.0	4.8
Palau	2000	1.7	…	…	…	…	[60]	…	…	…			…	…	…
Panama	1999	732	56.1		—	0.9	1.9	0.5	1.3	[41]	3.1	3.1		4.3	
Papua New Guinea	2000	318	…	…	…	…	…	…	…	…	…	…	…	…	…
Paraguay	2001	905	42.9	12.6	0.5	4.9	0.1	6.5	10.9	0.8	—	7.4	1.2	1.1	
Peru	1998	4,568	18.7	6.7		8.3	4.4	0.9	7.2		1.1	4.9	3.2	5.1	0.9
Philippines	2000	16,878	42.6	4.4	2.1	1.6	5.5		0.8	1.6	0.8	1.0		7.1	
Poland	1999	28,003	12.4	12.2	3.1	2.6	3.1	0.8	2.0	3.0	2.0	1.3	2.9	3.5	
Portugal	1997[3]	21,410	7.7	2.6	4.9	7.3	6.8	4.2	3.9	2.5[11]	3.2	4.9	2.2	1.6	2.0
Puerto Rico	1997[14]	36,427	4.0	5.7	…	0.2	1.9	0.6	…	0.1[11]	0.4	1.2	2.5	2.3	54.0
Qatar	1998	718	4.0	0.3	—	0.4	9.0	0.2	0.6	2.6	0.1	3.4	37.9	0.5	—
Réunion	1994	371	34.5	12.3	—	0.5		—	3.8		5.0[61]	6.3	…	3.7	
Romania	1997[62]	9,085	22.5	11.0	1.7	3.3	6.2	2.1	3.6	3.2[11]	1.0	1.7	2.3	1.5	1.2
Russia	1998	35,840[14]	16.4	4.2	1.5	1.3	1.0	0.4	1.9	0.9	2.4	1.1	5.6	2.3	1.5
Rwanda	1998	259		79.3		6.8	…	…	1.8		0.7			1.3	
St. Kitts and Nevis	2000[13]	30	9.3[64]	…	…	…	…	…	…	…	…	…	…	…	…
St. Lucia	1997	31	12.8	34.3	1.9	4.4	7.1	—	—	4.4	8.9	7.4	0.7	2.8	—
St. Vincent	2000[13]	15	…	…	…	…	…	…	…	…	…	…	…	…	…
Samoa	1998[15]	28	17.0	42.0	11.0	…	…	…	7.0	…	…	…	…	7.0	…
San Marino	…	…	…	…	…	…	…	…	…	…	…	…	…	…	…
São Tomé and Príncipe	2000[48]	2.5	…	…	…	…	…	…	…	…	…	…	…	…	…
Saudi Arabia	1998	12,542	7.9	2.8	—	1.0	0.1	0.2	0.3	0.8	2.5	1.3	26.7	4.0	
Senegal	1997[3]	341	36.6	4.1	3.1	5.2	—	—	0.2	0.1	1.9	2.5	19.8	4.3	2.1
Serbia and Montenegro	1999	3,591	28.6		2.4	4.6	3.5	2.3	2.2	6.1[34]	3.4	5.1		8.6	
Seychelles	1989	26[66]		79.6			0.6		2.1		6.0				4.1
Sierra Leone	1993[3]	92	37.0	21.6	10.5	—	1.0	0.1	0.3	1.2	0.2	2.2			20.2
Singapore	1998[7, 13]	23,162	2.7	0.8	—	0.2	0.6	0.1	0.2	0.5[11]	1.0	4.2	1.9	4.1	6.5
Slovakia	1998[35]	3,047	9.5	2.9	…	2.5[4]	3.6	1.6	1.6	1.6[11]	5.9	2.6	3.3	1.2	2.2
Slovenia	1998[3]	4,927		11.8		8.7		1.6	3.7	5.0[34]	8.4			11.2	
Solomon Islands	2000	9.0	…	…	…	—	…	—	…	…	—	…	—	—	—
Somalia	1990	36	21.6	6.3	37.5	10.5	0.8	2.0	—	7.3	–0.6	0.3	0.4	5.1	
South Africa	1999[13]	22,833	9.7	4.7	0.4	2.9	2.9	1.1	1.8	1.3	4.6	2.9	4.4	5.1	
Spain	1998	108,953	9.5	4.1	4.8	2.6	2.2	1.5	2.1	2.6[11]	2.5	5.0	3.3	2.7	2.4
Sri Lanka	2001	2,009		30.2			39.7		0.9		1.7				10.7
Sudan, The	1990	1,179	40.0	3.0	16.7	11.9	0.4	5.4	0.2	0.2	2.1	6.4	0.7	2.2	
Suriname	1992[2, 13, 44]	700	33.4	22.3	12.3	…	1.5	1.6	8.7	1.4	0.7	1.6	…	8.3	
Swaziland	1995[7, 13, 14]	335	27.5	42.0	…	0.4	3.0	…	1.2	0.8	17.9	1.1	—	0.2	…
Sweden	1999[3]	60,552	5.7	1.0	0.3	0.7	0.1	0.1	4.4	2.3[34, 69]	9.8	5.8	3.0	5.7	
Switzerland	1999	49,667		9.6		1.7	0.5	0.2	3.5	[41]	2.6	6.8			18.0
Syria	1995	3,805	12.0	5.8	3.8	20.2	1.2	2.1	2.2	0.2	0.4	0.8	0.2	0.9	
Taiwan	2001	70,798	5.8		1.2	5.3	1.5	0.4	0.2	1.0	2.0	0.9	7.3	2.6	
Tajikistan	1998[2]	679	35.8[4]	1.1[4]	0.1	18.3[4]	0.6	0.1[4]	—	—	…	0.1[4]	2.1[4]	…	…
Tanzania	1995	119	10.7	5.8	10.7	17.4	0.8	1.7	1.7	0.8	3.3	3.3	14.9	2.5	
Thailand	1996[3, 7]	39,380	11.4	7.0	3.1	4.7	2.4	1.6	1.5	1.4[11]	3.2	3.0[4]	2.8	2.5	0.6
Togo	1998	138		50.9			6.0		5.8		5.6				4.4
Tonga	1997[2, 3]	15	51.3		—	0.8	1.6	1.1	1.6	4.3[34]	—	6.0	—	20.5	
Trinidad and Tobago	1995	862	12.0	9.1	3.3	0.2	0.9	0.2	0.4	1.0	2.8	2.5	36.5	1.4	0.1
Tunisia	1998[3]	4,977	10.2	3.3	6.4	7.7	15.9	4.5	5.4		2.1		4.6	2.8	1.0
Turkey	1998	36,678	9.3	1.8	1.5	11.4	5.1	0.7	0.6	0.8	1.3	1.7	3.8	6.2	
Turkmenistan	1992[2, 14, 15]	801	13.3	…	…	18.9	1.2	0.4	0.3[16]		[16]		3.2[5]	[5]	[5]
Tuvalu	1998	0.55	…	—	—	—	…	—	—	…	—	—	—	…	—
Uganda	1997[4]	346	27.9[4]	15.2[4]	3.5	5.6[4]		0.4	3.6[4]	3.4	1.2	5.3[4]	[4]	6.7[4]	0.9
Ukraine	1998[2, 13, 14]	23,163	19.4	3.5	1.4	0.8	0.9	0.4	1.0	0.6	1.0	0.8	4.8	1.1	1.1
United Arab Emirates	1998[7]	5,498		7.5			11.9		1.6		3.9				50.0
United Kingdom	1998[13, 14]	243,567	9.7[4]	2.3	0.9	2.6	1.8	0.5	1.5	2.6[11]	2.7	9.6	3.5	3.4	3.0
United States	1999	1,962,644	9.1	1.5	1.9	1.9	1.6	0.2	1.9	2.0[11]	3.8	3.2	3.9	4.0	3.8
Uruguay	1997[19]	3,069	21.4	10.2	5.9	6.7	2.8	2.8	0.2	0.6	2.0	3.7	1.4	6.5	
Uzbekistan	1992[2, 14, 15]	2,147	12.6	…	…	21.4	3.1	1.9	1.3[16]		[16]		5.4[5]	[5]	[5]
Vanuatu	1995[14]	16		35.9			3.2		23.5		6.9				4.7[74]
Venezuela	1996[3, 19]	15,621	11.3	4.0	12.7	1.8	1.9	0.9	0.4	0.5	1.7	1.5	7.8	3.4	1.3
Vietnam	1998[3, 19, 75]	2,532	13.2	10.2	6.8	8.3	6.2	7.3	1.1	0.8[11]	2.1	2.8	3.0	3.0	1.3
Virgin Islands (U.S.)	1997[1, 14]	146		22.0		[46]	0.8	[46]	1.1	[46]	—	14.5			[46]
West Bank[40]	1998	479	12.8	0.9	0.3	1.4	19.5	3.0	1.1	7.6	1.5	1.2	0.1	4.4	
Western Sahara	…	…	…	…	…	…	…	…	…	…	…	…	…	…	…
Yemen	2000	426	32.3		14.5	1.3	2.6	0.6	3.2	2.3[11]	0.5	3.6		1.9	
Zambia	1995	450	19.2	17.1	6.7	9.8	1.1	0.7	3.3	1.1	0.9	2.2	4.9	10.5	
Zimbabwe	1998[13]	1,088	13.6	15.7	4.7	9.1	3.0	2.5	2.9	2.0	2.1	2.8	3.7[76]	5.1	

[1]Gross output in value of sales. [2]Gross output of production. [3]In producer's prices. [4]Sum of available data. [5]351 includes 352, 355, and 356. [6]37 includes 381. [7]Establishments employing 10 or more persons. [8]Value of manufactured exports. [9]Value of manufactured exports (excluding duty-free reexports). [10]390 includes 385. [11]Includes metal furniture. [12]Estimated figure includes agriculture. [13]In factor values. [14]Complete ISIC detail is not available. [15]Includes extraction of petroleum, natural gas, metals, and nonmetals. [16]33 includes 34. [17]355 and 356 include 361 + 362. [18]38 includes 39. [19]Establishments employing five or more persons. [20]Includes mining and quarrying in other than petroleum and natural gas sectors. [21]33 includes 341. [22]In factor values at 1992 prices. [23]Establishments employing 50 or more persons. [24]All state-owned industrial enterprises and privately owned industrial enterprises with annual sales of more than U.S.$604,000. [25]Excludes traditional sector. [26]390 includes 332. [27]Excludes petroleum refining. [28]Republic of Cyprus only. [29]Excludes establishments processing coffee or cotton. [30]Establishments employing 10 or more persons and using power-driven machines. [31]Excludes frozen and chilled fish and crustaceans. [32]Remainder. [33]369 includes 371. [34]332 includes 390. [35]Establishments employing 20 or more persons. [36]Excludes unavailable data for food, beverages, and tobacco. [37]Establishments employing 6 or more persons. [38]342 includes 32. [39]33 includes 39. [40]West Bank includes Gaza

			(36)		(37)		(38)								(39)	country
refined petroleum and products	rubber products	plastic products	pottery, china, and glass	bricks, tiles, cement, etc.	iron and steel	non-ferrous metals	fabricated metal products	nonelectrical machinery	office equip., computers	electrical equip.	radio, television	transport equip. exc. motor vehicles	motor vehicles	professional equip.	jewelry, musical instruments	
(353 + 354)	(355)	(356)	(361+ 362)	(369)	(371)	(372)	(381)	(382 exc. 3825)	(3825)	(383 exc. 3832)	(3832)	(384 exc. 3843)	(3843)	(385)	(390)	
—			10.7		...	...	4.8								...	Niger
—	1.9	2.8	0.4	5.8	1.0	1.9	3.7	1.1		2.0		9.8		—	0.5	Nigeria
[46]	[46]	[46]	2.8		—	—	—	—	—	—	—	0.2		—	[46]	Northern Mariana Islands
1.1	0.2	1.8	0.6[14]	2.7[14]	2.3	5.2	6.1	8.2	0.3	3.8	1.7	11.6	1.4	2.1[14]	0.7	Norway
16.8	—	2.7	2.5	17.2	0.1	4.0	6.6	1.9	0.1	2.6	—	0.1	0.1	—	0.5	Oman
3.1	0.9	0.4	0.5	7.2	4.2	—	0.7	1.6	—	5.0	2.7	0.8	2.7	0.2	0.8	Pakistan
...	...	...	...	...	...	...	...	...	...	...	...	...	...	...	...	Palau
9.5	4.9		6.8		1.8		2.2	—	—	0.4	—	1.5	0.1	0.2	1.4[41]	Panama
...	...	...	...	...	...	...	...	...	...	...	...	...	...	...	...	Papua New Guinea
2.1	—	2.8	0.1	4.7	0.1	0.1	0.4	0.1		—	—	0.4		—	0.2	Paraguay
0.9	2.4		7.6		3.1	17.8	2.4	0.7		1.5		0.6		...	1.6	Peru
8.9	0.7	...	2.7		1.6		1.7	1.3		11.6		1.1		...	3.0	Philippines
6.5	1.8	2.6	1.8	2.7	3.8	0.6	6.7	6.8		6.8		9.5		1.0	0.6	Poland
10.5	0.6	1.7	2.7	5.6	1.1	0.5	5.7	4.4	—	3.0	2.5	1.4	4.8	0.6	1.1	Portugal
2.3	—	1.0	1.6		0.2		1.1	7.3		2.6	5.4	—	0.3	4.2	0.4	Puerto Rico
4.4	...	0.8	13.5		17.6	—	3.8	...	...	0.3		0.3	—	...	0.3	Qatar
—	—	[61]	...	16.8	—	—	12.2	5.0							—	Réunion
2.7	1.1	0.9	5.2		6.6		4.2	5.9	0.5	2.8	1.7	2.0	3.7	0.7	0.7	Romania
6.1	1.1	0.5	1.0	5.1	8.3	11.4	1.8	8.0	0.5	2.8	[46]	2.1[63]	7.1	1.0	1.9	Russia
...	...	...	8.0		1.9[6]		[6]	...	...	...	...	...	...	...	0.2	Rwanda
...	...	...	...	...	...	...	...	...	...	...	...	...	...	...	...	St. Kitts and Nevis
—	0.4	3.8	—	—	—	—	5.6	—	—	3.3	0.9	—	—	—	1.3	St. Lucia
...	...	...	...	...	...	...	...	...	...	...	...	...	...	...	...	St. Vincent
...	...	...	...	10.0	...	...	1.0	...	...	...	...	...	...	...	5.0	Samoa
...	...	...	...	...	...	...	...	...	...	...	...	...	...	...	...	San Marino
...	...	...	...	...	...	...	...	...	...	...	...	...	...	...	...	São Tomé and Príncipe
14.4	0.1	3.6	1.7	12.0	4.9	0.1	9.0	2.3		2.4		1.0		0.2	0.7	Saudi Arabia
3.7	—	1.9	—	6.9	—	—	4.1	0.4	—	0.8	—	1.8	0.4	—	—	Senegal
–0.1	4.7		7.3		2.7		4.5	3.8	1.5	3.2	1.3	0.6	2.3	1.4	[34]	Serbia and Montenegro
—			5.2		—	—	2.4								—	Seychelles
—			3.5		...	...	2.1	...	...	...	...	...	...	...	0.1	Sierra Leone
4.9	0.3	2.2	0.4	1.4	0.4	0.1	5.7	6.7	24.2	2.4	17.8	6.6	0.8	2.9	0.4	Singapore
5.9	2.4	2.2	2.0	5.2	7.6	2.7	5.4	9.2	0.3	4.4[4]	1.9	2.5[4]	6.3	2.3	0.6	Slovakia
0.3	5.8		4.6		13.6[6]		[6]	9.8[67]		11.3		4.2		[67]	[34]	Slovenia
—	—	—	—	—	—	—	—	—	—	—	—	...	—	—	—	Solomon Islands
1.6	—	0.5	—	3.0	—	—	1.1	—	—	—	—	0.9		—	1.7	Somalia
5.9	1.2	2.4	1.4	3.3	9.7	5.4	6.1	5.4		5.9		9.2		0.7	1.6	South Africa
8.7[14]	1.5	2.8	1.5	5.3	2.8	1.1	7.9	6.0	0.8	3.4	1.3	1.8	8.1	0.9	0.9	Spain
—			8.9		0.7		4.9	2.3[68]							[68]	Sri Lanka
1.3	0.8	1.2	0.1	0.5	0.1	0.7	2.6	0.1		1.2		2.1		—	0.1	Sudan, The
...	0.7	0.6	5.3		...	...	...	...	...	...	...	0.9		0.2	0.5	Suriname
...	...	0.2	0.1	0.5	...	...	2.2	2.8	...	...	...	...	0.2	...	—	Swaziland
0.9	0.8	1.6	0.5	1.3	4.1	1.3	6.7	10.1	0.5	2.4	15.2	1.8	9.9	3.9	[34]	Sweden
—	3.2		2.3		2.2		10.5	14.5	5.8		3.1	1.4	0.5	10.7	3.0[41]	Switzerland
17.1	0.3	0.6	4.7	7.1	—	0.6	14.0	2.4		2.4		0.5		—	0.3	Syria
8.4	1.5	4.8	2.5		5.8		7.7	5.6		25.7		6.4		1.0	2.4	Taiwan
...	—	—	0.2[4]	1.1[4]	...	39.7	0.1[4]	0.3[4]	...	0.2[4]	...	...	0.2[4]	...	—	Tajikistan
4.1	0.8	1.7	—	5.8	1.7	2.5	4.1	0.8		1.7		3.3		—	—	Tanzania
3.3	3.6	2.7	1.3	5.2	1.5	0.3	3.5	3.9[4]	2.8	4.0	4.8	0.7[4]	14.0	1.2[4]	2.0	Thailand
—			10.4		—	...	14.8	2.1[68]							[68]	Togo
—	—	—	8.3		—	—	2.8	0.3	—	—	—	1.4	—	—	[34]	Tonga
10.5	0.2	0.5	1.2	3.6	8.2	—	1.4	0.3	—	1.4	0.3	0.1	0.1	[10]	1.9[10]	Trinidad and Tobago
14.5	0.9	1.4[70]	2.9	3.5	1.4	3.1[71]	[71]	0.4		3.9	[72]	2.1		[72]	1.9[72]	Tunisia
15.5	2.0	1.8	2.6	4.7	5.7	1.0	3.2	4.5		5.1		8.6		0.5	0.5	Turkey
55.7	[5]	[5]	4.0		0.1		0.8								...	Turkmenistan
—	—	—	—	...	—	—	—	—	—	—	—	—	—	—	...	Tuvalu
...	0.4[4]	1.1	4.9[4]	4.9[4]	...	10.9	...	...	...	3.7[4]	...	...	...	...	...	Uganda
5.4	2.0	0.5	1.0	4.4	25.6	1.9	5.1	6.6	0.1	2.2[4]	...	2.4	1.6	0.6[4]	0.1[4]	Ukraine
—			7.0		6.6		9.9								1.6	United Arab Emirates
1.5	1.1	4.2	1.2	2.0	2.0	1.2	8.4	8.9	2.2	3.6	4.1	1.0[4, 73]	6.3	3.2	1.3	United Kingdom
2.1	1.0	3.7	2.9		3.4		7.3	7.1	2.4	3.1	7.7	5.2	8.5	5.2	1.6	United States
18.8	0.9	2.9	0.9	2.9	1.9	0.2	2.8	0.7		1.2		1.5		0.6	0.5	Uruguay
12.4	[5]	[5]	5.4		12.2		13.2								...	Uzbekistan
—			[74]		21.0[6]		[6]	...	...	...	...	...	...	...	...	Vanuatu
15.8	2.2	1.6	2.3	2.9	7.0	6.1	2.7	1.7	—	1.7	0.1	0.3	5.9	0.3	0.3	Venezuela
0.3	1.1	2.5	1.0	9.2	2.7	0.3	2.3	2.4	0.7	2.6	3.5	2.3	1.8	0.4	0.9	Vietnam
—			15.0		—	—	2.3	[46]		—	—	3.4		19.8	1.9	Virgin Islands (U.S.)
—	0.1	4.7	0.5	25.4	0.1	—	11.7	1.1		1.9		0.3		0.2	0.2	West Bank[40]
...	...	...	...	...	...	...	...	...	...	...	...	...	...	...	...	Western Sahara
8.2	...	3.3	...	18.8	...	...	6.0	0.4		0.3		0.2		...	...	Yemen
4.2	1.8	1.3	–0.2	3.3	1.3	—	5.3	1.1		3.3		0.7		—	0.2	Zambia
[76]	2.7	1.6	0.4	5.8	7.9	0.7	5.9	1.1		3.4		2.8		0.1	0.5	Zimbabwe

Strip. [41]390 includes 332. [42]384 includes 390. [43]Represents export value of clothing articles made from fur. [44]Selected industries only. [45]Total manufacturing value added (2000): U.S.$26,000,000. [46]Data withheld for reasons of confidentiality. [47]332 includes 313 and 321. [48]Includes public utilities. [49]Sugar and rice manufacturing only. [50]Establishments with electric power and employing 10 or more workers and all establishments employing 20 or more workers. [51]390 includes 353 + 354. [52]38 includes 37. [53]Excludes exports destined for Switzerland. [54]Complete data not available for professional equipment. [55]351 includes 383. [56]382 includes 384. [57]Excludes government printing. [58]Derivatives of petroleum and coal only. [59]Excludes Transdniester area and city of Tighina (Bendery). [60]Garment manufacturing accounts for most of manufacturing value added. [61]341 includes 356. [62]State enterprises only; state enterprises account for about 80% of all industrial output. [63]Excludes shipbuilding and aircraft (data withheld for reasons of confidentiality). [64]Refined sugar only. [65]Sector percentages are estimated figures. [66]Figure for 1999 is U.S.$88,000,000. [67]382 includes 385. [68]382 through 385 includes 390. [69]Includes recycling. [70]Includes synthetic fibres. [71]372 includes 381. [72]390 includes 3832 and 385. [73]Excludes railway equipment and aircraft. [74]35 includes 36. [75]17 provinces only covering about 80% of total industrial output. [76]351 includes 353 + 354.

Energy

This table provides data about the commercial energy supplies (reserves, production, consumption, and trade) of the various countries of the world, together with data about oil pipeline networks and traffic. Many of the data and concepts used in this table are adapted from the United Nations' *Energy Statistics Yearbook.*

Electricity. Total installed electrical power capacity comprises the sum of the rated power capacities of all main and auxiliary generators in a country. "Total installed capacity" (kW) is multiplied by 8,760 hours per year to yield "Total production capacity" (kW-hr).

Production of electricity comprises the total gross production of electricity by publicly or privately owned enterprises and also that generated by industrial establishments for their own use, but it usually excludes consumption by the utility itself. Measured in millions of kilowatt-hours (kW-hr), annual production of electricity ranges generally between 50% and 60% of total production capacity. The data are further analyzed by type of generation: fossil fuels, hydroelectric power, and nuclear fuel.

The great majority of the world's electrical and other energy needs are met by the burning of fossil hydrocarbon solids, liquids, and gases, either for thermal generation of electricity or in internal combustion engines. Many renewable and nontraditional sources of energy are being developed worldwide (wood, biogenic gases and liquids, tidal, wave, and wind power, geothermal and photothermal [solar] energy, and so on), but collectively these sources are still negligible in the world's total energy consumption. For this reason only hydroelectric and nuclear generation are considered here separately with fossil fuels.

Trade in electrical energy refers to the transfer of generated electrical output via an international grid. Total electricity consumption (residential and nonresidential) is equal to total electricity requirements less transformation and distribution losses.

Coal. The term coal, as used in the table, comprises all grades of anthracite, bituminous, subbituminous, and lignite that have acquired or may in the future, by reason of new technology or changed market prices, acquire an economic value. These types of coal may be differentiated according to heat content (density) and content of impurities. Most coal reserve data are based on proven recoverable reserves only, of all grades of coal. Exceptions are footnoted, with proven in-place reserves reported only when recoverable reserves are unknown. Production figures include deposits removed from both surface and underground workings as well as quantities used by the producers themselves or issued to the miners. Wastes recovered from mines or nearby preparation plants are excluded from production figures.

Natural gas. This term refers to any combustible gas (usually chiefly methane) of natural origin from underground sources. The data for production cover, to the extent possible, gas obtained from gas fields,

Energy

country	electricity												coal		
	installed capacity, 1998 ('000 kW)	production, 1998		power source, 1998			trade, 1998		consumption				reserves, latest ('000,000 metric tons)	production, 1998 ('000 metric tons)	consumption, 1998 ('000 metric tons)
		capacity ('000,000 kW-hr)	amount ('000,000 kW-hr)	fossil fuel (%)	hydropower (%)	nuclear fuel (%)	exports ('000,000 kW-hr)	imports ('000,000 kW-hr)	amount, 1998 ('000,000 kW-hr)	per capita, 1998 (kW-hr)	residential, 1998 (%)	nonresidential, 1998 (%)			
Afghanistan	494	4,327	485	35.1	64.9	—	—	95	580	27	...	...	66	2	2
Albania	1,892	16,574	5,068	1.6	98.4	—	692	1,068	5,444	1,738	42.9[1]	57.1[1]	15[2]	59	39
Algeria	6,042	52,928	23,615	99.6	0.4	—	262	255	23,608	785	28.4	71.6	40	23	651
American Samoa	35	307	130	100.0	—	—	—	—	130	2,063	...	...	—	—	...
Andorra	...	...	...	...	...	...	...	...	...	...	...	...	—	—	...
Angola	462	4,047	1,063	10.0	90.0	—	...	...	1,063	88	29.4[1]	70.6[1]	...	—	—
Antigua and Barbuda	26	228	99	100.0	—	—	—	—	99	1,478	...	...	...	...	...
Argentina	23,032	201,760	74,135	54.1	35.9	10.0	1,080	6,434	79,489	2,201	47.3	52.7	430	289	1,415
Armenia	3,005	26,324	6,190	49.5	24.8	25.7	—	—	6,190	1,751	...	...	...	...	5
Aruba	90	788	470	100.0	—	—	—	—	470	5,000	...	...	...	...	...
Australia	39,694	347,719	194,834	91.6	8.4	—	—	—	194,834	10,520	...	...	82,090	284,559	126,327
Austria	18,258	159,940	57,437	32.6	67.4	—	10,467	10,304	57,274	7,036	...	...	25	1,140	4,632
Azerbaijan	5,239	45,894	17,985	89.2	10.8	—	648	903	18,240	2,378	19.5[1]	80.5[1]	...	...	1
Bahamas, The	401	3,513	1,532	100.0	—	—	—	—	1,532	5,176	...	...	...	—	—
Bahrain	1,120	9,811	5,773	100.0	—	—	—	—	5,773	9,703	53.1[1]	46.9[1]	...	...	...
Bangladesh	3,490	30,572	13,857	93.8	6.2	—	—	—	13,857	111	37.7	62.3	1,756[2]	...	173
Barbados	156	1,367	747	100.0	—	—	—	—	747	2,787	78.4	21.6	...	—	—
Belarus	7,498	65,682	23,492	99.9	0.1	—	2,073	12,747	34,166	3,312	17.1[1]	82.9[1]	...	—	730
Belgium	14,969	131,128	85,833	44.5	1.7	53.8	6,435	7,828	87,226	8,601	...	...	—	312	11,596
Belize	43	377	183	63.9	36.1	—	—	25	208	904	71.0	29.0	...	...	...
Benin	15	131	6	100.0	—	—	—	305	311	54	64.1	35.9	...	...	...
Bermuda	146	1,279	530	100.0	—	—	—	—	530	8,281	...	...	...	—	—
Bhutan	356	3,119	1,801	—	100.0	—	1,357	8	452	226	...	...	...	50	68
Bolivia	1,043	9,137	3,710	56.1	43.9	—	3	13	3,720	468	48.9	51.1	0.9	—	—
Bosnia and Herzegovina	2,719	23,818	2,538	38.8	61.2	—	199	423	2,762	752	...	...	...	1,794	1,794
Botswana	[3]	[3]	[3]	[3]	[3]	[3]	[3]	[3]	[3]	[3]	26.3	73.7	4,300	[3]	[3]
Brazil	65,209	571,231	321,588	8.4	90.6	1.0	8	39,412	360,992	2,177	26.7	73.3	11,929	5,516	17,636
Brunei	479	4,196	1,725	100.0	—	—	—	—	1,725	5,476	53.7	46.3	...	—	—
Bulgaria	12,088	105,891	41,711	51.5	8.0	40.5	4,211	564	38,064	4,566	53.1	46.9	2,711	30,111	33,220
Burkina Faso	78	683	298	60.4	39.6	—	—	—	298	26	...	...	...	...	...
Burundi	43	377	123	1.6	98.4	—	—	30	153	24	73.8	26.2	...	...	...
Cambodia	35	307	215	62.8	37.2	—	—	—	215	20	...	...	...	—	—
Cameroon	627	5,493	2,765	3.3	96.7	—	—	—	2,765	193	...	...	...	1	1
Canada	115,037	1,007,724	561,805	28.2	59.1	12.7	44,665	17,299	534,439	17,486	...	...	6,578	75,368	59,492
Cape Verde	7	61	41	100.0	—	—	—	—	41	100	...	...	...	—	—
Central African Republic	43	377	104	21.2	78.8	—	—	—	104	30	69.3	30.7	2.7	...	...
Chad	29	254	91	100.0	—	—	—	—	91	13	...	...	...	...	...
Chile	8,423	73,785	35,503	55.1	44.9	—	—	—	35,503	2,395	30.0	70.0	1,181	975	5,790
China	231,167	2,025,023	1,166,200	81.0	17.8	1.2	2,976	17	1,163,241	926	25.3	74.7	114,500	1,250,000	1,228,106
Colombia	11,736	102,807	45,960	33.0	67.0	—	64	85	45,981	1,127	70.9	29.1	6,748	33,671	4,195
Comoros	5	44	17	88.2	11.8	—	—	—	17	26	...	...	...	...	...
Congo, Dem. Rep. of the	3,197	28,006	5,429	0.4	99.6	—	1,045	52	4,436	90	33.2[1]	66.8[1]	88	96	142
Congo, Rep. of the	118	1,034	443	0.7	99.3	—	—	119	562	202	52.7[1]	47.3[1]	...	...	...
Costa Rica	1,474	12,912	5,788	7.7	81.0	11.3	148	77	5,717	1,488	71.1	28.9	...	...	...
Côte d'Ivoire	1,173	10,275	2,765	38.7	61.3	—	—	—	2,765	193	26.1	73.9	...	...	...
Croatia	3,825	33,507	10,899	49.8	50.2	—	428	3,782	14,253	3,181	68.0	32.0	39	51	394
Cuba	3,988	34,935	14,768	99.1	0.9	—	—	—	14,768	1,340	52.8	47.2	...	—	15
Cyprus	699	6,123	2,954	100.0	—	—	—	—	2,954	3,831	82.4	17.6	...	—	26
Czech Republic	13,852	121,344	65,112	76.9	2.9	20.2	10,844	8,383	62,651	6,093	...	...	5,678	67,529	59,274
Denmark	12,140	106,346	46,104	93.2	0.1	6.7[4]	7,610	3,280	41,774	7,927	...	...	—	—	9,311
Djibouti	85	745	187	100.0	—	—	—	—	187	300	...	...	...	...	...
Dominica	8	70	39	48.7	51.3	—	—	—	39	549	...	...	...	...	...
Dominican Republic	2,198	19,254	7,555	68.7	31.3	—	—	—	7,555	918	72.3	27.7	...	—	81
East Timor	...	...	...	...	...	—	...	...	...	...	...	...	...	...	...
Ecuador	3,935	34,471	10,896	33.6	66.4	—	—	—	10,896	895	56.8	43.2	24	...	...

petroleum fields, or coal mines that is actually collected and marketed. (Much natural gas in Middle Eastern and North African oil fields is flared [burned] because it is often not economical to capture and market it.) Manufactured gas is generally a by-product of industrial operations such as gasworks, coke ovens, and blast furnaces. It is usually burned at the point of production and rarely enters the marketplace. Production of manufactured gas is, therefore, only reported as a percentage of domestic gas consumption.

Crude petroleum. Crude petroleum is the liquid product obtained from oil wells; the term also includes shale oil, tar sand extract, and field or lease condensate. Production and consumption data in the table refer, so far as possible, to the same year so that the relationship between national production and consumption patterns can be clearly seen; both are given in barrels.

Proven reserves are that oil remaining underground in known fields whose existence has been "proved" by the evaluation of nearby producing wells or by seismic tests in sedimentary strata known to contain crude petroleum, and that is judged recoverable within the limits of present technology and economic conditions (prices). The published proven reserve figures do not necessarily reflect the true reserves of a country, because government authorities or corporations often have political or economic motives for withholding or altering such data.

The estimated exhaustion rate of petroleum reserves is an extrapolated ratio of published proven reserves to the current rate of withdrawal/production. Present world published proven reserves will last about 40 to 45 years at the present rate of withdrawal, but there are large country-to-country variations above or below the average.

Data on petroleum and refined product pipelines are provided because of the great importance to both domestic and international energy markets of this means of bringing these energy sources from their production or transportation points to refineries, intermediate consumption and distribution points, and final consumers. Their traffic may represent a very significant fraction of the total movement of goods within a country. Available data for petroleum pipelines are often incomplete and their basis varies internationally, some countries reporting only international shipments, others reporting domestic shipments of 50 kilometres or more, and so on.

For data in the hydrocarbons portions of the table (coal, natural gas, and petroleum), extensive use has been made of a variety of international sources, such as those of the United Nations, the International Energy Agency (of the Organization for Economic Cooperation and Development), the World Energy Council (in its *World Energy Resources* [triennial]); the U.S. Department of Energy (especially its *International Energy Annual*); and of various industry surveys, such as those published by the *International Petroleum Encyclopedia* and *World Oil.*

natural gas						crude petroleum							country
published proven reserves, 2002 ('000,000,000 cu m)	production		consumption			reserves, 2002		production, 1998 ('000,000 barrels)	consumption, 1998 ('000,000 barrels)	refining capacity, 2002 ('000 barrels per day)	pipelines (latest)		
	natural gas, 1998 ('000,000 cu m)	manufactured gas, 1998 (% of total gas consumption)	amount, 1998 ('000,000 cu m)	residential, 1998 (%)	nonresidential, 1998 (%)	published proven ('000,000 barrels)	years to exhaust proven reserves				length (km)	traffic ('000,000 metric ton-km)	
99	137	...	137	...	...	...	...	—	—	—	...	...	Afghanistan
3.8	17	65.5	17	13.0[1]	87.0[1]	206	86	2.4	2.4	26	251	8	Albania
4,955	79,762	29.1	28,074	11.9[1]	88.1[1]	9,200	30	310	159	450	6,910	...	Algeria
...	...	...	...	...	...	...	...	—	—	—	—	...	American Samoa
...	...	...	...	...	...	...	...	—	—	—	—	—	Andorra
113	565	5.4	565	...	...	5,970	22	270	14	39	179	...	Angola
...	...	...	...	...	...	...	...	—	—	—	—	—	Antigua and Barbuda
758	35,923	10.2	35,479	22.9[1]	77.1[1]	2,881	9.5	302	191	639	6,990	...	Argentina
...	...	...	1,454	...	...	...	...	—	...	—	—	—	Armenia
...	...	...	...	...	...	...	...	—	2.4	280	—	—	Aruba
2,265	33,224	19.2	22,168	...	...	2,828	17	165	218	848	3,000	...	Australia
24	1,615	12.7	8,352	...	...	86	13	6.8	65	209	777	8,165	Austria
850	5,400	3.1	5,400	...	...	1,178	14	83	83	442	1,760	1,705	Azerbaijan
...	—	—	...	...	...	...	...	—	—	—	—	—	Bahamas, The
91	7,957	3.2	7,957	...	...	125	8.9	14	91	249	72	...	Bahrain
292	8,344	0.2	8,344	40.3	59.7	57	...	...	5.4	33	—	—	Bangladesh
0.1	37	13.3	37	34.8	65.2	2.5	4.2	0.6	1.0	4	—	—	Barbados
2.8	271	4.0	16,513	8.1[1]	91.9[1]	198	15	13	84	493	2,570	...	Belarus
—	0.1	16.9	18,237	...	...	...	...	—	235	791	1,328	1,168	Belgium
...	...	...	...	...	...	...	...	—	—	—	—	—	Belize
1.2	...	...	...	...	...	8.2	21	0.4	...	—	—	—	Benin
...	...	...	...	...	...	...	...	—	—	—	—	—	Bermuda
...	...	...	...	...	...	...	...	—	—	—	—	—	Bhutan
775	3,444	20.0	1,578	0.1[1]	99.9[1]	441	32	14	14	63	2,380	...	Bolivia
...	—	...	284	...	...	...	...	—	...	...	174	—	Bosnia and Herzegovina
...	...	[3]	...	...	...	—	...	—	[3]	—	—	—	Botswana
222	6,100	49.8	6,100	2.6	97.4	8,465	24	360	562	1,786	7,742	...	Brazil
239	8,924	1.2	1,371	3.5[1]	96.5[1]	1,160	20	59	1.5	9	553	...	Brunei
1.5	31	15.2	4,142	...	...	15	75	0.2	41	115	525	244	Bulgaria
...	...	...	...	...	...	...	...	—	—	—	—	—	Burkina Faso
...	...	...	...	...	...	...	...	—	—	—	—	—	Burundi
...	...	...	...	...	...	...	...	—	—	—	—	—	Cambodia
110	—	95.6	...	...	...	400	9.3	43	3.7	42	—	—	Cameroon
1,691	177,211	29.9	86,315	...	...	4,858	7.6	641	510	1,944	23,564	99,908	Canada
...	...	...	...	...	...	...	...	—	—	—	—	—	Cape Verde
...	...	...	...	...	...	...	...	—	—	—	—	—	Central African Republic
...	...	...	...	...	...	...	...	—	—	—	—	—	Chad
38	1,819	24.7	3,636	8.7	91.3	150	79	1.9	68	205	1,540	...	Chile
1,212	25,902	49.3	22,540	31.8	68.2	24,000	20	1,179	1,268	4,528	12,397	60,132	China
142	6,524	22.5	6,524	29.9	70.1	1,850	7.0	264	111	286	4,935	...	Colombia
...	...	...	...	...	...	...	...	—	—	—	—	—	Comoros
1.0	—	...	—	—	—	187	22	8.5	0.6	15	390	...	Congo, Dem. Rep. of the
119	3.4	58.0	3.4	...	...	1,506	16	95	4.3	21	25	...	Congo, Rep. of the
...	—	—	—	—	—	...	...	—	0.4	15	176	...	Costa Rica
30	—	59.4	—	—	—	100	11	9.3	31	65	—	—	Côte d'Ivoire
34	1,529	20.3	2,575	16.3[1]	83.7[1]	92	7.7	12	39	293	690	951	Croatia
14	24	71.3	24	3.4[1]	96.6[1]	314	26	12	18	301	—	—	Cuba
—	—	71.8	—	—	—	...	...	—	7.9	27	—	—	Cyprus
2.1	239	20.1	10,825	...	...	15	13	1.2	46	198	736	2,078	Czech Republic
87	7,091	11.1	4,063	...	...	1,113	13	88	61	176	688	1,385	Denmark
...	...	...	...	...	...	...	...	—	—	—	—	—	Djibouti
...	...	...	...	...	...	—	—	—	—	—	—	—	Dominica
—	—	7.9	...	...	...	...	...	—	19	49	104	...	Dominican Republic
...	...	...	...	...	...	...	...	...	...	...	...	...	East Timor
109	318	30.4	318	—	—	2,115	14	147	57	176	2,158	...	Ecuador

Energy (continued)

country	electricity												coal		
	installed capacity, 1998 ('000 kW)	production, 1998		power source, 1998			trade, 1998		consumption				reserves, latest ('000,000 metric tons)	pro-duction, 1998 ('000 metric tons)	con-sump-tion, 1998 ('000 metric tons)
		capacity ('000,000 kW-hr)	amount ('000,000 kW-hr)	fossil fuel (%)	hydro-power (%)	nuclear fuel (%)	exports ('000,000 kW-hr)	imports ('000,000 kW-hr)	amount, 1998 ('000,000 kW-hr)	per capita, 1998 (kW-hr)	resi-dential, 1998 (%)	non-resi-dential, 1998 (%)			
Egypt	17,499	153,291	57,100	79.0	21.0	—	—	—	57,100	865	74.4	25.6	22	—	1,487
El Salvador	996	8,725	3,821	47.8	39.5	12.7[4]	23	61	3,859	640	67.4	32.6	...	...	...
Equatorial Guinea	5	44	21	90.5	9.5	—	—	—	21	49	...	...	...	...	...
Eritrea	[5]	[5]	[5]	[5]	[5]	...	...	...	[5]	[5]	[5]	[5]	...	...	...
Estonia	2,624	22,986	8,521	99.9	0.1	—	528	138	8,131	5,690	55.4	44.6	...	12,464	13,963
Ethiopia	456[5]	3,995[5]	1,676[5]	5.8[5]	94.2[5]	—	—	—	1,676[5]	27[5]	35.6[5]	64.4[5]	61	—	—
Faroe Islands	92	806	183	55.7	43.7	0.6[4]	—	—	183	4,256	...	...	...	—	—
Fiji	200	1,752	535	20.6	79.4	—	—	—	535	672	22.0	78.0	...	—	20
Finland	14,905	130,568	70,168	47.4	21.4	31.2	276	9,582	79,474	15,420	...	...	...	—	4,017
France	112,435[6]	984,931[6]	504,582[6]	9.8[6]	13.1[6]	77.1[6]	62,152[6]	4,590[6]	447,020[6]	7,613[6]	...	...	36	6,112[6]	25,001[6]
French Guiana	139	1,218	453	100.0	—	—	—	—	453	2,713	55.4	44.6	...	...	...
French Polynesia	89	780	361	62.6	37.4	—	—	—	361	1,648	...	...	...	...	...
Gabon	379	3,320	1,277	35.4	64.6	—	—	—	1,277	1,094	41.9	58.1	...	...	...
Gambia, The	29	254	77	100.0	—	—	—	—	77	63	...	...	...	...	...
Gaza Strip	...	...	...	...	...	...	...	...	...	...	...	...	...	...	...
Georgia	4,558	39,928	8,069	21.0	79.0	—	796	698	7,971	1,576	...	...	...	14	29
Germany	115,443	1,011,281	556,400	67.2	3.8	29.0	38,953	38,315	555,762	6,785	...	...	66,000	211,374	239,748
Ghana	1,187	10,398	6,662	0.1	99.9	—	232	4	6,434	336	7.2	92.8	...	—	3
Greece	10,146	88,879	46,363	91.1	8.7	0.2[4]	890	2,500	47,973	4,526	...	...	2,874	60,884	61,940
Greenland	106	929	260	100.0	—	—	—	—	260	4,643	...	...	183	...	...
Grenada	15	131	110	100.0	—	—	—	—	110	1,183	72.9	27.1	...	...	...
Guadeloupe	417	3,653	1,211	100.0	—	—	—	—	1,211	2,734	...	...	...	...	...
Guam	302	2,646	830	100.0	—	—	—	—	830	5,155	...	...	...	...	...
Guatemala	1,454	12,737	4,456	53.4	46.6	—	61	23	4,418	409	67.3	32.7	...	...	...
Guernsey	...	...	...	...	...	...	...	...	...	...	...	...	...	...	...
Guinea	186	1,629	545	65.1	34.9	—	—	—	545	74	...	...	...	...	...
Guinea-Bissau	11	96	53	100.0	—	—	—	—	53	46	...	...	...	...	...
Guyana	202	1,770	830	99.4	0.6	—	—	—	830	976	...	...	...	...	...
Haiti	264	2,313	691	59.8	40.2	—	—	—	691	87	44.1	55.9	13[2]	...	...
Honduras	518	4,538	3,690	47.5	52.5	—	1	42	3,731	607	69.5	30.5	21[2]	...	...
Hong Kong	11,312	99,093	31,414	100.0	—	—	610	7,760	38,564	5,790	25.2[1]	74.8[1]	...	—	7,102
Hungary	7,012	61,425	37,188	62.1	0.4	37.5	3,302	4,042	37,928	3,749	65.5	34.5	1,097	14,650	16,607
Iceland	1,245	10,906	6,281	0.1	89.5	10.4[4]	—	—	6,281	22,757	...	...	...	—	70
India	107,453	941,288	494,380	80.6	16.7	2.7	86	1,585	495,879	505	53.5	46.5	84,396	321,166	335,260
Indonesia	22,867	200,315	90,027	81.3	15.8	2.9[4]	—	—	90,027	436	46.9	53.1	5,370	60,321	14,034
Iran	30,627	268,293	103,412	93.2	6.8	—	—	—	103,412	1,573	31.6[1]	68.4[1]	1,710	1,169	1,466
Iraq	9,500	83,220	30,346	98.1	1.9	—	—	—	30,346	1,392	...	...	...	—	—
Ireland	4,412	38,649	21,387	94.3	5.6	0.1	73	152	21,612	5,871	...	...	14	—	2,918
Isle of Man	...	...	...	100.0	—	—	—	—	...	...	...	...	...	...	...
Israel	7,860	68,854	37,964	99.9	0.1	—	1,055	—	36,909	6,168	61.6	38.4	...	—	9,284
Italy	68,422[7]	599,377[7]	260,241[7]	80.2[7]	18.2[7]	1.6[4, 7]	901[7]	41,633[7]	300,973[7]	5,244[7]	...	...	34	189[7]	16,413[7]
Jamaica	1,182	10,354	6,480	97.8	2.2	—	—	—	6,480	2,553	36.2	63.8	...	—	71
Japan	245,258	2,148,460	1,046,294	58.1	9.8	32.1	—	—	1,046,294	8,285	...	...	773	3,681	132,849
Jersey	...	...	...	...	...	...	...	...	...	...	...	...	...	...	...
Jordan	1,295	11,344	6,745	99.8	0.2	—	4	...	6,741	1,069	66.1	33.9	...	...	...
Kazakhstan	18,960	166,090	49,144	87.5	12.5	—	3,441	7,252	52,955	3,245	10.6[1]	89.4[1]	34,000	69,773	47,310
Kenya	889	7,788	4,439	13.8	73.8	12.4[4]	—	146	4,585	158	38.8	61.2	...	—	65
Kiribati	2	18	7	100.0	—	—	—	—	7	86	...	...	...	—	—
Korea, North	9,500	83,220	30,989	35.7	64.3	—	—	—	30,989	1,327	...	...	600	84,910	86,583
Korea, South	47,983	420,331	240,587	60.2	2.5	37.3	—	—	240,587	5,218	41.8	58.2	78	4,361	55,892
Kuwait	6,997	61,294	30,514	100.0	—	—	—	—	30,514	16,849	93.3	6.7	...	...	...
Kyrgyzstan	3,690	32,324	11,615	14.4	85.6	—	7,125	6,399	10,889	2,345	25.4[1]	...	812	680	1,466
Laos	256	2,243	1,225	3.5	96.5	—	774	46	497	96	...	...	...	1	1
Latvia	2,103	18,422	5,796	25.5	74.5	—	385	914	6,325	2,609	59.5	40.5	...	—	146
Lebanon	1,400	12,264	9,011	91.3	8.7	—	—	300	9,311	2,918	54.5[1]	45.5[1]	...	—	121
Lesotho	[3]	[3]	[3]	[3]	[3]	[3]	[3]	[3]	[3]	[3]	...	...	...	[3]	[3]
Liberia	334	2,926	498	62.5	37.5	—	—	—	498	187	...	...	...	...	...
Libya	4,600	40,296	19,496	100.0	—	—	—	—	19,496	3,652	...	...	—	—	5
Liechtenstein	[8]	[8]	[8]	[8]	[8]	[8]	[8]	[8]	[8]	[8]	...	...	...	—	[8]
Lithuania	5,791	50,729	17,631	18.0	5.1	76.9	6,466	384	11,549	3,126	16.2[1]	83.8[1]	...	...	219
Luxembourg	1,268	11,108	1,159	9.9	90.1	—	924	6,338	6,573	15,576	...	...	...	—	152
Macau	352	3,084	1,539	100.0	—	—	1	173	1,711	3,728	87.2	12.8	...	—	—
Macedonia	1,494	13,087	7,048	84.6	15.4	—	2	—	7,046	3,525	44.5[1]	55.5[1]	...	8,176	8,501
Madagascar	220	1,927	785	34.9	65.1	—	—	—	785	52	31.7	68.3	1,075[2]	—	15
Malawi	185	1,621	877	2.2	97.8	—	2	—	875	85	67.4	32.6	1.8	—	17
Malaysia	13,604	119,171	60,471	92.1	7.9	—	5	—	60,466	2,824	48.4	51.6	3.6	351	2,633
Maldives	25	219	82	100.0	—	—	—	—	82	303	...	...	...	...	...
Mali	114	999	398	42.0	58.0	—	—	—	398	37	99.0	1.0	—	...	...
Malta	250	2,190	1,518	100.0	—	—	—	—	1,518	3,953	29.2[1]	70.8[1]	...	—	320
Marshall Islands	99[9]	867[9]	...	...	...	—	—	—	...	...	...	...	...	...	...
Martinique	396	3,469	1,080	100.0	—	—	—	—	1,080	2,776	...	...	...	...	...
Mauritania	105	920	155	81.3	18.7	—	—	—	155	61	...	...	...	—	6
Mauritius	364	3,189	1,283	91.7	8.3	—	—	—	1,283	1,122	64.7	35.3	...	—	68
Mayotte	...	...	...	...	...	—	—	—	...	...	...	...	...	...	...
Mexico	45,615	399,587	183,841	78.3	13.5	8.2[4]	272	1,705	185,274	1,933	36.9	63.1	1,211	11,232	12,034
Micronesia	...	...	...	...	...	—	...	...	...	...	...	...	...	...	...
Moldova	1,022	8,953	4,584	98.2	1.8	—	—	1,916	6,500	1,485	...	...	...	—	546
Monaco	[6]	[6]	[6]	[6]	[6]	[6]	[6]	[6]	[6]	[6]	...	...	...	[6]	[6]
Mongolia	901	7,893	2,745	100.0	—	—	60	367	3,052	1,183	...	...	24,000[2]	5,057	5,092
Morocco	4,037	35,364	13,440	86.9	13.1	—	—	705	14,145	517	54.5	45.5	5.4	269	3,497
Mozambique	2,383	20,875	7,345	7.1	92.9	—	5,677	350	2,018	107	33.2[1]	66.8[1]	212	18	34
Myanmar (Burma)	1,402	12,282	4,139	77.1	22.9	—	—	—	4,139	94	75.5	24.5	1.8	59	65
Namibia	[3]	[3]	[3]	[3]	[3]	[3]	[3]	[3]	[3]	[3]	...	...	...	[3]	[3]
Nauru	10	88	32	100.0	—	—	—	—	32	2,909	...	...	...	...	...
Nepal	327	2,865	1,202	13.2	86.8	—	63	210	1,349	59	59.5	40.5	1.8	16	339

natural gas						crude petroleum							country
published proven reserves, 2002 ('000,000,-000 cu m)	production		consumption			reserves, 2002		production, 1998 ('000,000 barrels)	consumption, 1998 ('000,000 barrels)	refining capacity, 2002 ('000 barrels per day)	pipelines (latest)		
	natural gas, 1998 ('000,000 cu m)	manufactured gas, 1998 (% of total gas consumption)	amount, 1998 ('000,000 cu m)	residential, 1998 (%)	non-residential, 1998 (%)	published proven ('000,000 barrels)	years to exhaust proven reserves				length (km)	traffic ('000,000 metric ton-km)	
1,533	12,356	11.9	12,356	5.1[1]	94.9[1]	2,948	10	292	213	726	1,767	...	Egypt
—	—	13.9	—	—	—	...	...	—	6.7	22	—	—	El Salvador
100	...	...	...	...	...	12	0.4	30	0.3	—	—	—	Equatorial Guinea
...	...	[5]	...	...	...	...	...	...	[5]	15	—	—	Eritrea
...	...	11.9	636	8.2[1]	91.8[1]	—	—	—	8.4	...	—	—	Estonia
25	—	100.0[5]	—	...	...	0.4	...	—	1.2[5]	—	—	—	Ethiopia
...	...	...	...	...	...	...	...	—	—	—	—	—	Faroe Islands
...	—	...	—	—	—	...	...	—	—	—	—	—	Fiji
—	—	28.8	4,027	...	...	...	...	—	84	239	—	—	Finland
14	2,279	17.8[6]	44,650[6]	32.4[1, 6]	67.6[1, 6]	149	12	12	661[6]	1,896	7,546	24,429	France
...	...	...	...	...	...	...	...	—	—	—	—	—	French Guiana
...	...	...	...	...	...	...	...	—	—	—	—	—	French Polynesia
99	654	1.7	654	19.7[1]	80.3[1]	2,499	19	133	5.3	17	284	...	Gabon
...	...	...	...	...	...	...	...	—	—	—	—	—	Gambia, The
...	...	...	...	...	...	...	...	—	—	—	—	—	Gaza Strip
8.5	—	...	820	...	...	35	39	0.9	0.4	106	670	...	Georgia
254	23,229	14.1	110,619	...	...	364	17	21	787	2,259	2,240	37,250	Germany
23	—	94.8	—	—	—	17	...	...	7.3	45	—	—	Ghana
1.0	47	65.5	864	...	...	9	4.3	2.1	133	407	573	...	Greece
...	...	...	...	...	...	...	...	—	—	—	—	—	Greenland
...	...	...	...	...	...	...	...	—	—	—	—	—	Grenada
...	...	...	...	...	...	...	...	—	—	—	—	—	Guadeloupe
...	—	—	—	—	—	...	...	—	—	—	—	—	Guam
2.8	11	2.8	11	...	...	526	57	9.2	6.7	16	275	...	Guatemala
...	...	...	...	...	...	...	...	—	—	—	—	—	Guernsey
...	...	...	...	...	...	...	...	—	—	—	—	—	Guinea
...	...	...	...	...	...	...	...	—	—	—	—	—	Guinea-Bissau
...	...	...	...	...	...	...	...	—	—	—	—	—	Guyana
...	...	...	...	...	...	...	...	—	—	—	—	—	Haiti
—	—	...	—	—	—	...	...	—	12	...	—	—	Honduras
...	—	18.2	2,590	—	—	...	...	—	—	—	—	—	Hong Kong
65	3,803	6.6	12,538	...	...	111	13	8.4	53	161	1,204	2,470	Hungary
...	...	...	...	...	...	...	...	—	7.3	—	—	—	Iceland
437	26,455	14.2	26,455	1.3[1]	98.7[1]	4,840	19	251	544	2,135	5,692	...	India
2,478	75,271	13.3	25,749	2.7[1]	97.3[1]	5,000	10	495	342	993	2,961	...	Indonesia
26,600	49,573	8.4	51,436	26.8[1]	73.2[1]	89,700	68	1,317	454	1,484	9,800	...	Iran
3,188	2,950	48.2	2,950	...	...	112,500	146	773	188	418	5,075	...	Iraq
20	1,645	3.5	3,278	...	...	—	...	—	22	71	—	—	Ireland
...	—	...	...	...	...	...	...	—	...	—	—	—	Isle of Man
42	12	118.7	12	—	100.0[1]	3.8	—	—	86	220	998	...	Israel
191	19,013	11.2[7]	62,438[7]	...	...	622	16	38	622[7]	2,283	3,851	13,981	Italy
—	—	26.0	—	—	—	...	...	—	8.8	34	10	...	Jamaica
40	2,301	30.1	71,037	...	...	59	18	3.3	1,560	4,786	406	...	Japan
...	...	...	...	...	...	...	...	—	—	—	—	—	Jersey
5.7	270	36.3	270	—	—	0.9	...	...	25	90	209	...	Jordan
1,841	7,679	2.0	8,400	...	...	5,417	31	176	56	427	6,965	26,581	Kazakhstan
—	—	100.0	—	—	—	...	...	—	16	90	483	...	Kenya
...	...	...	...	...	...	...	...	—	—	—	—	—	Kiribati
...	...	...	...	...	...	...	...	—	14	71	217	...	Korea, North
—	—	38.8	14,622	...	...	...	...	—	827	2,560	455	...	Korea, South
1,489	9,491	40.2	9,491	25.0[1]	75.0[1]	96,500	128	753	316	773	917	...	Kuwait
5.7	18	...	1,017	...	...	40	67	0.6	1.0	10	—	—	Kyrgyzstan
...	...	...	...	...	...	...	...	—	—	—	136	...	Laos
...	—	...	1,244	10.5[1]	89.5[1]	...	...	—	...	...	1,530	6,569	Latvia
—	—	...	...	...	...	...	...	—	...	38	72	...	Lebanon
—	—	[3]	—	...	...	...	...	—	[3]	—	—	—	Lesotho
—	—	...	—	...	...	...	...	—	—	15	—	—	Liberia
1,328	6,360	17.6	5,474	...	...	29,500	58	507	98	343	4,826	...	Libya
—	—	[8]	[8]	...	...	...	...	—	[8]	—	—	—	Liechtenstein
—	...	22.4	1,882	9.3[1]	90.7[1]	12	6.0	2.0	47	263	105	3,457	Lithuania
...	—	5.0	754	...	...	...	...	—	...	—	48	...	Luxembourg
...	...	...	...	...	...	...	...	—	—	—	—	—	Macau
...	—	34.6	...	...	...	...	...	—	5.6	51	—	—	Macedonia
2.8	—	75.0	—	...	...	...	...	—	1.6	15	—	—	Madagascar
...	—	—	—	—	—	...	...	—	—	—	—	—	Malawi
2,337	38,375	11.1	19,126	0.3	99.7	3,000	12	260	134	515	1,307	...	Malaysia
...	...	...	...	...	...	...	...	—	—	—	—	—	Maldives
...	...	...	...	...	...	...	...	—	—	—	—	—	Mali
—	...	—	...	...	...	...	...	—	—	—	—	—	Malta
...	...	...	...	...	...	...	...	—	—	...	—	—	Marshall Islands
—	—	161.5	...	...	...	...	...	—	5.8	17	—	—	Martinique
...	...	88.4	...	...	...	...	...	—	6.9	—	—	—	Mauritania
...	...	...	...	...	...	...	...	—	—	—	—	—	Mauritius
...	...	...	...	...	...	...	...	—	—	—	—	—	Mayotte
1,103	31,480	21.3	32,613	...	...	26,941	24	1,116	485	1,525	38,350	...	Mexico
...	...	...	...	...	...	...	...	—	—	...	—	—	Micronesia
...	—	...	3,373	11.6[1]	88.4[1]	...	...	—	...	...	—	—	Moldova
...	...	[6]	[6]	[6]	[6]	...	...	—	[6]	—	—	—	Monaco
...	...	...	...	...	...	...	...	—	3.3	—	—	—	Mongolia
1.3	37	23.4	37	—	100.0[1]	1.8	...	...	47	155	362	...	Morocco
57	—	—	—	...	...	...	...	—	—	...	595	...	Mozambique
346	1,641	1.2	1,641	0.3[1]	99.7[1]	50	19	2.7	7.3	32	1,343	...	Myanmar (Burma)
85	—	[3]	—	...	...	...	...	—	[3]	—	—	—	Namibia
...	...	...	...	...	...	...	...	—	—	—	—	—	Nauru
...	—	—	—	—	—	...	...	—	—	—	—	—	Nepal

Energy (continued)

country	electricity												coal		
	installed capacity, 1998 ('000 kW)	production, 1998		power source, 1998			trade, 1998		consumption				reserves, latest ('000,000 metric tons)	production, 1998 ('000 metric tons)	consumption, 1998 ('000 metric tons)
		capacity ('000,000 kW-hr)	amount ('000,000 kW-hr)	fossil fuel (%)	hydropower (%)	nuclear fuel (%)	exports ('000,000 kW-hr)	imports ('000,000 kW-hr)	amount, 1998 ('000,000 kW-hr)	per capita, 1998 (kW-hr)	residential, 1998 (%)	non-residential, 1998 (%)			
Netherlands, The	20,164	176,637	90,903	95.0	0.1	4.9	420	12,234	102,717	6,552	...	...	497	—	15,006
Netherlands Antilles	220	1,927	1,490	100.0	—	—	—	—	1,490	6,995	...	...	...	...	...
New Caledonia	253	2,216	1,568	69.5	30.5	—	—	—	1,568	7,612	...	...	1.8	—	165
New Zealand	7,960	69,730	37,566	28.4	64.9	6.7[4]	—	—	37,566	9,896	...	...	572	3,317	2,330
Nicaragua	614	5,379	2,153	50.3	19.1	30.6[4]	—	43	2,196	457	70.7	29.3	...	...	...
Niger	105	920	234	100.0	—	—	—	198	432	43	56.0	44.0	70	174	174
Nigeria	5,881	51,518	15,716	65.1	34.9	—	...	—	15,716	148	50.1[1]	49.9[1]	190	59	59
Northern Mariana Islands	...	...	...	...	...	—	...	...	...	...	...	...	...	...	...
Norway	29,277	256,467	117,043	0.6	99.4	—	4,415	8,046	120,674	27,277	...	...	0.9	328	985
Oman	2,135	18,703	10,672	100.0	—	—	—	—	10,672	4,480	...	...	...	...	...
Pakistan	15,658	137,164	62,104	63.9	35.5	0.6	—	—	62,104	419	72.3	27.7	2,265	3,159	4,119
Palau	62	543	208	85.6	14.4	—	—	—	208	10,947	...	...	—	—	—
Panama	1,094	9,583	4,498	29.0	71.0	—	23	57	4,532	1,638	79.5	20.5	...	—	59
Papua New Guinea	490	4,292	1,795	72.1	27.9	—	—	—	1,795	390	27.9	72.1	...	...	1
Paraguay	7,054	61,793	50,930	0.1	99.9	—	45,208	—	5,722	1,096	79.0	21.0	...	...	...
Peru	5,191	45,473	18,583	25.7	74.3	—	—	1	18,584	749	67.7	32.3	1,060	21	451
Philippines	11,601	101,625	41,192	65.5	17.8	16.7[4]	—	—	41,192	565	65.3	34.7	332	1,002	5,287
Poland	29,469	258,148	142,789	97.0	3.0	—	8,082	4,608	139,315	3,598	41.8	58.2	22,160	177,965	155,685
Portugal	9,787	85,734	38,985	66.1	33.5	0.4[4]	3,700	3,974	39,259	3,978	...	...	36	—	5,099
Puerto Rico	4,430	38,807	20,360	99.4	0.6	—	—	—	20,360	5,344	...	...	...	—	175
Qatar	1,899	16,635	8,170	100.0	—	—	—	—	8,170	14,111	74.9	25.1	...	...	...
Réunion	434	3,802	1,566	64.4	35.6	—	—	—	1,566	2,296	...	...	...	...	...
Romania	22,558	197,608	53,496	54.8	35.3	9.9	715	1,181	53,962	2,401	27.1	72.9	1,457	26,231	31,304
Russia	210,957	1,847,983	827,133	68.2	19.3	12.5	26,275	8,261	809,119	5,488	36.1	63.9	157,010	235,319	228,699
Rwanda	34	298	166	2.4	97.6	—	3	15	178	27	...	...	...	...	...
St. Kitts and Nevis	16	140	92	100.0	—	—	—	—	92	2,359	...	...	...	...	...
St. Lucia	22	193	116	100.0	—	—	—	—	116	773	...	...	...	...	...
St. Vincent and the Grenadines	16	140	85	74.1	25.9	—	—	—	85	759	...	...	...	...	...
Samoa	19	166	65	61.5	38.5	—	—	—	65	374	...	...	...	...	...
San Marino	[7]	[7]	[7]	[7]	[7]	[7]	[7]	[7]	[7]	[7]	...	...	...	[7]	[7]
São Tomé and Príncipe	6	53	15	46.7	53.3	—	—	—	15	106	...	...	...	...	...
Saudi Arabia	22,575	197,757	112,691	100.0	—	—	—	—	112,691	5,584	47.2[1]	52.8[1]	...	...	...
Senegal	235	2,059	1,252	100.0	—	—	—	—	1,252	139	16.7	83.3	...	...	...
Serbia and Montenegro	11,779	103,184	40,651	69.9	30.1	—	268	—	40,383	3,797	41.4[1]	...	16,255	44,072	44,124
Seychelles	28	245	159	100.0	—	—	—	—	159	2,092	24.3	75.7	...	...	...
Sierra Leone	126	1,104	242	100.0	—	—	—	—	242	53	...	...	...	—	—
Singapore	5,665	49,625	28,283	100.0	—	—	—	—	28,283	8,137	16.0[1]	84.0[1]	...	—	—
Slovakia	7,778	68,135	25,465	37.3	17.9	44.8	157	1,447	26,755	4,976	20.6[1]	79.4[1]	172	3,951	10,323
Slovenia	2,571	22,522	13,718	38.1	25.1	36.8	2,630	706	11,794	5,918	24.8[1]	75.2[1]	275	4,891	5,489
Solomon Islands	12	105	32	100.0	—	—	—	—	32	77	...	...	...	...	...
Somalia	79	692	278	100.0	—	—	—	—	278	30	...	...	...	...	...
South Africa	35,897[3]	314,458[3]	193,946[3]	92.2[3]	0.8[3]	7.0[3]	4,532[3]	3,078[3]	192,492[3]	4,221[3]	28.5	71.5	49,520	225,901[3]	159,436[3]
Spain	50,081	438,710	195,280	50.8	18.3	30.9	5,562	8,964	198,682	5,014	...	...	660	25,962	38,995
Sri Lanka	1,747	15,304	5,683	31.1	68.9	—	—	—	5,683	308	62.7	37.3	...	—	10
Sudan, The	606	5,309	1,346	29.4	70.6	—	—	—	1,346	48	18.6[1]	81.4[1]	...	—	—
Suriname	425	3,723	1,621	20.2	79.8	—	—	—	1,621	3,915	...	...	...	—	—
Swaziland	[3]	[3]	[3]	[3]	[3]	[3]	[3]	[3]	[3]	[3]	...	...	208	[3]	[3]
Sweden	33,949	297,393	158,277	6.3	47.0	46.7	16,799	6,102	147,580	16,629	...	...	0.9	...	2,917
Switzerland	16,692[8]	146,222[8]	62,909[8]	3.9[8]	55.1[8]	41.0[8]	29,561[8]	23,607[8]	56,955[8]	7,769[8]	...	...	...	—	108[8]
Syria	4,510	39,508	19,841	86.4	13.6	—	—	—	19,841	1,294	34.6[1]	65.4[1]	...	—	—
Taiwan	26,680	233,717	142,964	67.8	7.4	24.8	—	—	128,130	5,858	35.2	64.8	0.9	79	...
Tajikistan	4,443	38,921	14,422	1.9	98.1	—	3,724	3,969	14,667	2,438	14.6[1]	85.4[1]	...	20	126
Tanzania	543	4,757	1,747	13.8	86.2	—	—	—	1,747	54	36.6[1]	63.4[1]	200	5	5
Thailand	21,500	188,340	94,769	94.5	5.5	—	153	1,623	96,239	1,596	58.3	41.7	1,268	20,163	22,132
Togo	34	298	94	93.6	6.4	—	—	321	415	94	...	...	...	...	...
Tonga	7	61	34	100.0	—	—	—	—	34	347	...	...	...	...	...
Trinidad and Tobago	1,150	10,074	5,191	100.0	—	—	—	—	5,191	4,046	35.3	64.7	...	—	—
Tunisia	2,290	20,060	8,958	99.2	0.8	—	130	126	8,954	959	54.1	45.9	—	...	1
Turkey	23,351	204,555	111,022	61.9	38.0	0.1[4]	298	3,298	114,022	1,768	...	...	3,689	67,383	77,673
Turkmenistan	3,930	34,427	9,416	99.9	0.1	—	4,059	950	6,307	1,464	...	...	...	...	—
Tuvalu	...	...	...	...	...	...	...	...	...	...	...	...	...	...	...
Uganda	189	1,656	1,273	0.4	99.6	—	159	—	1,114	54	...	...	...	...	...
Ukraine	53,868	471,884	172,822	47.3	9.2	43.5	10,728	10,056	172,150	3,385	...	...	34,153	77,176	83,706
United Arab Emirates	5,710	50,020	31,392	100.0	—	—	—	—	31,392	13,341	...	...	...	...	...
United Kingdom	73,405	643,028	358,714	70.0	1.9	28.1	162	12,630	371,182	6,329	...	...	1,500	41,420	60,483
United States	792,839	6,945,270	3,833,979	72.4	8.4	19.2	12,730	39,513	3,860,762	14,089	...	...	248,257	1,013,383	926,634
Uruguay	2,179	19,088	9,570	9.5	90.5	—	2,234	78	7,414	2,254	76.0	34.0	...	—	1
Uzbekistan	11,709	102,571	45,900	87.5	12.5	—	5,100	6,000	46,800	1,985	...	...	4,000	2,923	2,920
Vanuatu	11	96	30	100.0	—	—	—	—	30	165	...	...	...	...	...
Venezuela	21,275	186,369	80,904	28.4	71.6	—	—	—	80,904	3,481	23.8	76.2	479	7,456	1,327
Vietnam	4,981	43,634	21,694	45.9	51.1	3.0[4]	—	—	21,694	280	32.6[1]	67.4[1]	150	11,672	6,162
Virgin Islands (U.S.)	323	2,829	1,082	100.0	—	—	—	—	1,082	11,511	...	...	...	—	254
West Bank	...	...	...	...	...	...	...	...	...	...	...	...	...	...	...
Western Sahara	56	491	87	100.0	—	—	—	—	87	316	...	...	...	...	...
Yemen	810	7,096	2,507	100.0	—	—	—	—	2,507	148	...	...	1[2]	...	...
Zambia	2,275	19,929	7,603	0.5	99.5	—	1,500	20	6,123	697	33.0	67.0	10	205	203
Zimbabwe	2,011	17,616	6,677	71.2	28.8	—	—	3,100	9,777	859	42.6	57.4	502	5,047	4,758

natural gas						crude petroleum							country
published proven reserves, 2002 ('000,000,000 cu m)	production		consumption			reserves, 2002		production, 1998 ('000,000 barrels)	consumption, 1998 ('000,000 barrels)	refining capacity, 2002 ('000 barrels per day)	pipelines (latest)		
	natural gas, 1998 ('000,000 cu m)	manufactured gas, 1998 (% of total gas consumption)	amount, 1998 ('000,000 cu m)	residential, 1998 (%)	nonresidential, 1998 (%)	published proven ('000,000 barrels)	years to exhaust proven reserves				length (km)	traffic ('000,000 metric ton-km)	
1,615	84,541	18.6	51,225	...	...	107	8.9	12	400	1,206	1,383	5,503	Netherlands, The
—	—	117.2	...	...	...	...	...	—	103	320	—	—	Netherlands Antilles
...	...	...	...	...	...	...	...	—	—	—	—	—	New Caledonia
59	4,457	9.0	4,456	...	...	90	5.3	17	40	106	160	...	New Zealand
—	—	51.3	—	—	—	...	...	—	6.2	20	56	...	Nicaragua
...	—	—	—	—	—	...	...	—	—	—	—	—	Niger
4,502	5,900	1.4	5,900	—	100.0[1]	24,000	34	709	58	439	5,042	...	Nigeria
...	...	...	...	...	...	...	...	—	—	...	—	—	Northern Mariana Islands
2,186	49,569	23.6	6,792	...	...	9,447	8.3	1,142	106	310	5,747	3,485	Norway
864	6,029	1.4	6,029	...	...	5,506	17	327	27	85	1,300	...	Oman
681	18,738	1.2	18,738	41.2	58.8	298	14	21	49	239	1,135	...	Pakistan
—	—	—	...	...	...	—	—	—	...	...	—	—	Palau
—	—	35.6	61	—	—	...	...	—	17	60	130	...	Panama
425	83	...	83	—	—	238	8.2	29	0.4	—	—	—	Papua New Guinea
—	—	—	...	—	—	...	...	—	1.1	8	—	—	Paraguay
245	724	36.1	724	61.4[1]	38.6[1]	323	7.7	42	60	182	800	...	Peru
105	—	44.8	—	—	—	178	593	0.3	121	420	357	...	Philippines
164	4,818	23.7	14,109	45.0[1]	55.0[1]	115	43	2.7	119	382	2,280	18,448	Poland
—	—	29.6	831	...	...	...	...	—	99	304	80	...	Portugal
—	—	127.8	...	...	...	...	...	—	48	49	—	—	Puerto Rico
21,456	19,580	7.6	19,580	—	100.0[1]	15,207	70	218	28	58	235	...	Qatar
...	...	...	...	...	...	...	...	—	...	—	—	—	Réunion
121	14,881	13.1	19,918	9.6[1]	90.4[1]	1,154	25	47	92	504	4,229	2,257	Romania
48,139	635,485	5.1	412,137	11.2[1]	88.8[1]	48,573	22	2,162	1,216	5,435	63,000	1,899,000	Russia
57	0.2	—	0.2	...	...	...	...	—	—	—	—	—	Rwanda
...	...	...	...	...	...	...	...	—	—	—	—	—	St. Kitts and Nevis
...	...	...	...	...	...	...	...	—	—	—	—	—	St. Lucia
...	...	...	...	...	...	...	...	—	—	—	—	—	St. Vincent and the Grenadines
...	...	...	...	...	...	...	...	...	...	—	—	—	Samoa
...	...	[7]	[7]	...	...	...	...	—	[7]	—	—	—	San Marino
...	...	...	...	...	...	...	...	—	—	—	—	—	São Tomé and Príncipe
6,349	46,819	42.5	46,819	...	...	261,750	83	3,135	670	1,745	6,550	...	Saudi Arabia
—	—	13.1	...	...	...	...	...	—	6.4	27	—	—	Senegal
48	665	2.0	2,370	...	...	78	11	6.8	21	158	545	...	Serbia and Montenegro
...	...	...	...	...	...	...	...	—	—	—	—	—	Seychelles
—	...	...	...	...	...	...	...	—	1.7	10	—	—	Sierra Leone
—	—	338.7	—	—	—	...	...	—	453	1,259	—	—	Singapore
14	284	10.1	8,066	20.9[1]	79.1[1]	9	23	0.4	40	115	...	...	Slovakia
3.4	7	...	877	7.7[1]	92.3[1]	7	...	...	1.8	14	290	128	Slovenia
...	—	—	—	—	—	...	...	—	—	—	—	—	Solomon Islands
5.7	—	...	...	...	...	...	...	—	...	10	15	...	Somalia
23	1,383	58.5[3]	1,383	...	...	16	0.3	54	167[3]	469	2,679	...	South Africa
0.5	118	24.6	13,348	...	...	21	5.3	4.0	449	1,294	2,059	6,872	Spain
—	—	39.8	—	—	—	...	...	—	15	50	62	...	Sri Lanka
113	—	58.3	...	...	...	563	—	—	7.6	122	815	...	Sudan, The
—	...	—	...	...	...	74	49	1.5	1.2	7	—	—	Suriname
...	...	[3]	...	...	...	...	...	...	[3]	—	—	—	Swaziland
—	—	39.7	849	...	...	...	...	...	145	424	—	—	Sweden
—	—	15.5[8]	2,884[8]	...	...	...	...	...	37[8]	132	318	234	Switzerland
241	5,125	5.2	5,125	...	...	2,500	13	189	87	242	1,819	...	Syria
76	929	...	6,400	37.5	62.5	4	4.4	0.9	308	920	3,400	...	Taiwan
5.7	29	...	767	...	...	12	120	0.1	0.1	...	—	—	Tajikistan
28	—	100.0	—	...	...	...	...	...	4.3	15	982	...	Tanzania
377	15,605	15.8	15,627	—	100.0[1]	516	52	10	249	682	67	...	Thailand
—	...	...	...	...	...	...	...	...	...	—	—	—	Togo
...	...	...	...	...	...	...	...	...	...	—	—	—	Tonga
557	8,492	6.3	8,492	1.8[1]	98.2[1]	716	16	45	52	160	1,051	...	Trinidad and Tobago
76	1,661	4.7	2,311	3.7[1]	96.3[1]	308	9.9	31	24	34	883	...	Tunisia
8.6	581	18.7	11,176	...	...	296	13	23	198	719	4,059	2,994	Turkey
2,860	12,808	...	9,891	...	...	546	12	47	40	237	250	694	Turkmenistan
...	...	...	...	...	...	...	...	...	...	—	—	—	Tuvalu
...	...	...	...	...	...	...	...	...	...	—	—	—	Uganda
1,121	17,967	4.5	70,925	...	...	395	14	29	100	1,026	8,500	38,402	Ukraine
6,006	37,069	29.6	30,349	...	...	97,800	121	808	89	515	830	...	United Arab Emirates
695	110,575	10.0	108,216	...	...	4,930	5.3	927	623	1,784	3,926	11,666	United Kingdom
4,889	581,153	16.4	655,388	21.3	78.7	22,045	9.8	2,261	5,608	16,564	276,000	843,586	United States
—	—	84.5	—	—	—	...	...	...	13	37	—	—	Uruguay
1,875	48,107	0.6	45,070	...	...	594	15	39	36	222	290	200	Uzbekistan
...	...	...	...	...	...	...	...	...	...	—	—	—	Vanuatu
4,225	36,032	18.0	36,032	13.1	86.9	77,685	66	1,186	388	1,282	6,850	...	Venezuela
193	13	...	13	...	...	600	6.7	89	0.3	—	150	...	Vietnam
—	—	101.4	...	...	...	...	...	...	121	525	—	—	Virgin Islands (U.S.)
...	...	...	...	...	...	...	...	...	...	—	—	—	West Bank
...	...	...	...	...	...	...	...	...	...	—	—	—	Western Sahara
481	...	100.0	...	...	...	4,000	28	142	40	130	676	—	Yemen
—	—	396.0	—	—	—	...	...	...	2.9	24	1,724	...	Zambia
...	—	78.5	—	—	—	...	...	...	...	—	212	...	Zimbabwe

[1]1995. [2]Estimated reserves in place. [3]South Africa includes Botswana, Lesotho, Namibia, and Swaziland. [4]Geothermally generated electricity. [5]Ethiopia includes Eritrea. [6]France includes Monaco. [7]Italy includes San Marino. [8]Switzerland includes Liechtenstein. [9]1993.

Transportation

This table presents data on the transportation infrastructure of the various countries and dependencies of the world and on their commercial passenger and cargo traffic. Most states have roads and airports, with services corresponding to the prevailing level of economic development. A number of states, however, lack railroads or inland waterways because of either geographic constraints or lack of development capital and technical expertise. Pipelines, one of the oldest means of bulk transport if aqueducts are considered, are today among the most narrowly developed transportation modes worldwide for shipment of bulk materials. Because the principal contemporary application of pipeline technology is to facilitate the shipment of hydrocarbon liquids and gases, coverage of pipelines will be found in the "Energy" table. It is, however, also true that pipelines now find increasing application for slurries of coal or other raw materials.

While the United Nations' *Statistical Yearbook, Monthly Bulletin of Statistics,* and *Annual Bulletin of Transport Statistics* provide much data on infrastructure and traffic and have established basic definitions and classifications for transportation statistics, the number of countries covered is limited. Several commercial publications maintain substantial databases and publishing programs for their particular areas of interest: highway and vehicle statistics are provided by the International Road Federation's annual *World Road Statistics;* the International Union of Railway's *International Railway Statistics* and Jane's *World Railways* provide similar data for railways; Lloyd's *Register of Shipping Statistical Tables* summarizes the world's merchant marine; the *Official Airline Guide,* the International Civil Aviation Organization's *Digest of Statistics: Commercial Air Carriers,* and the International Air Transport Association's *World Air Transport Statistics* have also been used to supplement and update data collected by the UN. Because several of these agencies are commercially or insurance-oriented, their data tend to be more complete, accurate, and timely than those of intergovernmental organizations, which depend on periodic responses to questionnaires or publication of results in official sources. All of these international sources have been extensively supplemented by national statistical sources to provide additional data. Such diversity of sources, however, imposes limitations on the comparability of the statistics from country to country because the basis and completeness of data collection and the frequency and timeliness of analysis and publication may vary greatly. Data shown in italic are from 1994 or earlier.

The categories adopted in the table also have special problems of comparability. Total road length is subject to wide international variation of interpretation, as "roads" can mean anything from mere tracks to highly developed highways. Each country also has individual classifications that differ according to climate, availability of road-building materials, traffic patterns, administrative responsibility, and so on. "Paved roads," by contrast, is a much more tightly definable category, but the proportion of paved to total roads may be distorted by the less comparable total road statistics. Automobile and truck and bus fleet statistics, which are usually

Transportation

country	roads and motor vehicles (latest)								railroads (latest)					
	roads			motor vehicles			cargo		track length		traffic			
	length		paved (per-cent)	auto-mobiles	trucks and buses	persons per vehicle	short ton-mi ('000,-000)	metric ton-km ('000,-000)	mi	km	passengers		cargo	
	mi	km									passen-ger-mi ('000,000)	passen-ger-km ('000,000)	short ton-mi ('000,000)	metric ton-km ('000,000)
Afghanistan	13,000	21,000	13	31,000	25,000	401	*1,993*	*2,910*	16	25	…	…	…	…
Albania	11,000	18,000	30	90,766	34,378	25	550	803	416	670	72	116	0.01	0.02
Algeria	63,643	102,424	69	725,000	780,000	19	*9,589*	*14,000*	2,451[2]	3,945[2]	1,135	1,826	1,465	2,139
American Samoa	*217*	*350*	*43*	*4,672*	*199*	*11*	…	…	—	—	—	—	—	—
Andorra	167	269	74	35,358	4,238	1.6	…	…	—	—	—	—	—	—
Angola	45,128	72,626	25	207,000	25,000	41	…	…	1,834[2]	2,952[2]	*203*	*326*	*1,178*	*1,720*
Antigua and Barbuda	155	250	…	13,588	1,342	4.3	…	…	—	—	—	—	—	—
Argentina	135,630	218,276	29	4,901,608	1,379,044	5.7	…	…	21,100[2]	33,958[2]	5,656	9,102	6,234	9,102
Armenia	5,238	8,431	100	1,300	4,460	655	146	213	516	830	29	46	201	324
Aruba	*236*	*380*	*100*	38,834	990	2.4	…	…	—	—	—	—	—	—
Australia	502,356	808,465	40	9,719,900	2,214,900	1.6	*786,643*	*1,148,480*	22,233[2, 7]	35,780[2, 7]	7,152	11,510	87,262	127,400
Austria	124,000	200,000	100	4,009,604	328,591	1.9	10,773	15,670	3,506	5,643	4,953[7]	7,971[7]	10,617[7]	15,500[7]
Azerbaijan	28,502	45,870	94	281,100	104,300	21	484	706	1,317	2,120	342	550	3,160	4,613
Bahamas, The	1,522	2,450	57	89,263	17,228	2.6	…	…	—	—	—	—	—	—
Bahrain	1,966	3,164	77	149,636	32,213	3.4	…	…	—	—	—	—	—	—
Bangladesh	126,773	204,022	12	54,784	69,394	991	…	…	1,699[2]	2,734[2]	3,094	4,980	567	828
Barbados	1,025	1,650	96	43,711	10,583	4.9	…	…	—	—	—	—	—	—
Belarus	33,186	53,407	99	1,132,843	8,867	8.9	6,323	9,232	3,410	5,488	10,485	16,874	20,911	30,529
Belgium	89,353	143,800	97	4,491,734	453,122	2.1	25,586	37,355	2,100[2]	3,380[2]	4,570	7,354	5,063	7,392
Belize	1,398	2,250	18	9,695	11,698	11	…	…	—	—	—	—	—	—
Benin	4,217	6,787	20	37,772	8,058	123	…	…	359	578	75.7	121.8	193.5	311.4
Bermuda	140	225	100	21,220	4,007	2.4	…	…	—	—	—	—	—	—
Bhutan	2,041	3,285	61	*2,590*	*1,367*	*348*	…	…	—	—	—	—	—	—
Bolivia	30,696	49,400	6	223,829	138,536	21	*1,133*	*1,654*	2,187[2]	3,519[2]	84.9	136.7	359.0	524.2
Bosnia and Herzegovina	13,574	21,846	52	96,182	10,919	30	*2,708*	*3,954*	641	1,031	19.3	31.1	63.6	92.8
Botswana	11,388	18,327	25	30,517	59,710	17	…	…	603	971	60	96	545	795
Brazil	1,030,652	1,658,677	9	21,313,351	3,743,836	6.5	*178,359*	*260,400*	18,458[2]	29,706[2]	8,676	12,667	96,741	141,239
Brunei	1,064	1,712	75	91,047	15,918	2.9	…	…	12[13]	19[13]	—	—	…	…
Bulgaria	23,190	37,320	92	1,730,506	251,382	4.2	4,300	6,278	4,020	6,470	2,341	3,767	3,071	4,484
Burkina Faso	7,519	12,100	16	38,220	17,980	190	…	…	386[2]	622[2]	126	202	31	45
Burundi	8,997	14,480	7	19,200	18,240	145	…	…	—	—	—	—	—	—
Cambodia	22,226	35,769	8	52,919	13,574	171	822	1,200	409	649	37	60	25	36
Cameroon	30,074	48,400	8	98,000	64,350	88	*175*	*255*	625[2]	1,006[2]	197	317	556	812
Canada	560,415	901,903	35	13,887,270	3,694,125	1.7	94,584	138,090	40,639	65,403	906	1,458	205,146	299,508
Cape Verde	680	1,095	78	3,280	820	94	…	…	—	—	—	—	—	—
Central African Republic	14,900	24,000	2	9,500	7,000	195	41	60	—	—	—	—	—	—
Chad	20,800	33,400	1	10,560	14,550	293	580	850	—	—	—	—	—	—
Chile	49,590	79,800	14	1,323,800	687,500	7.5	…	…	5,410[2]	8,707[2]	377	606	1,984	2,896
China	794,405	1,278,474	93	6,548,300	6,278,900	96	375,580	548,338	35,781	57,584	229,657	369,598	843,302	1,236,200
Colombia	71,808	115,564	12	762,000	672,000	27	21	31	*2,007*[2]	*3,230*[2]	*9.6*	*15.5*	504.3	736.2
Comoros	559	900	76	9,100	4,950	36	…	…	—	—	—	—	—	—
Congo, Dem. Rep. of the	95,708	154,027	2	787,000	60,000	55	…	…	3,193	5,138	18[14]	29[14]	121[14]	176[14]
Congo, Rep. of the	7,950	12,800	10	37,240	15,520	49	*46*	*67*	556	894	150	242	92	135
Costa Rica	22,119	35,597	17	294,083	163,428	7.6	2,103	3,070	590[2]	950[2]	3.7	5.9	45.8	66.8
Côte d'Ivoire	31,300	50,400	10	293,000	163,000	32	…	…	397[2]	639[2]	80[17]	129[17]	40[17]	58[17]
Croatia	17,475	28,123	82	1,124,825	117,794	3.4	1,774	2,590	1,694	2,726	619	996	1,321	1,928
Cuba	37,815	60,858	49	172,574	185,495	31	*2,482*	*3,623*	2,987	4,807	1,219	1,962	763	1,075
Cyprus	6,620	10,654	58	234,976	108,452	2.4	…	…	—	—	—	—	—	—
Czech Republic	78,234	125,905	44	3,695,792	426,684	2.5	23,227	33,911	6,469	9,444	4,323	6,957	11,447	16,713
Denmark	44,389	71,663	100	1,854,060	335,690	2.4	14,639	21,372	1,704[2]	2,743[2]	3,304	5,318	1,387	2,025
Djibouti	1,796	2,890	13	9,200	2,040	38	…	…	*66*	*106*	361	762	144	232
Dominica	485	780	50	6,581	2,825	7.8	…	…	—	—	—	—	—	—
Dominican Republic	7,829	12,600	49	224,000	151,550	21	…	…	1,083[2]	1,743[2]	…	…	…	…
East Timor	…	…	…	…	…	…	…	…	…	…	…	…	…	…
Ecuador	26,841	43,197	19	464,902	52,630	23	2,712	3,959	600[2]	966[2]	28	45	686	1,002

based upon registration, are relatively accurate, though some countries round off figures, and unregistered vehicles may cause substantial undercount. There is also inconsistent classification of vehicle types; in some countries a vehicle may serve variously as an automobile, a truck, or a bus, or even as all three on certain occasions. Relatively few countries collect and maintain commercial road traffic statistics.

Data on national railway systems are generally given for railway track length rather than the length of routes, which may be multitracked. Siding tracks usually are not included, but some countries fail to distinguish them. The United States data include only class 1 railways, which account for about 94 percent of total track length. Passenger traffic is usually calculated from tickets sold to fare-paying passengers. Such statistics are subject to distortion if there are large numbers of nonpaying passengers, such as military personnel, or if season tickets are sold and not all the allowed journeys are utilized. Railway cargo traffic is calculated by weight hauled multiplied by the length of the journey. Changes in freight load during the journey should be accounted for but sometimes are not, leading to discrepancies.

Merchant fleet and tonnage statistics collected by Lloyd's registry service for vessels over 100 gross tons are quite accurate. Cargo statistics, however, reflect the port and customs requirements of each country and the reporting rules of each country's merchant marine authority (although these, increasingly, reflect the recommendations of the International Maritime Organization); often, however, they are only estimates based on customs declarations and the count of vessels entered and cleared. Even when these elements are reported consistently, further uncertainties may be introduced because of ballast, bunkers, ships' stores, or transshipped goods included in the data.

Airport data are based on scheduled flights reported in the commercial *Official Airline Guide* and are both reliable and current. The comparability of civil air traffic statistics suffers from differing characteristics of the air transportation systems of different countries; data for an entire country may be two to three years behind those for a single airport.

Outside of Europe, where standardization of data on inland waterways is necessitated by the volume of international traffic, comparability of national data declines markedly. Calculations as to both the length of a country's waterway system (or route length of river, lake, and coastal traffic) and the makeup of its stock of commercially significant vessels (those for which data will be collected) are largely determined by the nature and use of the country's hydrographic net—its seasonality, relief profile, depth, access to potential markets—and inevitably differ widely from country to country. Data for coastal or island states may refer to scheduled coastwise or interisland traffic.

merchant marine (latest)				air					canals and inland waterways (latest)				country
fleet (vessels over 100 gross tons)	total deadweight tonnage ('000)	international cargo (latest)		airports with scheduled flights (latest)	traffic (latest)				length		cargo		
					passengers		cargo		mi	km	short ton-mi ('000,000)	metric ton-km ('000,000)	
		loaded metric tons ('000)	off-loaded metric tons ('000)		passenger-mi ('000,000)	passenger-km ('000,000)	short ton-mi ('000,000)	metric ton-km ('000,000)					
—	—	—	—	3	171.5[1]	276.0[1]	26[1]	38[1]	750	1,200	...	...	Afghanistan
24	*81.0*	120	2,040	1	2.2	3.5	0.22	0.32	46	74	*24*	*35*	Albania
149	*1,093.4*	*63,110*	*15,700*	28	1,803[3]	2,901[3]	12.5[3]	18.3[3]	...	...	...	...	Algeria
3	*0.1*	*380*	*581*	3	...	...	...	...	...	...	...	...	American Samoa
—	—	—	—	—	—	—	—	—	—	—	—	—	Andorra
123	73.9	*23,288*	*1,261*	17	385[4]	620[4]	60[4]	97[4]	805	1,295	...	...	Angola
292	*997.4*	*28*	*113*	2	157	252	*0.1*	*0.2*	...	...	...	...	Antigua and Barbuda
423	*1,173.1*	69,372	19,536	39	7,292[5]	11,735[5]	895[5]	1,307[5]	6,804	10,950	*19,326*	*28,215*	Argentina
...	...	...	...	1	356	572	5.9	9.5	...	...	...	...	Armenia
...[6]	...[6]	...	...	1	318	511	...	...	...	...	...	...	Aruba
695	*3,857.3*	35,664	43,360	400	46,647	75,071	1,156	1,688	5,200	8,368	*31,891*	*46,560*	Australia
26	*208.5*	1,479	5,766	6	7,742	12,460	247	361	218	351	7,938	11,590	Austria
69	...	...	...	3	1,025	1,650	125	183	...	...	3,112	5,008	Azerbaijan
1,061	*33,081.7*	*5,920*	*5,705*	22	87	140	0.32	0.455	...	...	...	...	Bahamas, The
87	*192.5*	*13,285*	*3,512*	1	1,762[8]	2,836[8]	81.3[8]	118.7[8]	...	...	...	...	Bahrain
301	*566.8*	948	10,404	8	2,154	3,466	95	139	5,000	8,046	...	...	Bangladesh
37	*84.0*	*206*	*538*	1	*93*[9]	*149*[9]	*0.8*[10]	*1.1*[10]	...	...	...	...	Barbados
...	*18,373.0*	...	...	1	864	1,390	7	10	1,092	1,757	71	103	Belarus
232	*218.5*	360,984	367,680	2	12,042	19,379	389	568	957	1,540	3,993	5,830	Belgium
32	*45.7*	255	277	9	...	...	...	...	513	825	...	...	Belize
12	*0.2*	339	1,738	1	160.5[11]	258.3[11]	8.4[11]	13.5[11]	...	...	...	...	Benin
94	*5,206.5*	*130*	*470*	1	...	...	...	...	...	...	...	...	Bermuda
—	—	—	—	1	29	46	...	...	—	—	—	—	Bhutan
1	*15.8*	...	...	14	1,223	1,968	28.7	41.9	6,214	10,000	*90*	*132*	Bolivia
...	...	...	...	1	25.1	40.4	0.29	0.43	...	...	...	...	Bosnia and Herzegovina
—	—	—	—	7	35.3[12]	56.8[12]	0.1[12]	0.2[12]	...	...	...	...	Botswana
635	*9,348.3*	239,932	146,452	139	21,765	35,028	891	1,031	31,069	50,000	*56,030*	*81,803*	Brazil
51	*349.7*	42	1,308	1	1,742	2,803	75.0	109.5	130	209	...	...	Brunei
107	391	*5,290*	*20,080*	3	1,259	2,026	18.9	30.4	292	470	487	711	Bulgaria
—	—	—	—	2	*134.9*	*217.2*	*23.4*	*34.2*	...	...	...	...	Burkina Faso
1	*0.4*	*35*	*188*	1	*1.2*	*2.0*	...	...	...	...	...	...	Burundi
3	*3.8*	*11*	*95*	8	26.1	42.0	0.3	0.4	2,300	3,700	51	75	Cambodia
47	*39.8*	2,385	2,497	5	348	560	57	91	1,299	2,090	...	...	Cameroon
1,185	*2,896.8*	187,716	94,536	269	42,379	68,202	1,224	1,787	1,860	3,000	...	...	Canada
42	*30.9*	*144*	*299*	9	106	171	13.2	19.2	...	...	...	...	Cape Verde
—	—	*53*	*126*	1	139.6[12]	224.7[12]	11.2[12]	16.4[12]	500	800	185	270	Central African Republic
—	—	—	—	1	145	233	25	37	1,240	2,000	...	...	Chad
392	*854.9*	29,532	18,144	23	6,618	10,651	1,443	2,107	450	725	*5,629*	*8,218*	Chile
2,390	*20,658.0*	1,146,084	*101,688*	113	49,725	80,024	2,291	3,345	68,537	110,300	1,329,187	1,940,580	China
101	*403.0*	49,332	15,288	43	3,723	5,991	573	836	11,272	18,140	1.7	2.5	Colombia
6	*3.6*	*12*	*107*	2	1.9	3.0	...	...	...	...	...	...	Comoros
27	*30.7*	*2,395*	*1,453*	22	173[15]	279[15]	29[15]	42[15]	9,300	15,000	*678*	*990*	Congo, Dem. Rep. of the
22	*10.8*	708	533	10	160[11]	258[11]	9.6	14	696	1,120	...	...	Congo, Rep. of the
24	*8.4*	3,017	3,972	14	2,167[16]	3,487[16]	61.9[16]	90.4[16]	454	730	...	...	Costa Rica
51	*98.6*	4,173	7,228	5	191[18]	307[18]	30[18]	44[18]	609	980	...	...	Côte d'Ivoire
203	*140.9*	4,416	7,680	4	474	763	2.0	3.0	580	933	43	63	Croatia
393	*924.6*	*8,092*	*15,440*	14	2,202	3,543	38.5	56.2	149	240	108	158	Cuba
1,416	*36,198.1*	1,344	4,308	2	1,685	2,711	26	38	...	...	...	...	Cyprus
18[19]	*514.1*[19]	759	409	2	2,705	4,354	21	30	413	664	627	915	Czech Republic
456	*7,589.1*	21,060	38,292	13	3,340[20]	5,376[20]	117[20]	171[20]	259	417	*1,100*	*1,600*	Denmark
10	*4.1*	*414*	*958*	1	*42*	*67*	*4*	*6*	...	...	...	...	Djibouti
7	*3.2*	*103*	*181*	2	...	...	...	...	...	...	...	...	Dominica
28	*10.4*	1,668	*4,182*	7	9.8	15.8	7.9	11.6	...	...	...	...	Dominican Republic
...	...	...	...	...	...	...	...	...	...	...	...	...	East Timor
154	*504.1*	*11,783*	*1,958*	14	574	924	79	116	932	1,500	...	...	Ecuador

Transportation (continued)

country	roads and motor vehicles (latest)								railroads (latest)					
	roads			motor vehicles			cargo		track length		traffic			
	length		paved (per-cent)	auto-mobiles	trucks and buses	persons per vehicle	short ton-mi ('000,000)	metric ton-km ('000,000)	mi	km	passengers		cargo	
	mi	km									passen-ger-mi ('000,000)	passen-ger-km ('000,000)	short ton-mi ('000,000)	metric ton-km ('000,000)
Egypt	39,800[21]	64,000[21]	78[21]	1,154,753	510,766	37	21,600	31,500	2,989	4,810	35,211	56,667	2,820	4,117
El Salvador	6,232	10,029	20	177,488	184,859	16	...	...	349[2]	562[2]	4.4	7.1	12	17
Equatorial Guinea	1,740	2,800	13	6,500	4,000	37	...	...	—	—	—	—	—	—
Eritrea	2,491	4,010	22	5,940	...	...	...	...	43	70	...	...	...	...
Estonia	10,209	16,430	51	451,000	86,900	2.7	2,691	3,929	636	1,024	149	238	4,808	7,020
Ethiopia	12,117	19,500	15	52,012	39,936	642	...	...	486[22]	782[22]	98	157	73	106
Faroe Islands	285	458	...	14,608	3,455	2.5	...	...	—	—	—	—	—	—
Fiji	3,200	5,100	20	49,712	33,928	9.4	...	...	370[13]	595[13]	...	...	...	...
Finland	48,340	77,900	65	2,069,055	300,048	2.2	19,884	29,030	3,626[2]	5,836[2]	2,122	3,415	6,680	9,753
France	547,200	893,500	100	27,480,000	5,610,000	1.8	114,382	166,995	19,486[2]	31,821[2]	40,100	64,500	37,000	54,000
French Guiana	*706*	*1,137*	*40*	*29,100*	*10,600*	*3.2*	...	...	—	—	—	—	—	—
French Polynesia	549	884	44	*37,000*	*15,300*	*4.0*	...	...	—	—	—	—	—	—
Gabon	4,760	7,670	8	24,750	16,490	28	...	...	506	814	53	85	345	503
Gambia, The	1,678	2,700	35	8,640	9,000	68	...	...	—	—	—	—	—	—
Gaza Strip	...	...	...	37,061	8,105	23	...	...	—	—	—	—	—	—
Georgia	12,862	20,700	93	427,000	41,510	11	288	420	961	1,546	219	349	2,150	3,139
Germany	143,372	230,735	99	42,323,672	2,550,222	1.8	176,337	257,447	54,188	87,207	41,321	66,500	48,875	71,356
Ghana	24,000	38,700	40	90,000	45,000	133	*873*	*1,275*	*592*[2]	*953*[2]	*731.4*	*1,177*	*93.9*	*137.1*
Greece	72,700	117,000	92	2,675,676	1,013,677	2.9	12,000	17,000	1,555[2]	2,503[2]	1,108	1,783	226	330
Greenland	93	150	60	2,242	1,474	15	...	...	—	—	—	—	—	—
Grenada	646	1,040	61	*4,739*	*3,068*	*12*	...	...	—	—	—	—	—	—
Guadeloupe	2,122	3,415	*80*	*101,600*	*37,500*	*2.9*	...	...	—	—	—	—	—	—
Guam	550	885	76	79,800	34,700	1.3	...	...	—	—	—	—	—	—
Guatemala	8,140	13,100	28	102,000	97,000	51	...	...	549[2]	884[2]	10.3	16.6	58.6	85.6
Guernsey	...	...	...	37,598	7,338	1.4	...	...	—	—	—	—	—	—
Guinea	18,952	30,500	16	14,100	21,000	219	...	...	411[2]	662[2]	25.8	41.5	5.0	7.3
Guinea-Bissau	2,734	4,400	10	7,120	5,640	91	...	...	—	—	—	—	—	—
Guyana	4,952	7,970	7	24,000	9,000	22	...	...	116[13]	187[13]	...	...	...	...
Haiti	2,585	4,160	24	32,000	21,000	121	...	...	—	—	—	—	—	—
Honduras	9,073	14,602	18	81,439	170,006	22	...	...	614	988	*4.8*	*7.7*	*20.7*	*30.2*
Hong Kong	1,183	1,904	100	332,000	133,000	14	...	...	21[2]	34[2]	2,231	3,591	68	99
Hungary	116,944	188,203	43	2,255,526	321,634	4.0	10,950	15,987	4,827[2]	7,768[2]	5,912	9,514	5,297	7,733
Iceland	7,691	12,378	25	151,409	19,428	1.6	*318*	*464*	—	—	—	—	—	—
India	2,062,727	3,319,644	46	4,189,000	2,234,000	148	656	958	39,028[2]	62,809[2]	261,254	420,449	209,259	305,513
Indonesia	212,177	341,467	56	2,734,769	2,189,876	41	*17,000*	*25,000*	4,013[2]	6,458[2]	11,548	18,585	3,449	5,035
Iran	102,976	165,724	50	1,793,000	692,000	24	*46,750*	*68,250*	3,915[2]	6,300[2]	3,792	6,103	9,863	14,400
Iraq	29,453	47,400	86	772,986	323,906	18	...	...	1,263[2]	2,032[2]	973	1,566	1,129	1,649
Ireland	57,477	92,500	94	1,269,245	188,814	2.6	4,041	5,900	1,209[2]	1,945[2]	870	1,400	342	500
Isle of Man	500	805	58	40,168	4,925	1.6	...	...	32[2]	52[2]	...	...	...	...
Israel	9,609	15,464	100	1,316,765	319,581	3.7	*2,993*	*4,370*	379[2]	610[2]	329	529	773	1,128
Italy	191,468	308,139	100	31,370,000	5,127,000	1.6	131,154	191,482	12,133	19,527	25,720	41,392	15,333	22,386
Jamaica	11,800	19,000	71	160,948	55,596	12	...	...	*129*[2]	*208*[2]	*12.1*	*19.5*	*1.7*	*2.5*
Japan	718,300	1,156,000	73	51,222,000	18,425,000	1.8	205,942	300,670	16,937	27,258	241,674	388,938	15,699	22,920
Jersey	346	557	100	58,491	9,922	1.3	...	...	—	—	—	—	—	—
Jordan	4,432	7,133	100	213,874	79,153	15	*19,133*	*27,934*	421[2]	677[2]	*3.7*	*6.0*	915	1,336
Kazakhstan	78,166	125,796	83	973,323	361,920	11	3,176	4,637	8,388[2]	13,500[2]	5,505	8,859	64,987	94,879
Kenya	39,600	63,800	14	278,000	81,200	78	*134*	*196*	1,885[2]	3,034[2]	239	385	813	1,309
Kiribati	416	670	5	222	115	260	...	...	—	—	—	—	—	—
Korea, North	14,526	23,377	8	*248,000*	...	...	...	...	5,302	8,533	*2,100*	*3,400*	*6,200*	*9,100*
Korea, South	55,162	88,775	76	8,084,000	3,938,000	3.9	51,031	74,504	4,165	6,703	18,686	30,072	8,704	12,708
Kuwait	2,765	4,450	81	747,042	140,480	2.3	...	...	—	—	—	—	—	—
Kyrgyzstan	11,495	18,500	91	146,000	...	...	695	1,015	264	424	58	93	323	472
Laos	13,870	22,321	14	16,320	4,200	242	16	23	—	—	—	—	—	—
Latvia	34,761	55,942	38	431,816	95,329	4.7	2,814	4,108	1,499	2,413	611	984	8,363	12,210
Lebanon	3,946	6,350	95	1,299,398	85,242	2.5	...	...	138	222	*5.3*	*8.6*	*29*	*42*
Lesotho	3,079	4,955	18	12,610	25,000	53	...	...	1.6	2.6	...	...	...	...
Liberia	6,600	10,600	6	9,400	25,000	59	...	...	304[2]	490[2]	...	...	534	860
Libya	50,704	81,600	57	809,514	357,528	4.0	...	...	—	—	—	—	—	—
Liechtenstein	201	323	...	21,150	2,684	1.4	...	...	12	19	...	...	...	...
Lithuania	44,350	71,375	91	980,910	105,022	3.4	3,843	5,611	1,241[2]	1,997[2]	463	745	5,376	7,849
Luxembourg	3,209	5,166	100	263,683	20,228	1.5	2,437	3,558	170[2]	274[2]	193	310	410	660
Macau	31	50	100	45,184	6,578	8.2	...	...	—	—	—	—	—	—
Macedonia	7,154	11,513	63	288,678	24,745	6.4	612	894	575	925	93	150	279	408
Madagascar	30,967	49,837	17	62,000	16,460	140	*220*	*321*	*680*[2]	*1,095*[2]	22	35	44	71
Malawi	10,222	16,451	19	27,000	29,700	171	—	—	495[2]	797[2]	16	26	34	49
Malaysia	41,282	66,437	76	3,517,484	644,792	5.1	...	...	1,384[2]	2,227[2]	828[31]	1,332[31]	625[31]	912[31]
Maldives	...	...	...	1,716	586	114	...	...	—	—	—	—	—	—
Mali	9,383	15,100	12	26,190	18,240	213	...	...	398[2]	641[2]	577.6	929.6	371	542.8
Malta	1,219	1,961	94	185,247	49,520	1.6	...	...	—	—	—	—	—	—
Marshall Islands	...	...	...	1,374	262	29	...	...	—	—	—	—	—	—
Martinique	1,299	2,091	*75*	*108,300*	*32,200*	*2.6*	...	...	—	—	—	—	—	—
Mauritania	4,760	7,660	11	18,810	10,450	82	...	...	437[2]	704[2]	...	...	1,603	2,340
Mauritius	1,184	1,905	93	46,300	12,100	20	...	...	—	—	—	—	—	—
Mayotte	145	233	77	6,553		20	...	...	—	—	—	—	—	—
Mexico	199,824	321,586	37	8,607,000	4,426,000	7.1	122,663	179,085	16,543[2]	26,623[2]	286	460	32,106	46,874
Micronesia	*140*	*226*	*17*	...	...	...	...	...	—	—	—	—	—	—
Moldova	7,643	12,300	87	166,757	67,638	18	697	1,018	819	1,318	213	343	816	1,191
Monaco	31	50	100	21,120	2,770	1.3	...	...	1	2	...	...	...	...
Mongolia	31,000	50,000	3	39,921	31,061	33	84.4	123.2	1,128	1,815	634	1,020	2,392	3,492
Morocco	35,921	57,810	52	1,018,146	278,075	21	1,429	2,086	1,099[2]	1,768[2]	1,104	1,776	3,258	4,757
Mozambique	18,890	30,400	19	4,900	7,520	1,431	75	110	1,940	3,123	317	510	781	1,140
Myanmar (Burma)	17,523	28,200	12	27,000	42,000	587	*71*	*103.7*	2,458[2]	3,955[2]	2,453	3,948	674	984
Namibia	40,526	65,220	8	74,875	66,500	12	...	...	1,480	2,382	21.6	34.7	738	1,077
Nauru	19	30	79	*1,448*		*6.3*	...	...	3[13]	5[13]	...	...	*4.7*	*6.8*
Nepal	4,785	7,700	42	47,541	29,371	306	*984*	*1,437*	37[2]	59[2]	...	...	...	...

merchant marine (latest): fleet (vessels over 100 gross tons)	merchant marine: total deadweight tonnage ('000)	merchant marine: international cargo (latest): loaded metric tons ('000)	merchant marine: international cargo (latest): off-loaded metric tons ('000)	air: airports with scheduled flights (latest)	air: traffic (latest): passengers: passenger-mi ('000,000)	air: traffic: passengers: passenger-km ('000,000)	air: traffic: cargo: short ton-mi ('000,000)	air: traffic: cargo: metric ton-km ('000,000)	canals and inland waterways (latest): length: mi	canals and inland waterways: length: km	canals and inland waterways: cargo: short ton-mi ('000,000)	canals and inland waterways: cargo: metric ton-km ('000,000)	country
444	1,685.2	15,012	22,044	11	5,638	9,074	185	270	2,175	3,500	452	660	Egypt
15	...	221	1,023	1	1,355	2,181	10.9	16.0	...	...	...	...	El Salvador
3	6.7	110	64	1	4	7	0.7	1.0	...	...	...	...	Equatorial Guinea
...	...	...	...	2	...	...	...	...	...	...	...	...	Eritrea
234	680.4	30,024	5,784	1	103.6	166.7	0.6	0.9	199	320	1.4	2.1	Estonia
27	84.3	234	1,242	31	1,190	1,915	225	328	...	...	...	...	Ethiopia
191	59.8	223	443	1	...	...	...	...	...	...	...	...	Faroe Islands
64	60.4	568	625	13	742	1,195	51.6	75.4	126	203	...	...	Fiji
263	989.3	39,312	38,052	27	8,026	12,916	216	316	3,880	6,245	127,945	186,797	Finland
729	4,981.0	64,704	189,504	61	55,344[23]	89,067[23]	3,271[23]	4,775[23]	3,562	5,732	5,436	7,936	France
7	0.7	73	447	8	...	...	...	...	286	460	...	...	French Guiana
41	16.5	15	666	17	...	...	...	...	...	...	...	...	French Polynesia
29	30.2	12,828	212	17	452	728	68	100	994	1,600	...	...	Gabon
11	2.0	185	240	1	31	50	3	5	250	400	...	...	Gambia, The
—	—	...	...	1	...	...	...	...	—	—	...	...	Gaza Strip
54	1,108	...	...	1	78.9	127.1	0.5	0.8	...	...	3,740	5,460	Georgia
1,375	6,832.3	74,568	138,864	35	55,219	88,867	4,520	6,599	4,188	6,740	44,019	64,267	Germany
155	131.0	2,424	2,904	1	407	655	20	30	803	1,293	75	110	Ghana
1,872	45,276.6	16,464	45,024	36	5,160	8,305	71	103	50	80	585	854	Greece
82	17.2	298	288	18	104	167	0.23	0.34	...	...	...	...	Greenland
3	0.5	21	193	2	...	...	...	...	...	...	...	...	Grenada
20	4.4	349	2,285	7	...	...	...	...	...	...	...	...	Guadeloupe
5	0.1	195	1,524	1	...	...	...	...	...	...	...	...	Guam
8	0.4	2,096	3,822	2	311	500	48	70	162	260	...	...	Guatemala
—	—	...	...	2	...	...	...	...	...	...	...	...	Guernsey
23	1.7	16,760	734	1	32	52	3	5	805	1,295	...	...	Guinea
19	1.8	46	283	2	6.2	10.0	0.7	1.0	...	...	...	...	Guinea-Bissau
82	13.5	1,730	673	1	154	248	2.3	3.3	3,660	5,900	...	...	Guyana
4	0.4	170	704	2	...	...	...	...	60	100	...	...	Haiti
966	1,437.3	1,316	1,002	8	212[24]	341[24]	23[24]	33[24]	289	465	...	...	Honduras
387	11,688.6	36,132[25]	80,820[25]	1	...	...	...	...	...	...	...	...	Hong Kong
15	93.2	...	...	1	2,183	3,513	38	56	853	1,373	1,069	1,561	Hungary
394	114.9	1,162	1,733	24	2,273	3,658	50.9	74.4	...	...	58	84	Iceland
888	10,365.9	61,880	102,630	66	11,456	18,436	329	481	10,054	16,180	202,000	295,000	India
2,014	3,130.2	310,246	208,871	81	7,698	12,389	234	341	13,409	21,579	17,000	25,000	Indonesia
403	8,345.3	32,148	37,404	19	3,871	6,229	49	72	562	904	...	...	Iran
131	1,578.8	97,830	8,638	...	976	1,570	37.4	54.6	631	1,015	...	...	Iraq
189	208.6	6,367	17,637	9	4,018	6,466	88.8	129.6	435	700	...	...	Ireland
101	2,836.5	6	203	1	526.1	846.8	0.1	0.2	...	...	...	...	Isle of Man
58	723.4	12,876	20,916	7	8,777[26]	14,125[26]	882[26]	1,288[26]	...	...	...	...	Israel
1,966	7,149.5	48,252	234,120	34	18,312[27]	29,471[27]	835[27]	1,219[27]	918	1,477	85,681	125,092	Italy
12	16.2	8,802	5,285	4	1,038[28]	1,670[28]	20.2[28]	29.5[28]	...	...	...	...	Jamaica
6,140	16,198	124,548	754,464	73	97,745	157,305	4,920	7,183	1,100	1,770	155,468	226,980	Japan
—	—	...	...	1	...	...	...	...	...	...	...	...	Jersey
5	113.6	7,308	5,328	2	2,526	4,065	150.1	219.2	...	...	19,202	28,035	Jordan
...	...	...	...	20	1,509	2,429	162	237	2,425	3,903	97	141	Kazakhstan
29	11.6	1,596	3,228	11	1,062[29]	1,709[29]	126[29]	203[29]	...	...	...	...	Kenya
7	2.7	15	26	9	4.4	7.0	0.6	1.0	3	5	...	...	Kiribati
100	951.2	635	5,520	1	178	286	19	30	1,400	2,253	...	...	Korea, North
2,138	11,724.9	255,888	448,416	14	29,647	47,712	4,987	7,281	1,000	1,609	22,920	33,462	Korea, South
209	3,188.5	51,400	4,522	1	3,813	6,137	151	243	...	...	...	...	Kuwait
...	...	...	...	2	2,739	4,408	44.7	65.2	290	466	41	6.0	Kyrgyzstan
1	1.5	—	—	11	30	48	3	5	2,850	4,587	68	100	Laos
261	1,436.9	45,144	3,888	1	185	298	6	9	66	106	19,241	28,091	Latvia
163	438.2	152	1,150	1	1,315	2,116	218	319	...	...	...	...	Lebanon
—	—	—	—	1	3.9	6.2	0.4	0.6	—	—	—	—	Lesotho
1,672	97,374.0	21,653	1,608	1	4.3	7.0	0.7	1.0	...	...	...	...	Liberia
150	1,223.6	62,491	7,808	12	264[30]	425[30]	23[30]	34[30]	—	—	...	...	Libya
—	—	—	—	—	—	—	—	—	...	...	...	...	Liechtenstein
52	373.9	12,864	2,796	3	190.5	306.6	1.8	2.6	229	369	8.9	13	Lithuania
54	2,603.6	—	—	1	79.5	232	606.9	886.1	23	37	205	300	Luxembourg
6	0.1	755	3,935	—	—	—	—	—	...	...	...	...	Macau
...	...	...	...	2	553.5	890.7	239.2	349.2	...	...	...	...	Macedonia
85	82.1	540	984	44	519	836	20.2	29.5	...	...	1.2	1.8	Madagascar
1	0.3	...	...	5	68	110	10	14	89	144	1,683	2,457	Malawi
552	2,916.3	39,756	54,852	39	20,945	33,708	976	1,425	4,534	7,296	...	...	Malaysia
44	79.0	27	78	5	44	71	...	...	...	...	...	...	Maldives
—	—	—	—	9	150	242	26	38	1,128	1,815	18	27	Mali
889	17,073.2	309	1,781	1	1,173	1,888	7.7	11.2	...	...	...	...	Malta
35	4,182.4	29	123	25	17	28	0.003	0.005	...	...	...	...	Marshall Islands
6	1.1	960	1,584	1	...	...	...	...	...	...	...	...	Martinique
126	23.9	10,400	724	9	160.5	258.3	9.2	13.5	...	...	...	...	Mauritania
35	152.2	966	2,753	1	2,398	3,859	561.2	819.4	...	...	...	...	Mauritius
1	1.1	158	31	1	...	...	...	...	...	...	...	...	Mayotte
635	1,495.3	134,400	67,500	83	14,864	23,922	1,779	2,597	1,800	2,900	14,806	21,616	Mexico
19	9.2	...	...	4	...	...	...	...	...	...	...	...	Micronesia
...	...	...	...	1	0.1	0.2	0.7	1.0	263	424	172	251	Moldova
1	...	...	...	—	—	—	...	...	...	...	...	...	Monaco
—	—	—	—	1	326	525	33	48	247	397	0.1	0.2	Mongolia
492	586.2	24,228	27,972	11	2,789	4,489	260	380	...	...	...	...	Morocco
107	31.6	2,800	3,400	7	239	384	6	9	2,330	3,750	57	83	Mozambique
144	1,354.0	1,788	3,456	19	272	438	2.2	3.2	7,954	12,800	240	351	Myanmar (Burma)
30	5.9	1,132	644	11	470	756	16	23	...	...	...	...	Namibia
2	5.8	1,650	59	1	151[32]	243[32]	15[32]	24[32]	...	...	...	...	Nauru
—	—	—	—	24	532	856	64	93	...	...	...	...	Nepal

Transportation (continued)

country	roads and motor vehicles (latest)								railroads (latest)					
	roads			motor vehicles			cargo		track length		traffic			
	length		paved (per-cent)	auto-mobiles	trucks and buses	persons per vehicle	short ton-mi ('000,-000)	metric ton-km ('000,-000)	mi	km	passengers		cargo	
	mi	km									passen-ger-mi ('000,000)	passen-ger-km ('000,000)	short ton-mi ('000,000)	metric ton-km ('000,000)
Netherlands, The	77,379	124,530	91	6,343,000	826,000	2.2	98,445	143,727	1,745	2,808	8,904	14,330	2,412	3,521
Netherlands Antilles	367	590	51	75,105	17,753	2.2	...	...	—	—	—	—	—	—
New Caledonia	3,582	5,764	52	56,700	21,200	2.6	...	...	—	—	—	—	—	—
New Zealand	57,213	92,075	62	1,831,118	351,494	1.7	...	...	2,431[2]	3,912[2]	*285*	*458*	2,712	3,960
Nicaragua	11,200	18,000	10	73,000	61,650	33	...	...	—	—	—	—	—	—
Niger	6,276	10,100	8	38,220	15,200	169	*1,044*	*1,524*	—	—	—	—	—	—
Nigeria	38,897	62,598	19	773,000	68,300	131	...	...	2,178	3,505	100	161	74	108
Northern Mariana Islands	225	360	100	12,113	6,479	3.0	...	...	—	—	—	—	—	—
Norway	56,470	90,880	74	1,813,642	447,583	2.0	10,086	14,726	2,489[2]	4,006[2]	1,609	2,589	1,467	2,142
Oman	20,518	33,020	24	229,029	110,717	6.9	...	...	—	—	—	—	—	—
Pakistan	149,679	240,885	55	1,167,635	251,407	95	66,304	96,802	5,452[2]	8,774[2]	11,908	19,164	2,753	4,020
Palau	*40*	*64*	*59*	4,271		3.8	...	...	...	...	...	...	...	...
Panama	7,022	11,301	33	203,760	74,637	9.4	...	...	220[2]	354[2]	242	389	1,096	1,600
Papua New Guinea	*12,263*	*19,736*	*6*	*13,000*	*32,000*	*93*	...	...	—	—	—	—	—	—
Paraguay	18,330	29,500	10	71,000	50,000	41	...	...	274[2]	441[2]	1.9	3.0	3.8	5.5
Peru	45,836	73,766	12	557,042	359,374	26	...	...	1,238[2]	1,992[2]	132	212	0.8	1.1
Philippines	124,243	199,950	39	745,144	263,037	73	...	...	557[2]	897[2]	7.5	12	452	660
Poland	234,286	377,048	66	9,283,000	1,762,000	3.5	47,632	69,542	14,280	22,981	16,279	26,198	37,994	55,471
Portugal	42,708	68,732	88	3,200,000	1,097,000	2.4	16,984	24,796	2,025[2]	3,259[2]	2,860	4,602	1,603	2,340
Puerto Rico	8,948	14,400	100	878,000	190,000	3.5	...	...	—	—	—	—	—	—
Qatar	764	1,230	90	126,000	64,000	2.9	...	...	—	—	—	—	—	—
Réunion	1,711	2,754	*79*	190,300	44,300	3.0	...	...	—	—	—	—	—	—
Romania	95,175	153,170	51	2,408,000	409,550	8.0	14,898	21,750	7,062	11,365	7,658	12,324	10,909	15,927
Russia	354,628	570,719	79	19,717,800	5,021,000	5.9	14,384	21,000	93,800	151,000	88,048	144,700	825	1,205
Rwanda	9,528	14,900	9	13,000	17,100	188	*140*	*200*	—	—	—	—	—	—
St. Kitts and Nevis	199	320	43	5,200	2,300	5.3	...	...	22	36	—	—	—	—
St. Lucia	750	1,210	5	14,783	1,020	9.5	...	...	—	—	—	—	—	—
St. Vincent and the Grenadines	646	1,040	31	6,089	3,670	11	...	...	—	—	—	—	—	—
Samoa	491	790	42	1,068	1,169	74	...	...	—	—	—	—	—	—
San Marino	157	252	...	25,571	2,636	0.9	...	...	—	—	—	—	—	—
São Tomé and Príncipe	199	320	68	4,040	1,540	24	...	...	—	—	—	—	—	—
Saudi Arabia	101,000	162,000	43	1,744,000	1,192,000	6.6	57,859	84,473	864[2]	1,390[2]	138	222	586	856
Senegal	9,134	14,700	29	85,488	36,962	72	*375*	*547*	761	1,225	*128*	*206*	*476*	*695*
Serbia and Montenegro	31,377	50,497	60	1,400,000	132,000	6.9	852	1,244	2,528	4,069	1,003	1,614	1,760	2,570
Seychelles	263	424	87	7,120	1,980	8.5	...	...	—	—	—	—	—	—
Sierra Leone	7,270	11,700	11	17,640	10,890	163	*36*	*53*	*52*	*84*	...	...	...	...
Singapore	1,875	3,017	97	413,545	147,325	5.8	...	...	73	117	[31]	[31]	[31]	[31]
Slovakia	10,953	17,627	...	1,135,914	100,254	4.4	5,804	8,474	2,282	3,673	1,844	2,968	6,753	9,859
Slovenia	7,771	12,507	81	829,674	67,111	2.2	1,986	2,900	746	1,201	388	625	1,907	2,784
Solomon Islands	845	1,360	3	*2,052*	*2,574*	*75*	...	...	—	—	—	—	—	—
Somalia	13,732	22,100	12	1,020	6,440	866	...	...	—	—	—	—	—	—
South Africa	205,838	331,265	41	3,966,252	2,069,536	7.2	*1,053*	*1,538*	12,626[2]	20,319[2]	1,103	1,775	71,142	103,866
Spain	215,335	346,548	99	16,847,000	3,659,000	2.0	85,801	125,268	8,595[2]	13,832[2]	11,525	18,547	7,959	11,620
Sri Lanka	61,640	99,200	40	107,000	150,160	71	21	30	899[2]	1,447[2]	2,028	3,264	90	132
Sudan, The	7,394	11,900	36	285,000	53,000	93	...	...	2,855[2]	4,595[2]	100	161	1,346	1,965
Suriname	2,815	4,530	26	46,408	19,255	6.4	...	...	187	301	...	...	...	...
Swaziland	2,367	3,810	29	31,882	32,772	17	...	...	187	301	*752*	*1,210*	*1,993*	*2,910*
Sweden	130,500	210,000	74	3,890,159	352,897	2.1	22,798	33,285	6,811	10,961	4,746	7,638	13,074	19,088
Switzerland	44,248	71,211	96	3,467,275	313,646	1.9	9,932	14,500	3,129	5,035	8,764	14,104	5,951	8,688
Syria	25,756	41,451	23	138,900	282,664	37	*1,075*	*1,570*	1,507[2]	2,425[2]	113	182	934	1,364
Taiwan	12,660	20,375	89	4,716,000	833,000	4.0	12,651	18,470	2,410	3,879	7,833	12,606	808	1,179
Tajikistan	8,500	13,700	83	680	8,190	667	34	50	295	474	77	124	1,449	2,115
Tanzania	54,805	88,200	4	23,760	115,700	229	...	...	2,218	3,569	*2,324*	*3,740*	927	1,354
Thailand	40,141	64,600	98	1,661,000	2,855,000	14	...	...	2,873[2]	4,623[2]	6,636	10,680	1,940	2,832
Togo	4,673	7,520	32	79,200	34,240	39	...	...	245[2]	395[2]	10.3	16.5	34	49
Tonga	423	680	27	1,140	780	51	...	...	—	—	—	—	—	—
Trinidad and Tobago	5,170	8,320	51	122,000	24,000	8.7	...	...	—	—	—	—	—	—
Tunisia	14,354	23,100	79	269,000	312,000	16	*678*	*990*	1,348[2]	2,169[2]	743	1,196	1,620	2,365
Turkey	238,380	383,636	25	4,283,080	1,488,016	11	104,255	152,210	5,388	8,671	3,804	6,122	6,871	10,032
Turkmenistan	8,500	13,700	83	220,000	58,200	16	335	489	1,317	2,120	1,307	2,104	4,643	6,779
Tuvalu	5	8	—	...	...	...	...	...	—	—	—	—	—	—
Uganda	16,653	26,800	8	35,361	48,430	249	...	...	771[2]	1,241[2]	17	27	162	236
Ukraine	107,111	172,378	95	4,885,691	...	...	12,534	18,300	14,021	22,564	29,577	47,600	107,081	156,336
United Arab Emirates	2,356	3,791	100	201,000	56,950	9.6	...	...	—	—	—	—	—	—
United Kingdom	231,096	371,914	100	23,393,000	2,368,000	2.3	117,504	171,553	23,518[45]	37,849[45]	23,800	38,300	12,603	18,400
United States	3,906,292	6,286,396	91	131,839,000	79,778,000	1.3	1,051,045	1,534,500	137,900	222,000	14,000	22,500	1,421,000	2,075,000
Uruguay	5,395	8,683	30	516,889	50,264	5.6	*500*	*730*	1,288[2]	2,073[2]	*87.4*	*140.6*	123	180
Uzbekistan	52,444	84,400	87	865,300	14,500	25	1,248	1,822	2,271	3,655	1,553	2,500	11,580	16,907
Vanuatu	665	1,070	24	4,000	2,600	27	...	...	—	—	—	—	—	—
Venezuela	59,443	95,664	36	1,505,000	542,000	11	...	...	390[2]	627[2]	93.1	149.9	37.3	54.5
Vietnam	58,000	93,300	25	*200,000*		*358*	1,462	2,134	1,952[2]	3,142[2]	1,694	2,727	958	1,398
Virgin Islands (U.S.)	532	856	100	*51,000*	*13,300*	1.7	...	...	—	—	—	—	—	—
West Bank	...	...	...	88,056	24,324	18	...	...	...	...	...	...	...	...
Western Sahara	*3,900*	*6,200*	*23*	*6,284*	*424*	*20*	...	...	—	—	—	—	—	—
Yemen	40,218	64,725	8	240,567	291,149	29	...	...	—	—	—	—	—	—
Zambia	24,170	38,898	18	157,000	81,000	37	...	...	787	1,266	166	267	316	462
Zimbabwe	11,395	18,338	47	323,000	32,000	31	...	...	1,714[2]	2,759[2]	253.6	408.2	3.2	4.6

[1]Ariana Afghan Airlines only. [2]Route length. [3]Air Algérie International flights only. [4]TAAG airline only. [5]Aerolineas Argentinas only. [6]Included in Netherlands Antilles. [7]Government railways only. [8]Portion of Gulf Air traffic. [9]Caribbean Airways only. [10]Caribbean Air Cargo only. [11]Air Afrique only. [12]Air Botswana only. [13]For industrial purposes only. [14]Zaire National Railways only. [15]Air Zaire only. [16]LASCA only. [17]Traffic between Ouagadougou, Burkina Faso, and Abidjan, Côte d'Ivoire. [18]Air Ivoire only. [19]Data refer to former Czechoslovakia. [20]Including SAS international and domestic traffic. [21]National roads only. [22]Includes 62 mi (100 km) of the Chemin de Fer Djibouti-Ethiopien (CDE) in Djibouti. [23]Air France and UTA only. [24]TAN and SAHSA airlines only. [25]Includes

merchant marine (latest)				air					canals and inland waterways (latest)				country
fleet (vessels over 100 gross tons)	total dead-weight tonnage ('000)	international cargo (latest)		airports with sched-uled flights (latest)	traffic (latest)				length		cargo		
		loaded metric tons ('000)	off-loaded metric tons ('000)		passengers		cargo		mi	km	short ton-mi ('000,000)	metric ton-km ('000,000)	
					passenger-mi ('000,000)	passenger-km ('000,000)	short ton-mi ('000,000)	metric ton-km ('000,000)					
399	2,874	91,920	305,232	6	36,109	58,112	2,679	3,911	3,135	5,046	27,887	40,714	Netherlands, The
154[33]	1,053.6[33]	215	517	6	234[34]	377[34]	1.2[34]	1.8[34]	...	...	...	...	Netherlands Antilles
17	18.1	1,040	930	11	145[35]	233[35]	3.4[35]	4.9[35]	...	...	...	...	New Caledonia
139	279.8	20,640	13,308	36	12,352	19,879	584	852	1,000	1,609	1,503	2,195	New Zealand
25	1.3	320	1,629	10	49	79	6	9	1,379	2,220	...	...	Nicaragua
—	—	—	—	6	160.5	258.3	9.3	13.5	186	300	14	20	Niger
271	733.3	86,993	11,346	12	70	112	1.3	2.1	5,328	8,575	...	...	Nigeria
2	0.9	33	205	2	...	...	...	...	...	...	...	...	Northern Mariana Islands
1,597	20,834	151,116	25,788	50	6,444[20]	10,371[20]	821[20]	1,199[20]	980	1,577	7,640	11,154	Norway
26	11.7	43,525	5,303	6	601[8]	968[8]	11[8]	18[8]	...	...	...	...	Oman
73	513.8	6,408	31,008	35	6,503	10,466	226	330	...	...	...	...	Pakistan
4	...	...	64	1	...	...	...	...	...	...	...	...	Palau
5,217	79,255.6	117,924	76,800	10	853	1,373	14.9	21.8	497	800	...	...	Panama
87	40.9	2,463	1,784	42	457	735	59	86	6,798	10,940	...	...	Papua New Guinea
38	38.5	...	...	5	134	215	13	19	1,900	3,100	...	...	Paraguay
623	615.6	10,197	5,077	27	1,637	2,634	172	251	5,300	8,600	...	...	Peru
1,499	13,807.1	16,980	52,596	21	6,395[36]	10,292[36]	165[36]	241[36]	2,000	3,219	...	...	Philippines
644	4,314.3	33,360	15,864	8	2,878	4,632	55	80	2,369	3,812	753	1,100	Poland
332	1,129.3	7,572	37,740	16	6,278	10,104	159	232	510	820	...	...	Portugal
13	...	...	...	7	...	...	...	...	...	...	...	...	Puerto Rico
64	744	18,145	2,588	1	1,776[8]	2,858[8]	72[8]	105[8]	...	...	...	...	Qatar
7	33.5	454	2,302	2	...	...	...	...	...	...	...	...	Réunion
439	4,845.5	11,676	18,972	12	1,446	2,327	33.8	49.4	1,002	1,613	2,947	4,302	Romania
4,543	16,592.3	7,092	744	75	33,181	53,400	1,575	2,300	55,357	89,089	44,962	65,643	Russia
—	—	—	—	2	1.2	2.0	...	...	...	...	...	...	Rwanda
1	0.6	24	36	2	...	...	...	...	...	...	...	...	St. Kitts and Nevis
7	2.1	138	547	2	...	...	...	...	...	...	...	...	St. Lucia
946	1,253	72	128	5	...	...	...	...	...	...	...	...	St. Vincent and the Grenadines
7	6.5	48	144	3	165	265	18	26	—	—	—	—	Samoa
—	—	—	—	—	—	—	—	—	—	—	—	—	San Marino
4	2.3	16	45	2	6	9	0.7	1.0	...	...	...	...	São Tomé and Príncipe
279	1,278	214,070	46,437	28	11,774	18,949	1,815	2,650	...	...	...	...	Saudi Arabia
183	27.5	1,396	2,894	7	139.6[30]	224.7[30]	11.2[30]	16.4[30]	557	897	...	...	Senegal
462[37]	5,173.1[37]	360	972	5	551	887	4,112	6,003	365	587	905	1,322	Serbia and Montenegro
9	3.3	47	543	2	389	626	48	70	...	...	...	...	Seychelles
62	18.4	2,310	589	1	68[38]	110[38]	1.4[38]	2.0[38]	500	800	447	652	Sierra Leone
946	14,929.2	326,040	188,234	1	40,096	64,529	3,755	5,482	...	...	...	...	Singapore
...	...	...	...	2	143.8	231.4	0.5	0.7	107	172	1,046	1,527	Slovakia
13	346.5	2,460	5,952	3	517	832	2.8	4.2	...	...	21,900	31,973	Slovenia
33	5.0	278	349	21	29[39]	47[39]	0.9	1.3	...	...	...	...	Solomon Islands
28	18.5	324	1,007	1	81	131	3.0	5.0	...	...	...	...	Somalia
219	282.5	114,331	22,203	24	12,005[40]	19,320[40]	464[40]	677[40]	...	...	...	...	South Africa
2,190	5,077.3	55,752	169,848	25	37,715	60,696	4,388	6,407	649	1,045	21,836[41]	31,880[41]	Spain
66	472.6	9,288	16,632	1	3,204	5,156	459	670	267	430	0.7	1	Sri Lanka
16	62.2	1,543	4,300	3	330[42]	531[42]	14[42]	20[42]	3,300	5,310	...	...	Sudan, The
24	15.7	1,595	1,265	1	549[43]	883[43]	66[43]	106[43]	746	1,200	...	...	Suriname
—	—	—	—	1	30.7	49.4	0.09	0.1	—	—	—	—	Swaziland
430	2,881	61,320	75,528	48	6,997[20]	11,261[20]	196[20]	286[20]	1,275	2,052	5,708	8,334	Sweden
24	602.8	...	...	5	19,739	31,767	1,216	1,776	13	21	34	49	Switzerland
94	210.4	2,136	5,112	5	884	1,422	14	21	541	870	...	...	Syria
649	9,241.3	182,127	301,275	13	24,369	39,218	2,828	4,129	...	...	274	400	Taiwan
...	...	...	...	1	1,386	2,231	140	205	...	...	...	...	Tajikistan
43	48.5	1,249	2,721	11	114	184	2.0	2.9	...	...	...	...	Tanzania
351	1,194.5	42,495	74,579	25	23,826	38,345	1,145	1,671	2,300	3,701	...	...	Thailand
8	20.6	391	1,274	2	139.6	224.7	11.2	16.4	31	50	...	...	Togo
15	13.7	15	104	6	7	11	0.7	1.0	...	...	...	...	Tonga
53	17.5	9,622	10,961	2	1,783	2,869	38	55	...	...	...	...	Trinidad and Tobago
77	443.3	6,792	13,152	5	1,674	2,694	13	21	...	...	...	...	Tunisia
880	7,114.3	24,756	78,168	26	10,248[44]	16,492[44]	260[44]	380[44]	750	1,200	189	276	Turkey
...	...	...	...	1	970	1,562	98	143	240	387	5.5	8.0	Turkmenistan
6	16.0	...	...	1	...	...	...	...	...	...	...	...	Tuvalu
2	8.6	...	...	1	32.4	52.1	3	5	...	...	...	...	Uganda
...	...	77,004	7,116	12	1,225	1,972	18	27	2,734	4,400	3,973	5,800	Ukraine
276	1,491.7	88,153	9,595	6	12,150[8]	19,553[8]	978[8]	1,428[8]	...	...	...	...	United Arab Emirates
1,631	4,355	177,228	178,572	57	99,628	160,336	3,373	4,925	716	1,153	36,302	53,000	United Kingdom
509	18,585	392,076[46]	713,880[46]	834	619,500	997,000	18,116	26,449	25,778	41,485	356,188	520,026	United States
93	172.5	710[47]	1,450[47]	1	398	640	42	62	1,000	1,600	...	...	Uruguay
...	...	...	...	9	2,150	3,460	220	321	684	1,100	...	...	Uzbekistan
280	3,259.6	80	55	29	110.8	178.3	1.3	1.9	...	...	...	...	Vanuatu
271	1,355.4	101,435	17,932	20	3,600	5,800	438	639	4,400	7,100	8.9	13	Venezuela
230	872.8	303	1,510	12	2,380	3,831	67	98	11,000	17,702	1,339	1,955	Vietnam
1	...	105.5	648.3	2	...	...	...	...	...	...	...	...	Virgin Islands (U.S.)
—	—	...	...	—	—	—	—	—	...	...	...	...	West Bank
—	—	40	15	1	...	...	...	...	...	...	...	...	Western Sahara
40	13.7	1,936	7,829	12	978	1,574	22	32	...	...	...	...	Yemen
—	—	—	—	4	192	308	6.8	9.9	1,398	2,250	...	...	Zambia
—	—	—	—	7	544	875	24	35	...	...	...	...	Zimbabwe

transshipments. [26]El Al only. [27]Alitalia only. [28]Air Jamaica only. [29]Kenya Airways only. [30]International traffic only. [31]Peninsular Malaysia and Singapore. [32]Air Nauru only. [33]Includes Aruba. [34]Antillean Airlines only. [35]Air Caledonie only. [36]Philippine Air Lines only. [37]Data refer to pre-1991 Yugoslavia. [38]Sierra Leone Airlines international traffic only. [39]Solair only. [40]SAA only. [41]Coastal shipping only. [42]Sudan Airways only. [43]Suriname Airways only. [44]Turkish Airlines only. [45]British Railways only; excludes Northern Ireland. [46]Includes Puerto Rico. [47]Port of Montevideo only.

Communications

Virtually all the states of the world have a variety of communications media and services available to their citizens: book, periodical, and newspaper publishing (although only daily papers are included in this table); postal services; and telecommunications systems: radio and television broadcasting, telephones (fixed and mobile), facsimile (fax) machines, personal computers (PCs), and access to the Internet. Unfortunately, the availability of information about these services often runs behind the capabilities of the services themselves. Certain countries publish no official information; others publish data analyzed according to a variety of fiscal, calendar, religious, or other years; still others, while they possess such data almost simultaneously with the end of the business or calendar year, may not see them published except in company or parastatal reports of limited distribution. Even when such data are published in national statistical summaries, it may be only after a delay of up to several years.

The data also differ in their completeness and reliability. Figures for book production, for example, generally include all works published in separate bindings except advertising works, timetables, telephone directories, price lists, catalogs of businesses or exhibitions, musical scores, maps, atlases, and the like. The figures include government publications, school texts, theses, offprints, series works, and illustrated works, even those consisting principally of illustrations. Figures refer to works actually published during the year of survey, usually by a registered publisher, and deposited for copyright. A book is defined as a work of 49 or more pages; a work published simultaneously in more than one country is counted as having been published in each. A periodical is a publication issued at regular or stated intervals and, in Unesco's usage, directed to the general public. Newspaper statistics are especially difficult to collect and compare. Newspapers continually are founded, cease publication, merge, or change frequency of publication. Data on circulation are often incomplete, slow to be aggregated at the national level, or regarded as proprietary. In some countries no daily newspaper exists.

Post office statistics are compiled mainly from the Universal Postal Union's annual summary *Statistique des services postaux.* Postal services, unlike the other media discussed earlier, tend most often to be operated by

Communications

country	publishing (latest)							postal services				telecommunications	
	books		periodicals		daily newspapers			post offices, 1998				radio, 1997	
	number of titles	number of copies ('000)	number of titles	number of copies ('000)	number	total circulation ('000)	circulation per 1,000 persons	number	persons per office	pieces of mail handled ('000,000)	pieces handled per person	receivers (all types; '000)	receivers per 1,000 persons
Afghanistan	2,795	3,741	...	...	12	113	6	373	50,400	0.5	—	2,750	132
Albania	381	5,710	143	3,477	5	116	34	698[2]	4,840[2]	3.2	0.6	810	259
Algeria	670	...	48	803	5	1,080	38	3,223[1]	9,140[1]	736[1]	21[1]	7,100	242
American Samoa	...	...	...	...	2	5.0	93	...	...	...	...	57	929
Andorra	57	...	...	...	3	4.0	58	...	...	...	...	16	227
Angola	22	419	...	...	5	128	11	80[1]	145,000[1]	1.2	0.1	630	54
Antigua and Barbuda	...	...	...	...	1	6.0	91	16[5]	4,375[5]	...	...	36	542
Argentina	9,850	39,663	...	...	181	4,320	123	6,678[1]	5,340[1]	472[1]	11[1]	24,300	681
Armenia	396[6]	20,212[6]	44	541	11	85	23	...	...	0.7[7]	0.2[7]	850	239
Aruba	...	...	...	...	13	73	852	4	17,500	10	90	50	557
Australia	10,835	...	...	...	65	5,730	297	3,922	4,780	4,732	225	25,500	1,391
Austria	8,056[8]	...	2,481	...	17	2,382	294	2,436	3,320	3,133[1]	372[1]	6,080	751
Azerbaijan	542	2,643	49	801	6	210	28	1,673[1]	4,560[1]	12[1]	1.3[1]	175	23
Bahamas, The	...	...	...	...	3	28	100	138	2,170	61[10]	51[10]	215	739
Bahrain	40[6]	...	26	73	4	67	117	13	49,200	55	50	338	580
Bangladesh	...	...	...	...	37	1,117	9.0	9,093[1]	13,400[1]	589[1]	4.3[1]	6,150	50
Barbados	...	...	...	...	2	53	199	16	16,900	39	114	237	888
Belarus	3,809	59,073	155	3,765	10	1,899	187	3,852	2,640	709	67	3,020	292
Belgium	13,913	...	13,706	...	30	1,625	160	1,637[5]	6,200[5]	3,713	346	8,075	797
Belize	70	—	...	...	4	23.5	0.5	134[1]	1,720[1]	4.0[1]	12[1]	133	591
Benin	84[6]	42[6]	...	...	1	12	2.2	178	32,500	9.6	1.2	620	110
Bermuda	...	...	...	...	1	17	270	14[2]	4,500[2]	15[2]	240[2]	82	1,296
Bhutan	...	...	...	...	...	...	...	106[1]	17,540[1]	1.8[1]	0.7[1]	37	19
Bolivia	...	...	...	...	18	420	55	171	46,500	9.9	0.7	5,250	675
Bosnia and Herzegovina	...	...	...	...	3	518	146	210	20,050	9.8	1.6	940	267
Botswana	158[6]	...	14	177	1	40	27	180	8,720	54	26	237	154
Brazil	21,574[11]	104,397	...	...	380	6,472	55	11,713	13,800	5,223	32	71,000	434
Brunei	45[6]	56[6]	15	132	1	21	69	18	17,200	20	52	93	302
Bulgaria	4,840	20,317	772	1,740	17	2,145	253	3,303	2,500	156[2]	18[2]	4,510	537
Burkina Faso	12[6]	14[6]	37	24	4	14	1.3	85	130,000	7.3[12]	...	370	34
Burundi	...	...	...	...	1	20	3.2	28	225,000	16	1.3	440	69
Cambodia	...	...	...	...	...	...	...	56	204,000	3.2	0.2	1,340	128
Cameroon	...	...	...	...	2	91	6.7	377[1]	37,000[1]	6.1[1, 13]	0.4[1, 13]	2,270	163
Canada	19,900	...	1,400	37,108	107	4,718	158	18,607[10]	1,570[10]	10,715[12, 14]	370[12, 14]	32,300	1,067
Cape Verde	...	...	...	...	...	...	...	54	7,780	1.6	2.1	73	183
Central African Republic	...	...	...	...	3	6.0	1.8	35	99,710	...	...	283	83
Chad	...	...	...	...	1	2.0	0.2	36	201,900	13	1.0	1,670	236
Chile	2,469	4,095	417	3,450	52	1,411	99	710	20,870	343[13]	23[13]	5,180	354
China	100,951	5,945[15]	6,486	205,060	44	48,000	42	112,204	11,200	6,967[1]	5.5[1]	417,000	335
Colombia	1,481	11,314	...	...	37	1,800	49	1,354	30,200	116[3]	2.2[1]	21,000	524
Comoros	...	...	...	...	...	...	...	37	17,800	0.4	0.3	90	141
Congo, Dem. Rep. of the	64[6]	535[6]	...	...	9	124	2.7	497	98,870	...	...	18,030	376
Congo, Rep. of the	...	...	3	34	6	20	7.8	114[2]	22,720[2]	1.8[2]	0.5[2]	341	126
Costa Rica	963	...	...	...	6	320	88	134	24,900	32[1]	6.9[1]	980	261
Côte d'Ivoire	...	...	...	...	12	231	17	373	38,300	31	1.9	2,260	161
Croatia	1,718	...	352	6,357	10	515	114	1,168	3,910	299	60	1,510	337
Cuba	932	4,610	14	285	17	1,300	118	1,855	5,990	12[13]	1.1[13]	3,900	352
Cyprus	930	1,776	39	338	9	84	111	777	990	64	67	310	406
Czech Republic	10,244	...	1,168	81,387	21	2,620	256	3,369	3,050	803	72	8,270	803
Denmark	12,352	...	157	6,930	37	1,628	311	1,169	4,530	1,828[2]	335[2]	6,020	1,145
Djibouti	...	...	7	6.0	...	...	...	12	51,700	16[2]	12[2]	52	84
Dominica	...	...	...	...	...	...	...	64[10]	1,090[10]	2.9[2]	30	46	647
Dominican Republic	...	...	...	...	12	416	52	239	33,900	9.8[16]	1.3[16]	1,440	178
East Timor	...	...	...	...	...	...	...	...	...	...	...	18	21
Ecuador	12[6]	19[6]	199	...	24	820	70	315	38,600	13	0.4	4,150	348
Egypt	2,215	92,353	258	2,373	17	2,400	38	7,488	8,810	317	3.3	20,500	317
El Salvador	...	...	45	774	5	278	48	289	20,900	18	1.9	2,750	465
Equatorial Guinea	...	...	...	...	1	2.0	4.9	23[10]	17,000[10]	...	...	180	428
Eritrea	106	420	...	...	...	...	...	37[5]	91,900[5]	2.3	0.5	345	100
Estonia	2,628	6,662	517	2,323	15	255	173	560	2,550	75	43	1,010	698

a single national service, to cover a country completely, and to record traffic data according to broadly similar schemes (although the details of *classes* of mail handled may differ). Some countries do not enumerate domestic traffic or may record only international traffic requiring handling charges.

Data for some kinds of telecommunications apparatus are relatively easy to collect; telephones, for example, must be installed, and service recorded so that it may be charged. But in most countries the other types of apparatus mentioned above may be purchased by anyone and used whenever desired. As a result, data on distribution and use of these types of apparatus may be collected in a variety of ways—on the basis of numbers of subscribers, licenses issued, periodic sample surveys, trade data, census or housing surveys, or private consumer surveys. Data on broadcast media refer to receivers; data on telephones to "main lines," or the lines connecting a subscriber's apparatus (fixed or mobile) to the public, switched net. Information on fax machines and PCs is estimated only, as noted above. "Users" refers to the number of people with access to computers connected to the Internet.

The *Statistical Yearbook* of Unesco contains extensive data on book, periodical, and newspaper publishing, and on radio and television broadcasting that have been collected from standardized questionnaires. The quality and recency of its data, however, depend on the completion and timely return of each questionnaire by national authorities. The commercially published annual *World Radio TV Handbook* (Andrew G. Sennitt, editor) is a valuable source of information on broadcast media and has complete and timely coverage. It depends on data received from broadcasters, but, because some do not respond, local correspondents and monitors are used in many countries, and some unconfirmed or unofficial data are included as estimates. The statistics on telecommunications apparatus and computers are derived mainly from the UN-affiliated International Telecommunication Union's *World Telecommunication Development Report* (annual).

... Not available.

— None, nil, or not applicable.

television, 1999		telephones, 2001		cellular phones, 2001		fax, 1999		personal computers, 2001		Internet users, 2001	country
receivers (all types; '000)	receivers per 1,000 persons	main lines ('000)	main lines per 1,000 persons	cellular subscriptions ('000)	subscriptions per 1,000 persons	receivers ('000)	receivers per 1,000 persons	units ('000)	units per 1,000 persons	number ('000)	
270[1]	12[1]	29	1.3	...	...	...	...	...	...	...	Afghanistan
430[3]	112[3]	198	64	350	113	18.3	4.8	30	10	10	Albania
3,300	107	1,880	61	100	3.2	7.0[1]	0.2[1]	220	7.1	60	Algeria
14[1]	212[1]	14	237	2.4	41	...	...	...	...	...	American Samoa
30[3]	400[3]	35	530	24[4]	356[4]	5.0[3]	67[3]	...	...	7.0[4]	Andorra
190	15	80	7.7	87	8.3	...	...	17	1.6	60	Angola
31[3]	413[3]	37	487	25	329	...	...	...	...	5[4]	Antigua and Barbuda
10,600	290	8,108	225	6,975	193	87[3]	2.4[3]	2,000	55.4	3,000	Argentina
840[3]	238[3]	529	175	25	8.3	0.4[5]	0.1[5]	30	9.9	50[4]	Armenia
20[1]	204[1]	37	408	53	582	0.5[2]	6.9[2]	...	...	...	Aruba
13,400	706	10,060	517	11,169	574	900[1]	48[1]	10,000	514	7,200	Australia
4,200[3]	514[3]	3,810	472	6,566	814	285[2]	35[2]	2,270[4]	282[4]	2,600	Austria
1,950[3]	253[3]	866	107	620	76	2.5[2]	0.1[2]	0.4[9]	—	25	Azerbaijan
67[1]	223[1]	123	403	61	198	0.5[2]	6.9[2]	...	...	17	Bahamas, The
270	406	174	266	300	457	6.9	10	100	153	140	Bahrain
940	7.4	514	3.9	520	4.0	40[2]	0.3[2]	250	1.9	150	Bangladesh
78	290	124[4]	460[4]	29[4]	106[4]	1.8[2]	6.7[2]	25	93	10[4]	Barbados
3,300	321	2,858	287	138	14	24	2.3	...	...	422	Belarus
5,300	522	5,074	494	7,960	775	190[5]	19[5]	3,500[4]	341[4]	2,881	Belgium
42	179	35	143	28	114	0.5[2]	2.6[2]	33	134	18	Belize
65[3]	11[3]	59	9.0	125	19	1.1[5]	0.2[5]	11	1.7	25	Benin
66[3]	1,031[3]	56	893	13	211	...	...	32	508	25[9]	Bermuda
13	20	14	20	...	...	1.5[3]	2.3[3]	4.0	5.7	2.5	Bhutan
960	118	514	62	744	90	...	...	170	21	120[4]	Bolivia
385[2]	100[2]	450	115	233	60	...	...	...	...	45	Bosnia and Herzegovina
33	20	150[4]	90[4]	278	166	3.5[1]	2.2[1]	65	39	25	Botswana
56,000	333	37,431	218	28,746	167	500[1]	3.0[1]	10,800	63	8,000	Brazil
205	637	81	234	95	276	2.0[2]	18[2]	25	73	35	Brunei
3,400[3]	411[3]	2,914	366	1,550	195	1.5[1]	1.8[1]	361[4]	45[4]	605	Bulgaria
120[3]	10[3]	58	4.7	75	6.1	0.1	—	17	1.4	21	Burkina Faso
100	15	20	3.2	20	3.2	4.0[5]	0.6[5]	...	...	6.0	Burundi
98	9.0	34	2.6	224	17	3.0[1]	0.3[1]	20	1.5	10	Cambodia
480[3]	33[3]	101	6.4	310	20	...	...	60	3.8	45	Cameroon
21,450[1]	703[1]	20,319	613	9,924	300	1,075[1]	36[1]	12,000	362	13,500[4]	Canada
2.0	4.8	62	140	32	71	1.0[5]	2.5[5]	...	...	12.0	Cape Verde
20	5.6	9.9	2.8	11.0	3.1	0.3[1]	0.1[1]	7.0	2.0	2.0	Central African Republic
10[3]	1.4[3]	11	1.3	22	2.5	0.2	0.03[1]	12	1.4	4.0	Chad
3,600	240	3,703	249	5,272	354	40[1]	2.7[1]	1,300	87	3,102	Chile
370,000	292	179,034	140	144,812	114	2,000[1]	1.6[1]	25,000	20	33,700	China
8,273	199	7,300	181	3,160	78	242	5.8	1,800	45	1,154	Colombia
1.0[1]	1.5[1]	8.9	15.7	...	...	0.2[2]	0.2[2]	4.0	7.1	2.5	Comoros
150[5]	3.0[5]	20	0.4	150	2.9	5.0[2]	0.1[2]	...	...	6.0	Congo, Dem. Rep. of the
33[1]	12[1]	22	7.7	150	53	0.1[2]	0.4[2]	12	4.2	0.5[9]	Congo, Rep. of the
900	229	945	243	311	78	8.5[1]	2.2[1]	700	180	384	Costa Rica
1,000[3]	69[3]	294	18	729	44	...	...	100	6.1	70	Côte d'Ivoire
1,250	285	1,700	388	1,755	400	50[1]	11[1]	400	91	250[4]	Croatia
2,750	246	573	51	8.1	0.7	...	...	220	20	120	Cuba
120	178	435	482	314	349	7.0[14]	11[14]	170	188.5	150	Cyprus
5,000	487	3,846	376	6,769	662	102	9.9	1,250[4]	122[4]	1,400	Czech Republic
3,300	621	3,882	724	3,954	738	250[2]	48[2]	2,300[4]	429[4]	2,400	Denmark
30	48	9.9	22	0.3	0.6	0.1	0.2	7.0	15.2	3.3	Djibouti
6.0[1]	79[1]	23[4]	303[4]	1.2	15.6	0.3[2]	4.0[2]	6.0	78	6.0[4]	Dominica
770[1]	92[1]	940	108	1,073	124	2.5[2]	0.3[2]	...	...	186	Dominican Republic
...	...	...	...	...	...	...	...	...	...	...	East Timor
2,500[3]	201[3]	1,336	104	859	67	...	...	300	23	328	Ecuador
11,400	183	6,650	102	2,794	43	34	0.5	1,000	15	600	Egypt
1,177	191	598	96	800	128	...	...	140	22	50[4]	El Salvador
4.0[1]	9.0[1]	6.9	14	15	31	0.1[2]	0.3[2]	3.0	6.2	0.9	Equatorial Guinea
60	16	32	8.4	92	24	0.8[2]	0.2[2]	7.0	1.8	10	Eritrea
800	555	504	369	651	477	13	8.7	250	183	430	Estonia

Communications (continued)

country	publishing (latest)							postal services				telecommunications	
	books		periodicals		daily newspapers			post offices, 1998				radio, 1997	
	number of titles	number of copies ('000)	number of titles	number of copies ('000)	number	total circulation ('000)	circulation per 1,000 persons	number	persons per office	pieces of mail handled ('000,000)	pieces handled per person	receivers (all types; '000)	receivers per 1,000 persons
Ethiopia	240	674	...	...	4	86	1.5	534	112,000	27	0.3	11,750	202
Faroe Islands	...	...	...	...	1	6.0	136	42[1]	1,190[1]	10[1]	161[1]	26	582
Fiji	401	2,256	...	...	1	40	50	318	2,520	40	35	500	636
Finland	13,104	...	5,711	...	56	2,332	455	1,601	3,220	1,614	305	7,770	1,498
France	34,766	1,041	2,672	120,018	117	12,700	218	17,038	3,450	26,115	436	55,300	946
French Guiana	...	...	...	...	1	2.0	7.0	...	...	...	...	104	650
French Polynesia	...	...	...	...	4	24	108	97	2,370	28	102	128	574
Gabon	...	...	...	...	2	33	30	108	11,000	5.9	2.2	208	183
Gambia, The	14[17]	10[17]	10	885	1	2.0	1.7	...	...	...	...	196	165
Gaza Strip	...	...	...	...	...	...	...	...	...	...	...	...	...
Georgia	581[6]	834[6]	...	...	9	84	111	1,190[1]	4,560[1]	1,025[10, 13]	188[10, 13]	3,020	590
Germany	71,515	...	9,010	395,036	375	25,500	311	14,500	5,650	21,105[1]	249[1]	77,800	948
Ghana	28	648	121	774	4	250	14	1,010	18,800	225	3.4	4,400	236
Greece	4,225	...	...	...	156	1,622	153	1,225	8,590	392[5, 12]	37[5, 12]	5,020	475
Greenland	...	...	...	...	2	1.0	18	75[1]	800[1]	7.8[1]	72[1]	27	483
Grenada	...	...	4	89	1[18]	4.0[18]	45[18]	58[10]	1,550[10]	...	...	57	615
Guadeloupe	...	...	...	...	1	35	81	...	...	...	...	113	258
Guam	...	...	...	...	1	26	180	...	...	...	...	221	1,400
Guatemala	...	...	...	...	7	338	33	540[10]	19,700[10]	79[10]	7.7[10]	835	79
Guernsey	...	...	...	...	...	...	...	18	3,440	10[12]	169[12]	...	...
Guinea	...	...	3	5.0	...	...	...	96	47,400	7.9	0.4	357	49
Guinea-Bissau	...	...	...	...	1	6.0	5.4	18[5]	60,600[5]	311[2, 19]	0.3[2, 19]	49	43
Guyana	42[6]	508[6]	...	...	2	42	50	85[1]	10,000[1]	4.0[1, 13]	4.7[1, 13]	420	498
Haiti	...	...	...	...	4	20	2.5	85	90,000	1.2[19]	0.2[19]	415	53
Honduras	22	80	...	...	7	320	55	435[2]	13,700[2]	35[2]	3.0[2]	2,450	410
Hong Kong	...	...	598	...	52	5,000	800	125	53,500	1,254	175	3,700[5]	586[5]
Hungary	9,193	53,194	1,203	14,927	40	1,895	189	3,236	3,120	1,046	103	7,010	690
Iceland	1,527	...	938	384	5	145	535	94[5]	2,870[5]	73[5]	254[5]	260	950
India	11,903	...	...	...	3,037	22,969	27	153,021	6,240	16,394	16	116,000	120
Indonesia	4,018[17]	8,103[17]	115	4,173	69	4,665	23	20,139	10,200	758	3.4	31,500	155
Iran	15,073	87,861	318	6,166	32	1,651	24	13,715	4,490	274	4.2	17,000	263
Iraq	...	...	...	...	4	407	20	...	...	69	2.1	4,850	229
Ireland	...	...	...	...	6	543	153	1,912	1,940	748	170	2,550	697
Isle of Man	...	...	...	...	...	...	...	36	1,940	21[5, 7]	300[5, 7]	...	...
Israel	2,310[20]	9,368[20]	...	...	34	1,650	291	664	8,990	601	95	3,070	524
Italy	35,236	278,821	9,951	80,469	74	5,985	105	13,967[1]	4,120[1]	5,850[1]	99[1]	50,500	880
Jamaica	...	...	...	...	3	158	63	688	3,690	67	19	1,215	483
Japan	56,221[6]	400,013[6]	2,926	...	122	72,705	580	24,678	5,120	25,731[1]	202[1]	120,500	956
Jersey	...	...	...	...	...	...	...	23[1]	3,650[1]	62[1]	468[1]	...	...
Jordan	511	2,673[6]	31	43	4	250	45	687	9,170	118[1]	17[1]	1,660	271
Kazakhstan	1,226	21,014	...	...	3	500	30	3,580	4,700	201[2, 12]	0.01[2, 12]	6,470	395
Kenya	300[6]	452	...	...	4	263	9.4	1,033	28,100	413	14	3,070	108
Kiribati	...	...	...	...	...	...	...	25[1]	3,200[1]	1.9[1]	1.2[1]	17	212
Korea, North	...	...	...	...	3	4,500	200	...	...	...	...	3,360	146
Korea, South	30,487[6]	142,804[6]	...	...	60	18,000	394	3,610	12,900	3,631	77	47,500	1,039
Kuwait	196[21]	6,107	...	...	8	635	376	51[1]	35,500[1]	99[14]	68[14]	1,175	678
Kyrgyzstan	351	1,980	...	...	3	67	15	914[1]	5,080[1]	39[1, 12]	8.5[1, 12]	520	119
Laos	88[6]	995[6]	...	...	3	18	4.0	106	48,700	5.2	0.9	730	145
Latvia	1,965	7,734	213	1,660	24	616	246	978	2,500	37	12	1,760	715
Lebanon	...	...	...	...	15	435	141	268[1]	11,700[1]	3.9[1]	1.2[1]	2,850	907
Lesotho	...	...	...	...	2	15	7.6	157	13,100	64	16	104	52
Liberia	...	...	...	...	6	35	16	34[5]	8,260[5]	...	...	790	329
Libya	26	2,645	...	...	4	71	14	342	15,600	39	3.5	1,350	259
Liechtenstein	...	...	...	...	2	19	606	12[5]	2,500[5]	17[10]	0.6[10]	21	658
Lithuania	3,645	14,915	269	...	19	344	92	978[1]	3,790[1]	51	11	1,900	513
Luxembourg	681	...	508	...	5	135	327	106	3,960	169	340	285	683
Macau	67	99	16	...	10	197	448	17	25,300	19	30	160	356
Macedonia	892	2,496	74	347	3	41	19	294	6,800	27	11	410	206
Madagascar	119	296	55	108	5	66	4.6	764	19,700	26	1.5	3,050	209
Malawi	117[6, 22]	9,174[6, 22]	...	...	1	25	2.6	314	34,100	44	3.4	2,600	258
Malaysia	5,843	29,040	25	996	42	3,345	163	1,382	7,490	993[7]	96[7]	9,100	434
Maldives	...	...	...	...	2	5.0	18	249[1]	1,080[1]	2.5	5.9	34	129
Mali	14[6]	28[6]	...	...	3	12	1.2	124	86,200	3.4	0.2	570	55
Malta	404	...	359	...	2	48	130	51[13]	7,450[13]	14[13]	34[13]	255	669
Marshall Islands	...	...	...	...	...	...	...	...	...	...	...	...	...
Martinique	...	...	...	...	1	30	78	...	...	...	...	82	213
Mauritania	...	...	...	...	2	1.0	0.5	61	41,500	4.2	0.5	360	146
Mauritius	80	163	62	...	6	85	76	101	11,500	63	47	420	371
Mayotte	...	...	...	...	...	...	...	...	...	...	...	50[5]	427[5]
Mexico	...	...	158	13,097	295	9,030	97	9,432	10,600	1,133	9.4	31,000	329
Micronesia	...	...	...	...	...	...	...	...	...	...	...	70[5]	667[5]
Moldova	921	2,779	76	196	4	261	59	1,276	3,430	41	8.1	3,220	736
Monaco	41	722	3	38	1	8.0	263	...	...	...	...	34	1,039
Mongolia	285[6]	959[6]	45	6,361	4	68	27	339[1]	7,050[1]	1.1[1]	0.3[1]	360	142
Morocco	918	1,836	...	...	22	704	27	1,469	18,900	240	7.7	6,640	247
Mozambique	...	3,490	...	...	2	49	2.7	353	47,900	6.8	0.1	730	40
Myanmar (Burma)	3,660	4,038	...	...	5	449	10	1,238	37,500	88[2]	1.9[2]	4,200	96
Namibia	106	...	...	...	4	30	19	115	14,400	66[12]	4.0[12]	232	143
Nauru	...	...	...	...	...	...	...	1[1]	10,000[1]	...	...	7.0	609
Nepal	...	...	...	...	29	250	11	4,156	5,260	29[5, 7]	1.4[5, 7]	840	38
Netherlands, The	34,067	...	367	19,283	38	4,753	305	2,387	6,580	7,009[23]	447[23]	15,300	980
Netherlands Antilles	...	...	...	...	6	70	334	16	12,625	...	...	217	1,031
New Caledonia	...	...	...	...	3	24	127	54	3,700	21	75	107	527
New Zealand	...	...	126	3,991	23	804	223	...	...	...	...	3,750	997
Nicaragua	...	...	...	...	4	135	30	183	26,300	8.3	1.2	1,240	265

television, 1999		telephones, 2001		cellular phones, 2001		fax, 1999		personal computers, 2001		Internet users, 2001	country
receivers (all types; '000)	receivers per 1,000 persons	main lines ('000)	main lines per 1,000 persons	cellular subscriptions ('000)	subscriptions per 1,000 persons	receivers ('000)	receivers per 1,000 persons	units ('000)	units per 1,000 persons	number ('000)	
350	5.7	310	4.7	28	0.4	3.1	0.1	75	1.1	25	Ethiopia
15[1]	333[1]	25[9]	556[9]	11[9]	244[9]	...	...	...	...	...	Faroe Islands
89	110	90	111	76	93	2.8	3.5	50	61	15	Fiji
3,320	643	2,845	548	4,044	780	198[1]	38[1]	2,200	424	4,303	Finland
36,500	623	34,033	575	35,922	607	2,800[1]	47[1]	20,000	338	15,653	France
30[1]	172[1]	49	293	18	108	...	...	...	...	...	French Guiana
43	186	53	221	67	282	3.0[3]	13[3]	...	...	16	French Polynesia
300	251	39	32	120[4]	98[4]	0.5[1]	0.4[1]	15	12	15[4]	Gabon
4.0	3.2	35	25	43	31	1.1[1]	0.9[1]	18	13	17	Gambia, The
...	...	...	...	...	...	...	...	...	...	...	Gaza Strip
2,580[3]	473[3]	868	174	295	59	0.5[10]	0.1[10]	0.7[9]	0.1[9]	25	Georgia
47,660	580	52,280	634	56,245	683	6,500	79	27,640[4]	336[4]	30,000	Germany
2,266	115	242	12	194	9.7	5.0	0.3	70	3.5	41	Ghana
5,100	480	5,608	511	7,962	725	40	3.8	860	78	1,400	Greece
22[1]	393[1]	26	468	17	298	...	...	...	...	20	Greenland
33	355	33	325	6.4	63	0.3	3.1	13	129	5.2	Grenada
118	262	205[4]	478[4]	293	682	3.4[2]	8.1[2]	100	233	8.0[4]	Guadeloupe
106	646	80[4]	508[4]	27[4]	172[4]	3.4	8.1	...	...	5.0[4]	Guam
660[3]	60[3]	756	65	1,134	97	10	1.0	150	13	200	Guatemala
...	...	55	873	32	500	0.7	11	...	...	20[4]	Guernsey
343	44	26	3.3	56	7.3	3.2	0.4	32	4.2	15	Guinea
...	...	12	9.1	...	...	0.5[3]	0.4[3]	...	...	4.0	Guinea-Bissau
60	70	80	103	40	51	...	...	23	30	95	Guyana
38	5.5	80	12	92	13	...	...	...	...	30	Haiti
600	95	310	48	238	37	...	...	80	13	40[4]	Honduras
2,884[3]	429[3]	3,926	584	5,702	848	390	58	2,600	387	3,100	Hong Kong
4,500	448	3,730	366	4,968	488	180	18	1,000	98	1,480	Hungary
145	520	191	669	235	826	4.1[14]	15[14]	120	421	195	Iceland
75,000	75	34,732	34	5,725	5.5	150[1]	0.2[1]	6,000	5.8	7,000	India
30,000	143	7,949	38	5,303	25	185	0.9	2,300	11	4,000	Indonesia
10,500	157	10,006	155	1,485	23	30	0.5	4,500	70	402	Iran
1,750[1]	78[1]	675[9]	29[9]	...	...	...	...	...	...	...	Iraq
1,505	406	1,860	480	2,800	722	100[1]	27[1]	1,500	387	895	Ireland
...	...	...	...	...	...	...	...	...	...	...	Isle of Man
2,000	328	3,100	497	5,260	842	140	25	1,600	256	1,500	Israel
28,000[3]	488[3]	27,303	472	48,698	841	1,800	31	11,300	195	16,000	Italy
480[3]	188[3]	513	197	700	268	1.6[14]	0.6[14]	130	50	100	Jamaica
91,000	719	76,000	598	72,796	573	16,000[1]	126[1]	44,400	349	57,900	Japan
...	...	74	849	61	706	0.7	8.0	...	...	8.0[4]	Jersey
540	83	660	129	746	146	52[3]	8.0[3]	170	33	212	Jordan
3,890[3]	239[3]	1,834[4]	124[4]	582	39	2.0	0.1	...	...	100[4]	Kazakhstan
660	22	313	10	500	16	3.8	0.1	175	5.7	500	Kenya
10[1]	122[1]	3.4[4]	38[4]	0.4[4]	4.5[4]	0.2	2.5	2.0	23	2.0	Kiribati
1,200	51	1,100[9]	50[9]	...	...	3.0	0.1	...	...	...	Korea, North
16,896	361	22,725	480	29,046	614	400	8.6	12,000	254	24,380	Korea, South
910	480	472	211	489	218	60	32	260	116	200	Kuwait
220[3]	47[3]	376[4]	76[4]	27	5.5	...	...	...	...	52[4]	Kyrgyzstan
51	10	53	9.3	30	5.3	0.5[10]	0.1[10]	16	2.8	10	Laos
1,808	741	725	307	657	279	0.9[2]	0.3[2]	360	153	170	Latvia
1,120[3]	346[3]	682[4]	188[4]	743[4]	205[4]	3.0[12]	1.1[12]	200	55	300[4]	Lebanon
33	16	22	10	33	15	0.6[2]	0.3[2]	...	...	5.0	Lesotho
70[1]	24[1]	6.6	2.0	...	...	...	...	...	...	...	Liberia
730[1]	133[1]	610	116	50	9.5	...	...	...	...	20	Libya
12[1]	375[1]	18	546	9.5	288	...	...	...	...	...	Liechtenstein
1,555	420	1,152	331	932	268	6.2[1]	1.7[1]	260	75	250	Lithuania
165[3]	385[3]	350	792	432	978	30	70	230	520	100[4]	Luxembourg
125	286	176	407	195	448	6.3	14	80	184	101	Macau
500[3]	249[3]	538	265	223	110	3.0	1.5	2.2[9]	1.1[9]	70	Macedonia
340[3]	22[3]	58	3.7	148	9.2	...	...	40	2.5	35	Madagascar
27	2.5	54	5.2	56	5.4	1.3	0.1	13	1.3	20	Malawi
3,800	174	4,738	199	7,128	300	175[3]	8.0[3]	3,000	126	5,700	Malaysia
11	40	27	99	18	67	3.5[2]	14[2]	6.0	21.7	10.0	Maldives
130[3]	12[3]	50	4.5	45	4.1	...	...	14	1.3	30	Mali
212	549	208	541	139	362	6.0[5]	16[5]	90	234	99	Malta
...	...	4.2	78	0.5	9.3	...	...	4.0	74	0.9	Marshall Islands
66[1]	168[1]	172[4]	447[4]	286	743	20[2]	52[2]	52	135	99[9]	Martinique
247	96	19	7.3	...	...	3.3	1.3	27	10	7.0	Mauritania
265	230	307	256	300	250	32	28	130	108	158	Mauritius
3.5[5]	30[5]	10	63	...	...	...	...	...	...	...	Mayotte
26,000	267	13,533	136	20,136	202	285[1]	2.9[1]	6,900	69	3,500	Mexico
2.4	21	10	93	...	...	0.5[3]	4.3[3]	...	...	4.0[4]	Micronesia
1,300	297	676	186	210	58	0.7	0.2	70	19.3	60	Moldova
25[1]	758[1]	33[3]	1,000[3]	12[3]	364[3]	...	...	...	...	...	Monaco
152[3]	58[3]	123	51	195	80	7.9	3.0	35	14	40	Mongolia
4,600	165	1,191	41	374	13	18[1]	0.6[1]	400	14	400	Morocco
95	5	89	5.1	170	9.6	7.2[10]	0.4[10]	70	4.0	15	Mozambique
323	7.2	281	6.7	14	0.3	2.5	0.1	55	1.3	10	Myanmar (Burma)
65	38	117	65	100	55	...	...	65	36	45	Namibia
0.5[1]	0.1[1]	1.7[3]	0.2[3]	0.8[3]	0.1[3]	...	...	...	...	...	Nauru
150	6.7	298	13	17	0.7	8.0	0.4	80	3.5	60	Nepal
9,500	600	10,000	623	11,900	742	600[1]	38[1]	6,900	430	5,300	Netherlands, The
69[1]	321[1]	79[9]	367[9]	16[3]	74[3]	...	...	...	...	...	Netherlands Antilles
101	481	51[4]	238[4]	50[4]	233[4]	2.2[10]	12[10]	...	...	24[4]	New Caledonia
1,975	518	1,834	475	2,417	626	65[2]	18[2]	1,500	389	1,092	New Zealand
340	69	159[4]	32[4]	156	32	...	...	50	10	50	Nicaragua

Communications (continued)

country	publishing (latest)							postal services				telecommunications	
	books		periodicals		daily newspapers			post offices, 1998				radio, 1997	
	number of titles	number of copies ('000)	number of titles	number of copies ('000)	number	total circulation ('000)	circulation per 1,000 persons	number	persons per office	pieces of mail handled ('000,000)	pieces handled per person	receivers (all types; '000)	receivers per 1,000 persons
Niger	5[6]	11[6]	...	...	1	2	0.2	53	190,000	3.4	0.3	680	70
Nigeria	1,314	18,800	...	...	25	2,740	27	3,971	26,800	391	2.0	23,500	226
Northern Mariana Islands	...	...	...	...	...	...	...	...	...	...	...	11[5]	190[5]
Norway	6,900[8, 20]	...	8,017	...	83	2,578	593	1,534[1]	210[1]	2,524[1]	555[1]	4,030	917
Oman	7[6]	21[6]	15	...	4	63	27	90[2]	23,700[2]	43	7.1	1,400	607
Pakistan	124	714	...	...	264	2,840	22	13,294	9,820	413	2.9	13,500	94
Palau	...	...	...	...	...	...	...	...	...	...	...	12	663
Panama	...	...	...	...	7	166	62	176	15,700	18	4.4	815	299
Papua New Guinea	122	...	...	...	2	65	15	108[24]	39,800[24]	39[24]	10[24]	410	91
Paraguay	152	...	...	...	5	213	43	326	16,000	4.6	0.5	925	182
Peru	612	1,836	...	...	74	2,000	85	963	25,800	43	1.3	6,650	273
Philippines	1,507	14,718[6]	1,570	9,468	47	5,700	82	3,023[10]	22,600[10]	3,205[5]	12[5]	11,500	161
Poland	14,104	80,306	5,260	75,358	55	4,351	113	7,836	4,930	2,503	63	20,200	522
Portugal	7,868[11]	26,942	984	10,208	27	740	75	3,712	2,660	1,201	117	3,020	306
Puerto Rico	...	...	...	...	3	475	127	...	...	...	...	2,700	714
Qatar	209[17]	2,205	11	47	5	90	161	26	20,800	20[13]	38[13]	256	450
Réunion	69	...	...	...	3	55	83	...	...	...	...	173	257
Romania	7,199	38,374	987	...	69	6,800	297	6,324	3,560	327	14	7,200	319
Russia	36,237	421,387	2,751	387,832	285	15,517	105	43,900[1]	3,350[1]	5,614[1, 7]	38[1, 7]	61,500	417
Rwanda	...	...	15	101	1	0.5	0.1	39	169,000	3.8	0.4	601	101
St. Kitts and Nevis	...	...	10	44	...	...	...	7	5,710	2.6	46	28	701
St. Lucia	...	...	...	...	...	...	...	63	2,380	2.3[12]	15[12]	111	746
St. Vincent and the Grenadines	...	...	...	...	1	1.0	9.0	41[1]	2,680[1]	...	...	77	690
Samoa	...	...	...	...	...	...	...	38	4,470	0.9	3.0	178	1,035
San Marino	...	...	15	9	3	2.0	72	10[5]	3,000[5]	...	...	16	610
São Tomé and Príncipe	...	...	...	...	...	...	...	18	7,780	0.3	0.6	38	272
Saudi Arabia	3,900[6]	14,493[6, 22]	471	...	13	1,105	59	1,421	14,200	1,246	45	6,250	321
Senegal	...	...	...	...	1	45	5.3	134	69,200	12	0.7	1,240	141
Serbia and Montenegro	5,367	16,669	395	...	18	1,128	110	1,783	5,940	242	19	3,150	296
Seychelles	...	...	...	...	1	3.0	46	5	16,000	5.2	49	42	560
Sierra Leone	...	...	...	...	1	20	4.7	54[2]	83,500[2]	1.1[2]	0.1[2]	1,121	253
Singapore	...	...	...	...	8	1,095	324	939	4,120	772[1]	184[1]	2,550	744
Slovakia	3,800	6,139	424	8,725	19	989	185	1,728	3,120	518	90	3,120	581
Slovenia	3,441	6,267	784	...	7	397	206	545	3,630	387	189	805	403
Solomon Islands	...	...	...	...	...	...	...	127	3,150	4.3[2]	11[2]	57	141
Somalia	...	...	...	...	2	10	1.2	...	...	...	...	470	53
South Africa	5,418	31,349	11	2,149	17	1,288	34	2,449	17,200	2,170[7]	52[7]	13,750	355
Spain	46,330	192,019	...	...	94	3,931	99	4,093	9,620	4,565	112	13,100	331
Sri Lanka	4,115	19,650	...	...	9	530	29	4,282	4,380	463	23	3,850	211
Sudan, The	...	...	...	...	5	737	27	491	57,600	4.4[5]	0.1[5]	7,550	272
Suriname	47[6]	21[6]	...	...	4	50	116	33	12,400	...	...	300	728
Swaziland	...	...	...	...	3	24	27	60[1]	15,200[1]	21[1]	18[1]	155	168
Sweden	13,496	...	373	19,242	94	3,933	446	1,720[5]	5,140[5]	4,570[5]	503[5]	8,250	932
Switzerland	15,371	...	60	4,561	88	2,383	330	3,630[5]	1,950[5]	4,230[10]	601[10]	7,100	979
Syria	598	310[5]	30	192	8	287	20	619	25,200	19	1.0	4,150	278
Taiwan	...	...	...	...	...	4,000	188	...	...	...	...	8,620[5]	402[5]
Tajikistan	132[6]	997[6]	11	130	2	120	20	706[1]	8,570[1]	3.0[1]	0.4[1]	850	143
Tanzania	172[6]	364[6]	...	...	3	120	3.9	612	52,400	55	1.3	8,800	280
Thailand	8,142	...	1,522	...	30	3,800	65	4,265	14,300	1,315	21	13,959	234
Togo	...	...	...	...	1	15	3.6	50[1]	86,400[1]	8.3[1]	0.7[1]	940	219
Tonga	...	...	...	...	1	7.0	71	1.8[14]	55,600[14]	4.0[14]	40[14]	61	400
Trinidad and Tobago	26	30	...	...	4	156	121	245	5,220	30[2]	16[2]	680	533
Tunisia	720	6,000[22]	170	1,748	8	280	31	947[2]	9,740[2]	117[2]	12[2]	2,060	224
Turkey	6,546	...	3,554	...	57	6,845	111	16,984	3,740	1,088	16	11,300	178
Turkmenistan	450[6]	5,493[6]	...	...	...	...	...	1,673[5]	2,730[5]	27[5]	6.0[5]	1,225	289
Tuvalu	...	...	...	...	...	...	...	...	...	...	...	4.0	384
Uganda	288	2,229[20]	26	158	2	40	2.1	313	67,200	18[1]	0.5[1]	2,600	130
Ukraine	6,225	68,876	717	2,521	44	2,780	54	15,227	3,320	374	6.3	45,050	882
United Arab Emirates	293[22]	5,117[22]	80	922	7	384	170	243	11,190	182	39	820	355
United Kingdom	107,263	...	...	...	99	19,332	332	18,760	3,130	19,556	325	84,500	1,443
United States	68,175	...	11,593	...	1,520	59,990	212	38,159	7,090	197,688	729	575,000	2,116
Uruguay	934	1,970	...	...	36	950	296	942	3,490	16	6.0	1,970	603
Uzbekistan	1,003	30,914	81	684	3	75	3.0	3,044[1]	7,700[1]	12[1]	0.4[1]	10,800	465
Vanuatu	...	...	...	...	...	...	...	...	...	...	...	62	350
Venezuela	3,468[6]	7,420[6]	...	...	86	4,600	206	407	57,600	141	5.1	10,750	472
Vietnam	5,581	83,000	338	2,710	10	300	4.0	3,075	25,200	...	...	8,200	107
Virgin Islands (U.S.)	...	...	...	...	3	42	326	9[1]	2,000[1]	3.6[10, 13]	0.2[10, 13]	107	1,119
West Bank	...	...	...	...	...	...	...	...	...	...	...	...	...
Western Sahara	...	...	...	...	...	...	...	...	...	...	...	56	211
Yemen	...	...	...	...	3	230	15	265	64,400	5.5	0.1	1,050	64
Zambia	...	...	...	...	3	114	14	195	45,000	16	0.8	1,030	120
Zimbabwe	232	...	28	680	2	209	19	296	42,800	137	9.4	1,140	102

television, 1999		telephones, 2001		cellular phones, 2001		fax, 1999		personal computers, 2001		Internet users, 2001	country
receivers (all types; '000)	receivers per 1,000 persons	main lines ('000)	main lines per 1,000 persons	cellular subscriptions ('000)	subscriptions per 1,000 persons	receivers ('000)	receivers per 1,000 persons	units ('000)	units per 1,000 persons	number ('000)	
285	27	22	2.1	1.8	0.2	0.3[2]	0.0[2]	6.0	0.6	12	Niger
7,200[3]	66[3]	500	3.9	330	2.6	6.8[2]	0.1[2]	800	6.3	200[4]	Nigeria
...	...	27[4]	383[4]	3.0[4]	43[4]	...	...	...	...	...	Northern Mariana Islands
2,900	648	3,262	723	3,737	828	220[1]	49[1]	2,300	510	2,700	Norway
1,415	575	235	95	325	132	6.4[1]	2.6[1]	85	34	120	Oman
16,000	119	3,400	24	800	5.6	268	2.0	600	4.2	500	Pakistan
...	...	...	...	...	...	...	...	...	...	20[9]	Palau
530[3]	188[3]	430	149	600	208	0.8	0.2	110	38	90[4]	Panama
60	13	65[4]	12[4]	8.6[4]	1.6[4]	0.8[10]	0.2[10]	300	57	135[4]	Papua New Guinea
1,100	205	289	51	1,150	204	1.7[14]	0.4[14]	80	14	60	Paraguay
3,700	147	2,022	77	1,545	59	15[2]	0.6[2]	1,250	48	3,000	Peru
8,200	110	3,100	40	10,568	135	50[3]	0.7[3]	1,700	22	2,000	Philippines
15,000	387	11,400	295	10,050	260	55[2]	1.4[2]	3,300	85	3,800	Poland
5,600	560	4,370	421	7,978	769	70	7.0	1,210	117	3,600	Portugal
1,250[3]	321[3]	1,330	346	1,211	315	543[14]	149[14]	...	...	600	Puerto Rico
490[3]	832[3]	167	280	179	300	10[3]	18[3]	100	168	40	Qatar
127[1]	184[1]	268	366	50	68.2	1.9[2]	2.9[2]	...	...	...	Réunion
7,000	312	4,094	188	3,860	177	21[2]	0.9[2]	800	37	1,000	Romania
62,000[3]	421[3]	35,700	247	5,560	39	53[3]	0.4[3]	7,300	51	4,300	Russia
10[1]	1.7[1]	22	2.9	65	8.9	0.5[2]	0.1[2]	...	...	20	Rwanda
10[1]	256[1]	22[4]	476[4]	1.2[4]	26[4]	...	...	8.0	174	2.0[9]	St. Kitts and Nevis
32[1]	208[1]	44[9]	286[9]	1.9[3]	12[3]	...	...	...	...	...	St. Lucia
18[1]	159[1]	25[4]	222[4]	2.4[4]	21[4]	...	...	13	116	3.5[4]	St. Vincent and the Grenadines
9.0[3]	51[3]	10	57	3.0	17	0.5[3]	2.8[3]	1	5.7	3.0	Samoa
9.0[1]	346[1]	20[9]	769[9]	9.6	356	...	...	...	...	...	San Marino
23[1]	160[1]	5.4	38	...	...	0.2[2]	15[2]	...	...	9.0	São Tomé and Príncipe
5,500	263	3,233	143	2,529	111	150[2]	8.2[2]	1,400	62	300	Saudi Arabia
370[3]	40[3]	237	25	391	41	...	...	180	19	100	Senegal
2,900[3]	273[3]	2,444	230	1,998	188	20	1.9	250	24	600	Serbia and Montenegro
16	200	21	261	44	538	0.6	7.5	12	146	9.0	Seychelles
60[3]	13[3]	23	4.9	27	5.8	2.5	0.5	...	...	7.0	Sierra Leone
1,200	308	1,949	472	2,859	692	100[3]	32[3]	2,100	508	1,500	Singapore
2,250	417	1,556	289	2,147	399	54[3]	10[3]	800	149	650[4]	Slovakia
710[3]	357[3]	800	406	1,516	770	21[3]	11[3]	550	279	600	Slovenia
6.0[3]	14[3]	7.4	17	1.0	2.3	0.8	1.9	22	52	2.0	Solomon Islands
135[1]	14[1]	15[9]	2.0[9]	...	...	...	...	...	...	...	Somalia
5,450[3]	124[3]	4,969	112	9,197	208	150[1]	3.4[1]	3,000	68	3,068	South Africa
22,000	547	17,427	427	26,494	649	700[5]	17[5]	6,800	168	7,388	Spain
1,900	102	828	44	720	39	11[10]	0.6[10]	150	8.0	150	Sri Lanka
5,000	173	453	13	105	2.9	25	0.9	115	3.2	56	Sudan, The
98[3]	236[3]	77	178	84	194	...	...	...	...	15	Suriname
110	112	32	29	66	60	1.2[5]	1.2[5]	...	...	14	Swaziland
4,700[3]	530[3]	6,585	740	6,867	772	450[5]	51[5]	5,000	562	4,600	Sweden
3,700	518	5,183	717	5,226	723	207[5]	29[5]	3,600[4]	498[4]	2,917	Switzerland
1,070	66	1,808	108	200	12	22	1.4	270	16	60	Syria
9,220	417	12,847	575	21,633	968	430[10]	20[10]	5,000	224	7,550	Taiwan
2,000	328	223	36	1.6	0.3	2.1	0.3	...	...	3.2	Tajikistan
690	21	148	4.1	427	13	2.0[14]	0.1[14]	120	3.5	300	Tanzania
17,600	289	5,974	95	7,550	120	150[1]	2.5[1]	1,700	27	3,536	Thailand
100	22	48	9.3	95	18	18	4.0	100	19	50	Togo
2.0[1]	20[1]	9.7[4]	97[4]	0.1[9]	1.0[9]	0.2[2]	2.0[2]	...	...	1.0[9]	Tonga
1,430	1,107	312	240	225	174	5.0[3]	3.9[3]	90	69	120	Trinidad and Tobago
1,800	190	1,056	109	389	40	31[1]	3.3[1]	230	24	400	Tunisia
21,500	332	18,901	276	20,000	292	108[1]	1.7[1]	2,700	39	2,500	Turkey
865[3]	197[3]	388	80	9.5[4]	1.9[4]	...	...	...	...	8.0	Turkmenistan
0.1[5]	9.1[5]	0.6[9]	55[9]	...	...	...	...	...	...	...	Tuvalu
580[3]	27[3]	64	2.7	323	14	3.0[5]	0.1[5]	70	3.0	60	Uganda
21,000[3]	415[3]	10,670	219	2,225	46	48	0.9	920	19	600	Ukraine
740	252	1,053	311	1,909	564	18	6.1	420	124	900	United Arab Emirates
38,800	652	34,710	579	47,026	784	1,992[5]	33[5]	22,000	367	24,000	United Kingdom
233,000	844	190,000	667	127,000	446	21,000[1]	78.0[1]	178,000	625	142,823	United States
1,760	531	951	283	520	155	0.6	0.2	370	110	400	Uruguay
6,700	276	1,663	66	63	2.5	2.2	0.1	...	...	150	Uzbekistan
2.0[1]	11[1]	6.8	34	0.3	1.5	0.6[2]	3.6[2]	...	...	5.5	Vanuatu
4,300[3]	181[3]	2,758	112	6,489	264	70[1]	3.0[1]	1,300	53	1,300	Venezuela
14,500	184	3,050	39	1,251	16	31	0.4	800	10	400	Vietnam
6.8[1]	57[1]	69[4]	562[4]	35[4]	321[4]	...	...	...	...	12[9]	Virgin Islands (U.S.)
...	...	257	72	40[1]	14[1]	...	...	...	...	60	West Bank
6.0[5]	24[5]	...	...	...	...	...	...	...	...	...	Western Sahara
5,000	286	423	22	152	8.1	2.8[2]	0.2[2]	37	2.0	17	Yemen
1,300	145	85	8.7	98	10	1.0	0.1	75	7.7	25	Zambia
2,074	180	254	22	329	29	4.1[3]	0.4[3]	165	15	100	Zimbabwe

[1]1997. [2]1995. [3]1998. [4]2000. [5]1996. [6]First editions only. [7]Domestic and foreign-dispatched only. [8]Not including school textbooks. [9]1999. [10]1994. [11]Including reprints. [12]Domestic only. [13]Foreign-dispatched and foreign-received only. [14]1993. [15]Millions of copies. [16]1985. [17]School textbooks and government publications only. [18]1980. [19]Foreign-received only. [20]Not including government publications. [21]Government publications only. [22]School textbooks only. [23]Domestic and foreign-received only. [24]1991.

Trade: external

The following table presents comparative data on the international, or foreign, trade of the countries of the world. The table analyzes data for both imports and exports in two ways: (1) into several major commodity groups defined in accordance with the United Nations system called the Standard International Trade Classification (SITC) and (2) by direction of trade for each country with major world trading blocs and partners. These commodity groupings are defined by the SITC code numbers beneath the column headings. The single-digit numbers represent broad SITC categories (in the SITC, called "sections"); the double-digit numbers represent subcategories ("divisions") of the single-digit categories (27 is a subcategory of 2); the three-digit number is a subcategory ("group") of the double-digit (667 is a subcategory of 66). Where a plus or minus sign is used before one of these SITC numbers, the SITC category or subcategory is being added to or subtracted from the aggregate implied by the total of the preceding sections. The SITC commodity aggregations used here are listed in the table at the end of this headnote. The full SITC commodity breakdown for the system used here is presented in the 1975 United Nations publication *Standard International Trade Classification, Revision 2.*

The SITC was developed by the United Nations through its Statistical Commission as an outgrowth of the need for a standard system of aggregating commodities of external trade to provide international comparability of foreign trade statistics. The United Nations Statistical Commission has defined external merchandise trade as "all goods whose movement into or out of the customs area of a country compiling the statistics adds to or subtracts from the material resources of the country." Goods passing through a country for transport only are excluded, but goods entering for reexport, or deposited (as in a bonded warehouse, or free trade area) for reimport, are included. Statistics in this table refer only to goods and exclude purely financial transactions that are covered in the "Finance" and "National product and accounts" tables. Gold for fabrication (*e.g.,* as jewelry) is included; monetary and reserve gold are excluded.

For purposes of comparability of data, total value of imports and exports is given in this table in U.S. dollars. Conversions from currencies other than U.S. dollars are determined according to the average market rates for the year for which data are supplied; these are mainly as calculated by the International Monetary Fund (IMF) or other official sources. The commodity categories are given in terms of percentages of the total value of the country's import or export trade (with the exclusions noted above). Value is based on transaction value: for imports, the value at which the goods were purchased by the importer plus the cost of transportation and insurance to the frontier of the importing country (c.i.f. [cost, insurance,

Trade: external

country	year	imports												
		total value ('000,000 U.S.$)	Standard International Trade Classification (SITC) categories (%)							direction of trade (%)				
			food and agricultural raw materials (0 + 1 + 2 – 27 – 28 + 4)	mineral ores and concentrates (27 + 28 + 667)	fuels and other energy (3)	manufactured goods: total[a] (5 + 6 – 667 + 7 + 8 + 9)	of which chemicals and related products (5)	of which machinery and transport equipment (7)	of which other[a] (6 – 667 + 8 + 9)	from European Union (EU)[b]	from United States	from Eastern Europe[c]	from Japan	from all other[d]
Afghanistan	1996[1]	359.0	— 19.9[2] —		2.7	77.4[3]	—	15.2	62.2[3]	16.5[4]	1.1[4]	8.3[4]	25.3[4]	48.8[4]
Albania	1998	840.8	28.4	0.3	3.9	67.4	8.9	16.3	42.2	81.6	1.0	6.3	0.1	11.0
Algeria	1999	9,161.9	30.1	0.2	1.7	68.1	11.7	33.1	23.2	56.2	8.4	4.8	3.9	26.7
American Samoa	1996[6]	499.0	— 40.5[2, 7] —		16.9[7]	42.6[3, 7]	2.3[7]	7.4[7]	32.9[3, 7]	0.1[7]	78.2[7]	—[7]	2.0[7]	19.6[7]
Andorra	1998	1,080.5	24.2	3.9	3.5	68.4	10.7	25.8	31.9	88.2	2.3	0.2	3.2	6.1
Angola	1999	2,143.0	— 33.6[2, 5] —		0.3[5]	66.1[3, 5]	9.1[5]	30.1[5]	26.9[3, 5]	46.0	13.2	4.3	0.7	35.8
Antigua and Barbuda	1998	357.5	— 15.7[2] —		8.4	75.9[3]	5.9	27.2	42.8[3]	10.1	26.6	—	—	63.3
Argentina	1999	25,508.0	6.4	1.0	2.8	89.7	17.5	46.4	25.8	29.1	19.6	1.4	4.2	45.8
Armenia	1999	810.9	26.7	10.5	21.6	41.3	10.1	13.9	17.3	31.1	10.9	22.2	0.2	35.5
Aruba	1998	832.5[10]	21.7	4.1	—	74.2	10.4	36.9	26.9	12.0	72.0	—	1.9	14.1
Australia	1999	65,514.5	5.9	0.7	5.9	87.5	11.1	47.0	29.3	22.4	20.5	0.2	13.2	43.6
Austria	1999	66,003.5	9.0	0.7	4.0	86.4	10.0	41.2	35.2	70.3	5.4	8.5	2.6	13.2
Azerbaijan	1999	1,035.7	21.2	1.0	6.3	71.5	6.1	41.5	23.9	18.4	8.0	29.4	5.4	38.9
Bahamas, The	1998	1,816.4	— 19.0[2] —		6.2	74.8[3]	8.8	30.6	35.4[3]	1.6[11]	91.5[11]	0.3[4, 11]	0.3[4, 11]	6.3[11]
Bahrain	1996	4,092.6	12.3	5.3	40.9	41.5	5.2	15.7	20.7	18.9	6.7	0.2	3.7	70.6
Bangladesh	1998[13]	7,018.0	20.7	0.6	7.5	71.2	8.7	19.6	42.9	12.3	4.3	1.7	6.8	74.9
Barbados	1999	1,067.3	19.1	0.9	6.2	73.8	10.3	32.0	31.6	16.4	42.5	0.1	7.9	33.2
Belarus	1999	6,673.7	15.0	1.7	23.0	60.2	12.8	20.4	27.0	19.8	1.9	70.4	0.5	7.3
Belgium	1999	160,708.4	11.8	8.7	6.0	73.6	16.0	31.1	26.5	70.6	7.5	2.5	2.6	16.8
Belize	1999	366.3	17.2	0.2	15.3	67.3	9.2	27.3	30.8	7.8	51.7	—	2.3	38.2
Benin	1998	807.0	29.8	0.8	20.8	48.6	7.9	17.2	23.5	45.7	5.9	2.9	4.4	41.2
Bermuda	1995	680.2	21.5	2.1	6.0	70.4	7.8	25.3	37.3	6.4	49.8	—	—	43.9
Bhutan	1997	137.4	22.8[8]	0.5[8]	11.4[8]	65.2[8]	8.5[8]	30.3[8]	26.5[8]	3.5	0.6	0.1	16.9	79.0[17]
Bolivia	1999	1,835.4	10.6	0.2	3.6	85.6	12.9	44.7	28.0	12.5	23.9	0.2	8.6	54.9
Bosnia and Herzegovina	1998	1,193.2	— 24.3[2] —		5.7	70.0[3]	10.5	28.2	31.3[3]	40.5	2.3	13.7[4]	1.0[4]	42.6[4]
Botswana	1997	2,261.9	16.6	2.7	5.6	75.0	7.3	37.6	30.2	8.2	...	—	...	91.8[20]
Brazil	1998	60,793.2	11.8	0.8	9.3	78.1	16.2	43.8	18.1	28.8	23.6	1.1	5.6	40.9
Brunei	1998	1,566.0	16.9	1.8	0.6	80.7	5.5	32.3	42.8	15.2	15.0	—	6.4	63.4
Bulgaria	1997	4,932.0	11.3	4.3	30.5	54.0	10.3	16.2	27.4	37.7	3.8	37.0	0.8	20.7
Burkina Faso	1997	529.9	— 25.6[2, 5] —		11.6[5]	62.8[3, 5]	18.5[5]	20.8[5]	23.5[3, 5]	46.1	4.2	1.8	5.5	42.3
Burundi	1999	132.0	13.0[22]	0.6[22]	12.4[22]	74.0[22]	14.1[22]	21.3[22]	38.6[22]	42.9	2.0	0.3	2.9	52.0
Cambodia	1998	1,080.3	17.2[22, 23]	...	11.7[22]	...	6.5[22, 23]	17.0[22, 23]	...	8.2	3.6	0.3	6.6	81.3
Cameroon	1999	1,315.8	16.2[25]	3.2[25]	15.7[25]	64.9[25]	14.6[25]	27.6[25]	22.7[25]	52.9	4.9	1.5	5.4	35.3
Canada	1999	215,554.9	6.6	1.3	3.4	88.7	8.2	53.2	27.3	10.2	67.0	0.4	4.7	17.6
Cape Verde	1997	261.0	37.1	0.1	5.9	56.9	5.2	27.0	24.8	69.7	10.0	2.2	3.2	14.9
Central African Republic	1996	179.9	25.9	0.4	8.1	65.6	7.9	37.4	20.3	48.6	1.7	—	8.7	41.1
Chad	1995	215.2	24.7	0.5	17.9	57.0	7.2	23.8	25.9	51.3	6.5	0.4	2.4	39.5
Chile	1999	13,891.5	9.4	0.7	13.5	76.4	13.4	36.6	26.4	20.4	21.5	0.6	4.5	53.0
China	1999	165,699.1	8.3	2.6	5.4	83.6	14.3	41.9	27.4	15.4	11.8	3.0	20.4	49.5
Colombia	1999	10,659.1	15.0	0.6	2.5	81.9	21.9	34.3	25.7	18.1	37.4	0.6	4.9	38.9
Comoros	1998	47.8	37.8[9, 23]	...	12.4[9]	49.8[9]	1.1[9, 23]	7.2[9, 23]	41.5[9]	47.3	0.2	0.2	3.8	48.5
Congo, Dem. Rep. of the	1995	889.2	— 20.0[27] —		13.8[27]	66.2[27]	4.4[27]	45.5[27]	16.3[27]	37.1	0.8[4]	0.3	1.3	60.5[4]
Congo, Rep. of the	1995	555.9	21.7	0.4	19.6	58.3	13.9	20.2	24.2	45.4	8.0	0.1	2.2	44.3
Costa Rica	1999	5,986.5	8.2	0.2	5.4	86.1	13.2	30.8	42.1	9.4	54.8	0.5	5.0	30.4
Côte d'Ivoire	1996	2,615.7	19.3	1.0	25.2	54.5	11.9	23.3	19.3	47.5	5.2	1.8	4.4	41.1
Croatia	1999	7,777.4	9.9	0.6	11.1	78.4	11.7	34.7	32.0	56.5	3.2	15.1	1.8	23.4
Cuba	1996	3,480.6	— 23.7[2] —		27.9	48.3[3]	8.7	16.1	23.5[3]	31.1	0.2	5.8	1.3	61.6
Cyprus	1999	3,618.0	20.7	0.5	8.7	70.0	9.2	27.4	33.5	52.6	10.8	5.3	6.7	24.5
Czech Republic	1999	28,837.4	7.7	1.0	6.6	84.7	11.2	40.3	33.2	64.0	4.1	17.1	2.0	12.8
Denmark	1999	44,316.6	15.0	0.5	3.1	81.4	9.7	35.8	35.9	71.3	4.5	3.9	1.9	18.4
Djibouti	1991	214.4	38.3	0.2	9.1	52.3	6.0	15.5	30.8	46.6	3.7	0.7[4]	7.2	41.8
Dominica	1999	132.8	25.3	0.2	6.4	68.1	12.6	25.9	29.6	14.5	41.5	0.1	7.2	36.7
Dominican Republic	1994	3,440.0	13.7[28]	0.3[28]	35.2[28]	50.7[28]	11.7[28]	23.2[28]	15.9[28]	2.0[4]	37.4[4]	—[4]	1.5[4]	59.1[4]
East Timor	...	...	...	...	...	...	...	...	...	...	...	...	...	...
Ecuador	1999	3,017.2	14.0	0.5	8.2	77.3	22.0	28.8	26.5	14.2	30.4	2.1	4.7	48.6

and freight] valuation); for exports, the value at which the goods were sold by the exporter, including the cost of transportation and insurance to bring the goods onto the transporting vehicle at the frontier of the exporting country (f.o.b. [free-on-board] valuation).

The largest part of the information presented here comes from the United Nations' *International Trade Statistics Yearbook.* This source is supplemented by the United Nations' *Commodity Trade Statistics* and by national and regional information. In some cases where the original data were only available for an alternative trade classification, an approximation has been made of the SITC commodity groupings. For some countries, where the amounts involved are very small, estimates have been made for selected categories.

The notes that follow further define the column headings.

a. Also includes any unallocated commodities.
b. EU of 15 countries (Austria, Belgium, Denmark, Finland, France, Germany, Greece, Ireland, Italy, Luxembourg, The Netherlands, Portugal, Spain, Sweden, and the United Kingdom).
c. Includes Albania, Bulgaria, Czech Republic, Hungary, Poland, Romania, Slovakia, and European republics of the former U.S.S.R. (Belarus, Estonia, Latvia, Lithuania, Moldova, Russia, and Ukraine).
d. May include value of trade shown as not available (...) in any of the four preceding columns. May include any unspecified areas or countries.

... Not available.
— None, less than 0.05%, or not applicable.
Detail may not add to 100.0 or indicated subtotals because of rounding.

SITC category codes

0	food and live animals chiefly for food
1	beverages and tobacco
2	crude materials, inedible, except fuels
27	crude fertilizers and crude minerals (excluding coal, petroleum, and precious stones)
28	metalliferous ores and metal scrap
3	mineral fuels, lubricants, and related materials (including coal, petroleum, natural gas, and electric current)
4	animal and vegetable oils, fats and waxes
5	chemicals and related products not elsewhere specified
6	manufactured goods classified chiefly by material
667	pearls, precious and semiprecious stones, unworked or worked
7	machinery and transport equipment
8	miscellaneous manufactured articles
9	commodities and transactions not classified elsewhere

exports													country
total value ('000,000 U.S.$)	Standard International Trade Classification (SITC) categories (%)							direction of trade (%)					
	food and agricultural raw materials (0 + 1 + 2 – 27 – 28 + 4)	mineral ores and concentrates (27 + 28 + 667)	fuels and other energy (3)	manufactured goods: total[a] (5 + 6 – 667 + 7 + 8 + 9)	of which chemicals and related products (5)	of which machinery and transport equipment (7)	of which other[a] (6 – 667 + 8 + 9)	to European Union (EU)[b]	to United States	to Eastern Europe[c]	to Japan	to all other[d]	
166.0	—— 63.0[2, 5] ——		...	37.0[3, 5]	...	...	...	19.3[4]	3.0[4]	8.4[4]	0.6[4]	68.7[4]	Afghanistan
207.7	18.6	10.5	1.2	69.9	0.4	2.8	66.6	92.5	1.7	0.7	—	5.1	Albania
12,525.3	0.4	0.2	97.1	2.3	1.0	0.5	0.8	63.9	14.0	0.3	0.5	21.2	Algeria
399.0	100.0[4]	—	—	—	—	—	—	—[5]	100.0[5]	—[5]	—[5]	—[5]	American Samoa
57.8	11.9	1.5	—	86.7	6.5	30.7	49.5	87.4	0.2	0.3	8.5	3.6	Andorra
4,404.0	0.3[8]	3.2[8]	96.5[8]	—[8]	—[8]	—[8]	—[8]	16.9	53.1	—	0.2	29.8	Angola
36.2	—— 5.1[2] ——		17.5	77.3[3]	7.9	28.9	40.5[3]	19.4[9]	24.7[9]	2.7[9]	—[9]	53.2[9]	Antigua and Barbuda
23,125.9	51.3	2.4	12.0	34.3	7.3	11.9	15.1	20.4	11.3	0.9	2.3	65.0	Argentina
231.7	11.4	48.0	8.3	32.3	0.9	8.7	22.7	46.0	6.9	16.8	0.2	30.1	Armenia
42.8[10]	23.4	2.8	—	73.7	1.9	44.9	26.9	10.2	55.1	0.1	0.1	34.5	Aruba
56,015.9	26.8	11.9	16.7	44.6	4.3	12.6	27.6	10.6	8.1	0.2	16.2	65.0	Australia
59,271.6	7.9	0.7	1.2	90.1	7.1	40.5	42.5	64.4	4.5	11.5	1.3	18.3	Austria
929.2	8.9	2.3	78.6	10.2	2.5	3.8	3.9	45.6	3.2	13.4	—	37.8	Azerbaijan
300.3	—— 38.8[2] ——		—	61.2[3]	22.3	26.1	12.9[3]	31.4	56.5	1.0[4]	0.3[4]	10.7	Bahamas, The
4,602.0	2.1	0.4	66.5	31.0	3.2	1.0	26.7	1.6	2.3	—	4.3	91.8[12]	Bahrain
5,057.0	8.9	—	0.2	90.8	0.9	1.1	88.9	43.0	39.4	0.9	2.4	14.2	Bangladesh
250.7	30.8	0.2	13.3	55.7	14.8	16.0	24.9	17.6	17.6	—	0.1	64.7	Barbados
5,908.9	—— 11.5[2] ——		9.1	79.4[3]	15.3	27.3	36.8[3]	8.9	1.4	73.7	0.1	15.9	Belarus
176,026.2	11.2	7.7	2.9	78.1	18.3	28.9	30.9	75.8	5.3	2.8	1.2	14.8	Belgium
175.7	81.7	—	0.9	17.4	1.9	1.5	13.9	38.1	48.4	—	0.1	13.4	Belize
332.9	63.6	30.0	1.4	5.1	0.3[4]	1.0	3.8[4]	37.1	0.8	0.1	0.2	61.9	Benin
62.9	5.6[14]	3.1[14, 15]	45.6[14]	45.8[14, 16]	9.5[14]	18.5[14]	17.8[14, 16]	6.4	49.8	—	—	43.9	Bermuda
117.9	30.9[8]	3.5[8]	25.6[8, 18]	40.1[8]	20.3[8]	—[8]	19.7[8]	0.2	0.1	—	0.3	99.5[19]	Bhutan
1,401.9	28.1	16.4	5.3	50.2	0.9	25.0	24.3	20.6	33.2	0.1	0.5	45.6	Bolivia
185.3	—— 37.3[2] ——		4.3	58.4[3]	3.9	11.0	43.5[3]	35.8	2.9	1.0[4]	0.1[4]	60.2[4]	Bosnia and Herzegovina
2,923.6	3.3	75.1	—	21.7	1.5	11.9	8.3	56.9	...	—	...	43.1[21]	Botswana
51,120.0	33.4	7.7	0.7	58.2	6.2	24.6	27.4	28.9	19.3	2.2	4.3	45.2	Brazil
2,306.8	—	—	88.6	11.4	0.2[4]	4.8	6.4[4]	2.0	9.1	—	53.1	35.7	Brunei
4,939.7	16.6	2.0	7.6	73.9	16.9	11.1	45.8	43.3	2.6	17.3	0.8	36.0	Bulgaria
194.1	83.5[5]	0.5[5]	—[5]	16.0[5]	0.1[5]	1.0[5]	14.9[5]	32.5	1.8	—	1.1	64.6	Burkina Faso
64.6	85.1[22]	—[22]	—[22]	14.9[22]	1.4[22]	—[22]	13.4[22]	59.9	2.8	0.2	0.3	36.8	Burundi
796.1	88.9[22, 24]	...	...	...	...	...	...	16.5	36.8	0.4	1.0	45.4	Cambodia
1,587.7	49.5[25]	0.1[25]	36.2[25]	14.3[25]	1.1[25]	1.1[25]	12.1[25]	70.6	2.5	0.2	0.3	26.3	Cameroon
238,778.0	13.6	1.5	8.5	76.4	5.2	42.6	28.6	5.6	85.9	0.2	2.4	6.0	Canada
81.5	5.3	0.5	28.8	65.4	0.2	51.2	14.0	55.2	1.1	—	—	43.7[26]	Cape Verde
115.1	25.4	60.1	0.2	14.3	—	7.5	6.8	95.1	—	—	—	4.8	Central African Republic
251.6	88.2[14]	—[14]	—[14]	11.9[14]	6.5[14]	3.1[14]	2.3[14]	76.6[4]	2.4[4]	0.8[4]	2.4[4]	17.7[4]	Chad
15,619.2	37.7	14.4	0.5	47.3	4.8	3.2	39.4	26.2	18.0	0.2	14.6	41.0	Chile
194,930.9	7.3	0.7	2.4	89.6	5.2	30.1	54.2	15.5	21.5	1.7	16.6	44.6	China
11,565.4	28.9	1.1	40.6	29.4	10.1	2.6	16.7	16.7	50.3	0.7	2.1	30.2	Colombia
4.0	57.9[9]	—[9]	—[9]	42.1[9]	21.0[9, 23]	—[9]	21.2[9]	80.0	2.5	—	—	17.5	Comoros
742.8	13.1[14]	58.5[2, 14, 15]	11.1[14]	17.3[3, 14, 16]	0.2[14]	1.2[14]	15.9[3, 14, 16]	23.3	14.5	—	—	62.1	Congo, Dem. Rep. of the
1,089.8	9.3	0.3	87.6	2.7	—	0.4	2.3	41.3	28.5	—	0.3	29.9	Congo, Rep. of the
6,283.1	30.8	0.2	0.4	68.6	3.7	46.5	18.4	22.4	51.9	0.9	2.0	22.7	Costa Rica
4,274.7	—— 69.3[2] ——		15.4	15.4[3]	3.7	2.0	9.6[3]	56.4	8.2	3.6	0.2	31.7	Côte d'Ivoire
4,279.7	14.4	0.8	7.8	77.1	11.7	29.1	36.3	48.8	2.4	5.2	0.1	43.4	Croatia
1,848.9	69.8	23.6[2]	0.2[4]	6.4[3, 4]	3.1	0.1[4]	3.2[3, 4]	25.8	—	32.0	3.9	38.2	Cuba
997.0	47.9	1.5	6.0	44.6	7.5	16.9	20.2	40.0	4.0	12.4	0.2	43.4	Cyprus
26,842.6	6.7	0.7	2.9	89.8	6.6	43.1	40.0	69.2	2.4	19.2	0.3	8.9	Czech Republic
49,027.8	23.4	0.4	3.8	72.4	10.7	27.9	33.9	61.6	4.5	4.3	2.9	26.7	Denmark
17.3	32.5	—	—	67.5	0.4	8.3	58.7	62.6	0.8	—	0.9	35.7	Djibouti
54.3	42.5	2.8	—	54.7	50.3	2.2	2.2	34.6	6.4	—	—	58.9	Dominica
2,007.8	20.7	0.1	—	79.2[29]	2.6	11.6	65.1[29]	8.7	84.6	—	0.8	5.9	Dominican Republic
...	...	...	...	...	...	...	...	...	...	...	...	...	East Timor
4,451.1	58.0	—	33.2	8.8	1.8	1.4	5.6	18.4	38.4	2.4	2.5	38.3	Ecuador

Trade: external (continued)

country	year	imports												
		total value ('000,000 U.S.$)	Standard International Trade Classification (SITC) categories (%)							direction of trade (%)				
			food and agricultural raw materials (0 + 1 + 2 – 27 – 28 + 4)	mineral ores and concen-trates (27 + 28 + 667)	fuels and other energy (3)	manufactured goods				from European Union (EU)[b]	from United States	from Eastern Europe[c]	from Japan	from all other[d]
						total[a] (5 + 6 – 667 + 7 + 8 + 9)	of which chemicals and related products (5)	of which machinery and transport equipment (7)	of which other[a] (6 – 667 + 8 + 9)					
Egypt	1999	15,962.1	27.2	1.9	6.1	64.8	11.5	26.2	27.1	35.5	14.4	6.6	3.3	40.3
El Salvador	1999	3,128.1	20.8	0.3	11.5	67.3	14.2	27.6	25.5	7.9	37.5	1.0	4.1	49.5
Equatorial Guinea	1990	61.6	13.5	3.4	7.7	75.4	3.9	58.2	13.3	31.5	39.9	—	0.3[4]	28.3
Eritrea	1998	526.8	—21.8[2]—		1.5	76.7[3]	5.7	38.3	32.7[3]	32.3[31]	4.2	—	4.0	59.5
Estonia	1999	4,107.4	16.2	1.4	6.9	75.5	10.6	34.3	30.6	57.8	4.4	22.5	4.7	10.6
Ethiopia	1995	1,141.0	15.7	0.2	11.1	73.0	14.0	35.5	23.5	39.6	12.9	0.6	8.4	38.4
Faroe Islands	1999	477.5	22.7	0.4	8.1	68.7	6.5	36.5	25.7	54.7	1.3	3.0	2.4	38.5
Fiji	1997	965.2	—16.6[2]—		14.1	69.3[3]	7.8	20.6	40.9[3]	4.6	5.2	0.1	6.9	83.2
Finland	1999	31,614.1	8.9	3.7	8.5	78.8	10.7	43.2	24.9	55.7	7.9	11.3	6.2	18.9
France[32]	1999	286,592.9	11.0	0.9	6.6	81.4	12.2	39.8	29.4	61.6	8.8	3.1	3.6	23.0
French Guiana	1995	783.3	18.8	0.1	5.3	75.8	8.0	42.2	25.6	76.9	3.3	0.5	1.4	17.9
French Polynesia	1994	880.7	20.4[33]	0.2[33]	5.4[33]	74.1[33]	6.4[33]	35.9[33]	31.8[33]	44.8	13.9	—	4.0	37.3
Gabon	1996	898.1	19.8	0.4	3.4	76.4	10.7	39.3	26.4	68.1	10.4	0.3	6.0	15.2
Gambia, The	1998	257.2	—45.5[2]—		6.3	48.2[33]	4.4	20.6	23.2[3]	48.4	5.5	0.9	2.8	42.3
Gaza Strip[34]	1994	339.3	...	...	...	...	...	...	...	...	...	...	...	100.0[35]
Georgia	1998	884.3	19.2	0.7	24.9	55.3	7.9	30.0	17.4	31.0	15.4[4]	26.2	0.5[4]	27.0
Germany	1999	464,318.0	9.5	1.3	5.7	83.5	8.7	36.5	38.3	52.4	8.1	9.5	4.9	25.1
Ghana	1999	3,003.8	14.7	0.2	17.7	67.3	10.3	37.7	19.4	43.6	8.7	0.9	2.8	43.9
Greece	1999	26,570.2	15.0	0.5	5.8	78.8	12.2	37.5	29.1	64.1	5.5	5.6	4.3	20.5
Greenland	1999	418.3	18.8	0.4	9.0	71.8	4.1	26.2	41.5	81.2	2.1	0.5	3.2	12.9
Grenada	1999	202.2	22.7	0.3	9.1	68.0	6.4	29.0	32.6	12.1	41.8	0.2	5.4	40.4
Guadeloupe	1995	1,901.3	22.6	0.3	5.8	71.3	9.5	32.0	29.8	77.8	3.3	0.3	2.2	16.5
Guam	1992	450.0	16.9[37]	0.1[37]	46.9[37]	36.2[37]	2.3[37]	19.1[37]	14.8[37]	...	23.4[37]	...	19.9[37]	56.6[37]
Guatemala	1999	4,554.3	14.1	0.2	9.9	75.9	16.3	35.4	24.2	9.0	41.6	0.9	4.0	44.5
Guernsey[38]	...	...	...	...	...	...	...	...	...	...	...	...	...	...
Guinea	1997	619.7	—25.1[2]—		10.3	64.5[3]	7.0	35.4	22.1[3]	54.5	7.6	1.5	5.7	30.6
Guinea-Bissau	1995	56.8	43.8	0.2	16.2	39.8	4.9	22.9	12.0	42.8[1]	0.7	0.9	9.3	46.3
Guyana	1993	483.8	9.0	...	16.7	74.3	5.1	44.5	24.7	21.9[4]	27.9[4]	0.4[4]	18.2[4]	31.6[4]
Haiti	1997[6]	706.5	—40.2[2]—		10.6	49.3[3]	7.3	15.8	26.1[3]	12.7[4]	57.5[4]	0.4[4]	4.5[4]	24.9[4]
Honduras	1999	2,651.9	17.3	0.2	9.3	73.2	14.6	31.4	27.2	7.1	48.8	0.6	4.0	39.4
Hong Kong	1999	180,710.6	6.2	2.2	2.1	89.6	6.3	38.5	44.7	9.3	7.0	0.3	11.6	71.8
Hungary	1999	28,008.2	4.6	0.4	5.9	89.1	9.0	49.8	30.3	64.4	3.5	13.5	4.1	14.5
Iceland	1999	2,315.5	11.5	3.8	5.5	79.3	7.7	41.8	29.8	55.9	10.9	4.8	5.6	22.7
India	1999[1]	42,425.0	10.9	11.5	19.0	58.5	12.3	15.8	30.5	25.3	8.6	2.0	5.8	58.3
Indonesia	1998	27,336.9	17.1	1.5	10.1	71.3	14.7	36.2	20.3	21.5	12.9	0.8	15.7	49.2
Iran	1999	12,621.8	23.2	1.5	1.7	73.6	14.8	38.3	20.4	40.9	0.5	5.7	4.7	48.3
Iraq	1990	4,833.9	—31.5[2]—		0.4	68.1[3]	8.8	30.3	28.9[3]	45.7[4]	10.8[4]	3.0[4]	4.6[4]	35.9[4]
Ireland	2001	51,165.5	7.6	0.5	3.9	88.0	11.1	52.8	24.1	58.1	15.2	1.5	3.5	21.6
Isle of Man[38]	...	...	...	...	...	...	...	...	...	...	...	...	...	...
Israel	1999	31,085.6	7.3	19.1	5.8	67.8	9.3	35.3	23.2	46.3	20.3	0.8	3.5	29.0
Italy[39]	1999	216,450.7	13.7	1.6	6.6	78.1	12.7	35.3	30.1	60.5	4.9	5.5	2.5	26.6
Jamaica	1997	3,112.9	18.4	0.1	13.1	68.3	9.0	28.2	31.1	12.8	49.3	0.3	6.4	31.2
Japan	1999	309,994.5	19.2	3.5	16.1	61.2	7.3	27.5	26.5	13.8	21.8	1.5	—	63.0
Jersey	1980	537.1	23.9	0.4	9.3	66.5	6.5	24.8	35.2	84.9[40]	...	...	...	15.1
Jordan	1998	3,828.5	25.1	0.8	9.3	64.8	12.6	28.6	23.7	32.7	9.5	4.8	5.9	47.1
Kazakhstan	1999	3,682.7	11.0	2.1	9.4	77.6	9.4	43.8	24.3	25.3	9.5	43.9	3.2	18.1
Kenya	1999	2,785.6	14.9	0.3	15.8	69.0	16.2	30.5	22.3	32.3	6.8	1.7	7.8	51.4
Kiribati	1995	34.1	40.5	0.3	10.3	49.0	7.0	14.7	27.3	1.1	3.1	—	7.6	88.2
Korea, North	1999	1,255.0[4]	...	...	...	...	...	...	...	14.7[4]	1.0[4]	5.7[4]	12.8[4]	65.7[4]
Korea, South	1999	119,751.3	9.2	3.1	19.2	68.6	9.1	36.4	23.0	10.5	20.8	1.7	20.2	46.7
Kuwait	1999	7,616.7	17.7	0.9	0.6	80.7	8.4	39.7	32.5	30.5	12.3	1.0	12.8	43.4
Kyrgyzstan	1999	599.7	14.0	1.3	20.3	64.4	10.8	30.4	23.1	18.3	9.0	22.0	2.0	48.7
Laos	1995	587.2	—36.8[2]—		6.1	57.1[3]	...	29.3	27.8[3]	2.0[4]	0.9	0.7[4]	11.8	84.6
Latvia	1999	2,946.8	14.4	1.0	10.8	73.8	12.8	29.8	31.2	54.5	2.0	35.6	0.2	7.6
Lebanon	1999	6,177.3	—21.9[2]—		9.0	69.1[3]	10.8	24.6	33.7[3]	46.4	8.1	5.8	4.2	35.5
Lesotho	1999	865.5	—39.2[2, 8]—		1.1[8]	59.7[3, 8]	10.0[8]	6.6[8]	43.1[3, 8]	1.6	0.1[4]	—[4]	0.1[4]	98.2[42]
Liberia	1999	209.6[44]	—36.5[2]—		24.2	39.2[3]	7.1	18.6	13.6[3]	23.6[4, 45]	1.5[4, 45]	3.2[4, 45]	24.8[4, 45]	47.0[4, 45]
Libya	1997	5,592.9	—23.9[2]—		0.2	75.9[3]	7.5	36.0	32.4[3]	55.4	1.4	0.9	8.1	34.2
Liechtenstein	1999	831.4	4.4[4]	0.3[2, 4]	1.0[4]	94.3[3, 4]	3.9[4]	45.2[4]	45.1[3, 4]	...	...	...	...	...
Lithuania	1999	4,834.5	13.8	1.8	14.8	69.6	12.3	25.9	31.4	49.7	2.9	41.0	1.6	4.8
Luxembourg	1999	9,888.7	12.3	3.4	4.0	80.2	8.8	39.5	31.9	82.9	9.8	0.9	1.4	5.0
Macau	1998	1,947.7	12.9	0.1	6.5	80.5	4.1	15.0	61.4	10.5	4.7	—	7.8	77.0
Macedonia	1998	1,914.7	18.6	0.7	8.5	72.1	10.5	19.1	42.5	36.3	5.3	20.0	0.9	37.5
Madagascar	1999	505.3	14.2	0.1	24.2	61.4	11.2	26.8	23.4	32.2	3.0	0.3	5.1	59.4
Malawi	1995	500.5	14.5	0.6	11.1	73.6	22.5	27.6	23.6	31.9	2.6	0.5	5.0	60.0
Malaysia	1999	64,939.2	6.8	0.9	3.1	89.2	7.3	61.7	20.2	11.7	17.6	0.7	21.0	49.0
Maldives	1997	348.8	25.3	1.7	11.1	61.9	4.6	28.1	29.2	12.7	1.5	0.1	3.2	82.7
Mali	1997	680.8	—20.2[2]—		20.9	59.0[3]	17.2	21.4	20.3[3]	35.7	3.5	2.6	3.0	55.1
Malta	1999	2,840.2	11.3	0.3	5.2	83.3	7.0	52.5	23.8	65.4	8.5	0.8	2.7	22.6
Marshall Islands	1996	72.7	—32.4[2]—		39.0	28.6[3]	0.1	10.7	17.8[3]	...	55.6	...	4.1	40.4
Martinique	1995	1,969.8	20.4	0.2	7.5	71.9	10.3	32.4	29.2	76.8	2.9	0.2	2.2	17.9
Mauritania	1996	426.7	—27.0[2]—		29.2	43.8[3]	3.0	24.8	15.9[3]	63.5	0.3	1.4	0.8	34.0
Mauritius	1999	2,275.9	15.8	2.1	7.1	74.9	6.5	31.1	37.3	32.5	4.2	0.3	5.9	57.1
Mayotte	1997	141.1	—23.8[2, 4]—		5.0	71.2[3, 4]	7.7	30.8	32.7[3, 4]	66.0[46]	...	...	...	34.0
Mexico	1999	145,556.2	6.8	0.5	2.1	90.6	8.2	50.3	32.0	9.0	74.4	0.3	3.5	12.8
Micronesia	1998	49.4	—37.3[2]—		8.9	53.8[3]	3.6	20.0	30.2[3]	...	45.7	...	14.0	40.4
Moldova	1999	573.1	7.9	0.6	37.5	54.0	9.1	15.4	29.6	27.3	3.9	61.6	1.0	6.3
Monaco[32]	...	...	...	...	...	...	...	...	...	...	...	...	...	...
Mongolia	1996	450.9	14.9	0.3	19.3	65.5	5.0	39.7	20.7	14.7	2.3	39.0	11.7	32.2
Morocco	1997	7,877.5	22.0	2.3	16.5	59.1	12.2	24.2	22.7	52.1	6.5	5.6	2.6	33.2
Mozambique	1998	817.3	26.7	1.1	8.1	64.1	7.7	35.0	21.4	18.2	5.3	0.2	4.0	72.3
Myanmar (Burma)	1996	1,914.0	—8.7[2]—		4.4	86.9[3]	8.6	27.0	51.3[3]	2.6	4.9	—	22.5	69.9
Namibia	1997	1,675.0	—23.3[2, 4]—		5.9	69.4[3, 4]	11.2	29.7	28.4[3, 4]	3.9[31]	4.1	1.0[31]	0.2	90.7[47]
Nauru	1994	31.8	87.8	...	...	12.2	...	2.8	9.3	...	...	...	...	...
Nepal	1998	1,313.2	12.2	1.1	12.5	74.3	6.9	16.0	51.4	7.7	1.6	0.6	3.2	86.9

exports total value ('000,000 U.S.$)	SITC categories (%): food and agricultural raw materials (0 + 1 + 2 – 27 – 28 + 4)	mineral ores and concentrates (27 + 28 + 667)	fuels and other energy (3)	manufactured goods: total[a] (5 + 6 – 667 + 7 + 8 + 9)	of which chemicals and related products (5)	of which machinery and transport equipment (7)	of which other[a] (6 – 667 + 8 + 9)	direction of trade (%): to European Union (EU)[b]	to United States	to Eastern Europe[c]	to Japan	to all other[d]	country
3,500.9	16.8	1.0	36.9	45.3	7.5	0.9	36.8	35.3	12.4	1.3	1.3	49.7	Egypt
1,164.2	42.8	0.1	4.7	52.4	14.4	3.5	34.5	14.2	21.3	1.2	0.7	62.5	El Salvador
61.7	48.6	—	—	51.4	0.1	39.8[30]	11.5	47.2	—	—	—	52.8	Equatorial Guinea
27.9	75.1[2]		...	24.9[3]	2.1	2.4	20.4[3]	10.0[31]	2.0	...	13.2	74.8	Eritrea
2,937.7	22.4	2.7	4.5	70.3	6.8	24.6	38.9	62.7	2.5	26.5	0.3	7.9	Estonia
421.9	86.0	—	2.9	11.2	0.3	—	10.8	51.7	6.4	0.5	13.0	28.5	Ethiopia
477.9	94.7	—	—	5.3	0.1	3.8	1.4	82.3	4.6	2.3	1.2	9.6	Faroe Islands
591.5	41.3[2]		—	58.7[3]	0.7	0.6	57.4[3]	22.5	10.7	—	5.0	61.8	Fiji
41,765.5	8.4	0.4	2.5	88.7	6.0	42.7	40.0	55.5	7.8	11.7	1.7	23.3	Finland
296,025.3	13.3	0.5	2.2	84.0	13.4	44.0	26.6	64.2	7.8	3.0	1.5	23.5	France[32]
158.2	33.6	0.1	0.2	66.1	1.4	33.0	31.7	77.6	1.0	—	—	21.3	French Guiana
226.2	5.9[33]	31.3[33]	—[33]	62.8[33]	1.6[33]	38.6[33]	22.6[33]	32.7	8.4	—	45.8	13.1	French Polynesia
3,145.6	13.3	2.0	82.7	1.9	0.4	0.4	1.1	11.5	64.1	0.1	2.1	22.3	Gabon
25.6	80.5[2]		—	19.5[3]	0.8	10.2	8.6[3]	72.3	0.4	2.3	0.8	24.2	Gambia, The
49.4	...	...	...	...	...	...	...	...	...	...	...	100.0[36]	Gaza Strip[34]
192.4	36.5	5.3	11.2	47.0	12.2	7.6	27.2	19.1	5.8	36.2	0.3[4]	38.7	Georgia
535,530.4	5.2	0.6	1.1	93.2	12.6	49.2	31.4	55.6	10.1	8.7	2.0	23.6	Germany
1,269.7	61.1	2.8	4.4	31.7	1.1	3.0	27.7	59.8	5.5	1.0	4.0	29.8	Ghana
10,149.8	31.5	1.8	10.1	56.6	6.8	10.1	39.7	49.7	5.9	13.8	0.6	30.1	Greece
289.5	95.2	—	1.4	3.4	—	0.5	2.9	85.4	1.7	—	8.3	4.5	Greenland
36.3	76.9	—	—	23.1	3.6	3.3	16.3	42.1	18.7	—	—	39.1	Grenada
162.0	52.3	0.6	—	47.0	1.1	36.5	9.4	77.0	3.4	—	—	19.6	Guadeloupe
86.1	69.5[2]		0.7	29.7[3]	0.7	3.8	25.2	2.3[4]	—	—	57.5	40.2	Guam
2,458.2	61.7	0.3	3.5	34.4	13.1	2.3	19.0	11.8	34.3	1.2	2.4	50.3	Guatemala
...	...	...	...	...	...	...	...	...	...	...	...	...	Guernsey[38]
684.5	6.8	67.1	1.3	24.8	9.7	2.1	13.1	63.5	20.7	1.9	—	13.8	Guinea
23.6	88.1	—	4.7	7.2	—	6.4	0.8	40.3	—	—	—	59.7	Guinea-Bissau
404.0	43.5[23]	47.3[23]	—	9.2	...	...	...	35.9[4]	22.8[4]	—[4]	2.1[4]	39.2[4]	Guyana
110.1	15.8[2]		—	84.2[3]	5.6	3.1	75.5[3]	11.5	86.3	—	0.2	2.0	Haiti
761.0	66.2	1.1	0.5	32.2	5.8	3.0	23.4	14.2	57.3	0.1	3.5	24.9	Honduras
174,402.8	3.1	1.4	0.4	95.1	5.3	34.8	55.0	16.1	23.8	0.4	5.4	54.3	Hong Kong
25,012.2	9.7	0.4	1.6	88.2	5.6	57.1	25.6	76.2	5.2	9.3	0.3	8.9	Hungary
2,009.7	70.4	0.7	0.1	28.8	0.5	7.0	21.3	64.1	15.1	0.8	5.0	15.0	Iceland
33,207.4	18.8	17.1	0.4	63.7	9.3	7.1	47.3	27.0	21.7	2.9	5.0	43.5	India
48,847.6	15.8	3.1	19.3	61.8	4.3	9.5	48.0	15.9	14.4	0.7	18.7	50.3	Indonesia
19,726.0	4.6	0.5	85.4	9.5	1.2	0.5	7.8	40.3[25]	—[25]	0.7[25]	17.1[25]	41.8[25]	Iran
6,659.0	0.8	0.3[15]	96.8	2.1[16]	1.2	0.2	0.7[16]	26.6[4]	33.6[4]	6.8[4]	9.5[4]	23.5[4]	Iraq
82,794.9	7.7	0.6	0.3	91.4	34.9	41.0	15.6	61.8	17.0	1.3	3.5	16.4	Ireland
...	...	...	...	...	...	...	...	...	...	...	...	...	Isle of Man[38]
25,839.9	5.0	31.8	0.5	62.6	14.1	30.4	18.1	29.7	35.5	2.2	3.2	29.4	Israel
230,093.8	7.4	0.3	1.2	91.1	8.6	38.8	43.7	57.0	12.9	5.8	1.6	22.8	Italy[39]
1,386.1	23.6	53.1	0.2	23.0	3.4	1.7	18.0	26.4	37.8	6.6	1.2	28.0	Jamaica
417,610.2	1.1	0.3	0.3	98.3	7.1	68.5	22.7	17.9	31.1	0.4	—	50.6	Japan
209.2	27.6	4.3[41]	—	68.0	1.2	31.1	35.7	67.3[40]	...	...	...	32.7	Jersey
1,382.3	16.9	27.0	0.1	56.0	32.4	4.6	19.0	7.0	0.6	0.9	1.0	90.5	Jordan
5,592.2	9.3	4.5	40.9	45.3	6.1	4.9	34.3	23.0	1.4	27.7	0.4	47.5	Kazakhstan
1,662.5	65.9	2.7	8.4	23.0	6.3	0.9	15.8	33.5	2.3	0.4	0.9	62.9	Kenya
7.2	85.3	—	—	14.7	—	—	14.7	2.2	10.4	—	—	87.4	Kiribati
782.0[4]	...	...	...	...	...	...	...	14.8[4]	—[4]	3.7[4]	23.3[4]	58.2[4]	Korea, North
143,685.4	2.9	0.1	4.1	92.9	7.4	54.2	31.3	14.1	20.6	1.6	11.0	52.6	Korea, South
12,140.1	0.6[4]	0.3[4]	90.6	8.5[4]	5.8	1.3	1.4[4]	11.8[4]	11.6[4]	—[4]	22.9[4]	53.7[4]	Kuwait
453.8	22.0	4.7	11.8	61.5	3.3	9.7	48.5	38.2	2.5	21.0	0.2	38.1	Kyrgyzstan
347.9	35.4[2]		7.0	57.5[3]	...	5.1	52.4[3]	9.7[4]	3.2	3.2[4]	0.6	83.3	Laos
1,723.8	36.5	2.3	2.9	58.3	6.0	6.1	46.2	62.6	5.7	26.1	0.2	5.4	Latvia
673.6	24.9[2]		0.1	75.1[3]	13.6	12.0	49.5[3]	26.0	6.2	1.2	0.6	66.0	Lebanon
172.5	15.3[2]		—	84.7[3]	0.5	10.6	73.6[3]	0.2	44.6[4]	—[4]	—[4]	55.2[43]	Lesotho
58.9[44]	99.3[2]		—	0.7[3]	—	—	0.7[3]	66.0[4, 45]	5.3[4, 45]	2.7[4, 45]	—[4, 45]	26.0[4, 45]	Liberia
9,028.7	0.4[4]	—[4]	94.8	4.9[4]	3.3	—[4]	1.6[4]	77.7	—	0.6	0.1[4]	21.6[4]	Libya
1,917.7	5.4[4]	0.2[2, 4]	0.1[4]	94.2[3, 4]	8.0[4]	61.0[4]	25.2[3, 4]	38.0[4]	...	...	...	62.0[4]	Liechtenstein
3,003.8	18.5	1.4	14.4	65.7	10.8	16.6	38.2	50.1	4.4	37.9	0.3	7.3	Lithuania
7,343.5	7.9	0.4	0.1	91.6	5.5	24.6	61.4	84.7	4.0	2.6	0.6	8.1	Luxembourg
2,134.7	2.3	—	0.4	97.3	0.8	5.0	91.6	30.5	47.7	0.1	0.7	21.1	Macau
1,310.7	18.3	2.2	0.8	78.8	4.8	7.5	66.5	44.1	13.3	8.3	0.2	34.2	Macedonia
232.8	42.0	10.4	2.4	45.2	2.9	0.9	41.5	56.7	5.4	0.9	1.4	35.5	Madagascar
433.4	90.2	—	—	9.8	0.4	2.0	7.4	47.7	13.2	3.5	5.0	30.6	Malawi
84,511.9	10.9	0.2	6.8	82.1	3.2	62.3	16.6	15.7	21.9	0.3	11.6	50.4	Malaysia
70.2	79.1	0.1[4]	—	20.9	0.1[4]	—	20.8	25.9	21.9	0.1	15.2	36.8	Maldives
302.4	92.5[2]		0.7	6.8[3]	—	0.7	6.1[3]	2.4	—	—	—	97.5	Mali
1,979.6	3.3	0.1	2.9	93.6	2.3	63.5	27.9	48.7	21.3	0.3	2.6	27.1	Malta
19.5	83.5[2]		—	16.5[3]	—	—	16.5[3]	...	80.0[4]	...	...	20.0[4]	Marshall Islands
241.9	62.3	1.0	17.8	18.9	2.1	13.0	3.8	78.0	2.6	—	—	19.3	Martinique
517.4	51.7	41.5	4.6	2.2	—	0.9	1.2	51.5	1.1	4.5	20.6	22.2	Mauritania
1,562.5	24.3	2.6	—	73.1	0.7	1.0	71.3	70.9	17.8	0.1	0.5	10.8	Mauritius
3.5	21.3[24, 25]	—[24, 25]	—[24, 25]	78.7[24, 25]	78.7[24, 25]	—[24, 25]	—[24, 25]	80.0[46]	...	...	...	20.0	Mayotte
136,262.8	6.1	0.5	7.1	86.3	3.2	59.6	23.4	3.8	88.4	0.1	0.6	7.1	Mexico
3.3	93.2[2]		—	6.8[3]	...	...	6.8[3]	...	...	...	94.6	5.4	Micronesia
462.3	65.3	3.5	0.2	31.0	2.9	7.4	20.7	20.5	3.1	70.5	—	5.8	Moldova
...	...	...	...	...	...	...	...	...	...	...	...	...	Monaco[32]
424.3	29.9	59.9	—	10.2	0.6	1.7	7.8	13.6	0.2	63.1	0.5	22.5	Mongolia
4,674.2	33.5	13.2	1.9	51.3	20.8	3.0	27.5	60.7	3.5	2.3	5.5	27.9	Morocco
244.6	63.5	0.5	15.4	20.6	0.4[4]	9.2	11.1	26.3	5.7	0.8	4.8	62.4	Mozambique
883.1	77.3[2]		0.6	22.2[3]	—	1.1	21.1[3]	4.3	4.9	—	7.3	83.5	Myanmar (Burma)
1,359.2	36.5	43.8	...	19.7	...	...	...	...	3.0[4, 5]	...	—[4, 5]	97.0[4, 5]	Namibia
31.2	—	100.0	—	—	—	—	—	...	...	...	...	...	Nauru
408.7	8.7	0.1	—	91.2	3.4	0.2	87.6	33.7	26.3	0.2	0.7	39.1	Nepal

Trade: external (continued)

country	year	imports												
		total value ('000,000 U.S.$)	Standard International Trade Classification (SITC) categories (%)							direction of trade (%)				
			food and agricultural raw materials (0 + 1 + 2 – 27 – 28 + 4)	mineral ores and concentrates (27 + 28 + 667)	fuels and other energy (3)	manufactured goods				from European Union (EU)[b]	from United States	from Eastern Europe[c]	from Japan	from all other[d]
						total[a] (5 + 6 – 667 + 7 + 8 + 9)	of which chemicals and related products (5)	of which machinery and transport equipment (7)	of which other[a] (6 – 667 + 8 + 9)					
Netherlands, The	1999	167,875.5	13.2	1.1	7.6	78.1	10.3	41.9	25.9	53.5	9.9	3.5	4.5	28.6
Netherlands Antilles	1995	1,832.5	—12.9[2]—		55.2	31.9[3]	4.5	12.7	14.7[3]	13.1	19.9	—	1.7	65.4
New Caledonia	1997	924.2	—20.3[2]—		11.7	68.0[3]	7.7	33.3	27.0[3]	41.9	5.3	—	4.3	48.5
New Zealand	1999	14,318.4	8.8	1.7	6.2	83.3	11.9	43.2	28.2	18.6	16.7	0.4	12.4	51.9
Nicaragua	1999	1,723.1	19.4	0.5	8.2	71.9	15.2	29.8	26.9	4.9	33.2	0.8	5.3	55.8
Niger	1998	420.0	42.2	2.2	14.9	40.7	9.8	13.2	17.7	43.0	7.3	1.3	3.2	45.3
Nigeria	1999	5,766.9	28.5	1.1	1.8	68.6	15.7	27.7	25.3	48.6	15.6	1.6	3.1	31.1
Northern Mariana Islands	1997	836.2	—11.8[2]—		8.2	80.0[3]	2.5[4]	6.0[4]	71.6[3, 4]	—[4]	7.6	—[4]	14.1	78.3
Norway	2001	32,936.6	9.2	4.7	4.2	81.9	9.5	42.1	30.2	65.7	7.1	5.5	3.7	17.9
Oman	1999	4,673.7	23.2	1.2	1.4	74.3	7.1	41.4	25.8	24.3	6.4	0.6	15.2	53.5
Pakistan	1999	10,159.1	22.3	1.2	20.8	55.7	18.7	22.2	14.8	17.3	6.4	1.4	7.6	67.3
Palau	1997	72.9	—25.4[2]—		12.0	62.5[3]	4.1	25.4	33.1[3]	...	44.1	...	14.8	41.1
Panama	1999	3,515.2	12.0	0.2	11.6	76.2	10.9	36.0	29.3	8.9	35.7	0.3	7.2	47.9
Papua New Guinea	1998	1,360.1	19.7	0.3	2.5	77.5	9.6	38.9	29.0	2.7	9.5	0.1	12.3	75.5
Paraguay	1999	1,905.9	17.3	0.2	11.6	70.9	11.9	36.0	23.0	14.0	13.7	0.2	6.1	66.0
Peru	1999	6,822.9	16.7	0.2	9.7	73.4	14.7	34.9	23.8	15.7	27.5	0.9	7.0	48.9
Philippines	1998	31,529.9	10.1	1.5	7.1	81.3	7.7	57.5	16.1	9.5	21.8	0.7	20.2	47.8
Poland	1999	45,876.1	8.4	1.1	7.2	83.2	13.5	37.7	31.9	65.0	3.6	13.7	2.0	15.6
Portugal	1999	39,828.6	14.8	0.5	6.8	77.8	9.3	39.1	29.5	78.1	2.8	1.3	2.7	15.0
Puerto Rico	1998[13]	27,308.7	17.3[14]	0.3[14]	10.6[14]	71.8[14]	25.4[14]	21.8[14]	24.7[14]	11.3	48.4	0.4[4]	4.3	35.6
Qatar	1994	1,927.4	15.8	2.7	0.6	80.8	7.0	39.7	34.2	33.9	10.6	1.4[4]	13.4	40.8
Réunion	1995	2,711.1	21.5	0.2	4.7	73.6	10.7	29.8	33.1	80.1	0.6	0.1	2.1	17.2
Romania	1999	10,395.3	8.8	2.2	10.1	78.9	10.6	26.3	42.0	60.4	3.5	16.9	1.1	18.1
Russia	1999	40,429.0	20.1	3.1[2]	2.0	74.8[3]	7.2	18.7	48.9[3]	36.6	7.9	25.9	1.5	28.0
Rwanda	1999	240.2	21.1[4]	2.5	16.8	59.5[4]	6.5	25.9	27.1[4]	27.6[4]	3.3	2.1[4]	13.1	54.0
St. Kitts and Nevis	1997	147.2	21.3	0.5	7.5	70.9	7.1	28.9	34.9	12.2	56.0	0.1	4.2	27.6
St. Lucia	1998	328.2	28.7	0.6	7.3	63.4	8.0	22.1	33.4	19.0	40.2	0.1	5.3	35.5
St. Vincent and the Grenadines	1999	200.7	25.5	0.4[4]	5.6	68.6	8.6	24.2	35.7	22.9	38.4	0.1	4.6	34.0
Samoa	1996	99.0	—35.0[2]—		11.8	53.2[3]	—[4]	16.9[4]	36.3[3]	2.1	14.0	—	3.8	80.0
San Marino[39]	1996	1,719.3	...	...	...	...	...	...	...	...	...	...	...	...
São Tomé and Príncipe	1999	21.9	—21.9[2, 23]—		17.4	60.7[3]	...	49.3	11.4[3]	63.0[31]	—	—	10.0	26.9
Saudi Arabia	1998	30,012.3	16.5	0.8	0.2	82.5	9.1	37.6	35.8	31.3	17.7	1.0	8.6	41.4
Senegal	1999	1,604.4	30.9	0.9	10.2	58.0	11.8	25.9	20.4	54.8	4.1	2.5	3.4	35.3
Serbia and Montenegro	1998	4,849.3	15.0	2.8	15.9	66.4	13.7	20.5	32.2	42.6	2.7	23.0	1.3	30.5
Seychelles	1998	383.1	24.9	0.1[4]	9.4	65.6	5.4	29.4[4]	30.9	42.9	3.3	—	3.5	50.4
Sierra Leone	1995	136.3	—47.9[2]—		17.4	34.8[3]	7.6	14.7	12.5[3]	48.4[4]	8.1[4]	2.8[4]	0.8[4]	39.8[4]
Singapore	1999	111,060.9	4.5	0.6	9.1	85.8	5.8	60.1	19.9	12.7	17.1	0.5	16.6	53.0
Slovakia	1999	11,300.4	7.9	1.9	9.1	81.0	10.3	36.8	34.0	51.7	2.6	35.5	1.6	8.6
Slovenia	1999	10,081.4	9.4	1.6	6.5	82.6	11.3	36.9	34.4	68.8	2.9	10.2	1.9	16.1
Solomon Islands	1997	184.5	—17.9[2]—		8.6	73.5[3]	4.9	37.7	30.9[3]	3.4	2.1	—	14.9	79.6
Somalia	1999	285.0[4]	30.3[51]	0.2[51]	4.6[51]	64.9[51]	5.1[51]	37.1[51]	22.7[51]	8.4[4]	1.1[4]	—[4]	—[4]	90.5[4]
South Africa	1999	26,694.9	6.9	3.1	10.2	79.8	12.2	38.2	29.4	42.7	13.7	0.5	7.8	35.3
Spain	1999	147,865.9	12.4	1.7	7.2	78.7	10.7	43.0	25.0	67.3	5.5	2.3	3.2	21.7
Sri Lanka	1999	5,338.2	16.4	3.2	5.7	74.7	8.4	23.2	43.2	15.9	4.0	0.3	10.5	69.3
Sudan, The	1998	2,058.6	16.2	0.5	10.4	72.9	11.0	30.2	31.7	29.4		1.7	7.1	61.8
Suriname	1998	540.8	14.9	0.6	11.3	73.2	14.4	31.9	26.8	28.6	41.2	—	5.5	24.8
Swaziland	1998	1,136.6[1]	22.5[1]	0.4[1]	11.4[1]	65.8[1]	11.3[1]	26.4[1]	28.0[1]	5.4[1]	0.9[1]	—[1]	1.9[1]	91.8[1, 52]
Sweden	1999	68,468.6	8.7	1.1	6.0	84.2	10.0	42.4	31.9	68.9	5.9	4.6	2.9	17.8
Switzerland[53]	1999	79,857.1	7.6	3.0	3.0	86.4	16.5	34.5	35.4	77.8	7.1	2.7	2.9	9.5
Syria	1999	3,611.3	24.1	0.8	2.5	72.5	9.9	19.7	42.9	32.1	4.8	14.5	4.3	44.2
Taiwan	2000	139,865.4	5.7	1.2	9.3	83.7	11.1	50.2	22.4	11.1	17.9	1.5	27.5	41.9
Tajikistan	1999	663.0	12.1	—58.6—		29.4	12.5	10.6	6.2	12.5	0.3	22.0	0.1	65.1
Tanzania	1999	1,588.0	18.4	0.3	8.0	73.2	10.4	39.4	23.4	30.6	5.1	0.4	8.2	55.7
Thailand	1999	50,309.1	7.9	2.2	9.7	80.2	10.8	43.1	26.3	11.7	12.8	1.2	24.4	50.0
Togo	1999	668.2	18.5	0.9	39.7	40.8	7.3	11.1	22.5	39.4	1.4	2.2	3.7	53.3
Tonga	1999	72.8	35.7	0.9	12.7	50.6	7.7	17.5	25.4	0.8	12.9	—	5.4	80.9
Trinidad and Tobago	1999	2,743.8	12.5	0.6[4]	21.0	65.9	9.0	34.0	22.9	12.7	40.3	0.4	5.1	41.5
Tunisia	1999	8,336.9	11.1	1.3	6.7	80.9	8.1	34.2	38.6	71.4	4.3	2.9	2.5	18.9
Turkey	1999	40,686.7	8.3	2.3	11.0	78.4	15.2	37.6	25.6	52.6	7.6	10.4	3.4	25.9
Turkmenistan	1998	980.7	9.1	0.8	7.2	82.9	10.1	45.7	27.1	16.1	7.4	36.5	0.8	39.2
Tuvalu	1999	8.1	35.0	—[2]	9.0	56.0[3]	5.0	25.0	26.0[3]	1.5	0.3	0.3	6.2	91.6
Uganda	1999	1,015.2	16.5	1.2	12.3	70.0	14.4	27.3	28.2	23.8	5.6	0.1	8.1	62.4
Ukraine	1999	11,846.1	8.9	3.4[2]	44.0	43.7[3]	9.2	17.5	16.9[3]	20.3	3.4	58.4	0.8	17.1
United Arab Emirates	1992	17,414.0	11.6	0.7	1.7	86.1	5.5	35.1	45.4	33.5	8.9	0.5	16.6	40.5
United Kingdom[38]	2001	327,576.1	9.9	3.3	4.4	82.3	10.4	44.0	28.0	50.5	13.3	3.1	4.1	29.0
United States[55]	1999	1,059,220.1	6.2	1.6	7.5	84.7	5.9	46.2	32.6	19.0	—	1.1	12.7	67.2
Uruguay	1999	3,356.3	13.6	0.5	11.3	74.7	17.2	31.2	26.3	18.7	11.3	2.2	2.1	65.8
Uzbekistan	1998	3,288.7	19.3[9]	1.3[9]	1.4[9]	78.0[9]	9.0[9]	43.1[9]	25.9[9]	17.9	7.5	23.6	0.3	50.8
Vanuatu	1999	95.6	—24.2[2]—		7.0	68.8[3]	5.8	30.2	32.8[3]	4.9	5.3	—	5.1	84.6
Venezuela	1999	13,554.0	14.2	0.7	2.6	82.5	11.8	43.1	27.6	25.8	38.5	0.3	3.4	32.0
Vietnam	1997	11,592.1	—8.1[2]—		10.3	81.6[3]	16.8	29.6	35.1[3]	11.0	2.2	2.0	13.0	71.8
Virgin Islands (U.S.)	1995	3,200.3	...	...	68.6[22]	...	...	...	...	...	32.7	...	...	...
West Bank[34]	1994	102.5[57]	...	...	...	...	...	...	...	...	...	...	...	...
Western Sahara	...	...	...	...	...	...	...	...	...	...	...	...	...	...
Yemen	2000	2,324.0	37.2	0.2[2]	12.0	50.7[3]	9.7	20.8	20.2[3]	17.5	4.4	0.9	3.2	74.0
Zambia	1995	708.3	12.2	1.8[2]	13.2	72.9[3]	13.3	37.9	21.7[3]	22.3	2.8	0.1	6.4	68.5
Zimbabwe	1999	2,126.2	10.5	1.5	11.6	76.4	16.8	35.2	24.4	22.2	4.8	0.4	4.1	68.5

[1]Year ending March. [2]Excluding precious stones, etc. (667). [3]Including precious stones, etc. (667). [4]Estimate. [5]1991. [6]Year ending September 30. [7]Percentage of the total excluding fish imports or the cannery (52.1% of the overall total), and government purchases (0.1%) in 1993. [8]1994. [9]1995. [10]Excluding mineral fuels; overall totals on a balance of payments basis, f.o.b.: imports U.S.$1,518,200,000, exports U.S.$1,164,800,000. [11]Percentage of non-oil imports. [12]Includes 66.5% for special categories. [13]Year ending June 30. [14]1992. [15]Including metals. [16]Excluding metals. [17]Includes 69.4% from India. [18]Mainly electricity. [19]Includes 94.6% to India. [20]Includes 72.2% from South Africa. [21]Includes 19.4% to Switzerland. [22]1993. [23]Main items only. [24]Domestic exports only. [25]1996. [26]Includes 24.9% for bunkers and ship stores. [27]1987. [28]1985. [29]Includes 9.1% for ferronickel. [30]Includes 38.7% for ships and boats. [31]Main countries only. [32]Figures for France include Monaco. [33]1988. [34]Total external trade for West Bank and Gaza Strip in 1999: imports U.S.$2,629,000,000, exports U.S.$372,100,000. [35]Includes 82.4% from

exports													country
total value ('000,000 U.S.$)	Standard International Trade Classification (SITC) categories (%)							direction of trade (%)					
	food and agricultural raw materials (0 + 1 + 2 – 27 – 28 + 4)	mineral ores and concentrates (27 + 28 + 667)	fuels and other energy (3)	manufactured goods				to European Union (EU)[b]	to United States	to Eastern Europe[c]	to Japan	to all other[d]	
				total[a] (5 + 6 – 667 + 7 + 8 + 9)	of which chemicals and related products (5)	of which machinery and transport equipment (7)	of which other[a] (6 – 667 + 8 + 9)						
170,538.3	20.7	0.8	6.8	71.8	13.5	36.2	22.0	72.5	4.3	3.2	1.1	19.0	Netherlands, The
1,355.8	6.9	2.0	85.1	6.0	1.0	1.7	3.3	14.3	13.9	—	0.2	71.5	Netherlands Antilles
529.4	—	39.5	—	60.5	—	—	60.5[48]	36.1[4]	11.3[4]	—[4]	29.8[4]	22.7	New Caledonia
12,474.0	58.8	0.4	2.2	38.6	7.1	10.2	21.3	17.7	13.6	0.6	12.6	55.5	New Zealand
508.5	84.5	0.3	0.9	14.2	1.7	1.1	11.4	22.9	36.3	2.7	0.7	37.4	Nicaragua
336.8	32.7	39.5	0.7	27.1	1.0	13.3	12.8	4.3	0.1	—	—	95.5	Niger
21,330.8	0.4	—	98.9	0.6	0.1	0.4	0.2	22.0	33.9	—	1.0	43.1	Nigeria
263.0[5]	—[5]	—[5]	—[5]	100.0[5]	—[5]	—[5]	100.0[5]	—[5]	100.0[5]	—[5]	—[5]	—[5]	Northern Mariana Islands
58,939.4	7.3	0.6	61.7	30.4	5.2	11.4	13.8	75.7	7.7	2.3	1.7	12.6	Norway
7,230.9	4.5	0.3	76.9	18.3	1.0	11.6	5.7	1.7	1.2	0.1	23.2	73.8	Oman
8,383.2	14.4	0.2	0.9	84.4	0.8	1.2	82.4	29.3	23.0	0.5	3.5	43.7	Pakistan
11.8	69.1[49]	—[49]	—[49]	30.9[49]	—[49]	—[49]	30.9[49]	—[49]	8.0[49]	—[49]	58.8[49]	33.2[49]	Palau
707.1	72.5	1.0	9.1	17.5	5.5	0.1	11.9	22.3	44.7	0.2	1.0	31.7	Panama
1,819.8	30.4	42.5	21.4	5.7	—	3.2	2.5	19.2[4]	3.6	0.9[4]	5.1	71.2[50]	Papua New Guinea
740.8	84.3	0.4	0.1	15.2	2.5	0.7	12.0	37.9	7.8	—	0.3	53.9	Paraguay
5,932.1	26.6	11.8	4.2	57.4	2.7	1.0	53.7	25.4	29.1	0.9	4.3	40.2	Peru
29,496.4	7.5	0.9	0.5	91.1	1.1	72.1	17.9	20.3	34.4	0.3	14.4	30.7	Philippines
27,375.0	11.0	0.7	5.0	83.3	5.8	29.6	47.9	70.6	2.8	16.6	0.2	9.8	Poland
24,493.6	10.1	1.1	1.8	87.0	4.8	34.1	48.1	83.2	5.0	1.0	0.4	10.4	Portugal
33,416.4	15.8[14]	0.1[14]	2.6[14]	81.5[14]	43.7[14]	21.7[14]	16.2[14]	2.7	82.0	—	0.7	14.6	Puerto Rico
3,212.9	0.5	0.2	73.8	25.4	15.9	1.4	8.1	1.9[4]	2.5[4]	—[4]	55.6[4]	40.0[4]	Qatar
208.7	78.6	0.5	0.2	20.7	1.7	12.7	6.2	79.9	0.6	—	6.1	13.4	Réunion
8,503.0	10.4	2.4	4.9	82.3	4.9	16.8	60.6	65.6	3.7	9.1	0.2	21.3	Romania
74,663.0	4.6	2.3[2]	41.8	51.4[3]	5.2	6.8	39.3[3]	33.3	6.3	26.0	2.8	31.5	Russia
54.5	83.3	—	—	16.7	—	—	16.7	14.7	—	—	—	85.3	Rwanda
41.1	58.2	—	—	41.8	0.2	37.2	4.4	33.7	57.4	—	4.6	4.4	St. Kitts and Nevis
53.9	72.5	0.1	—	27.5	1.5	6.9	19.1	63.2	15.6	—	0.4	20.8	St. Lucia
49.4	81.4	—[4]	—	18.6	0.8	8.7	9.1	42.3	3.2	—	—	54.5	St. Vincent and the Grenadines
10.1	—— 89.2[2] ——		...	10.8[3]	...	...	10.8[3]	16.8	18.8	—	2.0	62.4	Samoa
1,741.9	...	...	...	...	...	...	...	...	...	...	...	...	San Marino[39]
3.9	74.4[23]	...	...	25.6	...	...	25.6	100.0	—	—	—	—	São Tomé and Príncipe
39,807.0	1.5	0.2	84.3	14.0	9.2	1.4	3.4	18.3	15.9	—	14.5	51.3	Saudi Arabia
471.3	16.2	9.4	17.2	57.2	35.9	10.9	10.4	21.0	0.3	—	0.2[4]	78.5	Senegal
2,858.2	18.1	0.3	2.8	78.9	9.9	10.1	58.9	38.6	0.8	12.9	0.1	47.6	Serbia and Montenegro
121.4	75.0	0.1[4]	21.9	3.0	...	2.2	0.7	71.3	0.1	—	3.6	25.0	Seychelles
76.1	13.3	77.0	—	9.7	—	—	9.7	65.3[4]	13.3[4]	1.0[4]	1.5[4]	18.9[4]	Sierra Leone
114,681.8	3.4	0.3	8.0	88.3	7.8	66.2	14.3	15.2	19.2	0.3	7.4	57.8	Singapore
10,190.7	5.9	1.1	4.7	88.4	6.5	38.7	43.2	59.5	1.4	31.7	0.1	7.2	Slovakia
8,545.9	5.4	0.3	0.6	93.7	10.7	35.5	47.4	66.1	3.0	9.7	0.2	21.0	Slovenia
156.5	—— 96.5[2] ——		—	3.5[3]	—	—	3.5[3]	24.9	0.1	—	39.7	35.2	Solomon Islands
119.0[4]	95.4[14]	2.3[14]	—[14]	2.3[14]	—[14]	2.3[14]	—[14]	0.8[4]	0.1[4]	—[4]	—[4]	99.1[4]	Somalia
26,709.6	11.8	11.4	8.4	68.4	6.8	14.9	46.7	32.1	10.3	0.5	6.8	50.3	South Africa
111,493.0	15.9	0.8	2.2	81.1	8.7	43.3	29.1	72.2	4.4	2.4	1.0	20.0	Spain
4,467.3	22.9	3.4	0.3	73.4	0.6	4.2	68.6	29.4	39.9	2.9	3.5	24.3	Sri Lanka
534.7	80.5	0.3	—	19.2	—	4.5	14.7	33.6	—	0.7	2.7	63.0	Sudan, The
480.5	13.0	61.5	4.5	21.1	—	0.9	20.2	32.8	19.1	3.7	3.8	40.5	Suriname
965.6	54.5	1.3	1.0	43.2	16.4	9.4	17.3	10.5	5.2	—	—	84.2	Swaziland
84,784.5	7.0	0.9	2.3	89.7	8.9	47.3	33.4	58.4	9.2	4.7	2.4	25.3	Sweden
80,299.8	3.2	2.0	0.2	94.5	28.6	30.5	35.4	61.2	12.4	2.8	4.0	19.6	Switzerland[53]
3,389.0	19.4	1.0	68.4	11.3	0.4[4]	0.2[4]	10.6[4]	62.2	1.3	1.9	0.3[4]	34.3	Syria
148,129.3	2.4	0.1	1.1	96.4	6.2	58.4	31.7	14.9	23.5	0.6	11.2	49.8	Taiwan
689.0	4.0	—— 25.6 ——		70.3	1.3	1.0	68.0	35.4	0.2	20.5	0.1	43.7	Tajikistan
642.1	82.9	3.1	0.3	13.6	0.8	5.9	7.0	39.1	2.4	1.2	7.1	50.2	Tanzania
58,423.1	20.0	1.4	1.8	76.7	5.0	41.9	29.7	16.8	21.7	0.5	14.1	46.8	Thailand
360.3	46.2	18.3	3.7	31.8	0.6	4.9	26.3	13.6	0.6	2.1	—	83.8	Togo
11.3	91.9	—	—	8.1	1.5	2.2	4.4	0.9	25.5	—	55.0	18.6	Tonga
2,805.7	8.4	0.1[4]	54.1	37.4	18.9	3.7	14.8	10.9	41.4	0.1	0.2	47.4	Trinidad and Tobago
5,788.0	11.8	1.3	7.2	79.7	11.6	12.5	55.6	80.5	0.7	0.7	0.2	17.9	Tunisia
26,587.2	16.7	1.1	1.3	80.9	3.4	18.9	58.6	54.0	9.2	7.1	0.5	29.3	Turkey
614.1	32.6	0.8	58.5	8.1	0.7	0.2	7.2	7.8	0.5	6.1	—	85.5	Turkmenistan
1.4	92.2[54]	—[54]	—[54]	7.8[54]	—[54]	—[54]	7.8[54]	78.7	—	6.6	—	14.7	Tuvalu
505.7	89.3	0.7	0.2	9.7	0.6	1.5	7.7	35.2	1.8	4.2	3.8	55.0	Uganda
11,581.6	15.0	—— 10.1[2] ——		74.9[3]	11.0	11.5	52.4[3]	18.4	3.8	37.3	0.5	40.0	Ukraine
24,756.3	0.3	0.1	96.6	3.0	0.2	0.2	2.6	7.0[4]	3.2[4]	0.1[4]	35.7[4]	53.9[4]	United Arab Emirates
273,491.9	5.8	3.1	8.2	83.0	14.6	46.4	21.9	57.5	15.5	2.7	2.0	22.3	United Kingdom[38]
692,783.9	9.5	1.3	1.5	87.7	10.1	53.2	24.4	21.9	—	0.7	8.3	69.1	United States[55]
2,237.0	55.2	0.3	0.6	43.9	5.7	7.5	30.7	19.6	6.9	0.8	1.1	71.6	Uruguay
3,528.0	63.3[4, 9]	4.1[4, 9]	10.7[9]	21.9[9]	2.8[9]	2.4[9]	16.6[9]	23.8	1.8	20.7	1.1[4]	52.6	Uzbekistan
22.5	87.0[8]	—[8]	—[8]	13.0[8]	—[8]	1.0[8]	12.0[8]	43.6	4.4	—	19.6	32.4	Vanuatu
20,076.3	2.8	1.0	81.4	14.8	3.5	1.5	9.7	5.7	51.6	0.1	1.2	41.5	Venezuela
9,185.0	—— 34.1[2] ——		18.0	48.0[3]	1.2	8.2	38.6[3]	16.1	3.2	2.7	18.2	59.7	Vietnam
3,026.3	...	...	83.3[22, 56]	...	...	...	...	...	92.7	...	...	...	Virgin Islands (U.S.)
22.6[58]	...	...	...	...	...	...	...	...	...	...	...	...	West Bank[34]
...	...	...	...	...	...	...	...	...	...	...	...	...	Western Sahara
4,079.0	2.5	0.1[2]	96.5	0.9[3]	0.3	0.3	0.3[3]	1.2	6.1	—	2.1	90.6	Yemen
1,055.1	3.3	1.5	3.3	92.0	0.2	1.5	90.3	13.2	6.1	0.8	15.5	64.4	Zambia
1,887.2	60.4	5.7	1.8	32.0	2.6	2.3	27.1	34.6	5.8	3.0	7.1	49.4	Zimbabwe

Israel. [36]Includes 69.2% to Israel and 25.1% to Jordan. [37]1983. [38]Figures for United Kingdom include Guernsey, Isle of Man, and Jersey (data for Jersey is also shown separately). [39]Figures for Italy include San Marino and Vatican City State. [40]United Kingdom only. [41]Including coins. [42]Includes 89.5% from rest of Customs Union of Southern Africa. [43]Includes 53.9% to rest of Customs Union of Southern Africa. [44]Excluding external trade in ships. [45]Including external trade in ships. [46]France only. [47]Includes 84.3% from South Africa. [48]Includes 52.5% for ferro-alloys. [49]1984. [50]Includes 58.1% for areas not specified. [51]1986. [52]Includes 82.9% from South Africa. [53]Figures for Switzerland include Liechtenstein, also shown separately. [54]1989. [55]Figures for United States include American Samoa, Guam, Puerto Rico, and Virgin Islands (U.S.), also shown separately. [56]Exports of refined petroleum to United States only. [57]Excluding imports from Israel (90.9% in 1987). [58]Excluding exports to Israel (70.3% in 1987).

Household budgets and consumption

This table provides international data on household income, on the consumption expenditure of households for goods and services, and on the principal object of such expenditure (in most countries), food consumption (by kind). For purposes of this compilation, income comprises pretax monetary payments and payment in kind. The first part of the table provides data on distribution of income by households and by sources of income; the second part analyzes the largest portion of income use—consumption expenditure. Such expenditure is defined as the purchase of goods and services to satisfy current wants and needs. This definition excludes income expended on taxes, debts, savings and investments, and insurance policies. The third and last part of the table focuses on food, which usually, and often by a wide margin, represents the largest share of consumer spending worldwide. The data provided include daily available calories per capita and consumption of major food groups.

For both sources of income and consumption expenditure, the primary basis of analysis for most countries is the household, an economic unit that can be as small as a single person or as large as an extended family. For some of the countries that do not compile information by household, the table provides data on personal income and personal expenditure—*i.e.*, the income and expenditure of all the individuals constituting a society's households. When no expenditure data at all is available, the table reports the weights of each major class of goods and services making up a given country's consumer (or retail) price index (CPI). The weighting of the components of the CPI usually reflects household spending patterns within the country or its principal urban or rural areas.

The data on distribution of income show, collectively for an entire country, the proportion of total income earned (occasionally, expended) by households constituting the lowest quintile and highest decile (poorest 20% and wealthiest 10%) within the country. These figures show the degree to which either group represents a disproportionate share of poverty or wealth.

The data on sources of income illuminate patterns of economic structure in the gaining of an income. They indicate, for example, that in poor, agrarian countries income often derives largely from self-employment (usually farming) or that in industrial countries, with well-developed systems of salaried employment and social welfare, income derives mainly from wages and salaries and secondarily from transfer payments (*see* note a). Because household sizes and numbers of income earners vary so greatly internationally, and because the frequency and methodology of household and CPI surveys do not permit single-year comparisons for more than a few countries at once, no summary of total *household* income or expenditure was possible. Instead, U.S. dollar figures are supplied for *per capita* private final consumption expenditure (for a single, recent year) that are more comparable internationally and refer to the same date. The figures on distribution of consumption expenditure by end use reveal patterns of personal and family use of disposable income and indicate, inter alia, that in developing countries, food may absorb 50% or more of disposable income, while in the larger household budgets of the developed countries, by contrast, food purchases may account for only 20–30% of spending. Each category of expenditure betrays similar complexities of local habit, necessity, and aspiration.

The reader should exercise caution when using these data to make intercountry comparisons. Most of the information comes from single-country surveys, which often differ markedly in their coverage of economically or demographically stratified groups, in sample design, or in the methods

Household budgets and consumption

country	income (latest)						consumption expenditure						
	percent received by		by source (percent)				per capita private final, U.S.$ (1995)	by kind or end use (percent of household or personal budget; latest)					
	lowest 20% of households	highest 10% of households	wages, salaries	self-employment	transfer payments[a]	other[b]		food[c]	housing[d]	clothing[e]	health care	energy, water	education
Afghanistan	...	...	20.7	28.0	8.2	43.1	...	33.9	3.0	...	1.1	0.7	...
Albania	...	...	53.0	4.0	11.5	31.5	680	...	...	...	...	...	...
Algeria	7.0[1]	26.8[1]	43.1	38.3	18.6	1.8	810	52.3	6.7[2]	8.6	2.8	[2]	[3]
American Samoa	...	...	...	...	...	...	1,880[4]	32.9	20.4[5]	5.2	...	...	...
Andorra	...	...	...	...	...	...	...	...	...	...	...	...	...
Angola	...	...	...	...	...	...	370	74.1[6]	10.2[2, 6]	5.5[6]	1.8[6]	[2, 6]	2.7[6]
Antigua and Barbuda	...	...	...	...	...	...	4,050	*42.9*	*23.3*	*7.5*	...	5.5	...
Argentina	*4.4*	*35.2*	53.9	31.5	1.5	12.7	6,620	40.1	9.3	8.0	7.9	9.0	2.6
Armenia	...	...	24.5	13.6[7]	5.5	56.4	360	69.6	...	17.4	...	...	...
Aruba	...	...	...	...	...	...	11,190	26.9	9.9	8.4	2.9	8.5	1.9
Australia	5.9	25.4	72.7	7.5	13.0	6.8	12,040	18.7	18.5	5.6	7.1	2.2	1.6
Austria	*10.4*	*19.3*	55.7	[8]	24.4	19.9[8]	16,020	28.1	14.5	8.5	5.8	4.0	0.4
Azerbaijan	...	...	70.2	10.8[7]	19.0	—	460	42.2	—	13.6	4.8	—	—
Bahamas, The	3.6	32.1	...	...	...	...	3,950[9]	13.8	32.8	5.9	4.4	...	5.3
Bahrain	...	...	...	...	...	...	2,240	32.4	21.2	5.9	2.3	2.2	2.3
Bangladesh	8.7[1]	28.6[1]	18.7	48.3	7.5	25.5	170[10]	63.3	8.8	5.9	1.1	8.4	1.2
Barbados	*7.0*	*44.0*[11]	...	...	...	...	4,860	45.8	16.8	5.1	3.8	5.2	[3]
Belarus	11.4[1]	20.0[1]	47.1	7.3[9]	45.6	—	610	29.0	2.7	...	...	...	...
Belgium	*9.5*[12]	*20.2*[12]	49.6	10.9	20.7	18.8	16,550	18.3	11.4	7.0	10.5	6.2	[3]
Belize	...	...	*84.1*		——— *15.9* ———		1,780	34.0	9.0	8.8	1.6	9.1	2.3
Benin	*8.0*	*39.0*	26.3		——— 73.7 ———		240	37.0	10.0	14.0	5.0	2.0	4.0
Bermuda	7.2	24.7	65.3	9.0	3.3	22.4	12,690[13]	14.6	27.7	4.9	7.6	3.3	3.8
Bhutan	...	...	...	...	...	...	170	*72.3*	...	*21.2*	...	*3.7*	...
Bolivia	5.6[12]	31.7[12]	...	...	...	...	690	46.6	7.8	5.1	2.1	4.7	0.3
Bosnia and Herzegovina	...	...	53.2	12.0	18.2	16.6	1,890[14]	44.7	1.6	8.3	3.4	7.8	[3]
Botswana	3.7	42.9	73.3	15.4	10.8	0.4	1,030	39.5[15]	11.8	5.6	2.3	2.5	4.9
Brazil	2.5[12]	47.6[12]	62.4	14.7	10.9	12.0	4,420	25.3	21.3[2]	12.9	9.1	[2]	...
Brunei	...	...	...	...	...	...	...	*45.1*	*2.6*	*6.1*	...	*2.4*	[3]
Bulgaria	8.5[1]	22.5[1]	34.7	23.6[7]	14.8	—	1,470	47.0	4.1	7.4	3.2	4.3	[3]
Burkina Faso	5.5[1]	39.5[1]	...	...	...	...	220	38.7[6]	5.1[6]	4.4[6]	5.2[6]	13.7[6]	[3]
Burundi	7.9[1]	26.6[1]	...	...	...	...	190	59.6[6]	4.4[6]	11.1[6]	...	5.8[6]	...
Cambodia	6.9[1]	33.8[1]	...	...	...	...	280	...	...	...	...	...	...
Cameroon	...	...	41.4	52.6	3.0	3.0	570	49.1	18.0[2]	7.6	8.6	[2]	...
Canada	7.5[12]	23.8[12]	57.0	13.7	20.7	8.6	11,460	13.4	24.5[2]	5.3	4.7	[2]	3.1
Cape Verde	...	...	...	...	...	...	920	60.0	8.5	2.5	0.5	4.9	[17]
Central African Republic	2.0[1]	47.7[1]	...	...	...	...	350	70.5[6]	0.6[6]	9.5[6]	1.0[6]	6.5[6]	...
Chad	*8.0*	*30.0*	...	...	...	...	170	45.3[6]	...	3.5[6]	11.9[6]	5.8[6]	...
Chile	3.5[12]	46.1[12]	—— 75.1 ——		12.0	12.9	2,940	27.9	15.2	22.5	...	...	...
China	5.9[12]	30.4[12]	21.6	72.2	—— 6.2 ——		260	49.9[15, 18]	6.8[18]	13.7[18]	2.9[18]	...	2.3[18]
Colombia	3.0[12]	46.1[12]	45.1	35.4	14.2	5.3	1,540	45.0	7.8	4.5	6.4	2.2	1.7
Comoros	...	...	*25.6*	*64.5*	*8.7*	*1.2*	350	67.3	2.3	11.6	3.2	3.8	[3]
Congo, Dem. Rep. of the	...	...	...	...	...	...	190	61.7	11.5[2]	9.7	2.6	[2]	[3]
Congo, Rep. of the	*7.0*	*43.5*	...	...	...	...	870	37.0	6.0	6.0	6.0	3.0	8.0
Costa Rica	4.0[12]	34.7[12]	61.0	22.6	9.6	6.8	1,600	39.1	12.1[2]	9.4	3.7	[2]	[3]
Côte d'Ivoire	7.1[1]	28.8[1]	44.9	49.9	—— 5.2 ——		480	48.0	7.8	10.0	0.7	8.5	...
Croatia	9.3[1]	21.6[1]	40.2	40.8	12.1	6.9	3,790	37.8	2.9	8.6	4.3	7.6	[3]
Cuba	...	...	57.3		——— 42.7 ———		1,510[9]	26.7	...	...	...	2.5	...
Cyprus	...	...	76.3	5.9	14.4	3.4	8,300	22.7	5.5	10.0	3.1	1.3	1.4
Czech Republic	10.3[12]	22.4[12]	—— 66.7 ——		27.6	5.7	2,620	26.7	5.5[2]	7.3	[19]	[2]	...
Denmark	9.6[12]	20.5[12]	63.3	14.6	25.9	–3.8	17,730	17.9	22.9	5.2	2.2	6.1	1.9
Djibouti	...	...	*51.6*	*36.0*	*10.5*	*1.9*	590	50.3	6.4	1.7	2.4	13.1	...
Dominica	...	...	...	...	...	...	2,110	43.1	16.1	6.5	...	5.4	...
Dominican Republic	4.3[12]	37.8[12]	*41.7*	*31.8*	*1.5*	*25.0*	1,150	46.0	10.0	3.0	8.0	5.0	3.0
East Timor	...	...	...	...	...	...	...	...	...	...	...	...	...
Ecuador	5.4[1]	33.8[1]	17.4	76.9	3.6	2.1	1,040	36.1	9.0	10.1	4.2	3.3	[17]

employed for collection, classification, and tabulation of data. Further, the reference period of the data varies greatly; while a significant portion of the data is from 1980 or later, information for some countries dates from the 1970s. This older information is typeset in italic. Finally, intercountry comparisons of annual personal consumption expenditure may be misleading because of the distortions of price and purchasing power present when converting a national currency unit into U.S. dollars.

The table's food consumption data include total daily available calories per capita (food supply), which amounts to domestic production and imports minus exports, animal feed, and nonfood uses, and a percentage breakdown of the major food groups that make up food supply.

The data for daily available calories per capita provide a measure of the nutritional adequacy of each nation's food supply. The following list, based on estimates from the United Nations Food and Agriculture Organization (FAO), indicates the regional variation in recommended daily minimum nutritional requirements, which are defined by factors such as climatic ambience, physical activity, and average body weight: Africa (2,320 calories), formerly Centrally Planned Asia (2,300 calories), Far East (2,240 calories), Latin America (2,360 calories), Near East (2,440 calories).

The breakdown of diet by food groups describes the character of a nation's food supply. A typical breakdown for a low-income country might show a diet with heavy intake of vegetable foods, such as cereals, potatoes, or cassava. In the high-income countries, a relatively larger portion of total calories derives from animal products (meat, eggs, and milk). The reader should note that these data refer to total national *supply* and often do not reflect the differences that may exist within a single country.

In compiling this table, Britannica editors rely on both numerous national reports and principal secondary sources such as the World Bank's *World Development Report* (annual), the International Labour Organisation's *Sources and Methods: Labour Statistics vol. 1 Consumer Price Indices* (3rd ed.), the UN's *Yearbook of National Accounts Statistics* (annual) and *National Accounts Statistics: Compendium of Income Distribution Statistics,* and the FAO's *Food Balance Sheets.*

The following terms further define the column headings:

a. Includes pensions, family allowances, unemployment payments, remittances from abroad, and social security and related benefits.
b. Includes interest and dividends, rents and royalties, and all other income not reported under the three preceding categories.
c. Includes alcoholic and nonalcoholic beverages and meals away from home when identifiable. Excludes tobacco except as noted.
d. Rent, maintenance of dwellings, and taxes only; excludes energy and water (heat, light, power, and water) and household durables (furniture, appliances, utensils, and household operations), shown separately.
e. Includes footwear.
f. Furniture, appliances, and utensils; usually includes expenditure on household operation.
g. Includes expenditure on cultural activities other than education.
h. May include data not shown separately in preceding categories, including meals away from home (*see* note c).
i. Represents pure fats and oils only.
j. Consists mainly of peas, beans, and lentils; spices; stimulants; alcoholic beverages (when combined with "other"); sugars and honey; and nuts and oilseeds.

				food consumption, 1998										country
				daily available calories per capita	percent of total calories derived from:									
transportation, communications	household durable goods[f]	recreation[g]	personal effects, other[h]		cereals	potatoes, cassava	meat, poultry	fish	eggs, milk	fruits, vegetables	fats, oils[i]	other[j]	
…	…	…	61.3	1,716	83.4	1.1	4.1	—	2.4	2.6	3.8	2.6	Afghanistan
…	…	…	…	2,976	51.1	1.8	5.1	0.1	16.9	6.0	9.0	10.0	Albania
12.0	4.5	4.6[3]	8.5	3,020	60.3	2.2	2.7	0.3	6.1	5.1	13.8	9.5	Algeria
17.8	[5]	1.1	22.6	…	…	…	…	…	…	…	…	…	American Samoa
…	…	…	…	3,348	22.6	4.7	13.4	2.4	9.3	6.7	21.6	19.4	Andorra
3.9[6]	…	…	1.8[6]	…	…	…	…	…	…	…	…	…	Angola
10.0	…	…	*10.8*	2,450	25.8	1.0	15.8	1.7	11.3	7.9	16.4	20.2	Antigua and Barbuda
11.6	…	7.5	5.9	3,144	29.5	5.2	16.5	0.5	10.3	4.5	15.4	18.0	Argentina
…	6.6	…	28.7	2,356	52.3	6.7	5.3	0.1	7.0	6.5	11.7	10.4	Armenia
15.5	9.1	3.1	11.9	2,659	28.2	2.3	18.9	1.4	10.8	5.0	13.6	19.7	Aruba
15.1	7.0	7.5	16.7	3,190	22.7	3.2	15.5	0.8	11.8	5.3	17.0	23.5	Australia
16.3	7.8	7.1	7.5	3,531	20.7	3.1	13.8	0.6	11.4	5.5	21.5	23.4	Austria
5.1	6.5	0.7	27.1	2,191	66.6	2.7	4.6	0.1	9.7	5.1	2.8	8.4	Azerbaijan
14.8	8.9	4.9	9.2	2,546	30.1	1.4	18.8	1.1	5.9	8.6	9.3	24.9	Bahamas, The
8.5	9.8	6.4	9.0	…	…	…	…	…	…	…	…	…	Bahrain
0.9	…	…	10.4	2,050	81.6	1.3	0.8	0.9	1.5	1.1	5.6	7.2	Bangladesh
10.5	8.1	4.8[3]	—	2,978	31.6	3.9	12.6	2.3	6.6	3.4	12.8	26.8	Barbados
…	…	…	68.3	3,136	36.2	9.9	10.5	0.1	10.2	2.6	12.0	18.7	Belarus
13.4	10.6	6.8[3]	15.8	3,606	20.4	5.2	8.6	1.1	10.8	6.5	25.7	21.7	Belgium
13.7	8.0	…	9.4	2,922	34.0	1.4	6.3	0.4	7.5	9.6	10.2	30.7	Belize
14.0	5.0	…	9.0	2,571	37.5	36.9	2.2	0.7	0.8	2.6	5.3	14.0	Benin
7.3	16.6	10.8	3.4	2,921	22.8	2.6	15.7	2.7	7.8	12.4	15.2	20.8	Bermuda
…	*0.7*	…	*2.1*	…	…	…	…	…	…	…	…	…	Bhutan
17.7	9.7	2.7	3.3	2,214	40.7	6.6	11.2	0.1	3.7	8.6	11.4	17.7	Bolivia
6.0	4.1	3.5[3]	2.3	2,801	64.6	5.6	4.3	0.1	3.7	4.5	3.7	13.4	Bosnia and Herzegovina
13.1	13.8	3.1	3.4	2,159	46.9	1.8	6.3	0.5	8.9	2.5	11.6	21.6	Botswana
15.0	…	…	16.4	2,926	30.9	4.3	10.8	0.4	8.3	4.5	12.6	28.2	Brazil
17.2	*8.3*	*8.9*[3]	*9.4*	2,851	48.0	1.2	13.0	1.3	6.4	5.0	6.3	18.9	Brunei
6.6	4.0	3.0[3]	21.5	2,740	37.6	2.1	10.7	0.3	12.1	5.4	15.6	16.3	Bulgaria
18.6[6]	3.0[6]	2.3[3, 6]	9.0[6]	2,149	73.2	0.7	2.6	0.1	1.9	0.9	5.2	15.5	Burkina Faso
…	6.0[6]	…	13.1[6, 16]	1,578	16.7	30.0	1.3	0.4	0.8	10.3	1.5	39.0	Burundi
…	…	…	…	2,078	77.9	1.3	6.2	0.8	0.5	2.9	4.7	5.7	Cambodia
13.0	…	2.4	1.3	2,209	41.7	16.3	3.4	0.8	1.4	13.7	9.1	13.6	Cameroon
14.3	8.8	8.0	17.9	3,167	24.9	2.9	11.4	1.1	8.8	6.6	20.5	23.8	Canada
8.8	6.9	[17]	7.9[17]	3,099	40.3	2.5	5.8	1.5	4.9	3.1	17.6	24.2	Cape Verde
4.1[6]	0.8[6]	1.3[6]	5.7[6]	2,056	18.9	35.9	6.4	0.3	1.5	6.2	13.7	17.1	Central African Republic
…	…	…	33.5[6]	2,171	53.8	9.4	2.3	0.5	2.2	1.5	7.1	23.2	Chad
6.4	…	…	28.0	2,844	38.7	3.4	12.5	1.2	6.7	4.8	12.4	20.3	Chile
4.7[18]	5.3[18]	2.4[18]	12.0[18]	2,972	54.7	5.6	13.2	13.2	2.6	5.3	7.3	10.1	China
18.5	5.7	…	8.2	2,559	32.5	7.2	7.2	0.4	8.7	7.9	11.9	24.2	Colombia
2.2	3.0	2.5[3]	4.1	1,858	42.7	15.6	1.8	2.4	1.1	8.0	10.3	18.1	Comoros
5.9	4.8	3.8[3]	—	1,701	19.2	56.3	1.9	0.6	0.1	6.5	6.3	9.1	Congo, Dem. Rep. of the
15.0	4.0	…	15.0	2,241	25.4	37.9	3.1	2.2	1.5	6.2	11.7	11.9	Congo, Rep. of the
11.6	10.9	4.4[3]	8.8	2,781	32.9	1.9	5.3	0.5	9.5	5.0	14.1	30.9	Costa Rica
12.2	3.4	…	9.4	2,695	42.5	24.7	1.9	0.7	0.9	8.7	11.2	9.4	Côte d'Ivoire
9.3	4.5	4.1[3]	1.5	2,479	31.2	8.4	4.2	0.3	10.6	7.5	11.9	25.8	Croatia
5.4	…	…	65.4	2,473	37.3	5.3	5.3	0.8	4.9	5.1	9.6	31.7	Cuba
15.6	10.5	6.3	23.6	3,474	25.6	2.4	14.7	1.0	12.7	8.0	12.7	22.9	Cyprus
3.1	4.5	0.8[19]	52.7	3,292	27.6	4.4	10.1	0.7	9.6	4.3	17.9	25.4	Czech Republic
15.5	6.1	8.3	13.9	3,443	25.4	3.8	11.7	1.4	9.9	4.9	17.6	25.3	Denmark
…	1.5	…	24.6	2,074	51.3	0.2	4.5	0.2	4.8	1.6	17.9	19.4	Djibouti
11.6	6.0	…	11.3	2,996	23.9	9.1	10.6	1.6	8.7	12.5	6.9	26.7	Dominica
4.0	8.0	…	13.0	2,277	28.3	2.8	7.6	0.7	5.2	10.1	19.1	26.4	Dominican Republic
…	…	…	…	…	…	…	…	…	…	…	…	…	East Timor
12.8	5.5	[17]	19.0[17]	2,724	34.5	2.7	5.8	0.6	6.6	4.4	20.6	24.8	Ecuador

Household budgets and consumption (continued)

country	income (latest)						consumption expenditure						
	percent received by		by source (percent)				per capita private final, U.S.$ (1995)	by kind or end use (percent of household or personal budget; latest)					
	lowest 20% of households	highest 10% of households	wages, salaries	self-employment	transfer payments[a]	other[b]		food[c]	housing[d]	clothing[e]	health care	energy, water	education
Egypt	9.8[1]	25.0[1]	...	...	...	...	740	50.2	10.5[2]	10.9	2.7	[2]	[3]
El Salvador	*3.4*[12]	*40.5*[12]	...	...	...	...	1,520	37.0[18]	12.1[18]	6.7[18]	4.2[18]	3.6[18]	3.7[18]
Equatorial Guinea	...	...	57.0[6]	42.0[6]	—	1.0[6]	310	62.0[6]	...	10.0[6]	6.0[6]	...	...
Eritrea	...	...	...	...	...	...	170	...	...	...	...	...	...
Estonia	6.2[12]	26.2[12]	53.0	5.7	12.8	28.5	1,390	41.0	9.6	8.4	[19]	6.5	3.1
Ethiopia	7.1[1]	33.7[1]	0.2	79.5	—	20.3	87	49.0	7.0	6.0	3.0	7.0	4.0
Faroe Islands	...	...	88.3	11.7	—	—	...	40.9	11.0	8.0	...	18.9	...
Fiji	*3.7*	*37.8*	*81.5*	*9.1*	—	*9.4*	1,430[10]	34.7	15.6[2]	9.3	2.4	[2]	[3]
Finland	10.0[12]	21.6[12]	70.3	7.4	9.7	12.6	13,260	22.5	16.9	5.0	4.8	4.6	[3]
France	7.2[12]	25.1[12]	51.1	14.1	27.5	7.3	15,810	17.4	16.2	6.1	9.8	3.8	0.7
French Guiana	...	...	74.6	——	25.4	——	...	30.0[15]	16.1[2]	6.7	4.4	[2]	[3]
French Polynesia	...	...	61.9	18.5	16.6	3.0	4,310[20]	39.6	9.7	6.3	1.0	8.1	1.0
Gabon	*3.3*	*54.4*	...	...	...	...	4,060	...	...	...	...	...	...
Gambia, The	...	...	...	...	...	...	330	58.0[21]	5.1[21]	17.5[21]	...	5.4[21]	...
Gaza Strip	...	...	...	...	...	...	910[22]	...	...	...	...	...	...
Georgia	...	...	34.5	21.6[7]	21.7	22.0	430	38.3	...	14.8	...	0.3	...
Germany	8.2[12]	23.7[12]	57.9	[8]	21.3	20.8[8]	16,850	19.0	16.9	7.9	3.5	4.1	[3]
Ghana	8.4[1]	26.1[1]	41.6[23]	47.1[23]	—	11.3[23]	290	*57.4*	*11.5*[2]	*14.3*	*1.3*	[2]	[3]
Greece	7.5[12]	25.3[12]	34.0	22.8	17.0	26.2	8,140	29.9	14.1	6.5	3.1	3.3	0.5
Greenland	...	...	...	...	...	...	11,110	30.1	10.0	7.7	0.3	5.4	...
Grenada	...	...	...	...	...	...	1,650	40.7[15]	11.9	5.2	[24]	3.9	[3]
Guadeloupe	...	...	78.9	13.7	7.4	—	4,080[27]	31.6[15]	11.3[2]	9.3	4.6	[2]	[3]
Guam	...	...	...	...	...	...	...	*24.1*	*28.6*	*10.6*	*4.8*	...	...
Guatemala	2.1[12]	46.6[12]	...	...	...	...	1,180	64.4	16.0[2]	3.1	0.6	[2]	0.3
Guernsey	...	...	...	...	...	...	...	23.7	12.1	7.5	...	8.2	...
Guinea	6.4[1]	32.0[1]	...	...	...	...	510	*61.5*	*7.3*[2]	*7.9*	*11.1*	[2]	...
Guinea-Bissau	2.1[1]	42.4[1]	...	...	...	...	230	...	...	...	...	...	...
Guyana	4.0	40.0[11]	*73.0*	...	*6.3*	*20.7*	...	*42.5*[15]	*21.4*	*8.6*	...	*5.2*	[3]
Haiti	...	...	...	...	...	...	320	51.1[15]	4.3	8.7	2.2	...	[3]
Honduras	3.4[12]	42.1[12]	58.3	[8]	1.8	39.9[8]	450	44.4	22.4[2]	9.1	7.0	[2]	[3]
Hong Kong	...	...	...	...	...	...	13,880	15.1	15.7[2]	21.3	5.0	[2]	0.5
Hungary	8.8[12]	24.8[12]	—55.0—		19.2	5.8	4,270	38.1	5.7	7.4	1.5	6.1	0.7
Iceland	4.7	27.3	73.1	2.7	10.2	14.0	15,850	31.3	16.0	7.5	2.3	2.9	1.3
India	8.1[1]	33.5[1]	42.2	39.7	—18.1—		210	52.2	6.1[25]	10.0	2.4	4.7[25]	1.8
Indonesia	8.0[12]	30.3[12]	*42.1*	*41.5*	*2.5*	*13.9*	640	47.5[18]	20.1[2, 18]	5.5[18]	...	[2]	...
Iran	*3.8*	*41.7*	37.4[18]	30.5[18]	—32.1[18]—		1,040	42.6[15]	24.9[2]	11.8	3.9	[2]	[3]
Iraq	...	...	23.9	33.9	23.0	18.6	1,710[13]	50.2	19.9[2]	10.6	1.6	[2]	[3]
Ireland	6.7[12]	27.4[12]	58.6	13.3	19.9	8.2	9,650	30.5	7.1	7.4	3.2	6.1	2.4
Isle of Man	6.4	26.6	64.1	6.6	16.9	12.4	...	31.0	7.9	7.0	...	11.0	...
Israel	6.9[12]	26.9[12]	63.4[18, 26]	14.6[18, 26]	18.9[18, 26]	3.1[18, 26]	9,930	23.8	19.8	5.3	6.2	2.4	2.9
Italy	8.7[12]	21.8[12]	41.7	25.9	20.3	12.1	11,860	19.5	10.0	9.8	6.7	3.8	0.7
Jamaica	7.0[1]	28.9[1]	63.6	13.9	14.0	8.5	1,770	35.7	5.7	4.6	2.8	4.9	0.2
Japan	10.6[12]	21.7[12]	59.3	11.1	19.5	10.1	24,670	22.6	6.7	6.0	2.7	5.6	5.3
Jersey	...	...	...	...	...	...	...	*28.3*	*14.9*	*8.3*	...	*6.5*	...
Jordan	7.6[1]	29.8[1]	51.4	11.1	13.7	23.8	1,020	40.6	15.8	6.7	2.2	5.0	3.5
Kazakhstan	6.7[1]	26.3[1]	67.7	5.8[7]	16.9	9.6	1,290	29.6	2.6	...	...	...	...
Kenya	5.0	34.9	...	...	...	...	220	46.5	10.0	7.7	2.2	2.6	1.0
Kiribati	...	...	*69.7*	*21.4*	*6.0*	*2.9*	370[4]	50.0[15]	7.5[2, 5]	8.0	...	[2]	...
Korea, North	...	...	...	...	...	...	...	46.5[27]	0.6[27]	29.9[27]	...	3.3[27]	...
Korea, South	7.5[1]	24.3[1]	53.8	25.1	13.1	8.0	5,390	29.7	4.1	7.7	5.0	4.0	14.2
Kuwait	...	...	*53.8*	*20.8*	—*25.4*—		...	28.1[15]	15.5	8.1	0.7	9.6	[3]
Kyrgyzstan	6.3[12]	31.7[12]	67.3	——	32.7	——	670	33.5	2.2	...	...	...	...
Laos	9.6[1]	26.4[1]	...	...	...	...	140[9]	...	...	...	...	...	...
Latvia	7.6[12]	25.9[12]	67.0	5.4[7]	17.4	10.2	2,400	51.6	...	...	...	...	...
Lebanon	*5.0*	*45.0*	*27.9*	...	*3.0*	*69.1*	3,010	*42.8*[6]	*16.8*[6]	*8.6*[6]	*7.2*[6]	*4.5*[6]	*3.9*[6]
Lesotho	2.8[1]	43.4[1]	22.4	27.8	44.7	5.1	530	48.0[15]	10.1	16.4	...	...	...
Liberia	5.0	73.0[11]	...	...	...	...	330[9]	*34.4*[6]	*14.9*[6]	*13.8*[6]	...	*5.0*[6]	...
Libya	...	...	...	...	...	...	2,330[9]	*37.2*[15]	*32.2*[2]	*6.9*	*3.3*	[2]	[3]
Liechtenstein	...	...	...	...	...	...	...	21.3[15]	18.0	6.6	7.7	4.4	[3]
Lithuania	7.8[1]	25.6[1]	66.4	9.7	18.7	5.2	1,910	50.3	...	...	...	...	...
Luxembourg	10.0	34.0[11]	67.1	4.8	28.1	—	15,140[28]	12.8	13.7	5.9	7.3	6.1	[3]
Macau	...	...	65.0	18.1	7.0	9.9	5,480	39.2[15]	17.5	6.8	4.0	5.2	[3]
Macedonia	...	...	57.7	17.2	16.2	9.0	1,010	40.6	1.9	7.8	3.0	7.8	[3]
Madagascar	5.1[1]	36.7[1]	*58.8*[6, 29]	*14.1*[6, 29]	—	*27.1*[6, 29]	220	59.0	6.0	6.0	2.0	6.0	4.0
Malawi	*10.4*	*40.1*	83.3	6.0	—	11.7	109	30.0	4.0	9.0	4.0	5.0	10.0
Malaysia	4.5[12]	37.9[12]	...	...	...	...	2,090	28.7	10.2[2]	4.3	2.5	[2]	0.6
Maldives	...	...	...	...	...	...	270[9]	57.4	1.6	8.0	2.5	...	[3]
Mali	4.6[1]	40.4[1]	...	...	...	...	200	57.0	2.0	6.0	2.0	6.0	4.0
Malta	...	...	63.8	19.3	—	16.9	5,380	31.2	3.5	7.6	3.5	2.0	0.4
Marshall Islands	...	...	...	...	...	...	...	57.7	15.6[2, 5]	12.0	...	[2]	...
Martinique	...	...	80.0	...	...	20.0	4,840[6]	32.1[15]	10.6[2]	8.0	5.2	[2]	[3]
Mauritania	6.2[1]	29.9[1]	...	...	...	...	470	73.1	2.5	8.1	0.9	7.7	0.4
Mauritius	4.0	46.7	51.7	29.0	11.2	8.1	2,290	41.9	8.8	8.4	3.0	6.4	2.9
Mayotte	...	...	...	...	...	...	...	42.2	...	31.5	...	6.8	...
Mexico	3.6[12]	42.8[12]	61.5	29.1	7.8	1.6	2,110	36.6[15]	13.3[2]	8.4	3.4	[2]	[3]
Micronesia	...	...	51.8	23.0	2.1	23.1	...	73.5	...	...	...	...	...
Moldova	6.9[12]	25.8[12]	41.2	10.4	15.3	33.1	220	...	...	...	...	...	...
Monaco	...	...	...	...	...	...	...	...	...	...	...	...	...
Mongolia	7.3[1]	24.5[1]	72.1	9.5[7]	9.7	8.7	230	39.1	5.9[2]	23.4	0.5	[2]	2.9
Morocco	6.5[1]	30.9[1]	...	...	...	...	900	38.0	7.0	11.0	5.0	2.0	8.0
Mozambique	6.5[1]	31.7[1]	51.6	——	48.4	——	57	74.6	11.7	3.7	0.8	...	[3]
Myanmar (Burma)	*8.0*	*40.0*[11]	...	...	...	...	750[28]	*49.1*[6]	*10.4*[6]	*15.3*[6]	*2.4*[6]	*4.0*[6]	*5.9*[6]
Namibia	...	...	67.1	27.5	5.4	...	1,050	...	...	...	...	...	...
Nauru	...	...	...	...	...	...	...	...	...	...	...	...	...
Nepal	7.6[1]	29.8[1]	25.1	63.4	—11.5—		170	61.2	17.3	11.7	3.7	...	[3]

transpor-tation, com-munications	household durable goods[f]	recrea-tion[g]	personal effects, other[h]	food consumption, 1998: daily available calories per capita	percent of total calories derived from: cereals	potatoes, cassava	meat, poultry	fish	eggs, milk	fruits, vegeta-bles	fats, oils[i]	other[j]	country
4.7	5.0	3.3[3]	12.7	3,282	65.4	1.6	2.9	0.6	2.1	6.9	6.1	14.3	Egypt
10.2[18]	5.7[18]	4.3[18]	12.5[18]	2,522	53.4	1.5	2.6	0.2	6.3	3.5	7.7	24.9	El Salvador
...	...	...	22.0[6]	...	...	...	...	...	...	...	...	...	Equatorial Guinea
...	...	...	...	1,744	73.4	4.4	0.6	0.0	1.9	0.1	0.7	18.8	Eritrea
9.2	2.3	5.0[19]	15.0	3,058	38.5	5.3	8.9	1.6	12.7	4.3	13.3	15.4	Estonia
8.0	2.0	...	14.0	1,805	66.3	13.1	3.2	0.0	1.9	0.6	2.8	12.1	Ethiopia
...	6.6	...	14.6	...	...	...	...	...	...	...	...	...	Faroe Islands
13.8	9.3	4.3[3]	10.6	2,852	42.3	6.9	8.5	1.4	3.0	1.8	18.7	17.3	Fiji
14.8	6.3	9.5[3]	15.6	3,180	33.6	4.2	16.3	2.0	15.7	3.9	12.9	18.6	Finland
16.1	7.7	6.9	15.3	3,541	24.3	3.4	16.5	1.2	12.0	4.7	19.7	18.3	France
17.5	7.9	6.2[3]	11.2	2,818	32.4	7.9	13.2	2.1	7.5	7.0	10.5	19.3	French Guiana
16.4	4.4	4.0	9.5	2,924	33.6	4.0	13.3	4.4	6.1	3.0	13.6	22.1	French Polynesia
...	...	...	...	2,560	29.5	17.9	7.3	3.1	2.4	16.4	7.9	15.5	Gabon
...	...	...	14.0[21]	2,559	54.0	0.7	1.3	1.9	1.4	0.9	17.7	22.1	Gambia, The
...	...	...	...	...	...	...	...	...	...	...	...	...	Gaza Strip
...	5.9	...	40.7	2,252	60.5	4.8	4.9	0.2	7.6	4.8	3.0	14.2	Georgia
17.8	9.4	10.6[3]	10.8	3,402	22.5	4.1	11.7	0.8	10.3	5.7	21.6	23.3	Germany
3.3	3.8	3.9[3]	4.5	2,684	26.2	48.2	1.2	1.8	0.2	9.6	4.6	8.3	Ghana
17.5	6.9	5.2	13.0	3,630	29.1	3.5	8.9	1.2	11.8	8.6	20.0	16.8	Greece
8.0	9.2	15.5	13.8	...	...	...	...	...	...	...	...	...	Greenland
9.1	13.7	4.6[3]	10.9[24]	2,681	25.3	2.5	9.1	1.5	9.5	9.2	13.1	29.8	Grenada
20.5	9.3	4.7[3]	8.7	2,732	37.8	2.6	10.8	2.6	8.5	8.4	13.1	16.1	Guadeloupe
18.0	...	5.1	8.8	...	...	...	...	...	...	...	...	...	Guam
7.0	5.0	0.9	2.7	2,159	55.3	0.4	3.6	0.1	5.1	3.1	7.0	25.4	Guatemala
15.7	8.3	...	24.7	3,257	22.8	6.1	14.4	1.0	11.6	5.0	19.1	20.0	Guernsey
5.1	2.9	4.1	0.1	2,315	42.9	15.6	0.9	1.2	1.0	13.0	14.7	10.8	Guinea
...	...	...	...	2,411	61.2	7.4	4.6	0.2	1.4	4.2	13.0	8.1	Guinea-Bissau
4.8	2.9	6.4[3]	8.2	2,476	47.3	3.8	4.8	4.2	5.4	2.8	4.1	27.6	Guyana
7.6	9.2	5.3[3]	11.6	1,876	46.7	8.8	3.3	0.3	2.0	7.4	8.8	22.8	Haiti
3.0	8.3	2.4[3]	3.1	2,343	46.7	0.3	3.6	0.3	8.6	6.7	11.9	21.9	Honduras
8.4	17.5	8.1	8.4	3,200	27.1	1.6	20.0	3.3	5.2	4.0	19.7	19.2	Hong Kong
15.2	8.8	5.9	10.6	3,408	25.4	3.6	10.1	0.2	8.4	5.4	22.7	24.1	Hungary
14.5	7.6	9.6	7.0	3,222	20.7	3.2	14.3	3.6	14.6	4.0	13.4	26.2	Iceland
10.6	3.1	1.8	5.7	2,466	62.7	1.6	0.9	0.4	4.5	3.2	8.5	18.3	India
...	2.9[18]	...	24.0	2,850	64.6	5.8	2.2	1.3	0.6	2.3	7.8	15.4	Indonesia
5.0	6.4	1.7[3]	3.7	2,822	51.2	3.2	4.3	0.3	3.8	11.2	10.8	15.1	Iran
6.5	6.7	0.8[3]	3.7	2,419	59.4	1.2	1.4	0.1	1.9	8.0	19.5	8.6	Iraq
14.0	7.2	8.9	13.1	3,622	26.8	6.0	13.1	0.8	11.3	4.0	16.5	21.4	Ireland
14.9	5.7	...	22.5	3,257	22.8	6.1	14.4	1.0	11.6	5.0	19.1	20.0	Isle of Man
12.9	10.8	4.3	11.6	3,466	33.5	2.5	8.2	0.9	7.6	8.6	18.3	20.3	Israel
13.2	9.5	8.4	18.4	3,608	31.8	1.9	11.1	1.1	8.9	7.2	22.0	15.9	Italy
12.4	5.5	2.1	26.1	2,711	30.5	9.3	8.5	0.8	5.3	7.2	13.1	25.3	Jamaica
11.0	3.7	9.5	26.9	2,874	40.7	2.5	5.8	6.3	6.5	4.3	12.0	21.8	Japan
13.9	7.1	...	21.0	3,257	22.8	6.1	14.4	1.0	11.6	5.0	19.1	20.0	Jersey
11.2	6.1	4.0	4.9	2,791	52.7	1.1	5.1	0.2	5.4	3.9	15.3	16.3	Jordan
...	...	...	67.8	2,517	54.4	4.1	9.1	0.2	12.0	2.1	7.4	10.8	Kazakhstan
8.4	9.4	3.1	9.1	1,968	52.4	8.6	3.7	0.5	7.2	3.2	9.3	15.3	Kenya
8.0	[5]	...	26.5	2,977	34.7	8.3	4.6	4.6	1.6	4.6	7.2	34.4	Kiribati
...	3.8[27]	...	15.9	1,899	64.5	1.1	3.1	1.3	1.0	7.6	5.8	15.5	Korea, North
11.3	5.0	—— 19.0 ——		3,069	49.7	1.1	9.6	3.0	2.2	7.1	9.7	17.7	Korea, South
13.7	11.2	5.2[3]	7.9	3,059	36.8	1.9	11.2	0.5	9.8	8.4	10.2	21.2	Kuwait
...	...	...	64.3	2,535	58.3	6.7	8.7	—	13.0	2.1	3.6	7.6	Kyrgyzstan
...	...	...	...	2,175	77.7	3.8	4.4	0.7	0.5	2.2	2.3	8.5	Laos
...	...	...	54.8	2,994	32.7	8.4	6.0	0.9	12.9	3.8	15.3	20.0	Latvia
5.4[6]	2.6[6]	1.9[6]	6.3[6]	3,285	34.6	3.9	4.9	0.4	5.2	15.9	13.9	21.2	Lebanon
4.7	11.9	...	8.8	2,210	75.5	4.3	3.4	—	1.1	1.4	3.1	11.2	Lesotho
...	6.1[6]	...	25.8[6]	1,979	41.5	20.4	2.0	0.4	0.5	5.5	19.8	10.0	Liberia
9.4	4.6	8.5[3]	2.5	3,267	46.3	2.0	4.8	0.3	5.7	7.3	17.0	16.7	Libya
13.3	5.8	16.3[3]	6.6	3,222	22.1	2.3	14.8	0.8	12.5	6.1	18.7	22.7	Liechtenstein
...	...	...	49.7	3,104	45.5	7.8	8.9	0.9	6.9	5.3	10.1	14.6	Lithuania
19.1	10.8	4.2[3]	20.1	3,606	20.4	5.2	8.6	1.1	10.8	6.5	25.7	21.7	Luxembourg
8.2	3.0	8.8[3]	7.3	2,471	36.3	0.7	15.7	2.3	4.7	3.7	20.7	15.8	Macau
6.5	4.2	3.3[3]	1.8	2,938	39.7	3.3	7.0	0.3	5.2	6.9	15.7	21.8	Macedonia
4.0	1.0	...	12.0	2,001	53.0	21.1	5.5	0.7	3.1	3.8	4.4	8.3	Madagascar
10.0	3.0	...	25.0	2,226	59.0	15.8	1.3	0.4	0.5	4.2	4.0	14.7	Malawi
20.9	7.7	11.0	14.1	2,901	41.6	2.1	9.2	3.1	5.2	3.4	12.5	22.8	Malaysia
2.6	17.0	5.9[3]	5.0	2,451	43.5	3.2	1.4	13.1	4.3	5.6	5.2	23.7	Maldives
10.0	1.0	...	12.0	2,118	69.9	0.5	4.2	0.8	4.6	1.2	7.4	11.3	Mali
16.4	9.9	7.1	18.4	3,382	30.8	4.0	8.8	1.6	11.3	7.9	11.5	24.0	Malta
...	[5]	...	14.7	...	...	...	...	...	...	...	...	...	Marshall Islands
20.7	9.4	5.4[3]	8.6	2,865	30.0	4.2	12.1	2.9	8.5	11.0	8.7	22.5	Martinique
2.0	1.2	4.0	0.1	2,640	54.8	0.4	4.0	0.9	10.8	1.2	9.9	18.1	Mauritania
10.0	6.4	—	12.2	2,944	44.7	1.3	4.8	1.2	6.3	3.0	16.6	22.2	Mauritius
5.1	8.8	...	5.6	...	...	...	...	...	...	...	...	...	Mayotte
10.0	11.8	5.5[3]	11.0	3,144	46.2	0.8	8.2	0.7	6.0	4.0	11.3	22.8	Mexico
...	...	...	26.5	...	...	...	...	...	...	...	...	...	Micronesia
...	...	...	...	2,763	48.4	4.2	4.0	0.1	8.9	6.6	8.2	19.7	Moldova
...	...	...	...	3,541	24.3	3.4	16.5	1.2	6.3	3.0	16.6	22.2	Monaco
3.5	8.0	0.4	16.2	2,010	47.0	2.2	27.2	—	10.4	1.2	4.7	7.2	Mongolia
8.0	5.0	...	16.0	3,165	59.7	2.0	2.8	0.5	2.0	5.4	10.4	17.3	Morocco
...	...	1.4[3]	7.9	1,911	41.2	37.3	1.4	0.2	0.6	1.4	8.9	9.1	Mozambique
3.8[6]	0.5[6]	1.1[6]	7.5[6]	2,832	76.3	0.5	2.0	1.0	0.9	2.6	7.0	9.6	Myanmar (Burma)
...	...	...	...	2,107	48.6	13.9	5.6	0.6	3.4	1.9	5.1	20.9	Namibia
...	...	...	...	...	...	...	...	...	...	...	...	...	Nauru
1.2	...	2.9[3]	2.0	2,170	76.8	3.4	2.0	0.1	3.8	2.5	4.4	7.0	Nepal

Household budgets and consumption (continued)

country	income (latest)						consumption expenditure						
	percent received by		by source (percent)				per capita private final, U.S.$ (1995)	by kind or end use (percent of household or personal budget; latest)					
	lowest 20% of households	highest 10% of households	wages, salaries	self-employment	transfer payments[a]	other[b]		food[c]	housing[d]	clothing[e]	health care	energy, water	education
Netherlands, The	7.3[1]	25.1[1]	48.2	10.7	29.1	12.0	15,290	13.6	14.9	7.1	12.9	3.1	0.7
Netherlands Antilles	...	...	...	...	...	...	6,050[10]	24.4[30]	10.4[30]	8.7[30]	2.2[30]	8.3[30]	1.2[30]
New Caledonia	...	...	68.2	18.1	13.7	...	5,410[31]	25.9	23.3[2, 5]	3.5	3.2	[2]	...
New Zealand	2.7[12]	29.8[12]	65.8	9.8	15.2	9.1	10,300	20.0	19.4	4.4	2.9	3.2	1.5
Nicaragua	4.2[1]	39.8[1]	...	...	...	...	360	...	...	...	...	...	...
Niger	2.6	35.4	...	...	...	...	210	50.5	19.1[5]	7.3	...	...	...
Nigeria	4.4[1]	40.8[1]	30.2[18]	46.3[18]	0.9[18]	22.6[18]	350[32]	48.0	3.0	5.0	3.0	1.0	4.0
Northern Mariana Islands	...	...	...	...	...	...	...	49.2[15]	19.5[2, 5]	9.1	[19]	[2]	...
Norway	9.7[12]	21.8[12]	58.8	9.9	24.2	7.1	16,570	23.5	13.7	7.0	5.4	6.2	0.6
Oman	...	...	...	...	...	...	3,000	40.6	24.6	5.1	2.4	3.2	[3]
Pakistan	9.5[1]	27.6[1]	22.0	56.0	——22.0——		300	37.0	11.0	6.0	1.0	5.0	1.0
Palau	...	...	63.7	7.4	18.5	10.4	...	...	...	...	...	...	...
Panama	3.6[1]	35.7[1]	60.8[6]	12.8[6]	13.2[6]	13.2[6]	1,570	34.9	12.6[2]	5.1	3.5	[2]	[3]
Papua New Guinea	4.5[1]	40.5[1]	*57.3*	[8]	*1.1*	*41.6*[8]	1,140	40.9	12.5[5]	6.2	...	4.9	...
Paraguay	2.3	46.6	33.9	[8]	2.5	63.6[8]	1,590	48.7	16.4	9.7	3.4	—	1.5
Peru	4.4[12]	35.4[12]	31.2	65.1	3.7	...	1,820	44.1[15]	6.8[2]	10.1	2.7	[2]	[3]
Philippines	5.4[1]	36.6[1]	45.7	42.5	3.4	8.4	800	56.8	4.1[2]	3.9	...	[2]	...
Poland	7.7[12]	26.3[12]	34.0	4.3	20.7	41.0	1,940	41.2	2.8	10.9	8.1	1.0	[3]
Portugal	*7.3*[12]	*28.4*[12]	46.4	[8]	21.8	31.8[8]	6,860	34.8	2.0	10.3	4.5	3.0	1.4
Puerto Rico	*3.2*	*34.7*	56.3	6.4	29.5	7.8	5,640[10]	20.6	11.8[2]	7.4	11.6	[2]	3.1
Qatar	...	...	80.8	5.6	...	13.6	3,600[4]	24.5	35.1[5]	9.1	1.0	1.9	4.3
Réunion	...	...	68.9	[8]	16.0	15.1[8]	4,820[31]	22.4	11.8	7.9	2.2	2.2	[3]
Romania	8.9[12]	22.7[12]	62.6	————37.4————			1,570	51.1	16.4[2, 5]	15.7	1.2	[2]	[3]
Russia	4.4[1]	38.7[1]	68.5	6.4	15.7	12.1	1,180	34.8	2.7	22.3	...	...	...
Rwanda	9.7[1]	24.2[1]	10.4[33]	47.7[33]	13.9[33]	28.0[33]	130	32.1[33]	13.1[33]	9.4[33]	1.3[33]	1.2[33]	[33]
St. Kitts and Nevis	...	...	...	...	...	...	2,480[28]	*55.6*[15]	*7.6*	*7.5*	...	*6.6*	...
St. Lucia	...	...	...	...	...	...	...	49.6[15]	13.5	6.5	2.3	4.5	[3]
St. Vincent and the Grenadines	...	...	...	...	...	...	1,700	59.8	6.3	7.7	...	6.2	...
Samoa	...	...	*49.4*	*22.8*	...	*27.8*	710[1]	58.8	5.1[5]	4.2	...	5.0	...
San Marino	...	...	...	...	...	...	...	22.1	20.9[2]	8.0	2.6	[2]	[3]
São Tomé and Príncipe	...	...	...	...	...	...	270	...	...	...	...	...	...
Saudi Arabia	...	...	...	...	...	...	2,980	52.2[18, 34]	17.2[18, 34]	6.6[18, 34]	2.1[18, 34]	1.8[18, 34]	1.1[18, 34]
Senegal	6.4[1]	33.5[1]	51.6[6]	————48.4[6]————			380	49.0	7.0	11.0	2.0	4.0	6.0
Serbia and Montenegro	...	...	41.7	15.8	12.7	29.8	2,480[35]	51.6	1.4	7.4	5.2	8.4	[3]
Seychelles	4.1	35.6	*77.2*	*3.8*	*3.2*	*15.8*	3,410[32]	53.9	13.6	4.2	0.4	9.1	...
Sierra Leone	*1.1*[1]	*43.6*[1]	27.9	61.6	——10.5——		190	63.8	5.8[2]	7.3	4.5	[2]	[3]
Singapore	5.1	33.5	81.2	16.8	——2.0——		11,710	18.7	10.2[2]	7.1	4.6	[2]	1.4
Slovakia	11.9[12]	18.2[12]	76.7	[8]	8.7	14.4[8]	1,580	26.8	7.6[2]	8.9	...	[2]	...
Slovenia	8.4[12]	20.7[12]	52.4	13.0	23.4	11.2	5,460	30.8	18.3	8.5	5.0	7.3	[3]
Solomon Islands	...	...	74.1	————25.9————			820[4]	46.8	21.9[2, 5]	5.7	[19]	[2]	...
Somalia	...	...	...	...	...	...	...	62.3[6, 15]	15.3[6]	5.6[6]	...	4.3[6]	...
South Africa	2.9[1]	45.9[1]	73.6	[8]	4.9	21.5[8]	1,970	29.3	12.6[2]	7.5	4.5	[2]	1.4
Spain	7.5[12]	25.2[12]	48.5	27.5	19.5	4.5	8,840	21.6[15]	12.6[2]	8.6	4.7	[2]	[3]
Sri Lanka	8.0[1]	28.0[1]	48.5	[8]	9.7	41.8[8]	520	48.0	1.9	10.1	1.8	3.3	0.8
Sudan, The	*4.0*	*34.6*	...	...	...	...	1,050[35]	63.6	11.5	5.3	4.1	3.8	[3]
Suriname	...	...	*74.6*	...	*3.2*	*22.2*	5,960[10]	*39.9*[6]	*4.4*[6]	*11.0*[6]	*3.6*[6]	*6.9*[6]	*2.6*[6]
Swaziland	*2.8*	*54.5*	44.4	22.2	12.2	21.2	500	33.5[15]	13.4[2]	6.0	1.8	[2]	[3]
Sweden	9.6[12]	20.1[12]	58.9	9.7	25.8	5.6	13,680	21.3	19.9	8.6	3.2	4.9	0.1
Switzerland	6.9[12]	25.2[12]	63.6	[8]	16.5	19.9[8]	26,060	27.0[15]	13.1	4.4	9.9	7.7	[3]
Syria	...	...	40.7	...	25.1	34.2	2,210	58.8[15]	16.0[2]	7.5	...	[2]	[3]
Taiwan	7.1	25.5	64.5	19.7	4.5	11.3	12,230	26.8	22.5	5.6	7.8	3.0	5.6
Tajikistan	...	...	64.3	5.6[7]	30.1	—	340	65.3	...	...	...	...	...
Tanzania	6.8[1]	30.1[1]	28.1	34.2	3.5	34.2	150	66.7	8.3	9.9	1.3	7.6	...
Thailand	6.4[1]	32.4[1]	36.4	45.0	0.9	17.7	1,540	29.0	6.3	11.6	8.0	1.7	0.5
Togo	*8.0*	*30.5*	...	...	...	...	210	42.5[6]	13.4[2, 6]	11.5[6]	5.0[6]	[2, 6]	[3, 6]
Tonga	...	...	...	...	...	...	...	49.3	10.5	5.6	0.3	2.7	...
Trinidad and Tobago	*2.6*	*33.6*	...	...	...	...	2,050	25.5[15]	21.6	10.4	[19]	...	1.5
Tunisia	5.9[1]	30.7[1]	...	...	...	...	1,260	39.0	10.7	6.0	3.0	5.1	1.8
Turkey	5.8[1]	32.3[1]	24.1	51.4	10.8	13.7	1,940	38.5	22.8[2]	9.0	2.6	[2]	1.4
Turkmenistan	6.1[1]	31.7[1]	56.6	26.0[7]	14.4	3.0	570[10]	...	...	...	...	...	...
Tuvalu	...	...	*17.9*	*76.1*	...	*6.0*	...	45.5	11.5[5]	7.5	...	...	...
Uganda	6.6[1]	31.2[1]	...	...	...	...	260	57.1[6, 15]	...	5.5[6]	...	7.3[6]	...
Ukraine	8.6[1]	26.4[1]	66.4	9.3	13.4	10.9	490	41.3	1.7	...	...	...	[3]
United Arab Emirates	...	...	...	...	...	...	7,940	24.1	23.7	9.1	1.1	1.2	3.9
United Kingdom	6.6[12]	27.3[12]	66.2	9.8	13.9	11.0	12,020	17.1	21.7	6.0	...	4.6	...
United States	5.2[12]	30.5[12]	64.4	9.0	19.3	7.3	18,840	15.4	14.9	6.9	17.0	3.5	2.2
Uruguay	5.4[12]	32.7[12]	53.5	17.0	——29.5——		4,140	39.9	17.6[2]	7.0	9.3	[2]	1.3
Uzbekistan	7.4[12]	25.2[12]	59.8	18.5	21.7	...	950	...	...	...	...	...	...
Vanuatu	...	...	59.0	33.7	——7.3——		680	30.5[15]	29.0[2, 5]	4.7	[19]	[2]	...
Venezuela	3.7[12]	37.0[12]	...	...	...	...	2,490	30.4	11.5	10.6	2.9	3.0	0.8
Vietnam	8.0[1]	29.9[1]	17.2	64.6	17.6	0.5	280	62.4	2.5	5.0	...	...	2.9
Virgin Islands (U.S.)	...	...	65.7	2.6	13.0	12.7	...	25.3[36]	*24.9*[36]	*5.4*[36]	...	*6.5*[36]	...
West Bank	...	...	...	...	...	...	1,380[22]	...	...	...	...	...	...
Western Sahara	...	...	...	...	...	...	...	...	...	...	...	...	...
Yemen	6.1[1]	30.8[1]	...	...	...	...	310	61.0[37]	13.2[37]	...	1.1[37]	6.1[37]	...
Zambia	4.2[1]	39.2[1]	79.9	17.8	1.3	1.0	220	36.0	7.0	10.0	8.0	4.0	14.0
Zimbabwe	4.0[1]	46.9[1]	92.0	1.0	...	7.0	580	30.1[15]	6.5	10.3	7.1	8.9	6.0

[1]Data refer to consumption shares by fractiles of persons. [2]Housing includes energy, water. [3]Recreation includes education. [4]1988. [5]Housing includes household durable goods. [6]Capital city only. [7]Agricultural self-employment only. [8]Other includes self-employment. [9]1989. [10]1993. [11]Highest 20%. [12]Data refer to income shares by fractiles of persons. [13]1985. [14]1990. [15]Includes tobacco. [16]Includes wage taxes. [17]Personal effects, other includes education and recreation. [18]Urban areas only. [19]Recreation includes health care. [20]1984. [21]Low-income population in Banjul

transportation, communications	household durable goods[f]	recreation[g]	personal effects, other[h]	food consumption, 1998: daily available calories per capita	percent of total calories derived from: cereals	potatoes, cassava	meat, poultry	fish	eggs, milk	fruits, vegetables	fats, oils[i]	other[j]	country
13.3	7.1	9.7	17.6	3,282	17.1	4.5	15.0	1.0	15.0	6.1	16.1	25.1	Netherlands, The
19.5[30]	10.0[30]	4.2[30]	10.1[30]	2,659	28.2	2.3	18.9	1.4	10.8	5.0	13.6	19.7	Netherlands Antilles
16.1	[5]	6.7	21.3	2,812	30.9	6.1	13.1	1.5	8.6	3.9	16.0	19.9	New Caledonia
17.1	10.9	—— 20.6 ——		3,315	22.1	4.1	15.1	1.3	11.1	7.4	16.8	22.3	New Zealand
...	...	...	...	2,208	50.4	1.3	2.4	0.1	4.3	2.7	10.9	27.9	Nicaragua
...	[5]	...	23.1	1,966	70.5	3.2	2.6	0.1	2.2	1.7	4.4	15.2	Niger
3.0	6.0	...	27.0	2,882	45.8	18.6	2.4	0.4	1.0	4.4	14.1	13.3	Nigeria
8.3	[5]	13.9[19]	—	...	...	...	...	...	...	...	...	...	Northern Mariana Islands
12.8	6.9	8.8	15.1	3,425	27.4	4.3	10.7	3.5	12.2	4.9	17.7	19.2	Norway
8.9	7.1	4.1[3]	4.0	...	...	...	...	...	...	...	...	...	Oman
13.0	5.0	...	21.0	2,447	57.0	0.9	3.1	0.2	8.5	2.9	13.2	14.3	Pakistan
...	...	...	...	...	...	...	...	...	...	...	...	...	Palau
15.1	8.4	11.7[3]	8.7	2,476	37.0	2.7	7.5	1.1	7.4	5.7	16.1	22.5	Panama
13.0	[5]	...	22.5	2,168	31.2	25.4	7.7	1.3	0.6	17.6	6.2	9.9	Papua New Guinea
4.5	6.2	2.3	7.3	2,577	27.8	13.9	11.5	0.4	7.3	4.3	16.2	18.7	Paraguay
7.3	7.5	7.6[3]	13.9	2,420	35.7	13.4	4.3	1.8	4.5	6.4	11.6	22.4	Peru
5.0	12.8	...	17.3	2,280	51.7	4.2	8.8	3.0	2.2	8.3	5.9	15.9	Philippines
8.9	8.3	15.0[3]	3.8	3,351	34.4	7.4	10.4	1.0	8.6	4.5	15.6	18.0	Poland
15.4	8.6	4.4	15.6	3,691	28.6	6.3	10.8	2.4	8.3	7.1	17.0	19.6	Portugal
11.8	11.2	7.9	14.7	...	...	...	...	...	...	...	...	...	Puerto Rico
13.0	[5]	—— 11.1 ——		...	...	...	...	...	...	...	...	...	Qatar
24.9	6.0	10.1[3]	12.5	3,308	41.4	1.7	11.9	1.5	5.2	5.0	9.8	23.5	Réunion
6.6	[5]	4.5[3]	4.5	3,263	49.5	4.5	7.4	0.1	11.3	4.5	10.5	12.2	Romania
...	9.4	...	30.8	2,835	41.3	8.0	9.0	1.6	10.3	3.4	9.6	20.6	Russia
1.7[33]	5.3[33]	0.4[33]	35.5[33]	2,035	22.4	23.1	1.1	—	1.4	25.9	5.5	—	Rwanda
4.3	*9.4*	...	*9.0*	2,766	24.9	2.6	13.6	1.9	8.6	4.6	11.6	32.1	St. Kitts and Nevis
6.3	5.8	3.2[3]	8.3	2,842	34.3	4.8	14.0	1.3	6.8	9.3	6.9	22.7	St. Lucia
3.7	6.6	...	9.7	2,554	35.2	4.3	10.4	1.1	6.1	5.2	9.6	28	St. Vincent and the Grenadines
9.0	[5]	...	17.9	...	...	...	...	...	...	...	...	...	Samoa
17.6	7.2	7.1[3]	14.5	3,608	31.8	1.9	11.1	1.1	8.9	7.2	22.0	15.9	San Marino
...	...	...	...	2,201	28.3	15.4	1.4	2.1	0.8	17.0	10.6	24.3	São Tomé and Príncipe
4.5[18, 34]	5.9[18, 34]	...	8.6[18, 34]	2,888	46.6	1.1	7.3	0.4	4.9	10.1	11.4	18.2	Saudi Arabia
5.0	2.0	...	12.0	2,277	57.5	1.0	3.7	2.8	2.4	2.0	18.7	11.9	Senegal
5.7	1.6	2.4[3]	16.3	2,963	29.4	2.3	16.3	0.2	11.4	6.8	17.8	15.8	Serbia and Montenegro
6.4	6.6	1.4	4.4	2,462	37.3	1.2	5.6	5.1	6.5	5.8	11.5	27.1	Seychelles
4.4	3.9	3.8[3]	4.8	2,045	53.4	10.4	1.0	1.4	0.6	2.9	17.6	12.8	Sierra Leone
13.8	8.9	13.1	23.3	...	...	...	...	...	...	...	...	...	Singapore
...	3.9	...	26.2	2,953	27.3	4.3	10.5	0.3	8.9	4.7	20.8	23.2	Slovakia
12.7	3.3	6.1[3]	8.0	2,950	35.4	3.5	11.1	0.4	12.0	5.3	15.2	17.2	Slovenia
9.9	[5]	[19]	15.7	2,130	33.3	36.3	3.1	3.7	0.6	2.7	2.9	17.4	Solomon Islands
...	...	...	12.1[6]	1,531	33.4	1.5	8.7	0.2	28.4	2.8	7.4	17.5	Somalia
16.7	10.0	6.3	11.7	2,909	53.0	2.0	7.0	0.5	4.8	2.8	11.7	18.1	South Africa
15.3	7.1	7.0[3]	23.1	3,348	22.6	4.7	13.4	2.4	9.3	6.7	21.6	19.4	Spain
17.0	3.9	2.4	10.8	2,314	51.3	2.9	0.9	1.9	3.4	4.5	2.9	32.3	Sri Lanka
1.5	5.5	0.7[3]	4.0	2,444	56.5	0.6	5.1	0.1	13.3	2.9	9.5	11.9	Sudan, The
9.5[6]	*12.3[6]*	*5.8[6]*	*4.0[6]*	2,633	41.2	2.3	7.0	1.6	4.8	6.2	12.5	24.5	Suriname
8.8	12.8	3.3[3]	20.4	2,503	48.1	1.3	6.4	—	5.2	1.8	6.2	31.0	Swaziland
15.7	6.6	10.9	8.8	3,114	25.6	3.6	10.2	1.8	14.1	5.2	18.9	20.7	Sweden
12.9	5.1	9.8[3]	10.1	3,222	22.1	2.3	14.8	0.8	12.5	6.1	18.7	22.7	Switzerland
2.4	5.8	2.1[3]	7.4	3,378	53.9	1.2	3.8	0.1	6.6	5.6	12.9	15.9	Syria
10.7	2.2	1.1	4.7	...	...	...	...	...	...	...	...	...	Taiwan
...	...	...	34.7	2,176	67.9	0.1	2.8	—	3.4	4.3	12.2	9.2	Tajikistan
4.1	1.4	0.7	—	1,999	49.0	19.5	2.6	1.1	2.2	5.4	6.8	13.6	Tanzania
12.9	10.9	4.2	14.9	2,462	47.1	1.9	6.6	2.6	2.8	5.7	6.1	27.3	Thailand
9.5[6]	4.4[6]	5.1[3, 6]	8.6[6]	2,513	50.7	29.2	2.3	1.3	0.6	1.3	7.2	7.5	Togo
5.8	10.6	0.5	14.7	...	...	...	...	...	...	...	...	...	Tonga
15.2	14.3	[17]	6.2[17]	2,711	36.8	2.8	4.5	0.9	6.8	3.8	14.6	29.9	Trinidad and Tobago
9.0	11.2	7.1	7.1	3,297	52.9	1.8	3.0	0.5	4.6	6.2	15.8	15.3	Tunisia
8.8	9.0	5.6	2.3	3,554	48.4	3.7	2.5	0.4	6.9	7.9	15.1	15.1	Turkey
...	...	...	...	2,684	57.7	0.5	7.6	0.1	8.2	3.4	16.4	6.1	Turkmenistan
10.5	[5]	...	25.0	...	...	...	...	...	...	...	...	...	Tuvalu
5.9[6]	...	...	24.2[6]	2,216	20.4	23.4	3.2	0.8	1.9	25.8	2.2	22.3	Uganda
...	6.8	6.3[3]	43.9	2,878	44.5	8.8	5.8	0.7	10.3	3.4	10.8	15.7	Ukraine
14.1	11.6	4.7	6.5	3,372	33.8	1.6	11.5	1.4	9.5	14.3	10.3	17.7	United Arab Emirates
15.1	8.0	15.9	11.6	3,257	22.8	6.1	14.4	1.0	11.6	5.0	19.1	20.0	United Kingdom
13.9	1.5	5.8	18.9	3,757	23.6	2.9	11.9	0.8	11.7	5.2	17.9	26.1	United States
10.4	6.3	3.1	5.1	2,866	28.9	3.7	19.1	0.6	12.3	4.0	11.0	20.3	Uruguay
...	...	...	...	2,564	55.8	2.1	6.9	—	9.4	4.1	15.3	6.2	Uzbekistan
13.2	[5]	12.3[19]	10.3	2,737	21.4	30.7	9.2	1.6	1.5	6.4	8.9	20.3	Vanuatu
7.1	4.5	2.7	26.4	2,358	34.9	3.1	6.6	1.7	6.5	7.3	15.2	24.7	Venezuela
...	4.6	...	22.6	2,422	70.9	4.0	7.6	1.3	0.5	3.9	3.2	8.6	Vietnam
11.7[36]	*4.3[36]*	...	*21.9[36]*	...	...	...	...	...	...	...	...	...	Virgin Islands (U.S.)
...	...	...	...	...	...	...	...	...	...	...	...	...	West Bank
...	...	...	...	...	...	...	...	...	...	...	...	...	Western Sahara
1.9[37]	3.0[37]	...	13.7[37]	2,087	68.7	1.0	2.7	0.7	1.8	3.0	8.2	13.9	Yemen
5.0	1.0	...	15.0	1,950	64.9	14.5	2.7	0.8	1.3	1.5	3.4	10.9	Zambia
1.1	12.9	0.6	16.5	2,153	60.5	2.1	2.3	0.3	3.1	1.0	11.9	18.8	Zimbabwe

and Kombo St. Mary only. [22]1986. [23]Urban areas of Eastern region only. [24]Personal effects, other includes health care. [25]Housing includes water. [26]Wage earners only. [27]Workers and clerical workers only. [28]1992. [29]Malagasy households only. [30]Curaçao only. [31]1987. [32]1994. [33]Rural areas only. [34]Middle-income population only. [35]1991. [36]St. Thomas only. [37]Data refer to former Yemen Arab Republic.

Health services

The provision of health services in most countries is both a principal determinant of the quality of life and a large and growing sector of the national economy. This table summarizes the basic indicators of health personnel; hospitals, by kind and utilization; mortality rates that are most indicative of general health services; external controls on health (adequacy of food supply and availability of safe drinking water); and sources and amounts of expenditure on health care. Each datum refers more or less directly to the availability or use of a particular health service in a country, and, while each may be a representative measure at a national level, each may also conceal considerable differences in availability of the particular service to different segments of a population or regions of a country. In the United States, for example, the availability of physicians ranges from about one per 730 persons in the least well-served states to one per 260 in the best-served, with a rate of one per 150 in the national capital. In addition, even when trained personnel exist and facilities have been created, limited financial resources at the national or local level may leave facilities underserved; or lack of good transportation may prevent those most in need from reaching a clinic or hospital that could help them.

Definitions and limits of data have been made as consistent as possible in the compilation of this table. For example, despite wide variation worldwide in the nature of the qualifying or certifying process that permits an individual to represent himself as a physician, organizations such as the World Health Organization (WHO) try to maintain more specific international standards for training and qualification. International statistics presented here for "physicians" refer to persons qualified according to WHO standards and exclude traditional health practitioners, whatever the local custom with regard to the designation "doctor." Statistics for health personnel in this table uniformly include all those actually working in the health service field, whether in the actual provision of services or in teaching, administration, research, or other tasks. One group of practitioners for whom this type of guideline works less well is that of midwives, whose training and qualifications vary enormously from country to country but who must be included, as they represent, after nurses, perhaps the largest and most important category of health auxiliary worldwide. The statistics here refer to those midwives working in some kind of institutional setting (a hospital, clinic, community health-care centre, or the like) and exclude rural noninstitutional midwives and traditional birth attendants.

Hospitals also differ considerably worldwide in terms of staffing and services. In this tabulation, the term hospital refers generally to a permanent facility offering inpatient services and/or nursing care and staffed by at least one physician. Establishments offering only outpatient or custodial care are excluded. These statistics are broken down into data for general hospitals (those providing care in more than one specialty), specialized facilities (with care in only one specialty), local medical centres, and rural health-care centres; the last two generally refer to institutions that provide a more limited range of medical or nursing care, often less than full-time. Hospital data are further analyzed into three categories of administrative classification: public, private nonprofit, and private for profit. Statistics on number of beds refer to beds that are maintained and staffed on a full-time basis for a succession of inpatients to whom care is provided.

Data on hospital utilization refer to institutions defined as above. Admission and discharge, the two principal points at which statistics are normally collected, are the basis for the data on the amount and distribution of care by kind of facility. The data on numbers of patients exclude babies born during a maternal confinement but include persons who die before being discharged. The bed-occupancy and average length-of-stay statistics depend on the concept of a "patient-day," which is the annual total of daily censuses of inpatients. The bed-occupancy rate is the ratio of total patient-days to potential days based on the number of beds; the average length-of-stay rate is the ratio of total patient-days to total admissions. Bed-occu-

Health services

country	health personnel							hospitals									
	year	physicians	dentists	nurses	pharmacists	midwives	population per physician	year	number	kinds (%)				ownership (%)			hospital beds per 10,000 pop.
										general	specialized	medical centres	rural	government	private nonprofit	private for profit	
Afghanistan	1997	2,556	232	4,182	464	…	9,090	1988–93	…	…	…	…	…	…	…	…	3
Albania	1995	4,848	1,332	14,559	772[2]	9,936[2]	668	1993	40	…	…	…	…	100.0	—	—	31
Algeria	1996	27,650	7,837	…	3,866	…	1,015	1996[3]	186	…	…	…	…	…	…	…	12
American Samoa	1991	26	7[6]	140[6]	2[6]	1[6]	1,885	1990	1	100.0	—	—	—	100.0	—	—	27
Andorra	1998	166	35	188	59	6	434	1996	1	100.0	—	—	—	100.0	—	—	28
Angola	1997	736	…	10,942	…	411	13,228	1990	58	…	…	…	…	…	…	…	12
Antigua and Barbuda	1996	75	12	187	13	31	915	1998	3	50.0	50.0	…	—	100.0	—	—	42
Argentina	1992	88,800	21,900[8]	18,000[6]	…	…	376	1997	1,235	…	…	…	…	56.8	—43.2—		22
Armenia	1998	18,000[10]	[10]	18,258	144	1,750	292[10]	1998	183[11]	…	…	…	…	100.0	…	…	28
Aruba	1997	103	21	515	15	3	874	1999	2	50.0	—	50.0	—	100.0	—	—	32
Australia	1997–98	47,400	8,800	148,300	15,600	…	395	1996–97	1,222	…	…	…	…	61.0	—39.0—		95
Austria	1998	33,698	1,534	35,834	2,137[13]	1,056	240	1998	329	37.7	62.3	—	—	…	…	…	92
Azerbaijan	1998	28,850	2,426	62,213	2,560	10,843	274	1997	762	…	…	…	…	100.0	…	…	92
Bahamas, The	1996	419	72	648	52[4]	…	673	1997	5	60.0	20.0	20.0	—	60.0	—40.0—		38
Bahrain	1997	620	56	1,755	124	…	1,000	1994	12	58.3	42.7	—	—	75.0	16.7	8.3	30[14]
Bangladesh	1997	27,546	938	15,408	7,485[4]	13,211	4,627	1997	976	…	…	…	…	69.3	—30.7—		4
Barbados	1993	330	42	869	138[12]	377[12]	797	1995	9	66.7	33.3	—	—	80.0	—	20.0	74
Belarus	1999	39,007	4,522	47,343	3,152[13]	5,826	261	1999	276	55.4		——44.6——		100.0	…	…	68
Belgium	1998	39,420	7,360	109,187	14,597	6,602	259	1993	363	80.4	19.6	—	—	38.6	61.4	—	76
Belize	1998	155	26	404	30	230	1,542	1998	7	…	…	…	…	100.0	—	—	23
Benin	1995	312	16	1,116	85	432	17,538	1993	…	…	…	…	…	…	…	…	2
Bermuda	1996	96	22	522	29	…	639	1996	2	50.0	50.0	—	—	…	…	…	40
Bhutan	1997	101	9[4]	355[14]	5[4]	326[14]	6,128	1997	28	…	…	…	…	…	…	…	16
Bolivia	1996	4,346	444	2,062	…	…	1,747	1996	336	10.7[14]	8.9[14]	23.5[14]	56.8[14]	…	…	…	11
Bosnia and Herzegovina	1998	4,813	640	15,241	370	1,565[8]	699	1996	…	…	…	…	…	…	…	…	48
Botswana	1994	339	…	3,329	…	…	4,395	1994	30	53.3	3.3	43.3	—	…	…	…	23
Brazil	1997	205,828	137,600	67,760	51,847	…	774	1997	6,410	—100.0—		—	—	35.5	—64.5—		31
Brunei	1996	259	26	1,229	15[14]	278[14]	1,181	1995	10	90.0	—	—	10.0	90.0	—10.0—		33
Bulgaria	1998	28,823	5,324	47,434	1,230	5,923	286	1998	288	—71.2—		28.8	—	…	…	…	104
Burkina Faso	1991[15]	341	19	2,627	113	339	27,158	1993	78	—14.1—		85.9	—	100.0	—	—	5
Burundi	1996	329	9[4]	1,131	55[4]	…	16,507	1996	…	…	…	…	…	…	…	…	0.7
Cambodia	1998	3,464	210	8,608	262[12]	3,359	3,367	1988[3]	188	…	…	…	…	100.0	—	—	16
Cameroon	1996	1,031	56	5,112	206[6]	70	13,510	1988	629	—27.0—		—73.0—		72.3	—27.7—		27
Canada	1996	55,006	15,636	232,869	22,197	…	539	1989	1,079	81.8	16.6	1.6	—	95.8	—	4.2	54[11]
Cape Verde	1996	66	…	213	6	…	5,818	1996	65	8.0	—	92.0	—	100.0	—	—	19[16]
Central African Republic	1995	112	16	282	22[4]	157	28,600	1990	255	—21.1[17]—		—78.9[17]—		79.7[17]	—20.3[17]—		14[8]
Chad	1994	228	14	1,014	10	159	30,260	1994	…	…	…	…	…	…	…	…	13
Chile	1996	13,857	5,817	6,738	1,830[15]	5,369[15]	1,040	1994	198	…	…	…	…	89.4	—10.6—		31
China	1998	1,999,500[10, 18]	[10]	1,218,000	440,000	51,000	621[18]	1998	69,105	11.2	13.4	—75.4—		100.0	—	—	23
Colombia	1997	40,355	22,121	46,187	…	…	1,102	1997	1,657	…	…	…	…	…	…	…	1
Comoros	1997	64	6[4]	180	6[4]	74	7,765	1995	…	…	…	…	…	…	…	…	29
Congo, Dem. Rep. of the	1996	3,224	514	20,652	59[4]	…	14,492	1986	400	…	…	…	…	52.5	—47.5—		21
Congo, Rep. of the	1995	632	35[4]	4,663	175[4]	160	4,083	1990	…	…	…	…	…	…	…	…	33
Costa Rica	1997	5,500	1,420	3,720	1,362	…	641	1997	29	…	…	…	…	87.9	—	12.1	14
Côte d'Ivoire	1996	1,318	219[4]	4,568	135[4]	2,196	11,108	1993	…	…	…	…	…	…	…	…	5
Croatia	1998	9,766	2,802	20,216	1,940	1,407	436	1997	70	52.8	47.2	—	—	…	…	…	63
Cuba	1996	60,129	9,600	76,013	…	…	183	1993	244	…	…	…	…	100.0	—	—	65
Cyprus[19]	1997	1,725	594	2,942	668[14]	120[20]	486	1997[21]	103	71.8	22.1	—	6.1	10.0[20]	0.9[20]	89.1[20]	48
Czech Republic	1999	38,828	6,383	91,213	4,785	4,602	265	1999	365	59.2	40.8	—	—	70.7	—29.3—		67
Denmark	1995	15,175	4,605	36,944	747	1,046	345	1992	163	42.9	57.1	—	—	42.9	57.1	—	35

pancy rates may exceed 100% because stays of partial days are counted as full days.

Two measures that give health planners and policy makers an excellent indication of the level of ordinary health care are those for mortality of children under age five and for maternal mortality. The former reflects the probability of a newborn infant dying before age five. The latter refers to deaths attributable to delivery or complications of pregnancy, childbirth, the puerperium (the period immediately following birth), or abortion. A principal source for the former data was WHO's *The World Health Report* (annual) and for the latter, the UN Development Programme's *Human Development Report* (annual).

Levels of nutrition and access to safe drinking water are two of the most basic limitations imposed by the physical environment in which health-care activities take place. The nutritional data are based on reported levels of food supply (whether or not actually consumed), referred to the recommendations of the United Nations' Food and Agriculture Organization for the necessary daily intake (in calories) for a moderately active person of average size in a climate of a particular kind (fewer calories are needed in a hot climate) to remain in average *good* health. Excess intake in the many developed countries ranges to more than 40% above the minimum required to maintain health (the excess usually being construed to diminish, rather than raise, health). The range of deficiency is less dramatic numerically but far more critical to the countries in which deficiencies are chronic, because the deficiencies lead to overall poor health (raising health service needs and costs), to decreased productivity in nearly every area of national economic life, and to the loss of social and economic potential through early mortality. By "safe" water is meant only water that has no substantial quantities of chemical or biological pollutants—*i.e.*, quantities sufficient to cause "immediate" health problems. Data refer to the proportion of persons having "reasonable access" to an "adequate" supply of water within a "convenient" distance of the person's dwelling, as these concepts are interpreted locally.

The data on health care expenditure were excerpted from a joint effort by the WHO and the World Bank to create better analytical tools by which the interrelations among health policy, health care delivery systems, and human health might be examined against the more general frameworks of government operations, resource allocation, and development process. First published in the World Bank's *World Development Report 1993: Investing in Health* and, the following year, in the World Health Organization's *Global Comparative Assessments in the Health Sector* (edited by C.J.L. Murray and A.D. Lopez), the database and underlying methodology are expected to provide a continuing basis for international comparisons and policy analysis. The first two of ten volumes of the final results appeared in 1996 as *The Global Burden of Disease* and *Global Health Statistics* by the same editors.

Expenditures were tabulated for direct preventative and curative activities and for public health and public education programs having direct impact on health status—family planning, nutrition, and health education—but not more indirect programs like environmental, waste removal, or relief activities. Public, parastatal (semipublic, *e.g.*, social security institutions), international aid, and household expenditure reports and surveys were utilized to build up a comprehensive picture of national, regional, and world patterns of health care expenditures and investment that could not have been assembled from any single type of source. For reasons of space, public and parastatal are combined as the former.

Internet resources for further information:

- Most Recent Values of W.H.O. Global Health-For-All Indicators (for personnel and general indicators) http://www.who.int/htl/countrysup/countrye.htm

No comparable source exists for hospitals.

admissions or discharges: rate per 10,000 pop.	admissions or discharges: by kinds of hospital (%): general	special-ized	medical centres	rural	bed occu-pancy rate (%)	aver-age length of stay (days)	mortality: under age 5 per 1,000 live newborn 1997	mortality: maternal mortality per 100,000 live births 1990–97	popu-lation with access to safe water 2000 (%)	food supply (% of FAO require-ment) 1998	total health expenditures, 1990: as percent of GDP	per capita (U.S.$)	by source (percent): public	private	inter-national aid	country
...	...	...	...	...	...	...	257	...	13	73[1]	...	...	...	...	...	Afghanistan
...	...	...	...	...	...	...	40	65	97	124	4.00	26	84.0	16.0	—	Albania
371	...	...	...	...	49.3[4]	5[4]	39	220	89[5]	126	6.95	149	76.9	23.0	0.1	Algeria
965	100.0	—	—	—	38.4	4	...	...	...	...	...	...	...	...	...	American Samoa
...	...	...	...	...	...	...	6	...	100	...	...	...	...	...	...	Andorra
238	...	...	...	...	44.5[7]	16[7]	292	1,500	38	82	...	...	...	...	...	Angola
64[7]	...	...	...	...	50.0[7]	8[7]	21	150	91	99	4.55	241	59.1	37.3	3.6	Antigua and Barbuda
560[3]	...	...	...	...	52.0[3]	7[3]	24	44	81[9]	134	4.21	137	60.1	39.7	0.2	Argentina
...	...	...	...	...	...	...	30	35	...	92	4.17	152	59.8	40.2	—	Armenia
...	...	...	...	...	92.2[12]	...	...	...	...	...	...	...	...	...	...	Aruba
...	...	...	...	...	...	4.5	6	9	100	120	7.67	1,294	69.6	30.4	—	Australia
2,650	...	...	...	...	80.1	10	5	10	100[5]	134	8.38	1,711	66.4	33.6	—	Austria
...	...	...	...	...	...	...	46	37	78	86	4.27	99	61.2	38.8	—	Azerbaijan
837[3]	...	...	...	...	85.4[3]	12[3]	21	...	97	105	...	...	...	...	...	Bahamas, The
...	...	...	...	...	...	...	22	46	100	...	4.62	324	63.0	36.9	0.1	Bahrain
...	...	...	...	...	...	...	109	440	97	89	3.19	6	24.8	56.7	18.5	Bangladesh
810[12]	93.5[12]	6.5[12]	—	—	88.3[12]	32[12]	12	0	100[5]	123	5.04	323	64.3	33.8	1.9	Barbados
...	...	...	...	...	...	...	27	22	100	123	3.19	157	68.7	31.3	—	Belarus
1,963	96.0	4.0	—	—	84.4	12	7	10	100[5]	137	7.50	1,449	82.5	17.5	—	Belgium
...	...	...	...	...	...	...	43	140	92	129	5.88	23	48.4	41.0	10.7	Belize
...	...	...	...	...	...	...	167	500	63	112	4.32	19	26.3	36.4	37.3	Benin
1,313	97.0	3.0	—	—	75.0	8	...	...	...	116	...	...	...	...	...	Bermuda
...	...	...	...	...	...	...	121	380	62	...	5.05	10	41.1	30.4	28.5	Bhutan
250	...	...	...	...	48.0	6	96	390	83	93	4.01	25	39.9	39.6	20.5	Bolivia
529[6, 7]	...	...	...	...	82.4[6, 7]	11[6, 7]	19	10	...	110	...	...	...	...	...	Bosnia and Herzegovina
...	...	...	...	...	93.1[6]	...	49	330	95	93	6.19	139	61.8	21.6	16.5	Botswana
740	...	...	...	...	...	6	44	220	87	122	4.20	146	65.7	33.9	0.4	Brazil
...	...	...	...	...	...	...	10	0	90[5]	127	...	...	...	...	...	Brunei
...	...	...	...	...	...	...	19	15	100	110	5.36	121	81.4	18.6	—	Bulgaria
...	...	...	...	...	...	...	169	930	42	91	8.46	7	9.8	17.9	72.3	Burkina Faso
...	...	...	...	...	...	...	176	1,300	78	68	3.28	30	42.4	48.3	9.3	Burundi
...	...	...	...	...	...	...	167	470	30	94	...	...	...	...	...	Cambodia
...	...	...	...	...	...	...	145	550	58	98	2.62	27	26.4	61.7	11.9	Cameroon
...	...	...	...	...	...	14	7	6	100	119	9.05	1,945	74.1	25.9	—	Canada
...	...	...	...	...	...	...	73	55	74	132	6.32	64	20.7	25.5	53.7	Cape Verde
...	...	...	...	...	...	...	173	1,100	70	91	4.19	18	26.5	37.5	36.0	Central African Republic
...	...	...	...	...	...	...	198	830	27	91	6.22	12	27.6	24.7	47.7	Chad
749[3]	...	...	...	...	69.9[3]	7[3]	13	23	93	117	4.73	100	70.1	29.1	0.7	Chile
418[14]	60.4[14]		39.6[14]		66.9[14]	15[14]	47	60	75	126	3.51	11	58.5	40.9	0.6	China
614[6]	41.4[6]	16.7[6]	41.9[6]		57.2[6]	6[6]	30	80	91	119	3.98	51	44.0	54.4	1.6	Colombia
...	...	...	...	...	...	...	93	500	96	79	5.40	28	46.3	29.2	24.5	Comoros
...	...	...	...	...	...	...	207	870	45	77	2.38	5	8.5	64.8	26.7	Congo, Dem. Rep. of the
...	...	...	...	...	...	...	108	890	51	101	3.99	50	47.1	40.7	12.1	Congo, Rep. of the
958[8]	...	...	...	...	78.2[8]	6[8]	14	29	95	124	6.51	132	73.6	25.2	1.2	Costa Rica
...	...	...	...	...	...	...	150	600	81	117	3.35	28	48.7	47.9	3.4	Côte d'Ivoire
1,578	70.0	30.0	—	—	83.0	13	9	12	96[9]	98	...	...	...	...	...	Croatia
1,376[8]	...	...	...	...	...	...	8	24	91	107	...	...	...	...	...	Cuba
522	...	...	...	...	78.9	6	9	0	100[5]	140	3.96	64	62.9	26.8	10.3	Cyprus[19]
1,982	97.6	2.4	—	—	79.0[14]	9	7	9	100[5]	133	5.94[22]	169[22]	84.9[22]	15.1[22]	—	Czech Republic
1,253	92.9	7.1	—	—	80.4	8	6	10	100	128	6.30	1,588	84.2	15.8	—	Denmark

Health services (continued)

country	health personnel							hospitals									
	year	physicians	dentists	nurses	pharmacists	midwives	population per physician	year	number	kinds (%)				ownership (%)			hospital beds per 10,000 pop.
										general	specialized	medical centres	rural	government	private non-profit	private for profit	
Djibouti	1996	60	7	315	8	...	7,100	1993	8	— 25.0 —		— 75.0 —		100.0	...	...	27[6]
Dominica	1998	38	10	361	27[11]	...	2,000	1994	53	1.9	—	—	98.1	100.0	—	—	25
Dominican Republic	1997	17,315	1,879	8,600	372	...	464	1992[3]	723	— 7.9 —		— 92.1 —		...	...	...	12[11]
East Timor	...	...	...	...	...	...	...	...	...	...	...	...	...	...	...	...	...
Ecuador	1995	15,212	1,788	5,212	906[20]	802	753	1995	474	17.0	8.0	— 75.0 —		26.0	11.3	62.7	16
Egypt	1998	129,000	15,211	141,770	20,254[13]	...	490	1998	7,411	4.5	— 95.5 —			87.9	— 12.1 —		19
El Salvador	1997	6,177	5,604	12,851	...	1,940[8]	936	1993	78	...	...	...	...	61.5	1.3	37.2	17
Equatorial Guinea	1996	105	4	169	...	9	4,086	1988	...	...	...	...	...	...	...	...	29
Eritrea	1996	108	4	574	...	79	33,240	1993	10	...	...	...	...	...	...	...	9
Estonia	1998	4,471	987	9,088[23]	775	[23]	336	1998	78	...	...	...	...	87.2	— 12.8 —		73
Ethiopia	1988	1,466	...	3,496	364	...	30,195	1986–87	86	...	...	...	...	...	...	...	3
Faroe Islands	1995	85	40	412	10	19	529	1994	3	33.3	—	—	66.7	100.0	—	—	64
Fiji	1997	409	36	1,742	...	...	1,919	1997	25	...	...	...	...	...	...	...	23
Finland	1998	15,407	4,828	111,408	7,472	4,019	334	1994[7]	380	...	...	...	...	...	...	...	98
France	1997	177,585	39,736	291,287	58,609	12,718	330	1997	4,186	— 91.6 —			8.4	25.4	— 74.6 —		113
French Guiana	1994	213	38	495	47	40	669	1996	25	...	...	...	...	10	...	15	143
French Polynesia	1999	384	94	599	51	54[20]	599	1999	7	...	...	...	...	...	...	...	37
Gabon	1989	448	32	759	71	240	2,504	1988	27	...	...	...	...	...	...	...	51
Gambia, The	1997	43	...	155	6	102	28,791	1994	13	15.4	—	— 84.6 —		...	...	...	7
Gaza Strip	1993[24]	...	...	...	...	...	...	1995	6	...	...	...	...	83.3	— 16.7 —		9
Georgia	1998	22,236	1,800	24,174	469	1,586	229	1997	422[4]	...	...	...	...	100.0	...	...	48
Germany	1998	287,164	62,274	785,190	47,341	9,271	286	1996	2,269	...	...	...	...	49.2[20]	36.0[20]	14.8[20]	72
Ghana	1996[15]	1,117	36	12,970	67[6]	9,583	16,127	1991	121	90.9	9.1	—	—	60.3	— 39.7 —		16[11]
Greece	1995	40,995	10,667	30,967[11]	8,147[13]	1,837[11]	255	1996	356	49.7	50.3	—	—	...	...	...	50
Greenland	1997	83	28	528	10[8]	11	674	1990	16	6.3	—	—	93.7	100.0	—	—	75
Grenada	1996	96	14	232	47	...	582	1996[7]	3	100.0	—	—	—	100.0	—	—	35
Guadeloupe	1996	690	129	1,640	220	140	597	1995	29	...	...	...	...	44.8	— 55.2 —		76
Guam	1986	147	...	594[23]	...	[23]	823	1998	1	...	...	...	...	...	...	...	...
Guatemala	1997	9,812	1,367	13,247[20]	...	18,924[20]	1,072	1985	35[14]	...	...	...	...	...	...	...	11[14]
Guernsey	1993	79	...	...	...	...	804	1993	1	100.0	—	—	—	100.0	—	—	...
Guinea	1995	930	22[17]	3,983	197[8]	372	7,688	1991	38	— 100.0 —		...	...	100.0	—	—	5
Guinea-Bissau	1996	194	11	1,277	12[17]	148	6,015	1993	16	...	...	...	...	62.5	— 37.5 —		13
Guyana	1996	214	35	504	40	165	3,612	1994	30	...	...	...	...	83.3	— 16.7 —		30
Haiti	1996	773	95[11]	2,630	...	...	8,418	1994	49	...	...	...	...	...	...	...	10
Honduras	1997	4,896	989	6,152	975[20]	...	1,202	1994	61	...	...	...	...	47.5	— 52.5 —		9
Hong Kong	1999	9,580	2,052	38,320	1,368	...	714	1995	88	...	...	...	...	78.4	— 21.6 —		49
Hungary	1998	36,143	5,671	51,965	4,789	2,227	279	1998	167	...	...	...	...	...	...	...	83
Iceland	1998	893	288	2,370	228	235	307	1995	57	89.0	11.0	—	—	...	...	...	147
India	1998[25]	512,352	19,523[20]	449,351[20]	...	...	1,916	1998	15,067[8]	...	...	...	...	55.0[8]	— 45.0[8] —		27
Indonesia	1997	31,887[10]	[10]	155,911[23]	5,440[13]	[23]	6,267[10]	1997	1,090	...	...	...	...	...	...	...	6
Iran	1997	50,770	9,427	136,030	6,816	7,387	1,195	1997	685	...	...	...	...	83.5	— 16.5 —		16
Iraq	1998	11,769	1,220	50,499	2,525	...	1,818	1993	185	...	...	...	...	...	...	...	14
Ireland	1998	8,114	1,712	59,021	2,882	15,228	457	1996	62[3, 7]	100.0	—	—	—	100.0	—	—	33
Isle of Man	1998	117	26	...	25[13]	...	615	1986	3	33.3	33.3	—	33.3	100.0	—	—	...
Israel	1998	22,345	6,733	35,579	3,511	1,080	260	1995	259	18.5	81.5	—	—	12.0	51.7	36.3	61
Italy	1997	318,616	37,039	280,263	58,662	...	180	1997	1,589	91.5	8.5	—	—	59.2	— 40.8 —		65
Jamaica	1996	421	57	1,241	52	273	5,974	1996	24	75.0	25.0	—	—	75.0	— 25.0 —		24
Japan	1997	240,908	85,518	960,477	194,300	23,615	525	1997	9,413	88.7	11.3	—	—	73.5	— 26.5 —		131
Jersey	1995	95	...	...	...	...	895	1990	6	16.7	83.3	—	—	100.0	—	—	88
Jordan	1997	7,250	2,140	12,929	3,363	861[14]	602	1994	63	...	...	...	...	42.9	— 57.1 —		18[26]
Kazakhstan	1998	53,207	3,783	97,824	9,903	8,456	283	1996	1,518	...	...	...	...	100.0	...	...	123
Kenya	1995	3,606	600	24,610	605[20]	...	7,575	1994	846	— 35.1 —		— 64.9 —		...	...	...	14
Kiribati	1998	26	4	208	...	...	3,385	1990	1	...	...	...	...	...	...	...	40
Korea, North	1995	64,006	...	38,792	...	12,931	337	1989	...	...	...	...	...	...	...	...	135
Korea, South	1997	62,609	15,383	133,920	45,820	8,516	735	1997	6,446	70.0	30.0	—	—	...	...	...	47
Kuwait	1997	3,419	470	8,593	633[26]	19[14]	529	1995	24	...	...	...	...	66.7	—	33.3	31
Kyrgyzstan	1998	14,355	1,307	35,768	320	3,472	332	1994	348[14]	89.1	—	10.9	—	100.0	—	—	101[14]
Laos	1996	1,208	214	5,354	...	...	1,603	1995	25	0.7[4]	— 99.3[4] —			100.0	—	—	25[4]
Latvia	1998	6,900	1,064	13,445	292[11]	81	355	1998	150	51.2[11]	4.1[11]	28.8[11]	15.9[11]	97.5	2.5	—	94
Lebanon	1997	7,203	2,744	3,430	1,715	...	476	1995	153	...	...	...	...	10.5	— 89.5 —		22
Lesotho	1995	105	10	1,169	60[15]	914	18,524	1987	22	90.9	9.1	—	—	54.5	45.5	—	15
Liberia	1997	53	2	136	...	99	43,434	1988	92	— 37.0 —		— 63.0 —		...	...	...	...
Libya	1997	6,092	619[26]	17,136[26]	1,095[26]	...	781	1991	...	...	...	...	...	...	...	...	41
Liechtenstein	1997	41	18	...	2	...	764	1998	1	...	...	...	...	...	...	...	34
Lithuania	1999	14,578	2,316	37,448	2,143	1,611	254	1999	186	...	...	...	...	100.0	...	...	94
Luxembourg	1998	1,164	282	3,347	297	94	368	1994	34	50.0	50.0	—	—	...	...	...	109
Macau	1998	532	31	706	48	...	800	1994	30	6.7	—	93.3	—	46.7	— 53.3 —		22
Macedonia	1998	4,110	1,046	9,833	300	1,342	490	1994	58[26]	27.4	24.2	— 48.4 —		100.0	—	—	52[26]
Madagascar	1996	1,470	137	2,969	19[4]	1,471	9,351	1990	...	...	...	...	...	...	...	...	9
Malawi	1989	186	...	284	5	...	49,118	1987	395	12.2	0.8	— 87.0 —		59.2	— 40.8 —		16
Malaysia	1997	14,258	1,865	24,550	...	5,872	1,519	1997	337	...	...	...	...	35.1	— 64.9 —		20
Maldives	1995	100	...	281	134	461	2,533	1996	5	20.0	—	80.0	—	100.0	—	—	12
Mali	1994	419	9	1,167	57[28]	267	21,269	1987	...	...	...	...	...	...	...	...	4
Malta	1998	987	135	4,158	186	291	383	1996	7	...	...	...	...	71.4	— 28.6 —		57
Marshall Islands	1997	34	4	141	...	6	1,794	1997	2	100.0	—	—	—	100.0	—	—	21
Martinique	1996	680	130	1,700	230	150	547	1993	8[14]	...	...	...	...	...	...	...	56[14]
Mauritania	1995	323	47	1,461	6[8]	237	7,251	1990	16	...	...	...	...	100.0	—	—	7
Mauritius	1998	1,033	144	2,826[23]	250	[23]	1,117	1998	13	73.9[11]	17.4[11]	8.7[11]	—	60.9[11]	4.3[11]	34.8[11]	33
Mayotte	1985	9	1	51	1	2	7,427	1994	2	100.0	—	—	—	100.0	—	—	9
Mexico	1997	116,047	8,926	161,303	...	...	812	1993	1,888[26]	...	...	...	...	53.9	— 46.1 —		9[26]
Micronesia	1999	76	16	368	7[20]	...	1,737	1993	4	100.0	—	—	—	100.0	—	—	31
Moldova	1998	14,959	1,761	37,355	2,885	3,723	286	1996	312	...	...	...	...	100.0	...	...	125
Monaco	1997	188	22	500[14]	67[14]	11[14]	170	1997	1	100.0	—	—	—	100.0	—	—	173
Mongolia	1998	5,676	315	7,169	1,113[20]	...	411	1997	407	...	...	...	...	...	...	...	78
Morocco	1997	12,534	1,090	28,610	2,997	87[4]	2,173	1993[29]	201	48.8	—	51.2	—	100.0	—	—	10

admissions or discharges: rate per 10,000 pop.	by kinds of hospital (%): general	specialized	medical centres	rural	bed occupancy rate (%)	average length of stay (days)	mortality: under age 5 per 1,000 live newborn 1997	maternal mortality per 100,000 live births 1990–97	population with access to safe water 2000 (%)	food supply (% of FAO requirement) 1998	total health expenditures, 1990: as percent of GDP	per capita (U.S.$)	by source (percent): public	private	international aid	country
...	...	...	...	...	...	...	156	...	100	89	...	...	...	...	...	Djibouti
1,026	...	...	...	...	94.6	8	20	65	97	124	8.06	192	65.1	20.4	14.5	Dominica
470	...	...	...	...	...	...	53	230	86	101	3.72	38	52.7	43.3	4.0	Dominican Republic
...	...	...	...	...	...	...	...	...	...	...	...	...	...	...	...	East Timor
508	...	...	...	...	53.1	6	39	160	85	119	4.14	44	55.9	37.3	6.8	Ecuador
317	...	...	...	...	...	...	73	170	97	131	2.61	28	30.3	62.0	7.7	Egypt
...	...	...	...	...	54.9[3, 12]	6[3, 12]	36	160	77	110	5.86	58	29.7	55.6	14.7	El Salvador
...	...	...	...	...	...	...	172	...	44	68	7.60	28	36.6	20.7	42.7	Equatorial Guinea
...	...	...	...	...	...	...	116	1,000	46	75	...	...	...	...	...	Eritrea
1,952	76.7[11]	21.5[11]	—	1.8[11]	75.1	10	23	50	100[9]	120	3.62	228	53.0	47.0	—	Estonia
...	...	...	...	...	...	...	175	1,400	24	78	3.80	4	41.3	39.9	18.8	Ethiopia
...	...	...	...	...	86.4	12	...	...	...	...	...	...	...	...	...	Faroe Islands
...	...	...	...	...	...	...	24	38	47	125	3.76	70	54.9	38.3	6.9	Fiji
2,322	...	...	...	...	70.9	11	4	6	100	117	7.82	2,046	83.3	16.7	—	Finland
2,128	...	...	...	...	...	...	5	10	100	141	9.40	1,869	74.2	25.8	—	France
1,714[20]	...	...	...	...	70.3[20]	8[20]	...	...	84[9]	125	...	...	...	...	...	French Guiana
...	...	...	...	...	...	...	...	...	...	129	...	...	...	...	...	French Polynesia
...	...	...	...	...	...	...	145	500	86	109	4.10	164	52.7	40.9	6.4	Gabon
...	...	...	...	...	...	...	87	1,100	62	108	7.53	22	28.3	20.7	51.0	Gambia, The
752	...	...	...	...	74.9	3	...	...	...	...	...	...	...	...	...	Gaza Strip
...	...	...	...	...	...	...	23	60	79	88	4.45	152	62.5	37.5	—	Georgia
1,812[20]	...	...	...	...	82.8[20]	13[20]	5	8	100[5]	128	8.73	1,511	72.7	27.3	—	Germany
...	...	...	...	...	...	...	107	210	73	117	3.50	15	35.0	51.8	13.2	Ghana
1,370	81.0	19.0	—	—	66.0	9	8	10	99[5]	145	5.39	359	76.0	24.0	—	Greece
2,450	29.2	—	—	70.8	69.4	8	...	...	...	...	...	...	...	...	...	Greenland
774[8]	100.0	—	—	—	59.1[8]	7[8]	29	0	95	111	5.96	133	68.8	27.8	3.5	Grenada
2,154	...	...	...	...	84.0	10	...	...	90[9]	113	...	...	...	...	...	Guadeloupe
...	...	...	...	...	...	...	...	...	...	...	...	...	...	...	...	Guam
284	...	...	...	...	57.7	9	55	190	92	99	3.70	27	44.2	43.2	12.6	Guatemala
1,100	100.0	—	—	—	...	...	...	...	...	...	...	...	...	...	...	Guernsey
...	...	...	...	...	...	...	201	670	48	100	3.90	17	39.7	40.3	20.0	Guinea
...	...	...	...	...	...	...	220	910	56	104	8.15	16	31.3	18.9	49.8	Guinea-Bissau
...	...	...	...	...	...	...	82	180	94	109	10.37	42	40.7	15.1	44.2	Guyana
...	...	...	...	...	...	...	132	1,000	46	83	6.99	27	26.3	54.8	19.0	Haiti
459[20]	...	...	...	...	...	...	45	220	88	104	4.54	52	56.7	35.7	7.7	Honduras
1,811	...	...	...	...	...	...	6	7	100[5]	143	5.69	687	19.5	80.5	0.0	Hong Kong
2,502	...	...	...	...	77.0	10	11	15	99	130	5.95	185	84.4	15.6	—	Hungary
2,828[12]	94.0[12]	6.0[12]	—	—	86.5[12]	12[12]	5	6	100[5]	121	8.34	1,884	87.5	12.5	—	Iceland
...	...	...	...	...	...	...	108	440	84	112	6.00	21	20.0	78.4	1.6	India
...	...	...	...	...	...	...	60	450	78	132	2.01	12	25.6	66.7	7.7	Indonesia
...	...	...	...	...	...	...	35	37	92	117	2.54	244	56.9	43.1	0.0	Iran
645[4]	...	...	...	...	42.4[4]	4[4]	122	310	85	100	...	...	...	...	...	Iraq
1,470	100.0	—	—	—	82.2	7	7	10	100[5]	144	7.22	876	81.1	18.9	—	Ireland
...	...	...	...	...	...	...	...	...	...	...	...	...	...	...	...	Isle of Man
1,979	...	...	...	...	91.2	10	6	5	99[9]	135	4.20	480	49.3	50.6	0.1	Israel
1,743	90.4	9.6	—	—	72.0	9	6	7	100[5]	143	7.54	1,449	77.7	22.3	—	Italy
242[3]	81.7[3]	18.3[3]	—	—	53.7	5	11	120	92	121	5.04	83	57.4	33.2	9.5	Jamaica
...	...	...	...	...	...	...	6	8	97[9]	123	6.45	1,538	74.5	25.5	—	Japan
1,718	84.0	16.0	—	—	...	...	...	...	...	...	...	...	...	...	...	Jersey
478[3]	...	...	...	...	68.1[3]	4[3]	24	41	96	114	3.77	55	36.9	52.3	10.8	Jordan
...	...	...	...	...	...	...	44	70	91	98	4.44	154	62.3	37.7	—	Kazakhstan
...	...	...	...	...	...	...	87	370	57	85	4.33	16	40.0	37.9	22.1	Kenya
...	...	...	...	...	...	...	78[11]	...	48	131	...	...	...	...	...	Kiribati
...	...	...	...	...	...	...	30	110	100	81	...	...	...	...	...	Korea, North
629[14]	97.5[14]	2.5[14]	—	—	65.5[14]	13[14]	6	20	92	131	6.61	365	40.9	58.9	0.2	Korea, South
950[3, 11]	72.2[3, 11]	27.8[3, 11]	—	—	64.9[3, 11]	7[3, 11]	13	5	100[5]	126	4.86	541	64.2	35.6	0.1	Kuwait
1,775	95.5	—	4.5	—	75.6	15	68	65	77	99	4.97	118	66.7	33.3	—	Kyrgyzstan
...	...	...	...	...	...	...	122	650	37	98	2.53	5	17.4	60.7	21.9	Laos
2,210	78.4[11]	4.6[11]	13.8[11]	3.2[11]	76.5	13	22	45	100[9]	117	3.87	220	56.1	43.9	—	Latvia
...	...	...	...	...	...	...	37	100	100	132	...	...	...	...	...	Lebanon
221[7]	...	...	...	...	...	...	137	610	78	97	8.32	26	38.3	26.5	35.2	Lesotho
...	...	...	...	...	...	...	235	...	46[9]	86	8.24	4	19.9	11.8	68.3	Liberia
...	...	...	...	...	...	...	25	75	97	138	...	...	...	...	...	Libya
...	...	...	...	...	...	...	7	...	100[5]	...	...	...	...	...	...	Liechtenstein
2,001[14]	...	...	...	...	74.4[14]	15[14]	24	18	100	121	3.58	159	72.0	28.0	—	Lithuania
1,941	94.6	5.4	—	—	75.0	16	7	0	100[5]	137	6.56	1,662	91.4	8.6	—	Luxembourg
329	...	...	...	...	64.4	16	...	...	...	108	...	...	...	...	...	Macau
995	67.2	6.1	26.7 (medical centres and rural combined)		68.5	14	23	11	...	116	...	...	...	...	...	Macedonia
...	...	...	...	...	...	...	158	490	47	88	2.56	7	29.0	49.6	21.4	Madagascar
...	...	...	...	...	...	...	215	620	57	96	4.98	11	35.0	41.7	23.3	Malawi
717[3, 6]	...	...	...	...	...	...	11	39	78[9]	130	2.96	71	44.0	55.8	0.2	Malaysia
256[20, 27]	...	...	...	...	71.4[20, 27]	4[20, 27]	74	350	100	111	...	...	...	...	...	Maldives
...	...	...	...	...	...	...	239	580	65	90	5.19	15	24.9	46.7	28.4	Mali
...	...	...	...	...	...	...	10	...	100[5]	136	5.38	349	68.3	31.7	0.0	Malta
...	...	...	...	...	...	...	92[11]	...	82[9]	...	...	...	...	...	...	Marshall Islands
2,092	...	...	...	...	73.7	10	...	...	94[9]	118	...	...	...	...	...	Martinique
...	...	...	...	...	...	...	183	550	37	114	3.80	18	28.5	41.5	30.0	Mauritania
1,446[3, 11]	...	...	...	...	74.6[3, 11]	5[3, 11]	23	30	100	130	4.40	100	47.8	39.0	13.3	Mauritius
...	...	...	...	...	...	...	...	...	...	...	...	...	...	...	...	Mayotte
403[3, 8]	...	...	...	...	64.7[3, 8]	5[3, 8]	35	48	88	135	3.17	89	49.3	49.8	0.9	Mexico
...	...	...	...	...	...	...	24	...	100[5]	...	...	...	...	...	...	Micronesia
...	...	...	...	...	...	...	35	42	92	108	3.91	143	74.4	25.6	—	Moldova
...	...	...	...	...	...	...	5	...	100	140	...	...	...	...	...	Monaco
205	...	...	...	...	...	...	150	150	60	83	6.63	58	83.0	15.1	1.9	Mongolia
255	...	...	...	...	63.8	8	72	230	80	131	2.55	26	33.6	63.3	3.1	Morocco

Health services (continued)

country	health personnel							hospitals									
	year	physicians	dentists	nurses	pharma-cists	midwives	popu-lation per physi-cian	year	number	kinds (%)				ownership (%)			hos-pital beds per 10,000 pop.
										gen-eral	spe-cial-ized	medical centres	rural	govern-ment	private non-profit	private for profit	
Mozambique	1990	387	108	3,533	353	1,139	36,320	1990	238	4.2	0.8	— 95.0 —		100.0	—	—	8[20]
Myanmar (Burma)	1999	12,313	871	10,820	...	9,162	3,367	1996	737	...	...	...	...	...	...	...	7
Namibia	1997	495	67	2,817	91[8]	1,954	3,388	1992	47	...	...	...	...	91.5	— 8.5 —		45[8]
Nauru	1995	17	...	62	...	...	624	...	...	...	...	...	...	...	...	...	...
Nepal	1997	874	45[14]	3,845	18[14]	1,621[14]	26,316	1997	74	...	...	...	...	...	...	...	2
Netherlands, The	1997	33,618	7,319	124,000[20]	2,622	1,357	462	1998	222	64.4	35.6	—	—	...	...	...	53
Netherlands Antilles	1998	339	62	1,198	42	11	617	1998	11	38.3	36.3	25.4	—	...	...	...	70
New Caledonia	1996	362	107	852	74	61	549	1996	9	12.5[4]	12.5[4]	75.0[4]	—	62.5[4]	— 37.5[4] —		45
New Zealand	1997	12,399	1,467	29,000	3,634	2,114	303	1996	368	...	...	...	...	32.3	— 67.7 —		59
Nicaragua	1995	4,551	1,099	2,577	...	...	957	1994	56	46.4	7.1	46.4	—	...	...	...	11
Niger	1997	325	19	2,126	29[4]	511	28,560	1987	...	...	...	...	...	...	...	...	5
Nigeria	1993	21,739	1,335	80,186	6,474[12]	62,386	3,707	1985	11,588	6.6	0.5	— 92.9 —		81.4	— 18.6 —		7[14]
Northern Mariana Islands	1986	23	4	103	2	2	1,324	1988	1	100.0	—	—	—	100.0	—	—	19
Norway	1998	18,304	5,230	81,548	2,531	2,619	242	1994	...	...	...	...	...	...	...	...	51
Oman	1998	3,061	201	7,453	435	65	773	1998	62	— 8.1 —		— 91.9 —		25.8	— 74.2 —		36
Pakistan	1997	78,470	3,159	28,661	47,618[26]	20,869[14]	1,836	1997	5,118	— 7.6[11] —		— 92.4[11] —		...	...	...	6
Palau	1998	20	2	26	...	1	900	1998	1	...	...	...	...	...	...	...	37[4]
Panama	1998	3,518	784	3,203	756	...	773	1998	60	...	...	...	...	...	...	...	27
Papua New Guinea	1998	342	127	3,141	...	...	13,708	1993	...	...	...	...	...	...	...	...	34
Paraguay	1995	3,730	1,279	1,875	433	1,547	1,294	1995	...	...	...	...	...	...	...	...	14
Peru	1996	23,249	1,197	16,043	4,789	3,832	1,030	1996	472	...	...	...	...	50.2	— 49.8 —		13
Philippines	1996	36,375	1,668	5,663	...	13,750	1,923	1996	1,738	96.5	3.1	0.5	...	34.5	— 65.5 —		12
Poland	1998	91,121	17,869	215,295	20,139	25,014	424	1998	765	93.8	6.2	—	—	100	...	...	54
Portugal	1998	31,097	3,319	37,775	7,505	827	320	1993	335	43.0	18.8	38.2	—	74.3	14.7	11.0	41[14]
Puerto Rico	1989–92	6,269	902	19,666	2,111	120	558	1994	72	83.3	8.3	8.3	—	36.1	30.6	33.3	26
Qatar	1996[15]	703	117	1,612	285	...	793	1995	4	25.0	75.0	—	—	100.0	—	—	18
Réunion	1999	1,346	337	2,906	284	176	520	1998	19	85.5	—— 14.5 ——			71.0	— 29.0 —		39
Romania	1998	41,415	5,379	92,057	1,643	8,913	543	1995	414	...	...	...	...	99.5	— 0.5 —		77
Russia	1998	618,718	47,322	1,615,000	9,112	91,853	238	1998	11,200	37.4[11]	17.2[11]	—	45.4[11]	99.8	— 0.2 —		119
Rwanda	1989	272	7	835	25	...	24,697	1985[3]	220	— 13.6 —		— 86.4 —		100.0	—	—	9[6]
St. Kitts and Nevis	1998	50	8	274	21	...	846	1998	4	50.0	—— 50.0 ——			...	...	...	62
St. Lucia	1997	81	13	312	13	...	1,876	1998	6	25.0[12]	25.0[12]	—	50.0[12]	...	...	...	14
St. Vincent	1998	59	6	267	27[8]	...	2,075	1997	11	...	...	...	...	77.8[12]	— 22.2[12] —		19
Samoa	1996	62	7	281	6[12]	65	2,919	1992	36	2.8	—	—	97.2	100.0	—	—	34
San Marino	1998	84	...	...	...	...	309	1998	...	...	...	...	...	...	...	...	58
São Tomé and Príncipe	1996	61	7	167	1[6]	39	2,147	...	...	...	...	...	...	...	...	...	...
Saudi Arabia	1997	33,110	3,191	65,821	4,189	...	602	1996	290	...	...	...	...	74.1	— 25.9 —		22
Senegal	1996	649	93	1,876	322	588	13,656	1996	17	...	...	...	...	...	...	...	9
Serbia and Montenegro	1997	22,498	4,209	...	2,032	...	471	1997	...	...	...	...	...	...	...	...	55
Seychelles	1998	93	15	342	7	...	849	1997	7	14.3	14.3	71.4	—	100.0	—	—	54
Sierra Leone	1996	339	19	1,532	...	218	13,696	1998	219	— 25.6[16] —		— 74.4[16] —		...	...	...	8
Singapore	1998	5,147	914	15,570	858[26]	487[26]	615	1997	23	...	...	...	...	43.5	— 56.5 —		35
Slovakia	1998	19,030	2,598	38,168	1,822	2,119[14]	283	1991	111	72.1	27.9	—	—	100.0	—	—	92[14]
Slovenia	1998	4,501	1,201	3,125	887	...	440	1998	28	57.7	42.3	—	—	...	...	...	56
Solomon Islands	1997	31	...	464	...	283	13,258	1997	11	100.0	—	—	—	75.0	25.0	—	51
Somalia	1997	265	13	1,327	70	540[16]	25,034	1988	...	...	...	...	...	...	...	...	7
South Africa	1998	29,369	4,387	174,754	9,948	...	1,459	1998	704	...	...	...	...	51.1	— 48.9 —		34
Spain	1996	165,560	14,877	177,034	43,221	6,314	240	1994	783	57.5	18.5	— 24.0 —		42.5	— 57.5 —		40
Sri Lanka	1999	6,881	471	19,362	848	7,899	2,740	1995[3]	407	...	...	...	...	100.0	—	—	26
Sudan, The	1996	2,818	219	18,158	344	...	11,110	1986	...	...	...	...	...	...	...	...	8
Suriname	1996	305	31	631	14	40	1,373	1998	...	...	...	...	...	...	...	...	34
Swaziland	1996	149	7[4]	1,264[4]	13[4]	...	6,617	1986	24	— 41.7 —		— 58.3 —		...	...	...	...
Sweden	1997	27,511	13,446	72,625	5,953	6,351	322	1996	...	...	...	...	...	...	...	...	43
Switzerland	1998	22,965	3,470	55,387	4,373	1,884	310	1997	...	...	...	...	...	...	...	...	66
Syria	1998	22,293	11,456	29,259	8,205	6,063[14]	694	1995	294	...	...	...	...	20.5	— 79.5 —		12
Taiwan	1998	27,168	7,900	71,215	22,761	704	804	1998	700	...	...	...	...	13.7	— 86.3 —		57
Tajikistan	1998	12,291	1,125	29,597	734	3,999	498	1994	449	...	...	...	...	98.2	— 1.8 —		88
Tanzania	1995	1,277	218	26,536	...	13,953	24,389	1993	173[8]	...	...	...	...	...	...	...	10
Thailand	1995	14,181	2,920	54,262	5,867	9,713	4,192	1996	1,397	93.6	6.4	—	—	65.8	— 34.2 —		21
Togo	1995	320	29	1,252	65[8]	438	13,168	1990	...	...	...	...	...	...	...	...	16
Tonga	1997	43	9	309	...	30	2,279	1993	4	...	...	...	...	...	...	...	28
Trinidad and Tobago	1997	949	141	1,378[23]	518	[23]	1,339	1997	77	...	...	...	...	...	...	...	37
Tunisia	1997	6,464	1,200	26,409	1,570	...	1,429	1994[3]	163	— 13.5 —		— 86.5 —		100.0	—	—	18
Turkey	1998	77,375	13,428	69,701	21,486	41,181	826	1997	1,078	75.3[11]	8.8[11]	— 15.9[11] —		84.3[11]	— 15.7[11] —		23
Turkmenistan	1997	14,022	1,010	21,436	1,566	3,664	333	1994	368	...	...	...	...	100.0	...	...	115
Tuvalu	1999	8	1	33	...	10	1,375	1985	8	11.1	—	—	88.9	100.0	—	—	36
Uganda	1996	840[20]	42	3,897	...	2,835	22,399[20]	1989	81	...	...	...	...	...	...	...	12
Ukraine	1998	150,382	19,615	370,171	23,488	29,523	334	1997	3,400	...	...	...	...	100.0	...	...	99
United Arab Emirates	1997	4,749	644[26]	8,450[26]	2,007[26]	...	553	1996	50	...	...	...	...	72.0	— 28.0 —		29
United Kingdom	1998	82,803	20,216	299,010	33,759[12]	24,801[6]	716	1997	...	...	...	...	...	...	...	...	42
United States	1998	756,700	196,000	2,162,000	184,000[14]	3,000[14]	357	1998	6,097	88.0	12.0	—	—	25.3	49.2	25.5	38
Uruguay	1998	11,964	3,921	2,369	1,009	586	269	1997	118	...	...	...	...	75.4	— 24.6 —		35
Uzbekistan	1998	74,230	5,869	243,166	746	16,235	324	1995	192	...	...	...	...	100.0	...	...	84
Vanuatu	1997	21	3[14]	259[14]	6[14]	33[14]	8,524	1995	90	5.6	—	21.1	73.3	100.0	—	—	32
Venezuela	1997	53,818	13,000	46,305	8,571	...	423	1997	556	...	...	...	...	37.0	— 63.0 —		17
Vietnam	1998	36,683	...	42,797	6,500[20]	13,450	2,083	1994	12,500	...	...	...	...	...	...	...	27
Virgin Islands (U.S.)	1985	167	...	...	...	...	622	1985	...	...	...	...	...	...	...	...	49
West Bank	1993[24]	1,344	445	2,279	149	56	1,536	1995	17	...	...	...	...	52.9	— 47.1 —		9
Western Sahara	1994	100	...	...	24	...	2,504	...	...	...	...	...	...	...	...	...	...
Yemen	1998	3,883	245[26]	7,578[14]	613	385[11]	4,211	1998	81	...	...	...	...	...	...	...	55
Zambia	1995	601	26[4]	9,853	24[4]	311[4]	14,496	1987	965	8.2	0.3	19.0	72.5	80.9	19.1	—	29[20]
Zimbabwe	1995	1,522	142	14,095	411[20]	3,078	7,196	1993[3]	1,378	0.9	2.6	83.7	12.7	100.0	—	—	19[14]

[1]1997. [2]1987. [3]Government hospitals only. [4]1990. [5]Data refer to a period other than 1994–95, differ from the standard definition, or refer to only part of the country. [6]1989. [7]General hospitals only. [8]1991. [9]1994–98. [10]Physicians include dentists. [11]1994. [12]1992. [13]Number of pharmacies. [14]1995. [15]Government-employed personnel only. [16]1998. [17]1988. [18]Includes doctors of traditional Chinese medicine. [19]Republic of Cyprus only. [20]1993. [21]Excludes psychiatric hospitals. [22]Data refer to former Czechoslovakia. [23]Nurses include midwives. [24]West Bank includes Gaza Strip.

admissions or discharges					bed occupancy rate (%)	average length of stay (days)	mortality		population with access to safe water 2000 (%)	food supply (% of FAO requirement) 1998	total health expenditures, 1990					country
rate per 10,000 pop.	by kinds of hospital (%)						under age 5 per 1,000 live newborn 1997	maternal mortality per 100,000 live births 1990–97			as percent of GDP	per capita (U.S.$)	by source (percent)			
	general	specialized	medical centres	rural									public	private	international aid	
…	…	…	…	…	…	…	209	1,100	57	82	5.86	5	21.0	25.7	53.3	Mozambique
…	…	…	…	…	…	…	114	230	72	131	…	…	…	…	…	Myanmar (Burma)
…	…	…	…	…	…	…	75	230	77	92	3.92	45	47.8	41.3	10.9	Namibia
…	…	…	…	…	…	…	30	…	…	…	…	…	…	…	…	Nauru
…	…	…	…	…	…	…	104	540	88	99	4.54	7	23.0	51.7	25.4	Nepal
1,028	96.7	3.3	—	—	70.1	10	6	7	100	122	8.03	1,501	72.6	27.4	—	Netherlands, The
…	…	…	…	…	…	…	…	…	…	110	…	…	…	…	…	Netherlands Antilles
1,165[4, 7]	…	…	…	…	84.8[4, 7]	8[4, 7]	…	…	…	123	…	…	…	…	…	New Caledonia
1,332[3]	…	…	…	…	64.0[3]	6[3]	7	15	100[5]	126	7.37	925	81.7	18.3	—	New Zealand
769	—— 76.2 ——		23.8	—	…	…	57	160	77	98	8.61	34	56.9	22.5	20.6	Nicaragua
…	…	…	…	…	…	…	285	590	59	84	4.98	16	24.5	31.3	34.1	Niger
…	…	…	…	…	…	…	187	1,000	62	122	2.72	10	36.5	57.4	6.1	Nigeria
1,550	100.0	—	—	—	54.7	4	…	…	…	…	…	…	…	…	…	Northern Mariana Islands
1,515	96.4	3.6	—	—	83.0	10	4	6	100	128	7.35	1,835	95.7	4.3	—	Norway
911	…	…	…	…	…	…	18	21	85	…	4.22	209	59.5	40.1	0.5	Oman
…	…	…	…	…	…	…	136	340	90	106	3.48	12	47.4	47.1	5.5	Pakistan
1,582	…	…	…	…	48.5	6	34	…	88	…	…	…	…	…	…	Palau
1,239	…	…	…	…	52.5	8	20	85	90	107	7.13	142	72.6	23.1	4.3	Panama
…	…	…	…	…	…	…	112	370	42	95	4.44	37	59.1	36.1	4.8	Papua New Guinea
…	…	…	…	…	…	…	33	190	78	112	2.97	35	35.1	58.2	6.7	Paraguay
…	…	…	…	…	…	…	56	270	80	103	3.21	61	56.1	41.7	2.2	Peru
538	…	…	…	…	62.1	5	46	210	86	101	2.15	16	46.7	46.4	6.9	Philippines
1,288[12]	96.0[12]	4.0[12]	—	—	72.5[12]	14[12]	11	8	100[5]	128	5.07	84	80.3	19.7	—	Poland
1,146	86.3	10.5	3.2	—	74.5	10	8	8	100[5]	151	6.99	383	61.7	38.3	—	Portugal
1,101	94.0	4.3	1.7	—	63.1	5	…	…	…	…	…	…	…	…	…	Puerto Rico
…	…	…	…	…	71.7[12, 30]	7[12, 30]	20	10	100[5]	…	4.73	630	63.0	36.9	0.0	Qatar
1,951[11]	…	…	…	…	79.8[11]	7[11]	…	…	…	146	…	…	…	…	…	Réunion
…	…	…	…	…	…	…	26	41	58	123	3.87	58	61.4	38.6	—	Romania
2,320	…	…	…	…	85.0	14	22	49	99	111	3.02	159	66.8	33.2	—	Russia
85	…	…	…	…	42.8[28]	7[28]	170	1,300	41	88	3.44	10	15.0	45.2	39.8	Rwanda
1,068[7, 12]	…	…	…	…	49.3[7, 12]	9[7, 12]	37	130	98	114	5.99	212	58.1	27.8	14.1	St. Kitts and Nevis
890[12, 28]	…	…	…	…	…	…	29	30	98	117	7.18	169	75.6	23.0	1.4	St. Lucia
728	…	…	…	…	68.2	7	21	43	93	106	5.69	102	68.5	28.8	2.7	St. Vincent
894	70.8	—	—	29.2	32.9	5	27	…	99	…	2.94	20	6.1	54.2	39.7	Samoa
…	…	…	…	…	…	…	6	…	100[5]	…	…	…	…	…	…	San Marino
…	…	…	…	…	…	…	78	…	82[9]	94	9.22	38	28.8	17.0	54.2	São Tomé and Príncipe
…	…	…	…	…	…	…	28	130	95	119	4.76	260	64.3	35.7	0.0	Saudi Arabia
…	…	…	…	…	…	…	124	560	78	96	3.66	29	45.1	38.0	16.9	Senegal
1,154	…	…	…	…	72.0	12	21	10	98	117	5.11[31]	264[31]	80.4[31]	19.6[31]	—	Serbia and Montenegro
1,744[32]	…	…	…	…	76.4[32]	5[32]	18	…	97[5]	105	6.03	289	50.2	28.0	21.9	Seychelles
…	…	…	…	…	…	…	316	1,800	57	89	2.43	4	19.6	30.9	49.5	Sierra Leone
1,127[26]	…	…	…	…	73.1[11]	8[11]	4	6	100	…	1.87	215	58.3	41.6	0.1	Singapore
1,679[14]	94.9[14]	5.1[14]	—	—	73.2[14]	14[14]	11	9	100	120	…	…	…	…	…	Slovakia
1,643	…	…	…	…	78.4	10	6	11	100	116	…	…	…	…	…	Slovenia
…	…	…	…	…	…	…	28	550	71	93	2.18	117	43.2	50.5	6.3	Solomon Islands
…	…	…	…	…	…	…	211	…	31[9]	66	1.51	8	7.3	41.1	51.6	Somalia
…	…	…	…	…	…	…	82	230	86	119	5.56	77	57.5	42.5	0.0	South Africa
1,053	…	…	…	…	76.7[8]	12[8]	5	6	99[9]	136	6.59	831	78.4	21.6	—	Spain
1,464[4]	…	…	…	…	…	…	19	60	77	104	3.74	18	40.4	51.1	8.6	Sri Lanka
…	…	…	…	…	…	…	115	550	75	104	3.33	34	11.0	84.5	4.5	Sudan, The
766[33]	…	…	…	…	68.8[33]	10[33]	36	110	82	116	2.88	93	37.9	58.0	4.1	Suriname
…	…	…	…	…	…	…	94	230	50[9]	108	7.22	64	43.6	22.2	34.2	Swaziland
1,906[11]	…	…	…	…	82.2[11]	8[11]	4	5	100	116	8.79	2,343	89.3	10.7	—	Sweden
…	…	…	…	…	…	…	5	5	100	120	7.52	2,520	68.5	31.5	—	Switzerland
352[3, 20]	…	…	…	…	75.5[3, 20]	3[3, 20]	33	110	80	136	2.07	41	16.6	79.4	4.0	Syria
…	…	…	…	…	…	…	8	8	90[9]	…	4.30	323	53.0	47.0	0.0	Taiwan
1,492	…	…	…	…	70.2	15	76	85	60	85	5.98	100	72.6	27.4	—	Tajikistan
…	…	…	…	…	…	…	143	530	68	86	4.73	4	14.4	31.6	54.0	Tanzania
…	…	…	…	…	…	…	38	44	84	110	4.98	72	20.4	78.7	0.9	Thailand
…	…	…	…	…	…	…	125	640	55	109	4.10	18	40.4	38.5	21.2	Togo
622[12]	…	…	…	…	56.2[12]	10[12]	23	…	100	…	6.46	63	60.3	25.0	14.8	Tonga
1,114[3, 7]	…	…	…	…	70.7[3, 7]	6[3, 7]	17	90	90	112	4.54	180	62.4	36.9	0.6	Trinidad and Tobago
…	…	…	…	…	…	…	33	70	80	126	4.91	76	63.8	33.3	3.0	Tunisia
709	…	…	…	…	…	…	45	130	82	141	3.94	76	36.2	63.3	0.5	Turkey
…	…	…	…	…	…	…	78	110	74[9]	105	4.99	125	66.4	33.2	0.4	Turkmenistan
1,368	40.9	—	—	59.1	51.5[7]	12.2[7]	56	…	100	…	2.66	472	34.0	66.0	0.1	Tuvalu
…	…	…	…	…	…	…	137	510	52	95	3.40	8	13.3	53.0	33.7	Uganda
…	…	…	…	…	…	…	23	30	98	112	3.30	131	69.7	30.3	—	Ukraine
…	…	…	…	…	…	…	10	3	97[9]	132	2.66	472	34.0	66.0	0.1	United Arab Emirates
…	…	…	…	…	…	…	7	7	100	129	6.11	1,039	84.9	15.1	—	United Kingdom
1,180[34]	…	…	…	…	61.8[34]	6[34]	8	8	100	142	12.71	2,765	44.1	55.9	—	United States
477[3]	…	…	…	…	78.8[3]	9[3]	21	21	98	107	4.62	123	53.8	44.8	1.4	Uruguay
…	…	…	…	…	…	…	58	21	85	100	5.90	116	72.1	27.9	—	Uzbekistan
567	…	…	…	…	41.9	6	50	…	88	120	5.68	67	51.5	25.7	22.8	Vanuatu
601[3]	…	…	…	…	69.7[3]	6[3]	25	65	83	96	3.60	88	54.2	45.6	0.1	Venezuela
…	…	…	…	…	…	…	43	160	77	112	2.11	3	39.3	47.4	13.3	Vietnam
…	…	…	…	…	…	…	…	…	…	…	…	…	…	…	…	Virgin Islands (U.S.)
711	…	…	…	…	80.9	4	…	…	…	…	…	…	…	…	…	West Bank
…	…	…	…	…	…	…	…	…	…	…	…	…	…	…	…	Western Sahara
…	…	…	…	…	…	…	100	1,400	69	86	3.19	20	34.7	54.1	11.3	Yemen
1,249	—— 75.7 ——		—— 24.3 ——		68.5	7	202	650	64	84	3.16	17	65.4	30.6	4.1	Zambia
546	…	…	…	…	69.8	7	80	400	83	90	6.23	39	40.3	48.7	11.0	Zimbabwe

[25]Registered personnel; all may not be present and working in the country. [26]1996. [27]Central hospital only. [28]General and specialized hospitals only. [29]Public sector only. [30]Hamad General Hospital only. [31]Data refer to the former Socialist Federal Republic of Yugoslavia. [32]Victoria Hospital only. [33]Paramaribo hospitals (1,213 beds) only. [34]5,037 community hospitals only.

Social protection

This table summarizes three principal areas of social protective activity for the countries of the world: social security, crime and law enforcement, and military affairs. Because the administrative structure, financing, manning, and scope of institutions and programmed tasks in these fields vary so greatly from country to country, no well-accepted or well-documented body of statistical comparisons exists in international convention to permit objective assessment of any of these subjects, either from the perspective of a single country or internationally. The data provided within any single subject area do, however, represent the most consistent approach to problems of international comparison found in the published literature for that field.

The provision of social security programs to answer specific social needs, for example, is summarized simply in terms of the existence or nonexistence of a specific type of benefit program because of the great complexity of national programs in terms of eligibility, coverage, term, age limits, financing, payments, and so on. Activities connected with a particular type of benefit often take place at more than one governmental level, through more than one agency at the same level, or through a mixture of public and private institutions. The data shown here are summarized from the U.S. Social Security Administration's *Social Security Programs Throughout the World* (biennial). A bullet symbol (•) indicates that a country has at least one program within the defined area; in some cases it may have several. A blank space indicates that no program existed providing the benefit shown; ellipses [...] indicate that no information was available as to whether a program existed.

Data given for social security expenditure as a percentage of total central governmental expenditure are taken from the International Monetary Fund's *Government Finance Statistics Yearbook,* which provides the most comparable analytic series on the consolidated accounts of central governments, governmentally administered social security funds, and independent national agencies, all usually separate accounting entities, through which these services may be provided in a given country.

Data on the finances of social security programs are taken in large part from the International Labour Office's *The Cost of Social Security* (triennial), supplemented by national data sources.

Figures for criminal offenses known to police, usually excluding civil offenses and minor traffic violations, are taken in part from Interpol's *International Crime Statistics* (annual) and a variety of national sources. Statistics are usually based on the number of offenses reported to police, not the number of offenders apprehended or tried in courts. Attempted offenses are counted as the offense that was attempted. A person identified as having committed multiple offenses is counted only under the most serious offense. Murder refers to all acts involving the voluntary taking of life, including infanticide, but excluding abortion, or involuntary acts such as those normally classified as manslaughter. Assault includes "serious," or aggravated, assault—that involving injury, endangering life, or perpetrated with the use of a dangerous instrument. Burglary involves theft from the premises of another; although Interpol statistics are reported as "breaking and entering," national data may not always distinguish cases of forcible

Social protection

country	social security																
	programs available, 1999					expenditures, 1999 (% of total central govt.)[f]	finances										
	old-age, invalidity, death[a]	sickness and maternity[b]	work injury[c]	unemployment[d]	family allowances[e]		year	receipts					expenditures			
								total ('000,000 natl. cur.)	insured persons (%)	employers (%)	government (%)	other (%)	total ('000,000 natl. cur.)	benefits (%)	administration (%)	other (%)
Afghanistan	●	●	●		●	...	...	...	...	...	...	...	...	...	...	...
Albania	●	●	●	●	●	20.1	1990	967.0	—	—	88.8	11.2	1,440.0	99.5	—— 0.5 ——	
Algeria	●	●	●	●	●	...	1990	27,700.0	...	...	...	...	28,748.0	61.8	30.6	7.6
American Samoa	●	...	...	...	...	...	1990	...	...	...	...	...	13.0	100.0	—	—
Andorra	●	●	●	●	●	...	1993	11,832.2	...	...	...	...	7,937.2	90.2	4.6	5.2
Angola	...	...	...	...	...	...	...	...	...	...	...	...	...	...	...	...
Antigua and Barbuda	●	●	●			...	1983	13.0	29.2	48.7	—	22.1	4.2	66.1	33.9	—
Argentina	●	●	●	●	●	48.4	1989	1,015,837.0	28.8	45.0	16.6	9.6	989,009.0	95.0	5.0	—
Armenia	●	●	●	●	●	...	...	...	...	...	...	...	...	...	...	...
Aruba	●	...	●	...	...	[6]	1998	197.1	...	...	...	...	179.0	...	...	...
Australia	●	●	●	●	●	35.5	1998–99	...	...	...	...	1.9	41,825	99.6	0.3	—
Austria	●	●	●	●	●	42.0	1989	425,417.0	30.1	45.9	21.1	2.9	412,134.0	96.5	2.3	1.2
Azerbaijan	●	●	●	●	●	33.1	...	...	...	...	...	...	...	...	...	...
Bahamas, The	●	●	●			6.9	1989	95.9	22.9	38.5	2.1	36.5	43.5	71.1	27.2	1.7
Bahrain	●		●			4.8	1989	39.6	12.3	40.2	—	47.5	9.7	69.8	20.9	9.3
Bangladesh		●	●	●		...	1989	73.6	12.4	37.5	2.4	47.7	34.1	94.0	6.0	—
Barbados	●	●	●	●		...	1989	191.7	38.0	40.8	1.5	19.7	149.1	93.5	5.8	0.7
Belarus	●	●	●	●	●	33.3	1986	3,199.0	—	—	93.2	6.8	3,199.0	100.0	—	—
Belgium	●	●	●	●	●	...	1986	1,347,070.0	24.4	39.7	31.6	4.3	1,322,636.0	94.5	4.3	1.2
Belize	●	●	●			5.9[7]	1989	15.3	8.9	53.2	—	38.0	3.9	56.7	43.3	—
Benin	●		●		●	...	1989	3,551.9	16.8	81.4	—	1.8	4,500.9	69.3	28.1	2.6
Bermuda	●		●			...	...	...	...	...	...	...	...	...	...	...
Bhutan	...	...	...	...	...	...	1990	...	...	...	...	...	26.0[8]	...	...	...
Bolivia	●	●	●		●	25.0	1989	346.6	29.3	47.7	11.2	11.8	340.2	84.9	14.3	0.8
Bosnia and Herzegovina	●	●	●	●	●	...	...	...	...	...	...	...	...	...	...	...
Botswana	●		●			1.1[10]	1996	—	...	...	...	...	65.0[8]	...	...	...
Brazil	●	●	●	●	●	47.2[11]	1989	71,847.0	24.4	51.0	20.0	4.6	68,957.0	61.9	18.6	19.5
Brunei	●	...	...	...	...	...	1984	...	...	...	...	...	39.5	...	...	...
Bulgaria	●	●	●	●	●	32.8	1989	6,016.8	—	71.4	28.1	0.5	6,000.1	96.6	3.3	0.1
Burkina Faso	●		●		●	0.1[12]	1989	8,816.5	15.6	62.9	—	21.5	4,975.3	69.5	30.4	0.1
Burundi	●		●		●	5.1	1989	1,991.5	31.6	47.6	—	20.8	1,563.9	74.8	16.8	8.4
Cambodia	...	...	●	...	●	...	...	...	...	...	...	...	...	...	...	...
Cameroon	●		●		●	0.5	1989	41,331.8	13.1	64.8	—	22.1	41,332.0	70.6	28.8	0.6
Canada	●	●	●	●	●	53.2	1989	130,306.6	9.9	15.6	64.4	10.1	115,764.2	96.9	2.5	0.6
Cape Verde	●	●	●		●	...	1989	697.7	26.5	58.5	—	15.0	316.7	82.4	16.1	1.5
Central African Republic	●		●		●	...	1989	3,604.0	8.4	76.0	—	15.6	3,247.0	64.6	32.9	2.5
Chad	●		●		●	...	1989	1,172.8	12.6	77.6	—	9.8	634.5	43.0	51.4	5.6
Chile	●	●	●	●	●	35.7	1989	1,186,056.0	32.8	2.7	37.9	26.6	798,770.0	83.9	14.7	1.4
China	●	●	●	●		22.4	1989	57,446.2	—	99.4	—	0.6	54,654	98.4	0.6	1.0
Colombia	●	●	●		●	12.4	1989	294,438.0	24.8	56.0	0.2	19.0	257,455.0	85.5	11.5	3.0
Comoros	...	...	...	...	...	...	1983	40.7	100.0	—	—	—	54.3	17.4	62.3	20.3
Congo, Dem. Rep. of the	●		●		●	—	1986	1,238.3	28.6	60.2	—	11.2	1,044.2	27.9	72.1	—
Congo, Rep. of the	●		●		●	...	1983	15,272.8	12.1	80.2	—	7.7	7,256.7	66.6	21.3	12.1
Costa Rica	●	●	●		●	23.1	1989	36,407.3	33.2	44.4	1.2	21.2	31,049.8	89.0	4.1	6.9
Côte d'Ivoire	●		●		●	...	1989	27,288.4	19.3	75.4	—	5.3	20,593.5	100.0	—	—
Croatia	●	●	●	●	●	38.6	...	...	...	...	...	...	...	...	...	...
Cuba	●	●	●			...	1989	2,284.8	—	37.4	62.6	—	2,284.8	96.7	—	3.3
Cyprus[15]	●	●	●	●	●	24.5	1989	217.5	24.7	40.3	17.3	17.7	117.7	98.4	1.6	—
Czech Republic	●	●	●	●	●	37.7	1989[17]	132,748.0	—	3.9	96.1	—	132,748.0	99.7	0.3	—
Denmark	●	●	●	●	●	40.1	1989	225,965.6	4.3	5.0	88.2	2.5	218,258.2	97.0	3.0	—
Djibouti	●	...	...	...	●	...	1979	1,352.2	...	...	...	...	1,115.7	...	...	...
Dominica	●	●	●			...	1986	12.3	22.6	50.9	—	26.5	4.4	68.0	32.0	—
Dominican Republic	●	●	●			6.7	1986	77.9	20.1	72.9	—	6.8	74.3	75.9	24.1	—
East Timor[19]	...	...	...	...	...	...	...	...	...	...	...	...	...	...	...	...
Ecuador	●	●	●	●		1.9[3]	1988	71,286.0	37.0	50.0	—	13.0	52,032.4	86.0	14.0	—

entry. Automobile theft excludes brief use of a car without the owner's permission, "joyriding," and implies intent to deprive the owner of the vehicle permanently. Criminal offense data for certain countries refer to cases disposed of in court, rather than to complaints. Police manpower figures refer, for the most part, to full-time, paid professional staff, excluding clerical support and volunteer staff. Personnel in military service who perform police functions are presumed to be employed in their principal activity, military service.

The figures for military manpower refer to full-time, active-duty military service and exclude reserve, militia, paramilitary, and similar organizations. Because of the difficulties attached to the analysis of data on military manpower and budgets (including problems such as data withheld on national security grounds, or the publication of budgetary data specifically intended to hide actual expenditure, or the complexity of long-term financing of purchases of military matériel [how much was actually spent as opposed to what was committed, offset by nonmilitary transfers, etc.]), extensive use is made of the principal international analytic tools: publications such as those of the International Institute for Strategic Studies (*The Military Balance*) and the U.S. Arms Control and Disarmament Agency (*World Military Expenditures and Arms Transfers*), both annuals.

The data on military expenditures are from the sources identified above, as well as from the IMF's *Government Finance Statistics Yearbook* and country statistical publications.

The following notes further define the column headings:

a. Programs providing cash payments for *each* of the three types of long-term benefit indicated to persons (1) exceeding a specified working age (usually 50–65, often 5 years earlier for women) who are qualified by a term of covered employment, (2) partially or fully incapacitated for their usual employment by injury or illness, and (3) qualified by their status as spouse, cohabitant, or dependent minor of a qualified person who dies.
b. Programs providing cash payments (jointly, or alternatively, medical services as well) to occupationally qualified persons for *both* of the short-term benefits indicated: (1) illness and (2) maternity.
c. Programs providing cash or medical services to employment-qualified persons who become temporarily or permanently incapacitated (fully or partially) by work-related injury or illness.
d. Programs providing term-limited cash compensation (usually 40–75% of average earnings) to persons qualified by previous employment (of six months minimum, typically) for periods of involuntary unemployment.
e. Programs providing cash payments to families or mothers to mitigate the cost of raising children and to encourage the formation of larger families.
f. Includes welfare.
g. A police officer is a full-time, paid professional, performing domestic security functions. Data include administrative staff but exclude clerical employees, volunteers, and members of paramilitary groups.
h. Includes all active-duty personnel, regular and conscript, performing national security functions. Excludes reserves, paramilitary forces, border patrols, and gendarmeries.

crime and law enforcement (latest)						military protection								country
offenses reported to the police per 100,000 population					population per police officer[g]	manpower, 2002[h]		expenditure, 1999				arms trade, 1999 ('000,000 U.S.$)		
total	personal		property			total ('000)	per 1,000 population	total '000,000	per capita	% of central government expenditure	% of GDP or GNP	imports	exports	
	murder	assault	burglary	automobile theft										
…	…	…	…	…	540[1]	[2]	[2]	408[3]	…	…	…	0	0	Afghanistan
168.8	26.2	5.8	10.7	14.1	550	27.0	8.7	72	21	4.5	1.3	30	0	Albania
178.0	0.7	67.6	13.7	1.7	840	136.7	4.3	1,830	60	12.6	4.0	550	0	Algeria
3,006	8.0	494.0	588.0	6.0	460	[4]	[4]	—	—	—	—	…	…	American Samoa
2,616	0	16.7	515.2	110.6	220	—	—	…	…	…	…	…	…	Andorra
143.5	8.7	15.3	30.5	3.7	14[5]	100.0	9.4	2,460	248	41.1	21.2	350	0	Angola
4,977	4.7	475.0	1,984.4	35.9	120	0.2	2.6	…	…	…	…	…	…	Antigua and Barbuda
631.0	6.0	68.2	43.0	117.1	1,270	69.9	1.9	4,300	118	9.1	1.6	90	0	Argentina
264.4	4.1	4.7	16.6	0.7	…	44.6	14.8	570	170	20.2	5.8	10	0	Armenia
5,461	1.2	180.0	451.3	202.5	…	[4]	[4]	—	—	—	—	…	…	Aruba
7,003	3.7	708.5	2,926.2	684.8	438	50.9	2.6	7,060	372	7.6	1.8	1,100	550	Australia
6,095	1.4	3.0	944.0	34.7	470	34.6	4.2	1,690	208	1.5	0.8	30	30	Austria
176	4.2	2.4	10.3	0.4	…	72.1	8.8	927	120	24.4	6.6	10	0	Azerbaijan
4,870	27.1	61.5	1,560.2	415.7	125	0.9	2.9	…	…	…	…	…	…	Bahamas, The
1,390	1.6	0.5	380.1	207.6	180	10.7	15.9	415	666	18.9	8.1	70	0	Bahrain
90	2.8	4.3	4.3	1.1	2,560	137.0	1.0	624	5.0	10.1	1.3	80	0	Bangladesh
3,813	8.6	161.9	1,080.8	105.5	280	0.6	2.2	12	44	1.4	0.5	0	0	Barbados
1,282.4	11.6	20.6	197.9	59.9	…	79.8	8.0	925	89	4.1	1.3	0	310	Belarus
8,478	5.3	535.8	2,031.3	376.5	640	39.3	3.8	3,600	352	3.1	1.4	350	30	Belgium
…	12.8	20.0	600.0	4.0	290	1.1	4.3	11	47	5.4	1.6	0	0	Belize
297	5.1	102.0	4.6	0.6	3,250	4.6	0.7	34	5.0	8.3	1.4	5	0	Benin
8,871	5.1	221.7	1,949.2	…	370	[4]	[4]	—	—	—	—	…	…	Bermuda
…	…	…	…	…	…	…	…	…	…	…	…	0	0	Bhutan
660	28.6	59.4	0.9	…	…	31.5	3.7	148	18	8.0	1.8	10	0	Bolivia
402	2.5	2.6	…	…	…	19.8[9]	5.0[9]	276	75	24.3	4.5	40	0	Bosnia and Herzegovina
8,281	12.7	431.9	1.9	73.1	750	9.0	5.4	222	142	9.8	4.7	40	0	Botswana
779.1	11.2	255.7	5.2	61.2	…	287.6	1.6	9,920	58	5.5[7]	1.9	180	20	Brazil
932.9	1.5	1.2	79.8	57.5	100	7.0	19.9	295	897	11.5	4.0	20	0	Brunei
1,170.7	7.3	1.9	402.9	94.5	…	68.5	8.7	1,240	158	8.7	3.0	10	200	Bulgaria
9	0.4	1.7	—	—	…	6.0	0.5	42	4	5.9	1.6	0	0	Burkina Faso
156	9.7	10.8	2.0	0.2	…	40.0	6.2	49	8	26.7	7.0	60	0	Burundi
…	…	…	…	…	1,980	106	7.9	332	28	26.0	4.0	5	0	Cambodia
78	0.4	1.2	1.2	5.1	1,170	14.1	0.9	148	10	10.6	1.8	5	0	Cameroon
8,121	4.0	140.3	1,044.4	529.4	8,640	52.3	1.7	8,320	269	5.9	1.4	1,000	550	Canada
…	…	…	…	…	110	1.2	2.6	5	13	2.2	0.9	5	0	Cape Verde
135	1.6	22.8	2.7	…	2,740[1]	2.6	0.7	29	8	15.4	2.8	0	0	Central African Republic
…	…	…	…	…	990	25.4	2.8	37	5	12.7	2.4	10	0	Chad
1,366	4.5	84.8	488.0	12.9	470	80.5	5.3	1,990	133	12.3	3.0	100	10	Chile
128	0.2	5.2	45.2	6.9	1,360[13]	2,270.0	1.8	88,900	71	22.2	2.3	675	320	China
790	56.3	61.8	57.9	75.3	420	158.0	3.9	2,670	68	15.9	3.2	60	0	Colombia
…	…	…	…	…	960	—	[14]	…	…	…	…	…	…	Comoros
…	…	…	…	…	910	81.4	1.5	5,150	102	41.4[7]	14.4	110	0	Congo, Dem. Rep. of the
32	1.5	4.7	0.2	0.2	870	10.0	3.4	58	21	8.4	3.5	0	0	Congo, Rep. of the
868	5.3	11.1	232.4	23.1	480	—	—	69	19	2.0	0.5	0	0	Costa Rica
67	2.5	73.1	19.5	11.9	4,640	8.1	0.5	82	5	3.4	0.8	0	0	Côte d'Ivoire
1,216	6.1	24.1	290.9	38.6	…	51.0	11.6	2,090	491	14.2	6.4	10	10	Croatia
…	…	…	…	…	650	46.0	4.1	630	57	…	1.9	0	0	Cuba
689	1.9	17.7	203.3	3.0	180	10.0[16]	11.0[16]	309	411	9.3	3.4	340	0	Cyprus[15]
4,142	2.6	71.7	831.4	263.0	640[17]	49.5	4.8	3,000	292	6.3	2.3	220	80	Czech Republic
9,300	4.1	20.8	1,899	638.1	600	22.7	4.3	2,780	524	4.2	1.6	290	10	Denmark
252	4.2	124.2	45.0	0.5	…	6.0	12.7	23	51	12.7	4.3	0	0	Djibouti
9,567	7.9	682.4	1,736	77.6	300	[18]	[18]	…	…	…	…	…	…	Dominica
…	15.8	28.4	154.0	14.0	580	24.5	2.8	123	15	4.4	0.7	20	0	Dominican Republic
…	…	…	…	…	…	[20]	[20]	…	…	…	…	…	…	East Timor[19]
587	25.9	35.6	164.5	52.9	260	59.5	4.5	479	38	16.2	3.7	20	0	Ecuador

Social protection (continued)

country	social security															
	programs available, 1999					expenditures, 1999 (% of total central govt.)[f]	finances									
	old-age, invalidity, death[a]	sickness and maternity[b]	work injury[c]	unemployment[d]	family allowances[e]		year	receipts					expenditures			
								total ('000,000 natl. cur.)	insured persons (%)	employers (%)	government (%)	other (%)	total ('000,000 natl. cur.)	benefits (%)	administration (%)	other (%)
Egypt	●	●	●	●		0.5[7]	1989	2,443.5	22.8	41.0	2.0	34.2	1,685.6	93.4	6.6	—
El Salvador	●	●	●			2.7	1989	465.3	27.1	51.7	—	21.2	368.3	78.1	21.9	—
Equatorial Guinea	●	●	●		●	...	1989	141.0	7.1	92.9	—	—	134.0	49.3	50.7	—
Eritrea	...	...	...	...	...	...	...	...	...	...	...	...	...	...	...	...
Estonia	●	●	●	●	●	32.5	...	90.1	...	...	...	...	...	...	...	...
Ethiopia	●		●			5.0[10]	1989[21]	190.9	32.8	65.3	—	1.9	153.7	98.3	1.7	—
Faroe Islands	●	...	●	...	●	...	...	...	...	...	...	...	...	...	...	...
Fiji	●		●			4.1[10]	1989	153.5	20.9	33.8	0.8	44.5	75.47	95.3	4.7	—
Finland	●	●	●	●	●	36.4	1989	118,589.0	7.7	41.1	44.0	7.2	106,235	96.3	3.7	—
France	●	●	●	●	●	39.3[22]	1989	1,700,202.0	77.7	—	20.4	1.9	1,669,096.0	95.5	3.7	0.8
French Guiana	●	...	●	...	●	...	1991	1,071.5	...	...	...	...	997.1	...	...	...
French Polynesia	●	...	●	...	●	...	1990	19,268.0	...	...	...	...	17,832.0	...	...	...
Gabon	●		●		●	...	1989	3,415.0	—	44.3	29.3	26.4	2,737.0	55.2	44.8	—
Gambia, The	●		●			3.0[3]	1982	—	...	...	...	...	5.6	...	...	...
Gaza Strip	...	...	...	...	...	—	...	...	...	...	...	...	...	...	...	...
Georgia	●	●	●	●	●	33.9	...	...	...	...	...	...	...	...	...	...
Germany	●	●	●	●	●	50.0[10]	1989[23]	522,172.0	36.9	34.3	26.1	2.7	507,604.0	97.1	2.8	0.1
Ghana	●		●			4.3	1989	17,920.8	21.1	52.9	—	26.0	4,147.7	13.3	64.0	22.7
Greece	●	●	●	●	●	17.9[11]	1989	1,314,421.0	24.9	38.4	30.8	5.9	1,349,693.0	92.5	7.5	—
Greenland	●	...	...	...	●	...	...	...	...	...	...	...	...	...	...	...
Grenada	●	●				8.6[24]	1989	24.1	20.1	60.3	3.2	16.3	13.5	93.1	6.9	—
Guadeloupe	●	...	...	...	●	...	1994	2,607.3	...	...	...	...	5,883.4	...	...	...
Guam	●	...	...	...	●	...	1989	...	...	...	...	...	7.3	...	...	...
Guatemala	●	●	●			...	1989	348.5	29.1	54.8	—	16.1	279.7	82.7	14.6	2.7
Guernsey	●	●	●	●	●	...	1999	103,560	— 45.0 —		40.7	14.3	85,468	94.8	5.2	...
Guinea	●	●	●		●	...	1989	3,387.0	0.4	90.3	—	9.3	1,108.1	54.9	45.1	—
Guinea-Bissau	...	...	...	...	...	8.8[22]	1986	138.0	22.8	63.4	10.3	3.8	61.9	59.6	40.4	—
Guyana	●	●	●			...	1994	1,070.8	...	...	...	...	1,373.7	...	...	...
Haiti	●		●			5.1[25]	1977	60.5	— 26.6 —		69.9	3.5	52.4	92.7	7.3	—
Honduras	●	●	●			...	1986	166.2	23.9	40.8	3.3	32.0	76.8	84.6	15.4	—
Hong Kong	●	●	●	●	●	...	1998–99	...	...	...	...	...	26,939	...	...	...
Hungary	●	●	●	●	●	21.9	1994	798,000.0	—	—	—	—	737,000.0	—	—	—
Iceland	●	●	●	●	27	21.8	1997	14,799	—	—	—	—	96,094	98.2	1.8	—
India	●	●	●			...	1989	43,913.8	23.8	27.7	5.3	43.2	13,775.8	90.0	8.2	1.8
Indonesia	●		●			5.3	1989	239,477.0	50.7	49.3	—	—	181,499.0	12.3	15.8	71.9
Iran	●	●	●	●	●	15.9	1986	346,460.0	83.2	0.1	8.2	8.5	167,879.0	43.4	6.3	50.0
Iraq	●	●	●			...	1977	107.8	9.9	55.6	21.9	12.6	71.0	94.0	2.4	3.6
Ireland	●	●	●	●	●	27.1	1989	4,627.5	16.3	24.8	57.7	1.2	4,612.9	95.2	4.7	0.1
Isle of Man	●	●	●	●	●	...	1985	...	...	...	...	...	14.4	...	...	...
Israel	●	●	●	●	●	25.9	1989	13,851.1	31.1	27.7	35.0	6.2	13,593.3	81.7	15.4	2.9
Italy	●	●	●	●	●	...	1989	278,383.0	16.5	51.4	30.0	2.1	100,251.0	89.3	2.0	8.7
Jamaica	●		●			1.0	1989	374.3	11.5	13.6	43.8	31.1	273.6	92.6	7.4	—
Japan	●	●	●	●	●	36.8[24]	1989	59,571,299.0	27.4	31.6	24.4	16.6	46,684,159.0	94.3	1.7	4.0
Jersey	●	●	●	●	●	9.5[22, 25]	1991	60.9	— 63.8 —		23.4	12.8	52.8	...	...	...
Jordan	●		●			15.5	1986	53.6	28.7	55.3	—	16.0	9.5	77.4	14.0	8.6
Kazakhstan	●	●	●	●	●	46.3	...	...	...	...	...	...	...	...	...	...
Kenya	●		●			2.7	1989	4,262.0	18.2	13.7	10.0	58.1	1,857.8	53.8	46.1	0.1
Kiribati	●		●			...	...	...	...	...	...	...	...	...	...	...
Korea, North	...	...	...	...	...	...	...	...	...	...	...	...	...	...	...	...
Korea, South	●		●			10.8[7]	1996	7,425,400.0	—	62.2	—	—	9,656,600.0	...	...	...
Kuwait	●					20.4	1989	445.8	7.1	13.2	54.3	25.4	206.5	97.0	3.0	—
Kyrgyzstan	●	●	●	●	●	10.2	...	...	...	...	...	...	...	...	...	...
Laos	...	...	●	...	...	...	...	...	...	...	...	...	...	...	...	...
Latvia	●	●	●	●	●	43.1	...	...	...	...	...	...	...	...	...	...
Lebanon	●	●	●		●	5.2	...	...	...	...	...	...	...	...	...	...
Lesotho	...	...	...	...	...	1.1[29]	1992	—	...	...	...	...	12.0[8]	...	...	...
Liberia	●		●			...	1983	2.9	—	69.0	13.8	17.2	2.6	54.4	45.6	—
Libya	●	●	●			...	1989	314.3	21.6	25.4	50.2	2.8	260.0	77.5	19.5	3.0
Liechtenstein	●	●	●	●	●	...	...	...	...	...	...	...	...	...	...	...
Lithuania	●	●	●	●		36.3	...	...	...	...	...	...	24,981.7	...	...	...
Luxembourg	●	●	●	●	●	52.3[24]	1989	72,471.8	24.2	34.6	34.4	6.8	65,214.4	97.2	2.4	0.4
Macau	●	...	...	...	●	...	1998	223.2	...	...	...	...	207.4	...	...	...
Macedonia	●	●	●	●	●	...	1996	24,482	...	...	...	...	...	...	...	...
Madagascar	●		●		●	1.5	1989	15,229.0	22.2	77.8	—	—	14,542.0	81.2	18.8	—
Malawi			●			...	1986	—	...	...	...	...	5.4	...	...	...
Malaysia	●		●			7.0	1989	7,958.7	20.7	40.2	—	39.1	2,826.5	97.0	3.0	—
Maldives	...	...	...	...	...	2.8	1990	—	...	...	...	...	7.1	...	...	...
Mali	●		●		●	...	1986	8,128.8	16.6	74.3	—	9.1	7,924.6	63.7	34.7	1.6
Malta	●	●	●	●	●	34.4	1989	82.2	26.1	31.6	42.3	—	110.7	92.5	7.5	—
Marshall Islands	●					...	...	...	...	...	...	...	...	...	...	...
Martinique	●	...	...	...	●	...	1998	3,913.1	...	...	...	...	8,429.6	...	...	...
Mauritania	●		●		●	...	1989	808.4	1.5	90.4	—	8.1	735.2	63.5	31.2	5.3
Mauritius	●		●		●	12.3	1989	1,733.5	2.9	47.9	31.7	17.5	1,072.7	95.2	3.0	1.8
Mayotte	...	...	...	...	...	...	...	...	...	...	...	...	...	...	...	...
Mexico	●	●	●			20.6	1989	16,011,795.0	20.9	54.8	12.9	11.4	14,562,293.0	79.9	15.5	4.6
Micronesia	●					...	...	...	...	...	...	...	...	...	...	...
Moldova	●	●	●	●	●	40.2	...	...	...	...	...	...	...	...	...	...
Monaco	●	●			●	...	...	...	...	...	...	...	...	...	...	...
Mongolia	●	●	...	...	●	25.3	1989	2,431.6	—	—	20.8	79.2	2,304.6	100.0	—	—
Morocco	●	●	●		●	9.3	1989	4,660.5	20.6	47.5	12.9	19.0	3,040.7	94.8	5.0	0.2
Mozambique	●	...	...	...	...	...	1986	228.2	—	86.2	13.7	0.1	145.0	100.0	—	—
Myanmar (Burma)		●	●			1.6	1986	44.3	19.9	59.6	18.5	2.0	35.9	51.5	15.6	32.9
Namibia	●	...	...	...	...	6.8[12, 25]	...	...	...	...	...	...	...	...	...	...
Nauru	●	●	●	...	●	...	...	...	...	...	...	...	...	...	...	...
Nepal	●		●			2.3	1985	—	...	...	...	...	59.3	...	...	...

crime and law enforcement (latest)						military protection								country
offenses reported to the police per 100,000 population					population per police officer[g]	manpower, 2002[h]		expenditure, 1999				arms trade, 1999 ('000,000 U.S.$)		
total	personal		property			total ('000)	per 1,000 population	total '000,000	per capita	% of central government expenditure	% of GDP or GNP	imports	exports	
	murder	assault	burglary	automobile theft										
3,693	1.6	0.7	…	3.1	580	443.0	6.4	2,390	36	9.3[7]	2.7	700	0	Egypt
879	36.9	71.1	…	82.0	1,000	16.8	2.6	110	18	8.8	0.9	10	0	El Salvador
…	…	…	…	…	190	1.3	2.6	19	40	16.5	3.2	0	0	Equatorial Guinea
161.9	2.7	10.3	5.8	…	…	172.2	43.3	208	52	51.1	7.4	170	20	Eritrea
3,565	13.8	28.3	1,659.2	169.8	…	5.5	4.0	173	120	4.5	1.5	10	0	Estonia
258.3	6.5	77.8	1.4	1.4	1,100[21]	252.5	3.7	533	9	29.1	8.8	270	0	Ethiopia
…	…	…	…	…	…	[4]	[4]	—	—	—	—	…	…	Faroe Islands
2,370	2.9	44.1	427.9	44.4	407	3.5	4.2	35	42	5.4	2.0	0	0	Fiji
14,350	0.7	34.9	1,739.7	33.2	640	31.9	6.1	1,770	344	4.5	1.4	400	50	Finland
6,097	3.4	162.7	632.4	511.0	630	260.4	4.4	38,900	658	5.9	2.7	800	2,900	France
8,936	27.2	178.7	1,367.3	150.6	…	[4]	[4]	—	—	—	—	…	…	French Guiana
1,799	0.9	98.9	232.7	…	…	[4]	[4]	—	—	—	—	…	…	French Polynesia
114	1.4	17.9	2.3	7.5	1,290	4.7	3.8	93	78	7.3	2.4	0	0	Gabon
89	0.4	10.6	5.6	…	3,310	0.8	0.6	5	4	5.4	1.3	0	0	Gambia, The
4,355	…	…	…	…	…	—	—	…	…	…	…	…	…	Gaza Strip
286	4.7	99.5	21.1	0.8	…	17.5	3.5	165	33	7.0	1.2	10	30	Georgia
7,682	3.5	139.6	1,377.4	114.3	…	296.0	3.6	32,600	395	4.7	1.6	1,300	1,900	Germany
…	2.2	418.9	1.5	…	620	7.0	0.3	62	3	3.1	0.8	0	0	Ghana
3,641	3.0	68.2	356.8	166.5	380	177.6	16.2	6,060	573	16.4	4.7	1,900	90	Greece
9,360	18.1	845.0	1,883.5	…	340	[4]	[4]	—	—	—	—	…	…	Greenland
8,543	7.8	98.9	582.2	…	230	[18]	[18]	…	…	…	…	…	…	Grenada
5,793	13.2	215.2	821.5	453.9	…	[4]	[4]	—	—	—	—	…	…	Guadeloupe
10,080	7.9	169.3	634.2	333.6	…	[4]	[4]	—	—	—	—	…	…	Guam
510	27.4	77.1	27.9	58.1	670	31.4	2.6	121	10	5.0	0.7	0	0	Guatemala
…	…	…	…	…	…	[4]	[4]	—	—	—	—	…	…	Guernsey
18.4	0.5	0.7	0.7	0.1	1,140	9.7	1.2	54	7	7.4	1.6	0	0	Guinea
129	0.5	8.7	4.0	0.2	…	7.3	5.4	6	4	6.1	2.7	0	0	Guinea-Bissau
1,277	19.1	246.0	365.8	32.2	190	1.4	1.8	5	7	2.0	0.8	0	0	Guyana
701	…	…	…	…	400	[26]	[26]	…	…	…	…	0	0	Haiti
392	154.0	44.4	4.3	25.8	1,040	8.3	1.3	34	6	2.6	0.7	10	0	Honduras
1,122	1.0	117.1	133.4	15.3	221	[4]	[4]	—	—	—	—	…	…	Hong Kong
5,011	4.1	76.6	804.4	41.3	237	33.4	3.3	1,880	185	3.9	1.7	80	10	Hungary
31,332	0.7	15.8	920.3	…	940	—	—	—	—	—	—	10	0	Iceland
594	4.6	…	15.6	…	820	1,100.0	1.0	11,300	11	14.6	2.5	700	10	India
120.9	1.0	4.4	1.8	1.7	1,119	230	1.1	1,450	7	5.3	1.1	450	100	Indonesia
77	0.5	47.7	…	…	…	520.0	7.9	6,880	106	11.2	2.9	150	10	Iran
197	7.1	34.7	…	…	140	389.0	18.2	1,250	57	…	5.5	5	0	Iraq
1,696	1.4	12.4	479.8	16.3	310	10.5	2.7	779	208	2.6	1.0	40	0	Ireland
2,867	0.7	12.3	921.4	60.6	…	[4]	[4]	—	—	—	—	…	…	Isle of Man
6,254	2.2	491.8	990.1	501.7	210	161.5	25.3	8,700	1,510	18.5	8.8	2,400	600	Israel
4,214	4.4	46.4	…	537.0	680	216.8	3.7	23,700	412	4.7	2.0	700	380	Italy
1,871	37.2	511.4	135.7	7.2	430	2.8	1.1	51	19	2.1	0.8	10	0	Jamaica
1,773	1.0	16.0	206.0	34.0	480	239.9	1.9	43,200	342	6.1	1.0	3,000	20	Japan
…	…	…	…	…	…	[4]	[4]	—	—	—	—	…	…	Jersey
1,256	6.3	14.0	31.0	52.2	630	100.2	19.0	725	150	27.5	9.2	70	0	Jordan
932	15.9	…	…	3.4	…	60	4.0	671	40	5.3	0.9	160	10	Kazakhstan
484	6.4	54.1	76.9	9.7	1,500	24.4	0.8	200	7	7.1	1.9	5	0	Kenya
261	5.1	11.6	38.6	…	330	—	—	…	…	…	…	…	…	Kiribati
…	…	…	…	…	460	1,082.0	48.7	4,260	199	…	18.8	30	140	Korea, North
3,494	2.1	64.6	7.0	…	506	686.0	14.3	11,600	246	11.0	2.9	2,200	20	Korea, South
1,346	1.5	36.4	75.9	56.7	80	15.5	6.9	2,690	1,410	20.8	7.7	725	0	Kuwait
987	10.4[28]	12.6	482.4	…	…	8.5	1.7	285	62	14.0	2.4	0	0	Kyrgyzstan
…	…	…	…	…	280	29.1	5.0	28	5	11.1	2.0	0	0	Laos
2,097	9.3	18.6	56.1	129.0	…	5.5	2.4	144	59	2.5	0.9	5	0	Latvia
3,063	5.5	209.7	78.0	30.0	530	71.8	19.5	653	185	11.0	4.0	10	0	Lebanon
2,357	50.4	156.9	250.4	30.8	1,130	2.0	0.9	29	14	6.5	2.6	0	0	Lesotho
…	…	…	…	…	1,570	[30]	[30]	6	2	8.3	1.2	0	0	Liberia
1,065	2.1	5.4	…	…	…	76.0	14.2	1,490[7]	342[7]	19.7[7]	6.1[7]	20	30	Libya
…	…	114.3	614.3	153.6	660	[31]	[31]	—	—	—	—	…	…	Liechtenstein
2,029	9.0	10.4	585.6	96.7	…	13.5	3.9	314	87	3.9	1.3	20	0	Lithuania
6,280	17.2	89.0	1,152.8	182.0	829	0.9	2.0	141	326	2.0	0.8	50	0	Luxembourg
1,698	5.4	34.0	250.5	26.6	…	[4]	[4]	…	…	…	…	…	…	Macau
1,102	5.4	26.9	…	44.7	…	12.3	6.1	228	112	10.4	2.5	20	0	Macedonia
112	0.6	12.0	0.7	0.1	2,900	13.5	0.8	45	3	7.4	1.2	0	0	Madagascar
850	3.1	82.2	13.1	…	1,670	5.3	0.5	10	1	2.2	0.6	0	0	Malawi
604	3.1	25.9	155.6	20.8	760	100.0	4.1	1,660	78	9.3	2.3	925	0	Malaysia
2,353	1.9	3.3	36.1	…	35,710	—	—	…	…	…	…	…	…	Maldives
10.0	0.7	1.5	0.8	0.3	160	7.4	0.7	58	6	8.7	2.3	0	0	Mali
1,841	3.0	35.2	1,079.2	243.9	230	2.1	5.4	28	73	1.8	0.8	0	0	Malta
2,273	…	…	…	…	400	[32]	[32]	—	—	—	—	…	…	Marshall Islands
6,305	5.8	184.9	641.2	192.8	…	[4]	[4]	—	—	—	—	…	…	Martinique
95.4	0.8	27.0	7.3	2.5	710	15.7	5.9	37	14	18.9	4.0	0	0	Mauritania
2,712	2.9	7.8	116.0	…	240	—	—	9	7	0.9	0.2	0	0	Mauritius
…	…	…	…	…	…	[4]	[4]	—	—	—	—	…	…	Mayotte
108	7.3	30.2	…	…	…	192.8	1.9	2,700	27	3.8	0.6	160	30	Mexico
…	…	…	…	…	…	[32]	[32]	—	—	—	—	…	…	Micronesia
957	9.9	11.1	50.4	15.6	…	7.2	2.0	43	10	1.6	0.5	0	20	Moldova
3,430	—	46.7	106.7	70.0	…	—	—	…	…	…	…	…	…	Monaco
1,010	30.0	74.7	486.0	2.1	120	9.1	3.7	18	5	5.9	2.1	0	0	Mongolia
366	1.4	6.7	…	…	840	196.3	6.7	1,450	49	13.5	4.3	130	0	Morocco
166	4.2	9.2	45.9	…	…	[33]	[33]	94	5	9.1	2.5	5	0	Mozambique
64.5	1.9	26.9	0.1	0.1	650	325.0	7.7	4,650	112	189.3	7.8	60	0	Myanmar (Burma)
2,006	26.3	533.6	602.0	65.8	…	9.0	4.9	91	53	7.2	2.9	130	0	Namibia
…	25.0	400.0	100.0	…	110	—	—	…	…	…	…	…	…	Nauru
9	2.8	1.1	0.8	…	1,000	51.0	2.2	44	2	5.7	0.8	0	0	Nepal

Social protection (continued)

country	social security															
	programs available, 1999					expenditures, 1999 (% of total central govt.)[f]	finances									
							year	receipts					expenditures			
	old-age, invalidity, death[a]	sickness and maternity[b]	work injury[c]	unemployment[d]	family allowances[e]			total ('000,000 natl. cur.)	insured persons (%)	employers (%)	government (%)	other (%)	total ('000,000 natl. cur.)	benefits (%)	administration (%)	other (%)
Netherlands, The	•	•	•	•	•	37.4[7]	1989	154,427.0	37.3	30.3	19.0	13.4	135,609.0	96.9	3.1	—
Netherlands Antilles		...	•	•	...	12.9[6, 24]	1998	317.0	100.0	—	—	—	275.0	...	...	...
New Caledonia	...	...	...	...	•	...	1987	15,834.0	...	...	...	...	14,598.0	...	...	...
New Zealand	•	•	•	•	•	39.8	1989	14,266.0	1.0	4.7	92.5	1.8	14,372.3	95.6	2.8	1.6
Nicaragua	•	•	•		•	14.7[24]	1989	647,454.8	13.5	49.1	7.6	29.8	452,038.6	82.4	17.6	—
Niger	•		•		•	...	1989	5,634.9	9.4	90.6	—	—	3,804.2	62.5	—	37.5
Nigeria	•		•			...	1989	54.0	50.0	50.0	—	—	22.6	42.5	57.5	—
Northern Mariana Islands	•	...	...	...	...	...	...	...	...	...	...	...	...	...	...	...
Norway	•	•	•	•	•	39.0[11]	1989	158,105.0	18.3	31.4	46.6	3.7	131,578.2	98.7	1.3	—
Oman	•	...	•	...	...	6.0	1995	—	...	...	...	...	...	...	...	...
Pakistan	•	•	•			...	1989	9,321.4	1.3	8.0	84.3	6.4	8,092.0	97.4	1.2	1.4
Palau	•					...	...	...	...	...	...	...	...	...	...	...
Panama	•	•	•			18.7	1989	496.7	31.0	39.5	7.1	22.4	452.8	94.0	4.8	1.2
Papua New Guinea	•		•			2.3	1983	45.0	40.5	32.1	8.0	19.4	9.4	82.3	9.7	8.0
Paraguay	•	•	•			16.2[22]	1993	...	...	...	...	...	253,341	...	...	...
Peru	•	•	•			...	1989	1,363,280.6	30.2	65.1	4.7	—	1,435,134.1	78.5	21.5	—
Philippines	•	•	•			4.1	1989	19,213.6	22.2	32.3	—	45.5	7,878.3	87.3	12.3	—
Poland	•	•	•	•	•	51.2	1989	11,572,248.0	2.1	70.2	25.1	2.6	11,452,165.0	98.8	1.2	—
Portugal	•	•	•	•	•	27.3[3]	1989	833,442.5	31.3	50.1	13.4	5.2	756,410.8	94.6	4.2	1.2
Puerto Rico	•	•	•	•	•	...	1980	...	...	...	...	...	1,041.3	100.0	—	—
Qatar	...	...	...	...	...	...	1986	80.0	—	—	100.0	—	80.0	100.0	—	—
Réunion	...	...	...	...	...	...	1998	...	...	...	...	...	13,200.0	...	...	...
Romania	•	•	•	•	•	29.8	1989	90,561.2	—	48.9	51.1	—	90,561.2	100.0	—	—
Russia	•	•	•	•	•	37.4	...	...	...	...	...	...	...	...	...	...
Rwanda	•		•			...	1989	2,350.0	23.9	39.8	—	36.3	965.8	60.8	39.2	—
St. Kitts and Nevis	•	•	•			...	1989	14.3	...	...	...	...	7.9	...	...	...
St. Lucia	•	•	•			...	1986	14.6	28.6	28.6	—	42.8	3.4	61.4	38.6	—
St. Vincent and the Grenadines	•	•	•			10.7	1989	—	...	...	...	...	—	...	...	...
Samoa	•		•			—	...	—	...	...	...	...	—	...	...	...
San Marino	•	•	•		...	...	1983	51,673.0	12.0	48.7	36.1	3.2	46,179.0	95.7	3.7	0.6
São Tomé and Príncipe	•	•	•			...	1986	46.4	37.7	56.3	—	6.0	23.7	100.0	—	—
Saudi Arabia	•		•			...	1989	1,761.4	26.8	73.2	—	—	4,292.9	100.0	—	—
Senegal	•		•		•	2.6[12, 25]	1989	17,202.0	—	47.6	51.4	1.0	15,371.0	84.6	11.1	4.3
Serbia and Montenegro	•	•	•	•	•	6.0[38]	1986[38]	2,777,651.0	63.3	32.2	3.4	1.1	2,732,679.0	90.3	1.9	7.8
Seychelles	•	•	•			15.1	1983	69.1	30.1	60.2	—	9.7	42.7	69.6	4.9	25.5
Sierra Leone			•			2.3[3]	1990	...	...	...	...	...	153.00	100.00	—	—
Singapore	•	•	•			1.6	1989	7,531.9	49.1	35.3	0.1	15.6	5,045.8	78.0	0.6	21.4
Slovakia	•	•	•	•	•	29.2	1998	74,205	...	...	...	...	87,916	...	...	...
Slovenia	•	•	•	•	•	43.6	...	...	...	...	...	...	...	...	...	...
Solomon Islands	•		•			...	1989	20.9	27.8	41.1	—	31.1	17.4	89.7	10.3	—
Somalia			•			...	...	—	...	...	...	...	...	...	...	...
South Africa	•	•	•	•		3.5[7]	1994	2,034	—	100.0	—	—	2,260.0	...	...	...
Spain	•	•	•	•	•	38.5	1989	8,320,972.0	15.9	53.9	27.9	2.3	8,038,090.0	94.3	2.6	3.1
Sri Lanka	•		•		•	11.8	1989	15,399.9	22.0	24.4	29.1	24.5	5,819.0	98.5	1.3	0.2
Sudan, The	•		•			...	1989	62.0	24.9	0.5	—	74.6	14.7	37.5	62.5	—
Suriname	•	...	...	...	•	...	1989	73.0	24.7	75.3	—	—	70.6	100.0	—	—
Swaziland	•		•			0.4	1986	10.7	31.4	31.4	—	37.2	3.9	45.8	54.2	—
Sweden	•	•	•	•	•	46.3	1989	446,909.7	2.8	37.9	50.8	8.5	439,997.3	93.7	3.3	3.0
Switzerland	•	•	•	•	•	49.1	1989	45,800.1	45.6	22.6	25.9	5.9	41,745.7	91.5	3.0	5.5
Syria	•		•			5.4[11]	1989	3,147.9	30.4	60.9	...	5.6	1,455.9	95.7	4.2	0.1
Taiwan	•	•	•	•		13.8[3]	...	...	...	...	...	...	...	...	...	...
Tajikistan	•	•	•	•	•	18.7	...	...	...	...	...	...	...	...	...	...
Tanzania	•		•			...	1989	3,275.8	25.9	25.9	—	48.2	2,780.7	5.8	14.1	80.1
Thailand	•	•	•			5.8	1989	654.0	—	60.2	—	39.8	260.0	88.2	11.8	—
Togo	•		•		•	...	1989	10,162.0	8.1	61.5	—	30.4	5,844.0	77.5	22.5	—
Tonga	...	...	...	...	...	0.8[12]	...	...	...	...	...	...	...	...	...	...
Trinidad and Tobago	•	•	•		•	14.3[24]	1989	584.9	12.0	24.1	39.7	24.2	438.4	85.6	11.1	3.3
Tunisia	•	•	•	•	•	17.8	1989	325.3	36.9	63.1	—	—	358.3	...	...	...
Turkey	•	•	•		•	9.5	1989	12,075,809.0	28.5	32.9	22.8	15.8	10,241,427.0	97.2	2.2	0.6
Turkmenistan	•	•	•	•	•	...	...	...	...	...	...	...	...	...	...	...
Tuvalu	•	...	...	...	...	...	1981	...	...	...	...	...	0.1	67.6	32.4	—
Uganda	•		•			...	1989	265.9	32.1	64.3	1.1	2.5	145.0	0.3	76.8	22.9
Ukraine	•	•	•	•	•	50.1	1989	20,350.0	—	—	—	—	20,350.0	100.0	—	—
United Arab Emirates	...	...	...	...	...	3.4	1989	182.2	17.3	6.2	0.5	76.0	182.2	100.0	...	...
United Kingdom	•	•	•	•	•	36.5	1989	92,157.0	18.1	24.9	52.9	4.1	88,294.0	93.8	3.3	2.9
United States	•		•	•		28.7	1989	804,909.0	25.5	33.9	28.8	11.8	627,653.0	95.5	3.3	1.2
Uruguay	•	•	•	•	•	59.3	1989	535,507.0	31.4	37.3	26.0	5.3	548,591.0	93.6	5.4	1.0
Uzbekistan	•	•	•	•	•	...	...	...	...	...	...	...	...	...	...	...
Vanuatu	•					...	...	—	...	...	...	...	—	...	...	...
Venezuela	•	•	•	•		...	1986	7,457.6	21.3	40.7	12.7	25.3	6,355.7	86.1	14.9	—
Vietnam	•	•	•			10.6	...	...	...	...	...	...	...	...	...	...
Virgin Islands (U.S.)	•	...	...	•	•	...	...	...	...	...	...	...	...	...	...	...
West Bank	...	...	...	...	...	...	...	...	...	...	...	...	...	...	...	...
Western Sahara	...	...	...	...	...	...	...	...	...	...	...	...	...	...	...	...
Yemen	•	...	•	...	...	—	...	—	...	...	...	...	—	...	...	...
Zambia	•		•			1.2	1986	179.2	28.4	28.4	—	43.2	67.7	40.6	59.4	—
Zimbabwe	•		•			18.2[7]	1983	167.0	25.9	7.6	64.2	2.3	112.2	93.7	6.2	0.1

[1]Rural areas. [2]National army is being formed in early 2002. [3]1990. [4]Political dependency; defense is the responsibility of the administering country. [5]Includes civilian militia. [6]Netherlands Antilles includes Aruba. [7]1997. [8]Includes welfare. [9]In 2002 about 12,000 troops of the NATO Commanded Stabilization Forces were stationed in Bosnia and Herzegovina to assure implementation of the Dayton Accords. [10]1996. [11]1998. [12]1991. [13]Local officers only. [14]Military defense is the responsibility of France. [15]Republic of Cyprus only. [16]National Guard only. [17]Data refer to former Czechoslovakia. [18]Paramilitary unit of country participating in the U.S.-sponsored Regional Security System, a defense pact among eastern Caribbean countries. [19]Indonesia includes East Timor, except where noted. [20]UN forces of 5,199 troops including 117 observers are stationed in East Timor. [21]Ethiopia includes Eritrea. [22]1993. [23]Former West Germany. [24]1995. [25]Social Security only. [26]Haitian army was disbanded in 1995, and a National Police Force of 5,300 was formed in 2002. [27]Coverage is through the tax system. [28]Includes attempted murders. [29]1992. [30]As of 2002 there were between 11,000

crime and law enforcement (latest)						military protection								country
offenses reported to the police per 100,000 population					population per police officer[g]	manpower, 2002[h]		expenditure, 1999				arms trade, 1999 ('000,000 U.S.$)		
total	personal		property			total ('000)	per 1,000 population	total '000,000	per capita	% of central government expenditure	% of GDP or GNP	imports	exports	
	murder	assault	burglary	automobile theft										
7,808	10.9	242.8	3,100.4	239.0	510	49.6	3.1	7,030	445	5.9	1.8	775	140	Netherlands, The
5,574[34]	...	396	3,455	...	330	[4]	[4]	—	—	—	—	...	...	Netherlands Antilles
...	...	...	...	...	...	[4]	[4]	—	—	—	—	...	...	New Caledonia
13,854	3.9	546.3	2,352.9	788.6	630	8.7	2.2	587	156	3.5	1.2	575	0	New Zealand
1,069	25.6	203.8	110.7	...	905	14	2.8	24	5	2.9	1.2	0	0	Nicaragua
99	0.9	16.6	1.0	0.7	2,350[35]	5.3	0.5	24	2	6.4	1.2	0	0	Niger
312	...	...	...	...	1,140	78.5	0.6	1,560	13	8.1	1.6	0	0	Nigeria
245	3.8	92.6	73.7	20.8	...	[4]	[4]	—	—	—	—	...	...	Northern Mariana Islands
9,769	2.3	66.1	95.0	465.8	660	26.6	5.9	3,310	742	5.0	2.2	480	20	Norway
331	1.5	1.8	...	14.9	430	41.7	16.5	1,780	726	36.3	15.3	30	0	Oman
318	7.1	2.2	10.4	9.0	720	620.0	4.2	3,520	25	27.9	5.9	1,000	10	Pakistan
...	...	...	323.0	...	...	[32]	[32]	—	—	—	—	...	...	Palau
419	2.0	11.8	25.1	77.7	180	—	—	124	45	5.1	1.4	5	0	Panama
766	8.6	66.7	63	22.0	720	3.1	0.6	36	7	3.7	1.1	0	0	Papua New Guinea
418	11.5	54.2	21.4	30.5	310	18.6	3.2	84	15	3.9	1.1	10	0	Paraguay
218	3.2	24.1	7.8	3.6	730	110.0	4.1	1,200	45	12.3	2.4	30	0	Peru
...	13.1	14.9	...	3.3	1,160	106.0	1.3	1,110	14	7.3	1.4	110	0	Philippines
2,901	2.8	79.2	936.8	185.0	370	163.0	4.2	6,690	173	6.1	2.1	40	30	Poland
661	3.1	1.5	115.3	40.4	660	43.6	4.2	2,410	240	5.4	2.1	60	0	Portugal
2,339	16.2	101.8	412.4	1,521	380	[4]	[4]	—	—	—	—	...	...	Puerto Rico
1,079	2.1	7.1	34.1	11.5	...	12.4	20.5	1,060	1,470	22.9	10.0	120	0	Qatar
2,097	7.8	123.1	181.3	137.9	220	[4]	[4]	—	—	—	—	...	...	Réunion
2,206	7.1	5.8	367.8	30.4	...	99.2	4.6	2,190	97	4.7	1.6	200	40	Romania
20,514	21.3	32.6	669.1	25.6	...	988.1	6.9	35,000	239	22.4	5.6	470	3,100	Russia
...	45.1	114.3	...	0.3	4,650	[36]	[36]	87	12	22.7	4.5	30	0	Rwanda
3,808	12.0	434.0	1,790	...	300	[18]	[18]	...	...	...	...	...	...	St. Kitts and Nevis
4,386	17.0	1,193.0	778.0	...	430	[18]	[18]	...	...	...	...	...	...	St. Lucia
3,977	10.3	986.9	...	...	250	[18]	[18]	...	...	...	...	...	...	St. Vincent and the Grenadines
...	...	...	...	...	...	[37]	[37]	—	—	—	—	...	...	Samoa
...	4.1	...	...	...	...	—	—	...	...	...	...	...	...	San Marino
558	4.0	...	...	...	400	—	—	1	3	1.3	1.2	0	0	São Tomé and Príncipe
149	0.5	0.2	...	45.4	280	124.5	5.3	21,200	996	43.2	14.9	7,700	0	Saudi Arabia
123	0.5	8.8	2.1	8.2	730	9.4	0.9	81	8	8.2	1.7	0	0	Senegal
1,268	...	...	...	...	140[38]	74.5	7.0	1,200[7]	114[7]	55.0[3, 38]	4.9[3, 38]	10	0	Serbia and Montenegro
5,361	3.7	43.4	378.0	40.9	120	0.2	2.4	...	...	...	...	...	...	Seychelles
...	...	...	...	...	600	[39]	[39]	20	4	13.5	3.0	10	0	Sierra Leone
783	1.0	2.4	40.1	55.2	230	60.5	14.4	4,400	1,100	20.5	4.8	950	20	Singapore
1,740	2.4	204.6	504.3	142.4	...	26.2	4.9	1,010	187	4.4	1.8	20	10	Slovakia
3,138	3.6	20.7	427.3	25.6	...	9.0	4.6	436	227	3.4	1.4	10	0	Slovenia
...	...	...	...	...	620	—	—	...	...	...	...	0	0	Solomon Islands
144	1.5	8.0	31.2	...	540	[40]	[40]	18[3]	3[3]	...	0.9[3]	20	0	Somalia
7,140.8	121.9	595.6	896.6	262.7	870	60.0	1.3	1,960	45	5.0	1.5	50	30	South Africa
4,449	2.7	23.4	562.8	343.3	580	178.0	4.3	7,560	192	6.1	1.3	750	70	Spain
280	8.2	10.8	54.7	...	860	157.9[41]	8.4[41]	729	38	18.4	4.7	40	0	Sri Lanka
...	10.2	46.3	66.6	4.7	740	117.0	3.4	424	12	46.8	4.8	10	0	Sudan, The
17,819	7.6	1,824.4	...	...	...	1.8	4.1	14	33	5.4	1.8	10	0	Suriname
3,962	18.1	471.7	706.8	54.1	610	—	—	21	20	4.6	1.5	0	0	Swaziland
12,982	4.5	42.5	1,615.1	658.9	330	33.9	3.8	5,330	601	5.5	2.3	230	675	Sweden
7,030	2.7	73.3	1,065.9	1,065.5	640	3.5	0.5	3,400	469	5.1	1.2	1,100	50	Switzerland
42	1.0	—	15.6	2.7	1,970	319.0	18.6	4,450	280	25.1	7.0	210	0	Syria
799	8.2	...	...	124.9	720	370.0	15.2	15,200	690	23.8[7]	5.2	2,600	20	Taiwan
317	2.5	4.6	...	...	...	6.0	0.9	80	13	9.4	1.3	0	0	Tajikistan
1,714	7.7	1.7	96.6	0.9	1,330	27.0	0.8	122	4	10.1	1.4	5	0	Tanzania
351	7.7	25.4	9.9	3.3	530	306.0	4.8	2,040	34	6.1	1.7	330	0	Thailand
11	...	...	...	...	1,970	9.5	1.8	25	5	9.4	1.8	0	0	Togo
2,727	1.0	108.5	541.7	14.8	330	[37]	[37]	—	—	—	—	...	...	Tonga
1,170	9.7	31.0	452.7	80.6	280	2.7	2.0	92	78	5.5	1.4	0	0	Trinidad and Tobago
1,419	1.2	165.1	60.1	10.2	340	35.0	3.6	357	38	5.4	1.8	10	0	Tunisia
547	3.9	120.0	...	28.9	1,570	514.9	7.4	9,950	154	13.9	5.3	3,200	70	Turkey
...	...	...	...	...	...	17.5	3.5	542	122	16.0	3.4	10	0	Turkmenistan
...	...	...	...	—	290	—	—	...	...	...	...	...	...	Tuvalu
316	9.9	54.8	19.3	8.3	1,090	[42]	[42]	140	6	13.9	2.3	30	0	Uganda
1,115	10.0	14.7	224.3	7.6	...	302.3	6.3	5,110	103	8.2	3.0	10	550	Ukraine
2,604.7	3.0	10.1	5.1	23.0	140	41.5	11.7	2,180	935	39.6	4.1	950	0	United Arab Emirates
9,823[43]	2.8[43]	405.2[43]	1,832.7[43]	752.9[43]	350	210.5	3.5	36,500	615	6.9	2.5	2,600	5,200	United Kingdom
5,374	9.0	430.2	1,041.8	591.2	318	1,414.0	4.9	281,000	1,030	15.7	3.0	1,600	33,000	United States
3,002	7.7	162.5	52.3	130.1	170	23.9	7.0	275	83	4.1	1.3	10	0	Uruguay
328	3.2	3.0	33.2	2.3	...	[44]	[44]	933	38	5.3	1.7	0	10	Uzbekistan
...	...	...	...	...	450	—	—	...	...	...	...	...	...	Vanuatu
1,106	22.1	152.2	358.2	239.4	320	82.3	3.3	1,420	61	7.1	1.4	310	0	Venezuela
74	1.5	8.5	...	...	...	484.0	6.0	3,230[7]	44[7]	11.6[7]	2.5[7]	70	0	Vietnam
10,441	22.3	1,943.2	3,183.7	954	240	[4]	[4]	—	—	—	—	...	...	Virgin Islands (U.S.)
2,226	...	...	...	...	...	—	—	...	...	...	...	...	...	West Bank
...	...	...	...	...	...	[4]	[4]	—	—	—	—	...	...	Western Sahara
63[45]	5.3	3.2	1.2	3.6	1,940	66.5	3.4	374	22	18.0	6.1	30	0	Yemen
666	9.8	9.5	153.5	9.6	540	21.6	2.2	31	3	3.5	1.0	0	0	Zambia
5,619	9.0	198.4	435.9	13.4	750	36.0	3.2	263	23	12.1	5.0	10	0	Zimbabwe

and 15,000 in all armed forces. West African peacekeepers withdrew in January 1999 and the civil war resumed in some areas. [31]Military defense is the responsibility of Switzerland. [32]Military defense is the responsibility of the United States. [33]Forces are estimated between 10,000 and 11,150. [34]Curaçao only. [35]Includes paramilitary forces. [36]Forces are estimated between 60,000 and 75,000. [37]Military defense is the responsibility of New Zealand. [38]Data refer to Yugoslavia as constituted prior to 1991. [39]A new U.K.-trained national army was formed in 2002 and has an initial strength between 13,000 and 14,000. [40]Following the 1991 revolution, no national armed forces have yet been formed. [41]Includes 42,300 recalled reservists. [42]Forces estimated between 50,000 and 60,000. [43]England and Wales. [44]Forces estimated between 50,000 and 55,000. [45]Former Yemen Arab Republic.

Education

This table presents international data on education analyzed to provide maximum comparability among the different educational systems in use among the nations of the world. The principal data are, naturally, numbers of schools, teachers, and students, arranged by four principal levels of education—the first (primary); general second level (secondary); vocational second level; and third level (higher). Whenever possible, data referring to preprimary education programs have been excluded from this compilation. The ratio of students to teachers is calculated for each level. These data are supplemented at each level by a figure for enrollment ratio, an indicator of each country's achieved capability to educate the total number of children potentially educable in the age group usually represented by that level. At the first and second levels this is given as a net enrollment ratio and at the third level as a gross enrollment ratio. Two additional comparative measures are given at the third level: students per 100,000 population and proportion (percentage) of adults age 25 and over who have achieved some level of higher or post-secondary education. Data in this last group are confined as far as possible to those who have completed their educations and are no longer in school. No enrollment ratio is provided for vocational training at the second level because of the great variation worldwide in the academic level at which vocational training takes place, in the need of countries to encourage or direct students into vocational programs (to support national development), and, most particularly, in the age range of students who normally constitute a national vocational system (some will be as young as 14, having just completed a primary cycle; others will be much older).

At each level of education, differences in national statistical practice, in national educational structure, public-private institutional mix, training and deployment of teachers, and timing of cycles of enrollment or completion of particular grades or standards all contribute to the problems of comparability among national educational systems.

Reporting the number of schools in a country is not simply a matter of counting permanent red-brick buildings with classrooms in them. Often the resources of a less developed country are such that temporary or outdoor facilities are all that can be afforded, while in a developed but sparsely settled country students might have to travel 80 km (50 mi) a day to find a classroom with 20 students of the same age, leading to the institution of measures such as traveling teachers, radio or televisual instruction at home under the supervision of parents, or similar systems. According to UNESCO definitions, therefore, a "school" is defined only as "a body of students . . . organized to receive instruction."

Such difficulties also limit the comparability of statistics on numbers of teachers, with the further complications that many at any level must work part-time, or that the institutions in which they work may perform a mixture of functions that do not break down into the tidy categories required by a table of this sort. In certain countries teacher training is confined to higher education, in others as a vocational form of secondary training, and so on. For purposes of this table, teacher training at the secondary level has been treated as vocational education. At the higher level, teacher training is classified as one more specialization in higher education itself.

The number of students may conceal great variation in what each country defines as a particular educational "level." Many countries do, indeed, have a primary system composed of grades 1 through 6 (or 1 through 8) that passes students on to some kind of postprimary education. But the age of intake, the ability of parents to send their children or to permit them to finish that level, or the need to withdraw the children seasonally for agricul-

Education

country	year	first level (primary)					general second level (secondary)					vocational second level[a]	
		schools	teachers[c]	students[d]	student/ teacher ratio	net enroll-ment ratio[b]	schools	teachers[c]	students[d]	student/ teacher ratio	net enroll-ment ratio[b]	schools	teachers[c]
Afghanistan	1995	2,146	21,869	1,312,197	60.0	29	...	19,085	512,815	26.9	14	...	...
Albania	1996	1,782	31,369	558,101	17.8	102	162[1]	4,147	71,391	17.2	...	259[1]	2,174
Algeria	1997	15,426	170,956	4,674,947	27.3	94	3,954	151,948	2,618,242	17.2	56	...	...
American Samoa	1996	32	524[2]	9,971	...	...	9	245[2]	3,624	...	...	1	21[2]
Andorra	1997	12	...	5,424	...	...	6	...	2,655	...	...	...	...
Angola	1992	...	31,062[1]	989,443	...	...	...	5,138[1]	199,099	...	...	...	566[1]
Antigua and Barbuda	1997	58	559	12,229	21.9	...	13	389	4,260	11.0	...	1[3]	16[3]
Argentina	1997	22,437	309,081	5,153,256	16.7	96	7,623[4]	238,791[4]	2,463,608[4]	10.3[4]	42	[4]	[4]
Armenia	1998	1,407	61,965	602,600	9.7	...	...	57,325	365,025	6.4	...	69[5]	...
Aruba	1998	33	397	8,456	21.3	...	15[4]	470[4]	7,157[4]	15.2[4]	[4]	[4]	[4]
Australia	1998	7,709	104,603	1,869,852	17.9	95	2,468	104,477	1,329,000	12.7	89	...	28,900[3]
Austria	1998	3,680	38,491	385,207	10.0	87	1,837[6]	55,337	480,200	8.7	88	981	26,248
Azerbaijan	1998	4,515	36,800	700,900	19.0	...	...	85,300	905,500	10.6	...	78	...
Bahamas, The	1997	113	1,540	34,199	22.2	98	...	1,352	27,970	20.7	86	...	...
Bahrain	1997	124[3, 8]	3,536[3, 8]	72,876	...	98	...	2,305[3, 8]	49,897	...	83	...	820[3, 8]
Bangladesh	1996	75,595	242,252[5]	17,580,000	...	64	12,858	135,217[5]	5,788,000	...	18	156	8,800
Barbados	1996	79	994	18,519	18.6	78	21	1,263	21,455	17.0	74	...	...
Belarus	1998	4,835[9]	115,300[9]	1,580,000[9]	10.9[9]	85	[9]	[9]	[9]	[9]	...	150	...
Belgium	1996	4,401	82,168[10]	742,796	...	98	1,727	115,262	737,823	6.4	88	304[11]	...
Belize	1998	247	2,015	53,118	26.4	99	30	726	11,260	15.5	29	...	...
Benin	1997	3,072	13,957	779,329	55.8	63	145[5]	5,352	146,135	27.3	...	14[5]	283[5]
Bermuda	1997	26	478	5,883	18.3	...	...	355	3,726	10.5	...	...	...
Bhutan	1994	243	1,611	60,089	37.3	...	34	544	7,299	13.4	...	8	95
Bolivia	1995	...	51,763[12]	1,538,454	24.7[12]	91	...	12,434[4, 12]	293,158[4]	17.6[4, 12]	29	...	[4]
Bosnia and Herzegovina	1991	2,205	23,369	539,875	23.1	98	238	9,030	172,063	19.1	...	...	...
Botswana	1997	714	11,454	322,268	28.1	81	274	6,772	116,076	17.1	44	50	2,618
Brazil	1998	187,497	1,460,469	35,845,742	24.5	90	17,602	380,222	6,968,531	18.3	19	...	...
Brunei	1998	184[10]	3,858[10]	58,548[10]	15.2[10]	91	38	2,636	30,956	11.7	68	9	516
Bulgaria	1999	3,011[9]	65,885[9]	887,213[9]	13.5[9]	92	[9]	[9]	[9]	[9]	74	545	20,389
Burkina Faso	1996	3,568	14,037	702,204	50.0	31	252	4,152	137,257	33.0	7	41	731
Burundi	1993	1,418	10,400	651,086	62.6	52	113[12]	2,562	55,713	21.7	5	...	...
Cambodia	1998	5,026	43,282	2,011,772	46.5	100	440[11]	16,820	302,751	18.0	...	65[11]	2,315
Cameroon	1995	6,801	40,970	1,896,722	46.3	67	...	14,917	459,068	30.8	11	...	5,885
Canada	1996	12,685	148,565	2,448,144	16.5	95	3,780	133,275	2,505,389	18.8	91	...	...
Cape Verde	1994	370[12]	2,657	78,173	29.4	100	...	438	11,808	27.0	48	...	94[14]
Central African Republic	1991	930	4,004	308,409	77.0	53	46[4]	845[4]	46,989[4]	55.6[4]	...	[4]	[4]
Chad	1996	2,660	9,395	591,493	63.0	46	153	2,468	90,100	36.5	...	18	216
Chile	1995	8,702	80,155	2,149,501	26.8	89	...	51,042	679,165	13.3	58	...	...
China	1997	628,840	5,794,000	139,954,000	24.2	101	78,642	3,587,000	60,179,000	16.8	...	14,190	598,000
Colombia	1996	48,933	193,911	4,916,934	25.4	85	7,895[4]	165,976[4]	2,323,653	...	46	[4]	[4]
Comoros	1996	327	1,508	78,527	52.1	52	...	591	21,192	35.9	...	...	...
Congo, Dem. Rep. of the	1995	14,885	121,054	5,417,506	44.8	54	4,276[4, 11]	59,325[4, 11]	1,514,323[4]	...	17	[4]	[4]
Congo, Rep. of the	1997	1,612	6,926	489,546	70.7	96	...	5,466	190,409	34.8	...	...	1,746
Costa Rica	1998	3,711	19,235	529,637	27.5	89	353	10,943	202,415	18.5	40	...	...
Côte d'Ivoire	1996	7,401	40,529	1,662,285	41.0	55	147	15,959	489,740	30.7	...	...	1,424[3]
Croatia	1998	2,127	10,365	206,121	19.9	82	1,110	19,776	266,115	13.5	66	442	13,000
Cuba	1997	9,864[16]	78,625	1,028,880	13.0	101	...	71,025	778,028	11.0	59[16]	...	27,267[16]
Cyprus[17]	1997	376	4,159	64,761	15.6	96	125[4]	5,757[4]	61,266[4]	10.6[4]	93	[4]	[4]
Czech Republic	1998	8,067[18]	83,972[18]	1,186,246[18]	14.1[18]	91	367	11,658	83,010	7.1	89	1,776	54,204
Denmark	1996	2,536[3]	33,100	336,690	10.2	99	153[3]	37,000	321,448	8.7	88	237[3]	13,100

tural work all make even even a simple enrollment figure difficult to assess in isolation. All of these difficulties are compounded when a country has instruction in more than one language or when its educational establishment is so small that higher, sometimes even secondary, education cannot take place within the country. Enrollment figures in this table may, therefore, include students enrolled outside the country.

Student-teacher ratio, however, usually provides a good measure of the ratio of trained educators to the enrolled educable. In general, at each level of education both students and teachers have been counted on the basis of full-time enrollment or employment, or full-time equivalent when country statistics permit. At the primary and secondary levels, net enrollment ratio is the ratio of the number of children within the usual age group for a particular level who are actually enrolled to the total number of children in that age group (× 100). This ratio is usually less than (occasionally, equal to) 100 and is the most accurate measure of the completeness of enrollment at that particular level. It is not always, however, the best indication of utilization of teaching staff and facilities. Utilization, provided here for higher education only, is best seen in a gross enrollment ratio, which compares total enrollment (of all ages) to the population within the normal age limits for that level. For a country with substantial adult literacy or general educational programs, the difference may be striking: typically, for a less developed country, even one with a good net enrollment ratio of 90 to 95, the gross enrollment ratio may by 20%, 25%, even 30% higher, indicating the heavy use made by the country of facilities and teachers at that level.

Literacy data provided here have been compiled as far as possible from data for the population age 15 and over for the best comparability internationally. Standards as to what constitutes literacy may also differ markedly; sometimes completion of a certain number of years of school is taken to constitute literacy; elsewhere it may mean only the ability to read or write at a minimal level testable by a census taker; in other countries studies have been undertaken to distinguish among degrees of functional literacy. When a country reports an official 100% (or near) literacy rate, it should usually be viewed with caution, as separate studies of "functional" literacy for such a country may indicate 10%, 20%, or even higher rates of inability to read, or write, effectively. Substantial use has been made of UNESCO literacy estimates, both for some of the least developed countries (where the statistical base is poorest) and for some of the most fully developed, where literacy is no longer perceived as a problem, thus no longer in need of monitoring.

Finally, the data provided for public expenditure on education are complete in that they include all levels of public expenditure (national, state, local) but are incomplete for certain countries in that they do not include data for private expenditure; in some countries this fraction of the educational establishment may be of significant size. Occasionally data for external aid to education may be included in addition to domestic expenditure.

The following notes further define the column headings:

a. Usually includes teacher training at the second level.
b. Latest.
c. Full-time.
d. Full-time; may include students registered in foreign schools.

		third level (higher)							literacy[b]				public expenditure	country
students[d]	student/ teacher ratio	institutions	teachers[c]	students[d]	student/ teacher ratio	gross enroll- ment ratio[b]	students per 100,000 popula- tion[b]	percent of population age 25 and over with post- secondary education[b]	over age	total (%)	male (%)	female (%)	on education (percent of GNP)[b]	
...	...	...	...	12,800	...	2.0	165	3.0	15	36.3	51.0	20.8	2.0	Afghanistan
18,504	8.5	10[1]	2,348	34,257	14.6	12.0	1,007	...	10	91.8	95.5	88.0	3.1	Albania
...	...	...	19,910	347,410	17.4	10.9	1,236	...	15	63.3	75.1	51.3	5.1	Algeria
160[2]	7.6[2]	1	...	...	...	...	...	22.6	15	95.9	95.6	96.3	8.2	American Samoa
...	...	—	—	932	—	...	...	...	15	100.0	100.0	100.0	...	Andorra
22,401	...	1	787	6,.331	8.0	0.7	71	...	15	41.7	55.6	28.5	4.9	Angola
46[3]	2.9[3]	1	16	46	2.9	...	...	...	15	90.0	...	...	2.7	Antigua and Barbuda
[4]	[4]	1,831	117,104	936,832	8.0	38.0	3,117	12.0	15	96.9	96.9	96.9	3.5	Argentina
25,200[5]	...	15	4,420	38,500	8.7	12.0	976	...	15	98.8	99.4	98.1	2.0	Armenia
[4]	[4]	2	53	394	7.4	...	...	7.0	15	95.0	...	...	4.9	Aruba
985,000[3]	34.1[3]	92	32,663	671,853	20.6	80.0	5,552	...	15	99.5	...	...	5.5	Australia
307,548	11.7	77	20,356	232,377	11.4	48.0	2,970	6.1	15	100.0	100.0	100.0	5.4	Austria
23,500	...	23	17,900	120,870	6.6	17.0	1,516	...	15	97.3	98.9	95.9	3.0	Azerbaijan
...	...	1[7]	160[7]	3,463[7]	21.6[7]	18.0	...	13.5	15	96.1	95.4	96.8	4.0	Bahamas, The
7,287	...	...	558	7,011	12.6	20.0	1,445	10.3	15	87.6	91.0	82.7	4.4	Bahrain
29,923[5]	16.1[5]	1,268[5]	36,000[5]	1,032,635[5]	28.7[5]	4.0	399	1.3	15	40.8	51.7	29.5	2.2	Bangladesh
...	...	4	...	6,622	...	29.0	2,602	3.3	15	97.4	98.0	96.8	7.2	Barbados
125,600	14.3	59	16,300	224,500	13.8	44.0	3,177	12.5	15	99.4	99.7	99.2	5.9	Belarus
569,041	...	151	38,014	358,214	9.4	56.0	3,494	...	15	100.0	100.0	100.0	3.1	Belgium
...	...	12	228	2,753	12.1	...	...	6.6	14	70.3	...	...	5.0	Belize
4,873[5]	17.2[5]	16[5]	962	14,085	14.6	3.0	253	1.3	15	37.5	47.8	23.6	3.2	Benin
...	...	1	...	543	...	...	...	18.4	15	96.9	96.7	97.0	3.7	Bermuda
1,822[1]	12.2[1]	2[1]	57[1]	2,055	9.1[1]	...	...	...	15	47.3	61.1	33.6	4.1	Bhutan
[4]	[4]	...	4,261[2]	109,503[2]	25.7[2]	21.0	2,154	9.9	15	85.6	92.1	79.4	4.9	Bolivia
...	...	44	2,802	37,541	13.4	...	...	...	10	85.5	96.5	76.6	...	Bosnia and Herzegovina
9,829	3.8	1	1,001	9,660	9.6	6.0	596	1.4	15	77.2	74.4	79.8	8.6	Botswana
...	...	900	173,705[13]	1,948,200[13]	11.2[13]	15.0	1,094	...	15	85.3	85.5	85.4	5.1	Brazil
2,553	4.9	4	370	2,080	5.6	7.0	518	9.4	15	91.6	94.7	88.2	2.5	Brunei
201,736	10.0	86	42,829	258,240	6.0	41.0	3,103	15.0	15	98.5	99.1	98.0	3.2	Bulgaria
9,539	13.0	9	632	9,531	15.1	0.9	83	...	15	23.0	31.2	13.1	3.6	Burkina Faso
...	...	8	556	4,256	7.6	0.8	74	0.6	15	48.1	56.3	40.5	4.0	Burundi
16,350[11]	...	9[11]	784[11]	11,652[11]	14.9[11]	1.0	98	1.0	15	65.3	79.7	53.4	2.9	Cambodia
91,779	15.6	...	1,086[12]	33,177[12]	30.5[12]	3.0	289	...	15	75.4	81.8	69.2	2.9	Cameroon
...	...	265	64,100[5]	980,251[5]	14.4[5]	88.0	5,997	21.4	15	96.6	...	...	6.9	Canada
2,289	...	...	...	...	...	...	...	...	15	73.5	84.3	65.3	4.0	Cape Verde
[4]	[4]	1	136	2,823	20.8	1.0	131	2.0	15	46.5	59.6	34.5	2.3	Central African Republic
2,926	13.5	8	288	3,446	12.0	0.6	54	...	15	53.6	66.9	40.8	1.7	Chad
...	...	...	18,084[11, 15]	367,094	...	31.0	2,546	12.3	15	95.7	95.9	95.5	3.6	Chile
9,773,000	16.3	1,020	405,000	3,174,000	7.8	6.0	473	2.0	15	85.0	92.3	77.4	2.3	China
928,474	...	266	75,568	673,353	8.9	17.0	1,768	10.4	15	91.8	91.8	91.8	4.4	Colombia
...	...	...	...	348	...	0.6	57	...	15	56.2	63.5	49.1	3.9	Comoros
[4]	[4]	...	...	52,501	...	2.0	212	1.3	15	77.3	86.6	67.7	1.0	Congo, Dem. Rep. of the
23,606	13.5	...	1,341[3]	16,602[3]	12.4[3]	7.0	582	3.0	15	80.7	87.5	74.4	6.1	Congo, Rep. of the
...	...	40[13]	...	83,106[13]	...	30.0	2,919	...	15	95.6	95.5	95.7	5.4	Costa Rica
11,037[3]	7.8[3]	...	1,657[3]	43,147[3]	26.0[3]	6.0	396	8.7	15	46.8	54.6	38.5	5.0	Côte d'Ivoire
150,792	11.6	79	6,532	90,021	13.8	28.0	1,905	6.4	15	98.3	99.4	97.3	5.3	Croatia
244,253[16]	9.0[16]	35[1]	22,967[16]	104,595	5.3[16]	12.0	1,013	5.9	15	96.4	96.5	96.4	6.7	Cuba
[4]	[4]	35	812	9,982	12.3	23.0	1,383	17.0	15	96.9	98.7	95.0	4.5	Cyprus[17]
419,843	7.7	272	18,061	203,598	11.3	24.0	1,867	8.5	15	100.0	100.0	100.0	5.1	Czech Republic
123,234	9.4	158[3]	9,600	169,783	17.7	48.0	3,189	19.6	...	100.0	100.0	100.0	8.1	Denmark

Education (continued)

country	year	first level (primary)					general second level (secondary)					vocational second level[a]	
		schools	teachers[c]	students[d]	student/teacher ratio	net enrollment ratio[b]	schools	teachers[c]	students[d]	student/teacher ratio	net enrollment ratio[b]	schools	teachers[c]
Djibouti	1997	81[3]	1,005[3]	33,960	...	32	26[4, 12]	628[3, 4]	11,628[4]	...	12	[4]	[4]
Dominica	1998	63	587	13,636	23.2	...	15	293	5,455	18.6	...	...	...
Dominican Republic	1995	4,001	42,135	1,462,722	34.7	81	...	10,757	240,441	22.4	22	...	1,297
East Timor	...	...	...	...	...	...	...	...	...	...	...	...	...
Ecuador	1997	17,367	74,601	1,888,172	25.3	92	...	62,630[4, 11]	765,073[4]	...	...	...	[4]
Egypt[19]	1997	18,522[16]	310,116	7,499,303	24.2	93	7,307[5, 16]	259,618	4,835,938	18.6	64	1,351[5]	138,277
El Salvador	1996	5,025	34,496	1,130,900	32.8	78	...	9,255	143,588	15.5	22	...	...
Equatorial Guinea	1994	781	1,381	75,751	54.9	...	...	466	14,511	31.1	...	...	122
Eritrea	1996	537	5,828	241,725	41.5	30	86[11]	2,031	78,902	38.8	16	4[11]	174
Estonia	1996	727	...	125,718	...	87	...	9,299	95,342	10.3	83	84	1,793
Ethiopia	1995	9,276	83,113	2,722,192	32.8	32	...	22,779	747,142	32.8	...	...	826
Faroe Islands	1995	62	554[9]	4,898	...	...	6	[9]	3,041	...	...	...	...
Fiji	1997	697[5]	5,011	142,781	28.5	99	147[5]	3,519	70,098	19.9	...	35[5]	625[2]
Finland	1997	4,392	39,966	592,500	14.8	98	454	5,766	131,900	22.9	93	467	15,063
France	1995	41,244	216,962	4,071,599	18.8	100	11,212[4]	473,673[4]	6,003,797[4]	12.7[4]	95	[4]	[4]
French Guiana	1996	78[5]	802	17,006	21.2	...	22[12]	875	13,585	15.5	...	...	210
French Polynesia	1995	278	2,949	48,160	16.3	103	38	1,745	25,541	14.6	61	...	...
Gabon	1996	1,147	4,944	250,606	50.7	...	48	2,683	72,888	27.2	...	11	412
Gambia, The	1995	250[5]	3,158[5]	113,419	33.4[5]	65	32[4, 5]	1,126[4, 5]	31,567	24.1[4, 5]	20	[4]	[4]
Gaza Strip	1997	1,118	15,903	656,353	41.3	...	...	7,634	54,692	7.2	...	...	316
Georgia	1997	3,201	16,542	293,325	17.7	77	3,139	55,817	424,465	7.6	74	...	2,146
Germany	1998	17,829	198,116	3,697,806	18.7	86	19,668	413,993	5,720,092	13.8	88	9,754	110,185
Ghana	1992	11,056	66,068	1,796,490	27.2	...	5,540	43,367	816,578	18.8	...	57[1]	422[1]
Greece	1997	8,651	46,785	652,040	13.9	90	3,044	56,899	682,201	12.0	87	682	13,783
Greenland	1999	88	975	9,341	9.6	...	3	...	1,746	...	...	...	...
Grenada	1997	58	879	23,449	26.7	...	19[3]	381[3]	7,367	19.3	...	...	...
Guadeloupe	1999	348	2,936	38,092[5]	...	...	88[4]	3,392[4]	51,366[4, 5]	13.4[4, 5]	...	[4]	[4]
Guam	1998	24	469	20,248	43.2	...	11	622	17,091	27.5	...	2	370[1]
Guatemala	1995	11,495	43,731	1,470,754	33.6	72	2,308[4]	23,807[4]	372,006[4]	15.6[4]	10	626[12]	[4]
Guernsey	1993	22[2]	236	4,697	19.9	...	8[2]	276	3,642	13.2	...	...	...
Guinea	1998	3,723	13,883	674,732	48.6	42	239	4,958	143,245	28.9	9	55[16]	1,268[16]
Guinea-Bissau	1995	...	...	100,369	...	47	...	...	7,000	...	3	...	...
Guyana	1997	420	3,461	102,000	29.5	87	...	2,150	62,043	29.5	66	...	...
Haiti	1995	10,071	30,205	1,110,398	36.8	26	1,038	...	195,418	...	22	...	...
Honduras	1999	8,768	33,431	1,111,264	33.2	90	661[3, 4]	14,539[4]	189,000[4]	13.0[4]	21	[4]	[4]
Hong Kong	1998	832	20,038	476,682	23.8	90	507	23,077	455,392	19.7	69	9	...
Hungary	1999	3,732	83,404	964,248	11.6	97	1,545	40,130	504,829	12.6	86	1,245	26,344
Iceland	1997	198	3,877	31,100	8.0	98	37	1,454	17,970	12.4	87	...	...
India	1997	598,354	1,789,733	110,393,406	61.7	...	274,944	2,738,205	65,359,339	23.9	...	...	...
Indonesia	1997	173,883	1,327,218	28,236,283	21.3	95	41,847	863,389	12,442,813	14.4	45	3,894	123,505
Iran	1997	63,101	298,755	9,238,393	31.2	90	18,445[1]	280,309	8,776,792	31.3	71	...	20,418[3]
Iraq	1996	8,145	145,455	2,903,923	20.0	76	2,635[3]	49,884	1,075,490	21.6	37	310[3]	9,903
Ireland	1997	3,254	18,968	476,632	25.1	92	440	12,694	375,518	29.6	86	324	8,305
Isle of Man	1999	33	...	6,210	...	...	5	...	4,732	...	...	...	...
Israel	1998	1,651	57,738	532,070	9.2	...	653	62,054	414,405	...	...	338	17,141[11]
Italy	1997	19,890	289,504	2,809,699	9.7	100	16,973	315,920	2,648,535	8.4	67	7,732	305,582
Jamaica	1997	788[2]	9,512	293,863	30.9	95	126[3]	8,377[3]	228,533	...	64[3]	18[3]	950[3]
Japan	1997	24,376	420,901	7,855,387	18.7	103	16,753	546,337	8,852,840	16.2	99	62	4,384
Jersey	1990	32	...	5,794	...	...	14	...	4,405	...	...	1	...
Jordan	1996	2,531	51,721	1,074,877	20.8	89	741[5]	6,309	109,906	17.4	42	54[5]	2,306
Kazakhstan	1997	8,611[16]	262,000[16]	1,342,035	...	...	...	178,900[5]	1,743,623	...	...	239	...
Kenya	1995	15,906	181,975	5,544,998	30.5	91	2,878	41,484	632,388	15.2	11	62	1,147[14]
Kiribati	1997	86	727	17,594	24.2	...	9	215	4,403	20.5	...	...	23
Korea, North	1988	4,810[13]	59,000	1,543,000	26.2	...	4,840[13]	111,000	2,468,000	22.2	...	...	...
Korea, South	1997	5,721	138,670	3,783,986	27.3	93	4,612	202,335	4,517,008	22.3	97	166	13,282
Kuwait	1997	258	9,863	142,265	14.4	62	416	19,402	213,266	11.0	61	38	793
Kyrgyzstan	1996	1,885	24,086	473,077	19.7	95	1,474[5]	38,915	498,849	12.8	...	53[5]	3,371
Laos	1997	7,896	25,831	786,335	30.4	72	750[1]	10,717	180,160	16.8	22	...	1,600[16]
Latvia	1998	638	10,883	146,653	13.5	89	380	24,112	196,148	8.1	79	123	5,470
Lebanon	1997	2,160	...	382,309	...	76	...	...	292,002	...	...	275	7,745
Lesotho	1997	1,249	7,898	374,628	47.4	70	187[3]	2,817	67,454	23.9	18	9[5]	61
Liberia	1987	...	...	...	...	...	...	...	...	...	...	...	...
Libya	1996	2,733[5]	122,020	1,333,679	10.9	96	...	17,668	170,573	9.7	62	480	...
Liechtenstein	1998	14	134	2,021	15.1	...	10[4]	198[4]	4,121[4]	20.8[4]	...	[4]	[4]
Lithuania	1997	2,292	14,093	225,071	16.0	...	...	32,172	325,480	10.1	80	104	5,078
Luxembourg	1997	...	1,844	28,232	15.3	...	...	2,673	9,463	3.5	...	...	2,904[3, 14]
Macau	1998	81	1,744	47,235	27.1	...	47	1,577	28,280	17.9	53	2	47
Macedonia	1998	1,043	13,376	256,275	19.2	94	93[4]	5,226[4]	84,059[4]	16.1[4]	51	[4]	[4]
Madagascar	1996	13,325	44,145	1,638,187	37.1	61	...	16,795	302,036	18.0	...	...	1,150
Malawi	1996	3,706	49,138	2,887,107	58.7	103	...	2,948	139,386	47.2	2	...	475
Malaysia	1997	7,084	150,681	2,870,667	19.1	102	1,460	91,659	1,767,946	19.3	...	101	5,472
Maldives	1998	228	1,992	48,895	24.5	...	...	...	15,933[2]	...	...	...	...
Mali	1998	2,511	10,853	862,875	79.5	31	307[2]	4,549[16]	166,372	...	5	...	21,731
Malta	1998	99	1,457	35,261	24.2	100	75	2,458	27,178	11.1	79	22	626
Marshall Islands	1995	103	669	13,355	20.0	...	12	144	2,400	16.7	...	...	...
Martinique	1997	273	2,603	55,569	21.3	...	76[16]	2,888	36,605	12.7	...	...	896[16]
Mauritania	1997	2,392	6,225	312,671	50.2	57	...	1,865[16]	49,221[16]	26.4[16]	...	...	202
Mauritius	1998	285	5,065	130,505	25.7	98	133	4,820	94,364	19.6	33	13	1,170[13]
Mayotte	1997	88[1]	555[11]	25,805[10]	...	...	8	246[11]	6,190	...	...	2[1]	17[1]
Mexico	1996	94,844	516,051	14,623,400	28.3	101	25,000	467,686	7,589,400	16.2	51	6,571[11]	77,347[11]
Micronesia	1995	174	...	27,281	...	...	24	...	6,898	...	...	...	...
Moldova	1997	1,700[9]	14,097	320,725	22.8	...	[9]	28,615[4]	419,256	...	...	64	[4]
Monaco	1997	8	127	1,917	15.1	...	6	192	2,416	12.6	...	4	89
Mongolia	1997	308	7,587	234,193	30.9	81	337	12,503	184,100	14.7	53	36	668
Morocco	1998	5,730	116,638	3,317,153	28.4	74	1,406	82,589	1,328,789	16.1	20	71[14]	2,951[3, 14]

		third level (higher)							literacy[b]				public expenditure on education (percent of GNP)[b]	country
students[d]	student/ teacher ratio	institutions	teachers[c]	students[d]	student/ teacher ratio	gross enroll- ment ratio[b]	students per 100,000 popula- tion[b]	percent of population age 25 and over with post- secondary education[b]	over age	total (%)	male (%)	female (%)		
[4]	[4]	1[12]	13[12]	130[18]	...	0.2	26	...	15	51.4	65.0	38.4	3.6	Djibouti
...	...	2[11]	34[11]	484[11]	14.2[11]	...	...	1.7	15	90.0	...	...	5.5	Dominica
22,795	17.6	...	9,041[15]	176,995[15]	19.6[15]	23.0	...	...	15	83.8	84.0	83.7	2.3	Dominican Republic
...	...	...	...	...	...	...	...	...	...	...	...	...	...	East Timor
[4]	...	21	12,856[1]	206,541[1]	16.1[1]	20.0	2,012	12.7	15	91.9	93.6	90.2	3.5	Ecuador
1,912,040	13.8	16[15]	38,828[5, 15]	850,051	...	20.0	1,900	4.6	15	55.3	66.6	43.7	4.8	Egypt[19]
...	...	...	5,919	112,266	19.0	18.0	1,933	6.4	15	78.7	81.6	76.1	2.5	El Salvador
2,105	17.3	...	58	578	10.0	...	164	...	15	83.2	92.5	74.5	1.7	Equatorial Guinea
4,268	24.5	1	136	3,081	22.7	1.0	95	...	...	20.0	...	...	1.8	Eritrea
16,870	9.4	37	...	40,621	...	42.0	2,956	13.7	15	99.7	99.9	99.6	7.2	Estonia
9,103	11.0	...	1,937	32,671	16.9	0.6	62	1.0	15	38.7	43.9	33.4	4.0	Ethiopia
2,090[5]	...	1[12]	20[12]	91[12]	4.6[12]	...	...	...	15	99.0	99.0	99.0	...	Faroe Islands
7,283[2]	11.6[2]	...	277[12]	7,908[12]	28.5[12]	12.0	757	4.5	15	92.9	95.0	90.9	5.4	Fiji
251,600	16.7	29	8,134	168,996	20.8	74.0	4,190	15.4	15	100.0	100.0	100.0	7.5	Finland
[4]	[4]	1,062	52,613	2,083,129	39.6	51.0	3,600	11.4	...	98.8	98.9	98.7	6.0	France
2,404	11.4	1	...	324[11]	...	...	...	6.4	15	83.0	83.6	82.3	...	French Guiana
...	...	...	...	301[2]	...	1.0	...	...	15	95.0	94.9	95.0	9.8	French Polynesia
7,664	18.6	2[2, 15]	299[2, 15]	3,000[2, 15]	10.0[2, 15]	...	650	...	15	70.8	79.8	62.2	2.9	Gabon
[4]	[4]	...	155[5]	1,591[5]	10.3[5]	2.0	148	...	15	36.5	43.8	29.6	4.9	Gambia, The
1,775	5.7	5	2,473	49,599	20.0	...	...	...	...	...	...	...	...	Gaza Strip
19,593	9.1	23	25,549	163,345	6.4	30.0	3,002	...	15	99.5	99.7	99.4	5.2	Georgia
2,838,416	25.8	296	161,383	1,813,348	11.2	47.0	2,628	...	15	100.0	100.0	100.0	4.8	Germany
13,232[1]	31.4[1]	16[1]	700[1]	9,274[1]	13.2[1]	0.6	127	...	15	70.2	79.5	61.2	4.2	Ghana
135,365	9.8	18	16,057	363,180	22.6	47.0	3,149	8.7	15	97.2	98.6	96.0	3.1	Greece
...	...	...	...	...	...	...	...	...	15	100.0	100.0	100.0	...	Greenland
...	...	1[3]	66[3]	651[3]	9.9[3]	...	...	1.5	15	85.0	...	...	4.7	Grenada
[4]	[4]	1[5]	121[5]	4,673[5]	38.6[5]	...	...	5.2	15	90.1	89.7	90.5	...	Guadeloupe
4,369	...	1	192[1]	3,533	...	...	...	39.9	15	99.0	99.0	99.0	8.5	Guam
[4]	[4]	...	...	80,228	...	8.0	755	2.2	15	68.7	76.2	61.1	1.7	Guatemala
...	...	—	—	—	—	...	...	...	15	100.0	100.0	100.0	...	Guernsey
8,151[16]	6.8[16]	2[16]	947[16]	8,151[16]	8.6[16]	1.0	108	...	15	41.1	55.1	27.0	1.9	Guinea
...	...	...	...	...	...	...	...	0.1	15	36.8	53.0	21.4	...	Guinea-Bissau
...	...	...	612	8,965	12.5	11.0	954	1.8	15	98.5	99.0	98.1	5.0	Guyana
...	...	2[20]	817[20]	12,204[20]	14.9[20]	1.0	...	0.7	15	48.6	51.0	46.5	1.5	Haiti
[4]	[4]	8	3,676[3]	56,077	...	10.0	985	3.3	15	72.2	72.5	72.0	3.6	Honduras
42,003	...	18	...	91,748	...	22.0	1,635	14.5	15	93.4	96.5	90.0	2.9	Hong Kong
362,633	13.8	89	21,351	163,164	7.6	24.0	1,926	10.1	15	99.4	99.5	99.3	4.6	Hungary
...	...	10	508	7,972	15.7	37.0	2,787	...	15	100.0	100.0	100.0	5.4	Iceland
...	...	8,407[5]	286,000[5]	5,007,000[5]	17.5[5]	7.0	642	7.3	15	55.8	68.6	42.1	3.2	India
1,767,181	14.3	1,667	180,471	2,703,886	15.0	11.0	1,167	2.3	15	87.0	91.9	82.1	1.4	Indonesia
368,218[3]	18.0[3]	...	40,477	579,070	14.3	18.0	1,599	...	15	76.9	83.7	70.0	4.0	Iran
122,939	12.4	12	11,685	232,896	19.9	12.0	...	4.1	15	58.0	70.7	45.0	4.0	Iraq
96,821	11.7	30	4,872	107,501	22.1	41.0	3,618	13.1	15	100.0	100.0	100.0	6.0	Ireland
...	...	...	...	1,128	...	...	...	...	...	...	...	...	...	Isle of Man
106,393	...	7	9,546	181,038	19.0	41.0	3,598	11.2	15	96.1	97.9	94.3	7.6	Israel
2,597,449	8.5	56[15]	48,891[15]	1,595,642[15]	32.6	47.0	3,103	3.8	15	98.5	98.9	98.1	4.9	Italy
15,898[3]	16.7[3]	15[3]	...	24,200[3]	...	8.0	803	2.7	15	86.7	82.5	90.7	7.5	Jamaica
56,294	12.8	1,243	166,051	3,136,834	18.9	41.0	3,139	20.7	15	100.0	100.0	100.0	3.6	Japan
...	...	...	...	...	...	...	...	...	15	100.0	100.0	100.0	...	Jersey
35,579	15.4	55	4,821	99,020	20.5	27.0	2,542	...	15	89.8	94.9	84.4	7.9	Jordan
177,679	...	69[3]	27,189[3]	260,043[16]	...	33.0	2,806	12.4	15	97.5	99.1	96.1	4.4	Kazakhstan
11,700[14]	10.2[4]	14[11, 15]	4,392[1, 15]	88,180[11]	...	2.0	143	...	15	82.5	89.0	76.0	6.5	Kenya
333	14.5	—	—	—	—	...	...	...	15	90.0	...	...	6.3	Kiribati
220,000	...	519[13]	27,000	390,000	14.4	...	...	...	15	95.0	...	...	...	Korea, North
745,689	56.1	742	53,300	1,469,819	27.6	68.0	5,609	21.1	15	97.8	99.2	96.4	3.7	Korea, South
3,779	4.8	1	1,691	29,509	17.5	19.0	2,247	16.4	15	82.3	84.3	79.9	5.0	Kuwait
32,005	9.5	23	3,691	49,744	13.5	12.0	1,115	...	15	97.0	98.6	95.5	5.3	Kyrgyzstan
9,400[16]	5.9[16]	9[1]	1,369	12,732	9.3	3.0	253	...	15	61.8	73.6	50.5	2.1	Laos
45,672	8.3	28	4,486	56,187	12.5	33.0	2,244	13.4	15	99.7	99.8	99.6	6.3	Latvia
55,848	7.2	20	10,444	81,588	7.8	27.0	2,712	...	15	86.1	92.3	80.4	2.5	Lebanon
678	11.1	1	574	4,614	8.0	2.0	222	...	15	83.9	73.6	93.6	8.4	Lesotho
...	...	...	472	5,095	10.8	2.0	...	...	15	53.4	69.9	36.8	5.7	Liberia
155,483	...	13	...	126,348	...	17.0	1,358	2.7	15	79.8	90.9	67.6	7.1	Libya
[4]	[4]	...	...	...	...	...	...	...	15	100.0	100.0	100.0	...	Liechtenstein
56,400	11.1	15	13,136	83,645	6.4	31.0	2,244	12.6	15	99.5	99.7	99.4	5.5	Lithuania
19,346	...	1	200[3]	957	...	10.0	...	10.8	15	100.0	100.0	100.0	4.0	Luxembourg
699	14.9	7	818	7,682	9.4	28.0	1,700	5.9	15	93.2	96.4	90.1	...	Macau
[4]	[4]	30	1,385	36,167	26.1	20.0	1,415	6.7	10	89.1	94.2	83.8	5.1	Macedonia
8,479	7.3	...	921	18,458	20.0	3.0	174	...	15	80.2	87.7	72.9	1.9	Madagascar
2,228	4.7	6	531[3]	5,561	...	0.6	58	0.4	15	60.3	74.5	46.7	5.4	Malawi
36,573	6.9	48	14,960	210,724	14.1	12.0	971	6.9	15	87.5	91.5	83.6	4.9	Malaysia
452[2]	...	—	—	—	—	...	...	1.7	15	96.3	96.3	96.4	6.4	Maldives
7,200	3.0	7	796	13,847	17.4	1.0	73	...	15	40.3	47.9	33.2	2.2	Mali
4,159	6.6	1	770	7,146	9.3	29.0	1,595	...	15	92.1	91.4	92.8	5.1	Malta
...	...	...	...	...	...	...	...	...	15	91.2	92.4	90.0	...	Marshall Islands
11,101[16]	12.4[16]	1	99[5]	3,079	45.3[5]	...	...	5.6	15	97.4	96.0	97.1	...	Martinique
2,544	12.6	4	270	8,496	31.5	4.0	374	1.3	15	39.9	50.6	29.5	5.1	Mauritania
5,496	...	3	461	6,429	13.9	6.3	594	1.9	15	84.3	87.7	81.0	4.6	Mauritius
839[11]	...	—	—	—	—	...	...	...	15	91.9	...	...	...	Mayotte
1,076,700[11]	13.9[11]	10,341	163,843	1,532,800	9.4	16.0	1,586	9.2	15	91.0	93.1	89.1	4.9	Mexico
...	...	...	...	1,461[5]	...	...	...	...	15	76.7	67.0	87.2	...	Micronesia
26,245	...	20	8,814	93,759	10.6	27.0	2,110	11.3	15	98.9	99.6	98.3	10.6	Moldova
532	6.0	1	...	112	...	...	...	...	...	...	...	...	...	Monaco
11,308	16.9	86	4,471	44,088	9.8	17.0	1,753	23.4	15	99.3	99.2	99.3	5.7	Mongolia
22,415[14]	...	68	9,667	266,507	27.5	11.0	1,132	...	15	48.9	61.9	36.0	5.3	Morocco

Education (continued)

country	year	first level (primary)					general second level (secondary)					vocational second level[a]	
		schools	teachers[c]	students[d]	student/ teacher ratio	net enroll-ment ratio[b]	schools	teachers[c]	students[d]	student/ teacher ratio	net enroll-ment ratio[b]	schools	teachers[c]
Mozambique	1997	6,025	32,670	1,899,531	57.8	40	75	1,555	51,554	33.1	8	25	565
Myanmar (Burma)	1998	35,877	167,134	5,145,400	30.8	...	2,091	56,955	1,545,600	27.1	...	103[3]	2,462[3]
Namibia	1995	933[5]	10,912[2]	368,222	32.0[2]	91	114[5]	3,943[2]	101,838[5]	...	36	17[5]	56[2]
Nauru	1995	10	138	2,207	16.0	...	4	46	...	...	...	1	...
Nepal	1996	22,218	89,378	3,447,607	38.6	...	7,582[4]	36,127[4]	1,121,335[4]	31.0[4]	...	[4]	[4]
Netherlands, The	1999	7,238	99,031[12]	1,534,000	...	100	666	89,370[12]	856,000	...	84	143	18,613[12]
Netherlands Antilles	1998	85[16]	1,111	24,061	21.7	...	21	461[16]	8,372	...	...	33	623[16]
New Caledonia	1996	279	1,622	22,942	14.1	98	46	2,021[4]	20,360	...	72	14	[4]
New Zealand	1998	2,282	23,119	445,868	19.3	100	339	15,228	224,290	14.7	90	29	5,309
Nicaragua	1997	7,224	21,020[16]	783,002	...	77	451[5]	5,990[3]	220,670[3]	36.8[3]	18	...	...
Niger	1998	3,175	11,545	482,065	41.8	24	...	3,579	97,675	27.3	6	...	215
Nigeria	1995	38,649	435,210	16,191,000	37.2	...	6,074	152,596	4,451,000	29.2	...	...	...
Northern Mariana Islands	1993	18	183	4,666	25.5	...	9[4]	152[4]	3,044[4]	20.0[4]	...	[4]	[4]
Norway	1997	3,287	39,385	487,398	12.4	100	714[4]	21,105[4]	208,280[4]	9.9[4]	97	[4]	[4]
Oman	1997	429	11,925[16]	311,955	...	69	128[1]	11,896	205,046	17.2	49	25[1]	342[5]
Pakistan	1998	158,511[10]	346,000[10]	16,642,000[10]	48.0[10]	...	25,913	259,200	5,545,000	21.4	...	673	7,546
Palau	1997	...	172	1,450	8.4	...	...	60	490	8.2	...	...	...
Panama	1997	2,866	15,058	377,898	25.1	91	417	12,450	223,155	17.9	51	...	...
Papua New Guinea	1995	2,790	13,652	525,995	38.5	...	135[1]	2,415[2]	68,818	24.1[2]	...	117[1]	878[2]
Paraguay	1996	5,928	41,713	895,777	21.5	91	804[4]	17,668	293,651[4]	...	38	[4]	...
Peru	1997	33,017	153,951	4,163,180	27.0	91	8,085[3]	106,614	1,969,501	18.5	55	2,425[3]	12,293[3]
Philippines	1997	37,645	341,183	11,902,501	34.9	101	5,880[5]	154,705[4]	4,888,246[4]	31.6[4]	59	1,261[1]	[4]
Poland	1998	19,299	322,600	4,896,400	15.2	95	1,847	39,200	757,500	19.3	85	9,320	89,900
Portugal	1996	12,884	145,462[9]	1,339,744	...	104	664	[9]	477,221	...	78	262	6,895
Puerto Rico	1986	1,542	18,359	427,582	23.3	...	395	13,612	334,661	24.6	...	52	...
Qatar	1996[8]	174	5,864	53,631	9.1	80	123[3]	3,738[3]	36,964[3]	9.9[3]	69	3	120
Réunion	1998	351	...	76,364	...	...	111[4]	6,343	96,811	15.3	...	[4]	1,120[16]
Romania	1997	13,978[18]	175,426[18]	2,546,231[18]	14.5[18]	95	1,295[21]	64,485[21]	792,788[21]	12.3[21]	73	1,692	10,942
Russia	1999	69,613[9]	1,811,000[9]	21,966,900[9]	12.1[9]	93	[9]	[9]	[9]	[9]	...	3,590	...
Rwanda	1992	1,710	18,937	1,104,902	58.3	75	...	3,413[4]	94,586[4]	27.7[4]	8	...	[4]
St. Kitts and Nevis	1998	28	320	5,928	18.5	...	9	341	4,548	13.3	...	...	...
St. Lucia	1998	84	1,160	30,536	26.3	...	17	620	11,405	18.4	...	1[11]	34[11]
St. Vincent and the Grenadines	1998	60	1,007	21,347	21.2	...	21	379	7,775	20.5	...	3	32[16]
Samoa	1995	155	1,475	35,811	24.3	96	...	...	...	...	45	...	...
San Marino	1998	14	225	1,211	5.4	...	3	148	700	4.7	...	...	44[5]
São Tomé and Príncipe	1997	69	638	21,760	34.1	...	10	415	12,280	29.6	...	...	...
Saudi Arabia	1997	11,509	175,458	2,256,185	12.9	61	7,667	115,907	1,505,072	13.0	42	...	6,133
Senegal	1997	3,530	16,567	954,758	57.6	60	359[11]	6,219	206,934	33.3	16	19[11]	182[11]
Serbia and Montenegro	1999	4,431	52,294	864,199	16.5	69	561	27,766	367,587	13.2	62	...	...
Seychelles	1999	25	656	9,868	15.0	...	13	545	7,774	14.3	...	12	218
Sierra Leone	1993	1,643	10,595	267,425	25.2	...	167	4,313	70,900	16.4	...	44	709
Singapore	1997	196	11,189	280,108	25.0	93	165	10,673	209,835	19.7	44	10	1,315
Slovakia	1998	2,482	39,535	645,941	16.3	...	198	5,849	80,116	13.7	...	365	10,104
Slovenia	1997	824	7,283	98,866	13.5	95	153	8,665	131,573	15.2	...	...	5,908
Solomon Islands	1994	520	2,514	60,493	24.1	...	23	618	7,981	12.9	...	1	...
Somalia	1990	...	...	377,000	...	10	...	...	44,000		3	...	...
South Africa	1996	20,863[9]	224,896	8,159,430	36.3	103	[9]	128,611[5]	3,749,449[5]	29.2[5]	58	187[5]	10,807[5]
Spain	1997	16,540[5]	163,105	2,682,894	16.4	105	25,775[4, 11]	245,118[4]	2,946,191	...	74	[4]	[4]
Sri Lanka	1998	10,947[9]	194,823[9]	4,278,124[9]	22.0[9]	...	[9]	[9]	[9]	[9]	...	36	623
Sudan, The	1997	11,158	102,987	3,000,048	24.1	54	2,578[2]	15,504	405,583	26.2	...	...	761
Suriname	1996	304	3,611	75,585	20.9	...	104	2,286	31,918	13.9	...	1	...
Swaziland	1997	529	6,094	205,829	33.8	91	165[5]	2,954[16]	57,330[16]	19.4[16]	38	5[5]	228[5]
Sweden	1997	4,936	81,800	958,972	11.7	102	641	28,305	310,000	10.9	99	...	...
Switzerland	1998	...	...	462,262	...	100	...	...	421,025	...	79	...	...
Syria	1997	10,783	114,689	2,690,205	23.5	91	2,526[3]	52,182	865,042	16.6	38	292[3]	12,479
Taiwan	1998	2,540	92,104	1,905,690	20.7	...	1,151[4]	99,411[4]	1,874,747[4]	18.9[4]	...	[4]	[4]
Tajikistan	1997	3,432	27,172	638,674	23.5	...	...	112,532	688,150	6.1	...	75[3]	...
Tanzania	1996[22]	10,892[5]	108,874	3,942,888	36.2	48	491[5]	11,689	199,093	17.0	...	40[5]	1,062
Thailand	1997	34,412[11]	445,542[11]	5,909,618	...	...	2,318[11]	107,025[11]	3,267,449	...	...	679[11]	40,116[11]
Togo	1997	3,283[16]	18,535	859,574	46.4	81	314[11]	4,736[16]	169,178	...	18	...	653
Tonga	1994	115	701	16,540	23.6	...	47	809	15,702	19.4	...	9	67[1]
Trinidad and Tobago	1997	478	7,311	181,030	24.8	88	...	5,070[4]	104,349[4]	20.6[4]	65	...	[4]
Tunisia	1997	4,428	60,101	1,450,916	24.1	98	712[3]	45,411	882,730	19.4	...	...	237[16]
Turkey	1997	47,313	217,131	6,389,060	29.4	99	11,144	143,322	3,427,715	23.9	51	4,046	75,507
Turkmenistan	1995	1,900[9]	72,900[9]	940,600[9]	12.9[9]	...	[9]	[9]	[9]	[9]	...	78	...
Tuvalu	1994	12	72[1]	1,906	...	...	2	31	345	...	...	1	10[1]
Uganda	1995[8]	8,531	76,134	2,636,409	34.6	...	...	14,447	255,158	17.7	...	...	1,788
Ukraine	1996	21,900[9]	576,000[3, 9]	7,007,000[9]	12.4[3, 9]	...	[9]	[9]	[9]	[9]	...	782	...
United Arab Emirates	1997	...	16,148	259,509	16.1	78	...	12,388[3]	178,839	12.0	71	9	249[14]
United Kingdom	1997	23,312	283,492	5,328,219	18.5	99	...	312,038	4,435,000	13.2	91	...	152,098
United States	1998	88,223[8, 9]	1,874,000	34,681,000	18.5	95	[9]	1,217,000	17,494,000	14.4	90	...	...
Uruguay	1997	2,410	16,721	348,195	20.8	93	413	19,104	192,399	10.1	...	101	...
Uzbekistan	1996	9,300[9]	413,000[9]	5,090,000[9]	12.3[9]	...	[9]	[9]	[9]	[9]	...	248	22,164[11]
Vanuatu	1992	272	852	26,267	30.8	...	...	220	4,269	19.4	17	...	...
Venezuela	1997	15,894[11]	182,192	4,262,221	23.4	84	1,621[2, 4]	43,369[4]	377,984[4]	8.7[4]	22	[4]	[4]
Vietnam	1998	13,092[5]	324,431	10,431,337	32.2	...	6,298[5]	209,500	6,642,350	31.7	...	451[5]	9,336
Virgin Islands (U.S.)	1993[8]	62	790	14,544	18.4	...	...	541[12]	12,502	17.2[12]	...	—	—
West Bank	1997	1,193[9]	15,912[9]	431,565[9]	27.1[9]	...	[9]	[9]	[9]	[9]	...	...	...
Western Sahara	1995[8]	40	925	32,257	34.9	...	13	1,267	10,541	8.3	...	...	...
Yemen	1997[14]	11,013[5]	90,478	2,699,788	29.8	...	1,224[3]	13,787	286,405	20.8	...	125[3]	369[3]
Zambia	1996	3,907	38,528[3]	1,670,000	...	75	...	...	255,000	...	16	...	...
Zimbabwe	1996	4,659	63,718	2,493,791	39.1	...	1,536	28,354	751,349	26.5	...	25[2]	1,479[2]

students[d]	student/ teacher ratio	third level (higher): institutions	teachers[c]	students[d]	student/ teacher ratio	gross enroll- ment ratio[b]	students per 100,000 popula- tion[b]	percent of population age 25 and over with post- secondary education[b]	literacy[b]: over age	total (%)	male (%)	female (%)	public expenditure on education (percent of GNP)[b]	country
12,001	21.2	3	954	7,158	7.5	0.5	40	0.1	15	43.8	59.9	28.4	4.1	Mozambique
25,374[3]	10.3[3]	51	17,089	385,300	22.5	5.0	564	2.0	15	84.7	89.0	80.6	1.2	Myanmar (Burma)
1,503[5]	...	7[5]	331[12]	11,344	...	8.0	738	4.0	15	82.1	82.9	81.2	9.1	Namibia
...	...	...	...	...	...	...	...	...	15	99.0	...	...	...	Nauru
[4]	[4]	3[2]	4,925[12]	105,694	...	5.0	501	0.6	15	41.4	59.1	21.8	3.2	Nepal
517,000	...	13	...	147,000	...	47.0	3,176	...	15	100.0	100.0	100.0	5.1	Netherlands, The
8,524	...	1	97	686	7.1	...	...	8.8	15	96.6	96.6	96.6	...	Netherlands Antilles
5,916	...	4	79	1,749	22.1	5.0	...	7.5	15	57.9	57.4	58.3	13.5	New Caledonia
105,186	19.8	7	4,973	107,837	21.7	63.0	4,508	39.1	15	100.0	100.0	100.0	7.3	New Zealand
...	...	10[5]	3,840	48,758	12.7	12.0	1,231	...	15	64.3	64.2	64.4	3.9	Nicaragua
2,145	10.0	2	355	5,569	15.7	0.7	55	...	15	15.7	23.5	8.3	2.3	Niger
...	...	31	12,103	228,000	18.8	4.0	367	...	15	64.1	72.3	56.2	0.7	Nigeria
[4]	[4]	...	...	...	...	...	...	...	15	96.3	96.9	95.6	...	Northern Mariana Islands
[4]	[4]	89	11,515	181,741	15.8	54.5	4,164	18.7	15	100.0	100.0	100.0	7.4	Norway
2,350[5]	6.9[5]	5[1]	1,162	13,251	11.4	8.0	532	...	15	71.3	80.4	61.7	4.5	Oman
95,000	12.6	984	34,078	1,052,782	30.9	3.0	291	2.5	15	43.3	57.6	27.8	2.7	Pakistan
...	...	...	...	130	...	...	...	...	15	97.6	98.3	96.6	...	Palau
...	...	14	6,409	95,341	14.9	30.0	3,024	13.2	15	91.9	92.6	91.3	5.1	Panama
9,941	12.9[2]	2[1]	...	13,663	...	3.0	318	...	15	76.0	81.7	67.7	4.7	Papua New Guinea
[4]	...	2	742[11]	42,302	...	10.0	1,049	6.6	15	93.3	94.4	92.2	4.0	Paraguay
270,576[3]	22.0[3]	886	45,443	657,586	14.2	26.0	3,268	20.6	15	89.9	94.7	85.4	2.9	Peru
[4]	[4]	975[5]	56,880[12]	2,022,106[16]	...	29.0	2,981	22.0	15	95.4	95.5	95.2	3.4	Philippines
1,599,900	17.8	246	73,300	1,091,500	14.9	25.0	1,884	7.9	15	99.8	99.8	99.8	7.5	Poland
25,234	3.7	278	16,087	319,525	19.9	39.0	3,060	7.7	15	92.2	94.8	90.0	5.8	Portugal
149,191	...	45	9,045	171,625[16]	...	...	...	28.7	15	93.8	93.7	94.0	8.2	Puerto Rico
670	5.6	1	643	8,475	13.2	27.0	1,518	13.3	15	81.3	80.5	83.2	3.4	Qatar
13,547[16]	12.1[16]	1	286	8,663	30.3	...	...	...	15	87.1	84.8	89.2	...	Réunion
351,900	32.2	102	23,477	354,488	15.1	23.0	1,817	5.6	15	98.2	99.1	97.3	3.6	Romania
1,676,000	...	913	282,400	3,597,900	12.7	43.0	2,998	14.1	15	99.4	99.8	99.2	3.5	Russia
[4]	[4]	...	646[1]	3,389[1]	5.2[1]	0.4	...	...	15	67.0	73.7	60.6	3.8	Rwanda
...	...	1[11]	51[11]	394[11]	7.7[11]	...	...	2.3	15	90.9	90.0	90.0	3.8	St. Kitts and Nevis
808[11]	23.7[11]	1	157[16]	2,760[16]	17.6[16]	...	...	3.4	15	82.0	...	...	9.8	St. Lucia
415	...	...	...	...	...	...	...	1.4	15	96.0	...	...	6.3	St. Vincent and the Grenadines
...	...	...	...	...	...	...	...	5.6	15	100.0	100.0	100.0	4.2	Samoa
455[5]	10.3[5]	...	...	...	...	...	...	...	15	99.1	99.4	98.8	...	San Marino
...	...	...	...	...	...	...	...	0.3	15	54.2	70.2	39.1	3.8	São Tomé and Príncipe
51,916	8.5	68[15]	8,998[15]	165,262[15]	18.4[15]	16.0	1,455	...	15	77.0	84.1	67.2	7.5	Saudi Arabia
7,301[11]	40.1[11]	2	965[15]	24,081[15]	25.0[15]	3.0	297	...	15	37.3	47.2	27.6	3.7	Senegal
...	...	83	10,998	147,981	13.5	22.0	1,674	...	15	93.3	97.6	89.2	...	Serbia and Montenegro
2,002	9.2	...	...	...	...	...	...	4.6	15	84.2	82.9	85.7	7.9	Seychelles
7,756	10.9	1	257[12]	2,571[12]	10.0[12]	2.0	119	1.5	15	36.3	50.7	22.6	0.9	Sierra Leone
9,906	7.5	7	7,764	97,392	12.5	39.0	2,722	7.6	15	92.4	96.4	88.5	3.0	Singapore
116,681	11.5	18	8,544	83,942	9.8	22.0	1,903	9.5	15	100.0	100.0	100.0	5.0	Slovakia
80,885	13.7	37	3,907	51,009	13.1	38.0	2,775	10.4	15	100.0	100.0	100.0	5.7	Slovenia
...	...	...	...	...	...	...	...	...	15	54.1	62.4	44.9	3.8	Solomon Islands
10,400	...	1	549[12]	4,640[12]	...	0.5	...	...	15	24.0	36.0	14.0	0.4	Somalia
140,531[5]	13.0[5]	...	27,099[5]	617,897[5]	22.8[5]	19.0	1,664	1.5	15	85.1	85.8	84.5	8.0	South Africa
1,029,606	...	...	88,922	1,741,528	19.6	51.0	4,017	8.4	15	97.7	98.6	96.8	5.0	Spain
11,652	18.7	12	3,050	38,192	12.5	5.0	474	1.1	15	91.6	94.5	88.9	3.4	Sri Lanka
26,421	34.7	6	1,417	52,260	36.9	3.0	272	0.8	15	57.1	68.3	46.0	1.4	Sudan, The
1,462	...	1	155	1,335	8.6	...	1,124	...	15	94.2	95.9	92.6	3.5	Suriname
2,958[5]	13.0[5]	1	467	5,658	12.1	6.0	642	3.3	15	79.8	80.9	78.7	5.7	Swaziland
...	...	64	33,498[13]	275,217[13]	8.2[13]	50.0	2,972	21.0	15	100.0	100.0	100.0	8.3	Sweden
198,452	...	...	7,709[3]	151,021	...	33.0	2,066	11.5	15	100.0	100.0	100.0	5.4	Switzerland
92,622	7.4	...	4,733[3, 15]	215,734[3]	...	16.0	1,559	...	15	74.4	88.3	60.4	3.1	Syria
[4]	[4]	139	38,806	856,186	22.1	...	...	...	15	94.0	97.6	90.2	5.2	Taiwan
29,482[3]	...	10[3]	5,200[3]	76,613	...	20.0	1,864	11.7	15	99.2	99.6	98.9	2.2	Tajikistan
12,571	11.8	...	1,650	12,776	7.7	0.6	43	2.0	15	75.2	84.1	66.6	3.4	Tanzania
658,474	...	102	25,171[16]	481,936[16]	19.1[16]	22.0	2,096	5.1	15	95.6	97.2	94.0	4.6	Thailand
9,076	13.8	1	443	11,639	26.3	4.0	317	1.3	15	57.1	72.2	42.6	4.5	Togo
824	...	1	53	226[2]	...	...	...	2.8	15	92.8	92.9	92.8	4.7	Tonga
[4]	[4]	3	...	6,007	...	7.7	771	3.4	15	98.2	99.0	97.5	4.4	Trinidad and Tobago
3,839[16]	16.2[16]	...	6,641	121,787	18.3	14.0	1,330	2.8	15	70.8	81.4	60.1	7.7	Tunisia
1,333,177	17.6	863	53,805	1,222,362	22.7	21.0	1,960	10.8	15	85.2	93.6	76.7	2.2	Turkey
26,000	...	15	...	29,435[16]	...	22.0	2,072	...	15	97.7	98.8	96.6	3.9	Turkmenistan
58[12]	...	—	—	—	—	...	...	7.0	15	95.0	...	...	...	Tuvalu
36,063	20.2	...	2,006	29,343	14.6	2.0	154	0.5	15	67.3	77.7	57.1	2.6	Uganda
618,000	...	255[15]	...	922,800[15]	...	41.0	2,977	...	15	98.4	99.5	97.4	7.3	Ukraine
1,925[14]	7.7[14]	4	510[11]	17,950	...	12.0	801	...	15	76.5	75.5	79.5	1.8	United Arab Emirates
2,435,321	16.0	...	89,241	1,820,849	20.4	52.0	3,135	...	15	100.0	100.0	100.0	5.3	United Kingdom
...	...	5,758[11]	940,000	14,350,000	15.3	81.0	5,339	46.5	15	95.5	95.7	95.3	5.4	United States
58,246	...	2	7,165	62,026	8.7	30.0	2,487	10.1	15	97.8	97.4	98.2	3.3	Uruguay
240,100[13]	...	55[13]	...	272,300[13]	...	32.0	2,938	...	15	97.2	98.5	96.0	7.7	Uzbekistan
444	...	1	...	124[12]	...	...	...	...	15	52.9	57.3	47.8	4.8	Vanuatu
[4]	[4]	99[12]	36,232	717,192	19.8	28.0	2,820	11.8	15	93.0	93.3	92.7	5.2	Venezuela
179,907	19.3	104[5]	23,522	509,300	21.7	7.0	404	2.6	15	93.3	95.7	91.0	3.0	Vietnam
—	—	1	266	2,924	11.0	...	...	24.4	...	...	...	...	7.5	Virgin Islands (U.S.)
...	...	22	1,598	30,622	19.2	...	...	...	...	...	...	...	...	West Bank
1,222	...	—	...	...	...	...	...	...	...	...	...	...	...	Western Sahara
67,883	...	2	1,991[3]	65,675	...	4.0	419	...	15	46.4	67.4	25.0	7.0	Yemen
7,982[12]	...	2	640	4,470	7.0	2.0	241	1.5	15	78.0	85.2	71.2	2.2	Zambia
27,431[2]	18.5[2]	28[2]	3,581[3]	43,200[3]	12.1[3]	7.0[3]	638	4.9	15	92.7	95.5	89.9	7.1	Zimbabwe

[1]1990. [2]1992. [3]1995. [4]General second level includes vocational second level. [5]1994. [6]Includes upper primary. [7]College of the Bahamas only. [8]Public schools only. [9]First level includes general second level. [10]Includes preschool. [11]1993. [12]1991. [13]1997. [14]Excludes teacher training. [15]Universities only. [16]1996. [17]Republic of Cyprus only. [18]Includes lower secondary. [19]Data exclude 1,770 primary and 1,449 secondary schools in the Al-Azhar education system. [20]Port-au-Prince universities only. [21]Upper second level only. [22]Mainland Tanzania only.

BIBLIOGRAPHY AND SOURCES

The following list indicates the principal documentary sources used in the compilation of *Britannica World Data.* It is by no means a complete list, either for international or for national sources, but is indicative more of the range of materials to which reference has been made in preparing this compilation.

While *Britannica World Data* has long been based primarily on print sources, many rare in North American library collections, the burgeoning resources of the Internet can be accessed from any appropriately equipped personal computer (PC). At this writing, more than 100 national statistical offices had Internet sites and there were also sites for central banks, national information offices, individual ministries, and the like.

Because of the relative ease of access to these sites for PC users, uniform resource locators (URLs) for mainly official sites have been added to both country statements (at the end, in boldface) and individual Comparative National Statistics tables (at the end of the headnote) when a source providing comparable international data existed. Many sites exist that are narrower in coverage or less official and that may also serve the reader (on-line newspapers; full texts of national constitutions; business and bank sites) but space permitted the listing of only the top national and intergovernmental sites. Sites that are wholly or predominantly in a language other than English are so identified.

International Statistical Sources

Asian Development Bank. *Asian Development Outlook* (annual); *Key Indicators of Developing Member Countries of ADB* (annual).
Caribbean Development Bank. *Annual Report.*
Christian Research. *World Churches Handbook* (1997).
Comité Monétaire de la Zone Franc. *La Zone Franc: Rapport* (annual).
Eastern Caribbean Central Bank. *Report and Statement of Accounts* (annual).
Europa Publications Ltd. *Africa South of the Sahara* (annual); *The Europa Year Book* (2 vol.); *The Far East and Australasia* (annual); *The Middle East and North Africa* (annual).
Food and Agriculture Organization. *Food Balance Sheets; Production Yearbook; Trade Yearbook; Yearbook of Fishery Statistics* (2 vol.); *Yearbook of Forest Products.*
Her Majesty's Stationery Office. *The Commonwealth Yearbook.*
Instituts d'Émission d'Outre-Mer et des Départements d'Outre-Mer (France). *Bulletin trimestriel* (quarterly); *Rapport annuel.*
Inter-American Development Bank. *Economic and Social Progress in Latin America* (annual).
Inter-Parliamentary Union. *Chronicle of Parliamentary Elections and Developments* (annual); *World Directory of Parliaments* (annual).
International Air Transport Association. *World Air Transport Statistics* (annual).
International Bank for Reconstruction and Development/The World Bank. *Statistical Handbook 19**: States of the Former USSR* (annual); *World Bank Atlas* (annual); *Global Development Finance* (2 vol.; annual); *World Development Report* (annual).
International Civil Aviation Organization. *Civil Aviation Statistics of the World* (annual); *Digest of Statistics.*
International Institute for Strategic Studies. *The Military Balance* (annual).
International Labour Organisation. *Year Book of Labour Statistics; The Cost of Social Security: Basic Tables* (triennial).
International Monetary Fund. *Annual Report on Exchange Arrangements and Exchange Restrictions; Direction of Trade Statistics Yearbook; Government Finance Statistics Yearbook; International Financial Statistics* (monthly, with yearbook).
International Road Federation. *World Road Statistics* (annual).
International Telecommunication Union. *Yearbook of Statistics: Telecommunication Services* (annual).
Jane's Publishing Co., Ltd. *Jane's World Railways* (annual).
Keesing's Worldwide LLC. *Keesing's Record of World Events* (monthly except August).
Macmillan Press Ltd. *The Statesman's Year-Book.*
Middle East Economic Digest Ltd. *Middle East Economic Digest* (semimonthly).
Mining Journal, Ltd. *Mining Annual Review* (2 vol.).
Organization for Economic Cooperation and Development. *Economic Surveys* (annual); *Financing and External Debt of Developing Countries* (annual).
Organization of Eastern Caribbean States. *Statistical Booklet* (irreg.).
Oxford University Press. *World Christian Encyclopedia* (David B. Barrett, ed. [2001, 2 vol.]).
Pan American Health Organization. *Health Conditions in the Americas* (2 vol.; quadrennial).
PennWell Publishing Co. *International Petroleum Encyclopedia* (annual).
René Moreux et Cie. *Marchés tropicaux & Méditerranéens* (weekly).
Secretariat of the Pacific Community. *Population Profile* (assorted countries).
United Nations (UN). *Demographic Yearbook; Industrial Commodities Statistics Yearbook; Energy Statistics Yearbook; International Trade Statistics Yearbook* (2 vol.); *Monthly Bulletin of Statistics; Population Studies* (irreg.); *National Accounts Statistics* (2 parts; annual); *Population and Vital Statistics Report* (quarterly); *Statistical Yearbook; World Population Prospects 19*** (biennial).
UN: Economic Commission for Latin America. *Economic Survey of Latin America and the Caribbean* (2 vol.; annual); *Statistical Yearbook for Latin America and the Caribbean.*
UN: Economic and Social Commission for Asia and the Pacific. *Statistical Indicators for Asia and the Pacific* (quarterly); *Statistical Yearbook for Asia and the Pacific.*
UN: Economic and Social Commission for Western Asia. *Demographic and Related Socio-Economic Data Sheets* (irreg.); *National Accounts Studies of the ESCWA Region* (irreg.); *The Population Situation in the ESCWA Region* (irreg.); *Statistical Abstract of the Region of the Economic and Social Commission for Western Asia* (annual).
UN: Educational, Scientific, and Cultural Organization. *Statistical Yearbook.*
United Nations Industrial Development Organization. *Industrial Development Review Series* (irreg.); *Industrial Development: Global Report* (annual); *International Yearbook of Industrial Statistics.*
United States: Central Intelligence Agency, *The World Factbook* (annual); Dept. of Commerce, *World Population Profile* (biennial); Dept. of Health and Human Services, *Social Security Programs Throughout the World* (semiannual, 4 vol.); Dept. of Interior, *Minerals Yearbook* (3 vol. in 6 parts); Dept. of State, *Background Notes* (irreg.).
World Health Organization. *World Health Statistics Annual; World Health Statistics Quarterly.*
World Tourism Organization. *Compendium of Tourism Statistics* (annual).

Internet Resources

U.S. Census Bureau: International Data Base (World)
http://www.census.gov/ipc/www/idbprint.html
Thomas Brinkhoff: City Population (World)
http://www.citypopulation.de
GeoHive (World) http://geohive.com
The World Gazetteer (World)
http://world-gazetteer.com/home.htm

National Statistical Sources

Afghanistan. *Preliminary Results of the First Afghan Population Census (1979).*
Albania. *Population and Housing Census 2001; Statistical Yearbook of Albania.*
Algeria. *Annuaire statistique; Recensement général de la population et de l'habitat, 1998; Algeria: Recent Economic Developments* (IMF Country Staff Report [2001]).
American Samoa. *American Samoa Statistical Digest* (annual); *Report on the State of the Island* (U.S. Department of the Interior [annual]); *2000 Census of Population and Housing* (U.S.).
Andorra. *Anuari Estadístic* (annual); *L'Andorre en Chiffres* (annual); *Recull Estadístic General de la Població Andorra 90.*
Angola. *Angola—Recent Economic Developments* (IMF Staff Country Report [2000]); *Perfil estatìstico de Angola* (annual).
Antigua. *Antigua and Barbuda—Statistical Annex* (IMF Staff Country Report [1999]); *Statistical Yearbook; 1991 Population and Housing Census.*
Argentina. *Anuario estadístico de la República Argentina; Censo nacional de población, hogares y vivienda* 2001.
Armenia. *Recent Economic Development and Selected Issues* (IMF Staff Country Report [1999]); *Statisticheskii Yezhegodnik Armenii* (Statistical Yearbook of Armenia).
Aruba. *Statistical Yearbook; Central Bank of Aruba Bulletin* (quarterly); *Fourth Population and Housing Census October 14, 2000.*
Australia. *Monthly Summary of Statistics, Australia; Social Indicators* (annual); *Year Book Australia; 2001 Census of Population and Housing.*
Austria. *Grosszählung 2001* (General Census 2001). *Sozialstatistische Daten* (irreg.); *Statistisches Jahrbuch für die Republik Österreich.*
Azerbaijan. *Azerbaijan Republic: Selected Issues and Statistical Appendix* (IMF Staff Country Report [2002]); *Statistical Yearbook of Azerbaijan.*
Bahamas, The. *Census of Population and Housing 2000; Statistical Abstract* (annual); *Central Bank of The Bahamas Annual Report and Statement of Accounts.*
Bahrain. *Statistical Abstract* (annual); *The Population, Housing, Buildings and Establishments Census 2001.*
Bangladesh. *Bangladesh Population Census, 2001; Statistical Yearbook of Bangladesh; Bangladesh: Recent Economic Developments* (IMF Staff Country Report [2000]).
Barbados. *Barbados Economic Report* (annual); *Monthly Digest of Statistics; Barbados: Statistical Appendix* (IMF Staff Country Report [2000]).
Belarus. *Narodnoye Khozyaystvo Respubliki Belarus: Statisticheskiy Yezhegodnik* (National Economy of the Republic of Belarus: Statistical Yearbook).
Belgium. *Annuaire statistique de la Belgique; Recensement de la population et des logements au 1er mars 1991.*
Belize. *Abstract of Statistics* (annual); *Belize Economic Survey* (annual); *Central Bank of Belize Annual Report and Accounts; 2000 Population Census: Major Findings.*
Benin. *Annuaire statistique; Recensement général de la population et de l'habitation* (1992).
Bermuda. *Bermuda Digest of Statistics* (annual); *Report of the Manpower Survey* (annual); *The 2000 Census of Population and Housing.*
Bhutan. *Statistical Yearbook of Bhutan.*
Bolivia. *Anuario estadístico; Censo de población y vivienda 2001; Compendio estadístico* (annual); *Estadísticas socio-económicas* (annual); *Resumen estadístico* (annual).
Bosnia and Herzegovina. *Bosnia and Herzegovina: Statistical Appendix* (IMF Staff Country Report [2002]).
Botswana. *Statistical Bulletin* (quarterly); *2001 Population and Housing Census; Botswana—Selected Issues and Statistical Appendix* (IMF Staff Country Report [1999]).
Brazil. *Anuário Estatístico do Brasil; Censo Demográfico 2000.*
Brunei. *Brunei Statistical Yearbook; Brunei Darussalam Population and Housing Census 2001.*
Bulgaria. *Prebroyavaneto na naselenìeto kŭm 01.03.2001 godina* (Census of Population of March 1, 2001); *Statisticheskii godishnik na Republika Bŭlgariya* (Statistical Yearbook of the Republic of Bulgaria).
Burkina Faso. *Burkina Faso: Selected Issues and Statistical Annex* (IMF Staff Country Report [2002]); *Recensement général de la population du 10 au 20 decembre 1985.*
Burundi. *Annuaire statistique; Recensement général de la population, 1990; Burundi: Statistical Annex* (IMF Staff Country Report [2000]).
Cambodia. *1998 Population Census of Cambodia; Cambodia: Statistical Appendix* (IMF Staff Country Report [2002]).

Cameroon. *Cameroon—Statistical Appendix* (IMF Staff Country Report [2000]); *Recensement général de la population et de l'habitat 1987.*
Canada. *Canada Year Book* (biennial); *Census Canada 2001: Population.*
Cape Verde. *Cape Verde—Recent Economic Developments* (IMF Staff Country Report [2001]); *O Recenseamento Geral da População e Habitação 2000.*
Central African Republic. *Annuaire statistique; Central African Republic—Statistical Annex* (IMF Staff Country Report [2000]); *Recensement général de la population 1988.*
Chad. *Annuaire statistique; Recensement general de la population et de l'habitat 1993; Chad: Statistical Appendix* (IMF Staff Country Report [2002]).
Chile. *Chile XVII censo nacional de población y VI de vivienda, 24 de abril 2002; Compendio estadístico* (annual).
China, People's Republic of. *People's Republic of China Year-Book; Statistical Yearbook of China; 10 Percent Sampling Tabulation on the 1990 Population Census of the People's Republic of China.*
Colombia. *Colombia estadística* (annual); *Censo 93 informacion de vivienda; Colombia: Statistical Appendix* (IMF Staff Country Report [2001]).
Comoros. *Banque Centrale des Comoroes Rapport Annuel* (Central Bank of Comoros Annual Report); *Recensement général de la population et de l'habitat 15 septembre 1980.*
Congo, Dem. Rep. of the (Zaire). *Annuaire statistique* (irreg.); *Recensement Scientifique de la Population du 1er juillet 1984.*
Congo, Rep. of the. *Annuaire statistique; Recensement général de la population et de l'habitat de 1984.*
Costa Rica. *Anuario estadístico; Costa Rica at a Glance* (annual); *IX censo nacional de población y V de viviendas, 2001.*
Côte d'Ivoire. *Côte d'Ivoire—Selected Issues and Statistical Appendix* (IMF Staff Country Report [2000]); *Recensement général de la population et de l'habitat 1988.*
Croatia. *Census of Population, Households and Dwellings 31st March 2001; Statistical Yearbook.*
Cuba. *Anuario estadístico; Censo de población y viviendas, 1981.*
Cyprus. *Census of Industrial Production* (annual); *Census of Population 1992; Economic Report* (annual); *Statistical Abstract* (annual).
Czech Republic. *Statistická ročenka České Republiky* (Statistical Yearbook of the Czech Republic).
Denmark. *Folke-og boligtaellingen, 1981* (Population and Housing Census); *Statistisk årbog* (Statistical Yearbook).
Djibouti. *Annuaire statistique de Djibouti; Djibouti: Statistical Annex* (IMF Staff Country Report [1999]).
Dominica. *Dominica—Statistical Annex* (IMF Staff Country Report [2000]); *Population and Housing Census 1991; Statistical Digest* (irreg.).
Dominican Republic. *Cifras Dominicanas* (irreg.); *VIII censo nacional de población y vivienda, 2002.*
East Timor. *IMF Survey, June 10, 2002* (biweekly).
Ecuador. *Serie estadística* (quinquennial); *VI censo de población y V de vivienda 2001.*
Egypt. *Census Population, Housing, and Establishment, 1996; Statistical Yearbook.*
El Salvador. *Anuario estadístico* (irreg.); *Censos nacionales: V censo de población y IV de vivienda (1992); El Salvador en cifras* (annual); *Indicadores económicos y sociales* (annual).
Equatorial Guinea. *Censos nacionales, I de población y I de vivienda—4 al 17 de julio de 1983; Equatorial Guinea—Recent Economic Developments* (IMF Staff Country Report [1999]).
Eritrea. *Eritrea—Selected Issues* (IMF Staff Country Report [2000]).
Estonia. *2000 Population and Housing Census; Eesti Statistika Aastaraamat* (Estonia Statistical Yearbook).
Ethiopia. *1994 Population and Housing Census of Ethiopia; Ethiopia Statistical Abstract* (annual); *Ethiopia—Recent Economic Developments* (IMF Staff Country Report [1999]).
Faroe Islands. *Rigsombudsmanden på Færøerne: Beretning* (annual); *Statistical Bulletin* (annual).
Fiji. *Key Statistics* (annual); *Current Economic Statistics* (quarterly); *1996 Census of the Population and Housing.*
Finland. *Economic Survey* (annual); *Population Census 1990; Statistical Yearbook of Finland.*
France. *Annuaire statistique de la France; Données sociales* (triennial); *Recensement général de la population de 1999; Tableaux de l'Economie Française* (annual).
French Guiana. *Recensement général de la population de 1999; Tableaux economiques regionaux: Guyane* (biennial).
French Polynesia. *Résultats du recensement général de la population de la Polynésie Française, du 6 Septembre 1996; Tableaux de l'economie polynesienne* (irreg.); *Te avei'a: Bulletin d'information statistique* (monthly).
Gabon. *Recensement général de la population et de l'habitat 1993; Situation économique, financière et sociale de la République Gabonaise* (annual).
Gambia, The. *The Gambia—Selected Issues* (IMF Staff Country Report [2000]).
Gaza Strip. *Judaea, Samaria, and Gaza Area Statistics Quarterly; Palestinian Statistical Abstract* (annual).
Georgia. *Georgia—Recent Economic Developments and Selected Issues* (IMF Staff Country Report [2001]); *Narodnoye Khozyaystvo Gruzinskoy SSR* (National Economy of the Georgian S.S.R. [annual]).
Germany. *Statistisches Jahrbuch für die Bundesrepublik Deutschland; Volkszählung vom 25. Mai 1987* (Census of Population).
Ghana. *Ghana—Statistical Appendix* (IMF Staff Country Report [2000]); *Population Census of Ghana, 2000; Quarterly Digest of Statistics.*
Greece. *Recensement de la population et des habitations, 2001; Statistical Yearbook of Greece.*
Greenland. *Grønland* (annual); *Grønlands befolkning* (Greenland Population [annual]).
Grenada. *Abstract of Statistics* (annual); *Grenada—Statistical Appendix* (IMF Staff Country Report [2001]). *2001 Population and Housing Census.*
Guadeloupe. *Recensement général de la population de 1999: Guadeloupe; Tableaux economiques regionaux: Guadeloupe* (biennial).
Guam. *Guam Annual Economic Review; 2000 Census of Population and Housing (U.S.).*
Guatemala. *Anuario estadística; Censo nacional instituto nacional de estadística 1994: X nacional de población y V de habitación.*
Guernsey. *Guernsey Census 2001; Statistical Digest* (annual); *Economic and Statistics Review* (annual).
Guinea. *Guinea—Statistical Appendix* (IMF Staff Country Report [2000]).
Guinea-Bissau. *Guinea-Bissau—Statistical Appendix* (IMF Staff Country Report [2002]); *Recenseamento Geral da População e da Habitação, 1991.*
Guyana. *Bank of Guyana: Annual Report and Statement of Accounts; Guyana: Statistical Appendix* (IMF Staff Country Report [2001]).
Haiti. *Banque de la République d'Haiti: Rapport Annuel; Haiti: Selected Issues* (IMF Staff Country Report [2002]). *Résultats préliminaires du recensement général (Septembre 1982).*
Honduras. *Anuario estadístico; Censo nacional de población y vivienda, 2001; Honduras—Statistical Appendix* (IMF Staff Country Report [2000]); *Honduras en cifras* (annual).
Hong Kong. *Annual Digest of Statistics; Hong Kong* (annual); *Hong Kong 2001 Population Census; Hong Kong Social and Economic Trends* (biennial).
Hungary. *Statisztikai évkönyv* (Statistical Yearbook); *2001, Evi népszámlálás* (Census of Population 2001).
Iceland. *Hagtidhindi* (monthly); *Landshagir* (Statistical Yearbook of Iceland [annual]); *Iceland in Figures* (annual).
India. *Census of India, 2001; Economic Survey* (annual); *Statistical Abstract* (annual).
Indonesia. *Indonesia: An Official Handbook* (irreg.); *Hasil Sensus penduduk Indonesia, 2000* (Census of Population); *Statistical Yearbook of Indonesia.*
Iran. *National Census of Population and Housing, October 1996; Iran Statistical Yearbook; Islamic Republic of Iran: Selected Issues and Statistical Appendix* (IMF Staff Country Report [2002]).
Iraq. *Annual Abstract of Statistics.*
Ireland. *Census of Population of Ireland, 2002; National Income and Expenditure* (annual); *Statistical Yearbook of Ireland* (annual).
Isle of Man. *Census Report 2001; Isle of Man Digest of Economic and Social Statistics* (annual).
Israel. *1995 Census of Population and Housing; Statistical Abstract* (annual).
Italy. *Statistica agrarie; Statistiche demografiche* (4 parts); *Statistiche dell'istruzione; Annuario statistico Italiano; 13o Censimento generale della popolazione e delle Abitazioni 20 Ottobre 1991.*
Jamaica. *Economic and Social Survey* (annual); *Statistical Abstract* (annual); *Statistical Yearbook of Jamaica; Population Census 2001.*
Japan. *Japan Statistical Yearbook; Statistical Indicators on Social Life* (annual); *1995 Population Census of Japan.*
Jersey. *Report of the Census for 2001; Statistical Digest* (annual); *An Introduction to Jersey* (irreg.).
Jordan. *Population and Housing Census 1994; Central Bank of Jordan Report* (annual); *National Accounts* (irreg.); *Statistical Yearbook.*
Kazakhstan. *Statistichesky Yezhegodnik* (Statistical Yearbook); *1999 Population Census.*
Kenya. *Economic Survey* (annual); *Population Census 1999; Statistical Abstract* (annual); *Kenya—Selected Issues and Statistical Appendix* (IMF Staff Country Report [2002]).
Kiribati. *Annual Abstract of Statistics; Kiribati Population Census 2000; Kiribati—Statistical Appendix* (IMF Staff Country Report [1997]).
Korea, North. *North Korea: A Country Study* (1994); *The Population of North Korea* (1990).
Korea, South. *Korea Statistical Yearbook; Social Indicators in Korea* (annual); *2000 Population and Housing Census.*
Kuwait. *Annual Statistical Abstract; General Census of Population and Housing and Buildings 1995.*
Kyrgyzstan. *Statistichesky Yezhegodnik Kyrgyzstana* (Statistical Yearbook of Kyrgyzstan).
Laos. *Lao People's Democratic Republic: Selected Issues and Statistical Appendix* (IMF Staff Country Report [2002]).
Latvia. *Statistical Yearbook of Latvia; Latvijas Republikas 2000 Iedzivotāju Skaits* (2000 Census of Population of the Republic of Latvia).
Lebanon. *Lebanon: A Country Study* (1989).
Lesotho. *Lesotho—Statistical Annex* (IMF Staff Country Report [2002]); *Statistical Yearbook; 1996 Population Census.*
Liberia. *Economic Survey* (annual); *Liberia: Statistical Appendix* (IMF Staff Country Report [2002]).
Libya. *Libya Population Census, 1995.*
Liechtenstein. *Statistisches Jahrbuch; Volkszählung, 1990* (Census of Population); *Liechtenstein in Figures* (annual).
Lithuania. *Gyventojų ir Bustų Surašymu Skypĩus 2001* (Population and Housing Census 2001); *Lietuvos Statistikos Metraštis* (Lithuanian Statistical Yearbook).
Luxembourg. *Annuaire statistique; Bulletin du STATEC* (monthly); *Recensement général de la population du 15 février 2001.*
Macau. *Anuário Estatístico; XIV Recenseamento Geral da População, 2001.*
Macedonia. *Former Yugoslav Republic of Macedonia: Selected Issues and Statistical Appendix* (IMF Staff Country Report [2002]); *Statistical Yearbook of the Republic of Macedonia.*
Madagascar. *Madagascar: Selected Issues and Statistical Appendix* (IMF Staff Country Report [2001]); *Recensement général de la population et de l'habitat, aout 1993; Situation économique* (annual).
Malawi. *1998 Population and Housing Census; Malawi Statistical Yearbook; Malawi Yearbook; Malawi: Selected Issues and Statistical Appendix* (IMF Staff Country Report [2002]).
Malaysia. *Population and Housing Census of Malaysia 2000; Yearbook of Statistics; Malaysia: Statistical Appendix* (IMF Staff Country Report [2001]).
Maldives. *Population and Housing Census of Maldives 2000; Statistical Year Book of Maldives.*
Mali. *Annuaire statistique du Mali; Recensement general de la population et de l'habitat* (*du 1er au 9 mars 1998*); *Mali: Selected Issues and Statistical Annex* (IMF Staff Country Report [2002]).
Malta. *Annual Abstract of Statistics; Quarterly Digest of Statistics.*
Marshall Islands. *Marshall Islands Statistical Abstract* (annual); *Report on the State of the Islands* (U.S. Department of the Interior [annual]); *Population and Housing Census 1999.*
Martinique. *Recensement de la population de 1999. Martinique; Tableaux economiques regionaux: Martinique* (biennial).
Mauritania. *Recensement général de la population et de l'habitat 2000. Annuaire Statistique; Mauritania—Statistical Appendix* (IMF Staff Country Report [2000]).
Mauritius. *Annual Digest of Statistics; 2000 Housing and Population Census of Mauritius; Mauritius in Figures* (annual); *Mauritius: Selected Issues and Statistical Appendix* (IMF Staff Country Report [2002]).
Mayotte. *Bulletin Trimestriel* (quarterly) and *Rapport Annuel* (Institut d'Emission, France); *Recensement de la population de Mayotte: août 1997.*
Mexico. *Anuario estadístico; XII Censo general de población y vivienda, 2000; Anuario estadístico de los Estados Unidos Mexicanos.*
Micronesia. *Micronesia—Recent Economic Developments* (IMF Staff Country Report [1998]); *FSM Statistical Yearbook* (annual).
Moldova. *Republic of Moldova: Recent Economic Developments* (IMF Country Report [2001]); *Republica Moldova in Cifre* (annual).

Monaco. *Recensement general de la population 1990.*
Mongolia. *Mongolian Statistical Yearbook* (annual); *Mongolia: Selected Issues and Statistical Appendix* (IMF Staff Country Report [2002]); *2000 Population and Housing Census of Mongolia.*
Morocco. *Annuaire statistique du Maroc; Recensement général de la population et de l'habitat de 1994.*
Mozambique. *Anuário Estatístico; Republic of Mozambique—Statistical Appendix* (IMF Staff Country Report [2002]); *II Recenseamento Geral da População e habitação, 1997.*
Myanmar (Burma). *Myanmar—Statistical Appendix* (IMF Staff Country Report [2001]); *Report to the Pyithu Hluttaw on the Financial, Social, and Economic Conditions for 19**** (annual); *Statistical Abstract* (irreg.); *1983 Population Census.*
Namibia. *2001 Population and Housing Census; Statistical/Economic Review* (annual).
Nauru. *Population Profile* (irreg.).
Nepal. *Economic Survey* (annual); *Statistical Pocket Book* (irreg.); *Statistical Yearbook of Nepal; National Population Census* 2001.
Netherlands, The. *Statistical Yearbook of the Netherlands.*
Netherlands Antilles. *Fourth Population and Housing Census Netherlands Antilles 2001; Statistical Yearbook of the Netherlands Antilles.*
New Caledonia. *Images de la population de la Nouvelle-Calédonie principaux resultats du recensement 1996; Tableaux bilan economique* (annual); *New Caledonia Facts and Figures* (annual).
New Zealand. *2001 New Zealand Census of Population and Dwellings; New Zealand Official Yearbook.*
Nicaragua. *Censos Nacionales 1995; Compendio Estadístico* (annual); *Nicaragua—Statistical Appendix* (IMF Staff Country Report [2001]).
Niger. *Annuaire statistique; Niger—Statistical Annex* (IMF Staff Country Report [2002]); *2ème Recensement général de la population 1988.*
Nigeria. *Annual Abstract of Statistics; Nigeria: A Country Study* (1992); *Nigeria—Statistical Appendix* (IMF Staff Country Report [2001]).
Northern Mariana Islands. *CNMI Population Profile; Report on the State of the Islands* (U.S. Department of the Interior [annual]); *2000 Census of Population and Housing (U.S.).*
Norway. *Folke-og boligtelling 2001* (Population and Housing Census); *Industristatistikk* (annual); *Statistisk årbok* (Statistical Yearbook).
Oman. *General Census of Population, Housing, and Establishments* (1993); *Statistical Yearbook; Bank of Oman Annual Report.*
Pakistan. *Economic Survey* (annual); *Pakistan Statistical Yearbook; Population Census of Pakistan, 1998.*
Palau. *Statistical Yearbook; Census 2000; Republic of Palau: Recent Economic Developments* (IMF Staff Country Report [2002]).
Panama. *Indicadores económicos y sociales* (annual); *X censo nacional de poblacion y vivienda realizados el 14 de mayo del 2000; Panama en cifras* (annual).
Papua New Guinea. *Papua New Guinea: Recent Economic Developments* (IMF Staff Country Report [2000]); *Summary of Statistics* (annual); *2000 National Population Census.*
Paraguay. *Anuario estadístico del Paraguay; Censo nacional de población y viviendas, 1992; Paraguay: Recent Economic Developments* (IMF Staff Country Report [2001]).
Peru. *Censos nacionales; IX de población: IV de vivienda, 11 de julio de 1993; Compendio estadístico* (3 vol.; annual); *Informe estadístico* (annual); *Peru: Selected Issues* (IMF Staff Country Report [2001]).
Philippines. *Philippine Statistical Yearbook; 2000 Census of Population and Housing.*
Poland. *Narodowy spis powszechny 2002* (National Population and Housing Census); *Rocznik statystyczny* (Statistical Yearbook).
Portugal. *Anuário Estatístico; XIV Recenseamento Geral da População: IV Recenseamento Geral da Habitação, 2001.*
Puerto Rico. *Estadísticas socioeconomicas* (annual); *Informe económico al gobernador* (Economic Report to the Governor [annual]); *2000 Census of Population and Housing* (U.S.).
Qatar. *Annual Statistical Abstract; Economic Survey of Qatar* (annual); *Qatar Year Book; Qatar Central Bank Annual Report; Population and Housing Census 1993.*
Réunion. *Recensement général de la population de 1999; Tableau Economique de la Réunion* (biennial).
Romania. *Anuarul statistic al României* (Statistical Yearbook); *Census of Population and Housing March 27, 2002.*
Russia. *Demograficheskiy Yezhegodnik Rossii* (Demographic Yearbook of Russia); *Rossiysky Statistichesky Yezhegodnik* (Russian Statistical Yearbook).
Rwanda. *Bulletin de Statistique: Supplement Annuel; Recensement general de la population et de l'habitat 1991; Rwanda: Statistical Annex* (IMF Staff Country Report [2002]).
St. Kitts and Nevis. *Annual Digest of Statistics; St. Christopher and Nevis: Recent Economic Developments* (IMF Staff Country Report [2000]).
St. Lucia. *Annual Statistical Digest; St. Lucia: Selected Issues and Statistical Appendix* (IMF Staff Country Report [2002]); *2001 Population and Housing Census.*
St. Vincent and the Grenadines. *Digest of Statistics* (annual); *Population and Housing Census 2001; St. Vincent and the Grenadines: Statistical Appendix* (IMF Staff Country Report [2002]).
Samoa (Western Samoa). *Annual Statistical Abstract; Census of Population and Housing, 2001; Samoa: Statistical Appendix* (IMF Staff Country Report [1999]).
San Marino. *Bollettino di Statistica* (quarterly); *Annuario Statistico Demografico* (irreg.); *Republic of San Marino: Selected Issues and Statistical Appendix* (IMF Staff Country Report [2001]).
São Tomé and Príncipe. *1º Recenseamento Geral da População e da Habitação 1991; Sao Tome: Statistical Appendix* (IMF Staff Country Report [2002]).
Saudi Arabia. *Saudi Arabian Monetary Agency: Annual Report; Saudi Arabia Population and Housing Census 1992.*
Senegal. *Recensement de la population et de l'habitat 2001; Situation économique du Senegal* (annual); *Senegal: Selected Issues* (IMF Staff Country Report [2001]).
Serbia and Montenegro. *Popis stanovištva, domaćinstava, stanova i poljoprivrednih gazdinstava 1991 godine* (Census of Population, Households, Housing, and Agricultural Holdings 1991); *Statistical Pocket Book* (annual); *Statistički godišnjak Jugoslavije* (Statistical Yearbook of Yugoslavia).
Seychelles. *Statistical Abstract* (annual); *Seychelles in Figures* (annual); *National Population and Housing Census 1997.*
Sierra Leone. *Sierra Leone—Recent Economic Developments* (IMF Staff Country Report [1997]).
Singapore. *Census of Population, 2000; Singapore Yearbook; Yearbook of Statistics Singapore; Singapore: Selected Issues* (IMF Staff Country Report [2001]).
Slovakia. *Sčítanie Obyvatel'ov, Domov a Btov 2001* (Population and Housing Census 2001); *Statistical Yearbook of the Slovak Republic; Slovak Republic: Selected Issues and Statistical Appendix* (IMF Staff Country Report [2002]).
Slovenia. *Slovenija Popis 2002* (Slovenia Population Census 2002); *Statistični Letopis Republike Slovenija* (Statistical Yearbook of the Republic of Slovenia); *Republic of Slovenia: Statistical Appendix* (IMF Staff Country Report [2002]).
Solomon Islands. *Solomon Islands 1999 Population Census; Solomon Islands—Statistical Appendix* (IMF Staff Country Report [1998]).
Somalia. *The CIA World Factbook* (annual).
South Africa. *The People of South Africa Population Census, 1996; South Africa: Official Yearbook of the Republic of South Africa; Stats in Brief* (annual).
Spain. *Anuario estadístico; Censo de población de 2001.*
Sri Lanka. *Census of Population and Housing, 2001; Sri Lanka Statistical Abstract* (irreg.); *Statistical Pocketbook of the Democratic Socialist Republic of Sri Lanka* (annual); *Sri Lanka: Selected Issues and Statistical Appendix* (IMF Staff Country Report [2002]).
Sudan, The. *Sudan—Statistical Appendix* (IMF Staff Country Report [2000]); *Fourth Population Census, 1993; Sudan in Figures* (annual); *Sudan: Statistical Appendix* (IMF Staff Country Report [2000]).
Suriname. *General Population Census 1980; Statistisch Jaarboek van Suriname; Suriname—Recent Economic Developments* (IMF Staff Country Report [1997]).
Swaziland. *Annual Statistical Bulletin; Report on the 1997 Swaziland Population Census; Swaziland—Selected Issues and Statistical Appendix* (IMF Staff Country Report [2000]).
Sweden. *Folk-och bostadsräkningen, 1990* (Population and Housing Census); *Statistisk årsbok för Sverige* (Statistical Abstract of Sweden [annual]).
Switzerland. *Recensement fédéral de la population, 2000; Statistisches Jahrbuch* (Statistical Yearbook).
Syria. *General Census of Housing and Inhabitants, 1994; Statistical Abstract* (annual).
Taiwan. *The Republic of China Yearbook; Social Indicators of the Republic of China* (annual); *Statistical Abstract* (annual); *Statistical Yearbook of the Republic of China; Taiwan Statistical Data Book* (annual); *1990 Census of Population and Housing.*
Tajikistan. *General Population Census of the Republic of Tajikistan 2000; Republic of Tajikistan: Statistical Appendix* (IMF Staff Country Report [2001]); *Narodnoye Khozyaystvo Tadzhikskoy SSR* (National Economy of the Tadzhik S.S.R. [annual]).
Tanzania. *Tanzania—Statistical Annex* (IMF Staff Country Report [2000]); *Tanzania in Figures* (annual); *Tanzania Statistical Abstract* (irreg.); *1988 Population Census.*
Thailand. *Statistical Handbook of Thailand* (annual); *Statistical Yearbook; Population and Housing Census 2000; Thailand: Statistical Appendix* (IMF Staff Country Report [2001]).
Togo. *Annuaire statistique du Togo; Recensement général de la population et de l'habitat 1993; Togo—Selected Issues* (IMF Staff Country Report [1999]).
Tonga. *Population Census, 1996; Tonga—Statistical Appendix* (IMF Staff Country Report [2001]).
Trinidad and Tobago. *Central Bank of Trinidad and Tobago: Annual Economic Survey; 1990 Population and Housing Census; Trinidad and Tobago: Statistical Appendix* (IMF Staff Country Report [2001]).
Tunisia. *Annuaire statistique de la Tunisie; Recensement général de la population et des logements, 1994; Tunisia: Selected Issues* (IMF Staff Country Report [2002]).
Turkey. *2000 Genel Nüfus Sayımı* (2000 Census of Population); *Türkiye İstatistik Yilliği* (Statistical Yearbook of Turkey).
Turkmenistan. *1995 Population and Housing Census of the Republic of Turkmenistan; Turkmenistan v tsifrakh* (Turkmenistan in figures [annual]).
Tuvalu. *Tuvalu Country Profile 2000.*
Uganda. *2002 National Population and Housing Census; Uganda: Selected Issues and Statistical Appendix* (IMF Staff Country Report [1999]).
Ukraine. *Perepis Naselennya 2002* (Population Census 2002); *Statistichniy Shchorichnik Ukraini* (Statistical Yearbook of Ukraine).
United Arab Emirates. *Statistical Yearbook* (Abu Dhabi); *United Arab Emirates—Recent Economic Developments* (IMF Staff Country Report [1999]); *Central Bank of UAE Report* (annual).
United Kingdom. *Annual Abstract of Statistics; Britain: An Official Handbook* (annual); *Census 2001; General Household Survey* series (annual).
United States. *Agricultural Statistics* (annual); *Current Population Reports; Digest of Education Statistics* (annual); *Minerals Yearbook* (3 vol. in 6 parts); *Statistical Abstract* (annual); *U.S. Exports: SIC-Based Products* (annual); *U.S. Imports: SIC-Based Products* (annual); *Vital and Health Statistics* (series 1–20); *2000 Census of Population and Housing.*
Uruguay. *Anuario estadístico; VII Censo general de poblacion III de hogares y V de viviendas, 22 de mayo de 1996; Uruguay—Recent Economic Developments* (IMF Country Report [2001]).
Uzbekistan. *Narodnoye Khozyaystvo Respubliki Uzbekistan* (National Economy of Uzbekistan [annual]); *Republic of Uzbekistan; Uzbekistan—Recent Economic Developments* (IMF Staff Country Report [2000]).
Vanuatu. *National Population Census 1999; Vanuatu Statistical Yearbook; Vanuatu—Recent Economic Developments* (IMF Staff Country Report [2000]).
Venezuela. *Anuario estadístico; Censo general de la población y vivienda 2001; Encuesta de hogares por muestreo* (annual); *Encuesta industrial* (annual).
Vietnam. *Nien Giam Thong Ke* (Statistical Yearbook); *Tong Dieu Tra Dan So Viet Nam—1999* (*Vietnam Population Census—1999*); *Vietnam—Selected Issues and Statistical Appendix* (IMF Staff Country Report [2002]).
Virgin Islands of the United States. *2000 Census of Population and Housing* (U.S.).
West Bank. *Population, Housing and Establishment Census—1997; Palestinian Statistical Abstract.*
Western Sahara. *Recensement general de la population et de l'habitat* (1994 [Morocco]).
Yemen. *Population of Yemen: 1994 Census; Republic of Yemen: Selected Issues* (IMF Country Staff Report [2001]).
Zambia. *Zambia—Statistical Appendix* (IMF Staff Country Report [1999]); *2000 Census of Population, Housing, Agriculture.*
Zimbabwe. *Population Census 1992; Statistical Yearbook* (irreg.); *Zimbabwe—Statistical Appendix* (IMF Staff Country Report [2002]).

Index

This index covers both *Britannica Book of the Year* (cumulative for 10 years) and *Britannica World Data.* Biographies and obituaries are cumulative for 5 years.

Entries in **dark type** are titles of major articles in the *Book of the Year;* an accompanying year in **dark type** gives the year the reference appears, and the accompanying page number in light type shows where the article appears. References for previous years are preceded by the year in dark type. For example, **"Education 04:**187; **03:**204; **02:**206; **01:**204; **00:**191; **99:**209; **98:**201; **97:**203; **96:**191; **95:**174" indicates that the article "Education" appeared every year from **1995** through **2004.** Other references that appear with a page number but without a year refer to references from the current yearbook.

Indented entries in light type that follow **dark-type** article titles refer by page number to some other places in the text where the subject of the article is discussed. Light-type entries that are not indented refer by page number to subjects that are not themselves article titles. Names of people covered in biographies and obituaries from previous years are followed by the abbreviation "(biog.)" or "(obit.)" with the year in **dark type** and a page number in light type, e.g., Ritter, Jonathon Southworth ("John") (obit.) **04:**131. Biographies and obituaries for the current year appear under the main entry. In cases where a person has both a biography and an obituary, the words appear as subentries under the main entry and are alphabetized accordingly, e.g.:

Uhse, Beate
  biography **00:**71
  obituary **02:**146

References to illustrations are by page number and are preceded by the abbreviation *il.*

The index uses word-by-word alphabetization (treating a word as one or more characters separated by a space from the next word). Please note that "St." is treated as "Saint." "Mc" is alphabetized as "Mc" rather than "Mac."

A

B

C

D

E

Dark-type numbers refer to the yearly edition where the reference appears, e.g., **02:**324 for the 2002 edition, page 324.

G

Dark-type numbers refer to the yearly edition where the reference appears, e.g., **02**:324 for the 2002 edition, page 324.

H

Dark-type numbers refer to the yearly edition where the reference appears, e.g., **02:**324 for the 2002 edition, page 324.

Dark-type numbers refer to the yearly edition where the reference appears, e.g., **02:**324 for the 2002 edition, page 324.

J

L

Dark-type numbers refer to the yearly edition where the reference appears, e.g., **02:**324 for the 2002 edition, page 324.

Q

R

S

U

V

W

X

Y

Z

Index of Special Features in *Britannica Book of the Year,* 1995–2004

Special Reports and Spotlights